THEOLOGICAL DICTIONARY

OF THE

NEW TESTAMENT

EDITED BY

GERHARD FRIEDRICH

Translator and Editor

GEOFFREY W. BROMILEY, D. LITT., D. D.

Volume V

Ξ—Πα

WM. B. EERDMANS PUBLISHING COMPANY

GRAND RAPIDS, MICHIGAN

THEOLOGICAL DICTIONARY OF THE NEW TESTAMENT

Translated from
THEOLOGISCHES WÖRTERBUCH ZUM NEUEN TESTAMENT
Fünfter Band Ξ—Πα, herausgegeben von Gerhard Friedrich

Published by
W. KOHLHAMMER VERLAG
Stuttgart, Germany

Printed in the Netherlands
by Drukkerij Holland N.V., Amsterdam

Preface

When in November 1928 Gerhard Kittel began preliminary work on the Dictionary, he did not realise what difficulties were involved in producing such a work, or how long a period of time it would claim. In co-operation with 15 colleagues, he thought at first that he could complete the whole work in 3 years. From the very outset he was aware that a mere improvement of the older Cremer was not enough. In spite of his admiration for H. Cremer and J. Kögel he perceived the weaknesses of the older Dictionary. Hence no difficulties were allowed to deflect him from the original plan of creating a work consonant with modern requirements. Under his wise guidance there thus arose something quite new which found recognition both at home and abroad. With his organising skill and theological breadth he was able to assemble and co-ordinate a host of fellow-workers, so that the work came out steadily in the period from April 1, 1932 to the outbreak of the war. Kittel has not been privileged to see the completion of his life work. When he returned to his house in Tübingen after arrest and banishment, and planned to take up the task again, he was called away in the midst of his plans on July 11, 1948. If the name of Rudolf Kittel is most closely linked with the edition of the text of the OT, that of his son Gerhard Kittel is indissolubly associated with the Theological Dictionary of the New Testament.

The Dictionary did not merely lose its editor, for other contributors have also been snatched away by death during the past years, notably J. Schniewind, J. Behm, O. Grether, H. Preisker, and F. Hauck. We think of them with respect and gratitude.

After the war a new beginning had to be made. Records had been destroyed by bombing, contributors had in many cases moved to new addresses, and we also had to find out whether some authors would be allowed to take further part in the work. When Kittel wired me to come to his death bed, I was firmly resolved to refuse any invitation to take up the task of editing, for I realised how much time it would consume and how many difficulties it would involve. But when I saw the situation of the publishers and the original editor, I could not reject the appeal of Gerhard Kittel. I thus gave up other plans in order to take up and continue the work.

As with the earlier volumes published under Kittel's direction, loyal helpers have given solid and sacrificial service in reading manuscripts and correcting proofs. It is a pleasure to be able to mention these colleagues whose names hardly appear elsewhere. For all their help and trouble I pay grateful tribute to G. Bertram, J. Betz, E. Dammann, A. Debrunner, J. Fichtner, A. Hiller, A. Jehle, P. Katz, H. Kleinknecht, H. Krämer, K. G. Kuhn, E. Lochse, T. W. Manson, R. Meyer, E. Nestle, K. H. Schelkle, G. Schlichting, D. Schwertfeger, K. Staab, K. Steinwender, H. Traub, and E. Würthwein. These men have made a big contribution to the reliability of the work by additions in their special fields, by references, by checking quotations, and by proof-reading.

When H. Cremer compiled his Dictionary, he did not aim to write a dogmatics in alphabetical form. He had a purely philological concern to bring out the significance and bearing of the Greek words in the New Testament. He believed, of course, that fundamental philological research could aid theology and the practical ministry. G. Kittel shared this concern even though he adopted a different external form from that of Cremer's Dictionary. He hoped that the labours of the Theological Dictionary of the New Testament would also contribute to the history of religion and to philology. But in the first instance the findings were designed to serve the pastor in his preaching and teaching. If this has been done, at least to a modest degree, by the previous volumes, the Theological Dictionary has fulfilled its task in spite of all its defects.

G. Friedrich

Kiel, March 13, 1954.

Editor's Preface

The post-war volumes of the Theological Dictionary of the New Testament are distinguished from the first four by many special features. Gerhard Friedrich succeeds Gerhard Kittel as editor. The fall of Hitler has made possible wider international contacts, especially with scholars of the English-speaking world. The series begins to benefit not only from never developments in biblical and theological studies but also from exciting discoveries like the Dead Sea Scrolls.

These changes have certain important implications for the Dictionary. Some of the judgments in earlier articles have had to be reconsidered. A place has had to be found for additional material. Points not originally thought to be significant have had to be discussed. In a work extending over so many decades some of this would have been inevitable in any case. The break between the Kittel and the Friedrich volumes, however, has made an even more imperious demand, even at the risk of adding to the final size of the work.

Naturally the purpose, design and structure of the Dictionary remain the same. Nor is there any change in either its proper use or its enduring value. Added interest is imparted, however, by the fact that the post-war volumes bring us increasingly into the sphere of modern research and debate. Readers of the present version will also profit by the fact that few of even the most important articles in these later volumes have ever been offered previously in English translation.

A great debt is again owed to Professor F. F. Bruce of Manchester University for his invaluable and indefatigable labours in proof reading. If some errors still slip through the net — and we are grateful to readers who call attention to these — there is the consolation that Dr. Bruce in particular has been able to correct not a few errors in the original German.

In the present volume thanks are also expressed to the Student Christian Movement Press for their courtesy in allowing us to use, at the author's request, the revisions in the article παῖς θεοῦ which Dr. J. Jeremias made for the second edition of the English version, *The Servant of God, Studies in Biblical Theology*, 20, S.C.M. Press, London, 1965.

Pasadena, California, Ascension Day, 1967.   *G. W. Bromiley*

Contents

Page

Contents   XIII

Contributors

Editor :

Gerhard Friedrich, Kiel.

Contributors :

Otto Bauernfeind, Tübingen.
Johannes Behm †, Berlin.
Georg Bertram, Gieszen.
Hans Bietenhard, Bern.
Rudolf Bultmann, Marburg.
Gerhard Delling, Halle.
Johannes Fichtner, Bethel.
Werner Foerster, Münster.
Heinrich Greeven, Bethel.
Oskar Grether †, Erlangen.
Friedrich Hauck †, Erlangen.
Hans Wolfgang Heidland, Karlsruhe.
Johannes Horst, Marburg.
Joachim Jeremias, Göttingen.
Peter Katz, Cambridge.
Hermann Kleinknecht, Münster.
Karl Georg Kuhn, Göttingen.
Rudolf Meyer, Jena.
Wilhelm Michaelis, Bern.
Otto Michel, Tübingen.
Albrecht Oepke, Leipzig.
Herbert Preisker †, Jena.
Otto Procksch †, Erlangen.
Gottfried Quell, Rostock.
Gerhard von Rad, Heidelberg.
Bo Reicke, Basel.
Ernst Harald Riesenfeld, Uppsala.
Heinrich Schlier, Bonn.
Karl Ludwig Schmidt, Basel.
Martin Anton Schmidt, Basel.
Otto Schmitz, Münster, Wuppertal.
Johannes Schneider, Berlin.
Gottlob Schrenk, Zürich.
Heinrich Seesemann, Frankfurt a.M.
Erik Sjöberg, Johanneshof (Sweden).
Gustav Stählin, Mainz.
Helmut Traub, Stuttgart.
Walther Zimmerli, Göttingen.

| † ξένος, † ξενία, † ξενίζω, † ξενοδοχέω, † φιλοξενία, † φιλόξενος | (→ ἀλλογενής, ἀλλόφυλος, I, 266 f.; βάρβαρος, I, 546-553; ἔθνος, II, 364-372; παρεπίδημος, πάροικος, προσήλυτος, φίλος). |

Contents : A. The Tension in the ξένος Concept. B. Foreigner and Foreign in the Judgment of Antiquity : 1. Greeks and Romans : a. The Treatment of Foreigners ; b. The Evaluation of the Foreign in Religion ; 2. Israelites and Jews : a. Foreign Peoples, Resident Aliens and Foreigners Temporarily Present : (a) Linguistic Terms, (b) Basic Judgment ; b. Historical Survey : (a) The OT Period, (b) Later Judaism ; c. Graves of Foreigners ; 3. The Attitude of Christians to Foreigners. C. The Custom of Hospitality : 1. Greeks and Romans : a. Private ; b. Public ; c. Hospices and Inns ; 2. Israelites and Jews ; 3. Christians : a. The NT : (a) Terms, (b) In the Story and Message of Jesus, (c) In Exhortation. (d) Motives for Primitive Christian Hospitality ; b. The Early Church ; 4. Christ the Host. D. Foreign as a Religious Concept : 1. The Greek and Biblical View of Foreignness ; 2. Foreignness in Hellenistic Judaism ; 3. Foreignness in the NT : a. The Foreignness of God and Christ ; b. The Foreignness of Christians : (a) Legal Terminology, (b) OT Prototypes ; c. The Rejection of the Foreign, but without Exclusion of Foreigners ; d. The Devil as Foreigner ; 4. Fusions of Biblical and Greek Views of Foreignness : a. The Experience and Ethos of Foreignness in Gnosticism ; b. The Alien God of Marcion.

A. The Tension in the ξένος Concept.

1. Words from the stem ξεν- bear on the one side the concept of "foreign," "alien" (also "appearing strange" or "creating distaste") and on the other side that of "guest." Hence ξένος can be on the one hand par. to μέτοικος (Plut. De Exilio, 17; II, 607a),

---

ξ έ ν ο ς. Generally on A.: Moult.-Mill., Liddell-Scott, Pass., Pr.-Bauer[3], s.v., Cr.-Kö., 288 f. (παρεπίδημος), 781 f. (παροικέω, παροικία, πάροικος); O. Rühle, RGG[2], II, 773 f.: Art. "Fremde, 1"; V. Pappafava, Über d. bürgerliche Rechtsstellung d. Fremden (Germ. tr. M. Leesberg, 1884); A. H. Post, Grundriss d. ethnologischen Jurisprudenz, I (1894), 448-451; W. Schulze, Kleine Schriften (1934), 203 ff.; P. Thieme, "Der Fremdling im Rigveda," Abh.en f. d. Kunde des Morgenlandes, XXIII, 2, 1938); on the etym.: T. Benfey, "ξένος. κῶμος," Zschr. f. vergleichende Sprachforschung, 8 (1859), 81 ff.; Prellwitz, Etym. Wört, 318; Boisacq, 677 f. On B.: C. F. v. Nägelsbach, Homerische Theol.[2] (1861), 294-302; A. Dieterich, Nekyia[2] (1913), 163 ff.; F. Lübker, Reallexikon d. klass. Altertums[8] (1914), 385 (Art. "Fremdenrecht"), 866 (Art. "Proxenos"); G. Busolt-H. Swoboda, Gr. Staatskunde, I (1920), 292-303; II (1926), 1240-1264; C. Phillipson, The International Law and Custom of Ancient Greece and Rome (1911), esp. I, 39 ff., 122 ff., 300; U. v. Wilamowitz-Moellendorff, Staat u. Gesellschaft d. Griechen u. Römer[2] (1923), 39-41. J. Benzinger, Hebr. Archäologie[2] (1907), 284-286; also RE[3], 6, 262-265 : Art. "Fremdlinge bei d. Hebräern"; A. Bertholet, D. Stellung d. Israeliten u. d. Juden zu den Fremden (1896, quoted as Bertholet); also RGG[2], II, 774-776 : Art. "Fremde u. Heiden in Israel"; Bousset-Gressm., 75 ff., 89 ff.; F. Buhl, Die socialen Verhältnisse d. Israeliten (1899), 47-51; G. Boström, "Proverbiastudien : Die Weisheit u. d. fremde Weib in Spr. 1-9," Lunds Universitets Ársskrift, NF Avd. 1, XXX, No. 3; A. Geiger, Urschrift u. Übersetzungen d. Bibel in ihrer Abhängigkeit von d. inneren Entwickelung d. Judenthums (1857), 349-366; E. Grünebaum, "Die Fremden (Gerim) nach rabb. Gesetzen," Jüd. Zschr. f. Wissenschaft u. Leben, 8 (1870), 43-57; "Der Fremde (Ger) nach rabb. Begriffen," ibid., 9 (1871), 164-172;

πάροικος (Eph. 2; 19) etc. (also ἀνοίκειος, Suid. ξ 35), and on the other hand to
φίλος[1]; again, on the one hand it is the opp. of πολίτης (Jos. Vit., 372), ἐλεύθερος
(Demosth., 57, 45), ἀστός,[2] on the other of ξενοδόχος (Hom. Od., 8, 543), though it
can also be a synon. of this (Hom. Il., 21, 42).[3]

In the NT it is used predominantly in the sense of "strange" (adj. 3 Jn. 5; Hb. 13:9;
also Mt. 25:35 ff.; noun Eph. 2:19; Hb. 11:13), "foreign" (adj. Ac. 17:18, noun v. 21,
Mt. 27:7), also "surprising" (1 Pt. 4:12; Fr. of an Unknown Gospel, ed. H. I. Bell-
T. C. Skeat [1935], 13). It does not have the sense of "guest," though we find the less
common "host" (R. 16:23). The verb ξενίζω can mean in the NT both "to surprise," "to
be strange to" (Ac. 17:20; 1 Pt. 4:4, 12) and also "to entertain," "to lodge" (Ac. 10:23
etc.; Hb. 13:2). All the other derivates found in the NT (ξενία, ξενοδοχέω, φιλοξενία,
φιλόξενος) belong exclusively to the domain of hospitality → C. 3. a.

2. The linguistic data reveal already a distinctive cleavage. In the first instance
the ξένος is the "stranger." Between the stranger and those around him there is
reciprocal tension. He is a man from without, strange, hard to fathom, surprising,

---

G. Kittel, "Das Konnubium mit den Nichtjuden im antiken Judentum," FJFr, II (1937),
30-62; E. Kalt, Bibl. Reallexikon², I (1938), 558-560 : Art. "Fremde"; T. Nöldeke, Art.
"Fremde" in D. Schenkel, Bibellex., II, 298-302; Weber, 57-79. W. Brandt, "Die geringsten
Brüder," Jbch. d. Theol. Schule Bethel, 8 (1937), 1-28; A. Wikenhauser, "Die Liebeswerke
in dem Gerichtsgemälde Mt. 25:31-46," BZ, 20 (1932), 366-377. On C.: E. Buchholz, Die
homerischen Realien, II, 2 (1883), 38-53 (with older bibl., 38, n. 3); G. Egerer, "Die
homerische Gastfreundschaft" (Progr. Salzburg, 1881); L. Friedländer, Darstellungen aus
der Sittengesch. Roms⁹, I (1919), esp. 343 ff.; R. v. Ihering, "Die Gastfreundschaft im Altertum," Deutsche Rundschau, 51 (1887), 357-397 (quoted as v. Ihering); also Vorgeschichte
d. Indoeuropäer (1894), 275 ff.; R. Leonhard, Art. "Hospitium," Pauly-W., VIII (1913),
2493-2498 (with bibl.); H. Blümner, Die röm. Privataltertümer (1911), 450 ff.; Lübker, 401
(Art. "Gasthäuser"); O. Schrader-A. Nehring, Reallex. d. indogerm. Altertumskunde, I
(1923), 346-349. Benzinger, 124 f., 131 f.; Grundt, Art. "Gast," "Gastfreundschaft," in
Schenkel, II, 331-333; Kalt, 597 f.; Art. "Gastfreundschaft"; M. Löhr, "Gastfreundschaft im
Lande d. Bibel einst u. jetzt," PJB, 2 (1906), 52-63; O. Rühle, RGG², II, 863 f.: Art. "Gast-
freundschaft"; Str.-B., IV, 565-571; A. Wünsche, Neue Beiträge zur Erläuterung d. Evan-
gelien aus Talmud u. Midr. (1878), esp. 140 f., 322. H. Bolkestein, "Ξενών Gastverblijf,
Pelgrimsherberg, Armhuis" (Mededeelingen der Koninklijke Akademie van Wetenschappen,
Afdeeling Letterkunde, 84 B, 3 ; 1937); H. J. Cadbury, "Lexical Notes on Luke-Acts : III.
Luke's Interest in Lodging," JBL, 45 (1926), 305 ff.; Harnack, Mission u. Ausbreitung d.
Chrtts.⁴ (1924), 200-220, esp. 201, n. 1; D. W. Riddle, "Early Christian Hospitality : A
Factor in the Gospel Transmission," JBL, 57 (1938), 141-154; Wnd. Hb., 116 on 13:2; Krüll,
Art. "Gastfreundschaft" in F. X. Kraus, Real-Enzykl. d. chr. Altertümer, I (1882), 548-550;
W. Liese, Art. "Gastfreundschaft" in Lex. Th. K.², IV (1932), 297 f.; J. Sauer, Art. "Gast-
freundschaft" in M. Buchberger, Kirchl. Handlexikon, I (1907), 1596 f. (both Liese and
Sauer follow Krüll closely). On D.: Wnd. 2 K., 166 on 5:6; R. Bultmann, "D. Bedeutung d.
neuerschlossenen mandäischen u. manichäischen Quellen f. das Verständnis d. Joh.-Ev.,"
ZNW, 24 (1925), 119-123 (quoted as Bultmann); also Das Ev. d. Joh. (1941), passim
(42, 102, n. 1 etc.); A. v. Harnack, Marcion : Das Ev. vom Fremden Gott² (TU, 45, 1924),
esp. 1 ff., 118 ff.; H. Jonas, Gnosis u. spätantiker Geist, I : "Die mythologische Gnosis"
(1934), esp. 94 ff.; Rgg. Hb., 361 ff.

[1] Cf. the common combinations φίλος καὶ ξένος (Xenoph. An., II, 1, 5), φιλία καὶ
ξενία (Demosth., 18, 51 f., antonym μισθαρνία) etc.; originally specifically the "guest,"
then synon. with φίλος (cf. Suid. ξ 45 : ξένος ὁ φίλος, Philo Vit. Mos., I, 35). Already
in the older Aryan world the stranger received into protective table fellowship becomes a
friend, cf. Thieme, 15, also 102 ff. (ari = "stranger," aryá = "hospitable," aryamán =
"guest," "friend").

[2] ἀστοὶ καὶ ξένοι was a formal combination in class. tragedy (e.g., Soph. Oed. Col., 13)
and prose (e.g., Xenoph. Mem., I, 2, 60); it was taken up in similar formulae by later
rhetoric ; cf. Ac. 17:21 and E. Norden, Agnostos Theos (1913), 336; also Busolt-Swoboda,
II, 778 (further instances in n. 4), 878.

unsettling, sinister. But to the stranger his odd and different environment is also disturbing and threatening. There thus arises mutual fear, especially of the magical powers of what is foreign. [4] This is the first and basic mood associated with ξένος, no less in early antiquity than in other cultures. On the other hand, the ξένος is the "friend" (→ n. 1) who is associated with the other in the beautiful reciprocity of hospitality. This overcomes the distance of strangeness and the tension of being a foreigner. What the ξένος enjoys as a guest, *mansio et focus, panis et aqua*, and often more, he is obviously ready to repay just as generously as host. [5] The whole relation rests on mutual trust instead of fear. [6]

On closer investigation this strange contradiction in the concept of ξένος [7] resolves itself into a historical cultural sequence. [8] In all peoples the stranger is originally an enemy; this is why many nations have only a single word for both. [9] In the first instance, then, the stranger is an outlaw. [10] To kill him seems to be the easiest way to dispose of the sinister, unknown and threatening element in him. At a higher stage other ways were sought to achieve the same end. In particular, counter-magic was used reciprocally to dispel the sinister by the sinister. [11] But in any case the stranger was absolutely without any rights. [12]

Eventually men found a new, better and surprising way to master the hostile alien, namely, the way of friendship. In fact, animistic fear seems in many cases to have provided the first impulse for the noble custom of hospitality found among many primitive peoples. Even in Homer the basic feeling towards the guest is αἰδώς. [13] But then it came to be realised that the basic feeling was reciprocal, and that it was more deeply seated in aliens in a strange land than in natives of the land who encountered aliens. All peoples knew the wretchedness of being in an alien country. [14] Hence the stranger came to be granted the fellowship of table and protection, and instead of being an outlaw he became a ward of law and

---

[3] Cf. Pollux Onomast., 1, 74 : καλεῖται δὲ ὁ ὑποδεχόμενος καὶ ὁ ὑποδεχθεὶς ξένος· ἰδίως δὲ ὁ ὑποδεχόμενος ξενοδόχος. Further instances in Pass., Liddell-Scott, *s.v. Hospes* has the same twofold meaning, though "host" seems to be primary here : == *hostipots,* cf. Slav. *gospodi* == "lord" : What makes the lord a lord is his hospitality ; cf. A. Walde-J. B. Hofmann, *Lat. Etym. Wörterbuch*³, I (1938), 660 f.; Thieme, 81-89, 159, 138.

[4] Cf. Thieme, 42 f.

[5] Cf. Poll. Onom., 3, 60, *s.v.* ἰδιόξενος.

[6] For these ideas in the Rigveda, Thieme, 39 f., 68.

[7] For the same reason the Sanskrit *ari* can mean both friend and foe, Thieme, 8 ff., 150 f.

[8] v. Ihering, 368 f.

[9] The basic sense of *hostis* (identical with host, → n. 35), and perhaps also of ἐχθρός (probably by way of ἐχθός == ἐκτός from ἐκ, cf. Busolt-Swoboda, II, 1240, n. 5; Phillipson, I, 127; v. Wilamowitz-Moellendorff, 38; though cf. A. Vaniček, *Griech.-lat. etym. Wörterbuch* [1877], II, 1059 with n. 2), is "alien," "stranger," with the underlying sense of "enemy."

[10] Thus one of the most terrible punishments is to declare someone a stranger, i.e., to outlaw him ; giving succour to an outlaw is expressly forbidden (cf. Germany, Norway, Iceland); Schulze, 201 f.; also Thieme, 44 ff.

[11] Examples in J. G. Frazer, *The Golden Bough* (1928), 285 ff.; Rühle, "Fremde," 773.

[12] v. Ihering, *op. cit.,* shows convincingly that to leave the alien without rights was originally necessary to protect the rights of nationals, and was also needed to bind together the small emerging states of an early period.

[13] So Thieme, 156 (though cf. → n. 125); Thieme, 155 gives a striking example of religious fear as the driving force behind hospitality.

[14] Thus popular etym. derives *egens* from *ex-gens* (Festus, De Verborum Significatu, ed. W. M. Lindsay [Glossaria Latina, IV, 1930], *s.v.* 192 == 67 Teubn.); cf. also Plat. Leg., V, 729e : ἔρημος γὰρ ὢν ὁ ξένος ἑταίρων τε καὶ ξυγγενῶν ἐλεεινότερος ἀνθρώποις καὶ θεοῖς.

religion.[15] The obligation of the host to the guest, which is sometimes stronger than that to neighbours and relatives,[16] can even extend to the offering of life itself, → 25.

B. Foreigner and Foreign in the Judgment of Antiquity.

1. Greeks and Romans.

a. The Treatment of Foreigners.

Homer already divided the nations into savages who despised law and those who were hospitable and feared God, Od., 6, 119 ff.; 9, 175 f.: "Fear of God, hospitality and civilisation are co-extensive."[17] One of the distinguishing marks between Gks. and barbarians is that the former are kind to strangers ; on the other hand, we read in Strabo, XVII, 1, 19 : φησὶ δ᾽ Ἐρατοσθένης κοινὸν ... εἶναι τοῖς βαρβάροις πᾶσιν ἔθος τὴν ξενηλασίαν. Here, then, we have the proud consciousness of the Aryan self-designation as arya = hospitable,[18] → n. 1. How far this judgment was justified is open to question. For ancient Greece was marked by a definite reserve towards all aliens, cf. esp. the Spartans with their proverbial ξενηλασία, Xenoph. Resp. Lac., 14, 4; Thuc., 1, 144; Plut. Lycurgus, 27 (I, 56); Instituta Laconica, 20 (II, 238e), and the corresponding prohibition of foreign travel Plut. Lyc., loc. cit.; Instituta Lac., 19 (II, 238d e : ἵνα μὴ ξενικῶν ἐθῶν καὶ βίων ἀπαιδεύτων μετέχωσι), but cf. other states too.[19] This attitude is summed up in the one word βάρβαρος and in the principle : βαρβάρων δ᾽ Ἕλληνας ἄρχειν εἰκός, ὡς ταὐτὸ φύσει βάρβαρον καὶ δοῦλον ὄν, Aristot. Pol., I, 2, 1252b, 8 f.[20] Worth noting, too, is the avoidance of objects from abroad in cultic observance (Hdt., 5, 88) and the exclusion of aliens from the cultus → 10. On the other hand, there was also a definite attraction to the stranger, esp. in Athens, which Eur. proudly calls λιμένα τὸν εὐξεινότατον ναύταις, Hipp., 157.[21] This explains the large number of aliens always to be found in Athens, cf. Ac. 17:21, → n. 2, → 7, 10 ff.

In sum, one is forced to admit that in Aryan antiquity aliens for a long time had no rights,[22] nor was there any real international law. The statement of Livy (31, 29, 15):

---

[15] Löhr, 52 f.; on rules in the Rigveda cf. Thieme, 14 ff., among the Arabs, E. Glaser, "Zum altbiblischen Gebot d. Nächstenliebe," Ost u. West, 5 (1905), 647 ff. F. Rückert (Hamâsa [1846], III, 431; also VI, 724): the proud Bedouin says : I am the servant of the guest as long as he stays with me, but there is nothing else of the servant about me.

[16] Gellius, V, 13, 5 : In officiis apud maiores ita observatum est : primum tutelae, deinde hospiti, deinde clienti, tum cognato, postea affini ; cf. Hom. Od., 8, 546 ("as a brother").

[17] v. Ihering, 367; cf. also Thieme, 146 f., 18 ff.

[18] Thieme has tried to prove this derivation (esp. 145 ff.), but cf. A. Debrunner, Indogerm. Forsch., 57 (1940), 146 f., and esp. H. Siegert, Wörter u. Sachen, NF (1941/42), 85.

[19] Phillipson, I, 128 f. Naturally there were exceptions in Sparta, cf. Lichas who acc. to Xenoph. Mem., I, 2, 61 ταῖς γυμνοπαιδίαις τοὺς ἐπιδημοῦντας ἐν Λακεδαίμονι ξένους ἐδείπνιζε, and Teles (De Fuga, p. 28, 7 ff., Hense) even speaks of a special fairness towards foreigners.

[20] Ibid., 6, 1255a, 29; III, 14, 1285a, 20.

[21] The same pride in the friendliness of Athens to aliens may be seen in Aristoph. Ra., 457 ff.: εὐσεβῆ τε διήγομεν τρόπον περὶ τοὺς ξένους καὶ τοὺς ἰδιώτας. Cf. also Soph. Oed. Col., 562-8, though also the similar laudatory epithet which Emped. (Fr., 112, 3; I, 354, 16, Diels) uses of his own city Acragas: ξείνων αἰδοῖοι λιμένες κακότητος ἄπειροι. For further instances relative to Athens cf. Phillipson, 134 f.

[22] Cf. Lübker, 385; typical is the phrase ἀτίμητος μετανάστης ("a disregarded stranger") in Hom. Il., 9, 648; 16, 59; hence it was later thought to be noteworthy that the inhabitants of Lampsacos not only buried Anaxagoras even though he was a ξένος, but ἔτι καὶ νῦν τιμῶσιν (Aristot. Rhet., II, 23, 1398b, 15).

cum alienigenis, cum barbaris aeternum omnibus Graecis bellum est, is the exaggeration of a later and lofty sense of culture, but no less exaggerated is the self-designation of the race if *arya* does really mean hospitable. Among the Aryans we find the same twofold attitude towards foreigners as among the Semites, i.e., their treatment as enemies [23] and yet also a well-developed law of hospitality, → C. 1.

As relations between states constantly developed, together with trade and commerce, aliens came to have well-defined rights in all countries. All mankind was thus recognised to be fundamentally an area of law, and the foundation was laid for general international law. Religion played a primary part in this development. Among the Gks. first it ended the old defencelessness of the alien. [24] For the decisive pt. even among Gks. of an earlier period was that the stranger stood under the protection of the gods. Zeus himself, ὁ ἱκέσιος, is his defence, and the Furies are his avengers, → 17, 12 ff. [25]

The individual provisions of the Gk. law of aliens concerning πρόξενοι [26] and ξενοδίκαι, [27] μέτοικοι (πάροικοι) [28] and (παρ)επιδημοῦντες ξένοι, [29] belong to legal history. In relation to the NT it is more important that there developed a code of conduct towards ξένοι. In the old lists of vices, esp. in connection with judgment in the underworld, maltreating the ξένος comes just after ungodliness and impiety *vis-à-vis* parents, [30] and in the morality of popular philosophy in the Hell. period τὸ καθῆκον πρὸς ξένους has an assured place. [31] In this period, too, it is emphasised in the much-

---

[23] E.g., deporting and robbing (συλᾶν), cf. Hom. Il., 11, 669 ff.; Od., 14, 262 ff.; Nägelsbach, 294 ff., 303 ff. A late trace of this is to be found in the Athenian ordinance that the (resident) alien is subject to the polemarchos, the minister of war; cf. Aristot. Fr., 387, 1542b, 9 : δίκαι ξένων λαγχάνονται πρὸς τὸν πολέμαρχον (on this Busolt-Swoboda, II, 1093 ff.).

[24] Cf. Schulze, 203-205.

[25] It is unjust and foolish of Grünebaum (44) to conclude from Zeus' title as ἱκέσιος that foreigners helplessly begged for protection as though they had no rights among pagans, and that Jewish law was far in advance of that of antiquity in the matter of aliens. For basically the attitude is the same as that of the Gks. when Dt. 10:18 f. bases the laws relating to strangers on the love of God for strangers (for the same thought in Rabb. Judaism cf. M. Ex., 101a on 22:20 and Nu. r., 8 [148c], Str.-B., I, 355 f., also 928h), or when Philo in Vit. Mos., I, 36 derives the demand for righteous treatment of aliens as ἐλεύθεροι, ξένοι, ἱκέται and μέτοικοι from fear of the ἐλευθέριος καὶ ξένιος καὶ ἱκέσιος καὶ ἐφέστιος θεός, cf. also → c. 3. a (d). To be sure, the self-evaluation of the Gks. (→ 4) is just as narrow and self-righteous.

[26] Cf. Poll. Onom., 3, 59, and on this Lübker, 866; Busolt-Swoboda, II, 1246-1249, with bibl. 1246, n. 1.

[27] Cf. Ditt. Syll.³, II, 647, 38; Busolt-Swoboda, I, 487 and n. 2; A. Körte, "Die attischen ξενοδίκαι," Herm., 68 (1933), 238 ff. Elsewhere (Gortyn in Crete) the corresponding court was called ξένιος κόσμος (cf. Collitz, Gr. Dial. Inschr. 4981, 4; 4984, 15 etc.).

[28] The full expression is ξένοι μέτοικοι (Soph. Oed. Tyr., 452 etc.), but usually ξένοι is left out. Cf. H. Hommel, Art. "Metoikoi," Pauly-W., XV (1932), 1413-1458; U. v. Wilamowitz-Moellendorff, "Demotika d. attischen Metöken," Herm., 22 (1887), 107-128, 211-259; Phillipson, I, 157 ff.

[29] Cf. Ditt. Or., 268, 9; Syll.³, 1157, 80 f.; Harpokration, *s.v.* μετοίκιον, and esp. Ac. 2:9 f.: 17:21, → n. 203; also Just. Apol., 67, 6, → 24, 31 ff.

[30] Cf. Aristoph. Ra., 147: εἴ που ξένον τις ἠδίκηκε πώποτε κτλ., though often in such lists the ξένος must yield his place to the country (cf. Diog. L., 7, 108); there is a similar noteworthy shift in India from the Vedic to the epic period when the ideal of friendliness to strangers was replaced by that of friendliness to Brahmans; Thieme, 156, and on this whole question Dieterich, *op. cit.*; K. Weidinger, *D. Haustafeln* (1928), 27 ff.

[31] Epictet.'s ideal pupil asks (II, 17, 31) τί (μοι) πρὸς ξένους (ἐστὶ καθῆκον); (previously the same question is asked concerning the gods, parents, brethren, country). Cf. also Plut. Lib. Educ., 10, II, 7e : πῶς ἀλλοτρίοις ... χρηστέον ἐστίν. Already in Aesch. Suppl. (701 ff.) the three chief commands of Dike are for justice to strangers, and veneration for the native gods and for parents, cf. Eur. Fr., 311; TGF² (1926), 452.

cultivated literary genre of consolatory writings for the exiled (→ παραμυθέομαι) that only ἄφρονες treat the ξένος badly (Plut. De Exilio, II, 607a). On the other hand, a specific type of conduct is also expected from the alien, cf. the ideal picture in Eur. Suppl., 891-899, and if he settles he incurs certain obligations; he must ξενικὰ τελεῖν (Demosth., 57, 34) and render military service. In this respect foreigners gained such importance in Athens, which raised a kind of foreign legion, [32] that mercenaries were called ξένοι (Suid. ξ 20). [33] As distinct from these actual relations Plato in his ideal state (Leg., VIII, 845 ff.) sketched the basic outlines of a new order for ξένοι which would grant certain concessions but finally amount to a milder form of the Spartan ξενηλασία. [34]

The relation to aliens developed in much the same way in Rome. *Hostis* originally means a stranger, who is *eo ipso* an enemy. [35] Even up to the imperial period the alien was theoretically without protection or rights, [36] and only by finding a host could he secure accommodation, for inns were primarily for nationals, not aliens (→ 18, 24 ff.), and only by acquiring a *patronus* could he enjoy legal protection. As aliens had no legal

---

[32] Cf. Suid. ξ 34. The using of resident aliens as soldiers was extended to the raising of mercenaries abroad; the wars of the Hell. period were generally fought with troops of this kind, cf. Muson., p. 46, 14 f., Hense: ξενικὸν στράτευμα. The Maccabeans were familiar with this way of raising troops (ξενολογεῖν, 1 Macc. 4:35; 11:38; 15:3; ξενοτροφεῖν, 2 Macc. 10:14), and with wars with ξέναι δυνάμεις (1 Macc. 11:38; 2 Macc. 10:24), but only on the part of Greek leaders; Jos. reports the same of the Jews in Ant., 13, 373 etc., cf. Bertholet, 239 f.

[33] Cf. also Ditt. Syll.³, I, 409, 25; II, 684, 26 f.; 732, 5, though cf. Demosth., 18, 51 f. (→ n. 1), where the ξένος (= φίλος) is contrasted with the μισθωτός. A noteworthy analogous shift in meaning may be seen in the fem. ξένη, for as the ξένος becomes a mercenary by selling his person, so the ξένη becomes a harlot. There were many foreign prostitutes in antiquity, e.g., Chariton, 3, 2: εὐκαταφρόνητόν ἐστι γυνὴ μόνη καὶ ξένη. The same change of meaning takes place in Heb., for the נָכְרִיָּה of Prv. (2:16 = 7:5; 5:20; 6:24; 23:27) is a "harlot." If less emphasis is here placed on her alien origin (Bertholet, 195), there is a clear allusion which is reflected in the general evaluation of foreign women in Prv. (5:1 ff.; 22:14), cf. Bertholet, 24. In keeping with the attenuation of נכריה in Prv. ("another," → n. 48), the LXX uses ἀλλοτρία, but cf. Σ Prv. 2:16: ἀπὸ γυναικὸς ἀλλοτρίας, ἀπὸ ξένης ἧς οἱ λόγοι ὀλισθηροί, ΣΘ 6:24; Θ 23:27 (here Σ uses πόρνη just before, an obvious syn.). But the fact that the LXX was familiar with the equation "strange woman" and "harlot" may be seen from the materially good transl. of זרה by γυνὴ πόρνη in Prv. 5:3 (v. 20 again ἀλλοτρία, "another than one's own wife," cf. A. Kuenen, *Hist.-krit. Einleitung in d. Bücher des AT*, III [1894], 94 f.; W. Frankenberg, "Über Abfassungsort u. -zeit sowie Art u. Inhalt v. Prv. I-IX," ZAW, 15 [1895], 120). In this connection we should also mention the use of the ambiguous זרים for strange gods (Dt. 32:16; Jer. 2:25; 3:13; cf. also Is. 17:10). These are adulterous lovers and idolatry is πορνεία. Finally the Aram. verbal root גור takes on the sense "to have illicit intercourse," "to commit adultery," for any closer dealings of foreigners with Israel are regarded as fornication, cf. Geiger, 54, esp. n. ††, and the Aram. parallels גְּיוֹרָא "stranger" and גִּיוֹרָא "adulterer," and on these E. Glaser, 649. The same meaning as ξένη is reached by a different route — namely, *via* the dubious development of inns (→ n. 135; cf. Friedländer, 348 f.; Blümner, 454, n. 3) — in the case of ξενία, "hospitality," "hostess"; cf. bSanh., 107b (אכסניא → n. 137); on this H. Gressmann, "Vom reichen Mann u. armen Lazarus" (AAB, 1918), 88, n. 4; H. L. Strack, *Jesus, d. Häretiker u. d. Christen* (1910), 32* with n. 2. The same obviously applies to the Roman *hospita* in BGU, VII, 1690, 4 (131 A.D.), cf. *Glotta*, 17 (1929), 218.

[34] Cf. H. Hommel, *op. cit.*, 1455 f.

[35] *Hostis* is the same word as guest, cf. Festus, 224, Lindsay (91, Teubn.): *hostis apud antiquos peregrinus dicebatur*; cf. Cic. Off., 1, 37; *hosticus* is "strange" and "hostile"; *hostilis facies* in Verg. Aen., 3, 407 means "face of a foe." Cf. Walde-Pok., I, 640 f.; Walde-Hofmann, *s.v.*, *hostis*; → n. 9.

[36] v. Ihering, 362.

rights, so, with women (e.g., in Eleusis), they were often excluded from cultic fellowship [37] and troublesome aliens might be deported at any time, as in Sparta. Special officials were appointed, as in Greece, to exercise jurisdiction over aliens — the *praetor peregrinus* from 247 B.C. — and already the Law of the Twelve Tables, following Gk. models, granted the privilege of prompt treatment to a *hostis* who was accompanied to the courts by his host. [38]

With the formation of larger states in the Hell. period, there came about a change in the concept of ξένος, for the idea of the alien receded more and more into the background and foreign parts increasingly lost their terrors even though those who were exiled still needed comfort and assurance (cf., e.g., Teles, p. 21 ff.; 12, 1 ff.). In the Hell. cities well-to-do and cultured ξένοι lived alongside natives without any palpable distinction, and in centres of culture like Athens they formed a considerable proportion of the educated class. Thus in Ac. 17:21 there is no difference between Athenians and aliens, who are at one in their interest in what is newest and in ξενίζοντα.

b. The Evaluation of the Foreign in Religion.

The attitude of the Bible to all that is foreign in religion is one of outright rejection. That of Hellenism, however, is ambiguous. καινὰ δαιμόνια were resisted as not native, and, with some reason, as a threat to morals. Nevertheless, many alien cults gained a footing. If comedy derided ξενικοί and spoke contemptuously of ξέναι δεισιδαιμονίαι, [39] they were pursued with frank curiosity. For all the proud distinction from barbarians, altars were set up to the *dii peregrini*.

In investigation of the attitude of Paul's varied hearers at Athens (Ac. 17:18 ff.), their evaluation of the ξένον, esp. in religion, is vital. For the mark of the καινὴ διδαχή (v. 19) and the basis of the tense expectation of the Athenians is: ξενίζοντά τινα (v. 20) and even ξένα δαιμόνια. [40] As they see it, is this something good or not? The frequently noted analogy to the trial of Socrates, who was accused as ἕτερα καινὰ δαιμόνια εἰσφέρων, has led to an understanding in terms of accusation even in the technical sense, i.e., before a court. [41] It is intrinsically conceivable that one group of Athenians (τινές, v. 18) is introduced as mockers, another (οἱ δέ) as accusers. But to me it seems to make better sense to see a distinction between mockers and the intellectually curious. The strongly emphasised desire to know (v. 19, 20, 21) does not confront the ξενίζοντα accusingly, but with a more or less serious interest, as in the depiction of Strabo (10, 3, 18), acc. to which Ἀθηναῖοι ὥσπερ περὶ τὰ ἄλλα φιλοξενοῦντες διατελοῦσιν, οὕτω καὶ περὶ τοὺς θεούς. Important in this connection is the observation [42] that the description of Athens and the Athenians in Ac. 17:18 ff. is obviously composed with a view to the address which follows. But then, as the predicate κατείδωλος in v. 16 prepares for the δεισιδαίμων of v. 22, so the interest in alien

---

[37] Cf. Festus, 198, Lindsay (72, Teubn.): *Exesto, extra esto. Sic enim lictor in quibusdam sacris clamitabat : hostis* (the alien), *vinctus, mulier, virgo exesto, sc. interesse prohibebatur.*

[38] This is the presupposition of Plaut. Curculio, I, 1, 5 : *si status condictus cum hoste intercedit dies, tamen est eundum quo imperant ingratiis* (cf. also Festus, 410, Lindsay [416 Teubn.], *s.v. status dies* <*cum hoste*>).

[39] Plut. Praec. Coniug., 19; II, 140d. On this whole question cf. J. Leipoldt, *Antisemitismus in d. alten Welt* (1933), 6; O. Kern, *D. Religion d. Griechen*, II (1935), 225 ff.

[40] The phrase is used in a very different sense ("strange demons") in Cl. Al. Prot., 67, 1.

[41] So K. Bornhäuser, *Studien z. Ag.* (1934), 139 f.; also Pr. Ag. on v. 19. There had at times been laws imposing death for the introduction of strange gods ; so Jos. Ap., 2, 267: τιμωρία κατὰ τῶν ξένον εἰσαγόντων θεὸν ὥριστο θάνατος. Here we are also told of the execution of a priestess : ὅτι ξένους ἐμύει θεούς. But in general times had changed since the trial of Socrates : πολλὰ γὰρ τῶν ξενικῶν ἱερῶν παρεδέξαντο (Strabo, 10, 3, 18), without legal action being taken against anyone. Cf. also Jos. Ap., *loc. cit.*, and on the whole question Wendland Hell. Kult., 127 ff.

[42] Cf. M. Dibelius, "Pls. auf dem Areopag," SAH, XXIX, 2 (1939), 44 ff.

gods in v. 18 is a preparatory par. to the altar dedicated to an unknown god in v. 23. [43] Acc. to the explicit note of Jerome [44] the inscription on this read : *Diis Asiae et Europae et Africae diis ignotis et peregrinis.* Even though Ac. leaves out the decisive term, the serious interest of the Athenians in the ξένον is established. [45] Paul devotes himself to this in his famous address. It is a defence against ridicule, but above all it is God's answer to a serious question, like the no less specifically oriented address of Peter in Ac. 2 (v. 12 f.). The Athenians, of course, ask in the sense of a *religio eventualis,* whereas Paul proclaims, not the one unknown and true god of the philosophy of religion, [46] but the very different God who for the world is in fact a strange God in the ultimate sense (→ D. 3. a): εἰ ἄνθρωπον ἐκήρυσσεν ἐσταυρῶσθαι, οὐ ξένον ἦν τὸ λεγόμενον· εἰ δὲ θεὸν ἔλεγεν ἐσταυρῶσθαι καὶ ἐγηγέρθαι, ὄντως ξενίζοντα εἰσέφερεν εἰς τὰς ἀκοὰς αὐτῶν. [47]

2. Israelites and Jews.

a. Foreign Peoples, Resident Aliens and Aliens Temporarily Present.

(a) Linguistic Terms. The words for aliens in the Heb. text are 1. זָר, of another family (Dt. 25:5) or race (Job 15:19), an alien (Is. 61:5), barbarian (Is. 25:2, 5), even enemy (Jl. 3:17, → n. 9); 2. גֵּר, the resident alien (Ex. 22:20 etc.; the Israelites in Egypt, Lv. 17:12 etc.; the Canaanites in Israel; opp. אֶזְרָח, Lv. 19:34); 3. תּוֹשָׁב, the resident, not necessarily an alien, without civil rights (Gn. 23:4 etc.); 4. בֶּן־נֵכָר and נָכְרִי, the alien who is temporarily in another land (Dt. 14:21 etc.).

The main LXX equivalents are, for זָר ἀλλότριος (e.g., Lv. 10:1) and ἀλλογενής (Ex. 29:33), once even ἐχθρός (Prv. 6:1), [48] for תּוֹשָׁב πάροικος (Ex. 12:45 etc.), which is often used for גֵּר too (Gn. 15:13 etc.), for גֵּר προσήλυτος, esp. in Dt. and P (Dt. 1:16 etc.), which at a later date, though not for the translators themselves, helped to promote a restriction to the proselyte in the narrower sense, [49] for נֵכָר and נָכְרִי ἀλλότριος (Gn. 31:15 etc., → n. 48), for נֵכָר also ἀλλογενής.

ξένος, then, is not the chief equivalent for any of the Heb. terms. It occurs only 5 times for נָכְרִי (2 S. 15:19; Ps. 69:8; Rt. 2:10; Lam. 5:2; Qoh. 6:2) and once for גֵּר (Job 31:32), almost exclusively in the hagiographa; in the other passages the Heb. equivalent cannot be decided. Thus in discussing the theme of foreigners in Israel → πάροικος, → ἀλλογενής, → ἀλλόφυλος, → ἀλλότριος and esp. → προσήλυτος have to be taken into account as well as ξένος. The Heb. זָר can also have the sense of "astonishing" (Is. 28:21; Prv. 23:33) which we find for ξένον or ξενίζον in the NT at 1 Pt. 4:12; Ac. 17:20, though זָר does not anywhere seem to have ξένος as its equivalent.

---

[43] Cf. E. Norden, *Agnostos Theos* (1913), 31 ff.; Dibelius, *op. cit.,* 16 ff. and the bibl. which he gives, 16, n. 2.

[44] Comm. in Ep. ad Titum 1:12 : MPL, 26, 572 C (or 607 B), cf. also the θεὸς χσενικός in IG, I², 324, 91, and on this O. Kern, *op. cit.,* 241; also Kern, 317 f. on the ξένος ἰατρός, an anonymous hero-saviour.

[45] On the connection between καινά and ξένα cf. Norden, 53, n. 3. The governor in Act. Andr., 4 (quoted by Norden) shows the same serious interest in a ξένος θεὸς δι' οὖ δυνήσομαι ἐπιγνῶναι τὴν ἀλήθειαν.

[46] Harnack Marcion, 1-3.

[47] Anon. author in J. A. Cramer, Catena in Acta SS Apostolorum (1838), 285.

[48] In fact זָר both here and elsewhere, cf. also נֵכָר (נָכְרִי) has the weaker sense of "another" (cf. Bertholet, 195); hence the LXX rightly has ἀλλότριος or ἔτερος (Ex. 30:9; Sir. 14:4) or even πέλας, "neighbour" (Prv. 27:2).

[49] Cf. Cr.-Kö., 447; Schürer, III, 175, n. 71 (176 f.); Geiger, 353 f.; Str.-B., II, 716; though cf. W. C. Allen, "On the Meaning of προσήλυτος in the Septuagint," Exp., 10 (1894), 264-275.

(b) Basic Judgment. Israel distinguishes sharply between alien peoples, individual aliens in transit, and resident aliens. (1) Foreign peoples are in the first instance eo ipso enemies (e.g., Is. 29:5): a זר is a צר, ἀλλόφυλοι means traditional enemies, the classical example being the Philistines, whose name the LXX renders 153 times with the disdainful ἀλλόφυλοι. [50] Here already a religious evaluation accompanies the national, for ἀλλόφυλοι is a tt. for the Gentiles (cf. 2 Macc. 10:2, 5; Ac. 10:28). [51] On both counts, both because they are enemies and because they are heathen, it is a terrible thing for aliens to occupy the land, [52] as it is also for Israelites to go abroad (Jer. 5:19, also 30:8) [53] and even to have to die there, [54] but especially for them to be treated as strangers in their own land and by their own people (cf. ψ 68:8; Jos 19:15, where ξένος is used by 'ΑΘ, → n. 10).

(2) This shows already that for Israel, too, it is a wretched thing to be an alien. There are many instances of this in the OT, e.g., Gn. 19:4 ff.; Ju. 19; also Test. L. 6:9: ἐδίωξαν 'Αβραάμ τὸν πατέρα ἡμῶν ξένον ὄντα, cf. v. 10. But under the influence of various factors the attitude to foreigners underwent a radical change, and foreign visitors were received with kindness and hospitality (→ C. 2). [55]

(3) A basic reversal in the attitude to foreigners may be noted in respect of the alien who sought to settle in the land, i.e., to become גר or תושב rather than נכרי. This brought him under the protection of the people (Ex. 22:20), [56] and he was committed to its care as one who stood in need of help like the widow or orphan (Dt. 14:29 etc.). [57] But while the passing foreigner was highly esteemed as a guest, the resident alien was despised [58] and might even be subjected to

---

[50] Geiger, 53 with n.

[51] ἀλλόφυλος is still used in this way of the Philistines in 1 Cl., 4, 13 and Barn., 12, 2; cf. also Dg., 5, 17: (Christians) ὑπὸ 'Ιουδαίων ὡς ἀλλόφυλοι πολεμοῦνται. The double sense of enemy and pagan is also echoed in the expression ἡ παρεμβολὴ τῶν ἀλλοφύλων (1 Macc. 4:30; 11:68; 1 Cl., 55, 4), cf. also the passages in Str.-B., I, 368 on Mt. 5:44 [α].

[52] Cf. Lam. 5:2: κληρονομία ἡμῶν μετεστράφη ἀλλοτρίοις, οἱ οἶκοι ἡμῶν ξένοις, also Hos. 8:7; Is. 1:7; Ps. 109:11; Qoh. 6:2 etc.

[53] Cf. ἐπὶ τὴν ξένην πιπράσκεσθαι (Plut. Solon, 13) = peregre venum ire (Gellius, 20, 1, 47); in Israel, too, slaves were mostly foreigners.

[54] Cf. the prayer in 3 Macc. 6:3: ἔπιδε ἐπὶ ... λαὸν ἐν ξένῃ γῇ ξένον ἀδίκως ἀπολλύμενον, πάτερ, also 2 Macc. 9:28; 5:9: ὁ συχνοὺς τῆς πατρίδος ἀποξενώσας ἐπὶ ξένης ἀπώλετο. For antiquity it was a dreadful thing to be buried abroad, and philosophy sought diligently to offer consolation for this, cf. Ps.-Plat. Ax., 368d; Muson., p. 47, 5, Hense; Epict., I, 27, 5; Teles De Fuga, p. 29, 1-30, 9, Hense; Epicurus meets complaint concerning it with his "comfort of union" (→ παραμυθέομαι): the dead man does not feel anything any more, not even the alien soil; cf. Philodem. De Morte, IV; col. XXV, 38, ed. Mekler.

[55] The divergent attitude of the Egyptians, who would not extend table fellowship to strangers (Gn. 43:32; cf. 46:34) because they were viewed as criminals and savages, was regarded with annoyance (though the descendants of Israel were to put the Egyptians in the shade in this regard, → 11, 31 ff.). On many other grounds the Egyptians were regarded as paradigms of the ἄξενον (cf. Phil. Abr., 107; Wis. 19:14), by the Gks. too (Hdt., 2, 41; Diod. S., 1, 67; Strabo, 17, 1, 19), though Hom. tells of the fine hospitality of an Egyptian king (Od., 14, 279 ff.) and Hdt. (3, 39) of the hospitality between the Egyptian king Amasis and the Gk. tyrant Polycrates.

[56] The privilege of protection becomes a basic mark of גר and has remained so up to modern times in the Arab world, cf. E. Glaser, 648 ff.; W. Heffening, Das islamische Fremdenrecht (1925). For a par. from antiquity in N. Rhodokanakis, cf. D. Nielsen, Handbch. d. alt-arab. Altertumskunde, I (1927), 124.

[57] A. Jirku, Das weltliche Recht im AT (1927), 80d, 86 f., shows from the number of pertinent statutes how important a role aliens played in the life of Israel.

[58] Nöldeke, 300: The traveller is honoured, the resident alien at most tolerated. Cf. Bertholet, 27 ff.

violence (cf. Ps. 94:6). There are many examples of this in the OT (cf. Gn. 12:26, 29 ff. etc.; also Ruth's astonishment at the friendliness of Boaz [2:10], and even Sir. 29:22-28 : ὀνειδισμὸς παροικίας, v. 23). Nevertheless, there gradually developed in Israel, too, a kind of law pertaining to aliens. If the Gerim, like the resident aliens in Athens,[59] had fewer rights, they also had lesser obligations (cf. 2 S. 15:19).[60] As in Greece (→ 5), this law is fundamentally religious, for the one who guarantees the protection of aliens is God, who loves the stranger (Dt. 10:18), and as His vice-gerent the king (cf. 1 S. 22:3 f.); as in other lands the patron can also be a distinguished man or powerful family to which the alien in some sense belongs (cf. 1 S. 27; 29 f.). From the very earliest portions on (cf. the book of the covenant, Ex. 20:10; 23:9; also Lv. 19:33 f.; Dt. 10:18 f.),[61] the OT Law certainly puts the alien under legal protection,[62] and religiously the גר is increasingly integrated into the people until finally the proselyte becomes a full member.

b. Historical Survey.

(a) The OT Period. From what has been said already it may be seen that the concept "alien" underwent certain changes, and that there were parallel changes in approach.

The correlate of national greatness under the first kings is an obvious openness to foreigners. Solomon not only prayed to Yahweh for aliens (1 K. 8:41-43) but even built temples to their gods in Jerusalem (1 K. 11:7 f.). These aberrations, continued under the later monarchy (Ahab, Manasseh), naturally led to a reaction headed by the prophets and the Protestants of Israel, the Nazirites and Rechabites. These radically reject everything foreign in custom, marriage and cultus. In particular, they oppose strange gods,[63] mysteriously and ambiguously called זָרִים, i.e., aliens and paramours (→ n. 33). When they are openly described as אֱלֹהֵי הַנֵּכָר (e.g., Jer. 5:19), they appear almost by rote as the object of the hi of סור, "to put away" (Gn. 35:2, 4; Jos. 24:23; Ju. 10:16; 1 S. 7:3; 2 Ch. 33:15); Jer. and Dt. speak against אֱלֹהִים אֲחֵרִים in the same way. The basic thesis of the OT is : μὴ ἔστω ἐν σοὶ θεὸς ξένος (=אֵל זָר, Σ ψ 80:9), and not only gods, but also strange fire (Lv. 10:1; Nu. 3:4; 26:61) and incense (Ex. 30:9) are an abomination to Yahweh (→ 4, 21 f., n. 41).

---

[59] → n. 28, acc. to Schürer, III, 175 "גֵּרִים are the same as μέτοικοι in the Attic state," though some qualifications are needed.

[60] At many legal points, however, the rights and obligations of non-Israelites are the same as those of Israelites, e.g., in respect of the Sabbath (Ex. 23:12).

[61] The so-called Holiness Code applies the fundamental law of neighbourly love (Lv. 19:18) explicitly to the ger (v. 34), and expressly sets him as πλησίον alongside the αὐτόχθων; on Rabb. exposition → 14, 7 ff.

[62] The ger who prospered even had the right to buy and keep Jews as slaves (Lv. 25:47). Thus in the Samaritan form of the blessing of Jacob (Gn. 49:14) one of the tribes, Issachar, was called a beast of burden for strangers (חֲמוֹר גֵּרִים, Geiger, 359 ff.; Bertholet, 6, n. 1), though Gunkel describes this as a "hardly passable" reading (ad loc., 484). On the other hand, in Israel as elsewhere (e.g., Egypt), though aliens did not have to render military service (→ n. 32), heavy demands were made on them in forced labour (1 K. 9:20 f.; 2 Ch. 2:17; cf. Dt. 29:10). This was particularly true in the case of the remaining pre-Israelite inhabitants of Palestine, who, as distinct from individual aliens residing among the Israelites, were treated very much as pariahs, cf. Jos. 9:22 ff.; Grünebaum, 46; Buhl, 93.

[63] Cf. K. Holzhey, *Jahve, der Gott Israels. Sein Kampf gg. d. fremden Götter v. Mose bis Chr.* (1936); H. Rust, "D. fremden Götter," ZMR, 54 (1939), 75, 81 f.

From this standpoint the alien himself is the representative of his religion, i.e., a Gentile. Efforts are thus made to overcome his foreignness, but in two opposing ways, first, by complete exclusion, secondly, by full inclusion. The first line is adopted mainly in respect of the נכרי, the second in respect of the גר. That is, the נכרי is always definitely outside, the גר inside, the people as it increasingly develops into a religious entity.

Exilic prophecy takes a further significant step. On the basis of its universalism it raises a claim on the part of Yahweh to alien peoples too, and it calls for mission among them (cf. Is. 42:6 ff.; 66:19; Jon.; Zech. 14; Tob. 14:6).[64] But the distinctive duality remains. Gentiles far from God are to be won for him (cf. also Is. 45:14 ff.; 56:1-8) and aliens as well as Israelites will be heirs of the land in the great theocratic state projected by Ez. (47:22 f.). At the same time, however, ungodly Gentiles must be destroyed (cf. Jer. 46-51; Ez. 25-32).

In the post-exilic period the attitude stiffens. While more energetic attempts are made to integrate the gerim (cf. Is. 56:3 ff.), there is an increasingly firm rejection of the goyim. Nehemiah's wall symbolises the partition between the people of God and strangers: καὶ ἐχωρίσθησαν οἱ υἱοὶ ᾿Ισραὴλ ἀπὸ παντὸς υἱοῦ ἀλλοτρίου (2 Εσδρ. 19:2). All mixed marriages are forbidden, and those existing are dissolved (Ezr. 9 f.).[65] There also arises bitter opposition, which is to last for centuries, against an alien people in the land itself, namely, the Samaritans. But because land and people form a sacred unity for the theology of the time, represented by P, the individual resident alien is religiously counted in with the national community (cf. 2 Ch. 15:9). He is treated as a brother and regarded as a compatriot (Neh. 10:29).[66] Religion and soil rather than blood and soil (cf. Dt. 23:2 ff.) are the factors which constitute national unity.

The one distinguishing mark of the OT approach to foreigners is that it always has its roots in a final responsibility towards God. For God's sake mercy is shown to the stranger in the land, for God's sake foreigners, who are Gentiles, are bitterly opposed, for God's sake attempts are made to bring aliens into the people of God. OT φιλοξενία, which is rightly extolled, is a fruit of religious adherence no less than the μισοξενία which is rightly censured.

(b) Later Judaism. In the period which followed it was natural for Jews to reject all forms of the ξενικόν in the field of religion.[67] What gave offence to those outside, however, was the extension of this attitude of rejection to all non-Jews. Already Hecataeus says concerning Moses (Diod. S., 40, 3, 4): διὰ γὰρ τὴν ἰδίαν ξενηλασίαν ἀπάνθρωπόν τινα καὶ μισόξενον βίον εἰσηγήσατο. That the Gentile judgment was

---

[64] Cf. M. Löhr, D. Missionsgedanke im AT (1896); K. Axenfeld, "D. jüd. Propaganda als Vorläuferin u. Wegbereiterin d. urchr. Mission," Missionswissenschaftliche Studien, Festschr. f. G. Warneck (1904), 1-80; H. Gressmann, "Jüd. Mission in d. Werdezeit d. Christentums," ZMR, 39 (1924), 169-183; E. Sellin, "Der Missionsgedanke im AT," NAMZ, 2 (1925), 33-45, 66-72; Bertholet, 113 ff., 191 ff.

[65] In the period of Dt. there seemed to be no objection to foreign marriages, cf. J. Wellhausen, Israelitische u. jüd. Geschichte⁷ (1914), 88, n. 3. Later there was general opposition, cf. Jub. 30:7-17; Tob. 4:12 f.

[66] He did not have equal civil rights like the μέτοικοι in Athens or the peregrini in Rome (esp. in respect of acquiring land), but he did have such rights before the law (cf. Lv. 24:22; Nu. 35:15) and esp. in religious matters (except for the passover, Ex. 12:48 and perhaps the feast of tabernacles, Lv. 23:42). In the completed people of God of the future many aliens would even be priests and Levites (Is. 66:21).

[67] E.g., Aboda Zara, 3, 1-4, 7; cf. Schl. Theol. d. Judt., 51 f. etc.

that the Jewish way of life was hostile to strangers[68] may be seen from the LXX additions to Est. 3:13d e etc.[69] If any book of the Bible justifies the opinion it is Est. The additions did not achieve their purpose of eradicating the impression. In particular the Jewish practice of cultically based separation, e.g., in the ghettos provided by the Diadochi (cf. Jos. Bell., 2, 488) gave additional support to the view, along with the ostentatious avoidance of entering Gentile houses (cf. Jn. 18:28; Ac. 10:28) or having table fellowship with Gentiles (Jub. 22:16; Sanh., 63b; 104a; Str.-B., IV, 376; Gl. 2:12 ff.), and not least the sharp prohibition of all intermarriage (→ n. 65). The attempts at forceful conversion made by the Maccabeans and Hyrcanus worked in the same direction (cf. also Jos. Vit., 113), as did also the severe restrictions in commerce and trade with non-Jews (cf. Aboda Zara, 1, 1 and 8; 2, 1-4; 4, 8 ff.).

But this was only one side. In the final years of the 1st cent. B.C. there were already two parties in the Jewish people, the orthodox, which was hostile to foreigners and for which "alien," "pagan" and "ungodly" were parallel terms (cf. Ps. 69:8), and a broad and variegated party which was more open to foreigners. For some this openness consisted in a readiness to submit to foreign influences, as under Antiochus Epiphanes and Herod the Great with their supporters, whereas for others it consisted in a readiness for mission (cf. Ps. 119:46 etc.). Hostility finds literary expression esp. in the books of Joel, Est., Judith and the Ps. Sol. (cf. esp. 17:28 : καὶ πάροικος καὶ ἀλλογενὴς οὐ παροικήσει αὐτοῖς ἔτι), whereas openness finds expression in the Sib., Wis., Philo and Joseph.[70] The two latter are both motivated by opposition to μισοξενία, and they both fight for honourable equality for the Jews among their fellow-citizens. The apologetic motive may be seen in the deliberate statement in Jos. Ant., 8, 117: ἡμεῖς δ' οὐκ ἀπάνθρωποι τὴν φύσιν ἐσμὲν οὐδ' ἀλλοτρίως πρὸς τοὺς οὐχ ὁμοφύλους ἔχομεν (cf. also the example, ibid., 4, 234), while the other motive is expressed in Philo's basic discussion in Vit. Mos., I, 35 f., which, following Lv. 19:34, calls ξένοι "ὀλίγῳ τῶν αὐτοχθόνων διαφέροντες," and describes God as their special ἔφορος, cf. also esp. Sib., 2, 104 : ἔστωσαν δ' ὁμότιμοι ἐπήλυδες ἐν πολιήταις. The missionary zeal cuts right across the two parties, however, for even the most radical rejection of foreigners in Pal. Judaism is accompanied by the desire to make proselytes (cf. Mt. 23:15). The Jewish mission was mainly represented, of course, by the diaspora.[71] This took seriously the missionary summons of Dt. Is. and allowed Gentiles to attend synagogue worship (cf. Ac. 13:44 etc.), so that in addition to the narrow circle of full proselytes there was the wider group of σεβόμενοι or φοβούμενοι.

The treatment of semi-proselytes,[72] however, shows already that the rejection of non-Jews prevailed. Officially these were treated as Gentiles both in civil (cf. Ac. 10:28)

---

[68] This reproach is constantly made by the anti-Jewish voices quoted in Jos. Ap. Cf. inter al. Diod. S., 34, 1; Tac. Hist., 5, 5 of the Jews : adversus omnes alios hostile odium. But it seems that in spite of this the attitude to the Jews was not wholly unfriendly right up to the Hell. period, cf. F. Stähelin, Der Antisemitismus d. Altertums (1905), 3 ff.; Schürer, III, 156. The change in view and the widespread anti-Semitism of antiquity are traced back to the time of Antiochus Epiphanes (or the Jewish Tobiads who advised him), so H. Graetz, "Ursprung d. zwei Verleumdungen gegen d. Judentum vom Eselkultus u. von der Lieblosigkeit gegen Andersgläubige," MGWJ, 21 (1872), 193 f., 199 ff. It is plainer than in Hecataeus in Manetho's Egyptian history, cf. Jos. Ap., 1, 227 ff., and from then on increases in intensity, Stähelin, 9 ff. It was obviously caused in the first instance by the frictions in cities like Alexandria where Jews and Gentiles lived side by side (cf. Jos. Bell., 2, 487 ff.) and by numerous other matters, esp. the impression that the Jews hated foreigners ; cf. I. Heinemann, Art. "Antisemitismus," Pauly-W. Suppl., 5 (1931), 3 ff.; J. Leipoldt, Antisemitimus in d. alten Welt (1933), 16 ff. The Book of Esther itself give evidence of strong anti-semitic trends even in the Persian period.

[69] Cf. Bousset-Gressm., 91 f.; Bertholet, 306 ff.

[70] Bertholet, 266 ff., 271 ff., 274 ff., 291 ff.; but cf. Schl. Theol. d. Judt., 240 f.

[71] Cf. H. Gressmann, op. cit., 169 ff.

[72] The ירֵאי שמים were only rarely mentioned in Rabb. lit., cf. Str.-B., II, 716 f., 719 f.

and also in religious matters. [73] To be sure, Jerusalem was in fact a πόλις ἄπασι τοῖς ἀλλοφύλοις ἀναπεπταμένη εἰς θρησκείαν (Jos. Bell., 4, 275; examples, Jn. 12:20; Ac. 8:27). But in the temple these were allowed to go only to a certain pt. in the forecourt, beyond which they were threatened with death. [74] They might make sacrificial gifts and votive offerings. They might παρεῖναι κατὰ θρησκείαν, but not τῆς θυσίας μεταλαμβάνειν, Jos. Bell., 6, 42 f. At the beginning of the Jewish War (ibid., 2, 409) the laws were tightened, so that no more offerings would be received from the ἀλλότριος. This decision is symptomatic. [75] From this pt. on hostility to foreigners tends to predominate in Rabb. Judaism.

The main forces impelling in this direction were the destruction of the state and the treatment of the holy city [76] on the one side, and on the other the rise of Christianity, which released biblical religion from the bond of nationality. For Christians there were no longer any foreigners in the Jewish sense. Hence Christians themselves, even Jewish Christians, came to be treated by the Jews as foreigners, and even as heathen (Dg., 5, 17: ὡς ἀλλόφυλοι πολεμοῦνται). [77]

After the overthrow of the Jewish state Rabb. Judaism maintained both the national and the religious differentiation from foreigners (גּוֹיִם/נָכְרִים). [78] Only those who had entered the religio-national community by circumcision could be recognised as not foreigners, and they, too, were judged quite critically, [79] and not equated at all pts. with native Jews. [80] There was no longer the same urge to win foreigners. [81] Hillel's mildness, which attracted many foreigners, was forced to yield before the severity of Shammai. [82] The fine statement of Hillel's great-grandson Simon b. Gamaliel (Lv. r., 2, 8 [134b]): "If a stranger comes to become a proselyte, extend a hand to him to bring him under the wings of the Shekinah," is offset by the other statement (jSanh., 29b, 31; M. Ex., 66a) that one should repulse the proselyte with the left hand and bring him on with the right. [83] The Bar. Jeb., 46a (Str.-B., I, 106b) could say that the view that one who has received proselyte baptism is a proselyte, even though he has not been circumcised, was the general opinion, [84] but in fact the demand for both baptism and circumcision prevailed. [85] It was hoped that in the last time there would be a big influx of foreigners, [86] but in the present many were not interested in receiving proselytes, or at least entry was made more difficult. [87] In any case, after the last Jewish revolt full conversion to Judaism was forbidden by the state, cf., e.g., Spartianus, Septimius Severus, 17: Judaeos fieri sub gravi poena vetuit.

A distinction was now made between the ger-zedek, the true and genuine proselyte,

---

[73] Cf. Schürer, III, 166, n. 49; 172 f. on different degree of approximation to Judaism.

[74] Cf. Str.-B., II, 549, 761 f. (c); Schürer, II, 329 and n. 57 (text and bibl.).

[75] Cf. also the separation of Jews from ξένοι in the besieged fort of Machaerus, Jos. Bell., 7, 191.

[76] Cf. Dio C., 69, 12.

[77] → n. 51. For a typical example of this hostility to Christianity cf. T. Shab., 13, 5 (129), in Str.-B., I, 367 f.

[78] Cf. Str.-B., IV, 353 ff. = Exc. 15: "Die Stellung d. alten Synagoge zur nichtjüdischen Welt."

[79] Bertholet, 340 ff.; Grünebaum, 50 f.; Str.-B., I, 929 f. (q-v).

[80] → n. 66; Schürer, III, 186 f.; Bertholet, 343; Grünebaum, 168 f.

[81] Cf. Str.-B., I, 925 f.

[82] Cf. the well-known antitheses in Shab., 31b, Str.-B., I, 930 f.

[83] Bertholet, 344.

[84] Cf. the same attitude in Jos. Ant., 20, 38 ff. on the conversion of King Izates, and perhaps Sib., 4, 161 ff.; cf. Schürer, III, 173.

[85] Schürer, III, 181 ff. A proselyte who does not have both is a foreigner, Jeb., 46a; cf. Gerim, 1; Str.-B., I, 107 (b); also Schürer, III, 181 f., n. 81.

[86] Cf. Str.-B., III, 144 and 150 ff.

[87] Cf. Jeb., 24b; AZ, 3b; Str.-B., I, 929; for the increased difficulties, ibid., I, 925, 928 f. (k-n), esp. Gerim, 1 f.

and the *ger-toshab,* [88] and this distinction was decisive. The one was reckoned as a Jew and included in the law of love, the other was not. In contrast to the NT this thesis was reached by the momentous interpretation of the גר of OT legislation as the full proselyte, [89] and the Mishnah adopted the use of גר (without addition) in this sense. [90] The LXX, which is probably not responsible for this understanding (→ 8), made history here in dangerous fashion with its rendering of גר as προσήλυτος. Neighbourly love, restricted now to the Jewish people (רֵעַ = Jew), [91] is replaced by hostility. There are, of course, friendly directions in Rabb. lit., and these were assembled as proofs by the Talmud apologists, esp. some passages in the tractate Gittin (5, 8 f.; Bar. Git., 61a; Str.-B., I, 359). But apart from the fact that the monotonous "for the sake of peace" (i.e., in order that peaceful relations with alien residents should not be disturbed) empties these fine sayings of much of their value, they tend to be the exceptions which confirm the rule. More typical of Talmud Judaism are the longer lists of passages which show hostility to גרים. [92] What is presented in the Shulchan-Aruch of Joseph Qaro is simply a logical summary of this attitude; [93] these sayings, which in part derive from ancient pagan times, distinguish sharply between moral obligations to Jews and to foreigners (including Christians). [94] Jewish piety thus tends to revert to the earlier attitude adopted by barbarians in self-defence, i.e., one of hostility to everything foreign, and the rejection of foreigners can have eternal as well as temporal significance. [95]

c. Graves of Foreigners.

In this connection one should mention Mt. 27:7 in the NT. Here we are told that with the blood-money returned by Judas the high-priests purchased the potter's field εἰς ταφὴν τοῖς ξένοις. Who were these ξένοι, Jewish fellow-believers from abroad, proselytes who died while temporarily resident in Jerusalem, or Gentiles? Does this συμβούλιον of the council express φιλοξενία or μισοξενία? The comm. are silent on such matters. [96] Many simply refer to the קברי בני העם of Jer. 26:23 and 2 K. 23:6, the graves of those lower strata of the population who had no private burial-places. [97] As the relevant passages show, they were regarded as unclean. Criminals as well as

---

[88] Cf. Grünebaum, 165 ff.; Schürer, III, 178 ff.; Str.-B., II, 721 ff. (esp. c); the designation גר־השעׇר (Bertholet, 288, but cf. 325 f.) is of medieval derivation, Str.-B., II, 723; Schürer. III, 177 f., esp. n. 75.

[89] E.g., Dt. 10:18; → II, 580, n. 35. The only exception is necessarily made in respect of Dt. 14:21, Str.-B., II, 718.

[90] Cf. here esp. Schürer, III, 175, n. 71.

[91] Cf. Str.-B., I, 354 f.; in some passages (S. Dt. § 181 [108a] on 19:4 f. and § 112 [97b] on 15:2) the *ger-toshab* is expressly excluded from neighbourly love, as is the Samaritan and נכרי in M. Ex., 94b on 21:35 (*ibid.,* 356). In this respect the contrast with pagan antiquity is not too favourable, cf. the discussion, *ibid.,* 356 f.

[92] Cf. Str.-B., I, 359-363; III, 139-155; IV, 353-383; Weber, 57 ff., 65 ff.; Bertholet, 346 ff.; cf. also S. Bernfeld, *Die Lehren d. Judt.,* II (1922), 204 ff.; J. Weigl, *Das Judt.* (1911), 92 ff.; J. S. Bloch, *Israel u. d. Völker* (1922).

[93] Cf. G. Marx (= G. Dalman), *Jüdisches Fremdenrecht, antisemitische Polemik u. jüdische Apologetik* (= *Schriften d. Institutum Judaicum in Berlin,* No. 1, 1886), also the defence by D. Hoffmann, *Der Schulchan-Aruch u. die Rabb. über das Verhältnis d. Juden zu Andersgläubigen²* (1894).

[94] G. Marx, 38.

[95] All resident aliens and foreigners are excluded from the Messianic kingdom, Ps. Sol. 17:28; Jeb., 24b; Str.-B., I, 929; also Seder Elij. R., 20 (120); Str.-B., IV, 778; cf. 1066 f., also III, 63.

[96] Kl. Mt., *ad loc.* poses a relevant question, but without answering it.

[97] Cf. A. Bertholet, *Kulturgeschichte Israels* (1919), 140.

aliens could be buried here, for aliens had no hereditary burial-places in Israel; [98] the family grave was a sign of native rights. [99] Hence in Mt. 27:7 it is quite possible to think of Israelites who had no native rights in Jerusalem. This would agree with the ancient tradition, revived in the Middle Ages, [100] which led to Luther's rendering "pilgrims." [101] But this interpretation is surely wide of the mark, since pious Jews of the Dispersion would not have been allotted to a place burdened with this name and origin. The more likely interpretation is that an unclean place was set aside for unclean Gentiles. Hence the decision does not express hypocritical benevolence but a degree of μισοξενία which separates unclean aliens from nationals even in death, [102] thus helping to fulfil the promise to native Jews that they are to live apart from the Gentiles both here and hereafter, S. Dt. § 315 on 32:12.

3. The Attitude of Christians to Foreigners.

With the OT (→ 10) and Judaism (→ 11) newly emerging Christianity shares a revulsion against everything foreign in religion (e.g., Aristid., 15, 7). But in place of the imperfect and often distorted love for strangers in the contemporary NT world Jesus shows that unrestricted and unconditional love for the ξένος is a special instance of love for the neighbour (as the Holiness Code had already done in Lv. 19:18, 34, → n. 61). In many cases a ξένος will be ὁ πλησίον μου. Jesus presents this interpretation of the great commandment not merely in the form of a precept but 1. in the form of a parable in Lk. 10:30-35, where the answer to the question who was neighbour (cf. v. 36 f.) is undoubtedly that the neighbour was the foreigner, the Samaritan (cf. 17:18), and 2. in the form of the great judgment scene in Mt. 25, where one of the tests is that of conduct towards the ξένος, who in the NT, too, is eo ipso miserable and in distress, being placed between the thirsty and the naked. [103] Whether the foreigner is hospitably received or not (→ 20, 17 f. and n. 148) will help to fix one's eternal destiny.

This thought is not new. [104] In Parsee religion (Yasht, 22) hospitality to the man who comes from near or far is a criterion for the eternal destiny of the soul. [105] Again, in Gk. depictions of the hereafter men are punished for the wrongs done to foreigners [106] (→ 4; Aesch. Eum., 267 ff.; Aristoph. Ra., 147; Plut. Ser. Num. Pun., 30, II, 566 f; cf. Vergil. Aen., 6, 609). Among the Jews, too, we find the saying that hospitality to foreign travellers gives a share in the future world even for idolaters like Micah (Ju. 17; esp. 18:2 f.; cf. Sanh., 103b in Str.-B., IV, 567); for hospitality is one of the works whose interest is paid in this world and the capital in the world to come, Shab., 127a; ibid., 560, → 20, 5 f.

---

[98] Ibid., 85.

[99] It is thus shameful to be buried in a common grave, cf. J. Wellhausen, op. cit., 97.

[100] Cf. G. Dalman, Orte u. Wege Jesu² (1921), 265 f.; also Jerusalem u. sein Gelände (1930), 207 f.; here also on the question of location.

[101] So also Wünsche, 349.

[102] In the rule of Git., 61a Bar. that "one should bury the dead of aliens with the dead of Israelites," the "with," acc. to Raschi's exposition, means "at the same time" rather than "in the same place" (H. L. Strack, ThLZ, 19 [1894], 637; Str.-B., IV, 360).

[103] The combination "stranger and beggar" (πτωχός) is found already among the Gks. (cf. Hom. Od., 6, 208; 18, 106; → n. 118), for the ξένος was basically in the same position as the πτωχός and the ἱκέτης, i.e., forced to rely on the grace and mercy of others; Nägelsbach, 297 ff.

[104] Wikenhauser.

[105] Cf. H. Hübschmann, "Die parsische Lehre vom Jenseits u. jüngsten Gericht," Jbch. pr. Th., 5 (1879), 203 ff.

[106] Dieterich, 163 ff.; cf. C. C. van Essen, Did Orphic Influence on Etruscan Tomb Paintings Exist? (1927), 62 ff., esp. 66.

As compared with all these non-Christian examples, however, Mt. 25 has a new [107] reason why this is to be a criterion in the judgment, namely, that Jesus Himself is a ξένος.

All other religions to some degree placed the stranger under the direct protection of the deity. [108] The Greeks said that Zeus avenges the stranger (→ 17). Hence those who fear the gods will be gracious to strangers, Hom. Od., 8, 576; → 4. In the OT God loves the stranger, hence the Israelites are to love him too, Dt. 10:18 f. But Jesus says : I am Myself the stranger ; therefore demonstrate in him your love for Me, [109] Mt. 25:35, 43; cf. v. 38, 44. The link between the ξένος and the divine Lord is thus the most direct and personal conceivable. How sharp is the distinction from Judaism and even the OT may be seen by comparing Mt. 25:35 ff. with Prv. 19:17: δανίζει θεῷ ὁ ἐλεῶν πτωχόν. [110] Here care for the needy is a transaction with God ; for Jesus it is a gift personally received from Him. [111] Behind the saying stands the fundamental thought of the Gospel, namely, that the personal relation to Jesus decides in the judgment.

> The only remaining question is that of the identity of the ξένος with whom Jesus equates Himself, whether the Christian from abroad or any stranger. Are the ἐλάχιστοι (ἀδελφοί, v. 40, 45) only the disciples or all men in need of help ? [112] Our answer must be that, in distinction from the par. 10:40-42 with its μικροί (cf. 18:6 ff., → IV, 651 ff.), [113] the ref. in this final teaching of Jesus in Mt. is as universal (v. 31 f.) as in the first (5:3-10). [114] All the ethical concepts of mankind concerning love for strangers are "fulfilled" in the standard set by Jesus. In the ξένος, even in the most alien of aliens, Jesus Himself is loved, and herewith the ultimate and definitive decision is made.
>
> The situation is different in 3 Jn. 5. Here ξένος (as adj.) is expressly connected with ἀδελφός. The pt. is caring for Christians from abroad, esp. missionaries, who in their work depend on being received (ὑπολαμβάνειν, v. 8) by supporters in other congregations. [115] The author praises one such supporter in Gaius : ἀγαπητέ, πιστὸν ποιεῖς ὃ ἐὰν ἐργάσῃ εἰς τοὺς ἀδελφοὺς καὶ τοῦτο ξένους.

In the great judgment chapter Jesus makes hospitality to strangers a supreme commandment. The important role which it plays in apostolic writings is in keeping with this (→ C. 3).

---

[107] This is for Bultmann (Trad., 130) "perhaps the specifically Christian feature" in the whole pericope.

[108] Schulze, 203 ff.

[109] Popular fancy has twisted and coarsened this idea into the legend that Jesus Himself walks on earth and tests men in the garb of a stranger. It hereby gives Christian form to the myth of the gods clothed as strangers (→ 22). For examples of such legends cf. J. Bolte-G. Polivka, *Anmerkungen zu den Kinder- u. Hausmärchen der Brüder Grimm*, 2 (1915), 211, n. 1, 214, 218 f., 225 f.; M. Landau, "Die Erdenwanderungen d. Himmlischen u. d. Wünsche d. Menschen," *Zschr. f. vergleichende Litteraturgesch.*, 14 (1901), 14 f., 23 ff., 30.

[110] Rabb. Judaism took up and developed this thought, cf. Shab., 127a, → *supra*.

[111] This personal element is lost on an idealistic interpretation of the thought of Jesus, as though to act for the pure idea of the good were to act towards Jesus Himself, H. J. Holtzmann, *NTliche Theologie*² (1911), I, 394.

[112] Michel poses the question without answering it, → IV, 657, 2 ff., though → n. 41.

[113] In view of this most expositors decide for restriction, cf. *et al.* Kl. Mt. and *NT Deutsch* (Schniewind), *ad loc.*

[114] As Jesus sees it, both passages are primary examples of God-given action (→ 22) and the reward of grace ; cf. Schniewind, *loc. cit.*; Schl. Mt., 725 ff.

[115] Cf. G. Stählin, "Urchr. Missionspraxis," *Grundzüge d. Missionsarbeit in zwei Jahrtausenden*, I (= *Sendende Gemeinde*, No. 60, 1940), 10.

C. The Custom of Hospitality.

The foreigner who was originally denied all rights found rich compensation in the primitive custom of hospitality.

The root of this noble and world-wide custom is to be sought primarily in the sense of the mutual obligation of all men to help one another, for which there is divine sanction. This is indicated by many national traditions, and especially by the fact that temples and altars were places of asylum (cf. Diod. S., 13, 26). [116] The foreigner is the guest of God, and fear of God demands that he be protected. The hospitality of sanctuaries is shown by the fact that aliens preferably settled in their vicinity and became hierodules in the broader sense (cf. Ju. 17) or else placed themselves under the protection of a priestly family.

The Gks. and Romans [117] found in Ζεὺς Ξένιος, [118] who protects the oppressed foreigner, [119] or the host rewarded with ingratitude (cf. Hom. Il., 13, 623 ff.; 3, 350 ff.), from outrage, the supreme guardian of hospitality (Suid. ξ 37). Alongside him we also find the Dioscuri, [120] and esp. the Fury, who avenges offences against guests as well as against parents. [121]

1. Greeks and Romans.

a. Private. For the Gks. hospitality was a decisive mark of culture, although, as already mentioned (→ 5; n. 25), there could be no clear-cut differentiation, as though the Gks. themselves were hospitable [122] and non-Gks. the reverse. [123] The classical epics

---

[116] On asylum → n. 25. The Mohammendan *kaaba* also gives asylum, cf. *Handwbch. des Islam* (1941), 243.

[117] To the less plastic nature of Roman religious ideas there corresponds more the thought of a *hospitale numen* (Amm. Marc., 30, 1, 22) than that of *Juppiter hospitalis* (Cic. ad Quint. Fratr., II, 10, 3), and to the Roman differentiation of religious functions a plurality of *dii hospitales* (Liv., 39, 51; Tac. Ann., 15, 52) or *hospitii dii* (Ovid. Met., 5, 45); cf. also *diis hospitalibus et Jovi* in Servius, I, 736, and already Plat. Leg., V, 729e, 730a.

[118] Cf. 2 Macc. 6:2; Hom. Od., 14, 283 f.; Plat. Leg., 730a; Xenoph. An., 3, 2, 4; Ps.-Aristot. Mund., 7, 401a, 22; Plut. Amat., 20; II, 766c; Stob. Ecl., IV, 2, 24 (IV, 151, Hense); Cl. Al. Prot., 37, 1 etc.; cf. also esp. Hom. Od., 6, 207 f.: πρὸς γὰρ Διός εἰσιν ἅπαντες | ξεῖνοί τε πτωχοί τε, also the noteworthy interjection in Plut. De Exilio, 17, II, 607a : τὸν πτωχὸν λοιδόρημα ποιοῦντα ... καὶ νὴ Δία τὸν ξένον.

[119] Hom. Od., 9, 270 f.: Ζεὺς δ᾽ ἐπιτιμήτωρ ἱκετάων τε ξείνων τε | ξείνιος ὃς ξείνοισιν ἅμ᾽ αἰδοίοισιν ὀπηδεῖ, → Nägelsbach, 296 f.

[120] Cf. L. Weniger, "Theophanien, altgr. Götteradvente," ARW, 22 (1923/4), 39.

[121] Cf. Aesch. Eum., 267 ff. She pursues the violator of hospitality even to the underworld, where he is punished as a chief of sinners, cf. Plut. Ser. Num. Pun., 22; II, 566 f; also Plat. Leg., V, 730a.

[122] It is suspicious that the Gk. national hero Hercules, in a well-preserved story already offensive to the Homeric age, is represented as the one who οὐδὲ θεῶν ὄπιν ᾐδέσατ᾽ οὐδὲ τράπεζαν (Od., 21, 26 ff.; v. Ihering, 367 f.). As every human failing was projected by the Gks. into heaven, so Hercules finds an Olympian counterpart in the inhospitable Taurian Artemis, who φονεύει τοὺς ξένους (Athenag., 26, 1), a Scythian deity interpreted in Gk. terms, → n. 123.

[123] Hom. gives some examples of mythical inhospitality, Cyclops, who does not even fear Zeus Xenios, and represents the Gk. view of primitive culture (Od., 9, 275 ff.), the Laestrygones (10, 116 ff.), etc. Later, too, we find many instances of inhospitable brutality up to the stories of Christian martyrdom (e.g., Act. Andr. et Matth., 1 ff.; II, 1, 65 ff., Lipsius-Bonnet). Among historical peoples the Egyptians were renowned for inhospitability (→ n. 55), also the Scythians (cf. Hdt., 4, 64 f., 100-106; Strabo, 7, 298; Ps.-Luc. Toxaris, 8; Jos. Ap., 2, 269), from whose proverbial hostility to strangers the Black Sea perhaps took its name Πόντος Ἄξεινος (cf. M. Vasmer, *Reallex. d. Vorgeschichte*, 12 [1928], 241). Only through Gk. colonisation did it become a πόντος εὔξεινος.

of the Gks. and other sagas offer many examples of fine hospitality, including that extended by and to the poor. [124] An eloquent instance of freely given hospitality is also recorded in Ac. 28:7 on the part of the eminent Roman land-owner Publius in Malta : ὃς ἀναδεξάμενος ἡμᾶς ἡμέρας τρεῖς φιλοφρόνως ἐξένισεν.

The Gks. mention as the motive for hospitality, along with religion (→ 17), their natural sympathy and φιλανθρωπία. [125] Philosophical ethics calls for hospitality on this basis. [126] The hope of return is, of course, a third motive [127] (from this there developed a system of standing hospitality, cf. Hom. Od., 9, 18). But this could not be primary, since custom demanded that a stranger's name and origin should be asked only after the meal (e.g., Od., 3, 69 ff.; 4, 60 ff.; even Eumaios, 14, 45 ff.). This usage makes it plain that hospitality was to be extended, not to one's own profit, but out of fear of the gods and love of men. How seriously the duty was taken may be seen from the severe punishments for lack of hospitality both in this world (e.g., the saga of Philemon and Baucis, Ovid Met., 8, 613 ff.) [128] and in the world to come (→ n. 121), by human ordinance as well as divine (cf. Ael. Var. Hist., 4, 1).

b. Public. From the custom of extending hospitality as occasion offered there developed, with the growth of international dealings and the need for repayment, the system of standing hospitality which flourished among the Gks. already in the Homeric period and which continued to late antiquity, [129] practised also in the Jewish and Christian communities (→ n. 143; 23, 18 ff.).

Along with the private guest, the ἴδιος ξένος, there is the official guest, the πρόξενος (→ n. 26), along with the *hospitium privatum* the *hospitium publicum* (Liv., 1, 45), though this need not concern us further in relation to the NT.

c. Hospices and Inns. A brief word might be added about an institution which proved necessary with increasing commerce, that of the inn, [130] which is found from the 4th cent. [131] This, too, found its origin in religion, for the first hostelries were in the shadow of temples (Delos, Delphi etc.) and were open to pilgrims (πανδοχεῖα or ξενοτροφεῖα). The hospices connected with synagogues [132] and Christian places of pilgrimage [133] are a par. to this pagan institution, and a development of it. But soon the

---

[124] Cf. Hom. Od., 14, 45 ff.; Ovid Met., 8, 610 ff.; Fasti, 5, 499 ff.; Egerer, 23 ff.

[125] Both the religious and human motives may be found in class. combination in the words of the worthy swineherd Eumaios to Odysseus : Δία ξένιον δείσας, αὐτὸν δ' ἐλεαίρων (Hom. Od., 14, 389). They give rise together to the feeling of αἰδώς towards the stranger (→ 3), who is thus called αἰδοῖος (Hom. Od., 5, 447; 15, 373), Nägelsbach, 297.

[126] Cf. Aristot. Eth. Nic., 4, 5, 1122b, 19-1123a, 19 : μεγαλοπρέπεια is seen among other things in ξένων ὑποδοχαὶ καὶ ἀποστολαί κτλ. Cic. Off., 2, 18.

[127] Cf., e.g., Od., 1, 311 ff.; 24, 285 f.

[128] Only a modern would ask whether the punishment was not too hard (cf. M. Landau, *op. cit.,* 12, who gives further stories with this motif, 29 f.).

[129] On individual customs in the Homeric age, cf. Egerer, 11 ff.; Buchholz, 38 ff., and in the Roman period (with sources), M. Johnston, "Hospites Venturi," *The Class. Journal,* 28 (1932), 197-206. On this whole question cf. Leonhard ; Busolt-Swoboda, II, 1241 ff.

[130] Already in the Homeric period there were λέσχαι, public resting-places which, like the caravanserais of the East, offered only shelter for the night, and were strictly used only by the poor and beggars, cf. Hom. Od., 18, 329; Egerer, 24.

[131] Blümner, 450 ff.; Lübker, 401; Friedländer, I, 343 ff.; Mau, Art. "caupona," Pauly-W., III (1899), 1806-8; E. Ziebarth, "Beiträge zum gr. Recht," *Zschr. f. vergleichende Rechtswissenschaft,* 19 (1906), 291-298.

[132] Cf. Deissmann LO, 379 f., with n. 5.

[133] Bolkestein, cf. also the great pilgrim houses at Hindu shrines, with free reception and board.

vigorous commercial life of the Hell. period produced similar inns under many different names, [134] including πανδοχεῖον, [135] κατάλυμα, [136] and ξενία, [137] in the NT.

2. Israelites and Jews. [138]

Like the Gk. sagas, the biblical stories extol hospitality in many fine examples, cf. esp. Abraham, [139] Lot, Rebekah, and Job, who boasts (31:32): ἔξω οὐκ ηὐλίζετο ξένος, ἡ δὲ θύρα μου παντὶ ἐλθόντι ἀνέῳκτο (cf. Test. Zeb., 6, 4 f.). In sinister contrast [140] we find the Sodomites (Jos. Ant., 1, 194 : μισόξενοι), Benjamites (ibid., 5, 141 ff.) and Egyptians (→ n. 55, Wis. 19:13 f.: χαλεπωτέραν μισοξενίαν ἐπετήδευσαν etc. to εὐεργέται ξένοι, "worthy guests," vv. 22 ff.).

True hospitality is extended without commandment or reward. [141] It is a self-evident duty, given precedence, indeed, over neighbourliness, cf. 2 Βασ. 12:4, → 4 and n. 16. [142] The general acceptance of this duty in later Judaism is proved by

---

[134] ξενών (Ditt. Or., 609, 21), which passed into Lat. (Ziebarth, 298), ξενίδιον (P. Tebt., II, 335, 17), ξενοδοχεῖον (cf. Suid. ξ 40; in modern Gk. "hotel"), καταγώγιον, Lat. caupona and taberna (cf. Ac. 28:15), more fashionably deversorium and hospitium.

[135] Lk. 10:34. Inns were usually primitive, dirty and noisy ; ἐν τῷ πανδοχείῳ ἐλέπρησα καὶ αὐτὸς ἐγώ, says the leper in P. Lond. Christ., 1, 35 (Fr. of an Unknown Gospel, ed. H. I. Bell-T. C. Skeat [1935], 11), though lepers were usually excluded from public inns (ibid., 19). Comedy and art portray the conditions, Friedländer, II (1920), 113 and 116; cf. also the comparison of a πανδοχεῖον with a heart full of demons, Cl. Al. Strom., II, 114, 5; cf. also Aboda Zara, 2, 1.

[136] Lk. 2:7 might well be a public caravanserai, whereas a private house is called κατάλυμα in 22:11 (→ n. 143).

[137] Cf. Hesych. and Suid., s.v., perhaps also Sir. 29:27 B* (Rahlfs οἰκίας). This meaning is supported by the use as a loan-word (אכסניא) in Rabb. speech, bAr., 16b; Ex. r., 35, 5; cf. S. Krauss, Gr. u. lat. Lehnwörter im Talmud etc., II (1899), s.v.; bSanh., 107b uses in the same sense the Lat. loan word אושפיזא hospitium. ξενία seems to have much the same meaning as hospitium elsewhere. Originally it had the abstract sense of "hospitality" for which the NT uses the compound φιλοξενία, → 20, but it took on several concrete senses in Hell. Gk. (not mentioned in Pass.): 1. "guest-chamber" (P. Greci e latini, 1, 50, 16 f., also Phlm. 22); 2. "inn," → n. 33; 3. "quarters," "lodging," usually in private houses, as prob. in Ac. 28:23 (Liddell-Scott : "lodging"; cf. Cadbury, 320 ff., though not Moult.-Mill., et al.), hence materially the same as the more specific μίσθωμα (v. 30 : if Paul found lodging, not in the house of a friend, but in a hired room, this was not because the Roman Jews or Christians were wanting in hospitality, but because he was a prisoner under Roman guard, as against Riddle, 152, n. 10). ξενία often has this sense in Ps.-Cl. Hom., e.g., 14, 1, in the same phrase as Ac. 28:23 : ἐλθεῖν εἰς τὴν ξενίαν (the class. sense "to be received, to come to table, as an invited guest," cf. Pind. Nem., 10, 49; Jos. Ant., 5, 148 is not very likely here in view of Paul's situation), cf. also 12, 2 : τὰς ξενίας ἑτοιμάζειν, "to lodge" (Phlm. 22) etc. A special use 4. is for "soldiers' quarters" (Preisigke Sammelbuch, 3924, 8. 15. 17 in an edict of Germanicus; cf. SAB, 38 [1911], 796), then 5. "monks' cells" (Pall. Hist. Laus., p. 74, 7; 136, 16). Play on the loan-word ξενία in bSanh., 107 (→ n. 33) suggests also 6. "hostess."

[138] Grundt ; Löhr ; Benzinger, 131 f.; Bertholet, 22 ff.; also Kulturgeschichte Israels (1919), 135 f.

[139] Cf., e.g., 1 Cl., 10, 7; also Gk.-Byz. Fr. ed. G. Heinrici (ASGW, XXVIII, 8, p. 67, 20): God has given men 7 χαρίσματα after Adam, among them ... (τῷ) 'Αβραὰμ τὴν φιλοξενίαν. Jewish saga constantly embellished the exemplary hospitality of Abraham with new traits, cf. B. Beer, Das Leben Abrahams nach Auffassung d. jüd. Sage (1859), 37-43, 152-165; Landau, 6 f.

[140] Jael's deed (Ju. 4:17 ff.) is an unheard of breach of the law of hospitality in the cultural relations of the time, and can claim favourable judgment only in view of her ruthless dedication to the cause of God's people.

[141] Jos. Ant., 1, 250 f.: Eliezer, who offers μισθὸν τῆς ξενίας τελεῖν, receives from Rebekah the answer : πάντων ... ἀμισθὶ μεθέξειν.

[142] For details cf. Löhr, 58 f.

the Gospel stories. But there tended to arise among the Jews a severe restriction [143] which made considerable strides later.

In the Rabb. writings hospitableness is often commended as a work of mercy, and extolled in lofty terms. It is more than a vision of the Shekinah (Shebu., 35b); it is one of the most meritorious works, of which one enjoys the interest in this world and the capital in the next (Shab., 127a); a list of eulogies of the host on the basis of biblical texts is given in Ber., 63b. But it is worth noting that what was once practised spontaneously and ἀμισθί has now to be commanded (cf. already Is. 58:7) and also made acceptable with the promise of a reward. The worst limitation, however, is that the legitimate recipients of φιλοξενία are to be Jews rather than ξένοι. [144]

3. Christians.

a. The NT.

(a) Terms. The virtue of hospitality (φιλοξενία, not ξενία, in the NT, cf. R. 12:13; Hb. 13:2) makes the one who exercises it, the host (ξένος R. 16:23), the φιλόξενος (1 Tm. 3:2; Tt. 1:8; 1 Pt. 4:9), who practises it by ξενοδοχεῖν [145] (1 Tm. 5:10) or ξενίζειν, "to receive as a guest" [146] (Ac. 10:23; 28:7; Hb. 13:2; mid. "to dwell as a guest," 1 C. 16:19 vl.; Ac. 10:6, 18, 32; 21:16), [147] also συνάγειν [148] (Mt. 25:35 ff.), ὑπολαμβάνειν (3 Jn. 8), perhaps in a ξενία, "guest-chamber," Phlm. 22 (→ n. 137).

(b) In the Story and Message of Jesus. In the Gospels the custom of hospitality plays an extraordinarily important role. Lk. is the Evangelist who evinces an obvious interest in it (7:36 ff.; 9:51 ff.; 10:38 ff.; 14:1 ff. etc.). [149] From the external standpoint, the work of Jesus obviously rested to a large degree on the hospitality extended to Him (Mk. 1:29 ff.; 2:15 ff.; 14:3 ff. etc.). In the parables He plainly accords great significance to hospitality (cf. Lk. 10:34 f.; 11:5 ff.; 14:12 ff. etc.). What is even more important is that God's hospitality is an essential part of His message. Condescending generosity is one of the fundamental features in the biblical depiction of God (cf. Lk. 14:16 ff.; 12:37; 13:29; 15:23 ff. etc.).

(c) In Exhortation. ἀγάπη always implies φιλοξενία. Hence the latter plays a significant role in ethical instruction. Christian love is expressed according to Jesus (→ I, 44; II, 692, cf. Mt. 25:35 ff.). It is an expression of ἀγάπη (R. 12:9)

---

[143] Hell. Judaism borrowed two things from the pagan world : 1. the system of standing hospitality (cf. Tob. 5:6, often in Jos., e.g., Bell. 3, 436, perhaps in many cases in the work of the apostles, → 23), though non-Jews were unlikely to be welcome ; 2. the establishment of inns (Lk. 10:34), for up to the Gk. period there were only caravanserais, which also continued to exist (cf. Lk. 2:7). Palest. Judaism was also influenced by surrounding nations in this area, as may be seen 1. from the many loan-words (אכסנא = ξένος, "stranger" and "guest," אכסניא = ξενία, "hospitality," "hospice," "strange woman," "hostess" etc. (→ n. 33; examples in S. Krauss, op. cit.; → n. 137, s.v.), ξενισμός, (Midr. Ps. 116:10), πανδοχεῖον, πανδοχεύς (examples in Str.-B., II, 183 f.), πάροχος (jBik., 3c, 11), hospitium (→ n. 137 etc.), and 2. from the practice of the Essenes, who maintained a κηδεμών as a hostel for ξένοι in every city (Jos. Bell., 2, 125).

[144] Cf. Str.-B., IV, 565, 568; → 13, 34 ff.

[145] = Hell., rejected by Atticists (Moeris, Phryn., etc.; cf. also, e.g., Max. Tyr., 32, 9), for the class. ξενοδοκεῖν: Hdt., 6, 127; Eur. Alk., 552 (Codd.: ξενοδοχεῖν); Plat. Resp., IV, 419.

[146] Cf. Ps.-Clem. Hom., 8, 2 : οἱ ἀποδεχόμενοι καὶ ξενίζοντες, "hosts."

[147] Cf. Bl.-Debr. § 294, 5, 378.

[148] Cf. H. A. A. Kennedy, Sources of NT Greek (1895), 128; συνάγειν in the sense "to receive hospitably" seems to be a vox biblica developed in the LXX.

[149] Cadbury, op. cit.

and φιλαδελφία (v. 10) according to Paul (R. 12:13). The power of love to cover sins is fully worked out in it according to Peter (1 Pt. 4:8 f.). φιλοξενία is inseparable from φιλαδελφία in Hb. (13:1 f.).

In the vast majority of cases φιλοξενία, φιλόξενον εἶναι and ξενοδοχεῖν is thus included in the lists of virtues, and almost always with an imperative ref. in form or meaning. Only Jesus, e.g., in the Beatitudes, presents it as a fact in the life of His people, though this carries with it the strongest possible impulse towards action. As in antiquity, there are directions to guests as well as hosts (→ 6, 2 ff.). Thus Jesus speaks of the proper conduct of guests (Lk. 14:7 ff.; Mk. 12:39).

The command applies to all disciples (Mt. 25:35 ff.; R. 12:13 etc.). But in the Past. (1 Tm. 3:2; Tt. 1:8; 1 Tm. 5:10) φιλοξενία is in bishops and widows a special proof of fitness to serve the community (→ 24, 24 ff.).

φιλοξενία is also to be shown to all. It is striking that R. 12:13 f. puts it between duties to the ἅγιοι and the διώκοντες. [150] In Christ all barriers are removed. In practice, and according to the rule of Gl. 6:10, οἰκεῖοι τῆς πίστεως, ἀδελφοί, will in most cases be the ξένοι to be cared for, e.g., Hb. 13:2 (→ 22). This is expressly stated in 1 Pt. 4:9 (φιλόξενοι εἰς ἀλλήλους). In times of persecution, such as those underlying Hb. and 1 Pt., hospitality to refugees and exiles was most important. But in periods of peace, too, the hospitality of fellow-believers was often claimed in that travel-loving age, and he who came ἐν ὀνόματι κυρίου was to be received (cf. Did., 12). Part of the picture of the NT Christian is that he is always ready (Hb. 13:2: μὴ ἐπιλανθάνεσθε) to show hospitality, and to do so with zeal (R. 12:13: διώκω) and cheerfulness (1 Pt. 4:9: ἄνευ γογγυσμοῦ, cf. Prv. 15:17: ξενισμὸς ... πρὸς φιλίαν καὶ χάριν without expecting a reward (Lk. 14:12-14, → n. 141).

(d) Motives for Primitive Christian Hospitality. The basic motive is ἀγάπη, but there are also many subsidiary motives: 1. the charismatic, 2. the eschatological; 3. the metaphysical; and 4. the missionary.

(1) Hospitality is a divine χάρισμα of believers (→ n. 139) to be faithfully used (1 Pt. 4:9 f.). This is in accord with the profound NT concept that all the good works of the righteous are the work and gift of God (cf. Eph. 2:10 etc.). [151]

(2) Similarly, as recollection of their own distress as aliens in Egypt taught the Israelites to extend hospitality to the stranger (Lv. 19:34; Dt. 10:19), so Christians are obligated to fellow-strangers by the persecutions which they now endure and which precede the imminent end (1 Pt. 4:7), and by their own position as ξένοι on earth in the light of this end. [152]

Even more striking, however, are the two final motives.

(3) Hb. bases its exhortation to constant φιλοξενία (13:2) on the following ground: διὰ ταύτης γὰρ ἔλαθόν τινες ξενίσαντες ἀγγέλους. The author thus

<hr />

[150] It is expressly recorded of Polycarp that he showed hospitality to his persecutors (Eus. Hist. Eccl., IV, 15, 14); cf. also Conrad Ferdinand Meyer's poem: "Die Füsse im Feuer." This attitude is related to that of the Bedouin, who will show hospitality even to a mortal foe if he flees into his tent. Yet there is a profound difference, for, whereas the Bedouin will kill this foe if he meets him again at a certain distance from the tent, Christian φιλοξενία knows no such limitations.

[151] → n. 114. Cf. the close connection between φιλοξενία and πνεῦμα ἅγιον in P. Lond., 1912, 14, 4 (4th cent. A.D., H. I. Bell, Jews and Christians in Egypt [1924], 81 f.).

[152] So, e.g., Cl. Al. Strom., II, 41, 3 ff.; → D. 3b.

believes that there may be real angelic visitations such as those suggested to the faith of the time by stories both in the Bible and outside it.

This idea leads us to an important idea in religious history, that of sheltering and entertaining heavenly beings. Apart from open, popular visits of the gods to earth (cf. Hom. Od., 7, 201-203; Il., 1, 423 f.; Paus., VIII, 2, 2), ancient saga told of visits *incognito* which had the character of tests for men. [153] The best known example, [154] the story of Philemon and Baucis (Ovid Met., 8, 613-715), [155] finds detailed parallels in Gn. 19 and may have influenced Ac. 14:11 ff. The decisive motifs (variable in the OT) are sudden appearance, rejection by the many and reception by the few, epiphany and address, [156] reward [157] and punishment. With the incorporation of this type of narrative into the sphere of biblical monotheism, angels took the place of gods, [158] though in later Christian legend we find Christ or the apostles, [159] and in fairy tales God Himself or a dwarf etc. [160]

The use of this idea in Hb. 13:2 attracts attention, not to the reward, but to the possibility of contact with the metaphysical world which hospitality gives, and, of course, to the equally great possibility of throwing away this good fortune.

At Hb. 13:2 the Bible student is reminded of the experiences of Abraham and Lot (Gn. 18 f.) etc., of their unwitting entertainment of angels and of their reward. Neither here nor elsewhere in the NT is there any direct appeal to OT models of hospitality. For the hospitable harlot Rahab (cf. 1 Cl., 12, 3) is such a model only indirectly (Hb. 11:31; Jm. 2:25). On the other hand, in 1 Cl., 12, 1, a popular modification of Hb. 11:31, the hospitality of Rahab is used as an example: διὰ πίστιν καὶ φιλοξενίαν ἐσώθη, and almost in the same words so, too, are Abraham (10, 7) and Lot (11, 1).

Distinctively changed and in ultimate fulfilment, the same motive is used by Jesus Himself when He suggests that hospitality which is of no profit to oneself, i.e., to the poor and needy, is really proffered to Himself (Mt. 25:35 ff.; cf. 10:40). He Himself is lodged and entertained in the ξένος (→ 16, 8 ff.).

(4) Historically, however, the most important basis is that hospitality serves the Gospel, [161] as in 3 Jn. 8: ἡμεῖς οὖν ὀφείλομεν ὑπολαμβάνειν τοὺς τοιούτους (sc. the ἀδελφοὶ ξένοι, v. 5, who ὑπὲρ τοῦ ὀνόματος ἐξῆλθαν, v. 7, i.e., as missionaries, → 16). In the days of primitive Christianity the spread of the Gospel took place almost exclusively by word of mouth, and the evangel was carried by wandering messengers who were sustained by the hospitality of the brethren. Jesus Himself counted on this when He first sent out the disciples (Mt. 10:11 ff.;

---

153 Cf. Hom. Od., 17, 485 ff.:
  καί τε θεοὶ ξείνοισιν ἐοικότες ἀλλοδαποῖσιν
  παντοῖοι τελέθοντες ἐπιστρωφῶσι πόληας
  ἀνθρώπων ὕβριν τε καὶ εὐνομίην ἐφορῶντες,
and on this K. Latte, *D. Religion d. Römer* (1927), 54 f.
154 Cf. also Hom. Hymn. Cer., 218; Paus., I, 37, 2; III, 16, 3; Nonnus Dionys., XVIII, 35 ff.; further instances in E. Rohde, *Der griech. Roman u. seine Vorläufer*[2] (1900), 539, n. 2; Landau, 1 ff.
155 Cf. Wagner, Art. "Baukis 1," Pauly-W., III (1899), 153 f.
156 Cf. E. Stauffer, Art. "Abschiedsreden," RAC, I (1941), 30 ff.
157 The reward often consists in three wishes (cf. Landau, esp. 23 ff.; J. Bolte-G. Polívka, *op. cit.*, 210 ff.), or blessing of children (Abraham), or preservation from disaster (Lot); the Vulg. in its erroneous rendering of Hb. 13:2 imports this concept into the text: *latuerunt quidam* (some were sheltered from evil) *angelis hospitio receptis* (cf. Rgg. Hb., 429, n. 68).
158 Cf. H. Gunkel, *Genesis*[4] (1917), *ad loc.*
159 → n. 109; cf. Bolte-Polivka, 223 ff.
160 Cf. J. Grimm, *Deutsche Mythologie*, I[4] (1875), XXIX ff.; Bolte-Polívka, 210 ff.
161 Cf. Harnack Miss., 200 ff.; Riddle, *op. cit.*

Lk. 10:5 ff.), [162] and both His own work and that of the apostles rested on it (cf. Ac. 10:6, 18, 32, 48; 16:15, 34; 17:7; 18:2 f. with 1 C. 16:19 D; R. 16:23; Phlm. 22; Ac. 21:8 f., 16). In fact, whenever the hospitality of Christians is mentioned in the NT, the reference is primarily to that extended to apostles and missionaries. [163]

The words of the Lord in Mt. 25:35 ff. are related especially to apostles and teachers; these are to be received ὡς κύριον [164] (Did., 11, 2 and 4). But this applies only to genuine messengers (Did., 11; 2 Jn. 10 f.; cf. Herm. m., 11). For false teachers, self-seeking pseudo-prophets, and other mendicants (Did., 12) abuse the great hospitality of Christians. [165] On the other hand, hospitality is refused not only to such, but also on occasion to those of different parties in the Church (3 Jn. 9 f.). [166]

The hospitality extended to messengers of the Gospel was of far-reaching significance. It led to the baptism of whole families (e.g., Ac. 16:15, 33), and this to the house-churches which were so important in primitive Christianity. The connection between these churches and the hospitality given to Paul is obvious in the case of Priscilla and Aquila (cf. R. 16:4 f.), of Philemon (Phlm. 22), and especially of Gaius of Corinth (R. 16:23: ὁ ξένος μου καὶ ὅλης τῆς ἐκκλησίας, → 2, and n. 3). These instances presuppose that Paul used the system of standing hospitality (→ 18) on behalf of his missionary work, as Jesus had done before him (→ 20, e.g., in Capernaum, Mk. 1:29 ff.; 3:20; 9:33; in Bethany, 11:11; Jn. 11:1 ff.; Lk. 10:38 ff. etc.).

b. The Early Church.

One of the most prominent features in the picture of early Christianity, which is so rich in good works, is undoubtedly its hospitality. Witness is borne to this by both friend and foe alike; cf. on the one side 1 Cl., 1, 2 (τὸ μεγαλοπρεπὲς τῆς φιλοξενίας ἦθος) and Aristid. Apol., 15, 7: ξένον ἐὰν ἴδωσιν (sc. Christians), ὑπὸ στέγην εἰσάγουσι καὶ χαίρουσιν ἐπ' αὐτῷ ὡς ἐπὶ ἀδελφῷ ἀληθινῷ, [167] and on the other side Luc. Peregr. Mort., 11-13, 16, and the angry saying of Julian (Ep., 49) that ἡ περὶ τοὺς ξένους φιλανθρωπία μάλιστα τὴν ἀθεότητα (sc. Christianity) συνηύξησεν.

As in the NT, so later there was a distinctive tension between the actual practice of hospitality [168] and the exhortation thereto, and there were, of course, many Christians who refused it, provoking Origen (Hom., 5, 1 in Gen.; GCS, 29, 58) to the bitter (etym.) play on words: hospitem velut hostem vitatis.

---

[162] Riddle, 152 ff. thinks that there is a projection back of primitive custom into the words of Jesus in order to provide a basis in His teaching for the claim of the messengers to hospitality. But 1. hospitality to teachers was particularly enjoined in contemporary Judaism (Ber., 10b; Ket., 111b; other passages in Wünsche, 140 f.), and 2. Jesus obviously followed the same practice (→ 20 f.; cf. Cadbury, 308 f.: Cl. Al. [Quis Div. Salv., 13, 5] emphasises that Jesus claimed the hospitality of the well-to-do, ἐπιξενοῦσθαι).

[163] Cf. as a non-bibl. par. Ditt. Syll.³, 1025, 41 f. (4th/3rd cent. B.C.): ἱαροποιοὶ δὲ ξενιζό[ντω τὸν ἱ]ερῆ καὶ τὸς κάρυκας τ[αύτα]ν τὰν νύκτα.

[164] Cf. also the Brahman claim to be received as a god, Thieme, 155 f.

[165] Cf. already Sir. 11:29; perhaps Lk. 10:7 (which forbids changing lodgings) is already directed against a selfish exploitation of hospitality. Rules for receiving strangers which seek to preserve a mean between brotherly love and prudence may be found not only in Did., 11-13 but also in the strangers' hospice of the Nitrian monks (Pall. Hist. Laus., p. 25, 21-26, 3). The same abuse of hospitality, also by non-Christians, led the later churches to introduce letters of episcopal commendation (ἐπιστολαὶ συστατικαί), cf. already 2 C. 3:1, also R. 16:1.

[166] Like 3 Jn., Zoroaster bewails the refusing of hospitality (Yasna, 51, 12) and himself forbids the reception of liars, i.e., false believers, ibid., 46, 5 f.

[167] Cf. E. v. Dobschütz, D. urchr. Gemeinden (1902), 1.

[168] Cf. the journeys of Ignatius and also Peter in the Ps.-Clem. writings.

Thus Tert. (Ad Uxorem, 2, 4) argues against a mixed marriage on the ground that the Christian wife can no longer extend free hospitality to fellow-believers, and Ps.-Clem. Hom. (Ep. ad Jac., 9) admonishes : τοὺς ξένους μετὰ πάσης προθυμίας εἰς τοὺς ἑαυτῶν οἴκους λαμβάνετε (with other works of love from Mt. 25:35 ff.). The two Gn. Homilies 4 and 5 of Origen (GCS, 29, 50 ff., 59) concerning Abraham and Lot are devoted to exhortation to hospitality, and Melito of Sardis wrote a special work (now lost) περὶ φιλοξενίας (Eus. Hist. Eccl., IV, 26, 2). Such admonitions to unwearying hospitality like to appeal to the strong expression τὴν φιλοξενίαν διώκειν in R. 12:13 (cf. Hier. Ep., 125, 14, 2, CSEL, 56, 133, 6 ff.).

Herm. m., 8, 10, like the NT, emphasises φιλόξενον εἶναι in a list of virtues (cf. s., 9, 27, 2); the addition ἐν γὰρ τῇ φιλοξενίᾳ εὑρίσκεται ἀγαθοποίησίς ποτε obviously contains a ref. to the meritoriousness of the work. 1 Cl., 10, 7; 11, 1; 12, 1 also gives weight to the exhortation with the promise of reward ; here we have the striking combination of πίστις (or εὐσέβεια) and φιλοξενία as meritorious works. But the motive of Mt. 25 — in the stranger Christ is lodged — also had some influence, and continued to do so right on into the Middle Ages. [169]

With the great increase in hospitality ecclesiastical organisation soon became necessary, and we can see the beginnings of this even in the apostolic period. Those who had charge of the developing practice were on the one side the congregations as such, on the other officials specifically appointed for the purpose. Apart from the hospitality of the church at Corinth (1 Cl., 1, 2) we also know of that of Antioch, which in the days of Chrysostom (Hom. in Matth., 66, 3, MPG, 58, 630) cared daily for 3000 widows, sick (→ n. 174), strangers (ἀποδημοῦντες), etc. [170] We find rules about the hospitality of the churches in Const. Ap. (2, 58) and Canon. Ap. (13 and 32), also in the canons of the Synod of Elvira (25) and the Synod of Arles (9). The Past. stress the fact that the bishop must be hospitable (1 Tm. 3:2; Tt. 1:8; cf. also Herm. s., 9, 27, 2 : ἐπίσκοποι καὶ φιλόξενοι, οἵτινες ἡδέως εἰς τοὺς οἴκους ἑαυτῶν πάντοτε ὑπεδέξαντο τοὺς δούλους τοῦ θεοῦ ἄτερ ὑποκρίσεως). Alongside the bishops [171] we find women, [172] esp. widows. A widow can be a widow of the community only εἰ ἐξενοδόχησεν, says 1 Tm. 5:10. In such matters the leaders of the community would often act privately, but mostly as officials of the church, as Just. (Apol., 67, 6) emphatically shows. At the end of the service, the gifts which were gathered monthly (Tert. Apol., 39) by the members of the congregation were deposited παρὰ τῷ προεστῶτι, καὶ αὐτὸς ἐπικουρεῖ ὀρφανοῖς καὶ χήραις ... καὶ τοῖς ἐν δεσμοῖς οὖσι καὶ τοῖς παρεπιδήμοις οὖσι ξένοις καὶ ἁπλῶς πᾶσι τοῖς ἐν χρείᾳ οὖσι κηδεμὼν γίνεται. [173]

Later the bigger churches at important points of trade or famous sanctuaries established regular hospices for strangers, called ξενοδοχεῖα or ξενῶνες, [174] or hospit(al)ia (first

---

[169] Thus in an introductory letter (tracturia) for pilgrims, who undertook a long pilgrimage such as that of John Parricida on account of a crime, every Christian is to grant them for Christ's sake mansio et focus, panis et aqua ; for in ipso peregrino Christum pavistis seu suscepistis (Formulae Senonenses recentiores, 11, in Monumenta Germaniae historica. Legum sectio V: Formulae Merowingici et Karolini aevi, ed. K. Zeumer [1886], 217, 17 ff.; cf. also Formulae Salicae Lindenbrogianae, 17, ibid., 278, 32-279, 6). Cf. also Regula Benedicti, 53 : in hospitibus enim Christus adoratur et suscipitur.

[170] Obviously official ξενοδόχοι had to be appointed to take charge of this, cf., e.g., Pall. Hist.Laus., p. 15, 9 f.

[171] As an example cf. Polycarp's hospitality, → n. 150.

[172] Cf. Tert. Ad Uxorem, 2, 4; Pall. Hist. Laus., p. 146, 7 ff.; 163, 20 f.; it had long been the practice for a wife to discharge her duty esp. in the area of hospitality, Thieme, 86; Bertholet, 23.

[173] For a related organisation of ξενοδοχία cf. Pall. Hist. Laus., p. 127, 3 ff. This reminds us that the often extravagant hospitality of the Homeric heroes was supported by later collections from their peoples, cf. Od., 13, 14 f.; 19, 197 f. etc.

[174] Cf. Suid. ξ 52 : ξενῶνος· δόμου τοῦ ὑποδεχομένου τοὺς ξένους καὶ ἀρρωστοῦντας, also Chrys. Hom. in Matth., 66, 3, MPG, 58, 630 (... τοῖς ἐν τῷ ξενοδοχείῳ κάμνουσι); P. Masp., 151, 183 etc.; Bolkestein, loc. cit.

in Act. Archelai, 4). Groups of ascetics did the same, e.g., in the Nitrian desert, where the ξενοδοχεῖον was next to the church (Pall. Hist. Laus., p. 25, 20 ff.). The sick were cared for as well as strangers (→ n. 174), and since this aspect increasingly became the more important the original hospices gradually became hospitals. [175] This development is foreshadowed in Lk. 10:34.

4. Christ the Host.

It has been shown already (→ 20) that in Lk. especially Jesus is often shown at feasts, and that in His parables the image of the host plays a not insignificant role. Behind both these facts is a deeper meaning. Jesus comes to earth as a guest, and He expects to be received as such (→ 16).

At the same time, however, He is also the heavenly Host, as God is sometimes depicted already in the OT (cf. Ps. 15:1; [176] 23:5). Even before Christ the vital question for the righteous could be formulated as follows : Who may be the guest of the Lord (Ps. 15)? Whom will God receive into His αἰώνιοι σκηναί (Lk. 16:9)? Who may one day sit at His table with the patriarchs (Mt. 8:11) and eat His bread (Lk. 14:15)? As in the judgment, so in the eschatological banquet Jesus is now set alongside God or in His place. Indeed, judgment and the banquet are closely connected. The parable of the Great Supper (Mt. 22:2 ff.; Lk. 14:16 ff.) is also a picture of judgment when the righteous who have been invited decline and strangers are saved. Thus Christ's supper is a banquet for sinners. The psalmist had already seen in bold prophecy (Ps. 23:5) that God Himself prepares the table for His guests and anoints their heads. Jesus now fulfils this as the humble Host who not only entertains His guests lavishly (Mk. 6:41 ff.; 8:6 ff.) but who Himself serves them at table even though they are His servants (Lk. 12:37; 22:27), who with His own hands washes their feet (Jn. 13:1 ff.), [177] and who finally, as oriental hospitality requires in extreme cases, crowns His service by redeeming His guests with His own life (Mk. 10:45), giving Himself to His guests an an offering in a way which surpasses all human comprehension (Mk. 14:22 ff. and par.). What hospitality can be and achieve is thus fulfilled in all its greatness, and its true meaning is brought to light (→ II, 92).

D. Foreign as a Religious Concept.

1. The Greek and Biblical View of Foreignness.

Being foreign, becoming foreign, and overcoming foreignness are fundamentally significant concepts of experience and religious speech, both in classical antiquity

---

[175] Cf. W. Liese, Art. "Hospital" in Lex. Th. K.², V (1933), 152 f.

[176] Perhaps a primary thought here is that the man who is blameless is under Yahweh's protection, cf. R. Kittel, Die Psalmen³, ⁴ (1922), 44; A. Bertholet in Kautzsch, 135, ad loc.

[177] → IV, 947. Everywhere in antiquity, both in the East (cf. Gn. 18:4; 19:2; for Indian examples Thieme, 153, 155) and in the West (cf. Hom. Od., 8, 449 ff.; 19, 356 ff.; 3, 464 f.; 4, 48 f.; 17, 87 f.), washing the feet on arrival is a part of true hospitality. Jesus Himself expects this, and misses it when it is not offered (Lk. 7:44). To wash a guest's feet oneself is, of course, a donum superadditum (loc. cit.). Plut. (Sept. Sap. Conv., 3, II, 148c d) and Cl. Al. (Strom., IV, 125, 1) tell of the daughter of Cleobulos of Lindos who was not ashamed to wash the feet of her father's guests. Because Jesus set His disciples an example of this, it then became customary in the Church. It is one of the works of love of the proven widow (1 Tm. 5:10) and is often commended by the fathers (e.g., Cyr. Hom. in Joh., 10, MPG, 77, 1024 ff.; Hier. Ep., 125, 15, 2, CSEL, 56, 134, 10; cf. R. Knopf, D. nachapost. Zeitalter [1905], 442; Thalhofer, Art. "Fusswaschung," Wetzer-Welte, Kirchenlexikon, IV [1886], 2145-2148), though in the Roman church it simply became an empty demonstration of majestic humility on the part of the pope and other high ecclesiastics.

and also in the Bible. But the starting-point is different in the two spheres. The Greek thinks primarily of the foreignness of the soul in the world, whereas the Bible starts with the idea that God is foreign to the world. For the Greeks foreignness is an anthropological concept; for the Bible it is a theological concept. But where the two worlds come into contact, both in Hellenistic Judaism and in the early Church, the two outlooks combine and intermingle in various ways.

a. The Greek View. In the early period [178] the ἄνω μετοικία, transitory residence in the upper world, is the happier period as compared with the incorporeal existence of the soul in Hades (Soph. Ant., 890). But then the picture changes. The soul is brought into essential antithesis to the body, [179] and its home is found high above in the noetic world. The body, or the whole world, is a hospice in which the heavenly stranger, the soul, lodges for a time by divine ordinance. Hence its basic mood, especially in the wise who are aware of its origin, is one of anxiety in this alien world and longing for its heavenly home. [180]

b. The Biblical View. The biblical starting-point is quite different. [181] Here the world, which properly belongs to God the Creator, has been estranged from God by an alien power (→ 32), and man with it. The antithesis is not between man and the world; it is between man and God. The overcoming of this estrangement is the problem of salvation history.

We have already seen how strongly the OT resists that which is alien to God and His order, especially alien peoples and their religions (→ 10 f.). But God's action is to man strange and surprising, ξένον and παράδοξον (cf. Is. 28:21, → n. 183), [182] when it is seen in the world, whether it be a work of grace (cf. Wis. 16:2 f.) or of punishment [183] (cf. Wis. 16:16 [22א c]; 19:5). This alienation is provisionally

---

[178] Cf. Rohde, I, 3 ff. etc.; ²II, 161 ff.

[179] This basic theme in Gk. thought is expressed in various metaphors, e.g., the soul as a prisoner, as entombed (e.g., Orpheus Fr., 3 [I, 7, 1 ff., Diels]; Philolaos Fr., 14 [I, 414, 13 f., Diels]; Plat. Gorg., 493a; Crat., 400c; also Pos. etc.; cf. Überweg-Praechter, Grundriss d. Gesch. d. Philosophie, I¹² [1926], 481), as a passing guest, as an alien being in the body (cf. Heracl. in Sext. Emp. Hyp., 3, 231 etc.; Rohde², II, 161 f., 265 ff.; Cr.-Kö., 1137, → n. 180).

[180] Cf. the statement of Anaxag. (in Diog. L., II, 3, 7; also Diels⁵, II, 5, 14 ff.): "ἐμοὶ γὰρ καὶ σφόδρα μέλει τῆς πατρίδος" δείξας τὸν οὐρανόν, and the passages adduced in Wnd. 2 K., 166 on 5:6, esp. Plat. Phaed., 67b ff. (ἥ γε ἀποδημία ἡ νῦν μοι προστεταγμένη) and Epict. Diss., I, 9, 16 f.: ἐπὶ δὲ τοῦ παρόντος ἀνάσχεσθε ἐνοικοῦντες ταύτην τὴν χώραν, εἰς ἣν ἐκεῖνος (sc. God) ὑμᾶς ἔταξεν. ὀλίγος ἄρα χρόνος οὗτος ὁ τῆς οἰκήσεως καὶ ῥάδιος τοῖς οὕτω διακειμένοις (cf. 2 C. 4:17). Perhaps the idea that the soul is on a journey, and goes home at death, stands behind the Gk. and Roman custom of burying the dead on roads, e.g., the road from Athens to Eleusis, or the Via Appia, and cf. the following significant, because ambiguous, burial inscr. from Alexandria (1st-2nd cent. A.D.): Κεῖμαι δ' Εἰταλίδος γαίης νέκυς ἔνδεκα μησίν ξείνη ἐν ἀλλοδαπῇ χερσὶ ποριζόμενος (Preisigke Sammelbuch, 4313, 6 f.).

[181] One might find in the ἐνδημεῖν ἐν τῷ σώματι of 2 C. 5:6 an echo of the Gk. view of the soul as a stranger in the body, linked with the saying of Hillel (→ 28), but → n. 204.

[182] → ἔργον II, 640 f.; cf. A. Weiser, Glaube u. Geschichte im AT (1931), 90. There is a counterpart to Is. 28:21 in Jos. Ant., 1, 45: τὸν θεὸν ἐξένιζε τὸ πραττόμενον, sc. Adam's conduct after the fall, which marks the beginning of alienation between God and man. For a linguistic par. cf. Luc. Charon, 13: ξένον αὐτῷ δοκεῖ τὸ πρᾶγμα.

[183] Cf. also ξενίζουσαι τιμωρίαι, though in a secular sense, in 3 Macc. 7:3; ξένη ἡ δουλεία αὐτοῦ in 'A Is. 28:21 is also meant in this sense. Cf. R. Otto, Das Heilige ¹⁷⁻²² (1929), 32 f.

overcome for Israel by the fact that it is received into God's land as a *ger* of God, i.e., as a resident alien under His protection. [184] The land of Canaan belongs to God. Israel holds it only in fee, and it must not allow it to come into the possession of others; cf. Lv. 25:23: ἐμὴ γάρ ἐστιν ἡ γῆ, διότι προσήλυτοι καὶ πάροικοι ὑμεῖς ἐστε ἐναντίον μου. As a guest, the Israelite has no rights in relation to God. The most he can claim is protection (cf. Ps. 39:12 f.; 119:19; 1 Ch. 29:15). Nevertheless, it is a great privilege to be even a guest in God's sanctuary (Ps. 15:1; 61:4).

Because Israel as God's *ger* also keeps His Law, Israel itself becomes a foreign body in the world. Awareness of this both on the Gentile and Jewish side finds varied expression. Worth noting are the additions to Est., e.g., 3:13e: τόδε τὸ ἔθνος μονώτατον ... διαγωγὴν νόμων ξενίζουσαν παραφυλάσσον (for παραλλάσσον), "observing a strange (and hence repugnant) manner of life on the basis of its laws." [185]

2. Foreignness in Hellenistic Judaism.

Hellenistic Judaism, represented esp. by Philo (Conf. Ling., 76-82; Som., I, 180 f.), reads Gk. ideas into the Bible at this pt. Philo finds in Gn. 15:13 the idea that for the φιλάρετος the body is not an οἰκεία γῆ but an ἀλλοδαπὴ χώρα (Rer. Div. Her., 267, cf. 268: the desires = ξένα διανοίας, also 82) or ξένη (Conf. Ling., 81), a ξένη πόλις (Cher., 120), an alien (ὀθνεῖος) house (Agric., 65); here, then, there is permitted no κατοικεῖν but only a παροικεῖν (Rer. Div. Her., 267, Cher., 120, Agric., 64) or παρεπιδημεῖν (*ibid.*, 65). In keeping is the fact that ὁ σοφὸς ... κατοικεῖ ... ὡς ἐν πατρίδι νοηταῖς ἀρεταῖς (Conf. Ling., 81)[186] or that πᾶσα ψυχὴ σοφοῦ πατρίδα μὲν οὐρανόν (cf. the saying of Anaxag. → n. 180), ξένην δὲ γῆν ἔλαχεν (Agric., 65). A notable feature of these sayings is that the idea of the heavenly origin and earthly foreignness of the soul is restricted to the φιλάρετος and the σοφός. Philo means, of course, the κατὰ Μωϋσῆν σοφός (Conf. Ling., 77). Others, represented by the people of Babylon, κατῴκησαν ὡς ἐν πατρίδι, οὐχ ὡς ἐπὶ ξένης παρῴκησαν (*ibid.*, 76). In this distinction Philo shows himself to be a true Jew. Most noteworthy is the applying of Gk. categories to θεοῦ ἄνθρωποι, sc. ἱερεῖς καὶ προφῆται in Gig., 61, of whom it is said: ... εἰς τὸν νοητὸν κόσμον μετανέστησαν κἀκεῖθι ᾤκησαν ἐγγραφέντες ἀφθάρτων <καὶ> ἀσωμάτων ἰδεῶν πολιτείᾳ. They prefer to citizenship in this world citizenship in the spiritual world, in the state of imperishable and incorporeal ideas. They would rather be strangers in this world than κοσμοπολῖται. Gk. anthropology is thus impressed into the service of Judaism. In the poem of Ps.-Phocylides, an interesting testimony is borne to the fusion of Jewish and Gk. ideas;[187] there is again found in vv. 39 ff. (= Sib., 2, 104 ff.) the Gk. idea that men are strangers on earth (v. 40: πάντες γὰρ ξενίης πειρήσονται πολυμόχθου),[188] though here with the biblical emphasis that the whole man is afflicted by this fate. Perhaps NT interpolations may be discerned in what is said in Test. Abr. (Rec. A) 7, p. 84 (M. R. James, TSt, II, 2) about the heavenly stranger who will again πρὸς τὸν θεὸν ἐκδημεῖν (also *ibid.*, 15, p. 95, 23 ff.).

---

[184] Cf. Nöldeke, 301; Buhl, 113; Kalt, 559 f.; Geiger, 351. An Islamic par. to the גג יהוה is the *ğâr allâh*, the inhabitant of the *kaaba* in Mecca.

[185] Cf. Kautzsch Apkr. u. Pseudepigr., 203, n. c.

[186] Related is the thought of Test. L. 13:8: γενήσεται αὐτῷ σοφία ... ἐπὶ γῆς ἀλλοτρίας πατρίς, but in between there intrudes the further thought that the wise man οὐκ ἔσται ξένος, ὅπου ὑπάγει (v. 3), because wisdom alone makes him a → φίλος.

[187] Cf. W. Schmid-O. Stählin, *Griech. Lit. Geschichte*[6], II, 1 (1920), 622.

[188] The two following verses (ὡς ξένοι ἀλλήλων ξεῖνος δέ τοι οὔ τις ἐν ὑμῖν ἔσσετ' κτλ.) do not belong to the poem of Ps.-Phocylides; cf. J. Bernays, *Ges. Abh.* (1885), 255.

Ideas of clear Gk. origin are sometimes found in the Rabb., as when Hillel acc. to Lv. r., 34, 3 called his soul an אֲכְסַנְיָא (= ξένος) in his house, i.e., a guest in the body. [189]

3. Foreignness in the New Testament.

NT ideas about foreignness and alienation are a development of those of the OT. But there is a radical inversion of reference. Thus far man had been a member of a world estranged from God. Now he comes to God and hence he becomes alien to the world as God Himself is. This takes place by reason of the fact that on his behalf Christ goes into the land which is alien to God. [190] This great change is the content of the Gospel. Formally statements are made which are strongly reminiscent of what we find in the Greeks and Philo, but they are quite different in inner meaning.

a. The Foreignness of God and Christ.

The presupposition is the reciprocal foreignness of God and the world as found already in the OT. God literally confronts all that is world as the unknown God (Ac. 17:23 : one might almost say the Wholly Other), who is absolutely strange (Jn. 8:19). But this is because men themselves, especially Gentiles, are estranged from Him (ἀπηλλοτριωμένοι, Eph. 4:18; Col. 1:21), and this estrangement is so great that it becomes enmity ; at this level "foreign" again comes to mean "hostile" (→ n. 9). This hostile alienation between God and man is the mark of the world before Christ. Hence Christ Himself, who belongs uniquely to God, comes into the world as a foreigner, as already in the Synoptic parable (Mk. 12:1 ff. and par.; cf. esp. ἀπεδήμησεν, v. 1), and then especially in John's Gospel, where His origin is different from the world's, and is just as unknown as His goal (8:14, 25 ff.; 7:35). For He comes to it from the unknown God (7:27-29; 8:14; 9:29 f.; cf. 6:42; 7:41 f.). He thus lives as a stranger in a tent (Jn. 1:14; [191] cf. also Lk. 9:58), and what He thinks and says is subject to the misunderstanding of the world [192] (cf. Jn. 3:4; 2:20; 7:35 etc.). Even to His disciples, who know His origin (14:7) and goal (v. 4), who perceive ὅτι ὁ κύριός ἐστιν (21:7), He is alien as the One who already belongs again to the heavenly world, so that they can ask : σὺ τίς εἶ; (21:12). There may thus be said of the truth of God which came to earth with Christ (1:17; 14:6) what Tert. says in Apol., 1: "It knows that it simply sojourns as a stranger on earth, that enemies are easily found among strangers, and that it ... has its origin, home and hope ... in heaven." Like Himself, His royal dominion is also not ἐκ τοῦ κόσμου τούτου; it is alien to this world (18:36). In keeping with the same basic insight we are to understand the fact that in the Synoptic parable Jesus, as He came into an alien land (→ supra), is again to leave

---

[189] Cf. P. Fiebig, Altjüd. Gleichnisse u. d. Gleichnisse Jesu (1904), 112; also D. Gleichnissreden Jesu im Lichte d. rabb. Gleichnisse d. nt.lichen Zeitalters (1912), 8 f.; also Der Erzählungsstil d. Evangelien (1925), 64 f.

[190] Cf. J. Schniewind, Das Gleichnis vom verlorenen Sohn (1940), 32 f.; though cf. Wnd. 2 K., 166.

[191] In view of the preceding ἐγένετο, ἐσκήνωσεν cannot be construed along the lines of the Gk. image of the body as the tent of the soul (cf. Wis. 9:15 : βρίθει τὸ γεῶδες σκῆνος νοῦν πολυφρόντιδα) which has influenced 2 C. 5:1 and 2 Pt. 1:13 f. (cf. also Dg., 6, 8), but in terms of the view of earth as a foreign land, it has to be taken like the ἐν σκηναῖς κακοικήσας of Hb. 11:9. This is not to deny that there is in Jn. 1:14 a suggestion of the dwelling of God among men (Shechinah etc.) (cf. the comm., ad loc.). Nonnus (Metaphrasis Ev. Joh., 1, 31), rightly paraphrases the thought of Jn. 1:11: ὡς ξένον οὐκ ἐγέραιρον (→ n. 22).

[192] Cf. M. Dibelius in RGG², III, 359.

His people and go back to a far heavenly country (ἀπεδήμησεν, Mt. 25:15) to take the βασιλεία (Lk. 19:12). That the disciples now await their Lord's return from abroad is to the same effect (cf. ἄνθρωπος ἀπόδημος, Mk. 13:34).

b. The Foreignness of Christians.

The same is true of His own, His disciples and messengers. They are not just guests of God (→ 27), but members of His household: οὐκέτι ... ξένοι καὶ πάροικοι, ἀλλὰ ... οἰκεῖοι τοῦ θεοῦ (Eph. 2:19). Heaven is their home (Eph. 2:6; Hb. 12:22 f.; 13:14; Gl. 4:26; Phil. 3:20), as the Greek philosopher and the Jewish theologian had claimed for the sage, → n. 180 and → 28. The difference from these analogies, as also from later Gnostic fusions, is that the Christian is not returning to a home which he had left; [193] he is on the way to a home which has been newly given to him by God, cf. Hb. 11:15 f.

(a) Legal Terminology. To express this thought there developed in the language of Christianity a kind of constitutional terminology. In the NT, as in Philo (esp. Cher., 120; Gig., 61), the Stoic categories πόλις and πολιτεία are applied to the heavenly and earthly world, and in apocalyptic expectation these are fused with the city of God, [194] cf. Hb. 11:10, 16; [195] Eph. 2:12, 19; Phil. 3:20; Dg., 5, 9: ἐπὶ γῆς διατρίβουσιν, ἀλλ' ἐν οὐρανῷ πολιτεύονται, and esp. Hb. 12:22 f., the depiction of the Christian city with the festal community and the gathering of the first-born, cf. also Herm. s., 1, 1 ff. When a person becomes a believer, then he moves from the far country to the vicinity of God. [196] His former outlawry (Eph. 2:12: ἀπηλλοτριωμένοι τῆς πολιτείας τοῦ Ἰσραὴλ καὶ ξένοι [197] τῶν διαθηκῶν τῆς ἐπαγγελίας) is replaced by civil rights in heaven (Eph. 2:19: συμπολῖται τῶν ἁγίων, i.e., perhaps angels). [198] But this also means migration from the world to a place distant from the world. There now arises a relation of reciprocal foreign-ness and estrangement between Christians and the world. Comparison with the πνεῦμα brings this out very well in Jn. 3:8. Those born of the Spirit are just as unknown as Christ Himself as to their origin and goal. [199] In virtue of their ἄνωθεν γεννηθῆναι (Jn. 3:3), and in distinction from the worldly (cf. 1 Jn. 4:5), they are not ἐκ τοῦ κόσμου, but, like Christ, ἐκ τοῦ θεοῦ (cf. Jn. 15:19; 17:14, 16). This is the secret of their foreignness. Their life in the world is that of sheep among wolves (cf. Mt. 10:16; 2 Cl., 5, 2). This is well brought out by persecution. It is

---

[193] There springs to mind at once the antithesis to Hb. 11 in Philo Conf. Ling., 78 (the souls of the κατὰ Μωυσῆν σοφοί) ἐπανέρχονται ἐκεῖσε πάλιν, ὅθεν ὡρμήθησαν τὸ πρῶτον, πατρίδα μὲν τὸν οὐράνιον χῶρον ἐν ᾧ πολιτεύονται, ξένην δὲ τὸν περίγειον ἐν ᾧ παρῴκησαν νομίζουσαι.

[194] Cf. H. Weinel, Die Stellung d. Urchristentums zum Staat (1908), 23 and n. 68 (51-53); Rgg. Hb., 356, n. 17; Dib. Herm., 459 f. (on v., 3, 2, 4); K. L. Schmidt, Die Polis in Kirche u. Welt (1939).

[195] Expressed here is the distinctive idea of antiquity that πόλις and deity belong together. Believers have their πόλις in heaven not merely because they belong to God but also because God belongs to them, since He has created for them a πόλις; cf. Weinel, loc. cit.

[196] Cf. Philo Gig., 61 (→ 27).

[197] Dib., ad loc.: "without claim to"; ξένος with gen. is also found in Anth. Pal., 4, 3, 37; Heliodor., 10, 14; P. Oxy., 1154, 10; cf. Bl.-Debr. § 182, 3. The same construction is found with the Lat. hospes, e.g., urbis.

[198] With such images Cl. Al. Prot., 82, 4 ff. admonishes pagans to have themselves put on the citizens' rolls (ἐγγράφεσθαι καὶ πολιτεύεσθαι) and thus attain admission as children into the father's house: πῶς γὰρ εἰσελθεῖν ἐπιτέτραπται τῷ ξένῳ;

[199] Cf. Bultm. J., 101 f., ad loc.

thus worth noting that in 1 Pt. ξενίζω plays a particular role in the sense of the mutual alienation of the world and Christianity. The world is offended by the conduct of Christians, ἐν ᾧ ξενίζονται μὴ συντρεχόντων ὑμῶν εἰς τὴν ... τῆς ἀσωτίας ἀνάχυσιν (4:4), [200] and conversely: μὴ ξενίζεσθε τῇ ἐν ὑμῖν πυρώσει πρὸς πειρασμὸν ὑμῖν γινομένῃ ὡς ξένου ὑμῖν συμβαίνοντος (v. 12). Why should Christians be surprised? The hostility of the world is in some sense natural for those who live in it as aliens. [201]

Christians are in the world as a ξένον ἔθνος; their Christian name is a ξένον ὄνομα (Act. Joh., 3). Hence they cannot κατοικεῖν in this alien world (Cl. Al. Strom., III, 31, 3; cf. § 4). [202] They can only παροικεῖν, "reside as less privileged aliens," or strictly παρεπιδημεῖν, "sojourn temporarily as foreigners without rights" [203] (1 Pt. 2:11; 1:1, 17); for ἡ ἐπιδημία ἡ ἐν τῷ κόσμῳ τούτῳ τῆς σαρκὸς ταύτης μικρά ἐστιν καὶ ὀλιγοχρόνιος (2 Cl., 5, 5; cf. the strikingly similar words in Epict. Diss., I, 9, 16 f., → n. 180); hence they must always be ready to leave the παροικία τοῦ κόσμου τούτου (v. 1), since ἐνδημεῖν ἐν τῷ σώματι [204] means ἐκδημεῖν ἀπὸ τοῦ κυρίου (2 C. 5:6).

The foreignness of Christians in the world is described particularly impressively in Dg., 5, 5: πατρίδας οἰκοῦσιν ἰδίας, ἀλλ᾽ ὡς πάροικοι· μετέχουσι πάντων ὡς πολῖται, καὶ πάνθ᾽ ὑπομένουσιν ὡς ξένοι· πᾶσα ξένη πατρίς ἐστιν αὐτῶν, καὶ πᾶσα πατρὶς ξένη ..., and Herm. s., 1, 1: ἐπὶ ξένης κατοικεῖτε ὑμεῖς οἱ δοῦλοι τοῦ θεοῦ. Ἡ γὰρ πόλις ὑμῶν μακράν ἐστιν ἀπὸ τῆς πόλεως ταύτης. This s., 1, along with 2 Cl., 5, 1 and 5; 1 Pt. 2:11 etc., shows how the concept is worked out in early Christian exhortation. Each πόλις has its own νόμος. The Christian must live acc. to that of his city (→ 29). Otherwise there is no return to heaven (5 f., 2); ὡς ἐπὶ ξένης κατοικῶν he should not amass earthly possessions (1 and 6), for ταῦτα πάντα ἀλλότριά εἰσι, καὶ ὑπ᾽ ἐξουσίαν ἑτέρου [205] εἰσίν (3, cf. 11). The alien goods [206] of earthly possession and the alien desire of σαρκικαὶ ἐπιθυμίαι are not fitting for πάροικοι καὶ παρεπίδημοι (1 Pt. 2:11) who hope one day to return εἰς τὴν ἰδίαν πόλιν (Herm. s., 1, 2). Their deportment can only be τὸ ὁσίως καὶ δικαίως ἀναστρέφεσθαι καὶ τὰ κοσμικὰ ταῦτα ὡς ἀλλότρια ἡγεῖσθαι καὶ μὴ ἐπιθυμεῖν

---

[200] Cf. Pall. Hist. Laus., p. 20, 11 f.: δι᾽ ἀρετὴν ξενιτεύων.

[201] Cf. the strikingly similar thoughts in M. Ant., 8, 14 f.: when one is clear as to the basic principles of a man, οὐδὲν θαυμαστὸν ἢ ξένον μοι δόξει, ἐὰν τάδε τινὰ ποιῇ ... μέμνησο ὅτι ὥσπερ αἰσχρόν ἐστι ξενίζεσθαι εἰ ἡ συκῆ σῦκα φέρει, οὕτως, εἰ ὁ κόσμος τάδε τινὰ φέρει, ὧν ἐστι φόρος. In relation to the later loss of this fundamental biblical insight, it is worth noting that the Apologists tried to meet the charge of ξένον, which carried with it the implication of "despised," "atheistic" (cf. Tat., 33, 2).

[202] As the race of Gn. 11 did, representing intoxication with the world, cf. Philo Conf. Ling., 76: κατοικήσαντες ... βεβαίως καταμένειν εἰσάπαν ἔμελλον → πάροικος; → 27, 26 ff.

[203] → παρεπίδημος; cf. Böckh, CIG, I, 1338 = Collitz, Griech. Dial. Inschr., III, 2, 4520: καὶ τῶν ἄλλων ξένων κατοικοῦντες καὶ παρεπιδαμοῦντες ἐν Ἀμύκλαις, also the differentiation of three groups of residents in Ditt. Or., 339, 29: 1. πολῖται, 2. ἄλλοι οἱ κατοικοῦντες τὴν πόλιν, 3. οἱ παρεπιδημοῦντες ξένοι. Cf. also Busolt-Swoboda, I, 292, n. 1; Zahn, Einl., II, 4 f., 12 f.; Rgg. Hb., 355, n. 13.

[204] The body is here the σῶμα τῆς σαρκός which belongs to the world; cf. 2 Cl., 5, 5 (→ supra), where τῆς σαρκός is perhaps to be taken as an epexegetical gen. with κόσμος: in Gk. thought body and world are almost the same as the alien dwelling-place of the soul, cf. Philo Agric., 64 with § 65; Rer. Div. Her., 267 with Cher., 120 (→ 27).

[205] The primary ref. is to the Roman emperor, but the passage is intentionally ambiguous; behind the ἕτερος, the alien ruler, is the devil (→ 32); cf. Dib. Herm., ad loc.

[206] Here, too, Stoicism offers a distinctive par. which may have influenced the formulation (cf., e.g., Sen. Ep., 47, 10, also 28, 9; cf. Dib. Herm., 550). But there is obviously an essential difference, since the antithesis (ἴδια) is intellectual goods in the one case, heavenly in the other.

αὐτῶν (2 Cl., 5, 6). πονηρὸν γάρ ἐστιν ἀλλοτρίων ἐπιθυμεῖν (Herm. s., 1, 11). The prospect of return from abroad to their home, and a readiness for this (2 Cl., 5, 1; → supra), are thus a decisive motive in exhortation, not merely for admonitions along the lines of Mt. 6:33, but also for injunctions to a world-renouncing asceticism. This finds here its most powerful basis, taking the sayings of Jesus (Jn. 17:16, 11) about His own who are not ἐκ τοῦ κόσμου but ἐν τῷ κόσμῳ, who are indeed expressly sent into it (v. 18), and completely neglecting the latter aspect in favour of the former.

The thought of foreignness is even more strongly emphasised when the stay on earth is depicted as a journey on which Christians must sustain themselves with the provisions [207] (τὰ ἐφόδια) of Christ, the word and sacrament, 1 Cl., 2, 1.

(b) OT Prototypes. For this distinctive position of Christians in the world the NT finds prototypes (1) in the patriarchs, whose status as political aliens [208] is regarded as the outward form of a deeper homelessness (Hb. 11:8 ff.); [209] ὅτι ξένοι καὶ παρεπίδημοί εἰσιν ἐπὶ τῆς γῆς (v. 13), [210] (2) in Israel in Egypt when it was πάροικος ἐν γῇ ἀλλοτρίᾳ (cf. Ac. 7:6; 13:17), and especially (3) in the Jewish Dispersion, whose characteristic terminology was richly used by the NT in its new sense [211] — one aspect of the appropriation of Jewish prerogatives by the new Israel.

c. The Rejection of the Foreign, but without Exclusion of Foreigners.

The Christian, even though he has learned to regard the world as a foreign land, is always in danger of making it his homeland and treating as ἴδια the things of the world which ought to be ἀλλότρια for him. Here, then, constant vigilance is required. In particular, the ways and means of the world should not find entry into the Christian community. Thus στάσις (mutiny, revolution) is ἀλλοτρία καὶ ξένη τοῖς ἐκλεκτοῖς τοῦ θεοῦ (1 Cl., 1, 1). Even more important, everything foreign is to be kept at arm's length from the Gospel. It is obvious that Christians deos alienos non adorant (Aristid., 15, 7; → 15). As in the old covenant strange fire and incense were not to be brought to God's altar (→ 10), so διδαχαὶ ξέναι must not be given a place in Christian teaching, Herm. s., 8, 6, 5; [212] Hb. 13:9. Dg. (11:1) emphasises that he does not preach strange things, but faithfully presents what has been handed down. In doctrine there prevails the same law of mutual estrangement and oddity between the world and Christianity as in life, → 29. For the Gospel is at work as a foreign "import" into the world, cf. Ac. 17:20: ξενίζοντά τινα εἰσφέρεις, with Herm. s., 8, 6, 5: ὑποκριταὶ καὶ διδαχὰς ξένας εἰσφέροντες. Each perceives that the other has another spirit. [213]

---

[207] The same image is used by the Mandaeans in the myth of the strange man, → n. 234.

[208] Among relevant statements of the patriarchs cf. the explanation of the stem gersom in Ex. 2:22 LXX: πάροικός εἰμι ἐν γῇ ἀλλοτρίᾳ ('Α ξένη); cf. on this Philo Conf. Ling., 82.

[209] Cf. Rgg. Hb., 361 ff.

[210] In Philo, too, the patriarchs' sense of being aliens plays a significant role (e.g., Abr., 62), but along the lines of his anthropology it is allegorically related to the soul which is pre-existent in the other world and merely sojourns temporarily in this world of appearance (Conf. Ling., 79 ff.; Rer. Div. Her., 267 etc.); cf. Rgg. Hb., 362, n. 32.

[211] διασπορά (Jm. 1:1; 1 Pt. 1:1), παροικία (1 Pt. 1:17; 2 Cl., 5, 1: = "stay in an alien land"; Mart. Pol. Praef.; Eus. Hist. Eccl., 4, 23, 5 etc.: = "congregation of strangers), ἡ ἐκκλησία ἡ παροικοῦσα 'Ρώμην etc. (1 Cl. Praef.; Pol. Praef.; Mart. Pol. Praef.), πάροικος (1 Pt. 2:11; Dg., 5, 5), παρεπίδημος (1 Pt. 1:1; 2:11).

[212] Here the same teachings are also called διδαχαὶ μωραί because they proceed from the wisdom of the world which is μωρία to God (→ μωρός, IV, 845 ff.).

[213] An alien spirit, not just an alien tongue, speaks in the ξενοφωνεῖν of Montanus (Eus. Hist. Eccl., 5, 16, 7; cf. also Ac. 2:4, though here the individual singles out from the ἕτεραι γλῶσσαι, not a foreign language, but his own. The church in its judgment of ἐξενοφώνησεν against Montanus expresses the same feeling as against the διδαχαὶ ξέναι of all heretics, whom it eo ipso declares to be against God.

But while the Gospel with its total claim excludes everything foreign from its sphere, it does not exclude foreigners from the offer of salvation, in contrast to many other religions. Neither in Greece (Eleusis) nor Rome (→ n. 37) was the alien admitted to religious fellowship. In particular, later Judaism was very exclusive in this respect as compared with Christianity (→ 13), cf. already Test. Jud. 16 (disclosure of the secrets of God to foreigners is forbidden). This trait of openness to foreigners is a prominent characteristic of early Christianity as compared with contemporary missionary rivals, whether the Jews on the one side or the mystery religions on the other.

d. The Devil as Foreigner. Behind the world estranged from God stands a power which sums up all that is alien to God. The devil is the alien κατ᾽ ἐξοχήν. Here "foreign" still means "hostile," and in the NT the devil is the supreme enemy (cf. Mt. 13:39; Lk. 10:19). The early Church had many names for the devil (→ II, 79), among them ὁ ξένος. Traces of this may be found in the fr. of a Baruch Apc. which has undergone Christian revision, [214] in the fr. of a work of Porphyrius, [215] in a distinctive version of the doctrine of the two kingdoms in Ps.-Clem. Hom., 15, 6 ff.; 20, 2 f. [216] and esp. in the depiction of baptism and the preceding exorcism in the so-called Church Order of Hippolytus. [217]

4. Fusions of Biblical and Greek Views of Foreignness.

The NT idea of the foreignness of Christians established by Christ, and the Greek belief in the essential foreignness of the human soul, are rooted in very different views of God and man. But their fusion was made possible by the process of acute Hellenisation of Christianity, and far beyond anything found in orthodox theologians [218] we have Gnosticism and its further development in the Manichees

---

[214] In Cyprian Testimonia, III, 29 (CSEL, 3, I, 143); cf. the transl. in Hennecke, 390, also N. Bonwetsch, "Das slavisch erhaltene Baruchbuch," NGG, 1896, 91 ff., esp. 93 f.; believers are here called odibiles alieno.

[215] Porphyr. Christ. Fr., 72, p. 90, Harnack (AAB, 1916): τίς δὲ ἡ αἰτία τοῦ βληθῆναι τὸν ἄρχοντα ἔξω ὡς ξένον τοῦ κόσμου; καὶ πῶς ξένος ὢν ἦρξε;

[216] Cf. C. Schmidt, Studien z. den Pseudo-Clementinen (1929), 180 ff. For him who decides for the coming kingdom of the other aeon, and for its ruler Christ, the ruler of the other, present kingdom, the devil, is an ἀλλότριος βασιλεύς (15, 7), and earthly things are οὐκ ἴδια, but he himself, living ἐν ἑτέρου βασιλείᾳ, is a stranger in the world.

[217] At a second testing of catechumens before baptism, the unclean are to be weeded out, for it is impossible for the "alien" to remain hidden, i.e., the devil concealing himself in the candidate for baptism (Copt. text, 45, p. 25, Lagarde [Aegyptiaca, 1883], p. 315, 19 f., Horner [The Statutes of the Apostles or Canones Ecclesiastici, 1904], cf. H. Achelis, D. Canones Hippolyti, TU, 6, 4 [1891], 92; in the Eth. (34, p. 151, 24, Horner) and Arab. (33, p. 252, 10, Horner) the candidate who has an unclean spirit is called an alien, obviously in the same fig. sense, cf. Hennecke, 578. But those passed as suitable for baptism are also admonished to cleanse themselves and to liberate themselves, i.e., from the alien (only in the Copt., p. 25, Lagarde, p. 315, 22, Horner, p. 92, Achelis). In the solemn exorcism the day before baptism every foreign spirit (Arab., 33; Copt., 45 : all foreign spirits) are driven out (p. 252, 19 f.; 316, 1 f., Horner ; p. 25, Lagarde ; p. 579, Hennecke ; p. 93, Achelis). In baptism itself separation from everything foreign must be so complete that candidates are to go down naked into the water, the women without any adornment, in other words, without anything foreign (Eth., 35, p. 152, 30-153, 1; Arab., 34, p. 253, 14-17; Copt., 46, p. 316, 30 f., Horner ; p. 27, Lagarde ; p. 109, Funk [Didascalia et constitutiones apostolorum, II, 1905]; p. 95, Achelis ; p. 579, Hennecke ; cf. also Test. Domini, p. 127, Rahmani [1899] and Canones Hippolyti, 115, p. 94, Achelis : ne ... descendat in aquam regenerationis quidquam peregrinum de spiritibus peregrinis). Apart from notions that clothes and ornaments are the seat of demons there obviously stands behind this rule the conviction that all earthly things belong to the alien kingdom of the devil and are thus "foreign" goods in the special sense, cf. Herm. s., 1, 3; on this Dib. Herm., 551 f. and → 30, 24 ff.

[218] Cf. Dg., 6, 8 : ἀθάνατος ἡ ψυχὴ ἐν θνητῷ σκηνώματι κατοικεῖ· καὶ Χριστιανοὶ παροικοῦσιν ἐν φθαρτοῖς, τὴν ἐν οὐρανοῖς ἀφθαρσίαν προσδεχόμενοι. Cl. Al. Quis Div. Salv., 36, 2 : True Gnostics are the σπέρμα ... ὥσπερ ἐπί τινα ξενιτείαν ἐνταῦθα

and Mandaeans, who work out the Greek thought of foreignness with full consistency, and also in his own way Marcion, who one-sidedly exploits the original alienation of man from God.

a. The Experience and Ethos of Foreignness in Gnosticism.

One of the most influential starting-points of Gnostic thinking is undoubtedly a much deeper sense of the foreignness of the human soul than is found in Gk. philosophy. With this are linked at a higher level all the feelings which characterise the elemental experiences of being a civil alien (→ 3), namely, the sense of the strange and menacing, of defencelessness and of not being understood.

(a) This experience was the source of Gnostic theology in the narrower sense. For the inseparable correlate of this feeling of foreignness is an unquenchable longing for a home in the hereafter. [219] The soul as a being from another, heavenly world, and all such beings, are characterised by the fact that they are aliens in the eyes of this world. [220] This is especially true of God Himself. The view that "God is the great, first, strange life from the worlds of light" [221] is a basic Mandaean dogma. The idea of "strange life" [222] is also the "primary word" [223] of Gnosticism, in whose two parts the idea of God is pregnantly stated. The strangeness of the divine is most clearly evident where it enters into direct contact with the world in the heavenly Redeemer, among whose many names "the Stranger," [224] i.e., the man from another world, is perhaps the most divine. [225]

The soul as a stranger in the world, and the Redeemer as the Stranger from heaven, are the two chief characters in the Gnostic Redeemer myth. They share the same loftiness of origin and the same distress of foreignness in the world, so much so that they sometimes seem to be identical. [226] A complication of the myth is that the soul goes so far astray in the foreign land that it loses the sense of being abroad and becomes alien to its true home. [227] To redeem it from this twofold plight the strange man makes his way

---

πεμπόμενον ὑπὸ μεγάλης οἰκονομίας καὶ ἀναλογίας ("through the great harmonious world plan of God"). Thus the life of "Gnostics" in the foreign country of the world rests on God's special choice and sending. Jesus spoke indeed to His disciples of such a mission into the alien and hostile world (cf. Mt. 10:16; Lk. 22:35 f.; Jn. 17:18), but only after this world had through Him become an alien sphere for those whom He sent.

[219] Cf. for expressions of this homesickness in Manichean sources, Reitzenstein Ir. Erl., 3, 11 ff.; also Jonas, 98.

[220] Cf. Bultmann, 119, n. 1; Lidz. Ginza, 5, n. 2.

[221] Or "the first life before which nobody was, the strange life from the worlds of light" (Lidz. Liturg., 63, 11; 74, 11).

[222] Mandaean prayers (Lidz. Liturg., 44, 3; 18, 8), incense (11, 6) sacraments (85, 9; 22, 4 f.) and healing of the soul (25, 3; 35, 8) are all in this name; cf. also 6, 7; 15, 5 f.; 125, 3; 65, 7 f.; Ginza R., V, 2, p. 179, 19 f.; 5, p. 199, 20 f.; on this W. Brandt, *Mandäische Schriften* (1893), 3. The Mand. expression in Heb. is חייא נוכראייא, from the same stem as נכרי (→ 8).

[223] Jonas, 97.

[224] Cf. the passages in Lidz. Ginza, Index, s.v. "fremd," e.g., the solemn introduction R., V, 5, p. 197, 15 f.: In the name of that strange man who pressed on through the worlds, cf. also Liturg., 23, 1; 36, 7; 138, 3; Joh., 41, p. 166, 10 ff.; 54, p. 191 ff.; it is worth noting that in these sections the strange man (= Mandā d'Haijê) is the representative of the communities of life who opposes the non-Mandaean godhead Adonai and attacks Judaism and Islam.

[225] A truly divine claim is thus made when Mani calls himself "the first stranger, the stranger from the great glory, the ruler-child" (cf. F. W. K. Müller, AAB, 1904, 29, 108; Reitzenstein, Ir. Erl., 10, 8).

[226] The one who is to be redeemed, like the Redeemer, is often called "the strange man," e.g., Lidz. Ginza R., XII, 3, p. 273, 3 ff.; Liturg., 224, 10; Joh., 17, p. 67, 8 ff.

[227] Cf. Jonas, 96 f. Particularly graphic is the description of sinking into the sleep of the foreign land in Act. Thom. (109 → 34, 17 ff.).

through the alien world with all its distress and danger.[228] The rulers of the world, esp. the spiritual powers of the stars (cf. Col.), i.e., the seven planets, oppose his enterprise. These have already brought the soul under their dominion, and they seek to hold it fast. They first attempt to confuse the strange man, esp. in the intoxicating mysteries of the world.[229] They then try to kill him, and to reduce his party to confusion by saying that he is impotent and has fled, or by engulfing his summons in the clamour of the world.[230] But the strange man is victorious.[231] Unlike the soul, he does not allow himself to be alienated from his heavenly home.[232] He reminds the soul of its foreignness in the world.[233] He rekindles its homesickness for heaven. Realising once more that it is journeying abroad,[234] it attaches itself to the strange man,[235] and thus becomes foreign as he is,[236] so that worldly beings no longer recognise it.[237] At the end of the Gnostic way stands the triumph of the Stranger, when the soul and its Deliverer merge into one another.[238]

There are undoubtedly echoes of these views, and not just of ordinary Christian παροικία (→ 30), when disciples in the various Acts influenced by Gnosticism are called "strangers."[239] This title expresses victory over the alien world.

(b) But in these Acts, cf. the pearl-song of Act. Thom., or the Asc. Is., one may detect a modification of the Redeemer myth. The Stranger from heaven intentionally clothes himself in a garment of the earthly world, ἵνα μὴ, as he himself says, ξενίζωμαι (Act. Thom., 109, p. 221). He goes through the world, not merely as a stranger, but also without being recognised to be such (Asc. Is., 10, 29-11, 19). In so doing he incurs the danger, like the soul among the Mandaeans (but cf. also → 31), of forgetting his

---

[228] Cf. Jonas, 122-126.

[229] Lidz. Ginza R., III, p. 120 ff.; cf. Liturg., 184, 11-185, 2; Joh., 41, p. 166, 10 ff.; Reitzenstein Ir. Erl., 86, n. 3, 235 f.; Bultmann, 120, 122; Jonas, 117.

[230] Lidz. Ginza R., III, p. 101, 17 f., 33 f.; X, p. 244, 32 ff.: They must not hear the speech of the strange man who has come here.

[231] Lidz. Joh., 38, p. 161, 6; cf. the joyful conclusion to most parts of the Mand. Joh. and to many parts of the Liturg. The man who has come here, i.e., into the world, is victorious, cf. Lidz. Joh., 11, n. 3.

[232] Cf. Lidz. Ginza R., XI, p. 257 f., esp. 258, 15 f.

[233] Cf. Lidz. Ginza L., I, 3, p. 441, 4 ff.; R., XI, p. 258, 13, 28; Liturg., 224, 10. The sense of strangeness in which distress and pride, poverty and superiority intermingle, is very finely expressed in the prayers and songs of the alien soul in Lidz. Liturg., 208, 5; 223-227. Here (227, 1) the seven (planets) finally say : Hail to him who has alienated himself from the world.

[234] E.g., Lidz. Ginza R., XII, 3, p. 273, 3 ff.: "I am a strange man ; ... my food for the way comes from the strange man." For the metaphor of the spiritual viaticum (→ 31) cf. Lidz. Ginza, Index, s.v. "Reisezehrung."

[235] Of Adam and Eve, for the Mandaeans prototypes of the history of the human soul, it is said : He conceived love for the strange man, whose speech is foreign, who is estranged from the world (Ginza R., X, p. 244, 36 f.), and : Her alienated mind was brought back for her to the strange man (L., I, 3; p. 439, 33 and 440, 1). Re-recognition of home and return to the divine Stranger together constitute conversion in Gnosticism.

[236] Cf. n. 226; also O. Sol. 17:6 : "All who saw me were astonished ; I appeared as a stranger to them" (cf. 41:8); on this Reitzenstein Ir. Erl., 91; Bultmann, 123; H. Gressmann in Hennecke, 453; Lidz. Liturg., 138, 4 f.

[237] Cf. Lidz. Liturg., 224, 10; O. Sol., 28:16 (→ n. 238). But first the soul knows itself again, and its origin ; cf. Lidz. Liturg., 99 = Ginza L., III, 20, p. 543, 8 ff.; Liturg., 84 f.; cf. the (Gnostic) speech of the dead to the powers about the Demiurge in Iren., I, 21, 5; also G. P. Wetter, ZNW, 18 (1917/18), 49-63, esp. 59.

[238] In O. Sol. 17 and 28 Christ obviously speaks in the redeemed singer, cf. esp. 17:6 ("as a stranger I appeared among them") and 28:16, and on this H. Gunkel, "Die Oden Salomos," ZNW, 11 (1910), 306 ff.; Jonas, 125.

[239] Esp. in many passages in Act. Thom., e.g., 4, p. 106; 136, p. 242 (here "a stranger, and despised, and a beggar," → n. 103 and → n. 22), also Mart. Andr., 4, p. 39 (→ n. 250); Act. Pl. et Thecl., 19, p. 248; 26, p. 254 ("a stranger" = a handmaid of God).

origin and becoming worldly.[240] The Redeemer himself, then, must be redeemed, and this takes place through the letter from home[241] and the heavenly voice (Act. Thom., 110 f.). Only with the return of the Stranger to his heavenly home does there take place his recognition and the great ξενισμός of worldly powers (cf. Asc. Is., esp. 11, 23).[242]

It may be asked, however, whether this form of the story of the divine Stranger[243] could really arise without some knowledge of the Gospel, since it gives evidence of profound insight into the nature of divine revelation in concealment.

(c) Two basic distinctions mark off this whole complex of Gnostic thoughts about foreignness from those of the Bible. 1. In the Bible it is sin which estranges man and the whole world from God, whereas here it is only a half culpable assimilation to a world always hostile to God which alienates primal man, or the soul, from its heavenly home. 2. In the NT Christ makes the Christian a real stranger in the world for the first time by bringing him back to the Father's house, whereas in Gnosticism the Redeemer simply makes the soul aware that from the very outset its home was in the world beyond, and that it is only temporarily a stranger in this world. In other words, Christ redeems the soul from sin, Gnosticism only from ignorance. Behind this, however, is the basic difference that Gnosticism thinks anthropocentrically, the Bible theocentrically. For the starting-point of Gnosticism is the soul's experience of foreignness, whereas the Bible begins with the revelation of the holy and gracious God, whose holiness first gives the world and man an awareness of estrangement, and whose grace overcomes this estrangement.[244]

b. The Alien God of Marcion.

Between the Bible and Gnosticism is Marcion. For him man as a creation of the just God is by nature a stranger for the good God. Marcion thus reverses the thought of Gnosticism that man belongs essentially to God. He also corrects the Christian belief that Christians are strangers in the world. The God previously alien to them is the one who brings them into a new Father's house of which they had no inkling before.[245]

---

[240] Cf. Jonas, 320 ff., esp. 324, n. 1.

[241] Cf. also O. Sol. 23:5 ff.

[242] In a closely related myth the same event is depicted under the image of the strange star which with its full δόξα plunges all into terror and astonishment, cf. the traces in Ign. Eph., 19, 2 (... καὶ ξενισμὸν παρεῖχεν ἡ καινότης αὐτοῦ) and Cl. Al. Exc. Theod., 74, 2 (ἀνέτειλεν ξένος ἀστὴρ καὶ καινὸς καταλύων τὴν παλαιὰν ἀστροθεσίαν). Not without influence here was the star of the wise men (Mt. 2:2 ff., with the paraphrase of Orig. [Cels., I, 58]: καινὸν εἶναι νομίζομεν καὶ μηδενὶ τῶν συνήθων παραπλήσιον) which was even interpreted as a symbolical embodiment of the Redeemer; cf. H. Schlier, *Religionsgeschichtliche Untersuchungen zu den Ign.-Briefen* (1929), 28 ff.

[243] It is perhaps echoed 1 C. 2:8 and was later very plainly referred to Christ (cf. Asc. Is., 9, 13 ff.; Act. Thom., 45); obviously, too, there is a certain fusion with the τόπος of the *descensus ad inferos*; cf., e.g., Test. Domini, ed. Rahmani, 65 (death in the underworld asks: *quis est hic, qui terram est indutus, sed coelum est?*); for further examples cf. H. Schlier, *op. cit.,* 15 ff.; Bultmann, 120 f. (cf. 121, n. 1 for additional bibl. on the motif of the unknown Redeemer).

[244] If Jn. in phrases reminiscent of Gnosticism says that Jesus is a stranger unknown to the world, this is to be regarded, like much else, as a missionary accommodation to the concerns and thought-forms of the surrounding world (cf. *et al.* A. Oepke, "Das missionarische Christuszeugnis des Johannesevangeliums," *Evg. Missions-Zeitschr.,* 2 [1941], 4-26).

[245] This is why Marcion expunges from his NT the parable of the Prodigal Son. For how can the alien God be the father to whose house the penitent son returns if man did not previously have his home in heaven? Cf. Harnack, *op. cit.,* 126, n. 3, 225, and on the whole question 118 ff.; Jonas, 214-251.

Marcion, then, agrees with the NT against Gnosticism inasmuch as his starting-point is theocentric. His first thesis is that God is an absolute Stranger in relation to the world, [246] his second that in Christ this good God has come into the alien world to redeem it. The distinctive conception in Marcion is that the alien and unknown God has come in merciful love to redeem a world which is no concern of His, since He created nothing within it. [247]

But this undertaking of the alien God necessarily arouses the opposition of the creator of the world, cf. the opposition of the seven and of other spiritual beings in Gnosticism, and that of the ἄρχοντες τοῦ αἰῶνος τούτου in Paul. But the alien God is stronger than the world with its God, and He is the Victor. He comes down unhindered from His heaven through that of the creator of the world, and as the Redeemer takes from this creator his creatures.

The distinctive feature of the religious and philosophical outlook of Marcion is this combination of the radical foreignness of God with His radical goodness. In all languages the true name of Christ in the Marcionite churches is thus "the Stranger" or the "good Stranger." [248] The Marcionite is proud to proclaim a ξένη γνῶσις (Cl. Al. Strom., III, 12, 3) [249] and to call himself a γνώστης ξένου θεοῦ. [250]

In contrast, the Gospel, and the Church which builds on this alone, proclaims a God who intrinsically is no stranger to the world, but its Creator and Lord. It is the world's fault that it has become an alien kingdom for God, and hence also for those who are redeemed from it, and who as such are οὐκ ἐκ τοῦ κόσμου. Herein the religious sense of foreignness is, however, overcome; for those redeemed by Christ the world is a foreign land and their home is God.

Stählin

---

[246] This was in fact "a revolutionary idea" (Jonas, 247), though it came, not from a basic Gnostic conception also adopted by Paul, but from Paul himself. The only pt. is that in Marcion the alienation between God and the world is primary, whereas in Paul it is secondary, due to sin. The alien God of Marcion is a biblical concept worked out one-sidedly (Harnack, 1 ff.).

[247] *Deus processit in salutem hominis alieni* (Tert. Marc., 1, 23). On the basis of Lk. 10:22 Marcion emphasises (*ibid.*, 1, 2) that in Christ God has revealed Himself to the world for the first time; this is a *nova et hospita dispositio* (cf. Act. Thom., 72 : ᾽Ιησοῦ οὗ ἡ φήμη ξένη ἐν τῇ πόλει ταύτῃ, "of whom nothing has been heard in this world"). *Neque mundus per eum factus est, neque in sua venit, sed in aliena* (Iren., III, 11, 2). *Christus magis adamavit hominem, quando alienum redemit* (Tert. De Carne Christi, 4). These are typical sayings of Marcion, though the pointedly anti-NT understanding (esp. in Iren.) may be set to the account of the commentator.

[248] Cf. Harnack, 119.

[249] If later (III, 21, 2) Cl. ironically calls the Marcionite teachings ξένα δόγματα, there are three allusions : 1. a play on Marcionite statements ; 2. the suggestion that these doctrines derive from outwith the Bible (sc. from Plato); 3. the criticism that they are odd and unacceptable.

[250] This phrase occurs in Mart. Andr., 4 (also adduced in E. Norden, *Agnostos Theos* [1913], 53, n. 3). The strong emphasis on the stranger here — Andr. as a ξένος ἄνθρωπος who proclaims a ξένον θεόν — may be attributed to Marcionite influence (→ 34 ff.). It is certainly significant that only the stranger knows the strange God in whom alone truth and salvation are to be had ; hence there is need of one who knows the stranger.

---

† ξύλον

This word is not to be derived from ξύω, "to scrape." It is probably related to the Germ. "Säule,"[1] and denotes living wood or dead wood hewn from the stem. Living wood is rare. Cf. also Xenoph. An., 6, 4 and 5 : (ὄρος) δασὺ πολλοῖς καὶ παντο-7, 65 : Ἰνδοὶ δὲ εἵματα ἐνδεδυκότες ἀπὸ ξύλων πεποιημένα.[2] But the sense "living δαποῖς ξύλοις, Eur. Cyc., 572 : τὸ ξύλον τῆς ἀμπέλου, Callim. Hymnus in Cererem, 40 (41): ξύλον ἱερόν. We are referred to tree-felling (ξύλα κόπτειν) by P. Tebt., 5, 205 : καὶ τοὺς κεκοφότας τῶν ἰδίων ξύλα παρὰ <τὰ> ἐκ<κ>είμενα προστάγματα, and P. Flor., 152, 4 : ἵνα κόψῃ ξύλα. Much more often ξύλον means dead wood. ξύλον is wood for building, commercial timber, fuel.[3]

The word also means anything made from wood, esp. "stick," "cudgel," "club" (as a weapon). Cf. esp. Hdt., 2, 63; 4, 180; Plut. Lyc., 30, 2; P. Tebt., 304, 10. For the sense of "wood for shipbuilding" cf. Hes. Op., 808 (ξύλα νήϊα), Thuc., 7, 25 (ξύλα ναυπηγήσιμα). In Demosth., 45, 33 it means "bench" or "table," esp. "money-changers' table." In the popular assembly or theatre or court the first bench on which the πρυτάνεις and πρόεδροι sit is πρῶτον ξύλον, Aristoph. Ach., 25; Vesp., 90; Hermipp., 9, CAF, I, 227; Poll. Onom, 4, 121: πρῶτον δὲ ξύλον ἡ προεδρία (of the theatre).

The instrument of restraint and punishment used for slaves, madmen and prisoners has the name of ξύλον.[4] It is either a heavy wooden collar through which the head of the offender is put (cf. Aristoph. Nu., 592; Lys., 680) or the stocks in which the feet are fastened, Hdt., 9, 3, 7: ἐδέδετο ἐν ξύλῳ σιδηροδέτῳ. The typical phrase for this kind of punishment is δῆσαι ἐν ξύλῳ (Aristoph. Eq., 367, 394, 705; cf. Schol. Aristoph. Pl., 476 : ξύλα, οἷς τύπτονται ἐν τοῖς δικαστηρίοις οἱ τιμωρούμενοι, 606 : ὁ ξύλινος δεσμός, ἐν ᾧ δεσμεύονται οἱ ἐν τῇ φρουρᾷ), cf. also Polycel., 3, CAF, I, 790 : ξύλον ἐφέλκειν. The ξύλον πεντεσύριγγον is a special instrument of punishment combining the first two. As its name indicates, it contains 5 tubes or sleeves through which the head and limbs are put, Aristoph. Eq., 1049 : δῆσαι ἐν πεντεσυρίγγῳ ξύλῳ. Already, then, in secular Gk. the word ξύλον took on the sense of something disgraceful or shameful. From this, by way of the LXX, it is but a step to the NT sense of "cross."

ξύλον can also denote the "stake" or "tree" to which malefactors were fastened, Alexidos Tarantinoi, 222, 10, CAF, II, 379; Cratin., 341, CAF, I, 112. Finally, it is a measure of length (3 πήχεις = 4½ feet, Hero, Geometrica, 23, 4, 11).

The plur. occurs in Aristoph. Fr., 402, 403, CAF, I, 496 in the sense of wood market, ἐπὶ ξύλα ἰέναι.

Fig. ξύλον is a "wooden" or "unfeeling" person, Achill. Tat., 5, 22 : ὁ δὲ σίδηρός τις, ἢ ξύλον, ἤ τι τῶν ἀναισθήτων ἦν ἄρα πρὸς τὰς δεήσεις τὰς ἐμάς.[5] One may also refer to Anth. Pal., 9, 152, where the Trojan horse is called ἵπποιο κακὸν ξύλον.

In the LXX the sense of "living wood" ("tree") is much more common than in profane lit. Fruit-trees, forest-trees and trees of the field are called ξύλα. The tree is also a cultic site (Jer. 3:6, 13 : ξύλον ἀλσῶδες), though strongly attacked by the prophets because it is a place of idolatry (cf. ξύλα τοῦ ἄλσους, Ju. 6:26). ξύλον τῆς ζωῆς is

---

ξ ύ λ ο ν. [1] I owe this to A. Debrunner ; cf. Boisacq, 679; Walde-Pok., II, 503 f.

[2] εἵματα ἀπὸ ξύλου may be clothes of cotton, but also of bark or fibre. They are probably cotton. Cf. on this J. U. Fäsi, Progr. d. Zürich. Cantonsschule, 1838, 22, who rejects the sense of clothes of bark or fibre. To support his view he refers to Hdt., 3, 106.

[3] For detailed examples cf. Liddell-Scott and Pass. Cf. also C. G. F. Meineke, Comicae Dictionis Index (comp. H. Jacobi, 1857), V, 2, 666 (s.v. ξύλον) or Aristot., V, 494 (Index, s.v., ξύλον); cf. also BGU, 731, II, 8 and 10; 953, 6; 1028, III.

[4] Cf. on this whole section Fäsi, op. cit., 21 f.

[5] Acc. to ed. Hercher, Script. Erot. (1858) the quotation runs : ὁ δὲ σιδηροῦς τις ἢ ξύλινος <ἤ τι τῶν ἀναισθήτων> ἦν ἄρα πρὸς τὰς δεήσεις τὰς ἐμάς.

found in Gn. 2:9; 3:22, 24, also Is. 65:22; 4 Macc. 18:16. In Prv. 3:18 wisdom is ξύλον ζωῆς (ξύλον ζωῆς ἐστι πᾶσι τοῖς ἀντεχομένοις αὐτῆς). The expression ξύλον τοῦ παραδείσου occurs in Gn. 3:8 and Ez. 31:9 (ξύλον ἐν τῷ παραδείσῳ, Ez. 31:8). The meaning "wood" (for cultic and secular purposes) is common in the LXX; fairly common, too, is the combination ξύλα ἄσηπτα (esp. in Ex.).

The two basic meanings of "living wood" and "dead wood" are also found in the NT.

1. Wood. The saying on the way to Golgotha in Lk. 23:31 is dominated by the antithesis of ὑγρὸν ξύλον and ξηρὸν ξύλον. [6] This is a common figure of speech in later Judaism. [7] With Schlatter [8] we may assume that in spite of the par. in Ez. 17:24 ξύλον means wood rather than tree. [9] Jesus compares Himself with green (damp and sappy) wood, the Jewish people with dry. Sappy wood is not so easily burned as dry. Yet God has not spared Jesus; He goes on His way to the cross and death. How much more will Judaism, if impenitent, learn the seriousness of divine judgment. This is a hard prophetic saying which Jesus pronounces, and it takes away all illusions from Israel. Judgment will fall in full severity on the chosen people if it persists in unbelief and disobedience.

In 1 C. 3:12 Paul addresses seriously all who would be teachers in the Christian community. He refers to the judgment which will be passed on their whole activity. There is only one foundation, Jesus Christ. This is laid. No man may establish any other foundation for the community. Of decisive importance for the individual teacher, however, is the way in which he does his work and renders his service. What matters is the quality of what is built on the given foundation. Gold, silver, precious stones, wood, hay and stubble are possible building materials. The day of the Lord will reveal and test the work of each.

Among the wares of the merchants of the earth in Rev. 18:12, which they can no longer sell after the fall of Babylon, we find among many other luxuries ξύλον θύϊνον, i.e., wood from the North African thyia tree which was used to make costly vessels and inlaid work. [10]

2. Cudgels. Acc. to Mt. 26:47, 55 par. the host sent out by the high-priests and elders of the people to arrest Jesus was armed with swords and cudgels (μάχαιραι καὶ ξύλα). [11]

---

[6] ξύλον ξηρόν in the LXX Sir. 6:3; Is. 56:3; Ez. 17:24; 21:3.

[7] Cf. esp. Seder Elij. R., 14 (65), Str.-B., II, 263, where the saying is quoted as a proverb: If the fire takes hold of the fresh (sappy) wood (or tree), what will happen to the withered (dry)? Note should be taken esp. of the material par. in Gn. r., 65, 18 (Str.-B., II, 263 f.), where R. Jose b. Jo'ezer (c. 150 B.C.), going to crucifixion, says to the nephew riding beside him and scoffing: If this (crucifixion) happens to those who offend him (God), what of those who do his will! and: If this happens to those who do his will, what of those who offend him! It may be seen plainly that the Gospel depiction of the conduct and saying of Jesus on His last journey corresponds in every pt. to what, on the basis of Rabb. accounts, we should expect in such a situation of pious Jews aware of God's requirement. This is a strong pt. in favour of the historical fidelity of Lk. [Kuhn].

[8] Schl. Lk., 449.

[9] This is supported by the pars. from the Talmud and Midrash in Str.-B., II, 263.

[10] Loh. Apk., 147.

[11] Zn. Mt., 703 conjectures that the group which arrested Jesus consisted of Roman soldiers (μάχαιραι) and Sanhedrin police (ξύλα). But it is most unlikely that the Sanhedrin would have had Roman soldiers under its command. The text seems to refer only to Sanhedrin police armed with swords and staves. Cf. the par. in Lk. 22:52. Schl. Mt., ad loc. (753 f.) refers to T. Men., 13, 21, where it is said that the servants of the high-priest carried cudgels (מקלות) with which they beat the people.

3. Stocks. in Ac. 16:24 ξύλον is the wooden stocks in which the feet of prisoners were made fast. They were thus held secure. This treatment was accorded Paul and Silas when they were arrested at Philippi and put in the inner part of the prison. In the LXX ξύλον is only once used in this sense at Job 33:11: ἔθετο δὲ ἐν ξύλῳ (בַּסַּד) τὸν πόδα μου.

4. Cross. A distinctive NT use of ξύλον is in the sense "cross." This can be understood only against the background of the LXX. Primitive Christian preaching in Ac. (5:30; 10:39; 13:29) takes up the saying in Dt. 21:22, which says that if a man has done something worthy of death, and if after execution his body is hung on a tree, it should not be left on the tree overnight, but buried the same day. The person executed is regarded as accursed by God.[12] In Acts the description of the death of Jesus in terms of Dt. 21:22 serves to bring out the shame of the crucifixion. To crucify Jesus was to offer Him the greatest possible insult. But God revealed the whole majesty of the crucified Jesus, who died on this cross of shame, by raising Him from the dead and exalting Him to His right hand.

In Gl. 3:13 Paul uses the thought of Dt. 21:23: ἐπικατάρατος πᾶς ὁ κρεμάμενος ἐπὶ ξύλου, as the basis for his statement that Christ has redeemed us from the curse of the Law. In this he goes beyond the application of the OT saying in the primitive community according to the witness of Ac. By means of the verse he supports his views on the curse of the Law. The argument is as follows. A curse lies on the Jews, the people of the Law, because they have not kept the Law. This curse, if it is not lifted, will finally demand death. No curse lay on Christ Himself, for He was the righteous Son of God. But He became a curse for us. Herein consists His act of salvation. He who did not stand under the curse of the Law, because He did not sin, voluntarily and vicariously, in accordance with God's will, took upon Himself the curse and death. That He really took upon Himself the curse finds clear expression in the manner of His death. Crucifixion is death on the accursed wood. This is the deep significance of the crucifixion of Christ.

The figurative term ἐξαγοράζειν implies that for Paul transgressors of the Law lay in the curse as in a prison.[13] In the death of Christ, however, ransom took place.[14] Christ freed them from imprisonment. For individual Jews this fact was a reality of living experience through faith in Christ. For Christ's sphere of life means freedom from the Law, and consequently from its curse.[15]

Similarly, though with no reference to the Law, 1 Pt., under Pauline influence, declares that Christ bore our sins in His own body on the "wood" (1 Pt. 2:24). This is undoubtedly based on Is. 53:4, 12. Predominant here, too, is the idea of substitution. The sins of men are laid on the body of the sinless Christ, who bears them to the cross. With the crucifixion of His body, then, the sins which He voluntarily associated with His σῶμα are also crucified. The author's concern is to show that they are hereby set aside.[16] It could be that this conception is in-

---

[12] Jewish law does not prescribe crucifixion as a capital sentence, only Roman law. Hence Dt. 21:22 refers to the dead body, which after execution in some other way (stoning, beheading etc.) was hung to a tree or stake (κρεμάσητε αὐτὸν ἐπὶ ξύλου) in order to expose the condemned to the shame of public exposure even after death. Cf. also Str.-B., I, 1034 f.

[13] So also Zn. Gl., 157.

[14] On the concept of ransom cf. A. Deissmann, *Paulus²* (1925), 130 ff. and LO, 271 ff.

[15] On this whole section cf. Ltzm. Gl., 19; Zn. Gl., 158 ff., esp. 159.

[16] Cf. also Wnd. Kath. Br., 65: "The author is more concerned about the setting aside of sins than about their forgiveness."

fluenced by the idea of the scapegoat in Lv. 16:21 f. [17] (Cf. also Jn. 1:29.) Unlike the OT high-priests, Christ does not lay the sins on a scapegoat; αὐτός, ἐν τῷ σώματι, He takes them to Himself and cancels them on the cross. He Himself is both victim and priest in one. Sinless, He blots out the sins of sinners by His sacrificial death. The result is that we, dead to sin, live now to righteousness.

5. Tree (Tree of Life). In several verses (2:7; 22:2, 14, 19) Rev. speaks of the ξύλον τῆς ζωῆς. According to 2:7 this tree is in the heavenly Paradise of God. 22:2 tells us that trees of life [18] stand on both banks of the river of life in the heavenly Jerusalem, that they bear fruit 12 times a year, and that their leaves are for the healing of the nations. Entry into Paradise and a share in the fruits of these trees is gained by those who have been cleansed from their sins by the blood of Christ (22:14) and by the victors who in martyrdom have carried the day against earthly and satanic powers (2:7). This right is based on the divine sentence. But God can take away this share in the tree of life and the holy city from those who impugn the divinely given status of the prophetic word and do not give it unconditional recognition or due obedience (22:19).

The conception of the tree of life in Rev. goes back to later Jewish ideas. [19] In Jewish apocalyptic the return of the original conditions in Paradise plays an important role. Paradise is a heavenly place. It will be the future abode of believers. As in the original Paradise, so in that of the last time there will be the tree of life, and this will give believers the wonderful, supraterrestrial food of immortality (En. 25:4, 5). Eating of the tree of life is a reward for the blessed (Test. L. 18:11; cf. En. 24:4; 25:4 f.). The idea of the river of Paradise also occurs (Slav. En. 8:2 ff.; cf. already Ez. 47:1-12; Zech. 14:8). The concept of the heavenly city is closely linked with that of Paradise. Though originally it is quite distinct, the two concepts merge in apocalyptic (S. Bar. 4; 4 Esr. 8:52; Test. D. 5). They are directly associated in Rev. too. Rev. has taken over the ideas and conceptions of later Jewish apocalyptic. It uses them to present its thoughts on the future felicity of perfected believers. ξύλον τῆς ζωῆς is a figurative expression for the share of Christians in the glory of the heavenly world. [20]

Roberts [21] goes further. He believes that the expression ξύλον τῆς ζωῆς does not merely go back to Jewish lit., but receives a new content in Christian use. There is an allusion to the cross of Christ; the author of Rev. sets the cross in the Paradise of God. This view, however, implies a symbolism which was surely not in the mind of the author. ξύλον for δένδρον, and the expression ξύλον τῆς ζωῆς generally, is most simply explained in terms of LXX usage.

Of great interest in connection with the ideas expressed in Rev. 2:7; 22:14 is the Byzantine gravestone: κύριε ὁ θεὸς τῶν πατέρων ἡμῶν, ἐλέησον τὴν ψυχὴν τοῦ δούλου σου κτλ., ψώμισον αὐτῆς ἀπὸ τοῦ ξύλου τῆς ζωῆς. [22]

Early Christian art indicates a close relationship between the tree of life and the cross. The cross of Christ, the wood of suffering and death, is for Christians a tree of life. In the tomb paintings of the 2nd century it is thus depicted for the first time as the

---

[17] So also Wnd., loc. cit.

[18] In Rev. 22:2 ξύλον is collective (Heb. עֵץ). Cf. Loh. Apk., 173.

[19] Cf. the presentation in Bousset-Gressm., 282 ff., and for the Rabb. Str.-B., III, 792; IV, 1121 and 1123 f. under i; IV, 1132 and 1143 under x; IV, 1146 and 1152 under k.

[20] Cf. on the whole section EB, III, 3578 ff., s.v. "Paradise," 11 and Dict. of the Bible, IV, 809 ff., s.v. "Tree"; III, 668 ff., esp. 671, s.v. "Paradise."

[21] R. Roberts, "The Tree of Life (Rev. 2:7)," Exp. T., 25 (1913, 4), 332.

[22] Lefèbvre, Recueil des Inscr. Grecques-Chrétiennes de l'Égypte (1907), 67, 9; cf. Preisigke Wört., II, 148, s.v.

symbol of victory over death. It then recurs again and again. [23] The idea that the living trunk of the cross bears twigs and leaves is a common motif in Christian antiquity.

J. Schneider

---

† ὄγκος

In class. Gk. ὄγκος first means "mass," "weight," "compass." [1] Emped., 100, 13 (Diels, I, 200 : ἀέρος ὄγκος); Soph. El., 1142 : σμικρὸς ὄγκος ἐν σμικρῷ κύτει, Plat. Theaet., 155a : μήτε ὄγκῳ μήτε ἀριθμῷ, cf. also Aristot. Metaph. M, 9 (1085a, 12) and N, 2 (1089b, 14). Fig. it then means the inner spiritual weight which accrues to something, Philo Agric., 61: ὄγκος εὐτυχίας, Epict. Gnom. Stob., 9 : ἐν πλούτῳ καὶ ὄγκῳ τύχης. Philo esp. often uses it for "burden," Sacr. AC, 63 : σάρκινος ὄγκος, "fleshly burden"; acc. to Leg. All., II, 77 Egypt is σωματικὸς ὄγκος, cf. also Det. Pot. Ins., 27 and 113, where we find both the lit. and the fig. senses : ἄθλιοι δ' ὧν μεστοὶ μὲν οἱ ὄγκοι, κεναὶ δ' αἱ ἐπιθυμίαι καὶ ἔτι διψῶσαι. Related to this is the sense of "dignity," "worth," Eur. Phoen., 717: ἔχει τιν' ὄγκον "Αργος Ἑλλήνων πάρα, Philo Jos., 65 : ὄγκῳ καὶ σεμνότητι πρὸς ἄπαντα χρώμενον, but also "pride," "conceit," i.e., self-ascribed worth : Plut., I, 526b : συμπεριτιθεὶς ὄγκον αὐτῷ, cf. I, 154b. The term is relatively common in Philo, who also uses it fig. — also in the sense of ὕβρις — e.g., Ebr., 128 : οὐ διὰ μεγαλαυχίας κενοῦ φυσήματος ὑπόπλεων ὄγκον; Decal., 43. The LXX does not use it.

The only NT occurrence of ὄγκος is at Hb. 12:1: ὄγκον ἀποθέμενοι πάντα. [2] In connection with the metaphor of the contestant, ὄγκος unquestionably has the sense of the weight which he must put off to be able to attain his goal unhampered. [3] It is hardly possible to define more closely what kind of a burden the author has in mind. [4] By using the adj. πάντα he himself abandons any such attempt. In view of the great host of witnesses who have preceded him, the Christian must not try to do other than emulate them. He must enter the appointed track and allow nothing to hamper or distract him. [5]

Seesemann

---

[23] Cf. L. v. Sybel, Ξύλον ζωῆς, ZNW, 19 (1919/20), 85 ff. Cf. also J. Schneider, *Die Passionsmystik des Paulus* (1929), 128, 135.

ὄ γ κ ο ς. [1] Etym.: ἐν-εγκ-εῖν, "to bear," hence the basic sense is "burden," Boisacq, 684; Walde-Pok., I, 129 [Debrunner].

[2] 𝔓 13 links ὄγκον with the preceding word μαρτύρων, which is surely incorrect ; *v.* Michel Hb., *ad loc.*

[3] Of exegetes, Bengel and A. Seeberg opt for the sense of "pride," "arrogant disposition," but this is unconvincing, since it does not take the metaphor sufficiently into account.

[4] Severian of Gebala : "Ογκος ἐστὶν ἡ ἁμαρτία τῆς κατὰ τὴν σάρκα ἀπολαύσεως, ἐξ ἧς ἡ εὐπερίστατος ἁμαρτία τίκτεται. εὐπερίστατον δὲ εἶπε τὴν ἁμαρτίαν τὴν εὐκόλως ἡμᾶς περιϊσταμένην καὶ ἄγουσαν εἰς τὸ ἑαυτῆς θέλημα (K. Staab, "Pauluscommentare d. gr. Kirche," *NTliche Abhandlungen*, XV [1933], 351).

[5] In the comm. of Rgg., Moffatt and Michel ref. is made in elucidation to Philo Vit. Cont., 3, which acc. to Moffatt has αἰσθήσεων καὶ αἰσθητῶν ὄγκος in view. The passage occurs in c. 3 § 27, but the text has ὄχλος, ὄγκος being a weaker vl. Hence this ref. ought not to be included in the comm. on Hb. 12:1.

ὁδός, ὁδηγός, ὁδηγέω, μεθοδία,
εἴσοδος, ἔξοδος, διέξοδος, εὐοδόω

---

† ὁδός.

Contents : A. ὁδός for the Greeks : 1. General ; 2. The Prodicus Fable, Parallels and Precursors ; 3. ὁδός in Statements Significant from the Standpoint of the History of Religion. B. ὁδός in the LXX and Judaism : 1. LXX ; 2. The Influence of OT Usage in the Pseudepigrapha and Rabbinic Writings ; 3. Philo and Josephus. C. ὁδός in the New Testament : 1. ὁδός in the Literal Sense ; 2. The Metaphorical Use : a. The Metaphor of the Two Ways in Mt. 7:13 f., b. The Way into the Sanctuary in Hb. 9:8; 10:20, c. Jesus as the Way in Jn. 14:4 ff.; 3. The Figurative Use. D. Christian Usage up to the Apologists.

A. ὁδός for the Greeks.

1. General.

ὁδός means a. from Hom. on (as a place) the "way" or "street" in its many possible forms, e.g., the narrow path trodden by those who have gone before, or the broad roads made for traffic, on which chariots can travel (Hom. Il., 7, 340; ὁδός ἀμαξιτός, Pind. Nem., 6, 54), troops can march (the common βασιλικὴ ὁδός is usually a road for armies), and processions can be held (ἰόντες τὴν ἱρὴν ὁδόν, Hdt., 6, 34, of the pilgrims' road to Delphi). The word can also be used for the route taken by ships (Hom. Il., 6, 292), the course of a river, its bed (ποταμοῦ ὁδός, Xenoph. Cyrop., 7, 5, 16).[1] The sense of way or street is also attested in inscr.; Ditt. Syll.³, 57, 27 (450/449 B.C.) and 313, 19 ff. (320/319 B.C.) refer to viae sacrae; in the building inscr. on the Astyages tower in Ephesus, the later so-called prison of Paul, the importance of ὁδοί in the plan is mentioned (Ditt. Syll.³, 936, n.; 1182). Services in building streets are extolled in Ditt. Or., 606, 5 (1st cent. A.D.); 701, 8 (2nd cent. A.D.).[2] In the pap. the sense "way" or "road" is predominant ; there are many instances of βασιλικὴ ὁδός, δημοσία ὁδός (national road) (both from the 3rd cent. B.C. on), πεδιακὴ ὁδός (footpath) (from the 1st cent. A.D. on), cf. also πεζῇ ὁδός, P. Tebt., 5, 29 (2nd. cent. B.C.).[3]

ὁδός κτλ. Cr.-Kö., 776-8, s.v.; J. Alpers, Hercules in bivio. Phil. Diss. Göttingen (1912), O. Becker, "Das Bild d. Weges u. verwandte Vorstellungen im frühgr. Denken," Hermes, Einzelschriften, 4 (1937); J. Pascher, "Η ΒΑΣΙΛΙΚΗ ΟΔΟΣ. Der Königsweg zu Wiedergeburt u. Vergottung bei Philon v. Alexandreia," Studien z. Gesch. u. Kultur d. Altertums, XVII, 3/4 (1931); E. Käsemann, "Das wandernde Gottesvolk. Eine Untersuchung zum Hebräerbrief," FRL, NF, 37 (1939); K. Bornhäuser, "Die Bergpredigt. Versuch einer zeitgenössischen Auslegung," BFTh, 2. Reihe, 7. Bd. (²1927), 201 ff.; R. Bultmann, "D. Bedeutung d. neuerschlossenen mandäischen u. manichäischen Quellen f. das Verständnis d. Johannesevangeliums," ZNW, 24 (1925), 100 ff., 133 f.; E. Schweizer, "Ego eimi . . . D. religionsgeschichtliche Herkunft u. theologische Bedeutung d. joh. Bildreden, zugleich ein Beitrag zur Quellenfrage des vierten Evangeliums," FRL, NF, 38 (1939), Etym. ὁδός ⸗ Old Slav. chodŭ "course," Walde-Pok., II, 486; it replaces in Gk. the missing abstract of ἰέναι, e.g., ἔξοδος for ἐξ-ι-σις (cf. Lat. ex-i-tus), hence ὁδός is fem., cf. A. Debrunner, Indogerm. Forschungen, 48 (1930), 71. For this reason sense b. does not have to be deduced from a., but rather vice versa [Debrunner]. Cf. also Becker, 15 f.

[1] For further information, also on b., cf. Pass. and Liddell-Scott, s.v., with details also on prepositional phrases like πρὸ ὁδοῦ, κατὰ τὴν ὁδόν etc. Already from the 5th cent. B.C. ἄνθρωπος ἐξ ὁδοῦ is found for the man from the street (in the comic poet Eupolis, 25d). The goal of a way, in Hom. then generally, is indicated by εἰς, e.g., Od., 22, 128, though later the gen. is used as well as εἰς, ἐπί τι, e.g., Eur. Hipp., 1197: τὴν εὐθὺς Ἄργους . . . ὁδόν. In many combinations ὁδός is left out, cf. also Mayser, II, 1 (1926), 27.

[2] For details cf. Ditt. Syll.³ and Or., Index, s.v.

[3] Cf. Preisigke Wört., II, 151; I, 339; Moult.-Mill., 438, s.v.

ὁδός also means b., from the time of Hom. on (as action), the "way" which someone takes, the "course," "journey," by land or water, e.g., Hom. Od., 2, 256, 273, 404; "departure," *ibid.*, 2, 285; also a "military march." In inscr. and pap. this sense is very rare, e.g., Ditt. Or., 629, 88 (2nd cent. A.D.); ἄρτος εἰς ὁδόν, P. Tebt., 121, 33, 41 (1st cent. B.C.); σκυλμὸς τῆς ὁδοῦ, "hardship of the journey," P. Fay., 111, 5 (95/96 A.D.). Meanings a. and b. cannot always be differentiated : Ἀμφιάρεως ... κρατύνων ... οἰωνῶν ὁδοῖς, Soph. Oed. Col., 1314, can refer either to the flight of birds or their lines of flight. Similarly, as regards the expression ἡμέρας ὁδός ("day's journey"), e.g., Hdt., 4, 101, it may be debated whether this does not refer to the stretch of the way. Decision between the two is esp. hard in the fig. use, e.g., τὰν νεάταν ὁδόν στείχειν, "to go the final way," i.e., "to die," Soph. Ant., 809 (cf. ἐξιοῦσαν ὑστάτην ὁδόν, Eur. Alc., 610, and the late example in P. Masp., 151, 259 : ἐγὼ εἰς ὁδὸν πόντων πορεύσομαι).

Metaphorical or fig. use is early. Cf. μέσην ὁδὸν ἔρχεσθαι, Theogn., 220, 231; ἐν εὐθείαις ὁδοῖς στείχειν, Pind. Nem., I, 25. ὁδός often has the sense "way and means" to achieve or do something, "measure," "procedure," or "manner" of doing something. Cf. already Heracl. Fr., 135 (I, 181, 13 f., Diels⁵): συντομωτάτην ὁδὸν ἔλεγεν εἰς εὐδοξίαν τὸ γενέσθαι ἀγαθόν, "the shortest way to renown is to show oneself to be a worthy man"; πολλαὶ δ' ὁδοὶ σὺν θεοῖς εὐπραγίας, Pind. Olymp., 8, 13 f.; ὑπάρχουσι δὲ καὶ ἄλλαι ὁδοὶ τοῦ πολέμου ἡμῖν, "other military circumstances may improve our situation," Thuc., 1, 122, 1. Life is simply compared with a way, not called a way, in Democr. Fr., 230 (II, 191, 11 f., Diels⁵): βίος ἀνεόρταστος μακρὴ ὁδὸς ἀπανδόκευτος, "a life without leisure is like a long road (or journey) without a place to halt." The phrase ὁδὸς βίου, found in Plat. Resp., X, 600a : τοῖς ὑστέροις ὁδόν τινα παρέδοσαν βίου Ὁμηρικήν (par. to the Πυθαγόρειον τρόπον ... τοῦ βίου which follows), means the characteristic manner of life which a ἡγεμὼν παιδείας exemplifies for his followers ; cf. Isoc. ad Demonicum, 3 : ὅσοι τοῦ βίου ταύτην τὴν ὁδὸν ἐπορεύθησαν, "who have decided for this manner of life." In such cases ὁδός means "manner," and ὁδὸς βίου does not mean "path of life" (life, destiny) but "form of life." The phrase ἄδικον ὁδὸν ἰέναι (Thuc., 3, 64, 4) refers to conduct, not in general, but in a specific case, so that the meaning is "conduct," or even perhaps "measure," rather than "way of life." As a philosophical tt. in the sense of "way of enquiry or knowledge," "method," ὁδός is often found in Parm., e.g., Fr. 7, 3 (I, 234, 33, Diels⁵); cf. here ὁδῷ or καθ' ὁδόν, "methodically," Plat. Phaedr., 263b; Resp., IV, 435a. ⁴

2. The Prodicus Fable, Parallels and Precursors.

In view of the presence of the metaphor of the two ways in Jewish and Christian lit., particular attention must be paid to the fable of Hercules at the cross-roads, which is traced back to the Sophist Prodicus and recounted in Xenoph. Mem., 2, 1, 21-34. This deals with the thesis, which Socrates defended against Aristippus and proved from lit., that he who would side with ἀρετή must accept toil and trouble. Ref. is first made in 2, 1, 20 to Hes. Op., 287 ff., then to two verses in Epicharmus, of which the first expresses the main thought clearly and succinctly : τῶν πόνων πωλοῦσιν ἡμῖν πάντα τἀγάθ' οἱ θεοί, "only at the price of effort do the gods sell us the good." The Hes. passage is esp. important because it speaks of two ways :

> τὴν μὲν γὰρ κακότητα καὶ ἰλαδὸν ἔστιν ἑλέσθαι
> ῥηιδίως· λείη μὲν ὁδός, μάλα δ' ἐγγύθι ναίει.
> τῆς δ' ἀρετῆς ἱδρῶτα θεοὶ προπάροιθεν ἔθηκαν
> 290 ἀθάνατοι· μακρὸς δὲ καὶ ὄρθιος οἶμος ἐς αὐτὴν
> καὶ τρηχὺς τὸ πρῶτον· ἐπὴν δ' εἰς ἄκρον ἵκηαι,
> ῥηιδίη δὴ ἔπειτα πέλει, χαλεπή περ ἐοῦσα.

---

⁴ The sense of "means," "procedure," does not seem to occur in inscr. and is rare in the pap., P. Lond., 897, 10 (84 A.D.): ἐὰν δὲ μὴ ἦσ<θ>α εὑρηκώς τινα ὁδὸν γράψον μοι κτλ., cf. P. Tor., I, 6, 13 (116 B.C.): κατὰ νόμους ὁδῶι πορευόμενος, "taking the legal path."

This passage is obviously quoted because of v. 289; this alone is a quite adequate proof in the context. The emphasis is not on the two ways, which serve only as an illustration. It is possible that the Hes. passage is given in full because two ways are also mentioned in the Prodicus fable which follows the Epicharmus verses. It should be noted, however, that the procedure here is very different. In Hes. the short way (obviously to κακότης, subj. of ναίει) is only briefly mentioned, whereas the way to ἀρετή (ἐς αὐτήν) is fully depicted : it is long and steep, then reaches a height; at first it is rugged and difficult, but on the height smooth [5] (the way to κακότης is obviously level and easy as well as short). Very different are the two ways mentioned in the introduction to the Prodicus fable : φησὶ γὰρ (sc. Πρόδικος ὁ σοφός) [6] Ἡρα-κλέα ἐπεὶ ἐκ παίδων εἰς ἥβην ὡρμᾶτο, ἐν ᾗ οἱ νέοι ἤδη αὐτοκράτορες γιγνόμενοι δηλοῦσιν εἴτε τὴν δι' ἀρετῆς ὁδὸν τρέψονται ἐπὶ τὸν βίον εἴτε τὴν διὰ κακίας, ἐξελθόντα εἰς ἡσυχίαν καθῆσθαι ἀποροῦντα ποτέραν τῶν ὁδῶν τράπηται. The two ways which confront young people as soon as they attain to years of discretion are not now said to be short or long, easy or hard, on level ground or leading upwards. So one may well ask what force there is in the figure of the ὁδός. The ways both have the same goal, namely, life itself (ὁδός, then, is not strictly the way of life); they are not, as in Hes., roads which lead to ἀρετή or κακία. The relation of ἀρετή and κακία to these ways is indicated very generally by a διά, though it is manifest that ἀρετή and κακία are not personified, e.g., as guides on these two ways ; the point is rather whether one takes the way to life which consists in virtuous or vicious conduct. Since the character of the ὁδοί as ways with a course and form etc. is not plain, one cannot answer the question whether young people have already been on a way from which the two are forks ; [7] the expression "cross-roads" is too graphic to be used here. Similarly, one should hesitate to take the expression used of Hercules, namely, ποτέραν τῶν ὁδῶν τράπηται, and derive from it the idea of a cross-roads, since here, too, the plastic or spatial aspect is by no means clear (cf. 23 : ποίαν ὁδὸν ἐπὶ τὸν βίον τράπῃ). Since Hercules is expressly depicted as sitting, it must be assumed that neither the way he has come thus far, nor the way which he will take when he gets up, is of any significance. Probably one should conclude that he will simply go home again the same way that he has come (not allowing later versions of the story to influence one's inter-

[5] οἶμος occurs as a masc. as well as fem. elsewhere, though it is odd that there should be alternation of gender within 3 verses. One might consider, then, whether the subj. of v. 292 is not ἀρετή, in which case one should read ἵκηαι (as in Xenoph.) rather than the ἵκηται of the Hes. MSS at v. 291. We need not discuss here the question how far κακότης and ἀρετή are personified in Hes. Cf. Becker, 57 ff.

[6] For details on the authorship of Prodicus cf. Alpers, 9 ff., with older bibl.

[7] Alpers, 7 ff. refers to the late interpretation (in a schol. on Persius [1st cent. A.D.] Satirae, III, 55 f.) of the so-called Y Pythagoreum : Pythagoras invented the letter Y and made it a picture of human life. The lower stroke represents unbroken childhood sheltered by parents and teachers. Then there are forks to left and right (→ II, 38), which represent vice and virtue. Alpers finds here one of the presuppositions of the whole Prodicus fable, though there is affinity at most only with the introduction, and it may be asked whether the restrained presentation there is really to be understood in the light of this more developed form of the idea. Even if the interpretation of the Y really does go back to Pythagoras (cf. Rohde [7, 8], II, 221 n.), it is a special form rather than the starting-point of the in-trinsically older image of the two ways. The earlier history of the *littera pythagorica* is even more complicated if W. Schultz, "Herakles am Scheidewege," *Philol.*, NF, 22 (1909), 488 f., is right in his conjecture that the Y was originally a sign of the tree of life, and was related to the way of life as such ; though for a different view cf. A. Brinkmann, "Ein Denkmal des Neupythagoreismus," *Rhein. Museum*, NF, 26 (1911), 616 ff. Standing at the cross-roads is also used as a figure for choice between two possibilities in Theogn., 911 f.: ἐν τριόδῳ δ' ἕστηκα. δύ' εἰσὶν πρόσθεν ὁδοί μοι· φροντίζω τούτων ἥντιν' ἴω προτέρην. Since the image does not underlie the ensuing description of the possibilities : ἢ μηδὲν δαπανῶν τρύχω βίον ἐν κακότητι, ἢ ζώω τερπνῶς ἔργα τελῶν ὀλίγα (913 f.), it is obviously not related directly to the ethical field. Cf. Hdt., 1, 11, 2 and Becker, 130 ff., 59, n. 24.

pretation; cf. Just. Epit., 11, 3: τὸν Ἡρακλέα ἐπὶ τρίοδόν τινα ἔφη ὁ Ξενοφῶν βαδίζοντα κτλ.).

While Hercules was sitting lonely and perplexed, he had a vision: φανῆναι αὐτῷ δύο γυναῖκας προσιέναι μεγάλας (22). We are not told that these two women, who, as we are shown, are Ἀρετή and Κακία, came to him along two ways, nor should we assume this, and it is certainly not meant that in the vision Hercules saw the two courses between which he found it so hard to decide as two actual ways in front of him.[8] This is further proof that in the introduction the two ways could not be clearly envisaged as such, and it is understandable that the more abstract ref. to the two ὁδοί in the introduction should not take concrete form in the description of the vision. This insight is unshaken by the fact that in later authors features not present in Prodicus found their way into the fable. It is certainly noteworthy that the main influence here was not the introduction itself but the preceding quotation from Hes., for in later versions the two women sit on two hills or mountains involving an easier or harder ascent.[9] As concerns the original fable of Prodicus, the image of the two ways is not a constituent part. The essential thing is the appearing of the two women, who in heated debate seek to win Hercules to their respective sides. This ἀγών between Ἀρετή and Κακία, with Ἀρετή as the winner, forms the framework and content of the fable. The detailed description of it in 22-34 forces the introduction (21) more and more into the background.

Ref. is, of course, made to the ways within the fable. Mention has been made already of the expression used by Κακία: ὁρῶ σε, ὦ Ἡράκλεις, ἀπορoῦντα ποίαν ὁδὸν ἐπὶ τὸν βίον τράπῃ (23). In the next sentence Κακία continues: ἐὰν οὖν ἐμὲ φίλην ποιήσῃ, τὴν ἡδίστην τε καὶ ῥᾴστην ὁδὸν ἄξω σε (23). Later Ἀρετή says: εἰ τὴν πρὸς ἐμὲ ὁδὸν τράποιο (27). Hence the comparison is used here in a different way. Κακία is guide on the one way, Ἀρετή is the goal of the other. The ways are contrasted in the saying of Κακία: ἐννοεῖς, ὦ Ἡράκλεις, ὡς χαλεπὴν καὶ μακρὰν ὁδὸν ἐπὶ τὰς εὐφροσύνας ἡ γυνή σοι αὕτη διηγεῖται; ἐγὼ δὲ ῥᾳδίαν καὶ βραχεῖαν ὁδὸν ἐπὶ τὴν εὐδαιμονίαν ἄξω σε (29; it should be pointed out that acc. to 26 Κακία seeks to present herself as Εὐδαιμονία). But these sayings are too small a part of the whole context to be regarded as the main thread of the fable. They have only supportive significance, and the same ideas are more commonly expressed without the use of ὁδός.[10] Hence they can hardly invest the image of the two ways in the introduction with greater weight than it properly has, and we are thus driven to the conclusion that the usual title of the fable, i.e., Hercules at the cross-roads, lays too

---

[8] As against Alpers, 18, 43, who even combines the introduction and vision to the pt. of saying that the two ways in which Prodicus has the women come to Hercules run *in planitie deserta* (a distinctive difference from Hes., for whom one at least leads up a mountain). But surely ἐξελθόντα εἰς ἡσυχίαν is simply saying that Hercules sought isolation in order to find clarity without being influenced by his surroundings. Furthermore, solitude is accepted as the right place for visions. This does not have to mean that the solitary place was level, and it certainly does not mean that in the vision he saw a plain with two roads before him. For the same reason Alpers is on flimsy ground when he argues (46 f.) that the Prodicus fable influences the depiction of the two ways, to παιδεία on the one side and ψευδοπαιδεία on the other, in Ceb. Tab., 11 ff. This hardly follows from the fact that in 15 it is said of the τόπος of παιδεία: ὅπου οὐδεὶς ἐπικατοικεῖ, ἀλλ' ἔρημος δοκεῖ εἶναι.

[9] Cf. the instances in Alpers, 27. The fable went through many changes, even in authors who appeal expressly to Prodicus or Xenoph. The meaning of the women varies (*ibid.*, 34 ff.), the figure of Hermes is introduced (47 f.), etc. In Ceb. Tab., 11 ff., which is nearer to Hes. than Prod. (→ n. 8), the metaphor of a way is combined with that of a tower, C. 2. b.

[10] Since the sayings which speak of the ways are not emphasised much, it is also unwise to deduce different sources from the inangularities to be found in them. Alpers, 18 f. suggests that the statement in which Κακία is guide (23, 29) come from Prod. himself, while the idea that Ἀρετή is the goal (27) is borrowed by Xenoph. from Hes.

great emphasis on the metaphor unless later versions are taken into account. [11] The two ways are not even the framework within which the ethical ideas of the fable are presented. These are deduced independently from the qualities of the two disputants. This is not to say that the fable, and esp. its introduction, is not an important instance of the metaphor of the two ways. Nevertheless, in the secular Gk. of the following period the passages which apply this figure of speech to the ethical decisions of man cannot all be regarded as under the influence of the Prodicus fable. The metaphor is older than the fable (→ n. 17) and has its own life alongside and after it. [12] Similarly, there is no methodological justification for jumping to the conclusion that the fable influenced the use of the metaphor in Jewish and Christian writings. [13]

3. ὁδός in Statements Significant from the Standpoint of the History of Religion.

With the metaphor of the two ways as dealt with under A. 2 one should not over-hastily associate the common idea that there are two ways in the underworld, the one on the right leading to the χῶρος εὐσεβῶν, that of the left to the place of punishment for the ἄδικοι, [14] or, as in Verg. Aen., VI, 540 ff., the one to Elysium, the other to Tartarus. The difference is that these two ways imply no possibility or necessity of decision or choice, but represent different destinies after death. Another pt. is that they are thought of as true ways. It should not be overlooked that the topography of the underworld can take other forms, e.g., with three ways. [15] Only where the ref. is to two ways might there be a connection with the customary metaphor. It seems, however,

---

[11] Alpers does not say how old the title is, and the later refs. to the fable which he adduces do not have it. In keeping is the fact that in such brief refs. and descriptions as those in the schol. on Aristoph. Nu., 361; Philostr. Vit. Soph., I, 12 the two ways are not mentioned. They are not the distinctive feature of the fable. This is to be found in the debate between the two women as they try to win over Hercules (not for nothing Athen., 510c links the fable with the decision of Paris ; cf. also Schultz, op. cit., 490, 498); Philostr., loc. cit. uses the expression τὴν Ἡρακλέους αἵρεσιν. Xenoph. himself finally describes the content as follows : οὕτω πῶς διώκει Πρόδικος τὴν ὑπ' Ἀρετῆς Ἡρακλέους παίδευσιν (2, 1, 34), and in acc. with the passage from Hes. and the verses of Epicharmus his main thought was surely as follows : τῶν γὰρ ὄντων ἀγαθῶν καὶ καλῶν οὐδὲν ἄνευ πόνου καὶ ἐπιμελείας θεοὶ διδόασιν ἀνθρώποις (28). Basil in Sermo de legendis libris gentilium, 4 (MPG, 31, 573a-c) admirably grasps the pt. of the fable when he merely mentions the two ways in introduction, and in the following form : (τῷ Ἡρακλεῖ βουλευομένῳ ποτέραν τράπηται τῶν ὁδῶν, τὴν διὰ τῶν πόνων ἄγουσαν πρὸς ἀρετὴν ἢ τὴν ῥᾴστην, προσελθεῖν δύο γυναῖκας κτλ.
[12] The influence of the fable is present for certain only where there is express ref. to it. There are many such cases on into the Christian period, cf. Just. Epit., 11, 3; Cl. Al. Strom., II, 20, 107; V, 5, 31; Bas., op. cit. On the other hand Bas. in his discussion of the two ways in Hom. in Ps. 1:5 (MPG, 29, 221c/d) mentions the fable only in the introduction (he refers to the position of the young beyond κακία and ἀρετή without speaking of the ways); in what follows he discusses the metaphor of the two ways of Ps. 1 in terms of Mt. 7:13 f. with a few touches from Hes. Op., 287 ff. There is also influence when the main features of the fable recur unmistakably. Thus it is correct to say that Silius Italicus (1st cent. A.D.) Punica, XV, 18 ff. transmitted the fable to P. Cornelius Scipio (Alpers, 11 f., 34), though there is no mention of the two ways, and Virtus and Voluptas approach dextra laevaque per auras allapsae, 20 f. Other instances are less plain, e.g., Diog. L., 30; cf. Alpers, 35 f., and the use of the metaphor of the two ways in popular philosophy has only a remote connection with the fable. Cf. Wendland, Hell. Kult., 85, n. 5; E. Norden, Die antike Kunstprosa (1898), 467; C. F. G. Heinrici, Beiträge zur Gesch. u. Erklärung d. NT, III (1905), 89. What applies to the two ways applies also to the confrontation of ἀρετή and κακία. Here, too, the fable was undoubtedly a stimulus, but its influence should not be overestimated.
[13] → n. 16 f., 36, 51, 57, 105, 189.
[14] Cf. Rohde [7, 8], II, 220, n. 4, who thinks the idea "might derive from the imaginings of sects in Lower Italy." Cf. Plat. Gorg., 524a; Resp., X, 614c.
[15] Cf. Rohde, loc. cit., and esp. A. Dieterich, Nekyia (1893), passim, who strongly emphasises the Orphic-Pythagorean influence.

that this is not so. The two ways in the underworld are nowhere directly described as continuations of the other two ways. [16] The ideas arose independently of one another. [17]

Particular note should be taken of ὁδός when used of the ascent of the soul to the heavenly world. Already in the proem to the didactic poem Parmen. Fr., 1 (I, 228 ff., Diels[5]) the way to truth is depicted as a way to heavenly light "which carries the man of knowledge above all habitations." If the way is described as a real road which one may travel with horse and chariot, this is mythical and poetical imagery ; the way is right thinking. Later in the Hermetic writings *gnosis* is viewed as a way : μία γάρ ἐστιν εἰς αὐτό (to νοεῖν of the καλὸν καὶ ἀγαθόν, i.e., God) ἀποφέρουσα ὁδός, ἡ μετὰ γνώσεως εὐσεβία, Corp. Herm., VI, 5 (cf. VI, 6 : οἱ ἀγνοοῦντες καὶ μὴ ὁδεύσαντες τὴν τῆς εὐσεβείας ὁδόν). Cf. also (though ὁδός is not used) X, 15 : τοῦτο μόνον σωτήριον ἀνθρώπῳ ἐστί, ἡ γνῶσις τοῦ θεοῦ, αὕτη εἰς τὸν Ὄλυμπόν ἐστιν ἀνάβασις (= ἡ πρὸς τὰ ἄνω ὁδός, IV, 11); also XI, 21: ἡ γὰρ τελεία κακία τὸ ἀγνοεῖν τὸ θεῖον, τὸ δὲ δύνασθαι γνῶναι καὶ θελῆσαι καὶ ἐλπίσαι ὁδός ἐστιν εὐθεῖα, διὰ τοῦ ἀγαθοῦ φέρουσα καὶ ῥᾳδία ὁδεύοντι. [18] In Gnosticism we find the idea of the heavenly journey of the soul which takes the way from its heavenly home to earth and then after death takes the same way back home. Here the way as such plays an important part. [19] Nevertheless, many typical examples are from Christian Gnostic texts (cf. the Naassene hymn in Hipp. Ref., V, 10, 2 : σφραγῖδας ἔχων καταβήσομαι, αἰῶνας ὅλους διοδεύσω, μυστήρια πάντα δ' ἀνοίξω, μορφὰς δὲ θεῶν ἐπιδείξω, τὰ κεκρυμμένα τῆς ἁγίου ὁδοῦ γνῶσιν καλέσας, παραδώσω), and in Gnosticism the concept of the way or path hardly ever seems to have the same independent and comprehensive significance as in the Mandaean texts (→ n. 141). [20]

---

[16] Lact. Inst., VI, 3 ff. (cf. Epitome, 59) associates the two conceptions, both familiar to him from ancient lit., but he bases this on the fact that he already understands in Christian terms the *duae viae per quas humanam vitam progredi necesse est : una quae in caelum ferat, altera quae ad inferos deprimat.* A changing of the original idea of two ways in a real underworld into the metaphor of two ways representing different spiritual destinies after death may be seen in Cic. Tusc., I, 30, 72; cf. F. Cumont, *After Life in Roman Paganism* (1922), 152 f. But this is not to view life on earth under this image of the ways. On the other hand, the Prodicus fable in Xenoph. does not refer to the underworld. In Mem., 2, 1, 34 we are simply told that he who follows after virtue, his memory will remain alive after his death, whereas he who follows after vice will be forgotten.

[17] Even though there is much to support the view that the idea of ways in the underworld is older, this is not the basis of the earthly cross-roads or moral fork (even Dieterich, *op. cit.,* 192, who uses these expressions, does not establish a clear line of development). The metaphor of the two ways, as found in Hes. and the Prod. fable, arose independently in this form. It was simply preceded by a more general form in which only the idea of decision between two possibilities was stated (cf. the Theogn. passage, → n. 7), and later the figure was transferred to the ethical field. Becker, 41 ff. pursues the development of the ways as a mental image (also κέλευθος, πόρος etc.) from Hom. by way of Pind., Hdt. and the philosophers (Parm., Heracl., Emped.) to Aesch. and Soph.

[18] Cf. W. Scott, Hermetica, IV, ed. A. S. Ferguson (1936), Index, 524, *s.v.*; J. Kroll, *Die Lehren d. Hermes Trismeg.* (1914), 380 f.; Reitzenstein Hell. Myst., 294 f. → I, 694, n. 21. Cf. also what is said about ἡ πρὸς ἀλήθειαν ὁδός in the Hermetic section in Stob. Ecl., 1, 41, 1a (p. 273 f.): σεμνὴ αὕτη ὁδὸς καὶ λεία, χαλεπὴ δὲ ψυχῇ ὁδεῦσαι ἐν σώματι οὔσῃ. There are no grounds for changing λεία to θεία (Scott, I [1924], 392, *ad loc.*).

[19] Cf. W. Bousset, "Die Himmelsreise d. Seele," ARW, 4 (1901), 136 ff., 229 ff.; H. Jonas, *Gnosis u. spätantiker Geist.* 1. "Die mythologische Gnosis" = FRL, NF, 33 (1934), esp. 101, 124, n. 2, 135, 207, n. 1.

[20] The origin of these ideas is to be sought in the Orient. Originally the ref. is simply to an ascent of the dead to the stars ; only later do we find the idea of a descent and reascent of the soul. An early Babylonian form is noted already by W. Anz, *Zur Frage nach dem Ursprung des Gnostizismus,* = TU, XV, 4 (1897); cf. W. Cumont, *Die orient. Religionen im röm. Heidentum*[3] (1931), 114 ff., 272 f. Jonas, *op. cit.,* 207, n. 1 rightly observes that Anz overestimates the concept of the way in his definition of *gnosis* as γνῶσις ὁδοῦ.

It is well known that the figure of the way extends far beyond the segment of religious history treated here (one need only think of the eight-branched way of Buddhism and the Chinese Tao = way). This suggestive and easily understandable metaphor offered itself independently in many different places when there was a need to illustrate spiritual processes and religious and ethical developments.

B. ὁδός in the LXX and Judaism.

1. The LXX.

In the LXX ὁδός is found some 880 times (100 in Prv., 81 in Ps., 73 in Ez., 67 in Is., 61 in Jer.). Where there is a Mas. original (700 cases), it corresponds predominantly (some 600 instances) to דֶּרֶךְ. Of other equivalents one may refer to אֹרַח in 35 passages, חוּץ in 15, מְסִלָּה in 12. Conversely, דֶּרֶךְ is predominantly transl. ὁδός. There are a few noteworthy exceptions. At 3 Βασ. 18:27, when Elijah mocks the prophets of Baal because their god does not answer them, the וְכִי־דֶרֶךְ לוֹ remains untranslated, unless one is to assume that καὶ ἅμα μήποτε χρηματίζει αὐτός is a rendering of this and not the preceding וְכִי־שִׂיג לוֹ. [21] In Gn. 19:31 the LXX renders כְּדֶרֶךְ כָּל־הָאָרֶץ by ὡς καθήκει πάσῃ τῇ γῇ and in 31:35 כִּי־דֶרֶךְ נָשִׁים לִי by ὅτι τὸ κατ᾽ ἐθισμὸν τῶν γυναικῶν μοί ἐστιν (cf. also the rendering of אֹרַח in the related 18:11). In Job 38:19 אֵיזֶה הַדֶּרֶךְ יִשְׁכָּן־אוֹר is transl. ποίᾳ δὲ γῇ αὐλίζεται τὸ φῶς (did the LXX read הָאָרֶץ?). In Job 40:19 הוּא רֵאשִׁית דַּרְכֵי־אֵל (of Behemoth) is transl. τοῦτ᾽ ἔστιν ἀρχὴ πλάσματος κυρίου, though in Prv. 8:22 רֵאשִׁית דַּרְכּוֹ is ἀρχὴν ὁδῶν αὐτοῦ. For the oath חֵי דֶרֶךְ בְּאֵר־שָׁבַע in Am. 8:14 the LXX has ζῇ ὁ θεός σου, Βηρσαβεε (par. to the preceding ζῇ ὁ θεός σου, Δαν = חֵי אֱלֹהֶיךָ דָן.) [22] It is worth noting that in Ex. 33:13 הוֹדִעֵנִי נָא אֶת־דְּרָכֶךָ is rendered ἐμφάνισόν μοι σεαυτόν. For the annexed וְאֵדָעֲךָ the LXX has γνωστῶς ἴδω σε. The Mas. is thinking of the divine purpose to which Moses is to devote himself, but the LXX relates the verse to the ensuing request of Moses that he may be allowed to see God.

In numerous passages ὁδός is used lit. for a way, path or street which carries ordinary traffic, along which one may go, travel or march (πορεύεσθαι, ἀπέρχεσθαι, etc.), on which one may pass someone (παραπορεύεσθαι, ψ 79:12; 88:41; Job 21:29; Lam. 1:12; 2:15), from which one may deviate or which one may leave (e.g., ἐκκλίνειν, Nu. 22:23). In many cases the ref. may be to the network of roads across a land to connect the villages and towns (e.g., Gn. 38:14; 1 Βασ. 13:17 f.). The direction or goal may be added in the gen. (e.g., ὁδὸν γῆς Φυλιστιιμ, Ex. 13:7), or linked by a prep. (e.g., ὁδὸν τὴν εἰς Βασαν, Dt. 3:1; ὁδὸν ἐπὶ θάλασσαν ἐρυθράν, Nu. 21:4; ὁδὸν τὴν ἐπὶ τῆς ἐρυθρᾶς θαλάσσης, Dt. 1:40). [23] Ways of all kinds are ὁδοί, so that

---

[21] Here, though not elsewhere in the LXX and NT, χρηματίζει means "he has something to do," "he is occupied." Cf. Ges.-Buhl, s.v., שִׂיג and E. Nestle, ZAW, 23 (1903), 338, → III, 435.

[22] It is not certain that דֶּרֶךְ here has to mean "pilgrimage," "cultus" (so Kautzsch, ad loc.). It seems more likely that it comes to means cultus from "nature and manner" (cf. Jer. 12:16 : אֶת־דַּרְכֵי עַמִּי = LXX τὴν ὁδὸν τοῦ λαοῦ μου = the special form of the cultus of Israel). But it is open to question whether דֶּרֶךְ is the original. E. Nestle, Philologica sacra (1896), 7 f. is right, of course, that we cannot postulate אֱלֹהֶיךָ on the basis of the LXX (he considers צְרֶךְ, or no change). It might be that there is an underlying divine name Dod, with דֹּדְךָ the original of the LXX. In this case one could hardly draw a line from Am. 8:14 to the use of ὁδός in Ac. 9:2; 19:9 etc. (→ C. 3).

[23] It is surely a Semitism when the adv. דֶּרֶךְ, "in the direction of" (Ges.-Buhl, s.v., 1. d) is rendered ὁδόν, e.g., Dt. 1:19; ὁδὸν δυσμῶν ἡλίου, 11:30; προσεύξονται ἐν ὀνόματι κυρίου ὁδὸν τῆς πόλεως ... καὶ τοῦ οἴκου, 3 Βασ. 8:44; ἐπίβλεψον ὁδὸν τῆς θαλάσσης, 18:43; ὁδὸν θαλάσσης, Is. 8:23. Cf. Johannessohn Kasus, 75.

clear differentiation from τρίβοι is not always possible. We are not often to think of well constructed roads. Only the great international trade routes would come in this category (cf. ὁδὸς βασιλική in Nu. 20:17; 21:22).[24] City streets, in many cases πλατεῖαι (often with τῆς πόλεως, e.g., Ju. 19:15; Zech. 8:5), are called ὁδοί in Jer. 14:16 א B; Lam. 1:4; Ez. 11:6, etc.[25] It is a bad sign if the streets are deserted, Lv. 26:22; Is. 33:8; Zeph. 3:6; Sir. 49:6, and when men must avoid the streets and choose the by-ways, the days are evil, ἐξέλιπον ὁδοὺς καὶ ἐπορεύθησαν ἀτραπούς, Ju. 5:6 Cod. B. A way blocked by stakes (φράσσω τὴν ὁδὸν αὐτῆς ἐν σκόλοψιν, Hos. 2:8) or walled up (ἀνοικοδομεῖν, Hos. 2:8; Lam. 3:9) is an apt metaphor for God's punitive action, just as His promise can make good use of the image of making a way in the desert (Is. 43:19) or making mountains into ways (49:11; cf. 35:8 f.; 57:14; 62:10). The metaphor is of greatest significance when the ref. is to God's way (Is. 40:3; cf. Mal. 3:1; → C. 2).

ὁδός is often linked with verbs of going in phrases which do not speak of a specific way or road, e.g., "to go on one's way" (Gn. 32:1: ἀπῆλθεν εἰς τὴν ἑαυτοῦ ὁδόν, 1 Βασ. 25:12; 3 Βασ. 1:49 etc.), "to let someone take a good path," i.e., to let him go unhindered (ἐκπέμψαι αὐτὸν ἐν ὁδῷ ἀγαθῇ, 1 Βασ. 24:19). In many cases the meaning is almost that of "journey," "course," "trip," for which there are many instances, e.g., ἐν ὁδῷ μακρᾷ, Nu. 9:13; ποιῆσαι τὴν ὁδὸν αὐτοῦ, Ju. 17:8; ἑτοίμασον τὰ πρὸς τὴν ὁδόν, Tob. 5:17 א; δοῦναι αὐτοῖς ἐπισιτισμὸν εἰς τὴν ὁδόν, Gn. 42:25.[26] The phrase ὁδὸν ἡμέρας, "a day's journey," "a day long," is also fairly common, Gn. 30:36; 31:23; Ex. 3:18; 3 Βασ. 19:4; 1 Macc. 5:24 etc. In Ιωβ 33:29 (cf. vl. to Θ in Cod. A) ὁδοὺς τρεῖς seems to mean three times.

Animals have their ὁδοί as well as men, the eagle and the snake (Prv. 30:19), locusts (Jl. 2:7), though the ὁδοί of ants which sluggards should take as a pattern in Prv. 6:6 are their manner of life. In ψ 18:6 the ref. of δραμεῖν ὁδὸν αὐτοῦ is not directly to ἥλιος, but in the first instance to γίγας. Thunders take the course which God has ordained for them acc. to Job 28:26; 38:25. It is not advisable to pay too much attention to wind and weather, for man does not know τίς ἡ ὁδὸς τοῦ πνεύματος, Qoh. 11:5. In the depiction of the majestic coming of God to judgment in Nah. 1:3 it is said: ἐν συντελείᾳ καὶ ἐν συσσεισμῷ ἡ ὁδὸς αὐτοῦ. On the other hand the statement in ψ 76:19: ἐν τῇ θαλάσσῃ ἡ ὁδός σου, καὶ αἱ τρίβοι σου ἐν ὕδασι πολλοῖς, mythological though it sounds, refers, like the hymn in vv. 16 ff. (esp. v. 20), to God's act at the Red Sea. Though ὁδός is not used in Ex. 14:21 f., there is a plain ref. to this in Is. 43:16 (διδοὺς ὁδὸν ἐν θαλάσσῃ); 51:10 (ὁδὸν διαβάσεως); Wis. 19:7 (ἐξ ἐρυθρᾶς θαλάσσης ὁδὸς ἀνεμπόδιστος); cf. also Is. 11:16 vl.[27]

The fig. use of ὁδός is very common in all parts of the LXX, including the apocrypha, though special expressions are peculiar to specific books. In many cases it is hard to say how far the metaphor is felt to be such. Even when ὁδός

---

[24] Cf. K. Galling, Art. "Handel und Verkehr," *Bibl. Reallexikon* (1937), 260 ff.; for the later period S. Krauss, *Talmudische Archäologie*, II (1911), 323 ff.

[25] The city streets were seldom paved, cf. Galling, Art. "Stadtanlage," *op. cit.*, 499. Their cleanliness left much to be desired; cf. the expressions πηλὸς ἐν ταῖς ὁδοῖς etc., Mi. 7:10; Zech. 9:3; 10:5, and κοπρία ἐν μέσῳ ὁδοῦ, Is. 5:25.

[26] On εἰς or κατὰ τὴν ὁδόν cf. Johannessohn Präpos., 296, 300 f., 247 f. בְּדֶרֶךְ, "on the way," is rendered ἐν τῇ ὁδῷ in the LXX, e.g., Gn. 45:24; Ex. 18:8; Nu. 21:4. בְּדֶרֶךְ מִצְרַיִם, "after the manner of, exactly like, the Egyptians," is transl. ἐν ὁδῷ Αἰγύπτου in Am. 4:10 (ὁδός is also used in the similar expression in Is. 10:24, 26, though the transl. is so free that the original sense is obscured).

[27] Cf. the passage in the great Paris magic pap., Preis. Zaub., IV, 3054 f.: Ἐρυθρὰ θάλασσα ἣν ὥδευσεν Εἰσραὴλ καὶ ἔσται (= ἔστη) ἀνόδευτος. Whether Wis. 14:3: ἔδωκας καὶ ἐν θαλάσσῃ ὁδὸν καὶ ἐν κύμασι τρίβον ἀσφαλῆ, is to be referred to Noah (cf. 14:6) (so Kautzsch Apkr. u. Pseudepigr., *ad loc.*) is questionable.

is used with verbs of going, it does not have to indicate the retention of a spatial concept, for the figure of speech can be much weakened even in these verbs.

Thus in Dt. 8:2 : μνησθήσῃ πᾶσαν τὴν ὁδόν, ἣν ἤγαγέν σε κύριος ὁ θεός σου ἐν τῇ ἐρήμῳ, ὁδός certainly does not have to be the route taken, nor even the journey as such (so Dt. 24:9; 25:17). It may well refer to the desert march, both as a whole and in detail, as a witness to God's dealings with Israel.

How far the original figure of a way can fade into the background may be seen clearly in Prv. 1:31: ἔδονται τῆς ἑαυτῶν ὁδοῦ τοὺς καρπούς, or Is. 33:15 : λαλῶν εὐθεῖαν ὁδόν, or 3 Βασ. 8:32 (cf. 2 Ch. 6:23): δοῦναι τὴν ὁδὸν αὐτοῦ εἰς κεφαλὴν αὐτοῦ (cf. Ez. 9:10; 11:21; 16:43; 22:31). Nor is it always possible to differentiate the individual meanings within a fig. use, nor to assign specific meanings to the various instances. Nevertheless, specific types emerge, so that with the reservation already made one can review the most important examples.

Both as a totality and in its individual sections human life can be viewed as a way.

To be sure βίου ὁδός does not occur. Only in Prv. 4:10 is there added to the statement from the Mas.: καὶ πληθυνθήσεται ἔτη ζωῆς, the clause : ἵνα σοι γένωνται πολλαὶ ὁδοὶ βίου. That God holds all men's ways in His hand is emphasised in Da. 5:23 Θ (πᾶσαι αἱ ὁδοί σου par. to ἡ πνοή σου); cf. also Job 31:4; Jer. 10:23; Prv. 20:24 (here one may ask whether the ref. is to destiny in general or to specific conduct). [28] Is. 40:27 may also be mentioned in this connection. The people (Jacob and Israel) should not say : ἀπεκρύβη ἡ ὁδός μου ἀπὸ τοῦ θεοῦ; God knows their situation well and has His own plan (ὁδός embraces both present and future destiny). With respect to the future of the individual, the metaphor is found in Job's complaint that his way is hidden, 3:23 (acc. to the Mas., but only A). Yet God has known man's way from of old, Job 23:10; ψ 36:18 (τὰς ὁδοὺς τῶν ἀμώμων, Mas. תמימם).[29] If we read in ψ 138:3 : πάσας τὰς ὁδούς μου προεῖδες, this does not refer to future destiny, but to present decisions and plans (cf. διαλογισμοί in v. 2, also the linking of βουλαί, διανοήματα and ὁδοί in Is. 55:8 f., of ὁδοί and ἐνθυμήματα in Ez. 14:22 f. and the usage in Ju. 18:5 f., where ὁδός connotes "plan"; cf. also 1 Βασ. 9:6, 8). A man does well to commit his way to God : the LXX translates the גֹּל עַל־יהוה דַּרְכֶּךָ of Ps. 37:5 by ἀποκάλυψον πρὸς κύριον τὴν ὁδόν σου at 36:5 (deriving גֹּל from גלה instead of גלל), but even so, in accordance with the context, powerful expression is given to the thought that man cannot arrogantly shape his own destiny. God keeps a man's way (Jdt. 13:16; Prv. 2:8), or commissions angels to do so (ψ 90:11; Ex. 23:20; cf. the opposite in ψ 34:5). Dying is called the way which all must go (Jos. 23:14; 3 Βασ. 2:2) and by which none can return (Job 16:22). Related, though with a different orientation, is Prv. 14:12 : ἔστιν ὁδὸς ἣ δοκεῖ ὀρθὴ εἶναι παρὰ ἀνθρώποις, τὰ δὲ τελευταῖα αὐτῆς ἔρχεται εἰς πυθμένα ᾅδου (cf. 16:25; 7:27: ὁδοὶ ᾅδου ... κατάγουσαι εἰς τὰ ταμιεῖα τοῦ θανάτου).

In many passages ὁδός means "walk," "conduct," "manner of life." Cf. the parallelism of ὁδοί and ἔργα, e.g., Ex. 18:20; Ιερ. 33:13, or the correspondence between τὴν ὁδὸν αὐτοῦ and αὐτὸς ἐποίησεν in Job 21:31, or the combining of ὁδοί with ἐπιτηδεύματα ("behaviour") in Ιερ. 4:18, or the relation between

---

[28] This thought is also present in Sir. 33(36):13, though the primary ref. of the parenthesis in v. 13b is to πηλός and κεραμεύς : πᾶσαι αἱ ὁδοὶ αὐτοῦ κατὰ τὴν εὐδοκίαν αὐτοῦ, "the destiny of the clay is as the potter wills."

[29] In the blasphemous speech of the wicked in Jer. 12:4 : οὐκ ὄψεται ὁ θεὸς ὁδοὺς ἡμῶν, ὁδοί does not have to mean actions (as against Kautzsch, ad loc.) but may refer to their present situation or future end.

τρόπος and ὁδός in Dt. 5:32 f. In a large group of references a man's actual conduct is called his ὁδοί in a purely factual manner, with no ethical evaluation, though this will often be plain from the context.

Along with passages like 1 Βασ. 18:14; 3 Βασ. 2:4; 8:25, 32 (cf. 2 Ch. 6:16, 23); ψ 48:13; Job 17:9; 22:3 (cf. also Qoh. 11:9), one may refer esp. to the stereotyped saying that a king walked in the way or ways of his father or predecessor, e.g., 1 Βασ. 8:3, 5; 3 Βασ. 15:26, 34; 16:2, 19, 26, 28b; 22:43, 53; 4 Βασ. 8:18, 27; 16:3; 21:21; 2 Ch. 20:32 (it is because of the historical facts that in these verses the ref. is always to a reign not pleasing to God; for the reverse cf. 4 Βασ. 22:2; 2 Ch. 11:17; 17:3). This phrase occurs for the most part in 3 and 4 Βασ. and 2 Ch., but it is also used in Ju. 2:17; Bar. 2:33; Ez. 18:11; 23:31 and Jdt. 5:8; Sir. 48:22.

Much more numerous, and of significantly greater material significance, are the passages in which the use of ὁδός is made to serve the proclamation of God's will. Attention should first be paid here to verses which speak of the way or ways of God or the Lord. The same expressions can be used for the ways which God Himself takes, i.e., His dealings, purposes and acts (→ 55), but the context always makes it clear whether this is the sense or whether one is to think of human conduct. The ways which men walk can be called the ways of the Lord because they are ways which He has commanded. This is the use in Jer. 7:23: πορεύεσθε ἐν πάσαις ταῖς ὁδοῖς μου, αἷς ἂν ἐντείλωμαι ὑμῖν; also Dt. 5:33: κατὰ πᾶσαν τὴν ὁδόν, ἣν ἐνετείλατό σοι κύριος ὁ θεός σου πορεύεσθαι ἐν αὐτῇ, and Ex. 32:8: παρέβησαν ταχὺ ἐκ τῆς ὁδοῦ ἧς ἐνετείλω αὐτοῖς, cf. Dt. 9:12, 16; 11:28; 13:6; 31:29. The way of the Lord is the walk which God requires of man. In many instances the sense approximates to that of the command of the Lord relating to human conduct; ὁδός is almost synonymous with → ἐντολή. [30]

This may be seen in verses like ψ 118:15: ἐν ταῖς ἐντολαῖς σου ἀδολεσχήσω καὶ κατανοήσω τὰς ὁδούς σου (cf. Job 23:11: ἐξελεύσομαι δὲ ἐν ἐντάλμασιν αὐτοῦ, ὁδοὺς γὰρ αὐτοῦ ἐφύλαξα) and Dt. 8:6: φυλάξῃ τὰς ἐντολὰς κυρίου τοῦ θεοῦ σου πορεύεσθαι ἐν ταῖς ὁδοῖς αὐτοῦ (cf. Dt. 10:12 f.; 11:22; 19:9; 30:16; Jos. 22:5; 3 Βασ. 2:3; 3:14; 2 Ch. 17:6, 4; ψ 118:3 f., 168; Zech. 3:7; cf. also the parallelism of οὐκ ἀπειθήσουσιν ῥημάτων αὐτοῦ with συντηρήσουσιν τὰς ὁδοὺς αὐτοῦ in Sir. 2:15). The same use emerges when ὁδός is combined with verbs also used with ἐντολή etc., esp. φυλάσσω: ἐφύλαξα ὁδοὺς κυρίου, 2 Βασ. 22:22 (cf. Gn. 18:19; Ju. 2:22; Job 23:11; ψ 16:4; 17:21; 36:34; 38:1; Prv. 25:10a; 10:17), also τηρέω, Prv. 23:26, and συντηρέω, Sir. 2:15. Cf. also the phrases ὁδοὶ ἐντολῶν θεοῦ, Bar. 4:13; ψ 118:32, and ὁδός or ὁδοὶ δικαιωμάτων, ψ 118:27, 33; Prv. 2:8; cf. 8:20. Finally, though the expression πορεύεσθαι ἐν ταῖς ὁδοῖς αὐτοῦ (apart from passages already mentioned, cf. 3 Βασ. 11:33, 38; 4 Βασ. 21:22; ψ 80:13; 127:1; Is. 42:24; Bar. 3:13) retains the sense of "ways" and thus presents a uniform picture, it may be pointed out that πορεύεσθαι is not used in quite the same way with ἐντολαί, but it is with προστάγματα (3 Βασ. 3:3; Ιερ. 39:23; Ez. 11:20; 18:9, 17 etc.), δικαιώματα (Ez. 36:27), νόμιμα (Lv. 18:3; Ιερ. 33:4; Ez. 5:6 f.; 1 Macc. 6:59 etc.),[31] νόμος or νόμοι (4 Βασ. 10:31; ψ 77:10;

---

[30] At ψ 118:151 א has the vl. ὁδοί for ἐντολαί. At Prv. 19:16, presupposing the correspondence of the two words, the divine ἐντολή confronts man's own ὁδοί. At ψ 118:59 the LXX has διελογισάμην τὰς ὁδούς σου (the Mas. would give μου), undoubtedly under the influence of τὰς ἐντολάς σου in v. 60, τὸν νόμον σου in 57, and τὰ μαρτύριά σου in 59.

[31] Jer. 10:2: κατὰ τὰς ὁδοὺς τῶν ἐθνῶν (אֶל-דֶּרֶךְ הַגּוֹיִם) μὴ μανθάνετε, also belongs here. It might seem natural to find the sense of "walk" or "manner" in this verse, but 10:3: ὅτι τὰ νόμιμα τῶν ἐθνῶν μάταια, shows that the ὁδοί implies the commandments or laws accepted among the Gentiles (as distinct from Am. 4:10 → n. 26).

Da. 9:10 Θ). Hence one should not take the phrase "to walk in God's ways" in a purely general sense, but one should relate it strictly to observing His commandments.

How far the reference is to the commandments of the Law, however, is debatable.

There seems to be a plain ref. to these in passages like Dt. 5:33; 9:12 (cf. 5:8); 11:28, where there is relation with the more precise commandments mentioned in the narrower context. Cf. also 3 Βασ. 2:3; ψ 102:7 (though in ψ 118:1: μακάριοι οἱ ἄμωμοι ἐν ὁδῷ, οἱ πορευόμενοι ἐν νόμῳ κυρίου, the ἐν ὁδῷ does not seem to refer to the ὁδὸς κυρίου, cf. v. 5). Elsewhere the ὁδοὶ κυρίου are not directly equated with the νόμος. In keeping is the fact that when we are told wherein the ὁδοὶ κυρίου consist, more general, though no less binding, explanations are given: ποιῆσαι τὸ εὐθὲς ἐνώπιον ἐμοῦ, 3 Βασ. 11:33 (cf. 38); ποιεῖν δικαιοσύνην καὶ κρίσιν, Gn. 18:19; cf. also the equation with ἀγαπᾶν κύριον τὸν θεόν, λατρεύειν κυρίῳ τῷ θεῷ, φοβεῖσθαι αὐτόν, and other requirements, Dt. 8:6; 11:13, 22 etc.

The ὁδοὶ κυρίου as the walk commanded by God are further characterised by the fact that there is a series of obviously synonymous expressions.

Among these is ὁδὸς ἀγαθή, 1 Βασ. 12:23; 3 Βασ. 8:36 (cf. 2 Ch. 6:27); Jer. 6:16; cf. Prv. 16:7: ἀρχὴ ὁδοῦ ἀγαθῆς τὸ ποιεῖν τὰ δίκαια. What is meant is a way which is good, or right, because it is commanded by God. Related are ὁδὸς εὐθεῖα (1 Βασ. 12:23; Is. 33:15) and ὁδὸς δικαία (ψ 2:12; cf. Prv. 10:17), also ὁδὸς or ὁδοὶ δικαιοσύνης (at least in Job 24:13; Prv. 8:20; 21:16, though not Prv. 11:5; 12:28; 13:6; 17:23; 21:21, and perhaps the ref. in 16:17, 31, too, is to the proof or practice of δικαιοσύνη rather than to a walk which is commanded and right). ὁδὸς ἀληθείας (ψ 118:30; Wis. 5:6; Tob. 1:3) is also to be taken as the true and right way commanded by God. Cf. ὁδὸς ἄμωμος (ψ 100:2, 6) and ὁδὸς αἰωνία (ψ 138:24). In the Wis. lit. the expression ὁδοὶ σοφίας (always plur.) is a clear synon. of ὁδὸς κυρίου. The ref. is to the ὁδοί ordered or advised by a personified σοφία. Of these the same statements are made as of the ὁδοὶ κυρίου, Prv. 3:17; 4:11; 8:34; Sir. 6:26; 14:21 f. (though the sing. ὁδὸς σοφίας in Job 28:13, 23; Bar. 3:23, 31 denotes the way which σοφία itself takes, i.e., its conduct and works; cf. also ὁδὸς ἐπιστήμης, Bar. 3:20, 27). [32] Another par. is ὁδοὶ ζωῆς in ψ 15:11; Prv. 5:6; 10:17. These are not primarily (as in Prv. 6:23; 15:24; cf. 21:21) the possibilities of attaining to life but the ways commanded by God (cf. ψ 118:37: ἐν τῇ ὁδῷ σου ζῆσόν με) which ensure men of life [33] (on Jer. 21:8 → 54).

There are not wanting passages which assume that men can really follow these ways of God. In most cases, however, these are self-protestations like Job 23:11: ὁδοὺς γὰρ αὐτοῦ ἐφύλαξα καὶ οὐ μὴ ἐκκλίνω; ψ 16:4; 17:21; 36:34; 38:1 and 118:15; perhaps also ἐν ὁδοῖς δικαιοσύνης περιπατῶ (Prv. 8:20) and πᾶσαν ὁδὸν ἄδικον ἐμίσησα (ψ 118:128 = ἐμίσησα πᾶσαν ὁδὸν ἀδικίας, v. 104; cf. 29; Tob. 4:5; Prv. 8:13; Jer. 3:21). But there is an impressive number of passages painting a different picture. Men (including Israel, to which most of the passages refer) do not observe the ways of God (Mal. 2:9) and will not know them (Jer. 5:4 f.; Wis. 5:7). They want nothing to do with the ὁδὸς δικαία (Job 24:11; cf. 24:4; 28:4) or δικαιοσύνης (24:13). They turn aside from the ὁδὸς ἀληθείας

---

[32] A singular expression is ὁδὸς καλῶν ἔργων in the gloss Sir. 11:15. It obviously corresponds to γνῶσις νόμου in the first part of the verse and denotes its practice (cf. σοφία and ἐπιστήμη on the one side, ἀγάπησις on the other).

[33] A doctrine is called a way of life in Egyptian Wis. lit. too; cf. L. Dürr, "Heilige Vaterschaft im antiken Orient," *Heilige Überlieferung, Ausschnitte aus d. Gesch. d. Mönchtums u. des heiligen Kultes ... Ildefons Herwegen dargebracht = Beiträge z. Gesch. d. alten Mönchtums u. d. Benediktinerordens*, Suppl. Vol. (1938), 18 f. Cf. also → II, 845, n. 95.

(Wis. 5:6) and leave the ὁδὸς εὐθεῖα (Prv. 2:13, 16; cf. also Is. 30:11). Instead, they take other ways, their own ways (Is. 56:11), ways of which it is ironically said that they believe or state them to be ὀρθαί (Prv. 12:15; 14:12; 16:25, cf. the evil counsellor in Sir. 37:9 : καλὴ ἡ ὁδός σου).

Their ὁδός is οὐ καλή (Is. 65:2 vl.), οὐκ ἀγαθή (ψ 35:4; cf. Prv. 6:12; 16:29). It is a ὁδὸς κακή (Prv. 2:12; 4:27; 22:14a; 28:10; Ez. 20:44; cf. Prv. 8:13; 25:19, and the very striking reading ἡ κακία [the Mas. would yield ἀκακία] τῆς ὁδοῦ σου, Job 4:6), a ὁδὸς σκληρά (Ju. 2:19; ψ 16:4), σκολιά (Prv. 21:8; 22:5, 14a; 28:18). Esp. common is the expression ὁδοὶ πονηραί (usually plur.) (1 Βασ. 3:21; 4 Βασ. 17:13; ψ 118:101; Jonah 3:8, 10; Zech. 1:4; Jer. 23:14; Ez. 13:22 etc.). Worth noting is the no. of refs. to the ὁδοὶ (τῶν) ἀσεβῶν (ψ 1:6; Prv. 2:22; 4:14, 19; 12:26; 15:9; Jer. 12:1; Ez. 33:11; cf. Is. 55:7; Ez. 33:8 f.), the ὁδὸς ἁμαρτωλῶν (ψ 1:1; 145:9; Sir. 21:10; cf. ὁδὸς ἁμαρτίας, Sir. 47:24), the ὁδοὶ ἀφρόνων (Prv. 12:15) or παρανόμων (4:14; cf. ὁδὸς ἀνομίας, ψ 106:17; 138:24; Job 34:8). But there are very few instances of ὁδὸς εὐσεβῶν (only Is. 26:7) or ὁδὸς δικαίων (only ψ 1:6; cf. Prv. 4:18; 15:28a [Mas. 16:7]). The result is ὁδοὶ διεστραμμέναι (Prv. 8:13; 11:20; cf. 10:9), ὁδοὶ σκότους (Prv. 2:13; cf. 4:19), σύντριμμα καὶ ταλαιπωρία ἐν ταῖς ὁδοῖς αὐτῶν (Is. 59:7). The example of another does not remove personal guilt (cf. Prv. 3:31; 4:14; 22:25), and the seducing of others increases it (cf. Job 24:4). The question : τί ἐπλάνησας ἡμᾶς, κύριε, ἀπὸ τῆς ὁδοῦ σου; in the penitential liturgy in Is. 63:17 is not designed to diminish the responsibility of Israel.

It may thus be said : ἀποστρέψατε ἀπὸ τῶν ὁδῶν ὑμῶν τῶν πονηρῶν (Zech. 1:4; Jonah 3:8, 10; often in Jer. and Ez.). These are ὁδοί of which one can only be ashamed (Ez. 16:61; 20:43; 36:31). Conversion is necessary, for God punishes such ὁδοί (ἐκδικεῖν, Hos. 4:9; Ez. 7:7) and repays κατὰ τὰς ὁδούς (3 Βασ. 8:39 [cf. 2 Ch. 6:30]; Zech. 1:6; Jer. 17:10; 39:19; Ιεζ. 7:5-8, 27; 18:30; 24:14). In this connection it is a serious thought that God's eyes see all the ways of men (Ιερ. 16:17; 39:19; Prv. 5:21; Sir. 17:15; Job 31:4).

Man cannot turn from ὁδοὶ πονηραί unless God helps him. Confidence that He can and will help is expressed in various forms. The common theme is the promise : δώσω αὐτοῖς ὁδὸν ἑτέραν καὶ καρδίαν ἑτέραν, Ιερ. 39(32):39.

God will not grow weary of showing man His way, i.e., of teaching him His commandments ; He practises δεικνύειν (Is. 48:17; the LXX also has δείξουσιν at Mi. 4:2; cf. ψ 49:23), διδάσκειν (ψ 24:9; Prv. 4:11), γνωρίζειν (ψ 24:4; 15:11; 142:8; Prv. 22:19), ἀναγγέλλειν (Is. 2:3; Ιερ. 49[42]:3), συμβιβάζειν (ψ 31:8), νομοθετεῖν (ψ 24:8, 12; 26:11; 118:33). Cf. the δηλοῦν of the good way, 3 Βασ. 8:36 and par., and ψ 85:11: ὁδήγησόν με, κύριε, τῇ ὁδῷ σου, also 138:24; 5:9. God's help is also needed and expected in respect of man's way as his walk and state, as may be seen from many instances, e.g., Wis. 10:17; Ιερ. 38:9; Is. 42:16; Jdt. 12:8; 2 Βασ. 22:33 (cf. ψ 17:32); Tob. 4:19. Similar statements are made regarding σοφία (cf. Prv. 3:6; Wis. 10:17) and δικαιοσύνη (cf. Prv. 11:5; 13:6). The many imperatives, however, show that man is fully responsible for taking God's way and for his own way. Yet the thought of divine assistance is always present. Sir. 2:6 is a kind of motto : εὔθυνον τὰς ὁδούς σου καὶ ἔλπισον ἐπ' αὐτόν. It should not go unnoticed that there is emphasis on pastoral responsibility for the way of another (cf. Prv. 28:23). He who, instructed by God (→ supra), knows the ὁδοὶ κυρίου, should also proclaim them. Cf. the vl.: τὰς ὁδούς σου ἐξήγγειλα, ψ 118:26 אA and ψ 50:13 : διδάξω ἀνόμους τὰς ὁδούς σου (also 1 Βασ. 12:23).

A special question is how far the motif of the two ways, which became so important later (→ 57; 61; C. 2. a; D), is already to be found in the OT or LXX as a figure of speech for two lines of conduct between which a man must choose.

It is evident that the ὁδός passages mentioned thus far are all in some way antithetical, that the ways commanded by God are contrasted with those of man's own choice, and that each expression relating to the ways of men has, or can have, its counterpart, even if only by way of negation (e.g., ὁδός ἀγαθή / ὁδός οὐκ ἀγαθή). The reason for this is that all these statements help forward the task of developing the necessity, urgency and scope of decision for or against God. But for the same reason the schema of the two ways is not yet found in them. One can speak of this only where two opposing ways are mentioned together. The strong use of parallelism in the OT and apocrypha naturally helps to develop such a schema. But in fact there are not many passages in which the metaphor is clearly present. [34]

The most important of these is ψ 1:6 : ὅτι γινώσκει κύριος ὁδὸν δικαίων καὶ ὁδὸς ἀσεβῶν (cf. ὁδὸς ἁμαρτωλῶν, 1:1) ἀπολεῖται. Related, and worth noting because of the use of the category of light and darkness, is Prv. 4:18 f.: αἱ δὲ ὁδοὶ τῶν δικαίων ὁμοίως φωτὶ λάμπουσιν, προπορεύονται καὶ φωτίζουσιν, ἕως κατορθώσῃ ἡ ἡμέρα· αἱ δὲ ὁδοὶ τῶν ἀσεβῶν σκοτειναί, οὐκ οἴδασιν πῶς προσκόπτουσιν. The construction of the antitheses in Prv. 15:19 also yields a plain contrast : ὁδοὶ ἀεργῶν ἐστρωμέναι ἀκάνθαις, αἱ δὲ τῶν ἀνδρείων τετριμμέναι, though here the fig. character of ὁδός is stronger than elsewhere, and the ref. is to a particular question. The schema is also present in ψ 118:29 f., though it does not stand out in the context : ὁδὸν ἀδικίας ἀπόστησον ἀπ᾽ ἐμοῦ καὶ τῷ νόμῳ σου ἐλέησόν με. ὁδὸν ἀληθείας ᾑρετισάμην, τὰ κρίματά σου οὐκ ἐπελαθόμην. Prv. 4:26 introduces the metaphor of the ὁδοί (though in synon. parallelism with τροχιαί : ὀρθὰς τροχιὰς ποίει σοῖς ποσίν καὶ τὰς ὁδούς σου κατεύθυνε), and then to 4:27: μὴ ἐκκλίνῃς εἰς τὰ δεξιὰ μηδὲ εἰς τὰ ἀριστερά (cf. Dt. 5:32 f.; Is. 30:21 etc.), ἀπότρεψον δὲ σὸν πόδα ἀπὸ ὁδοῦ κακῆς, the LXX adds the not wholly apposite 4:27a : ὁδοὺς γὰρ τὰς ἐκ δεξιῶν οἶδεν ὁ θεός, διεστραμμέναι δέ εἰσιν αἱ ἐξ ἀριστερῶν, which causes a clash of imagery, so that the metaphor of the two ways already present in 4:27a loses its clarity and force (→ III, 478 f.). One might also refer to ψ 138:24 : καὶ ἰδὲ εἰ ὁδὸς ἀνομίας ἐν ἐμοί, καὶ ὁδήγησόν με ἐν ὁδῷ αἰωνίᾳ, and Prv. 2:13 : ὦ οἱ ἐγκαταλείποντες ὁδοὺς εὐθείας τοῦ πορεύεσθαι ἐν ὁδοῖς σκότους.

Finally, Prv. 11:20 is important : βδέλυγμα κυρίῳ διεστραμμέναι ὁδοί, προσδεκτοὶ δὲ αὐτῷ πάντες ἄμωμοι ἐν ταῖς ὁδοῖς αὐτῶν, also 12:28 : ἐν ὁδοῖς δικαιοσύνης ζωή, ὁδοὶ δὲ μνησικάκων εἰς θάνατον (the Mas. is different). The latter verse is worth noting because, even if not precisely in this formulation, it speaks of the way of life and that of death (5:5 f. almost has the metaphor too). In this connection we should also mention Jer. 21:8 : ἐγὼ δέδωκα πρὸ προσώπου ὑμῶν τὴν ὁδὸν ζωῆς καὶ τὴν ὁδὸν τοῦ θανάτου, though acc. to 21:9 this advice refers to the fact that those of the besieged inhabitants of Jerusalem who go over to the Chaldeans will be delivered,

---

[34] It should be pointed out that ὁδός can be used in the most varied ways in antithetical statements without involving the schema of the two ways. ὁδός may be only in the one half (e.g., Prv. 11:5 : δικαιοσύνη ἀμώμους ὀρθοτομεῖ ὁδούς, ἀσέβεια δὲ περιπίπτει ἀδικίᾳ, 13:15; Tob. 4:5), or the ref. may be only to the one kind of way which is taken or not (e.g., Hos. 14:10; Prv. 14:8; cf. also Wis. 5:7; ψ 106:40), or which may help to decision in some other manner (e.g., Sir. 39:24 : αἱ ὁδοὶ αὐτοῦ τοῖς ὁσίοις εὐθεῖαι, οὕτως τοῖς ἀνόμοις προσκόμματα, cf. also Is. 35:8). Prv. 14:2 forms a transition to the image of the two ways : ὁ πορευόμενος ὀρθῶς φοβεῖται τὸν κύριον, ὁ δὲ σκολιάζων ταῖς ὁδοῖς αὐτοῦ ἀτιμασθήσεται. So, too, does Prv. 28:18; the related 28:6 is transl. differently in the LXX. It is hardly accurate to say that the two ways are already a stereotyped expression in the last two passages (so Str.-B., I, 460). Alpers, 60 thinks the earliest ref. to the two ways is in the Song of Deborah in Ju. 5:(, but this is really recalling evil days when, as the LXX puts it, the ὁδοί (the recognised ways were avoided and ἀτραποί (hidden paths) had to be found.

whereas those who remain in the city will perish by sword, famine and pestilence. Only formally, then, is this par. to the schema of the way of life and death. In content, it bears no relation to it. [35]

Reviewing the passages cited, one may say that the number is not very great in comparison with the lavish use of ὁδοί elsewhere, nor are all the verses of the same value. The metaphor of the two ways is certainly present in the OT, though restricted to Ps. and Prv. if one does not count Jer. 21:8. Yet it is in no sense primary. [36] The expression "two ways" does not occur in this connection, [37] and when there is reference to two ways this is not a comprehensive schema into which further hortatory material is integrated but only an obvious and effective form in which the figurative use of ὁδοί can be presented. [38]

A final group is constituted by passages which speak of the ὁδοί (rarely sing.) which God Himself takes.

The combination with ἔργα (Dt. 32:4; Tob. 3:2; ψ 144:17; Da. 3:27, also Prv. 8:22 and ψ 94:10, cf. 9) shows that ὁδοί has here the sense of "acts" or "dealings," and the combination with βουλαί (Is. 55:8 f.) shows that it may also connote "purpose," "plans" (cf. also Is. 58:2). This is supported rather than contradicted by the fact that in 2 Βασ. 22:31 = ψ 17:30 there is mention of the ῥῆμα κυρίου (cf. also the vl. λόγου for ὁδοῦ, Job 26:14), for God's action and speech are one (hence God's way in these verses is not His commandment, but His Word in general). It is stressed that the ways of God are ἔλεος καὶ ἀλήθεια (ψ 24:10, Mas. חֶסֶד וֶאֱמֶת, cf. ἐλεημοσύναι καὶ ἀλή-θεια, Tob. 3:2). They are εὐθεῖαι, Hos. 14:10; Ez. 33:17, 20 (cf. 18:25, 29); Da. 3:27. What is meant is not that they are straight, but right. In Sir. 39:24 (→ n. 34) the ref. is again, not to the commandments of God, but to His leadings and dispensations, which are acknowledged by some but cause others to stumble. Again, in Job 21:14 : ὁδούς σου εἰδέναι οὐ βούλομαι, acc. to the par. 22:17, the ref. is to God's judicial dealings rather than His commandments. Cf. ψ 9:25. God is δίκαιος in all His ὁδοί, ψ 144:17, His way is ἄμωμος, 17:30 (cf. 2 Βασ. 22:31) and ἐν τῷ ἁγίῳ, ψ 76:13(one may see from v. 14 ff. that this refers to His works). Cf. also the use of κρίσεις (Dt. 32:4) → III, 941 f.; Is. 26:8 : ἡ γὰρ ὁδὸς κυρίου κρίσις, can be taken in the same sense in the free LXX rendering (cf. 9), though the meaning "judgment" is demanded by the Mas. Common to all these statements is the conviction that God's ways are not to be criticised by men (cf. Is. 40:14). This conviction presupposes that God's work is acces-

---

[35] Naturally the verse may have influenced the development of the metaphor of the two ways, esp. in the form of the way of life and that of death. Indeed, it obviously did so to a very high degree, → 59. The refs. adduced in → II, 855, n. 182 (Sir. 15:17; 33:14; 37:18) do not have the image of the two ways.

[36] All the passages mentioned are so embedded in the usage and thinking of the OT that one can nowhere assume extraneous influence. Alpers, 62 f. believes Prv. 7-9 is affected by the Prodicus fable. Prv. 7, however, is not to be taken fig. The γυνὴ ἀλλοτρία καὶ πονηρά of 7:5 is a real harlot or adulteress (cf. 6:24 ff.). Hence one cannot discern in 7 f. any echo of the Prodicus debate between virtue and vice. The confrontation between Lady Wisdom and Lady Folly in 9:1 ff., 13 ff. certainly reminds us of the two women in the Prodicus fable, but there is no ref. here to the two ways (the figure of speech in 9:15 is different, and the בְּדֶרֶךְ בִּינָה of 9:6 is otherwise rendered by the LXX).

[37] Sir. 2:12 οὐαὶ ... ἁμαρτωλῷ ἐπιβαίνοντι ἐπὶ δύο τρίβους can hardly be taken as an instance of the metaphor of the two ways (as suggested by Str.-B., I, 461), for the ref. is obviously to a man who halts between two opinions (cf. 3 Βασ. 18:21).

[38] Kn. Did. on 1, 1 writes : "The metaphor of the two ways, or of one of the two (that of God and men, of the just and the unjust, or righteousness and unrighteousness) is extra-ordinarily common in the LXX ; there are hundreds of examples ... The way of life and that of death are mentioned together in Jer. 21:8; cf. also Prv. 12:28 and Ps. 1:1 f." The above discussion shows that each individual ref. needs to be checked.

sible only to a fraction of human knowledge (ἰδοὺ ταῦτα μέρη ὁδοῦ αὐτοῦ, Job 26:14), and it finds classical expression in the comparison between the ways of God and those of man in Is. 55:8 f. [39]

The LXX gives evidence of a very varied use of ὁδός even within its figurative usage. Nevertheless, as we have sought to show, the material may be seen under specific aspects which present decisive ideas in the biblical understanding of God and man. The distinctiveness of these ὁδός statements comes out when one compares them, e.g., with Philo. Not only are important elements in the OT message absent from Philo (→ n. 61), but features characteristic of Philo are also absent from the LXX (including the apocrypha). Thus the idea that there are ways to virtue is quite alien to the LXX; apart from the fact that ἀρετή is found only in Wis. and 2-4 Macc., there is no reference whatever to the belief that ways exist whereby man may come to possess a perfection with which he can stand before God. In the LXX the metaphor of the way is not controlled by a goal which man should seek and to which he may attain. The metaphor presupposes that the command of God stands at the beginning of the way. In particular, we do not find at all in the LXX the idea that there are ways which lead to God or to heaven. Only once in 4 Macc. 14:5, and thus on the very margin of the LXX, do we find an expression reminiscent of the usage of Philo, namely, ὥσπερ ἐπ' ἀθανασίας ὁδὸν τρέχοντες.

2. The Influence of OT Usage in the Pseudepigrapha and Rabbinic Writings.

When the pseudepigrapha speak of ways (they do so less commonly than the OT, and it is noticeable that ὁδός plays no part in Ep. Ar.), the influence of OT usage is unmistakable. There is hardly a reference for which a parallel may not be found in the OT or LXX.

The lit. use is rare, e.g., S. Bar. 22:3 (III, 3, 3, Violet). There is ref. to the course of the years in Jub. 6:34, or the path of the stars in Eth. En. 41:6 f. (cf. 69:20 ff., 25; 83:11), or, again in heavenly topography, the way of the angels in Eth. En. 18:5 (not Gk. En.), the ways upwards to the firmament and the ways (doors) into Paradise, 4 Esr. 4:7 (I, 7, 7, Violet), also the way to hell-fire, S. Bar. 85:13 (VIII, 8, 2, Violet). The sense of "walk" is commonly attested, e.g., Jub. 5:19; Gk. En. 8:2; Eth. En. 108:13; Ps. Sol. 10:1, 3 f.; 4 Esr. 7:122 (III, 16, 8, Violet); S. Bar. 77:6 (VII, 3, 6, Violet); Test. L. 2:3; in parallelism with "works," e.g., Jub. 22:16; Eth. En. 61:8 f.; Sib., 3, 233 (ὁδούς τ' ἀγαθὰς καὶ ἔργα δίκαια, though τρίβος is usually preferred in Sib.); cf. also the correspondence between καρδίαι and ὁδοί in Test. Sim. 5:2. The expression "way of the father" etc. (→ 51) had some influence, e.g., Mart. Is. 3:3; 5:4; Heb. Test. N. 1; cf. Test. R. 1:3: ἐγὼ ἀποθνῄσκω καὶ πορεύομαι ὁδὸν πατέρων μου. [40] There is also ref. to the ways which God takes in the sense of His dealings, plans, or decisions, esp. in 4 Esr., which wrestles with the question how we are to understand what it mostly calls the

---

[39] When Stauffer Theol., 184 (cf. on this n. 684) uses the expression "ways of God" as a biblical title for the historico-theological principles which he discusses in what follows (184 ff. § 51: "The Ways of Providence"), it is only loosely that he groups the material under this heading, since the principles are not strictly related to the biblical instances of "ways of God." This seems to call in question the legitimacy of using the phrase as Stauffer does.

[40] The ref. is to the way which the fathers took, not the way which leads to them. The sense is different in S. Bar. 44:2 (IV, 8, 2, Violet): I go hence to my fathers by the way of all flesh (on this last expression, which presupposes a Heb. כְּדֶרֶךְ־כָּל־הָאָרֶץ, cf. 4 Esr. 10:13 [IV, 5, 8b, Violet], and → 43, 12, also → n. 26).

"ways of the Most High," 3:31 (I, 6, 3, Violet); 4:2 (I, 7, 2); 4:10 f. (I, 7, 10 f.); 5:34 (II, 3, 5); 12:4 (V, 6, 2); cf. S. Bar. 14:8 (II, 4, 8, Violet); 20:4 (II, 8, 2). [41]

In particular, the important OT concept of the ways which God has commanded for man, the ways of God, finds a solid place in these works, cf. Jub. 5:13; 20:2 f.; 21:2; 4 Esr. 7:24 (III, 4, 7, Violet), 79 (III, 11, 3), 88 (III, 12, 1); 8:56 (III, 26, 56); 9:9 (III, 27, 8); 14:31 (VII, 5, 6); S. Bar. 14:5 (II, 4, 5, Violet); Test. Jud. 26:1; Damasc., 3, 15; cf. 1, 11: "the way of his heart." "The way" is also found in the absolute, e.g., 4 Esr. 14:22 (VII, 3, 5c, Violet); Damasc., 1, 13; 2, 6. In many passages the way of the Lord stands in parallelism with His commandments or Law; it is the way of the Law, S. Bar. 44:3 (IV, 8, 3, Violet), and is called the way of righteousness, Jub. 1:20; 23:26; Gk. En. 99:10 (ed. Bonner, ἐν ὁδοῖς δικαιοσύνης αὐτοῦ); Eth. En. 82:4 (cf. 91:4); Damasc., 1, 16, also the way of truth, Jub. 23:21; Gk. En. 104:13 (ed. Bonner); cf. Eth. En. 105:2. Cf. the "straight way" of the Son of Man in Eth. En. 71:17.

As is to be expected, the metaphor of the two ways is used. [42]

4 Esr. 7:12 f. (II, 3, 12 f., Violet) is, of course, to be ruled out. In 7:6 ff. (III, 3, 6 ff.), after the parable of the broad sea to which there is only narrow access, there comes the parable of the city on a plain reached only by a narrow path along a ridge between abysses of fire and water; then in 7:12 (III, 3, 12) the ways in this world are contrasted with those in the world to come, the great aeon, 7:13 (III, 7, 13). The former are "narrow, full of sighs and toil, few and evil, rich in dangers, beset by sufferings," whereas the others are "broad and protected and bring the fruits of immortality." But man cannot choose between these different kinds of ways, as the metaphor of the two ways demands. The ways succeed one another in time and space, the former leading to the latter. [43] At most the only choice man has is whether or not to tread the narrow ways in this life. But this is not the point of the image, which rather seeks to explain why it is that the ways in this world or aeon demand walking on a dangerous ridge. Hence the metaphor of the two ways is not to be found here. [44] There is close similarity in 4 Esr. 7:48 (III, 6, 4), but even this is not a valid instance. We read here of "the wicked heart which has led us from life and seduced us to destruction and onto the way of death" (cf. III, 6, 5a); there is no direct ref. to the way of life. [45]

The metaphor of the two ways occurs plainly in Eth. En. 91:18 f., where the ways of righteousness are enjoined and there is warning against the ways of violence. Even clearer is Slav. En. 30:15: "I called his name Adam and showed him two ways, light and darkness, and said to him: 'This is good and that evil,'" cf. also 42:10b: "Blessed is he who turns from the crooked way and walks on the straight way" (Sib., 8, 399 f.: αὐτὸς ὁδοὺς παρέθηκα δύο, ζωῆς θανάτου τε, καὶ γνώμην προέθηκ' ἀγαθὴν ζωὴν προελέσθαι, must be regarded as Christian). Older than Slav. En. is Test. A., where we read in 1:3-5: δύο ὁδοὺς ἔδωκεν ὁ θεὸς τοῖς υἱοῖς τῶν ἀνθρώπων, δύο

[41] The phrase "the upper ways" (4 Esr. 4:23, I, 9, 2, Violet) is also to be taken in this sense, cf. 4:21 (I, 8, 12); though cf. Gunkel in Kautzsch Apkr. u. Pseudepigr., ad loc.
[42] In Jub. 12:21 the right way is contrasted with confusion (of heart); cf. Sib. Fr., 1, 23 ff. (ed. Geffcken): τρίβον ὀρθὴν εὐθεῖαν προλιπόντες ἀπήλθετε καὶ δι' ἀκανθῶν καὶ σκολόπων ἐπλανᾶσθε. The metaphor also occurs in Jub. 7:26, which contrasts the ways of corruption with a walk in righteousness. It also underlies the admonition in S. Bar. 85:12 (VIII, 8, 1a, Violet); at the end there is no more place for repentance and no changing of ways, in the sense that one cannot alter one's way and enter upon another.
[43] Violet renders "entries" (εἴσοδοι) rather than "ways," but his explanation that "entries in this world" means "entries through this world to that" seems most unlikely, and what are the "entries in the future world"?
[44] As against Str.-B., I, 461.
[45] 4 Esr. 7:129 (III, 17, 3, Violet) also refers to the way of life only indirectly, so that it is not a true instance of the metaphor of the two ways.

διαβούλια καὶ δύο πράξεις καὶ δύο τόπους καὶ δύο τέλη. διὰ τοῦτο πάντα δύο
εἰσίν, ἓν κατέναντι τοῦ ἑνός. ὁδοὶ δύο, καλοῦ καὶ κακοῦ, ἐν οἷς εἰσι τὰ δύο
διαβούλια ἐν στέρνοις ἡμῶν, διακρίνοντα αὐτάς. This passage must be accepted
as the oldest example of the metaphor of the two ways in Judaism. Yet, though the
image has the character of an introductory thought, it does not serve as a framework
for more precise expositions showing wherein the ὁδοὶ δύο καλοῦ καὶ κακοῦ consist.
The theme of what follows is to be found rather in the statement πάντα δύο εἰσιν. It
is demonstrated that man can conjoin good and evil within himself, and that consequently
everything διπρόσωπόν ἐστιν. There are men who are half pure but in actuality
impure (c. 2), others who are half impure but in totality pure (c. 4). Everything, then,
has two sides ; what matters is *intentio*. If the antithesis of virtue and vice is the basis,
and if everything leads up to the admonition not to be schizophrenically both good
and bad, but to cleave only to good (3:1), the metaphor of the two ways is developed
here in a manner which cannot be harmonised with the role which it plays later as an
introduction to lists of virtues and vices.

If, then, we are not to assume — and there is no cause to do this — that the
expositions in Test. A. have a polemical intent, showing that it is too schematic
to treat virtue and vice merely as antitheses, the only remaining conclusion is that
in the days of Test. A. the metaphor of the two ways had not yet become a constituent part in a tradition of exhortation which was built up on the arrangement
suggested by it. Test. A. seems to have little if anything to do with a catechism
for Jewish proselytes following the schema of the two ways. [46]
Such a catechism would inevitably have left traces at least in the Rabbinic
writings. But no such traces are to be found.

The metaphor of the two ways occurs here, though not too commonly. [47] It is surprising, indeed, that the number of passages, of which many are pars. or doublets, is
comparatively so great. For, whereas in the OT the metaphor is supported by a wide
and varied fig. use of way in the sense of "walk," there seems to be nothing corresponding to this in the Rabb. lit. [48] There must be specific reasons why the metaphor
of the two ways appeared at all, and occupied the place it did, and it seems obvious

---

[46] It is hard to see to what extent Fr. 1 of the Apc. Zeph. (L. Stern, "Die koptische
Apokalypse d. Sophonias," *Zschr. f. ägyptische Sprache u. Altertumskunde*, 24 [1886],
115 ff.) offers support for the assumption that "in the first cent. of our era or even earlier
there was a course for proselytes under the title 'The Two Ways'" (as against A. Harnack,
*Die Apostellehre u. d. jüdischen beiden Wege*² [1896], 29, n. 1). If in this Fr. the angel
in Hades has a scroll on which sins are inscribed, and later a second angel produces another roll on which presumably (the Fr. breaks off here) good works are entered, this is
an instance of the Jewish conception of the two books (→ I, 620, n. 23), but it has nothing
to do with the two ways.
[47] Cf. Str.-B., I, 461 ff.; IV, 1080. Str.-B., I, 462 f. also adduces passages which speak of
keeping the mean between two ways, but this is a totally different metaphor which cannot
be regarded as a variation on the usual figure of the two ways.
[48] The no. of instances of "straight way," "way of life," "way of God" quoted by
Str.-B., I, 462 f. is trifling. The Rabb. obviously like to speak of works as a way, and it
is worth noting that when ψ 1:6 is quoted the formulation of the psalmist is replaced by
"works of the righteous or the wicked," cf. Str.-B., I, 239; II, 427. On the other hand we
often find דַּרְכֵי הָאֱמֹרִי, "ways of the Amorites," i.e., heathen customs, cf. Str.-B., I, 511, 682;
III, 492; IV, 412; esp. II, 690; III, 599 f. The only OT par. is הַגּוֹיִם (or דֶּרֶךְ (מִצְרַיִם (→ n. 26,
31); cf. the sing. דֶּרֶךְ אַחֶרֶת in the Rab., Str.-B., II, 690. Sometimes there is ref. to the ways
of the Samaritans (Str.-B., I, 539) and the ways of the congregation (II, 20). In the sense
of "manner" or "behaviour" דֶּרֶךְ is a favourite tt. of the Rabb., partly in a very weakened
form. Cf. S. Krauss, *Talmudische Archäologie*, III (1912), Index, s.v.; G. Klein, *Der älteste
christl. Katechismus u. d. jüd. Propaganda-Lit.* (1909), 61 ff. This is perhaps the usage in
4 Esr. 4:3 (I, 7, 3, Violet) and esp. 7:79 ff., 88 (III, 11, 3 ff.; 12, 1); cf. Violet on 7:80 (III,

that passages of Scripture provided the basis for it. In fact the influence of Dt. 11:26
and esp. 30:19 is unmistakable. To be sure, these verses are not instances of the metaphor in the OT. But the Rabb. take them to mean that when God set life and death,
blessing and cursing, before the people, He propounded two ways. [49] Jer. 21:8 undoubtedly influenced this interpretation, for here the phrase נָתַן לִפְנֵי, also used in Dt.
11:26; 30:19, is combined with דֶּרֶךְ הַחַיִּים and דֶּרֶךְ הַמָּוֶת Jer. 21:8 certainly does not refer
to life and death in the same sense as Dt. 11:26 and 30:19 (→ 54), nor is it quoted
by the Rabb. in this connection, [50] but the above exposition can hardly be explained in
any other way. [51] Once it became established, this exposition for its part explains why
the concepts life and death came to have an almost exclusive position in the metaphor
of the two ways. [52]

Except in this combination the metaphor occurs only in bBer., 28b [53] and bAb,
2, 13 f. [54] The first ref. records that when Jochanan b. Zakkai lay weeping on his death-
bed he said: "Before me are two ways, the one to Paradise, the other to Gehinnom,
and I do not know which I shall be told to take; why should I not weep?" This is
quite a different use, for the ref. is not to the decision which man must take in his
conduct but to the destiny ordained by God after death. In contrast, bAb, 2, 9 speaks
of the two ways between which man must choose: Rabban Jochanan b. Zakkai asks
his disciples first concerning the good way and then concerning the evil (דֶּרֶךְ טוֹבָה
or דֶּרֶךְ רָעָה; → 52 f.). In turn they answer: a good or evil eye, a good or evil neighbour
etc., until we come at last to the answer of R. Eleazar: "A good or bad heart," and
this is praised as the best because it includes all the others. This is not told in order
to give a correct definition of the good or bad way, but to show the superiority of
R. Eleazar or the wisdom of R. Jochanan b. Zakkai. Although the story contains in the
unfolding answers a list of good and bad qualities or decisions, this has not much to do
with catechetical exposition. Indeed, the very fact that the question can be put, and
different answers received, implies that there is as yet no solid and generally recognised
schema of the two ways. It is significant, however, that we have here an exposition

---

11, 5); on XXXVI f. Violet incorrectly expounds other passages from 4 Esr. in the same
way. The Rabb. חֲלָכָה (cf. Strack, Einleitung, 4 f.; Weber, 95 ff.) should be mentioned in
this connection, though the metaphor of a way underlies it only indirectly (cf. Joh. W.
1 K., 119) and the sense of "rule," "teaching," "precept," goes far beyond the basic sense
of "walk."

[49] Cf. S. Dt. 11:26 § 53 (86a) and other instances in Str.-B., I, 461 ff.

[50] The passages already discussed (→ 53) can hardly have affected Rabb. lit. as discussed by Str.-B. acc. to the Index, IV, 1279 ff.

[51] As against Str.-B., I, 460, where Dt. 11:26; 30:15 are called the biblical basis of the
metaphor because, "after the words 'I lay before you blessing and cursing, life and death,'
there is immediate ref. to the way or ways of God." It should be noted that Dt. 11:28 is
not quoted by the Rabb. in this connection, nor is 30:16 (the ref. to ways here is hardly
appended to 30:19). Both S. Dt. 11:26 § 53 (86a): "Like one who sat at the cross-roads
and had two ways before him etc.," and Ex. r., 30 (90b): "Like a king who built two ways
etc.," enable us to see something which is hardly surprising, namely, that the metaphor of
the two ways has an assured place in popular imagery. It is more than doubtful whether
we are to see here the influence of the Prodicus fable (so Str.-B., IV, 408 f., Qoh. r. on
1:14) → n. 196. Qoh. r. on 12:14 (Str.-B., I, 463) speaks lit. rather than fig. of two different
ways.

[52] Apart from passages which quote Dt. 11:26; 30:19 (→ n. 49) we may refer to bMen.,
99b, 39 (men seduce one another from ways of life to those of death, whereas God does
the opposite; Str.-B., IV, 1080; cf. also bSanh., 55a); bChag., 3b and par. (the words of
the Torah direct those who learn them from the ways of death to those of life; Str.-B.,
I, 461; IV, 178 f.). Cf. also the exposition in Gn. r., 21 (14b) and par., reminiscent of
Slav. En. 30:15 (→ 57), which has God set two ways before Adam, one to death and
one to life (Str.-B., I, 461; IV, 8). Cf. Volz Esch., 306.

[53] Cf. the par. M. Ex., 14, 28; Str.-B., I, 461.

[54] Cf. the par. Ab. R. Nah., 14; Str.-B., I, 461.

by concrete examples of that in which the two ways consist. Ab., 2, 9 is the first instance of content being given to the two contrasting ways.

3. Philo and Josephus.

Philo uses ὁδός frequently. Only rarely, however, is he influenced by the OT in so doing (the most important instances in which this is true, and in which Philo is especially concerned to expound ὁδός, are mentioned in what follows). In the main, Philo shows himself to be dependent on the general, philosophical and hortatory use, and it is impressive to see from his works what rich and varied possibilities the theme offered a skilful and imaginative writer such as he was.

In the first place, note should be taken of certain passages which contain a use rare in Philo. ὁδός is used lit. in Vit. Mos., I, 177: at the passage through the Red Sea ὁδὸς εὐρεῖα καὶ λεωφόρος (the army road, → 63) γίνεται, cf. also Vit. Cont., 86. We also read of ways by land and sea in Philo Spec. Leg., IV, 154, and of ways in the sea or water in Op. Mund., 114; Spec. Leg., I, 335; IV, 111. The stars, too, have their ways or courses: the moon, Op. Mund., 101; the sun, Rer. Div. Her., 149, the στοιχεῖα, Aet. Mund., 109 f. (cf. also Som., I, 156). The sense of "procedure" or "method" is found in Poster. C., 7: τὴν δι᾽ ἀλληγορίας ὁδόν; related is Deus Imm., 180, where the world of lofty and pure conceptuality is denoted by ὑψηλαὶ καὶ ὁρικαὶ ὁδοί (with χρᾶσθαι and not a verb of going).

Philo frequently views human life from the standpoint of a way, and with the help of ἀτραπός, e.g., Gig., 64, he speaks of the way of life. The writing Leg. All. closes (III, 253) with a resigned ref. to the fact that acc. to Gn. 3:19 the beginning and end link man with the corruptible materials of the earth: τελευτήσεις δὲ πάλιν εἰς ἐκεῖνα τὴν μεταξὺ τοῦ βίου τρίψας ὁδὸν οὐ λεωφόρον, ἀλλὰ τραχεῖαν, βάτων καὶ τριβόλων κεντεῖν τε καὶ τιτρώσκειν πεφυκότων μεστήν. On the other hand, Philo Deus Imm., 61 counts on it that those to whom an εὔμοιρος φύσις and an ἀγωγὴ ἐν πᾶσιν ἀνυπαίτιος are imparted fare better: τὴν ... ὁδὸν τοῦ βίου λεωφόρον καὶ εὐθεῖαν εὑρίσκοντες. Vit. Mos., I, 195 has the expression: εἶτα καὶ εἰς ᾄδου προπέμπων, τὴν τοῦ βίου τελευταίαν ὁδόν.

Very numerous are the passages in which ὁδός (sing. and plur.) is used in the context of exhortation.

It occurs often with the gen., e.g., ἀδικημάτων, Jos., 212; Spec. Leg., I, 243; ἁμαρτημάτων, I, 192; ἐγκρατείας, Det. Pot. Ins., 19; δεισιδαιμονίας, 24; φρονήσεως, Plant., 98; Agric., 104; σοφίας, Plant., 97, though other constructions are also found, e.g., τὰς ἐπ᾽ ἀλήθειαν ἀγούσας ὁδούς, Exsecr., 148; διὰ πασῶν ἰέναι τῶν εἰς ἀρέσκειαν ὁδῶν, Spec. Leg., I, 300; τὴν πρὸς εὐδαιμονίαν ἄγουσαν ὁδόν, Vit. Mos., II (III), 189. These statements [55] occur throughout Philo's ethical teaching. He speaks of ways which men should take (βαίνειν and πορεύεσθαι are used, often βαδίζειν), which they should not miss, from which they should not stray (πλανᾶσθαι, e.g., Det. Pot. Ins., 21; commonly ἐκτρέπεσθαι, e.g., Spec. Leg., I, 215), but also of ways on which we should not walk nor lead others (ἀφηγεῖσθαι, Ebr., 125).

In keeping with the great significance of ἀρετή for Philo (→ I, 458 f.) it is natural that he should often speak of the way to virtue, Congr., 10; Fug., 21; Som., I, 179 and 246; with καλοκἀγαθία (cf. also Som., I, 209), Spec. Leg., I, 215. That the way to virtue is for the ἄφρων τραχεῖα καὶ δύσβατος καὶ ἀργαλεωτάτη is emphasised in Ebr., 150 (Hes. Op., 289 ff. is quoted here, → 43), but Philo realises that at first ἀσκηταί (→ I, 494 f.) too regard the way to virtue as rugged and difficult, though later (by God's help, → 64) it becomes a broad way, Poster. C., 154. In Leg. All., I, 57 philosophy is considered a way to virtue. When Philo speaks of two ways, he never omits the way to virtue (→ 61, 27 ff.). In comparison with the host of refs. to this way, very few speak

---

[55] Cf. the comprehensive section in Leisegang, *s.v.*

of the way to εὐσέβεια, Det. Pot. Ins., 21; Spec. Leg., I, 132; III, 29; Agric., 177; Leg. Gaj., 216.

Particular note must be taken of the few passages which speak directly of the way to God.

Because God is the πρῶτος καὶ μόνος τῶν ὅλων βασιλεύς, acc. to Poster. C., 101 ἡ πρὸς αὐτὸν ἄγουσα ὁδός bears the name ἡ βασιλικὴ ὁδός (→ infra). In Deus Imm., 140 ff. it is deduced from Gn. 6:12 LXX : ὅτι κατέφθειρε πᾶσα σάρξ τὴν ὁδὸν αὐτοῦ ἐπὶ τῆς γῆς, that the passage is to be referred to τὴν τοῦ αἰωνίου καὶ ἀφθάρτου τελείαν ὁδὸν τὴν πρὸς θεὸν ἄγουσαν (142) whose goal is the γνῶσις καὶ ἐπιστήμη θεοῦ (143; in what follows we again have the description as a royal way). In Exsecr., 167 the goal of the way of those who have found peace and reconciliation is εὐαρεστεῖν τῷ θεῷ καθάπερ υἱοὺς πατρί. Acc. to Conf. Ling 95 it is incumbent on τοῖς λογισμοῖς to ascend the way πρὸς τὸ αἰθέριον ὕψος where God dwells. Knowledge of self (ἐπίσκεψις ἑαυτοῦ) opens to man the way which leads from self to the knowledge of God, Migr. Abr., 195. Once Philo also speaks of the way to heaven, Poster. C., 31 (in the strict sense, i.e., with ref. to Hom. Od., 11, 315 f., Conf. Ling., 4 speaks of the way to heaven ; the biblical story of the building of the tower does not give Philo any occasion to use this expression).

In many of the passages mentioned thus far, even though the express reference is only to one way, there stands in the background the conception that along with the right way, the ὀρθὴ ὁδός as it is often called (e.g., Det. Pot. Ins., 22; Agric., 101), there is also a wrong way, that there is thus a choice between different ways, and that man has to decide. But Philo also speaks frequently and directly of two ways.

We cannot, of course, include Som., I, 237, the only place where the expression δύο ὁδοί occurs, since here the ref. is to the two methods of νομοθεσία, the positive which leads to truth and the negative which is meant to deter. The most important passage is Spec. Leg., IV, 108 : ἐπεὶ τοῦ βίου διττὴ ὁδός, ἡ μὲν ἐπὶ κακίαν, ἡ δ᾽ ἐπ᾽ ἀρετὴν ἄγουσα, καὶ δεῖ τὴν μὲν ἀποστρέφεσθαι, τῆς δὲ μηδέποτε ἀπολείπεσθαι. The antitheses κακία (→ III, 474) and ἀρετή, with → πάθος also in Leg. All., II, 98; Abr., 204, are found also in Vit. Mos., II (III), 138 : οὐ τὴν τραχεῖαν κακίας ὁδὸν ἤ κυριώτερον εἰπεῖν ἀνοδίαν (→ 62), ἀλλὰ τὴν δι᾽ ἀρετῆς λεωφόρον, and Plant., 37, where the combination with θάνατος / ζωή is particularly to be noted : ἡ μὲν πρὸς ἀρετὴν ὁδὸς αὕτη ζωὴν καὶ ἀθανασίαν ἔχουσα τὸ τέλος, ἡ δὲ πρὸς κακίαν φυγήν τε τούτων καὶ θάνατον. [56] One might also refer to Abr., 269, which differentiates between two groups of men, those who, riveted to the material and external, follow a slippery way, δι᾽ ὀλισθηρᾶς ὁδοῦ, and those who, cleaving to the ἀρεταί, are on a dry and smooth way, διὰ ξηρᾶς καὶ λεωφόρου. In what is said about the king's way in Deus Imm., 140 ff., 159 ff., though this is controlled by other thoughts, the idea of the two ways occurs later (180). Edom, representing the earthly, seeks to block τὴν οὐράνιον καὶ βασιλικὴν ἀρετῆς ὁδόν, but the divine Logos counters this by making impassable the way of Edom and its ὁμόζηλοι, to which there has been no previous ref. [57]

---

[56] The observation of A. Vögtle, "Die Tugend- und Lasterkataloge im NT," Nt.liche Abh., XVI, 4/5, 114, n. 116, that Philo "never speaks of the way of good and evil" is correct, but one should not overlook the fact that the idea of the two ways is attested in Philo, → n. 58.

[57] Pascher, op. cit., 11 f. wrongly introduces the theme of the two ways into the passage on the royal way in Deus Imm., 140 ff. I can only regard it as confusing to say that because Philo takes Gn. 6:12 to mean that πᾶς ὁ σαρκῶν ἑταῖρος hates the way which leads to the γνῶσις and ἐπιστήμη θεοῦ (οὐδενὶ οὕτως οὐδὲν ἀντίπαλον ὡς ἐπιστήμη σαρκὸς ἡδονῇ), he therefore has in view "the antithesis between the flesh and the spirit."

How far from schematic is the idea of the two ways in Philo, and how small a place it occupies in the totality of related statements, may be seen from the many other possibilities which he knows and uses to express the same thought. One may refer first to the common use of the antitheses ὁδός/ἀνοδία (ἀνοδία does not occur in the LXX, but is found in Σ at Job 12:24, also ἀνόδευτος at ᾽Α Jer. 18:15), cf. Praem. Poen., 117; Spec. Leg., I, 215; II, 23; III, 29; IV, 155; Vit. Mos., II (III), 138 : the way of κακία is better described as ἀνοδία, no way at all ; Agric., 101; Som., II, 161; Exsecr., 167. There can also be ref. to one way which is traversed either forwards or backwards, Praem. Poen., 62; Fug., 25, or to ways which go uphill or down, Abr., 59, or to a way which can be followed (Deus Imm., 143) or which is impassable and blocked (144, 180), or to a way which some can follow and others avoid, Abr., 204. On the basis of Nu. 20:17 we can be told not to stray from the way either on the right hand or the left, Poster. C., 101; Deus Imm., 145; Migr. Abr., 146; alongside the right way are threatening clefts and chasms, φάραγγες καὶ βάραθρα, Agric., 101. In the same connection we read of the middle way, Spec. Leg., IV, 167 f.; Deus Imm., 162 and 164; Poster. C., 101 f.; Migr. Abr., 133 and 146. This is not the middle way of many, but the middle of the right way. In the background is the high estimation of the μεσότης in Gk. philosophy. The definition of Philo in Spec. Leg., IV, 168 : βασιλικὴν δ᾽ εἴωθε Μωυσῆς ὀνομάζειν ὁδὸν τὴν μέσην, ὑπερβολῆς καὶ ἐλλείψεως οὖσαν μεθόριον, reminds us of what is said about → μετριοπάθεια in Aristot. Eth. Nic., II, 6, 1107a, 2 f.: μεσότης δέ δύο κακιῶν, τῆς μὲν καθ᾽ ὑπερβολήν, τῆς δὲ κατ᾽ ἔλλειψιν. This review confirms the impression that Philo, even though he uses the idea of the two ways, is not to be regarded as the pronounced champion of a two-ways-schema.[58]

Reference has been made to the concept of the king's way, and Philo can sometimes speak of this in important and even extended expositions. Even when he does not quote Nu. 20:17 directly, he has this verse in view. This may be seen in Gig., 64, and even more plainly in Migr. Abr., 146 f. One may also see from Spec. Leg., IV, 168 (→ supra; εἴωθε) that Philo did not overlook Nu. 21:22, though he never quotes or expounds this. There is definite exposition of Nu. 20:17 in Poster. C., 101 f. and especially Deus Imm. (140 ff.), 144 ff., 159 ff. How closely the expression βασιλικὴ ὁδός is linked with its OT basis may be seen from the fact that no connection is ever made with the term βασιλεία or with the idea of the sage as βασιλεύς (→ I, 575), though this would otherwise be a natural combination. This implies also that the influence of contemporary philosophy (cf. Epict. Diss., III, 21, 19) cannot have been very great. Indeed, in Poster. C., 101 f. Philo plainly sets aside non-biblical views and orientates the concept βασιλικὴ ὁδός exclusively to the experiences of the OT congregation, the ἀρχαῖος ἀσκητῶν θίασος. The king's way is identical with the Word of God: τὴν βασιλικὴν γοῦν ταύτην ὁδὸν ... ὁ νόμος καλεῖ θεοῦ ῥῆμα καὶ λόγον, as may be deduced from the fact that Dt. 28:14 as well as Nu. 20:17 speaks of not going aside either on

indeed, between the way of the flesh and the way of the spirit," and this way of the flesh and way of the spirit do not constitute an ethical theme but are religio-mystical concepts. In the very passages in which Philo actually presents the schema of the two ways it is clear that this is in fact an ethical theme. One cannot assume any direct influence of the Prodicus fable (→ A. 2) in these passages. How little Philo followed specific models in his use of the schema may be seen from the fact that he quotes Hes. Op., 287 ff. in a passage which deals, not with the two ways, but only with the way of virtue (→ 60). He certainly knew the Prodicus fable, but he drew from it, not the schema of the two ways, but the great debate between ἀρετή and ἡδονή in Sacr. AC, 20 ff., which can hardly be undertood apart from the fable.

[58] In this we agree with Vögtle, and draw special attention to the fact that the passages in which Philo speaks of the two ways do not contain lists of virtues and vices.

the right hand or on the left. [59] In Deus Imm., 143, however, the royal way is equated with σοφία, and in 180 it is the way of virtue. Inasmuch as Philo regards Edom as the representative of the earthly, the context of Nu. 20:17 also implies that walking on the king's way is understood as τὰ γήινα παρέρχεσθαι, Deus Imm., 159. If in these passages great emphasis is laid on the concept, its significance is limited to these passages. It can hardly be made a slogan for the whole of Philo's religion. [60] In the concept (as in μέση ὁδός, → 62) the term ὁδός has. however, an independent force which it does not have in the many other combinations in which we find it.

Another OT verse which occupied Philo [61] is Gn. 49:17: γενηθήτω Δαν ὄφις ἐφ' ὁδοῦ, ἐγκαθήμενος ἐπὶ τρίβου. The expositions which he offers in Leg. All., II, 97 f. and Agric., 101 ff. are not in full harmony, though this is a feature found elsewhere in Philo. [62] They agree in not regarding ὁδός and τρίβος as wholly synonymous. ὁδός is the right way, the way of virtue, whereas τρίβος is τετριμμένη τρίβος, the worn and heavily travelled street. The much used path of κακία and πάθος is thus contrasted with the little used way of virtue: ἄτριπτος μὲν ὁ ἀρετῆς χῶρος, ὀλίγοι γὰρ βαίνουσιν αὐτόν, τέτριπται δὲ ὁ κακίας, Leg. All., II, 98; αἱ δὲ φρονήσεως καὶ σωφροσύνης καὶ τῶν ἄλλων ἀρετῶν ὁδοί, καὶ εἰ μὴ ἄβατοι, ἀλλά τοι πάντως ἄτριπτοι· ὀλίγος γὰρ ἀριθμός ἐστι τῶν αὐτὰς βαδιζόντων, Agric., 104. It is worth noting that the idea that only few follow the right way is found only here, in connection with an OT verse which does not really suggest it, and that it does not occur in what is said about the two ways or the king's way. The rarity of the concept is hardly surprising in view of Philo's tendency to stress that the right way is a broad and comfortable road, a ὁδός λεωφόρος, a road for mass transit, a military road.

---

[59] When Bau. J.[3] on 14:6 (the self-designation of Christ as the way) refers to this passage in Poster. C., 102 where the λόγος is the way, it should be noted that Philo does not have in view a personal Logos but the Word of God (cf. Dt. 28:14) which in the next sentence can be called ῥῆμα rather than λόγος : ταὐτό ἐστι τῇ βασιλικῇ ὁδῷ τὸ θεοῦ ῥῆμα. Cf. also F. Büchsel, Joh. u. d. hell. Synkretismus (1928), 53, n. 6.

[60] As against Pascher, 9, who finds here the basic theme which can serve as the starting-point and leading motif in his reconstruction of the mystery system supposedly espoused by Philo. But explanation of the concept βασιλικὴ ὁδός is possible if regard is had to the use of ὁδός elsewhere in Philo. Pascher, however, does not even consider all the passages in which βασιλικὴ ὁδός itself occurs, e.g., Poster. C., 101 f. (→ 62), which is characterised by the fact that even though Philo uses terms from the cults (though not only the mystery cults), e.g., θίασος, the OT flavour of βασιλικὴ ὁδός is emphasised. On Pascher's general interpretation of Philo cf. W. Völker, "Fortschritt u. Vollendung bei Philo v. Alexandrien," TU, 49, 1 (1938), 35, n. 1. Käsemann, 45 ff. follows Pascher too closely. The passage in Vit. Mos., II (III), 134, which he adduces (46) in the same way as Pascher, does not mean by the Son of God the Logos, but the world as the perfect creation of God (cf. 135; Spec. Leg., I, 96; also Deus Imm., 31). As the context shows, the passage is to be taken ethically ; it does not refer to a mystical journey to God. Cf. N. A. Dahl, Das Volk Gottes = Skrifter utgitt av Det Norske Videnskaps-Akademi i Oslo, II. Hist.-Filos. Klasse, 1941, No. 2 (1941), 112 f.

[61] The few OT verses which Philo quotes are not typical within the OT itself. The truly significant lines of OT usage are not followed up in Philo. In particular, it is important that the many passages where the ref. is to the ways of God which men should follow (→ 51) had not the slightest influence on Philo. For him the literary and rhetorical utilising of ὁδός was obviously more important than continuing the OT proclamation of the commandments of God. Hence the conjecture (→ IV, 665) that Conf. Ling., 63 : μιμούμενος τὰς τοῦ πατρὸς ὁδοῦς, refers to obedience can hardly be sustained. This use of ὁδός is not found elsewhere in Philo.

[62] It is thus hardly accurate to say that two interpretations of ὁδός stand in violent contradiction in Agric., 101 ff. (I. Heinemann, Philos Werke, IV [1923], 132, n. 3). The contrast is between the exposition of ὁδός and that of τρίβος.

It is true that Philo quotes approvingly the Pythagorean watchword : ταῖς λεωφόροις μὴ βαδίζειν ὁδοῖς (e.g., Diog. L., VIII, 17; Ael. Var. Hist., IV, 17; Diels⁵, I, 464, 23 ff.; 465, 32; 466, 19) — which he interprets in terms of τὸ μήτε λόγοις μήτ' ἔργοις δημώδεσι καὶ πεπατημένοις χρῆσθαι — but in the main λεωφόρος is a favourite term to denote the right way. In Leg. All., III, 253 (→ 60) he does, of course, call the way of life οὐ λεωφόρον, ἀλλὰ τραχεῖαν, but in Vit. Mos., II (III), 138 the way of κακία is τραχεῖα, that of ἀρετή λεωφόρος. In Op. Mund., 144, too, virtues make broad streets ; acc. to Virt., 51 the same is true of φιλανθρωπία, acc. to Abr., 7 of ἐλπίς (→ II, 529 f.), and acc. to Rer. Div. Her., 70 of ἀλήθεια (→ I, 241). The middle way (→ 62) is λεωφόρος in Spec. Leg., IV, 167, and the royal way of σοφία in Deus Imm., 143. The commandments on the tables of the Law open up εὐρείας ὁδοὺς καὶ λεωφόρους, Decal., 50.

In one portion of these statements we find the thought that the broad ways are established only by the things mentioned (ἀνατέμνειν is often used in this connection), and that divine aid is hereby given. It is then plainly said in Poster. C., 31 that God Himself makes the way to heaven a broad road (cf. also 154); similarly Migr. Abr., 146. With an allusion to ψ 90:11 f. the divine Logos is in Deus Imm., 182 called an angel who frees the way ἵνα ἄπταιστοι διὰ λεωφόρου βαίνωμεν τῆς ὁδοῦ. Related are passages in which Philo speaks of the need for a ἡγεμὼν τῆς ὁδοῦ. Of himself man does not know the way : ψυχῇ δι' ἑαυτῆς ἀγνοούσῃ τὴν ὁδόν, Migr. Abr., 170. Hence he needs a guide. In Conf. Ling., 95 Moses is the guide on the way, in Som., I, 168 ab φύσις, ἄσκησις and μάθησις are guides to the καλόν (cf. Abr., 52; → III, 542; I, 494 f.), but then in Migr. Abr., 174 the Logos is called the ἡγεμὼν τῆς ὁδοῦ (cf. ἡγούμενος τῆς ὁδοῦ) whom man needs so long as he is not made perfect and has not attained πρὸς ἄκραν ἐπιστήμην. Above all, however, God is the ἡγεμὼν τῆς ὁδοῦ, Migr. Abr., 171; Det. Pot. Ins., 114 (ἡγεμὼν τῆς ἀνόδου). Acc. to Som., I, 179 the promise of Gn. 28:15 : ἐγὼ μετὰ σοῦ διαφυλάσσων σε ἐν τῇ ὁδῷ πάσῃ, refers to the fact that God is the συνοδοιπόρος on the way to virtue ; acc. to Det. Pot. Ins., 29 God is the συνοδοιπόρος καὶ ἡγεμὼν τῆς τε ὁδοῦ καὶ τῆς ψυχῆς. Because He is ὁ σωτὴρ ἐλεῶν, He leads the νοῦς on the right way, Praem. Poen., 117; He ensures that the ascent ἐκ τοῦ τῶν παθῶν ᾅδου πρὸς τὸν ὀλύμπιον χῶρον ἀρετῆς will succeed ποδηγετοῦντος ἐμοῦ under His guidance, Poster. C., 31 (cf. also the passages on guidance by the Spirit adduced s.v. → ὁδηγέω). In Philo, then, we find statements which exclude unbiblical synergism in the use of ὁδός. ⁶³

In Joseph., as is to be expected in a historian, ὁδός is always used in the lit. sense. All kinds of ways and streets are denoted by it. They criss-cross the land, e.g., Ant., 8, 235, 330; 9, 84; Bell., 2, 212, and are watched and barricaded in war, e.g., Ant., 2, 324; Vit., 108, 118, 241, 253. Public roads are called δημοσία ὁδός, Ant., 20, 113; sometimes ὁδός is left out in such phrases, e.g., κατὰ τὰς λεωφόρους πάσας, Bell., 4, 380. The roads are named by the starting-point or destination, e.g., διὰ μόνης τῆς ἐπὶ Τιβεριάδα φερούσης ὁδοῦ, Bell., 3, 537; διὰ πάσης δὲ τῆς ὁδοῦ τῆς ἀπὸ Ταριχεῶν εἰς Τιβεριάδα φερούσης, Vit., 276; cf. ἡ διὰ τῆς χώρας ὁδός, Ant., 18, 121. Particular note is taken if a mountain is ὑπὸ τραχύτητος ὁδῶν ἄπορον, Ant., 2, 325. The streets in villages (Bell., 1, 338) and towns (Ant., 5, 28) are ὁδοί; town streets are also πλατεῖα ὁδός (Bell., 6, 149). When a great street is flanked by στοαί (Ant., 16, 148), the carriage-way in the middle is ἡ ὕπαιθρος ὁδός, the open street. Processional roads are ὁδοί in Ant., 3, 141, 148. But the passages or corridors in a palace are also ὁδοί

---

⁶³ Völker, op. cit., 204. We have dealt so fully with Philo's usage because there are expressed in it many characteristic features of his religion and thought which separate him from both the OT and NT and whose presence in the ὁδός passages has not been sufficiently noticed in the works on Philo. There is also need to correct the arbitrarily selective use of certain ὁδός passages by Pascher. If Philo is to be regarded as "a political and theological propagandist on behalf of the Judaism of later antiquity" (cf. G. Bertram, ThLZ, 64 [1939], 193 ff.), then in respect of the use of ὁδός the OT is much less typically Jewish than Philo.

(Ant., 19, 103, 116). The way of Israel through the Red Sea is also mentioned (Ant., 2, 338, cf. 348; 3, 86, → 49, 60). It is called θεία ὁδός in 2, 339. Joseph. never speaks of the way of animals, ships etc. The stars have κινήσεις and δρόμοι, Ant., 1, 32. The sense "journey," "(military) march," is also common in Joseph., e.g., Ant., 2, 133, 175 (God as ὁδοῦ ταύτης ἡγεμών); 6, 157; 8, 227; 12, 198; Bell., 2, 544, 551. πορεία is if anything more common in the same sense, e.g., Ant., 2, 315; 9, 31; Bell., 1, 345; Ap., 1, 204; Vit., 57, 90, 126, 269. [64] There are many prepositional phrases : καθ' ὁδόν, "on the way," e.g., Ant., 14, 53; in the same sense κατὰ τὴν ὁδόν, 1, 254; 4, 108; 6, 281; 11, 134 (also plur. 6, 135; 14, 440); καθ' ὁδὸν ἑτέραν, Vit., 138; καθ' ἑκάτερον τῆς ὁδοῦ, Bell., 2, 542; παρὰ τὴν ὁδόν, 6, 283; ἐπὶ τῆς ὁδοῦ, 7, 287; ἐκ τῆς ὁδοῦ, Bell., 1, 158; ἐν τῇ ὁδῷ, Ant., 6, 55; cf. οἱ ὁδῷ βαδίζοντες, "those who pass by," 4, 234. Common also are μιᾶς ἡμέρας ὁδός etc., e.g., 3, 318; 15, 293; Ap., 2, 21, 23, 116.

The fig. use is very rare in Joseph. The sense of "walk" or "manner of life" occurs in the following passages : τῶν γὰρ τοῦ πατρὸς ἐπιτηδευμάτων ἐκτραπόμενοι (→ 51) καὶ τὴν ἐναντίαν ὁδὸν ἀπελθόντες, Ant., 6, 34; ξένας καινοτομεῖτε κακίας ὁδούς, Bell., 5, 402 (Hyrcanus to the Pharisees) ἠξίου γε μήν, εἴ τι βλέπουσιν αὐτὸν ἁμαρτάνοντα καὶ τῆς ὁδοῦ τῆς δικαίας ἐκτραπόμενον εἰς αὐτὴν ἐπαναγαγεῖν καὶ ἐπανορθοῦν, Ant., 13, 290. Less common is the sense "means," "purpose," "possibility" : τρέπεται ταύτης τολμηροτέραν ὁδόν, "he resorts to a more effective means than before," Ant., 7, 33; ὅπως τῷ ἁμαρτήματι σκέψηταί τινα τοῦ λαθεῖν ὁδόν, "he should seek a way in which the offence may remain concealed," 7, 131; πᾶσαν θεμιτὴν ὁδὸν ἐποίει τὸ κέρδος, "the prospect of winning seemed to make every means legitimate," Bell., 6, 432; δεινὰς βασάνων ὁδούς, "terrible methods of torture," 5, 435; cf. also σωτηρίας ὁδός, "a possibility of deliverance," 5, 415, and φυγῆς ὁδός, Ant., 2, 233. In Joseph., as in Philo, expressions which characterise OT usage (ὁδοὶ κυρίου etc.) seemed not to find any echo.

C. ὁδός in the New Testament.

1. ὁδός in the Literal Sense.

The literal use of ὁδός in the NT is the same as that found elsewhere. Most of the instances are in the Synoptic Gospels.

It is in keeping with the distinctive character of the Gospel narratives, and in turn helps to characterise them, that, though Jesus led a life of constant wandering during His earthly ministry, we are never told which roads or streets He used. Whenever it is possible to locate the sites and routes with any accuracy, it is as a result of careful investigation of the Gospel data combined with topographical knowledge gleaned from the OT and Rabbinic writings, and also with archaeological findings. [65] For the tradition itself the routes were not important, [66] nor was it concerned to praise the fine network of roads which the Romans had con-

---

[64] Joseph. also uses some terms seldom found in the NT, i.e., ὁδοιπορέω (Ant., 14, 226; Vit., 157, not in the LXX), ὁδοιπορία (Ant., 2, 231; 3, 3 and 193, in the LXX only in Wis. and 1 Macc.), also ὁδοιπόρος (Ant., 8, 241, not in the NT and only 6 times in the LXX). He makes frequent use of ὁδεύω (Ant., 1, 244; 2, 185 and 247; 13, 252; Ap., 2, 21; Vit., 115 and 241, in the NT only at Lk. 10:33, in the LXX only 3 Βασ. 6:12; Tob. 6:6; Wis. 5:7 vl.); cf. also the compounds διοδεύω, παροδεύω etc.; also ὁδοποιέω (Bell., 6, 243, in the NT only Mk. 2:23 vl.).

[65] Cf. G. Dalman, Orte u. Wege Jesu³ (1924), which also deals with material concerning roads, ET Sacred Sites and Ways (1935).

[66] Even later when the sacred sites began to be visited — it may be questioned whether this is already so in Jn., cf. K. Kundsin, "Topologische Überlieferungsstoffe im Joh.-Ev.," FRL, NF, 22 (1925) — the sacred routes claimed little interest. Even the Via Dolorosa in Jerusalem was no exception ; cf. Dalman, 289 and 364 f.

structed in Palestine and the territory covered by the first Christian missions. [67]

In the whole of the NT roads are mentioned in terms of ὁδός only in two passages. Jesus Himself in the parable of the Good Samaritan refers to the road from Jerusalem to Jericho. Here the phrase ἐν τῇ ὁδῷ ἐκείνῃ (Lk. 10:31) is not meant to draw the hearer's attention to the dangerous nature of the road (i.e., "on this very dangerous road"). It refers back to 10:30, emphasising that the priest and Levite were proceeding in the same direction down it, i.e., from Jerusalem to Jericho and not *vice versa*. [68] The second ref. to a great trade-route is in Ac. 8:26 : ἐπὶ τὴν ὁδὸν τὴν καταβαίνουσαν ἀπὸ Ἰερουσαλὴμ εἰς Γάζαν. This road (not Gaza) is more closely described in the clause which follows (αὕτη ἐστὶν ἔρημος) with ref. to the incident recounted, [69] and κατὰ μεσημβρίαν gives the location in relation to Samaria. [70]

Many incidents in the Synoptic tradition take place during the larger and smaller journeys undertaken by Jesus. In these circumstances it is surprising that the general reference ἐν τῇ ὁδῷ, which tells us that the event took place *en route*, is not more common, and that when it is used in this way it has not been preserved by the tradition as a whole. Thus in the story of Peter's confession at Caesarea it is only Mk. (8:27b) who emphasises that Jesus questioned the disciples ἐν τῇ ὁδῷ. This note is orientated to 8:27a, and it is designed to tell us that what follows does not happen in one of the previously mentioned κῶμαι Καισαρείας, i.e., in the proximity of strangers or the bustle of village life, but in the solitude of the journey and hence within the small familiar circle. Mt. does not describe the situation otherwise in the par. 16:13, but by speaking more generally of the μέρη Καισαρείας he makes it unnecessary to add ἐν τῇ ὁδῷ. Lk. 9:18 seems to be set in quite a different locality. [71]

In the introduction to the third intimation of the passion ἐν τῇ ὁδῷ occurs in Mk. 10:32 and again, at a different point, in Mt. 20:17 (Lk. 18:31 is much shorter), but in these cases it is not meant, or not meant only, that Jesus spoke what follows during the journey. It implies that the road to Jerusalem will take Jesus to the place where the passion, which He again intimates in this situation ἐν τῇ ὁδῷ,

---

[67] Jesus and His disciples must have passed many of the Roman milestones which still remain. The roads which Paul used in his missionary journeys — on their relation to the great trade-routes of antiquity cf. A. Deissmann, *Pls.*[2] (1921), 190 and 261 f. — are also of no great importance in Ac. (as compared with the later Act. Pl. et Thecl., 3, 23). If we had for the journeys of the apostle by land (the phrase in 2 C. 11:26 refers to these, cf. v. 25) the same diaries as for the sea journeys in Ac. 20:13 ff., 27 f. we should know a great deal more about the roads which he used and his experiences *en route*.

[68] Cf. W. Michaelis, *Das hochzeitliche Kleid, Eine Einführung in d. Gleichnisse Jesu über d. rechte Jüngerschaft* (1939), 193, 196.

[69] Cf. M. Dibelius, "Stilkritisches zur Apostelgeschichte," *Eucharisterion,* II (1923), 40, n. 2.

[70] O. Bauernfeind, *Die Apostelgeschichte* (1939), ad loc. thinks there is no intention to fix the exact location, so that we do not even know which of the two possible roads is meant (cf. Zn. Ag., ad loc.). The context suggests, however, that the road nearer to Samaria is meant, i.e., the northern route (cf. also the mention of Ashdod, which is north of Gaza, in 8:40). One cannot link this directly with Mt. 10:5 (cf. ZNW, 39 [1940], 126). ὁδός means "road" in 8:36, "journey" in 8:39.

[71] Cf. K. L. Schmidt, *Der Rahmen d. Geschichte Jesu* (1919), 216. It is surely a mistake to say that "ἐν τῇ ὁδῷ is a typical Marcan indication of locality which serves to set the portion of the tradition in its proper place (cf. 10:17, 32; 9:33 ff.)," Bultmann Trad., 276. For one thing, there is no reason to separate 8:27b from 8:27a, which introduces it into the story (Bultmann for not very good reasons links 8:27a with the preceding pericope, cf. op. cit., 68). Then ἐν τῇ ὁδῷ is too infrequent to be typical. It is certainly not used to indicate locality in the passages adduced by Bultmann.

is to take place. (In the two preceding intimations the journey to Jerusalem is mentioned only in the secondary Mt. 16:21.) Here ἐν τῇ ὁδῷ has a stronger material relation to what follows than in the previous instance. It is more than a marginal topographical note.

Nor is it a mere indication of locality in Mk. 9:33 f., which shifts the account of the dispute about rank to Capernaum. "The ἐν τῇ ὁδῷ is firmly connected with the preceding journey, to which it refers back." [72] The ἐν τῇ ὁδῷ is thus a graphic touch such as is particularly characteristic of Mk. The reader may well imagine that on a journey, when Jesus might be alone at certain times, the disciples would find natural opportunities for disputing πρὸς ἀλλήλους in the belief that they were alone. On the other hand, πορευομένων αὐτῶν ἐν τῇ ὁδῷ in Lk. 9:57 is a topographical note in the narrower sense. It is here designed to integrate into the Lucan journey an event which in Mt. 8:19 is set in Capernaum. [73] In contrast, the ἐκπορευομένου αὐτοῦ εἰς ὁδόν which introduces the story of the rich young ruler in Mk. 10:17 is not to be regarded as an intimation of place ; [74] like προσδραμών (which Mt. and Lk. consequently did not include), it serves to characterise the rather excited zeal of the young man, who "hastily seeks to use the last few minutes before Jesus sets off on a journey to get Jesus' decision on the crucial issue of salvation." [75] In the story of the healing of the blind in Jericho Mt. 20:34 and Lk. 18:43 leave out the ἐν τῇ ὁδῷ which Mk. 10:52 added after the ἠκολούθει αὐτῷ. This is probably because they construed ἀκολουθεῖν differently, though Mk., too, is thinking of discipleship and not just of following in a spatial sense. [76] In this case ἐν τῇ ὁδῷ is not just the customary scenic note, but carries an emphasis on the fact that Jesus is going to Jerusalem. [77] The reader who knows from the prophecy of the passion what consequences this journey will have for Jesus has to consider what the decision to follow Him must have meant at this particular juncture for the beggar who had received his sight. Even as He goes to His passion Jesus still finds disciples.

Apart from the passages mentioned, ἐν τῇ ὁδῷ also occurs in the sense *"en route"* in Mt. 5:25 par. Lk. 12:58, for, although the saying demands eschatological exposition, to find in ἐν τῇ ὁδῷ an image for our life on earth [78] is an allegorical exaggeration of this aspect. Ref. should also be made to Mt. 15:32 par. Mk. 8:3 ("on the way," before reaching their dwelling, though it could also imply "collapsing on the road out of exhaustion, lying down by the edge of the road"). Again, the risen Lord appears *"en route"* to the two who went to Emmaus in Lk. 24:32, 35 (the only account which depicts the exalted Christ as a traveller). [79] He appears similarly to Saul in Ac. 9:17, 27. At 9:17 the addition ᾗ ἤρχου suggests that the whole phrase is an indication of time rather than locality, i.e., on the journey just completed, recently. In 9:27, however, the sense

[72] Schmidt, *op. cit.*, 230.
[73] *Ibid.*, 248.
[74] If it were, it would be rather forlorn. Schmidt, *op. cit.*, 241, rightly emphasises how difficult is the task of exegetes who try to construe it thus. ὁδός means here "way," "journey," not "road" or "street." It cannot be linked with the εἰς τὴν οἰκίαν of 10:10.
[75] Hck. Mk., *ad loc.*; cf. also Schl. Mk., *ad loc.*
[76] In Mt. and Lk., too, accompanying is included, since Jesus is on a journey. To the Gk. ear the two meanings would both be suggested by the term.
[77] Kl. Mk., *ad loc.* correctly interprets ἐν τῇ ὁδῷ ("i.e., to Jerusalem") but fails to see any religious significance in the expression.
[78] So J. Schniewind Mt. (*NT Deutsch*, 2), *ad loc.* Cf. Schl. Mt., *ad loc.* and → n. 26.
[79] The vl. at Ac. 10:41: καὶ συνανεστράφημεν, is not to be linked with Lk. 24:13 ff. The underlying thought is that of the unbroken forty days of fellowship between the risen Lord and the disciples.

is "on the way," before the real objective was reached, in the middle of a journey undertaken for very different ends, hence quite unpreparedly. κατὰ τὴν ὁδόν is used with the same intent (→ n. 26, and 65) in the par. account in Ac. 26:13. This "expression depicts the surprising element in the appearance which excluded all self-deception." [80] κατὰ τὴν ὁδόν bears the same sense of "on the way" in Ac. 25:3 and Lk. 10:4 as well. [81]

ὁδός occurs in several parables of Jesus without having any special (allegorical) significance. In the parable of the sower (Mt. 13:4 par. Mk. 4:4; Lk. 8:5) there is reference to the seed which ἔπεσεν παρὰ τὴν ὁδόν. This phrase is briefly repeated in the interpretation in Mt. 13:19 par. Mk. 4:15; Lk. 8:12, where it is related to a particular group of listeners, but the ὁδός itself has no more significance than the Lucan addition in 8:5: καὶ κατεπατήθη, which does not add to the meaning, or the reference to the birds, which are not to be taken as a direct figure of speech for Satan. [82] The general picture suggests a path along the edge of the field, or possibly through the middle of it, on which one can go διὰ τῶν σπορίμων (Mt. 12:1 par.) when the grain is ripe. παρὰ τὴν ὁδόν does not mean, as in Mt. 20:30 par. Mk. 10:46; Lk. 18:35, [83] "by the side of the path," "near it," "by it," but "on it," "along it."

In the parable of the great supper the servant is first bidden in Lk. 14:21 to go εἰς τὰς πλατείας καὶ ῥύμας τῆς πόλεως, and then he receives from his master the command in 14:23: ἔξελθε εἰς τὰς ὁδοὺς καὶ φραγμοὺς κτλ. It is evident that whereas the first order refers to the streets and lanes of the city [84] the second has in view, not streets in outlying sections of the city, but highways, or at least main roads running out into the country from the city which is the scene of the parable. This is supported by the fact that the φραγμοί are the enclosures around vineyards (cf. Mt. 21:33 par. Mk. 12:1) or gardens, which would not be located in the city but on its outskirts. Since the use of ὁδοί (and φραγμοί) shows that different places are in view in Lk. 14:23 and 14:21, it follows that hearers and readers of the parable are to think of two different types of new guests, on the one hand the poor and sick among those who live in the same city as the host (14:21), and on the other strangers from the streets (14:23) (not servants or day-labourers working in the enclosed gardens, for the fences are mentioned, not because the host's messenger is to call over them, but because those moving along the roads

---

[80] B. Weiss, Das NT, III² (1902), ad loc. ("on the way as the road was followed unsuspectingly"). Rightly Wdt. Ag., 166, n. 1 rejects the view of, e.g., J. Jüngst, Die Quellen d. Apostelgeschichte (1895), 89 f., who sees behind ἐν τῇ ὁδῷ in Ac. 9:17, 27, which he sharply differentiates from κατὰ τὴν ὁδόν (26:13) and compares with the ἐν τῇ ὁδῷ of Lk. 24:35, a tradition that Paul's conversion involved, not an appearance of light, but an appearance of the risen Lord such as is recounted in Lk. 24.

[81] In Ac. 8:36, however, κατὰ τὴν ὁδόν has a different sense (→ n. 70), though this does not mean that 26:13 is referring to the road as the place where the phenomenon is to be localised.

[82] Cf. W. Michaelis, Es ging ein Sämann aus, zu säen. Eine Einführung in die Gleichnisse Jesu über das Reich Gottes u. d. Kirche (1938), 44 ff.

[83] The sense "on the road," which Pr.-Bauer, s.v., III, 1. d regards as possible in these verses, is ruled out not only by Mk. 10:49 but also by the fact that Mt. 20:32 and Lk. 18:40 also seem to presuppose some distance between Jesus and the blind man. The position is obviously that the crowd which accompanied Jesus could come between the two. Hence the beggar was on the edge of the road, possibly pitched by a house wall or a fence.

[84] Even without the τῆς πόλεως πλατεῖα (sc. ὁδός) would here denote city streets, as also in Rev. 11:8; 21:21 (cf. αὐτῆς, 22:2; Lk. 10:10); cf. Mt. 6:5 etc., → 48; 64. ῥύμη (cf. in the NT Mt. 6:2; Ac. 9:11; 12:10) is usually the narrow street or lane as distinct from πλατεῖα, the broad road. On ἄμφοδον in Ac. 19:28 vl. cf. Pr.-Bauer³, s.v.

pass by these fences and sometimes rest at them). To put it plainly, Gentiles are invited as well as publicans and sinners. In the Matthean version only one group of new guests is mentioned, but in 22:9 the charge is : πορεύεσθε οὖν ἐπὶ τὰς διεξόδους τῶν ὁδῶν (cf. 22:10 : εἰς τὰς ὁδούς). It thus confirms our conclusion (→ 108).[85]

In the parable of the friend and his request in Lk. 11, the visitor who arrives unexpectedly at midnight is said to have come ἐξ ὁδοῦ (v. 6), i.e., "in his journey," "during the course of a journey which did not have this visit as its goal" (→ 65).

The other passages in which ὁδός is used lit. in the NT may be mentioned briefly. The sense of "road" or "way" occurs at Mt. 10:5 : εἰς ὁδὸν ἐθνῶν μὴ ἀπέλθητε. The ref. is to a road leading to the Gentiles or to Gentile territory. The disciples would have to take this if they regarded the winning of the Gentiles as their present task.[86] Cf. also Mt. 21:8 par.: δι' ἄλλης ὁδοῦ, Mt. 2:12 (cf. ἑτέρᾳ ὁδῷ, Jm. 2:25; the original in Jos. 2:16 is stated differently); Mt. 8:28; 21:19;[87] Rev. 16:12. In respect of the ὁδὸν θαλάσσης of Mt. 4:15 (quoting Is. 8:23) it is hard to say how this expression is to be understood. The LXX, which glosses the Heb. and in part must have followed a different reading, also has ὁδὸν θαλάσσης, but the ὁδόν is obviously used prepositionally for "towards the sea," → n. 23. Mt., however, does not follow the LXX here (or in 4:16), and yet he does not keep strictly to the Heb. either (in any case דֶּרֶךְ הַיָּם means the road to the sea).[88] ὁδός is used in the sense of "journey" in Mt. 10:10 par., and in 1 Th. 3:11, though "way" seems to be suggested, "journey" is also possible (the use of κατευθύνω with ὁδός in the LXX by no means restricts the sense to "way," for we find "walk" in ψ 118:5 and "purpose" in Jdt. 12:8). Ὁδὸν ποιεῖν in Mk. 2:23 does not mean "to make a way" but "to traverse, to travel, a way."[89] In Lk. 2:44 ἡμέρας ὁδός means "a day's journey" (→ 43; 49; 65). In Ac. 1:12 the Mt. of Olives is said to be a Sabbath journey (σαββάτου ὁδός) from Jerusalem.[90]

2. The Metaphorical Use.

The metaphorical and figurative use of ὁδός is also important in the NT. Whereas the literal sense is for the most part limited to the Synoptists, the metaphorical and figurative is to be found in all the writings. It is not always easy to estimate how far the idea of a road is still present. This is clear in the quotation

---

[85] Cf. Michaelis (→ n. 68), 31 f., 54, 56.

[86] Kl. Mt., ad loc.; Str.-B., I, 538. In what follows we read : καὶ εἰς πόλιν Σαμαριτῶν μὴ εἰσέλθητε. Schl. Mt., ad loc. refers this to the fact that in passing from Galilee to Jerusalem the disciples could not avoid going through Samaritan territory. On the other hand, the command surely does not imply going through Samaria for other reasons, but going to the Samaritans themselves. In any case, it was quite possible to reach Jerusalem without touching Samaria. The change from ὁδός to πόλις is thus to be explained as stylistic variation.

[87] On ἐπὶ τῆς ὁδοῦ in the sense of "on the way" cf. Schl. Mt., ad loc.

[88] Cr.-Kö., s.v. 1. b; Schl. Mt., ad loc.; Bl.-Debr. § 161, 1.

[89] Schl. Mk., ad loc.; Wbg. Mk., 91 f.; Wellh. Mk., 20 ("en passant"). For the unusual ὁδὸν ποιεῖν — though cf. Ju. 17:8 : τοῦ ποιῆσαι (τὴν) ὁδὸν αὐτοῦ for לַעֲשׂוֹת דַּרְכּוֹ — there is found as a vl. ὁδοποιεῖν, which does not occur elsewhere in the NT and which means "to make a way," as in LXX ψ 79:9; Is. 62:10. ὁδεύω is rare in the NT (Lk. 10:33, also LXX), as are also ὁδοιπορέω (Ac. 10:9), ὁδοιπορία (Jn. 4:6; 2 C. 11:26, also LXX, cf. ὁδοιπόρος), and πορεία (Lk. 13:22; Jm. 1:11; → 65).

[90] Cf. Str.-B., II, 590 ff. Bauernfeind, op. cit., rightly criticises the view that this note justifies us in assuming that the ascension took place on the Sabbath (so Pr. Ag., ad loc.; cf. Zn. Ag., 41, n. 78). He himself thinks that the "narrative likes sometimes to use sacred measures for the sacred story." But it could be that the author had found it in his materials (cf. Lk. 1:3), and that just because it was strange to him he could not keep it from his readers.

from Is. 40:3 (→ 49), which occurs in the same wording in Mk. 1:3 and Lk. 3:4. The whole verse is here reproduced, so that the parallelism of ὁδός and τρίβοι [91] is preserved. [92] The verse is given as in the LXX [93] except that the final τοῦ θεοῦ ἡμῶν is changed into αὐτοῦ. This suggests that the preceding κυρίου is to be referred to Jesus rather than to God (as in Is.). [94] John the Baptist had the task of a fore-runner preparing the way for Jesus. He was to proclaim the coming of Jesus, and to prepare men for it by calling on them to repent and summoning them to be baptised. [95] This means that in the quotation from Mal. 3:1 [96] which precedes Is. 40:3 in Mk. 1:2 the τὴν ὁδόν σου is the way of Jesus, at least in the mind of the one who put the quotation here. [97] In the same wording, but with ἔμπροσθέν σου at the end, the same quotation is used in Mt. 11:10 par. Lk. 7:27 (→ I, 83). Since Jesus uses the quotation, the reader who relates the (threefold) σου to Jesus can see that this verse of Scripture helps Jesus clarify the relation of the Baptist to Him. [98] The picture of the way is not so clearly preserved here as in Mt. 3:3 and par. In the version in Mk. 1:2 at least ὁδός might already have the sense of "plan," "enterprise," "work."

a. The Metaphor of the Two Ways in Mt. 7:13 f.

Jesus uses the metaphor of the two ways in a saying which is found in the Sermon on the Mount at Mt. 7:13 f. There is a material parallel in Lk. 13:24, though it is debatable whether this is another version of the same saying as in Mt. 7:13 f. For there are considerable differences between the two. The choice of

---

[91] τρίβος, which is often a synon. of ὁδός in the LXX, but which Philo sharply differentiates from it (→ 63), occurs in the NT only at Mt. 3:3 and par.

[92] Is. 40:3 is also quoted in Jn. 1:23 on the lips of the Baptist, but this is a shorter form. Either the last half is omitted and the ἑτοιμάσατε changed into εὐθύνατε (Bultmann J., 62, n. 6), or the two halves are merged and εὐθύνατε betrays the influence of εὐθείας ποιεῖτε.

[93] Lk. appends Is. 40:4 f. to 3:5 f., but here changes the LXX. The εἰς ὁδοὺς λείας of 3:5 is peculiar to him (LXX εἰς πεδία).

[94] The reader of Lk. is prepared for this interpretation by 1:76, for here in the intimation concerning John the Baptist : προπορεύσῃ γὰρ ἐνώπιον κυρίου ἑτοιμάσαι ὁδοὺς αὐτοῦ, the κυρίου or αὐτοῦ is referred directly to Jesus, even though the statement, like 1:15 ff., might have originated amongst followers of John who had God in mind (→ II, 936 f. and n. 71).

[95] The Synoptists do not say that John the Baptist applied Is. 40:3 to himself, and Jn. 1:23 is hardly adequate proof in view of the distinctive nature of the Johannine presentation. It is also doubtful whether the Baptist, who can hardly have read the OT in the LXX version, would even take the passage Messianically or find in it the figure of the "one crying in the wilderness" (from the instances in Str.-B., I, 97 f. on Mt. 3:3 it by no means follows that in the time of the Baptist Is. 40:3 had to be taken exclusively in this sense). It is thus useless to ask what the Baptist himself really meant by the way of the Lord. What matters is how the verse was understood in the Synoptic tradition. → I, 625; II, 659, n. 9; 706.

[96] In view of the importance of Mal. 3:1 in Elijah expectation (→ II, 931; 936, n. 65), one has to think esp. of this passage. The relation with Ex. 23:20 LXX is intrinsically so strong that the question has to be put which exerted the greater influence (ὃς κατασκευάσει τὴν ὁδόν σου occurs in this form in neither). It is incorrect to say that the two merge into one another in Rabb. tradition (E. Lohmeyer Mk. [1937], ad loc.). In Ex. r., 32 (93d) they are quoted after one another and independently (Str.-B., I, 597 on Mt. 11:10).

[97] The quotation is obviously introduced from Mt. 11:10 and par., cf. Kl. Mk. and Hck. Mk., ad loc., as against Lohmeyer, 11, n. 2, who thinks the quotation is original in Mk. 1:2, and who refers the σου to the people (on the basis of Ex. 23:20).

[98] Jesus speaks here and in Mt. 11:10 and par. In itself the quotation also expresses the conviction of the community (cf. Hck. Lk., ad loc.).

θύρα in Lk. 13:24 (rather than the πύλη of Mt.; → III, 178) may be controlled by 13:25 (though in what follows the reference is to a closed door rather than a narrow door). But the principal difference is that Lk. speaks only of the στενὴ θύρα and not also of the πλατεῖα θύρα, and that the parallel statements about the two ways are not found at all in his version. [99] It is quite possible, however, that both versions go back to Jesus and represent independent developments (the introduction in Lk. 13:23 could come from the Evangelist). If so, there is no point in asking whether Mt. 7:13 f. or Lk. 13:24 is the original, and in the present context we may limit our discussion to Mt. 7:13 f., which alone speaks of the two ways.

The saying begins : εἰσέλθατε διὰ τῆς στενῆς πύλης. Only in what follows do we then read of the two πύλαι and two ὁδοί. But this is no reason for doubting the original connection between the introduction and what follows, and it is also no reason for following the few textual witnesses which do not have ἡ πύλη in 7:13 or 7:14 or both. [100] We must begin by assuming that πύλη and ὁδός are found together in both verses. If πύλη comes first on both occasions, this should not lead us to the conclusion that these are gates through which one must first pass in order to reach the respective ways (e.g., city gates leading on to the streets of the city). [101] This is contradicted by the fact that entry through the narrow gate is presented in the introduction in such a form as apparently to exclude going through the gate on to a street which will then later bring to the desired goal. On the contrary, he who passes through the narrow gate has already entered and is at the goal. Hence we must either assume that the two gates are at the end of the two ways, which is against the order πύλη/ὁδός, or we are to see in πύλη and ὁδός synonymous metaphors which are not to be interrelated but which stand side by side, supplementing and strengthening one another. The latter possibility is to be preferred, for only thus can one explain without difficulty the fact that the εἰσέρχεσθαι of 7:13 can be linked both with πύλη and with ὁδός. δι᾽ αὐτῆς plainly refers to ἡ ὁδός unless one is to say that, like the αὐτήν of 7:14, it refers back to both ἡ ὁδός and ἡ πύλη. In effect, then, we have a double metaphor. The πύλη neither follows the ὁδός nor *vice versa*. This also means that in the saying there is nothing peculiar in the fact that the narrow road is not linked with the broad gate, nor the broad road with the narrow gate. The narrow gate and way, and the broad gate and way, go together, since way and gate are interchangeable in the saying.

---

[99] Kl. Mt., *ad loc.* thinks that Lk. "has essentially preserved the original form as compared with the symmetrical parallelism of Mt.," who expanded the original. H. Huber, *Die Bergpredigt* (1932), 157, believes that the version in Mt. is "definitely more original, for the double metaphor is in keeping with Jesus' manner of teachiing."

[100] Acc. to Kl. Mt., *ad loc.* the image of the πύλη is first introduced in 7:14. That is, ἡ πύλη in v. 13 is a later addition, in v. 14 original. The argument is that in v. 14 ἡ πύλη is missing in only a few witnesses. In fact, however, it is missing in only a few witnesses (though these include ℵ*⁾ at v. 13 as well. If the number is even fewer than in v. 14, this is obviously because it is harder to justify the elimination of ἡ πύλη after the στενή of v. 14 than the πλατεῖα of v. 13. The introduction supports the expression στενὴ πύλη.

[101] So Kl. Mt., *ad loc.* Acc. to Zn. Mt., *ad loc.* πύλη and ὁδός together are meant to convey the idea of the "gateway." Acc. to Bornhäuser, 209 there is a "similar, if not wholly identical complex" "in the Rabbis too." The house of instruction is the house of the gate, which in ψ 117:19 f. symbolises the Law. But from the house of instruction also goes forth the Halacha, i.e., the way. "Hence the Rabbis can say : Go through the broad gate (the gate of righteousness = the Torah) and walk on the broad path which we show you (keep the hălāchā), and you will live. In contrast, Jesus says : ..." → n. 112.

Nevertheless, it is right and important to point out that the saying is in no sense trying to convey the thought that initial effort will bring later alleviation, and *vice versa*. We should have to construe it thus if the narrow way were linked with the broad gate, and the broad way with the narrow gate. The fact that this is not so distinguishes the saying in Mt. 7:13 f. from all the versions of the metaphor of the two ways which have this thought more or less explicitly as a basis. [102] For the rest, one can only say that the characterisation of the two ways as εὐρύχωρος [103] or τεθλιμμένη [104] does not force us to assume any direct dependence on one of the older forms of the metaphor. Nowhere is there exact agreement with Mt. 7:13 f., [105] quite apart from the fact that material parallels for the reference to ἀπώλεια or ζωή are found at best only in the OT and later Jewish writings. Naturally, Jesus' use of the figure of the two ways is not to be regarded as wholly original, for the metaphor as such was widespread. Jesus, however, took over only the metaphor as such, and He probably did so from the Jewish world around Him. [106]

This conclusion is not affected by research into the origin of the linking of πύλη and ὁδός, for, if these are interchangeable, all other parallels are ruled out. In Ceb. Tab., 11 ff. (→ n. 9) we certainly find both θύρα and ὁδός in the image of the two ways, but they are plainly differentiated : cf. οὐκοῦν καὶ θύραν τινὰ μικρὰν καὶ ὁδόν τινα πρὸ τῆς θύρας, ἥτις οὐ παροχλεῖται, ἀλλ' ὀλίγοι πάνυ πορεύονται ὥσπερ δι' ἀνοδίας τινὸς καὶ τραχείας καὶ πετρώδους εἶναι δοκούσης, 15 (to the little, not narrow, gate there leads, not a narrow way, but one which is difficult and little used). The parable in 4 Esr. 7:6 f. (III, 3, 6 f., Violet, → 57) speaks of a narrow path leading to a city, and elsewhere it refers to a narrow entrance, but this is the same as the path, not the city gate, so that there is no combination of gate and way. [107] PRE1, 15 is late (9th cent. A.D.), and in any case it is no true par., for here, though we find gates in the parable of the two ways, these gates are four in number, they are located

---

[102] Cf. passages like Hes. Op., 287 ff. (→ n. 2), also the corresponding trains of thought in Philo (→ 60; 64). This idea was alien to the OT. One cannot object that the beginning and end are contrasted in Mt. 7:13 f., for the eschatological ζωή which God gives to those who take the narrow way is not compared with the repose in virtue which beckons those who strive hard. Cf. also Stob. Ecl., 274, 4 f. and on this G. Heinrici, *Die Hermes-Mystik u. das NT* (1918), 115.

[103] Only here in the NT; not linked with ὁδός in the LXX or, as it appears, Joseph. (cf. Pass. and Liddell-Scott, *s.v.*). It is in any case unusual to speak of a broad way, though the contrast with τεθλιμμένη shows that εὐρύχωρος does not mean "long" (covering a wide stretch of territory). I have been unable to find any other example of the category broad/narrow among the instances of the parable of the two ways (on 4 Esr. 7:12 f. [III, 3, 12 f., Violet] cf. → 57). The ἀνάβασις στενὴ πάνυ of Ceb. Tab., 15 is only a partial par. The refs. of Bornhäuser, 207 f. to ψ 118:45, 96 (if the equivalent ὁδός is put for ἐντολή in v. 96, the statement runs : Thy way is very broad) hardly stand up to closer examination.

[104] → III, 139; Bornhäuser, 205 f.; Kl. Mt., ad loc.

[105] Cf. the instances discussed in A. and B. E. Wechssler, *Hellas im Evangelium* (1936), 246, states : "In Hesiod, and in the well-known story of Prodicus about the choice of a way of life by Heracles, we read of the narrow way to virtue and the broad way to ruin (cf. Mt. 7:13)." But the passages quoted are inaccurately reproduced, and the differences are blurred over.

[106] Cf. also Clemen, 227 (with bibl.). The antithesis ἀπώλεια/ζωή (→ I, 396 f.) is not found in the OT and later Jewish pars. This is related to their predominant lack of eschatological orientation.

[107] As against Kl. Mt., ad loc., who also wrongly adduces the passage as an instance of the metaphor of the two ways. This occurs only in 7:12 f. (III, 3, 12 f., Violet), and on it → 57. Other combinations of way and gate which have no connection with the metaphor cannot be regarded as pars., e.g., Parmen. Fr., 1 (I, 228, 17 ff., Diels⁵).

on the way of death, and they form stations where guardian angels deal with those traversing this way. [108]

It is unlikely that the saying in Mt. 7:13 f. is to be related to 7:12, or that the narrow gate or way refers to the law of love in the Golden Rule. [109] The par. in Lk. 13:24, whether this is another version of the same saying or an independent development (→ 71), shows in any case that Mt. 7:13 f. is a self-enclosed saying. Another argument against an original connection between Mt. 7:13 f. and 7:12 is the fact that Mt. 7:12 is given another context in Lk. (6:31). Finally, though the significance of the Golden Rule is not to be underrated, it is surely overestimated if ζωή and ἀπώλεια depend on keeping or not keeping it. The force of the either-or of Mt. 7:13 f. is too great for a mere reference to 7:12. It must be taken much more radically and generally than that. The point that in the par. Lk. 13:24 the narrow door has to do with entry into the kingdom of God [110] is not much help, for, while this is true, Mt. 7:13 f. says the same when it speaks of ζωή, since ζωή and βασιλεία θεοῦ are interchangeable. The main problem remains, namely, why this entrance into the kingdom is compared to a narrow door or way, and what is meant by walking on the two ways.

It is surely correct that the broad way is not just the way of frivolity and vice, nor is the narrow way simply that of a pious and virtuous life in the current sense. [111] Along these lines the saying could be construed easily enough as a summons to μετάνοια, and on this view it would be profoundly serious. If, however, one presupposes that Jesus in His preaching was constantly opposing the fundamentally false orientation of the piety represented by His contemporaries, and that the moral demands which He Himself laid on His disciples went far beyond the ordinary rules, it would seem that one can refer the saying to virtue and vice only on a level much below that on which the preaching of Jesus, including His preaching of μετάνοια, moves. Certainly it is inadvisable to expound the saying exclusively in terms of Jesus' opposition to the Pharisaic understanding of the Law, as though the πολλοί were the Pharisees and their supporters. [112] If Jesus could be just as severe as He would have to be to pass the judgment of Mt. 7:13 on the Pharisaic position, the structure of the saying shows that what is to the fore is not the inadequacy of the attitude which one is to avoid, but the indispensability of the attitude which is required. To be sure, the first reference is to the broad gate and the broad way, and only then to the narrow gate and narrow way. But before either reference comes the single, positive demand to enter in at the strait gate (the introduction is not: Do not enter in at the broad gate, nor is this warning added as a second member). This implies that the aim of Jesus in this saying is not primarily polemical. It is the positive one of wooing

---

[108] Str.-B., I, 463.

[109] So Bornhäuser, 205 ff., whose discussion merits attention even if it is not wholly convincing.

[110] So Kl. Mt., ad loc.

[111] R. Luther, NT.liches Wörterbuch[11] (1937), 203. ὁδός here does not mean "walk," but is a figure of speech (like πύλη).

[112] Bornhäuser, 207 ff. tries to produce a whole series of connections with the world of thought and OT exposition of the Pharisees. But he does not carry full conviction, cf. also → n. 101, 103, 118. O. Schmitz, "Thurneysens christologische Deutung d. Bergpredigt," Jahrb. d. Theologischen Schule Bethel (1938), 20, 31, rightly objects against relating the broad way to self-righteousness on the basis of works of the Law ("it is obviously not Christ's intention to speak the language of Romans in the Sermon on the Mount").

and winning. The form of the introduction shows us that the gate through which we are to enter is narrow quite irrespective of the existence of a wide gate. (The par. in Lk. 13:24 refers only to the strait gate, and then mentions as the two possibilities either entering in by this gate or not.)

Thus Mt. 7:13 f. is a summons to discipleship. In the foreground is the unconditional severity of the requirements which Jesus puts to His disciples. Because it is so hard to be a disciple of Jesus, the gate is strait and the way narrow. But there is no other way to life than the one on which Jesus leads His disciples (Mt. 7:24, 26; 11:27). Since the way is narrow, there are few who enter on it. This is not because there is no room on it for passers-by. A crowd can throng on to a narrow path, and a broad street can be empty of people. But men like a broad street which brings them securely and comfortably to their destination, rather than a narrow path to which it is difficult to keep. The broad and narrow ways are symbolical of the easy on the one side, the hard on the other. It is easy not to be a disciple of Jesus, but it leads to destruction. It is hard to be a disciple of Jesus, but it alone leads to life. [113] Whether the clauses καὶ πολλοὶ κτλ. or καὶ ὀλίγοι κτλ. are to be construed as dependent or autonomous is difficult to decide. Only in the former case can one infer from the admonition that the disciples are not to be offended by the few who travel with them on the same road, but "are rather to see here a proof that they are on the right road to life." [114] In the latter case, the clauses are more of an estimate: How many (or few) are there (or will there be) who reach the one destination or the other, cf. Mk. 10:24. The ὀλίγοι are the disciples of Jesus. The πολλοί are not particularly the scribes and Pharisees, nor the Jewish people, but more generally all those who refuse to become disciples of Jesus. [115]

As ὁδός does not have here the sense of "walk" (→ n. 111), so the life, future, or destiny of the disciples is not depicted under the image of the way. Certainly, ὁδός can have this signification (→ 50; 60). But the narrow way is not so much a figure of the difficult way of life which the disciples must accept. It rather symbolises the severity of the demands which are laid on the disciples. Like πύλη, ὁδός denotes entry. Hence the destination is mentioned along with the way. This is ζωή on the one side, ἀπώλεια on the other. [116] We thus find in 7:13, not οἱ πορευόμενοι αὐτήν, but οἱ εἰσερχόμενοι δι' αὐτῆς. An expression is used which can apply both to ὁδός (on δία cf. Mt. 2:12; 8:28) and to πύλη. Special emphasis

---

[113] One should consider that discipleship and self-denial are demanded, and temptation, persecution and the cross are to be expected, cf. J. Schniewind Mt. (NT Deutsch, 2), ad loc. In this light one can see again how inadequate it is simply to refer to the Golden Rule of Mt. 7:12 (→ 73).

[114] Zn. Mt.⁴, 313. Cf. Huber, op. cit., 154 f.: "Herewith the demand for a certain separation between disciples and non-disciples is plainly stated ... We have here the profound thought of the religious right of the minority which stands with Jesus. The disciples are here contrasted with the people, the small flock with the multitude."

[115] πολλοί/ὀλίγοι may be linked with Mt. 20:16 inasmuch as there, too, the ὀλίγοι are those who accept the demands of discipleship. On the other hand, one can hardly think of the πολλοί of Mk. 10:45 par.; 14:24 par. (Schniewind, loc. cit.), since in these passages πολλοί = πάντες and is not contrasted with ὀλίγοι. Ceb. Tab., 15 (→ 72) and Philo Leg. All., I, 98; Agric., 104 (→ 63) are only formal parallels.

[116] On ἡ ὁδός ἡ ἀπάγουσα, Dalman WJ, I, 130 f. emphasises that "in the OT there is never ref. to a way which 'leads' to a place," and he adduces some examples from postbibl. lit., e.g., S. Bar. 85:13 (VIII, 8, 3, Violet) and Gn. r., 9 (7ᵃ); cf. also Str.-B., I, 463. But

is laid on the entering, with orientation to the goal. οἱ εὑρίσκοντες αὐτήν can then be used in 7:14 in so far as the reference is plainly to a single happening, not a lasting state.

It may still be asked, however, whether εὑρίσκοντες keeps faithfully to the metaphor of the gate and the way. The possibility must be ruled out that it is a matter of finding the right way among many, or of trying to find the way in difficult terrain. Completely alien images and categories would be introduced on such interpretations. More likely is the consideration that a wide city gate is easily found, whereas a narrow concealed entry through a wall is not so easily discovered. In all cases the assumption is that finding comes only after strenuous search. Nevertheless, one can hardly appeal to Mt. 7:7 in support of this view. For if we are not to see a connection with 7:12 (→ 73), it is hardly legitimate to assume a link with 7:7. [117] Nor can we turn to the par. Lk. 13:24, for ζητεῖν there is obviously a fruitless searching, not the right search, and it cannot simply be equated with ἀγωνίζεσθαι (→ I, 137, 611); indeed, it might even be that ζητεῖν has the sense "to wish," "to desire." [118] Finding in Mt. 7:14 is not to be regarded as a reward for previous searching. Here, as so often (→ II, 769 f.), it is connected with the mystery of the divine action. Those who find the gate and way to life are those to whom access to life is given. [119] To this extent the ὀλίγοι are like the little flock to whom the Father has resolved to give the kingdom (Lk. 12:32), though this does not weaken the seriousness with which the introductory admonition : εἰσέλθατε διὰ τῆς στενῆς πύλης, summons man to exert all his own powers.

That the way to life is found in Christ, and that Christ makes possible entry upon it, is a thought which may be deduced from the claim underlying the whole of the Sermon on the Mount, though not directly expressed in Mt. 7:13 f. itself. The fact that the saying is incorporated into the schema of the two ways, so that the wrong way is set alongside the right, prevents the term "way" from taking on the pregnant sense which is later found on the one side in Hb. 9:8; 10:20 and on the other in Jn. 14:4 ff.

b. The Way into the Sanctuary in Hb. 9:8; 10:20.

Hb. 10:19 f. is linked with 9:8 (→ III, 276). Hence one may suspect that the uses of ὁδός in 9:8 and 10:20 are also related. In 9:8, though τὰ ἅγια obviously refers to the true sanctuary in heaven, one is at once inclined to interpret the phrase τὴν τῶν ἁγίων ὁδόν [120] in terms of the topography of the earthly sanctuary, the

---

one might mention Prv. 7:27: דַּרְכֵי שְׁאוֹל בֵּיתָהּ יֹרְדוֹת אֶל־חַדְרֵי־מָוֶת = LXX ὁδοὶ ᾅδου ὁ οἶκος αὐτῆς κατάγουσαι εἰς τὰ ταμιεῖα τοῦ θανάτου, cf. also 14:12 : τὰ δὲ τελευταῖα αὐτῆς (sc. τῆς ὁδοῦ) ἔρχεται εἰς πυθμένα ᾅδου. Philo commonly uses ἄγουσα with ὁδός (→ 60; 61), Joseph. φέρουσα (→ 64).

[117] Huber, op. cit., 155 appeals to 7:7, and he derives from 7:13 f. the thought that if a man perishes, i.e., does not succeed in finding, it is his own fault, since he has not engaged in the necessary search. "Failure to search means no finding. This imparts profound seriousness to the saying of Jesus, and lays on the disciple full personal responsibility for his own eternal future."

[118] In → II, 893 Lk. 13:24 is wrongly grouped. Bornhäuser, 207 f. associates εὑρίσκειν with דרשׁ in ψ 118:45, but this is too violent an attempt to introduce the vocabulary of Rabb. legal piety into Mt. 7:13 f.

[119] Schniewind, ad loc. Parallelism with 7:13 does not allow us to relate αὐτήν to εἰς τὴν ζωήν. Nor does the NT ever speak of finding (attaining to) life.

[120] Rgg. Hb. [2, 3], 249, n. 93; Bl.-Debr. § 166. The transl. "way of the saints" in Käsemann, 19 is surely mistaken.

temple of the old covenant. It is hard to think that ὁδός might be part of a vocabulary independent of the earthly conceptions presupposed in 9:1 ff. (as one has to consider in respect of 10:20, → 77). If ὁδός in 9:8 is to be linked with the εἰσίασιν of 10:19, then ὁδός is surely the noun which corresponds, not to the way leading into the sanctuary, but to the possibility of εἰσιέναι, i.e., access in the sense of being able or permitted to enter. ἡ τῶν ἁγίων ὁδός is then fully equivalent to the ἡ εἴσοδος τῶν ἁγίων of 10:19, since εἴσοδος here means, not entrance in the architectural sense of a gate, but entry or access (→ 106). The relative clause in 10:20: ἣν ἐνεκαίνισεν ἡμῖν ὁδὸν πρόσφατον καὶ ζῶσαν κτλ., is thus related to εἴσοδος rather than παρρησία, [121] and there thus arises the question of the interrelationship of εἴσοδος and ὁδός.

If εἴσοδος is not to be taken spatially, does it follow unconditionally that ὁδός is also not to be taken spatially (whether lit. or fig.) as a way, but has here the sense of access, like εἴσοδος? That it may have this sense can be seen from 9:8. The εἴσοδος of 10:19, however, corresponds already in this passage to the ὁδός of 9:8. The ἐνεκαίνισεν also gives rise to difficulties (→ III, 454), and the senses "to re-establish" and "to dedicate" (i.e., "use for the first time") would seem to favour a spatial understanding of ὁδός. The construction supports this, for ἐνεκαίνισεν takes the double acc., so that, while the ἣν certainly takes up again the preceding εἰς τὴν εἴσοδον, ὁδός is in independent juxtaposition with εἴσοδος as a predicative acc. [122] The διὰ τοῦ καταπετάσματος which follows (→ III, 630) also makes the spatial understanding probable, and the πρόσφατος and ζῶσα are neutral in this respect, since πρόσφατος fits both senses and ζῶσα is equally surprising in either. If, however, "with a slight shift of the metaphor," i.e., "inasmuch as the reference is now, not to access, namely, the right of entry, but to the topographical possibility of entry," [123] ὁδός means "way," this cannot be based simply on the occurrence of εἴσοδος in 10:19, and certainly not on the use of ὁδός in 9:8, but has to be for a special reason. One might put it thus. ὁδὸν πρόσφατον καὶ ζῶσαν might be left out without destroying the completeness of the relative clause. Or one might have εἴσοδον instead of ὁδόν in the relative clause. Since, however, the author wrote ὁδὸν πρόσφατον καὶ ζῶσαν, he must have had a particular reason for so doing, unless we are to assume that the slight alteration of the metaphor is of no material significance, but is due to a conscious or unconscious desire for stylistic variation.

If it is a material change, it is possible that the reason for referring to a way is provided from outside the context, so that ὁδός, even though understood spatially, is to be separated from the spatial conceptions of a heavenly sanctuary which dominate the context. In this case, it should be considered that διὰ τοῦ καταπετάσματος does not have to belong unconditionally to the relative clause, but may be appended to εἰς τὴν εἴσοδον τῶν ἁγίων and ἐν τῷ αἵματι Ἰησοῦ, just as 10:21 still depends on the ἔχοντες at the beginning of 10:19. [124] If so, the

---

[121] As against Rgg., 313. As the relation of ἣν to εἴσοδος "is not controlled by the topographical understanding of the term" (Rgg., n. 73), so the non-topographical understanding of εἴσοδος does not compel us to relate ἣν to παρρησίαν.

[122] Cf. Hb. 1:2: ἐν υἱῷ, ὃν ἔθηκεν κληρονόμον πάντων, and Bl.-Debr., § 157, 1. Wnd. Hb., ad loc. refers to 2 C. 10:13, but the constr. there is to be taken differently (cf. Bl.-Debr., § 294, 5), and this apparent par. is no argument for taking ὁδός as a repetition of εἴσοδος.

[123] H. Strathmann Hb. (NT Deutsch, 9), ad loc.

[124] On this construction the two phrases ἐν τῷ αἵματι Ἰησοῦ and διὰ τοῦ καταπετάσματος or διὰ τῆς σαρκὸς αὐτοῦ enter into a new relation to one another. The

way is not a way which leads through the veil into the ἐσώτερον τοῦ κατα-πετάσματος (6:19). It is not to be regarded as ὁδὸς τῶν ἁγίων. The gift of Jesus, namely, to have granted us the right of free access into the sanctuary, is depicted in the relative clause under the additional and quite independent metaphor of the opening of a new and living way. What makes it hard to assume the complete independence of the metaphor is that it is connected by the ἥν to εἴσοδος τῶν ἁγίων. [125] If its independence is to be affirmed all the same, the question arises how the author came to adopt this particular figure of speech.

Though we are not told where the way leads, the whole context shows that it is to be understood as the way to God, as a figure of the possibility of attaining to fellowship with Him. Nowhere in the OT do we read of a way in this special sense. The same is true of Philo to the degree that in the various expressions at his disposal (way to God, royal way etc. → 61) he never develops an absolute sense which allows him simply to speak of the way. The only NT parallel is Jn. 14:6 (→ C. 2. c). But there is the notable distinction, of course, that one cannot conclude from Hb. 10:20 that Jesus Himself is the way. The wording does not suggest any such equation, though it does not expressly rule it out. Nor does the addition διά ... τῆς σαρκὸς αὐτοῦ (if it belongs to the relative clause), nor the description of the way as a living way, make any difference, though the predicate ζῶσα shows that the way "is bound to the living person of Jesus Christ." [126] It is hardly conceivable that a description of Jesus as the way, as in Jn. 14:6, is a preliminary stage to the use of ὁδός in Hb. 10:20, for Hb. 10:20 would then be

question also arises whether it is correct to say that the curtain is understood as the σάρξ of Jesus, or whether conversely the σάρξ of Jesus is equated with the curtain, but the latter is mentioned first because this is suggested by the idea of a heavenly sanctuary evoked by (εἴσοδος) τῶν ἁγίων. If the meaning is not that Jesus as fore-runner has taken the way through the curtain (which is intrinsically possible in the context, cf. 6:19), it is also no longer possible or necessary to ask what διὰ τῆς σαρκὸς αὐτοῦ meant for Him on this way. Only of us is it true that we have access to the sanctuary διὰ τῆς σαρκὸς αὐτοῦ. That this could not be meant in the sense of the διὰ τῆς προσφορᾶς τοῦ σώματος Ἰ. Χρ. of 10:10 is evident, for διά, having the same sense in both τοῦ καταπετάσματος and τῆς σαρκὸς αὐτοῦ, has to be used locally, not instrumentally, in 10:20. This is not to say, however, that the curtain must be understood as an obstacle which He had to over-come. In the two passages in which the curtain is mentioned in Hb. (6:19; 9:3), it is not designed to bar access but to mark off the innermost part of the sanctuary, cf. Ex. 26:33. Consequently the ref. in 9:7 f. is not to the curtain (as a previous barrier). The thought is that there can be access only after the first tent is set aside (the curtain, which is the second curtain in 9:3, does not belong to the first tent at all). It thus seems advisable not to take the curtain as a hostile barrier but as the border beyond which the sanctuary begins (and to take the σάρξ of Jesus similarly : beyond His σάρξ = after His death). If this view is correct, it is hardly possible to agree with the exposition of Käsemann, 145 ff., who interprets 10:19 f. in Gnostic terms : The curtain corresponds to the partition between heaven and earth, which encloses the sphere of matter and prevents the ascent of souls to God, and the σάρξ of Jesus represents matter, so that when He freed Himself from the physical body in death He destroyed the curtain and breached the envelope of matter for His people. Rgg., 315 f. links διὰ τοῦ καταπετ. κτλ. only with ἐνεκαίνισεν (not ὁδόν), so that the statement applies only to Jesus and not to believers also.

[125] Though Ephr. seems to have read ἥ (Rgg., 313, n. 73), ἥν is virtually unanimous. It is highly debatable to conjecture instead of ἥν a ὅς (referring to Jesus), though this would remove some of the difficulties.

[126] O. Michel Hb. (1936), ad loc.; Rgg., 314; Strathmann, ad loc.; → II, 862 n. 251. The designation of the way as πρόσφατος (only here in the NT; the adv. in Ac. 18:2) does not contrast it with an old way. For this antithesis Hb. uses καινός or νέος, and in any case there was no previous access at all acc. to 9:8.

a weaker retrogression. What happened is surely the reverse, namely, that from the special use of ὁδός in Hb. 10:20 there developed later the designation of Jesus as the way (though cf. → n. 147). The special use in Hb. might well be a creation of the author, or a creation of primitive Christianity, this being the only instance, or a borrowing from the surrounding world, though this has not as yet been demonstrated. [127] In view of the uncertainty of the derivation of a special use it would be very much simpler to keep to the idea of a slight shift in metaphor without any particular significance (→ 76).

c. Jesus as the Way in Jn. 14:4 ff.

The statements about the ὁδός in Jn. 14:4 f., 6 grow out of the context of the beginning of the parting discourses. Jesus is not speaking about His own future destiny after death. He is speaking about the situation in which His disciples will be left. When He refers to the μοναί πολλαί in God's house in 14:2a, it is true that the expression οἰκία τοῦ πατρός μου contains the thought that Jesus as the Son "possesses an inalienable and never forfeited right to dwell in this house of God" [128] (cf. 8:35), but, as the wording shows, He is speaking about these many dwellings, not because His return to God is to be interpreted as a homecoming to the Father's house (and because one of these dwellings is reserved for Him), but solely and simply because these many dwellings will be at the disposal of His disciples. [129] The dwellings represent the goal of salvation (→ IV, 580; II, 705). "'The Father's house' and 'the kingdom of God' cannot be separated from one another"; "the entry of the disciples into the Father's house takes place through the parousia." [130] No matter how we understand 14:2b in relation to 14:3, in 14:3 the emphasis is not on what the going away and the returning of Jesus will mean for Jesus Himself but on what they will mean for His disciples. He will prepare a place and receive them to Himself (πρὸς ἐμαυτόν = into the house of His Father = πρὸς τὸν πατέρα, 14:6). As Jesus is not ranged alongside His disciples in 14:2, as the μοναί are for them, not also for Him, so in 14:3 His going into the house of God is not parallel to theirs. Jesus alone "goes." There is no reference to any independent going on the part of the disciples. They are received by Him (the ἔρχεται of 14:6 does not obliterate this distinction, but is to be understood in the light of 14:3). Jesus' going is His death. We are not also to think of the death

---

[127] Käsemann, 145 ff., in his discussion of Hb. 10:19 f. (→ n. 124), sees both εἴσοδος and ὁδός (147, n. 2) from the standpoint of the Gnostic motif of the ascent of souls to God. Similarly, these verses, with 9:8, are claimed (op. cit., 19) for the motif of the wandering people of God. The idea of wandering is, however, quite alien in 10:19 f. and 9:8. The ref. is to entry into the sanctuary (the entry of the priests and high-priest in 9:6 f. is no wandering). Furthermore, when the idea of the wandering people of God occurs in Hb. ὁδός is not used at all (it is found in Hb. only at 3:10 apart from 9:8 and 10:20, → 87). These points do not favour any decisive influence of the Gnostic motif of the way or of wandering. Käsemann has many examples to show how widespread such ideas were, but not all his instances are of the same value. Thus in O. Sol. 33:6 f. (op. cit., 31 f.) the idea of wandering is not present; "ways" has the well-known sense of "walk" or "commandments" (on the examples from Philo → n. 60).

[128] Zn. J. 5, 6, 552.

[129] One might say that, as God does not live in these μοναί but is the owner of the whole house, so the Son does not live in them, since the whole house belongs to Him too. Zn. on 14:2a, however, argues that "the statement refers primarily to Jesus," "but He cannot and will not be the only one to find an abiding dwelling there," etc.

[130] Schl. J., 292: We are not to think of heaven, hence not of the going away of Jesus, which is an ascension into heaven.

of the disciples, and certainly not of their martyrdom. For no parallel is suggested (He does not take them with Him at His going, but receives them at His *parousia*), and the proximity of the intimation of 13:36 (which applies primarily to Peter alone) is no adequate reason for bringing in this idea. [131] The conclusion of 14:3: ἵνα ὅπου εἰμὶ ἐγὼ καὶ ὑμεῖς ἦτε, confirms our exposition, since it suggests, not a similarity of going, but simply a being together at the same goal (cf. 17:24; on the other hand 12:26, if it hints at the passion of His disciples, does not justify us in finding the idea of martyrdom in 14:3).

From what has been said, it may be seen that in the light of 14:2 f. one cannot argue that the decisive presupposition of 14:4 ff. is the similarity of the going, or way, of Jesus on the one side and the disciples on the other. To understand what is meant by οἴδατε one should appeal neither to 13:36 nor to 12:26. Jesus Himself tells us in 14:6 what is meant in 14:3. But it is not necessary to anticipate. The explanation may be gathered quite adequately from 14:3 (it is no accident that 14:4 is linked by a καί). The disciples know where Jesus is going, because He has told them, and they know the way, for He has spoken of this too. But to whose way does 14:4 refer? The first exclusive and unmistakable reference to that of the disciples is hardly to be found in 14:6, for the question in 14:5: πῶς οἴδαμεν τὴν ὁδόν; can only refer to the way of the disciples if 14:6 is an answer to it. Did Thomas with his question misunderstand the words of Jesus in 14:4? He did not understand how he was to know the way, but surely he understood that the reference was to the way of the disciples. Even if we read: καὶ ὅπου ἐγὼ ὑπάγω οἴδατε τὴν ὁδόν, this interpretation is still to be upheld. If, as we have seen, the emphasis in 14:2 f. is not on the going and coming again of Jesus as such, but on the significance which this going and coming again would have for the disciples, the ὅπου ἐγὼ ὑπάγω, notwithstanding the emphatic ἐγώ, cannot refer only to the destiny of Jesus (as in 13:36). Furthermore, the ὑπάγω, after the prior mention of the coming again, cannot be a mere equivalent of the πορεύομαι of 14:2. It embraces the new going away, after the coming again, when Jesus will take the disciples with Him according to 14:3. No special emphasis, however, is laid on this second going, since ὅπου ἐγὼ ὑπάγω is linked with ὅπου εἰμὶ ἐγώ.

The context is plain enough if in 14:4 the reading: καὶ ὅπου ἐγὼ ὑπάγω οἴδατε καὶ τὴν ὁδὸν οἴδατε, is to be accepted as original. [132] What is meant in this case is that from what Jesus previously said the disciples know where He is going, namely, that they, too, will attain to the house of God, and they also know the way which leads there, namely, that He will take them. In this double form 14:4 is still a unity. The first clause prepares the way for the second. It refers to the going away of Jesus only because this is the presupposition of the promised being together of the disciples with Him. The same applies to what Thomas says in 14:5. Only the second clause is put in the form of a question. That is, the question relates only to the way which the disciples should know. The preceding clause: οὐκ οἴδαμεν ποῦ ὑπάγεις, mentions the presupposition. It has no independent force, and should not be compared with the question in 13:36: ποῦ ὑπάγεις;

---

[131] As against Zn. J., 555. How unimportant here was the death of the disciples may be seen best from the fact that there is no mention whatever of a question which was to occupy the minds of believers in the days of Paul, namely, whether they would be privileged to experience the *parousia*. It is worth noting that the problem of the delay of the *parousia* does not seem to arise at all in this passage.

[132] Zn., 555 f. and n. 17.

In both 14:4 and 14:5 the reference is to the way of the disciples. Similarly, the answer of Jesus in 14:6 refers, not to His own way, but to the way of the disciples.

Thus, if we leave aside the concepts "truth" and "life," 14:6 is part of a series of sayings which embraces 14:2 f. and 14:4 f. The statement in 14:6 is equivalent to what has been said already, and puts it even more plainly. What is meant by ἐγώ εἰμι ἡ ὁδός is explained in 6b. Even though, in respect of the δι᾽ ἐμοῦ, one should not perhaps recall that ὁδός, too, can be used with διά (cf. Mt. 2:12; 8:28; → 69), even though δι᾽ ἐμοῦ bears a predominant instrumental sense (the local can also be implied, → II, 67), it is quite evident that what is said in 6b is materially the same as the παραλήμψομαι ὑμᾶς of 14:3. The πρὸς τὸν πατέρα of 6b also corresponds to the πρὸς ἐμαυτόν of 14:3. This equation, already visible in 14:2 in the rank which Jesus takes in the house of His Father, is further developed in 14:7 ff. The exclusiveness of the ἐγώ εἰμι is underlined in 6b. Nor is the validity of 6b verbally restricted to the circle of the disciples who are addressed just before and just after; we find, not οὐδεὶς ἐξ ὑμῶν, but οὐδείς (cf. Mt. 11:27). Nor is the general application of the saying invalidated by the assumption that in the context it is addressed in the first instance only to the disciples. If the saying polemically excludes other attempts to reach God, it is primarily directed, not against the attempts of others, but against other attempts by the disciples. It is possible, however, that the negative side of the statement is less important than the positive side, and that the saying is simply designed to support the claim of 6a. Indeed, this is necessarily so if 14:6 is strictly meant only as an answer to 14:5. For Thomas is not considering whether or not there might be other ways to the Father. He merely confesses that he does not know the one way to which Jesus had already referred. He now receives the answer that Jesus, and He alone, is for His disciples the way to the Father, because He alone, as the Son, has full authority to receive them into the house of His Father. To know the way is to know that one must be received by Jesus, that one must be ready to be placed by Him in the fellowship with Him which will find its consummation in the being together with Him mentioned at the conclusion of 14:3. [133]

In one respect 14:6 might seem to diverge from what goes before. 14:2 ff. looks forward to the *parousia,* and says that after the *parousia* Jesus will receive the disciples to Himself in the Father's house. 14:6, however, is so formulated that, if 14:2 ff. did not come first, the two parts of the saying would appear to have a present application in every age. Coming to the Father would then have to be construed as generally attaining to fellowship with God. This interpretation seems to be suggested by 14:7 ff. inasmuch as knowing and seeing the Father, here referred to as a possession mediated by Jesus, are equivalent to coming to the Father. Nevertheless, it is inadvisable to let 14:6 be controlled exclusively by thoughts present in 14:7 ff. The connection with 14:2 ff. is too strong for this. Either the change into a statement about the present comes only with 14:7 and 14:6 is to be taken in an exclusively eschatological sense, or 14:6, as an answer to the question

---

[133] Since the reference is to Jesus alone, there is no thought of anything that the disciples must do. Certainly, they cannot attain to the Father by their own efforts, but one recalls that Jesus Himself lays requirements on those who acknowledge Him to be the way. There is no ref. to these, however, in 14:6, and it is thus out of place to find in 14:4 the thought of a verification of discipleship. Zn., 556, appealing to 13:36; 12:26, introduces the idea of discipleship and its sufferings, and Schl. J., 293, suggests that 14:4 states the commitment "to deed and service."

of Thomas, is eschatologically orientated like the question, but 14:4, as is materially apposite, has a present and general reference, and thus prepares the way for 14:7 ff. To decide which of these two possibilities is to be preferred, it is essential to determine the relation of ἀλήθεια and ζωή to ὁδός.

If it has been stressed thus far that the statement: ἐγώ εἰμι ἡ ὁδός (and the explanation which follows in 14:6b), grows naturally out of the sayings in 14:2 ff., the same hardly seems to be true of the continuation: καὶ ἡ ἀλήθεια καὶ ἡ ζωή, for what has preceded thus far provides no apparent reason for mentioning these terms as well. It is true that the three concepts are not of equal worth; ὁδός takes precedence of the others. This may be seen clearly from the fact that v. 6b again refers exclusively to ὁδός. [134] A possible explanation seems to be that ὁδός is related to ἀλήθεια and ζωή in such a way that ἀλήθεια and ζωή state the goal to which the way leads. In this case the saying cannot be taken to mean that Jesus is simply the way to this goal. The wording prevents this, for it refers the ἐγώ εἰμι equally to all three terms. Hence one is forced to say that on this reading Jesus is called the goal as well as the way. This exposition cannot rely, of course, on the argument that what Thomas says in 14:5 refers to both way and goal. [135] For we have seen that the two statements in 14:5 are both to be referred to the way of the disciples (→ 80). This observation is another reason for giving precedence to ὁδός in 14:6. Intrinsically ἀλήθεια and ζωή can represent the goal. Both terms carry an eschatological reference, and so they might be regarded here (par. πρὸς τὸν πατέρα) as descriptions of the goal of salvation. [136] Nevertheless, our deliberations have made it clear that ὁδός is the predominant concept which establishes the link with what precedes. If ἀλήθεια and ζωή are added to it, their function is surely one of elucidation for which no preparation is necessary in the preceding verses. What is meant is that Jesus is the way inasmuch as He is the truth and the life. [137]

If this is the interrelation of the three concepts, it is right that they should be linked by καί ... καί, and one can also understand why the choice has fallen on the two terms ἀλήθεια and ζωή, for these are important words frequently used in Jn. to denote the gifts of Christ, even though there are no sayings corresponding directly to ἐγώ εἰμι ἡ ἀλήθεια or ἐγώ εἰμι ἡ ζωή (yet cf. 11:25). One has certainly to consider that in Jn. both ἀλήθεια and ζωή, though ζωή is not without an emphatic eschatological flavour (cf. 11:25: ἐγώ εἰμι ἡ ἀνάστασις καὶ ἡ ζωή), refer to that which is even now given to believers through Christ (→ I, 246; II, 825). Nevertheless, this feature in ἀλήθεια and ζωή is not to be set in anti-

---

[134] Even if δι' ἐμοῦ is to be taken only instr. (though cf. → 80), this expression in connection with ἔρχεται is so strongly orientated to the figure of the way that there is no place for a corresponding reference to ἀλήθεια and ζωή. The other ἐγώ εἰμι sayings in Jn. all contain only one term, though usually with an addition (τῆς ζωῆς, τοῦ κόσμου, or adj. καλός, ἀληθινός). The only exception is the double statement in 11:25 (the omission of ἡ ζωή is secondary). But since ὁδός takes precedence in 14:6, this saying is closer to the single formulae than to 11:25.

[135] Cf. Bau. J., ad loc., who suggests that in reply to the "double question" of Thomas (neither materially nor formally is this really a double question) Jesus "answers separately the question of the goal and that of the way."

[136] It is surely impossible that ἀλήθεια should be the master-concept, or that it should bear so strong an emphasis that one can say: "Hence revelation is not the means to an end; it is itself both the way and the goal (ζωή)" (R. Bultmann, → I, 246).

[137] Cf. Schl. J., 294; F. Büchsel J. (NT Deutsch, 4), ad loc.; Schweizer, 166: "The way whose character is described in terms of ἀλήθεια and ζωή."

thesis to the fact that ὁδός in 14:2 ff. is orientated to eschatological salvation, and it actually corresponds to the fact that statements about the present are made in 14:7 ff. One may thus assume that it is this use of the explanatory concepts ἀλήθεια and ζωή in 14:6 which brings about the redirection to the present which is so prominent in 14:7 ff. Jesus will one day take the disciples to Himself in the house of His Father, and He will then show Himself to be the way. But He is already the way, for even now He gives truth and life. No one either then or now comes to the Father except by Him.

Consequently the mention of ἀλήθεια and ζωή does not disrupt nor destroy the unity of thought in 14:2 ff. (→ 80). The ideas introduced into ὁδός by ἀλήθεια and ζωή are new but not alien or remote. The use of ὁδός itself in 14:6 obviously grows out of what precedes. In these circumstances there is no cause to assume that the choice of the terms ἀλήθεια and ζωή is due to some influence from outside the context. The attempts and proposals which can and have been made along these lines are thus unsatisfactory. There can be no question of OT influence, for ὁδός is not used there in the absolute, and expressions like ὁδὸς ἀληθείας (→ 52) and ὁδοὶ ζωῆς (→ 52) are not direct parallels. The corresponding phrases in Philo (→ 60; 61) are even further removed from the content of the Johannine declaration (cf. also → n. 59). A more likely suggestion is that in Jn. 14:6 there is antithesis to the Torah, the more so as statements about the Torah are transferred to Jesus elsewhere in Jn. (→ IV, 136). In fact, the Torah is called way, truth and life, [138] but in the examples thus far adduced we never find more than one of the terms at a time. [139] Hence it is inadvisable to suppose that Jn. 14:6 as a whole is directed against the Torah. The sequence of ὁδός, ἀλήθεια and ζωή is better understood in terms of the meaning which the terms bear individually in the Johannine world of thought. To assume that ὁδός alone is used in antithesis to the Torah would carry greater cogency only if the ὁδός of 14:6 were not so strongly linked as it is with the ὁδός of 14:4 f. and the ideas underlying 14:2 f.

If the unity of the section 14:2-6 can be argued against the idea of a polemic against the Torah in 14:6, the same unity might be alleged in support of the view that the Gnostic idea of a heavenly journey of the soul has influenced the section (→ 47). Now there can be no doubt that the influence of this idea is to be seen elsewhere in Jn. [140] This interpretation is distinguished by the fact that it does not isolate the section, nor think that Gnostic influence is to be found in it alone. Nevertheless, even though we cannot and should not decide the question whether and how far one might truly speak of a Gnostic impact on Jn. along these lines, the following objection must be lodged against this understanding. If the idea of the way, which is already in the background in 14:2 f. and dominant in 14:4 ff., and which comes to expression in the use of ὁδός, is genuinely connected with the Gnostic conception of the heavenly journey of the soul, one might have ex-

---

[138] → IV, 135; I, 245, n. 34; Str.-B., Index, s.v.

[139] K. Bornhäuser, *Das Johannesevangelium eine Missionsschrift für Israel* (1928), 84 refers to ψ 118:1, 30, 37, but these three verses, though contained in the same psalm, do not meet the requirements which would qualify them as pars. to Jn. 14:6 referring to the Torah. In v. 1 ὁδός has the sense of "walk" (and only in 1b do we read of the νόμος κυρίου); this is also the sense in the ὁδὸς ἀληθείας of v. 30 (in antithesis to ὁδὸς ἀδικίας in v. 29); in v. 37: ἐν τῇ ὁδῷ σου ζῆσόν με, ὁδός is the way which God has commanded, the divine commandment (→ 52).

[140] Bau. J. on 14:6; Bultmann, 100 ff., esp. 133 f.

pected that elsewhere in Jn. the term ὁδός would play a significant role, and that
it would be especially favoured in sources where the Gnostic conception may be
perceived. [141] Outside 14:4-6, however, ὁδός occurs in the Gospel only in 1:23
(a quotation from Is. 40:3, → n. 92), and the idea of a way is not presented in
other terms. This fact shows plainly that, no matter what may be the Gnostic
influence on Jn., the use of ὁδός in 14:4-6 cannot be generally orientated to the
usage and thought of Gnosticism. It must owe its origin to another and more
specific cause, i.e., to one which belongs to the narrower context.

It may be added that the context itself, i.e., the section 14:2 ff., clearly differs
from the Gnostic circle of ideas in various matters which are by no means unimportant. Perhaps one should not stress too greatly the fact that the going of
Jesus is represented as a return to God only indirectly, i.e., by the expression ἐν
τῇ οἰκίᾳ τοῦ πατρός μου. For the thought that Jesus came from God and goes
back to Him belongs intrinsically to Jn. It is in keeping with the character of the
parting discourses that our gaze is directed, not to the heavenly origin of Jesus,
but to His future destiny. More important, however, is the fact that no reference
whatever is made to the heavenly origin of souls. Certainly, the μοναί have been
long since ready for the disciples (cf. 2 C. 5:1). But that the disciples originally
came forth from these heavenly dwellings, that they had left them and were now
returning to them, is obviously not the meaning (the ἑτοιμάσαι τόπον shows that,
while the dwellings had been long since ordained for the disciples, they had still
to be made ready or furnished for them).

It should also be noted that according to the Gnostic view souls begin their
journey after death. [142] Here, however, attention is not focused exclusively on the
death of the disciples (→ 78 f.). Everything is orientated to the *parousia*. This is
also important inasmuch as the meaning which the *parousia* has for Jesus Himself finds no parallel in the Gnostic world of thought. If the πορεύεσθαι or ὑπά-
γειν of Jesus might be equated with the homecoming of the Gnostic Redeemer,
there is no convincing equivalent for His πάλιν ἔρχεσθαι, which is so constituent
a part not only of the Johannine but also (terminology apart) of the whole NT
understanding. These differences are perhaps counterbalanced by the fact that in
Gnosticism, too, the Redeemer has the task of pointing out the way to his people,
or of preparing it for them. [143] It should be remembered, however, that the Gnostic

---

[141] Bultmann, 133 f.; Käsemann, 52 ff.; → 47. The Mandaean texts abound in examples
(cf. Lidz. Ginza, Index, 615, *s.v.* "Weg"; 612, *s.v.* "Pfad"; 607, *s.v.* "Geheimnisse des
Weges"; cf. 392, 29). They mostly use עוהרא, also דירכא, much less frequently שבילא,
"footpath." But as E. Percy points out in his *Untersuchungen über den Ursprung d. joh.
Theologie, zugleich ein Beitrag zur Frage nach d. Entstehung des Gnostizismus* (1939),
228, n. 63, it should be noted that in the Mandaean texts the Redeemer himself is never
called the way. It may be assumed that Jn. 14:6 has influenced the verses in Act. Thom.
(quoted in Bultmann, 134) where Jesus is called the way.

[142] This is esp. emphasised by Käsemann, 54.

[143] Cf. the examples in Bultmann, 133 f. There is also the distinction that in spite of the
underlying topography in 14:2 f. there is little of the spatial about the way in Jn., as
distinct from the Mandaean texts, which refer to "laying," "levelling" and "treading" the
way (e.g., Lidz. Liturg., 68, 89, 134; cf. also Percy, → n. 141). Nor do we find in Jn. an
idea which is typical of the Gnostic teaching of the heavenly journey, namely, that the way
is long and traverses various heavens and aeons (in the Gnostic texts this idea is the presupposition of the belief that the way must be specially prepared and indicated). In Pist.
Soph. "way of the centre" is a fixed term for the way beneath the sphere which the soul
must take past the various archontes of the way of the centre.

conception of the Redeemer as leader and guide [144] finds no echo in the vocabulary of Jn. The παραλήμψομαι ὑμᾶς of 14:3 presents a different picture, and it is highly debatable whether the ἐγώ εἰμι ἡ ὁδός (and δι' ἐμοῦ) can be rendered "I lead you." For the concrete spatial sense is of little acount here. Predominant is the thought of attachment to the person of Jesus in the sense of commitment in faith. This is shown by the use of non-spatial concepts ἀλήθεια and ζωή, [145] and also by the additional ideas of seeing and knowing the Father in 14:7, 9.

The only possible conclusion is that the Gnostic myth of the heavenly journey of the soul cannot be regarded as the basis of 14:2 ff. It is true that, though no specific foreign influence can be proved at this point, one cannot rule out the possibility that the ἐγώ εἰμι of the Johannine declaration might be a conscious antithesis to the corresponding claims of other entities in the world around the Evangelist. [146] A strong argument against this, however, is that the use of the ὁδός is in fact adequately explained by the context, so that such a hypothesis is superfluous. The independence of the Johannine use of ὁδός is thus to be upheld. The uniqueness of the position of Jesus is brought to expression in 14:6. [147]

3. The Figurative Use.

In the figurative use the spatial idea of a way is often very strong, as may be seen from the verbs used with ὁδός (though these are also used fig., → 49). [148] Cf. Lk. 1:79 : τοῦ κατευθῦναι τοὺς πόδας ἡμῶν εἰς ὁδὸν εἰρήνης. The reference is to the attainment of Messianic salvation (→ II, 412 f.), yet ὁδός does not signify "means," but the whole saying keeps graphically to the picture of a way. [149] In spite of the OT flavour of the Benedictus, there can be no certainty that ὁδός

---

[144] Bau. J. on 14:6; Bultmann, 133 f. How far Philo's statements about God or the Logos as ἡγεμὼν τῆς ὁδοῦ (→ 64) should be associated with the Gnostic myth depends on our general assessment of Philo's relation to Gnosticism (→ n. 60). The OT, too, has the thought that God shows the right way, but it first says that God has commanded the way, and it links terms of proclamation with ὁδός (→ 53). → ὁδηγέω.

[145] It is unlikely that the mention of ἀλήθεια and ζωή is to be explained by the fact that in Mandaean writings "the three concepts of way, truth and life stand in equally close connection with the heavenly Redeemer" (Bau. J. on 14:6), for here truth and life indicate the goal of the way (as distinct from Jn. 14:6).

[146] → II, 871 f. Cf. esp. Schweizer, 167, who thinks the Johannine figures of speech are controlled "by opposition to the religious answers of men (which are also the natural answers)." He, too, recalls the Mandaean and Gnostic writings, but only as examples : he is hesitant to connect them too directly with Jn. He does not deal specifically with 14:6 (166; cf. 161). It is worth considering whether the liking for the idea of the "way" in the Mandaean writings is not in fact to be explained in terms of the influence of Jn. 14:6.

[147] The Johannine use of ὁδός is also independent of Hb. 9:8; 10:20. The difference between Hb. and Jn. is not merely that Hb. does not call Jesus the way nor Jn. refer to the topography of the heavenly sanctuary. The main distinction is that the idea of the parousia of Jesus is not present in Hb. Hence there is in Hb. nothing to correspond to the παραλήμψομαι ὑμᾶς of Jn. 14:3. The exclusive commitment to the person of Jesus distinguishes Jn.'s declaration from the later principle : extra ecclesiam nulla salus (Bau. J., ad loc. refers to this, but the saying in Jn. is not controlled by the claim of the Church in his day). Cf. also W. Oehler, "Zum Missionscharakter d. Joh.-Ev.," BFTh, 42, 4 (1941), 52 f. Unfortunately it was not possible to consult Bu. J., 462 ff. until this art. had gone to press, and interaction with him is thus impossible for technical reasons.

[148] Stauffer Theol., 10 ff., appealing to passages in which verbs of going are used, regards the way of Jesus as the decisive category, but the same objections apply to this as mentioned in → n. 39.

[149] Cf. Schl. L., 181.

εἰρήνης derives from Is. 59:8. On the other hand, this verse (καὶ ὁδὸν εἰρήνης οὐκ οἴδασιν) is definitely quoted by Paul in R. 3:17. Neither the Mas. nor LXX has in view the way which leads to Messianic salvation, [150] but a walk in which one strives to be at peace with those around. Paul, too, links 3:17, not with 3:18, but with 3:15 f. (= Is. 59:7): ἐκχέαι αἷμα is the obvious antithesis of εἰρήνη. Ac. 2:28, in a passage (2:25-28) which quotes ψ 15:8-11, adduces ψ 15:11: ἐγνώρισάς μοι ὁδοὺς ζωῆς. In the Mas. and LXX the reference is to the walk which God has commanded and which will ensure man of (eternal) life, → 52; → II, 854; 864, n. 279). It is tempting to suppose that Lk. quoted this final verse of ψ 15, in which v. 10 was for him the most important saying (= Ac. 2:27), because it seemed to him to refer to the resurrection of Jesus. As he sees it, the verse means: "Thou hast already shown me long before how thou wilt lead me from death to life, i.e., raise me up again." In this case ὁδός is the "means" or "possibility" of attaining to or achieving something. ὁδός bears the same meaning in Ac. 16:17: καταγγέλλουσιν ὑμῖν ὁδὸν σωτηρίας. Apostolic proclamation answers the question how one can be saved (cf. 16:30). It is unlikely that the sense here is that of "teaching" (the "doctrine of salvation"), → 90.

In 1 C. 12:31b Paul writes: καὶ ἔτι καθ᾽ ὑπερβολὴν ὁδὸν ὑμῖν δείκνυμι. Though καθ᾽ ὑπερβολήν is linked attributively with ὁδός, the meaning of ὁδός is to be sought independently of an obviously stereotyped phrase like καθ᾽ ὑπερβολήν. [151] ὁδός can hardly be the way along which spiritual gifts may be sought (cf. 12:31a). It is certainly not the way in which true ζηλοῦν can be achieved. The context shows this. This is not to say, however, that ὁδός cannot be regarded formally as the "means," "possibility" or "manner," but has to have a definite content as the "manner of life, walk or action." [152] The meaning "attitude" is intrinsically possible (the incomparably better, because Christian, attitude or *habitus* of love is contrasted with that of ζηλοῦν τὰ χαρίσματα), but it is more natural to give ὁδός the formal sense of "way and means," namely, "the way of reaching the goal which is elsewhere sought by this ζηλοῦν." [153]

The sense of "walk," "conduct," is plain in many passages: ἀκατάστατος ἐν πάσαις ταῖς ὁδοῖς αὐτοῦ, Jm. 1:8; [154] εἴασεν πάντα τὰ ἔθνη πορεύεσθαι ταῖς ὁδοῖς αὐτῶν, Ac. 14:16; σύντριμμα καὶ ταλαιπωρία ἐν ταῖς ὁδοῖς αὐτῶν,

---

[150] As against Cr.-Kö., *s.v.*, 1. b.

[151] Schl. K., ad loc. goes back to the root meaning of ὑπερβολή: "A ὑπερβολή is a throw which goes beyond that of others." "What takes place καθ᾽ ὑπερβολήν is done with surpassing force and *élan*." He thus concludes: "The phrase is hard to link with the idea of a 'way,' " and he believes that it should be taken with ὁδὸν δείκνυμι rather than ὁδός. For the reading εἴ τι for ἔτι cf. Bl.-Debr. § 272.

[152] As against Cr.-Kö., *s.v.*, 3. a/b, where only two possibilities are considered, the formal relation to ὁδός, and the understanding in terms of content.

[153] Bchm. 1 K.³, ad loc. The goal to which the way leads is not easily stated, and the Corinthians do not have to have had the same goal in view. Joh. W. 1 K., ad loc. rightly rejects the view that the edification of the community is the goal which Paul is trying to set before the Corinthians, who had not previously considered it. But he himself stresses too much the Corinthian standpoint when he states as the goal the "enhancement of their whole being," "the consummation of Christian life." Paul surely regarded the eschatological consummation as the goal (cf. 13:8 ff.). On δείκνυμι → II, 26 f. Bornhäuser combines 1 C. 12:31b with his interrelating of Mt. 7:13 f. and the law of love in Mt. 7:12 (→ n. 109).

[154] Cf. Dib. Jk., ad loc.; Schl. Jk., 117: "Whatever he may undertake." The sense of "walk," "action," "activity," is also present in Jm. 1:11: ἐν ταῖς πορείαις αὐτοῦ, cf. Dib. Jk., ad loc.

R. 3:6 (= Is. 59:7). These examples have the plur. ὁδοί, but in others we find the sing. Jm. 5:20 : ὁ ἐπιστρέψας ἁμαρτωλὸν ἐκ πλάνης ὁδοῦ αὐτοῦ, maintains the unity of the metaphor, even though ἐπιστρέφειν and πλάνη are also used figuratively. The linking of πλανᾶσθαι etc. and ὁδός is common in the OT (cf. Dt. 11:28 etc.); this is perhaps why, in the preceding verse (Jm. 5:19), א 33 etc. have the vl.: ἐάν τις ἐν ὑμῖν πλανηθῇ ἀπὸ τῆς ὁδοῦ τῆς ἀληθείας (cf. Wis. 5:6 : ἐπλανήθημεν ἀπὸ ὁδοῦ ἀληθείας). [155] It is hard to decide whether ὁδὸς τῆς ἀληθείας in this vl. simply has the OT sense of the "right way" (→ 52; cf. → 57) or whether ἀλήθεια denotes the Gospel. The same expression occurs in 2 Pt. 2:2 : δι' οὓς ἡ ὁδὸς (δόξα א³ A) τῆς ἀληθείας βλασφημηθήσεται. It is by no means certain that the meaning here is "genuine Christianity," and that ὁδός thus has the sense of "teaching" or "doctrine." [156] But the exhortatory aim of the context seems rather to demand the sense of "walk," so that what is meant is the Christian way of life which alone corresponds to the divine revelation. [157] This is supported by the use of ὁδός in this sense elsewhere in 2 Pt. Thus in 2:15 we read : καταλείποντες εὐθεῖαν ὁδόν ("the right way," → 52) ἐπλανήθησαν, ἐξακολουθήσαντες τῇ ὁδῷ τοῦ Βαλαὰμ τοῦ Βεώρ. The metaphor of the way is strong here, but it is plain that the reference is to practical conduct or walk, not to teaching or error. The parallel in Jd. 11 certainly uses τῇ πλάνῃ τοῦ Βαλαάμ, but this is preceded by τῇ ὁδῷ τοῦ Κάϊν ἐπορεύθησαν. Hence πλάνη is "erroneous way" or "aberration" rather than "error," and the ὁδὸς τοῦ Βαλαάμ of 2 Pt. 2:15 is not a direct equivalent of the διδαχή Βαλαάμ in Rev. 2:14, but means "walk" rather than "view" or "teaching." Similarly, 2 Pt. 2:21: κρεῖττον γὰρ ἦν αὐτοῖς μὴ ἐπεγνωκέναι τὴν ὁδὸν τῆς δικαιοσύνης, is not describing Christianity as the "way of righteousness," [158] nor is δικαιοσύνη used in this phrase as a slogan for Christianity, but ὁδὸς τῆς δικαιοσύνης (par. εὐθεῖα ὁδός, 2:15) means "the right way" (→ 52; cf. → 57), "the true Christian walk." Indeed, the ensuing ὑποστρέψαι ἐκ τῆς παραδοθείσης αὐτοῖς ἁγίας ἐντολῆς gives to ὁδὸς τῆς δικαιοσύνης the sense of "the way which is right because God has commanded it" (→ II, 199). This may also be the meaning in Mt. 21:32 : ἦλθεν γὰρ 'Ιωάννης πρὸς ὑμᾶς ἐν ὁδῷ δικαιοσύνης : John came on the right way, i.e., on God's commission. [159] The usage of Mt. elsewhere, however, suggests that δικαιοσύνη should be construed as "righteousness of life in accordance with the will of God," (→ II, 199). Even so, the reference is not to the Baptist's requiring of this way of life from his hearers. [160] The construction ἦλθεν ἐν ὁδῷ demands that ὁδός be referred to the Baptist himself. What is meant is that he came to you on the

---

[155] Dib. Jk., 238, n. 1.
[156] Wnd. Kath. Br., ad loc.; Pr.-Bauer³, s.v., 2. c.
[157] Wbg. Pt., ad loc.
[158] As against Wnd. Kath. Br., ad loc.
[159] So Zn. Mt.⁴, ad loc.
[160] As against G. Schrenk, → II, 199; Str.-B., I, 866 f. and Kl. Mt., ad loc., who accordingly translates : "John came to you with the way of righteousness." But how can ἐν ὁδῷ have this meaning with a verb of going ? The ἐν of accompanying circumstance (as in ἔρχεσθαι ἐν ῥάβδῳ, 1 C. 4:21, → II, 538, can hardly be used with ὁδός itself when it has the sense of "walk." Cf. also Zn. Mt.⁴, 628, n. 27. E. Lohmeyer, *Johannes d. Täufer* (1932), 102 f. regards ὁδὸς δικ. as a term for baptism itself (as the way to eschatological salvation), but Mt. 21:32 (unlike Lk. 7:29 f.) does not in fact speak of baptism.

way of righteousness, as a righteous man, and yet you did not believe him. [161]

The sense of "(divinely) commanded walk," which is common in the OT or LXX (→ 51) and which has been considered in relation to 2 Pt. 2:21 (→ 86), is perhaps to be found also in Hb. 3:10 in the quotation from ψ 94:10 : αὐτοὶ δὲ οὐκ ἔγνωσαν τὰς ὁδούς μου, [162] though it is possible that both in the OT and Hb. (par. ψ 94:9 = Hb. 3:9b : εἶδον τὰ ἔργα μου) the reference is to God's dealings and saving purposes. [163] The meaning is undoubtedly "commanded walk" in Mk. 12:14 par. Lk. 20:21; Mt. 22:16. When the Pharisees say to Jesus : ἐπ' ἀληθείας τὴν ὁδὸν τοῦ θεοῦ διδάσκεις, they mean the proclamation of the divine will, of the walk which God requires. [164] "What is commanded by God" could also be the sense in Ac. 13:10 : οὐ παύσῃ διαστρέφων τὰς ὁδοὺς τοῦ κυρίου τὰς εὐθείας; esp. since ὁδός in this sense is often combined with εὐθεῖα in the OT (→ 52), and this is the meaning in Prv. 10:9 in the expression ὁ διαστρέφων τὰς ὁδοὺς αὐτοῦ. On the other hand, it should be considered that the αὐτοῦ of Prv. 10:9 refers to ὁ διαστρέφων, so that in spite of the use of διαστρέφειν this verse cannot have been of decisive influence on Ac. 13:10. Furthermore, the OT often says of God's own ὁδοί that they are εὐθεῖαι (→ 55). Hos. 14:10 : εὐθεῖαι αἱ ὁδοὶ τοῦ κυρίου, which with Da. 3:27 : αἱ ὁδοί σου εὐθεῖαι, is the closest formal par. to Ac. 13:10, clearly has in view God's dealings, dispensations or leadings. The saying in Hosea : καὶ δίκαιοι πορεύσονται ἐν αὐταῖς, would permit us to think of the walk which God requires of man, but the next sentence : οἱ δὲ ἀσεβεῖς ἀσθενήσουσιν ἐν αὐταῖς, forbids this, for it cannot be said of this walk that it would ever be in any circumstances to anyone's hurt. It is thus possible that Ac. 13:10 is referring to the divine plans, and especially to God's missionary purposes. This makes good sense in the context of the charge against Elymas. With his opposition to the Christian missionaries he is trying to hamper God's foreordained purposes in the propagation of the Gospel.

When in 1 C. 4:17 Paul says of Timothy : ὃς ὑμᾶς ἀναμνήσει τὰς ὁδούς μου τὰς ἐν Χριστῷ Ἰησοῦ, καθὼς πανταχοῦ ἐν πάσῃ ἐκκλησίᾳ διδάσκω, the καθώς clause shows that the reference is not to the apostle's personal way of life, for this was not the content of his διδάσκειν. [165] The relation of the καθώς clause

---

[161] Though the father issues commands to his sons in the preceding parable in Mt. 21:28 ff., this does not justify us in relating ὁδὸς δικαιοσύνης to demands made by the Baptist, since there is no original connection between 21:32 and the parable, cf. Michaelis, Sämann, 239 f.

[162] So Rgg. Hb. [2, 3], 83, n. 16 : "Less an understanding of God's acts of revelation and guidance than a reference to God's commands."

[163] → 55, and H. Gunkel, Die Psalmen (1926), 420, ad loc.: "Yahweh's ways, i.e., His gracious rule which one can trust."

[164] The sing. is rare in the OT. Hck. Mk., ad loc. renders the expression by "religion," and Kl. Mk., ad loc. regards this as a possible meaning. But the ref. to ethical practice is predominant.

[165] No appeal can be made to 4:16 as an example to the contrary, → IV, 668. Schl. K., ad loc. who defines the "ways of Paul" as "the manner in which he acts and obeys the will of God in each new situation," fails to make it clear how this definition is related to a phrase which he uses later : "the teaching accepted in Corinth." His statement : "He who speaks about the 'ways' of man 'teaches,'" conceals rather than elucidates the problem. Joh. W. 1 K., ad loc. is right when he says : "If we omitted the καθώς clause we should undoubtedly think of the ways which I walk in the fellowship of the Lord Jesus," but he concludes : "All these considerations which constantly crowd in upon us are, however, ruled out by the final clause, which forces us, for good or ill, to understand the ὁδοί of Paul as his doctrines," → IV, 677, n. 12.

to 1 C. 7:17; 11:16; 14:33 also enables us to see that he is thinking, not of his own conduct, but of that of the Corinthians or of all his churches. In the light of this clause the μου means that these are called his ways because he teaches them. [166] There is a parallel in R. 2:16 when Paul writes τὸ εὐαγγέλιόν μου, though normally he has εὐαγγέλιον θεοῦ etc. This parallel for its part supports the conjecture, to which one would be inclined in any case, namely, that behind αἱ ὁδοί μου lies the OT usage αἱ ὁδοὶ τοῦ κυρίου in the sense of the walk which God requires of man. In view of the parallel it is not in the least surprising that these ὁδοί, which one would expect to be called ὁδοὶ τοῦ κυρίου etc., [167] can be described by Paul as his ways, and the OT usage mentioned above shows us that the thought of commanded ways can be so dominant in ὁδοί that they can be adopted fairly self-evidently as the theme of διδάσκειν (cf. also ψ 24:9; Prv. 4:11; → 53). In so far as ὁδός has in the OT the sense of "the commandment" (relative to human conduct), so that it is almost synonymous with ἐντολή (→ 51), the question arises whether this is to be taken as the meaning in 1 C. 4:17: [168] αἱ ὁδοί μου, "my commandments," "principles," "rules." There is no reason not to answer this question in the affirmative. [169] This does not mean, of course, that the description of the principles of Christian life taught by Paul as ways is connected with the existence of a Jewish proselyte catechism entitled "The Ways" or "The Two Ways," nor does it mean that the hortatory material in Pauline proclamation was assembled catechetically under the title "Ways." It has not been proved that there ever was a Jewish catechism with this title (→ 57 f.; 59 f.; 94 ff.), and though the hortatory material in Paul's epistles is often stereotyped and presupposes a fixed tradition, it does not come from a primitive Christian catechism. [170]

While the usage in 1 C. 4:17 points back to the sense of "walk" and displays an ethical orientation, it cannot be immediately accepted as a parallel (or preparatory stage) to Ac. 9:2; 19:9, 23; 22:4, 14, 22, where ὁδός is distinctively used to describe "the mode of life which comes to expression in the Christian fellowship." [171] Here ὁδός is always in the sing. and mostly absolute. From Ac. 24:14 : κατὰ τὴν ὁδὸν ἣν λέγουσιν αἵρεσιν οὕτως λατρεύω τῷ πατρῴῳ θεῷ, one is

---

[166] It is evident that only the ways, not the ἀναμιμνήσκειν of Timothy, can be the content of διδάσκειν. On the syntactical connection of the καθώς clause cf. Bchm. 1 K. and Ltzm. K., ad loc.

[167] Cf. Joh. W. 1 K., ad loc.: The addition τὰς ἐν Χρ. ᾿Ι. characterises the ways rather than mentioning the one who makes the requirement, → II, 541.

[168] It is perhaps surprising that Paul does not use ἐντολή for his own exhortation. Perhaps ὁδός is used instead, though it has this sense, of course, only in 1 C. 4:17. διδαχή is synon. in R. 6:17; 16:17, → I, 129.

[169] Cf. Joh. W. 1 K. and Ltzm. K., ad loc. The transl. "my Christian doctrines" (Pr.-Bauer³, s.v., 2. c) is possible only if one thinks exclusively of ethical instruction. The rendering "my procedure" (Bchm. 1 K., ad loc.) is not wholly felicitous.

[170] These questions have been much agitated since the days of A. Seeberg, cf. esp. his writings Der Katechismus d. Urchristenheit (1903); Die beiden Wege u. das Aposteldekret (1906), esp. 37 f. Note should be taken of Seeberg's explanation that by catechism he means only catechetical material (Das Ev. Christi [1905], 103, n. 2). The significance of his theses is weighed by K. Weiss in his "Urchristentum u. Geschichte in d. nt.lichen Theol. seit d. Jahrhundertwende," BFTh, 40, 4 (1939), 20 ff. Cf. also O. Moe, Pls. u. d. evangelische Geschichte (1912), 66 f.; K. Weidinger, Die Haustafeln (UNT, 14) (1928), 5; P. Feine, Die Gestalt d. apostolischen Glaubensbekenntnisses in d. Zeit d. NT (1925), 76; Vögtle, op. cit., 3 ff.; M. Dibelius, Die Formgeschichte d. Ev.² (1933), 240 ff.; Dib. Thess.³ (1937), 19 f. (Exc.).

[171] Cr.-Kö., s.v., 3. c.

forced to conclude that ὁδός is the Christian term for the same phenomenon as the Jewish opponents of the Gospel call αἵρεσις (the construction κατὰ τὴν ὁδόν ... λατρεύω obviously corresponds to the expression in 26:5 : κατὰ τὴν ... αἵρεσιν ... ἔζησα). Though αἵρεσις means "school" (as a group) in many verses in Ac. (5:17; 15:5; for Christians on the lips of Tertullus, 24:5), this cannot be the sense in 24:14, since this would mean that ὁδός would then have to refer to Christians as a fellowship, which is hardly possible. αἵρεσις, however, can also mean "teaching," i.e., the view represented by a group or school (in Ac. cf. 26:5; 28:22). This must be the sense in 24:14, and accordingly ὁδός has the same meaning. It cannot be contested that, though αἵρεσις does not exactly have a bad sense ("heresy"), it is used disparagingly. [172] If Jewish opponents do not call the Christian message a false doctrine, they certainly state it to be one view among others, a view which is held only by a small, unauthorised group, and which has no binding force. [173] Christians, however, believe that they are in the right, and this is expressed by the use of ὁδός. This sense of "doctrine," "view," is found in other verses in Ac.; it is quite clear in 19:9, 23; 24:22, and possible also in 9:2 and 22:4. [174] From 22:4 : ταύτην τὴν ὁδὸν ἐδίωξα, one can hardly conclude for certain that the author of Ac. uses ὁδός for other views or presupposes a general use of this kind. ταύτην is not so much a demarcation as a more specific definition of what is meant. The use is thus uniform in Ac. inasmuch as it always relates to Christian proclamation or teaching and calls this ὁδός in the absolute. Where does this usage come from?

Reference to Ac. 18:25 f. does not help much. It is said of Apollos here : οὗτος ἦν κατηχημένος τὴν ὁδὸν τοῦ κυρίου, and in 18:26 we read of Priscilla and Aquila : ἀκριβέστερον αὐτῷ ἐξέθεντο τὴν ὁδὸν τοῦ θεοῦ. Neither the fact that some MSS leave out τοῦ κυρίου or τοῦ θεοῦ (obviously under the influence of the usage elsewhere) nor the parallelism with 24:22 established by ἀκριβέστερον constitutes a reason for construing the expressions used in 18:25 f. otherwise than they would be if there were no abs. use in Ac. The "way of the Lord (or God)" is here the divine plan and work of salvation, the way which God took, as the γραφαί (18:24) teach and τὰ περὶ τοῦ Ἰησοῦ (18:25) make plain. The phrase is related to the ὁδοὶ τοῦ κυρίου of 13:10 (→ 88), and it is hard to see how the abs. use can be equated with these expressions. [175] Nor does it seem possible that

---

[172] As against H. Schlier, → I, 182.

[173] Cf. Pr.-Bauer³, s.v., 2. c : "after the doctrine which they call the opinion of a school."

[174] 9:2 and 22:4 are the two places where ὁδός might best be regarded as the designation of Christians as a group (Gl. 1:13 is perhaps a par. to 22:4). Pr. Ag. uniformly has "teaching" for the refs. in Ac. Bauernfeind, op. cit. keeps "way" with his "way of faith" (though usually with some addition, e.g., the new or Christian way of faith). H. W. Beyer Ag. (NT Deutsch, 5) usually has "teaching," but prefers "trend" in 9:2 and "movement" in 22:4. The latter rendering seems at first sight to be a happy one, and one might be inclined to prefer it in other verses too, but it is best avoided in view of the false associations it might evoke (the connection between the German Weg and Bewegung has no significance for modern readers). If, of course, ὁδός denotes a group and is thus a sociological term, the idea of a political movement is a semasiological par.

[175] As against H. W. Beyer, who comments on 18:25 : "This (sc. the way of the Lord) is a designation for Christian teaching frequently found in Ac." In fact, this phrase does not occur in the other verses. Zn. Ag., 321 f. also mentions 18:25 (on 18:26, 668, n. 83) and declares : "The use of ἡ ὁδός in the sense of manner of doctrine or life demands, if it is to be intelligible, either an attributive gen. like τοῦ κυρίου in 18:25 (18:26 τοῦ θεοῦ vl.), or a demonstrative referring back to what has gone before, as in 22:4, or an equivalent relative clause, as in 24:14. Only when there is repetition after a brief interval, e.g., 24:22

the abs. use should have developed out of these expressions, for in them ὁδός does not mean "doctrine," "command" (or "commanded walk"), but "walk," and the reference is to God's way rather than man's. For the same reason the phrases in 13:10; 18:25 f. are to be differentiated from ὁδὸς τῆς ἀληθείας in 2 Pt. 2:2 (→ 86) and ὁδὸς τῆς δικαιοσύνης in 2 Pt. 2:21 (→ 87). In particular, one cannot link Ac. 18:25 f. with 2 Pt. 2:2, 21 or Ac. 16:17 (→ 85) and Lk. 20:21 (→ 87), and draw therefrom the conclusion that "it makes sense that Christianity as the religion of 'the way' to God should be called ἡ ὁδός." [176] In these verses we are dealing with many different senses of ὁδός which cannot be brought under the common denominator of "way to God" and from which the absolute use cannot, then, be smoothly derived. Moreover, if the sense of "doctrine" is not present in ὁδὸς τῆς σωτηρίας (Ac. 16:17), ὁδὸς τῆς ἀληθείας (2 Pt. 2:2) and ὁδὸς τῆς δικαιοσύνης (2:21) (→ supra), the abs. use in Ac. finds no parallel whatever in the NT. Nor does there seem to be any influence of the OT [177] or later Jewish usage. [178] The only possible par. is the way in which Damasc., I, 13; II, 6 (→ 57) speaks of the way. In II, 6 apostates are described as "those who deviate from the way and despise the law." In I, 13 this community of the faithless is equated with those who "diverge from the way." Along with other connections between Damasc. and the NT [179] this use might call for notice, but until these connections are more firmly established it is best not to overestimate the agreement. If one might conclude from Luc. Hermot., 46 that from the sense of (philosophical) "method" (→ 43) ὁδός acquired the broader sense of "system" or "school," [180] this would still be an isolated instance, and in any case it is most improbable that Luke would be so influenced by a philosophical use of ὁδός as to call the Christian message the way. The only possible conclusion is that there is no solid explanation of the origin of this unique usage, which in the NT is limited to Ac., and which found no immediate imitators in the period which followed (→ 93; 96).

The verses 18:25 f. and 13:10, which we have discussed already (→ 89; 87), relate ὁδός to the ways which God Himself takes. In 18:25 f. the reference is to His whole plan of salvation, in 13:10 to its fulfilment through mission. The two other verses which speak of God's ways in this sense stand in a similar context. In the rapt exclamation in R. 11:33: ὡς ἀνεξερεύνητα τὰ κρίματα αὐτοῦ καὶ ἀνεξιχνίαστοι αἱ ὁδοὶ αὐτοῦ, Paul has in view God's past, present and future plan for the Jewish people; His judgment is indicated by κρίματα (→ III, 942), His deliverance by ὁδοί. [181] In Rev. 15:3, on the basis of OT statements like

after 24:14, probably also 18:26 after 18:25, and then immediately again 19:9, 23, does the mere ἡ ὁδός suffice." This elimination of the abs. use will hardly do in 22:4; 24:14; 24:22, and is quite impossible in 19:9, 23. One should assume at once that the abs. use does occur in Ac., and that 18:25 is thus no true par.

[176] Wbg. Pt., 215, n. 31.

[177] Cr.-Kö., s.v., 3. c rightly opposes any appeal to Am. 8:14. Cf. also → n. 22.

[178] Zn. Ag., 322: "We are obviously dealing with a Jewish concept which has its roots in the OT and which finds expression in the common Rabb. combination דֶּרֶךְ אֶרֶץ." Cf. Str.-B., II, 690 on Ac. 9:2 and → n. 48. This would yield the sense "manner," "particular attitude," but not the abs. use.

[179] Cf. H. Preisker, "Jerusalem u. Damaskus — ein Beitrag zum Verständnis d. Urchristentums," ThBl, 8 (1929), 49 ff.

[180] Cr.-Kö., s.v., 3. c, who adduces the passage in full, believes that this is so, though the sense "method" is also supported.

[181] The sense "ways and means" (cf. P. Althaus R. [NT Deutsch, 6] ad loc.) is not necessary here; the ref. may well be to God's guidance in history and salvation history, i.e., to His way through history, → 55.

Dt. 32:4; ψ 144:17 (→ 55), the song of those who overcome contains the saying: δίκαιαι καὶ ἀληθιναὶ αἱ ὁδοί σου.

D. Christian Usage up to the Apologists.

ὁδός in the lit. sense is comparatively rare in the post-apost. fathers. ἡ ὁδὸς ἡ Καμπανή is mentioned in Herm. v., 4, 1, 2, and it is called ἡ ὁδὸς ἡ δημοσία (→ 42). [182] Again, the allegory of the building of the tower in v., 3, 2, 9 refers to the stones which fall from the tower on to the way, yet do not remain on the way, but roll ἐκ τῆς ὁδοῦ εἰς τὴν ἀνοδίαν. In the interpretation in 3, 7, 1 it is said of these stones: οὗτοί εἰσιν οἱ πεπιστευκότες μέν, ἀπὸ δὲ τῆς διψυχίας αὐτῶν ἀφίουσιν τὴν ὁδὸν αὐτῶν τὴν ἀληθινήν, and it is added: δοκοῦντες οὖν βελτίονα ὁδὸν δύνασθαι εὑρεῖν, πλανῶνται καὶ ταλαιπωροῦσιν περιπατοῦντες ἐν ταῖς ἀνοδίαις. The interpretation is not in full accord with the allegory, since it expounds only the second part. The antithesis of ὁδός and ἀνοδία (common in Philo, → 62) is exploited. The supposedly better way which was expected later proves to be no way at all, a trackless land. The previous way is thus called the only true way (their true way, because they were already on it). To leave this way is to renounce faith. What is not explained, however, is leaving the tower, which would seem to involve both abandoning the faith and leaving the community. The fact that the stones fall from the tower shows that they are unserviceable, and even if they had remained on the way they would not have been in their proper place. Hence in the allegory the way is already the sphere of apostasy in comparison with the tower, which is interpreted as the ἐκκλησία in 3, 3, 3. In the interpretation, however, it is the sphere of faith. Whether or not this later view of the way influenced its mention in the allegory itself, the fact that the way could take on this independent significance as compared with the tower can be explained only on the assumption that ὁδός was in common use in the sense presupposed in the interpretation. In the context the ref. is not so much to the way of life; though ὁδός does not have to mean "religion" or "religious teaching," [183] it denotes a man's religious attitude or development.

In Ign. R., 9, 3 we read: καὶ γὰρ αἱ μὴ προσήκουσαί μοι (sc. ἐκκλησίαι) τῇ ὁδῷ τῇ κατὰ σάρκα, κατὰ πόλιν με προῆγον. This saying expounds the ἀγάπη τῶν ἐκκλησιῶν τῶν δεξαμένων με κτλ. which precedes. It seeks to emphasise that the churches (Ephesus, Magnesia, Tralles) which lay apart from the route taken by Ignatius' escort through Asia Minor have also received him inasmuch as their delegations were waiting for him in towns through which he passed (e.g., Smyrna). [184] Though no μου is used, the ὁδός is obviously the way of Ign. The thought is not very clearly expressed, since the delegations of these churches crossed his path at the places where they waited for him. It would have been clearer to say that the churches which I did not come to on my way have nevertheless brought about a meeting with me. If the way of Ign. is called one κατὰ σάρκα, this is controlled by the fact that the μὴ προσήκουσαί μοι is not meant so exclusively as it first sounds. What he is making clear in this addition is in what connection these churches did not exercise προσήκειν, namely, τῇ ὁδῷ τῇ κατὰ σάρκα, i.e., in such a way that they could greet Ign. in their own cities. His way κατὰ σάρκα did not lead him to them. This does not mean that there was another way, or that his way might be considered from another standpoint. Nor does the meaning have to be that contrasted with his way κατὰ σάρκα is "an-

---

[182] Cf. Dib. Herm., ad loc.

[183] Pr.-Bauer³, s.v., 2. b quotes this passage among examples of the sense "walk." Dib. Herm. on v., 3, 7, 1 regards the seeking of a better way as seeking of a new, non-Christian mystery of salvation.

[184] Cf. Bau. Ign., ad loc.

other ὁδός, or other ὁδοί, on which every believer could meet him." [185] The addition κατὰ σάρκα is not meant to differentiate this way from another, but to describe the way at issue. It is a way on which Ign. is no longer a free agent, a way whose external course is wholly under the control of earthly powers. The sense of way or route perhaps contains a hint of "journey," which occurs elsewhere in the post-apost. fathers only at 1 Cl., 12, 4 (the story of Rahab, Jos. 2; → 69).

In the post-apost. fathers ὁδός is mostly used fig., though the idea of a way is strongly present. In Ign. Eph., 9, 1 ἀγάπη is described as ὁδὸς ἡ ἀναφέρουσα; just before πίστις is described as an ἀναγωγεύς ὑμῶν. The two images belong together. ἀναγωγεύς does not correspond to the previously mentioned μηχανή. It is not a device for lifting (nor can ὁδός have the sense of "means," since this implies a possibility rather than an instrument). ἀναγωγεύς is the one who leads above, [186] just as the way is one which leads upwards (cf. the preceding metaphor of the movement εἰς τὰ ὕψη which controls the stones). "Way to God" is an expression found neither in the OT nor the NT, but it has pars. in Philo (→ 61). The summons in 1 Cl., 31, 1: ἴδωμεν τίνες αἱ ὁδοὶ τῆς εὐλογίας, does not refer to the ways of God, to the possibilities which He has of blessing (if so, this would be the only ref. to the ways of God in the post-apost. fathers). It speaks of the ways in which men can attain to the blessing of God, unless the sense is that of "walk" or "conduct" (the walk which can count on God's blessing). ὁδός can also mean "behaviour" in 1 Cl., 36, 1, though the clause: ἐν ᾗ εὕρομεν τὸ σωτήριον ἡμῶν, seems to favour the sense of "nature and manner." [187]

The sense "walk," "conduct," occurs in 1 Cl., 16, 6 (= Is. 53:6); Herm. v., 2, 2, 6. How far the original sense can fade into the background may be seen in 1 Cl., 57, 6 (= Prv. 1:31; → 50) and Barn., 4, 10 : τὰ ἔργα τῆς πονηρᾶς ὁδοῦ. The term "way of God" (the walk which God requires of man ; cf. 1 Cl., 53, 2 = Ex. 32:8) is found in

---

[185] As against Bau. Ign., ad loc. A big argument against this view is that the ref. is to the way of Ign., not of the community, so that one would expect the thought to be worked out more fully. Moreover, one would have to assume that this other way, which would be incomparably more important, would be known to the readers in these terms. ὁδός, however, is found elsewhere in Ign. only in Eph., 9, 1; Magn., 5, 1 (→ 92; 93). Bau. refers to the use of ὁδός in verses like Mt. 22:16; Ac. 18:26; 1 C. 4:17 etc., but these hardly seem to have influenced Ign. (quite apart from the fact that the usage in these passages is not uniform). If in R., 9, 3 Ign. is alluding to other possibilities of a meeting between bishop and congregation one could supplement κατὰ σάρκα by, e.g., κατὰ πίστιν, κατὰ ἀγάπην (Eph., 2, 1) or κατὰ ὁμόνοιαν (cf. the list in Phld., 11, 2). H. Schlier, "Religionsgeschichtliche Untersuchungen zu den Ignatiusbriefen," Beihefte zur ZNW, 8 (1929), 136 believes that to the ὁδὸς κατὰ σάρκα "there corresponds a ὁδὸς κατὰ πνεῦμα after death," but this could not be a way on which every believer could meet Ign. In any case, the allotting of σάρξ and πνεῦμα to the times before and after death is without par. in Ign. Schlier, 136 ff. tries to see in Ign. the idea of the heavenly journey of the martyr or pneumatic which begins already on earth. It should be noted, however, that this idea finds no expression in a corresponding use of ὁδός.

[186] Cf. Bau. Ign., ad loc.; Pr.-Bauer³, s.v.; Iambl., II, 7 (p. 84, Parthey): μετὰ τοῦ ἀναγωγοῦ ἡγεμόνος. Schlier, op. cit., 136 f. also relates Eph., 9, 1 to the heavenly journey of the martyr or believer, but the context does not refer to martyrdom, and no strong emphasis is laid on the image of the way. The σύνοδοι in 9, 2 (only here in Ign. and the post-apost. fathers) relates to the practice of love and fulfilment of the commands of Jesus Christ, and the added epithets, though taken from the vocabulary of processions, weaken the idea of the way. Cf. H. W. Bartsch, "Gnostisches Gut u. Gemeindetradition bei Ign. v. Antiochien," BFTh, 2. Reihe, 44 (1940), 30, 74 f., 80, n. 2.

[187] 36, 1 is linked with the preceding quotation from ψ 49:23 in 35, 12, which is quoted in the form ἐκεῖ ὁδός, ἣν δείξω αὐτῷ κτλ. The LXX has ᾗ δείξω (though cf. the vl. ἥν in A. Rahlfs, Psalmi cum Odis [1931], ad loc.); whereas the Mas. has in view the "walk," the LXX perhaps uses ὁδός in the sense of "nature and manner." On 1 Cl., 31, 1 cf. for another view Stauffer Theol., 184, 188; n. 684, 775 (cf. → n. 39, 148).

1 Cl., 18, 13 (→ ψ 50:13); Apc. Pt., 34. In the same connection one might mention ὁδὸς τῆς ἀληθείας, the way or walk which is prescribed and therefore right (→ 52; 86), 1 Cl., 35, 5; in the same sense ὁδὸς δικαιοσύνης, Barn., 1, 4; ὁδὸς δικαία, 2 Cl., 5, 7; Barn., 12, 4 (= Is. 65:2, with the synon. ὁδὸς ἀληθινή or οὐ καλή in what follows). In 2 Cl., 7, 3 ὁδὸς εὐθεῖα is fitted into the context with its picture of the race, but one may also discern the influence of the OT ὁδὸς εὐθεῖα, "the way commanded by God" (→ 52; 86); cf. Herm. v., 3, 5, 3 : ἐπορεύθησαν ἐν τῇ εὐθύτητι τοῦ κυρίου (= κατωρθώσαντο τὰς ἐντολὰς αὐτοῦ). If in some of these passages, as elsewhere when the ref. is to the walk demanded by God, ὁδός approximates to the sense of "command," this (→ 51; 88) special use may be seen more clearly in Apc. Pt., 1: ὁδοὺς καὶ δόγματα ποικίλα τῆς ἀπωλείας διδάξουσιν. [188]

In this Apc. one also finds a use of ὁδός of which there is no certain example in the NT in view of the fact that ὁδὸς (τῆς) δικαιοσύνης or τῆς ἀληθείας cannot be regarded as designations of the Christian religion (→ 86) and the abs. use in Ac. (→ 88 ff.) is a phenomenon *sui generis*. Apc. Pt., 2, 2 speaks of οἱ βλασφημοῦντες τὴν ὁδὸν τῆς δικαιοσύνης; cf. οἱ βλασφημήσαντες καὶ κακῶς εἰπόντες τὴν ὁδὸν τῆς δικ. 28. What is in view is obviously not the "walk," but the Gospel or the Christian faith. ὁδὸς τῆς δικαιοσύνης might mean the "right way" (→ 52; 86 supra), here in the sense of the "right faith" or "right religion." Yet the use of δικαιοσύνη in 22, and the description of Christians as οἱ δίκαιοι in 5, 13 f., 20, 25, 27 seems to support the view that δικαιοσύνη means "righteousness," "piety," so that ὁδὸς τῆς δικ. is "the religion of (Christian) δικαιοσύνη," "the δικαιοσύνη religion" ("the Christian religion which alone can be claimed as ὁδός"). In both cases ὁδός would then mean "teaching," "religion," "faith," as a total position. Did., 6, 1: ὅρα, μή τίς σε πλανήσῃ ἀπὸ ταύτης τῆς ὁδοῦ τῆς διδαχῆς, is to be taken differently. Here ὁδός does not mean "teaching," but διδαχή is the way. This figure is linked with the use of πλανᾶν.

The metaphor of the two ways occupies a special place in the post-apost. fathers. One can hardly adduce Barn., 4, 10, which mentions only the πονηρὰ ὁδός (→ 92), nor is Herm. v., 3, 7, 1 (→ 91) an example. [189] Again, while the metaphor of going is present in Ign. Magn., 5, 1: ἕκαστος εἰς τὸν ἴδιον τόπον μέλλει χωρεῖν, there is no actual ref. to two ways ; death and life are simply the two destinations. On the other hand, the use of ψ 1:1 in Barn., 10, 10 might be mentioned, esp. as ψ 1:6 is quoted in 11, 7. Barn., 5, 4 is also relevant : δικαίως ἀπολεῖται ἄνθρωπος ὃς ἔχων ὁδοῦ δικαιοσύνης γνῶσιν ἑαυτὸν εἰς ὁδὸν σκότους ἀποσυνέχει. Here ὁδός cannot mean "teaching," and ὁδὸς δικαιοσύνης seems to mean more than the "right way" (cf. 1, 4, → supra), for ὁδὸς σκότους points too strongly to 18, 1. Hence ὁδὸς δικ. has a par. in the ὁδὸς φωτός of 18, 1, and it denotes a walk which takes place in righteousness and stands under its sign. Similarly, ὁδὸς σκότους in 5, 4 does not denote a way which leads to darkness, but a walk in darkness. The close connection between the senses "way" and "walk" may be seen precisely in the two passages which are the most important examples of the metaphor of the two ways in the post-apost. fathers, Barn., 18-20 and Did., 1-6. [190]

---

[188] Pr.-Bauer³, *s.v.* 2. a wrongly associates this passage with Mt. 7:13.

[189] As against C. Taylor, "The Two Ways in Hermas and Xenophon," *The Journal of Philology*, 21 (1893), 249, who finds in Herm. v., 3, 7, 1 "an express ref. to the Two Ways." In fact, the contrast is between ὁδός and ἀνοδία; only to the false hopes of apostates does ἀνοδία seem to be βελτίων ὁδός. Taylor, 251 links Herm. s., 8, 9, 1: αὕτη ἡ ὁδός (dealings with pagans) ἡδυτέρα αὐτοῖς (the censured rich Christians) ἐφαίνετο, with the expression τὴν ἡδίστην ... ὁδόν from the Prodicus fable in Xen. Mem., 2, 1, 23; but the Herm. passage is not a true example of the two ways. Apc. Pt. does not refer to two ways, but to Paradise and hell as two τόποι, as against Dieterich, *op. cit.*, 193.

[190] On the interrelation of the two passages cf. Wnd. Barn. and Kn. Did. On the title *Duae viae* in Rufinus, which can hardly refer to Herm. (rather Did.), cf. Zahn Kan., II, 243; Hennecke, 143; A. Hilgenfeld, Evangeliorum secundum Hebraeos ... quae supersunt (1884), 110 ff.

In both cases hortatory material is integrated into a two ways schema. The form in which this is done in the Did. is much more consistent and strict. The introduction in 1, 1: ὁδοὶ δύο εἰσί, μία τῆς ζωῆς καὶ μία τοῦ θανάτου, διαφορὰ δὲ πολλὴ μεταξὺ τῶν δύο ὁδῶν, is followed by the description of the way of life beginning in 1, 2 with the statement : ἡ μὲν οὖν ὁδὸς τῆς ζωῆς ἐστιν αὕτη, and closing in 4, 14 with the corresponding αὕτη ἐστὶν ἡ ὁδὸς τῆς ζωῆς. In 5, 1 the depiction of the ὁδός τοῦ θανάτου begins with the par. ἡ δὲ τοῦ θανάτου ὁδός ἐστιν αὕτη, but there is no par. ending in 5, 2, and in 6, 1 ὁδός is used in a way which is no longer orientated to the schema (→ 93, 23 ff.). Hence 6, 1 as well as 6, 2 f. is supplementary. In 1, 1 etc. ὁδός means "way." The ref. is to two opposing ways, the one to life and the other to death. The sense of "walk" is implied only in so far as the two ways relate to the walk. In the related passage in Barn., 18-20 there is no ὁδός (τῆς) ζωῆς, and though ὁδός θανάτου occurs, it is not a true catchword for the schema (cf. 19, 2 : οὐ κολληθήσῃ μετὰ τῶν πορευομένων ἐν ὁδῷ θανάτου; 20, 1: ὁδός γάρ ἐστιν θανάτου αἰωνίου). The schema itself is controlled by the antitheses φῶς and σκότος. The intr. corresponding to Did., 1, 1 in Barn., 18, 1 runs as follows : ὁδοὶ δύο εἰσὶν διδαχῆς καὶ ἐξουσίας, ἥ τε τοῦ φωτὸς καὶ ἡ τοῦ σκότους. διαφορὰ δὲ πολλὴ τῶν δύο ὁδῶν. Accordingly the description of the ὁδός τοῦ φωτός begins with the statement in 19, 1: ἡ οὖν ὁδὸς τοῦ φωτός ἐστιν αὕτη, and closes in 19, 12 : αὕτη ἐστὶν ἡ ὁδὸς τοῦ φωτός. In the description of the ὁδός τοῦ σκότους, however, there is no introductory sentence which uses the expression. Instead, in 20, 1 we find a sentence which already describes the way : ἡ δὲ τοῦ μέλανος ὁδός ἐστιν σκολιὰ καὶ κατάρας μεστή, to which is added : ὁδός γάρ ἐστιν θανάτου αἰωνίου κτλ. While ὁδός θανάτου is the way which leads to death, ἡ τοῦ μέλανος ὁδός (τοῦ μέλανος is masc., → IV, 551) is the way (or walk) which is ruled by the black one, the way of subjection to the devil (cf. ἐξουσία, 18, 1). Similarly, ὁδός τοῦ φωτός or τοῦ σκότους is not the way which leads to light or darkness but the way which is controlled by light or darkness. That this is the true interpretation is shown by the sentence which follows the introductory 18, 1: ἐφ᾽ ἧς μὲν γὰρ εἰσιν τεταγμένοι φωταγωγοὶ ἄγγελοι τοῦ θεοῦ, ἐφ᾽ ἧς δὲ ἄγγελοι τοῦ σατανᾶ. The angels of God are called φωταγωγοί because they dispense light, not because they lead to it. The ref. to the two groups of angels has no par. in the Did., but there is assimilation to Barn., 18, 1 in the Lat. version of Did., 1, 1: *viae duae in saeculo, vitae et mortis, lucis et tenebrarum. In his constituti sunt angeli duo, unus aequitatis, alter iniquitatis* (cf. Herm. m., 6, 2, 1 ff. → 95, 11 ff.). Though the idea of ways underlies Barn., the fact that φῶς and σκότος are not the goals means that the sense "walk" is also implied (Barn., 19, 1: ἐάν τις θέλων ὁδὸν ὁδεύειν ἐπὶ τὸν ὡρισμένον τόπον, also applies the metaphor of the way to the walk).

Barn. is much further from Mt. 7:13 f. (→ C. 2. a) than Did., for ὁδός (τῆς) ζωῆς does not occur, and the antithesis of φῶς and σκότος is not related in any way to Mt. 7:13 f. Nevertheless, the Did. also diverges from the saying of Jesus by not echoing the ἀπώλεια which is there the antithesis of ζωή. Quite apart from the failure to combine πύλη and ὁδός as in Mt., both Did. and Barn. also differ from Mt. in the fact that detailed exhortation does not follow the dominical saying in Mt., and also in the fact that the Matthean description of the ways as broad and narrow is not reproduced in any form in either Did. or Barn. It is thus unlikely that Mt. 7:13 f. is the decisive influence behind the use of the schema of the two ways in Did. and Barn. The question thus arises where to seek other influences. The use of φῶς/σκότος in Barn. is perhaps connected, not so much with the liking for this antithesis in primitive Christian writings, but rather with the fact that Prv. 4:18 f. (→ 54) already links the category of light and darkness with the metaphor of the two ways, and that the same combination is found in Sl. En. 30:15 (→ 57) (cf. also the statement in Test. Lev., 9:1: ἐκλέξασθε ἑαυτοῖς ἢ τὸ φῶς ἢ τὸ σκότος ἢ τὸν νόμον κυρίου ἢ τὰ ἔργα τοῦ Βελιάρ, which, though it does not use the fig. of the two ways, is reminiscent of Dt. 11:26; 30:19). Barn., then, follows a definite Jewish tradition. Did., too, stands in this tradition inasmuch as the concepts death and life are also firmly linked with the metaphor of the two ways in

Judaism, → 59.[191] On the other hand, we have no proof that Judaism had a proselyte catechism containing the schema (and also the concepts life and death); indeed, observations have been made already to the effect that such an assumption is most improbable (→ 58; 59 f.). Whether one can deduce the existence of such a catechism merely from Did. and Barn. is certainly open to question.[192]

Jewish influence, which cannot be contested, is not impugned by the ref. to the ἄγγελοι τοῦ θεοῦ or τοῦ σατανᾶ in Barn., 18, 1. For, though it is tempting to see here the influence of the two women in the Prodicus fable (→ n. 2), one should not overlook differences which rule out any direct influence, in particular, the fact that the motif of the women is dominant in the fable, that of the two ways in Barn., 18, 1 f. Furthermore, the two angels appear also in Herm. m., 6, 2, 1 ff. in a form which manifests no relation whatever to the fable. To be sure, the schema of the two ways is present in m., 6, 1, 2 ff., but the two angels are independent of this, and in any case the schema here gives no evidence of the influence of the fable and related forms, → *infra*. The appearance of the two angels in Barn., 18, 1 is thus to be derived from a Jewish rather than a non-Jewish view.[193]

This feature, which found its way into the Lat. version of the Did. (→ 94), was readily maintained, varied, and combined with motifs from the Prodicus fable and Hes. Op., 287 ff. (→ 43 f.) in the period which followed. The depiction of the two ways in Ps. Cl. Hom., VII, 6 ff. combines features from Mt. 7:13 f., Hes. and the Prodicus fable. Πίστις and Ἀπιστία are mentioned instead of the angels [194] (in XX, 2, however, the metaphor of the two ways is linked with the idea of βασιλεῖαι, and we have two kings instead of the angels). Cf. also Ps. Cl. Recg., VIII, 54. In Bas. Homilia in Ps. 1:5 (→ n. 12) the description of the two ways is orientated to Mt. 7:13 f. and Hes.: καὶ δύο ὁδηγοί, ἑκάτερος πρὸς ἑαυτὸν ἐπιστρέφειν ἐπιχειρῶν. These two ὁδηγοί (cf. Lact., *loc. cit.* → n. 16: *utrique* [*sc. viae*] *praepositum esse ... ducem utrumque immortalem*) are then called the δαίμων πονηρός and ἄγγελος ἀγαθός. The fact that the two figures try to entice men to themselves reminds us of the Prodicus fable. In the hortatory compilation Ps.-Athanasius Syntagma Doctrinae (MPG, 28, 836 ff.; cf. also 1637 ff.), which is related in many details to the material in Barn., 19 f.; Did., 1 ff., the schema of the two ways plays no part.

As already pointed out, the metaphor does occur in Herm. m., 6, 1, 2 ff., and the ways are described (cf. Mt. 7:13 f., unlike Barn. and Did.). The sense of walk is thus less prominent. After the introduction of the antithesis of τὸ δίκαιον and τὸ ἄδικον in 6, 1, 1 there follows in 6, 1, 2 the admonition: σὺ οὖν πίστευε τῷ δικαίῳ, τῷ δὲ ἀδίκῳ μὴ πιστεύσῃς (on the basis: τὸ γὰρ δίκαιον ὀρθὴν ὁδὸν ἔχει, τὸ δὲ ἄδικον

---

[191] Corp. Herm., I, 28 f. is only a general par., since there is no special use of the metaphor. To be sure, we read in I, 29: τῇ τοῦ θανάτου ὁδῷ ἑαυτοὺς ἐκδεδωκότες, but I, 28 does not have the fig.: τί ἑαυτούς, ὦ ἄνδρες, εἰς θάνατον ἐκδεδώκατε, ἔχοντες ἐξουσίαν τῆς ἀθανασίας μεταλαβεῖν; (though cf. οἱ συνοδεύσαντες τῇ πλάνῃ in what follows). It should be noted that light and darkness are also used here as well as θάνατος/ἀθανασία: ἀπαλλάγητε τοῦ σκότους, ἅψασθε τοῦ φωτός (this conjecture of W. Scott, I, 132, *ad loc.* is surely correct, though cf. IV, 360).

[192] Cf. A. Seeberg and Dibelius (→ n. 170); Wnd. Barn.; Kn. Did.; Harnack, esp. 26 ff.; C. Taylor, *The Teaching of the Twelve Apostles with Illustrations from the Talmud* (1886). I cannot share the confidence with which these writers assume that there was a Jewish proselyte catechism under the title "The (Two) Ways."

[193] On the Jewish origin of the ref. to the two angels cf. Dib. Herm. on m., 6, 1, 1 and 6, 2, 1. Test. Jud. 20:1, of course, is not very convincing. But cf. bShab., 119b (Str.-B., I, 781).

[194] Taylor, *op. cit.* (→ n. 189), 257 conjectures that this version was much older, and that Herm. knew the two ways in this form, but the use of Πίστις and Ἀπιστία in a very different connection in s., 9, 15, 2 f. cannot weaken the objection that Herm. uses the metaphor differently even when he has it.

στρεβλήν). The advice: ἀλλὰ σὺ τῇ ὀρθῇ ὁδῷ πορεύου καὶ ὁμαλῇ, τὴν δὲ στρεβλὴν ἔασον is followed in 6, 1, 3 f. by a vivid description of the two ways. The crooked way has no τρίβοι, no specific paths; it offers only ἀνοδίαι and προσκόμματα πολλά; it is τραχεῖα καὶ ἀκανθώδης. The straight way, however, is level. It is neither rough nor overgrown, so that one does not stumble. It is thus best, συμφορώτερόν ἐστιν, to choose the straight way. This description is in its detail very reminiscent of Hes. (the ways are not portrayed so graphically in the fable), though the vocabulary is different (apart from τραχύς). It bears no relation to Mt. 7:13 f. A distinctive feature is that the way one should take if one would cleave to the δίκαιον is described as smooth and easy. [195] For this there are no par. in the use of the schema; only in Philo is there anything comparable (→ 61; 64), and there is no reason to assume that Philo had any influence on Herm. This peculiarity is an argument against any relation to Hes., the Prodicus fable, Mt. 7:13 f., Barn. or Did. Herm. is also shown to be independent of Barn. and Did. by the way in which he moves directly to the theme of the two angels in what follows in m., 6, 2, 1 ff. → 95. [196]

In comparison with the rich and manifold use in the post-apost. fathers ὁδός is of no significance in the Apologists. [197] Just. uses it some 50 times, but the vast majority of these refs. are quotations from the NT and esp. the OT (cf. ψ 2:12; 18:6; 49:23; Prv. 8:22; Is. 40:3; 55:8, in some cases more than once). Biblical usage is to be noted in some of the few instances of ὁδός in Just. outside quotations: Dial., 8, 2; 39, 2; the way of the stars in 85, 5. Worth noting is 88, 2 which says of John the Baptist: τὴν τοῦ βαπτίσματος ὁδὸν προϊών; what is meant is that his way as precursor is characterised by his baptising. Since Just. also uses δι' ἧς or ταύτης τῆς ὁδοῦ in 44, 4; 100, 4, in the final statement of the Dial. in 142, 3 διὰ ταύτης τῆς ὁδοῦ has thus the sense of "in this way." Here, then, ὁδός is not a term for Christianity or Christian teaching. Nor is this the sense (→ 88; 93) in Tert. De Oratione, 11. [198] If here, in exposition of Gn. 45:24: et ne irascimini in via, we read: nos scilicet monuit. Alias enim via cognominatur disciplina nostra, the alias obviously refers to other biblical passages which speak of the way and which also relate to the Christian walk, cf. the statement which follows: tum ne, in via orationis constituti, ad patrem cum ira incedamus. Inasmuch as the passage does not refer to ecclesiastical use at the time, it is an indirect witness to the fact that in Tert.'s day "way" was not a current term for Christian teaching, though this sense finds attestation in the letter of the churches of Vienne and Lyons in Eus. Hist. Eccl., V, 1, 48: διὰ τῆς ἀναστροφῆς αὐτῶν βλασφημοῦντες τὴν ὁδόν.

---

[195] Dib. Herm., ad loc. rightly points out that "the ethos of the dominical saying in Mt. 7:13 and that of the Prodicus fable" are missing, and that instead "a certain opportunism" is "the presupposition."

[196] Dib. Herm. quotes Qoh. r. on 1:14 (→ n. 51) and says in conclusion: "Here we obviously have a combination of teaching on the ways with this type of variation on the Prodicus fable, but the use of the metaphor is opportunist and rationalistic." The Rabb. passage, which speaks of ways in the lit. sense, refers to an old man who sits at the crossroads and earns the thanks of passers-by by showing them that what seems at first to be the way is later full of thorns and cedars and reeds, whereas the other way which at first seems to be blocked is later smooth. This is, however, a distinctive development which is closer to Hes. than the fable, but hardly influenced by either. It is best not to try to relate either this Rabb. ref. or the Herm. passage to literary variations on the fable. They are independent versions on the basis of the popular use of the idea of two different ways.

[197] Cf. E. J. Goodspeed, Index apologeticus (1912), s.v.

[198] As against Harnack (→ n. 46), 38.

† ὁδηγός, † ὁδηγέω.

The noun ὁδηγός (the Doric ὁδαγός is also found even in Atticists), and the derived verb ὁδηγέω, are mostly used lit., more rarely fig. ὁδηγός has the sense of "leader" (on a way), fig. "teacher," "guide," ὁδηγέω (always with acc. of person) "to lead on a way," "to show the way," fig. "to guide," "to instruct." ¹ Neither word seems to be attested on inscr., but both occur on pap. (from the 3rd cent. B.C.), usually lit. ² The fig. sense is prominent, however, when in Preis. Zaub., XIII, 523 ff. the soul is promised : πάντα κινήσεις καὶ πάντα ἱλαρυνθήσεται Ἑρμοῦ σε ὁδηγοῦντος. The word does not occur in connection with psychopompous deities etc., ³ nor does it play the prominent role one would expect in the Herm. lit. In Corp. Herm., 7, 2 we find the summons : ζητήσατε χειραγωγὸν τὸν ὁδηγήσοντα ὑμᾶς, ἐπὶ τὰς τῆς γνώσεως θύρας, and acc. to 10, 21 this task falls to the *nous* : εἰς δὲ τὴν εὐσεβῆ ψυχὴν ὁ νοῦς ἐμβὰς ὁδηγεῖ αὐτὴν ἐπὶ τὸ τῆς γνώσεως φῶς. The context of 7, 2 esp. shows how greatly spatial conceptions underlay this statement. ⁴ This is particularly so when the idea of the heavenly journey of the soul is present. 12, 12 refers to the ascent after death : ἐξελθὼν (sc. ὁ ἄνθρωπος) ἐκ τοῦ σώματος, ὁδηγηθήσεται ὑπὸ ἀμφοτέρων (sc. νοῦς and λόγος) εἰς τὸν τῶν θεῶν καὶ μακάρων χορόν; ⁵ cf. also 4, 11: εὑρήσεις τὴν πρὸς τὰ ἄνω ὁδόν (→ 47). μᾶλλον δὲ αὐτή σε ἡ εἰκὼν ὁδηγήσει (what is meant is ἡ τοῦ θεοῦ εἰκών, of which it is previously said : αὕτη σοι ... ὑπογέγραπται). ὁδηγός does not occur in Corp. Herm., but we find καθοδηγός, though in 1, 26 and 29 this is used for the author in the function transmitted to him by Poimandres to say to others (τοῖς ἀξίοις, 1, 26), πῶς καὶ τίνι τρόπῳ σωθήσονται (1, 29); hence the sense of "guide" or "teacher" is better than "leader" (→ III, 699 f.).

ὁδηγός is rare in the LXX. It is used for guides in 1 Macc. 4:2; 2 Macc. 5:15; 2 Εσδρ. 8:1, and in the same sense for the pillar of fire which showed the way by night during the wilderness journey, Wis. 18:3 (→ 98, 2 ff.). Wis. 7:15 says of God : αὐτὸς καὶ τῆς σοφίας ὁδηγός ἐστιν καὶ τῶν σοφῶν διορθωτής. ὁδηγέω occurs much more often, namely, 42 times (27 in Ps.). In 25 instances it is used for the Mas. נחה q or hi. In the overwhelming majority of cases ὁδηγεῖν is ascribed to God. Apart from verses from Prv., Qoh. and Wis., which we shall mention later, the only exceptions are Ex. 32:34 (Moses at God's command); ψ 44:4 (the king's right hand); Job 31:18 (here, as in the previous verse, the HT caused the translator some difficulty). Israel experienced God's

---

ὁ δ η γ ό ς, ὁ δ η γ έ ω. Etym. ὁδηγός from *ὁδο-αγός to ἄγω like στρατηγός from *στρατο-αγός etc. Cf. Debr. Gr. Wortb. § 118. On the connection between ἄγω and ὁδός Xen. Mem., 2, 1, 23 : ἐπὶ τὴν ῥάστην ὁδὸν ἄξω σε, though we also find ἡγήσασθαι ὁδόν (Hom.) [Debrunner].

¹ Cf. Pass., Liddell-Scott, Pr.-Bauer³, *s.v.*

² Preisigke Wört. has no instance of ὁδηγός, though cf. Preisigke Sammelbuch, 7173, 16 (as adj.: ὁδηγὰ πλοῖα, pilot boats); Preis. Zaub., XII, 224 (4th cent. A.D.): ὦ τῶν ἀνέμων ὁδηγοί; Mayser, I, 3² (1936), 164; *ibid.*, 262 συνοδηγός. On ὁδηγέω, cf. Preisigke Wört., II, 150 *s.v.*

³ The usual term is ἡγεμών, cf. F. Cumont, *Die orientalischen Religionen im röm. Heidentum*³ (1931), 271 f.; "Les vents et les anges psychopompes," *Pisciculi* (= *Antike u. Christentum,* Suppl. 1) (1939), 70 ff.; Rohde ⁷, ⁸, II, 387 f. Acc. to O. Eissfeldt, *Tempel u. Kulte syrischer Städte in hell.-röm. Zeit* (AO, 40) (1940), 54 the idea of guides of the dead is non-Semitic.

⁴ J. Kroll, *Die Lehren d. Herm. Trism.* (1914), 380 f. even thinks that "*gnosis* is thought of as a spatially understood kingdom."

⁵ Cf. on this W. Scott, Hermetica, IV, ed. A. S. Ferguson (1936), 384 f. νοῦς and λόγος are not thought of as persons but as divine powers lent to man. In Corp. Herm., 9, 10 it is said of the νοῦς of the adept that it is led beyond the λόγος (i.e., the τέλειος λόγος, the teaching of Herm. Trism. who instructs it, cf. 9, 1), ὑπὸ τοῦ λόγου μέχρι τινὸς ὁδηγηθείς, and that it thereupon comes independently to the truth.

ὁδηγεῖν at the Exodus, Ex. 13:17; 15:13; Nu. 24:8; ψ 76:20; 77:53; 105:9; cf. also Is. 63:14 and 2 Βασ. 7:23 (= 1 Ch. 17:21). For God's preceding and showing the way by means of the cloud and pillar of fire, for which ἡγεῖσθαι is used in Ex. 13:21, Dt. 1:33; 2 Εσδρ. 19:12, 19; ψ 77:14 have ὁδηγεῖν. Lit. (as in the preceding verses), ὁδηγέω is also used of Abraham's wanderings in Jos. 24:3. On the other hand, in ψ 66:5 we find the fig. sense "to lead," "to guide," "to help" (ἔθνη ἐν τῇ γῇ ὁδηγήσεις). This dominates all the other refs. in Ps., which speak of God's care for the righteous. Along with some plur. expressions (ψ 24:9; 77:72; 106:7, 30; cf. 89:16) we also find statements in which the individual confesses that he has experienced, or hopes to experience, the ὁδηγεῖν of God (ψ 22:3; 30:3; 60:2; 72:24). In particular, the individual prays for God's ὁδηγεῖν, ψ 5:8; 24:5; 26:11; 85:11; 118:35; 138:24 (cf. also the question in ψ 59:9 [= 107:10]; cf. 59:10 [= 107:11]). The spatial sense comes out in various ways when ὁδηγέω is used with ὁδός or τρίβος or par. terms (which are also fig.) in ψ 22:3; 26:11; 85:11; 106:7; 118:35; 138:24. It occurs with ποιμαίνω in ψ 77:72; 79:1 (cf. also 22:3 with v. 1). On the other hand, it is par. to διδάσκω in ψ 24:5, 9; 142:10, and to νομοθετέω in 26:11. Hence the meaning "to teach," "to instruct," is strong. In addition to passages which mention God there are also some indirect expressions: ἡ χείρ σου ὁδηγήσει με, ψ 138:10; αὐτά (sc. God's φῶς and ἀλήθεια) με ὡδήγησαν, 42:3; τό πνεῦμά σου τὸ ἀγαθόν (vl. ἅγιον) ὁδηγήσει με ἐν γῇ εὐθείᾳ 142:10. [6]

Different from all the verses in which God is the subject of ὁδηγεῖν is Prv. 11:3 BS: τελειότης εὐθείων ὁδηγήσει αὐτούς. Related is Qoh. 2:3: καρδία μου ὡδήγησεν ἐν σοφίᾳ, which is also close to Wis. 9:11; 10:10, 17, where σοφία is the subject. This again corresponds to the high estimation of σοφία. "For the author of Wis. it can take the place of God, it has become a hypostasis, or is at least on the way to doing so." [7] As ὁδοὶ σοφίας is in the Wis. lit. par. to ὁδοὶ κυρίου (→ 52), so ὁδηγεῖν is ascribed to σοφία in Wis. The ὁδηγήσει με ἐν ταῖς πράξεσί μου σωφρόνως of 9:11 finds a par. in many OT verses in which ὁδηγεῖν is used for God's care and guidance (→ supra). In 10:17 there is a clear allusion to Ex. 13:21 when we read: ὡδήγησεν αὐτοὺς ἐν ὁδῷ θαυμαστῇ; this verse, too, finds a par. in the instances given → supra. Finally the αὕτη φυγάδα ὀργῆς ἀδελφοῦ δίκαιον ὡδήγησεν ἐν τρίβοις εὐθείαις of 10:10 has in view Jacob's flight, cf. Jos. 24:3 (→ supra). Since the ὁδηγέω verses in Wis. all have OT pars. which make the same statements of God, it may be seen that this is simply a development within the OT itself. It is thus not only unnecessary, but mistaken, to link the usage of Wis. with statements like that in Preis. Zaub., XIII, 523 ff. (→ 97) rather than with its OT pars. [8]

ὁδηγός occurs only once in Philo at Vit. Mos., I, 178 (ἡ ὁδηγὸς νεφέλη, hence as adj. → n. 2). Philo has ἡγεμὼν τῆς ὁδοῦ both lit. in Virt., 7, where he speaks of those who lean on a blind man and use a blinded man as guide ἡγεμόνι τῆς ὁδοῦ χρώμενοι πεπηρωμένῳ, and also fig. in places where he speaks of those who lead to virtue etc., God esp. being the ἡγεμὼν τῆς ὁδοῦ (→ 64). He does not have ὁδηγέω, though several times we find ποδηγετέω (from πούς and ἡγέομαι). [9] Thus in Deus Imm., 182 he calls the θεῖος λόγος an ἄγγελος ποδηγετῶν καὶ τὰ ἐν ποσὶν ἀναστέλλων, an angel who leads and who sets aside that on which our feet might stumble (ψ 90:11 f.). In Poster. C., 31 it is God Himself who promises guidance to the soul in search of help (ποδηγετοῦντος ἐμοῦ). In respect of Jn. 16:13 Vit. Mos., II (III), 265 is also worth noting: ὁ γὰρ νοῦς οὐκ ἂν οὕτως εὐσκόπως εὐθυβόλησεν, εἰ μὴ καὶ θεῖον ἦν πνεῦμα τὸ ποδηγετοῦν πρὸς αὐτὴν τὴν ἀλήθειαν, cf. Gig., 55: τούτῳ (sc. Moses)

---

[6] Cf. L. Köhler, Theol. d. AT (1936), 98. On πνεῦμα ἀγαθόν cf. Lk. 11:13 P [45] L etc.

[7] J. Fichtner, "Weisheit Salomos," Handb. z. AT, II, 6 (1938), 31 on 7:15-21. If in 7:15 God is described as τῆς σοφίας ὁδηγός (→ 97, 27 ff.), in 7:21 σοφία is the teacher.

[8] As against Reitzenstein Poim., 23 and n. 5; also Zwei religionsgeschichtliche Fragen (1901), 111 and n. 14.

[9] Cf. Leisegang, s.v. (ποδηγός occurs in Leg. All., III, 109). ποδηγετέω is rare outside Philo; ποδηγέω is found already in Plato. Cf. Pass. and Liddell-Scott, svv.

μὲν οὖν τὸ θεῖον ἀεὶ παρίσταται πνεῦμα πάσης ὀρθῆς ἀφηγούμενον ὁδοῦ. Joseph. uses ὁδηγός in Ant., 6, 362; 12, 305; 15, 348 of guides who know the way in military expeditions; cf. also 1, 217 of Hagar : ὁδηγῷ τῇ ἀνάγκῃ χρωμένην. ὁδηγέω is also used lit. in, e.g., Vit., 96; Ant., 3, 309 (here very unusually with the dat.); Bell., 5, 417: ἐπὶ ταῦτά τις ὁδηγεῖ φλόγα; "will someone show by torch the way to such glories ?" The rare noun ὁδηγία [10] occurs in Ant., 15, 347: εἰ μὴ τρίβῳ χρῷτό τις ἐξ ὁδηγίας, "in case one cannot use a way with the help of direction."

The idea of angels guiding a man on his way and in his actions is common in the Rabb. writings. These are called accompanying angels, e.g., bShab., 119b, but mostly ministering angels. [11] Later they have the task of fetching the souls of the righteous after death. [12] It is evident that this is a development from the presuppositions of Jewish angelology and has nothing to do with non-biblical ideas on conductors of souls (→ 97) cf. esp. Lk. 16:22.

ὁδηγέω occurs several times in Test. XII : R. 2:9; Jud. 14:1; 19:1; G. 5:7: true μετάνοια ... ὁδηγεῖ τὸ συμβούλιον πρὸς σωτηρίαν; B. 6:1: ὁ δὲ ἄγγελος τῆς εἰρήνης ὁδηγεῖ τὴν ψυχὴν αὐτοῦ; cf. D. 5:4. In S. Bar. 83:7 (VIII, 4, 8, Violet) one should perhaps conjecture ἡγούμενος or ὁδηγός for "ruler" (God as ruler of the world).

ὁδηγός is found in the NT only in the lit. sense of "leader," "escort." Judas is called this in Ac. 1:16 because he led the police to the place where they could arrest Jesus. When Jesus calls the Pharisees ὁδηγοὶ τυφλοί, which is used twice in the speech against them in Mt. 23 (v. 16, 24), both ὁδηγός and → τυφλός are fig., but the meaning is the lit. one of "guides" rather than "teachers." The Pharisees make out that they are the guides of others, but they themselves are blind. They will necessarily miss the right way and lead astray those who trust in them (cf. the twofold charge in 23:13b). It does not need to be assumed that the Pharisees regard those whom they seek to lead as blind and in need of leaders, for even those who see can seek guides when they do not know the way. Nevertheless, the judgment on the Pharisees in Mt. 15:14a : τυφλοί εἰσιν ὁδηγοὶ τυφλῶν, [13] shows that Jesus is probably thinking of blind leaders of the blind in 23:16, 24. [14] This is further suggested by the fact that Paul's description (of the Ἰουδαῖος) in R. 2:19 : πέποιθάς τε σεαυτὸν ὁδηγὸν εἶναι τυφλῶν, surely owes its origin to the judgment of Jesus, which Paul must have known. [15] Even if

---

[10] Pass. and Liddell-Scott have examples only from the 6th and 12th cent. A.D.

[11] Cf. Str.-B., IV, 1230, Index, s.v., "Geleitsengel," esp. I, 781 ff.; III, 437 ff. Cf. → I, 82, IV, 231, 28 f. It is understandable that there are no similar statements about the Messiah, who is not an angelic being.

[12] Str.-B., II, 223 f.

[13] τυφλῶν does not occur in אBD et al. (cf. Zn. Mt.⁴, 521, n. 30). It might have been deduced from what follows, though even if this is an independent saying (→ n. 16) it shows how familiar to Jesus was the metaphor of the blind leading the blind.

[14] The proverbial idea that one should not choose a blind guide is found elsewhere. Cf. the par. in Kl. Mt. on 15:14. Plato has ἡγεμὼν τοῦ χοροῦ in this connection (Resp., VIII, 554b), and Philo ἡγεμὼν τῆς ὁδοῦ (Virt., 7, → 98). It is presupposed also in Test. Reub. 2:9 that a blind man cannot prevent himself from being led to destruction. There are in the NT and primitive Christian exhortation no instances of the admonition to help and lead the blind (e.g., Ps.-Phocylides, 24 = Sib., 2, 84 : τυφλὸν ὁδήγει). This positive injunction is to be distinguished from the negative one in Lv. 19:14; Dt. 27:18 (cf. Philo Spec. Leg., III, 107 ff., IV, 197 f.), namely, that one should not put obstacles in the way of a blind man, or lead him astray.

[15] There are no par. which would permit us to assume that Paul is here characterising himself as a Jew. The promise of Is. 42:7 which Lagrange quotes (cf. Ltzm. R., ad loc.) refers to the granting of sight to the blind, not to their finding of a guide. The passage in Sib., III, 195 : οἳ πάντεσσι βροτοῖσι βίου καθοδηγοὶ ἔσονται (cf. Eth. En. 105:1), which

ὁδηγὸς τυφλῶν is par. and largely synonymous with the predicates παιδευτής ἀφρόνων and διδάσκαλος νηπίων in 2:20, yet within the image it has the meaning "guide" rather than "teacher."

ὁδηγέω is used in the lit. sense at Mt. 15:14b par. Lk. 6:39 of leading or escorting the blind, [16] cf. also Rev. 7:17 (alluding to ψ 22:2 f.). [17] The fig. sense "to instruct" is found in Ac. 8:31 in the question of the treasurer: πῶς γὰρ ἂν δυναίμην ἐὰν μή τις ὁδηγήσει με;

ὁδηγέω also occurs in Jn. 16:13. Here, in the fifth and last of the Paraclete sayings, we read: ὅταν δὲ ἔλθῃ ἐκεῖνος, τὸ πνεῦμα τῆς ἀληθείας, ὁδηγήσει ὑμᾶς εἰς τὴν ἀλήθειαν πᾶσαν. This reading suggests that ὁδηγέω should be taken in the sense "to lead," "to guide"; the full truth — under the influence of the spatial metaphor of the way — is the goal to which the Spirit will lead the disciples. ψ 24:5 and 142:10 might be adduced in support of this interpretation. Nevertheless, it should not be overlooked that at ψ 24:5: ὁδήγησόν με ἐπὶ τὴν ἀλήθειάν σου, א A read ἐν τῇ ἀληθείᾳ, which corresponds to the HT, where the underlying figure of the way or walk is clearer (הַדְרִיכֵנִי בַאֲמִתֶּךָ). On the other hand, in ψ 142:10, which is important because ὁδηγεῖν is here, too ascribed to the πνεῦμα (→ 98), it should be noted that the spatial metaphor predominates far more clearly than in Jn. 16:13 (the same could be said of the instances from Philo quoted → 98). One certainly cannot argue against the above interpretation of Jn. 16:13 that a promise "that the Spirit will successfully lead the disciples to a knowledge of all truth, and keep them from all error," is ruled out by the fact that "successful direction and guidance" demands "not only the expert and reliable guide but also the obedient traveller." [18] But one would certainly have thought that the idea of the way and goal and direction would have played a greater role than it does in Jn.'s Gospel, and especially in the Paraclete sayings. When one notes that אD et al. read ἐν τῇ ἀληθείᾳ πάσῃ at Jn. 16:13, and when one considers that this was probably the original wording, [19] the question arises whether ὁδηγέω does not have here the sense "to instruct." It cannot be contested that the task of instruction can here be ascribed to the Spirit. As may be seen from what follows, He exercises ὁδηγεῖν as a λαλεῖν and ἀναγγέλλειν (cf. also the λέγειν of 16:12), and there is indeed a direct par. in 14:26: ἐκεῖνος ὑμᾶς διδάξει πάντα. [20] This instructing or teaching of the Spirit continues, supplements and completes the proclamation

---

is adduced by Str.-B., III, 105, ad loc.; Zn. R., 137, n. 67a, and which deals with the future of the Jewish people, does not say at all that the blind need a guide. The content of the par. cited by Str.-B., I, 721 on Mt. 15:14 is also quite different.

[16] The original form of the saying is perhaps better preserved in Lk. with no ref. to the Pharisees ; cf. Kl. Mt. and Hck. Lk., ad loc.; Bultmann Trad., 103.

[17] Cf. W. Jost, ΠΟΙΜΗΝ (1939), 44 f.

[18] Zn. Jn. [5],[6], ad loc. The same objection may be brought against Jn. 14:26, which Zn. regards as a par. Successful teaching needs not only an expert and reliable teacher but also an obedient pupil (Zn. takes the fut. ὁδηγήσει to imply success).

[19] The reading with ἐν is unquestionably the more difficult, and in view of the idea of leading it is natural to turn the ἐν into εἰς. Cf. Schl. J., ad loc.; Zn. J. [5],[6], 593, n. 22. The solution of F. Büchsel, Der Geist Gottes im NT (1926), 500, n. 1, that the ἐν was probably original but that ἐν here = εἰς (on the infrequency of the change cf. Bl.-Debr. § 218) is unsatisfactory. Cf. also Bu. J., 442, n. 2.

[20] The reading διηγήσεται ὑμῖν τὴν ἀλήθειαν πᾶσαν, supported by a few fathers and also some it. MSS (cf. also Vulg.: docebit vos omnem veritatem), is undoubtedly secondary, though it shows how the saying was taken in the early period.

of Jesus (16:12). The πάντα of 14:26 is par. to the ἐν τῇ ἀληθείᾳ πάσῃ of 16:13. This expression may be construed as "within the whole sphere of the truth," so that the theme of instruction is mentioned (cf. the πολλά of 16:12 as the content of the message which is no longer proclaimed by Jesus).[21] This does not rule out the fact that ἐν τῇ ἀληθείᾳ πάσῃ denotes the manner in which the Spirit leads the disciples as the πνεῦμα τῆς ἀληθείας.[22] 16:13 does not merely repeat 14:26; it develops it. Whereas 14:26 refers more to confirmation of the preaching of Jesus, 16:13 has in view its deepening and definitive completion. Common to both, however, is the predominance of the kerygmatic aspect, which is expressed in 16:13 by the use of the term ἀλήθεια in so far as this is the truth revealed by the λαλεῖν of the Spirit, but which finds supreme expression in the use of ὁδηγέω in a sense related to the διδάσκω of 14:26, namely, the sense "to instruct," "to teach."

This conclusion is important in a specific connection. If the ὁδηγέω of Jn. 16:13 meant "to lead," if there were ascribed to the Spirit the task of a ὁδηγός in the sense of "leader" or "guide," then one might find in this verse the idea of the Spirit preceding believers on their way as a "leader," with the further suggestion that, since the Spirit has the task of the ἄλλος παράκλητος, Jesus Himself is a ὁδηγός of this kind. To explain the religious derivation of this view all kinds of combinations would then be possible.[23] It is true that this one verse would perhaps be too slender a basis for such far-reaching conclusions. The possibility is ruled right out, however, if ὁδηγέω has here the sense "to teach."[24] It is possible, of course, to discern the influence of non-biblical ideas in Jn. 16:13 even if it does bear this meaning.[25] Nevertheless, it should be noted that if the interpretation favoured above is correct Jn. 16:13 differs plainly from the examples from the Corp. Herm. quoted → 97), where ὁδηγέω has in any case the sense "to lead," and at points a spatial basis is plainly evident. The fact that this is the only occurrence of ὁδηγέω in Jn. is no reason for suspecting alien influence.[26] It is enough to point out that elsewhere in biblical Gk. ὁδηγέω is common in the sense "to instruct," "to teach."

ὁδηγός does not occur in the post-apost. fathers (nor καθοδηγός).[27] On the other hand, ὁδηγέω is used in Did., 3, 2-6 in admonitory sayings which are all constructed in the same way and designed to show to what great offences and transgressions sinful

---

[21] Only with reservation may one cite constructions like ψ 5:8 : ὁδήγησόν με ἐν τῇ δικαιοσύνῃ σου, since the meaning here is plainly "to lead."

[22] Schl. J., ad loc. takes ἐν instr. (though he takes ὁδηγέω in the sense "to lead"). Perhaps one might compare the ἐν with that of ψ 72:24; Qoh. 2:3.

[23] Cf. Bu. J., 442, n. 4. From Mandaean texts one should note Lidz. Ginza L., 510, 27 ff. (the Redeemer as guide); 514, 23; though cf. 545, 19. But the concept seemed to be so unimportant to Lidz. that he did not list "Geleiter" in the index.

[24] Cf. → 83 f. A question is whether the idea of the Redeemer as leader as we find it in Gnostic writings (cf. E. Käsemann, Das wandernde Gottesvolk [1939], 55 etc.) should be linked with the ἀρχηγός sayings of Hb. if they cannot be connected with any NT ὁδηγός passage. Cf. Käsemann's criticism (79 ff.) of Delling's art on ἀρχηγός, → I, 487 f. Jesus is never called ἡγεμών (→ n. 3; → 98) in the NT.

[25] E. Gaugler, Die Bedeutung d. Kirche in den joh. Schriften, Diss. Bern (1925), 43 ff., is too readily inclined to find in Jn. 16:13 an analogy to the language of the mysteries.

[26] διδάσκω, too, is used in the sayings of Jesus in Jn. only at 14:26, apart from 18:20. Nevertheless, there is no assimilation to non-biblical terminology in 14:26.

[27] The angels which Barn., 18, 1; Herm. m., 6, 2 associate with the image of the two ways (→ 93 f.) are not called ὁδηγοί (this occurs for the first time in the quotation from Bas.,

impulses and passions may lead even though at first they seem trivial. 3, 2 may be taken as an example : μὴ γίνου ὀργίλος, ὁδηγεῖ γὰρ ἡ ὀργὴ πρὸς τὸν φόνον, and 3, 5 : μὴ γίνου ψεύστης, ἐπειδὴ ὁδηγεῖ τὸ ψεῦσμα εἰς τὴν κλοπήν. Here, then, ὁδηγέω is used in the same sense (i.e., not presupposing the image of a way) as ἄγω is used, not in the NT (for it has greater weight in R. 2:4; Hb. 2:10), but in Prv. 18:6; 1 Cl., 9, 1. On ὁδηγέω in this sense cf. already Test. Jud. 19:1: ἡ φιλαργυρία πρὸς εἰδωλο-λατρίαν ὁδηγεῖ. In the Apologists ὁδηγός does not occur and ὁδηγέω is rare, Just. Dial., 38, 3 (= ψ 44:4); 132, 3 (lit.); also Tat. Or. Graec., 13, 2 (in a discussion of the fate of the ψυχή after death : ἀνέρχεται δὲ πρὸς ἅπερ αὐτὴν ὁδηγεῖ χωρία τὸ πνεῦμα; cf. Corp. Herm., 12, 12, → 97, though the spatial idea is only fig.).

† μεθοδεία.

μεθοδεία is not attested prior to the NT, though μέθοδος and the derived verb μεθοδεύω are older. [1] μέθοδος has the sense of "treatment" (of a matter), "procedure," esp. planned and conscious "method," e.g., ἡ διαλεκτικὴ μέθοδος, Plat. Resp., VII, 533c; Aristot. Rhet., 1358a, 4, then the premeditation and art expressed in method, esp. in a bad sense, "cunning," "deception," "craftiness" (first in Plut.). μέθοδος has this sense in later pap. [2] This is the meaning, too, in the two LXX instances : πολυπλόκοις μεθόδων παραλογισμοῖς, Est. 8:12 n; κατεπείρασεν διὰ μεθόδων (through the use of military cunning) τοὺς τόπους, 2 Macc. 13:18. Philo, on the other hand, uses μέ-θοδος in the neutral sense, regularly with τέχνη, Spec. Leg., II, 99; plur., Leg. All., III, 15; Fug., 168. The same development may be seen in the case of μεθοδεύω. It first has the sense "to treat methodically," "to handle acc. to plan," e.g., the gathering of taxes. This sense of collecting taxes or debts is found in the pap. [3] But the word then takes on the nuance of "handling craftily," "overreaching," "deceiving." Older than Polyb., 38, 12, 10 (mid.) is 2 Βασ. 19:28 : καὶ μεθώδευσεν ἐν τῷ δούλῳ (vl. τῷ δούλῳ or ὁ δοῦλος) σου πρὸς τὸν κύριόν μου τὸν βασιλέα (Mas. רגל pi, "to go

---

→ 95). Barn., 1, 4 is singular : ἐμοὶ συνώδευσεν (this word is not used in the NT and occurs in the post-apost. fathers only here) ἐν ὁδῷ δικαιοσύνης κύριος. The general thought of divine help finds here particularly graphic expression in connection with the expression ὁδὸς δικαιοσύνης (→ 93, 3) (Wnd. Barn., ad loc. refers to ψ 22:4). But the verse is not an example of the special view of the divine leader or escort on the heavenly journey (this is not the issue in Barn., 1, 4). In relation to this view ὁδηγός and ὁδηγέω are first used in Act. Thom. Cf. R. Bultmann, "Die Bedeutung d. neuerschlossenen man-däischen u. manichäischen Quellen für das Verständnis d. Joh.-Ev.," ZNW, 24 (1925), 134; H. Schlier, "Religionsgeschichtliche Untersuchungen zu den Ignatius-Briefen," Beih. ZNW, 8 (1929), 137 f., who emphasises (138, n. 1): "The concrete image of leading should not be read out of expressions which are already weak" (he refers to Is. 63:14; ψ 24:5 etc.). It should not be overlooked, however, that the description of Jesus as ὁδηγὸς ἐν χώρᾳ πλάνης in Act. Thom., 156 (p. 266, 1, Bonnet) is not with ref. to the heavenly journey of the soul, and that the addressing of Jesus as διδάσκαλε καὶ ὁδηγὲ τῶν ψυχῶν in Act. Phil., 93, p. 36, 15 f. carries a hint of the meaning "instructor." Furthermore, the use of ὁδηγέω in Act. Thom., 103, p. 216, 7 f. is already par. to the weak expressions, and finally the leaders in the pearl song in Act. Thom., 109, p. 220, 12, 6 are called ἡγεμόνες (not ὁδηγοί). ὁδηγός and ὁδηγέω are plainly connected with the heavenly journey only in Act. Thom., 167, p. 281, 7.

μ ε θ ο δ ε ί α. [1] Cf. Pass. and Liddell-Scott, s.v.

[2] Cf. Preisigke Wört., II, 62, s.v. Mayser, I, 3² (1936), 47 adduces from a pap. of 257 B.C. μεθόδιον in the sense of "money for a journey," but this is obviously a form (constructed like ἐφόδιον) which has nothing whatever to do with the other development of the word group ; cf. also Ditt. Or., 229, 31 (3rd cent. B.C.). Ditt. Syll.³ and Or., Index, s.v. list no instances of μέθοδος or μεθοδεύω on inscr.

[3] The late examples (5th and 6th cent. A.D.) found in Preisigke Wört., II, 62, s.v. may be added to Preis. Zaub., XIII, 713 (2nd/3rd cent. A.D.), cf. Moult.-Mill., 394.

about as a calumniator"). Philo uses μεθοδεύω 4 times (cf. also Eus. Praep. Ev., 8, 14, 59). He knows the neutral sense (e.g., Agric., 25 : ἐργασάμενοι καὶ μεθοδεύοντες), but in Vit. Mos., II (III), 212 he speaks disparagingly of the manner of philosophising ὅπερ μεθοδεύουσιν οἱ λογοθῆραι καὶ σοφισταί. It is thus no surprise that μεθοδεία (formed from μεθοδεύω and synon. to μέθοδος) is used in a bad sense in the NT, while late instances in the pap. use the word in the neutral sense for procedures in gathering taxes etc. [4]

In the NT μεθοδεία occurs only in Eph. Eph. 4:14 warns against the activities of men who have not attained to assurance of faith. These are subject to changing influences, and their goal and end is described in the closing expression : πρὸς τὴν μεθοδείαν τῆς πλάνης. [5] In 6:11 the readers are summoned to put on the whole armour of God πρὸς τὸ δύνασθαι ὑμᾶς στῆναι πρὸς τὰς μεθοδείας τοῦ διαβόλου. Since there is here no alternative, it is plain that μεθοδεία cannot be meant in the neutral sense for the method or procedure as such, but has to carry with it a closer definition of the activity. The word can thus be meant only sensu malo or sensu diabolico. The reference is to machinations or (in military terms) attacks against which one must be armed. The nature of the attacks (the plur. suggests that they are constantly repeated or are of incalculable variety) constitutes their great danger, against which the armour of God is the only defence. They are distinguished not so much by technique or strategy as by refinement and insidiousness (Vulgate translates insidiae, Luther "cunning attacks," A.V. "wiles"). If this be so, however, μεθοδεία is also used in a bad sense in 4:14. What is meant is not "methodical confusion of truth," [6] but a cunning process which seeks to deliver up to error, or such as is proper to error. [7]

In the post-apost. fathers only μεθοδεύω occurs, the sense being "to distort" : ὃς ἂν μεθοδεύῃ τὰ λόγια τοῦ κυρίου πρὸς τὰς ἰδίας ἐπιθυμίας, Pol., 7, 1. [8]

† εἴσοδος, † ἔξοδος, † διέξοδος.

εἴσοδος and ἔξοδος, often used together, are complementary in meaning, mostly by way of antithesis. [1] In the spatial sense εἴσοδος (from Hom.) means "entry," "ap-

---

[4] Cf. Preisigke Wört., II, 62 and Moult.-Mill., 394, s.v. The oldest instance in P. Oxy., VIII, 1134, 9 is from the year 421 A.D. The pap. have the itacistic spelling μεθοδία, which also predominates in the older NT MSS. Cf. Bl.-Debr. § 23. For the lexicographers cf. Cr.-Kö., 778, s.v.

[5] On the integration of the expression into the constr. of the sentence, cf. the comm.

[6] So Ew. Gefbr., ad loc. Ew. starts by assuming that "μεθοδία is simply the abstract of μεθοδεύειν, 'to handle artistically,' 'to arrange methodically,' so that the meaning is simply 'artistic arrangement.'" He overlooks the fact that μεθοδεύω (and μέθοδος) are both attested in a bad sense in bibl. Gk. At 6:11 he does actually translate "artifices," so that it is in no sense neutral here. Dib. Gefbr. renders 4:14 by "tricks," and 6:11 by "dodges." J. Schmid, "Der Epheserbr. d. Ap. Paulus," Bibl. Studien, XXII, 3/4 (1928), 146 suggests "deceit," "craftiness." He is right when he says (142) that in the case of μεθοδεία and other Eph. hapax legomena also found in the LXX we are not to think in terms of direct LXX influence, but that "the LXX simply attests that these words were current in the koine."

[7] The gen. τῆς πλάνης is hard to determine. Cf. Cr.-Kö., loc. cit.

[8] The word group does not occur in the Apologists. On μεθοδεία in Iren., Cl. Al. etc. cf. Sophocles Lex., s.v.

εἴσοδος κτλ. [1] Cf. Pass. and Liddell-Scott, svv.; Dit. Syll.³, Index, svv.; Preisigke Wört., I, 431 f., 518; Moult.-Mill., 188 and 224.

proach" to a place or building, the "forecourt" to a temple, the "door," while ἔξοδος (from Aesch., Thuc.) means "exit," "door," "mouth" of a river etc., e.g., οἰκία σὺν εἰσόδοις καὶ ἐξόδοις, P. Oxy., 1, 104, 13 (1st cent. A.D.); both words are also used fig. Esp. in the verbal sense εἴσοδος (= εἰσιέναι) means "entry," "access," "moving in," e.g., ἔσοδον εἶναι παρὰ βασιλέα ἄνευ ἀγγέλου, Hdt., 3, 118; εἴσοδον ἐπί τε βουλὴν καὶ ἐκκλησίαν, Ditt. Syll.³, 426, 25 f. (3rd cent. B.C.); πυλωρὸς ὢν ἀποκλείσω τὰς εἰσόδους τῶν κακῶν καὶ αἰσχρῶν ἐνεργημάτων, τὰς ἐνθυμήσεις ἐκκόπτων, Corp. Herm., 1, 22. In the case of ἔξοδος the corresponding use is even more rich and varied, "exodus," "going away," e.g., τῆς πατρίδος, "banishment," Plat. Leg., IX, 856e; "dissolution of marriage," BGU, IV, 1105, 24, 28 (1st cent. A.D.); fig. "disappearance," e.g., λήθη ἐπιστήμης ἔξοδος, Plat. Symp., 208a. Often in a military sense, "marching out," "campaign" (Hdt.), or of festal processions, esp. women, cf. Ditt. Syll.³, 1219, 15 ff. (3rd cent. B.C.); 695, 26 f. (2nd cent. B.C.).² Commonly "end": ἐπ᾽ ἐξόδῳ εἶναι, "to come to an end," Thuc., 5, 14; of the result of an enquiry, the conclusion of a tragedy etc. The sense of the "end of life," "death," is rare (attested in LXX, Joseph., NT): ὅρα ὅτι δεῖ σε δουλεύειν ἀεὶ τῷ δυναμένῳ σοι διαπράξασθαι τὴν ἔξοδον, Epict., 4, 4, 38.³ Both terms are common (both sing. and plur.) on inscr. and pap. in the commercial sense of "receipts," "income," and "expenditure,"⁴ cf. Polyb., 6, 13, 2: ἔξοδον ποιεῖν εἴς τι.

εἴσοδος occurs in the LXX some 50 times (12 in 1-4 Βασ., 8 in 1 and 2 Ch., 8 in Εz.). In the Mas. forms of בּוֹא are the equivalent in 20 cases, the noun מָבוֹא in 10. In many verses the sense is architectural, "entrance," "gate," "door," e.g., 4 Βασ. 11:16; 16:18; Prv. 8:3, 34; in the spatial sense it is also a geographical term, e.g., Jos. 13:5; 1 Βασ. 17:52; Jdt. 4:7. The verbal sense of "entry" into a city or house is less common, e.g., Gn. 30:27; 1 Βασ. 16:4; 3 Macc. 3:18; for the entry of a woman into the house or family of her husband (or the beginning of marital fellowship), Ju. 1:14 (A has εἰσπορεύεσθαι, cf. Jos. 15:18); of the arrival of birds of passage, Jer. 8:7; a military attack, 1 Εσδρ. 8:60; the coming of God, Mal. 3:2: τίς ὑπομενεῖ ἡμέραν εἰσόδου αὐτοῦ (cf. Is. 66:11); also with ἔξοδος (→ infra). ἔξοδος is used in over 70 verses; in the Mas. forms of יָצָא q correspond in 20 instances, the noun מוֹצָא in 13, קִיר in 14. Here, too, we find the spatial sense, whether geographical (e.g., ψ 64:8) or architectural (e.g., Εz. 42:11, also water installations, e.g., Prv. 25:26). The common use in the sense of a (city) "street" or "lane" (e.g., 2 Βασ. 1:20; Prv. 1:20; Lam. 2:21) deserves special mention; the ref. is obviously not to the street as arterial road, but to the outside street as distinct from the houses = חוּץ; cf. 3 Βασ. 21:34 of bazaars. The use in a verbal sense is highly varied, e.g., leaving a room, Jdt. 13:3; departure of an army, 1 Ch. 20:1; export, 3 Βασ. 10:28 f.; the sprouting of grass, Job 38:27 etc. One might also mention that it can be used as an astronomical term, e.g., Ju. 5:31 B; ψ 18:6; 74:6. Special note should be taken of the customary use of the term for the exodus from Egypt, e.g., Ex. 19:1; Nu. 33:38; 3 Βασ. 6:1; ψ 104:38. We often find it with εἴσοδος. Thus going out and coming in denote constant fellowship in 1 Βασ. 29:6; 2 Ch. 16:1, or total action and activity in 2 Βασ. 3:25; 3 Βασ. 3:7; 4 Βασ. 19:27; ψ 120:8; Is. 37:28 (the underlying Mas. יָצָא and בּוֹא or מוֹצָא and מָבוֹא are elsewhere translated as verbs). In all the verses mentioned ἔξοδος comes first. In Wis. 7:6 the two words are used for birth

---

² In Ditt. Or. we find in the same sense the abstract ἐξοδεία (from ἐξοδεύω), e.g., 90, 42, in the Rosetta inscr.: ἐξοδεῖαι τῶν ναῶν (of miniature temples carried round in processions).

³ The use in the will of Bishop Abraham of Hermonthis, P. Lond., I, 77, 57: κελεύω μετὰ τὴν ἐμὴν ἔξοδον τοῦ βίου κτλ. (cf. Mitteis-Wilcken, II, 2, 372) is late (6th cent. A.D.) and also Christian. → 107.

⁴ Cf. also P. M. Meyer, Juristische Pap. (1920), Index, svv.; also ἐξοδιάζω, ἐξοδιασμός, "payment." Cf. also R. Tautenschlag, "Das Recht auf εἴσοδος u. ἔξοδος in den Pap.," APF, 7 (1927), 25 ff.

and death : μία δὲ πάντων εἴσοδος εἰς τὸν βίον ἔξοδός τε ἴση. Here one might suppose that ἔξοδος means departure (from life), but one may see from 3:2 : καὶ ἐλογίσθη κάκωσις ἡ ἔξοδος αὐτῶν (τεθνάναι corresponds in the first clause) that the meaning is "end" (cf. Ex. 23:16; 2 Ch. 23:8 in chronological data). These are the two oldest instances of ἔξοδος for death. In Sir. 40:1 the day of birth is described as ἡμέρα ἐξόδου ἐκ γαστρὸς μητρός, in 38:23 that of death as ἔξοδος πνεύματος. ἔξοδος ζωῆς (→ II, 854) occurs in Prv. 4:23 (for תּוֹצָאוֹת) and 8:35 (for מֹצָא read as מֹצָא).

Both terms are rare in Philo in a spatial sense (in Fug., 183 πυλῶνες are taken as εἰσόδου τῆς πρὸς ἀρετὴν σύμβολον). Philo uses εἴσοδος in Deus Imm., 132; Spec. Leg., I, 261 of the entry (of the priests) into the temple. We often find the two words together, Deus Imm., 60; Sacr. AC, 96 to denote "coming" and "going"; Op. Mund., 119, with ref. to Plat. Tim., 75d, describes the human mouth as θνητῶν ... εἴσοδος, ἔξοδος δ' ἀφθάρτων. In Sacr. AC, 135 and also Ebr., 9 the passage in Gn. 27:30 (Jacob goes, Esau comes) is taken to mean that when κακία stages its ἔξοδος, ἀρετή can stage its εἴσοδος. ἔξοδος is also used in Rer. Div. Her., 273 for release from prison. It is par. with φυγή in Poster. C., 9. It is also used for the exodus from Egypt in Migr. Abr., 15, 151; Vit. Mos., I, 105, 122; II (III), 248. In Vit. Mos., I, 268 ἔξοδος means "departure." This is also the sense in Virt., 77 (= de humanitate or caritate, 4, ed. Mangey). The ref. here, however, is to the death of Moses, his μεταβάλλειν ἐκ θνητῆς ζωῆς εἰς ἀθάνατον βίον, 76. When in 77 we read : εἶθ' ἑτοιμασάμενος τὰ πρὸς ἔξοδον οὐ πρότερον ἐστείλατο τὴν ἀποικίαν κτλ., death is for Philo "departure on a journey." This is shown esp. by the use of the synon. ἀποικία (cf. also ἔξοδος in Rer. Div. Her., 97 and the corresponding ἀποικία in the par. Abr., 77). Nevertheless, Virt., 77 is not an instance of ἔξοδος in the sense of death, the more so as this meaning develops from "end" when it is actually present (→ 104; → infra ; → 107 f.).

Joseph. makes frequent use of nouns formed out of ὁδός,[5] and this applies to εἴσοδος and ἔξοδος (sometimes together : Ant., 15, 154; Bell., 5, 423). εἴσοδος is used spatially of, e.g., entrances into a house, Ant., 1, 202, or a cave, 12, 274, the tabernacle, 3, 124, the temple, 15, 394; also geographically, 2, 325; Vit., 240. It is more common with verbal significance, e.g., entry or penetration into a land, Bell., 7, 246, a city, Ant., 5, 247; Bell., 5, 346, a building, Ant., 9, 148; the marching in of troops, Bell., 4, 270, but also the visiting of prisoners, Ant., 18, 203, audiences with the emperor, 18, 164. In Bell., 2, 547; Ant., 18, 240 ἔξοδος is used for escape (δυσέξοδος for difficult escape in Bell., 7, 293), in Ant., 4, 156 for a military undertaking, in Bell., 2, 8 for departure, in Ant., 18, 166 for walks, in 18, 228 for going out (to the bath), in 8, 237 for riding out, in 8, 186 for setting off ; often for the exodus from Egypt, 2, 271; 3, 305; 5, 72; 8, 61; Ap., I, 230 etc. (ἄφιξις is the opp. in Ap., I, 223). In Ant., 7, 76 ἔξοδος means "end," "issue" (of a battle); in 4, 189 ἔξοδος τοῦ ζῆν means "end of life," "death."

In Ep. Ar., 120 εἴσοδος means intrusion into a land.[6] In Test. Sol. 23:3 εἴσοδος is used for entry into the temple. In 20:15 it has the sense of "entry" or "entrance" : αἱ γὰρ ἀρχαὶ καὶ ἐξουσίαι καὶ δυνάμεις ἄνω ἵπτανται καὶ τῆς εἰσόδου τοῦ οὐρανοῦ ἀξιοῦνται. In 25, 5 ἔξοδος is used for the Exodus, cf. also Test. S. 8:4; 20:6 (c. Charles); B. 12:3 (β; Charles alters to εἴσοδος), 4; of exodus from life, N. 1:1. Sib. Or., 2, 150 : τοῦτο πύλη ζωῆς καὶ εἴσοδος ἀθανασίης, is hardly Jewish.

---

[5] In Joseph. we find (apart from the compounds in this art.) ἄνοδος, ἄφοδος, δίοδος, ἐπάνοδος, ἔφοδος, κάθοδος, πάροδος, περίοδος, πρόοδος, πρόσοδος, σύνοδος. Of these only σύνοδος occurs in the NT at 1 C. 16:7. The συνοδία of Lk. 2:44 is found in Jos. Ant., 6, 243; Bell., 2, 587.

[6] The verb εἰσοδεύω in Ep. Ar., 182 is not as rare as would appear from H. G. Meecham, The Letter of Aristeas. A Linguistic Study with Special Reference to the Greek Bible (1935), 50, 235 (cf., e.g., Preisigke Wört., I, 431, s.v.), but the passage in Ep. Ar. is the oldest example.

In the NT both εἴσοδος and ἔξοδος are rare (and they never occur together; cf. the verbal expressions in Ac. 1:21; 9:28; on Jn. 10:9 → III, 178 f.). There is no instance of the spatial use. τῶν ἁγίων is certainly neuter in Hb. 10:19 (cf. 9:8; → ὁδός, n. 120), and the reference is to the heavenly sanctuary as a building. But the statement: ἔχοντες οὖν, ἀδελφοί, παρρησίαν εἰς τὴν εἴσοδον τῶν ἁγίων, shows plainly, no matter whether παρρησία be understood as "confidence" or better as "permission" or "right," that the reference cannot be to the porch of this temple, but that εἴσοδος has to have the sense of "entry" or "access." It is true that in this sense εἴσοδος is nearly always used with εἰς; only rarely do we find ἐπί (cf. Ditt. Syll.³, 426, 25 f. → 104) and — when the access is to persons — παρά (cf. Hdt., 3, 118, → 104) and πρός (cf. Jos. Ant., 18, 164). The construction with the gen. must be regarded as unusual. [7] All the same, it is attested at least in Test. Sol. 20:15 as well (→ 105). On the relation of the εἴσοδος of Hb. 10:19 to the ὁδός of 10:20 → 76. [8]

The usual construction with εἰς occurs in 2 Pt. 1:11: οὕτως γὰρ πλουσίως ἐπιχορηγηθήσεται ὑμῖν ἡ εἴσοδος εἰς τὴν αἰώνιον βασιλείαν κτλ. Here the noun expresses what is commonly called εἰσελθεῖν εἰς τὴν βασιλείαν in the Gospels. [9]

The construction with πρός, which is used for access to persons (cf. Jos. Ant., 18, 164), is found in 1 Th. 1:9; 2:1. The statement in 2:1: αὐτοὶ γὰρ οἴδατε, ἀδελφοί, τὴν εἴσοδον ἡμῶν τὴν πρὸς ὑμᾶς, ὅτι οὐ κενὴ γέγονεν, shows that the meaning here has to be the *actus ingrediendi,* for only thus is the use of κενός appropriate. [10] Moreover it is apparent that εἴσοδος itself cannot include the positive result, and hence it cannot denote already a successful debut. It thus appears that in 1:9: ὁποίαν εἴσοδον ἔσχομεν πρὸς ὑμᾶς the thought of success is contained only in ὁποίαν, [11] while εἴσοδος is a simple statement denoting entry,

---

[7] That ὁδός is also constr. with the gen. as well as prep. is a par. inasmuch as this constr. is found not merely with the spatial sense (cf. the example in Hb. 9:8), → 75 f.

[8] Wbg. Th.², 37 f., strives to establish the local significance of εἴσοδος in all the NT refs. including Hb. 10:19 (though he does not use the odd constr. as an argument). Rgg. Hb. ², ³, 313 rightly takes a different course.

[9] Wbg. Pt., *ad loc.,* objects to Wnd. Pt.¹, *ad loc.* (also Pt.²) speaking of a "brilliant entry." In fact the πλουσίως does not refer to the splendour of the entry but the nature of the ἐπιχορηγ., and εἴσοδος means access rather than entry. But the local view of Wbg. himself: "What is meant is simply that readers have a broad and comfortable place for entering," is to be rejected. The stress falls on the fact that there is to be no doubt as to the guarantee of entry. Access is richly, i.e., assuredly, provided. We cannot presuppose too unreservedly that the access is linked with the fulfilment of certain conditions (cf. Wnd. Pt.², *ad loc.*). It is simply said that the access must be guaranteed, and that without this guarantee it is forbidden. The introductory οὕτως is to be taken in the same way. In so far as it pts. back to what precedes, it certainly takes on the character of a condition to be fulfilled, but ἐπιχορηγ. shows that there is an authority (God or Christ) on which the guarantee decisively depends.

[10] Wbg. Th.² believes that εἴσοδος should be taken in a concrete, local sense, suggests "entrance" or even "gate" as a transl., and recalls the common NT image of the door. But when he then construes 1:9 as saying "that the apostles found an entry, acceptance, among the Thess." he is himself abandoning the "lit. and local sense." On p. 43 on 2:1 he again fails to keep to this sense. If one adopts the local sense, one has necessarily to think of a door which is empty or not empty. But it is evident, nor does Wbg. contest this, that κενός is used fig.

[11] The statements which follow show that ὁποίαν relates to the success, not to difficulties (as against Wbg., 38).

the first appearance of the apostle in Thessalonica (ἐγενόμην πρὸς ὑμᾶς is a corresponding verbal form in 1 C. 2:3). [12]

The sense of "appearance" is to be found in Ac. 13:24, where it is said of the preaching and baptising of John the Baptist that he did it πρὸ προσώπου τῆς εἰσόδου αὐτοῦ (sc. Jesus). In distinction from the previous passages there is here no indication of goal. The reference is not to the coming of Jesus into the world (hence εἰσερχόμενος εἰς τὸν κόσμον in Hb. 10:5, cf. 1:6 is no true parallel), but to His public appearance, the beginning of His ministry. [13]

ἔξοδος occurs only 3 times. It refers to the Exodus in Hb. 11:22 (→ 104 f.). In the two other instances it means the end of life (Lk. 9:31; 2 Pt. 1:15). The expression in 2 Pt. 1:15 : μετὰ τὴν ἐμὴν ἔξοδον, corresponds to the passages from the pap. quoted in → n. 3, though these are, of course, later, and the addition τοῦ βίου does not occur in 2 Pt. Lk. 9:31 does not have any corresponding addition either. NT usage is thus closer to Wis. 3:2; 7:6 (→ 104) and Epict., 4, 4, 38 (→ 104) than to Jos. Ant., 4, 189 (→ 105). As in the Wis. verses, ἔξοδος is also to be taken here in the sense of "end" of life rather than "departure" from it. Thus, when it is said in Lk. 9:31 that on the Mount of Transfiguration Moses and Elijah ἔλεγον τὴν ἔξοδον αὐτοῦ, ἔξοδος does not mean His going out of life or the world (cf. ἐξέρχεσθαι ἐκ τοῦ κόσμου, → II, 680, n. 5), nor is there any reference to the destination of Jesus after His death, but ἔξοδος simply means the "end," "conclusion," of His life and work. It is quite erroneous to see any reference to the resurrection as a coming out of the grave. Certainly the reference to the resurrection immediately before in 9:22 suggests that this is in view as well as death as the end of life. [14, 15] The only point is that the resurrection is not regarded as part of the conclusion of the earthly life of Jesus.

In the post-apost. fathers εἴσοδος is found only in Herm. s., 9, 12, 6 : ἡ δὲ πύλη ὁ υἱὸς τοῦ θεοῦ ἐστιν· αὕτη μία εἴσοδός ἐστι πρὸς τὸν κύριον; the par. shows that the meaning here is the spatial one of "entrance," "gate" (though αὕτη should be taken to refer to εἴσοδος, not πύλη). ἔξοδος, too, occurs only once at Herm. v., 3, 4, 3 : ἤθελον γνῶναι τῶν λίθων τὴν ἔξοδον κτλ. It has to have here the sense of "end" and hence of future destiny (what will be their end or fate). Among the Apologists Just. uses both terms frequently. εἴσοδος occurs in quotations in Dial., 61, 5 (Prv. 8:34);

---

[12] Dib. Th.³, ad loc. believes that "coming" is the sense in 2:1, but that the pass. "acceptance" is appropriate in 1:9. There are, however, no instances of a pass. use of εἴσοδος, and it is unlikely, if not impossible, inasmuch as ὁδός is the noun of ἰέναι. In a free transl. one might, of course, render 1:9 : "What kind of reception we had among you," but εἴσοδος does not really mean "reception." When Wbg., 38 argues that only the local sense of εἴσοδος fits ἔχειν, one might at least refer to the corresponding Lat. expression, which indicates a verbal sense : ideo peto a te ut habeat introitum ad te, P. Oxy., I, 32, 14 f. (cf. Deissmann LO, 164).

[13] πρὸ προσώπου is unusual even as a Semitism (cf. Bl.-Debr. § 5, n. 1), for of some 90 instances in the LXX the gen. always denotes a person except at 2 Ch. 1:13 vl. (Johannessohn Praepos., 184 ff.; cf. 357). Although one might expect a note of time as with προκηρύξαντος (→ III, 717 f.), πρὸ προσώπου, following the clear usage of the LXX with πρόσωπον, keeps a spatial sense : before the appearance of Jesus (as His forerunner preparing the way for Him). Wbg., 37, n. 1, errs, however, when he takes εἴσοδος itself in a local sense by regarding the Baptist as the θυρωρός who opens the door for Jesus.

[14] Kl. Lk., ad loc. simply asks whether such an understanding is possible ; Zn. Lk. ³, ⁴, 383 champions it without further ado.

[15] One can hardly refer to 9:26 (so Zn., loc. cit.), for ἔξοδος in 9:31 relates to events in Jerusalem.

85, 9 (Is. 66:11), and also in the phrase ἔν τινι εἰσόδῳ κώμης, Apol., 32, 6; Dial., 53, 2 (for the εἰσπορευόμενοι of Mk. 11:2 and par.). ἔξοδος is also found in quotations in Dial., 61, 5 (Prv. 8:35), 64, 8 (ψ 18:6), also in the phrase ἔξοδος τοῦ βίου in Dial., 105, 3, then in the same sense without the τοῦ βίου in Dial., 105, 3, 5 (i.e., "end of life," "death"). This meaning is found in later Christian authors, e.g., Iren., III, 1, 1; Eus. Hist. Eccl., V, 1, 36; 2, 3. [16]

In the parable of the royal marriage-feast the king's order to his servants in Mt. 22:9 runs : πορεύεσθε οὖν ἐπὶ τὰς διεξόδους τῶν ὁδῶν κτλ. These διέξοδοι can hardly be cross-roads in the town or country, [17] nor can they be city squares where many streets converge. [18] The use of διέξοδος elsewhere suggests that the meaning is "end," [19] so that the διέξοδοι τῶν ὁδῶν are the points where the streets of the town give way to country roads. [20] The charge in the parable of the great feast in Lk. 14:21 does not correspond to that of Mt. 22:9, since it refers specifically to the streets and lanes of the city. Nor does the further order in Lk. 14:23, which refers to the roads outside the city. As compared with Lk., Mt. 22:9 seems intentionally to try to combine the two orders in Lk. 14:21, 23. [21] This means that we must rule out an idea which might be suggested if Mt. 22:9 corresponded to Lk. 14:21, namely, that Lk. 14:23, construed as an invitation to the Gentiles, [22] goes beyond the Matthean version and is thus a secondary feature. In fact, the view that the Gospel is ordained for the Gentiles too is part of the original content of the parable. Hence we cannot deny this concept to Jesus ; it is a part of His message, → 68 f.

διέξοδος is found from the time of Hdt. in the sense of "going through," "going into through" a gate etc., "passage," "gateway," "way out." Sometimes there is greater stress on the δι-, sometimes on the -εξ-. In the second case διέξοδος = ἔξοδος, and shares its various senses. In Hdt., 1, 199 διέξοδοι are passages (in the temple precincts). The hierodules sit on the sides of these (δι' ὧν οἱ ξεῖνοι διεξιόντες ἐκλέγονται). The verbal sense is rare, though Celsus uses the word for the heavenly journey of the soul, its passage through the sphere of the planets and fixed stars, in his description of Mithraism, Orig. Cels., VI, 21: καὶ τῆς δι' αὐτῶν τῆς ψυχῆς διεξόδου; cf. Stob.

---

[16] For further instances cf. Sophocles Lex., s.v.

[17] The meaning "intersection" (cross-roads) is not attested. But we also do not find "starting-point" (from which streets begin), hence "fork" or "junction." Schl. Mt., ad loc. is thus wrong when he renders the Rabb. פְּרֶשֶׁת דְּרָכִים ("parting of the ways") (e.g., S. Dt., 11, 26 § 53 [86a] → ὁδός, n. 51) by the Gk. διέξοδος τῶν ὁδῶν. Cf. also Str.-B., I, 881: "διέξοδοι τῶν ὁδῶν roughly = פַּרְשִׁיּוֹת דְּרָכִים." The expression in Mt. 22:9 obviously cannot be explained as if διέξοδος τῶν ὁδῶν were put in the plur. The sing. would have to be διέξοδος τῆς ὁδοῦ, so that the different διέξοδοι of the various ὁδοί are in view.

[18] So Kl. Mt., ad loc. with ref. to Lk. 14:21 as par.

[19] But for the τῶν ὁδῶν, διέξοδος might simply mean "street." διέξοδος has a whole range of meanings like the simple ἔξοδος (cf. Pass. and Liddell-Scott, s.v.). Thus, as ἔξοδος can mean "street" (→ 104), so might διέξοδος, though there is no instance in the LXX. Only in respect of ψ 1:3; 118:136 (cf. the Mas. פֶּלֶג in both cases) might one ask whether the translator with his διέξοδοι τῶν ὑδάτων was perhaps thinking of "canals" or "waterways." The sense of "gateways" [Debrunner] is not easily proved from usage elsewhere.

[20] Cf. also Pr.-Bauer³, s.v.

[21] On the thoroughly secondary character of the Matthean version cf. W. Michaelis, Das hochzeitliche Kleid. Eine Einführung in d. Gleichnisse Jesu über d. rechte Jüngerschaft (1939), 11 ff.

[22] Cf. Michaelis, 55 ff.

Ecl., II, p. 171, 1: τοῦ πρώτου βίου ἡ διέξοδος διὰ τῶν ἑπτὰ σφαιρῶν γιγνομένη. In the pap. the word has thus far been found only once for the "end" or "issue" of a lawsuit, P. Magd., 12, 11 (218 B.C.).[23] In the LXX διέξοδος is used in 18 verses in Nu. 34 and Jos. 15-19 as a geographical tt. for the endpoints of a boundary (always sing. except at Jos. 19:33; always תֹּצְאוֹת in the Mas.). At 4 Βασ. 2:21 (sing.); ψ 1:3; 106:33, 35 vl.; 118:136 we then find the expression διέξοδοι (τῶν) ὑδάτων. The ref. is obviously always to the pt. where a covered watercourse breaks through the earth and runs in the open, e.g., "spring";[24] cf. Sir. 25:25 : μὴ δῷς ὕδατι διέξοδον. The ref. in ψ 67:20 : καὶ τοῦ κυρίου κυρίου αἱ διέξοδοι τοῦ θανάτου, is obviously to escape from the danger of death. ψ 143:14 is not a good transl. and the exact meaning is thus hard to ascertain.[25] Joseph. has διέξοδος in Ant., 12, 346; Bell., 4, 378 in the sense of "exit" which can be blocked by the enemy. In Ep. Ar., 105 (where the context is uncertain) διέξοδοι seem to be ways through towers or streets which go through the wall of a city into open country.[26] (In 251 διέξοδος is the course kept by the helmsman of a ship.) The idea of "passing or coming through" is present in Test. Jud. 62.

From the time of Plat. and Arist. διέξοδος is also used for an "express depiction," "exposition," "discussion." The adj. διεξοδικός has the same sense of "explicit," "comprehensive," the adv. διεξοδικῶς also being found in Jos. Bell. prooem, 18 (cf., too, inscr., Ditt. Syll.[3], 694, 38 [129 B.C.]). There are no instances of the noun in this sense in bibl. and early Christian writings. Philo, however, who uses διέξοδος in many senses (spatial, Spec. Leg., IV, 111; Poster. C., 79; for "course," "result," Deus Imm., 34; Plant., 49; with βίος for "conduct," Migr. Abr., 100; Vit. Mos., II [III], 150), often has it in the sense of "exposition," "elucidation," Spec. Leg., I, 272 and 342; Poster. C., 53; Conf. Ling., 14; Migr. Abr., 117; Det. Pot. Ins., 130; Vit. Mos., I, 23 (cf. διεξοδικός, Congr., 30 and 33). Flacc., 124 uses ἐπέξοδος in the sense of "exit," "way out."

† εὐοδόω.

εὐοδόω, though a correct formation,[1] is rare outside the Bible, possibly not used at all prior to the LXX. The oldest example might be Soph. Oed. Col., 1435 : σφῶν δ' εὐοδοίη Ζεὺς τάδ' εἰ τελεῖτέ μοι, with the sense "to show a good way," "to lead on a good path," "to guide well." But it should be noted that along with other conjectures (the changing of σφῶν to σφώ, or the reading σφῶν δ' εὖ διδοίη), σφὼ δ' εὖ ὁδοίη has been proposed, and this might well be the original reading. In this case the basis might well be ὁδόω, "lead or bring on the right way," which is known to us

---

[23] Cf. Preisigke Wört., I, 375, s.v.; Mayser, I, 2[2] (1938), 17; I, 3[2] (1936), 175; Moult.-Mill., 160, s.v.

[24] Pr.-Bauer[3], s.v. Also in ψ 1:3; 118:136 (elsewhere the Mas. is מוֹצָא) one must assume that the meaning is "place where water gushes forth" (→ n. 19). The only instances of διέξοδος in the post-apost. fathers and Apologists are quotations from ψ 1:3 in Barn., 11, 6; Just. Apol., 40, 9; Dial., 86, 4.

[25] It seems διέξοδος is linked with κατάπτωμα φραγμοῦ rather than κραυγή. Is the meaning that the previously mentioned βόες do not break any fences, do not break out, and do not disturb by their lowing? Ju. 5:17 B has διέξοδοι (A διακοπαί). ᾽ΑΣΘ all have διέξοδοι at Ez. 48:30 (LXX διεκβολαί). On בֵּית נְתִיבוֹת "the place where the ways intersect," at Prv. 8:2 Ges.-Buhl, s.v. alludes to Mt. 22:9.

[26] What Meecham says on p. 237 sheds little light on this passage.

εὐοδόω. [1] Like the intrans. εὐοδέω, cf. Liddell-Scott and Pass., s.v., εὐοδόω derives from the adj. εὔοδος, which means "easy to travel" (e.g., Xenoph. An., 4, 8, 10), fig. "easy," "without difficulty," but also "favouring travel" (cf. the name for Pan, Ditt. Or., 38, 3; 70, 1; 71, 2, and in the pap., Preisigke Wört., I, 617, s.v.). εὔοδος, like the noun εὐοδία ("good way," "smooth journey"), occurs in the LXX (→ 112). A later development is εὐόδωσις; εὐοδιάζω and εὐοδιασμός also derive from εὐοδία.

from Aesch. Prom., 498 and 813; Ag., 176; Eur. Ion, 1050. [2] In Hdt., 6, 73 also ὡς Κλεο-μένεῖ εὐωδώθη τὸ πρῆγμα is the less well attested reading ; ὡδώθη is probably the original (ὁδόω is also used in 4, 139). Finally, the τὸ εὐοδοῦν in Theophr. De Causis Plantarum might be read as τὸ εὖ ὁδοῦν. The few instances from the pap. are all from the Christian period. εὐοδοῦσθαι, P. Oxy., XIV, 1680, 4 (3rd/4th cent. A.D.), is in any case an uncertain reading, and the context of ἡ οἰκο[θε]ν εὐοδ[ω]θῶ, P. Jandanae, 62, 3 (6th cent. A.D.) is very corrupt. On the other hand, we have a clear instance in P. Greci e Latini, IV, 299, 11 f.: ἄρχεις οὗ ἄν με θεὸς εὐοδώσῃ [πρὸς] ὑμᾶς, also line 13 f.: ἕως οὗ ἄν με πάλιν πρὸς ὑμᾶς εὐοδώσῃ (3rd cent. A.D.). [3]

It thus seems as if εὐοδόω is one of those not very numerous constructs first found in the LXX. Even if this is not so, one is astonished by the frequency with which it occurs there. Including Da. Θ, there are 75 instances [4] ('ΑΣΘ and other transl. also have the word, often in agreement with LXX). Both meaning and construction vary greatly, so that it may be asked whether the different understanding of the Mas. and the caprice of translation are the only influences, or whether there is a specific development. [5] An obvious starting-point is the relation between εὐοδόω and צלח, which is very plain. Of the 75 instances (including those in Sir.), there is a Mas. original in 50 cases, and behind 44 of these are forms of צלח: in 39 passages the original is hi הִצְלִיחַ in the 3 verses Is. 54:17; Jer. 12:1; Da. LXX 11:27 it is q צָלֵחַ, in 2 Εσδρ. 5:8 the Aram. צְלַח ; in 2 Ch. 35:13 צְלֵחוֹת is misunderstood as a form of צלח. Other equivalents are less significant : נָחָה q in Gn. 24:27 and hi 24:48, רָצָה in Jer. 14:10, [6] also 1 Ch. 13:2 (cf. BHK[3]), קָרָה hi in Gn. 24:12, and שָׂכַל hi in Prv. 17:8. On the other hand, it appears that הִצְלִיחַ and also q צָלֵחַ (in the present sense "to succeed," "to progress") are pre-dominantly rendered by εὐοδόω, κατευοδόω and εὔοδος. Where this is not so, it is due either to omission (Jer. 5:28; 22:30; 32:5; Ez. 16:13) or mistranslation (Is. 53:10, where there is confusion with נצל ; Σ has εὐοδόω) in the LXX, or to translation with the help of related words. [7]

That other possibilities of transl. are not better exploited, but εὐοδόω is preferred, can hardly be due to the fact that εὐοδόω was in current use in the sense "to cause

_____

[2] Cf. E. Fraenkel, Griech. Denominativa (1906), 145. I owe important insights to A. Debrunner, esp. in this par. Aesch. Pers., 656 offers no example, for the conjectured εὐώ-δωσεν for ἐποδώκει (from ἐφοδόω) is unnecessary.

[3] Cf. on this W. Döllstädt, Griech. Papyrusprivatbriefe in gebildeter Sprache aus den ersten vier Jahrhunderten nach Christus (Diss. Jena) (1934), 38 f.; also Preisigke Wört., I, 617 and Moult.-Mill., 263, s.v.

[4] Acc. to Hatch-Redp. εὐοδόω also occurs as a vl. at Gn. 24:35; Ju. 15:18; Sir. 43:26, though only weakly attested. The first two are not mentioned in Rahlfs, but cf. Swete and Brooke-McLean (also Schleusner, II, 562 ff., s.v.); on the other hand Rahlfs adopts εὐοδοῖ as the reading in Sir. 43:26.

[5] Anz, 34 (Diss. phil. Hal., XII [1894], 290) and Helbing Kasussyntax, 94 f. already gave attention to this question, though Anz was hampered by the fact that he dealt only with the Pent.

[6] א A read ηὐδόκησεν for εὐώδωσεν (→ II, 738); cf. also Jer. 2:37 א*. On the other hand εὐοδόω also competes with εὐδοκέω at Ju. 15:18 (→ n. 4) and with εὐδοκία at Sir. 43:26 (→ n. 4), and הִצְלִיחַ is rendered εὐδοκηθῆναι at 1 Ch. 29:23 (so Αλλ.). This is probably very largely a matter of faulty transcription (due to the similarity of εὐοδ- and εὐδοκ-), though it would be assisted by the relationship in meaning.

[7] Thus Gn. 39:2 (Schleusner, II, 499, s.v.) has ἐπιτυγχάνων for מַצְלִיחַ (Σ εὐοδούμενος, 'Α κατευθυνόμενος). The pass. χράομαι or χρήσιμόν ἐστιν is used at Jer. 13:7, 10; Ez. 15:4. Particularly worth noting is the use of κατευθύνω at Ez. 17:9 f., 15, for κατευ-θύνω is also par. to the LXX εὐοδόω at Da. Θ 8:24 f.; 11:27, 36 and Is. 55:11 'Α, and it is used elsewhere in the LXX for צלח, sometimes in a different sense ; cf. also Hesych., s.v.: εὐοδώσει· κατευθυνεῖ.

to succeed" (pass. "to succeed"). This idea is not supported by use outside the Bible. Hence we may conjecture that the selection or reapplication of εὐοδόω is due to the fact that הִצְלִיחַ (also צָלֵחַ in Jer. 12:1) is often linked with דֶּרֶךְ. If הִצְלִיחַ, on the basis of "to prevail" (also "to succeed") for צָלַח, had the meaning "to carry out," "to bring to a good end," then along with דֶּרֶךְ it could mean "to bring a way to a good conclusion," "to make a journey successfully," and εὐοδόω seemed to offer a good rendering, while the simultaneous retention of דֶּרֶךְ as ὁδός also yielded an effective fig. etym. Thus the act. εὐοδόω is used with the acc. ὁδόν or ὁδούς in Gn. 24:21, 40, 42, 56; Dt. 28:29; Jos. 1:8; Tob. 5:17 BA; 10:14; Is. 46:11 (LXX addition); 48:15; 55:11 (cf. also Gn. 24:48), and ὁδός is the subj. of the pass. εὐοδοῦσθαι in Ju. 18:5 B; Tob. 5:22; 11:15 א; Jer. 12:1; where there is Mas., we always find הִצְלִיחַ or (Jer. 12:1) צָלֵחַ and דֶּרֶךְ (except Is. 55:11, which is a free rendering). Only in Dt., Jos., Jer. is the use of ὁδός fig. On the other side this fig. etym. gives εὐοδόω itself the meaning "to cause to succeed," and this opens up all the other possibilities of use for forms of צלח.

When not used in the abs., as it often is, הִצְלִיחַ is constructed with the acc. of the object (e.g., דֶּרֶךְ) which is brought to a good end. When there is indication of a person to whom success accrues, this is effected by לְ (Neh. 1:11; 2:20) or suffix (2 Ch. 26:5; in 14:6 acc. to BHK³ this should be altered to לָנוּ on the basis of the LXX). In such cases the LXX has the dat. (which is original in Neh. 2:20 as opposed to the acc. in B). This corresponds to the Mas. and is to be expected in the light of secular Gk. Tob. 7:12 BA, 13 א; Sir. 38:14 have a dat. of person as well as acc. of obj.; this is a dat. comm., so that intrinsically these are examples of the constr. with the acc., which is the usual one in the LXX. [8] Mostly this is an acc. of object; cf. the examples with ὁδόν or ὁδούς, → supra; also Gn. 39:3, 23, τὰ κάλλιστα Tob. 7:12 BA, εἰρήνην 7:13 א, ἔργον Wis. 11:1, αὐτόν (= αἶνον) Sir. 15:10, [9] ἀνάπαυσιν 38:14, also Is. 54:17. But we also find the acc. of person, cf. Gn. 24:27 (נָחָה q, with an indication of destination εἰς οἶκον, → 110, ἄγγελον Ju. 4:8 (LXX addition) and Tob. 7:12 א; 10:11 B, also the vl. noted in → n. 8 at Gn. 24:48; 1 Macc. 4:55. The act. εὐοδόω is used in the abs. at 3 Βασ. 22:12, 15; 1 Ch. 22:11, 13; 2 Ch. 18:14; ψ 117(118):25 and Jer. 14:10 (→ n. 6); cf. also Gn. 24:12 (קָרָה hi).

Corresponding to the strong trans. use of the act. εὐοδόω, the pass. is also of frequent occurrence (38 times). [10] As one would expect from the act., ὁδός is often the subj. of εὐοδοῦσθαι, → supra, and other things can also be the subj., 2 Ch. 7:11; 1 Εσδρ. 6:9; 2 Εσδρ. 5:8; Tob. 4:19; Sir. 11:17; Da. LXX 8:25; 1 Macc. 3:6. But we often have a construction with personal subj., giving the sense "I am successful," cf. je réussis: Jos. 1:8 (→ n. 11); 2 Ch. 18:11; 20:20; 24:20; 32:30; Tob. 4:6 א; 5:17 BA (as a parting greeting); 10:13 א; Prv. 28:13; Sir. 41:1; Jer. 2:37; Da. LXX 6:4; 8:11 f., 24; 11:27, 36;

---

[8] Helbing, 94 has rather an inclination to allow more scope for a constr. with the dat. But the only pure instance, not controlled by the Mas., is 1 Macc. 4:55, where the acc. is also attested. נָחָה hi underlies Gn. 24:48, and here, too, the acc. is attested as a later reading, a plain assimilation to the accepted rule of constr. with the acc.

[9] Acc. to Rahlfs ὁ κύριος εὐοδώσει αὐτόν (neither Rahlfs nor Swete gives vl.). Zn. R., 58, n. 11 notes that εὐοδέω is used here, but since he does not say that the text is disputed this must be an error. V. Ryssel in Kautzsch Apkr. and Pseudepigr., II, 306 concludes from the Lat. and Syr. the Gk. original: ὁ κυριεύων δώσει αὐτόν, but this might be faulty copying, since the HT has הִצְלִיחַ, and this is also rendered εὐοδόω at Sir. 11:17; 38:14; 41:1.

[10] Helbing, 94 f. speaks in such cases of the med., but at most one can only assume a deponent use. It is more correct to see in εὐοδοῦσθαι a passive even when the basic Mas. is act.

Da. Θ 8:12; 2 Macc. 10:23 (where we have the Mas. it is הִצְלִיחַ) and Prv. 17:8 (שָׂכַל hi). [11] The impersonal εὐοδοῦται etc. is also attested ("it turns out well"), with dat. 2 Ch. 13:12; Tob. 10:14 א, abs. 1 Ch. 13:2; 2 Ch. 31:21 (a personal understanding is also possible); 35:13 (→ 110); 1 Macc. 14:36; 16:2; an inf. follows in Tob. 10:14; 1 Macc. 14:36; 16:2 (an inf. is also used with the act. εὐοδόω at Gn. 24:48; 2 Macc. 10:7). [12] → n. 16.

The rich use of εὐοδόω, whose significance may be seen from the fact that in some 40 instances God is directly or indirectly the one to whom true success is ascribed, finds a counterpart in the use of the compound κατευοδόω, which was fashioned by the LXX as a stronger form, perhaps under the influence of κατευθύνω, → n. 7. It occurs in the act. (with dat.) only at ψ 67(68):20 for עָמַס (elsewhere the Mas., if present, is צלח mostly hi), and we must assume either a scribal error or another original. It is found in the abs. "to succeed" at Ju. 18:5 A (εὐοδοῦσθαι, B). The other instances are all pass.: ψ 1:3; 36(37):7; 44(45):4; Prv. 17:23; Da. Θ 8:11 (dat.), 12 A (for LXX εὐοδοῦσθαι, either under the influence of v. 11 or dittography due to the preceding καί); 1 Macc. 2:47 (cf. also Gn. 39:2 Σ). εὔοδος also occurs in the LXX : Nu. 14:41 for צלח Prv. 11:9 obvious confusion of חלץ and צלח; elsewhere no Mas., 1 Εσδρ. 7:3; Prv. 13:13a; also εὐόδως, Prv. 30:29 (24:64) = par. καλῶς (in both cases יָטַב hi). εὐοδία "fortune," "success," occurs in Sir. 43:26 (→ n. 4), also 10:5; 20:9; 38:13 (vl. εὐωδία, though for מְצֻלָחַת), with no Mas. 1 Εσδρ. 8:6, 50; Tob. 4:6 BA, freely for פָּתָה pu, Prv. 25:15.

Joseph. would not appear to have εὐοδόω. In his accounts of OT stories he misses out εὐοδόω passages (cf. e.g., Ant., 1, 249 and 254; 7, 338; 8, 125, 402, 404; 11, 95; 12, 323). [13] From Test. XII one should mention : ἐὰν δὲ εἷς ὑπὲρ ὑμᾶς εὐοδῶται, "if one is more favoured by fortune than you," G. 7:1; also κατευοδούμενος or καὶ εὐοδούμενος in the same sense, Jud. 1:6.

In the NT εὐοδόω occurs only in R. 1:10; 1 C. 16:2; 3 Jn. 2 (twice), and is always passive. The small number of instances does not allow us to draw far-reaching conclusions, but the history of the term outside the NT shows us that εὐοδόω would not have occurred even in these verses if it had not enjoyed so uncommonly rich a usage in the LXX as compared with that elsewhere. In keeping is the fact that the meaning and construction in the NT occurrences finds in the LXX parallels which are not available in other writings.

---

[11] תַּשְׂכִּיל follows in Jos. 1:8. This is also transl. by the LXX (though not very well as συνήσεις; הִשְׂכִּיל is never construed as "to have success" in the LXX), so that the additional εὐοδωθήσῃ of the LXX cannot be attributed to it. Rather εὐοδωθήσῃ καὶ εὐοδώσεις τὰς ὁδούς σου must be regarded as a double transl., which also shows that the act. and pass. use were strongly felt to be related.

[12] Often the sphere of success is indicated by ἐν (HT בְּ: ἐν πᾶσι τοῖς ἔργοις αὐτοῦ, 2 Ch. 32:30, also Tob. 10:13 א: Sir. 41:1; Jer. 2:37 (לְ); Da. LXX 6:4; cf. also ἐν ὁδῷ ἀληθείας, Gn. 24:48 (the ἐν of Jer. 14:10 [→ n. 6] is controlled by εὐδοκέω). In Gn. 39:3 the בְּיָדוֹ alongside הִצְלִיחַ which means "for him" or takes up again "all that he did," does not contain any idea of mediation ; cf. also 2 Εσδρ. 5:8. Hence we should not render the par. phrase in 1 Macc. 3:6; 14:36; 16:2; 2 Macc. 10:23 (here also with acc. of relation) by "through him" (so E. Kautzsch in Kautzsch Apcr. u. Pseudepigr. on the verses from 1 Macc. — incorrectly not even construed with εὐοδώθη at 16:2). What it means is "for him" or "in all that he took in hand" (so A. Kamphausen on 2 Macc. 10:23). Cf. also Sir. 38:13.

[13] As concerns Philo, Leisegang does not have εὐοδόω, though εὐοδέω occurs 16 times. Philo has this for εὐοδόω in his rendering of Gn. 39:2 in Poster. C., 80. εὐοδόω is a vl. for εὐοδέω in Jos., 150, 213; it has also been conjectured at Som., II, 200; Leg. Gaj., 126.

The active use finds no place in the NT. [14] The thesis that the passive is not used in the NT "in the literal sense of being led on a good way" [15] can hardly be sustained with such certainty in view of R. 1:10. The infinitive which follows here [16] (ἐλθεῖν πρὸς ὑμᾶς) suggests [17] that we should take εὐοδωθήσομαι in the sense "I will succeed." It is also correct that even in the LXX the passive is usually figurative. Nevertheless, this is not always so. [18] Thus the context of εὐοδωθείητε in the parting greeting in Tob. 5:17 BA shows that the sense is either exclusively or predominantly "to be led on a good way," "to have a good journey," and in some of the passages in which ὁδός is the subject of the passive (→ 111 f.) the meaning "to succeed" is less prominent in the framework of the fig. etym. (so Ju. 18:5 B, cf. 6; Tob. 5:22; 11:15 א). Again, at Gn. 24:48 we find the active εὐοδόω in the literal sense (חצל hi is the original) with an infinitive construction. It has thus to be considered whether the meaning at R. 1:10 is not "to have a way made," "to receive a possibility of travel as a gift from God" etc. [19] The infinitive could easily enough be taken with this. There is an OT parallel for the apostle's submitting the fulfilment of his plan to God (→ III, 59; → 112).

1 C. 16:2 reads : κατὰ μίαν σαββάτου ἕκαστος ὑμῶν παρ' ἑαυτῷ τιθέτω θησαυρίζων ὅ τι ἐὰν εὐοδῶται. It would first appear that εὐοδῶται is here used with a personal subject which takes up again the preceding ἕκαστος, and that the ὅ τι is to be construed as an accusative of object. [20] In the light of the LXX, however, this seems most unlikely, for the passive εὐοδοῦσθαι, even when it might be taken as a deponent (→ n. 10), is not used with an accusative of object in the LXX (only at 2 Macc. 10:23 is there an accusative of relation, → n. 12). One might assume a personal subject at 1 C. 16:2 only if the ὅ τι as an accusative were under the influence of θησαυρίζων or τιθέτω, or if one might supply εὐοδῶται with an infinitive on which the accusative ὅ τι would depend. [21] This is not impossible, but on the basis of LXX usage (→ 111) it seems better to take ὅ τι as the material subject of εὐοδῶται. [22] This gives the sense of gathering "all that he can (as much as possible)." It is improbable that the reference is to the

---

[14] κατευθύνειν τὴν ὁδόν is used at 1 Th. 3:11 for "to direct a way (or journey) successfully to its goal." This, too, is common in the LXX : Jdt. 12:8; ψ 5:8; 118(119):5; Prv. 4:26; 9:15; 13:13a; 29:27; Ez. 18:25; Sir. 49:3 A. Cf. also → 69.

[15] Pr.-Bauer³, s.v.

[16] Cf. Bl.-Debr. § 392, 3. This constr. is found already with εὐοδόω or εὐοδοῦμαι in the LXX (→ 111). Only at Gn. 24:48 can there have been any influence of the HT, though Tob. 10:14 could have had a Semitic original. The examples from Macc. are wholly Gk. in formulation.

[17] Ltzm. R., ad loc. is too dogmatic when he says that "if εὐοδ. were here used in the lit. sense there could be no ἐλθεῖν."

[18] So B. Weiss R.⁹ (1899), ad loc.

[19] Cf. also Zn. R., 58 and Schl. R., 28.

[20] So the transl. "what he can," e.g., Ltzm. K., ad loc., which here presupposes the idea of gain or profit, cf. Ltzm. R. on 1:10. Joh. W. 1 K., 381 admits that thus far no instances have been found of the sense "to have something over," "to make a profit."

[21] So Bchm. K., 473, n. 1 with a ref. to R. 1:10; he supplies the inf. τιθέναι.

[22] This is considered as a possibility in Pr.-Bauer³, s.v., though "so far as he may succeed" is preferred. Liddell-Scott, s.v. equates εὐοδῶται with εὐπορῇ, refers expressly to Ac. 11:29 : καθὼς εὐπορεῖταί τις, and assumes a personal subj. in 1 C. 16:2. But in Ac. 11:29 the mid. εὐπορεῖσθαι (cf. Bl.-Debr. § 101, s.v. ἀπορεῖν) is used in the abs. with a personal subj., and there is thus no syntactical par. (the Attic εὐπορεῖν is also intr. in this sense ; on the use in the pap. cf. Döllstädt, op. cit., 43 f.).

yield or profit of gainful activities. [23, 24] The idea of success is linked rather with the result of gathering or saving. The demand of the apostle is not directed only to members of the congregation who might fairly cheerfully forego unexpectedly high business profits in favour of the collection. It is expressly laid upon all (cf. ἕκαστος ὑμῶν). That is to say, the Corinthian Christians, who are mostly poor (cf. 1:27 f.), should without exception make a real sacrifice week by week.

In 3 Jn. 2 : περὶ πάντων εὔχομαί σε εὐοδοῦσθαι καὶ ὑγιαίνειν, καθὼς εὐο-δοῦταί σου ἡ ψυχή, we see the obvious influence of a wish for health which is very common in the letters of antiquity, though this is the only instance in the NT. The basic form of this wish is (πρὸ μὲν πάντων) εὔχομαί σε ὑγιαίνειν. [25] But the wish is used here in a very distinctive way. [26] The ὑγιαίνειν is retained, but it is given second place after εὐοδοῦσθαι, and this, not the ὑγιαίνειν, is taken up again in the καθώς clause. [27] One can hardly be wrong in supposing that the addition and pre-eminence of εὐοδοῦσθαι are due to the fact that, thanks to its prior history in the LXX, εὐοδοῦσθαι is further removed from secular use than ὑγιαινεῖν, and necessarily carries with it the thought of God, on whom all success and health depend. Without this presupposition the clause would seriously trivialise the position of Gaius as a believer (that he walks in the truth, v. 3 f.). With this presupposition, however, both writer and recipient are united in thanksgiving to God for the spiritual gifts which God has given Gaius in and since his con-version. [28]

In the post-apost. fathers Herm. s., 6, 3, 5 excuses unsuccessful planners : ἑαυτοὺς μὴ εὐοδοῦσθαι ἐν ταῖς πράξεσιν αὐτῶν, "but they had no luck in their enterprises" ; on the other hand, it is said of them after their repentance : εὐοδοῦνται ἐν πάσῃ πράξει αὐτῶν (6). The pass. is thus used with a personal subj. in a sense which does not maintain the high level of the NT, namely, "to enjoy success" in business ventures ; on the constr. with ἐν → n. 12. In the Apologists Just. uses εὐοδώσω in Dial., 14, 6 quoting Is. 55:11; in Epith., 7, 8 he uses εὐοδοῦν himself in the sense "to find oneself on a good path," "to be well advised," more synon. with εὐοδεῖν, → n. 13.

Michaelis

---

[23] Cf. B. Weiss, *Die paul. Briefe im berichtigten Text* (1896), *ad loc.*: "Whatever is given him by fortune"; W. M. L. de Wette, *Das NT,* II (1885), *ad loc.*: "What he has won by successful enterprise."

[24] The vl. εὐοδωθῇ (AC 1739) presupposes this understanding, but it is secondary.

[25] Cf. O. Roller, "Das Formular d. paul. Briefe," BWANT, 4. *Folge, Heft* 6 (1933), 62 ff.

[26] Roller, *loc. cit.* does not particularly consider the context of 3 Jn., but his rich collec-tion of materials (cf. also 460 ff., and 449 ff. on ὑγιαίνειν in epistolary salutation) do not include a single example which is even an approximate par. to 3 Jn. 2.

[27] This prevents us from relating ὑγιαίνειν to sickness or ill-health on the part of the recipient. In any case the conventional nature of the wish for health seems to rule this out. Cf. Bü. J., *ad loc.*; Deissmann LO, 147, n. 2.

[28] καθώς (as often in Jn., cf. Bu. J., 291, n. 3 etc.) might have more than comparative force and denote the basis, not in the sense that a *mens sana* underlies a *corpus sanum,* but in the sense that the God who upholds the ψυχή can be trusted to maintain the whole outward life. There is no LXX par. referring to εὐοδοῦσθαι of the ψυχή, but we might recall verses like ψ 40:4; 65:9; 93:18. The ὑγιαίνειν τῇ πίστει of Tt. 1:13; 2:2 may be compared with the περιπατεῖν ἐν ἀληθείᾳ of 3 Jn. 3 f.; 2 Jn. 4.

† ὀδύνη, † ὀδυνάομαι

[1] ὀδύνη : a. of "physical pain," Hom. Od., 9, 440; common in Il.: 11, 268, 398, esp. of severe sudden pains due to a wound or fracture, and felt as stabbing, piercing, or cutting. [2] ὀδύνη is common in the plur., since pains of this kind are often felt individually, Il., 5, 397, 399; 4, 117. [3] The physical sensation then affects the soul and fills it with great anguish, Il., 15, 60, hence b. "mental distress," "grief" etc., Hom. Od., 1, 242; 2, 79, esp. in the plur., which is also common after Hom.

ὀδυνάω, "to cause pain or sorrow," Eur. Hipp., 247; Aristoph. Eccl., 928; Menand. Fab. Inc., 113, CAF, III, 51: μὴ ὀδύνα τὸν πατέρα. Pass. "to feel pain," "to suffer," Soph. El., 804; Plat. Resp., 9, 583d; Dio Chr. Or., 38, 46; 43, 2; 66, 16.

The LXX use is similar. ὀδύνη occurs 60 times for 33 different Heb. words, ὀδυνάομαι 8 times for 7 counterparts. [4] The predominant use is for profound and violent grief of soul, esp. for יָגוֹן: Gn. 44:31; ψ 12:2; 30:10; with θλῖψις ψ 106:39; with λύπη and στεναγμός, Is. 35:10; 51:11, or for √ מרר, which denotes bitter sorrow of heart: Zech. 12:10 (at the loss of a firstborn son, הֵמֵר); Is. 38:15; Am. 8:10 (מַר, bitterness of soul); Prv. 17:25 (מֶמֶר, vexation); Ez. 21:11 (מְרִירוּת, distress), or אוֹן, Gn. 35:18 (בֶּן־אוֹנִי, son of misfortune); Dt. 26:14; Job 20:10, also for עָמָל: Job 4:8; 7:3; 15:35, עֶצֶב: ψ 126:2, דְּוֶה דְּוַי: ψ 40:3; Lam. 5:17 B; 1:13 (ὀδυνᾶν LXX in the fig. sense of "sick at heart").

ὀδύνη occurs in the NT (with λύπη μεγάλη) at R. 9:2 for Paul's deep distress that his fellow-countrymen are shut off from salvation. It is found also at 1 Tm. 6:10 for the severe and piercing (περιπείρω) self-accusations and pangs of conscience which will smite those who have defected out of love of money. ὀδυνάομαι occurs in the NT 4 times in the Lucan writings: in Lk. 2:48 of deep agitation and anxiety for a beloved child, in Ac. 20:38 of the deep sorrow at parting from the apostle as he goes forward to death, then in Lk. 16:24 f. with reference to violent pain or grief at exclusion from salvation, the physical torments of the damned in Lk. 16:24: ἐν τῇ φλογὶ ταύτῃ, and the spiritual torture of remorse in v. 25 (opp. παρακαλεῖται).

Hauck

ὀδύνη κτλ. J. H. H. Schmidt, *Griech. Synonymik,* II (1878), 574 ff., 596 ff.

[1] Etym. dependence of ὀδυν- on ἔδω ("gnawing pain"): E. Fränkel, *Satura Berol.,* 24, *Glotta,* 15 (1926), 198, or δύη, "misfortune," "affliction, of body or soul," Boisacq, 685, is unlikely or uncertain acc. to Walde-Pok., I, 768.

[2] So also of the pain caused by burning or cutting of physicians, Plat. Prot., 354b.

[3] On the plur. cf. K. Witte, *Glotta,* 2 (1910), 18 f. On the plur. of intensive feeling cf. also W. Havers, *Festschrift f. P. Kretschmer* (1926), 41 f. Unlike ὀδύνη, ἄλγος is more used for general and more lasting pain, Hom. Il., 12, 206; Od., 9, 121, ἄχος denotes the violent pain of soul which fills with anger and stirs to action, Il., 12, 392 ff.; 16, 581 ff., and πένθος the sorrow expressed, e.g., in tears and lamentation at the death of relatives, Od., 11, 195, and often on burial inscr., IG, II, 3, 2116, 2477, 2892. → Schmidt, II, 576 ff.

[4] 17 times in Job for 13 different Heb. words, 9 in Jer. and Lam. for 7 different equivalents.

(ὀδύρομαι,) † ὀδυρμός

ὀδύρομαι a. intr. "to wail," "to lament," "to grieve," "to be distressed," esp. for outward expressions of grief, often with tears, Hom. Od., 9, 13 (ὀδυρόμενος στεναχίζω); 14, 129 (ὀδυρομένη βλεφάρων ἄπο δάκρυα πίπτει); 16, 144 f. (στοναχῇ τε γόῳ τε); 18, 203 (κατὰ θυμόν); b. trans. "to bewail," "to bemoan," Hom. Il., 24, 714 (δάκρυ χέοντες); Soph. Ant., 693; Muson., p. 41, 4; 43, 2 (the exile). ὀδυρμός, "wailing," "lamentation," "weeping," Eur. Tro., 609; Plat. Resp., 3, 398d (with θρῆνοι); Isoc. Panegyricus, 169 (δυστυχίας ἀνδρῶν); Plut. Demetr., 47, 3 (τῆς τύχης); Philo Migr. Abr., 156.

In the LXX the verb occurs only in 'Ιερ. 38:18 (31:18) for נוד hithp (lit. "to shake," shaking the head as a sign of grief), "to lament." For the noun ὀδυρμός cf. 'Ιερ. 38:15 (31:15) (with θρῆνος and κλαυθμός, Heb. בְּכִי תַמְרוּרִים, bitter weeping) for the loud (ἠκούσθη) and violent lamentation of the mother at the loss of her children; also 2 Macc. 11:6 (μετὰ ὀδυρμῶν καὶ δακρύων ἱκέτευον).

The only NT examples of ὀδυρμός are in Mt. 2:18 (quoting 'Ιερ. 38:15 [31:15] → supra) for loud and grievous lamentation at a most bitter loss, and 2 C. 7:7 for violent expressions of bitter remorse.

Hauck

οἶδα

οἶδα is an Indo-Eur. perf. of the root εἰδ-, ἰδ- (→ εἶδος, εἰδέναι, ἰδεῖν), though always used in the pres.: "to have realised, perceived" = "to know." [1] It often replaces the perf. ἔγνωκα (→ I, 689), "to have experienced, learned to know" = "to know." But it can also be synon. with γινώσκω; in the abs. use in the koine it is hard to establish any distinction of meaning. [2] This is esp. so when the inchoative element in γινώσκω is subsidiary or absent. Cf. as LXX examples: Est. 4:17d: σὺ πάντα γινώσκεις, σὺ οἶδας, Sir. 34:9 f.: ἀνὴρ πεπλανημένος ἔγνω πολλά ... ὃς οὐκ ἐπειράθη, ὀλίγα οἶδεν, Is. 59:8: ὁδὸν εἰρήνης οὐκ οἴδασιν (vl. ἔγνωσαν), and as NT

ὀδυρμός. J. H. H. Schmidt, *Griech. Synonymik,* III (1879), 384 f.

οἶδα. Cr.-Kö., 388 f.; B. Snell, "Die Ausdrücke f. den Begriff des Wissens in der vorplatonischen Philosophie" (*Philol. Unters.,* 29 [1924]).

[1] Walde-Pok., I, 236 ff.

[2] So correctly Moult.-Mill., *s.v.,* as against Cr.-Kö., *s.v.* On the relation of γινώσκω and οἶδα in class. Gk. cf. Snell, *passim,* esp. 24 ff. → I, 691. For examples of a very weak use of οἶδα in the apocr. Acts, cf. H. Ljungvik, *Uppsala Univ. Årsskrift,* 1926, *Filosofi, språkvetenskap och historiska Vetenskaper,* 8, 55-64.

examples : Mt. 16:3 : γινώσκετε διακρίνειν with Lk. 12:56 : οἴδατε δοκιμάζειν, Jn. 7:27: τοῦτον οἴδαμεν πόθεν ἐστίν· ὁ δὲ Χριστὸς ὅταν ἔρχηται, οὐδεὶς γινώσκει πόθεν ἐστίν, 8:55; 14:7 (note the vl.); 21:17: πάντα σὺ οἶδας, σὺ γινώσκεις ὅτι φιλῶ σε, R. 7:7: τὴν ἁμαρτίαν οὐκ ἔγνων ... τήν τε γὰρ ἐπιθυμίαν οὐκ ᾔδειν, 2 C. 5:16 : νῦν οὐδένα οἴδαμεν ... νῦν οὐκέτι γινώσκομεν. One must thus beware of pressing the distinctive senses. Thus in Mk. 4:13 : οὐκ οἴδατε τὴν παραβολὴν ταύτην, καὶ πῶς πάσας τὰς παραβολὰς γνώσεσθε, one can hardly demonstrate any difference, [3] and it is hard to see any distinction in nuance as between Mt. 7:23 : οὐδέποτε ἔγνων ὑμᾶς [4] (cf. Lk. 13:27 οὐκ οἶδα πόθεν ἐστέ) and Mt. 25:12 : οὐκ οἶδα ὑμᾶς (cf. Lk. 13:25). [5]

There are few peculiarities in the NT use of the term. 1. In most of the 320 passages where οἶδα occurs it has the sense "to know" as indicated above, and only rarely is it interchangeable with related senses of "know," e.g., knowing a person (Mk. 14:71; Mt. 26:72 : Peter in the court of the high-priest : οὐκ οἶδα τὸν ἄνθρωπον, 2 C. 5:16 : ὥστε ἡμεῖς ἀπὸ τοῦ νῦν οὐδένα οἴδαμεν κατὰ σάρκα), or ability to understand (Mt. 7:11; Lk. 11:13 : οἴδατε δόματα ἀγαθὰ διδόναι, cf. Jos. Bell., II, 91: φέρειν οἴδασιν μετρίους ἡγεμόνας, Lv. r., 5, 8 : אִיתְּתָא דְּחָכִימָא לְמִשְׁאַל, a woman who knows how to borrow. εἰδέναι = חָכַם = "to be able." Cf. Phil. 4:12; Jm. 4:17: εἰδότι οὖν καλὸν ποιεῖν; cf. Jos. Ant., VI, 167: παῖδα ... ψάλλειν εἰδότα), or understanding in the sense "to apprehend" (Eph. 1:18 : εἰς τὸ εἰδέναι ὑμᾶς τίς ἐστιν ἡ ἐλπὶς τῆς κλήσεως αὐτοῦ, Mt. 26:70 : Peter at the denial : οὐκ οἶδα τί λέγεις, cf. the par. in Mk. 14:68 : οὔτε οἶδα οὔτε ἐπίσταμαι σὺ τί λέγεις). [6] Unusual, though understandable, is the use for "to recognise" ("to know about someone") in 1 Th. 5:12 : εἰδέναι τοὺς κοπιῶντας, cf. as a par. Ign. Sm., 9, 1: καλῶς ἔχει θεὸν καὶ ἐπίσκοπον εἰδέναι.

2. Of theological significance is the phrase "to know God (or Christ)" or "not to know God (or Christ)." The NT use is influenced by the OT concept of a culpable ignorance of God, [7] which is echoed in Paul under the slogan εἰδέναι. The Gentiles are characterised by the fact that they "do not know (a) God," "they know nothing about a God"; Gl. 4:8 : τότε μὲν οὐκ εἰδότες θεόν ..., cf. Tt. 1:16 and the adoption of OT sayings in 1 Th. 4:5 and 2 Th. 1:8 (Jer. 10:25, cf. ψ 78:6). Cf. also Hb. 8:11 (= Jer. 31:34).

The demons have a knowledge of Jesus in Mk. 1:24, 34 (Lk. 4:34, 41). By supernatural knowledge they can see the purpose of His coming. Hence, realising that their very existence is threatened, they seek to defend themselves against Jesus

---

[3] As against Loh. Mk., ad loc.: "For this (εἰδέναι) is used for a knowledge which comes from inspiration or one's own insight, whereas that (γινώσκειν) applies to the knowledge which comes by experience or outside teaching." This is a distinction which can hardly be justified in the light of the examples quoted.

[4] Acc. to Str.-B., I, 469 this was used by the Rabb. as a formula of excommunication.

[5] As against Cr.-Kö., s.v.: Mt. 25:12 means that you stand in no relation to me, but Mt. 7:23 that I have never stood in relation to you. Cf. Kl. Mt. on 7:23.

[6] Cf. Schl. Mt., ad loc.

[7] Cf. the express discussion of this concept → I, 696 f., also W. Reiss, "Gott nicht Kennen im AT," ZAW, NF, 17 (1940/41), 70-98. Some OT examples are Is. 5:13 : τοίνυν αἰχμάλωτος ὁ λαός μου ἐγενήθη διὰ τὸ μὴ εἰδέναι αὐτοὺς τὸν κύριον, 26:13; Jer. 24:7; Job 18:21: οὗτος δὲ ὁ τόπος τῶν μὴ εἰδότων τὸν κύριον, 36:12.

by declaring His true name and nature : Mk. 1:24 : οἶδά σε τίς εἶ, ὁ ἅγιος τοῦ θεοῦ. [8] This is not to be taken as a confession, but as a defensive formula. [9]

In distinction from γινώσκω and γνῶσις (→ I, 708 f.), the thought of knowing Jesus plays no very significant role in Paul in connection with the term εἰδέναι. We simply find the term in the Corinthian letters where Paul is wrestling with the penetration of Gnostic ideas into Christianity. Thus 1 C. 2:2 : οὐ γὰρ ἔκρινά τι εἰδέναι ἐν ὑμῖν εἰ μὴ 'Ιησοῦν Χριστόν, καὶ τοῦτον ἐσταυρωμένον, is a demarcation against Gnostic attempts to change the message of Christ into wisdom speculation. 2 C. 5:16 : ὥστε ἡμεῖς ἀπὸ τοῦ νῦν οὐδένα οἴδαμεν κατὰ σάρκα, is also a demarcation, though here obviously directed against Judaisers who made the apostle's ignorance of the earthly Jesus an occasion for agitation against him. [10]

3. Only in the Fourth Gospel can one say with certainty that Gnostic usage has intruded into εἰδέναι. To the same degree that the unity of Jesus with God is expressed in the Johannine writings by the term γινώσκειν (→ I, 711), the same is true in respect of εἰδέναι, especially in the repeated statement of Jesus that He has knowledge of, or knows, God : 7:28 f.: καὶ ἀπ' ἐμαυτοῦ οὐκ ἐλήλυθα, ἀλλ' ἔστιν ἀληθινὸς ὁ πέμψας με, ὃν ὑμεῖς οὐκ οἴδατε· ἐγὼ οἶδα αὐτόν, ὅτι παρ' αὐτοῦ εἰμι κἀκεῖνός με ἀπέστειλεν. 8:55 : ἐγὼ δὲ οἶδα αὐτόν. κἂν εἴπω ὅτι οὐκ οἶδα αὐτόν, ἔσομαι ὅμοιος ὑμῖν ψεύστης· ἀλλὰ οἶδα αὐτὸν καὶ τὸν λόγον αὐτοῦ τηρῶ (cf. 8:14). This knowledge is not abstract. In 7:28 f. it is a knowledge of the goal and purpose of His mission, and according to 8:55 it takes concrete shape in His obedience to the word and commandment of His Father. His union with God explains His knowledge of the divine plan of salvation which is fulfilled in His mission, and especially in His death : 13:3 : εἰδὼς ὅτι πάντα ἔδωκεν αὐτῷ ὁ πατήρ . . . καὶ ὅτι ἀπὸ θεοῦ ἐξῆλθεν καὶ πρὸς τὸν θεὸν ὑπάγει. To this extent His death does not catch Him unawares, cf. 13:1: . . . εἰδὼς ὁ 'Ιησοῦς ὅτι ἦλθεν αὐτοῦ ἡ ὥρα ἵνα μεταβῇ ἐκ τοῦ κόσμου τούτου πρὸς τὸν πατέρα, cf. 18:4; 19:28 : μετὰ τοῦτο εἰδὼς ὁ 'Ιησοῦς ὅτι ἤδη πάντα τετέλεσται. [11]

To the same degree that there is expression of this knowledge of Jesus concerning His Father and His mission, it is also true that the Jews do not recognise Jesus as the Son of God ; they do not know Him, because they "are of this world" (8:23). Even the Baptist, to whom knowledge of Jesus had to be imparted by divine revelation (1:31 ff.), says to them : μέσος ὑμῶν στήκει ὃν ὑμεῖς οὐκ οἴδατε (1:26), and in what follows the Fourth Gospel continually refers to this lack of knowledge : 7:28; 8:14 : ὑμεῖς δὲ οὐκ οἴδατε πόθεν ἔρχομαι ἢ ποῦ ὑπάγω, 8:19; 8:54 f.; 9:29; cf. 4:10, 22. The disciples are also described as men

---

[8] The reading οἴδαμεν, which is attested by ℵ al and preferred by Hck. Mk., ad loc., is theologically more correct, cf. Loh. Mk., ad loc., but for this very reason is to be regarded as a correction of the better attested οἶδα.

[9] Cf. O. Bauernfeind, Die Worte der Dämonen im Mkev. (1927), 3 ff., esp. 13 ff.

[10] Cf. Ltzm. K., ad loc.

[11] Cf. on this the knowledge of the Gnostics, e.g., Ign. Eph., 12, 1: οἶδα, τίς εἰμι καὶ τίσιν γράφω, or Iren., I, 21, 5 : ἐγὼ οἶδα ἐμαυτὸν καὶ γινώσκω ὅθεν εἰμί. Cf. also the warning in Corp. Herm., XI, 21a against the closing of the soul to revelation, which will necessarily result in the insight : οὐκ οἶδα τίς ἤμην, οὐκ οἶδα τίς ἔσομαι. Here one may see plainly the proximity of Gnostic-Hell. use to that of the Fourth Gospel. Cf. G. P. Wetter, ZNW, 18 (1917/18), 49-63; Bau. J. on 8:14; H. Schlier, "Religionsgesch. Untersuchungen zu den Ignbriefen," Beih. ZNW, 8 (1929), 141 f.; also esp. Bultmann Joh. on 8:14 etc., Index, s.v. εἰδέναι. For more remote par. cf. also L. Bieler, ΘΕΙΟΣ ΑΝΗΡ, I (1935), 73 ff.

who do not know, cf. 4:32 : ἐγὼ βρῶσιν ἔχω φαγεῖν ἣν ὑμεῖς οὐκ οἴδατε, and especially 14:7: εἰ ἐγνώκειτέ με, καὶ τὸν πατέρα μου ἂν ᾔδειτε. But to the disciples, who are not of the world (15:19; 17:14, 16), full knowledge is promised when Jesus has gone away and sent to them the Paraclete (14:15 ff.; 16:7 ff., 25 ff.).

Seesemann

οἶκος, οἰκία, † οἰκεῖος, † οἰκέω, † οἰκοδόμος, † οἰκοδομέω, † οἰκοδομή, † ἐποικοδομέω, † συνοικοδομέω, † οἰκονόμος, † οἰκονομία,
κατοικέω, † οἰκητήριον, † κατοικητήριον, † κατοικίζω, † οἰκουμένη

οἶκος → οἰκία.

Contents : 1. General Greek and Hellenistic Usage. 2. "House" and "House of God" in the Old Testament. 3. "House of God" in Jesus and the Gospels. 4. The Heavenly "Father's House" in Gnosticism and Philo. 5. Early Christian Sayings about the Earthly Temple, and Contacts with Oriental Symbolical Use. 6. "House of God" as an Early Christian Image for the Community. 7. The Related Symbolism of Later Jewish Apocalyptic and the Rabbinate. 8. "House" as Family and Race. 9. The "House" as a Group in the Structure of the Christian Community.

1. General Greek and Hellenistic Usage.

οἶκος (etym. stem ϝοἶκος, Sanskr. *vêças,* Lat. *vicus*) means "house," "dwelling."[1] The noun is common in Gk. from the time of Hom.[2] and is in current use, cf. Hom. Il., 15, 497 f.: ἀλλ᾽ ἄλοχός τε σόη καὶ παῖδες ὀπίσσω, καὶ οἶκος καὶ κλῆρος ἀκήρατος. It can also denote the cave of Cyclops (Od., 9, 478) or the chamber of Penelope (Od., 1, 356; 19, 514 and 598). Sometimes specific houses are meant, e.g., a "temple" (Hdt., 8, 143 : ἐνέπρησε τούς τε οἴκους καὶ τὰ ἀγάλματα), a "treasure-house," a "palace," even "graves" (Diod. S., 1, 51: τοὺς δὲ τῶν τετελευτηκότων τάφους ἀϊδίους οἴκους προσαγορεύουσιν, ὡς ἐν ῞Αιδου διατελούντων τὸν ἄπειρον αἰῶνα). Ditt. Syll.³, 987 tells of the Κλυτίδαι (φρατρία Χίων): Κλυτίδαις εἶναι ἐν τῷ τεμένει τῶν Κλυτιδῶν οἶκον τεμένιον ἱερὸν οἰκοδομήσασθαι καὶ τὰ ἱερὰ τὰ κοινὰ ἐκ τῶν ἰδιωτικῶν οἰκιῶν εἰς τὸν κοινὸν οἶκον ἐνεγκεῖν, θυσαμένοις ἐκαλλιέρησεν (to sacrifice with favourable omens, to get favourable omens) οἰκοδομήσασθαι καὶ τὰ ἱερὰ τὰ κοινὰ ἐκ τῶν ἰδιωτικῶν οἰκιῶν εἰς τὸν κοινὸν οἶκον ἐνεγκεῖν.[3] Very often οἶκος means a "temple" : ἐν τῷ οἴκῳ τοῦ ῎Αμμωνος (Wilcken Ptol., 79, 4), i.e., "house or temple of Ammon" (transl. from the Egyptian?); P. Oxy., XI,

---

ο ἶ κ ο ς. A. Fridrichsen, "Ackerbau u. Hausbau," ThStKr, 94 (1922), 185 f.; also "Exegetisches zu den Paulusbriefen," ThStKr, 102 (1930), 291-301; also in *Serta Rud- bergiana, Symbolae Osloenses Fasc. Supplet.,* IV (1931), 25 f.; A. Deissmann, *Paulus*² (1924); H. Jonas, *Gnosis u. spätantiker Geist,* I (1934); P. Vielhauer, *Oikodome, Das Bild vom Bau in d. chr. Lit. vom NT bis Cl. Al.* (1939).

[1] Liddell-Scott, 1204 f.

[2] On Hom. *v.* H. Ebeling, *Lexicon Homericum,* II (1880), 34 f.

[3] Ch. Michel, *Recueil d'inscr. Grecques* (1900), 786 (No. 997, end of the 4th cent. B.C.).

1380, 2 : τὴν ἐν τῷ Ἡφαίστου οἴκῳ, probably the main temple of Hephaestus. It is a common Egyptian practice to call the temple the "house" of a deity. [4] οἶκος βασιλέως is found in Hdt., 5, 31; οἶκος κηρύκων, Ditt. Syll.[2], 587, 24 : ὁ Σεβαστὸς οἶκος, Ditt. Syll.[3], 799, 10; ὁ ἱερεὺς τοῦ Δεκελειῶν οἴκου, *ibid.*, 921, 41. οἶκον ἱκάνεται occurs in Hom. Od., 23, 7 (cf. εἰς or πρὸς οἶκον, Aesch. Eum., 459; Ag., 867). In the pap., too, οἶκος means "house," "dwelling," P. Amh., 54, 3 : οἶκος καθειρημένος, ἧς (read οὗ) οἱ τοῖχοι περίεισιν, P. Oxy., XIV, 1755, 2 : ἐρωτᾷ σε Ἀπίων δειπνῆσαι ἐν τῷ οἴκῳ Σαραπείου εἰς κλείνην τοῦ κυρίου Σαράπιδος. οἱ ἐν οἴκῳ (P. Tebt., 58, 63) are the household, cf. P. Lips., 104, 12; P. Gen., 51, 35 (ἀσπάζομαί σε καὶ πάντας τοὺς ἐν τῷ οἴκῳ σου). But οἶκος can also mean "domestic affairs," "wealth," "possessions" (P. Lond., 1309, 3 : ποιήσατε ἐπ' ἀσφάλειαν εἶναι τοὺς οἴκους αὐτῶν, "confiscated their whole property"), also the "family" or "family property": P. Ryl., 76, 10 : κατ' οἶκον εἶναι τὴν διαίρεσιν τῶν κτημάτων καὶ μὴ κατὰ πρόσωπον, "division should be by families, not by heads." οἶκος can also be the "chest": P. Tebt., 120, 53 : καταλείπονται ἐν οἴκῳ δραχμαὶ χ = "there remain in the chest *x* drachmas." Sometimes we find the expression ἀπέχειν διὰ χειρὸς ἐξ οἴκου, which denotes payment from the chest at home, not from the bank, cf. the examples in Preisigke Wört., 2, 163, 10 ff. οἶκος Καίσαρος, δεσποτικὸς οἶκος, θεῖος οἶκος means the supervision of the goods of the imperial household, P. Lips., 96, 3; P. Strassb., 23, 75; P. Lond., 234, 6; P. Masp., 2, 2; P. Soc., 196, 1; 197, 1; 238, 3. A striking sense is the astrological one, "the station of the planets," P. Oxy., 235, 8 etc.

2. "House" and "House of God" in the Old Testament.

In the LXX οἶκος is mostly used for the Mas. בַּיִת, e.g., Gn. 7:1; 12:1, 15, 17, though it is also the rendering of other terms, e.g., אֹהֶל (Gn. 9:21, 27; 24:67), הֵיכָל (Da. 1:4), or לִשְׁכָּה (Ἰερ. 43[36]:12, 20, 21). It is a favourite LXX word. [5] Fig. it can denote the "family," "race" (e.g., Gn. 7:1). Hence the Heb. phrase עָשָׂה בַיִת ("to found a dynasty," 2 S. 7:11; 1 K. 2:24) is rendered οἶκον οἰκοδομεῖν or ποιεῖν in the LXX. [6] οἶκος θεοῦ is a fixed term for the sanctuary in the LXX; it is used for בֵּית אֱלֹהִים in Gn. 28:17 and for בֵּית־אֵל in Gn. 28:19, [7] and is quite common (Ju. 17:5; 18:31; 2 S. 12:20), cf. also οἶκος κυρίου (3 Βασ. 5:14a; 6:1c). We also find other gen. constr. in biblical Gk., e.g., οἶκος δουλείας (Ex. 13:3, 14; Dt. 6:12); οἶκος τοῦ δεσμωτηρίου (Ju. 16:21, 25). The expression "houses of high places" (בָּתֵּי בָמוֹת) finds an equivalent in the LXX : καὶ ἐποίησεν οἴκους ἐφ' ὑψηλῶν (1 K. 12:31). For מִשְׁפָּחָה we find οἶκος πατριᾶς (Ex. 6:17, 19). The rich use of οἶκος is strengthened by οἰκία, which can also represent the Heb. בַּיִת. [8] Prv. 9:1 refers to the house which wisdom has built for itself : ἡ σοφία ᾠκοδόμησεν ἑαυτῇ οἶκον ... Originally the text speaks fig. of the way that Lady Wisdom has built her house and adorned it with seven pillars. Similarly Lady Folly sits at the door of her house high in the street and entices in the honest traveller (9:14). This metaphor leads to the idea of the house of wisdom, and the similar house

---

[4] Grenfell-Hunt, 203 recall that Memphis itself is called Ha-t-ka-ptah, "temple of the divine person of Ptah," obviously after the main temple in the city. Cf. A. Wiedemann, *Herodots zweites Buch* (1890), 47; Wilcken Ptol., 367.

[5] Cf. Hatch-Redpath, 973-982.

[6] The well-known command to Noah in Gn. 7:1 runs : εἴσελθε σὺ καὶ πᾶς ὁ οἶκός σου εἰς τὴν κιβωτόν, ὅτι σὲ εἶδον δίκαιον ἐναντίον μου ἐν τῇ γενεᾷ ταύτῃ. The LXX rendering οἶκος seems rather weaker than the Heb. אֹהֶל: Gn. 9:21, 27; 31:33; Lv. 14:8; Nu. 9:15 (ἐκάλυψεν ἡ νεφέλη τὴν σκηνήν, τὸν οἶκον τοῦ μαρτυρίου).

[7] Gn. 28:19 LXX : καὶ ἐκάλεσεν Ἰακὼβ τὸ ὄνομα τοῦ τόπου ἐκείνου Οἶκος θεοῦ, 28:22 : καὶ ὁ λίθος οὗτος, ὃν ἔστησα στήλην, ἔσται μοι οἶκος θεοῦ ...

[8] Hatch-Redp., 969 f.

of the Torah : "Acc. to the judgment of their fellows, who sit with the scorners, they will be judged, for they have preached revolt against the statutes and have despised the covenant which they have established in the land of Damascus — this is the new covenant — and neither they nor their kin shall have a portion in the house of the Torah" (Damasc., 20, 11-13). Is the "house of the Torah" here a term for the community itself ? Unique, too, is Damasc., 3, 18 ff.: "But God ... remitted their guilt and took away their sin, and he built for them a permanent house (בית נאמן) in Israel." The expression "permanent house" is obviously metaphorical, but it carries an allusion to 1 S. 2:35; 2 S. 7:16; 1 K. 11:38. In the Damasc. teaching there was obviously a specific use of "house," "house of the Torah," "permanent house." Apocalyptic speaks similarly : "And then will the righteous and elect cause to appear the house of his congregation" (En. 53:15). This is obviously connected in some way with the NT understanding of the community as the "house of God" (Hb. 3:1-6).

3. "House of God" in Jesus and the Gospels.

In the NT, too, we find both οἶκος and οἰκία; the gen. τοῦ θεοῦ is usually linked with οἶκος, not οἰκία (though cf. Jn. 14:2 : ἐν τῇ οἰκίᾳ τοῦ πατρός μου). As in the LXX, οἶκος τοῦ θεοῦ is used in honour of the earthly sanctuary of Israel. No other sacred or ecclesiastical structure is called by this term in the NT sphere. But the Christian community itself is the → ναὸς τοῦ θεοῦ, the οἶκος τοῦ θεοῦ (Hb. 3:6; 1 Pt. 4:17; 1 Tm. 3:15) and the οἶκος πνευματικός (1 Pt. 2:5). It may be supposed that this usage was common to primitive Christianity and became a permanent part of the preaching tradition.

In the Synoptists we find οἶκος τοῦ θεοῦ in Mk. 2:26 and par. Jesus is here alluding to the story of David's meeting with the priest Ahimelech in Nob (1 S. 21:1-10). It is true that the OT narrative itself does not refer to an οἶκος τοῦ θεοῦ in Nob, but the NT adds other features too. [9] In another tradition Jesus at the cleansing of the temple taught : "Is it not written, My house shall be called of all nations the house of prayer ? but ye have made it a den of thieves" (Mk. 11:17 and par.). Jesus is alluding primarily to Is. 56:7 (LXX: ὁ γὰρ οἶκός μου οἶκος προσευχῆς κληθήσεται πᾶσιν τοῖς ἔθνεσιν). [10] The term "house of prayer" is attested elsewhere for the temple (Is. 56:7; 60:7 LXX; cf. 1 K. 8:29); it also seems to have been used for Jewish synagogues. [11] Lohmeyer comments on the special significance of Mk. 11:17: "(The temple) is the 'house of God' and is thus holy in all its parts and chambers. But this general description is not based on the fact that a holy offering is continually made there or priests discharge a holy ministry. It is due to the fact that this is a 'place of prayer' where each of the righteous can and should pray to God. Plainly to be seen here is the view of the Galilean layman who works and lives far from the cultic centre of the Jewish faith, and venerates the temple merely as the chief synagogue ; for 'house of prayer' is a fixed expression for the synagogue of the Jewish congregations. Also to be seen is the ancient prophetic antithesis between prayer and sacrifice, between a godly and pious life and sacred ministry. But the view is first given its strict significance by the final definition :

---

[9] "David takes and eats the forbidden holy bread, the disciples pluck and eat what is permitted but at a forbidden time" (Loh. Mk., 64). "The οἶκος τοῦ θεοῦ is naturally the tabernacle" (Loh., 64, n. 4).
[10] The continuation in Is. 56:8 LXX is not without importance : εἶπεν κύριος ὁ συνάγων τοὺς διεσπαρμένους Ἰσραήλ, ὅτι συνάξω ἐπ' αὐτὸν συναγωγήν. As compared with Mt. 21:13; Lk. 19:46, Mk. adopts the πᾶσιν τοῖς ἔθνεσιν of Is. 56:7 LXX. Bultmann Trad., 36, Joh., 87 conjectures that the original story is expanded in Mk. 11:17.
[11] Cf. Loh. Mk., 236, n. 1, referring to Abrahams, Stud., I, c. 11.

'of all nations.' In the 'forecourt of the nations,' as one might interpret it, the peoples, let alone 'the people,' must not buy and sell, but 'all nations' must 'worship' there." [12] In Jn. 2:16 the rebuke of Jesus runs : "Take these things hence ; make not my Father's house an house of merchandise." This form, too, seems to have arisen out of the situation, but it recalls the prophecy in Zech. 14:21: καὶ οὐκ ἔσται Χαναναῖος οὐκέτι ἐν τῷ οἴκῳ κυρίου παντοκράτορος ἐν τῇ ἡμέρᾳ ἐκείνῃ. Jn. himself refers to ψ 68(69):9: ὁ ζῆλος τοῦ οἴκου σου καταφάγεταί με. Jn. does not mean that Jesus is consumed by inner zeal for His Father's house, but that His zeal will lead Him to death (hence fut. καταφάγεταί με, cf. ψ 68:9 in R. 15:3). [13]

Jesus often spoke of "my Father's house." Sometimes He had in view the earthly temple (Lk. 2:49 : τὰ τοῦ πατρός μου, Jn. 2:16 : ὁ οἶκος τοῦ πατρός μου), sometimes the heavenly home (Jn. 14:2 : ἡ οἰκία τοῦ πατρός μου). In Jn.'s imagery the "house" can imply God's kingdom (8:35). [14]

4. The Heavenly "Father's House" in Gnosticism and Philo.

Gnosticism, too, is fond of the picture of the "dwelling" or "house." In Mandaean writings we often find the address : "To you I say and declare, you elect and perfect, who dwell in the world." [15] The world itself is a "dwelling" or "house," though "lower," "dark" and "perishable," and differentiated from the house of consummation. (ביתא באיתא) is often used in Mandaean writings for the cosmic structure, [16] though the same metaphor is found among the Persians. [17] Typically Mandaean is Lidz. Ginza, 499 f.: "When Adam heard this (the words of the helper, the uthra), he no longer asked concerning the transitory. He no longer asked concerning those who built the perishable house ; he endured and dwellt therein. But soon he flew upwards and came to his place, the place whence he had been made, the place whence he was made and where his figure was illumined. Adam rejoiced in his mind, he brightened in his mind : How wonderful is

---

[12] Loh. Mk., 236.

[13] In the LXX (as opposed to Rahlfs) this is already an eschatological prophecy which points back to a tradition.

[14] "The 'Father's house' and 'the kingdom of God' cannot be separated. The term 'house' corresponds to the name 'father,' the term 'kingdom' to the name 'king.' In 8:35, too, the idea of the 'house of God' is par. to God's kingdom even though not related to heaven" (Schl. J., 292 f.).

[15] Lidz. Joh., 54, 179; Ginza R., 376, 25 : "I say and declare to you, you souls, which dwell in the perishable house," cf. Lidz. Liturg., 4, n. 3. On Gnostic thinking cf. Jonas, 101: "The stay in this world is a 'dwelling' — with the implication of changeability as well as confinement — and the world itself is a 'dwelling' or 'house.' In antithesis to the dwellings of light it is the 'lower dwelling,' the 'dark dwelling,' the 'perishable house.' In the idea of dwelling there is the sense of a temporary sojourn which has come about by destiny or choice and which can be ended in principle — one may leave a dwelling, exchange it for another, or let it perish behind one — and yet with this impermanent aspect there is also the constitutive aspect, the importance that the place has for life, the reference of existence to it : Life has to dwell somewhere and is linked with the Where; this is essential to it ; it is determined by the Where, that is, it is itself a spatial phenomenon and lives in terms of its place. Hence it can only exchange dwelling for dwelling, and even life outside the world is dwelling, i.e., in the habitations of light and life which are an infinity of circumscribed places outside this world. If, however, 'life' settles in the world, it can lead its established temporal relation thereto to the point of becoming a 'son of (earthly) life' — the danger of dwelling. But 'you were not from here, your root was not from this world' (Lidz. Ginza, 379)." It is hardly possible, however, to understand the distinctive elements of Jn. 8:35 f. in terms of Gnostic thought.

[16] Lidz. Joh., 7, n. 5.

[17] Cf. Bundehiš <Justi>, 58, 17.

what my father has said to me, how wonderful what the great life has taught me. Go, go, you planets, be a portion of your own houses. Go, be a portion of your own houses, and your houses be your portion ! I rise up with the root of my father, while the house is left to you." The believer, too, is admonished to keep in mind his otherworldly origin : "You were not from here, your root was not from this world. The house in which you dwell, this house life has not built." [18] The elect are promised : "You will shine in the house of your Father as the uthras of light shine at the place of light." [19] There is longing for the Father's house : "When will I put off the bodily garment and go to the place of life, to the place of the house of good, to the world in which my house stands ? I will set forth and go to my Father's house, I will not return to my house here." [20]

Metaphorically Philo also (Som., 1, 256) can sometimes speak of the return of the soul to the Father's house (εἰς τὸν πατρῷον οἶκον) to flee the long and unceasing storm abroad. As it was possible for paganism to speak of a "house of God" (οἶκος τοῦ θεοῦ, the house of Aphrodite, Herond. Mim., 1, 26) or "house of the gods" (οἶκος τῶν θεῶν, W. R. Paton and E. L. Hicks, Inscr. of Cos [1891], No. 8, 4), so in later Judaism οἶκος τοῦ θεοῦ remained in use as a name for the temple in Jerusalem (Jos. Bell., 4, 281). [21] Philo likes to spiritualise this as he does ναὸς τοῦ θεοῦ, and to apply it to the individual soul : "Hasten, my soul, to become God's house, a holy sanctuary, the most beautiful abode. For perhaps you also will acquire as master of the house the master whom the whole world has, and who is concerned for his house that it should always be kept safe and undamaged" (Som., 1, 149). Even plainer is Sobr., 62-64 : "It must be considered, however, who is to dwell in the house of Shem after this blessing ; for Holy Scripture does not tell us precisely. One can only say : the Governor of the universe. Is there then to be found in creation a more worthy house for God than a soul which is perfectly purified and which regards only the morally beautiful as a good, but counts everything else which is held to be such only among satellites and subjects ? But God's dwelling in a house is not meant in a spatial sense — He embraces all things while embraced by none — but in the sense that He lavishes special care and protection on this place ; to every owner of a house there necessarily attaches concern for it. Hence may everyone upon whom God has poured love for Him as a good pray to God that he may acquire as a resident the ruler of the world who will raise this paltry building (τὸ βραχὺ τοῦτο οἰκοδόμημα), the soul, from earth up aloft, and bind it to the ends of heaven." Widespread in Hell. and Gnostic literature is the movement of thought from building to builder, work of art to artist, creation to God. In this sense Philo, too, can compare the cosmos with a house (οἰκία) or city (πόλις). Thus, in order that a house or city may be built, one asks what must be assembled. A builder, stone, wood and tools are needed. What is the builder (δημιουργός) but the author by whom the building is erected ? What are stone and wood but the materials from which it is made ? What are the tools but the things by which it is constructed ? But for what purpose is the building put up if not for shelter and protection ? Now turn from individual buildings and consider the great dwelling or city, this world (ἴδε τὴν μεγίστην οἰκίαν ἢ πόλιν, τόνδε τὸν κόσμον). You will recognise as its author God, by whom it is built, as the material the four elements, from which it is made, as the tool God's reason,

---

[18] Lidz. Ginza, 379, 24-27.
[19] Ibid., 20, 21 f.
[20] Lidz. Ginza, 560, 4-9; a portion of Ginza is called "The Book of Silmai, 'the lord of the House.' " The term (מרא ביתא) has the same meaning as elsewhere in the Mandaean writings ; it refers to the Lord of the earthly world. The Evil One can bear this designation, and Silmai seems to belong to the underworld.
[21] "We Idumeans will protect the house of God, put ourselves at the head in the fight for the common fatherland, and resist both enemies from without and traitors from within" (Jos. Bell., 4, 281).

through which it was constructed, and as the ground the goodness of the Creator (τῆς δὲ κατασκευῆς αἰτίαν τὴν ἀγαθότητα τοῦ δημιουργοῦ). Cf. Philo Cher., 126 f., also Leg., 3, 99 : the same comparison of the cosmos with a house or city. [22] Philo can sometimes quote a philosophical view of life acc. to which the body is the "house" of the soul (οὐκ οἰκία ψυχῆς τὸ σῶμα; Det. Pot. Ins., 33). But for him the soul, too, can be a house which lodges holy and pious thoughts (Conf. Ling., 27) or which receives the *logos* itself (Deus Imm., 135). In such cases the term οἰκία is either metaphorical or it comes from another exegetical context in the OT (e.g., Leg. All., 3, 1-3). [23]

5. Early Christian Sayings about the Earthly Temple, and Contacts with Oriental Symbolical Use.

According to Lk. 11:51 the priest Zacharias was struck down by a godless mob in the temple itself, between the temple house or entrance (Lk. οἶκος, perhaps אוּלָם) and the altar of burnt offering. [24] In Stephen's speech in Ac. 7:2 ff. we find a distinction between the tabernacle (σκηνὴ τοῦ μαρτυρίου) and Solomon's temple (οἶκος). David received permission to build for the house of Jacob a dwelling-place (σκήνωμα) for God, but Solomon built Him a house (οἶκος). God does not dwell in the works of men's hands (7:48); what house will you build for me ? (7:49). In accordance with the present form of the text one might ask whether the tabernacle and the dwelling-place of David's prayer (σκηνὴ τοῦ μαρτυρίου, σκήνωμα) are pleasing to God (cf. Hb. 8:2) while the house (οἶκος) is the occasion of false conceptions, or whether σκήνωμα and οἶκος finally amount to the same and are equally unobjectionable so long as 1 K. 8:27; 2 Ch. 6:18 (God's trans-

---

[22] "Similarly when one enters into the great palace of the world, and sees the all-embracing vault of heaven moving in a circle, the planets and fixed stars with their similar, steady, harmonious and rhythmical movement so beneficial to the universe, one will surely come to the conclusion that all this has not been made without perfect art, but that God was and is the Creator of all these things. He who draws this conclusion perceives the deity through the shadow, since he moves on from the works to the Master" (Leg. All., 3, 99). In Gnostic lit. Lidz. Ginza, 379 : "The man who brought me here will tell me why he has brought me. The house in which I dwell will tell me who built it. The seven who live in it will tell me whence they come." Related, yet different, are the statements in Hb. 3:1-6 about the οἶκος and the κατασκευάσας αὐτόν.

[23] For Philo the wicked man is homeless (φυγάς), without city and house (ἄπολις καὶ ἄοικος), as shown by the example of Jacob and Esau. "For wickedness, which follows after the passions and full of unreason pursues to rustic boorishness, cannot inhabit the city of virtue. But Jacob, full of wisdom, is a full citizen (πολίτης) and inhabits virtue as his dwelling (οἰκίαν τὴν ἀρετὴν κατοικεῖ), for of him it is said : And Jacob was a simple man, who lived in a house" (Leg. All., 3, 2). The inter-relating of πόλις and οἶκος should be noted here. Cf. also Deus Imm., 94-95 with its association of cities, houses, wells, vineyards and oliveyards on the basis of Dt. 6:10 ff.: "The general and specific virtues are symbolically depicted as cities and houses, for the genus (τὸ γένος) may be compared with a city, since it is presented in broader outline and is common to many, whereas the species (τὸ εἶδος) is like a house, since it is restricted to a smaller space and excludes generality."

[24] Cf. E. Nestle, "Über Zacharias in Mt. 23," ZNW, 6 (1905), 198-200 : "In a small contribution to the Exp. T., 13, 562 I have shown with ref. to Ez. 8:16; Joel 2:17; 1 Macc. 7:36; Prot. Ev. Jc., 23 that ναός (οἶκος) is a transl. of אוּלָם, so that there is no contradiction with 2 Ch. 24 (on the Syr. קסטרומא v. also Merx, ad loc.)." Ez. 8:16 LXX : καὶ εἰσήγαγέν με εἰς τὴν αὐλὴν οἴκου κυρίου τὴν ἐσωτέραν, καὶ ἰδοὺ ἐπὶ τῶν προθύρων τοῦ ναοῦ κυρίου ἀνὰ μέσον τῶν αιλαμ καὶ ἀνὰ μέσον τοῦ θυσιαστηρίου ὡς εἴκοσι ἄνδρες ...

cendence over space) are not forgotten.[25] It may be suspected that a radical antithesis is concealed behind the text (ἀλλ' οὐχ ὁ ὕψιστος ἐν χειροποιήτοις κατοικεῖ), with an appeal to Is. 66:1.[26] Distinctive is the prophetic threat of Jesus in Mt. 23:38 : "Behold, your house will be left unto you desolate." At a first glance it might appear that the "house" (ὁ οἶκος ὑμῶν) refers to the temple at Jerusalem,[27] but it is not impossible that in accordance with prophetic and apocalyptic usage (En. 89:50 ff.; Test. L. 10) the city and people themselves are rushing onward to destruction.

Metaphorical, but linguistically not unusual, is the use in Mt. 12:44; Lk. 11:24. The unclean spirit which has gone out of a man wanders through dry places, and, finding no rest, says : "I will return to my house from which I went out," and when he comes he finds it empty, swept and garnished. That demons pursue their unnatural activities in shrines and houses finds attestation also in Babylonian and later Jewish texts : the sick man is the "house" of the evil spirit.[28]

6. "House of God" as an Early Christian Image for the Community.

In a midrash on Nu. 12:7 LXX : οὐχ οὕτως ὁ θεράπων μου Μωυσῆς· ἐν ὅλῳ τῷ οἴκῳ μου πιστός ἐστιν, Hb. 3:1-6 shows that Moses was a faithful servant in the whole house of God but that Christ as the Son has been set over the house of God (ἐν ὅλῳ τῷ οἴκῳ αὐτοῦ, 3:2, 6; 10:21: ἐπὶ τὸν οἶκον τοῦ θεοῦ). In the OT "my house" refers to Israel itself, so that the NT exegesis reminds us of the equation of "house of God" and the community. Indeed, the midrash presupposes

---

[25] Cf. the comm. on Ac.; O. Bauernfeind (1939), 118 f.; earlier Wendt (1913), 149, though his own judgment is that "he is pointing, not to the valuelessness, but to the purely relative value of the temple." Yet surely Ac. 7:48 is not so restricted.

[26] On Is. 66:1 cf. Mt. 5:34 f.

[27] Cf. in this sense 'Ιερ. 33:6 (26:6): καὶ δώσω τὸν οἶκον τοῦτον ὥσπερ Σηλωμ καὶ τὴν πόλιν δώσω εἰς κατάραν πᾶσιν τοῖς ἔθνεσιν πάσης τῆς γῆς, Syr. Bar. 8:2 (a voice from within the temple calls): "He who keeps the house has left it." Though cf. Jer. 12:7: ἐγκαταλέλοιπα τὸν οἶκόν μου, where the ref. is to the people ; Jer. 22:5 : ἐὰν δὲ μὴ ποιήσητε τοὺς λόγους τούτους, κατ' ἐμαυτοῦ ὤμοσα, λέγει κύριος, ὅτι εἰς ἐρήμωσιν ἔσται ὁ οἶκος οὗτος. Cf. esp. the great allegory of the house and the tower in En. 89:50 ff. (→ 128): the house is Jerusalem, the tower the temple. The way is already prepared for the equation of the house and Jerusalem in some prophetic texts, but it is basically apocalyptic. Cf. Test. L. 10 : "For the house which the Lord will choose for himself will be called Jerusalem, as the book of Enoch the Just has it." Cf. NT Deutsch (Schniewind) Mt., 231: "The temple will be destroyed ; it is also possible that 'your house' means 'your state and people' (v. on Mk. 3:24 f.); both interpretations fit in with what actually happened in 70 A.D. According to both the saying views the destruction of Jerusalem and the last judgment together, as in the address on the return which follows in c. 24."

[28] H. Gunkel, Zum religionsgeschichtlichen Verständnis d. NT (1910), 29 : "This is the real point where foreign material entered Judaism in full flood." "Demonology, which, as the Synoptics show, plays a great role in the age of Jesus, and which plainly recalls ancient Babylon ..." "The priest-exorcist of Babylon also knows how to cast out demons from the sick, and for this reason, in what became a well-known conjuration, as I learn from H. Zimmerli, he calls himself : 'He who destroys the sanctuaries (shrines) which are in the body of the sick.' Hence wicked demons set up 'their temple' in the body of the sick, cf. Mt. 12:44 f.; 1 C. 3:16; 2 C. 6:16; Eph. 2:22 etc." In later Judaism cf. bChul., 105b; bGit., 52a : (Satan laments concerning R. Meïr, or the demon of poverty says): "Woe is me, he has driven me out of my house" (quoted in Str.-B., I, 217; 652, and Kl. Mt., 113).

theologically that the community is the "house of God." [29] According to Hb. 3:3 the glory of Moses the servant stands in the same relation to that of Christ the Son as does the glory of the building to that of the builder. It is on the basis, not of the OT text itself, but of Hellenistic tradition, which likes to link the house with the builder, that the comparison between Moses and Christ is developed along these lines (3:2). κατασκευάζειν might very well be taken as a verb in the sense "to erect a building." [30] Christ in His dignity as the Son (υἱός) and Lord (κύριος) is thus the builder of the OT community of God (οἶκος τοῦ θεοῦ, 3:3). As the Son He is set over the house (3:6), and we cannot boast of being God's house unless we keep the confidence and boasting of our hope firm to the end (3:6). This train of thought shows on the one side that the equation of community and God's house is made quite naturally, and on the other side how developed is the Christology of Hb. The idea that the community is God's house is obviously related to, and grows out of, the early proclamation that the community is God's temple (1 C. 3:16; 6:19). Here, too, it may be plainly seen that the NT is not, like Philo, espousing an individualistic piety in which the pure soul of the individual becomes God's house. In the NT it is the community as such which is first called God's house or temple. In Eph. and 1 Pt. the early motif of the spiritual temple is taken up and expounded along basically similar lines : "You are fellow-citizens with the saints, and of the household of God, built upon the foundation of the apostles and prophets, in whom Jesus Christ is the head of the corner ; in him you are built up to be a dwelling-place of God in the Spirit" (Eph. 2:19-22). "Come to him (Christ), the living stone, rejected indeed by men, but chosen by God and precious, and build up yourselves as living stones to be a spiritually wrought house for a holy priesthood, to offer spiritual sacrifices which are acceptable to God, through Jesus Christ" (1 Pt. 2:3 ff.). How natural the term is as thus applied to the community may be seen from 1 Pt. 4:17: "For it is time that judgment begin at the house of God," and 1 Tm. 3:15 : "In case my coming is delayed, you should know what should be the order in the house of God, that is, in the church of the living God, which is the pillar and bulwark of truth." One may well say that this traditional material is an integral part of the primitive Christian κήρυγμα. The

---

[29] The older comm., in connection with the בַּיִת of Nu. 12:7, refer to "the whole complex of institutions set up by Yahweh to guide His people, or His economy of salvation" (Baentsch [1903], 513), or else they speak of the "nation and kingdom in which Moses has to arrange and rule everything" (Dillmann [1886], 66). But בַּיִת can hardly be so greatly spiritualised. The obvious ref. is to Israel as the possession of God : "When an Israelite spoke of his house, he did not refer only to the four walls of his dwelling, but rather to his children and grandchildren, to his family. Thus the house of God is His community, His people, the host of those who are bound to Him and whom He has called to be His possession" (Schl. Erl., III, 270). H. Windisch refers to the tabernacle, to the community established by the pre-historical Jesus, or to the world created by the Son (cf. Philo Post. C., 5; Plant., 50; Som., 1, 185; Wnd. Hb., 29). E. Käsemann, Das wandernde Gottesvolk (1939), 97 adduces Gnostic pars. in explanation of this by no means simple οἶκος concept : "The only pt. is that Hb. does not refer to the body of the Anthropos, but to his house, which is the same in Gnosticism. Thus myth describes the process of redemption as οἰκοδομή; the Anthropos is the οἰκονόμος, and the host of the redeemed are his 'house' in the heavenly home, or proleptically already on earth." Cf. also H. Schlier, Christus u. d. Kirche im Eph. (1930), 49 f.

[30] κατασκευάζειν == "to establish," "to set up," cf. Hb. 9:2, 6; 11:7; 1 Pt. 3:20; κατα-σκευάζειν in relation to a building "to erect," Jos. Vit., 65; Ap., I, 127; 193; 228; II, 12. For the divine creating Is. 40:28; 45:7; Wis. 9:2; 11:24; 13:4; Bar. 3:32; 4 Macc. 2:21; Philo Op. Mund., 149.

motif of the οἶκος τοῦ θεοῦ is referred to the community, yet it is not really a metaphor for the *familia dei*, but οἶκος remains an actual house, a spiritual, supraterrestrial, divine, and heavenly structure. This οἶκος πνευματικός is contrasted with the stone temple in Jerusalem and the sanctuaries of paganism. Christ is the living stone (1 Pt. 2:4: λίθος ζῶν) who is on the one side the valuable cornerstone underlying the whole building (Is. 28:16; Ps. 118:22; Mk. 12:10) and yet on the other the stone of stumbling and rock of offence (Is. 8:14; R. 9:33). Christians are fitted into the building as living stones (λίθοι ζῶντες, 1 Pt. 2:4 f.; Eph. 2:22); indeed, the metaphor can then change and on an OT basis embrace the priesthood as well as the sanctified people (1 Pt. 2:5, 9; Hb. 13:15 f.). The series of concepts: heavenly temple, holy priesthood, acceptable sacrifices, fuses and intermingles, though the roots are different and there is no material unity. [31] The saying in 1 Pt. 4:17 takes up an ancient prophetic idea (Jer. 25[32]:29; Ez. 9:6), namely, that the divine plagues and judgments will smite the sanctuary and the city first to purify and sanctify them; they are thus part of the eschatological plan. [32] The admonition in 1 Tm. 3:15 obviously seeks to express a fixed catechetical truth, namely, that the Church is the house of God, the support and stronghold of truth.

---

[31] Schlier, *op. cit.*, 49, n. 1: "That Christ is the ἀκρογωνιαῖος is often maintained in primitive Christian lit. on the basis of Is. 28:16; Ps. 118:22, cf. Ac. 4:11; 1 Pt. 2:4-7; Barn., 6, 2-4; Act. Pt. Verc., 24. How are we to explain it that a Jewish Gnostic sect gave the same title to Adam? Cf. the Naassene sermon, c. 14. This passage is not a later interpolation (cf. Reitzenstein-Schaeder, *Studien zum antiken Synkretismus aus Iran u. Griechenland*, 1926, 105). Is, then, a title of the Anthropos transferred to Jesus by the primitive Christian community? As regards Eph. 2:19 ff. this might well be true so far as investigation has thus far shown, esp. since Is. 28:16 is not really quoted here, but use is simply made of a traditional term from it (ἀκρογωνιαῖος). As far as the other passages are concerned I leave it an open question." 50: "The term 'building,' 'palace,' or 'house' is common in Mandaean lit. for the human body, cf., e.g., LG, 506, 31; 539, 20; 507, 20; 520, 26 ff.; 537, 30; 590, 15; Joh., 242, 12. We also find here refs. to the building of Adam, cf. RG, 242, 25 ff.; 245, 21. It is beyond my competence to say whether this goes back to Indian speculations, as alleged by L. Troje, "Ἀδάμ und ζωή," SAH, 17. *Abh.* (1916), 27 f. But in the present connection we are dealing, not with the earthly body of man, but with the heavenly body of the Anthropos." 50: "To find the explanation we seek, it is necessary to recall the ἀνὴρ τέλειος. This is the Anthropos who dwells in the heavens and to whom believers attain, or whose σῶμα grows. This ἀνὴρ τέλειος is, however, in Act. Arch., 8, 7 (p. 13) the στῦλος τῆς δόξης or στῦλος τοῦ φωτός, the place of light of saved souls, the heavenly building. But this pillar of light or splendour is also the cloud of light or splendour which is the abode of heavenly beings and which is called the world of light generally. Here again, however, the heavenly building is erected, or it is itself the abode of the redeemed to which they return. One may thus see that in the Act. Arch. the Anthropos (i.e., the σῶμα of the Anthropos) is identified as the heavenly building." On the one side the NT writings have some points of contact with Gnostic ideas and concepts, as H. Schlier and E. Käsemann (→ n. 29) can show. But on the other the lit. which has come down to us presupposes Christian thought and the tradition of Christian Gnosticism. It is thus very hard to delineate the historical background of the NT so far as the Gnostic sphere is concerned.

[32] Cf. Wnd. Kath. Br., 78; *NT Deutsch* (Hauck) on 1 Pt. 4:17 (III, 202). Str.-B., III, 767 adduces Rabb. pars., cf. Midr. Qoh. r., 9, 15 (45a): "The men of his age said to Noah: Where will the punishment begin? It will begin at the house of this man (i.e., at thy house). When Methuselah died, they said to Noah: Has not his punishment begun at the house of this man?" Test B. 10: "The Lord will first judge Israel on account of its ungodliness against him ... And then he will judge all the Gentiles." bBQ, 60a: "R. Shemuel b. Nachman (c. 260) has said, R. Jonathan (c. 220) has said, A judgment comes only when there are ungodly in the world, but it begins only with the righteous first ..." Thus the prophetic legacy lives on in the Rabb. as in apocalyptic, though it is set in a new light by the Christ event of the NT.

Though οἶκος can be used in the Greek world not only for a place of meeting but also for a religious society, [33] this verse suggests primarily the spiritual structure, which then attracts further images to itself (στῦλος, ἑδραίωμα). The Church is the house of God, the pillar, the bastion, because the Spirit dwells within it, revelation is committed to it, and the tradition is proclaimed by it. [34]

7. The Related Symbolism of Later Jewish Apocalyptic and the Rabbinate.

The concept of "house" is also fairly common in later Jewish lit. It is a common metaphor in the historical allegories in En. 83-90, with the special sense of sanctuary. Thus En. 89:36 refers to the tabernacle : "I saw in this vision until each sheep became a man and the lord of the sheep built a house and caused all the sheep to enter into the house." The sheep come to a good place and a pleasant and glorious land, "and that house stood among them in the pleasant land" (89:40). Sometimes the house can also be Jerusalem, and the tower the temple : "But that house became big and broad, and a high and tall tower was built for those sheep. That house was lowly, but the tower was high and lofty, and the lord of the sheep stood on the tower, and there was set before him a full table" (89:50). "But the sheep fell away and beasts of prey came upon them, so that the lord of the sheep left their house and their tower, and gave them all up to the lions to tear them to pieces" (89:56). [35] "The lions and tigers ate and consumed the greater part of the sheep, and wild boars ate with them, and they set the tower on fire and destroyed that house" (89:66). Then three sheep came back and began to build up again the ruins of the house (89:72). [36] A tower was also erected and a table set before the tower, "but all the bread was spotted and unclean" (89:73). Then the new Jerusalem was put in place of the old : "I stood up to see until he folded up that house. All the pillars were dismantled and the beams and decorations were wrapped up with it. It was taken away and set in a place in the south of the land. I saw until the lord of the sheep brought a new house, bigger and higher than the first, and set it up on the site of the first, which had been folded up. All its pillars were new, even its decorations were new and greater than those of the first and old house which he had dismantled ; and the lord of the sheep was in it" (90:28 f.). Here the concept of the new house is related to the heavenly Jerusalem in which all the slain and scattered sheep appear (90:32). The sword which was entrusted to the sheep is laid up in this house (90:19, 34). All the sheep were invited into this house, but it did not hold them, though it was big and roomy (90:34). [37] Tob., too, speaks of the destruction and rebuilding of the house of God (14:4 f.). As the text stands, it seems as if Jerusalem and the temple were to lie waste until the times of the aeon were fulfilled ;

---

[33] A. Wilhelm, "Beiträge zur gr. Inschriftenkunde," *Sonderheft d. Österr. Arch. Institutes,* VII (1909), 51; M. Fränkel, *Rhein. Museum,* 57 (1902), 153, 1; Inschr. von Magnesia, 94, 5 ff.: ἀρετῆς ἕνεκεν καὶ εὐνοίας [ἧς ἔχ]ων διατελεῖ εἴς τε τὸν οἶκον τὸν ἱερὸν καὶ εἰς τὸ[ν δῆμον].

[34] Rightly perceived by B. Weiss, *Die Briefe Pauli an Timotheus u. Titus* (1902), 152 n.; also Schl. Past., 111 f.

[35] En. 89:56 is quoted in Barn., 16, 5 : καὶ ἔσται ἐπ' ἐσχάτων τῶν ἡμερῶν, καὶ παραδώσει κύριος τὰ πρόβατα τῆς νομῆς καὶ τὴν μάνδραν καὶ τὸν πύργον αὐτῶν εἰς καταφθοράν (ἡ μάνδρα : from Soph., also pap., LXX = "hurdle," "pen," cf. Pr.-Bauer[3], s.v.).

[36] One cannot be sure who are the three sheep ; Zerubbabel, Joshua and Nehemiah (or Ezra) are mentioned. Cf. Schürer, III, 199.

[37] "En. 90 speaks particularly explicitly of the new 'house'; the direct divine origin, but not a preceding heavenly existence of the house, is maintained." "This house is Jerusalem, not just the temple, since the whole depiction fits the place of the saved community better than a single building." "Nevertheless, Jerusalem and the temple merge into a single picture in this section" (Volz Esch., 373).

only then would come the return from captivity and the building up of Jerusalem. [38] Here, then, there is expected a temple in glory which is ordained for all peoples. Test. L. 10:5 makes express appeal to En. 89:50 ff.: "For the house which the Lord will choose for himself will be called Jerusalem, as the Book of Enoch the Just has it." In Rabb. teaching a sevenfold heaven arches over the earth ; the highest heaven is called Araboth and is the dwelling of God, the righteous, and the angels which serve the Lord (Chag., 12b). Ref. is thus made to a special dwelling of God in the highest sphere of heaven ; cf. the idea of the Mechiza (מְחִיצָה), BB, 98a. [39] A curtain conceals the dwelling, the throne and the glory of God, and makes the dwelling of God inaccessible, but the righteous dead always approach and ministering angels do so at command, and hear the voice of God behind the curtain, though they do not see God Himself face to face. Acc. to Chag., 5b the dwelling of God is differentiated as an "inner chamber" (בתי גואי) from the "outer chamber" of heaven (בתי בראי). Both parts are together called "His place." [40] In Heb. En. we have an express description of the heavenly household, the upper court of judgment, and the most important angelic powers. Here, too, there is division into seven spheres, of which the highest is Araboth. A named angelic power is set over each (16:1). [41]

8. "House" as Family and Race.

Distinctive Hebrew modes of expression explain the fairly common NT phrase "house of Israel" = οἶκος Ἰσραήλ, Mt. 10:6; 15:24; Ac. 2:36; Hb. 8:8, 10. It derives from בֵּית יִשְׂרָאֵל, Ex. 16:31; 2 S. 1:12 (also without art. in the LXX at 3 Βασ. 12:21; ψ 113:17). On an OT basis the "house of David" (οἶκος Δαυίδ) is also used in Lk. 1:27, 69; 2:4. What is meant is the royal race (*gens*) of David. The term occurs especially in the story of the nativity (cf. 1 S. 20:16; 1 K. 12:16; 13:2). Two OT quotations speak of the "house of Jacob" (οἶκος Ἰακώβ) in Lk. 1:33 and Ac. 7:46. The reference is to the whole people of Israel. Another quotation (from Jer. 31:31 ff.) gives us the "house of Judah" (οἶκος Ἰούδα), which is in the first instance historical and speaks of the political disruption of the people (note "house of Israel" and "house of Judah" in Jer. 31:31), but which seems to be parallel to "house of Israel" in the NT (Hb. 8:8 ff.). The statement : "Pharaoh made him (Joseph) governor over Egypt and all his house," is also reminiscent of the OT (Ac. 7:10; cf. ψ 104:21).

---

[38] For an analysis of the text cf. Volz Esch., 26, 75 etc. "Probably the ἕως πληρωθῶσιν καιροὶ τοῦ αἰῶνος is to be detached from what immediately precedes and regarded as a direct continuation of, or explanatory addition to, the μέχρι χρόνου of v. 4. Thus the return from captivity and the rebuilding of Jerusalem would take place when the times of the aeon are fulfilled" (26).

[39] R. Jehuda said in the name of Rab : "He who adorns himself with the mantle of a scribe without being a scribe will not be brought into the circle of the Holy One, blessed be He, for it is written here : He does not dwell, and it is written there (Ex. 15:13): Unto the habitation of thy sanctuary" (bBB, 98a). On this whole section cf. Weber, 162-165. Cf. En. 14:10 (οἶκος μέγας); 14:15 (οἶκος μείζων) of the dwelling-place of God.

[40] "This is no objection, the one refers to the inner rooms and the other to the outer," bChag., 5b with ref. to 1 Ch. 16:27: "Beauty and glory are before him ; strength and gladness in his dwelling-place."

[41] On the text cf. H. Odeberg, *3 Enoch or the Hebrew Book of Enoch* (1938). Cf. the concept of the divine household : פמליא = פְּמַלְיָא, *familia*. Odeberg translates "heavenly household." 3 En. 27:2; 28:9; 30:1 speaks of a great synagogue in the highest heaven (Araboth-Raqia) under the direction of God and made up of the most important angels.

All these expressions remind us of basic OT ideas. The *natio, gens,* or *familia* has an ancestor or leader from whom the whole group receives its name and after whom it calls itself. Originally the proper name is a gen. behind οἶκος, but it then becomes the name of the group as such.

9. The "House" as a Group in the Structure of the Christian Community.

Primitive Christianity structured its congregations in families, groups and "houses." The house was both a fellowship and a place of meeting. Thus we read of the house of Stephanas in 1 C. 1:16, the house of Philemon in Phlm. 2, the house of Cornelius in Ac. 11:14, the house of Lydia in Ac. 16:15, the house of the prison governor at Philippi in Ac. 16:31, 34. Ac. 18:8 also refers to the faith of Crispus and his whole house. It is also likely that the house of Onesiphorus in 2 Tm. 1:16; 4:19 is a house fellowship of this kind. In this regard we read expressly in Ac. 2:46 that they broke bread by house (κατ' οἶκον), and the summary in Ac. 5:42 says that they taught and proclaimed the good news in the temple and in houses (κατ' οἶκον). It is explicitly emphasised that the conversion of a man leads his whole family to the faith; this would include wife, children, servants and relatives living in the house. [42] The use of οἶκος for "house," "family," is found elsewhere in primitive Christianity. This is especially evident in the fact that Christian life is lived in this kind of "house." One has only to think of the directions in the Past. The bishop must rule his own house well (1 Tm. 3:4), for if he cannot do this, how can he take care of the whole congregation (1 Tm. 3:5)? Deacons, too, should take good care of their children and houses (1 Tm. 3:12). [43] Hence it is no surprise that Tt. 1:11 complains of false teachers leading whole houses astray and ruining them, while 2 Tm. 1:16 and 4:19 stress the particular relation of the house of Onesiphorus to the imprisoned apostle. The house and family are the smallest natural groups in the total structure of the congregation. There is an interesting observation in Ac. 20:20 : "And how I kept back nothing that was profitable unto you, but have shewed you, and have taught you publicly, and from house to house (δημοσίᾳ καὶ κατ' οἶκους)." Along with public preaching the apostle also gave instruction in the house meetings of the community.

We find the same state of affairs and the same usage in the post-apost. writings. There is an interesting ref. in Ign. Sm., 13, 1: "I greet the houses of my brothers with

---

[42] It seems to me that the importance of the οἶκος and *familia* in the structure of the Christian community has not yet been fully recognised, though there is ref. to it in J. Jeremias, *Hat die älteste Christenheit die Kindertaufe geübt?* (1938), 15. Paul's admonitions and the household tables call for consideration. J. Weiss, *Urchristentum* (1917), 486 thinks these house churches are of the nature of conventicles, but this is not the meaning. We have here a natural growth of congregations which runs counter to the individualistic process of disintegration.

[43] Cf. Dib. Past., 33 f.: "The inference from house to office is also found in Gk. paraenesis, *v.* Isocrates Ad Nicoclem, 19 (text not very certain): οἴκει τὴν πόλιν ὁμοίως ὥσπερ τὸν πατρῷον οἶκον ταῖς μὲν κατασκευαῖς λαμπρῶς καὶ βασιλικῶς, ταῖς δὲ πράξεσιν ἀκριβῶς, ἵν' εὐδοκιμῆς ἅμα καὶ διαρκῆς, Ps.-Isoc. Ad Demonicum, 35 : ὅταν ὑπὲρ σεαυτοῦ μέλλῃς τινὶ συμβούλῳ χρῆσθαι, σκόπει πρῶτον πῶς τὰ ἑαυτοῦ διῴκησεν. ὁ γὰρ κακῶς διανοηθεὶς περὶ τῶν οἰκείων οὐδέποτε καλῶς βουλεύσεται περὶ τῶν ἀλλοτρίων, cf. also Euphr. Fr., 4, III, p. 320, Kock : ὁ γὰρ τὸν ἴδιον οἰκονομῶν κακῶς βίον, πῶς οὗτος ἂν σώσειε τῶν ἔξω τινά." At this pt., then, the Past. adopt the widespread popular wisdom of Hellenism.

[44] Herm. v., 1, 1, 9; 1, 3, 1; 2, 3, 1; s., 7, 1 f.; 7, 5; m., 12, 3, 6; s., 5, 3, 9.

wives and children, also the virgins, who are called 'widows.' " The virgins here are outside the houses of the brothers, and are perhaps not directly connected with them. In Pol., 8, 2 the bishop greets the widow of Epitropos "with her whole house and children"; here the wife is head of the household. Herm. likes to use οἶκος for "family." [44] It is striking that children are specifically mentioned in the post-apost. writings ; they are not just included in the οἶκος.

οἰκία → οἶκος.

Originally Gk. distinguished between οἶκος and οἰκία, cf. Xenoph. Oec., 1, 5 : οἶκος δὲ δὴ τί δοκεῖ ἡμῖν εἶναι; ἆρα ὅπερ οἰκία, ἢ καὶ ὅσα τις ἔξω τῆς οἰκίας κέκτηται, πάντα τοῦ οἴκου ταῦτά ἐστιν, Hdt., 7, 224 : ὃς καὶ ἐκδιδοὺς τὴν θυγατέρα Δαρείῳ τὸν οἶκον πάντα τὸν ἑαυτοῦ ἐπέδωκε. οἶκος had then a broader range than οἰκία, being the whole of a deceased person's possessions, what he leaves behind, whereas οἰκία is simply his residence. οἰκία occurs from the time of Hdt. (1, 17; 114 etc.) and is in common currency, also inscr. and pap. Ditt. Syll.[3], 306, 16 : τὰν δὲ οἰκιᾶν τιμὰν κομιζέσθω τῶ οἴκω ἑκάστω δύο μνᾶς, τὰν δὲ τιμασίαν ἦναι τᾶν οἰκιᾶν κατάπερ ἀ πόλις νομίζει. In other places, too, οἶκος is sometimes distinguished from it, P. Tebt., I, 46, 9. [1] In the LXX οἰκία is used for בַּיִת, בֵּית etc., but in the same sense as οἶκος.

In the NT οἰκία is used 1. lit. for "house" (Mt. 5:15; 7:24 ff.; 10:12a etc.), then fig. for "family," "household" (Mt. 10:12b; 12:25; Mk. 6:4). Worth noting is the precedence given it in Mk. 10:29 f. and par.: ὃς ἀφῆκεν οἰκίαν ἢ ἀδελφοὺς ἢ ἀδελφὰς ἢ μητέρα ἢ πατέρα ἢ τέκνα ἢ ἀγρούς. It is not impossible that the first and last in the series (οἰκία-ἀγροί) include the other members, though οἰκία could also mean the "household" or familia.

At Mt. 24:17: ἆραι τὰ ἐκ τῆς οἰκίας αὐτοῦ, it is probable that a later reading has ousted the original text : ἆραί τι ἐκ τῆς οἰκίας αὐτοῦ (DΘ lat Ir Or, cf. Mk. 13:15). [2]

οἰκία can also mean "possession" (= τὰ ὑπάρχοντα), as shown by a striking expression which is not uncommon in Gk., namely, κατεσθίειν τὰς οἰκίας τῶν χηρῶν (Mk. 12:40 and par.). [3] In Mk. 13:35 we find ὁ κύριος τῆς οἰκίας, equivalent to ὁ οἰκοδεσπότης in Mt. 24:43. οἰκία can also be used fig. Thus the independent parabolic saying in Jn. 8:35 tells us that the servant does not stay in the house eternally, but the son does. It could be that there is a mysterious reference to the kingdom of God in the ἐν τῇ οἰκίᾳ. [4] According to Mk. 3:24 f. βασιλεία and οἰκία are associated, and in Mt. 12:25, along with βασιλεία, we have the favourite Hellenistic pair πόλις and οἰκία; the point is to show that a society cannot be inwardly divided and hence Jesus cannot invade the kingdom

---

οἰκία. [1] Liddell-Scott, 1203; Moult.-Mill., 441. On the etym. Walde-Pok., I, 231. On the formation of οἰκ-ία (orig. collective ?) cf., e.g., ν(ε)οσσία "nest with young (νεοσσοί), brood," v. P. Chantraine, Formation des noms (Paris, 1933), 82; E. Schwyzer, Griech. Grammatik, I, 469, 4 and 5 [Debrunner].

[2] "ἆραι τὰ ἐκ τῆς οἰκίας αὐτοῦ. Was the clause hellenised ? Is D the original : ἆραί τι ἐκ τῆς οἰκίας αὐτοῦ ? Materially, too, τι is stronger than τά. There can be no question of his trying to take all that is in the house. τὰ ἐκ τῆς οἰκίας is par. to the Gk. of Jos." (Schl. Mt., 705).

[3] Cf. Hom. Od., 2, 237 f.: κατέδουσι βιαίως οἶκον 'Οδυσσῆος, Plut. Aud. Poet., 22d : καὶ γὰρ 'οἶκον' ποτὲ μὲν τὴν οἰκίαν καλοῦσιν 'οἶκον ἐς ὑψόροφον' ποτὲ δὲ τὴν οὐσίαν 'ἐσθίεταί μοι οἶκος', καὶ 'βίοτον' ποτὲ μὲν τὸ ζῆν ...

[4] So Schl. J., 213.

of Satan with satanic power. The term οἰκία does not refer to a ruling house, but simply to a family.⁵ Mk. 6:4 links three circles which deny recognition to the prophet, his native city (πατρίς), kin (συγγενεῖς) and family (ἡ οἰκία αὐτοῦ).⁶

2. Distinctive is Jesus' word of revelation in Jn. 14:2 f.: "In my Father's house (οἰκία τοῦ πατρός μου) are many dwellings (resting places). If it were not so, would I have told you that I go to prepare a place for you? And when I have gone and prepared a place for you, I will come again and receive you to myself, that where I am you may be also." This saying, which would seem to have lost its original form, is fairly isolated in the context, and is perhaps older than the sayings around it. The expression ἡ οἰκία τοῦ πατρός μου reminds us of such parallels as the Rabb. mechiza and the Gnostic abode of light.⁷ As the earthly temple is an asylum for fugitives, so the Father's dwelling has places of rest for the afflicted disciples of Jesus. The same apocalyptic tradition may be clearly seen in Eth. En. 45:3: "Your dwellings will be without number."

Acc. to Schlatter⁸ Jesus is referring to the ascension when He speaks of going away to prepare a place for them, but the conducting of the disciples into God's house will take place only at the parousia. The expression οἰκία τοῦ πατρός cannot be seen in isolation from οἶκος τοῦ θεοῦ and ναὸς τοῦ θεοῦ; hence it can hardly be heaven in general.

3. New questions are raised by what Paul says in 2 C. 5:1-10. Here the metaphorical οἰκία τοῦ σκήνους denotes first the corruptible body which we have on earth; its counterpart is οἰκοδομὴ ἐκ θεοῦ, οἰκία ἀχειροποίητος, αἰώνιος, οἰκητήριον ἐξ οὐρανοῦ, which denotes the future heavenly body.

The use of "house" fig. for the body is very common, and it can convey the idea of perishability. Thus Job complains in 4:19: "And especially the man of a house of clay, mortal man, built of dust ..." (τοὺς δὲ κατοικοῦντας οἰκίας πηλίνας), cf. 1 Cl., 39, 5. In the Rabb. however, בַּיִת is not commonly used for the body, though Ber., 44b might be an exception.⁹ The Lat. domus has rather a different ring in Sen. Epist. Moral., XX, 3, 14: nec domum esse hoc corpus, sed hospitium et quidem breve hospitium ... Philo, on the other hand, is not wholly pessimistic: "For God wished to assign to the virtuous man in reward a well-built house finely appointed from foundation to roof —

⁵ To this saying of Jesus there are many pars. in the popular wisdom of antiquity, e.g., from Derech Erez Zuta, 5: "A house in which there is disunity will assuredly be destroyed at the last" (Str.-B., I, 635). Soph. Ant., 672: ἀναρχίας δὲ μεῖζον οὐκ ἔστιν κακόν· αὕτη πόλεις τ' ὄλλυσιν ἥδ' ἀναστάτους οἴκους τίθησιν. Cic. Lael., 7, 23: quae enim domus tam stabilis, quae tam firma civitas est, quae non odiis et discidiis funditus possit everti?
⁶ In analysis cf. Bultmann Trad., 30 ff. and Loh. Mk., 111. There is an important par. to the saying of Jesus in P. Oxy., I, 1, 9: οὐκ ἔστιν δεκτὸς προφήτης ἐν τῇ πατρίδι αὐτοῦ, οὐδὲ ἰατρὸς ποιεῖ θεραπείας εἰς τοὺς γινώσκοντας αὐτοῦ.
⁷ Lidz. Liturg., II Oxford Collect. 10: "This is the prayer and praise which have come to us from the great place of light and the radiant dwelling," p. 179. But the world itself is the house acc. to this Gnostic view: "Above the four corners of the house and above the seven sides of the firmament rests silence, peace and splendour" (Qol., 5, p. 9).
⁸ Schl. J., 292.
⁹ Ber., 44b: "Woe to the house through which vegetables (λάπαθον) pass," cf. Levy Wört., I, 224, Str.-B., III, 517. In Rabb. בַּיִת can mean dwelling, temple, school, house of instruction, and it can also denote the relation of pupils to a teacher (the "school" of Shammai or Hillel), but esp. the wife as the "house" of the husband in a sexual sense.

the body is indeed the house of the soul, which has grown up in close association with it (οἰκία δὲ ψυχῆς συμφυεστάτη σῶμα), both with regard to many other things useful and indispensable to life and also with regard to our spirit purged by perfect expiations" (Praem. Poen., 120). This picture seems to have been familiar to Philo in this anthropological sense. But only in Gnosticism proper can it really be worked out. Here the body is the abode of evils, "the abode in which the planets dwell." The soul mounts up to its original home and "curses this place of the house of thy guardians" (Lidz. Liturg., 160).

Paul shares to some degree this general idea, espoused especially by Gnosticism: οἰκία δὲ ψυχῆς σῶμα. Related is 1 C. 6:19. The idea of the tent is only a modification of the general anthropological conception, and denotes particularly the transitory nature of the earthly body. [10] 2 Pt. 1:13 refers to a σκήνωμα.

This image, too, was common in Hellenism, and is linked with a specific anthropological conception. There is an early instance already in Is. 38:12: ἐξῆλθεν καὶ ἀπῆλθεν ἀπ' ἐμοῦ ὥσπερ ὁ καταλύων σκηνὴν πήξας, though here σκηνή is only a simile. Cf., however, Wis. 9:15: φθαρτὸν γὰρ σῶμα βαρύνει ψυχήν, καὶ βρίθει τὸ γεῶδες σκῆνος νοῦν πολυφρόντιδα. [11]

4. According to Phil. 4:22 there are around Paul "slaves from the imperial palace" (οἱ ἐκ τῆς Καίσαρος οἰκίας). This expression (domus Caesaris, Caesarum, Augusta, Augustana, Augustiana, later divina) might mean the ruling family with all its members, but the more likely reference is to the staff of the imperial household, both slaves and freedmen. Though the expression alone does not prove that Paul wrote Phil. from Rome, when taken with other hints in the epistle it suggests a Roman origin. [12]

Herm. s., 1, 1 f. and 8 f. demands Christian resolution and the renunciation of the earthly world. The passage raises objections to Christian possessions in this world (lands, expensive establishments, houses, perishable dwellings). He who possesses these earthly goods, and on account of them is expelled from the heavenly city, cannot be

---

[10] Wnd. 2 K., 158: "The pitcher goes to the water until it breaks, and the tent is pulled down as soon as circumstances do not allow of any longer stay."

[11] Wnd. 2 K., 158, Excurs. "Das Bild vom Zelt" mentions Plat. Phaed., 81c as a passage with a Hellenistic feel. But the image of the σκηνή or σκῆνος is pre-Platonic, Diels, Index. It is common after Plato, cf. Ps.-Plat. Ax., 365e; 366a; Cl. Al. Strom., 5, 94, 3: ὃ γήϊνόν φησιν ὁ Πλάτων σκῆνος. Corp. Herm., 13, 15: καλῶς σπεύδεις λῦσαι τὸ σκῆνος, is important. In Chr. lit. cf. Dg., 6, 8; Tat. Or. Graec., 15, 3.

[12] Cf. esp. Zahn Einl.², I § 31, 389, n. 1: "Though domus Caesaris (Caesarum, Augusta, Augustana, Augustiana, later divina) commonly denotes the imperial house in our sense of the ruling family with all its members, the expression here (ἐκ τῆς οἰκίας, ex domo) as constantly used does not mean relatives of the emperor — this would be οἱ ἐκ γένους (or πρὸς γένους, Clem. Hom., 4, 8; 12, 8 and 15) or ἀφ' αἵματος (Philo Leg. Gaj., 11; Jos. Bell., I, 18, 4) or συγγενεῖς τοῦ Καίσαρος (Acta Pl. et Thecl., 36) — but persons of lower or higher rank belonging to the imperial household, always slaves or freedmen in earlier days: Philo Flacc., 5; Act. Pt. et Pl., p. 104, 9; 106, 15; 193, 5; Hipp. Ref., 9, 12; Inscr. R. Neapol., No. 6912 ex domo Caesarum libertorum et servorum etc.; CIL, 6, No. 8645; 8653 f.; 10, No. 1745. In the will of Gregory (Migne, 37, 389) ἐκ τῆς οἰκίας μου γενόμενος is my former slave. It should also be remembered that from an early time οἰκέται, domestici in the imperial period (Suet. Otho, 10 extr.; Tert. Apol., 7; 39), means "domestics." Cf. Dib. Ph., 75: "The expression οἱ ἐκ τῆς Καίσαρος οἰκίας refers to imperial slaves, who were to be found in Rome (cf. the inscr. of the slave Narcissus and his Christian descendants in de Waal, Röm. Quartalschrift, 26 [1912], 161 ff.), but also throughout the empire."

happy about these earthly possessions (1, 4). "Thus, seek to win oppressed souls instead of fields, each according to his abilities, visit widows and orphans and do not neglect them, and direct all your riches and all your possessions which you have received from God to fields and houses of this kind" (1, 8). The terms ἀγροί, παρατάξεις, οἰκοδομαί, οἰκήματα, οἰκήσεις, οἰκίαι, are here depreciated and parodied ; we are to win fields and houses of another kind.

† οἰκεῖος.

(Adj., in Ion. οἰκήϊος), from οἰκεύς, "member of the household," "household slave." [1] Hence the basic meaning of οἰκεῖος is "belonging or standing in relation to the household" [Debrunner]. The opp. is ἀλλότριος. The word occurs as an adj. from Hes., Hdt., cf. also inscr., pap. and LXX. In the LXX we find such expressions as οἰκεῖα σαρκὸς αὐτοῦ (Lv. 18:6); οἰκεία πατρός or μητρός (Lv. 18:12 f.); γείτονες οἰκεῖοι θεράποντες (Job 19:15 A); ὃς δὲ μισεῖ κρύπτειν, διίστησιν φίλους καὶ οἰκείους (Prv. 17:9); ἀπὸ τῶν οἰκείων τοῦ σπέρματός σου οὐχ ὑπερόψῃ (Is. 58:7), cf. Barn., 3, 3. Epict. Gnom. Stob., 11: ὅπερ οὖν σοι φυσικὸν καὶ συγγενές, ὁ λόγος, τοῦτο καὶ οἰκεῖον ἡγησάμενος τούτου ἐπιμελοῦ. The meaning "belonging to the house" [2] is secondary ; from it (cf. familiaris : 1. "pertaining to the family ," 2. "intimate," "familiar") comes οἰκεῖος "fitting," "suitable" [Debrunner], cf. Polyb., 5, 87, 3 : οὐκ ἀλλότριος ἦν τῆς ἡσυχίας, ἀλλ᾽ ὑπὲρ τὸ δέον οἰκεῖος, 4, 57, 4 : ἅτε λίαν οἰκείους ὄντας τῶν τοιούτων ἐγχειρημάτων, 14, 9, 5 : πάντα δ᾽ ἦν οἰκεῖα μεταβολῆς τὰ κατὰ τὴν χώραν, Diod. S., 13, 91: οἰκείους ὄντας ὀλιγαρχίας, 19, 70 : ὡς ὄντας οἰκείους τυραννίδος, Strabo, 1, 1, 11: οἰκεῖοι φιλοσοφίας (cf. 1, 1, 20).

In the NT the adjective, partly used as a noun, is found in the Pauline corpus, and is obviously controlled by the understanding of the community. This is the οἶκος τοῦ θεοῦ in Hb. 3:1-6; hence Christians are members of the household, the familia Dei. Gl. 6:10 demands that good should be done to all men, but chiefly to the household of faith (πρὸς τοὺς οἰκείους τῆς πίστεως). Understanding of the "neighbour" recognises a particular obligation to fellow-believers. [2] πίστις is here obviously objective as elsewhere in Paul (cf. Gl. 3:2, 25). The gen. dependent on οἰκεῖος is not taken by Zahn in the strict sense of "intimate with" but in the more general sense of a member of the household "with reference to, or in the sense of, faith." [3] Eph. 2:19 has a solemn, almost liturgical ring : "Ye are no more strangers (ξένοι) and foreigners (πάροικοι), but fellow-citizens with the saints, and of the household of God (οἰκεῖοι τοῦ θεοῦ)"; here again the Hellenistic combination of οἶκος and πόλις is worth noting. The image of the "house of God" (οἶκος τοῦ θεοῦ), transferred spiritually to the community, is echoed here and developed in what follows, 2:20-22. This circle of images is a common motif particularly beloved in primitive Christianity. Closely related is the Gnostic conception of the heavenly building and the building up of believers into it. [4] The gen. is to be taken as a subj. gen.; Christians are members of the familia Dei. Gl. 6:10 and Eph. 2:19 undoubtedly presuppose the concept and metaphor of a spiritual building. οἰκεῖος is used in a very different and secular sense in 1 Tm. 5:8:

οἰκεῖος. [1] Chantraine, Formation des noms (1933), 52; Liddell-Scott, 1202; Moult.-Mill., 440.

[2] Later Jewish pars. which simply recognise the privilege and precedence of those who are nearest may be found in Str.-B., III, 578.

[3] Zn. Gl., 276, n. 1.

[4] H. Schlier, Christus und die Kirche im Eph. (1930), 49 f.

"But if any provide not for his own (οἱ ἴδιοι), and specially for those of his own house (μάλιστα τῶν οἰκείων) ..." We have here the didactic style of legal exposition (εἰ δέ τις ...) and ethical admonition, which lends the support of a divine command to a general moral norm. It is interesting that the term ἴδιοι is broader here, while οἰκεῖοι is taken more narrowly. [5]

† οἰκέω.

This word, linked with οἶκος and οἰκία, can mean intrans. "to dwell," "to live" (from Hom., also inscr. and pap., cf. Hom. Il., 14, 116; Od., 9, 200, 400; Hdt., 1, 56; 2, 166), and also trans. "to inhabit," "to take as one's abode" (Hom. Il., 20, 218; Hdt., 1, 1 and 175). [1] In the LXX it is often used for יָשַׁב. οἰκεῖν μετά τινος means "to live with a woman," cf. Soph. Oed. Tyr., 990 : Μερόπης, γεραιέ, Πόλυβος ἧς ᾤκει μέτα. Cf. also 1 C. 7:12 : καὶ αὕτη συνευδοκεῖ οἰκεῖν μετ' αὐτοῦ, and 7:13 : καὶ οὗτος συνευδοκεῖ οἰκεῖν μετ' αὐτῆς. In a general sense Dg., 6, 3b can say of Christians : καὶ Χριστιανοὶ ἐν κόσμῳ οἰκοῦσιν, οὐκ εἰσὶ δὲ ἐκ τοῦ κόσμου (cf. Jn. 17:11, 14), or 5, 5 : πατρίδας οἰκοῦσιν ἰδίας, ἀλλ' ὡς πάροικοι· μετέχουσι πάντων ὡς πολῖται, καὶ πάνθ' ὑπομένουσιν ὡς ξένοι (note that the stems οἶκος and πόλις are again used together).

More important, however, is the fact that οἰκεῖν is used to describe inward psychological and spiritual processes. Thus Dg., 6, 3a can say metaphorically : οἰκεῖ μὲν ἐν τῷ σώματι ψυχή, οὐκ ἔστι δὲ ἐκ τοῦ σώματος ... (as the soul lives in the body, but does not derive from the body, so is the relation of Christians in the world). Similarly we read in R. 7:18 : "For I know that in me (that is, in my flesh) dwelleth no good thing" (οὐκ οἰκεῖ ἐν ἐμοί ... ἀγαθόν), and 7:20 goes on to say that sin dwells in me (ἡ οἰκοῦσα ἐν ἐμοὶ ἁμαρτία). The dwelling of sin in man denotes its dominion over him, its lasting connection with his flesh, and yet also a certain distinction from it. [2] The sin which dwells in me (ἡ οἰκοῦσα ἐν ἐμοὶ ἁμαρτία) is no passing guest, but by its continuous presence becomes the master of the house (cf. Str.-B., III, 239). Paul can speak in just the same way, however, of the lordship of the Spirit. The community knows (οὐκ οἴδατε, a reference to catechetical instruction, 1 C. 3:16) that the Spirit of God dwells in the new man (ἐν ὑμῖν οἰκεῖ, 1 C. 3:16; R. 8:9, 11). This "dwelling" is more than ecstatic rapture or impulsion by a superior power. The spiritual part of man is not set aside, but impressed into service. [3] The use of the same formula πνεῦμα θεοῦ οἰκεῖ ἐν ὑμῖν in 1 C. 3:16 and R. 8:9, 11 suggests that it was one of the permanent catechetical and didactic elements in Paul's theology.

---

[5] On οἰκεῖος cf. also Whitaker, Exp., VIII, Ser. 23 (1922), 76 f.

ο ἰ κ έ ω. [1] Liddell-Scott, 1202; Moult.-Mill., 440.

[2] W. Gutbrod, Die paul. Anthropologie (1934), 158 thinks the local use in 7:18 ("in my flesh dwelleth no good thing") is a figure of speech, but it could be that there is here not merely a mythological but also a literal signification. The οἰκεῖν of R. 7:17 ff. reminds us of the idea of the οἶκος of demons ; the human body is their οἶκος (Mt. 12:43-45). The Paul. οἰκεῖν also corresponds to the Johannine μένειν (cf. Jn. 8:35), and it has a strong sense, as the later Jewish pars. in Str.-B., III, 239 show. He who abides has a right to do so ; he is not a guest, but master of the house. The Rabb. point out the psychological development. Sin is first a guest and then becomes the master, Gn. r., 22 (15a). Paul's thinking is perhaps more mythological here.

[3] Here again Jn.'s μένειν corresponds to Paul's οἰκεῖν, cf. Jn. 1:33 : καταβαῖνον καὶ μένον ἐπ' αὐτόν. The new possession of the Spirit is more than ecstatic.

The expression in 1 Tm. 6:16: "God dwells in light inaccessible" (φῶς οἰκῶν ἀπρόσιτον) has an antique ring.

One is reminded of apocalyptic depictions of the heavenly throne of God, e.g., in En. 14:10 ff., where a sphere of light and glory surrounds God, but the NT description is in comparison very reticent. Acc. to En. 14:10 ff. the seer first enters a great house (οἶκος μέγας) built of hailstones: "It was as hot as fire and as cold as snow; and there was nothing there of the joy of life; fear enveloped me and trembling laid hold of me; and shaken and trembling I fell down on my face and looked in the vision, And lo, there was another house, greater than this, and the door wide open before me; and it was built of tongues of fire, and in all its parts so overpowering in glory and splendour and greatness that I can give no description of its glory and greatness." 14:21 ff.: "And none of the angels could enter into this house and look on his countenance for majesty and glory, and none who is of flesh could see him. Flaming fire was about him, and a mighty fire stood before him, and none of those around him approached him. Ten thousand times ten thousand were before him, but he needed no counsel." A comparison between 1 Tm. 6:16 and En. 14:10 ff. leaves us in some surprise that in this apocalyptic *gnosis* δόξα and πῦρ rather than φῶς play the decisive role. It should also be noted, however, that in its use of φῶς 1 Tm. 6:16 differs from Hellen. and primitive Christian usage elsewhere. [4]

† οἰκοδόμος.

"Builder of a house" (cf. δέμω, "build"), "architect." [1] Cf. Hb. 3:4: πᾶς γὰρ οἶκος κατασκευάζεται ὑπό τινος. It occurs already in Hdt., 2, 121; Ditt. Or., 770, 6; pap.; [2] LXX (e.g., Is. 58:12: καὶ κληθήσῃ Οἰκοδόμος φραγμῶν).

The only NT use is at Ac. 4:11 in a quotation: ὁ λίθος ὁ ἐξουθενηθεὶς ὑφ' ὑμῶν τῶν οἰκοδόμων, ὁ γενόμενος εἰς κεφαλὴν γωνίας = ψ 117:22. The LXX reads: λίθον, ὃν ἀπεδοκίμασαν οἱ οἰκοδομοῦντες (cf. Lk. 20:17). Ac. paraphrases in order to make a personal reference to those addressed.

οἰκοδομέω.

Contents: A. οἰκοδομέω outside the NT. B. οἰκοδομέω in the NT: 1. In the NT apart from Paul; 2. The Pauline Concept: a. οἰκοδομεῖν as a Specific Apostolic Activity; b. οἰκοδομεῖν as a Spiritual Task of the Community; c. οἰκοδομεῖν in Contrast to κατα-λύειν. C. οἰκοδομέω in Post-Apostolic Literature. D. Summary.

---

[4] Dib. Past., 56: "The rich styling makes use of both Jewish and Hell. materials. In both Hell. and Christian writings φῶς is more generally used for the being of God or Christ (as ἀπρόσιτον φῶς, Cl. Al. Exc. Theod., 12, 3) and for the inheritance of Christians (Col. 1:12; *lumen inaccessibile,* Act. Pl. cum Simone, p. 66, Lipsius); it is used here of the divine dwelling, cf. the depiction in En. 14:15 ff." On En. 14:15 ff. cf. H. Kittel, "Die Herrlichkeit Gottes," *Beih.* ZNW, 16 (1934), 168.

ο ἰ κ ο δ ό μ ο ς. [1] [Debrunner].

[2] Moult.-Mill., 442; Preisigke Wört., II, 158 f.

ο ἰ κ ο δ ο μ έ ω. H. Cremer, *Ueber d. bibl. Begriff der Erbauung* (1863); H. Bassermann, "Über d. Begriff 'Erbauung,'" *Zschr. f. prakt. Theol.,* 4 (1882), 1-22; P. C. Trossen, "Er-bauen," *Theol. u. Glaube,* 6 (1914), 804 ff.; A. Deissmann, *Paulus²* (1924), 163 ff.; E. Käse-mann, *Leib u. Leib Christi* (1933), 171 ff.; P. Vielhauer, *Oikodome, Das Bild vom Bau in d. chr. Lit. vom NT bis Cl. Al.* (1939).

A. οἰκοδομέω outside the NT.

This word (Hdt., 1, 21; 2, 121 etc., inscr., pap., LXX for Heb. בָּנָה, rarely כּוּן hithp and עָשָׂה) is first used externally and literally for building houses, temples, pyramids, but it already has a fig. sense in Gk., cf. Xenoph. Cyrop., 8, 7 and 15 : μὴ οὖν ἅ οἱ θεοὶ ὑφήγηνται ἀγαθὰ εἰς οἰκειότητα ἀδελφοῖς μάταιά ποτε ποιήσητε, ἀλλ' ἐπὶ ταῦτα εὐθὺς οἰκοδομεῖτε ἄλλα φιλικὰ ἔργα. This metaphorical use may be found also in the LXX : ψ 27:5 : ὅτι οὐ συνῆκαν εἰς τὰ ἔργα κυρίου καὶ εἰς τὰ ἔργα τῶν χειρῶν αὐτοῦ· καθελεῖς αὐτοὺς καὶ οὐ μὴ οἰκοδομήσεις αὐτούς, Ἰερ. 40(33):7: καὶ ἐπιστρέψω τὴν ἀποικίαν Ἰούδα καὶ τὴν ἀποικίαν Ἰσραὴλ καὶ οἰκοδομήσω αὐτοὺς καθὼς τὸ πρότερον.

In the LXX we find the expression οἰκοδομεῖν τινα, which is important for the NT. "To plant" and "to build" are here related concepts (opp. "to root up," "to tear down," "to destroy"). God can build, plant, set up or convert Israel, and in judgment He can also overthrow and destroy His work. [1] The image of building is also common in later Judaism, perhaps because it is suggested by the idea of the "house of Israel." In the Rabb. God is the builder of the world, cf. also Hb. 3:4 : ὁ δὲ πάντα κατασκευάσας θεός. [2] There is a good par. to Mt. 7:24-27 in Ab. R. Nat., 24 : Elisha b. Abuja (c. 120) said : "A man who has many good works and has learned much of the Torah, with whom is he to be compared ? With a man who below (i.e., the foundation) builds with stones and then with (unfired, only dried in the sun) bricks ; even though many waters come and stay at their sides, they will not pry them (the solid stones) from their place. But a man who has no good works and learns the Torah, with whom shall he be compared ? With a man who first builds with bricks and then with stones ; even though only few waters come, they will at once overthrow them." The parable demands that one should build in such a way that the building itself will stand in time of disaster ; thus regard must be had to a good relation between good works and study. In a fig. sense "builders of the Torah" is an honorary title for the scribes, and "builders" can also be used as a description for students. [3] Acc. to bShab., 144a students are occupied in building up the world by studying and expounding the Torah. bBer., 64a repeats a Rabb. tradition which appeals to Is. 54:13 : "R. Eleazar (c. 270) has said, R. Chanina (c. 225) has said : Students of the scribes advance peace in the world acc. to Is. 54:13 : All thy builders (students) will be pupils of Yahweh, and great shall be the peace which the builders bring. Do not read בָּנַיִךְ, thy children, but בֹּנַיִךְ, thy builders." The term בָּנָה, "to study," "to expound," is thus common in the Rabb., and may underlie NT use.

ἐποικοδομεῖν is fig. but more theoretical in Epict. Diss., 2, 15, 8 : οὐ θέλεις τὴν ἀρχὴν στῆσαι καὶ τὸν θεμέλιον τὸ κρίμα σκέψασθαι πότερον ὑγιὲς ἢ οὐχ ὑγιές, καὶ οὕτως λοιπὸν ἐποικοδομεῖν αὐτῷ τὴν εὐτονίαν, τὴν ἀσφάλειαν; Acc. to

---

[1] The OT οἰκοδομέω tradition is important, Jer. 1:10: ἰδοὺ κατέστακά σε σήμερον ἐπὶ ἔθνη καὶ βασιλείας ἐκριζοῦν καὶ κατασκάπτειν καὶ ἀπολλύειν καὶ ἀνοικοδομεῖν καὶ καταφυτεύειν. Jer. 24:6: καὶ ἀνοικοδομήσω αὐτοὺς καὶ οὐ μὴ καθελῶ καὶ καταφυτεύσω αὐτοὺς καὶ οὐ μὴ ἐκτίλω. Cf. also Ἰερ. 38(31):4 : οἰκοδομήσω σε καὶ οἰκοδομηθήσῃ, παρθένος Ἰσραήλ, Ἰερ. 40(33):7: οἰκοδομήσω αὐτοὺς καθὼς τὸ πρότερον, Σειρ. 49:7: (Jeremiah) ἡγιάσθη προφήτης ἐκριζοῦν καὶ κακοῦν καὶ ἀπολλύειν, ὡσαύτως οἰκοδομεῖν καὶ καταφυτεύειν.

[2] For Rabb. sources cf. Str.-B., I, 733, esp. Gn. r., 66 (42b), where R. Huna (c. 350) in the name of R. Acha (c. 320) opened with Ps. 75:3 : "Though the earth dissolves with all its inhabitants, ... I, I have established (its pillars)." Jelammᵉdenu in Jalkut, 1 § 766, quoted by Str.-B., I, 733 on Mt. 16:18. On God as builder of the world cf. also M. Ex., 15, 11 (49b) and Gn. r., 1 (2a).

[3] Str.-B., I, 876; III, 379.

J. Weiss [4] it might perhaps be possible to prove a Gnostic use of οἰκοδομεῖν in circles connected with the mystery religions. [5]

The imagery of the Mandaean writings seems to be significant. Here believers are chosen, planted and built up (in the building of life); they are integrated into the fellowship of life. [6]

Philo is close to Gk. modes of thought. In Leg. All., 2, 6 he compares the leading part of the soul with the total soul, and uses as an analogy the relation of the heart to the body. It is formed before the whole body, "like a basic pillar or the keel of a ship," and on it the rest of the body is built (οἰκοδομεῖται τὸ ἄλλο σῶμα). Here the term οἰκοδομεῖσθαι seems to be a stock image. Som., 2, 284 f. has the expression δόγμα οἰκοδομεῖν (Post. C., 51: δόγμα κατασκευάζειν); fools raise on high like a tower the building of their untenable doctrine. Philo has in view the tower of Babel, and has God destroy this thought-structure of fools. Leg. All., 3, 228 allegorises Nu. 21:27 ff.: "But if we wholly trust our own calculations, we erect and build the city of the spirit which destroys truth." Leg. All., 1, 48 has the expression φυτεύειν καὶ οἰκοδομεῖσθαι τὰς ἀρετάς; it is for God alone to create virtues, while man must cherish them as creations of God. Leg. All., 3, 3 speaks similarly of the fulfilling of works of virtue (οἰκοδομεῖν τὰ ἀρετῆς πράγματα). Cher., 101 takes up the fairly common picture of building with all its different aspects (foundation stones, ornamentation); good dispositions and instruction are the foundation stones of a solid and magnificent house. Philo and Epict. probably adopted and used the common imagery of the diatribe. The Gk. use is obviously not the same as that of the OT. It finds no place either for the genuinely historical work of God (His building) or esp. for the motif of the building up of a people. In Joseph. οἰκοδομεῖν and οἰκοδομή are used only lit., and οἰκοδομή is only a *nomen actionis,* i.e., "building," not "a building." [7]

B. οἰκοδομέω in the NT.

1. In the NT and post-apostolic writings we find οἰκοδομέω both in the literal sense and also combined with various objects in a fig. use.

Thus οἰκία is the obj. in Lk. 6:48 (ἄνθρωπος οἰκοδομῶν οἰκίαν), cf. πύργον in Mk. 12:1 and Mt. 21:33 quoting Is. 5:2 (καὶ ᾠκοδόμησα πύργον), and in Lk. 14:28 in another parable of Jesus (τίς γὰρ ἐξ ὑμῶν θέλων πύργον οἰκοδομῆσαι). καθαιρεῖν and οἰκοδομεῖν (pull down and build) are antonyms in the parable of the rich fool (obj. τὰς ἀποθήκας, Lk. 12:18). In Lk. 11:47 the Jews build the sepulchres of the prophets (τοὺς τάφους τῶν προφητῶν). The great similitude of the tower in Herm. makes frequent use of οἰκοδομεῖν, cf. s., 9, 3, 1 and 4; 9, 12, 6; v., 3, 2, 4 ff.; 3, 3, 3; 3, 5, 5; 3, 8, 9 etc. In later ecclesiastical writings the use of οἰκοδομεῖν is not uniform. The various authors either have in view a heavenly building or temple, perhaps the Church as a whole (Herm.) or individuals (Barn.), or they are influenced by the specific

---

[4] Joh. W. 1 K., 215.

[5] Cf. the material in J. Weiss 1 K. (1910), 215, n. 3, and the conclusion : "No matter how we derive the concept of 'edification,' it is certainly not new in Paul, but is already a fixed expression which the Corinthians could readily understand."

[6] "I built them up into the building of life and integrated them into the fellowship of life. I illumined them with an illumination, an illumination, wonderful and unending" (RG, 16, 1; 381, 33-36). (The uthra of life) "was full of goodness towards him and let him build a building. He let him build a building and let him plant a planting" (RG, 3, 113, 19-21). In the Gnost. myth the heavenly Anthropos is ἀνὴρ τέλειος, στῦλος τῆς δόξης, στῦλος τοῦ φωτός, the place of light, the cloud of splendour, which is the seat of heavenly beings. "But on this again the heavenly building is erected, or it is itself the seat of the redeemed, to which they return" (H. Schlier, *Christus u. d. Kirche im Eph.* [1930] 51).

[7] Schl. Mt., 694.

Pauline idea of edifying or edification, Pol. Phil., 3, 2. The phrase ναὸν οἰκοδομεῖν is important, cf. Mk. 14:58 and par.; Jn. 2:20; Barn., 16, 3 (= Is. 49:17); 16:6.

Building is primarily an apocalyptic and Messianic concept. Through Easter, or the *parousia,* Christ will build the heavenly temple. Related is the word of revelation to Peter in Mt. 16:18 : καὶ ἐπὶ ταύτῃ τῇ πέτρᾳ οἰκοδομήσω μου τὴν ἐκκλησίαν. As here, so also in Mk. 14:58 οἰκοδομήσω denotes an eschatological act of Christ, a new authorisation by God. The Messiah will build the future temple and the new community. The exact connotation of the future is uncertain. Will the Son of Man gather the elect at the *parousia* (cf. Mk. 13:27), or is there reference to the power of the resurrection of Christ in building up the community, which would agree with the charismatically historical prerogative of Peter and the Pentecost narrative in Ac. 2:1 ff.? The fut. οἰκοδομήσω in Mk. 14:58 and Mt. 16:18 certainly points to an act of eschatological power, perhaps also denotes a spiritual element which may be found equally well in the *parousia* and the Easter event, and possibly has its own particular part in the widespread primitive Christian image of the heavenly building. [8]

The puzzling saying about the ναὸς ἀχειροποίητος in Mk. 14:58 is related materially and theologically to another tradition in Ac. 7:47, 49 : ποῖον οἶκον οἰκοδομήσετέ μοι (= Is. 66:1). Because God is exalted above heaven and earth — heaven is His throne and earth the footstool of His feet — men are in no position to build Him a house (Mt. 5:34; Ac. 7:49). The "house" which corresponds to God's glory must come from God Himself and it must be miraculous in character (ἀχειροποίητος).

The word οἰκοδομεῖν is of Messianic significance, but from a very early time it also has a typically ecclesiastical ring, and it becomes a central concept in religious speech. Ac. 9:31 is characteristic : ἡ μὲν οὖν ἐκκλησία ... εἶχεν εἰρήνην οἰκοδομουμένη καὶ πορευομένη τῷ φόβῳ τοῦ κυρίου. Similarly Ac. 20:32 says : τῷ δυναμένῳ οἰκοδομῆσαι καὶ δοῦναι τὴν κληρονομίαν ἐν τοῖς ἡγιασμένοις πᾶσιν. One might also recall the promise in Ac. 15:16 : μετὰ ταῦτα ἀναστρέψω καὶ ἀνοικοδομήσω τὴν σκηνὴν Δαυὶδ τὴν πεπτωκυῖαν, καὶ τὰ κατεστραμμένα αὐτῆς ἀνοικοδομήσω καὶ ἀνορθώσω αὐτήν. This is a free quotation which borrows from Am. 9:11 and Jer. 12:15 ff. The ἀνοικοδομεῖν obviously denotes the eschatological restoration of the people of Israel. Ac. has an absolute use of οἰκοδομεῖν = ἀνοικοδομεῖν under the influence of the OT. The subject is God, the object Israel or the community. The reference is to a fellowship. The totality grows and is built up with a spiritual and eschatological reference. We are not to think too readily of the idea of the heavenly building. God Himself rather than the Messiah is the subject. Hence the usage in Ac. is not an echo of the Synoptic tradition. It is to be regarded as a new and independent development on an OT foundation. [9]

---

[8] E. Lohmeyer, *Galiläa u. Jerusalem* (1936), 79, n. 2, thinks that he can sift and differentiate territorially : "The absence of the term ἐκκλησία need only show that there (in Galilee) the theological idea of an accomplished establishment of the ἐκκλησία was not yet known, or, positively, that this establishment will take place only on the day when the Son of Man will come in manifest glory." It seems to me that Messianic οἰκοδομήσω is linked with the motif of the Son of Man, and that οἰκοδομήσω conceals a certain eschatological tension, since it may be linked equally well with both the *parousia* and Easter. As I see it, the territorial distinction is not adequately supported at this point, and lacks cogency.

[9] ᾽οἰκοδομεῖν and ἀνοικοδομεῖν in Ac. are in their special theological use eschatologico-soteriological terms in the OT sense of 'God's action in grace.' Even when

2. The Pauline Concept.

The term οἰκοδομεῖν is particularly important in Paul.

a. οἰκοδομεῖν as a Specific Apostolic Activity. In Paul's letters the term denotes a specific apostolic activity. Perhaps he had before him the saying at the call of Jer. (1:10) and the divine promise to the same prophet (24:6).

The term is used in this way to denote a particular apostolic task in relation to the community, cf. 2 C. 10:8 : εἰς οἰκοδομὴν καὶ οὐκ εἰς καθαίρεσιν ὑμῶν, 13:10 : εἰς οἰκοδομὴν καὶ οὐκ εἰς καθαίρεσιν, 12:19 : τὰ δὲ πάντα, ἀγαπητοί, ὑπὲρ τῆς ὑμῶν οἰκοδομῆς.

Paul may destroy (καθαιρεῖν, 2 C. 10:4), but this is not his true work. It is forced upon him, and is ultimately only a necessary presupposition for his true work, which is to be found in the establishment and building up of the community. Dt. Is. and Jer. helped to shape his sense of calling, so that this apostolic οἰκοδομεῖν draws strength from these sources too. In the great allegory in 1 C. 3:10-15 the image is given a new turn. One apostle lays the foundation (θεμέλιον τιθέναι), another builds on it (ἐποικοδομεῖν). The use of the metaphor of the foundation and building for spiritual activity is not uncommon ; the same allegory or comparison is found in Philo and Epict. as well. [10] Paul uses this allegory because he wants to adopt familiar usage. Yet it is also not impossible [11] that even in 1 C. 3:10-15 Paul had in view an actual building, for the mysterious saying about the spiritual temple continually affects the imagery and crops up in a new form quite close to the passage (3:16). It is certainly probable that the origin of this form of the metaphor is to be sought in Jewish Hellenism. The related image of planting is also found in this passage (3:6, 7, 9); the combining of these two images is common to antiquity (OT, Judaism, the Greek world, Hellenism, Philo, Gnosticism). But the metaphor of the building is preferred because it fits the point better. In time as well as materially Paul laid the foundation of the community by his missionary preaching, then another continued the preaching and promoted the further building of the community in a new way. So many essential and formative features are linked up with laying the foundation that this activity cannot be compared with any other, cf. the rather different metaphor in Gl. 4:19 : οὓς πάλιν ὠδίνω. It is the special pride of the apostle that he did not preach where another had already laid the foundation (ἵνα μὴ ἐπ' ἀλλότριον θεμέλιον οἰκοδομῶ, R. 15:20). But this principle is for him a rule rather than an absolute law (R. 1:11, 14 f.).

b. οἰκοδομεῖν as a Spiritual Task of the Community. οἰκοδομεῖν also seems to be for Paul an important task of the Spirit of God in the community. οἰκοδομεῖσθαι is indeed a term for the process of the growth and development of the community in salvation history. In this sense the term "edification" is very early in Paul. It is not just suggested by polemical or other usage. It has a more charismatic

---

not expressly stated the subj. is always God and the obj. the community or the coming community. The use is 'verbal,' hence it is not controlled by the image of a building. It is not coined in Ac., but presupposed, and already fixed. It is no different from that of Paul" (Vielhauer, 113).

[10] Cf. Joh. W. 1 K., 79 : "The metaphor of laying a foundation seems to be common in the diatribe ; Epict. Diss., 2, 15; 8, 9; cf. Hb. 6:1; Philo Gig., 30; Mut. Nom., 211; Som., II, 8."

[11] In spite of Vielhauer, 79.

and spiritual ring than the ecclesiastical word based upon it. This spiritual and charismatic concept of edification is certainly connected with other forms of the metaphor, but cannot be traced back directly to them.

1 Th. 5:11: διὸ παρακαλεῖτε ἀλλήλους καὶ οἰκοδομεῖτε εἷς τὸν ἕνα, καθὼς καὶ ποιεῖτε. Here the pastoral exhortation of the individual is the form in which he participates in the upbuilding of the community and the development or spiritual growth of the brother. The individual helps to edify the community by receiving for himself the exhortation of the Gospel and then passing it on to others. Important, then, in relation to the term is 1. the relation of the individual to the whole, 2. the mutual interrelationship of the individual members, 3. the spiritual and charismatic character of the process of growth, which aims at fulness and perfection and is not to be limited to morality or wrongly construed in sentimental or emotional terms, and 4. the theological comprehension. The individual Christian contributes to the building and upbuilding because this is ultimately the true work of God or Christ. The derivation of the word from the standpoint of the history of religion, and its detailed figurative meaning, may point us in different directions, but theologically and materially these finally constitute a single whole. The interrelating of παρακαλεῖν and οἰκοδομεῖν is plainly to be seen elsewhere in Paul. Thus 1 Th. 5:11 points forward to 5:14 : νουθετεῖτε, παραμυθεῖσθε, ἀντέχεσθε, μακροθυμεῖτε. Similarly 1 C. 14:3 relates οἰκοδομή, παράκλησις and παραμυθία. By the prophetic word the community is built up in its life of faith, i.e., it is inwardly promoted and strengthened, and the ἰδιώτης or ἄπιστος present in the gatherings of the congregation is also won, that is, he is convinced, judged and tested, and the secrets of his heart are made manifest (1 C. 14:24 f.).

οἰκοδομή refers, then, to the spiritual furtherance both of the community and also of the individual by Christ. The term reflects the manifoldness of the primitive Christian understanding of the Church. A spiritual, theological and cultic or congregational element is concealed in it. οἰκοδομή denotes the goal of knowledge, yet also the inner growth of the community and the content and purpose of its liturgical life and its meetings. The word can thus carry many different nuances. The Pauline slogan : ἡ γνῶσις φυσιοῖ, ἡ δὲ ἀγάπη οἰκοδομεῖ (1 C. 8:1b), has the force of an axiom. Originally a Pauline term (cf. 1 Th. 5:11), οἰκοδομεῖν was perhaps taken up and understood in a new way by the Gnostics in Corinth. It occurs in 1 C. 8:1, 10; 10:23, being used in 8:10 in a different way from the other two verses. According to 8:10 the conscience is edified to eat meat offered to idols. Perhaps Paul is ironically referring to a Corinthian expression and practice whereby the weak should be encouraged to act in the way shown him by the strong. Possibly there was in Corinth an enthusiastic but dangerous slogan : ἡ γνῶσις οἰκοδομεῖ, which Paul revises : ἡ γνῶσις φυσιοῖ, ἡ δὲ ἀγάπη οἰκοδομεῖ. There can be no doubt that he takes the catchword : πάντα ἔξεστιν, and adds the correction : ἀλλ᾽ οὐ πάντα οἰκοδομεῖ. The spiritual and enthusiastic element in Hellenistic piety must be given a centre, impulsion and meaning in ἀγάπη. φυσιοῦν becomes the opposite of οἰκοδομεῖν. The absolute use of the term must again be related to the community of which the individual is a member. The community as a whole, and each member in it, is advantaged and prospered by love ; in 1 C. 8:1 οἰκοδομεῖν takes on the same sense as συμφέρειν (cf. 10:23). It is thus wrong for the man who speaks in tongues to edify himself (1 C. 14:4). This act is not orientated to the community and the brother (14:17), it is not regarded as service, and consequently it is not dictated by love, but is self-directed. The case is different with the man who proclaims God's Word, the προφητεύων. This man edifies the community (ἐκκλησίαν οἰκοδομεῖ). The term edification comprises two aspects, on the one side inner strengthening in might and knowledge, and on the other outer winning and convincing. It corresponds to the congregation's process of growth, but this is to be understood in terms of Christ, the Spirit and the act of faith. Though the idea of οἰκοδομή and οἰκοδομεῖν has general presuppositions in the history of religion, and plays a certain role in the life of the primitive community and the spiritual movements of Hellenistic enthusiasm, it is understood by Paul christocentrically, filled with ἀγάπη, and exalted to be a critical element in the possession of the Spirit. [12]

c. οἰκοδομεῖν in contrast to καταλύειν. Paul, however, can also use οἰκοδο- μεῖν in a general metaphorical sense in contrast to καταλύειν: εἰ γὰρ ἃ κατέλυσα ταῦτα πάλιν οἰκοδομῶ, παραβάτην ἐμαυτὸν συνιστάνω (Gl. 2:18). The object of καταλύειν or οἰκοδομεῖν is here the Law, or the distinction between Jews and Gentiles established by the Law. What Peter has first pulled down is the wall of partition between Jews and Gentiles. With his yielding to the party of James he is now building this up again and characterising his previous attitude as παρά- βασις, and himself as παραβάτης. There is in the Rabbinic world a similar ex- pression which contrasts סָתַר = καταλύειν and בָּנָה = οἰκοδομεῖν.

Cf. bBer., 63a : "They spoke to him : Thou has built up (by praising us), thou canst not now tear down (by calumniating us ; thy tearing down would contradict thy building up); thou hast already fenced around, thou canst not make a break." bNed., 40a, Bar.: "R. Shimeon b. Eleazar (c. 190) said : When the young men say to thee : Build, and the old : Tear down, listen to the old men and not to the young ; for the building of the young is a tearing down, and the tearing down of the old a building ; a sign of this is Rehoboam, the son of Solomon."

It may be seen that the antithesis of building up and tearing down has a certain academic ring in Rabbinic usage, and for all the special sense — Gl. 2:18 is con- cerned with more than a thesis — there is a hint of this in the Pauline use too. In this more formal understanding, with no particular reference to content, the usage in Gl. 2:18 is on the whole unique in Paul. [13] The image of "building oneself on" (οἰκοδομεῖσθε, א C ἐποικοδομεῖσθε) ... is found again in a great primitive Christian allegory in 1 Pt. 2:5 with express Scripture references (Is. 28:16; ψ 117:22; Is. 8:14; Ex. 19:6). The OT passages are the origin and basis of the allegory. The christological witnesses to the corner-stone and stone of stumbling underlie the whole passage, but then the house is understood as the community : οἶκος is both house and household, and the eschatological temple is the new community ac- cording to En. 91:13 and Jub. 1:17. οἰκοδομεῖσθαι, then, is not just metaphorical. It is to be taken as a reference to the spiritual integration of the individual into the community. Apocalyptic, Synoptic and Pauline motifs come together in this allegory, and thus demonstrate in a later Christian writing how they can co- operate with one another.

---

[12] Cf. Vielhauer, 91: "Ecstatic manifestations of religious life have no independent aim or value ; from the standpoint of the edification of the ἐκκλησία they are relativised as means to an end, the benefit of the community."

[13] Ibid., 89 : "οἰκοδομεῖν, in distinction from Pauline usage elsewhere, has here a negative character ; it is not a soteriological term ; for it signifies the restoration and con- fession of the ancient order of the Law, the very opposite of its ordinary sense. The use of οἰκοδομεῖν in Gl. 2:18 is in every way unique and not at all typical."

C. οἰκοδομέω in Post-Apostolic Literature.

In post-apost. writings, too, οἰκοδομεῖν is fairly common. It has an assured place in the allegory of the tower in Herm. In mythological terms Herm. s., 9, 3, 1 ff. tells how men have the task of building a tower over a rock and over a gate (οἰκοδομεῖν ἐπάνω τῆς πέτρας <καὶ ἐπάνω τῆς πύλης> πύργον τινά). In s., 9, 12, 6 it is then explained that the multitude who build the tower are all glorious angels who surround the Lord like a wall. In the related description in v., 3, 2, 4 it is emphasised that the tower over the waters is built of shining four-cornered stones (πύργον μέγαν οἰκοδομούμενον ἐπὶ ὑδάτων λίθοις τετραγώνοις λαμπροῖς). The "lady" explains in v., 3, 3, 3 : "I am the tower which you see being built, I, the Church, who have appeared to you, both now and earlier." Now is the time in which conversion is possible, while the tower is being built ; when the tower is finished, sinners will have no more place but will be excluded, v., 3, 5, 5. The question of the end of times is very closely related to the building of the tower : "Only when the tower which is being built is finished is the end there," v., 3, 8, 9. The question why the tower is not yet finished is answered in s., 9, 5, 2 : "The tower cannot be finished unless the Lord comes first and tests this building, so that if He finds that some of the stones have weathered He can replace them, for the tower is built in accordance with His will." The image in s., 9, 9, 7 also deals with the building of the tower : "But when the Shepherd saw that the tower was finely built, He was very glad. For the tower was so beautifully built that on seeing it I was filled with longing to live in it. For it was built as from one stone ; it did not have a single joint. And it looked as though it had been chiseled out of the rock. It seemed to me to be of a single stone." Herm. is obviously using ancient mythological material (οἰκοδομὴ τοῦ πύργου, v., 3, 2, 6; 3, 4, 1; 3, 5, 1; 3, 12, 3 etc.) which he relates to the metaphor of the Church as a building. The Church is the tower and rock. individual Christians are built into the building as stones. [14]

Barn., too, develops primitive Christian ideas, along with some from Hellenism. The section on the baptismal water in 11, 1 has a strange ring. Israel does not accept baptism, which brings remission of sins, but builds for itself (ἀλλ' ἑαυτοῖς οἰκοδομήσουσιν). What Barn. has in view is that Judaism tries to evade the claim of baptism by its legal washings ; as in Philo οἰκοδομεῖν is an attempt to set up a structure of teaching (cf. δόγμα οἰκοδομεῖν or κατασκευάζειν). Instructive, too, is the discussion of the true and false temple in 16, 1 ff. This continues the ancient biblical polemic against the temple made with hands (Is. 66:1 = Ac. 7:49 f.). The Jews have set their hopes on the temple as a building (οἰκοδομή) as though it were really God's dwelling (οἶκος θεοῦ). There is, however, a temple of God which He Himself promises to make and prepare (ὅπου αὐτὸς λέγει ποιεῖν καὶ καταρτίζειν, 16, 6). A composite quotation from Scripture follows : "And it will come to pass when the week is fulfilled that the temple of God will be gloriously built in the name of the Lord" (En. 91:13; Tob. 14:5; 2 Βασ. 7:13 = the catchword οἶκος). "Being built" is elucidated in what follows. Before man believed in God his heart was exposed to corruption and subject to decay. It had to be built on the name of the Lord. "By receiving forgiveness of sins and setting our hope on his name, we have become new men and have been created anew. Thus God really dwells in us in our innermost beings," 16, 8. The image of the temple (ναός) is combined with that of "building" (οἰκοδομεῖν) as in Mk. 14:58. "Being built" (οἰκοδομεῖσθαι) is in Barn. an inward spiritual act related to conversion ; it is not meant so

---

[14] Vielhauer, 159 : "Though we can only indicate it, Dib. has shown in a minute analysis that Herm. adopts mythological material — astral and cosmic ideas and terms about the heavenly city and building — without understanding its context, and uses it to make statements about the Church." Cf. also 162 : "His usage is controlled by the thought of οἰκοδομή as a building (the tower); only rarely in him does οἰκοδομή denote the act of building. The thought of the Church as a heavenly building determines and dominates the usage."

mythologically or ecclesiastically as in Herm. Indeed, the figure is much more subjective in Barn. The individual is primarily God's temple, whereas Paul applies the image in the first instance to the community (cf. 1 C. 3:16; 6:19; 2 C. 6:16).

Thus the image of the building is still found with many different nuances. It is not surprising, then, that οἰκοδομεῖσθαι is also found in the specifically Pauline sense of spiritual edifying. Polycarp in Phil., 3, 2 tells how Paul taught the word of truth and wrote letters "by which, if only you immerse yourselves in them, you may be built up in the faith which is given you" (εἰς ἃς ἐὰν ἐγκύπτητε, δυνηθήσεσθε οἰκοδομεῖσθαι εἰς τὴν δοθεῖσαν ὑμῖν πίστιν). οἰκοδομή has the same meaning in 13, 2 : The letters of Ign. treat of faith and patience and the edifying which concerns the Lord (περιέχουσιν γὰρ πίστιν καὶ ὑπομονὴν καὶ πᾶσαν οἰκοδομὴν τὴν εἰς τὸν κύριον ἡμῶν ἀνήκουσαν). Though the term denotes spiritual strengthening as in Pl., there is no ref. here to the brother or to the community as a whole. The concept of edification loses its true centre and comprises only the growth of the individual.

D. Summary.

οἰκοδομεῖν is understood teleologically, spiritually, cultically and ethically. It is a typical community concept and arises very early in primitive Christianity, but Paul especially plays an essential role in its development.

A. Deissmann has pointed out [15] that ancient temples, like medieval cathedrals, constantly needed to be built up : "This explains the favourite Pauline concept of edifying, which is particularly significant in 1 and 2 C." P. C. Trossen, too, thinks [16] that οἰκοδομεῖν is borrowed from the sphere of architecture ; Paul noted many details, spiritualised them, and then used them fig. of spiritual building ("abstraction"). W. Bousset [17] regards the assembled congregation as the basis and context of the ideas of σῶμα, ναός and οἰκοδομή. He thinks the community is primarily a sociological unity, and only then a spiritual and ecstatic entity. H. Gunkel [18] refers to the apocalyptic origin of the image of a building. R. Reitzenstein [19] and E. Käsemann [20] see close connections between Pl. and Gnostic usage; οἰκοδομεῖν belongs to the established aeon vocabulary. H. Cremer, [21] E. Schwartz [22] and P. Vielhauer [23] emphasise the underlying OT ideas, cf. Vielhauer : [24] "In the Pauline concept of οἰκοδομεῖν the OT view has been adopted and modified, as may be seen from a comparison of exegesis of the verses in Pl. and Ac. with the section on the OT." He admits, however, that one has to assume Stoic influence in 1 C. 3:10-15 and Gnostic in 2 C. 5:1. [25]

† οἰκοδομή.

The formation οἰκοδομή is rejected by Atticists, [1] but occurs in Aristot. Eth. Nic., 1137b, 30; Diod. S., 1, 46; Plut. Lucull., 39; Philo Vit. Mos., I, 224; Spec. Leg., I, 73; per-

---

15 Deissmann, 163 ff.
16 Trossen, 804 ff.
17 W. Bousset, Kyrios Christos² (1921), 89.
18 H. Gunkel, Schr. NT, II, 546.
19 Reitzenstein Ir. Erl., 167.
20 E. Käsemann, 171 ff.
21 Cremer, passim.
22 E. Schwartz, GGA (1911), 664.
23 Vielhauer, op. cit., 120 ff.
24 Ibid., 121.
25 Ibid., 122.
οἰκοδομή. Bibl. → οἰκοδομέω.
1 C. A. Lobeck, Phrynichi eclogae nominum et verborum Atticorum (1820), 421, 487 ff.:

haps also Joseph.;[2] it is common in the *koine*, e.g., IG, XIV, 645, 146; 150 (Doric); Ditt. Or., 655, 2; P. Grenf., I, 21, 17; BGU, 699, 3; 894, 2; it also occurs in the LXX, sometimes with a gen., e.g., 1 Ch. 26:27: τοῦ μὴ καθυστερῆσαι τὴν οἰκοδομὴν τοῦ οἴκου, 1 Esr. 2:26 : ἤργει ἡ οἰκοδομὴ τοῦ ἱεροῦ, 4:51: εἰς τὴν οἰκοδομὴν τοῦ ἱεροῦ δοθῆναι, also elsewhere. Cf. Sir. 40:19 : τέκνα καὶ οἰκοδομὴ πόλεως στηρίζουσιν ὄνομα; Ez. 16:61; 17:17; 40:2 etc. But οἰκοδομή is not common in the LXX. [3]

1. οἰκοδομή denotes in the first instance the act of building : Herm. s., 9, 5, 1: ἐτελέσθη ... ἡ οἰκοδομή (οὐκ ἀπετελέσθη δὲ ὁ πύργος), s., 9, 14, 2 : τῆς οἰκοδομῆς ἀνοχὴ ἐγένετο. In Pauline usage the primary reference is to spiritual furtherance. 1 C. 14:12 : πρὸς τὴν οἰκοδομὴν τῆς ἐκκλησίας, 2 C. 12:19 : ὑπὲρ τῆς ὑμῶν οἰκοδομῆς. Without obj. gen. we find οἰκοδομή in the same sense πρὸς οἰκοδομήν, R. 15:2; 1 C. 14:26; Eph. 4:29. Whatever takes place in the community should contribute to this edifying. Apostolic authority should serve it, 2 C. 10:8; 13:10. It is given and received by the individual member of the community. Paul admonishes in R. 14:19 : ἄρα οὖν τὰ τῆς εἰρήνης διώκομεν καὶ τὰ τῆς οἰκοδομῆς τῆς εἰς ἀλλήλους. He lauds the gift of prophecy : ὁ προφητεύων ... λαλεῖ οἰκοδομήν, 1 C. 14:3. The decisive criterion in judging charismata is whether the community receives edification : ἵνα ἡ ἐκκλησία οἰκοδομὴν λάβῃ, 1 C. 14:5. The image of the growth of the body of Christ is a related one ; hence the two are used together : τὴν αὔξησιν τοῦ σώματος ποιεῖται εἰς οἰκοδομὴν ἑαυτοῦ ἐν ἀγάπῃ, Eph. 4:16.

2. οἰκοδομή can then mean the finished building which is the result of building. In the first instance this is thought of in external and concrete terms. In Mk. 13:1 f.; Mt. 24:1 the reference is to the temple buildings. Barn., 16, 1 refers in this sense to the error of the Jews who set their hope on the temple building, εἰς τὴν οἰκοδομὴν ἤλπισαν. In the NT οἰκοδομή is a familiar figure of speech which is primarily used for the community, cf. 1 C. 3:9 : θεοῦ γάρ ἐσμεν συνεργοί· θεοῦ γεώργιον, θεοῦ οἰκοδομή ἐστε. Here we have a common double metaphor of antiquity, i.e., husbandry and building. Then the image of building is given a new turn, 3:10 ff. οἰκοδομή becomes a mysterious catchword whose content is known but which can adopt new embellishments and motifs. [4] Eph. 2:21 also starts with the ancient traditional κήρυγμα of a divine house. This οἰκοδομή becomes the holy temple in which Jesus Christ is the corner-stone and which is built on the foundation of the apostles and prophets. The vocabulary and thought of Eph. are related to familiar Gnostic ideas, e.g., the σῶμα of the Redeemer and a heavenly οἰκοδομή. [5]

οἰκοδομή οὐ λέγεται· ἀντ' αὐτοῦ δὲ οἰκοδόμημα. W. Schmidt, *Der Attizismus in seinen Hauptvertretern,* III (1893), 248. On οἰκοδόμημα cf. Liddell-Scott, 1204.

[2] On Joseph. cf. W. Schmidt, "De Flavii Josephi elocutione," *Jbch. f. klass. Philol. Suppl.,* 20 (1894), 528 f. οἰκοδομή seems to me to be not too well attested in Joseph., since other readings are more probable.

[3] P. Vielhauer, *Oikodome* (1939), 14 f.

[4] "I have sought the material presupposition of the combination of the two images in the fact 'that the two activities mentioned typify life in the country on the one side and life in the town on the other,' " A. Fridrichsen, "Exegetisches zu den Paulusbriefen," ThStKr, 102 (1930), 298 ff., cf. also "Ackerbau u. Hausbau," ThStKr, 94 (1922), 185 f.; "Exegetisches zu d. Paulusbriefen," *Serta Rudbergiana = Symbolae Osloenses fasc. supplet.,* IV (1931), 25 f. On the metaphor in 1 C. 3:10 cf. O. Eger, *Rechtsgeschichtliches zum NT* (1919), 37 ff.; W. Straub, *Die Bildersprache d. Apostels Pls.* (1937), 87 ff.; Vielhauer, 78 ff.

[5] H. Schlier, *Christus u. d. Kirche im Eph.* (1930), 57 f.: "If these conjectures are correct, we have discovered beneath the confusion of Gnostic ideas the Anthropos who consists of

Worked out rather differently, the same imagery is found in Ign. Eph., 9, 1: ὡς ὄντες λίθοι ναοῦ πατρός, ἡτοιμασμένοι εἰς οἰκοδομὴν θεοῦ πατρός ... Already in Eph. 2:21 the two images of the ναὸς θεοῦ and the οἰκοδομή occur together. They are also combined in Ign., and show how primitive Christian material is related to the Gnostic tradition. [6]

The position is the same in Herm., who in the similitude of the tower unites mythological motifs with the Christian concept of οἰκοδομή. In Herm. οἰκοδομή denotes the finished building, though in some passages the question arises whether it might not be the act of building. Cf. v., 3, 2, 6 : τοὺς μὲν ἐκ τοῦ βυθοῦ λίθους ἑλκομένους πάντας οὕτως ἐτίθεσαν εἰς τὴν οἰκοδομήν ... ἐφαίνετο δὲ ἡ οἰκοδομὴ τοῦ πύργου ὡς ἐξ ἑνὸς λίθου ᾠκοδομημένη. v., 3, 4, 1: διὰ τούτων οὖν τελεσθήσεται ἡ οἰκοδομὴ τοῦ πύργου. v., 3, 5, 1: περὶ τῶν λίθων τῶν ὑπαγόντων εἰς τὴν οἰκοδομήν. v., 3, 12, 3 : καὶ διὰ τοῦτο ἐδήλωσεν ὑμῖν τὴν οἰκοδομὴν τοῦ πύργου. The following combinations are characteristic in Herm.: s., 9, 9, 3 : τὰ ἐξώτερα μέρη τῆς οἰκοδομῆς, the external side of the tower ; v., 3, 5, 5; 3, 6, 1 and 6 : εὔχρηστοι (ἔσονται) εἰς τὴν οἰκοδομήν, the stones which are serviceable for building ; cf. also s., 9, 15, 6 : οὐκ ἂν εὔχρηστοι γεγόνεισαν τῇ οἰκοδομῇ τοῦ πύργου τούτου, v., 4, 3, 4 : χρήσιμοι ἔσεσθε εἰς τὴν οἰκοδομὴν τοῦ πύργου, s., 9, 8, 3 : Stones are brought into the building (εἰς τὴν οἰκοδομὴν ἀπενεχθῆναι) or rejected from it (ἀπεβλήθησαν ἀπὸ τῆς οἰκοδομῆς τοῦ πύργου). A singular expression is ἀπέρχεσθαι εἰς τὴν οἰκοδομήν, of stones which find their way into the building, s., 9, 5, 3 f.; 9, 7, 4 ff.; 9, 10, 2. ἀποδοκιμάζειν ἐκ τῆς οἰκοδομῆς, to remove from the building as unserviceable, s., 9, 12, 7; pass. (again of the stones) οὗτοι οὖν ἀπὸ τοῦ πύργου ἀπερρίφησαν καὶ ἀπεδοκιμάσθησαν τῆς οἰκοδομῆς αὐτοῦ, s., 9, 23, 3. ἁρμόζειν εἰς τὴν οἰκοδομήν, to fit into the building, v., 3, 6, 5; 3, 7, 5; pass. s., 9, 4, 3; 9, 8, 5 ff.; 9, 9, 4; 9, 15, 4. Also βάλλειν εἰς τὴν οἰκοδομήν, s., 9, 7, 4 ff.; 9, 8, 2; pass. 9, 7, 5; 9, 10, 1; 9, 30, 2. δοκιμάζειν τὴν οἰκοδομήν, s., 9, 5, 2. Also εἰσέρχεσθαι εἰς τὴν οἰκοδομήν, s., 9, 12, 4; 9, 13, 4. ἐκλέγειν εἰς τὴν οἰκοδομήν, s., 9, 9, 3. ἐπιθυμεῖν τὴν οἰκοδομήν, s., 9, 9, 7. ἐργάζεσθαι εἰς τὴν οἰκοδομήν, s., 9, 6, 2; εὑρεθῆναι εἰς τὴν οἰκοδομήν, s., 9, 6, 4. [7] Though there are some doubtful passages, one is forced to say that in the imagery of Herm. οἰκοδομή is predominantly the building, the tower, and that the use of οἰκοδομή for the act of building is secondary.

3. In Paul too, however, οἰκοδομή is a figure of speech for man's corporeality. According to 2 C. 5:1 the earthly body is a tent (οἰκία τοῦ σκήνους) which can be dismantled (ἐὰν ... καταλυθῇ ...). But then we have a house from God (οἰκοδομὴ ἐκ θεοῦ) which is not made with hands (ἀχειροποίητος), which is eternal, and which is ready in heaven (αἰώνιος ἐν τοῖς οὐρανοῖς). The very

---

κεφαλή and σῶμα and who himself or his σῶμα (as σοφία) is the heavenly οἰκοδομή." Vielhauer, 125 : "In keeping with his theme, i.e., interpretation in terms of Christians and the Church, the author says of this building, however, that it is still in process of arising, that it is growing into a holy temple. We thus have the architecturally impossible picture of an unfinished building whose foundation is laid, whose walls and pillars are partly erected and partly still to be erected (vv. 21-22), and yet whose key-stone is already in place and exercising its integrating function."

[6] Vielhauer, 155 : "Here the Gnostic terminology is quite plain. The words and the process described remind us of Act. Arch., 8, cf. the synopsis of the two texts in Schlier (Religionsgesch. Unters. zu den Ignatiusbriefen [1929], 112)." "This gives us the background in the history of religion ; it is the same as that of the Act. Arch. The image of the building and stones points especially to Mandaean ideas. In short, the background is 'Iranian,' though the idea of the temple is Jewish Christian in origin. The building of the father is interpreted as a 'temple.'"

[7] For further examples Pr.-Bauer³, 927.

wording of this eschatological passage is most striking. Perhaps we are to think of Mk. 14:58 : καταλύειν, οἰκοδομεῖν, ἀχειροποίητος. In what relation does Mk. 14:58 stand to 2 C. 5:1? The οἴδαμεν which introduces the passage presupposes that the apocalyptic teaching of 2 C. 5:1 is not peculiar to Paul but is an article of belief which he shares with the congregation, so that appeal can be made to it.

The image of the tent finds many pars., more esp. in Hell. rather than strictly biblical thought, though cf. Is. 38:12; Wis. 9:15; 2 Pt. 1:13 f. Later Jewish apocalyptic has also been adduced in explanation of it, though the distinctive change from the metaphor of the house to that of the garment suggests comparison with Gnostic Mandaean ideas. Judaism did not use the thought of a "building" or "house" anthropologically ; even in the Rabb. "house" did not become a current term for the body. [8] The wording and context of 2 C. 5:1 suggest an Iranian origin for the related imagery.

† ἐποικοδομέω.

"To build on something," "to build further." In Gk. from Thuc. (7, 4 : ἐποικοδομήσαντας αὐτὸ <= τὸ τεῖχος> ὑψηλότερον), also Xenoph., inscr. and pap. καὶ ἐμβατεύειν [καὶ ἐποι]κοδομεῖν καὶ ἐγμισθοῦν [καὶ] ἑτέροις παραχωρεῖν, BGU, IV, 1130, 14. οὐκ ἐπῳκοδομήσαμεν ταῖς κέλλαις, "we have not built anything over the rooms" (P. Giess., 1, 67, 12, Preisigke Wört., I, 589). Also Epict. Diss., 2, 15, 8 : ἐποικοδομεῖν αὐτῷ τὴν εὐτονίαν, τὴν ἀσφάλειαν. [1] The word does not occur in the LXX, but cf. Jos. Ant., 11, 79 of the κατασκευή of the temple (καὶ τοὺς θεμελίους ἐγείραντες τῇ νουμηνίᾳ τοῦ δευτέρου μηνὸς τοῦ δευτέρου ἔτους ἐπῳκοδόμουν).

In the NT we find the term in the allegory in 1 C. 3:10 : ὡς σοφὸς ἀρχιτέκτων θεμέλιον ἔθηκα, ἄλλος δὲ ἐποικοδομεῖ. Here the further building thereupon continues the apostolic work of laying the foundation, but it does not mean the same as laying the foundation (θεμέλιον τιθέναι). The one who builds further must recognise only the responsibility which is his (εἰ δέ τις ἐποικοδομεῖ ἐπὶ τὸν θεμέλιον, 3:12; εἴ τινος τὸ ἔργον μενεῖ, ὃ ἐποικοδόμησεν, 3:14). Cf. Ditt. Or., 483, 117: μὴ ἐξουσία δὲ ἔστω ἐπὶ τοὺς τοίχους μήτε ἐποικοδομεῖν μήτε διορύσσειν μήτε ἄλλο καταβλάπτειν μηθέν, ἐὰν μὴ πείσωσιν τοὺς κυρίους. Cf. also the sense in Herm. s., 9, 5, 1: καὶ ἐτελέσθη τῇ ἡμέρᾳ ἐκείνῃ ἡ οἰκοδομή, οὐκ ἀπετελέσθη δὲ ὁ πύργος· ἔμελλε γὰρ πάλιν ἐποικοδομεῖσθαι, v., 3, 8, 9 : ὡς ἐὰν οὖν συντελεσθῇ ὁ πύργος οἰκοδομούμενος, ἔχει τέλος. ἀλλὰ ταχὺ ἐποικοδομηθήσεται. Eph. 2:20 uses the same figure of building on a foundation as in 1 C. 3:10 : "You are built up (ἐποικοδομηθέντες) on the foundation of the apostles and prophets." [2] Cf. also 1 Pt. 2:5 : καὶ αὐτοὶ ὡς λίθοι ζῶντες ἐποικοδο-

---

[8] Str.-B., III, 517. For religious historical material on 2 C. 5:1 cf. Wnd. 2 K., 158; 264 ff. and Ltzm. K., 119 f. Cf. esp. Slav. En. 22:8 ff. (longer recension)? Asc. Is. 7:22; 8:26; 9:2, 8, 9; En. 62:15; Corp. Herm., 10, 17; 13, 3 and 14; Stob. Frag., I, 276 f. Cf. also Iranian contacts in Reitzenstein Hell. Myst., 355; Ir. Erl., 164 and 167. On this whole matter v. the judgment of Vielhauer, 107 ff. ("The Mandaean pars. to 2 C. 5:1 are naturally only pars.; as such they are very striking, but they are not the source of Paul's ideas. Since, however, there is no dependence of Paul on Mandaean concepts, the pars. point to a common source for both, the 'Iranian.' Thus the Mandaean pars. indirectly reveal the 'pre-history' of the Pauline concepts and images"). W. Straub's Die Bildersprache des Ap. Pls. (1937), 84 f. is not very adequate.

ἐ π ο ι κ ο δ ο μ έ ω. Bibl. → οἰκοδομέω.
[1] Moult.-Mill., III, 251.
[2] ἐπί with dat., cf. Xenoph. An., 3, 4, 11: ἐπὶ δὲ ταύτῃ ἐπῳκοδόμητο πλίνθινον τεῖχος ...

μεῖσθε (א C vg) οἶκος πνευματικὸς εἰς ἱεράτευμα ἅγιον.[3] The ἐπι-, which is more chronological in Herm., is used materially in Paul, but it can be very weak, so that the image is blurred, cf. Col. 2:7: ἐρριζωμένοι καὶ ἐποικοδομούμενοι ἐν αὐτῷ (= Χριστῷ). We again find together the two metaphors of planting and building, as elsewhere in Paul (1 C. 3:9), the Odes of Solomon (38:17), and the Mandaean writings (Ginza, 495, 12; 500, 9; 536, 1). In this interrelation they are controlled by an ancient tradition. Nevertheless, they do not attract attention to themselves but to the ἐν Χριστῷ. "In Christ" is our root and foundation.[4]

The great primitive Christian image of building has had some influence on Jd. 20, though the ἐπι- here has no special significance : "But ye, beloved, building up yourselves on your most holy faith" (ἐποικοδομοῦντες ἑαυτοὺς τῇ ἁγιωτάτῃ ὑμῶν πίστει). What is meant is that the holy content of faith should be the foundation of the life of the individual Christian.[5]

† συνοικοδομέω.

Attested in Gk. from Thuc., συνοικοδομεῖν occurs in Plut., inscr., pap. Ditt. Syll.[3], 913, 16 : ἐπειδὴ ἡ νῦν οὖσα ἀγορὰ συνῳκοδόμηται, P. Oxy., 1648, 60 : τὰ συνῳκοδομημένα βαφικὰ ἐργαστήρια. Diod. S., 13, 82, 3 : συνῳκοδομοῦντο οἱ κίονες τοῖς τοίχοις. The act. means "to build together," the pass. "to be built together, or into." The only instance in the LXX is at 1 Esr. 5:65 : καὶ προσελθόντες τῷ Ζοροβάβελ καὶ Ἰησοῦ καὶ τοῖς ἡγουμένοις τῶν πατριῶν λέγουσιν αὐτοῖς Συνοικοδομήσομεν ὑμῖν.

In the NT we simply have the fig. use at Eph. 2:22 : εἰς ναὸν ἅγιον ἐν κυρίῳ, ἐν ᾧ καὶ ὑμεῖς συνοικοδομεῖσθε εἰς κατοικητήριον τοῦ θεοῦ ἐν πνεύματι. The community, with Christ as corner-stone, is built up together with the apostles and prophets into one building and temple. συνοικοδομεῖσθε should not be taken as an imperative (Calvin), nor does the συν- denote the mutual fellowship of believers. The reference is to the unity and totality of the structure, in which Christ and the apostles and prophets are united with believers.[1]

The same verb also occurs in the image in Herm. s., 9, 16, 7: The righteous of the old covenant are led to life by the apostles and teachers of the new, and learn to know the name of the Son of God : "Hence they rose up with them, fitted into the building of the tower, and could be built in without being hewn" (καὶ συνηρμόσθησαν εἰς τὴν οἰκοδομὴν τοῦ πύργου καὶ ἀλατόμητοι συνῳκοδομήθησαν). The biblical metaphor also influences the mythological and allegorical material in Herm.

---

[3] Vielhauer, 145 : "The variant in v. 5 : ἐποικοδομεῖσθε (אC al s vg) is secondary."

[4] Loh. Kol., 97 f.: "The metaphor of 'being rooted,' found only here, is not very vivid and tends to merge into the image of building. The two participles, which are linked by a common 'in him,' express the incontestable certainty with which each believer is grounded in Him. Hence it is not born of the unyielding necessity of an 'I can do no other,' but of a divine event for which the believing heart is a stone which can be fitted into the structure of the community."

[5] Wnd. Kath. Br., 46 : "The holy faith, the foundation, which gives stability to the individual, and from which heretics have fallen away (v. 3)."

συνοικοδομέω. [1] On this cf. A. v. Harless, Kommentar über den Brief Pauli an d. Ephesier[2] (1858), 264 f.

† οἰκονόμος.

In Gk. used like οἰκοδεσπότης for the "steward," attested from Aesch. Xenoph. Oec., 1, 2 : δοκεῖ γοῦν, ἔφη ὁ Κριτόβουλος, οἰκονόμου ἀγαθοῦ εἶναι εὖ οἰκεῖν τὸν ἑαυτοῦ οἶκον, Plat. Resp., 3, 417a : οἰκονόμοι μὲν καὶ γεωργοὶ ἀντὶ φυλάκων ἔσονται. [1] Not uncommon in inscr. and pap. P. Tebt., II, 402, 1: Μαρτι [...] οἰκονόμῳ Φλαυίας 'Επιμάχης κα[ὶ] τῶν πρότερον 'Ιουλίας Καλλίνιδος παρὰ Διδύμου οἰκοδόμου, P. Oxy., VI, 929, 25 : Νιννάρῳ οἰκονόμῳ 'Απίωνος στρατηγοῦ, P. Fay., 133, 2 : ἀπέστειλα τὸν οἰκονόμον 'Ηρακλείδην πρὸς σὲ καθὰ ἠξίωσας ἵνα τὴν διαταγὴν τῆς τρύγης (harvest, vintage) ποιήσηται. οἱ Καίσαρος οἰκονόμοι can even be used for the Lat. office of procurator, P. Tebt., II, 296, 12 : διέγραψε Σεκούνδῳ τῷ τοῦ κυρίου Καίσαρος οἰκονόμῳ (procurator) (δραχμὰς) <'A>φ, P. Oxy., IV, 735, 6 : Καισάρων οἰκονόμου οὐικαρίου, inscr. of Priene, 6, 30 : τὸ δὲ ἀνάλωμα ὑπηρετῆσαι τὸν οἰκονόμον. [2] οἰκονόμος can thus be the one in charge of separate branches of a household, "steward," "inspector of goods," "chief cook" etc. [3] Also fig., Aesch. Ag., 155 : οἰκονόμος δολία, μνάμων μῆνις τεκνόποινος. Here οἰκονόμος occurs as fem. The word is used in the LXX, for אֲשֶׁר עַל־הַבַּיִת (3 Βασ. 4:6; 16:9; 18:3; 4 Βασ. 18:18, 37; 19:2; Is. 36:3, 22; 37, 2), for רַב בַּיִת (Est. 1:8), or פֶּחָה (Est. 8:9). οἰκονόμος means in the Rabb. the "steward" (בֶּן בַּיִת), a kind of chief slave who super-intended the household and even the whole property of his master ; בֶּן בַּיִת can also be sometimes the child or son of the house, jSanh., 28d, 10. [4] οἰκονόμος then becomes the loan-word אִיקוֹנוֹמוֹס and is used for city officials, e.g., the treasurer, cf. R. 16:23 : οἰκονόμος τῆς πόλεως. Finally οἰκονόμος can be used for a kind of "house-keeper," "estate manager," or "accountant" (= גִּזְבָּר, Aram. גִּזְבְּרָא, cf. Lk. 16:1). [5]

Close study of both the Gk. and Heb. is needed to fix the precise sense. 1. For בֶּן בַּיִת, cf. Pesikt. r., 10 (35b): After a parable of master of the house and steward : Thus God is a householder, for the whole world is His, v. Ps. 24:1; and Moses is His steward, v. Nu. 12:7: He is trustworthy in all my house (cf. Hb. 3:1-6). Lv. r., 12 (113d): R. Pinechas (c. 360) has said in the name of R. Levi (c. 300): "Like a king who had a faithful steward (בֶּן בַּיִת נֶאֱמָן)." For בֶּן בַּיִת נֶאֱמָן cf. Mt. 24:45 : ὁ πιστὸς δοῦλος Simi-larly δοῦλος φρόνιμος corresponds to עֶבֶד פִּקֵּחַ bShab., 153a. [6] 2. On the loan word אִיקוֹנוֹמוֹס: TBM, 9, 14 : "If anyone takes over a field from another, he reaps it, binds the sheaves, and winnows. Then come the surveyors, the diggers, the overseer and the treasurer (community official) and take their share" (of the whole, before it is divided among lessees and contractors). [7] TBB, 3, 5 (402): "When a town is sold, then acc. to R. Jehuda (c. 150) the overseer of the boundaries is sold along with it, but not the treasurer (איקונומוס)." For further instances cf. bBB, 68b; jBM, 11d, 13. [8] 3. For the

---

οἰκονόμος. [1] Further material in Liddell-Scott, 1204.
[2] Further material in Moult.-Mill., V, 443; Preisigke Wört., III, 137 f., 216, 403.
[3] Ltzm. Gl. on 4:2.
[4] Cf. Str.-B., I, 967 f.; II, 192, 217; III, 564.
[5] Cf. the fine comparison in Shab., 31a (Str.-B., I, 737): "Rabba b. Huna (c. 300) has said : He who possesses the Torah, but has no fear of God, is like a treasurer who was given the inner keys but not the outer. How will he get in ?"
[6] Cf. the great parable of Shab., 153a (Str.-B., I, 878): "R. Jochanan b. Zakkai (d. c. 80) has said : Like a king who invited his servants to a feast without fixing a time. The clever among them dressed and settled themselves at the entrance to the palace. They said : Can anything be lacking in the house of a king ? (In his house everything is always ready, so the meal can begin any minute). The foolish went on with their work. They said : Can there be any feast without laborious preparation ?"
[7] Str.-B., I, 871.
[8] Ibid., II, 218.

treasurer, bBB, 9c : R. Eleazar (c. 270) has said : Even when a man has a reliable steward (treasurer) in his house, he should bind up and count his own money (2 K. 12:11: They bound up and counted the money). In Test. Jos., 12 Joseph is an οἰκονόμος in sense 1. = בֶּן בַּיִת: Potiphar's wife says to her husband : Take the young man as your steward, then the God of the Hebrews will bless you, for grace from heaven rests on him.

In the NT the οἰκονόμος occurs first in the parables of Jesus. Lk. 12:42 refers to a πιστὸς οἰκονόμος ὁ φρόνιμος, cf. Mt. 24:45 : ὁ πιστὸς δοῦλος καὶ φρόνιμος. [9] As the interchangeability of οἰκονόμος and δοῦλος in Lk. 12:42, 43, 45 f. shows plainly, the reference both here and in Mt. 24:45 ff. is to a בֶּן בַּיִת, a steward from among the slaves, who is over the whole household (θεραπεία) and sometimes the whole property of his master (τὰ ὑπάρχοντα). [10] In Lk. 16:1, 8 the οἰκονόμος is a free treasurer (→ supra); ὁ οἰκονόμος τῆς ἀδικίας is a Heb. gen. qual. [11] Cf. Erastus in R. 16:23 : ὁ οἰκονόμος τῆς πόλεως.

This title is common on inscr., Ditt. Syll.³, 1252 : πόλεως Κῴων οἰκονόμος, Ditt. Or., II, 669, 22.

Paul, too, adopts οἰκονόμος and likes to use it metaphorically. Gl. 4:2 associates ἐπίτροποι and οἰκονόμοι; the heir, while still a minor, is in their hands.

Perhaps the term οἰκονόμος is meant to amplify and elucidate ἐπίτροπος. It is part [12] of the task of the guardian to see to the support and education of minors, but also to administer the whole inheritance to their benefit and advantage. ἐπίτροπος, which is also a loan word in the Rabb., is thus the steward. "In the popular mind the guardian and steward was one and the same." [13]

But Paul also used the word οἰκονόμος as a figure for apostolic authority and knowledge in 1 C. 4:1 f. Neither here nor in Gl. 4:2 is there any concern as to the social position of the οἰκονόμος. The steward is entrusted with the treasures of the Gospel ; he has knowledge of God's plan of salvation. The expression οἰκονόμοι μυστηρίων θεοῦ reminds us of Mt. 13:11: τὰ μυστήρια τῆς βασιλείας τῶν οὐρανῶν. [14] While 4:1 links "ministers of Christ" and "stewards of the mysteries

---

[9] ὁ φρόνιμος, Lk. 12:42 (om syrˢ) is amplified by ὁ ἀγαθός D itᵛᵃʳ syrᶜ. Perhaps this addition is based on Mt. 25:23. Cf. Kl. Lk., 139.

[10] Str.-B., II, 192.

[11] Bl.-Debr.⁷ § 165. On the parable of the unjust steward cf. Bultmann Trad., 190, 216; Kl. Lk., 161-166; Schl. Lk., 362-374; NT Deutsch, III (Rengstorf), 172-175; Jülicher Gl. J., 495-514; P. Fiebig, D. Gleichnisreden Jesu im Lichte d. rabb. Gleichnisse d. nt.lichen Zeitalters (1912), 210-212; J. Kögel, BFTh, 18, 6 (1914); E. Riggenbach in Schlatter-Festschrift (1922), 17 ff.; F. Tillmann, BZ, 9 (1911), 171-184; Gerda Krüger, ibid., 21 (1933), 170-181; F. Hüttermann in Theologie u. Glaube, 27 (1935), 739-742; for further bibl. Pr.-Bauer³, 928.

[12] Str.-B., III, 565.

[13] Loc. cit. οἰκονόμος can thus elucidate ἐπίτροπος, cf. also ἐπίτροπος in Mt. 20:8; Lk. 8:3. The steward can be a higher slave, but there is nothing in the text to suggest that οἰκονόμος should be taken in this sense.

[14] "As the head of the house (Mt. 13:52) brings forth from his treasures things both old and new, so it is perhaps suggested here that the steward has control of the hidden treasures of his master, which would lie dead and unprofitable if he did not dispense them. In this case we should not enquire too closely why Paul speaks of the Gospel in this way. The expression reminds us of μυστήρια τῆς βασιλείας τῶν οὐρανῶν in Mt. 13:11. As the ref. there is to the as yet undisclosed counsels of God for the establishment of His kingdom, so the ref. here is to God's purposes of salvation, which would be hidden from mankind if the apostles did not bear witness to them" (Joh. W. 1 K., 94).

of God," 4:2 enunciates the principle that the chief thing required in a steward is faithfulness (Lk. 12:42; 16:10 f.; Mt. 25:21, 23).

It may be conjectured that under the influence of the parabolic material in the Synoptic Gospels οἰκονόμος came to have a place in the common legacy of primitive Christian proclamation. We find it again in the charge to the bishop in Tt. 1:7: "For a bishop must be blameless, as the steward of God." As faithfulness is demanded in the older Pauline letters, so Tt. 1:7 requires of the office-bearer a life consonant with the mysteries of the Gospel. 1 Pt. 4:10 calls every Christian a recipient of the divine gift of grace, and consequently a steward of the manifold grace of God. The continuation in 4:11 teaches that office-bearers in particular are recipients of grace and stewards of God. But Ign. Pol., 6, 1 also admonishes the community : "Labour together, fight, run, suffer, sleep, watch with one another as God's stewards, companions, and servants" (ὡς θεοῦ οἰκονόμοι καὶ πάρεδροι καὶ ὑπηρέται). The influence of early usage may be seen in this challenge too.

Schlatter [15] refers to Jos. Ant., 8, 164 : Solomon sends the sailors dispatched by Hiram μετὰ τῶν ἰδίων οἰκονόμων, 12, 199 : δοῦναι ἐπιστολὴν πρὸς τὸν ἐν Ἀλεξανδρείᾳ οἰκονόμον. [16] In Philo Praem. Poen., 113 we find the combination πολιτικὸς καὶ οἰκονόμος, "namely, because the wise man merits praise in all his movements and in all situations, in the house and outside, as statesman and ruler of the house, because he rules well in the house and acts in a statesmanlike way outside, as is beneficial to the improvement of society."

† οἰκονομία.

In Gk. from the time of Xenoph. and Plat.: Xenoph. Oec., 1, 1; Plat. Ap., 36b; Resp., 6, 498a; 3, 407b. Inscr. and pap. use the word. P. Tebt., I, 27, 21 describes the office of the οἰκονόμος : φρόντισον ὅπως ... πρὸς ταῖς οἰκονομίαις καὶ ἀρχιφυλακειτείαις προχειρισθῶσιν ἀξιόλογοι. P. Eleph., 11, 7: ὃν δ' ἂν πράξῃς γ' οἰκονομιῶν. The term relates primarily to household administration, and applies generally to "direction," "administration," "provision." It is no longer a specific τέχνη among others, as in Xenoph., but comes into general parlance.

BGU, III, 926, 3 : ὅσα δέεται γενέσθαι ἐν τῷ ὑπὸ τὴν οἰκονομίαν σου βαλανείῳ. In P. Lond., 904, 25, the rescript of the prefect is important in relation to the settling of men in their homeland : ἵνα καὶ τὴν συνήθη οἰκονομίαν τῆς ἀπογραφῆς πληρώσωσιν. P. Rein., 7, 34 : μηδεμίαν οἰκονομίαν κατ' ἐμοῦ ποιεῖσθαι. P. Tebt., I, 30, 18 : τῶν δὲ πρὸς ταῖς γραμματείαις ἀγνοούντων τὴν γεγονυῖαν περὶ ἐμοῦ οἰκονομίαν, II, 318, 19 : τὸ εἰς με δίκαιον οἰκονομείας, P. Oxy., I, 56, 17: ἐπιγραφῆναί μου κύριον πρὸς μόνην ταύτην τὴν οἰκονομίαν Ἀμοιτᾶν. Also Cic. Att., 6, 1, 1; Epict. Diss., 3, 24, 92; M. Ant., 4, 19. [1] In the LXX (= מִמְשַׁלְתּ) in Is. 22:21 (τὴν οἰκονομίαν σου δώσω εἰς τὰς χεῖρας αὐτοῦ) and (= מַצָּב) Is. 22:19 (ἀφαιρεθήσῃ ἐκ τῆς οἰκονομίας σου). Jos. Ant., 2, 89 : This advice commended itself to Pharaoh just as much as the interpretation of the dream, and he charged him with the whole execution of the matter (αὐτῷ τὴν οἰκονομίαν παραδίδωσιν).

In the NT οἰκονομία first means 1. the office of household administration and the discharge of this office : Lk. 16:2 ff.: ἀπόδος τὸν λόγον τῆς οἰκονομίας σου·

---

[15] Schl. Lk., 372.
[16] In Schl. Lk., 372 the wrong figures are given.

ο ἰ κ ο ν ο μ ί α. [1] For further material cf. Liddell-Scott, 1204; Moult.-Mill., 442; Preisigke Wört., II, 160; III, 137.

οὐ γὰρ δύνῃ ἔτι οἰκονομεῖν, ... τί ποιήσω, ὅτι ὁ κύριός μου ἀφαιρεῖται τὴν οἰκονομίαν ἀπ᾽ ἐμοῦ; ... ἵνα ὅταν μετασταθῶ ἐκ τῆς οἰκονομίας. Paul uses the term for the apostolic office, 1 C. 9:17: οἰκονομίαν πεπίστευμαι. He is entrusted with an office ; he does not preach the Gospel of his own accord ; he does what he has to do, cf. 1 Th. 2:4 : δεδοκιμάσμεθα ὑπὸ τοῦ θεοῦ πιστευθῆναι τὸ εὐαγγέλιον.[2] The word also occurs, with paraphrases and embellishments, in the Prison Letters : Col. 1:25 : κατὰ τὴν οἰκονομίαν τοῦ θεοῦ τὴν δοθεῖσάν μοι εἰς ὑμᾶς, according to the divine office towards you with which God has commissioned me ; Eph. 3:2 : τὴν οἰκονομίαν τῆς χάριτος τοῦ θεοῦ τῆς δοθείσης μοι εἰς ὑμᾶς, you have heard of the office of divine grace which has been laid upon me in service towards you. A distinctive feature in these epistles is that there is room for doubt whether οἰκονομία denotes office or the divine plan of salvation ; the two are closely linked in the Prison Letters.[3] Ign. Eph., 6, 1 says of the bishop : πάντα γὰρ ὃν πέμπει ὁ οἰκοδεσπότης εἰς ἰδίαν οἰκονομίαν, οὕτως δεῖ ἡμᾶς αὐτὸν δέχεσθαι ὡς αὐτὸν τὸν πέμψαντα. The one who is sent by the master of the house to his household must be received like the one who has sent him. Dg., 7, 1: οὐδὲ ἀνθρωπίνων οἰκονομίαν μυστηρίων πεπίστευνται. No administration of human mysteries is entrusted to Christians, 1 C. 9:17.

2. The word also means "plan of salvation," "administration of salvation," "order of salvation." In this sense it has both a religious and a general significance. In the magic pap. (e.g., I, 4, 293) we read of measures by which one can secure the help of heavenly powers.[4] The ordinances and decrees of the authorities are also described by this term, P. Turin, I, 9, 2. In Eph. 1:10 the reference is to God's plan of salvation which He has undertaken to execute in the fulness of times (εἰς οἰκονομίαν τοῦ πληρώματος τῶν καιρῶν). Eph. 3:9 also refers to the actualising of the mystery which was hidden in God, the Creator of all things, before the times (τίς ἡ οἰκονομία τοῦ μυστηρίου τοῦ ἀποκεκρυμμένου ἀπὸ τῶν αἰώνων ἐν τῷ θεῷ τῷ τὰ πάντα κτίσαντι).

The concept finds a place in the tradition of the community. Ign. likes it. In a christological context in Eph., 18, 2 he speaks of this divine plan of salvation : ὁ γὰρ θεὸς ἡμῶν ᾽Ιησοῦς ὁ Χριστὸς ἐκυοφορήθη ὑπὸ Μαρίας κατ᾽ οἰκονομίαν θεοῦ ἐκ σπέρματος μὲν Δαβίδ, πνεύματος δὲ ἁγίου. Cf. also 20, 1: προσδηλώσω ὑμῖν ἧς ἠρξάμην οἰκονομίας εἰς τὸν καινὸν ἄνθρωπον ᾽Ιησοῦν Χριστόν, "I will also enlighten you further on that with which I began, namely, the plan of salvation which relates to the new man, Jesus Christ." Perhaps Gnostic usage had some influence here.[5]

---

[2] "If, however, I do this unwillingly, by constraint, I have no claim whatever to a reward or to thanks (Lk. 17:9), but I am and act only as one who is entrusted with the office of keeping a house (1 Th. 2:4), of whom it is simply expected ἵνα πιστὸς εὑρεθῇ, and who does ὃ ὀφείλει (Lk. 17:10); for an οἰκονόμος is usually a slave who is not specifically renumerated for his services" (Joh. W. 1 K., 240).

[3] Dib. Gefbr., 17: οἰκονομία has a wide range of meanings in the koine. Possible senses here are 1. God's plan in respect of the μυστήριον, v. on Eph. 3:9; 2. divine office. δοθεῖσα decides in favour of 2., though Loh. Kol., 79 f. takes a different view.

[4] Preis. Zaub., I, 4, 293 : ἐὰν ἀπορηθῶ τῇσδε τῆς οἰκονομίας, in case I enjoy no success with this magical action.

[5] H. Schlier, Religionsgesch. Untersuchungen zu d. Ignatiusbriefen (1929), 32 : "The concept οἰκονομία itself, as used in Eph., 18, 2 and 20, 1, means God's order of salvation, and is to be found as a soteriological and dynamic concept in the NT only at Eph. 1:10 and 3:9, and in the post-apost. fathers as a verb only in Dg., 9, 1. On the other hand, as is well-known, it also occurs in Just. (e.g., Dial., 30, 3; 45, 4) and Iren. (e.g., I, 10, 3; IV, 33, 7;

3. In 1 Tm. 1:4 it is said of the false teachers that they proclaim fables in which there is more questioning than godly instruction in faith, αἵτινες ἐκζητήσεις παρέχουσιν μᾶλλον ἢ οἰκονομίαν θεοῦ τὴν ἐν πίστει. [6]

οἰκονομία is often used by the fathers in this sense, e.g., Cl. Al. Paed., I, 8 § 64, 3; 70, 1; Orig. Tat. (rec. E. Schwartz, TU, IV, 1, 1888, Index).

κατοικέω.

This is a common Gk. word, Soph. Phil., 40; Hdt., 7, 164; inscr. and pap.: P. Fay., 98, 14; P. Oxy., VIII, 1102, 12. [1] It also occurs in the LXX for many Heb. terms, e.g., שָׁכַן and יָשַׁב. The geographical or local sense is not really very important, but cf. the fig. intellectual or religious meaning. This occurs already in Judaism, cf. Wis. 1:4: ὅτι εἰς κακότεχνον ψυχὴν οὐκ εἰσελεύσεται σοφία οὐδὲ κατοικήσει ἐν σώματι κατάχρεῳ ἁμαρτίας, Test. D. 5:1: ἵνα Κύριος κατοικήσει ἐν ὑμῖν καὶ φεύξεται ἀφ᾽ ὑμῶν ὁ Βελίαρ, Test. Jos. 10:2: ὁ κύριος κατοικήσει ἐν ὑμῖν, ὅτι ἀγαπᾷ τὴν σωφροσύνην, 10:3: ὅπου δὲ κατοικεῖ ὁ ὕψιστος; ὁ κύριος κατοικῶν ἐπ᾽ αὐτὸν διὰ τὴν σωφροσύνην. There is originally hidden in these statements a cultic element; acc. to the OT view God "dwells" in the temple. Cf. Jos. Bell., 5, 458 f.: καὶ ναοῦ [ἀπολλυμένου] ἀμείνω τούτου τῷ θεῷ τὸν κόσμον εἶναι. σωθήσεσθαί γε μὴν καὶ τοῦτον ὑπὸ τοῦ κατοικοῦντος, ὃν καὶ αὐτοὶ σύμμαχον ἔχοντες πᾶσαν χλευάσειν ἀπειλὴν ὑστερούσαν ἔργων. Also the usage in Philo Sobr., 63: κατοικεῖν δὲ ἐν οἴκῳ λέγεται ὁ θεὸς οὐχ ὡς ἐν τόπῳ. Philo obviously uses the word in an extended sense. Fug., 102: ὁ μὲν οὖν ἀνεὺ τροπῆς, ἑκουσίου μὲν ἄπαγε, ἀλλὰ καὶ τῆς ἀκουσίου γεγονώς, αὐτὸν τὸν θεὸν κλῆρον ἔχων, ἐν αὐτῷ μόνῳ κατοικήσει. He speaks of a κατοικεῖν of man in God. Leg. All., 3, 244: ὁ γὰρ μελετῶν ἐν ἀρετῇ τελείᾳ κατοικεῖν, who will dwell in perfect virtue. Conf. Ling., 81 says of the wise man (σοφός): ὅτι παροικεῖ μὲν ὁ σοφὸς ὡς ἐν ξένῃ σώματι αἰσθητῷ, κατοικεῖ δ᾽ ὡς ἐν πατρίδι νοηταῖς ἀρεταῖς. The wise man dwells in the perceptible body like an alien resident in a foreign land, but in spiritual virtues he dwells like a native in his own country. Leg. All., 3, 2 says of Jacob: ὁ δέ γε σοφίας μεστὸς Ἰακὼβ καὶ πολίτης ἐστὶ καὶ οἰκίαν τὴν ἀρετὴν κατοικεῖ. Leg. All., 3, 115 is to the same effect: ἐνταῦθα γὰρ κατοικεῖ ἐπιθυμία, ὄρεξις ἄλογος of a dwelling of desire (cf. R. 7: 17). κατοικεῖν in the spiritual, religious and psychological sense is thus already adequately attested in Judaism.

In the NT the verb is used intrans. (= to dwell ἔν τινι, Ac. 1:20 = ψ 68:25; Ac. 2:5; 7:2, 4, 48 etc.) and also trans. (= to inhabit τι, Lk. 13:4; Ac. 1:19; 2:14; 4:16). We find current expressions like κατοικεῖν ἐπὶ τῆς γῆς, Rev. 3:10; 6:10; 8:13; 11:10; 13:8, 12, 14; 17:8; οἱ κατοικοῦντες τὴν γῆν, Rev. 17:2. It is strengthened at Ac. 17:26: κατοικεῖν ἐπὶ παντὸς προσώπου τῆς γῆς.

---

also Bousset, *Kyrios Christos*[2] [1921], 350, n. 3 and 4; Lightfoot, *Notes on the Epist. of St. Paul ad Eph.* 1:10). It is common in Gnosticism, with which Iren. is concerned. Here οἰκονομία is partly God's order of salvation generally or the order which finds expression in the saving event of redemption, as in Act. Andr., 45, 25; Act. Pt. et Pl., 198, 5; Exc. ex Theod., 5, 4; Iren., I, 15, 3; partly God's (or Christ's) order of salvation as 'completed' by the Redeemer (or the apostle), as in Act. Joh., 204, 5; Epist. Ap., 12, c. 13 (24); 18, c. 21 (39), and Act. Joh., 213, 14; Act. Phil., 23, 17; Act. Pl. (C. Schmidt), 82 (51), 3 ff.; partly the administration of salvation, the order as executed, Act. Joh., 190, 29; Act. Thom., 177, 16; identified with God's will in O. Sol. 23:5; Act. Andr. et Matth., 67, 1; Mart. Mt., 241, 12 f.; Treasure Cave, 57." Cf. *ibid.*, 32, n. 3: "In the Valentinians οἰκονομία is also the kingdom and world government of the Demiurge; it is the upper world too."

[6] The vl. οἰκοδομίαν D and οἰκοδομήν D* are softenings; Pr.-Bauer[3], 928.

κ α τ ο ι κ έ ω. [1] Liddell-Scott, 928; Moult.-Mill., 338; Preisigke Wört., I, 778.

Cf. Herm. s., 1, 6 : ὡς ἐπὶ ξένης κατοικῶν μηδὲν πλέον ἐτοίμαζε σεαυτῷ ... Dg., 5, 2 : οὔτε γάρ που πόλεις ἰδίας κατοικοῦσιν (οὔτε ...).

κατοικεῖν can then take on spiritual and religious significance. Demons dwell in man (Mt. 12:45; Lk. 11:26 : πνεύματα ... κατοικεῖ ἐκεῖ), according to the ancient oriental view (→ οἰκέω, 132 f.). Barn., 16, 8, on the basis of 1 C. 3:16, says : ὁ θεὸς κατοικεῖ ἐν ἡμῖν. The human heart, which has accepted the word of faith, the summons of the promise, the wisdom of the demands and the commandments of the doctrine, becomes the temple of God in us. The question again arises whether the temple at Jerusalem may rightly be accorded the dignity of a divine abode. God dwells in the temple according to Mt. 23:21 : καὶ ὁ ὀμόσας ἐν τῷ ναῷ ὀμνύει ἐν αὐτῷ καὶ ἐν τῷ κατοικοῦντι αὐτόν. In tension with this general belief is the prophetic and Hellenistic message in Ac. 7:48 : ἀλλ' οὐχ ὁ ὕψιστος ἐν χειροποιήτοις κατοικεῖ, and 17:24 : οὗτος οὐρανοῦ καὶ γῆς ὑπάρχων κύριος οὐκ ἐν χειροποιήτοις ναοῖς κατοικεῖ. Rev. 2:13 has a definite political and legal ring (θρόνος τοῦ σατανᾶ): ὅπου ὁ σατανᾶς κατοικεῖ. Satan has here set up his seat as ruler.

Biblical already is the idea of Christ dwelling in our hearts by faith, Eph. 3:17: κατοικῆσαι τὸν Χριστὸν διὰ τῆς πίστεως ἐν ταῖς καρδίαις ὑμῶν. It is said of Christ in Col. 1:19 : ὅτι ἐν αὐτῷ εὐδόκησεν πᾶν τὸ πλήρωμα κατοικῆσαι, 2:9 : ὅτι ἐν αὐτῷ κατοικεῖ πᾶν τὸ πλήρωμα τῆς θεότητος σωματικῶς. This obviously belongs to the fixed liturgical and kerygmatical stock of the community. Christ is also the temple in whom God dwells (Jn. 2:19), though the usage in the Prison Epistles is Gnostic or anti-Gnostic. 2 Pt. 3:13 says of the new heaven that righteousness dwells in it (ἐν οἷς δικαιοσύνη κατοικεῖ).

In this connection we should perhaps recall that acc. to En. 42 wisdom found no place where it could dwell on earth, but a dwelling was given to it in the heavens. [2] Herm. m., 5, 2, 3 runs : αὕτη οὖν ἡ μακροθυμία κατοικεῖ μετὰ τῶν τὴν πίστιν ἐχόντων ὁλόκληρον, as patience dwells among those who have undiminished faith, so Herm. can also speak of God dwelling in patience, but the devil in anger (m., 5, 1, 3 : ἐν γὰρ τῇ μακροθυμίᾳ ὁ κύριος κατοικεῖ, ἐν δὲ τῇ ὀξυχολίᾳ ὁ διάβολος). [3] Herm. often refers to the Holy Spirit dwelling in man, and these statements are shot through with older mythological colours : m., 5, 2, 5 : "For if these spirits dwell in the same vessel in which the Holy Spirit dwells (οὗ καὶ τὸ πνεῦμα τὸ ἅγιον κατοικεῖ), there is no

---

[2] En. 42 : "Wisdom found no place where it could dwell, so a dwelling was assigned to it in the heavens. Wisdom went out to dwell among the children of men, but found no dwelling ; then wisdom returned to its place and took its seat with the angels. And unrighteousness came forth from its chambers, found those who had not sought it and dwelt among them like rain on the desert and dew on the thirsty earth." "The new world is the great aeon of the righteous" (Slav. En. 65:8). Wnd. Kath. Br., 104.

[3] On Herm. m., 5, 1, 3 and 5, 2, 3, cf. Dib. Herm., 516 on m., 5, 2, 3 : "But there is lacking here, esp. in the second sentence, the idea which is so strongly represented there, namely, that the μακροθυμία is a πνεῦμα τρυφερόν which dwells in man. Here, then, the Christian, working over the pre-Christian tradition, strongly moderates the πνεῦμα concept." Ibid., 517 Exc.: "The least Christian view is roughly as follows : To man (m., 3, 1: ἐν τῇ σαρκὶ ταύτῃ, not ἐν τοῖς δούλοις τοῦ θεοῦ) there has been given by God a tender Holy Spirit which indwells him like a vessel. This Spirit must be kept from dwelling with other spirits, for He needs plenty of room to be able to live in peace and joy (m., 5)." On the question of the origin of this view of the Spirit and demons Dib. refers to W. Bousset in ARW (1915), 134 ff., and suspects an Iranian origin ("Hell. tradition under oriental Persian influence").

more room in the vessel but it overflows." m., 10, 2, 5 : "So cast sadness from thee and do not grieve the Holy Spirit who dwells in thee (τὸ πνεῦμα τὸ ἅγιον τὸ ἐν σοὶ κατοικοῦν). This doctrine of the Spirit, which has strong mythological roots, is important in the Christology of Herm., cf. s., 5, 6, 5 : "God caused the pre-cosmic Holy Spirit, who created the whole world, to dwell in a fleshly nature which He had selected (κατῴκισεν ὁ θεὸς εἰς σάρκα ἣν ἠβούλετο). "This fleshly nature, in which the Holy Spirit dwelt (ἐν ᾗ κατῴκησε τὸ πνεῦμα τὸ ἅγιον), served the Spirit well by a holy and honourable walk, and did not stain the Spirit in any way." Perhaps s., 5, 6, 7 displays a practical anti-Gnostic interest in the doctrine of the Spirit with its more general teaching : "For each fleshly nature in which the Spirit has dwelt (ἐν ᾗ τὸ πνεῦμα τὸ ἅγιον κατῴκησεν) will receive a reward if it is found unspotted and faultless." We have here in Herm. a distinctive demonology and doctrine of the Spirit which either gives evidence of Stoic elements or, more probably, stands under oriental Persian influence. [4] The formalised nature of the statements is worth noting.

† οἰκητήριον.

This is used in Gk. for "dwelling-place," "abode" [1] (Democr., 171, Diels, I, 416; Eur. Or., 1114; Ps.-Aristot. Mund., 393a, 4; Fr., 482; Strabo, 12, 5, 3; Plut. Pomp., 28; P. Oxy., II, 281, 11; BGU, IV, 1167, 33; P. Tur., II, 3, 23; inscr. from a shrine of Isis ('Ἰσιδεῖον): [2] σὺν τοῖς περὶ αὐτὸ κατῳκοδομημένοις οἰκητηρίοις, Ceb. Tab., 17; 2 Macc. 11:2. [3] In En. 27:2 it is used for the place of punishment of the eternally accursed : ὧδε ἐπισυναχθήσονται, καὶ ὧδε ἔσται τὸ οἰκητήριον. In Jd. 6 : ἀγγέλους τε τοὺς μὴ τηρήσαντας τὴν ἑαυτῶν ἀρχὴν ἀλλὰ ἀπολιπόντας τὸ ἴδιον οἰκητήριον εἰς κρίσιν ... τετήρηκεν. Cf. the similar ideas in En. 12:4 : εἶπε τοῖς ἐγρηγόροις τοῦ οὐρανοῦ, οἵτινες ἀπολιπόντες τὸν οὐρανὸν τὸν ὑψηλόν, τὸ ἁγίασμα τῆς στάσεως τοῦ αἰῶνος ..., the watchers have left the high heaven, the holy eternal city; 15:3 : διὰ τί ἀπελίπετε τὸν οὐρανὸν τὸν ὑψηλὸν τὸν ἅγιον τοῦ αἰῶνος; 15:7 : καὶ διὰ τοῦτο οὐκ ἐποίησα ἐν ὑμῖν θηλείας· τὰ πνεύματα τοῦ οὐρανοῦ, ἐν τῷ οὐρανῷ ἡ κατοίκησις αὐτῶν. οἰκητήριον is thus used esp. for the seat of the angels in heaven.

We find the word in an anthropological context in 2 C. 5:2 : ... στενάζομεν, τὸ οἰκητήριον ἡμῶν τὸ ἐξ οὐρανοῦ ἐπενδύσασθαι ἐπιποθοῦντες. οἰκητήριον ἐξ οὐρανοῦ is thus used here in development of the metaphor of the building (οἰκοδομὴ ἐκ θεοῦ, v. 1). We are obviously dealing with an older Gnostic Persian view in which the human body is compared with a building or dwelling-place.

† κατοικητήριον.

This occurs not infrequently in the LXX for זְבוּל, יֵשֵׁב (מוֹשָׁב), מָעוֹן or מְעוֹנָה, Aram. מְדָר, e.g., Ex. 12:20; 15:17; 3 Βασ. 8:13, 39, 43, 49; 2 Ch. 30:27; ψ 32:14; 75:2; 106:4, 7; Na. 2:12, 13; Jer. 9:10; 21:13; Da. 2:11; 3 Macc. 2:15 A.

It is as an LXX term that it seems to have come also into NT usage. Rev. 18:2 : καὶ ἐγένετο κατοικητήριον δαιμονίων καὶ φυλακὴ παντὸς πνεύματος ἀκα-

---

[4] Cf. on this whole question Dib. Herm., pp. 517-519, Exc. "Die πνεῦμα-Vorstellung der Mandata."

οἰκητήριον. [1] οἰκη-τήριον, "the place of dwelling," cf. Debr. Griech. Wörtb., § 283; P. Chantraine, Formation des noms (1933), 63.
[2] G. Plaumann, Ptolemais (1910), 35.
[3] Liddell-Scott, 1203; Moult.-Mill., 441; Preisigke Wört., II, 156. Also Jos. Ap., I, 153 : καὶ δοὺς οἰκητήριον αὐτῷ Καρμανίαν ἐξέπεμψεν ἐκ τῆς Βαβυλωνίας.

θάρτου καὶ φυλακὴ παντὸς ὀρνέου ἀκαθάρτου καὶ μεμισημένου. The description of this fall of Babylon is based on Is. 13:21 f. ('Ιερ. 27:39 [50:39]; Zeph. 2:14; Bar. 4:35), though the wording is independent. It may be conjectured that the terms κατοικητήριον and φυλακή are chosen not merely on the basis of the LXX but also in connection with Gnostic apocalyptic ideas (→ οἰκητήριον). The great metaphor of the spiritual building and temple at the end of Eph. 2 also leads to the use of the word : ἐν ᾧ καὶ ὑμεῖς συνοικοδομεῖσθε εἰς κατοικητήριον τοῦ θεοῦ ἐν πνεύματι, "in him ye also are builded together for an habitation of God through the Spirit," Eph. 2:22. As in 2 C. 5:1 the concept κατοικητήριον τοῦ θεοῦ takes up the image of the building (οἰκοδομή) and temple (ναός). The reference is to the spiritual edification of the whole community.

Barn., on the other hand, favours an application to individual Christians : 6, 15 : ναὸς γὰρ ἅγιος, ἀδελφοί μου, τῷ κυρίῳ τὸ κατοικητήριον ἡμῶν τῆς καρδίας, 16, 7 : πρὸ τοῦ ἡμᾶς πιστεῦσαι τῷ θεῷ ἦν ἡμῶν τὸ κατοικητήριον τῆς καρδίας φθαρτὸν καὶ ἀσθενές, 16, 8 : διὸ ἐν τῷ κατοικητηρίῳ ἡμῶν ἀληθῶς ὁ θεὸς κατοικεῖ ἐν ἡμῖν. The idea of the chamber of the heart as a temple of God is almost stereotyped in Barn.

† κατοικίζω.

In Cret. καταϝοικίδδω ; [1] from Hdt., 2, 154; Soph. Ant., 1069; Aristoph. Pax, 205; Plat. Resp., 2, 370e etc. [2] The verb came into current usage in the sense "to make to dwell," "to assign a dwelling." Cf. P. Oxy., IV, 705, 24 and the LXX, where it is used for a series of Heb. verbs. [3] Gn. 3:24 : κατῴκισεν αὐτὸν ἀπέναντι τοῦ παραδείσου, 47:6 : ἐν τῇ βελτίστῃ γῇ κατοίκισον [Α : κατοίκησον] τὸν πατέρα σου, ψ 4:8 : σύ, κύριε, κατὰ μόνας ἐπ' ἐλπίδι κατῴκισάς με, Ez. 26:20; 29:14; 36:11, 33; 38:12, 14; 39:6 A, 26 etc.

In the NT we find the term, used almost like a formula (as comparison with Herm. shows) at Jm. 4:5 : τὸ πνεῦμα ὃ κατῴκισεν ἐν ἡμῖν, "the Spirit to whom God has assigned a dwelling in us." [4] Cf. Herm. m., 3, 1 : τὸ πνεῦμα ὃ ὁ θεὸς κατῴκισεν ἐν τῇ σαρκὶ ταύτῃ, s., 5, 6, 5 : τὸ πνεῦμα τὸ ἅγιον τὸ προόν, τὸ κτίσαν πᾶσαν τὴν κτίσιν, κατῴκισεν ὁ θεὸς εἰς σάρκα ἣν ἠβούλετο. Cf. m., 5, 2, 5 : ὅταν γὰρ ταῦτα τὰ πνεύματα ἐν ἑνὶ ἀγγείῳ κατοικῇ, m., 10, 2, 6; 3, 2. Perhaps one should also recall Test. B. 6:4 : κύριος γὰρ ἐν αὐτῷ κατοικεῖ. [5] On the basis of the biblical doctrine of creation or conversion the Holy Spirit is regarded as sent into us by God, though a precise understanding of Jm. 4:5 is not possible.

κ α τ ο ι κ ί ζ ω. [1] E. Schwyzer, Dialectorum Graecarum Exempla Epigraphica Potiora (Leipzig, 1923), 175, 2.
[2] Examples in Liddell-Scott, 928. Etym. either from κατά and οἰκίζω, "make a dwelling," or κάτοικος, "make to be a dweller" [Debrunner].
[3] Hatch-Redp., 755.
[4] Dib. Jk., 205, n. 3 : "The koine reading κατῴκησεν is to be rejected as easier, since it supplies a subj. for the relative clause and is easily reached by itacistic pronunciation."
[5] Ibid., 206, n. 2 : "This sense of πνεῦμα, i.e., 'the divinely sent good spirit in man,' is possible in the apocryphal text of our quotation, and indeed very likely in view of the agreement of the relative clause with Herm." Wnd. Kath. Br., 27.

† ἡ οἰκουμένη.

In Gk. a part. used as noun (γῆ to be supplied). The word occurs already in Hdt., 4, 110 (ὁδοιπόρεον ἐς τὴν οἰκεομένην); cf. also Demosth., Aristot., inscr. and pap. [1] What is meant from the very first is the inhabited world as distinct from the (relatively) uninhabited ; so Hdt., also Aristot. Meteor., 362b, 26. Limitation to the world of (Gk.) culture is secondary [Debrunner]. The term then embraces the Roman Empire (P. Oxy., 7, 1021, 5 ff.: ὁ δὲ τῆς οἰκουμένης καὶ προσδοκηθεὶς καὶ ἐλπισθεὶς Αὐτοκράτωρ ἀποδέδεικται, ἀγαθὸς δαίμων δὲ τῆς οἰκουμένης [ἀρ]χὴ ὢν [μέγισ]τε πάντων ἀγαθῶν Νέρων Καῖσαρ ἀποδέδεικται. Ditt. Or., 666, 3 ff.: ἐπεὶ [Νέρων] Κλαύδιος Καῖσαρ Σεβαστὸς Γερμανικὸς αὐτοκράτωρ, ὁ ἀγαθὸς δαίμων τῆς οἰκουμένης ..., 668, 5 : Νέρωνι Κλαυδίωι Καίσαρι Σεβαστῶι Γερμανικῶι αὐτοκράτορι τῶι σωτῆρι καὶ εὐεργέτηι τῆς οἰκουμένης. These formulae in the imperial style are stereotyped, cf. Preisigke Sammelbuch, 176, 2 with ref. to Marcus Aurelius : τὸν εὐεργέτην καὶ σωτῆρα τῆς ὅλης οἰκουμένης, 1070 (Abydos) with ref. to a deity [Besa?]: ἄψευστον καὶ δι' ὅλης οἰκουμένης μαρτυρούμενον. Also magical invocations : P. Lond., 121, 704 : σὲ καλῶ τὸν καταλάμποντα τὴν ὅλην οἰκουμένην, P. Leid., 5, 2, 9 : ἧκέ μοι ο (= ὦ) δέσποτα τοῦ οὐρανοῦ, ἐπιλάμπων τῇ οἰκουμένῃ. For further material CIG, II, 2581; III, 4416.

ἡ ο ἰ κ ο υ μ έ ν η. Liddell-Scott, 1205; Moult.-Mill., 443; J. Kaerst, Die antike Idee der Oikumene in ihrer politischen u. kulturellen Bdtg. (1903); J. Vogt, Orbis Romanus, Zur Terminologie d. römischen Imperialismus (1929); Preisigke Wört., II, 163 f. (where we also find οἰκουμενικός, "relating to the Roman world").

[1] The concept of the οἰκουμένη is first geographical, but then becomes cultural and political. Religion, philosophy and politics (e.g., the concept of dominion in Alexander the Gt.) combine to create the idea of a generally binding human society. There thus arises the cosmopolitanism of later Hell. culture with its philosophical understanding of humanity : "The ideally Hellenic is as such the cosmopolitan, which represents true humanity ; severed from its specific local background, it embraces the world." "Even the originally non-Hellenic, understood as the generally human, is now assimilated into the Hellenic ; under the concept of the rational it is elevated into the sphere of the ideally Hellenic. The antithesis between the Hellenic and the barbarian shifts. The Hellenic gives up its national restriction to rule over the oecumene. The world of culture is identical in principle with the oecumene ; non-culture is on the frontiers of the oecumene" (Kaerst, 18). In Hellenism the οἰκουμένη takes the place of the ancient πόλις, the νόμος κοινός or λόγος ὀρθός that of the ancient νόμοι. In the imperial period the philosophical concept of the Hellenic οἰκουμένη fuses with the political and legal structure of the Roman Empire ; the idea that the Empire embraces the οἰκουμένη is a Gk. conception. "While Roman political leaders after the Second Punic War allowed the almost unavoidable extension of Roman power in the East almost unwillingly, apart from a few bold innovators like the older Scipio, the Gks. were quick to recognise the Roman expansion in its total significance. The invasion of Asia, the third continent, by Roman power, seemed to them to be a decisive step on the way to world conquest, and the victory over Antiochus of Syria an epoch in the history of the known world. Under the impress of this event envoys from the East greeted the Romans as lords of the oecumene. Others proclaimed in inspiring visions the dawn of a universal Roman empire replacing Macedonian dominion" (Vogt, 10, with refs. to C. Trieber, Herm., 27 [1892], 337 ff.; W. Weber, Der Prophet u. sein Gott [1925], 57 ff.). The oldest Roman ref. to Roman dominion over the earth is Rhetorica ad C. Herennium, ed. F. Marx (1894), 4, 9, 13 : nedum illi imperium orbis terrae, cui imperio omnes gentes, reges, nationes partim vi, partim voluntate consenserunt, cum aut armis aut liberalitate a populo Romano superati essent, ad se transferre tantulis viribus conarentur. An important witness for this view is Cic. pro Murena, 9, 22 : haec (sc. rei militaris virtus) nomen populo Romano, haec huic urbi aeternam gloriam peperit, haec orbem terrarum parere huic imperio coegit ... Off., 2, 27: illud patrocinium orbis terrae verius quam imperium poterat nominari. For further material cf. Vogt, 12 ff.

The word also occurs in the LXX for Heb. אֶרֶץ, חֶלֶד, יָשֵׁב, תֵּבֵל. Cf. ψ 17:15; 18:4: 23:1; 32:8; 48:1; 49:12 etc.; Is. 10:14, 23; 13:5, 9, 11; 14:17, 26 etc. Philo, too, uses it frequently, e.g., Leg. Gaj., 10; Vit. Mos., I, 157, 195, 255, though with him it has primarily a general rather than a political sense, i.e., inhabited land as distinct from uninhabited, and even the universe.[2] Cf. Jos. Ant., 11, 196, 292; Bell., 1, 633; 5, 187. The word occurs sometimes in the Rabb.: יקומיני (ikumini? read iekumini), "the inhabited earth": Gn. r., 32, 5; Jalkut Gn. § 56; Qoh. r. on 6:3.[3]

The word is fairly common in the NT. We find it in the prophecy at Mt. 24:14 : καὶ κηρυχθήσεται τοῦτο τὸ εὐαγγέλιον τῆς βασιλείας ἐν ὅλῃ τῇ οἰκουμένῃ εἰς μαρτύριον πᾶσιν τοῖς ἔθνεσιν. This is more solemn and liturgical in comparison with Mk. 13:10; the formula ἐν ὅλῃ τῇ οἰκουμένῃ derives from current Hellenistic usage.[4] It is certainly not to be linked here with political imperial style. The reference is simply to the glad message which is for all nations and the whole earth.

On the other hand Lk. 2:1 perhaps has in view the Roman claim to tax the whole world (ἀπογράφεσθαι πᾶσαν τὴν οἰκουμένην).[5] Lk. likes the term and uses it again in 4:5 : ἔδειξεν αὐτῷ πάσας τὰς βασιλείας τῆς οἰκουμένης ἐν στιγμῇ χρόνου (Mt. 4:8 : πάσας τὰς βασιλείας τοῦ κόσμου). In 21:26 he has ἀπὸ φόβου καὶ προσδοκίας τῶν ἐπερχομένων τῇ οἰκουμένῃ in the apocalyptic prophecy. Behind this is the Aram. אָתֵא עַל עָלְמָא = "come on the whole earth" (Heb. בּוֹא לְעוֹלָם).[6] Perhaps the same Aram. or Heb. tradition underlies Ac. 11:28 : ἐσήμαινεν διὰ τοῦ πνεύματος λιμὸν μεγάλην μέλλειν ἔσεσθαι ἐφ' ὅλην τὴν οἰκουμένην, and Rev. 3:10 : κἀγώ σε τηρήσω ἐκ τῆς ὥρας τοῦ πειρασμοῦ τῆς μελλούσης ἔρχεσθαι ἐπὶ τῆς οἰκουμένης ὅλης. That οἰκουμένη is current Gk. may be seen from Ac. 17:6 : βοῶντες ὅτι οἱ τὴν οἰκουμένην ἀναστατώσαντες οὗτοι καὶ ἐνθάδε πάρεισιν, though the LXX has had an influence here, as may be seen plainly from 17:31 : ἐν ᾗ μέλλει κρίνειν τὴν οἰκουμένην ἐν δικαιοσύνῃ.[7] Also in keeping with current usage is Ac. 19:27 : ἣν ὅλη ἡ 'Ασία καὶ ἡ οἰκουμένη σέβεται, cf. 24:5 : καὶ κινοῦντα στάσεις πᾶσιν τοῖς 'Ιουδαίοις τοῖς κατὰ τὴν οἰκουμένην.[8]

It is worth noting that Paul does not use the term except in the quotation from ψ 18:4 in R. 10:18 : καὶ εἰς τὰ πέρατα τῆς οἰκουμένης τὰ ῥήματα αὐτῶν.

---

[2] E.g., Philo Som., 2, 180 : "But you will find this, not by traversing long and untrodden paths or journeying across unnavigable seas or hastening with breathless speed to the borders of earth and sea, for it has not moved off to the far distance or fled from the frontiers of the inhabited land, but as Moses says (Dt. 30:12-14) the good is nigh thee and is closely linked with thee, made up of three most important parts." Jos. Bell., 1, 633 adopts the political style : 'Ρώμη μοι μάρτυς τῆς εὐσεβείας καὶ ὁ τῆς οἰκουμένης προστάτης Καῖσαρ, ὁ φιλοπάτορα πολλάκις με εἰπών.

[3] S. Krauss, Griech. u. lat. Lehnwörter in Talmud, Midrasch u. Targum, 2 (1899), 281.

[4] Jos. Ant., 11, 196 : ζητῆσαι δὲ περιπέμψαντα καθ' ὅλην τὴν οἰκουμένην παρθένους εὐπρεπεῖς.

[5] Kl. Lk., 31: "Hyperbolically of the orbis terrarum comprised in the Roman Empire."

[6] Str.-B., II, 255; IV, 799-976.

[7] Preuschen Ag. (1912), 110 : "v. 31 is a quotation from ψ 9:8 = 95:13 = 97:9, though elsewhere the address, in accordance with its purpose, has very few quotations from the OT."

[8] Cf. Jos. Ant., 12, 48 : βουλόμενος δὲ καὶ τούτοις χαρίζεσθαι καὶ πᾶσι τοῖς κατὰ τὴν οἰκουμένην 'Ιουδαίοις τὸν νόμον ὑμῶν ἔγνων μεθερμηνεῦσαι. To the last-named, as to all Jews scattered in the world, I will render a service.

On the other hand Hb. 1:6 : ὅταν δὲ πάλιν εἰσαγάγῃ τὸν πρωτότοκον εἰς τὴν οἰκουμένην, and 2:5 : οὐ γὰρ ἀγγέλοις ὑπέταξεν τὴν οἰκουμένην τὴν μέλλουσαν, betray the influence of current Hell. usage. Hb. 2:5 clearly represents the old apocalyptic phrase אבֹֽ םלֹ֑וֹע. Also to be seen as a rendering of ancient apocalyptic tradition into current Hellenistic usage are Rev. 12:9 : ὁ πλανῶν τὴν οἰκουμένην ὅλην, and 16:14 : ἃ ἐκπορεύεται ἐπὶ τοὺς βασιλεῖς τῆς οἰκουμένης ὅλης. There is within the NT no disputing of the political οἰκουμένη understanding of the Roman Empire, not even in Rev.

In prayer 1 Cl., 60, 1 equates the concept οἰκουμένη with the κόσμος understanding : σύ, κύριε, τὴν οἰκουμένην ἔκτισας. Perhaps the term includes not only the world of men and living creatures, but also that of spirits and angelic powers. [9] The LXX provided a basis for the adoption and interpretation of οἰκουμένη in this sense in 1 Cl., 60.

Michel

☩ οἰκτίρω, ☩ οἰκτιρμός, ☩ οἰκτίρμων

A. Greek Usage.

If ἔλεος (→ II, 477 f.) denotes the emotion of compassion or sympathy, οἶκτος is in the first instance "grief" or "lamentation," [1] esp. "lamentation" at the misfortune or death of a man, [2] then often "sympathetic lamentation," "sympathy," "pity." [3] If οἶκτος (like οἴκτισμα, οἰκτισμός) primarily denotes the expression of emotion, the lament, the rarer οἰκτιρμός is used for the emotion of sympathy itself. [4] οἰκτίρειν thus means "to be sympathetic" in the sense of grief or sorrow, [5] but also in that of the sympathy which is ready to help. [6] Οἰκτίρειν can thus have the same meaning as ἐλεεῖν. [7] The accused who seek to arouse the ἔλεος and οἶκτος of the judge [8] pray : οἴκτιρόν με. [9] Sympathetic lamentation is a sign of weakness, and therefore acc. to Plat. Resp., III, 387c ff. all passages which deal with the ὀδυρμοί and οἶκτοι of heroes should be ex-

---

[9] Pr.-Bauer³, 931.

οἰκτίρω κτλ. On the orthography cf. Bl.-Debr., § 23; Liddell-Scott, *s.v.*; further bibl. Pr.-Bauer³, *s.v.*

[1] Aesch. Choeph., 411; Eum., 515; Sept. c. Theb., 51; Soph. Trach., 864.

[2] Soph. El., 100; Plat. Resp., III, 387d e.

[3] Aesch. Prom., 239; Soph. Ai., 525; Phil., 965, 1074.

[4] Pind. Pyth., I, 85 (opp. φθόνος); P. Masp., 7, 19.

[5] Hom. Il., 11, 814; 16, 5; Aesch. Prom., 352; Ag., 1241; Soph. Ai., 652; Xenoph. An., I, 4, 7; Oec., 2, 4 and 7; 7, 40.

[6] Aesch. Suppl., 209; Soph. El., 1410 ff.; Oed. Col., 109, 242; Phil., 507, 756.

[7] Cf. Soph. Phil., 309 f.; also 501 with 507; 967 with 1071; Epict. Diss., IV, 6, 18 f. with 21. The two verbs are combined in Plat. Euthyd., 288d; Philo Fug., 95; Virt., 91. They are par. in Antiphon, III, 1, 2 (p. 29, 4 f., Thalheim). Cf. Aristot. Poet., 14, p. 1453b, 14 (οἰκτρός) with b, 1 (ἐλεεινός).

[8] → II, 478; cf. Plat. Ap., 37a, also Aristot. Rhet., III, 16, p. 1417a, 13.

[9] Aristoph. Vesp., 555 f., 975 f.

punged from the poets. [10] Nevertheless compassion and mercy are not reprehensible. Mercy is invoked from the deity, [11] or οἰκτίρειν is predicated of it. [12] For Stoicism, however, οἶκτος is an εἶδος of λύπη [13] and hence a reprehensible πάθος, though the term οἶκτος plays no part in Stoic discussion. [14] Οἶκτος is not found at all in Epict. or M. Ant., and οἰκτίρειν only at Epict. Diss., IV, 6, 21. The adj. οἰκτρός means both "lamenting" and "lamentable"; οἰκτίρμων, "sympathetic," is rare. [15]

B. οἰκτίρω etc. in the LXX (and Judaism).

Οἰκτίρειν is used in the LXX almost always for חנן pi (10 times) and רחם pi (12 times), also once each for ידע and שׁוּב pi, and 9 times with no Heb. equivalent. ἐποικτίρω is also found once and κατοικτίρω twice. οἶκτος is rare, being used twice for נְהִי (both times vl. οἰκτρός) and 4 times with no Heb. On the other hand οἰκτιρμός is common, occurring 25 times for רַחֲמִים, once for תַּחֲנוּנִים. and 6 times with no Heb.; in most cases it is plur. (οἰκτιρμοί), [16] only 6 times sing. (3 in Zech.). οἰκτίρημα occurs once. Among adj. formations we find οἰκτρός (4 times, also 3 as vl.), οἴκτιστος (twice), and much more often οἰκτίρμων (18 times, 12 for רַחוּם, 3 for forms of חנן). The word group is most common in the Ps., but rare in the historical books.

The stem οἰκτ- is thus used predominantly for derivates of the stem רחם, also for formations of חנן. The meaning is always "sympathy," "pity." There is no palpable distinction between οἰκτίρειν and ἐλεεῖν or οἰκτιρμοί and ἔλεος; חנן and רחם are rendered by both οἰκτίρειν and ἐλεεῖν (→ II, 478), and in the LXX οἰκτίρειν and ἐλεεῖν are combined or used as par. like the Heb. רחם pi and חנן. [17]

οἰκτίρειν etc. may denote human compassion, [18] but in most cases the ref. is to divine compassion, cf. materially ⊢→ II, 480 f.

Under the influence of the Ps. invocation of God's compassion (רַחֲמִים) became a characteristic feature in Jewish prayer. [19] As distinct from ἐλεεῖν etc. (→ II, 481), οἰκτίρειν etc. obviously did not become eschatological terms in Gk. speaking Judaism. The words are completely absent from Wis. and Ep. Ar. [20] οἰκτίρειν [21] and οἰκτιρμοί [22]

---

[10] Cf. Plat. Leg., VII, 800d; XII, 949b.

[11] Aesch. Suppl., 209; Soph. Oed. Col., 109; Phil., 1042; Eur. Alc., 251; Aristoph. Vesp., 327 f.

[12] Plat. Leg., II, 653c d.

[13] v. Arnim, III, 100, 43.

[14] As distinct from ἔλεος, → II, 477.

[15] Gorg. Pal. in Diels, II, 262, 25; Theocr., 15, 75; Anth. Pal., VII, 359, 1; Preisigke Sam- melbuch, 3923 (I, 263).

[16] This must be regarded as a Semitism, v. Bl.-Debr., § 142.

[17] Ex. 33:19; 4 Βασ. 13:23; Is. 27:11; ψ 122:2 f. οἰκτίρειν and ἐλεεῖν also occur together with no Heb. equivalent at Prv. 13:9a; 2 Macc. 8:2 f. At Da. 9:18 the LXX has ἔλεος but Θ οἰκτιρμοί. The common רַחוּם וְחַנּוּן is almost always transl. οἰκτίρμων καὶ ἐλεήμων in the LXX, Ex. 34:6; Jl. 2:13; Jon. 4:2; ψ 85:15; 102:8; 110:4; 111:4; 2 Ch. 30:9. Also at Sir. 2:11. ἔλεος (ἐλέη) is used with οἰκτιρμοί in the rendering of combinations of חֶסֶד (חֲסָדִים) with רַחֲמִים, e.g., ψ 24:6; 39:11 f.; 50:1; 68:16 etc.

[18] Οἰκτίρω 3 Βασ. 8:50; ψ 36:21; 101:15; 111:5; Prv. 12:10; 21:26 etc.; οἰκτιρμοί, 3 Βασ. 8:50; Zech. 7:9; ψ 105:46; 2 Ch. 30:9; 2 Esr. 11:11; 4 Macc. 6:24; οἰκτίρμων, ψ 108:12; 111:4; Lam. 4:10.

[19] G. Harder, Paulus u. das Gebet (1936), 88 f.

[20] Only Wis. 18:10 : οἰκτρός "lamenting."

[21] 2 Macc. 8:2; 3 Macc. 5:51; God is always subj.

[22] 1 Macc. 3:44; 3 Macc. 2:20; 6:2 (both times God's mercy).

occur a few times in Macc., but the eschatological sense of divine pity can be detected only at 3 Macc. 2:20. On the other hand οἰκτίρειν is used in an eschatological promise in Test. L. 16:5 : ... ἕως αὐτὸς (God) πάλιν ἐπισκέψηται καὶ οἰκτειρήσῃ καὶ προσδέξηται ἡμᾶς.

C. οἰκτίρω etc. in Primitive Christian Writings.

In the NT the verb οἰκτίρειν occurs only at R. 9:15 in a quotation from Ex. 33:19, and, as in the original, it stands parallel to ἐλεεῖν (→ II, 484). It does not occur at all in the post-apostolic fathers or Apologists, whereas ἐλεεῖν is common in the NT, the post-apostolic fathers and Justin.

Of the nouns the NT uses only οἰκτιρμός, always plur. except at Col. 3:12. In 2 of the 5 instances God's οἰκτιρμοί are meant, and both times the OT concept of God's רַחֲמִים is adopted. Thus in R. 12:1 Paul admonishes the congregation διὰ τῶν οἰκτιρμῶν τοῦ θεοῦ, and in 2 C. 1:3 he calls God the πατὴρ τῶν οἰκτιρμῶν. The latter designation is a common one in Judaism.[23] The gen. in this case is not gen. qual., but gen. auct., like the par. θεὸς πάσης παρακλήσεως and the Jewish בעל הרחמים, which is parallel to the אב הרחמים:[24] God is the Father from whom all compassion comes and it is imparted to us.[25] 1 Cl., 9, 1; 18, 2 (based on ψ 50:1); 20, 11 also speak of God's οἰκτιρμοί.

In the introduction to Paul's admonition Phil. 2:1: ... εἴ τις σπλάγχνα καὶ οἰκτιρμοί, σπλάγχνα[26] and οἰκτιρμοί are obviously a hendiadys: "heartfelt sympathy." The reference is to the sympathy of the Philippians, to which Paul appeals in order to give emphasis to his admonition.[27] Mercy as a human attitude is also at issue in Col. 3:12 : ἐνδύσασθε οὖν ... σπλάγχνα οἰκτιρμοῦ, χρηστότητα κτλ. also denotes Christian sympathy in 1 Cl., 56, 1. The pity of the law or the judge is meant in Hb. 10:28 : ἀθετήσας τις νόμον Μωϋσέως χωρὶς οἰκτιρμῶν ... ἀποθνῄσκει.

The only adj. found in the NT is οἰκτίρμων, used of God in Jm. 5:11 in an expression which is a variation on the description of God in ψ 102:8; 110:4. οἰκτίρμων is found as a description of God in 1 Cl., 23, 1, and also in the invocation in 1 Cl., 60, 1, where it is combined with ἐλεήμων in OT fashion. The word denotes the divine mercy in the saying in Lk. 6:36, where it serves as the basis of the admonition to show mercy.[28] There is a variation on this admonition in Just. Apol., 15, 13 : γίνεσθε δὲ χρηστοὶ καὶ οἰκτίρμονες, ὡς καὶ ὁ πατὴρ ὑμῶν χρηστός ἐστι καὶ οἰκτίρμων, cf. also Just. Dial., 96, 3.

Bultmann

---

[23] Harder, 88 f.; A. Marmorstein, *The Old Rabbinic Doctrine of God*, I (1927), 56.
[24] Marmorstein, *op. cit.*, 80 f.
[25] Cf. Ltzm. K. and Wnd. 2 K., ad loc.
[26] Like οἰκτιρμοί, σπλάγχνα is often used for רחמים in the LXX.
[27] Though cf. Loh. Phil.: "So assuredly is God love and mercy."
[28] On the question whether the Lucan γίνεσθε οἰκτίρμονες is original rather than Mt.'s ἔσεσθε ... τέλειοι, or whether Lk. emends to link the passage with what follows, cf. the comm.

---

† οἶνος

The vine is one of the oldest of cultivated plants, dating back to pre-historic times. Wine is found very early both as a means of enjoyment and also as a constituent part of the cultus.[1] In antiquity it is used esp. in sacrifices; it is presented as a sacrifice of petition, thanksgiving and expiation, and also as a sacrifice for the dead. Libations of wine occur along with other offerings. They play a special part in feasts, where at the beginning or end drink is offered to the deity, or it is perhaps thought that there is celebration or drinking together with the deity, and that this leads into particularly close fellowship with it.[2] Wine has a very prominent place in the cult of the god Dionysus, who is equated with wine.[3]

Wine is very significant in Palestine. Acc. to Gn. 9:20 Noah, the forefather of the new race, is also the first to cultivate the vine. In the OT there are many sayings in praise of wine. In Ju. 9:13 it is the drink which makes glad both men and gods, cf. Ps. 104:15. Fulness of wine is a special blessing from God, Gn. 27:28, 37; Jl. 2:23 f. Abstinence from wine (cf. the position of the Rechabites in Jer. 35, or Hos. 2:10-14; 3:1, where wine is linked with Baal worship) is rare. The common use of the metaphor of the vine supports this, → I, 342 f. On the other hand there are many warnings against over-indulgence, cf. Is. 5:11 f.; Prv. 20:1; 21:17; Sir. 19:1 ff. As in the ancient world generally, wine has cultic significance in the OT too, and there are precise regulations for offering the sacrifice of wine (Ex. 29:38-41; Nu. 15:2-15 etc.).[4] Sacred temple wine is mentioned in Jos. Bell., 5, 565. Wine is specifically mentioned as an integral part of the passover meal no earlier than Jub. 49:6, but there can be no doubt that it was in use long before. Pes., 10 gives precise directions as to the four cups at the passover (→ III, 733 f.) and explanations of their meaning.[5]

οἶνος. Walde Pok., I, 226; P. Thomsen, Art. "Wein" in *Reallexikon d. Vorgeschichte*, 14 (1929), 265-269; J. Hempel, L. Köhler, RGG², V, 1796-1798; K. Kircher, "D. sakrale Bedeutung des Weines im Altertum," RVV, IX, 2 (1910); H. F. Lutz, *Viticulture and Brewing in the Ancient Orient* (1922); J. Hempel, "Mystik und Alkoholekstase," *Die Alkoholfrage in d. Religion*, I, 3 (1926); J. Benzinger in RE³, XXI, 58-62; V. Zapletal, "Der Wein in d. Bibel," BSt, XX, 1 (1920); E. Busse, "Der Wein im Kult d. AT," *Freiburger Theol. Studien*, 29 (1922); G. Dalman, *Arbeit u. Sitte in Palästina*, IV (1935), 291-413; J. Döller, "Der Wein in Bibel u. Talmud," *Biblica*, 4 (1923), 143-167, 267-299; H. Schmidt, "Die Alkoholfrage im AT," *Die Alkoholfrage in d. Religion*, I, 1 (1926). J. Boehmer, "Das NT und d. Alkohol," *Die Studierstube*, 22 (1926), 321-364; E. Zurhellen-Pfleiderer, "Die Alkoholfrage im NT," *Die Alkoholfrage in d. Religion*, II, 2 (1927); I. W. Raymond, *The Teaching of the Early Church on the Use of Wine and Strong Drink* (1927).

[1] Kircher, *passim*.

[2] Cf. Ltzm. K., Exc. on 1:10, 21 f., and as an individual example a festal liturgy from the period 2000-1600, discovered in Ras Shamra and discussed by G. A. Barton, JBL, 53 (1934), 61-78. This contains an invitation to drink with the gods.

[3] Cf. J. Leipoldt, "Dionysos," *Angelos, Beih.* 3 (1931), 38; W. F. Otto, *Dionysos* (1933), 136-141.

[4] Busse, 18-28; Döller, 279-286.

[5] Cf. G. Beer, *Pesachim* (1912), 187-199; Zapletal, 58-66; esp. G. Dalman, *Jesus-Jeschua* (1922), 134-137.

In the NT οἶνος is mainly used in the literal sense of "wine," and never in a cultic relation. A characteristic of the Baptist is that he abstains from wine, Lk. 1:15; cf. 7:33 (Mt. 11:18). As those dedicated to God in the OT refrained from wine or intoxicating drinks (Nu. 6:3; cf. Ju. 13:4, 7), so John, fully consecrated to God, must be controlled solely by the fulness of the Holy Spirit.

In distinction from the Baptist Jesus drank wine, as may be seen from Mt. 11:19; Lk. 7:34 (Jesus as οἰνοπότης). According to Mk. 2:18-22 and par. Jesus justified His conduct on the ground that the time when the bridegroom is present is one of festivity. Jesus is more than a Nazirite; hence the corresponding OT regulations do not apply to Him. He explains this in the parable of the new wine and the old skins, Mk. 2:22 and par. The new which he brings cannot be mixed with the old. Lk. 5:39 added the difficult saying: καὶ οὐδεὶς πιὼν παλαιὸν θέλει νέον· λέγει γάρ· ὁ παλαιὸς χρηστός ἐστιν.

Cf. Sir. 9:10: οἶνος νέος φίλος νέος· ἐὰν παλαιωθῇ, μετ' εὐφροσύνης πίεσαι αὐτόν. Ber., 51a: "Is not the old wine more wholesome?" There are similar sayings among the Gks. and Romans, cf. Luc. De Mercede Conductis, 26: τῶν ἄλλων ἥδιστόν τε καὶ παλαιότατον οἶνον πινόντων ..., Plut. Mar., 44 (I, 431d); Plaut. Casina. 5: qui utuntur vino vetere, sapientes puto. [6] The saying in Lk. 5:39 seems to contradict what goes before, since it favours the retention of the old. In the context of Lk., however, it is to be regarded as a warning against over-estimation of the old. [7]

Only the Fourth Gospel records the miracle at Cana of Galilee (Jn. 2:1-11, cf. 4:46), [8] where according to the account Jesus changes a vast amount of water into wine (6 pots of 39 litres each). The significance of the miracle, which is peculiar to this Gospel, [9] depends on our total understanding of the Gospel. On the one side decisive attention may be paid only to the literal account, [10] while on the other reference is made to the need to take into account the nature of the Johannine miracles as signs (→ σημεῖον), and a deeper meaning is sought. On the latter view the question of historicity is secondary and the main point is to understand the symbolism which seems to be present in the miraculous provision of wine.

There seems to be already a movement in this direction in the monarchian preface to Jn. [11] which says of Jn. 2:1-11 that it shows that veteribus immutatis nova omnia, quae a Christo instituuntur, appareant. Along the same lines is the interpretation which sees in the contrast between water and wine the antithesis between Law and Spirit, [12] or that which refers the wine to the blood of Jesus proffered at the Last Supper. [13]

---

[6] For many more instances cf. Wettstein on Lk. 5:39.

[7] So L. Fendt, Der Christus d. Gemeinde (1937), 76: "Thus the saying of Lk. is a sermon ... to the conservatives of his day." For other interpretations cf. the comm.

[8] For bibl. cf. the comm., also K. L. Schmidt, "Der joh. Charakter d. Erzählung vom Hochzeitswunder in Kana," Harnack-Ehrung (1921), 32-43; J. Grill, Untersuchungen über d. Entstehung des 4. Ev., II (1923), 73-95, 107-119; H. Schmidt, "D. Erzählung von der Hochzeit zu Kana," Die Alkoholfrage in d. Religion, IV, 1 (1931).

[9] Cf. E. Schweizer, Ego Eimi (1939), 100.

[10] Cf. the exegesis in F. Büchsel, Das Ev. nach Jn. (NT Deutsch, 1937), ad loc.

[11] Kl. T., 1, 13.

[12] Cf. K. L. Schmidt, op. cit.; also E. Hirsch, Das 4. Ev. in seiner urspr. Gestalt (1936), 125 f.: "The purity of legal worship is swallowed up by the gift of the Holy Spirit." But Jn. nowhere equates wine and Spirit.

[13] So R. Eisler, "Das Rätsel d. Joh.-Ev.," Eranos Jbch. (1935), 487 f. O. Cullmann, "Urchristentum u. Gottesdienst," Abh. z. Theol. des A u. NT, 3 (1944), 41-46. Cf. the correct rejection of this equation in Bu. J., 84, n. 1.

On the other side, attempts have been made to explain the miracle in terms of analogies from comparative religion. The idea found in Philo that the *Logos* is God's gift of wine [14] offers one possibility if Philo's *Logos* is replaced by the person of Jesus, while invocation of the wine miracles of Dionysus [15] finds esp. in Jn. 2:1-11 Dionysiac features in the Johannine picture of Christ. [16]

In the accounts of the Last Supper the term οἶνος occurs neither in the Synoptists nor Paul. It is obvious, however, that according to custom Jesus was proffering wine in the cup over which He pronounced the blessing; this may be seen especially from the solemn γένημα τῆς ἀμπέλου (Mk. 14:25 and par.) which was borrowed from Judaism. [17] In this final saying before the passion Jesus looks forward triumphantly to the consummation in the kingdom of God which He often describes elsewhere (cf. Mt. 8:11; 22:1-14) in the image of a common meal. [18]

In the story of the passion Mk. 15:23 records that prior to the crucifixion Jesus was handed wine mingled with myrrh (Mt. 27:34 changes this into μετὰ χολῆς μεμιγμένον in allusion to ψ 68:22). The point of this was to stupefy Him, but He refused it.

> Cf. Sanh., 43a : Rab Chisda has said : "To him who went forth to be executed there was given a little frankincense mixed with wine to deprive him of consciousness." [19] Jesus' rejection of the drink shows that He accepted the suffering of the cross to the full. Wine is a means of healing in Lk. 10:34. [20]

Paul does not use the term much. In R. 14:21 he recommends total abstinence from flesh and wine should the weaker brother be upset about eating and drinking. [21] In Eph. 5:18, on the basis of Prv. 23:31: μὴ μεθύσκεσθε οἴνῳ (Β ἐν οἴνοις), he warns against excessive drinking of wine, ἐν ᾧ ἐστιν ἀσωτία. [22] In contrast, he calls for surrender to the fulness of the Spirit, cf. Lk. 1:15. There is

---

[14] Som., II, 249 : τίς ἐπιχεῖ τοὺς ἱεροὺς κυάθους τῆς πρὸς ἀλήθειαν εὐφροσύνης, ὅτι μὴ ὁ οἰνοχόος τοῦ θεοῦ καὶ συμποσίαρχος λόγος, cf. Leg. All., III, 82.

[15] On these miracles cf. Athen., I, 61 (34a b): τῆς Ἠλείας τόπος ἐστὶν ἀπέχων ὀκτὼ στάδια, ἐν ᾧ οἱ ἐγχώριοι κατακλείοντες τοῖς Διονυσίοις χαλκοῦς λέβητας τρεῖς κενοὺς παρόντων τῶν ἐπιδημούντων ἀποφραγίζονται καὶ ὕστερον ἀνοίγοντες εὑρίσκουσιν οἴνου πεπληρωμένους, Diod. S., III, 66; Paus., VI, 26, 1 and 2. Cf. also Bau. J., Exc. on 2:12; H. Schmidt, *op. cit.*; W. F. Otto, 133 ff.

[16] So esp. Grill, 107-120; Bu. J.: "In fact this is the motif of the story ... a typical motif in the Dionysus legend" (83, esp. n. 3 on Jn. 2:6-11). Cf. J. Leipoldt, 51. On the glorifying of wine in Syrian cults cf. H. Schlier, "Religionsgeschichtliche Untersuchungen zu den Ignatiusbriefen," NZW, *Beih.* 8 (1929), 54, n. 1. Cf. also Lidz. Joh., 4, n. 4; 5, n. 1; Lidz. Ginza, Index, *s.v.* "Wein," also W. Brandt, *D. mandäische Religion* (1889), 110. The so-called rule in 2:10 is found neither in antiquity nor elsewhere. The examples adduced by H. Windisch, ZNW, 14 (1913), 248-257, do not fit the sense of 2:10.

[17] → I, 685; III, 733 f.; Dalman, *op. cit.*, 137.

[18] Jewish par. in Str.-B., IV, 1154-1159. That wine is a symbol of the age of salvation does not follow from the sources, as against J. Jeremias, *Jesus als Weltvollender* (1930), 27-31; Hck. Lk. on 5:33-39. The common meal is the symbol of this age.

[19] For further information cf. Str.-B., I, 1037.

[20] *Ibid.*, 428 f. Döller, 277 f. tells us that a mixture of oil and wine, called Samaritan balsam, is still used as a medicine in the Orient.

[21] On the abstinence in principle of the Therapeutae cf. Philo Vit. Cont., 74. For them wine was ἀφροσύνης φάρμακον. Cf. also Ltzm. R., Exc. on 14:1 ff.; H. Lewy, "Sobria Ebrietas," ZNW, *Beih.* 9 (1929), *passim*, cf. Index, *s.v.* "Wein." Cf. also Raymond, *passim*.

[22] → I, 507 and Str.-B., III, 609.

also a warning against over-indulgence in 1 Tm. 3:3, 8; Tt. 2:3.[23] A moderate use of wine can be beneficial to health, 1 Tm. 5:23; if, however, one assumes a non-Pauline authorship, there is perhaps an anti-Gnostic note here.[24]

The word οἶνος is common in Rev., but only once, at 18:13, is it used literally. Here οἶνος is one of the commodities which the merchant fleet can no longer sell. In Rev. 6:6 οἶνος is used as *effectus pro causa*, i.e., for vineyard. The sparing of the wine and oil in the plague which follows the breaking of the third seal is to be interpreted in terms of the understanding of the book as a whole. The most simple explanation is that the fruits of one season of the year (wheat and barley) are to be destroyed in this plague.[25] In the remaining passages in Rev. οἶνος is used fig. in two senses. At 14:10; 16:19; 19:15 it denotes the wrath of God. The clearest and fullest passage is 14:10 : καὶ αὐτὸς πίεται ἐκ τοῦ οἴνου τοῦ θυμοῦ τοῦ θεοῦ τοῦ κεκερασμένου ἀκράτου ἐν τῷ ποτηρίῳ τῆς ὀργῆς αὐτοῦ.

The picture of the cup as an expression of God's wrath and punishment is taken from the OT, where it was developed in prophecies of judgment against Judah and the nations, Jer. 25:15 f., 27 f. Cf. also Is. 51:17, 22; Jer. 49:12; Ez. 23:31-35; Hab. 2:16; Ps. 75:8; Lam. 4:21, and Ps. Sol. 8:14.[26] To emphasise how great and dreadful the wrath of God is, the wine is called ἄκρατος and κεκερασμένος. ἄκρατος indicates the unmitigated effect of wine (= wrath) unadulterated by water.[27] As far as κεκερασμένος is concerned there are two possibilities. κεράννυμι means either "to pour"[28] or "to mix," i.e., with stupefying herbs which accentuate its intoxicating character.[29] The second of the two seems to fit better. In Rev. 19:15 the metaphor of the wine of God's wrath is combined with that of the wine-press (14:19), → IV, 257. There is another combination, namely, that of the cup and the sword, in Jer. 25:15 f. This shows that the metaphor was already well-worn in the time of Jer., for otherwise it could not have been brought into an unorganic connection of this kind.

Rather different is the figurative use at Rev. 14:8 : ἔπεσεν ἔπεσεν Βαβυλὼν ἡ μεγάλη, ἣ ἐκ τοῦ οἴνου τοῦ θυμοῦ τῆς πορνείας αὐτῆς πεπότικεν πάντα τὰ ἔθνη (cf. 17:2, where we simply have οἶνος τῆς πορνείας, and 18:3).

---

[23] Cf. 1 Pt. 4:3 with its warning against drunkenness (οἰνοφλυγία). Cf. v. Arnim, III, 397: οἰνοφλυγία δὲ ἐπιθυμία οἴνου ἄπληστος.

[24] Cf. Dib. Past., *ad loc.*; Str.-B., III, 654 f.; cf. 1 Tm. 3:3; Tt. 1:7 (πάροινος).

[25] For attempts at interpretation cf. → II, 471 f. A contemporary understanding was first suggested by S. Reinach, *Revue archéologique*, 39 (1901), 350-374 = *Cultes, Mythes et Religions*,³ II (1928), 356-380, then in another form by S. Krauss, "Schonung von Öl u. Wein in d. Apk.," ZNW, 10 (1909), 81-89. Cf. also J. Moffatt, Exp., 7, Series VI (1908), 359-369. Cf. also F. Boll, *Aus d. Offenbarung Joh.* (1914), 84-87 and the comm., *ad loc.* On the combining of oil and wine among the Gks. cf. C. Bezold-F. Boll, "Reflexe astrologischer Keilinschriften bei gr. Schriftstellern," SAH (1911), 7. *Abh.*, 19 ff.

[26] H. Gressmann, *Der Ursprung d. isr.-jüd. Eschatologie* (1905), 129-136 has investigated the development of this distinctive image. He believes that the cup was originally a symbol of joy, but then the prophets changed it into one of terror in their messages of doom. A different view is found in P. Volz, *Der Prophet Jeremia* (1928), 392 f., who thinks the origin of the image is to be sought in a mantic use which has still to be investigated (cf. Gn. 44:5): "The cup as a means of prophecy is the power of destiny, and there thus arises the idea that the cup is destiny, and drinking it implies and brings its fulfilment."

[27] For an example of the power of undiluted wine cf. 3 Macc. 5:2.

[28] Cf. Pr.-Bauer³, *s.v.*

[29] Cf. Loh. Apk. on 14:10. Cf. P. Oxy., VIII, 1088, 53 ff.: μετὰ γλυκέως καὶ μέλιτος καὶ στροβίλων κ<εκ>[ρ]αμένων δὸς πεῖν. ψ 74:8 : ποτήριον ... οἴνου ἀκράτου πλῆρες κεράσματος. Ps. Sol. 8:14 : διὰ τοῦτο ἐκέρασεν αὐτοῖς ὁ θεὸς πνεῦμα πλανήσεως, ἐπότισεν αὐτοὺς ποτήριον οἴνου ἀκράτου εἰς μέθην.

It might seem natural enough to link these passages with 14:10; 16:19; 19:15. The wine of fornication is on this view the wine of God's wrath, since the nations who yield to the seductions of Babylon fall victim thereby to the wrath of God. [30] Nevertheless, esp. in the light of 17:2, the independence of the image seems to be supported by the passage which the author has in mind, 'Ιερ. 28:7 f. (51:7 f.): ποτήριον χρυσοῦν Βαβυλὼν ἐν χειρὶ κυρίου, μεθύσκον πᾶσαν τὴν γῆν· ἀπὸ τοῦ οἴνου αὐτῆς ἐπίοσαν ἔθνη ... Cf. Hos. 7:5 : ... ἤρξαντο οἱ ἄρχοντες θυμοῦσθαι ἐξ οἴνου. It may be conceded, of course, that in 14:8 and 18:3, as in 19:15, the two metaphors merge into one another.

Seesemann

---

† ὀκνηρός

Like ὄκνος, [1] which means "hesitation" through weariness, sloth, fear, bashfulness, or reserve, ὀκνηρός is used a. of persons in the sense of "showing ὄκνον," "hesitating," "anxious," "negligent," "slothful." It thus denotes one who for various reasons or difficulties does not have the resolution to act. Pind. Nem., 11, 22 : ἐλπίδες; Thuc., IV, 55, 2 : ἐς τὰ πολεμικά, along with ἀπρόθυμος Plut. De Tuenda Sanitate Praecepta, 14 (II, 129b); Them., 2, 3 (I, 112c); opp. τολμήρος (cf. R. 15:15), θρασύς (cf. Luc. Epistola ad Nigrinum, 38); Aristot. Hist. An., 9, p. 608b, 13 : τὸ θῆλυ ... ὀκνηρότερον, Eth. Nic., 4, p. 1125a, 24; Menand. Peric., 127: ὡς ὀκνηρῶς μοι προσέρχε[ι], Δᾶε (cf. Ac. 9:38; Nu. 22:16 מאן; Ju. 18:9 עצל ni); Plut. Lib. Educ., 16 (II, 12c d): δύο γὰρ ταῦθ' ὡσπερεὶ στοιχεῖα τῆς ἀρετῆς ἐστιν, ἐλπίς τε τιμῆς καὶ φόβος τιμωρίας· ἡ μὲν γὰρ ὁρμητικωτέρους πρὸς τὰ κάλλιστα τῶν ἐπιτηδευμάτων, ἡ δ' ὀκνηρούς πρὸς τὰ φαῦλα τῶν ἔργων ἀπεργάζεται. Plut. Cicero, 5 (I, 863a): ταῖς ἀρχαῖς ὀκνηρῶς προσῄει. Philo Rer. Div. Her., 254; Spec. Leg., I, 99; cf. the expression in epistolary style, P. Eleph., 13, 7 (223/2 B.C.): μὴ ὀκνῶν γράφειν, Procl. de Forma Epist. in R. Hercher, Epistolographi Graeci (1873), 8 ε. It is also used b. of things, "causing ὄκνον," "awakening suspicion, dislike, fear," Soph. Oed. Tyr., 834 : ἡμῖν ... μὲν ταῦτ' ὀκνηρά ...

In the OT ὀκνηρός is often used in connection with rules of practical wisdom. [2] Industry and work are here part of pious but prudent conduct. Thus ὀκνηρός (pre-

---

[30] So Bousset Apk., 385; Loh. Apk. on 14:8.

ὀ κ ν η ρ ό ς. Moult.-Mill. and Liddell-Scott, *s.v.*

[1] Hom. Il., 5, 817; 10, 122; 13, 224; Plat. Soph., 242a : εἰ τοῦτό τις εἴργει δρᾶν ὄκνος, Leg., II, 665d : πᾶς που γιγνόμενος πρεσβύτερος ὄκνου πρὸς τὰς ᾠδὰς μεστός, Ps.-Isoc. Demonicon, 7: ἡ δὲ τῆς ἀρετῆς κτῆσις ... τὸν μὲν ὄκνον ψόγον, τὸν δὲ πόνον ἔπαινον ἡγουμένη, Plut. Cato Minor, 49 (I, 783c): ὄκνου καὶ μελλήσεως ἀτόλμου ... ὑπόπλεως. The rope of the ὄκνος, who became an allegorical figure, was proverbial. Paus., 10, 29, 2; Prop., IV, 3, 21, cf. L. Schmidt, *Die Ethik d. alten Griechen*, I (1882), 102, 381, n. 39. On ὀκνεῖν cf. Suid., *s.v.* ὀκνεῖ· εὐλαβῶς ἔχει. Hesych.: ὀκνῶν· ἀναδυόμενος, φοβούμενος. *Ibid.*, ὀκνεῖ· δέδοικε, δειλιᾷ, εὐλαβεῖται, οὐ βούλεται. Plut. Apophth. Pomp., 6 (II, 204c): *Mulierum virtutes*, 19 (II, 257b): ὤκνει ... αἰδεσθείς.

[2] The OT at this pt. follows ancient oriental wisdom, cf. J. Fichtner, "Die altorientalische Weisheit in ihrer isr.-jüd. Ausprägung," ZAW, Beih. 62 (1933). H. Gressmann, *Israels Spruchweisheit im Zshg. der Weltlit.* (1925); W. Baumgartner, *Isr. u. altorientalische Weisheit* (1933); W. Zimmerli, "Zur Struktur d. at.lichen Weisheit," ZAW, NF, 10 (1933), 177-204.

dominantly for the Heb. עָצֵל) depicts the slothful man who lacks the resolve to get to work (Prv. 6:6, 9), who lets inconveniences stop him (Prv. 20:4), or who, having no resolution, never moves on from the will to the deed (Prv. 21:25). In contrast the continually active wife, who takes pleasure in work, is extolled (Prv. 31:27 for Heb. עֲצַלּוּת). ³ Cf. also Sir. 22:1 f.; 37:11 (שׁוא).

In the NT a. occurs at Mt. 25:26 in an eschatological context. The slothful servant, who cannot overcome his distaste for responsible effort, is an image of the Christian who hesitates to put his divinely imparted gift actively to work during the testing period of earthly life. This sloth is a serious matter because it ignores and neglects the responsibility which the righteous must display in face of God's eternal judgment. In R. 12:11 Paul significantly relates the warning against sloth to the admonition to be inspired and directed by the Spirit. To yield to the promptings of carnal indolence is for Christians an offence against the Spirit who enables and obligates them to overcome themselves.

Sense b. occurs at Phil. 3:1, "arousing dislike or displeasure." ⁴ Impelled by the Spirit to equip Christians adequately for salvation, Paul overcomes the dislike or distaste which might arise through repetition of his admonition.

Hauck

> ὀλεθρεύω, ὄλεθρος,
> ὀλοθρευτής, ἐξολοθρεύω

† ὀλεθρεύω.

"To corrupt," "to destroy," derived from ὄλεθρος with -εύω, cf. φόνος φονεύω. ὄλεθρος ὀλοθρεύω (vowel assimilation) is normal; ὀλεθρευ- is an artificial readjustment to ὄλεθρος. ¹

The word occurs only in later lit. Philo in Leg. All., II, 34 says in allegorical exposition of Ex. 12:23 : ἐᾷ μὲν γὰρ τὸν ὀλοθρεύοντα — ὄλεθρος δὲ ψυχῆς ἐστιν ἡ τροπή — εἰσελθεῖν εἰς τὴν ψυχήν, ἵνα τὸ ἴδιον ἐνδείξηται τοῦ γενητοῦ, "God causes the corrupter — the corruption of the soul is its alteration — to enter into the soul to show the fate of what is mortal." Test. L. 13:7 advises that wisdom be received

---

³ The Mas. text is often greatly altered in the LXX, e.g., Prv. 10:26; 24:30 ff., cf. G. Bertram, "Die religiöse Umdeutung d. altorientalischen Lebensweisheit in d. griech. Übersetzung d. AT," ZAW, NF, 13 (1936), 153-167, esp. 157 f.
⁴ Probably formal, cf. οὐκ ὀκνῶ etc., Dib. Th., 66; Ew. Gefbr., 149; Theod. Mops., ad loc. (230 f., Swete).

ὀ λ ε θ ρ ε ύ ω. ¹ I owe this to Debrunner, cf. E. Fränkel, Gr. Denominativa (1906), 192. Acc. to K. Buresch, "Γέγοναν u. anderes Vulgärgr.," Rheinisches Museum, 46 (1891), 216, the formation of the verb ὀλεθρεύω from ὄλεθρος (with other constructs like ὀλεθρευτής, ἐξολέθρευσις, -ευμα, -ευτικός) is a "child of Alexandria," "unheard of in ancient secular lit." But, as Debrunner points out, this insight has no more than historical importance : ὀλε/οθρεύω is a Hell. word, cf. Bl.-Debr. § 32, 1 App. On ὀλοθρεύειν, -ευτής in the Ps. Clem. cf. Reinhold, 30 f.

in the fear of God. Wisdom cannot be destroyed when material values are brought to nothing. Vett. Val., II, 39 (123, 11, Kroll) speaks of the influence of certain constellations : Κρόνος μετὰ ῎Αρεως τυχὼν ὀλεθρεύει ἀδελφοὺς ἢ ἀσθενικοὺς ποιεῖ. Cf. also Schol. Eur. Hipp., 535 : μὴ τιμῶντες τὸν ῎Ερωτα, ... τὸν πορθοῦντα καὶ ὀλοθρεύοντα τὸν τῶν ἀνθρώπων βίον. Anth. Pal., I, 57: ὀλοθρεύων, φεῦγε, μὴ ἐγγὺς ἴθι. The word occurs 18 times in the LXX with the same meaning as elsewhere. גּוֹי כְּרֵתִים in Zeph. 2:5 is transl. πάροικοι Κρητῶν in the LXX, though ᾽ΑΣΘ give כְּרֵתִים a general sense (᾽Α ἔθνος ὀλέθριον; Σ ἔθνος ὀλεθρευόμενον; Θ ἔθνος ὀλεθρ(ε)ίας).

Regarding the spelling of ὀλεθρεύω and ὀλοθρεύω in the LXX, B usually has ὀλεθρεύω, while Bᶜᵒʳʳ has the more correct ο. א and Aˡ also have ὀλεθρεύω. At Is. 9:14 (13) ᾽ΑΣ have ὀλοθρεύσει or ἐξολοθρεύσει; ἐξολοθρευθήσεται also occurs in ᾽Α at Is. 56:5.

In the form ὀλοθρεύω the term passed into the Byzantine, though only ξολοθρεύω occurs in modern parlance.

The only NT instance is Hb. 11:28. According to the judgment of Hb. the observance of the passover and the sprinkling of blood on the lintel and sideposts of the door were an act of faith. The cultic acts prescribed in Ex. 12 were designed to prevent the ὀλεθρεύων [2] (= הַמַּשְׁחִית, "the angel of destruction"), which slew the firstborn of men and beasts, from touching the Israelites. [3]

† ὄλεθρος. [1]

a. "Corruption," esp. "destruction," "death." ὄλεθρος ψυχῆς, "destruction of life" (Hom. Il., 22, 325; Philo Leg. All., II, 34); ὄλεθρος χρημάτων, "loss of money" (Thuc., VII, 27, 3); [2] ὄλεθρος καὶ διαφθορά (Plat. Resp., VI, 495a); ὄλεθρος καὶ φθορά (Philo Som., I, 86); ἐπ᾽ ὀλέθρῳ ἐκκλησιάζειν (to speak in the assembly) (Aristoph. Thes., 84). b. "That which brings corruption," Hes. Theog., 326 f.: ἣ δ᾽ ἄρα Φῖκ᾽ ὀλοὴν τέκε Καδμείοισιν ὄλεθρον ῎Ορθῳ ὑποδμηθεῖσα Νεμειαῖόν τε λέοντα. Esp. of men who corrupt others, cf. Hdt., III, 142, 5 : γεγονώς τε κακῶς καὶ ἐὼν ὄλεθρος, Soph. Oed. Tyr., 1343 : Oedipus calls himself τὸν μέγ᾽ ὀλέθριον. Aristoph. Lys., 326 : ὑπό τε γερόντων ὀλέθρων. Plat. Resp., VI, 491b: πολλοὶ ὄλεθροι καὶ μεγάλοι. In Demosth. ὄλεθρος is a term of abuse. Demosth. in Or., 9, 31 calls Philip of Macedonia ὄλεθρος Μακεδών, and in 18, 127 Aeschines is ὄλεθρος γραμματεύς, cf. also 21, 209 : τὸν δὲ βάσκανον, τὸν δ᾽ ὄλεθρον, 23, 202 : ἀνθρώπους οὐδ᾽ ἐλευθέρους ἀλλ᾽ ὀλέθρους καὶ τοιαῦτα πεποιηκότας, οἷα λέγειν ὀκνήσειεν ἄν τις εὖ φρονῶν. Cf. also BGU, IV, 1027, 11: οἴου ὀλέθρου πίρας (ἐποεῖτε), Ditt. Syll.³, 527, 82 : κακίστῳ ὀλέθρωι ἐξόλλυσθαι.

The word is common in the LXX. In the prophets it often has the sense of "eschatological destruction." ᾽Ιερ. 31(48):3 : ὄλεθρος καὶ σύντριμμα μέγα. Wis. 1:14 : "The creatures of the world bring salvation, and there is in them no draught of corruption (καὶ οὐκ ἔστιν ἐν αὐταῖς φάρμακον ὀλέθρου). 4 Macc. 10:15 (an oath by the blessed death of my brothers and the eternal destruction of the tyrant : μὰ ... τὸν αἰώνιον τοῦ τυράννου ὄλεθρον).

---

[2] vl. ὀλοθρεύων.

[3] Cf. on this Rgg. Hb., 373, n. 50 : "The הַמַּשְׁחִית of Ex. 12:23 is rightly understood personally in the LXX and also in Jewish tradition, cf. Jub. 49:3 : Mechiltha on Ex. 12:22 f. (Winter-Wünsche, 37 f.)." Cf. also Str.-B., III, 412 f.

ὄλεθρος. [1] ὄλεθρος from ὄλλυμι ὀλέ-σαι. The sense "bringer of destruction" is perhaps the older, cf. P. Chantraine, La formation des noms en grec ancien (1933), 373.
[2] Cf. H. Richards, Classical Quarterly, 6 (1912), 227.

The word occurs twice in the NT in eschatological sayings. In 1 Th. 5:3 it is said of those who do not expect Christ's *parousia* that precisely when they brag of peace and safety inescapable destruction (αἰφνίδιος ὄλεθρος) will suddenly overtake them. In 2 Th. 1:9 it is stated that on the revelation of Christ from heaven those who do not know God and who have refused to obey the message of salvation will be allotted eternal destruction (ὄλεθρος αἰώνιος) as a punishment. [3] In 1 Tm. 6:9 the conscience of those who desire to be rich is seared. They are in danger of succumbing to the temptations and lusts which plunge men into corruption and ruin (εἰς ὄλεθρον καὶ ἀπώλειαν), i.e., into complete destruction. [4] The most important NT instance is 1 C. 5:5. This has to do with the case of incest. Paul demands that the congregation should meet to judge the incestuous man. He himself will be there in spirit. In the power of the Lord at work in the assembled congregation, the community should then pronounce the solemn curse : "We deliver thee up [5] to Satan." [6] This handing over to Satan is εἰς ὄλεθρον τῆς σαρκός. In line with ancient ideas of the religio-cultic curse and its effect, [7] Paul obviously believes that the curse will be followed by the (sudden) death of the person thus condemned. [8] Death is a punishment for the flesh which has sinned. But the spirit, i.e., the πνεῦμα which God has put in Christians, will in some unknown way escape destruction, so that the Christian who has sinned will be saved on the day of judgment.

There is an NT par. in Ac. 5:5, 10 (Ananias and Sapphira), [9] also further par. in apcr. Acts (Act. Pt. Verc., 2, 15, 32; Act. Joh., 41 f., 86; Act. Thom., 6). [10] Instructive as regards the idea of the divine power at work in the community is Ign. Eph., 13, 1: "When the community assembles often, the powerful spirits of Satan are destroyed and the corruption which he threatens does not develop (καὶ λύεται ὁ ὄλεθρος αὐτοῦ)."

† ὀλοθρευτής. [1]

This term is peculiar to Christian lit., cf. Act. Phil., 130 (59, 9, Bonnet): ἐπλήγητε ὑπὸ τοῦ ὀλοθρευτοῦ.

It is found only once in the NT at 1 C. 10:10. [2] Paul points to the warning example of the people of Israel. The Israelites murmured against God in the

---

[3] On αὐτοῖς ἐφίσταται ὄλεθρος (1 Th. 5:3) cf. 1 Cl., 57, 4 : ἡνίκα ἂν ἔρχηται ὑμῖν ὄλεθρος (quoting Prv. 1:26).
[4] Cf. Pr.-Bauer³, 246.
[5] Cf. παραδίδωμι, → II, 170.
[6] Cf. on this Deissmann LO⁴, 256 f.; Ltzm. K., ad loc.; C. Bruston, "L'Abandon du Pécheur à Satan," *Revue de Théologie et des Questions religieuses*, 21 (1912), 450 ff.; L. Brun, *Segen u. Fluch im Urchr.* (1932), 106-108.
[7] Cf. K. Latte, *Heiliges Recht* (1920), 61-88 and the bibl. in E. v. Dobschütz, *Die urchr. Gemeinden* (1902), 270 f. Cf. also R. Wünsch, *Antike Fluchtafeln* (Kl. T., 20).
[8] So also v. Dobschütz, op. cit., 271; Ltzm. K., ad loc.; Pr.-Bauer³, 934; → παραδίδωμι, II, 170, n. 9. Acc. to the view of the Gk. fathers (Theod. Mops. and Severian of Gabala ; cf. K. Staab, *Pauluskommentare aus d. griech. Kirche* [1933], 178 and 243 f.) ὄλεθρος τῆς σαρκός does not refer to the death of the sinner but to severe punishments in his earthly life. If he repents because of these, the spirit in him, the divine χάρισμα, will be saved.
[9] Cf. also 1 Tm. 1:20 (Hymenaeus and Alexander).
[10] Ltzm. K. on 1 C. 5:5.

ὀλοθρευτής. [1] ὀλοθρεύτρια, the normal fem. of ὀλοθρευτής, occurs in Hesych. acc. to Liddell-Scott.
[2] ὀλοθρευτοῦ is best attested, אABCDᶜEKLP etc.; ὀλεθρευτοῦ D.

wilderness, and they were destroyed by the destroyer. In good OT fashion[3] Paul is thinking of the angel of destruction as the agent of divine punishment. Thus ὁ ὀλοθρευτής = ὁ ἄγγελος ὁ ἐξολεθρεύων הַמַּלְאָךְ הַמַּשְׁחִית (1 Ch. 21:12, 15).[4]

Dibelius[5] thinks the art. indicates, not the avenging angel of God, but a specific person, namely, Satan, to whom the destruction of sinners is ascribed. This is possible. But in 1 C. 10:10 Paul is moving in the sphere of ideas which are plainly influenced by the OT.[6] He probably had in view not only Nu. 14:2 ff.; 17:6-15; but also Wis. 18:20-25, the punishment of the murmuring people by the destroyer.

In the Rabb. מַשְׁחִית became a proper name for a specific angel.[7] This is one of the angels of destruction (מַלְאֲכֵי חַבָּלָה) which in the first instance personify God's will of wrath and punishment, but gradually become independent angels whose task is to bring destruction on the ungodly. Though fundamentally these are ministering angels, they soon come to be reckoned among the bad angels and are thus counted among the angels of Satan.[8] On 1 C. 10:10 Str.-B. rightly observes : "Whether the apostle Paul when he speaks of the ὀλοθρευτής in 1 C. 10:10 is thinking specifically of the angel of judgment Mashchith or more generally of one of the many angels of destruction, is hard to decide. The definite art. before ὀλοθρευτής favours the former view, the fact that in 2 C. 12:7 the apostle speaks generally of an angel of destruction as an angel of Satan favours the latter."[9]

† ἐξολοθρεύω.

"To destroy completely," "to extirpate."[1] This word is comparatively rare.[2] An exception is the LXX, where it is very common in the form ἐξολεθρεύω. It is used for 20 different Heb. terms, כרת being the most common. The Heb. words have a special place in apocalyptic. The history and cultus fix the use and content of individual expressions. Their rendering in Gk. depends on the changing understanding of the translators. The word is often used in the LXX in statements which intimate God's will to root out men for their sins or to cast off the chosen people for their disobedience. It occurs a few times in Test. XII : Test. S. 6:3; Jud. 6:5; 7:3; 21:1; Jos. 5:2. It occurs once in Test. Sol. D., VI, 2 (94 McCown): ἐξολόθρευσον τοῦτον ἀπὸ τῆς τοιαύτης χώρας.[3] There is also only one example on pap., P. Masp., 2, III, 28 (67002, III, 18) (Byzantine): ἐξαλεῖψαι καὶ ἐξολοθρεῦσαι αὐτὴν (κώμην). Finally H. Usener, Legenden d. hl. Pelagia (1879), 23, 15 : εἰσαγαγεῖν σε ἐν τῷ οἴκῳ μου οὐ τολμῶ, μή πως ἀκούσῃ ὁ ὁρμαστός σου καὶ παγγενῇ με ἐξολοθρεύσῃ, 24, 18 : ἄγγελον ἐξαποστελεῖ καὶ ἐξολοθρεύσει πᾶσαν τὴν στρατιάν.

---

[3] So Ltzm. K., ad loc.
[4] In Ex. 12:23 the angel of destruction is ὁ ὀλεθρεύων (הַמַּשְׁחִית), cf. also Hb. 11:28; cf. Wis. 18:25 (B ὁ ὀλεθρεύων; AC ὁ ὀλοθρεύων).
[5] M. Dibelius, Die Geisterwelt im Glauben des Pls. (1909), 44 f.
[6] Cf. on this O. Everling, Die paul. Angelologie u. Dämonologie (1888), 24.
[7] Cf. Str.-B., III, 412.
[8] Ibid., 412 f.
[9] Ibid., 413, with Rabb. examples.
ἐ ξ ο λ ο θ ρ ε ύ ω. [1] In modern Gk. we now find only ξολοθρεύω.
[2] Rather oddly the word does not occur in Philo. In Joseph. it is a vl. (ἐξολοθρεύσω) for ἐξολέσω, Ant., 8, 270.
[3] For the use with ἀπό cf. also 1 Macc. 2:40; Jdt. 6:2 (ἐξολεθρεύειν ἀπὸ τῆς γῆς).

The NT has the word only once at Ac. 3:23. [4] After the healing of the lame man in Solomon's porch, Peter turns to the people. He proclaims Christ as the prophet promised by Moses, [5] and quoting Lv. 23:29 and Dt. 18:19 declares that rejection of Jesus as the Messiah will be followed by destruction from among the redeemed people.

The term is common in the post-apost. fathers, usually in OT quotations. 1 Cl., 53, 3 (ἔασόν με ἐξολεθρεῦσαι αὐτούς) is a quotation from Dt. 9:14; 1 Cl., 15, 5 : ἐξολεθρεύσαι κύριος πάντα τὰ χείλη τὰ δόλια = ψ 11:3; 1 Cl., 22, 6 : τοῦ ἐξολεθρεῦσαι ἐκ γῆς τὸ μνημόσυνον αὐτῶν = ψ 33:16; 1 Cl., 14, 4 : οἱ δὲ παρανομοῦντες ἐξολεθρευθήσονται ἀπ' αὐτῆς, cf. ψ 36:38 : οἱ δὲ παράνομοι ἐξολεθρευθήσονται ἐπὶ τὸ αὐτό, τὰ ἐγκαταλείμματα τῶν ἀσεβῶν ἐξολεθρευθήσονται.

J. Schneider

ὀλιγοπιστία, ὀλιγόπιστος → πιστεύω.

ὀλίγος

ὀλίγος means a. "small," "few," to denote a small number or group, opp. πολύς. Infrequently it can also mean b. "little" to denote a small quantity, opp. μέγας. The meanings merge into one another when both number and quantity are at issue, e.g., Hom. Il., 12, 452 : ὀλίγον ἄχθος. From the time of Hom. on we often find the adverbially used neut. ὀλίγον, "little," "a little," either abs. or in stereotyped expressions. [1]

In the LXX the concept of "little" takes on theological significance in certain recurrent trains of thought. Thus God can work much with few means, 1 Βασ. 14:6; 2 Ch. 14:10, and so can the righteous with God's help. They are on God's side. What matters is not that they have little but that they know how to use it, Tob. 4:8; 12:8; Job 8:7; ψ 36:16; Prv. 15:29a. In any case a poor man who is wise can do much with little, Qoh. 9:14 f. A little wisdom means much, 10:1; cf. also Sir. 19:1; 31:19. If in such sayings there is primarily reflected a sober experience of life and the practical wisdom of the world, under the influence of an eschatologically orientated piety each of these statements can take on a new and radical sense. They express the transvaluation of all values before God and in His kingdom. Thus characterisation by the term ὀλίγος is part of the biblical typology of the poor — the righteous.

We are pointed in a different direction by the thought that man is limited to a brief span of life, Job 10:20; Wis. 2:1; 12:2; 15:8; Sir. 18:10. For the sinner brevity of life is a punishment, ψ 36:10; 108:8. The fact that only a few remain in times

---

[4] AB*CD ... read ἐξολεθρευθήσεται, אB³ al ἐξολοθρευθήσεται. Cf. Bl.-Debr. § 32, 1. App.

[5] Dt. 18:15.

ὀλίγος. [1] Cf. Pass. and Liddell-Scott, *s.v.*

of distress is also a punishment, Dt. 4:27; 4 Βασ. 14:26; Is. 21:17; 24:6; Ιερ. 20:24; 49(42):2; 51(44):28; Bar. 2:13. It is a punishment, too, when in spite of every effort little is left of the harvest of the fields, Dt. 28:38; Hag. 1:6, 9.

As compared with the punishment which smites the ungodly, and the awaited reward, the punishment, chastisement, suffering, toil and temptation of the righteous is of little account, Wis. 3:5; 16:3, 6; 12:2; 13:6; cf. also Sir. 6:19; 51:16, 27; Zech. 1:15. This thought is altered somewhat in the primarily very secular saying at Sir. 34:10 : ὃς οὐκ ἐπειράθη, ὀλίγα οἶδεν, though the LXX reader could easily take this in the sense of religious πειρασμός. [2] A severe judgment is passed at Job 15:11. In many cases, e.g., the friends of Job, men will find the punishment which overtakes the sinner too small. [3]

In the NT ὀλίγος is common in the sense mentioned above. ὀλίγον is used both adverbially and in expressions such as ἐν ὀλίγῳ at Eph. 3:3 and πρὸς ὀλίγον at Jm. 4:14. [4] Only the following verses are significant.

Lk. 7:47: When the Pharisee had not been able to conceal his displeasure at the Lord's attitude to the woman who was a great sinner, Jesus said to him : οὗ χάριν λέγω σοι, ἀφέωνται αἱ ἁμαρτίαι αὐτῆς αἱ πολλαί, ὅτι ἠγάπησεν πολύ· ᾧ δὲ ὀλίγον ἀφίεται, ὀλίγον ἀγαπᾷ. D omits the words from ὅτι on, an obvious softening which shows very clearly how difficult is the exegesis of v. 47b. [5] The question is : Does Jesus address the final words to the Pharisee, so that He is saying indirectly : You, of course, are righteous, and need little forgiveness, but for this very reason you love so little? [6] Or is the concluding statement to be taken more formally and theoretically? [7] If Jesus Himself spoke the words — and there is no reason to dispute this — then He was surely aiming them at the Pharisee. In other words, He is here again assessing Pharisaic righteousness and showing how defective it is (→ δίκαιος, II, 189 f.). Where this righteousness which differentiates itself from the sinner is in the ascendent, love is small, and consequently the chief commandment is transgressed (Mk. 12:29 ff.).

Mt. 25:21, 23 : The saying of Jesus to the faithful servant : ἐπὶ ὀλίγα ἦς πιστός, ἐπὶ πολλῶν σε καταστήσω. Lk. himself offers an exegesis of the ἐπὶ ὀλίγα when he gives the saying in a strengthened and therefore secondary form : ἐν ἐλαχίστῳ πιστὸς ἐγένου (19:17): Even faithfulness in little, in the very least, will be rewarded at the judgment. [8]

Cf. Ex. r., 2 on 3:1: "God gives a man greatness only when he has tested him in a little thing ; then he exalts him to greatness."

---

[2] ℵ reads ἐπειράσθη. Cf. J. H. Korn, πειρασμός, Die Versuchung des Gläubigen in der griech. Bibel (1937), 27 f.

[3] These three paragraphs are by Bertram.

[4] Cf. Pr.-Bauer³, s.v., where all the passages are listed and the most important secular pars. and literary refs. are given. A favourite expression of the author of Ac. is οὐκ ὀλίγος = πολύς, 12:18; 14:28; 15:2 etc. Cf. on this expression, which is fairly common in the pap., Preisigke Wört., II, 168 and Moult.-Mill., s.v.

[5] On the textual problem v. Zn. Lk., ad loc., 325 n.

[6] So Schl. Lk., 261; Zn. Lk.; J. Weiss, Das Ev. des Mk. u. Lk.⁸ (1892). The Pharisee is reproached for the little love which he showed Jesus on entering his house.

[7] So, e.g., Hck. Lk.; also a possibility acc. to Kl. Lk.

[8] Cf. also Lk. 16:10, where D reads ἐν ὀλίγῳ for the second ἐν ἐλαχίστῳ.

In Lk. 12:48 Jesus says : ὁ δὲ μὴ γνούς (sc. τὸ θέλημα τοῦ κυρίου αὐτοῦ), ποιήσας δὲ ἄξια πληγῶν, δαρήσεται ὀλίγας. This saying is connected with what precedes. In a parable Jesus is calling for faithfulness to Himself, for the following of His will. The only point is that He seems to make some exception for those who do not know His will and are thus unable to do it. In contrast to those who knowingly disregard it these are threatened by a small punishment. Whether our Lord is thinking of the people (the ὄχλος) or the Gentiles when He refers to those who do not know His will, we cannot say, since we do not know in what situation the saying was delivered. [9]

Seesemann

ὀλιγόψυχος → ψυχή.
ὀλοθρευτής, ὀλοθρεύω → 167 ff.
ὀλοκληρία, ὁλόκληρος → III, 766 f.

| † ὀλολύζω | → ἀλαλάζω, I, 227, → θρηνέω, III, 148 ff., → κόπτω, III, 830 ff. |

Onomatopoeic, [1] "to make a loud and inarticulate cry" in expression of very great stress of soul, esp. in the sacral field : [2] shrill outcries at the Dionysiac mysteries [3] (Eur. Ba., 689) and at sacrifices (Hom. Od., 3, 450), [4] esp. at the epiphany of a god (Eur. Fr., 353 [Nauck²]; Aristoph. Eq., 1327; Xenophon Ephesius, 5, 13; Callim. Hymn., 4, 258; 5, 139). In this sense it is uttered by women — along with dancing (Aesch. Eum., 1043) — and is a sign of jubilation (Aesch. Sept. c. Theb., 268).

The term does not occur in Philo, Joseph. [5] or pap. (apart from P. Lond., 125, 30 [5th cent. A.D.]), but is found in the LXX in prophecies of judgment (only here, 19 times, 12 in Is. and 16 for ילל hi) [6] as an impressive description of the effect of

---

[9] Cf. A. Loisy, *L'évangile selon Luc* (1924), 355. The saying of Jesus to Martha as given in א ὀλίγων δέ ἐστιν χρεία ἢ ἑνός, makes no true sense. The text must have been corrupted here at a very early date. Cf. the comm., ad loc. on the meaning of the saying. → εἷς, II, 435.

ὀ λ ο λ ύ ζ ω. C. Theander, "Ὀλολυγή and ἰά," *Eranos*, 15 (1915), 99-160; Wegner, Art. "Ololyge," Pauly-W., XVII (1937), 2493 f.; L. Deubner, "Ololyge u. Verwandtes," AAB (1941).
[1] Cf. Moult.-Mill., *s.v.* Acc. to Theander from pre-Gk. cults and synon. with ἀλαλάζω (→ I, 227 f.), *v.* P. Kretschmer, *Glotta*, 9 (1918), 228 f.
[2] Hesych, *s.v.* ὀλολυγή differentiates clearly between the sacral and the profane use : the one : φωνὴ γυναικῶν, ἣν ποιοῦνται ... εὐχόμεναι, the other : ποιά φωνὴ λυπηρά, ὀδύνην καρδίας ἀσήμῳ τινὶ φθόγγῳ παριστῶσα.
[3] Cf. W. F. Otto, *Dionysos* (1933), 86 f.
[4] Not to be understood as an explicit prayer (so Wegner). Where there is such, ὀλολύζω is not an introductory *verbum dicendi*, but is added to this : ὡς εἰποῦσ' ὀλόλυξε, Hom. Od., 4, 767. This does not denote speaking loud ; there is a special act of ὀλολύζειν.
[5] Schl. Jk. on 5:1.
[6] ילל hi (31 times), only in prophecies ; perhaps the sound suggested the rendering ὀλολύζειν (18 times, also 4 in Σ, 1 in 'A) and ἀλαλάζειν ('Ιερ. 4:8; 29[47]:2; 32[25]:34), also 6 times θρηνεῖν. It is worth nothing that for הֵילִילוּ in Ez. 30:2 LXX has the cry itself : ὦ ὦ, while ΣΘ use ὀλολύζετε.

judgment on those smitten by it[7] (crying in terror). There can be a present call for ὀλολύζειν (imp. Is. 13:6; 14:31; 23:1, 6, 14; 'Ιερ. 31(48):20; Ez. 21:17; Zech. 11:2), since the "day" is immediately present to prophetic vision. In this crying there is thus reflected in two ways the great change which comes. As an inarticulate expression of emotion it shows how the self-glorying of worldly power is brought to nothing in face of the revealed lordship of God, and as a cry of dread it shows how the self-intoxication of ecstasy becomes horror at oneself (Am. 8:3). Positively there is a demand for the true prayer of the heart rather than ecstatic crying as the proper attitude before God (Hos. 7:14).

Jm. 5:1 corresponds externally to the prophetic message,[8] but behind the words there stands Christ as the fulfilment. Only now when the last and total possibility of repentance has gone and self-glorifying has reached its climax in the crucifixion will there be the full ὀλολύζειν of the rich at the return of the crucified Lord.

Heidland

ὅλος, ὁλοτελής

ὅλος.

ὅλος = "whole," "complete," "undivided," "intact," in the NT mostly with a noun, and to express its totality. Whether it comes before or after the substantive makes no decisive difference to the sense, cf. ὅλη ἡ πόλις (Mk. 1:33; Lk. 8:39) and ἡ πόλις ὅλη (Ac. 21:30) or ὅλον τὸ σῶμά σου (Mt. 5:29 f.; 6:22 f.; 1 C. 12:17) and τὸ σῶμά σου ὅλον (Lk. 11:36).[1]

The use of ὅλος in the NT is theologically significant only in a few instances. In Jn. 7:23 Jesus says to the multitude: εἰ περιτομὴν λαμβάνει [ὁ] ἄνθρωπος ἐν σαββάτῳ ἵνα μὴ λυθῇ ὁ νόμος Μωϋσέως, ἐμοὶ χολᾶτε ὅτι ὅλον ἄνθρωπον ὑγιῆ ἐποίησα ἐν σαββάτῳ;

The most natural interpretation is suggested by T. Shab., 15, 16: "Circumcision sets aside the Sabbath; why? Because on account of it, if it is not performed at the appointed time, one can incur the penalty of extirpation. And is not conclusion from the easier to the harder justified? He sets aside the Sabbath for the sake of one member, and may be not set it aside altogether (when life is in danger)?"[2] It seems too narrow, however, to find expressed in ὅλον ἄνθρωπον ὑγιῆ ἐποίησα merely the contrast between the healing of the whole man and that of one member which is made sound by circumcision. There are also no instances of the Jew either regarding or expounding circumcision as healing. Hence we have to look wider for a true interpretation. Cf.

---

[7] Without ref. to the day of judgment only Is. 52:5; Hos. 7:14.

[8] There is an inner reason for the rather plerophoric κλαύσατε ὀλολύζοντες (as compared with the OT, → III, 724 f.).

ὅ λ ο ς. [1] Linguistically cf. Pass., Liddell-Scott, Pr.-Bauer³, *s.v.* Analysis and definition of ὅλον in Aristot. Metaph., IV, 26, p. 1023b, 26-1024a, 10.

[2] Str.-B., II, 488; cf. Schl. J., *ad loc.*

Jn. 13:10 : ὁ λελουμένος ... ἔστιν καθαρὸς ὅλος. How we understand foot-washing is not at issue here ; it seems most likely that the λελουμένος is the baptised person. [3] If so, then regardless of the context the meaning is that he who is baptised is wholly clean, i.e., he is fully, through and through pure before God.

In this light Jn. 7:23 means that by healing Jesus has made the sick man healthy in his whole being. [4] The healings which Jesus performs are healings of the whole man (→ ἰάομαι, III, 212 f.). Similarly, forgiveness of sins is a healing of the whole man (→ ἀφίημι, I, 512). Hence we have to take the ὅλος of Jn. 7:23 in this broad sense. [5]

The claiming of the whole man by God is plainly expressed by Jesus in His answer to the question concerning the chief commandment, Mk. 12:30 par. ... ἀγαπήσεις κύριον τὸν θεόν σου ἐξ ὅλης τῆς καρδίας σου καὶ ἐξ ὅλης τῆς ψυχῆς σου καὶ ἐξ ὅλης τῆς διανοίας σου καὶ ἐξ ὅλης τῆς ἰσχύος σου (Dt. 6:5). [6] Man must yield wholly and utterly to God. In keeping, negatively, is the admonition to stake everything on the whole body (= man, → σῶμα) not being cast into Gehenna (Mt. 5:29 f.), and positively, the admonition to care for the health, i.e., the integrity [7] and clearness of the whole body (man) (Mt. 6:22 f.; Lk. 11:34-36). Only the man who serves God in this totality can render true service (Mt. 6:24).

† ὁλοτελής. [1]

A strengthened form of ὅλος, "wholly and utterly," "through and through." The basic meaning is "having reached the full end or goal (τέλος)" or "having fully met the taxes (τέλος)." Naturally a rare word! Cf. Aristot. Plant., I, 2, p. 817b, 38 : ὁ κόσμος ὁλοτελής ἐστιν καὶ διηνεκής (probably not authentic, the received text being undoubtedly a transl. from the Lat.). The oldest instance is Ditt. Syll.³, 814, 45 (67 A.D.): ἀνεισφορία ὁλοτελής (complete exemption from the war tax). The LXX does not have the word.

In the NT the only instance is at 1 Th. 5:23 : ὁ θεός ... ἁγιάσαι ὑμᾶς ὁλοτελεῖς. Paul's blessing, which is especially warm and full, is given emphasis by the use of the rare word ὁλοτελής.

---

[3] Cf. Schl. J. and Zn. J., ad loc., also H. v. Campenhausen, "Zur Auslegung von Jn. 13:6-10," ZNW, 33 (1934), 259-271.

[4] Cf. also Jn. 5:14.

[5] Cf. Zn. J., ad loc. ὅλος is used in the same way in Jn. 9:34, where the Pharisees say to the man born blind : ἐν ἁμαρτίαις σὺ ἐγεννήθης ὅλος = wholly and utterly.

[6] In acc. with the biblical concept of God this formulation, found in many different contexts in various parts of the OT, denotes man's full and absolute commitment to God.

[7] → ἁπλοῦς, I, 386.

ὁ λ ο τ ε λ ή ς. [1] Cf. Trench, s.v. ὁλόκληρος, 47-51.

[2] ὁλοτελής is synon. to ὁλόκληρος, which in Philo Dec., 110 corresponds to a ἡμιτελής τὴν ἀρετήν (here is a usage related to Paul's use of ὁλοτελής), and also to παντελής, which is more common, but also more stereotyped, in the Gk. Bible and Philo. On λίθοι κολοβοὶ καὶ οὐχ ὁλοτελεῖς in Herm., cf. the λίθοι ὁλόκληροι in Dt. 27:6, Jos. 9:2b (8:31); 1 Macc. 4:47, which are used in building the altar. In 'A Dt. 13:17 ὁλοτελῶς is used for the archaic concept of the total offering (בָּלִיל) with ref. to war booty brought under the ban. The LXX has πανδημεί. The translators no longer understood the cultic sense of בָּלִיל cf. Trench, 47 ff. [Bertram].

In the post-apost. fathers the term occurs 4 times in Herm. in the sense "unbroken" (m., 9, 6; v., 3, 10, 9; 3, 13, 4), or "complete" (v., 3, 6, 4 : [λίθοι] κολοβοὶ καὶ οὐχ ὁλοτελεῖς). The pars. adduced above, and all those mentioned in the dictionaries, correspond more to the use in Herm. There seems to be no other instance of the use of ὁλοτελής found in Paul.

Seesemann

---

† ὁμείρομαι.

The meaning, etym. and breathing are doubtful, [1] since the word is attested only 4 times. Hesych. equates it with ἐπιθυμεῖν, though the term is better taken med. as "to feel oneself drawn to something," with strong intensification of the feeling. Thus ὁμειρόμενο[ι] περὶ παιδό[ς] (of the sorrowing parents) on a burial inscr. [2] probably means "with intense longing," cf. also LXX Job 3:21 (AB, for הכה pi [= μένειν, Is. 8:17; ὑπομένειν, Is. 64:3]); perhaps the strength of the longing suggested the rare word (changed to ἱμείρονται in B^corr). The meaning and vl. are similarly related in Σ ψ 62:1 (שחר LXX ὀρθρίζω). This sense is also in keeping with the metaphor of the nurse in 1 Th. 2:8. [3]

The rarity of the term selected in 1 Th. 2:8 brings out the peculiar nature of the relation of the apostle to the community. This consists in a "warm inward attachment." The apostle is impelled by it to serve, not only in unconditional obedience to his commission, but also in heartfelt love for the community.

Heidland

| ὀμνύω | → ὅρκος.
|---|

ὀμνύω means "to swear," "to affirm (confirm) by an oath." It is the new form of ὄμνυμι which came to predominate in Hell. usage. Etym. it probably belongs to the Sansk. root *am-,* which can mean not only "to swear," but also "to press," "to afflict," "to fasten," "to torment." The basic meaning is "to grasp firmly," ὅρκον ὀμνύναι, "to grasp the sacred object," with the idea of linking assurance with a sacred material. [1] The tragic poets and Aristot. use only ὄμνυμι for the ind. pres.; Hdt., Attic prose

---

ὁ μ ε ί ρ ο μ α ι. [1] Bibl. in Pr.-Bauer³, *s.v.*; Bl.-Debr. § 101. With ἱμείρομαι (vl. Job 3:21 B^corr; 1 Th. 2:8 minusc., Chrys.) a similarity only externally and in meaning, *v.* A. Debrunner, *Indogerm. Forschungen,* 21 (1907), 204. Also derived from μείρομαι (then ὁ as derelict prep., so Westcott-Hort, *Notes²,* 151; Moulton-Mill., *s.v.*), but this very doubtful, Bl.-Debr.

[2] CIG, III, 4000, 9 f.; Boekh-Franz change to ὁ[δυ]ρόμενο[ι].

[3] Dib. Th., *ad loc.* In view of the LXX it is very doubtful whether ὁμείρομαι is a tt. in the vocabulary of nurses (Wbg. Th., *ad loc.*).

ὀ μ ν ύ ω. [1] E. Bickermann, *Revue des études juives,* 99 (1935), 104. Cf. W. Neister in (Bezzenberger's) *Beiträge zur Kunde d. indogermanischen Sprachen,* 30 (1906), 299-304; E. Benveniste, *Revue de l'histoire d. religions,* 134 (1948), 81-94; Walde-Pok., 1, 178 f.

writers, inscr., pap. [2] and LXX [3] also have ὀμνύω. In the NT the older form occurs only as the inf. ὀμνύναι at Mk. 14:71 B etc., while ℵ with ℵ AC *et al.* reads ὀμνύειν. [4] ὀμνύω is usually found with the acc. of person or object by which the oath is taken, in prose also with the prep. κατά τινος, [5] ἐπί τινος, εἰς τινα. Those to whom one swears are in the dat., in Hom. also πρός τινα, cf. Lk. 1:73. The matter sworn is in the acc. or inf., usually fut. inf.: to swear one wishes something; often with ἤ μέν (Attic ἤ μήν) which precedes the inf., e.g., Hom. Il., 1, 76 f.: καί μοι ὄμοσσον ἤ μέν μοι ... ἀρήξειν. In the NT the acc. of what is sworn is still found only at Jm. 5:12; elsewhere we have ἔν τινι (Heb. בְּ) (Mt. 5:34 ff.; 23:16 ff.), εἰς τι (Mt. 5:35), or κατά τινος (Hb. 6:13, 16). [6] The dat. of person, Ac. 7:17 ℵ; apart from this only the OT quotation at Ac. 2:30.

In the LXX [7] ὀμνύειν is normally used for the ni of שׁבע, while the hi is regularly ὁρκίζειν, derivates or compounds. Sometimes we have the acc., e.g., Gn. 21:23 (Heb. בְּ). But we also find the following constructions : often κατά τινος, also ἔν τινι, the dat. ὀνόματι; ἐν and ὀνόματι, 1 Βασ. 20:42. [8] The Heb. formula חַי or חֵי (by the life of) is often translated by ζῆ. When God swears by Himself the first person is used : ζῶ ἐγώ (Nu. 14:28; Dt. 32:40; Ἰερ. 26[46]:18). [9] In two verses (Gn. 42:15, 16) the particle νή comes first : [10] νή τὴν ὑγίειαν Φαραω (חֵי פַרְעֹה) by the life of Pharaoh.

In antiquity swearing is usually by the gods [11] (e.g., ὄμνυμι θεοὺς καὶ θεάς, Xenoph. An., VI, 6, 17), who are invoked as witnesses of the truth (→ ὅρκος). In the Hell.-Roman period, on the basis that divine honours should be paid to rulers, we have oaths by the king and emperor as well. Often these are linked with oaths by the gods. These oaths figured prominently in public life. [12] Later, esp. in the Byzantine period, we find many formulae ; oaths were taken not only by the emperor but also by his νίκη, διαμονή, εὐσέβεια, τύχη (genius). The pap. offer rich materials. [13] Examples : P. Oxy., XII, 1453, 10 f.: ὁ. Καίσαρος θεὸν ἐκ θεοῦ, BGU, 936, 6 : ὁ. θεὸν τὸν παντοκράτορα καὶ τὴν σωτηρίαν (of the emperor); P. Lond., 992, 15 : ὁ. τόν τε παντοκράτορα θεὸν καὶ τὴν θείαν καὶ οὐράνιον τύχην (of the emperor). [14] The oath has to be strengthened, since the individual formula no longer suffices. This is a sign that its force has declined.

1. Theologically the most important NT passage is Mt. 5:33-37. [15] What Jesus says about oaths is preceded by a saying which on the basis of the OT Law

---

[2] For the form ὄμνυμι, which is rare in the pap., v. BGU, 543, 2 : ὄμνυμι Καίσαρα Αὐτοκράτορα θεοῦ υἱόν. Cf. Mayser, I, 351 f.; II, 2, 303 f.

[3] On the use of the word in the LXX cf. Thackeray, 279.

[4] Cf. on this Pr.-Bauer³, 938; Bl.-Debr. § 92.

[5] For instances of the use of κατά τινος cf. Pr.-Bauer³, 938.

[6] κατά τινος also Herm. v., 2, 2, 5 and 8.

[7] Cf. Johannessohn Kasus, 77; Helbing, 107.

[8] The tradition vacillates between ὀνόματι and ἐν ὀνόματι at Jer. 12:16, ὀνόματι and ἐπὶ ὀνόματι at Dt. 6:13; 10:20. Acc. to W. Heitmüller, *Im Namen Jesu* (1903), 25 and 45 ὀμνύειν ἐν or ἐπὶ (τῷ) ὀνόματι is to swear by the name, in conjunction with the name, or with mention of the name of the κύριος. ὀμνύειν εἰς τὸ ὄνομα, Herodian Hist., II, 2, 10; 13, 2 (Heitmüller, *op. cit.*, 101). → ὄνομα.

[9] In Nu. 14:21 the translator adds to ζῶ ἐγώ : καὶ ζῶν τὸ ὄνομά μου.

[10] Cf. also 1 C. 15:31: νή τὴν ὑμετέραν καύχησιν.

[11] Cf. the detailed examples in Liddell-Scott, 1223.

[12] Cf. Mitteis-Wilcken, I, 1, 107.

[13] Cf. esp. Preisigke Wört., II, s.v. ὄμνυμι or ὀμνύω.

[14] Along with these oaths the pap. often have the ὅρκος πάτριος, the oath by one's ancestors, e.g., P. Petr., 56d, 10 ff.: ὤμοσά σοι τὸν πάτριον ὅρκον.

[15] Cf. the comm. and monographs on the Sermon on the Mount, also H. Müller, *Zum Eidesverbot d. Bergpredigt* (1913).

forbids perjury (Lv. 19:12) and demands the fulfilment of vows [16] (Nu. 30:3; Dt. 23:22 ff.; ψ 49:14; cf. also S. Nu., 30, 5 § 153). [17] The thesis and antithesis are not brought into sharp contrast, since v. 33 does not deal directly with swearing.

In the Law the oath is an essential element in jurisprudence. As shown by Ned., 2, 2 f. and Shebu., 3, 1-9 it was also so much an integral part of daily life that there was a tendency to enforce any statement with an oath. Scribal circles exerted themselves to limit this abuse. Thus an oath lightly taken and not always kept could be punished by scourging, Shebu., 3, 7. The same purpose was served by the admonition which preceded judicial swearing and which was meant to check the frivolous taking of oaths, *ibid.*, 6, 1-4 (39b). A similar tendency may be seen in Rabb. lit. [18]

The Mosaic Law sought to safeguard the sanctity of the oath. No false oaths were to be taken, and oaths and vows had to be kept. Jesus as the new Messianic Lawgiver establishes a new order. In the order of life ruled by the kingdom of God there is no further place for the oath. It makes sense only when there is reason to question the veracity of men. Bringing in and proclaiming the kingdom of God, Jesus does not merely attack the misuse of the oath; He rejects it altogether. This radical attitude to oaths is to be explained, therefore, by His preaching of the kingdom of God. [19] He who already belongs to the kingdom, and is controlled by its concepts and powers, may not act as though he were still bound to this aeon. He must be truthful in all things; hence he stands under the requirement not to swear at all.

Attempts have been made to limit the μὴ ὀμόσαι ὅλως of Jesus, e.g., to promises rather than affirmations. [20] It has also been explained that Jesus was simply rejecting the swearing in daily life so common among the Jews of His day. [21] But these interpretations hardly do justice to His true intention. Jesus issues a new commandment binding on His disciples. [22] They are to be so truthful that no oaths are needed to back their statements. Hence the μὴ ὀμόσαι ὅλως applies to all oaths, whether in daily life or in judicial cases. [23]

Similar statements are found prior to Jesus and outside the NT. [24] Soph. [25] and later

---

[16] God's name was not invoked in vows, but it was in oaths, Str.-B., I, 327.

[17] J. Schniewind, *Das Ev. nach Mt.* (*NT Deutsch*), *ad loc.* thinks the ref. in Mt. 5:33 is to one of the ten commandments. The older Synagogue related the prohibition of Ex. 20:7 to empty swearing, and to the prohibition thus understood the corresponding command was added in Nu. 30:3 etc. Cf. the examples in Str.-B., I, 326 f. But this interpretation is questionable. Mt. 5:33 certainly refers only to the provisions of the Law, not to Rabb. exposition.

[18] For details *v.* Str.-B., I, 328 ff.; P. Fiebig, *Jesu Bergpredigt* (1924), 63-92.

[19] Cf. on this H. Asmussen, *Die Bergpredigt* (1939), 25 f.

[20] So, e.g., E. Rietschel, "Das Verbot des Eides in d. Bergpredigt," ThStKr, 79 (1906), 393; 80 (1907), 609-618. In answer cf. O. Procksch, "Das Eidesverbot Jesu Christi," *Thüringer kirchliches Jbch.*, 13 (1907), 15 ff. Bengel, *ad loc.* takes the same view as Rietschel : *imprimis promissoriis juramentis interdicit Christus, quum homines de futuro per ea confirmant, quorum nil in eorum potestate est.*

[21] So, e.g., Kl. Mt., *ad loc.*; H. J. Holtzmann, *Nt.liche Theol.*, I² (1911), 191 f.; J. Müller, *D. Bergpredigt²* (1908), 150; P. Fiebig, *Jesu Bergpredigt* (1924), 67; R. Seeberg, *Zur Ethik d. Bergpredigt* (1934), 39; H. Huber, *Die Bergpredigt* (1932), 94 f. etc.

[22] J. Schniewind, *op. cit., ad loc.* states emphatically that Jesus means : "I command you not to swear at all."

[23] So Str.-B., I, 328. Cf. also Schl. Mt., 181 f.; also J. C. Gspann, "Der Eid in d. Bergpredigt," *Der Katholik*, 35, 1 (1907), 34.

[24] Cf. esp. R. Hirzel, *Der Eid* (1902), 109-123.

[25] Oed. Col., 650; Phil., 811 f. (shaking hands instead of an oath).

Plut. [26] declare that an oath is unworthy, since it constrains the spirit of a free man. As originally Delphic Apollonian wisdom we find the principle : ὅρκωι μὴ χρῶ, Ditt. Syll.³, 1268, I, 8. The Pythagoreans [27] acc. to Diog. L., VIII, 22, also demanded : μηδὲ ὀμνύναι θεούς, ἀσκεῖν γὰρ ἑαυτὸν δεῖν ἀξιόπιστον εἶναι. [28] Among the Stoics Epict. Ench., 33, 5 (ὅρκον παραίτησαι, εἰ μὲν οἷόν τε, εἰς ἅπαν, εἰ δὲ μή, ἐκ τῶν ἐνόντων) forbade his pupils to swear. Nor does the prohibi..n apply only to the student days of the young philosopher. The Stoic sage will do nothing unworthy or unnecessary throughout his life. Acc. to M. Ant., 3, 5, too, the sage has no need of oaths. The Essenes rejected the oath unconditionally, though a fearful oath was exacted of novices entering the order. [29]

In Jewish exhortation Sir. 23:9 ff. forbids frivolous and habitual swearing. [30] Sir. censures πολύορκος. We read in 23:9 : "Do not accustom thy lips to swearing and do not accustom thyself to mentioning the name of the Holy One," then in v. 11 : "A man who swears often will commit unrighteousness in plenty." Ps.-Phocylides simply forbids perjury (16).

In Philo [31] we find the most diverse injunctions. He deals most explicitly with the oath in Spec. Leg., II, 2-38. [32] He demands that one should avoid oaths, or swear with the utmost circumspection if forced to do so. [33] In Decal., 84-93 he says that it is best not to swear, second best to swear aright, worst to commit perjury. In the main Philo draws on Stoic sources for what he says about swearing. [34] His ideal is the sage who does not swear at all because his words have the force of oaths. [35] It would be most in accord with reason not to swear at all if a man learned to be so truthful in all his statements that they could be accepted as oaths. [36] In this the wise man would be more like God, whose λόγοι are ὅρκοι. [37] Philo rejects swearing by God. [38] But in spite of strong Stoic influence he does not wholly reject the oath. If there is need for swearing, one should proceed carefully and take an oath only after fully examining the situation. He who takes an oath should ask whether he has the right moral qualities for swearing, whether he is "pure in body, soul and tongue," for "it would be sinful if

---

[26] Quaest. Rom., 44 (II, 127d). Cf. also Quint. Inst. Orat., IX, 2, 98 : *in totum jurare, nisi ubi necesse est, gravi viro parum convenit.*

[27] Cf. Hirzel, 99 f., 109-123, 120, n. 2. A. Bonhöffer first believed (*Die Ethik d. Stoikers Epict.* [1894], 113, n. 31) that Epict. was following Pythagoreanism, but in his book *Epict. u. d. NT* (1911), 30 he no longer saw so close a link between Pythagoreanism and Stoicism on this matter of the oath.

[28] So also Iambl. Vit. Pyth., 47 (cf. A. Bonhöffer, *D. Ethik d. Stoikers Epict.*, 113 f.).

[29] Cf. Bousset-Gressm., 464 and Schürer, II⁴, 658. Jos. Bell., 2, 135 declares : "The given word had for them (the Essenes) more validity than an oath ; indeed, they renounced swearing because they regarded it as worse than perjury. He who finds no credence without calling on the Godhead is, they say, already judged." Cf. also Jos. Ant., 15, 371 f.

[30] Sir. mentions three kinds of oaths, the false, the careless and the unnecessary. Cf. G. Dalman, *Der Gottesname Adonaj* (1889), 61.

[31] Cf. on Philo J. Heinemann, "Philos Lehre vom Eid," *Judaica, Festschr. zu H. Cohen's 70. Geburtstag* (1912), 109-118; Dib. Jk., 229; Dalman, *op. cit.*, 60.

[32] Philo gives the following definition of an oath : ὅρκος οὐδὲν ἄλλο ἢ μαρτυρία θεοῦ περὶ πράγματος ἀμφισβητουμένου, "the oath is a witness of God in disputed matters," Spec. Leg., II, 10; Sacr. AC, 91; Plant., 82; Decal., 86; cf. also Leg. All., III, 205. For invocation of God as witness, the heart of the matter in Philo, cf. also Cic. Off., III, 104.

[33] Decal., 85.

[34] So also Heinemann, *op. cit.*, 110.

[35] Cf. L. Cohn, *D. Werke Philos*, III (1919), 151.

[36] Decal., 84.

[37] Leg. All., III, 204; Sacr. AC, 93 : God's words are in themselves as sure as oaths.

[38] Spec. Leg., II, 5; Leg. All., III, 207. Men should not swear by God because they do not know His essence ; they should swear only by His name. On the question why God swears in the OT cf. Leg. All., III, 203-207 and Sacr. AC, 91 ff. God can swear only by Himself since there is none even equal to Him, let alone better.

abominable things were to pass through the mouth with which one pronounces the most holy name." [39] Philo allows substitute oaths which, apart from that by parents, [40] are of Gk. origin. [41] One may swear by the life and memory of parents, by the earth, the sun, the stars, heaven, the whole world. [42]

The absolute prohibition of swearing is followed in Mt. 5:34b-36 by four statements which set aside any misunderstanding of the principle μὴ ὀμόσαι ὅλως. Jesus excludes the common Jewish practice of avoiding the name of God because of its sanctity but substituting equivalents (→ III, 93). He exposes the insincerity of this habit, showing that the reference is really to God even though His name is avoided.

The sayings introduced by μήτε amplify the general prohibition which resides in the ὅλως. Hence μήτε-μήτε should not be rendered "neither-nor." It has rather the sense of "not-not." [43] The man who swears by heaven and earth overlooks the fact that God is Lord of heaven and earth. Acc. to Is. 66:1 heaven is His throne [44] and earth the footstool of His feet. [45] Similarly swearing εἰς Ἱεροσόλυμα [46] is rejected. Jerusalem is the centre of the cultus. Oaths are taken by it because it is the city of God. [47] Hence God is really in view. Even swearing by one's own head [48] is indirectly swearing by God, for life is in God's hands alone. Thus all substitutes for swearing by God have in them an element of subterfuge. Though an attempt is hereby made to avoid misusing God's name in everyday swearing, the misuse is not in fact avoided. Any attempt to weaken the requirement of Jesus is thus futile.

In Mt. 5:37a Jesus adds to the prohibition the command: ἔστω δὲ ὁ λόγος ὑμῶν ναὶ ναί, οὖ οὔ. In the context this can mean only that Jesus replaces swearing by a simple Yes and No. All oaths are thus ruled out.

---

[39] Decal., 93.

[40] Swearing by parents derives from Gn. 31:53.

[41] There is something similar in the so-called elliptical oath which Schol. Aristoph. Ra., 1374 (cf. Suid., s.v. μὰ τόν) counsels us to swear: ἐλλειπτικῶς ὀμνύει· καὶ οὕτως ἔθος ἐστὶ τοῖς ἀρχαίοις ἐνίοτε μὴ προστιθέναι τὸν θεόν· εἰώθεισαν δὲ τοῖς τοιούτοις ὅρκοις χρῆσθαι ἐπευφημιζόμενοι, ὥστε εἰπεῖν μὲν μὰ τόν, ὄνομα δὲ μηκέτι προσθεῖναι. Cf. also Plat. Apol., 22a with Schol.

[42] Spec. Leg., II, 5. Philo adds: "But not by the final and supreme cause of all being, God." Cf. ibid., II, 2-5: One should swear by health, fortune and memory of parents, or simply say νὴ τόν and μὰ τόν and stop. The Pythagoreans swore by the elements, cf. H. Diels, Elementum (1899), 48. Acc. to J. Heinemann, 113 Philo's proposal of the heavenly bodies as surrogates for God is based on his view of these as θεοὶ ὁρατοί, cf. Plat. Tim., 40d. Swearing by heaven and earth are also mentioned as weaker formulae in Shebu., 4, 13. Cf. on this A. Wünsche, Neue Beiträge u. Erläuterung d. Ev. (1878), 59.

[43] So Str.-B., 328. Cf. also T. Soiron, D. Bergpredigt (1941), 272.

[44] Dalman WJ, I, 168 f. thinks Jesus is emphasising that this oath is better avoided altogether but not objecting to the wording as such. This is incorrect. He is completely rejecting swearing by heaven. If all swearing is rejected, there is no place for swearing by heaven.

[45] On ὑποπόδιον v. Deissmann NB, 50; it is a new koine construct.

[46] There is no such oath in Rabb. texts, though the name Jerusalem occurs in abjurations (Str.-B., I, 333) and there are Gk. and Rom. analogies.

[47] πόλις τοῦ μεγάλου βασιλέως, cf. ψ 47:2. God has chosen Jerusalem to set up His kingdom there: "There echo here the hopes of 'God's royal dominion'" (J. Schniewind, ad loc.). Schniewind even thinks the saying belongs to a logia tradition "which, unlike the main Synoptic tradition, is oriented to Jerusalem."

[48] Cf. Sanh., 3, 5: "Vow to me by the life of his head."

It may be conceded that the text of Mt. is not wholly clear. The twofold ναί and
οὔ is striking. It has been pointed out that acc. to the Rabb. the twofold Yes or No
was itself an oath, [49] and the conclusion has been drawn that Jesus was allowing a
new and simpler oath in place of the usual formulae. [50] There are also passages in the
Rabbinic tradition, however, in which the twofold Yes or No simply serves to strengthen
or confirm the simple Yes or No. [51] This is how we are to understand the second ναί
and οὔ in the saying of Jesus. [52] The oath is replaced by the simple affirmation of the
man who is inwardly truthful. [53]

Mt. 5:37b expresses the thought that the disciples are forbidden to say anything
beyond the simple Yes and No : τὸ δὲ περισσὸν [54] τούτων ἐκ τοῦ πονηροῦ ἐστιν.
The gen. τοῦ πονηροῦ can be derived from ὁ πονηρός. If so, the meaning is that
the inclination to confirm what is said by an oath comes from the devil. [55] If τοῦ
πονηροῦ is taken as a neut., swearing is a consequence of the evil present in the
world. [56] It is most likely that ἐκ τοῦ πονηροῦ does in fact derive from τὸ πονηρόν.

2. Perhaps the authentic form of the saying of Jesus is preserved in Jm. 5:12
rather than Mt.: μὴ ὀμνύετε, μήτε τὸν οὐρανὸν μήτε τὴν γῆν μήτε ἄλλον τινὰ
ὅρκον· [57] ἤτω δὲ ὑμῶν τὸ ναὶ ναί, καὶ τὸ οὒ οὔ. [58] The wording here, of course,

---

[49] Cf. Str.-B., I, 336 f. Shebu., 36a : "R. Eleazar has said : 'No' is an oath and 'Yes' is
an oath." Acc. to M. Ex., 20, 1 the Israelites at the giving of the Law responded with
No (לֹא) to a negative (לָאו) command, Yes (הֵן) to a positive (הֵן). Cf. also Slav. En. 49:1:
"Let them swear in a word Yes Yes or No No." Cf. also 2 C. 1:17, and the double ναί in
Preis. Zaub., I, 90.

[50] J. Schniewind, ad loc. contends earnestly for the view that we have an oath in v. 37.
Cf. also A. Meyer, Das Rätsel d. Jk. (1930), 85, who argues that the Yes Yes and No No
of Mt. are oaths.

[51] Cf. also Str.-B., I, 336. Bl.-Debr. § 432, 1 regards ἔστω δὲ ὁ λόγος ὑμῶν ναὶ ναί,
οὒ οὔ as an incorrect reading compared with the true and commonly attested (also by
the Koridethi Ev.) reading ἔστω δὲ ὑμῶν τὸ ναὶ ναὶ καὶ τὸ οὒ οὔ. Cf. also Dib. Jk.,
229, n. 7.

[52] So also Schl. Mt., 183 : "The repetition of the particles makes the positive or negative
statement an emphatic and earnest assurance." Cf. Wellh. Mt., 17: "Let your speech be
Yes for Yes and No for No." Cf. also C. C. Torrey, The Four Gospels (1933), 291, acc. to
whom the second Yes and No are predicates. (On this E. Littmann, "Torreys Buch über
d. vier Ev.," ZNW, 34 [1935], 23 f.) Torrey refers to Jm. 5:12, which he regards as a
correct transl. of the Aram. original.

[53] Cf. also Dib. Jk., 230.

[54] τὸ περισσὸν τούτων = τὸ πλέον τούτων, Bl.-Debr. § 60, 3. K. Bornhäuser, D. Bergpredigt (1923), 89 thinks v. 37 means that superfluity of such asseverations, their overuse,
has its roots in evil. But τὸ περισσὸν τούτων says that all statements which contain more
than Yes or No are of evil.

[55] So Schl. Mt., 183 f. Also H. Huber, op. cit., 96 on the ground that "the opp. of the
true God is not evil but the evil one, the devil." Cf. also H. J. Holtzmann, Nt.liche Theol.,
I² (1911), 191.

[56] So Zn. Mt., 245 and Kl. Mt., 47. Cf. also J. Schniewind, op. cit., ad loc.

[57] Jerusalem is not found among the examples introduced by μήτε. Wnd. Jk., ad loc.,
thinks this is accidental or because Jm. is after 70 A.D. "Jerusalem was no longer of any
significance for Christians living in the diaspora." This is very likely the reason why
Jerusalem does not occur.

[58] The Rabb. made a demand similar to that of Jm. 5:12. E.g., S. Lv., 336a (on Lv. 19:36):
The לָאו must be a true one and the הֵן a true one. Midr. Ruth, 3, 18 : The הֵן of the just is a
הֵן and their לָאו a לָאו. Cf. also Str.-B., 336 and A. Meyer, Das Rätsel des Jk. (1930),
162, n. 2. Even more striking is the similarity of Slav. En. 49:1 ff.: "I swear to you, my
children, but I do not swear this with any single oath, neither by heaven nor the earth
nor any other creature which God has made ; for the Lord says : In (by) me an oath

does not enable us to say with certainty whether the prohibition applies only to frivolous swearing in daily life or to all swearing. But the prohibition of Jm. 5:12 does seem to have a certain absoluteness. [59] This may be seen from the second half of the saying. There is no excuse for swearing in the Christian community. It is necessary only where truthfulness can no longer be presupposed as a norm of all speech. It is expected of the Christian, however, that his word will be unconditionally rivetted to the truth. Hence his Yes or No is enough. By the radical statement μὴ ὀμνύετε the Christian community is detached from the Jewish practice of swearing.

The relation between Jm. 5:12 and Mt. 5:34-37 is probably as follows. Jm. is not dependent on Mt. in his formulation of the saying. He probably derives it from an independent tradition. This is shown already by the fact that many ancient Chr. texts [60] quote the saying in a form similar to that of Jm. [61] That this form is simple and "ethically purer" is an argument in favour of the priority of Jm. [62] Jm. does not introduce the statement as a saying of Jesus but as his own admonition. But the absence of a quotation formula is no argument "that the statement about swearing was not regarded as a dominical saying in the time of Jm." [63] Other sayings of Jesus "of more assured derivation" are used in paraenetic texts without being expressly characterised as dominical sayings. [64] It may be accepted that in sense there is agreement between the saying of Jesus in Mt. and the saying of James.

---

is no longer unrighteousness (untruth) but truth. If there is no truth among men, they should swear with the saying Yes Yes or No No." Cf. also BM, 49a : "But learn only this, that thy Yes and thy No must be true."

[59] So Dib. Jk., 228, though cf. Wnd. Jk., ad loc.: "Here, too, the ref. can be only to swearing in matters over which the brethren have free control." Cf. Hck. Jk., ad loc., also Hck., Die katholischen Briefe (NT Deutsch) on Jm. 5:12.

[60] Just. Apol., I, 16, 5 (το μὴ ὁμόσητε ὅλως· ἔστω δὲ ὑμῶν τὸ ναὶ ναί, καὶ τὸ οὖ οὖ, Just. adds : τὸ δὲ περισσὸν τούτων ἐκ τοῦ πονηροῦ). He obviously mixed the two forms. Dib. Jk., 320, n. 2 thinks that "since Just. shows no other acquaintance with Jm., his knowledge of the form outside the Gospel must come from another source"; Cl. Al. Strom., V, 99, 1; VII, 67, 3; Ps.-Clem. Hom., 3, 55; 19, 2; Epiph. Haer., 19, 6, 2. Cf. also Dib. Jk., 230.

[61] On the literary relations between Jm. 5:12 and Mt. 5:34-37 cf. esp. Dib. Jk., 230 f.

[62] So also Dib. Jk., 231. A. Meyer, op. cit., 162 agrees at least that Jm. is not dependent on Mt. Jm. was written either before the Gospel, or at a distance from it, or with an independent tradition and outlook. Hence it was not influenced by the wording of Mt. Acc. to Meyer Jm. 5:12 is one of the Chr. intrusions made into an original Jewish writing. Meyer thinks that a Chr. copyist or translator introduced Jm. 5:12 quite mechanically into the text, since the passage "is not speaking about oaths at all, let alone forbidding them, but giving an assurance by oath concerning the destiny of the soul in the life to come and in this life" (162). F. Hauck, D. katholischen Briefe (NT Deutsch) on Jm. 5:12 conjectures that there is a tacit ref. to the saying in Mt. or that there is common dependence on a similar Jewish rule. The words μήτε τὸν οὐρανὸν μήτε τὴν γῆν μήτε ἄλλον τινὰ ὅρκον were possibly interpolated by a Chr. redactor (in Jk., 231, n. 83 Hck. decides for the independence of Jm. in relation to Mt.). Schl. Jk., 278 takes the opp. view that Jm. 5:12 is based on the dominical saying in Mt. Schniewind Mt. (NT Deutsch), ad loc. also argues for the priority of Mt. He thinks the form in Jm. is a softening of the original saying of Jesus.

[63] Dib. Jk., 231.

[64] E.g., R. 12:14. Cf. Did., 1, 3 ff. Cf. also M. Dibelius, Die Formgeschichte d. Ev.² (1933), 241 f. A. Meyer, op. cit., 162 regards Jm. 5:12 as a dominical saying or a saying of Chr. origin. He conjectures that the logion in Mt. is one of the sayings which Mt. added to the source from the treasury of proverbial Jewish wisdom. Acc. to Wnd. Jk., 32 the saying in Jm. "developed entirely out of Jewish connections." The view of Meyer, 253 f., 284, that Jm. 5:12 is perhaps a Zebulon saying, because acc. to Jerome (P. de Lagarde, Onomastica Sacra, I [1870], 12) Zebulon et al. were interpreted in terms of jus jurandum, is adopted in Wnd. Jk., 32.

3. A self-enclosed series of sayings in Mt. 23:16-22 reminds us of Mt. 5:33-37. It is directed against the casuistical treatment of oaths and vows by the scribes and Pharisees. Jesus explains that it is meaningless to say that we are bound by an oath by the gold of the temple [65] or by the offering, whereas an oath by the temple or the altar is without significance. The temple [66] and the gold, the offering and the altar, go together. They are consecrated to God. Hence God is always in view in such oaths. In v. 22 a statement is added which introduces the thought of Mt. 5:34 and gives the impressive sequence of altar - temple - heaven. The oath takes in everything belonging to the altar, the temple and heaven. The concern of Jesus here is simply to reduce the casuistry of the scribes and Pharisees ad absurdum. The basic question of the legitimacy of oaths is not at issue. [67] The chapter does not contain an address to the disciples but a sharp polemic against Pharisaism.

No Rabb. examples have been found of the distinctions mentioned by Jesus between oaths by the temple and by its gold, by the altar and by the sacrifice. [68] But there are par. sayings which may be adduced in interpretation. Vows in which the words temple and altar occur are binding (Ned., 1, 3), but "he who says Jerusalem has said nothing." [69] Cf. also Ned., 14b : "He who vows by the Torah has said nothing ; but he who vows by what is written in it, his words count."

Oaths were made at first in God's name. But when uttering the name of Yahweh was forbidden on the ground of Ex. 20:7, a subsidiary designation was used. Apart from the formulae mentioned in Mt. (5 and 23) we also find the following in Rabb. writings : by omnipotence, by this house (the temple), by the ministry of the temple, by the covenant, by the Torah, by Moses, by the oath, by (thy) life etc. [70] How strong was the inclination of the Jewish people to confirm all possible statements by an oath may be seen esp. from Ned., 2, 2 f. and Shebu., 3, 1-9.

4. The strict line laid down by Jesus was not always kept in primitive Christianity. Hb. in its statements about swearing uninhibitedly follows the Jewish Hellenistic tradition also found in Philo. We shall leave aside the OT quotations and investigate only Hb. 6:13, 16 and 7:20 ff. Hb. 6:13 speaks of the oath of God which accompanied the promise to Abraham. The author regards it as natural that God should swear. He sticks to the exegetical findings and does not feel that such a view is impossible according to the NT concept of God. [71] Like Philo [72] he

---

[65] The temple gold is the ornamentation rather than the treasury (Schl. Mt., 677: The gold sheets which covered the walls and which were dedicated to God). Perhaps there is also a ref. to the golden vessels, Kl. Mt., 185.

[66] Schniewind, ad loc. thinks the ref. to the temple presupposes that it was still standing. The sayings must come from South Palestine, since they are based on an exact knowledge of the temple.

[67] Kl. Mt., 185 sees in Mt. 23:16-22 further teaching on swearing which supplements 5:34-37 and which is "perhaps secondary."

[68] Str.-B., I, 931.

[69] This means that his oath is not binding, loc. cit.

[70] Ibid., I, 334 ff. for details.

[71] It is worth noting that the idea of God swearing does not occur elsewhere in the NT except in OT quotations (e.g., Ac. 2:30; 7:17 𝔖). Acc. to Wnd. Hb. on 6:16 the author of Hb. knew of no objections to swearing such as those in Mt. 5:33-37 and Jm. 5:12. Mi. Hb. on 6:16 thinks the trains of thought of Jesus and Hb. do not intersect because they start with different presuppositions. This view is hardly in accord with the facts.

[72] Leg. All., III, 203 f. Philo expressly calls the oath which God swears good : "It is excellent that the promise is confirmed by an oath, and indeed by an oath appropriate to God ; for God swears, as you see, not by another, since there is none stronger than He, but by Himself, the best of all beings." Cf. also Sacr. AC, 91; Abr., 273. Cf. Herm. v., 2, 2, 8.

also sees in the oath of Gn. 22:16 a confirmation of the promise. [73] God swears by Himself since He is the supreme being and can swear by none higher. [74] In this respect the divine oath differs from human oaths. Men confirm their words by referring their statements to someone more powerful as a witness and guarantor. But God takes an oath by Himself to vouch for it that the will expressed in the promise will remain unchanged. The divine oath is the guarantee which rules out all doubt and gives faith assurance of the promise. [75] In Hb. 7:20-22 the divine saying confirmed by an oath is again contrasted with the simple word of God. The oath binds God and gives His word unconditional and impregnable validity. This is a biblical insight taken by Hb. from ψ 109:4. The Levitical priesthood cannot claim a divine oath. In ψ 109:4, however, God appoints His eternal priest, Christ, by an oath. He thereby sets aside the ancient priesthood. [76]

Rev. 10:6 uses the image of the angel taking an oath. This is closely related to Da. 12:5-7, [77] and the content of the oath is also based on Da. The angel is sent to make new prophecies. In so doing he swears a solemn oath by the living and eternal God, the Creator of all things. [78] This assurance by oath shows that there will be no further delay in the unfolding of eschatological events. The hour of redemption dawns. [79]

5. How little the conduct of the disciples was at first influenced by Jesus' prohibition of swearing may be seen from the example of Peter in Mk. 14:71 (par. Mt. 26:74). [80] Peter maintains that he does not know Jesus. He swears this; indeed, he goes further and invokes the divine ban on himself and what he says. [81], [82] Peter will fall under the ban (חֵרֶם) if he lies, and so will they if they call him a disciple. [83]

Only apparently is there tension between Jesus' own conduct and the prohibition of Mt. 5:33-37. He often introduced His sayings with a solemn ἀμὴν λέγω ὑμῖν and thereby confirmed them. [84] But the ἀμήν is not an oath. Nor does Jesus make a declara-

---

[73] Philo and Hb. probably follow the same exegetical tradition. In Philo this is "philosophically broadened" (Mi. Hb.[7], 70, n. 2). Rabb. exegesis, too, posed the question what it means that God swears by Himself, cf. Shemoth rabba on Ex. 32:13.

[74] εἰ μήν in v. 14 is Hell. for ἦ μήν vl. This oath particle occurs only here in the NT; it comes from the LXX (for אִם לֹא). Cf. Deissmann NB, 33-36; Bl.-Debr.[7] § 24; 441, 1.

[75] J. Schneider, Der Hb. (1938), 54. Cf. Mi. Hb.[7], 71.

[76] The OT priesthood loses its basis with the institution of the new priestly order, cf. Schneider, op. cit., 63.

[77] Da. 12:7: καὶ ὤμοσε τὸν ζῶντα εἰς τὸν αἰῶνα θεόν. Θ reads (like Rev.): καὶ ὤμοσεν ἐν τῷ ζῶντι τὸν αἰῶνα.

[78] Loh. Apk., ad loc.: "v. 5 f. introduces a solemn oath in sweeping statements with a liturgical ring."

[79] So also Had. Apk., ad loc., though cf. Loh. Apk., ad loc.: As Da. 12:7 deals with the kingdom of Antichrist, "so it is said here that the hour of this kingdom begins with the 7th trumpet." More generally J. Behm, Die Offenbarung d. Joh. (NT Deutsch), ad loc.: "The content of the oath is the promise that there will now be no more time or period of delay up to the end of the world."

[80] The Ev. Hb. reads: ... καὶ ἠρνήσατο καὶ ὤμοσεν καὶ κατηράσατο.

[81] ἀναθεματίζειν in Mk., like καταθεματίζειν in Mt., has no obj. The obj. is to be supplied from the context.

[82] ὀμνύναι is with ἀναθεματίζειν a hendiadys. Cf. also Loh. Mk., ad loc.; → I, 355; also Schl. Mt., 764.

[83] So Schl. Mt., 764.

[84] J. Schniewind, op. cit. on 5:37a (cf. his Ev. nach Mk. [NT Deutsch] on 8:12) thinks this confirmation is the "supreme oath." This is not what Jesus intends. The ἀμήν is more like a confirmatory Yes. Dalman WJ, I, 187 is right when he says that "this is no oath ... His own demand that the oath should be replaced by a simple Yes, Yes is met by Him

tion on oath in Mt. 26:64; this is a simple statement which, in answer to the question of the high-priest and in acceptance of its content, contains an open Messianic confession on the part of Jesus (cf. → ἐξορκίζω).

The principle of Jesus is observed by Paul inasmuch as he does not use any of the formulae rejected by Jesus. But he does come near to asseverations in the form of oaths. He often feels moved to confirm the truth of what he says by invoking God (R. 1:9; 2 C. 1:23) or his conscience (R. 9:1) as a witness. Esp. strong is his affirmation that he is speaking the truth in R. 9:1. The statement νὴ τὴν ὑμετέραν καύχησιν ("by my pride in you") in 1 C. 15:31 is very close to an oath. Here we have the acc. of that by which one swears, [85] and the sense of νὴ τὴν ὑμετέραν καύχησιν demands that an ὀμνύω be supplied. [86]

6. Mk. 6:23 sets before us the practice of the non-Christian world. [87] At the birthday feast [88] Herod swears [89] after the manner of "a great oriental prince [90] that he will give his stepdaughter up to the half of his kingdom. [91] This frivolous promise, made when his senses were intoxicated, seals the fate of John the Baptist.

J. Schneider

---

† ὁμοθυμαδόν. [1]

This word denotes the inner unity of a group of people engaged in an externally similar action. It can thus be rendered "with one mind." Worth noting is the fact that it often occurs along with statements about the number and place of participation, e.g., πάντες (Philo Leg. Gaj., 356; Ac. 1:14; 2:1 ᾳ; 5:12) and ἐπὶ τὸ αὐτό (Ac. 2:1). The θυμός in which the unanimity consists may be anger (Philo Flacc., 144), fear (Jdt. 15:2), gratitude (Wis. 10:20), etc. The earliest (e.g., Aristoph. Av., 1015) and later the most common use (e.g., Ditt. Syll.³, 742, 14; 1104, 28 f.) is in the political field (Ac. 12:20). Here it confers particular weight on the decision of a corporate body (Ac. 15:25). In

---

(Jesus) in this way. But since Jesus in prohibiting oaths wishes to guard the divine name against abuse, one can also speak here of an intentional avoidance of the name of God." → ἀμήν, I, 337 f.

[85] Pr.-Bauer³, 890.

[86] Bl.-Debr. § 149. Cf. P. Giess., 19, 11: νὴ τὴν σὴν σωτηρίαν, P. Oxy., VI, 939, 20 : Gn. 42:15 f.: νὴ τὴν ὑγίειαν Φαραω.

[87] Mt. 14:7 has μεθ' ὅρκου ὡμολόγησεν.

[88] On the historical background v. Loh. Mk., 117 f.; Kl. Mk., ad loc.

[89] The oath of Herod reads like the promise of Ahasuerus to Esther, Esth. 5:3 : καὶ εἶπεν ὁ βασιλεύς Τί θέλεις, Εσθηρ, καὶ τί σού ἐστιν τὸ ἀξίωμα; ἕως τοῦ ἡμίσους τῆς βασιλείας μου καὶ ἔσται σοι. A adds to 5:6 : τί τὸ αἴτημά σου καὶ δοθήσεταί σοι καὶ τί τὸ ἀξίωμά σου ἕως τοῦ ἡμίσους τῆς βασιλείας.

[90] Loh. Mk., 120. Herod as a tetrarch dependent on Rome could not really dispose of his own kingdom.

[91] ℵ ACL read : καὶ ὤμοσεν αὐτῇ ὅτι· ὃ ἐάν με αἰτήσῃς (so also Tischendorf and v. Soden); B has ὤμοσεν αὐτῇ· ὅ τι ἐάν με αἰτήσῃς. Loh. Mk., n. ad loc. accepts the reading of ℵ ACL because ὅ τι does not occur elsewhere in Mk.; εἴ τι ἄν D is impossible because εἴ τι is never followed by ἄν in the Gospels. Cf. H. Pernot, Études sur la langue d. Évangiles (1927), 175.

ὁμοθυμαδόν. [1] On the etym. ὁμό-θυμος, "with the same emotion," "with the same mind," "unanimously"; on adv. in -αδον cf. Debr. Griech. Wortb. § 107; E. Schwyzer, Griech. Grammatik, I (1936), 626.

the religious field it occurs in Judaism (Philo Flacc., 122; 3 Macc. 5:20²) and the NT, only Ac. apart from R. 15:6.

Varied though the use is, two common observations may be made, first in respect of secular Gk., then in respect of the NT, where they are of theological significance. First. the term does not denote the personal sympathy of those participating, but material interest in a specific action. Demosth. (Or., 10, 59) calls upon the people to set aside personal feelings and instead work ὁμοθυμαδόν to resist the plans of Philip. Secondly, this common material concern is not based upon a similarity of inclination or disposition but upon an event which comes on a group from without (e.g., the hostility of Philip in Demosth.) and provokes a common reaction.

In the NT ὁμοθυμαδόν is used to stress the inner unanimity of the community. The term occurs in connection with the actions which constitute the community of the risen Lord, namely, listening to apostolic teaching (Ac. 8:6; 20:18 vl.) ³ and prayer (1:14; 2:1, 46; 4:24; 5:12; R. 15:6). ὁμοθυμαδόν is here almost a fixed term in the vocabulary of the community, and its use in the life of political communities forms a significant background. Christian unanimity, too, has its root elsewhere than in a similar disposition on the part of Christians. We are well acquainted with the many personal and material tensions in the first congregations. But these tensions are continually transcended when the community addresses itself to the magnifying of the one Lord (R. 15:6). Unanimity is an event; it constantly needs a new γίγνεσθαι (Ac. 15:25). This unifying worship is not the expression of a religious disposition of man; it is the response to God's action for the world and the community in Christ (e.g., the ascension in Ac. 1:14; liberation from prison in 4:24). ⁴ Unanimity is thus a gift of God to the praise of God.

Heidland

ὁμοιοπαθής → πάσχω.

ὅμοιος, ὁμοιότης, ὁμοιόω, ὁμοίωσις, ὁμοίωμα, ἀφομοιόω, παρόμοιος, παρομοιάζω

ὅμοιος.

From ὁμός, which is related to ἅμα (Lat. *simul, similis*; Old High Germ. *sama. samt*; Sansk. *sama*, like). From the time of Hom. common in all types of Gk.

a. "Of the same kind," "like"; it should be differentiated from → ἴσος (→ III, 343 f.). ¹ The words are so close that they can often be used interchangeably or com-

---

² In the LXX 36 times, 14 in Job, 16 in the Apcr. In Job it occurs always for יַחַד and יַחְדָּו, elsewhere rendered ἅμα (Is. 43:9) and ἐπὶ τὸ αὐτό (Jos. 11:5). Its common use in Job is due to the poetic love of sonority.

³ Cf. Corp. Herm., I, 28.

⁴ Conversely proclamation of the saving act can provoke unanimity in rejection, Ac. 7:57; 19:29; 18:12.

ὅμοιος. ¹ Cf. on this R. Hirzel, *Themis, Dike u. Verwandtes* (1907), 421-423. Cf. also Class. Rev., 16 (1902), 19b; 19 (1905), 106b; 27 (1912), 48a. *Classical Quarterly*, 6 (1912), 217.

bined for added strength, e.g., Plat. Parm., 140a b. Οἱ ἴσοι καὶ ὅμοιοι (Thuc., Demosth. etc.), "those who have the same position and rights." b. "Of like disposition." Οἱ ὅμοιοι "men of the same mind or party." Among the Spartans and in other aristocratic and oligarchical constitutions citizens with the same claim to high office and the same share in government are called ὅμοιοι, Xenoph. Hist. Graec., III, 3, 5; cf. Aristot. Pol., V, 7, p. 1306b, 28 ff. Soph. Ai., 1366 : ἢ πάνθ᾽ ὅμοῖα· πᾶς ἀνὴρ αὑτῷ πονεῖ, it is all the same, all men are equally egoistic. Also "the same," expressing the closest agreement, Hom. Od., 16, 182 etc. Ἕν καὶ ὅμοιον, "one and the same," Plat. Phaedr., 271a; Xenoph. Cyrop., VI, 1, 37 (cf. Hist. Graec., IV, 2, 11): καὶ ταῦτα ὅμοιος εἰ οἷόσπερ καὶ τἆλλα, "the same as usual." c. In relation to possessions, "belonging equally, in common"; esp. Hom. Then "accruing equally to all, general" (e.g., γῆρας ... ὁμοίϊον, "age which is common to all men," i.e., approaching all equally, Hom. Il., 4, 315; ὁμοίϊος θάνατος, Od., 3, 236; ὁμοίη μοῖρα, Il., 18, 120). d. In geometry, "similar," of figures (Euclid, 6, Def. 1 etc.; of triangles, in the sense of equal, Aristot. Cael., II, 14, p. 296b, 20; 297b, 19; IV, 4, p. 311b, 34 etc.); of numbers (the square of a number as the product of two equal factors) Plot. Enn., 6, 2, 21 (p. 323, 14, Volkmann). Ὅμοιος thus emphasises the agreement by which one thing is similar or equal to another. [2]

The word has the same meaning in the LXX. It is common in the question : Who is like such and such ? and presupposes a negative answer. Or it occurs in the corresponding statements that none is like God, Abraham, Elijah, Saul, Josiah etc. In this sense it is usually found in the Gk. OT for כְּמוֹ, its most common equivalent. The word is also used in comparisons etc. as a sign of likeness. In similar passages in the law concerning sacrifices in Lv. 11 and Dt. 14 the Mas. original is 13 times מִין. Each time here it refers, with the addition "and its kind," to animals which may not be eaten. [3] In Sir. 13:15(19) it means beings of the same kind. In Tob. 7:2 (ὡς ὅμοιος ὁ νεανίσκος Τωβιτ τῷ ἀνεψιῷ μου) ὅμοιος means "of like appearance."

The word is common in the pap., [4] always in the sense of "similar." The only phrases worth noting are ἐπὶ τῶν ὁμοίων, "in view of similar circumstances," P. Oxy., VI, 889, 21, and ὡς ἐπὶ τῶν ὁμοίων, e.g., P. Tebt., II, 325, 18, "according to known similar processes"; P. Ryl., II, 105, 20 : "as in similar (the same) cases." In P. Oxy., I, 124, 2 (Ἄδραστος ... γήμας ἐκ τῶν ὁμοίων ἔσχεν θυγατέρας δύο) [5] ὅμοιος means one who belongs to the same social stratum. Often we find ἴσος and ὅμοιος together, e.g., BGU, 1123, 8 : μέρη ἴσα καὶ ὅμοια τρία, "three equal and similar parts"; P. Magd., 29, 5 : διειρῆσθαι ἴσως καὶ ὁμοίως, "to divide in parts of equal size and worth." P. Tebt., II, 300, 11 ff.: διὸ ἐπιδίδομι ὅπως περιερεθῇ [τ]οῦτο τὸ ὄνομα ταγῆναι ἐν τῇ τῶν ὁμο[ίων] τάξι, "I charge that his name be put on the list of those in a similar position" (i.e., to put the dead on the official list of the dead).

The word [6] is very common in the NT in a formula which introduces images and parables (Mt., Lk., Rev.), especially in Jesus' parables of the kingdom of God. This is the formula ὁμοία ἐστὶν ἡ βασιλεία τῶν οὐρανῶν. [7] In the comparison

---

[2] Cf. Cr.-Kö., 790 : "ὅμοιος does not denote the similarity which leaves a place for distinction, i.e., mere similarity, but the similarity which consists in congruity."

[3] I owe this to Bertram.

[4] Cf. the examples in Preisigke Wört., II, 175 f.

[5] Cf. also Stob. Ecl., III, 113, 5 f.

[6] ὅμοιος is usually found with a dat. in the NT; the gen. occurs only once at Jn. 8:55 vl. (cf. Is. 13:4). Cf. Bl.-Debr. § 182, 4.

[7] Cf. on this esp. Jülicher Gl. J., I, 43 f. and J. Jeremias, "D. Gleichnisse Jesu," Abh. z. Theol. d. A. u. NT, 11 (1947), 65 f. Among the Rabb. we find the introduction : "I will tell you a parable. Wherewith may it be compared ?" or : "Let us tell a parable. Wherewith may it be compared ?" or more briefly : "A parable of such and such," or simply : "Like a man (לְאָדָם)ו"; "like a king (לְמֶלֶךְ)ו". Cf. Str.-B., I, 653 ff.; II, 7 ff.

a thought is clarified by associating with it a statement or story which is similar but which belongs to a field directly known to the listeners. [8]

Only a few NT instances are of theological significance. In Jn. 8:55 Jesus declares that He alone has true knowledge of God. If He were to say the opposite He would be like the Jews who have not known God; He would be a liar. In his Areopagus address in Ac. 17:29 Paul quotes the saying of the poet that "we are divine offspring" as a basis for his observation on the cultic view of deity: the Godhead cannot be represented by a likeness, since it is not like gold or silver or stone or a statue graven by the art and device of man. It cannot be set forth with the help of earthly or human means.

In 1 Jn. 3:2 ὅμοιος is linked with an insight which is important in Johannine theology, namely, that divine sonship is not the highest stage in the being and nature of the Christian. Fulfilment is reached only when Christians are like Christ. This likeness will be achieved when Christ is manifested. [9] The parousia of Christ thus brings perfection to Christians. Then the transfiguration of Christians will enable them to see the transfigured Christ as He is.

In Rev. 1:13 the divine sees among the candlesticks a figure which he describes as ὅμοιον υἱὸν [10] ἀνθρώπου. Jn. is building on Da. 7:13, where ὡς υἱὸς ἀνθρώπου represents the kingdom of the saints as opposed to the four empires represented by the four beasts. For Jn. ὅμοιος υἱὸς ἀνθρώπου is a Messianic designation. [11] The Messiah is here the exalted Christ in divine majesty. [12] The same expression occurs again in Rev. 14:14. [13]

In the sense "of equal value" the word is found in Mt. 22:39, where it is said that the command to love one's neighbour is equal in importance and validity to the command to love God. Cf. also Rev. 18:18: τίς ὁμοία τῇ πόλει τῇ μεγάλῃ (Babylon); "where is a city so great (powerful) as this?" and Rev. 13:4: τίς ὅμοιος τῷ θηρίῳ; "who is like the beast (in power)?"

In Gl. 5:21 τὰ ὅμοια τούτοις is a kind of comprehensive phrase. Paul has listed the works of the flesh. He then breaks off and closes with the words "and such like," which enable the reader to continue the catalogue in thought.

† ὁμοιόω.

a. "To make equal," "to make alike" (Eur. Hel., 33; Plat. Parm., 148b; Isoc., 9, 75). In the LXX for דמה, e.g., Is. 46:5: τίνι με ὡμοιώσατε; "to whom would you make

---

[8] Cf. the def. of "comparison" and "parable" in Jülicher, I, 80.

[9] Here there is a basic connection between the parousia and creation, cf. Gn. 3:5. The parousia of Christ gives Christians what God originally had in view when He created man.

[10] ὅμοιον υἱὸν ἀνθρώπου אB is a solecism. Cf. Bl.-Debr. § 182, 4 App. ACP al read υἱῷ, so also many exegetes, e.g., Zn. Apk., 198, n. 40, who regards υἱόν as a scribal error.

[11] Cf. Had. Apk., 35.

[12] Here Jn. follows quite strictly the view of the Messiah found in Da. The Messianic expectation linked with Da. was given a different form in Mk., then in Mt. and Lk. The designation has a twofold ref., first to Jesus in His manifestation on earth and in history, then to His coming in glory. Cf. E. C. Hoskyns-F. N. Davey, The Riddle of the NT (1957), pp. 108-115, esp. p. 112: "The whole tradition concerning Jesus, as it is presented by a critical separation of sources, emphasizes two comings, the first in humility, and the second in glory. These are held together by the application of the title 'Son of Man' to Jesus himself."

[13] Loh. Apk., 124 thinks the designation ὅμοιος υἱὸς ἀνθρώπου is not commensurate with "the ultimate and deepest nature of the one who bears it." This is true only of τὸ ἀρνίον figuratively and ὁ λόγος τοῦ θεοῦ literally. But this is hardly the view of Rev.

me like ?" The word does not occur in this sense in the NT. b. "To liken," "compare."
Very rare in this sense. Plut. Cimonis et Luculli Comparatio, 1, 5 (I, 521c): οὐ γὰρ
ἄξιον ὁμοιῶσαι τῷ νοτίῳ τείχει τῆς ἀκροπόλεως ... τοὺς ἐν Νέᾳ πόλει θαλάμους κτλ. In the mid. Hdt., I, 123. c. Most common is the pass. in the sense "to be
made like," "to be like," so Hom., Plat., Hdt., Thuc., Emped., Isoc.

In the LXX a. = דמה q, Is. 1:9 : ὡς Γομορρα ἂν ὡμοιώθημεν (quoted R. 9:29);
ψ 143:4 : ἄνθρωπος ματαιότητι ὡμοιώθη, ψ 88:6 : τίς ὁμοιωθήσεται τῷ κυρίῳ ἐν
υἱοῖς θεοῦ; b. = משל ni, ψ 27:1; 142:7; c. = אות, "to accede to" ni Gn. 34:15 : ἐν
τούτῳ ὁμοιωθησόμεθα ὑμῖν, 22 : μόνον ἐν τούτῳ ὁμοιωθήσονται ἡμῖν οἱ ἄνθρωποι. In LXX similes and parables = דמה q "to be like" (Cant. 2:17; 7:8; 8:14;
Ez. 32:2 ni ; Sir. 13:1; 25:11; 1 Macc. 3:4). "Of imitated likeness but no full equality" [1]
only Ep. Jer. 38 : τοῖς ἀπὸ τοῦ ὄρους λίθοις ὡμοιωμένοι εἰσὶν τὰ ξύλινα καὶ τὰ
περίχρυσα καὶ τὰ περιάργυρα, οἱ δὲ θεραπεύοντες αὐτὰ καταισχυνθήσονται.

In the NT the word serves most commonly in Mt. to introduce parables of the
kingdom of God [2] (ὡμοιώθη ἡ βασιλεία τῶν οὐρανῶν, Mt. 13:24; 18:23; 22:2;
ὁμοιωθήσεται, Mt. 25:1). In Mt. 11:16 (par. Lk. 7:31) Jesus introduces the parable
of the children at play, which concludes His witness to the Baptist, with the
question : τίνι ὁμοιώσω τὴν γενεὰν ταύτην; "to whom shall I liken the present
generation ?" Similarly in Mk. 4:30 He introduces the parable of the mustard seed
(Lk. 13:18, 20 the parables of the mustard seed and the leaven) with the stereotyped question : πῶς ὁμοιώσωμεν τὴν βασιλείαν τοῦ θεοῦ; "whereunto shall
we liken the kingdom of God ?" or : τίνι ὁμοιώσω αὐτήν; "with what shall I
compare it ?" In Mt. 6:8 the disciples are told not to do as the Gentiles do when
they pray, cf. Mt. 7:24.

When Paul healed the lame man at Lystra, the crowd, overcome with astonishment at the miracle, cried out : οἱ θεοὶ ὁμοιωθέντες ἀνθρώποις, "the gods have
taken the form of men" (Ac. 14:11).

In Hb. 2:17 the point of Christ's humiliation is explained as follows : Christ had
to be made like His brethren in all things (ὤφειλεν ... τοῖς ἀδελφοῖς ὁμοιωθῆναι) to be able to be merciful. The author is showing that Christ was a true
man, for only as such could He do His high-priestly work. But the ὁμοιωθῆναι
does not indicate full equality, only likeness. For the eternal Spirit abode in
Christ, 9:14.

† ὁμοιότης.

"Likeness," "correspondence," the resultant "similarity." So from the time of the
pre-Socratics, Isoc., Plat., Polyb., Epict., Luc. etc. "Everywhere, even where there is
difference, attention is directed not to this but to the agreement." [1]
In the LXX Wis. 14:19 : ἐξεβιάσατο ... τὴν ὁμοιότητα ἐπὶ τὸ κάλλιον. 4 Macc.
15:4 : "We marvellously set the stamp of similarity with our own soul and form (ψυχῆς
τε καὶ μορφῆς ὁμοιότητα) on the tender being of children."
καθ' ὁμοιότητα, Gn. 1:11, 12; Philo Fug., 51; Corp. Herm., 464, 29; 518, 13; BGU,
IV, 1028, 15; P. Oxy., II, 237; VI, 6; IX, 1202, 24; P. Greci e Latini, I, 107, 2; P. Flor.,
279, 22.

ὁμοιόω. [1] Cr.-Kö., 793.
[2] ὅμοιος → 187, 38 ff.
ὁμοιότης. [1] Cr.-Kö., 792.

The only NT instance is in Hb. At Hb. 4:15 it is said of Christ that He was tempted καθ' ὁμοιότητα. This emphasises the similarity of His temptation to ours. [2] But it is stressed that there is a difference between Him and us. Even in the time of temptation, which embraced His whole life (κατὰ πάντα), [3] Christ was without sin. In Hb. 7:15 Christ is called a priest κατὰ τὴν ὁμοιότητα Μελχισέδεκ. He is like Melchisedec, for He is a high-priest, not on the basis of descent and law, but in virtue of the indwelling power of indestructible life (v. 16). The expression is like κατὰ τὴν τάξιν Μελχισέδεκ in v. 11, but κατὰ τὴν ὁμοιότητα is the correct rendering of עַל־דִּבְרָתִי, Ps. 110:4. [4]

† ὁμοίωσις.

This word is not very common. It means a. "making similar or like," Ps.-Plat. Epin., 990d : τῶν οὐκ ὄντων ὁμοίων ἀλλήλοις φύσει ἀριθμῶν ὁμοίωσις. Cf. also Plat. Resp., V, 454c. It also means b. "being like," "correspondence," Plat. Theaet., 176b : φυγὴ δὲ ὁμοίωσις θεῷ κατὰ τὸ δυνατόν· ὁμοίωσις δὲ δίκαιον καὶ ὅσιον μετὰ φρονήσεως γενέσθαι. In Aristot. De Plantis, II, 6, p. 826b, 32 f. (πολλάκις δὲ καὶ ἐν φυτοῖς ἄλλο φυτὸν γεννᾶται οὐ τοῦ αὐτοῦ εἴδους καὶ τῆς αὐτῆς ὁμοιώσεως) it obviously means "species" or the "concept of species." It is used by grammarians c. for "comparison," Dion. Thr. Art. Gramm., 642, 6. d. καθ' ὁμοίωσιν means "after the analogy," Sext. Emp. Pyrrh. Hyp., 75.

In the LXX it is mostly used for דְּמוּת [1] in the sense of "similarity." καθ' ὁμοίωσιν means "after the manner." So esp. Gn. 1:26 : "Let us make man κατ' εἰκόνα ἡμετέραν καὶ καθ' ὁμοίωσιν." Cf. ψ 57:4 : θυμὸς αὐτοῖς κατὰ τὴν ὁμοίωσιν τοῦ ὄφεως. But the word does not mean "image"; there is a fundamental distinction from εἰκών, → II, 395. εἰκών presupposes an original from which there is derivation, whereas ὁμοίωσις, like ὁμοιότης and ὁμοίωμα, simply denotes the likeness, which has not arisen by derivation; [2] it may be quite accidental, just as one egg resembles another, or as there may be similarity between two men who are in no way related. [3] Thus even in Ez. 1:10 : ὁμοίωσις τῶν προσώπων αὐτῶν· πρόσωπον ἀνθρώπου κτλ., the meaning is not "image" but "similarity of species" or "species" (in the sense of Aristot.), unless one simply renders : "Their faces look like ..." The same is true of Da. 10:16 Θ : ὡς ὁμοίωσις υἱοῦ ἀνθρώπου, "like one who belongs to the sons of men." [4] Cf. also Ez. 8:10 A : πᾶσα ὁμοίωσις ἑρπετοῦ καὶ κτήνους, "every species (or form) of creeping things and fourfooted beasts." [5]

The only NT instance is at Jm. 3:9, where, on the basis of Gn. 1:26, [6] it is said : ἐν αὐτῇ (γλώσσῃ) εὐλογοῦμεν τὸν κύριον καὶ πατέρα, καὶ ἐν αὐτῇ καταρώμεθα τοὺς ἀνθρώπους τοὺς καθ' ὁμοίωσιν θεοῦ γεγονότας. He who curses man turns against God Himself, who created man after His own similitude.

---

[2] Wnd. Hb., ad loc. thinks κατὰ τὴν ὁμοιότητα might be referred to the persons : "corresponding to the likeness between Him (Christ) and us." But this view is rendered impossible by the words χωρὶς ἁμαρτίας.

[3] Cf. Mi. Hb.[7], 55.

[4] Cf. Wnd. Hb., ad loc.

ὁμοίωσις. [1] דְּמוּת = 1. "copy," "imitation"; 2. "form," "appearance." Cf. Ges.-Buhl, s.v.

[2] ὅμοιος → 187, 38 ff.

[3] Loc. cit.

[4] So Cr.-Kö., 794.

[5] Loc. cit.

[6] The Gn. verse is quoted word for word in 1 Cl., 33, 5; Barn., 5, 5; 6, 12; cf. also Ps.-Clem. Hom., XI, 4; III, 17; Cl. Al. Strom., V, 5. 29, 1. On Jewish exposition cf. the material in Wnd. Barn., 327 f.

The verse in Gn. (1:26): ποιήσωμεν ἄνθρωπον κατ' εἰκόνα ἡμετέραν καὶ καθ' ὁμοίωσιν, played an important part among the fathers, esp. in the Arian controversy. [7] Gregory of Nyssa devoted a treatise to the question of the relation between εἰκών and ὁμοίωσις. With several fathers he argued for a real distinction between the two. The great Alexandrian theologians taught that εἰκών is something wherein men were created, which is common to all, and which remains after the fall (Gn. 9:6), whereas ὁμοίωσις is something for which man was created, that he should strive after it and attain to it. [8] We are probably to see here the influence of Plat. Theaet., 176b : ὁμοίωσις θεῷ κατὰ τὸ δυνατόν, to which Philo refers in Fug., 63 and which is also used by Cl. Al. in his discussion of the question in Strom., II, 22, 136, 6. Cf. also Iren. and Tertullian. The Schoolmen, too, distinguished between the twofold imprint of man. [9]

† ὁμοίωμα.

ὁμοίωμα is "what is made similar," "copy." The word is rare in secular Gk. It occurs in Plat., Aristot., Epicur., and occasionally pap., [1] and always has the concrete sense of "copy" rather than the abstract sense of likeness or correspondence. [2] It is thus synon. to εἰκών (= II, 388). [3] εἰκών and ὁμοίωμα are often used as equivalents, e.g., Plat. Phaedr., 250b; ὁμοιώματα and εἰκόνες are in Plat. the earthly copies of the heavenly prototypes. But there is often a distinction between the two words. This may be formulated as follows : εἰκών represents the object, whereas ὁμοίωμα emphasises the similarity, but with no need for an inner connection between the original and the copy. [4]

The word is common in the LXX. It is used for דְּמוּת,[5] תַּבְנִית,[6] תְּמוּנָה,[7] and infrequently צֶלֶם. [8] Dt. 4:16; Is. 40:19; Ex. 20:4 show that ὁμοίωμα means the "copy" which is made like something else and is congruent with it (cf. Is. 40:18 : τίνι ὁμοιώματι ὡμοιώσατε αὐτόν; "where is something like, with which you may compare him ?"). This leads to a transition to the sense of "form," with no further thought of a copy, e.g., Dt. 4:12 : ἐλάλησεν κύριος πρὸς ὑμᾶς ἐκ μέσου τοῦ πυρὸς ... καὶ ὁμοίωμα οὐκ εἴδετε κτλ. It is common in Ez., e.g., 1:26 : ὁμοίωμα ὡς εἶδος ἀνθρώπου, 23:15 : ὁμοίωμα υἱῶν Χαλδαίων. [9] There are thus 2 senses in the LXX : a. "copy" ("image" in the sense of "similitude," Dt. 4:16 ff.; ψ 105:20 : ὁμοίωμα μόσχου, "similitude of a bull") and b. "form."

In the NT ὁμοίωμα has at Rev. 9:7 the sense of "form" (τὰ ὁμοιώματα τῶν ἀκρίδων ὅμοιοι ἵπποις, "the forms of the locusts are like horses"). [10]

---

[7] On this cf. Trench, 36 f.
[8] Trench, 36.
[9] For examples cf. Trench, 36.

ὁ μ ο ί ω μ α. [1] Plat. Parm., 132d; 133d; Phaedr., 250a; 250b; Soph., 266d. Cf. Class. Rev., 10 (1896), 131. Aristot. Rhet., I, 2, p. 1356a, 31. Ditt. Or., 669, 52 : ἐξ ὁμοιώματος, "after the analogy"; P. Fay., 106, 20.
[2] Cf. Cr.-Kö., 794.
[3] Cf. Trench, 33-37.
[4] Ibid., 34. Cf. Moult.-Mill., 449 : "As distinguished from εἰκών, which implies an archetype, the 'likeness' or 'form' in ὁμοίωμα may be accidental, as one egg is like another."
[5] דְּמוּת is seldom transl. ὁμοίωσις, only once each ὅμοιος, ἰδέα and εἰκών.
[6] For תַּבְנִית ὁμοίωμα is used 10 times, occasionally παράδειγμα, once each τύπος, ῥυθμός and μορφή.
[7] תְּמוּנָה is twice transl. δόξα, once μορφή.
[8] צֶלֶם is mostly εἰκών, rarely ὁμοίωμα.
[9] Cf. the detailed instances in Cr.-Kö., 794.
[10] So Loh. Apk., ad loc.; Pr.-Bauer³, 941; Had. Apk., ad loc. translates : "Their appearance is like horses."

The NT verses which are of theological significance are in R. and Phil.

1. On R. 1:23 → II, 395. The cultic images of the Gentiles are contrasted with the δόξα of God which cannot be represented plastically. It is said of these empty idolatrous figures (όμοιώματα) that they are fashioned in the form of human and animal bodies (εἰκόνες). [11]

2. R. 6:5 is important in relation to Paul's understanding of baptism. Paul says : εἰ γὰρ σύμφυτοι γεγόναμεν τῷ όμοιώματι τοῦ θανάτου αὐτοῦ, ἀλλὰ καὶ τῆς ἀναστάσεως ἐσόμεθα.

The meaning is much debated. There are two main views. Acc. to the one — which corresponds to the direct wording — we are to render : "to grow with the copy (or imitation) of his death." [12] It is here assumed that Paul is using an abbreviated and imprecise formulation. [13] What is meant is : "By imitation of his death we have grown together with his death," [14] or : "We have grown together with a death like his death." Acc. to the second and less common view σύμφυτοι has to be filled out by an αὐτῷ (on the analogy of v. 4 : συνετάφημεν αὐτῷ) and τῷ όμοιώματι τοῦ θανάτου αὐτοῦ is to be taken instrumentally. [15] Hence the translation is : "We have grown together with him by imitation of his death" (or "by the same death as he"). The first view is quite definitely to be preferred, since there is no αὐτῷ in the text.

The decisive question is that of the meaning of όμοίωμα τοῦ θανάτου αὐτοῦ. Acc. to H. Schlier [16] όμοίωμα means an image which is like its object but not equivalent. Acc. to S. Stricker [17] it is something intrinsically similar in another form. But does όμοίωμα mean baptism, or does it mean Christ's death sacramentally present ? In other words, is baptism a representation of the death of Christ, or is it the likeness which contains the original ? [18] Here the views of expositors diverge.

a. A first opinion is that όμοίωμα refers to baptism. For baptism represents the death of Christ. So Cr.-Kö., 795 : "The experience which in the eyes of the apostle is equivalent to Christ's death is baptism." Similarly Wikenhauser : [19] "Baptism is for the apostle a reproduction or similitude of the death and resurrection of Christ." [20] Barth, [21] too, relates όμοίωμα to our baptism, which is thereby described as an image

---

[11] So esp. Ltzm. R., ad loc. R. 1:23 is based on ψ 105:20 : καὶ ἠλλάξαντο τὴν δόξαν αὐτῶν ἐν όμοιώματι μόσχου ἔσθοντος χόρτον.
[12] So Ltzm. R., ad loc.; R. A. Lipsius R., ad loc. in Handkomm. z. NT; P. Althaus, D. Brief an d. Römer (NT Deutsch), ad loc.; Schl. R., 205; A. Wikenhauser, D. Kirche als der mystische Leib Christi (1937), 124; also W. Sanday-A. C. Headlam, (ICC [1930]), The Epistle to the Romans[5], ad loc. prefer a direct connection between σύμφυτοι and τῷ όμοιώματι. A. Schweitzer, Die Mystik d. Ap. Pls. (1930), 120 has the general formulation : "planted in Christ's death." Cf. also W. Bousset, Kyrios Christos[4] (1930), 107, who speaks of the "cultic and sacramental growing together of the Christian with Christ effected in baptism."
[13] So, e.g., Ltzm. R.; Sanday-Headlam ; M. J. Lagrange, St. Paul, Épitre aux Romains[3] (1922), 146 ("une construction elliptique"); Wikenhauser, 124.
[14] Ltzm. R.; Wikenhauser, 124 : "By imitation of his death we have grown together with his death (= the dead and buried Christ)."
[15] So Pr.-Bauer[3], 941; J. Weiss, Das Urchr. (1917), 356, n. 1; Lagrange, 145 f.
[16] H. Schlier, "Zur kirchlichen Lehre von d. Taufe," ThLZ, 72 (1947), 324.
[17] S. Stricker, "Der Mysteriengedanke d. heiligen Pls. nach R. 6:2-11," Liturgisches Leben, 1 (1934), 285-296. Cf. Jbch. f. Liturgiewissenschaft, 14 (1934), 372.
[18] H. Schlier, loc. cit.
[19] Wikenhauser, 124.
[20] Stauffer Theol., 276 understands the όμοίωμα in R. 6:5 as follows : We die with him, we live with him — we are like him. Cf. 131: "We are crucified and buried in likeness to his death, to awaken like him to new life." But this hardly does justice to the thought in σύμφυτοι.
[21] K. Barth, "D. kirchliche Lehre von d. Taufe," Theologische Existenz heute, NF, 4 (1947), 6.

of Christ's death. On the other hand H. W. Bartsch [22] thinks it important that in baptism we are brought into likeness to a similitude of Christ's death, which can only be the baptism of Jesus. [23] This is, however, quite impossible exegetically, for Paul never refers to the baptism of Jesus, and has indeed little interest in the life of the historical Jesus at all. [24]

b. A second view relates ὁμοίωμα τοῦ θανάτου αὐτοῦ to our death in baptism. We have grown together with the death which we have experienced in baptism and which is like the death of Christ. Schlatter took this as his starting-point : "The likeness of the death of Jesus is that by baptism the believer is set in a position which is like the death of Jesus, the position of one on whom the divine judgment on sin has been visited, with the result that entrance into life is opened up for him. Hence Paul says that the likeness of Jesus does not adhere to the baptised externally, but that they have grown together with it." [25] Similarly Zahn : "Not the act of baptism, but the ἀποθανεῖν τῇ ἁμαρτίᾳ (v. 10) effected by baptism, is the likeness of the death of Christ." [26] Acc. to Zn. Christ's death is the "type" whose reflection is the death experienced by us in baptism.

c. A third and Roman Catholic understanding emphasises the mystical character of the process indicated by the word ὁμοίωμα. S. Stricker [27] claims that the person baptised dies mystically the death of Christ. "Baptism is ὁμοίωμα τοῦ θανάτου αὐτοῦ, i.e., of Christ, not of the subject of baptism ; and because Christ's death was the death on the cross, the person baptised dies this death (v. 6 : συνεσταυρώθη)." "The death of Christ is present, not naturally, but sacramentally." Stricker admits that in the first instance it is the candidate's death which is depicted, but he then declares that indirectly Christ's death is also represented, for the candidate dies with Christ and Christ has made baptism a likeness of His death. The conclusion of Stricker is that in the similitude of baptism the once for all crucifixion of Christ is brought so close to the subject of baptism that the latter dies the death of Christ with Him. O. Casel [28] relates the ὁμοίωμα even more strongly to the death of Christ present in the sacrament. He equates βαπτισθῆναι εἰς Χριστόν and βαπτισθῆναι ἐν Χριστῷ, and thus understands the βαπτισθῆναι as being baptised in the sphere of Christ. Thus baptism is for him in the ultimate and decisive sense a spiritual process which takes place in the sphere of Christ, and specifically in that of His death. "The ὁμοίωμα τοῦ θανάτου thus consists in this burial of the candidate in water, which, since it takes place in the sphere of Christ and His death, signifies burial in Christ." The decisive thing for Casel is that in baptism we have "the immediate presence of the death of Christ in the sacrament." "The death and burial of Christ are necessarily present in the sacrament, since otherwise one could not speak of being crucified and buried with Him."

d. This view has found a place in Protestant exposition. Its main champion is H. Schlier, [29] who adopts the sacramental rather than the mystical understanding of

---

[22] H. W. Bartsch, "D. Taufe im NT," *Evangelische Theol.,* NF, 3 (1948/49), 91.

[23] Bartsch *loc. cit.* says : "Our likeness with the death of Christ is obviously not brought about directly but by way of the baptism of Jesus. Inasmuch as we in our baptism take on us the baptism of Jesus, and this signifies his death and resurrection, we in our baptism are like the death and resurrection of Jesus." This idea is quite impossible in Paul.

[24] Cf. 2 C. 5:16.

[25] Schl. R., 206.

[26] Zn. R., 300, cf. 299 : "With baptism, to which alone there can be ref., the candidate does not grow together to a unity, but receives it, lets it happen to him, and thereby, acc. to v. 3, enters into relation to Christ, and specifically to His death." Schlier, 324 thinks it likely that the ὁμοίωμα does not denote baptism itself but as a single concept with τοῦ θανάτου αὐτοῦ denotes the singularity of Christ's death.

[27] Acc. to O. Casel, *Jbch. f. Liturgiewissenschaft,* 14 (1934), 372.

[28] *Loc. cit.*

[29] Schlier, 324.

ὁμοίωμα. Acc. to Schlier we are by nature integrated into Christ's death in baptism. But the ref. of baptism is not to the experience of the person baptised, whose death is understood as a likeness of the death of Christ. It is to Christ's death present in baptism, and hence sacramentally. This means that the ref. is not to the crucifixion as such, as it took place historically at Golgotha. As we in baptism grow together with the death of Christ sacramentally present, the contemporaneity of our (baptismal) death and the death of Christ is achieved. [30]

The second part of the verse reads ἀλλὰ καὶ (σύμφυτοι τῷ ὁμοιώματι) τῆς ἀναστάσεως (αὐτοῦ) ἐσόμεθα, and this allows of just as many different interpretations as the first half. In the first instance there are two main lines of exposition acc. to the text. It may refer to (mystical-sacramental) resurrection with Christ in the act of baptism, [31] or to the future resurrection of the baptised. [32] Both views are possible according to the wording and context. But it is most natural to think in terms of a present event. [33] v. 11 (ζῶντας δὲ τῷ θεῷ ἐν Χριστῷ 'Ιησοῦ) supports this. If Christians, having died to sin, are alive for God in Christ Jesus, then they must have passed already through a resurrection which has awakened them from death to life. Through baptism they have thus taken part in a resurrection like that of Christ. They have indeed so grown together with this resurrection which is like that of Christ that this event lays its impress on their lives from now on. The following explanations have been advanced in exegesis of the passage.

a. ὁμοίωμα τῆς ἀναστάσεως αὐτοῦ is the likeness of the resurrection of Christ in the sense that the candidate who comes up out of the watery tomb experiences a spiritual or mystical resurrection corresponding to that of Christ. Zahn [34] speaks of a process in the life of the baptised analogous to the resurrection of Christ as the "type." Schlatter says [35] that "a likeness of the life now enjoyed by the risen Lord will grow together with us."

b. Roman Catholic exegetes take a different view. Stricker [36] maintains that the candidate participates sacramentally in Christ's resurrection. It is thus assumed that the resurrection of Christ is sacramentally present as well as His death. Stricker does not make the gen. τῆς ἀναστάσεως dependent on ὁμοιώματι, but sees in it a gen. of relationship : "Then we shall be (partakers) of the resurrection." "Baptism is thus a likeness only of Christ's death, participation in the resurrection being a result of dying with Christ." There seems to be little doubt, however, that the sense demands σύμφυτοι τῷ ὁμοιώματι after καί. Paul is saying that as we grow together with the likeness of the death of Christ, so we grow together with the likeness of His resurrection. Casel

---

[30] Schlier speaks of the conforming of our nature to Christ's. So, too, does Stricker, who sums up the results of his exposition of R. 6 in the following main points : "1. The fate of the baptised person is par. to that of Christ. 2. There is also a dying with Christ. 3. The person baptised dies with Christ because he dies in Christ, in His death ; he does not die his own death with Christ, but dies Christ's death with Him. 4. The death (and resurrection) of the baptised with Christ takes place sacramentally, in the ὁμοίωμα of the death of Christ." Cf. Casel, op. cit., 371.

[31] So Wikenhauser, 124; Zn. R., 300 f.

[32] So, e.g., Schl. R., 206; Lipsius R., ad loc. (Handkomm. z. NT).

[33] The fut. is thus a logical fut. Zn. R., 300 also takes the ἐσόμεθα as a fut. exactum. "It expresses the logical requirement of an event belonging to the past." Cf. 301: "The conviction that the baptised are linked with the resurrection of Christ is stated to be a deduction from the link with Christ's death."

[34] Zn. R., 301: "If the baptised have by baptism entered into an inner union with the death of Christ as the type of something which happens to them, they must also have entered into an inner union with the resurrection of Christ as the type of an analogous process in their own lives."

[35] Schl. R., 206.

[36] Cf. Jbch. (→ n. 27), 371.

is closer to the mark : [37] "When we grow together with the likeness of His death, it follows that we are (mystically) dead. But things cannot stop here. Since death is only a transition to a new (mystical) life, we shall also partake of the resurrection." [38] The thought that the baptised cannot remain in death suggests that we have in the ἐσόμεθα a logical future.

We are forced to the following conclusions. 1. Paul does not say that in baptism we have grown together with the death and resurrection of Christ, but with the likeness of His death and resurrection. The term ὁμοίωμα rules out any idea of mystical relation to the historical saving acts. 2. Since Paul expressly emphasises that we are organically linked with the likeness of the death and resurrection of Christ, we fail to do justice to his view if we say that the death which we have experienced in baptism, and the resurrection which has been imparted to us in baptism, are copies of the death and resurrection of Christ. 3. What Paul really has in view is the death and resurrection of Christ present in baptism. The sacramentally present death and resurrection of Christ are the ὁμοίωμα of His historical death and resurrection. This means that we are very closely linked with the saving realities of Christ's death and resurrection as these are present in baptism. This is a further development or more precise formulation of the thought of v. 3, namely, that we are baptised into Christ and His death. For in v. 3, too, the death of Christ is for Paul a present saving reality.

3. In R. 5:14 Paul declares that in the time from Adam to Moses, when there was no Law, death held sway even over those who had not sinned according to Adam's transgression (ἐπὶ τῷ ὁμοιώματι τῆς παραβάσεως 'Αδάμ). ὁμοίωμα here means "copy." The meaning is that the sin of those who lived after Adam did not copy the sin of Adam. It would have done so if they had been given a law like that given to Adam. They did, of course, sin, though not after the manner of Adam. They thus fell victim to death. [39]

4. Certain difficulties arise in passages in which Paul uses ὁμοίωμα in connection with Christ's manifestation on earth, R. 8:3 and Phil. 2:7. In R. 8:3 Paul says that God sent His Son into the world in the form of sinful flesh (ἐν ὁμοιώματι σαρκὸς ἁμαρτίας). [40] He is emphasising that Christ was really man. He bore a physical body fashioned according to the human body which is infected with sin. In outward form He was in no way different from other men. But Paul does not say that He came ἐν σαρκὶ ἁμαρτίας. With his ἐν ὁμοιώματι Paul is showing

---

[37] *Ibid.,* 373.

[38] Casel puts it even more plainly, *ibid.,* 246 : For Paul "death is primarily important in baptism as the sacrament of transition from death to life." From participation in the death of Christ there follows "directly ... participation in the life of the risen Lord." The pneumatic-aeonic life is "present at once in the baptised." (Cf. R. 6:11.) "At bodily resurrection this new life will simply assert itself definitively for the whole man."

[39] Zn. R., 269, 273 is not materially incorrect when he sees in Adam's sin the type or model which others who sinned after him followed. Zn. takes the gen. here as a *gen. appositivus.* Cr.-Kö., 796 attacks Zn. but comes to much the same view. "Since there was no Law for those living in the epoch from Adam to Moses prior to its impartation, these men were not guilty of a transgression comparable with the sin of Adam." Cf. also Schl. R., 189 : "In the first generations of mankind there took place nothing comparable to the fall of Adam, for no divine command was given to them."

[40] In concrete things ὁμοίωμα means "form," "appearance." Cf. Schl. R., 256 : "Ὁμοίωμα is meant concretely ; it says of Christ's body that it was made just like ours. Docetic ideas should not be intruded."

that for all the similarity between Christ's physical body and that of men there is an essential difference between Christ and men. Even in His earthly life Christ was still the Son of God. This means that He became man without entering the nexus of human sin. The words ἐν ὁμοιώματι keep us from a deduction which Paul did not wish to make, namely, that Christ became subject to the power of sin, and did in fact sin. [41] For Paul Christ is sinless. [42] Sin, which clung to the physical body He assumed, had no power over Him. The ὁμοίωμα thus indicates two things, first the likeness in appearance, and secondly the distinction in essence. Why did God send His Son into the world in the form of sinful flesh? Paul answers : With this body the intrinsically sinless Christ became the representative of sinful mankind. Hence God, by giving up Christ to death, could condemn sin by destroying His body, and thus cancel it. [43] Christ took the likeness of σάρξ ἁμαρτίας in order that God in Christ might achieve the liberation of mankind from sin.

J. Weiss [44] devotes special attention to R. 8:3. He concludes that ἐν ὁμοιώματι σαρκὸς ἁμαρτίας is an ambiguous expression which Paul formulated "under the pressure of an antinomy." On the one hand the thought of R. 8:3 f. (that sin was judged in the flesh in the crucifixion of Christ) demands that sin be present in Christ's flesh. For only so could it be put to death in His death. On the other hand, however, it is quite inconceivable for Paul that Christ should be under the sway of sin. He tries to overcome the difficulty, though not very convincingly acc. to Weiss, by choosing "this middle term." "He accepts this in order to leave the thought of incarnation in a certain vacillation between true humanity and the purely external acceptance of a human body, so that the inner core of Christ's personality is unaffected by genuine earthly humanity and sinfulness." Weiss thinks that Paul is here close to Docetism. The real reason for the tension is that Paul is controlled by different traditions. On the one side is the view of the heavenly Messiah found in later Jewish apocalyptic, on the other the earthly Jesus of primitive Christian tradition. Paul was faced by the impossible task of uniting the two conceptions. But this criticism is highly rationalistic. Paul is confronted by mystery of the person of Christ and His redeeming act. The problem is that human terms are inadequate to express a mystery which cannot be grasped in human concepts.

To support his thesis Weiss refers to certain LXX passages [45] where ὁμοίωμα means the form in which a divine entity, God or angel appears on earth. He mentions esp. Ez. 8:2 f.: "And I beheld, and lo a likeness as the appearance of a man or a human form (ὁμοίωμα ἀνδρός) ..., and he stretched out something like a hand (ὁμοίωμα χειρός). "The seer knows that it is not the real hand of a real man, but that a heavenly being appears in the form of a man." Weiss also refers to Da. 10:16, 18 and Rev. 1:13 (ὅμοιον υἱὸν ἀνθρώπου). But these refs. are not very convincing. For Paul is saying more than that the heavenly Christ in His earthly form simply took on the form of a man. Jesus Christ was a definite, concretely apprehensible individual who felt and

---

[41] So all exegetes, cf. esp. Schl. R., 256 and Zn. R., 381 f. Zn. does not think this is an appositive gen. since this would produce the unacceptable thought "that sinful flesh is a form similar and corresponding to the being of God or the Son of God. What is meant is simply that God sent His own Son and caused Him to be manifested in the world in a form like that of sinful flesh." 382 : "If Christ had human nature as a nature infected by sin we should have to maintain identity rather than likeness with the nature common to man." But the "hereditary infection of human nature by sin was not passed on to Jesus."
[42] Cf. Ltzm. R.⁴, ad loc. Cf. 2 C. 5:21.
[43] Cf. W. Wrede, Pls. (1906), 60 f.: "With the destruction of his flesh the total mass of flesh, with the sin clinging to it, is as it were abolished."
[44] J. Weiss, Das Urchr. (1917), 376 f.
[45] Op. cit., 376, n. 2.

thought as a man, though distinguished from other men by the divine mystery concealed in Him : sin had no power over Him.

There is a similar statement in Phil. 2:7: Christ took the form of a servant, came into the world in the form of a man (ἐν ὁμοιώματι ἀνθρώπων γενόμενος), [46] and was found in fashion as a man. Paul shows that Christ has undertaken a μεταμόρφωσις. He has renounced the form of God and assumed that of a slave [48] (→ IV, 750 f.). He truly became man, not merely in outward appearance, but in thought and feeling. He who was the full image of God became the full image of man. [49] But even in this passage, where ὁμοίωμα so obviously means "form," there is still in the background the idea of the "image" which is not identical with the original (the form of men) but like it. For in His humanity Christ differed from all other men by virtue of His consistent obedience. [50] It is thus said in Phil. 2:7 that Christ changed His form and assumed an appearance which made Him like men. The divine figure entered history. This is only another way of saying what Jn. says in 1:14 : ὁ λόγος σὰρξ ἐγένετο. Paul does not say with any clarity how far the being of Christ was affected by this change. The words ἑαυτὸν ἐκένωσεν in v. 7 (→ III, 661) could suggest that He retained nothing of His divine nature. But the fact that as man He accomplished what no other man could do, i.e., perfect obedience, leads necessarily to the conclusion that even as man He remained at the core of His being what He had been before. [52] The earthly μορφή is also the husk which encloses His unchanging essential existence, though as such it is, of course, a real human body. Docetic ideas are quite alien to Paul. But as man Christ is in the depths of His essence a being of another kind.

Ign. uses ὁμοίωμα once to confirm the resurrection of Christians. He says in Tr., 9, 2 : οὗ (sc. Χριστοῦ) καὶ κατὰ τὸ ὁμοίωμα ἡμᾶς ... οὕτως ἐγερεῖ ὁ πατὴρ αὐτοῦ, "corresponding to whose likeness (like Him) the Father will raise us up too." [53] In the Sacramentarium Serapionis the sacramental bread is called the ὁμοίωμα of Christ's body, [54] and the offering of the bread is τὸ ὁμοίωμα τοῦ θανάτου ποιεῖν. [55] The point

---

[46] Cf. in transl. of this difficult expression Weiss, 376 f.: "He took an appearance like that of men," or : "He came in human form," or : "He appeared as man."

[47] Acc. to E. Lohmeyer, *Kyrios Jesus* (1928), 36 the word ὁμοίωμα contains no suggestion of mere appearance ; it denotes "a biological actuality." 37: "ὁμοίωμα, like μορφή, to which it is par., is defined by ref. to the nature of man, but σχῆμα by ref. to history." In Phil. 2:7, however, ὁμοίωμα too has a historical ref.

[48] ἐν ὁμοιώματι ἀνθρώπων stands in juxtaposition to ἐν μορφῇ θεοῦ ὑπάρχων (v. 6).

[49] Cf. Cr.-Kö., 796.

[50] Cf. Mich. Ph., 38.

[51] So also Lohmeyer, *op. cit.,* 36 f.

[52] Cf. J. Weiss, *op. cit.,* 376, n. 2; 377. Pr.-Bauer³, 941 also takes this possibility into account. Loh. Phil., 94 states : "Thus here, too, the little word 'in' serves to change this 'human appearance,'' which in itself embraces the fulness of human existence, into an envelope which mysteriously conceals something obscure and indefinable." Zn. goes furthest when he says that even in the form of man Christ remained God ("Altes u. Neues z. Phil. Brief," ZWL, 6 [1885], 262).

[53] The word is used in a general sense in Herm. m., 4, 1, 9 (ὃς ἂν τὰ ὁμοιώματα [= τὰ ὅμοια] ποιῇ τοῖς ἔθνεσιν, "he who does what resembles the deeds of the heathen) and m., 4, 1, 1 (περὶ τοιούτων τινῶν ὁμοιωμάτων πονηρῶν [the thought] of certain wickednesses which are of the same kind).

[54] Sacram. Serapionis, XIII, 12 (Funk, Didaskalia, II, 174, 10 f.): ὁ ἄρτος οὗτος τοῦ ἁγίου σώματός ἐστιν ὁμοίωμα.

[55] *Ibid.,* XIII, 13 (Funk, II, 174, 15 f.): διὰ τοῦτο καὶ ἡμεῖς τὸ ὁμοίωμα τοῦ θανάτου ποιοῦντες τὸν ἄρτον προσηνέγκαμεν.

is that the bread is an indication of what took place in the body of Christ, of Christ's crucifixion. [56]

† ἀφομοιόω.

"To copy." Common in Plat., Xenoph., Aristot., Plut. (Plat. Crat., 427c : ὡς ἀφομοιῶν τοῖς γράμμασι τὰ ἔργα, "thus to restore reality by letters"). But also "to make similar" (τινί Xenoph. Eq., 9, 9; Plat. Resp., III, 396a; always πρός τι in Plut.). Wis. 13:14 : ζῴῳ τινὶ εὐτελεῖ ἀφωμοίωσεν (Β ὡμοίωσεν) αὐτό, "the woodcarver fashions the wood in the likeness of an ordinary animal" (showing the folly of idolatry). Occasionally, but infrequently, "to compare" (Plat. Resp., VIII, 564b).

Pass. "to be similar," "to represent oneself as similar." In the aor. "to become like," perf. "to be like," so Plat., Aristot., Ep. Jer. 4 : εὐλαβήθητε οὖν μὴ καὶ ὑμεῖς ἀφομοιωθέντες τοῖς ἀλλοφύλοις ἀφομοιωθῆτε "take care that you do not become like an alien"; 62 : ταῦτα δὲ οὔτε ταῖς ἰδέαις οὔτε ταῖς δυνάμεσιν αὐτῶν ἀφωμοιωμένα ἐστίν, "these (the gods) are like them neither in form nor strength." Similarly in conflict with idolatry 70 : ὡσαύτως δὲ καὶ νεκρῷ ἐρριμμένῳ ἐν σκότει ἀφωμοίωνται οἱ θεοὶ αὐτῶν ξύλινοι καὶ περίχρυσοι καὶ περιάργυροι, "so their wooden, gilded and silvered gods are like a corpse thrown into the darkness of the grave."

The only NT instance is at Hb. 7:3 of Melchisedec : ἀφωμοιωμένος δὲ τῷ υἱῷ τοῦ θεοῦ, "he is like the Son of God." [1]

Exegesis has mainly followed Chrys. (Hom. in Hb.) who called the Son of God τύπος. ἀφωμοιωμένος has been expounded accordingly (e.g., Bengel, Bleek, Riggenbach). Thus Riggenbach states : "In the fact that his life is without beginning or end Melchisedec is a counterpart of the Son of God and in his person represents in likeness what the Son possesses as prototype." [2] The text, however, does not expressly relate Melchisedec here to Christ. More likely is the suggestion that the OT narrative is to be understood as a ref. to Christ, as a Messianic prophecy. Thus Michel : "What took place in ancient time was a sign pointing forward to Christ." [3] So also Windisch, who refers to Philo Fug., 109; Abr., 31: "Melchisedec and the Son of God are both like the high-priestly *logos* in Philo, and are thus like one another." [4]

† παρόμοιος.

"Similar," from the time of Hdt., but rare. Poll. Onom., IX, 130 explains as follows : ὁ γὰρ παρόμοιος παρ' ὀλίγον ὅμοιός ἐστιν. παρόμοιος [1] thus means lit. "almost alike," but the difference from the simple form is not always clear. In Xenoph. Hist. Graec., III, 4, 13 παρόμοιος means "nearly equal" (παρόμοιοι τοῖς Ἕλλησι τὸν ἀριθμόν), cf. also Polyb., VI, 3, 11 (ὀλιγαρχικὰ πολιτεύματα ... δοκοῦντα παρόμοιον ἔχειν τι τοῖς ἀριστοκρατικοῖς).

---

[56] Cf. H. Lietzmann, *Messe u. Herrenmahl* (1926), 192.

ἀφομοιόω. [1] Epiph. Haer., 67, 7 distinguishes between ὅμοιος and ἀφωμοιωμένος (οὐ γὰρ εἶπεν ὅμοιον τῷ υἱῷ τοῦ θεοῦ, ἀλλ' ἀφωμοιωμένον), but this is overfine. Cf. Rgg. Hb. n., ad loc.

[2] Rgg. Hb., 185; cf. n. 6 : The reason why the Son of God is the original, Melchisedec the copy, is to be found in the matter rather than the phrase. Cf. Cr.-Kö., 797, who renders ἀφωμοιωμένος ... "as a reflection resembling the Son of God."

[3] Mi. Hb.[8], ad loc.

[4] Wnd., ad loc. Wnd. rightly dismisses the view that the ἀφωμοιωμένος is only in Scripture (Rgg., Cr.-Kö.). It is in reality as well as Scripture, "for distinction between the historical Melchisedec and the presentation which Scripture gives of him is inadmissible for Hb."

παρόμοιος. [1] Cf. πάρισος etc., E. Schwyzer, *Griech. Grammatik*, II (1949), 492.

In the NT — apart from Mk. 7:8 $\Re^2$ — it occurs only once at Mk. 7:13. In the debate about what is clean and unclean Jesus declares that God's moral command takes precedence of cultic vows. After Jesus has given an example to show how the Pharisees think and act, He continues: "And you do many similar things" (παρόμοια τοιαῦτα πολλὰ ποιεῖτε).

† παρομοιάζω.

Only Mt. 23:27: "to be like" (τινί). In His great address against Pharisaism Jesus is here declaring that the Pharisees are like whited (→ κονιάω, III, 827) sepulchres.

J. Schneider

---

† ὁμολογέω, † ἐξομολογέω, † ἀνθομολογέομαι,
† ὁμολογία, † ὁμολογουμένως

Contents: A. The Word Group in Secular Greek Usage. B. The OT-Oriental and Hellenistic-Gnostic Liturgy of Thankoffering. C. The Word Group in the LXX and Post-biblical Judaism: 1. LXX; 2. Extrabiblical Later Jewish Literature; 3. Philo; 4. Apocalyptic. D. The Word Group in the NT: I. ὁμολογεῖν: 1. "to assure," "to promise," "to admit," "to concede"; 2. judicially, "to make a statement," in the legal sense "to bear witness"; 3. "to make solemn statements of faith," "to confess something in faith". II. ὁμολογουμένως. III. ἀνθ- and ἐξομολογεῖσθαι τῷ θεῷ: 1. ἀνθομολογεῖσθαι; 2. ἐξομολογεῖσθαι. IV. ἐξομολογεῖσθαι τὰς ἁμαρτίας. V. ὁμολογία. E. The Word Group in Post-Apostolic Writings: 1. ὁμολογεῖν: a. "to assure," "to promise," "to admit," "to

---

² A, some *koine* uncials, almost all minusc., vg syr arm go aeth add after ἀνθρώπων Mk. 7:8 the following sentence: βαπτισμοὺς ξεστῶν καὶ ποτηρίων καὶ ἄλλα παρόμοια τοιαῦτα πολλὰ ποιεῖτε.

ὁ μ ο λ ο γ έ ω κ τ λ. Liddell-Scott, 1226. G. Bornkamm, "Ὁμολογία, zur Geschichte eines politischen Begriffes," *Herm.*, 71 (1936), 377-393; also "Die Offenbarung des Zornes Gottes," ZNW, 34 (1935), 239-262; also "Das Wort Jesu vom Bekennen," *Monatsschrift f. Pastoraltheol.*, 34 (1938), 108-118; also "Das Bekenntnis im Hb.," ThBl (1942), 56-66; H. Grimme, "Der Begriff von Heb. הוֹדָה und תּוֹדָה," ZAW, 17 (1940/41), 234-240; E. Norden, *Agnostos Theos* (1913), 143-206; 263-276; I. Elbogen, *Der jüdische Gottesdienst in seiner Entwicklung*² (1924), 24 f., 235 f.; M. Pohlenz, *Die Stoa*, I (1948), 116-119; II (1949), 67 f.; F. K. Schumann, "Vom Sinn evangelischen Bekennens," *Um Kirche u. Lehre* (1936), 67-77; also "Die Bekenntnisse u. d. Bekenntnis," ThStKr, 108 (1937/38), 181-205; O. Michel, "Kirche u. Bekenntnis," *Evangelisches Westfalen*, 11 (1934), 307 f.; also "Bibl. Bekennen u. Bezeugen," *Evangelische Theol.*, 2 (1935), 231-245; O. Procksch, *Das Bekenntnis im AT* (1936); A. Seeberg, *Der Katechismus d. Urchristenheit* (1903), 96-99; 142-151; O. Cullmann, "D. ersten christlichen Glaubensbekenntnisse," *Theol. Studien*, 15 (1943); Stauffer Theol., 212-216; G. Harder, *Pls. u. das Gebet* (1936), 25-64; E. Käsemann, *Das wandernde Gottesvolk* (1939), 105-110; Steinleitner; I. Schnitzer, "Die Beichte im Lichte d. Religionsgesch.," *Zeitschrift f. Völkerpsychologie*, 6 (1930), 94-105; R. Pettazzoni, *La confessione dei peccati*, II (1935), 252; Reitzenstein Ir. Erl., 251-268; H. Gunkel, *Einleitung in d. Psalmen* (1933), 27-31; E. Sjöberg, *Gott u. die Sünder im palästinischen Judt.* (1938), 125-266; T. Arvedson, *Das Mysterium Christi, Eine Studie zu Mt. 11:25-30* (1937), 10-76; "Über die Geltung d. Bekenntnisse in d. evangelischen Kirche," *Gutachten d. Leipziger Fakultät, Evangelisch-Lutherische Kirchenzeitung*, 1 (1947), 2-5; H. Rheinfelder, "confiteri, confessio, confessor im Kirchenlatein u. in d. romanischen Sprachen," *Die Sprache* (1949), 56-67.

concede"; b. "to make legal statements," "to bear witness" in the legal sense ; c. "to make solemn statements of faith, or to confess something in faith"; 2. ἐξομολογεῖσθαι τῷ θεῷ or τὰς ἁμαρτίας; 3. ὁμολόγησις, ἐξομολόγησις; 4. ὁμολογουμένως; 5. The Word Group in Cl. Al.

A. The Word Group in Secular Greek Usage.

ὁμολογεῖν with the compounds ἀνθομολογέομαι (LXX also ἀνθομολόγησις) and ἐξομολογέω (LXX also ἐξομολόγησις) and the related noun ὁμολογία (cf. also ὁμολόγησις, Herm. s., 9, 28, 7) is a common term in Gk. and Hell. speech, of esp. significance in law and religion. The group is found from the 5th cent. B.C. (ὁμολογέω from Soph. and Hdt., ὁμολογία from Hdt. and Thuc.), is very common in Plat. and Xenoph., and occurs both generally and legally on pap. and inscr. [1] Lit. ὁμολογεῖν means "to say the same thing," "to agree in statement." Hence of a majority, Xenoph. Sym., VIII, 36 : ὁμόλογοι γενέσθαι, "to agree on the statement," Hdt., I, 142, 4 : κατὰ γλῶσσαν ὁμολογεῖν, "to speak the same language." Often pass.: ὁμολογεῖται, ὁμολογούμενος, ὁμολογουμένως, "all men are agreed on the statement." From one side a. "to agree to the statement of another (or others)," "to accept his affirmation," specifically "to admit a charge," "to make a confession of guilt" (from Soph. Phil., 980); b. "to confirm the receipt of money" (often in pap.); c. "to agree to a proposal" (Hdt., Thuc.), even "to submit to it"; d. "to agree to a wish," "to promise" (with inf. fut.). Then transferred to things, to which the -λογ- does not really apply : a. Words and deeds "agree" (Thuc., V, 55, 1; Demosth. Or., 18, 14; Stoa : ὁμολογουμένως τῇ φύσει ζῆν, ὁμολογία τοῦ βίου); b. "agreement" of customs (Hdt.), character (Lys.). Basic to ὁμολογεῖν, ὁμολογία is 1. what is common (ὁμο-), 2. the word (-λογ-), hence a common statement. Sometimes the agreed persons are to the fore, sometimes the thing at issue. [2] In modern Gk. ἐξομολογοῦμαι, "do penance," act. ἐξομολογῶ, "hear penance."

The noun ὁμολογία, as agreement through a common *logos,* is esp. significant in the Platonic Socratic dialogue and is the opp. of the average opinion adopted uncritically (δόξα). ὁμολογία implies consent to some thing felt to be valid, and in such a way that it is followed by definite resolve and action, by ready attachment to a cause. The aim in ὁμολογία is not a theoretical agreement which does not commit us, but acceptance of a common cause ; cf. συνθῆκαι καὶ ὁμολογίαι, Crito, 52d. [3] As regards the material orientation of the word the use of the pass. in Aristot. is also significant (ὁμολογεῖσθαι, ὁμολογούμενόν ἐστιν = *constat*); this denotes the agreement of one thing with another. In Aristot. Pol., II, 9, p. 1270b, 31 there is a depiction of the poor character of the *ephori* ; their manner of life is not in keeping with the purpose of the constitution (ἔστι δὲ καὶ ἡ δίαιτα τῶν ἐφόρων οὐχ ὁμολογουμένη τῷ βουλήματι τῆς πόλεως). [4] In the diatribes of Epictet. we still find the use in dialogue, though

---

[1] Liddell-Scott, 1226; Preisigke Wört., II, 177-180.

[2] The section after → n. 1 is by Debrunner.

[3] "Hence the establishment of homology in dialogue never means that the speakers find themselves on a middle line and come together by compromise ; the agreement expresses the fact that the one who agrees is vanquished by the matter itself and gives it place," Bornkamm, *Herm.,* 71, 381. Debrunner in a written communication is more cautious : "I do not see so sharp a distinction between δόξα and ὁμολογία; in the Socratic dialogues we often find that a ὁμολογία achieved earlier in the dialogue has to be given up. ὁμολογία is simply the basis of discussion whose tenability has to be tested in the dialogue." True homology, which is agreement on a moral demand, necessarily includes action, Plat. Crito, 49e; 51e; Gorg., 488a. The opp. of serious διαλέγεσθαι and ὁμολογεῖν is the childish prattle which does not even take itself seriously. Any discussion of ἀρετή which does not take itself seriously is childish prattle.

[4] In Aristot. the ordinary use is also important : ὁμολογεῖν = "to agree with someone in something," Pol., VII, 3, p. 1325a; Eth. Nic., V, 10, p. 1135b; ὁμολογίαι = "affirmative answers," Rhet., 37, p. 1444b, or ὁμολογία = "harmony between persons, valid treaty,"

now with a definitie Stoic impress. Acc. to Epictet. ὁμολογία expresses the typical Stoic sense of freedom, Diss., III, 22, 42; Socrates is the model, for he kept what was in his power and was always seeking to become better.[5] The verb has only a minor role in the Stoics, but we find the adv. ὁμολογουμένως. Ὁμολογουμένως ζῆν is the real Stoic formula (with or without τῇ φύσει). It is traced back to Zeno and Cleanthes and variously interpreted and paraphrased (e.g., κατ᾽ ἀρετὴν ζῆν and ἕπεσθαι θεοῖς).[6] Chrysipp. explains Zeno's formula with the help of the definition ἐμπειρίαν τῶν φύσει συμβαινόντων, Stob., II, 76, 8; Diog. L., VII, 87 [53]). Stoic tradition thus equates a natural life with a virtuous life, Stob., II, 78, 1; Diog. L., VII, 87 [53]). Acc. to Epict. Diss., III, 1, 25 λογικῶς = φύσει ὁμολογουμένως = τελέως ζῆν.[7] This ὁμολογουμένως ζῆν of Stoicism is no longer actual conduct but a state of life, Plut. De Virtute Morali, 3 (II, 441c). "The life brought into harmony with nature is the integrated life which is passed in unbroken constancy and harmony."[8] Man must direct himself by the divine *logos*, but the *logos* is also the power which permeates the world ; thus man may τηρεῖν τὸ ἡγεμονικὸν κατὰ φύσιν ἔχον (Epict. Diss., I, 15, 4) in so far as this is in his power. "The goal is a life of inner resolution under the direction of the *logos*. Herein is the enduring integration of conduct, but also as its presupposition the spiritual harmony which is at every moment man's guarantee of certainty of action."[9]

Alongside the philosophical sphere of use, however, we also find a broader though varied general use. ὁμολογέω means that "I agree with someone on something"; it embraces both the fact and event and also the act and action in which I bear witness to the agreement.[10] From the very outset it denotes both the understanding and the candid declaration, Soph. Phil., 980 : ὁμολογῶ τάδε, Eur. Fr., 265 (TGF, 437): ὁμολογῶ δέ σε ἀδικεῖν. It can take on the sense "to engage oneself," "to promise," Plat. Symp., 174a; Phaedr., 254b. It plays quite a role in court in the sense "to admit," "to acknowledge," P. Magd., 23, 6; P. Hibeh, 72, 18; P. Petr., II, 13, 1, 2; P. Oxy., X, 1255, 11. We also find in the pap. the sense "to consent to," "to agree to," P. Magd., 1, 14; P. Oxy., I, 138, 21. There are many instances in which it denotes acknowledgment of a debt, P. Hibeh, 97, 5; P. Hamb., 26, 10; P. Amh., 149, 7; 150, 17; P. Flor., 336, 7. An important phrase is χάριτάς σοι ὁμολογήσω, "I would be much obliged to you," P. Amh., 142, 19; P. Gen., 47, 18; P. Lips., 34, 21; 35, 23; P. Oxy., I, 67, 22; VI, 939, 6. ὁμολογεῖν can also be used of a declaration in court, e.g., withdrawal of a charge, P. Hibeh, 96, 5.

Eth. Nic., IV, 13, p. 1127a. Aristot. also has an ἐξ ὁμολογίας διαλέγεσθαι, but this is not so closely linked with the dialogue as in Plato. In Aristot. homology supports the συλλογισμός, An. Pri., I, 23, p. 41a.

[5] Bornkamm, *Herm.*, 71, 388.

[6] O. Rieth, "Über das Telos d. Stoiker," *Herm.*, 69 (1934), 13-45, investigates the meaning and development of the Stoic formula ὁμολογουμένως τῇ φύσει ζῆν from the time of Zeno and Cleanthes. A. C. Pearson, *The Fragments of Zeno and Kleanthes* (1891), Fr. 120 and 123 (p. 162-164) in Zeno, Fr. 72 (p. 296-297) in Cleanthes, cf. Pohlenz, I, 116 f.; II, 67. On Zeno, Diog. L., VII, 87 (53); Lact. Inst., III, 7 f.; Stob. Ecl., II, 75, 11 ff.; Plut. Comm. Not., 23, 1 (II, 1069 f.); Cic. Fin., 3, 21; 4, 14; 4, 72; Cl. Al. Strom., II, 21, 129, 1; Epict. Diss., I, 20, 14 ff. On Cleanthes, Stob. Ecl., II, 76, 3 ff.; Diog. L., VII, 87; Cl. Al. Strom., II, 21, 129, 1. Cf. on the whole question v. Arnim, I, Fr. 179 ff., 552.

[7] ἄνθρωπος εἶ· τοῦτο δ᾽ ἐστὶ θνητὸν ζῷον χρηστικὸν φαντασίαις λογικῶς. τὸ δὲ λογικῶς τί ἐστιν; φύσει ὁμολογουμένως καὶ τελέως.

[8] Bornkamm, *Hermes*, 71, 391.

[9] Pohlenz, I, 116.

[10] The philosophical use is simply a development of the true meaning of the Gk.; on this connection between language and the philosophy of Socrates cf. J. Stenzel, Art. "Sokrates" in Pauly-W., 2, Ser. III, 1 (1927), 822 : "Language is the starting-point of the teaching of Socrates." 829 : "The reciprocal exchange of knowledge is a characteristic of the dialectic of Socrates, of the conversations which are conducted in an attitude of ignorance and which seek to call forth from the other the power of the λόγος." On the original sense of ὁμολογεῖν cf. Hdt., I, 23; I, 171, 5; IV, 154, 1 (agreement with someone in a statement).

τὰ ὁμολογούμενα are agreements by contract, BGU, IV, 1123, 11; 1160, 7. ὁ ὁμολογῶν is the one who makes such an agreement, the party in a compact, BGU, I, 297, 22; 339, 23. ὁμολόγημα is the agreement or compact, CPR, 232, 2; P. Oxy., II, 237; IV, 6. Worth noting is the contractual ratification ἐπερωτηθεὶς ὡμολόγησα. [11]

ὁμολογία has in the pap. the sense of "compact" or "agreement," P. Eleph., 2, 2 : συγγραφὴ καὶ ὁμολογία, P. Ryl., II, 178, 13; P. Fay., 91, 1; P. Tebt., II, 392, 23; P. Oxy., XIV, 1627, 20; P. Strassb., I, 40, 27. The homology is a solemn and public declaration by which a legal relation is contractually established, Ditt. Syll.³, 472, 16 ff.; 647, 65; 945, 42 and 47.

Obviously so varied and general a term is to be found in the religious sphere. One confesses sins (ἁμαρτίαν ὁμολογεῖν), commits oneself to vows (εὐχὴν ὁμολογεῖν). Cf. IG, IV, 542; Plut. Quomodo Quis Suos in Virtute Profectus, 11 (II, 82a) and De Cohibenda Ira, 16 (II, 464b). ὁμολογεῖν — ὁμολογία is not primarily a religious term ; it simply acquires a religious sense. All the same, the usage of a later age betrays the influence of predominantly eastern cultic practices. In the imperial period a series of Lydian and Phrygian inscr. testify to a confession of sin in which a man comes before the priest as the representative of a deity and seeks to propitiate the deity in order to find relief from sickness and infirmity. [12] These oriental inscr. are supported by literary witness, Plut. Apophth. Lac.: Antalcidas, 1 (II, 217d) and Lysander, 10 (II, 229d); Plut. Superst., 7 (II, 168d); Menand. Fr., 109 (CAF, III, 33); Apul. Met., III, 28 and Juv., VI, 532-541 all give evidence of the same oriental piety and outlook. [13] On the inscr. the act of penance before the priest and the ensuing public confession are described as ἐξομολογεῖσθαι and ὁμολογεῖν. [14] Plut. Superst., 7 (II, 168d) has the similar ἐξαγορεύειν τὰς ἁμαρτίας, which is fairly common in Hell. Gk. Juv., VI, 532 ff. speaks of the intercession and penitential requirement of the priest of Isis after a Roman lady has transgressed a specific rule of chastity.

B. The OT-Oriental and Hellenistic-Gnostic Liturgy of Thankoffering.

1. Biblical homology developed originally out of the cultus and liturgy. Here we find both confession of human guilt and also the biblical praise of God. An investigation of the liturgies of sin-offering and thankoffering must take into account not only the literature of Israel but also oriental, Hellenistic and Gnostic songs.

A series of OT psalms like 22; 30; 34; 40; 116, also hymnic pieces outside the Psalter, e.g., 1 S. 2:1-10; Is. 38:9-20; Jon. 2:3-10; Tob. 8:15-17; Sir. 51:1-12 and Lk. 1:46-55, may be regarded as psalms of thankoffering. These are originally psalms which were offered in prayer after deliverance and which accompanied the true sacrifice of thanksgiving. Job 33:26-28 describes how God takes pity on a man in serious danger. Sickness has brought him to the verge of death, but God has mercy. He may see God's face with joy and receives "righteousness." He thus

---

[11] Preisigke Wört., I, 537 f.; Mitteis-Wilcken, II, 1, 76.

[12] Steinleitner, 40; 48; 53. "In the sacral justice administered by the priests of the Maionian cults in the name of the deity, the trial thus ends here as follows. The condemned man, as a sinner, makes confession and writes this confession of his wrongdoing on a stele in public expiation and in praise and thanks for divine power and justice, the stele being then set up in the sacred precincts for everyone to see" (116).

[13] Ibid., 70-74, 75 f.; Schnitzer, 94-105; Pettazzoni. A distinction must be made between public penance and confession of sin as an affront to the deity. In both cases ὁμολογεῖν-ὁμολογία is found on inscr. We also find ἐξαγορεύειν, ἐξομολογεῖν ═ ἐξομολογεῖσθαι.

[14] The confession itself is called ὁμολογία : πενφθεὶς εἰς ὁμολογίαν (Steinleitner, 57, No. 26).

comes before the people and confesses: "I sinned indeed, and violated the law, but was not requited as I deserved. He redeemed my soul from going down into the grave, and my life may see the light with joy" (27 f.). Here is an oriental custom found also in Babylon and Egypt. [15] Confession is similarly found in psalms of complaint both in and outside Israel. To be stricken with sickness is to be punished for sin. It is possible for a man unwittingly to arouse the divine displeasure and thus to be delivered up to evil powers. The one affected turns to the deity and confesses his sin or protests his innocence. He invokes the mercy of God and promises to offer a sacrifice and song of thanksgiving if delivered. [16] The vow is fulfilled and the תּוֹדָה sung at the feast of thankoffering. The hymn begins with invocation of God or a short introductory song. There then follows a description of the distress, the prayer, and the salvation which was its answer, cf. Ps. 116:4; Sir. 51:10; Is. 38:14. The sacrifice as well as the psalm is called תּוֹדָה. Some psalms are directed against a false estimation of sacrifice, cf. 40:6 ff.; 50:8 ff.; 51:16 ff.; 69:31 f. The thanksgiving closes with a summons to those present to magnify Yahweh (Jer. 33:11). This thanksgiving is a duty and takes place only in prescribed sacred words (Ps. 51:15; En. 71:11). It is sometimes emphasised that a new song must extol Yahweh (Ps. 33:2; 40:3 etc.). In this case a song newly inspired by God is sung rather than one already to hand (Ps. 40:3).

2. The history of the liturgy of thanksgiving did not end with the popular religions of the Semitic and oriental world. It entered on a new phase in the Hellenistic religions of redemption. The religious centre is here the myth of the redeemer and belief in the union of redeemer and redeemed. This is new in comparison with the ancient national religions. The soteriological drama is enacted in the cultus.

A good example of Gnostic liturgics is to be found in the song in the Act. Thom. Before this is sung, the apostle prays: "I extol thee, Jesus, that thou hast made me worthy not only of faith but also of bearing many things for thy sake." [17] The connection between this prayer and the hymn which follows is not wholly clear. [18] We find something of the same in the Syr. Acta of the martyrs Cyriacus and Julica (5th cent.). The former is thrown into a vessel full of burning pitch, but then begins to pray. "This is the gate of the Lord; the righteous shall enter in through it." The prayer then breaks off and a new section tells of a myth. Elsewhere, too, the liturgy of Ps. 118 plays a role in Gnostic circles. In the Baruch Book of the Gnostic Justin it is recounted

---

[15] On this whole matter cf. Gunkel, 284-290; Reitzenstein, esp. 157 f., 251-268; Arvedson, 11-20; Grimme, 235. H. Grimme finds in הוֹדָה the two senses of "to confess": "to acknowledge" (sin as obj.) and "to proclaim" (Yahweh or His name as obj.). The meaning "to praise" is not primary in his view, 235. An important non-biblical par. is the text found in the library of Assurbanipal (a thankful song of deliverance with an express description of the earlier affliction), cf. E. Lehmann-H. Haas, Textbuch zur Religionsgeschichte (1922), 311-316; AOT, 273-281. The song begins: "I will praise the Lord of wisdom." Acc. to Grimme the concept of confession did not arise on Israelitish soil, but is of ancient Semitic origin. Is "confession of the name of Yahweh" confession of the names of Yahweh?

[16] Sacrifices are offered acc. to Ps. 116; 118; Jon. 2:10. "When only the psalm is mentioned and not the sacrifice, this does not usually mean that there was no offering, though the psalm is emphasised at the expense of it." Arvedson, 15; S. Mowinkel, Psalmenstudien, VI (1924), 51-58.

[17] Act. Thom., 107 (Hennecke, 277).

[18] E. Preuschen, Zwei gnostische Hymnen (1904); R. Reitzenstein, Hell. Wundererzählungen (1906), 107-111; 117-122; Ir. Erl., 70-76; H. Jonas, Gnosis u. spätantiker Geist, I (1934), 320-326; Arvedson, 46-53.

that the Creator God Elohim cried out when he returned from earth to heaven : "Open the door that I may go in and thank the Lord ; for I believe that I am a lord." Then a voice spoke out of the light : "This is the gate of the Lord ; the righteous shall enter in through it." [19]

In this connection special ref. should be made to the hymns and songs of praise in the Corp. Herm., I and XIII, though the group ὁμολογεῖν — ὁμολογία is not actually used here. [20] I, 31 has the prayer : δέξαι λογικὰς θυσίας ἁγνὰς ἀπὸ ψυχῆς καὶ καρδίας πρὸς σὲ ἀνατεταμένης, ἀνεκλάλητε, ἄρρητε, σιωπῇ φωνούμενε. For the one who prays the words of the hymn are obviously "pure and reasonable sacrifices of the heart." I, 32 concludes with the assurance of faith and witness, with magnifying of the Father who has given all power to the Anthropos. The whole life of the righteous can be described as λογικὴ θυσία, but in particular the inspired hymn of thanks merits this name, though in XIII it is an effusion of the *logos*. When healing, transfiguration and the heavenly journey are completed, the righteous must draw near to God with gifts. But it is the hymn esp. which opens the gate of heaven. The idea of λογικὴ θυσία expresses two motifs : first, it gives inwardness and depth to the concept of thankoffering, since one must offer oneself as a sacrifice ; and secondly it gives special force to the hymn, since this bears witness to God and His *logos*. [21]

C. The Word Group in the LXX and Post-Biblical Judaism.

1. In contrast to profane Gk., ἐξομολογεῖσθαι (noun ἐξομολόγησις) and ἀνθομολογεῖσθαι (noun ἀνθομολόγησις) are more common in the LXX than ὁμολογέω, ὁμολογία, ὁμόλογος, ὁμολογουμένως. Outside the Bible ἐξομολογεῖσθαι can mean only "open" ("public" : ἐξ), "admit" (esp. sins), then "acknowledge," "grant," but never "extol." On the other hand the Heb. יָדָה (hi and hithp) means both "to confess sins" and "to praise God." In transl. the ὁμολογία group is given less prominence because its legal and commercial sense seemed too profane. The noun ὁμολογία occurs in the LXX for נֶדֶר or נְדָבָה, e.g., Lv. 22:18; Dt. 12:6 (B), 17; 1 Εσδρ. 9:8 (δότε ὁμολογίαν δόξαν τῷ κυρίῳ "makes confession of sin"); Am. 4:5; 'Ιερ. 51:25; Ez. 46:12. The verb ὁμολογεῖν as a rendering of תְּנוּ תוֹדָה in Ezr. 10:11 : (often for יָדָה hi, נֶדֶר, שָׁבַע ni) occurs in 1 Εσδρ. 5:58 A (Ezr. 3:11); Job 40:14; 'Ιερ. 51:25; Ez. 16:8 B; with no Heb. original 1 Εσδρ. 4:60; Wis. 18:13; 1 Macc. 6:61 vl.; 2 Macc. 6:6; 4 Macc. 6:34; 9:16; 13:5. For the Semitic linking of confessing sin and praising God cf. 1 K. 8:33, 35; Neh. 9:3; Da. 9:4, 20; Ezr. 10:11. The LXX, too, presupposes that sin is publicly confessed before the congregation, the guilty person is blessed, and the power of God is glorified. Thus the works of God are proclaimed, Ps. 118:17 ff. Perhaps we are to think of the related aretalogy which expresses the power of deity in Hellenism (= δόξα). [22] ὁμολογεῖν and ἐξομολογεῖσθαι in the

---

[19] In the Baruch Book of Justin (Hipp. Ref., V, 26, 15): ἀνοίξατέ μοι πύλας, ἵνα εἰσελθὼν ἐξομολογήσωμαι τῷ κυρίῳ· ἐδόκουν γὰρ ἐγὼ κύριος εἶναι. The ἐξομολογήσωμαι thus becomes a fixed term in oriental and Hell.-Gnostic hymnology, cf. Reitzenstein, 252, n. 1; 251-268; Act. Thom., 107.

[20] W. Scott, *Hermetica*, IV (1936), Index Graecitatis.

[21] On λογικὴ θυσία cf. the exc. in Ltzm. R. on 12:1; Reitzenstein Hell. Myst., 38; Arvedson, 232 f.; → θύω, III, 180.

[22] Helbing Kasussyntax, 242-245. Reitzenstein, 252, n. 1 points out the connection with Hell. aretalogy and thinks the general sense "to praise" (praise of God, esp. LXX) developed out of "to confess." Cf. also Pr.-Bauer³, 459 on ἐξομολογεῖν. In fact the two grew up together from the very first, and it would be hard to show the derivation of the one from the other. On OT confession cf. esp. Gunkel, 265 f. and Arvedson's description of the liturgy of thanksgiving in Israel and the ancient Orient, 11-20. On הוֹדָה = ὁμολογεῖν-ἐξομολογεῖσθαι, Reitzenstein, 258 : "I readily believe that in Israel, too, the song of thanksgiving was at first really offered in the temple ; but this was not always possible.

sense "to praise," "to thank," "to confess," "to extol" (הוֹדָה) are true lexical Hebraisms which had found a home in the usage of the Jewish world to which the LXX belonged, and which raised no difficulties for the Jewish reader.

Invocation of the name (ἐπικαλεῖσθαι τὸ ὄνομα, → III, 499) is an act of prayer and confession in the OT (Jl. 2:32 = R. 10:13). The word for this ἐπικαλεῖσθαι is קָרָא ("to invoke," "to confess," also "to recite"). קָרָא is also a fixed term for the saying of the daily confession. To call on the name of the Lord is to confess the Lord. The name embraces also God's acts and counsel. In the prayers of the OT and Judaism we also find δοξάζειν, ἐπικαλεῖσθαι, εὐλογεῖν, ἐξομολογεῖσθαι, ὑψοῦν, verbs which play a part in the usage of the NT too. One should not overlook the fact that the Jewish prayer is built on the hymn and constantly uses benedictions ("Praised be thou ..."). Since prayer replaced sacrifice in synagogue worship, prayer is called sacrifice (cf. Jos. Ant., 8, 111 f.); in particular the *schema* is sacrifice. [23]

2. In the lit. of later Judaism the group ὁμολογεῖν — ἐξομολογεῖσθαι is often used for penance and confession of sin, cf. Δα. 9:4 and Ps. Sol. 9:6. Jos. maintains: "The Godhead is easily reconciled for those who confess and convert" (ἐξομολογουμένοις καὶ μετανοοῦσιν, Bell., 5, 415). Acc. to Jos. the history of Israel constantly shows that such acknowledgment protects against divine judgment, Ant., 8, 129, 256 f., 362. There is everywhere in Judaism an awareness that penitence and confession go together; thus the whole congregation says penitential prayers on the great Day of Atonement. [24] The penitential prayer is a specific literary genre and a fixed form of prayer. The great men of the past publicly confess their sins before the congregation. e.g., Da. 9:1-19; Jdt. 9:1-14; Bar. 1-3; Tob. 3:1-6, 11-15; Est. 4:17¹-17ᶻ; 3 Macc. 2:2-20; 6:2-15. Even an ungodly king like Manasseh humbles himself before God and utters a prayer of penitence under the stress of divine judgment, cf. 2 Ch. 33:12, 13, 18. This prayer does, of course, tend to become a definite human possibility, a necessary religious exercise which is evaluated and rewarded as such by God. Here human confession is not so much personal testimony to a powerful act of God but rather acknowledgment of the judicial majesty of God and one's own sinfulness. It is futile to try to conceal sins: "Do not be ashamed to confess sins, and do not try to force the flow of the river," Sir. 4:26, 28. What is meant is obviously that God will establish the truth. Sir. 51:1-12 contains a grateful confession of God for His help in deliverance from mortal sickness, and in the Heb. concludes with a long song of praise which has been shortened in the Gk. and Syr. transl. [25] In Philo and Jos. the usage is much the same, since behind ὁμολογεῖν — ἐξομολογεῖσθαι there stands not only penitential practice (confession of sins is included in תְּשׁוּבָה) but also the benediction of the Synagogue and its liturgy of thanksgiving. In Jos. Bell., 7, 418, however, we find the new expression Καίσαρα δεσπότην ὁμολογεῖν, cf. 419: Καίσαρα δεσπότην ἐξονομάζειν. This ὁμολογεῖν Καίσαρα has political and perhaps even religious traits. Its opposite is confession of the one God, 2 Macc. 7:37.

3. In Philo the philosophical influence is plain. On the basis of the Stoic ideal of the ὁμολογουμένως τῇ φύσει ζῆν he demands from the soul a constancy and harmony

---

and not all songs which took this form were rendered thus, or even publicly." On the psalm of Jonah, *loc. cit.*: "Even if we ascribe this psalm to an interpolator, the important question has still to be answered how he could insert as a prayer for deliverance a song of thanks for deliverance — a song which, as long since noted, is not even orientated to the prophet himself or composed with ref. to him."

[23] Harder, 35. On the praise of God in later Judaism, bBB, 14b: "R. Jochanan said she was called Ruth because from her sprang David, who satisfied the Holy One, blessed be He, with songs of praise and thanksgiving." Acc. to the teaching of later Rabb. theology, Hezekiah did not become the Messiah because he did not strike up a song of praise after being delivered from Sennacherib. On eschatological praise cf. Volz Esch., 168, 224.

[24] Cf. Weber, 317, 320; Bousset-Gressm., 389 f.; Sjöberg, 216, 254.

[25] Norden, 277-308; Meyer Ursprung, I, 281; Arvedson, 10 ff. Cf. on what follows Schl. Theol. d. Judt., 147.

like that of God Himself. The saying in Dt. 5:31 applies to the soul : "But as for thee, stand thou here by me." Human acts must be consistent, Deus Imm., 25 : ἐν ὁμολογίᾳ τῶν κατὰ τὸν βίον πράξεων ἔχει τὸ τέλος. Philo thus follows the terminology of Stoicism. More strongly reminiscent of the OT is Ebr., 117: "For concord and harmony there is an important proof in the fact that they offer God the gift, i.e., they appropriately honour being by clear confession." The two kinds of insight are embodied in Judah and Issachar : the former, seeking divine insight, gratefully confesses God, who has given the good in generous measure ; the latter also performs fine acts, Leg. All., I, 80. That Leah bears no more children after the birth of Judah shows that confession of God is a stage of virtue which cannot be transcended. "Thus Judah, the spirit which thanks God and continuously sings Him songs of praise, is itself the holy and honoured fruit, not of a tree of the earth, but of a disposition which is sound and loyal to reason. For this cause it is said of the disposition which bare him that it ceased to bear ; for it had nowhere to turn when it had attained the limit of perfection. For of all the acts which we can bear the best and most perfect product is the hymn to the Father of all things," Plant., 135; cf. Leg. All., II, 95; III, 26. In Leg. All. we find a significant meditation on ὁμολογεῖν : "Judah, the confessing nature (ὁ ἐξομολογητικὸς τρόπος), is immaterial and incorporeal ; for his name, that of the confessor, shows that he confesses something outside himself. For only when the spirit goes out of itself and offers itself to God like the laughing Isaac does it confess true being. But as soon as it regards itself as the cause of something it is far from yielding to God and confessing Him. Confession must not indeed be viewed as a work of the soul, but as a work of God, who brings the sense of gratitude to expression in it. Hence the confessor Judah is immaterial," I, 82. A rich vocabulary (ἐξομολογεῖσθαι, ἐξομολογητικὸς τρόπος, ὁμολογεῖν, ὁμολογία) points to the liturgical and cultural background of the word group.[26] But apart from these solemn expressions we often find confessions of the soul in Philo : that all actions and designs are effected by God, and nothing takes place in its own strength (Leg. All., II, 95); that God is the cause only of the good, not of all things (Agric., 129); that God is merciful and grants man all things when he achieves perfection and reaches the goal (Sacr. AC, 42, cf. Gen., 33, 11). In Philo ὁμολογεῖν can mean God's "solemn declaration" in Scripture (Det. Pot. Ins., 60; Abr., 275; Leg. All., III, 77, 187; Gig., 29) as well as man's promise towards God (Sacr. AC, 72). The prophets too (e.g., Moses) make such express and solemn declarations in Scripture (Op. Mund., 25; Sacr. AC, 118; Abr., 203). The word naturally occurs with ref. to "confession of sin" (Leg. All., II, 78; III, 66 f.; Exsecr., 163; Conf. Ling., 116). We also find ὁμολογεῖν as "to admit," not in the sense of rhetorical dialogue, but in that of agreement and affirmation, the opp. being to suspend judgment (ἐπέχειν) or to negate a statement (ἀρνεῖσθαι), cf. Ebr., 192, 200. The noun ὁμολογία (plur. ὁμολογίαι) corresponds to the verb ὁμολογεῖν. A religious use is reflected here too, Mut. Nom., 220 : τὰς εὐχαρίστους ὁμολογίας ποιεῖσθαι, Vit. Mos., I, 253 : χαριστήριοι ὁμολογίαι. In Ebr., 39 ὁμολογίαι θεοῦ are God's solemn promises to man, though ὁμολογίαι can also be used for man's promises and commitments to God, Ebr., 107; Congr., 177; Leg. All., I, 82; Mut. Nom., 57. In the profane sense ὁμολογία means "engagement" or "contract" (Spec. Leg., I, 107; III, 72; Vit. Mos., I, 242), and in a more Gk. sense it can express the agreement of one thing with another, Sacr. AC, 3; Spec. Leg., III, 155; Vit. Mos., II, 140; Deus Imm., 25.

4. The praise of God also plays a role in apocalyptic and in the eschatologically orientated writings of later Judaism. En. 61:9-12 tells how the praise of God will ac-

---

[26] For details of Philo's use of ὁμολογεῖν, ὁμολογία, ὁμολογουμένως, ἐξομολογεῖσθαι, ἐξομολόγησις, ἐξομολογητικός (τρόπος) cf. Bornkamm, Zorn Gottes, 247. The concept has extraordinary significance for Philo ; he can unite in it his Stoically coloured ideal of harmony, his synagogue's confession of the God of the patriarchs, and his form of expression in rhetorical dialogue. Each of these components contributes positively to his concept of ὁμολογεῖν-ὁμολογία. Cf. the use in 4 Macc. 6:34; 9:16; 13:5. In 9:16 there is a forensic nuance, in the other two a philosophical (Hellenistic).

company the just judgment of the Lord of spirits : "Then all will speak with one voice and extol, exalt and praise the name of the Lord of spirits. He will summon the whole host of the heavens, all the saints in the heights, the host of God, the cherubim, seraphim and ophanim, all the angels of strength, all the angels of dominions, the elect and the other powers which are on dry land and above the water. And in that day they will lift up one voice and praise, extol, laud and magnify in the spirit of faith, wisdom, patience, mercy, right, peace and goodness, and all will say with one voice : Praise him, and the name of the Lord of spirits be praised to all eternity." In other places, too, the coming of the Judge of the world is accompanied by this praise : "All who dwell on dry land will fall down before him and worship and praise, extol and sing praise to the name of the Lord of spirits," En. 48:5. "They lauded him (the Messiah) with one voice, exalted and extolled him with wisdom, and showed themselves wise in speech and in the spirit of life," En. 61:7. These traditions in En. bear some relation to Is. 45:23 = Phil. 2:10 f. But such praises are also the sign of a transformation in man. In rapture Enoch falls on his face, his whole body dissolves, and his spirit changes : "I cried with a loud voice, with the spirit of power, and blessed, extolled and exalted him. But these praises which came forth from my mouth were well-pleasing to the Ancient of days," En. 71:11 f. For other instances of this eschatological praise cf. En. 39:7; Sib., 5, 428.

D. The Word Group in the NT.

I. ὁμολογεῖν.

1. ὁμολογεῖν = "to assure," "to promise," "to admit," "to concede."

Mt. 14:7: ὅθεν μεθ᾽ ὅρκου ὡμολόγησεν αὐτῇ δοῦναι. The compound ἐξομολογεῖν is used in the same way in Lk. 22:6 : καὶ ἐξωμολόγησεν. Ac. 7:17: τῆς ἐπαγγελίας ἧς ὡμολόγησεν ὁ θεὸς τῷ Ἀβραάμ (ἐπηγγείλατο P⁴⁵ DE; ὤμοσεν ℵ). Agraph., 18 : ὁ ὁμολογήσας μὴ γῆμαι ἄγαμος διαμενέτω. A solemn ὁμολογεῖν of this kind binds the speaker to his word. This general use is in the first instance Hellenistic and not cultic ; ὁμολογεῖν shades into ἐπαγγέλλεσθαι and ὀμνύναι (Ac. 7:17; Hb. 6:13). It is not always easy, however, to fix the precise sense in a given case, especially in view of the fact that primitive Christian usage can often influence the term. The antithesis ὁμολογεῖν-ἀρνεῖσθαι is already Hellenistic and general (cf. Ael. Nat. An., II, 43; Jos. Ant., 6, 151), but in Jn. 1:20 it must be understood in the light of the Gospel. The Greek sense "to state solemnly," "to affirm," "to attest" (Plat. Symp., 202b; 4 Macc. 13:5; Dg., 2, 1) calls for notice, but the distinctiveness of Johannine theology has also to be taken into account in our interpretation. We must not make too strong a differentiation from the word group μαρτυρεῖν-μαρτυρία (Jn. 1:7, 15, 19). These solemn declarations belong to the circle of witness to Christ.

Primitive Christian usage may be discerned also in Hb. 11:13 : ὁμολογήσαντες ὅτι ξένοι καὶ παρεπίδημοί εἰσιν ἐπὶ τῆς γῆς. On the one side ὁμολογεῖν is admission and solemn confirmation in the Hellenistic sense, on the other (cf. Ac. and Hb.) it is solemn declaration of faith in the Christian sense of proclamation. Note should be taken of, e.g., 1 Jn. 1:9 : ἐὰν ὁμολογῶμεν τὰς ἁμαρτίας ἡμῶν. In the first instance this ὁμολογεῖν is the opposite of the contesting of sin in 1:8. We admit that we are sinners and disclose specific sins in confession ; there is an obvious connection with the general expression ἐξομολογεῖσθαι τὰς ἁμαρτίας. We are thus in a distinctive tradition shaped by the OT and LXX.

2. ὁμολογεῖν = judicially "to make a statement," in the legal sense "to bear witness."

The legal sense of ὁμολογεῖν is perhaps the most important in the NT tradition.

It is shaped by the Gospel tradition and presupposed and adopted in the apostolic and post-apostolic writings. Q has preserved a saying of Jesus which in strictly parallel members sets the disciple's confession or denial under eschatological promise or eschatological judgment, Lk. 12:8; Mt. 10:32.[27] Whereas in the Q tradition confession and denial are mutually related as positive and negative members, in Mk. 8:38 the admonition is purely negative in form, ὁμολογεῖν does not occur, and ἀρνεῖσθαι is replaced by ἐπαισχύνεσθαι. In Q Jesus demands that the disciple confess Him in the hour of trial (before the judgment, publicly, before men); He rejects denial of discipleship. In the last judgment the confession or denial of the disciple will be rewarded by the Son of Man as Judge of the world (Lk. 12:8), or it will be confirmed and disclosed to the Father by Jesus as the eschatological Witness (Mt. 10:32). In all the sayings importance is attached to the correspondence between human conduct here on earth and the eschatological word of the Judge or Witness, though ὁμολογεῖν can take on different nuances according to the metaphor used. The decisive thing is the correspondence, not the nuance determined by the metaphor. In this context ὁμολογεῖν denotes an act of proclamation in which the concrete relation of man to Jesus is expressed in binding and valid form. Definitive importance is thus ascribed to the disciple's confession here on earth. Rev. 3:5 takes up this saying of the Lord, without altering the Palestinian Semitic peculiarities, in a victorious cry. Similar sayings in which Jesus refers to Himself as eschatological Witness or Judge may be found elsewhere, e.g., Mt. 7:23 (using a form of synagogue excommunication): καὶ τότε ὁμολογήσω αὐτοῖς ὅτι οὐδέποτε ἔγνων ὑμᾶς (cf. Mt. 25:12).[28] In this word of testimony Jesus breaks off all fellowship with the disciple.[29]

---

[27] Worth noting in this Q saying are a pronounced Aramaism (Heb. לְ הוֹדָה,, Jewish Aram. אוֹדִי Chr. Syr. אַוְדִי) and the Palestinian Semitic colouring (ἔμπροσθεν). ὁμολογεῖν ἐν in Mt. 10:32; Lk. 12:8 is in keeping with Aram. and Syr. speech forms, Moulton, 169; Bl.-Debr. § 220, 2; E. Nestle, ZNW, 7 (1906), 279 f.; 8 (1907), 241; 9 (1908), 254; Pr.-Bauer³, 943; cf. also ἔμπροσθεν (Rev. 3:5 ἐνώπιον). ἔμπροσθεν used prepositionally is a standard expression for standing before the judge. In form the saying about confession is like the "rules" in Mt. 5:22, 28; 7:8, 24, more esp. those modelled on the schema of correspondence, Mt. 6:14 f.; 7:1, Bornkamm, Wort Jesu, 112. In the view linked with the saying there is ref. to a heavenly judgment scene corresponding to the earthly. In the NT ἐπαισχύνεσθαι or ἀπαρνεῖσθαι is often the antonym of ὁμολογεῖν, just as μὴ αἰσχύνεσθαι is often used for ὁμολογεῖν. Cf. Mk. 8:38 (Lk. 9:26): ὃς γὰρ ἐὰν ἐπαισχυνθῇ με καὶ τοὺς ἐμοὺς λόγους, R. 1:16: οὐ γὰρ ἐπαισχύνομαι τὸ εὐαγγέλιον, 2 Tm. 1:8: μὴ οὖν ἐπαισχυνθῇς τὸ μαρτύριον τοῦ κυρίου ἡμῶν μηδὲ ἐμέ, Hb. 2:11: οὐκ ἐπαισχύνεται ἀδελφοὺς ... καλεῖν, 11:16: οὐκ ἐπαισχύνεται αὐτοὺς ὁ θεὸς θεὸς ἐπικαλεῖσθαι αὐτῶν. In all these instances the point at issue is not psychologically caused shame but the refusal or non-refusal of witness. Is the usage influenced by the dominical saying in Mk. 8:38 (Lk. 9:26)? Or is it better to speak of the influence of a specific Synoptic usage?

[28] The judgment saying in Mt. 7:23 finds a par. in Mt. 25:12 (and 25:41) though ὁμολογήσω is not used here. On the meaning of Mt. 7:23; 25:12 in the Palestinian Rabb. tradition, cf. Str.-B., I, 469. In general one has not only to seek the occurrences of ὁμολογεῖν but also to consider passages which deal with the essential point at issue. Thus in Peter's confession in Mk. 8:27-30 and par. there is no ref. to the word group but the point at issue is the same. In Mk. 8:38 and par. we have a warning pointing in the same direction as Mt. 10:32 f. even though the term is not used.

[29] Bornkamm, Wort Jesu, 113: "Hence confessing and denying have nothing whatever to do with mere acquaintance — Peter does not even accept this in answer to the maid (14:68) — but include a previous relationship of obedience and fidelity." Cf. H. Schlier, → ἀρνεῖσθαι, I, 470.

John's Gospel continues an ancient usage when it says that the Jews expel from the synagogue those who publicly confess Jesus as the Messiah (αὐτὸν ὁμολογεῖν Χριστόν), 9:22; 12:42. Refusal of public witness in the hour of trial, if due to fear, is tantamount to denial (μὴ ὁμολογεῖν = ἀρνεῖσθαι) according to Jn. [30] It is assumed that public confession of Christ leads to honour with God, whereas denial or refusal of witness is grounded in the desire for honour among men, Jn. 5:44; 12:43. Honour with God and honour among men are just as mutually exclusive in Jn. as are God and Mammon in the Synoptists (Mt. 6:24; Lk. 16:13; cf. Mt. 23:6-8). Here again we are in the sphere of Palestinian Judaism. [31] Judicial admission is also at issue in Ac. 24:14: ὁμολογῶ δὲ τοῦτό σοι, ὅτι ... οὕτως λατρεύω τῷ πατρῴῳ θεῷ. Paul confesses that as a Christian he serves the God of the fathers, interprets the Law and the prophets, and expects the resurrection of the just and the unjust. According to this verse Christianity is a particular way of confessing the God of the fathers.

3. ὁμολογεῖν = "to make solemn statements of faith," "to confess something in faith."

In R. 10:9-10 (expounding Dt. 30:14) Paul refers to the connection between confession and faith: "If thou confess with thy mouth the lordship of Jesus, if thou believe in thine heart that God has raised him from the dead, thou shalt be saved. For with the heart man believes and receives righteousness, with the mouth he confesses to salvation." [32] Faith and confession are similarly related elsewhere in Paul (2 C. 4:13). Confession and the word of proclamation grow out of faith. The reverse sequence is presented by the quotation (mouth and heart). In a special way, however, confession stands under eschatological responsibility (2 C. 4:14) and the promise of eschatological salvation (R. 10:9-10). That it confers eschatological salvation corresponds to the Synoptic tradition. Ac. 23:8 states that there was a difference of opinion between the Sadducees and the Pharisees. The Sadducees contested the resurrection (λέγουσιν μὴ εἶναι ἀνάστασιν) but they were opposed by the Pharisees with their doctrinal confession of eschatological truths relating to the world to come (ὁμολογοῦσιν τὰ ἀμφότερα). The related use in Hb. 13:15 is perhaps to be construed in the same way: "The fruit of the lips which

---

[30] Here is a contact with Gk. and Hell. usage, where ὁμολογία or ὁμολογίαι can denote the contract, agreement or ratification, → 202 and Preisigke Wört., I, 537 f. But even as a final word ὁμολογεῖν never loses the positive character of "ministering witness," for "it is also penitence and praise, witness and prayer." "It is that until, in extremes, the saying of Jesus applies: Shake off the dust from your feet (Mt. 10:14). Then, of course, there is only silence" (F. K. Schumann, ThStKr, 108 [1937/38], 190).

[31] Str.-B., II, 553-556. On the Johannine ὁμολογεῖν Χριστόν cf. K. Bornhäuser, Das Joh.-Ev., eine Missionsschrift für Israel (1928), 49: "Note the formula: ὁμολογεῖν Χριστόν, i.e., to speak ἐν παρρησίᾳ. Mere allusion to Him as the Christ which does not expressly name Him as such makes the danger of being expelled from the synagogue less acute, just as in the case of Jesus Himself references to His being the Messiah did not bring about the catastrophe, but only the open confession: I am the Christ." In Jn. ὁμολογεῖν is in fact connected with candid speech (= ἐν παρρησίᾳ λαλεῖν) in 7:13, 26; 10:24; 11:14; 16:25, 29; 18:20. → παρρησία is a sign of genuine confession and true proclamation of God's Word, Ac. 2:29; 4:29, 31; 28:31.

[32] Concrete confession is emphasised in B by the reading τὸ ῥῆμα ἐν τῷ στόματί σου ὅτι Κύριος 'Ιησοῦς. What is meant is the primitive Christian confession of Christ's lordship, 1 C. 12:3. R. 10:13 = Jl. 2:32 corresponds also to the high estimation of confession, esp. the shᵉma, in later Judaism. He who says the shᵉma correctly, at the right time, is a son of the future world, Sheq., 47c, 45; bBer., 61b, Harder, 14.

confess his name" (καρπὸν χειλέων ὁμολογούντων τῷ ὀνόματι αὐτοῦ). [33] God's name is mentioned, proclaimed, acknowledged and extolled in prayer and the offering of praise. Tt. 1:16 is to be taken in the same way. The false teachers claim to know God, but their word and work contradict one another. Their word confesses God, their work denies Him (θεὸν ὁμολογοῦσιν εἰδέναι, τοῖς δὲ ἔργοις ἀρνοῦνται).

The style of the Johannine Epistles especially belongs to the sphere of primitive Christian confession. ἀρνεῖσθαι is here used to express the disputing of a christological tenet, whereas ὁμολογεῖν denotes the acceptance and proclamation of a specific anti-heretical thesis. He who denies that Jesus is the Christ is a liar; he who denies the Father and the Son is antichrist (1 Jn. 2:22). We have before us a didactic style which defines and distinguishes afresh the terms ψεύστης and ἀντίχριστος in the concrete contemporary situation of the community. These theses, fashioned in the conflict with Gnosticism and Judaism, presuppose a specific confessional use of the two terms ὁμολογεῖν and ἀρνεῖσθαι. ὁμολογεῖν is acceptance of a specific christological understanding, while ἀρνεῖσθαι is the contesting of an acknowledged ecclesiastical truth. According to 1 Jn. 4:2 f. the spirits must be tested whether they are from God or not, cf. 1 C. 12:3. Only the spirit which affirms the christological truth that Jesus Christ has come in the flesh is from God. But the spirit which does not confess Jesus (πᾶν πνεῦμα ὃ μὴ ὁμολογεῖ τὸν Ἰησοῦν) [34] is not from God. In these Johannine theses we obviously have a solemn proclamatory statement; they seek to express a specific truth, the only possible relation to Christ. The anti-heretical understanding of ὁμολογεῖν is very closely linked with the cultic and liturgical understanding. 1 Jn. 4:15 shows that these kerygmatic statements are in no sense to be taken intellectualistically. Only he who confesses that Jesus is the Son of God has true fellowship with God. 2 Jn. 7 ff. (οὗτός ἐστιν ...) as well as 1 Jn. 2:22 f. shows that Jn. defines both men and concepts in a fixed way. It is stated apocalyptically in 2 Jn. 7 that false teachers who do not accept the christological *kerygma* (οἱ μὴ ὁμολογοῦντες) have gone forth. ὁμολογία, then, has divisive power. Jn. is not seeking to define a specific doctrine dogmatically, but by a firm formulation of the *kerygma* to overcome the error of false teaching, to bring the opponent to decision, and so to proclaim the old truth in a new situation that its full saving significance is expressed. The real point in the act of confession is the whole truth attested in individual confessional formula. Though confession divides and distinguishes as solemn proclamation, it is still praise and acknowledgment of the work of Christ; it does not express the self-assertion of the Church. Confessions in the anti-heretical liturgical sense are new only in form. In substance they are still concrete ecclesiastical truth unfolded in solemn proclamation.

The witness of Jesus at His trial is also viewed as confession (1 Tm. 6:13: τοῦ μαρτυρήσαντος ἐπὶ Ποντίου Πιλάτου τὴν καλὴν ὁμολογίαν). The false

---

[33] Perhaps the offering of praise in Hb. 13:15 is to be seen as an answer to Christ's sacrifice present at the celebration of the Lord's Supper. "The addition is obviously designed to say that the community's offering of praise consists for God in the worshipping confession of the name which is given Christ by God, i.e., that of the Son (1:4)" (Bornkamm, *Bekenntnis*, 61). But Hb. 13:15 refers to God, not Christ.

[34] In 1 C. 12:3 as well as 1 Jn. 4:2-3 an existing formula of confession in the Church is used to divide the spirits in the community. A specific ὁμολογία in the community is the judge of prophetic claims (hence πνεῦμα). At 1 Jn. 4:3 the Lat. witnesses (vg Iren), also Cl. Al. and Orig., read λύει instead of μὴ ὁμολογεῖ. For bibl. cf. Wnd. Kath. Br., *ad loc.*

witness of His opponents (ψευδομαρτυρεῖν, Mk. 14:56) and the denial of the disciple (ἀρνεῖσθαι, Mk. 14:68) stand in sharp contrast to the καλὴ ὁμολογία of Jesus Christ (Mk. 14:62; 15:2). The καλὴ ὁμολογία, i.e., the confession which is ordained, accepted and confirmed by God, consists in a solemn and binding statement that Jesus is the Christ, the Son of God, Mk. 14:62, cf. Mk. 8:29; Mt. 16:16; Mk. 15:39; Mt. 27:54; Jn. 11:27. ὁμολογεῖν and μαρτυρεῖν are very closely related, 1 Tm. 6:12, 13; Jn. 1:19, 20. [35] This confession of Christ, which is judicially pronounced before the authorities, is the model of forensic confession to which the Christian is called in discipleship (Mt. 10:32; Lk. 12:8), the example of public declaration which the one who bears witness knows that he is obliged to make (Jn. 1:20; 9:22; 12:42), and also the basic constituent in the liturgical and cultic baptismal confession which is solemnly recited at reception of the sacrament and ordination. Here, too, a decisive role is played by the fact that this confession is public (1 Tm. 6:12: ἐνώπιον πολλῶν μαρτύρων, Mt. 10:32: ἔμπροσθεν τῶν ἀνθρώπων, ἔμπροσθεν τοῦ πατρός μου, Lk. 12:8: ἔμπροσθεν τῶν ἀγγέλων τοῦ θεοῦ), binding (the apostle in his command [παραγγέλλω] refers back to the confession already made by Timothy, 1 Tm. 6:12 f.), and definitive (Mt. 10:32; Lk. 12:8; 1 Tm. 6:12 f.). [36] Just because Timothy has made this binding confession he is committed to passing on the proclamation, keeping the commandment and walking without blame until Christ is manifested.

Confession is often the answer to a question. Thus in baptism it is a reply to the question put by the minister. In the teaching conversation between Jesus and the disciples recorded in Mt. 16:13-20 (which does not contain the liturgical and confessional ὁμολογεῖν) Jesus Himself is the questioner. In Jn. 1:19-34 we also find alongside one another witness in the form of answer and sayings embedded in a particular situation. At Ac. 8:37 some MSS record an express dialogue between the minister and the candidate, obviously in a fixed form of words. [37] The authentic confession: σὺ εἶ ὁ Χριστὸς ὁ υἱὸς τοῦ θεοῦ τοῦ ζῶντος (Mt. 16:16), is answer to a question, rejection of other human possibilities, insight of the Holy Spirit, revelation (ἀποκάλυψις), commitment to discipleship, scriptural exposition in power, final and definitive word, subscription and seal. If the disciple is always questioned personally, he answers representatively in the name and on the commission of the community. Even though Peter's saying is the personal gift of God in a specific situation, it becomes the saying of the community. Peter speaks as the first among the μαθηταί, as a member of the Messianic ἐκκλησία.

---

[35] It should be noted that this confession of Jesus, too, is the expounding or revealing of something hidden, so that confession becomes public as an event which is not just significant as the convincing of opponents (in this case they were not in fact convinced). The καλὴ ὁμολογία, then, is not καλή because it has persuasive power but because God demands it and man fulfils this command of His. Here, too, Jesus bears witness to the truth, Jn. 18:37.

[36] Bornkamm, Bekenntnis, 58 on the concept of confession: "Homology has here the connotation of a binding public declaration by which a legal relation is contractually established. It always has as content that around which the relation of two partners moves, i.e., is newly ordered with legal force. In the act of homology a binding and definitive affirmation is freely given, beyond which there is nothing further to say which might be of importance for the legal relation here established."

[37] O. Cullmann, Die Tauflehre d. NT (1948), 65-73 sees in Ac. 8:36 f. the oldest baptismal ritual (οὐδὲν κωλύει = nihil obstat). The variety and growth of christological confessional formulae in the NT is significant, cf. Mt. 16:16 and par.; Ac. 8:37; Jn. 6:69; 1 Jn. 4:2 f., Norden, 143-206; Stauffer Theol., 92-96.

It must be conceded, of course, that knowledge of the message does not as such include genuine confession (Mt. 10:19; Jn. 12:42), and indeed that true confession is no protection against future denial. [38] In openly confessing the authority of Jesus, one takes His side in the battle of spirits. The word of confession thus has divisive force, 1 C. 12:3. [39] If Israel in the shema confesses the lordship of God (Dt. 6:4), Paul weaves the "one God" and "one Lord" into a unity, 1 C. 8:6; Eph. 4:5 f. Confession of Christ's lordship has in view especially His resurrection and exaltation (R. 10:9; Phil. 2:11). The confession is thus linked with a series of christological formulae which developed historically and bear different senses. Behind every act of confession stands Christ Himself as the true Witness (Rev. 1:5) who as the prototype of history, the bearer of God's Spirit, and the eschatological Witness and Judge, sustains the community's confession.

New insights are yielded by the very fact that primitive Christian proclamation (κήρυγμα) and teaching (διδαχή) are described and depicted as confessing (ὁμολογεῖν) and witnessing (μαρτυρεῖν). All such terms as κηρύσσειν, εὐαγγελίζεσθαι, ὁμολογεῖν, μαρτυρεῖν have a proclamatory character which expresses a commitment and an obligation, a bond and a claim. [40] They all find their starting-point in an event of history vouched for by a specific tradition. They interpret this event and prevent its evaporation into myth and theory. In the confession of the community is a new and genuine historicity far surpassing all false traditionalism and intellectualism, all the non-obligatoriness of mere opinion and all mythology. In the last resort there is in the variety of meaning a theological unity which confers on man a true self-understanding and which at the same time integrates him into an eschatological fellowship to the praise of God.

---

[38] This is taught not merely by the story of Peter in the NT but also by the history of the Church in times of special trial.

[39] "In 1 C. 12:3 Paul sets alongside the call ἀνάθεμα Ἰησοῦς the further call κύριος Ἰησοῦς. This makes sense, as it seems to me, only if ἀνάθεμα and κύριος are words which occur in the language of acclamation. This can be shown," E. Peterson, Εἷς θεός (1926), 147, n. 1. On the whole passage cf. L. Brun, Segen u. Fluch im Urchr. (1932), 118-124. The connections between prayer and confession are worked out in Harder, 105-108. "Judaism developed a special form of confessional prayer, the schema. It is important to note that in Pauline prayers not only does there begin to crystallise a primitive form of Christian confession : 'The Lord is Jesus,' but also that confession as such is highly regarded by Paul, and furthermore that it is thought of along Jewish lines. What Paul, quoting Joel, says about calling on the name in R. 10 is related to the confession mentioned by him in 1 C. 12 : 'The Lord is Jesus.' He says of this confession that it guarantees salvation, deliverance (R. 10:9)," Harder, 107. On 1 C. 15:3-5 as confession cf. A. Seeberg, 54 ff.: "It may be shown that in 1 C. 15:3-5 we have the record of a formula" (54). "At one time and place it had a very specific wording" (55). "In the apostolic age the formula was for all a norm of preaching" (56). In fact this might well be an ancient and originally Aram. tradition which Paul reproduces and in some sense expounds and interprets, but he does not call it a "confession" or the "norm of evangelical proclamation."

[40] Acc. to Dt. Is. events of the last time are to take place which will bring with them a new proclamation (διηγεῖσθαι, Is. 43:21), a new acknowledgment of God (ἐξομολογεῖσθαι, 45:23), and a new witness (43:10, 12; 44:8). On the relation of ὁμολογεῖν and μαρτυρεῖν in the NT (→ IV, 497, n. 63), esp. in Jn., there is need for more precise enquiry, since the two terms are used similarly and even synon. in Hell. Gk. In the vocabulary of Jn. μαρτυρεῖν often represents the Synoptic εὐαγγελίζεσθαι (→ II, 717), though ὁμολογεῖν cannot always be used in quite so comprehensive a sense as μαρτυρεῖν. Cf. Jn. 18:28-37; 1 Tm. 6:13.

II. ὁμολογουμένως.

Adv. of the pres. part. pass. of ὁμολογεῖν, "with common consent," "acc. to the judgment of all," Thuc., VI, 90, 3; Xenoph. An., II, 6, 1; Plat. Menex., 243c; Diod. S., 13, 27, 4; Epict. Diss., I, 4, 7; Vett. Val., 168, 17; Ep. Ar., 24; Jos. Ant., 1, 180; 2, 229; 4 Macc. 6:31; 7:16; 16:1; P. Par., 15, 66; P. Tor., I, 5, 32; W. Crönert, Memoria Graeca Herculanensis (1903), 241.

The common Hellenistic term ὁμολογουμένως occurs only once in the Past., where it serves to introduce the hymn to Christ in 1 Tm. 3:16: ὁμολογουμένως μέγα, "confessedly great" (Vg manifeste magnum) is the mystery of the Christian faith. The mystery of Jesus Christ is declared in the worship of heaven and earth, angels and men. [41] Perhaps there is here for primitive Christianity an echo of the concept of ὁμολογία.

III. ἀνθομολογεῖσθαι and ἐξομολογεῖσθαι τῷ θεῷ.

1. ἀνθομολογεῖσθαι occurs in profane Gk. with many meanings (mid. "to agree," "to reach agreement," "freely to admit," "to express thanks for something"): Plut. Aem., 11 (I, 260b); Diod. S., 1, 70, 6; Polyb. and pap. In the LXX: τῷ θεῷ ψ 78:13; Da. 4:37 (alongside ἐξομολογοῦμαι); 3 Macc. 6:33: ἀνθομολόγησις with ἐξομολόγησις, Sir. 17:27 f.

Lk. 2:38 is closest to OT use with its ἀνθωμολογεῖτο τῷ θεῷ (only here in the NT). The praise of Anna is an answer to the act of God (ἀντι-) which she has experienced in her old age. It implies "acknowledgment," "obedience," "proclamation." Along the lines of the piety of the Psalter there is a linking of prayer to God with witness to men. Lk. himself shows what he means by this ἀνθομολογεῖσθαι τῷ θεῷ in 1:46-55, 68-79; 2:29-32. Formally these are psalms of thanksgiving and hymns of praise in the strict sense, but in content they speak of eschatological fulfilment.

2. ἐξομολογεῖσθαι occurs from the 3rd cent. B.C. with various nuances, "to admit," "to confess," "to acknowledge" (act. Lk. 22:6: "to promise"). Subst. ἐξομολόγησις. ἐξομολογεῖσθαι in Plut. Numa, 16, 3 (I, 71a); Eumenes, 17, 7 (I, 594b); Anton., 59, 3 (I, 943d); Luc. Hermot., 75; Jos. Bell., 1, 625; Ant., 8, 256; P. Hibeh, 30, 18 f.; P. Tebt., I, 183; P. Oxy., XII, 1473, 9; P. Flor., I, 86, 11.

NT usage follows the various senses (e.g., ἐξομολογεῖσθαι τὰς ἁμαρτίας, Jos. Ant., 8, 129), but adopts especially the cultic use in divine worship ("to confess," "to extol"). Worth noting is the Pauline usage in R. 15:7-13. Paul himself leads in cultic and liturgical prayer, joining with the Gentiles in praise. [42] All such

---

[41] On the Stoic equation of λογικῶς = φύσει ὁμολογουμένως = τελέως ζῆν (Epict. Diss., III, 1, 25) cf. Bornkamm, Herm., 71, 390. ὁμολογουμένως here always means ὁμολογουμένως τῇ φύσει. A. Seeberg, 113 rejects the transl. "correspondingly great" (as the Church) or "confessionally great" (D ὁμολογοῦμεν ὡς) and thinks that we simply have an interjection "truly." The distinction from 4 Macc. 6:31; Jos. Ant., 1, 180 is incontestable.

[42] All these verbs describe the cultic and hymnic praise which takes place in the community; there is enacted here ἐξομολογεῖσθαι, εὐφραίνεσθαι, αἰνεῖν, ἐλπίζειν ἐπ' αὐτῷ in fulfilment of OT prophecy. Cf. Hb. 2:12, where Christ is the speaker (= Ps. 22:22). On the question of the subj. of ἐξομολογήσομαι cf. M. J. Lagrange, St. Paul Epitre aux Romains (1922), 347; on the language used by Paul in prayer, cf. Harder, 33, 61, 65.

terms as ἐξομολογεῖσθαι, ψάλλειν, εὐφραίνεσθαι, (ἐπ-) αἰνεῖν derive from the OT, especially the Psalms. [43] All genres of Scripture combine to make one solemn witness, as in Rabbinic usage. Also reminiscent of the OT are R. 14:11 and Phil. 2:11, with express reference to Is. 45:23. In the last judgment every tongue will confess God (ἐξομολογήσεται τῷ θεῷ). This confession can mean various things. According to Phil. 2:11 every tongue will acknowledge the lordship of Christ, to the glory of God the Father. That this confession is to God's glory (δόξα) is in keeping with the form and content of homology. [44] Undoubtedly the confession refers to the worship of the community and confession of Christ made in the Holy Spirit, 1 C. 12:3. Where members of the community make this confession, then, they are harbingers of this all-embracing heavenly and cosmic scene. The earthly kahal broadens out into that of the last time.

It should also be recalled that in Rev. solemn songs of praise describe the glory of God and His Christ, 4:8, 11; 5:9, 10, 12, 13; 11:15, 17 f.; 12:10-12; 15:3-4; 19:1 f., 5, 6-8. These songs, too, are homology, though the word group does not occur. A heavenly kahal speaks or sings to God's glory, but its words and songs are a special form of proclamation for the Church militant. These fixed and developed songs express God's Spirit. They are a pledge of final victory and comfort in present affliction. Hence homology is a summons to join in the rejoicing : 12:12 (εὐφραίνεσθε); 19:5 (αἰνεῖτε); 19:7 (χαίρωμεν καὶ ἀγαλλιῶμεν). Christ Himself as Redeemer stands in the midst of the community, prays to God and proclaims His name to the brethren (Hb. 2:12 = Ps. 22:22). The Psalter and the OT generally thus lay down in large measure the form and content of homology. We are pointed in the same direction by the angels' song of praise (Lk. 2:14) and the blessing of Simeon (Lk. 2:29-32) in the nativity stories of Lk.

As psalms often begin with praise to God (ψ 74:1; 110:1, 3; 137:1, 2, 4; Sir. 51:1), so does Jesus' cry of jubilation in Mt. 11:25; Lk. 10:21. Lk. refers to a rejoicing in the Holy Spirit (ἠγαλλιάσατο τῷ πνεύματι τῷ ἁγίῳ), cf. Ac. 2:26; Hb. 1:9 as quotations from the Ps.

> Worth noting in the present tradition is the threefold structure in Mt.: 11:25 f. praise of God who has hid these things (ταῦτα) from the wise and prudent and revealed them to babes ; 11:27 revelation of the authority and knowledge of the Son in disclosure of Christ's uniqueness to the disciple ; 11:28-30 summons to hearers to accept the refreshment of eschatological wisdom. The summons is replaced in Lk. by the blessing of eye-witnesses (10:23 f.). The researches of E. Norden show that the threefold division is not accidental. [45] In distinction from the revelations of oriental Hellenism, which also relates thanksgiving, reception of revelation and an appeal to the hearers (Sir., O. Sol.,

---

[43] On the use of ἐξομολογεῖσθαι as the most important in the group, 1 Ch. 16:4, 8, 34; 23:30; 29:13; 2 Ch. 5:13; 6:24; 7:6; 20:21; 23:12; 30:22; 31:2. Note should be taken of similar and synon. verbs (e.g., αἰνεῖν, εὐλογεῖν, ᾄδειν, διηγεῖσθαι, ἀγαλλιᾶσθαι). In 2 Ch. 23:12 the king is the object of praise. ἐξομολογεῖσθαι is common in Tob. (12:6, 20; 13:3, 7, 8, 10; 14:1, 2, 7). Basic is the use in Ps. (ψ 6:5; 7:17; 9:1; 17:49; 27:7; 29:4, 9; 104:1; 105:1; 117:1 etc.). For the language of prayer cf. also Da. 2:23; 3:25, 89, 90; 4:37; 9:4, 20.
[44] Cf. E. Lohmeyer, Kyrios Jesus, eine Untersuchung zu Phil. 2:5-11 (1928), 57; Harder, 59. Since the text of Is. 45:23 is uncertain (ὁμεῖται along with ἐξομολογήσεται), Phil. 2:10 f. may indicate a different original. In the Jewish alenu prayer, too, the Is. verse is altered, and there is an expression corresponding to the εἰς δόξαν θεοῦ. The conclusion of Phil. reminds us of the heritage of Jewish prayer, Harder, 59.
[45] E. Norden, 277-308; Bultmann Trad., 171 f.

Corp. Herm.), note should be taken of the distinctive feature in the Gospel tradition, namely, that the scribes reject the claim of Jesus (1 C. 1:19 f.). The authority and knowledge of Jesus do not have the same significance as in oriental mysticism. The wisdom to which the hearer is summoned is not a wisdom of the Law (cf. Sir. 51:23 ff.; 24:1 ff.) but of the Gospel. It thus bears within it the marks of the preaching of Jesus. The historical integration and interrelation of the three strophes are debated, but there is an Aram. basis, esp. for the first strophe.

IV. ἐξομολογεῖσθαι τὰς ἁμαρτίας.

In primitive Christian literature the formula ἐξομολογεῖσθαι τῷ θεῷ is not unambiguous. In Phil. 2:11 Paul takes Is. 45:23 in the sense of God's praise, but in R. 14:11 the same quotation denotes the eschatological confession of sins which each must make before the judgment throne of God. Prayer and praise are, of course, closely linked with the confession of sin. From the time of the preaching of John the Baptist public confession of sin is a mark of the conversion which God demands (μετάνοια) and a part of the baptismal act, Mk. 1:5; Mt. 3:6; Ac. 19:18 : ἐξομολογούμενοι καὶ ἀναγγέλλοντες τὰς πράξεις αὐτῶν. It was also a custom to make confession of sin in times of sickness, Jm. 5:16. It is possible that in all these cases free public confession of personal guilt accompanied the use of set penitential prayers.[46]

V. ὁμολογία.

ὁμολογία is a free act of confession of the Gospel or a traditional liturgical form of confession in the community.

In the one occurrence in the basic Pauline corpus (2 C. 9:13) the term is response to the Gospel of Christ, obedience to its message, acceptance of its claim and expression of commitment. The churches will see in the gift of the Corinthians an open witness and confession of this kind, and they will praise God for it. There thus arises a particular occasion for thanksgiving (διὰ πολλῶν εὐχαριστιῶν, 2 C. 9:12) and praising God (δοξάζοντες τὸν θεόν, 9:13). The term, which does not occur at all in the Gospels, is used very broadly here, and has no precise sense. A specific free act of brotherly love can become ὁμολογία to the Gospel. ὁμολογία is also two-sided. It is an answer to God's action in the community, and it is also a witness of the community to the public.

The situation is very different in Hb. Hb. contains the admonition — this is its distinctiveness — to hold fast to the confession : 3:1; 4:14 (κρατῶμεν τῆς ὁμολογίας); 10:23 (κατέχωμεν τὴν ὁμολογίαν τῆς ἐλπίδος). The ὁμολογία of Hb. is a firmly outlined, liturgically set tradition by which the community must abide. We are to think of an ecclesiastical confession of faith or baptismal confession[47] to which the hearers are already committed — the formula of divine sonship (4:14; 6:6; 10:29) is frequently enough attested as the content of the baptismal confession — or possibly of a liturgy of praise which is connected with the various predicates of Christ (3:1; 4:14 f.). In this case the ὁμολογία is identical

---

[46] Ancient Jewish confessions of sin, Yoma, 3, 8; 4, 2; 6, 2. On the discussion whether individual sins should be enumerated on the great Day of Atonement cf. Str.-B., I, 113.

[47] A. Seeberg, 142-151; Bornkamm, ThBl, 56-59. Typical of the context is the assurance that God or Christ will keep His Word and thus keep faith with the confessor, Hb. 10:23; 2 Tm. 2:13; 1 Jn. 1:9.

with the εὐχαριστία which has a firm place in the Lord's Supper in the form of a hymnic confession of Christ, Hb. 1:3; 13:15. Liturgical connections between Hb. and 1 Cl. (36; 61, 3; 64) are quite probable.[48] In any case, ὁμολογία is in Hb., too, a binding word, an expression of obligation and commitment, the answer of the community to the promise of God. The new and distinctive thing in Hb. is the reference to a fixed ὁμολογία which sums up the beliefs of the community as a living word and which has to be held fast.

1 Tm. 6:12 f. describes a primitive Christian gathering in which Timothy has made a good confession (τὴν καλὴν ὁμολογίαν) before many witnesses. The obvious reference is to ordination in which the good confession is made before the congregation.[49] Perhaps the words which follow recall this good confession, for in a solemn liturgical formula the letter speaks of God, who calls all things into life (τοῦ ζῳογονοῦντος τὰ πάντα), and of Jesus Christ, who Himself made a good confession before Pontius Pilate (τοῦ μαρτυρήσαντος ἐπὶ Ποντίου Πιλάτου τὴν καλὴν ὁμολογίαν, → IV, 499). Echoed here are both the forensic form of the confession and also its liturgical and cultic form. At baptism and ordination this solemn commitment before many witnesses has an established place. The hymn in 2 Tm. 2:11-13 is reminiscent of the language and ideas of Mt. 10:32 f.: Christ, who Himself summons to confession, and who Himself made confession, is and remains faithful. "If we deny him, he also will deny us; if we are unfaithful to him, yet he abides faithful; he cannot deny himself." Perhaps the concept of witnesses is also significant in this passage, 1 Tm. 6:12; Hb. 12:1; Rev. 1:5. The μάρτυρες guarantee the solemn and public nature of the scene. They hear and accept the commitment. They will thus speak for or against him who makes confession in the final judgment.

2 Tm. 2:11-13 is a four-membered hymn whose style suggests a Jewish Christian author. The two first and two last members obviously belong together, the two first being orientated to the eschatological promise, the two last to the future attitude of Christ. The third and fourth seem to be in logical contradiction; the third adopts the concept of correspondence in the form of a warning (Lk. 12:9 and par.; Mk. 8:38) whereas the fourth breaks it. That God's faithfulness is greater than man's unfaithfulness is stated elsewhere in R. 3:3; 1 C. 10:13. It is possible, of course, that Christ will put His judgment into effect, i.e., that His faithfulness will be faithfulness to His word. The interpretation that He will keep faith with us is, however, more likely. Perhaps this is an ancient Christian hymn which in the third member is not only bound by tradition but also emphasises the decisive character of faith, thus protecting the promise of covenant faithfulness and forgiveness (fourth member) against abuse. The hymn in

---

[48] P. Drews, Untersuchungen über d. sog. klementinische Liturgie (1906), 23-34; Kn. Cl., 106 f.; Käsemann, 107.
[49] A. Seeberg, 98 and W. Michaelis, Pastoralbr. u. Gefangenschaftsbr. (1930), 89 think in terms of a baptismal confession. J. Jeremias, D. Pastoralbr. (NT Deutsch, ad loc.) favours an ordination confession. The witnesses are not just hearers but men who themselves stand under the confession and embody the community. Cullmann, 20 f. takes a different view: "The whole of the accompanying text shows that this is a judicial process, that Timothy has already made a first appearance in court and 'made a good confession before many witnesses.'" On the twofold structure of the formula cf. Lietzmann, "Symbolstudien," ZNW, 22 (1923), 269; Cullmann, 31, 36: Such formulae owe their existence to the battle against paganism. For primitive Christianity confession of God, who calls all things into life, is not made for its own sake but as a presupposition for what is confessed in the Christian declaration (cf. Herm. s., 11, 23, 4). Cf. J. Jeremias, op. cit., ad loc.

2 Tm. 2:11-13 shows that the saying of Jesus in Lk. 12:8 f. and par. was not misunderstood casuistically.

The point of Jm. 2:14 ff. (πιστεύειν = ὁμολογεῖν) is that confession, far from releasing from obedience, actually demands it.

E. The Word Group in Post-Apostolic Writings.

1. ὁμολογεῖν.

a. "To assure," "to promise," "to admit," "to concede." Dg., 2, 1: καθάπερ καὶ αὐτὸς ὡμολόγησας, "as you yourself have also granted"; Ign. Mg., 8, 1: "If we still live to-day after the manner of Jews, we admit that we have not received grace," ὁμολογοῦμεν χάριν μὴ εἰληφέναι.

b. "To make legal statements," "to bear witness" in the legal sense. Ign. Sm., 5, 1: ὅν τινες ἀγνοοῦντες ἀρνοῦνται, μᾶλλον δὲ ἠρνήθησαν ὑπ' αὐτοῦ, "some deny him (Christ) out of ignorance, or better, they are denied by him, since they are advocates of death rather than truth." The man who does not recognise Christ as "flesh-bearer" denies Him and is thus denied by Him. Hence we have another version of the correspondence between denial and being denied (Mt. 10:33; Lk. 12:9). The eschatological movement is anticipated in the present. The situation of confession and the saying of Jesus with ref. to it (Mt. 10:32 f. and par.) occupy the community a great deal in other places too. Herm. s., 9, 28, 1-8 speaks of believers who have suffered for the name of the Son of God, and of the duty of confession : "All who were led before the authorities and who did not deny in the hearing, but willingly accepted suffering, are glorious to a higher degree in the eyes of God. But all who were fearful and hesitant and considered in their hearts whether they should deny or confess, yet accepted suffering, their fruits are less beautiful, because this thought rose up in their hearts ; for the mere thought of a servant being ready to deny his own master is wicked" (v. 4). The striking thing here is the psychological recasting of the concept as compared with the NT saying. The duty of legal confession is explained in terms of the servant who must not deny his own lord. "Confess that you have a master, that you be not cast into prison as a denier" (v. 7). [50] Herm. thus regards confession as a legal obligation, as an expression of ownership, as relation to a master, and he finds here the basis of the duty. Elsewhere, too, the saying of Jesus in Mt. 10:32 f. and par. keeps alive the fear of denial. 2 Cl., 3, 1-4 contains an admonition not to deny the Lord but to confess Him with works by loving others and keeping the commandments. Acc. to 2 Cl. true confession is not the word of the lips but the work of the heart. The usage in Mart. Pol. is formal : 6, 1: ὧν τὸ ἕτερον (sc. παιδάριον) βασανιζόμενον ὡμολόγησεν, 9, 2 : τοῦ δὲ ὁμολογοῦντος ἔπειθεν ἀρνεῖσθαι, 12, 1: Πολύκαρπος ὡμολόγησεν ἑαυτὸν Χριστιανὸν εἶναι.

c. "To make solemn statements of faith, or to confess something in faith." Reminiscent of Johannine usage is Ign. Sm., 5, 2 : μὴ ὁμολογῶν αὐτὸν σαρκοφόρον; ὁ δὲ τοῦτο μὴ λέγων τελείως αὐτὸν ἀπήρνηται, ὢν νεκροφόρος. ὁ μὴ ὁμολογῶν = ὁ μὴ λέγων is the false teacher who does not agree with the liturgical confession that Jesus is "flesh-bearer" (cf. 1 Jn. 4:2 f.: πᾶν πνεῦμα, ὃ ὁμολογεῖ or ὃ μὴ ὁμολογεῖ). It is probable that in Jn. and Ign. a formula is linked with this liturgical ὁμολογεῖν (ἐν σαρκὶ ἐληλυθότα or αὐτὸν σαρκοφόρον, cf. Cl. Al. Strom., V, 6 and 34). Because there is refusal to participate in this liturgical homology, or to agree to the formula, this μὴ ὁμολογεῖν is also an ἀντιλέγειν, Ign. Sm., 7, 1. False teachers stay away from

---

[50] Dib. Herm., 636 : "δεσμωτήριον is said with intentional ambiguity of the world to come." In Herm. s., 9, 28, 8 ἐάν τις ἀρνήσηται τὸν κύριον ἑαυτοῦ is worth noting ; ἀρνεῖσθαι τὸν κύριον means to contest legal ownership.

the Lord's Supper and common prayer because they do not confess that the Supper is the flesh of our Saviour Jesus Christ which suffered for our sins and which the Father in His goodness raised again, 7, 1. Here, too, we have a fixed liturgical form which found a place in the *eucharistia* of the Supper, cf. the eucharistic sayings in Jn. 6:51 ff., which are liturgical in form. Contradiction of this confession is for Ign. contradiction of the gift of God. It thus brings death ; they die of their disputing (συζητοῦντες ἀπο-θνήσκουσιν, Sm., 7, 1). The man who excludes himself from the Lord's Supper excludes himself from life. Contradiction of the confession kills. Contesting of the liturgical confession is also at issue in Pol., 7, 1, where 1 Jn. 4:2 f.; 2 Jn. 7 are quoted as a basis, and then the corresponding formulae of excommunication are added (ὃς ἂν μὴ ὁμολογῇ τὸ μαρτύριον τοῦ σταυροῦ ..., ὃς ἂν ... λέγῃ μήτε ἀνάστασιν μήτε κρίσιν ...). The opp. in 7, 2 is the doctrine handed down from the very first along with prayer and fasting, which overcome temptation. Christological gainsaying is a temptation, cf. already Jn. 6:66. The confession is the stone of offence which runs contrary to carnal thinking. The community must keep to the word which has been solemnly handed down (προσ-καρτερῶμεν τῇ ἐλπίδι ἡμῶν, Pol., 8, 1, cf. Hb. 10:23 : κατέχωμεν τὴν ὁμολογίαν τῆς ἐλπίδος. Jesus Christ is hope in the absolute). 2 Cl., 3, 2 ff. quotes the dominical saying in Mt. 10:32 and interprets it as the claim to a new work and a fulfilment of the divine commands (ἐν τοῖς ἔργοις αὐτὸν ὁμολογῶμεν, 4, 3). 2 Cl. thus stands in some tension to solemn liturgical homology. It is not enough merely to honour Christ with the lips ; He must be honoured with the whole heart and mind, 3, 4.

2. ἐξομολογεῖσθαι τῷ θεῷ or τὰς ἁμαρτίας.

Like ἀγαλλιᾶσθαι, ἐξομολογεῖσθαι τῷ θεῷ found a place in the liturgy and cultus, as its use in post-apost. lit. shows. 1 Cl., 26, 2 quotes : καὶ ἐξαναστήσεις με, καὶ ἐξομολογήσομαί σοι. The miracle of the resurrection is acknowledged and proclaimed. Instructive is 1 Cl., 52, 1-3. The thesis is first advanced that the Lord needs nothing but the bringing of praise (ἐξομολογεῖσθαι αὐτῷ).[51] This is based on biblical quotations (the Ps. as in 1 Cl., 48, 2 and Barn., 6, 16). Then follows an enumeration of various acts (the Ps.), such as bringing to God the sacrifice of praise, fulfilling vows to God, calling on Him in the day of trouble, or extolling Him, which can all be brought under the concept of ἐξομολογεῖσθαι (52, 1 and 2). In this passage we can see plainly the idea of praise to God and the usage based on the Ps. and the OT generally. How fixed this ἐξομολογεῖσθαι is may be seen in Barn., 6, 16 (= ψ 21:22), where, as distinct from LXX and Hb. 2:12, ἐξομολογήσομαι can even replace διηγή-σομαι (or ἀπαγγελῶ). 1 Cl., 61, 3 is perhaps an indication of the christological style of homology : "We praise thee through the High-priest and Guardian of our souls, Jesus Christ, through whom glory and majesty belong to thee, now and from generation to generation and from eternity to eternity, Amen." Herm. m., 10 orders that sorrow should be rooted out as the sister of doubt and anger. In the mode of Hell. wisdom there is here a description of the way that sorrow drives out the Holy Spirit on the one side but unites with penitence to bring deliverance on the other. In the contrast between the cheerful man and the melancholy man in 10, 3, 1 f. it is said that the latter troubles the Holy Spirit but neither prays to the Lord nor gives Him thanks (ἐξομολο-γούμενος τῷ κυρίῳ).[52]

---

[51] In Hennecke the transl. ἐξομολογεῖσθαι = "to confess sins" at 1 Cl., 52, 1 (p. 498) can hardly be right.

[52] Orig., too, shows acquaintance with the equating of ἐξομολογεῖσθαι and εὐχα-ριστεῖν when he says in Orat., 14, 5 : "An example of thanksgiving (εὐχαριστία) is finally the saying of the Lord : I thank thee, O Father, Lord of heaven and earth, that thou hast hid these things from the wise and prudent, and hast revealed them unto babes ; for the word ἐξομολογοῦμαι is equivalent to εὐχαριστῶ." [J. Betz.]

1 Cl., 50-51 extols the remission of sins and recommends that it is better for a man to confess his sins (ἐξομολογεῖσθαι περὶ τῶν παραπτωμάτων) than to harden his heart (51, 3), so that this confession precedes the praise of God in 52, 1 f. This ἐξομολογεῖσθαι is a further sign that confession of sins is closely linked with praise of God. 2 Cl., 8, 1 ff. contains a summons to conversion and adds that after death it is possible neither to make confession of sin nor to repent, 8, 3. Acc. to Did., 4, 14 == Barn., 19, 12 it is an ancient commandment to make personal confession of sin in the congregation prior to the prayer of intercession, so that one should not come before God with a bad conscience. In Did., 14, 1, too, it is expressly ordered that there should be confession of sin before the breaking of bread and the Eucharist, that the offering may be pure (προεξομολογησάμενοι τὰ παραπτώματα ὑμῶν). Confession of sin is thus an act preparatory to the Eucharist on the Lord's Day. The original προεξομολογησάμενοι carries the sense "as you therein confess your sins." Herm., too, connects prayer and confession of sin, though in another way. In different situations v., 5, 1, 3 and 3, 1, 5 show prayer and confession before God, but in literary connection with the revelation which follows rather than autonomously. s., 9, 23, 4 perhaps points to specific liturgical formulae related to the word of forgiveness : "When our God and Lord, who rules over all things and has power over His whole creation (cf. 1 Tm. 6:13), does not impute to them the sins which they have confessed, but has mercy on them, can man, corruptible and laden with sins, impute evil to another man as though he could condemn or save him ?"

3. ὁμολόγησις, ἐξομολόγησις.

Neither of the 2 nouns occurs in the NT. a. ὁμολόγησις "confession" as act (opp. ἄρνησις) is found in Diod. S., 17, 68; Herm. s., 9, 28, 7: ταῦτα ὑμῖν λέγω τοῖς διστάζουσι περὶ ἀρνήσεως ἢ ὁμολογήσεως, "I say all this to you who are hesitating whether to deny or confess." b. ἐξομολόγησις "avowal or praise of God," cf. Dion. Hal., Plut., esp. LXX for יוֹה, תּוֹדָה, תְּהִלָּה, תְּרוּעָה, e.g., Jos. 7:19; 1 Ch. 25:3; 2 Ch. 20:22; 2 Εσδρ. 22:27 S; Tob. 14:1 S; Jdt. 15:14; Job 8:21; common in Ps., e.g., ψ 41:4; 94:2; 95:6; 99:1, 4; 103:1; 110:3; 146:7; 148:13; Sir. 17:28; 18:28; 39:15; 47:8; 51:10. Herm. uses the noun in his own sense : s., 2, 5 : καὶ λίαν μικρὰν ἔχει τὴν ἐξομολόγησιν καὶ τὴν ἔντευξιν πρὸς τὸν κύριον. The rich man can bring little in the way of thanksgiving or petition before God, but it is different with the poor man : ὅτι ὁ πένης πλούσιός ἐστιν ἐν τῇ ἐντεύξει καὶ τῇ ἐξομολογήσει ("the poor man is rich in prayer and thanksgiving").

4. ὁμολογουμένως.

Dg., 5, 4 : θαυμαστὴν καὶ ὁμολογουμένως παράδοξον ἐνδείκνυνται τὴν κατάστασιν τῆς ἑαυτῶν πολιτείας ("in their whole manner of life they exhibit a wonderful and admittedly most unusual nature").

5. The Word Group in Clement of Alexandria.

Later in Cl. Al. we find ὁμολογεῖν and ὁμολογία used in a way closer to the Gk. sense. ὁμολογεῖν in Cl. Al. means a. "to agree," "to belong together," e.g., Strom., I, 13, 57, 4 : τῷ γένει γε καὶ ὅλῃ τῇ ἀληθείᾳ ὁμολογοῦντα, b. "to concede," "to admit," Strom., IV, 4, 16, 3 : ὅπερ καὶ ἡμεῖς ὁμολογοῦμεν, c. "to promise," Strom., III, 15, 97, 4 ὁ κατὰ πρόθεσιν εὐνουχίας ὁμολογήσας μὴ γῆμαι ἄγαμος διαμενέτω, d. "to confess," Strom., IV, 9, 73, 1 : ὅτι εἰ καὶ μὴ πράξει τινὲς καὶ τῷ βίῳ ὡμολόγησαν τὸν Χριστὸν ἔμπροσθεν τῶν ἀνθρώπων, τῷ μέντοι κατὰ φωνὴν ὁμολογεῖν ἐν δικαστηρίοις καὶ μέχρι θανάτου βασανιζομένους μὴ ἀρνεῖσθαι ἀπὸ διαθέσεως πεπιστευκέναι φαίνονται. In the same way ὁμολογία means "agreement," Strom., VI, 11, 90, 4 : ὁμολογιῶν τε καὶ ἀναλογιῶν εὑρετικήν, "assent," "acceptance," "compact," Strom., IV, 4, 15, 3 : εἰ τοίνυν ἡ πρὸς θεὸν ὁμολογία μαρτυρία ἐστί, πᾶσα ἡ καθαρῶς πολιτευσαμένη ψυχή ... μάρτυς ἐστὶ καὶ βίῳ καὶ λόγῳ. In Strom., IV, 9, 70-73 there is an express exposition of the sayings of the Lord about confession. First Cl. introduces the view of Heracleon, then he adds his own deliberations. [53] ἐξομολογεῖσθαι and ἐξομολόγησις are also fairly common in Cl. Al. Strom. [54]

Michel

---

† ὄναρ

Contents : A. The Dream in the World around Primitive Christianity : I. Dreams and the Interpretation of Dreams in Antiquity : 1. The Problem of Belief in Dreams and Criticism ; 2. The Most Important Books of Dreams ; 3. The Importance of Dreams in the Life of Antiquity : a. The Cultic Dream ; b. The Political Dream ; c. The Dream and Personal Destiny ; 4. The Metaphysics of Dreams ; 5. The Interpretation of Dreams as a Science ; 6. The Dream as a Literary Form ; 7. The Dream Life as a Mirror of the Man of Antiquity. II. Dreams and the Interpretation of Dreams in the OT : 1. The Dream and History ; 2. The Dream as a Regular Means of Revelation in Yahwism ; 3. The Prophetic Criticism of Dreams. III. Dreams and the Interpretation of Dreams in Judaism : 1. Philo ; 2.Hagiography and Apocalyptic ; 3. Josephus ; 4. Rabbinic Judaism. B. The Dream and

---

[53] Cl. Al. Strom., IV, 9, 71, 1: ὁμολογίαν εἶναι τὴν μὲν ἐν πίστει καὶ πολιτείᾳ, τὴν δὲ ἐν φωνῇ, 73, 2 : διάθεσις δὲ ὁμολογουμένη καὶ μάλιστα ἡ μηδὲ θανάτῳ τρεπομένη ὑφ' ἐν ἁπάντων τῶν παθῶν, ἃ δὴ διὰ τῆς σωματικῆς ἐπιθυμίας ἐγεννᾶτο, ἀποκοπὴν ποιεῖται ("This mind declared by confession, esp. if not changed by death, sets aside at a stroke all the emotions which arise by physical desire"). Cf. Herm. s., 9, 28, 7.
[54] Cf. O. Stählin, Cl. Al., IV (1936), 399 (Index of words and subjects, s.v.).

ὄ ν α ρ. Pass., Liddell-Scott, Moult.-Mill., Preisigke Wört., Pr.-Bauer, Prellwitz Etym. Wört., Walde-Pok., s.v. also ὄνειρος, ὀνειρόμαντις, ἐνύπνιον, ἐνυπνιοκριτής κτλ. J. v. Negelein, Art. "Traum" in RGG², V, 1258-1261; Türk, Art. "Oneiros," Roscher, III, 900-910; C. v. Orelli, Art. "Träume bei d. Hebräern," RE³, XX, 13 ff.; Encycl. of Religion and Ethics, V (1912), 28-40, Art. "Dreams and Sleep"; T. Hopfner, Art. "Traumdeutung," Pauly-W., 2. Reihe, VI (1937), 2233-2245; G. van d. Leeuw, Phänomenologie d. Religion (1933), Index, s.v. "Traum"; G. Jacob, "Märchen u. Traum," Beiträge z. Märchenkunde d. Morgenlandes, ed. G. Jacob and T. Menzel, I (1923) (material and bibl.); A. de Buck, De godsdienstige Opvatting van den Slaap inzonderheit in het oude Egypte (Leiden, 1939); A. Volten, "Demotische Traumdeutung" (Pap. Carlsberg XIII and XIV verso), Analecta Aegyptiaca, 3 (Copenhagen, 1942); A. Wikenhauser, "D. Traumgeschichte d. NT in religionsgesch. Sicht" in Pisciculi, Antike u. Christentum, Suppl. Vol. I (1939), 320-333; S. Laukamm, "Das Sittenbild d. Artemidor v. Ephesus," Angelos, 3 (1930), 32-71; J. Hänel, Das Erkennen Gottes bei den Schriftpropheten (1923), 128-142; G. v. Rad, "Die falschen Propheten," ZAW, NF, 10 (1933), 109-120, esp. 118; H. Lewy, "Zu dem Traumbuche d. Artemidoros," Rheinisches Museum, NF, 48 (1893), 398-419; Str.-B., I, 53-63; IV, 326 f. etc. (v. Index); W. Lang, Das Traumbuch des Synesius v. Kyrene (1926); M. Förster, Beiträge z. mittelalterlichen Volkskunde, IV, Archiv f. d. Studium d. neueren Sprachen u. Literaturen, 64 (1910), 39-70; S. Freud, Die Traumdeutung⁷ (1945). For a review of books of dreams → 222 f. Cf. Grösstes u. vollständigstes illustriertes ägyptisches Universal-Traumbuch nach d. ältesten chald., pers., ägypt. u. griech. Hdschr., sowie nach d. bewährtesten mündlichen Überlieferungen zusammengestellt u. mit den dazu gehörigen Figuren versehen. Nebst einem vollständigen Planetenbuch u. allen d. Lotterie betreffenden Erklärungen u. Tabellen (Vienna).

the NT : 1. The Tradition ; 2. The Uniqueness of the NT Understanding of Dreams : a. Paucity of Mention ; b. Absence of Allegorical Dreams and Interpretation ; c. Lofty Nature of Dream Life in the NT. C. Dreams and the Interpretation of Dreams in the Post-Apostolic Period.

The word is used only in the nom. and acc. The other cases are replaced by corresponding forms of ὄνειρος and ὄνειραρ. In the NT we find only the phrase κατ' ὄναρ, Mt. 1:20; 2:12, 13, 19, 22; 27:19 (peculiar to Mt.). On its significance → 224; 235. The etym. is not known. Deriv. from ἀνά Aeol. ὀν "up above" (apparently) and suffix αρ as opp. to ὕπαρ from ὑπό "below" (in reality, cf. ὑπάργυρα χρυσία, gold which in reality, below, is silver),¹ is quite impossible. The initial vowel, though α in Cret., Armen. and Albanian, is an Indo-Europ. o, since the first syllable is unlikely to be Aeolian for ἀν-.² But the meaning is certain enough. Hesych., s.v.: καθ' ὕπνον φαντασία. In the NT only Lk. mentions dreams in addition to Mt. (though cf. Jd. 8), and only in Ac. Lk., however, uses → ὅραμα, not ὄναρ (Ac. 16:9 f.; 18:9), ὅρασις and ἐνύπνιον in the quotation at 2:17. The latter is the usual LXX word for dream, Gn. 37:5 ff.; 41:1 ff.; Ju. 7:13; 3 Βασ. 3:15; ψ 72:20; Jl. 2:28; Δα. 4:5(2) ff. etc. We also find → ὅρασις (Gn. 40:5), → ὅραμα (Nu. 12:6), also the simple → ὕπνος (Gn. 20:3; 3 Βασ. 3:5 etc.), ἐνυπνιάζεσθαι (Is. 29:7 etc.), ὄνειρος only at Wis. 18:17, 19; 2 Macc. 15:11; 4 Macc. 6:5 (Symm. ψ 72:20; Qoh. 5:2, 6), but ὄναρ does not occur. ὄναρ and ἐνύπνιον are gen. synon. The distinction in Artemid. (→ infra) is late and isolated.

A. The Dream in the World around Primitive Christianity.

I. Dreams and the Interpretation of Dreams in Antiquity.

1. The Problem of Belief in Dreams and Criticism.

Belief in the significance of dreams is widespread in antiquity. It is anchored in the metaphysics of dreams. This also explains the tenacity with which belief in dreams is still maintained in the world of modern man, who is so critical in other matters. Yet there was always a note of criticism even in antiquity.

In the very earliest times attempts were made to differentiate between significant dreams and those which were not significant or could not be interpreted. The hieratic book of dreams³ divides dreamers into companions of Horus and Seth, the pious and the ungodly, and gives different interpretations of the same dream for the different classes. This method helps to explain away wrong interpretations. But behind it there stands the final problem whether at least some dreams are not inspired by demonic powers, so that they deceive, or by physical causes (eating, wine, eroticism), so that they are meaningless. Such distinctions are found already in Babylonian interpretation. They are fully worked out by the Gks. Homer sees two gates of dreams, the first of ivory, the second of horn. Dreams which comes out of the former deceive, the others are true.⁴ In the same way Lucian (Vera historia, II, 33) has his travellers find two temples on the island of dreams, one to 'Απάτη and one to 'Αλήθεια. Artemid. distinguishes sharply between the ἐνύπνιον which is to be explained psychologically or physiologically and which is thus without significance, and the ὄνειρος which intimates the future (Oneirocr., I, 1b [3, 1 ff.]). Dietary rules for the regulation of the dream life occur

---

¹ Prellwitz, s.v. ὕπορ.
² Walde-Pok., I, 180; cf. E. Hermann, NGG (1918), 284-286.
³ Pap. Beatty, III, ed. A. H. Gardiner, Hieratic Pap. in the British Museum, III, 1 (1935).
⁴ Od., 19, 562-567. Note the etym. punning : κέρας-κραίνω ("to execute"), ἐλέφας-ἐλεφαίρω ("to deceive").

from the time of Pythagoras. [5] The Mohammedan doctrine of dreams attributes those which intimate destiny to the archangel Gabriel; mere phantoms are traced back to the *dews* (demons), [6] → 233.

Philosophy puts the problem most acutely. Aristot. is mainly sceptical. Cic. De Divinatione is a veritable mine in this regard. [7] In I, 39-65 he advances the arguments for the reliability of intuitions and esp. of dreams, but then in II, 119-148 be opposes to this his own keen-sighted rationalism. As casting lots can give the desired result for all the element of pure chance, and can do so repeatedly, so it may be with the interpretation of dreams. But there is no way of distinguishing between truth and deception. There are three possibilities for the genuineness of dreams, II, 124. The first is direct divine inspiration. But it is more worthy of deity to reveal itself to those who are awake than merely to snorers, among them despisers. In fact dreams spring from the fact that the soul is never wholly at rest even in sleep, but, without direction, arbitrarily produces all kinds of notions. [8] Another possibility is the immanent sympathy of the soul with events. But the uncertainty of interpretation, of which there are graphic instances, is against this. Finally, there is the possibility of an empirical derivation. But attempts in this direction are frustrated by the unmanageably great number of instances. Hence Cic. dismisses the metaphysics of dreams in any form. One does not believe a liar even when he speaks the truth. Should one believe dreams because of occasional prophecies? Cic. is not hereby attacking religion (II, 148): *nec vero ... superstitione tollenda religio tollitur.*

The very criticism shows how deeply belief in dreams was in the blood of the men of antiquity. Even more so do the books of dreams, of which only a few have come down to us.

2. The Most Important Books of Dreams.

Our knowledge in this field has been much extended recently by important findings and publications, but is still far from complete. Even more than elsewhere it is difficult in the Babyl. texts [9] to distinguish sharply between the interpretation of omens and that of dreams. Where completely unimaginable situations are presupposed, we are in the sphere of dreams. Babyl. interpretation undoubtedly influenced Artemid., Oneirocr., II, 68 (158, 19 ff.): on flying. Even more inaccessible is Indian dream manticism. [10] We have more light on Egypt. The British Museum has a hieratic book of dreams, [11] and the museums at Cairo [12] and Berlin [13] have several demotic texts. Cf. also the demotic

---

[5] The Pythag. advised against beans, which make the spirit heavy (Cic. Divin., I, 62; Pease, *ad loc.*), cf. also Eleusinian and Orphic rules. For other recommendations cf. Ps.-Hippocr. De Insomniis. On moderation before going to sleep Plat. Resp., IX, 571c-572b; Artemid. Oneirocr., I, 7 (13, 22 ff.); Max. Tyr., 10, 1 f.; Philostr. Vit. Ap., 3, 42. Autumn is unfavourable because of its fruitfulness, Plut. Quaest. Conv., VIII, 10, 2-3 [II, 735b ff.]. Many ascribe significance only to morning dreams when the process of digestion is complete.
[6] Volten, 11.
[7] On Aristot. cf. Index, *s.v.* ἐνύπνιον. For Cic. cf. the ed. of A. S. Pease *Univ. of Illinois Studies in Lang. and Literature*, VI, 2-VIII, 3 (1920-1923), which is esp. valuable for its many comments and index.
[8] Cic. was probably more correct than the experimental psychology which tries to trace back dreams predominantly to external sense stimuli, though these obviously play some part. Cf. W. Wundt, *Grundriss d. Psychologie*[15] (1922), 335-340.
[9] A. Boissier, *Choix de textes relatifs à la divination Assyro-Babylonienne* II (1906).
[10] J. v. Negelein, "D. Traumschlüssel d. Jagaddeva," RVV, XI, 4 (1912).
[11] Pap. Beatty, III, ed. A. H. Gardiner, *Hieratic Pap. in the Brit. Museum*, III (1935), Vol. I, 9-23; II, 5-8a, 12-12a.
[12] W. Spiegelberg, *Demotische Inschr. u. Pap., D. demotischen Denkmäler*, 3 (1932).
[13] W. Spiegelberg, *Demot. Pap. aus d. königlichen Museen zu Berlin* (1902), Pap. 8769.

pap. Carlsberg, XIII in Copenhagen, [14] written in the 2nd cent. A.D. or later. Agreements with Babylon may be due to parallelism. On the other hand, Egypt. interpretation strongly influenced that of Greece, Hdt., II, 82; Artemid., II, 44 (148, 20 ff.). Through Artemid. and his disciples quite a few Egyptian interpretations have come into more modern books and have continued to our own time, cf. the popular German and Danish belief that dreams of teeth falling out signify the death of close relatives. [15] The first Gk. book of dreams of which we have knowledge comes from a contemporary of Socrates, Antiphon. [16] Around the same period Lysimachos prophesied from a πινάκιον ὀνειροκριτικόν, Plut. Aristid., 27 (I, 335d). There is little pt. in listing the many lost books of dreams before Artemid. [17] We have fragments of the 4 books of Philochoros (inspector of sacrifices at Athens from 306), Περὶ μαντικῆς. [18] The first Gk. book to come down to us in full is that of Artemidorus of Ephesus or Daldis, written under Commodus (180-192) directly or indirectly from Babyl., Egypt., esp. Gk., perhaps also Jewish (→ 234) sources. The portrayal of Artemid. [19] is of interest from the standpoint of cultural history. The book of the later Chr. Neo-Platonist Synesius of Cyrene takes a platonist turn. [20] The Byzantine dream book of Achmet [21] (c. 820) derives from Arabian sources. All the other extant books are apocryphal. A dream book of the first Pythia Phemonoë (in hexameters) was forged at the end of the Alexandrian period, and that of Epicharm. (5th cent. B.C., Syracuse) in the Hell. age. In the Byzantine period, perhaps earlier, a book in 101 alphabetically arranged hexameters, which exists in 2 versions, [22] was attributed to the Persian magus Astrampsychos. Enlarged to 200 verses, it was then passed on as the dream book of the patriarch Nicephoros (d. 829). [23] In spite of the imposing name it is a poor piece of work, but was much loved because of its brevity and easy arrangement. It formed a source for the Ps.-Daniel book of dreams composed c. 960, [24] which with the widespread dream alphabets of Joseph of Egypt is extant in a Lat. transl., in one manuscript with Old English glosses [25] — a proof of the lasting popularity of this lit. On Jewish books → 234.

3. The Importance of Dreams in the Life of Antiquity.

a. The Cultic Dream. New cults and sanctuaries were established by visions and old ones renewed. Rê-Harmachis, the god of the great Sphinx at Gizeh, orders the later Thotmes IV (1420-1411 B.C.) to have the Sphinx opened again. In a dream the king who had brought an Egyptian statue to his country to heal his daughter is told to send it back to its own country. [26] Hera orders the building of a temple in Hierapolis (Ps.-Luc. Syr. Dea, 19). On the basis of a dream Ptolemy Soter has the colossus of Pluto brought from Sinope and establishes the cult of Sarapis in Alexandria (Tac. Hist., IV,

---

[14] Cf. A. Volten.

[15] Volten, 76, due to similarity of sound. This interpretation, passed on to the Gks. by Aristandros of Telmessos, interpreter to Alexander the Gt., was worked out in detail by him or by Artemid. (I, 31 [31, 3 ff.]).

[16] Cf. Diels[5], II, 367 f. for fragments.

[17] For the fullest possible list cf. Pauly-W., 2. Reihe, VI (1937), 2236-2241, which has 40 titles.

[18] For fr. cf. FHG, I, 415 f.

[19] Cf. Laukamm.

[20] MPG, 66, 1281 ff.; cf. W. Lang.

[21] Ed. F. Drexl (1925); also Drexl, Achmets Traumbuch, Einleitung u. Probe eines kritischen Textes (Diss. Munich, 1909).

[22] Cf. append. to the ed. of Artemid. and Achmet by N. Rigaltius (Paris, 1603) and the ed. of Sib. by S. Gallaeus (Amsterdam, 1689).

[23] Ed. F. Drexl, Festgabe f. A. Ehrhard (1922), 94-118.

[24] Gk. text: Revue de philologie, de littérature et d'histoire anciennes, 33 (1909), 93-111.

[25] Förster, p. 40 on the books of Joseph.

[26] T. Hopfner, Plut. über Isis u. Osiris, II (1941), 128.

83 f.; Plut. Is. et Os., 28 [II, 361 f.]). Zoïlos is advised to set up a shrine of Sarapis in his dwelling with the help of the Egypt. minister of finance, Apollonius. By an order given in a dream the god prevents someone else from pursuing the same intention, P. Greci e Latini, IV, 435. [27] An unknown deity demands that its document of revelation be transl. into Gk., P. Oxy., XI, 1381. In the three last instances the dilatory are prodded by repetition of the dream and punishments. Common in votive inscr. is the phrase κατ' ὄναρ "on the basis of a dream," Anth. Pal., 11, 253; Ditt. Syll.[3], 1147, 1148, 1149; Inscr. Perg., 357, 8; IG, XII, 1, 979, 4 f. Directions are often very specific. Sophocles is summoned by a repeated vision to show who was the thief of a golden vessel from the temple treasury of Heracles the Areopagite, Cic. Divin., I, 54. The gods very often complain about neglect. Capitoline Jupiter protests against the fact that Augustus has taken worshippers from him by the excessive promotion of Jupiter Optimus Maximus, Suet. Augustus, 91. Only he who is summoned by a vision may enter the sanctuary of Isis, Apul. Met., XI, 21. These dreams are often accompanied by threats and penalties. But mostly the gods are benevolent. During incubation the sick in a dream receive healing which is later shown to be real. [28] Isis comes to them and gives them the means of healing, Diod. S., I, 25. The formal relation of patronage is common in the dream tradition. Sethos in his patron's temple is encouraged by him against the Arabs, Hdt., II, 141. The worse, then, when the protective deity shows displeasure and withdraws assistance. Domitian before his death dreamed that his protective goddess Minerva threw away her weapons and plunged into the abyss on a chariot drawn by black horses (Dio C., 67, 16, 1), or that she left his domestic chapel and declared that she had been disarmed by Jupiter (Suet. Domitian, 15, 3). Even when the content seems to lead us away from the cultic sphere, cultic connections may be seen. To the leader of the army of the Plataeans Zeus Soter appeared before the battle in a grotto of nymphs and a shrine of Demeter Kora (Plut. Aristides, 11 [I, 325c ff.]). This helps us to understand better the many votive offerings "on the basis of a dream," → supra. The personal experience behind them makes Epigr. Graec., 839 quite plain: a man who had been blind sets up two stelae of gratitude to Aesculapius for healing dreams (δοιοὺς ὀνείρους) because he has been cured in both eyes.

b. The Political Dream. Commonly attested, but of disputed authenticity, are dreams which intimate the future greatness of political personages. The mother of Pericles dreamed during pregnancy that she was bringing a lion into the world, Hdt., VI, 131. The mother of Augustus dreamed that her entrails flew up toward heaven and covered heaven and earth, while his father dreamed that the sun's radiance was shining forth from her womb, Suet. Augustus, 94. Generals like Xerxes (Hdt., VII, 19) and Caesar (Suet. Divus Julius, 7, 2) were promised victory and deliverance in dreams. Often such dreams influenced political decisions. Hannibal was called to Italy in this way (Cic. Divin., I, 49), and Caesar at the Rubicon dreamed he held converse with his mother (Plut. Julius Caesar, 32 [I, 723 f.]), traditionally taken to signify a happy homecoming (Hdt., VI, 107) or even world dominion. But dreams are equivocal. Hamilcar's dream that he would eat in Syracuse on the evening of the following day was fulfilled by his capture, Cic. Divin., I, 50. Dreams before turning-points in history are often vaticinia ex eventu, tendentious legends or literary reflections. Nero in the last days of his reign is supposed to have been told in a dream to lead the chariot of Jupiter Optimus Maximus out of the sanctuary into the house of Vespasian, and then to the circus, Suet. Vespasian, 5. Vespasian saw the equally long rule of his predecessors and the Flavians in the form of a balanced scales in the forecourt of his palace, Suet. Vespasian, 25. Hadrian and Marc. Aurel. were given intimation of their accession by descending fire and the gift of ivory members which were still flexible, Dio C., 69, 2, 1; 71, 36, 1. Thus the people said — or propaganda.

---

[27] Deissmann LO, 121-128.
[28] On the healings at Epidauros → III, 194 ff.

c. The Dream and Personal Destiny. As politics and destiny are closely related, so, too, are political dreams and those which intimate destiny. Naturally enough tradition is here predominantly linked with figures in public life. But it is presupposed that the people, too, have such dreams. The dream which announces individual destiny is usually symbolical and allegorical. Sometimes it promises good fortune, but mostly bad. When Xenophon, concerned about the fate of his comrades, finally sleeps, in a dream he sees lightning strike and light up his father's house — a sign both of good fortune and bad, An., III, 1, 11 f. On another occasion he dreams that chains fall from his feet, IV, 3, 8. Croesus saw his son Atys transfixed by the point of a lance, which happened in spite of every precaution, Hdt., I, 34, 38-40, 43. Intimations of one's own death by dreams are common. Hipparchus dreamed the night before his death of a tall handsome man who spoke enigmatic words to him, Hdt., V, 55 f., 62. Death was announced to Cimon by a bitch barking in a human voice, Plut. Cim., 18 (I, 490c). Caesar the night before his assassination felt himself hover over the clouds and reach out his hand to Jupiter, Suet. Divus Julius, 81, 3, cf. the continuation. To rulers who were esp. hated wild dreams were attributed symbolising the pangs of conscience. Caligula on his last night dreamed that Jupiter kicked him down from heaven to earth, Suet. Caligula, 57. After his mother's murder Nero, who had never dreamed before, saw the rudder of a ship which he was steering slip out of his hands. He was also cast into oppressive darkness by his patron goddess. He was covered by a swarm of winged ants and encircled by idols. His favourite stallion was changed into an ape with a neighing horse's head, Suet. Nero, 46, 1. The dream books show that the dream played just as large a part in the lives of ordinary people as in those of more important figures. If ὄναρ has not been found in the pap. this is probably because the sources have not yet been systematically investigated. We certainly find an ἐνυπνιοκριτής for the shrine of Sarapis at Memphis in the 2nd cent. B.C., P. Par., 54, III, 78. The ὀνειρόμαντις is obviously a not wholly unimportant personage, P. Lond., 121, 795. The following eloquent compounds are found : ὀναραίτητος, "concerning the divine direction given by a dream" (P. Lond., 121, 222 etc.), and ὀνειροπομπέω, "to send direction in a dream" (ibid., 46, 488; 121, 877).

4. The Metaphysics of Dreams.

The dream is a complete enigma to primitive man. The further he is from rational explanation, the more he feels that in dreams he is in contact with the suprasensual world. The figures encountered there are real in a higher transcendental sense. Modern religion has generally ceased to see this primitive belief in terms of animism. The argument of primitive man is not : I see the dead and gods in dreams, therefore they exist, but rather : I see the dead and gods, therefore I am caught up into their sphere, the hereafter, or they have come to me. [29]

We see this best in Egypt. Here the hereafter is called Nun. This is the ocean around our world. The sun-god traverses it by night in his boat, and comes up again refreshed in the morning. Man experiences the same refreshing in sleep, which takes him to the sphere of Nun. From Nun comes the annual, fructifying overflowing of the Nile, also the life-giving water of the cultus. In dreams man comes into physical contact with this other world. Presupposing that it is genuine and received aright, what he experiences in this condition is thus unconditionally correct and extremely valuable.

In the Gk. world sleep and death are not just connected by external analogy. Νύξ gave birth to both — and to the people of dreams, Hes. Theog., 211 f. Hom. Od., 24, 11-14 describes how Hermes Psychopompos leads the souls of slain suitors to the floods of the ocean, the gates of the sun, and the people of dreams. Acc. to Vergil Aen., VI, 282 ff. dreams hang like bats among the leaves of a giant elm in the underworld. [30] It is not by chance that the dead appear so often in dreams (Varus : Tacit. Ann., I, 65; the shades of Galba : Suet. Otho, 7; Agrippina : Suet. Nero, 34, 4; on the Somnium

---

29 On what follows cf. de Buck.
30 For details cf. Volten, 47.

Scipionis → 227; also gods, → 223 f.). Oneiros is even the object of a cult, a deity. In Balawit there is a special temple dedicated to Makhir, the god of dreams. It is visited by those who want favourable dreams. Of Epaminondas we read in Paus., IV, 26, 8. εὐξάμενος τῷ πεφηνότι ὀνείρατι. Dreams are often messages from the other world, the hereafter, or more strictly they are rapture. The dream is ecstasy. Though the word ἔκστασις originally has a different sense, [31] it takes on that of rapture. Because of its dualism, this metaphysics of dreams was naturally felt to be sympathetic by Platonism (under Orphic influence) and by all the movements which derived from it. Logically the true mantic situation of the soul is seen in the few moments directly before departing, and there is close approximation to Indian thought. In the formulation of the apologist for a metaphysics of dreams in Cic. we read : *Appropinquante morte [animus] multo est divinior*, Divin., I, 63. On this basis the last speeches of Socrates in Plato appear in a new light, and it is again consistent that a dream occurs in each of them. A manifestation of deity when one is awake counts for even more than such a manifestation in a dream. The priest of Kronos in Luc. Kronosolon, 10, says : "Kronos has not merely come to me in a dream (οὐκ ὄναρ ἐπιστάς), but has spoken with me lately when I was already awake (ἐναργὴς συγγενόμενος). Cf. Corp. Herm., XIII, 4 : <ἵνα εἰδῆς, μὴ> ὡς οἱ ἐν ὕπνῳ ὀνειροπολούμενοι (those visited by dreams), <ἀλλὰ> χωρὶς ὕπνου. Cf. Nu. 12:6 ff. → 230.

The two other possibilities whereby dreams might have significance (cf. Cic. and in part Poseidonius → 222) are compromises between the older metaphysics of dreams and the rational thought to which the Gks. inclined. In the first case aid is sought from an immanent soul mysticism, in the second from the empirical sphere, though the background of an admittedly indefinite transcendence is still required.

5. The Interpretation of Dreams as a Science.

Dreams in which the subject receives an unequivocal impartation or direction, or in which a personally relevant instance of good or evil fortune is enacted, need no interpretation. Theory, however, sought to derive meaning from the many other dreams which do not meet this presupposition. These demanded and even invited interpretation. The meaning might be sought along intuitive and speculative lines. A base was offered by the most varied relations, especially puns, in the use of which the Egyptians were already masters. On the other hand, interpretation might be put on an empirical foundation. It would be assumed that the sequence of a certain dream and a striking event rested on a law and would thus be repeated again and again. To support this idea it was necessary to collect the most comprehensive possible historical material. In fact, however, the course of events was far from uniform, so that far-reaching distinctions had to be made (→ 221), which would then be supported in turn by examples. The reference books had to try to cover every conceivable case. Thus the material grew to monstrous proportions. Only the expert could handle correctly the two methods, which in actuality were always connected. Hence the interpretation of dreams became a science.

So it was in ancient Babylon and Egypt. Native sources also bear witness to the soothsayers, Chaldeans, wise men and scribes who are said to be interpreters of dreams in Da. 2:2 ff.; 5:7 ff.; Gn. 41:8. We have particularly good knowledge of the situation in Egypt. In the Bohairic transl. of Gn. 41:8, 24 חַרְטֻמִּים (LXX ἐξηγηταί) is rendered "scribes of the house of life." This house of life [32] was a highly regarded corporation to which many of the king's descendants belonged and whose task it was to protect the life of pharaoh. It was an *universitas litterarum*, and in this university there was a faculty for the interpretation of dreams. This existed originally only to interpret pharaoh's dreams, but later it was open to all and the science was popularised. The books consulted were systematically arranged lexicons, sometimes of inordinate bulk.

---

[31] → II, 449 ff., cf. also F. Pfister, "Ekstasis" in Pisciculi, *Antike u. Christentum*, Suppl. Vol. 1 (1939), 178-191.
[32] Volten, 17-44.

The Gk. interpreters very zealously used the accounts of allegedly fulfilled dreams collected in the shrine of Sarapis. Artemon of Miletus assembled 22 books in this way (Artemid. Oneirocr., II, 44 [148, 20 ff.]), and though Artemid. resisted this, he himself was no mean compiler. Not only did he borrow widely from the Egyptians. He also bought all the relevant books he could lay hands on, and travelled through Greece, Asia Minor and Italy gathering material. Nor did he disdain to learn from market-criers and magicians (I, 1a [2, 10 ff.]), He expounded esp. his own principles of inter-pretation (I, 1b-12 [3, 1-17, 13] and IV, 1-4 [201, 13-207, 22]). Dreams which occur suddenly and unexpectedly are to be regarded as divinely sent visions (IV, 3 [206, 23]) and they can be interpreted only if the whole context is remembered. Artemid. is very systematic and scientific. Theorematic dreams, e.g., a ship-wreck, need no interpretation. This is required only with allegorical dreams (I, 2 [4, 9 f., 18 ff.]; IV, 1 [201, 13 ff.]). The same dream may have many interpretations acc. to age, sex, health, situation, national customs etc. I, 9 [15, 5 ff.]). [33] The art of the interpreter is to find the allegory which fits a given case. Ability and mother wit are needed for this (I, 12 [16, 16 f.]). But it can also be learned to some degree. Artemid. seeks a solution in the joint develop-ment of the empirical and rational method (IV, 20 [212, 3 ff.]).

Pleasant dreams, e.g., good food, usually signify good things, unpleasant dreams the reverse. But it can work out the opposite way too. Drinking one's own urine, by associa-tion with the sperm, denotes the blessing of children. Excrement denotes possession, that of animals landed property. Dreams of animals are variously interpreted acc. to their estimation. In Egypt the crocodile denotes a rapacious official (Pap. Beatty, III, verso 2, 22), in Artemid. a pirate, murderer, or no less wicked person. The puns greatly used already by the Egyptians rest originally on the assumption that language is directly divine. Translated, they are meaningless, and can be explained only by ref. to the original. They thus bear all the stronger witness to a chain of tradition. The ref. of teeth falling out to dying relatives (→ 223) comes by way of Artemid. (I, 31 [31, 6 ff.]) into ancient Jewish interpretation (Bar Chadia, bBer., 56a), Achmet (26, 13 ff.), Nicephoros (217), Ps.-Daniel (263) and the Old English paraphrase (193), Abdor-rahman and popular modern belief. [34] While the Egyptians go by arbitrarily related key-words (drink, bring forth, wreath, swim), Artemid. has a well-arranged system: birth, education, parts of the body, instruction in the arts, contests, washings, means of nourishment, sleep, waking, dirt, heavenly phenomena, the chase, fishing, voyages etc. Interpretation is so detailed that not only does harvest generally refer to progeny, but wheat to sons and barley to daughters (a hierarchy of sex). Fruits in husks are mis-carriages. This is a baroque world. But we must not fall too easily into the absolute negation of rationalism. It may be that in the realistic symbolical sensitiveness of belief in dreams there is an element of truth for which the modern investigation of dreams has given us once again a sharper eye.

6. The Dream as a Literary Form.

While this whole sphere was a popular one in antiquity, it is to be noted that the dream also became an independent form of literary composition. Cic. in his own develop-ment of the mysterious end of Plato's Rep. (X, 614 ff.) brought the six books of his Dialog. Rep. to an effective conclusion with the famous Somnium Scipionis (preserved only in Macrob. Comm. in Somnium Scipionis). A transcendent idealism of state is here embodied in Scipio Africanus Maior, who appeared to his grandson.

---

[33] Cf. Achmet, 240, 8 ff.: τὰ ὀνείρατα ... εἰς διάφορα κρίνονται πρόσωπα δια-φόρως. ἐφ᾽ ἑνὶ γὰρ ὀνείρατι ἄλλη ἡ κρίσις ἐπὶ βασιλέως καὶ ἄλλη ἐπὶ λαοῦ, ἄλλη γεωργοῦ καὶ ἄλλη στρατιώτου, ἑτέρα τοῦ μεγιστάνου καὶ ἑτέρα τοῦ πένητος, ἄλλη κρίσις ἐν ἀνδράσιν καὶ ἄλλη ἐν γυναιξίν, ἄλλη ἐν θέρει καὶ ἑτέρα ἐν χειμῶνι, ἑτέρα ἐν τῇ αὐξήσει τῆς ἡμέρας καὶ ἑτέρα ἐν τῇ μειώσει, ἄλλη ἐν αὐξήσει σελήνης καὶ ἄλλη ἐν μειώσει. καὶ ἄλλα τῶν ὀνειράτων ταχέως καὶ ἄλλα βραδέως κρίνονται (are fulfilled).

[34] Universaltraumbuch, 227.

Lucian described his eventful life in a vision which is modelled on the account of Hercules at the cross-roads by the Sophist Prodikos. On another occasion he uses the same form in a witty dialogue between the cobbler Micyllos and his cock. This is able to convince the cobbler that his penurious existence is better than that of the envied rich. These dreams display an idealistic tendency. But they are artistic constructs. The reality was otherwise.

7. The Dream Life as a Mirror of the Man of Antiquity.

Hardly anywhere else can we see the man of antiquity so unadorned as in dreams. The books of dreams enable us to construct an almost perfect mosaic of ancient culture. If we seek to work through the colourful exterior to the inner life, the result is for the most part horrifying. We do find harmless and even sympathetic themes in dreams. Life means work (Artemid., IV, 40 [225, 13 ff.]): ὅτι τὸ ἐργάζεσθαι τῷ ζῆν τὸν αὐτὸν ἔχει λόγον, the dream of a spinner that her thread broke signified death because she had no more to do. Good fortune is denoted by steering, cobbling and carpentering in a dream πᾶσι τοῖς κατὰ νόμον ζῶσι on account of the μέτρα (I, 51 [49, 10 ff.]). [35] But in the main the picture is one of wild and riotous fantasy. There is no place here for censorship or false moralising. The dream life is unregulated and unchecked, and the books, as works of reference, construct the most unlikely cases in the interests of completeness, though this does not prove that they actually happened. [36] Disgusting themes like the eating of one's own excrement or that of others or even animals, the drinking of urine, sexual intercourse, esp. in unlawful and even perverted forms, incest, homosexuality and sodomy, are all to the fore. The Pap. Carlsberg, XIII has a whole chapter on this type of sexual life. We also find male pregnancies and animal births. Nor are things much better in the Gk. interpreters for all the progress in enlightenment. Interpretation neither is nor seeks to be anything more than an egocentric reading of destiny. Curiosity seeks satisfaction, eudaemonism must have its due. A bourgeois view of life in the worst sense is widespread. If this is true of the cultic and political dream (→ 223 f.), how much more of the private! Only occasionally do we find a higher goal. In general the concern is with the trivialities of daily life: becoming poor or rich, sickness or health, slavery or freedom, shipwreck or a safe voyage, fortune in work or love, sexual fulfilment, a right choice of spouse, and dear children. What difference does it make that Artemid. speaks highly of philosophy? [37] His Stoicism is a very thin veneer. The unfavourable interpretations, which perhaps predominate, show sober realism in relation to the actualities of life, but pessimistically and without pity they leave those concerned to their fate. There is no deeper content, no real meaning or stability, to life. For all its scientific aspirations the ancient interpretation of dreams is little more than a mixture of fatalism, superstition and filth. In a wholly different sense from that of ancient belief, the saying is true: *in somnio veritas*. Nowhere is man so unmasked as in dreams.

II. Dreams and the Interpretation of Dreams in the OT.

1. The Dream and History.

At a first glance the OT findings convey much the same impression as the surrounding world. We again find the cultic, the political and the personal dream.

---

[35] The seams of cobblers, as a binding element, are against the interests of those who desire marriage. The tanner, who has to do with cadavers and bad smells, and lives outside the city (Ac. 10:6), is a bad sign, esp. for physicians.

[36] Volten, 13 is right, but goes too far, when he says: "Yet the adverse content should not give us a wrong impression of Egypt. morality. The text is simply an interesting example of how far academic pedantry could go even among the ancients. The interpretation of dreams was a science which had to presuppose all possible dreams, even the most scabrous.

[37] II, 34 (131, 26 ff.); II, 37 (141, 29 ff.): οἱ κατὰ νόμον ζῶντες καὶ μέτριοι ἄνθρωποι καὶ φιλόσοφοι, the opp. the lawless, persecutors of others, those who seek great things; cf. also against hubris II, 68 (159, 6 ff.).

Through the dream of the heavenly ladder, the fundamental revelation to the patriarch Jacob, Yahweh founds the sanctuary at Bethel (Gn. 28:11 ff.). He reveals Himself to the young Solomon at Gibeon (1 K. 3:5 ff.). The dreams of the boy Joseph (Gn. 37:5 ff.) remind us of ancient intimations of coming greatness (→ 224). Gideon overhears the account of a Midianite's dream of the delivering of the host into the hands of the much smaller army of Israel (Ju. 7:13 ff.), and this confirms his confidence of victory and nerves him for powerful action. Purely personal are the dreams of the butler and baker in the Egypt. prison (Gn. 40:8 ff.). Though there are some theorematic dreams, the allegorical predominate (Gn. 20:6; 28:11 ff.; 31:11 ff.; 1 K. 3:5 ff. — Gn. 37:5 ff.; 40:8 ff.; 41:1 ff.; Ju. 7:13 ff.; Da. 2:1 ff.). Hence interpretation plays no insignificant role. It follows the traditional lines. In the Egypt. interpreters of the Joseph stories we recognise the scribes of the house of life (→ 226). Joseph in a sense takes their place, as does Daniel that of the Chaldeans, but the agreement goes deeper, for cows as a sign of years is Egyptian and also Persian. In the Gk. period the word "year" was ideographically represented by a cow, and Achmet says with ref. to Joseph, yet obviously also from living tradition, that the interpreter should relate cows to years, the fat to fat years, the lean to lean. [38] In the OT, too, one can sometimes find an almost ludicrous eudaemonism (Gn. 31:11 f.). Of the OT sources E is most inclined to dreams (Gn. 20:6 f.; 28:11 f.; 31:11 ff., 24; 37:5 ff.; 40:8 ff.; 41:1 ff.). But there are dreams in J (Gn. 28:13 ff.) and P (Nu. 12:6) as well. Only D (13:2 ff.) is hostile or critical.

Is the view of dreams found in the OT as primitive as that in the world around? There are differences. The sobriety of atmosphere is striking. The OT, as is well-known, is not prudish in historical matters. But in dreams we seek in vain for obscene or scabrous motifs. Conversely, where do we find in antiquity any parallel to the dream of Solomon (1 K. 3)? The metaphysics, if one may use this term, is also different. The psychological experience, intrinsically common to all men, that the dream is evanescent, that it is shown to be deception on wakening, is emphasised with a force and universality which threaten the primitive metaphysics of dreams, Is. 29:7 f.; Job 20:8. Particularly striking is Ps. 73:20: "Like a dream after awakening, so, O Lord, when thou awakest, thou despisest their image." The idea that dreams come from the realm of the dead, from a better hereafter, would seem strange to the Israelite. For him *sheol* is the place of night and dread, where even the power of Yahweh does not seem to reach, or where at least He is not praised (Ps. 6:5; though cf. Am. 9:2; Ps. 139:8). The thought of Yahweh Himself finding fresh strength by night in the sphere of the dead, in the land of dreams, is too ridiculous even to be considered (→ III, 435). Significant dreams, even among the Gentiles, are all without exception attributed to Yahweh (Gn. 20:6; 28:10 ff.; 31:10 ff., 24; 41:1 ff.; Ju. 7:13 ff.; Da. 2:1 ff.; 7:1 ff.). The dream as such is not necessary to revelation. But the transcendent God can, if He so chooses, use this method too to declare Himself to men. In so far as dreams need interpretation, this is not accessible to human art or science. Even God's special vessels do not command it. God gives it to whom He wills (Gn. 40:8; 41:16, 39; Da. 2:17 ff.). When these presuppositions are fulfilled, the dream is in supreme measure an event, a part of history. It is not by chance that the dreams of the OT do not stand alone but are integrated into the chain of the history of God's people. This is evident in the case of such dreams as Gn. 41:1 ff.; Ju. 7:13 ff.; Da. 2:1 ff.; 7:1 ff. But dreams like Gn. 20:6; 31:10, 24; 40:5 ff. are also told, not because of purely personal concerns, but in the interests of the patriarchs as part of salvation history in the broadest sense of the term. The God of history is the Holy One of Israel.

---

[38] Volten, 70. Cf. Achmet, 189, 24 ff.; 190, 9 ff.; 191, 24.

Sanctifying power goes forth from Him, and so the ring closes. Even what the OT says about revelation in dreams is all given a distinctive stamp by the biblical belief in God.

2. The Dream as a Regular Means of Revelation in Yahwism.

Within the limits hereby set one can speak of a positive approach to dreams found throughout the OT from the earlier period to the later. Not only are there isolated intimations of the living God through dreams; the dream is a regular means of revelation, a legitimate part of the religion of Yahweh. There is no need to speak of syncretistic influences when the friends of Job (4:13 ff.), Elihu in his added speeches, [39] and Job himself (7:14), for all their awareness of the fleeting nature of dreams (20:8), regard the dream as a message which, if for the most part dreadful, nevertheless comes from Yahweh. As the ancient sanctuaries have dreams in the legends of their founding (Gn. 28:10 ff.), so there are signs that at cultic centres visionary revelations were sought through incubation (1 S. 3:1 ff.; 1 K. 3:4 ff.; → III, 434). The dreams thus induced rank with the oracle and prophetic direction, and if Yahweh rebuffs the seeker this is a sign of severe displeasure and a reason for despair (1 S. 28:6). There are strong links between the dream and prophecy. This may be seen in its own way in the criticisms of Jeremiah (→ infra). In P the dream is a current mode of receiving revelation, though not the highest (Nu. 12:6 f.; → infra). In Jl. 2:28 the unrestricted gift of visions to the people is held out as a prospect for the age of salvation. Daniel's well-known vision of the kingdom and the Son of Man is called חֵלֶם, with חֶזְוֵה רֵאשֵׁהּ (7:1) as a parallel. We are here very close to the state of soul known as a trance. The visions of the night in Zechariah are no longer thought of as dreams. It is clear, however, that in broad circles in Israel, even those which are incontestably theocratic, the dream was regarded as a regular means by which Yahweh revealed Himself. [40]

3. The Prophetic Criticism of Dreams.

The dream, however, comes in for criticism. This has nothing whatever to do with enlightenment or scepticism. It has its source in the most inward impulses of Yahwism. According to P God spoke to Moses directly rather than through dreams (Nu. 12:6 ff.). Dt. distrusts revelations by dreams even though ostensibly prophetic (Dt. 13:2 ff.). Signs and wonders, even when they occur, are not the distinguishing marks of genuine revelation. The criterion is confirmation of faithfulness to the redeeming God.

This immanent criticism reaches its climax in the prophet Jeremiah (23:16-32; 27:9 f.; 29:8 f.). [41] Jer. has to struggle against such prophets as Hananiah, who, appealing to dreams, preach salvation to the apostate people and deceive it as to the seriousness of judgment. Yahweh says concerning them: "I hear what the prophets say, that prophesy lies in my name, I have dreamed, I have dreamed ... Do they wish to cause my people to forget my name by their dreams which they tell one another? ... The prophet that hath a dream may tell a dream; but he that hath my word, let him speak my word faithfully" (23:25-28). Here is no

---

[39] 33:15 f.: "In a dream, in a vision of the night, when deep sleep falleth upon men, in slumberings upon the bed: Then he openeth the ears of men, and sealeth their instruction."

[40] Cf. Hänel.

[41] Cf. v. Rad.

gradual depreciating of revelation by dreams on the ground that the true prophet does not need them. The situation at that time demanded absolute rejection. Here, then, the metaphysics of dreams is uprooted as completely as possible, not by unbelieving, but by believing criticism, by reason of the earnestness of a conscience which is bound to Yahweh. Nor does this criticism of Jer. stand alone. The same situation of conflict called forth a similar saying in Dt. Zech. (10:2): "For the teraphim spoke vanity, and the diviners had lying visions; they speak only false dreams (יְדַבֵּ֔רוּ חֲלֹמוֹת) and give only empty comfort." The current eudaemonistic belief in and interpretation of dreams is here rightly unmasked as part of paganism.

On more general grounds the Wisdom literature reaches similar conclusions. Qoh. 5:3, 7: "For dreams come where there is much care, and foolish speech where there are many words. For in many dreams and words there is much that is vain. [42] Rather fear God." Sir. 34:5 ff.: "Predictions and dreams are empty, and the heart is full of imaginings like a woman in labour. If they are not sent from the Most High visiting the dreamer, set not thy heart on them. For dreams have led many men astray, and, hoping in them, they lost hope. The law will be put into effect without deception, and so, too, wisdom is perfect only on truthful lips." Sir. 40:5 ff. and Wis. 18:17, 19 describe the anxious dreams of the ungodly which God may nevertheless use as messengers, yet as messengers of judgment.

III. Dreams and the Interpretation of Dreams in Judaism.

The inwardly based criticism of dreams was increasingly lost to view in Judaism. In Hellenistic Judaism it was overpowered by a Platonic-Stoic belief in dreams.

1. Philo.

Philo knows the emptiness of dreams. Flacc., 164 (Flaccus to himself): κοιμώμενος ὄναρ εἶδον τὴν τότ' εὐθυμίαν, εἴδωλα κατὰ κενοῦ βαίνοντα, πλάσματα ψυχῆς ἴσως ἀναγραφούσης τὰ μὴ ὑπάρχοντα ὡς ὄντα. But through dreams God gives knowledge of heavenly things to the pure soul, Aet. Mund., 2. The spirit, having removed everything alien in sleep, τὰς περὶ τῶν μελλόντων ἀψευδεστάτας διὰ τῶν ὀνείρων μαντείας ἐνθουσιᾷ, Migr. Abr., 190. In this connection the word φαντασία does not denote what is unreal but the miracle by which there is prophecy of the future through dreams, Spec. Leg., I, 29. In dreams, i.e., those of the Therapeutae, only the beauties of divine virtues and forces are disclosed (φαντασιοῦσθαι). πολλοὶ γοῦν καὶ ἐκλαλοῦσιν ἐν ὕπνοις ὀνειροπολούμενοι (the sage who dreams or interprets dreams) τὰ τῆς ἱερᾶς φιλοσοφίας ἀοίδιμα δόγματα, Vit. Cont., 26. Of Philo's five tractates (γραφαί) on dreams (Eus. Hist. Eccl., II, 18, 4; Hier. De viris illustribus, 11), [43] three have been lost. The title of the two which remain (Som., I; II): Περὶ τοῦ θεοπέμπτους εἶναι τοὺς ὀνείρους, though it is not Philo's own, accurately shows the drift. Like Poseidonios (Cic. Divin., I, 64), but in reverse order, the Jewish philosopher distinguishes three kinds of dreams sent by God: those in which God speaks directly to the sleepers (Abimelech in Gn. 20:3?), those mediated by immortal souls in the air (symbolised by the heavenly ladder in Gn. 28:12 ff.; cf. also Gn. 31:11 ff.), and those which have their origin in the soul's own power of divination (the dreams of Joseph, the butler and baker, and Pharaoh himself, Gn. 37; 40; 41). So I, 1 and II, 1. The dreams of the last category are particularly obscure and in need of interpretation: αἱ δὲ κατὰ τὸ τρίτον εἶδος φαντασίαι μᾶλλον τῶν προτέρων ἀδηλούμενοι διὰ τὸ βαθὺ καὶ κατακορὲς ἔχειν τὸ αἴνιγμα ἐδεήθησαν καὶ τῆς ὀνειροκριτικῆς ἐπιστήμης, II, 4.

---

[42] Acc. to the texts as emended by Delitzsch.
[43] On Philo's writings about dreams cf. Schürer, III, 659.

Interpreters of dreams have special authority and responsibility as those who declare the divine word. So Joseph to the butler and baker: ἐπειδὴ τοῖς ὀνείρων κριταῖς ἀληθεύειν ἀναγκαῖον θεῖα λόγια διερμηνεύουσι καὶ προφητεύουσι, λέξω μηδὲν ὑποστειλάμενος, Jos., 95. The more odd it is, then, that Philo himself does not keep to the authentic interpretations, but even in respect of dreams which Scripture itself interprets, as with others, he indulges in diffuse and discursive allegorical exposition. At root his one exclusive concern is his own philosophical thinking.

2. Hagiography and Apocalyptic.

It is not surprising that popular religious lit., esp. in Palestine, should continue even more strongly the line of belief in dreams. In Esther the LXX adds a dream of Mordecai about two battling dragons and a spring which wells up from the tears of the righteous people. This is later interpreted in terms of the struggle between Mordecai and Haman, and of Queen Esther ('Εσθ. 1:1a ff.; 10:3a ff.). In 2 Macc. 15:11 ff. Judas Maccabeus, before the battle with Nicanor, encourages his men by telling them a "wholly (ὑπέρ τι, vl. ὕπαρ τι) reliable" divinely given dream. In answer to the prayer of the high-priest Onias there appeared to him a man distinguished by gray hair and a glorious figure, encircled by wonderful and glorious majesty, the prophet Jeremiah. This man handed him a golden sword with the words: "Take this holy sword, which God gives thee; with it thou shalt smite thine enemies." This dream reminds us of the political dreams of antiquity (→ 224), but with characteristic toning down. [44]

In apocalyptic the border between dream and ecstasy is fluid. Dreams are usually spun out into extensive and complicated visions which are then interpreted allegorically and always have as their theme the history of God's people. Enoch in a vision sees the sanctuary and the holy of holies of heaven, and therein God on His throne, and he receives the commission to intimate judgment to fallen spirits (Gn. 6), Eth. En. 14 f. He tells his son Methuselah how in two visions he has seen the flood and the whole of world history from the beginning to the establishment of the Messianic kingdom, 83-90. These dreams are simply literary constructs with no real experience behind them. Esp. rich in dreams are the Test. XII. Levi in a vision sees the seven heavens and receives orders for the priestly ministry of his tribe and revelations of the coming Redeemer, Test. L. 2-5. Naphthali on the Mt. of Olives sees two visions which allegorically intimate the prerogatives of the Davidic kingdom, the exile, the return, the struggle for pre-eminence between Levi and Judah, and the victory of the former, Test. N. 5-7. All this reflects the Maccabean reading of history. Test. N. 5-7 (Heb.) narrates the same dreams with the further embellishments of the contest for sun, moon and stars, and the sinking ship. The remark of Jacob: "This is a bad dream, which will be followed by neither good nor evil, for it was not repeated" (4:1), seems at first glance to hint at criticism, but in reality it simply underlines the dreadful nature of the repetition which follows, and hence the belief in dreams. Test. Jos. 6:2 records a waking vision rather than a dream. Test. Jos. 19 contains a dream which proclaims the overthrow of Joseph. i.e., the northern kingdom, and intimates the ascendancy of Levi and Judah, i.e., the Maccabeans. [45]

3. Josephus.

Jos. combines Palestinian and Hell. credulity. Apart from some rationalising, there is in him little trace of criticism. He not only records the dreams narrated in the OT but adds new ones in accordance with Hell. taste. To Amram, father of Moses, there is shown in a dream (God ἐφίσταται κατὰ τοὺς ὕπνους αὐτῷ) the future greatness of

---

[44] Worth noting is the paucity of material in Jub. The Gn. dreams are soberly recounted if not shortened or even omitted. Fantastic additions like the visions of Jacob on the basis of Gn. 35:9 ff. (32:21 ff.) are rare.

[45] The text is undoubtedly a Christian interpolation, but opinions differ as to the extent of the interpolation, cf. R. H. Charles on 19:8 (210, 27).

the son who will be born to him, Ant., 2, 212 ff. God charges the prophet Nathan φανεὶς κατὰ τοὺς ὕπνους to punish David, 7, 147; cf. 2 S. 12:1. Post-canonical history is richly adorned by dreams. In Ant., 11, 327 God encourages the high-priest Jaddus against the approaching Alexander. In 12, 112 the Gentile Theopompos, temporarily smitten by madness, learns in a dream that he will be chastised for his lack of respect for the Jewish Law, cf. Ep. Ar., 315.[46] In 13, 322 Hyrcanus in a dream asks God concerning his successor. In 14, 451 ὀνείρων ὄψεις proclaimed to Herod the Gt. the death of his brother, cf. Bell., 1, 328. In 17, 345 ff. Archelaus before being recalled to Rome saw oxen eating up ten full ears of wheat. The interpreters disagreed. One Essene took the oxen to signify trouble, the unsettled earth imminent change, and the ears years. The rule of Archelaus was soon at an end, cf. Bell., 2, 111 ff. In 17, 351 Archelaus' daughter, Glaphyra, saw her deceased first husband in a dream; he announced her death because she had remarried, and she died, cf. Bell., 2, 116. In 20, 18 Monobazos of Adiabene, when he touched the body of his pregnant wife in sleep, heard a voice that he should not harm the child, it would have a happy destiny (Helena and Izates went over to Judaism). Jos. himself is guided by dreams. One such encourages him to assume command in Galilee, Vit., 208. Before going over to the Romans nightly dreams come to his recollection in which God revealed to him the approaching misfortune of the Jews and the future destiny of the Roman emperors. He claims that as the son of a priest he has the gift of explaining even ambiguous dreams, Bell., 3, 351 ff.

4. Rabbinic Judaism.

The enlightenment makes strides among the Rabb., but these strides are only modest, and they are accompanied by the increasingly stronger infiltration of Hell. interpretation, though this is, of course, reciprocal. Scarcely a trace remains of the prophetic criticism.

A familiar quotation attributed esp. to R. Meïr (c. 150), though also found on the lips of other scholars, is to the effect that "the words of dreams neither exalt nor abase," i.e., they are of no importance, bGit., 52a; bHor., 13b; jMS, 4, 55b, 38; Str.-B., I, 56 f. Dreams are explained psychologically: One (God) causes man (in a dream) to see only the thoughts of his heart (which have occupied him by day), bBer., 55b; Str.-B., I, 57. But a distinction is made between valid and invalid visions. As by the Egyptians, the former are traced back to angels, the latter to demons, bBer., 55b; Str.-B., I, 54, 58. In particular there was belief in a specific angel of dreams (ish ha-chalôm, ba'al ha-chalôm, ba'al ha-chalomôth), Ramaël acc. to S. Bar. 55:3. The dream of revelation is a sixtieth part of prophecy, or a degenerate form (a weak counterpart), bBer., 57b; Gn. r., 17 (12a); 44 (27d); Str.-B., I, 53. A man may dream twenty-two years for the fulfilment of a good dream, bBer., 55b; Str.-B., I, 59. Others again think that no dream is ever wholly fulfilled. R. Shim'on b. Jochai (c. 150): As there can be no grain without straw, so there can be no dream without vain words, bBer., 55a; Str.-B., I, 54, 59. But in any case profit could be humorously extracted from this principle. When R. Shemu'el (d. 254) had a bad dream he used to say: "Dreams speak vanity" (Zech. 10:2). But when he had a good dream he used to say: "Do dreams speak vanity?" (No, acc. to Nu. 12:6), bBer., 55b; Str.-B., I, 53.

The dream plays in practice no less important a role than in paganism. The concerns are essentially the same, questions of destiny, money, health, marriage etc., Str.-B., I, 57 f. Filth is rarely mixed with religion. He who in a dream sleeps with his mother, let him hope for reason (Prv. 2:3); he who sleeps with one betrothed, for the Torah (Dt. 33:4 acc. to the al-tiqri method (→ 234); he who sleeps with his sister, for wisdom (Prv. 7:4). He who sleeps with a married woman, let him be assured that he is a child of the world to come, so long as he does not know her and has not thought of her the evening before, bBer., 57a. Only rarely do less egocentric concerns appear, e.g., rain, a greater number of pupils, once the forgiveness of sins (before migration from Babylon to Palestine), Str.-B., I, 57 f.

---

[46] Ep. Ar., 213 ff. explains dreams psychologically.

There are expert interpreters of dreams, supposedly twenty-four in Jerusalem, and also books of dreams, bBer., 55b, 56a. But there are also popular interpretations, mostly emanating from Rabb. circles and gradually becoming stereotyped. To see a well or wheat denotes peace, barley the forgiveness of sins, a white horse good, a red horse trotting misfortune, an ass (Zech. 9:9) Messianic salvation etc. These traditional interpretations and related materials are collected in bBer., 55a-57b in the form of a book of dreams. Str.-B., I, 55, 63. The methods of interpretation are the familiar ones. Puns are to the fore. A goose (אַוָּז) denotes wisdom, for wisdom cries on the street (חוּץ), Prv. 1:20. Intercourse with it means promotion to be head of a school, bBer., 57a. Lat. *platea* means both street and stuffed goose. For this *al-tiqri* method beloved in the exposition of Scripture (Str.-B., I, 93 f.), which produces an unexpected sense by a slight shift in construction, Hebrew offers unsuspected possibilities. In the light of puns which are Semitic in conception, there is every likelihood that Artemid. too used Jewish sources. [47] The equation of raven and malefactor (Artemid., II, 20 [113, 15] and bBer., 56b) rests on the similarity of עֹרֵב and עָרֵב, used in Jalqut, I, 261a of illegitimate dealings. bBer., 56a : I saw the outer door collapse. Answer : Thy wife will die. Artemid., II, 10 (97, 17 f.): burning doors signify the death of one's wife.

Apparently peculiar to Judaism is the idea that a dream acquires its force only when interpreted. bBer., 55a b; Str.-B., I, 60 : "A dream which is not interpreted is like a letter which is not read," i.e., without results. Hence the common principle : "All dreams are governed by the mouth," i.e., the interpretation, bBer., 55b; Str.-B., I, 60; cf. Gn. 41:13. When twenty-four interpreters differ, all the interpretations come true, bBer., 55b; Str.-B., I, 54. Thus interpretation becomes a terrible weapon. Frivolous interpretation can kill a man, jMS, 4 (55c), 14; Str.-B., I, 59. Interpretation is often for sale, as Juvenal (VI, 546 f.) realised :

Implet et illa manum, sed parcius ; aere minuto
Qualiacumque voles Iudaei somnia vendunt.

There are various more or less clever ways of guarding against the evil consequences of dreams. Thus we have dream fasting, or getting three persons to confirm a favourable interpretation, or reciting suitable texts of Scripture, or prayer, almsgiving and penitence, Str.-B., I, 55, 61.

The whole treatment of dreams is religiously unfruitful. Some circles tried to apply them morally, as a means of leading to repentance (Qoh. 3:14 referred to dreams). Thus a bad dream is better than a good one. God does not let the good man see good dreams or the bad man bad dreams. David never had a good dream, nor Ahithophel a bad. In the case of a bad dream concern averts the evil consequences, in that of a good dream joy arrests the good consequences. The man who passes seven nights without a dream is an ungodly man (Prv. 19:23 with *al-tiqri* interpretation). Cf. the mosaic of quotations in bBer., 55a b; Str.-B., I, 56. In such statements we find elements of biblical piety, but developed in baroque fashion.

B. The Dream in the New Testament.

1. The Tradition.

In the NT we have at least one tradition which bears the clear stamp of authenticity. The account of Paul's dream at Troas, which launched the mission to Europe (Ac. 16:9 f.), stands at the head of the first longer We-passage, and thus comes from a travelling companion to whom the apostle recounted his dream. [48] The colour and simplicity bear witness to accurate recollection. The same is true of Ac. 27:23 f. If this shows that Paul had special dreams at turning-points in his

---

[47] Cf. Lewy.
[48] The context makes it clear that this is a dream.

life, and that he attributed some significance to them, it is hard to see why Ac. 18:9 and 23:11 should not also be regarded as historical in the special or even the most general sense. Elsewhere we find accounts of dreams only in Mt. 1:20 f.: Joseph's dream prior to the birth of Jesus; 2:12: the warning to the wise men not to go back to Herod; 2:13, 19, 22: instructions to Joseph regarding the flight to Egypt, and finally 27:19: the dream of Pilate's wife.[49] That all these come from the same hand, that of the Evangelist, is shown by the stereotyped regularity of the recurrent, linguistically late[50] κατ' ὄναρ, "in a dream." This special tradition in Mt. has come under the suspicion of being legendary and apologetic in tendency. If this is so, it has source value only in relation to the thinking of later antiquity. Beyond this there are only scattered references. The paucity of material, however, does not make it hopeless to try to single out the distinctiveness of the NT understanding of dreams, for this stands out clearly from the surrounding world with its correspondingly greater wealth of sources.

2. The Uniqueness of the NT Understanding of Dreams.

a. Paucity of Mention. There is an inner reason for this paucity, not just an outer. To be sure, Christians dreamed no less than other men of their age, though to some extent there might be psychological reasons why they should not have done so. The point is, however, that they regarded much fewer dreams as significant. The line found in the OT is now fully developed. Dreams are not wholly ruled out as a means of divine revelation. Jl. 2:28 can be approvingly quoted in Ac. 2:17, nor does it matter whether Peter used it in his address or it was added later by the community as a proof from Scripture.[51] The metaphysics of dreams, however, is even more fully uprooted than in the OT. Even in the latest NT writings we still find the same sobriety in face of insurgent Hellenism. In Jd. the lowest marks are given to libertinistic Gnostics who appeal to dreams (ἐνυπνια-ζόμενοι). Primitive Christianity is not hostile to dreams, but it is strongly critical. Even when significance is accorded to a dream, it remains peripheral, limited to individual instances of divine leading. Paul in his letters mentions none of the notable dreams which he had in Ac.[52] He seems to regard dreams as less worth noting than ὀπτασίαι καὶ ἀποκαλύψεις when awake, and even these he refers to only hesitantly and for a special reason (2 C. 12:1). No NT witness ever thought of basing the central message, the Gospel, or an essential part of it, on dreams.

b. Absence of Allegorical Dreams and Interpretations. All the dreams mentioned in the NT are theorematic, not allegorical (→ 226).[53] The Kurios appears to the person dreaming (Ac. 18:9; 23:11), or a divine messenger appears, or an angel (Ac. 27:23; Mt. 1:20; 2:13, 19), or a man (Ac. 16:9), and unequivocal direction is

---

[49] Cf. E. Fascher, "Das Weib des Pilatus," ThLZ, 72 (1947), 201-204; A. Oepke, "Noch einmal das Weib d. Pilatus," ThLZ, 73 (1948), 743-746.

[50] Phot. Lex., s.v. calls it βάρβαρον παντελῶς. Cf. Phryn. Ecl., ed. Lobeck (1820), 421-424. It is common in votive inscr. in the sense "on the basis of a dream," E. Schweizer, Grammatik d. pergamenischen Inschr. (1898), 157, → 224. Achmet constantly uses it in the other sense: ἐάν τις ἴδῃ κατ' ὄναρ, 18, 6; 19, 19; 54, 10 etc.; ἐν ὀνείρῳ, 3, 26; καθ' ὕπνους, 4, 5; 5, 19. So also Strabo, IV, 1, 4; Diog. L., X, 32.

[51] It is perhaps not wholly without deeper significance that Ac. 2:17 puts dreams second as compared with Jl. 2:28.

[52] Gl. 2:2 might refer to a dream, but if so it is worth noting that this is not given special prominence by Paul.

[53] For allegorical visions cf. Ac. 10:11 f.; Rev. 10:8 ff. etc.

given as to what will take place or what is to be done. Where the first is not
expressly stated, the second is indicated (Mt. 2:12, 22). For this reason there is
no interpretation of dreams at all in the NT. This is a simplification far beyond
that of the inspired interpretation of the OT. This simplification rests on the
unique confidence of the righteous man of the NT in his God. God is indeed the
hidden God for him too (R. 11:33 ff.; 1 Tm. 6:16). But when God comes forth
from His hiddenness and declares Himself, He speaks, not ambiguously, but openly.
He means to be understood.

c. Lofty Nature of Dream Life in the NT. The lofty nature of dream life in the
NT is unique. To come from the dream life of antiquity to the NT is to leave a
very profane and, for all its religion, very filthy world, and to enter the sanctuary.
The OT is the forecourt. There we see already the purifying power of the biblical
belief in God, a development beyond the limitations of the individual, and the close
connection between dreams and salvation history. The NT is the inner shrine,
but a shrine in which to live. It is in truth quite the reverse of self-evident —
even though it appears this, and that in itself is worth noting — that in a collection
of ancient writings which contain references — though few — to dreams, there
should be a complete exclusion of everything scabrous, vulgar, base, disgusting,
sexual, unnatural or egocentric. The things which dominate the ordinary dream
world of antiquity, the riotous superstition, curiosity, perversion, the half hopeful,
half despairing questioning as to one's personal fate, are all completely obliterated,
swallowed up in the peace of God. God is at the centre. His kingdom stands pre-
eminent. All the records of dreams in the NT are properly only variations on the
one theme of Christ. In keeping is the fact that there are no terrifying dreams in
the NT. [54] God gives His children direction (Mt. 1:20; 2:13 etc.; Ac. 16:9). The
Lord speaks words of consolation and strength to His disciples (Ac. 18:9; 23:11;
27:23 f.). If He chooses, He does this in dreams. [55] Thus the clash between superstition and enlightenment, which could not be resolved in antiquity, is now replaced by a higher synthesis. This solution is in a sense a paradigm on such NT
sayings as 2 C. 5:17; Mt. 6:33; 2 Tm. 1:7.

C. Dreams and the Interpretation of Dreams in the Post-Apostolic Period.

Early Christianity did not succeed for long in staying on the high level thus
achieved. The traditional understanding of dreams soon began to flourish again
in the Church, in detail to very different degrees and in very different ways.

The relevant terms do not occur in the post-apost. fathers. ὅραμα and ὅρασις are
partly used in Herm. for night visions, v., 3, 10, 6 : ἐν ὁράματι τῆς νυκτός, cf. 3, 1, 2,
not 3, 2, 3. But it may be doubted whether there is any basis in experience. It is difficult
to draw a sharp line between trance and dream. The lexical data suggest caution. The
words are also rare in the Apol., and here the dream is simply an instance of something
vain and empty, Athenag. Suppl., 13, 1: The heathen do not know οὐδ' ὄναρ, what
God is ; Tat. Or. Graec., 21, 1 — the text is hopelessly corrupt. Tat. Or. Graec., 1, 1
ironically recounts the things which the Gks. have taken over from the barbarians,
among them the δι' ὀνείρων μαντική of the Telmessians. He waxes merry about the

---

[54] Mt. 27:19 is to some degree the exception, but this is conditioned by special circumstances.
[55] Cf. A. Wikenhauser, "Doppelträume," Biblica, 29 (1948), 100-111; F. Smend, "Untersuchungen zu den Acta-Darstellungen von der Bekehrung des Paulus," Angelos, 1 (1925),
34-45, esp. 37 f.

gods which bind men by sickness to cure them δι' ὀνείρων, 18, 3. Just. Apol., 14, 1 links ὀνείρων ἐπιφάνεια and the magical pranks of demons as means to enslave man. Here, then, dream manticism is unmasked as paganism. But the same Just. makes dangerous apologetic use of spiritist phenomena, among them οἱ λεγόμενοι παρὰ τοῖς μάγοις ὀνειροπομποὶ καὶ πάρεδροι.

In the Gnostic Acts of the 2nd cent. visions and dreams abound. To Lycomedes, local leader in Ephesus, it is intimated in a dream that John will come to heal his wife, Act. Joh., 19, 21; 161, 16 f.; 162, 19. Early in the morning John ὄναρ θεασάμενος is present at the gates of the city to raise up one smitten by his son and to prevent further evils, 48; 175, 7. Mnesara, wife of Vazan, son of the king, who was converted by Thomas, is sent to him through a dream, Act. Thom., 154; 263, 13. The only historical value of these accounts is in relation to the milieu. Belief in dreams is already knocking at the door again.

We are on firmer ground in the accounts of martyrdom. Here the reports come from the immediate circle of the martyrs, or from their own hands. The dreams recorded are best understood in terms of agitation of spirit prior to martyrdom. Polycarp three days before his death saw his pillow in flames and said: "I must be burned alive," Mart. Pol., 5, 2. The account first suggests a trance : προσευχόμενος ἐν ὀπτασίᾳ γέγονε ... στραφεὶς εἶπεν πρὸς τοὺς σὺν αὐτῷ, but since it is expressly stated that he prayed day and night (5, 1), it is possible, esp. in view of his great age, that this was a dream. Mention of the pillow supports this. Perpetua in a dream sees her seven-year old brother Dinocrates, who died of cancer, as a saint, Mart. Perpetuae, 7, 3 ff.; [56] this was on the day before her death in the arena. Saturus in a dream has a vision of the Son of Man, and also sees the martyrs who have gone before with Him, and the entrance into Paradise, 11. Cyprian escaped arrest by fleeing to the estate of Curubis. Here he told the author of the Vita, his deacon Paulinus, how half-asleep he asked and received from the pro-consul a one-day postponement of his execution. Cheered by this, he came to himself again (resipisco). But the uncertainty of interpretation caused him palpitation of heart (metu tamen interpretationis incertae sic tremebam, ut reliquiae formidinis cor exultans adhuc toto pavore pulsarent, Vita, 12, CSEL, 3, 3, CIII, 6 ff.). It is significant that all these accounts are in the first person. While the theorematic element is predominant, an allegorical element may be detected again. This complicates interpretation and leads to burdensome anxiety for a right understanding. The biographer of Cyprian rejoiced that the intimation was fulfilled to the letter. For a year later Cyprian was crowned. In a divine intimation a day is a year. But the contorted considerations which he links with it, and the example of his hero, show plainly the difficulties experienced.

The dream metaphysics of paganism now begins to infiltrate Christianity with increasing force. Synesius of Cyrene, a disciple of Hypatia on the bishop's throne, is the author of a book of dreams. [57] This is quite distinctive. Synesius has only gentle contempt for current books because they do not give individual interpretations, 151b ff. The express purpose of his work, supposedly written in one night (Ep., 153, MPG, 66, 1556d), is, however, to protect dream manticism against contempt, 143a. He sets his view on a broad metaphysical and epistemological foundation, uniting Platonic-Aristotelian, atomistic, Stoic (Poseidonius) and Neo-Platonic (Porphyrius, Chald. oracle) in a confused eclecticism. Theorematic dreams, which need no interpretation, are esp. valued, 149a. In interpretation of most of the rest the principle applies : Like follows like, 150c d. To try to gain a personal empirical basis for application, Synesius recommends the keeping of a book of day-dreams and dreams (ἐφημερίδες, ἐπινυκτίδες, 153a). The level of his work is above the average. Since dream manticism is at the

---

56 O. v. Gebhardt, Acta Martyrum selecta (1902), 73.
57 → 223. Quoted acc. to the arrangement of Lang, which is not exactly the same as MPG, loc. cit.

disposal of rich and poor alike without unwieldy apparatus, it is to be accorded special respect, 143d ff. It affords the opportunity of timely protection against misfortune, sickness etc., and of a double enjoyment of good fortune by anticipation. It helps equally in hunting, writing, and the performance of difficult diplomatic tasks, 146a ff.; 148a ff. This one-sided optimism is rooted in the metaphysics of dreams ; dream manticism smooths the way to God (143b), and the promise given in dreams is a divine pledge (146d). The only question is how far the Christianity of the time is responsible for this hodge-podge. Synesius undoubtedly wrote the book before his baptism. [58] But there is also no doubt that he knew Christianity well enough at the time, and his election as bishop, though it has political undertones, shows how little offence was taken at his Neo-Platonic syncretism. He himself, with full subjective sincerity, felt no break at this point, and merely regretted losing his leisure.

In the period which followed, the situation became quite unequivocal. The fact that dream books could be ascribed to men of the Bible and high ecclesiastics (→ 223) is very illuminating. In Achmet (→ 223) a religious medley and crass superstition are closely related and engage in unrestricted orgies. Achmet traces the beginning of interpretation to God (1, 1), and grounds dream manticism on the dreams of Joseph and Daniel, and indeed on Jn. 14:23 (2, 1 ff.). But he draws his wisdom, and the interpretation of dreams about the Trinity, the resurrection of the dead, angels, paradise and hell, prophets and apostles, from what seem to be Indian, Persian and Egypt. sources (3 ff.). An appearance of Christ signifies great good fortune and for sinners repentance and salvation (105, 13 ff.). The main ingredients, however, are trivial interpretations of everyday things, as in Artemid., but at a much lower level : Mottled hair denotes a position of honour (15, 1 ff.), the cutting of side-hairs poor management of income (15, 18 ff.), urinating in an alabaster vessel, if by a poor man, his wife's pregnancy, if by a king, the pregnancy of a commoner with miscarriage, because of the fragility (29, 5 ff.).

Thus the muddy waters of antiquity, not without a misuse of holy things, nor without the guilt of the Church, debouch into the sink of new superstition.

Oepke

ὀνάριον → ὄνος.

ὄνειδος, ὀνειδίζω, ὀνειδισμός

† ὄνειδος.

ὄνειδος belongs etym., not to ὄνομαι, but to an Indo-Eur. root *neid-* "to revile," "to reproach." [1] On a deriv. from ὄνομαι the -ειδος would be inexplicable. The idea of "good repute" is rightly rejected by Liddell-Scott. When used thus by the poets (e.g., Eur. Med., 514 : καλὸν ὄνειδος, Phoen., 821 : κάλλιστον ὄνειδος) the word is meant ironically. The predominant sense is "disgrace," "shame," "scandal," then "abuse," "objurgation." The word is usually found with the verbs λέγειν, προφέρειν or ἐπιφέρειν, βάζειν etc.: ὄνειδος ὀνειδίζειν, Soph. Phil., 523. ὄνειδος is also the "object of disgrace or shame." In this transf. sense the word denotes "one who is covered by shame or brings disgrace on others." Thus the daughters of Oedipus are called (Soph. Oed. Tyr., 1494) τοιαῦτ' ὀνείδη. Cf. also Aristoph. Ach., 855 : Λυσίστρα-

---

58 Cf. Lang, 33.

ὄνειδος. [1] [So Debrunner.] Cf. Walde-Pok., II, 322.

τος . . ., Χολαργέων ὄνειδος and Lyc., 5 : τῆς τε πατρίδος ὄνειδος καὶ πάντων ὑμῶν.

In the LXX[2] the group ὄνειδος, ὀνειδίζω, ὀνειδισμός embraces a number of experiences whose common factor is a relation to God disrupted by sinful man. For this reason the whole of man's earthly life stands under the shame to which God subjects man as a sinner (cf. esp. Jer. and Ps.). The hope of deliverance is orientated especially to liberation from this, e.g., Is. 25:8; Jl. 2:19. Man in his earthly life is in many ways subject to the shame which, whether he despises or is despised, is the basis and result of sin. This may be seen in the fact that he heaps opprobrium on others, especially the righteous. This is how Israel views its history and the righteous their destiny. The human passion for abuse is finally directed against God, who avenges the insults brought against Him and subjects the ungodly, the enemies of the chosen people, to shame. This is true of wrong-doers, whether individual or national, who transgress divine and human law and offend against morality. Sin is a reproach to a people, Prv. 14:34 (Mas., Σ; not the LXX). Violating the Law is a disgrace before both God and man. But this is also true of the righteous, whom God delivers up to reproach for testing, training and chastisement (Is. 37:3), but whom He finally delivers from it. In this respect the righteous are on God's side. They bear the shame which would fall on God Himself (ψ 68:7, 9). This is the final explanation of their destiny. Their piety is a piety of suffering which gives joy and power in affliction and which in the assurance of faith (ψ 72:23-28) finds security in the world and the courage for action. In suffering, then, lies deliverance and liberation from all shame.

As in secular lit., so in the LXX one may note a transition from abstract to concrete use. In several passages ὄνειδος means "one who is covered with shame." The word thus has the sense of ὀνειδιζόμενος. The neutr. takes the place of the masc. form. Ez. 16:57 is clearest in this respect : νῦν ὄνειδος εἶ θυγατέρων Συρίας. The borders of ὄνειδος and ὀνειδισμός are fluid in the LXX. The same is true in the other transl. Σ sometimes prefers ὄνειδος where LXX has ὀνειδισμός (ψ 68:10; 73:22). 'Α, however, seems to prefer ὀνειδισμός, e.g., Job 19:5; ψ 68:10, 20; 'Ιερ. 38:19.

In the NT ὄνειδος occurs only at Lk. 1:25. Elisabeth, wife of Zacharias, feels her childlessness to be a disgrace. When, after the miraculous intimation of the angel to Zacharias, she becomes pregnant, she rejoices : οὕτως μοι πεποίηκεν κύριος . . . ἀφελεῖν ὄνειδός μου ἐν ἀνθρώποις.

† ὀνειδίζω.

ὀνειδίζειν, "to upbraid," "scold," "revile," "bring reproaches against someone," "lay something to a person's charge," "raise a complaint against something." In gen. with acc. of obj.,[1] but also περί τινος, ἔκ τινος, εἴς τι[2] with dat. of person, more rarely acc. In the LXX most common in Ps., esp. of opponents ; then common in Sir. Mostly for pi of חרף. The objects of ὀνειδίζειν are God, Israel, the righteous, or men of the nearest and closest circle of life. Several times in Test. XII : Test. S. 4:6; Jud. 13:3; Jos. 17:4. In the NT with acc. of obj. or person ; also without acc. obj.

---

[2] Detailed examples in Liddell-Scott and Pass., s.v.
ὀ ν ε ι δ ί ζ ω. [1] In pap.: BGU, IV, 1024 VII, 20 f.: αἰσχρῶς τὴν ἐπ' ἀ[ν]θρώποις τύχην ὀνειδίζουσαν.
[2] In this section I owe a great deal to G. Bertram.

Included in the authority of the earthly Jesus is ὀνειδίζειν. When His work is unsuccessful in the cities of Galilee, and His acts of power do not lead to faith and conversion, Jesus condemns the cities, Mt. 11:20. In the inauthentic Marcan ending (Mk. 16:14) the disciples are also reproached by the risen Lord for their unbelief and hardness of heart. This is because they did not believe those who had seen Jesus after His resurrection.

But the passion of Jesus also includes being despised even by those who were crucified with Him, Mk. 15:32; Mt. 27:44. The disciples share with their Master the fate of having to suffer. Jesus shows them in Mt. 5:11 that they will be reviled and persecuted for His sake. But above their sufferings stands the word μακάριοι, → IV, 368. In this paradox is enclosed the uniqueness, mystery and glory of discipleship. [3] In Lk. 6:22 ἀφορίζειν is used instead of διώκειν. The disciples have to reckon with the fact that they will be excluded from all fellowship with their fellow-men. A similar thought occurs in 1 Pt. 4:14, where we again find ὀνειδίζεσθαι and μακάριοι in juxtaposition. Because Christians separate themselves from the world to live for the will of God, there arises hatred, contempt and persecution. Blessedness in suffering is based on the fact that the "Spirit of glory" rests on them. According to Heitmüller [4] ἐν ὀνόματι Χριστοῦ means the same as ὡς Χριστιανός. Thus the thought of Christ's passion is echoed in the whole phrase ὀνειδίζεσθαι ἐν ὀνόματι Χριστοῦ. [5]

In Jm. 1:5 a statement about God is made in connection with ὀνειδίζειν. To be generous in giving is of the very essence of God. Men often accompany their gifts with discontented utterances which degrade and wound the recipient. [6] But God gives and does not upbraid.

Paul in R. 15:3 quotes Ps. 69:9 : οἱ ὀνειδισμοὶ τῶν ὀνειδιζόντων σε ἐπέπεσαν ἐπ᾽ ἐμέ, [7] with a view to setting before the community the example of the unselfish and humble mind of Christ.

ὀνειδίζειν occurs as vl. in Mk. 15:34 and 1 Tm. 4:10. In Mk. 15:34 the Evangelist renders the saying of Jesus on the cross : ἐλωΐ ἐλωΐ λαμὰ σαβαχθάνι (which comes from ψ 21[22]:2 Messianically interpreted), by ὁ θεός μου ὁ θεός μου, εἰς τί ἐγκατέλιπές με. But this expression of dereliction seems to have caused offence at quite an early date. It does not occur in Lk. or Jn. D it^var Macarius Magnes I 12 weaken ἐγκατέλιπες to ὠνείδισας. [8] At 1 Tm. 4:10 our text reads : εἰς τοῦτο γὰρ κοπιῶμεν καὶ ἀγωνιζόμεθα. The reading ὀνειδιζόμεθα found in many witnesses, e.g., א^c D vg syr^utr arm aeth, hardly fits the context. Paul is speaking of the γυμνασία of the piety which is the goal of his own and Timothy's efforts and exertions.

---

[3] Cf. Schl. Mt., 142 : "Discipleship brings sufferings and therewith the reason for exultant joy."
[4] W. Heitmüller, Im Namen Jesu (1903), 87: "ἐν ὀνόματι Χριστοῦ denotes the category in which, or the title under which, Christians are reviled."
[5] On 1 Pt. 4:14 T. Spörri, Der Gemeindegedanke im 1 Pt. (1925), 69, 88, 202, 207; Wnd. Pt., 77; J. Schneider, Die Passionsmystik d. Pls. (1929), 122.
[6] Cf. the sayings in Sir.: 20:15 : ὀλίγα δώσει καὶ πολλὰ ὀνειδίσει, the admonition in 41:25 : μετὰ τὸ δοῦναι μὴ ὀνείδιζε. Cf. also Plut. Adulat., 22 (II, 64a): πᾶσα μὲν γὰρ ὀνειδιζομένη χάρις ἐπαχθὴς καὶ ἄχαρις καὶ οὐκ ἀνεκτή.
[7] וְחֶרְפּוֹת חוֹרְפֶיךָ נָפְלוּ עָלָי.
[8] Kl. Mk., 185. A. v. Harnack, "Probleme im Texte d. Leidensgeschichte Jesu," SAB (1901), 261-265.

† ὀνειδισμός.

ὀνειδισμός "insult," "abuse," "reproach," is a late word, a construction of the *koine*. [1] It occurs in Dion. Hal., Ep. ad Pompeium, 785 : προσλαμβάνων (τινὰ) τοῖς ἀναγκαίοις ὀνειδισμοῖς, Menander Protector, 37[2] : ἡ γὰρ ἐπιστολὴ ὕβρεώς τε μεστὴ καὶ ὀνειδισμοῦ καὶ μεμεθυσμένων ῥημάτων ὑπῆρχε, Plut. Artaxerxes, 22, 6 (I, 1022e): τοῦτο δ' ἦν ὀνειδισμὸς εἰς προδοσίαν μᾶλλον ἢ χάριτος ὑπόμνησις, Vett. Val., 65, 7: ἐξ ὀνειδισμῶν γὰρ καὶ κακῶν, 73, 10 f.: ἐξ ὀνειδισμῶν καὶ ἐνέδρας καὶ δόλου καὶ ἐπιθέσεως.

It is fairly common in the LXX, usually for חֶרְפָּה. Cf. the expression λόγος (λόγοι) ὀνειδισμοῦ, Sir. 23:15; 31:31; 41:25. With ὀνειδισμοὺς ἀκούειν, λαμβάνειν, ὑποφέρειν, we also find the strong χορτάζεσθαι ὀνειδισμῶν, Lam. 3:30. πονηρία and ὀνειδισμός occur together at Neh. 1:3, ἐμπαιγμός and ὀνειδισμός at Sir. 27:28, ἄβατον and ὀνειδισμός at Bar. 2:4. Even more characteristic is the heaping up of synon. in the description of a יוֹם צָרָה at Is. 37:3 : ἡμέρα θλίψεως καὶ ὀνειδισμοῦ καὶ ἐλεγμοῦ καὶ ὀργῆς. As with ὄνειδος, there is a concrete use at Tob. 8:10 : μήποτε γενώμεθα ... ὀνειδισμός. Yet even more common is ἔσεσθαι εἰς ὀνειδισμόν, Jdt. 5:21; Ἰερ. 24:9; 30:7. In Test. XII cf. R. 4:2; 4:7: ὀνειδισμὸν ἑαυτῷ φέρει καὶ πρόσκομμα, L. 10:4 : ἔσεσθε εἰς ὄνειδος καὶ εἰς κατάραν, Jud. 23:3. In Jos. Ant., 19, 319.

In 1 Tm. 3:7 blamelessness of walk is required of the ἐπίσκοπος. This is to find expression in the testimony of those who do not belong to the Christian community, lest the ἐπίσκοπος should come under reproach and defamation (ἵνα μὴ εἰς ὀνειδισμὸν ἐμπέσῃ).

The fullest use is in Hb. At 10:33 we find ὀνειδισμοί and θλίψεις together. The author reminds the readers that in earlier times of affliction they were made a spectacle by reproaches and oppressions (θεατριζόμενοι, → III, 43). At 11:26, in a distinctive combination of widely separated historical events, there is reference to the ὀνειδισμὸς τοῦ Χριστοῦ in the life of Moses. The suffering of the people of Israel which Moses is willing to share is closely related by the author to the (future) suffering of the Messiah. There is a mysterious connection between all the sufferings which occur according to God's plan of salvation. The resolve of Moses to accept the afflictions of his people rather than enjoy sinfully the treasures of Egypt is regarded as an act of faith. The expression ὀνειδισμὸς τοῦ Χριστοῦ recurs at 13:13. The author demands from his readers a separation from the world, and from earthly life in general, according to the example of Jesus. As Jesus suffered outside the camp, so Christians are to differentiate themselves from the profane world and bear the reproach of Christ necessarily involved in such action and conduct. This reproach is the suffering which Christians must endure as such. The nature of the ὀνειδισμός is more precisely indicated by the gen. τοῦ Χριστοῦ. [3] In a fellowship of suffering with Christ — the expression ὀνειδισμὸς τοῦ Χριστοῦ

ὀ ν ε ι δ ι σ μ ό ς. K. H. Schelkle, *Die Passion Jesu in d. Verkündigung d. NT* (1949), 108 f.
[1] Cf. Bl.-Debr.[7] § 109, 1.
[2] Historici Graeci Minores, II, 76, 5 ff.
[3] Cf. O. Schmitz, *Die Christusgemeinschaft d. Pls. im Lichte seines Genetivgebrauchs* (1924), 229-233.

unites Christ and Christians — Christians are to be "Messianic bearers of the cross" [4] (cf. ὀνειδισμὸν φέρειν already in Test. R. 4:7).

ὀνειδισμός as well as ὀνειδίζειν occurs in the quotation at R. 15:3 (οἱ ὀνειδισμοὶ τῶν ὀνειδιζόντων), → 240.

J. Schneider

ὄνομα, ὀνομάζω, ἐπονομάζω, ψευδώνυμος

Contents: A. Religio-Historical Background. B. The Greek World and Hellenism: 1. Usage; 2. The Significance of ὄνομα in the History of Greek Thought; 3. The Name of God; 4. The Magic Papyri. C. The Old Testament: 1. Lexical and Statistical Data; 2. The Significance of the Name; 3. Proper Names and Meaningful Names; 4. שֵׁם יהוה; 5. בְּשֵׁם, especially בְּשֵׁם יהוה. D. Hellenistic Judaism: 1. LXX; 2. Philo; 3. Josephus;

---

[4] Wnd. Hb., 119.

ὄνομα κτλ. On A: H. Schmidt-E. Wissmann, Art. "Namenglaube," RGG², IV, 408-412; G. van der Leeuw, *Phänomenologie d. Religion* (1933), 129-142; L. Lévy-Bruhl, *D. Seele d. Primitiven* (1930), 205, 216-220, 335, 339; F. Freiherr v. Andrian, "Über Wortaberglauben," *Correspondenzblatt d. deutschen Gesellschaft f. Anthropologie, Ethnologie u. Urgeschichte*, 27 (1896), 109-127. On B: R. Hirzel, "Der Name, ein Beitrag zu seiner Geschichte im Altertum u. bes. bei d. Griechen," ASG, 36, 2 (1918); W. Nestle, *Vom Mythos zum Logos* (1940), 103, 112, 197 f., 271 f., 302, 349, 467, 494; F. Heinimann, "Nomos u. Physis," *Schweizerische Beiträge zur Altertumswissenschaft*, 1 (1945); H. Usener, *Götternamen*³ (1948); Rohde ⁹, ¹⁰, I, 206 f.; II, 346 f.; T. Hopfner, *Griech.-ägyptischer Offenbarungszauber*, I (1921), §§ 147 f., 413, 489, 569, 680, 686-706, 718, 767, 775, 777; E. Norden, *Agnostos Theos* (1913), 57, 71, 145, 164 f., 179; H. Steinthal, *Gesch. d. Sprachwissenschaft bei d. Griechen u. Römern*², I (1890), II (1891); M. Pohlenz, "Die Begründung d. abendländischen Sprachlehre durch d. Stoa," NGG, I, NF, 3 (1939), 155-190; F. Preisigke, *Das Girowesen im griech. Ägypten* (1910), 75, 120, 142, 147, 149-151. On C: J. Boehmer, *Das bibl. "Im Namen," eine sprachwissenschaftliche Untersuchung über das hbr. בְּשֵׁם u. seine gr. Äquivalente* (1898); also "Zwei Kapitel aus d. bibl. Hermeneutik," BFTh, 5, 6 (1901), 49-127; F. Giesebrecht, *D. at.liche Schätzung d. Gottesnamens* (1901); B. Jacob, *Im Namen Gottes* (1903); O. Grether, "Name u. Wort Gottes im AT," ZAW Beih., 64 (1934); M. Noth, "D. isr. Personennamen im Rahmen d. gemeinsemitischen Namengebung," BWANT, 3, F. 10 (1928). On D: Helbing Kasussyntax, 51; J. Pascher, ʿΗ Βασιλικὴ ʿΟδός, *Der Königsweg zu Wiedergeburt u. Vergottung bei Philon v. Alex.* (1931), 16 f.; A. F. Dähne, *Geschichtliche Darstellung d. jüdisch-alexandrinischen Religionsphilosophie*, I (1834), 73, 138 f., 149 f.; Schl. Theol. d. Judt., 60-62, 112, 155, 245. On E: Bousset-Gressm., 307-319, 349 f.; Moore, I, 424-431; J. Bonsirven, *Le Judaïsme Palestinien au temps de Jésus-Christ*, I (1935), 30, 138-145; L. Blau, *Das altjüdische Zauberwesen* (1898), 30, 118-146; Bacher Term., I, 85, 159, 186-189; II, 217 f.; M. Grünbaum, "Über Schem Hammephorasch als Nachbildung eines aram. Ausdrucks u. über sprachliche Nachbildungen überhaupt," ZDMG, 39 (1885), 543-616; 40 (1886), 234-304; H. Odeberg, *3 Enoch or the Hebrew Book of Enoch ...* (1928). On F: Cr.-Kö., Pr.-Bauer, *s.v.*; Deissmann B, 143 ff.; Deissmann NB, 24 f.; Deissmann LO, 97 f.; W. Heitmüller, "Im Namen Jesu," FRL, I, 2 (1903); A. Seeberg's review of Heitmüller, ThLBl, 25 (1904), 602-606; Dalman WJ, I², 149 f.; Clemen, 164-168; C. Weizsäcker, *Das apostolische Zeitalter d. Kirche*² (1892), 551 f.; H. J. Holtzmann, *Lehrbuch d. nt.lichen Theol.*, I² (1911), 452; II² (1911), 196-199; H. Weinel, *Bibl. Theol. d. NT*⁴ (1928), 203; Stauffer Theol., 128-140; R. Reitzenstein, *D. Vorgeschichte d. chr. Taufe* (1929), 28-30, 139, 156 f., 161, 165, 179; A. J. H. W. Brandt, "ʿΟνομα en de Doopsformule in het NT," ThT, 25 (1891), 565-610.

4. Later Judaism: I. The Pseudepigrapha; II. Rabbinic Sources: (1) Usage; (2) The Name of God; (3) Belief and Magic. F. The New Testament: 1. Usage; 2. ὄνομα as the Name of God or Jesus Christ. 3. Other References.

A. Religio-Historical Background.

There was and is a world-wide belief that the name of an object, man, or higher being is more than a mere label only incidentally associated with the one who bears it. The name is an indispensable part of the personality. One might say that a man is constituted of body, soul and name. [1] Various rites are used to seek, find and give a name to a child. If a man has the name of an ancestor, he represents this ancestor in his social group. [2] When a child receives the name of a deceased person, he fills in his clan the gap caused by the death. Often a new name is given in puberty rites, for the man himself is made new by the rites. [3] "The name is not just a designation but an expressed essentiality." [4] Experience of power and will is reflected in the name. The name is not abstract; it gives clear form and solid content to the will. Only when the gods have names do they acquire personality, history and myth. Only when men know the name of a god can they call upon him, have dealings with him, or bring him into play by magic. Men can have this magical power over the god only because in the case of the gods, too, the name is essentially linked with the one who bears it. Of both men and gods it is finally true that the name contains *mana*. [5] When the name is invoked or pronounced, the one invoked appears or works whether desired or not, or the one who invokes affects the one invoked. This explains the reluctance to state or give a name, and the corresponding desire to know a name, which is a desire to enjoy the protection or help of the power linked up with the name. Associated with this, of course, is the exact knowledge of a name, or the knowledge of all names. This is important when gods or demons have secret names. Possession of these ensures their freedom, but when other gods or even men learn them, they come to be fully dependent on them.

The name is thus a power which is very closely associated with the bearer and which discloses his nature. Pronouncement or invocation of the name sets in operation the energy potentially contained in him.

B. The Greek World and Hellenism.

1. Usage.

ὄνομα [6] (Aeol. and Doric ὄνυμα, poetic οὔνομα by metrical extension) is common in all secular Gk.

a. "Name" of a person or thing, used only with ref. to men in Hom.; each man has a name given him by his parents, Od., 8, 550-554. There is in the name-giving an attempt to awaken good *omina*. [7] A stranger must give his name if he claims the right of hospitality, Od., 9, 16-20; only then can a gift be given him, 9, 355 f. The name is a constituent part of a man. Only when it is lost is his whole nature destroyed, 4, 710. To be without a name (ἀνώνυμος) is abnormal acc. to Hdt., IV, 184.

---

[1] Lévy-Bruhl, 217.
[2] *Ibid.*, 335.
[3] *Ibid.*, 220.
[4] van der Leeuw, 129-141.
[5] A. Bertholet, "Religionsgeschichtliche Ambivalenzerscheinungen," *Theol. Zeitschrift*, 4 (1948), 5.
[6] Etym. Lat. *nomen*, Germ. *Name*, Eng. "name," Sanskr. *nāma* etc.; a link with ὄνομαι, "scold," "blame" is unlikely (Walde-Pok., I, 132, 180, cf. E. Schwyzer, *Griech. Grammatik*, I = *Hndbch. AW*, II, 1, 1 [1939], 352d, 523) [Debrunner].
[7] J. Burckhardt, *Griech. Kulturgeschichte*, IV (1902), 9 ff.

The most important grammatical combinations are ὄνομα τίθεσθαί τινι (Od., 19, 403 f.; Plat. Crat., 393e) or ἐπί τινι (Od., 8, 554), "to give someone a name"; cf. ὄνομα φέρειν ἐπί τι (Aristot. Eth. Nic., III, 12, p. 1119a, 33 f.); ὄνομα καλεῖν τινα, "to call someone by name," "to name" (Od., 8, 550), τινί "to give someone a name" (Plat. Polit., 279e), or ἐπί τινι (Plat. Parm.,147d). Πόλις ὄνομα Καιναί "of the name" (Xenoph. An., II, 4, 28), rarely ὀνόματι in this sense, e.g., Xenoph. Hist. Graec., I, 6, 29. With prep. κατ' ὄνομα, ἐπ' ὀνόματος, "by name," "specifically." [8] ἐκ τοῦ τῶν βασιλέων ὀνόματος "in the name" (Diod. S., 18, 60, 6; cf. 18, 57, 3). [9] The Gk. language does not have ἐν τῷ ὀνόματι with gen. of person as modal definition. [10] Very rarely we find ἐπὶ τῷ ὀνόματί τινος, "with mention, indication, or invocation of the name of someone," e.g., Demosth. Or., 20, 126 : εἰ γὰρ ἃ κατὰ μηδέν' ἄλλον ἔχουσι τρόπον δεῖξαι δίκαιον ὑμᾶς ἀφελέσθαι, ταῦτ' ἐπὶ τῷ τῶν θεῶν ὀνόματι ποιεῖν ζητήσουσι, Isaeus, 11, 13 : ἐπὶ δὲ τοῦ παιδὸς ὀνόματι πράγματ' ἐμοὶ παρέχειν, Demosth. Or., 34, 36 : ἐπὶ τῷ τῆς πόλεως ὀνόματι, Luc. Piscator, 15 : ἐπὶ τῷ ἡμετέρῳ ὀνόματι, but cf. Isaeus, 6, 21: ἐπὶ τῷ αὐτοῦ ὀνόματι, "under his own name." On the other hand εἰς τὸ ὄνομα with gen. of person is first found on pap. in the Hell. period (→ 245). [11]

b. "Name" in the sense of "repute," Hom. Od., 24, 93 f.; synon. with κλέος. Thuc., II, 64, 3 : ὄνομα μέγιστον ἔχειν, Strabo, IX, 1, 23 : ἐν ὀνόματι εἶναι "to have a name," "to be known." Xenoph. Cyrop., VI, 4, 7: ἐν ἀτίμῳ ὀνόματι "in an unnoticed position" (as secondary wife). Polyb., 15, 35, 1: οἱ ἐν πράγμασιν ἐπ' ὀνόματος γεγονότες. Athen., VI, 39 (p. 241a): δι' ὀνόματος. εἰς ὄνομα in the abs. "to the honour." [12]

c. "Name" as opp. to thing, opp. ἔργον (Eur. Or., 454; Thuc., VIII, 78; 89, 2), opp. πρᾶγμα (Demosth. Or., 9, 15); opp. φύσις (Thuc., IV, 60, 1). Thuc., VI, 10, 2 : ὀνόματι σπονδαὶ ἔσονται, "nominally" (not in reality), cf. III, 10, 6. ἐν τῷ ὀνόματί τινος "under the pretext": Dio C., 38, 44 : ταῦτ' ἐκεῖνος ἔν τε τοῖς τῆς φιλίας καὶ ἐν τοῖς τῆς συμμαχίας ὀνόμασιν ἐξείργασται, cf. 42, 24.

d. ὄνομα with gen. = the actual thing or person. Eur. Iph. Taur., 905 f.: τὸ ὄνομα τῆς σωτηρίας λαβόντες = τὴν σωτηρίαν λαβόντες, Phoen., 1702 : ὦ φίλτατον δῆτ' ὄνομα Πολυνείκους ἐμοί. [13]

---

[8] κατ' ὄνομα : Strato, 1, 14 (CAF, III, 362); Epigr. Graec., 983, 4. ἐπ' ὀνόματος, Polyb., 18, 45, 4; Monumentum Ancyranum, 21: θέατρον ... ἀνήγειρα ἐπὶ ὀνόματος Μαρκέλλου = theatrum ... feci, quod sub nomine M. Marcelli ... esset (the transl. of Apollonia has ὀνόματι).

[9] ἐκ τοῦ δεῖνα ὀνόματος, "to the account," "on the commission," "at the instance" of NN (BGU, I, 300, 7; σύμβαλε αὐτῷ ἐξ ὀνόματός μου, "go to him on my commission" (P. Oxy., VII, 1063, 3).

[10] On this and what follows cf. Heitmüller, 47-51.

[11] Ibid., 101-109. The formula in Herodian Hist., II, 2, 10; 13, 2 : ὀμνύναι εἰς τὸ ὄνομά τινος, which reminds us of the NT, is late (2nd/3rd cent.): Latinism iurare in nomen principis (from Sueton.) [Debrunner].

[12] Plut. Sertorius, 3 (I, 569b); Pericl., 4 (I, 153 f.); Philostr. Vit. Ap., 3, 22; Heitmüller, 101.

[13] From the 1st cent. A.D. we find many pap. instances of ὄνομα for person, cf. Preisigke Wört., s.v.; P. Flor., III, 373, 2 : πολλὰ ὀνόματα δούς (3rd cent. A.D.); Mitteis-Wilcken, I, 28, 19 : ἕτερα ὀνόματα ἀντ' αὐτοῦ εἰς τὴν χρέαν πέμψαι, "to propose substitutes for service" (2nd cent. A.D.); P. Oxy., III, 533, 21: ὀνόματα πέμπειν ... εἰς κλῆρον τῆς πρακτορείας, to present suitable names for drawing for service in raising taxes (2nd/3rd cent. A.D.); BGU, II, 390, 8 : ἀπορικὰ ὀνόματα καὶ ἄλλα τετελευτηκότα, those who have inadequate income or who are dead (3rd cent. A.D.); C. Wessely, Studien z. Paläographie u. Papyruskunde, I (1902), 71, 439 : ὀνόματα ιβ', number of heads 12 (1st cent. A.D., Jewish taxation list). Semitic Gk. possibly exerted some influence on this common use of ὄνομα for person, cf. Hirzel, 11 and 13.

e. ὄνομα as tt. in grammar : "word," "noun," "substantive," Plat. Soph., 262a.

f. The pap. extend the usage at some points. Thus ὄνομα is "the name of a person in books or on lists establishing its owner's rights and obligations." [14] ἑκάστῳ ὀνόματι παράκειται δικαιώματα, BGU, I, 113, 11 the documents of authorisation are always deposited in the "names" of those concerned. βαρέσαι (= βαρῆσαι) τὸ ἐμὸν ὄνομα, P. Oxy., I, 126, 8, "to charge to my account." Administratively ὄνομα has the sense of "legal title" or "item in an account." [15] τὸ τῶν δημοσίων ὄνομα, Ditt. Or., II, 669, 18, "public title," "taxes." γίνονται ὀνόματι ἰδιωτικῆς ἄρουραι Χ, x measures of land in the "class" private land. [16] περὶ πράγματος ἀνήκοντος τῷ ὀνόματι τῶν γονέων, P. Par., 20, 22, with regard to property belonging to the title of parents. γεωργῶ δημοσίαν γῆν ὀνόματι τοῦ δεῖνα, P. Oxy., VII, 1031, 12, "to the account," "on the responsibility of someone" (3rd cent. A.D.). ἔχω ἐμμισθώσει ἀπὸ ὀνόματος Νόννου, [17] from the property of Nonnos (4th cent. A.D.). Payment is made to the account of the recipient : μετρήσομαι εἰς τὸ ὄνομα τοῦ δεῖνα, P. Tebt., II, 577 (1st cent. A.D.); διάστειλον εἰς ὄνομα τοῦ δεῖνα ἀρτάβας Χ [18] (2nd cent. A.D.); σύμβολον εἰς τοῦ Κλεομάχου ὄνομα, P. Hibeh, 74, 3 ; permit in the name of Kleomachos (3rd cent. B.C.); ἔντευξις εἰς τὸ τοῦ βασιλέως ὄνομα, P. Petr., II, 2, 1, 3; P. Hal., 9, 2, petition to the authorities in the name of the king. The expression εἰς (τὸ) ὄνομα is a tt. in the business world. At root is the idea of entry in an account under the name of the holder. εἰς with the name can be used instead of εἰς (τὸ) ὄνομα. [19] We find it esp. in banking : Make a credit in the name (εἰς ὄνομα) of Eponychos ... to the amount of C artabas of wheat [20] (2nd/3rd cent. A.D.). A specialised expression in banking is πρόσθες εἰς ὄνομα τοῦ δεῖνα. [21] Here εἰς ὄνομα does not just mean in the name but refers to the account over each of whose divisions the name of the owner stands. Hence we read ἐποίσω μέ[τ]ρησιν καθαρὰ[ν] [ε]ἰς [ὄ]νομά σου, P. Lond., III, 938, 10 : "I will enter the payment in the section of the account which bears your name." διάστειλον ἐκ τοῦ ἐμοῦ θέματος εἰς ὄνομα Λουκιλλᾶτος (πυροῦ) τρίτον ὄγδον [22] (2nd/3rd cent. A.D.); here εἰς ὄνομα is expressly used to denote unequivocally payment or credit in the account under the name of Lukillas. If εἰς (τὸ) ὄνομα τοῦ δεῖνα occurs, the thought is that of payment by credit, while use of εἰς τὸν δεῖνα denotes cash payment. [23] Changes of meaning occur in respect of certain prep. phrases. ἀπὸ τῶν κατηντηκότων εἰς με ἐξ ὀνόματος τοῦ πατρός μου, P. Oxy., I, 75, 5 f. (the inheritance which has come to me by (testamentary) disposition of my father (2nd cent. A.D.). Entered ἐν ὀνόματι, under the name, is used in the βιβλιοθήκη ἐγκτήσεων (property office), where the name of the owner is always put at the head of inventories and in the record book. With the name the relevant data are entered or the title is recorded. [24] τῆς οἰκίας οὐ διακειμένης ἐν ὀνόματι τῆς ἀποδομένης, P. Lips., 3, II, 25, the information relating to the house is not entered under the name of the woman who sells it. ἐπ' ὀνόματος τοῦ δεῖνα, rights or duties transferred to the name of NN ; πάντα τὰ ἐπ' ὀνόματος τῆς μητρός μου ὑπάρχοντα (BGU, I, 226, 15), all the assets transferred to the name of my mother (1st cent. A.D.). ἐπ' ὀνόματι

---

[14] Preisigke Wört., s.v.
[15] Loc. cit.
[16] F. Preisigke, Gr. Urkunden d. ägypt. Museums zu Kairo (1911), 47, 10.
[17] B. Grenfell, An Alexandrian Erotic Fragment and Other Gk. Papyri (1896), 54, 7.
[18] P. M. Meyer, Griech. Texte aus Ägypten (1916), Ostracon, 56, 2.
[19] Mayser, II, 2, 415.
[20] U. Wilcken, Griech. Ostraka aus Ägypten u. Nubien, II (1899), 1159; Preisigke, Girowesen, 149.
[21] Preisigke, Girowesen, 120; there is no actual transaction.
[22] Wilcken, op. cit., 1164.
[23] Preisigke, op. cit., 149 f.
[24] Preisigke Wört., II, 186, 31 ff.

τοῦ δεῖνα, to execute an act in the name of NN ; ἐποίησεν τὰς ὠνὰς ἐπὶ τῷ Διονυσίου τοῦ υἱοῦ ὀνόματι (2nd cent. A.D.). [25]

2. The Significance of ὄνομα in the History of Greek Thought.

Epic poetry shares the common belief in the significance of the name (→ 243), but already seems to be aware of the problem which later occupied philosophy, namely, whether human speech with its names for things is a true reflection of reality ; for some things have two names (Hom. Il., 24, 315 f.; 18, 487 = Od., 5, 273). Hector calls his son Σκαμάνδριος, but to the Trojans he is 'Αστυάναξ, because they seek by this name to invoke the essence of his father, Hom. Il., 6, 402 f.; 22, 506 f.). Many things have one name among men, another among the gods. The latter is correct ; the significance and etymology are here apparent, Il., 1, 403 f.; 2, 813 f.; 14, 291; 20, 73 f. The etym. interest goes back to belief in the magical power of the name.

In 6th and 5th cent. philosophy rational consideration brings out the acuteness of the problem of speech. [26] The philosophers of this age reject the names, the καλεῖν of men ; these express false notions and concepts. For Parmenides ὄνομα is the direct opp. of ἀλήθεια : "Hence all is mere name that mortals have established in their speech, convinced that it is true." [27] Man's blind confidence in experience leads to false designation as a second error. The name is something conventional, [28] an expression of appearance. But the Eleatics want to pierce through the δόξα and know the truth ; language interests them only as an expression of the δόξα, the world of appearance to which it belongs. The name does not express the true essence of a thing. Heraclitus thinks along the same lines : τῷ οὖν τόξῳ ὄνομα βίος, ἔργον δὲ θάνατος. [29] The names of the gods simply express one side of the one God and are therefore incomplete and false. Thus the name of Zeus is for him an inadequate expression of the deity. [30] He is saying dialectically that the name both is and is not the thing itself.

The recognition of a contradiction between the conventional name and the true essence is expressed by the Sophists in the antitheses ὄνομα-ἔργον, ὄνομα-πρᾶγμα or ὄνομα-φύσις. Eur. and Thuc. (→ 244) are influenced by this line of thought. Fundamentally Hermogenes expresses the view in Plat. Crat., 384d : οὐ γὰρ φύσει ἑκάστῳ πεφυκέναι ὄνομα οὐδὲν οὐδενί, ἀλλὰ νόμῳ καὶ ἔθει τῶν ἐθισάντων τε καὶ καλούντων. But the Sophists also contrast ὄνομα with νοῦς, σῶμα, τέχνη and even οὐσία. The antithesis ὄνομα-φύσις seems to be esp. clear in Eur. : ὀνόματι μεμπτὸν τὸ νόθον, ἡ φύσις δ' ἴση. [31] The *physis* is the inborn nature ; a mere name cannot change it. We thus find already the depreciation of the name which is often found in the work De Arte in the Corpus Hippocraticum. [32] The view constantly gains ground that the ὄνομα belongs only νόμῳ and not φύσει. This leads to rejection of the ὄνομα as a mere sign, as seen first in a medical context — under the influence of reflection on the φύσις — in the work De Natura Hominis, 5 (VI, 40, Littré), which is ascribed to Polybos. ὀνόματα belong to the νόμος, but ἰδέαι to the φύσις. Language is a product of συνθήκη and ὁμολογία, Plat. Crat., 384d; 435a. The view of Protagoras is to the same effect. [33] The Sophist Prodikos [34] investigates the ὀρθότης ὀνομάτων and becomes the founder of the study of synonyms.

Plato dealt with the problem of the philosophy of language esp. in Crat. In his day the view was still widespread that the nature of things is best known from their names.

---

[25] T. Reinach, *Pap. grecs et démotiques* (1905), 44, 15.
[26] Cf. on this and on what follows Heinimann, 46-56.
[27] Parm., 8, 38 f. (Diels[5], I, 238).
[28] Nestle, 112.
[29] Heraclit., 48 (Diels[5], I, 161, 6 f.); on what follows cf. 67 (I, 165).
[30] *Ibid.*, 32 (I, 159, 1 f.).
[31] Fr. 168, cf. 377 (TGF, 408, 476); Heinimann, 108.
[32] On this and what follows Heinimann, 157-162.
[33] Nestle, 286 f., 302.
[34] Plat. Crat., 384b; Nestle, 349.

This led to an arbitrary playing about with etymologies. In opposition Plato had to put the deeper question of the relation between word and concept, between thought and speech. Thus Crat. tackles the great problem of the age whether ὀνόματα arose by nature (φύσει) or by arrangement (θέσει). Against the assertion of Cratylos (435d) that to know the name is to know the thing it is objected that the creator of names might have erred in his view of things when he made the choice. Many bad things have names which on etym. examination prove to be good, and *vice versa*. Thus Plato declares in Crat. that it is impossible to reach knowledge by way of names and their etymologies. [35] Plato stated here his definitive view that words are tonal signs (σημεῖα τῆς φωνῆς) which acquire their meaning by thought, association and custom (ὁμολογίᾳ καὶ ἔθει). Thus, while they are not products of individual caprice, they belong to general δόξα and are irrelevant to true knowledge. The same applies in respect of the ideas. For them, too, names are simply signs by means of διάνοια. Nevertheless, there can be no philosophy without language, Soph., 260a; 261d-262d. [36] With ref. to names and speech, then, Plato occupied middle ground between the antitheses of φύσει and νόμῳ. [37]

Aristot. shared generally the view of Plato. He stated more plainly, however, that the sound does not itself bear the meaning but thought has first to appropriate it as a sign. The sounds of animals mean something, but they are not ὀνόματα. The fact that a sound becomes a sign, and the way in which it does, is subjective and contingent: ὁ γὰρ λόγος αἴτιός ἐστι τῆς μαθήσεως ἀκουστὸς ὤν, οὐ καθ' αὑτὸν ἀλλὰ κατὰ συμβεβηκός· ἐξ ὀνομάτων γὰρ σύγκειται, τῶν δ' ὀνομάτων ἕκαστον σύμβολόν ἐστιν. [38] In De Sophisticis Elenchis, 1, p. 161a, 6 ff. Aristot. says: "Since it is not possible in conversation to produce the thing itself, since we use names as signs instead of things, we believe that what is true of the names is true of the things, as with numbers in counting. But the situation is not quite the same. For names and the number of speeches are limited, but things themselves are innumerable. Hence the same speech and one and the same word necessarily has to mean more than one thing." [39] Aristot. finds concepts for which there is no corresponding term (ἀνώνυμα). [40] Since operations of thought and the contents of thought are known only in the form of speech, his teaching on logical thinking has to deal with this, esp. with words which denote philosophical objects. Changes in the meaning of such words and their etymologies have to be investigated: μεταφέρειν τοὔνομα ἐπὶ τὸν λόγον, i.e., to take the word in its original sense as distinct from common usage: ὡς κεῖται τοὔνομα. [41] In Aristot. linguistic research stands in the service of logic. ὄνομα is the verbal sign (σύμβολον) of the thing, προσηγορία the application of the ὄνομα to the thing denoted.

Stoicism shaped the further development of the Gk. philosophy of language. [42] The four main parts of speech acc. to Zeno[43] — ὄνομα, ῥῆμα, σύνδεσμος, ἄρθρον —

---

[35] Cf. F. Ueberweg, *Grundriss d. Geschichte d. Philosophie,* I[12] (1926), ed. K. Praechter, 256 ff.; U. v. Wilamowitz-Moellendorff, *Platon,* I[2] (1920), 287-295. M. Warburg, "Zwei Fragen zum 'Kratylos,'" NPhU, 5 (1929), 23; ref. is made here to Polit., 261e and Ep., VII, 342a-b, and it is stressed that the ὄνομα is for Plato the lowest agent of knowledge. Cf. A. Debrunner, *Germanisch-Romanische Monatsschrift,* 14 (1926), 321 ff.

[36] In Soph., 262 Plato dealt for the first time with the nature of the terms ὄνομα and ῥῆμα: ῥῆμα describes the action, ὄνομα is a linguistic sign for the one who acts. Judgment arises formally from their union, Pohlenz, 155.

[37] Steinthal, I, 111 f. The question was raised whether words (ὀνόματα) denote things (πράγματα) correctly (φύσει) or only νόμῳ, ἔθει and ξυνθήκη. Xenoph. Mem., III, 14, 2 suggests that this question of the ὀρθότης τῶν ὀνομάτων was often discussed by the educated.

[38] De Sensu, 1, p. 437a, 12 ff.; Steinthal, I, 187.

[39] Steinthal, I, 190 f.

[40] Cf. Plat. Polit., 260e.

[41] Topic., II, 6, p. 112a, 32 f.; Steinthal, I, 193.

[42] Steinthal, I, 304.

[43] Diogenes of Babylon Fr., 22 (v. Arnim, III, 213 f.); Pohlenz, 163, 165 f.; Steinthal, I, 297.

were increased by Chrysipp. when he divided ὄνομα into ὄνομα κύριον (*nomen proprium*) and ὄνομα προσηγορικόν (or προσηγορία, *nomen appellativum*). [44] This is related to the sharp distinction which Stoicism made between specific things, which alone exist, and general predicates. The Stoics explain that language arose φύσει from the soul of man ; the word represents the thing acc. to its nature and is thus true and moves (κινεῖ) the hearer by its significance. [45] In content thing, concept and spoken word are the same. This view established itself in the philosophy of antiquity. Acc. to it ὀνόματα are also ἔτυμα. Hence the art of ἐτυμολογία has the task of demonstrating the ἐτυμότης, the truth of words, by showing how the word agrees with the object which it denotes. But etymology must also unfold the moral, metaphysical and religious contents in the ἔτυμα. In the word is a wisdom which science and thought bring to light. By the art of etymology the Stoic can also take over popular religion with its gods and myths. He finds his truth and wisdom here once he etymologises the many names. For unconsciously developed speech is just as direct and valid as the religion and morality which reside directly in the popular consciousness. [46] As an expression of thought it is part of universal reason. [47] For the Stoics a main proof that words copy things is onomatopoeia. [48] The Stoics instituted a scientific doctrine of speech. It is important in this connection that leading Stoics had other native tongues and began to compare these with Gk. Dionysius Thrax. (2nd cent. B.C.) as a philologist developed the Stoic doctrine περὶ φωνῆς into τέχνη γραμματική, which became determinative in the age which followed. Shortly after there appeared another "techne" [49] which in a revised form the Romans made the basis of their language and which has dominated elementary instruction up to our own time.

3. The Name of God. [50]

Herodot., II, 52, records as a tradition of the priestesses at Dodona that the Pelasgians worshipped gods without giving one of them a cognomen (ἐπωνυμίη) or name (ὄνομα). The names of the gods came from Egypt, and an oracle allowed their use. The Gks. later took the names of the gods from the Pelasgians. Hom. and Hesiod created the theogony of the Gks. and gave the gods their names. This account of Herodot. sheds light on a preliminary stage of Gk. religion. [51] Later it would have been regarded as a sign of godlessness for the gods to have no names. Strabo, III, 4, 16, following Poseidonios, tells of a Celtic-Iberian tribe of the Callaici who were atheists (ἄθεοι), who at the time of the full moon sacrificed to an anonymous god (ἀνωνύμῳ τινὶ θεῷ), i.e., their gods, and those of other tribes, had no proper names.

In historical time, at the higher stages of religion, the gods of the Gks. had names. Since these names esp. are full of significance, they primarily and supremely are regarded as *etyma* and are explained accordingly. The Gks. constantly sought to learn about the nature and essence of the gods from their names, and Hesiod made a beginning

---

44 Pohlenz, 163. The medieval problem of universals is not at issue here. As opp. to Chrysipp. Dionysius refused to make this differentiation : ἡ γὰρ προσηγορία ὡς εἶδος τῷ ὀνόματι ὑποβέβληται, 23, 2, though he distinguished as εἴδη of the ὄνομα the κύριον as τὸ τὴν ἰδίαν οὐσίαν σημαῖνον and the προσηγορικόν as τὸ τὴν κοινὴν οὐσίαν σημαῖνον (33, 6) and thus remained within the Stoic def., Pohlenz, 181 f. The Stoic def. of ὄνομα as a part of speech is as follows in Dion. (24, 3): μέρος λόγου πτωτικόν, σῶμα ἢ πρᾶγμα σημαῖνον, Pohlenz, 182.

45 The Stoic thesis was the "source of monstrous errors," P. Barth, *Die Stoa* (1903), 76 f. It was contested by the Sceptics, who pointed out that in this case all men would understand one another, Steinthal, I, 330.

46 Steinthal, I, 330 f.

47 A. Schmekel, *D. Philosophie d. mittleren Stoa* (1892), 205 ff.

48 P. Barth, *op. cit.*, 78.

49 Pohlenz, 157, 190.

50 → III, 71-79.

51 Usener, 277-279. On the question of gods without names cf. Norden, 57, n. 1; O. Kern, *D. Religion d. Griechen*, I (1926), 125-134.

in this direction with an etymology of Aphrodite, Theog., 188-198. [52] In his great list of names it may be seen that the name contains myth, and that the etym. itself has its roots in myth. [53] In contrast, philosophical thought splits the identity of name and person or thing, and in respect of divine names concludes accordingly that no name can wholly correspond to the god, cf. Heraclit., → 246. Plato puts it thus in Crat., 400d-401a : The true names of the gods are those which the gods call themselves ; since we men cannot know these, we must be content with the names with which we are wont to call on the gods in prayer ; hence an etym. investigation of the divine names can at best give us information only on the thoughts by which men were led when they gave the gods names. Nevertheless, even the philosophers were aware of the great significance of the divine names. Thus for Democrit. (Fr., 142, Diels⁵, I, 170, 9) these names are ἀγάλματα φωνήεντα, "speaking statues." The name is an εἶδος of the being thereby denoted. To the name as ἄγαλμα φωνῆεν there belongs, as to the statue, an element of the unapproachable and terrible. Plato has Socrates say in Phileb., 12c that he hesitates to give etymologies of the divine names, and he points out in Crat., 403a that men φοβούμενοι τὸ ὄνομα would rather call the god Hades Pluto. The euphemism widespread in Greece, however, is not just awe of gods and demons ; it is also an expression of the desire to order the world.

In contrast to the primitive anonymity of the gods is another stage of religion, namely, that which heaps as many names as possible on the god which is worshipped. On the magical view that the utterance of the right word, in this case the use of the appropriate divine name, is an indispensable condition for achieving the desired effect, "names are heaped up, and it is felt better to go too far than to run the risk of missing the decisive word." [54] Already in Hom. Il., 1, 37 ff. the offended priest of Apollo calls upon his god with many names. The aim here, however, is to pay the god special honour. The greater his power, the greater should be the number of epithets and ἀνακλητικὰ ὀνόματα. [55] A later instance (2nd cent. A.D.) is Aristid., 43, 29 f. (1, 8, Dindorf): Ζεὺς πάντων πατὴρ καὶ οὐρανοῦ καὶ γῆς καὶ θεῶν καὶ ἀνθρώπων ..., καὶ διὰ τοῦτον ὁρῶμεν καὶ ἔχομεν ὁπόσα καὶ ἔχομεν. οὗτος ἀπάντων εὐεργέτης ... οὗτος δοτὴρ ἀπάντων, οὗτος ποιητής, οὗτος ἐν μὲν ἐκκλησίαις ... ᾿Αγοραῖος κέκληται, ἐν δὲ μάχαις Τροπαῖος, ἐν δὲ νόσοις ... Σωτήρ, οὗτος ᾿Ελευθέριος ..., πάνθ᾿ ὅσα αὐτὸς εὗρεν μεγάλα καὶ ἑαυτῷ πρέποντα ὀνόματα. [56] This heaping up of names for the one god can easily lead religion to the conclusion that language no longer has the resources to name the god adequately, e.g., Aesch. Ag., 160 ff.: Ζεὺς ὅστις ποτ᾿ ἐστίν, εἰ τόδ᾿ αὐτῷ φίλον κεκλημένῳ, τοῦτό νιν προσεννέπω. This is not philosophical resignation ; the religious thinker is pressing forward in profound faith to acceptance of the θεῖον and θεός. [57]

For Stoicism the bearing of many names is an honorary predicate of universal deity. Thus Diog. L., VII, 1, 68 tells us that Poseidonios taught : "God is a single being, reason, destiny, Zeus, but he is called by many names." "According to his mode of operation he is called by different names : He is called Δία because all things are by (διά) him, Ζῆνα because he is the author of life (ζῆν) etc. ..., and they invested him with other names with ref. to specific characteristics" (VII, 1, 72). Polytheism was to be vanquished in this syncretistic fashion. [58] The pantheism of Stoicism finds expression in Ps.-Aristot. Mund., 7, p. 401a, 13 ff.: The one God has many names : εἷς δ᾿ ὢν πολυώνυμός ἐστι, κατονομαζόμενος τοῖς πάθεσι πᾶσιν ἅπερ αὐτὸς νεοχμοῖ.

---

[52] Cf. U. v. Wilamowitz-Moellendorff, Der Glaube d. Hellenen, I (1931), 33. Since the greatest of the Gk. gods have non-Gk. names, etym. could not always help.
[53] On this and what follows Warburg, 70-81.
[54] Usener, 336; cf. Kern, I, 152; for further examples from tragedy, Norden, 145, n. 3.
[55] Menandros (2nd/3rd cent. A.D.), Rhet. Graec., III, 445, 25 f.
[56] On this cf. Norden, 164 ff.
[57] O. Kern, II (1935), 39.
[58] Pascher, 116 f.

There follows a long list of all the epithets of the universal God Zeus, who is himself the all : πάσης ἐπώνυμος ὢν φύσεώς τε καὶ τύχης ἅτε πάντων αὐτὸς αἴτιος ὤν (26 f.). All the names of gods denote the same one God. The same thought occurs in Apul. Met., XI, 5, where the goddess Isis says : "My deity is one, but the whole earth venerates it in many forms, with many cults, under many names." Various names follow. Here the many names express fulness of being.

In the Hermetic writings [59] the many names of deity turn into anonymity : ὁ δὲ θεὸς εἷς. ὁ δὲ εἷς ὀνόματος οὐ προσδέεται· ἔστι γὰρ ὁ ὢν ἀνώνυμος. [60] God is too lofty to have a name. [61] No name names him definitely. [62] The universal father and lord is without a name, or rather, all names fit him ; in his unity he is all things, so that one must call him by the name of all things, or call all things by his name. [63] The same thought is present when it is said that the name of deity cannot be uttered by human lips ; [64] that God is the ἄφραστον ὄνομα. [65] The name of the lord is honoured (σεβαστόν) among the gods, but concealed (κρυπτὸν) among all men. [66] The anonymity of deity, however, is also connected with its incorporeality, for language itself is corporeal. In addition, names serve to differentiate distinct things, and this is unnecessary with the one and all. [67] οὐδέν ἐστιν [οὗτος] ὃ οὐκ ἔστιν (οὗτος). πάντα γὰρ ἃ ἔστι καὶ οὗτός ἐστιν. καὶ διὰ τοῦτο αὐτὸς ὀνόματα ἔχει ἅπαντα, ὅτι ἑνός (αὐτοῦ πάντα) ἐστὶ πατρός. καὶ διὰ τοῦτο αὐτὸς ὄνομα οὐκ ἔχει, ὅτι πάντων ἐστὶ πατήρ (Corp. Herm., V, 10a).

Celsus is thinking along these lines when he regards the names of the one God as irrelevant, Orig. Cels., I, 24 f.; Origen contradicts him on this point. The Gnostics teach the same doctrine. For Basilides God is ὑπεράνω παντὸς ὀνόματος ὀνομαζομένου, Hipp. Ref., VII, 20, 3; for others the supreme principle is ἀκατονόμαστος, ἄρρητος, ineffabilis. [68] Finally the idea may also be seen in Christian works : οὐδὲν γὰρ ὄνομα ἐπὶ θεοῦ κυριολογεῖσθαι δυνατόν· τὰ γὰρ ὀνόματα εἰς δήλωσιν καὶ διάγνωσιν τῶν ὑποκειμένων κεῖται πραγμάτων, πολλῶν καὶ διαφόρων ὄντων. θεῷ δὲ οὔτε ὁ τιθεὶς ὄνομα προϋπῆρθεν, οὔτε αὐτὸς ἑαυτὸν ὀνομάζειν ᾠήθη δεῖν, εἷς καὶ μόνος ὑπάρχων, ὡς αὐτὸς διὰ τῶν ἑαυτοῦ προφητῶν μαρτυρεῖ λέγων· (Is. 44:6 as quotation). [69] In a hymn of Gregory of Nazianzus it is said of God : καὶ πάντων τέλος ἐσσί, καὶ εἷς καὶ πάντα καὶ οὐδείς. οὐχ ἓν ἐών, οὐ πάντα· πανώνυμε, πῶς σε καλέσσω. [70] This unbiblical doctrine of late antiquity that God has no name has found champions up to the modern period, cf. Goethe, Faust, I, 3432 ff. "Who may name him ?"

4. The Magic Papyri.

The magic pap. are full of expressions showing belief in the power and efficacy of names. Expressed here is the primitive belief that knowledge of names gives power over their bearers, that the simple utterance of a name puts a spell on its owner and brings him under the power of the speaker. Sometimes the name of a person one wishes

---

[59] God is also ἀνώνυμος in Max. Tyr., 2, 10a.
[60] Corp. Herm. Fr., 3 (Scott, I, 534).
[61] Ibid. Excerpt 6, 19 (Scott, I, 418, 23).
[62] Ibid., Asclepius, 20a (Scott, I, 330, 26 f.).
[63] Loc. cit. (I, 332, 9 f.).
[64] Fr., 11 (I, 536).
[65] Asclepius, 41b (I, 374, 3).
[66] Excerpt, 23, 55 (I, 486, 31).
[67] J. Kroll, D. Lehren des Herm. Trismeg. (1913), 20.
[68] Ibid., 20 f.
[69] Ps.-Just., Cohortatio ad gentes, 21. The idea is already present in the 2nd cent. Apologists, Just. Apol., I, 10, 1; 61, 11; II, 6, 1-3, 6; Minucius Felix, 18, 10; Cl. Al. Strom., V, 12, 78, 3.
[70] Anthologia Graeca carminum Christianorum, ed. W. Christ-M. Paranikas (1871), 24.

to harm has only to be written on a piece of paper or elsewhere along with magical formulae, Preis. Zaub., II, 51 and 53.

If a man utters the name of a god and then demands or asks something, it will be fulfilled as and because he speaks the name. The mystic even identifies himself with the god: "For thou art I and I am thou, thy name is mine and mine is thine. For I am thy image. If something happens to me it happens to the great god (magical words) who is written in front on the holy ship," ibid., II, 47; cf. 123. Identity with the god confers protection. As in the mystical pantheism of philosophical religion, so here, too, the many names of the god who is invoked play a role. If the god is invoked as πολυώνυμος, this emphasises his particular honour, power and dignity. Thus the magician makes the god favourable to him. [71] In specific acts at a specific time and hour each of the many names of the god must be uttered, ibid., I, 50. The one who knows the names of a god, which often differ at each hour, can conjure up the god, I, 52/54. [72] The syncretism of the age is to be seen in the fact that the names come from all languages and are used in the original forms (Gk., Egypt., Phrygian, Persian, Syr., Heb.). Barbaric names have particular power, but must be pronounced exactly as the are (no transl.) if they are to have the desired effect. One may see this in Origen, acc. to whom even the names of the patriarchs should not be translated, Cels., I, 24; V, 45. We thus have the prayer for hearing: "Because I invoke ... the names which have never yet found entry into mortal nature and were not pronounced in articulated utterance by the human tongue ...," Preis. Zaub., I, 92-95. Close to these alien and barbaric names are the sequences of letters and esp. vowels which give force to magic. Examples may be found everywhere in Preis. Also related is the writing of the names on a sheet in a specific order, e.g., in the form of a heart, ibid., I, 24. Gentile and Jewish magic intermingled freely in Egypt. This may be seen in the fact that the efficacious vowel sequences often echo Yahweh, or the name Ιαω often appears, in many cases alongside Σαβαωθ, Αδωναι. [73] In one place it is said explicitly that the name of God was given to the prophets of Israel, I, 184. In order that the magic may work the true name (ἀληθινόν or αὐθεντικὸν ὄνομα) must be named, the one made known by the god himself. [74] Thus the initiate sometimes appeals to a previous encounter with the god in which he learned his name, I, 38. There are also requests for a revelation of the name: "What is thy divine name (τὸ ἔνθεόν σου ὄνομα)? [75] Tell it me truly, that I may invoke him," I, 10. But usually knowledge of the name or names is already present. The magician simply addresses the god: "Thy name is ... (ὄνομά σοι)," and lays his hand on the god. In address the name is honoured by many predicates. [76] The god has a great name; he is μεγαλώνυμος. One must invoke his true name or the magical name (τὸ φυσικὸν ὄνομα). [77] The name works of itself; it is a powerful essence, a hypostasis of the god, [78] which, invoked, is set in motion and operation. Here non-Gk., i.e., Jewish, influence may be seen. The god is himself the name: "... thou art the holy and strong name which is sanctified by all angels ...," I, 112. The secret name invoked presses through all heavenly worlds to earth, I, 12. Before the sound of this name the earth opens, the rivers and rocks burst, the demons tremble and flee, I, 84; II, 122, 145. By the utterance of his supreme name God holds

---

[71] For examples Preis. Zaub., I, 26, 160 ff.; II, 34 and 46.

[72] Cf. Reitzenstein Poim., 6 f., 259.

[73] E.g., Preis. Zaub., I, 56, 84, 122, 192; II, 53, 164.

[74] Ibid., I, 38, 67, 71, 80, 184; II, 116, 158.

[75] As in the Herm. writings (→ 250), God has an ἄφραστον ὄνομα. "God" is simply the address by which he is honoured, Preis. Zaub., I, 56/58.

[76] For examples cf. Preis. Zaub., passim.

[77] Ibid., II, 109 f. Invocation formulae: II, 31: ἐπικαλοῦμαί σε τοῖς ἁγίοις σου ὀνόμασιν, I, 12: ἐπικαλοῦμαί σου τὸ κρυπτὸν ὄνομα, cf. 124. Conjurations: II, 39: ἐξορκίζω σε τοῖς μεγάλοις ὀνόμασίν σου, II, 67: ἐξορκίζω σε τὰ τξε' (365) ὀνόματα τοῦ μεγάλου θεοῦ, I, 80: ἐξορκίζω σε κατὰ τοῦ ἀμιάντου ὀνόματος τοῦ θεοῦ, cf. 184.

[78] Reitzenstein Poim., 17, n. 6.

fast the whole world, I, 38. Gods are created when the great God utters the ὄνομα μέγα καὶ θαυμαστόν. [79] The initiate himself has protection or works for the name's sake (διὰ τὸ ὄνομα). [80]

From the 4th cent. Christian magic pap. are found. These mention the names of Mary, John the Baptist and the Trinity as efficacious along with other *voces mysticae* like Jaô, Sabaôth etc., II, 190-200.

Even on pagan soil, of course, there were always those who opposed this belief in names and name magic. Thus Lucian scoffed at the stupidity of those who think that a boil or a fever will vanish through awe at an ὄνομα θεσπέσιον. In this, too, he brought down on himself the objections of believers against his scepticism. They supposed that anyone who doubted the power of names did not believe in the gods at all, Luc. Philops., 9 f., 12, 17.

C. The Old Testament.

1. Lexical and Statistical Data.

שֵׁם [81] — which occurs in the OT same 770 times in the sing. and 84 times in the plur. — has not been fully explained etym.; it originally denotes an external mark to distinguish one person or thing from others. [82] It then means "name," *nomen proprium,* of gods, men and animals [83] (שְׁמוֹ צְבָאוֹת יהוה, Jer. 10:16; וַיִּקְרְאוּ בְשֵׁם הַבַּעַל, 1 K. 18:26; וּשְׁמוֹ שָׁאוּל, 1 S. 9:2; שֵׁמוֹת לְכָל־הַבְּהֵמָה, Gn. 2:20), of geographical entities, towns, mountains, rivers etc. (e.g., קָרָא שְׁמָהּ בָּבֶל, Gn. 11:9; הַנָּהָר הַשֵּׁנִי גִּיחוֹן, וְשֵׁם, Gn. 2:13), and sometimes of things and times (altar, Ex. 17:15; pillar, 2 S. 18:18; stars, Is. 40:26; cf. שֵׁם הַיּוֹם date? Ez. 24:2, also Est. 9:26 פּוּרִים). [84] Then with ref. to the acts of the persons mentioned it can means a "good" (Qoh. 7:1; Prv. 22:1) or "bad" (Dt. 22:14; cf. Ez. 23:10?) "reputation," and in the abs. "repute" or "esteem" (Dt. 26:19 and Jer. 13:11 alongside תְּהִלָּה and תִּפְאֶרֶת; cf. Is. 55:13; Zeph. 3:19 etc.); thus men of repute are called אַנְשֵׁי הַשֵּׁם (Gn. 6:4) or אַנְשֵׁי שֵׁמוֹת (1 Ch. 5:24; 12:31), and unknown or dishonourable folk בְּנֵי בְלִי־שֵׁם (Job 30:8). Then שֵׁם, like זֵכֶר, of which it is sometimes a par., means "memory," "remembrance," "fame" even after death (Dt. 9:14; Jos. 7:9; Job 18:17; cf. the expression שֵׁם וּשְׁאֵרִית, 2 S. 14:7 and שֵׁם וּשְׁאָר, Is. 14:22). Whether שֵׁמוֹת in Nu. 1:2, 17, 20 (and *passim*) is used metonymically for person, like נֶפֶשׁ (e.g., Ex. 1:5), [85] is contested. Similarly there is no general acceptance of its use in the sense of "memorial," "sign," as sometimes suggested for passages like Gn. 11:4 (נַעֲשֶׂה־לָּנוּ שֵׁם), Is. 55:13 (שֵׁם par. to אוֹת), 56:5 (alongside יָד) and 2 S. 8:13. [86]

In prep. combinations [87] שֵׁם occurs mostly with בְּ and לְ. We also find בַּעֲבוּר once (1 S. 12:22), מִן 3 times (partitive and comparative Ex. 28:10; 1 K. 1:47), כְּ 7 times, ("as," e.g., Gn. 4:17; 2 S. 7:9), עַל 16 times (usually "according to," e.g., 1 K. 16:24)

---

[79] A. Dieterich, "Abraxas. Studien z. Religionsgeschichte d. späteren Altertums," *Festschrift H. Usener* (1891), 19.

[80] Preis. Zaub., II, 123.

[81] Etym. not related to שֵׁם Shem, nor to the divine name (אֵ)שֵׁם, which is a theophorous element in יִשְׁמָאֵל, M. Noth, 123 f.

[82] Ges.-Buhl, *s.v.* שֵׁם and Boehmer, *Im Namen,* 20-27.

[83] As regards animals we have the names of species.

[84] In the few cases where things are named in the OT it is usually by means of קָרָא לְ, cf. Gn. 1:5: וַיִּקְרָא אֱלֹהִים לָאוֹר יוֹם Later שֵׁם approximates to the sense of "concept," cf. Sir. 6:22: "The truth is כִּשְׁמָהּ."

[85] So E. König, *Hbr. u. Aram. Wörterbuch zum AT* [6, 7] (1936).

[86] R. Gottheil, "Hizzib Yad," ZAW, 26 (1906), 277-280.

[87] J. Boehmer, *Im Namen,* 2-9.

and לְמַעַן 16 times ("for the sake," e.g., 1 K. 8:41; Ps. 23:3; Is. 66:5), and always of the name of God. To these 43 verses should be added 56 in which לְשֵׁם is used, mostly with ref. to the name of Yahweh; the לְ here normally serves to denote the nearer or remoter obj. (23 times in the expression: "to build a house for my (Yahweh's) name" or the like, e.g., 2 S. 7:13). Esp. common, more than 130 times, is the prep. בְּ with שֵׁם in the st. c. or with suffix. Apart from the few verses in which the ref. is to speeches, greetings or written communications in the name of a man, the name of Yahweh is usually meant by בְּשֵׁם. Often בְּשֵׁם יהוה is combined with the verbs "to invoke," "to speak," "to prophesy," "to bless," but we also find "to walk," "to serve," "to tread down enemies," "to raise the banner" etc. in isolated instances. The expression בְּשֵׁם יהוה is specifically dealt with under C. 5.

2. The Significance of the Name.

In Israel as among other peoples there was awareness of the significance attached to a name, and of the power which resided in it. [88] The first and later utterance of a name means more than formal endowment with, and use of, a means of naming someone. By giving someone a name, one establishes a relation of dominion and possession towards him.

Thus acc. to Gn. 2:19 f. Adam names all the animals. This means that he exercises dominion over creation and relates it to his own sphere. To name a conquered city (2 S. 12:28) or lands (Ps. 49:11) is to establish a right of possession and to subject them to one's power. In times of distress forsaken and threatened women ensure male protection by requesting the name of a man and thereby seeking to become his possession (Is. 4:1). Yahweh gives the stars their names as their Creator and Lord (Ps. 147:4); He also calls Israel by name and thereby establishes His claim to it (Is. 43:1). Conversely, Yahweh's name is named over Israel, and it thus becomes the people of His possession (Is. 63:19; 2 Ch. 7:14). The name of Yahweh is named over the temple (Jer. 7:10), over the ark (2 S. 6:2), and also over Jerusalem; this makes the city holy (Jer. 25:29; Da. 9:18). God knows Moses by name, i.e., He has called Him to His service (Ex. 33:12, 17). What Jer. says about his prophetic call is to be understood along similar lines (Jer. 15:16).

The significance of the name also finds expression in the idea that a man's name lives on in his descendants. Children are a blessing because they keep alive the name of their father (Gn. 21:12; 48:16; 2 S. 18:18). By Levirate marriage (Dt. 25:5-10; cf. Nu. 27:1-11) the name of an Israelite who died without sons is kept alive in his family (cf. Rt. 4:5: לְהָקִים שֵׁם־הַמֵּת עַל־נַחֲלָתוֹ). In default of this, the name of the deceased is blotted out from the midst of his brethren. Again, the one whose son is killed has neither name nor continuing life on the earth (2 S. 14:7; cf. 1 S. 20:15 f.). If a man has many descendants, his name lives on for ever (cf. Ps. 72:17). By war and esp. by the ban the name of a whole people can be blotted out, Jos. 7:9; Is. 14:22; cf. Ex. 17:14. The familiar thought of later Judaism and the NT that the names of the righteous are written in the book of life has an OT basis in Ex. 32:32 f.; Ps. 69:28; cf. Is. 4:3; Ez. 13:9. → I, 619 f.

3. Proper Names and Meaningful Names.

For "to give a name," "to call," Heb. uses קָרָא with the acc. of the name and לְ of the person or thing (Gn. 1:8; 31:47), sometimes also the double acc. (Is. 60:18), but mostly קָרָא (אֶת־) שֵׁם (Gn. 2:20; 5:2), and rarely שִׂים שֵׁם (לְ), lit. "to confer a name" (2 K. 17:34; Da. 1:7).

---

[88] Giesebrecht, 17 f.

Throughout the OT there is a sense of the significance of the proper name.[90] The name denotes the person, establishes its identity, and is a part of it. It can often be said: "As a man is named, so is he."

The best-known example is that of Nabal; he is a fool, as his name tells us (1 S. 25:25). To this context belong many etymologies of proper names given esp. in Gn. — though elsewhere in the OT too — when important persons and places are named (e.g., Gn. 28:17, 19). In the very earliest records the names of Eve (Gn. 3:20), Cain (4:1) and Noah (5:29) are explained etym., and the city of Babel bears in its name an eternal reminder of God's punishment on human hubris (11:9). The stories of the patriarchs are rich in etymologies. Isaac recalls the laughter of Abraham (17:17) and Sarah (18:12; 21:6), Jacob is the cunning holder of his brother's heel (25:26; 27:36; cf. Hos. 12:4), Esau is Edom because he is ruddy (אַדְמוֹנִי, Gn. 25:25) and eats a red dish (25:30). Either the decisive total significance (Eve, Noah) or a single distinctive aspect of the person named is considered and expressed. In this connection we may also mention the many theophorous names whereby those who originally give the names denote their relation to the tribal deity (or its relation to them) but which later seek to express a special Godward wish for the child thus named.[91] In the names of the twelve patriarchs the parents, esp. the mothers, bear witness to the assistance of Yahweh (Gn. 29:31-30:24; 35:18; cf. 1 S. 1:20).

The significance of the name for the bearer and those around is also attested by the many secondary names which the OT records.

Thus Pharaoh calls Joseph Zaphnath-paaneah (Gn. 41:45), Nechoh when he sets up Eliakim renames him Jehoiakim (2 K. 23:34), Nebuchadnezzar calls Mattaniah Zedekiah (2 K. 24:17), and Daniel and his companions are also given new names in the Babylonian court (Da. 1:7). The new names express the changed position of those concerned, either their exaltation to special dignity or their reduction to a state of dependence.[92] Thus Yahweh, too, alters the names of His elect when He sets them in a new position, with a particular reference to the future. Jacob's name is changed to Israel because he has wrestled with God (Gn. 32:29). Abram becomes Abraham as the father of nations, and Sarai Sarah as a princess (Gn. 17:5, 15). In the future the new Jerusalem will have a new name (Is. 62:2; cf. Zech. 8:3). Similarly, the righteous in the age of salvation will bear a new name which Yahweh will determine, while the name of sinners will become a curse (Is. 65:15).

The name has meaning for more than its bearer. In Abraham's name there is blessing for all the races of eath (Gn. 12:2 f.).[93] What this connotes may be seen from Gn. 48:20: "With thy name (lit. 'in' or 'with thee')[94] will Israel wish blessing and say: God make thee as Ephraim and Manasseh" (cf. Zech. 8:13). In this connection one should also mention the symbolical names[95] which prophets give their children: לֹא רֻחָמָה and לֹא עַמִּי (Hos. 1:6, 9; cf. יִזְרְעֶאל 1:4), שְׁאָר יָשׁוּב and מַהֵר שָׁלָל חָשׁ בַּז (Is. 7:3; 8:3). These names indicate God's judgment and even bring it. God's curse smites Pashur when his name is changed to "Fear (round about)" (Jer. 20:3 f.). But God's grace is also guaranteed by the names of those who bear salvation: עִמָּנוּ אֵל (Is. 7:14), פֶּלֶא יוֹעֵץ, אֵל גִּבּוֹר, אֲבִי־עַד and שַׂר שָׁלוֹם (Is. 9:5), יהוה צִדְקֵנוּ (Jer. 23:6) and צֶמַח (Zech. 6:12); cf. Hos. 2:2 f.

---

89 Cf. A. R. Johnson, *The One and the Many in the Israelitic Conception of God* (1942), 7 f.

90 Cf. M. Noth.

91 Noth, 66-131; also (for the etym. of place-names too) C. v. Orelli in RE, XIII, 626 f.

92 J. Pedersen, *Israel, Its Life and Culture,* I-II (1926), 250-252.

93 On the universalist significance of the formula cf. G. v. Rad, "Das formgeschichtliche Problem d. Hexateuchs," BWANT, 4, 26 (1938), 60 f.

94 Acc. to the versions בְּךָ should be בָּכֶם, "with your (plur.) name."

95 This common term is used here even though it is subject to rationalistic misinterpretation.

4. שֵׁם יהוה.

In all religions knowledge of the names of the gods is of special significance for dealings with them (→ 243). To be able to honour the deity and to secure divine help one must know the divine name. This explains the request of Jacob to the powerful being which wrestled with him (Gn. 32:30), and that of Manoah to the mysterious divine messenger (Ju. 13:17 f.), that they might learn their names. In both cases the request is rejected with a counter-question: "Why askest thou thus after my name?" to which the angel adds in Ju. 13:18: הוּא פֶלִאי ("it is wonder- ful, secret"). Elsewhere in the OT, however, God reveals Himself by disclosing His name, e.g., to Abraham: אֲנִי אֵל שַׁדַּי (Gn. 17:1 P), to Moses: אֲנִי יהוה (Ex. 6:2 P) and אֶהְיֶה אֲשֶׁר אֶהְיֶה (Ex. 3:14 E), → III, 1067-1081. The expression קָרָא בְּשֵׁם יהוה which originally signified: "To invoke (the deity) with the name Yahweh," still bears traces of the idea of a magical constraint which can be exercised on the deity by utterance of the name. In the OT, of course, the invocation bears the weaker sense of "calling on Yahweh," i.e., worshipping Him (Gn. 4:26; 12:8; 13:4; 26:25; Zeph. 3:9; cf. 1 K. 18:24),[96] and the magical notion disappears. Indeed, mis- using the name of God in magic and incantation is expressly forbidden in the Decalogue (Ex. 20:7; Dt. 5:11). Yahweh refuses to be conjured up by the utterance of His name. He promises His coming at the appointed shrines when He is called upon there: בְּכָל־הַמָּקוֹם[97] אֲשֶׁר אַזְכִּיר[98] אֶת־שְׁמִי אָבוֹא אֵלֶיךָ (Ex. 20:24 Book of the Cove- nant).[99] The blessing of the people by the priests, which originally in the history of religion was dominated by magical ideas (cf. שִׂים שֵׁם יהוה עַל), is also completely purged of magic in its present OT form, and the granting of blessing is at the disposal of the God who has freely linked it to the priestly action.[100] Thus the name of Yahweh is not an instrument of magic; it is a gift of revelation. This does not rule out the fact that uttering or calling on Yahweh's name implies faith in His power; this is true also of use not directly connected with the cultus. When a man swears (1 S. 20:42; Lv. 19:12), curses (2 K. 2:24), or blesses (2 S. 6:18) בְּשֵׁם יהוה, i.e., with mention of the name of Yahweh, the name thus pronounced guarantees Yahweh's presence, attention, and active intervention. This use, at- tested here in early examples, is found throughout the OT.

There is also found from an early period a use of שֵׁם יהוה which is not con- nected with utterance of the name of Yahweh but which also bears witness to the fact that this name is so strongly filled with content, and so plainly denotes the personal rule and work of Yahweh, that it may be used as an alternative term for Yahweh Himself. Instances are perhaps to be seen in the older part of the Holiness Code in which there is reference to desecrating the holy name of Yahweh (Lv. 18:21; 20:3; 21:6; 22:2),[101] and also in certain prophetic sayings (Am. 2:7; Mi. 5:3; Is. 29:23?). Furthermore, even in the pre-Deuteronomic period שֵׁם יהוה could

---

[96] Utterance of the divine name played a special role in the cultus.

[97] Originally בְּכָל־מָקוֹם ("in each place"), Mas. ("in all the place") is "a dogmatic correction for the sake of harmonisation with Dt. 12" (G. Beer, Exodus [1939], ad loc.).

[98] Perhaps we are to read תַּזְכִּיר with the Syr. ("thou art mindful of my name").

[99] Cf. J. J. Stamm, "Zum Altargesetz im Bundesbuch," Theol. Zeitschrift, 1 (1945), 304-306.

[100] Cf. the blessing in Nu. 6:24-26; cf. also v. 27.

[101] In other verses quoted by Grether, 27 there are plain hints of a relation to uttering the name (Lv. 19:12; 24:16).

occasionally be regarded as an independent form of revelation used by Yahweh, though the only certain example is Ex. 23:20 f. if Is. 30:27 (הִגֵּה שֵׁם יהוה בָּא מִמֶּרְחָק) is not to be ascribed to the 8th cent. prophet. [102] In the Ex. passage the question is raised who will accompany and protect the people on the wilderness journey. The answer is: "Behold, I send an (my) Angel before thee, to keep thee on the way, and to bring thee into the place which I have appointed; take heed to thyself before him, and obey his voice, provoke him not; [103] for he will not pardon your trangsressions כִּי שְׁמִי בְּקִרְבּוֹ", Ex. 23:21. In the Angel who is to go with the people the שֵׁם of Yahweh is thought to be present, guaranteeing the personal presence of Yahweh. [104] This gives the Angel full divine authority (he pardons or retains sins). The *shem* here is Yahweh in His revelatory action towards Israel. It is true, of course, that only Yahweh's name, not Yahweh Himself, is in the Angel. He is thus a temporary manifestation of Yahweh, and does not fully embrace His being and majesty.

Dt. further develops these ideas of the שֵׁם יהוה, With the help of the *shem* concept it answers the question how Israel may have dealings with Yahweh and be sure of the presence of its God. [105] Yahweh Himself dwells in heaven (Dt. 4:36; 26:15), but He chooses a place (מָקוֹם) to cause His *shem* to dwell there (לְשַׁכֵּן, Dt. 12:11; 14:23; 16:11 etc.), to set it there (לָשׂוּם, 12:5; 14:24). [106] Thus Dt., and the historical books inspired by it, work out to its logical conclusion what is first suggested in Ex. 20:24. With a presence which is almost material the *shem* is in the house which is built for it (2 S. 7:13; 1 K. 3:2; 5:17; 8:17 etc.). Yahweh sets His name in the house which He sanctifies for it (1 K. 9:3, 7; 2 K. 21:7). The presence of the *shem* in the temple denotes in terminologically distinctive form the proximity of God from the standpoint of salvation history. The *shem* guarantees God's presence in the temple in clear distinction from Yahweh's throne in heaven. [107] A glance at the Deuteronomic form of Solomon's prayer at the dedication of the temple shows what a change was wrought by Dt. The older version of the prayer in 1 K. 8:12 f. speaks of the dwelling of Yahweh in the darkness (of the temple); the Deuteronomic continuation in 8:14 ff. speaks only of the dwelling of the *shem* of Yahweh in the temple and gives a negative answer to the question whether Yahweh might dwell on earth, 8:27. To seek the ultimate background of this *shem* concept in Dt. would take us beyond the limits of the present article. It might be that prophetic lines of thought are taken up and developed in opposition to the dominant popular view. [108] Or it might be that Dt. stands here "in the tradition of the ancient Israelitish Yahweh amphictyony." [109] One thing, however, is clear. By having the *shem* and not Yahweh Himself dwell

---

[102] O. Procksch, *Jesaja*, I (1930) supports the authenticity of Is. 30:27 ff., while Eichrodt Theol. AT, II, 17 regards the שֵׁם as later.

[103] Read הָמֵר for תָּמֵר ("embitter") BHK.

[104] "The 'Name' is an important 'extension' of Yahwe's personality analogous to that which is observable in the case of man," Johnson, 21.

[105] G. v. Rad, "Deuteronomium-Studien²," FRL, 40 (1948), 26.

[106] Only the later Deuteronomistic historical works identify this place as the city of Jerusalem (1 K. 11:36; 2 K. 21:4 etc.).

[107] M. Schmidt, *Prophet u. Tempel. Eine Studie zum Problem d. Gottesnähe im AT* (1948), 93 f.

[108] So, e.g., Grether, 33 f.

[109] G. v. Rad, 27 f.

in the temple, both a high and a low estimation of the temple is secured. Yahweh
is not tied to the temple; He is enthroned in heaven. But the significance of the
cultic site is safeguarded by the fact that He causes His *shem* to dwell there, in
whom the people of God may find Yahweh. The older idea that Yahweh simply
sends his *shem* to earth for temporary purposes (Ex. 23:20 f.; Is. 30:27?) is thus
revised, and according to the view of Dt. the *shem* is permanently localised in the
temple.

In the period after Dt., and especially after the Exile, we find a rich and varied
use of the *shem* concept in relation to Yahweh, in which older thoughts are taken
up and developed. As occasionally earlier (cf. Ex. 9:16; Jos. 9:9), [110] שֵׁם יהוה is now
more commonly used for the glory or praise of Yahweh, cf. Is. 55:13; Ps. 48:10;
Is. 26:8. As a parallel to שֵׁם יהוה we find כָּבוֹד (Is. 59:19; Ps. 102:15) or תְּהִלָּה
(Ps. 106:47; 145:21). The formulae לְמַעַן שֵׁם יהוה and יהוה שְׁמוֹ [111] might also be mentioned in this connection. The latter is used in magnifying the power of Yahweh
as Creator (Am. 4:13; Jer. 10:16) and also with reference to His aid in the Exodus
(Ex. 15:3), to intimation of vengeance on Babylon (Is. 47:4), and to the redemption
and glorifying of Israel (Is. 51:15; 54:5). It is finally used as the conclusion to
threats, where it forms a kind of Amen, a divine confirmation of the saying (Jer.
46:18; 48:15). The formula לְמַעַן שֵׁם יהוה (e.g., Jer. 14:7; Ez. 20:9; Is. 48:9; Ps. 23:3;
79:9; 109:21) also refers to Yahweh's claim to lordship and glory in the world
among the peoples, for the sake of which He is disposed, or is implored, to be
gracious to Israel, that His holy name might not be dishonoured among the nations
(Ez. 20:9, 14, 22; Ps. 79:9 f.). Neither in the formula "for his name's sake" nor in
the expression "Yahweh is his name" is there intended any reference to the
(etymological) interpretation of the name of Yahweh in Ex. 3:13 f. On the contrary, there is an attempt to call to remembrance herewith the knowledge, linked
with this name of God, of Yahweh's historical acts, His power and glory. [112]

Much more commonly than before, שֵׁם יהוה is used after the Exile, especially
in parallelism in the Ps. and prophets, as an alternative for Yahweh; the name
stands for the person. Only a few of the many instances may be mentioned:
Ps. 7:17; 9:10; 18:49; 68:4; 74:18; 86:12; 92:1; Is. 25:1; 26:8; 56:6; Mal. 3:16. [113]
The action of the verbs used is here referred to the שֵׁם as to Yahweh Himself.
There is no longer any distinction between Yahweh in heaven and His *shem* at the
cultic site. Yahweh Himself reveals Himself in the *shem*. It is the side of Yahweh
presented to man.

From this use of the *shem* concept it is only a small step to the hypostatisation
of the *shem*. [114] In fact it is often hard to draw a line between the use of the *shem*
interchangeably for Yahweh and its use as a hypostasis standing over against
Yahweh in greater independence. In some passages the *shem* is the acting subject,
in others it is a means or instrument, sometimes in the hand of Yahweh. Its
character as a hypostasis is plainer in the latter verses. Thus Ps. 54:1 reads:

---

[110] Jos. 7:9; 1 S. 12:22; cf. שֵׁם גָּדוֹל 2 S. 7:9.
[111] Or (ךְ) לְמַעַן שְׁמִי and יהוה שְׁמִי etc.
[112] Giesebrecht, 31 f.; Grether, 53-58.
[113] The verbs here used to denote the honouring or despising of Yahweh's name (e.g.,
to seek, love, honour, thank, rejoice in, or to desecrate, despise, shame) have שֵׁם as acc. or
dat. obj.; in the constr. combination we find כְּבוֹד־שֵׁם e.g., Ps. 29:2.
[114] Giesebrecht, 123-126; Grether, 44-52.

"O God, help me by thy *shem*, and establish justice for me by thy strength," or Ps. 89:24 : "My faithfulness and my mercy be with him, and by my *shem* his horn be exalted"; cf. also Ps. 20:5; 44:5; 118:10-12; (124:8 ?). The righteous of the old covenant confess herein that they find help and protection through the *shem* of Yahweh, which seems here to be an independent power. [115] The same is true of verses where שֵׁם יהוה is the subject : Jer. 10:6 : "Great art thou (Yahweh), and great is thy *shem* in might" ; Ps. 20:1 : "Yahweh hear thee in the day of trouble, and the *shem* of the God of Jacob defend thee" ; but especially Prv. 18:10 : "A strong tower is the *shem* of Yahweh ; the righteous runneth into it and is safe" [116] (cf. also Mal. 1:11, 14; 2:5; Ps. 54:6 f.; 148:13 ?). It is true that in these and other verses the demands of parallelism play an important role in the use of שֵׁם יהוה alongside יהוה. Nevertheless, the use of *shem* is here more conscious and considered than previously. Thus the Mal. verses obviously speak intentionally of the honouring of the *shem* rather than Yahweh Himself by the Gentiles, and the author of Ps. 54:6 f. confesses that it is Yahweh's *shem* which has rescued him from trouble. The *shem* is thus a transcendent entity at work in the world, or an instrument by which Yahweh works. This is the last turn in the outworking of the concept, and it is connected with the general post-exilic tendency to heighten the transcendence of God and increasingly to transfer His immanent working to intermediary beings. [117]

In the use of שֵׁם יהוה in the OT the following points emerge. In the testimony of the period before Dt. the name of Yahweh is essentially a naming of God, who reveals Himself (and His name), and who causes Himself to be called upon by His people, in order that He might bless them, protect them, and be present to them in many different ways. But already there are in this period the seeds of a use of שֵׁם יהוה which is not connected with calling upon or pronouncing the divine name (שֵׁם as the glory or honour of Yahweh, as an alternative word for Him, perhaps even as an independent form of revelation). In Dt. Yahweh Himself, who dwells in heaven, is fairly clearly differentiated from His *shem*, which is localised in the holy place and which is His earthly representative. This theologoumenon facilitates the increased later use of שֵׁם יהוה as an alternative for Yahweh and also prepares the way finally for the hypostatisation of the *shem* as a relatively independent force compared with Yahweh.

5. בְּשֵׁם, especially בְּשֵׁם יהוה. [118]

The many possible ways of using the prep. בְּ, [119] which originally always denotes a connection, a special link or contact, suggest from the very outset that in the term בְּשֵׁם it will not be possible to give a uniform rendering of the בְּ. There is no room for doubt when lists of names are given. Thus in Jos. 21:9 we read : "Those cities which are called by name (בְּשֵׁם)." The same applies when names are given, e.g., Ju. 18:29 : "And they called the name of the city Dan בְּשֵׁם דָן אֲבִיהֶם, i.e., in connection with or

---

[115] Cf. Grether, 51.
[116] The text is uncertain in v. b.
[117] Eichr. Theol. d. AT, II, 17, 27, 40-43; with an interesting historical par. (17) from the Eshmunazar inscr. (AOT, 446 f.), which offers שֶׁם־בַּעַל as another name for the goddess Astarte.
[118] Cf. Boehmer, 4-63; Giesebrecht, 24-27; Jacob, 25-48; Heitmüller, 19-43; Grether, 18-24, 47-50.
[119] L. Koehler and W. Baumgartner, Lexicon in Veteris Testamenti libros (1948), 102-105.

according to the name of their father Dan." [120] Here the בְּשֵׁם is only loosely related to the verb as a more precise definition of the obj., cf. Is. 44:5. In secular use, however, the expression בְּשֵׁם פְּלֹנִי is sometimes found adv. with the verbs "to write (a letter or decree)," "to greet," "to speak." Here there are two possibilities as regards בְּשֵׁם. We might simply have the naming, or, more generally, the use of the name of another without express commission. Thus Jezebel writes a letter to the men of the city of Samaria — obviously behind the king's back — בְּשֵׁם אַחְאָב, i.e., "under his name," using both his name and seal (1 K. 21:8). Here, then, there is no question whatever of any commission. But the situation seems to be different in Est. 3:12; 8:8, 10, where it is said of written decrees: בְּשֵׁם הַמֶּלֶךְ אֲחַשְׁוֵרֹשׁ נִכְתָּב. In this instance there is undoubtedly a commission, but this does not finally rule out the possibility that the בְּשֵׁם הַמֶּלֶךְ does not express this commission, but simply denotes the use of the king's name. In Est. 2:22 as well one might ask whether the rendering should be "with mention of the name of Mordecai" [121] or "on the commission of Mordecai." [122] The context, esp. in the first instances, certainly suggests "on the commission." That this not only could develop from the possibly more original "with mention of the name of," [123] but actually did so, or was implicit in it from the very first, may be seen plainly in two further instances. Thus, after express commissioning of the messengers by David, we read in 1 S. 25:9 that "when David's young men came, they spake to Nabal all these words בְּשֵׁם דָּוִד, i.e., on the commission of David." [124] Acc. to Jer. 29:25 the prophet threatens Shemaiah with the words: "Because thou hast sent a letter בְּשִׁמְכָה," i.e., tua auctoritate, not on that of Yahweh. It is particularly significant that in v. 26 this letter began with the words: "The Lord hath made thee ...," for this shows that one could actually write in one's own name even when expressly mentioning the name of Yahweh. It is thus plain that in the secular sphere the expression בְּשֵׁם פְּלֹנִי is not always linked with, nor is it necessarily to be interpreted in terms of, the mention or use of the name; it can be used in the sense of "on the authority" or "on the commission," like the English "in the name." [125]

בְּשֵׁם is much more commonly combined with the OT name of God than with human names [126] — also with בַּעַל, 1 K. 18:26; cf. Jer. 2:8; 23:13, אֱלֹהִים אֲחֵרִים, Dt. 18:20 — so that one is left with the impression that this is a fixed and much used formula. [127] In keeping, perhaps, is the fact that this formula is an element in cultic speech, and is used in the general vocabulary of religion, [128] though one has to ask, of course, whether its meaning is to be deduced exclusively from its cultic use, or whether various translations and interpretations are not possible in view of the multiple sense of בְּ.

---

[120] The בְּ of the MSS is a smoothing.

[121] So Kautzsch.

[122] M. Haller, Esther (Hndb. z. AT, I, 18 [1940]), ad loc.

[123] So W. Heitmüller, 40.

[124] 1 S. 25:9; in v. 5 (וּשְׁאֶלְתֶּם־לֹו בִּשְׁמִי לְשָׁלֹום) the בִּשְׁמִי should be rendered "on my commission," though the other view is not impossible.

[125] As against Heitmüller, 40.

[126] Almost always בְּשֵׁם יהוה, sometimes supplemented appositionally by אֱלֹהֵינוּ, אֱלֹהָיו or the like; we never find in relation to Yahweh an original בְּשֵׁם אֱלֹהִים (Ps. 44:5; 54:1; 63:4 are in E psalms in which an original יהוה has been replaced by אֱלֹהִים. But cf. בְּשֵׁם אֱלֹהֵינוּ in Ps. 20:5 and בְּשֵׁם אֱלָה יִשְׂרָאֵל in Ezr. 5:1, also similar occasional expressions.

[127] But cf. verses in which the בְּ introduces an obj., e.g., Is. 50:10: יִבְטַח בְּשֵׁם יהוה (cf. Ps. 33:21).

[128] Heitmüller, 24.

The meaning of בְּשֵׁם יהוה in its cultic and generally religious use is undoubtedly linked with the solemn invocation, mention and utterance of the name Yahweh (→ 255), e.g., in the expression קָרָא בְּשֵׁם יהוה (more rarely הִזְכִּיר), to call on the deity by the name Yahweh, to invoke Yahweh. This is a common phrase for to worship Yahweh cultically (Gn. 4:26; 12:8; Zeph. 3:9 etc.). [129] Particularly worth noting in this connection is Ex. 33:19 (34:5), since here obviously Yahweh declares His own name before Moses (וְקָרָאתִי בְשֵׁם יהוה לְפָנֶיךָ) and thus makes known His presence. [130] If there is cause to fear His proximity, one must avoid naming Him (Am. 6:10). To this sphere also belongs the use of בְּשֵׁם יהוה in oaths (Dt. 6:13; Lv. 19:12; 1 S. 20:42; Jer. 12:16), or in blessing (Dt. 10:8; 2 S. 6:18; Ps. 129:8) and cursing (2 K. 2:24), which involve express mention of the name of Yahweh. → 255. [131]

Apart from the *verba dicendi* already mentioned, or similar terms, other verbs are occasionally used with בְּשֵׁם יהוה at an early period, and more often later. Thus David comes to Goliath בְּשֵׁם יהוה (1 S. 17:45), Elijah builds an altar in the name of Yahweh, [132] and in the Ps. it can be said that בְּשֵׁם יהוה one is strong (20:7; [133] cf. 124:8), one sets up a banner (20:5), one treads underfoot (44:5) and crushes (118:10-12) one's enemies. In the older of these verses, and in some of the later, בְּשֵׁם יהוה can be construed as calling on the name of Yahweh. In the Ps., however, one has to take into account the fact that שֵׁם is an alternative for Yahweh (→ 257), so that בְּשֵׁם יהוה is not just utterance or invocation of the name of Yahweh, but is usually set in parallelism to Yahweh Himself.

Most keenly debated is the use of בְּשֵׁם in the sense of "in the name" or "on the commission." We believed it possible to find instances of this in a secular sense (→ 259), and for בְּשֵׁם יהוה, too, it may be accepted in connection with דִּבֶּר and נִבָּא. One of the most important of the relevant passages here is the promise of Yahweh to Moses in Dt. 18:18 f.: "I will raise them up a prophet from among their brethren, like unto thee, and will put my words in his mouth; and he shall speak unto them (דִּבֶּר) all that I shall command him. And it shall come to pass, that whosoever will not hearken unto his (my) words which he shall speak in my name (בִּשְׁמִי), I will require it of him." Here the rendering "on my commission" seems to be demanded by the context, and is the most natural interpretation. [134] The matter is more complicated when the same formula is used, not of the message of the prophets of Yahweh, but of the utterances, indeed, the lying speeches, of false prophets. Thus we read on in Dt. 18:20: "But the prophet which shall presume to speak a word in my name which I have not commanded him to speak, or that shall speak in the name of other gods, shall die." Again, we read in Jer. 14:14: "The prophets prophesy lies in my name: I sent them not" (cf. 14:15; 23:25; 29:9). In these

---

[129] Also used more narrowly of calling on Yahweh in a special case (e.g., with the request for healing): 2 K. 5:11; cf. 1 K. 18:24 ff.

[130] Here קָרָא בְּשֵׁם יהוה is a formula unless the בְּ is taken to introduce an obj.; cf. W. Koehler, *s.v.* No. 17.

[131] With "to lift up the hands" (Ps. 63:4) and "to minister" (שָׁרֵת, Dt. 18:5, 7) בְּשֵׁם יהוה may also be understood as calling upon God in prayer and priestly ministry.

[132] 1 K. 18:32, text uncertain.

[133] Read נַזְכִּיר for נַגְבִּיר.

[134] Cf. also Jer. 11:21 (prophesy not בְּשֵׁם יהוה!) and Jer. 20:9.

verses בִּשְׁמִי certainly cannot denote a genuine commissioning of these prophets by Yahweh, for this is expressly repudiated (Jer. 14:14; 29:9; Dt. 18:20). It thus seems that "naming my name" is the only possibility. Nevertheless, it might be that בִּשְׁמִי is, as it were, in quotation marks ("ostensibly in my name and on my commission"[135]), and if this is found a little too bold, and "with appeal to my name" is preferred, [136] even this goes rather beyond mere invocation and approximates to an interpretation in which the name is an alternative for Yahweh Himself. In Ex. 5:22 f. (cf. v. 1), where Moses negotiates with Pharaoh in Yahweh's name for the liberation of the Israelites, בִּשְׁמֶךָ, referring to Yahweh, again means "on thy commission."

Thus the formula בְּשֵׁם יהוה, controlled by the various possible meanings of the preposition בְּ and the שֵׁם concept, is capable of various senses. It often signifies mention or utterance of the name Yahweh, then action on His commission or with appeal to His name, and finally it is used in parallelism with Yahweh, either as an alternative or for a hypostatised שֵׁם (Ps. 54:1). [137]

D. Hellenistic Judaism.

1. LXX.

In the LXX ὄνομα occurs in over 1000 verses, of which some 100 are in the Apocrypha. It is used almost always for the Heb. שֵׁם (Aram. שֻׁם). Other Heb. words rendered by it are זֵכֶר (Dt. 25:19); נֵכֶר (Gn. 21:23); שָׁמַע (Gn. 19:13; Nu. 14:15; Dt. 2:25; 3 Βασ. 10:1; 2 Ch. 9:1; Is. 66:19); שָׁמַע (Jos. 6:27; 9:9). In many cases שֵׁם is not rendered by ὄνομα, e.g., Est. 8:8 : τοῦ βασιλέως ἐπιτάξαντος (בְּשֵׁם); 4 Βασ. 21:4 (A): ἐν Ιερουσαλημ θήσω τὸν θρόνον μου (B τὸ ὄνομά μου); Prv. 21:24 (καλεῖν); Dt. 26:19 (καύχημα?); Ez. 23:10 (λάλημα); Sir. 49:1 (μνημόσυνον). ὀνομαστός occurs in the expression ἄνδρες ὀνομαστοί (or οἱ ἄνθρωποι οἱ ὀνομαστοί) for אַנְשֵׁי שֵׁם (הַשֵּׁם); Gn. 6:4; Nu. 16:2; 1 Ch. 5:24; 12:31, and also for שֵׁם and לְשֵׁם mostly in the sense of "fame": Is. 56:5; Dt. 26:19; Zeph. 3:19 f.; Jer. 13:11; Ez. 22:5. For וְעָשִׂיתִי לְךָ שֵׁם גָּדוֹל we read in 2 Βασ. 7:9 καὶ ἐποίησά σε ὀνομαστόν, for וְנִקְרָאָה בְשֵׁם in Est. 2:14 ἐὰν μὴ κληθῇ ὀνομαστί (A; ὀνόματι B). [138] Sometimes for stylistic polish the LXX adds ὄνομα before mentioning the name of a person or place, e.g., Gn. 21:31; Ju. 8:14 (B); 1 Βασ. 20:16; 1 Ch. 2:1. Here it can hardly have read שֵׁם in the Mas., though elsewhere, where there is strong divergence between LXX and Mas., this is a problem, e.g., Jos. 19:48 (Mas. 47); [139] Est. 2:22; 9:26. In many instances the LXX ὄνομα is due to

---

[135] As against B. Jacob, 32.

[136] Heitmüller's note that in this connection the word *Berufung* must be taken literally does little to clarify matters (39). As against this cf. Grether, 24, n. 1.

[137] Section 5. was revised by J. Fichtner.

[138] There is deliberate alteration — avoidance of the name of a strange god — in Mi. 4:5 : ὅτι πάντες οἱ λαοὶ πορεύσονται ἕκαστος τὴν ὁδὸν αὐτοῦ, כִּי כָּל־הָעַמִּים יֵלְכוּ אִישׁ בְּשֵׁם אֱלֹהָיו. At Job 30:8 : ἀφρόνων υἱοὶ καὶ ἀτίμων ὄνομα, καὶ κλέος ἐσβεσμένον ἀπὸ γῆς : בְּנֵי־נָבָל גַּם־בְּנֵי בְלִי־שֵׁם נִכְּאוּ מִן־הָאָרֶץ; ὄνομα is a transl. of שֵׁם, but is par. to υἱοί = bearers of the name, posterity (cf. Gn. 21:23) and stands for the בְּנֵי of the Mas., while בְּלִי־שֵׁם is replaced by ἄτιμοι. Perhaps there is double transl. here, for the LXX adds κλέος in the second half of the verse [Bertram].

[139] The translator had our text, but misread לְלֶשֶׁם דָּן as Λασενδακ, left out the last three words as inappropriate, and added ὄνομα for the sake of smoothness. Does Λασενδακ go back to a mistaken transcription לֶשֶׁם דָּן = λασενδαν ? [Bertram.]

a false reading or interpretation of the Heb., e.g., τὸ ὄνομα αὐτοῦ (שְׁמֹה) for שְׁמָה Nu. 33:54 [140], cf. Dt. 17:12; Is. 33:21; Jer. 46(26):17. In Job 19:14 the addition of τὸ ὄνομα rests on dittography and wrong copying from שכחוני (שכ=שם?). Also due to a slip is Ps. 130(129):4 f., where in תּוֹרָא לְמַעַן the תורא is understood as νόμος (ΣΘ), which becomes ὄνομα in SA al. Cf. Ps. 119(118):165, perhaps also Is. 42:4, though in Ps. 59(58):12 (Mas. עם) the Gk. νόμος (BS) for ὄνομα (Sᶜ) is preceded by a Heb. שם for עם. The Mas. is supported by the three Hexapla translators. ὄνομα for στόμα in ψ 62:5 is due to an error in copying, cf. Prv. 9:18a : ὄμμα-ὄνομα, while misreadings are responsible in Is. 33:21; ψ 39:4; 43:26; 71:14; Zeph. 1:4. Double translation occurs in ψ 12:5; 24:14, cf. Nu. 33:54. In 2 Ch. 1:9 דבר is rendered by ὄνομα : instead of the ref. to David confidence is grounded in the name of Yahweh. ὄνομα also occurs in words or verses in which the LXX goes beyond the Heb., e.g., 2 Βασ. 23:24; 3 Βασ. 8:16; Job 42:17b-d. If the occurrence here raises questions of textual criticism, the issues in what follows are those of translation technique.

The Heb. בְּשֵׁם especially seems to have caused difficulties. "To do something in someone's name" is variously rendered : ἐκ τοῦ ὀνόματος at Est. 8:8; διά without ὄνομα at Est. 3:12; 8:10; ἐπὶ τῷ ὀνόματι at 1 Βασ. 25:5; 3 Βασ. 20(21):8; ἐν τῷ ὀνόματι at 1 Βασ. 25:9. The common LXX formula ἐν τῷ ὀνόματι is unusual in classical Greek, → 244; it is an attempt to render the Heb. בְּשֵׁם literally and exactly. It is in a way like the instrumental use of the preposition ἐν, which is attested in secular Greek from the classical period. But it is to be regarded as real translation Greek, corresponding more to Semitic linguistic sense. [141]

"To call by name" in Ex. 31:2 is rendered ἀνακέκλημαι ἐξ ὀνόματος, cf. Ex. 35:30; Nu. 1:17. "By their name" is ἐξ ὀνομάτων αὐτῶν (בְּשֵׁמֹתָם) in Nu. 3:17, cf. 32:42 : ἐκ τοῦ ὀνόματος αὐτοῦ (= בִּשְׁמוֹ). The acc. occurs in Is. 43:1: ἐκάλεσά σε τὸ ὄνομά σου, cf. 45:3. But we find the dat. in Is. 45:4 : καλέσω σε τῷ ὀνόματί σου (S; μου B). קָרָא בְּשֵׁם יהוה, "to call on Yahweh," can be rendered transit. in the LXX : (ἐπι-)κα-λεῖσθαι τὸ ὄνομα, Gn. 4:26; 13:4; 21:33; 26:25; ψ 78:6; 79:18; 104:1; 114:4; 115:4; Is. 64:6; Jer. 10:25, though one also reads: ἐπικαλεῖσθαι ἐν ὀνόματι, 3 Βασ. 18:24, 25, 26; 4 Βασ. 5:11; 1 Ch. 16:8, or : ἐπικαλεῖσθαι ἐπὶ τῷ ὀνόματι, Gn. 12:8. Along with βοᾶν ἐν ὀνόματι at 3 Βασ. 18:24 we find βοᾶν τὸ ὄνομα αὐτοῦ at Is. 12:4. The same vacillation between the simple dat., ἐν with dat. and ἐπί with dat. may be seen in respect of the verbs "to swear" (cf. 1 Βασ. 20:42 with Dt. 6:13), "to praise" (1 Ch. 16:10; ψ 104:3), "to bless" (cf. 2 Βασ. 6:18; ψ 71:17; 117:26; 128:8 etc. with Dt. 21:5), "to speak" (cf. 3 Βασ. 22:16 with Ex. 5:23; 33:19; Dt. 18:19, 20, 22; Jer. 20:9). בָּא בְּשֵׁם יהוה (הָלַךְ) is rendered ἐν ὀνόματι at 1 Βασ. 17:45; Mi. 4:5, but ἐπὶ τῷ ὀνόματι at 2 Ch. 14:10, בֹּא לְשֵׁם is ἐν ὀνόματι at Jos. 9:9, but הֵכִין לִשְׁמוֹ is ἐπ' ὀνόματι αὐτοῦ at Sir. 47:13. At Dt. 17:12 the LXX renders שָׁרֵת שָׁם אֶת־יהוה by λειτουργεῖν ἐπὶ τῷ ὀνόματι κυρίου, at 2 Βασ. 22:50 לְשִׁמְךָ אֲזַמֵּר by ἐν τῷ ὀνόματί σου ψαλῶ, at 4 Βασ. 2:24 וַיְקַלְלֵם בְּשֵׁם יהוה by κατηράσατο ... ἐν ὀνόματι κυρίου.

On this basis we may now examine the thesis that ἐν or ἐπί (τῷ) ὀνόματι in the OT and then the NT means only "in," "with mention of," "with utterance or invocation of the name." In the Heb. OT we have already come across passages where this is not an adequate rendering of בְּשֵׁם, but where the term means rather "on the commission of." We have also seen that the element of actual utterance gradually loses

---

[140] In 1 Ch. 12:24 the LXX substitutes for וְאֵלֶּה מִסְפְּרֵי the more common καὶ ταῦτα τὰ ὀνόματα.

[141] A. Dieterich, Eine Mithrasliturgie² (1910), 115; on Semitism and the instrumental ἐν generally cf. Bl.-Debr. § 4, 195, 219.

significance, and esp. that in Dt. the *shem* represents Yahweh in the temple. In addition, שֵׁם יהוה becomes an alternative for Yahweh. [142] How ἐν or ἐπί (τῷ) ὀνόματι is used in the LXX for this varied use of שֵׁם יהוה in the Mas. may best be seen in each case from the basic text followed by the LXX. The prep. ἐπί is used to express calling after something : Gn. 4:17 ἐπωνόμασεν τὴν πόλιν ἐπὶ τῷ ὀνόματι τοῦ υἱοῦ, Heb. כְּשֵׁם. Gn. 48:6 ἐπὶ τῷ ὀνόματι τῶν ἀδελφῶν αὐτῶν κληθήσονται, Heb. עַל־שֵׁם, "according to the name," so also 2 Εσδρ. 17:63, though in the par. 2 Εσδρ. 2:61 (B) ἐκλήθη ἐν ὀνόματι αὐτῶν. Cf., however, 1 Macc. 14:43 : ὅπως γράφωνται ἐπὶ τῷ ὀνόματι αὐτοῦ πᾶσαι συγγραφαί. In transl. of נִקְרָא שֵׁם עַל ("the name of someone is named over a thing or person") ὄνομα is sometimes used with ἐπί and dat.: ἐπικέκληται τὸ ὄνομά σου ἐπ' ἐμοί, Ιερ. 15:16; cf. Ιερ. 7:10, 11, 14; 39(32):34; 41(34):15. ἐπί with acc. is also common, e.g., 2 Βασ. 12:28; 3 Βασ. 8:43; 2 Ch. 7:14; Am. 9:12; Is. 4:1; 63:19; Jer. 7:30; 14:9; Da. 9:19; Bar. 2:15; ἐπ' αὐτοῦ (Α ἐπ' αὐτόν) at 1 Macc. 7:37. Only 3 times in the LXX do we find εἰς ὄνομα for לְשֵׁם (with verbs of becoming or making): Is. 55:13 : καὶ ἔσται κύριος εἰς ὄνομα, cf. 2 Εσδρ. 16:13; 1 Ch. 22:5. In Jer. 13:11 לְשֵׁם is transl. ὀνομαστόν, → 261; in Ez. 34:39 φυτὸν εἰρήνης is used for Heb. מַטָּע לְשֵׁם. [143] In all these verses שֵׁם (ὄνομα) means reputation or renown, not name. At 2 Macc. 8:4 and 3 Macc. 2:9 we find εἰς τὸ ὄνομα with no Heb. original.

If שֵׁם יהוה often occurs alongside Yahweh in the Mas., the LXX seems occasionally to have carried this further (unless it had a different Heb. text), cf. Nu. 14:21; 1 Ch. 22:6 (A); 2 Ch. 6:2; ψ 12:6; Is. 12:5; 19:18 (?). Along the same lines is the idea of Yahweh choosing a city or house "to cause his name to dwell there" (2 Εσδρ. 6:12; 11:9) or "to set his name there" (3 Βασ. 11:36; 14:21; 4 Βασ. 21:4, 7). In these verses the Mas. is transl. lit. by the LXX, but the expressions can be paraphrased : ὁ τόπος, ὃν ἂν ἐκλέξηται κύριος ὁ θεὸς ὑμῶν ἐπικληθῆναι τὸ ὄνομα αὐτοῦ ἐκεῖ, Dt. 12:11, cf. 12:26; 14:23 f.; 16:2, 6, 11, 15 (A); 17:8 (AS); 26:2; 2 Ch. 6:20; cf. 12:13. Similarly, at 3 Βασ. 3:2; 5:17, 19; 8:17, 20; 2 Ch. 6:7, 8, 9 the LXX has the lit. τῷ ὀνόματι for the expression "to build a house for the name of the Lord," though at 1 Ch. 28:3 we find : οὐκ οἰκοδομήσεις ἐμοὶ οἶκον τοῦ ἐπονομάσαι τὸ ὄνομά μου ἐπ' αὐτῷ. In Nu. 14:21 the LXX adds καὶ ζῶν τὸ ὄνομά μου after ζῶ ἐγώ. ὄνομα is often combined with ζάω in Sir : 37:26; 39:9; 44:14. The ref. is to the ὄνομα αἰώνιον, Sir. 15:6; Is. 56:5. On the other hand, in the strongly anthropomorphic Ez. 43:7 the LXX prefers to speak of God's name rather than of God Himself. In Mal. 3:5 those who swear falsely (Mas.) are those who swear falsely in my name (LXX). Particular note should be taken of two verses from Lv. At 24:11 the Mas. reads : "And the son blasphemed (וַיִּקֹּב) ... the name (אֶת הַשֵּׁם) and cursed ; LXX : ἐπονομάσας ὁ υἱός ... τὸ ὄνομα κατηράσατο. At 24:16 : "And whosoever blasphemes the name of Yahweh shall die the death," LXX : ὀνομάζων δὲ τὸ ὄνομα κυρίου θανάτῳ θανατούσθω. The Heb. forbids blaspheming the name of Yahweh, but the LXX goes further and forbids naming the name.

Though ὄνομα is common in the LXX, the verb ὀνομάζειν is rare. Of the 30 or so instances, a dozen are in the Apocrypha. The verb seems to have been replaced by καλεῖν, perhaps because the Heb. שֵׁם has no verb. It is a transl. of זָכַר at Jer. 3:16; 23:36; hi Jos. 23:7; Am. 6:10; Is. 19:17; of נָקַב at Lv. 24:16; Is. 62:2; ni 1 Ch. 12:32; 2 Ch. 31:19; of קָרָא at Gn. 26:18 (A); Ιερ. 32(25):29.

---

[142] Heitmüller tries to use only one principle of exposition and thus engages in exegesis which "can only be called rather artificial" (Bousset-Gressm., 349).

[143] Probably on the basis of Heb. שָׁלֵם. Ex. 32:25 'A reads εἰς ὄνομα ῥύπου. לְשִׁמְצָה, whose meaning is not certain, is taken as לְשֵׁם צָאָה "that they count as filth." Σ, too, read שֵׁם and changed צה to רע, so that we have κακωνυμία. At Ιερ. 40(33):9 'A and Σ have εἰς ὄνομα εὐφροσύνης for לְשֵׁם שָׂשׂוֹן, while the LXX simply has εἰς εὐφροσύνην. Here, too, there is combination with a verb of becoming [Bertram].

ἐπονομάζειν [144] occurs in the LXX some 36 times. It is a rendering of שֵׁם קָרָא only at Gn. 4:17 and 26:18 (BS); Jos. 7:26. ἐπονομάζειν τὸ ὄνομα is used for the simple קָרָא at Gn. 21:31; for זָכַר hi at Ex. 20:24; for נָקַב at Lv. 24:11; for שׂוּם שֵׁם at Dt. 12:5; 2 Ch. 12:13; with no Heb. equivalent at 1 Ch. 28:3. In the other instances it is a transl. of קָרָא.

2. Philo.

What the name means for Philo is most plainly stated in Decal., 82 : "The name is a second thing attaching to the basic matter, like a shadow which accompanies the body." Hence there is first ref. to God, then to His name. The name is a the mirror of the thought (Vit. Cont., 78). If we have clear and plain thoughts, our speech has a great wealth of illuminating and suitable expressions (ἐμφαντικωτάτων καὶ κυρίων ὀνομάτων); on the other hand, an unclear thought is unable to choose fitting expressions (ὀνόματα, Det. Pot. Ins., 131; Migr. Abr., 79). Moses was a prototype of those who have full knowledge and an exact grasp of concepts ; hence he never exercised the θέσις τῶν ὀνομάτων wrongly (Agric., 1 f.; Cher., 56). There is the danger, however, that the ambiguity of words (κοινότητι τῶν ὀνομάτων, Rer. Div. Her., 72) will prevent an object of knowledge from being defined exactly, and the great majority of men do not name things accurately. Hence Philo praises the LXX because in it the Gk. text is so brought into harmony with the Heb. that the words fully correspond to the things denoted, Vit. Mos., II, 37 f., 40. The θέσις τῶν ὀνομάτων is in the Bible ascribed to the first man, Op. Mund., 148; Quaest. in Gn., I, 20 f. This is the origin of speech. Acc. to Philo the Bible has here a more accurate view of things than the Gk. philosophers, who ascribe the giving of names to many men. From the beginning confusion is thus avoided and names correspond to things, Leg. All., II, 14 f. Philo interprets many OT proper names allegorically ; for him they express the nature of persons or contain some other deep significance (Mut. Nom., 64-121) which he brings out for his readers by transl. them into Gk. The Bible itself expounds many proper names (→ 254), and Philo shares the etym. interest of Stoic philosophy, which he may also count on in his readers. Examples of explanations of words and proper names after the Gk. manner may be found throughout his writings. Philo is in close touch with the linguistic teaching of his age, and can tell of those who occupy themselves with the exact meanings of words, the ζητητικοὶ τῶν κυρίων ὀνομάτων (Deus Imm., 86; Det. Pot. Ins., 76). He himself has a long discussion of homonyms and synonyms, Plant., 150-155. On the other hand, though he aims at exactness in the choice of words and in expression, he censures the pedantic zeal of those who occupy their whole lives, not with questions of philosophy and ethics, but with ὀνόματα and ῥήματα, as though their whole fate depended on them, Congr., 53. Man's idolatry is expressed in the fact that false names (ψευδώνυμος) are given to the parts of the universe and the one true God is thus obscured, Decal., 53.

As concerns the name of God, Philo moves in Stoic circles. In calling God "the one who is" (ὁ ὤν) he borrows from LXX Ex. 3:14. But he has God say to Moses : "For me, to whom alone being belongs, there is no name appropriate to my nature," Vit. Mos., I, 75. Being itself (τὸ ὄν) cannot be named ; it simply "is"; hence God is called "he who is" in order that man may grasp what can be grasped in God alone, existence, Som., I, 230 f. Since being is ineffable, its proper name is unknown to creatures, Rer. Div. Her., 170. Acc. to Mut. Nom., 11 f. the divine name given to men is κύριος ὁ θεός. God also has a relative name by which men may call upon Him : "I am the God of Abraham, Isaac, and Jacob, this is my name for ever," Abr., 51, cf. Ex. 3:15. Hence

---

[144] προσονομάζειν occurs in 2 Macc. 6:2. We also find ὀνομαστί (only Est. 2:14 [A]) and twice ὀνομαστός (2 Βασ. 7:9 for גָּדֹל שֵׁם). ὀνομασία occurs in ψ 67:5 (Aquila) in the sense of "naming a name," cf. also Sir. 23:9 of naming the divine name as a par. to frivolous swearing. We also find ὀνοματογραφία (1 Εσδρ. 6:11; 8:48), ἐπώνυμος (Est. 8:12 u), μεγαλώνυμος (Ιερ. 39[32]:19); ἀνώνυμος (Wis. 14:27). There are no Heb. equivalents for these Hell. constructions ; εὐώνυμος occurs as a transl. but the etym. connection is lost [Bertram].

God has no proper name. [145] The names in the Gk. Bible, κύριος and θεός, simply denote powers in God. [146] κύριος, as illustrated by Gk. etym., means the power of rule, θεός that of grace. [147] Philo realised, of course, that on the diadem of the high-priest four letters were inscribed which indicated the name of God (μηνύεσθαι, Vit. Mos., II, 132). He also knew that in their temple ministry the priests had a golden tablet (πέταλον): τέτταρας ἔχον γλυφὰς ὀνόματος, ὃ μόνοις τοῖς ὦτα καὶ γλῶτταν σοφίᾳ κεκαθαρμένοις θέμις ἀκούειν καὶ λέγειν ἐν ἁγίοις, ἄλλῳ δ' οὐδενὶ τὸ παράπαν οὐδαμοῦ (Vit. Mos., II, 114). He does not say expressly that this name was the tetragrammaton, and his statements about the utterance of the divine name in temple worship are not very feasible. [148] He also has very hazy ideas about the connection between the tetragrammaton and the κύριος of the LXX. [149] He stands in the Stoic tradition with his assertion that the powers of Him who is have many names (Som., II, 254), just as wisdom does (Leg. All., I, 43). This honour of having many names then passes to the *logos,* which is among other things the name of God, Conf. Ling., 146. Though men do not know God's name, but only given designations, these are still to be held holy, Mut. Nom., 11-13. Philo often speaks of God's "improper name"; it should not be invoked lightly, Spec. Leg., II, 3. One cannot swear by God Himself, since one knows only His name, not His essence, Leg. All., III, 207 f. To swear falsely is to sully the unspotted name of God, Spec. Leg., IV, 40. Philo warns against the use of blasphemous names, for it is sin for the lips to pronounce the most holy name (τὸ ἱερώτατον ὄνομα) as well as vile words, and yet many use the many-formed name (πολυώνυμον ὄνομα) in an unfitting and sinful manner, Decal., 93 f. Instead of praising God, men utter the most solemn names (φρικωδεστάτας ὀνομάζουσι κλήσεις), heap many ὀνόματα together, and think that they will attain their purpose thus, Spec. Leg., II, 8.

3. Josephus.

Joseph.'s use of ὄνομα [150] stands in closer relation to the Gk. world than to the OT and Semitic Gk. His usual rendering of "in the name" is ἐξ ὀνόματος, Ant., 2, 275; 14, 138. Not ungreek (→ 244), but found mainly in the LXX, is the expression ἐπ' ὀνόματι: The Israelites were not going to worry about Moses, who hindered them "under the pretext of the name of God (ἐπ' ὀνόματι τοῦ θεοῦ) ..." (Ant., 4, 5). ἐπ' ὀνόματι τοῦ 'Ιακώβου denotes the animals falling to Jacob, 1, 321. Jos. follows the OT when he has Samuel say to Saul: τὸ 'Αμαλήκου ὄνομα ... ἐξαλείψαι, 6, 133. Only the Jews refused to swear by the name of Gaius: μόνους τούσδε ἄδοξον ἡγεῖσθαι ... ὅρκιον αὐτοῦ τὸ ὄνομα ποιεῖσθαι, 18, 258. Herod began the war when "thy name, too, O Caesar, was desecrated with the other gods," ἠσεβημένου δὲ μετὰ τῶν ἄλλων θεῶν καὶ τοῦ σοῦ, Καῖσαρ, ὀνόματος, 16, 346.

In relation to God's name Jos. is very reserved. "Since Jos. extended the banishment of God's name from speech even to κύριος, literal quotations from the biblical books are almost completely absent. Not once in the Apologies does he support by quotations ordinances said to be valid." [151] He puts the third commandment as follows: "The third commandment teaches that one is not to swear lightly by God" (ἐπὶ μηδενὶ φαύλῳ τὸν θεὸν ὀμνύναι, Ant., 3, 91). In the revelation of God in Ex. 3 Jos. has Moses ask God not to withhold from him knowledge of His name (μηδὲ ὀνόματος αὐτῷ γνῶσιν τοῦ ἰδίου φθονῆσαι) after he heard the voice, καὶ τὴν προσηγορίαν εἰπεῖν, ἵνα θύων ἐξ ὀνόματος αὐτὸν παρεῖναι τοῖς ἱεροῖς παρακαλῇ. "And God declared

---

[145] W. W. Graf Baudissin, *Kyrios als Gottesname* ..., II (1928), 179 f.
[146] Som., I, 163; Plant., 85 f.; Leg. All., III, 73.
[147] For Philo, then, the LXX κύριος was simply God's second "name" alongside θεός, Schl. Theol. d. Judt., 61, n. 1.
[148] Baudissin, 177 f.
[149] *Ibid.,* 179-181.
[150] On Joseph. cf. Schl. Theod. d. Judt., 60-66, 112, 155, 245.
[151] *Ibid.,* 61.

to him His name (προσηγορία, not ὄνομα) which had not previously come to men, and about which it is not permissible to say anything," 2, 275 f. Since Jos. was a priest, he knew how to pronounce the name, but kept the well-known command which forbade its utterance. The name (προσηγορία) of God is inscribed with holy signs on the head-band, 3, 178. The high-priest Jaddus comes before Alexander fully robed ; he bears the head-band on which τὸ τοῦ θεοῦ ἐγέγραπτο ὄνομα. [152] Alexander the Gt. προσεκύνησεν τὸ ὄνομα, 11, 331.

God's name is dreadful. In certain crises "they invoked the terrible name of God" (τὸ φρικτὸν ἐπικαλουμένων ὄνομα τοῦ θεοῦ, Bell., 5, 438). This does not have to be the tetragrammaton. If it is said in Dt. that God's name dwells in the temple, Jos. has Solomon say at the dedication : σοὶ κατεσκεύακα τὸν ναὸν ἐπώνυμον, Ant., 8, 108. The divine transcendence is strengthened now that part of God's Spirit rather than the name of God is thought to dwell in the temple, 8, 114. Perhaps Jos. also puts it thus because he was writing for Gks. who would have thought it odd for God's name to dwell in the temple. Not the temple only bears God's name (= ἐπώνυμον). Coins too, can be ἐπώνυμα of God : "They destroyed coins which we collect for God as marked with His name (ἐπώνυμα), and thus openly robbed the temple," 16, 45. Pagan sanctuaries are also ἐπώνυμα of the gods concerned ; the Law orders that "alien sanctuaries should not be robbed, nor any jewel taken if it is named for a god" (ἐπωνομασμένον, 4, 207). To honour one's father is a religious duty because he has the same name as God, 2, 152; 4, 262.

E. Later Judaism.

I. Pseudepigrapha.

The pseudepigr. lit. is not particularly rich in statements about the name ; there are hardly any new features as compared with the OT. The comprehensive knowledge of the author of Slav. En. [153] includes knowledge not only of the meaning of human names but also of the names of plants and animals, 40:7. Adam's name has profound significance, and obviously characterises him as a cosmic being, 30:13 f. (A). Eve's name is taken from Adam as well as Eve herself : "And I took his last letter and gave her the name of mother, i.e., Eve," 30:17 (A). [154] As in the OT the name of the forefather lives on in the children (→ 253), so also in Jub. 16:16; 17:6; 19:16, 24; 25:21. In Eth. En. 108:3 the wicked are threatened that their names will be blotted out of the book of life [155] (→ I, 619 f.), → 253. This will mean eternal perdition and death. In the Last Judgment the deeds of sinners will be disclosed, and the names of the righteous will appear, 4 Esr. 14:35; cf. Eth. En. 65:12.

Apocalyptic instruction contains revelations about saints and angels and their names. In Eth. En. 43 the apocalyptist sees (lightnings and) stars of different degrees of brightness, and receives from the interpreting angel the explanation : "These are the names of saints who dwell on the earth and who believe in the name of the Lord of spirits." [156] There is special interest in the names of the fallen angels, Eth. En. 6:7; 8:3; 69:2-13. In the astronomical book of Eth. En. the names of the leaders of the heavenly host (of stars) are mentioned, 82:13 f., 17, 20. As in the OT (Is. 40:26; Ps. 147:4) the stars have names (Eth. En. 78:1 f.; Slav. En. 30:6 [A]; 40:3 f. [A]), and so do the chambers of heaven acc. to 4 Esr. 6:4.

The pseudepigr. lit. often refers to the name of God. In this respect it usually follows the OT, and here again the various expressions cannot be sharply differentiated from

---

[152] Though cf. Ant., 8, 93 : The head-band εἰς ἣν τὸν θεὸν Μωυσῆς ἔγραψε.
[153] N. Bonwetsch, TU, 44, 2 (1922): "D. Bücher der Geheimnisse Henochs".
[154] This is to be explained in terms of the Gk. Ἀδάμ — μήτηρ.
[155] Acc. to another reading "from the book of the saints."
[156] "The name of the righteous seems here to be their (pre-existent) heavenly essentiality ..., their soul, their ego (name = person)," Bousset-Gressm., 350.

one another. It is not expressly emphasised that knowledge of God's name is an in-dispensable prerequisite of worship. [157] Acc. to 4 Esr. 7:132-139 seven divine names are known ; these denote qualities, cf. 8:31 f. Since Israel is called by God's name (10:22), there arises in respect of its destiny the question what God will do for His name (4:25). for His name is not honoured by the overthrow of Jerusalem (S. Bar. 67:3). To know God's name is to praise Him ; thus the angels extol Him : "Magnified be thou, and blessed be the name of the Lord to all eternity," Eth. En. 39:13. But sinners worship idols and thus deny the name of God, 46:7 f. They misuse it, and hence come into judgment, 60:6; cf. 46:6. On the other hand, in the day of affliction the righteous will overcome in the name of the Lord of spirits, and they will be delivered by His name, 50:2. At the Last Judgment the Son of Man will be brought before God and His name before the Ancient of Days ; before the creation of the stars His name was named before the Lord of spirits, 48:2 f. The pre-existence of the name herein mentioned denotes the pre-existence of the Son of Man Himself, since name and person are very closely related (→ III, 489, 13 ff., 26 ff.; cf. Eth. En. 69:26; 70:1 f.). After the judgment God swears by His great name : "From now on I will no longer do thus to any dweller on earth" (55:2). In these and similar passages about God's name it is often hard to decide whether the ref. is to naming the name or to God Himself. Sometimes the sense is that of repute or glory. Only Jub. continues the *shem* concept of Dt. (→ 256 f.) acc. to which the name of God dwells in the temple, e.g., Jub. 32:10; 49:21. On the other hand there is a series of verses in which God's name is a mysterious and mighty potency which is revealed to men by angels. Men swear by it (Jub. 36:7); indeed the strange idea is found that it is the oath itself (Eth. En. 69:13 ff.), and everything in heaven and on earth was created by this name and oath (Eth. En. 69:13-21; Jub. 36:7). The mysterious divine name men-tioned in the oath is the power which creates and sustains the cosmos, a hypostasis. Thus OT ideas are taken up and developed, → 257 f.

II. Rabbinic Sources.

(1) Usage.

The meanings of the Heb. שֵׁם are upheld in the Rabb. writings too. [158] A man acquires one name from his parents, people give him a second, and he wins the third [159] for himself. [160] Thus R. Jochanan (d. 279) says : "Well with him who ... leaves the world with a good name," Ber. 17a. A good name runs from one end of the earth to the other. [161] It is said of R. Meir that he took note of the names of men — *nomen est omen* — and acted accordingly, Yoma, 83b. If in Scripture the name of a man is doubled, then acc. to R. Abba b. Kahana (c. 310) he has a share both in this world and in the world to come. [162] Good works and observance of the commandments make a name great in the world. [163]

Like the OT בְּשֵׁם (→ 260 f.), מִשֵּׁם, מִשּׁוּם and also בְּשֵׁם, בְּשׁוּם are used in Rabb. lit. for "in virtue of the name," "on the basis of the name," "with appeal to the name." Thus we find in parallels to the stories of healing in the name of Jesus : "Ja'akob came from Kephar Sama to heal R. El'azar in the name of a certain person (בְּשׁוּם פְּלוֹנִי)," Midr.

---

[157] The words of Test. L. 5:5 : "I pray thee, lord, tell me thy name that I may call upon thee in the day of trouble," refer to the name of an angel (cf. the answer to the prayer) not to the name of God.

[158] In New Heb. שֵׁם, שְׁמָא and שׁוּם, the last two from Aram.

[159] Cf. also Midr. Qoh., 7, 1 (31b); Str.-B., II, 712.

[160] Tanch. ויקהל, 121b; Str.-B., II, 107.

[161] Midr. Qoh., 7, 1 (31a); Str.-B., II, 547.

[162] Gn. r., 30 (18b); Str.-B., II, 258.

[163] Str.-B., I, 986; Midr. Cant., 1, 3 (85a).

Qoh., 1, 8 (8b). [164] There is also occasional ref. to "prophesying in the name (בְּשֵׁם) of a false god." [165] S. Dt., 177 on 18:19 f. shows how this is to be taken : That is one who says : "Thus has the false god said."

The term מְשׁוּם is important in Jewish tradition. [166] R. Meir speaks a parable in the name (מִשּׁוּם) of the Rabban Gamaliel, TBQ, 7, 2. He who heard something in the house of instruction and passed it on was obliged to quote the authority to which he appealed, in whose name he passed on the tradition. One of the 48 conditions for acquiring the Torah is that "one pronounces every saying in the name of its author (בְּשֵׁם אוֹמְרוֹ)," Ab., 6, 6; cf. Meg., 15a. This shows what or how much authority the statement has.

In relation to the NT the expression לְשֵׁם is particularly important. It has a final sense : "with respect to the fact that something is to happen." [167] Thus sacrifice is made לְשֵׁם הַשֵׁם, i.e., to offer it to Yahweh, not to a heathen god. But the nature of the sacrifice is also denoted by לְשֵׁם. [168] The bath, too, takes place לְשֵׁם. The slave takes it לשם בן חורין (Jeb., 45b), "in the name of a free man," to become a free man. Similarly, Gentile slaves, when entering a Jewish house, take it לשם שפחות (Jeb., 47b), "in the name of the status of slave," i.e., the bath puts them in this position. The circumcision of a proselyte is done לשם גר (TAZ, 3, 12 f. [464]), "in the name of the proselyte," to receive him into Judaism. This circumcision takes place לשם ברית (loc. cit.), "in the name of the covenant," to receive him into the covenant. The person circumcised is also engaged hereby to keep the statutes of the covenant. לְשֵׁם also has causal significance : "with respect to the fact that something is," "on account of," "for the sake of." [169] "All who exert themselves for the community should do so for the sake of God (לְשֵׁם שָׁמַיִם) "all thine acts should be done for the sake of God" (Ab., 2, 12; cf. 2, 2).

(2) The Name of God (→ III, 92 ff.).

In Scripture reading in synagogue worship the tetragrammaton was read as Adonai, but in the schools הַשֵׁם was used in quotations from Scripture. [170] Sometimes this is also used for Elohim, cf. Meg., 4, 3 with Ber., 7, 3. In reading the Law the Samaritans put שְׁמָא for the tetragrammaton. [171] The tetragrammaton יהוה is the name par excellence. More specifically the tetragrammaton is שֵׁם הַמְיוּחָד, "God's own name," or שֵׁם הַמְפֹרָשׁ, "the separated, special name peculiar to God," His proper name as distinct from designations (כִּנּוּי), the name which is generally kept secret and uttered only on special occasions. ברכת השם is blaspheming of God, Sanh., 56a. Whosoever curses father or mother with pronouncement of the tetragrammaton comes under penalty of death, Sanh., 7, 8. Acc. to S. Nu., 43 on 6:27 the shem hamm\u1ebdphorash was used by the priests in the temple in benediction ; otherwise another designation was employed. [172] The use of שֵׁם for the tetragrammaton occurs already in Lv. 24:11, 16. [173] It is to be noted that the

[164] Str.-B., I, 468; cf. AZ, 2, 40d, 35 : "in the name of Jeshu ben Pandera."

[165] S. Dt., 177 on 18:19 f.; Sanh., 11, 1 and 5; 89a.

[166] In the language of the schools שֵׁם often means the biblical ground for a legal ruling (Bacher Term., I, 121 and 188 f.). Cf. Mak., 1, 2.

[167] On this section cf. Str.-B., I, 590 f., 1054 f.

[168] Ibid., 591; Zeb., 4, 6.

[169] The distinction between the final and causal meanings which לְשֵׁם can have is decisive in respect of Heitmüller's polemic (123-126) against Brandt.

[170] Str.-B., II, 316.

[171] Dalman WJ, I², 149.

[172] So also Mishnah Tamid, 7, 2; on what follows cf. Bacher Term., I, 186 f.

[173] Dalman WJ, I², 149 f. On this basis the tetragrammaton was vocalised יְהוָה (cf. BHK³), to be read as שְׁמָא = name.

Rabb. in quoting Scripture increasingly used הַשֵּׁם rather than Adonai for Yahweh. Ancient witnesses are Sanh., 7, 5 : פֵּרֵשׁ הַשֵּׁם "to pronounce the tetragrammaton exactly"; Ber., 9, 5 : שָׁאַל שָׁלוֹם בְּשֵׁם, "to greet with use of the tetragrammaton." Acc. to Yoma, 3, 8; 4, 2; 6, 2 the high-priest on the Day of Atonement even began the confession of sins with אָנָּא הַשֵּׁם instead of אָנָּא יהוה. [174] It is told that after the death of Simon the Just the priests ceased to bless with the שֵׁם, i.e., with the name Yahweh. [175] In S. Nu., 39 on 6:23 the matter is discussed by R. Josia and R. Jonathan. Both agree with the Mishnah and attest that the tetragrammaton was pronounced in temple worship. [176] Acc. to the Tannaitic tradition (Abba Shaul) he who pronounces the name will lose his portion in the hereafter. [177] The sharp commands of the Rabbis against uttering the name led in time to a forgetting of the original pronunciation of the tetragrammaton.

In time, then, the שֵׁם הַמְּפֹרָשׁ really became the ineffable name, [178] the secret name of God. There happened to the name of Yahweh precisely what the OT had said should not happen. Yahweh became a God with a secret name like any other god. Knowledge of this name became an instrument of power and magic, → 251; infra. The command not to utter the name is explained by the Rabbis, not as a rule of tradition, but as a biblical command. The נקב of Lv. 24:11, 16 was taken to mean "to utter." Ex. 3:15 : "This is my name for ever, and thus will I be called upon from generation to generation," was referred to non-pronouncement of the tetragrammaton. A defectively written לְעֹלָם was read as לְעַלֵּם, "(this is my name) to conceal it."

The tt. for the tetragrammaton in Rabb. writings is "the name of four letters" (שֵׁם ארבע אותיות). Alongside it are divine names of 12 or 42 letters, Qid., 71a. Only in the Midrash is there ref. to the name consisting of 72 letters. [179] On the hallowing of God's name → I, 98 f.

(3) Belief and Magic.

Belief in the wonder-working power of the secret name of God may be seen at many points in the Jewish tradition. [180] Thus the prayer for rain made by Choni, the drawer of circles : "Lord of the world ... I swear by thy holy name that I will not stir from here until thou hast had pity on thy children," Taan., 3, 8. There are accounts of miracles worked with the help of the plainly pronounced tetragrammaton. A shem was inscribed on the jaws of the bull of Jeroboam so that he could speak, Sota, 47a. Isaiah under persecution spoke a shem, was swallowed up by a cedar, and was thus delivered, Jeb., 49b. Asmodai, prince of the demons, was bound by a chain and a seal-ring on which a divine name was written, Git., 68b. [181] With the help of the tetragrammaton it is even possible to gain knowledge of the future and the future world, Tg. Qoh., 3, 11. The magic pap. from Gk. Egypt contain many divine names, among which Ιαω, Ιαη and Ιαοηλ occur frequently, → 251. In the syncretistic magic of the time the names of pagan gods are intermingled and associated with Jewish names. Jewish tradition, too,

---

[174] But cf. Levy Wört., IV, 569 s.v.

[175] T. Sota, 13, 8; Yoma, 49b; Sota, 38b.

[176] Cf. Nu. r., 11 (163b); Sota, 38a; Qid., 71a; jJoma, 3, 40d; Midr. Cant., 3, 11; v. K. G. Kuhn, S. Num. (1933 ff.), 122 f.

[177] Sanh., 10, 1; T. Sanh., 12, 9; as against A. Marmorstein, "The Old Rabbinic Doctrine of God," Jews' College Publications, 10 (1927), 19, who says R. Levi (3rd cent.) was the author of the prohibition. Tg. O. on Lv. 24:16 agrees here with Mishnah and Tosefta, while Tg. J. I says : "He who utters the name and blasphemes will be put to death."

[178] Cf. Grünbaum (1885), 545.

[179] Gn. r., 44 on 15:14; Lv. r., 23 on 18:3; Pesikt. r., 76b.

[180] Schürer, III⁴, 407-420.

[181] Cf. M. J. bin Gorion, Der Born Judas², I (1919), 320 f.; II (1919), 47-57.

can tell of this combination of God's name with the names of pagan deities. Thus in the sin of the golden calf the Jews used the name of Yahweh with the names of false gods. [182] In this connection we should also cite the assertion of the Rabb. that God has associated His name with the names of creatures ; the divine name *ēl* is part of the names of angels, e.g., Michael, Gabriel, Uriel ; the name is written on a tablet over their hearts. [183] Similarly, God's name is bound up with Israel, jTaan., 65d. The tradition called this שתף. Involved is a transfer of power ; the power of God is made over to the one whose name is a compound of *ēl* or *yah*. Official Judaism led the struggl⁼ against magic. He who prophesies in the name of an idol is strangled, Sanh., 11, 1, and Abba Shaul says that he who whispers over a wound loses his portion in the world to come, T. Sanh., 12, 10 (433). R. Acha b. Sera said : "He who does not observe magic keeps his place in the circle of the angels," jShab., 6, 8 (23a). Already in the Talmud, however, not merely the names of God but the individual letters of the names and indeed of the whole Heb. alphabet are regarded as magically potent, cf. Men., 29b. This trend may be seen in Heb. En. [184] Certain divine names hold together the opposing elements in the cosmos, its polar forces. They thus guarantee the harmony of the universe, Heb. En. 42:2-7. [185]

F. The New Testament.

1. Usage.

a. Name of a Person. In the NT a proper name is usually integrated into the sentence construction, e.g., Mk. 3:16 : ἐπέθηκεν ὄνομα τῷ Σίμωνι Πέτρον, Ac. 27:1: ἑκατοντάρχῃ ὀνόματι Ἰουλίῳ. Only rarely is the construction broken by a name in the nominative, e.g., Rev. 9:11: ὄνομα ἔχει Ἀπολλύων. The nominative is used with an intercalated ὄνομα αὐτῷ in Jn. 1:6 : ἐγένετο ἄνθρωπος ... ὄνομα αὐτῷ Ἰωάννης, but we usually find ᾧ (ῇ, οὗ) ὄνομα or ὀνόματι. [186] An isolated use is the acc. of relation τοὔνομα in Mt. 27:57: "by the name." [187] Heb. influence may be seen at Lk. 1:5 (cf. v. 27): καὶ τὸ ὄνομα αὐτῆς, cf. 1 S. 1:1; also at Mt. 1:21, 23, 25; Lk. 1:13, 31; 2:21; καλεῖν τὸ ὄνομα αὐτοῦ Ἰησοῦν etc.; [188] and again (→ 252; 263) at Lk. 1:59: ἐκάλουν αὐτὸ ἐπὶ τῷ ὀνόματι τοῦ πατρὸς αὐτοῦ Ζαχαρίαν.

b. Name as "reputation" also occurs in the NT. At Mk. 6:14 Jesus is widely known. At Rev. 3:1 the church of Sardis has the name (reputation) that it lives.

c. Name for "person" occurs 3 times in the NT. Ac. 1:15 : "And there was a group of about 120 persons (ὀνομάτων ═ people) together." Rev. 3:4 : "But thou hast few people (ὀνόματα) who have not defiled their garments ..." Rev. 11:13 : "And in the earthquake 7000 men (ὀνόματα ἀνθρώπων) were slain." The phrase seems too full here as compared with 3:4, since either ὀνόματα or ἀνθρώπων is dispensable. Possibly Ac. 18:15 is to be construed similarly : "But if it be a matter of teaching and persons (ὀνομάτων) and your law, see to it yourselves." [189] Gallio assumes that amongst other things it is a matter of party differences, which are often about leading personalities. On ὄνομα for person in Paul → 275.

---

[182] S. Dt., 43 (81b) on Dt. 11:16 and Ex. 22:19; Sanh., 63a; Ex. r., 42.

[183] Pesikt. r., 108b; Tanch. יתרו (Buber, p. 77); Blau, 118.

[184] Cf. Odeberg, 172 (c. 41).

[185] Cf. the par. in Odeberg, 130-132.

[186] Bl.-Debr.⁷ § 143; 144.

[187] *Ibid.*, § 160.

[188] *Ibid.*, § 128, 3; 157, 2.

[189] Pr.-Bauer, *s.v.*; ὄνομα for "person" perhaps also Lk. 6:22 : ... ὅταν ἀφορίσωσιν ὑμᾶς καὶ ὀνειδίσωσιν καὶ ἐκβάλωσιν τὸ ὄνομα ὑμῶν ὡς πονηρὸν ἕνεκα τοῦ υἱοῦ τοῦ ἀνθρώπου. Confession of Jesus means excommunication from the community, cf. Jn. 9:22, 34. But cf. Pr.-Bauer, *s.v.* ἐκβάλλω : "to treat the name disparagingly," "to despise"; Str.-B., II, 159 : to use the name as an oath or curse. For the linguistic form of the saying cf. Dt. 22:19; Schl. Lk., 246.

d. A review of the prepositional combinations in the NT shows wide Semitic influence. In the quotations in Mt. 7:22; 12:21 the simple dat. is used in deviation from the LXX ἐπί with dat. On the other hand ἐν (τῷ) ὀνόματι occurs some 40 times, εἰς (τὸ) ὄνομα 9 times, διὰ τὸ ὄνομα 4, διὰ τοῦ ὀνόματος 3, περὶ (τοῦ) ὀνόματος(ων) twice, κατ' ὄνομα twice ("individually by name"), and πρὸς τὸ ὄνομα once. [190] Of the 40 instances with ἐν (τῷ) ὀνόματι 8 definitely refer to God, 28 to Christ. Paul has this only at 1 C. 5:4; 6:11; Eph. 5:20; Phil. 2:10; Col. 3:17; 2 Th. 3:6.

The expression ἐν τῷ ὀνόματι occurs with the following verbs : ἔρχεσθαι, Mt. 21:9 and par.; 23:39 and par. (as OT quotation); Jn. 5:43; εὐχαριστεῖν, Eph. 5:20; ποιεῖν, Jn. 10:25; Ac. 4:7; Col. 3:17; δαιμόνια ἐκβάλλειν, Mk. 9:38; 16:17; Lk. 9:49; τὰ δαιμόνια ὑποτάσσεται, Lk. 10:17; λαλεῖν, Jm. 5:10; κρίνειν, 1 C. 5:4; παρρησιάζεσθαι, Ac. 9:27 f.; παραγγέλλειν, Ac. 16:18; 2 Th. 3:6; πᾶν γόνυ κάμπτει, Phil. 2:10; δικαιοῦσθαι, 1 C. 6:11; ἀλείφειν, Jm. 5:14; αἰτεῖν, Jn. 14:13, 14; 15:16; 16:23 f., 26; πέμπειν, Jn. 14:26; ὀνειδίζειν, 1 Pt. 4:14; ποτίζειν, Mk. 9:41; ζωὴν ἔχειν, Jn. 20:31; τηρεῖν, Jn. 17:11; ἐγείρειν καὶ περιπατεῖν, Ac. 3:6; σῴζεσθαι, Ac. 4:12; παρέστηκεν ὑγιής, Ac. 4:10; βαπτίζεσθαι, Ac. 10:48 (?). We have to reckon here not merely with LXX influence but also with translation Gk.: Heb. (Aram.) בְּשֵׁם or מִשּׁוּם was rendered ἐν (τῷ) ὀνόματι analogously to LXX. [191] A glance at the miracles said in Rabb. writings to be done beshem (mishum) Jeshua' (→ 267 f.) confirms this. But the expression cannot be transl. in precisely the same way in every instance. The most general meaning of ἐν (τῷ) ὀνόματι is "with invocation of" (→ 276). He who says or does something in the name of someone appeals to this one, claims his authority. This gives us various nuances acc. to context. It may mean "with calling upon" or "with proclamation of the name" (→ 278), or "on the commission" (→ 273; 278), or "in fulfilment of the will" (→ 273; 276), or "in obedience" (→ 278). But ἐν ὀνόματι can also mean "in the sphere of power" (→ 272; 274), "in the power" (→ 277), "in the presence" (→ 277). 1 Pt. 4:14 is difficult : εἰ ὀνειδίζεσθε ἐν ὀνόματι Χριστοῦ (→ 240). Perhaps לְמַעַן שֵׁם הַמָּשִׁיחַ lies behind it. [192] Mk. 9:41 and Jn. 14:26 are ultimately to be understood in this way too.

ἐπὶ τῷ ὀνόματι is linked with the following verbs : δέχεσθαι, Mt. 18:5 and par.; δαιμόνια ἐκβάλλειν, Lk. 9:49 (vl. ἐν); ποιεῖν δύναμιν, Mk. 9:39; ἔρχεσθαι, Mt. 24:5 and par.; λαλεῖν, Ac. 4:17; 5:40; διδάσκειν, Ac. 4:18; 5:28; κηρύσσεσθαι, Lk. 24:47; βαπτίζεσθαι, Ac. 2:38. Sometimes the expressions are identical with ἐν (τῷ) ὀνόματι, sometimes closely related. Semitic originals must again be assumed. ἕνεκεν τοῦ ὀνόματος, Mt. 19:29; Lk. 21:12, and διὰ τὸ ὄνομα, Mt. 24:9; Mk. 13:13; Lk. 21:17; Jn. 15:21; 1 Jn. 2:12; Rev. 2:3, cf. Heb. לְמַעַן שֵׁם (→ 252; 257). [193] διὰ τοῦ ὀνόματος has instrumental significance, Ac. 4:30 : σημεῖα καὶ τέρατα γίνεσθαι, and causal, Ac. 10:43 : ἄφεσιν ἁμαρτιῶν λαβεῖν; 1 C. 1:10 : παρακαλεῖν. Four times in the Johannine writings we find πιστεύειν εἰς τὸ ὄνομα, Jn. 1:12; 2:23; 3:18; 1 Jn. 5:13. It corresponds to the Rabb. הֶאֱמִין לְשֵׁם. [194] Cf. → 276, 30 ff.

2. ὄνομα as the Name of God or Jesus Christ.

In the NT the name, person and work of God are — with various differentiations — inseparably linked with the name, person and work of Jesus Christ. This applies also in respect of OT quotations and allusions, cf. Mk. 11:9 f. and par. (Ps. 118:26); Mt. 23:39 (Ps. 118:26); Lk. 1:49 (Ps. 111:9, Lk. omits two words); Ac. 15:17 (LXX Am. 9:12); R. 9:17 (Ex. 9:16); R. 10:13 (Joel 2:32); R. 15:9 (2 S. 22:50 = Ps. 18:49); 2 Tm. 2:19

[190] Synoptic par. counted only once.
[191] Bl.-Debr.[7] § 206, 2.
[192] Boehmer, 66.
[193] Dalman WJ, I[2], 100.
[194] Schl. J., 19; → II, 432.

(Is. 26:13); Ac. 2:21 (Joel 2:32); Rev. 11:18 (Ps. 102:15; 115:13); Rev. 15:4 (Jer. 10:7. not in LXX; Ps. 86:9).

a. The name of God belongs to His manward side, the side of revelation. In this respect — especially in Jn. — it is linked with δόξα. ὄνομα thus expresses the concrete connection between God and man, the personal relationship which declares itself in a specific approach of God and which demands a specific approach from man. When Jesus prays : "Father, glorify thy name," and God answers : "I have glorified it, and will glorify it again," Jn. 12:28 (note 12:23), [195] the three words → πατήρ, δοξάζω (→ II, 253 f.) and ὄνομα are so closely connected with one another that they have to be expounded together. The prayer of Jesus and God's answer do not have as their goal merely God's self-glorifying. God is addressed as Father, and He reveals Himself as Father, as the loving God (Jn. 3:16; 17:12, 26), by glorifying His name in the life and work of Jesus, and by glorifying it again in the death and resurrection of Jesus. The glorifying of God's name is effected by Christ's work, and to this again it belongs that Jesus should reveal God's name to men as that of the Father [196] (Jn. 17:6; cf. v. 26 and 12:28). [197] God's name is obscure to men; it is strange and general. But to those whom the Father has given Him Jesus makes this name manifest, certain and plain, so that it again acquires specific content: Father. In His Son, Jesus Christ, God is the Father and Reconciler of the world. A mark of the divine sonship of Jesus is His ability to make known this name of God to men. [198] To be received ἐν τῷ ὀνόματι is to stand in the sphere of the love of the Father and the Son. This is to stand in the sphere of a force which unites the disciples in relationship with one another, Jn. 17:11, 12, 21. [199] The declaration of the name finds its goal in the presence of the Father's love for the Son in those who believe in Him (Jn. 17:26), in the demonstration in them of its power to awaken life (1 Jn. 4:7), in the presence of the Son in them in the love of the Father. From this standpoint the glorification and declaration of the Father's name are the supreme work of Christ. They characterise this work as the Father's work of revelation and salvation in the work of the Son. As the Church is grounded in Jesus' work of revelation, so it stands constantly under the promise that His work will be continued in it: "And I have declared thy name, and will declare it (γνωρίσω)," Jn. 17:26.

b. The fulness of the being and work of Jesus Christ may be seen in His name. At God's command He receives the name of Jesus (Mt. 1:21 and par.), which expresses His humanity (→ III, 287) and also His divine mission: αὐτὸς γὰρ σώσει τὸν λαὸν αὐτοῦ ἀπὸ τῶν ἁμαρτιῶν αὐτῶν. [200] The significance of this

---

[195] The two verses Jn. 12:23 and 12:28 are perhaps an indication of the equation of Jesus with the name of God, which is not elsewhere attested in the NT, cf. Grether, 182.
[196] Schl. J., 319; Bu. J., 327, n. 6.
[197] In the background (as against Bu. J., 380, n. 2) is ψ 21:22 : διηγήσομαι τὸ ὄνομά σου τοῖς ἀδελφοῖς μου.
[198] Schl. J., 326. In Jesus is fulfilled the Jewish expectation that the new world of God will bring the revelation of His name, → 279.
[199] Schl. J., 321. Linguistically the ἐν before ὀνόματι denotes the means by which God or Jesus (v. 12) keeps. Bau. J.³ on 17:11; Bu. J., 385, n. 1, who also emphasises (as against Heitmüller, 84) that the keeping is not by the mere uttering of God's name. The revelation of God brought by Jesus is that which keeps the community from perishing in the world.
[200] Acc. to Philo Mut. Nom., 121 the name Joshua means σωτηρία κυρίου. Str.-B., I, 67 collects 18 names of the Messiah from later Jewish lit. I, 63 f. gives examples of the way in which names were generally felt to be significant in Judaism. I, 64 gives the meanings of the name Jᵉhoshua' from Rabb. writings.

name is more fully elucidated in v. 23. It implies "God with us" (μεθ' ἡμῶν ὁ θεός), i.e., that with the presence of Jesus God's presence is given to the community.[201] The exalted name which Jesus receives according to Hb. 1:4 is the name of Son (cf. v. 5: υἱός μου εἶ σύ). The name κύριος, which in the LXX is either a translation or a paraphrase of the divine name Yahweh (→ III, 1058), is also His name (Phil. 2:9 f.).[202] It denotes His divine equality (Is. 42:8; → III, 1088). Because the essence of the Most High is in it, because the name of Lord belongs to both God and Jesus Christ, it is the name above all other names, i.e., beings (cf. Eph. 1:21). In His divine equality He is ΚΥΡΙΟΣ ΚΥΡΙΩΝ (Rev. 19:16). The divine dominion is revealed in Him : ΒΑΣΙΛΕΥΣ ΒΑΣΙΛΕΩΝ (Rev. 19:16; cf. Dt. 10:17). The unity of nature and name may also be seen in Rev. 19:13 when taken with Jn. 1:1: He not only bears the name, but is ὁ λόγος τοῦ θεοῦ, i.e., He alone has the communion with God which is described in Jn. 1:1 and remains a mystery in every revelation. The being of the Lord who is exalted over all also remains a mystery; He bears a name which no one knows apart from Himself, Rev. 19:12. "He possesses a relationship with God which none can perceive."[203]

Sometimes ὄνομα in the abs. can be used instead of Jesus. Ac. 5:41: "They departed from the presence of the Sanhedrin, rejoicing that they were counted worthy to suffer shame for the name (ὑπὲρ τοῦ ὀνόματος).[204] This is perhaps the meaning in 3 Jn. 7, where it is said of missionaries that "for the name (ὑπὲρ γὰρ τοῦ ὀνόματος) they went forth."[205]

Jesus' action is action in God's name. His coming takes place ἐν ὀνόματι κυρίου, i.e., He alone has the communion with God which is described in Jn. 1:1 and remains a mystery in every revelation. The being of the Lord who is exalted over all also the Χριστός promised by God, Jn. 10:24 f.; 5:43. His coming again brings His work to completion; He comes ἐν ὀνόματι κυρίου, in the service of divine grace with God's saving help, Mt. 23:39.[206] Thus the name of Jesus takes on the significance that it embraces the whole content of the saving acts revealed in Jesus. "In (or through) the name of the Lord Jesus Christ and in the Spirit of our God" the Corinthians are "washed, sanctified and justified," 1 C. 6:11.[207] The fulness of Christ's saving work is contained in His name and is present to the community, → 272; 277. The purification, sanctification and justification of Christians does not consist in the fact that they pronounce the name of Jesus[208] but in baptism, which means ultimately in the death and resurrection of Jesus Christ, R. 6:1-11 etc. By His name (διά) believers receive remission of sins, Ac. 10:43; 1 Jn. 2:12.

---

[201] "Undoubtedly the revelation of God by name and word is condescension. A name which can be spoken in human speech serves to denote the God who is exalted above all the capacities of human understanding," Grether, 165.

[202] O. Cullmann, "Königsherrschaft Christi u. Kirche im NT," Theologische Studien, 10 (1941), 5-10; also Christus u. d. Zeit (1946), 164-186; Stauffer Theol., 95.

[203] Schl. Erl., ad loc.

[204] Bau. Ag., on 5:41.

[205] Str.-B., III, 779. This usage is still found in the post-apost. fathers, e.g., Barn., 16, 8; Ign. Eph., 3, 1; Phld., 10, 1.

[206] Schl. Mt., 691.

[207] "The name of Jesus made their baptism a purifying bath ... ; it names for them the One who has forgiveness for them; and the name of Jesus declares to them that they are called and brought to God, whereby they are sanctified; and the name of Jesus shows them the One who has cancelled their guilt and who makes God's righteousness efficacious for them and in them," Schl. K., 197.

[208] Heitmüller, 74 f.

This is to be understood in the light of 1 Jn. 1:7: "The blood of Jesus his Son cleanseth us from all sin." Those who believe in His name as that of the Son (1 Jn. 5:13) have life ἐν τῷ ὀνόματι αὐτοῦ, i.e., by entry into His sphere of action, the sphere of His person, Jn. 20:31. They thus escape judgment, Jn. 3:18. In connection with the healing of the lame man, which plainly shows in a sign whence salvation comes, Peter embraces the whole content of the message of salvation in the word : "Neither is there salvation in any other : for there is none other name given under heaven for men, whereby (ἐν ᾧ) we must be saved," Ac. 4:12. [209] In 2 Th. 1:12 the echo of Is. 66:5 shows that, as in the OT glorification of the name of God is the goal of God's people, so God's people of the new covenant has the goal of glorifying the name of the author of the new covenant. The whole life of the Christian stands under the name of Jesus. "And whatsoever ye do in word or deed, do all in the name of the Lord Jesus, giving thanks to God the Father by him," Col. 3:17. The fulness of the divine gifts of grace for which the community must thank God is embraced in the name of Jesus. The name of Jesus is the ground of thanksgiving : "Giving thanks always for all things unto God the Father in the name of our Lord Jesus Christ," Eph. 5:20. The prophecy of the Servant of the Lord in Dt. Is. is fulfilled in Jesus : "And in his name shall the Gentiles trust" (Mt. 12:21 = Is. 42:4). The name of Jesus is the hope of the world, for it brings salvation to the world. It is also an expression of His sending in judgment. He who does not believe in the name of the only-begotten Son of God, i.e., he who withholds recognition from this name and thus fails to understand His nature and mission, "is judged already," Jn. 3:18. Of particular significance is Jn. 14:26. Not only does Jesus act in the name of the Father, but the Father, too, does the will of Christ by sending the Holy Spirit in the name of Jesus Christ, [210] thus executing Christ's work in accordance with the prayer of Jesus (14:16) and in unity of will and action with the risen Lord (16:26; cf. 15:7; 20:22).

c. Mt. 28:19 combines the name of Father and Son and Holy Ghost. Only through this link with the name of Son and Holy Ghost does the name of Father acquire its fulness. The common name (ὄνομα occurs only once) also expresses the unity of being. Baptism into the name means that the subject of baptism, through fellowship with the Son who is one with God, receives forgiveness of sins and comes under the operation of the Holy Spirit. [211]

The expression εἰς (τὸ) ὄνομα creates difficulties. It is fairly generally recognised that in some places the formula is to be regarded as a lit. rendering of the Semitic לְשֵׁם, לְשׁוּם (→ 268). εἰς (τὸ) ὄνομα means "with respect or regard to," "because ... is." Mt. 10:41 f. is to be expounded thus : "He that receiveth a prophet in the name of, i.e., with respect to the fact that he is, a prophet" (εἰς ὄνομα προφήτου); also Mk. 9:41: "Whosoever shall give one of these little ones to drink in the name of, i.e., because he is, a disciple" (εἰς ὄνομα μαθητοῦ); [212] also Mt. 18:20: "For where two or three are gathered together in my name, i.e., in relation to me" (εἰς τὸ ἐμὸν ὄνομα); Hb. 6:10 :

---

[209] "The name which in the eyes of the questioner seems to be a kind of secret property of a sectarian quasi-magician and his assistant is in reality the only name in the cosmos which is of saving significance for all, and for all evils," Bau. Ag., 76.

[210] As against Heitmüller, 83 : "At the naming of the name of Jesus, i.e., when they name the name of Jesus in their prayers (cf. 16:23)."

[211] Schl. Mt., 799.

[212] Cf. Pr.-Bauer, s.v. ὄνομα; Heitmüller, 114. Cf. also Ign. R., 9, 3 : ἀσπάζεται ὑμᾶς ... ἡ ἀγάπη τῶν ἐκκλησιῶν τῶν δεξαμένων με εἰς ὄνομα Ἰησοῦ Χριστοῦ.

"For God is not unrighteous to forget your work and labour of love, which ye have showed toward his name, i.e., for his sake" (εἰς τὸ ὄνομα αὐτοῦ). As in Mt. 18:20 Christ is the basis on which the two or three meet, so in Hb. 6:10 God is the basis of the acts of love. In the verses mentioned εἰς (τὸ) ὄνομα has causal significance, → 268. The derivation of the baptismal formula βαπτίζειν εἰς τὸ ὄνομα in Mt. 28:19; Ac. 8:16; 19:5; 1 C. 1:13, 15 is debatable. Mt. 18:10 : συνηγμένοι εἰς τὸ ἐμὸν ὄνομα,[213] corresponds linguistically to Mt. 28:19 : βαπτίζοντες αὐτοὺς εἰς τὸ ὄνομα τοῦ πατρὸς καὶ τοῦ υἱοῦ καὶ τοῦ ἁγίου πνεύματος, but difficulties arise on a causal understanding. Recourse is thus had to the usage of the pap., → I, 539 f.; → 245. Mt. 28:16-20 has a Semitic flavour. Paul too, who knew the formula, was bilingual, Ac. 21:40; 22:2; 26:14; Phil. 3:5. One might also refer to Ign. R., 9, 3, which, though Gk. in form, has to be explained in Semitic terms,[214] since it echoes Mt. 10:41 f. The expression εἰς τὸ ὄνομα in the baptismal formula must be explained along the lines of the לְשֵׁם of the Rabb. schools ; לְשֵׁם = εἰς τὸ ὄνομα has a final sense. We have seen that Judaism knew sacrifices and baths which were for a specific end or with a particular intention,[215] → 268. In just the same way Christians baptised εἰς τὸ ὄνομα 'Ιησοῦ Χριστοῦ, or, acc. to Mt. 28:19 : εἰς τὸ ὄνομα τοῦ πατρὸς καὶ τοῦ υἱοῦ καὶ τοῦ ἁγίου πνεύματος. The formula εἰς (τὸ) ὄνομα is thus to be regarded as translation Gk. by origin,[216] and the final element in the underlying לְשֵׁם finds expression in it. No mystical ideas are connected with the phrase.[217] A forensic understanding is nearer the mark.[218] In itself βαπτίζειν εἰς τὸ ὄνομα is rare in the NT. Mt. 28:19 is the triadic version. εἰς τὸ ὄνομα τοῦ κυρίου 'Ιησοῦ is used in Ac. 8:16; 19:5. Paul uses a related expression only where he must show the Corinthians that they are not baptised in his own name : εἰς τὸ ὄνομα Παύλου ἐβαπτίσθητε; (1 C. 1:13), μή τις εἴπῃ, ὅτι εἰς τὸ ἐμὸν ὄνομα ἐβαπτίσθητε (1 C. 1:15).

Paul does not use βαπτίζειν εἰς τὸ ὄνομα ('Ιησοῦ) Χριστοῦ, but on the basis of 1 C. 1:13, 15 one might conclude that he was familiar with it. Elsewhere he simply refers to baptism εἰς Χριστὸν 'Ιησοῦν (R. 6:3) or εἰς Χριστόν (Gl. 3:27). Constructed similarly is the phrase in 1 C. 10:2 : The Israelites εἰς τὸν Μωϋσῆν ἐβαπτίσαντο. Materially εἰς τὸ ὄνομα is equivalent to the simple εἰς. It may even be asked whether Paul does not intentionally render the Hebraism εἰς τὸ ὄνομα by the more Greek εἰς, → 245. If he uses εἰς τὸ ὄνομα in 1 C. 1:13, 15 it might be that he is asking : "Were you baptised into the person (ὄνομα = person) of Paul ?" "That none might say he was baptised into my person."

Since the formula can be shown to have a Semitic origin, its derivation from popular Hellenistic usage[219] is improbable. To try to derive it from Hellenistic commercial life (→ I, 539 f.) creates great difficulties. The idea is that of charging to an account over which stands the name of the owner, → 245. Now it is true that the NT speaks of a heavenly book in which the names of believers are written, → I, 619 f.; → 281. But can one relate βαπτίζειν ("to dip in water") with this idea ? If the formula is connected with Hellenistic commercial life it has completely lost its original content ; this has been replaced by the simple concept of appropriation. But this still brings us back to the

---

[213] Even Heitmüller, 97 thinks the verse could be expounded as thought it had a Semitic original, though he himself does not think this. He construes it in the light of Gk. expressions, esp. in the pap., 123-126. He appeals (115 f.) to the Gk. speaking Paul, who also uses the formula.

[214] Cf. Heitmüller, 113 f.; Brandt, 591-603; Str.-B., I, 1054 ff.; Schl. Mt., 352, 799.

[215] J. Jeremias, Hat d. Urkirche die Kindertaufe geübt ?² (1949), 20 f.

[216] As against A. Dieterich, Eine Mithrasliturgie² (1910), 114.

[217] In the Jewish ritual bath undertaken לְשֵׁם we find the same elements as in baptism : dipping in water, the purpose, the one to whom the person baptised is assigned.

[218] Deissmann B., 143 ff.; NB, 25; Heitmüller, 103-109; cf. also Pr.-Bauer, s.v., who leaves open both possibilities of derivation; → I, 539 f.

[219] Heitmüller, 108.

meaning of the formula in Rabb. usage. It is self-evident that in baptism the name of Jesus is mentioned as the name of the one to whom the candidate is made over. [220]

Ac. 2:38 : βαπτισθήτω ἕκαστος ὑμῶν ἐπὶ (vl. ἐν) τῷ ὀνόματι Ἰησοῦ Χριστοῦ εἰς ἄφεσιν τῶν ἁμαρτιῶν, and 10:48 : προσέταξεν δὲ αὐτοὺς ἐν τῷ ὀνόματι Ἰησοῦ Χριστοῦ βαπτισθῆναι stand alone in the NT. It is possible that here, too, a Heb. שֵׁם‎ (Aram. שֻׁם‎) stands behind the ἐπὶ (ἐν) τῷ ὀνόματι, cf. LXX Jos. 9:9; 2 Βασ. 22:50; Sir. 47:13, where the original has שֵׁם‎. In Ac. 2:38, however, the ἐπί with dat. may denote the basis of repentance and baptism. The hearers receive the message of Christ, and on this account they repent and are baptised. The ἐν τῷ ὀνόματι of 10:48 can be taken in the same way. The people in the house of Cornelius have received the Spirit. They know who Jesus is. They must be baptised on the basis of the name of Jesus.

d. The first petition which Jesus frames, building on ancient Jewish prayers [221] (cf. Is. 29:23; Ez. 36:23), refers to the name of God: ἁγιασθήτω τὸ ὄνομά σου, Mt. 6:9 and par. The dawn of God's kingdom brings about a situation in which God's name will no longer be desecrated and blasphemed by sin. The reference is not to the intrinsically biblical thought that men sanctify God's name, e.g., by a life of faith and obedience. The prayer to God is that He will accomplish the hallowing of His name in spite of all sin and all adversaries, → I, 111.

The prayer of the community is made in the name of Jesus, Jn. 14:13 f.; 15:16; 16:23, 26. To pray in His name means here to pray according to His will and at His commission in fulfilment of the mission given to the disciples. [222] But it also means with invocation of His name. This prayer in the name of Jesus is an expression of the belief that He came forth from God, that He is God's Son, and for the sake of this belief the Father will hear such a prayer, Jn. 16:26 f., 23 f.; 15:16. The unity of the Son with the Father finds expression in the fact that prayer in the name of Jesus can be directed to either Father or Son : "And whatsoever ye shall ask in my name, that will I do, that the Father may be glorified in the Son," Jn. 14:13 f.

e. To believe in His name (Jn. 2:23) is to believe in His Messianic mission, to believe in Him as the Christ, as the only-begotten Son of God, 3:18. [223] This belief arises through the manifestation of God's power in His acts. Acting in the Father's name He shows Himself to be the Son, 10:25. To believe in the Son (τοῖς πιστεύουσιν εἰς τὸ ὄνομα αὐτοῦ) is to acquire a right relation to the Father (ἔδωκεν αὐτοῖς ἐξουσίαν τέκνα θεοῦ γενέσθαι, Jn. 1:12). God commands that we should believe in the name of His Son Jesus Christ, 1 Jn. 3:23; cf. 5:13. To put it more simply, we are to believe in the Son of God, 1 Jn. 5:10.

---

[220] The same formula as in Mt. 28:19 is found in Did., 7, 1: βαπτίσ(τε εἰς τὸ ὄνομα τοῦ πατρὸς καὶ τοῦ υἱοῦ καὶ τοῦ ἁγίου πνεύματος. The def. articles do not occur in 7, 3. A simpler formula reminiscent of Paul occurs in 9, 5 : οἱ βαπτισθέντες εἰς ὄνομα κυρίου. So also Herm. v., 3, 7, 3. Just. Apol. I, 61, 3 (cf. 10, 13): "For in the name (ἐπ' ὀνόματος) of God the Father and Lord of all things and of our Saviour Jesus Christ and the Holy Ghost they then take a bath in water." Acc. to Tert. Bapt., 6 and 13 baptism is in nomen, acc. to Cyprian Epistula, 73, 5 it is in nomine (cf. Itala and Vulgata).

[221] Str.-B., I, 408 f.

[222] "There takes place in Jesus' name only that which is according to His command. He who acts and prays in His name desires to do His will, and His commands declare this to the disciples," Schl. J., 296.

[223] "In the formula πιστεύειν εἰς τὸ ὄνομα the Jew is thinking of God's name," Schl. J., 19. With no alteration of sense we may simply have πιστεύειν εἰς, Jn. 2:11; 3:16, 36; 7:5, 31, cf. Bu. J., 31, n. 3; 37, n. 4.

f. As the disciples are set in His sphere of power (→ 272; 274), they for their part can act in His name, i.e., on His commission and also in His power. They find that in such action His power works in them: "Lord, even the devils are subject unto us in thy name," Lk. 10:17. But the possibility of working miracles in the name of Jesus is not restricted to the circle of disciples. In Mk. 9:38 John tells of a man who does not belong to this circle and yet who works miracles with the name of Jesus (ἐν [Lk. 9:49 vl. ἐπί] τῷ ὀνόματί σου). Jesus defends him against the exclusivism of the disciples: "There is no man which shall do a miracle in my name (ἐπὶ τῷ ὀνόματί μου, on the basis of my name), that can speak lightly of me," Mk. 9:39. Works of mercy as well as miracles are done in the name of Jesus: Mt. 18:5 and par.: "And whoso shall receive one such little child in my name (ἐπὶ τῷ ὀνόματί μου) receiveth me." [224] The power of the name of Jesus is seen after Easter. Peter heals the lame man in the name of Jesus, Ac. 3:6 (cf. also 14:10). This passage shows how the cure was accomplished: "But such as I have give I thee. In the name (ἐν τῷ ὀνόματι) of Jesus Christ rise up and walk." In the later explanation it is said that "his (Jesus') name hath made this man strong" because he believed in the name of Jesus (3:16). Power (δύναμις) and name (ὄνομα) are parallel concepts, cf. already Ps. 54:1; → II, 311. "By what power, or by what name, have ye done this?" (Ac. 4:7). [225] The members of the council who put this question suspect idolatry behind the act of the apostles. They think that a sinister power is at work and that the name of a false god was named at the healing. But the apostles assure them, too, that the name of Jesus was the efficacious force in the healing, Ac. 4:10. Paul expels a spirit of soothsaying in the same way: "I command thee ἐν ὀνόματι Ἰησοῦ Χριστοῦ to come out of her," Ac. 16:18. This kind of healing does not take place through the use of magic formulae — ἐν (τῷ) ὀνόματι Ἰησοῦ is not to be interpreted thus — nor does it stand in the power or at the whim of the healer. It is Jesus Himself who heals, → III, 213. This may be seen plainly in the healing of Aeneas at Lydda. to whom Peter says: "Aeneas, Jesus Christ maketh thee whole; arise, and make thy bed," Ac. 9:34. This instance shows that ὄνομα Ἰησοῦ is to be understood as the presence of Christ, → 273.

With few exceptions there are no adjurations in the NT. One of the exceptions is at Mk. 5:7 (a demon speaking); the other equally noteworthy example is at Ac. 19:13-16. Encouraged by Paul's success in healing Jewish exorcists also try to heal in the name of Jesus by naming His name over those who have evil spirits. They use the right formula: ὁρκίζω ὑμᾶς τὸν Ἰησοῦν ὃν Παῦλος κηρύσσει, but the result is the very opposite of that expected. The evil spirit knows Jesus and Paul, "but who are you?" Instead of driving out the spirit, the exorcists themselves are attacked by it. In the light of Mt. 7:21 f. and Mk. 9:38 f. one is forced to say that the name of Jesus shows its power only where a man joins Jesus in faith and obedience, and does the will of God. Use of the name of Jesus

---

[224] Cf. LXX, where ἐν and ἐπί are used interchangeably for בְּשֵׁם, → 262. "The name names the one who orders the action, by whose will it is done," Schl. Mt., 546. But Mk. 13:6 and par. cannot be explained in this way: "Many shall come in my name (ἐπὶ τῷ ὀνόματί μου), saying, I am Christ ..." False christs do not appeal to Jesus Christ but claim the name of Christ. One should thus translate "under my name." Cf. Heitmüller, 63.

[225] Here the name of Jesus Christ is almost a hypostasis. In Herm. s., 9, 14, 5 the name of Christ is a hypostasis: τὸ ὄνομα τοῦ υἱοῦ τοῦ θεοῦ μέγα ἐστὶ καὶ ἀχώρητον καὶ τὸν κόσμον ὅλον βαστάζει. But the continuation runs: εἰ οὖν πᾶσα ἡ κτίσις διὰ τοῦ υἱοῦ τοῦ θεοῦ βαστάζεται. Cf. also Herm. s., 9, 12, 4. 5. 8; 9, 13, 2 f.; 1 Cl., 58, 1; 60, 4 etc.

for independent ends is a misuse and condemns to failure. The NT knows no theurgy which forces God or Jesus. Jesus is the *Kyrios*; He stands above all magical compulsion. In Ac. 4:30 the primitive community beseeches God that He will stretch forth His hand, that healings, signs and wonders may take place διὰ τοῦ ὀνόματος of His holy Servant Jesus. [226] Again, there is in the NT no belief in magically potent names; in fact, there are no mysteriously dreadful words or names at all, → 269. In healings the Lord acknowledges His disciples and the task which He has given them. [227] It is in obedience to Jesus (ἐν τῷ ὀνόματι τοῦ κυρίου) that the sick in the Church are healed by anointing with oil (Jm. 5:14 f.), for Jesus has pledged His disciples to mutual assistance. Healing does not take place by pronouncing a set formula, but through the Lord in answer to the prayer which calls upon Him in faith.

g. The name of Jesus Christ is the foundation and theme of proclamation. Philip declares the glad tidings of (περί) the kingdom of God and the name of Jesus Christ, Ac. 8:12. According to Lk. 24:47 Scripture promises that repentance will be preached to the Gentiles on the basis of the name of Christ. Jesus says to Ananias concerning Paul: "He shall bear my name before the Gentiles, and kings, and the children of Israel," Ac. 9:15. Paul himself bears witness that he has received grace and apostleship from Jesus Christ to establish the obedience of faith among all nations for His name, R. 1:5. Paul has no ambition to do missionary work where Christ is already named (ὅπου ὠνομάσθη Χριστός), i.e., where the Gospel, whose content is Christ, has already come, R. 15:20. Missionaries all go out "for the name," 3 Jn. 7. When Paul describes his activity as a persecutor he says that he thought he should do many things against the name of Jesus of Nazareth, Ac. 26:9. His persecution was directed against the message of the community concerning Christ. Immediately after his conversion, however, Paul came forth proclaiming the name of Jesus (ἐν τῷ ὀνόματι Ἰησοῦ) both in Damascus and in Jerusalem, Ac. 9:27 f. Because Jesus and His work are the central content of early Christian proclamation, the Jewish authorities in Jerusalem tell the apostles they must not speak or teach any more on the basis of this name (ἐπὶ τῷ ὀνόματι τούτῳ). In other words, they are not to proclaim the message of Christ, Ac. 4:17 f.; 5:28, 40.

Paul is called to be an apostle by Jesus Christ, R. 1:5; 1 C. 1:1; 2 C. 1:1; Gl. 1:1. He can thus admonish ἐν ὀνόματι τοῦ κυρίου Ἰησοῦ Χριστοῦ, i.e., on His commission, with His authorisation (2 Th. 3:6). "In the name of the Lord Jesus" Paul has already pronounced sentence on the incestuous person, 1 C. 5:4; he has done so as an apostle, in obedience to the Lord. [228] He beseeches the Corinthians διὰ τοῦ ὀνόματος τοῦ κυρίου ἡμῶν Ἰησοῦ Χριστοῦ, 1 C. 1:10. The name of Christ is an instrument of admonition, and Paul also maintains that he speaks on Christ's

---

[226] The borderline begins to get fluid in Just. Apol. II, 6, 6: "But many of us ... a whole host of possessed in the whole world ... were healed through adjuration in the name of Jesus Christ (ἐπορκίζοντες κατὰ τοῦ ὀνόματος Ἰησοῦ Χριστοῦ) ... and they still heal ...," cf. Just. Dial., 85. Justin also tells of healings in or through the name of Jesus in Apol. II, 8, 4; Dial., 30, 49, 76. Cf. Iren. Haer., II, 32, 4.

[227] "... the ὄνομα implies the real presence of the Lord and denotes His very own person," Boehmer, 40.

[228] There is much debate as to the ref. of ἐν τῷ ὀνόματι τοῦ κυρίου. Schlatter seems to grasp best the parallelism: "While ἐν τῷ ὀνόματι τοῦ κυρίου Ἰησοῦ belongs to κέκρικα, σὺν τῇ δυνάμει τοῦ κυρίου ἡμῶν Ἰησοῦ is appended to συναχθέντων, Schl. K., 176. The ὄνομα of Jesus is again par. to the δύναμις of Jesus.

commission. [229] But the admonition may be simply ἐν κυρίῳ, 1 Th. 4:1. Thus the expression ἐν ὀνόματι τοῦ κυρίου ᾽Ιησοῦ Χριστοῦ is very close to Paul's common ἐν Χριστῷ, → II, 541 ff.

h. Belief in the name of Jesus Christ and proclamation lead to confession of the name (Hb. 13:15), which cannot be separated from suffering for the name of Jesus Christ. Mk. 10:29 : "And Jesus answered and said, Verily I say unto you, There is no man that hath left house, or brethren, or mother, or wife, or children, or lands, for my sake, and the gospel's ..." In the parallel in Mt. 19:29 "for my name's sake" is used instead of "for my sake and the gospel's." [230] In this connection reference should also be made to Mt. 10:22; 24:9 and par.; Jn. 15:21: the disciples will be hated, persecuted and brought to judgment "for my name's sake" (διὰ τὸ ὄνομά μου), i.e., because of their confession of Jesus Christ. The disciples are put to shame for (ὑπέρ) the name of Jesus (Ac. 5:41), because they believe in Jesus and proclaim Him. Paul must suffer for the name of Jesus (Ac. 9:16) and is ready to die for His name (Ac. 21:13). Paul and Barnabas both risked their lives "for the name of our Lord Jesus Christ" (Ac. 15:26). In Rev. 2:13 Christ praises the church of Pergamos : "And thou holdest fast my name." The church has not allowed itself to be turned aside from confession of its Lord or from the Christian message. Similarly the church at Philadelphia, though weak, has not denied the name of Jesus, 3:8. If believers are reproached with the name of Christ (ἐν ὀνόματι Χριστοῦ), blessed are they; for the name of Christ carries δόξα with it, and guarantees the presence of God's Spirit to those who are willing to bear its reproach, 1 Pt. 4:14. He who is punished as Χριστιανός need not be ashamed, δοξαζέτω δὲ τὸν θεὸν ἐν τῷ ὀνόματι τούτῳ, 1 Pt. 4:16. He must use the opportunity to glorify God with this name. By his conduct he may confess this name even in this situation, and magnify God. The relation of the community to God finds consummation in reverence (φοβέομαι) for the name of God (Rev. 11:18) and praise (δοξάζω) of His name (15:4).

He who calls on the name of the Lord will be saved, Ac. 2:17-21; cf. R. 10:13; Jl. 2:32. He belongs to the community, 1 C. 1:2; cf. Ac. 9:14, 21; → III, 499 f. [231] The name of Christ is the worthy name which is named over Christians as the possession of their Lord, Jm. 2:7. They are called Χριστιανοί after Him, Ac. 11:26; cf. 26:28. In the new creation those who overcome will bear, with the name of God and the name of the new Jerusalem, [232] the new name of the Lamb as well, Rev. 3:12; cf. 14:1; 22:4. Investing with the new name of Jesus (cf. Rev. 19:12) [233] is a sign of entry into the new world order (cf. Is. 56:5; 62:2 f.; 65:15).

As the position of believers is declared in a specific attitude to the name of God and of Jesus Christ (in prayer, faith, healing, proclamation, admonition, confession,

---

[229] Ltzm. K., ad loc.; Schl. K., 67.

[230] Cf. H. J. Holtzmann, Lehrbuch d. nt.lichen Theol.², II (1911), 532; Seeberg, 604.

[231] Cf. LXX Jl. 2:32; R. Bultmann, Theol. d. NT (1948), 124 f.

[232] Gn. r., 49 (31a): "R. Pinᵉchas (c. 360) has said in the name of R. Shᵉmuel (c. 260): Abraham also knew the new name by which God will one day name Jerusalem, as it is said : At that time Jerusalem will be called the 'throne of Yahweh' (Jer. 3:17)." BB, 75b: "Rabbah (d. 331) has said, R. Jochanan (d. 279) has said : One day the righteous will be called by the name of God, for it is said : All who call themselves by my name and whom I have created, fashioned and made to my glory (Is. 43:7). Again, R. Shᵉmuel b. Nachman (c. 260) has said, R. Jonathan (c. 220) has said : Three will be called by the name of God, and these three are : the righteous, the Messiah and Jerusalem." The righteous acc. to Is. 43:7, the Messiah acc. to Jer. 23:6, and Jerusalem acc. to Ez. 48:35. Cf. Str.-B., III, 795 f.

[233] Loh. Apk., on 3:12.

suffering, reverence and praise), so unbelief is manifested in βλασφημεῖν, R. 2:24; 1 Tm. 6:1; Jm. 2:7; Rev. 13:6; 16:9; → I, 622 f., 624.

3. Other References.

a. ὄνομα with θηρίον (→ III, 134) and πόρνη is an expression of ungodliness. The beast (θηρίον is in antithesis to ἀρνίον, Rev. 5:6) bears on its heads ὀνόματα βλασφημίας, Rev. 13:1. These ὀνόματα are names and titles which belong to God. When the beast usurps them, they become names of blasphemy, [234] self-deification and ungodliness, → I, 624; cf. ἀντικείμενος, 2 Th. 2:4; → ἀντίχριστος, 1 Jn. 2:18; → ψευδόχριστοι, Mt. 24:24. Attempts to solve the riddle of the number and to find in it the name of a specific man yield no assured results. [235]

> The heart of the theological problem is that the name of the beast is concealed behind an enigma, and that it is then said of the number equivalent to the name : ἀριθμὸς γὰρ ἀνθρώπου ἐστίν. The explanatory statement does not force us to conclude that the ref. is to the number, and therewith to the name, of a specific man of the time. It is simply to the effect that the beast has a human name. The true being of the beast is concealed behind an ἀριθμὸς ἀνθρώπου. To see the true nature of the bearer of this name which is equivalent to the number, i.e., to know the ἀριθμὸς ἀνθρώπου as ἀριθμὸς τοῦ θηρίου, is the task for which wisdom and understanding are needed. This is true whether or not one makes a link with 17:11 with the help of the triangular numbers (666 ⩵ 36 ⩵ 8), or, on the basis of the context of theological meaning, one views all the statements about the beasts in Rev. as a disclosure of their demonic character. [236] The name or equivalent number is a χάραγμα, a mark of the beast (13:17); it shows to whose sphere of influence those marked thereby belong. They stand contrasted with those who are steadfast in the war against the beast : τοὺς νικῶντας ἐκ τοῦ θηρίου καὶ ἐκ τῆς εἰκόνος αὐτοῦ καὶ (ἐκ τοῦ χαράγματος αὐτοῦ καὶ) ἐκ τοῦ ἀριθμοῦ τοῦ ὀνόματος αὐτοῦ, Rev. 15:2. ἐκ can thus be taken to mean that those who overcome are taken out of the sphere of the beast. [237]

The names of the great harlot (→ πόρνη, Rev. 17:1, 3, 5 in contrast to γυνή, Rev. 12) denote her ungodliness. She bears the name of Babylon (the centre of idolatry [→ I, 514 ff.] as compared with Jerusalem), ἡ μήτηρ τῶν πορνῶν (πόρνων, πορνειῶν) καὶ τῶν βδελυγμάτων τῆς γῆς, the abominations connected with idolatry, → I, 599 f. Bearing also ὀνόματα βλασφημίας, like the beast, she violates the purity and majesty of God. The name of the whore is described as a μυστήριον, → IV, 823. If this is referred primarily to Babylon, the mystery of the name lies in the fact that it does not state directly what she is. If it is referred to the whole name up to γῆς, one might see in it an antithetical reference to the ὄνομα of the λόγος τοῦ θεοῦ, ὃ οὐδεὶς οἶδεν εἰ μὴ αὐτός, Rev. 19:12. [238] The names of death and death-bringing Hades (6:8) also denote forces which are opposed to life as God's true nature, → III, 15; I, 148 f. Similarly, the names Abaddon and Apollyon (Rev. 9:11; → I, 4, 397) for the angel of the abyss characterise the nature and function of this figure as the destroyer. The spirits, too, have names. The man who knows these has power over them. In Mk. 5:9 the power of Jesus is displayed in the fact that the spirit cannot conceal its name when confronted by

---

[234] Loh. Apk., ad loc.
[235] J. Behm Apk. (NT Deutsch), ad loc.; but cf., e.g., E. Stauffer, Coniectanea Neotestamentica XI in honorem Antonii Fridrichsen (1947), 237-241.
[236] Loh. Apk., 115 f., 110 ff.
[237] Ibid., 128.
[238] Ibid., 139.

Him. The name Legion does not denote only the nature and greatness of the unclean spirit, but also the plenitude of the power of Jesus. [239]

b. Further reference need be made here to the names of men only in so far as they also express their relation to God. Jesus gives three disciples new names. Simon is called Peter, the sons of Zebedee Βοανηργές, Mk. 3:16, 17. The meaning of the names is not to be sought in the fact that they give prominence to natural qualities. [240] This is certainly not true in the case of Peter, and hardly so in that of James and John. The names have rather the character of promises. Their significance lies in the fact that Jesus gives them. He tells Simon how He will use him when as Lord of the Church He builds the community. He credits the sons of Zebedee, as the one name shows, with unbreakable fellowship, and perhaps also allots to them a mighty power of witness. [241] In Rev. 21:14 the names of the twelve apostles of the Lamb are described as the twelve foundation stones of the new Jerusalem, → II, 328. The connection between the OT community and the NT community is plainly set forth in Rev., for in 21:12 the names of the twelve tribes of Israel are written on the gates of the new Jerusalem.

The names of those who belong to God and to Christ have especial significance. Jesus shows Himself to be the Good Shepherd by the fact that He knows all His sheep personally; He calls them by name, embracing the man in that which constitutes his ego, Jn. 10:3. [242] That their names are written in heaven (Lk. 10:20) means that "they are received by God Himself and belong to His kingdom of grace." [243] In the book of life (→ I, 619 f.) stand the names of those who are destined for eternal life, Rev. 3:5; cf. 13:8; 17:8. Paul shares this view when in Phil. 4:3 he speaks of those ὧν τὰ ὀνόματα ἐν βίβλῳ ζωῆς, cf. also Hb. 12:23. Christ promises to him who overcomes (Rev. 3:5) that He will not blot out his name. [244] The standing of these names before God rests on the fact that Christ confesses them and thus bears witness before God and the angels to His fellowship with those who bear them. With the handing over of the white stone (Rev. 2:17) a new name is given to the victor, i.e., he is set in a new situation in which the old guilty nature has perished. [245] If no one knows the new name except the one who receives it, this describes the unexchangeable fellowship of each member of the community with Christ.

---

[239] Schl. Mk., 113.
[240] J. Schniewind Mk. (NT Deutsch) on 3:17.
[241] Cf. Schl. Mk., 86 f.
[242] Schl. J., ad loc.; Erl., 167.
[243] K. H. Rengstorf Lk. (NT Deutsch), ad loc.
[244] Acc. to OT and later Jewish teaching, if a man's name is blotted out of the book of life, this means that he dies. In this connection name and person are interchangeable concepts, as the following example shows: "And now, if you will forgive their sins, forgive; but if not, blot me out of the book of the righteous in which thou hast written my name. And Yahweh said to Moses: It is not just to blot out your name, but he who has sinned before me, him will I blot out of my book." Tg. pal. on Ex. 32:32 f.; Str.-B., II, 169.
[245] Acc. to the Rabb. view a man who repents acquires a new name, Str.-B., III, 794. In the Roman forces a non-Roman entering the (naval) service received a Roman name, Deissmann LO, 148; Harnack Miss.⁴, 437 and 439 f.

† ὀνομάζω.

Its occurrence in the Gk. world is similar to that of ὄνομα in the senses "to name," "to call by name," "to number," "to express," "to denote," "to promise."

It is found only 9 times in the NT : Lk. 6:13, 14; Ac. 19:13; R. 15:20; 1 C. 5:11; Eph. 1:21; 3:15; 5:3; 2 Tm. 2:19 (as vl. also 1 C. 5:1). As in the LXX, so in the NT καλεῖν is much more common (→ III, 487 ff.). Jesus called the twelve "apostles"; both name and ministry come from Him (Lk. 6:13). He called Simon "Peter" (Lk. 6:14). On Ac. 19:13 → 277; on R. 15:20 → 278; on Eph. 1:21 → 273. If a man bears the name of brother (ἀδελφὸς ὀνομαζόμενος) but lives unworthily or is a covetous man, an idolater, a railer, a drunkard, or an extortioner, he is to be refused table fellowship, 1 C. 5:11. The name of brother imposes moral obligations in the community. The community is so sharply separated from sin that there is not even to be mention of it : "But fornication, and all uncleanness, or covetousness, let it not be once named among you (μηδὲ ὀνομαζέσθω), as becometh saints," Eph. 5:3. As the context shows, the admonition is primarily directed against sins of the tongue. Eph. 3:14 f. is theologically important : "For this cause I bow my knees unto the Father of our Lord Jesus Christ, of whom every family (→ πατριά) in heaven and earth is named (ὀνομάζεται) ..." God names all families, and is thus Father of all ; for it is the father's affair to give names. The saying describes the fatherhood of God in relation to angels and men. [1]

† ἐπονομάζω.

The meaning is "to name after," "to give a nickname," "to give a second name." For LXX → 264.

The only NT occurrence is at R. 2:17: "If thou callest thyself a Jew (ἐπονομάζῃ) ..." What the name "Jew" means Paul shows in vv. 17-20, which describe the religious legacy of the Jew. But Paul is overturning any pride associated merely with the name. The Jew stands under divine judgment like the Gentile, and is thus referred equally to grace in Jesus Christ. (ἐπονομάζειν is also a vl. at Lk. 6:14 D.)

† ψευδώνυμος. [1]

Attested in Gk. from Aesch., made up from ψευδο- and ὄνομα, with the sense : "bearing a false name," "named falsely, inaccurately, not in accordance with the facts." Aesch. Prom., 85 f.: ψευδωνύμως σε δαίμονες Προμηθέα καλοῦσιν. Prometheus is

---

ὀ ν ο μ ά ζ ω. [1] Dib. Gefbr., 57; Ew. Gefbr., 169. Cf. E. Percy, "Die Probleme d. Kolosser-u. Epheserbriefe." Acta Regiae Societatis Humaniorum Litterarum Lundensis, Vol. 29 (1946), 277, n. 30 : "But then the thought in this passage is obviously that God as the Father of believers is Himself the prototype of every fatherly relationship and therewith of every fatherly disposition throughout creation, so that every other fatherly relationship is only a reflection of that in which God stands to His children." For Percy the question whether there are πατριαί in heaven is irrelevant ; the verse simply says that every fatherly relationship has its prototype in God. In contrast H. Odeberg, "The View of the Universe in the Epistle to the Ephesians," Lunds Universitets Arsskrift, NF, I, Vol. 29, 6 (1934), 20, thinks the πατριά in heaven is the "upper family" (the world of angels), which in Rabb. speculation stands over against the "lower family" (Israel).

ψ ε υ δ ώ ν υ μ ο ς. [1] Liddell-Scott, Pass., Pr.-Bauer, s.v. On compounds with ψευδο-in general cf. Debrunner Gr. Wortb. § 114.

mocked on account of his name because he does not consider what it means ; he thus has a false name. Aesch. Prom., 717: ἥξεις δ᾽ Ὑβριστὴν ποταμὸν οὐ ψευδώνυμον : The river is turbulent, hence its name is not incorrect. Both examples relate to the etym. of the names. Aesch. Sept. c. Theb., 670 f.: ἦ δῆτ᾽ ἂν εἴη πανδίκως ψευδώνυμος Δίκη, ξυνοῦσα φωτὶ παντόλμῳ φρένας, Dike, whose name means "right," would bear her name wrongly if she were to help Polyneikes. Philo Decal., 53 : Men make parts of the universe into gods and give them false names (ψευδωνύμους προσρήσεις), i.e., they call that God which by nature is not God.

The only NT instance is at 1 Tm. 6:20 : "Avoid profane babblings, and oppositions of science falsely so called (τῆς ψευδωνύμου γνώσεως)." Paul is warning Timothy against a movement which gives the lie to its name, since it leads away from faith to false paths, and thus to error rather than to knowledge, v. 21 (→ I, 709).

Bietenhard

┌─────────────────────────┐
│ † ὄνος, † ὀνάριον │
└─────────────────────────┘

ὁ or ἡ ὄνος "the ass." In the Mas. = אָתוֹן, חֲמוֹר, עַיִר, פֶּרֶא and עֲרוֹדֶ (cf. the LXX combinations ὄνος ἄγριος, ὄναγρος, ὄνος ἐρημίτης and ὄνος θήλεια). The word is found from Homer, and generally in inscr., pap. and LXX. A secondary form (properly diminutive) is τὸ ὀνάριον, Diphilus, 89 (CAF, II, 570); Macho in Athen., 13 (582c); Epict. Diss., II, 24, 18; IV, 1, 79; P. Oxy., I, 63, 11; ὀναρίδιον, P. Ryl., 239, 21. [1] עַיִר acc. to Gn. 32:16; Ju. 10:4; Is. 30:24 is probably the male (Accadian *uru*). [2]

A. The Ass in Palestine and Judaism.

1. In Egypt and Palestine there are early refs. to the ass. Gn. 12:16; 22:3, 5; 24:35 tell us that Abraham and the patriarchs had asses. The ass is used metaphorically in Gn. 49:14 (strongboned ass); Ez. 23:20 (lust like an ass). [3] Acc. to Ex. 13:13; 34:20 the ass was not sacrificed (cf. late antiquity). [4] Only in emergencies was its flesh eaten

---

ὄ ν ο ς. F. Olck, Art. "Esel" in Pauly-W., VI (1909), 626-676; I. Benzinger, RE³, 5, 496 f.; A. Jeremias, *Das AT im Lichte d. Alten Orients,* 306, 406, 672; Schürer, III, 152, 532, 549; Harnack Miss., 432; E. Bickermann, "Ritualmord u. Eselskult," MGWJ, 71 (1927), 255-264; A. Jacoby, "Der angebliche Eselskult d. Juden u. Christen," ARW, 25 (1927), 265-282; K. Kerényi, *Die griech.-orientalische Romanlit.* (1927), 151-205; L. Köhler, *Kleine Lichter* (1945), 52-57.

[1] In Preisigke Wört., II, 181-183 we find ὀνικός, ὄνιον, ὀνάριον, ὀναρίδιον, ὀνάγριον, ὀνάγρινος, ὀνηλατέω, ὀνηλάτης (ὀνελάτης), ὀνηλατικός, ὀνηλασία, ὀνηλάσιον, ὀνοθήλεια.

[2] Köhler, 6.

[3] Gn. 16:12 : "He will be a man like a wild ass ; his hand against every man, and every man's hand against him ; and he shall dwell in defiance of all his brethren." Acc. to Artemid., the interpreter of dreams, the ass refers to a ruthless enemy or to the overcoming of opponents, Oneirocr., II, 12 (103, 21 ff.). On the strong sexual impulse of the ass cf. Cornut. Theol. Graec., 61, 1; Ps.-Luc. Asin., 32; Dio Chrys. Or., 78, 658, 32; Script. Hist. Aug., VII, 10, 9. Cf. the corresponding murals W. Helbig, *Waldgemälde der vom Vesuv verschütteten Städte Campaniens* (1868), 383, No. 1548; also pictures on the vases of antiquity, Pauly-W., VI, 670-672.

[4] For 300 A.D. cf. the assertion of Porphyr. Abst., 2, 25; Arnobius, VII, 16, that the ass was not sacrificed to the gods.

(2 K. 6:25). It is used for riding (Nu. 22:22 ff.; Ju. 10:4; 12:14), as a beast of burden (1 S. 25:18; Is. 30:6) and for ploughing (Is. 30:24; Dt. 22:10) and threshing (Jos. Ap., 2, 87). It is grouped with camels and oxen (Job 1:3; 42:12). In OT stories the usual ref. is to the she-ass (אָתוֹן = ὄνος θήλεια), e.g., Job 1:3, 14; 42:12; עַיִר (LXX πῶλος = young animal) probably denotes the male ass.

The poetic tradition of the OT often speaks of the wild ass (Job 6:5; 11:12; 39:5 ff.; Jer. 14:6). Its urge for freedom is extolled; the steppes and deserts are its home (Job 39:5-8). [5] The prophet's word of judgment on King Jehoiakim is that he will be given the burial of an ass, Jer. 22:19. It is often taken for granted in antiquity that the ass is stubborn and averse to work. [6] Thus Sir. 33:25 apportions to it provender, stick and burden. Jos. defends Judaism against the charge of Apion that the head of an ass was set up and worshipped in the temple, Ap., 2, 80. From the beginning of the 3rd century the same calumny was directed against Christians. [7]

2. According to Gn. 49:11 and Zech. 9:9 the king of the last time, who will establish peace among the nations, will appear on an ass (עַיִר), the riding animal of antiquity. Zech. 9:9 Mas. has three terms, whereas LXX has only two (עַיִר חֲמוֹר בֶּן־אֲתֹנוֹת ὑποζύγιον καὶ πῶλος νέος). What is meant in both texts is a young male animal, not a foal. Neither in the parallelism of Gn. 49:11 nor in that of Zech. 9:9 is the reference to two animals (the LXX at Zech. 9:9: ἐπὶ ὑποζύγιον καὶ πῶλον νέον, is not clear). Rabb. exegesis understood the Semitic form of expression correctly when it consistently spoke of only one animal. If Gn. 49:11f. seems to emphasise the fruitfulness and blessing of the Messianic age (wine and milk), the Messianic king of Zech. 9:9 is righteous (צַדִּיק) and meek (עָנִי), and "will be helped" (Mas. נוֹשָׁע), LXX: "he delivers, is the Saviour" (σῴζων). Chariots, bows and horses will be done away. He will ordain (וְדִבֶּר שָׁלוֹם) peace among the nations. His kingdom stretches from sea to sea, from the Euphrates to the ends of the earth.

The Rabb. worked at the exposition of the Messianic prophecy in Zech. 9:9 ff. Midr. Qoh., 1, 9 (9b) drew an express par. between the first and the last redeemer: "R. Berekiah (c. 340) has said in the name of R. Jizchak (c. 300): As the first redeemer (Moses), so the last redeemer (the Messiah). As it is said of the first redeemer (Ex. 4:20): Moses took his wife and his sons and had them ride on an ass, so of the last redeemer (Zech.

---

[5] For records of the various districts in which the wild ass was found in antiquity cf. Pauly-W., VI, 630; cf. F. Altheim, Die Krise d. alten Welt, I (1943), 27 f.

[6] Lazy (Hom. Il., 11, 558 f.), stubborn (Horat. Sat., I, 9, 20), unteachable (Plut. Is. et Os., 50 [II, 371c]), persistent (Xenoph. An., V, 8, 3), unreceptive to music (Plut. Sept. Sap. Conv., 5 [II, 150 f.]).

[7] The charge takes the three forms of worshipping an ass, a man in the form of an ass, or the head of an ass. Acc. to Plut. Quaest. Conv., IV, 5, 2 (II, 670e) (Tac. Hist., V, 3-4) the Jews nearly perished from thirst on the exodus from Egypt. They then came on the tracks of wild asses and found springs. At a later date they thus worshipped the likeness of an ass in the temple. Pagans thought that Christians, too, worshipped the head of an ass, Minucius Felix, 28, 7; Tert. Apol., 16, 1-5; Nat., I, 11. As there are proverbs about the ass, so we find caricatures. A wall scribbling in the paedagogium of imperial slaves on the Palatine in Rome depicts an ass turning a mill with the caption: Labora, aselle, quomodo ego laboravi, et proderit tibi. Perhaps this is in mockery of a slave Asellus. In the same building (first half of the 3rd cent.?) there is a graffito of a crucified slave with the head of an ass, and of another slave worshipping, with the inscr.: Ἀλεξάμενος σέβετε (σέβεται) θεόν. In another graffito the same Alexamenos calls himself fidelis, i.e., a Christian, F. Haug, Berliner philolog. Wochenschrift, 16 (1896), 562; Pauly-W., VI, 676. On cameos with figures having the head of the ass cf. C. A. Kaufmann, Hndbch. d. chr. Archäologie (1922), 614.

9:9): "Poor and riding on an ass." [8] That the last redeemer acc. to Zech. 9:9 would come poor and riding on an ass was, of course, a theological difficulty. Acc. to Sanh., 98a a contradiction was seen between Zech. 9:9 and Da. 7:13 : "R. Alexandrai (c. 270) has said : R. Jehoshua b. Levi (c. 250) has contrasted Da. 7:13 : 'Lo, with the clouds of heaven came one like a son of man,' with Zech. 9:9 : 'Poor and riding on an ass.' If they (Israel) have merits, he comes with the clouds of heaven ; if they have no merits, poor and riding on an ass." Pesikt. r., 34 (159b) expounds Zech. 9:9 similarly : "Riding on an ass — for the sake of the ungodly who have no merit, he does this, and recalls (by his riding on an ass) the merit of the fathers (of an Abraham, who in obedience to God's command undertook to saddle his own ass, Gn. 22:3)." Ber., 56b : "He who sees an ass in a dream, let him hope for Messianic salvation" (with a quotation from Zech. 9:9). [9]

B. The Ass in Antiquity, Hellenism and Gnosticism.

In Egypt the ass was dedicated to the god Typhon (Plut. Sept. Sap. Conv., 5 [II. 150 f.]), and was thus hateful to the inhabitants (Apul. Met., 11, 6; Ael. Nat. An., X, 28). It seems to have been brought to Greece from Asia Minor ; the etym. of ὄνος lends support to this view. [10] In Hom. Il., 11, 558-562 (the only instance of ὄνος in Hom.) Ajax in his resistance to the enemies who throng him is compared to an ass who in spite of blows will not leave a field of corn until he has eaten his fill. On a Mycenean mural three demons are depicted with the heads of asses. Dionysus and his followers ride on asses. The god is put in a chest on the back of an ass to be carried to Euboia, Ps.-Oppian Cyn., IV, 256; cf. the proverb ὄνος ἄγων μυστήρια (Aristot. Ra., 159), which is related to the Eleusinian cult. In gratitude Dionysus is supposed to have set an ass amongst the stars, Schol. of Germanicus on Arat. Phaen., ed. Buhle, II (1801), 51; Lact. Inst., I, 21, 27. Asses were used in Dionysiac processions ; Silenus rides on an ass, Ovid Fast., I, 399; III, 749; VI, 339. Originally it was perhaps esp. valued because it saved Lotis from the snares of Priapus, Ovid Fast., I, 433-436. But later it was regarded as a lusty animal, Cornut. Theol. Graec., 61, 1, and there are many accounts of intercourse with an ass or she-ass. [11] The ass romance of a later period (Ps.-Luc. Asin.) contains fabulous elements but shows how the ass was regarded at this time. [12] Possibly ancient mythological ideas had some influence (the ass, dedicated to Typhon, is the enemy of Isis). [13] Depictions on Gk. vases often portray ithyphallic asses. [14]

In Epiph. Gnostics are later characterised as worshippers of the Egyptian Typhon. [15]

---

[8] For the same saying under the name of R. Levi (c. 300) cf. Midr. S., 14 § 9 (45b); Str.-B., I, 843.

[9] J. Klausner rightly concludes : "A messianic interpretation of G. 49:11 and Zech. 9:9 was given very early in the Tannaitic period," Die messianischen Vorstellungen d. jüdischen Volkes im Zeitalter d. Tannaiten (1904), 45 f.

[10] ὄνος, like asinus, is a loan word from a language of Asia Minor in the south of Pontus, Walde-Pok., I, 113; A. Walde-J. B. Hofmann, Lat. etym. Wörterbuch, I (1938), 73. On the findings at Mycenae cf. Pauly-W., VI, 627; on the ass in the Dionysus cult, cf. W. F. Otto, Dionysos (1933), 154 f.

[11] A noble youth of Ephesus, son of Demostratus, has intercourse with a she-ass and this bears a girl called Onoskelia (bone of an ass), cf. Aristocles Rhod. in Stob., IV, 473. In the time of Juvenal (6, 334) noble ladies in Rome had intercourse with asses in the orgies of the Bona Dea. Cf. the description in Ps.-Luc. Asin., 50; Apul. Met., X, 19.

[12] On the Gk. source of the Luc. corpus and Apul. Met., cf. Kerényi, 151 ff. (on the metamorphosis of the ass man, his adventures, and his liberation from the spell).

[13] Beating the ass is an old Egyptian motif linked to the character of the Typhonic animal. Lucius as an ass is beaten no less than 14 times, Kerényi, 185.

[14] Pauly-W., VI, 671 f.

[15] Acc. to Epiph. Panarion, 26, 10, 6 Gnostics maintain that the archon Sabaoth, creator of the world, has the form of an ass. In a Gnostic work the prophet Zacharias (Mt. 23:35) discovers that temple worship is addressed to a man with the figure of an ass. He tries to

The Mandaeans speak of a mystery and sacrament of the she-ass with four bones, in polemic against Christianity.[16]

C. The Ass in the NT.

In the NT ὄνος occurs at Mt. 21:2, 5, 7 (with πῶλος and ὑποζύγιον), and also at Jn. 12:15 (with πῶλος and ὀνάριον), as a constituent part of the story of the triumphal entry. Along with βοῦς (cf. the OT) it is also found in Lk. 13:15 (and one reading of Lk. 14:5).

1. Mk. 11:1-11, though it does not refer expressly to Zech. 9:9 like Mt. 21:4 f.; Jn. 12:14 f., is already full of mysterious links (11:2 : εὑρήσετε) and not wholly unequivocal allusions (e.g., πῶλος, 11:2, 4, 5, 7; ὁ κύριος, 11:13; ὁ ἐρχόμενος, 11:9). The "coming one" (Mk. 11:9), the "king of Israel" (Jn. 12:13), was seen in Jesus, the prophet of Galilee (Mt. 21:11),[17] but the secret of the עָנִי = עָנָו and צַדִּיק of Zech. 9:9 was not yet perceived. "It is the secret of the lowly king — who goes to his death."[18] Many scholars assume that there are legendary embellishments in the story of the entry.[19] Mk. and Lk. lay special stress on the fact that the disciples find a "foal" on which no one has ever yet sat, Mk. 11:2; Lk. 19:30. The general principle that an animal or vessel provided for sacred ministry should not be put to ordinary human use applies also in the Bible, Nu. 19:2; Dt. 21:3; 1 S. 6:7.[20] If Mk. and Lk. interpret the OT πῶλος motif in their own way, Mt. understands Zech. 9:9 along very different lines peculiar to himself.[21] From the OT parallelism he deduces that two beasts were impressed into the Lord's service, an ass and its foal (ὄνον δεδεμένην καὶ πῶλον μετ' αὐτῆς, 21:2).

It is possible that he did not correctly understand the OT text. Methodologically it is not impossible to separate the two members of a parallelism in interpretation, cf. Ps. 22:18 with Jn. 19:23 f., though the Rabb. saw no cause to distinguish between ass and foal in the commonly quoted verse Zech. 9:9. Such disjunction of parallelism necessarily results in a special sense and a new understanding. But Mt. with his interpretation is confronted by various material difficulties which are not easily solved and which may have influenced the textual history of 21:7: Do the disciples put their clothes on both animals (καὶ ἐπέθηκαν ἐπ' αὐτῶν τὰ ἱμάτια) or is one to read the sing. ἐπ' αὐτόν with D it Chrys? Does Jesus sit on both, or only on the clothes of the one

---

teach the Jews: "Woe to you, whom you worship!" but is put to death by them. Cf. R. Wünsch, *Sethianische Verfluchungstafeln aus Rom* (1898), 108.

[16] Lidz. Ginza, 227, 21 ff.; Jacoby, 266.

[17] Acc. to A. Schweitzer, *Gesch. d. Leben-Jesu-Forschung*[4] (1926), 440 (cf. J. Klausner, *Jesus v. Nazareth*[2] [1934], 426) the entry is for Jesus a Messianic action in which His self-awareness breaks through, as in the sending out of the disciples, the declaration that the Baptist was Elijah, and the feeding of the multitude.

[18] J. Schniewind, *Das Ev. nach Mt.* (*NT Deutsch*), on 11:10.

[19] Cf. Bultmann Trad., 281: "One can only ask whether the entry as such is historical but is made Messianic by legend, or whether it derives wholly from the prophecy." H. Gressmann, *Das religionsgeschichtliche Problem des Ursprungs d. hell. Erlösungsreligion*, I (ZKG, NF, 3 [1922], 189) conjectures that Menahem's solemn entry into Jerusalem as king was perhaps a model for the similar event in the life of Jesus. Cf. Jos. Bell., 2, 262 and 433 f.

[20] "For no stranger shall sit on his throne, and the atoning red heifer of the Bible must not have carried the yoke," J. Klausner, 424.

[21] The end of the quotation is obviously assimilated to the Mas. and has a strong flavour of Jewish Gk., Deissmann B, 158 f.; Kl. Mt. on 21:4 f.

(ἐπάνω αὐτῶν)? Is the sing. to be preferred here too (ἐπάνω αὐτόν, ἐπάνω αὐτοῦ, or simply ἐπάνω)? Entry on two animals does not seem to agree with the prophecy and is difficult in practice. [22] It is an open question why Mt. should think it important to mention the ass along with the "foal" (πῶλος). [23]

The details and structure in Jn. do not wholly correspond to the Synoptic account. The little ass (ὀνάριον, Jn. 12:14) which Jesus Himself finds according to divine plan is a reference to the foal (πῶλος ὄνου) to which Zech. 9:9 refers. It is stated expressly that only after the glorification of Jesus do the disciples understand the significance of this saying and their own earlier action (12:16). It is surprising that Jn. emphasises only the agreement of the prophecy with the Messianic event and not with the character of Him who comes (δίκαιος, πραΰς). [24]

2. In the OT the ox (μόσχος, βοῦς) and the ass (ὄνος, ὑποζύγιον) are often mentioned together in stories and injunctions. [25] It is natural, then, that the two should also occur together in a saying of Jesus at Lk. 13:15: "Doth not each one of you on the sabbath loose his ox or ass from the stall, and lead him away to watering?" Textually Lk. 14:5 is more difficult; the true reading is probably τίνος ὑμῶν υἱὸς ἢ βοῦς (AB it). [26] Translation back into Aram. gives the following play on words: "Who of you, if a son (bᵉra) or ox (beʿira) falls into the well (bera), hesitates to pull him out at once even on the sabbath?" [27] In this case other possibilities, e.g., ὄνος ἢ βοῦς (א it vg), βοῦς ἢ ὄνος (syˢ) or πρόβατον ἢ βοῦς (D), are to be dismissed. [28] Even at a later date it is still presupposed that the ass is a riding animal, Mart. Pol., 8, 1: ὄνῳ καθίσαντες.

Michel

---

[22] Zn. Mt., 610 thinks, however, that there is a historical basis.

[23] Köhler, 56: "Jesus, when He entered Jerusalem, did not ride on a foal, nor on a war-horse, but, acc. to ancient custom (Ju. 10:4; 12:14), on an ass."

[24] Several questions of exposition remain open: 1. Did Jesus Himself understand His entry in the light of Zech. 9:9, or did the community interpret it thus? 2. In what sense and to what degree did Jesus seek to fulfil the prophecy? Why do both Mt. and Jn. cut short the verse if the original was perhaps significant for Jesus? Does this involve simplification? Cf. Bultmann Trad., 281; H. Gressmann, 189.

[25] Ex. 21:33; 22:3; 23:4; Dt. 22:10 etc. On "beast of burden" (ὑποζύγιον) for "ass" cf. A. Geiger, *Urschrift u. Übers. d. Bibel*² (1928), 360 f., 442; Bickermann, 260. The NT does not mention the ass in the Christmas story. But from the time of Origen the fathers refer Is. 1:3 and Hab. 3:2 LXX to the birth of the Lord. In the early Middle Ages Ps.-Matth. introduced the motif into literature. It is found in Christian art from the 4th cent., and spread into the whole of the medieval West from the 7th. In the Legenda Aurea the ox and ass symbolise the birth-place. Cf. K. Künstle, *Ikonographie der chr. Kunst*, I (1928), 346-348; W. Molsdorf, *Chr. Symbolik* (1926), No. 55, p. 25 f. and No. 967, p. 155 f.; K. L. Schmidt, "Prudentius u. Erasmus über die Christuskrippe mit Ochs u. Esel," *Theologische Zeitschrift*, 5 (1949), 469 ff. [G. Bertram].

[26] Acc. to the stricter legislation of Damasc., 11, 13 f., 16 f. it is permissible to pull a man out of a pit on the sabbath, but no implements, ladders, or rope must be used. On the other hand, pulling out an animal is roundly forbidden. Acc. to the Rabb. Halacha pulling out a man is allowed without any restrictions except that the prohibition of work on the sabbath should not be violated more than necessary. It is again forbidden, however, to pull an animal out of a pit, though a cover may be thrown in so that it may get a footing and spring out of the hole, Str.-B., I, 629. Pulling out a son would thus be permissible, but not pulling out an ox [K. G. Kuhn].

[27] M. Black, *An Aramaic Approach to the Gospels and Acts* (1946), 126; cf. J. Jeremias, "Die aram. Vorgeschichte unserer Evangelien," ThLZ, 74 (1949), 530.

[28] On the whole problem cf. F. Schulthess, "Zur Sprache der Evangelien," ZNW, 21 (1922), 225; Kl. Lk., ad loc.

† ὄξος

Etym., to ὀξύς, "sharp," "sour," as βάθος to βαθύς etc.; hence strictly "sharpness," "sourness," then "sour wine," the popular drink of hot countries (Heb. חֹמֶץ), [1] given with meals to soldiers and workers, good for quenching thirst and for refreshment. With a stronger content of sourness ("vinegar") it is used as seasoning in the preparation of foods and at table, cf. Ruth 2:14. It is to be noted that vinegar prepared from good wine (cf. Nu. 6:3) is far less sharp and if mixed with water is regarded as a good drink. ὄξος is recommended by doctors for its qualities in reducing fever, giving refreshment, and helping the digestion. There is no example of its hostile use as a torture. The only torture in Aristoph. Ra., 620 is that it is poured into the nose and thus irritates the mucous membrane. Prv. 10:26, too, is simply referring to the unpleasant effect of the bitterness on the teeth, and this is disputed in bShab., 111a. If it is sometimes used in a bad sense, this is in relation to οἶνος, Eubulus Fr., 65 (CAF, II, 186); Antiph. Fr., 240 (cf. 116): σφόδρ' ἐστὶν ἡμῶν ὁ βίος οἴνῳ προσφερής· ὅταν ᾖ τὸ λοιπὸν μικρόν, ὄξος γίνεται (Kock, loc. cit., refers to Anth. Pal., II, 43, though ὀξύχολος is used here in clarification). The same applies in ψ 68:21, which is quoted in connection with the passion in Jn. 19:29. Complaint is here made about the giving of ὄξος to drink only because it is mean and sour in comparison with wine. [2] Cf. finally Midr. Rt. 2:14 (132b). where a ref. to the sufferings of the Messiah is seen in the taking of חֹמֶץ, though bShab., 113b simply says in connection with the same verse that חֹמֶץ is good for heat. In any case this isolated and late relating of ὄξος to the sufferings of the Messiah must not be regarded as testimony to a widespread view in the pre-Christian or early Christian period.

The passion narrative (Mk. 15:36 and par.) tells us that a drink of ὄξος was given to Jesus on the cross. This can refer only to the wine of the people. That this was available at the place of execution seems quite natural to the Evangelists. Jn. mentions specifically a vessel with ὄξος, and according to Lk. a soldier hands it to our Lord. These details also point to the popular drink, whereas there would have to be some special reason for the sudden appearance of vinegar in this context. [3] The Gospels vary in their placing of the incident and also in their interpretation. Mk. 15:36 realistically supposes that it was given for its refreshing effect. Possibly prompted by the cry Eloi, Eloi, one of those standing around [4] benevolently hands Him the wine to soothe the fever of the wounds and to quench His thirst.

Many comm. [5] mistakenly suppose that this was a sharp drink which like modern vinegar would cause strong nervous stimulation even when taken in small quantities. In this case taking the ὄξος would delay death and prolong the agony of the cross. Handing the ὄξος would thus be a gruesome act. This line of exposition is refuted by the very

---

ὄ ξ ο ς. H. Stadler, Art. "Essig," Pauly-W., VI (1907), 689-692; J. Behrendes, Die Pharmazie bei den alten Kulturvölkern, I (1891), 14, 68, 94; G. Dalman, Arbeit u. Sitte in Palästina, IV : "Brot, Öl u. Wein" (1935), 403; Str.-B., II, 264.

[1] Nu. 6:3; Rt. 2:14; with emphasis on the sourness Ps. 69:21; Prv. 10:26; 25:20; LXX, apart from Prv. 10:26, ὄξος (and only in these verses).

[2] Cf. Str.-B., II, 580; G. Dalman, Der leidende u. sterbende Messias (1888), 49.

[3] For the idea of an irritating drink at Mk. 15:36 cf. Wbg. and Kl. Mk., ad loc.; at Lk. 23:36 Kl. Lk., K. H. Rengstorf, Das Ev. nach Lk. (NT Deutsch), ad loc.; at Jn. 19:29 F. Büchsel, Das Ev. nach Jn. (NT Deutsch), ad loc.

[4] We are not told whether this was a soldier or one of the people.

[5] → n. 3.

fact that no such effect is known even in the case of ὄξος as a seasoning. Nor is Mk. consciously referring to Ps. 69:21, [6] since the drink is given for refreshment.

Mt. 27:48 emphasises even more strongly the kindly nature of the action. It is motivated by the cry, Eli, Eli, and those standing around explicitly try to restrain the giver by referring to the possible help of Elijah. Lk. 23:36 f., on the other hand, has in view the lesser value of ὄξος as a cheap popular drink, and the incident comes before the cry as an act of mockery. The drink itself is contemptuous — sour wine offered to the King of the Jews. Jn. 19:28-30 goes beyond this and stresses the fact that the drink was sour and bitter. In particular, ὄξος is set in the light of the verse in Ps. 69:21 which speaks of the innocent sufferer being given vinegar to drink. To fulfil this saying is the last desire (διψῶ) of the crucified Jesus. [7] Even to this detail the connection between the faithfulness and the suffering of the Son of God is thus demonstrated to the Evangelist.

The addition μετὰ χολῆς (sy^h lat Ferrar) is made to bring this out, since it is not wholly clear from the nature of ὄξος, [8] and also to clarify the ref. to Ps. 69:21. Barn., 7, 3 goes even further in this direction : ἐποτίζετο ὄξει καὶ χολῇ, and esp. Ev. Pt. 5:15 : ποτίσατε αὐτὸν χολὴν μετὰ ὄξους, designed to accelerate death like a poison.

Apart from the ὄξος Mk. 15:22 f.; Mt. 27:34 speak of a stupefying drink customarily given before crucifixion. [9] The actions are quite different, and are thus independent. When the account in Mt. tells us that the drink was made up of οἶνον (אBD) μετὰ χολῆς, it is possibly alluding to Ps. 69:21, and this conjecture is strengthened by the reading ὄξος (AEF sy^v h). Understood thus, the account can be regarded as a par. to that of the ὄξος drink, and it is thus eliminated in Lk. and Jn.

Heidland

---

† ὀπίσω, † ὄπισθεν

1. The stem ὀπισ- undoubtedly derives from the Indo-European *epi, *opi "thereon," "thereby." ὀπί(σ)σω is constructed as an instrumental adv., ὄπι(σ)θε(ν) as an adv. of place. [1]

In general usage ὀπίσω is an adv., usually with ref. to place or time, "behind," "after," "later," also "again." [2] In answer to the question "where," it is used in the

---

[6] Kl. Mk.; J. Schniewind, *Das Ev. nach Mk.* (*NT Deutsch*), ad loc.

[7] Zn. J., ad loc. refers the fulfilment of Scripture to the death and sees in the drink a fortifying for conscious dying, cf. also Bau. J.[3], ad loc.; Behm → II, 226. On the relation of ὄξος and χολή cf. G. Bertram, *Die Leidensgeschichte Jesu u. d. Christuskult* (1922), 82 f.

[8] Acc. to G. Dalman, *Jesus-Jeschua* (1922), 188 f. the drink is here, too, given for refreshment, but it is the lowest point of the passion, since He who dispenses water is now Himself thirsty. This cannot be linked, however, with a ref. to Ps. 69.

[9] G. Dalman, 375, 400; Str.-B., I, 1037.

ὀ π ί σ ω, ὄ π ι σ θ ε ν. Cf. Pass., Pape, Liddell-Scott, Pr.-Bauer, *s.v.,* the comm. on the various verses, and the bibl. under ἀκολουθέω (→ I, 210).

[1] Boisacq compares ἐπί to the Lat. ob and other non-Gk. words ; cf. on this A. Walde-J. B. Hofmann, *Lat. etym. Wörterbuch*[3], II (1949), *s.v. ob.* On the word construction and meaning cf. E. Schwyzer, *Griech. Grammatik* (*Hndbch. AW,* II, 1), I (1939), 550 with n. 7, 618, 628; II (1950), 465, 540 f.

[2] Cf. the dict.

NT only in subst. form, as already in Plato, LXX and Philo.[3] Phil. 3:13 : τὰ μὲν ὀπίσω ἐπιλανθανόμενος, "what lies behind me." Cf. Jn. 6:66 : πολλοὶ ... ἀπῆλθον εἰς τὰ ὀπίσω in the sense "to withdraw," also Jn. 18:6; 20:14; Lk. 9:62 : βλέπειν εἰς τὰ ὀπίσω, "to look back," cf. Gn. 19:26. With ἐπιστρέφειν, Mk. 13:16; Lk. 17:31. As an adv. answering the question "whither ?" ὀπίσω occurs in the NT only at Mt. 24:18 and Lk. 7:38.

In LXX and NT usage ὀπίσω is also used improperly as a prep. with the gen., mostly of person.[4] The origin of this use, found over 25 times in the NT, is undoubtedly to be sought in the LXX transl. of the Heb. הָלַךְ אַחֲרֵי by πορεύεσθαι ὀπίσω.[5] The NT develops the use, though only in the Gospels, Ac., Past., 2 Pt., Jd. and Rev. It does not occur in Pl. or Hb.

2. Ὄπισθεν, used prepositionally from the time of Hom., means adverbially and prepositionally "behind."[6] The prep. use is common in the LXX, cf. Jos. 6:13 : ὄπισθε τῆς κιβωτοῦ τῆς διαθήκης, Ιερ. 31(48):2 : ὄπισθέν σου βαδιεῖται μάχαιρα. א reads ὀπίσω, a common variant, cf. Jl. 2:3 (twice); Ez. 2:10.[7] In the LXX ὄπισθεν is the transl. of אַחַר, אַחֲרֵי, and even more often מֵאַחַר, מֵאַחֲרֵי, though there is no fixed rule for the rendering of any of these words by ὀπίσω or ὄπισθεν. It is probable that the usual combination of ὄπισθεν with the gen. of person in the translation Gk. of the LXX led to ὀπίσω with the gen. of person, which jars the linguistic sense of the Gks.

The NT uses ὄπισθεν only 7 times, as an adv. "from behind," Mk. 5:27 (Mt. 9:20; Lk. 8:44),[8] "behind" : Rev. 4:6 and 5:1;[9] as a preposition, "behind" : Mt. 25:23; Lk. 23:26.

3. In the NT ὀπίσω is generally of theological significance when combined with the genitive of person or a verb of motion.

Exceptions are Lk. 9:14 : ἀπέστειλαν πρεσβείαν ὀπίσω αὐτοῦ, Rev. 12:15 : ἔβαλεν ... ὀπίσω τῆς γυναικὸς ὕδωρ, cf. Rev. 1:10. Here there is no theological import. Again, when Jesus is called ὀπίσω μου ἐρχόμενος by the Baptist (Jn. 1:15, 27, 30; cf. Mk. 1:7 and Mt. 3:11),[10] the ὀπίσω is not theologically significant, but simply indicates the time.

In all the other expressions in which ὀπίσω occurs with a genitive of person or verb of movement a very close relation is expressed between the persons in

---

[3] Cf. Plat. Phaedr., 254b, LXX concordance, and Leisegang, II, 586.

[4] In non-biblical Gk. this prep. use has been found (Schwyzer, II, 541) in Ditt. Or., 56, 62 : ταύτης δ' ὀπίσω (237 B.C.), GDI, III, 3246, 10, 12 : ὀπίσω τοῦ Κορείου, "behind the temple of Kore," P. Oxy., I, 43 B IV, 3 (3rd cent. A.D.): ὀπίσω Καπιτολείου. Cf. Bl.-Debr. § 215, 1 with appendix. Radermacher², 145 speaks in terms of Semiticising substitution.

[5] → I, 211. In a temporal sense ὀπίσω with gen. occurs in the LXX at, e.g., 1 Βασ. 24:22; 3 Βασ. 1:24; Jl. 2:14 etc.

[6] Cf. Bl.-Debr. § 214-217 for the many adv. used as improper prep. In Hom. Od., 8, 527; 15, 34 = 5, 167 the meaning "from behind" is possible, but not very likely in view of the many other instances where it plainly means "behind."

[7] In Ez. 2:10 the LXX alters the original sense of the Mas. The statement that the roll is written from before and behind (i.e., within and without) is rendered γεγραμμένα ἦν τὰ ὄπισθεν καὶ τὰ ἔμπροσθεν, and ὄπισθεν is thus given a temporal sense : "In it was written the past and the future." In general the LXX uses the prep. μετά to express what comes after.

[8] This sense of "from behind," which is very uncommon in class. Gk. (cf. Xenoph. An., IV, 1, 6 : ἐκ τοῦ ὄπισθεν), is a Semitism deriving from the transl. Gk. of the LXX.

[9] On ὄπισθεν in Rev. 5:1 cf. W. Bousset, Offenbarung Johannis (1906), n. ad loc.

[10] On Jn. 1:15, 27, 30 → II, 672; O. Cullmann : "ὁ ὀπίσω μου ἐρχόμενος," Coniectanea Neotestamentica, 9 (1947), 26-32. On Mt. 3:11 cf. Schl. Mt., ad loc.; E. Lohmeyer, "Zur joh. Überlieferung v. Joh. dem Täufer," JBL, 51 (1932), 311-316.

question. In the Synoptists it is usually Jesus who, by the call: δεῦτε ὀπίσω μου (Mk. 1:17; Mt. 4:19), summons the disciples to follow Him and binds them to Himself. Though the origin of this expression is to be sought formally in the Gk. translation of אַחֲרֵי הָלַךְ, the NT use on the lips of Jesus is much broader and deeper.

The OT expression is first used in many instances for "going after" other gods (Ju. 2:12: ἐπορεύθησαν ὀπίσω θεῶν ἑτέρων, cf. also Dt. [4:3] 6:14; 3 Βασ. 11:2; Jer. 11:10; 13:10; 16:11; Hos. 2:7; 2:15), and this gives it the simple sense "to walk," "to belong to," "to follow." It is then used for the opposite demand to walk after Yahweh (Dt. 13:5: ὀπίσω κυρίου τοῦ θεοῦ ὑμῶν πορεύεσθε, 3 Βασ. 14:8; 18:21: εἰ ἔστιν κύριος ὁ θεός, πορεύεσθε ὀπίσω αὐτοῦ· εἰ δὲ ὁ Βααλ αὐτός, πορεύεσθε ὀπίσω αὐτοῦ, 4 Βασ. 23:3). It is obvious that this simply means "to follow," "to be obedient to." The Rabb. world did not develop the usage further. [11]

Jesus certainly calls the disciples to be His followers. But this involves more than simply following. Otherwise He would summon them to follow God — a call which, surprisingly, is never sounded in the NT as distinct from the OT. The summons of Jesus implies more than this. It is a demand for full commitment to Him. [12] Going after Jesus is a decisive precondition of participation in the glory of the βασιλεία. But it means a complete renunciation of one's own will, Mk. 8:34 (Mt. 26:24; Lk. 9:23): εἴ τις θέλει ὀπίσω μου ἐλθεῖν, ἀπαρνησάσθω ἑαυτὸν καὶ ἀράτω τὸν σταυρὸν αὐτοῦ, καὶ ἀκολουθείτω μοι. To follow the Lord Jesus, who must one day bear His cross, means for His disciples a readiness for the full surrender of oneself to the Lord. Cf. also Mt. 10:38: ὃς οὐ λαμβάνει τὸν σταυρὸν αὐτοῦ καὶ ἀκολουθεῖ ὀπίσω μου, οὐκ ἔστιν μου ἄξιος (Lk. 14:27: οὐ δύναται εἶναί μου μαθητής). Once one has heard the call of Jesus δεῦτε ὀπίσω μου (Mk. 1:17 and par.) — cf. Mk. 1:20: John and James ἀπῆλθον ὀπίσω αὐτοῦ (cf. Lk. 5:11) — there is no going back; Lk. 9:62: οὐδεὶς ἐπιβαλὼν τὴν χεῖρα ἐπ' ἄροτρον καὶ βλέπων εἰς τὰ ὀπίσω εὔθετός ἐστιν τῇ βασιλείᾳ τοῦ θεοῦ. When the supreme crisis comes, disciples must guard against ἐπιστρέφειν εἰς τὰ ὀπίσω (Mk. 13:16; Mt. 24:18; Lk. 17:31). Commitment to Jesus, which includes full surrender, rules out any looking back. Discipleship means belonging exclusively to Him. When Jesus tells Peter to get behind Him (Mk. 8:33; Mt. 16:23: ὕπαγε ὀπίσω μου, σατανᾶ) because he does not think the things of God, this rejection implies a requirement of complete separation from all that is satanic, from all that does not come from God. [13]

The great number of Jesus' disciples — in spite of Jn. 6:66 — aroused the anger and envy of the Pharisees, Jn. 12:19: ἴδε ὁ κόσμος ὀπίσω αὐτοῦ ἀπῆλθεν. But Jesus knew that the decision would be made only after His going out of this world. According to Mk. 13:6 ff. and par. one of the signs of the *parousia* is the appearance of many false Christs ... καὶ πολλοὺς πλανήσουσιν. The more relevant, then, is the admonition to the disciples in Lk. 21:8: μὴ πορευθῆτε ὀπίσω αὐτῶν, "go ye not after them!"

The other verses in which ὀπίσω occurs in the NT offer no difficulties in the light of what has been said. In Ac. 5:37 Gamaliel says of Judas: ἀπέστησεν λαὸν ὀπίσω αὐτοῦ. In Ac. 20:30 Paul sees false teachers coming ... τοῦ ἀποσπᾶν τοὺς μαθητὰς

---

[11] → ἀκολουθέω, I, 210-216, esp. 211-213, where there are numerous examples.
[12] → ἔρχομαι, II, 669.
[13] It is probably from this passage that the same expression ὕπαγε ὀπίσω μου, σατανᾶ made its way into the MS tradition of the temptation story, Mt. 4:10; Lk. 4:8 𝔅D al.

ὀπίσω ἑαυτῶν. In 1 Tm. 5:15 there is ref. to Christians who ἐξετράπησαν ὀπίσω τοῦ σατανᾶ. In Rev. 13:3 : καὶ ἐθαυμάσθη ὅλη ἡ γῆ ὀπίσω τοῦ θηρίου, the ὀπίσω is weakened by the controlling verb, which is not a verb of motion.[14] Jd. 7 calls the sin of licentiousness an ἐκπορνεῦσαι καὶ ἀπελθεῖν ὀπίσω σαρκὸς ἑτέρας.[15] Cf. 2 Pt. 2:10 : μάλιστα δὲ τοὺς ὀπίσω σαρκὸς ... πορευομένους, which is probably dependent on Jd.

Apart from 1 Tm. 5:15 Pl. uses ὀπίσω only at Phil. 3:13 : ἓν δέ, τὰ μὲν ὀπίσω ἐπιλανθανόμενος τοῖς δὲ ἔμπροσθεν ἐπεκτεινόμενος, (14) κατὰ σκοπὸν διώκω εἰς τὸ βραβεῖον τῆς ἄνω κλήσεως τοῦ θεοῦ ἐν Χριστῷ ᾽Ιησοῦ. The formal use here is different from that of Jesus in the Synoptists, but the material reference is the same. Commitment to the Lord means a full surrender which completely abandons that which lies behind in favour of fellowship with Jesus and the prize of victory for which Paul is contending.

Seesemann

| ὅπλον, ὁπλίζω, πανοπλία, ζώννυμι, διαζώννυμι, περιζώννυμι, ζώνη, θώραξ, ὑποδέω (ὑπόδημα, σανδάλιον), θυρεός, περικεφαλαία | → μάχαιρα, IV, 524 ff.; → στρατιώτης. |

† ὅπλον.

Orig. "implement,"[1] then specialised : 1. "ship's tackling" (sing. and plur.) in Hom. only Od. (14, 346; 2, 390); Hes. Op., 627; "cable," "rope" : Hdt., VII, 25; IX, 115; 2. "tool" of any kind ; the smithy tools of Hephaistos (Hom. Il., 18, 409, 412), the sickle (Anth. Pal., VI, 95, Antiphilos), the staff of age (Callim. Epigrammata, 1, 7, ed. O.

---

[14] Cf. the comm. and Bl.-Debr.[7] § 196 App.: "pregnant for ἐθαύμασεν ἐπὶ τῷ θηρίῳ καὶ ἐπορεύθη ὀπίσω αὐτοῦ."
[15] Cf. for ἐκπορνεῦσαι ὀπίσω LXX Ex. 34:15, 16; Lv. 17:7 etc.

ὅπλον κτλ. Preliminary Note : In the light of Eph. 6:14 ff. it has seemed advisable to deal with all the individual parts of the panoply under this common term. Thus words from other stems are to be found under the stem ὁπλ-.
Liddell-Scott, Preisigke Wört., Pr.-Bauer³, *s.v.*; M. Ebert, *Reallexikon d. Vorgeschichte.* IV, 2 (1926), 577 ff., *s.v.* "Gürtel," X (1927/28), 32-36, *s.v.* "Panzer," VI (1926), 380-394, *s.v.* "Kleidung," XI (1927-28), 255-262, *s.v.* "Schild," V (1926), 290-298, *s.v.* "Helm"; BW, *s.v.* "Kleidung," "Waffen"; P. Volz, *Die bibl. Altertümer²* (1925), 510-513; K. Galling, *Bibl. Reallexikon* (1937), *s.v.* "Kleidung," "Panzer," "Schild," "Helm"; AOB, AOT *passim*; E. Schwyzer, "Profaner u. heiliger Gürtel im alten Iran," *Wörter u. Sachen,* 12 (1929), 20-37, 302; J. Kromayer-G. Veith, *Heerwesen u. Kriegführung d. Griechen u. Römer, Hndbch. AW,* IV, 3, 2 (1928), 18 f., 38 f., 50 f., 108 ff., 134, 278 f., 324 ff., 409 ff., 521 ff.; L. Lindenschmit, *Tracht u. Bewaffnung d. römischen Heeres während d. Kaiserzeit* (1882); on the orendistic and magical use of the girdle E. Schuppe, "Gürtel u. Orendismus," *Oberdeutsche Zeitschrift f. Volkskunde,* 2 (1928), 128-146; cf. bibl. in F. Pfister, "D. Religion d. Griechen u. Römer," *Jahresbericht über d. Fortschritte d. klassischen Altertumswissenschaft,* Suppl. Vol., 229 (1930), 112, 261 f.; K. Marti, *Das Buch Jesaja* (1900); B. Duhm, *Das Buch Jesaja³* (1914); O. Procksch, *Js.* I (1930), P. Volz, *Js.* II (1932): on Is. 11:5; 52:7; 59:17; F. Baethgen, *D. Ps.³* (1904), R. Kittel, *D. Ps.⁵,⁶* (1929) on Ps. 7:10; 35:1 ff.; Wettstein on Eph. 6:11 ff.; Str.-B., I, 98, 121, 435 f., 565-569; II, 11, 586 f.; III, 616 ff.; Kl., Hck., Loh. Mk.

Schneider, I [1870], 68); 3. "weapon," mostly plur., in Hom. only Il. (18, 614 etc.); Pind. Nem., 8, 27; in the tragedians, Eur. Herc. Fur., 161 etc.; in prose Hdt., IV, 23; Plat. Resp., V, 474a; Xenoph. Cyrop., VII, 4, 15; common on inscr. (Ditt. Or., 90, 22, 39 [2nd cent. B.C.]: ὅπλον νικητικόν, panoply of the victorious king; Ditt. Syll.³, v. Index) and in pap., P. Tebt., 48, 19 (2nd cent. B.C.): Λύκος σὺν ἄλλοις ἐν ὅπλοις. Sing. as one piece of equipment, esp. the "shield," Ditt. Syll.³, 706, 18: εἰκόνα γραπτὴν ἐν ὅπλῳ etc. Also weapons of animals, Aristot. Part. An., IV, 10, p. 687a, 25, cf. b, 4. 4. "Troops," Soph. Ant., 115: πολλῶν μεθ' ὅπλων, Thuc., IV, 74, 3: ἐξέτασιν ὅπλων ποιεῖσθαι, or "camp," Thuc., III, 1, 1: ἐκ τῶν ὅπλων προϊέναι. Well-known expressions are ἐνδύεσθαι τὰ ὅπλα, Hdt., VII, 218; ἐν ὅπλοισ(ι) εἶναι or γενέσθαι, Eur. Ba., 303; Thuc., VI, 56, 2; μένειν ἐπὶ τοῖς ὅπλοις, Xenoph. Cyrop., VII, 2, 8.

It is used fig. esp. by comedians and philosophers without distinction between weapons of defence and offence: ποτὶ πονηρὸν οὐκ ἄχρηστον ὅπλον ἁ πονηρία, Epicharm. Fr., 275 (CGF, I, 142), τῆς πενίας ὅπλον ἡ παρρησία, Nicostrat. Fr., 29 (CAF, II, 227), ὅπλον μέγιστόν ἐστιν ἡ ἀρετὴ βροτοῖς (Menand. Mon., 433, Fr. Comicorum Graecorum, ed. A. Meineke, IV [1841], 352). For Stoicism cf. esp. Epict. Diss., III, 22, 94: While kings and tyrants are furnished with spearbearers and weapons to reprimand some and to smite malefactors, though they themselves are wicked, for the cynic ἀντὶ τῶν ὅπλων καὶ τῶν δορυφόρων conscience (τὸ συνειδός, previously τὸ ἡγεμονικόν) gives the authority to punish others. Metaphorically Epict. speaks of concepts which are rusted ὡς ὁπλάρια ἀποκείμενα, Diss., IV, 6, 14.

Of the words for which ὅπλον is used in the LXX the closest, כְּלִי (Jer. 21:4; Ez. 32:27) and נֶשֶׁק (2 K. 10:2; Ez. 39:9, 10), are the rarest. In general the Gk. tends to think less concretely than the Semite, so that individual weapons are replaced in the LXX by the general term, e.g., ὅπλον for spear (חֲנִית, ψ 45:9 etc.), for various types of shields (מָגֵן, 1 K. 10:17 etc.; צִנָּה, ψ 5:12 etc., though Am. 4:2 צִנּוֹת, "fishhooks," misunderstood by the LXX; שֶׁלֶט, 2 Ch. 23:9), for armour (סִרְיוֹן, 'Ιερ. 28[51]:3) and missiles (שֶׁלַח, 2 Ch. 23:10; 32:5). Often ὅπλον occurs with no obvious Heb. equivalent, 2 Ch. 21:3 etc., and esp. Macc. It is seldom used fig., cf. ψ 56:4 (חֲנִית) of the teeth of the ungodly, Prv. 14:7 (a complete change of sense): ὅπλα δὲ αἰσθήσεως χείλη σοφά, Wis. 18:21 of prayer (and incense) as weapons of Moses against the Egypt. plagues, ψ 90:4 (צִנָּה) of the protective faithfulness of God. Yahweh uses the weapons of men for His purposes, often in judgment (Jer. 21:4). But when He wishes He destroys them (Ps. 46:9; 76:3) and lends His people His own weapons (Ps. 35:2). These ideas, fully developed already in the Heb. OT, are similar to those of the Stoics, for all the distinctive differences, → supra.

Philo achieves a synthesis. In his works the fig. use is predominant. How should we fear, τὸ φόβου καὶ παντὸς πάθους λυτήριον σὲ τὸν ὑπερασπιστὴν ὅπλον ἔχοντες (Som., I, 173)? Why, O soul, dost thou pursue vain things and not follow the ascetic (Jacob), τὰ κατὰ τοῦ πάθους καὶ τῆς κενῆς δόξης ἀναλαβεῖν ὅπλα καὶ παλαίσματα μαθησομένη (Som., I, 255)? The logos is given to men as ὅπλον ἀμυντήριον against excess (Leg. All., III, 155; Som., I, 103; also in the plur. Sacr. AC, 130).

---

on 1:6; 6:8 f.; Kl., Schl. Mt. on 3:4, 11; 10:9 f.; Zn., Bau. J. on 13:4; 21:7, 18; Wdt. Ag. on 21:11; Haupt, Ew., Dib. Gefbr. on Eph. 6:11 ff.; Dob., Dib. Th. on 1 Th. 5:8; Bss., ICC, Loh., Had. Apk. on 1:13; 15:6; E. Lohmeyer, "Joh. der Täufer," Urchr., I (1932), 49 ff., 99 and Index, s.v. "Kleidung"; P. Joüon, "Le costume d'Elie et celui de Jean Baptiste," Biblica, 16 (1935), 74-81; D. Buzy, "Pagne ou ceinture?" Recherches de science religieuse, 23 (1933), 589 ff.; H. Windisch, "Die Notiz über Tracht u. Speise d. Täufers," ZNW, 32 (1933), 65-87; S. Krauss, "D. Instruktion Jesu an d. Ap.," Angelos, I (1925), 96-102, esp. 101; W. Straub, D. Bildersprache d. Ap. Pls. (1937), 91 f.; K. Barth, "Des Christen Wehr und Waffen," Eine Schweizer Stimme 1938-1945 (1945), 123-132.

1 From √ sep "to push forward" something with inner participation, Sanskrit sapati "to caress," "to urge on," Gk. ἕπω (with ἀμφι etc.), to be distinguished from ἕπομαι = "to follow," cf. Walde-Pok., II, 487.

In the NT and early Christian literature ὅπλον is always in the plur. (except at Barn., 12, 2) and it is always used in sense 3. ("weapon"), lit. only in Jn. 18:3; Barn., 12, 2; Mart. Pol., 7, 1; Cl. Al. Strom., I, 24, 159, 3, otherwise fig., in the NT only in Paul. Paul repeatedly describes his missionary service as *militia Christi* (→ στρατιώτης). In 2 C. 10:4 he emphasises the efficacy of his weapons: τὰ γὰρ ὅπλα τῆς στρατείας ἡμῶν οὐ σαρκικὰ ἀλλὰ δυνατὰ τῷ θεῷ πρὸς καθαίρεσιν ὀχυρωμάτων. The use of ὅπλα for siege-engines, though not common, is understandable in view of the basic sense. In 2 C. 6:7 the stress is on moral blamelessness: διά (= with, → II, 66) τῶν ὅπλων τῆς δικαιοσύνης τῶν δεξιῶν καὶ ἀριστερῶν (weapons of offence and defence). But the *militia Christi* is the task of all the baptised. Hence the admonition: "Yield not your members as weapons [2] of unrighteousness (gen. qualitatis = unrighteous weapons) unto sin, but yield yourselves unto God, as those that are alive from the dead, and your members as weapons of righteousness unto God," R. 6:13. Cf. also R. 13:12: "Let us therefore cast off the works of darkness, and let us put on (on ἐνδύεσθαι τὰ ὅπλα → 293) the weapons [3] of light," i.e., the weapons which are in keeping with the dawning day, cf. 1 Th. 5:8. The proximity of the *parousia* does not mean feeble peace but final conflict. This fig. use, though prepared in many ways → 293, is characteristic of the NT. The reference is not to the constant battle in the world between reason and what is unnatural, and on that ground immoral, though this may be found in Paul (1 C. 11:13 ff.). It is rather to the transcendental conflict between God and satanic powers, in which man is both passively and actively involved.

The fathers keep close to the NT. Ign. in Pol. 6, 2 writes: τὸ βάπτισμα ὑμῶν μενέτω ὡς ὅπλα (→ πανοπλία). Cl. Al. Prot., 11, 116, 3 f. reproduces Eph. 6:14 ff. and continues: ταῦτα ἡμῶν τὰ ὅπλα τὰ ἄτρωτα· τούτοις ἐξοπλισάμενοι παραταξώμεθα τῷ πονηρῷ, cf. Exc. Theod., 85, 3. But the eschatological aspect fades into the background; it is replaced by Stoicising rationalism. On Pol., 4, 1 → 295. Herm. m., 12, 2, 4 commends as weapons the desire for righteousness and the fear of the Lord: ἡ ἐπιθυμία ἡ πονηρὰ ἐὰν ἴδῃ σε καθωπλισμένον τῷ φόβῳ τοῦ θεοῦ καὶ ἀντεστηκότα αὐτῇ, φεύξεται ἀπὸ σοῦ μακράν, καὶ οὐκέτι σοι ὀφθήσεται φοβουμένη τὰ ὅπλα σου. Cl. Al. Strom., VII, 11, 66, 1 finds in the Gnostic the only brave man because he has the right standard of goods and evils — in the true sense. Knowing that wickedness is his enemy and tears down what leads to *gnosis,* he fights against it, armed with the weapons of the Lord (τοῖς ὅπλοις τοῦ κυρίου πεφραγμένος). Stoic ideas are thus given a Christian tinge.

† ὁπλίζω.

Common from the time of Hom., rare in inscr. (Ditt. Syll.[3], 13, 10 [Athens, 6th cent. B.C.]), not in pap., LXX (though Σ Jer. 52:25). The basic sense is "to prepare": provisions for the way, Hom. Od., 2, 289, a meal, Eur. Ion, 852, sacrifice, *ibid.,* 1124, horses, Hom. Il., 23, 301, ships, Od., 17, 288, lamps, Aesch. Sept. c. Theb., 433. Used of men, esp. soldiers, "to equip with weapons," Hdt., I, 127; ὁπλίζει τὸν δῆμον πρότερον ψιλὸν ὄντα, Thuc., III, 27, 2; Jos. Ant., 20, 177; but also, in acc. with the basic sense, "to exercise," Hdt., VI, 12. Mid. and pass. also "to prepare oneself," for dancing, of women

---

[2] Pr.-Bauer[3], *s.v.,* considers sense 2. ("instruments" whereby to establish unrighteousness or righteousness), but he himself points out that account must be taken of the exclusive sense of "weapons" in Paul and early Christian literature.

[3] The vl. ἔργα (A D 88. 321) is an obvious assimilation to what precedes.

Hom. Od., 23, 143; with inf.: τοὶ δ' ὁπλίζοντο ... νέκυάς τ' ἀγέμεν, ἕτεροι δὲ μεθ' ὕλην (to fetch wood to the funeral pile), Il., 7, 417 f. Mostly "to arm oneself," "to arm" abs. ὁπλιζώμεθα θᾶσσον, Hom. Od., 24, 495, with acc. of object ὁπλίζεσθαι χέρα, "to arm one's hand," Eur. Or., 926, with instrum. dat. χαλκῷ, Hdt., II, 152, both together : ὁπλιζώμεσθα φασγάνῳ (sword) χέρας, Eur. Or., 1223, fig. abs. ὁπλίζου, καρδία, Eur. Med., 1242, or with acc. of reference ὁπλίζεσθαι θράσος, "to arm oneself with courage," Soph. El., 995 f.; cf. Anth. Pal., V, 92.

The word is used only fig. in the NT : 1 Pt. 4:1: Χριστοῦ οὖν παθόντος σαρκὶ καὶ ὑμεῖς τὴν αὐτὴν ἔννοιαν ὁπλίσασθε, "arm yourselves likewise with the same mind." It is best not to keep to the more general basic sense "prepare yourselves," since the specialised sense predominates in current usage. Furthermore, 1 Pt., even if in a less precise form, is still using the motif of the *militia Christi* (→ στρατιώτης, cf. 2:11). Materially the reference is to unavoidable sufferings. There is thus an intentional element of paradox in the expression. On the construction → *supra*.

Pol., 4, 1 offers a more didactic comparison : ὁπλισώμεθα τοῖς ὅπλοις (→ *supra*) τῆς δικαιοσύνης καὶ διδάξωμεν ἑαυτοὺς πρῶτον πορεύεσθαι ἐν τῇ ἐντολῇ τοῦ κυρίου. Cl. Al. Quis Div. Salv., 34, 2 classes χήρας πραότητι ὡπλισμένας among the divinely led στρατὸς ἄοπλος, which the rich man who is saved chooses for himself.

† πανοπλία.

Contents : 1. Linguistic Data ; 2. Archaeological Data ; 3. Data from the History of Religion : a. The Military Equipment of Deity ; b. Man as One who has a Share in this Equipment ; c. The πανοπλία of the Community according to Hebrew Manuscripts recently discovered in Palestine ; 4. πανοπλία in the New Testament ; 5. πανοπλία in the Vocabulary of the Church.

1. Linguistic Data.

The full equipment of the heavily armoured foot-soldier (from Hdt., poetic only in Aristoph., though cf. Tyrtaios Fr., 8, 38, Diehl, I, p. 13 πάνοπλοι, inscr. but not pap.), as war material πανοπλίαι χίλιαι, Polyb., 4, 56, 3; as booty τριακόσιαι πανοπλίαι, Thuc., III, 114, 1; the reward of a soldier who fought so bravely ὥστε στεφανωθῆναι καὶ πανοπλίαν λαβεῖν παρὰ τοῦ στρατηγοῦ, Isoc., 16, 29; also the prize in contests : (Hannibal) προέθηκε πανοπλίας Γαλατικάς, οἵαις εἰώθασιν οἱ βασιλεῖς αὐτῶν, ὅταν μονομαχεῖν μέλλωσι, κατακοσμεῖσθαι, Polyb., 3, 62, 5. Fig. only in bibl. lit. and that influenced by it. Epict. has the concept, though not the word, in a very different sense from Eph. 6:11 ff. when he speaks of animals having been given by nature all the things which they need in the service of men : ὥσπερ οἱ στρατιῶται ἕτοιμοί εἰσι τῷ στρατηγῷ ὑποδεδεμένοι ἐνδεδυμένοι ὡπλισμένοι, εἰ δ' ἔδει περιερχόμενον τὸν χιλίαρχον ὑποδεῖν ἢ ἐνδύειν τοὺς χιλίους, δεινὸν ἂν ἦν, οὕτω καὶ ἡ φύσις πεποίηκε τὰ πρὸς ὑπηρεσίαν γεγονότα ἕτοιμα παρεσκευασμένα μηδεμιᾶς ἐπιμελείας ἔτι προσδεόμενα (Diss., I, 16, 4). On the LXX → 296; on Philo → 298.

2. Archaeological Data.

The parts of the panoply remained much the same for centuries. But there is development both as a whole and in details. The shield becomes smaller. Body armour becomes heavier up to the Macedonian period, then lighter.[1]

π α ν ο π λ ί α. [1] For the panoply in the Mycenean, Homeric, Persian, and Macedonian-Hell. periods cf. Kromayer-Veith, Plates 1-5, 8.

We have two full descriptions of the equipment of the Roman legionary around the NT period. Pieces which have been found also help us to visualise it.[2] Polyb., 6, 23 tells us that the πανοπλία of the *hastati,* the *principes* and the *triarii* (who, however, carried lances instead of throwing spears) included the shield (θυρεός), the sword (μάχαιρα), two javelins (ύσσός = *pilum*), the helmet (περικεφαλαία) with crest, greaves (προκνημίς) and breastplate (καρδιοφύλαξ), or coat of mail for the wealthy (ἁλυσιδωτὸς θώραξ). Later the greaves, lance and heavy *pilum* were abandoned. Jos. Bell., 3, 93 ff. says that the legionaries of Titus (πεζοί) were equipped with armour, helmet (κράνος, mostly without crest), and shield (θυρεὸς ἐπιμήκης for the ranks, ἀσπίς oval or round shield for the general's bodyguard) as defensive weapons, sword (on the left), dagger (on the right) and javelin (the bodyguard, lance), as offensive weapons, also entrenching tools and provisions. Greaves disappeared ; they are heard of later, but only as items worn by officers on parade. On the other hand there is significant emphasis on the shoe (→ 311). The later imperial period tried to lighten the defensive weapons in order to make the offensive weapons more effective.

In the Orient the picture was much the same from an early period.[3] In the OT the defensive weapons are the shield (שֶׁלֶט[?] 2 S. 8:7; small מָגֵן 2 S. 1:21, big צִנָּה Jer. 46:3), the helmet (כּוֹבַע Ez. 27:10; קוֹבַע Ez. 23:24), armour (שִׁרְיָן 1 S. 17:38 or סִרְיוֹן Jer. 46:4), sometimes greaves (מִצְחוֹת 1 S. 17:6), finally the shoe (סְאוֹן Is. 9:4); the offensive weapons were the sword (חֶרֶב Ju. 8:10), the spear (חֲנִית 1 S. 18:11, רֹמַח Ju. 5:8, כִּידוֹן 1 S. 17:6, 45), and esp. for the lightly armed the bow (קֶשֶׁת 2 S. 1:22), the arrow (חֵץ Jer. 51:11) and finally the sling (קֶלַע 1 S. 17:40). Often the weapons are listed together in fairly full descriptions : helmet, armour, greaves, spear, shield and sword in 1 S. 17:5 ff., 45, 51 (Philistine); big and little shield, helmet, spear, armour, Jer. 46:3 f. (Egyptian); tunic, helmet, armour and sword, 1 S. 17:38 f. (Israelite); shield, lance, helmet, armour, bow, sling 2 Ch. 26:14 (the same). But there is no general term in Heb. In 2 Βασ. 2:21 LXX πανοπλία is used for חֲלִיצָה, which means clothing (*exuviae*), but includes civilian dress (στολάς at Ju. 14:19). πανοπλία is also used in error for אַרְבֶּה (locust) at Job 39:20. With no Heb. equivalent it occurs at Jdt. 14:3; Wis. 5:17; Sir. 46:6; 1 Macc. 13:29; 2 Macc. 3:25; 10:30; 11:8; 15:28; 4 Macc. 3:12 (A), and in 'Α (2 Βασ. 8:7; ψ 90:4) and Σ (4 Βασ. 11:10; ψ 90:4) for individual weapons in the Heb. The Semite thinks more concretely than the Greek. Jos. is a Hellenist in his use of the word (Ant., 4, 88 : τὰς πανοπλίας ἀναλαβόντες, 20, 110).

3. Data from the History of Religion.

a. The Military Equipment of Deity. Since man thinks of his gods as like himself, though omnipotent, the idea of armed deity is a natural one in the mythological thinking of all peoples. It is esp. coloured by meteorological phenomena. The Babylonian creation myth[4] mentions the following items of equipment used by Marduk (originally Enlil ?) to subdue Tiâmat : bow, arrow, quiver, club (? = lightning ?), net (= hurricane ?), mailed shirt, helmet (brightness) and war chariot (storm). An alabaster bas-relief[5] from the Ninurta temple in Nimrud (c. 880 B.C.) depicts a god with armour, helmet and sword, wielding triple pointed forked lightning in each hand. A relief from Boghazköi[6] (15th-13th cent. B.C. ?) depicts a war-god with a pointed helmet, armour (?), loin cloth, battle-axe and sword. The many representations of Teshub[7] with axe, sword and lightning are in the Hell. period transferred to Jupiter Dolichenus[8] (with Roman armour,

---

[2] Cf. Lindenschmit, also Kromayer-Veith, Plates 34-37.
[3] AOB, No. 9.
[4] c. 2000 B.C. AOT, 117, 35 ff.; 118, 57 f.
[5] AOB, No. 380.
[6] No. 341.
[7] No. 339, 340.
[8] No. 356.

double-headed axe, sword and lightning). In Gk. mythology the cloud is the helmet and shield of Zeus (→ IV, 903 f.), lightning his weapon of attack. Apollo as the god of pestilence has a bow and arrows. Athena esp. is depicted in full armour with the weapons of her father Zeus (Hom. Il., 5, 733-747; 8, 384-391; Plat. Leg., VII, 796c : πανοπλία παντελεῖ κοσμηθεῖσα, Athena of Aegina). ⁹

In the OT Yahweh, too, appears fully armed (cf. Is. 42:13, Yahweh as a man of war). But in the texts as we have them the concept is spiritualised. Among the oldest is Is. 59:17: "Yahweh put on righteousness as a breastplate (כַּשִּׁרְיָן ὡς θώ- ρακα), and (put on) the helmet of salvation (כּוֹבַע יְשׁוּעָה περικεφαλαίαν σωτη- ρίου) on his head." A post-exilic psalmist prays : "Yahweh ... fight against them that fight against me. Take hold of target (מָגֵן ὅπλου) and shield (צִנָּה θυρεοῦ, which the shieldbearer carries before the battle), ... draw also the spear (חֲנִית LXX inaccurately ῥομφαίαν) and battle-axe (? Mas. סְגֹר, LXX σύγκλεισον, read perhaps סַגָּר, cf. σάγαρις, the battle-axe of the Scythians, Hdt., I, 215) against them that persecute me," Ps. 35:1 ff. Both passages are poetic. They do not try to give a full description, but a fairly complete picture emerges when they are combined. Repeated mention is also made of Yahweh's sword, javelin and bow (Is. 34:6; Ez. 21:8 ff.; Ps. 7:12 f.; Hab. 3:9 ff., ¹⁰ → III, 340). Finally there is an explicit and comprehensive depiction in Wis. 5:17-22, where creation — this ancient view is surprising in so late a document — is presented as Yahweh's levy against the powers of the deep : λήμψεται πανοπλίαν ... καὶ ὁπλοποιήσει τὴν κτίσιν εἰς ἄμυναν ἐχθρῶν· ἐνδύσεται θώρακα δικαιοσύνην καὶ περιθήσεται κόρυθα κρίσιν ... λήμψεται ἀσπίδα ἀκαταμάχητον ὁσιότητα, ὀξυνεῖ δὲ ... ὀργὴν εἰς ῥομφαίαν ... πορεύσονται ... βολίδες ἀστραπῶν καὶ ὡς ἀπὸ εὐ- κύκλου τόξου τῶν νεφῶν ἐπὶ σκοπὸν ἁλοῦνται, καὶ ἐκ πετροβόλου θυμοῦ πλήρεις ῥιφήσονται χάλαζαι. Off-shoots may still be found in Rev. 1:16; 2:12, 16; 6:1 ff.; 19:11-21.

b. Man as One who has a Share in this Equipment. The idea that man is secure and invincible because of weapons given him by deity is very old. Often connected with magic, it finds reflection in the myths of various peoples. It takes on new content in the OT where it is related to the omnipotent and holy God. But even outside the Bible it is often spiritualised and moralised. It finds a special niche in the idea of the one who fights for God (→ στρατιώτης).

In this connection we might mention Odin's helmet as a cap of invisibility, also the invincibility of Achilles and Siegfried, the former by virtue of the armour forged by Hephaistos, the latter by virtue of the sword Balmung. In the OT Yahweh intervenes with His weapons on behalf of the upright against ungodly foes (Ps. 35:1 ff.). He also holds the shield of the righteous, wields his sword for him, and shoot his arrows (Ps. 7:11 ff.). His faithfulness is a shield and buckler (Ps. 91:4). Sir. 46:2 ff., on the basis of Jos. 8:18, 26, depicts Joshua as God's champion to whose lance God gives miraculous power and who acc. to Jos. 10:11 is aided by God's own weapons hurled down from heaven. ¹¹ Even more strongly mythological, though with ethical depth, is the presenta-

---

⁹ To-day in the Munich collection, Photo Giraudon, 5010. Cf. also Haas, 13/14 (1928), No. 5, 50, 81, 82, 150, 153, 175. The many breasts of the Ephesian Artemis (Haas, 9/11 Leipoldt [1926], No. 130) are perhaps misunderstood buckles. The regular absence of the sword is worth noting.

¹⁰ Though the text is uncertain, the ref. is plain.

¹¹ The LXX has introduced the term by error in v. 6c. The original was probably : "... that the peoples of destruction might see (cf. 16:9a גּוֹי חֶרְמוֹ read as חַרְבּוֹ "גּ?, R. Smend, D. Weisheit d. Jesus Sirach erklärt [1906], 441; αὐτοῦ from the inauthentic 16:9c ?) that the Lord detected (צוֹפֶה) their war (read αὐτῶν, Smend)" [Katz].

tion of this thought in Test. XII. Levi receives from an angel a shield and sword (ὅπλον καὶ ῥομφαίαν) to avenge the wrong done to Dinah (Gn. 34), Test. L. 5:3; cf. 6:1. But Joseph, too, is in rapture given a sword whereby to resist the temptations of Potiphar's wife, so that her magical plots do not hurt him, Test. Jos. 6:2. Behind the lustful woman is Beliar (7:4), and the chief weapon with which to fight him is prayer (3:3; 8:1; 9:4). The spiritualising is expressly emphasised in Mandaean Gnosticism : "My elect! Arm yourselves with an armour which is not of iron. Let your armour be Nāṣāreanship, and the true speeches of the place of light." [12]

The Persian moralises completely : (It is possible to win Ahuramazda and heaven, and to escape Ahriman and hell) "if one makes the spirit of wisdom one's rearguard, and carries the spirit of content with life as weapon and armour and defence, and takes the spirit of truth as a shield, the spirit of gratitude as a club, the spirit of full vigilance as a bow, the spirit of generosity as an arrow ; and if one takes the spirit of moderation as a spear, the spirit of steadfastness as a gauntlet and the spirit of (belief in) destiny as armour." [13] The allegorising of the items of equipment is not always clear, but perhaps it is intentionally paradoxical in parts.

In Philo the ideas of nature philosophy are very much attenuated. Nature has equipped every living creature to protect itself against attack καὶ ἀνθρώπῳ μέγιστον ἔρυμα καὶ φρουρὰν ἀκαθαίρετον λόγον (speech) δέδωκεν, οὗ κραταιῶς οἷα πανοπλίας ἐνειλημμένος οἰκεῖον καὶ προσφυέστατον ἕξει δορυφόρον, Som., I, 103. As the horse neighs and the dog barks, so man speaks rationally. The creature most dear to God has had rational speech given to him as ἔρυμα, περίβλημα, πανοπλία, τεῖχος, Som., I, 108.

Oepke

c. The πανοπλία of the Community according to Hebrew Manuscripts recently discovered in Palestine. [14]

In the Dead Sea Scrolls [15] we are made acquainted with a sect of Palestinian Judaism which belongs to the 1st cent. B.C. and which in its understanding of itself and its forms of expression shows surprising affinities to the NT community. This sect understands its existence in the world as a situation of conflict. Its members, the sons of light (בני אור), are engaged in battle against the world, the sons of darkness (בני חושך), the kingdom (ממשלת) of Belial, of Satan. Thus in the *Manual of Discipline* (col. 1, lines 9-11), in a series of rules and ethical demands for him who enters the sect, covenant (ברית), or community (עדה; יחד), we read :

[12] Lidz. Ginza, 27, 4 f.; cf. 45, 4 f.

[13] Dînâ-î Moînôg-î Khirad, 43 (SBE, 24, 84, c. 600 A.D.), cf. H. Junker, "Über iranische Quellen d. hell. Aion-Vorstellung," *Vorträge d. Bibliothek Warburg*, I (1923), 140, 164, n. 54.

[14] Editor's Note : In view of the new discoveries this section was contributed by K. G. Kuhn and incorporated into Oepke's already completed art. so as to present these important contemporary parallels to the NT concept of the *militia Christi* and the Christian's πανοπλία.

[15] Extracts from the *The Manual of Discipline*, the *Habakkuk Commentary*, the *Psalms of Thanksgiving* and the *Book of the War of the Sons of Light against the Sons of Darkness* are used. In part these have not yet been transcribed and in this account, written in January, 1950, use has been made of the text thus far published by Sukenik and, as regards the *Manual of Discipline*, a reduced photographic reproduction. Some of the readings on which my renderings are based may thus be uncertain.

Abbreviations in this section : Sukenik = E. L. Sukenik, מגילות גנוזות, *Bialikfond Jerusalem* (1948) (quoted by page and line); BASOR = *Bulletin of the American Schools of Oriental Research*, Jerusalem-Baghdad ; *Hodajot*, מגילת ההודיות, *The Psalms of Thanksgiving* (quoted from Sukenik); *Milhama* מגילת מלחמת בני אור בבני חושך, *The Book of the War of the Sons of Light against the Sons of Darkness* (quoted by column and page acc. to Sukenik's rendering); *The Manual of Discipline* (quoted by col. and p. of the MS acc. to the photographic reproduction of col. 1 by J. C. Trever, BASOR, 111 (1948), 10.

"And to love all the sons of light, each corresponding to his lot in the council of God, [16] and to hate all the sons of darkness, each corresponding to his guilt by virtue of the wrath of God." The sect's task in the world is to be steadfast, cf. col. 1, line 17 f.: "And not to yield for any fear or anxiety or purgation (i.e., test: מצרף) in life [17] in the kingdom of Belial." [18] Cf. also *Milhama*, col. 13, lines 8-9, where what remains of the text contains the demand not to yield; also Sukenik, p. 20, line 5.

As the world is here the kingdom of Satan, and the existence of the righteous within it is מצרף = πειρασμός, [19] so the enemies who must be fought are the sons of darkness (*Manual of Discipline* and *Milhama*), the host of Belial (חיל בליעל) (*Milhama*, Sukenik, 19, 7), or the community of Belial (עדת בליעל) *Hodajot*, Sukenik, 29, 5), the community of falsehood (סוד שוא) (*ibid.*, 29, 5), the community of iniquity (עדת רשעה) (*Milhama*, Sukenik, 20, 6). In *Milhama* according to Sukenik, 19, 6 they are also described historically and nationally (though the question arises whether the references are literal or figurative) as "the hordes of Edom and Moab and the Ammonites ... the land of the Philistines and the hordes of the Assyrian Kittians." [20]

By contrast the community is יחד אל the community of God (*Manual of Discipline*, col. 1, line 12), ברית אל covenant of God (*Milhama*, col. 12, line 4; cf. also Damasc. 7:5; 14:2), סוד עולם the eternal fellowship (*Hodajot*, Sukenik, 31, 7), צבא קדושים the host of the saints (*ibid.*, 31, 9), עדת בני שמים the community of the sons of heaven (*ibid.*, 31, 10); [21] also עם קודשכה thy sacred people in *Milhama*, e.g., col. 12, line 12 and in the portion in Sukenik, 21, 5. In *Milhama* (Sukenik, 19, 4 f.) they are also "the sons of Levi and the sons of Judah and the sons of Benjamin" who have gone out from "the desert of the nations (עמים) to the camp (חנה) in the desert of Jerusalem." Similarly in *Milhama* (Sukenik, 24, 5 from the bottom) the host of the sons of light goes to the camp (מחנה) after the battle and there gives praise for God's help in a service of thanksgiving. The concept מחנה thus bears the double sense of the military camp and the camp in the desert (cf.

---

[16] On this expression and concept (גורלו בעצת אל) cf. Eph. 5:5 οὐκ ἔχει κληρονομίαν ἐν τῇ βασιλείᾳ ... θεοῦ, also κλῆρος in Ac. 26:18; Col. 1:12 etc. The expression ב גורלו = ἔχειν κληρονομίαν or κλῆρον ἐν is common in these texts.

[17] It is uncertain whether לחיים is the right reading.

[18] ממשלת בליעל occurs also in the *Manual of Discipline*, col. 1, lines 23-24: "All committals of their (i.e., those who enter the covenant) iniquity and their sin in the kingdom of Belial"; cf. also *Milhama*, col. 12, lines 9 and 10. Cf. Test. Dan. 6:2, 4, where the kingdom of the enemy is used in the same sense. In the NT Mt. 12:26; Lk. 11:18; Ac. 26:18: ἡ ἐξουσία τοῦ σατανᾶ.

[19] Cf. Damasc. 20:27: "All those who do evil to Judah (i.e., the people) בימי מצרפותיו in the days of his testings." As here the sing occurs along with the plur., so the NT speaks of both πειρασμός and πειρασμοί with the same ref. to life in the world as in the kingdom of Satan: Lk. 22:28: ἐν τοῖς πειρασμοῖς μου, 8:13 πειρασμός = Mk. 4:17 and Mt. 13:21 θλῖψις ἢ διωγμός, also Lk. 4:13; Jm. 1:2 alongside 1:12; cf. already Sir. 2:1-5.

[20] The last are perhaps the Seleucids; cf. O. Eissfeldt, "Der gegenwärtige Stand d. Erforschung der in Palästina neugefundenen hbr. Handschriften, 2" ThLZ, 74 (1949), 97.

[21] Members of this community thus bear the self-designations בני שמים (cf. ἐπουράνιοι, 1 C. 15:48) and קדושים = ἅγιοι (so also in *Milhama* in the verse which Sukenik uses as a heading on his dedication page: קדושי עמו, the saints of thy people) and בחורי אל = ἐκλεκτοὶ θεοῦ (Habakkuk Comm., col. 10, line 13); hence the same titles as the NT community.

the camp of the children of Israel in the wilderness wandering). Highly significant in this connection is the fact that in the Damascus Document the individual settlement or congregation is regularly called מחנה or camp.

In Milḥama the war between these opponents is presented in the form of an explicit though schematic description of the regular actions in a battle. This is where the equipment as well as the composition and disposition of the army of the sons of light is so important. According to Sukenik 20, 1 f. it consists of חניתות (lances), זרקות (darts), כידונים (throwing spears), מגינים (shields). There is specific mention in Milḥama, col. 7, line 1 of the אנשי הקלע, the slingers, who have to throw seven times ; in line 4 of the שלושה דגלי בינים, the three sections of advance troops ; in line 4 f. of the אנשי הרכב מימין ומשמאול the cavalry on the right hand and on the left (are we to think here of 2 C. 6:7: διὰ τῶν ὅπλων τῆς δικαιοσύνης τῶν δεξιῶν καὶ ἀριστερῶν?); in lines 7-8 : On the approach of the hostile line they are to grasp their weapons ; line 11: זרקות המלחמה.

To understand these sources it is important to note that Hodajot, too, often uses military imagery. Thus in one psalm (Sukenik, p. 32, lines 7-8) we read : "When all the arrows of destruction fly, so that no resistance is possible, and they shoot so that there is no hope." Another psalm (p. 29, last line — p. 30, line 3) refers plainly, from the context, to the situation of the righteous in the world : "Mighty men have pitched (חנו) their camp against me. They encompass me with all their weapons, and shoot arrows hopelessly,[22] and their flaming spear is like fire consuming trees" (וירו חצים ... ולהוב חנית כאש).

If one compares Eph. 6:16 (πάντα τὰ βέλη τοῦ πονηροῦ τὰ πεπυρωμένα) the great similarity both of the image and also of the sense is immediately apparent. In the light of the new discoveries verses like R. 13:12 (ἐνδυσώμεθα δὲ τὰ ὅπλα τοῦ φωτός)[23] and Eph. 6:11 (πρὸς τὸ δύνασθαι ὑμᾶς στῆναι πρὸς τὰς μεθοδείας τοῦ διαβόλου) acquire a new vividness and a rich background.

4. πανοπλία in the New Testament.

In the NT the word occurs only in metaphor and allegory. In the parable of the overcoming of the strong man Lk. (11:22) introduces the concept of an armed conflict and thus brings in the word πανοπλία. In this respect he shows himself to be a Hellenist.

The word occurs twice in the allegory of our spiritual armour in Eph. 6:10 ff.: v. 11: ἐνδύσασθε τὴν πανοπλίαν τοῦ θεοῦ πρὸς τὸ δύνασθαι ὑμᾶς στῆναι πρὸς τὰς μεθοδείας τοῦ διαβόλου, v. 13 : διὰ τοῦτο ἀναλάβετε τὴν πανοπλίαν τοῦ θεοῦ, ἵνα δυνηθῆτε ἀντιστῆναι ἐν τῇ ἡμέρᾳ τῇ πονηρᾷ καὶ ἅπαντα κατεργασάμενοι στῆναι. Paul likes to sound a manly note, especially in the concluding exhortations of his epistles (cf. 1 C. 15:58; 16:13; R. 13:11 ff.; 16:20). Here the concept of the militia Christi (→ στρατιώτης) is worked out far more graphically than anywhere else.[24] The verbs used are taken from military speech (→ 294;

---

[22] לאין מרפא means the same as לאין תקוה: in the previous verse : "so that there is no deliverance."

[23] The first and related part of R. 13:12 (ἀποθώμεθα οὖν τὰ ἔργα τοῦ σκότους) finds exact equivalents in these new texts : Milḥama, quoted in Sukenik, p. 20, line 6 : ובחושך כל מעשיהם = Gk. καὶ ἐν σκότει πάντα τὰ ἔργα αὐτῶν.

[24] That OT knowledge here replaces the vivid observation of Pl. in 1 Th. 5:8 (Holtzmann NT, ad loc.) is a hazardous judgment.

313). This is, or is almost, the last hour, ἡ ἡμέρα ἡ πονηρά. The enemy is making a particularly severe attack. Hence one must be ready to fight. Six items of equipment, grouped 3 + 3, are then listed in vv. 14-17 in a free but realistic order. First we have the girdle, breastplate and shoes, then the shield, helmet and sword. The absence of the spear cannot be explained archaeologically, but no effort was made to be complete (→ 297), and in any case it would be hard to give a separate interpretation for the lance as compared with the sword. The demons fight artfully from a distance (βέλη, v. 16). The believer, however, must fight hand to hand (πάλη, v. 12). Hence no *pilum* is needed. Except in points of detail (e.g., the dagger), the items correspond exactly to the equipment of the Roman legionary of Paul's day. Characteristic is the absence of greaves, the long four-cornered shield, the *caliga* (→ ὑποδέω). According to the monuments the latter is part of the equipment only from the Roman period, when long marches were required (→ 311). Paul, then, is not romancing; he has in view the harsh and stern reality of the soldier's life. [25] This does not mean that OT motifs are not also present, for in the main OT equipment is much the same. The apostle sees these earlier examples with contemporary eyes.

Since the demons are not creatures of flesh and blood and cannot be fought with the weapons of this world (v. 12), it is necessary to put on the πανοπλία τοῦ θεοῦ. The gen. is an elastic subj. gen. The OT allusions (→ 297, 309) [26] lead strongly to the idea that God gives believers parts of His own personal armour. This mythical concept is in the background. [27] But possibly it is not wholly clear even to Paul himself. One is rather given the impression that God is the supreme commander who sees to it that the soldiers are provided with the weapons which they are to use in His service. [28] The allegorising implies spiritualising, though not evaporation. This raises the question of the distinctive theology of the passage.

At a first glance one seems to be in the world of late Hellenistic superstition. Is not the conflict simply against the *heimarmene*, the στοιχεῖα or δαιμόνια, which bring sickness and all other evils on man and against which he is defenceless? In general one fights demons by means of conjurations. But there is no mention of these here. Even the ῥῆμα θεοῦ (v. 17), if not exactly the same as ὁ λόγος τοῦ θεοῦ, cannot be regarded as a magic formula. We must also remember that the passage is the impressive conclusion to the wholly ethical exhortation of 4:17-6:9. The concern, then, is that believers should not yield to the assault of temptation and to all the evils which this brings in its train if successful. That the battle is thus religious and moral is also shown by the description of the spirits as πνευματικὰ τῆς πονηρίας (v. 12), and also by the exhoration to prayer and intercession (vv. 18 ff.). To this degree there is some relation to the ancient Persian text quoted earlier (→ 298), and yet the flavour

---

[25] Paul would have had excellent opportunities to see Roman legions at least in Syria and Palestine (cf. the review of the distribution of the legions in Kromayer-Veith, Plate 52 and 474). But the *provinciae pacatae*, too, were not entirely denuded of military strength.

[26] The influence of Wis. 5:17 ff. is probable. Cf. E. Grafe, "Das Verhältnis d. paul. Schriften zur Sap.," *Festschr. Weizsäcker* (1892), 278 f.; Haupt Gefbr., ad loc.

[27] This is considered in Dib. Gefbr. Exc. ad loc. The suggestion of Haupt Gefbr., on v. 11: "Armour which corresponds to the nature of God," is weak. Better Ew. Gefbr., ad loc.: "The total equipment which comes from God."

[28] It is unwise to press the δέξασθε of v. 17 in this sense (Haupt Gefbr., ad loc.). For one thing, it is textually a little uncertain. For another, δέχεσθαι can simply mean "to take" (Lk. 22:17). Cf. Pr.-Bauer³, *s.v.* δέχομαι 2.

of the passage is quite different, not merely because it is much more vivid and
life-like, but also because the reference is to protective divine realities (→ the
individual articles which follow) rather than to moral qualities. The Bible tracks
down the conflict between God and evil to its transcendental depths, and it
realises far better than Parseeism that man's existence depends absolutely on the
decision in this conflict. Man can triumph in the struggle against the threatening
powers of darkness only "in the Lord, and in the power of his might" (v. 10).

5. πανοπλία in the Vocabulary of the Church.

In the lit. of the Church the word disappears almost with out a trace. Ign., in a
passage which contains several technical military terms (→ στρατιώτης), writes :
τὸ βάπτισμα ὑμῶν μενέτω ὡς ὅπλα, ἡ πίστις ὡς περικεφαλαία, ἡ ἀγάπη ὡς
δόρυ, ἡ ὑπομονὴ ὡς πανοπλία, Pol., 6, 2. The influence of Eph. 6 is possible, though
not certain. The expression is less vivid and to some degree alien. Love armed with a
spear is perhaps an intentional paradox. In this he goes beyond Paul. Oddly enough
πανοπλία is one item amongst others, as though it meant armour ; the comparison with
patience would fit in with this. As a catalogue of virtues the passage is closer to Persian
moralism (→ 298) than Eph. Cl. Al. often quotes from Eph. 6:10 ff., but he uses πανοπλία only once in a very Stoic context, Strom., II, 20, 109, 2.

† ζώννυμι (ζωννύω), † διαζώννυμι, † περιζώννυμι (περιζωννύω), † ζώνη.

I. Girdle and Girding in Graeco-Roman Antiquity.

The girdle fulfils many purposes in antiquity. 1. It is a means of fastening the articles
of clothing, or of shortening the undergarment, esp. in the case of women (putting on
the girdle is part of dressing, Hom. Od., 5, 231; 10, 544; Il., 14, 181; Hdt., I, 51, 5 etc.),
but also men, often ζωστήρ, though ζώνη of, e.g., the girdle of Orion (Aristot. Meteor.,
I, 6, p. 343b, 24). The verbs, esp. the simple form, are rare in Attic. The act. is used
with acc. of person : περιζῶσαι τὸ παιδίον, Rufus in Oribasius Incerta, 20, 1 (ed.
U. C. Bussemaker and C. Daremberg [1851 ff.], III, 154, 12); also with material obj.:
νῆα ... ἔζωσαν πάμπρωτον εὐστρεφεῖ ἔνδοθεν ὅπλῳ, Apoll. Rhod., I, 367 f. of
shipbuilding, though cf. in Appian Bell. Civ., V, 91 διαζώννυσθαι τὰ σκάφη in the
sense of Ac. 27:17. The pass. sometimes means "to be fastened" : πύργοι ... ἐζωσμένοι
(on elephants), 1 Macc. 6:37. Most common is the middle "to gird oneself" abs.: Κλέων
... περιζωσάμενος (setting himself in position), ἐδημηγόρησε, Aristot. Res Publica
Atheniensium, 28, 3; of a cook : περιζωσάμενος, with fastened apron, Alexis Fr., 174, 11
(CAF, II, 363); with dat. Odysseus ζώσατο ... ῥάκεσιν, had girded himself with
rags, Od., 18, 67; often with acc. of obj., "to gird on something," "to tie on something,"
ἐσθῆτα, Plut. Romulus, 16 (I, 27b); τήβεννον (the toga, to free the left arm), Plut.
Coriolan., 9 (I, 217d); the shirt up to the thigh, Plut. Anton., 4 (I, 917d); διαζώννυσθαι
τριβώνιον (little mantle), Luc. Quomodo Historia Conscribenda Sit, 3; also with acc.
of the part of the body and instr. dat.: ζώννυσθαι τὰς κοιλίας ζώναις, Theopompus
Historicus Fr., 39a (ed. B. Grenfell and A. Hunt in Hellenica Oxyrhynchia [1909]).
People girded themselves for going out (Hes. Op., 345), for work (Aristoph. Av., 1148 f.
jokingly : rumours, girded high, bore tiles περιεζωσμέναι ἐπλινθοφόρουν); ἐπὶ βουσίν,
Apoll. Rhod., I, 425 f.; for dancing, Polyb., 30, 22, 10; for athletic contests, Od., 24, 89.
Activity is denoted by girding oneself, rest by ungirding, Hdt., VIII, 120. This applies
also to a traveller during involuntary rest : ἀπέδησε τὴν ζώνην ἑαυτοῦ, Epigr. Graec.,
482, 3.

ζ ώ ν ν υ μ ι κ τ λ. Note : If Paul in Eph. 6:14 ff. mentions the parts of the panoply in
the order in which they were put on, this leads among other things to certain inferences
as to the nature of the items in view. It is thus as well to deal with the following individual
pieces in the order of the text.

2. The golden, richly decorated and often colourful girdle is for adornment, esp. in the case of women (→ 302). A marriage contract of 127 A.D. mentions among the bride's portion ζώνας δύο σανδυκίνην ροδίνην (red and pink), P. Oxy., III, 496, 4, cf. I, 109, 11.

3. The girdle, originally the roll of clothing caused by it, but apparently also the girdle specially made for the purpose, serves as a pocket, a place to keep valuables, esp. money : ζώνη χρυσίου (purse with gold), Luc. Fugitivi, 31; ζώνη χάλκους (with copper coins), Plut. Quaest. Conv., IV, 2, 3 (II, 665b); P. Ryl., II, 127, 32 (29 A.D.): ζώνη ἐν ᾗ κέρματ(ος) (δραχμαὶ) δ, 141, 22 (37 A.D.): robbed ἀργ(υρίου) (δραχμὰς π̄ καὶ ζώνην, also a place where the barbarian kept his dagger, Xenoph. An., I, 6, 10; IV, 7, 16.

4. The girdle is an item of military equipment. In this sense it was used in different ways at different times. a. In the Mycenean period, whose customs are partly presupposed in Hom., there was no armour, but only a leather body-girdle, which was fairly broad, and which was often furnished with metal studs and clasps, partly for adornment and partly for strength. [1] The tt. for it is μίτρη "band" (→ IV, 605). As distinct from this the ζωστήρ is usually the simple girdle and the ζῶμα a kind of loin cloth ; neither is for protection. Yet the distinction is not maintained strictly. The related verb undoubtedly means putting on the military girdle. ζώννυσθαι ζωστῆρι (II., 10, 77 f.) is synon. with the abs. ζώννυσθαι (11, 15; 23, 685 [683 ζῶμα], 710), ζώννυσθαι μίτρη (5, 857) or χαλκόν (23, 130). b. With the coming of armour the body girdle disappears. Instead, to protect the thighs there is worn a kind of apron which hung under the armour, which was made of loose or sewn thongs of leather, and which was like breeches in the Roman period. [2] c. The Roman legionary also wore above his armour a broad leather belt studded with metal which with its hanging ends, issuing in strong metal strips, protected the lower body, cf. P. Petr., III, 6a, 27 (3rd cent. B.C.): θώρακα καὶ τὴν ζώνην θωρακῖτιν. In many cases this belt serves also as a sword-belt, [3] while in others the sword, or more rarely the dagger, is carried in a special strap running over the right or left shoulder. [4] 4. The body belt — conspicuously marked ? — was a sign of rank and thus a kind of cingulum. οἱ ὑπὸ ζώνην are officers (Suid. s.v. αὐθεντήσαντα, Codex Justinianus, I, 5, 12; 6, 11). Among the Persians seizing by the belt denotes the death sentence on an unfaithful officer, Xenophon. An., I, 6, 10.

In a transf. sense ζώνη is used in many different ways. Among women it is a sign of virginity. λύειν παρθενίην ζώνην is a veiled description of intercourse (Hom. Od., 11, 245), med. of the bride, to have loosed the girdle to only one man, Anth. Pal., VII, 324. Hence ζώνη can mean "marriage" (Eur. Iph. Taur., 204) or sexual intercourse (Philostr. Vit. Ap., VII, 6). The word is also used for the ocean as the girdle of the earth, Plut. Fac. Lun., 21 (II, 935a), then fig. for the zones of the earth, exclusively so in Philo, Leg. All., III, 171; Rer. Div. Her., 147; Vit. Mos., I, 114. The purposeful establishment of zones plays a great part in the nature theology of antiquity. [5] Finally there is ref. to the planetary spheres (Corp. Herm., I, 25), the zodiac (Porphyr. in Ptolemaei Tetrabiblon, ed. Basel [1559], p. 186), or the personified watchers, the angels of the

---

[1] Kromayer-Veith, Plate 1, No. 3.

[2] Ibid., Plate 4, No. 18-21; 5, No. 23; 34, No. 104/5; 36, No. 111; Lindenschmit, Plate 2, No. 1; 3, No. 1; 4, No. 1. When, however, Polyb., 6, 25, 3 refers to the περίζωμα rather than the θώραξ of older Roman cavalry he is not thinking just of the loin cloth but of a white garment fastened by a strap. This often occurs on monuments, Lindenschmit, Plate 4, No. 2; 5, No. 1 and 3; 6, No. 1 and 2; 7, No. 2.

[3] Lindenschmit, Plate 3, No. 2; 4, No. 2.

[4] Ibid., 4, No. 1. We also find two crossing hip-straps, ibid., Plate 5, No. 1 and 3. Jos. Ant., 6, 184 has the current περιζωννύναι τινὶ τὸ ξίφος for the LXX ἔζωσεν τὸν Δαυιδ τὴν ῥομφαίαν αὐτοῦ (1 Βασ. 17:39; Appian Rom. Hist. Hannibal, 20).

[5] M. Dibelius, "Pls. auf dem Areopag," SAH, 1938/39 (1939), 8-14 makes a convincing attempt on this ground to substitute a "philosophical" explanation of Ac. 17:26 f. for the usual "historical" understanding.

zones (Damascius De Principiis, 96, ed. Ruelle [1889], p. 241, 19). The verbs, however, are seldom used fig. ζωννύναι may be used for an embrace in wrestling (Paus., VIII, 40, 2), or of the ocean (Anth. Pal., IX, 778), περιζωννύναι with personal obj. Aristoph. Pax, 686 f.: ἀπορῶν ὁ δῆμος ἐπιτρόπου καὶ γυμνὸς ὢν τοῦτον τέως τὸν ἄνδρα περιεζώσατο, or with dat. τοῖς ἐντέροις τινός, to hang oneself around with someone's entrails (Philodem. De Ira, ed. C. Wilke [1914], 26, 16 f.). Pass. in a magical connection : ὄνομά μοι καρδία περιεζωσμένη ὄφιν (words of the demon Akephalos : my name is "a heart girt about with a serpent," Preis. Zaub., V, 157).

II. Girdle and Girding in the Old Testament and Judaism.

For ζώνη the OT has a whole list of equivalents (מֵזַח ,אַבְנֵט ,אֵזוֹר ,אֵזֵן ,חֲגוֹר ,חֲגוֹרָה) [6] which are used with no apparent distinction except for אַבְנֵט, exclusively the girdle of the high-priest and princes, and אֵזֵן, whose meaning is uncertain, possibly armour. (מֵזִיח) מֵזַח Ps. 109:19 — elsewhere fig.: dam, Is. 23:10 (Job 12:21?) — is an Egyptian loan word. The LXX often has other renderings : περίζωμα = חֲגוֹרָה Gn. 3:7; = חֲגוֹר, Prv. 31:24; = אֵזוֹר, Jer. 13:1, 2, 4, 6 f., 10 f.; παραζώνη = חֲגוֹרָה, 2 Βασ. 18:11; ποίκιλμα = אֵזוֹר Ez. 23:15, cf. also ἐζωσμένος = אֵזוֹר, Is. 11:5. Since it is more a question of loose rendering than exact equivalents with חָבַשׁ ,כִּרְבֵּל שִׂים and אָסַר ζώννυμι and περιζώννυμι [7] are used only for the verbs אֵזֵר and חָגַר, the former also in the ni, pi and hitp. The person girded is in the acc. (ζώσεις αὐτούς, Ex. 29:9), with the pass. the nom. (καὶ ἔσται ἐζωσμένος, Is. 11:5), the part of the body covered with the med. and pass. in the acc. (ζῶσαι ... τὴν ὀσφύν σου, Job 38:3; ἐζωσμένος τὴν ὀσφὺν αὐτοῦ, Ez. 9:11). What is put on is usually in the acc. [8] (ἔζωσεν τὸν Δαυιδ τὴν ῥομφαίαν αὐτοῦ, 1 Βασ. 17:39; ζώνην δερματίνην περιεζωσμένος τὴν ὀσφὺν αὐτοῦ, 4 Βασ. 1:8; περιεζώσαντο σάκκους ἐπὶ τὰς ὀσφύας αὐτῶν, 3 Βασ. 21:32), but often the dat., ζώνῃ λινῇ ζώσεται (Lv. 16:4), or in Hebraic fashion the instr. ἐν (Δαυιδ περιεζωσμένος ἐν στολῇ βυσσίνῃ, 1 Ch. 15:27; περιεζωσμένος ἐν δυναστείᾳ, ψ 64:6: נֶאְזָר בִּגְבוּרָה). Other renderings are ἀναζώννυμαι = חָגַר, Prv. 31:17, very freely κυρτός = חָגַר 3 Βασ. 21(20):11, and obscurely ἑορτάσει for תַּחְגֹּר ψ 75:11; the text is corrupt.

The significance of the girdle is much the same as in Graeco-Roman antiquity. 1. It is an article of clothing of linen or leather, Prv. 31:24; 2 Βασ. 18:11; Jer. 13:1. To gird up one's loins, to fasten one's clothes by a girdle, is to prepare for hasty departure (4 Βασ. 4:29; 9:1). The first passover was to be eaten with loins girded, Ex. 12:11. People also gird themselves for work (Prv. 31:17), for prophetic ministry (Jer. 1:17) and for debate (Job 38:3; 40:7 → supra, unless fig. = sense 4. → 305). The leather girdle of the prophet Elijah (4 Βασ. 1:8) is perhaps made of raw leather. [9] At any rate, his apparel marks him as a follower of the stern God of the desert as distinct from the voluptuous Baal. In keeping is the picture of the fine runner who, high-girded, [10] runs before the king's chariot, 1 K. 18:46.

2. It is used for adornment e.g., of the marshal of the royal court, Is. 22:21; the girdle woven of blue, purple and scarlet is part of the raiment of the high-priest, Ex. 39:29; cf. 28:4; 29:5, 9; Lv. 8:7, 13; 16:4; 1 S. 2:18; the golden girdle is also part of the adornment of the angel, Da. 10:5. On the other hand, it can denote disgrace or deep sorrow to be girded with a grass-rope (Is. 3:24) or with sackcloth, i.e., coarse, hairy material

---

[6] Cf. also חֵשֶׁב for the girdle on the ephod and the high-priestly vestment, and קִשֻּׁרִים for the bridal girdle. קֶסֶת (ζώνη at LXX Ez. 9:2, 3, 11) does not mean girdle but inkstand.

[7] διαζώννυμι in the LXX only at Ez. 23:15 A (probably dittography).

[8] Cf. Helbing Kasussyntax, 47.

[9] Cf. H. Gressmann, D. Schriften d. AT, I (1910), 281. Joüon suggests a kind of girdle used in modesty when there is no undergarment.

[10] The term has come down in a corrupt form.

(2 S. 3:31; 1 K. 20:32; Is. 3:24; 15:3; Lam. 2:10 etc.). [11]

3. It is also a pocket, though not for valuables, since impressed coins came only in the Persian period, and noble metals used for exchange were kept elsewhere. In Ez. 9:2, 3, 11, however, the prophet in a vision sees a man who carries pen and ink (not understood by LXX) at his side, i.e., on or in a girdle. זוֹן, זוֹנֵי, זוֹנִין are Rabb. loan words for the girdle, which is also called פּוּנְדָּא = *funda* (purse for money), Str.-B., I, 564 f.

4. It is also an item of military equipment, a. to fasten undergarments and also for adornment and to distinguish officers ; b. to protect the lower part of the body as a ringed girdle supplementing armour, 1 K. 22:34, misunderstood by LXX → 309, n. 7; c. mostly as a sword belt clasped round the tunic, 1 S. 17:39; 18:4; 25:13; Neh. 4:12; 2 S. 20:8, [12] also on parade, Ps. 45:3. "Each who bore the girdle" (כֹּל חֹגֵר חֲגֹרָה, πᾶς περιεζωσμένος ζώνην, 2 K. 3:21) is a short designation for men able to bear arms. מְפַתֵּחַ, he who opens (the sword belt) is the one who after victory puts off his armour, (1 K. 20:11, LXX very freely ὁ ὀρθός).

Fig. [13] the close tie offers a term of comparison. Thus Yahweh bound Israel closely to Himself like a girdle. But this produced no results, so it was symbolically delivered up to judgment in the form of Jeremiah's girdle, Jer. 13:11. To the ungodly enemy the curse is a girdle with which he is continually girded, Ps. 109:19. But usually the metaphor is more positive, so that one may ask whether there is an echo of senses 2. and 4. as well as 1. Yahweh is girded with might, Ps. 65:6. He girds the righteous with strength, Ps. 18:32, 39 (different in 2 S. 22:33, 40). He also girds them with joy (Ps. 30:11), and the hills with rejoicing (Ps. 65:12). Is. 11:5 is to be understood in the same way ; there it is said of the king (Messiah?): וְהָיָה צֶדֶק אֵזוֹר מָתְנָיו וְהָאֱמוּנָה אֵזוֹר חֲלָצָיו, LXX : καὶ ἔσται δικαιοσύνη ἐζωσμένος τὴν ὀσφὺν αὐτοῦ καὶ ἀληθείᾳ εἰλημένος (held together) τὰς πλευράς. [14] What is meant in the first instance is that the ideal king of David's house will be closely bound up with righteousness and trustworthiness, truly royal qualities which stand in a close functional relation, Gn. 15:6; Hab. 2:4. [15] But this leads to further implications. The least prominent of the senses in this connection is 3. → *supra*. More active are 1. (→ 304), 2. [16] (→ 304) and 4 (→ *supra*), the last in form a., with possible though not certain echoes of b. and c. [17] "People gird themselves for battle or for work. Hence the girdle denotes strength and readiness. The king is strong and efficient because he is just and faithful. And so his country prospers ; good government bears good fruits." [18]

The prophetic targum translates Is. 11:5 lit. and incorrectly, yet in such a way that the origin of the metaphor is instructively brought to light : "Those who show faithfulness will be close to him." [19] The fig. use in Judaism associates with the main concept of girding oneself the secondary one of strength and readiness. bBer., 16b: [20] "May it be

---

[11] Diod. S., I, 72, 2 tells of a 72 day mourning for the Egypt. king : καταπεπλασμένοι δὲ τὰς κεφαλὰς πηλῷ καὶ περιεζωσμένοι σινδόνας ὑποκάτω τῶν μαστῶν ὁμοίως ἄνδρες καὶ γυναῖκες περιῆσαν ἀθροισθέντες.

[12] The text is corrupt. Joab's cunning is that he intentionally let fall the usually girded sword, so that in the embrace he seemed to be unarmed, but in fact he had a second sword in his left hand, concealed under the tunic.

[13] We may leave aside the obscure Job 12:18.

[14] The original would seem to have used two terms for girdle, one of them חֲגוֹר.

[15] The comm. largely overlook the fact that this is the basis of the metaphor.

[16] O. Procksch, *Js.*, I (1930), ad loc.: "The girdle ... gives dignity, character and figure to the appearance."

[17] The context might seem to suggest armour or sword belt, but neither is intended, since v. 4b shows that the Messianic king needs no weapons.

[18] B. Duhm, *Das Buch Js.*³ (1914), ad loc.

[19] Str.-B., III, 617.

[20] *Ibid.*, II, 301; III, 617.

thy will, O Lord ... that thou clothest thyself with mercy and deckest thyself with power, that thou robest thyself in thy love and girdest thyself (תְּאַזֵּר) with thy grace." Nu. r., 2 (138a): "Immediately (after the sin with the golden calf) Moses girded (חָגַר) his loins with prayer." [21]

III. Girdle and Girding in the New Testament.

In the NT all the known meanings recur, often in a metaphorical or transferred sense.

1. An article of clothing. According to Mt. 3:4 John the Baptist showed himself to be the Elias of the last days by wearing a garment of leather and hair. [22] The fastening of one's undergarment for work is a graphic touch in several of the parables of Jesus, Lk. 17:8; 12:37. [23] The dominical saying in Lk. 12:35: ἔστωσαν ὑμῶν αἱ ὀσφύες περιεζωσμέναι καὶ οἱ λύχνοι καιόμενοι, while reminiscent of Ex. 12:11, has in view the readiness of the disciples to serve their Lord on His unexpected return. [24] At the last supper in Jn. the Lord girds Himself with the slave's apron (→ 302; 308) to wash the disciples' feet (Jn. 13:4, 5; cf. Suet. Caligula of slaves: succincti linteo). On the meaning of this parabolic story → IV, 305. Jn. uses the same word διαζώννυμι of Peter when he puts on his overgarment, Jn. 21:7: τὸν ἐπενδύτην διεζώσατο. It is not clear whether the girdle was sometimes used to fasten this (→ 302) or whether we simply have an extension of the term. Peter is motivated by a sense of decorum [25] and perhaps of cultic modesty (→ I, 774). Girding oneself can also denote setting forth in the NT, Ac. 12:8: the mantle is thrown loosely over the fastened shirt. This expression is used by Jn. at 21:18 to give vividness to a saying of Jesus which is rich in implications. It is of the nature of the impetuous youth to gird himself, and the fate of the tired old man to be led. The temperamental Peter needs to be reminded of this because, though already past his first youth, he has not yet overcome the youthful desire to be his own master. But the saying takes on its deepest significance [26] as an intimation of the crucifixion of Peter. Girding in this sense is

---

[21] Ibid., III, 617.

[22] At Mk. 1:6 the relevant terms do not occur in D it. They perhaps came in from Mt. It is an open question how far they were fashioned by the theology of the community. The complete absence of this feature in Lk. is hard to explain. Peculiarities of dress are also found among the Gk. philosophers. Pythagoras is said to have worn a white stole, Menedemos a black chiton down to the feet and a purple girdle (ζώνη φοινικῆ), Diog. L., VIII, 1, 19; VI, 9 and 102. Depiction of such things is a stylistic feature of biographies of saints and founders of orders. But there is no reason to think there was any literary connection. The par. with Elijah is more likely in the case of John. It is worth noting that there is nothing comparable recorded of Jesus. Cf. E. Lohmeyer, Joh. d. Täufer (Das Urchr., I [1932]), 49 ff., 99 and Index, s.v. "Kleidung"; Windisch; Loh. Mk. on 1:6 (who suggests an apron of skins in place of the usual undergarment [→ n. 9] and introduces the rather remote par. with Adam); Hck. Mk., ad loc. On the girdle as bearer of magical potency cf. Pfister, though this is not applicable here.

[23] Cf. Kl., Hck., Lk., ad loc. The comparison is not abandoned in v. 37b, but since the presupposed situation is impossible in real life the paradox is emphasised. There is no suggestion of the Roman Saturnalia when masters waited on their servants; this would weaken the force of the saying. Though there may be a literary connection with Lk. 22:27; Mk. 10:41 ff.; Jn. 13:4, 5, there is only a remote relation of sense.

[24] Kl. Lk., ad loc. Cf. Philo Sacr. AC, 63: "τὰς ὀσφῦς περιεζωσμένους" ἑτοίμως πρὸς ὑπηρεσίαν ἔχοντας. Hck. Lk., ad loc. includes the motif of departure.

[25] Cf. Soran, ed. Jlberg, CMG, IV (1927), II, 70a of a midwife: περιζωσαμένη κοσμίως ἄνωθεν καὶ κάτωθεν.

[26] Zn. J., ad loc. rightly perceives the double sense. Cf. also Bau. J., ad loc.; Wdt. Ag. on 21:11. The opposition of Schl. J., ad loc. to Zahn's view is not convincing.

simply a euphemism for chaining. The stretching out of the hands precedes the march to the place of execution. Bound to the *patibulum*, the criminal bore this to the place of execution. The prophet Agabus uses Paul's girdle in the same sense as a symbolical intimation of the apostle's imprisonment, Ac. 21:11.

2. Adornment. In Rev. the divine sees the angels who bring the last plagues clothed in linen, i.e., priestly garments and girded with a golden girdle about their breasts, Rev. 15:6; cf. Ez. 9:2 LXX, Da. 10:5 Θ. Similarly the exalted Christ appears in a long garment and is "girt about the paps with a golden girdle," Rev. 1:13; cf. Da. 7:13; Ez. 1:26; 9:2, 11 LXX; Da. 10:5 Θ. [27] The high girdle is similar to that worn by the high-priests. [28]

3. Pocket. When Jesus sends out the disciples He charges them μὴ (αἴρωσιν) εἰς τὴν ζώνην χαλκόν (Mk. 6:8). Strictly, Mt. 10:9 forbids only gain rather than possessions : μὴ κτήσησθε χρυσὸν μηδὲ ἄργυρον μηδὲ χαλκὸν εἰς τὰς ζώνας ὑμῶν. But the distinction cannot be pressed as though in Mt. Jesus were simply forbidding payment for the healings. [29] This is forbidden already in v. 8b, and in general Mt. is more rigorous than Mk. (→ 311). The essential point is the same as in Mk. and Lk. 9:3 : μήτε (αἴρετε) ἀργύριον. [30] Jesus wills that provision for the disciples in their preaching should be made, not by human foresight, but by divine providence. [31]

4. Armour. The only instance is the fig. use in Eph. 6:14 : στῆτε οὖν περιζωσάμενοι τὴν ὀσφὺν ὑμῶν ἐν ἀληθείᾳ. There is an obvious echo here of Is. 11:5 LXX (→ 305). But the quotation is not exact. What was there said of the Messiah is now transferred to believers, and the two halves of the verse are shortened and combined. The context shows that an item of military equipment is intended. Since putting on the armour is not mentioned until v. 14b, the reference can hardly be to the protective girdle worn over the armour or to the sword belt (→ 303; 305). The separate protective girdle, the ancient μίτρη (→ 303), was no longer used in Paul's day. The Roman legionary, who serves as a model for the whole description, did not need to fasten his undergarment. If Paul had such details in view, it would seem, then, that he is referring to the breech-like apron worn by the Roman soldier (→ 303). ἀλήθεια is not, as in Heb. Is., reliability, and certainly not subjective truthfulness, [32] or real fighting as distinct from mere skirmishing. [33] All these interpretations are ruled out, partly by the meaning of ἀλήθεια in Paul, partly by the context. In what follows the reference is always to objective realities which alone can serve as weapons for the Christian. One

---

[27] To bear the golden clasp is the privilege of kings and their relatives.

[28] Jos. Ant., 3, 153 f.: ποδήρης χιτὼν ..., ὃν ἐπιζώννυνται κατὰ στῆθος ὀλίγον τῆς μασχάλης ὑπεράνω τὴν ζώνην περιάγοντες πλατεῖαν μὲν ὡς εἰς τέσσαρας δακτύλους, διακένως ὑφασμένην.

[29] This is considered, but rightly rejected, in Kl. Mt., *ad loc.* Schl. Mt., *ad loc.* thinks Mk. has perhaps abbreviated Mt., who has the further idea of a forbidding of voluntary gifts. But the term κτήσησθε lends no support to this interpretation, which is in any case doubtful in the light of Jn. 12:6. What is meant is that the disciples are not to be concerned in the least about earning a living.

[30] Cf. Lk. 10:4 : μὴ βαστάζετε βαλλάντιον.

[31] The Rabb. par. that one must not approach the temple hill with a staff, in shoes, with a purse, or with dusty feet (Ber., 9, 5, cf. Tos. Ber., 7, 19; Str.-B., I, 565) are for the most part external and perhaps literary. More genuinely relevant are the Rabb. refs. to renunciation of stipend (Str.-B., I, 561-564) and pious lack of material concern (*ibid.*, I, 435 : The Torah is given for interpretation only to those who eat manna).

[32] No longer espoused by exegetes.

[33] B. Weiss acc. to Haupt Gefbr., *ad loc.*

might think in terms of the Gospel as the embodiment of supreme truth, [34] but this is not advisable in view of the absence of the article. The paraphrase : "ἀλήθεια is what is, as it should be by nature," [35] is too abstract and again leads to subjectivity. It is best, then, to remember the basic biblical view of ἀλήθεια = אֱמֶת (→ I, 232 ff., esp. 235 ff., 243) as divine reality. Dependable divine reality, which has in fact come to men in the Gospel, is something which the believer can put on like the protective apron of the soldier. He can make active use of it in withstanding the assaults of evil. The ἐν added by the author is instrumental (→ II, 538). It softens a little the difficult conception of God's actuality as a girdle.

IV. Girdle and Girding in the Early Church.

The words are not much used in the early Church. It is noted of the aged Polycarp that he took off his clothes and loosed his girdle before his fiery martyrdom : λύσας τὴν ζώνην, Mart. Pol., 13, 2. In Herm. abstinence is strongly girded (περιεζωσμένη, v., 3, 8, 4), the heavenly virgins are finely girded (περιεζωσμέναι εὐπρεπῶς, s., 9, 2 and 4), but so, too, are vices (s., 9, 9, 5, if authentic). Herm. puts himself at the disposal of the Shepherd with a clean apron of sackcloth (περίζωσαι ὠμόλινον ... ἰδὼν δέ με περιεζωσμένον καὶ ἕτοιμον ὄντα τοῦ διακονεῖν αὐτῷ, s., 8, 4, 1 and 2). Cl. Al. says of Satan : οὐ παρὰ βασιλέως ἐζώσατο λαβὼν τὴν μάχαιραν, ἑαυτῷ δὲ ἐξ ἀπονοίας ἁρπάσας, Exc. Theod., 72, 2. He also refers his readers to Jeremiah, who was content with a linen girdle (→ 305), to John the Baptist, who wore a leather girdle, and to the Lord Himself who girded Himself with the apron of a slave (σαβάνῳ περιζωσάμενος) to wash His disciples' feet. These are all models of contentment and humility, Paed., II, 3, 38, 1; 10, 112, 3 f.; Strom., III, 6, 53, 5. The girding of the tunic in liturgical use is understood as an admonition to continence, since the loins are the seat of sexuality. [36]

† θώραξ.

1. Armour.

In the Greece of the Mycenean and epic period there were leather and linen doublets (λινοθώρηξ) with metal studs. Hom. mentions already bronze (χάλκεος, Il., 23, 560 f.) hollow (γυάλοισιν ἀρηρώς, 15, 529 f.) armour, so broad that the one who wears it can avoid a spear-thrust even within it. The bronze statuette of Dodona displays a slimmer type. [1] The Athenians even later prefer the leather doublet with metal studs and shoulder pieces. [2] The classical period develops armour which conforms to the body, which no longer sticks out but covers the lower body and back, and which protects the upper thighs by an attached apron of leather. [3] The Romans of the 2nd cent. B.C. use not only full armour or the leather doublet with breastplate, [4] but also coat of mail. Strength and lightness are the two qualities required in good armour. In relation to strong armour weighing only 2 minas (17.600 kg.) [5] (early in the 3rd cent. B.C.) Plut.

---

[34] A. Klöpper, Der Brief an d. Eph. (1891), ad loc.: the truth objectively contained in Jesus ; more subjectively Haupt Gefbr., ad loc.: agreement with what is inwardly true (cf. 1:13; 4:24; 5:9).

[35] Ew. Gefbr., ad loc.

[36] L. Eisenhofer, Hndbch. d. katholischen Liturgik, I (1932), 422 f.

θ ώ ρ α ξ. [1] For ill. cf. Ebert, X, Plate 12a, the so-called bell armour.

[2] On a vase, cf. Kromayer-Veith, Ill. 21. Cf. also the Aristion stele, Ill. 17.

[3] Ibid., Plate 8, Ill. 33 (Pergamon).

[4] καρδιοφύλαξ Polyb., 6, 23, 14. It may be assumed as self-evident that a strong garment was worn under it.

[5] Full equipment usually weighed a talent (26.196 kg.), though a particularly strong man might carry double (Plut. Demetr., 21 [I, 898d]). Perhaps in this case the πανοπλία is simply the armour.

Demetr., 21 (I, 898c) estimates that a catapulted arrow from 20 paces distant left only a light scratch on it.

In Egypt armour was known only from the 18th dynasty (1580 B.C.). It was first introduced as booty taken from defeated Asiatic princes or as tribute from Asiatic vassals (coat of mail). The Egyptian army was then equipped with it. Something of the same took place in Assyria in the 9th cent. The warrior vase of Megiddo [6] seems to show that a leather doublet was also used, perhaps with metal plates. The Philistine Goliath wore coat of mail (שִׁרְיוֹן קַשְׂקַשִׂים, LXX θώρακα ἀλυσιδωτόν), with the monstrous, perhaps exaggerated, weight of 5000 shekels = 60 kg. (1 S. 17:5 → 296; 314). Armour, at first the privilege of the nobility, was used in the army of Israel, 1 S. 17:38. [7] It came into more general use under Uzziah, 2 Ch. 26:14; cf. Neh. 4:10. The name (שִׁרְיָה, שִׁרְיוֹן, סִרְיוֹן = that which shines) suggests metal armour or coat of mail. (נֶשֶׁק בַּרְזֶל) (Job 20:24; 39:21 etc.) would seem in contrast to denote very strong armour (not understood by the LXX). When the LXX translates סִרְיוֹן by θώραξ it undoubtedly has coat of mail in view. The term תַחְרָא in Ex. 28:32; 39:23, however, denotes a leather doublet (= Egypt. dhri' leather). Philo Spec. Leg., I, 86 speaks of ὕφασμα θωρακειδές in relation to the high-priestly vestments. In the NT θώραξ is used lit. at Rev. 9:9, 17.

2. θώραξ = Chest, Trunk, Thorax.

In a transf. sense the term is used for the part of the body covered by armour, i.e., the chest or trunk, Aristot. Hist. An., I, 13, p. 493a, 17, κεφαλῆς καὶ θώρακος καὶ τῆς κάτω κοιλίας, Aristot. Probl., 33, p. 962a, 34, also below the midriff, Plat. Tim., 69e, ἀπ' αὐχένος μέχρι αἰδοίων, Aristot. Hist. An., I, 7, p. 491a, 29, also the armour of crustaceans [8] (Aristot. Hist. An., VIII, 13, p. 601a, 13). Aristoph. Vesp., 1194 f. puns on the lit. and fig. senses. Philo thinks it meaningful that nature has assigned to the second human quality, i.e., courage, the thorax, which is formed of strong bones, Leg. All., III, 115; Spec. Leg., I, 146; IV, 93.

3. The Metaphorical Use in the Bible.

a. The Old Testament.

The metaphorical use in the Bible goes back to Is. 59:17 (→ 297): "And Yahweh put on righteousness as a breastplate" (וַיִּלְבַּשׁ צְדָקָה כַּשִּׁרְיָן, LXX καὶ ἐνεδύσατο δικαιοσύνην ὡς θώρακα). [9] In plain terms this means that Yahweh will deploy His full moral consistency to bring salvation to His community and the nations, and to destroy the evil will which withstands Him whether within or without. With no abstract separation the concept of righteousness embraces the penal justice of the judge, a concern for the poor and afflicted (Am. 5:7; Is. 5:16), and faithfulness and mercy in giving help (Ps. 5:8; 22:31; 89:16; 98:2; 145:7). These aspects are all combined in the concept of the one who judges and for that reason

---

[6] AOB, No. 24.

[7] Cf. also 1 K. 22:34; 2 Ch. 18:33. The note that the arrow smote Ahab בֵּין הַדְּבָקִים וּבֵין הַשִּׁרְיָן (LXX certainly incorrect: between lung and armour) is to be rendered: between girdle and armour, and thus suggests short armour and belt.

[8] That the image in Rev. 9:3 ff. is partly inspired by this is quite possible. On the other hand, there is no reason to think that the first θώρακας in v. 9 is used in the transf. sense for scales or breasts (the latter is considered by Pr.-Bauer[3], s.v.). The same words are always used in the same sense in vv. 7-9. At Job 41:5b the LXX wrongly thinks in terms of the armour of the crocodile.

[9] Since Wis. 5:18 (→ 297) is almost lit. the same as Is. 59:17, Paul surely has the latter alone in view (→ infra). He knows Wis., however, so that it might have had a secondary influence (→ 301). Dob. Th. on 1 Th. 5:8 wrongly argues that there was no OT basis for (the authentic) Paul.

genuinely establishes (2 S. 8:15 as a general evaluation of the reign of David). [10] It is not very obvious why this should be expressed in the imagery of armour. Certainly the context does not support the view that emphasis is laid on the inviolability of the divine action. The point of the metaphor is more likely to be sought in the fact that this is part of the equipment whose putting on denotes military initiative. Righteousness is thus understood in an activist sense.

b. In the New Testament.

In the two passages in which Paul alludes to the OT saying (→ n. 9) he does not quote it but makes free reference. In both instances he is engaged in exhortation and believers are the subject. [11] 1 Th. 5:8: νήφωμεν, ἐνδυσάμενοι θώρακα πίστεως καὶ ἀγάπης, Eph. 6:14 : ἐνδυσάμενοι τὸν θώρακα τῆς δικαιοσύνης. In the first verse the idea is worked out only in terms of two items, and in this form it is rather artificially connected with the Pauline [12] triad of faith, love and hope. The relationship with righteousness is abandoned. Nor is there any connection here between the image of armour and what is signified. Certainly the emphasis is not that faith and love encompass believers like protective armour. It is rather that believers, as milites Christi, should make ready for the final conflict by putting on their armour. The situation is different in Eph. 6:14. Here the concept of δικαιοσύνη is taken over, and the construction connects it closely with the metaphor. The analogy of the other images makes it likely that δικαιοσύνη is deliberately presented as a defensive piece of equipment. The reference is not, of course, to the divine attribute, as in Is. 59:17. In view of the ethical context it might seem best to think exclusively in terms of human uprightness. Subjective righteousness, however, is not very well adapted to be called an item in the πανοπλία τοῦ θεοῦ, and the aorist part. does not fit this view either. Here, too, one must think of the right use of a means of protection which is truly adapted to the Christian as such. According to Paul this is righteousness before or from God by faith in Christ. R. 3:22. [13] Enclosed by this, believers are secure against all the assaults of evil spirits, R. 8:38 f. But this cannot be abstractly separated from righteousness of life. [14] Just because it issues in the latter, it gives protection against temptation. There is need to make full use of this armour which God gives (→ 301) in courageous warfare.

† ὑποδέω († ὑπόδημα, † σανδάλιον).

"To bind underneath," "to furnish with footgear," with acc. of person (ἐνέδυσαν αὐτοὺς καὶ ὑπέδησαν [= ‏בַעֵל‎ hi] αὐτούς, 2 Ch. 28:15), also dat. of thing (ὑπέδουν τοῖς καλκίοις (= calceus, half-boot) αὐτόν, Plut. Pomp., 24 [I, 631e]) or with double acc. (Ez. 16:10 : ὑπέδησά [= ‏בַעֵל‎ qal] σε ὑάκινθον), often med. "to put on soles or sandals," abs. (ὅσοι δὲ ὑποδεδεμένοι ἐκοιμῶντο ... Xenoph. An., IV, 5, 14), with acc. of object fastened (κέλευε δέ σφεας ... κοθόρνους ὑποδέεσθαι, Hdt., I, 155;

---

[10] Cf. Ges.-Buhl, s.v. צְדָקָה; Eichr. Theol. AT, esp. I, 121-126.

[11] Rabb. exegesis refers the verse to men, but with a distinctive narrowing of the concept צְדָקָה. bBB, 9b (statement of R. Eleazar, c. 270): "It says, he put on well-doing as a breastplate ; this means that as the individual plates are joined to form a big piece of armour, so in benevolence the individual perutas (pennies) are joined to constitute a big contribution."

[12] → I, 51 f. The artificiality of the connection shows that the triad was already a formula in Paul.

[13] So Ew. Gefbr., ad loc.

[14] Rightly emphasised by Haupt Gefbr., ad loc.

κούκινα [sandals of coconut fibre, prophetic garb] Preis. Zaub., IV, 934; λύκεια [wolf leather] ὑποδήματα, ibid., VII, 729; Ac. 12:8 : ὑπόδησαι τὰ σανδάλιά σου [sign of departure]), or acc. of the part of the body covered, τὸν ἀριστερὸν μόνον πόδα ὑποδεδεμένοι, Thuc., III, 22, 2. In several of these constructions it occurs in Epict. (act. abs., Diss., III, 26, 21, with acc. I, 16, 4; IV, 1, 37; mid. abs., I, 16, 3 f.), but not Philo.

In the Orient and Greece people usually went about barefoot or else wore sandals (נְעָלִים, σανδάλια : [1] Ac. 12:8; Mk. 6:9; ὑποδήματα : Mt. 3:11 and par.; 10:10 and par.; Lk. 15:22; 22:35). These were put off in the sanctuary [2] or for mourning, fasting, or the ban. [3] A slave fastens and unfastens the thongs of his master's sandals, Epict. Diss., III, 26, 21; bQid, 22b; Str.-B., I, 121; Mk. 1:7; Lk. 3:16; Jn. 1:27; Ac. 13:25. He also carries his sandals for him, e.g., on a journey when they can be dispensed with, or at the baths, Mt. 3:11. In Lydia wearing a high shoe (κόθορνος) is regarded as extravagant and effeminate, Hdt., I, 155 → supra. On the other hand the Assyrian soldier (not the Jewish) wears laced boots which reach to the calf and which are covered by nails (סְאוֹן Is. 9:4, not understood by the LXX). [4] In Rome shoes of leather, often expensive, were generally worn. The calceus is so typically Roman that Pontic pirates in the days of Pompey mockingly clad captured Romans in it, and then threw them into the sea, Plut. Pomp., 24 (I, 631e). The legionary wears the caliga, a low half-boot with a strong sole and open leather work above. [5]

John the Baptist does not feel worthy to carry the shoes or unloose the latchets of the sandals of the mightier one who comes after him, → supra (Mt. 3:11 and par.). According to Mt. 10:10; Lk. 10:4; 22:35 Jesus did not allow His disciples to use ὑποδήματα on their preaching mission, though according to Mk. 6:9 (ἀλλὰ ὑποδεδεμένους σανδάλια → supra) He did allow, even if He did not expressly enjoin, the use of sandals. Attempts to reconcile the apparent contradiction have not been very successful. [6] Nor can it be said for certain either that Mk. is

---

ὑ π ο δ έ ω κτλ. [1] The sandal is distinguished from the mere solea (Rabb. loan word סוּלְיָם). It has a heel strap or heel, Str.-B., I, 567.

[2] (Ex. 3:5; Jos. 5:15; Ac. 7:33; Ditt. Syll.³, 338, 25 f.; 999, 7 f.). J. Heckenbach, "De Nuditate sacra," RVV, IX, 3 (1911), 40 ff. In Andania only felt shoes or shoes from the leather of sacrificial animals (δερμάτινα ἱερόθυτα) were permitted. Ditt. Syll.³, 736, 22 f. The cultic practice of wearing a shoe only on the right foot (e.g., παῖς μυούμενος ἀφ' ἑστίας in the Palace of the Conservatory at Rome, Haas, 9/11, Leipoldt, No. 190) is usually explained as an attempt to approach the gods of the underworld, W. Amelung, Dissertazioni della Pontifica Academia Romana di Archeologia, II, 9 (1907), 113-135. Thuc., III, 22, 2 (→ supra) explains the clothing of only the left foot as a protection against slipping. It is hard to say whether this is an accidental par. or whether the military practice has a religious basis (or the cultic a military).

[3] Str.-B., I, 569. The legal practice of taking off the shoe, perhaps originally a pledge on the purchase of property (Rt. 4:7), but later found only in cases of Levirate marriage, is already interpreted in Dt. 25:9 f. and later Test. Zeb. 3:4 f. (in strange conjunction with the story of Joseph) as a public shaming of those who refuse such marriage.

[4] Ill. in Galling, 359.

[5] Ill. of a caliga, Kromayer-Veith, Plate 40, No. 123; monuments of legionaries often emphasise the caliga, ibid., Plate 34, No. 104/6; 35, No. 108; 36, No. 110/2; 37, No. 113/4; 38, No. 115 etc. The third Roman emperor is usually called Caligula, the nickname given him in his father's camp.

[6] There is little to commend the conjecture of F. Spitta (ZwTh, 55 [1913], 39 ff., 166 f.) that we should read ὑπενδύματα or ὑποδύματα for ὑποδήματα, so that Lk., simply forbids underclothes (cf. 9:3 : μήτε ἀνὰ δύο χιτῶνας) whereas Mt. developed the double prohibition. Wellh. Mk. (1903) suggested an error in transl.: אלא (only) instead of לא (Allen ולא), but he changed his mind in the 2nd ed. (1911). Quite impossible is the view of Str.-B., I, 569 that Jesus in Mt. and Lk. is demanding that the disciples should not acquire more than the one pair of sandals which they wear. Nor does the distinction between soles

softening the demand in the light of the apostolic mission (Roman custom?) or that Q is romantically sharpening it. [7] In any case Jesus is requiring full commitment from His disciples, with the renunciation of all non-essentials. [8]

Paul figuratively lists shoes in the divine panoply. Eph. 6:15 : καὶ ὑποδησάμενοι τοὺς (→) πόδας ἐν ἑτοιμασίᾳ τοῦ εὐαγγελίου τῆς εἰρήνης. In explanation it is sufficient to refer to the equipment of the Roman legionary, though Is. 52:7 may have had some influence on the formulation. Paul has in mind the joyful proclamation of the Gospel in the Messianic NT period, cf. R. 10:15; → II, 719, 731 f. The ἑτοιμασία τοῦ εὐαγγελίου τῆς εἰρήνης is not the readiness for conflict given by the Gospel [9] but the readiness for active propagation of the Gospel, which is the most effective means of combatting satanic powers, and which naturally cannot be restricted to missionary preaching as a vocation. ἐν has the force of an instrumental dat., with or by. The connection with the verb is not as close as in the usual construction with the accusative, → 310 f. Hence the danger of a dubious literalness is avoided. That the battle is waged with the message of peace is a fine paradox and is in full keeping with the general outlook of Eph. (2:14 ff.).

Ign. Pol., 6, 2 does not mention shoes in his depiction of our spiritual armour. Herm. v., 4, 2, 1 in a vision sees the Church as the bride of Christ arrayed in white clothes καὶ ὑποδήμασιν λευκοῖς. Cl. Al. fights the luxury which led esp. the women of his day to wear shoes embroidered with gold, richly embossed and adorned with erotic sayings. He would have women wear white shoes except on a journey, when they should use nailed shoes. Feminine modesty demands that the foot should be covered. The man, however, ought to go barefoot when not on military service. This is healthy and makes for simplicity. Cl. Al. compares the talkative Sophists to old shoes which are weak except for the tongue. Paed., II, 7, 59, 3; Strom., I, 2, 22, 5. Comparison and contrast between this Christian Stoicism and the NT give rise to exciting lines of thought.

† θυρεός.

θυρεός is the four-cornered long shield which covers the whole man like a door (צִנָּה).[1] Along with it lighter shields were used, mostly round or oval, e.g., among the Hittites, Phoenicians, [2] Philistines and Israelites (מָגֵן masc. or fem., 1 K. 10:16 f.; 2 Ch. 9:15 f. etc.); cf. also the Mycenean-Aegean culture in Hellas (the ἀσπίς, 80-100 cm. across ; the Etruscans and Romans in Italy, the clipeus. Very light shields included that

---

and sandals help much, since the sandal is the more comfortable. For details cf. Kl. Mk., ad loc.

[7] Longer journeys were hardly possible in Palestine without footgear. Outside cities mourners and the banned were freed from the law that they should go barefoot (bTaan., 13a, cf. Str.-B., I, 569). The Cynics, however, went barefoot, Diog. L., VI, 34. The staff and sandals in Mk. express equipment and readiness for the journey.

[8] S. Krauss, "Die Instruktion Jesu an die Ap.," Angelos, 1 (1925), 96-102, esp. 101. For further bibl. cf. Pr.-Bauer³, s.v. ὑπόδημα; Hck. Lk. on 10:4; Kl. Mk. on 6:8 f.

[9] So Ew. Gefbr., ad loc., who contests dependence on Is. 52:7. But Paul leans constantly on Is. in the preceding verses. A connection between shoes and the readiness for battle given by the Gospel is less immediately relevant. The paradox (→ infra) would then be pointless and ἑτοιμασία would be weak without an obj. gen. Hence the train of thought derives from the πόδες εὐαγγελιζομένου ἀκοὴν εἰρήνης of Is. 52:7. One must remember the active element in the εὐαγγέλιον. In Paul the term denotes active propagation as well as the objective message.

θυρεός. [1] Apart from its epic use, the word means "door-stone," late. The oldest instance, if correctly reproduced, is the inscr. Plut. Pyrrhus, 26 (I, 400d). Then P. Cairo, 9, 40; P. Greci e Latini, IV, 428, 36; Polyb.; Dion. Hal. etc.; also LXX and Jos. Ant., 8, 179; not in Philo, but a loan word in the Rabb.

[2] Ill., also for what follows, Galling, s.v. "Schild," with refs. to AOB.

adopted by the Scythians, originally half-moon, later round (the πέλτη, *pelta*), also the *parma* of 3 ft. diameter and the *cetra* of only 2. These do not apply here. The long shield itself takes various forms. It is rounded at the top among the Egyptians, Assyrians, Israelites (1 K. 10:16; 2 Ch. 9:15 etc.) and perhaps the Philistines (הַצִּנָּה אִישׁ גָּ, 1 S. 17, 7, 41), violin shaped or eight-cornered among the Hittites and in the Aegean, finally rectangular, level or concave. This form alone is of interest to us. It, too, is very old. In a smaller form it occurs already among the Hittites. ³ In the Mycenean period it has the form of the so-called tower shield which is more a portable wall than a weapon. Hom., too, presupposes this though he does not use the term (ἀσπὶς ποδηνεκής reaching to the feet, Il., 15, 646; ἀμφιβρότη, covering the whole man, half-cylindrical in form, 2, 389). From the 7th cent. on it disappears completely. No connection has been proved between it and the later forms of the long shield. The Romans c. 340 B.C. exchanged the round shield for the long shield, Liv., 8, 8, 3 : *postquam stipendiarii facti sunt, scuta pro clipeis fecere*. The latter then came to characterise the Roman legionary, ⁴ and only in the age of Constantine was it again replaced by the round or oval form.

The ideals of strength and lightness were hard to reconcile. The tower shield might consist of seven layers of oxhide (ἑπταβόειος = 15-30 kg.). Then there were wooden struts and metal studs. For curvature the shield of the Roman legionary was made of two wooden pieces glued together and covered with linen and then with calf leather, Polyb., 6, 23, 2 f.; Liv., 23, 19, 13. Polyb., 6, 23, 2 f. gives the following measurements : breadth in the curve, 2½ ft.; length 4 ft. The thickness could be up to a hand's breadth. Jos. Bell., 3, 95 speaks of the θυρεὸς ἐπιμήκης. A strong boss gave it added power of resistance. Large but thinner metal shields were used only on parade. There is no transf. or fig. use in secular Gk. ⁵

The LXX sometimes renders צִנָּה inexactly by ἀσπίς (Jer. 46:3) and מָגֵן quite often (12 times) by θυρεός (used only 10 times for צִנָּה). When distinction is made it is usually correct ⁶ (Ez. 23:24; ψ 34:2; 2 Ch. 9:15 f.: ἀσπίς = מָגֵן half as heavy as θυρεός = צִנָּה; cf. also 2 Ch. 23:9, though not Cant. 4:4). The idea is often used by the OT in a transf. sense with ref. to Yahweh. In the Heb. it is then almost always מָגֵן (צִנָּה only Ps. 5:12; 91:4 LXX ὅπλον). But the LXX never uses θυρεός or even ἀσπίς (apart from Wis. 5:19 [→ 297, of God's panoply]; Sir. 29:13 [of almsgiving], and 37:5 proverbially). ⁷ It seeks rather to give the sense by more or less abstract expressions (ὑπερασπιστής ψ 17:2, 30 = 2 Βασ. 22:3, 31; 27:7; 32:20; 58:11; 83:9; 113:17-19; 143:2; ὑπερασπισμός, ψ 17:35 = 2 Βασ. 22:36; ὑπερασπίζω, Gn. 15:1; Dt. 33:29; Prv. 30:5; ἀντιλήμπτωρ, Ps. 3:3; ψ 118:114; βοήθεια, Ps. 7:10. We see evidence here of a feeling for Gk. and also of the individual theology of the LXX.

In the NT θυρεός is used only fig., Eph. 6:16 : ἐν πᾶσιν ⁸ ἀναλαβόντες τὸν θυρεὸν τῆς πίστεως, ἐν ᾧ δυνήσεσθε πάντα τὰ βέλη τοῦ πονηροῦ τὰ (not in BD*G) πεπυρωμένα σβέσαι. The shield of faith must be taken up in addition to the items already mentioned. There is no specific OT model for this requirement. But the verb is a military tt. (Hdt., III, 78; Ditt. Syll.³, 742, 45 and 49 [Ephesus, c. 85 B.C.]), used already in the OT (→ IV, 8, cf. also Ιερ. 26:3: ἀναλάβετε ὅπλα καὶ ἀσπίδας [וְצִנָּה מָגֵן], 2 Macc. 10:27; Jdt. 5:7; 14:3). Materially the thought of ψ 34:2 : ἐπιλαβοῦ ὅπλου καὶ θυρεοῦ (used of Yahweh, → 297) is transferred to

---

³ Ill. in Galling, 217, 4; AOB, 62 and 106.

⁴ Ill. in Lindenschmit, Plate 4, No. 1.

⁵ Cf. Liddell-Scott, *s.v.*

⁶ Cf. also Jos. Bell., 3, 95; the bodyguard of the general carries the ἀσπίς, the ordinary legionary the θυρεός.

⁷ Note need not be taken here of the description of the crocodile in Job 41:7.

⁸ The vl. ἐπὶ πᾶσιν is attested by AℜDG Orig, but is a softening acc. to the evidence of אB Plat syrP. The meaning is roughly the same, Dib. Gefbr., *ad loc.*; Lk. 16:26; → II, 538. ἐν πᾶσιν is not to be taken with v. 15, Haupt Gefbr., *ad loc.*

believers, → 297. Faith, described as a shield, is not just the subjective attitude, but an objective, divinely given reality (1 C. 13:13; 1 Th. 5:8).[9] All the attacks of Satan are hurled back by the fellowship with God granted to believers. The metaphor is not consistent, since the shield does not in fact quench fiery darts,[10] but at best can only cause them to fall harmlessly to the ground. Materially cf. 1 Jn. 5:4; 1 Pt. 5:9.

The term does not occur in ecclesiastical authors. No mention is made of the shield in the account of spiritual equipment in Ign. Pol., 6, 2. Faith is here compared to a helmet (→ infra). Cl. Al. has the term only in an archaeological note on the inventor of the θυρεός, the Samnite Itanos, Strom., I, 16, 75, 7.

† περικεφαλαία.

"Head covering,"[1] usually military, "helmet"; it can serve as a weapon in a sally by night (Aen. Tact., 24, 6); it is to be covered in an ambush (τὰς περικεφαλαίας ὑποτιθέναι τοῖς ὅπλοις, Polyb., 3, 71, 4); because of its pressure gladiatorial combat was medically suspect (Antyllus in Oribasius, VI, 36, 3, ed. U. C. Bussemaker and C. Daremberg [1851 ff.]); with three lances or a spear it is a prize for the pugilist (Ditt. Syll.³, 958, 29 and 30). In the LXX 1 Βασ. 17:5 (כּוֹבַע), 38 (קוֹבַע, cf. Jos. Ant., 6, 184), 49 (added in illustration); 2 Ch. 26:14; Ιερ. 26:4; Εz. 23:24 (added by A) etc. The word does not occur in Philo.

The Mycenean-Homeric age speaks only of the κόρυς, the leather morion, often with a plume (Hom. Il., 6, 470 etc.), covered with rows of boar's teeth or metal plates. Goliath's helmet was probably like this, so that only in part did it merit description as a "helmet of brass" (1 S. 17:5). In Israel, too, metal helmets on the Assyrian-Babylonian rather than the Egypt. pattern are rare (1 S. 17:38), though they seem to have been generally introduced later (2 Ch. 26:14). In Greece the city soldier always carried a bronze helmet with a long hoop or two cross hoops containing the plumes, a protection for the forehead, nose and neck, and two hinged cheek-pieces fastened by a chin-band. In Rome Camillus († 365 B.C.) tried to replace the bronze helmet by an iron helmet, but without success. Even later the helmet of the legionary was made of bronze (χαλκή, Polyb., 6, 23, 8) with no true vizor but offering some protection to neck, cheeks and chin.[2] On marches it was slung on a strap. Putting on the helmet marked the beginning of battle. There is no fig. use in secular Gk.

---

[9] Wettstein refers to Silius Italicus Punica, XI, 206: armatumque fide pectus, but there is no true par. of sense.

[10] In antiquity a favourite weapon in sieges: חִצִּים דֹּלְקִים, Ps. 7:13; זִיקוֹת Is. 50:11; זִקִּים Prv. 26:18 (always of the ungodly, no longer understood by the LXX). πυρφόροι ὀϊστοί, Thuc., II, 75, 5; Lat. malleoli. Servius (ed. H. A. Lion [1826], I, 540 f.). In the Aen. IX, 705: "The burning arrow is a powerful weapon, made of turned iron, which has iron an ell long, on it a ball whose weight is increased by lead; it has, as we have said, fire attached, being surrounded by tow and daubed with pitch; when kindled it destroys the enemy either by wounding or burning." Amm. Marc., 23, 4 gives the following description of smaller burning arrows: the arrow is made of cane articulated between tip and shaft by fissured iron; it is curved like a weaver's spindle on which linen threads are spun, and stands fine and abundantly open with its cavity, and takes into its belly fire with combustible material. And when, shot fairly slowly from a not too taut bow, for it would be extinguished by too rapid flight, it strikes somewhere, it burns stubbornly, and if water is poured on it, causes stronger bursts of flame, and can be put out by no other means than sand spread over it. For further material cf. Wettstein on Eph. 6:16.

περικεφαλαία. [1] Of fox fur acc. to Callias Comicus Fr., 1 (Suppl. Com., 27). P. Petr., III, 140a, 3 (3rd cent. B.C.) among household articles: price with theke 50 drachmas. Preisigke Wört.: "head-cloth," "cap," perhaps "wig" with case? Cf. Liddell-Scott, s.v.

[2] Ill. in Kromayer-Veith, Plate 1-5, 8, 34-41; Lindenschmit Plate 3, 4, 9, 12; Guthe Ill. 41, 208; AOB, No. 9, 341 etc.

In contrast, the only use in the NT is figurative. 1 Th. 5:8 : ἐνδυσάμενοι ... περικεφαλαίαν ἐλπίδα σωτηρίας, Eph. 6:17: καὶ τὴν περικεφαλαίαν τοῦ σωτηρίου δέξασθε. Both passages are based on Is. 59:17,³ where Yahweh is the subject: καὶ περιέθετο περικεφαλαίαν σωτηρίου (מְשׁוּעָה כּוֹבַע) ἐπὶ τῆς κεφαλῆς, → 297. Yahweh makes His entry, wholly clad in aid and salvation, that He might represent the cause of His community against its oppressors. The Synagogue referred the passage to the Messiah: "in that hour God will adorn the Messiah with a crown and put the helmet of salvation on His head ... and set Him on a high hill to proclaim to Israel that salvation is nigh."⁴ Paul adopts only the idea of the helmet of salvation, and gives it a completely new turn. Believers are now the subject. The indicative becomes an imperative or cohortative. Salvation is given the passive and fully NT sense of σωθῆναι. In 1 Th. 5:8 the eschatological element is particularly strongly emphasised (ἐλπίδα σωτηρίας), but the intention is the same in Eph. The final deliverance which is assured to the baptised by the putting on of God's salvation encompasses the head (περι-κεφαλαία) like a protective shield. The putting on of the helmet means that, trusting in the given salvation, one can and should commit oneself fully to the commencing (→ 314) struggle against the sinister powers which seek to prevent salvation.

Something similar is in view when Ign. compares faith to a helmet in Ign. Pol., 6, 2. But now the human attitude rather than the divine gift is to the fore. In the later vocabulary of the Church the word plays no further part.

Oepke

> ὁράω, εἶδον, βλέπω, ὀπτάνομαι, θεάομαι, θεωρέω, ἀόρατος, ὁρατός,
> ὅρασις, ὅραμα, ὀπτασία, αὐτόπτης, ἐπόπτης, ἐποπτεύω, ὀφθαλμός,
> καθοράω, προοράω, προεῖδον

ὁράω, εἶδον, βλέπω, † ὀπτάνομαι, † θεάομαι, † θεωρέω.

Contents : A. Usage among the Greeks : 1. The words : a. ὁράω and εἶδον, b. βλέπω, c. ὀπτάνομαι, d. θεάομαι, e. θεωρέω. 2.Seeing in the Greek World and Hellenism. B. Usage and Concept in the Septuagint and Judaism : I. Septuagint : 1. Meanings of the Terms : a. ὁράω and εἶδον, b. βλέπω, c. ὀπτάνομαι, d. θεάομαι, e. θεωρέω. 2. The Significance of Seeing in OT Proclamation : a. Visionary-Ecstatic Prophetic Seeing ; b. Seeing God in Theophanies etc.; 3. Seeing God in a Transferred Sense. II. Philo and Josephus : 1. Philo : a. The Words ; b. The Significance of Seeing ; 2. Josephus. III. Pseudepigrapha and Rabbinism : 1. The Pseudepigrapha ; 2. Rabbinism. C. Usage and Concept in the New Testament : 1. Review of the Words : a. ὁράω and εἶδον; b. βλέπω, c. ὀπτάνομαι, d. θεάομαι, e. θεωρέω. 2. The Significance of Seeing in NT Proclamation : a. General, b. Eye-witness ; Faith and Sight, c. Visionary-Ecstatic Prophetic Seeing, d. The Resurrection Appearances, e. Johannine Seeing, f. The Vision of God. D. Usage and Concept in the Post-apostolic Fathers.

---

³ In Wis. 5:18 (→ 297) honest judgment is κόρυς. There is no apparent dependence of Paul on this verse, → 309, n. 9.
⁴ Beth ha-Midr., 3, 73, 17, Str.-B., III, 618.

A. Usage among the Greeks.

1. The Words.

If we ignore the rare ἀκροάομαι, also ἔκλυον, which occurs only in the epic sphere and is not found in the LXX and NT, and verbs like πυνθάνομαι etc., which are synon. only in respect of one aspect of the meaning of ἀκούω, the Gk. language has for the concept of hearing only ἀκούω and its compounds, whereas for seeing it has a whole series of verbs at its command. This interrelation shows us already that seeing was more important for the Gks. than hearing (→ 319). The individual words for seeing are not, of course, simple synon., but denote different forms of seeing. [1] On the other hand, in course of time there took place an interchange of meaning, so that different verbs which originally denoted specific actions and were related to specific tenses were combined into a single system of conjugation (ὁράω, ὄψομαι, εἶδον). The following picture emerges when we review the use of the individual verbs which are also of particular importance in the NT.

a. ὁράω, from Hom., abs. "to see," "to look" (also with εἰς, "to look at something"), and trans. with acc. "to see or perceive something." [2] To see is to take part in life itself; often in Hom. ζώειν καὶ ὁρᾶν φάος ἠελίοιο, Od., 4, 540 etc.; already we see the meaning "to experience," Soph. Oed. Tyr., 831 f. (ἰδεῖν). For seeing in dream or vision cf. the healing inscr. of Epidauros (4th cent. B.C.), Ditt. Syll.³, 1168, 98; 1169, 2, 5, 28 with ἐνύπνιον, 1168, 11, 118 with ὄψις, "apparition," also pap. [3] Quite early transf. for spiritual sight ("perceiving," "considering") and also for perception with the other senses, so that ὁράω can even be used for ἀκούω. In the sense "to take note," "to see to" (with ὅπως, Thuc., V, 27, 2) commonly "to take care," "to be on guard," esp. imper. ὅρα or ὅρᾶτε, with εἰ (from Aesch.) or μή and conj. (from Soph.), also interrogative pron. [4] Pass. ὁράομαι (Hom. only mid.) also in intrans. sense "to be visible," "to appear" (as φαίνομαι), in this case with ὑπό τινος rather than τινί, the dat. signifying the person concerned rather than the active person, i.e., the one who perceives. [5] The two tense-forms missing from ὁράω are taken either from the stem

---

ὁ ρ ά ω κτλ. → ἀκούω, I, 216 ff.; Cr.-Kö., 387 s.v. εἴδω I. εἶδον (the other verbs of seeing are not dealt with in Cr.-Kö.); W. W. Graf Baudissin, "'Gott schauen' in d. at.lichen Religion," ARW, 18 (1915), 173-239; J. Hänel, "Das Erkennen Gottes bei d. Schriftpropheten," BWAT, 2. F. 4 (1933); E. v. Dobschütz, "Die fünf Sinne im NT," JBL, 48 (1929), 378-411; R. Bultmann, "Untersuchungen zum Joh.-Ev. θεὸν οὐδεὶς ἑώρακεν πώποτε," ZNW, 29 (1930), 169-192; E. Fascher, "Deus invisibilis," Marburger Theol. Studien, 1 (1931), 41-77; G. Kittel, Religionsgesch. u. Urchr. (1932), 95-106; O. Becker, Plotin u. d. Problem der geistigen Aneignung (1940); G. Rudberg, "Hellenisches Schauen," Classica et Mediaevalia, 5 (1942), 159-186; W. Michaelis, Die Erscheinungen des Auferstandenen (1944); M. Barth, Der Augenzeuge (1946).

[1] On these distinctions in Homeric usage cf. B. Snell, Die Entdeckung des Geistes (1946), 15-19. In the NT note esp. ἀτενίζω ("to look at intently" cf. Pr.-Bauer³, s.v.). On κατοπτρίζομαι → II, 696. In certain senses many verbs have a relation to seeing, e.g., κατανοέω → IV, 975, → παρακύπτω.

[2] With the rise of βλέπω and θεωρέω, ὁράω ceases to expand, but Moult.-Mill., 455 rightly rejects the view that it was dead after the 1st cent. A.D. Etym. [Debrunner] ὁράω is related to the Gothic war, "careful" (Germ. wahr-nehmen, gewahr, wahren, Eng. "ware," "beware"), thus orig. "to take note." Cf. Walde-Pok., I, 284; G. Curtius, Grundzüge d. gr. Etym.⁵ (1879), 101: "wary, cautious seeing."

[3] Cf. Moult.-Mill., 455; Preis. Zaub., IV, 200, 236 f., 3089 f.

[4] ὅρα and ὅρα μή common in pap.; cf. Preisigke Wört., II, 192 f., s.v.

[5] Cf. Bl.-Debr. § 313; Mayser, II, 1 (1926), 122, n. 2; II, 2 (1934), 273. On the constr. with ὑπό (along with dat.) Act. Thom., 24 (Bonnet, 139, 13 ff.): ἄξιος γενέσθαι τῶν ὀφθέντων μοι ὑπὸ τῶν ἀγγέλων (cf. Mart. Mt., 16 [Bonnet, 237, 3]). The meaning "to be shown" (so Reinhold, 100: quasi in verbo ὁρᾶν notio monstrandi insit) does not arise here. Cf. H. Ljungvik, Studien zur Sprache der apkr. Apostelgeschichten (Uppsala Universitets Årsskrift [1926]), 34, cf. also → n. 117.

ὁπ- (e.g., fut. ὄψομαι always act., aor. pass. ὤφθην) [6] or from the stem ϝιδ-, aor. act. εἶδον.

The range of meaning is much the same in the case of ἰδεῖν ("to see") as in that of ὁράω. It denotes seeing as sense-perception, hence eye-witness : μάρτυρας παρίστημι τοὺς ἰδόντας, APF, 2 (1902), 125b, 13, cf. 26 f. (2nd cent. B.C.) : ὃ ἄν <μὴ> ἴδῃς, μὴ λέγε, saying of Solon (Diels⁵, I, 63, 21). Seeing implies being there, participating ; cf. the (inauthentic) saying of Democr. Fr., 115 (Diels⁵, II, 165, 7 f.) : ὁ κόσμος σκηνή, ὁ βίος πάροδος· ἦλθες, εἶδες, ἀπῆλθες. Hence ἰδεῖν τινα also means "to visit someone," "to meet someone" (Thuc., Xenoph.), "to speak with someone." From the time of Hom. generally for "to perceive," "to note," "to grasp," also "to consider." [7]

b. βλέπω "to see," from Aesch. and Pind., with a stronger emphasis on the function of the eye than in ὁράω. [8] Hence abs. often the opp. of "to be blind," e.g., βλέπων ἀμφοῖν ἐξῆλθε, Ditt. Syll.³, 1168, 78, cf. 75 (4th cent. B.C., Epidaurus); cf. ὀλίγον βλέπων, "short-sighted," P. Oxy., I, 39, 9 (52 A.D.) and διὰ τὸ μὴ βλέπειν τὰς νύκτας, P. Hal., I, 8, 4 (232 B.C.). φάος or ἥλιον βλέπειν common in the tragedians, e.g., Aesch. Pers., 261; also a simple βλέπειν in this sense, e.g., Aesch. Ag., 677. Though the sensual aspect is to the fore, βλέπω also took over in large part the other senses of ὁράω. With reference to the sense "to note something," "to be intent on," e.g., Democr. Fr., 96 (Diels⁵, II, 162, 9 f.), we should note the constr. of the imper. with μή [9] (common in the pap.) and also the constr. with ἀπό (outside the NT → n. 149 only BGU, IV, 1079, 24 [41 A.D.]) : βλέπε σατὸν (= σεαυτὸν) ἀπὸ τῶν 'Ιουδαίων. [10] βλέπω can also be used for conceptual perception, "to perceive," even abs. in the sense "to have insight," Soph. Phil., 110 etc. Not attested in the case of the other words is the use in geographical orientation, Xenoph. etc.: τὸν τοῖχον ... τὸν βλέποντα πρὸς νότον, Ditt. Syll.³, 691, 17 f. (131 B.C.); Preis. Zaub., IV, 138 f. [11]

c. ὁπτάνομαι, rare and late, only pass. : [12] the pres. P. Par., 49, 33 == Wilcken Ptol., 62, 33 (164-158 B.C.); P. Tebt., I, 24, 5 (117 B.C.); Corp. Herm., III, 2b; the aor. ὁπτανθέντα, P. Par., 574, 3033 f. == Preis. Zaub., IV, 3033 f. (4th cent. A.D.). The meaning corresponds to the pass. of ὁράομαι (→ 316), "to be visible," "to appear." [13]

d. θεάομαι, dep. [14] used from the time of Hom., abs. and with acc. to denote

---

[6] Root oqᵘ "to see," Lat. oculus. On the rare ὡράθην etc. cf. Mayser, I, 2² (1938), 189.
[7] On the imper. ἰδού used as interjection, cf. Pr.-Bauer³, s.v.; Bl.-Debr. § 101 s.v. ὁράω. On the etym. of ἰδεῖν [Debrunner]: root weid- wid- "to perceive," Lat. videre ; perf. woida (οἶδα "know" → 116), "have seen, recognised," "know." Cf. Walde-Pok., I, 236 ff. For linguistic observations esp. on ὁράω (more intentional) and εἶδον (more perceptional), but also βλέπω and θεάομαι, cf. A. Bloch, Zur Gesch. einiger suppletiver Verba im Griech., Diss. Basel (1940), 91-111.
[8] No certain etym. [Debrunner]. There is an emphasis on the sensual aspect in the compounds too, e.g., ἀναβλέπω, "to look up," "to regain sight" (after being blinded).
[9] Cf. Preisigke Wört., I, 271 and Moult.-Mill. 113 s.v.
[10] Cf. Deissmann LO, 96.
[11] βλέπω hardly seems to be adapted for visionary seeing, though cf. P. Par., 44, 6 == Wilcken Ptol., 68, 6 (153 B.C.).
[12] ὁπτάνομαι is hardly a new pres. construction from the pass. aor. ὤφθην (so Pr.-Bauer³, s.v.). It is rather a development of the verbal adj. ὁπτός (cf. also ἄοπτος → ἀόρατος, n. 1), perhaps by way of *ὁπτανός (so E. Schwyzer, Griech. Grammatik, I, Hndbch. AW, II, 1, 1 [1939], 700 and n. 2), so that an independent aor. ὡπτάνθην could be formed (→ infra). Cf. Preisigke Wört., II, 191; Moult.-Mill., 454, s.v.; Mayser, I (1906), 404, 465 == I, 3² (1935), 149; Deissmann LO, 65, 290, n. 3. Very late, e.g., Eustath. Thessal. Comm. in Il., 14, 101, we also find ὁπταίνω; cf. also ὁπτάζομαι in the LXX.
[13] Constr. with dat. (→ n. 5). In P. Tebt., I, 24, 5 : καὶ μηδαμῶς ὁπτανομένων ὑπ [. . . one can hardly supplement to form ὑπό; over 20 letters are missing at the end of the line].
[14] Aor. ἐθεάθην not found before the 1st cent. A.D. On the very late act. θεάω cf. Liddell-Scott, s.v. Etym. [Debrunner]: θεάομαι from θέα, "looking at," "view," which is related to θαῦμα, "astonishment," "surprise," "admiration." Cf. Walde-Pok., I, 832. With ref. to Hom. Snell, 18 says : "θεᾶσθαι is in some sense to see and in so doing to gape."

astonished or attentive seeing, "to look (at or upon)," "to behold." Cf. οἱ θεώμενοι, "spectators," Aristoph. Nu., 518, etc. (cf. θέατρον); Ditt. Syll.³, 730, 20 (1st cent. B.C.); Democr. Fr., 194 (Diels⁵, II, 185, 16).¹⁵ The term has a certain loftiness and even solemnity (cf. "to behold" and "to see"). It is thus used for visionary seeing¹⁶ and also in the Hermet. writings, where the ref. is usually to a spiritual and even visionary apprehension of higher reality, e.g., τὸ κάλλος τῆς ἀληθείας, Corp. Herm., VII, 3; cf. the link with νοέω, IV, 11b; X, 6 and the parallelism with κατανοέω, XI, 6b.

e. θεωρέω, from Aesch., is to be derived from the noun θεωρός, first found in Aesch., but it must be older. θεωρός (Arcad. θεαορός, Dor. θεαρός) reminds us in constr. of θυρωρός, πυλωρός (→ n. 20) and presupposes "tending," "charge," "care" (the same root as ὁράω, "to be aware of," [Hom., for *ὄρος] "watcher," → n. 2). Thus θεωρός might have come from *θᾱ𐅵ᾱ-𐅵ωρός, deriving from θέα (orig. θᾱ𐅵ᾱ), "show."¹⁷ In this case the basic sense would be "giving attention to a spectacle." In keeping is the fact that Aesch. uses θεωρός for spectator at a festival (these were all religious festivals), and esp. for a participant, one who visits the feast as the accredited representative of a friendly state. The use of θεωρός elsewhere fits in with this history of its meaning, esp. the oldest attested sense of θεωρέω, "to look at," "to view something." It is true that already the peripatetic school¹⁸ derived θεωρός from θεός (rather than θέα) in the sense of watching over the god, with primary ref. to cultic officials. This view has recently been revived.¹⁹ But there are serious etym. objections to it,²⁰ and it makes the transition to the sense of "(mere) spectator" hard to explain.²¹ Hence the former derivation is to be preferred. It should be emphasised, however, that in this case too, since the ref. is to spectators at a religious festival, the word must have had from the very first a sacral ring.²² The result is that the primary use of θεωρέω too must have been for watching religious festivities; θεωρέω has this

---

¹⁵ In the pap. (from the 3rd cent. B.C.) θεάομαι often means simply "seeing" (as frequently elsewhere, cf. Hdt., I, 8; 11, 3). Cf. Preisigke Wört., I, 666; Moult.-Mill., 285, s.v.
¹⁶ With Corp. Herm., VI, 6: μηδὲ ὄναρ θεασάμενον εἴ τί ἐστιν ἀγαθόν, cf. Philo Agric., 43: οὐδ᾽ ὄναρ ἰδόντι, "wholly unsuspecting," Poster. C., 22, and the phrase: "Not even in my wildest dreams (did I think of it)," et al.
¹⁷ The Dor. θεαρός and Arcad. θεαορός must be later dialect forms of the Ion.-Att. θεωρός (the hypothesis of P. Kretschmer, Zschr. f. vergleichende Sprachforschung, 31 [1890], 289 f.), which is quite possible. On θυραωρός and πυλαωρός, however, cf. E. Risch, Wortbildung d. homer. Sprache (1937), 195; P. Chantraine, Grammaire homérique (1942), 160 f. [Debrunner].
¹⁸ Cf. P. Boesch, ΘΕΩΡΟΣ. Untersuchung zur Epangelie griech. Feste, Diss. Zürich (1908), 1, n. 1.
¹⁹ Becker, 61 and the section 59-72: "Die Grundbedeutung von θεωρία." W. Krause, 61, n. 4 accepts this derivation.
²⁰ πῠλᾱ-ωρός (shown to be old by the ᾱ), Hom. Il., 8, 177 f.: οὐδενόσωρα (τείχεα) "not worth notice" = οὐδενὸς ὥραν ἔχων, "without regard for anyone or anything" and θυραωρός are the only ones with -ωρός in Hom. (there are none with -ορός or -ουρός). If θεωρός is related to θεός, we should have to have *θεο-𐅵ωρός, and it would have to be shown how this developed into θεαορός or θεωρός. *θεο-𐅵ωρός is unlikely, since this would give *θεουρός, cf. κηπουρός from *κηπο-𐅵ορός. The suggestion that because of the sequence of three short sounds *θεο-𐅵ορός became *θεᾱ-𐅵ορός *θηορός is unlikely, since κηπουρός is against it, and the supposedly analogous θεηκόλος (cf. Becker, 61 f., n. 6) comes from epic and like θανατηφόρος ἐλαφηβόλος etc. could have arisen by metrical expansion [Debrunner]. Rudberg, 162, n. 1 also rejects Becker's derivation.
²¹ Becker, 63 f. tries to explain the transition by giving θεωρία the basic sense of "divine service," "feast," "festivity." He then says of the participation of the spectator in sacrifices, processions, contests and games: "This participation of the individual in all these public actions was simply that of inwardly involved and solemn watching — the festival consisted simply of things to be watched. 'Watching,' then, meant the same as 'celebrating the feast,' and this was the same as 'serving the god.'"
²² Boesch, 4 wrongly concludes that the religious element is to be ruled out if there can be no question of derivation from θεός.

sense even more strongly than θεάομαι, though the term quickly passed into use for watching in general. [23] Cf. Ditt. Syll.[3], 1168, 23 f. (4th cent. B.C.) for looking at the πίνακες in a temple, and Xenoph. An., I, 2, 16 etc. for the military sense "to muster," "to review." In the general sense "to see," "to perceive," "to discover," "to recognise," [24] θεωρέω then became a synon. of θεάομαι and ὁράω and largely replaced ὁράω in the *koine*. [25] The fig. sense became particularly significant, "to contemplate," "consider," "investigate." Cf. already Democr. Fr., 191 (Diels[5], II, 184, 13), esp. Plato and Aristot., Corp. Herm., I, 7; XIII, 21, with ἐν τῷ νοΐ. This sense, which is shared by θεωρία (elsewhere "spectacle," "procession") and θεώρημα (elsewhere "spectacle"), and which is predominant in the case of the adj. θεωρητικός, leads to the use of θεωρέω, θεωρία etc. as tt. for scholarly treatment and understanding (theory as distinct from practice).

2. Seeing in the Greek World and Hellenism.

The fact that there are so many verbs of seeing, and that they cover such a wide and varied range of meaning, is an indication of the high estimation of seeing (→ 316), and corresponds to its indisputable importance for man. In a very special way the Greeks were "a people of the eye." [26] Hence it is no surprise that seeing should have taken on a very strong religious significance in the Greek world, or conversely that Greek religion may be regarded as a religion of vision. [27]

This insight would control the whole section if θεωρός could be derived from θεός and if the word group were thus to prove that this highly important seeing developed originally out of the cultus. But this thesis cannot be sustained (→ 318), nor does the strong emphasis on seeing, which is found already in the very earliest lit. (both epic and lyric), rest solely on this slender basis of religion and the cultus. These served only to foster and focus this aspect of seeing. [28]

From a very early period seeing and hearing were regarded as the most important instruments of perception, and of the two seeing was obviously given the palm: ὀφθαλμοὶ γὰρ τῶν ὤτων ἀκριβέστεροι μάρτυρες, Heracl. Fr., 101a (Diels[5], I, 173, 15 f.); Plat. Phaedr., 250d: ὄψις ... ἡμῖν ὀξυτάτη τῶν διὰ τοῦ σώματος ... αἰσθήσεων. [29] That verbs of seeing underwent an early transition from sensual to intellectual perception shows that at this stage the close relation between the two forms of perception was not contested. If what is perceived by the senses must be worked over by the νοῦς, and if in the last analysis

---

[23] Becker, 69 thinks this is a definite secularisation, with a full self-sublimation of the religious element which had characterised the word. But one can speak of secularisation only in a limited sense. For one thing, there was no lengthy development, but both uses were present together. For another, there was never any great distance between the sense of serving the god and that of watching, for watching was at issue in both cases, the one with a religious tinge, the other without.

[24] So also inscr., e.g., Ditt. Syll.[3], 590, 33 (196 B.C.); 630, 7 (182 B.C.); with acc. cum part., Ditt. Or., 751, 9 (2nd cent. B.C.), also pap. of the 3rd/2nd cent. B.C. (cf. Preisigke Wört., II, 675).

[25] Cf. Moult.-Mill., 290, *s.v.*; Preis. Zaub., I, 102, 185; IV, 164 f., 2364.

[26] "The Hellenes enjoyed in high measure the gift of seeing, of contemplating. They were a people of the eye, with a fine sense for what was seen in different forms and at different spiritual levels," Rudberg, 162.

[27] K. Kerényi, *Die antike Religion* (1940), 120.

[28] Rudberg, 166. Rudberg devotes 166-180 to this theme, and only 180-182 to seeing in the narrower religious sense.

[29] For further examples Rudberg, 178 f. Often seeing is used for the other senses, cf. 179 f. On the precedence of the eye over the ear among the Gks., and the profound reasons for this, cf. R. Bultmann, "Zur Geschichte d. Lichtsymbolik im Altertum," *Philologus*, 97 (1948), 16-23.

the νοῦς is thus decisive, no contradiction was felt between the νοῦς and the senses. [30] On the other hand, it was not overlooked that seeing and hearing, like all sensual perception, have their limits. There are many complaints about the inadequacy of the senses. [31] In many ways the insight is expressed that the senses are unable to grasp the true nature of things. Thus Melissos Fr., 8 (Diels[5], I, 274, 12) shows that things present themselves to the senses in constant flux, and he draws the deduction that their immutable nature is necessarily concealed from us: ὥστε συμβαίνει μήτε ὁρᾶν μήτε τὰ ὄντα γινώσκειν.

The same applies to the answer to the question whether and how far deity or the divine can be seen. In mythology, and the poetry which uses its themes, an anthropomorphic idea of the gods allows the assumption that they can be seen by human eyes. [32] But even here there are reservations.

In Hom. the god usually (though cf. Il., 1, 194-200) draws near only in human garb (Od., 1, 96-105; 2, 267 f.; 22, 205 f.; he may disappear in the form of a bird, thus making himself known, 1, 319 f.; 3, 371 f.; 22, 239 f.). In Od., 16, 161 it is emphasised: οὐ γάρ πως πάντεσσι θεοὶ φαίνονται ἐναργεῖς, cf. Il., 20, 131. Only to a few elect do the gods show themselves (with this reservation cf. also Od., 7, 201 ff.), and even then in such a way that they are present to these and not to others, cf. also Il., 1, 198 ff.; Od., 16, 159-162. If this seems to show that the ref. is to supernatural, visionary perception, [33] the naive poetic style does not allow us to be more precise about the nature of the seeing in these theophanies. There can be no doubt, however, that it is depicted with great restraint, cf. Od., 1, 321 ff.; 19, 33-43. Stress is often laid on the fear and terrible astonishment which seize men when the deity discloses itself, Il., 1, 199; 24, 170; Od., 1, 323; 19, 36; → III, 4. Nevertheless, we do not find in Hom. the idea that he who has seen the deity must die.

It may be added that in other texts which speak of the appearing of gods to men [34] these theophanies are visionary and hallucinatory experiences which are usually felt to be such even by those who have them. In relation to the accompanying circumstances as distinct from the actual declaration, what is seen is stressed rather than what is heard. [35] A special group is constituted by incubation visions at a sacred place, though

---

[30] Cf. Epicharmos Fr., 12 (Diels[5], I, 200, 16): νοῦς ὁρῆι καὶ νοῦς ἀκούει· τἇλλα κωφὰ καὶ τυφλά. The question how seeing arises was often discussed. For the Pre-Socratics cf. Index in Diels[5], III, 329, s.v. ὄψις. → II, 376, n. 9.

[31] Heracl. already called sight deceptive, cf. Fr., 46 (Diels[5], I, 161, 3 f.): ἔλεγε ... τὴν ὅρασιν ψεύδεσθαι. Fr., 107 (I, 175, 1 f.): κακοὶ μάρτυρες ἀνθρώποισιν ὀφθαλμοὶ καὶ ὦτα βαρβάρους ψυχὰς ἐχόντων, shows, of course, that the fault is not always with the senses, but may be with the "souls of those who, like barbarians, cannot understand aright the statements of the senses" (Diels, ad loc.).

[32] "The non-philosophical Gk. world from Hom. to Hellenism presupposes that deity can be known by seeing rather than by thinking," Kittel, 95. When it is said that the deity sees itself, this is usually an uninhibited, intentional or permissible anthropomorphism, though it may clothe a deeper insight, e.g., Emped. Fr., 24 (Diels[5], I, 135, 7): οὖλος ὁρᾶι, οὖλος δὲ νοεῖ, οὖλος δέ τ' ἀκούει, "God is wholly eye, wholly spirit, wholly ear." The deity is said to be all-seeing when there is a desire to stress omniscience, cf. Hes. Op., 267; Soph. Ant., 184 etc.

[33] It is thus doubtful whether the presupposition in Hom. is "that human eyes can see the deity, but may not do so because the deity does not will that they should," Bultmann, 171.

[34] It is connected with the concept of the stay of the dead in Hades that the early Gk. period did not believe that it is granted to man to see the gods after death.

[35] F. Pfister, Art. "Epiphanie," Pauly-W., Suppl. IV (1924), 277-323, lays the main stress on epiphanies in a wakeful state (279) and adduces only a few instances of other revelations, esp. in dreams, or described as dreams. His division into epic, mythical and legendary epiphanies is not wholly convincing. Ref. is often made to the NT material (cf. esp. 321 f.) but its distinctive features are not adequately noted (the OT material is ignored).

these are not always theophanies and may have a very different content. [36]

If even in mythology there is no direct reference to the visibility of the gods, in philosophy there were from the very outset those who emphasised the invisibility of the gods. Thus Emped. Fr., 133 (Diels[5], I, 365, 9 f.) emphasises :

οὐκ ἔστιν πελάσασθαι ἐν ὀφθαλμοῖσιν ἐφικτὸν
ἡμετέροις ἢ χερσὶ λαβεῖν

("one cannot bring the deity near to oneself as accessible to our eyes, or touch it with the hands"). This conviction took on added depth once the world of sense perception was seen in express antithesis to the spiritual world, as in Plato's doctrine of "ideas." Here ὁρᾶν was necessarily contrasted with νοεῖν. The world of the senses, the αἰσθητόν, can be ὁρατόν, but that of ideas, the true reality, is ἀόρατον, it is only νοητόν, only accessible to the νοῦς. [37] Hence the νοῦς alone can comprehend God. [38] Nevertheless — and this is worth noting — for the Greeks even supreme and purely intellectual striving is always a seeing. [39]

In particular θεωρεῖν, θεωρία and θεᾶσθαι are preferred for this. The questions arises once again whether this is because θεωρεῖν and θεωρία derive originally from the cultic and religious world. Since this is not at all certain (→ 318), and the other verbs of seeing are used in the same way, it seems rather that the significance of seeing for the Gks., [40] and the fig. use which developed on this basis, formed the starting-point for the concept of a purely intellectual seeing independent of the senses. As to the great importance of this pure seeing in Gk. philosophy and religion there can be not the slightest doubt.

Already in the introduction to Metaph., I, 1, p. 980a, 24 ff. Aristot. speaks of the pre-eminence of ὁρᾶν: τὸ ὁρᾶν αἱρούμεθα ἀντὶ πάντων ὡς εἰπεῖν τῶν ἄλλων. Plat. Tim., 47a-b extols the ability to see as a gift of God and the source of philosophy. In Resp., V, 475e he calls true philosophers τοὺς τῆς ἀληθείας φιλοθεάμονας. As the most spiritual sense, related to light, seeing gives access to true being. This contemplation (θεωρῶν) of πολὺ πέλαγος τοῦ καλοῦ (Symp., 210d) is something pure, reverent, disinterested, solemn and religious. Nor is it just θεωρεῖν, for we go on at once to read: βλέπων πρὸς πολὺ ἤδη τὸ καλόν. Plato uses θεᾶσθαι, too, in the same sense (Symp., 210c-212a). [41] The instrument

---

[36] Cf. L. Deubner, De incubatione, Diss. Giessen (1899). For the appearance of the deity ἐφίστασθαι is common (11), for the disappearance ἀναπέτεσθαι or ἀφανῆ γενέσθαι (13).

[37] This is almost a contradiction, since intrinsically ἰδέα and εἶδος (→ II, 373 ff.) mean "perceptible form," "image." The use of ἰδέα etc. for the "ideas" is not so much linked with the fact that νοεῖν is an intellectual seeing which has no need of the senses (Bultmann, 172). In the background for Plato himself is the mythical concept that prior to their earthly life souls did in fact contemplate the ideas, the pure forms of the higher world, cf. Phaedr., 246 ff.

[38] Bultmann, 171 ff.; Fascher, 61-64; Kittel, 95; 369, 1 ff. On the idea that God may be known from His works, cf. → III, 73 and n. 36. The problem of seeing God takes a particular form in the ruler cult, since here the divine ruler may be seen physically in a way for which there are no direct par. in other theophanies. Kleinknecht draws attention to the hymn of the Athenians for the cultic reception of Demetrios Poliorketes : the other gods ἢ οὐκ εἰσὶν ἢ οὐ προσέχουσιν ἡμῖν οὐδὲ ἕν, σὲ δὲ παρόνθ' ὁρῶμεν, οὐ ξύλινον οὐδὲ λίθινον, ἀλλ' ἀληθινόν. εὐχόμεσθα δή σοι, Athen., 6, 63 (253e). → (ἐπιφάνεια) φῶς.

[39] This section (A. 2) owes a great deal to the notes and refs. of Kleinknecht. The next main paragraph follows him almost word for word.

[40] For him "seeing and thinking were united from the very first, on a more primitive 'pre-logical' level," Rudberg, 183.

[41] Cf. Becker, 72-87: "Das Motiv des Schauens bei Plato"; F. Boll, Vita Contemplativa[2] (1922), 6 f., 26-30.

for this seeing of the divine is for Plato the "eye of the soul" (τὸ τῆς ψυχῆς ὄμμα, Resp., VII, 533d), which is better than ten thousand eyes, for with it alone is the truth perceived (μόνῳ γὰρ αὐτῷ ἀλήθεια ὁρᾶται, Resp., VII, 527d-e). At the end or climax of the loving ascent to the divine-beautiful itself (αὐτὸ τὸ θεῖον καλόν) there is only one thing which gives full meaning to life: θεᾶσθαι μόνον καὶ ξυνεῖναι, Symp., 211d-e. [42] This is contemplated with that wherewith alone it allows itself to be contemplated (ὁρῶντι ᾧ ὁρατὸν τὸ καλόν, ibid., 212a), the eye of the soul. This world of the prototype of being, in which the philosopher delights to tarry, is by no means easy to see because of its radiance. For most men cannot bear for long to gaze at the divine (πρὸς τὸ θεῖον ἀφορῶντα, Soph., 254a-b). [43] From this point it is only a step to the express religious formulation of Aristot. Eth. Eud., VII, 15, p. 1249b, 16 ff.: In contemplative self-giving to God, in τοῦ θεοῦ θεωρία, there is achieved the true purpose of human life, which is thus worship of God (τὸν θεὸν θεραπεύειν καὶ θεωρεῖν). To contemplate God is the way in which man should seek, so far as possible, to be like the immortals (ἐφ' ὅσον ἐνδέχεται ἀθανατίζειν, Eth. Nic., X, 7, p. 1177b, 33). For the divine mode of being and working consists in pure θεωρία, ibid., 8, p. 1178b, 20 ff. This line is continued and brought to supreme fulfilment in Plotinus. [44] Very typically for the Greeks the θεῖον is not something to be believed or heard; it is something to be seen, something revealed only to contemplation. This fact, first worked out in Greek philosophy, is also the core and essence of Greek religion. Ἡ τοῦ ὄντος θέα (Plat. Phaedr., 248b), τὸν θεὸν θεωρεῖν (Plot. Enn., V, 3, 7), understood as piety and worship — in this central idea Greek philosophy is simply transposing into an intellectual key something which had been a historical reality in the religious life of the Greek people.

In the mysteries, too, the visual plays an important role: ὄλβιος ὅστις ἰδὼν κεῖν' (= ἐκεῖνα), "Happy is he who has seen," says Pind. Fr., 137 in the fr. of the rites handed down in Cl. Al. Strom., III, 3, 17, 2; cf. also Hom. Hymn. Cer., 481: ὄλβιος ὃς τάδ' ὄπωπεν, → IV, 364, n. 28.

The ref., as at Eleusis (→ I, 217), is to the seeing of sacred actions, or, as in the Isis rites, Apul. Met., XI, 23 (→ I, 217), to seeing and worshipping at close proximity (de proxumo) the dii inferi and dii superi. Whether the initiate was taken on a nocturnal tour through various chambers of the sanctuary to representations of the gods or priests dressed up as gods, or whether these experiences were enjoyed in visionary and ecstatic

---

[42] This formulation is repeated in Symp., 211e-212a: ἆρ' οἴει ... φαῦλον βίον γίγνεσθαι ἐκεῖσε βλέποντος ἀνθρώπου καὶ ἐκεῖνο ᾧ δεῖ θεωμένου καὶ ξυνόντος αὐτῷ; Kleinknecht suggests: "θεᾶσθαι καὶ ξυνεῖναι, this is literally the same view of the relation of man to God as expressed already in Hom. (in the ideal sphere of Phaeacian life), Od., 7, 201 ff., cf. also Hes. Fr., 82 (Rzach)." In Hom. this θεᾶσθαι καὶ ξυνεῖναι is granted to only a favoured few, and Kleinknecht sees a par. here to the fact that in Plat. it is only for philosophers. He thus concludes that "in the cultic, poetic and philosophical world there lives on the same basic Gk. view of θεᾶσθαι καὶ ξυνεῖναι, though progressively spiritualised and refined in these areas." That the statements are par. can hardly be contested. Nevertheless, Plat. is not just a spiritualising of what is to be found already in Hom. His thought is a development of the unity of seeing and thinking (cf. → n. 40) which is not yet present in the same way in Hom.

[43] In Plat. Phaedr., 247d it is said on the other hand that the θεοῦ διάνοια itself contemplates the ideas from time to time: ἰδοῦσα διὰ χρόνου τὸ ὂν ἀγαπᾷ τε καὶ θεωροῦσα τἀληθῆ τρέφεται.

[44] Cf. particularly III, 8 and the interpretation of Becker, 87-106. Kleinknecht refers esp to Plot. Enn., V, 3, 17; 5, 11; VI, 7, 35 f. (cf. on this Bultmann, 33 f.).

states, is an enigma which has not yet been solved. [45] On the other hand, in the so-called Mithras Liturgy (Preis. Zaub., IV, 475-723) the ref. is plainly to ecstatic vision, to κατοπτεύειν ... τοῖς ἀθανάτοις ὄμμασι (516 f.) imparted to the one who is νοήματι μεταγεννηθείς, born again in spirit (cf. 508). [46]

In Hellenistic Gnosticism the conviction that God is invisible by nature is widely held, [47] as in other circles of later philosophy. Cf., e.g., Sen. Naturales Quaestiones, VII, 30, 3: *ipse ... qui totum hoc fundavit deditque circa se ... effugit oculos: cogitatione visendus est;* the Neo-Pythagorean Onatas in Stob., I, 48, 12 f.: ὁ μὲν ὢν θεὸς αὐτὸς οὔτε ὁρατὸς οὔτε αἰσθητός, ἀλλὰ λόγῳ μόνον καὶ νόῳ θεωρατός. [48] Nevertheless, Gnosticism appended the further idea that when man approximates to the divine nature and is deified he can see God. This essential change in man is brought about by *gnosis:* γνῶσις makes possible θέα, the vision of God; indeed, it is itself vision of God. [49]

The Herm. writings combine different strains of thought, but Gnostic statements predominate. It is expressly emphasised that God is not accessible to the senses: οὐ γὰρ ἐστιν ἀκουστός, οὐδὲ λεκτός, οὐδὲ ὁρατὸς ὀφθαλμοῖς, ἀλλὰ νῷ καὶ καρδίᾳ, Corp. Herm., VII, 2a; cf. VI, 4b, 5; XIII, 3, 11a. God is ἀόρατος and ἀφανής, V, 1 f., but also τῷ νοΐ θεωρητός, V, 10a. [50] Acc. to some passages this possibility of seeing God τῷ νοΐ is given to man only after death. Cf. Corp. Herm., X, 5 and the excerpt 6, 18 from Stob., I, 194 (Scott, I, 418, 12 ff.). [51] Acc. to other passages the vision of God is already fully possible for the Gnostic. Cf. Corp. Herm., V, 2; XII, 20b. The liberation from the world of sense and the subjection to the νοῦς or ψυχή, which make man a new creature (cf. XIII, 11a, if with Scott we are to read οὐσία καινὴ γενόμενος ὑπὸ τοῦ θεοῦ), are obviously an ecstatic experience: ἐγένετο γὰρ ὁ τοῦ σώματος ὕπνος τῆς ψυχῆς νῆψις, καὶ ἡ κάμμυσις τῶν ὀφθαλμῶν ἀληθινὴ ὅρασις, I, 30. [52] The preponderance of the visual element is incontestable in Corp. Herm. too. Hearing mostly refers to listening to and following the instructions of the mystagogue, → I, 695. These prepare the way for ecstatic vision (hence the order: hearing and seeing, e.g., I, 1). But there is also a very different line of thought, namely, that God becomes visible in His ποιήματα, cf. R. 1:20. Cf. XIV, 3: ἐπεὶ δὲ τὰ γεννητὰ ὁρώμενά ἐστι, κἀκεῖνος δὴ ὁρατός. διὰ τοῦτο γὰρ ποιεῖ, ἵνα ὁρατὸς ᾖ. ἀεὶ οὖν ποιῶν, ἀεὶ ὁρατός ἐστιν. It is true that the MSS here have ἀόρατος 3 times, but to read ὁρατός with Scott is critically sound (thus the context demands that the third ἀόρατος be read as ἀ<εἰ> ὁρατός) and is also suggested by XI, 21b, which says that it is wrong to call God ἀόρατος, for ὁ νοῦς ὁρᾶται ἐν τῷ νοεῖν, ὁ θεὸς ἐν τῷ ποιεῖν. We have here Stoic thoughts developed in a form which is partly rationalistic, partly pantheistic.

The magic pap. show with what practices and formulae attempts were made to force gods and demons to manifest themselves and subject themselves to control. αὔτοπτος (λόγος) is the tt. for prayers which are meant to lead to direct personal vision, e.g., Preis. Zaub., V, 54; VII, 319; cf. III, 699.

---

[45] L. Deubner, *Attische Feste* (1932), 83. Cf. J. Dey, ΠΑΛΙΓΓΕΝΕΣΙΑ = Nt.liche Abh., 17, 5 (1937), 64, 92, n. 14; H. Preisker, *Nt.liche Zeitgesch.* (1937), 142.

[46] Dey, 104-109.

[47] For details cf. Bultmann, 173 f.

[48] For further examples cf. J. Kroll, *D. Lehren d. Herm. Trism.* (1914), 18 f.

[49] → 318; I, 693, esp. 694 and n. 19 (ὁράω etc. and γινώσκω are often used synon.). → III, 569.

[50] Dobschütz, 408 f. and n. 25.

[51] Cf. Scott, III, 386, ad loc.

[52] Dey, 119-122; Bultmann, 174; K. Deissner, *Pls. u. d. Mystik seiner Zeit*[2] (1921), 30 f., 66 ff.

Along with φαίνεσθαι (φάνηθί μοι, IV, 999; VII, 331 etc.; cf. II, 115) we find esp.
ὀφθῆναι (ὄφθητί μοι, e.g., IV, 236; cf. 3089 f.), but also θεωρεῖν (e.g., I, 185; III,
512 f.; IV, 164 f.). When the deity in V, 101 f. is addressed : σὺ εἶ 'Οσοροννωφρις,
ὃν οὐδεὶς εἶδε πώποτε, no profound insight lies behind this expression, which is reminiscent of Jn. 1:18; it is simply meant to extol the efficacy of the formula, cf. also
XIII, 69 f. We have a weak and broken echo of philosophical terminology when
ἀόρατος is also to be found among the many divine attributes, e.g., V, 123; VII, 961;
XII, 455; XIV, 117; cf. τὸν πάντα ὁρῶντα καὶ μὴ ὁρώμενον, XIII, 163.

B. Usage and Concept in the Septuagint and Judaism.

I. Septuagint.

1. Meanings of the Terms.

a. ὁράω. With εἶδον this covers most of the refs. to seeing, ὁράω being used some
520 times, εἶδον some 930 (and 35 in Da. Θ). The frequency of the fut. ὄψομαι calls
for notice : 178 times. The pres. and perf. act. are balanced, 110 and 97 times (the rare
imp. 14). As aor. and fut. pass. ὤφθην and ὀφθήσομαι (77 and 32 times) are accompanied by ὡράθην in Ez. 12:12; 21:29; also Prv. 26:19 אּ*B and Da. Θ 1:15, also
'ΑΣ, and by ὁραθήσομαι in Job 22:14. [53] As perf. pass. ἑώραμαι, Lv. 14:35; Ju. 19:30 B
and ὦμμαι, Ex. 3:16; 4:1, 5; Ju. 13:10. The pres. pass. only Wis. 13:1: ἐκ τῶν ὁρωμέ-
νων ἀγαθῶν (cf. τὰ βλεπόμενα, 13:7; 17:6; → n. 68). In so far as we have the Mas.
(over 400 of the 520 instances) the main equivalent is רָאָה (over 350 times, 273 q,
77 ni). In 27 cases we have the Heb. חָזָה and in 7 the Aram. חֲזָה or חֲזָה הֲוָה (many
different words are used in the few remaining refs.). Things are much the same as
regards εἶδον : 670 instances רָאָה (almost always q), 17 or 19 הָוָה or חָזָה. In Gn. חָלַם
is 7 times the original of εἶδον, and יָדַע also occurs in nearly 20 instances, sometimes
when εἶδον is a vl. for various forms of εἰδέναι, e.g., Ex. 8:6; 33:13; Dt. 34:6; Job 19:14;
Jer. 10:25.

Fig. ψ 76:16 can speak of water seeing, ψ 113:3 of the sea, ψ 96:4 of the earth (though
the ref. in ψ 97:3; Is. 52:10 is to men). In Tob. ὁράω (like βλέπω) is often used for
the ability to see as distinct from blindness, cf. 3:17 א; 5:10 א; 11:8 א in the expression
"to see the light (of God or heaven)." In the sense "to live" (→ 316 f.) this expression
is used negatively in ψ 48:19 of the dead, in Job 3:16 of the unborn, and positively in
Job 33:28 of being delivered from death, cf. 33:30. Probably ἐν τῷ φωτί σου ὀψόμεθα
φῶς in ψ 35:9b (cf. 9a) is to be taken in the same way, unless the ref. is not just to
mere existence, but to full salvation both outward and inward. [54] In most cases ὁράω
does not mean only sense perception as such (as very commonly βλέπω) but also
intellectual perception. When seeing and hearing are mentioned together, the ref. is only
infrequently to sense perception (so in the judgments on idols, Dt. 4:28; ψ 113:13 f.;
134:16 f.). In most cases what is meant is recognition or understanding, e.g., Job 13:1;
Is. 52:15; Ez. 40:4 (also of God, 4 Βασ. 19:16; 20:5; Is. 37:17; 38:5; Da. 9:18). In this
combination seeing sometimes comes first (e.g., Qoh. 1:8; Sir. 17:13; Ez. 40:4) and sometimes hearing (e.g., Bar. 3:22; Is. 64:3; 66:8). The two functions are equal; God has
created both, Prv. 20:12. But seeing can denote true experience as distinct from mere
hearsay, e.g., ψ 47:8; Job 42:5; cf. also 4 Βασ. 7:13 f.

In the intrans. pass. use, in the sense "to cause oneself to be seen," "to show oneself," "to appear," "to be found," "to be there," the ref. is only seldom to perception

---

[53] Cf. also 'ΑΣ. Cf. Helbing, 96 f. → n. 6.
[54] H. Gunkel, Ps. (1926), 151, ad loc. In the "seeing of light" there is no echo of the
mysteries, as against R. Kittel, Die hell. Mysterienreligion u. d. AT = BWANT, NF, 7
(1924), 91 f. Cf. also the conjecture in Gunkel, 153. The promise in Is. 9:1 is obviously
a figure of speech.

with the eye. In verses like Nu. 23:21 (ἔσται / ὀφθήσεται), Ju. 19:30 (ἐγενήθη / ὤφθη or ἐόραται); 3 Βασ. 10:12 (ἐληλύθει / ὤφθησαν; cf. 2 Ch. 9:11) the parallelism makes it quite plain that ὀφθῆναι simply means "to be present." [55] Also stereotyped are expressions which speak of appearing before God or His presence in the temple (cf. ψ 62:2) etc. In such cases the LXX uses ὀφθῆναι with ἐνώπιον or ἐναντίον, or with the dat. If in places in the Heb. where רָאָה ni is construed with the acc. we should read an original רָאָה q, [56] then an original "see the face of God" in the HT was later felt to be objectionable and changed. The LXX went a step further and by the use of ἐνώπιον etc. avoided mention of God's πρόσωπον. [57] Here ὀφθῆναι means that man comes face to face with God in a religious and spiritual encounter. At ψ 16:15; 41:2, however, the LXX does use ὀφθῆναι with the dat. τῷ προσώπῳ (God's) (cf. ἐν προσώπῳ κυρίου, Sir. 35[32]:4), and it could also use the act. "to see the face." The expression "to see God's face" (on the seeing of God gen. → 331) is, of course, very rare, only Ex. 33:20, cf. 23 (→ 332), at Ps. 11:7 only the Mas. (the LXX goes its own way, on ψ 10:7 cf. 16:2), also Gn. 33:10 (at Job 33:26 the LXX renders differently, cf. also ψ 16:15a). [58] The phrase "to see the face" is common when the ref. is not to God; apart from instances like Gn. 31:2, 5 (cf. also Ex. 34:35 and 4 Βασ. 14:8, 11 par. 2 Ch. 25:17, 21); Gn. 46:30; 32:21, it has esp. the sense "to (be allowed to) visit someone," "to be received," Gn. 33:10; 43:3, 5; 44:23, 26 (cf. 1 Macc. 7:28, 30, "to have a personal encounter"), in the language of court "to be granted an audience," Ex. 10:28 f. etc.; 4 Βασ. 25:19 : οἱ ὁρῶντες τὸ πρόσωπον τοῦ βασιλέως as the title of a court official (cf. also Jer. 52:25; Est. 1:14). The simple ἰδεῖν (without πρόσωπον) can also be used for "to visit" (2 Βασ. 13:5 f.; 4 Βασ. 8:29; 9:16) and "to discuss with" (1 Macc. 10:56), cf. also ’Ιερ. 39(32):4; 41(34):3.

ὁράω and εἶδον are often used for spiritual perception. In the sense "to establish," "to observe," "to note," Gn. 16:4 f.; Ex. 8:11; Is. 29:15 (33:11) etc.; almost always in this sense in 1-4 Macc.; also of God, Gn. 1:4, 8; 7:1; 29:31 f.; Ex. 3:7; Dt. 9:16; 1 Βασ. 24:16; ψ 52:2; 118:159; Is. 30:19; Jer. 23:11, 13 (ἴδε with acc. is common in prayers in the sense "to regard," "to observe," sometimes par. with "to hear" : ψ 9:13; 24:18 etc.). In the sense "to recognise," "to perceive," Gn. 26:28; 37:20; 1 Βασ. 12:17; 2 Εσδρ. 14:5 etc.; also of God, Gn. 18:21; ψ 93:7; Is. 59:16 etc. Seeing is often the basis of spiritual perception, though other senses, e.g., hearing, are also mentioned, e.g., Gn. 2:19; 42:1; Hab. 2:1. Since רָאָה, like ὁράω (→ 317), can include other senses, the LXX follows the Heb. original even when another rendering would have been natural, cf. Ex. 20:18; Is. 44:16. The HT also underlies the very common use of the imper. in the sense "to take note" as an introduction to admonitions etc. (negatively "to guard against"), also as an interjection in direct speech etc. ὅρα (ὁρᾶτε) and ἴδε (ἴδετε) correspond here to

---

[55] Cf. Michaelis, 151, n. 147.

[56] Baudissin, 181 ff. Barth, 308 f., n. 133 doubts the possibility of such emendation, but his ref. to the distinction between an act. and pass. sense of פָּנִים (71, 308, n. 130) is questionable in this form.

[57] Cf. Johannessohn Präpos., 190-197. When ἐνώπιον is used the etym. connection with "face" is no longer clearly sensed.

[58] In the HT the no. of instances is, of course, much greater if "to appear before God's face" is a correction of "to see God's face," → n. 56. On Bab. pars. cf. Baudissin, 189 ff.; F. Nötscher, "Das Angesicht Gottes schauen" nach bibl. u. babylon. Auffassung (1924), 62-76. If the orig. ref. is to worship before a statue, the cultic situation may often be detected in the OT, but with no ref. to a statue (→ II, 381 ff.). To the fore in the OT is the sense of God's spiritual proximity. Cf. Gunkel, 41; Hempel, Gott u. Mensch im AT = BWANT, 3, F. 2 H² (1936), 267; L. Köhler, Theol. d. AT (1936), 108 ff. On Canaanite influences cf. Baudissin, 192-196; Bultmann, 178, n. 1; 181, n. 1; cf. also E. G. Gulin, "Das Angesicht Jahves im AT," Annales Academiae Scientiarum Fennicae B, XVII, 3 (1923), 5 ff., 22, n. 5.

הִנֵּה or רְאֵה (וּרְאוּ); there is often approximation to the sense "to recognise," e.g., ἴδετε καὶ γνῶτε, ἐρευνήσατε καὶ ἴδετε etc. [59]

The LXX again follows the HT in using the word for "to experience" through one-self or others, "to learn to see," "to detect," "to realise" etc. This is one of the senses of רָאָה; only at Est. 9:26 does the LXX have the apt ὅσα πεπόνθασιν for מָה־רָאוּ. In most cases the context makes the meaning plain enough : [60] thus to see sword and famine (Jer. 5:12; 14:13) is to experience war and hunger ; to see good, Job 7:7; [61] ψ 26:13; [62] Jer. 17:6; ψ 33:12 (ἡμέρας ἀγαθάς) is to experience good things, cf. to see evil (ψ 89:15), to see διαφθοράν or καταφθοράν (ψ 15:10; 48:9), [63] death (ψ 88:48), life (Is. 26:14; cf. 53:10 : σπέρμα μακρόβιον). In verses like Ex. 34:10; Dt. 3:21; 4:3, 9; 11:7 (cf. Sir. 42:15) the ref. is not to the recollection of experiences but seeing God's ἔργα means encounter with the God who is at work in history, cf. Sir. 36(33):2; Mi. 7:9; Is. 62:2; also Tob. 13:17 א. In ψ 62:2 the aim of visiting the temple is : τοῦ ἰδεῖν τὴν δύναμίν σου καὶ τὴν δόξαν σου (in the HT we first have בַּקֹּדֶשׁ חֲזִיתִיךָ, "in the sanctuary I have seen thee"; on the LXX version → 333). [64] If the ref. is to proclamation of the saving acts of Yahweh in which His δύναμις is manifest, ψ 62:2 is an example to show that what the righteous see in worship is not subjective. In a passage like Is. 52:10 the parallellism of ἀποκαλύψει κύριος and ὄψονται shows that in such cases man's seeing is complementary to God's revealing.

This helps us to understand how the expression "to see God's glory" is to be taken. In ψ 96:6; Is. 26:10; 35:2; 66:18 f.; [65] Sir. 42:25 (on ψ 62:2 → supra) it is impossible to think in terms of sense perception, but one can also speak of spiritual perception and personal experience only in the sense of seeing as the receiving of the revelation of God in His δόξα. Further examples are Ex. 16:7; Nu. 14:22 (on Nu. 12:8 → 331). In close proximity to these passages we often find refs. to the ὀφθῆναι of the δόξα κυρίου (Ex. 16:10; Lv. 9:6, 23; Nu. 14:10; 16:19; 17:7; 20:6) in connection with a rather more concrete understanding of the δόξα κυρίου (→ II, 240, 244 f.). But the concreteness is not to be sought exclusively or even especially in the use of ὀφθῆναι. It rather resides in the special use of δόξα κυρίου, and finds particular expression in the mention of the νεφέλη (→ IV, 905, 36 ff.). But the cloud, which is mentioned with the δόξα κυρίου in other verses too (e.g., Ex. 24:15 ff.), is only a veil, and if "a manifestation of the glory of God" is in view (→ II, 240; cf. Ex. 24:17), one cannot finally deduce from the use of ὀφθῆναι

---

[59] The imp. ἴδε (ἴδετε) can also introduce dependent clauses with ὅτι, ὡς, εἰ or interr. pronoun. Cf. M. Johannessohn, "Der Wahrnehmungssatz bei d. Verben d. Sehens in d. hbr. u. gr. Bibel," Zschr. f. vergleichende Sprachforschung, 64 (1937), 145-260. Semitic narrative style is to be seen in the common εἶδον καὶ ἰδού (esp. frequent in Ez. in depicting visions). Cf. M. Johannessohn, "Das bibl. καὶ ἰδού in d. Erzählung samt seiner hbr. Vorlage," ibid., 66 (1939), 145-195; 67 (1942), 30-84.

[60] In Qoh. 8:16; Lam. 3:1; even more so Qoh. 9:9; 2:1 the sense is obscured by lit. transl.

[61] Though the eye is mentioned here (cf. ψ 16:2), in Qoh. 1:16 it is the καρδία which has seen σοφία and γνῶσις, i.e., which has come to share them ; in Is. 53:10 seeing is ascribed to the ψυχή.

[62] On the constr. with בְּ cf. Gunkel, 118, ad loc.

[63] In both passages the HT has שַׁחַת, "grave" (= sheol); the LXX obviously connected שַׁחַת (related to שׁוּחַ, "to sink") with שָׁחַת, "to perish" (cf. Ges.-Buhl, s.v. שַׁחַת). In Job 38:17b: וְשַׁעֲרֵי צַלְמָוֶת תִּרְאֶה, the ref. is not to real experience of death, i.e., dying, but to learning the situation of sheol (the LXX read וְשֹׁעֲרֵי).

[64] "It is evident that 'seeing' does not refer to cultic actions perceptible to the senses, since power cannot be perceived by them, even if glory can," Baudissin, 176. → II, 241.

[65] In Is. 66:19 οὐδὲ ἑωράκασιν τὴν δόξαν μου comes after οὐκ ἀκηκόασίν μου τὸ ὄνομα, but as the one denotes receiving the message, so the other denotes a share in the revelation of δόξα which constitutes the content of the message.

the manner in which the δόξα κυρίου made its presence known ; the ὀφθῆναι simply denotes its presence as such. In these passages ὀφθῆναι is thus to be regarded as a term in the vocabulary of revelation. [66] Hence Ex. 16:7; Nu. 14:22 remain in the sphere of the use of "to see God's glory" elsewhere. In the case of Ex. 16:7 this is made perfectly clear by the parallelism with 16:6 (in both verses the sense is roughly "to attain to conviction," "to reach certainty"). The statements in Is. 40:5 (HT וְנִגְלָה; cf. 60:2); ψ 16:15, where δόξα is not meant concretely, also show that ὀφθῆναι simply denotes the presence of revelation as such with no necessary reference to its sensual perceptibility, → II, 238 ff.; 242 ff.

b. βλέπω occurs over 130 times, 38 in Ez. In 35 of the instances in Ez. we have a use, attested also in Nu. 21:20; Jos. 18:14; 2 Ch. 4:4, [67] for geographical or architectural directions (→ 317). Where there is a Mas. original it is mostly פָּנָה q, in 9 cases the noun פָּנֶה, "front." Otherwise βλέπω corresponds in the Mas. almost exclusively to רָאָה (nearly always q). In the LXX, too, βλέπω more than other verbs of seeing denotes ability to see, e.g., Gn. 48:10; 1 Βασ. 3:2 etc.; cf. Ex. 4:11 and fig. 23:8. [68] In Qoh. 11:7: ἀγαθὸν τοῖς ὀφθαλμοῖς τοῦ βλέπειν σὺν (rendering of the acc. after the manner of ᾽Α) τὸν ἥλιον the Gk. reader can catch the expression ἥλιον βλέπειν (→ 317) and thus grasp the tenor of the saying. βλέπω is often combined with ἀκούω, but in Dt. 29:3; Is. 6:9; 44:18; Jer. 5:21; Ez. 12:2, also Da. Θ 5, 23, the ref. is obviously to spiritual perception. Very occasionally it can be used of God, ψ 9:31, 34; Sir. 15:18 (cf. 19); also Da. LXX 3:55. In 1 Βασ. 9:9, 11, 18; 1 Ch. 9:22; 29:29 the predicate of Samuel (הָרֹאֶה) is rendered ὁ βλέπων; it is left untranslated in 1 Βασ. 9:19 (at 16:4 the LXX also read, or misread, בֹּאֲךָ as הָרֹאֶה and added ὁ βλέπων; for רֹאֶה προφήτης is used at 1 Ch. 26:28; 2 Ch. 16:7, 10; Is. 30:10). βλέπω is also used for prophetic vision in the question τί σὺ βλέπεις; Am. 8:2; Zech. 4:2; 5:2, also Ez. 13:3, 6. βλέπω does not occur in the expressions "to see God," "to see God's δόξα or πρόσωπον" (though τὸ πρόσωπον βλέπειν occurs in court style at 2 Βασ. 14:24).

c. ὀπτάνομαι occurs twice, both times impf., also pres. in an addition in Sir. after 1:10 or later (→ 333). In 3 Βασ. 8:8 the first יֵרָאוּ is rendered ἐνεβλέποντο, while the second time we read : οὐκ ὠπτάνοντο ἔξω "(the ends of the staves of the ark) were not seen without" (pass.). It is most unlikely that the ref. in Tob. 12:19 AB : πάσας τὰς ἡμέρας ὠπτανόμην ὑμῖν, καὶ οὐκ ἔφαγον οὐδὲ ἔπιον, ἀλλὰ ὅρασιν ὑμεῖς ἐθεωρεῖτε, is already to a manifestation in the sense of a ὅρασις, since this idea is not developed in what follows. The constr. of θεωρέω with ὅτι in א leads us to suppose that ὠπτανόμην ... καί in AB faithfully renders a co-ordinating constr. of the Heb. original, with the meaning : "All the days I was visible to you (you saw) that I neither ate nor drank." ὀπτάζομαι is an intrans. pass. at Nu. 14:14 : ὅστις (sc. God) ὀφθαλμοῖς κατ᾽ ὀφθαλμοὺς ὀπτάζῃ (HT רָאָה ni).

d. θεάομαι, which occurs 8 times, also 4 in other transl., has a Heb. original only at 2 Ch. 22:6 (רָאָה); the meaning here is "to visit." At Tob. 2:2 AB the ref. is to seeing with astonishment, cf. 2 Macc. 2:4. In Jdt. 15:8; Tob. 13:7; 2 Macc. 3:36 the ref. is to contemplation of God's acts leading to praise, in Tob. 13:16 AB to seeing the future δόξα of Jerusalem, in Jdt. 15:8 to personal convincing, though the combinations with

---

[66] When in 2 Macc. 2:8 (→ II, 245; IV, 905, 47) the ref. back to the adduced passages is made with the clause ὡς ἐπὶ Μωυσῇ ἐδηλοῦτο, a revelation term is rightly inserted, → II, 61; 30.

[67] Cf. also Prv. 16:25 LXX (not 14:12).

[68] Liddell-Scott, s.v. pt. out that τὰ βλεπόμενα in Wis. 13:7 is an (isolated) instance for "the visible world," but it means, not the whole visible world, but only what is offered to the ὄψις. "What is seen," "what is before our eyes," is a better rendering, cf. also 17:6 → 324. The pass. of βλέπω is rare in the LXX, cf. Wis. 2:14; 2 Ch. 5:9 (twice); mid. fut. βλέψομαι, Dt. 28:32, 34; Job 10:4; Is. 29:18.

ὑπ' ὄψιν at 2 Macc. 3:36 and κόραις ὀφθαλμῶν at 3 Macc. 5:47 show that θεάομαι does not have to include eye-witness.

e. θεωρέω occurs 56 times, 13 in Da. LXX (17 also in Da. Θ), 12 in 1-4 Macc., 8 in Ps., 6 in Wis. (no instances in Pent., 1-4 Βασ., Job, or the prophets, except Da.). Often other verbs of seeing contest the place of θεωρέω as vl. Where there is a Mas. equivalent it is 11 times רָאָה, but this occurs in Da. LXX only at 8:15, elsewhere in Da. either Aram. הֲזָה חֱזָה or חֱזָה (Heb. חָזָה at ψ 26:4). The ref. in Da. is to visionary seeing except at 3:91 LXX; 3:94 LXX Θ (cf. Sus. 37 LXX, 8:20 Θ). Mostly θεωρέω denotes sense perception, Jos. 8:20; Ju. 13:19 f. etc.; "to see the sun or the light" == "to live" at Qoh. 7:11; Tob. 5:10 א. In line with the sense of participation in a festival θεωρέω is used in Ju. 16:27 B for the spectators of Samson's making sport, and in ψ 67:24 (here also 'ΑΘΣ, where the term is uncommon) for watching processions; at 26:4, too, the LXX suggests cultic participation more strongly than the Heb. Less common are meanings remote from actual seeing, e.g., ψ 72:3; Tob. 9:3 א etc.; also ψ 65:18. Only in Wis. 6:12; 13:5 does the word mean "to perceive"; on 6:12 cf. προγνωσθῆναι in 6:13; in 13:5 there occurs a thought similar to R. 1:20: ἐκ γὰρ μεγέθους καὶ καλλονῆς κτισμάτων ἀναλόγως ὁ γενεσιουργὸς αὐτῶν θεωρεῖται.

2. The Significance of Seeing in OT Proclamation.

As regards the distinction between sensual and spiritual seeing, the compass of verbs of seeing is much the same in Greek and Hebrew, so that the LXX translators were not in the main confronted by any very serious difficulties (exceptions are Gn. 39:23; 41:33; Sir. 7:22; Is. 5:12).[69] In the many instances in which God is said to see,[70] one should remember how far the verbs of seeing can move away from the idea of sense perception (→ 324; 325; 327; 328). Anthropomorphisms in the narrower sense are extremely rare.

Plain instances are Gn. 6:12; 11:5; Ex. 12:13, 23; but in Gn. 9:16, inasmuch as the LXX (intentionally?) does not transl. the suffix in רְאִיתִיהָ, ὄψομαι τοῦ μνησθῆναι may be taken in the sense "and I will pay heed to it to remember." At Ex. 3:4 εἶδεν means "he noted." In 1 Βασ. 16:7 the distinction between human and divine seeing is very plain, and there is already a suggestion of the fig. sense "to observe," "to judge" (on Job 10:4 → 379). Refs. to God seeing are common in the poetic diction of the Ps., prophets etc. In ψ 13:2 the meaning is more "to ascertain," but just before we read: κύριος ἐκ τοῦ οὐρανοῦ διέκυψεν, cf. also Lam. 3:50; Is. 63:15. Also Job 31:4; Sir. 1:9; Jer. 23:24, with ἐπιβλέπειν ψ 32:13; Lam. 1:11; 2:20; 5:1; though here already in the sense "to look at," "to observe," "to pay attention," cf. also ἴδε → 325. It is worth noting that even a later age did not think it inappropriate to speak of God seeing.[71] Thus the LXX has no reason to make alterations. In Job 35:13 f. God is called ὁρατής contrary to the HT, perhaps under the influence of 34:21.[72] The pertinent instances with ὀφθαλμός (→ 376) and ἐπόπτης (→ 374) fit into the total picture. On βλέπειν of God → 327; θεᾶσθαι and θεωρεῖν are not ascribed to God.

---

[69] Bertram pts. out that the many compounds of verbs of seeing used in the LXX often correspond to Heb. words which have nothing whatever to do with seeing. He refers specifically to ἀνα-, ἐπιβλέπειν, παρ-, ὑπεριδεῖν.
[70] Cf. H. Middendorf, *Gott sieht. Eine terminologische Studie über das Schauen Gottes im AT*, Diss. Freiburg i.Br. (1935).
[71] Cf. Köhler, 6 on the function of anthropomorphisms in the OT.
[72] ὁρατής only as a vl. (for ὁρατός) at 2 Βασ. 23:21.

On the question of the position of seeing as such in the OT, especially as contrasted with hearing, it is important that the verbs of seeing embrace a whole series of meanings which have little to do with seing, that the very common verbs of hearing (e.g., ἀκούω in some 1080 verses) are also used for spiritual processes, and that words like ἀγγέλλω, γινώσκω, διδάσκω, κηρύσσω, μανθάνω may be related to either seeing or hearing. As concerns theologically significant statements about the relation of man to God and His revelation, it seems that greater importance is attached to hearing in the OT, cf. also → I, 217 f. In what follows we shall discuss this in relation to two particularly relevant questions, that of visionary-ecstatic prophetic seeing, and that of whether God may be seen, and, if so, how.

a. Visionary-Ecstatic Prophetic Seeing. [73]

ὁράω and εἶδον, for רָאָה and חָזָה, are the characteristic words used for visionary-ecstatic prophetic seeing (cf. also → 327 and n. 59). חֹזֶה as a title refers usually to a professional seer in the service of a king, and it is rendered ὁ ὁρῶν in the LXX : 2 Βασ. 24:11 (= 1 Ch. 21:9); 4 Βασ. 17:13; 2 Ch. 9:29; 12:15; 29:25; 33:18 f.; also Am. 7:12; [74] for הָרֹאֶה, however, ὁ βλέπων is selected, → 327. In relation to these seers the OT does not record any visions ; in 2 Βασ. 24:11; 2 Ch. 29:25 we have revelations by word. There may be a ὁρᾶν in revelations during sleep, Gn. 31:10; 41:22; cf. Nu. 24:4, 16, also the combination with ἐνύπνιον, Gn. 37:9; 40:5, 8 etc.; Est. 1:1a; 10:3b; Mi. 3:7; Da. passim. These dreams are purely visual, [75] so that the pictures and images seen have to be interpreted by individuals specially endowed therefor (by God). [76] Though not without reservations (→ III, 434 f.), such dreams are accepted as revelation, as an impartation of the divine will and knowledge, → 230. They are not called an ὀφθῆναι of God ; they represent a different type from the revelations by night in, e.g., 3 Βασ. 3:5 (→ 333). Gn. 28:10 ff. (→ n. 92) also stands apart.

The so-called night visions of Zech. (1:8 etc.) are not to be regarded as dreams (cf. 4:1). They belong to the second category of prophetic visions, [77] i.e., hallucinatory or inner perceptions which may occur either by day or by night. [78] If in the HT the use of רָאָה or חָזָה depends on whether the visions are genuine visions which come from God or deceptions which come only from one's own heart, [79] this distinction is effaced in the LXX. ὁράω is used indiscriminately for רָאָה, e.g., Am. 7:8; 8:2 A; Zech. 5:1; Ez. 8:17 (also with חִזָּיוֹן Jl. 2:28), and for חָזָה, e.g., Am. 1:1; Mi. 1:1; Ez. 12:27; 13:9; Lam. 2:14. The marks of the authenticity of visions are the same as those of the authenticity of the prophetic message of revelation in general, → III, 575. In particular, the principle holds good that man is always the recipient and never the author of revelation. There is no human

---

[73] This is more in the nature of a general term embracing different types. Ref. may be made to the perspicacious researches of Hänel. Cf. also F. Haeussermann, "Wortempfang u. Symbol in d. at.lichen Prophetie," ZAW, Beih., 58 (1932). The material is treated rather too much on the one level in Köhler, 86-91. → προφήτης.

[74] In the LXX alone Is. 29:10 (cf. 47:13); 30:10; Nu. 24:3, 15. Mantic ὁρᾶν (רָאָה): 1 Βασ. 28:12 f.

[75] One part of the ἐνύπνια in Da. is an exception, cf. Michaelis, 151, n. 143.

[76] On Gn. 31:11 cf. Michaelis, 151, n. 144.

[77] Hänel, 115-122.

[78] It is debatable how far one may speak of ecstatic experiences, cf. → II, 454 f.; Hänel 61-64, 80; Hempel, 96, n. 9.

[79] Baudissin, esp. 207 ff.; Hänel, 7-13.

process, whether prayer, sacrifice, or a specific technique, whereby man can bring about a theophany. [80] God Himself shows the prophets visions, e.g., Am. 7:1, 4, 7; 8:1; Ez. 40:4 (→ II, 29; HT ראה hi). Here is an important distinction from the mystery religions and the native Gnostic attempt to attain to vision by contemplation or more external methods.

There is no tt. for audition, [81] and חָזוֹן, מַרְאֶה etc. as well as ὅρασις etc. are used even when the ref. is not, or not only, to visual impressions. The consistency of this usage indicates that the visual element might have been predominant originally ; the more significant, then, is the development to a predominance of the auditive aspect. In the prophets, especially the great writing prophets, the material preponderance of hearing over seeing is quite unmistakable. Mostly revelation by word is also to the fore ; revelation by picture is more and more a framework for revelation by word, → I, 218. [82] Furthermore, the theme and content of the visual side of prophetic visions is not God Himself. What is to be heard is God Himself, who gives His Word to the prophet in the vision. But what is to be seen is not God Himself. As in dreams, it is persons, animals, objects, processes such as occur in nature and life, sometimes with mythological or heavenly features, but never God Himself. It is commensurate with the OT view of God that God reveals Himself with (relative) immediacy in what can be heard, but not in what can be seen.

Unless the structure demands a different constr., the content of what is seen is introduced as an acc. obj. of ὁράω or by expressions like εἶδον καὶ ἰδού (→ n. 59), but not with ὤφθη (the only exceptions are 2 Macc. 3:25 and Da. 8:1 Θ). In keeping is the fact that ὤφθη is for its part the characteristic term to denote the (non-visual) presence of the self-revealing God, → 333.

The principle that God Himself is not seen in visions is not qualified by what is said about the δόξα κυρίου in the visions of Ez. The δόξα is not described, and in 1:28 there is only a general ref. to the ὅρασις ὁμοιώματος δόξης κυρίου, cf. 1:26; 3:23; 8:1 ff.; → II, 241, n. 32. He who speaks with the prophet is not described and is obviously not even seen, cf. 43:5 f.; [83] 44:4 f. Only later in Da. 7:9 is there in a vision a description of God, and even this is not very explicit. Nor is this depiction of the Ancient of Days the real point of the vision 7:1-28. What it is really presenting is the fate of the four empires. It is also significant that the no less important figure of the Son of Man is not described. Above all, the visions in Da. 7 ff. are only a literary device and do not present genuine prophetic visions. Am. 9:1 is obviously only introductory and not a report, of equal importance with the divine Word, that the prophet has seen God in a vision, cf. also the introductory 7:1, 4, 7; 8:1, also the LXX version of 7:7. In the vision at the call of Is. (6:1 ff.) the εἶδον τὸν κύριον of 6:1 is certainly given emphasis by the addition τοῖς ὀφθαλμοῖς μου in 6:5, but here, too, there is no description of the figure of God, → II, 381. Nevertheless, Is. 6:1 stands apart. There is nothing par. in any other prophet (cf. Jer. 1:9), nor is there any repetition in any of the other visions in Is. Finally, in 3 Βασ. 22:19 (= 2 Ch. 18:18) Micaiah ben Imlah says that he has seen God on His heavenly throne and been a spectator of what took place between Him and His servants. This ancient witness, however, is more a poetic garb, closer to Job 1 than Zech. 3, for the Word of the Lord which Micaiah is to deliver to Ahab.

---

[80] Köhler, 87; → II, 455.

[81] שְׁמוּעָה does not mean "audition" but "report," "message," Hänel, 82, n. 2, 67-71, 74-80. The LXX has the good renderings ἀγγελία at Is. 28:9 and ἀκοή at 53:1; Ἰερ. 30:8 (Mas. 49:14); Ob. 1; Is. 28:19; → I, 221.

[82] Köhler, 87: "Even revelation in visions is revelation by word." Cf. esp. → IV, 98; I, 218. For a completely different view cf. Barth, 62 ff., 68, 308, n. 124.

[83] At Ez. 43:7 the LXX transl. שָׁכֶן־שָׁם אֲשֶׁר by κατασκηνώσει τὸ ὄνομά μου (= שָׁם). The idea of seeing God is thus kept at a distance.

b. Seeing God in Theophanies etc.

In Nu. 12:8 the direct seeing of God in theophanies is not brought into relation to the visionary seeing of God by the prophets. 12:6 already makes it plain that the prophets — the verse reflects later reflection, so that the reference is to the writing prophets of the 8th and 7th centuries — do not see God in their visions, but that God declares His will in visions, speaking therein to the prophets. Moses is magnified in 12:8 by reason of the unique fact that only with him did God speak פֶּה אֶל־פֶּה, στόμα κατὰ στόμα. [84] The comparison, then, is between the way in which God spoke to Moses on the one side and the way He spoke to the prophets on the other.

That speaking פֶּה אֶל־פֶּה does not have to mean that Moses saw God directly may be learned from Ex. 33:11 (cf. 33:18 ff.) and Dt. 34:10 (cf. Nu. 14:14). The statement which follows Nu. 12:8 : וּתְמֻנַת יהוה יַבִּיט, is perhaps a gloss. There is nothing comparable in 12:6, the words used are rare, and in particular God is spoken of in the third person. If the statement is original, the relation of נָבַט to Ex. 3:6 and of תְּמֻנָה to Ps. 17:15 and esp. Dt. 4:12, 15 makes it doubtful whether we are to think of an actual seeing of God. From the transl. καὶ τὴν δόξαν κυρίου εἶδεν the LXX reader understands that Moses perceived the δόξα κυρίου or experienced the revealed presence of God, → 326.

At the burning bush in Ex. 3:2 the angel of Yahweh appeared to Moses (וַיֵּרָא ... אֵלָיו ὤφθη δὲ αὐτῷ). From 3:4 on God Himself is referred to rather than the angel, → I, 77 f. 3:6 says expressly, however, that Moses veiled his face because "he was afraid to look upon God." (This is softened in the LXX rendering : εὐλαβεῖτο γὰρ κατεμβλέψαι ἐνώπιον τοῦ θεοῦ, "to look before God, in God's presence," i.e., at the burning bush.) It might appear that God could have been seen but that Moses did not avail himself of the opportunity. Though Moses did not see God, it can be said in 3:16 : "The Lord, the God of your fathers, נִרְאָה אֵלַי ὦπταί μοι" (cf. 4:1, 5). This makes it quite evident that the intrans. ὀφθῆναι does not mean "to present oneself to the eyes for sense perception," but "to manifest oneself as present." This is particularly clear in 6:3, where it is said that God appeared (וָאֵרָא אֶל καὶ ὤφθην πρός) to Abraham, Isaac and Jacob, for there are no accounts of theophanies to Isaac (the reference is not to the angelophany of Gn. 22:11 ff.). Comparison of 6:3 with the mention of the patriarchs in 3:16; 4:5 shows that the emphatic ὀφθῆναί τινι means "to attest oneself to someone as God." This is surely the sense in 3:4 as well.

It is probably meant as a higher form of the manifestation to all the people at Sinai when we are told in Ex. 24:10 f. (→ III, 109) that a select group of men was allowed to ascend the mountain with Moses and that there they saw God (רָאָה in v. 10, חָזָה in v. 11). The reference in 24:1, of course, is only to worship from a distance, but originally 24:10 f., as the other contents show, belongs to a very ancient stratum in which there is uninhibited reference to a seeing of God tale quale (though God is not described either here or in 24:12 ff.). The LXX softens the realism. In 24:10 it reads : εἶδον τὸν τόπον οὗ εἱστήκει ἐκεῖ ὁ θεὸς

---

[84] In what follows we should probably read וְלֹא בְמַרְאֶה וְלֹא בְחִידֹת, "and neither by visions nor by riddles." On the LXX version → II, 374, n. 7. Rabb. exposition (→ I, 178 f.) laboriously seeks to harmonise the traditional version of 12:8 with 12:6.

τοῦ Ἰσραήλ, [85] and the conclusion of v. 11 is as follows: καὶ ὤφθησαν ἐν τῷ τόπῳ τοῦ θεοῦ καὶ ἔφαγον καὶ ἔπιον.

Much more restrained are the statements in Ex. 33:18 ff. In v. 18 Moses expresses the wish that God might let him see His δόξα. As compared with הַרְאֵנִי the sensual element is far less in δεῖξόν μοι (δείκνυμι is a common rendering of ראה, → II, 29). The direct answer to the wish is in v. 19, and perhaps the continuation in vv. 20-23 or 20, 22 f. (E) is not originally related to v. 18 (J), though the δόξα is mentioned again in v. 22. [86] The statement in v. 20a that Moses was not allowed to see the face of God sounds at first very general ("to see my face" = "to see myself"; cf. יִרְאַנִי, v. 20b). Then in v. 23, with the help of the use of פָּנִים for "front," [87] distinction is made between the front of God which it is forbidden to see and the back which may be seen. The more noteworthy it is, then, that although the element of realistic mythology is not completely eliminated (→ II, 239 f.), nevertheless the thought is present that even Moses was not allowed to see God directly. [88] The basic principle of Ex. 33:20b, namely, that he who sees God must die, is not thinking of death as a fixed penalty for violation of a corresponding prohibition, for no such prohibition is stated either here or elsewhere. Rather the holiness and majesty of God on the one side, and the unworthiness of man on the other, mean that man cannot see God without being completely destroyed, cf. Is. 6:5.

The same principle is affirmed briefly in Ex. 19:21 (cf. 24; Lv. 16:2; Nu. 4:20): "He who sees God must perish" (acc. to some texts "he who hears God's voice," cf. Ex. 20:19; Dt. 5:24 f.; 18:16). Hence Moses (Ex. 3:6, cf. 33:22) and Elijah (3 Βασ. 19:13) hide their faces (that the seraphim do so too in Is. 6:2 is designed to prevent the viewing of God; the prohibition in Gn. 19:17, 26 is simply against looking round, and does not refer to the seeing of God). If men come upon God unawares they are later seized by thankful astonishment that they have escaped with their lives (Gn. 32:30; cf. also 16:13), [89] or by anxiety lest they must die (Ju. 6:22 f.; [90] cf. also 13:22). Since in other theophanies it is not recalled that he who has seen God must really die, one might ask whether the passages mentioned are not to be regarded as a harmonisation between naively related theophanies and the insight of Ex. 33:20. Their age is against this. In spite of their naive and plastic character even the other theophanies are in no sense examples of a completely unbroken view that God may be seen quite easily by man. Implicitly the thought is common to all of them that these are special tokens of grace, and that the few men

---

[85] May one conclude from the Hebrasim οὖ ... ἐκεῖ (שָׁם ... אֲשֶׁר; cf. Gn. 10:14; 2 Ch. 6:11) that the LXX already had before it a different HT? Cf. other deviations in the HT: Dt. 5:5 as compared with Ex. 19:19; Dt. 4:12, 15, 33; 5:4, 22 ff.; 18:16, also Dt. 4:12, 15 in relation to Ex. 19:21 (LXX κατανοῆσαι = לִרְאוֹת).

[86] It depends on source analysis how far Ex. 34:5 ff. is to be seen in the light of 33:20 ff., though 34:5 ff. does not speak of seeing God. On the LXX version of 33:13, 18 B cf. Michaelis, 119. Proclamation of the name of God in 33:19 (J) is in itself an important part of the answer to the request of v. 18, but it can hardly be put on the same level as seeing the back of God in v. 23 (as against Barth, 64; cf. esp. 34:5b).

[87] The expression "to see the face of God" cannot, then, have been an established one (in the sense "to see God"), → 325.

[88] The Gk. idea that God may be perceived, not by the senses, but by the νοῦς, remained an alien one to the OT, Bultmann, 117 f.

[89] Cf. Fascher, 46 f.; Hempel, 8, n. 6.

[90] The address: "Be not afraid" (Ju. 6:23, though not 13:23) establishes a connection with the many verses where this formula removes awe of the numinous, but this awe cannot be construed as fear of death. In terrifying visions too (cf. Is. 21:3 ff.; Job 4:12 ff.) exclamations of fear are to be taken more generally.

to whom they are granted are dispensed by God Himself from the intrinsically valid
rule that those who have seen God must die, cf. Ex. 24:11a. [91]

A special type is constituted by the instances where we have the brief introduction: ὤφθη κύριος τῷ ... καὶ εἶπεν (αὐτῷ), and then we are simply told what
God had to say: Gn. 12:7; 17:1; 26:2, 24; 35:9 f. (cf. 48:3); 3 Βασ. 3:5 (= 2 Ch.
1:7); 9:2 (= 2 Ch. 7:12); cf. 11:9. Ιερ. 38(31):3 is related to these passages; here
ὤφθη even includes God's speaking. [92] When the ὀφθῆναι takes place by night
or in a dream (Gn. 26:24; 3 Βασ. 3:5), we are not on this account to think in
terms of dreams, → 329. In none of these instances is God seen. He is simply
heard, and the ὤφθη marks the beginning of the revelation by word, i.e., it indicates the presence of the God who reveals Himself in His Word. [93]

> The ref., then, is not to exceptionally brief (or abbreviated) theophanies. The LXX
> often introduces an ὀφθῆναι of God independently (Gn. 16:13; 31:13; Ju. 6:26 A; cf. also
> the LXX versions of ψ 83:7 [cf. 101:16]; Is. 66:5), and it could hardly have done this
> if ὀφθῆναι had meant that God was actually seen, for its own tendency is the very
> opposite; cf. the weakenings already quoted, Ex. 3:6; 19:21; 24:10 f.; Nu. 12:8, also
> → 325, 326 on the expressions "to see the πρόσωπον or δόξα of God"; on ψ 16:15;
> 62:2; Is. 38:11 → infra and n. 98.

c. Seeing God in a Transferred Sense.

> In some passages there is ref. to seeing God in a transf. sense. We need not consider
> the poetic expression in ψ 76:16 (on 2 Βασ. 22:11 cf. the par. Ps. 18:10: וַיֵּרָא). In
> ψ 16:15a; 62:2a the seeing of God refers to certainty of His proximity, → 326, 327. [94]
> In both verses the LXX emends: ὀφθήσομαι τῷ προσώπῳ σου or ὤφθην σοι. In
> Sir. 15:7b: ἄνδρες ἁμαρτωλοὶ οὐ μὴ ἴδωσιν αὐτήν (sc. σοφία, which here stands
> for God), the meaning is "to perceive," "to grasp," cf. καταλήμψονται in 15:7a.
> Similarly, in the addition which is a vl. after Sir. 1:10 or elsewhere: ἀγάπησις κυρίου
> ἔνδοξος σοφία· οἷς δ' ὀπτάνηται, μερίζει αὐτὴν εἰς ὅρασιν αὐτοῦ, [95] the meaning
> is that God is seen, i.e., His nature is known, by those who love Him, cf. the par.
> Wis. 6:12; → II, 769. In Sir. 43:31(35): τίς ἑόρακεν αὐτὸν καὶ ἐκδιηγήσεται (cf.
> 42:15) it is intrinsically possible [96] that we have a basic challenge to the whole idea of
> seeing God, but the reason given in 43:32 (→ II, 639) shows that what is meant is
> that the little bit which man can see does not allow Him to know all there is to know
> about God from His works. In the heartfelt sigh of Job 23:9 the "I see him not" means
> that Job sees no sign of God taking any note of him; cf. also 9:11; 35:14 (the LXX

---

[91] The same questions arise in relation to angelophanies. Where there is appearance
to the senses, angels take the form of (unknown) men, Gn. 18:2; Jos. 5:13; Ju. 6:11 ff.;
13:3 ff. — just like God in Gn. 32:25. It is also true that he who has seen an angel must
die, cf. Ju. 6:22 f. On the "literary theologisation" which dissolves God into angels, → I,
77 f.; Fascher, 46-51. In Job 5:1 the LXX translates: ἢ εἴ τινα ἀγγέλων ἁγίων ὄψῃ,
"whether thou come to see a holy angel who can help thee" (i.e., experience the help of
an angel).
[92] Cf. also Gn. 28:13-16 (E); also 31:13; 35:1. For details, Michaelis, 105 f.
[93] On ὀφθῆναι to denote presence (not Barth, 305, n. 106) → 324 f. and Michaelis, 151,
n. 147 f. When in Gn. 20:3, 6; 31:24; 46:2; Nu. 22:20; Ju. 6:25 God comes by night and
speaks (cf. also Gn. 28:13; 1 Βασ. 3:10), these revelations seem to be just the same as
those in which ὤφθη is used. They do not belong to other strata, but show that ὀφθῆναι
can mean "to come (to speak the word of revelation)." Cf. also Gn. 15:1; 2 Βασ. 7:4
(= 1 Ch. 17:3); 1 Βασ. 15:16.
[94] → I, 95; on ψ 62:2 cf. Baudissin, 175, 199; R. Kittel, 91.
[95] Cf. V. Ryssel in Kautzsch Apkr. u. Pseudepigr., ad loc.
[96] Ryssel, ad loc. regards the verse as a gloss.

remoulds v. 13 f.). In Job 34:29b (HT corrupt) "to see God" is to be certain of His nearness or grace, cf. 33:26. Job 42:5 : "I have heard of thee by hearsay, but now mine eye hath seen thee," refers to the fact that through the divine instruction commencing in 38:1 his eye (in the spiritual sense of full understanding) has been opened, so that through creation and its marvels he now realises his own impotence and stupidity and God's almightiness and sovereignty. Cf. the examples on → 326 which show that seeing the acts of God is to be taken as submission to His revelation in His dealings with men, [97] and cf. also Wis. 13:1. Hellenistic Stoicism is reflected in Wis. 13:5 (→ 328). [98]

Job 19:26 f. (→ III, 109) raises the question whether God is seen after death. The wording itself suggests a seeing in this life, for in keeping with 23:9; 35:14; also 34:29 (→ supra) the meaning is that God will again be gracious to Job. The view that the reference is to the time after death (→ II, 848) also has to meet the difficulty that there is little place for the hope of life after death in the OT. Yet even on this interpretation the seeing of God might be a fig. way of expressing the conviction that God's grace sustains us even after death. In ψ 16:15 the expression "when I awake" can hardly refer to awaking out of the sleep of death [99] (the LXX leaves it untranslated). In the OT, then, there is no sure attestation of the promise that man will be granted a vision of God after death. [100] If in passages like Is. 60:2, which hold out the prospect of an ὀφθῆναι of God or His δόξα in the future (or the last time), the real reference is to revealing presence rather than visibility, [101] then it is only with qualification that we can say that "seeing God is an eschatological event" (→ I, 218). The promise of Mt. 5:8 and the certainty of 1 Jn. 3:2 find no direct precursors in the OT.

II. Philo and Josephus.

1. Philo.

a. The Words.

In Philo ὁράω (including εἶδον) occupies the most important place among the verbs of seeing. [102] It is surely due to his non-eschatological outlook that the fut. ὄψομαι occurs only in Leg. All., II, 5; III, 56. The pass. is also rare : 21 times ὁρᾶσθαι, 12 ὀφθῆναι (4 ὁραθῆναι inf. and part.: Spec. Leg., II, 165; III, 189; Leg. All., III, 57, 170, → n. 102). There is ref. to the ὀφθῆναι of God only in connection with OT citations, Mut. Nom., 1 f., 6 (Gn. 17:1); Som., I, 189, 227 ff. (Gn. 31:13); it is emphasised in Mut. Nom., 3 that

---

[97] → I, 218, n. 11; Hänel, 223 ff.; Köhler, 83-86.

[98] Is. 38:11: "I shall not (no longer) see Yah Yah in the land of the living" (LXX . οὐκέτι μὴ ἴδω τὸ σωτήριον τοῦ θεοῦ, → III, 109) also refers to the knowledge of God in the ordinary and extraordinary phenomena of nature and history, which the dead can no longer have. Hänel, 226 f.; Baudissin, 179 f. The use in Is. 64:3 LXX is transf. ("to learn to know").

[99] Baudissin, 176 f.; R. Kittel, 88 f.; Gunkel, ad loc.

[100] The Rabb. idea that man will see God immediately on death (→ n. 125) finds no basis in the OT.

[101] In Is. 60:2 this is proved by the parallelism of זָרַח (not a verb of seeing) and יֵרָאֶה. Is. 40:5 (וְנִגְלָה ὀφθήσεται) refers to revelation as a proof of the gracious presence of God ; hence the statement which follows : "And all flesh shall see it," carries no thought of sense perception. In 52:10 the return of the exiles is called a return of God, so that this is not an instance of seeing God either.

[102] In Leisegang we have over 300 of the more important refs. On the vl. ὡράθη in Deus Imm., 131 (for ἑώραται, so also Lv. 14:35 LXX) cf. P. Katz, Philo's Bible (1950). 29 f.

there can be no question of perception with the senses, and in Som., I, 228 ff. that God is represented by an angel (ἐν τόπῳ θεοῦ = in God's place, 228). Along with βλέπω Philo also uses ὁράω for sensual seeing, e.g., ὁρᾶν and ἀκούειν are the παιδία of αἴσθησις in Cher., 73; cf. Leg. All., III, 216 and his use of → ὅρασις. But ὁράω denotes esp. the spiritual seeing which is so important for Philo (as does ὁρατικός exclusively). Even when he compares seeing and hearing he takes seeing in this sense, Conf. Ling., 148; Migr. Abr., 38 f.; Som., I, 129. In Migr. Abr., 47 ff. he takes it that in verses like Ex. 20:18; Dt. 4:12, where ראה means "to perceive," the words and voice of God are described as visible, so that seeing is to be regarded as the instrument of the knowledge of God's world. For "to see God" he uses ὁράω (and θεωρέω); only in Leg. All., II, 46, 93; III, 81; Som., I, 114 does he call Israel ὁ βλέπων (elsewhere ὁ τὸν θεὸν ὁρῶν etc., → n. 113). In Migr. Abr., 38 (not Rer. Div. Her., 78) he calls the prophets οἱ βλέποντες along with the LXX, but for his own part he prefers ὁράω, e.g., with ref. to dreams in Jos., 6, 8, 90 etc.; Som., II, 113, 137 (on Agric., 43; Poster. C., 22 cf. → n. 16). ὁράω is also used of God in Cher., 96; Jos., 236, 255; Leg. All., II, 17; Op.Mund., 149. ὀπτάνομαι does not occur.

βλέπω (64 times, in alternation with other verbs of seeing, e.g., Rer. Div. Her., 78; Praem. Poen., 45; Abr., 70) has primary ref. to sense perception, e.g., Leg. All., II, 67; Rer. Div. Her., 55; Jos., 58, hence in enumerations of the senses, Conf. Ling., 123; Poster. C., 36; Mut. Nom., 157; Decal., 74; cf. Jos., 126. It is seldom used of God, Mut. Nom., 40; cf. Jos., 265. In relation to considering or taking note of heavenly prototypes (Decal., 101; Conf. Ling., 63; cf. Gig., 31; Vit. Mos., I, 190) some part is played by the transf. sense of the spiritual seeing of νοητά. βλέπειν in this sense is ascribed to the νοῦς in Op. Mund., 53, to the ψυχή in Plant., 38; Jos., 147; Ebr., 157; Poster. C., 21; Migr. Abr., 52, 191, also to the διάνοια in Migr. Abr., 222; Vit. Mos., I, 188; Leg. Gaj., 109; Plant., 58, and the λογισμός in Leg. All., III, 110; Congr., 81. In the expression ὁ βλέπων (opp. τυφλός) πλοῦτος, e.g., Agric., 54; Sobr., 40; Rer. Div. Her., 48; Jos., 258; Vit. Mos., I, 153; Spec. Leg., II, 23; Virt., 85; Vit. Cont., 13; Praem. Poen., 54, Philo is dependent on Plat. Leg., I, 631c : πλοῦτος οὐ τυφλὸς ἀλλ' ὀξὺ βλέπων, → 379, 33.

θεάομαι (64 times, also pass.: Deus Imm., 78; Gig., 15; with dat. in the interpolation, Som., I, 188) is used for intensive looking, e.g., Spec. Leg., III, 160; Abr., 197, θεασώμεθα in Leg. All., II, 5, 61 etc., of dreams and visions, e.g., Som., II, 6; Jos., 10; Praem. Poen., 58. It is thus used esp. for perceiving of νοητὴ φύσις, Abr., 70; Spec. Leg., IV, 157; Op. Mund., 46; also for seeing God, Abr., 88; Conf. Ling., 96; Poster. C., 168; Spec. Leg., I, 45. Though θεάομαι is hardly ever combined with ἀκούω, we often find θέα with ἀκοή and θέαμα with ἄκουσμα, though rarely θεατής with ἀκροατής; θέα is common, also φιλοθεάμων "liking to see," "desirous of seeing" (cf. Plat. Resp., V, 475e → 321), always with ref. to the divine world.

θεωρέω (57 times, 32 of these pass.) is very rarely used for sense perception (Op. Mund., 67), often for "to consider," "to perceive," e.g., Op. Mund., 131, also of God, Decal., 97; Virt., 57; Mut. Nom., 217; pass. "to show, to prove oneself as," Leg. All., I, 74; II, 38 etc. Mostly of spiritual seeing, as exercised by οἱ ψυχῇ μᾶλλον ἢ σώματι ζῶντες (Abr., 236), hence, e.g., often with ψυχή, Op. Mund., 54; Vit. Cont., 78; Gig., 52 etc.; with διάνοια, Abr., 161 f.; with σοφία, Migr. Abr., 39. For "seeing God," Mut. Nom., 82; Praem. Poen., 40, 45 f.; Som., I, 66. θεωρία is common in the sense of "perception," "consideration," e.g., Migr. Abr., 77; Abr., 131, also as the opp. of πρᾶξις, Leg. All., I, 57 (cf. θεωρητικός as the anton. of πρακτικός), several times in the sense of (spiritual) "contemplation." θεωρία (τοῦ) θεοῦ is not used, though cf. Sacr. AC, 120 : θεωρίας δὲ τῆς τοῦ μόνου σοφοῦ (sc. God). θεώρημα (with one exception always plur.) is common in the sense of "view," "doctrine."

b. The Significance of Seeing.

The distinction between the κόσμος νοητός and the κόσμος αἰσθητός, which Philo takes over from Gk. philosophy, esp. Plato, leaves him with a poor view of the senses, which relate only to αἰσθητά. [103] Among the senses ὅρασις and ἀκοή are the ἡγεμονι-κώταται αἰσθήσεις, Vit. Mos., II, 211 (cf. Conf. Ling., 72; Migr. Abr., 103), the most philosophical senses, Abr., 150 (cf. Spec. Leg., I, 337, 339 f.); hence they always come first in enumerations, e.g., Op. Mund., 62; Migr. Abr., 119; Leg. All., I, 25. Sight is ἡ ἡγεμονὶς τῶν αἰσθήσεων(Abr., 164, cf. Spec. Leg., III, 195; Op. Mund., 53) even as compared with hearing, Fug., 208 ff. (→ I, 217); Mut. Nom., 102 etc. (on hearing cf. Conf. Ling., 148; Vit. Mos., I, 274; Abr., 60). While perception of the κόσμος νοητός is ascribed to seeing, this seeing is obviously greatly superior to hearing unless this be metaphysical, cf. Migr. Abr., 39. By means of allegorical interpretation Philo proves the inferiority of hearing from the OT itself ; thus in Conf. Ling., 72 etc. Jacob as σύμβολον ἀκοῆς is contrasted with Israel as σύμβολον ὁράσεως. [104] Again, in Fug., 208 (cf. Mut. Nom., 202) Ishmael, as ἀκοὴ θεοῦ, is adduced as an instance of the lesser value of hearing. Naturally Philo was inwardly at odds with the orientation of the OT message to hearing, and its consequent call for decision. Even his seeing, then, is not bound up with the attitude to revelation. It is an agent in man's development to per-fection. This seeing has nothing whatever to do with sense perception : τὰ ὄντα ὄντως ὁρᾶν is possible only δίχα αἰσθήσεως, i.e., ψυχῇ μόνῃ, Conf. Ling., 105; it is a seeing with the help of the ψυχή, the διάνοια, the ἐπιστήμη, the λογισμός etc., esp. the νοῦς, as Philo never tires of emphasising, cf. already → 334 f. [105] Does this mean that in Philo seeing is visionary and ecstatic ? [106] Is he influenced by the piety of the mysteries ? [107]

The question must be raised whether he really has in view a vision of God, and if so, how far. In this respect his way of handling the relevant OT statements is particularly instructive. He does not deal with Gn. 32:30. No commentary on this passage has survived, nor did he ever write any. Indeed, even in the works we have he does not mention it. He quotes Nu. 12:6, 8 LXX in Leg. All., III, 103; Rer. Div. Her., 262, but in both cases he breaks off at οὐ δι᾽ αἰνιγμάτων in 12:8. Ex. 24:10a is adduced in Som., I, 62; II, 222 acc. to the LXX (→ 331 f.), also Ex. 24:11b (→ 332) in Quaest. in Ex., 39 ff. Acc. to Vit. Mos., I, 66 there was in the burning bush of Ex. 3:2 a wonderfully beautiful and completely unearthly μορφή like an εἰκὼν τοῦ ὄντος, but this was not God (καλείσθω δὲ ἄγγελος). On the other hand Ex. 33:13 LXX (→ n. 86) in Leg. All., III, 101; Poster. C., 13, 16; Mut. Nom., 8; Spec. Leg., I, 41, and Ex. 33:18 in Spec. Leg., I, 45 (Philo softens this : τὴν γοῦν περί σε δόξαν), are for him classical examples of the justifiable desire of every philosopher to see God (cf. also Conf. Ling., 97; Abr., 58, 88). or, as he says with greater caution in Leg. All., III, 101, to behold the ἰδέα of God (in a mirror, → II, 696) (Poster. C., 13 the φύσις of God), cf. also the descending line in Conf. Ling., 97. Acc. to Poster. C., 16 Ex. 33:13 bears witness that such seeing depends on God's initiative, cf. also Abr., 59 and the note on Gn. 12:7: οὐχ ὅτι ὁ σοφὸς εἶδε θεόν, ἀλλ᾽ ὅτι "ὁ θεὸς ὤφθη" τῷ σοφῷ, Abr., 80. From Ex. 33:23 Philo deduces that only πάνθ᾽ ὅσα μετὰ τὸν θεόν (the δυνάμεις which follow or accompany God) is κατάληπτα, αὐτὸς δὲ μόνος ἀκατάληπτος (Poster. C., 169), and he adds in

---

[103] On the 5 senses in Philo and their allegorical significance cf. Dobschütz, 380 ff.
[104] Τὸ ἀκοή belongs μάθησις, τὸ ὅρασις ἄσκησις (→ I, 494 f.). This obviously leads to a lower view of μάθησις (cf. also Conf. Ling., 148), though → IV, 406.
[105] In Spec. Leg., III, 185 ff. sensual perception of the ὄψις is the basis of the philo-sophical process and enquiry (191: ἔρευνα). In the case of ἐπιστήμη etc. the ref., however, is to specially given and more intuitive faculties which make man a σοφός, one who sees (cf. Migr. Abr., 38; Rer. Div. Her., 78).
[106] Acc. to Plant., 36 allegorical exposition of the OT is esp. important for ὁρατικοὶ ἄνδρες. But does this mean that "perception of the symbolical meaning" (so Leisegang, Art. "Philo" in RGG², IV, 1194) can be attained "only in the state of ecstasy"?
[107] Affirmed by J. Pascher, Η ΒΑΣΙΛΙΚΗ ΟΔΟΣ, Der Königsweg z. Wiedergeburt u. Vergottung bei Philon v. Alex. = Studien z. Gesch. u. Kultur d. Altertums, 17, 3/4 (1931), but not W. Völker, Fortschritt u. Vollendung bei Philo v. Alex. = TU, 49, 1 (1938), esp. 285, n. 5, 314, 317.

Mut. Nom., 10 that it cannot be otherwise where even ὁ ἐν ἑκάστῳ νοῦς is ἄγνωστος, cf. Abr., 74. In Quaest. in Ex., 39 ff., though Philo follows the LXX version of Ex. 24:11 (as of v. 10, cf. 37), there is ref. to a vision of God, a deification of the holy soul, in the unmistakable language of the mysteries. But this line of thought is interrupted even in Quaest. in Ex. itself, for in blatant contrast [108] other passages emphasise the inaccessibility of God. Elsewhere, too, Philo has statements which seem to speak without qualification of the vision of God (in Leg. All., II, 81 he even relates the ἰδὼν αὐτόν of Nu. 21:8 to God instead of ὄψις), but these are accompanied by many refs. to the basic invisibility and unknowability of God. Does this mean that rational considerations invade mystical ideas ? Has Philo "here allowed his concept of transcendence to adulterate the notion of the royal way" ? [109] On the contrary, his statements are all governed primarily by the concept of God's invisibility. [110] This may be seen from the numerical relation and material importance of the two sets of utterances. Furthermore, it is emphasised in Poster. C., 168 (on the basis of Dt. 32:39) that to see God can only mean to see the ὕπαρξις or existence of God. Hence the most important expositions in Praem. Poen., 36 ff. [111] culminate in the saying that one can see only the fact and not the nature of God's existence (cf. also 44 : οὐχ οἷός ἐστιν ὁ θεός — τοῦτο γὰρ ἀμήχανον, ὡς ἔφην —, ἀλλ' ὅτι ἔστιν and the appeal to Ex. 3:6 in Fig., 141). Only in this sense is Moses called ὁ τῆς ἀειδοῦς φύσεως θεατής in Mut. Nom., 7. There is thus no decisive reason not to think that Philo himself added θεόπτης here. [112] The word occurs only in this passage (θεοπτία and θεοπτικός are attested elsewhere, though they are late). But Philo could very well use it in the sense developed in the context. The ref. in Praem. Poen., 44 to the equation Χαλδαϊστί : Ἰσραήλ = Ἑλληνιστί : ὁρῶν θεόν (cf. Leg. Gaj., 4) shows that this fairly common expression in Philo can also indicate the vision of God as qualified above. [113] Even the intellectual vision of God is only a

---

[108] So even Fascher, 244, though in 239-259 he believes the expositions in the comm. on Ex. are the crowning confirmation of his understanding.

[109] Fascher, 162 f. → 62 and 63, n. 60.

[110] Fascher, 161 writes : "Directly alongside the joyfully affirming mystic there is in Philo the pitilessly negating philosopher," and he ascribes to the latter the belief in God's abs. transcendence. In fact, however, the passages which regard vision as possible betray philosophical influence, their basis being Plato's contemplation of the ideas rather than mystical vision of God. It is true, of course, that the emphasis on God's invisibility also derives from philosophical presuppositions, Fascher, 60; Bultmann, 189-192. The idea that man may not see God is alien to Philo ; his slogan is ἀμήχανον, e.g., → infra. He ignores Ex. 33:20, and 20:19 is rendered innocuous in Poster. C., 143; Som., I, 143; cf. Rer. Div. Her., 19.

[111] Fascher disregards this passage, and refers only briefly to Mut. Nom., 8 ff. (166, n. 2).

[112] L. Cohn excises θεόπτης, P. Wendland conjectures καὶ θεοπρόπος, cf. Fug., 139. Baudissin, 229, n. 2 thinks θεόπτης is original because it expresses the thought of Nu. 12:8; Philo, however, always avoids this verse, → 336.

[113] (ὁ) ὁρῶν (τὸν) θεόν (always masc. and sing.), in Abr., 57; Congr., 51 etc. expressly for Ἰσραήλ, either Jacob (Fug., 208; cf. Migr. Abr., 201) or the people (Leg. All., III, 38, 172, 186, 212); often for friends of virtue and philosophers (Poster. C., 92; Conf. Ling., 56; Rer. Div. Her., 78; Mut. Nom., 81); also the νοῦς (Som., II, 173); the ψυχῆς ὀφθαλμός (Conf. Ling., 92), the λόγος (146). Cf. also the simple ὁ ὁρῶν (cf. ὁ βλέπων, → 335; ὁ βλέπων τὸν ὄντα, Leg. All., III, 172) in the same sense (e.g., Leg. All., II, 34). also expressions like ὁρατικὸν γένος (e.g., Deus Imm., 144). The statement (→ III, 372) that Ἰσραήλ means for Philo ἄνθρωπος ὁρῶν θεόν is open to question. He does not use the formulation ; it is only a deduction from the conjecture (cf. L. Cohn/I. Heinemann, D. Werke Philos v. Alex., V [1929], 116, n. 7; I [1909], 108, n. 2) that יִשְׂרָאֵל is etym. explained as אִישׁ רָאָה אֵל; but then we should somewhere find אִישׁ in Gk. as ἄνθρωπος or ἀνήρ (Schl. Theol. d. Jdt., 56, n. 2), which is not so. On the other hand derivation from אֵל and רָאָה alone (cf. L. Cohn, D. Werke Philos, III [1919], 258, n. 2; V, 158, n. 2) leaves the יָשׁ unexplained. Nor can there be any question of a connection with the explanation of the name Pniel in Gn. 32:31. Philo ignores the etym. of יִשְׂרָאֵל in Gn. 32:29

πόρρωθεν ... θεωρεῖν, Som., I, 66. Cf. Leg. All., II, 81: He who has seen τὸ σωφροσύνης κάλλος (even ψυχικῶς) has seen διὰ τούτου τὸν θεὸν αὐτόν, cf. 82; so also
Deus Imm., 3. Acc. to Poster C., 15 the goal can only be ἰδεῖν ὅτι ἐστὶν (sc. God)
ἀόρατος.

2. Josephus.

In Joseph., in keeping with the nature of his works, the verbs of seeing are predominantly used for sensual or the related mental perception. βλέπω and θεωρέω
are not so common, and ὀπτάνομαι does not occur. The aor. pass. of ὁράω is ὁραθῆναι : inf. after adj. Ant., 2, 81; 3, 9 and 13; also 3, 76; 5, 280 and 284; 9, 109, part.
11, 51, ind. ἑωράθην, Ap., 2, 291. Pass. occasionally with ὑπό τινος, e.g., Ant., 7, 298;
Bell., 2, 82, but mostly with dat. even when one would not expect an intr. pass., e.g.,
Ant., 5, 330; 6, 112; 9, 109; Bell., 4, 190 (also intr. pass. of βλέπω with dat., Ant., 11, 165;
abs. 6, 169). βλέπω is often fig. "to note," "to observe," "to judge"; of God, Ant., 1, 35;
6, 159. θεάομαι can often denote special vision (Ant., 1, 163; 6, 340; 7, 327; Vit., 208
and 210) but is usually synon. with ὁράω, Ant., 1, 90, 141, 196. Eye-witness (e.g.,
Bell., 6, 297) is more strongly suggested by the subst. θεατής (Ant., 2, 23 with μάρτυς,
275 with ἀκροατής, though it also has the sense of "observer" (1, 19) or (mere)
"spectator" (Bell., 4, 371). θεωρέω often means "to see," "to look at," "to view"
(as a witness), e.g., Ant., 17, 326; 19, 35, "to be present as a spectator," 14, 210; 19, 75;
also transf. "to perceive," 20, 75 etc.

When men receive directions in dreams, it is not said that they have seen God :
Jos. is always brief and restrained at this pt., e.g., Ant., 5, 215. He omits the ὤφθη
passages Gn. 12:7; 17:1; 26:2, 24; 35:9 f., [114] also Ex. 33:20, 23, and for Ju. 13:22 f.
(Ant., 5, 284) has ὄψις τοῦ θεοῦ ("vision of God") and τὸν θεὸν αὐτοῖς ὁραθῆναι
(cf., 280). Acc. to Ant., 2, 264 ff. only the τέρας θαυμάσιον of the burning bush was
to be seen at Ex. 3:2 ff.; God was only heard, 267 ff. Ant., 3, 75 ff. deals with Ex. 19 f.;
the ref. is to the παρουσία of God (80; cf. πάρεστι, 84), and Moses' encounter with
God is paraphrased (84). Hence the statement : τῷ θεῷ γὰρ εἰς ὄψιν ἐλθὼν ἀκροατὴς
ἀφθάρτου φωνῆς ἐγενόμην (88), does not mean that Moses saw God but that God
received him (cf. 84). [115] Jos. qualifies the OT theophanies in this way because he
believes that God is intrinsically invisible, cf. Bell., 7, 346 (ἀόρατος → 369), and, in
different phraseology, Ap., 2, 167 (→ I, 120) and 190. In waiting for the fulfilment
of God's promises (Jos. did not take this thought from his basis in 1 K. 8:15 ff.) what
has already been fulfilled, and may be seen, can strengthen faith : πιστεύοντας ἐκ τῶν
ἤδη βλεπομένων, Ant., 8, 110. [116]

(cf. Jos. Ant., 1, 333). He mentions the verse in Ebr., 82 (and briefly in Mut. Nom., 44) but
combines it at once with ὅρασις θεοῦ as the supposed meaning of the name Israel (cf. 83;
he never refers to Gn. 35:10). Better than these derivations is the proposal of A. Adler
(Cohn/Heinemann, V, 116, n. 7) who suggests יְשֻׁר אֵל (from שׁוּר "to look"). Here no connection is made with אִישׁ and the י is taken as a preformative of the impf. (cf. Gn. 16:11;
32:29). Perhaps the אֲשׁוּרֶנּוּ of Nu. 24:17 fixed the etym. for Philo and his unknown predecessors.

[114] On the use of φαίνεσθαι etc. cf. Schl. Theol. d. Judt., 53.

[115] Ant., 2, 171: εἰς ὄψιν Ἰωσήπου παραγενέσθαι certainly means "come to see
Joseph" (cf. also 303), but in Ant., 19, 35 we have a subj. gen. (εἰς τὴν ὄψιν τὴν Γαΐου),
and εἰς ὄψιν αὐτῷ μὴ παραγίνεσθαι in Ant., 5, 354 means "not come under his eyes"
(i.e., Eli will see his sons, or they will see him, no more); cf. also Ant., 2, 164 and 261; 8, 10.

[116] Ep. Ar.: ὁράω occurs for certain only in 182 (though cf. the vl. ὁρᾶται for ὁρμᾶται, 270, and the conjecture ὁρῶντι for ὁρᾶν τι, 194; also compounds of ὁράω).
θεωρέω occurs in ten times, βλέπω 3 (of direction, 88); also θεάομαι (96). H. G. Meecham,
The Letter of Aristeas. A Linguistic Study with Special Reference to the Greek Bible (1935),
267 pts. out that ὁράω was now less common in current usage (→ n. 2); but θεωρέω is
in place in the description of architectural and other details (e.g., 65, 67), and also in the
sense "to consider," "to ponder."

III. Pseudepigrapha and Rabbinism.

1. The Pseudepigrapha. The attitude of later Judaism to seeing and hearing is not uniform. In apocal. seeing is strongly to the fore, → I, 218. But in, e.g., Eth. En. an interpreting angel explains the visions, 18:14 etc.; cf. 1:2. In Jub. 32:17 ff. we have a type which approximates closely to OT models, though Gn. 35 is, of course, much extended : God speaks with Jacob by night ; in a vision an angel then lets the patriarch read (not see) his future and that of his posterity. Jub. 44:3 suggests that in Gn. 46:1 Jacob waited a week for a vision (Jos. Ant., 2, 170 f. also has a postponement with rational considerations).[117] In Eth. En. 14:15 ff. the author sees the house in heaven where the throne of God stands ; he also sees God Himself. But the climax of the vision is in v. 24 when God speaks to him : "Come here, Enoch, and hear my word"; God then addresses him, 15 f.; cf. Test. L. 5:1. In apocal. the vision of God is nowhere regarded as an unqualified goal to be pursued. In Gr. Bar. 6 the seeing of God's δόξα is simply the seeing of heavenly wonders (the sun, the Phoenix bird etc.). In Eth. En. 89:30 f., a paraphrase of Ex. 19 f., the use of terms like sheep, Lord of the sheep, softens the problem of seeing God (cf. Ex. 19:21; 20:18 f.). In a few statements, however, the vision of God is regarded as an eschatological possibility. Thus we read in 4 Esr. 7:87 (Violet, III, 11, 14) that after death sinners will be in an intermediate state for seven days (cf. 100 f., III, 13, 1 f.), and that as the final torment "they must see the glory of the Most High before whom they sinned during their lifetime and by whom they will be judged at the last day." Similarly we read in 7:91 (III, 12, 3; → II, 247), and esp. 7:98 (III, 12, 12), that the righteous will one day see the glory, or the face, of God. cf. Apc. Mos. 31 f. In passages like 4 Esr. 6:25 (II, 10, 9); 9:8 (III, 27, 7b) the ref. is to seeing God's salvation, not God Himself. In Ps. Sol. 17:31 (→ II, 247) only experience of the δόξα attested in the blessing of Israel is intended, cf. 17:44; 18:6.[118] That in the last time God will appear to all eyes is promised, however, in Jub. 1:28; cf. Sib., 5, 426 f., seeing the servant of God in 4 Esr. 13:52 (VI, 9, 2b), and the two versions of Test. Zeb. 9:3.

2. Rabbinism. In contrast to apocal. the Rabbis develop the OT view with a greater emphasis on hearing (→ I, 218). There is thus great restraint in relation to ecstatic vision, and even abhorrence of it.[119] Nevertheless, many statements speak of the vision of God. "To greet the face of the Shekinah," "to greet the face of the King of all kings," "to see the face of the Shekinah," etc. are customary phrases[120] (only in OT quotations do we find the expressions "to see God, God's countenance or glory"). The vision of God is esp. eschatological. In the intermediate state of Gan Eden the righteous will see the face of the Shekinah,[121] while the ungodly will be excluded.[122] Only after

---

[117] Cf. the OT ὤφθη ... καὶ εἶπεν (→ 333) in Jub. 44:5; cf. also Test. Iss. 2:1 and N. 5:8 : καὶ ἰδοὺ γραφὴ ἁγία ὤφθη ἡμῖν λέγουσα κτλ. In Test. L. 1:2 we even find ὤφθη γὰρ αὐτῷ ὅτι μέλλει ἀποθνήσκειν as though we had a trans. verb of revelation (= ἀπεκαλύφθη αὐτῷ, → n. 5). In the sense "to perceive" ἰδεῖν in G. 1:9 is used with both δι' ὀφθαλμῶν and δι' ἀκοῆς, and in S. 5:4 it refers to reading. Cf. also 4 Esr. 4:4 (Violet, I, 7, 4), 43 (I, 11, 13); also 4:26 (I, 10, 1) where "seeing" means experience rather than referring to comfort in future vision, Baudissin, 221.

[118] Test. Zeb. 9:8 is an interpolation (also the twofold mention of ἐπὶ γῆς φανείς in Test. B. 10:7, 9). On Mart. Is. 5:1 cf. Baudissin, 222, n. 2.

[119] → II, 453 f. On the (probably speculative rather than ecstatic) entry of 4 rabbis into Paradise (bChag., 14b-16a), cf. Kittel, 101; → I, 219, n. 18. The dying have the gift of visionary seeing, Str.-B., I, 30; II, 226. Shortly before death God lets them see their future destiny, III, 218 ff.; hence those around try to read their fate from their expressions, III, 220 f.; IV, 502, 526, 1037, 1043.

[120] Str.-B., I, 206.

[121] I, 207, 209-212.

[122] III, 601 f.; IV, 1057.

the resurrection is felicity in the future world a true vision of God. [123] Later emphasis on the period of the days of the Messiah already sets the vision of God here. [124] The ref. now is always to direct or proper vision, as in the idea of an appearance before God for judgment immediately after death. [125] In his lifetime no man can see God. For God is invisible. No man can or may see Him. [126] Not even the angels who are with God see Him. [127] If the expression "to greet the face of the Shekinah" is also referred to coming up to the temple for feasts, or attending the synagogue, or praying, or studying the Torah, [128] or even giving alms, [129] the sense is fig., [130] though it should be noted that it involves a tendency to bring down the concept of seeing God to the level of a righteousness of works, and hence to turn grace into merit. [131]

C. Usage and Concept in the New Testament.

1. Review of the Words.

a. ὁράω and εἶδον.

In the NT, too, ὁράω and esp. εἶδον are the most common verbs of seeing. εἶδον occurs some 350 times, esp. in the Gospels, Ac. and Rev. The lesser role in Jn. (only 36 instances) is due only in part to the fact that there is less narrative (for in Jn. εἶδον is also used in sayings and addresses). The main reason is the preference for the perf. ἑώρακα; of the 33 examples of this in the NT (within the 113 occurrences of ὁράω), 19 are in Jn. (also 7 in 1 and 3 Jn.). In many cases the perf. is designed to show the effect of seeing on the subj., [132] but in the main ἑώρακα is simply used for εἶδον in Jn. [133] The pres. ὁράω is not used by Jn. at all (he has θεωρέω instead), and it is

---

[123] I, 207, 212 f.; IV, 480 f., 926. The passages from Tanch. במדבר, 20 (Buber, p. 18) and bBer., 17a (not 34a; → II, 246, 250, n. 66) mentioned → II, 249, also refer to the coming aeon.

[124] Str.-B., I, 207 f., 213 f.; IV, 884, 924 ff. In this the Messianic age will be like that of the law-giving at Sinai, IV, 926, 939 f. Acc. to Midr. Ps. 149 § 1 (270a) the Israelites were allowed to see God at the Red Sea and in the tabernacle, I, 213.

[125] I, 207 f.; IV, 1036 ff. This is to be distinguished from the vision of one's own destiny shortly before death, → n. 119. While the ungodly are excluded from the vision of God in Gan Eden and the future world (→ n. 122 f.), they have to appear before God after death. It is unlikely that the associated vision of God simply means their destruction. The argument in Midr. Ps. 22 § 32 (99a) is not to this effect (Str.-B., I, 209); cf. also Jalkut Shimoni on Ps. 17:15 in P. Fiebig, "Jesu Bergpredigt," FRL, NF, 20 (1924), 11. There is need to correct → I, 219, n. 17 in this respect.

[126] Str.-B., II, 362; I, 783, 916. A common thought is that God sees but is not seen, ibid., II, 362 f.; III, 31 f. The contrast between God, who sees but cannot be seen, and a blind man, who is seen but cannot see (bChag., 5b, 32 par.; Str.-B., III, 32, 778; I, 916), does not mean that "the invisible God is represented by our fellow-men" (Bultmann, 187, n. 2, who compares 1 Jn. 4:20 f.). The Rabb. did not stress the fact that God is visible and knowable in creation Str.-B., III, 33.

[127] → IV, 651, n. 15. The highest class of angels is an exception, Str.-B., I, 783 f. Cf. Eth. En. 14:21; Asc. Is. 9:37 ff.

[128] Str.-B., I, 206 f.

[129] Jalkut Shimoni on Ps. 17:15, Fiebig, 10 f. bBB, 10a (Str.-B., I, 207) also refers more to almsgiving than prayer.

[130] So Str.-B., I, 206. In the comparison "like one who greets the face of the Shekinah" (cf. also → I, 219) the connection with the lit. meaning is, however, stronger.

[131] Bultmann, 185 f.

[132] Cf. Bl.-Debr. § 342, 2.

[133] The fact that Jn. takes a different course with ἀκούω, and usually has ἤκουσα, but only rarely ἀκήκοα, does not permit us to conclude that he thinks more highly of seeing than hearing, for in seeing he has in view only the effect as expressed by the perf. Nor should too much be read into the ἑώρακα and ἤκουσα of Jn. 3:32 (whether intrinsically or in comparison with 5:37; 1 Jn. 1:1, 3). Cf. Bl.-Debr. § 342, 2; Bu. J., 118, n. 2; Bau. J., ad loc.

generally rare in the NT (often replaced by βλέπω). The impf. occurs only at Jn.
6:2 ℵ; hence the reading ἐθεώρουν ℌ is to be preferred. ὄψομαι occurs 33 times
(βλέψω and θεωρήσω are extremely rare), 10 of these in Jn. There are 23 instances
of ὤφθην (not in Jn.), but ὀφθήσομαι occurs only at Ac. 26:16; Hb. 9:28.

ὁράω and εἶδον have a broad range of meaning in the NT. It is said of God
in Ac. 7:34 (= Ex. 3:7) that He sees ἰδὼν εἶδον (transf. "to observe," "to note");
cf. also ὁ πατήρ σου ὁ βλέπων ἐν τῷ κρυπτῷ or κρυφαίῳ, Mt. 6:4, 6, 18 [134]
(neither θεάομαι nor θεωρέω is used of God). In relation to verbs of seeing
anthropomorphisms are no problem in the NT, → 328. Outside narrative sections
Jn. uses ὁράω for the seeing of Christ at 3:11; 6:46; 8:38 [135] (in the specific
Johannine sense, → C. 2. e.; on 5:19 → 343). When men see the earthly Jesus, no
special terms are used to emphasise the significance of the encounter. [136] In
Jn. 12:21 "to see" means "to speak to" (cf. Lk. 8:20; λαλῆσαι, Mt. 12:46 f.; → 325).
Hence the importance of seeing the earthly Jesus is not emphasised, nor is there
any natural testimony to the fact "that the Greeks give precedence to seeing." [137]
There are other NT examples of this usage. [138]

The distinction in Phil. 1:27, 30; 4:9, where seeing means knowledge by personal
presence and hearing that gained from other sources, does not imply any antithesis between seeing and hearing (cf. also R. 15:21). On the other hand, seeing is
more highly estimated than hearing in Jn. 8:38; cf. 6:45 f. (→ 364). Often seeing
and hearing together constitute the totality of sensual and spiritual perception [139]
which underlies eye-witness, personal experience and individual certainty. So
Mk. 4:12 and par.; Mt. 13:14 f.; Mk. 8:18; Ac. 28:26 f.; R. 11:8 (→ 378); cf. also
the negative statement in 1 C. 2:9, which is meant to exclude all possibilities of
human apprehension (the heart is mentioned here along with the eye and ear;
cf. the eye and heart in the quotation at Jn. 12:40). Mostly seeing is put before
hearing in these cases; cf. also Lk. 7:22; Jn. 3:32 (→ n. 133); Ac. 4:20 etc. Hearing
comes first at, e.g., Lk. 2:20; Jn. 5:37. With few exceptions (e.g., Ac. 22:14 f.) the

---

[134] → 343; III, 960, 974. Can one tacitly supply an acc. obj. "it" (cf. Pr.-Bauer⁴, s.v.
βλέπω 1. c.)? Is the meaning that God, previously called a God in concealment (→ III, 960,
n. 3), sees in concealment (→ III, 974)? Or is this an instance of the (rare, cf. Bl.-Debr.
§ 218) use of ἐν for εἰς (perhaps under the influence of an original Aram. בְּ)? 4 Macc. 15:18
does not throw much light on the constr. in Mt.

[135] Inasmuch as the Jews (Jn. 8:57) misunderstand the saying of 8:56 the meaning of
ὁράω in v. 57 is not dependent on v. 56 (ἑώρακας is to be preferred); cf. Bu. J., 248, n. 3.
On Jn. 16:10, 16 f., 19, 22 → 362.

[136] The part. in Lk. 17:14; Ac. 3:12 (cf. D) and also 16:40 (Pr.-Bauer³, s.v. 6 thinks the
main meaning here is "to visit") is simply transitional to the main verb (Aramaism; cf.
Mk. 5:22 par. Lk. 8:41); in Lk. 5:8; 10:31 ff., however, seeing is an independent process.
βλέπω in Jn. 1:29 means that Jesus came into the Baptist's circle of vision, and John saw
him (cf. ἐμβλέπω, 1:36, 42).

[137] As against Dobschütz, 396. Cf. Schl. J. and Bau. J., ad loc.

[138] Jn. 16:22; Ac. 19:21; 28:20 (on 16:40 → n. 136); Gl. 1:19; in travel plans, R. 1:11;
1 C. 16:7; Phil. 2:26 (cf. 28); 1 Th. 3:6; 2 Tm. 1:4; Hb. 13:23; 3 Jn. 14, with πρόσωπον
1 Th. 2:17; 3:10. "To see the face" also Ac. 20:25, 38 (θεωρέω); Col. 2:1 and with ref.
to God Mt. 18:10 (βλέπω, → 343); Rev. 22:4 (→ 366); on 1 C. 13:12 → 344. Only formally
does the comparison in Ac. 6:15 (considering the expression on his face) recall Est. 5:2a.

[139] Cf. H. Riesenfeld, "Accouplements de termes contradictoires dans le NT," Coniectanea
Neotestamentica, 9 (1944), 10; R. Morgenthaler, Die lukanische Geschichtsschreibung als
Zeugnis (1948), I, 33 f.; II, 13, 27 f. Seeing is only seldom mentioned along with the other
senses; cf. seeing and touching in Lk. 24:39; 1 Jn. 1:1.

order makes no odds ; cf. the alternation in 1 Jn. 1:1, 3; Mt. 13:13 ff.; Lk. 7:22 par. Mt. 11:4. Putting seeing first simply expresses in an unreflecting way the natural precedence of seeing over hearing. For brevity seeing can be mentioned alone, Jn. 12:40; R. 11:10 (cf. v. 8); Lk. 10:23 (cf. Mt. 13:16 and Lk. 10:24 par. Mt. 13:17); Ac. 26:16 (cf. 22:14 f.); 1 Jn. 1:2 (cf. 1:1, 3). [140] The great material significance which hearing undoubtedly has in the NT cannot be fully expressed when it is combined with seeing.

Whereas in Ac. 8:6 seeing σημεῖα is in some sense equivalent to hearing the preaching of the apostles, elsewhere seeing, or desiring to see, σημεῖα demonstrates resistance to hearing the message, Mt. 12:38; Lk. 23:8; Jn. 4:48; 6:26; cf. also 4:45; 6:14, 30; Ac. 14:11 and (with θεωρέω) Jn. 2:23; 6:2; Ac. 8:13. On the other hand, the reference in Jn. 11:45 (θεάομαι!) seems to be to a faith resulting from being convinced by what one has seen (cf. Lk. 19:37; Hb. 3:9 [quotation] etc.).

The general meaning "to perceive," e.g., Mt. 5:16; 27:54, is part of the considerable transf. use of ὁράω and εἶδον, whose nuances cannot always be differentiated with precision. Very common is the group of meanings "to bring to knowledge," "to experience," "to note," "to establish," "to know" (cf. also the vl. εἰδώς Mt. 9:4; Lk. 9:47 and the par. ἐπιγνούς Mk. 2:8; Lk. 5:22). The constr. in such cases is with an acc.; Mt. 9:2 and par. (πίστιν); 26:58; Mk. 12:15; Lk. 9:47; Ac. 11:23; Jm. 5:11, [141] or an ὅτι clause : Mt. 2:16; Lk. 17:15; Gl. 2:7, 14; Jm. 2:24; Rev. 12:13, or an acc. c. part.: Jn. 19:33; Ac. 7:24; Hb. 2:8, also as part. referring back to a preceding sentence : Mt. 9:11 and par.; [142] 12:2; 21:32. [143] The δεῦτε ἴδετε of Mt. 28:6 and Jn. 4:29 denotes lit. seeing (cf. 4 Βασ. 7:14), but ἔρχου καὶ ἴδε in Jn. 11:34 carries the further sense "to come to realise," "to learn to know," and in Jn. 1:46 "to judge." The sense "to know" is also included in the ἔρχεσθε καὶ ὄψεσθε of 1:39, [144] cf. also 7:52. Other formulations with the imp. at Ac. 13:41; R. 11:22; Gl. 6:11 show an inclination towards the sense "to pay heed," "to mark," which is present in ὅρα (ὁρᾶτε), "see to it," "pay attention," and with a negative "watch out," "be on guard." [145] The fut. ὄψη (ὄψεσθε) in Mt. 27:4, 24; Ac. 18:15 ("see thou to it") seems to be a Latinism. [146] The sense "to come to see," "to experience," (→ 326), perhaps present in Mk. 2:12 and par., is common : life or death, Jn. 3:36; Lk. 2:26; Hb. 11:5, διαφθοράν, Ac. 2:27, 31; 13:35 (ψ 15:10), πένθος, Rev. 18:7, ἡμέρας ἀγαθάς, 1 Pt. 3:10 (ψ 33:12). In the wish of Lk. 17:22 : μίαν τῶν ἡμερῶν τοῦ υἱοῦ τοῦ ἀνθρώπου ἰδεῖν, this experience implies participating in the

---

[140] Dobschütz, 399 f. attributes the change in order in 1 Jn. 1:1, 3 to a redactor. But since the passage seems to be original in its totality (cf. R. Bultmann, "Analyse d. 1 Jn.," Festgabe A. Jülicher [1927], 138), one should rather conclude that the ἑωράκαμεν of 1:2 (in spite or perhaps just because of the ἐφανερώθη) includes the hearing mentioned before and after, so that it is used more comprehensively than ἑωράκαμεν in 1:1, 3; cf. τεθεάμεθα 4:14. → 345; 348.

[141] Cf. Dib. Jk., 225 f. If we are not to think in terms of eye-witnesses of the passion, the sense is fig., and the verse is not an example of the combining of seeing and hearing.

[142] The Pharisees do not have to be regarded as curious spectators of the feast in the house of Levi (so Hck. Mk. on 2:16). The sense may be "to learn" (cf. also Mt. 18:31).

[143] Pr.-Bauer⁴, s.v. εἶδον thinks these are instances in part of perception mediated by seeing. Under 1. c. he also adds examples of the constr. with an indirect question following ; but in the case of Mk. 5:14; 15:36 and even Lk. 19:3 one has to ask whether (on the basis of perception by appearance) the meaning is not "to learn by experience" etc. Cf. on the constr. with verbs of seeing in the NT Johannessohn, Wahrnehmungssatz, 234-250.

[144] Cf. Bl.-Debr. § 442, 2; Bu. J., 69, n. 8. On καὶ ἰδού cf. Johannessohn, 234 f., 249 f. (Rev.), also his Das bibl. καὶ ἰδού, 67 (1942), 30-62 : "καὶ ἰδού im NT."

[145] Examples and details of constr. in Pr.-Bauer³, s.v. 2. b. and c. → 316.

[146] Cf. Bl.-Debr.⁶, 310 (App. on § 349); ⁷ § 362.

Messianic age of salvation; cf. also Jn. 8:56. [147] In Jn. 1:50 μείζω τούτων ὄψῃ refers to experience of the revelation increasingly disclosed for the believer in fellowship with Jesus. [148] Cf. also → 361 f.

b. βλέπω.

βλέπω occurs 137 times (not in Th., Past. and some Catholic Ep.). Fut. βλέψω only in the quotation (Is. 6:9) at Mt. 13:14 and Ac. 28:26, impf. Jn. 13:22 (as vl. Ac. 22:11; Rev. 22:8), aor. Ac. 3:4; Rev. 22:8. Otherwise always pres. (pass. only R. 8:24; 2 C. 4:18; Hb. 11:1, 3, 7), which is not just used as a synon. in lively alternation with ὁράω and individual moods of εἶδον (e.g., Mt. 11:4 par. Lk. 7:22; Mt. 13:16 f. par. Lk. 10:23 f.; Hb. 2:8 f.; Jm. 2:22, 24), but also very commonly in place of the pres. ὁράω (→ 341), e.g., Lk. 7:44; 9:62; 1 C. 13:12 cf. with 1 Jn. 3:2. [149] βλέπω is also used interchangeably with θεωρέω, Lk. 21:6 and par. (cf. also 24:12 with Jn. 20:6). [150]

In the NT, too, βλέπω denotes sense perception, e.g., being able to see as distinct from blindness: Mt. 12:22; 15:31; Mk. 8:23 f.; Lk. 7:21; Jn. 9 passim; Ac. 13:11; fig. Jn. 9:39; Rev. 3:18 (cf. ἀναβλέπω in healings of the blind); cf. also Lk. 8:16 par. 11:33; Jn. 11:9 etc. The βλέπειν of the βιβλίον in Rev. 5:3 f. obviously includes reading (= "to examine"). βλέπειν εἰς πρόσωπόν τινος in Mt. 22:16 par. Mk. 12:14 (not Lk. 20:21) refers to inquisitive scrutiny of those to whose judgment one is exposed. [151] βλέπω in Mt. 6:4, 6, 18 (→ 341) might seem to be an anthropomorphism, but it is qualified by the fact that the term κρυπτόν implies inaccessibility to human perception. Much more striking is Jn. 5:19: ἂν μή τι βλέπῃ (sc. ὁ υἱός) τὸν πατέρα ποιοῦντα, for here there is a material par. to verses like 8:38 (ἑώρακα παρὰ τῷ πατρί) → 363. Elsewhere in Jn. θεωρέω is used for the pres. of ὁράω, → 345. [152] If the saying of Jesus in Mt. 18:10 stands in antithesis to the Jewish view that the angels cannot see God (→ n. 127; I, 82), then βλέπω admirably expresses the view of Jesus that the guardian angels of the

---

[147] In the Rabb. view that God let Abraham see the furthest future and eschatological salvation (Str.-B., II, 525 f.) there is no promise that Abraham would personally experience it. On the other hand the εἶδεν of Jn. 8:56 could refer to prophetic vision (Stauffer Theol., n. 246) only if this, previously intimated, were already a subject of joy. What is meant is probably that in heaven Abraham longed for the coming of the age of salvation, and actually experienced it as promised. εἶδεν as aor. shows that (unlike Lk. 17:22) the ref. is not to the Day of Judgment (as against → II, 951) but to the coming of Jesus (cf. Bu. J., 247 f.).

[148] Cf. Jn. 11:40. Also in 12:41, even if αὐτοῦ is to be related to God (vl. τοῦ θεοῦ), the ref. is to the δόξα manifested in the story of Jesus, though here (unlike 8:56 → n. 147), we have prophetic vision, not the contemporaneity of the prophet with Jesus, but at most that of the pre-existent Christ with the prophet, cf. Bu. J., 346, n. 6. One should not think exclusively of the vision of Is. 6 since otherwise ἐλάλησεν would have to refer only to this.

[149] Hence βλέπε, βλέπετε (cf. βλεπέτω in 1 C. 3:10; 10:12) are more common than ὅρα, ὁρᾶτε (→ 342) in the same sense; the 26 instances in Pr.-Bauer⁴, s.v. βλέπω 4-6 are fairly complete (in addition cf. only Mk. 13:23; Hb. 3:12). Thus far there is only 1 non-NT example (→ 317) of the constr. with ἀπό found in Mk. 8:15; 12:38 (Bl.-Debr.⁷ § 149 App.).

[150] If βλέπω is used in Jn. 21:20 and θεάομαι in 1:38 this has no bearing on the question of authorship, esp. as θεωρέω occurs also at 20:14 (cf. M. E. Boismard, "Le Chapître XXI de Saint Jean," Rev. Bibl., 54 [1947], 487). On Lk. 24:12 cf. J. Jeremias, Die Abendmahlsworte Jesu² (1949), 74.

[151] A connection with הִכִּיר פָּנִים (cf. Kl. Mk. on 12:14) is by no means certain, for the LXX transl. this differently, Dt. 1:17; 16:19; Prv. 24:23; 28:21. Cf. also Schl. Mt., ad loc. on Rabb. par.

[152] In Jn. βλέπω seems to share with other verbs of seeing a use which has no connection with sense perception (→ C. 2. e.), though this is the only possible meaning in 5:19.

little ones really do see the face of God. βλέπω is very much in place to denote seeing processes in the world of empirical phenomena as distinct from religious certainty, which has to do with things invisible : R. 8:24 f.; 2 C. 4:18; Hb. 11:1, 3, 7 (→ n. 174). On Ac. 27:12 → 327.

In alternation with other verbs of seeing βλέπω can be used fig. It can thus mean "to perceive," "to note" etc., e.g., R. 7:23; 2 C. 7:8; Col. 2:5; Hb. 2:9; 10:25; [153] as a tt. in argument, Hb. 3:19; Jm. 2:22 (cf. ὁράω, 2:24). It is rare for visionary seeing, Ac. 12:9; Rev. 1:11 f.; 22:8 (cf. the weakly attested vl. 6:1, 3, 5, 7). It is not used for the appearances of the risen Lord. In Ac. 1:9, 11 βλέπω is hardly meant to show that the event could be perceived by the senses, but rather, in alternation with ἀτενίζω, to denote the full and tense participation of the disciples. Nor is βλέπω used for the vision of eschatological fulfilment. [154] βλέπω certainly occurs in 1 C. 13:12, but here the metaphor of the mirror demands a figurative reference to sense perception.

By constr. βλέπομεν applies also to the second half of the saying, but it is open to question whether Paul would have called eschatological vision a βλέπειν if he had presented the thought of the second half of the verse independently. Furthermore, there is no mention of an obj. (πρόσωπον πρὸς πρόσωπον is adverbial), and even if God is to be inferred from ἐπεγνώσθην, the passage is not an express example of seeing God. The seeing relates rather to the whole of God's saving work and its consummation, and though πρόσωπον πρὸς πρόσωπον denotes the immediacy of this vision, it does not force us to conclude that the obj. will be a person, → 365.

Apart from Mt. 18:10 (→ 343) and the very different Jn. 5:19 (→ 343), the vision of God is never described as a βλέπειν in the NT (cf. also → 327).

c. ὀπτάνομαι.

This is found only in Ac. 1:3 with reference to the resurrection appearances : δι᾽ ἡμερῶν τεσσεράκοντα ὀπτανόμενος αὐτοῖς. The choice of the term does not reflect a peculiar understanding different from that found in other statements (→ C. 2. d.). ὀπτάνομαι is used here only because a pres. part. was demanded to denote an appearing which comprises πολλὰ τεκμήρια, → 341.

d. θεάομαι.

There are only 22 instances : 3 each in Lk. and Ac., 6 in Jn., 3 in 1 Jn., 4 in Mt., 2 in the inauthentic Marcan ending, 1 in Paul. At Mt. 6:1; 23:5; Mk. 16:11 the aor. pass. is used (→ n. 14), elsewhere the aor. med., also the perf. in Jn. 1:32; 1 Jn. 4:12, 14 (no pres. or fut.).

Among the verbs of seeing the term has its own nuance. It is colourless only when there is alternation between θεάομαι (cf. Ac. 22:9) and θεωρέω (Ac. 9:7). In R. 15:24, as compared with ἰδεῖν in 1:11 etc. (→ n. 138), the visit suggested is longer, more warm and intimate. In Mt. 22:11 θεάσασθαι has the distinctive sense

---

[153] βλέπω can be used for perceptions with the other senses, Mt. 15:31; perhaps also 14:30 and Mk. 5:31 (the abbreviated expression in Rev. 1:12 means, however, that the seer would like to see whose voice he has heard). In Mk. 4:24 par. Lk. 8:18 (Dobschütz, 399) the sense is "to pay heed." There is hardly alternation between βλέπω and κατανοέω in Mt. 7:3 par. Lk. 6:41, for one cannot "see" a beam in one's own eye (cf. Lk. 6:42; κατανοέω is again used for considering with the eye in, e.g., Ac. 7:32; Jm. 1:23 f.).

[154] In Hb. 10:25 the meaning is "to observe" (on the basis of specific indications ; cf. Mi. Hb., ad loc.).

"to look over," whereas εἶδεν in the same verse means "to spot," "to discover" while looking around. In 11:8 and par. the twofold ἰδεῖν is a mere variation which is perhaps less graphic than the θεάσασθαι of v. 7. θεάομαι in Lk. 23:55 as compared with θεωρέω in Mt. 28:1 par. Mk. 15:47 lays stress on the element of love and intimacy in the regarding (cf. the explicit description of the obj. in Lk.). ἐθεάσατο in Lk. 5:27 for εἶδεν in Mk. 2:14 par. Mt. 9:9 is designed to emphasise the importance of the encounter. [155] In Ac. 21:27 what is meant is that perhaps with surprise, but certainly with attentive regard, they caught sight of the hated opponent. In 1:11 the θεάομαι does not take up again the βλέπω and ἀτενίζω of 1:10 f. but the βλεπόντων αὐτῶν of 1:9: The disciples are reliable witnesses because they have seen what has taken place. Nevertheless, the word is not a tt. for seeing the risen Lord either here or elsewhere (the obj. in Ac. 22:9 is φῶς, and the use in Mk. 16:11, 14 helps to show that this is not the true ending to Mk.). [156]

In Jn., too, one cannot say that there is no distinction [157] between θεάομαι and other verbs of seeing. On 11:45 → 342.

The θεασάμενος of Jn. 6:5 corresponds to the εἶδεν of Mt. 14:14 par. Mk. 6:34; we owe its use to the solemnity of the introduction. Cf. τεθέαμαι in Jn. 1:32 with εἶδεν in Mk. 1:10 and par. The ἐθεασάμεθα of 1:14 is not just a simple equivalent of εἴδαμεν (cf. 11:40; 12:41; → n. 148). The use of lofty speech is meant to indicate the unique impression made by this seeing. Even if this is a seeing of faith, [158] this alone does not rule out the element of eye-witness. On the other hand, it is significant that in 1 Jn. 1:1 the emphasis on eye-witness is not implicit in θεάομαι as such. For throughout 1 Jn. θεάομαι is like ἑώρακα, cf. 1 Jn. 4:12 with Jn. 1:18 (cf. 1 Jn. 4:20) and 1 Jn. 4:14 with Jn. 1:34 (cf. 3:11, 32; 19:35). It is true that the ἐθεασάμεθα of 1 Jn. 1:1 stands alongside the ἑωράκαμεν and ἀκηκόαμεν of 1:1, 3, but the combination with ἀκηκόαμεν finds a par. in Jn. 3:32 and with ψηλαφάω a par. in Lk. 24:39 (ἴδετε). Hence 1 Jn. 1:1 is not in itself enough to show that eye-witness is necessarily denoted by ἐθεασάμεθα in Jn. 1:14. [159]

Neither the Johannine nor any other NT writings use θεάομαι for seeing God, → 335. The absence of θέα (and θεατής) from the NT is also worth noting.

e. θεωρέω.

θεωρέω occurs 58 times, 24 of these in Jn. and 14 in Ac. Impf. Mk. 3:11; 12:41; 15:47; Lk. 10:18; Jn. 6:2. Fut. only Jn. 7:3, aor. Mt. 28:1; Lk. 23:48; Jn. 8:51; Rev. 11:12, otherwise always pres. Since ἑώρων does not occur in the NT (→ 340 f.), and the pres. ὁράω does not occur in Jn. (only 8:23 in Ac.), while other tenses of ὁράω and εἶδον are used 66 times in Jn., it would appear that in the NT ἐθεώρουν is used for ἑώρων, and at least in Jn. the pres. θεωρέω is used for ὁράω. It is unlikely that θεωρέω is used as the pres. and impf. of θεάομαι (no pres. or impf. in the NT), [160] for in Jn.,

---

[155] θεάομαι can hardly be called a "favourite word of Luke's" (Hck. Lk. on 5:27), for at 7:24 he shares it with Mt. 11:7, and where he alters (5:27; 23:55) it is for material reasons. One might with greater justice call it a favourite word of Matthew's (3 of the 4 instances here are peculiar to Mt.).
[156] Cf. also the constr. with ὑπό, Mk. 16:11, cf. Michaelis, 150, n. 140; Bl.-Debr. § 191, 1.
[157] So Bu. J., 45, n. 1.
[158] Cf. ibid., 45.
[159] For a different view cf. F. Torm, "Die Psychologie d. 4. Ev.: Augenzeuge oder nicht?", ZNW, 30 (1931), 125 f. Cf. also W. Oehler, "Zum Missionscharakter d. J.," BFTh, 42, 4 (1941), 23 ff. and O. Cullmann, Urchr. u. Gottesdienst² (1950), who emphasises that physical seeing is undoubtedly meant here as well (p. 42).
[160] Bl.-Debr. § 101, s.v. θεωρέω.

e.g., ἐθεασάμην etc. occur only 6 times as compared with 36 instances of εἶδον and 20 of ἑώρακα. Furthermore, it is only rarely that θεωρέω and θεάομαι are used interchangeably, → 344, whereas θεωρέω often alternates with ὁράω or εἶδον (e.g., Mk. 5:15, cf. 16; 5:38 par. Mt. 9:23) and also βλέπω (e.g., Lk. 21:6 par. Mt. 24:2 and Mk. 13:2; Jn. 20:5 f.; cf. Lk. 24:12; with εὑρίσκω Mk. 5:15 par. Lk. 8:35, cf. also Lk. 24:2 par. Mk. 16:4).

In Mt. 27:55 par. Mk. 15:40; Lk. 23:35, 48 (cf. 14:29) θεωρέω is used in its original sense, "to watch something" (as a spectator) (cf. 23:48 θεωρία "spectacle," "sight"). θεωρέω is not a tt. for visionary seeing in Lk. 24:37 (cf. Mt. 14:26 and par.) [161] nor in Ac. 9:7; 10:11 (in 7:56 it is chosen as a pres.). The chief sense in Ac. is "to perceive," "to recognise," 4:13; 17:16, 22 etc.

In Jn. 6:19; 20:6, 12, 14, where θεωρέω is used interchangeably with other verbs of seeing, the reference is to sense perception (even in the first instance in 20:12, 14), cf. also 2:23; 6:2 (→ 342; cf. 7:3). The plain meaning in 4:19; 12:19; 14:17, perhaps also 9:8; 10:12, is "to perceive," "to recognise." On the other hand, in 6:40, 62; 12:45; 14:19; 16:10, 16 f., 19 θεωρέω shares the specific Johannine use with other verbs of seeing, → C. 2. e. In Jn. 8:51 we have the transf. sense "to experience," "to know": θάνατον οὐ μὴ θεωρήσῃ, → 342. Does 17:24: ἵνα θεωρῶσιν τὴν δόξαν τὴν ἐμήν, refer similarly to the fact that the disciples of Jesus are to experience His δόξα themselves in fellowship with Him (cf. 11:40, → n. 148)? The expression ὅπου εἰμὶ ἐγώ, which relates to the heavenly mode of existence in 12:26; 14:3 (cf. the concept ζωὴ αἰώνιος [12:25], which is shown to be more narrowly eschatological by its antithesis to ἐν τῷ κόσμῳ τούτῳ, and the connection with 14:3; → 78, 7 ff.), points to the fact that we are to think along these lines in 17:24, and that the μετ' ἐμοῦ refers to fellowship with Jesus in the heavenly consummation. But if so, then the clause ἵνα θεωρῶσιν τὴν δόξαν τὴν ἐμήν means "to see His glory in eschatological fulfilment," "to see Him in His future δόξα," cf. 1 Jn. 3:2. [162] Hence this is a different seeing of the δόξα of Jesus from that of 1:14. Only in 17:24 does Jn. speak of an eschatological seeing.

2. The Significance of Seeing in New Testament Proclamation.

a. General.

Numerically the NT relation between verbs of seeing and verbs of hearing is much the same as in the LXX, → 329. With 680 instances the verbs of seeing have a clear majority over ἀκούω with roughly 425 instances. This does not mean, however, that seeing is necessarily more decisive as regards revelation. In this respect greater significance is ascribed to hearing, → 341; n. 133; I, 219 f., also the proofs which follow. No particular attention is paid in the NT to seeing as a physiologico-psychological process, cf. also → 377. Because no distinction is made between the sensual and spiritual worlds as in Gk. philosophy and Hellenism, there is no complaint (as in Philo, → 335 f.) that sense perception cannot give knowledge of spiritual reality. Seeing is simply accepted as a fact of creation, and its value as a function in revelation is evaluated accordingly.

In the NT, too, the numerical ascendancy of seeing over hearing is largely due to the fact that seeing has a natural superiority among sense perceptions. Nevertheless,

---

[161] Visionary seeing is not denoted by the word alone in Lk. 10:18. Is the impf. used here in the iterative sense? It should be remembered that this saying of Jesus is undoubtedly a transl. from the Aram., and in Aram. there is only one past tense [Kuhn]. Does this seeing really take place in Christ's pre-existent life? Cf. → IV, 130, n. 220; W. Bousset, *Kyrios Christos*[2] (1921), 16.

[162] Bu. J., who ascribes 17:24 to the author, not a redactor (397, n. 6), relates the passage to "a being with the Revealer after death," "to a Then after death" (399), though he does not associate it with "ancient Jewish-Christian apocalyptic eschatology" (397 f.).

the fact that there are in the Gospels more healings of the blind (Mt. 9:27 ff.; Mk. 8:22 ff.; 10:46 ff. and par.; Jn. 9:1 ff.) than the deaf, and that the blind but not the deaf are mentioned in Lk. 14:13, 21; Jn. 5:3 (though not Mt. 15:30) can hardly be explained by saying "that we attach greater significance to the eye than the ear" and "the blind play a greater role in human life and thought than the deaf." [163] The real reason is that blindness and eye-afflictions were very common in Palestine, and hence Jesus often healed the blind. In these healings (for a theological appraisal → III, 211 f.) there is no thought in the background that sight must be given to the blind in order that they might have a part in the work of Jesus as eye-witnesses. The parallels with other healings are of themselves enough to refute this, and in addition it would involve a blatant over-estimation of seeing as a prerequisite of eye-witness.

b. Eye-witness ; Faith and Sight.

The saying in Mt. 13:16 (cf. Lk. 10:23): ὑμῶν δὲ μακάριοι οἱ ὀφθαλμοὶ ὅτι βλέπουσιν, καὶ τὰ ὦτα [ὑμῶν] ὅτι ἀκούουσιν, sounds at first like a commendation of eye-witness in the realistic sense. But several reservations must be made.

Mention of eyes and ears (cf. Lk. 11:27 → IV, 367) does not mean emphasis on sense perception. It is a graphic Semitic (cf. Job 19:27; 42:5) mode of expression found also in Lk. 2:30 (cf. 4:20); 1 C. 2:9; Rev. 1:7. In Lk. 10:23 the ref. is simply to the eyes, but 10:24 par. Mt. 13:17 shows that this is an abbreviation of the original tradition, which is better preserved in this respect in Mt. Since Jewish expectations of the experience of the age of salvation are always in terms of seeing, [164] the ref. to hearing in Mt. 13:16 f. is explicable only on the assumption that hearing is esp. significant in Jesus (and the NT) as hearing and receiving the message of salvation. But seeing too, at least in 13:16, is a prerequisite of the knowledge of salvation. In Mt. we have the train of thought that, in contrast to prophets and righteous men (13:17), you have the unmerited privilege of seeing and hearing (v. 16); how terrible if, in spite of this, you still do not attain to true seeing and hearing (v. 14 f.)! This sequence seems to have been imposed by Mt., but it is closer to the original meaning of the saying than the order in Lk., who, unlike Mt., seems to make 10:23 f. rather over-rich by combining it with 10:21 f. Furthermore, the Lucan form seems to suggest that the μακάριοι applies directly only to the eyes of the eye-witnesses, and the eyes of the disciples alone are surely meant in 10:24 again. In Mt., on the other hand, the statements ὅτι βλέπουσιν or ἀκούουσιν claim attention ; without 13:17 it would not be apparent to what 13:16 refers. Neither Mt. nor Lk. probably has the original wording. There is much to be said for the view that this is an admonition [165] not to play around with the opportunity offered by seeing and hearing ; the ref. to prophets and righteous men then finds a par. in Mt. 11:20 ff.; 12:41 f. The person of Jesus is not mentioned as the obj. in 13:16 and par. because this is not the immediate ref.; the obj. of seeing, as in 11:20 ff., is the δύναμις, and that of hearing acc. to 12:41 f. the κήρυγμα or σοφία of Jesus.

Underlying Mt. 13:16 f. par. is the conviction that the awaited time of salvation has come in Jesus, → IV, 368. Hence we may conclude that eye-witness as such is not extolled, but emphasis is laid on the increased obligation to make a right decision in the light of it. In this sense the saying fits in well with the estimation of eye-witness elsewhere in the NT.

---

[163] So Dobschütz, 397; cf. 396. The order to the lame man in Ac. 3:4 : βλέψον εἰς ἡμᾶς, shows the significance which seeing has for the establishment and continuance of spiritual relations, but there is no thought of influencing the sick man by suggestion. For this view cf. M. Dibelius, "Stilkritisches zur Ag.," *Eucharisterion*, II [1923], 39 and n. 2; Bau. Ag., 59.

[164] Cf., e.g., → 339; Str.-B., II, 139; Lk. 2:30; 3:6 (Is. 40:5); Jn. 8:56 (→ n. 147). Cf. also W. G. Kümmel, *Verheissung u. Erfüllung* (1945), 69 and n. 174.

[165] Cf. W. Michaelis Mt., II (1949), 201; though cf. also Bultmann Trad., 114; Kümmel, *op. cit.*, 68 and n. 172.

According to Lk. 1:2 the ἀσφάλεια (→ I, 506) of the primitive Christian proclamation of Christ depends on the fact that it reaches back without a break to the eye-witnesses of the πράγματα. Lk. will accept as true agents of the tradition only those αὐτόπται (→ 373), or he will accept as αὐτόπται only those who were also ὑπηρέται τοῦ λόγου (→ IV, 121, 124 f.). In so doing, he makes it plain in what sense eye-witness, and hence the historicity of the events, is to be understood. The reference is to seeing which leads to the proclamation of the Word by the believing community because it is not limited to the perception and contemplation of what has taken place, but has come to see its meaning, and understood it as revelation which must be encountered in faith, cf. also Jn. 20:31. Eye-witness is genuine only when the imperative of faith is present as well as the privilege of sight. For this reason, while the Gospels are certainly based on the tradition of eye-witnesses, they are more than the reports of eye-witnesses.

> Luke, too, saw no guarantee of ἀσφάλεια in the subjective form which distinguishes eye-witness accounts, nor did he think the objective form of his own presentation was any hindrance to its effectiveness as witness of faith. How far Mk. reproduces the actual wording of an account by Peter may be left undecided. The emphasis on eye-witness in 2 Pt. 1:18 (cf. ἐπόπται in 1:16; → 375) is without par. in the NT and is thus regarded as an argument against the authenticity of this epistle ; [166] on μάρτυς in 1 Pt. 5:1 → IV, 494 (in the NT the element of testimony to facts in this concept is increasingly accompanied by that of witness in the sense of a confession which is sought, → IV, 489). The ἐθεασάμεθα of Jn. 1:14 does not force us to think in terms of eye-witness ; [167] at any rate, it does not introduce a Gospel in eye-witness style. [168] 1 Jn. 1:5 (cf. 3:11) shows that what follows is indeed the passing on of a message, yet not just as a report, but in independent form and exposition. The strong emphasis on eye-witness in 1:1-3 is simply designed to accredit the author in his task as an expositor. [169]

If in the Gospels we are not told what Jesus looked like (→ I, 219), if no descriptions are given of others (apart from notes like Lk. 19:3), if there is hardly any reference at all to the whole world of colour (→ IV, 246), if there are no descriptions of the scenery, if topographical recollections are often very trite etc., the reason is not that such details had dropped away before the Gospels were written. The real point is that for the eye-witness accounts what was to be seen, and what had to be described as visible, was the actions of Jesus, His deeds, encounters with Him. From the very first what was handed down included not merely His words (→ IV, 140 f.) but also His acts. This is connected with the fact that both word and work, and hence both hearing and seeing, constitute the full historicity and totality of the event of revelation. There can be no doubt as to the primacy of hearing : the οἱ ἀκούσαντες of Hb. 2:3 shows this when one considers that it is par. to the οἱ αὐτόπται of Lk. 1:2 (→ I, 219). But seeing is also a kind of hearing ; that is to say, it, too, is a receiving of revelation. Like

---

[166] Characteristically there is sometimes in apocr. gospels a taste for the eye-witness account. Cf. Ev. Pt., 59 f. and the fragments of Ev. Hb. which are adduced in Hennecke, 45-48 as Nos. 7, 21 f., 25, 38, 48, 56, 59 f.

[167] Cf. → 345 and Bu. J., 45 f. (46, n. 1: *plur. ecclesiasticus*).

[168] This does not mean that the author cannot be the son of Zebedee. If this is to be accepted on other grounds (cf. W. Michaelis, *Einl. in d. NT* [1946], 93-99), it is the more noteworthy that he does not write in the I or We style.

[169] The view that in 1 Jn. we have a "readoption of the situation of contemporaries by the new generation of the time" (Bu. J., 46, n. 2) hardly does justice to the tenor of 1:1 ff. As an introduction to the whole epistle 1:1 ff. is not exclusively connected with the polemic which began only later against those who contested "the corporeality of the revelation of the Eternal in Jesus" (so Bü. J., 10).

hearing, it can and should lead to faith, Jn. 11:40; 20:8. Hence it is a fault if faith is not reached through seeing, 6:36 (→ 342), though there can also be a dependence of faith on seeing which is unbelief, Mk. 15:32; Jn. 20:25, 27.

In Jn. 20:24 ff. the reference is indeed to an encounter with the risen Lord, but the saying in 20:29 : μακάριοι οἱ μὴ ἰδόντες καὶ πιστεύσαντες, has a general and basic validity beyond this particular context. It is addressed to contemporaries of the Evangelist who have to believe without seeing for themselves, 1 Pt. 1:8 makes the same point in the simple statement: ὃν (sc. Ἰησοῦν Χριστὸν) οὐκ ἰδόντες ἀγαπᾶτε, and Jn. 20:29 shows that this faith without seeing is fully equal to faith on the basis of seeing. [170] The primitive Christian tradition takes the place of personal eye-witness. Nevertheless, as the eye-witness of the contemporaries of Jesus was from the very first orientated to the *kerygma* of the community (→ 347), so the tradition of the community must rest on this eye-witness; only thus can the significance of the historicity of the revelation in Jesus be safeguarded. [171] In a new form seeing thus becomes hearing. Paul bases faith only on hearing apostolic preaching, R. 10:16 ff. (→ I, 221), and he realises that he himself is a link in the chain of tradition, 1 C. 15:3 etc. Perhaps opponents of the apostle made special claims that they had been eye-witnesses of the earthly life of Jesus, cf., e.g., 2 C. 5:12. If Paul rejected such claims this does not mean that he attached no importance to the historicity of the life of Jesus in the factual and empirical world, cf. 1 C. 15:3 ff.

2 C. 4:18 must also be regarded as a contribution to the question of the relation between sight and faith. Is the invisible here really that which is as yet still invisible, that which is to come, the eschatological? [172]

> 5:7 does not throw any light on this, since διὰ εἴδους does not mean "in sight" (→ II, 374), and there is thus no linguistic relation to the τὰ (μὴ) βλεπόμενα of 4:18. Nor does the αἰώνιος of 5:1 justify explanation of 4:17 f. in terms of c. 5. The decisive pt. is the connection between 4:17 and 4:16. One can hardly fail to see that τὸ παραυτίκα ἐλαφρὸν τῆς θλίψεως in v. 17 corresponds to the διαφθείρεσθαι of the ἔξω ἄνθρωπος in v. 16. The question is whether αἰώνιον βάρος δόξης in v. 17, independently of v. 16, is simply an internal antithesis to τὸ παραυτίκα ἐλαφρὸν τῆς θλίψεως, or whether the expression does not necessarily correspond to the ἀνακαινοῦσθαι of the ἔσω ἄνθρωπος in v. 16. If so, τὰ βλεπόμενα and τὰ μὴ βλεπόμενα in 4:18 are par. to v. 16 : What is before our eyes is the perishing of the outer man, and what escapes present perception is the renewal and growth of the inner man.

Though αἰώνιον βάρος δόξης in 2 C. 4:17 is eschatologically orientated (→ I, 554 f.), the τὰ μὴ βλεπόμενα of v. 18 refers, not to that which comes, and which

---

[170] A fundamentally higher estimation of faith without sight (cf. Schl. J., ad loc.: "The ... saying sets the community of believers above the apostles") can hardly be deduced from the μακάριοι, since the form of the saying is determined by the comparison with Thomas, whose faith was based on eye-witness. Cf. Tanch. לך לך 17a in Str.-B., II, 586.

[171] Cf. Bu. J., 46 on the contemporaneousness of disciples with the eye-witnesses, and his objections in ThLZ, 65 (1940), 244 f. to dissociation from the apostolic Easter witness as proclaimed by E. Hirsch, *Die Auferstehungsgeschichten u. der chr. Glaube* (1940); on this cf. also P. Althaus, "Die Wahrheit des kirchlichen Osterglaubens," BFTh, 42, 2² (1941), 64 ff. Cf. further Cullmann, *op. cit.*, 40-46 on sight and faith in Jn.; also his "Εἶδεν καὶ ἐπίστευσεν, La vie de Jesus, objet de la 'vue' et de la 'foi,' d'après le quatrième Evangile," *Aux sources de la tradition chrétienne. Mélanges offerts à M. M. Goguel* (1950), 53-58, 60. On Ac. 1:21 f. → I, 436.

[172] Cf. Bchm. K., Ltzm. K., Schl. K., ad loc. Cf. also → III, 463 f. and G. Delling, *Das Zeitverständnis d. NT* (1940), 142 f.

is not yet visible, but to that which is already present, and still not visible. This thing which is not visible is called αἰώνια because in this world, by the operation of the Spirit through whom renewal of the inner man takes place (Eph. 3:16; Tt. 3:5), there come into play the δυνάμεις μέλλοντος αἰῶνος (Hb. 6:5) whose work will outlast that which is visible, which belongs only to this world, and which is consequently πρόσκαιρα. [173] The renewal of the inner man, though a reality, i.e., a spiritual reality, is not διὰ εἴδους; it does not have a form which is visible, which can be grasped by sensual or intellectual perception. To be certain of it, to direct σκοπεῖν on it alone, is πίστις.

In R. 8:24 f. Paul shows that hope is possible as an attitude to the future only if its object is not yet present (cf. → II, 531, 12 f.). He adds this definition of hope to the statement: τῇ γὰρ ἐλπίδι ἐσώθημεν, which for its part relates to the fact that in 8:23 Paul has added to the υἱοθεσία which is already given by possession of the ἀπαρχὴ τοῦ πνεύματος (cf. 8:15) the eschatological υἱοθεσία which is still awaited. If υἱοθεσία is still awaited and is not yet visible, if it is thus an object of hope, the υἱοθεσία already given in faith cannot be regarded as a visible entity. Neither faith nor hope relates to that which is already visible.

In the definition of faith in Hb. 11:1, which describes it as ἐλπιζομένων ὑπόστασις (→ II, 531), the addition πραγμάτων ἔλεγχος οὐ βλεπομένων refers to the future πράγματα (cf. μηδέπω, 11:7). In 11:3 τὸ βλεπόμενον (cf. plur., → n. 68) is the visible world (= τοὺς αἰῶνας, → I, 204). An antithetical relation to the πράγματα οὐ βλεπόμενα of 11:1 is not intended, but it arises from the fact that the ῥῆμα θεοῦ, by which, as faith alone realises, the visible world was created, does not belong to the φαινόμενα. [174]

c. Visionary-Ecstatic Prophetic Seeing.

Revelations by dreams, [175] common in the OT (→ 230; 329), are rare in the NT (→ 234 f.). According to Mt. 1:20; 2:13, 19 an ἄγγελος κυρίου (i.e., of God) appeared (always φαίνεσθαι) to Joseph κατ᾽ ὄναρ (cf. also 2:12, 22, 27 and 27:19) to give him instructions. These are not true dreams of a visual kind (→ 329) but a variation on the OT type (→ 333) introduced by ὤφθη κύριος τῷ ... καὶ εἶπεν (αὐτῷ) and conveying only revelation by word.

This OT form may be found in the NT at Ac. 7:2 f. (= Gn. 12:1, 7) and even more purely Lk. 1:11 (ἄγγελος κυρίου). Cf. also Ac. 9:10; 18:9 (in both cases εἶπεν alone); 23:11 (ἐπιστὰς ... εἶπεν); 27:23 (παρέστη ... λέγων, → n. 93), also 16:9: ὅραμα διὰ νυκτὸς τῷ Παύλῳ ὤφθη (the visual element — the direction is given by a

---

[173] For a not exclusively eschatological use of αἰώνιος cf. in Paul 2 Th. 2:16 as well as 2 C. 4:18 (and perhaps 4:17).

[174] Cf. Mi. Hb., ad loc. In 11:1 the negative οὐ comes before the part. βλεπομένων, perhaps because it is closely related and has the effect almost of an α privativum (cf. Bl.-Debr. § 426, 430, 3; "because = ἀόρατος ?"). Nevertheless, it is no accident that the author does not use ἀόρατος here or in 11:7 (as in 11:27), for οὐ βλεπόμενα, in accordance with the meaning of βλέπω (→ 343), is better adapted to express inaccessibility to sense perception. Paul uses forms of βλέπω, not ἀόρατος (R. 1:20 etc.), in R. 8:24 f.; 2 C. 4:18.

[175] On ἐνύπνιον in Ac. 2:17 cf. Michaelis, 152, n. 151. A. Wikenhauser, "Die Traumgesichte d. NT in religionsgeschichtlicher Sicht," Pisciculi = Antike u. Christentum, Suppl. Vol. 1 (1939), 320-333, describes visions in dreams as "symbolic dreams" (→ 329), and he distinguishes between visions given during sleep and visions given while awake (→ 372 and n. 4).

Macedonian who is known to be such from his clothes, not his speech — simply supports the revelation by word). Inasmuch as the instructions in 16:9; 18:9; 23:11; 27:23 are given by night, it might be — though we are not told this — that Paul was asleep and dreaming (the use of ὄραμα in 16:9; 18:9 does not prove the contrary, though in 9:10 and elsewhere this is used for visions by day). At any rate, it is evident that ὄραμα, and in connection therewith ὤφθη in 16:9 and εἶδεν in 16:10, can refer to pure revelation by word. In the NT, as distinct from the OT, God Himself does not speak directly. In the infancy stories in Mt. it is an angel who speaks, in Ac. 9:10; 18:9; 23:11 the κύριος, i.e., the Lord Jesus (cf. 9:17; the ref. in 27:23 is obviously to an ἄγγελος τοῦ θεοῦ, cf. θεός 27:24 f., → I, 85. On the other hand, there is no suggestion that the recipients of such revelations are afraid, nor do we find the allaying of such fears by a μὴ φοβοῦ, which is rare even in the OT accounts, → 333; n. 93. Again, there is no ecstatic element. [176] The instances in Ac. are obviously not angelophanies or epiphanies of the κύριος in the strict sense, but revelations by word (the directions of the Spirit in Ac. 16:6 f. perhaps have something of the same character).

Apart from the quotation in Ac. 7:2 (→ 350) there are no theophanies (→ 331) at all. [177] The instances in which God's voice is heard belong to the sphere of revelation by word, though only in Ac. 7:31 (cf. Ex. 3:4 ff.) is this described as such; in Mt. 3:17 and par. (cf. Jn. 12:28) the reference is to a → φωνή from heaven or from a cloud (→ I, 219). [178]

Angelophanies are more frequent (→ I, 84). In the story of Jesus they occur especially in the infancy stories in Lk. (on the stories in Mt. → 350) and in the resurrection stories. The appearance of Gabriel in Lk. 1:11 ff. is described in 1:22 as ὀπτασία, but this lays no special emphasis on the visual or visionary aspect, → 372. ὤφθη is used in 1:11 (→ 350), εἰσελθών in 1:28, and ἐπέστη in 2:9 (→ 350). In these three instances the angels are "simply heralds of the divine action" (→ I, 84). On Lk. 2:13 f. → I, 84 f.; II, 247 f.; 413. When Lk. 22:43 f., which is peculiar to Lk. (though cf. Mt. 4:11 and par.; 26:53, → I, 84), begins: ὤφθη δὲ αὐτῷ ἄγγελος, the ὤφθη here simply denotes the coming and presence of the angel (and αὐτῷ does not mean that Jesus saw an angel, but that the angel came to help Him). In the resurrection narratives the angels are agents of proclamation (here again the angelophany is called → ὀπτασία in Lk. 24:23, though the reference is simply to revelation by word). It is no surprise that in the secondary Mt. 28:2 ff., which is peculiar to this Gospel, both the action and the appearance of the angel are described, though we do not have any such description elsewhere, apart from the white clothes, → I, 84 and n. 67; IV, 255. A parallel to the Synoptic resurrection stories may be found in Jn. 20:12, though there are no angelophanies elsewhere in Jn. [179] Jn. 12:29, which is not a true par. to Lk. 22:43, shows how naturally the angel was regarded as a bearer of divine messages. It is presupposed here that in some circumstances an angel may be heard (by anyone), but not seen (by anyone).

Ac. 1:10 is to be reckoned among the resurrection stories; the v.l. ὤφθησαν for παρειστήκεισαν in arm Cat is in full keeping with the OT and NT use of ὤφθη to denote presence. The angel whom Cornelius sees ἐν ὀράματι (10:3, cf. v. 30; 11:13) comes with a message. The relation to the brief type of angelic message in Mt. 1:20

---

[176] Michaelis, 152 f., n. 155.
[177] On Ac. 7:35, ibid., 153, n. 156.
[178] In Ac. 10:13, 15; 11:7, 9 the voice of the κύριος Jesus is meant (though cf. Zn. Ag., 349, n. 49). On Jn. 5:37 cf. Bu. J., 200, n. 6; → 364.
[179] On 1:51 cf. Bu. J., 75, 74, n. 4; → I, 84.

etc. is plain to see, cf. also Ac. 8:26. In Ac. 5:19 f.; 12:7 ff. the angels bring liberation
from prison and an explanatory message, though in these instances one may appreciate
how hard it is to infer the underlying historical events from the realistic depiction.
12:9 is instructive: οὐκ ᾔδει ὅτι ἀληθές ἐστιν τὸ γινόμενον διὰ τοῦ ἀγγέλου,
ἐδόκει δέ ὅραμα βλέπειν. For here ὅραμα does not mean imagination or deception,
since ἀληθής has the sense of "real" (→ I, 248), and the result is that a ὅραμα, both
here and elsewhere in Ac., does not take place in the realm of that reality which can
be perceived by the natural senses, i.e., the ref. is not to normal sense perception. [180]

Whereas other ὁράματα are simply revelations by word, the ὅραμα of Ac.
10:11 ff. (→ n. 176; 372) — whose distinctiveness is apparent from the fact that
Peter is expressly said to be in a state of ἔκστασις in 10:10; 11:5 (→ II, 457) —
is the only instance outside Rev. where there is revelation by symbol (on 16:9
→ 350 f.; on 7:55 f. → 353). In this respect the vision of Peter is like the dreams
and prophetic visions of the OT, → 329. Revelations of the future by visions in
which the future events of the last times are "seen" occur in the NT only in
Rev. [181] Rev. as a whole is a record of such visions, 1:2. In the letters communications about the future (e.g., 2:10) are embedded in prophetic proclamation which
tells what the Spirit has to say to the churches especially in respect of past and
present, 2:7 etc. The later visions are of a different type. [182] After his ascent
ἐν πνεύματι (cf. 1:10) into heaven (4:1 f.), the author now sees the heavenly world
and learns the course of eschatological events (c. 4 ff.). The relation to OT and
later Jewish apocalyptic (→ 333; 339) is manifest. Nevertheless, according to its
own testimony in 1:3; 22:7 etc. Rev. is intended to be → προφητεία, and in the last
analysis revelation by word predominates, 22:6, 8. [183]

Paul, though capable of ecstatic experiences, does not seem to have had visions
after the manner of Rev. [184] If to clear up detailed eschatological questions he
appeals to special revelations, his reference is to the words of the exalted Lord
(1 Th. 4:15) or to disclosed μυστήρια (1 C. 15:51). That is to say, he always
has in view revelation by word, which can include theological intuition. The
rapture in 2 C. 12:2 ff., which as a heavenly journey may be compared with Rev.
4:1 f., [185] is not designed to make possible a disclosure of coming events. Otherwise the ἄρρητα ῥήματα of 12:4, like the ἀποκάλυψις of Rev. 1:1, would have
played an introductory role. It is true that one cannot speak of revelation by

---

[180] For details cf. Michaelis, 112 f.

[181] In Ac. 9:12 par. v. 10 we simply have revelation by word, ibid., 152, n. 152. Cf. 146,
n. 123 on predictions like Ac. 11:28, → n. 147 on Jn. 8:56, → n. 148 on 12:41.

[182] The author uses only the verb εἶδον (on ὤφθη in 11:19; 12:1, 3 → n. 192; on βλέπω
→ 344), not the nouns ὅραμα or ὀπτασία. On ὅρασις in Rev. → 371 with n. 6. On the
relation of vision and reflection in Rev. cf. F. Torm, Hermeneutik d. NT (1930), 161-168.

[183] → II, 458; III, 588 f. On the preponderance of the acoustic element over the optic in
Rev. cf. C. Schneider, D. Erlebnisechtheit d. Apk. d. Joh. (1930), esp. 136 ff. Rev. (cf.
22:4 → I, 220; Kittel, 103 f.) can be adduced as an instance of the fact that in the NT
"eschatology is described in terms of seeing rather than hearing" only with the qualification
that the importance of seeing in this book derives from the apocal. tradition. Hence instances
from the other NT books are of greater theological relevance.

[184] On what follows cf. also Deissner, op. cit., 83-87. On Col. 2:18, → II, 536.

[185] There is in 2 C. 12 no literary garb as in the heavenly journeys of apocal., Eth. En.
17 ff. etc. The Gnostic heavenly journey of the soul is also of a different kind, → 82;
I, 521; very different phenomena are grouped together in the Exc. in Ltzm. K., ad loc.
It is, however, an important feature of the experience of Paul that it cannot be induced
by Paul himself, cf. the κυρίου of 12:1 (→ 357) and also ἁρπαγέντα in 12:2; cf. v. 4.
On the Jewish or at least not Hell. background of 2 C. 12 cf. F. Büchsel, Der Geist Gottes
im NT (1926), 269, n. 1 (on bChag., 14b-16a cf. → n. 119).

word in the narrower sense, though it is striking enough that Paul mentions only the ῥήματα. Again, one cannot deduce from the → ὀπτασία of 12:1 that the reference is predominantly or exclusively to visual experiences. Since Paul speaks only of ἀποκαλύψεις in 12:7, ὀπτασίαι and ἀποκαλύψεις in 12:1 seem to be interchangeable (perhaps relating to the subjective and objective aspects of the same thing). In any case ἀποκαλύψεις is the chief concept ("ὀπτασίαι and other ἀποκαλύψεις"). The plur. shows that what is recorded in 2 C. 12 is a selected example. Since other ὀπτασίαι or ἀποκαλύψεις are not mentioned in 2 C. 12, it is hard to say what these might have been. One thing which is certain is that the Damascus experience is not to be placed in this category, → 357.

Paul does not mention the Spirit in 2 C. 12:2 ff., though he might have used the formulation of Rev. 1:10; 4:2 : ἐγενόμην ἐν πνεύματι. This aspect is plainly stressed in Stephen's vision to the degree that ὑπάρχων δὲ πλήρης πνεύματος ἁγίου in Ac. 7:55 is not just a reference back to 6:5, 8, 10. [186] The primary thought is not that of the vision of God as a foretaste of eschatological vision. [187] In this case there would be no need for an explanatory revelation by word, since the appearance of Stephen as he looked on the Son of Man would be unmistakable. [188] It might well be that there is a relation here to the Jewish idea that the dying are granted a view of their future destiny, → n. 119.

That no corresponding vision is granted to Jesus in the hour of death would surprise us only if Jesus had been a typical visionary or ecstatic. But this is not so, → II, 456. Along with Lk. 10:18 (though cf. → n. 161) the only example which might be quoted is the baptism story.

> Lk. completely suppresses the visionary aspect by eliminating the εἶδεν of Mk. 1:10 in his alteration of the constr., so that the whole event mentioned in 3:21 f. is on the ordinary level. Mt. in 3:16 separates the opening of heaven from the constr. with εἶδεν, so that the εἶδεν which follows can refer only to non-visionary seeing. In Mk., however, the wording of the voice from heaven in the 2nd person would seem to suggest that originally Jesus alone was thought to have seen and heard something. Since the Baptist at least must have been present too, this forces us to the conclusion that the ref. is not to ordinary seeing and hearing.

What Jesus saw was the descent of the Spirit. Certainty of receiving the Spirit found visionary expression in the perceiving of a coming. [189] Vision and audition are not so attuned to one another that the voice from heaven interprets the vision. Their relation is that of the two sides of a common event. To Jesus, as Messiah, there is imparted the Spirit at the beginning of His earthly activity — this is the one side. Related to it is the other — the certainty of Jesus that He is the elect Son of God. To the degree that His Sonship includes His Messiahship (and not

---

[186] On what follows cf. Michaelis, 114 ff.

[187] It is not unintentionally that the δόξα θεοῦ is mentioned only in 7:55 and not in the cry of 7:56; more significant, then, is the fact that Stephen sees the Son of Man standing on the right hand of God.

[188] The Son of Man stands because He has already risen to welcome Stephen. Cf. Bau. Ag., 120, ad loc.

[189] Cf. W. Michaelis, Reich Gottes u. Geist Gottes nach dem NT (1931), 38, n. 22. The coming of the Spirit in Ac. 2:2 f. also involves "visionary accompanying phenomena" (→ I, 724). Yet ὤφθησαν in 2:3 does not have to emphasise the visual side ; it is par. to the more abstract ἐγένετο in 2:2. The tongues were suddenly there (→ n. 93, 192). βλέπειν and ἀκούειν in 2:33 do not refer to the γλῶσσαι and ἦχος of 2:2 f.

vice versa) [190] the revelation by word enjoys material primacy over the revelation by image.

The transfiguration of Jesus in Mk. 9:2 ff. and par. is not to be regarded as an ecstatic experience of Jesus Himself, → II, 456 and n. 40. If so, the participation of the disciples would have to be very different from that recorded, or, in fact, non-existent. Account must be taken of the appearance of Moses and Elijah and the voice from the cloud when we try to decide whether the voice whole event was a real experience of Jesus or a visionary experience of the disciples. [191]

> Since ὤφθη is very often neutral and denotes presence, [192] the expressions ὤφθη αὐτοῖς in Mt. 17:3 par. Mk. 9:4 or ὀφθέντες in Lk. 9:31 seem to leave open the question what form of seeing is intended. ὅραμα in Mt. 17:9 and par. can mean "what is seen" (cf. Ac. 7:31); cf. the verbal phrases in Mk. 9:9 par. Lk. 9:36. If it is a peculiarity of Lk. that in 9:31 ff. the disciples are awakened out of sleep, this indicates that in what follows he had in view seeing (and hearing) while they were awake.

The transfiguration was obviously not necessary for Jesus' own sake. Nor did Moses and Elijah appear on His account, as Lk. 9:30 f. might seem to suggest. [193] The voice from the cloud, being in the 3rd person (unlike that at the baptism, → 353), also makes it quite evident that the disciples alone need to be taught by this revelation. This supports the view that we have a visionary process, though with no implied material disparagement. It is not surprising that three persons share the same vision, for other visions can be available for more than one person at once. [194]

> As the disappearance of Moses and Elijah is not described, [195] so it is not expressly stated that the transfiguration was reversed at the end. In the tradition it is quite natural that, if the transfiguration was real, it could be only temporary, while what is seen in a vision obviously cannot outlast the vision. The eschatological form of the features in which the transfiguration is presented (→ IV, 247) and the purely eschatological orientation of the whole story rule out any possibility of regarding the transfiguration as an emergence of the pre-existent δόξα of Jesus (→ IV, 758, n. 18), esp. since ideas of pre-existence do not occur in the Synoptics. The transfiguration is rather the "anti-

---

[190] Cf. W. Michaelis, "Der Messias als Gottes Sohn ?" *Deutsches Pfarrerblatt*, 41 (1940), 365 f.; also "Das Urchr.," *Mensch u. Gottheit in den Religionen*[2] (1942), 326 f.

[191] → IV, 758 seems to be at fault in this respect. A careful, though in its very fulness rather confusing review of the various expositions of the pericope both as a whole and in detail is to be found in the (Roman Catholic) monograph of J. Höller, *D. Verklärung Jesu* (1937). Cf. also H. Riesenfeld, "Jésus transfiguré," *Acta Seminarii Neotestamentici Upsaliensis*, 16 (1947), 243-306.

[192] On Ac. 2:3 → n. 189. ὤφθη is used with the dat. for the coming of a man in Ac. 7:26 (not Ex. 2:13); cf. also the logion of Jesus in P. Oxy., I, 1, verso 11 ff.: ἔστην ἐν μέσῳ τοῦ κόσμου καὶ ἐν σαρκὶ ὤφθην αὐτοῖς κτλ. (cf. Hennecke, 36). On Rev. 11:19; 12:1, 3 → Michaelis, 152, n. 150.

[193] Cf. W. Michaelis, *Mt.* II (1949), 382.

[194] The absence of the pericope from Jn. is to be linked with the author's view of δόξα. The strongly limited, if emphatic, Johannine view of the manifestation of the δόξα in the earthly life of Jesus (→ II, 249) would accord better with the idea that certainty of the δόξα dignity of Jesus is mediated by visionary seeing than with the assumption of a real transfiguration.

[195] Acc. to Lk. they were obviously received by the cloud in so far as the αὐτούς of 9:34b (vl. ἐκείνους) refers to Moses and Elijah (cf. Höller, *op. cit.*, 123 ff.). But this can hardly have been the original idea, → IV, 908; Michaelis (→ n. 193), 384.

cipation and guarantee of an eschatological reality" (→ IV, 758), [196] though the voice from the cloud does not stress this aspect. [197] If "Jesus appears to His disciples in the form which He will have as the Messiah-Son of Man," [198] the primary reference is not to the resurrection (and resurrection appearances), but to the *parousia*. [199]

d. The Resurrection Appearances.

The question now to be considered is that of the significance of seeing in the resurrection appearances. What are the appearances? Are they ὁράματα, visions etc., or not? We have such appearances in Mt. 28:9 f., 16 ff.; Lk. 24:13 ff., 36 ff., 50 ff.; Jn. 20:14 ff., 19 ff., 24 ff.; 21:1 ff.; Ac. 1:4 ff. We should also include the accounts of Paul's conversion in Ac., the apostle's own refs. to this event, and the brief summaries in Lk. 24:34; 1 C. 15:5 ff. The material is thus comparatively rich. A difficulty is that there can be no reconstructing the originals by comparing two or more versions of the same pericope, since, with the exception at very most of Mt. 28:9 f.; Jn. 20:14 ff., the stories are all available only in the one form. [200]

When the accounts in the Gospels and Acts are reviewed, there are several points of agreement which are important for an understanding of the nature of the appearances. In the first place — and this is particularly clear when several appearances are recorded one after the other in Lk. — the individual appearances are obviously self-contained and isolated events separated from one another in time and place. Whereas the commencement of the appearances is always noted (cf. ἔστη ἐν μέσῳ αὐτῶν in Lk. 24:36 etc.), their end is seldom indicated except by the beginning of a new pericope. [201] There is never anything to suggest that the appearances are to be regarded as part of a lasting stay of Jesus with His disciples. [202] Nor is there any evidence for the view that in the times between the appearances He was somewhere else on earth, though not with the disciples. The appearance outside Damascus is depicted as an appearance of the risen Lord

---

[196] The ref. is not to visionary seeing of the fut., since Moses and Elijah are mentioned, not in virtue of the future position, but in virtue of their present status as prominent members of the heavenly world.

[197] That this voice is meant to be proclamation of Jesus as Messiah (Bultmann Trad., 278; Riesenfeld, 250-253) is unlikely, as shown by the special connection of the voice at baptism with Sonship rather than Messiahship, → 353 f. Son of God and Messiah are not simple equivalents, → n. 190.

[198] J. Schniewind, *Mk.* (*NT Deutsch*), ad loc.; → IV, 248.

[199] The pericope is hardly an original resurrection story. The reasons for this view (cf. Bultmann Trad., 278 ff. and bibl.) are not convincing. In particular the tradition in Apc. Pt. is not to be rated above the Synoptic account. Cf. also the differentiation in M. Albertz, "Zur Formengeschichte d. Auferstehungsberichte," ZNW, 21 (1922), 263.

[200] Michaelis, 5-10; there is here a criticism of the thesis of Hirsch (→ n. 171) etc. that behind Mk. 16:8, in an ending later excised, there is an original appearance to Peter. In part Hirsch follows R. Hartstock, "Visionsberichte in d. synpt. Ev.," *Festgabe f. J. Kaftan* (1920), 130 ff., though Hartstock goes much further than Hirsch in trying to explain the most varied sections in the Synoptic tradition (e.g., the finding of the empty tomb) as originally visions.

[201] There are special reasons for the exceptions in Lk. 24:31, 51; Ac. 1:9 ff., Michaelis, 85 f.

[202] Cf. also ἐν πολλοῖς τεκμηρίοις, Ac. 1:3. The expression δι' ἡμερῶν τεσσερά-κοντα in Ac. 1:3 means spread over 40 days rather than uninterruptedly for 40 days. Cf. W. Michaelis, "Zur Überlieferung d. Himmelfahrtsgeschichte,'" ThBl, 4 (1925), 101-109; A. Schneider, *Gesammelte Aufsätze* = *Jbch. d. Theol. Seminars d. Unierten Evangelischen Kirche in Polen,* 1 (1929), *passim* ; W. Künneth, *Theologie d. Auferstehung* (1933), 69 f.; P. Benoit, "L'Ascension," *Rev. Bibl.,* 56 (1949), 161-203.

from heaven. It is true that in the first instance the phrase ἐκ τοῦ οὐρανοῦ in Ac. 9:3; 22:6 (cf. οὐρανόθεν, 26:13) refers to the light. But it also tells us whence the whole occurrence originates (cf. also τῇ οὐρανίῳ ὀπτασίᾳ, 26:19). The under-lying thought is not that the risen Lord has been in heaven since the ascension. On the contrary, His resurrection is itself exaltation to God (→ I, 370 f.). As may be seen from 5:30 f., the τῇ δὲ δεξιᾷ οὖν τοῦ θεοῦ ὑψωθείς of Ac. 2:33 refers, not to the ascension, but to the resurrection mentioned in 2:32. As compared with the resurrection, the ascension is not a further alteration in the mode of existence of the risen Lord. We are thus to think of the appearances between Easter and the ascension (certainly in Ac. and hence in Lk., but also in the Synop-tists generally) as appearances of the risen Lord from heaven. [203] This is true even when their commencement is not actually described as an appearing from heav-en. [204]

Again, there is consistent agreement that none of the appearances recorded in the Gospels and Ac. (Paul's statements are similar) is said to have taken place during sleep, in a dream, or even simply by night. [205] Thus the appearances are not dreams, whether in the sense of exclusively visual dream-visions, which do not occur in the NT, or in that of revelations κατ' ὄναρ, such as we find in Mt., → 350 and 234 f. They are never referred to in this way. If on the one side this implies some similarity to angelophanies, which usually take place by day (there are always special reasons for exceptions like Lk. 22:43; Ac. 5:19 ff.; 12:7 ff.) it also implies on the other side a distinction from the revelations by night which are recorded in Ac. 16:9; 18:9; 23:11; 27:23 and which in the first two instances are described as ὁράματα. In fact, the appearances are never called ὁράματα, and nowhere is it said that in them the risen Lord spoke ἐν ὁράματι. Thus analogies are not to be found, not merely in nocturnal visions, but in any ὁράματα (on ὀπτασίαι in 2 C. 12:1 → 357). Inasmuch as it is a mark of ὁράματα that they do not occur in a reality which can be perceived by the natural senses (→ 352), the fact that the appearances do not belong to this category suggests that they occur in a reality to which ὁράματα do not belong and which is characterised by the antithesis of ὅραμα and ἀληθές in Ac. 12:9, → 359.

A further point is that the appearances are always associated with revelation by word. The visual aspect is never stressed. The Damascus appearance is no exception. The revelation by word is thus a constitutive element in the appearances; it is particularly significant in some instances, → n. 217.

Along with these common features there are also, of course, some notable differences between the individual Gospels and Acts. The result is that some questions are difficult to answer in the light of these writings alone.

---

[203] Cf. Michaelis, 73-96. Even the distinctive appearance in Jn. 20:19 is in agreement.

[204] Cf. angelophanies, where the appearance of angels, who are undoubtedly heavenly beings, is described as ἐπέστη, εἰσελθών etc. like that of the risen Lord. ὤφθη, which serves as an introduction in angelophanies (→ 351, 25. 28 ff.), is not used thus in Christophanies, for in Lk. 24:34; Ac. 9:17; 13:31; 26:16; 1 C. 15:5 ff., it refers to the appearances as a whole. The fact that the beginning of the appearances is not described as a coming from heaven rules out any idea that the ref. is to the *parousia*, and conversely the conclusion of the last appearance before Pentecost takes the form of an ascension because of the connection between the parting character of this appearance and expectation of the *parousia*, cf. Ac. 1:10 f. and Michaelis, 86-89.

[205] On the chronology of Lk. 24:13 ff., and esp. on 24:29, cf. Michaelis, 113 f.

Some of these questions need not be dealt with here (number, order, location of the appearances). [206] Note should be taken, however, of the fact that the corporeality of the risen Lord sometimes seems to be viewed more spiritually (passing through closed doors in Lk. 24:36; Jn. 20:19, 26 is an example of this, → III, 176) and sometimes very literally (Lk. 24:39 f.; Jn. 20:20, 25, 27; cf. the eating in Lk. 24:41 ff.; Ac. 10:41). In view of post-canonical developments (→ II, 335) we must regard the more literal view as later, but both are closely intermingled in the same stories. Another question is what we are to infer from the ὀπτασία of Ac. 26:19 in relation to the Damascus appearance. Again, in connection with the account of Paul's conversion in Ac. 22 we have the record, not attested elsewhere, of a visionary experience which he had in the temple at Jerusalem. Are we to deduce from Ac. 22:17 f.: γενέσθαι με ἐν ἐκστάσει καὶ ἰδεῖν αὐτὸν λέγοντά μοι κτλ., that the Damascus experience itself was ecstatic, and that the author of Ac. equates seeing of the risen Lord with the ecstatic-visionary seeing of 10:10; 11:5, → II, 457 ?

Though it is difficult to achieve an understanding in the light of the accounts in the Gospels and Acts, there is the advantage that theological evaluation is decisively helped by the statements of the apostle Paul. Basic here is the observation that in 2 C. 12:1 Paul does not reckon the Damascus experience among ὀπτασίαι and ἀποκαλύψεις κυρίου. [207] In 12:2 ff. Paul says nothing about seeing the κύριος in his rapture, and the passages in which he does speak about seeing the Lord always refer to the one experience, i.e., that on the Damascus road. One may thus conclude that the plural in 12:1 necessarily refers to experiences of a different kind from the Damascus experience, and that the gen. in 12:1 (cf. Gl. 1:12) can be regarded simply as a gen. auct. rather than an obj. gen., → III, 583 f., 585. Paul did not call the Damascus appearance an ὀπτασία, as Ac. 26:19 did. He uses ὀπτασία only at 2 C. 12:1 and ὅραμα not at all. Hence he would reckon the ὁράματα of Ac. 9:10; 16:9 f.; 18:9 among ὀπτασίαι or ἀποκαλύψεις, but would distinguish them thereby from the Damascus experience. To the degree that the rapture of 2 C. 12:2 ff. was definitely an ecstatic experience, we are forced to conclude, in line with his own judgment as to the special role of the ecstatic element in the pneumatic life (→ II, 458), that the Damascus experience could not have for him the characteristics of ecstatic rapture. Consequently the statement in Ac. 22:17 (→ supra) is not too well adapted to promote a correct understanding of the Damascus experience itself. [208]

What positive statements does Paul make about this experience? He nowhere gives an express description. In 1 C. 9:1 we have the brief reference : οὐχὶ Ἰησοῦν τὸν κύριον ἡμῶν ἑόρακα;

The use of the act. ὁράω suggests the form of expression in Mk. 16:7 and par.; Mt. 28:10, 17, also Jn. 20:18, 25, 29 (→ n. 214) and the use of Ac., which is familiar with the act. (9:27; 22:14) as well as the pass. (9:17; 26:16) for the Damascus event. It should be noted, however, that in the two short questions which precede in 1 C. 9:1 Paul is the subj., so that balanced sentence construction demanded an act. verb. Along

---

206 Cf. on this Michaelis, 11-72. On E. Lohmeyer, Galiläa u. Jerusalem (1936), cf. ibid., 137 f., n. 58 and 139, n. 64.

207 On what follows cf. Deissner, op. cit., 138 f.; E. Käsemann, "Die Legitimität des Ap.," ZNW, 41 (1942), 64 (bibl., n. 174).

208 ἰδεῖν in Ac. 22:18 can only mean "to perceive," "to receive"; unlike 22:14 this verse has hearing rather than seeing in view. Nor can 26:16 refer to further appearances (as against → IV, 493, 34). For details cf. Michaelis, 147 f., n. 127.

with the uniqueness of the event (if there had been other instances they would not have gone unmentioned) one can conclude from 1 C. 9:1 merely that Paul saw in it the basis of his apostleship, → I, 438.

This common early Christian link (→ I, 430) may be seen also in Gl. 1:16.[209] The only difference is that here we have an express statement of the view that in the last analysis God and not Christ (and certainly not Paul) is to be regarded as "the subject of the process," → I, 438. Since Paul here uses ἀποκαλύπτω and not a verb of seeing, the passage also teaches that the event is to be understood as revelation, as the disclosure of divine truth and reality. Hence this thought is present even when verbs of seeing are used. Verbs of seeing (→ 326, 333) can become terms to express the event of revelation, and they can do so in such a way that the implied reference to (more sensual or more spiritual) perception is enhanced by the concept of openness to the event of revelation. In this sense the verbs of seeing may rightly be added to the revelational verbs discussed → III, 590.

In the confessional list in 1 C. 15:3 ff., which is taken over from the primitive community, Paul uses ὤφθη (in such a way that Χριστός can remain the subj.) for the various appearances. In 15:8 Paul uses this for the Damascus appearance too; he does not adopt an act. formulation as in 9:1. Pars. for this use of ὤφθη in the NT may be found with reference to the resurrection appearances at Lk. 24:34; Ac. 9:17; 13:31; 26:16, and with reference to angelophanies at Lk. 1:11; cf. 22:43. But, as attested in the NT at Ac. 7:2, 30, 35, it already has great significance in the LXX, and indeed in such a way that ὤφθη or ὀφθῆναι is a tt. for the presence of revelation as such without reference to the nature of its perception (→ 327), or to the presence of the God who reveals Himself in His Word (→ 333).[210] It thus seems that when ὤφθη is used as a tt. to denote the resurrection appearances there is no primary emphasis on seeing as sensual or mental perception. The dominant thought is that the appearances are revelations, encounters with the risen Lord who herein reveals Himself, or is revealed, cf. Gl. 1:16. The distinctive intr. pass. (→ 316) is thus of even stronger theological relevance than in the OT. The relation of ὤφθη in 1 C. 15:5 ff. to the act. of 9:1 does not involve a simple replacing of the act. by the corresponding passive form. If so, the significance attached to seeing would be the same in both instances. The important point about ὤφθη with the dative, however, is that the one who constitutes the subject is the one who acts, i.e., appears, shows himself, with no special emphasis on the resultant action of the person in the dative, namely, that he sees or perceives. ὤφθη Κηφᾷ etc. does not mean in the first instance that they saw Him, with an emphasis on seeing, e.g., in contrast to hearing. It means rather: παρέστησεν αὐτοῖς ἑαυτὸν ζῶντα (cf. Ac. 1:3), or even better: ὁ θεὸς ἀπεκάλυψεν αὐτὸν ἐν αὐτοῖς (cf. Gl. 1:16). He encountered them as the risen, living Lord; they experienced His presence. In the last resort even active forms like ἑόρακα in 1 C. 9:1 means the same thing (cf. the Johannine concept of seeing,

---

[209] On ἐν ἐμοί cf. Oe. Gl., 25; → II, 539.

[210] ὤφθη is not used to introduce the appearances (→ n. 204), though cf. Lk. 1:11; 22:43; Ac. 7:2, 30, also Mt. 17:3 and par. As in the LXX (→ 324 f.), so in the NT (→ n. 189; Michaelis, 152, n. 150) ὤφθη can denote presence in the secular sense. Pfister, op. cit. (→ n. 35), 301 pts. out that ἐπιφανής (cf. ἐπήκοος for a similar development) can often simply have the sense of praesens. Whether this is a "weakened" sense is open to question, since it can go hand in hand with greater profundity in the understanding of epiphanies.

→ 361). Since this is the guiding thought, the question of the way in which He could be perceived is notably neutralised or subordinated to theological evaluation, so that it cannot be answered correctly if the supremacy of the thought that the appearances are revelation is thereby prejudiced.[211] When Paul classifies the Damascus appearance with the others in 1 C. 15:5 ff. this is not merely because he regards it as equivalent (especially in relation to his apostleship, and in spite of his own unworthiness, 15:8 ff.). It is also because he regards this appearance as similar in kind.[212] In all the appearances the presence of the risen Lord is a presence in transfigured corporeality, 1 C. 15:42 ff. It is the presence of the exalted Lord from heaven, → 356.[213] This presence is in non-visionary reality; no category of human seeing is wholly adequate for it, cf. also → 378.[214] On this ground, too, the appearances are to be described as manifestations in the sense of revelation rather than making visible.

As specifically shown in Gl. 1:16 (→ 358), the object of the revelation is the risen Lord Himself (in distinction from all other ὀπτασίαι or ἀποκαλύψεις κυρίου, which

---

[211] This view, which is also that of Michaelis, 103-109, is resolutely opposed by Barth, esp. 298, n. 58; 310, n. 140; 317 f., n. 185. He for his part accepts the "sensually real significance of the biblical statements," 318, n. 185. His pt. is that those to whom the appearances came experienced a "miracle of seeing." They were singled out from the human race, 171. "The seeing of the witnesses of the appearances" is to be understood "as a gift and work of Jesus Christ," 174. The question arises, however, whether this is sensually real seeing. Again, can one list this ability to see the risen Lord (Lk. 24:31 notwithstanding) with the power of sight given to the blind when they were healed, or to Paul when his sight was restored in Ac. 9:18 (173)? It is legitimate to call the appearances a miracle. But the NT teaches us to seek the miracle more on the side of the appearing of the risen Lord than on that of the seeing of the witnesses. There is no need for us to engage in full debate with M. Barth (for a review of his book cf. E. Käsemann in ThLZ, 73 [1948], 665-670). The thesis which he advanced already in his work Das Abendmahl. Passamahl, Bundesmahl u. Messiasmahl (1945), 43-46, namely, that the appearances, and esp. the Easter meals, are a fulfilment of the imminent expectation of Mk. 9:1 par. etc. and the intimation of Mk. 14:25 par., and that these sayings of Jesus had them in view, is in itself an untenable one. Cf. Käsemann, op. cit., 669; E. Gaugler, Internationale kirchliche Zschr., 36 (1946), 254 ff.; W. Michaelis, "Karfreitags- oder Ostercharakter des Abendmahls?" Das Wort sie sollen lassen stahn. Festschr. f. A. Schädelin (1950), 61-66.

[212] Can one conclude from the ἔσχατον of 1 C. 15:8 that in Paul's view "from the time of this ἔσχατον there can be no similar or equivalent events" (→ II, 697)? One can say with certainty only that Paul (he wrote 1 C. some 25 yrs. after the Damascus experience) had not heard of any further appearances (there is surely no polemic against opponents raising similar claims for themselves). The material connection between the appearances and the resurrection certainly sets a temporal limit to the appearances, which, while extended by the special time of the Damascus experience, is not removed. Events like those in Act. Pt. Verc. 35; Act. Andr. 14 cannot be regarded as appearances in the sense of 1 C. 15, nor are they thought of as such.

[213] Paul's use of → σῶμα expresses the same interest in the reality of the mode of existence of those raised from the dead as is found in the appearances as intimations of the reality of the resurrection of Jesus. The more realistic statements in the accounts (→ 357), which appear to harmonise so badly with the presupposition of a transfigured corporeality, are to be regarded as yet another attempt to underline rather dramatically the reality of the somatic, cf. Michaelis, 91-96 (also on Lk. 24:39).

[214] The act. formulations of seeing in Ac. 9:27; 22:14 in no way crowd out the revelation by word. In general act. verbs of seeing are avoided in the resurrection narratives. On this, and on ἔδωκεν αὐτὸν ἐμφανῆ γενέσθαι in Ac. 10:40 cf. Michaelis, 117 ff. It must be regarded as a reflection of the inaccessibility of transfigured corporeality to human sight that in some stories the risen Lord is not immediately recognised because He has the garb of a travelling stranger (Lk. 24:15 f.) or an unknown gardener (Jn. 20:14 f.), cf. ἐν ἑτέρᾳ μορφῇ in the inauthentic Marcan ending, 16:12.

are revelations given by Him, → 357). This is connected with the purpose of the appearances, viz. to reveal and bear witness to the resurrection or exaltation of Jesus. [215] If the appearances are personally of supreme importance to the witnesses because they help them to conversion and faith, [216] their significance goes far beyond this. In the appearances Jesus manifests Himself as the risen and exalted One, and also as κύριος and Χριστός (as the Son, cf. Gl. 1:16; R. 1:4). To this broader context belongs the significance of the appearances for the genesis of the community [217] (on their relation to the apostolate → 358; 359). In this function the appearances, like Easter and Pentecost generally, stand in strong tension to expectation of the parousia.

An essential mark of the appearances is that they could not be misunderstood as the awaited parousia, → n. 204. On the contrary, their task was to steer away from too close expectation of the parousia and the kingdom of God to the age of the Church and the work of the Holy Spirit. Hence it is as well not to regard the visual element which, even if in a very limited way, is present in the appearances (→ n. 214), as an analogy to the visual element in expectation of the parousia, or even to deduce the one from the other. The linguistic agreement is not too great. [218] Only at Hb. 9:28 is ὀφθῆναι used of the parousia: ἐκ δευτέρου χωρὶς ἁμαρτίας ὀφθήσεται κτλ.; ἐκ δευτέρου, however, refers not so much to the resurrection appearances as to the earthly life of Jesus, which is herewith indirectly called an ὀφθῆναι — a singular NT use which also shows how strongly ὀφθῆναι has the sense of "coming on the scene." [219] The ἴδωσιν of Mt. 16:28 par. Mk. 9:1; Lk. 9:27 certainly means that those concerned will be

---

[215] On the question of the empty tomb and the material priority of the appearances cf. Michaelis, 123-128. The angelophanies at the tomb are secondary to the appearances (22, 117. 125), though cf. K. Barth, K.D., III, 3 (1950), 594 f. (C.D., III, 3 (1961), 507 f.).

[216] Thomas believes through seeing, Paul is converted through an appearance, also James acc. to 1 C. 15:7; again, the other disciples do not first believe and then see, but see and then believe (the most one can draw from Jn. 21:7 is that love, or the sense of being loved, gives a disposition for seeing the appearing Lord). In no appearance is possession of the Spirit a prerequisite. Pl. is baptised after conversion (Ac. 9:18); the other appearances are all before Pentecost (→ II, 457, n. 43). Stephen's vision is linked with possession of the Spirit (→ 353), but cannot be regarded as an appearance, Michaelis, 114 ff.

[217] If we cannot think in terms of an Ev. quadraginta dierum (cf. R. Seeberg, Aus Religion u. Gesch., I [1906], 42-58 and the bibl. → n. 202) as ongoing instruction of the disciples by the risen Lord, we certainly have to take seriously the possibility that the decisive impulses at work in the period which followed derive from the revelation by word in the time between Easter and the ascension, as typically expressed in such condensed statements as Mt. 28:16 ff. and Ac. 1:6 ff. Cf. also W. Michaelis, "Geist Gottes u. Mission nach dem NT," Evangel. Missionsmagazin, NF, 76 (1932), 5-16. M. Albertz, Die Botschaft d. NT, I, 1 (1946), 97-105 lays gt. stress on the fact that auditio rather than visio is to the fore in the resurrection narratives.

[218] Michaelis, 122 f.

[219] In 9:26 πεφανέρωται is used for Jesus' coming to earth, cf. 1 Tm. 3:16; 1 Pt. 1:20; 1 Jn. 3:5, 8. φανερωθῆναι is used for the appearances in Jn. 21:14 (cf. v. 1) and Mk. 16:12, 14. ὤφθη ἀγγέλοις in 1 Tm. 3:16 does not refer to the appearances, since ἄγγελοι does not mean the apostles as messengers (as against Wbg. Past., ad loc.). On the basis of Asc. Is. 11:23 Dib. Past.², ad loc. refers the saying to the exaltation of Christ as His triumph over spiritual powers (cf. also O. Cullmann, D. ersten chr. Glaubensbekenntnisse [1943], 54). But it is not clear from the context that the ἄγγελοι are hostile powers. L. Brun, Die Auferstehung Christi in d. urchr. Überlieferung (1925), 94 ff., who also quotes Asc. Is. 11:23 ff., thinks in terms of angels and powers which "recognise and greet the risen Lord on His approach and arrival in the heavenly world," but ὤφθη does not demand the pass. transl. "seen by angels." E. Käsemann, Das wandernde Gottesvolk (1938), 66 refers the passage to the presentation before angels described by εἰσάγειν in Hb. 1 ("obviously also in the parousia," 60), but there is no thought of the parousia in 1 Tm. 3:16. The constr. ἐν πνεύματι ὤφθη ἀγγέλοις cannot be considered.

eye-witnesses of the *parousia,*[220] but the important thing is the coming of the Son of Man, the *parousia* itself, not their seeing. In the Lucan version the sense is almost "to experience," "to have a share in," → 342.[221] As concerns ὄψεσθε in Mt. 26:64 par. Mk. 14:62, the par. in Lk. 22:69 shows that there is no intention of emphasising the visual aspect. Indeed the context suggests the sense "to perceive," "to know" (cf. Lk. 13:28). Seeing is perhaps more important at Mt. 24:30 and par., as also at Rev. 1:7, which is related to Mt. 24:30 by its use of Zech. 12:10 f., unless the meaning here (cf. ἐπιβλέψονται πρός με, LXX) is "to pay attention to," "to take note of" (Jn. 19:37, which also adduces Zech. 12:10, is not eschatological). On the whole, there is little emphasis on seeing in relation to the *parousia,*[222] and even where there is some stress the meaning is not so specific as in statements like 1 Jn. 3:2. Hence the visual element in the appearances is not to be regarded as either proleptic of or even influenced by the seeing of eschatological events.[223]

e. Johannine Seeing.

Among the verses in Jn. special attention must be devoted to a group of statements in which seeing Jesus, which can sometimes include seeing God, is either demanded or promised. The verse Jn. 6:62 : ἐὰν οὖν θεωρῆτε τὸν υἱὸν τοῦ ἀνθρώπου ἀναβαίνοντα ὅπου ἦν τὸ πρότερον; reminds us in the first instance of Ac. 1:11: ἐθεάσασθε αὐτὸν πορευόμενον εἰς τὸν οὐρανόν. Apart from the fact that the one reference is to the *parousia,* the other to pre-existence, this saying to the disciples — the circle is not the same as in Ac. 1:4 ff. — is not intimating that they will be eye-witnesses of the ascension ; ἀναβαίνειν does not refer to the ascension as an isolated event but to the ascent of the Son of Man, by the ὑψωθῆναι and δοξασθῆναι of the cross, to His heavenly home, so that the reference is to the offence of the cross.[224] Hence θεωρεῖν does not here denote sense perception or eye-witness, but a spiritual perception of the offence which necessarily gives rise to debate and decision (the decision of faith). Perhaps one might paraphrase it thus : "When you see yourselves confronted by the offence that ..." This use of "to see" for "to see oneself confronted (by a message of revelation) and to have to believe" is found again in other verses, e.g., in the

---

[220] The decision of the Papal Office, July 19, 1944, *Christum Dominum ante finale judicium ... visibiliter in hanc terram regnandi causa esse venturum ... tuto doceri non posse,* refers to the millennial coming of Christ. For details cf. W. Michaelis, "Katholische Kirche u. Wiederkunft Christi," *Der Kirchenfreund,* 82 (1948), 312-316.

[221] On the par. expression in Jn. 3:3 cf. Bu. J., 95, n. 3; Cr.-Kö., 388. Acc. to Barth, K.D., III, 2 (1948), 600 (C.D., III, 2 (1960), 499) it is presupposed in Mk. 9:1 par. that the kingdom of God has already come, and what is proclaimed is simply that this kingdom which has come is shortly to be seen. But the ref. in the saying is to seeing the coming ; the two are simultaneous. Again, Barth suggests that we think of seeing the transfiguration, the resurrection and the second coming of Jesus. Apart from the difficulty of a multiple ref. of this kind, the main objection here is that the deaths intimated in the saying did not take place in the time up to the resurrection, and certainly not in that up to the transfiguration.

[222] If ἐκεῖ αὐτὸν ὄψεσθε in Mk. 16:7 par. originally refers to the *parousia* (cf. 14:28 par.; Michaelis, 61-65), the idea of meeting or encounter is more important than the purely visual aspect. The situation is different in the question of the disciples in the agraphon P. Oxy., IV, 655, 19 ff.: πότε ἡμῖν ἐμφανὴς ἔσει καὶ πότε σε ὀψόμεθα; (Hennecke, 58).

[223] Kittel, 104 : "The Easter event and the resurrection appearances are clothed in the form of eschatological manifestation. This shows that they are regarded as an event of the other world ... as the 'breaking in of eschatology' " (→ also I, 220). The eschatological orientation of the appearances is incontestable, but it does not find expression in a predominance of the visual side.

[224] Bu. J., 341.

related 6:40 and 12:44 f. According to 6:40 : ἵνα πᾶς ὁ θεωρῶν τὸν υἱὸν καὶ πιστεύων εἰς αὐτὸν ἔχῃ ζωὴν αἰώνιον the seeing here referred to should lead to faith, or rather, since the goal is the receiving of life, and the construction relates θεωρῶν to πιστεύων, seeing is defined as the encounter with the Son which finds fulfilment in faith. In 12:44 f., too, seeing and faith are interrelated, faith coming first; cf. also the shift in order between seeing and perceiving in 14:7, 9 (on 12:45; 14:9 → 363).

In contrast, the seeing of Jesus in 16:10, 16 f., 19 refers to the time up to His going to the Father and to the time after His return, i.e., to the seeing of His earthly life and to eye-witness of the resurrection or the *parousia*. This is undoubtedly the most natural explanation within the parting discourses, and yet all these statements are transparent and have a further meaning. The ὄψεσθέ με of 16:16 f., 19, embracing both Easter and Pentecost, refers to the time in which the Spirit will have come as the Paraclete.[225] For this reason this seeing is neither sensual nor mental perception. It is the encounter with Jesus which takes place in faith under the work of the Holy Spirit. Similarly, there lies in the οὐκέτι θεωρεῖτέ με of 16:10, 16 f., 19 (the present is not without significance) a reference to the time when the Spirit no longer works and there can be for the disciples no more seeing, no more meeting Jesus, no more believing.[226] Again, the fact that the world does not see Jesus while the disciples do (the present once more) does not mean that only the disciples will have seen the resurrection appearances; 14:22 ff. makes it plain that the reference is not to the appearances, and also that the "coming" of 14:18 and the "that day" of 14:20 (cf. 16:23) refer, not to the *parousia*, but to the age of the Spirit (both 14:18 ff. and 16:16 ff. come directly after sayings about the Paraclete). If the world does not see Jesus in this age, this means that it resists the Spirit's work and persists in unbelief. Both positively and negatively the same view underlies all the verses 6:40; 12:44 f.; 14:19; 16:10, 16 f., 19. The reference is not merely to sense perception (eye-witness of the story of Jesus) or intellectual perception (consideration of this story) but also to a further seeing, namely, the decision which is taken in encounter with Jesus and which is a turning to faith.

If in 16:22 an ὄψομαι ὑμᾶς corresponds to the ὄψεσθέ με (16:16 f., 19), the ref. is not to the *parousia*, but, as with the coming of 14:18, 23, to the fellowship with Jesus which is achieved in the Holy Spirit (cf. 14:25 f.) and which includes love for Jesus and keeping His commandments (14:21, 23). As the ὄψομαι ὑμᾶς of 16:22 supplements and elucidates the ὄψεσθέ με of 16:16 f., 19, so does the ἐμφανίσω αὐτῷ ἐμαυτόν of 14:21

---

[225] E. Fascher, "J. 16:32," ZNW, 39 (1940), 223 ff. (cf. already 189, n. 8) emphasises too strongly a ref. to the *parousia*. Bu. J., 447 f. wrongly supposes that the Johannine statements are a rejection of Jewish and primitive Christian apocal. (cf. also 479 : "The Easter experience as a fulfilment of the promise of the *parousia*").

[226] Perhaps [Kuhn] it would be more consistent to abandon any temporal limitation (Easter, Pentecost, *parousia*) and take the οὐκέτι θεωρεῖτέ με to refer to the situation which might arise at any time in the life of the disciples, namely, that of being left in the world without the assistance of the Spirit, the antithesis in the ὄψεσθέ με being the newly granted possibility of overcoming the world in unity with Jesus within it. Bu. J., 448 also sees here a description of the stages "through which the life of believers must go and at which it may founder." For the Evangelist, however, the parting discourses as the setting of all these statements were not just fiction. What was true then is that which will always and ever again be true.

the θεωρεῖτέ με of 14:19. To see Jesus means that He reveals Himself; to encounter Him means that He encounters us.

In verses which speak of seeing the Father, stating that Jesus Himself sees the Father, and that those who see Jesus see the Father, it is noteworthy that this seeing cannot be integrated into the parallelism of seeing and hearing found elsewhere in Jn.

In 5:24; 8:43; 10:16, 27 (cf. 3:8); 12:47; 18:37 we have (with individual variations) the same demand to hear the φωνή, ῥήματα, λόγος of Jesus (cf. also 14:24); cf. also the hearing of the φωνή or ῥήματα of God in 5:37 f.; 8:47. It is striking that there is no par. statement to 12:45; 14:9 to the effect that he who hears the Word of Jesus hears God Himself, though the command to hear the Word of Jesus corresponds to the thought that the Son Himself hears the Father (with ἀκούω παρά c. gen. 8:26, 40; 15:15; cf. also 3:32; 5:30 and — with another subj. — 6:45; 16:13). One cannot, of course, take 12:45; 14:9 to mean that he who has seen Jesus has seen God because Jesus for His part has seen God, for what another has seen can be received from him only by hearing, not seeing. This means, however, that 12:45; 14:9 cannot be understood in terms of 6:46 or 1:18. Apart from 6:46; 1:18 (→ 364), however, we never read that Jesus Himself has seen God. In 3:32 (where seeing is linked with hearing) God is not the content (cf. 3:11), and ἑώρακα παρά c. dat. in 8:38a corresponds to the ἠκούσατε παρά c. gen. in 8:38b and does not refer to seeing the Father. But then 5:19 (→ 343) is also not an example of seeing the Father, for it is to be grouped materially with the verses which use ἑώρακα παρά or ἤκουσα, 8:26, 38, 40; 15:15. [227]

If the usual parallelism between seeing and hearing is here fully abandoned in all decisive points, the statements in 12:45; 14:9 necessarily speak of a relation of the disciple to the Son and the Father which — more exclusively than in statements which refer to hearing — is in no way comparable to the relation of the Son to the Father. If Johannine seeing in 12:45; 14:9 (and also 6:40; 14:19; 16:10, 16 f., 19) always refers to our relation to the Son and the Father, but never to the inner relation between Father and Son (the description of Jesus as εἰκών in 2 C. 4:4; Col. 1:15 has in view, not His relation to God, but His manward quality as Revealer), then the verbs of seeing are here very definitely terms used in connection with the event of revelation.

Jn. does not use ἀποκαλύπτω (→ III, 587). In the context of verses which illustrate Johannine seeing this term is replaced by words which lightly touch on the visual aspect, namely, ἐμφανίζω in 14:21 f. (→ 362 f.; n. 214) and δείκνυμι in 14:8 f. (→ II, 27 f.; in Ac. 7:44 we have ὃν ἑωράκει for the τὸν δεδειγμένον of Ex. 25:40), and to these there correspond on man's side the verbs of seeing (including θεωρέω as the pres. of ἑώρακα and ὄψομαι, → 345).

Whereas in 12:45 (corresponding to v. 44; cf. 13:20; Mt. 10:40) there is more emphasis on the fact that Jesus is the Revealer who makes God manifest in a unique way (cf. Mt. 11:27 and par.), in 14:9 (cf. v. 8) the stress is on the fact that God has revealed Himself in Jesus, and only in Jesus. Johannine seeing involves a submission in faith to the revelation of God in Jesus Christ. On the one side this means that the history, the incarnation of the Revealer, is maintained;

---

[227] Dobschütz, 400, n. 6 rightly criticises L. Brun, "Die Gottesschau des Joh. Christus," *Symbolae Osloenses*, 5 (1927), who takes 5:19 as a starting-point for understanding seeing in Jn.

on the other side pre-existence and post-existence (cf. 6:62; → 361) are included, and this revelation is also set specifically in the light of Easter and Pentecost.

Does John — following his strong inclination to use originally eschatological terms in the present — proleptically describe as sight that which strictly deserves only to be called faith? Sight is for him the seeing of faith, → n. 158. Indeed, it is itself faith. But this does not mean that it is an anticipation of future sight, i.e., that he pays no heed to the borders which separate faith from eschatological seeing (cf. 17:24; → 346). On the other hand, the significance which the Easter event has for the Johannine picture of Christ (→ I, 220) could have led him to prefer verbs of seeing only if independent significance were accorded to the visual aspect in what the NT says about the Easter event, which is not so (→ C. 2. d.). While the terms used for the events of revelation (ἀποκαλύπτω, δείκνυμι, φανερόω etc., whose use is more figurative than literal) are nearer to the visual side than the auditive, Jn. probably chose verbs of seeing because with their help he could the better emphasise the personal and existential character of the encounter with Jesus. [228]

f. The Vision of God.

If according to Jn. 12:45; 14:9 God is to be seen only in His revelation in Christ, [229] Jn. 1:18 is not in the first instance aimed polemically against other assertions that God has been seen in theophanies or visions or ecstatic journeys to heaven, [230] but with the help of the words of seeing found also in 12:45; 14:9 it is maintaining that God has revealed Himself exclusively in His Son. The ἐκεῖνος ἐξηγήσατο is not a record similar to the accounts of theophanies etc.; it is a "manifesting" corresponding to the showing of 14:8 f. (→ n. 233; II, 908; for the link with Sir. 43:31 [35] cf. → 333; II, 908). That the Son for His part has seen the Father is not directly stated in 1:18, though we find it in another connection in 6:46. If the seeing of 6:46 denotes immediate access to God as compared with the ἀκούειν and μανθάνειν of 6:45 (cf. 8:38), 5:37 f. shows that seeing and hearing (in spite of the concrete understanding in 5:37b seeing and hearing are not meant literally here, as may be seen from 5:38a) can be regarded as equally valid forms of receiving revelation. The master concept common to all the passages mentioned is that man of himself has no access to God, but is referred to the fact that God reveals Himself to him. If in 6:46 there is greater emphasis on the fact that even revelation does not make possible immediate access to God, or sight, but only hearing and believing, in 1:18 the whole emphasis is on the uniqueness of the revelation in Jesus Christ, which is also stressed in 6:46. [231] In so far as the

---

[228] In the Mandaean lit. a considerable part is played by seeing light, e.g., Lidz. Ginza 22, 4 f.; Liturg., 193, 4, or life, e.g., Ginza, 272, 15 f., or Manda dHaijē, e.g., Liturg., 136, 5 ff.; 184, 1; 234, 11; 273, 6. But there is not even a remote par. here to Johannine seeing.

[229] 3 Jn. 11 shows the influence of this view. The ἑώρακεν of 1 Jn. 3:6, though it refers to seeing Jesus, is not orientated to the ἐφανερώθη of 3:5 (→ n. 219); the combination of ἑώρακεν and ἔγνωκεν reminds us rather of Jn. 14:7, 9. The related 3 Jn. 11 (→ III, 486), which refers to seeing God, also shows that 1 Jn. 3:6 cannot be a specific polemic against Gnostics who allege that "they have had appearances of the spirit manifested in Jesus" (as against Bü. J., ad loc.); → n. 236.

[230] As against Schl. J., 34, ad loc., who finds this thrust in the statement. Cf. his exposition of 6:46.

[231] That this uniqueness implies exclusiveness is very strongly emphasised here, even in relation to the OT (cf. Bu. J., 53 on 1:17). Acc. to 5:37 f., however, revelation can be found in Judaism (with Christ as goal, cf. 5:39).

concept of revelation is not orientated to the category of visibility/invisibility, the issue in these passages is not whether the intrinsically invisible God is in some way visible, but whether the God who is completely beyond man's grasp reveals Himself to him. [232]

1 Jn. 4:12 — formally closely related to Jn. 1:18 — stands apart by virtue of the fact that there is no express thought of the function of Jesus Christ as Revealer. [233] The same may be said of 1 Jn. 4:20 (→ n. 126). Nor do we find in either passage (cf. also 1 Jn. 3:6; 3 Jn. 11) the Johannine idea that God may be seen; they are content to maintain the factual invisibility of God, cf. 1 Tm. 6:16, and verses like 1 Tm. 1:17; Hb. 11:27, which call God ἀόρατος, → 369. On the other hand, in Col. 1:15, in keeping with Johannine lines of thought, the invisibility of God is linked with the description of Christ as the εἰκών of God, and in R. 1:19 f. Paul calls the works of creation a revelation of God by which He seeks to be seen, → 369. In both these verses (as in Jn. 12:45; 14:9) it is clear that there can be no thought of removing or penetrating the divine ineffability. As in all revelation, this is the abiding presupposition.

Even though God will be seen in the eschatological consummation, His ineffability will not be abolished nor the border between God and man effaced. On the contrary, revelation will then be perfect and immediate. It is true that expectation of eschatological union with God, for which other categories and images are used elsewhere (e.g., divine sonship in Mt. 5:9; table fellowship in Rev. 3:20), is seldom related to a vision of God. In 1 C. 13:12 God is not expressly named as the object of future sight, → 344. Nor is He self-evidently the object of present sight δι᾽ ἐσόπτρου ἐν αἰνίγματι, except along the lines of Col. 1:15 or Jn. 12:45; 14:9, though the object of this sight is the present rather than the future act of salvation. On the other hand there is no antithesis between the present βλέπειν of 1 C. 13:12 and the present walk διὰ πίστεως of 2 C. 5:7. Present sight (and γινώσκειν ἐκ μέρους) is itself faith. Thus, though the βλέπομεν of 1 C. 13:12 is accompanied by ἄρτι and is to be supplemented (in the fut.) by τότε, it should not be concluded from this verse that eschatological seeing, as seeing, will be a direct continuation and enhancement of the seeing which is already possible. [234] Future vision — like everything eschatological — will be totally different from anything possible now.

In Mt. 5:18; 1 Jn. 3:2 as well the eschatological vision of God is seen to be a possibility which can be actualised only in the future. In keeping is the fact that the beatitude next to 5:8 (5:9) refers only to eschatological sonship (cf. Lk. 20:36;

---

[232] Cf. Bu. J., 54 f., also W. Köhler, Dogmengesch.[2] (1943), 92.

[233] 4:9 f. refers to a revelation of the love of God in the mission and death of Jesus, and thus adds an important thought to what is found in other Johannine passages — a thought which obviates the danger that more importance will be attached to the word than to the work of Jesus in the ἐξηγεῖσθαι of Jn. 1:18 and the δεικνύναι of 14:8 f. But 1 Jn. 4:12 does not refer back to 4:9 f. (nor forward to 4:14), nor is 4:9 f. emphasising that in spite of 4:12 a seeing of God is possible in the sense of Jn. 12:45; 14:9.

[234] In 2 C. 3:18 (→ II, 696) there is no direct ref. to eschatological vision. In relation to the question how far this teaches change through vision, and what contacts there are with Hell. mysticism (→ IV, 758; there is a good emphasis on the material differences, 758, l. 31 ff.), it should not be overlooked that Paul does not use any of the verbs commonly employed for the Hell. vision of God. Cf. also Bchm. 2 K.[3], 176, n. 1.

Mt. 5:45, [235] though also R. 8:15 f., 23). While the vision of God and divine sonship are parallel in Mt. 5:8 f., in 1 Jn. 3:2 sonship is present, as in Paul, but vision remains a purely eschatological promise, as in Mt. 5:8. Mt., it would seem, does not regard the vision of God as the greatest of all the promises, but equates it with sonship in 5:9 and membership of the kingdom of God in 5:10 (cf. 5:3; also the parallelism of οὐ μὴ εὕρητε τὴν βασιλείαν τοῦ θεοῦ and οὐκ ὄψεσθε τὸν πατέρα in the agraphon in P. Oxy., I, 1, verso 6 ff.). [236]

In 1 Jn. 3:2 the reference is to the vision of God, not to the seeing of Christ at His *parousia* (cf. 2:28). [237] τί ἐσόμεθα should be supplied as the subject of φανερωθῇ, and αὐτόν as well as αὐτῷ is linked with τέκνα θεοῦ (there is a ref. to Christ with the help of ἐκεῖνος in 3:3, cf. 3:5). καθώς ἐστιν (cf. Sir. 43:31[35] → 333) underscores the immediacy and fulness of this vision. Since here as elsewhere the author wishes to make full use of the preaching of Jesus in answering his opponents, the statement ὅτι ὀψόμεθα αὐτόν, "we shall see him," is an intentional reference to the promise of Mt. 5:8 (in some sense the sanctification of 1 Jn. 3:3 corresponds to the purity of heart in Mt. 5:8). The presupposition of this vision, namely, the divine likeness expected only in the eschatological consummation, makes it clear why the vision of God can come only with the consummation. There is obviously no thought of deification by the vision of God as in the piety of the mysteries. [238]

The combination of sanctification and the vision of God [239] in Hb. 12:14 is reminiscent of 1 Jn. 3:2, but the constr. and context show that the motive here is hortatory, and that as such it is related in form and content to 1 C. 6:9 f. and par. In Rev. 22:4 the vision of God is spoken of in a book orientated to the visual, so that it does not form so great a climax, but the reader may measure its significance by the fact that one day there will be granted to the servants of God that which had previously been a privilege of the heavenly creatures around God's throne, cf. 4:2 ff.; Mt. 18:10 → 343 f.

The restraint with which the NT speaks of the vision of God in only a few passages plainly differentiates the NT from the piety of the mysteries and from Gnosticism. Inasmuch as the OT offers hardly any support for expectation of an eschatological vision of God (→ 334), and the corresponding Jewish hopes take rather a different direction (→ 339 f.), it is the plainer that what we have here is a promise which is possible only on a NT basis and with the authority of Jesus (cf. Mt. 5:8). The insurpassable greatness of this promise is that it is not lightly repeated nor arbitrarily varied, but rings out only infrequently and with quiet joy, as in 1 Jn. 3:2.

---

[235] W. Michaelis, "Gotteskindschaft u. Gottessohnschaft," *Deutsches Pfarrerblatt*, 44 (1940), 133; *Das Urchristentum*, 319 ff.; W. G. Kümmel, *Das Bild des Menschen im NT* (1948), 19.

[236] Mt. 5:8; 1 Jn. 3:2 and other NT statements avoid the concept of the vision of God found in later Judaism (→ 339 f.). The hortatory statements in 1 Jn. 3:6; 3 Jn. 11 (→ n. 229) are not to be misinterpreted by analogy with later Jewish ideas.

[237] As against Stauffer Theol.⁴, 196, who also relates 1 C. 13:12; 2 C. 5:7 to seeing the "glory of the Son of God" (cf. on the other hand 209); → 188.

[238] Cf. Bü. J., *ad loc.*; J. Leipoldt, *Jesu Verhältnis zu Griechen u. Juden* (1941), 118 f.

[239] τὸν κύριον is to be referred to God, cf. Rgg. Hb., *ad loc.* Bultmann, 178, 182 relates the verse too closely to Mt. 5:8.

D. Usage and Concept in the Post-Apostolic Fathers.

In the post-apostolic fathers the use of verbs of seeing, their relation to one another, and the distribution of individual meanings are all much the same as in the NT.

As compared with some 170 instances of ἀκούω there are about 265 examples of verbs of seeing, many of them in Herm. The pres. ὁράω is relatively uncommon. [240] εἶδον unites almost half the instances of verbs of seeing to itself. The imp. ἴδε is a common rhetorical expression, e.g., Barn., 6, 14; 12, 10 (often also ἴδωμεν, 1 Cl., 7, 3; 19, 3; 21, 3 etc.). The intr. pass. ὤφθη c. dat. for appearing in visions occurs 5 times in Herm. (v., 3, 1, 2; 3, 3, 3; 3, 10, 3 and 7; 3, 11, 2). βλέπω often occurs for the pres. ὁράω (some 80 instances, 60 in Herm.); the pass. only 1 Cl., 28, 1. βλέπετε ind. or imp. as an epexegetical flourish in Scripture refs., Barn., 10, 11; 13, 6; 1 Cl., 56, 16 (cf. Barn., 4, 14; 1, 7 and 10, 11: καλῶς εἶπεν βλέπων τὴν ἐντολήν, "in respect of"). ὀπτάνομαι does not occur. θεάομαι is rare (interchangeably with other verbs of seeing in 2 Cl., 17, 7; Herm. v., 3, 8, 1, also 2 Cl., 1, 7 of God and Dg., 10, 7). So is θεωρέω, in quotations, 1 Cl., 16, 16 (ψ 21:8); 35, 8 (ψ 49:18). Pass. "to become visible," "to appear," Mart. Pol., 2, 2, cf. also Ign. Mg., 6, 1, with ἐν and acc. "to see another in someone" (as a representative), i.e., in the delegates the whole church ; similarly θεωρεῖσθαι in Tr., 1, 1 (med. vl. θεωρῆσαι).

That God sees is stated in 1 Cl., 28, 1: πάντων οὖν βλεπομένων καὶ ἀκουομένων only indirectly on the basis of the quotation from ψ 18:3 (which uses ἀκούονται) in 27, 7 (εἶδον in Barn., 6, 12; 1 Cl., 55, 6; Herm. v., 3, 12, 3; s., 8, 6, 2; 9, 24, 3, and θεάομαι in 2 Cl., 1, 7 are used in the transf. sense "to perceive," "to note" etc.). Man cannot see God, who is often called ἀόρατος (→ 370) in the post-apost. fathers. Only fig., then can there be ref. to the vision of God : ἀνθρώπων δὲ οὐδεὶς οὔτε εἶδεν οὔτε ἐγνώρισεν, αὐτὸς δὲ ἑαυτὸν ἐπέδειξεν. ἐπέδειξε δὲ διὰ πίστεως, ᾗ μόνῃ θεὸν ἰδεῖν συγκεχώρηται, Dg., 8, 5 f.; 1 Cl., 19, 3 reminds us of Hell. terminology and Philo: ἴδωμεν αὐτὸν κατὰ διάνοιαν καὶ ἐμβλέψωμεν τοῖς ὄμμασιν τῆς ψυχῆς εἰς τὸ μακρόθυμον αὐτοῦ βούλημα. Men alone among all creatures enjoy this privilege : οἷς μόνοις ἄνω πρὸς αὐτὸν ὁρᾶν (in prayer etc.) ἐπέτρεψεν, Dg., 10, 2. That God may be known from His works in the visible world is stated in 1 Cl., 60, 1 when God is described as ἀγαθὸς ἐν τοῖς ὁρωμένοις, cf. Wis. 13:1; → 324. It is said of the incarnation in Barn., 5, 10 : εἰ γὰρ μὴ ἦλθεν ἐν σαρκί, οὐδ' ἄν πως ἐσώθησαν οἱ ἄνθρωποι βλέποντες αὐτόν (men could not have stood a direct view). Seeing Jesus at the *parousia* is emphasised with the help of ὄψεσθαι in Barn., 7, 9; 2 Cl., 17, 5; Did., 16, 8 (cf. Mt. 24:30; 26:64, → 361). Eschatological fellowship with Jesus is called seeing in Barn., 7, 11: οὕτω, φησίν, οἱ θέλοντές με ἰδεῖν καὶ ἅψασθαί μου τῆς βασιλείας ὀφείλουσιν θλιβέντες καὶ παθόντες λαβεῖν με. [241] Unusual in comparison with Jn. 3:3 and Lk. 9:27 is the distinction in Herm. s., 9, 15, 3 : ταῦτα τὰ ὀνόματα ὁ φορῶν τοῦ θεοῦ δοῦλος τὴν βασιλείαν μὲν ὄψεται τοῦ θεοῦ, εἰς αὐτὴν δὲ οὐκ εἰσελεύσεται (cf. v. 2).

---

[240] 19 times altogether. Apart from the passages listed in Pr.-Bauer³, *s.v.* 1 a β; 1 c α and β; 2 b β, cf. also 1 Cl., 10, 4; 60, 1 (the only pres. pass.); Dg., 10, 2.
[241] A saying of Jesus obviously composed by the author (with the help of Ac. 14:22). Cf. Wnd. Barn., *ad loc.*

† ὁρατός, † ἀόρατος.

1. The verbal adj. ὁρατός, "to be seen," "visible" (from Hippocr.) and its opp. ἀόρατος "unseen," "invisible" (only later — in Polyb. — trans. "not seeing") [1] came to have special significance for the Gk. world in the vocabulary of philosophy. Cf. Diog. L., VIII, 30 (Diels⁵, I, 450, 21 f.); Gorg. Fr., 3, 86 (ibid., II, 282, 35 f.). In Plato they are slogans to denote the world of sense perception on the one side and that of the ideas on the other. ὁρατός is the opp. of νοητός, Resp., VI, 509d; VII, 524c etc.; synon. of ἀόρατος are ἀειδής, ἀφανής (also quite frequently οὐχ ὁρατός). The sing. θεὸς ἀόρατος does not occur in Plato. [2] Cf. also → 320; 323; 324. [3]

2. The two words are very rare in the LXX. In 2 Βασ. 23:21 the noun מַרְאֶה is rendered by ὁρατός (of a man), "imposing," "fine-looking" (cf. the addition of ὁρατός in the par. 1 Ch. 11:23). ὁρατός also occurs in Job 37:21; 34:26; also ὁρατικός (a mistransl. Prv. 22:29) and ὁρατής (→ 328 and n. 72). None of these 3 occurs in ᾿ΑΘΣ (nor ἀόρατος). There are only 3 instances of ἀόρατος. תֹּהוּ, rendered very differently elsewhere, is transl. ἀόρατος at Gn. 1:2. ἀοράτους in Is. 45:3 corresponds to מִסְתָּרִים, perhaps originally (cf. its absence in A) as an alternative for ἀποκρύφους (cf. ψ 9:28 f.; 16:12; 63:4). In 2 Macc. 9:5 it is used of a sickness whose seat is ἔνδον. God is not called ἀόρατος. [4] In 6 passages ἀορασία means "blindness" (→ n. 3).

3. In Philo ἀόρατος is used over 100 times, and ὁρατός over 70, though often with a negative, thus materially adding to the instances of ἀόρατος (cf. also the many examples of ἀειδής and esp. ἀφανής). Philo adopts and extends the view and terminology of Plato. [5] To the κόσμος αἰσθητός, which is often called ὁρατός (Op. Mund., 12, 16, → III, 77; Rer. Div. Her., 111; Som., I, 188; Abr., 88) belongs the ὁρατὴ ἅπασα οὐσία, heaven and earth, Op. Mund., 111, the sun, Som., I, 73, also the human σῶμα, Migr. Abr., 51. τὸ ὁρατόν or τὰ ὁρατά is often a comprehensive expression, less frequently τὸ ἀόρατον or τὰ ἀόρατα. Everywhere invisible δυνάμεις are at work, e.g., Ebr., 192; Spec. Leg., I, 46 ff. (equated with the ἰδέαι in 48). For Philo the νοῦς esp. is ἀόρατος (Migr. Abr., 51; Abr., 73 f.; Spec. Leg., I, 18; Omn. Prob. Lib., 111; Vit. Cont., 78; Op. Mund., 69), since it is the organ which relates us to the invisible world, and invisible like it, cf. also the ψυχή, e.g., Som., I, 73 and 135; Jos., 255; Virt., 57 and 172. But ἀόρατος is esp. used of God (→ 336; 338; → III, 972), of His φύσις, Leg. All., III, 206; Rer. Div. Her., 115, of the divine πνεῦμα, Plant., 18; cf. Som., II, 252; of the θεῖος λόγος, Rer. Div. Her., 119; cf. Op. Mund., 30 f., in predications like ἀόρατος ἐπιστάτης, Mut. Nom., 14, as a term for θεός, Som., I, 72 etc., in the expression ὁ ἀόρατος, Decal., 120; Sacr. AC, 133 etc. (for this reason εἰκονογραφεῖν is forbidden, Leg. Gaj., 290; cf. 318). In Migr. Abr., 47 ff. Philo, ignoring the sense "to perceive" which ἑώρα has in the LXX, wrestles with the wording of Ex. 20:18; cf. also Vit. Mos., II, 213; Decal., 47. As the ἀόρατος κόσμος is the παράδειγμα of the ὁρατὸς κόσμος (e.g., Spec. Leg., I, 302), so God has impressed the τύποι of His invisible θειότης on

---

ὁρατός κτλ. Cf. Bibl. on → ὁράω.

[1] Cf. Pass. and Liddell-Scott, s.v. On ἄοπτος cf. Antiphon the Sophist Fr., 4, 7 (Diels⁵, II, 339, 12 f., 21).

[2] Fascher, 63; Bultmann, 172 ("chance"; on the reading of Tim., 92c, ibid., n. 2, though cf. → II, 389).

[3] Both words are rare or only late in inscr. and pap.; cf. Preisigke Wört., I, 149; Moult.-Mill., 51, 454. ἀορασία for "blindness" in Ditt. Syll.³, 1240, 14 (2nd cent. A.D.) is influenced by Dt. 28:28 LXX; cf. Deissmann LO, 18, n. 2.

[4] Bultmann, 178 : "The Gk. ἀόρατος has no Heb. equivalent ; it is a characteristic of Heb. thinking that verbal adjectives of this kind are not formed." ὁρατός, too, has no Heb. equivalent.

[5] Bultmann, 189 ff.; Fascher, 59 ff.

the soul of man in order that even the earthly sphere should not be without the εἰκὼν θεοῦ, Det. Pot. Ins., 86, cf. Cher., 101. Since the divine ἀρχέτυπον is ἀειδές, the εἰκών too, namely, the human ψυχή, can only be οὐχ ὁρατή, Det. Pot. Ins., 87 (though in Op. Mund., 146 man is described as ὁρατὴ εἰκών). Thus man is mortal κατὰ τὴν ὁρατὴν μερίδα, but immortal κατὰ τὴν ἀόρατον, Op. Mund., 135. [6]

Joseph., who often uses ἀόρατος of places etc. which are not, or ought not, to be seen (e.g., Ant., 12, 76; Bell., 1, 152; 3, 160; cf. also ἀθέατος, 1, 354; 5, 219, and ἀθεώρητος, 5, 212), [7] refers in Bell., 7, 340 ff. to the fact that the soul, as long as it is in the body, cannot be seen, but nevertheless ἀοράτως moves the σῶμα as its ὄργανον, 345; then after death τότε δὴ μακαρίας ἰσχύος καὶ πανταχόθεν ἀκωλύτου μετέχει δυνάμεως, ἀόρατος μένουσα τοῖς ἀνθρωπίνοις ὄμμασιν ὥσπερ αὐτὸς ὁ θεός, 346 (→ 338). On Test. R. 6:12 → II, 859, n. 210. In Test. L. 4:1 the downfall of ἀόρατα πνεύματα is depicted ; cf. Test. Sol. 1:2 L. On the invisibility of God cf. Sib. Prooemium, 8 ff.; Test. Sol. Recensio C, Prologue 2. There are obviously no Rabb. equivalents for ἀόρατος and ὁρατός, though cf. → 340.

4. In the NT ὁρατός occurs only in Col. 1:16 along with ἀόρατος in the phrase τὰ ὁρατὰ καὶ τὰ ἀόρατα, which, like ἐν τοῖς οὐρανοῖς καὶ ἐπὶ τῆς γῆς, is intended to show the unrestricted validity of the statement ἐν αὐτῷ ἐκτίσθη τὰ πάντα. The addition εἴτε θρόνοι εἴτε κυριότητες κτλ. supports the conjecture that τὰ ὁρατά denotes the whole of the earthly sphere (including that which is of the soul), also the stars and other heavenly phenomena, while τὰ ἀόρατα refers exclusively to the powers. [8] Although these seek to rule the world (→ III, 914), and are active in the υἱοὶ τῆς ἀπειθείας (Eph. 2:2), they have their being ἐν τοῖς ἐπουρανίοις (or in the ἀήρ, → IV, 550, n. 9) and are πνευματικά (Eph. 6:12). In spite of the invisibility which they share with God (cf. Col. 1:15), they are still to be regarded as beings created in Christ.

All the other instances of ἀόρατος relate to God, → 365. In the doxology in 1 Tm. 1:17 ἀόρατος, too, is one of the predicates of God. The designation of God as "the Invisible" (→ 368) is found in Hb. 11:27b : τὸν γὰρ ἀόρατον ὡς ὁρῶν ἐκαρτέρησεν. [9] This is not directly orientated to the definition of faith in 11:1 (cf. 11:27a) inasmuch as the πράγματα οὐ βλεπόμενα of 11:1 are also ἐλπιζόμενα (→ 350), whereas in 11:27b God is described as invisible not merely with a future reference (nor does the ἀόρατος refer, e.g., to the Christ who had not yet come in this age). Yet what is described in 11:27b as the power to accept God as supreme reality in His demands and promises certainly helps us to characterise faith in its quality as ὑπόστασις in 11:1. Paul in R. 1:20 calls God's invisible being τὰ ἀόρατα αὐτοῦ. [10] He does not say that it becomes visible in the ποιήματα, for νοούμενα καθορᾶται does not imply seeing, → 380. God does not become visible ; He is revealed, cf. also ἐφανέρωσεν in 1:19. 2 C. 4:4 shows that Christ can be called the εἰκὼν θεοῦ without any express emphasis on God's invisibility

---

[6] The view of N. A. Dahl, Das Volk Gottes (1941), 108 ff., that Philo was the first to distinguish between a visible and an invisible community can hardly appeal to instances of ὁρατός or ἀόρατος.

[7] In Ep. Ar., 90 ἀοράτως ἔχειν is used with the dat.: "to be invisible to someone" (of structural works); cf. ἀθέατος, 71.

[8] Cf. Ew. Gefbr., 322, ad loc.

[9] The author is not interested in the question whether Moses ever saw God or not, → 331. Philo Migr. Abr., 183 : ἀόρατος ὡς ἂν ὁρατὸς ὤν, is no par.

[10] → I, 719. The plur. is used (though the sing. is possible ; cf. τὸ γνωστὸν τοῦ θεοῦ, 1:19) because of the two nouns (δύναμις and θειότης) in what follows. On the neut. v. Fascher, 72.

as in Col. 1:15. The concept εἰκὼν θεοῦ is not based solely on God's invisibility (there are other presuppositions, → II, 395), and the being of Christ as εἰκών is not to be understood as a making of God visible, or a removing of His invisibility. [11] Jn. 12:45 and 14:9 are to be regarded as parallels (→ II, 395); in both, Johannine seeing means encounter with revelation, → 361. [12]

5. In the post-apost. fathers God is called ἀόρατος in the doxology in 2 Cl., 20, 5 (cf. 1 Tm. 1:17) and in Dg., 7, 2 etc. (cf. His ἀόρατος δύναμις, Herm. v., 1, 3, 4; 3, 3, 5). In distinction from the earthly ἐπίσκοπος, called βλεπόμενος, God is also the ἀόρατος (sc. ἐπίσκοπος) in Ign. Mg., 3, 2. [13] In Ign. Pol., 3, 2 the earthly life of Jesus is a making visible of the pre-existent Christ, who was ἀόρατος. Without par. in NT anthropology is the view in Dg., 6, 4 that the ἀόρατος ψυχή is guarded in the ὁρατὸν σῶμα; similarly, the world knows Christians, but their θεοσέβεια is ἀόρατος. Only at a distance does the correspondence between σαρκικός or πνευματικός and φαινόμενα or ἀόρατα in Ign. Pol., 2, 2 remind us of 2 C. 4:18, → 349. In Sm., 6, 1; Tr., 5, 2 (as distinct from Col. 1:16, → 369) differentiation is made between the visible and invisible angelic powers; on the other hand, Ign. R., 5, 3 is closer to Pol., 2, 2. [14] Barn., 11, 4 quotes Is. 45:3 LXX, → 368.

† ὅρασις.

ὅρασις, which is synon. to ὄψις, [1] has the same sense of "seeing," "sight," plur. "eyes" (sing. Ditt. Or., 56, 56 [3rd cent. B.C.], as a term of endearment, "apple of the eye"). The meaning "appearance" is rare and late, P. Leid. W, 13, 36 = Preis. Zaub., XIII, 582 (4th cent. A.D.). [2] The sense "vision" occurs for the first time in the biblical sphere. [3]

In the LXX ὅρασις is used some 110 times (38 in Ez., 18 in Da.), also 49 times in Da. Θ (including the lists of visions in Cod. A; elsewhere, too, more common in Θ than in ᾿ΑΣ). [4] Where there are Mas. originals the most common are מַרְאֶה (38 times) and חָזוֹן (31). The meanings are "sense of sight," "sight" (e.g., Lv. 13:12; 1 C. 17:17; Qoh. 11:9; Wis. 15:15), more commonly "appearance" (e.g., Gn. 2:9; Ju. 13:6 A; Sir. 11:2; also Ez. and Da.; on Is. 52:14 ᾿Α → IV, 751, n. 53); also with obj. gen. "view" in Sir. 41:22 (on the addition after Sir. 1:10 → 333); cf. also Is. 66:24 (דְּרָאוֹן "aversion" construed as a derivate of רָאָה). Mostly "vision," with ἐνύπνιον, e.g., Gn. 40:5; Sir. 34(31):3, with μαντεία, Mi. 3:6; Jer. 14:14, with gen. auct. θεοῦ, Nu. 24:4, 16; Ez. 1:1 (cf. παρὰ

---

[11] → 365. In Philo, too, the εἰκών for its part is mostly called οὐχ ὁρατή, → 369.

[12] Although "the question whether Paul calls the pre-existent or only the exalted Christ εἰκὼν τοῦ θεοῦ is quite irrelevant" (→ II, 396, n. 97), it is wrong to relate Christ's being as εἰκών exclusively to the earthly life of the man Jesus, so Fascher, 74 f.

[13] Pr.-Bauer³, s.v. wrongly refers the verse to Christ.

[14] Bau. Ign., 249 links R., 5, 3 with Tr., 5, 2 (and this with Pol., 2, 2, cf. 235).

ὅρασις. Cf. Bibl. → ὁράω.

[1] In the NT ὄψις means "face" in Jn. 11:44, "appearance" in 7:24, either the one or the other, Rev. 1:16. For details cf. Pr.-Bauer, s.v.

[2] Cf. Pass. and Liddell-Scott, s.v.; Preisigke Wört., II, 192, s.v.; Moult.-Mill., 455, s.v.; Mayser, I, 3² (1935), 69.

[3] As regards ὁρασεία "vision" in P. Strassb., 35, 5 (4/5th cent. A.D.) the reading is uncertain and the form ὁρασεία is very dubious. The use of ἀορασία (→ 368) is no proof to the contrary; cf. κρίσις but ἀκρισία, αἴσθησις but ἀναισθησία etc. [Debrunner].

[4] ὄψις is used about 60 times in the LXX, always "appearance" (in this sense preferred to ὅρασις in Sap. and Lv.). βλέμμα for "view" occurs in the NT only at 2 Pt. 2:8, and not at all in the LXX.

κυρίου, Lam. 2:9), καρδίας, Sir. 40:6. This use is later restricted to writings dependent on the vision terminology of the OT.

Philo already uses ὅρασις (over 70 times) only for the sense or process of sight (examples, → 335), seldom transf., e.g., ἡ ἐν ψυχῇ ὅρασις, Migr. Abr., 49, cf. Abr., 57. Cf. ὅρασις θεοῦ, Leg. All., I, 43; Praem. Poen., 27, 36 (cf. 51) and the explanation of the name Ἰσραήλ, Ebr., 82; Conf. Ling., 72; Fug., 208 (→ 337, n. 113), also Ἱερουσαλήμ (Som., II, 250, 254) as ὅρασις θεοῦ. ὄψις is used much more in Philo for "seeing," also "countenance" (occasionally "vision," e.g., Jos., 103). Joseph. obviously prefers ὄψις, → 338 and n. 115; commonly "vision," Ant., 1, 279; 2, 10 ff., 65). In Ep. Ar., 142 we find ὅρασις with ἀκοή; cf. Test. R. 2:4; L. 8:16 (Gn. 2:9), though ὄψις in S. 5:1 (Gn. 39:6). [5]

In the NT ὅρασις is twice used in the sense of "appearance" in Rev. 4:3 (cf. Ez. 1:27; → n. 1), and also in the sense of "vision" in Rev. 9:17: εἶδον ... ἐν τῇ ὁράσει (cf. Da. 9:21 Θ; 8:1 LXX) [6] and Ac. 2:17 (= Jl. 2:28). [7]

In the post-apost. fathers it means "eyesight" in 2 Cl., 1, 6 (transf.), "sight," "spectacle" in the quotation of Is. 66:24 (→ 370) in 2 Cl., 7, 6; 17, 5, also "vision" 13 times in Herm. v., 2-4.

† ὅραμα.

ὅραμα is "that which is to be seen," "appearance," "spectacle" (from the time ot Xenoph.), also outside the Bible tt. for "vision," P. Par., 51, 37 = Wilcken Ptol., 78, 37 (160 B.C.); Ditt. Syll.³, 1128, 3 (2nd cent. B.C.); P. Goodspeed, 3, 5 (3rd cent. B.C.); [1] cf. also Corp. Herm., IX, 2.

There are 43 instances in the LXX, 7 in Is. (mostly for מַשָּׂא "saying," elsewhere rendered ὅρασις, λῆμμα, ῥῆμα, χρηματισμός, ᾠδή), and 25 times in Da., mostly חָזוֹן and חֵלֶם; also 4 times in Da. Θ (though Da. Θ usually prefers ὅρασις). [2] In Da. the sense is usually "vision," and this is often the meaning elsewhere, Job 7:14; Is. 30:10; of pure revelation by word, Gn. 15:1; 46:2; Is. 21:2, and the מַשָּׂא passages in Is. (sometimes vl. ῥῆμα); on Nu. 12:6 → 331. The meaning can often be "what is seen" (in a natural way), Dt. 28:34, 67; Qoh. 6:9; Sir. 43:1, also ἐν βραχίονι ὑψηλῷ καὶ ἐν ὁράμασιν μεγάλοις, Dt. 4:34; 26:8; Ἰερ. 39(32):21 (here מוֹרָא, meaning a miracle which arouses terror, rightly rendered τὰ θαυμάσια in Dt. 34:12, is derived from רָאָה rather than יָרֵא). Ref. might also be made at this pt. to Ex. 3:3, where ὅραμα = מַרְאֶה means "what is to be seen," though with no implication as to the kind of seeing. [3]

---

[5] Violet's division of 4 Esr. into σημεῖα, ὁράσεις, ἐντολαί keeps to the LXX use of ὅρασις. Ps. Sol. 6:3 : seeing of ἐνύπνια.

[6] Loh. Apk., ad loc. derives from the consistent usage of Rev. the sense of "appearance." But the constr. is against this (cf. Had. Apk., ad loc.), and 4:3, which is dependent on Ez., seems to tell against consistency of usage. Neither ὅραμα nor ὀπτασία occurs in Rev.

[7] Michaelis, 152, n. 151.

ὅ ρ α μ α. Bibl. → ὁράω and Wikenhauser, → 350, n. 175.

[1] E. J. Goodspeed, Gk. Papyri from the Cairo Museum (1902). Cf. Preisigke Wört., II, 192 s.v.; Moult.-Mill., 454 f., s.v.; Mayser, I, 3² (1935), 60.

[2] ὅραμα occurs a few times in ᾿ΑΘΣ, also the derivates (not attested elsewhere) ὁραματίζομαι (usually natural seeing) 7 times in ᾿Α and once in Θ, ὁραματισμός (visionary) 8 times in ᾿Α, also ὁραματιστής once in Σ.

[3] Leisegang does not list ὅραμα in Philo (in Vit. Mos., I, 65 θέαμα is used for ὅραμα at Ex. 3:3; cf. Jos. Ant., 2, 267: ὄψις παράδοξος). Test. Jud. 3:10; L. 9:3; 11:5 use ἐν ὁράματι ("in the vision"). Cf. Gk. En. 99:8 (C. Bonner).

In the NT ὅραμα (always sing.) occurs, outside Ac., only in Mt. 17:9. Here the verb in the par. Mk. 9:9; cf. Lk. 9:36 suggests "what is seen," even though the reference is to a vision, → 354; cf. also Ac. 7:31 (ref. to Ex. 3:3). In the other 10 passages in Ac. (9:10, 12; 10:3, 17, 19; 11:5; 12:9; 16:9 f.; 18:9) the meaning is "vision," though it is only formally that the phrases ἐν ὁράματι in 9:10, 12; 10:3 and δι' ὁράματος in 18:9 emphasise the visionary aspect, this being suggested elsewhere more by the content.[4] On the ὁράματα → 350; 351; 356; 357 (on Col. 2:18 → II, 535 f.).

In the post-apost. fathers the τὰς ἀποκαλύψεις καὶ τὰ ὁράματα of Herm. v., 4, 1, 3 reminds us of 2 C. 12:1 (→ 353, 357). Elsewhere ὅραμα (= ὅρασις, "vision," → 371) occurs only 4 times in Herm. v., 3 f. (twice plur.; at night only in 3, 10, 6).[5]

† ὀπτασία.

ὀπτασία, a noun deriving from ὀπτάνομαι or ὀπτάζομαι (→ 317 and n. 12), is attested only in Anth. Pal., VI, 210, 6 outside the LXX and Christian writings.[1] It occurs 4 times in the LXX, 6 in Da. Θ (Da. LXX ὅρασις, once ὅραμα).[2] Except in Da. Θ ("vision") the meaning is "appearing," etc., always non-visionary. In ἐν ἡμέραις ὀπτασίας μου at Est. 4:17w the ref. is to the public appearance of Esther as queen.[3] ἐν ὀπτασίᾳ in Sir. 43:2 refers (par. ἐν ὁράματι δόξης in 43:1) to the appearance of the sun on rising, ἐν ὀπτασίᾳ (B plur.) αὐτοῦ in 43:16 to the manifestation of God in storms. In Mal. 3:2 וּמִי הָעֹמֵד בְּהֵרָאוֹתוֹ ἢ τίς ὑποστήσεται ἐν τῇ ὀπτασίᾳ αὐτοῦ; the ref. is to God's appearing on the ἡμέρα εἰσόδου αὐτοῦ. ὀπτασία can hardly be called a fixed tt. for visions.[4]

In the NT ὀπτασία in Lk. 1:22; 24:23 refers to angelophanies. These could be called visions only if the sense "visionary appearance" were firmly established, but this is not so. The appearance outside Damascus is called an οὐράνιος ὀπτασία in Ac. 26:19. In terms of current usage Lk. is not calling this a vision, and he commonly uses ὅραμα for it, → supra. Less, or even no emphasis at all is placed on the visual element as compared with the revelation by word and its

---

[4] Wikenhauser, 320 f. distinguishes Ac. 16:9; 18:9; 23:11; 27:23, which he calls dreams and among which he also groups the directions κατ' ὄναρ in Mt. (→ 350), from the ὁράματα in 9:10, 12; 10:3, 11 f., which he thinks are waking visions, and with which he associates Mt. 17:9; Lk. 1:11, 22; 24:23; Ac. 7:31; 22:17; 26:19; 2 C. 12:1. But many different processes are brought together in these two categories (on Mt. 17:9; Ac. 7:31 → supra; on Ac. 22:17 → 357; on the special nature of Ac. 10:11 ff. → 352; on Lk. 1:22; 24:23; Ac. 26:19; 2 C. 12:1 → ὀπτασία). Furthermore, it is never said that revelation by night came during sleep. Hence the revelations called ὅραμα are best taken as a separate group distinct from directions κατ' ὄναρ. With different categories the many religious pars. assembled by Wikenhauser may be put to profitable use.

[5] To what the very imperfectly preserved apocr. fr. in P. Oxy., X, 1224 Fr. 2 recto II, line 2: Ἰη(σοῦ) [ἐ]ν ὁράμα[τι λέγει (cf. also Kl. T., 8³, 26, 10) is referring is very uncertain (it can hardly be a par. to the Synoptic story of the transfiguration, but seems to be an appearance to Peter).

ὀπτασία. Bibl. → ὁράω.

[1] On the derivation cf. P. Chantraine, La formation des noms en grec ancien (1933), 185.

[2] Θ has ὀπτασία at Ez. 1:1, also 'Α, cf. Σ Ez. 1:5, and the gen. sing. ὀπτασίας, Gn. 22:2 (τὴν ὑψηλήν LXX, τὴν καταφανῆ 'Α, הַמֹּרִיָּה HT).

[3] Liddell-Scott, s.v. incorrectly suggests "vision" here.

[4] Even ὀπτάνομαι does not steer ὀπτασία in this direction, → 327.

demand for obedience. Paul himself could hardly have called this appearance an ὀπτασία, → 357. [5] On 2 C. 12:1 → 353; 357.

In the post-apost. fathers Mart. Pol. 5, 2 records a vision of Polycarp in which his approaching martyrdom is fig. shown to him shortly before his death. We read here : προσευχόμενος ἐν ὀπτασίᾳ γέγονεν (cf. ἐγενόμην ἐν πνεύματι in Rev. 1:10). There is further ref. to this ὀπτασία in 12, 3.

† αὐτόπτης.

αὐτόπτης, which combines αὐτός with the stem ὀπ-, means "seeing, or having seen, something for oneself," "eye-witness" (cf. αὐτήκοος "ear-witness"). It is found from the time of Hdt., and occurs in the pap.: αὐτόπτης γάρ εἰμι τῶν τόπων, P. Oxy., VIII, 1154, 8 (1st cent. A.D.). [1] The term does not occur in the LXX. Joseph. uses it in Ant., 18, 342; 19, 125; Bell., 3, 432; Ap., 1, 55, with μάρτυς in Bell., 6, 134. [2]

The only NT use is in Lk. 1:2 : οἱ ἀπ' ἀρχῆς αὐτόπται καὶ ὑπηρέται γενόμενοι τοῦ λόγου. On the one side this reference to eye-witness in terms of αὐτόπτης is one of the stylistic features of Lk.'s preface for which there are parallels in the world around. [3] On the other side, the distinctiveness of the Lucan statement is incontestable. [4] Hence there must have been in the history of the tradition an inner necessity demanding that eye-witnesses should here be mentioned as normative bearers of the tradition. [5] Cf. also the phrase ὑπηρέται τοῦ λόγου, → 348; IV, 115; I, 219. [6]

† ἐπόπτης, † ἐποπτεύω.

The noun ἐπόπτης [1] has first the sense of "one who sees and notes something," "observer," "(attentive) spectator," e.g.: καὶ σὺ δὴ πόνων ἐμῶν ἥκεις ἐπόπτης, Aesch. Prom., 298 f.; Preis. Zaub., VII, 351 (4th cent. A.D.). Then the "overseer" who sees to something or controls it, Apollo and Artemis as Πυθῶνος ἐπόπται, Pind. Nem., 9, 5; Epicharmos Fr., 23 (Diels⁵, I, 202, 9): αὐτός (sc. God) ἐσθ' ἁμῶν ἐπόπτης, Hecate as τῶν τριόδων ἐπόπτις, Cornut. Theol. Graec., 34. As the epiclesis of deities

---

[5] For further details cf. Michaelis, 148 f., n. 128 (as against E. Hirsch, "Zum Problem d. Osterglaubens," ThLZ, 65 [1940], 298).

α ὐ τ ό π τ η ς. [1] Cf. Pass. and Liddell-Scott, s.v.; Moult.-Mill., 93, s.v.; Preisigke Wört., I, 241, s.v. On αὔτοπτος in the magic pap. → 323.

[2] Leisegang does not list αὐτόπτης in Philo. αὐτήκοος is almost synon. to αὐτομαθής, with which it is always combined in Philo.

[3] Cf. Kl. Lk., 1 f., Exc.; H. J. Cadbury, "Commentary on the Preface of Lk.," F. Jackson-K. Lake, The Beginnings of Christianity, I, 2 (1922), 489-510.

[4] Elsewhere "it is not customary indirectly to support the works of others like one's own with anonymous eye-witness, as is done here," M. Dibelius, Die Formgeschichte d. Ev.² (1933), 11. In Jos. Ap., 1, 55 αὐτόπτης is less significant than αὐτουργός, cf. Polyb., 3, 4, 13. Cf. also → 375, n. 15.

[5] Cf. R. Asting, Die Verkündigung des Wortes im Urchr. (1939), 82 f.; W. Michaelis, Einl. in d. NT (1946), 14 f.

[6] αὐτόπτης does not occur in the post-apost. fathers.

ἐ π ό π τ η ς κτλ. [1] Formed from the root ὀπ- and belonging to ἐπόψομαι; cf. also ἐπίσκοπος ἐπι-σκέψασθαι [Debrunner]. ἐφοράω is common (ἐπεῖδον only twice in the NT, cf. Pr.-Bauer³, s.v.).

also in inscr. and pap.; the Egyptian sun god as ἐπόπτης καὶ σωτήρ, Ditt. Or., 666, 25 (1st cent. A.D.); Preisigke Sammelbuch, 1323 (2nd cent. A.D.); Preis. Zaub., XII, 237; also of Augustus : πάσης γῆς καὶ θαλάσσης ἐπόπτην, Inscr. Perg., 381, 2.[2] In the mysteries it is used of initiates of higher degree, e.g., τοῖσι μύστεσιν καὶ τοῖς ἐπόπτεισιν, Ditt. Syll.[3], 42, 48 ff. (Eleusis c. 460 B.C.); with μύστης, 1052, 3 ff.; 1053, 3 ff. (both inscr. from Samothrace, end of the 1st cent. A.D.) and Plut. Alkibiades, 22 (I, 202e). The sense here is obviously not "overseer" (though this might be used for a higher initiate), but "one who comes to have a share in vision."[3] ἐποπτεύω can also mean "to hold the degree of, to be, an *epoptes*," e.g., Plat. Ep., VII, 333e; Plut. Demetr., 26 (I, 900e).[4] In constr. with the acc., however, even with ref. to the mysteries (cf. φάσματα, Plat. Phaedr., 250c; ἐποπτεύσω τὴν ἀθάνατον ἀρχὴν τῷ ἀθανάτῳ πνεύματι, Mithr. Liturg., 4, 10 f. = Preis. Zaub., VII, 504 f.), we find the gen. sense "to view" (from Hom. onwards); cf. of ἔργα, "to inspect," Hom. Od., 16, 140; οἱ περὶ νόμους ἐποπτεύοντες, Plat. Leg., XII, 951d; (intellectually) "to consider," "to ponder," Emped. Fr., 110, 2 (Diels[5], I, 352, 21).

ἐποπτεύω does not occur in the LXX,[5] but we find ἐπόπτης 4 times, always of God, → 328. Acc. to 2 Macc. 3:39 : ἐπόπτης ἐστὶν καὶ βοηθὸς ἐκείνου τοῦ τόπου, a desecrating of the temple, as by Heliodorus, does not go unnoticed by God.[6] Cf. also Est. 5:1a : ἐπικαλεσαμένη τὸν πάντων ἐπόπτην θεὸν καὶ σωτῆρα : the peril of Esther and her people, or the conduct of those who accuse them, does not escape God's attention. God's omniscience is also indicated by ἐπόπτης in 2 Macc. 7:35 and ὁ πάντων ἐπόπτης θεός in 3 Macc. 2:21. That πάντων is neuter is shown both by the τοῦ πάντα ἐφορῶντος of 2 Macc. 12:22; 15:2 (cf. Job 34:23 A) and the τοῦ τὰ πάντα κατοπτεύοντος ἀεὶ θεοῦ of Est. 8:12d.[7] Cf. also παντεπόπτης (vl. πανεπόπτης) in 2 Macc. 9:5.[8]

Philo does not use ἐπόπτης or ἐποπτεύω.[9] ὃς ἐφορᾷ πάντα καὶ πάντων ἐπακούει in Jos., 265 is undoubtedly a quotation from Hom. (→ n. 2); cf. also Spec. Leg., IV, 32; Som., I, 140, but also Decal., 90; Spec. Leg., I, 279. τοῦ πάντα ἐφορῶντος in Leg. Gaj., 336 seems to echo the LXX (→ *supra*); cf. Aet. Mund., 83. In Jos. Ap., 2, 187

---

[2] Though Augustus is previously called θεοῦ υἱός and θεὸς Σεβαστός, ἐπόπτης is not to be regarded as a divine predicate, Deissmann LO, 295. It is a military or imperial title, cf. also the Cyzikus inscr., JHS, 27 (1907), 64 : Pompey as ἐπόπτης γῆς τε καὶ θαλάσσης. Preisigke Wört., I, 590 thinks the sense in Ditt. Or., 666, 25 etc., cf. also ὁ ἀγαθὸς κύριος ἐπόπτης θεός, P. Masp., 4, 20 (6th cent. A.D.), is "protector," but this can hardly be so in Ditt. Or., 666, 25. Again, πάντων ἐπόπτης in Preisigke Sammelbuch, 1323 does not mean "who protects all things," but "who sees or notes all things," in the sense "whom nothing escapes," cf. ὃς πάντ' ἐφορᾷ καὶ πάντ' ἐπακούει of Helios Hom. Od., 11, 109; 12, 323 etc. It is not clear whether Preisigke Wört., I, 590 and III, 118 thinks that "protector" is meant when a police official is called ἐπόπτης εἰρήνης in P. Oxy., VI, 991; XII, 1559, 3 (both 341 A.D.), but the obvious meaning is "one who has regard for the peace, for law and order." Cf. also ἐπόπται for tax-inspectors in Mitteis Wilcken, I, 1, 228.

[3] Mostly abs. In ἱεροποιοὶ καὶ μυστηρίων ἐπόπται, Rec. IG, 1141, 1 (2nd cent. B.C.) the gen. gives the ref. Cf. also O. Kern, Art. "Epoptes 2.," Pauly-W., VI (1907), 248 f. esp. on the relation of ἐπόπτης to μύστης, artistic representations etc.

[4] Cf. ἐποπτεία, e.g., Plut. Demetr., 26 (I, 900 f.); Schol. on Aristoph. Ra., 757.

[5] Σ has the word at ψ 9:34 (Mas. 10:14; LXX κατανοέω) and ψ 32[33]:13, LXX ἐπιβλέπω.

[6] For the sense "to inspect" cf. ἐποπτικὴ δύναμις in 4 Macc. 5:13.

[7] τὸν κατόπτην in 2 Macc. 15:21 does not occur in Cod A or the ed. of A. Rahlfs.

[8] If חי ראי in Gn. 16:14 means "the living one of seeing," i.e., "the divine being who graciously beholds those who confess him" (cf. R. Kittel, Die hell. Mysterienreligion u. d. AT = BWANT, NF, 7 [1924], 11), this can hardly be rendered ἐπόπτης in Gk.

[9] Acc. to Leisegang. If Philo was really close to the piety of the mysteries (→ 337), could he have failed to use ἐπόπτης as a title? On θεόπτης → 337.

the priests are ἐπόπται πάντων καὶ δικασταί (overseers), and God is ἐποπτεύων, 294. [10] Jos. commonly uses compounds like κατοπτεύω, e.g., Ant., 3, 128, κατόπτης, 18, 320, κάτοπτος, 1, 226, ὑπερόπτης, 9, 160, ὑποπτεύω, 4, 43, ὕποπτος, 1, 263, ἀνύποπτος, 7, 34. The influence of the LXX may be seen in Ep. Ar., 16 : τὸν γὰρ πάντων ἐπόπτην καὶ κτίστην θεόν, [11] cf. also παντεφόπτου in the tablet of Hadrumetum, line 36 (3rd cent. A.D.), IG, III, 3, p. XVIII, παντεπόπτης, [12] also Sib. Fr., 1, 4, ἐποπτεύω, 12, 167 and Gr. En. 104:8 (C. Bonner).

In the NT ἐποπτεύω occurs only at 1 Pt. 2:12; 3:2. The verses are related (hence ἐποπτεύοντες in 2:12 has partly replaced ἐποπτεύσαντες as a vl. in 3:2). The Gentiles take note (cf. ἴδωσιν, Mt. 5:16) of the walk of Christians or Christian couples, and cannot fail to see the καλὰ ἔργα (2:12) or ἐν φόβῳ ἁγνὴ ἀναστροφή (3:2). This observing thus includes an evaluation and persuasion which leads to δοξάζειν (2:12) or κερδαίνεσθαι (3:1), → III, 673. [13] There is no relation whatever to the usage in the mysteries. Nor does ἐπόπτης in 2 Pt. 1:16 force us to suppose dependence on this terminology. [14] The statement does not lose its forcefulness if we take the word in the general sense of "observer," "spectator." Eye-witness is not too strongly emphasised in ἐπόπτης alone, and 1:17 f. as a whole seems to suggest pseudonymity, → 348. Hence, even though 2 Pt. is to be regarded as part of the NT *kerygma* in virtue of its acceptance into the Canon, there are definite limits to the value of 1:16 (→ IV, 784; 789; 792), and other statements have higher worth in clarifying the relation between Gospel and myth. [15]

In 1 Cl., 59, 3 we find τὸν ἐπόπτην ἀνθρωπίνων ἔργων (God), who beholds the deeds of men, to whom they are all known ; [16] God as παντεπόπτης, 1 Cl., 55, 6 (cf. 2 Macc. 9:5 → 374); 64, 1, also Pol., 7, 2. [17]

ὀφθαλμός.

1. ὀφθαλμός, first "apple of the eye," then "eye," from Hom. and Hes. (mostly plur.). The gt. significance of the eye as the main agent relating man to his environment is variously reflected in sayings like ἐλθεῖν ἐς ὀφθαλμούς τινος, Hom. Il., 24,

---

[10] Schl. Theol. d. Judt., 188 thinks ἐφοράω means "to inspect" in Bell., 2, 164. For other instances of God's ἐφορᾶν, Ant., 4, 114; 19, 61; Bell., 1, 630 (hardly a variation of the Homeric expression, → n. 2); 5, 413; Ap., 2, 181.

[11] P. Wendland in Kautzsch Apokr. u. Pseudepigr. translates "ruler."

[12] Cf. Pr.-Bauer³, s.v.

[13] Perhaps ἐκ τῶν καλῶν ἔργων in 2:12 should be linked with ἐποπτεύοντες. Cf. Wbg. Pt. and Wnd. Pt., ad loc.; Pr.-Bauer³, s.v. ἐκ 3 g β (though cf. s.v. ἐποπτεύω).

[14] So Wnd. Pt., ad loc., who transl. Weihezeuge, appealing to Pr.-Bauer, s.v.; → IV, 542. Cf. also J. Höller, D. Verklärung Jesu (1937), 136; S. Eitrem, "Orakel u. Mysterien am Ausgang d. Antike," Albae Vigiliae, NF, 5 (1947), 70.

[15] The verdict of Wbg. Pt. does not refer to αὐτόπτης, which is not synon. and which is also a tt. in the mysteries. Again, μῦθοι and ἐπόπται do not correspond in 2 Pt. 1:16, but ἐξακολουθήσαντες and ἐπόπται γενηθέντες; the opp. of μῦθοι is the μεγαλειότης of Christ.

[16] Kn. Cl., ad loc. transl. "who ... seeks out," but God sees without any long search. Pr.-Bauer, s.v. transl. "observes" or "supervises."

[17] Kn. Cl., on 1 Cl., 55, 6 is mistaken when he says that the word does not occur in the LXX, → 374. If Deissmann B, 47 does not have the example, this is because the relevant section of Hatch-Redpath had not yet appeared.

ὀ φ θ α λ μ ό ς. Bibl. → ὁράω.

203 f., γενέσθαι ἐξ ὀφθαλμῶν τινος, Hdt., V, 106, [1] in accounts of healings of the blind, e.g., Ditt. Syll.[3], 1169, *passim* (4th cent. B.C.), fig. "what is most dear or precious," [2] in the admonition of the Praecepta Delphica ὀφθαλμοῦ κράτει, Ditt. Syll.[3], 1268, II, 9. On the impossibility of perception with the eyes, → 319, esp. 321; 323; more important, then, are the eyes of the νοῦς, Corp. Herm., X, 4b; XIII, 14 and 18, or the καρδία, IV, 11; VII, 1a. [3] Cf. also ὄμμα τῆς ψυχῆς, Plat. Resp., VII, 533d; Soph., 254a; → 322.

2. In the LXX ὀφθαλμός occurs c. 700 times ; where there is a Mas. original it is almost always עַיִן. [4] The frequency is noteworthy, esp. as compared with → οὖς (about 175 times). [5] It rests on the poetic usage which has eyes for the person who sees, even in a transf. sense ("to perceive," "to note," "to judge" etc.). Cf. the common ἐν ὀφθαλμοῖς, "acc. to the judgment of someone," [6] to find χάρις or ἔλεος in someone's eyes, Gn. 33:8 A; Ju. 6:17 etc. Often there is ref. to God's eyes, Dt. 11:12; Ju. 6:17; 2 Βασ. 11:27; ψ 32:18; 33:15; Prv. 15:3; Sir. 15:19; Am. 9:8; Is. 1:15 etc. (→ 328; on Job 10:4 → 379). It is correspondingly used of the relation of man to God, e.g., ψ 24:15; 118:82, 123; 122:2; 140:8; 144:15; on Job 42:5 → 334. It is often used fig. for the ability to judge or perceive, e.g., Ex. 23:8; cf. Sir. 20:29; the LXX takes a different path at Prv. 29:13. When φωτίζω is used in 2 Εσδρ. 9:8; ψ 12:3; 18:8; Sir. 34(31):17 the ref. is rather to the spirit expressed in clear eyes. The eye can be the seat of evil impulses, e.g., Prv. 6:17; 10:10; 30:17; Sir. 14:9; 27:22; Jer. 22:17, esp. pride, e.g., ψ 17:27; Prv. 30:13; Is. 5:15, also carnal desire, Job 31:1, 7; Prv. 23:33 LXX; Sir. 9:8; 26:9; Is. 3:16; cf. Ez. 24:16, 21, 25. ὀφθαλμὸς πονηρός, "envious eye" (cf. ὀφθαλμὸς πλεονέκτου, Sir. 14:9), occurs at Sir. 14:10; 31(34):13a; in both cases the Heb. is רַע עַיִן which is rendered βάσκανος at Prv. 23:6; 28:22; Sir. 14:3 (on βασκαίνων ὀφθαλμῷ, 14:8, cf. Dt. 28:54, 56). On טוֹב־עַיִן at Prv. 22:9 = ἱλαρός LXX 22:8a → III, 298. ἀγαθὸς ὀφθαλμός occurs at Sir. 35(32):7, 9. Though God has formed the eye (πλάσας, ψ 93:9), its sinful inclination leads to the heartfelt sigh of Sir. 31(34):13b : πονηρότερον (רַע) ὀφθαλμοῦ τί ἔκτισται;

3. Philo uses ὀφθαλμός about 130 times, over 100 of these being in the lit. sense with ref. to sight or seeing (e.g., → 336), often by way of example or to clarify the relation of the eye to the πάθη or ἡδονή. ὀφθαλμοὶ σώματος, e.g., Decal., 60; Conf. Ling., 100; Sobr., 4, has as its opp. in Spec. Leg., I, 49 διανοίας ὄμματα and in Rer. Div. Her., 89; Congr., 135; Mut. Nom., 3 ψυχῆς ὄμμα. Philo uses ὄμμα fig. (over 60 times) when he speaks of the mental eyes (9 times with διάνοια, 28 with ψυχή). But cf. ὀφθαλμὸς τῆς ψυχῆς, Spec. Leg., III, 6; Conf. Ling., 92 (cf. Congr., 145; Spec. Leg., III, 161) or διανοίας, Poster. C., 118; Spec. Leg., IV, 191 (cf. Conf. Ling., 100; the διάνοια as ὀφθαλμὸς ὀφθαλμῶν, Congr., 143; cf. Migr. Abr., 77). ὀφθαλμὸς τοῦ νοῦ does not occur (Philo is closer to Plato → line 6 f. than the Hermet. writings → line 5). He seldom speaks of the eyes of God : ἀκοιμήτῳ γὰρ ὀφθαλμῷ βλέπει πάντα, Mut. Nom., 40; Cher., 96 f.; Det. Pot. Ins., 61; ὀφθαλμῶν γε μὴν οὐκ ἐδεῖτο ..., ἑώρα δὲ ὁ θεὸς καὶ πρὸ γενέσεως φωτὶ χρώμενος ἑαυτῷ, Deus Imm., 58. There is nothing distinctive about the usage of Joseph.

In the pseudepigr. we can see the influence of OT expressions like ἐν ὀφθαλμοῖς

---

[1] Cf. Ditt. Or., 210, 8 (3rd cent. B.C.); Preisigke Wört., II, 214 f.; Moult.-Mill., 469, *s.v.*
[2] For examples and other meanings cf. Pass. and Liddell-Scott, *s.v.*
[3] → III, 608; Dobschütz, 397; J. Kroll, *Die Lehren d. Herm. Trism.* (1914), 352, n. 4.
[4] The more choice ὄμμα occurs 10 times in Prv., Wis., 4 Macc. That its use in Wis. 15:15 recalls ψ 113:13a with its echoing of στόμα (J. Fichtner, "Der AT-Text d. Sap. Sal.," ZAW, NF, 16 [1939], 184, n. 2) is hardly likely.
[5] Dobschütz, 395 estimates a proportion of 4 to 2, but it is almost exactly 4 to 1.
[6] On this and other prepos. phrases with ὀφθαλμός cf. Johannessohn Präpos., Index, *s.v.*

κυρίου, Test. Jud. 13:2; 4 Esr. 4:44 (Violet, I, 12, 1). [7] The eyes reveal an adulterous nature, Ps. Sol. 4:4 f.; Test. Iss. 7:3 (μετεωρισμός also B. 6:3; cf. Sir. 23:4; 26:9), also covetousness, Ps. Sol. 4:9, 12. In Test. Iss. 3 f. the ἁπλότης ὀφθαλμῶν is extolled, → I, 387; cf. Test. B. 4:2 : ὁ ἀγαθὸς ἄνθρωπος οὐκ ἔχει σκοτεινὸν ὀφθαλμόν. It is said of true μετάνοια in Test. G. 5:7: φωτίζει τοὺς ὀφθαλμοὺς καὶ γνῶσιν παρέχει τῇ ψυχῇ, → I, 702, n. 59. The Rabbis could also speak of seeing the seducer in the eye, [8] and there is often ref. to the evil (envious) or good eye. [9]

4. In the NT ὀφθαλμός occurs 100 times (ὄμμα only at Mk. 8:23; Mt. 20:34). → οὖς occurs 36 times, so that the ratio has slightly increased in its favour as compared with the LXX, → 376. [10] The eye is usually mentioned as the organ of sight, → 346. Cf. the ἐπαίρειν of the eyes as a sign of taking note, Lk. 6:20; 16:23; Jn. 4:35; 6:5 [11] (cf. also Mt. 17:8), blinding, Ac. 9:8 (cf. 18), [12] healing the blind (→ 347), Mt. 9:29 f.; 20:33; Mk. 8:25; Jn. 9 passim (cf. 10:21; 11:37), the stirring of one raised from the dead, Ac. 9:40; cf. also the heaviness of the eyes, Mt. 26:43 par. Mk. 14:40 (→ I, 558 f.) and the wiping away of tears, Rev. 7:17; 21:4. [13] The thought that "no man has the right to judge another" (→ III, 939) is emphasised in Mt. 7:3-5 par. Lk. 6:41 f. by the parable of the mote in the eye of another and the beam in one's own eye, → 344, n. 153. The OT rule of an eye for an eye (ὀφθαλμὸν ἀντὶ ὀφθαλμοῦ, Ex. 21:24; Lv. 24:20; Dt. 19:21) is quoted in Mt. 5:38, and by contrast restraint from retaliation is commanded, cf. also R. 12:17; 1 Th. 5:15; 1 Pt. 3:9 with no reference to the OT saying.

The function which the eye has by creation as a member of the body (cf. 1 C. 12:16 f., 21) forms the basis of the parable (Mt. 6:22 f. par. Lk. 11:34) in which the eye is described as λύχνος τοῦ σώματος (→ IV, 326) and the implications of the possibility that the eye might be ἁπλοῦς or πονηρός (→ I, 386) are explored. That ἁπλοῦς and πονηρός are used as moral concepts may be seen in Test. Iss. 4:6. It is said there of the one who πάντα ὁρᾷ ἐν ἁπλότητι (cf. ἐν ἁπλότητι ὀφθαλμῶν, 3:4) that he is μὴ ἐπιδεχόμενος ὀφθαλμοῖς πονηρίας (acc. plur.) ἀπὸ τῆς πλάνης τοῦ κόσμου, and ἁπλότης ὀφθαλμῶν and the πονηρίαι of the world lead to a completely different relation to the ἐντολαὶ τοῦ κυρίου mentioned in what follows. The ἁπλοῦς and πονηρός of Mt. 6:22 f. and par. are, of course, used in a broader sense [14] than that of ὀφθαλμὸς πονηρός in the sense of evil or envious eye, as in the NT at Mt. 20:15; Mk. 7:22. [15] That the eyes entice to sin is stated generally in 1 Jn. 2:16 (→ III, 171), though ἐπιθυμία τῶν ὀφθαλμῶν is more specific than ἐπιθυμία τῆς σαρκός; there is then special reference to sexual desire in 2 Pt. 2:14, → IV, 734. The possibility of → σκανδαλίζειν is ascribed to the eye in Mt. 5:29; 18:9 par. Mk. 9:47. On ὀφθαλμοδουλία → II, 280.

---

[7] In the comprehensive note of Violet, ad loc. (cf. also his Intr. XXXV) Ιερ. 41:15 B is overlooked (cf. Johannessohn Präpos., 186).

[8] Str.-B., I, 302, 722.

[9] Str.-B., s.v. Auge and Blick.

[10] There are only 15 instances of ὁ ἔχων ὦτα ἀκουέτω etc. (cf. Dobschütz, 395).

[11] As a gesture of prayer Lk. 18:13; Jn. 11:41 → I, 185 and n. 1; 186; Str.-B., II, 246 f.

[12] → III, 820. On Gl. 4:15 → loc. cit.

[13] Is. 25:8 is obviously in the background ; there is no need to look for Mandaean pars. (cf. Loh. Apk. on 7:17). For the OT background of Rev. 1:14 (cf. 2:18; 19:12); 5:6 and 4:6, 8 cf. the comm.

[14] Schl. Mt., 222, ad loc. suggests generosity or avarice.

[15] Sometimes the Rabb. use, too, is broader (→ n. 9), cf. Str.-B., I, 833.

Sometimes, under OT influence (→ 376), the eyes are mentioned with reference to eye-witness, Mt. 13:16 par. Lk. 10:23 (→ 347); Lk. 2:30; 1 Jn. 1:1; Rev. 1:7 (→ 361). When the eyes of the recipients of the revelation are mentioned in connection with the resurrection appearances, there is no implication that sight is singled out in any way. This is immediately apparent in Ac. 1:9; 9:8, but also in Lk. 24:16, 31 (→ III, 911; I, 704), since the two disciples see the risen Lord between 24:16 and 31, and it thus follows that no particular power of vision is at issue (hence 4 Βασ. 6:17, 20 is no parallel). The real distinction here is between seeing as sensation and seeing as the basis of understanding or as understanding; cf. also the sayings which utilise Is. 6:10, i.e., Mt. 13:15; Mk. 8:18; Jn. 12:40; Ac. 28:27; cf. R. 11:8 (Dt. 29:3; Is. 29:10), 10 (ψ 68:23).[16] Further examples of the transf. use of ὀφθαλμός are to be found in the prepositional phrases [17] with ἐν, Mt. 21:42 and par. (ψ 117:23; → III, 39), ἀπέναντι R. 3:18, ἀπό Lk. 19:42 (→ III, 973) and κατά Gl. 3:1 (→ I, 771). Along with Ac. 26:18; 1 Jn. 2:11, Eph. 1:18: ὀφθαλμοὶ τῆς καρδίας, deserves special mention (→ III, 612 and n. 23; IV, 966, n. 14). It is for God to grant enlightened [18] eyes of the heart εἰς τὸ εἰδέναι ὑμᾶς κτλ. [19] The reference in Rev. 3:18 is more to the achieving of ethical standards, cf. R. 12:2. Only rarely, and always fig., is there reference to the eyes of God, 1 Pt. 3:12 (ψ 33:15; → 376) and Hb. 4:13, → I, 774. [20]

5. In the post-apost. fathers ὀφθαλμός is rare apart from 10 instances in 1 Cl. 1 C. 2:9 (→ n. 16) is quoted in 1 Cl., 34, 8; 2 Cl., 11, 7; Mart. Pol., 2, 3. Prepositional phrases (→ supra), ἀπέναντι, 1 Cl., 8, 4 (Is. 1:16); Pol., 6, 2, πρό, 1 Cl., 2, 1; 5, 3; 39, 3 (Job 4:16); Mart. Pol., 2, 3. [21] God's eyes, 1 Cl., 22, 6 (ψ 33:15; → supra); Pol., 6, 2. The phrase ὀφθαλμοὶ τῆς καρδίας (→ supra), also 1 Cl., 36, 2; 59, 3 (both times with ἀνοίγω, cf. Ac. 26:18), is applied in Mart. Pol., 2, 3 to martyrs, who in the hour of death ἐνέβλεπον τὰ τηρούμενα τοῖς ὑπομείνασιν ἀγαθά with the eyes of the heart. ὀφθαλμοί and φρόνησις are contrasted in Dg., 2, 1. ὄμματα (τῆς ψυχῆς) occurs only in 1 Cl., 19, 3, → 376.

---

[16] With the exception of Jn. 12:40; R. 11:10 the ear is always mentioned too, cf. also 1 C. 2:9 (→ 341; Dobschütz, 391, 395). This verse ((apparently an apocr. quotation, → III, 612, 988 f.), seems to be used in Lidz. Liturg., 77, 3 ff. The Mandaean writings often speak of the lifting up of the eyes on high etc. (tt., e.g., Liturg., 15, 3; 47, 4; 48, 2, 11; 65, 1; 162, 11; 193, 4; Ginza, 510, 23 f.; 546, 31 f.; Joh., 63, 13), of the raising of the eyes (Liturg., 38, 2; Ginza, 378, 10 ff.), of the filling of the eyes with light (Liturg., 155, 3; Ginza, 58, 25 f.; 59, 6 f., 21 f.), of open eyes (Liturg., 138, 3 f.; Ginza, 466, 27 f.) etc. Lidz. attaches so little significance to these passages that he does not even list Auge (or Gesicht, sehen) in the index, → 364, n. 228.

[17] For details cf. Pr.-Bauer³, 599, s.v.

[18] The LXX instances (→ 376) have a different bearing. There is no connection with the πατὴρ τῆς δόξης of Eph. 1:17.

[19] ἐν ἐπιγνώσει αὐτοῦ in 1:17 is not to be taken with πεφωτισμένους (as against Ew. Gefbr., 96 f.). πεφωτισμένους ... καρδίας is in apposition, and not, as argued by Dib. Gefbr., ad loc. with a mistaken appeal to Bl.-Debr. § 468, 2, one of the free part. connections (the cases with the nom. in Eph. 3:17; 4:1 ff. are different); on the art. in πεφωτισμένους τοὺς ὀφθαλμούς cf. Bl.-Debr. § 270, 1.

[20] αὐτοῦ is to be taken with God; cf. Rgg. Hb. ², ³, 115; → IV, 103, 21 ff.

[21] For further details cf. Pr.-Bauer³, 999, s.v. 2.

† καθοράω.

1. First "to look down," abs. ἐξ "Ιδης καθορῶν (Hom. Il., 11, 337) or with acc. ὁπόσους ἥλιος καθορᾷ (Theogn., 168, Diehl, II, 125), then generally "to view," "to consider." Early transf. "to perceive," "to note," "to look over," e.g., ὅ τι μέλλει, ... εὖ καθορᾷς, Pind. Pyth., 9, 48; ἔν τινι, "to give attention to someone," e.g., Plat. Gorg., 457c; Resp., IV, 432b; Leg., X, 905b. [1]

2. καθοράω occurs 4 times in the LXX, also κατεῖδον 4 times. Sense perception is indicated by καθοράω at Nu. 24:2; Job 39:26, and by κατεῖδον at Ex. 10:5. This is also the primary ref. of κατεῖδον in Dt. 26:15; Bar. 2:16 and Jdt. 6:19, though since it is used anthropomorphically of God the meaning is "to take note of," "to observe." Job 10:4a : ἤ ὥσπερ βροτὸς ὁρᾷ καθορᾷς (sc. God), is similar. It corresponds to HT 10:4b, cf. LXX 10:4b : ἤ καθὼς ὁρᾷ ἄνθρωπος βλέψῃ, an apparent doublet of 10:4a, though it is possible that this corresponds to HT 10:4b and LXX 10:4a is a free rendering of HT 10:4a. Since in HT 10:4a עֵינֵי בָשָׂר (cf. 1 Βασ. 16:7) does not mean sense perception as such, e.g., in antithesis to intellectual perception, but the human, sinful mode of perceiving, and since עַיִן can also stand for intellectual perception (→ 376), one cannot dismiss the possibility that καθοράω is used in the free rendering in 10:4a because this term seemed to the translator to emphasise, not exclusively sense perception, but rather intellectual. It is in any case most unlikely that the translator used it to suggest God's looking down from heaven after the manner of Dt. 26:15 etc. Either καθοράω is here synon. with ὁράω or βλέπω (HT רָאָה in both cases), or καθοράω already has the transf. sense "to judge." In 3 Macc. 3:11: οὐ καθορῶν τὸ τοῦ μεγίστου θεοῦ κράτος, we obviously have the transf. sense "to perceive," "to ponder" (in spite of the obj. there is no direct par. to R. 1:20).

3. Philo uses καθοράω 34 times. [2] The relation to sense perception is here less prominent (only Det. Pot. Ins., 87; Agr., 95; Op. Mund., 45, 54; Leg. All., II, 26; Sobr., 6). Elsewhere the ref. is to intellectual perception, as may be seen partly from the obj. (e.g., Leg. All., II, 57; Ebr., 83), partly from God as subj. (e.g., Migr. Abr., 135; Spec. Leg., I, 330, cf. τὸ θεῖον, Som., I, 91), partly from the use which connects ὀφθαλμός and ὄμμα with διάνοια (Spec. Leg., I, 54; Poster. C., 118) or ψυχή (Conf. Ling., 92; Congr., 145; Gig., 44; Plant., 22; cf. Leg. All., III, 171, ψυχικῶς II, 81). There is also a plain connection with intellectual perception in the common phrase ὀξὺ καθορᾶν, Deus Imm., 63; Fug., 19, 121 etc.; Virt., 5 shows dependence on Plat. Leg., I, 631 c; → 335. Since God is subj. when there is a link with ἀόρατα in Deus Imm., 29 and ἀθέατα in Migr. Abr., 115, there is no par. to R. 1:20 (Sobr., 6, where we have ἀθέατα, is obviously not a par.). That there is no connection with νοῦς (par. to that with διάνοια or ψυχή, → supra), seems to be plainly linked with the fact that Philo does not use ὀφθαλμὸς τοῦ νοῦ, → 376. καθοράω and νοῦς are even in antithesis in Leg. All., II, 26. When we turn to Joseph., the use of καθοράω, as one would expect from the mostly narrative character of his writings, is predominantly for sense perception, e.g., Ant., 8, 106; 9, 84; Bell., 1, 59; 3, 241 and 286; 6, 64. The sense "to look down," still to be seen in Ant., 15, 412, is so far lost in 3, 36 that καθορᾶν can be used of seeing Moses as he came down from the mount. But we also find the transf. sense "to perceive," "to inspect," e.g., Bell., 2, 523; 3, 130 and 331; 4, 307; 7, 171.

κ α θ ο ρ ά ω. Bibl. → IV, 948 s.v. νοέω under 2., also n. 2.
[1] Cf. Pass.; Liddell-Scott, s.v. Rare in pap., Preisigke Wört., I, 718 and Moult.-Mill., 314, s.v.
[2] Acc. to Leisegang, s.v.

4. In the NT καθοράω is used only at R. 1:20 : τὰ γὰρ ἀόρατα αὐτοῦ (sc. τοῦ θεοῦ) ἀπὸ κτίσεως κόσμου τοῖς ποιήμασιν νοούμενα καθορᾶται, ἥ τε ἀΐδιος αὐτοῦ δύναμις καὶ θειότης (→ 369 and n. 10; → I, 719; II, 307; IV, 950 and n. 9). The participle construction νοούμενα καθορᾶται rules out the possibility that Paul means a consideration with the eyes prior to νοεῖν. [3] νοεῖν must either come before καθορᾶν, or take place at the same time. [4] If νοεῖν can here denote only a purely intellectual process (→ IV, 950), [5] the first possibility must be discarded, for it leaves unanswered the question wherein there is a distinction between the mental process of νοεῖν and that of καθορᾶν which only follows it, and which is thus itself mental. Within the second possibility we are thus left to choose between a sense process of καθορᾶν which is at the same time intellectual νοεῖν [6] and a process which is expressly and unequivocally shown to be intellectual by the addition of νοούμενα. [7] The two views are very close if νοούμενα is a modal rather than a conditional participle, so that the καθορᾶν is at the same time a νοεῖν. This is surely what is intended. Because καθορᾶν, as LXX usage shows, is not restricted to intellectual perception, the addition νοούμενα is designed to show unambiguously that an intellectual proces is in view. In this regard the constr. with the dat. τοῖς ποιήμασιν is close to the common constr. with ἕν τινι when καθοράω is used fig., → 379. [8]

The ποιήματα, then, are not phenomena or processes which are primarily noted by sense perception, and which call for this. [9] On the contrary, the ποιήματα which the apostle has in mind may well be phenomena or processes which, if they are to be perceived at all, must be considered in a way which combines καθορᾶν and νοεῖν. If the ref. is to nature, it cannot be to the side of it which offers itself primarily for apprehension by the senses ; the ref. might well be specifically to history including providences in individual life. There is thus a marked distinction between R. 1:20 and the otherwise closely related (→ IV, 951) verse Wis. 13:5 (→ 328), which is referring specifically to the κτίσματα accessible to sense perception (cf. also Corp. Herm., XIV, 4; XI, 21b, → 323). That the ref. of the καθορᾶν conjoined with νοεῖν in R. 1:20 is not to a

---

[3] The statement in Schl. R., 57, quoted in → IV, 950, does not clearly rule out this interpretation ; cf. also → n. 6 f. The emphasis would here be on νοεῖν, but καθορᾶν would not be superfluous ; in this case, however, νοεῖν would have to be the main verb, cf., e.g., Wis. 13:5 (→ 328); Ps.-Aristot. Mund., 6, p. 399b, 22 (cf. Pr.-Bauer³, s.v. καθοράω). where θεωρέω is used exclusively in the sense "to perceive."

[4] Cf. Bl.-Debr. § 418, 5.

[5] This cuts out the view of, e.g., Zn. R., 92, ad loc. that Paul puts καθορᾶν for intellectual perception after νοεῖν for sense perception (cf. also → IV, 948 f., n. 2; 950, n. 11).

[6] We are pointed in this direction by the following statements in Schl. R., 57: "who sees them with understanding"; "that perception of something which is shown us does not come through the eye, but through our power of thought."

[7] Schl., loc. cit., can still finally relate καθορᾶν to perception by the eye, → n. 6. Hence he reckons with the possibility (58) that man with his νοεῖν, with the thoughts formed by him, can nullify or even falsify perception. Nevertheless, the νοεῖν which Paul has in view, and which is simultaneous with καθορᾶν, is either present or absent with καθορᾶν, just as νοεῖν in Jn. 12:40 bears a religious and moral impress (→ IV, 950) or is not there at all, or at least cannot bear any other impress. R. 1:20 would have to be stated differently if the guilt of men consisted in the fact that they exercise καθορᾶν but forget or falsify νοεῖν. As the passage stands, the guilt can only be that they do not exercise the καθορᾶν bound up with νοεῖν.

[8] τοῖς ποιήμασιν is to be taken with καθορᾶται (and not exclusively with νοούμενα).

[9] Cf. the statement in Zn., loc. cit. (→ n. 5): "so that one may say that it is seen with the eyes."

possibility always available to man, but to one which is opened up for him by God (in individual cases ?), seems to be clear from the context, cf. v. 19; → 369. The expression πεφωτισμένοι ὀφθαλμοὶ καρδίας (→ 378) in Eph. 1:18, which is used of the special revelation of God in Christ, if transposed *mutatis mutandis* to the level of general revelation, is well designed to bring out the nature of this καθορᾶν; [10] R. 1:20 is also closer to Hb. 11:3 than would appear from → IV, 951. [11]

† προοράω, † προεῖδον.

προοράω, aor. προεῖδον, has in the act. and mid. the sense "to see before one" (spatially), e.g., Hom. Od., 5, 393; Xenoph. Hist. Graec., IV, 3, 23; Ditt. Syll.³, 569, 13 (3rd cent. B.C.), also "to see ahead" (in time), "to have seen earlier," "to see what is future in advance," "to know in advance," etc., e.g., ἐσσόμενον, Pind. Nem., 1, 27. Also (with gen.) "to provide for," so also pap. [1]

The mid. is used spatially, though fig., in ψ 15:8 : προωρώμην (שִׁוִּיתִי pi "to set") τὸν κύριον ἐνώπιόν μου διὰ παντός, "to hold before one's eyes"; act. "already to have seen earlier," 1 Εσδρ. 5:60 A; "to have seen someone already πρὸ τοῦ ἐγγίσαι αὐτόν, Gn. 37:18 (רָאָה); transf. of God, who knows all the ways of men beforehand, ψ 138:3 (הִסְכַּנְתָּה simply tells us that God is acquainted with these ways).

There are 9 instances in Philo, all mid., only Sacr. AC, 29 not temporal, mostly for the foreseeing of dangers, Praem. Poen., 72; Ebr., 160; Spec. Leg., I, 99; Som., I, 27 (cf. Spec. Leg., IV, 165). With ref. to the foreseeing of the future, and indeed of future πράγματα and γνῶμαι of others, Philo declares that this is impossible for man but possible for God as a result of His πρόνοια, Deus Imm., 29. Joseph. usually has it for the foreseeing of perils, etc., e.g., Ant., 13, 189; Ap., 1, 77; Bell., 2, 649; Vit., 19; often "to note in advance," e.g., Ant., 2, 245; Bell., 1, 42; 5, 271 and 273, also "to make provision for," Ant., 16, 378; 17, 101. A true prevision of the future, though possible for the prophets (Bell., 1, 69; cf. Ap., 1, 204 and 258) is barred to man on account of his ἄγνοια and ἀπιστία, Ant., 10, 142.

In the NT προοράω or προεῖδον occurs only 3 times in Ac. and at Gl. 3:8. In the latter verse Paul speaks of the προϊδεῖν of γραφή (→ I, 753 f.) as the presupposition of its προευαγγελίζεσθαι, → II, 737. If Scripture is here personified, [2] Ac. 2:31 says of David as the author of ψ 15 that he προϊδὼν ἐλάλησεν κτλ. This can hardly mean that he prophetically (cf. 2:30) "saw" the future resurrection of Jesus in advance ; [3] what is meant is that as a prophet he had advance knowledge of it ("to know in advance" is also a suitable rendering in Gl. 3:8). Ac. 2:25 quotes ψ 15:8 (→ *supra*); the sense in 21:29 is "already to have seen beforehand." προβλέπομαι in Hb. 11:40 means "to contemplate something in advance."

---

[10] The paraphrase "to see with (the eyes of) the reason" (transl. of Ltzm. R., ad loc., cf. Pr.-Bauer³, s.v. καθοράω) rightly grasps the unity of Paul's statement and relates it to a mental process, but on the other hand it wrongly brings it into close proximity to the corresponding philosophical terminology (→ 376) which for its part relates to νοητόν as the world of the ideas, cf. Schl., op. cit.

[11] καθοράω does not occur in the post-apost. fathers.

π ρ ο ο ρ ά ω κ τ λ. [1] Cf. Pass., Liddell-Scott, Preisigke Wört., II, 381, s.v.

[2] Cf. the Rabb. personification of the Torah, → I, 754, n. 20; Str.-B., III, 538. But the exegetical use of רָאָה by the Rabb. (loc. cit.) is only a distant par.

[3] Somewhat after the analogy of the foreseeing of the future which acc. to the Rabb. view (cf. Str.-B., II, 525 f.) God granted to Abraham, also Adam and Moses.

In the post-apost. fathers προορῶν τὰς ἐνέδρας τοῦ διαβόλου is used in Ign. Tr.,
8, 1 for the foreseeing (and taking into account) of undoubtedly approaching dangers.

Michaelis

| † ὀργή, † ὀργίζομαι, † ὀργίλος, † παροργίζω, † παροργισμός |

(→ ἅγιος, I, 92 ff.; θυμός, III, 167 f.; κρίνω, III, 921-941; μακροθυμία, IV, 374-387).

Contents : A. Wrath in Classical Antiquity : I. The Meaning of ὀργή; II. The Wrath of
the Gods in the Greek World ; III. *Ira deum* in the Roman World. B. The Wrath of Man
and the Wrath of God in the OT : I. The Hebrew Terms for Wrath and Being Wrathful ;
II. The Wrath of Man : 1. Against Other Men ; 2. Against God ; 3. Evaluation ; III. The
Wrath of God : 1. Linguistic Discussion ; 2. Objects ; 3. Exercise ; 4. Motives ; 5. Outbreak,
Duration and Turning Aside ; 6. God's Wrath in relation to His Holiness, Righteousness
and Pity. C. The Wrath of God in the LXX : I. Usage ; 1. ὀργή and θυμός; 2. ὀργίζω,
(θυμόω,) παροργίζω, παροργισμός; 3. ὀργίλος and θυμώδης; 4. (κότος,) χόλος
and μῆνις; II. Interpretations and Paraphrases. D. The Wrath of God in Later Judaism :
I. Apocrypha and Pseudepigrapha ; II. Rabbinism ; III. Philo ; IV. Josephus. E. The Wrath
of Man and the Wrath of God in the NT : I. The Wrath of Man : 1. Relative Justification :
2. Negative Appraisal ; II. The Wrath of God : 1. Differentiation from the World Around ;
2. Wrath in the NT View of God ; 3. The Revelation of the Divine Wrath : a. In Jesus
and His Message ; b. In its Historical and Eschatological Outworking ; 4. The Wrath of
God in NT Imagery ; 5. The Objects and Instruments of Wrath : a. Objects ; b. Instruments ; c. The Position of the Christian. 6. The Causes and Effects of the Divine Wrath .
a. Causes ; b. Inseparability of Causes from Effects ; c. Effects ; 7. Liberation from God's
Wrath : a. In the World Around ; b. Conversion and Baptism ; c. Jesus the Deliverer.

ὀ ρ γ ή κ τ λ. Introductory Note : O. Procksch was originally assigned this art. After
his death (1947) H. Kleinknecht, O. Grether, E. Sjöberg, and G. Stählin shared the task.
When Grether suddenly died in the summer of 1949 J. Fichtner completed the section on
the OT. The portions signed by Procksch are taken from his MS, which was in part
available to the authors.
        Cr.-Kö., Liddell-Scott, Pape, Pass., Pr.-Bauer, *s.v.*; J. H. H. Schmidt, *Synonymik d. griech.*
Sprache, III (1879), 551-572; R. C. Trench, *Synonyms of the NT*[15] (1906), 123-127 (§ 37
θυμός, ὀργή, παροργισμός); A. Rüegg, "Zorn Gottes" in RE³, 21, 719-729; A. Bertholet,
H. Gunkel, W. Mundle, "Zorn Gottes" in RGG², V (1931), 2133-2136. A. Ritschl, *De Ira*
Dei (1859); also *Die chr. Lehre v. der Rechtfertigung u. Versöhnung,* II³ (1889), 119-156;
R. Bartholomäi, "Vom Zorn Gottes," *Jahrbücher f. Deutsche Theologie,* 6 (1861), 256-277;
F. Weber, *Vom Zorne Gottes* (1862), A. Dieckmann, "Die chr. Lehre vom Zorne Gottes,"
ZwTh, NF, 1, II (1893), 321-377; R. Otto, *Das Heilige*²⁶⁻²⁸ (1947), 18-20, 91 f., 101, 116-
118; also *Gottheit u. Gottheiten der Arier* (1932), 50-54. Orig. Cels., IV, 71-73 (GCS,
Orig. I, 340-343); Lact. De Ira Dei (CSEL, 27, 1, 65-132); on this W. Kutsch, "In Lactanti
de ira dei librum quaestiones philologae," *Klassisch-philologische Studien,* 6 (1933); M.
Pohlenz, "Vom Zorne Gottes," FRL, 12 (1909). On A : Aristot. Rhet., II, 2, p. 1378a, 31-
1380a, 4; Stob. Ecl., III, 20 (Wachsmuth-Hense, III, 539-556): περὶ ὀργῆς; Philodem.
Philos. De Ira (ed. Wilke [1914]); Plut. De Ira Cohibenda (II, 452e-464d); Sen. De Ira.
J. Irmscher, *Götterzorn bei Homer* (1950); W. Marg, "Der Charakter in der Sprache der
frühgriech. Dichtung," *Kieler Arbeiten zur klass. Philologie,* 1 (1938), 13 f.; R. Camerer,
Zorn u. Groll in d. sophokleischen Tragödie, Diss. Freiburg (1936), esp. 52-64; K. Latte,

A. Wrath in Classical Antiquity.

I. The Meaning of ὀργή.

ὀργή, post-Homeric, first found in Hes. Op., 304, then common in poetry and prose, is related in stem to ὀργάω/ὀργάς, [1] and thus means the "lavish swelling of sap and vigour," "thrusting and upsurging" in nature, originally gener. a. the "impulsive nature" of man or beast, esp. the impulsive state of the human disposition, which in contrast to more inward and quiet ἦθος (Plat. Leg., X, 908e : ἄνευ κάκης ὀργῆς τε καὶ ἤθους) breaks forth actively in relation to what is without. When ὀργή is used of the mind and nature of man, animal and other comparisons point expressly to the natural side of the concept : ὅς κεν ἀεργὸς ζώῃ κηφήνεσσι (drones) ... εἴκελος ὀργήν, Hes. Op., 303. The female type which God created from the fox ὀργὴν δ᾽ ἄλλοτ᾽ ἀλλοίην ἔχει, Semonides Fr., 7, 11 (Diehl); another is best likened to the changeable sea in its nature (ὀργήν, ibid., 41 f.). The characters of men are distinct, hence Theogn., 213-215 (Diehl) advises : φίλους κατὰ πάντας ἐπίστρεφε ποικίλον ἦθος ὀργὴν συμμίσγων ἥντιν᾽ ἕκαστος ἔχει· πουλύπου ὀργὴν ἴσχε. Pindar can even speak of a μείλιχος and γλυκεῖα ὀργά (Pyth., 9, 43; Isthm., 2, 35 f.). In war, says Thuc., III, 82, 2, the ὀργαί of the masses rise acc. to the given relations : ὁ δὲ πόλεμος ... πρὸς τὰ παρόντα τὰς ὀργὰς τῶν πολλῶν ὁμοιοῖ, on which the Schol. has the gloss τὰς γνώμας καὶ τοὺς τρόπους, cf. Suid., s.v. ὀργῇ. Cf. Hdt., VI, 128, who sets ὀργή, man's natural disposition, character and bent, in the same category as his ἀνδραγαθίη, παίδευσις and τρόπος, cf. Theogn., 964 (Diehl).

In the general and broader sense of individual nature or disposition ὀργή is esp. important in Attic tragedy [2] where it became a tragic element. In ὀργή there is actualised the true or false insight of man which impels him to decisive deeds : παυσανέμου γὰρ θυσίας παρθενίου θ᾽αἵματος ὀργᾷ περιόργως ἐπιθυμεῖν θέμις· εὖ γὰρ εἴη ... ἀνάγκας ἔδυ λέπαδνον, Aesch. Ag., 214-218; cf. 68-71. [3] In Soph. [4] the chorus passes judgment on the fate of Antigone : σὲ δ᾽ αὐτόγνωτος ὤλεσ᾽ ὀργά, Soph. Ant., 875, and Electra has the self-judgment : δείν᾽ ἐν δεινοῖς ἠναγκάσθην· ἔξοιδ᾽, οὐ λάθει μ᾽ ὀργά, El., 221 f.; cf. 1011. Not blind anger, but a demonic excess of will in the nature of the tragic person, goes hand in hand with ἀνάγκη, necessity and fate.

"Schuld u. Sünde in der griech. Religion," ARW, 20 (1920/21), 257-260; R. Hirzel, Themis, Dike u. Verwandtes (1907), 138, 416-418. On B : C. v. Orelli, "Einige at.liche Prämissen zur nt.lichen Versöhnungslehre," ZWL, 5 (1884), 22-33; J. Böhmer, "Zorn," ZAW, 44 (1926), 320-322; P. Volz, Das Dämonische in Jahwe (1924); also OT Theologies by E. König[3, 4] (1923), 173-177; W. Eichrodt, I[3] (1948), 124-131; E. Sellin (1936), passim. On D: Weber, 155, 161, 172, 314; Bousset-Gressm., 350 f.; Str.-B., III, 30 f.; E. Sjöberg, "Gott u. die Sünder im palästinischen Judentum," BWANT, F. 4, H. 27 (1930), Index, s.v. Zorn Gottes. On E. I.: Str.-B., I, 276-278; III, 645; Dib. Jk., 104-106; Hck. Jk., 74 f., n. 30; T. Rüther, "Die sittliche Forderung der Apatheia in den beiden ersten chr. Jhdten u. bei Cl. Al.," Freiburger Theol. Studien, 23 (1949). On E. II.: Dob. Th., 79; Schl. R., 46-54; G. P. Wetter, Der Vergeltungsgedanke bei Pls. (1912), 16-55; F. V. Filson, St. Paul's Conception of Recompense (1931), 39-48; H. Braun, Gerichtsgedanke u. Rechtfertigungslehre bei Pls. (1930), esp. 41-44; G. Bornkamm, "Die Offenbarung des Zornes Gottes (R. 1-3)," ZNW, 34 (1935), 239-262; G. Schrenk, Unser Glaube an den Zorn Gottes nach dem R. (1944); A. v. Jüchen, Der Zorn Gottes (1948); also NT Theol., esp. by H. J. Holtzmann, II[2] (1911), 57 f.; H. Weinel[3] (1928), 109, 260 f., 322 f.; P. Feine[7] (1936), 206-208; R. Bultmann (1948), 76, 283 f.

[1] Cf. Sanskrit ūrj(ā), "fulness of power"; to be distinguished are ὀρέγω and Lat. urgeo, cf. Walde-Pok., I, 289; II, 363 [A. Debrunner].

[2] ὀργῆς νοσούσης εἰσὶν ἰατροὶ λόγοι, Aesch. Prom., 378; ἀστυνόμους ὀργάς, Soph. Ant., 355 f.

[3] For Aesch. cf. W. Nestle, "Menschliche Existenz u. politische Erziehung in der Tragödie d. Aischylos," Tübinger Beiträge zur Altertumswissenschaft, 23 (1934), esp. 56 ff.

[4] Camerer, esp. 51-53 (n. 1).

As compared with the older use, ὀργή in tragedy has already become more restricted and specialised. ὀργή now has more of the sense of a specific reaction of the human soul. It takes on the sense b. of anger as the most striking manifestation of powerful inner passion, θυμός. [5] The two terms can now supplement one another (ὀργαί τε ... καὶ θυμοί, Plat. Tim. Locr., 102e; Luc. De Calumniis, 23), and yet on the other hand ὀργή, in distinction from θυμός, is essentially and intentionally orientated to its content, namely, revenge or punishment : ὀργή· παράκλησις τοῦ θυμικοῦ εἰς τὸ τιμωρεῖσθαι, Ps.-Plat. Def., 415e; Aristot. Rhet., II, 2, p. 1378a, 31. [6] ὀργή, which already in tragedy is always seen to be protecting something recognised to be right, becomes in the political life of the following period the characteristic and legitimate attitude of the ruler who has to avenge injustice : οἱ ... νόμοι ... διδόασιν αὐτοῖς ἀκούσασιν, ὁποῖον ἄν τι νομίζωσι τὸ ἀδίκημα, τοιαύτη περὶ τοῦ ἠδικηκότος χρῆσθαι τῇ ὀργῇ, μέγα μεγάλῃ, μικρὸν μικρᾷ, Demosth. Or., 24, 118. A fixed formula in pronouncement of judgment is thus δεινὸν καὶ ὀργῆς ἄξιον, ibid., 9, 31; 19, 7 etc.; ὀργή here relates, not to the verdict (Aristot. Rhet., I, 1, p. 1354a, 16 ff.) but only to the sentence. [7] In virtue of this ὀργή itself acquired the meaning c. "punishment" (ἅπαντα μὲν ... τάσεβήματα τῆς αὐτῆς ὀργῆς δίκαιον ἀξιοῦν, Demosth. Or., 21, 147; cf. Lyc. Contra Leocratem, 138).

Apart from the moral wrath which protects against evil [8] and which is sometimes expressly called δικαία ὀργή (Demosth. Or., 16, 19; Dio C., 40, 51, 2; Ditt. Syll.³, 780, 22), ὀργή in Gk. came under a predominantly negative judgment. [9] Already in tragedy as "irritation" (Soph. Ant., 280, 766; Oed. Tyr., 337, 404 f.) it was linked with the blind [10] thought and fancy by which man allows himself to be impelled, and thus opposed to γνώμη (Soph. Oed. Tyr., 523 f.), λόγος and λογισμός (Menand. Fr., 630 [CAF, III, 188]; Thuc., II, 11, 4 f.; Aristot. Fr., 661 [ed. Rose]), σοφόν (Eur. Fr., 760 [TGF, 597]). It is not just itself an ἀμήχανον κακόν (Eur. Med., 446 f.), but necessarily leads to many other κακά (Chairemon Fr., 28 [TGF, 789]). The moral demand of philosophy, then, is that man should master this irrational emotion which does not stop short even before the gods (ὀργιζόμεθα καὶ πολεμίοις καὶ φίλοις καὶ τέκνοις καὶ γονεῦσι καὶ θεοῖς, Plut. De Ira Cohibenda, 5 [II, 455d]): ὀργῆς γὰρ ἀλογίστου κρατεῖν ... μάλιστα τὸν φρονοῦντα δεῖ (Menand. Fr., 574 [CAF, III, 175]). While Academicians and Peripatetics explain that anger is natural and even necessary for great acts and virtues, and esp. for military valour, and simply seek its moderation and control by

---

[5] → θυμός, III, 167 f. cf. Camerer, 3-5 and J. Böhme, Die Seele u. das Ich im homerischen Epos (1930), 69 ff.

[6] Linked with this is the Stoic def. of ὀργή, which is also set in conceptual relation to the various Gk. synonyms as sub-divisions : ὀργὴ μὲν οὖν ἐστιν ἐπιθυμία <τοῦ> τιμωρήσασθαι τὸν δοκοῦντα ἠδικηκέναι παρὰ τὸ προσῆκον· θυμὸς δὲ ὀργὴ ἐναρχομένη· χόλος δὲ ὀργὴ διοιδοῦσα· μῆνις δὲ ὀργὴ εἰς παλαίωσιν ἀποτεθειμένη ἢ ἐναποκειμένη· κότος δὲ ὀργὴ ἐπιτηροῦσα καιρὸν εἰς τιμωρίαν· πικρία δὲ ὀργὴ παραχρῆμα ἐκρηγνυμένη (Chrysipp. Fr., 395, cf. Fr. 396 f. [v. Arnim, III, 96, 14 ff.]). The various forms of wrath, for which the Gks., though not the Romans, have special terms, are discussed in Sen. De Ira, I, 4. A comparison of the two lists of vices in Col. 3:8 and Eph. 4:31 with this and with Gk. categories of ὀργή and its εἴδη, Chrysipp. Fr., 394 (v. Arnim, III, 96, 3 ff.), shows that the enumeration of πικρία, θυμός, ὀργή, κραυγή (cf. Sen. loc. cit.: irae, quae intra clamorem considant), κακία, βλασφημία, αἰσχρολογία (cf. Ariston Chius Fr., 395 [v. Arnim, I, 89, 15 f.]: τὴν κακολογίαν ἡ ὀργὴ φαίνεται ἀπογεννῶσα, Sen. loc. cit.: irae ... in verborum maledictorumque amaritudinem effusae) displays an inner unity in the two NT writings. These are irarum differentiae (Sen., I, 4) in which current Stoic synonyms and systematisation may well be reflected.

[7] Hirzel, 416-418; Pohlenz, 15, n. 3.

[8] Cf. Theophr. in Sen. De Ira, I, 14 : non potest fieri, ut non vir bonus irascatur malis.

[9] Cf. the many examples in Stob. Ecl.

[10] Cf. Chrysipp. Fr., 390 (v. Arnim, III, 94, 43 ff.): τυφλόν ἐστιν ἡ ὀργὴ καὶ πολλάκις μὲν οὐκ ἐᾷ ὁρᾶν τὰ ἐκφανῆ.

reason, [11] the Stoa regards ὀργὴ καὶ τὰ εἴδη αὐτῆς as one of the chief πάθη [12] which must be completely eradicated. [13] This moral ideal was then maintained very particularly by philosophy in face of the concept of the wrath of deity.

II. The Wrath of the Gods in the Greek World.

Wrathful deities are so vividly present to the consciousness of all peoples that attempts have even been made to explain every cult as an effort to anticipate or soften the anger of the gods. This factor is present in pre-Homeric religion. [14] The pre-Greek gods of earth and of cursing, like the Furies, show by their very name ("the wrathful ones") that wrath is their nature. [15] Unswerving, pitiless and terrible as nature itself, they appear always where the unbreakable ties of nature — especially of blood and family, later of law too [16] — are violated and call for retribution. From the time of Homer divine wrath is in Greek mythology and poetry "a powerful force in the interplay of the powers which determine destiny," [17] i.e., the reality which seeks to enforce itself. This anger appears in two forms in so far as it may be either anger between the gods or anger directed against man. In both cases it is a form of self-assertion and protest, whether in the clash of specific divine claims which conflict with one another (Hom. Il., 8, 407 and 421) or as a reaction against transgressions on the part of men, perhaps as arrogance in face of the gods (Il., 24, 606), the neglect of sacrifices (5, 177 f.; 9, 533-538), disregard for the priest (1, 44 and 75), for hospitality (Od., 2, 66 f.; 14, 283 f.), for honouring the dead (Il., 22, 358; Od., 11, 73) etc. All such things evoke divine wrath, which is hard to placate, which leads to no good result (Od., 3, 135 and 145) and before which it is best to yield (Il., 5, 443 f.). Anger and resentment are not here anthropomorphic characteristics but for the most part something to which the god has a kind of right in virtue of the infringement of a claim. By it order is restored, assertion made good and destiny achieved. Hence the wrath of the gods is not just blind rage. It is seeing anger, and even in regard to man, *via negationis,* it confers dignity on him by marking him out or putting him in the limits set for him, thus making him what he is.

At first this was not expressed by ὀργή, which is not a Homeric word, but by χόλος, [18] κότος, [19] and especially by a word which comes from the sacral sphere and is almost exclusively reserved for it, namely, μῆνις [20] and its associated

---

[11] ὁ μὲν οὖν ἐφ᾽ οἷς δεῖ καὶ οἷς δεῖ ὀργιζόμενος, ἔτι δὲ καὶ ὡς δεῖ καὶ ὅτε καὶ ὅσον χρόνον, ἐπαινεῖται, Aristot. Eth. Nic., IV, 11, p. 1125b, 31 f.; Cic. Tusc., IV, 43; Sen. De Ira, III, 3.

[12] Chrysipp. Fr., 397 (v. Arnim, III, 96, 35 ff.); *ibid.,* 459 (III, 111, 32 ff.): καὶ γὰρ ἐπιθυμίαν καὶ ὀργὴν ... δόξας εἶναι καὶ κρίσεις πονηράς.

[13] *Stoici ... voluerunt eam* (sc. *iram) penitus excidere, ibid.,* 444 (III, 108, 34 ff.).

[14] Cf. U. v. Wilamowitz, *Der Glaube d. Hellenen,* I (1931), 35.

[15] From ἐρινύω, which Paus., VIII, 25, 5 explains as an Arcadian word by θυμῷ χρῆσθαι, and which is rendered ὀργίζεσθαι by Etym. M. For other etym. suggestions cf. Boisacq, 297; Walde-Pok., I, 140; II, 349.

[16] Heracl. Fr., 94 (Diels⁵, I, 172, 9) calls the Furies Δίκης ἐπίκουροι.

[17] W. Schadewaldt, *Iliasstudien* (1938), 154, n. 1.

[18] Hom. Il., 15, 122 : πὰρ Διὸς ἀθανάτοισι χόλος καὶ μῆνις ἐτύχθη. Cf. Apoll. Rhod., III, 337.

[19] Hom. Od., 11, 101 ff. (Teiresias to Odysseus): οὐ γὰρ ὀΐω λήσειν (σε) ἐννοσίγαιον, ὅ τοι κότον ἔνθετο θυμῷ χωόμενος, ὅτι οἱ υἱὸν φίλον ἐξαλάωσας. Cf. Aesch. Ag., 1211.

[20] Hom. Il., 5, 177 f.: εἰ μή τις θεός ἐστι κοτεσσάμενος Τρώεσσιν ἱρῶν μηνίσας· χαλεπὴ δὲ θεοῦ ἔπι μῆνις. Il., 21, 523 has the image of a city which the wrath of the

verbs. [21] Only in tragedy does ὀργή come to be used for the wrath of the gods. [22] It is frequently used by Euripides in this sense: ὅταν γὰρ ὀργὴ δαιμόνων βλάπτῃ τινά, | τοῦτ' αὐτὸ πρῶτον, ἐξαφαιρεῖται φρενῶν | τὸν νοῦν τὸν ἐσθλόν· εἰς δὲ τὴν χείρω τρέπει | γνώμην, ἵν' εἰδῇ μηδὲν ὧν ἁμαρτάνει, Adespota Fr., 296 (TGF, 896). [23] Whereas in Hesiod (Op., 47, 53) Zeus in his anger against Prometheus causes the punishment to follow the fault immediately, for Solon it is a sign of the power and greatness of the god that he does not punish at once. There is a distinction between divine and human wrath: τοιαύτη Ζηνὸς πέλεται τίσις, οὐδ' ἐφ' ἑκάστῳ ὥσπερ θνητὸς ἀνὴρ γίγνεται ὀξύχολος, Solon Fr., 1, 25 f. (Diehl). [24] With reference to ὀργαί (though this is used here in the broad sense a. → 383), Eur. Ba., 1348 says that it is not seemly that gods should resemble mortals: ὀργὰς πρέπει θεοὺς οὐχ ὁμοιοῦσθαι βροτοῖς. The ethical rational concept of θεοπρεπές, which was discovered by Xenophanes, is directed especially against the μυθεύματα of the poets, who depict the dwelling-place of the gods ὡς τοιαύτης τινὸς τῷ μακαρίῳ καὶ ἀθανάτῳ διαγωγῆς μάλιστα πρεπούσης, αὐτοὺς δὲ τοὺς θεοὺς ταραχῆς καὶ δυσμενείας καὶ ὀργῆς ἄλλων τε μεστοὺς παθῶν ἀποφαίνοντες οὐδ' ἀνθρώποις νοῦν ἔχουσι προσηκόντων, Plut. Pericl., 39 (I, 173 d-e). [25] Criticism of myth is raised especially in the philosophical demand that by its true nature the θεῖον must be free from every πάθος: δόγμα μέντοι φιλοσόφων ... ἀπαθὲς εἶναι τὸ θεῖον, Sext. Emp. Pyrrh. Hyp., I, 162. Cicero can thus say that freedom from anger is common to the concept of God in all the philosophical schools: *num iratum timemus Iovem? At hoc quidem commune est omnium philosophorum ... numquam nec irasci deum nec nocere*, Off., III, 102. [26] Epicurus begins the Κύριαι δόξαι in 1. with the affirmation (Fr., 139): τὸ μακάριον καὶ ἄφθαρτον ... οὔτε ὀργαῖς οὔτε χάρισι συνέχεται· ἐν ἀσθενεῖ γὰρ πᾶν τὸ τοιοῦτον. [27] The same contrast between ὀργή and χάρις (Demosth. Or., 19, 92) may be seen in Plut. Suav. Viv. Epic., 22 (II, 1102 e): οὐ τοίνυν ὀργαῖς καὶ χάρισι συνέχεται τὸ θεῖον ἅμα, ὅτι χαρίζεσθαι καὶ βοηθεῖν πέφυκεν, ὀργίζεσθαι δὲ καὶ κακῶς ποιεῖν οὐ πέφυκεν. The distinction from Epicurus is that while the Stoic, too, denies ὀργή, he clings to the χαρίζεσθαι and βοηθεῖν, the

gods causes to go up in smoke and flames: ἄστεος αἰθομένοιο θεῶν δέ ἑ μῆνις ἀνῆκεν. Hence the divine wrath can strike a city and a whole people as well as individuals.

[21] The etym. and meanings of the many Homeric words for the wrath of the gods are finely discussed by Irmscher, 3-26. Cf. 29-36 for the various manifestations of this wrath in Homer.

[22] Cf. the ὀργαί of the Furies in Aesch. Eum., 847 and 936. Soph. Ai., 776 f. ἀστεργῆ θεᾶς (sc. Athena) ἐκτήσατ' ὀργὴν οὐ κατ' ἄνθρωπον φρονῶν.

[23] Characteristically Gk. here is the way the divine wrath works, beginning in man's νοῦς: *eadem ira deorum hanc eius satellitibus iniecit amentiam,* Cic. Mil., 86. Cf. Eur. Iph. Taur., 987: δεινή τις ὀργὴ δαιμόνων ἐπέζεσε, Med., 129 f.; Hipp., 438: ὀργαὶ δ' ἐς σ' ἀπέσκηψαν θεᾶς, 1417 f.

[24] The thought appears in Christian guise in Lact., 20 f.

[25] Cf. Cic. Nat. Deor., I, 16 (42): *qui* (sc. *poetae*) *et ira inflammatos ... induxerunt deos;* II, 28 (70): *et perturbatis animis inducuntur* (sc. *dei*); *accepimus enim deorum ... iracundias ... ut fabulae ferunt ... Haec et dicuntur et creduntur stultissime et plena sunt futtilitatis summaeque levitatis.*

[26] Luc. Jup. Conf., 14 has the motif: ἦν τις ... τῷ 'Απόλλωνι ὀργῆς αἰτία κατὰ τοῦ Κροίσου, opines Zeus, to receive from Cyniscos the answer: ἐχρῆν μὲν μηδὲ ὀργίζεσθαι θεὸν ὄντα, cf. Luc. Prometheus, 8 and 10.

[27] For further development cf. Lucretius De Rerum Natura, II, 651; Philodem. Philos. De Ira, col. 43 (ed. Wilke, p. 85-87); Pos. in Cic. Nat. Deor., I, 44 (124); I, 17 (45); Epic. Fr., 363, 365 f. (ed. H. Usener, p. 242-244).

εὐμένεια of deity : θεὸς τὸν πάντα κόσμον διοικεῖ μετ' εὐμενείας καὶ χωρὶς ὀργῆς ἁπάσης, Ep. Ar., 254. [28]

We should not allow the teachings of the philosophical schools to create a false impression. In fact, they show how widespread must have been the idea, not only in poetry but also in popular belief, that the wrath of the gods demands expiation and expresses itself especially in punishments. Plato speaks of particularly severe sicknesses and sufferings which for various reasons fell on this or that race as a result of ancient divine wrath, and which could be healed only by the μανία of consecrated priests who had recourse to vows and prayers, to ministerial acts, to rites of expiation and dedication. [29] Otherwise Lucretius would not have contended so passionately for liberation from the related anxiety, cf. De Rerum Natura, V, 1194 ff.; VI, 71 f.; Cic. Nat. Deor., I, 17 (45): *metus omnis a vi atque ira deorum pulsus esset,* nor would Plutarch have needed to wrestle with the sceptical question : αἱ δὲ τῶν θεῶν ὀργαὶ τίνι λόγῳ παραχρῆμα δυόμεναι καθάπερ ἔνιοι τῶν ποταμῶν εἶθ' ὕστερον ἐπ' ἄλλους ἀναφερόμεναι πρὸς ἐσχάτας συμφορὰς τελευτῶσιν; (Ser. Num. Pun., 12 [II, 557e]). For even if God punishes, He does not act out of anger : οὐ γὰρ ἀμύνεται τὸν ἀδικήσαντα κακῶς παθὼν οὐδ' ὀργίζεται τῷ ἁρπάσαντι βιασθεὶς οὐδὲ μισεῖ τὸν μοιχὸν ὑβρισθείς, ἀλλ' ἰα- τρείας ἕνεκα ... κολάζει [30] πολλάκις, Plut. Ser. Num. Pun., 20 (II, 562 d). Plutarch's main attack is on the popular mythological tradition, but he is also against cultic ideas in which ὀργή and ὀργίζεσθαι have a firm place as the judgment of the gods in spite of philosophical criticism. Hence Paus. can say of the primitive period : οἱ γὰρ δὴ τότε ἄνθρωποι ξένοι καὶ ὁμοτράπεζοι θεοῖς ἦσαν ὑπὸ δικαιοσύνης καὶ εὐσεβείας, καί σφισιν ἐναργῶς ἀπήντα παρὰ τῶν θεῶν τιμή τε οὖσιν ἀγαθοῖς καὶ ἀδικήσασιν ὡσαύτως ἡ ὀργή (VIII, 2, 4); his reference is to the judicial ὀργή of the gods, but the expressions alternate, with no very clear distinction of meaning, when he goes on to say in 5 that later it was different because οὔτε θεὸς ἐγίνετο οὐδεὶς ἔτι ἐξ ἀνθρώπου, ... καὶ ἀδίκοις τὸ μήνιμα τὸ ἐκ τῶν θεῶν ὀψέ τε καὶ ἀπελθοῦσιν ἐνθένδε ἀπόκειται. The same alternation of ὀργή and μήνιμα or μῆνις, which is the true word for the wrath of deity that demands cultic propitiation, [31] may be seen, e.g., in the

---

[28] Cf. Lact., 5, 1: *existimantur Stoici ... aliquanto melius de divinitate sensisse, qui aiunt, gratiam in deo esse, iram non esse.* Lact. himself accepts the view that both wrath and grace are necessary as the punishment of evil and reward of good if the being of God and all religion are not to be undermined. The Chr. Apologists (Aristid. Apol., 1, 6; Athenag. Suppl., 21) used the philosophical view in their criticism of pagan religion and mythology (cf. J. Geffcken, *Zwei gr. Apologeten* [1907], 40), but philosophy for its part made τὰ περὶ ὀργῆς θεοῦ a charge against Christians : ἢ γὰρ οὐ καταγέλαστον· εἰ ἄνθρωπος μὲν ὀργισθεὶς Ἰουδαίοις πάντας αὐτοὺς ἡβηδὸν ἀπώλεσε καὶ ἐπυρπόλησεν, οὕτως οὐδὲν ἦσαν· θεὸς δ' ὁ μέγιστος, ὥς φασιν, ὀργιζόμενος καὶ θυμούμενος καὶ ἀπει- λῶν πέμπει τὸν υἱὸν αὐτοῦ, καὶ τοιαῦτα πάσχει; Orig. Cels., IV, 73. On the rebuttal of Orig., who had intrinsically the same ideal of God's ἀπάθεια (VI, 65), cf. Pohlenz, 31-36.

[29] Phaedr., 244 d-e : ἀλλὰ μὴν νόσων γε καὶ πόνων τῶν μεγίστων, ἃ δὴ παλαιῶν ἐκ μηνιμάτων ποθὲν ἔν τισι τῶν γενῶν, ἡ μανία ἐγγενομένη καὶ προφητεύουσα, οἷς ἔδει ἀπαλλαγὴν ηὕρετο, καταφυγοῦσα πρὸς θεῶν εὐχάς τε καὶ λατρείας, ὅθεν δὴ καθαρμῶν τε καὶ τελετῶν τυχοῦσα ἐξάντη ἐποίησε τὸν ἑαυτῆς ἔχοντα πρός τε τὸν παρόντα καὶ τὸν ἔπειτα χρόνον, λύσιν τῷ ὀρθῶς μανέντι τε καὶ κατασχομένῳ τῶν παρόντων κακῶν εὑρομένη. On this F. Pfister, "Der Wahnsinn des Weihepriesters," *Festschr. Cimbria* (1926), 55-62.

[30] Cf. the related idea in Cl. Al. Paed., I, 8, 68, 3 (cf. I, 8, 74, 4; 133, 23): τὴν κόλασιν ὁ θεὸς οὐχ ὑπὸ ὀργῆς ἐπιφέρει, ἀλλὰ τὸ δίκαιον σκοπεῖ.

[31] Cf. Hdt., VII, 134 and 137; Plat. Leg., IX, 880e; Paus., III, 4, 6; Dio Chrys. Or., 4, 90. It is thus impossible to secure a total picture of the wrath of deity among the Gks. if we

aetiological myth of Demeter Erinys in Oncai, with whom Poseidon lived in the form of a stallion : τὴν Δήμητρα ἐπὶ τῷ συμβάντι ἔχειν ὀργίλως,[32] χρόνῳ δὲ ὕστερον τοῦ τε θυμοῦ παύσασθαι ... ἐπὶ τούτῳ καὶ ἐπικλήσεις τῇ θεῷ γεγόνασι, τοῦ μηνίματος μὲν ἕνεκα Ἐρινύς, ὅτι τὸ θυμῷ χρῆσθαι καλοῦσιν ἐρινύειν οἱ Ἀρκάδες, Paus., VIII, 25, 6.[33] ὀργίζεσθαι is an equivalent of δαιμόνιος χόλος in Dio Chrys. Or., 33, 50 : Λημνίων ταῖς γυναιξὶ τὴν Ἀφροδίτην ὀργισθεῖσαν λέγουσι διαφθεῖραι τὰς μασχάλας.

On the one side, then, the ὀργὴ θεοῦ is an essentially mythological concept, e.g., when it is said of Artemis in relation to Actaion : ὁμολογουμένη καὶ δικαίαν ὀργὴν ἔσχε πρὸς αὐτὸν ἡ θεός (Diod. S., 4, 81, 5), or when it is told of Orpheus : τὸν μὲν Διόνυσον οὐκ ἐτίμα ... ὅθεν ὁ Διόνυσος ὀργισθεὶς αὐτῷ ἔπεμψε τὰς Βασσαρίδας who tore Orpheus in pieces.[34] On the other side, however, the equation with the tt. μήνιμα or μῆνις in aetiological legends, and statements like Apollodor. Bibliotheca, II, 1, 3 (οὐκ ἐπισπᾶσθαι τὴν ἀπὸ τῶν θεῶν ὀργὴν γινομένους ὅρκους ὑπὲρ ἔρωτος) in later Gk. show at least that there were solid connections with the cultus.[35] Paus., I, 32, 4 tells of an appearance by night at the grave of Miltiades. Anyone who goes there deliberately ἐς ἐναργῆ θέαν does not come away unpunished, ἀνηκόῳ δὲ ὄντι καὶ ἄλλως συμβὰν οὐκ ἔστι ἐκ τῶν δαιμόνων ὀργή.[36] In a burial ordinance on a 3rd cent. inscr. any who offend against it are threatened for their ἀσεβεῖν with the ὀργὴ μεγάλη τοῦ μεγάλου Διός, Ditt. Syll.[3], 1237, 5. With a similar reference to the δαιμόνων ὀργὴ καὶ θεῶν ἁπάντων King Antiochus of Commagene (1st cent. B.C.) seeks to protect for all time the cultic statute issued by him, Ditt. Or., 383, 210.

Especially in extraordinary natural events like pestilence, storm and hail, deformity and sickness, popular belief sees the operation of the ὀργή of gods and demons : λέγουσι δ᾽ οὖν τινες λοιμούς τε καὶ χαλάζας καὶ θυέλλας καὶ τὰ παραπλήσια ... κατά τινα δαιμόνων ἢ καὶ ἀγγέλων οὐκ ἀγαθῶν ὀργὴν φιλεῖν γίνεσθαι, Cl. Al. Strom., VI, 3, 31, 1. Thus in Cleonai magi can avert such disasters by sacrifices and magical songs. Cl. Al., who tells us this (ibid., 2; cf. Plut. Ser. Num. Pun., 12 [II, 557 a-e]), naturally accepts the philosophical view : οὐκ ὀργίζεται τὸ θεῖον, Paed., I, 8, 68, 3, and censures the Greeks for whom the gods καθάπερ ὀξύχολον γραΐδιον[37] εἰς ὀργὴν ἐρεθιζόμενον ἐκπικραίνονται ᾗ φασι (Hom. Il., 9, 533-538) τὴν Ἄρτεμιν δι᾽ Οἰνέα Αἰτωλοῖς ὀργισθῆναι (Strom., VII, 4, 23, 2), so that men δεισιδαίμονες περὶ τοὺς εὐοργήτους (sc. θεούς) γινόμενοι πάντα σημεῖα ἡγοῦνται εἶναι τὰ συμβαίνοντα καὶ κακῶν αἴτια (ibid., 24, 1; cf. Tac. Historiae, II, 1). The final thought displays a religious attitude

---

restrict ourselves to the word ὀργή. All the Gk. terms which are interchangeably used for it have to be taken into account.

[32] Aristid. Apol., 8, 2 calls the Gk. gods Ὀργίλους; ὀργίλος is attested for Dionysus at least in the anon. hymn, Anth. Pal., 524, 16, and for Priapus in Anth. Pal., 240, 3.

[33] Cf. Paus., X, 32, 10 f.: ἐδήλωσε μὲν ὡς ἡ Ἀντιόπη δι᾽ ὀργὴν ἐκ Διονύσου μανείη. καὶ κατὰ αἰτίαν ἥντινα ἐπεσπάσατο ἐκ τοῦ θεοῦ τὸ μήνιμα.

[34] Ps.-Eratosthenes, Catasterismi, 24 (Mythographi Graeci, III, 1, p. 29, 6 ff.), cf. Apollodor. Bibliotheca, III, 4, 1 etc.

[35] In spite of the poetic term the Ζηνὸς ἱκεσίου κότος which is so strongly emphasised in Aesch. Suppl. (385, 343, 478, 616) must be regarded as a cultic concept; it recurs frequently in Paus., I, 20, 7; VII, 25, 1 as τὸ δὲ τοῦ Ἱκεσίου μήνιμα.

[36] Cf. the story of the placating of the ὀργή of the murdered Cleonike in the Nekyomanteion at Heraclea by Pausanias Plut. Cim., 6 (I, 482c).

[37] Though cf. Solon Fr., 1, 25 f. (Diehl), → 386.

such as is found especially among the Romans in their understanding of the *ira deum*.

III. *Ira Deum* in the Roman World.

In their writings the Romans at first accepted to a very large degree the same ideas about the wrath of the gods as are found in Greek poetry and mythology from the time of Homer. [38] The philosophical criticism then brought to bear against these is also much the same as in Greece. [39] Even the *manifesta caelestium ira* which inspires the moving of the statue of Serapis from Sinope to Alexandria derives from a Hellenistic cultic legend according to the explicit report of Tacitus (Hist., IV, 84). Nevertheless, there is among the Romans an original idea of the *ira deum* which is independent of Greek influence. This has its roots in the peculiar nature of their ancestral *religio*. It finds expression in the belief in prodigies, in which, according to Roman views, some divine wrath always comes openly into appearance and action: [40] *priore anno intolerandam hiemem prodigiisque divinis similem coortam, proxumo non prodigia sed iam eventus, pestilentiam agris urbique inlatam haud dubia ira deum, quos pestis eius arcendae causa placandos esse in libris fatalibus inventum sit*, Liv., 5, 14, 3. Usually aroused by *neglegentia caerimoniarum auspiciorumque* (Liv., 22, 9, 1), the *ira deum* is the cause of natural disasters, famine, sickness and plague in both town and country, 4, 9, 3. Of mass deaths in Rome Livy says in 40, 37, 2: *postremo prodigii loco ea clades haberi coepta est. C. Servilius pontifex maximus piacula irae deum conquirere iussus*. To avert disaster and re-establish the *pax deum* (27, 23, 4), i.e., good terms with the gods, there must be *piacula irae deum*, to use the tt., in the form of *preces, vota, dona, supplicationes* etc., 22, 9, 1; Lucan., I, 683. The expiatory rites and formal usage show that the *ira deum* is a concept and expression of the Roman cultus. Hence Cicero, though he knows and gives utterance to the general denial of the divine wrath by philosophy (→ 386), can find a place, in his sketch of ideal laws pertaining to relations with the gods, for the following statute for auguries: *divorumque iras providento* (i.e., before they find expression in punishments) *isque* (= *iisque*) *apparento* (De Legibus, II, 21); and it is generally accepted that *impius ne audeto placare donis iram deorum* (22), [41] because the wrath of deity falls specifically on the *impius*. [42] As one may call on the gods in prayer to direct their anger against the wicked and against enemies, [43] so in the solemn oath he who swears asks that in case of perjury the wrath of Father Jupiter, Mars Gradivus

---

[38] Lucretius De Rerum Natura, V, 399 ff.; Cic. Tusc., IV, 29 (63); Vergil Aen., 7, 305 (cf. Hom. Il., 9, 533 ff.); Georgica, III, 152 f.; Horat. Epodi, 10, 13 f.; Tacitus Ann., 3, 61.

[39] Lucretius De Rerum Natura, VI, 753 f.; V, 1194 ff.; VI, 70 ff.; II, 651; Cic. Nat. Deor., I, 16 f. (42, 45); III, 38 (91); Off., III, 102; Sen. De Ira, II, 30, 2.

[40] On what follows cf. H. Kleinknecht, "Laokoon," *Herm.*, 79 (1944), 82, 108 f.

[41] There are many refs. to the wrath of the gods in Cicero's speeches, Mil., 86; Pro Q. Roscio, 46; Pro Caelio, 42; In Pisonem, 59.

[42] Cf. Horat. Epodi, 10, 13 f.; *Pallas usto vertit iram ab Ilio in inpiam Aiacis ratem*; Carmina, I, 3, 38 ff.: *neque per nostrum patimur scelus iracunda Iovem ponere fulmina*. Tac. Ann., 1, 30: *durabat et formido caelestis irae, nec frustra adversus impios hebescere sidera, ruere tempestates*.

[43] Cf. Liv., 9, 1 and 8: *precabor, ut iras suas vertant in eos* ...; Horat. Epodi, 5, 53 f.: *nunc nunc adeste, nunc in hostilis domos iram atque numen vertite*. But cf. the criticism of Seneca: *deus est: tam perdis operam cum illi irasceris, quam cum illum alteri precaris iratum*, De Ira, II, 30, 2.

and other gods will fall on him: *si fallat, Iovem patrem Gradivumque Martem aliosque iratos invocat deos,* Liv., 2, 45, 15. In particular, the *ira deum* which falls on those who despise the gods has an established place in cultic legends and stories of visitation, Liv., 2, 36, 5; 9, 29, 11; Tac. Ann., 14, 22. Pious faith often embellished such stories so that sometimes the historian leaves the truth open: *et vera esse et apte ad repraesentandam iram deum ficta possunt,* Liv., 8, 6, 3. In general, both among the populace and in the army, religion, i.e., the scrupulous observing of signs, often became superstition, especially in times of crisis, when even contingent and purely natural happenings could be interpreted as signs of divine anger: *quod in pace fors seu natura, tunc fatum et ira dei vocabatur,* Tac. Hist., IV, 26. Thus, e.g., at the burning of the corpse of the murdered Britannicus there was such a cloudburst *ut vulgus iram deum portendi crediderit adversus facinus,* Tac. Ann., 13, 17.[44] Finally, Minucius Felix traces back to fear of the gods the ready acceptance of all possible cults by the Romans in the course of their history.[45] There may also be seen here a proof of their distinctive religiosity as decisively affected by the concept of the *ira deum.*

According to the Roman view, however, the stability of state and government rested essentially on *religio.* Hence the *procuratio* of prodigies and the related placating of the *ira deum* were not just a matter of very widespread public concern. Disastrous events in political and historical life, e.g., inner dissension, the strife of classes, civil war and mutiny (Tac. Ann., 1, 39; Hist., II, 38) were also brought into connection with *irae deum* or *numinum: factiones ... bella externa ... fames morbique, quaeque alia in deum iras velut ultima publicorum malorum vertunt,* Liv., 4, 9, 3. The wrath of the gods was seen to be particularly at work in *cladibus exercituum aut captivitate urbium,* and references to it are part of the style of Roman historical description, Tac. Ann., 16, 16. The divine anger brought about the destruction of Corinth and Carthage,[46] the defeats at Trasimenus (Liv., 22, 9, 1), at Cannae[47] and in the Teutoburger Wald.[48] It was also responsible for the reign of terror of a Sejanus or Nero (Tac. Ann., 4, 1), or the destruction of the Capitol in 69 A.D. (Tac. Hist., IV, 54).

Religious guilt, *neglegentia caerimoniarum auspiciorumque,* but also *temeritas* and *inscitia,* are mostly responsible for bringing down the wrath of the gods, who themselves will often point to or even directly command[49] the seeking of ways and means of expiation. The supreme way, and the climax of older Roman *religio* and *virtus,* is the sacrifice of one's own life in the rite of devotion, which according to tradition was performed for the first time by the consul of 340 B.C., P. Decius Mus, in the decisive battle of the Latin War. In this case animal sacrifices aver-

---

[44] Cf. Tac. Ann., 1, 30 and the philosophical criticism in Sen. De Ira, II, 27, 2: *dementes itaque et ignari veritatis illis* (sc. *dis immortalibus, qui nec volunt obesse nec possunt) imputant saevitiam maris, inmodicos imbres, pertinaciam hiemis.*

[45] Octavius, 7, 2: *eos* (sc. *maiores) deprehendes initiasse ritus omnium religionum, vel ut remuneraretur divina indulgentia vel ut averteretur imminens ira aut iam inruens et saeviens placaretur,* → 385.

[46] Cf. Cic. Nat. Deor., III, 38 (91).

[47] Liv., 25, 6, 6; cf. Valerius Maximus, I, 1, 16: *creditum est Varronem consulem apud Cannas cum Carthaginiensibus tam infeliciter dimicasse ob iram Iunonis.*

[48] Dio C., 56, 24, 2: τό τε γὰρ πάθος οὐκ ἄνευ δαιμονίου τινὸς ὀργῆς ... ἐδόκει οἱ (sc. Augustus) γεγονέναι.

[49] Liv., 22, 9, 7 f.: *quaeque piacula irae deum essent ipsos deos consulendos esse,* is the view of the dictator Q. Fabius Maximus after the disaster of Lake Trasimenus.

runcandae deum irae were ineffectual. Hence the consul solemnly devoted himself and the hostile army to death. His figure appeared to all as more exalted than a purely human frame. He seemed to be sent from heaven as an expiation for *all* divine wrath, which thus fell on the enemy and destroyed them : *augustior humano visu, sicut caelo missus piaculum omnis deorum irae, qui pestem ab suis aversam in hostes ferret*, Liv., 8, 9, 10. By means of the image *sicut caelo missus* which interprets the event, the voluntary, substitutionary, sacrificial death which enraged deity demands is changed for Livy into an act of divine grace which obviously wills that religious guilt should be expiated inasmuch as it sends, at the supreme moment of the crisis, a man who *omnis minas periculaque ab deis superis inferisque in se unum vertit* (Liv., 8, 10, 6), [50] so that the *pax deum*, [51] good relations between the gods and men, are restored.

In Roman historians this cultic and religious form of thought took on a historical significance which it had never had for the Greeks. The *ira deum*, closely bound up with *fatum*, [52] plays a momentous role in the whole of Roman history. In close inner tension Tacitus always finds the same *hominum rabies* and *deum ira* at work, Tac. Hist., II, 38. He constantly speaks of this because the very existence of Rome is threatened thereby : *ira illa numinum in res Romanas fuit, quam non, ut in cladibus exercituum aut captivitate urbium, semel edito transire licet*, Ann., 16, 16. It is thus more than a poetic device adopted from the great model, Homer, when in Verg. Aen. [53] the divine wrath is a controlling motive behind the action and an impelling force in the fulfilment of the destiny which has led Aeneas to Latium *fato profugu(m) ... multum iactatu(m) ... vi superum saevae memorem Iunonis ob iram*, Aen., 1, 2 ff.; cf. 1, 130; 5, 781. The proeomium closes with the question : *tantaene animis caelestibus irae?* (1, 11). Divine beings and human seers constantly refer to this wrath of the heavenly ones : *omnem cursum mihi prospera dixit religio et cuncti suaserunt numine divi Italiam petere ...; .. sola novum dictuque nefas Harpyia Celaeno prodigium canit et tristis denuntiat iras*, 3, 362-366. This is based on the Roman outlook, as may be seen from the related cultic usage, the connection with the *prodigium*, and the rite which in what follows is designed to implore the *pax deum*, 369 ff. *Ira deum* and *fata* are the negative and positive sides of one and the same thing. Hence they cannot be separated, whether it be that Athena proclaims to Aeneas through her priest Nautes : *vel quae portenderet ira magna deum vel quae fatorum posceret ordo* (Aen., 5, 706 f.), or whether it be that the anger of the gods smites the enemies of the Trojans and thereby gives them to understand : [54] *fatalem Aenean manifesto numine ferri*, 11, 232 f. When Aeneas is at the goal, there appears to him in a dream the god of the Tiber river with the consolation and direction : *irae concessere deum ... Iunoni fer rite preces iramque minasque supplicibus supera votis*, 8, 50 f., 60 f.; cf. Liv., 8, 33, 7: *preces ... deorum iras placant*. The wrath of the gods or of Juno, which is here appeased, is simply a metaphysical expression for the severe reverses and more than

---

[50] Cf. G. Stübler, "Die Religiosität des Livius," *Tübinger Beiträge zur Altertumswissenschaft*, 35 (1941), 181-201; on the historicity cf. F. Altheim, "Der Opfertod der Decier," *Forschungen u. Fortschritte*, 17 (1941), 112 f.

[51] This is the true counterpart to the *ira deum*, cf. *deum benignitas* (Tac. Ann., 12, 43; Hist., V, 85), *indulgentia numinum* (Ann., 13, 57), *favor erga nos deorum* (Germania, 33).

[52] Cf. Liv., 25, 6, 6; Tac. Hist., IV, 26 and 54; Ann., 1, 39.

[53] Cf. in the novel : *me ... sequitur gravis ira Priapi* (Petronius Satirae, 139; cf. 134), Chariton, VIII, 1, 3 (Erotici Scriptores Graeci, II, 136, 4 f.).

[54] *Admonet ira deum*, cf. Liv., 2, 36, 6.

human opposition [55] with which the actualisation of destiny has to wrestle in its temporal and historical course. In Vergil, then, an epic form taken from the poetic tradition of the Greeks is filled with the religious content of a genuinely Roman understanding which, by virtue of its explicit reference to history, represents a new and essential feature in the ancient view of the wrath of the gods.

Kleinknecht

B. The Wrath of Men and the Wrath of God in the Old Testament.

I. The Hebrew Terms for Wrath and Being Wrathful.

Hebrew is rich in terms for wrath, each of which originally denotes a specific aspect of anger. a. The most common of these words is אַף, which derives from אָנַף "to be angry," originally "to snort," [56] so that the basic meaning may well be "snort." [57] Hence the meaning "nose," "nasal cavity." In the OT the nose is less the organ of smell (Am. 4:10; Ps. 115:6) than that of wrath; when God's anger waxes hot (חָרָה אַף) there comes smoke from His nostrils, Ps. 18:8. אַף and the much rarer אַפַּיִם [58] occur some 210 times in the OT, 170 times for divine wrath and 40 for human. The combination חָרָה אַף is found in the most varied OT books, but predominantly in the older Pentateuch sources and the historical books. [59] The verb אָנַף occurs only 14 times, 8 in the q and 6 in the hitp. It is always used of God. Though this might seem to suggest a specific usage, the fact that אַף or אַפַּיִם can be used for human anger, and the rare occurrence of אָנַף, are reasons for caution. b. The most common synonym of אַף is חֵמָה, from the root יָחַם, "to be hot," "passionate." This can be used for the "heat" of wine (Hos. 7:5), "excitement" of spirit (Ez. 3:14), and the "poison" of serpents (Dt. 32:24; Ps. 58:4; 140:4) or poisoned arrows (Job 6:4). But it most commonly (115 times) denotes the "wrath" or "rage" of God (90 times) or man (25). c. Exclusively for God's wrath the Mas. has חָרוֹן, which in 33 of 39 occurrences [60] is used in the expression חֲרוֹן אַף. On the other hand, the related חֳרִי, which occurs only 6 times and always in the expression חֳרִי אַף, can denote the anger of man (4 times) as well as that of God (2). The nouns חָרוֹן and חֳרִי derive from חָרָה, which in the q relates only to wrath (divine or human, some 80 times), and which in derived stems can have the sense "to be zealous," "to act with zeal." The basic sense is probably "to burn," "to glow." Hence the nouns, with אַף, denote the "burning of wrath," the "fire of anger." On the basis of the exclusive ref. of the q of חָרָה to wrath, [61] חָרוֹן is to be interpreted as wrath in the few instances in which it occurs without אַף d. עֶבְרָה in the sense of "anger" does not come from the common root עָבַר I "to overflow," "to go over," with Arab. ʿAjin, [62] but from עָבַר II, the less common root, Arab. ğabira, which seems to mean "to be angry," "to be full of rage." עֶבְרָה "wrath" is used 24 times with ref. to God, 6 with ref. to men. The verb עָבַר II occurs in the OT only in the hitp and in the sense "to be angry" (of both God and

---

[55] Cf. Vergil Aen., 7, 315 : *at trahere atque moras tantis licet addere rebus.*

[56] L. Köhler, *Lexicon in Veteris Testamenti libros* (1948 ff.), 70.

[57] *Ibid.,* 75, or is the noun original, the verb derived from it ?

[58] This is used for "wrath" in, e.g., Ex. 15:8 and Prv. 30:33, but esp. in the expressions קְצַר אַפַּיִם and אֶרֶךְ (אֹרֶךְ) אַפַּיִם.

[59] Cf. on חָרָה what is said about חָרוֹן and חֳרִי → *infra.*

[60] Ps. 58:9 and Jer. 25:38 are not included, since the text is uncertain ; Ps. 88:16 חֲרוֹנֶיךָ.

[61] חָרָה occurs with אַף 50 times, without אַף with a dat. of person (e.g., וַיִּחַר לוֹ) 26 times, elsewhere with בְּעֵינַיִם (Gn. 31:35; 45:5).

[62] Whence עֶבְרָה I "presumption," "arrogance" (Is. 16:6; Jer. 48:30; Prv. 21:24).

men, 7 times in all). e. The verb קָצַף (in the q 28 times),[63] whence קֶצֶף perhaps has the basic sense "to break out," from which it is an easy step to "to fly out," "to be angry."[64] While the verb is used for both divine and human anger, the noun is predominantly employed for God's wrath (26 times) and only twice (Qoh. 5:16; Est. 1:18, both late writings) for man's anger or annoyance.[65] f. The verb זָעַם (OT 12 times), which means "to address angrily," "to scold," "to chide," but also "to curse," gives us the noun זַעַם which orig. denotes anger expressed in words of chiding.[66] Thus it can be said of the lips of Yahweh in Is. 30:27: שְׂפָתָיו מָלְאוּ זַעַם. In 5 of the 6 passages in which it is used of God[67] the verb unequivocally denotes His wrath, and even in the 6th this is possible (Nu. 23:8), though one cannot rule out here the sense "to curse." In the 5 instances in which it is used of men, it never seems to demand the sense "to chide."[68] In Mi. 6:10 the pass. part. q is used of an obj., the abominably scant ephah. Thus the verb is used only for the divine wrath. In keeping is the noun זַעַם, which in its 22 occurrences denotes exclusively God's wrath.[69] Furthermore the verb and noun are used only in poetic texts, mainly later. זַעַם finds a special use in apocalyptic writings, where it can perhaps mean the "time of wrath," cf. Is. 26:20; Da. 8:19; 11:36, → 405. g. The related root זָעַף is very much less common. In the 4 instances of the verb זָעַף (basic meaning "to storm," "to rage"?) it is used of men and things. Only at Prv. 19:3; 2 Ch. 26:19 does it mean "to chide." The verbal adj. זָעֵף "cross," "angry," is found in 1 K. 20:43; 21:4. The noun זַעַף is twice used in relation to God, 4 times in relation to men, and fig. for the raging of the sea in Jon. 1:15. Like the verb זָעַף (except for Gn. 40:6) it occurs only in post-exilic writings. h. כָּעַס has in the q (6 times) the sense "to be annoyed," "to be reluctant," "to be angry," and in the pi (twice) and hi (almost 50 times) the causative sense "to anger," "to annoy," "to provoke to wrath," almost always with God as obj. The hi is predominant in Dt., in the historical books edited along the lines of Dt. (Ju. and K.), and in the parts of Jer. submitted to similar revision. The pt. is that Israel provokes God to anger by its apostasy and idolatry. The noun כַּעַס — always in the form כַּעַשׂ in Job (cf. 5:2; 6:2; 10:17; 17:7) — is used 8 times of God, 17 of man, and means "annoyance," "displeasure" ("anger"?).[70] i. Since the verb רָגַז means "to be disturbed," "unsettled" — also once in the hi (Job 12:6) "to provoke to wrath" — the much less common noun רֹגֶז means "raging," "unrest," also "anger." As distinct from the verb, which can be used for joyful stimulation (Jer. 33:9), it is more restricted in sense. רֹגֶז occurs only 7 times, and it is fig. for the unrest of life and the raging of man against God. Only in Hab. 3:2 does it denote God's wrath. The verb occurs some 40 times in works of all periods, the noun only in later writings.

---

[63] hi (5 times) "to provoke to anger."

[64] Hos. 10:7 uses קֶצֶף in the concrete sense ("shavings" or "froth"); does this perhaps come from another stem (Ges.-Buhl קֶצֶף II)?

[65] Unlike the verb, it occurs almost always in later writings, esp. P and the Chronicler (though cf. 2 K. 3:27); on the abs. use → 396.

[66] Köhler's rendering "to curse," "to berate" (262) is too restricted; the same is true of his transl. of זַעַם as simply "cursing"; cf. Is. 10:5, where זַעַם is par. to אַף.

[67] Is. 66:14; Zech. 1:12; Mal. 1:4; Ps. 7:11; Prv. 22:14.

[68] Nu. 23:7 par. אָרַר, Nu. 23:8 and Prv. 24:24 par. קָבַב; Prv. 25:23 "cross," Da. 11:30 "to curse."

[69] This is also true of Jer. 15:17 (cf. 6:11). There is a textual error in Hos. 7:16 (cf. LXX); acc. to T. H. Robinson, Die zwölf kleinen Propheten (1938), 30 זַעַם can here perhaps mean "insolence." זַעַם יהוה does not occur, but זַעַם with suffix in relation to Yahweh 11 times; otherwise (without or with art.) abs. (e.g., Is. 26:20; Da. 8:19; but also Ez. 22:24; Ps. 78:49), very typical of the later period.

[70] Qoh. 2:23; 5:16; 7:3; 11:10 "trouble."

k. רוּחַ is hardly to be called a true term for wrath, though in the nuance "snort" it comes close to this sphere ; cf. קְצַר־רוּחַ par. אֶרֶךְ אַפַּיִם Prv. 14:29. [71] רוּחַ is found along with אַף in Job 4:9 (מֵרוּחַ אַפּוֹ).

Grether-Fichtner

II. The Wrath of Men.

Though in essence the same terms are used for divine and human wrath, there are considerable material differences between the two conceptions. We shall deal first with human anger in the OT. The usual objects of this in the OT are individuals — whether Israelites [72] or not [73] — though sometimes also groups of men and nations [74] or their rulers. [75] As far as other nations are concerned, the ref. is to their raging, their arrogant military wrath, against God's people. [76] This is a threat (Am. 1:11; Is. 51:13; Ez. 35:11), but it is declared to be puny in face of the protection of Yahweh (Is. 7:4; Ps. 124:3).

1. Against Other Men. The anger of men is mostly against other men. [77] This is a just and holy anger in so far as it is not concerned only with maintaining one's own rights. [78] Thus David, when Nathan appeals to him as supreme judge, is furious with the unjust rich man of the story (2 S. 12:5). So, too, is Nehemiah when confronted by the abuses in Jerusalem (Neh. 5:6). Cf. also Saul's wrath against the Ammonites, which is attributed to the Spirit of Yahweh (1 S. 11:6). Things are much the same in the case of Shechem's offence against Dinah, which provokes the anger of her brothers (כֵּן לֹא יֵעָשֶׂה), who exact a terrible revenge (Gn. 34:7). [79] Again, one might refer to David's anger against Amnon when he raped Tamar (2 S. 13:21), though in this and the previous instance the anger is not quite so disinterested, since the honour and even the existence of the clan are at stake. On the other hand, one can speak esp. of holy and righteous anger when it is a matter of directly championing the cause of Yahweh against the violation of His claim to lordship or the disregarding of His holiness. Thus Moses grows angry at the Israelites' lack of trust in God (Ex. 16:20), at their apostasy at the mount of God (32:19, 22), at the forbidden sparing of the Midianite women (Nu. 31:14), and at cultic transgression (Lv. 10:16). There are similar reasons for the wrath of Elijah (2 K. 13:19) [80] and Elihu (Job 32:2, 3, 5). In particular, however, one must refer to the prophets as the messengers of God's anger, and among them esp. Jer. and Ez. [81] Jer. has to say of himself : "I am full of the fury of the Lord" (6:11; cf. 15:17), and this wrath is expressed in many of his sayings, and those of other prophets, against God's people or the Gentiles. [82]

The anger of men can also be purely selfish when they feel that their actual or supposed claims are violated. [83] Examples are Cain against Abel in Gn. 4:5, Esau against

---

[71] Cf. Is. 30:28 (God snorts with anger); 25:4; Prv. 16:32; 29:11 (of men).

[72] E.g., Moses in Ex. 32:19; Samuel, 1 S. 15:11; David, 2 S. 6:8; Uzziah, 2 Ch. 26:19.

[73] Potiphar in Gn. 39:19; Pharaoh, 40:2; Naaman, 2 K. 5:12; Sanballat, Neh. 4:1; Haman, Est. 3:5.

[74] Princes of the Philistines, 1 S. 29:4; enemies of the righteous, Ps. 7:6; Edom, Am. 1:11; Babel, Is. 51:13.

[75] Nebuchadnezzar, Da. 3:13; Ahasuerus, Est. 1:12.

[76] Or against other nations, Is. 14:6; Da. 11:44.

[77] Only once do we hear of anger or annnoyance at an animal (Balaam's ass), Nu. 22:27.

[78] The verse from Ps. 4:4 quoted in Eph. 4:26 (ὀργίζεσθε καὶ μὴ ἁμαρτάνετε) hardly belongs to this context. It does not envisage the possibility of righteous anger, but warns against allowing annoyance to become sin in word or act.

[79] In the blessing of Jacob it is interesting that this anger of Dinah's brothers is condemned, Gn. 49:5-7. This is perhaps because it exceeded all due bounds, H. Gunkel, *Genesis*[5] (1922), *ad loc.*

[80] Cf. also Elijah's measures against the prophets of Baal (though without the tt. wrath), 1 K. 18:40.

[81] → n. 121, 122.

[82] Sometimes there seems to be here a tendency to overhasty identification of the national cause with that of God, esp. in post-exilic prophecy.

[83] The boundary between wrath and displeasure is hard to fix. Sometimes the ref. seems

Jacob in 27:44 f., Balak against Balaam in Nu. 24:10, Saul against Jonathan, 1 S. 20:30, the tribes of Israel against Judah, 2 S. 19:43, Pharaoh against his servants, Gn. 40:1 f., Potiphar against Joseph, Gn. 39:19, Ahasuerus against Queen Vashti, Est. 1:12. The anger of those concerned can also be kindled against the demand or threat of a man of God, [84] e.g., Ahab against Elijah, 1 K. 20:43, Asa against the reproach of the seer, 2 Ch. 16:10, Uzziah against the prohibition of the priests, 2 Ch. 26:19.

2. Against God. Man's anger or displeasure can also be directed against God Himself when His dealings seem to be enigmatic and incomprehensible, and cannot be brought into harmony with His righteousness, e.g., Samuel on the rejection of Saul, 1 S. 15:11, [85] David on the death of Uzzah, 2 S. 6:8, Job under his undeservedly severe affliction, Job 11:2 f.; 18:4, and Jonah at God's showing mercy to Nineveh, Jon. 4:1, 4, 9. [86] At root the anger of the righteous at the prosperity of the wicked is also directed against God and His rule, Ps. 37:1, 7 f.; Prv. 3:31 f. [87]

3. Evaluation. Only the Wisdom literature attempts a true evaluation of human anger. [88] The sages of Prv. measure it by utilitarian standards in accordance with the general view of chokma. Anger is dangerous because it does mischief and has evil consequences, Prv. 6:34; 15:1; 16:14; 19:19; 27:4. It is thus to be avoided and placated, 15:18; 22:24; 29:8, 11. There is warning against even understandable anger at the prosperity of the wicked, whose punishment will come, 24:19 f.; Ps. 37:7-9. Hence the longsuffering man (אֶרֶךְ אַפַּיִם or אֶרֶךְ־רוּחַ) is lauded as the true sage (Prv. 14:29; 15:18; 16:32; Qoh. 7:8), while the angry man (קְצַר־רוּחַ or קְצַר־אַפַּיִם)[89] is condemned as a fool, Prv. 14:17, 29. The wise are naturally aware that the wrath of man leads to injustice, (Prv. 14:17: אִוֶּלֶת; 29:22 : פֶּשַׁע). The Epistle of James, which is close to the Wisdom literature, takes up this theme in 1:20 : ὀργὴ γὰρ ἀνδρὸς δικαιοσύνην θεοῦ οὐκ ἐργάζεται, → 421. The antithesis angry man — sage, which occurs in Prv., does not have its roots in Gk. philosophy but in Egyptian wisdom, [90] where the fool can be called a hot-headed person. [91] Job's anger against God is sharply condemned by his friends because Job not only damages himself thereby (18:4) but also undermines the fear of God (15:4) and attacks God's justice (8:2 f.; cf. 11:2 f. etc.). God's speeches formally endorse this verdict, though at much greater depth (Job 38 ff.), and Job repents of the disrespectful speeches he made in his anger, and humbles himself (42:6).

III. The Wrath of God.

1. Linguistic Discussion.

In the OT the terms for wrath more often indicate the wrath of God than that of men. [92] Some words are used in the OT writings exclusively for God's wrath, i.e., חָרוֹן

---

to be not so much to an elemental outburst of anger but rather to an expression of vexed displeasure at an unexpected and unwelcome event, Gn. 30:2; 31:35 f.; 44:18; 1 S. 29:4; 1 K. 21:4; 2 K. 5:12.

[84] This is basically against God Himself by whom these men realise that they are sent.
[85] Kittel's alteration of וַיִּחַר to וַיֵּצֶר (Kautzsch) is unnecessary.
[86] In 1 and 2 S. the LXX has ἀθυμεῖν for חָרָה לְ, in Jon. 4 λυπεῖσθαι.
[87] Note in Prv. 3:31b דְּרָכָיו; for תִּבְחַר read תִּתְחַר (hitp of חרה).
[88] לֹא־תִטֹּר in Lv. 19:18 forbids vengefulness and vindictiveness.
[89] Cf. בַּעַל אַף, אִישׁ חֵמוֹת (Prv. 22:24) and בַּעַל חֵמָה, אִישׁ־אַף (29:22).
[90] Cf. J. Fichtner, Die altorientalische Weisheit in ihrer isr.-jüdischen Ausprägung (1933), 20 f.
[91] Cf. Amenemope : "Associate not with the hot-headed man," AOT, 41, c. 9; cf. J. Hempel, Althbr. Lit. (1930), 51.
[92] Nouns for wrath are used some 375 times for the wrath of God, 80 times for that of men.

or חֲרוֹן אַף, זַעַם and the verb אָנַף, others are used predominantly in this way, namely, קֶצֶף [93] and עֶבְרָה, while אַף and חֵמָה and the rarer זַעַף (and רֹגֶז) denote both divine and human anger. It is possible that חֲרוֹן or חֲרוֹן אַף [94] and זַעַם [95] were in fact reserved for the wrath of God in the living use of the spoken language, but there is too little to go on to be certain about this. What is significant is that combinations of terms for wrath are used only to denote the wrath of God. [96] Apart from the constructions חֲרוֹן אַף (33 times), [97] זַעַף אַף (Is. 30:30), זַעַם־אַף (Lam. 2:6), and עֶבְרוֹת אַף (Job 40:11), we find syndetic associations of two or three terms: אַף and חֵמָה (15 times), עֶבְרָה וַחֲרוֹן אַף (Is. 13:9), מִפְּנֵי־זַעְמְךָ וְקִצְפֶּךָ (Ps. 102:10), בְּאַף וּבְחֵמָה וּבְקֶצֶף גָּדוֹל (Dt. 29:7, cf. Jer. 21:5: 32:37) and חֲרוֹן אַפּוֹ עֶבְרָה וָזַעַם וְצָרָה (Ps. 78:49); there are related forms in Dt. 9:19; Ez. 5:15; 13:13. The accumulations, in which אַף or חֲרוֹן אַף is always the chief term except at Ps. 102:10, express the qualitative difference between God's wrath and man's by vividly showing the power of the divine anger, before which no one can stand, Ps. 76:7; Nah. 1:6. When a term for wrath is combined with a designation of God we usually find יהוה. Over 50 times אַף, חֵמָה, עֶבְרָה and קֶצֶף are associated with this. [98] Only twice do we find אַף־אֱלֹהִים, Ps. 78:31 — in the E Psalter (Ps. 42-89) where אֱלֹהִים is used for יהוה [99] — and Nu. 22:22, where other witnesses have יהוה. [100] In Ezr. 10:14 אֱלֹהֵינוּ, which is in fact almost identical with יהוה, is linked with חֲרוֹן אַף, and finally we find חֲמַת שַׁדַּי in Job 21:20, which is not surprising in view of the avoidance of the name Yahweh in the dialogue sections of Job. The consistent linking of nouns for wrath with Yahweh, the covenant God, is of supreme theological significance. It shows that the idea of wrath is closely bound up with belief in the covenant. [101]

At a later period there is obviously an attempt to loosen and even dissolve too close an association of God with wrath. This may be seen linguistically in the abs. use of the word, cf. esp. קֶצֶף in the post-exilic period, and particularly the Priestly writers. In P קֶצֶף יהוה does not occur at all. We once have יָצָא הַקֶּצֶף מִלִּפְנֵי־יְהוָה (Nu. 17:11), and elsewhere only קֶצֶף (Nu. 1:53; 18:5; Jos. 9:20; 22:20; probably also 22:18 [102] and Lv. 10:6). [103] The Chronicler has קֶצֶף יהוה twice (2 Ch. 29:8; 32:26), but also the indeterminate קֶצֶף (1 Ch. 27:24; 2 Ch. 19:2; [104] 19:10; 24:18; 32:25). Satan is used at 1 Ch. 21:1 for the wrath of God which in 2 S. 24:1 provokes David to hold a census. In both authors, of course, we find אַף יהוה, but in the Chronicler this is mainly in material from older sources. Distinctive in both is the abs. use of the term, and this calls for notice. Very infrequently, and only later, other words are used without direct ref. to Yahweh. [105]

---

[93] The verb קָצַף for both divine and human wrath.

[94] Perhaps in conscious differentiation from חֳרִי אַף.

[95] Cf. also the verb זָעַם.

[96] We are not counting the occurrence of synonyms in parallelism (40 times, only 3 for human anger).

[97] חֳרִי אַף is used 4 times for human anger.

[98] Of these אַף יהוה some 40 times.

[99] The basic Nu. 11:33 has אַף יהוה.

[100] 1 MS of Mas., Samaritanus, LXX F and N (Targ Onk).

[101] In Gn. there is no term for the wrath of God.

[102] For יִקְצֹף read יִהְיֶה קֶצֶף acc. to the LXX (ἔσται θυμός) Syr, Targ (cf. v. 20), but not M. Noth, Das Buch Josua (1938), ad loc., who more recently has come to see in Jos. 22:9-34 a very late addition, Überlieferungsgeschichtliche Studien (1943), 232.

[103] Here, too, LXX reads ἔσται θυμός, Mas. עַל כָּל־הָעֵדָה יִקְצֹף.

[104] Here with מִלִּפְנֵי־יהוה.

[105] J. Boehmer, "Zorn," ZAW, NF, 3 (1926), 320-322 mentions many other instances of the unrelated use of terms for wrath, but these need not concern us here.

Thus we find חֲרוֹן אֶל כָּל־הֶהָמוֹן at Ez. 7:12, [106] חֲרוֹן אַף עַל־יִשְׂרָאֵל at 2 Ch. 28:13, and אַתֶּם מוֹסִיפִים חֲרוֹן עַל־יִשְׂרָאֵל at Neh. 13:18. [107] In Is. 63:5 the wrath of Yahweh is singularly distinguished from Yahweh : וַתּוֹשַׁע לִי זְרֹעִי וַחֲמָתִי הִיא סְמָכָתְנִי; though the next v. shows that this is no more than poetic personification. On זַעַם in the abs. → n. 69.

2. Objects.

The idea of God's wrath in the OT is particularly characterised by the fact that in Israel there was basically only one God, [108] so that there could be no invoking of a pantheon or demons, [109] and also by the fact that there was a special relation to this God, established by His holy righteousness and electing love. For the righteous of the old covenant, therefore, the source of wrath was not an unknown deity or a merely sensed power of fate, but one "unequivocally distinct divine person." [110] This does not mean that the irrational element was completely excluded from the concept of God — closer examination of the idea of divine wrath will make this plain — but it does mean that the OT knowledge of faith and control of life are in their backward look to history, their attitude to the present and their forward glance to the future, fundamentally set in one direction. Nowhere do they encounter an obscure or indeterminate power, but the personal will of Yahweh with which it is necessary to come to terms. The personal element in the OT view of God shapes in a special way the anthropopathic form of what is said about wrath, but also gives it its urgent vitality. [111] The danger that too strong anthropopathisms will erase the borders between God and man is averted by the strong sense of distance which the righteous of the OT feels in relation to God [112] and also by the profound insight into the nature of divine wrath. The result is a differentiation from human anger, which has its root predominantly in the domineering ego of man. [113]

In the OT the message of the wrath of God is not identical with the depiction of His judicial acts. [114] It has in view not merely an action but a process in God Himself, an "emotion" on the part of God. [115] It is true, however, that this emotion does not affect the being of God as such. [116] It relates only to the being which He has established outside Himself, i.e., the world and its entities. Hence when the OT speaks of the wrath of God it is proper to ask concerning the objects against which it is directed.

---

[106] The words do not occur in LXX B; they are found also in v. 14, but with חֲרוֹנִי.

[107] J. Boehmer's thesis (321) that the abs. use of terms for wrath gives evidence of an original belief in "demons which are not yet subdued and assimilated by the supreme deity" is refuted by the late development of this use.

[108] Though cf. M. Jastrow, Die Religion Babyloniens u. Assyriens, I (1905), 362, 477-479; only in 2 K. 3:27 does the OT plainly refer to the anger of another god, Chemosh of the Moabites : וַיְהִי קֶצֶף גָּדוֹל עַל־יִשְׂרָאֵל (LXX καὶ ἐγένετο μετάμελος [!] μέγας ἐπὶ Ισραηλ), → IV, 627, n. 4.

[109] → II, 10 ff.; cf. F. Baumgärtel, Die Eigenart d. at.lichen Frömmigkeit (1932), 36.

[110] G. Quell, → III, 1062.

[111] Cf. W. Eichrodt, 98-100.

[112] Cf. J. Hempel, Gott u. Mensch im AT² (1936), 198, 267 f.

[113] On the holy and righteous anger of man → 394.

[114] The wrath of God does, of course, embody itself in judgment, cf. wrath and judgment : Ez. 5:15 שְׁפָטִים par. תּוֹכְחוֹת חֵמָה; Mi. 7:9; Ps. 7:6; wrath and vengeance : Ez. 24:8 לְהַעֲלוֹת חֵמָה לִנְקֹם נָקָם; Nah. 1:2.

[115] Cf. F. Weber, 11.

[116] Such an idea is never even considered in the OT.

a. In the first instance God's anger is directed against Israel itself. Even at the concluding of the covenant it threatens those who might infringe the majesty of Yahweh (Ex. 19 JE), and in the story of the wilderness wanderings it plays an important role in both J and E [117] and also in D and P. [118] It is also a recurrent factor in the story of the people from the conquest (cf. Jos. 7 JE ?; 22:20 P) to the exile (1 S. 6:19; 15; 28:18; 2 S. 6:7; 24:1). The Deuteronomistic view of history portrays this period wholly from the standpoint of continual provocations of God's wrath (→ 403), and the Chronicler, too, can speak of this wrath (1 Ch. 13:10; 27:24; 2 Ch. 19:2; 24:18; 29:8), as can also the historical psalms (e.g., 78:31; 106:32). [119] In this respect, especially in the earlier period, the collective solidarity of the individual with the totality of the people is plain. God's wrath is directed against the individual in his specific function in the people of God, e.g., against Moses (Ex. 4:14, 24; Dt. 1:37), Aaron (Dt. 9:20), Miriam (Nu. 12:9), Nadab and Abihu (Lv. 10:6), also kings and prophets (1 S. 15; 2 K. 23:26; 2 Ch. 29:8; Jer. 21:1-7). On the other hand, wrathful judgment may come on the whole people because of the sins of individuals (Achan's theft in Jos. 7, David's census in 2 S. 24). The collective link was weakened later (cf. Ps. 6:1; 27:8; 38:1).

Among the prophets those who came before the exile were the ones who especially made God's wrath against His people the central theme of their message, though they do not all use the term wrath, cf., e.g., Amos. [120] The conflict of these men is against the false assurance of the people which is grounded in the sense of election and which feels secure against wrath and judgment (Am. 3:2; 5:18; Hos. 13:9-11; Is. 5:18 f.; 28:14-22; Mi. 3:11; Zeph. 2:2; Jer. 7:4; 28:1-17; Ez. 5:13; 16:38). Among them Jeremiah [121] and Ezekiel [122] can be numbered as prophets of God's wrath against His people. The prophets during and after the exile see in the exile an outworking of the wrath of Yahweh; [123] they speak less than their predecessors of the destructive pouring out of this wrath on the people, but they realise, especially after the return, that the wrath of Yahweh is still upon His people (Hag. 1:5-11; Zech. 1:3, 12), or still threatens it (Jl.; Is. 64:8), and we catch the same note in the laments of the period (Ps. 74:1-8; 85:4, 6).

b. Along with Israel the nations and their rulers are also objects of God's wrath. Prophetic threats are aimed at them in the so-called Gentile oracles of Am., Is., Jer. and Ez. and the prophecies of Zeph., Ob., Nah., Hab., Jl., cf. also Jonah. [124] In particular the prophets of the exilic and post-exilic period proclaim God's wrath against the nations, Is. 13:3, 5, 9, 13; 30:27; 59:18; 63:3, 6; 66:14; Jer. 50:13, 15; 51:45; Ez. 25:14; 30:15; Jon. 3:9 etc. [125] Similarly the psalms which sing of the eschatological victory of Yahweh and His anointed threaten the nations with God's wrath, Ps. 2:5, 11; 110:5. When this breaks forth, the whole earth (cf.

---

[117] Ex. 32; Nu. 11:1, 10, 33; 12:9; 13:25-14:38; 25:3, 4.
[118] Dt. 1:34, 37; 9:8, 19 f.; Nu. 17:11; 18:5; 25:7-13; 32:10-14; Lv. 10:6.
[119] Cf. also the exhortations in Dt. (6:15; 7:4; 11:17; 29:19 ff.) and the corresponding sections of the Priestly tradition (Lv. 26:28; Nu. 1:53; Jos. 22:18; 2 Ch. 19:10). It is highly significant that in the legal corpora of the Pentateuch the impending wrath of God is only rarely made a reason for obedience, Ex. 22:23; Lv. 26:28.
[120] A basic pt. is that we refer primarily to passages which use the tt. wrath, but occasionally also to those which have the concept without the tt.
[121] Jer. 4:4, 8, 26; 7:20, 29 (דּוֹר עֶבְרָתוֹ); 17:4; 32:31; 36:7 etc.
[122] Ez. 5:15; 6:12; 7:8; 8:18; 14:19; 16:38; 20:8 etc. Cf. A. Ruegg, RE³, 21, 720.
[123] Is. 42:25; 47:6; 51:17; 54:8; 60:10; Zech. 1:2, 12.
[124] Cf. H. Gressmann, Der Messias (1929), 97-148.
[125] Sometimes specific nations are mentioned, sometimes just the nations in general.

Dt. 32:22) and all mankind (Jer. 10:10; Is. 13:9, 11; Zeph. 3:8) will be affected, just as His wrath smote all men in primitive antiquity, Gn. 3; 6-8; 11.

3. Exercise.

To depict the sway of God's wrath, its effects and instruments, very different parts of the OT tradition have to be considered. [126] One thing connects the various aspects of God's sovereign anger. When it threatens or breaks forth, the existence of those concerned is at stake. Conversely, when existence is at stake, the man of the old covenant detects the wrath of his God.

The destructive power and irresistible force of the divine wrath may be seen in the metaphors and figurative expressions used to portray it. We must distinguish here between metaphors which, taken from a different sphere from that of anger, illustrate a typical feature of God's active wrath, and conceptions which are not merely used as figures but represent the concrete manifestations of this wrath. A good example of the latter is the predominant picture for God's wrath, which vividly expresses its destructive effect, namely, fire. When Yahweh's holiness is infringed, His anger is kindled, [127] fire burns in His nose (Jer. 15:14; 17:4; cf. Is. 65:5), smoke comes forth from it (Ps. 18:8), [128] His tongue is כְּאֵשׁ אֹכֶלֶת, Is. 30:27. [129] Nor does burning and consuming fire merely depict God's anger; it also portrays its concrete operation. "The breath of the Lord, like a stream of brimstone, will burn in it (Tophet)," Is. 30:33, cf. Dt. 32:22; Ez. 22:31. The fig. use and concrete depiction of the fire of wrath may fuse directly into one another, cf. Ez. 21:36 f.; Is. 30:27-33. It is thus plain that these biblical statements are not just fig. in our sense. What applies to fire applies no less to the storm, which portrays the power to devastate. This is less common than the image of fire, Jer. 30:23; cf. Is. 30:30; Ps. 83:15 [130] and also Is. 2:6-22. Related to the idea of the storm is that of Yahweh snorting; this lies behind the use of רוּחַ (→ 394) and may be seen in the etym. of אָנַף and אַף, → 392.

Along with the thought of God's wrath as fire or storm is that which depicts it in as a fluid. This occurs in the image of the pouring out (שָׁפַךְ and נָתַךְ) and drinking of wrath. Yahweh also pours out His anger over His people and the Gentiles like water: עֲלֵיהֶם אֶשְׁפּוֹךְ כַּמַּיִם עֶבְרָתִי Hos. 5:10; cf. Jer. 10:25; Ps. 69:24 and esp. Ez. 7:8; 14:19; 20:8 etc. The figure of pouring can be combined with that of fire: חֲמָתוֹ נִתְּכָה כָאֵשׁ, Nah. 1:6; cf. Lam. 2:4 and in parallel verses or their members Ez. 21:36; 22:31. Whether the ref. here is to fire and brimstone (Ez. 38:22) or to streams of pitch (cf. Is. 30:33; 34:9), or whether the accumulation of images is meant to bring out the greatness and horror of judgment, it is hard to say. On the other hand, the metaphor of drinking wrath is purely fig., cf. Job 21:20 [131] and esp. the wine of wrath in Jer. 25:15 [132] and the cup of wrath in Is. 51:17, 22; Jer. 25:15 (→ III, 168; V, 165). [133] This expresses very vividly the

---

[126] Cf. 2 S. 6:7; 24:1 with Jer.'s preaching of wrath or Nu. 1:53; 17:11 with the experience of God's wrath in Job.

[127] Mostly חרה, also בער Ps. 2:11; יצת 2 K. 22:13 and יקד, Jer. 65:5.

[128] In Dt. 29:19 and Ps. 74:1 "to smoke" means "to chide."

[129] Cf. also the etym. of חָרָה and → 392.

[130] It is worth noting that the LXX renders סוּפָה (ψ 82:15) as well as סַעַר and סְעָרָה (Ιερ. 37:23) by ὀργή.

[131] "He shall drink of the wrath of the Almighty."

[132] הַיַּיִן הַחֵמָה occurs only here; the words are sometimes regarded as a gloss. But the LXX (τοῦ οἴνου τοῦ ἀκράτου) is against this; did it read חֶמֶר (fermenting wine) for חֵמָה?

[133] The LXX transl. כּוֹס חֲמָתוֹ in Is. 51:17, 22 by τὸ ποτήριον (or τὸ κόνδυ) τοῦ θυμοῦ (Rev. 14:10 has τὸ ποτήριον τῆς ὀργῆς (!) αὐτοῦ along with ὁ οἶνος τοῦ θυμοῦ).

ineluctability of wrath and its draining even to the dregs.[134] The prophet who hands over the cup (Jer. 25:15-28) brings judgment irrevocably on Jerusalem and the nations.[135]

The weapons of God's wrath and agents of His chastisements are the nations when there is ref. to them as the כְּלֵי זַעַם (Is. 13:5; Jer. 50:25),[136] or as שֵׁבֶט אַף or מַטֶּה זַעַם (Is. 10:5).[137] This vivid image expresses the common OT view that God vents His wrath through earthly powers. We also find the more abstract view that His arm serves as the instrument of His anger, Is. 30:30; 63:5; Jer. 21:5; cf. Ez. 20:33; Is. 9:11.

There is in the expressions for the beginning and ending of God's wrath something of the ambiguity of the terms for wrath. If the ref. is to the emotion, one reads for the most part of the kindling or rising of wrath, or of Yahweh stilling it, Ez. 5:13; 6:12; Lam. 4:11. If the ref. is to the act, one reads of the bringing (2 Ch. 36:16), sending (Job 20:23; Ps. 78:49), or executing of His wrath (1 S. 28:18; Hos. 11:9). Perhaps the same duality is to be seen in the varied use of שׁוב for the ending of wrath : Yahweh ceases from His anger (Ex. 32:12; 2 K. 23:26; Jon. 3:9, often with נָחַם) or diverts it (הֵשִׁיב, Jer. 18:20; Job 9:13; Ezr. 10:14), or His anger turns aside (Jer. 4:8; Is. 5:25; Jos. 14:5). But this last expression can also mean that the anger has abated (not merely that judgment has ceased), so that caution is required in relation to the usage now before us. For the coming of anger the later period (P and the Chronicler) uses the weaker expression הָיָה קֶצֶף (Nu. 1:53; 18:5; Jos. 22:20; 1 Ch. 27:24 etc.).

In its radical operation the wrath of Yahweh aims at destruction, at full extirpation. Thus we read in the exhortations of Dt.: וְחָרָה אַף יְהֹוָה בָּכֶם וְהִשְׁמִידְךָ מַהֵר Dt. 7:4 (cf. 9:8, 19, 25 etc.), or in P : וַאֲכַלֶּה אֹתָם כְּרֶגַע, Nu. 16:21; 17:10. The prophets, too, proclaim to Israel and the Gentiles the all-destructive wrath of Yahweh, Ez. 22:31; 43:8; Is. 30:28; 34:2, 5; 63:1-3; Jer. 50:13. It should be noted in this connection that the prophets[138] do not merely depict God's anger in powerful images of cosmic proportions, impressing all creation into service to this end (Is. 13:13; 30:30; 34:2-4; 66:15 ff.; Ez. 38:22 etc.), but also set it in concrete relation to historical occurrence and its magnitudes. Thus they interpret national oppression and defeat, both past and present, as the sway of Yahweh's wrath manifested to Israel in individual blows. Is. closes his great poetic threat with the refrain : בְּכָל־זֹאת לֹא שָׁב אַפּוֹ וְעוֹד יָדוֹ נְטוּיָה 9:11, 16, 20; 10:4; 5:25,[139] and according to him Yahweh delivers up the people of His anger to the Assyrian, His rod, 10:5 f.; cf. 9:10 f.[140] For Israel judgment takes especially the form of banishment from the land (passim). In the predictive and retrospective preaching of the prophets the exile is the main example of God's sovereign and judicial wrath. Similarly, the ancient traditions revised and interpreted in the history books tell of the destructive force and terrible scale of Yahweh's wrath, which finds expression in drought and famine, plague and pestilence, high mortality and deliverance up to enemies, Nu. 11:1, 10, 33; 12:9; 17:11; 1 S. 6:19; 2 S. 24 etc. With sinister and elemental power

---

[134] Is. 51:17 מָצִית (thou hast emptied).

[135] The picture of the winepress of wrath is also found ; Is. 63:1-6.

[136] Ιερ. 27:25 literally transl. τὰ σκεύη ὀργῆς, Is. 13:5 — in view of the ἔθνος ὁπλομάχον of v. 4 — οἱ ὁπλομάχοι.

[137] שֵׁבֶט עֶבְרָתוֹ is a figure of speech for wrath in Lam. 3:1; cf. Job 9:34 שִׁבְטוֹ and 21:9 שֵׁבֶט אֱלוֹהַּ; Prv. 22:8 שֵׁבֶט עֶבְרָתוֹ (of human anger).

[138] Cf. the Deuteronomistic interpretation of history, → supra.

[139] Cf. Am. 4:6-12 (no tt. for wrath).

[140] The nations are also instruments of His wrath against other nations to execute judgment, i.e., to destroy them, Is. 13:5; Jer. 50:25.

this wrath is kindled and snatches away thousands [141] or smites individuals who have dared to draw near to the Holy One, Ex. 19; 2 S. 6:7. That there is not here the same concrete historical reality as in the prophetic interpretation of history is of lesser significance in this context.

Prophetic preaching, perhaps adopting earlier national expectations, [142] increasingly looks beyond historical interpretation to the message of eschatological wrath and judgment in which Yahweh will make good His claim in face of all opposing powers and bring history to an end. The earlier prophets proclaim this judgment not merely on the Gentiles but also on the people of God which has turned aside from Him. [143] In this sense they can speak of the day of Yahweh, the day of wrath, as an eschatological event, Am. 5:18-20; Is. 2:6-21; Zeph. 1:15, 18. For Israel there is no escaping it, except that individuals may be sheltered by timely conversion, Zeph. 2:1-3. For this judgment will come ineluctably. Only by Yahweh's love and covenant grace will it come about that wrath will not be fully executed against Israel but a time of salvation will be ushered in by judgment and will avert God's wrath. In the post-exilic period, and especially in later Judaism, the coming judgment of wrath is to be primarily on the Gentiles (Ps. 9:16 f.; 56:7; 79:6-8) and on the wicked and ungodly in the congregation (Ps. 7:6; 11:5 f.; 28:4; 94:2), while the righteous within God's people believe they are protected from approaching wrath by experienced forgiveness of sins, Ps. 30:5; 65:3 ff.; 103:3. Even in this period, however, there can be no question of assurance of salvation, of solid confidence that coming wrath will be escaped. For all the experience of forgiveness, the wrath which rests on the community and its members can never permit a satisfactory answer to the question of the final pacification of the divine anger, → 408.

In the destiny of the righteous as individuals the wrath of God, as may be seen especially in later witnesses, [144] is experienced in various handicaps and mortal threats. Sickness, persecution by personal enemies, the threat of premature death, the sense of remoteness from God, are all signs of wrath, e.g., Ps. 88:16; 90:7, 9 f.; 102:8, 10 f., 23. This may be seen very impressively in Job. Here the righteous man feels that he is smitten by the wrath of God, who has taken from him not only goods and health but also justice and honour, [145] and who displays to Him His hiddenness in His wrath, → infra and 406, 33 ff.

4. Motives.

The question of the motives for the divine wrath leads to a discussion of its innermost nature, and hence to an integration of the concept of the wrath of God into the total view of God according to OT belief. A series of witnesses in the OT writings makes it apparent that the wrath of Yahweh was fundamentally an irrational and in the last resort inexplicable thing which broke out with enigmatic,

[141] Nu. 17:14, 14,700; Nu. 25:9, 24,000; 1 S. 6:19, 50,070; 2 S. 24:15, as many as 70,000.
[142] Cf. H. Gressmann, Der Ursprung der isr.-jüdischen Eschatologie (1905), 144 f.
[143] In the prophets one cannot always distinguish clearly between the historical and the eschatological dominion of wrath; cf. → 405.
[144] We are not considering here the individual acts of wrath mentioned → supra, e.g., 2 S. 6:7.
[145] Cf. F. Baumgärtel, Der Hiobdialog (1933), 174.

mysterious and primal force. [146] This insight may be gathered from Gn. 32:23-33 (Jacob's wrestling at Jabbok) and Ex. 4:24 f. (Yahweh's falling on Moses). It may also be seen in various places where we have the sinister and death-dealing intervention of the holy God whom man may not behold face to face (Ex. 33:20; Ju. 13:22; Is. 6:5), and who destroys everything which violates His holiness (Ex. 19:9-25; 20:18-21; Nu. 1:52 f.; 1 S. 6:19; 2 S. 6:7). In 2 S. 24:1, where Yahweh tempts David to hold the census, the motif of the unfounded and incomprehensible wrath of Yahweh is plain (cf. also 1 S. 26:19 : אִם־יְהוָה הֱסִיתְךָ בִי). It is placated according to 2 S. 21:14, but breaks out afresh in 24:1, cf. also 1 K. 22:20 f. How strongly a later period resisted this interpretation of wrath may be seen from the Chronicler's modification of 2 S. 24:1; Satan now replaces the wrath of God as the author of David's temptation, 1 Ch. 21:1. The complaints of individuals in the Psalter, and especially the Book of Job, also bear testimony to the feeling of the righteous that they are often delivered up without cause to the wrath of Yahweh. Thus the author of Ps. 88, who has no guilt to confess, complains before Yahweh that he has suffered His terrors from his youth : עָלַי עָבְרוּ חֲרוֹנֶיךָ, v. 15, and Job accuses God with the words : "His wrath teareth me and attacketh me (אַפּוֹ טָרַף וַיִּשְׂטְמֵנִי), he gnasheth upon me with his teeth" (16:9); "he hath also kindled his wrath against me (וַיַּחַר עָלַי אַפּוֹ) and he counteth me as one of his enemies" (19:11). It is true that one cannot place these later witnesses directly among those of earlier accounts of sinister outbreaks of divine wrath, since the post-exilic righteous measure their lot by the standard of strongly individual retribution, and this was not so consistently applied earlier. Nevertheless, there is in both instances an awareness of being exposed to an act of God which in its incomprehensibility borders closely on caprice and in which, as one might better put it, there is encounter with the incalculable One, the Wholly Other, the *tremendum*. [147] Here the element of inconceivable power and holiness in Yahweh outweighs the other motives of action. This incomprehensible and awe-inspiring action is not to be explained in terms of an absorption of the ancient belief in demons (→ n. 107). It must be clearly affirmed that the "demonic element" in Yahweh "is not in the last resort imported into His nature, but is there from the very first . . ., it is bound up with the innermost being of this God and His religion." [148]

Increasingly, of course, Yahweh's dealings are lifted out of the sphere of the incalculable, and there is closer investigation of the reasons for His wrath. [149] This is seen to be a reaction to the acts or failures of men. In relation to Israel Yahweh is the God who has declared His will to save in promise and guidance, and who demands full consecration from His people, i.e., exclusive worship, perfect trust and the observance of prescribed requirements. He is the covenant God who has given promise and Law and therewith bound Israel exclusively to Himself.

Thus, according to all the Pentateuch sources, His wrath smites the people or groups within it when they rebel against His saving will, when they murmur against His guidance in the wilderness (Nu. 11:1 [E]; 17:6-15 [P]; 13:25-14:38 [JE]; Dt. 1:34-36). The failure of Achan to observe the ban (Jos. 7:1; 22:20) and the

---

[146] P. Volz, 7-17.

[147] Otto, 21, 97; cf. Volz, 12 etc.

[148] Volz, 33.

[149] Job's speeches in the first phase of the discussion are shot through by the search for a reason for God's anger, (3:11;) 7:20; 10:18; 13:24.

sparing of Agag, king of the Amalekites, by Saul (1 S. 15), provoke Yahweh's wrath. [150] In particular, the obvious apostasy of the people from its God, its turning to other gods, is a constantly recurring reason for divine wrath against Israel. [151] From Ex. 32 (the golden calf) by way of Nu. 25 (Ba'al Pe'or) we move through the exhortations of D (Dt. 11:16 f.; 12:23-13:19; 29:15-17; Jos. 23:16) to the depiction of history in Judges and Kings according to the Deuteronomic pattern, [152] and we find the well-known scheme of the apostasy of the people, which provokes (הִכְעִיס) Yahweh thereby, so that in His wrath He sells Israel to other peoples etc. [153]

This brings us to the central motive for God's wrath against Israel. It is found in all its breadth and depth in the prophets. These never weary of emphasising what Yahweh has done for Israel with His election and guidance, [154] and this is the background against which they bring their message of the wrath of Yahweh. [155] At the back of every individual prophetic charge, whether it refers to the cultus [156] or to social injustice, [157] to a policy which trusts in armaments and alliances, [158] or even to the worship of other gods, [159] there stands finally the one great complaint, namely, that the people has forgotten its God, turned from Him, and despised His love. [160] This is the deepest root of the concept of wrath, and in this light one can understand the overwhelming force of the message. It is Yahweh's wounded love which awakens His wrath. [161] The wrath of God is correlative to His קֹדֶשׁ, to His חֶסֶד, to the turning of Yahweh to Israel, which is the basis of the covenant relationship. This point is clarified by the fairly common linking of the idea of Yahweh's zeal (קִנְאַת יהוה, → II, 878-880) with that of His chiding. [162] קִנְאַת יהוה is grounded in the relation of the holy God to the elect people. [163] But the election carries within it God's gracious turning to Israel and His demand for the loyalty and obedience of this people. If Yahweh's love is not reciprocated by the people, if it turns aside to other gods, His jealousy burns. This finds expression in wrath (Dt. 32:20 f.; cf. Ps. 78:58; 79:5), and it casts out Israel, the unfaithful wife (Ez. 16; 23). As may be seen in post-exilic writings, however, the same expression קִנְאָה can also denote Yahweh's zeal for His people, in which He interposes Himself as a loving husband when Israel is threatened by other nations

---

[150] In the historical presentation and exhortation of P the whole field of cultus and ritual is fenced off by God's wrath. Nadab and Abihu, who offer אֵשׁ זָרָה (an improper burnt offering ?), are destroyed by the fire of Yahweh's wrath (Lv. 10:1 f.). A wrong attitude on the part of the priests can easily bring down wrath on the congregation (Lv. 10:6). This is also provoked by desecration of the Sabbath (Neh. 13:18).

[151] A. Ritschl has rightly pointed out that the true reason for God's wrath is *defectus a foedere*, though he has overworked the thesis.

[152] Dt. 4:25; 9:18; Ju. 2:14; 3:8; 10:7; 1 K. 14:15; 16:33; 2 K. 17:17; 21:6; 22:17 etc.

[153] There are similar motifs in the Chronicler, 2 Ch. 12:1-7; 16:7-12; 25:14-18 etc.

[154] Cf. Am. 2:9-11; 3:2; Hos. 11:1-6; Is. 1:2; 5:1 f.; 17:10; Jer. 2:1-3; 31:1-3; Ez. 16:4-14.

[155] E.g., Hos. 5:10; 8:5; 13:11; Is. 9:11; Jer. 4:4; 17:4; Ez. 5:13; 7:3; 20:8 etc.

[156] Am. 5:21-27; Hos. 6:6; Is. 1:10-17; Jer. 6:20; 7:21-28.

[157] E.g., Am. 5:7, 10-12; Is. 1:15-17; Mi. 3:1; Jer. 5:28 etc.

[158] Cf. Hos. 5:13; 7:11; Is. 30:1-5; 31:1-3; Jer. 2:35-37; Ez. 16:23 etc.

[159] Or the supposed worship of Yahweh in alien cultic forms.

[160] → n. 154.

[161] Eichrodt, 125.

[162] קִנְאָה is sometimes linked with terms for wrath : Dt. 29:19; Ez. 16:38; 36:6 and parallel to them : Dt. 6:15; Ez. 5:13; 16:42; Zeph. 3:8; Ps. 79:5; Nah. 1:2 (אֵל קַנּוֹא par. וּבַעַל חֵמָה).

[163] Cf. F. Küchler, "Der Gedanke des Eifers Jahves im AT," ZAW, 28 (1908), 42-52.

(Is. 42:13; 59:17; 63:15), and zealous in His wrath destroys the nations, but brings salvation to His own people (Zech. 1:14 f.; 8:2 f.; Nah. 1:2).

Great sections of the message of God's wrath against the Gentiles may be brought under this motive. This is particularly clear in the post-exilic period, which experienced the attack of the nations on Israel's existence, the hatred of Edom, and the destructive urge of Babylon and other nations. [164] An attack on Israel was an attack on Yahweh Himself; the honour of the people was His honour, Is. 48:9-11 and esp. Ez. Though perhaps exaggerated and expressed one-sidedly in the post-exilic period, this is a genuine concern of prophecy. The same theme dominates the older historical writing when it seeks to portray the execution of Yahweh's redemptive purpose in face of the enemies of His people, Ex. 23:27-30; Jos. 24:12; Nu. 24:18. [165] The sustaining basis of this motive for Yahweh's anger against the nations is His absolute claim to dominion over the whole world, which is directed against the arrogance of the nations (cf. Gn. 11) and their rulers, against their self-glorying, and also against transgressions of commandments which are of general validity. Thus Is. proclaims Yahweh's judgment on the Assyrian who is the rod of His anger, because in his own power he has gone beyond the limits set for him, Is. 10:5-15; cf. 14:4-6; 16:6; Ez. 25:15-17; 28:1-17; Zech. 1:15. Similarly, His anger (Dt. 29:22) is directed against the immorality of Sodom and Gomorrah (Gn. 19), the irreverence of the Moabites (Am. 2:1), and the wickedness of Nineveh (Jon. 1:2). [166] In the final judgment of the world Yahweh's holiness will finally be set up on the whole earth, → 401.

We also find in the OT proclamation of the rule of God's wrath over the whole of human life. The burden and finitude of human life is explained in terms of the divine wrath provoked by the pride of men and the consequent burden of guilt. From the fall of the first man (Gn. 2-3) this line leads through primitive history by way of the first murder (fratricide, Gn. 4), the increasing corruption of men (Gn. 6-8), and their heaven-storming plans (Gn. 11) to the final judgment of the Psalmist: כִּי כָלִינוּ בְאַפֶּךָ וּבַחֲמָתְךָ נִבְהָלְנוּ (Ps. 90:7), which finds its basis in the reference to human guilt: שַׁתָּ עֲוֹנֹתֵינוּ לְנֶגְדֶּךָ, v. 8; cf. also Job 14:1-4: "Man that is born of woman is of few days, and full of trouble ... How could a clean thing come out of an unclean?" [167] Here all human life, being sinful, stands under the constant operation of the wrath of God.

5. Outbreak, Duration and Turning Aside.

When we ask concerning the outbreak, duration and turning aside of wrath, a distinction has again to be made between its historical and its eschatological exercise. In this section we shall concentrate for the most part on wrath in history (on the eschatological aspect, cf. → 401. In the history of His people Yahweh's wrath takes effect in individual acts and especially in the banishment of the people. In this sense there can be reference to the day of wrath which is expected, or

---

[164] Jer. 10:25 (late): "Pour out thy fury on the heathen that know thee not ... for they have eaten up Jacob"; cf. Zech. 2:1-4; Mal. 1:3 f. etc.

[165] Cf. Ritschl, *Rechtfertigung u. Versöhnung*, II, 128.

[166] The detailed ethical motives for Yahweh's wrath against the nations are comparatively rarely given in the OT.

[167] G. Hölscher, *Das Buch Hiob, Hndbch. z. AT*, I, 17 (1937), ad loc., strikes out the last words on rhythmic grounds ("metrical deficiency"), but he can hardly be right, cf. Job 4:17.

which has already dawned, as a historical event, → II, 944 f. The application may be to the fate of the people (Ez. 7:19; 22:24; Lam. 1:12, 21; 2:1, 21 f.) or to that of the individual (Job 20:28; 21:30; Prv. 11:4). [168] Not infrequently, and mostly in the historical books of the OT, there is reference to the sudden nature of the outbreak of wrath, to its direct onslaught. It smites like lightning those who have sinned against Yahweh, Ex. 19:12; Nu. 11:33; 12:9; 17:6-11; 25:9-11; 2 S. 6:7.

On the other hand, the OT bears ample testimony to Yahweh's longsuffering (→ IV, 376-379) in which He does not give free rein to His anger but restrains Himself and waits, Ex. 34:6 f.; Nu. 14:18; Nah. 1:3; Is. 48:9; Ps. 103:8. By individual blows He warns and admonishes Israel to turn before His wrath involves complete destruction. The prophetic writings all bear witness to this both in wrath-sayings (cf. Am. 4:6-11; Is. 9:11 and par.; Jer. 4:4) and also in those about Yahweh's wooing love already referred to above (→ n. 154). In His merciful turning to Israel [169] Yahweh either refrains from giving effect to His wrath (cf. especially Hos. 11:9) [170] or exercises clemency towards His people. [171] In His longsuffering He gives Israel space for repentance and conversion. This is also true of His long-suffering towards Nineveh about which Jonah complains (4:2). Elsewhere Yahweh's restraint towards the enemies of His people (Jer. 15:15; Ps. 7:6; 77:9 etc.) is for the purpose of testing and chastising His people on the one side and bringing out the guilt of their enemies the more plainly on the other.

The question of the duration of wrath in its historical exercise is repeatedly put by those who sigh under its outworking. Jer. already has the people ask: הֲיִנְטֹר לְעוֹלָם אִם יִשְׁמֹר לָנֶצַח (3:5), and he proclaims to it the saying of Yahweh: שׁוּבָה... כִּי חָסִיד אֲנִי.. לֹא אֶטּוֹר לְעוֹלָם (3:12). [172] In the exile there awakens the hope that God's anger at His people is at an end (Is. 40:2; cf. Ps. 103:9). The reason for this is given in the well-known words of Dt. Is.: "In a little wrath I hid my face from thee for a moment, but with חֶסֶד עוֹלָם [173] will I have mercy on thee ... I have sworn not to be wroth with thee," 54:8-10. And yet even after the exile the question of the duration of wrath recurs constantly in the Psalter (Ps. 79:5; 85:5; 89:46) and in prophetic sayings (Hag. 1:5-11; Zech. 1:3, 12). More strongly than before the exile the community of God detects in its existence, and the individual in his destiny, the divine anger resting upon it. This experience later produces in apo-calyptic the insight that there is a time of wrath which must run its course before the time of grace can dawn, Is. 26:20; Da. 8:19; 11:36; → 393. This will bring, it is hoped, the end of wrath. On the other hand, in relation to Yahweh's enemies out-side Israel the message is proclaimed that His anger against them is eternal: נֹקֵם יְהוָה לְצָרָיו וְנוֹטֵר הוּא לְאֹיְבָיו (Nah. 1:2), and in Mal. 1:4 Edom is even described as הָעָם אֲשֶׁר זָעַם יְהוָה עַד־עוֹלָם. Here the historical and the eschatological views of wrath overlap. At the same time there is expressed here the fact that Yahweh's wrath against the nations is the reverse side of His gracious turning to Israel. The op-

---

[168] At Job 21:30 read בְּיוֹם עֶבְרָתוֹ.

[169] Yahweh's longsuffering has its basis in חֶסֶד and רַחֲמִים, → II, 479-482.

[170] "I will not execute the fierceness of mine anger ...; for I am God, and not man; a Holy One in the midst of thee; I do not come to destroy."

[171] Cf. Ex. 34:6 f.; Nu. 14:18; Nah. 1:3 ("and leave not wholly unpunished").

[172] The verses do not belong to the same context, but are materially related.

[173] The Is. scroll has חסדי עולם (to be pointed חַסְדֵי עוֹלָם), "with eternal demonstrations of grace"; cf. The Dead Sea Scrolls of St. Mark's Monastery, I (1950), Plate 45.

ponents of Yahweh (and His people), who hamper His plan of salvation, are destined for complete destruction.

To avert the destructive wrath of Yahweh and to maintain for Israel the good-pleasure and mercy of its God is the aim of the Law and also of prophetic preaching. [174] For Yahweh is an אֵל קַנָּא who punishes sins. Thus a Deuteronomic exhortation concludes with the words : "Yahweh, thy God, might otherwise be angry with thee, and destroy thee from off the face of the earth," Dt. 6:15. The later period ascribes to the cult and its ministers the decisive role in protecting the people from the impending wrath of God. The Levites are to encamp as a protective wall about the מִשְׁכַּן הָעֵדוּת "that there be not wrath upon the congregation of the children of Israel," Nu. 1:53. [175]

On the other hand, when the wrath of Yahweh strikes, the people has no such means to placate it as are known and used in the world around. There are no magical practices wherewith to conjure the deity. [176] Everywhere the point is plain that the turning aside of wrath depends finally on the free will of Yahweh and must be an act of merciful giving. [177] Prayer for an averting or mitigation of wrath is addressed to the mercy of Yahweh ; [178] we find examples already in the question as to the duration of wrath (→ 405), and also elsewhere — cf. the Deuteronomistic schema. [179, 180] Intercession for those threatened or already smitten by wrath appeals similarly to God's mercy. This is how Moses prays for the apostate people (Ex. 32:11 f., 31 f.; Nu. 11:1 f.; 14:11-13; Dt. 9:19; Ps. 106:23) or for guilty individuals (Nu. 12:13; Dt. 9:20). This is also how Amos prays for Israel (7:2, 5), Jeremiah for Judah (14:7-9; 18:20), or Job for his friends (42:7 f.). Such intercession is heard by Yahweh, and wrath is limited in its outworking (Nu. 14; Dt. 9) or completely turned aside (Nu. 11; 2 S. 24). But the time may come when Yahweh will no longer give heed to intercession (Am. 7:8; 8:2; Ez. 14:14) or even forbid His servant to engage in it (Jer. 7:16). Then nothing can avert wrath, and it is exercised relentlessly and irresistibly (Ez. 8:18; 14:14). The decisive ground of intercession — reference to Yahweh's total commitment to Israel (Ex. 32:12; Nu. 14:15 f.; Ps. 74:2), His mercy and His covenant faithfulness (Nu. 14:18; cf. Dt. 13:18) — is sometimes amplified by a depiction of the weakness and creatureliness of those smitten by wrath. Thus Amos bases his request for Israel on the words : מִי יָקוּם יַעֲקֹב כִּי קָטֹן הוּא (7:2, 5), and the Psalmist : כִּי דַלּוֹנוּ מְאֹד (79:8). [181] In the Book of Job the creatureliness and impotence of man stand in particularly marked contrast

---

[174] Even the proclamation of ineluctable wrath always includes an appeal for conversion and penitence, in which alone there is hope of being preserved in the judgment of wrath.

[175] This provision certainly does not mean that the sphere of cultus and ritual is particularly exposed to the wrath of God, Cr.-Kö., 812.

[176] Eichrodt, 126; M. Jastrow, Die Religion Babyloniens u. Assyriens, I (1905), c. 16; Nu. 16:44 ff. contains a rite of atonement prescribed by Moses.

[177] This does not rule out the possibility that Yahweh will demand punishment and expiation for the fault committed.

[178] Cf. F. Heiler, Das Gebet² (1920), 87.

[179] "And when the children of Israel cried unto the Lord, the Lord raised up a deliverer to the children of Israel," Ju. 3:9 etc., → 403.

[180] Cf. also the prayer for the mitigation of wrath, Is. 64:8; Jer. 10:24; Ps. 6:1; 38:1, and the promise of Yahweh, Jer. 30:11.

[181] Cf. the reasons why Yahweh refrains from wrath in Is. 57:16; Ps. 78:39; cf. also F. Hesse, Die Fürbitte im AT, Diss. Erlangen (1950).

to the onslaught of divine wrath. It is true that in Job's speeches the main reference is to the hopeless abandonment to wrath of the man who does not know the divine love which is ready to pardon, but can see only God's terrible omnipotence, so that in his weakness he beseeches God to leave him alone, Job 7:1-20, 21; 9:18-22; 13:13-22; cf. 14, esp. vv. 1-6. In this connection it should be noted with reference to the present composition of the book that the reader is shown from the very first that in the enigmatic plight of Job we do not have the outworking of blind rage, but that there is a special reason for the severity of his lot. [182]

Since the wrath of Yahweh manifests His holiness, which is violated by defection from His covenant and the transgression of His statutes, He can link the turning aside of His wrath and His gracious turning to the people with punishment and expiation. Thus after the apostasy to Ba'al Pe'or His wrath against Israel is pacified when the guilty have been put to death (Nu. 25:1-5 [JE]) or when Phinehas set an example and thrust through two who were caught in the very act (25:6-11 [P]). [183] The same holds good when Achan and his family, who had taken what was under the ban, have been destroyed, Jos. 7:1, 25 f.; cf. 2 S. 21:14. Comparatively infrequently in the OT there is reference to the turning aside of divine wrath by expiatory offerings, Nu. 16:46; 2 S. 24:(17 ff.); Ps. 78:38 and also 1 S. 26:19; → III, 302-310. The prophets preach that the wrath of Yahweh may perhaps be averted only by complete turning from a wrong path, conversion, and repentance, Jer. 4:4, 8; 36:7; cf. Da. 9:16 etc. Dt. Is. promises the exiled people the ending of divine wrath when it has atoned for its guilt, "emptied the cup of wrath" (51:17, 22), and "received double for its sins," 40:2.

6. God's Wrath in relation to His Holiness, Righteousness and Pity.

Only once is Yahweh's wrath described as an essential trait in God, and in this case the wrath is against the enemies of Yahweh, not His people, Nah. 1:2: נֹקֵם יְהוָה וּבַעַל חֵמָה. [184] This fact should not blind us, however, to the indissoluble link between the proclamation of God's wrath and the whole message of the OT. The wrath of God is the onslaught of the holy God asserting and establishing His absolute claim to dominion. If, linguistically, the holiness of God is comparatively seldom brought into direct combination with His wrath (cf. Ps. 78:38-41), [185] the connection is materially incontestable. It may be seen in the fact that the wrath of God is constantly presented in expressions and metaphors which are related to those of theophany (cf. Ps. 18; Ex. 19; Is. 30; Hab. 3). Thus the divine wrath is understood and presented, not as the work of an objective power of fate, but as that of a personal subjective will. It describes an "emotion" in God [186] and its expression in attacks on all forces which oppose the holy will of God. This formula comprises Yahweh's wrath against Israel and the nations, against individuals and all mankind. In relation to the people of God, of course, the wrath

---

[182] J. Fichtner, "Hiob in der Verkündigung unserer Zeit," *Jbch. d. Theologischen Schule Bethel* (1950), 71 ff., 88.

[183] Hereby Phinehas expresses Yahweh's zeal among the people, Nu. 25:11.

[184] More common is אֵל קַנָּא (5 times in Ex. and Dt.) and קַנּוֹא (twice). The expression וְאֵל זֹעֵם בְּכָל־יוֹם in Ps. 7:11 is none too sure textually (cf. the LXX).

[185] Cr.-Kö., 810; holiness stands opposed to wrath in Hos. 11:9.

[186] Weber, 11.

of Yahweh has a very profound basis in the fact that it is proclaimed as an expression of the wounded holy love of Yahweh, as a reaction against the ingratitude and unfaithfulness of Israel towards His gracious turning to it. [187]

Naturally this does not mean that the wrath of Yahweh is identical with His justice. On the contrary, it is noteworthy that Yahweh's justice is never linked with His wrath, though in countless passages the reason for the exercise of divine wrath is to be found in the acts or failures of Israel (or men) which violate God's claim to lordship and transgress His demands. [188] Job even turns from the wrathful God who attacks him to the God who as his attorney will vindicate him, i.e., to the God of justice (Job 16:20 f.). [189] This makes it plain that the man of the old covenant is aware of the irrationality, incalculability and subjectivity of the divine wrath, and in relation to Yahweh's justice he is referred increasingly to His revealed will. There is good cause and reason for Yahweh's wrath, but it is hard to understand, let alone calculate or measure, its exercise, duration or end. Even the cause and reason may sometimes be enwrapped in complete obscurity, [190] so that to the eye of man, e.g., in the dialogues in Job or some of the Psalms, wrath and injustice seem very close to one another. In this light one may perhaps understand the varied request (Jer. 10:24; Ps. 6:1; 38:1) that Yahweh will be moderate in His wrath, i.e., that His anger will be within the framework of His justice and will not simply boil over. In the same light one may also understand the concern lest wrath will gain the upper hand in God, as in the question of the psalmist: "Has God forgotten to be gracious? Has he in anger shut up his tender mercies?" Ps. 77:9. [191] One can hardly take these or similar sayings as a basis for stating that "it is typical of the OT view of God that love and wrath in God are close to one another as in an oriental ruler, with no mutual adjustment." [192] On the contrary, the wrath of God against Israel is the reverse side of His love, with which it is very closely associated in the concept of His zeal, → 403. And if Dt. Is. gives us a glimpse into the conflict between wrath and pity in the heart of God, we are not looking into the heart of a tyrant who assigns anger and love capriciously. We see rather how חֶסֶד and רַחֲמִים restrain the surging wrath of Yahweh and cause mercy finally to have the upper hand in Him, Is. 54:8-10; cf. Jer. 31:20. Thus the psalmist can confess in his prayer: "A man stands but a moment under his wrath, but a life long in his favour" (Ps. 30:5), [193] and the song of praise in Is. 12 thanks Yahweh for turning aside His anger. Alongside these confessions of the divine pity there are of course, especially in the earlier period, intimations of ineluctable judgment on the people of God. Even in the later period after the exile, which expects God's

---

[187] Though this may well provide a common denominator for God's wrath in the OT, it should not be overlooked that its depiction varies considerably at different times and in the different OT witnesses.

[188] Eichrodt, 129.

[189] J. Hempel's observation: "God, being now controlled by wrath, needs to remember His true nature" ("Das Problem des Hiob," ZSTh, 7 [1929], 675, n. 2) is correct only in the sense of Job, who does not see the reason for his plight, and attributes it to the (unjustifiable) wrath of God.

[190] Or are yet to be sought, e.g., Jos. 7.

[191] Cf. Hab. 3:2: "In wrath remember mercy."

[192] J. Lindblom, "Zur Frage der Eigenart der at.lichen Religion," ZAW, Beih. 66 (1936), 135.

[193] Unless with Halevy we are to read נֶגַע for רֶגַע (H. Gunkel, Ps.⁴ [1926], 126).

wrath especially on the nations and the ungodly, there is even for the community no certainty of deliverance from the wrath to come, to which all transgressors are subject, cf., e.g., Jer. 30:24; Is. 13:11.

Fichtner

C. The Wrath of God in the LXX.

I. Usage.

1. ὀργή and θυμός.

In rendering the various Hebrew terms for wrath (→ 392-394), the LXX turns primarily to ὀργή and θυμός. [194] In etym. and meaning these words are originally distinct. The difference is that "θυμός denotes the emotion, ὀργή its manifestation and expression, θυμός the wrath which boils up, ὀργή the wrath which breaks forth." [195] In LXX usage, however, this distinction is completely lost. This will be proved by the following review of the use of ὀργή and θυμός and related verbs. In this regard there is no fundamental need to consider whether the terms denote God's wrath or man's. Only in special cases will express ref. be made to this.

a. ὀργή and θυμός are used together: in Dt. 9:19 Moses says with ref. to God's wrath on Israel: ἔκφοβός εἰμι διὰ τὴν ὀργὴν (אַף) καὶ τὸν θυμόν (חֵמָה); ψ 77:49 combines θυμὸν (עֶבְרָה) καὶ ὀργὴν (זַעַם) καὶ θλῖψιν (צָרָה) cf. also ψ 101:10; Mi. 5:14; Is. 13:9; Jer. 7:20; Ez. 5:13 etc. b. In parallelism the two terms are used interchangeably in half-verses acc. to the laws of Heb. poetry: Hos. 13:11: ἔδωκά σοι βασιλέα ἐν ὀργῇ (אַף) μου καὶ ἔσχον ἐν τῷ θυμῷ (עֶבְרָה) μου, Is. 34:2: θυμὸς (קֶצֶף) κυρίου ἐπὶ πάντα τὰ ἔθνη καὶ ὀργὴ (חֵמָה) ἐπὶ τὸν ἀριθμὸν αὐτῶν, cf. also Ez. 7:5; 22:31; ψ 2:5; 6:1; 37:1; 89:11; Prv. 15:1; 27:4 etc. The corresponding adj. and verbs are also found in parallelisms, e.g., Prv. 22:24: ἀνὴρ θυμώδης (בַּעַל אַף) and φίλος ὀργίλος (אִישׁ חֵמוֹת). c. The gen. constructions θυμὸς τῆς ὀργῆς (or θυμὸς ὀργῆς) and ὀργὴ τοῦ θυμοῦ (or ὀργὴ θυμοῦ) are used interchangeably, mostly for חֲרוֹן אַף, Ex. 32:12; Nu. 32:14; Jer. 4:26; ψ 68:24 etc., though sometimes for a single Heb. term, Job 3:17; 37:2 רֹגֶז; Ez. 23:25: חֵמָה, Is. 9:18; 13:13 עֶבְרָה. d. We often find θυμοῦσθαι ὀργῇ (Gn. 39:19; Jos. 7:1; Is. 5:25), more rarely ὀργὴ θυμοῦται (1 Βασ. 11:6; 4 Βασ. 23:26), the one always, the other almost always, for חָרָה אַף. The fig. etym. θυμοῦσθαι θυμῷ or θυμόν does not occur in the LXX acc. to Hatch-Redpath. More common than θυμοῦσθαι ὀργῇ is ὀργίζεσθαι θυμῷ, e.g., Ex. 22:23; Dt. 7:4; Ju. 2:14; ψ 105:40, and like the rare θυμὸς ὀργίζεται (Ju. 6:39; ψ 73:1; 123:3) this is almost always a rendering of חָרָה אַף. The fig. etym. ὀργίζεσθαι ὀργήν in Zech. 1:2, 15 corresponds to קָצַף קֶצֶף Mas.; in the form ὀργίζεσθαι ὀργῇ it occurs for הָיָה קֶצֶף in 2 Ch. 29:8. e. Quite astonishing is, in acc. with the Heb. original, the number of expressions with ὀργή or θυμός. We shall give only a selection and treat the two words as almost complete equivalents. [196] With either as subj. it may be said: ἀναβαίνειν (ψ 77:21; Ez. 24:8), γίνεσθαι (Jos. 22:20; Lam. 3:47), εἶναι (2 Ch. 19:10; Lv. 10:6), ἔρχεσθαι (Job 3:26;

---

[194] The ὀργή of God is mentioned over 200 times, that of man about 50, while the θυμός of God occurs 200 times, that of man 70. It is worth noting that in the LXX θυμός is used so often for God's wrath, and synon. with ὀργή, for the word does not denote God's wrath in profane Gk., Irmscher, 3 ff.

[195] Cr.-Kö., 807; cf. → 383.

[196] The first ref. offers an example of ὀργή (or ὀργὴ θυμοῦ), the second of θυμός (or θυμὸς ὀργῆς).

36:18 A), [197] ἐκκαίεσθαι (Dt. 29:19; Ιερ. 51:6), παύεσθαι (Job 14:13; Is. 1:24), ἀποστρέφειν (intr. Hos. 14:5; Jer. 23:20), ἀποστρέφεσθαι (Nu. 25:4; Da. 9:16), ἐκχεῖσθαι (4 Βασ. 22:13; Jer. 7:20 A) etc. As acc. obj. ὀργή and θυμός occur in dependence on ἐγείρειν (Prv. 15:1; Sir. 36:6), ἐκκαίειν (ψ 77:38; Job 3:17 B al), ἐξαποστέλλειν (ψ 77:49 a and b), ἀποστρέφειν (Prv. 29:8; ψ 77:38), συντελεῖν (Ez. 5:13; Lam. 4:11), ἐκχεῖν (Zeph. 3:8; Ez. 9:8). Other expressions with the words as obj. are infrequent; they both occur in dependence on the adj. πλήρης in Is. 30:27; Wis. 5:22, [198] and are also attributes of the nouns ἡμέρα (Job 20:28; Zeph. 2:2), [199] καιρός (Sir. 44:17; Jer. 18:23), πῦρ (Ez. 21:36; 36:5), πλῆθος (ψ 9:25; Is. 31:4) and ῥάβδος (Is. 10:5).

In contrast to this considerable number of constructions with both terms, there are much fewer with ὀργή and not θυμός or *vice versa*. None of these, nor all of them together, can support a distinction between the two words. Hence we shall not list them *in extenso*. [200] There is a surprising alternation between the words in the LXX MSS. [201] If there were any material or linguistic distinction, this would hardly have been possible. We may thus conclude that ὀργή and θυμός and the related verbs can be used *promiscue*, and are actually used in this way in the LXX.

2. ὀργίζω, (θυμόω), παροργίζω, παροργισμός.

Active forms of ὀργίζω and θυμόω, both in the sense "to make angry," "to enrage," occur for certain only once each (Job 12:6 A; Hos. 12:15), but we find pass. forms of ὀργίζω almost 80 times and of θυμόω over 60, often strengthened by θυμῷ or ὀργῇ (→ 409), always in the sense "to become angry," "to be angry." The subj. may be either God or man. The act. παροργίζω, [202] used more than 50 times, also means "to make angry." The nouns παροργισμός (6 times) and παρόργισμα (3, not in the NT), are surprisingly rare in the LXX. They mean "provocation to anger" (3 Βασ. 15:30; 2 Ch. 35:19c), but can be used more broadly for an action provoking to anger (2 Εσδρ. 19:18; 3 Βασ. 16:33). Except in Dt. 32:21 [203] man is the subj.; παροργισμός and παρόργισμα are also used in the act. only of man. παροργισμός is twice used in the pass. sense, 4 Βασ. 19:3; Jer. 21:5.

3. ὀργίλος and θυμώδης.

As an adj. ὀργίλος occurs 4 times (ψ 17:48 and 3 times in Prv.), as an adv. once (4 Macc. 8:9). θυμώδης is found 8 times (5 in Prv., 2 Sir., 1 Ιερ. 37:23). Both terms are thus found mainly in the Wisdom lit. They mean "wrathful," "angry," and, except at Ιερ. 37:23 (30:23) they are used only for the human attribute.

4. (κότος), χόλος and μῆνις.

These three words, used in secular Gk. for divine anger, [204] are not used for God's wrath in the LXX. κότος does not occur here at all, χόλος is used only 5 times (Prv. 16:28 א; Qoh. 5:16; 2 Macc. 3:28 A; 3 Macc. 5:1, 30), and the verb (ἐκ-) χολᾶν is found only at 3 Macc. 3:1. In all 6 instances the ref. is to human anger. [205] Μῆνις occurs

---

[197] Compounds of ἔρχεσθαι also occur.
[198] Both words are also found with the same prep.
[199] ἡμέρα θυμοῦ only at Zeph. 2:2 and Prv. 11:4 (LXX Bא om), elsewhere, including other verses in Zeph., always ἡμέρα ὀργῆς.
[200] Mostly the expressions occur only once.
[201] Cf. Is. 10:4; Jer. 10:25; Lam. 4:11; 2 Chr. 29:8 etc.
[202] Only Da. 11:36 and Sir. 4:3 not in the act.
[203] Here controlled by the antithesis to Israel's provocation.
[204] In secular Gk. they are almost exclusively poetic words [Kleinknecht].
[205] Qoh. 5:16 for קֶצֶף, Prv. 16:28 without Heb. original; the other passages in 2 and 3 Macc.

4 times (Gn. 49:7; Nu. 35:21; Sir. 27:30; 28:5), μηνίαμα or μήνιμα [206] only once at Sir. 40:4, while the related verb μηνίειν is found 5 times (Lv. 19:18; Jer. 3:12; ψ 102:8; Sir. 10:6; 28:7). Of the 10 refs. 8 speak of human anger ; only in Jer. 3:12 and ψ 102:8 is the verb set in relation to God, though here, remarkably, in such a way that an implacable μηνίειν of God is expressly denied. From all this it may be concluded that the Gk. translators thought the 3 terms and their derivates were too heavily freighted as expressions used for the wrath of the (Gk.) gods, so they deliberately avoided them as unsuitable when they wished to speak of the wrath of the biblical God.

II. Interpretations and Paraphrases.

In general the LXX translators correctly rendered the Heb. original in OT passages referring to God's wrath. They replaced the Heb. words for wrath by Gk. terms. In some cases they did this rather mechanically. Thus חֵמָה, one of the main Heb. words for wrath, [207] is transl. θυμός even when it means the poison of serpents or arrows (Dt. 32:24; Ps. 58:4; Job 6:4; the expected ἰός only at ψ 139:4). Again, כַּעַס or כַּעַשׂ, which occurs 25 times in the OT and usually means "displeasure," "vexation," "grief," is almost always transl. ὀργή (9 times), [208] θυμός (8 times), παροργισμός (twice) or παρόργισμα (once) in the LXX. Thus typical words for wrath are used, and other renderings are very rare : 1 Βασ. 1:6, 16 A ἀθυμία, Prv. 21:19 γλωσσώδης (with ὀργίλος), and Qoh. 1:18 γνῶσις. רוּחַ is sometimes rendered ὀργή (Prv. 16:32) or θυμός (Zech. 6:8; Prv. 29:11), sometimes, where this might at least seem to be suggested, πνεῦμα (Ju. 8:3; Is. 25:4; 30:28). מֵרוּחַ אַפּוֹ in Job 4:9 is ἀπὸ πνεύματος ὀργῆς. Sometimes the LXX replaces concrete means or operations of the exercise of divine wrath by the abstract "anger," so Ιερ. 37:23 (30:23), where ὀργή κυρίου is used for חֲמַת יְהוָה and ὀργή for עַף also — and this is perhaps more noteworthy, since the context is not referring to God's anger — ψ 82:16 : בְּסוּפָתְךָ תְבַהֲלֵם for ἐν τῇ ὀργῇ σου ταράξεις αὐτούς.

Esp. characteristic is the transl. of אַף in two instances where it means "nose" rather than "wrath." When the ref. is to the nose of man (Prv. 30:33) or snout of an animal (11:22), the LXX can say μυκτήρ or ῥίς; even of idols it may be said : ῥῖνας ἔχουσιν, ψ 113:14. [209] On the other hand the עָלָה עָשָׁן בְּאַפּוֹ of Ps. 18(17):8 — used of Yahweh — obviously creates difficulties for the LXX translators, and they use ἀνέβη καπνὸς ἐν ὀργῇ αὐτοῦ. For the מִנִּשְׁמַת רוּחַ אַפֶּךָ of v. 15 : "at the blast of the breath of thy nostrils," they similarly use ἀπὸ ἐμπνεύσεως πνεύματος ὀργῆς σου. Obviously the anthropopathic "wrath" is more tolerable for them than the anthropomorphic "nose" of the Heb. In other verses the antipathy of the LXX translators for πάθη leads them to replace the idea of God's wrath by other concepts. Thus, instead of speaking of God's wrath, they refer to the human sin which provokes it, cf. Job 42:7; Nu. 1:53; also Is. 57:17; 1 Εσδρ. 6:14, → I, 287; [210] cf. also the paraphrase in Mal. 1:4, where the apocalyptic penal name : "The people with which Yahweh is continually wrathful," is replaced by λαὸς ἐφ᾽ ὃν παρατέτακται κύριος ἕως αἰῶνος, "the people against which the Lord stands ready for battle as long as the world endures." In Is. 66:14 the Mas. runs : וְזָעַם אֶת־אֹיְבָיו, "and he (Yahweh) will rage against His enemies," but the LXX alters both terms in favour of the more ethical and rationalistic Hellen. idea of God : (κύριος) ... ἀπειλήσει τοῖς ἀπειθοῦσιν. The most violent paraphrase is at

---

[206] LXX has μήνιμα (א and A) or μηνίαμα (B).
[207] In the sense wrath θυμός 70 times, ὀργή 25 times.
[208] Also ὀργίλος once.
[209] In Am. 4:10 the words "the stink of the camp in your nostrils," due to confusing בְּאֹשׁ and בְּאַשׁ, are taken very differently (ἐν τῇ ὀργῇ μου for וּבְאַפְּכֶם).
[210] On such paraphrases in the Targum cf. Weber, 155.

Zech. 1:12: κύριε παντοκράτωρ, ἕως τίνος οὐ μὴ ἐλεήσῃς τὴν Ιερουσαλημ καὶ τὰς πόλεις Ιουδα, ἃς ὑπερεῖδες (for וְזָעַמְתָּה) τοῦτο ἑβδομηκοστὸν ἔτος; here national pride plays a certain role along with the changed view of God. In the Mas. we have a hymn to the God of wrath; the LXX replaces this by the revelation of the Word. A double transl. (? cf. BHK³) of בְּרֹגֶז רַחֵם (+ בְּרֹגֶז יְחִי) gives us in v. 2 the statement: ἐν τῷ ταραχθῆναι τὴν ψυχήν μου ἐν ὀργῇ ἐλέους μνησθήσῃ, "when my soul has been confused by (God's) wrath, then wilt thou remember mercy." Thus the parenthetical observation of the Mas., which is perhaps only a gloss, is made a main clause. In v. 5 דָּבָר, revelation in the λόγος, replaces דֶּבֶר, pestilence as one of God's terrible weapons. Whereas in the Mas. Yahweh is the subject throughout the c., in the LXX λόγος is the chief word in vv. 5-9. Only later are the sayings put on the lips of God with the λέγει κύριος of v. 9. V. 12 here reads: ἐν ἀπειλῇ ὀλιγώσεις γῆν καὶ ἐν θυμῷ κατάξεις ἔθνη. ἀπειλή is used for זַעַם (also for זַעַף in Prv. 19:12, the wrath of the king), so that the ref. is not to an emotion in God, but to an utterance (revelation) in relation to the earth. The θυμός in the second half-verse is to be construed accordingly. The ref. is to the will or purpose of God. The meaning imparted to the verse by the LXX corresponds to Ps. 33:8: "With (thy mere) threatening thou reducest the earth (to submission), with (thy mere) will thou overthrowest the peoples." Not the God who reveals Himself from Sinai in natural disasters, but the Spirit-God is extolled here. The LXX sometimes seeks to express its knowledge of God by not writing (Dt. 32:22): "A fire is kindled in mine anger" (כִּי־אֵשׁ קָדְחָה בְאַפִּי) but ἐκ τοῦ θυμοῦ μου, i.e., as a result of my anger, or more generally acc. to my will. The LXX has simply taken over statements in the Psalter, cf. ψ 2:12; 77:38 (God does not let His anger run its full course); 78:5; 88:46. Sir. 48:1 treats directly of the revelation of God's wrath: καὶ ἀνέστη Ηλιας προφήτης ὡς πῦρ, καὶ ὁ λόγος αὐτοῦ ὡς λαμπὰς ἐκαίετο. It is true that this refers in the first instance to Elijah. But in what follows it may be seen that God is really the one who speaks and acts: ἐν λόγῳ κυρίου ἀνέσχεν οὐρανόν (v. 3). Thus the verse corresponds to the prophetic description of the revelation of the wrath of God in Is. 30:27: καιόμενος ὁ θυμός, ... τὸ λόγιον ὀργῆς πλῆρες, καὶ ἡ ὀργὴ τοῦ θυμοῦ ὡς πῦρ ἔδεται. Cf. Is. 65:5; Ιερ. 4:4; 7:20; 15:14; 51(44):6. In these verses also there is ref. to the operation of wrath. [211]

Grether/Fichtner

D. The Wrath of God in Later Judaism.

I. Apocrypha and Pseudepigrapha.

Post-canonical Jewish lit., both in the dispersion and in Palestine, continues along the same lines as are found in the OT.

a. In so far as we have Heb. originals (Sir. and Damasc.), the words for wrath (of God) are אַף (Sir. 5:6 etc.; Damasc. 1:21 [1:17] etc.); חֵמָה (Sir. 16:6, 11; 36:6; Damasc. 2:5 [2:4]); זַעַם (Sir. 5:7; 39:23); רֹגֶז (Sir. 5:6). In the Gk. text God's wrath is usually denoted by ὀργή and derivates, [212] though with no essential difference of meaning and as an equivalent for the same Heb. words we also find θυμός [213] (evidently preferred in 4 Macc.) with θυμόομαι (only Sib.). The combinations ὀργὴ θυμοῦ (1 Macc. 2:49;

---

[211] The latter half of this paragraph is by Bertram (from → 411, 34).

[212] ὀργίζομαι Ps. Sol. 7:5; Gk. En. 18:16; Gr. Bar. 4:8; 9:7; Apc. Mos. 8, 16, 18, 21; ἀπ-οργίζομαι, 2 Macc. 5:17; ἐποργίζομαι, 2 Macc. 7, 33; παροργίζω, Jdt. 8:14; 11:11; Test. L. 3:10 etc.; παροργισμός, Ps. Sol. 8:9; διοργίζομαι, 3 Macc. 3:1; 4:13.

[213] Cf. R. Smend, *Gr.-syr.-hbr. Index zur Weisheit d. Jesus Sirach* (1907), *s.v.* ὀργή and θυμός, → 419. θυμός has a rather narrower compass of meaning than ὀργή inasmuch as it does not develop also the sense of wrathful judgment, → 414, 424.

Gk. En. 5:9) or θυμὸς καὶ ὀργή (Sir. 45:18) correspond to the double חֲרִי אַף (Damasc. 9:4, 6; 10:2, 4 etc.) and are to be regarded like those in Eph. (τὸ κράτος τῆς ἰσχύος, 1:19; 6:10 etc.; ἀρχὴ καὶ ἐξουσία κτλ., 1:21; 6:12 etc.) as a rhetorical heaping up of terms. Other words are rare : ἀγανακτέω, 4 Macc. 4:21, παροξύνω, Bar. 4:7; Ps. Sol. 4:21; Test. A. 2:6, χόλος, Wis. 18:22, μηνίω, Prayer of Man. 13. The two last, with their derivates, are obviously preferred to ὀργή and θυμός in the epic speech of Sib. [214]

b. Human anger is judged in different ways ; it depends on whether the relation to God serves as a criterion or alien standards take its place. Even in the first case there may be righteous anger, e.g., at transgression of the Law or blasphemy, esp. in Macc. (1 Macc. 2:24, 44; 6:59; 2 Macc. 4:40; 10:35). The anger of a pagan ruler may be justified when it flares up against a sinner, cf. 2 Macc. 4:38; 1 Macc. 9:69; 3 Macc. 6:23, → n. 269. It can even be inspired by God, 2 Macc. 13:4; cf. Gk. Bar. 16:2. Indeed, the righteous anger of a king, as in the Rabbis (→ 416), can serve as an illustration of the divine wrath, Slav. En. 46:1. On this view only unrighteous anger is judged adversely, Sir. 1:22. In the majority of instances, however, anger is adjudged a passion which leads to sin and ruin, cf. Sib., 3, 377; Ps. Sol. 16:10; Wis. 10:3; Damasc. 9:4, 6 (10:2, 4). This is esp. so in Sir., e.g., 10:18; 20:2, and Test. XII, D. 1-6; G. 5:1; Jud. 14:1; S. 4:8; cf. also 2:11; Zeb. 4:11. If the fierce anger of heathen rulers is often condemned, [215] this is esp. because it is directed against the people of God, but also because it is a sign of the foolish arrogance of man ; for strictly anger is proper only to God, Sir. 10:18. Hence it is precisely man's anger which arouses the wrath of God to a particular degree, Da. 11:36; [216] Sir. 45:18 f.; Slav. En. 44:2; Apc. Abr. 17 (Bonwetsch, p. 28); if God turns aside, this is always a mark of His wrath, → 446, cf. Sir. 28:3, 5 : The wrathful person can expect neither ἴασις nor ἐξιλασμός from God, for μῆνις καὶ ὀργή are βδελύγματα before God, Sir. 27:30.

Even when rational criteria cover the religious, the assessment is usually negative, e.g., Sir. 30:24. Acc. to Gk. En. 8:3 Semiaza, a leader of the fallen angels, has taught men "anger against reason." Wis. esp. (10:1 ff.) sets ὀργή in total antithesis to σοφία. On the other hand it is distinctive of 4 Macc. that θυμός is subject to λογισμός (2:15 ff.), which can cure it (βοηθῆσαι, 3:3). 4 Macc. shares the problem of mastering anger with Hell. philosophy (cf. Sen. De Ira, II, 2, 1 ff.) and also the Ep. Ar. in the one place in which it speaks of anger, 253 f. Along with critical and positive judgments there are in this literature many neutral statements about human anger. [217]

c. In view of the predominantly negative estimation of human anger, it is surprising that almost all apocr. and pseudepigr. writings speak quite uninhibitedly of the wrath of God (though → 414). The only fundamental exception is the Stoically coloured Ep. Ar.: God governs the world without any wrath, 254. [218] It is more accidental that Tob. and 3 Macc. do not refer to God's wrath. What is esp. striking is that a work so strongly tinged by Hellenism as 4 Macc. reckons quite freely with God's righteous anger (4:21; 9:32; → 414), and that the most passionate depiction of divine wrath in these writings is in Sib. (4, 159 : χόλῳ βρυχῶν).

---

[214] χόλος : 3, 51; 556; 561; 4, 160 and 169; 5, 130; 373; 456; 508; Fr., 3, 19; χολόομαι : 3, 766; μηνίω : 4, 51; μῆνις : 4, 135; μήνιμα : 3, 632; 811; ὀργή : 4, 162; 5, 76; θυμός : 3, 309; Fr., 3, 19; θυμόομαι : 5, 298 and 358.

[215] Tob. 1:18; Jdt. 5:2; Ps. Sol. 2:23 f.; 17:12; S. Bar. 48:37; 63:2; Sib., 3, 660 f., but esp. Macc.

[216] The Gk. translator introduces the play on words, which is rather more than a play : παροργισθήσεται (sc. Antiochus IV) ... ἕως ἂν συντελεσθῇ ἡ ὀργή (sc. of God). Here, too, post-canonical apocalyptic simply follows the same line as the Canon.

[217] E.g., Tob. 5:14; Sir. 25:15; 4 Esr. 10:5 and esp. Jub. (26:8; 27:3, 6; 28:4 etc.).

[218] In later centuries this view shapes the Alexandrian tradition in Philo (→ 417), Cl. Al. (→ 388) and Origen (Cels., IV, 71 ff.).

Like θυμός, μῆνις and χόλος, and their verbal derivates, ὀργή denotes the passion of anger itself, whether the ref. be to the outbreak (e.g., Sir. 16:6) or mitigation (48:10) or it be said (Eth. En. 99:16) that the Lord will kindle the spirit of His anger, → infra. One might speak here of anthropopathism, but is should be recalled that the phrase expresses the personal nature of God on the one side, [219] and His righteous opposition to all evil on the other. In not a few cases, however, ὀργή denotes the effects of God's anger in the judgment which smites men, i.e., God's wrathful judgment, e.g., when His great wrath in Apc. Mos. 14 is explained to be the death which rules over the whole race, or when in Vit. Ad. 49 it refers to the disasters of fire and flood which come on the posterity of Adam and Eve, → 437, or when Jub. 36:10 refers to a daily renewal of judgment in rage and anger. In particular eschatological wrath often means judgment, Jub. 24:30 and esp. Gr. En. 13:8 : ἴδον ὁράσεις ὀργῆς, [220] cf. also a hendiadys like "wrath and punishment," Eth. En. 55:3; 91:7, 9; Jub. 41:26. More frequently, however, ὀργή suggests both the upsurge of God's wrath and also the resultant punishment, e.g., Jdt. 9:9; 1 Macc. 3:8; Sir. 7:16; 47:20; Ps. Sol. 15:4; Test. R. 4:4; Test. L. 6:11; Sib., 5, 76. [221] This is particularly so in instances in which the wrath of God is personified in different ways, being sent in Eth. En. 101:3, going forth in Sir. 5:7, [222] and resting in Sir. 5:6. In other places these personifications serve to detach the reactions of anger from God Himself, so Eth. En. 99:16 (the spirit of His anger); Damasc. 2:5 (2:4 : חמה גדולה as the angel of destruction, → 416); cf. Wis. 18:22, 25 (anger as the κολάζων and ὀλεθρεύων fought and conquered by Moses). [223] ὀργή can also be the occasion as well as the effect of wrath, as obviously in Sir. 26:8; cf. 25:22.

The motifs of theodicy may be discerned both in what has been presented and also in many other statements about God's anger, including those about its relation to God's mercy, patience and longsuffering, → 407; 425-427. Sir. (5:6; [224] 16:11) links wrath and mercy as a unity in tension in God : ἔλεος καὶ ὀργὴ παρ' αὐτῷ, cf. Prayer Man. 5 f. Towards Israel esp. God's wrath can be regarded as an outworking of His chiding mercy and love. [225] This is the view of, e.g., 2 Macc. 5:17, 20; 7:33; Wis. 11:9; 16:5; 18:20-25 (cf. Ps. Sol. 7:5). Yet restraint of anger [226] is also a sign of God's patience, S. Bar. 59:6; cf. R. 9:22; → 425 f. The divine wrath kindled by the transgressions of sinners can also be viewed as in full accord with His righteousness ; [227] indeed, it can be called a function of the divine righteousness, as is esp. plain in 4 Macc. 4:21; cf. 9:32.

Only for apocalyptists do God's righteousness and mercy exclude the work of His wrath. Thus 4 Esr., whose view of God is controlled by passionate righteousness on the one side and unlimited mercy on the other, sees various reasons for holding wrath in check, e.g., the small number of righteous (8:30), the → ἄγνοια of the masses who are like cattle, and universal sinfulness, which seems to make anger pointless and unjust (8:34; cf. v. 35). [228] Related are the thoughts in S. Bar. (48:14, 17): man's absolute weak-

---

[219] This is suggested esp. by the phrase "to provoke the name of God" (Palaea on Apc. Abr. 29; v. N. Bonwetsch, Die Apk. Abr. [1897], 63 f., n. 1; cf. also p. 63).

[220] Cf. also Bar. 4:9, 25; 1 Macc. 1:64; Gk. En. 10:22; Eth. En. 106:15; Ass. Mos. 8:1; in Sib. χόλος (3, 51; 5, 130 etc.) and μήνιμα (3, 811) are to be taken in the same way. θυμός in Sir. 48:10, if original, obviously means eschatological judgment too.

[221] The same is true of χόλος in Sib. 3, 556; 561 and θυμός in Sir. 18:24.

[222] Cf. also v. 6c if we are in fact to read ἐλεύσεται for ἔλεος καί, cf. V. Ryssel in Kautzsch Apkr. u. Pseudepigr., I, 253.

[223] Cf. also the obscure Apc. Abr. 25, where God says : "The image which you saw is my wrath with which the people which comes to me from you (sc. Abraham) provokes me."

[224] Though cf. → n. 222.

[225] An ἀνελεήμων θυμός, however, obtains against the Gentiles (Wis. 19:1).

[226] Cf. on the other hand Sir. 7:16 : μνήσθητι ὅτι ὀργὴ οὐ χρονιεῖ.

[227] Cf. Sjöberg, 197 f., 224-227.

[228] 4 Esr. 4:29 is not relevant here whether one prefers the reading comminatio or in-dignatio, because what is meant is God's mighty working in cosmic catastrophes (there

ness and vanity rule out wrath, though it is not clear whether the appeal here is to God's righteousness or His mercy. The question of God's righteousness also lies behind Apc. Abr.: Why is God angry at the evil which He Himself has subordinated to His own counsel ? (→ 426).

God's wrath breaks forth in two phases, first as historical wrath, then as eschatological, → 430. [229] Sir. (cf. 18:24) [230] and Damasc. speak only of the former. Its victims are all men (cf. Eth. En. 84:4; Damasc. 2:21 [3:7]); individuals (thus Cain the first υἱὸς ὀρ-γῆς, [231] Apc. Mos. 3, [232] but esp. Adam and Eve, Rev. Mos. 8 f.; Vit. Ad., 3, 34); in-dividual groups and nations (so the Egyptians, Wis. 19:1, or the mocker, the man of derision with his host, Damasc. 1:21 f. [1, 17]; 5:16 [7, 17]; 8:13 [9, 22] = B. 19:26; 8:18 [9, 26] = B. 19:31); in particular Israel, whose main offence to provoke wrath is idolatry, Apc. Abr. passim ; Eth. En. 89:33. But while God's wrath remains on others to the very last (cf. Wis. 19:1), it is limited in the case of Israel [233] (cf. 16:5; 18:20), and does not bring destruction, cf. Gr. En. 5:9 : οἱ ἐκλεκτοὶ ... οὐ μὴ ἀποθάνωσιν ἐν ὀργῇ θυμοῦ, though cf. S. Bar. 64:4 and esp. Jub. 15:34, which even speaks of an eternal wrath (cf. also 36:10) on Israel. Other creatures are also objects of wrath, e.g., the vine (Gr. Bar. 4:9) because of its seductive effect, [234] the moon (Gr. Bar. 9:7) [235] and the stars (Gr. En. 18:16), ungodly beings such as the devil (Vit. Ad. 15 f.; Jub. 3:23), the hosts of Azazel (Eth. En. 55:3), the fallen angels (Gr. Bar. 4:8; Eth. En. 68:4 : ... "because they act as though they were equal to the Lord"; Jub. 5:6), and perhaps the disobedient sons of God in Gn. 6 (Gr. En. 16:4; 21:6). [236]

All historical wrath points forward to eschatological ; all historical periods of wrath (Sir. 44:17; Damasc. 1:5 : חרון קץ) are types of the day of wrath (e.g., Jub. 24:28, 30; 36:10, → 430), of ὀργὴ πυρός (Sir. 36:8) in the καιρὸς συντελείας (39:28). Eschato-logical wrath smites two groups as the national or individual aspect predominates. It is directed against the Gentiles (Sir. 36:6; Ass. Mos. 10:3; Apc. Abr. 24, though also Eth. En. 90:15, 18, and esp. Jub. 24:28, where the Philistines are objects of both historical and eschatological wrath), [237] and also against sinners who do not repent, whether Gentiles or Israelites, the mighty of earth on whom the wrath of the Lord of spirits rests (Eth. En. 62:12), the oppressors of orphans, widows and strangers (Slav. En. 50:5 A etc.; cf. Wis. 5:17-23; Ps. Sol. 15:5; Jub. 36:10 etc.). Those who are objects of God's wrath in history may also be its instruments, men, esp. heathen oppressors and persecutors (4 Macc. 4:21; Ass. Mos. 8:1), various creatures (Wis. 5:22; [238] 16:5; cf. 11:18), also angels set up in opposition to the fallen angels (Jub. 5:6).

---

is no suggestion that these are a form of God's wrathful judgment); cf. also S. Bar. 21:6; 48:8 (chiding is the original here rather than threatening); Ryssel, op. cit., II, 428 uses a conjecture of Charles as the basis of his rendering, though without acknowledging it as such.

[229] Both together, more by accident than in principle called ὀργή and θυμός, Sir. 48:10, though → 422.

[230] Cf. V. Ryssel, ad loc.

[231] Cf. Sib., 3, 309; Eph. 2:3.

[232] If the ref. is not to Cain's own anger against Abel (קין from קנא!); cf. the textual variants in C. Tischendorf, Apocalypses apocryphae (1866), 2.

[233] Its goal is conversion (Gr. Bar. 16:2, though this could be a Christian interpolation from R. 10:19, unless there is allusion to Dt. 32:21).

[234] This view intertwines with another which derives from a Christian interpolation in which there is allusion to the Lord's Supper.

[235] Acc. to the Gk. text because the moon shone when Adam was tempted by the serpent, acc. to the Slavic because it laughed when the serpent tempted Adam and Eve and made them aware of their nakedness.

[236] Cf. Stauffer Theol., 199.

[237] In this wrath there is a touch of national anger.

[238] There is here described a remarkable "arming" of the wrathful God, → 297, 18 ff.

Judaism, too, was occupied with the question how God's wrath can be overcome and averted. It found many answers, though not the one decisive answer (→ 444-447), e.g., prayer (Apc. Abr. 20 [p. 31, Bonwetsch; cf. p. 62]), worship (Slav. En. 18:8 A; cf. Wis. 18:20 ff.), righteousness (Sir. 44:17), the substitutionary intercession of Moses and Elijah (Wis. 18:21; Sir. 48:10), vicarious suffering (2 Macc. 7:38), the wrath of the elements acting as an antidote (Sir. 39:28), God's own saving advocacy (Wis. 16:5; Nu. 21). In the last analysis Judaism very close to the NT, but the veil is not yet taken away.

Sjöberg/Stählin

II. Rabbinism.

In Rabbinic literature, too, the concept of the wrath of God is very common. There is no trace of aversion to the idea. It is one of the things which are taken for granted theologically. OT passages about it are adduced without any attempt at reinterpretation. In this connection comparisons are used which depict God's wrath in terms of human anger, as when a father is angry with his son, a king with his subjects, a man with his wife. [239] There is no hesitation even to include in descriptions of the divine wrath the irrational arbitrariness which characterises human anger. Like this, it perhaps flares up furiously at first, and then after a while subsides. [240] Sometimes God is more angry, sometimes less. [241] These depictions are linked to expositions of biblical verses, and it is worth noting that the expositions, though they could be evaded, are freely given. This is the more surprising in that Rabbinism condemns anger against one's neighbour [242] (though allowing righteous indignation against the sinner). [243]

If in some — fairly late — passages anger is hypostatised in various angelic forms, [244] what has been said shows that this is not due to fear of anthropopathisms. It rests on the one hand on the love of a concrete and plastic mode of depiction which is distinctive of Rabbinism, and on the other on the general growth of angelological speculations.

In spite of the freedom with which God's wrath is depicted after the model of human anger, it is a fundamental principle in Rabbinism that the divine anger does not set aside righteousness. That God never acts contrary to righteousness is essential in Rabbinism as in all Judaism, → 426. Thus we read on Dt. 32:41: "'If I sharpen the lightning of my sword,' that is, if judgment goes forth from me, it is as swift as lightning, but nevertheless: 'And my hand holds fast to right.'" [245]

The wrath of God differs from human anger in another respect too. An angry man might lay about him uncontrollably in his rage, but God, even in the hour of chiding, does not forget His good and merciful care for the world. [246] If sin is in the world, so, too, is divine wrath. [247] But this is not alone. The divine mercy is also at work. This does not simply mean that in punishing those who provoke Him God does not forget His kindness to the righteous. His mercy is toward sinners too. This is seen esp. in His patience and in the good gifts which He gives sinners in spite of their sin, so that there is often reason to exclaim: If God acts thus toward those who provoke Him, how

---

[239] Cf. e.g., jTaan., II, 65b, 43 (Str.-B., III, 30); M. Ex., 14, 15 (Horovitz, 98); S. Lv., 9, 4 f. (Weiss, 43c); cf. Sjöberg, 63.

[240] Cf. the above refs., and also Str.-B., III, 409, 685, 687.

[241] M. Ex., 17, 4 (Horovitz, 174); S. Nu., 90 on 11:10. Cf. also S. Dt., 305 on 31:14; R. Nathan: Because of His love for Israel, God does not get angry at their deeds.

[242] Str.-B., I, 276 ff.

[243] *Ibid.*, III, 602 f.; cf. also I, 365 f. (b and c).

[244] *Ibid.*, III, 30 f.

[245] S. Dt., 331 on 32:41. Cf. Sjöberg, 4.

[246] M. Ex., 15, 3 (Horovitz, 130).

[247] Midr. Tannaïm on Dt. 13:18 (Hoffmann, 69); S. Dt., 96 on 13:18.

much more toward those who do His will ! [248] If He acts thus in the hour of wrath, how much more in that of good-pleasure ! [249]

The idea that wrath is linked with mercy is not always present. Often it is simply said that sin arouses God's wrath and brings righteous punishment. At times it can even be said that sin makes the merciful One terrible. [250] In particular it is held that at the last judgment, after death, or on the day of judgment, sinners are smitten by God's wrath without finding mercy. [251] The judgment of Gehinnom is one of wrath, [252] and the day of judgment is a day of wrath — though this expression is rare. [253] Nevertheless, the concept of the righteousness of judgment is much more to the forefront than that of judgment in wrath.

Sjöberg

III. Philo.

Philo's position between the OT and the Stoa, or rather his attempt to live and think in both, is reflected also in what he says about wrath. But here, too, his Stoic Alexandrian thinking is predominant. With biblical and non-biblical antiquity he recognises a righteous anger of man at evil and at evildoers. [254] But fundamentally, like Ep. Ar. and Stoicism, he counts anger among the passions which are to be suppressed and controlled by reason.

It is thus understandable that there should be some tension in what he says about God's wrath. When he speaks of ἄξια ὀργῆς, Philo can refer to God's anger as well as man's, Som., II, 179. In such cases one may rightly speak of God's chiding, [255] and Philo sees the outworking of God's wrath in earthly events [256] and human destiny. [257] But on the other side — and this is the predominant line in Philo — God's ὀργαί are not for him a reality, but, so far as pagan statements are concerned, an ascription, [258] like all the ἀνθρωποπαθές which pagans ascribe to the divine, Sacr. AC, 95. For there is no real πάθος with God. [259] Such features are indeed no more than ἀσεβῶν μυθοποιίαι, Deus Imm., 59. This interpretation will not do, however, when Moses himself ζῆλον, θυμόν, ὀργάς, ὅσα τούτοις ὅμοια ἀνθρωπολογῶν διεξέρχεται (Deus Imm., 60), i.e., in relation to the OT. The many passages in which the OT speaks along these lines are a difficulty, a theological problem, for Philo. He finally explains them as an accommodation of the divine Word to the capacity of those without understanding who

---

[248] So M. Ex., 15, 1 (Horovitz, 122 f.); 16, 13 (165); S. Dt., 43 on 11:16; 320 on 32:19. Cf. Sjöberg, 62-71, 86-94, 110-117.

[249] S. Nu., 105 on 12:10; 137 on 27:14. The ref. here is to those who are generally righteous but who have provoked God's wrath by a sin.

[250] M. Ex., 15, 6 (Horovitz, 134); S. Nu., 157 on 31:16.

[251] Mek. R. Sim. on Ex. 20:5 (Hoffmann, 105): "'A jealous God' : This teaches us that they saw the form which in the future age will be called for by sinners ; 'a jealous God' : a judging God, a hard God, a terrible God."

[252] S. Dt., 320 on 32:22; cf. also Str.-B., I, 115 f.

[253] Str.-B., III, 804 does not adduce any Rabb. refs. on R. 2:5 and Rev. 6:17, though → 430.

[254] Cf. Leisegang, II, 591 f.

[255] Som., II, 177: οἱ μὲν ὑπαιτίως ζῶντες παραπικραίνειν καὶ παροργίζειν ἐνδίκως λέγοιντ᾽ ἂν θεόν. Cf. also the εἴρηται καλῶς in Spec. Leg., I, 265.

[256] Vit. Mos., I, 6 (bad harvests in Egypt); cf. *ibid.*, 119.

[257] Som., II, 179 : μηδὲν μὲν τῶν ὀργῆς ἀξίων ἐπ᾽ ὀλέθρῳ κίνει τῷ σεαυτῆς.

[258] Sacr. AC, 96 : ... χεῖρας πόδας εἰσόδους ἐξόδους ἔχθρας ἀποστροφὰς ἀλλοτριώσεις ὀργὰς προσαναπλάττομεν.

[259] Abr., 202 : παντὸς πάθους ἀμέτοχος ἡ τοῦ θεοῦ φύσις. Cf. Cl. Al. Strom., V, 11, 68, 3 (note the formal similarity to Philo Sacr. AC, 96 → n. 258; Som., I, 235 → n. 261).

are incapable of true knowledge of God. These are instructed thereby. [260] Hence there is no reality corresponding to the statements. They simply serve the needs of learners. [261]

Sjöberg/Stählin

IV. Josephus.

As distinct from Philo, Jos. is influenced by the OT and contemporary Rabbinism. [262] Like the LXX he uses ὀργή for divine and human anger. He also has χόλος (e.g., Bell., 7, 34 and 332), μήνιμα and μῆνις (Ant., 15, 243; cf. 15, 299: τοῦ θεοῦ μηνίσαντος), which in the LXX occur almost exclusively in Sir. and which betray the influence of Gk. thought. On the other hand, he does not use θυμός and θυμοῦσθαι, [263] perhaps because θυμός = חֵמָה seemed to him to be unworthy of God, unless, as with Philo, we are to think of the psychological meaning of the Platonic θυμός, though this is less likely. He takes the ὀργὴ θεοῦ from the OT, where it is connected with transgression and violation of the Law, Ant., 11, 141: μὴ κοινὴν ἐπὶ πάντας ὀργὴν λαβὼν πάλιν αὐτοὺς εἰς συμφορὰς ἐμβάλῃ, 11, 127: ὅπως δὲ μηδεμίαν ὀργὴν ἐπ' ἐμὲ λάβῃ τὸ θεῖον, cf. 3, 321: δεδιὼς τὸν νόμον καὶ τὴν ὀργήν. Acc. to a popular view the house of Herod is under the divine wrath, Ant., 15, 376: ταῦτα δ' οὐκ ἂν λάθοι τὸν θεὸν ἐπὶ τῇ καταστροφῇ τοῦ βίου τῆς ἀντ' αὐτῶν ὀργῆς ἀπομνημονευομένης. 15, 243: Herod's sickness παρέσχεν ἅπασιν ἐξυπονοῆσαι κατὰ μῆνιν τοῦτο συνενεχθῆναι. The misfortune of Herod the Gt. in the 13th year of his rule seems to be εἴτε ... θεοῦ μηνίσαντος ἢ καὶ ... οὕτως ἀπαντήσαντος τοῦ κακοῦ (Ant., 15, 299); his sickness ἐνεπικραίνετο δίκην ὧν παρανομήσειεν ἐκπρασσομένου τοῦ θεοῦ (Ant., 17, 168). Of course, in Jos., under Gk. influence, the personal wrath of God is often replaced by impersonal δίκη, which "like εἱμαρμένη becomes an independent force." [264] Party division in Jerusalem ἄν τις ὡς ἐν κακοῖς ἀγαθὸν εἴποι καὶ δίκης ἔργον, Bell., 5, 2. On the punishment of Simon bar Giora it is said: οὐδὲ γὰρ διαφεύγει πονηρία θεοῦ χόλον, οὐδὲ ἀσθενὴς ἡ δίκη, Bell., 7, 34. Σίμωνα ... εἰς δίκην τῆς κατὰ τῶν πολιτῶν ὠμότητος ... ἐποίησεν ὁ θεός, Bell., 7, 32. Hyrcanus asked the Pharisees τίνος αὐτὸν ἄξιον ἡγοῦνται τιμωρίας ... τῷ μέτρῳ τῆς δίκης, Ant., 13, 294. Belief in God's wrath is everywhere fundamental, but this finds its criterion in δίκη. In the time of Jos. the Romans are its instrument; their world power is in the plan of God.

Procksch

---

[260] Deus Imm., 52: ... τοῦ νουθετῆσαι χάριν τοὺς ἑτέρως μὴ δυναμένους σωφρονίζεσθαι. Cf. also Orig. Cels., IV, 71 f.: God's wrath is simply an expression which the Bible uses for the uneducated, for one cannot ascribe to God what is prohibited in man.

[261] Som., I, 235: πρόσωπον ... καὶ χεῖρας καὶ βάσεις ... ὀργάς τε καὶ θυμοὺς ... περιέθηκεν, οὐ πρὸς ἀλήθειαν τὸ κεφάλαιον τοῦτο τῶν λόγων ἀναφέρων, ἀλλὰ πρὸς τὸ λυσιτελὲς τῶν μανθανόντων. Cf. also Deus Imm., 53 f. with its juxtaposition of the statements: "God is not as a man," and: "God is as a man," and the added note: The first statement expresses the reality, but the second πρὸς τὴν τῶν πολλῶν διδασκαλίαν εἰσάγεται.

[262] Cf. B. Brüne, *Flavius Josephus* (1913), 151-153.

[263] Schl. Theol. d. Judt., 40.

[264] Schlatter, *op. cit.*, 40 f., from whom the following examples are taken.

E. The Wrath of Man and the Wrath of God in the NT. [265]

I. The Wrath of Man.

Apart from the stem word ὀργή, all the derivates of the stem οργ- are used only of human wrath in the NT. [266] Where ὀργή itself is used thus, it is generally interchangeable with θυμός (→ n. 6; 409; 422). But θυμός is preferred for the passionate rage which boils up suddenly, Lk. 4:28; Ac. 19:28, even though ὀργή seems by derivation to be particularly well adapted to express this, → 383. This term, however, contains an element of awareness and even deliberation absent from θυμός; in Jm. 1:19 (βραδὺς εἰς ὀργήν), e.g., θυμός could hardly be used instead of ὀργή. Παροργίζω and παροργισμός go beyond ὀργή in denoting an angry outburst which threatens to become lasting bitterness, [267] cf. Eph. 6:4; 4:26, where the change from ὀργίζομαι to παροργισμός is surely intentional. But elsewhere παροργίζω, as mostly in its common use in the LXX, can simply be the act of ὀργίζομαι, so R. 10:19.

1. Relative Justification.

The assessment of human anger in the NT is not uniform. A purely negative judgment, as in Stoicism, is not possible wherever the wrath of God is taken seriously. For if anger is ruled out a limine, what is said about God's wrath has to be explained away. [268] Conversely, when this is taken seriously, a limited anger has to be accepted in the human sphere too, cf. of course R. 12:19, → 420, 433. The NT recognises a holy anger which hates what God hates and which is seen above all in Jesus Himself (Mk. 3:5 : μετ᾽ ὀργῆς, cf. Jn. 11:33, 38, both times ἐμβριμᾶσθαι; of Paul, Ac. 17:16 : παρωξύνετο τὸ πνεῦμα αὐτοῦ ἐν αὐτῷ); but in the anger of Jesus there is revealed God's own wrath, → 427 ff. Whereas this is a δικαία ὀργή (→ 383; 426), as shown by close links with derivates of the stem δικ- (R. 1:18; 3:5; 12:19; 13:4), human anger is never described in this way in the NT. [269] Wrath is right for God, but not for man (Jm. 1:20, → 420). [270] God's love includes wrath (→ 425), but love and anger are mutually exclusive in man, cf. 1 C. 13:5 : ἀγάπη . . . οὐ παροξύνεται. Only twice in the NT is human anger estimated positively : R. 10:19 : ἐπ᾽ ἔθνει ἀσυνέτῳ παροργιῶ ὑμᾶς. In distinction from the meaning of the verse quoted here (Dt. 32:21), [271] this παροργισμός is a salutary wrath; God Himself induces it to cause Israel to think. In 2 C. 7:11

---

[265] In what follows, refs. with the synonyms → θυμός, θυμομαχέω, θυμόομαι, ἀγανακτέω, ἀγανάκτησις, ἐμβριμάομαι, παροξύνομαι etc. are considered, so that we should not be confined to the sometimes purely contingent use of words from the stem ὀργ-, but gain as full a picture as possible of the NT statements about the wrath of man and the wrath of God.

[266] As regards ὀργίζομαι human anger is used to depict divine wrath in Mt. 18:34 and 22:7; παροργίζω occurs only twice (R. 10:19; Eph. 6:4), παροργισμός and ὀργίλος only once each (Eph. 4:26; Tt. 1:7), as also θυμόομαι, which is used only for the wrath of man, Mt. 2:16.

[267] Cf. Philo Som., II, 177: . . . παραπικραίνειν καὶ παροργίζειν.

[268] As in Stoicism (→ 386), Philo (→ 417) and Orig. (Cels., IV, 71 ff.) etc.

[269] On the other hand, one finds a justification of righteous anger among the Gks. (→ 384), in the OT (→ 394) and among the Jews, and here not merely against the ungodly (cf. the refs. in Str.-B., III, 602 f.), but also — in accordance with the Jewish attitude to ξένος (→ 11 ff.), against non-Jews, cf. S. Lv. 19, 18 (352a) in Str.-B., I, 366.

[270] The same applies to ἐπιτιμᾶν (→ II, 623 ff.), one of the forms in which ὀργή finds expression.

[271] Cf. also Ez. 32:9 and esp. Gr. Bar. 16, a verse possibly interpolated from R. 10:19 (→ n. 233), though here the impotent wrath of the Jews does not have, as in Paul, the prospect of leading them back to God.

ἀγανάκτησις (used only here in the NT) stands alongside ἐκδίκησις among the seven καρποὶ τῆς μετανοίας; it obviously denotes well-founded anger at the ἀδικήσας (v. 12) or at one's own previously corrupt attitude. [272]

2. Negative Appraisal.

Elsewhere the judgment of the NT on human wrath is always negative. This is shown by the sombre depiction of anger (except when the ref. is to Christ or God, → 428; 429) in parables, stories and visions. Cf. the elder son in Lk. 15:28, who is the very opposite of Jesus, since his anger is pitiless as compared with the holy wrath of mercy (Mk. 3:5). God's wrath is that of wounded love (→ 425; 442; 428); human wrath is that of aroused self-seeking (cf. Lk. 4:28).

This selfish wrath is necessarily directed against God Himself. This is so in Lk. 15:28 (the image is very clear) and 4:28: ἐπλήσθησαν πάντες θυμοῦ. It is esp. so in respect of the wrath of the Gentiles, Rev. 11:18; cf. Ac. 19:28: γενόμενοι πλήρεις θυμοῦ, Hb. 11:27: (Moses) μὴ φοβηθεὶς τὸν θυμὸν τοῦ βασιλέως. The final concentration of this wrath against God is that of the devil, Rev. 12:17; cf. v. 12: ἔχων θυμὸν μέγαν. The devil is angered by the victorious establishment of salvation by God, [273] and also by the frustration of his own plan of destruction. The historical antitype of the angry devil is Herod, Mt. 2:16: ἐθυμώθη λίαν, again because his anti-godly plan, which was designed to frustrate God's plan of salvation, did not succeed. [274] The anti-godly background of human wrath is not the least reason why the judgment of Jesus is that of Jm. 1:20: ὀργή ... ἀνδρὸς δικαιοσύνην θεοῦ οὐκ ἐργάζεται, i.e., the angry man will not stand before God. Perhaps already the saying of Jesus about anger in the Sermon on the Mount (Mt. 5:22: πᾶς ὁ ὀργιζόμενος τῷ ἀδελφῷ αὐτοῦ ἔνοχος ἔσται τῇ κρίσει) is to be taken in this sense, unless v. 22b and c were added later; then ἔνοχος τῇ κρίσει would mean "to fall victim at the last to divine judgment." But since the three-membered logion must be accepted as genuine on various grounds, κρίσις means local judgment, and the logion has the grotesque character of many sayings in the Sermon on the Mount, for what human judge can arraign anger unless it find concrete expression (as many think is the idea of Jesus)? But the grotesqueness, as elsewhere, lies precisely in the absoluteness of the demand of Jesus. Even anger which does not find expression in a single word is compared to a fatal blow. Anger is the first step to murder. [275] For Jesus even more than for the OT (→ 395) ὀργή has the full gravity of sin. This judgment is shared by Paul and his followers. In Col. 3:8 and Eph. 4:31 ὀργή stands under the verdict of κακία, and here again, as in Jm. 1:19 (with λαλῆσαι), it is obviously in the main a sin of the tongue. [276] While to refrain from anger is to give place to God (R. 12:19), [277] anger can be

---

[272] Cf. Wnd. 2 K., ad loc.

[273] A kind of prototype is the wrath of the devil at attempts of the first men to attain to salvation again, Vit. Ad., 9.

[274] The NT has another angry Herod (Ac. 12:20), though it does not give the reason for his θυμομαχεῖν. If this is to be linked with what immediately precedes, we again have anger at the frustration of an ungodly plan.

[275] Cf. among others H. Huber, Die Bergpredigt (1932), 76-85.

[276] Similarly θυμοί in Gl. 5:20 are among the ἔργα τῆς σαρκός, and in 2 C. 12:20 they are in a list of vices, esp. sins of the tongue. In this respect the sayings differ from Mt. 5:22, where ὀργή and sins of the tongue are plainly distinct.

[277] 1 Pt. 2:23 paradigmatically shows the fulfilment of R. 12:19 in Jesus acc. to His own sayings in Mt. 5:38 ff., 44.

a giving place to the devil (Eph. 4:26 f.). Indeed, if it becomes revenge, it can be an infringing of God's rule of wrath (→ 434) and prerogative of judgment (R. 12:19). Thus the wrath of God is the response to man's wrath (cf. Col. 3:8 with v. 6, and esp. Rev. 11:18, → 439) [278] in the *kairos* of judgment. [279] Hence the exhortations neither to be angry oneself (Col. 3:8; Eph. 4:31, → n. 6) nor to provoke others to anger (Eph. 6:4), which is to seduce into sin (→ σκανδαλίζειν) and is just as bad as ἁμαρτάνειν, if not worse, cf. Mt. 18:6. Hence anger esp. is banished from the near presence of God, so 1 Tm. 2:8 : βούλομαι ... προσεύχεσθαι τοὺς ἄνδρας ... χωρὶς ὀργῆς καὶ διαλογισμοῦ, [280] Tt. 1:7: δεῖ ... τὸν ἐπίσκοπον ἀνέγκλητον εἶναι ... μὴ αὐθάδη, μὴ ὀργίλον. In a θεοῦ οἰκονόμος wrath is incompatible with ministering in the sanctuary, [281] for where there is anger God will not dwell, Ign. Phld., 8, 1.

This almost exclusively negative judgment of anger in man explains why the NT is so much more restrained in its concessions than the world around. These are to be found at most in Eph. 4:26 and Jm. 1:19. In Eph. 4:26 (ὀργίζεσθε καὶ μὴ ἁμαρτάνετε) ὀργίζεσθε by no means has the full force of an imperative, for it is a quotation (Ps. 4:4) according to the sense given by the LXX. [282] Thus it is better to translate, not : "Be angry for my sake but do not sin," but : "If you are angry, be careful not to sin." Anger is not called sin here, but there lies in the background the thought that when one is angry sin couches at the door. [283] For this reason there is added : ὁ ἥλιος μὴ ἐπιδυέτω ἐπὶ παροργισμῷ ὑμῶν. The quotation is to be read in the light of the saying five verses later (v. 31), with its repudiation of πᾶσα ὀργή. The continuation in v. 26b forms a counterpart to Jm. 1:19 : ἔστω δὲ πᾶς ἄνθρωπος ... βραδὺς εἰς ὀργήν (cf. v. 20) inasmuch as here, too, there is no absolute negating of anger, and the thoughts in the two verses complement one another, for if in Jm. one is to be slow to anger, in Eph. one is to be quick to overcome it. [284] The expression βραδὺς εἰς ὀργήν might be taken as a par. and equivalent of אֶרֶךְ אַפַּיִם along with μακρόθυμος (→ 395; 432). In this case μίμησις of God and His μακροθυμία is commended, and since this is very close to His χάρις (→ 425), the exhortation is more a demand to forgive than to be angry. Here too, as in Eph. 4, the apparent concession is followed at once by the verse (20) which rejects anger : "Anger does not build up the righteousness which matters before God." [285]

---

[278] There is a fine par. in Liv., 8, 6, 2 f., where Annius is angry with Jupiter and is himself smitten by the wrath of the gods.

[279] Cf. the same thought in bNed., 22a (Str.-B., I, 277): "He who is angry, over him rule all the punishments of Gehinnom;" for Gehinnom is the place of wrathful judgment. On the other hand, in Gr. Bar. 16 the wrath of God finds a response in that of man.

[280] In the case of ὀργή, as in that of διαλογισμός, one may doubt whether it is against God (cf. Plut.. De Ira Cohibenda, 5 [II, 455d, → 384]: "We are angry against the gods") or against men, in which case there is a par. to Mk. 11:25 (cf. Mt. 5:23 f.); Rabb. parallels (Str.-B., III, 645) make the latter more likely in the case of ὀργή (so also Wbg. Past., 112).

[281] Materially Ign. Phld., 1, 2 says the same : τὸ ἀόργητον αὐτοῦ (sc. the bishop). But the neuter form and the neighbouring expressions (τὸ ἀκίνητον, ἐνάρετος, ἐπιείκεια) suggest Stoic influence on the thoughts ; cf. Bau. Ign., ad loc.

[282] For other interpretations cf. Str.-B., III, 602.

[283] Cf. bBer., 29b: "Do not flare up, that thou sin not."

[284] ὀργῆς ταμίαι δίκαιοι, as which Joseph. lauds the Essenes in Bell., 2, 135, act in this twofold sense.

[285] For the meaning of δικαιοσύνη θεοῦ here cf. the comm. Related to Jm. 1:19 f. is the thought of Ab., 5, 11: "He who is slow to anger and inclined to be friendly is a righteous

II. The Wrath of God.

1. Differentiation from the World Around.

a. Linguistic Differentiation. In distinction from Joseph., [286] though in the train of the LXX, [287] the NT never uses the terms of Gk. poetry for the implacable wrath of the gods, μῆνις [288] and χόλος [289] (→ n. 6; 384; 410 f.), but employs for God's wrath only ὀργή and θυμός, [290] and the latter only in R. 2:8 and Rev. (14:10, 19; 15:1, 7; 16, 1, 19; 19:15). [291] Whether in the choice of the word by the apostle Paul or John the Divine there is some sense of a qualitative distinction between θυμός and ὀργή [292] it is hard to decide. The heaping up of terms in many of these passages (R. 2:8 f.: ὀργή καὶ θυμός, [293] θλῖψις καὶ στενοχωρία, Rev. 16:19 : τὸ ποτήριον τοῦ οἴνου τοῦ θυμοῦ τῆς ὀργῆς, cf. 19:15; 14:10), which serves to enhance the shattering impression of the reality of the divine wrath (→ 396; 412 f.), leaves no sharp distinction between θυμός and ὀργή. But one might very well say that θυμός, to which there clings the concept of passionate outburst, was well adapted for describing the visions of the seer, but not for delineating Paul's concept of the wrath of God.

The meaning of ὀργή may be fixed more precisely by considering the terms which are placed alongside it or contrasted with it in the NT (→ 430). The fact that it is set side by side with ἐκδίκησις (Lk. 21:22; R. 12:19, → II, 445 ff.) and δικαιοκρισία (R. 2:5, → 419; II, 224 f.) rules out the thought of unbridled and hence unrighteous revenge when applied to God. If → θλῖψις (Mk. 13:9 and par.; R. 2:8 f.), → στενοχωρία (R. 2:8 f.) and → ἀνάγκη (Lk. 21:23) are par., this shows that in the meaning of the term in most NT verses the effect is of more significance than the emotion, → 424 f.; cf. 397.

b. Material Differentiation. Jesus and the Baptist (Lk. 3:18) bring a Gospel which includes the proclamation of the ὀργὴ θεοῦ (cf. Mt. 3:7 and par.; Lk. 21:23). Similarly Paul and the Gospel and Revelation of John declare a message which proclaims not merely grace and mercy but also the wrath of God, cf. R. 1:18; Jn. 3:36; Rev. 14:10. In the NT, then, the wrath of God is in no sense regarded as an inconsistent bit of OT religion which has been dragged in, as though reference to God's wrath belonged only to the OT and reference to His love were confined to the NT. For the OT, too, proclaims God's love and mercy just as impressively as His wrath, and the NT preaches His wrath as well as His mercy, → 425, 10 ff.

---

man." In respect of such statements one must realise how very different were the criteria in the world which stood outside biblical categories, cf. Athenag. Suppl., 21: ἐγὼ μὲν γὰρ ... ἀνθρώπους ἀμαθεῖς καὶ σκαιοὺς (uncultured and boorish) λέγω τοὺς ὀργῇ καὶ λύπῃ εἴκοντας. On the one side, the question is that of culture, on the other that of righteousness ; on the one side the interest is in man, on the other in God.

[286] Cf. A. Schlatter, Wie sprach Josephus von Gott? (1910), 59.

[287] Cf. Wetter, 16.

[288] The LXX, however, also uses the verb μηνίζω (μηνίω) for God, ψ 102:8.

[289] Though notably in Sib., VIII, 93 : ἀπαραίτητος (pitiless) χόλος.

[290] Cf. v. Jüchen, 49 f. If the reason is not just the linguistic one that μῆνις, χόλος, κότος etc. were then mainly poetic and were felt not to be suitable in prose, it is to be sought, not in a weakening (Wetter, 16), but in a purifying of the concept and in awareness of the essential difference between the anger of the gods and the wrath of God.

[291] → III, 167. On the use of the derivates → 419 and n. 266; also 410, 17-33.

[292] → 384, cf. esp. Philodem. De Ira, 45, 32 ff. (Wilke, p. 90), and in the textual apparatus, ad loc. the note on the meaning of ὀργή and the distinction between it and θυμός; cf. also Trench, 123 ff.

[293] So also Ael. Var. Hist., 13, 2 (A. Fridrichsen, "Observationen zum NT aus Ael. Var. Hist.," Symb. Osl., 5 [1927], 63); Isoc., 12, 81 etc.

Though the world from which the men of the NT come, and to which they speak, reckons with the wrath of God as a given factor, the NT differs distinctively at this point from the world before and around it. It is true that a profound reason for the wrath of God is the same in both, namely, the human hubris which basically despises God and seeks to live without Him, cf. R. 2:4 ff.; 1:18 ff.; → 432; 431. But whereas in the pagan world the result is eternal hostility between gods and men, [294] in the NT there stands alongside and above God's wrath His love, whose violation is an ever new occasion of His wrath (→ 420). In keeping is the fact that nowhere in the NT is God's wrath portrayed with the colours of psychical or natural passion, as often in the OT. We never find in it enigmatic and irrational outbursts of divine anger. Nor does the wrath of God last to eternity (→ 433 f.), as in the OT. A theological concept of ὀργή plainly outweights the psychological concept in the NT. [295] This goes hand in hand with the fact that the thought of operation or effect is much stronger than that of psychical reaction, → 424, 28 ff.

2. Wrath in the NT View of God.

a. Wrath is an essential and inalienable trait in the biblical and NT view of God. When it is realised, as everywhere in the NT, that it is a fearful thing to fall into the hands of the living God (Hb. 10:31), that He has power to save and to destroy (Jm. 4:12), and when He is feared because, beyond the death of the body, He has the power to destroy both body and soul in hell (Lk. 12:5; Mt. 10:28), [296] awareness of God's wrath is at the root. [297]

b. Sometimes, to be sure, the wrath of God even in the NT (→ 396; 416) seems, as it were, to be detached from God as an independently operating force, personified, almost, as a terrible demon. It is undoubtedly striking that in 15 out of 18 passages Paul has ὀργή without the qualifying (τοῦ) θεοῦ. [298] On the basis of this and other observations the thesis has been advanced [299] that in Paul, as in Judaism, ὀργή is an autonomous entity alongside God.

The beginning of this "absolute" use of ὀργή are found in the OT (cf. Ezr. 7:23; Da. 8:19). The personification of ὀργή is also prefigured in the OT in the concept of the instruments of wrath (Is. 13:5; Jer. 50:25; → 400) [300] and also in the many figurative

---

[294] Cf. v. Jüchen, 33, 47 f.

[295] This is shown by expressions like ἐπιφέρω ὀργήν (R. 3:5), ὀργὴ ἔρχεται (Rev. 11:18), or φθάνει (1 Th. 2:16), θησαυρίζω ὀργήν (R. 2:5) et al.; cf. Pohlenz, 14.

[296] There seems to me to be no doubt that in this logion Jesus has God in view, not the devil; cf. the comm., ad loc.

[297] In many verses this wrath seems to have numinous features, e.g., Mk. 11:14; Hb. 12:29. Hence Otto, 99 ff. seeks to incorporate into his view of the phenomenon of numinous anger a series of NT passages and stories, esp. the incident in Gethsemane, → 445; n. 386. But divine wrath as an irrational *mysterium tremendum* finds no place in the NT view of either Jesus or God; in all such passages the ref. is in reality to the holy wrath of Jesus Christ and His Father, cf. P. Althaus, *Die chr. Wahrheit*, II (1948), 163.

[298] In some cases the tradition — Western witnesses in 1 Th. 2:16, Chrys. in R. 12:19 — supplies the missing θεοῦ, while Marcion suppresses it in R. 1:18, since it does not fit in with his view of God.

[299] Wetter, 16-55, with hints also in Pohlenz, 15. Böhmer, 320-322 discusses the same observations and similar conclusions in respect of the OT.

[300] Hbr. כְּלִי זַעַם, LXX Jer. 27:25 (Mas. 50:25): σκεύη ὀργῆς, obviously weapons which God takes from His armoury (θησαυρός); cf. also Is. 10:5: ῥάβδος τοῦ θυμοῦ μου καὶ ὀργῆς. But in Is. 13:5 the LXX has ὁπλομάχοι for כלי זעם. which symbolise God's host at the judgment of the world. On this whole question cf. Böhmer, 320 ff.

refs. to the sending, coming and passing of wrath (e.g., Is. 10:6; 26:20; cf. → 414), or when God says in Is. 63:5 : "Then my fury helped me." Judaism, however, goes much further along these lines, as already in many passages in the apocr. and pseudepigr., e.g., Wis. 18:21: (Moses) ἀντέστη τῷ θυμῷ. Apc. Abr. speaks rather obscurely of an image of the divine wrath [301] "with which the people which comes to me from you (Abraham) provokes me." For Rabb. Judaism wrath is on the one side one of the two basic powers (*middoth*) in God, [302] while on the other אַף and חֵמָה or מַלְאָךְ זַעַף [303] are independent angels of destruction, → n. 354; 414. The "absolute" view of the NT is thought to be on the one hand a continuation of this development, but on the other a form of the fatalism of antiquity, a counterpart to Gk. Εἱμαρμένη and Roman fate, though it is allowed that in distinction from the gods of fate NT ὀργή always stands under God and is directed by Him. [304]

Over against these supposed prefigurations and counterparts of NT ὀργή it must be affirmed 1. that the idea of transcendent embodiments of wrath (like the prophetic instruments of wrath → 400; 436 or the angels of wrath) is unknown to the NT, for the angels of Rev. which pour out the vials of wrath etc. are simply messengers and executors of the divine will, as is the nature of all NT angels ; 2. that while the NT often speaks of the coming of wrath (though not the sending etc.), in this context coming is simply a tt. for the coming of things to come, i.e., the last things ; [305] 3. that the NT does not share the two basic motifs of contemporary religion, namely, fatalism and dualism, since it may easily be shown that nowhere in the NT is ὀργή a principle which operates rigidly and independently of God, but that everywhere it is very closely linked to God, to the God who acts personally therein. [306] The common absence of θεοῦ does not support the conclusion that even Paul felt ὀργή to be an independent hypostasis. It simply shows us how strong was the awareness of God in all things. [307] The independent use of ὀργή corresponds fully to the use of → χάρις in Pl. and his disciples ; [308] it is self-evident here that the ref. is to the grace of God.

c. Nevertheless, though NT ὀργή is indissolubly related to God, there can be no evading the question whether this ὀργή is in any sense an emotion in God (→ 397). Is it not rather the punishment ordained by God in His wrath (→ 384; 414; 422)? [309] Now there is no doubt that Origen is right (Cels., IV, 72); one cannot heap up a passion (R. 2:5 f.). In most NT passages ὀργή is in fact the divine work, destiny or judgment of wrath (so Mt. 3:7 and par.; R. 2:5; 3:5; 12:19 etc.). All the same, the idea of an actual attitude of God cannot be disputed in respect of many NT

---

[301] Obviously this image lasts to the very end as a monument for the judge, for human sacrifices to idols are called a witness at the last judgment.

[302] Cf. Bousset-Gressm., 350 f. The wrath corresponds to מִדַּת הַדִּין. Acc. to S. Nu., 71a; Tg. Ps. 56:11 and other passages the name Elohim belongs here, while the name Yahweh belongs to מִדַּת הָרַחֲמִים; cf. also Weber, 154, 259. Within this view it is not only possible but it makes sense that the midrash Ps. 7:7 has the form : "Stand up, Yahweh, against thy wrath (not in thy wrath)," and that bBer., 7a has God "pray" : "May it be my will that my mercy subdue my wrath."

[303] Cf. bShab., 55a; Dt. r., 3 (200c); jTaan., 2, 65b, 43 (→ 432) in Str.-B., III, 30 f.; cf. Bousset Gressm., 350 f.; Weber, 154 and 172; Böhmer, 321. Tanch. תזריע, 155b (Str.-B., III, 30).

[304] Wetter, 46-55.

[305] Cf. Cr.-Kö., 445 f., *s.v.* ἔρχομαι; → II, 666 ff.

[306] Cf. Braun, 42.

[307] So Schl. Mt., 71.

[308] Cf. esp. R. 5:20 f.; 6:14 f.; Phil. 1:7; Hb. 4:16, also the introductions and conclusions of epistles, so 1 Pt. 1:2; Col. 4:18; 1 Tm. 6:21; 2 Tm. 4:22; Hb. 13:25.

[309] So Bultmann, 283 f.

verses, any more than this is possible in respect of → ἀγάπη and ἔλεος, [310] cf. R. 1:18; 9:22; Rev. 6:16, and most clearly the OT quotation in Hb. 3:11; 4:3. As in the OT (→ 400), so in the NT ὀργή is both God's displeasure at evil, His passionate resistance to every will which is set against Him, [311] and also His judicial attack thereon.

d. Objections are continually raised against the thesis that the ὀργή θεοῦ is an integral part of biblical proclamation. They are chiefly based on belief in God's love. If God is truly love, He cannot be angry. [312] But even prior to the NT it was realised that wrath and love are mutually inclusive, not exclusive, in God. [313] In the NT as in the OT, in Jesus as in the prophets, in the apostles as in the rabbis, the preaching of God's mercy is accompanied by the proclamation of His wrath, → 422. Only he who knows the greatness of wrath will be mastered by the greatness of mercy. The converse is also true : Only he who has experienced the greatness of mercy can measure how great wrath must be. For the wrath of God arises from His love and mercy, → 403. Where mercy meets with the ungodly will of man rather than faith and gratitude, with goodwill and the response of love, love becomes wrath, cf. Mt. 18:34; Mk. 3:5; R. 2:5. In Christ mankind is divided into those who are freed from wrath inasmuch as they are ready to be saved by His mercy, and those who remain under wrath because they despise His mercy. This is what was proclaimed from the very first concerning Jesus by Simeon (Lk. 2:34) and John the Baptist (Mt. 3:12). This is how Jesus Himself regarded the operation of His word and work (cf. Lk. 20:18; Mk. 4:12). And He finally illustrated His divisive power by dying between two malefactors (Lk. 23:39 ff.).

e. What is the relation of God's ὀργή to His μακροθυμία, → IV, 376 f. ? This is a crucial issue in the exegesis of R. 9:22 : εἰ δὲ θέλων ὁ θεὸς ἐνδείξασθαι τὴν ὀργὴν κτλ. The μακροθυμία θεοῦ stands in rather a different light if we take the θέλων causally on the one side, [314] or concessively on the other. [315] Is it a servant of wrath or an instrument of mercy ? It probably has a double function. Primarily it is an outflowing of love (cf. 1 C. 13:4) and mercy, which gives the sinner space for μετάνοια (cf. R. 2:4; Rev. 2:21; 2 Pt. 3:9), and is thus a help to salvation (2 Pt. 3:15; cf. 1 Tm. 1:16) by which even σκεύη ὀργῆς may become σκεύη ἐλέους, [316] so that it is a way to the final manifestation of glory for the vessels

---

[310] Cf. Althaus, op. cit., II, 164.

[311] Cf. P. Kalweit, Art. "Zorn Gottes," IV in RGG², V, 2137. The Enlightenment called such ideas "the crude anthropopathisms of an uncultured age" (Rüegg in RE³, 21, 719, 43 f.), but they are no more anthropopathic than what the Bible says about the fatherly love of God ; like this they belong inalienably to the biblical concept of the personal God.

[312] This was the conclusion of, e.g., Marcion in respect of his good God, cf. Tert. Marc., I, 27: Deus melior inventus est, qui nec offenditur nec irascitur nec ulciscitur.

[313] Cf. Prayer of Man. 5 f.: ἀνυπόστατος ἡ ὀργὴ τῆς ἐπὶ ἁμαρτωλοὺς ἀπειλῆς σου, ἀμέτρητόν τε καὶ ἀνεξιχνίαστον τὸ ἔλεος τῆς ἐπαγγελίας σου, and twice in the brief summary Sir. 5:6 = 16:11: ἔλεος ... καὶ ὀργὴ παρ' αὐτῷ (the par. half-verse shows this to be original at least in the second ref., → 414 and n. 222). For a discussion cf. Barth K.D., II, 1² (1946), 407, 442-446 (C.D., II, 1 [1957], 362 ff., 396-8); Althaus, op. cit., II, 32 f.

[314] Zahn, Schlatter, Kühl, Lietzmann, Althaus etc.

[315] So B. Weiss R.⁹ (1899), A. Jülicher in Schr. NT, ad loc. and transl. by Weizsäcker, Menge, Zurich Bible etc.

[316] The σκεύη ὀργῆς, like the τέκνα φύσει ὀργῆς of Eph. 2:3 (→ 435), may count on this possibility, which becomes a reality in μετάνοια. The NT knows no rigid predestination to eternal perdition. A different view is taken on the specific question in Zn. R., 459 (though cf. 461), Ltzm. R. on 9:22, et al. (→ n. 318).

of mercy. But when the patience of God is despised and misused (cf. 1 Pt. 3:20),
it serves to sharpen the wrath of God and to confirm the destruction ordained
for the σκεύη ὀργῆς (cf. Ign. Eph., 11, 1). The longsuffering of God has the same
enigmatic dual operation as all God's tokens of grace, e.g., the miracles of healing,
the parables, and even Jesus Himself, → 429. On the one side it leads to falling,
on the other to raising up. Thus we may paraphrase R. 9:22 as follows: "But if
God tolerated in great longsuffering the vessels of wrath which were made for
destruction, because He willed to manifest His wrath and declare His power in
them, (he did it) also [317] in order that he might make known the riches of his glory
in the vessels of mercy, which he had prepared long before for glory." Here, too,
we have the underlying thought of R. 1:17 f. and 3:23 that the revelation of wrath
is the indispensable foil to the revelation of mercy. [318]

f. The tension between wrath and righteousness, of which antiquity, too, was
aware in spite of its admission of the judge's right to wrath, [319] is a particular
problem in the theological thinking of the NT. God's wrath is on human sin according to the NT. But it is precisely the ἀδικία of man which serves the triumph
of God's δικαιοσύνη (R. 3:4 f. ὅπως). Without sin there could not be the miracle
of *sola gratia* on which not only our salvation but also God's δόξα rests (v. 7).
The question, then, seems to be justified (R. 3:5): μὴ ἄδικος ὁ θεὸς ὁ ἐπιφέρων
τὴν ὀργήν; Indeed, further insight into the implications of the causes and effects
of ὀργή forces us to broaden the question: Is God right to be angry at the chaos
of sin to which He Himself delivers up godforsaken humanity [320] (→ 440; 443;
444)? Paul's answer to these difficult questions is primarily (R. 3:6) an argument
of Jewish theology. God is the world's Judge, hence He cannot be other than
righteous. We might restate the argument as follows. He who realises that he is
a sinner deserves from God nothing other than wrath, and in the judgment nothing
other than rejection. For him God's righteousness is beyond question. For he sees
that God's ὀργή, like His resistance to ἀδικία, is simply an expression of His
δικαιοσύνη. [321]

This thought is the basis of Paul's deliberations in R. 1:18 ff. But in the parallelism of v. 17 and v. 18 there is contained a very different answer to the question
which affirms that God's wrath and righteousness are united in a surprising way
which man could never have thought of. [322] For precisely (γάρ, v. 18) because
God has to be wrathful against the whole world, not just the Gentiles but also the
Jews, and also against each individual (c. 2), for this very reason He gives righteousness ἐκ πίστεως εἰς πίστιν (1:17; 3:21 ff.) and shows Himself to be the righteous Judge in the acknowledgment of this righteousness, 3:26.

---

[317] καί is absent in B vulg etc.; if it is taken in the sense of "also," the construction is
hard, but it is not disrupted, so also Zn. R., 458, n. 24, P. Althaus R. (*NT Deutsch*), ad loc.,
et al.
[318] For a rather different view cf. J. C. K. v. Hofmann, *D. heilige Schrift NTs*, III (1868),
401-406 and → μακροθυμία κτλ. (Horst), IV, 377 ff., esp. 385, 15 ff.; both reject the
possibility considered in n. 316.
[319] → 384; Pohlenz, 15, n. 3 and Hirzel, 417 refer to Demosth., 24, 118 and Aeschin.,
3, 197, which speak of a righteous correspondence between transgression and judicial wrath.
[320] Cf. Apc. Abr., 27 (Bonwetsch, p. 36) with 25 (p. 35), where the image of God's
wrath against Israel imperceptibly becomes the idol wherewith Israel provokes God. In
plain terms, God's wrath continually causes new wrath, → 443, 15 ff.
[321] Cf. Althaus, *op. cit.* (→ n. 297), II, 163.
[322] Schrenk, 14 ff.

This very answer, however, raises the problem afresh. If God is angry at those who do not go the way of faith, is this righteous? This problem is only one of many in the general biblical dialectic, which is not capable of rational resolution, that everything is grounded in God's will and plan, and yet the guilt of everything that is against God is not thereby diminished, so that wrath thereat is righteous without qualification. From this conclusion there is only one refuge, namely, Christ and faith in Him, → 445, 4 ff.

3. The Revelation of the Divine Wrath.

a. In Jesus and His Message.

Wrath is an integral characteristic of the Jesus of the Gospels.[323] To be sure, express reference to it is rare (ὀργή, Mk. 3:5; ὀργίζομαι, Mk. 1:41 vl.; cf. ἐμβριμάομαι, Mt. 9:30; Mk. 1:43; Jn. 11:33, 38), but essentially the thing itself is often present.

The wrath of Jesus is in the first instance a sign that He was a man of flesh and blood.[324] Nevertheless, this is not just human anger. It always has about it something of the nature of God's wrath. We see this especially from the things which made Jesus angry. He was angry at various forces and powers of will set against God. He addressed Satan with imperious anger (Mt. 4:10; 16:23).[325] He angrily threatened (ἐπιτιμάω) demons (Mk. 1:25; 9:25; Lk. 4:41). He was angered (ὀργισθείς)[326] by the terrible disease of leprosy (Mk. 1:41). He was deeply incensed by the devilish nature of men (Jn. 8:44), especially the Pharisees (as πονηροὶ ὄντες, Mt. 12:34, as those who put to death the one sent by God, 23:33, as untruthful hypocrites, 15:7 etc.). This is the wrath of the Ruler of the world provoked by rebels against God. Jesus is also angered (ἐμβριμάομαι) by healed persons

---

[323] Cf. J. Ninck, Jesus als Charakter (1925), 22-32; P. Feine, Jesus (1930), 245 f.

[324] He is not like the Stoic with his inhuman (cf. Sen. Ep., 99, 15: inhumanitas, non virtus) ἀταραξία; hence there is nothing artificial about His anger, as some have tried to deduce from the reflexive ἐτάραξεν ἑαυτόν of Jn. 11:33; cf. Aug. in Joh. Ev. Tract., 49, 18; W. Heitmüller in Schr. NT, ad loc.; Bau. J.², ad loc.; H. J. Holtzmann, Lehrbuch d. nt.lichen Theol., II² (1911), 463, n. 1; cf. Bu. J., 310, n. 4 and esp. the completely erroneous interpretation of H. J. Holtzmann in Handcommentar zum NT, IV³ (1908), ad loc. The expression denotes just the same as the reading of the Western text (also v P⁴⁵) ἐταράχθη τῷ πνεύματι (also 13:21) ὡς ἐμβριμούμενος, namely, a strong and direct personal reaction (for the reasons → 428 and n. 329). On the other hand, we can hardly agree with Zn. J., ad loc. in taking the τῷ πνεύματι with ἐμβριμᾶσθαι or ταράττεσθαι so pregnantly that God Himself is said to be angry in Jesus.

[325] Jesus sees in Peter an instrument of Satan in whom the latter is concealed, cf. G. Stählin, Skandalon (1930), 162 f.

[326] The reading ὀργισθείς in D it (a ff² r) Tat is to be preferred to the more common and easier σπλαγχνισθείς (perhaps the rise of the one or the other is due to the interchange of gutturals [אתרחם-אתרעם] cf. E. Nestle, Philologica sacra [1896], 26; R. Harris, "Artificial Variants in the Text of the NT," Exp., 24 [1922], 259-261); so also J. Schniewind Mk. (NT Deutsch), ad loc.; ὀργίζεσθαι denotes Jesus' embittered struggle against deathlike sickness, and is thus equivalent to ἐμβριμᾶσθαι, Jn. 11:33, 38, and στενάζειν, Mk. 7:34. That He was angry at the leper because he approached Him contrary to the Law (cf. J. Weiss, Schr. NT on Mk. 1:41) or because he said, doubtingly, "if thou wilt" (Ephr. Evangelii concordantis expositio, transl. by J. B. Aucher [1876], 144), or that the wrath was originally that of the leper (a change of subject only after ἥψατο, so K. Lake, 'Εμβριμησάμενος and ὀργισθείς Mk. 1:40-43," HThR, 16 [1923], 197 f.), is most unlikely.

whose disobedience He foresees [327] (Mk. 1:43; [328] Mt. 9:30), and by the disciples and their lack of faith (17:17). He is provoked by unbelieving Jews who in His presence give way to unrestricted grief even though He proclaims Himself to be the resurrection and the life (Jn. 11:33), and He makes severe remarks about their lack of faith and understanding (v. 38). [329] This is the wrath of the Lord whose majesty is affronted by unbelief and disobedience. In particular Jesus is full of angry sorrow (μετ' ὀργῆς συλλυπούμενος, Mk. 3:5) [330] at the Pharisees. There are two reasons for this. It is first the wrath of the merciful Lord at legalists who will not accept the new way of mercy and salvation, and who thus allow themselves to be carried away by mercilessness and even mortal enmity (v. 6). [331] It is secondly the wrath of love, which seeks to win even the Pharisees for the kingdom of mercy and which encounters only hate because they want law, not love. There is thus mixed with holy wrath a divine pity [332] for their piety which is so far from God. This wrath is the same as that which Jesus in the parable attributes to the lord of the feast (Lk. 14:21: τότε ὀργισθεὶς ὁ οἰκοδεσπότης) when his magnanimous invitation is despised by those invited. Incomparably more severe, however, is wrath at the wicked servant (Mt. 18:34: καὶ ὀργισθεὶς ὁ κύριος αὐτοῦ) who responded with inconceivable mercilessness to the unlimited mercy which he had himself experienced. [333] In all these cases we have outbursts of the holy wrath of despised mercy and wounded love. Finally, Jesus is full of terrible anger at the cities which refused the summons to conversion (Mt. 11:20 ff.) and at the dealers in the temple who by their desecration of the house of God showed that they did not take God Himself

---

[327] It is also possible that Jesus is angry because He sees that many will be led into a superficial faith in miracles by those healed.

[328] It is tempting to see an inner connection between the ὀργίζεσθαι before the healing of the leper and the ἐμβριμᾶσθαι after, attention being drawn to the unheard of expenditure of spiritual energy in the θέλω (v. 41) and the ἐξέβαλεν (v. 43). But these are hardly considerations which concern Jesus (→ supra and n. 326, 327). On the other hand, one cannot expunge the ἐμβριμησάμενος of v. 43 because it does not fit the theory of prophetic frenzy (which has to precede a miracle), cf. C. Bonner, "Traces of Thaumaturgic Technique in the Miracles," HThR, 20 (1927), 178-181, who regards ἐμβριμησάμενος as the original reading in v. 41; in the Itala this then became iratus, and by retranslation then became ὀργισθείς in D.

[329] There has been much discussion of the reason for Jesus' anger in the Lazarus story. For the many conjectures cf. F. Godet, Commentar zu dem Ev. Joh.³ (1890), 401; H. J. Holtzmann, op. cit., ad loc.; Bau. J., ad loc.; Bu. J., ad loc., who, with Bonner, op. cit., 176 ff., regards ἐμβριμάομαι (also ταράσσω and στενάζω) as vox mystica for the pneumatic transport of the θεῖος ἄνθρωπος. The most natural interpretation is that of anger at unbelief, since the wrath of Jesus is in both cases linked with the conduct of the Jews.

[330] Cf. Schl. Mk., ad loc. In the par. there is no ref. to the ὀργή and λύπη of Jesus. On the other hand, there is a related combination of grief and anger in Jos. Ant., 16, 200.

[331] An astonishing par. to the relation of the Pharisees to Jesus is that of the Romans to Caesar, whom they do not want and finally kill because he is lenissimus (cf. his own statement, Cic. Att., 9, 7 C 1; also pro sua humanitate, indulgentia etc., loc. cit. A 2, also Sen. De Clementia). They will not have the new way of kindness and reconciliation, as Caesar himself strongly emphasises; cf. E. Stauffer, "Clementia Caesaris," Schrift u. Bekenntnis, Zeugnisse lutherischer Theol. (1950), 174-184, esp. 182 f.

[332] This is shown by the compound συλλυπέομαι, cf. Pr.-Bauer, s.v.

[333] John the Baptist (cf. Mt. 3:8) and Jesus Himself both leave the door open for the Pharisees. The divine love of Jesus sorrows at everyone who is lost (cf. Lk. 19:41 ff.; perhaps also Jn. 11:38). The promise of salvation is still held out, cf. Lk. 13:35. On the other hand, final judgment overtakes the blessed but graceless disciple. The reason for judgment in Mt. 18:34 is the same as in Hb. 6:4-6.

seriously (Mt. 21:12 ff.; cf. Jn. 2:13 ff.). [334] Again, in a strange parabolic action [335] He manifests His wrath against those who withhold from Him the fruits of repentance (Mk. 11:14; cf. Lk. 13:7). This is the wrath of the eschatological Judge who has full power to destroy, to cut off from divine fellowship (ἐκβάλλω, Mt. 21:12; cf. 22:13; 25:30; Lk. 13:28), and to cast into Hades (Mt. 11:23), and who has already used this power.

From what has been said it is obvious already that Jesus was aware, and often showed by word and act, that His anger basically reveals even now the eschatological wrath of God. Wrath is a feature in the varied picture of the last things fulfilled in the coming of Jesus. Jesus is the provoked Lord of the Last Judgment (cf. Ps. 2:12), [336] who repudiates all connection with those against whom He is angry (Mt. 7:23; 25:12; Lk. 13:27), [337] who in wrath destroys His foes (Lk. 19:27; 12:46 and par.; cf. Mt. 22:7), and who casts the rejected εἰς τὴν κάμινον τοῦ πυρός (Mt. 13:42; cf. v. 49 f.; 25:41) and εἰς τὸ σκότος τὸ ἐξώτερον (22:13; 25:30) or into hopeless imprisonment (18:34). Even though the word ὀργίζομαι occurs in only two of the passages quoted (Mt. 18:34; 22:7), this must be mentioned here, the more so because in polar correspondence to the first parts of the NT the last book takes up again in its own forceful and vivid way this picture of the wrathful King and Judge of the last days. Thus Rev. 19:15 portrays the King of kings and Lord of lords who in blood-drenched garments, and with a sword proceeding from His mouth, treads the winepress of the wrath of Almighty God (→ 431; 437 f.), and Rev. 6:16 has the particularly striking expression ὀργὴ τοῦ ἀρνίου, cf. also 14:10. [338] In relation to this apparently impossible mixture of images one should remember first that, in distinction from the → ἀμνός of Jn. 1:29 etc., the → ἀρνίον can also denote the young and strong ram, and secondly, and supremely, that the same Christ who once as Lamb fell defencelessly victim to the judgment of men will then as wrathful Judge exercise terrible judgment on men, cf. esp. Rev. 19:11 ff.; His wrath is particularly against those who despised the self-sacrifice of the Lamb.

---

[334] The φραγέλλιον of v. 15 is both the sign and weapon of the divine wrath which already in the prophets is directed against every commercialised cultus.

[335] With the wrathful cursing of the fig-tree there arises even for Jesus Himself the question of the justice of His anger, for the time of ripe figs was long since over (cf. the comm.). Here is one of the difficult features in the parables and parabolic actions of Jesus whose only point is to draw attention to what is taught and impressively to bring out its true seriousness.

[336] On the other hand Jesus in Lk. 13:9 rather strangely says ἐκκόψεις, not ἐκκόψω. In this historical judgment the roles of angry Judge and merciful Advocate are allotted to the Father and the Son.

[337] Something similar is expressed by the sevenfold οὐαί of Mt. 23. Jesus hereby exercises as present Judge the judgment of the wrath of God.

[338] The authenticity of the καὶ ἀπὸ τῆς ὀργῆς αὐτοῦ is disputed (E. Vischer, D. Offenbarung Joh. [1886], 40 f.; E. Spitta, D. Offenbarung des Joh. [1889], 27 f.; J. Weiss in Schr. NT on Rev. 6:16; E. Sievers, D. Johannesapk. klanglich untersucht u. hsgg. in ASG, 38, 1 [1925], 31, et al., also Procksch in the first draft of the art.), first, because it echoes ἀπὸ προσώπου τοῦ καθημένου ἐπὶ τοῦ θρόνου, and secondly, because in v. 17 most witnesses read αὐτοῦ for αὐτῶν. Nevertheless, it seems to me that a later addition is most unlikely. The phrase "wrath of the lamb" succinctly and forcefully expresses the fact that Christ is both Saviour and Judge, and that the day of judgment is the day of His (αὐτοῦ) wrath, v. 17.

b. In Its Historical and Eschatological Outworking.

Like many other NT terms and values — βασιλεία, δικαιοσύνη, σωτηρία — ὀργή is a concept which can have a distinctly eschatological as well as a distinctly present character. [339] In the case of ὀργή, as of the other terms, the present manifestations are provisional as compared with the eschatological. Both forms of manifestation occur in the NT more or less equally from the material, if not the numerical, standpoint.

(a) Eschatological ὀργή is characterised as such esp. by certain typical accompanying words, antonyms and images. Eschatological terms used with ὀργή are the verbs ἔρχομαι (1 Th. 1:10; cf. Eph. 5:6; Rev. 11:18) and μέλλω (Mt. 3:7), esp. in the pres. part. (→ II, 666 ff.), also → σῴζω (R. 5:9) and ἀποκαλύπτω (R. 1:18; → III, 583, but cf. also → 431 and n. 345), and esp. ἡμέρα in the sense of the day of Yahweh as already fixed by the prophets [340] (e.g., Zeph. 1:15; cf. ψ 109:5 etc., → 401; 417; but also 404 f.), then used in the pseudepigr. (e.g., Jub. 24:28, 30) and Talmud (bAZ, 18b; bBB, 10a; → n. 374) and finally adopted in the NT (R. 2:5; Rev. 6:17). Antonyms to eschatological ὀργή are ζωὴ αἰώνιος (R. 2:7; cf. v. 5) and περιποίησις σωτηρίας (1 Th. 5:9). Of NT images for the wrath of God (→ 436-439) the fire (Mt. 3:10-12), the cup (Rev. 14:10) and the winepress (19:15) are esp. eschatological in thrust.

The significance of eschatological wrath in NT proclamation comes out most plainly in the fact that the NT, directly following the OT prophets, begins with the message of ὀργὴ μέλλουσα (Mt. 3:7) and also closes with it (Rev. to c. 19). John the Baptist sets the tone with his preaching of the coming wrath of God [341] (Mt. 3:7, 10-12) and his baptism with its aim of liberation therefrom (→ 436; 444), and Jesus follows him in this regard. Only seldom does Jesus speak expressly of the divine wrath (cf. → 422). The noun ὀργή occurs only once in the Lucan form of the address on the future (21:23), and the verb ὀργίζομαι only twice in this eschatological sense in the parable (Mt. 22:7; Lk. 14:21 is rather different; cf. also Mt. 18:34). But the thing itself is an integral part of Jesus' view of the future as in that of His apostles, esp. Paul and John the Divine (→ 431). There are two points in the future where eschatological ὀργή has a place, first, in the tribulation before the end, then in the final judgment itself.

In the one ὀργή saying of Jesus (Lk. 21:23) it belongs to the period of the Messianic woes and is almost synonymous with ἀνάγκη, [342] for which the Synoptic par. have θλῖψις (Mt. 24:21; Mk. 13:19). These are tt. for the eschatological tribulation whose climax is the destruction of Jerusalem, cf. v. 21, 24. The reference, then, is to the historical outworking of wrath, and hence to wrath of limited duration, v. 24: ἄχρι οὗ πληρωθῶσιν καιροὶ ἐθνῶν.

---

[339] Cf. L. Pinoma, "Der Zorn Gottes," ZSTh, 17 (1940), 590; Ritschl (Rechtfertigung u. Versöhnung, 153) thought he could show that the idea of God's wrath in the NT has only an eschatological reference and is no longer used, as in the OT (→ 400-402) and Judaism (→ 415) to appraise present phenomena, so that it is no longer binding on Christian faith. But this type of consistent eschatological understanding is one-sided and leads to wrong conclusions, cf. F. Weber, passim; Cr.-Kö., 813-816; P. Feine, 207; Bu. J., 121, n. 4.

[340] Sometimes in the OT ἡμέρα ὀργῆς is used of historical disasters, cf. 4 Βασ. 19:3 and the par. Is. 37:3; also Job 20:28; 21:30.

[341] Acc. to the account in Jn. the last words of the Baptist as well as the first speak of God's wrath (3:36).

[342] Cf. in this regard the close connection between ira deum and fatum among the Romans, e.g., Tac. Historiae, IV, 26, → 390.

Already in the Rabb. wrath is sometimes used for the judgment of Gehinnom. [343] Similarly in Paul it can be the same as the ἀποκάλυψις δικαιοκρισίας τοῦ θεοῦ (R. 2:5), and in Rev. it is equated with καιρὸς τῶν νεκρῶν κριθῆναι (11:18). Obviously here wrath is not so much the righteous anger of the Judge of the world as what He imposes (→ 424), ἐκδίκησις (cf. Lk. 21:22 f.), the opposite of δικαίωσις, the denial of salvation. [344] Thus, in accordance with its predominant characteristic, the Last Day is called the ἡμέρα ὀργῆς (R. 2:5; Rev. 6:17). From the first reference to ὀργή in Rev.: ἦλθεν ἡ ἡμέρα ἡ μεγάλη τῆς ὀργῆς (6:16 f.), it may be seen that the whole drama of wrath in the Apc. takes place on this one "day" of judgment. In ever new disasters wrath is poured out with the breaking of the sixth seal (6:12 ff.), the last trumpet (11:18), each of the seven vials (c. 15 f.), the judgment on Babylon (16:19) and the *parousia* of the Lord and Judge, who Himself treads the winepress of wrath (19:15).

(b) In varied relation to the eschatological judgment of wrath, there is found in the NT a present exercise of wrath. We have seen already (→ 428) how the wrathful Jesus of the Gospels is constantly manifested in the present as the One in whom the Messiah and Judge of the earth, indeed, the holy God Himself, is here. Furthermore, Jesus in His sayings portrays in various ways the wrath which is at work in history (e.g., Lk. 13:2 ff.), and Paul, too, in different connections speaks unequivocally of a historical outworking of the wrath of God. We may refer first to R. 1:18: ἀποκαλύπτεται γὰρ ὀργὴ θεοῦ ἀπ' οὐρανοῦ ἐπὶ πᾶσαν ἀσέβειαν καὶ ἀδικίαν ἀνθρώπων τῶν τὴν ἀλήθειαν ἐν ἀδικίᾳ κατεχόντων. There can be not the slightest doubt that a present revelation of God's wrath is proclaimed here. [345] It is revealed at the same time and in detailed parallelism [346] with the δικαιοσύνη θεοῦ, and the two revelations are linked by a significant γάρ. That outside πίστις there is for all mankind (cf. 3:9 ff., 23) only ὀργή is the indispensable presupposition of the fact that δικαιοσύνη is revealed only ἐκ πίστεως. [347] The logic of this γάρ is the same as that of the twofold γάρ in 3:22 f. or the ἵνα of Gl. 3:22. The twofold revelation of the wrath and righteousness of God, however, is bound exclusively to Christ. Since He came into the world there takes place the eschatological judgment of the world, both pardon (justification) and the sentence of wrath. [348] For the term "ἀποκαλύπτω characterises the message as an event of eschatological salvation." [349] In both instances ἀποκαλύπτω denotes here a revelation in concealment, i.e., one which is manifest only to the believer. This is just as strictly true of the ἀποκάλυψις ὀργῆς as of the ἀποκάλυψις δικαιοσύνης. The ἐν αὐτῷ of R. 1:17, of course, is not formally related to 1:18, but only in the sphere of the Gospel is it clear that the abysmally deep

---

[343] Cf. Str.-B., I, 115 f., → n. 374.
[344] Cr.-Kö., 814.
[345] The pres. here is to be taken neither as a living "presentation" of the future nor as the gnomic pres. of the doctrine of things to come derived from prophecy (so Ritschl, *op. cit.*, 142-147), as is the case in 1 C. 3:13 (ἡ ἡμέρα ... ἐν πυρὶ ἀποκαλύπτεται); since this is not possible in 1:17, it has to be rejected in the case of the v. which immediately follows (Cr.-Kö., 815).
[346] Cf. esp. Schl. R., 46 and on the dialectic of the relation of the two revelations W. Elert, *Der chr. Glaube* (1940), 170-176.
[347] Cf. Schl. R., 52; → 426, 30 ff.
[348] Cf. present judgment in Jn. and on this G. Stählin, "Zum Problem der joh. Eschatologie," ZNW, 33 (1934), 238; Cr.-Kö., 814 f.
[349] Bornkamm, 239.

sinfulness of the world is a revelation of the wrath of God. [350] Every such temporal revelation in concealment, however, points forward to the full manifestation at the end. Hence proclamation of the present revelation of wrath is always accompanied by that of future wrath (2:8), just as the promise of future justification (3:30) goes along with the message of present justification (v. 24, 28).

Hence in the other verses in which Paul speaks of the ὀργή (θεοῦ) (R. 2:5, 8; 9:22) a present element accompanies the eschatological, and whenever he speaks of present wrath (R. 3:5; 4:15; 13:4 f.; 1 Th. 2:16) an eschatological perspective is not entirely absent. [351] In R. 3:7 we have τί ἔτι κἀγὼ ὡς ἁμαρτωλὸς κρίνομαι; par. to v. 5 μὴ ἄδικος ὁ θεὸς ὁ ἐπιφέρων τὴν ὀργήν; The present ἐπιφέρων refers to the present revelation of wrath as in 1:18; but the present yet undoubtedly eschatological κρίνομαι confers on ὀργή the quality of eschatological wrath. [352]

(c) In the NT there is a noteworthy delaying of the judgment of wrath. God Himself does what He asks of man: ἔστω πᾶς ἄνθρωπος ... βραδὺς εἰς ὀργήν, Jm. 1:19. This explains why there is often no execution of wrath even when one might expect it.

The motif of delay is found in many forms even prior to the NT, among the Gks. (Homer, Solon, → 386), in the OT, esp. in the vivid expression ארך אפים = μακρό-θυμος κτλ., → IV, 378; → n. 58; 405; 421), [353] and in Judaism (e.g., S. Bar. 59:6), though here with a more particularist restriction, whether as a one-sided means to save Israel (e.g., jTaan., 2, 65b, 44 ff., esp. 50-58), [354] or as a means to bring θυμός on the Gentiles (e.g., 2 Macc. 6:14), or both together (b. Er., 22a: "Slow in wrath against the righteous, slow in wrath against transgressors"). [355]

In the NT the thought of delayed wrath lies behind three verses in R., [356] in two of which may be seen the same dual operation as in Rabbinic statements: in R. 9:22 (→ 425; 436) the delaying of wrathful judgment serves on the one side to demonstrate the more forcefully the power of God's wrath on the σκεύη ὀργῆς, and on the other to reveal the more gloriously His mercy on the σκεύη ἐλέους; in R. 2:4 it is plain that this double function of the delaying of divine wrath (ἀνοχὴ

---

[350] Bultmann, 271; Elert, 181.

[351] Though cf. Hb. 3:11; 4:3, where the ref. of the quotation from Ps. 95:11 is to the thoroughly non-eschatological divine wrath of the OT, which burst forth now against Israel and now against the Gentiles.

[352] Wetter, 29 thinks Paul's argument is as follows: If God is already the future Judge of the world (v. 6), His present judicial sway (ἐπιφέρων ὀργήν) is undoubtedly just. Hence there is a conclusion a maiori ad minus. But the present and future work of judgment cannot be divided in this way, cf. Zn. R., ad loc.

[353] Cf. also Jer. 51:33 (עוד מעט denotes the span of time which God's wrath allows itself before breaking forth in judgment), perhaps also Na. 1:2 f.

[354] ארך אפים (Jl. 2:13) is here taken in the sense of "holding wrath at a distance" and associated with the personification of wrath as two angels (→ 424), the angels of destruc-tion, who are two on account of the dual אפים ("wrath" and "fury") and who are set at a distance; hence Israel can repent in the long period before they come forth from afar, cf. Str.-B., III, 30.

[355] Here the twofold אפים is referred to the twofold countenance of God, a friendly and an angry, L. Goldschmidt, Der babylonische Talmud II (1930), 69, n. 132.

[356] Cf. also some of the parables of Jesus. Thus the delay of judgment in Mt. 13:24 ff. serves to preserve the δίκαιοι, while in Lk. 13:8 it provides opportunity for repentance.

καὶ μακροθυμία) applies not only to different people but may also be worked out in one and the same person, for on the one side it may lead him to μετάνοια, and hence to δικαιοσύνη ἐκ πίστεως, and then also to ἔργον ἀγαθόν, but on the other it may lead to an increase in the capital of wrath which will be paid in full on the ἡμέρα ὀργῆς καὶ ἀποκαλύψεως δικαιοκρισίας τοῦ θεοῦ, → 438. Finally in R. 12:19 man is warned not to anticipate the delayed wrath of God by exercising retribution himself, though → n. 403.

(d) Faith, then, views history as follows. There are two periods of salvation history, the one characterised by ὀργή, the other by the δικαιοσύνη θεοῦ. There are two αἰῶνες, οὗτος and ἐκεῖνος, though these overlap in the age of Christ between the comings. In this age there takes place at one and the same time the twofold revelation of R. 1:17 f. The revelation of wrath turns one's gaze in a twofold direction. On the one side it shows that the history of mankind stands under ὀργή from the fall onwards. On the other it shows that herein world history is an anticipation of world judgment, and the fuse which kindles ὀργή in the aeon of wrath is the Law: ὁ νόμος ὀργὴν κατεργάζεται, R. 4:15. Like the Gospel, the Law is a gift of the love of God. [357] Again, as wrath is provoked by despising the goodness and longsuffering of God in the Gospel, so it is by despising the Law. This is not the purpose of the Law. [358] Only from the standpoint of the transgressor does it look like this. If God is angry because of transgression of the Law, this is the reaction of spurned love, which sought to benefit man through the Law. [359]

(e) The anticipating of eschatological events in history implies a transposition from the punctual to the linear. Events become states, μέλλουσα ὀργή becomes ὀργὴ μένουσα. Jn. 3:36: ὁ ἀπειθῶν τῷ υἱῷ οὐκ ὄψεται ζωήν, ἀλλ᾽ ἡ ὀργὴ τοῦ θεοῦ μένει ἐπ᾽ αὐτόν. What does this mean? Does wrath remain to the end or for ever? The second view would mean that contemplation of present wrath wholly absorbs the prospect of future wrath. But the eschatological views of Jn. are not exhausted by the images of realised eschatology. [360] Hence we have to say that μένουσα ὀργή will one day be swallowed up by μέλλουσα ὀργή. [361] Over and above this, however, the question still remains whether there is according to the NT an eternal ὀργή.

The answer of the Gk. world to this question is in the affirmative, that of the OT in the negative. The eternal fury of the divine μῆνις may be seen, e.g., in the myths of Sisyphos and Prometheus. [362] By contrast the Lord of the Bible says: "I will not keep anger for ever" (Jer. 3:12; cf. Ps. 103:9 ff. etc.). [363] Judaism sometimes speaks of eternal wrath, so Sib., III, 309 (conjecture of Geffken): καὶ θυμοῦ τέκνοις αἰώνιος ἐξολό-θρευσις, and Jochanan b. Zakkai (Ber., 28b): "The king of kings whose anger, when

---

[357] The Law is still regarded in this way by orthodox Jews.

[358] Nor is it an unalterable decree, Wetter, 39; though cf. on Paul → 443.

[359] v. Jüchen, 33 ff. and → 403.

[360] Cf. G. Stählin, 253-257.

[361] So also Procksch; Cr.-Kö., 814.

[362] Ancient definitions distinguish between θυμός and ὀργή as πρόσκαιρος and πολυ-χρόνιος (Ps.-Ammon. Adfin. Vocab. Diff., s.v.), but the ref. here is not to the eternal duration of ὀργή. The same is true of the related def.: θυμὸς ὀργὴ ἀρχομένη, Diog. L., VII, 1, 63 : ὀργὴ θυμὸς ἐμμένων, Greg. Naz. Carmina, II, 34, 44; διὰ τοῦ θυμοῦ τὸ ταχὺ δεδήλωκε, διὰ δὲ τῆς ὀργῆς τὸ ἐπιμόνιον, Thdt. in Ps. 68 (Mas. 69): 25.

[363] But cf. → 405. On the common OT ref. to wrath which lasts εἰς τέλος, → n. 367.

it flames forth, is an eternal anger." But Jewish voices are not uniform in this respect. Thus acc. to Sanh., 10, 6d the fire of divine wrath will remain only so long on the world as there are transgressors in it, [364] and bBer., 7 develops the view that though God is angry every day His wrath is only for a fleeting moment.

In the NT itself there are passages which clearly limit the duration of wrath (so Lk. 21:23, → 430) and others which seem to envisage an eternal burning of anger (so Mt. 3:12 : the πῦρ ἄσβεστον is here a picture of ὀργή, cf. Mk. 9:43 ff.; also the πῦρ αἰώνιον of Mt. 18:8; 25:41; Jd. 7). In Mt. 18:34 the anger of the king at the wicked servant is such as to imply eternal duration, for how can he pay his infinite debt in prison ? So, too, the wine of wrath in Rev. 14:10 (etc.) is obviously par. to the torments of the lake of fire, which last εἰς αἰῶνας αἰώνων (v. 11; 20:10). In all these latter quotations, however, the reference is not to wrath itself but to the punishment, which according to the main tenor of the NT (→ I, 392 : apokatastasis ?) is certainly of eternal duration. Only in this sense can one speak of eternal wrath in the NT. [365] Nevertheless, God's wrath also has something of a lasting character, since it is not just a swiftly passing emotion but His holy resistance to everything unholy. It lasts until every will opposed to God is overcome, Rev. 20:10, 14; 21:8. The question of the eternity of the ὀργὴ θεοῦ is posed directly in 1 Th. 2:16, where it is said of the Jews : ἔφθασεν (or ἔφθακεν) ἐπ' αὐτοὺς ἡ ὀργὴ εἰς τέλος. What does εἰς τέλος mean ? "To the end" (and then no longer) [366] or "for ever" ? It might mean that because of continuing serious transgressions on the part of the Jews the wrath of God has been at work up to the last time which has now dawned. But the probability is that this is only the common and often rather weak εἰς τέλος which the LXX uses for נצח. [367] εἰς τέλος can certainly mean εἰς τὸν αἰῶνα, e.g., ψ 102:9 : οὐκ εἰς τέλος ὀργισθή- σεται οὐδὲ εἰς τὸν αἰῶνα μηνιεῖ, but 1 Th. 2:16 means "for ever," yet with no implication of the eternity of this wrath. [368] The idea of eternal wrath might well be suggested by the consideration that the Jews had fallen eternal victim to the ὀργὴ θεοῦ by rejecting Christ and therewith salvation from it. [369] But in this case the verse would stand in irreconcilable contradiction to R. 11, where Paul works out his fundamental eschatological ideas concerning the Jews. These are surely to be regarded as normative in the interpretation of other passages about the Jews like 1 Th. 2:14 ff. Hence the passage cannot be made to support ideas of an ὀργή which lasts for ever.

---

[364] Sometimes in a way which is not tenable theologically the Rabb. count on an abate- ment of wrath, cf. the various sophisms on Ps. 95:11 whereby they apparently seek to evade the conclusions of Hb. 4:3 ff.: Nu. r., 14 (177c) in Str.-B., III, 685; T. Sanh., 13, 10 f. (435), ibid., 409; Midr. Qoh., 10, 20 (49b), ibid., 678.

[365] Cf. Althaus, op. cit. (→ n. 297), II, 31.

[366] τέλος in the sense of destruction as in the par. (original or copy ?) in T. Lv., 6, 11: "The wrath of the Lord came on them (the men of Shechem) to destruction"; with destruc- tion, wrath is also at an end.

[367] How εἰς τέλος can be used in purely rhetorical fashion may be seen from the common combination with ἕως πότε, e.g., ψ 78:5 : ἕως πότε, κύριε, ὀργισθήσῃ εἰς τέλος;

[368] Cf. Jub. 24:28 : "Cursed be the Philistines to the day of wrath and fury." Here the idea of the end of the curse is of no significance. The meaning is simply : "So long as the world lasts," "for ever."

[369] So Pr.-Bauer, s.v.; Dib. Th., ad loc.

4. The Wrath of God in NT Imagery.

NT statements about God's wrath, like those of the OT (→ 399), are sometimes extremely figurative. As in the case of many other NT concepts, images are used to convey a clearer picture of the related concepts, though by reason of their constant use many of the figures of speech become weak and conventional.

a. In some of the parables of Jesus we find images for the wrathful God, Mt. 18:34; 22:7; cf. Lk. 14:21. In such instances the ὀργίζεσθαι of the king or lord marks a turning-point in the story and denotes the rejection of the Jews and those who go the same way. The anger of the judge, even though ὀργή or ὀργίζομαι is not used, may also be seen in the parable of the fig-tree (Lk. 13:6 ff.; Mk. 11:13 f., → 429) and the great parables of judgment in Mt. 25. In the latter the ref. is esp. to wrath at the despising or insulting of God (v. 24, 26, 30) and the complete lack of love (vv. 41 ff.).

b. Images are also used for those smitten by wrath. That of the σκεύη ὀργῆς in R. 9:22 (→ 432) derives from the LXX (Ιερ. 27:25) and is found also in Symmachus (Is. 13:5). In accordance with the wide range of meaning enjoyed by the original כלי, however, σκεῦος (ὀργῆς) means in the Gk. OT the vessel whereby God executes His anger, while in the NT it means the vessel on which He executes it. On the one side it points to the weapons in God's arsenal (Ιερ. 27[50]:25), the soldiers in His army at the judgment of the world (Is. 13:5), on the other to the vessel into which His anger is poured so that it is wholly filled therewith and bound to fall victim to destruction. [370] The opposites are the σκεύη ἐλέους which are filled with mercy, though a change of content is possible before the τέλος, the final execution of ὀργή, since Christians know that they were once τέκνα φύσει ὀργῆς and are now τέκνα θεοῦ (Eph. 2:3), and conversely the wicked servant obviously became a σκεῦος ὀργῆς instead of a σκεῦος ἐλέους, and the Jews who once were υἱοὶ τῆς βασιλείας (Mt. 8:12) may become υἱοὶ γεέννης (23:15). [371]

There are pre-NT models for the phrase τέκνα ὀργῆς in Eph. 2:3. [372] It is one the great group of phrases which use → τέκνον or → υἱός to denote belonging, so that in the strict sense it is not really figurative. The impf. ἤμεθα τέκνα φύσει ὀργῆς tells us that though → φύσις seems to express the original and essential aspect of the being which has fallen victim to wrath (cf. Gl. 2:15; R. 11:21, 24), it has become the past, since in a new ζωοποίησις it has been replaced by another φύσις. Before God there has been a change of family (Jn. 1:12; Mt. 23:15) by adoption. There is a new υἱοθεσία, and with this a change of φύσις (cf. R. 6:5). [373]

---

[370] On this distinction in the meaning of σκεῦος ὀργῆς cf. v. Hofmann, op. cit. Zn. R., ad loc. takes a different view, but there can be no doubt that mention of the potter naturally suggests vessels. It is true, however, that there is an imperceptible transition from the act. sense — σκεῦος εἰς τιμήν (v. 21; cf. 2 Tm. 2:20) — vessel for an honourable use — to the pass. A vessel from which wrath is poured out over others, like Pharaoh, is itself always under the operation of this wrath, and is thus esp. marked for the final judgment of wrath.

[371] Cf. Elert, 563 : " 'Children of wrath,' which are just the same as the 'vessels of wrath,' may be 'set in heavenly places in Christ Jesus' " (Eph. 2:3-6).

[372] Apc. Mos. 3 (Tischendorf, p. 2 : Cain is ὀργῆς υἱός; Sib., III, 309 (→ 433): καὶ θυμοῦ τέκνοις αἰώνιος ἐξολόθρευσις, i.e., "eternal perdition comes for the children of Babel." Zn. R., 457, n. 23 compares the completely non-fig. ἀνὴρ ἐπιθυμιῶν of Da. 10:11 Θ.

[373] σύμφυτος, "of like nature" (Plat. Phileb., 16c), "fashioned like" (συμμορφιζόμενος, Phil. 3:10), as took place in prototype in Stephen (Ac. 6:15; 7:59 f.). When a man has a share in the death of Christ, he will also share in the form of His resurrection, cf. R. 8:29; Phil. 3:21; → 192. This interpretation of → σύμφυτος has at least to be considered along with the more common "grown together."

c. The images for wrath itself are taken in the main from three circles.

(a) The first is that of the fire (→ πῦρ), originally for the passion of an outbreak of anger (→ 392; 399), then for the judgment of wrath. Several ideas are united here : the thought of the terrors and torments of the end, a concept of the Last Judgment itself (e.g., 1 C. 3:13, 15), and that of the fires of hell (Mt. 5:22; 18:9), πῦρ αἰώνιον (Mt. 18:8; 25:41; Jd. 7). This is the threefold background of the threefold image of fire which the Baptist uses for his saying about μέλλουσα ὀργή (v. 7) in Mt. 3:10-12. [374] Closely related is the saying about the axe in Mt. 3:10 and par. This is another metaphor for the divine wrath which is so immediately imminent. While the ref. in Mt. 3:10 is to eschatological wrath, Lk. 13:7 D (cf. v. 9) is speaking of historical wrath, → n. 336.

(b) As sometimes in the OT, the metaphor of fire is accompanied by that of flood in the Baptist's address, cf. Ez. 21:36; 22:31, → 399. This combination of images was suggested by the twofold tradition of the Flood and the raining of fire on Sodom and Gomorrah, and also by the expectation of a great universal fire and flood at the end [375] in accordance with the basic biblical view that the last time is like the first time. [376] These things are brought to mind when we note that the Baptist connects his water baptism as well as the baptism of fire with μέλλουσα ὀργή, Mt. 3:7. Like beneficial as well as terrible fire and other elemental forces [377] water has an ambivalent character. It can be the water of death and also the water of life. [378] On this, and not merely on the rite of immersion, reposes the fact that baptism can be for Jesus a figure of death, i.e., His own death (Mk. 10:38; Lk. 12:50), [379] just as its saving significance can be suggested by the thought of the water of life and not just by the symbolical act of coming up out of the water as a type of resurrection or new birth. Baptism is one of the many symbolical actions in the Gospel which not only are capable of many interpretations but do in fact often have a twofold or manifold sense. Obviously baptism is for Jn. the Baptist both a prefiguring of spiritual baptism and also an anticipatory sign of the final judgment. [380] In the first sense it promises the gift of salvation in the last time (εἰς ἄφεσιν ἁμαρτιῶν, Mk. 1:4; cf. Ac. 2:38, where we find the same chain of baptism, forgiveness and the gift of the Spirit), while in the second it refers to deliverance from the fiery baptism [381] of the Last Judgment. Hence he who desires baptism hopes to

---

[374] V. 9 disrupts the train of thought and can hardly be original. On the other hand v. 8 is the presupposition of v. 10, and with ἤδη a direct link is made with the μέλλουσα ὀργή of v. 7. How closely Judaism connected fire and wrath may be seen from Rabb. sayings in which "(day of) wrath" is referred to the fires of hell, cf. bAZ, 18; bBB, 10 and n. 360 in Goldschmidt, VIII, 38; also bNed., 22a (ibid., V, 410). On baptism with fire cf. C. M. Edsman, Le baptême de feu (1940).

[375] Cf. Vit. Ad., 49. Contradiction arises between the expectation of an eschatological flood and the promise of Gn. 9:11 only if one misses the emphasis on the pass. "neither any more all," for in the last flood a portion of men will be saved. Cf. R. Eisler, Ἰησοῦς βασιλεὺς οὐ βασιλεύσας (II, 1933), 101 f.

[376] Cf. H. Gunkel, Schöpfung u. Chaos in Urzeit u. Endzeit² (1921).

[377] Cf. ὀσμή (2 C. 2:16), λίθος (Lk. 20:17 f.) etc.

[378] This interchangeability is the main pt. in the Adapa Myth (AOT¹, 36 f.; cf. Chant. de la Saussaye, I, 600; K. Galling, Art. "Wasser," RGG², V, 1770 f.).

[379] This idea, found in the Marcan tradition as well as in the special Lucan material, is intrinsic to the original form of the sayings of Jesus. Like the ransom saying in Mk. 10:45 par. it must not be detached from the bed-rock of the tradition by critical manipulations.

[380] This is the pt. of Mt. 3:11 where, at least acc. to the interpretation of the Evangelist (πῦρ in v. 11 as in v. 10 and v. 12 has to mean the fire of judgment), water baptism contrasts with the twofold baptism which will be given by Him who is to come. The heavenly voice (v. 17) also seems to presuppose the relation of Jn.'s baptism to the judgment of wrath at the end. He who came voluntarily under ὀργή stands in truth under εὐδοκία, → 446.

[381] On the expectation of a fiery flood (ποταμὸς πυρός, diluvium ignis) at the end cf. also Sib., II, 196 ff., 315, 252 f.; Ps.-Melito, 12 in J. C. T. v. Otto, Corpus Apologetarum Christianorum Saeculi Secundi, IX (1872), 432 and on this Eisler, 109.

escape future wrath, Mt. 3:7. It is still not shown on what the saving power of baptism rests from the very first, namely, on its link with the death of Jesus and His saving power. Because Jesus in His death took on Himself the whole wrath of God against the world (→ 445), the power of deliverance from this wrath is set in the sacrament of death, i.e., in baptism. But while this gift is only promised in John's baptism, it is actually conferred in Christian baptism.

(c) In certain connections a third image is added to that of fire and water, namely, that which embraces the cup or vial of wrath, the wine or winepress. [382] In the NT (→ 399) the metaphor of the cup [383] or wine of wrath is a favourite one in Rev., and there is ref. to two different cups or wines acc. to the twofold operation of the wrath of God, → 443 f. The one symbolises the punishment of the βασανισμός (Rev. 14:10, here as epexegetical par. βασανισθήσεται ἐν πυρὶ καὶ θείῳ, cf. 16:19), the other the judgment of apostasy acc. to the principle that God's wrath punishes sin with sin, so Rev. 14:8 : (Babylon) ἣ ἐκ τοῦ οἴνου τοῦ θυμοῦ τῆς πορνείας αὐτῆς πεπότικεν πάντα τὰ ἔθνη, "who has given all nations to drink of the wine of wrath [384] of her licentiousness," cf. 18:3. [385] This is the stupefying wine or cup of the OT (e.g., Ps. 60:3; 75:8; Is. 51:17, 22) which has here come to its eschatological fulfilment. God Himself is at work when Babylon in its ungodliness takes the cup of God's wrath, cf. the same pt. in the same image in Jer. 51:7: "Babylon was a golden cup in the Lord's hand, that made all the earth drunken : the nations have drunken of her wine ; therefore the nations are mad." This means that God's wrath itself gives the cup of licentiousness, of apostasy from God, and punishes all who drink it. R. 1:18-32 is an exposition of the saying. [386]

To the figure of the cup (= βασανισμός) corresponds that of the seven vials of wrath [387] (Rev. 16:1 ff.) which are poured out on the earth as the third of the great apocalyptic series of sevens. The content of the ἑπτὰ φιάλαι τοῦ θυμοῦ τοῦ θεοῦ is "the wrath of the God who lives to all eternity" (15:7) in the form of the seven last plagues in which God's wrath is consummated, 15:1.

Rev. makes twofold use of the image of the winepress of God. [388] In 19:15 it is again the wine of God's wrath (cf. 14:10; 16:19) which the returning Christ, who Himself

---

[382] The common idea of pouring out wrath is to be understood in terms of the imagery discussed under (b) and (c); in the NT cf. esp. Rev. 16:1 ff.

[383] The metaphor also occurs in the Dead Sea Scrolls, Midr. Hab. col. 11; cf. O. Eissfeldt, "Der gegenwärtige Stand der Erforschung d. in Palästina neugefundenen Hdschr. 2," ThLZ, 74 (1949), 96; on the development of the figure cf. H. Gressmann, *Der Ursprung d. isr.-jüd. Eschatologie* (1905), 129 ff. and P. Volz, *Der Prophet Jeremia* (1928), 392 f.; → 165, n. 26.

[384] The interpretation advanced here is not uncontested. θυμός is usually taken in the sense of passion : "the wine of their passionate ungodliness." But 18:6 : ἐν τῷ ποτηρίῳ ᾧ ἐκέρασεν κεράσατε αὐτῇ διπλοῦν, makes it likely that οἶνος τοῦ θυμοῦ is one concept in 14:8, 10. There is certainly some confusion of images, but the cup is the same, though filled with different wines. The idea that θυμός is poison (cf. Dt. 32:33) is not likely, for, while this is possible in Rev. 14:8; 18:3, it does not fit 14:10; 16:19; 19:15, cf. Bss. Apk., 385; Loh. Apk., 121 f.; Büchsel, → III, 168; though for a different view Seesemann, → 165 f.

[385] In 17:2, however, the wine (οἶνος τῆς πορνείας) merely symbolises the seductive and bemusing power of ungodliness.

[386] Is the cup which the Almighty Father passes on to Jesus (Mk. 14:36 : παρένεγκε τὸ ποτήριον τοῦτο ἀπ' ἐμοῦ) also that of God's wrath ? If so, by taking it Jesus fears a disruption of the loving fellowship in which His existence rests. And the sign that He still must drink it is the cry of dereliction on the cross (Mk. 15:34 and par.; so Procksch, → 445 f.). Now in the OT a cup which is not more precisely defined can be the cup of wrath (e.g., Jer. 49:12). But it is hard to differentiate between the cup of wrath and that of suffering (→ III, 168), and acc. to Jesus' own use of the metaphor (Mk. 10:38; Jn. 18:11) it is more likely that in Gethsemane He has in view the cup of death. Cf. also Asc. Is. 5:13.

[387] The OT prototype is the threat of sevenfold punishment in Lv. 26:18, 21, 24, 28, cf. also the six men of Ez. 9:2.

[388] The OT prototype is Is. 63:1-6; cf. Jl. 3:13. Cf. G. Bornkamm, → IV, 255-257.

treads the press, prepares. In 14:19 f., however, the ref. is to the sin-ripe grapes of men which are pressed in the ληνὸς τοῦ θυμοῦ τοῦ θεοῦ, and the wine is their blood, which, streaming from the press, becomes a sea, v. 20.

(d) Finally, we find θησαυρίζειν ὀργήν in R. 2:5 (→ 433), with its paradoxical suggestion of a capital of wrath [389] heaped up in heaven. This is the opp. of the very different treasure in heaven in Mt. 19:21; 6:20; Lk. 12:33 f. While the interest on this capital (קֶרֶן), acc. to the Jewish view, is already enjoyed on earth in the form of merit and reward, and only the capital will be paid back at the end, the capital of wrath grows until the Last Judgment and will then be paid with compound interest; hence this day is the ἡμέρα ὀργῆς, R. 2:5. [390]

5. The Objects and Instruments of Wrath.

a. Objects.

In the NT, too, God's anger is never unrelated. Wrath is not part of the divine essence, → 397. As in the ancient depictions of wrath and in the prophets (→ 397 f.), the first object of wrath is God's ancient people, the Jews. The Baptist's sermon refers to this, Mt. 3:7 and par.: "Do you think that you can escape the wrath to come?" Jesus takes up the thought in Lk. 21:23: ἔσται ἀνάγκη μεγάλη ἐπὶ τῆς γῆς καὶ ὀργὴ τῷ λαῷ τούτῳ, "Messianic tribulation comes for the whole earth, [391] and God's wrath precisely on this people." So elsewhere when Jesus speaks of wrath, it is directed against the Jews (cf. Mk. 3:5; Lk. 14:21; Mt. 22:7 and 18:34). Paul sees things in the same light, cf. 1 Th. 2:16 (→ 434), also R. 2:5: The Jews primarily are the impenitent who despise God's μακροθυμία, and R. 4:15: The Jews primarily are the men of the Law which ὀργὴν κατεργάζεται for them.

But the reference is not to the Jews alone. Before God's wrath all men are equal. From the very first the same φύσις is common to all. All are bound to the ἐπιθυμίαι and θελήματα τῆς σαρκός, and hence all have fallen victim to ὀργή. For this reason all men were originally τέκνα φύσει ὀργῆς (Eph. 2:3), [392] and by analogy σκεύη ὀργῆς, like σκεύη ἐλέους, come οὐ μόνον ἐξ Ἰουδαίων ἀλλὰ καὶ ἐξ ἐθνῶν, R. 9:22 ff. Rev. gives us a particularly rich picture of the execution of wrath. [393] All nations are affected (Rev. 11:18; 14:8; 18:3; 19:15), and all classes

---

[389] Cf. the Rabb., e.g., jPea, 1, 15d, 64: "... four things for which a man is punished in this world, and the capital remains in that world: idolatry, adultery, incest and calumny"; cf. also T. Pea, 1, 2 (cf. W. Bauer on Pea, 1, 1b; G. Schlichting, Der Toseftatraktat Pea, Diss. Tübingen [1936], ad loc.).

[390] There is a terrible irony in many of the metaphors. Treasure is really an object of joy (Mt. 6:21 and par.; 13:44); harvest (Mt. 3:12), esp. the vintage (Rev. 14:18 ff.), is a time of joy (cf. Is. 9:2); wine makes glad the heart of man (Ps. 104:15); the cup is a type of joy and salvation (Ps. 116:13). But when linked with ὀργή all are turned into their dreadful opp. This is a common feature in biblical imagery.

[391] It is an open question whether the γῆ of v. 25 is the whole earth or the land, → I, 677 f., i.e., Palestine, as in 4:25 (cf. Hck. Lk., ad loc.). The parallelism suggests the second view, but I still think the first is correct, 1. because of the proximity of v. 25, which makes a different understanding of v. 23 most unlikely, and 2. because the land is often referred universalistically to the whole earth in the Messianic promises of Judaism.

[392] The ἡμεῖς here means either "we Jewish Christians — in this case οἱ λοιποί are Gentile Christians — or "we Christians," in which case ὡς καὶ οἱ λοιποί means "as other men" (sc. those who are not yet Christians).

[393] In Rev. ὀργή occurs only in 6:16 f.; 11:18; 14:10; 16:19 and 19:15 of the verses mentioned; the others have θυμός, which is preferred in Rev. → 422.

(esp. the high and mighty and the rich, 6:15 ff.). Wrath falls on the whole earth (14:19; 16:1) because all worship antichrist (14:9 ff.). But it falls esp. on Babel, the embodiment of ungodly, arrogant, total power, 14:8; 16:19.

Babel is so closely related to the beast (e.g., 17:3), however, that it has itself the character of an ungodly power of the other world. One of the marks of the richness of the depiction in Rev. is that God's wrath is also against devils and powers which oppose God, as is made plain by the revelation of God in Christ, → 427. Indeed, the *dies irae* applies already to them primarily, and in this connection we are given the picture of two antithetical forces of wrath. The devil with his θυμὸς μέγας (→ 420) — Rev. 12:17 has the image of the angry dragon (καὶ ὠργίσθη ὁ δράκων) — and along with him the angry nations (11:18) fight against God and His kingdom. This is the great eschatological wrath which opposes the wrath of God. It is described in colours taken from the Psalter. The drama of revelation can thus be understood in large measure as a battle between two ὀργαί.

b. Instruments.

This struggle between ὀργαί in Rev. 11 f. arises because God Himself in wrath at man causes the demons to rage. This means that ungodly forces become instruments of the wrath of God against the world. [394] "The power and authority of Satan and his hosts are grounded in God's wrath." [395]

It is by a detour that devilish wrath comes to serve the wrath of God. At the first stage ungodly powers independently take the place of God's wrath, and only at the second are they subordinated to it. The first stage is that of an attempt to separate as widely as possible from God the disasters which are a sign of His wrath, → 399. The second is that of a concern to bar the door against the dualism which threatens at the first stage. For the first stage cf. 1 Ch. 21:1 with 2 S. 24:1 (→ 402); Jub. 49:4 with Ex. 12:12; 1 C. 10:10 [396] with Nu. 14:34 ff.; Hb. 2:14 with Gn. 3:19b. [397] For the second cf. Sir. 39:28 ff.: ἔστιν πνεύματα [398] ἃ εἰς ἐκδίκησιν ἔκτισται καὶ ἐν θυμῷ αὐτοῦ ἐστερέωσεν μάστιγας αὐτῶν· ἐν καιρῷ συντελείας ἰσχὺν ἐκχεοῦσιν καὶ τὸν θυμὸν τοῦ ποιήσαντος αὐτοὺς κοπάσουσιν. The spirits are represented as God's bailiffs who have made their scourges firm and strong with His wrath. But in the divine hour of world consummation, i.e., manifestly in the end time immediately before the Last Judgment, they will pour out their whole power and mitigate the wrath of their

---

[394] In rather a different sense, though hardly correctly, the impressing of these powers into the service of wrath has been detected in R. 13:4, → n. 401.

[395] Althaus, *op. cit.* (→ n. 297), II, 260.

[396] The ὀλεθρευτής is either an angel of destruction (→ 424; n. 354; cf. 414) or the devil himself, → 169.

[397] Cf. Apc. Mos. 14: God's wrath is death, → n. 418. Vacillation in interpreting the δυνάμενος καὶ ψυχὴν καὶ σῶμα ἀπολέσαι ἐν γεέννῃ of Mt. 10:28 (→ n. 296) is thus grounded in the ambivalent judgment of the Bible itself. We find the same dual statements not only about death but also about temptation etc. On the other hand, God Himself can assume the role of prosecutor at the judgment, though this is the *opus proprium* of Satan, the accuser κατ᾽ ἐξοχήν (cf. Rev. 12:10); cf. Gn. r., 93 (59b) on 45:3 (Wetter, 49, n. 1; Str.-B., III, 220): "How will men stand then before the Holy One ..., who is both Judge and Accuser ?"

[398] The ref. is not to winds — along with other natural forces mentioned in the same verse — but to spirits, i.e., personifications of these powers, which are depicted in personal terms in v. 31 as well: ἐν τῇ ἐντολῇ αὐτοῦ εὐφρανθήσονται κτλ., "they fulfil the judgment of God's wrath with delight" etc.

Creator.[399] Here, then, it would seem that the thought is that of an anticipation of the Last Judgment in the fury of these subservient spirits, by which the final paroxysm of the wrath of God in the judgment itself is softened. The second evaluation and classification of the wrath of the devil lies behind the NT statements, and this is true even where the devil seems to stand independently alongside and in opposition to God. The devil is never more than God's bailiff. Unwittingly and unwillingly he is an instrument of the wrath of God whose functions he has only apparently taken under his own wing, cf. 1 C. 2:8.[400]

But the devil is also an object and victim of divine wrath, → 439, also 415. We see here a basic principle of the divine governance. To be an instrument of God's wrath is eo ipso to be also its victim. A σκεῦος ὀργῆς in the act. sense (Ιερ. 27:25) is also as such a σκεῦος ὀργῆς in the pass. sense (R. 9:22; → 435). In the old covenant this is true of the great powers (cf. Is. 10:5-19 with 5:25-30 and 1 Ch. 27:24 with 2 S. 24:1) in relation to Israel. In the new it is true of the Jews in relation to Christians and the new Israel (→ 443). It is also true of Judas (cf. Lk. 17:1) and esp. of the devil himself, who, as will set in absolute opposition to God, is the act. and pass. σκεῦος ὀργῆς of God κατ' ἐξοχήν for the cosmos in this aeon. Here again we see affinity between the first time and the last. Like the two disasters at the beginning and the end of world history (→ 436), a judgment of wrath on the devil at the beginning (cf. Vit. Ad., 15 f.; Apc. Mos. 26; Jd. 6) finds its counterpart in a similar judgment at the end (Rev. 20:10).

Finally, the relation of political power to the wrath of God is to be seen in the same light. In R. 13:4 the ἐξουσία[401] is called θεοῦ διάκονος εἰς ὀργήν[402] ἔκδικος τῷ τὸ κακὸν πράσσοντι. It has been found difficult that political power is presented as the executor of divine wrath, but we should not on this account excise the almost universally attested εἰς ὀργήν,[403] nor see in it a reference to the

---

[399] The trans. use of κοπάζω (mentioned neither by Pass. nor Liddell-Scott) seems to be peculiar to Sir. (cf. 43:23; 46:7 and esp. 48:10); cf. Helbing Kasussyntax, 79.

[400] Cf. the excursus on the deceiving of the spirit world by Christ in Ltzm. K. on 1 C. 2:6.

[401] Though otherworldly powers can have the role of διάκονοι εἰς ὀργήν and of ἔκδικοι in God's service (→ 439), this seems to me to be a very questionable interpretation of the ἐξουσίαι of R. 13 (G. Dehn, "Engel u. Obrigkeit" in Festschr. f. K. Barth [1936], 90-109; K. Barth, Rechtfertigung u. Recht [1944], 14-21 [though not in the comm. on R., even the last ed.]; O. Cullmann, Königsherrschaft Christi u. Kirche im NT [1941], 44-48; Christus u. d. Zeit [1946], 169-186, with bibl. 182 f. [E.T. 191-210, 205 f.]; W. Schweitzer, Die Herrschaft Christi u. der Staat [1949]). On a simple reading the ref. of expressions like ἕξεις ἔπαινον ἐξ αὐτῆς, τὴν μάχαιραν φορεῖ, φόρους τελεῖτε, is always first to political powers, as Iren. (Haer., V, 24, 1) rightly perceived. That behind them are other forces is plain in the NT, esp. in Rev., but that these are also in view in R. 13 cannot be proved in spite of 1 C. 2:8 (cf. G. Kittel, Christus u. Imperator [1939], 48-54; F. J. Leenhardt, Le chrétien doit-il servir l'Etat? [1939], 36 ff.; E. Brunner, "Zur christologischen Begründung des Staats," Kirchenblatt f. d. reformierte Schweiz, 99 [1943], 2-5, 18-23, 34-36; M. Dibelius, Rom u. d. Christen im 1. Jhdt. [1942], 6 ff.; W. Elert, "Pls. u. Nero," Zwischen Gnade u. Ungnade [1948], 42, n. 1; H. v. Campenhausen, "Zur Auslegung von R. 13 : d. dämonistische Deutung d. ἐξουσία-Begriffes," Festschr. f. A. Bertholet [1950], 97-113; G. Bornkamm, "Christus u. d. Welt in d. urchr. Botschaft," ZThK, 47 [1950], 224; → II, 565 art. ἐξουσία, though this was written before the discussion started by Dehn).

[402] In spite of the better attestation of the usual order, I believe that given above is the original. διάκονος εἰς ὀργήν is par. to διάκονος εἰς τὸ ἀγαθόν (cf. the same antithesis — εἰς ἀγαθόν-θυμός — in 2 Esr. 8:22), and ἔκδικος goes better with the dat. than with εἰς ὀργήν: "as a servant in matters of God's rule of wrath the state is for the evil-doer an avenger." The change was made because offence was taken at the idea of being God's deacon for wrath.

[403] So Procksch acc. to the Western text. It is not wrong to set the nearby 12:19 in direct relation to 13:4 f.: The power of state is entrusted with this service for the ὀργὴ θεοῦ which the individual is not arbitrarily to take into his own hands (cf. Cullmann, Christus u. d. Zeit [1946], 177 f. E.T. 200).

wrath of the authorities. [404] The Bible regards many pagan peoples and rulers as executors of God's wrath (→ 400 and n. 140; 404). They are this even when, like the devil, they consciously fight against God and His people. In so doing they unconsciously rage in truth against themselves as διάκονοι εἰς ὀργὴν ἔκδικοι τῷ τὸ κακὸν πράσσοντι. This is the picture of political powers in Rev., and it is here that we may see the inner unity between R. 13 and Rev. 13 ff. [405] At all times the ἐξουσίαι may fall from their position as ministers. If they do, they become servants of the devil rather than servants of God, as the images of Rev. show. Like their master, they then fall even more under the wrath of God whose instruments they were chosen to be.

c. The Position of the Christian.

No one is unaffected by God's wrath (R. 3:23). There is only liberation from it. The particular position of the third race as compared with others, whether Jew or Gentile, is that though, like others, they must set themselves under the wrath of God, nevertheless through Christ they are delivered from ὀργή (1 Th. 1:10; R. 5:9) and κατακρίνεσθαι (1 C. 11:32; 2 Th. 1:5 ff.), so that, in retrospect from Christ, they can confess: We were never destined for wrath, we were prepared from the very outset (προετοιμάζω, R. 9:23) as σκεύη ἐλέους.

6. The Causes and Effects of the Divine Wrath.

a. Causes.

As in the OT (→ 403), so also in the NT all the causes of divine wrath may be traced back to a basic cause, man's despising of God. [406] Paul shows that the whole world, both Gentile and Jewish, stands under the ὀργὴ θεοῦ (R. 1:18-3:20). The reason is ἀδικία and ἀσέβεια, the despising of God in the form of disregard for the revelation of His being (δύναμις καὶ θειότης) in creation (R. 1:18, 21 ff.) and also the disdaining and transgression of the revelation of His will in the Law (R. 2:17 ff.; 3:19 f.). This divine wrath is echoed in Paul's wrath in Ac. 17:16 (παρωξύνετο). He is angered by the dishonouring of God in false worship, cf. the ζῆλος of Jesus in Jn. 2:15 ff. The view that ὀργή is anger at evil (R. 12:19; 13:4), παράβασις (4:15), ἀδικία (3:5) is one which NT proclamation obviously has in common with that of the OT, cf. esp. Hb. 3:11; 4:3 with the motivation in 3:10: ἀεὶ πλανῶνται τῇ καρδίᾳ, and the par. passages Eph. 5:6 and Col. 3:6, where the ὀργὴ τοῦ θεοῦ, perhaps in dependence on a kind of catechetical tradition, [407] is directly linked with a list of vices in which we also find ὀργή, i.e., that of man. Expressly related to the OT is the ὀργή of the ἡμέραι ἐκδικήσεως in Lk. 21:22 f., along with other refs. to ὀργὴ ἐρχομένη or μέλλουσα (→ 430). Wrath has still to come because it is foretold by the prophets, in whose vision of the future the revelation of wrath is an integral element. But in both cases the real reason is that men are ἁμαρτωλοί, ἐχθροὶ θεοῦ (R. 5:8, 10 etc.), apostates. In two ways Rev. further develops this reason for the wrath of God. In Rev. 14

---

[404] J. C. K. v. Hofmann R. (1868), ad loc.

[405] Hence this inner unity is not brought out only by attempting to establish a so-called "Christological basis for the state," Cullmann, 179 (202).

[406] That this is in fact the common denominator may be seen esp. from the parables of Jesus, e.g., Mt. 22:11 ff.; 25:24 ff.; 21:37 ff.

[407] Cf. Loh. Kol., ad loc.

wrath is kindled by apostasy from God, not merely to the creature as in R. 1, but to the power which is opposed to God, the beast. Wrath is executed by delivering up not merely to sin but to apostasy itself. For πορνεία is the wine of God's wrath (→ 437). It is thus an act of divine wrath in which this achieves its supreme dimension.

The reason for the ὀργή θεοῦ is even more profound and serious when this wrath is at ἁμαρτία against God not merely as a despising of His holy will in the Law (or creation), but as the despising of His holy love in the Gospel (R. 2:4; → 403). But there is still a detailed parallel to the despising of God in the Law. [408] For while on the one side the line to wrath is νόμος-παράβασις-ὀργή, it is here ἐπαγγελία-ἀπιστία-ὀργή, and while the counter-movement is there ὑπακοή-τιμή, it is now πίστις-χάρις-δόξα. Despising God's goodness, patience and forbearance (R. 2:4) is the decisive cause of ὀργή in the NT. Jesus makes the same point when He speaks of the scornful rejection of the invitation (Lk. 14:16 ff., esp. 21), which in the version in Mt. (22:2 ff.) can become hatred and murder. Paul has a similar picture when referring to the Jews in 1 Th. 2:14 ff. Their No to Jesus is answered by God's No in the form of His ὀργή.

Another NT reason for ὀργή is lovelessness as a reply to God's love, or mercilessness, which can becomes hatred and murder (cf. Mk. 3:5 f.; Mt. 18:23 ff.: ἔπνιγεν, v. 28), as a reply to His mercy. This, too, is a despising of God and His χρηστότης. Apart from Mk. 3:5 and Mt. 18:34 [409] it is a cause of ὀργή in R. 2:5 also to the degree that judging (v. 1) is a lack of love and also an expression of impenitence. [410] Here it is plain that the two reasons for ὀργή, the despising of God and lack of love for one's brother as a reply to the Gospel, are at root one and the same. For the ἀμετανόητος is eo ipso unmerciful. Cf. the Jews in the Gospels, esp. the Pharisees. [411] The NT calls this attitude → πώρωσις τῆς καρδίας (Mk. 3:5) or → σκληρότης (R. 2:5). The ὀργή θεοῦ as an answer thereto (R. 12:19) is the "vengeance" of wounded love (12:19), which is the same as His judicial righteousness. [412]

The motivation of God's wrath already mentioned intersects with a final reason which is hard to define. Paul seems to suggest that behind all the other reasons the true and normative ground of ὀργή is God's own will. There here lurks in the background the dark possibility of a predestination to wrath when Paul refers in R. 9:22 to σκεύη ὀργῆς κατηρτισμένα εἰς ἀπώλειαν in which God wills to demonstrate the power of His wrath. For κατηρτισμένα does not simply means that they were meet or ripe (for destruction). [413] In the light of the parallel ἃ προητοίμασεν in v. 23 it means that they were prepared thereto by God. A similar

---

[408] Both can be called ἀπειθεῖν-ἀπείθεια, the one more in the sense of disobedience (Eph. 5:6), the other of unbelief (Jn. 3:36). R. 2:8 marks the transition, or rather the relation: ἀπειθεῖν τῇ ἀληθείᾳ, πείθεσθαι τῇ ἀδικίᾳ, cf. also 1:18: τὴν ἀλήθειαν ἐν ἀδικίᾳ κατέχειν, and the close connection between ἀπιστία and ἀδικία in R. 3:3, 5.

[409] On the other hand, in the second part of the parable of the Prodigal Son we read only of the ὀργή of the unloving brother (Lk. 15:28); there is no ref. at all to a natural reaction of anger on the part of the father. On the contrary, we find τέκνον in v. 31; cf. also Mt. 20:13-15.

[410] Cf. Schrenk, 20 f.

[411] Cf. J. Schniewind, Das Gleichnis vom verlorenen Sohn (1940), 35-38.

[412] Cf. P. Althaus (→ n. 317) on R. 12:19.

[413] So v. Hofmann, op. cit., 401.

ordination to divine wrath seems to be indirectly intimated in 1 Th. 5:9 too : οὐκ ἔθετο ἡμᾶς ὁ θεὸς εἰς ὀργήν, ἀλλὰ εἰς περιποίησιν σωτηρίας, "God has appointed us (i.e., Christians) to attain to salvation," but only us. For others there is indeed a θέσθαι of God εἰς ὀργήν. The same thought lies behind Paul's view of the Law in R. 4:15 : ὁ γὰρ νόμος ὀργὴν κατεργάζεται. Nor is this for Paul a parergon of the Law ; it is its *opus proprium*. The Law is given in order that man might be set unequivocally under wrath : ἵνα πᾶν στόμα φραγῇ καὶ ὑπόδικος γένηται πᾶς ὁ κόσμος τῷ θεῷ, R. 3:19. These statements are not isolated. They are embedded in sayings about ἐκδίκησις and the like. This means, however, that in such cases we are to think always and supremely of the guilt of man. Human guilt and the divine will form here a no less inextricable web than devilish temptation on the one side and original sin and new and actual transgressions on the other, Eph. 2:2 f.

b. Inseparability of Causes from Effects.

We come into the final impenetrable obscurity of the wrath of God when we perceive that its most serious causes are also its own effects, so that all the great acts of divine wrath are so many reasons for new outbreaks of wrath. What the Jews did, and what was so severely reckoned against them, had to take place according to God's own plan. In putting Jesus to death they were instruments of this plan of love and salvation, and yet the wrath of God overtook them. The ground of wrath is itself the punishment, the rejection of Christ. [414] We are thus plunged into what to human logic seems to be a vicious circle of guilt and punishment which is one of the most terrible insights of the Bible. Sin and unbelief, the two main causes of the ὀργὴ θεοῦ, are also its effect. Paul points this out in R. 1, and it is also the meaning of R. 9:22 : God demonstrates His wrath in the hardening of the σκευή ὀργῆς which He has tolerated so long, e.g., Pharaoh, but also the Jews. [415] It is quite impossible to distinguish between sin and punishment. The wrath of God works according to the divine principle [416] which repays like with like, so that the doer's act falls on his own head. [417]

c. Effects.

In the last point we have already anticipated the deepest answer of the NT to the question of the effects of God's wrath. In answering this question the non-biblical world and the OT world were surprisingly close, → 388 ff.; 400 f. In both cases disasters in nature and national life were traced back to God's wrath. The OT is especially impressive in the way in which it establishes the fundamental

---

[414] Cf. Filson, 43.

[415] "The reality of hardening displays the power of God's wrath, which is a match for man even in his sin," Althaus, *op. cit.* (→ n. 317) on R. 9:17 f. Though the word wrath is not used, 1 Pt. 2:8 finely and succinctly shows that the unity of guilt and fall is established by God, so that basically we have here a depiction of the operation of His wrath in unbelievers : προσκόπτουσιν τῷ λόγῳ ἀπειθοῦντες, εἰς ὃ καὶ ἐτέθησαν, cf. G. Stählin, *Skandalon* (1930), 197 f.

[416] Without actually being this principle, as against Wetter, 20.

[417] Cf. also Mt. 26:52b; 27:25. Judaism had some sense of this, though not with the full profundity of the NT insight, cf. Ab., 4, 2 : "One fulfilment of duty brings with it another, and one transgression another, since the reward of a fulfilment is fulfilment, and of a transgression transgression."

relation between the wrath of God and death (e.g., Ps. 90:7-11). [418] The NT follows it here, [419] cf. particularly R. 1:18 ff. (v. 32 ἄξιοι θανάτου) and R. 13:1 ff. (μάχαιρα-ὀργή).

In the NT picture of eschatological wrath, however, the link between ὀργή and θάνατος is replaced by that between ὀργή and ἀπώλεια (cf. R. 9:22; Rev. 14 ff.). The destruction of Jerusalem, as an execution of wrath, is a type of this (Lk. 21:23 and cf. the par. in the parable at Mt. 22:7). But eschatological ἀπώλεια in its most terrible form is not, of course, annihilation or extinction of being; it is eternal βασανισμός [420] (Rev. 14:10 f.; 20:10 etc.; also Mt. 18:34). Wrathful judgment is not less unbounded than mercy, cf. v. 27, 24.

The most proper NT outworking of wrath, however, is unbelief, apostasy, and its consequences according to the NT equation of μὴ πιστεύοντες and ἀπολλύμενοι. Thus that which is a cause of wrath becomes its effect. In this respect R. 1 goes far beyond the OT statements, though here, too, Paul's train of thought might be called a more profound application of the Deuteronomic schema of retribution (→ 398). The moral chaos of antiquity, and indeed of the whole race, is an order of the ὀργὴ θεοῦ in the revelation granted to faith. Even formally this is indicated by the careful construction of the section. A threefold παρέδωκεν corresponds to the threefold (μετ)ήλλαξαν (v. 23, 25, 26). Here cause and effect are one and the same. The schema of the nexus of cause and effect as the outlook of modern man is broken by the power of the divine wrath.

7. Liberation from God's Wrath.

a. In the world around. The desire to escape or turn aside God's wrath is one which the NT shares with the non-biblical [421] and OT world. [422]

b. Conversion and baptism. Since in the NT the prospect of future wrath controls the scene, the question of deliverance therefrom is raised and answered at the very outset in the message of the Baptist. The answer is as follows: μετανοεῖτε ... ποιήσατε οὖν καρπὸν ἄξιον τῆς μετανοίας, Mt. 3:2, 8, and the promise of deliverance is baptism inasmuch as this anticipates the judgment of wrath in a figure which is more than a figure, and which in this anticipation promises the averting of judgment, → 436. [423] This deliverance, however, is not attained ex opere operato. This seems to be the error of the Pharisees, and the Baptist inveighs sharply against this first baptismal heresy: γεννήματα ἐχιδνῶν, τίς ὑπέδειξεν ὑμῖν φυγεῖν ἀπὸ τῆς μελλούσης ὀργῆς; Mt. 3:7. As the brood of the serpent,

---

[418] Acc. to one of the pseudepigr., in keeping with the equation of wrath and punishment, God's wrath is even identical with the general condemnation of death. In Apc. Mos. 14 Adam says to Eve: τί κατηργάσω ἐν ἡμῖν καὶ ἐπήνεγκας ἐφ' ἡμᾶς ὀργὴν μεγάλην, ἥτις ἐστὶν θάνατος κατακυριεύων παντὸς τοῦ γένους ἡμῶν;
[419] Cf. Bartholomai, 258 et al.
[420] Cf. Wis. 11:9: ἔγνωσαν πῶς μετ' ὀργῆς κρινόμενοι ἀσεβεῖς ἐβασανίζοντο.
[421] → 387; 388 ff., cf. F. Heiler, Das Gebet³ (1921), 87-89 etc.
[422] → 406-407; also Cr.-Kö., 811 f.
[423] The same idea — baptism as the pacifying of wrath — stands behind the legend in Vit. Ad., 6-11: Adam and Eve undertake to baptise themselves in the Jordan or the Tigris with a view to deliverance from God's anger. The alternatives — pacifying of wrath by baptism or judgment by fire — are also stated in Sib., IV, 165, 169, 173. Here "baptism" in rivers is equated with open prayer for forgiveness (cf. 1 Pt. 3:21), whereas Adam and Eve mutely ask for deliverance (in Vit. Ad.).

or children of the devil (→ ὄφις), they are τέκνα ὀργῆς, destined for eternal fire, Mt. 25:41. Who has advised you — if anyone, it can only be the devil — to accept baptism insincerely, i.e., to feign conversion and therewith surreptitiously to obtain protection against the judgment of wrath?[424] The *opus operatum* of baptism does not save. Everything depends on the genuine μετάνοια which accepts the verdict of God and whose genuineness is demonstrated in the καρπός, vv. 8-12. This is the only legitimate and hopeful way of flight from judgment, nor are the Pharisees themselves debarred from it, v. 8.[425]

c. Jesus the Deliverer. The apostolic *kerygma* relates deliverance from God's wrath inseparably to Jesus. Jesus is the One who already saves, 1 Th. 1:10. Jesus it is who will then deliver us from the wrath to come, R. 5:9. Only through Him can we have assurance that we are not destined for wrath, 1 Th. 5:9 f. Through Him we are already σῳζόμενοι, as He is already the ῥυόμενος. Salvation is both present and future in accordance with the dual character of eschatology. Why is deliverance from wrath bound up with Jesus? Because we are justified by His blood, reconciled by His death (R. 5:9 f.), which means that we are no longer under condemnation (8:1), no longer enemies (5:10). Or are we to say: Because Jesus tasted God's wrath for us? Various attempts have been made to show that we are to say this,[426] especially on the basis of the scene in Gethsemane and the saying on the cross in Mt. and Mk.

R. Otto[427] would view the conflict in Gethsemane in terms of the numinous with its *mysterium* and *tremendum*. He thus teaches that it is most closely related to the wrestling of Jacob at Jabbok and the attack on Moses in the inn, → 401. It is above all a struggle with the wrath of God, and victory in the struggle is decisive in this regard too. Similarly, Procksch thinks that the cup which Jesus prays may be taken from Him (Mk. 14:36) is the cup of wrath (→ n. 386). Jesus is shrinking from the ultimate depths of dereliction, as impressively depicted in Lk. 22:44. The angel, who appears in the Gospels only at crises, embodies the nearness of God in imminent dereliction, v. 43.[428] But He is not spared this final horror. His prayer is not answered.[429] This is shown by his last cry in Mt. and Mk.: Eli eli lama asabthani? For to be forsaken by God is to stand under His

---

[424] Related is the rejection of a sacrifice offered by the ungodly with a view to placating the *ira deorum* in Cic. De Legibus, II, 22; → 389.

[425] Cf. Zn. Mt., 133 f.; Schl. Mt., 69 ff. On the other hand, Jesus counts upon it that during the Messianic woes His people may literally escape wrath by flight, Lk. 21:21. In sum, acc. to the Baptist, and later Jesus and the apostles, the principle of no salvation by baptism without conversion is just as important as the principle of no salvation by conversion without baptism. One might say that Jn.'s baptism, like the Passover, is a genuine pre-Christian sacrament in which the operation is related to God's command and the external fulfilment to the assent of the recipient.

[426] Cf., e.g., J. T. Beck, "Der Zorn Gottes," Chr. Reden, V² (1871), 200; H. J. Holtzmann, *Lehrbuch d. nt.lichen Theol.*² (1911), II, 122 : The wrath under which the dying Christ seems to be set is truly exhausted with His death ; so also Procksch : The wrath of God is broken with the sacrificial death of Christ ; also K. Barth, K.D., II, 1² (1946), 444 (C.D., II, 1, 397), who speaks of His suffering the eternal wrath of God. A different view is taken by Ritschl, *Rechtfertigung u. Versöhnung*, II, 155 f.; also W. Hasenzahl, *Die Gottverlassenheit des Christus* (1938), 138-148, though there is hardly any allusion here to the equation of ὀργή, cf. also Althaus, *op. cit.* (→ n. 297), II, 259-261.

[427] *Das Heilige* 26-28 (1947), 106.

[428] Cf. E. Schick, *Die Botschaft der Engel*³ (1949), 128-130.

[429] Hb. 5:7: οὐκ εἰσακουσθείς (acc. to Harnack's conjecture). Gl. 3:13 says something similar.

wrath. This is the consistent view of the OT. God turns from the one with whom He is angry, and *vice versa* (cf. Dt. 31:17; 32:19 f.; Is. 54:8; Ps. 27:9; 89:46).

It may be granted that the passion is never directly related to God's wrath. We are never told expressly that Jesus stood under wrath. [430] Indeed, we are explicitly told (Lk. 2:40, 52; Mk. 1:11; Mt. 12:18; 17:5) that from beginning to end the εὐδοκία and χάρις of God rested on Him. Nevertheless, the heavenly voice at the baptism may itself be regarded as an indication that by accepting baptism, the figure of wrathful judgment, Jesus entered under this judgment, → n. 380. This was the πρέπον that the Baptist could not understand, and to this Jesus, who innocently took the wrath of God upon Himself, the voice ascribed, not ὀργή, but εὐδοκία. What was granted Him in this anticipation of His substitutionary work on the cross was denied on the cross itself, in order that He might take away God's wrath for us by bearing it Himself (cf. R. 5:9, also the par. αἴρειν ἁμαρτίαν in Jn. 1:29).

It is certainly an inalienable part of the NT message that deliverance from the wrath to come was achieved in the death of Christ. There is thus liberation from present wrath as well, and this is decisive, for is the true destructive force. [431] In Christ alone has eternal wrath been breached. Only in Him can we see the solution to the unparalleled tension between God's wrath and His love. [432]

If there is deliverance from eternal wrath in Christ alone, [433] then everything depends on whether a man rejects Christ or appropriates, or more correctly, lets himself be appropriated to, what Christ is and brings. To reject Him is to abide under wrath. To receive Him is to be free. "Either we must fear future wrath or love present grace — one of the two" (Ign. Eph., 11, 1). Liberation from God's wrath is bound up with faith in Christ, Jn. 3:36. In faith in Him we have the eschatological gift of freedom from wrath as a present reality. In water baptism as anticipatory judgment we recognise the legitimacy of the true baptism of judgment or fire, and so this ἀντίτυπον of outpoured wrath saves us from wrath. [434] The power of the ἀντίτυπον, however, reposes in the fact that the candidate receives a portion in Christ, who Himself bore and cancelled wrath. By the Christ-power of baptism we become σκεύη ἐλέους instead of σκεύη ὀργῆς. Whereas we were νεκροί, we are now alive. This view of baptism is thus very close to that of R. 6. The two interpretations are not mutually exclusive; they are complementary.

---

[430] Jesus is perhaps alluding to this in his fig. saying about the fire in Lk. 23:31: Even Jesus, though "green wood," is delivered up (sc. by God) to the fire, i.e., the judgment, → 436.

[431] Althaus, II, 260 in debate with the Gk. theologians and K. Heim. It seems to me, however, that the two propositions: "Christ is the Deliverer from divine wrath and its sentence of condemnation," and: "Christ's act is the great divine counteraction to the revolt of Satan," are equally important acc. to the total view of the NT; cf. Stauffer Theol.³ (1947), 4 etc., esp. 127-130.

[432] Cf. Althaus, II, 32; R. Bultmann, *Theol. d. NT* (1948), 283.

[433] There are in antiquity no true analogies to Christ, who as Judge is the bearer of wrath and yet also the only deliverer from it. Three passages, in different ways, stand relatively closest to the NT concepts: 1. Liv., 8, 9, 10 (→ 391), where the idea that the deity itself sends an offering to placate wrath is only a beautiful notion, but there is an analogy in the free readiness of Decius to sacrifice himself; 2. The offer of Moses to give himself up to divine wrath in place of the people (Ex. 32:32); and 3. the version of Ps. 7:6 in the Midr. (→ n. 302), in which there is appeal to God Himself to fight against His wrath. Cf. also the interpretation of Nu. 21 in Wis. 16:5 ff.

[434] Cf. Schl. Mt., 71.

Nevertheless, deliverance from wrath by pure grace is not a possession which cannot be lost. Even after total forgiveness, even after total acceptance into the fellowship of the kingdom of God, total rejection is still possible, cf. Mt. 18:34; 22:13. Herewith the rejected fall victim to an eternal outworking of God's wrath (→ 434), where "their worm dieth not, and their fire is not quenched." This, too, is part of the NT *kerygma* (cf. R. 2:16),[435] though the final testimony is not to the fiery lake of wrath but to the well-spring of mercy in Christ.

Stählin

---

† ὀρέγομαι, † ὄρεξις

ὀρέγω,[1] "reach out," e.g., the hands to heaven, Hom. Il., 15, 371; hence mid. ὀρέγομαι "reach for something," e.g., Hector for his child, Hom. Il., 6, 466. ὄρεξις occurs only in a transf. sense.

Transf. the group means 1. striving as a faculty of the soul. There is no intrinsic evaluation of the striving. a. Gen., e.g., "to seek the fellowship of Socrates," Xen. Mem., I, 2, 15. b. Philosophically, the pre-Socratics use the term in a comparatively simple sense. Nor does Plato attach any special weight to it, though he can use it to define philosophy : φιλοσοφία τῆς τῶν ὄντων ἀεὶ ἐπιστήμης ὄρεξις, Def., 414b; Resp., VI, 485d; Phaed., 65c.[2] Only with Aristot.[3] and esp. in the Stoic schools[4] is there a special doctrine of ὄρεξις, Epict. Diss., IV, 4, 16. In general ὄρεξις is here the seeking of the soul as something which depends on a decision of the will, so that it is in man's power and accessible to reason.[5] If reason is the measure of ὄρεξις, this striving becomes βούλευσις (= ὄρεξις εὔλογος, Stob., II, 87, 21 f.), and as such it is calm and prudent, Epict. Diss., IV, 1, 84. If ὄρεξις does not follow reason, it becomes desire (ἐπιθυμία = ὄρεξις ἀπειθὴς λόγῳ, Stob., II, 90, 7 f.). The word group can even become the epitome of man's whole attitude to life. The supreme goal of man is ὀρέγεσθαι κατὰ φύσιν (Epict. Diss., I, 21, 2; cf. II, 17, 24 f. [Διὶ] συνορέγεσθαι, and χαρίσασθαι τὴν ὄρεξιν). Philo uses the group in the same way, though within the context of a different philosophical system. His ref. is to the homesickness of the soul pre-existent in the world of ideas. Typical is Som., I, 140, where in contrast to the earthly minded soul are μειζόνων φρονημάτων καὶ θειοτέρων ἐπιλαχοῦσαι, μηδενὸς μὲν τῶν περιγείων ... ὀρεχθεῖσαι (cf. also Abr., 96; Gig., 35; Virt., 218).

---

435 Though cf. W. Michaelis, *Versöhnung des Alls* (1950), esp. 55 f.

ὀρέγομαι κτλ. A. Bonhöffer, *Epict. u. die Stoa* (1890), 233-249; 255-257; *Epict. und d. NT* = RVV, 10 (1911), esp. 122, 209; P. E. Matheson, *Epict.* (1916); H. v. Arnim, "Die drei aristot. Ethiken," *Sitzungsberichte d. Akademie d. Wissenschaften in Wien, phil.-hist. Klasse*, 202, 2 (1925), 26-39; R. Walzer, "Magna Moralia u. aristot. Ethik," NPhU, 7 (1929), 99 f., 136, n. 3, 199.

1 Lat. *rego, erigo*, Germ. *recken* etc., cf. Walde-Pok., II, 362 ff.

2 ὄρεξις, then, is not limited, like θυμός and ἐπιθυμία, to the original faculty of desire, so Walzer, 136, n. 3.

3 Cf. v. Arnim, 27.

4 Bonhöffer, *Epict. u. d. Stoa*, 233-249, 255-257.

5 Thus animals do not have ὄρεξις, ibid., 247.

2. Infrequently the transf. sense is used for physical craving (for nourishment, e.g., Wis. 16:2 f.). The Stoics use προθυμία for this, esp. when the impulse is common to animals too. When Philo and the apcr. [6] use the group in this sense, they emphasise in the context that the physical craving either should be repressed altogether by reason (Sir. 23:6) or can be mastered thereby (4 Macc. 1:33, 35). But the term itself is still *vox media,* and derives its quality only from the subj. or obj. of striving.

It is not without significance for our assessment of the relationship of the NT to the Stoa that the word group occurs in the NT only 4 times, that only twice is there reminiscence of the philosophical use, and that even there only the formal structure of the concept is maintained. [7] According to Hb. 11:16 faith is an ὀρέγεσθαι of the future, better home. In accordance with the common use we are not to see in this seeking an emotional excitement which tries to set itself above reality, but a clear and concentrated will which in all sobriety takes reality into account. But this reality — and here is the distinction from Stoicism and Philo — is not φύσις or λόγος, but ἐπαγγελία, Hb. 11:9, 13. [8] One's attitude to the promise decides the direction which ὄρεξις takes. This attitude is no longer a matter of reason, but of faith. If a man has the obedience of faith (Hb. 11:8, 17), his life is orientated to the city which is to come. If he turns aside from the promise, his life becomes a lust for filthy lucre (1 Tm. 6:10; [9] note the ἀποπλανᾶσθαι in this connection). Either way ὀρέγεσθαι embraces man in his totality. If true ὀρέγεσθαι was already for the philosopher an attitude of life, the eschatological orientation of man genuinely permeates for the first time all his functions and spheres of life.

In R. 1:27 ὄρεξις denotes the sexual impulse, but here again formal similarity to the apocrypha should not be allowed to mask the material distinction. There is for Paul a natural use of the gift of sex. Physical ὄρεξις, then, is not in itself to be depreciated in a dualistic sense. [10] Only when man perverts the truth of God (v. 24 f.) is ὄρεξις corrupted in punishment. For the justified, however, ὄρεξις integrates itself into the reasonable service of God to which he is to dedicate his body. Decision is made concerning physical needs, too, in the conflict of faith.

Heidland

---

[6] In the canonical part of the Gk. transl. act. only in Σ at Job 8:20; Ez. 16:49 etc. in the lit. sense. In the LXX apcr. the noun occurs only 8 times, and never in the philosophical and technical sense.

[7] R. 1:27; Hb. 11:16. On the other hand, the usage of the Apologists gives evidence of even material affinity to philosophical terminology, e.g., Just. Apol., 12, 5 : οἵ γε εὐσεβείας καὶ φιλοσοφίας ὀρέγεσθε, and also to the derogatory manner of the apcr., Athenag., 21, 1: οὔτε γὰρ ὀργὴ οὔτε ἐπιθυμία καὶ ὄρεξις οὐδὲ παιδοποιὸν σπέρμα ἐν τῷ θεῷ.

[8] Cf. Mi. Hb., *ad loc.*

[9] The general wisdom of v. a (Dib. Past., *ad loc.*) is set in the light of revelation in v. b. On the other hand, seeking the episcopate in 1 Tm. 3:1 is not shown to be an unworthy ambition either by the context or the concept.

[10] Only by the addition εἰς ἀλλήλους are the impulses characterised as corrupt.

ὀρθός, διόρθωσις, ἐπανόρθωσις, ὀρθοποδέω

† ὀρθός.

a. "Standing straight up," "upright," Hom. Od., 18, 241; Il., 23, 271; Hdt., VII, 64; Pind. Pyth., 4, 267: σὺν ὀρθαῖς κιόνεσσιν (pillars), transf. Pind. Pyth., 3, 53 : τοὺς δὲ τομαῖς ἔστασεν, "set up again," "put on its feet"; Aesch. Eum., 294; Soph. Ant., 994 : δι' ὀρθῆς τήνδ' ναυκληρεῖς πόλιν, "to direct the state successfully." It is used of buildings for "standing" as opp. to ruinous, Thuc., V, 42; P. Lond., III, 735 B 48 : στῦλοι ὀρθοί, P. Oxy., III, 490, 16; fig. Plat. La., 181b: ὀρθὴ ἂν ἡμῶν ἡ πόλις ἦν, Soph. Oed. Tyr., 1385 : ὀρθοῖς ... ὄμμασιν ... ὁρᾶν, Epict. Diss., III, 26, 35 : ἀντιβλέπειν ... ὀρθοῖς τοῖς ὀφθαλμοῖς. b. "Moving in a straight direction or line," Hes. Op., 727; Soph. Ai., 1254 : ὀρθὸς εἰς ὁδὸν πορεύεται. c. "Right," "correct," "true," Pind. Olymp., 6, 90 : ἄγγελος ὀρθός, Pind. Pyth., 4, 279 : δι' ἀγγελίας ὀρθᾶς, 10, 68 : νόος ὀρθός, 3, 96 : ὀρθὰν καρδίαν, Plat. Phaed., 73a : ὀρθὸς λόγος, Plat. Leg., II, 660a : ὁ ὀρθὸς νομοθέτης, Epict. Diss., I, 11, 13; I, 11, 19 with καλός; II, 23, 27 of the power of will ; I, 18, 20 with ἐλεύθερος; M. Ant., III, 5, 4; IV, 18; V, 9, 1; BGU, I, 248, 9 : ἐν ὀρθῷ μέλλει γείνεσθαι, P. Masp., 151, 209 : ὀρθῷ καὶ ἀγαθῷ συνειδότι. d. "Stretched," "taut," Isoc., 5, 70 : αἰσθάνῃ δὲ τὴν Ἑλλάδα πᾶσαν ὀρθὴν οὖσαν, with expectation, cf. 16, 7; Polyb., 28, 17, 11: ὀρθοὶ καὶ μετέωροι ταῖς διανοίαις ἐγενήθησαν οἱ Ῥόδιοι. Adv. ὀρθῶς, Aesch. Prom., 1000 : ὀρθῶς φρονεῖν, Choeph., 526; Plat. Phaed., 67b; Xen. Cyrop., II, 2, 14 : ὀρθῶς λογίζεσθαι, Epict. Diss., I, 11, 5; II, 15, 6 : ὀρθῶς κρίνειν, M. Ant., X, 3 : ὀρθῶς καὶ φιλοσόφου ἀξίως ἔφη, Iambl. Vit. Pyth., 30, 174 : ὀρθῶς λέγειν, 30, 183 : μὴ ληφθείσης ὀρθῶς τῆς ἀρχῆς, cf. in the NT Mk. 7:35; Lk. 7:43; 10:28; 20:21.

In the LXX ὀρθός means a. "straight," "upright," 1 Esr. 9:46 : πάντες ὀρθοὶ ἔστησαν, fig. Mi. 2:3 : οὐ μὴ πορευθῆτε ὀρθοὶ ἐξαίφνης, 4 Macc. 6:7: ὀρθὸν εἶχεν καὶ ἄκλινῆ τὸν λογισμόν, b. "in a straight direction," Jer. 38:9 : ἐν ὁδῷ ὀρθῇ, Ez. 1:7; transf. Prv. 4:25 : οἱ ὀφθαλμοί σου ὀρθὰ βλεπέτωσαν, 4:26 : ὀρθὰς τροχιὰς ποίει σοῖς ποσίν, 14:12; 15:14 : καρδία ὀρθή (opp. ἀπαίδευτος) "understanding"; 16:25, c. "right," "correct," "true" to denote a recognised norm, esp. in Prv.: 8:6 : ἀνοίσω ἀπὸ χειλέων ὀρθά, 8:9 : πάντα ... ὀρθὰ τοῖς εὑρίσκουσι γνῶσιν, 11:6; 12:6 opp. ἀσεβής; 12:15; 16:13 par. δίκαιος; 21:8 par. ἁγνός, 23:16; 31:5 "in accordance with what is right"; Mi. 3:9; 4 Macc. 1:15. Jos. Ant., 6, 13 : τὴν ὀρθὴν ὁδόν. Very common in Philo, usually in sense c., e.g., Som., II, 97: ἐπ' ὀρθὸν βίον καὶ λόγον, Conf. Ling., 52 : ὀρθῆς γνώμης, Virt., 39 : παιδείας ὀρθῆς etc.

In the NT ὀρθός is used in the healing of the lame man at Ac. 14:10 in the sense of "standing up straight." Paul sees the faith of the sick man and orders him : "Stand up straight on your feet." Hb. 12:13 quotes Prv. 4:26 (→ supra), but in the context ὀρθός undergoes a distinctive change of sense. In Prv. it refers to right conduct under the direction of divine wisdom. In Hb. it refers to the perseverance of members of the community through even the most stringent tests of faith, not merely in orientation to a doctrine, but with eyes on the martyrs and

---

ὀρθός κτλ. Pape, Liddell-Scott, s.v.

especially on Jesus, who, exalted to dominion, assures His disciples of the goal of their conflict of faith. Strengthened thus, faith cannot waver, but moves in a straight direction, sure of its goal. There is no question of making straight paths, but of pursuing ways which are directed straight to their goal. [1] The term ὀρθός has been brought into line with the eschatology of primitive Christianity. It is not just used ethically, as in classical Greek, Stoicism, and Jewish Wisdom literature, but indicates the orientation of life to χαρά, and the pledge of this χαρά. ὀρθός thus expresses the eschatological attitude of the disciples of Jesus.

† διόρθωσις.

διόρθωσις denotes the "making straight of what has shifted from its true position"; hence in Hippocr. the setting of a dislocated member, De Officina Medici, 16; Mochlicum, 38; also the repairing and restoring of what is shattered : καὶ τῶν πιπτόντων οἰκοδομημάτων καὶ ὁδῶν σωτηρία καὶ διόρθωσις, Aristot. Pol., VI, 5, 3, p. 1321, b. 21; Plat. Leg., I, 642a uses it as a word for "planned arrangement," cf. often in Polyb., for whom it is the antonym of, e.g., βλαβή, 5, 88, 2; fig. "correction of an error," Polyb., 3, 58, 4; gen. of human relationships, Polyb., 3, 118, 12 : πρὸς τὰς τῶν πολιτευμάτων διορθώσεις, "to the setting up of states"; cf. Aristot. Pol., VI, 1, 5, p. 1317a, 35; Preis. Zaub., XIII, 707: πρὸς διόρθωσιν βίου, of the "payment of debts," Polyb., 5, 50, 7; 11, 25, 9; "payment of taxes," BGU, IV, 1022, 13; P. Lond., IV, 1349, 9. The word does not occur in the LXX (only διορθωτής, διορθοῦν) and is found only once in Philo, Sacr. AC, 27. Jos. Ap., 2, 183 : τὰ γὰρ μὴ τοῦτον ἔχοντα τὸν τρόπον αἱ πεῖραι δεόμενα διορθώσεως ἐλέγχουσιν.

In accordance with the general line of thought in Hb. we read of the sacrificial ministry of the OT in 9:10 that the offerings and the whole cultus could affect only the external man, but not the inner being. [1] Hence the cultus was only a temporary plan in God's dealings with man. It lasted until the setting up of the order of the fulfilled time, until the time when the Law and the prophets were replaced by the καιρὸς διορθώσεως, i.e., until the time of the true order. From this time on there is in force the order of the dawning time of consummation in the fashioning of the relation between God and man. Thus διόρθωσις is a witness to the fulfilment of Judaism in Christianity and an expression of the eschatological faith of primitive Christianity.

† ἐπανόρθωσις.

ἐπανόρθωσις, "restoration" (ἐπανορθόω, "to raise up again," "to reform"), "re-establishment," "correction," "reformation": Demosth. Or., 24, 22 τῶν νόμων, Aristot. Eth. Nic., IX, p. 1165b, 19; Polyb., 1, 66, 12 : μεγάλας εἶχον ἐλπίδας καὶ μεγάλην προσδοκίαν τῆς ἐσομένης περὶ αὐτοὺς ἐπανορθώσεως, 1, 35, 1: ἐπανόρθωσιν τοῦ τῶν ἀνθρώπων βίου, Plut. Aud., 16 (II, 46d): πρὸς ἐπανόρθωσιν ἤθους, Epict. Diss., III, 21, 15 : ἐπὶ παιδείᾳ καὶ ἐπανορθώσει τοῦ βίου, of the mysteries ; Iambl. Vit. Pyth., 6, 30 : εἰς ὠφέλειαν καὶ ἐπανόρθωσιν τοῦ θνητοῦ βίου. In the LXX 1 Esr. 8:52 of God's assistance to the returning exiles ; [1] 1 Macc. 14:34 of the improvement of the

---

[1] So correctly Rgg. Hb., ad loc.; Mi. Hb.8, ad loc. A different view is taken in Wind. Hb., ad loc.

δ ι ο ρ θ ω σ ι ς. [1] Wnd. Hb., ad loc.

ἐ π α ν ό ρ θ ω σ ι ς. [1] Mas. Ezr. 8:22 לְטוֹבָה = 2 Esr. 8:22 εἰς ἀγαθόν; 1 Esr. 8:52 may well be the original freer transl. εἰς πᾶσαν ἐπανόρθωσιν [Bertram].

situation of the Jews in Joppa. Common in Philo, e.g., Conf. Ling., 171: ἁμαρτημάτων ... κώλυσις καὶ ἐπανόρθωσις, Leg. Gaj., 369 τῶν νομίμων, Mut. Nom., 70 ἠθῶν etc.

In 2 Tm. 3:16 we are told that Scripture can teach us how the believer may attain to salvation. Since Scripture originates from God's Word, it is profitable for teaching, for the conviction of the sinner, and for instruction in righteousness. There is obviously a planned sequence in this list of nouns. If between the conviction of the sinner and his instruction in righteousness there is a reference to ἐπανόρθωσις, this can only mean that the convicted sinner receives the restoration, i.e., the amendment in conversion εἰς σωτηρίαν (2 Tm. 3:15), which only God can give. Hence here, too, there is an eschatological determination of ἐπανόρθωσις, though, in accordance with the general structure of the Pastorals, we have a stronger orientation to ethical outworking.

† ὀρθοποδέω.

ὀρθοποδέω (from ὀρθόπους, "with upright feet") "to stand erect on the feet," "not to waver," "not to tumble," is found only in the NT and early Christian writings. In the assessment of the situation at Antioch the conduct of Peter and the followers of James is characterised in Gl. 2:14 as follows, ὅτι οὐκ ὀρθοποδοῦσιν πρὸς τὴν ἀλήθειαν τοῦ εὐαγγελίου. They deny freedom from the Law and justification by faith alone, v. 16. To walk firmly according to the truth of the Gospel is thus to be obedient to the reality of salvation as accomplished by God in Christ.

It is thus true of this whole word group that it deals with the new relation established by God, and with man's conduct towards God. Everywhere — only 2 Tm. 3:16 is a qualified exception — we are directed by it to the fact that the human situation is eschatologically determined.

Preisker

ὀρθοτομέω → τέμνω.

ὀ ρ θ ο π ο δ έ ω → τέμνω. [1] Luther's "walk correctly" does not give the true sense [Debrunner].

ὁρίζω, ἀφορίζω, ἀποδιορίζω, προορίζω

† ὁρίζω.

The simple derives from ὁ ὅρος, "boundary," which does not occur in the NT (though cf. τὸ ὅριον in the same sense, only plur. τὰ ὅρια "territory," also ἡ ὁροθεσία). It thus means "to limit," "to set the limit," and then fig. "to fix," "to appoint." The verb, which is found from the time of Aesch. and Hdt., and which later belongs to the literary *koine*, occurs in the NT 6 times in Luke's historical writing and once each in Pl. and Hb. [1]

In the lit. sense it occurs also in the LXX: Nu. 34:6; Jos. 13:27; 15:12; 18:20 (Mas. גבל; fixing of the borders on the occupation of Israel). [2] Time can be limited as well as space: χρόνου τοῦ ὂν ὁ νόμος ὥρισεν, Plat. Leg., IX, 864e; ὁ νόμος τὸν χρόνον ὥρισεν, Demosth., 36, 26; εἰς τὸν ὡρισμένον καιρόν, Jos. Ant., 6, 78 etc.

The limitation is temporal at Hb. 4:7: πάλιν τινὰ ὁρίζει (God) ἡμέραν. [3] It is both temporal and spatial at Ac. 17:26 f.: ὁρίσας (God) προστεταγμένους (vl. προτ-) καιροὺς καὶ τὰς ὁροθεσίας [4] ("limitations," "limits") τῆς κατοικίας αὐτῶν (sc. men), ζητεῖν τὸν θεόν. In both instances one might use the more general "appoint." This is the sense elsewhere in the NT. Ac. 11:29: ὥρισαν ἕκαστος αὐτῶν (sc. τῶν μαθητῶν) with inf. following, as in classical Gk.: [5] "They determined ..."; Lk. 22:22: ὁ υἱὸς ... τοῦ ἀνθρώπου κατὰ τὸ ὡρισμένον πορεύεται ... "according to what has been determined (by God), according to the counsel (of God)." Similarly Ac. 2:23: τοῦτον (sc. Ἰησοῦν) τῇ ὡρισμένῃ βουλῇ καὶ προγνώσει τοῦ θεοῦ ἔκδοτον ... "delivered according to the deter-

---

ὁ ρ ί ζ ω. [1] Cf. esp. Pr.-Bauer³, *s.v.* Note should be taken of the 4 passages (Pr.-Bauer has only the 4th) in which there is ref. in profane Gk. to ὁρίζειν by the gods: Zeus and Dike in Soph. Ant., 452: οἳ τούσδ᾽ ἐν ἀνθρώποισιν ὥρισαν νόμους, Eur. Fr., 218 (TGF, 424): τὸ δοῦλον ὡς ἁπανταχῇ γένος πρὸς τὴν ἐλάσσω μοῖραν ὥρισεν θεός. Epict. Diss., I, 12, 25: ἐκεῖνος (sc. Ζεύς) μετὰ τῶν Μοιρῶν παρουσῶν καὶ ἐπικλωθουσῶν σου τὴν γένεσιν ὥρισεν καὶ διέταξεν, and Meleager in Anth. Pal., 12, 158: σὲ γὰρ θεὸν ὥρισε δαίμων [Kleinknecht].

[2] In the LXX ὁρίζειν ὁρισμόν (περὶ [κατὰ] τῆς ψυχῆς αὐτοῦ) is used 8 times in Nu. 30 for אֱסָר אָסַר "to lay a bond on oneself," i.e., "to take a vow." At Prv. 18:18 פרד ("to separate") is rendered ὁρίζειν. At Prv. 16:30b ὁρίζειν is par. to λογίζεσθαι in 30a and means "to plan," "to devise" [Bertram].

[3] Cf. Mi. Hb.⁷, *ad loc.*: "God is the Lord of time: acc. to 4:7 He appoints (ὁρίζει) a day (cf. Ac. 17:31 ἡμέραν ἔστησεν); over against an earlier 'day' there is set a 'to-day' (σήμερον).

[4] R. Morgenthaler, *Die lukanische Geschichtsschreibung als Zeugnis*, I (1949), 19, like A. v. Harnack, *Sprüche u. Reden Jesu* (1907), 83, sees in the phrase ὁρίσας ὁροθεσίας an "etymological figure," and says (69): "At Ac. 17:26 Zn. thinks ὁρίσας-ὁροθεσίας is dreadful tautology ... *De gustibus non est disputandum.*"

[5] Cf. Liddell-Scott, *s.v.* III, 1.

minate counsel and decree of God." ⁶ Christ Himself was appointed by God to do the work of salvation, Ac. 17:31: God ἔστησεν ἡμέραν ἐν ᾗ μέλλει κρίνειν τὴν οἰκουμένην ἐν δικαιοσύνῃ, ἐν ἀνδρὶ (vl. + ᾽Ιησοῦ) ᾧ ὥρισεν ... "by a man (Jesus) whom he has appointed (thereto)." Even more significantly we read in Ac. 10:42 : οὗτός (vl. αὐτός, sc. Jesus Christ) ἐστιν ὁ ὡρισμένος ὑπὸ τοῦ θεοῦ κριτὴς ζώντων καὶ νεκρῶν ... "the judge of the quick and the dead determined, appointed, instituted by God." This pass. construction presupposes for the act. a construction with double acc.: ὁρίζειν τινά τι, "to determine someone as something" (cf. Xenoph. Mem., IV, 6, 4, in the pass.), or "to appoint someone as something." So R. 1:4 : (Χριστοῦ ᾽Ιησοῦ) τοῦ ὁρισθέντος (lat Irᶦᵃᵗ : προορ-) υἱοῦ θεοῦ ἐν δυνάμει κατὰ πνεῦμα ἁγιωσύνης ἐξ ἀναστάσεως νεκρῶν ... "who was instituted as Son of God in power." The prepositional ἐν δυνάμει is not an adverbial qualification of ὁρισθέντος but an attribute of υἱοῦ θεοῦ, → II, 304. ⁷ Similarly, in Ign. Eph., 3, 2 we read of bishops that they are κατὰ τὰ πέρατα ὁρισθέντες.

The exegetical dispute ⁸ whether R. 1:4, according to usage attested elsewhere, is a declaration or decree concerning Christ, or His appointment and institution to a function or relation etc., is not a matter of great urgency, since a divine declaration is the same as a divine appointment : God's *verbum* is *efficax*. But behind the dispute there is an important point, for in the christological passages adduced, Ac. 10:42 and 17:31 as well as R. 1:4, the appointment of Jesus (Christ) as what He is to be must be equated with what He already is from the very beginning of the world, from all eternity in God's decree. It is no accident that προορισθέντος is attested at R. 1:4 as a pertinent interpretation of ὁρισθέντος, that the ὡρισμένη βουλή and πρόγνωσις are mentioned together at Ac. 2:23, and that we find the reading προτεταγμένους for προστεταγμένους (καιρούς) at Ac. 17:26. The reference is always to the predestination of the Christ event by God. A feature of the 8 ὁρίζω passages in the NT is that with the exception of Ac. 11:29 they are all emphatically theological and christological ; they describe the person and work of Jesus Christ.

---

⁶ The part. ὡρισμένος is esp. common in the pap. (*v.* Preisigke Wört.) and seems to be an old legal term [Debrunner].

⁷ So correctly Zn. R., *ad loc.*: "He who was indeed a Son of God, but also a weak human image, was destined to become a Son of God in power. τοῦ ὁρισθέντος υἱοῦ θεοῦ ἐν δυνάμει cannot mean anything else." On the other hand cf. Ltzm. R., *ad loc.*: "Whether ἐν δυνάμει goes with υἱοῦ θεοῦ ... or with ὁρισθέντος on the analogy of 2 C. 13:4, cannot be said for certain." As against this, the question is not really a grammatical one, which undoubtedly cannot be answered for certain, but a christological one. An adverbial qualification would imply an erroneous adoptionism. Cf. E. Gaugler, *Der Brief an d. Römer*, I (1945), *ad loc.* and O. Cullmann, *Christus u. d. Zeit* (1946), 210, 215 (E.T. 236, 241). For patristic exegesis cf. K. Staab, *Pauluskommentare aus d. alten gr. Kirche* (1933), 57: Apollinaris of Laodicea : ... κατὰ τὸ πνεῦμα καὶ τὴν δύναμιν υἱὸς ἀναδείκνυται θεοῦ ..., 470 : Phot.: ἐπιγνωσθέντος, εἰς γνῶσιν ἀνθρώποις ἐλθόντος, cf. BZ, 18 (1928), 77: Orig. ... υἱὸς δὲ ὡρίσθη εἶναι θεοῦ τουτέστιν ἐκυρώθη τοῦτο ὤν ...

⁸ On this *v.* Cr.-Kö., 819 f. and Ltzm. R., *ad loc.*

† ἀφορίζω.

This compound, attested from the time of Soph., Plat., occurs 10 times in 9 NT texts and means "to separate," "to sever." In connection with what was said about ὁρίζω, it seems that at the heart of the NT we find the principle of God separating, i.e., marking off for His service. So R. 1:1: κλητὸς ἀπόστολος ἀφωρισμένος εἰς εὐαγγέλιον θεοῦ, ὃ προεπηγγείλατο, where the divine separating to the Gospel underlines the divine call of the apostle, → I, 438 f.; III, 494. It does this, indeed, with reference to the message which God promised beforehand (προ-). Both materially and formally Gl. 1:15 is to the same effect: God is ἀφορίσας με ἐκ κοιλίας μητρός μου καὶ καλέσας διὰ τῆς χάριτος αὐτοῦ, with a combination once again of separation and calling. When Paul calls God an ἀφορίσας in Gl. 1:15 and himself an ἀφωρισμένος in R. 1:1, this can be related to his Pharisaism (→ Φαρισαῖος), for ἀφωρισμένος is the current transl. of the Heb. פָּרוּשׁ and Aram. פְּרִישׁ, of which Φαρισαῖος is the transcription. [1]

By God's commission the Son of Man will divide the good from the bad as a shepherd separates the sheep from the goats, Mt. 25:32. The same function will be given to the angels, who will divide the wicked from the righteous, Mt. 13:49. [2] Hence the attitude of Christians must be as follows: If God separates, believers have to accept this and separate themselves, as a people of salvation, from the people of perdition. The exclusive God demands this exclusiveness. In 2 C. 6:17, as in the OT (Is. 52:11; cf. Jer. 51:45), we read: ἐξέλθατε ἐκ μέσου αὐτῶν καὶ ἀφορίσθητε, λέγει κύριος. The Holy Spirit demands the same separation for the work of the apostolate, saying in Ac. 13:2: ἀφορίσατε δή μοι τὸν Βαρναβᾶν καὶ Σαῦλον εἰς τὸ ἔργον ὃ προσκέκλημαι αὐτούς. Paul differentiates the community from the Israel which understands or misunderstands itself in physical terms, Ac. 19:9: ἀποστὰς ἀπ' αὐτῶν (sc. τῶν Ἰουδαίων) ἀφώρισεν τοὺς μαθητάς. Peter on one occasion reversed this by separating himself from Gentile Christians even though they belong to spiritual Israel, Gl. 2:12: ἀφώριζεν ἑαυτόν. [3] The world replies with its own ἀφορίζειν, Lk. 6:22: "Blessed are ye when men hate you and ὅταν ἀφορίσωσιν ὑμᾶς καὶ ὀνειδίσωσιν." [4]

As 2 C. 6:17 = Is. 52:11 shows, the separation between the Christian and the world is prefigured in that between Israel and the world in the OT. In the LXX ἀφορίζω does not correspond to a single, definite Heb. term. פרד in Gn. 2:10; 10:5 means cleavage, spatial separation; בדל in Lv. 20:25 (twice), 26; Dt. 4:41; Jos. 16:9; Is. 56:3 means "division," "separation." סגר is used for the separation esp. of lepers. Otherwise pre-

---

ἀφορίζω. [1] Zn. R. on 1:4 pts. this out expressly: "... he is always a Pharisee in a higher sense; even as a Christian and apostle he said ἐγὼ Φαρισαῖός εἰμι in Ac. 23:6 ..." H. Schlier, *Der Galaterbrief* (1949) on 1:15 is more cautious: "Perhaps there is a pun on (the Heb.) פָּרוּשׁ or (Aram.) פְּרִישָׁה (better א for ה), i.e., Pharisee, though the readers would hardly detect this. Paul would then be noting in his membership of the Pharisees a symbolical relationship." Cf. also Str.-B., III, 4.
[2] Moult.-Mill., 98: "For the word, as in Mt. 13:49, we may add a citation from the *Pelagia-Legenden*, p. 6, 5: μή με ἀφορίσης ἀπὸ τοῦ οὐρανίου σου θυσιαστηρίου."
[3] Luther esp. emphasised Peter's sin here, cf. K. L. Schmidt, *Die Kirche des Urchristentums*[2] (1932), 308 f.
[4] Jn. 9:22; 12:42; 16:2 use → ἀποσυνάγωγος for the same thing. Liddell-Scott renders the ἀφορίζω of Lk. 6:22: "set apart for rejection, cast out, excommunicate."

dominantly cultic terms are the originals : עבר, חרם, מקדש, רום, נוף, which are all used for the bringing of sacrifices and the dedication of fields and land to religious and cultic purposes, and which all involve separation from everyday life from the LXX standpoint. The same is true of ברר when on occasion it is rendered by ἀφορίζειν. The dividing out of the unclean or unholy is an esp. important matter in the legal statutes concerning purity and holiness, → I, 91 and 100 f. Lv. 13:4 f.: ἀφοριεῖ ... ὁ ἱερεὺς ἑπτὰ ἡμέρας the leper, because he is ἀκάθαρτος (unclean), cf. v. 11, 21, 26, 31, 33, 54; 14:38, 46. In Nu. 12:14 f. Miriam was cast out (ἀφωρίσθη) of the camp 7 days because of her revolt. In Dt. 4:41 Moses separated (ἀφώρισεν) 3 free cities. In Jos. 16:9 the territories of the Ephraimites were separated (ἀφορισθεῖσαι) in the inheritance of the children of Manasseh. Is. 56:3 : "The son of the stranger, that hath joined himself to the Lord, shall not speak, saying, the Lord will separate (ἀφοριεῖ) me from his people." Materially relevant is also 2 Esr. 10:8 : "If anyone does not obey the commandment given by Ezra, his whole possessions will fall under the ban, [5] and he himself shall be cast out of the congregation of those who have returned (διασταλήσεται, בדל for this as for ἀφορίζω).

If in the NT separation is by God for a specific and express purpose, there are OT models for this too. The separation of holy men or things taken place ἔναντι κυρίου or τῷ κυρίῳ, cf. the refs. to the so-called heave offering (votive offering) in Ex. 29:24, 26; Lv. 10:15; 14:12; Nu. 18:24; Ez. 45:13; 48:9. The Levites are an offering (ἀπόδομα) of this kind ; Aaron is to separate them (ἀφοριεῖ) from the other Israelites. In the so-called Holiness Code we find the admonition : "And ye shall be holy unto me, for I the Lord am holy," with the statement : "And I have severed you (ὁ ἀφορίσας ὑμᾶς) from other people, that ye should be mine," Lv. 20:26.

† ἀποδιορίζω.

Double compounds with ἀπό and διά are rare, and being formed to meet special needs they have often to be explained from the context. In secular Gk. the only instance of this word is in Aristot. Pol., IV, 4, p. 1290b, 25 : εἰ ζῴου προηρούμεθα λαβεῖν εἴδη, πρῶτον ἂν ἀποδιωρίζομεν ὅπερ ἀναγκαῖον πᾶν ἔχειν ζῷον. Here ἀποδιορίζω means "to define more exactly." It is a stronger form of διορίζω, "to define." The ἀπό emphasises the separation of different details, and thus underlines the διά. [1]

It is open to question whether the only NT occurrence can or should be expounded in terms of the ref. in Aristot. Jd. 18 f.: ἐπ' ἐσχάτου τοῦ χρόνου ἔσονται ἐμπαῖκται κατὰ τὰς ἑαυτῶν ἐπιθυμίας πορευόμενοι τῶν ἀσεβειῶν. Οὗτοί εἰσιν οἱ ἀποδιορίζοντες ψυχικοί, πνεῦμα μὴ ἔχοντες. One might relate τῶν ἀσεβειῶν to ἀποδιορίζοντες as an obj. gen., and then translate and expound as follows : "Who make ungodly things the subject of an activity of thought which defines all things." [2] But in a more natural and literal sense διορίζω means "to separate" as well as "to define." [3] Along these lines the false teachers combatted in Jd. 18 f.

---

[5] Cf. Str.-B., IV, 293 ff., Exc.: "Der Synagogenbann." Distinction is here made between the ban as discipline within the synagogue and excommunication from it (→ ἀποσυνάγωγος). Cf. also Schl. Lk. on 6:22. In the Christian Church ἀφορίζειν is excommunicare, ἀφορισμός excommunicatio ; v. the instances in E. A. Sophocles, Gk. Lexicon of the Roman and Byzantine Periods (1888), s.v.

ἀ π ο δ ι ο ρ ί ζ ω. [1] ἀποδια-, in Mayser, I, 3² (1936), 242 only 3 verbs.

[2] Cr.-Kö., 821 mentions and rejects this acute and not wholly impossible exposition of J. C. K. v. Hofmann on the ground that there is too narrow a restriction and that the usage attested only once in Aristot. is not binding.

[3] So, e.g., R. Wünsch, Antike Fluchtafeln = Kl. T., 20 (1907), 12 : ἐξορκίζω ὑμᾶς κατὰ τοῦ ἐπάν[ω] τοῦ οὐρανοῦ θεοῦ, τοῦ καθημένου ἐπὶ τῶν Χερουβί, ὁ διορίσας τὴν γῆν καὶ χωρίσας τὴν θάλασσαν.

are those who cause splits or divisions by their teaching. [4] This fits in well with v. 20, where believers are addressed as those who build up themselves (ἐποικοδο-μοῦντες ἑαυτούς): The building up of a community is the exact opposite of its disruption. Materially apposite is 2 Pt. 2:1, where the false teachers παρεισάξουσιν αἱρέσεις. One might also mention the castigation of the spirit of contention and division in the primitive lists of vices (Gl. 5:20; 1 Tm. 4:1 ff.). There is nothing odd in the fact that ἀποδιορίζοντες has no obj. in Jd. 19. For any trans. verb can be used without a specific obj. when emphasis is to be laid simply on the pt. at issue in it. [5] The whole verse acquires a distinctive aspect if the ἀποδιορίζειν is to be related to the content of the false teaching, namely, that it splits up men into psychics and pneumatics. [6]

† προορίζω.

This comparatively rare and late word is used in the Gk. Bible only 6 times in the NT in the sense "to foreordain," "to predestinate." Since God is eternal and has ordained everything before time, προορίζειν is a stronger form of ὁρί-ζειν, [1] → 453. The synonyms and textual history show that the ref. in προγι-νώσκειν is the same. R. 8:29: οὓς προέγνω, καὶ προώρισεν συμμόρφους τῆς εἰκόνος τοῦ υἱοῦ αὐτοῦ, R. 8:30: οὓς ... προώρισεν (Α: προέγνω), τούτους καὶ ἐκάλεσεν, → I, 715; II, 396. The omniscient God has determined everything in advance, [2] both persons and things in salvation history, with Jesus Christ as the goal. [3] When Herod and Pilate work together with the Gentiles and the mob against Jesus Christ, it may be said: ἡ χείρ σου (God's) καὶ ἡ βουλὴ προώρισεν γενέσθαι, Ac. 4:28. Herein lies the hidden wisdom of God in a mystery, ἣν προ-ώρισεν ὁ θεὸς πρὸ τῶν αἰώνων εἰς δόξαν ἡμῶν, 1 C. 2:7, → IV, 819. The goal of our predestination is divine sonship through Jesus Christ: προορίσας ἡμᾶς εἰς υἱοθεσίαν διὰ Ἰησοῦ Χριστοῦ, Eph. 1:5. That we have our inheritance in Christ rests in the fact that we are προορισθέντες κατὰ πρόθεσιν τοῦ τὰ πάντα ἐνεργοῦντος, Eph. 1:11. [4]

K. L. Schmidt

---

[4] So the Zurich Bible: "Who provoke divisions," and Luther: "Who form sects."

[5] On this ground we are to reject the externally poorly attested vl. (Cod C Vg: *qui segregant semetipsos,* Aug. *et al.*) which adds ἑαυτούς. Thes. Steph.: *Schismatici.*

[6] Cf. Wnd. Kath. Br., *ad loc.* (following older exegetes): "ἀποδιορίζειν, 'to make distinc-tions,' thus refers, not to the splits they cause in the communities, but to the content of their teaching." C. Weizsäcker seems to have the same in view in his rendering: "These are they who make classes."

π ρ ο ο ρ ί ζ ω. [1] Cf. also E. v. Dobschütz, "Prädestination," ThStKr, 106 (1934/35), 9-19, and K. Staab, *Pauluskomm. aus d. alten gr. Kirche* (1933), 76 (Orig.), 95 (Diodore of Tarsus).

[2] The OT prophets also speak of what is determined far in advance, cf. esp. 2 K. 19:25; Is. 22:11 [v. Rad].

[3] R. Liechtenhan, "D. göttliche Vorherbestimmung bei Pls. u. in d. Posidonianischen Philosophie," FRL, NF, 18 (1922). 17-24.

[4] If, acc. to Cr.-Kö., 822 "προορίζειν is a purely formal concept, and not (like προ-γινώσκειν in R. 8:29), one which is independent and self-contained," we have to remember that the decisive subj., i.e., God, overrides any such distinction.

ὅρκος, ὀρκίζω, ὀρκωμοσία, ἐνορκίζω, ἐξορκίζω (ἐξορκιστής), ἐπίορκος, ἐπιορκέω	→ ὀμνύω, 176.

† ὅρκος.

a. "Oath." Possibly the word ἕρκος ("hedging in") underlies the noun.[1] Usually an oath is taken by the gods, who are invoked as witnesses to the truth of the statement. For the Gks. the supreme oath is by the Styx[2] (Στυγὸς ὕδωρ, ὅς τε μέγιστος ὅρκος δεινότατός τε πέλει μακάρεσσι θεοῖσι, Hom. Il., 15, 38; cf. Hes. Theog., 400, 784; 805; Aristot. Metaph., I, 3, p. 938b, 31). The oath usually contains the words μέγας, καρτερός (Hom. etc.). The expressions ὅρκον διδόναι and ὅρκον λαμβάνειν are common, e.g., Aristot. Rhet., I, 15, p. 1377a, 7 f. ὅρκῳ ἐμμένειν, Eur. Med., 754; ὅρκον τηρεῖν, Democr. Fr., 239 (Diels⁵, II, 193, 6). b. Ὅρκος is also a personified figure (the son of Eris) which punishes false swearing and perjury, Hes. Op., 804, 219; Theog., 231; Hdt., VI, 86, 3. Διὸς Ὅρκος, Soph. Oed. Col., 1767.[3]

In the pap.[4] βασιλικὸς ὅρκος, an oath by the king, BGU, VI, 1214, 11 etc., by the emperor, P. Oxy., II, 382, 395; θεῖος ὅρκος, by the emperor (3rd or 4th cent. A.D.), P. Flor., 32 B 16, or by God (6th and 7th cent. A.D.), P. Oxy., VI, 393, 4. 5. 8; σεβάσμιος θεῖος ὅρκος, by the emperor, ibid., X, 1265, 15; φρικτὸς ὅρκος, "dreadful oath" (i.e., one which kindles dread and reverence before God), P. Masp., 200, 4; φρικωδέστατος ὅρκος, "the most dreadful oath," P. Lond., I, 77, 52. From the 6th cent. on oaths by the Trinity (ἁγία Τριάς)[5] and by relics (σωματικὸς ὅρκος), P. Masp., 151, 163 (6th cent. A.D.). Oaths increase steadily in intensity and compass, e.g., ὁ φρικτὸς καὶ σεβάσμιος ὅρκος κατὰ τῆς ἁγίας καὶ ὁμοουσίου τριάδος καὶ νίκης καὶ δια-

---

ὅ ρ κ ο ς. E. Ziebarth, Art. "Eid" in Pauly-W., V, 2075-2083; J. Köstlin, I. Benzinger, Art. "Eid" in RE³, V, 239-244; A. Bertholet, L. Köhler, F. K. Schumann, E. Ruck in RGG², II, 49-55; K. Hilgenreiner in Lex. Th. K., III, 586-591; G. Ferries, Art. "Oath" in Hastings DB, III, 575-577; M. A. Canney, T. K. Cheyne, Art. "Oath" in EB, III, 3451-3454; A. E. Crawley, E. Beet, M. A. Canney, Art. "Oath" in ERE, IX, 430-438; R. Hirzel, Der Eid (1902); J. Pedersen, Der Eid bei den Semiten (1914); E. Seidl, D. Eid im römisch-ägyptischen Provinzialrecht, I (1933); II (1935); W. Luther, "Wahrheit" u. "Lüge" im ältesten Griechentum (1935); G. Glotz, Art. "Jusjurandum" in Darembg.-Saglio; M. P. Nilsson, Geschichte d. gr. Religion, I (1941), 128 f.
[1] So Eustath. Thessal. Comm. in Il., 2, 339 : γίνεται δὲ ὁ ὅρκος ὅθεν τὸ ἕρκος. "For a new and better explanation cf. M. Leumann, Homerische Wörter (1950), 91 f. ὅρκος 'staff' (which is taken and raised at an oath) = Lat. surcus (from surculus, 'twig'); thus ὅρκον ὄμνυμι, 'I take the (oath) staff.' Cf. Hom. Il., 1, 234 : ναὶ μὰ τόδε σκῆπτρον (233 : μέγαν ὅρκον), 7, 411: ὅρκια δὲ Ζεὺς ἴστω . . ., 412 : τὸ σκῆπτρον ἀνέσχεθε πᾶσι θεοῖσιν, 10, 321, 328 : ἐν χερσὶ σκῆπτρον λάβε καὶ οἱ ὄμοσσεν" [Debrunner].
[2] On the oath by the Styx cf. esp. Hirzel, 171-175.
[3] As the son of Eris Horcos has the character of a demon of the underworld, as a servant of Zeus he is a god of the upper world of light. Two distinct mythological ideas are obviously at work here. Hirzel thinks that if the gods swear their supreme oath by a being of the underworld this can only be a "relic of earlier life and religion which has lost its original point in the new age and its theology," 174.
[4] Cf. in detail Preisigke Wört., s.v.; Fachwörter, s.v., with bibl.
[5] A. Heisenberg-L. Wenger, Byzant. Pap. in d. königlichen Hof- u. Staatsbibliothek zu München (1914), 6, 56 (6th cent. A.D.). Oath by the Gospels, P. Lond., V, 1708, 228 (567 A.D. ?): ἑκάστου τούτων ἐνωμότως θεμένου ὅρκον ἐπάνω τῶν σεπτῶν μεγαλί(= ει)ων. Cf. on this Moult.-Mill., 457 f., s.v. ὅρκος.

μονῆς τῶν ... Αὐτοκρατόρων, "the dreadful oath by the Trinity and the oath by the triumphant and enduring nature of the imperial government." [6] In this period ecclesiastical and political oath forms are thus found united.

A. The Oath in the Greek World and Judaism.

The oath is primarily self-cursing should one not be speaking the truth. It strengthens the human word and is meant to give an assurance that what is said is true. [7] This may be done by swearing by what is held to be valuable and sacred. Usually to strengthen a statement the witness of a higher being, generally a deity, is invoked. [8] In any case a witness whose testimony cannot be impugned is needed. The oath is thus a declaration which backs up a human statement, which guarantees its veracity, and which is affirmed by divine co-operation. Distinction is made between assertions and promises referring to what is past or present on the one side (a fact) and what is future on the other (a promise). The assertive oath is especially a means of proof in legal cases. The promissory oath is common in private life. The theory of antiquity dealt essentially with the latter.

1. In the Gk. world the oath took the most varied forms from the simple νὴ Δία to the Cretan formulae in which as many as 16 deities might be mentioned. [9] The basis of the variety is the richness of the Gk. world of the gods. Linked with this is the fact that a man would not call on the same gods as his wife, or a young man on the same gods as an old. Individual cities and states had their official gods in oaths. [10]

In public life the formula (ὁ νόμιμος ὅρκος or ὁ ἐγχώριος ὅρκος) and the appropriate deities were fixed by the legislator. This means that the oath in public life gives religious sanction and a divine basis to the political order. The official gods of oaths were witnesses which linked men together more effectively than other gods. Usually one god was invoked, though two or three gods might be mentioned. At the end of an agreement we find the invocation of the θεοὶ ὅρκιοι on both sides. [11] In the ὅρκος βασιλικός the deities of the Ptolemies, Seleucids etc. were taken up into the formula during the Hellenistic period.

The βασιλικὸς ὅρκος is first an oath by the person of the king. We have a series of such formulae from the early Ptolemaic period (Philadelphos and Euergetes). These proclaim the importance of the royal oath for the political and economic life of the Ptolemaic kingdom. Then the whole dynasty in its existing state was taken up into the oath, and finally the deities particularly related to the royal house. [12] In the kingdom of the Seleucids, too, we find examples of oaths by the person of the king. [13]

---

[6] Heisenberg-Wenger, op. cit., 4, 4 (6th cent. A.D.).

[7] Cf. the general religious definition of the oath in Bertholet, RGG², II, 49 : "The oath is a solemn statement whose force is enhanced by being linked with a particular source of power."

[8] Cf. Hirzel, 4. Acc. to Philo Spec. Leg., II, 10; Sacr. AC, 91; Plant., 82; Decal., 86; Leg. All., III, 205 the oath is μαρτυρία θεοῦ περὶ πράγματος ἀμφισβητουμένου, "a calling upon God as witness in disputed matters." Cf. also Ammonius in Aristotelis de Interpretatione, p. 4a, 21, who distinguishes the oath from a simple statement by the fact that it includes μαρτυρία τοῦ θείου.

[9] Cf. Pauly-W., V, 2076.

[10] Loc. cit.

[11] From the 3rd cent. A.D. a single formula was adopted for almost all agreements, and both parties had to swear by it, ibid., 2078.

[12] Cf. J. Kaerst, Gesch. d. hell. Zeitalters, II (1909), 344, n. 3.

[13] Cf. in the reign of Seleucos II Callinicos (246-226 B.C.) the inscr. (political treaty between Smyrna and the colonists of Magnesia) in Ditt. Or., 229. In the oath which gives force to the treaty we find the tyche of the king as well as the gods.

When the Gk. states passed under the dominion of Rome, they maintained the oaths by the old deities, but adopted into their formulae, already broadened by the βασιλικὸς ὅρκος, the oath by the genius of the emperor. Along with official and civil oaths the judicial oath takes on particular significance ; the judge gives force to his sentence by an oath. For the contesting parties as well as for the judge the oath is a means to find the right. But it was used only when there were no witnesses or proofs. It was usually administered to the defendant, though sometimes also to the plaintiff. In addition the oath was also used at the conclusion of all kinds of legal dealings, particularly in political administration, taxation, and public documents. [14]

The oath often becomes an agreement setting a fixed punishment in case of perjury. Honour, possessions and even life may be pledged. There are different degrees of oaths in the Gk. world. As faith in the force of an oath declined, the oath was strengthened, repeated (preferably acc. to a sacred number), taken by different deities, or by deities in conjunction with other beings, and united with other oaths to form one grand oath. An impressive picture of this development is given in the pap. of the Hell. and Roman period, → ὀμνύω, 176.

The dwindling force of the oath also led, however, to reflection on its nature and attempts to reform it. The oldest of these attempts is connected with the name of Rhadamanthys (Ῥαδαμάνθυος ὅρκος, Ῥαδαμάνθυος κρίσις). The frivolous abuse of the oath was to go ; oaths which invoked the gods were to be banned from everyday matters in order to give them greater force and sanctity. Hence Socrates felt obliged εὐλαβείας χάριν ("out of religious awe") to swear intentionally by trivial things rather than by the gods. [15]

Movements to abolish the oath (Sophocles, Pythagoreans, → 178 f.) were not able to carry the day in the Gk. world. Judicial and political oaths maintained their validity even when the oath was lightly esteemed. [16]

2. The OT has 2 words for "to swear" : a. שָׁבַע. שֶׁבַע, "seven," is from the same root. שָׁבַע originally means "to come under the influence of 7 things." Acc. to Hdt., III, 8 the Arabs when reaching an agreement smeared 7 stones with the blood of those concluding it. Comparison of Gn. 21:31 with 15:10 and Jer. 34:18 suggests that there was an offering of 7 animals when solemn oaths were taken. [17] b. אָלָה, which lit. means "to curse." In many cases the two words occur together, Nu. 5:21; cf. 1 K. 8:31; 2 Ch. 6:22; Neh. 10:30. The force of the oath is enhanced by adding a curse.

In Israel the Law prescribed (Dt. 6:13; 10:20) that oaths should be by Yahweh. Israel's monotheism found expression here in the fact that only the oath by Yahweh was permitted ; all other gods were excluded. [18] Hence the oath is a solemn confession of the one God, cf. Is. 19:18; 45:23; 48:1; Jer. 12:16. False swearing was condemned as an abuse of the name of God, Ex. 20:7; Lv. 19:12. Swearing by other gods was idolatry, Jer. 5:7; 12:16; Zeph. 1:5; Am. 8:14; Hos. 4:15. The most common formula, first found in Ju. 8:19 and then particularly in the Books of Samuel, is חַי־יְהֹוָה, "so truly as Yahweh lives." Less common is the oath "Yahweh is witness between me and thee," Gn. 31:50; 1 S. 20:12; Jer. 42:5. [19]

---

[14] Cf. Pauly-W., V, 2081, 2083, and v. esp. Seidl, I, 44-91; also 92-118.

[15] Cf. Plat. Ap., 22a with Schol.: Ῥαδαμάνθυος ὅρκος οὗτος ὁ κατὰ κυνὸς ἢ πλατάνου ἢ κριοῦ ἤ τινος ἄλλου τοιούτου ... κατὰ τούτων δὲ νόμος ὀμνύναι, ἵνα μὴ κατὰ θεῶν οἱ ὅρκοι γίγνωνται, τοιοῦτοι δὲ καὶ οἱ Σωκράτους ὅρκοι.

[16] Attic orators (e.g., Lys., 25, 28) extol the oath as the strength and stay of democracy.

[17] So Benzinger, RE³, V, 243.

[18] Cf. Pedersen, 159, 142.

[19] In swearing the hand was lifted up to heaven, Gn. 14:22; Dt. 32:40; Ez. 36:7; Ps. 106:26. Hence "to lift up the hand" means "to give a sworn assurance," Ex. 6:8; Nu. 14:30. In

The oath is strengthened by self-cursing: "Yahweh do to me, and more also, if ..." The punishment is usually only implied, but sometimes it is stated more precisely, and the strongest curses are pronounced for breaking the oath, cf. Is. 65:15; Jer. 29:22; Nu. 5:21; Job 31:8, 10, 22, 40. As there are oaths by the life of Yahweh, so we find some by the life of the king or of the one addressed ("so truly as thou livest," 1 S. 1:26; 17:55; 2 S. 11:11).[20] The ancient Israelites did not have the oath "by my life." Man cannot swear thus, for his life is not in his own hands.

Yahweh swears as well as man, and He can swear only by Himself.[21] He can even stake His life as a pledge ("as I live ..., if the men of the land see," Nu. 14:21-23). God guarantees with His oath the truth of His Word. He backs the declaration of His will by His majesty and holiness, and even by His very existence.[22] Particularly significant are the divine cursings and blessings, e.g., Nu. 14:21, 28. Yahweh's most dreadful curse is on Eli and his house, 1 S. 3:11 ff. God has made a sworn covenant with His people. As marriage is regarded as a covenant entered into with an oath (cf. Rt. 4:7-12), so the relation of God to His people is viewed as a formal marriage by oath, cf. Is., Jer., and esp. Ez. (c. 16) and Hosea (1-3). God Himself establishes the covenant. He takes up men into it. He remains faithful to it even though the people is guilty of unfaithfulness and apostasy. He punishes its violation. Thus the greatest significance of OT oaths is in contracts and treaties,[23] but esp. in the one unique covenant between God and His people.

Neither biblical nor Talmudic law uses the oath of witness to support a court statement. Instead we find the oath of purification which the accused takes when legal proof of innocence is not possible because of lack of witnesses, Ex. 22:8, 10; cf. also Nu. 5:11-28. This oath takes the form either of self-cursing or of a protestation of innocence.[24]

The earlier period took the binding nature of an oath seriously. If an ill-considered oath was taken the Law (Lv. 5:4 ff.) demanded a trespass offering. The Law forbade perjury, but laid down no penalties for the perjurer, simply delivering him up to divine retribution, 1 K. 8:31 f.; Zech. 5:3; Mal. 3:5. Scourging was first introduced as a penalty by Talmudic law.

---

2 instances (Gn. 24:9; 47:29) we find the ceremony whereby he who takes the oath touches the genital organ of the one to whom he takes it, cf. Pedersen, 150 f. This ceremony is still found among many Arab tribes.

[20] He is thus set alongside or in place of God as a witness and avenger of the truth, as is quite clear when the oath is both by the life of God and also of a man, 1 S. 20:3; 25:26; 2 K. 2:2 ff.

[21] For early witness to God's oaths in the OT cf. Am. 6:8; 8:7; also Gn. 22:16; Ex. 32:13; Is. 45:23; very common in Jer. The formula by which Yahweh invokes Himself as witness and judge is חַי־אָנִי, "I live." Yahweh swears by His right arm (i.e., His strength) in Is. 62:8; by His great name in Jer. 44:26; by His holiness in Am. 4:2.

[22] Cf. Pedersen, 157. "That He swears by Himself implies that He is dependent on none other" (158). Cf. also J. Happel, Der Eid im AT (1893), 15.

[23] Cf. Pedersen, 108 ff.

[24] Cf. R. Press, "Das Ordal im alten Israel, I," ZAW, NF, 10 (1933), 137. Press states: "In detail the oath seems to have been taken as follows. The accuser pronounced a curse, and in the holy place the accused accepted this curse as a specific self-curse, whether by repeating it or by ... appropriating the curse with an Amen. When the suspect had pronounced the oath, it was believed that Yahweh had heard it in heaven, and in case of perjury would have to bring into effect the cursing annexed thereto" (138).

In the history of Israel and Judah, too, we observe a decline in the oath. The prophets were already complaining about this, e.g., Jer. 5:2; 7:9; Zech. 5:3, 4; Mal. 3:5. Related was the excessive use of the oath in daily life. Sir. 23:9 ff. attacks πολύορκος, → 179. When the strict ancient view of the world and life began to break up with the influx of Hellenistic ideas, the significance of the oath was questioned. Qoh. 9:2 refers to hesitation in taking the oath, not to its refusal. Finally, Pharisaic casuistry debased the oath by making gradations and denying binding force to many formulae.

3. The Damascus document has a section on the oath (9:9-10:3) in the part dealing with the ordering of the religious life of the community of the new covenant, 9:1-15:16. Here it is laid down that the oath of cursing which serves to unmask a thief may be demanded only by the judges, 9:11, 12. [25] On the position of the Essenes regarding oaths → 179.

In the Mishnah we find 1. the oath which is the same both to confirm and to assert (שְׁבוּעַת בִּטּוּי); 2. the vain, deceptive and false oath (שְׁבוּעַת שָׁוְא) which, when deliberate, is to be punished by scourging, but when unintentional, to be without penalty ; 3. the oath of witness which serves to confirm rejection of a testimony (שְׁבוּעַת הָעֵדוּת); 4. the deposition oath which is to be taken as an oath of purification by an accused person (שְׁבוּעַת הַפִּקָּדוֹן); and 5. the judicial oath (שְׁבוּעַת הַדַּיָּנִים). The so-called Rabbinic oath (שְׁבוּעַת הֶיסֵּת) arises only in the Talmudic period. [26]

B. The Oath in the New Testament.

1. In Jm. 5:12 ὅρκος is the object of ὀμνύω. [27] The general principle μὴ ὀμνύετε is elucidated by the three-membered statement μήτε τὸν οὐρανὸν μήτε τὴν γῆν μήτε ἄλλον τινὰ ὅρκον. The final member shows that Jm. has in view an absolute prohibition of oaths, → 181.

2. Twice ὅρκος appears in OT quotations. In the Benedictus (Lk. 1:73) it is par. to διαθήκη, and διαθήκη [28] is elucidated by ὅρκος. [29] Declaring His will to Abraham, God has given him a sworn promise which refers to events in the time of salvation. [30] In this time the people of God shall serve Him "in holiness and

---

[25] We read in 9:11, 12 : "If someone loses something, and it is not known who stole it, the ephor of the camp in which it was stolen shall exact from its owner an oath with a curse, and he who hears it — if he knows and does not tell — is guilty." There follow regulations concerning the validity of witness, the age of a witness in criminal cases, and the credibility of a notorious offender in court. Cf. on this W. Staerk, "Die jüdische Gemeinde des Neuen Bundes in Damaskus," BFTh, 27, 3 (1922), 11 f. On the rite of the curse cf. L. Ginzberg, "Eine unbekannte jüdische Sekte," MGWJ, 57 (1913), 284 f.

[26] For details on this section cf. Str.-B., I, 321-325.

[27] ὅρκῳ ὀμνύειν, "to swear with an oath," occurs also in Test. Jud. 22:3.

[28] E. Lohmeyer, Diatheke (1913), 150 points out the parallelism between ὅρκος and διαθήκη. Hence in Lk. 1:73 διαθήκη means "a sacred promise or inviolable and gracious undertaking." J. Behm, Der Begriff Διαθήκη im NT (1912), 58 relates διαθήκη to ὅρκος as a declaration of God's will which also contains a promise and self-commitment." Cf. → II, 132 f.

[29] ὅρκον ὃν ὤμοσεν is attractio inversa for τοῦ ὅρκου ὃν ὤμοσεν, cf. Bl.-Debr. § 295. There is strong Hebraic influence here. Cf. also Schl. Lk., 180, who finds a material par. in M. Ex., 29b on 13:19.

[30] The content of the promise sworn to Abraham is given with the explicative inf. τοῦ δοῦναι κτλ., cf. Kl. Lk., ad loc. On the construction cf. Legenden d. Pelagia, ed. H. Usener (1879), p. 13, 9 : ἐν ὅρκῳ εἶχεν τοῦ μὴ γεύσασθαί τι.

righteousness." What God promised Abraham has been fulfilled in Christ. Ac. 2:30 refers to the oath which God gave David. Peter in his Pentecost sermon finds in Ps. 132:11 (cf. Ps. 89:3 f.) a prophetic saying about the resurrection of the Messiah, Jesus.[31] As the promised son of David Christ has ascended the Messianic throne.

On the basis of OT sayings Mt. 5:33 shows that the legislator of the old covenant demanded performance of oaths taken to God (ὅρκοι),[32] → 177 f.

3. Theologically the most important passages regarding oaths are in Hb. It is said in Hb. 6:16 : It belongs to the nature of the oath that it invalidates any contradiction of the statement confirmed by it. The oath is a definitive and binding confirmation of the spoken word.[33] In 6:17 the author deals with God's oath, → 183; IV, 620, 23 ff.

4. The connecting of statement and oath in the expressions ὁμολογεῖν μεθ' ὅρκου and ἀρνεῖσθαι μετὰ ὅρκου may be found in Mt. 14:7 and 26:72.[34] Mk. 6:26 (par. Mt. 14:9) brings out the serious consequences of a lightly taken oath. Herod is troubled διὰ τοὺς ὅρκους.

† ὁρκίζω.

1. "To cause someone to swear." Not accepted by the Atticists, but found from Xenoph. (Sym., 4, 10), Demosth., Polyb., etc.; inscr., pap., LXX. 2. "To adjure someone by something" a. ὁρκίζειν τινὰ κατά τινος, P. Masp., 295, II, 15;[1] Jos. Vit., 258; LXX 3 Βασ. 2:42; 2 Ch. 16:13; Audollent Def. Tab., p. 473 ff. (cursing tablets); Preis. Zaub., III, 36 f.; IV, 289; VII, 242; Mt. 26:63 D; with ἵνα, Herm. s., 9, 10, 5. b. with double acc., Orph. Fr. (Kern), 313, Fr. 299 : οὐρανὸν ὁρκίζω σε. Clay tablet from Hadrumetum,[2] 1 ff.: ὁρκίζω σε, δαιμόνιον πνεῦμ[α], ... τὸν θεὸν τοῦ Αβρααμ κτλ.[3] c. with double acc. and following acc. and inf., 1 Th. 5:27 ℵ,[4] with dat. 1 Εσδρ. 1:46 : ὁρκισθεὶς τῷ ὀνόματι τοῦ κυρίου. For an express adjuration cf. also Preis. Zaub., IV, 3007 ff.

In Mk. 5:7[5] the demoniac of Gerasa[6] adjures Jesus with the words : ὁρκίζω σε τὸν θεόν, μή με βασανίσῃς.[7] The sick man sees the superior power of Jesus

---

[31] Cf. Wdt. Ag., ad loc.; H. Beyer, Ag. (NT Deutsch), ad loc.
[32] ἀποδιδόναι τινὶ ὅρκον can also mean "to free oneself from an oath," i.e., by performing it, Demosth., 19, 318; Aeschin. Adversus Ctesiphontem, 74; Ditt. Syll.³, 150, 16. Cf. Pr.-Bauer, s.v. ὅρκος.
[33] On εἰς βεβαίωσιν in Hb. 6:16, cf. Deissmann B, 100-105; NB, 56; Mitteis-Wilcken, II, 1, 188 f., 269; O. Eger, Rechtsgeschichtliches zum NT (1918), 38-42; H. Schlier, → I, 600 ff. εἰς βεβαίωσιν is a legal formula (Egyptian) which persisted for centuries, cf. also LXX Lv. 25:23; P. Par., 28, 8. It is a tt. for the legal guarantee in a transaction.
[34] Cf. the par. in Jos. Ant., 2, 3 : παραχωρεῖ τῶν πρεσβείων αὐτῷ μεθ' ὅρκων.

ὁ ρ κ ί ζ ω. [1] Cf. Preisigke Wört. and Moult-Mill., s.v., also Mayser, II, 2, 304 f.
[2] IG, III, 3, p. XVII; Deissmann B, 28. The tablet contains a love charm : "the invocation of a departed spirit who is to lead Urbanus to the Domitiana who has fallen in love with him. The god whose power is summoned has purely Jewish attributes taken from the LXX." Wendland Hell. Kult. 194.
[3] For details cf. R. Wünsch, Antike Fluchtafeln, Kl. T., 20² (1912), 13 ff. (No. 4, 1 ff.).
[4] Cf. Bl.-Debr. § 392, 1d.
[5] Cf. on Mk. 5:7 O. Bauernfeind, Die Worte der Dämonen im Mk. (1927), 23-26.
[6] On the whole pericope Mk. 5:1-20 cf. Loh. Mk., 93-99.
[7] J. C. K. v. Hofmann, ZWL, 2 (1881), 352 and Zn. J., 154, n. 85 relate the words 'Ιησοῦ υἱὲ τοῦ θεοῦ τοῦ ὑψίστου, not to the question introduced by τί, but to the adjuration. Hence this is given particular force : "Jesus, thou Son of the Most High God, I adjure thee by God," not : "What have I to do with thee, Jesus, thou Son of the Most High God ?"

and tries to keep Him at a distance. But mention of the name of Jesus does not have the expected effect. Jesus, the opponent of demons, is not robbed of His power thereby. Hence the sick man uses the strongest adjuration there is. He calls on God to protect him. But the adjuration is useless. For Jesus is the Son of the Most High God. [8]

Ac. 19:13 tells of the enterprising exorcists [9] who try to cast out demons with the help of the name of Jesus. [10] Their formula is: ὁρκίζω [11] ὑμᾶς τὸν Ἰησοῦν ὃν Παῦλος κηρύσσει. They believe there is such power in the name of Jesus that mention of the name will drive out demons. [12] But for them the name is significant only as the strongest magic. Acts makes it plain that the name of Jesus has force only when pronounced on His commission and in faith in Him. [13] The unbelieving exorcists are simply magicians. [14] They thus come to grief with their adjuration.

† ὁρκωμοσία.

"Confirmation by oath." A rare word. [1] Apart from Poll., I, 38 only LXX : 1 Εσδρ. 8:90; Ez. 17:18 f.; Jos. Ant., 16, 163. [2] In the pap. ὁρκομοσία, P. Lond., V, 1728, 9 ("taking of an oath"). [3] The neut. ὁρκωμόσιον, Ditt. Syll.[3], 1007, 30; plur. τὰ [ὁρ]κω-μόσια, Ditt. Or., 229, 82. [4]

In spite of the par. adduced by Bauernfeind, op. cit., 25 (Audollent Def. Tab., p. 208, 226, 338), it is unlikely, however, that the one invoked should be mentioned before the adjuration. βασανίζειν probably refers to eternal torment. This thought is suggested by Mt., who adds πρὸ καιροῦ in 8:29. The demon asks not to be delivered up to eternal punishment. So also Loh. Mk., 95; similarly Wbg. Mk., ad loc. On βασανίζειν → I, 561 ff.

[8] For a vivid example of the way in which the non-Christian magic-believing world set about healing a demoniac cf. Preis. Zaub., IV, 3007-3086. A charm is hung about the sufferer, and then follows the invocation with a series of formulae. The first of these is: ὁρκίζω σε κατὰ τοῦ θεοῦ τῶν Ἑβραίων Ἰησοῦ, 3019 f.

[9] The wandering Jewish exorcists are called sons of the high-priest Sceva, though no record of such a high-priest has been found.

[10] Jülicher, RGG[2], II, 475 thinks the story in Ac. 19:13 throws light on "the early form of an exorcism much practised in primitive Christianity, and on its development." Cf. also W. Heitmüller, Im Namen Jesu (1903), 56 : The καί in v. 13 points to the fact that the Jewish exorcists were doing what they had seen Paul do.

[11] ὁρκίζομεν ℵ, ἐξορκίζομεν 𝔓[38], 614 etc. Pr. Ag., 116 thinks that since we do not have after ὁρκίζω the expected statement of what the demons were to be forced to do, we should add with the Armenian Catena, p. 339 ἐξ αὐτῶν ἐξέρχεσθαι. But these words are self-evident in the context.

[12] Acc. to Jos. Ant., 8, 45 ff. there may be traced back to Solomon "sayings for the healing of the sick and invocations with whose help one can subdue and drive out spirits so that they do not return."

[13] For primitive Christianity too (Ac. and Gospels) pronouncing the name was the means for driving out demons, W. Heitmüller, 56. But only the believer in Christ might use the name.

[14] Cf. Bau. Ag., 232 : "Since he (the exorcist) seeks to make use of a holy thing with which no faith connects him, he is a magician, and no more than a pagan magician."

ὁρκωμοσία. [1] Acc. to E. Fraenkel, Gesch. d. gr. Nomina agentis auf -τηρ, -τωρ, -της, I (1910), 200 ὁρκωμότης is perhaps koine Doric, but (loc. cit.) "ὁρκωμοτεῖν is good Attic (or Ionic ?) ... The same is true of ὁρκωμόσια ..., ὁρκωμοσία." There is no Doric example of ὁρκωμοσία [Debrunner].

[2] Cf. Bl.-Debr., § 2; 119, 3; Sophocles Lex., 817. Cf. also Fraenkel, loc. cit.

[3] Cf. Preisigke Wört., s.v.

[4] Cf. Moult.-Mill., 458.

In the NT ὁρκωμοσία occurs only in Hb. (7:20 f., 28). In Hb. 7:28 the Law and God's oath are contrasted. The latter was given after the Law. The Law appointed weak and sinful men as high-priests, but the oath has instituted the Son of God as the High-priest who has the power of an endless life and who is perfect to all eternity.

† ἐνορκίζω.

From ἔνορκος, "bound by an oath" : [1] a. "To adjure someone by something," often with double acc., CIG, IV, 9288, 6 : ἐνορκίζω ὑμᾶς τὸν ὧδε ἐφεστῶτα ἄγγελον, μή τίς ποτε τολμῇ ἐνθάδε τινὰ (a corpse in the grave) καταθέσθε, ibid., 9270, 4 (on a Jewish Christian gravestone): ἐνορκιζόμ[ε]θ[α] τὸν παντ[ο]κράτο[ρ]α θεόν. Cf. also IG, XII, 3, 1238; Audollent Def. Tab., p. 26, 15 : ἐνορκίζω ὑμῖν τὸν βασιλέα τῶν δαιμόνων. LXX 2 Εσδρ. 23(13):25 Α : ἐνώρκισα αὐτοὺς ἐν τῷ θεῷ. b. "To invoke in petition," e.g., P. Masp., 5, 25. Uncertain restoration, ibid., 188, 1; P. Lond., V, 1677, 40. There is a late form ἐνορκέω in, e.g., BGU, III, 836, 9. c. Mid. "to cause someone to swear something," IG, XII, 5, 697, 4 (Cyrus); IX, 1, 643 (Kephallenia).

In the NT it occurs only at 1 Th. 5:27. [2] Paul adjures the community by the Lord (ἐνορκίζω ὑμᾶς τὸν κύριον) to read the letter to all the brethren. [3]

† ἐξορκίζω († ἐξορκιστής).

From the time of Demosth.; also inscr., [1] pap., [2] LXX (Gn. 24:3; Ju. 17:2 A; 3 Βασ. 22:16 B). a. "To cause to swear," "to put on oath" (so usually, then = ἐξορκόω); b. "to invoke someone." Very common in magic pap., with ὁρκίζω, of invoking a god or demon, [3] Preis. Zaub., XVI, 1 ff.; XXXV, 13 ff. etc. Usually with simple acc., Preisigke Sammelbuch, 4947, 7 (love charm): ἐξορκίζω τὸν πάντα συνέχοντα κύριον θεὸν ... ποίησον 'Απλωνοῦν ... φιλεῖν με. With double acc. BGU, IV, 1141, 10 : ἐρωτῶ σε οὖν καὶ παρακαλῶ καὶ τὴν Καίσαρος τύ[χη]ν σε ἐξορκίζω, LXX : Gn. 24:3 : ἐξορκιῶ σε κύριον τὸν θεόν. With κατά and gen., Preis. Zaub., III, 10, 119; IV, 1240 ff.: ἐξορκίζω σε, δαῖμον, ὅστις ποτ' οὖν εἶ, κατὰ τούτου τοῦ θεοῦ. Cf. also P. Lond., I, 46, 76 ff.: ἐξορκίζω σε κατὰ τῶν ἁγίων ὀνομάτων ... καὶ κατὰ τῶν φρικτῶν ὀνομάτων ... παράδος τὸν κλέπτην κτλ. With ἐν, Preis. Zaub., XIII, 233 f.: ὡς ἐξώρκισά σε, τέκνον, ἐν τῷ ἱερῷ τῷ ἐν 'Ιερωσολύμῳ. [4] Jos. Ant., 2, 200; 11, 145. c. "To deny upon oath," P. Rev., 56, 12.

ἐξορκιστής. The "exorcist" who expels demons by magical formulae. [5] The word is rare : Luc. Epigrammata, 23 = Anth. Pal., 11, 427; Claudius Ptolemaeus, Tetrabiblos (ed.

ἐ ν ο ρ κ ί ζ ω. [1] So Debrunner.
[2] On the constr. v. Bl.-Debr. §§ 149; 155, 7; 392, 1 d. 4.
[3] The solemn direction is surprising. It is quite erroneous, however, to think that the formality is a sign of non-authenticity. Possibly the community was not a tightly-knit fellowship (Dib. Th., ad loc.) and so Paul spoke with emphasis. It is also conceivable that neither Paul nor the readers had any experience of letters to communities (Dob. Th., ad loc.). In this case the adjuration is to be taken as the mark of a new practice. In this first letter known to us Paul lays on the Thessalonians the duty of making the contents of the epistle known to every member of the community.

ἐ ξ ο ρ κ ί ζ ω. [1] For details v. Liddell-Scott, s.v. There are also examples in E. Fraenkel, Gr. Denominativa (1906), 147.
[2] Cf. Preisigke, Moult.-Mill., s.v., also Mayser, I¹, 405.
[3] Examples in R. Wünsch, Antike Fluchtafeln = Kl. T., 20² (1912), 13 ff. (No. 4, 1 ff.).
[4] Further instances in Preisigke Wört., s.v.
[5] So Pr.-Bauer³, 459.

Melanchthon, 1553), 182. Acc. to Jos. Ant., 8, 42 ff. Solomon was the great exorcist of early days : "God taught him the art of driving out evil spirits to the profit and salvation of men." [6]

In the NT ἐξορκιστής is used only in Ac. 19:13 for the wandering exorcists, → 463. ἐξορκίζειν is used for the conjuring of evil spirits in Ac. 19:13 vl.; 14 D. [7]

In Mt. 26:63 the high-priest at the trial demands an oath from Jesus. He adjures Him [8] by the living God to tell the simple truth and express Himself plainly on His claim to be the Messiah and Son of God. [9] Jesus gives a definite affirmation in answer to the high-priest's question. He confesses that He is the Messiah and declares that there will be granted to Him the supreme dignity of the Messiah, that of the world Judge who comes from heaven.

There is much debate as to the exposition of the words σὺ εἶπας in v. 64. The following views are held. 1. It has the significance of a declaration on oath. Jesus takes the oath demanded by the high-priest and thus recognises as legitimate the oath demanded by the authorities ; [10] 2. Jesus makes a declaration instead of taking the oath ; [11] He swears no oath, but issues a statement in the form of an admission ; [12] 3. Jesus gives an evasive answer, with the emphasis on the pronoun : "*Thou* hast said it"; [13] 4. Jesus rejects the oath : "*Thou* hast said this ; I will not accept this oath." [14] Merx considers yet another possibility, namely, that Jesus leaves the answer to the conscience of the high-priest : "On the contrary, I tell you that from now on you will see the Messiah, i.e., the judgment, coming." In fact, Jesus does not take an oath. He makes a simple declaration which contains His Messianic witness. Hence Mt. 26:64 stands in tension, but not contradiction, with Mt. 5:33-37. Jesus does not invoke God as witness ; He uses no oath formula, → 180.

In the post-apostolic period [15] baptism was regarded as an exorcism too. [16] In Just.

---

[6] Jos. Ant., 8, 45 ff. gives an explicit description of exorcism in his day : "The healing took place as follows. He (the exorcist Eleazar) held under the nose of the possessed a ring in which was one of the roots which Solomon had prescribed, caused the sick man to smell it, and thus led the evil spirit out through the nose. The demoniac then collapsed, and Eleazar, invoking the name of Solomon and the proverbs composed by him, adjured the spirit never to return into the man."

[7] On the constr. cf. Bl.-Debr. §§ 149; 392, 1 d.

[8] Adjuration means "to engage someone by an oath to do something" (cf. Ex. 13:19; 2 Ch. 36:13; esp. 1 K. 22:16: "I have often engaged thee by an oath to tell me the truth"). Cf. A. Merx, *Das Ev. Mt.* (1902), 391. The older Halachah recognises three forms of adjuration : 1. in the oath of witness ; 2. in that of deposition ; 3. in the judicial oath. The declaration on oath demanded of Jesus may best be understood, acc. to Str.-B., I, 1005 f., as שְׁבוּעַת הָעֵדוּת (oath of witness), though there is something unusual about it, since Jesus was to make it in His own case. On this whole question *v.* the explanations in the text.

[9] Messiah and Son of God are here equated as in Mt. 16:16, cf. also Jn. 1:49; 11:27. Already in Jewish exposition of the OT the Son of Man in Da. 7 was equated with the Messiah.

[10] B. Weiss, *Das Mt.*[10] (1910), ad loc.; Str.-B., I, 1006; J. Schniewind, *Das Ev. nach Mt.* (*NT Deutsch*), ad loc.; cf. on 5:37b.

[11] Zn. Mt., 705 f.

[12] Dalman WJ, I, 256.

[13] Kl. Mt., *ad loc.* Bl.-Debr. §§ 149; 392, 1 d; Dausch Synpt., 347.

[14] Merx, *op. cit.*, 392.

[15] W. Heitmüller, *Im Namen Jesu* (1903), 310. In particular the name of Jesus is supposed to have been important in exorcism, 304, 311.

[16] Heitmüller, 331 goes so far as to say that for primitive Christianity the solemn use of the name Jesus was an exorcism in baptism. This is debatable.

exorcism and the baptismal symbol are linked. [17] We read in Dial., 30 : τὰ δαιμόνια ... ἐξορκιζόμενα κατὰ τοῦ ὀνόματος 'Ιησοῦ Χριστοῦ τοῦ σταυρωθέντος ἐπὶ Ποντίου Πιλάτου. Even plainer is Dial., 85 : κατὰ γὰρ τοῦ ὀνόματος αὐτοῦ τούτου τοῦ υἱοῦ τοῦ θεοῦ καὶ πρωτοτόκου πάσης κτίσεως καὶ διὰ παρθένου γεννηθέντος καὶ παθητοῦ γενομένου ἀνθρώπου καὶ σταυρωθέντος ἐπὶ Ποντίου Πιλάτου ὑπὸ τοῦ λαοῦ ὑμῶν καὶ ἀποθανόντος καὶ ἀναστάντος ἐκ νεκρῶν καὶ ἀναβάντος εἰς τὸν οὐρανὸν πᾶν δαιμόνιον ἐξορκιζόμενον νικᾶται καὶ ὑποτάσσεται. [18]

† ἐπίορκος.

"Perjured," [1] from Hom., usually in the expression ἐπίορκον ὀμόσσαι, "to commit perjury," "to swear falsely." [2] Of men, Hes. Op., 804; E. Schwyzer, Dialectorum Graecarum Exempla Epigraphica Potiora (1923), 179a; Eur. El., 1355; Aristoph. Nub., 399 etc. Also LXX Zech. 5:3 ὁ ἐπίορκος. Philo Decal., 88 (on the nature of the perjurer); Spec. Leg., II, 27 (on his punishment); also ibid., IV, 40.

1 Tm. 1:8 ff. deals with the relation of the Christian to the Law. To the righteous man, i.e., the justified man set in the new life, the requirement of the Law does not apply. Only where sins arise, which are enumerated in a catalogue of vices [3] in v. 9 and v. 10, are the strictness and severity of the Law relevant. [4] Perjurers are among the enemies of the Law and the gainsayers. [5]

† ἐπιορκέω.

This means "I am an ἐπίορκος." From Hom.; [1] also inscr.: IG, II, 2, 1126, 9; Ditt. Or., 229, 69; pap.: BGU, III, 783, 11; P. Oxy., III, 251, 26 etc. 1 Εσδρ. 1:46; Wis. 14:28.

---

[17] Ibid., 251 f.; cf. also F. Kattenbusch, Das ap. Symbol, II (1900), 288-298, 628-630.
[18] Heitmüller, 251 finds the first beginnings of this trend already in the NT at Ac. 3:6; 4:10.
ἐπίορκος. [1] "How exactly the word ἐπίορκος came to denote the perjurer was obscure even to the ancients, and the desperate attempts to explain it (e.g., Eustath. Thessal. Comm. in Il., 10, 333) are in fact only a confession of ignorance," R. Hirzel, Der Eid (1902), 151, Hirzel, 152 bases his own attempted explanation on Ὅρκος ("hedger in") as a demon. More illuminating is that of E. Schwyzer, Etymologisch-kulturgeschichtliches, 2, Indogermanische Forschungen, 45 (1927), 255-258 : ἐπίορκος = ὃς ἐπὶ ὅρκῳ ἔβη, cf. Archiloch., 79, 13 (Diehl², 3, 36): λάξ δ' ἐφ' ὁρκίοισ' ἔβη. Acc. to E. Benveniste, Revue de l'Histoire des Religions, 134 (1948), 89 ἐπίορκος πρὸς δαίμονος = "qui attire le ὅρκος (de la part d'un dieu)." The best explanation of ἐπίορκος is in M. Leumann, Homerische Wörter (1950), 79-90 (→ 457, n. 1): 1. ἐπὶ δ' ὅρκον ὄμοσσε etc., "and for this (statement) he grasped the staff," hence 2. ἐπίορκον ὄμοσσε "to commit perjury," cf. Hes. Op., 282 f.: ἐπίορκον ὀμόσσας ψεύσεται, 193 f.: μύθοισιν σκολιοῖς ἐνέπων, ἐπὶ δ' ὅρκον ὀμεῖται). "Hence ἐπίορκος is basically an artificial poetic term, and all later use derives from the passages in Hom. and esp. in Hesiod," 89 [Debrunner].
[2] Cf. for details Liddell-Scott, 649.
[3] On this list of vices cf. Dib. Past., ad loc. and J. Jeremias, Die Briefe an Tim. u. Tit. (NT Deutsch), ad loc.
[4] Since the list enumerates transgressors of the Ten Commandments, the νόμος of v. 8 is the Law of Moses, so esp. J. Jeremias, also Schl. Past., 47: "The fact that νόμος has no art. does not generalise the concept." For another view cf. J. Weiss, D. Briefe Pauli an Tim. u. Tit.⁷ (1902), 88 : νόμος does not mean the Mosaic Law, but a law in general.
[5] The ἐπίορκοι are those who swear what is untrue, not those who break a sworn oath.
ἐπιορκέω. [1] For details cf. Liddell-Scott, 649, s.v. On the concept of perjury in the Gk. world R. Hirzel, Der Eid (1902), 75-79. The question of perjury was particularly discussed by the Stoics Cleanthes and Chrysipp. Acc. to the former a man commits perjury when he swears with the intention of not keeping his oath, Stob., III, 28, 14. The latter,

Philo : Spec. Leg., I, 235 on the basis of Lv. 5:21 ff.; *ibid.,* II, 26 (Lv. 5:1). a. "To swear falsely," "to commit perjury" (the usual sense); b. "to break a sworn oath," "to transgress a vow" : Chrysipp. Fr., 197 (v. Arnim, II, 63); Herodian Hist., III, 6, 7; 1 Εσδρ. 1:46; c. = ὄμνυμι, "to swear," very rare, e.g., Lys., 10, 17.

Mt. 5:33 maintains that the law-giver of the old covenant forbade false swearing, Lv. 19:12; Nu. 30:3, 4. In contrast, the Law-giver of the Messianic age of salvation issues a commandment which prohibits swearing altogether, → 177 f.

The Didache (2, 3 : οὐκ ἐπιορκήσεις) forbids perjury, but not swearing. [2] It has not been influenced, then, by the prohibition of Jesus : μὴ ὀμνύναι ὅλως. The OT ruling is still normative.

J. Schneider

> ὁρμή, ὅρμημα, ὁρμάω, ἀφορμή

† ὁρμή, † ὅρμημα, † ὁρμάω.

A. Extra-biblical Usage.

1. ὁρμή seems to be linked to the Indo-European root *ser,* "to stream," Sanskrit *sárma-h,* "flowing." [1] The word develops many meanings [2] which mostly denote the beginning of a swift and even hostile movement, i.e., "start" or "starting." It is often used psychologically with ref. to various impulses and strivings. The derived ὅρμημα (Hom., Hell., LXX) can also denote psychical as well as physical processes, emotions of anger or temper. The verb ὁρμάω means trans. "to set in rapid motion," "to impel," intr. "to go out from," "to storm out," "to originate." The group is common in description of military and other movements, Xenoph. Hist. Graec., I, 6, 20; An., IV, 3, 31; Ditt. Syll.[3], 700, 24 (117 B.C.); P. Strassb., 100, 17 (2nd cent. B.C.); P. Oxy., IX, 1216, 20 (2nd/3rd cent. A.D.); VI, 906, 6 [3] (336 A.D.). Trans. ἐφορμάω, Hom. Od., 7, 272; Il., 3, 165. For psychological movements, Il., 13, 74; 21, 572 (inspiration); Od., 8, 499 : ὁρμηθεὶς θεοῦ, Soph. Ant., 133 : νίκην ὁρμῶντ᾽ ἀλαλάξαι, cf. Fr., 619 (TGF, 279) ἐφορμᾶν κακά. In Plato we read in Leg., IX, 875b : ἐπὶ πλεονεξίαν ... φύσις αὐτὸν ὁρμήσει (cf.

---

however, thinks that such a man only swears falsely (ψευδορκεῖ); he becomes a perjurer only when he fails to do what he has vowed in the oath, *ibid.,* line 18. Later, as in Chrysipp., ἐπιορκεῖν and ἐπιορκία were used esp. for breaking an oath. "But finally special words were formed for this (παρορκεῖν and παρορκία)," Hirzel, 78.

[2] Cf. Kn. Did., 11 f.; Pr.-Bauer[3], 493. Cf. also Sib., II, 68 f.: μηδ᾽ ἐπιορκήσῃς μήτ᾽ ἀγνῶς μήτε ἑκοντί᾽ ψεύδορκον στυγέει θεός, ὅττι κὲν ἄν τις ὁμόσσῃ. In almost literal agreement Carmen Phocylideum 12, 16 f. (J. Bernays, *Gesammelte Abh.,* I [1885], 254 f.).

ὁ ρ μ ή κ τ λ. [1] Walde-Pok., II, 497, *s.v.*

[2] Cf. the dict., esp. Liddell-Scott and Pass., *s.v.* For a survey cf. F. Dornseiff, *Der deutsche Wortschatz nach Sprachgruppen geordnet* (1934), *s.v.* "Wille." On Gnostic usage cf. F. M. Sagnard, *La gnose valentinienne* (1947), Index, *s.v.,* p. 650.

[3] There is an accidental par. to Mk. 5:13 when the text speaks of 2 swine breaking into a plot (τὴν ὁρμὴν ποιούμενοι).

Ep. Ar., 270); [4] Symp., 181d ὁρμᾶσθαι ὑπὸ ἔρωτος. Gorg., 502c refers, not to impulses, but to the essential determination of tragedy (ὥρμηται). For impulse to virtue cf. Xenoph. An., III, 1, 24, for the natural demand for a response of love Mem., II, 6, 28, for preparation for sickness, or even striving after it, Epict. Diss., II, 6, 10. The verb is used for ordered motion in the cosmos, Plato Pol., 273a; intellectual striving is denoted in Soph., 228c; Parm., 135d. ὁρμή is often used of divine or demonic power which impels man irresistibly, Soph. Ant., 135 f.: μαινομένᾳ ξὺν ὁρμᾷ βακχεύων ἐπέπνει, Hdt., VII, 18 : δαιμονίη ὁρμή, Plat. Phaedr., 279a : ὁρμὴ θειοτέρα. ὁρμή seems almost synon. with ἐπιθυμία in Phileb., 35d. For the further development of the term in Gk. philosophy Plato's basic def. of θυμός as ὁρμὴ βίαιος ἄνευ λογισμοῦ in Def., 415e is important. Aristot. often uses ὁρμή for unconscious impulses. He thus explains the famous fundamental principle ἄνθρωπος φύσει πολιτικὸν ζῷον in Pol., I, 2, p. 1253a, 29 : φύσει μὲν οὖν ἡ ὁρμὴ ἐν πᾶσιν ἐπὶ τὴν τοιαύτην κοινωνίαν. ὁρμή is also associated with φύσις in An. Post., II, 11, p. 95a, 1. Whereas ὁρμή is impulsive will, προαίρεσις denotes the considered activity of the will, preference and choice, Metaph., IV, 5, p. 1015a, 27. In the sphere of ὁρμή there is no free decision, Eth. M., I, 16, p. 1188b, 25 : ὁρμή is the same as ὄρεξις which divides into εἴδη τρία : ἐπιθυμία, θυμός, βούλησις, ibid., I, 12, p. 1187b. Even the last is no true expression of free will, for uncontrolled men take up what they desire into their will, I, 13, p. 1188a, 28. Their longings are also set on what is contradictory, Eth. Nic., I, 13, p. 1102b, 21. On the basis of Hom. Eth. Nic., III, 11, p. 1116b, 30 elucidates the nature of θυμός, cf. VII, 7, p. 1149a, 31, and on the other hand De Virtutibus et Vitiis, 4, p. 1250a, 41 on πραότης. As it may be said of θυμός : ὁρμᾷ πρὸς τὴν τιμωρίαν, so of ἐπιθυμία : ὁρμᾷ πρὸς τὴν ἀπόλαυσιν, Eth. Nic., VII, 7, p. 1149a, 35; cf. De Virtutibus et Vitiis, 2, p. 1250a, 11; 5, p. 1250b, 13.

ὁρμή is also used gen. in Aristot. for "inclination," Eth. M., II, 16, p. 1213b, 17, and particularly for the "striving" for what is good and beautiful, ibid., X, 10, p. 1197b, 7. There is constant ref. to non-capricious dedication as the presupposition of all virtues, Eth. M., I, 20, p. 1191a, 21 f.; I, 35, p. 1197b, 39; 1198a, 8 f., 15-17, 20 f.: πράξαι ... ἄν τις τὰ δίκαια ... ὁρμῇ τινι ἀλόγῳ ... ἀλλὰ βέλτιον ... τὸ μετὰ λόγου εἶναι τὴν ὁρμὴν πρὸς τὸ καλόν. Cf. also II, 7, p. 1206b, 20 ff.; Eth. Nic., III, 11, p. 1116b, 35. In Aristot., then we may see already the possibilities of both positive and negative philosophical development. These may be traced esp. in the use in Stoic philosophy. Zeno already uses ὁρμή in the def. of πάθος as ἡ ἄλογος καὶ παρὰ φύσιν ψυχῆς κίνησις, ἡ ὁρμὴ πλεονάζουσα (Diog. L., VII, 110; v. Arnim, I, 205). [5] ὁρμή is man's faculty of pursuing, even in opposition to reason or nature, that which his striving or aspiration (ὄρεξις alongside ὁρμή in Epict. Ench., 1, 1) demands. [6]

2. Philo is fond of the word in this sense. With its derivates it is relatively common in his works. ὁρμή and φαντασία distinguish beings with souls, Leg. All., I, 30; cf. II, 23; Mut. Nom., 257; Som., I, 136; Deus Imm., 41. The Stoic def. of pathos is worked over in Spec. Leg., IV, 79, [7] cf. also Deus Imm., 44; Rer. Div. Her., 245; Congr., 55 and 60; Fug., 158; Som., II, 276; Mut. Nom., 173; Praem. Poen., 48; Spec. Leg., I, 305; Leg. All., III, 118. 185. 229. 248 f.); Sacr. AC, 80; Ebr., 98; Conf. Ling., 90; Exsecr., 154; Op. Mund., 81; Poster. C., 74 etc. Over against it the logos has the task of ἐπέχων and ἀνακόπτων, Spec. Leg., I, 343. The fig. of the charioteer or helmsman is common in

---

[4] ὃς γὰρ ἐπὶ τὸ πλεονεκτεῖν ὁρμᾶται, προδότης πέφυκε.

[5] W. Völker, Fortschritt u. Vollendung bei Philo v. Alexandrien (1938), 80.

[6] Acc. to Kleinknecht. Cf. also M. Ant., XI, 37: ἐν τῷ περὶ τὰς ὁρμὰς τόπῳ = "in the branch of Moral Philosophy called περὶ ὁρμῆς." So A. S. L. Farquharson, The Meditations of the Emperor Marcus Antoninus (1944), who quotes Diog. L., VII, 84 : τὸ δ' ἠθικὸν μέρος τῆς φιλοσοφίας διαιροῦσιν εἴς τε τὸν περὶ ὁρμῆς καὶ εἰς τὸν περὶ ἀγαθῶν καὶ κακῶν τόπον ... εἰς τὸν περὶ τέλους περί τε τῆς πρώτης ἀξίας [T. W. Manson].

[7] Völker, 80, cf. also 86 f., 129; L. Cohn, Die Werke Philos v. Alex., II [1910], 270, n. 2.

this connection. [8] ὁρμή is used with it in a good sense partly for natural orientation (Abr. 275 : οὐ γράμμασιν ἀναδιδαχθείς, ἀλλ' ἀγράφῳ τῇ φύσει σπουδάσας ὑγιαινούσαις καὶ ἀνόσοις ὁρμαῖς ἐπακολουθῆσαι, cf. Cher., 114) and partly for the striving for immortality (Omn. Prob. Lib., 117), for perfect virtue (Leg. All., III, 244; Op. Mund., 79; Vit. Mos., II, 139; Abr., 38), for piety (Spec. Leg., II, 209 etc.).

B. The Word Group in the Old Testament.

In Heb. there is no term for will, [9] let alone any differentiation between its various motions and impulses. Even in the Gk. OT the group is hardly used at all in the psychological sense. It is sometimes used to describe quick movements; here a decisive role is played by Gk. usage and by the ideas of the translator rather than the Heb. original. The original meaning comes out best when the ref. is to flowing water, Prv. 21:1; ψ 45:4 פֶּלֶג; Jos. 4:18 שׁוּב; Job 38:34 ΑΣΘ (LXX τρόμος) שִׁפְעָה. Other verbs of movement are also rendered by the group, Hab. 1:8 בּוֹא; Gn. 31:21 שׂוּם אֶת־פָּנָיו; Ju. 20:37 A (Β ἐκινήθη) חוּשׁ; Dt. 33:22 Allos (LXX ἐκπηδήσεται) זָנַק; ψ 77:26 Ἀ (LXX ἀπῆρε, Σ ἧρεν) נָסַע; Nu. 17:7 פָּנָה: here it seems acc. to the LXX, not that Moses and Aaron flee, but that the mob hurls itself on them or on the tent of revelation; Ju. 5:22 Ἀ (LXX σπουδῇ ἔσπευσαν) דָּהֲרָה; Jer. 8:6 Σ Syr. (LXX ὡς ἵππος κάθιδρος, Ἀ καλπάζων) שָׁטַף; Dt. 28:49; Jer. 48(31):40 Θ דָּאָה (ὡς ἀετός); 1 S. 15:19 עִיט, "to break loose"; Ju. 7:3 A (Β ἐκχωρείτω) צָפַר; Jer. 6:1 Ἀ עוּז (LXX ἐνισχύσατε : עוּז); Na. 3:16 פָּשַׁט; [10] Nu. 11:11 LXX Θ (A ὀργή, Ἀ ἄρμα, Σ βάρος); 11:17 מֶשֶׁךְ; Jos. 6:5, no Mas. [11] In 2-4 Macc. the group is used for violent, often hostile movement. παρορμᾶν in 2 Macc. 15:17; 4 Macc. 12:6 means "to inflame," "to incite." [ἐφ-] ὁρμᾶν is often used with ref. to the spirit which seizes a man, 1 S. 10:6, 10; 16:13 Σ; Ju. 14:6 Σ צָלַח; Ez. 1:12, 20 Σ הָלַךְ. The instances are only in Σ, who here, as elsewhere, follows classically select usage and thus stands out from the other witnesses. ὁρμή is used for (sexual) desire in Gn. 3:16 Σ; 4:7 Σ for תְּשׁוּקָה (LXX ἀποστροφή) and Ez. 23:5, 11 Θ for עֲגַב (LXX ἐπιτίθημι, ἐπίθεσις); 23:20 Σ ὅρμημα for זִרְמָה (LXX αἰδοῖα, ὁ Ἑβραῖος : αἱ διεγέρσεις); in Cant. 8:6, where the Mas. refers to sparks of love, Σ substitutes ὁρμή. If in LXX Gn. 39:7 the ref. is to Potiphar's wife casting her eyes on Joseph, Jos. Ant., 2, 53 speaks of Joseph trying to restrain her ὁρμή. LXX alters the sense of Prv. 3:25. The Mas. refers to the destruction (שׁוֹאָה) of the ungodly, the LXX, however, to the assaults (ὁρμή) of the ungodly on the righteous. The verb is sometimes used when the Mas. refers to the roaring of the lion (Is. 5:29 A S; Β ὀργιῶσιν) or the stamping of the horse (Ιερ. 29[47]:3). In Jer. 4:28 the verb is used in the sense "to cause" for זָמַם "to aim," "to plan (evil)" with ref. to God's purpose to punish Israel. In Ez. 3:14 the LXX puts in place of the psychological emotion of wrath (חֵמָה) the spiritual impulse (ὁρμή), as in passages already mentioned where the Heb. original is different, so that here, too, there seems to be ref. to spirit possession. In Da. Θ 8:6 חֵמָה is again transl. ὁρμή (LXX θυμός). In Zech. 7:12 A ὁρμή is used for קֶצֶף (Β ὀργή), and at Hos. 11:9 Q 407 has ὁρμή for the ὀργή of Β (Mas. חֲרוֹן אַפִּי). Jer. 4:28 shows that this is not just a simple slip in copying. [12] The translator avoids speaking of the

---

[8] → 471, 4 ff. on Jm. 3:4.

[9] → θέλειν, III, 44. Cf. R. Asting, *Die Verkündigung des Wortes im Urchr.* (1939), 15 f., who mentions רוּחַ, נֶפֶשׁ, לֵב, also רָצוֹן as substitutes.

[10] Meaning uncertain : "to plunder"? "burst forth"? "make an onslaught"? Cf. Ges.-Buhl, *s.v.* and F. Horst, *Die 12 kleinen Propheten* (1938), ad loc.

[11] Perhaps the term is suggested by the Mas. נֶגֶד, which is in this case transl. twice.

[12] → supra Nu. 11:11 A; Is. 5:29 B.

wrath of God, → I, 287; *infra.* He speaks of the storm which is sent by God on the people. Similarly, ὅρμημα is often used for עֶבְרָה. Thus Hab. 3:8 speaks of God's wrath against the sea. ὅρμημα is here synon. with ὀργίζειν and θυμός, cf. Am. 1:11; Hos. 5:10; Ex. 32:22 [13] with ref. to the attitude of the people. In ʼA ὅρμημα is regularly used for רַהַב as an emblematic name for Egypt, Is. 30:7; 51:9; ψ 86:4. ὅρμημα act. might be understood of the turbulence of Babel; thus Σ uses ὑπερηφανία in ψ 86:4, ἀλαζονεία in Is. 51:9 and ταραχαί in 30:7 as act. terms for רַהַב. But the ref. can also be pass. to the overthrow of Babel, as in Rev. 18:21. In this case ʼA seems to derive רַהַב from the root רהב, "to assault," which is rendered παρορμᾶν by ΣΘ at Prv. 6:3, LXX παροξύνειν. In 1 Macc. 4:8, 30; 6:33, 47 ὅρμημα is used for violence in attack.

Even where the LXX uses the group to express emotion, this is not in the strict psychological sense. It denotes an uncontrollable power of violent effort which goes beyond the conscious will and reflective reason, and against which all resistance is useless. Hence it accords well with the true understanding of the OT concept of God that the group should sometimes be used to describe divine intervention, so long as there is no reference to God's emotions in the spirit of the Hellenistic view of God.

C. The Word Group in the New Testament.

The NT, too, avoids using ὁρμή κτλ. as a psychological term. In the few passages where it occurs the group denotes violent movement uncontrolled by human reason. In the story of the casting of the demons into the swine (Mk. 5:13; Mt. 8:32; Lk. 8:33) it is used in this sense to describe the senseless flight of the animals into the water. They were gripped by demonic terror and irresistibly propelled by their own mass. [14] The case is similar in mob action such as that recounted in Ac. 7:57; 19:29. In Ac. 14:5 there seems to be reference to a planned stroke, but there is no responsible subject. [15] The different circles of both people and government are stirred up against Paul and his companions. In the two other passages we have descriptions of direct mob action. This leads to the death of Stephen in 7:57, though there is some contradiction between the tumultuous outcry at the end of the hearing and the scrupulous observance of the laws of stoning. [16] 19:29 is followed in v. 36 by the corresponding warning μηδὲν προπετὲς πράσσειν, which is obviously successful.

ὅρμημα occurs in the NT only at Rev. 18:21: οὕτως ὁρμήματι βληθήσεται Βαβυλὼν ἡ μεγάλη πόλις, καὶ οὐ μὴ εὑρεθῇ ἔτι. In the context of OT verses which use ὅρμημα for עֶבְרָה the passage is obviously to be construed of the wrath which overtakes Babylon. [17] But as a psychological understanding is neither possible nor necessary in the OT, it is better to refer the word in Rev. 18:21 either act.

---

[13] Cf. the conjecture in BHK³, *ad loc.*

[14] Cf., e.g., in the novel of K. Hamsun, *Nach Jahr u. Tag* (1934), 488 f. the plunge of a herd of sheep in the concluding scene. O. Bauernfeind, "Die Worte d. Dämonen im Mk." = BWANT, 3 F. 8 (1927), 40-44; on the other hand Bultmann Trad., 224, n. 4; Loh. Mk., *ad loc.*; Wettstein quotes Longus (c. 200) Past., 1, 32 : ἡ δὲ Χλόη λαβοῦσα τὴν σύριγγα ... ἐσύριζε μέγιστον ... καὶ αἱ βόες ἀκούουσι, καὶ τὸ μέλος γνωρίζουσι, καὶ ὁρμῇ μιᾷ μυκησάμεναι πηδῶσιν εἰς τὴν θάλασσαν.

[15] Not syʰᵐᵍ, where the ref. is to a new persecution stirred up by the Jews.

[16] Pr. Ag., *ad loc.*

[17] Loh. Apk., *ad loc.*

(cf. Dt. 28:49) to the storm against Babylon or pass. to its fall. Cf. also the image of the throwing or fall of Satan into the sea, and on this Neh. 9:11 = 2 Εσδρ. 19:11; Jer. 51(28):63 f.

Behind Jm. 3:4 stands a theme of popular Hell. ethics. [18] ὁρμή denotes neither the physical pressure on the rudder which directs the powerful stern of the ship, nor the rational purpose of the helmsman who is trying to keep to a set course ; it expresses the free caprice [19] with which man technically controls nature, without this optimistic line of thought being disturbed by knowledge of the storm and the hazards of the voyage.

The two images of the bridle and the rudder have behind them a long common history. [20] Philo esp. uses them in various ways. There is the negative possibility that the *logos* will not be able to establish itself as ruler, so that ἄκριτοι ὁρμαί gain the upper hand, Leg. All., III, 118 and 128; cf. II, 99; Spec. Leg., IV, 99; Ebr., 111 and esp. Leg. All., I, 73 : ὅταν δὲ ἔμπαλιν ἀφηνιάσῃ καὶ ἀναχαιτίσῃ ὁ θυμὸς καὶ ἡ ἐπιθυμία καὶ τὸν ἡνίοχον, λέγω δὲ τὸν λογισμόν, τῇ βίᾳ τῆς ὁρμῆς κατασύρῃ καὶ ὑποζεύξῃ, ἑκάτερον δὲ πάθος λάβηται τῶν ἡνιῶν, ἀδικία κρατεῖ. The terminology prefigured in Aristot. and developed by Stoicism is obviously exerting an influence here. The optimistic interpretation of biblical sayings (cf. Stoicism) [21] has greatly affected exposition of Jm. 3:4, which has frequently tried to work out the ethical application. Thus we read already in the Cat., ad loc.: εἰ χαλινῷ θράσος ἵππου ἀνακόπτομεν, καὶ πηδαλίῳ μικρῷ ὁρμὴν πλοίου μεταφέρομεν, πολλῷ μᾶλλον τὴν γλῶτταν εἰς τὸ εὖ ἔχον τῷ ὀρθῷ λόγῳ μετάγειν ὀφείλομεν. [22] A similar understanding is to be found in Theophylactus (7th cent. A.D.), Ep., 70. [23]

In fact, however, the images are taken pessimistically in Jm. 3:4. As the horse cannot resist the bridle or the ship the rudder, so man is helpless against the ὁρμή or caprice of the tongue (→ I, 721), little though the member is. The fate of the whole man is dependent on it. In spite of the various possibilities of interpretation and translation, [24] the meaning here is ultimately quite definite. The word denotes the *cupiditates, quae rationi non obtemperant,* [25] and this is the sense in Jm. 3:4.

D. The Post-Apostolic Period.

In primitive Christian writings outside the NT ὁρμή and ὁρμᾶν are rare. Athenag. takes up the Philonic formula ἄλογοι ὁρμαὶ τῆς ψυχῆς καὶ ἐπιθυμίαι, Suppl., 36, 1 and 2, cf. also Just. Apol., 2, 3. The word is used for caprice in Dg., 4, 5. In the Apologists it can also denote striving ἐπὶ θεωρίαν θείων or περὶ τὸ θεῖον (Just. Apol., 58, 3; Dial., 8, 3) or πρὸς τὸ καλόν (Apol., 1, 2), cf. also Apol., 29, 4 : ὡς θεὸν διὰ φόβου

---

[18] Cf. esp. Dib. Jk., ad loc.
[19] Cf. Ez. 1:12 Σ : ὅπου ᾖ ἡ ὁρμὴ τοῦ πνεύματος. The freedom and caprice of the one who sets the course are expressed, e.g., in Ps.-Aristot. Mund., 6, p. 400b, 11 f.: [θεὸς] πάντα κινεῖ καὶ περιάγει, ὅπου βούλεται καὶ ὅπως. For similar phrases in Philo cf. Leg. All., III, 223; Op. Mund., 88 (Dib. Jk., ad loc.). Cf. also Calvin and Bengel, ad loc. and the 𝔎 reading : ἂν ... βούληται.
[20] Dib. Jk., ad loc.
[21] Dib. Jk., ad loc. quotes Aristipp. acc. to Stob., III, 493, 15 ff.: κρατεῖ ἡδονῆς οὐχ ὁ ἀπεχόμενος ἀλλ᾽ ὁ χρώμενος μέν, μὴ παρεκφερόμενος δέ· ὥσπερ καὶ νεὼς καὶ ἵππου οὐχ ὁ μὴ χρώμενος, ἀλλ᾽ ὁ μετάγων, ὅποι βούλεται.
[22] Catenae Graecorum Patrum in NT, ed. J. A. Cramer (1844), ad loc.
[23] Dib. Jk., ad loc.
[24] Vg, Erasmus : *voluntas, impetus* ; Calvin : *arbitrium, affectus.*
[25] Calvin, ad loc.

σέβειν ὥρμηντο. The verb can also mean "to derive from," Athenag. Suppl., 2, 2; Just. Apol., 26, 6. Here too, then, the specific philosophical meaning exerts no direct influence. On the other hand, we do not find the distinctive aversion which is consistently felt for the term in biblical or more specifically NT usage.

† ἀφορμή.

This is in Gk. a purely formal term for "start," "origin," "cause," "stimulus," "impulse," "undertaking," "pretext," "possibility," "inclination," also as a Stoic word "aversion" as the opp. of ὁρμή. Aristot. Cael., II, 12, p. 292a, 16 has it for "means of assistance." In Pol., VI, 5, p. 1320a, 39, b, 8 it means "opportunity" for trade or agriculture, or more generally for work with a view to overcoming unemployment. "Logical starting-point" is the sense in Ps.-Aristot. Rhet. Al., 3, p. 1423a, 33; b, 14, 32; 39, p. 1445b, 29; in Eur. Hec., 1238 f. we also find the sense "pretext" : βροτοῖσιν ὡς τὰ χρηστὰ πράγματα χρηστῶν ἀφορμὰς ἐνδίδωσ' ἀεὶ λόγων, cf. also Phoen., 199 f. In the commonly quoted Polyb., [1] 3, 7, 5; 32, 7; 4, 58, 8 the term is used in the sense of "cause" or "starting-point." Similarly in an edict of Caracalla (215 A.D.) in P. Giess., I, 40, 2, 11 there is ref. to ἐπηρείας ἀφορμή alongside δειλίας αἰτία. [2] In a derogatory sense ἀφορμή occurs along with δόλος in a 3rd cent. pap., [3] and in P. Oxy. I, 34, III, 1 f. (127 A.D.) we read : τοὺς παραβάντας καὶ τοὺς διὰ ἀπειθίαν καὶ ὡς ἀφορμὴν ζητοῦντας ἁμαρτημάτων τιμωρήσομαι. [4] In particular in the pap. the word has the sense of "occasion," "cause," "suitable opportunity." In many cases it is hardly or not at all distinguishable from ὁρμή. Thus in Poimandres, 25 [5] the ἀφορμαὶ κακαί are obviously the same as the ὁρμαὶ ἄλογοι in Philo. It is also worth noting that θυμός and ἐπιθυμία are mentioned in the same context. But the word can have many different meanings in Philo : [6] Decal., 17: πρὸς τὸ εὖ ζῆν, Migr., 2 : εἰς σωτηρίαν, Jos., 258 : εἰς ἀργυρισμόν, Leg. All., III, 66 : εἰς ἀπολογίαν. It means "logical starting-point" in Plant., 36. It is used with ἀρχή in Conf. Ling., 68 and with πηγή in Op. Mund., 47.

The only OT occurrence with a Heb. original is at Ez. 5:7. Here it stands for הֲמָנְכֶם. The Mas. means : "On account of your raging more than the Gentiles ..." [7] The Gk. translators, however, establish a connection with the Gentiles (syr-hex): ἀνθ' ὧν τὸ πλῆθος ὑμῶν ἐγένετο ἐκ τῶν ἐθνῶν, cf. Hier.: quia multitudo vestra fuit e gentibus. 'A : eo quod numerati estis in gentibus. In the LXX, too, ἀφορμή refers here not merely to orientation of thought (Θ λογισμοί) under Gentile influence, but to origin. Herewith the historical fact of the derivation of many of the Jews of the Hell. Roman period from the Gentiles is at least correctly perceived. [8] In Prv. 9:9 the LXX adds ἀφορμή in elucidation : δίδου σοφῷ ἀφορμὴν καὶ σοφώτερος ἔσται. In 3 Macc. 3:2 the word is used in the sense of "cause," so, too, Sir. Prologue, 29 vl.: μικρὰν παιδείας ἀφορμήν.

In the NT ἀφορμή occurs in the usual texts only in the Pauline corpus. In D there is also a vl. at Lk. 11:54 : ζητοῦντες ἀφορμήν τινα λαβεῖν αὐτοῦ = occasio-

---

ἀ φ ο ρ μ ή. Moult.-Mill., Liddell-Scott, s.v.; A. Bonhöffer, Epikt. u. das NT (1911), 110, 177. Preisigke Wört., s.v.

[1] Pr.-Bauer, s.v.; Ltzm., Zn. R. on 7:8.
[2] Moult.-Mill., s.v.
[3] Preisigke Sammelbuch, 5671, 16.
[4] Moult.-Mill., s.v.
[5] Reitzenstein Poim., 336, 9 ff.
[6] Cf. Leisegang, I, s.v.
[7] The text is much emended, cf. A. Bertholet, Hesekiel = Hndbch. z. AT, I, 13 (1936), ad loc.
[8] G. Rosen-G. Bertram, Juden u. Phönizier (1929), esp. 64, 68.

nem aliquam invenire de illo (it syr^c). [9] This is an old reading [10] in which the word has the same derogatory sense as in Paul. This negative sense, however, is not present in 2 C. 5:12, where Paul says that his aim in the passage is to give the Corinthians ἀφορμὴν καυχήματος, a "basis" or "possibility" of boasting. ἀφορμή is thus "the 'occasion' or 'starting-point' of something inasmuch as it evokes a movement of will and also provides the material which is exploited in this movement." [11]

On the other hand 2 C. 11:12: ἐκκόψω τὴν ἀφορμὴν τῶν θελόντων ἀφορμήν, offers a clear par. to the use in Lk. 11:54 D. All kinds of deceptive "pretexts" are sought in the attack on Paul as in that on Jesus. Paul disarms these by his conduct. What the content of these was, is not wholly clear, so that textual corruption has been considered. [12] What his opponents boast about, i.e., the apostolic right to support by the churches, Paul ought to claim. For the churches, in view of wandering preachers and their avarice, [13] interpret in Paul's favour renunciation of this right. [14] If he were to claim it, however, he would give occasion for calumny, [15] as though he also preached for gain. In fact, as Paul ironically affirms, he would then be doing exactly what his adversaries boast of doing. Calvin [16] sees in Paul's conduct an example which teaches Christians to avoid all evil appearance (Luther 1 Th. 5:22): *caeterum hic utilis est admonitio de praecidenda improbis occasione, quoties aliquam captant, hic enim unus est vincendi modus, non autem quum eos nostra impudentia armamus.*

In Gl. 5:13 the σάρξ occupies the position of the malicious opponent and seeks a "pretext" in ἐλευθερία. In 1 Tm. 5:14 it is ἀντικείμενος and in R. 7:8, 11 ἁμαρτία. What offers a "starting-point" or "occasion" is not in itself bad, whether it be the apostolic right to support (2 C. 11:12), widowhood (1 Tm. 5:14), Christian freedom (Gl. 5:13) or the Law, God's commandment (R. 7:8, 11). In 1 Tm. 5:14, on the analogy of the other verses, that which gives an "occasion" or "pretext" for Jewish or Christian opponents to slander the Christian community or to take other hostile action is not a possible seduction of the young widows, [17] but the state of widowhood itself, which offers Satan [18] an occasion for tempting widows. This alone justifies the radical requirement that widows should marry again. In this

---

[9] The usual text (cf. Nestle) is: ἐνεδρεύοντες αὐτὸν θηρεῦσαί τι.
[10] B. and J. Weiss, *Die Ev. d. Mk. u. Lk.*⁹ (1901), *ad loc.* accept this as the original.
[11] Bchm. K., *ad loc.*
[12] Wnd. 2 K., *ad loc.*
[13] Cf. esp. Did., 11, also 12 and 13, and on this Kn. Did., *ad loc.* Paul exercises discretion in handling the collection, 2 C. 8:20, 21. Cf. what he says in 12:16-18 and Wnd. 2 K. on both passages.
[14] Cf. on this the Cat., K. Staab, *Pls.-Kommentare aus d. gr. Kirche* (1933), *ad loc.*, 297: ἵνα τῶν κατηγόρων ἐκκόψω τὴν πρόφασιν (Severian of Gabala) and Ign. Tr., 8, 2: "Give the pagans no material, that the divine community be not slandered for the sake of a few without understanding" (cf. Bau. Ign.).
[15] Cf. esp. Ltzm. K. and Wnd. 2 K., *ad loc.*; on the other hand, Bchm. K. translates "point in support," seeing it as the intention of the adversaries that they might appeal to Paul if he were maintained by the community as they were.
[16] *Ad loc.*
[17] So Bengel, Grotius and most modern expositors, cf. B. Weiss, *Die Briefe Pauli an Tm. u. Tit.* (1902), Wbg., Dib. Past., *ad loc.*, who all think the adversaries are earthly opponents.
[18] Bengel, though of a different view, pts. out that in Σ ψ 37:20 ἀντίκειμαι is used for שׂטן, and that Satan is mentioned in 5:15.

way barriers are set up which eliminate the occasion and thus remove the danger outwardly, though they do not overcome it inwardly. R. 7:8, 11 tells us once and for all that neither the erection of such barriers nor any law can act as a safeguard against the abuse of freedom. The very Law itself, God's commandment, can be an occasion for sin. In this respect the Law has a specific task : *detexit in me omnem concupiscentiam, quae dum lateret, quodam modo nulla esse videbatur.* [19] Desire is thus unmasked in its true colours. As Origen expressed it in familiar Philonic terms, ὄρεξις ἄλογος γινομένη κατὰ ὁρμὴν πλεονάζουσαν παράλογον. From its opposition to the commandment sin receives an impetus to lead men astray into covetousness. [20] God's commandment with its authority incites sin to open resistance to God. [21] In so doing the Law is as little guilty of the instigation of sin by its coming as is the tree in Paradise guilty of the disobedience of Adam, or the coming of Christ guilty of the sin of those who rejected Him (Jn. 15:22; cf. also Hb. 10:29). An ancient Greek commentator, [22] who already draws attention to these parallels, has in view especially the greatness of the punishment. In fact the opponents of the Christian community, the power of Satan, sin and the flesh which lies behind them, take the good gifts of God in creation, or indeed the Christian freedom which is the dawn of eternal salvation, and make them into a deceitful occasion [23] for leading men astray. In this way they themselves are given a fresh impulse to resist God. [24] The devil in some sense uses the precepts of the Law as materials with which to work. [25] It belongs to the inscrutability of the divine counsel that the good gifts of God, including the gift of salvation itself, begin by giving a fresh impetus to sin so that they can then unmask it as such. In this way, however, the formal concept of ἀφορμή takes on in the NT a specifically material character. It comes to be grouped with "offence" and "temptation" and figures of speech like "nets" and "snares." [26]

Bertram

---

[19] Calvin, *ad loc.*

[20] Acc. to an expository note which is wrongly ascribed to Origen in Cramer Cat. (→ n. 22), and in which ancient (Stoic) ascetic and legalistic motifs may be discerned, sin suggests to men that the desire for wealth, fame, wives etc. is good. This distorts Paul's view.

[21] This is not the same as the psychological insight that a prohibition incites men to transgress it. For examples in antiquity cf. Wettstein, e.g., Ovid Amores, III, 4, 17: *Nitimur in vetitum semper cupimusque negata.*

[22] Cramer Cat. 167 wrongly ascribes this to Chrysostom.

[23] Cf. also Herm. m., 4, 1, 11; 3, 3, where proclamation of an opportunity for repentance can be an incitement. This abs. use of the word is to be understood in terms of Pauline statements. Elsewhere the word occurs in early Christian lit. esp. in the Apologists, though with no notable Pauline influence. Materially the development of rigorist and libertine sects provides the examples.

[24] Photius in Staab, *op. cit.* (→ n. 14), 504, cf. also Gennadius, *ibid.,* 370.

[25] Diodore of Tarsus, Staab, 88 : τὰ παραγγέλματα τοῦ νόμου ὥσπερ ὕλην τινὰ τῆς ἑαυτοῦ τέχνης ποιησάμενος, cf. also Severian of Gabala, *ibid.,* 219.

[26] → σκάνδαλον, πειρασμός, cf. also βρόχος, Prv. 7:21; 22:25.

| ὄρος | → Σινᾶ, Σιών. |

τὸ ὄρος denotes the (individual) "mountain" or "hill," Dio C. often of the hills of Rome, e.g., 53, 27, 5 : ἐν τῷ Παλατίῳ ὄρει, and also the "mountain range," Hdt., I, 104 : τὸ Καυκάσιον ὄρος, Demosth. Or., 55, 10 : ὄρους δὲ περιέχοντος κύκλῳ, Xenoph. An., I, 2, 22; III, 4, 30; Cornut. Theol. Graec., 6 : τὴν Ἴδην ... μετέωρον ὄρος. The plur. means "individual mountains," Xenoph. An., IV, 1, 11: πυρὰ πολλὰ ἔκαιον κύκλῳ ἐπὶ τῶν ὀρέων, and also "mountain range," Xenoph. Cyrop., III, 1, 2 : ἔπεμπεν εἰς τὰ ὄρη τὸν νεώτερον υἱὸν Σάβαριν καὶ τὰς γυναῖκας.

A. The Mountain in Antiquity.

1. The striking natural phenomenon of the mountain has attracted attention, and awakened religious concepts,[1] in all ages and among all peoples. First, the power of the mountain has caused it to be honoured as divine, along with rivers, springs, waterfalls, and the earth.[2] Then mountains and high places were peopled with spirits.[3] In lofty religions the soaring up of the mountain led to its being viewed as the abode of the gods or to the cultic worship of higher beings on its peaks. "Above" and "below" in their symbolical content are not interchangeable in religion and mythology. With the upward movement is associated heaven, the world of light, of day, and of consciousness. Hence the gods of light and the day are connected with the peaks, while those of death and the unconscious are linked with the inside of the mountain, though also with the nocturnal darkness of mountain forests or with the mountain wilderness.[4] Finally, the mythological concept of the primal mountain is widespread.[5] This is connected with the direct impression that the mountain, being hard and stony as compared with the soft earth and the changing course of rivers, is the oldest part of the earthly world. The more detailed ideas attached by individual peoples to hills vary considerably, and are related to the size and form and the proximity or distance of mountains in the various lands, also to the question whether they are covered with vegetation, or bare, or mantled by eternal snow. Further differences arise according to the differing endowment of the peoples and their particular intellectual and religious world.

2. The peoples of Mesopotamia were very conscious of the height and power of

---

ὄ ρ ο ς. Chant. de la Saussaye, Index, s.v. "Berg"; G. van d. Leeuw, Phänomenologie d. Religion (1933), 35 f.; F. v. Andrian, Der Höhenkultus asiatischer u. europäischer Völker (1891); J. Jeremias, Der Gottesberg (1919); R. Frieling, D. heilige Berg (1930); M. Rohrer, Berglieder d. Völker (1928); B. Meissner, Babylonien u. Assyrien, II (1925), 110-112; R. Beer, Heilige Höhen d. alten Gr. u. Römer (1891); O. Kern, Die Religion der Griechen, I (1926), 74-81; G. Westphal, "Jahves Wohnstätten nach den Anschauungen d. alten Hebräer," ZAW Beih., 15 (1908), 98-118.

[1] Van d. Leeuw, 35 f.
[2] Ibid., 370 f.; Chant. de la Saussaye, I, 174. Cf., e.g., the invocation of "mountains, rivers, springs" etc. in a Hittite treaty, J. Friedrich, Aus dem hethitischen Schrifttum, 1 (AO, 24, 3) (1925), 18.
[3] Hes. Theog., 129 f.: (Γαῖα) ... γείνατο δ᾽ οὔρεα μακρά, θεῶν χαρίεντας ἐναύλους Νυμφέων, αἳ ναίουσιν ἀν᾽ οὔρεα βησσήεντα.
[4] Van der Leeuw, 120.
[5] Ibid., 36, cf. H. Schärer, Die Gottesidee d. Ngadju-Dajak in Südborneo (1946), acc. to the review in Theol. Zschr., 4 (1948), 57 f.

mountains. [6] This is often expressed figuratively. [7] From this it is only a small step to use "mountain" as a fig. for "power," and this is just as firmly established here, and for the same reason, as the use of "horn" in the OT. [8] The Accadian *shadu* means "mountain," "refuge" (?), "lord." [9] Adad is called "mountain (i.e., lord), of the four quarters of the earth," [10] Enmesharra "mountain of the Anunnaki," [11] and we also find "mountain of the Igigi." [12] Ninib carries among other weapons "a mountain whose power none can escape," [13] and says of himself : "From me, the lord, the high mountains all flee." [14] Several theophorous personal names are linked with *shadi* = my mountain. [15] Enlil means "mountain" or "great mountain," [16] a name which was transferred also to other gods. [17] This fig. use of "mountain" is not Gk., but occurs among the Mandaeans. [18] Since mountains encircled the Babylonian plain only at a distance, it is understandable that Babylonian lit. should emphasise the remoteness and inaccessibility of mountains. [19] This geographical situation of Babylon led also to the idea of two (twin-peaked) [20] mountains in east and west on which the arch of heaven rested and where the sun rose and went down. [21] On the eastern range is found the Kammer Duku = bright mountain, where the gods fix destiny on New Year's Day. [22] In the west is Mashu, where heaven and the underworld meet [23] and where is also the entrance to the realm of the dead. [24]

---

[6] "Mighty" (*gashru*) is a common name for mountains, C. Bezold, *Babylonisch-assyrisches Glossar* (1926), s.v. "*gaschru*"; A. Ungnad, *Die Religion d. Babylonier u. Assyrer* (1921), 185, lines 6, 19.

[7] Istar, "mistress of the field of battle, who casts down the mountains," Ungnad, 217, line 11; "the pain in the head which like a mountain does not waver," 277; "When Adad is angry, ... the great mountains fall down before him," 194; cf. also the god of pestilence, Irshum, 158; Marduk's word is "high as the mountains," 213 f.; he who dreams he carries a mountain on his head will have no adversary, Meissner, 266.

[8] → III, 669 f.

[9] K. Tallquist, *Akkadische Götterepitheta* (1938), 221; J. J. Stamm, "Die akkadische Namengebung," *Mitteilungen d. vorderasiatisch-ägyptischen Gesellschaft*, 44 (1939), 82, 198, n. 1. Shadu is thus related to the Heb. צוּר in its extension of meaning.

[10] Tallquist, 221.

[11] Meissner, 157.

[12] Tallquist, 221.

[13] M. Jastrow, *Die Religion Babyloniens u. Assyriens*, I (1905), 461.

[14] M. Witzel, *Der Drachenkämpfer Ninib* = *Keilinschriftliche Studien*, 2 (1920), 82.

[15] W. W. Graf Baudissin, *Kyrios als Gottesname*, III (1929), 565; Stamm, 82, 211, 226; Jeremias, 31 f.

[16] Tallquist, 221, 296, 344.

[17] *Loc. cit.*; also *Reallexikon d. Assyriologie*, I (1928), 197b; II (1938), 383a.

[18] Lidz. Ginza, 82, 14; → n. 25. With the orientation of their thinking to eternal duration, the Egyptians, when they used the image of the mountain, emphasised esp. its solidity and indestructibility, H. Grapow, *Die bildlichen Ausdrücke des Ägyptischen* (1924), 52 f.

[19] "Your lord stays there (in the city) no longer, ... your lord climbs up with loud roars into the mountains," Ungnad, 208; head pains "have come down from the middle of the mountains into the land," 275; the storm bird Zu flies to the "inaccessible mountains," "the far abode," 153; 154. The inaccessibility and barrenness of mountains made them a refuge for demons : the "seven demons were born in the mountains of the west," Meissner, 199; in the myth of the Huluppu tree the bird Zu flies to the mountains, while Lilith goes into the wilderness (both mountains and desert are here abodes of demons), S. N. Kramer, *Sumerian Mythology* (1944), 34; "He caused many spirits of the dead to return to the mountain," A. Jeremias, *Die ausserbiblische Erlösererwartung* (1927), 61.

[20] A. Jeremias, *Handbuch d. altorientalischen Geisteskultur*² (1929), 132.

[21] *Ibid.*, 368; Meissner, 108 ff.; H. Gressmann, *Der Messias* (1929), 170. Cf. the legend of the birth of Sargon and Assurbanipal II, Gressmann, 32.

[22] Meissner, 111.

[23] Ungnad, 89.

[24] Meissner, 112; K. Tallquist, *Sumerisch-akkadische Namen der Totenwelt* = *Studia Orientalia*, V, 4 (1934), 23 ff. "The god has gone to the mountain" = "he had died," *loc. cit.* and Meissner, 98.

Among the Mandaeans the two pure and the two dark mountains echo these ideas. There is also an indistinct reminiscence in the Rabb. [25] We may also think of the varied notion of the cedar mountain, the abode of the gods, [26] the mountain of the lands where "Ea, Sin, Shamash, Nebo, Adad and Ninurta were lawfully born," [27] the mountain of assembly where the gods meet, [28] the "mountain of the world," "bond of heaven and earth," from which Enlil rules, [29] the "mount of winds whose top reaches to heaven and whose foundation is laid in the pure watery depths." [30] It is not certain whether these mountains are equated with earthly hills. [31] Localisation of the mythical mount of the gods in the north is as little attested in Babylonian sources as the idea of a mountain of Paradise. [32] What notions were originally linked with the designation of Enlil as "great mountain" [33] or of his temple in Nippur as "mountain house" [34] it is difficult to say. In the historical period "great mountain" denotes great power, the great lord, and "mountain house" became a common name for temple. [35] This term, and the bulding of the zigurrat, remind us of the mountain as the place of divine proximity or abode of the gods. [36] The hill of sunset in the west, and its inside, is associated with the dark side of life, with death and judgment, and here, too, the judgment of the dead will take place. [37]

3. The natural relation of the Gks. to mountains differs already from that of the Babylonians. Greece is a land of wooded mountains. If these were dangerous for

---

[25] The dark mountains, Lidz. Ginza, 314, 37-315, 1; 501, 7 f.; the hill of darkness in the sing., Lidz. Joh., 90, 13; 98, 7 and 10; 100, 6; 174, 30; 180, 15; 199, 28. The pure mountains, Lidz. Ginza, 326, 34; 380, 18 f.; 309, 6 f.; Joh., 189, 13; 229, 21; cf. also Joh., 116, 11 and 184, n. 4. The pure mountains in Mandaean writings remind us of the bright mountains which the storm demon Pazuzu lays waste, Meissner, 205. The Rabb. speak of the dark mountains which Alexander had to cross when he wanted to go into Africa, Lv. r., 27 on 22:27; bTamid., 32a, cf. b; Gn. r., 33, 1 on 8:1.

[26] Gilgamesh Epic, V, 6 (Ungnad, 78).

[27] Meissner, 111, 119; Kramer, 72.

[28] Meissner, 111.

[29] *Ibid.*, 7; Jeremias (→ n. 20), 108.

[30] Tallquist, *Totenwelt,* 31; *Epitheta,* 221.

[31] B. Alfrink, "Der Versammlungsberg im äussersten Norden," *Biblica,* 15 (1933), 41-67; A. Deimel, *Sumerisches Lexikon,* III, 1, *sumerisch-akkadisches Glossar* (1934), 18b, *s.v.* "*areli/a*"; the mountain of the lands is the atmosphere with the vault of heaven.

[32] T. C. Vriezen, *Onderzoek naar de paradijsvoorstelling bij de oude semietische volken,* Diss. Utrecht (1937); cf. Jeremias, 464.

[33] → n. 17.

[34] Tallquist (→ n. 24), 26; the sanctuary of the temple of Assur is the "house of the great mountain of the lands," Meissner, 111.

[35] Meissner, 7.

[36] There are many comparisons of the temple with a mountain, C. Frank, *Studien zur babyl. Religion,* I (1911), 187; Chant. de la Saussaye, I, 524; Vriezen, *op. cit.,* 50 (temple founded as the hill of abundance). The temple is "built toward heaven like the great world mountain," Jeremias, 115. The temple tower in Nippur is called the world mountain, *ibid.,* 132. H. J. Lenzen, *Die Entwicklung der Zikurrat-Ausgrabungen d. Deutschen Forschungs-gemeinschaft in Uruk-Warka,* 4 (1941), concludes that "the zigurrats with their high temples were always the altar and abode of the distant god," 60. "On the basis of their development I no longer think it possible to regard them as copies of mountains," 55. But it is hard to separate the idea of the mountain from an elevated place of sacrifice for the distant god. For the mountain as a place of sacrifice and of divine proximity cf. Gilgamesh Epic, XI, 157; cf. Ungnad, 107 (offerings of incense on the mountain peak); Meissner, 87; hills as dwelling-places of the gods, Meissner, 119 f.

[37] Meissner, 98; Jeremias, 290, 462.

travellers, [38] the Greek extols them as an adornment of his homeland. [39] The unspoiled mountain forests, and the untouched peaks of mountains soaring up into the regions of eternal snow, gave both Gks. and Romans a sense of divine power. [40] Of the many peaks on or in which gods and nymphs and muses lived [41] Olympus soon came to be distinguished as the supreme home of the gods and was idealised as such [42] and equated with heaven (→ οὐρανός). [43] This view of Olympus is a typical expression of the Gk. sense that the upper world is the pure world of stars, aether, and fire, i.e., the divine, and Olympus soars up into this world. [44] Hence this mountain takes on supreme significance for the Gks. as the symbol of natural and ethical perfection. [45] On the other hand we do not find, or find only on the margin, such mythological ideas as that of the mountain of sunrise and sunset, or the origin of the gods on a mythological mount of the gods, or the location of this mountain in the north, or the link between the inside of the mountain and the world of death. Equally absent is the connection between the mountain and harmful spirits. [46]

4. In Asia Minor worship of the "great mother," the "mountain mother," [47] is always associated with a mountain. [48] The mother of nature is here sensed in the storm wind

---

[38] In Artemid. Oneirocr., II, 28 (124, 15), 68 (160c, 2), the mountain with its valleys and ravines is sinister, but cf. Ael. Arist. on the *pax Augusta*, Or. 35, 37: οὐ τὰ μὲν ὄρη τὴν αὐτὴν ἔχει τοῖς ὁδεύουσιν ἥνπερ αἱ πόλεις τοῖς οἰκοῦσιν αὐτὰς ἀσφάλειαν. Hence this is not self-evident.

[39] Cf. the texts in Rohrer, 183-200, esp. Odysseus on his country, Hom. Od., 9, 21 f.; also Soph. Ant., 1127-1136; Eur. Tro., 1060-1070; Catull., 34, 9-12.

[40] Sen. Ep., 41, 3 : *si quis specus saxis penitus exesis montem suspenderit, non manu factus, sed naturalibus causis in tantam laxitatem excavatus, animum tuum quadam religionis suspicione percutiet.* Silius Italicus, *Punica* (ed. L. Bauer, I [1890]), III, 500 ff.:

> at miles dubio tardat vestigia gressu
> impia ceu sacros in finis arma per orbem,
> natura prohibente, ferant divisque repugnent

(of Hannibal's crossing of the Alps).

[41] Kern, 74; M. P. Nilsson, *Gesch. d. gr. Religion*, I = *Hndbch. AW*, V, 2 (1941), 367-374; Chant. de la Saussaye, II, 301 f., 416; H. Schmidt, *Der Heilige Fels in Jerusalem* (1933), 93 f.

[42] Hom. Od., 6, 43-46 of Olympus :

> οὔτ' ἀνέμοισι τινάσσεται οὔτε ποτ' ὄμβρῳ
> δεύεται οὔτε χιὼν ἐπιπίλναται ἀλλὰ μάλ' αἴθρη
> πέπταται ἀνέφελος, λευκὴ δ' ἐπιδέδρομεν αἴγλη·
> τῷ ἔνι τέρπονται μάκαρες θεοὶ ἤματα πάντα.

[43] In Vergil Ecl., V, 56 f. the deified Daphnis sees from Olympus *sub pedibus ... nubes et sidera.* J. Schmidt, Art. "Olympos," Pauly-W., XVIII (1939), 278 etc. But sometimes they are distinguished later, *ibid.*, 290.

[44] Max. Tyr., II, 1 f. ἐπεφήμισαν δὲ καὶ Διῒ ἀγάλματα οἱ πρῶτοι ἄνθρωποι, κορυφὰς ὀρῶν, Ὄλυμπον, καὶ Ἴδην, καὶ εἴ τι ἄλλο ὄρος πλησιάζει τῷ οὐρανῷ.

[45] Schmidt, 300 : "It was easy to see in Olympus, the abode of the gods attainable only by supreme virtue, the epitome of an ideal of the greatest perfection," also 301: "It is characteristic of the conquering Roman that he uses Olympus for comparison when speaking of outstanding human deeds, whereas the Gk. sets the ethical and religious aspect to the fore by showing the distinction between mortals and the eternal gods in Olympus."

[46] Perhaps a remnant of these ideas is to be found in imprecation on hills, though O. Weinreich, "Gebet u. Wunder," *Genethliakon W. Schmid = Tübinger Beiträge zur Altertumswissenschaft*, 5 (1929), 176 regards ἀποπομπὴ εἰς ὀρέων κεφαλάς as an "indulgent form" in isolated places. For the German sphere cf. *Handwörterbuch d. deutschen Aberglaubens*, ed. H. Bächtold-Stäubli, I (1927), s.v. "Berg," "Bergentrückte," "Berggeister," 1043-83.

[47] μήτηρ ὀρεία, Eur. Hipp., 144.

[48] F. Schwenn, Art. "Kybele," Pauly-W., XI, 2251-2298; cf. also E. Ohlemutz, *D. Kulte u. Heiligtümer d. Götter in Pergamum* (1940), 174-183.

which rages around the mountain and through the forest. She is experienced in ecstatic dancing by night through the woods. Here the mountain with its forest darkness and night belongs to the dark side of life. This is reflected also in the connecting of the mother of the gods, Cybele, with mountain caves. [49]

5. In Syria and Palestine we first find divine honours paid to the mountain itself, [50] then cultic worship on mountain tops and hills. [51] The Ras Shamra texts [52] show that Zaphon, a hill north of Ras Shamra, was regarded as an abode of Baal; [53] the parallelism equates sitting on Zaphon with "sitting on the throne of glory." [54] Furthermore, there are also hints of mountain myths in these texts. The gods assemble on Mt. Ll, [55] and we read of mountains among which is the entry to the underworld. [56] Perhaps the Heb. word for north, צָפוֹן, is related to Mt. Zaphon as the mount of the gods in the north. [57] Finally, it is to be noted that "mountain" is used fig. for power in the Ras Shamra texts too. [58]

B. The Mountain in the OT and Judaism.

1. The LXX almost without exception has ὄρος for the Heb. הַר. [59] This means in the sing. a "mountain," e.g., Ebal or Gerizim, Dt. 11:29, or Zion, cf. also in the Rabb. הַר מִשְׁחָה, the Mt. of Olives, [60] or Aram. טורא for Mt. Gerizim, → n. 78; Jos. Vit., 188: τὸ Ἰταβύριον ὄρος. But it can also mean a "range": הַר־הָהָר אֶת־עֲלִיתֶם = ἀναβήσεσθε εἰς τὸ ὄρος, Nu. 13:17; Aram. טורא : טורא לטורא פוק, Gn. r., 50, 20 on 19:19 (angel to Lot), ὄρος in this sense, Sir. 50:26: οἱ καθήμενοι ἐν ὄρει Σαμαρείας, Jos. Ant., 2, 337: τὸ περικλεῖον ἡμᾶς ὄρος, cf. Ant., 4, 83. [61] The plur. denotes either individual mountains or a range. In 2 S. 1:6, 21 the Mas. and LXX vacillate between the sing. and the plur. to denote Mt. Gilboa.

2. The cartography of Palestine is reflected in the many refs. to hills in the OT. In later days the mountains, most of which are not much over 3000 ft., were in general

---

[49] Kern, 34, 78. For a similar relation to the mountain cf. the Dionysus cult.

[50] Tac. Hist., II, 78: *Carmelus, ita vocant montem deumque;* Etym. M., *s.v.*, "Libanon": δοκοῦσι γὰρ αὐτὸν οἱ Ἰουδαῖοι ὅλον εἶναι πνεῦμα καὶ θεόν ... ὅθεν καὶ αὐτὸν σέβονται. Eus. Onomastikon, *s.v.* Ἀερμών (ed. E. Klostermann [1904], 20, 10 f.) φασίν δὲ εἰς ἔτι νῦν Ἀερμών ὄρος ὀνομάζεσθαι καὶ ὡς ἱερὸν τιμᾶσθαι ὑπὸ τῶν ἐθνῶν. In the sacrificial lists of Ras Shamra there is offering to Zaphon himself as well as Mt. Zaphon, C. H. Gordon, *Ugaritic Literature* = Scripta Pontificii Instituti Biblici, 98 (1949), 113 f. (Text, 9, 4. 7). Cf. Philo of Byblos in Eus. Praep. Ev., I, 10, 9.

[51] O. Eissfeldt, *Baal Zaphon, Zeus Kasios u. der Durchzug d. Israeliten durchs Meer* (1932), 31 f.; cf. the myth of Krt, 74 ff. = Gordon, 68 f. In the passage in → n. 50 Jerome's transl. of Eus. Onomastikon has: *dicitur esse in vertice eius insigne templum, quod ab ethnicis cultui habetur.*

[52] The quotations are given as in Gordon.

[53] Anat., III, 26 f. in Gordon, 19: Baal to Anat.: Come and I shall show it in the midst of the mountain of me, God of Sapan, in the sanctuary in the mountain of mine inheritance.

[54] Text, 76, III, 12-15; Gordon, 51.

[55] Text, 137, 14, Gordon, 13: Toward the convocation of the assembly in the midst of the mountain of Ll.

[56] Text, 51, VIII, 1-9, Gordon, 37.

[57] Eissfeldt, *op. cit.*, 16 ff.

[58] Text, 127, 31 f., Gordon, 82: Dost thou administer like the strongest of the strong, and govern (like) the mountains?

[59] G. Bertram, "Der Sprachschatz d. LXX u. der des hbr. AT," ZAW, NF, 16 (1939), 88.

[60] → n. 100.

[61] הַר קָדְשִׁי in Is. 11:9 etc. is used of the land of Canaan. Westphal, 93. Similarly in Arabic to-day the sing. *ǧebel* is used for the mountain country round Jerusalem, G. Dalman, "Jerusalem u. sein Gelände," BFTh, II, 19 (1930), 3.

denuded of trees. For the earlier period cf. Jos. 17:18; Ju. 6:2. In the main we find only pasture, Ps. 147:8; Sib., III, 788 f.; 6 Esr. 1(15):58, Riessler, 322. The hills are thus very suitable for beacons, Is. 13:2; 30:17; the feet of the messengers of peace can also be seen on the hills from afar, Na. 2:1; Is. 52:7. [62] Indeed, the mountains offer extensive views in general, Dt. 34:1 ff.; Ps. Sol. 11:2. The voice also carries in them, Ju. 9:7; 2 S. 2:25 f.; 2 Ch. 13:4; O. Sol. 33:3. But the mountains of Palestine with their ravines were then, as now, an obstacle to communications, 2 K. 19:23; cf. Is. 37:24; Jos. Ant., 2, 333 and 337. They are lonely (1 S. 23:14), so that it is a disgrace to be killed and lie unburied on the mountains ('Hσ. 14:19; Ps. Sol. 2:26). The lonely hills are also a place of refuge, Ju. 6:2; 'Hσ. 22:5; ψ 10:1; 1 Macc. 2:28; 4:5; 9:38, 40.

3. In the OT the mountains are particularly mentioned in prophecy and poetry to show the superior power of God over all things on earth. God is exalted above the hills, the oldest (Ps. 90:2), highest (Ps. 95:4) and most solid things on earth. God establishes the mountains (Ps. 65:6). He weighs them, Is. 40:12; cf. 2 Macc. 9:8. They tremble before Him, Ju. 5:5; Na. 1:5; Jer. 4:24; Sir. 16:19; 43:16. They break in pieces, 1 K. 19:11; Ez. 38:20; Hab. 3:6. God grinds and crushes them, Is. 41:15. He turns them around, Job 9:5; Ιωβ 18:4; Jos. Ant., 2, 337. He levels them, Is. 40:4; Jos. Ant., 2, 333. They are consumed by God's fire, Dt. 32:22; 'Hσ. 10:18; Ep. Jer. 61; Ps. 83:14; 104:32; Sir. 43:4. They melt before Him, Mi. 1:4; Is. 63:19 f.; Eth. En. 1:6; 4 Esr. 8:23. The solidity of the mountains, which is important in this connection, finds typical expression in the OT in their being seen as rooted in the earth, Job 28:9; Jdt. 6:13; 7:12; cf. Herm. s., 9, 30, 1.

In the later prophecies, also the Rabb. and pseudepigr., we find that the mountain is a symbol of power, as in Babylonian usage and on into the Mandaean writings. In Jer. 51:25 Babylon is described as הַר הַמַּשְׁחִית, i.e., as a destructive (political) force. Cf. Zech. 4:7: "Who art thou, O great mountain? before Zerubbabel thou shalt become as a plain." In Da. 2:44 the mountain which fills the whole earth (v. 35) is described as the kingdom which shall not be destroyed to all eternity. Important here is the firm and enduring nature of the mountain as well as its power. [63] In the vision in S. Bar. 36-40 a forest of trees around high and wild mountains is a figure of the nations of the world and their power. [64] In Eth. En. 18:13; 21:3; 108:4 the fallen angels are represented as burning mountains; the metaphor shows that they are powers. In Cant. 8:14 R. Simon reads הָרֵי בַשָּׁמַיִם (Mas. הָרֵי בְשָׂמִים) and takes this to refer to angel princes. [65] Eth. En. 52:2, 6 f. depicts the power of iron and gold under the metaphor of iron and gold mountains. In Gr. Bar. there flies before the sun a bird as large "as nine hills." For a similar use cf. Eth. En. 98:4: "No slave has or will become as a mountain, no maid-servant as a hill, and in the same way sin is not sent on the earth, but men have made it themselves." In bSukka, 52a R. Jehuda shows that the evil impulse is like a great mountain for the righteous; they ask then: How can we overcome (כבש) such a great mountain? Commonly in the Rabb. "mountain" is used for someone prominent. We once find [66] the exegetical principle: אֵין הֶהָרִים אֶלָּא הַזְּקֵנִים. "Mountains of the world" is a title of honour for rabbis. [67] Authoritative sayings are also compared with mountains. [68]

---

[62] For the Rabb. use of the passages → II, 715 f.
[63] The fig. of the mountain in 4 Esr. 13:6 does not have the same force, since we are referred at once to Mt. Zion.
[64] Cf. the par. in Test. Sol. 23:1: ὄρη μεταστῆναι and βασιλεῖς καταβαλεῖν.
[65] Midr. Cant., 8, 14 in Str.-B., III, 50.
[66] Ex. r., 15, 5 on 12:1 f.
[67] Midr. Cant., 23b on 7:12; Bacher Tannaiten, I², 128, n. 3.
[68] jJeb., 3a, 54 f.: "You bring my head between the two high mountains (ההרים הגבורים), between the words of the house of Shammai and those of the house of Hillel."

4. The mountainous nature of Palestine is a hindrance to the development of human life. Hence in the last time, when the nature of beasts of prey will be altered, there is also expected an alteration of inanimate nature. The hills will then be dripping with wine (Am. 9:12; Jl. 3:18; hyperbolically Test. Job 13:1; [69] Book of Elijah 6:4); [70] they will be negotiable (Sib., III, 777 f.), or they will disappear from the earth. [71] The levelling of hills and valleys is mostly associated with the return of the exiles, for whom a way is thus made, Is. 40:4; 45:2; 49:11; Bar. 5:7; Ps. Sol. 11:4. The symbolising of power by the mountain is found again in the expectation that one day the Mt. of Olives, which overlooks the temple hill, will disappear (Zech. 14:4; Leqach tob, → n. 71) and Mt. Zion will be higher than all other hills (Mi. 4:1; Is. 2:2). [72] Its influence is also seen in the fact that the destruction of the earth in its present form is primarily seen as a shaking of the mountains, the most solid and powerful of earthly things, Eth. En. 1:6; 83:4; Ass. Mos. 10:4; Asc. Is. 4:18. [73]

5. The OT, too, associates the mountain with a sense of God's nearness, → Σινᾶ. From Mt. Ebal and Mt. Gerizim God's blessing and curse are invoked on the Israelites, Dt. 11:29; 27:12 f.; Jos. 8:33. Isaac is to be offered on a mountain, Gn. 22:2. [74] During the battle against the Amalekites Moses prays on the top of the hill, Ex. 17:9 f. Elijah climbs to the top of Carmel to pray, 1 K. 18:42; Jos. Ant., 8, 344. The circumcision of the Israelites takes place on the hill Haaraloth, Jos. 5:3. The ark is set on a hill, 1 S. 7:1; 2 S. 6:3. The high-place of sacrifice (בָּמָה) [75] is for the Israelites in Canaan the oldest cultic site; Samuel offers there, 1 S. 9:12 ff., 19, 25. In Gibeon was the great high-place of sacrifice, 1 K. 3:4. Here was the dwelling-place of Yahweh (1 Ch. 16:39) and the altar of burnt offering (1 Ch. 21:29; 2 Ch. 1:3, 13). [76] David then captured the fortress of the Jebusites and made it his own residence. On the projecting height which overlooked it to the north Solomon then built the temple. The hill of Zion gradually became the only legitimate place of sacrifice and the sign of God's presence. The prophetic protest against the cult in the high-places, which led to cultic centralisation in Jerusalem

---

[69] Ed. M. R. James, TSt, V, 1 (1897), 111.

[70] Riessler, 237.

[71] This idea is Iranian (Plut. Is. et Os., 47 [II, 370b]; Gressmann, op. cit., 186; Loh. Apk. on 16:20) and is found also in Sib., VIII, 236 and Leqach tob, Nu. 24:17, Str.-B., II, 298.

[72] Eissfeldt, op. cit., 16; G. v. Rad, "Die Stadt auf dem Berge," Evangelische Theologie, 8 (1948/9), 439-447.

[73] One might also mention the idea of judgment by molten metal, another Iranian concept, cf. Chant. de la Saussaye, II, 254; Eth. En. 52:2, 6 ff.; 67:4 (on this cf. Volz Esch., 23).

[74] The LXX renders אֶרֶץ הַמֹּרִיָּה by ἡ γῆ ἡ ὑψηλή, and thus strengthens the idea of height.

[75] The etym. of בָּמָה (Accadian bamtu, "height," "eminence") is obscure, but the בָּתֵּי בָמוֹת were mostly on the tops of mountains and heights, 1 K. 14:23; 2 Ch. 21:11; the LXX often has ὑψηλόν for בָּמָה, → n. 76. A בָּמָה in the Vale of Hinnom, Jer. 7:31. Cf. L. H. Vincent, "La notion biblique du haut-lieu," Rev. Bibl., NS, 55 (1948), 245-278, 438-445.

[76] It is worth noting that the LXX does not transl. בָּמָה, but transcribes it as Βαμα, when the ref. is to a legitimate cult of Yahweh, 1 S. 9:12 ff., 19, 25; 1 Ch. 16:39; 21:29; 2 Ch. 1:13. Only at 2 Ch. 1:13 does it have ἡ ὑψηλή for בָּמָה, and at 1 K. 3:4 ὑψηλοτάτη καὶ μεγάλη (no subst.) for "the great height." When, however, בָּמָה is used for the disowned cultic sites of Israel and Canaan the LXX transl. τὰ ὑψηλά, βουνός, θυσιαστήριον, στήλη, βωμός etc. and never simply transcribes. It may be suspected that even the temple site was an ancient Canaanite high-place of sacrifice, Schmidt, 84 f.

(Dt. 12:2-9), was not directed against the siting of cultic centres on mountains, but against the Canaanite ideas and acts associated with the centres. The view that the God of Israel is a mountain God is specifically repudiated in 1 K. 20:23, 28 f. There remain only two lawful places of revelation in the OT, Mt. Sinai (→ Σινᾶ) and Mt. Zion (→ Σιών). These are not as such sacred mountains. It is not in keeping with the OT view when Philo calls Sinai ὄρος ὑψηλότατον καὶ ἱερώτατον τῶν περὶ τὸν τόπον, [77] or when the Samaritans refer to Mt. Gerizim as the holy and blessed hill. [78] Zion is the mountain which God has chosen. [79]

There is a similar reduction of the significance of the mountain in prophecy. Balaam comes from the mountains of the east (Nu. 23:7) and utters his prophetic sayings from a hill (Nu. 22:41; 23:9, 14, 28). The bands of prophets in Israel come from the high-place (1 S. 10:5) [80] and we are given the impression that Elijah and Elisha live in the hills (2 K. 1:9; 4:25). But we cannot show any connection between the writing prophets and the mountains. [81] The link is plain again in the pseudepigr. In S. Bar. 13:1 Baruch hears the word of coming judgment on Mt. Zion; in Apc. Abr. 9 [82] God wants to show Abraham the aeons from a high mountain; in Test. N. 5:1 we read of a vision on the Mt. of Olives; in Test. L. 2:5 ff. Levi is installed in the priestly office on the high mountain Aspis; acc. to Apc. Eliae 2 Elijah has a revelation on Mt. Seir. [83] The same is true of the NT apocrypha. [84]

6. Nor is there much mountain mythology in the OT. We find many mythical motifs, e.g., the fruitful primal mountain, perhaps the mount of the gods, Gn. 49:26; Dt. 33:15; Ps. 36:6; [85] the divine hill of Bashan, Ps. 68:15; the idea of a hill of the gods in the extreme north at least reflected in the wording of Ps. 48:2; [86] perhaps the twin-peaked mountain of the sunrise behind Zech. 6:1. [87] The clearest allusions to mythological divine mountains, however, are in the related songs in Is. 14:12 ff. and Ez. 28:11-19, [88] where

---

[77] Vit. Mos., II, 79; Spec. Leg., III, 125.

[78] Dt. r., 3, 8 on 7:14 : טורא קדיש; Gn. r., 32, 16 on 7:18 = Gn. r., 81, 3 on 35:4 : טורא בריכא; Jos. Ant., 18, 85 : τὸ Γαριζεὶν ὄρος ... ὃ ἀγνότατον αὐτοῖς ὁρῶν ὑπείληπται. Cf. Volz Esch., 330.

[79] The motif of the holy hill of Zion may be found in Ez. (the navel of the earth in 38:12); cf. also Jub. 8:19 and esp. the Treasure Cave; also Jos. Bell., 3, 52.

[80] Here, too, the LXX transcribes בָּמָה as Βαμα.

[81] Only in Ez. 40:2 is the prophet in his vision brought to a very high hill from which he can see the new temple. This very high hill is the elevated temple hill of Is. 2:2 and Mi. 4:1.

[82] G. N. Bonwetsch, Die Apk. Abrahams (1897), 21, 6.

[83] G. Steindorff, Die Apk. des Elias = TU, XVII, 3a (1899), 39.

[84] Cf. also the Book of Elijah 3, Riessler, 234; Apc. Esr. 6:12, Riessler, 135. NT Act. Andr. et Matth. 21; Act. Petri et Andreae 1; Act. Joh. 97; Herm. s., 5, 1, 1; 9, 1, 4.

[85] The exposition of Ps. 36:6 in Gn. r., 33, 1 on 8:1 = Lv. r., 27, 1 on 22:27 shows that the Rabb. connected supreme height, depth and fertility with the mountains of God in Ps. 36:6; here at most are echoes of mythological notions.

[86] LXX has τὰ πλευρὰ τοῦ βορρᾶ. This rests on another linguistically possible understanding of the Heb. יַרְכְּתַיִם. Cf. Nu. 23:7, where מֵהַרְרֵי־קֶדֶם = ἐξ ὀρέων ἀπ᾽ ἀνατολῶν suggests more than the dwelling of Balaam. Similarly Jdt. 16:3 in the song on the death of Holofernes : ἦλθεν Ασσουρ ἐξ ὀρέων ἀπὸ βορρᾶ. Cf. Gressmann, op. cit., 165. Eissfeldt, 15 refers to Mt. Zaphon.

[87] Gressmann, 170; on the hills of metal → n. 73.

[88] It is worth noting that with its rendering ἐν ὄρει ὑψηλῷ ἐπὶ τὰ ὄρη τὰ ὑψηλὰ τὰ πρὸς βορρᾶν the LXX obscures the allusion of בְּהַר מוֹעֵד בְּיַרְכְּתֵי צָפוֹן, perhaps intentionally. Cf. Gressmann, 164-170; A. Jeremias, Das AT im Lichte d. alten Orients⁴ (1930), 80, 635; Vriezen, 219-225; A. Bertholet, Hesekiel, Handbuch z. AT, I, 13 (1936) on 28:11-19.

the ref. is to the mount of the gods rather than the mount of Paradise. [89] But the decisive pt. is that here the pagan myth is used ironically in songs mocking the downfall of pagan rulers. Elsewhere pagan mythology is deliberately pushed into the background. The original idea to be deduced, perhaps, from Gn. 2:10-14, namely, that Paradise was on a hill, is of no consequence whatever to the author of the present account. Again, expectation that the mountain of the Lord in the last time will be higher than all other mountains does not mean that Mt. Zion will become Paradise on the mount of God. [90] In the OT eastern and western Semitic mountain mythology is all consciously avoided or set on the margin. In no way does the OT link the inside of the mountain with death, with the dark side of life, or with hurtful spirits.

The pseudepigr., however, take up again these motifs which had been suppressed in the course of Israel's history. In Jub. 4:26 there is ref. to 4 places which belong to God on earth : the Garden of Eden, the Mount of the East, Mt. Sinai and Mt. Zion ; it is fairly obvious that the author located Paradise, too, on a hill. The mount of God and that of Paradise are also equated in Eth. En. 24 f. and 87:3. [91] Brief mention may also be made of other speculations connected in these works with biblical mountains : with Ararat (called Lubar), Jub. 5:28; 6:1; 7:1; with the mountain on which Isaac was offered = Mt. Zion, cf. already 2 Ch. 3:1 HT, not LXX ; then esp. Treasure Cave, but not Apc. Abr. 12 f.; the fall of angels on Mt. Hermon, Slav. En. 18:4; the hiding of the holy vessels on a mountain, 2 Macc. 2:4 f.; Jos. Ant., 18, 85. If increasingly in the OT the idea that mountains suggest the suprasensual world fades from the scene, this is not because it is denied or contested. Mt. Zion is constantly called the holy mountain of God, → Σιών, and there is expectation that it will be higher than all hills. The battle is not between a sensually related and a purely spiritual view of God. It is not for an emancipation proceeding from man. What is at issue is an elevation above the world of imagery in relation to the God who acts in history. [92]

C. The Mountain in the NT.

1. As in Gk. generally, and like הַר in the OT, ὄρος in the NT means both the single "mountain" (Gerizim, Jn. 4:20 f., Sinai, Ac. 7:30 etc., Zion, Hb. 12:22 etc.) and also the "mountain range" (Mk. 5:11 etc.). In many instances the plur. is used for a "range" (Mt. 18:12; Mk. 13:14 etc.).

2. The cartography of Palestine is often reflected in the Gospels. More than one concrete illustration of the city set on a hill could be found in Palestine (Mt. 5:14). [93] In the parable of the lost sheep (Mt. 18:12) the shepherd leaves the 99 ἐπὶ τὰ ὄρη, [94] i.e., in dangerous isolation. The saying about the faith which moves mountains (Mk. 11:23 and par.; Mt. 17:20) must have been uttered in face of an actual mountain. [95] Lk. 23:30 (Hos. 10:8) also presupposes the topography of Judaea, cf. Rev. 6:15 f. [96] Similarly, Hb. 11:38 relates to events in Palestine. [97] The

[89] O. Eissfeldt, *Einleitung in d. AT* (1934), 36, 108.
[90] As against Bousset-Gressm., 283 f. Cf. v. Rad, 481 on Is. 2:2-5 : "The vision has full historical immanence and is without supporting mythology" even though the oriental myth of the mount of God lies behind it.
[91] Volz Esch., 415.
[92] Cf. M. Schmidt, *Prophet u. Tempel* (1948), 9-17.
[93] Str.-B., I, 238. Sepphoris in particular was such a city. It is unlikely that the comparison echoes Is. 2:2 (God's city on the mountain), as v. Rad suggests (*op. cit.,* 447).
[94] Materially identical with the wilderness of Lk. 15:4, G. Dalman, *Orte u. Wege Jesu³* (1924), 166 f.
[95] The demonstrative is always found, even in the related saying in Lk. 17:6. Paul alludes to the Lord's saying in 1 C. 13:2.
[96] The wish is for speedy death, so Kl., Schl., Hck. Lk. and K. H. Rengstorf Lk. (*NT Deutsch*) on 23:30. The thought in Rev. 6:15 (Loh. and Had. Apk., *ad loc.*) is that of flight from God's wrathful glance ; this is also possible in Lk.
[97] The ref. is to affliction in the Syr. persecution, the battles of the Hasmonean period (Ps. Sol. 17:17), or the flight of David or Elijah, so Rgg. and Mi. Hb., *ad loc.*

injunction of Jesus in Mk. 13:14 and par. to flee Jerusalem and go into the mountains was carried out with the flight to Pella in 66 A.D. [98] The range on the Gentile east coast of Lake Gennesaret is mentioned in Mk. 5:11. Only this verse tells us that the demoniac lived in the mountains and not just in the tombs.

Specific mountains are named : Gerizim in Jn. 4:20 f.; the hill on which Nazareth lay, Lk. 4:29; [99] the Mt. of Olives. [100] Mention of this in Lk. 19:37 and Mk. 13:3 and par. shows topographical knowledge. [101] There is not sufficient attestation for a Jewish view that the Messiah would manifest himself on the Mt. of Olives. [102] With regard to the question whether the Last Supper was the Passover it is not unimportant that one part of the Mt. of Olives (Bethphage), including Gethsemane, was in the precincts of Jerusalem, so that on the Passover night even those who had eaten the Passover might go there. [103]

3. Repeatedly the Gospels tell us that Jesus went εἰς τὸ ὄρος, Mt. 5:1 (8:1); Mk. 3:13 = Lk. 6:12; Mt. 15:29; Jn. 6:3, 15; Mk. 6:46 = Mt. 14:23; Lk. 9:28. In all these verses the transl. "he went up into the mountains" is linguistically just as good as "he went up the mountain," → 475, 479. [104] When we are told that Jesus prayed (Mk. 6:46 = Mt. 14:23; Lk. 6:12; 9:28), the related Mk. 1:35 makes it at least probable that by going εἰς τὸ ὄρος He was seeking solitude, for which there was plenty of opportunity in the high country of Galilee or Judah. [105] Else-

---

[98] Rengstorf, op. cit., on 21:20 ff.

[99] The depiction in Jn. 4:20 f. shows first-hand knowledge : "Someone who had not seen the place could not have invented it," Schl. J., 124. On Gerizim as the Samaritan place of worship v. Bau. J. and Schl. J., ad loc., also the refs. → n. 78. Whether the note on Nazareth is first-hand is disputed, cf. Dalman, 83 f.; M. Brückner, "Nazaret, die Heimat Jesu," PJB, 7 (1911), 82-84.

[100] τὸ ὄρος τῶν ἐλαιῶν is the form of the name in Mk., Mt. and Jn. 8:1; Lk. 19:37; 22:39; Act. Joh. 97. In Ac. 1:12, however, we find Ἐλαιών, gen. Ἐλαιῶνος. If this is also present in Lk. 19:29; 21:37, one would expect πρὸς τὸ ὄρος τὸ καλούμενον Ἐλαιῶνα. But we are to read ἐλαιῶν in these vv.; on the gen. in such constructions cf. Ac. 3:11; 6:9. Test. N. 5:1 has ἐν τῷ ὄρει τοῦ Ἐλαιῶνος. Jos. has the declined proper name in Ant., 7, 202, elsewhere the gen. ἐλαιῶν, Ant., 20, 169; Bell., 2, 262; 5, 70. 135. 504; 6, 157 (not 137, as in Schl. Mt. on 21:1 and Lk. on 19:29). הַר הַזֵּיתִים is biblical, Zech. 14:4 (cf. 2 S. 15:30), LXX τὸ ὄρος τῶν ἐλαιῶν. Older Rabb.[7] הַר הַמִּשְׁחָה, Schl. Mt. on 21:1 and Dalman, 278, n. 3; Bl.-Debr.[7] § 143, App.

[101] Dalman, 275; Schl. Lk., 408.

[102] The Mt. of Olives plays a role in certain ritual discussions of the Rabb., Str.-B., I, 841 f.; Dalman, 279 f. Under David there was a place of worship there (2 S. 15:32); under Solomon a high-place for Chemosh (1 K. 11:7); in Ez. 11:23 the glory of God alighted there when it had left the temple (cf. Ez. 43:2 and Rabb. speculations on this, Str.-B., I, 841 f.). Zech. 14:4 says that "in that day" God will come forth from the Mt. of Olives. But the hill will be split, and one part will fall into the Vale of Hinnom (Is. 40:4). Thus the hill which overtops the mount of the Lord will be lowered. One cannot agree with Loh. Mk. on 11:1 that this is evidence of a Jewish view that the Messiah will appear on the Mt. of Olives. Nor is this view proved by Jos. Ant., 20, 169 f. = Bell., 2, 261 f. and the Rabb. passages adduced by Lohmeyer.

[103] G. Dalman, Jesus-Jeschua (1922), 87-89; Joachim Jeremias, Die Abendmahlsworte Jesu² (1949), 30; Str.-B., II, 833 f.

[104] The art. is no obstacle, P. Fiebig, Der Erzählungsstil d. Ev. (1925), 74; examples, ibid., 68 f., 78 f., 106; Zn. Mt.⁴ (1922), 177, n. 4; J. Wellhausen, Einl. in die drei ersten Ev.² (1911), 19; Joachim Jeremias, "Die Zinne d. Tempels," ZDPV, 59 (1936), 206 and n. 3 (with additional bibl.); M. Black, An Aramaic Approach to the Gospels and Acts (1946), 68-70, and on this Jeremias, ThLZ, 74 (1949), 530.

[105] Jesus, then, does not go to the anonymous mount of God, as Jeremias suggests, op. cit., 143.

where the picture presented is certainly not that of Jesus standing alone on a mountain top, [106] for there is no hint of this at all. Mt. 28:16 does not expressly say that He went up the mountain, and nowhere is the κορυφὴ τοῦ ὄρους even mentioned, let alone emphasised. Nor do the Evangelists seem to have attached particular significance to the mountain because of the events connected with it. [107] It could be that Jesus went into the hills for the Sermon on the Mount because the voice carries well in mountain country, → 480. [108] But this would only be a secondary reason. It is more likely that Jesus went into the mountains because this made the crowds decide whether or not they would follow Him. [109] Possibly, too, the psychological effect of leaving everyday surroundings played some part. [110] More important is the fact that Jesus Himself withdraws by going up εἰς τὸ ὄρος. This is plain in Mt. 5:1 and the par. 8:18. [111] Lk. also understood it thus in 6:12. Solitude plays a part in the transfiguration and also in the last appearance of the risen Lord in Galilee, Mt. 28:16. It must be seriously asked, and is hard to decide, whether the Evangelists, esp. Mt., had more in view when they mentioned the mountain. Were they perhaps thinking of specific mountain incidents in the OT? [112] Thus the introduction to the Sermon on the Mount has often raised the question whether the choice of a mountain by Mt., and indeed by Jesus Himself, [113] was intended as an antithetical ref. to the mount of the Law in the OT, esp. in view of the antitheses in the Sermon on the Mount. One is also tempted to go further and set all the mountain references in Mt. in a systematic relationship. [114] But Mt. himself did nothing to clarify any such connections. As a parallel to Moses one would expect ἀνέβη εἰς τὴν κορυφὴν τοῦ ὄρους, Ex. 19:20. To a Palestinian ἀνέβη εἰς τὸ ὄρος could hardly mean any more than that He went up into the mountains. [115] That the ascension took place on the Mt. of Olives is only hinted at in Lk. 24:50 and Ac. 1:12.

4. The transfiguration took place on Mt. Tabor acc. to an ancient ecclesiastical tradition. In favour of this is the fact that when He came down not only the crowd but scribes, too, were gathered around the disciples who had been left behind. But Tabor is not isolated, [116] and one would expect an isolated place for the transfiguration. Nor is it likely that from Caesarea Philippi Jesus would go to Tabor, where He could hardly expect concealment. If the transfiguration did in fact take place on Tabor, this is not important for the Evangelists, since they do not give the name of the mountain. It is not for them a holy mountain, as 2 Pt. 1:18 calls it. They find it worth noting that the mountain was high. This suggests that they climbed to the top. Jesus was not merely

---

[106] K. L. Schmidt, Der Rahmen d. Gesch. Jesu (1919), 109, cf. 194.

[107] So Loh. Mk. on 3:13: "The site of this call is 'the mountain,' not just an elevation in 'the mountains'; it is the theatre of special divine mysteries and special divine revelation, as already in the OT and also in other ancient religions; it is holy, and is known by what took place on it."

[108] J. Sickenberger, Leben Jesu nach d. vier Ev. (1932), II, 15: "The mountain as a natural pulpit." Cf. Mk. 4:1.

[109] Schl. Mt., 128 f.

[110] Cf. the appearing of the Baptist in the desert.

[111] Schl. Mt., 128.

[112] L. Goppelt, Typos = BFTh, II, 43 (1939), 84, n. 1: "It seems that Jesus and the Evangelists, in the choice of localities, had also in view the typological significance of the hour. We have thus to think of the role of the mountain in the stories of Moses and Elijah, and also in the Gospels." P. Feine-J. Behm, Einl. in das NT⁹ (1950), 52.

[113] Cf. → A. J. Wilkens, Der König Israels, I, "Die urchr. Botschaft," 1 (1934), 83.

[114] Wilkens, op. cit., 209, 210 f.

[115] Cf. Dalman, op. cit. (→ n. 94), 166 f.

[116] Dalman, 204; Zn. Mt. and Schl. Mt., on 17:1; but cf. T. Soiron, Das Ev. u. die heiligen Stätten in Palästina (1929), 110.

seeking solitude; He also wanted to bring the feelings and thoughts of the disciples closer to the world of God. Jesus is thus using the evocative significance of the mountain. The mount of temptation mentioned in Mt. 4:8, though not expressly in Lk., is not a mountain which can be localised in the wilderness of Judah. Indeed, no single mountain in Judah stands out as a ὑψηλὸν λίαν. Surveying all the kingdoms of the world is naturally represented as looking out from a high mountain. [117] The simple ἀναγαγών of Lk. 4:5 is obviously a more spiritual nuance. Rev. 21:10 (with allusion to Ez. 40:2) is clearly a looking ἐν πνεύματι. Here the idea of being on a great and high mountain serves to suggest the surveying of an event which encompasses both heaven and earth. There is no relating of the mountain to prophetic vision; this is completely absent from Rev. [118]

5. Important are the sayings about mountains in an eschatological context. Lk. 3:4 f. gives a wider range to the verses in Is. 40:3 ff., which are also adduced in Mk. and Mt. The reason for this extension is to be found in the last clause καὶ ὄψεται πᾶσα σάρξ τὸ σωτήριον τοῦ θεοῦ. This is why there is also quotation of the saying which promises the levelling of the monutains for the return of the exiled Israelites, → 481. As concerns the "great mountain burning with fire" in Rev. 8:8, there is no need to look for contemporary events like the eruption of Vesuvius in 79 A.D. [119] On the other hand, the formal analogies in Eth. En. (→ 480) are materially quite different. The mountain expresses power. If it burns with fire, this means that its power is destructive. Rev. 6:14; 16:20 goes beyond the OT expectation that the mountains will be levelled. A specific state of the earth is not altered; the shaking of the mountains and islands in 6:14 announces the approaching shaking of heaven and earth. In 16:20 the mountains and islands disappear altogether, and the climax comes in 20:11 when heaven and earth perish. [120]

> For the disappearance of heaven and earth there are par. in Persian eschatology (→ n. 71), but not for that of the islands. Mountains and islands are typical parts of the ancient earth. In the OT the isles symbolise the Gentiles living far off in ungodly security; the mountains are signs of earthly power, → n. 2; 480. Hence the shaking of mountains and islands in 6:14 is the shaking of pagan power and security, and their destruction in 16:20 is a symbolical anticipation of judgment on Babylon. The eschatological disappearance of the mountains in Rev. is not balanced by the appearing of a mountain of God or Paradise. The expectation of Mi. 4:1 f. and Is. 2:2 is not taken up. In view of the many OT echoes in Rev., and its highly symbolical language, this can hardly be an accident. It may be compared with Jn. 4:20-24, which does not contrast the cultic worship of God with spiritual worship, but which has in view the eschatological consummation which has begun on earth in Christ. [121] The temple and altar have no place in the new world where God dwells among men (Rev. 21:3) and they may see His face (22:4). But with the temple and altar the mountain also disappears as the symbol of the worship of the distant God, → n. 36. But since the consummation has still to come, the evocative character of the mountain is as little disputed as in the OT, → 483. Thus Jesus takes the three disciples up the mount of transfiguration, → 485 f.

---

[117] For examples cf. A. Meyer, "Die evangelischen Berichte über d. Versuchung Jesu," *Festgabe f. H. Blümner* (1914), 460 f.; S. Bar. 76:3.

[118] Gressmann, 166, 181 is wrong when he says that the great and high hill is to uphold the holy city, Jerusalem. There is no such idea. H. Gunkel, *Zum religionsgeschichtlichen Verständnis d. NT* (1910), 49 is also wrong when he says that this mountain is originally the mount of heaven. Clemen, 404 rightly sees a standard feature; he refers to Luc. Charon, 2.

[119] Zn. Apk., *ad loc.*

[120] This progression is emphasised in Had. Apk. on 16:20. Loh. Apk. on 6:14 wrongly suggests the levelling of mountains.

[121] Bu. J. on 4:23.

The seven hills of Rome are called ὄρος, → 475. If the seven hills of Rev. refer to these (Rev. 17:9), no more need be said about the use of ὄρος here. Now 4 Esr. 12:11 says that the 4th beast of Da. 7 is Rome, thus giving the beast a definite place in temporal history. Rev. 13:2, however, gives the beast the features of all the beasts in Da. and thus rules out a ref. to temporal history. Within this framework the explanation that the hills are the hills of Rome does not fit too well. In Rev. statements are constantly made about Babylon which refer, not to a single empire, but to a power which spans the centuries. [122] Emphasis is also placed, not on the political power of the sword, but on the seductive power of the culture, wealth, earthly self-security and worldly pleasure-seeking of Babylon. It is also hard to interpret the ten horns of 17:12 historically, → III, 670 f. Hence an understanding of the hills is to be sought in some other direction. In the ancient Orient (→ n. 2; 479), and also in the Rabb. (→ 480), mountain is a common expression for power, including political power. Since seven is in Rev. the number of fulness and completeness (→ II, 632 f.), the seven hills are seven, i.e., the totality of, world powers, and these are identical with the seven kings. [123] Rev. 16:20 points in the same direction, → 486. Babylon symbolises the Johannine κόσμος. The detailed description of Babylon in Rev. 17 f., as noted above, reminds us strongly of 1 Jn. 2:16. The world is enthroned on all the world powers, the hills, and antichrist, the beast, has the nature of these powers (= ἐκ τῶν ἑπτά ἐστιν, 17:11). [124]

Foerster

---

† ὀρφανός

1. ὀρφανός, Lat. *orbus,* "bereaved," "without parents or children," is mostly used in class. Gk. in the lit. sense of "orphaned," "orphan," so from Hom. Od., 20, 68. The word is used as both adj. (two or three endings) and noun. Of children Eur. El., 914: ὀρφανὴ φίλου πατρός, Plat. Leg., XI, 926c; Plut. Aetia Graeca, 12 (II, 293d). Of parents, Eur. Hec., 149: ὀρφανὸς παιδός, Plat. Leg., V, 730c-d: ὥστε ζώντων καὶ μὴ ἑταίρων καὶ παίδων σχεδὸν ὁμοίως ὀρφανὸν αὐτῷ γενέσθαι τὸν βίον. Common on pap., esp. petitions: τοὺς ἀδικουμένους ὀρφανο[ύς], ἡγεμὼν δέσποτα, ἐκδικεῖν εἴωθεν τὸ μεγαλεῖον τὸ σόν· ἑαυτὸς το[ί]νυν ὀρφανὸς καταλελιμμένης στερηθεὶς ἑκατέρων τῶν γονέων οὐκ ὀλίγ[ον] ἀδικοῦμαι. [1]

In the LXX ὀρφανός (Mas. יָתוֹם) is usually associated with χήρα, Is. 1:17: κρίνατε ὀρφανῷ καὶ δικαιώσατε χήραν, Ez. 22:7: ὀρφανὸν καὶ χήραν κατεδυνάστευον ἐν σοί, and many other verses where the peculiar helplessness of orphans and widows brings them together. So often in Philo, e.g., Spec. Leg., II, 108; Som., II, 273; Decal., 42.

ὀρφανός is also used in a transf. sense for "abandoned," "left," "deprived," "destitute." But this use is not common. Ps.-Plat. Alc., 147a: ὀρφανὸς ἐπιστήμης; epigram in Paus., 1, 13, 3: ὀρφανὰ κεῖται σκῦλα, cf. also Philo Spec. Leg., IV, 179: σχεδὸν δὲ καὶ τὸ σύμπαν Ἰουδαίων ἔθνος ὀρφανοῦ λόγον ἔχει [2] ... τῷ δ' ἥκιστά τις συναγωνίζεται νόμοις ἐξαιρέτοις χρωμένῳ.

---

[122] 14:8: πάντα τὰ ἔθνη, cf. also 17:4 f.; 18:3; and again 17:6; 18:24.
[123] On the equation of kingdom and ruler v. W. Foerster, *Die Bilder in Offenbarung,* 12 f., 17 f.; ThStKr, 104 (1932), 297; → n. 64.
[124] This means that antichrist does not come during the empire under which the divine lives. This agrees with Paul, Foerster, *op. cit.,* 300 f.

ὀ ρ φ α ν ό ς. [1] Pap. de Théadelphie, ed. P. Jouguet (1911), 19, 4 ff. (4th cent. A.D.). For further examples cf. Preisigke Wört., *s.v.*
[2] I.e., to be regarded as orphaned = abandoned. Cf. ψ 9:38, where ὀρφανός is used fig. alongside ταπεινός; cf. 1 Εσδρ. 3:19; Is. 47:8.

2. ὀρφανός occurs twice in the NT.[3] The first instance is in Jm. 1:27, which is under OT influence : θρησκεία καθαρὰ καὶ ἀμίαντος παρὰ τῷ θεῷ καὶ πατρὶ αὕτη ἐστίν, ἐπισκέπτεσθαι ὀρφανοὺς καὶ χήρας ἐν τῇ θλίψει αὐτῶν. Jm. is here making a common OT demand, namely, to protect orphans and widows, as in Ex. 22:21: πᾶσαν χήραν καὶ ὀρφανὸν οὐ κακώσετε, Dt. 24:17: οὐκ ἐκκλινεῖς κρίσιν προσηλύτου καὶ ὀρφανοῦ καὶ χήρας.[4]

Later Judaism regards caring for an orphan as a meritorious work : bSanh., 19b : "... this teaches thee that if anyone brings up an orphan in his house Scripture reckons it to him as if he had begotten it." Midr. Est., 2, 5 (93a): "Who is he then who at any time shows mercy (does a good work)? Say : it is he who brings up an orphan in his house."[5] In Judaism orphans were under special legal protection and had a series of special privileges, some of which go back to ancient times, while some arose in later Judaism.[6] Jm. 1:27 is the first admonition to care for orphans in a Chr. writing. We then find many such admonitions in post-NT works, Barn., 20, 2; Herm. m., 8, 10; s., 1, 8; 5, 3, 7; 9, 26, 2; Pol., 6, 1 etc.[7]

The other NT occurrence of ὀρφανός is at Jn. 14:18 : οὐκ ἀφήσω ὑμᾶς ὀρφανούς, ἔρχομαι πρὸς ὑμᾶς.

This use reminds us of many passages in Gk. lit.[8] Plat. Phaed., 116a depicts the feelings of the pupils left behind by Socrates : ἀτεχνῶς ἡγούμενοι ὥσπερ πατρὸς στερηθέντες διάξειν ὀρφανοὶ τὸν ἔπειτα βίον, i.e., when left by their teacher they feel completely orphaned or bereaved.[9] For a similar use cf. Epict. Diss., III, 24, 15 : ᾔδει γάρ, ὅτι οὐδείς ἐστιν ἄνθρωπος ὀρφανός, ἀλλὰ πάντων ἀεὶ καὶ διηνεκῶς ὁ πατήρ ἐστιν ὁ κηδόμενος.

Acc. to Jn. 14:18 the Lord assures His disciples in His final words that even though He is going from them He is not really leaving them. We are not to suppose that Jesus is here representing Himself as a father and His disciples as children who will be orphaned when He leaves them. ὀρφανός is simply used in a fig. sense for "abandoned." There is also, perhaps, a hint of the defencelessness of the orphan : "I will not leave you unprotected." For the thought of ἔρχομαι πρὸς ὑμᾶς, and the exegetical difficulties of the verse, esp. in relation to non-abandonment and coming, cf. the comm. → II, 673.

Seesemann

---

[3] In Mk. 12:40 only D and few other witnesses have καὶ ὀρφανῶν after τῶν χηρῶν; this is surely a secondary interpolation.
[4] Cf. also Dt. 10:18; 27:19; Job 29:12; ψ 9:34; 67:5; 145:9; Is. 1:17; Jer. 5:28; 22:3; Ez. 22:7; Zech. 7:10; Sir. 4:10; 35:14.
[5] Cf. also Str.-B., IV, 536-558 on the private altruism of ancient Judaism, 559-610 on works of charity in ancient Judaism, *passim* ; also Schl. Jk., *ad loc.*; cf. also 1 Tm. 5:10.
[6] Cf. M. Cohn, "Jüdisches Waisenrecht," *Zschr. f. vergleichende Rechtswissenschaft,* 37 (1920), 417-445; M. Grunwald, "Jüdische Waisenfürsorge in alter u. neuer Zeit," *Mitteilungen zur jüdischen Volkskunde,* 23 (1922), 3-29; M. Cohn, Art. "Waise" in Jüd. Lex., V, 1281-1283.
[7] For many other instances cf. O. Gebhardt-A. Harnack-T. Zahn, *Patrum Apostolicorum Opera,* III (1877) on Herm. m., 8, 10.
[8] Cf. Pr.-Bauer[3], *s.v.* ὀρφανός 2. and Bau. J. on 14:18 and 16:32.
[9] Cf. also the similar saying in Luc. Pergr. Mort., 6.

ὅσιος, ὁσίως, ἀνόσιος, ὁσιότης

† ὅσιος, ὁσίως.

1. ὅσιος in Greek Usage.

a. Of actions which by ancient sanction are regarded as "sacred," "lawful" and "acc. to duty," cf. Lat. *sanctus*. [1] ὅσιος is perhaps connected with the root found also in ἔθος and ἦθος. [2] It makes no odds whether the sanctioning force is divine precept, natural law or ancient custom. ὅσιος thus corresponds (cf. the German *fromm*) to what a man does by disposition in accordance with his inward attitude and the inner acceptance of what is felt to be binding. [3] This is more than cultic, legal, opportunist, or forced action. [4] Nor is it limited to action *vis-à-vis* the gods. [5] In content it is what is right and good from the standpoint of morality and religion. [6] ἡ ὁσία is "holy custom," "divine or natural law." [7] There may be severe conflicts between obedience to a human commandment and what is felt to be truly moral. ὅσια πανουργήσασα Antigone gives her brother burial, Soph. Ant., 74. Acceptance of what is demanded by ancient custom can lead to ὅσιος φόνος, Demosth., 23, 74; Philo Sacr. AC, 130. ὅσιος often refers to pious duty to relatives, Hdt., III, 19, 65. Thus by Gk. judgment incest violates the eternal ordinances and hence is one of the things which are μηδαμῶς ὅσια, θεομιση δέ, Plat. Leg., VIII, 838b. More restricted than ὅσιος is → ἱερός (Lat. *sacer*), i.e., what is holy to the gods, the holy in a priestly sense, [8] and also νόμιμος, what is right by human law, Plat. Leg., IX, 861d. ὅσιος is often used along with θέμις, what is established and

---

ὅ σ ι ο ς. J. H. H. Schmidt, *Synonymik d. gr. Sprache*, IV (1886), 321-345; L. Schmidt, *Die Ethik d. alten Griechen*, I (1882), 308, 338 etc. (*v.* Index, *s.v.*); E. Meinke, "Der platonische u. der nt.liche Begriff d. ὁσιότης," ThStKr, 57 (1884), 743-768; Trench, 307 ff.; Cr.-Kö., 822-825; J. Kalitsunakis, Ἡ ἐν τῷ Εὐθύφρονι Πλατωνικὴ ἐκδοχὴ τοῦ ὁσίου καὶ ἡ χρονολόγησις τοῦ διαλόγου, Πρακτικὰ καὶ Ἀκαδημίας Ἀθηνῶν, 5 (1930), 395-420; cf. also Bibliotheca philologica classica, 57 (1930), 53; U. v. Wilamowitz-Moellendorff, *Der Glaube der Hellenen*, I (1931), 15 ff., 204 ff.; II (1932), 76-81, 118, 328, n. 2, Index, *s.v.*; J. C. Bolkestein, *Ὅσιος en Εὐσεβής*, Diss. Utrecht (1936); L. Gulkowitsch, "Die Entwicklung des Begriffes *hāsīd* im AT," Acta et Commentationes Universitatis Tartuensis, Vol. 32, 4 (1934); also "Die Bildung des Begriffes *hāsīd*, I (1935), Acta et Commentationes Universitatis Tartuensis (Dorpatensis), Vol. 37, 6 (1936); W. J. Terstegen, *Εὐσεβής en ὅσιος in het Grieksch taalgebruik na de IVe eeuw*, Diss. Utrecht (1941); N. Glueck, "Das Wort *ḥesed* im at.lichen Sprachgebrauche als menschliche u. göttliche gemeinschaftsgemässe Verhaltungsweise," ZAW Beih., 47 (1927); M. H. A. L. H. van der Valk, "Zum Worte ὅσιος," *Mnemosyne*, III, 10 (1941/2), 113-140; H. Jeanmaire, "Le substantif Hosia et sa signification comme terme technique dans le vocabulaire religieux," *Revue des Études Grecques*, 58 (1945), 66-89.

[1] Acc. to Aug. De Fide et Symbolo, 19 *sanctus* = *quod sanctione antiqua et praecepto firmatum*.

[2] H. Ehrlich, *Zur indogermanischen Sprachgeschichte* (1910), 52; Boisacq, 721, 291 conjectures dependence on a stem *soto*, cf. ἐτάζω.

[3] Plat. Euthyphr., 6e : τὸ μὲν τοῖς θεοῖς προσφιλὲς ὅσιον, Leg., IV, 716e-717a. To worship the gods is not the whole of piety ; temple inscr. of Epidaurus, Theophr. in Porphyr. Abst., II, 19 : ἀγνεία δ' ἐστὶ φρονεῖν ὅσια.

[4] Philo Det. Pot. Ins., 21: θρησκείαν ἀντὶ ὁσιότητος ἡγούμενος.

[5] Thuc., I, 71, 6 : loyalty to allies ; Aesch. Sept. c. Theb., 1010 f.: death for one's country; Hippocr. De Jusiurando, CMG, I, 1, p. 6, 3 : conscientiousness of the doctor ; Eur. Cyc., 125 : φιλόξενοι δὲ χὤσιοι περὶ ξένους.

[6] Theogn., 132 (Diehl², I, 2, p. 12): ὁσίη δίκη, Isoc., 12, 187: οὐδὲν οὔθ' ὅσιον οὔτε καλόν ἐστι τῶν μὴ μετὰ δικαιοσύνης καὶ λεγομένων καὶ πραττομένων.

[7] Hom. Od., 16, 423; 22, 412.

[8] Plat. Leg., IX, 857b: ἱερὰ ἢ ὅσια, divine or human property ; Thuc., II, 52, 3 : ἱερὰ καὶ ὅσια, divine and human ordinances. Cf. Plut. Thes., 25 (I, 11d). → βέβηλος, I, 604.

sacred by origin, [9] and εὐσεβής, what is done in fear of the gods, esp. in knowledge of and obedience to cultic demands. [10] Very commonly we find ὅσιος and δίκαιος together ; the combined expression indicates that which corresponds to divine and human statute (*fas et jus*). [11] ὅσιος is frequently used of loyal and conscientious discharge of office in inner commitment to eternal laws, Ditt. Syll.[3], 91, 16 : ταμιεύειν.

b. As a quality of persons who feel inward awe before the gods and eternal laws, and who act accordingly, "pious." Eteocles is ὅσιος when he falls fighting for his country, Aesch. Sept. c. Theb., 1010. Socrates was δίκαιος ... τὰ πρὸς ἀνθρώπους καὶ ὅσιος τὰ πρὸς θεούς, M. Ant., VII, 66, 3. [12] In a narrower sense ὅσιος is used of initiates (Aristoph. Ra., 336 : ὅσιοι μύσται, 327: ὅσιοι θιασῶται), esp. Orphic initiates (οἱ ὅσιοι, Plat. Resp., II, 363c), perhaps because of the purification which confers consecration. [13] Of the judge, who in the view of antiquity discharges a religious function, Jos. Bell., 1, 622 says : πᾶς δικαστὴς ὅσιος. [14] οἱ ὅσιοι is used by Philo for the Essenes, Omn. Prob. Lib., 91. Only rarely is ὅσιος used of God Himself. We find this esp. in Orphic circles in the sense of "holy," "pure," [15] though it should not be forgotten that the Gk. world did not attain to the strict biblical concept of holiness.

c. Of things, "sanctified," "pure," "absolved" : χεῖρες, Aesch. Choeph., 378 esp. in prayer ; στόμα, Emped. Fr., 3, 2 (Diels[5], I, 30, 1); Sib., IV, 23.

2. Septuagint.

In the LXX ὅσιος is used predominantly for חָסִיד. which for its part is used only of persons (24 times in Ps., Dt. 33:8; 2 Βασ. 22:26). [16] ὅσιος is never used in the LXX for קָדֹשׁ (→ ἅγιος, I, 91 f.) or צַדִּיק (→ δίκαιος, esp. II, 186, 185), and it is plainly distinct from καθαρός (→ III, 417), θρησκός (→ III, 158) and → εὐσεβής. חָסִיד, an intr. construct, denotes the one who exercises חֶסֶד (→ II, 479). The latter term is correlative to בְּרִית and means conduct acc. to right and duty, as where there is a bond (relatives, allies, guests etc.). In this respect it differs from voluntary favour. [17] חָסִיד is the one who observes such obligations. It can thus be used of God (Ps. 145:17; in Dt. 32:4 ὅσιος is used for יָשָׁר), but it is much more frequently used of men. In the

---

[9] Hes. Op., 136 f.; Aristot. Eleg., 3 (Diehl[2], 1, 116); Eur. Iph. Taur., 1035 ff.; Philo Leg. Gaj., 194.
[10] In the dialogue Euthyphron Plat. distinguishes between ὅσιος and δίκαιος, εὐσεβής; 12d : μέρος τὸ ὅσιον τοῦ δικαίου, 15b : thus the ὅσιον seems to be τὸ τοῖς θεοῖς φίλον, 14d : ἐπιστήμη ἄρα αἰτήσεως καὶ δόσεως θεοῖς ὁσιότης, cf. O. Kern, *D. Religion d. Griechen,* I (1926), 273 f.; J. Geffcken, *Griech. Lit.-Gesch.,* II (1934), 66, though cf. 51 f., n. 186; F. Überweg-K. Praechter, *Grundriss d. Gesch. d. Philosophie d. Altertums*[12] (1926), 234-236; O. Kunsemüller, *Die Herkunft der platonischen Kardinaltugenden,* Diss. Munich (1935), 17 and n. 58.
[11] Ditt. Syll.[3], 800, 21: πρός τε θεοὺς καὶ πάντας ἀνθρώπους ὁσίως καὶ δικαίως, Plat. Gorg., 507b : καὶ μὴν περὶ μὲν ἀνθρώπους τὰ προσήκοντα πράττων δίκαι᾽ ἂν πράττοι, περὶ δὲ θεοὺς ὅσια, Polyb., 22, 10, 8 (v. Pr.-Bauer[3], s.v.); Xenoph. Hist. Graec., I, 7, 19.
[12] Jos. Ant., 10, 83 : μήτε πρὸς θεὸν ὅσιος μήτε πρὸς ἀνθρώπους ἐπιεικής, 19, 332 : Only the ὅσιος may draw near to the temple (with εὐαγής).
[13] Cf. ὁσιοῦν of ritual cleansing and expiation, Eur. Or., 515; βάκχος ἐκλήθην ὁσιωθείς, Eur. Fr., 475, 15 (TGF, 505); τὰς ὁσίους ἁγιστείας, of Eleusinian consecrations, Ps.-Plat. Ax., 371d; but Bolkestein, 157 contests the view of Rohde, *Psyche*[3], I, 288, n. 1 that the basic meaning of ὅσιος is "pure," from which by no means all the instances can be derived, esp. the oldest in Theogn., 131 f. (Diehl[2], I, 2, p. 12).
[14] For further examples in Jos. and Philo cf. Schl. Theol. d. Judt., 99 f.
[15] Orph. Hymni (ed. Quandt), 77, 2 : ἡ Μούσας τέκνωσ᾽ ἱεράς, ὁσίας, Orph. Argonautica, 27; CIG, 3830, 3594.
[16] Elsewhere once each rendered ἐλεήμων (Jer. 3:12), εὐλαβούμενος (Prv. 2:8), εὐλαβής (Mi. 7:2, vl. εὐσεβής), οἱ υἱοί μου (vl. ψ 88:20; 2 Ch. 6:41).
[17] Glueck, 13, 20 f., 31 ff.

cultus the righteous are pledged to obedience to God (Ps. 50:5). Since חָסִיד as used in religion expresses the relation of faithfulness to Yahweh, it is used predominantly with gen. or suffix. The חֲסִידֵי יהוה or οἱ ὅσιοι αὐτοῦ [18] are originally the whole cultic community of Israel, Ps. 149:1 f.; 79:1 f.; 132:9, 16 = 2 Ch. 6:41. Nevertheless, in the course of a development which showed that the community also included some who were ungodly, the concept narrowed itself to a smaller circle of those who for their part were willing to fulfil the obligations of the covenant. The word becomes a self-designation of the righteous who call themselves οἱ ὅσιοι in the abs., Ps. 12:1; 18:26; 32:6. [19] חָסִיד is an ideal, and thus acquires an ethico-religious content. It is par. to תָּמִים (Ps. 18:26) [20] and close to צַדִּיק. But if in the latter the main pt. is uprightness in fulfilment of God's demands, what counts in חָסִיד - ὅσιος is rather what follows from dutiful acceptance of relationship to others (men or God). [21] Toward the end of OT development the חֲסִידֵי יהוה are the core of the people which remains loyal to Yahweh. [22] They are the quiet ones in the land who are faithful to the Law and who oppose the Philhellenic party, esp. in the Syrian period. In the Maccabean age they are an organised group, 1 Macc. 2:42 : συναγωγὴ Ασιδαίων, cf. Ps. 149:1: קְהַל חֲסִידִים. For the sake of their faith they are prepared to give up their quiet love of peace and enter the struggle for freedom, the Hasideans in 1 Macc. 7:13; 2 Macc. 14:6. But they withdraw again from the political struggle when this begins to serve other than religious ends. Their spiritual descendants in NT days are the Pharisees.

In the 8 other instances of its use in the LXX ὅσιος is (a) personal, twice for תָּמִים (Prv. 2:21; Am. 5:10), once each for תָּם (Prv. 29:10), טָהוֹר (Prv. 22:11), זַךְ (Prv. 20:11), יָשָׁר (Dt. 32:4 of God), and (b) neuter, for חֶסֶד at Is. 55:3 : διαθήσομαι ὑμῖν ... τὰ ὅσια Δαυιδ τὰ πιστά, i.e., the unassailable proofs of grace which Yahweh will give in faithfulness to His promises (cf. 2 S. 7:8-16; 2 Ch. 6:42), for שָׁלוֹם (Dt. 29:18), and for תֹּם (Prv. 10:29).

We read again of the group of ὅσιοι τοῦ θεοῦ in Ps. Sol. 8:23; 13:10; 14:3, 10. [23]

3. The New Testament.

It is surprising that ὅσιος, which became a tt. in the OT, should occur only 8 times in the NT (5 in quotations), also once as an adv. in the current phrase ὁσίως καὶ δικαίως, 1 Th. 2:10. [24] ὅσιος does not occur in the Gospels, the main Pauline epistles, or the Catholic epistles. With ἀνόσιος, it is common only in the Pastorals whose vocabulary is more strongly Hellenistic. ὅσιος, which has no eschatological core (→ εὐσεβής), which has its historical roots elsewhere (→ 490), and whose content is more self-righteous than is in keeping with the NT community, is not a leading concept in the vocabulary of this community, and in particular it is not a term which believers use for themselves, → ἅγιος, I, 105-109.

a. As a quotation (Dt. 32:4; ψ 144:17), ὁ ὅσιος is used for God in two hymns in Rev., 16:5, and in the stronger form ὁ μόνος ὅσιος 15:4. God is righteous and

---

[18] ψ 4:3; 30:23; 36:28; 49:5; 78:2 (cf. 1 Macc. 7:17); 84:8; 96:10; 115:6 etc.
[19] Cf. R. Kittel, Die Ps. [5, 6] (1919), 217 ff., Exc. on Ps. 64.
[20] Gulkowitsch, Entwicklung, 25 : antonym רְשָׁעִים ψ 36:28 (ἄνομοι, ἀσεβεῖς).
[21] Gulkowitsch, Entwicklung, 38; ψ 84:8 with ἐπὶ τοὺς ἐπιστρέφοντας πρὸς αὐτὸν καρδίαν, ψ 85:2 with τὸν ἐλπίζοντα ἐπὶ σέ, ψ 144:17 with δίκαιος, 96:10 with οἱ ἀγαπῶντες τὸν κύριον.
[22] The circles of the 'anawim are their spiritual ancestors, R. Kittel, op. cit., Exc. on Ps. 86:5.
[23] Cf. 9:3; synon. 4:23 οἱ φοβούμενοι τὸν κύριον, 4:25 οἱ ἀγαπῶντες θεόν, the opposing party 14:6 οἱ ἁμαρτωλοί, παράνομοι.
[24] Twice ἐν ὁσιότητι καὶ δικαιοσύνῃ, Lk. 1:75; Eph. 4:24; twice ἀνόσιος, Past.

holy in the fact that He vindicates persecuted believers and exercises judgment on malefactors. He and He alone is worthy to be praised and perfectly blameless, maintaining righteousness and truth without abridgment or disruption, and bringing salvation by His acts.

b. ὅσιος occurs three times in quotations in the speeches in Ac. In 2:27 and 13:35, in Messianic interpretation of Ps. 16, [25] the sing. τὸν ὅσιόν σου is used of Christ, the Messiah. He is in the full sense the "holy one of God." In Ac. 13:34 Is. 55:3 (→ 491) is referred to Christ. To Him, the promised shoot of David, are given the demonstrations of grace (τὰ ὅσια Δαυίδ) promised to the forefathers, and especially preservation from corruption and exaltation over death. In Hb. 7:26 Jesus as perfect High-priest is called ὅσιος, ἄκακος, ἀμίαντος. In mind and conduct He perfectly fulfils the divine requirements. Hence, as one who is wholly free from sin, He does not need to bring an atoning offering for Himself, like the imperfect priests of the OT.

c. The word group ὅσιος is in the NT predominantly applied to men, four times alongside δίκαιος. Echoed here is not the old חָסִיד, with its roots in the covenant, but the general Gk. use for "what is right and good before God and man." Only once in 1 Th. 2:10 does Paul use the current ὁσίως καὶ δικαίως (strengthened by ἀμέμπτως) of his conscientious discharge of office, which satisfies both divine and human law, fas et jus (→ 490). In the Past., where alone in the NT ὅσιος (→ ἀνόσιος, infra) is common, the Hellenistic use and content predominates. Thus in the list of positive qualities required in a bishop we find ὅσιος alongside δίκαιος (Tt. 1:8). The bishop must have a mind which is committed to God if he is to be able to fulfil his office faithfully. 1 Tm. 2:8 also follows Gk. usage with its command to lift up ὁσίους χεῖρας to God in prayer. [26] These symbolise freedom from ungodly thought and action (cf. v. 8: χωρὶς ὀργῆς καὶ διαλογισμοῦ) → ἀνόσιος.

4. In the post-apost. fathers ὅσιος and ἀνόσιος occur only in 1 and 2 Cl.

† ἀνόσιος.

1. Of "impious" acts which transgress ancient laws, Plat. Leg., VIII, 831d ruthless avarice, Eur. Med., 796 murder of children, Eur. Hec., 714 f. violation of the law of hospitality, Soph. Ant., 1070 f., not burying the dead, Ep. Ar., 167 planning murder (with κακοποιεῖν), Philo Vit. Mos., II, 199: βεβήλων καὶ ἀνοσίων ἐνθυμημάτων, cf. 1 Cl., 1, 1 (στάσις). 2. Of "impious" persons, Aristot. Pol., I, 3, p. 1253b, 18 (without ἀρετή man is ἀνοσιώτατον καὶ ἀγριώτατον [ζῷον]); Ep. Ar., 289 (τύραννος); Philo Spec. Leg., I, 327 (with ἀσεβής); 1 Cl., 45, 4 (with ἄνομος); Porphyr. Abst., II, 50 (of one who because of his impious state is excluded from visiting the temple). Similarly in the LXX 1. of acts, Ez. 22:9 (זִמָּה, ἀνόσια ἐποίουν ἐν μέσῳ σου); Wis. 12:4: ἔργα φαρμακειῶν καὶ τελετὰς ἀνοσίους, 2. of persons, 2 Macc. 7:34; 8:32.

In the NT it occurs twice in the Past. for "impious" persons who impiously reject sacred obligations. In 1 Tm. 1:9 (with → βέβηλος, I, 604; cf. 3 Macc. 2:2) it seems to have the sense of "ungodly," but in 2 Tm. 3:2 the sequence (γονεῦσιν ἀπειθεῖς, ἀχάριστοι, ἀνόσιοι, ἄστοργοι) suggests the sense of "impious," "devoid of piety."

---

[25] Jewish theology, too, can sometimes interpret Ps. 16 Messianically, Str.-B., II, 618.
[26] Examples in Dib. Past. The expression, originally cultic (cultically clean, absolved), is already ethical in its use prior to and outside Christianity.

† ὁσιότης.

Of "personal piety," which acts out of regard for eternal ordinances. [1] This pious disposition does not have to be towards God. ὁσιότης is also piety to parents. [2] As an inner disposition ὁσιότης is found with εὐσέβεια, the external piety expressed esp. in cultic worship of the gods, [3] with θρησκεία (→ III, 156), the cultic worship of the gods, [4] or, as piety esp. toward God, with δικαιοσύνη (→ II, 192 ff.), the keeping of human laws, Philo Abr., 208. In the proclamation of Antiochus ὁσιότης is the rendering of the Zoroastrian aša (right, righteousness ; Ditt. Or., 383, 20).

In the LXX, where it occurs only 3 times, ὁσιότης is "personal piety," Dt. 9:5 (τῆς καρδίας, יֹשֶׁר), Prv. 14:32; 3 Βασ. 9:4 (תֹּם). It is common in the Apocrypha in Wis., [5] for perfect godliness, 9:3 : καὶ διέπῃ τὸν κόσμον ἐν ὁσιότητι καὶ δικαιοσύνῃ.

The word occurs in the NT only twice in the current phrase ἐν ὁσιότητι καὶ δικαιοσύνῃ. The meaning is personal piety (Lk. 1:75 the life of the righteous in the age of salvation ; Eph. 4:24 the nature of the new man). Whereas Plato, in true Gk. fashion, defines ὁσιότης as an ἐπιστήμη of right conduct toward the gods, the NT regards it as a consequence of the new birth.

Hauck

---

† ὀσμή

A. The Meaning of ὀσμή outside the NT.

ὀσμή, Ionic ὀδμή, related to the Lat. *odor,* almost always for רֵיחַ in the LXX, means "smell," a. predominantly pleasant (in the LXX, apart from sacrifices, esp. of flowers, ointments etc.), but then b. bad (Is. 34:3 of corpses, 2 Macc. 9:9 f., 12 of the rotting body of Antiochus), and finally c. neuter, Gn. 27:27 smell of clothes, Da. 3:27 (94) smell of burning, hence transf. Ex. 5:21 = "reputation."

1. The distinctive NT use cannot be understood without some knowledge of the ideas of antiquity about animal and plant physiology. These were obviously widespread in the most diverse geographical and cultural regions. Thus we find in Palestine the view that a withered tree can derive from the scent of water new powers of growth, ἀπ᾽ ὀσμῆς ὕδατος ἀνθήσει, Job 14:9. Again, Aristot., though he contests it, mentions the Pythagorean tradition, τρέφεσθαι ... ἔνια ζῷα ταῖς ὀσμαῖς, De Sensu, 5, p. 445a, 17. Scientific investigation justifies this outlook at least to the degree that it affirms

ὁ σ ι ό τ η ς. For bibl. → ὅσιος.
[1] Stob., II, 68, 9 : τὴν γὰρ ὁσιότητα ὑπογράφεσθαι δικαιοσύνην πρὸς θεούς.
[2] Diod. S., 7, 4 : τῆς τε πρὸς γονεῖς ὁσιότητος καὶ τῆς πρὸς θεοὺς εὐσεβείας.
[3] Philo Vit. Mos., I, 190; with εὐσέβεια a main virtue, Spec. Leg., IV, 135; the chief virtue of all, II, 259.
[4] Philo Det. Pot. Ins., 21 (→ 489, n. 4).
[5] 2:22; 5:19 : λήμψεται ἀσπίδα ἀκαταμάχητον ὁσιότητα, 14:30 : ἀδίκως ὤμοσαν ἐν δόλῳ καταφρονήσαντες ὁσιότητος.

ὁ σ μ ή. E. Lohmeyer, "Vom göttlichen Wohlgeruch," SAH, Vol. 10, 9 (1919); Wnd. 2 K. on 2:14-16a; E. Nestle, "Der süsse Geruch als Erweis des Geistes," ZNW, 4 (1903), 272; 7 (1906), 95 f.; H. W. Bartsch, Gnostisches Gut u. Gemeindetradition bei Ign. v. Antiochien (1940), 134-136. Cf. also H. Vorwahl, ΕΥΩΔΙΑ ΧΡΙΣΤΟΥ, ARW, 31 (1934), 400 f.; F. Pfister, Art. "Epiphanie," Pauly-W., Suppl. Vol. 4 (1924), 316; also Art. "Rauchopfer," Pauly-W., 2. Ser., I (1914), 267-286; R. O. Steuer, Über das "wohlriechende Natron" bei den alten Ägyptern (1937), 21 f., 27 f., 34-36, 42 f., 91, 95 f.; H. Bonnet, "Die Bedeutung d. Räucherungen im ägyptischen Kult," Zschr. f. ägyptische Sprache, 67 (1931), 20-28.

odours to be transitional products, exhalations made up of mist and vapour (εἰσὶ δὲ ὀσμαὶ ξύμπασαι καπνὸς ἢ ὀμίχλη), hence thinner than water but more compact than air (λεπτότεραι μὲν ὕδατος, παχύτεραι δὲ ... ἀέρος, Plat. Tim., 66e). Odours are thought of in such material terms that the idea of their power to give life (or death) is self-explanatory. The thought of energies received from scent derives ultimately from the sphere of nature.

2. These statements throw a vivid light on religious sayings about the sweet savour of the gods. [1] In accordance with what has been said these are to be taken seriously. In Gk. religious history the idea of a scent going forth from deity plays no small role in theophanies. [2] In the accounts we find a lively sense "that the odour is the agent and cause of divine life," [3] that "divine life is kindled ... by the scent, in its very breath." [4] Apart from Egyptian sources, which yield similar results, [5] Hell. burial inscr. testify esp. to this idea of the lifegiving power of ὀσμή. An example is IG, XIV, 1362, 8 ff.: [6] ἀπ' εὐόδμου χρωτὸς ἰοῦσα δρόσος ἀγγέλλη τὸν παῖδα θεοῖς φίλον ἔνδοθι κεῖσθαι, λοιβῆς καὶ θυέων ἄξιον, οὐχὶ γόων, "the fresh green which goes forth from the sweet-smelling skin shows that the boy lies there beloved by the gods, and that libations and incense are more suitable for him, not lamentation." From the deified boy there go forth scents which give living force to flowers growing out of his grave. Participation in divine life is itself mediated by odours, cf. Gk. En. 25:4, 6 : [7] The life of the righteous and pious will be given them in the blessed last time by a δένδρον εὐωδίας, a tree, from which a sweet savour goes forth (and whose fruits serve them as food, v. 5), in the proximity of God : αἱ ὀσμαὶ αὐτοῦ (sc. the tree) ἐν τοῖς ὀστέοις (the seat of life) αὐτῶν. In Mandaean writings the bringer of salvation is called "the tree of praise from whose scent each receives life," Lidz. Ginza, 59, 19 f. [8] Lidz. Liturg., 199 f. emphasises that the divine messenger is the scent which gives life to the dead.

3. The concept of living power given by scents enables us to understand the OT view that deity inhales the savour of sacrifice (this is not an attempt on the part of those who bring it to explain how the distant deity may enjoy their offering). In this sense ὀσμή is used in the LXX mainly in Gn.-Nu. The savour of sacrifice kindles in God a favourable disposition towards man (Gn. 8:21). If the sacrifice of God's people has no savour, this is a supreme sign of rejection (Lv. 26:31). Esp. in the sacrificial regulations of the Pentateuch we constantly find the statement that the offering serves as a sweet savour to God, εἰς ὀσμὴν εὐωδίας κυρίῳ (e.g., Lv. 2:12; Da. 4:37a), that it is an ὀσμὴ εὐωδίας τῷ κυρίῳ (e.g., Lv. 1:9, 13, 17). Both expressions are common and they are correlative. Ez. 6:13; 16:19; 20:28 speaks of the ὀσμή of sacrifices to idols. The original idea was that the deity was nourished by the ascending savour of the burning offering ; the scent gives power. In the OT, of course, this natural concept of God had already been superseded. Thus on the one side הריח (Lv. 26:31; Am. 5:21) takes on the very general sense of accepting the offering, and on the other it is made clear in some passages that Yahweh is not referred to the presenting of the ὀσμή. [9] In other instances a scent prevents evil powers from developing their force. Thus in Tob. 8:2 f. the hostile demon is banished by the smoke from the burning of certain inner parts of a certain fish, cf. 6:8. Fig. wisdom says of itself that it gives out a sweet savour, i.e., vitality,

---

[1] Lohmeyer.
[2] Examples in Lohmeyer, 4-7, cf. Eur. Hipp., 1391: Hippol. is made aware of the coming of Artemis by the θεῖον ὀδμῆς πνεῦμα.
[3] Lohmeyer, 13.
[4] Ibid., 3.
[5] Ibid., 18-22. Scent as the stuff of life in a realistic sense is of decisive importance in the deification of the dead, cf. the vivid examples in Steuer, 42 f., 91. "Incense" as the "scent of God"; → Bonnet.
[6] Lohmeyer, 10 f.
[7] Cf. 24:3 ff., → Lohmeyer, 26 f.
[8] Cf. Lidz. Ginza, 58-60; → Bartsch, 134 f.
[9] I owe this ref. to Würthwein, cf. E. Würthwein, "Am. 5:21-27," ThLZ, 72 (1947), 146.

the capacity for true living, Sir. 24:15. Spiritualisation of the concept of sacrifice is the basis when the righteous are summoned to give out a sweet savour in praise of God, Sir. 39:14. Nevertheless, in this formulation the more literal background is still to be seen. On the other hand, the spiritualising is emphatic in Test. L. 3:6, where the reconciling angels of the face of the Lord present ὀσμὴν εὐωδίας λογικήν in the fifth heaven.

B. ὀσμή in the NT.

There is a threefold use in the NT.

1. We find the literal sense at Jn. 12:3.

2. The idea that the scent of sacrifice is pleasing to God is increasingly taken fig. as biblical thinking frees itself from an anthropomorphic concept of God. Thus ὀσμὴ εὐωδίας simply becomes another term for sacrifice, → III, 184 ff. In the deepest sense the self-offering of Christ in death is a pleasing sacrifice, Eph. 5:2. The decisive combination with the concept of love rules out any idea that God's pleasure in the death of Jesus is aroused by a demand for the punishment of men which is satisfied herein. On the contrary, the pleasure is in the love which sacrifices itself on behalf of men. [10] The naturalistic basis of the metaphor is completely forgotten when Paul calls the financial contribution made by the Philippians an ὀσμὴ εὐωδίας, Phil. 4:18. He means that it is a sacrifice to God (cf. the conclusion of the verse), that it is pleasing to Him, again as a demonstration of love.

3. Paul also takes up the idea of the power of ὀσμή to dispense life (and death), 2 C. 2:14-16. [11] Such life-giving ὀσμή is given out by the knowledge of God in Christ. It quickens the apostle, through whom it is now effectively declared, v. 14. Thus Paul himself carries the savour which is shed abroad by Christ. In virtue of this he does God's work among those who through him are confronted by decision before God, v. 15. He carries this scent further and thereby mediates divine life. He thus becomes a carrier of this life to others through the power of God working in him, v. 16 : ἐκ ζωῆς εἰς ζωήν. In accordance with the character of the Gospel as decision he also, as its messenger, brings judgment to those who oppose it, so that the subjection to death which characterises their present existence becomes definitive. Thus the ὀσμή carries eternal death to those who do not free themselves from the power of death at work in them, ἐκ θανάτου εἰς θάνατον. Paul uses the traditional physiological [12] idea of ὀσμή to symbolise the power of God which gives life to the believer and creates the new man in him. [13]

In later development [14] the concept is naturalised again. Thus we find the idea that the outpouring of the Holy Spirit was linked with a shedding abroad of the divine savour — an obvious continuation of the line of thought last mentioned. In other connections, too, we find that the sweet scent is a demonstration of the Spirit. [15]

Delling

---

[10] The thought of Paul is thus very different from the Rabb. view that the savour of the sufferings of martyrs is well-pleasing to God, cf. for examples Str.-B., III, 497.

[11] There is no connection with the view mentioned in → n. 10. Nor is there any material link with θριαμβεύοντι (→ III, 160) in v. 14.

[12] This is not perceived by Wnd. et al.

[13] The idea is thus very different from that found elsewhere in antiquity. Thus for the Egyptians a bad smell was a symbol of death, indicating the kingdom of Satan and demons, → Vorwahl, op. cit., 400 [Bertram].

[14] On Ign. Eph., 17, 1: Christ exudes (πνέῃ) ἀφθαρσία for the Church, Bartsch, op. cit., 134-136.

[15] Nestle (1903), 272 and (1906), 95 f. with examples.

† ὀσφύς

The "hip." So lit. in class. Gk. from Aesch. (Prom., 497, opp. κῶλα); cf. Hdt., II, 40; Aristot. Hist. An., I, 13, p. 493a, 22; Ditt. Syll.³, 57, 9 (5th cent. B.C.); 1037, 2 (4th-3rd cent. B.C.).

The word is common in the LXX, e.g., 4 Βασ. 1:8 : καὶ ζώνην δερματίνην περιεζωσμένος τὴν ὀσφὺν αὐτοῦ, Ez. 9:3 : ὃς εἶχεν ἐπὶ τῆς ὀσφύος αὐτοῦ τὴν ζώνην. Esp. common is the phrase (περι)ζωννύναι τὴν ὀσφύν etc., e.g., Ex. 12:11; αἱ ὀσφύες ὑμῶν περιεζωσμέναι, Jer. 1:17: καὶ σὺ περίζωσαι τὴν ὀσφύν σου καὶ ἀνάστηθι, cf. 4 Βασ. 4:29; 9:1; Job 40:7; Jer. 13:4; Ez. 9:11. The expression "to gird up one's loins" means to belt the garment which is worn ungirdled in the house or in times of relaxation, with a view to greater mobility for work,[1] for travel, for battle etc. This is so much a current phrase in the OT that it can be said of the Messiah in Is. 11:5 : καὶ ἔσται δικαιοσύνη ἐζωσμένος τὴν ὀσφὺν αὐτοῦ καὶ ἀληθείᾳ εἰλημένος τὰς πλευράς, where ὀσφύς loses its lit. significance and is used fig., like the Heb. חֲלָצַיִם. The phrase can thus a take on also the sense of girding on ornaments or armour.[2] In the LXX ὀσφύς is also a common figure of speech for "power," Dt. 33:11; Na. 2:2; Da. Θ 5:6 etc. A distinctive use found only in the LXX and, in dependence on it, the NT, is for loins as the place of generation,[3] corresponding to the Heb. יֹצְאֵי מֵחֲלָצָיו כִּי = ἐξέρχεσθαι ἐκ τῆς ὀσφύος τινός as in Gn. 35:11: βασιλεῖς ἐκ τῆς ὀσφύος σου ἐξελεύσονται, 2 Ch. 6:9 : ὁ υἱός σου, ὃς ἐξελεύσεται ἐκ τῆς ὀσφύος σου.

Philo seems to have the term only in OT quotations, cf. Sacr. AC, 63 on Ex. 12:11: "τὰς ὀσφῦς περιεζωμένους" ἑτοίμως πρὸς ὑπηρεσίαν ἔχοντας, also Leg. All., III, 154.

In the NT ὀσφύς occurs in 8 passages which are wholly controlled by the OT or by LXX usage. In Mk. 1:6 and Mt. 3:4 it is said of the Baptist : ἐνδεδυμένος τρίχας καμήλου καὶ ζώνην δερματίνην περὶ τὴν ὀσφὺν αὐτοῦ.[4] There is no doubt that with this description Mk. and Mt. are comparing him with Elijah — or equating him with the returning Elijah — concerning whose clothing 4 Βασ. 1:8 has a statement which is almost word for word the same, → supra. It seems more likely that the description of the Baptist's garb goes back to the saying of Jesus in Mt. 11:14 : καὶ εἰ θέλετε δέξασθαι, αὐτός ἐστιν Ἠλίας ὁ μέλλων ἔρχεσθαι, than that it is the actual description of an eye-witness.[5] Lk. 12:35-40, the section on the vigilance and loyalty of the disciples, opens in v. 35 : ἔστωσαν ὑμῶν αἱ ὀσφύες περιεζωσμέναι. The LXX examples already quoted, esp. Ex. 12:11 (→ supra), show both the derivation and meaning of the admonition, → 306, 11 ff.

In Eph. 6:14, Is. 11:5 is quoted, except that a prophecy of the Messiah is now an exhortation to the warring Christian. As in Is. 11:5 the use of ὀσφύς is transf. or fig., → 307, 20 ff. More strongly fig. is the sense in 1 Pt. 1:13 : διὸ ἀναζωσάμενοι τὰς ὀσφύας τῆς διανοίας ὑμῶν. Though the use here is hardly good Gk.,

---

ὀ σ φ ύ ς. Acc. to Bl.-Debr. § 13 the accentuation ὀσφῦς in the NT is not quite certain ; there is a good case for ὀσφύς as well.

[1] For girding up the garment for work cf. G. Dalman, Arbeit u. Sitte in Palästina, II (1932), 151 f. and Ill. 25-27; III (1933), 28; V (1937), 232 f.

[2] → 306-308, where there are further examples. On the construction cf. Helbing Kasussyntax, 47.

[3] Cf. Pr.-Bauer³, s.v. ὀσφῦς 2.

[4] D a b ff² t leave out the words from καὶ ζώνην on in Mk. 1:6, but this can hardly be right, since the rest of the tradition has them.

[5] So Wbg. Mk., on 1:6.

and translation is none too easy, the meaning is perfectly clear. We have an admonition to watchfulness and readiness for battle. Anything that might impair mind or sense (→ IV, 967) is to be girded up high, i.e., set aside.

The last three passages are based on the OT יָצָא מֵחֲלָצָי פּי. Hb. 7:5 : καίπερ ἐξεληλυθότας ἐκ τῆς ὀσφύος Ἀβραάμ, is a direct echo of Gn. 35:11 and 2 Ch. 6:9. This also gives us the sense of Hb. 7:10 : ἔτι γὰρ ἐν τῇ ὀσφύϊ τοῦ πατρὸς ἦν, which means, before he was yet begotten. Ac. 2:30 : ὤμοσεν αὐτῷ ὁ θεὸς ἐκ καρποῦ τῆς ὀσφύος αὐτοῦ καθίσαι ἐπὶ τὸν θρόνον αὐτοῦ, is a quotation of ψ 131:10 = one of his descendants. [6]

Seesemann

οὐρανός, οὐράνιος, ἐπουράνιος, οὐρανόθεν

† οὐρανός.

Contents : A. Greek Usage : 1. The Basic Idea ; 2. οὐρανός in the Cosmological Sense ; 3. In the Mythological Sense : a. The God Uranos ; b. The Abode of the Gods ; c. Orphic Writings ; d. The Magic Papyri ; 4. Gnosticism ; 5. Philo. B. The Old Testament : 1. Heaven in the World Picture of Ancient Israel ; 2. Yahweh and Heaven ; 3. Heaven as the Place of Salvation. C. The Septuagint and Judaism : I. The Septuagint : 1. Additions ; 2. The Plural οὐρανοί. II. Judaism. D. The New Testament : 1. Heaven and Earth ; 2. God in Heaven ; 3. Heaven and Jesus Christ ; 4. Heaven Opened ; 5. Heaven as the Starting-point of the Event of Revelation ; 6. Heaven and the Blessings of Salvation ; 7. Heaven and the Angels ; 8. Heaven as the Firmament ; 9. Heaven in the Plural. E. The Post-Apostolic Fathers.

A. Greek Usage.

1. The Basic Idea.

οὐρανός, [1] in class. Gk. almost without exception [2] in the sing., always means "heaven." The word always has a double reference. Heaven is the firmament, the

---

[6] ψ 131:10 has ἐκ καρποῦ τῆς κοιλίας, not ὀσφύος. From Ac. 2:30 ὀσφύος came into the LXX Codex R saec VI.

ο ὐ ρ α ν ό ς κ τ λ. Note : H. Sasse undertook the art. οὐρανός along with the arts. on γῆ and κόσμος. Because of his departure for Australia he was not able to get the work ready for the press. On the basis of his extensive preparatory labours H. Traub has written the art. Bibl.: Cr.-Kö., Moult.-Mill., Liddell-Scott, Pass., *s.v.*; K. Barth, K.D., III, 3 (1950), 426-623 (C.D., III, 3 [1960], 369-531); G. Bertram, "Die Himmelfahrt Jesu vom Kreuz," *Festgabe f. A. Deissmann* (1927), 187-217; F. Boll, *Sphaera, Neue gr. Texte u. Untersuchungen zur Gesch. der Sternbilder* (1903); also *Aus der Offenbarung Johannis, Hell. Studien zum Weltbild der Apokalypse* (1914), 30-56; F. Cumont, *Die orientalischen Religionen im römischen Heidentum* (1931), 245, 296, n. 70; H. Cremer, Art. "Himmel," *RE³*, 8, 8-84; G. Dalman, *Worte Jesu* (1930), Index, *s.v.*; H. Diels, "Himmels- u. Höllenfahrten von Homer bis Dante," *N. Jbch. Kl. Alt.*, 50 (1922), 239-252; R. Eisler, *Weltenmantel u. Himmelszelt* (1910); T. Flügge, *Die Vorstellung über den Himmel im AT*, Diss. Königsberg (1937); H. Gebhardt, "Der Himmel im NT," *ZWL*, 7 (1886), 555-575; H. Gressmann, "Die hell. Gestirnsreligion," *OA Beih.*, 5 (1925); C. Hönn, "Studien zur Gesch. d. Himmelfahrt im klass. Altertum," *Programm Mannheim* (1910); R. Holland, "Zur Typik der Himmelfahrt," *ARW*, 23 (1925), 207-220; J. Kroll, "Gott u. Hölle," *Studien der Bibliothek Warburg*, 20 (1932); W. Michaelis, "Zur Überlieferung der Himmelfahrtsgeschichte," *ThBl*, 4 (1925), 101-109; A. Oepke, "Unser Glaube an die Himmelfahrt Christi," *Luthertum*, 5 (1938), 161-186; E. Pfister, *Der Reliquienkult im Altertum*, II (1912), 480-489; A. C. Rush, *Death and Burial in Christian Antiquity*, Diss. Washington (1941); Weber, 162-165, 398-400; H. Westphal, "Jahves Wohnstätten," *ZAW Beih.*, 25 (1908), 251-273.

[1] Ionic, Attic, Boeotic : οὐρανός, Doric ὠρανός, Aeolic ὄρανος. The etym. is much

arch of heaven over the earth. But it is also that which embraces all things in the absolute, a θεῖον. In the historical development of the two insights or ideas the definitions change, but the indissoluble duality remains. We find it in the very ancient view, preserved in Orphic writings, of a cosmic egg which bursts open. The upper shell becomes the envelope of the world (→ 500), but it also becomes the God-heaven elevated above the earth and moistening and fructifying it. We also find the double understanding in Homer's mythical view of the brazen, iron, starry heaven which rests on pillars (→ infra), but which also serves as a habitation for the heavenly beings, especially Ζεὺς οὐράνιος (→ 500). The same duality underlies the use in Plato, who equates οὐρανός with the πᾶν, the κόσμος, but who also regards it as that which embraces all conceivable life, so that it is seen to be a figure of the absolute and perfect (→ 499). Plato, then, can have the gods mount up to the ἐπουράνιος ἁψίς : θεωροῦσι τὰ ἔξω τοῦ οὐρανοῦ to the final perception of pure being. In Aristot., too, we find both the cosmological sense and also the use of οὐρανός to express the θεῖον. Further development does not follow his attempt to differentiate the various aspects in his definitions of the concept (→ 499). For Stoicism, too, regards heaven both as the physical limit of the aether and also as τὸ ἡγεμονικὸν τοῦ κόσμου. [3] Finally, heaven is in Gnosticism ἀήρ and αἰθήρ, and does not lose its substantiality, and yet it also expresses the freedom, knowledge and immortality of God, → 501. [4] In the enlightened imperial age we still find representations of the god Uranos right up to the 3rd cent. (→ 500). The reason why the concept οὐρανός cannot be given clearly separated meanings is to be sought in the fact that it is always an expression both for the natural and physical givenness of what is above and embracing, and also for corresponding speculative data. The heaven which is the firmament, the heaven of μετέωρα, is the same as the heaven of the gods, the heaven which can be thought of as idea, direction, or revelation. It makes no difference to the concept whether the relationship was originally understood in realistic or in symbolical or figurative terms. For antiquity the term gives expression to the unity of the world, of the cosmos which is not only physical but also psychical and metaphysical.

2. οὐρανός in the Cosmological Sense.

In Hom. the vault of heaven is a hollow half-globe resting above the earth on pillars and held up by Atlas, Hom. Od., 1, 53 f.; Aesch. Prom., 348 ff. The solidity of the vault is expressed by such words as brazen (χάλκεος, Hom. Il., 17, 425 etc.; Pind. Pyth., 10, 27; πολύχαλκος, Hom. Il., 5, 504) or iron (σιδήρεος, Hom. Od., 15, 329; 17, 565). It is often called starry (ἀστερόεις, Hom. Il., 6, 108; 5, 769; so also Orphic writings, Diels[5], I, 13, 5). [5] The antithesis Tartarus-heaven is the supreme one, Hom. Il., 8, 16. The sense is weaker in phrases like κλέος οὐρανὸν ἵκει (Hom. Od., 9, 20), ὕβρις τε βίη

---

contested, cf. Walde-Pok., I, 281; A. Debrunner, *Indogermanische Forschungen,* 53 (1935), 239; F. Specht, Z. *Vgl. Spr.,* 66 (1939), 200 f.

[2] We find the plur., e.g., οὐρανοὺς καὶ κόσμους, esp. in some late traditions about Anaximander, cf. Ps.-Plut. Stromateis, 2 (Diels[5], I, 83, 29); Hipp. Ref., I, 6, 2 (*ibid.,* I, 84, 5); Aetius De Placitis Philosophorum, I, 7, 12 (I, 86, 13). It also occurs in a passage in Aristot. referring to Idaios, Cael., IV, 5, p. 303b, 13 (cf. Diels[5], II, 51, 11). On the question of the plur. *v.* F. Torm, "Der pluralis οὐρανοί," ZNW, 33 (1934), 48-50; P. Katz, *Philo's Bible* (1950), 141-146.

[3] Cf. Poseidonios in Diog. L., VII, 139.

[4] Exc. 11, 2, 25-29 (Scott, I, 428, 25 ff.; 430, 1 ff.).

[5] Cf. ἄστρα οὐρανοῦ, Eur. Phoen., 1; ἀστέροι, οἵ εἰσιν οὐρανοῦ σπλάγχνα, P. Lond., I, 121, cf. Reitzenstein Hell. Myst., 177.

τε σιδήρεον οὐρανὸν ἵκει (15, 329). When mythical ideas disintegrate, [6] the sense of "firmament" remains. An attempt is now made, however, to understand the origin, constitution and movement of οὐρανός [7] in terms of thought or experience. The equation οὐρανός = ἡ περιφορὰ ἡ ἐξωτάτω τῆς γῆς comes down from Anaximenes. [8] With γαῖα and θάλασσα it is understood as the world (cf. Orph. Fr., 16, Diels⁵, I, 14, 31), and along with four-membered formulae we find the basic γῆ τε καὶ οὐρανός (Plat. Soph., 232c), πρὶν οὐρανὸν καὶ γῆν γενέσθαι (Plat. Euthyd., 296d). Mention should also be made of ὑπὸ τὸν οὐρανόν = "on earth" (Plat. Ep., 7, 326c). In Parmenides we already find the equation οὐρανός = κόσμος, Diels⁵, I, 225, 13. This is then expanded by Plato (Tim., 28b : [9] οὐρανὸς ἡ κόσμος ἡ καὶ ἄλλο ὅ τί ποτε ὀνομαζόμενος μάλιστ' ἂν δέχοιτο). Heaven is the cause of origination and the prototype of all that is. It embraces all conceivable life and can be equated with πᾶν and κόσμος, as already in Pythagoras. [10] For the sake of this heavenly perfection there is only εἷς ὅδε μονογενὴς οὐρανὸς γεγονὼς ἔστι τε καὶ ἔτ' ἔσται (Plat. Tim., 31b, cf. a), and Proclus declares this : ὡς ὁρῶντα τὰ ἄνω καὶ θεώμενον τὸ νοητὸν καὶ ὡς νοερᾶς οὐσίας μετέχοντα (Procl. Tim., II, 83e), and therewith as τὴν μοναδικὴν αἰτίαν ... καὶ τὴν πάντων περιεκτικὴν τῶν δευτέρων καὶ τὴν τῶν ὅλων ἐπικρατοῦσαν οὐσίαν (II, 139b); it reflects the eternal Apeiron or the Apeiron of time : the one heaven is the reflection of absolutely all being. Thus for Plato the starry heaven (Plat. Resp., VI, 488d; Theaet., 173e) is the heaven of the gods (Resp., VI, 508a; Phaedr., 246e) and the starting-point of the contemplation of being and absolute knowledge (Phaedr., 247b). On the other hand, Aristot. (Cael., I, 9, p. 278b, 11 ff.), distinguishing the various senses, attempts the following formulation : ἕνα μὲν οὖν τρόπον οὐρανὸν λέγομεν τὴν οὐσίαν τὴν τῆς ἐσχάτης τοῦ παντὸς περιφορᾶς, ἡ σῶμα φυσικὸν τὸ ἐν τῇ ἐσχάτῃ περιφορᾷ τοῦ παντός (= universe). εἰώθαμεν γὰρ τὸ ἔσχατον καὶ τὸ ἄνω μάλιστα καλεῖν οὐρανόν, ἐν ᾧ καὶ τὸ θεῖον πᾶν (= the divine all) ἱδρῦσθαί φαμεν. ἄλλον δ' αὖ τρόπον τὸ συνεχὲς σῶμα τῇ ἐσχάτῃ περιφορᾷ τοῦ παντός, ἐν ᾧ σελήνη καὶ ἥλιος καὶ ἔνια τῶν ἄστρων· καὶ γὰρ ταῦτα ἐν τῷ οὐρανῷ εἶναί φαμεν. ἔτι δ' ἄλλως λέγομεν οὐρανὸν τὸ περιεχόμενον σῶμα ὑπὸ τῆς ἐσχάτης περιφορᾶς· τὸ γὰρ ὅλον καὶ τὸ πᾶν (= totality of the world and universe) εἰώθαμεν λέγειν οὐρανόν. Stoicism formulates οὐρανός as αἰθέρος τὸ ἔσχατον· ἐξ οὗ καὶ ἐν ᾧ ἐστι πάντα ἐμφανῶς· περιέχει γὰρ πάντα πλὴν αὐτοῦ, Zeno Fr., 115 (v. Arnim, I, 33, 28), ... ἔξω δὲ τοῦ οὐρανοῦ εἶναι κενόν, ibid., 96 (v. Arnim, I, 26, 32 f., cf. 34). [11] Transposition from the religious to the philosophical sphere (περιέχειν) finds expression such as this : οὐσίαν δὲ θεοῦ ... τὸν ὅλον κόσμον καὶ τὸν οὐρανόν, Zeno Fr., 163 (v. Arnim, I, 43, 6). Acc. to the interpretation of Minucius Felix Iovem = caelum, and in Chrysipp. Fr., 644 (v. Arnim, II, 194, 13) οὐρανός becomes the guiding principle (ἡγεμονικόν). It is theologically important that along these lines Cicero could find in the aequalitas motus ... caeli the fourth basis for the animis hominum informatae deorum notitiones (Nat. Deor., II, 15), and also that Cl. Al. could call οὐρανὸν κυρίως πόλιν, Strom., IV, 26, 172, 2. [12]

---

[6] On the destruction of the Homeric world picture by Anaximander, and on further developments, cf. I. L. Heiberg, Gesch. der Mathematik u. Naturwissenschaften im Altertum = Handbuch AW, V, 1, 2 (1925), 50 ff.

[7] For the pre-Socratics cf. Diels⁵, III, s.v. οὐρανός.

[8] Doxographi Graeci² (1926), 339; Diels⁵, I, 93, 22 f.

[9] → III, 872. On the origin of the equation cf. Diog. L., VIII, 48 (Diels⁵, I, 225, 13 f.).

[10] Pythagoras in Diog. L., VIII, 48 (Diels⁵, I, 225, 13). Cf. also Anaxim. and Parm. in Aetius De Placitis Philosophorum, II, 11, 1 (Diels⁵, I, 93, 23). On the applying of number speculation to heaven by Pythagoras cf. Aristot. Metaph., I, 5, p. 986a, 3 : τὸν ὅλον οὐρανὸν ἁρμονίαν εἶναι καὶ ἀριθμόν, also ibid., I, 5, p. 986a, 21; VII, 6, p. 1080b, 18.

[11] The μετέωρα could also be regarded here as οὐράνια, cf. M. Pohlenz, Die Stoa, I (1948), 218; II (1949), 108.

[12] Cf. esp. the οὐρανός speculations of Plotinus : πᾶσαι (sc. ψυχαί) μὲν δὴ καταλάμπουσιν τὸν οὐρανόν, Enn., IV, 3, 17.

3. In the Mythological Sense.

a. The God Uranos. Uranos (Anth. Pal., 9, 26, 9; Hes. Theog., 176) [13] is one of the gods of pre-Homeric religion : Γαῖα ... ἐγείνατο ἶσον ἑατῇ Οὐρανὸν ἀστερόεντα, ἵνα μιν περὶ πάντα καλύπτοι, Hes. Theog., 126 f.; cf. Hom. Od., 5, 184; Il., 15, 36. Earth brings forth heaven from itself [14] to fructify it in the ἱερὸς γάμος. [15] In the myth Uranos was then emasculated and overthrown by his son Cronos, and he in turn by his son Ζεὺς οὐράνιος. The great gods of antiquity [16] were then completely crowded out by the Olympian gods. [17] How strong was the impression made by the god Uranos may be seen from his depiction not only on the Pergamon altar but also in the imperial period, e.g., on the Prima Porta statue of Augustus and above all on the sarcophagus of Junius Bassus (300 A.D.): on his head are the feet of the youthful Christ, the arched veil of heaven stretched out above.

b. The Abode of the Gods. Heaven as the abode of the gods is identical with Olympus. [18] The Olympian gods are called Οὐρανίωνες, "dwellers in heaven," Hom. Il., 1, 570, though there may be a suggestion here of their descent from Uranos, ibid., 5, 373 and 898. The setting of the gods in heaven means that "the lord of heaven is the lord of the universe ... and hence a universal god." [19] This is esp. true of Zeus. [20] Prayer is made χεῖρ' ὀρέγων εἰς οὐρανὸν ἀστερόεντα, Hom. Il., 15, 371; cf. 24, 307; Od., 9, 527; Pind. Pyth., 538; Aesch. Sept. c. Theb., 442 f. Oaths are also taken νὴ τὸν οὐρανόν, Aristoph. Pl., 267, 366, cf. μαρτυρόμεθα ... τὸν οὐρανόν, Jdt. 7:28. Crime can also reach to heaven, Hom. Od., 15, 329; 17, 565.

c. Orphic Writings. Here we find a unity of heaven and earth far beyond a mere interrelation, cf. ὡς Οὐρανός τε Γαῖα τ' ἦν μορφὴ μία, Eur. Fr., 484 (TGF, 511). On this view of the world there is, as it were, the breaking of an egg, and heaven is constituted of the upper shell. [21] The Orphic initiate can recapture this deepest unity and thus, even as man, become a divine being : Γῆς παῖς εἰμι καὶ οὐρανοῦ ἀστερόεντος, αὐτὰρ ἐμοὶ γένος οὐράνιον, Orph. Fr., 17 (Diels⁵, I, 15, 26 f.). Here, too, we find the lofty view of heaven as the mantle of the world, which is possibly Babylonian in origin : τῶν παλαιῶν καὶ τὸν οὐρανὸν βηλὸν εἰρηκότων οἷον θεῶν οὐρανίων περίβλημα, Porphyr. Antr. Nymph., 14. [22]

d. The Magic Papyri. Here, too, οὐρανός is common : as the firmament which includes the heavenly ocean οἱ καταράκτοι τῶν οὐρανῶν, cf. the OT, Preis. Zaub.,

---

[13] Cf. U. v. Wilamowitz-Moellendorff, Der Glaube d. Hellenen, I (1931), 342 f.; W. F. Otto, Die Götter Griechenlands³ (1947), 37 f., 93; E. Peterich, Die Theologie der Hellenen (1938), 119, 195-197; J. Schmidt, Art. "Uranos," Roscher, VI, 106-116.

[14] He is also said to be the son of Erebos.

[15] οὐρανῷ καὶ γῆ προτελεῖν τοὺς γάμους, Procl. in Tim., 293c; cf. Eur. Fr., 839 (TGF, 633).

[16] There was never a cult of heaven, cf. Wilamowitz-Moellendorff, op. cit., 212, also n. 1. But heaven was mentioned constantly as chief of the elemental gods, cf. Reitzenstein Hell. Myst., 224 f.

[17] Peterich, 278.

[18] Wilamowitz-Moell., I, 333. Even Emped. Fr., 44 (Diels⁵, I, 330, 24) substitutes Ὄλυμπος for οὐρανός. This equation is first fully made in the Homeric world. In the ancient Hell. period there is a close connection between the mount of storms and the storm-god Zeus, cf. Wilamowitz-Moell., I, 224 f.; M. P. Nilsson, Gesch. d. gr. Religion, I = Handbuch AW. V, 2, 1 (1941), 330, 490. Ancient and widespread mythological ideas of the mount of the gods are also at work here.

[19] Wilamowitz-Moell., I, 334.

[20] So also Plato : ὁ μέγας ἡγεμὼν ἐν οὐρανῷ Ζεύς, Phaedr., 246e.

[21] Cf. οὗτος ὁ Ἡρακλῆς ἐγέννησεν ὑπερμέγεθες ᾠόν, ὃ συμπληρούμενον ὑπὸ βίας τοῦ γεγεννηκότος ἐκ παρατριβῆς εἰς δύο ἐρράγη· τὸ μὲν οὖν κατὰ κορυφὴν αὐτοῦ Οὐρανὸς εἶναι ἐτελέσθη, τὸ δὲ κάτω ἐνεχθὲν Γῆ, Athenag., 18 (Diels⁵, I, 12, 26 ff., cf. 11, 11 ff. and 20 f.). For further material cf. Eisler, II, 420 f.; O. Kern, Die Religion der Griechen, II (1935), 151; cf. also W. Staudacher, Die Trennung von Himmel u. Erde. Ein vorgr. Schöpfungsmythus bei Hesiod u. d. Orphikern, Diss., 1942, esp. 61 f.

[22] Cf. φᾶρος ἶσον οὐρανῷ θεῶν, Aesch. Fr., 216 (TGF, 72).

15, 5; 15b, 2 (Vol. II, p. 204), λέγε ... εἰς οὐρανὸν βλέπων (ibid., XIII, 40), with a picture of Uranos. [23] In the initiation of Monos the invocation of the sun-god is: ἐγώ εἰμι, ὁ ... ἀνὰ μέσον τῶν δύο φύσεων, οὐρανοῦ καὶ γῆς (ibid., XIII, 255). We read of the eternal aeon κατ' οὐρανὸν ἀνυψωθείς (I, 209). The deity is invoked as οὐράνιος (I, 300), ὁ μέγας ἐν οὐρανῷ (II, 102; III, 130), indeed, as ὁ κύριος τοῦ οὐρανοῦ καὶ τῆς γῆς (IV, 641), cf. Mt. 11:25. [24]

4. Gnosticism.

In Hell. Gnosticism as found in the Corp. Herm. [25] the — πολυστεφής [26] — heaven [27] is divided into 7 κύκλοι (Corp. Herm., III, 2b) corresponding to the 7 spheres of the planets. It was created by the demiurge and serves as his dwelling. [28] It is above αἰθήρ, ἀήρ, γῆ, [29] and in keeping with its fiery nature is ἔκπυρος. [30] The θεὸς ἐν οὐρανῷ [31] is evil — the planetary deities became demons. Hence the μυστήρια are shut up in heaven, [32] and there rules the compulsion of necessity, ἀνάγκη and heimarmene in the heavens, which close off the earth: οὐδεὶς ... τῶν οὐρανίων θεῶν ἐπὶ γῆν κατελεύ- σεται, οὐρανοῦ τὸν ὅρον καταλιπών (Corp. Herm., X, 25). Heaven is distinguished by immutability, freedom, blamelessness, gnosis, the earth closed off by it by the op- posite, for οὐ κοινωνεῖ τὰ ἐν οὐρανῷ τοῖς ἐπὶ γῆς. [33] This demonic heaven has a demonic soul; those who dwell in heaven seek to deceive. To be liberated from it man is illumined by φῶς which enables him to see πρὸς οὐρανόν, [34] ὅπως ἐγὼ μόνος αἰητὸς οὐρανὸν βαίνω, as we read in the introduction to the Mithras Liturgy. It is man: ὁ δὲ ἄνθρωπος καὶ εἰς τὸν οὐρανὸν ἀναβαίνει (Corp. Herm., X, 25). If he begins the heavenly journey of the soul, man perceives in παλιγγενεσία by the νοῦς: ἐν οὐρανῷ εἰμι (XIII, 11b). As he puts down the burden of the planets with his own σῶμα — for otherwise εἰς τὸν οὐρανὸν ἀναβῆναι οὐ δύναμαι (XI, 21a) — he can stride through the heavenly spheres: ἀνοίγητε οὐρανοί (XIII, 17). It is thus true of the somatically dead: ὑμῖν οὐρανὸς ... ὁ μισθός. [35] In the Corp. Herm. heaven or the heavens are a sign of dualism and the most profound pessimism. They denote a lost world, and they are the mark of a new world consciousness. [36]

5. Philo.

The decisive pt. in Philo's use of οὐρανός is that he combines the Platonic doctrine of ideas, Stoic speculation and biblical statements. Heaven and earth are God's ἀνά- θημα (votive offering), Som., I, 243 = πρὸς ἀλήθειαν ἱερὸν θεοῦ, Spec. Leg., I, 66. οὐρανός represents in this cosmos τὸ ἁγιώτατον τῆς τῶν ὄντων οὐσίας μέρος

---

[23] Cf. among signs for heaven: ☉ Preis. Zaub., XIII, 255, 269, 284 etc. and Ø XIII, 867, also both, II, p. 214, s.v. Cf. XIII, col. XIX; Vol. II, Ill. 8.

[24] On the heavenly letters (ἐπιστολαὶ ἀπὸ τοῦ τῶν θεῶν προσώπου, Diog. L., VI, 101), also βίβλος ... ἐξ οὐρανοῦ, cf. A. Dieterich, Kleine Schriften (1911), 234-251.

[25] Cf. H. Jonas, Gnosis u. spätantiker Geist, I (1934), 181 f., 344 f. For bibl. on the soul's heavenly journey cf. A. Dieterich, Eine Mithrasliturgie (1903), 197-205; Reitzenstein Hell. Myst., 47.

[26] Exc. 23, 2 (Scott, I, 456, 14).

[27] Exc. 23, 51 and 68 (Scott, I, 484, 35; 494, 3). Cf. A. Festugière, "La création des âmes dans la Koré Kosmou," Pisciculi = Antike u. Christentum, Suppl. Vol. I (1939), 105, n. 17.

[28] Exc. 24, 1 (Scott, I, 494, 27).

[29] Exc. 23, 11 (I, 462, 24).

[30] Exc. 25, 13 (I, 512, 27). There are, however, some minute distinctions here; thus the ἐπουράνιοι are under the ἐμπύριοι, Scott, IV, 32, 9.

[31] Corp. Herm., XIV, 10; θεοί in Exc. 23, 53 (I, 486, 12).

[32] Dieterich, op. cit. (→ n. 25), 2, reading as in Reitzenstein Hell. Myst., 174.

[33] Exc. 11, 2, 25 ff. (I, 428, 25 ff.).

[34] Corp. Herm., XVI, 8; Exc. 4b, 4 (I, 406, 19).

[35] Exc. 23, 17 (I, 466, 22).

[36] It is in this light that we are to see the burial inscr. of Antiochus IV of Commagene: πρὸς οὐρανίους Διὸς Ὠρομάσδου θρόνους θεοφιλῆν ψυχὴν προπέμψαν, Ditt. Or., 383, 40 ff.

(*loc. cit.*). Here heaven is the νοητὸς οὐρανός and κυρίως (Stoic) οὐρανός, Spec. Leg., I, 302, with appeal to Dt. 10:14. It is ἀσώματος or ἰδέα, Op. Mund., 29; Decal., 102. It is quite distinct from the αἰσθητὸς οὐρανός — the second heaven acc. to Philo's doctrine of the double creation (→ III, 877 f.) — though there is a paradigmatic bond between them, Spec. Leg., I, 302. Philosophically, then, it seems to be absurd to reserve heaven for gods, Virt., 212. In this great typological scheme the second heaven is dependent on the first, and earthly things on heavenly things, Op. Mund., 117. The οὐράνιος ἄνθρωπος is also the prototype of the physical and historical Adam, Leg. All., I, 31. Man himself is as an οὐρανός, Op. Mund., 82 — the Pythagorean and Stoic doctrine of the macrocosm and microcosm. As οὐρανός man carries many star-like natures as life within himself: πολλὰς ἐν αὐτῷ φύσεις ἀστεροειδεῖς ἀγαλματοφοροῦντα (Op. Mund., 82). Hence the νοερὸν καὶ οὐράνιον τῆς ψυχῆς γένος πρὸς αἰθέρα ... ὡς πατέρα ἀφίξεται, from which come οἵ τε ἀστέρες καὶ ὁ σύμπας οὐρανός (Rer. Div. Her., 283). Philo can thus call dying εἰς οὐρανὸν στέλλεσθαι (Vit. Mos., 288). In stark contrast to the Hermetic use, οὐρανός is here a sign of the unity and co-ordination of the whole cosmos. Indeed, it effects this unity. There are no distinctive features in the usage of Joseph. (always sing.), which corresponds to the Hellenistic. [37]

Traub

B. Old Testament.

The word for heaven, שָׁמַיִם in Heb., שמם in Phoenician, šmm (or šmym) in Ugaritic, שמין in Aram., is obviously from a root šmw (y). The abnormal Heb. plur. (it should be pronounced šamayim) can only be regarded as a secondary shortening. In Western Semitic the use is plur., in Eastern Semitic sing. The plur. has been explained as that of "spatial extension." [38] Etym. the word is obscure, though the view that it is a compound of the *nota relativa* ša and *mayim,* i.e., the "place of water," [39] is undoubtedly erroneous.

1. Heaven in the World Picture of Ancient Israel.

If we seek examples to show precisely what Israel understood by שָׁמַיִם, we first come across statements which speak of it as something fixed and material: heaven is stretched out, [40] it has windows, [41] also pillars (Job 26:11) and foundations, [42] and can be torn etc. [43] This is not just the language of poetry and symbol, for it seems that שָׁמַיִם is in large measure another word for רָקִיעַ, "firmament." This is the huge, luminous bell of heaven which has above it the heavenly ocean and whose orb arches over the circle of the earth, → 498. [44] The heavenly ocean (מַבּוּל), whose blue may be seen on the firmament from below, was naturally of great significance both because it blessed the earth (rain) and could also destroy it (flood). [45] To what degree שָׁמַיִם could be used as a synon. for רָקִיעַ may be seen in Ps. 148:4-6, which refers to the "waters above the heaven." The definition of P in Gn. 1:8 (he called the firmament heaven) pts. in the same direction. Finally the phrase "shaking of heaven and earth" makes sense only if

---

[37] Heaven is God's creation, Jos. Ant., 8, 107; it belongs to the φύσις τοῦ παντός, 3, 184. God is Judge from heaven, and He sees all things therefrom, Bell., 1, 630. "Pure and obedient souls ... attain (after death) to the most sacred place of heaven," Bell., 3, 374.

[38] Ges.-Buhl²⁸, 415.

[39] Cf. T. K. Cheyne, *The Book of Is.* == *The Sacred Books of the OT*, 10 (1899), 157; H. Bauer-P. Leander, *Historische Grammatik der hbr. Sprache des AT* (1922), 621.

[40] Is. 40:22; 44:24; 45:12; 48:13; 51:13, 16; Jer. 10:12; 51:15; Ps. 104:2; Zech. 12:1.

[41] Gn. 7:11; 2 K. 7:2, 19; Mal. 3:10.

[42] 2 S. 22:8.

[43] Is. 63:19.

[44] On the orb or circle of heaven and earth (חוּג) cf. Is. 40:22; Job 22:14; Prv. 8:27.

[45] On מַבּוּל for the heavenly ocean cf. J. Begrich, "Mabbul," *Z. Sem.,* 6 (1928), 135-153.

heaven is regarded as something solid, 2 S. 22:8. The distinction is that רָקִיעַ was a technical cosmological term, while שָׁמַיִם was in ordinary cultic and general use, and was thus
essentially much more fluid ; it had a much bigger range of meaning. Emphasis has been
put on the fact that שָׁמַיִם denotes the atmosphere between firmament and earth, as
plainly suggested by the very common "fowls of heaven."[46] But the word was in no
sense restricted to this sphere. In very many instances it has the more general meaning
of the cosmic sphere above the earth with no thought of upper limitation. This is esp.
so when the ref. is to God's dwelling in heaven or to His coming thence.[47] In such
cases שָׁמַיִם is the dimension above the firmament.

Israel seems not to have been acquainted with the idea of many intersecting heavenly
spheres. Perhaps there is an echo of this part of the Babylonian view in the phrase
"heaven of heavens," שְׁמֵי הַשָּׁמַיִם.[48] But though there may be general connections, the
phrase could well be regarded in Israel as no more than rhetorical hyperbole. Sometimes
we read of the "four ends of heaven," Jer. 49:36; cf. Zech. 2:10; 6:5; Da. 7:2; 8:8; 11:4.
This is meant horizontally, cf. Dt. 4:32 : "from one end to the other." The height of
heaven cannot be climbed by men, Dt. 30:12; Prv. 30:4.[49] Proverbially heaven is also
the quintessence of lasting duration, cf. the "days of heaven," Dt. 11:21; Ps. 89:29.

The commandment in Ex. 20:4 divides the cosmos into three parts, heaven, earth and
the chaotic waters under the earth. The same division is found in Ps. 115:15-17. The
universe is much more frequently described, however, as heaven and earth, → III, 881.
This formula is not based on the sacral picture of the world, like that of Ex. 20:4, but
simply on elementary observation. It seems that there never was a sacrally canonised
view of the world in Israel. The basis of this surprising fact is to be sought in the
complete absence of a myth uniting and quickening the elements. Only occasionally do
we find fragmentary mythical ideas, and these are rather used with poetic freedom as
ancient ways of making things vivid, cf. the idea of the two world mountains in Zech.
(1:8 textus emendatus ; 6:1), which is close to Babylonian as well as Egyptian notions.[50]
There can be no question of any more comprehensive mythical connections in the world
of Israel's thinking. Along with such echoes we do, of course, find free poetic imagery.
Thus it was easy to present the cosmos as a house with the balcony (עֲלִיָּה) as a cover
(Ps. 104:3; Am. 9:6), or as an outstretched tent.[51] Heaven is also compared with the
stretched out roll of a book (Is. 34:4) on which the stars are obviously the writing.[52]
In heaven, i.e., above the firmament (רָקִיעַ), are chambers for snow and hail (Job 38:22),
the winds (Jer. 49:36; Job 37:9, 12; Ps. 135:7), and the water (Ps. 33:7; Job 38:37), which
in a cycle, when it has fallen on the earth as rain, returns thither (Job 36:27; Is. 55:10).
In these and other instances we are struck by the wholly non-mythological and rational
understanding which has made heaven and its laws the subject of sober observation.[53]

Heaven is also the place of special signs [54] and calendar points of reference to fix the
festivals. Gn. 1:14, with its emphasis on the purposiveness of the heavenly bodies, is
another instance of the cool and almost rational observation of these things. At all
events, there is in P and OT wisdom a complete demythologisation of this part of the

---

[46] Gn. 1:26, 28, 30; 2:19 f.; 6:7; 7:3 etc.; L. Köhler, Theol. d. OT (1936), 139.
[47] Examples → 505.
[48] Dt. 10:14; 1 K. 8:27; Ps. 148:4; Neh. 9:6; 2 Ch. 2:5; 6:18.
[49] On the other hand, heaven is not infinitely high above the earth. To build a tower
"whose top may reach unto heaven" (Gn. 11:4) is on the extreme limit of the sphere of
human capabilities. Nevertheless, the pt. of the tower story in J is not that deity is threatened
by man. For a correct criticism of this common line of exposition cf. Flügge, 16-19.
[50] On the idea of the two world mountains cf. B. Meissner, Babylonien u. Assyrien, II
(1925), 108-110. On the so-called heavenly ladder → 504.
[51] Is. 40:22; Ps. 104:2.
[52] On the stars as writing cf. Meissner, op. cit. (→ n. 50).
[53] Jer. 33:25; Job 38:33 speak of the laws of heaven (חֻקּוֹת).
[54] C. A. Keller, Das Wort Oth als Offenbarungszeichen Gottes (1946).

world. It is also plain that only occasionally and on the periphery did the whole sphere of astrology make assault on the belief in Yahweh, Dt. 18:9 ff.; Is. 47:13; Jer. 10:2.

2. Yahweh and Heaven.

Yahweh created heaven. [55] The different verbs used (בָּרָא קָנָה כּוּן עָשָׂה) are of detailed interest for the various ideas and circles of tradition (→ κτίζω, III, 1007 ff.), but have no particular importance here. קָנָה (Gn. 14:19, 22), "to acquire by work," enshrines a vocabulary which belongs to the world outside Israel. [56] Most of the references to heaven which are important for Israel's faith speak of Yahweh's dwelling in heaven. A simple presentation of the relevant instances, however, would give a very one-sided picture. For there are in fact other statements which call, not heaven, but the innermost sanctuary of the temple, or Sinai, or the ark, or other sacral places, the place of the presence or even of the dwelling of Yahweh, and which cannot be brought under the slogan שָׁמַיִם. In this respect the OT tradition is in fact very complicated. For after the conquest the ideas of primitive faith in Yahweh, which we find hard to grasp, combined closely with notions from the Canaanite cult. Furthermore, exposition has in some cases to take into account the noteworthy distinction between the temple of dwelling and that of manifestation.

This important distinction has been worked out on the basis of the sacral architecture of Babylonia and Assyria. [57] In temples of dwelling, esp. the ziggurats (towers), the deity dwells in heavenly heights far removed from the human sphere. In temples of manifestation the deity is embodied in the cultic symbols and may be found and worshipped by men. We thus have two distinct cultic ideas relating to one and the same god. [58] There does not have to be a ziggurat. In such cases the true dwelling of the god is behind or above the temple of manifestation. This corresponds to a more developed religion with an inclination to the abstract. [59] Naturally these ideas, which developed in a very ancient culture with stable sacral relationships, cannot be presupposed at once in the primitive faith of Israel which was much more volatile and the history of whose tradition is so complicated. There is no doubt, however, that, through the medium of the ancient religious forms of Canaan, belief in Yahweh also came to move in these circles, or that it does at least give evidence here and there of their influence. Thus the ark in the sanctuaries at Shiloh and Jerusalem, which we have to think of as an empty throne and perhaps even as a non-Yahwistic processional shrine, is to be interpreted in terms of this circle of thought. The ark as an empty throne is thus no more than the place of a temporary presence and manifestation of Yahweh. [60] The Bethel story (Gn. 28:10 ff.) also shows plainly that the question of the dwelling of Yahweh involves more than the traditional alternative of heaven or earth. Jacob says : "Here is the house of Elohim and here is the gate of heaven." In the "ladder" (better סֻלָּם = "staircase" from סָלַל "to heap up") there may even be seen a distant recollection of the steps of a ziggurat. [61] Thus one may conjecture that in the original elements of Canaanite tradition

---

[55] Gn. 1:1; 2:4; Is. 42:5; 45:18; Ps. 33:6; Prv. 3:19; 8:27 etc.

[56] Thus the word is found in Ugaritic in this sense, C. H. Gordon, *Ugaritic Handbook* = *Analecta Orientalia*, 25 (1947), Glossary, 1800 (p. 267) (*qnyt* = fem. creator). On the meaning of קָנָה cf. L. Köhler, ZAW, NF, 11 (1934), 160.

[57] W. F. Andrä, *Das Gotteshaus und die Urformen des Bauens im alten Orient* (*Studien zur Bauforschung*, ed. the Koldeweygesellschaft, H. 12 [1930]). On the ziggurat cf. T. Dombardt, "Der babylonische Turm," AO, 29, 2 (1930), and → 477, n. 36.

[58] Andrä, 15.

[59] *Ibid.*, 16.

[60] K. Galling, *Bibl. Reallexikon* (1937), 343.

[61] A. Jeremias, *Das AT im Lichte d. Alten Orients*[4] (1930), 360-364.

the ancient Babylonian idea is more influential than in the genuine Yahweh traditions, or at least in the traditions which come from the pre-Mosaic religion of the patriarchal gods. [62] But one can hardly go beyond a more or less, for in the literature as we now have it the traditions are already so closely interfused that it is no longer possible to distinguish them historically. It could be that even the ancient and common oriental idea of the dwelling of deity on the distant and high mountain of God has in some OT sayings surreptitiously fused with the idea of Yahweh's dwelling in heaven when this is not transferred to Zion (cf. Is. or Ps. 48:2) and has not become a belief of central importance. [63]

Historically, then, we cannot fix a sequence of the different views of Yahweh's dwelling, least of all in the sense of showing that the idea of His dwelling in heaven arose only later or is simply the commutation of a very different notion. [64] The vision of Yahweh with a radiant building of sapphire stones at His feet (Ex. 24:9-11 J) is a very ancient tradition, and it contains already the idea of a God of heaven enthroned above the firmament. To the same effect is the tradition that Yahweh comes down to Sinai (Ex. 19:18 J). The concept of Yahweh as the God of heaven is well-known indeed, not merely to J, but to the traditional material worked over by him (Gn. 11:5, 7; 19:24; 24:3, 7). It is hardly possible to separate Canaanite material from the original J material at least (until we come to descriptions of the holy wars). It may be stated, however, that the idea which became so popular in Israel, namely, that of Yahweh as the heavenly king enthroned in the midst of the heavenly host, may be traced back to the influence of the Canaanite pantheon. [65] In particular, Yahweh in the course of His invasion took over important functions from the heavenly Baal (בעל שמם) long since known to us from inscr. [66]

The idea of Yahweh as the God of heaven is in some sense predominant over others. We have here a self-contained circle of concepts. Yahweh is the King enthroned over earth in heaven (cf. the stock-title מֶלֶךְ in Is. 6:5; Ps. 29:10). His palace, established over the heavenly ocean (Ps. 104:3), is the heavenly sanctuary, which is sometimes more the seat of world government, sometimes more a cultic centre. [67] The idea is presented particularly vividly in the vision of Micaiah ben Imlah (1 K. 22:19-22) and the prologue to Job (Job 1:6-12), for here we read also of the host of heaven which is around the throne of the heavenly King to serve Him and also to share in Yahweh's government of the world.

Traditions of diverse origin have perhaps combined in this idea of the heavenly host, which is also called the host of Yahweh. The decisive contribution probably came from the religion of Canaan, for this host is simply the Canaanite pantheon demoted and adapted to the belief in Yahweh. From Ugarit, too, we have the ṣbu špš, the "host of the sun," and also a mlk ṣbu špš, a "king of the host of the sun." [68] The special ref. here,

---

[62] A. Alt, Der Gott der Väter = BWANT, III, 12 (1929).

[63] On the mountain of God — linked with Paradise in Ez. 28:2, 13 f. — cf. O. Eissfeldt, Baal Zaphon, Zeus Kasios u. der Durchzug der Israeliten durchs Rote Meer (1932), 1-30.

[64] So Westphal, 270.

[65] So A. Alt in a duplicated paper "Vom Königtum Gottes im AT."

[66] Cf. the Baal who rides on the clouds in the Ras Shamra texts (rkb 'rpt Gordon, op. cit., 51: III : 11. 18 and V: 122; 67: II : 7) with Dt. 33:26; Ps. 68:4 רֹכֵב בָּעֲרָבוֹת (also Ps. 18:10; Is. 19:1). Inscr. which refer to the heavenly Baal have been collected and interpreted by O. Eissfeldt, "Baalšamem u. Jahve," ZAW, 57 (1939), 1-31.

[67] 1 K. 22:19-22; Is. 6:1 ff.; Job 1:6 ff.; Da. 7:9 ff.; G. Westphal, "ṣebā haš-šamaim," Orientalische Studien Nöldeke-Festschrift, II (1916), 719-728.

[68] Gordon, op. cit. (→ n. 56), Glossary, 1709 (p. 264).

of course, is to stellar deities. But the OT, too, can speak of the host of heaven with this specific astral signification, cf. Dt. 4:19.

It is not surprising that these ideas of the host of heaven remain fluid. Sometimes one has to think of supraterrestrial spirits which Yahweh employs on different errands (1 K. 22:19), sometimes of the host of stars (Gn. 2:1; Ju. 5:20). The heavenly host is like an earthly army with its leader and fiery horses and chariots (Jos. 5:14; 2 K. 2:11). Probably under later influences due to political dependence on Assyria a cult of the host of heaven came in during the later monarchy. This was resisted as a serious transgression by the belief in Yahweh. [69] In Dt. 4:19 alone, in an isolated instance of toleration, is it condoned as a religious practice for the Gentiles. But according to the understanding of belief in Yahweh only a small sphere of operation was granted to heavenly beings in the direction of history and destiny, → ἄγγελος, I, 78.

> To show how strongly Israel appropriated the idea of Yahweh as the God of heaven one might refer to the prayer of Dt. 26:15 ("look down from heaven, thy holy habitation"), [70] for the prayer formulae of Dt. 26 are much older than the book itself. Or again one might refer to the uplifting of the hands in oaths (Dt. 32:40) or their outstretching in prayer (Ex. 9:29, 33), since both point to the same concept of Yahweh dwelling in heaven.

If in ancient times such ideas were freely accompanied by the thought of Yahweh's dwelling and presence on earth [71] (which cannot be wholly ruled out even according to the basic understanding of the ancient Orient), in the Deuteronomic theology we find an open attempt to clarify the problem of Yahweh's transcendence and yet of His commitment to Israel along the lines of a precise theological definition of the relationship. Fundamental for this theological school is the idea that heaven is Yahweh's dwelling-place. The need to achieve a more consistent view leads the school, e.g., to reconstruct the old tradition of the revelation at Sinai. Yahweh did not speak from the mountain (cf. E in Ex. 19:20), but from heaven. [72] And when the individual or the congregation lifts up its voice in prayer, God hears from heaven. With this emphasis on Yahweh's remoteness from earth is very closely linked the idea of His relation to the cultic site. Yahweh has set His name there (שִׂים) and also made it to dwell there (לְשַׁכֵּן), → 256. [73] One can hardly describe this theologoumenon of the name present at the cultic site as a break with the idea of dwelling. It is rather to be regarded as an incisive theological spiritualising. For the name is in some sense a part of Yahweh, i.e., the side which is turned to man in revelation, → 257. [74] Clearly the ancient distinction between the place of dwelling and the place of manifestation, which was alien to the most primitive belief in Yahweh, has provided the Deuteronomist with the material for his theological understanding. The new thing in the Deuteronomic school is not, then, the idea of Yahweh's dwelling in heaven as such. It is the rise of powerful reflection in an attempt at theological clarification. How far the distinction came in practice to be accepted inwardly by the generality of cultic participants is another question. In the literature available to us it is at all events a turning-point. For apart from the considerable Deuteronomic writings (including

---

[69] 2 K. 17:16; 21:3, 5; 23:4 f.; Zeph. 1:5; Jer. 8:2; 19:13. Cf. also the repudiation of the cult of the queen of heaven, Ishtar, Jer. 7:18; 44:17 f.

[70] Cf. also 1 K. 8:30; Is. 63:15.

[71] Yahweh in the temple, 1 K. 8:12; 2 K. 19:14.

[72] Dt. 4:36. In JE Yahweh comes down on to Sinai, Ex. 19:11, 18, 20.

[73] Dt. 12:5, 11, 21; 14:23 f.; 26:2, 6, 11; 26:2.

[74] O. Grether, "Name u. Wort Gottes im AT," ZAW Beih., 64 (1934), 1-58.

Deuteronomic redactions), it also affected the work of the Chronicler. The various references to the name of Yahweh in later cultic lyricism may also be regarded as a powerful popularisation of this Deuteronomic movement. [75] In daily cultic practice, and especially in prophecy, interest in Yahweh's true dwelling-place had, of course, to yield to concern as to His manifestation, sphere of power etc. Ez. certainly sees the throne-carriage of Yahweh (Yahweh above the רָקִיעַ, 1:25) coming forth from transcendence (the heavens open, 1:1). But his whole prophetic proclamation is then exclusively concerned with the revealed and present Yahweh and His dealings with Israel and the Gentiles. In so far as the question is not so much that of the dwelling-place of Yahweh, but rather of His sphere of power and dominion, the Deuteronomist, too, must say that "Yahweh alone is God in heaven above, and upon the earth beneath" (Dt. 4:39; 10:14), and that "the heaven and heaven of heavens cannot contain" Him (1 K. 8:27). This view, with its many tensions, is finely expressed in Ps. 113:5 f.: Yahweh is He "who is enthroned on high and looks down below, who raiseth up the poor out of the dust." [76] In times of affliction there broke in on this belief the consoling certainty that Yahweh is always at work in the world too. We find complaints that He has wrapped Himself impenetrably in the clouds (Lam. 3:44), and prayer that He will rend the heavens and come down (Is. 63:19). Sometimes, perhaps, there is a certain scepticism. Thus Eliphaz sees in Job one who thinks that God cannot judge through the cover of clouds which separates Him from men: "Thick clouds are a covering to him, that he seeth not; and he strolleth on the vault of heaven" (Job 22:13 f.; cf. Ps. 10:4). Ecclesiastes is not far from this dangerous notion in his admonition: "God is in heaven, and thou upon earth ..." (Qoh. 5:2; Ps. 115:16). But such ideas are on the periphery of the OT belief. If in the post-exilic period the concept of heaven as the habitation of Yahweh was increasingly confirmed, this is linked almost always with the belief that Yahweh is mightily at work in this world too. Daniel is an instance of this. He uses the expression "God of heaven," which came in during the Persian age. But with it he bears witness to the God who in historical omnipotence controls the destinies of world empires and carries through His plans for the world. [77]

3. Heaven as the Place of Salvation.

If, for all the awareness of God's action in this world, heaven was still regarded as the sphere of Yahweh in a special sense, it was natural to regard this place, which in any event was the source of all blessings (Gn. 49:25; Dt. 33:13; 1 K. 8:35), as the setting of the eternal life inaccessible to man, and indeed as the place where God's planned salvation is already present prior to its working out on earth.

> Obvious here is the influence of distinctive ancient oriental notions of the pre-existence of everything earthly in heaven. "The view is accepted that according to the law of correspondence between the macrocosm and the microcosm the prototypes of all lands, rivers, cities and temples existed in heaven in certain constellations, while these earthly things are only copies thereof." [78] This correspondence, in terms of which what is below

---

[75] For statistics cf. Grether, op. cit., 35-38.

[76] The statement that Yahweh is present also in Sheol (Ps. 139:8) is, however, most unusual.

[77] The use of אֱלָהּ שְׁמַיָּא for the name of God itself, not in apposition to Yahweh (cf. Gn. 24:3, 7: יְהֹוָה אֱלֹהֵי הַשָּׁמַיִם), is first found in Ezr. 5:11 f.; 6:9 f.; 7:12, 21, 23; Da. 2:18 f., 28, 37, 44.

[78] Meissner, op. cit., 110.

is only a copy of what is above, [79] finds expression in the building inscr. of the Sidonian kings Bodaštart and Ešmunazar, in which *šmm rmm* ("high heaven") and *šmm 'drm* ("glorious heaven") are used as names for sections of the city. The earthly Sidon is simply a copy of the heavenly prototype. [80] This speculative view of the world was obviously alien to the older belief in Yahweh. Its influence may be seen only in writings which are clearly later.

The idea of rapture (→ ζωή, II, 848) shows some affinity to this concept. Elijah goes up into heaven in a whirlwind, 2 K. 2:11. Whenever the OT refers to rapture, it always has in view heavenly chambers in which men, rescued from death, are set in a state of perpetual nearness to God. [81] But the reference here is only to very isolated events. The statement in Ps. 119:89 goes much further, for here is a word of salvation which applies to the whole community : "Eternal is, Yahweh, thy word ; it is settled in heaven." There is a very similar thought in Ps. 89:2 : "Grace was built up for ever in heaven, thy faithfulness was grounded in it." [82] Such doxological and hymnic statements do not permit us to fix their theological content with precision. But we clearly find the same idea very sharply developed in the P tradition of the תַּבְנִית, the heavenly model of the earthly tabernacle, which was shown to Moses by God on Mt. Sinai (Ex. 25:9, 40). Finally we might think of Ez. 2:1 ff., the roll of the book already pre-existent in heaven, or Is. 34:5. [83]

The night visions of Zech. should be mentioned in this connection. In the first and last visions Zech. sees the gate of heaven, that is, the two mountains where the heavenly and earthly worlds meet, to which the messengers of God return at evening, and from which they come forth in the morning to accomplish the salvation which God has planned. The content of the vision, which is received during the night between the return and the going forth of the divine messengers, is that the whole kingdom of God is already prepared in heaven, that, though the earth still lies in undisturbed and wicked peace, Yahweh is glowing with zeal, that even down to the last details He has made full provision, that He has indeed considered all possible contingencies. [84] From here the way is fairly direct to the vision of the Son of Man in Da. (→ υἱὸς τοῦ ἀνθρώπου). The question of some Persian influence on the idea of the Son of Man who comes with the clouds of heaven has not yet been settled. Whether we keep to the vision itself, which in original form undoubtedly referred to the taking over of world dominion by a single figure, or whether we prefer the collective interpretation (Da. 7:17 ff.), there can be no doubt that that which comes down from above "with the clouds of heaven" stands in sharp contrast to the empires which have come up from below, from the sphere of chaos.

This is no place to enter into a critical discussion of the various ways in which Da. 7:14 can be expounded or of the conjectural historical background of the statement about the Son of Man. Who is the בַּר אֱנָשׁ, the man, who is so solemnly enthroned in v. 14 ?

---

[79] *Ibid.*, 107.

[80] O. Eissfeldt, *Ras Schamra u. Sanchunjaton* (1939), 62-66, 109-127.

[81] Gn. 5:24; but also Ps. 73:24. Cf. G. v. Rad, " 'Gerechtigkeit' und 'Leben' in der Kultsprache der Ps.," *Festschr. Bertholet* (1950), 426-437.

[82] We do best to read בַּשָּׁמַיִם with the LXX. In exposition cf. B. Duhm, *Die Psalmen*[2] (1922), *ad loc.*

[83] On the "heavenly book" cf. G. Widengren, *Literary and Psychological Aspects of the Hebrew Prophets* (1948), 74 f.

[84] In Zech. 1:8 (cf. 6:1) הָרִים is to be read for הַדַּסִּים. On the night visions as a whole cf. F. Horst in T. H. Robinson-F. Horst, *Die zwölf kleinen Propheten = Handbuch z. AT*, I, 14 (1938).

The most natural solution is still the theory that for the Jewish author ancient Messianic ideas were linked with the prophecy, though in a new and distinctive way.[85] But between v. 13 and v. 14 there is an obvious break in both form and content, for in v. 14 we no longer have the poetic form of the throne vision (Da. 7:9, 10, 13, materially distinct from the vision of the beasts), and the judgment scene is changed into a *translatio imperii*. It is thus evident that existing material is here adapted to a special concern of belief in Yahweh, namely, that of v. 14.[86]

Since heaven is plainly on the same level as earth in view of its creaturehood, and can very commonly be mentioned along with it in this respect, reference may sometimes be made to the shaking of heaven, which is always regarded as an act of judgment by Yahweh. Thus the story of the flood in P depicts a complete collapse of the structure of the world as God established it in Gn. 1-2:4a. In the prophets, too, heaven is affected by the divine judgment, cf. Am. 8:9; Jer. 4:23-26. When Dt. Is. says that heaven "is dispersed like smoke" (Is. 51:6; cf. Job 14:12 *textus emendatus*), he is obviously prophesying a universal cosmic catastrophe, a kind of end of the world.[87] Tr. Is. goes on to speak of the creation of a new heaven and a new earth, Is. 65:17; 66:22. Thus heaven is drawn increasingly into soteriological ideas. On the other hand, one should remember that heaven could not be of central interest for the faith of Israel. Even it it was sometimes depicted as the place of the salvation prepared for Israel, this was a salvation which comes to earth. OT Israel did not, of course, regard heaven as the place of the blessed after death.

The substitution of heaven for the name of God takes place only once in the OT on the very margin of the Canon (Da. 4:23). It may be asked, however, whether such verses as Ps. 73:9 or Job 20:27 did not prepare the way for the well-known later practice, → III, 93. For swearing by heaven (not in place of the name of God etc.), cf. the stele of Sudshin (c. 740 B.C.).[88]

v. Rad

C. The Septuagint and Judaism.

I. The Septuagint.

1. Additions.

In the LXX οὐρανός is used 667 times, almost exclusively for שָׁמַיִם or Aram. שְׁמַיָּא. In only a few instances is it added to the original of the Heb. books.

a. First of all we have additions designed to give greater vividness. Thus εἰς τὸν οὐρανόν is added to the ascent of the smoke in Jos. 8:21, the cry of Elijah in 3 Βασ. 18:36, the stretching out of the hands in Ex. 9:29 A, and of the staff in Ex. 10:13. ἕως τοῦ οὐρανοῦ is added to the burning fire in Dt. 9:15 B (cf. 4:11), ἀπ᾽ οὐρανοῦ to the

---

[85] Cf. A. Bentzen, *Messias-Moses redivivus-Menschensohn* (1948), 72-74.

[86] Materially the throne vision in Da. 7:9, 10, 13 does not originally constitute a unity with the vision of the beasts (Da. 7:1-8, 11-12). M. Noth, "Zur Komposition des Buches Da.," ThStKr, 98/99 (1926), 144-153. On the various derivations of the concept of the Son of Man from Egyptian, Babylonian, Ionic, Iranian, even Indo-Aryan or purely OT presuppositions, cf. the survey in W. Staerk, *Die Erlösererwartung in d. östlichen Religionen* (1938), 422-435; W. Baumgartner, "Ein Vierteljahrhundert Danielforschung," ThR, NF, 11 (1939), 217-222.

[87] Cf. Is. 13:13; 34:4; 50:3; Jl. 2:30 f.; Hag. 2:6, 21; Ps. 102:26 f. On the destruction of the world in the message of the prophets cf. E. Sellin, *Der at.liche Prophetismus* (1912), 122; W. Staerk, "Zu Hab. 1:5-11. Geschichte oder Mythos?" ZAW, 51 (1933), 12.

[88] Text ed. H. Bauer, *Archiv für Orientforschung* (1932), 8, 1-16. Cf. also J. Hempel, ZAW, NF, 9 (1932), 182.

cloud in Job 7:9, ἐκ τοῦ οὐρανοῦ to the fire which falls in 3 Βασ. 18:38, cf. 4 Βασ. 1:10, 12. At Ez. 37:9 A has ἀνέμων τοῦ οὐρανοῦ (רוּחוֹת) instead of πνευμάτων. To fill out the picture ἕως ἄκρου τοῦ οὐρανοῦ is added to ἀπ' ἄκρου τοῦ οὐρανοῦ in Dt. 30:4, cf. also 2 Εσδρ. 11:9 S (Neh. 1:9) and the τοῦ οὐρανοῦ added to τοῦ οὐρανοῦ in 2 Ch. 6:23 B, unless this is a scribal error. To make the "all" of ψ 113:11 (Ps. 115:3) more concrete, ἐν τοῖς οὐρανοῖς καὶ ἐν τῇ γῇ is added, cf. Is. 5:30. On the other hand, the adding of τοῦ οὐρανοῦ to describe the birds in Gn. 40:17, 19; Is. 18:6; ψ 49:11 is based on the stereotyped formula τὰ πετεινά (ὄρνεα) τοῦ οὐρανοῦ. This is newly brought into the LXX text in Hos. 2:14 (cf. Mas. v. 12); Ez. 34:5 A; 3 Βασ. 12:24m (cf. 14:11). In repetitions as compared with the Mas. οὐρανός occurs in Gn. 1:9; Dt. 5:14 B (cf. Ex. 20:11); Job 1:6 A (cf. 1:7).

b. Another reason for adding οὐρανός or using it in transl. of more general terms in the original is to make what is "above" or "on high" more concrete. Thus in Δα. 12:3 LXX הָרָקִיעַ is rendered τοῦ οὐρανοῦ (as compared with Θ τοῦ στερεώματος). Is. 8:21 reads εἰς τὸν οὐρανὸν ἄνω for לְמָעְלָה, Is. 24:18 ἐκ τοῦ οὐρανοῦ for מִמָּרוֹם, Is. 24:21 ἐπὶ τὸν κόσμον τοῦ οὐρανοῦ for בַּמָּרוֹם עַל־צְבָא הַמָּרוֹם (cf. the addition in 13:10), and Is. 38:14 εἰς τὸ ὕψος τοῦ οὐρανοῦ for לַמָּרוֹם.

Earth as the theatre of human history is regarded in the same concrete way, esp. in Job, as ἡ ὑπ' οὐρανόν (γῆ), so for אֶרֶץ Job (1:7); 2:2; 9:6; 18:4; 38:18, 24, 33; 42:15, for חוּצוֹת Job 5:10 (ἀποστέλλοντα ὕδωρ ἐπὶ τὴν ὑπ' οὐρανόν), for תֵּבֵל Job 34:13; Prv. 8:26, for תְּהוֹם Prv. 8:28 (the sea on which the earth rests); at Job 9:13 עֹזְרֵי רָהַב = κήτη τὰ ὑπ' οὐρανόν (addition?). In such instances we do not have a distinctive LXX view or mode of expression, but usage found already in the Mas., cf. Qoh. 1:13; 2:3; 3:1; Job 28:24; 37:3; 41:3; but also שֶׁמֶשׁ for שָׁמַיִם, Qoh. 1:3, 9, 14; 2:11 etc.

c. Finally, the OT belief that God, as Creator of heaven and Ruler of heaven, is linked with heaven, is itself the occasion for the adding of οὐρανός to the original text. Thus שַׁדַּי is rendered ὁ θεὸς τοῦ οὐρανοῦ in Ps. 91:1. The phrase became the most expressive description of God in Hell. Judaism, cf. 2 Εσδρ. 1:2; 5:11 f.; 6:9 f. etc. Witness to God as Creator and Ruler of the world found transcendent expression in it. In Is. 14:13 מִמַּעַל לְכוֹכְבֵי־אֵל becomes ἐπάνω τῶν ἄστρων τοῦ οὐρανοῦ, and in Job 22:26 אֶל־אֱלוֹהַּ is εἰς τὸν οὐρανόν. Though for no dogmatic reason, there may be seen here an anticipation of the later replacement of the name of God by the concept of heaven, 1 Macc. 4:10; 12:15; 2 Macc. 7:11 etc., → III, 93. The case is similar with the ἐν οὐρανῷ of ψ 88:37 for בַּשַּׁחַק. On the other hand, there may be dogmatic reasons for the fact that in Ex. 19:3 B God calls to Moses, not from the mount, but ἐκ τοῦ οὐρανοῦ, since this safeguards the divine transcendence. In Hos. 13:4 ὁ θεός σου στερεῶν οὐρανὸν κτλ. [89] (cf. ψ 32:6; Is. 45:12) is added, and to the protestation in Dt. 8:19 : τόν τε οὐρανὸν καὶ τὴν γῆν (cf. Dt. 4:26; 30:19; 31:28). Additions are also found at 3 Βασ. 8:53a : ἐν οὐρανῷ κύριος, Δα. 3:17: θεὸς ἐν οὐρανοῖς, 9:3 ΘΑ : θεὸν τοῦ οὐρανοῦ. These reflect the Hell. predilection for the phrase "God of heaven" or "God in heaven."

2. The Plural οὐρανοί.

In the LXX οὐρανός occurs 51 times in the plur. This use is almost completely alien to profane Gk. (→ 498, n. 2) and came into Gk. usage by way of the LXX. The model of the Heb. plural makes possible its use in the transl. of the OT. Finding a basis in the plerophory of hymnic and doxological style, it occurs almost exclusively in the Ps. or similar pieces, e.g., 1 Βασ. 2:10; 2 Βασ. 22:10; Hab. 3:3; Dt. 32:43 εὐφράνθητε οὐρανοί cf. Is. 44:23; 49:13, though 1 Ch. 16:31 sing. Parallelism and poetic considerations determine the plur. of Job 16:19. The only prose instance — and this is in a prophetic

---

[89] Cf. Gn. 1:8 : the def. οὐρανός = στερέωμα, with 1:14 : ἐν τῷ στερεώματι τοῦ οὐρανοῦ. Also Plut. De Placitis Philosophorum, II, 11 (II, 888b): στερέμνιον ... τὸν οὐρανόν.

saying — is at 2 Ch. 28:9. In later writings, even when it does not rest on the transl. the plur. takes its place increasingly alongside the sing, cf. 2 Macc. 15:23; 3 Macc. 2:2; Wis. 9:10, [90] 16; [91] 18:15; Tob. 8:5 etc. In its pure use it serves to express the idea of a plurality of heavens which came in from the Orient, along with the associated speculations. Hence the plur. in the phrase ἔκτισεν τοὺς οὐρανοὺς καὶ τὴν γῆν (Jdt. 13:18; cf. 9:12; ψ 68:34; 135:5; Prv. 3:19) is to be regarded as a true plur.

The phrase הַשָּׁמַיִם וּשְׁמֵי הַשָּׁמַיִם (Dt. 10:14; 1 K. 8:27; 2 Ch. 2:5; 6:18; Neh. 9:6) is rendered ὁ οὐρανὸς καὶ ὁ οὐρανὸς τοῦ οὐρανοῦ in the LXX (cf. Sir. 16:18); the status constructus construction is copied here in a way which is not originally Gk. The phrase is also found in the intrinsically incorrect transl. of Ps. 68:34 בִּשְׁמֵי שְׁמֵי, also Ps. 115:16 (ψ 113:24) הַשָּׁמַיִם שָׁמַיִם, and in the plur. ψ 148:4 (cf. also 2 Ch. 6:23 B, though here the repetition may probably be attributed to a scribal error). Though the concepts may be hazy and ambivalent in the transl. of the formula, its use presupposes the idea of several heavens, perhaps a plurality. [92] This presupposition, however, did not determine the development of the phrase, but the desire to express by plerophory the comprehensiveness of the universe.

The fact that the Heb. שָׁמַיִם was used to express in the same way the same ancient view of the world as the Gk. οὐρανός made the Gk. term basically well fitted to serve as a rendering of the Heb. The LXX, however, contributed to the Gk. word the status constructus form and the plural use. Hence it gave to Hellenistic thought the possibility of expressing more easily and quickly the ideas and speculations of the Orient about a plurality of heavens.

II. Judaism.

In Judaism [93] the further use of שָׁמַיִם [94] is characterised on the one hand by burgeoning speculation about heaven under oriental and esp. Babylonian [95] influences, and on the other by the use of heaven as a synon. for God.

a. In the different systems which sometimes appealed to the same sayings (heaven of heavens, heaven and heaven of heavens, Dt. 10:14; 1 K. 8:27; 2 Ch. 2:5; 6:18), distinction was made between 2 to 10 heavens. The notion of 7 heavens, however, was the usual one. [96] A biblical basis was sought for each and a corresponding name developed. [97] "All (these) sevens are beloved before God," Ab. R. Nat., 37 (9d); Pirke R. Eliezer, 154b. A frequently repeated story tells of the ascent of the divine Shekinah from the

---

[90] Once σοφία is said to be derived ἐξ ἁγίων οὐρανῶν.

[91] Comparison of Wis. 18:15 with 16 raises the question whether the sing. of v. 16 is used for the firmament as the visible side of the chambers of heaven, which are envisaged and expressed in the plur. in v. 15, cf. Asc. Is. 7. In Wis., which was originally written in Gk., half the instances of οὐρανός are in the plur.

[92] The greatness of the distance was vividly portrayed in later Judaism, Ber., 9, 13a: "R. Levi (c. 300) has said: From the earth to the firmament is a way of 500 years, and from one firmament to the other (there are 7 altogether) another way of 500 years, and the thickness of each firmament amounts to another way of 500 years" (Str.-B., I, 451). The same view, attributed to R. Jochanan b. Zakkai (d. c. 80), may be found in Chag., 13a (v. Str.-B., I, 606, 975).

[93] Cf. Levy, IV, 574.

[94] שָׁמַיִם can also be used for "height" in Judaism, e.g., bYom., 53a: "Smoke mounts up on high to the highest rafter," cf. Pes., 8b; Ber., 48a.

[95] Cf. Bousset-Gressm., 500, n. 1, with bibl.

[96] So, e.g., Midr. Ps. 114 § 2 (236a) R. Eliazar; Pesikt. r., 5 (18b) R. Shimeon b. Jochai; Pesikt. r., 17b Shimeon b. Josena; RH, 32a; Men., 39a; Ex. r., 15 (78a); Pesikt., 7b; Midr. Ps. 92 § 2 (201b); Tanch. תיומה, 101b; Ab. R. Nat., 37 (9d); Ber., 13a; Pesikt. r., 20 (98a): "God opened seven heavens to Moses." Cf. Str.-B., III, 533. Test. L. 2 f.; Slav. En. 8-22.

[97] Chag., 12b in Str.-B., III, 532. שמיה as a name for the 1st and 6th heaven in Pesikt., 154b; Lv. r., 29 (127c).

1st to the 7th heaven in aversion from the sin of men, and then of its descent from the 7th heaven beyond the first to the tabernacle in view of the piety of the patriarchs and Moses. [98] The idea of 2 heavens (more commonly firmaments) occurs in En. 1:3; 71:5, cf. 1 K. 8:27 and Midr. Ps. 114 § 2 (236a); Chag., 12b; Dt. r., 2 (199b) on the basis of Dt. 10:14; appeal was also made to Ps. 68:34. We also find 3 heavens in 1 K. 8:27; Midr. Ps. 114 § 2; Test. L. 2:9; 3:1-4; Slav. En. 8 (B). Acc. to this ref. Paradise is in or by the third heaven. There are 5 heavens in Gr. Bar. 1:1, unless we follow Orig. Princ., II, 3, 6 : *denique etiam Baruch prophetae librum in assertionis huius testimonium vocant, quod ibi de septem mundis vel caelis evidentius indicatur.* Slav. En. (A) 20:8; 22 f. speaks of 10 heavens. In the uppermost is the throne of God, and hence there is direct access to God there. [99] A vivid depiction of heaven may be found in En. 71:5-10 : "Then the spirit caught up Enoch into the heaven of heavens, and I saw there in the midst of that light a building of crystal stones, and between those stones tongues of living fire. My spirit saw how a fire ran around that house, on its four sides streams of living fire which encircled that house. Round about were seraphim, cherubim and ophanim ; these are they who never sleep but guard the throne of his glory. I saw countless angels, thousands of thousands and ten thousands of ten thousands, around that house. Michael, Gabriel, Raphael and Phanuel and the holy angels up aloft in the heavens go in and out of that house. From that house came forth Michael, Gabriel, Raphael and Phanuel, and innumerable holy angels. And with them came the Ancient of Days ; his head white and pure as wool, and his garment indescribable. Then I fell on my face ..." Cf. also in En. 14:9-23 the description of heaven all aflame to express the fact that "I cannot give any description of its glory and greatness," v. 16. [100] The distance between the individual firmaments, and their individual extent, is said to be a way of 500 years. [101] It can also serve to denote abs. separation, e.g., between man and woman, Ned., 11, 12.

b. Acc. to the Rabb. understanding of the third commandment שָׁמַיִם was used as a paraphrase or concealing concept for God, → 509. [102] The most common phrases are מַלְכוּת שָׁמַיִם "rule of God"; מוֹרָא שָׁמַיִם, "respect for God," Ab., 1, 3; כְּבוֹד שָׁמַיִם "honour of God," Ber., 13a; בִּידֵי שָׁמַיִם, "in God's hand," Ber., 33b; שֵׁם שָׁמַיִם, "name of God," Ab., 4, 4 and 11; לָצֵאת יְדֵי שָׁמַיִם, BM, 37a. רַע לַשָּׁמַיִם וְרַע לַבְּרִיּוֹת in BM, 37a recalls Lk. 15:18. As a name for God שָׁמַיִם was later detached from הַמָּקוֹם.

c. A new creation was expected in the last time. On the one hand this was simply to be a kind of transfiguration which would leave the substance of the old creation intact : "When heaven and earth and all their creatures will be renewed (to new life) like the powers of heaven and all the creatures of earth," Jub. 1:29; when "I shall transform heaven," En. 45:1. Tg. J., I on Dt. 32:1 specifically rejects any destruction of heaven, cf. also Lv. r., 29 (127c). On the other hand there is to be a new creation in the strict sense after complete destruction of the old world : "The first heaven will disappear and pass away, a new heaven will appear, and all the powers of heaven (= stars, Is. 30:26) will shine sevenfold for evermore," En. 91:16. [103]

d. In the Tg. the צְבָא הַשָּׁמַיִם (stars, Is. 34:4) become חֵילֵי שְׁמַיָּא (angels, Tg. Ps. 96:11).

---

[98] So Pesikt. r., 5 (18b). Cf. Tanch. פְקוּדֵי, 129b; Tanch. (Buber) נשא § 24 (19a, 18); cf. Str.-B., III, 172 f.

[99] Cf. Pesikt., 54b, Bar.; Chag., 13a, Bar.; Chag., 12b (in the 7th heaven).

[100] R. Meïr equates blue — sea — firmament — heaven — throne of glory, Sota, 17a, Str.-B., I, 977.

[101] jBer., 9, 13a, 15, cf. bChag., 13a, Bar., Str.-B., I, 605 f., 975.

[102] Cf. Str.-B., I, 863 f.; II, 209. One might say much the same of שְׁמַיָּא; thus מִילֵי דִשְׁמַיָּא means "divine concerns" in Ber., 7b (Da. 4:8). Perhaps because there is a reason for using heaven as a synon. of God — God dwells in heaven — heaven can also be regarded as the fixed setting of the reward allotted to the righteous, e.g., 4 Macc. 17:5 : καὶ ἐστήρισαι ... ἐν οὐρανῷ. Str.-B., III, 584 refers in this connection to Philo Exsecr., 6 : τὴν ἐν οὐρανῷ τάξιν βεβαίαν.

[103] Cf. En. 72:1, also Tg. Ps. 102:27; Tanch. (Buber) בראשית § 20 (8a) v. Str.-B., III, 846.

D. New Testament.

The word occurs in the NT 284 times (94 plur.), 84 in Mt. [104] (plur. 58), [105] 37 in Lk. (plur. 5), [106] 26 in Ac. (plur. 2), 54 in Rev. (plur. 1), [107] 11 in Hb. (plur. 8), 6 in 2 Pt. (plur. 5), 10 in Paul (plur. 3, or 4 with 2 C. 12:2), thus comparatively rare, 9 in Eph. and Col. (plur. 8), [108] no instances in the Past., Phlm., 1, [109] 2 or 3 Jn., 19 in Jn., no plur. [110] The plur. is common in Mt., Eph., Col., Hb. and 2 Pt. Only in the sing. is the word used with ὑπό, ἕως, ἄχρι, almost always in the sing. with ἐκ (plur. Mt. 3:17 par.; 1 Th. 1:10), ἀπό (plur. Hb. 12:25) and εἰς (plur. Ac. 2:34), and only in the plur. with ἐπί and ὑπεράνω. In the Synoptists it is often combined with ἐν in the plur., and only in the plur. in the Epistles apart from 1 C. 8:5. The common occurrence in Mt. is due to two formulae, πατήρ μου (σου, ὑμῶν, ἡμῶν only 6:9) ὁ ἐν τοῖς οὐρανοῖς, 15 times [111] — twice in Mk. [112] — and ἡ βασιλεία τῶν οὐρανῶν 32 times, [113] found only in Mt., [114] → I, 581 f. In both cases the plur. is a Semitism. [115] Esp. to be understood in the plur. are the verses which stand under the linguistic and material influence of Jewish apocr. and Rabb. writings or Hellenistic Gnosis, [116] → 534. It is not necessary to appeal to the latter for an understanding of the Pauline use [117] apart from Eph. 1:10; 4:10; 6:9; Col. 1:16, 20. How far it may have influenced Hb. 4:14; 7:26; 9:23 is very doubtful. The formula ἐν (τῷ, τοῖς) οὐρανῷ (-οῖς) (ἄνω) καὶ ἐπὶ (τῆς) γῆς (κάτω) [118] is OT and corresponds to LXX usage. [119] In the Rabbis, too, it serves to indicate the world as a totality. [120]

[104] At 16:3 D reads ἀήρ for οὐρανός.

[105] In 18:10; 19:21; 24:30 vl. plur.

[106] In 10:20; 21:26 vl. sing.; 18:22 vl. plur.

[107] 12:12 a quotation from Is. 49:13 LXX, cf. 44:23.

[108] Apart from Col. 1:23 cf. 4:1 vl. sing., 𝔖 D G it plur., perhaps under the influence of Eph. 6:9.

[109] Though cf. ἐν τῷ οὐρανῷ at 1 Jn. 5:7 in the comma johanneum.

[110] At Jn. 3:5 ℵ reads τῶν οὐρανῶν for τοῦ θεοῦ.

[111] Mt. 5:48; 23:9 vl. for → οὐράνιος in 𝔖DΘ. In 6:1; 7:21; 10:32, 33 the art., absent elsewhere, is read in 𝔖DΘ. At Mt. 23:8 Blass, on the basis of 𝔖, conjectures ὁ Χριστός: ὁ ἐν τοῖς οὐρανοῖς. This is unlikely, since it is construed acc. to 9a and never occurs elsewhere, cf. Dalman, 155; → II, 537 f.

[112] Mk. 11:25 and v. 26 𝔖 Θ. The phrase is added to Lk. 11:2 in C 𝔖 D Θ by textual assimilation to Mt. Lk. 11:13 reads πατὴρ ὁ ἐξ οὐρανοῦ, for which P⁴⁵ 579 have → οὐράνιος.

[113] At Mt. 5:10 Cl. Al. reads ἔσονται τέλειοι; 13:11 vl. incorrectly θεοῦ; 19:24 uncertain, λ 33 lat sy read τῶν οὐρανῶν.

[114] Elsewhere only Jn. 3:5, where ℵ pc Orig Just erroneously read τῶν οὐρανῶν for θεοῦ. Cf. Ev. Hebr. Fr., 11.

[115] Cf. on the βασιλεία formula → I, 571, on the πατήρ formula → πατήρ, Str.-B., I, 395; E. Lohmeyer, Vater Unser² (1947), 20. Cf. ὁ θεὸς (κύριος) τοῦ οὐρανοῦ, e.g., 2 Εσδρ. 5:11 f.; 6:9 f.; 7:12, θεὸς ἐν οὐρανῷ Da. 2:28; θεὸς ἐν οὐρανοῖς Da. 3:17 LXX, cf. 2 Ch. 20:6 : σὺ εἶ θεὸς ἐν οὐρανῷ.

[116] Cf. Bl.-Debr. § 141, 1.

[117] On 2 C. 5:1 and 12:2 cf. Wnd. 2 K., ad loc.; Str.-B., III, 531; → 534 f. 1 Th. 1:10 is a Semitism, cf. the sing. 1 Th. 4:16; 2 Th. 1:7 (→ 522), but there might be Hell. influences at Phil. 3:20, esp. if with Loh. Phil., ad loc. ἐξ οὗ cannot be related to οὐρανοῖς.

[118] Mt. 6:10; 16:19; 18:18 (23:9 οὐράνιος, 𝔖 D Θ τοῖς οὐρανοῖς); 28:18 (Lk. 2:14 ἐν ὑψίστοις; 19:38 ἐν ὑψίστοις, ἐν οὐρανῷ; 11:2 C[𝔖]DΘ); Ac. 2:19; 1 C. 8:5; Eph. 1:10 (vl. for ἐπί : ἐν AG 69); 3:15; Col. 1:16, 20; Rev. 5:3, 13. Mt. 16:19; Eph., Col. in the plur., reverse order in Col. 1:20. At Col. 3:2 we have ἄνω (→ I, 376 f.) for ἐν (τῷ) οὐρανῷ. Cf. Ign. Sm., 11, 2. Note Rev. 5:3 (three-membered like Ex. 20:4; Dt. 5:8; also ἐπουρανίων — ἐπιγείων — καταχθονίων in Phil. 2:10) and 5:13 (four-membered). On the formula in Judaism, cf. Str.-B., I, 744, n. 1.

[119] Two forms in Heb.: Dt. 3:24; 1 Ch. 29:11; Ps. 113:6; 135:6; Jl. 2:30 : בַּשָּׁמַיִם וּבָאָרֶץ: Dt. 4:39; Jos. 2:11; 1 K. 8:23; Qoh. 5:1: בַּשָּׁמַיִם (מִמַּעַל) וְעַל־הָאָרֶץ (מִתָּחַת); Da. 6:28 : בִּשְׁמַיָּא וּבְאַרְעָא. In LXX the sing. ἐν (τῷ) οὐρανῷ (ἄνω) ... ἐπὶ τῆς γῆς (κάτω). Only ψ 112:6; 134:6 do we have the lit. ἐν instead of ἐπί, cf. Eph. 1:10 vl. Cf. Wis. 9:16, v. Str.-B., II, 424.

[120] On the absence of art. with οὐρανός cf. Bl.-Debr. § 253, 3.

The use of οὐρανός in the NT is determined on the one side by the view of the world which dominates the whole of antiquity, though with variations in detail. According to this picture heaven is the strong, firm vault which secludes the flat earth. Orientals often thought of it as a tent, → 527; 533. The stars were fastened to it, → 534. On the other side, however, the use is also controlled by the idea, self-evident to Judaism, Hellenism and primitive Christianity, that God is above and comes down from thence. Heaven is so much God's sphere that it can be regarded as a synonym for God, → 512; 521. There is hardly an οὐρανός reference to which both these dominant factors have not contributed. οὐρανός in relation to God involves the cosmic meaning, while conversely οὐρανός as a cosmic term involves the relation to God. In the NT, in continuity with OT usage, οὐρανός is the upper [121] and controlling [122] part of the universe, which is always [123] described as οὐρανὸς καὶ γῆ. [124, 125] This expression is not a term for the world not yet understood in cosmological unity. Indeed, the Gk. tt. κόσμος came into use only hesitantly under Hellenistic influence. [126] The integration of heaven and earth is not regarded as immanent; it is understood to be the work of the divine Creator. Heaven and earth, both in their relationship and also in the superiority of heaven over earth, are a symbolical representation of the relation of God as Lord and Creator to His lordship and creation. Thus at no point, not even when used in the sense of firmament and atmosphere, does the term οὐρανός lose this symbolical character (cf. Is. 55:9), which is very evident in its use for the "home of the divine." [127]

1. Heaven and Earth.

οὐρανός is used with γῆ in four main groups of statements.

a. With the earth, heaven was created by God : [128] ὁ ποιήσας τὸν οὐρανὸν

---

[121] Cf. in Jn. 3:31 ἄνωθεν with ἐκ τοῦ οὐρανοῦ, Jn. 19:11 ἄνωθεν with Jn. 3:27 ἐκ τοῦ οὐρανοῦ (φ adds ἄνωθεν); Jm. 1:17 ἄνωθεν with Mt. 7:11 ἐν τοῖς οὐρανοῖς; Jm. 3:15 ἄνωθεν — ἐπίγειος; on ἄνω cf. οὐρανὸς ἄνω Ac. 2:19 (Rev. 5:3 vl.); cf. ἐγὼ ἐκ τῶν ἄνω εἰμί Jn. 8:23 with ἐγώ εἰμι . . . ἐκ τοῦ οὐρανοῦ Jn. 6:51; ἄνω Jn. 11:41 with οὐρανός Jn. 17:1 etc.; ἡ δὲ ἄνω Ἰερουσαλήμ Gl. 4:26 with Ἰερουσαλήμ . . . ἐκ τοῦ οὐρανοῦ Rev. 21:2; Luther renders the ἄνω of Phil. 3:14 by "heavenly." The quotation ψ 109:1 in Col. 3:1 f. shows that ἄνω is identical with οὐρανός; cf. Mt. 26:64; Ac. 2:34; Hb. 8:1 etc. → ἄνω, I, 376; κάτω, III, 640.

[122] Usually heaven comes before earth, cf. the typical ὡς of Mt. 6:10, which cannot be omitted with D Tert Cypr. → n. 163.

[123] Cf. the three-membered form οὐρανός, γῆ, θάλασσα (Rev. 14:7) with τὰ ἐν αὐτῷ (αὐτῇ) (Rev. 10:6; also 5:3; 21:1; Ac. 4:24; 14:15). The four-membered form οὐρανός, γῆ, θάλασσα, πάντα τὰ ἐν αὐτοῖς occurs in Ac. 4:24; 14:15; cf. Rev. 5:13.

[124] Cf. Mt. 5:18, 34 f.; 11:25 and par.; 24:35 and par.; Lk. 12:56; Ac. 17:24; Hb. 12:26; Rev. 20:11; 21:1 and the formula ἐν (τῷ) οὐρανῷ [καὶ] ἐπὶ (τῆς) γῆς → n. 119.

[125] τὰ πάντα cannot be regarded as a consistently used NT expression for the universe. It occurs in a modified way in Col. 1:16, 20; Eph. 1:10, 11, 23 (→ 517 f.). We also find it in R. 11:36; 1 C. 8:6, and cf. Hb. 1:3; 2:10; Rev. 4:11.

[126] Cf. Ac. 17:24 : ὁ ποιήσας τὸν κόσμον καὶ πάντα τὰ ἐν αὐτῷ, οὗτος οὐρανοῦ καὶ γῆς ὑπάρχων κύριος, where the Hell. κόσμος is defined in OT fashion as οὐρανὸς καὶ γῆ. For a similar explanation cf. 1 C. 8:4 and v. 5; → III, 884, 6 ff.; 886, 19 ff.

[127] So Pr.-Bauer, s.v. 2.

[128] 2 Pt. 3:5 : οὐρανοὶ ἦσαν ἔκπαλαι καὶ γῆ ἐξ ὕδατος καὶ δι' ὕδατος (vl. πνεύματος on the basis of Gn. 1:2) συνεστῶσα τῷ τοῦ θεοῦ λόγῳ, cannot be adduced in this connection. The emphasis here is on τῷ τοῦ θεοῦ λόγῳ and the witness is to the creation of heaven and earth by the Word of the Creator in terms of Gn. 1. In spite of grammatical difficulties συνεστῶσα is to be preferred to the συνεστῶτα of א Ψ and the συνεστώσης of B. We are to see here an attraction so that it embraces the plur. and masc. οὐρανοί.

καὶ τὴν γῆν, Ac. 4:24; cf. 14:15; 17:24; Rev. 14:7; [129] ὃς ἔκτισεν τὸν οὐρανὸν ...
καὶ τὴν γῆν, Rev. 10:6; [130] cf. also Hb. 1:10 (= ψ 101:25). [131] A notable feature
here is that we find the statement only as an OT quotation and only in Ac. and
Rev. Thus Ac. 17:24 : ὁ θεὸς ὁ ποιήσας τὸν κόσμον ..., οὗτος οὐρανοῦ καὶ
γῆς ὑπάρχων κύριος. To the creation of heaven and earth corresponds, in fulfilment of prophetic promise (Is. 65:17; 66:22 → 509; 512) their eschatological new
creation : οὐρανὸν καινὸν καὶ γῆν καινήν, Rev. 21:1; καινοὺς δὲ οὐρανοὺς
καὶ γῆν καινήν, 2 Pt. 3:13, cf. Is. 65:17; 66:22. The word καινός (→ III, 449, 6 ff.)
denotes an act of creation which excludes evolution. The addition in 2 Pt. 3:13 :
ἐν οἷς δικαιοσύνη κατοικεῖ, shows that the present temporal heaven has been
essentially disrupted by the ἀδικία of man and has become old (= πρῶτος,
Rev. 21:1), → 520, 4. This new creation is already achieved in God, i.e., in His
saving purpose. The divine can say εἶδον, and to this corresponds κατὰ τὸ ἐπάγ-
γελμα αὐτοῦ προσδοκῶμεν in 2 Pt. 3:13; cf. R. 8:21 ff. [132] The awaited eschatological consummation does not extend, then, to heaven alone. Along with heaven
it includes earth as well.

b. Not earth alone passes away. With it and before it heaven also passes away :
ὁ οὐρανὸς καὶ ἡ γῆ παρελεύσονται, Mk. 13:31 and par.; [133] cf. Rev. 21:1; Hb.
12:26 (= Hag. 2:6; cf. v. 21); [134] 1:11 f. (= ψ 101:26 f.); [135] similarly 2 Pt. 3:10,
12. [136] Heaven and earth are kept for this destruction (2 Pt. 3:7), and both experience the eschatological terror of flight from God's manifestation, Rev. 20:11. [137]
Mt. 5:18 and par. shows how much this stock announcement, which is rooted in
the OT (→ 509) and Jewish apocalyptic (→ 512), is taken for granted. [138] In the
saying here the validity of the Law is linked with the existence of the πρῶτος
οὐρανός and the πρώτη γῆ, while according to Mk. 13:31 only the words of
Jesus cannot be affected by the passing away of heaven and earth. [139] Hence the
existence of heaven and earth testifies to man that he cannot escape the demand
of the νόμος. The passing away of heaven and earth shows that it too, being

---

There is no emphasis on water as the original cosmogonic material ; the ref. here is to the
primal sea of Gn. 1:2, 6. On corresponding cosmogonies cf. the material in Kn. Pt., ad loc.
and H. Gunkel, Genesis⁵ (1922) on 1:2 (102-107).

[129] Quoting Ex. 20:11; 2 Εσδρ. 19:6; ψ 145:6.

[130] Quoting Gn. 14:9; 1 Εσδρ. 6:12; Bel 5.

[131] The κύριος (= יהוה) here addressed as Creator is Christ; cf. Col. 1:16 : ἐν αὐτῷ
(sc. υἱῷ θεοῦ, v. 13) ἐκτίσθη τὰ πάντα (τὰ ACℜ) ἐν τοῖς οὐρανοῖς καὶ (τὰ ACℜDG)
ἐπὶ τῆς γῆς. ἐν αὐτῷ does not describe Christ strictly as Creator, but as "the possibility
in which all being is grounded ... which fashions 'everything' to the reality of its own
purpose, to the entelechy of its own being," Loh. Kol., 56 f. As the formula ἐν-ἐπί already
shows, this is strictly a saying about salvation rather than creation, → 517. It bears witness
to the NT understanding of creation as the "external basis" of the ecclesia.

[132] There is no sea in this new creation. We find neither a first nor a new sea, but only
the sea, and since this is a name and habitation for powers which are hostile to God (Δα.
7:3; Rev. 13:1) it cannot be granted a place in the eschatological consummation.

[133] א omits Mt. 24:35.

[134] Hb. omits the two last members of Hag. 2:6 LXX : καὶ τὴν θάλασσαν καὶ τὴν
ξηράν, and binds the first two, οὐρανός and γῆ, closer together by μόνον-ἀλλά.

[135] αὐτοί (= חֵמָּה) in v. 27 is not to be restricted to οὐρανοί but embraces both heaven
and earth. In Rev. 6:14 (= Is. 34:4) the passing away of heaven is described as the rolling
up of a scroll, though this, too, is connected with earthly events (σεισμός) in v. 12.

[136] Do the στοιχεῖα represent γῆ here, or is it left out ? Cf. v. 10.

[137] οὐρανός here is worked into a combined quotation from ψ 113:7 and 3.

[138] Acc. to Wellh. Mt., ad loc. the saying Lk. 16:17 is even harsher.

[139] Cf. J. Schniewind, Mt. (NT Deutsch), ad loc.

created, [140] is subject to the judgment of God as Lord. But what is said about the passing away of heaven and earth is not the true content of the NT *kerygma*. It is never more than the negative background for the true and positive proclamation of that which endures [141] and is unshakable (Hb. 12:27), i.e., of that which comes. [142]

c. With earth, heaven stands under the same lordship of God. Jesus calls on God as πάτερ, κύριε τοῦ οὐρανοῦ καὶ τῆς γῆς, Mt. 11:25 and par. [143]

Though the expression is uncommon in the OT, [144] Gn. 24:3 (J) [145] shows that it is old and did not simply arise under Persian influence. [146] Esp. in connection with πατήρ, [147] as here, it refers primarily, not to God as Creator, but to the covenant God as the Lord of the world who brings salvation. [148] The emphasis is different in Rev. 17:24 : ὁ θεὸς ὁ ποιήσας τὸν κόσμον καὶ πάντα τὰ ἐν αὐτῷ, οὗτος οὐρανοῦ καὶ γῆς ὑπάρχων κύριος (cf. Is. 42:5). Here the statement about the Lord is bound up with, if not grounded in, that about the Creator. Col. 1:16 (→ n. 131) does not belong to this group ; it is to be expounded along with Eph. 1:10; cf. also Eph. 6:9; Col. 4:1 (→ 517, 5 f.).

With Is. 66:1, Mt. 5:34 [149] and Ac. 7:49 describe heaven and earth as the absolute sphere of God's dominion. His power is manifested at the coming of the Son of Man in the gathering of the elect ἐκ τῶν τεσσάρων ἀνέμων ἀπ' ἄκρου γῆς ἕως ἄκρου οὐρανοῦ, Mk. 13:27.

We have here a combination of three current phrases : ἐκ τῶν τεσσάρων ἀνέμων (Zech. 2:10); ἀπ' ἄκρου τῆς γῆς (Dt. 13:8; 28:64; Is. 5:26 etc.); ἕως ἄκρου τοῦ οὐρανοῦ (Dt. 4:32; 30:4). As in the OT refs., also Mt. 24:31: ἀπ' ἄκρων οὐρανῶν ἕως (τῶν) ἄκρων αὐτῶν, one would expect either earth both times or heaven both times. Since the paradox in Mk. is obviously intentional, [150] the phrase is simply an

---

[140] Probably the plur. in 2 Pt. 3 is meant to show that heaven is to be understood in its totality, in all its zones.

[141] The words of Jesus in Mk. 13:31, Christ (κύριος) in Hb. 1:12b, the θρόνος μέγας λευκός in Rev. 20:11.

[142] The verses in 2 Pt. 3 bear witness to the coming again of Christ ; Rev. 20:11 prepares the way for 21:1; so also Loh. Apk., *ad loc.*

[143] At Lk. 10:21 P 45 and Marcion omit καὶ τῆς γῆς.

[144] Cf. κύριον τὸν θεὸν τοῦ οὐρανοῦ καὶ τὸν θεὸν τῆς γῆς, Gn. 24:3, 7 LXX (in v. 7 the LXX repetitively adds καὶ κτλ.); ὁ κύριος τοῦ οὐρανοῦ καὶ τῆς γῆς, Tob. 7:17 BA; cf. also Jos. Ant., 4, 40; τοῦ θεοῦ τοῦ οὐρανοῦ καὶ τῆς γῆς, 2 Εσδρ. 5:11; ὁ θεὸς ... δέσποτα τῶν οὐρανῶν καὶ τῆς γῆς, Jdt. 9:12. Cf. also θεὸς τοῦ οὐρανοῦ esp. in Δα. LXX 2:44; 4:31, 34, 37 etc.; Θ 2:18, 19; 2 Εσδρ. 5:12; 6:9, 10; 7:12, 21, 23; 11:4; 12:4, 20; cf. Tob. 8:15 א; 10:11. κύριος τοῦ οὐρανοῦ, Δα. LXX 2:37; 4:17; Tob. 6:18 א; 10:13. κύριος θεὸς τοῦ οὐρανοῦ, Jon. 1:9; Δα. 4:33a, 37b; Θ 5:23; 9:3 (A); 2 Ch. 36:23; 2 Εσδρ. 1:2; 11:5, *v.* Gunkel, *op. cit.,* on 24:3. The refs. in Str.-B., I, 607; II, 176; Schl. Mt., 381 do not fully correspond. But *v.* Str.-B., I, 173. ὁ κύριος τοῦ οὐρανοῦ καὶ τῆς γῆς, Preis. Zaub., IV, 641.

[145] Cf. S. Dt., 313 on 32:10 in Str.-B., I, 173 : "Before our father Abraham came into the world God was in some sense king only over heaven, as it is said in Gn. 24:7: 'Yahweh, the God of heaven.' But after our father Abraham came into the world, he made him king over heaven and earth, *v.* Gn. 24:3."

[146] Cf. O. Eissfeldt, "Ba'al Samem u. Jahve," ZAW, 57 (1939), 1-31.

[147] Cf. Schl. Mt., *ad loc.*

[148] So also Bousset-Gressm., 313, but not Lohmeyer, *op. cit.* (→ n. 115), 77. The Rabb. examples in Str.-B., I, 173, acc. to which God as Creator of the world is called its Lord or King, are not par., since there is no ref. to → πατήρ.

[149] Cf. Jm. 5:12 and Mt. 23:22, where Jesus affirms in opposition to Pharisaic casuistry that to swear by heaven is to swear by God, → 180, 5 ff.

[150] The tradition is uniform here. Only a few unimportant MSS have ἄκρου and οὐρανοῦ in the plur. acc. to Mt.

emphatic expression for a gathering which embraces the universe. The end of earth coincides with that of the world. [151]

d. Through the saving event in Jesus Christ heaven and earth acquire a new relation to one another expressed in the formula ... ἐν (τῷ, τοῖς) οὐρανῷ (-οῖς) — ἐπὶ (τῆς) γῆς. [152] In the first instance this can serve to denote an embracing of heaven and earth, as in Eph. 1:10 and Col. 1:16, 20.

Here the formula is added to a preceding → τὰ πάντα [153] to show that this is absolutely exhaustive and all-comprehensive. The plerophoric mode of expression is not merely based on the hymnic liturgical style but is also designed to make the τὰ πάντα more concrete. This is esp. plain in Col. 1:16, where the formula adds to the spatial description of the universe (= τὰ πάντα) a substantial [154] description whose interest centres in the series εἴτε θρόνοι κτλ. which obviously goes with τὰ ἀόρατα, → 369. Probably the whole series — certainly the τὰ ἀόρατα — is to be referred to the ἐν τοῖς οὐρανοῖς. The ascribing of invisibility to heaven is connected with its creaturely function of concealing and enveloping, → 523. [155] Under Gnostic influence (→ 501) the heavens of Eph. and Col. are thought to be filled with demonic forces which subjugate man and his destiny, cf. Eph. 1:20-23. The universe, understood in this concrete way, is in Col. 1:16 f. seen each time (thrice) in strict relation to Christ. The ἐκτίσθη τὰ πάντα ἐν τοῖς οὐρανοῖς καὶ ἐπὶ τῆς γῆς [156] in Col. 1:16, with the abruptly preceding ἐν αὐτῷ (sc. Ἰησοῦ Χριστῷ), is also meant to set creation in the light of salvation history (cf. 16c : τὰ πάντα δι᾽ αὐτοῦ καὶ εἰς αὐτὸν ἔκτισται). The basis of the possibility of being of all things in heaven and on earth is to be found from the very beginning "in Him" through whom — this is the close connection in the text — the work of reconciliation and peace is absolutely accomplished for the totality : "All things in heaven and on earth are drawn into the work of reconciliation and peace," Col. 1:20. [157]

In these verses the τὰ πάντα ἐν τοῖς οὐρανοῖς καὶ ἐπὶ τῆς γῆς denotes the totality in Christ. The formula thus serves as a phrase for the σῶμα concept, cf. v. 18. "Everything in heaven and on earth" is the body of which Christ is the Head. [158] The same thoughts are similarly expressed in Eph. 1:10, where it is pro-

---

[151] Loh. Mk., 279 gives good reasons for a different view : "... the elect are to be assembled on the point of the earth, i.e., its sacred and lofty centre, and from there conducted to the supreme point of heaven, where God is enthroned." He renders ἐπισυνάξει ("to bring together") by "to conduct." But cf. Ass. Mos. 10:8 : "Thou, Israel, shalt rise up on the neck and wings of the eagle ..., and God will exalt thee and cause thee to float in the starry heaven ...," cf. also Philo Migr. Abr., 181: ἀπὸ γῆς ἐσχάτων ἄχρις οὐρανοῦ περάτων, but conversely Cher., 99; v. also En. 104:2, 6.

[152] → n. 118, 119; on Hb. 12:25 (ἐπὶ γῆς — ἀπ᾽ οὐρανοῦ) → 531, 5 f.

[153] Cf. Loh. Kol., 57, n. 4.

[154] Loc. cit., though we also read there : "The concept of the universe is simply expressed in a loose Jewish formula in which heaven and earth represent the thought of a spatial order."

[155] The breach of this order is an indication of the incursion of eschatological events, cf. Ac. 7:55; 2 C. 12:2 ff.; Rev. 4:1; 12:1, 7; 15:1; 21:1, → 529. On heaven opened → 530; cf. Loh. Kol., 54, n. 2. Note should be taken of the Nicene use of this passage.

[156] ACℜ have a τὰ before ἐν τοῖς οὐρανοῖς, ACℜDG before ἐπὶ τῆς γῆς.

[157] Loh. Kol., ad loc. (68). It is worth noting that πᾶς is used 8 times (7 neut.) in the 6 vv. Col. 1:15-20; cf. Eph. 1:21-23 (6 times). In both passages, however, the σῶμα concept is central.

[158] E.g., Loh. Kol., 68; cf. loc. cit. " 'all things' the body ... the community the body of this aeon which overthrows ancient chaos," ibid., 149 : "Only because this peace between 'upper and lower, heavenly and earthly' is established in Christ and is eternal, i.e., because there is one body, is the believer called to peace in one body." Cf. ibid., 144 on Col. 3:12. But on the other hand cf. P. Leid. W., 17, 23 ff. (II, 141) on Serapis : ᾧ οὐρανὸς κεφαλή, αἰθὴρ δὲ σῶμα, γῆ δὲ πόδες, τὸ δὲ περὶ σὲ ὕδωρ ... ὁ ἀγαθοδαίμων· σὺ εἶ ὁ ὠκεανός, ὁ γεννῶν ἀγαθὰ καὶ τρέφων τὴν οἰκουμένην.

claimed as the mystery of the saving divine will that τὰ πάντα ἐν τῷ Χριστῷ, τὰ ἐπὶ (AG ἐν) τοῖς οὐρανοῖς καὶ τὰ ἐπὶ τῆς γῆς, are to be gathered together ἐν Χριστῷ as in a head. Everything that exists in the heavens (cf. the more concrete statement in v. 21) and on earth is integrated as a body whose head is Christ (cf. v. 22), so that here τὰ πάντα τὰ ἐπὶ κτλ. serves to denote the world of Christ.

1 C. 8:5 f. tells us that before the one God and Lord the θεοὶ πολλοὶ καὶ κύριοι πολλοί ... εἴτε ἐν οὐρανῷ, εἴτε ἐπὶ γῆς, on the basis of their genesis and entelechy, which means on the basis of the event of salvation, will become for us no more than λεγόμενοι, i.e., beings without reality. What is in heaven and on earth is defined for us by the one God and the one Lord. There is no other definition of what is in heaven and on earth. In Eph. 3:15 the heavens and earth are combined as spheres in which there may be "families." Their existence is grounded, not just in God or the Creator, but, with emphasis on the work of salvation, in the Father of Jesus Christ, ἐξ οὗ πᾶσα πατριὰ ἐν οὐρανοῖς [159] καὶ ἐπὶ γῆς ὀνομάζεται. [160] In Rev. 5:3 the seer, taught by the revelation of Jesus Christ, realises that there is none in heaven or on earth [161] who has the power or worth to open the sealed book, and in 5:13 he hears all creation in heaven and on earth, also under the earth and on the sea, praising the Lamb who alone is worthy; the Lamb is not one of the all things in heaven and on earth. The presence of the last days, which began in Christ and was manifested in the outpouring of the Spirit (Ac. 2:17), displays itself in the fact that creation is filled with signs and wonders: ἐν τῷ οὐρανῷ (here = in the heavens) ἄνω καὶ ... ἐπὶ τῆς γῆς κάτω (= Jl. 2:30 LXX, where there is no ἄνω, κάτω). The inclusion of heaven and earth in the saving event in Jesus Christ means that no entity in heaven or on earth can possess autonomy: πᾶσα ἐξουσία ἐν οὐρανῷ (-οῖς D) καὶ ἐπὶ τῆς (BD, not א ℵ Θ) γῆς, Mt. 28:18. [162] By the resurrection all power has been placed exclusively in the hands of the risen Lord. Heaven and earth are made more concrete by the text from Da. (7:14) which is taken up in this saying. To earth belong πάντα τὰ ἔθνη τῆς γῆς κατὰ γένη (LXX) or πάντες οἱ λαοί, φυλαί, γλῶσσαι (Θ), to heaven is ascribed αἰώνιος ἐξουσία, and excluded is all decay or destruction, i.e., death, in whose overthrow the power of the resurrection consists.

Not only does the Mt. formula comprehend heaven and earth. It also implies a new interrelation of heaven and earth effected by God's saving action. This is reflected in the expression γενηθήτω τὸ θέλημά σου, ὡς [163] ἐν οὐρανῷ καὶ ἐπὶ

---

[159] The families in heaven are angels. It is not enough to refer to the sons or children of angels in En. 69:4; 71:1; 106:5. En. 69:3 : Heads of their angels, leaders over hundreds, fifties and tens, is more apposite. Cf. Str.-B., I, 744; III, 594 on the "upper family."

[160] Though the content is the same, i.e., that God's fatherhood is the only one, the form is very different in Mt. 23:9 : ... πατέρα μὴ καλέσητε ... ἐπὶ τῆς γῆς· εἷς γάρ ἐστιν ὑμῶν ὁ πατὴρ ὁ οὐράνιος (ℵDΘ ἐν τοῖς οὐρανοῖς). Here οὐράνιος or ἐν τοῖς οὐρανοῖς is fully a part of the designation of God. The saying that true fatherhood is God's alone implies that heaven and earth are not seen together, but are brought into a relation rich in tension, since the Father in heaven is also the true Father for men on earth. This use of the formula is preponderant in Mt., → line 32. Here ὁ οὐράνιος or ἐν τοῖς οὐρανοῖς is also the basis for the removal of all limitations on God, esp. national.

[161] Here three or four-membered formulae are used, → n. 123. ὑποκάτω τῆς γῆς may be equated with θάλασσα; in v. 13 : ἐπὶ τῆς θαλάσσης has a different sense. τὰ ἐν αὐτοῖς relates to all four members. Cf. Loh. Apk., ad loc.

[162] On Mt. 28:18 cf. Bultmann Trad., 169.

[163] ὡς is read also in BGU, III, 954, 18 (6th cent. A.D.). That ὡς (→ n. 165) — καί is certain in spite of D (which does not have ὡς), is shown in Lohmeyer, op. cit. (→ n. 115), 77.

γῆς [164] in Mt. 6:10. [165] Heaven is here described as "the creaturely sphere in which the will of God, which we pray should be done on earth, takes place already, and has always done so." [166] This doing in heaven is an example; it determines the doing on earth. The formula ὡς ἐν — καὶ ἐπί expresses herewith the new participation of heaven in earth which in the saving work of Jesus Christ has replaced the division of heaven and earth. This finds concrete shape in the idea of an eschatological taking up of earth into heaven, or descent of heaven to earth. [167] For all the participation, however, the superiority of heaven over earth is plainly expressed here. But this has a very different basis from the Stoic ἡγεμονικόν of heaven, → 499. It is grounded first in the fact that God's will is done in heaven, which is a par. to the idea of God's throne in heaven (→ 522); cf. on this Hb. 8:1: ἀρχιερέα ... ἐν τοῖς οὐρανοῖς, and 8:4: εἰ μὲν οὖν ἦν ἐπὶ γῆς, οὐδ᾽ ἂν ἦν ἱερεύς (→ 528; n. 246). It is also grounded in the fact that the superiority is designed to reflect God's relation to creation: ὡς ... ὁ οὐρανὸς ἀπὸ τῆς γῆς, οὕτως ... ἡ ὁδός μου ἀπὸ τῶν ὁδῶν ὑμῶν, Is. 55:9. Only in appearance is this contradicted [168] by the promise: ὃ ἐὰν δήσῃς ἐπὶ τῆς γῆς ἔσται δεδεμένον ἐν τοῖς οὐρανοῖς, καὶ ὃ ἐὰν λύσῃς ἐπὶ τῆς γῆς ἔσται λελυμένον ἐν τοῖς οὐρανοῖς, Mt. 16:19. According to this, acts performed on earth will have the power and right to have validity in heaven. Cf. Mt. 18:19: ... ἐπὶ τῆς γῆς ... γενήσεται ... παρὰ τοῦ πατρός μου τοῦ ἐν οὐρανοῖς. The reference here is not to the influencing or control of God's will in heaven by the will on earth; it is to the agreement of the two wills. The division between heaven and earth has been set aside, the third petition is assumed to be granted, [169] and here in the community eschatological fulfilment rules, so that what is found is not power over heaven but right over against the Father through the community. Hence these promises apply to the eschatological saved community of the heavenly dominion, in which God's will is done as in heaven. It should be noted in this connection that the promises are made by Jesus with reference to His "Father in heaven." This means that within creation heaven maintains its prerogative over earth as the starting-point of the divine act of salvation.

The formula εἰς τὸν οὐρανὸν καὶ ἐνώπιόν σου in Lk. 15:18, 21 thus resembles the formula ἐν-ἐπί to the degree that it is meant to comprehend heaven and earth; for earth is represented by the σου, which relates to the earthly father. In this passage οὐρανός is usually taken as a substitute for God, [170] for since εἰς τὸν οὐρανόν is not alone (as, e.g., in Rev. 18:5: αἱ ἁμαρτίαι ἄχρι τοῦ οὐρανοῦ, cf. Ιερ. 28:9: εἰς οὐρανόν), but is accompanied by ἐνώπιόν σου, one cannot argue for the meaning "up to heaven" on the basis of 2 Εσδρ. 9:6: ἕως εἰς οὐρανόν, [171] or 2 Ch. 28:9: ἕως τῶν οὐρανῶν. [172] The meaning "against" rather than "up to" is thus demanded. Hence it is

---

[164] 𝔓DΘ read τῆς; "both nouns are also defined without art.," Schl. Mt., 210.

[165] At Lk. 11:2 א 𝔓DΘ it vg add the third petition in the Mt. version, and D has ὡς. One has thus to consider that a scribal error is perhaps responsible for the omission of ὡς in Mt. 6:10 D. To strengthen the ὡς before καί א adds a οὕτω.

[166] K. Barth, op. cit., 519 (ET, 445).

[167] Acc. to the meaning of βασιλεία τῶν οὐρανῶν in Mt. we must assume the latter. Cf. Lohmeyer, 87; also Barth, loc. cit.

[168] Lohmeyer, op. cit., 77.

[169] In this sense the statements in the two liturgical passages at Lk. 2:14: ἐπὶ γῆς εἰρήνη; 19:38b: ἐν οὐρανῷ εἰρήνη, may perhaps be regarded, not as a contradiction, but rather as an elucidation of the fact that in fixing the relation of heaven to earth the point at issue is the process of salvation in Jesus. Cf. Barth, op. cit., 520 (ET, 446).

[170] Cf. Dalman WJ, I, 178; Str.-B., II, 217.

[171] Zn. Lk., ad loc.; Str.-B., II, 217.

[172] Barth, 493 (ET, 424).

apparent that heaven is used for God. Nevertheless, even though heaven symbolically takes the place of the divine Father (→ 521), [173] it does not cease to be heaven as the counterpart of earth and the starting-point of the divine work of salvation. He who sins on earth sins also against this heaven ; sin can disrupt earth and heaven, cf. 2 Pt. 3:13.

2. God in Heaven.

a. God is called ὁ θεὸς τοῦ οὐρανοῦ (strikingly only in Rev. 11:13; 16:11). [174] According to this designation God, who dwells in heaven (Ps. 2:4 → 504), has a strong affinity to it, though heaven does not have a corresponding affinity to God, since is it God's work. The meaning of the expression is to be sought along the lines of the concept of heaven as the starting-point of the divine work of salvation.

Hence it does not just denote divine transcendence, God's lofty character high above everything earthly. [175] On the contrary, this expression of absolute world dominion [176] is used for cosmic rule over heaven and hence over all the powers which are opposed to God and hostile to man. God as the God of heaven, ruling over heaven, governs earth from heaven.

The same sense is borne substantially by the formula πατήρ μου (σου, ἡμῶν, ὑμῶν) ὁ ἐν τοῖς οὐρανοῖς, [177] Mt. 5:16, 45, 48 vl.; 6:1, 9; 7:11, 21; 10:32, 33; 12:50; 16:17; 18:10, 14, 19; 23:9 vl.; Mk. 11:25, 26 vl.; Lk. 11:2 vl. It is worth noting that in Lk. 11:13 we find ἐξ instead of ἐν, → 521. But the use of πατήρ for θεός emphasises more strongly God's approach to man. The thesis that the name of Father is "a substitute for the name God" [178] does justice neither to the expression nor to the material adduced. In place of the gen. in the sense of "over" we now have ἐν, and heaven is plur. as in Aram., → 510. [179] In two thirds of the instances the designation of God as Father — this shows its significance — carries with it a mention of heaven. [180] More than half of the other instances are statements of Jesus about His Father (Mt. 11:27; 20:23; 24:36 vl.; 25:34; 26:29, 39, 53), so that there is no need of the addition. The specific sense of "in heaven" as applied to God, namely, to denote a complete lack of any earthly or spatial restriction, [181] may be seen in the Sermon on the Mount, which uses the formula particularly : "Father who is in heaven," 5:16, 45, 48 vl.; 6:1, 9; 7:11, 21; the heavenly Father, 5:48; 6:14, 26, 32; "Father who sees into what is concealed," 6:4, 6, 18; "Father who knows," 6:8, 32. Now the statements obviously cannot be equated, but they

---

[173] → 512.

[174] This phrase, which does not denote the "god of heaven" (the gen. means "over") — cf. also Ac. 7:42, → 533 —, is a favourite one in Jewish apocalyptic. It derives from the OT (J) and with the adoption of Canaanite features (→ n. 146) came into widespread use under Persian influence. We find ideas of the dwelling of the gods in heaven among the Babylonians (M. Jastrow, Die Religion Babylons u. Assyriens, I [1905], 218; II [1912], 801; H. Zimmern, Babylonische Hymnen u. Gebete, II [1905], 5), among the Egyptians (A. Erman, Die Ägyptische Religion [1905], 79; G. Roeder, Urkunden d. Religion d. alten Ägypten = Religiöse Stimmen d. Völker, 4 [1915], 5-12); Bousset-Gressm., 312, n. 4; → n. 144 and 505, 26 ff.

[175] Rabb. exegesis regards the designation "God of heaven" (Gn. 24:7) as a limitation of God's sovereignty, cf. → n. 145. The addition καὶ ὁ θεὸς τῆς γῆς in LXX Gn. 24:7 follows v. 3, but has a material basis.

[176] So Bousset-Gressm., 313.

[177] Cf. Lohmeyer, 20; on אֲבוּנָא דְבִשְׁמַיָּא cf. Schl. Mt., 151.

[178] Str.-B., I, 394 f.

[179] θεὸς ἐν (τῷ) οὐρανῷ is rare in the OT, e.g., Δα. 3:17; 4:27; Δα. Θ 2:28. For the same sense cf. Ps. 2:4 יוֹשֵׁב בַּשָּׁמַיִם (LXX ὁ κατοικῶν ἐν οὐρανοῖς).

[180] → οὐράνιος, Mt. 5:48; 6:14, 26, 32; 15:13; 18:35; 23:9.

[181] Acc. to Lohmeyer, 39 f. this is the true meaning as opposed to the "God of Seir" or the "Lord on Zion." If one might mention the restriction of the Samaritans to Gerizim, the definition of the Father as "God in heaven" or "the heavenly One" is par. to the πνεῦμα and ἀλήθεια of Jn. 4:23; cf. ἀληθινός and ἐκ τοῦ οὐρανοῦ in Jn. 6:32 ff.

agree that "the heavenly Father is the God who, unhampered by earthly restrictions, knows all things, sees all things, can do all things, and is thus accessible to all." [182] Hence one may say that what is concealed on earth may be seen from heaven, and that what man needs on earth is known from heaven. It is worth noting in this connection that there is no definition of the nature of heaven, but a clear definition of its function. Heaven is not defined as a place or state. It is a dynamic point of departure.

In Solomon's prayer in the temple one may compare אֶל־הַשָּׁמַיִם (1 K. 8:30, par. 2 Ch. 6:21 מִן־הַשָּׁמַיִם), also בַּשָּׁמַיִם (v. 32, 34, 36 etc., par. 2 Ch. 6:23, 25, 27 etc. מִן־הַשָּׁמַיִם) with the LXX 3 Βασ. 8:30 : ἐν οὐρανῷ, v. 32; 2 Ch. 6:21, 23 : ἐκ τοῦ οὐρανοῦ, though the similarly constructed and closely related מִמְּקוֹם is rendered by ἐν τῷ τόπῳ. This shows that what is said about God's activity in heaven could be understood as action from heaven. The change from ἐν in Mt. 7:11 to ἐκ in Lk. 11:13 is to be explained along the same lines.

b. In Rabb. writings שׁמים (שׁמיא) became a substitute for יהוה, → I, 571; III, 93.

This use is commonly assumed [183] in Lk. 15:18, 21; Mk. 11:30 par. [184] The same supposedly applies also to Mt. 6:20 par.; 51:12 par., also Lk. 10:20. Hence βασιλεία τοῦ θεοῦ in Mk. is preferred to the literal βασιλεία τῶν οὐρανῶν of Mt. But even in the oldest strata NT proclamation gives no hint whatever of any fear of pronouncing directly the name of God. [185] Again, τῶν οὐρανῶν adds a material definition which corresponds linguistically to the material context, → line 6. Though the missionary preaching of the NT can often use expressions from the surrounding world, it has still to be asked whether Mt.'s τῶν οὐρανῶν rather than τοῦ θεοῦ is of no significance in understanding the βασιλεία. This could be true only if οὐρανός were an arbitrary cipher. But the term not only has its own meaning ; it has a meaning which is closely related in content to what it is seeking to state. This may be seen in the fact that heaven could later be distinguished from the wholly neutral הַמָּקוֹם (also הַשֵּׁם, → III, 93). This could not have happened if heaven had adequately screened the term God against misuse. It is said that heaven itself then became "sacred" as a substitute. But logically the same should then have happened in the case of the new substitute הַמָּקוֹם, and it did not. It has thus to be considered whether heaven did not always and necessarily, since there could be no concealment, relate to the concept of God in OT and Jewish proclamation. Surely, even before it was a substitute, when the name of God could be used freely, heaven helped to define the sovereignty of God, cf. Is. 63:15, 19; → 506. [186] It has to be remembered that "what is referred to here is the lordship which comes down from heaven into this world" (better "on to this earth"). [187] Even if the gen. denotes the name of

---

[182] J. Haussleiter, "Vaterunser," RE, XX, 436. He points to Jewish usage acc. to which it is the heavenly Father on whom we rely, and may rely, because He hears Israel's prayer. Hence we read in the Kaddish : "The prayer and supplication of all Israel is accepted before their heavenly Father." Cf. Dalman WJ, I, 153.

[183] Kl. Lk., Kl. Mk., ad loc., with ref. also to Mk. 10:21.

[184] On Lk. 15:18, → 519. On Mk. 11:30 (→ 531): The origin, basis and authority of Jn.'s baptism are either from men or ἐξ οὐρανοῦ (D -ῶν), undoubtedly from God, but no less undoubtedly from the God who in this baptism comes down with His heavenly dominion from heaven. What is at issue is the more precise definition of God which denotes eschatological saving action. This is why we should transl. "heaven" here rather than "God."

[185] Cf. Zn. Mt., 128.

[186] Kuhn → III, 93, n. 148 derives the substitute from the designation of God as אֱלָהּ שְׁמַיָּא in Da. In this case the implied ideas and assertions are preserved.

[187] Cf. K. L. Schmidt, → I, 582; also art. "Jesus Christus," RGG, III, 126. Str.-B., I, 181 regards heavenly dominion as God's gift to men ; hence it comes from heaven as distinct from שׁמים מלכות in the Rabb., over against which man has to act. Cf. Zn. Mt., 126. That God's lordship is understood as a cosmic event is also established by the concept of heavenly lordship, cf. R. Bultmann, Nt.liche Theologie (1948), 3; K. Barth, 506 (ET, 434): ". . . He steps down from the heaven created by Him . . . and He moves from these heavens in the direction of earth."

God, the reason for its use in this sense is palpable. God's kingdom breaks in from heaven. It sets heaven itself in motion : ἤγγικεν ἡ βασιλεία τῶν οὐρανῶν, Mt. 3:2 etc.

Thus the use of "heaven" in these verses is more than a substitute. It is a term for God's name which refers to God's dealings and action. God's work, which is sovereign and which brings sovereignty, is an active lordship coming down from heaven.

c. In keeping is another idea taken from the fixed proclamation of the OT, namely, that heaven itself (Mt. 5:34; 23:22; Ac. 7:49 = Is. 66:1 LXX), or in heaven [188] (Hb. 8:1), [189] is the throne of God. [190]

> But this is not par. to Babylonian, Egyptian or even Gk. ideas, which in various forms are familiar with a dwelling of God or the gods in heaven. Expression of the sovereign action of God always without exception underlies this persistent theme. [191, 192] The ref. is not to a "being" of God in heaven. Throne means dominion, and implies that God's being in heaven is in the full sense His activity in heaven. [193] Heaven is His "official seat." [194] The obedient man will not separate God, His throne and heaven. In his perspective they go together, Mt. 23:22. This is confirmed by the fact that what the NT says about heaven as God's throne, or God's throne in heaven, has no independent significance. It is always used as a traditional way of proclaiming the inviolability and absoluteness of the divine lordship.

3. Heaven and Jesus Christ.

a. In the NT kerygma what is said about the sovereign saving action of God characterised by heaven takes on more concrete shape in statements concerning Christ and heaven. The oldest of these await Christ Jesus, the risen Lord, from heaven as the manifestation of the end : ἀναμένειν τὸν υἱὸν αὐτοῦ (sc. θεοῦ) ἐκ τῶν οὐρανῶν, ὃν ἤγειρεν ἐκ τῶν νεκρῶν, Ἰησοῦν ..., 1 Th. 1:10 (cf. 4:16; 2 Th. 1:7; Phil. 3:20).

In stock apocalyptic images the coming of the Son of Man, which Jesus was believed to be, is also awaited from heaven μετὰ τῶν νεφελῶν τοῦ οὐρανοῦ, Mt. 14:62. [195] οὐρανός is not to be understood here as the atmosphere in which the clouds move. [196] νεφέλη (→ IV, 907; 909) is not a natural cloud, but stands for an event of transfiguration, theophany and apotheosis. Hence οὐρανός, too, is regarded as the absolute starting-point of the apocalyptic process. [197] The same is true of the σημεῖον τοῦ υἱοῦ τοῦ ἀνθρώπου ἐν οὐρανῷ, Mt. 24:30. [198] Since the

---

[188] Cf. ψ 10:4 : ἐν οὐρανῷ ὁ θρόνος αὐτοῦ, also ψ 102:19.

[189] Also to be mentioned here are the refs. in Rev. 4:9, 10; 5:1, 7, which are to be taken in the light of 4:1 ("saw ... in heaven"), just as 5:13 is to be understood in terms of 5:11 and 6:16 in terms of 6:12; "I saw" always means "I saw in heaven."

[190] Cf. ψ 44:6; Song of the Three Children 32 (Δα. 3:54); 4 Esr. 8:20 f.; → III, 162, 26 ff.; 164, 18 ff. The idea of God's right hand is closely bound up with that of His throne in heaven, cf. the quotation of ψ 109:1 in the NT at Mk. 12:36 and par.; 14:62 and par.; (16:19); Ac. 2:34; (7:55); Eph. 1:20; Col. 3:1; Hb. 1:3, 13; 10:12; (12:2).

[191] Cf. H. Gunkel-J. Begrich, Einl. in d. Ps. (1933), 73.

[192] Cf. Ps. 11:4; 14:2; 33:13; 53:2; 68:33; 80:14; 102:19; 113:6; 115:3, 16; Am. 9:6; Is. 40:22; 57:15 etc.

[193] Cf. Mi. Hb.⁸, 184.

[194] Barth, 510 (ET, 438).

[195] Da. 7:13 Θ; LXX ἐπὶ τῶν νεφελῶν, so Mt. 26:64; 24:30 → 508, 30 ff.

[196] So Pr.-Bauer ; the νεφέλαι τοῦ οὐρανοῦ are also to be distinguished from the cloud as a vehicle of ascension (Ac. 1:9; Rev. 11:12).

[197] Cf. 4 Esr. 13:3 ff.

[198] א with art.: D, on the other hand, has τοῦ ἐν οὐρανοῖς to denote the Son of Man as a heavenly being; cf. 1 C. 15:47: ὁ δεύτερος ἄνθρωπος ἐξ οὐρανοῦ (G: ὁ οὐράνιος). Hell. ideas have played some part here, → 528, 17.

promise is that the Son of Man will come from heaven, His sign, which in mysterious fashion is identical with Him, will be visible in the heavens. [199] The absence of speculation as to whether this takes place after the heavenly catastrophe shows most significantly that, though it is still believed that the created heaven will pass away, heaven is very closely linked to the event of eschatological manifestation. Fulfilment of the prophecy in Da. is normative here. [200] In Mk. 14:62 and par., where Da. 7:13 is connected with ψ 109:1, ἐκ δεξιῶν τῆς δυνάμεως (LXX μου) is the *terminus a quo* of the ἔρχεσθαι. Since the right hand of God [201] is identical with His throne, this confirms the idea that the Son of Man comes from heaven as in some sense a localising of the initiative of the divine sovereignty.

In 1 Th. 1:10 — probably a community formula [202] — ἐκ τῶν νεκρῶν corresponds to ἐκ τῶν οὐρανῶν. That is, the resurrection of Jesus from the dead corresponds to His coming from heaven for the resurrection of all the dead. This interconnection plainly underlies 1 C. 15. Χριστὸς ἐγήγερται ἐκ νεκρῶν (v. 20) involves both ὁ δεύτερος ἄνθρωπος ἐξ οὐρανοῦ in v. 47 and ἐν τῇ παρουσίᾳ αὐτοῦ in v. 23, where ἀπ' οὐρανοῦ is a self-evident presupposition (1 Th. 4:16; 2 Th. 1:7). [203] Nothing is said here about an ascension of Jesus. Christ's resurrection from the dead is the basis of the possibility of His *parousia*, which is awaited as a coming from heaven. [204] In keeping is the use of ἐκ, which as compared with the more spatial ἀπό emphasises the idea of origin, coming from, or breaking forth. When it is said in 1 Th. 4:16 that the Lord, i.e., the risen Lord, comes ἀπ' οὐρανοῦ, this again implies : καὶ οἱ νεκροὶ ἐν Χριστῷ ἀναστήσονται. [205] Similarly 2 Th. 1:7 says : ... ἐν τῇ ἀποκαλύψει τοῦ κυρίου Ἰησοῦ ἀπ' οὐρανοῦ ... Here the concept of being concealed in heaven lies behind that of being revealed. What is in heaven cannot be grasped. [206] Heaven conceals. Also in this concealment lies the πολίτευμα ἐν οὐρανοῖς ... ἐξ οὗ καὶ σωτῆρα ἀπεκδεχόμεθα κύριον Ἰησοῦν Χριστόν, Phil. 3:20. [207] The coming of Jesus Christ, which means eschatological manifestation, is regarded in all these passages as a penetration or opening up of the heaven which conceals, → n. 261.

---

[199] Cf. Rev. 1:7. Cf. Wellh. Mt., *ad loc.*; J. Schniewind, *Mt.* (*NT Deutsch*), *ad loc.*: "He (Christ) Himself will ... be in the full sense the sign in His coming from heaven ..." For other explanations cf. Kl. Mt., *ad loc.*

[200] Cf. Loh. Mk. on 13:24-27.

[201] → n. 204 and II, 39, 5 ff.

[202] So A. Seeberg, *Der Katechismus d. Urchristenheit* (1903), 82-85, though cf. Dib. Th., *ad loc.*

[203] παρουσία = ἀποκάλυψις ἀπ' οὐρανοῦ, cf. 1 Th. 4:16 with 2 Th. 2:1.

[204] Cf. v. 52 with 1 Th. 4:16; in R. 8:34 ἐγερθείς denotes being ἐν δεξιᾷ τοῦ θεοῦ, which in R. 10:6 corresponds to ἐν οὐρανῷ.

[205] It is to be noted that ἀπ' οὐρανοῦ is not to be equated with ἐπὶ τὴν γῆν. The texts might suggest that the Messiah comes only so far out of heaven as to be visible on earth. This would presuppose that the promised renewal of heaven had taken place already (with the resurrection?). But there are no speculations about this. What is expected is the coming of Christ from heaven, not the renewal of heaven.

[206] Cf. Dib. Th., 245; Barth, 494 ff. (ET, 424): "Heaven is the boundary which is clearly and distinctly marked off for man." On the doubtful use of the concept of invisibility cf. Col. 1:16.

[207] ἀπεκδέχεσθαι (→ II, 56, 17 ff.) indicates expectation of the *parousia*. Linguistically the first ref. of ἐξ οὗ must be to the πολίτευμα (Loh. Phil., G. Heinzelmann, *Phil.* [*NT Deutsch*], *ad loc.*, but not K. Barth, *Erklärung d. Phil.* [1928], 113, who transl. "from there [heaven]"; Dib. Gefbr., *ad loc.*: "We are at home in heaven ; from thence ..."), but there are no material parallels, and the thought is hard to grasp. At all events we seem to have here a general idea so that, even though the construction refers only to the first part, the

b. The firm expectation of the primitive community that the *Kurios* Jesus would come from heaven in virtue of His resurrection might have led to the formation of a theologoumenon about the *Kurios* in heaven.[208] That this did not happen shows not only the intensity of the expectation but above all the force and significance of the central and original kerygmatic construct : He is risen, that is, He is coming from heaven. He is regarded, not as the One who is, but basically as the One who comes ; hence ἐξ οὐρανοῦ. Only when this force and intensity began to slacken, and the question of ordered life in the world was raised, do we find in the household tables, in admonition to earthly κύριοι, the flourish : ... εἰδότες ὅτι καὶ ὑμεῖς ἔχετε κύριον ἐν οὐρανῷ, Col. 4:1; cf. Eph. 6:9.[209] These exhortations, and the statement about the *Kurios*, simply adopt the established ideas of Hellenism or Judaism, so that no distinctive Christian formulation or view is to be found in the ἐν οὐρανῷ.[210] In a weakened sense the ἐν οὐρανῷ probably denotes not more than simply "over you." In a more emphatic sense it points to the sway of the Judge who knows and perceives all things from — because in — heaven, → 520, 30. There is certainly no ref. to place or state ; we never find any such elsewhere.

c. When later in the primitive *kerygma* the resurrection of Jesus was distinguished[211] from His exaltation and the immediate expectation of His coming from heaven, place was found for the proclamation of the ascension.[212] In Ac. the primitive *kerygma* is still to be seen in Peter's address at Pentecost : τοῦτον τὸν Ἰησοῦν ἀνέστησεν ὁ θεός, 2:32 = τῇ δεξιᾷ οὖν τοῦ θεοῦ ὑψωθείς, 2:33, with the elucidation immediately after in v. 34 : ἀνέβη εἰς τοὺς οὐρανούς = κάθου ἐκ δεξιῶν μου (ψ 109:1). The equation of heaven, δεξιὰ τοῦ θεοῦ and the exaltation[213] is maintained, though the ἀνέβη εἰς τοὺς οὐρανούς implies a slight disjunction of the resurrection and the exaltation. Already in Lk. 24:51 vl.: καὶ ἀνεφέρετο εἰς τὸν οὐρανόν,[214] there is intimation of the external understanding found in the true ascension story in Ac. 1, where heaven itself is set in the foreground :[215] ἀτενίζοντες ... εἰς τὸν οὐρανὸν ..., (ἐμ- ACℵD) βλέποντες εἰς τὸν οὐρανόν, ... Ἰησοῦς ὁ ἀναλημφθεὶς ... εἰς τὸν οὐρανὸν (not D) ..., πορευόμενον εἰς τὸν οὐρανόν, Ac. 1:10 f.[216] The disciples look up to where Jesus

---

material connection is with both. The plur. here is for the Hebrew-speaking Paul the Hebrew plur., to be taken in the sing. This is not impossible in Gk. Materially the ἐξ οὗ certainly refers to heaven. The coming of the Saviour-Lord out of His concealment is awaited.

[208] Naturally Christ dwells in heaven as does God in Rev. 13:6. But there is no emphasis on this insight, perhaps expressed also in Ac. 3:21.

[209] The Lord in heaven is not here, as in Col., the judging Lord, but the Protector of slaves. On the question of the dependence of Eph. on Col. cf. Dib. Gefbr., Exc. after Eph. 5:14.

[210] Cf. Loh. Gefbr. on Col. 4:1.

[211] Cf. R. Bultmann, Art. "Urgemeinde," RGG², V, 1409.

[212] The main influence in the development of this story was neither the Gnostic concept of the redeemer, nor the heavenly journey of the soul (→ 502), nor the Jewish idea of rapture (Elijah, Enoch and Moses). What Bultmann Trad., 310 calls the "ascension legend" arose out of a need to link the resurrection and the expectation from heaven once realistic appearances of the risen Lord were proclaimed. The ascension marks the end of the appearances. Michaelis (ὁράω, → 359) thinks the appearances of the risen Lord were also from heaven.

[213] → n. 190; 528; II, 39, 5 ff.; III, 164, 18 ff.; 442, 16 ff.; IV, 8, 18 ff.

[214] ﬡℜΘ, which Zn. Lk., ad loc. wrongly takes to be original (cf. Kl. Lk., ad loc.), and which, as he sees it, was later omitted by D only in the light of Ac. 1.

[215] Bultmann Trad., 310 f. thinks this is the work of a redactor of Ac. He quotes epistola apostolorum (ed. C. Schmidt [1908], 154): "The heavens opened, and there appeared a light cloud which carried him up." On the eschatological figure of the tearing apart of heaven → 529, 33.

[216] ἀνελήμφθη εἰς τὸν οὐρανόν also in the non-authentic Marcan ending at 16:19 and πορευθεὶς εἰς οὐρανόν in 1 Pt. 3:22 suggest kerygmatic formulations of the primitive

disappears, to heaven, which means in effect the sky. It is very hard to think that in the narrow context of two verses οὐρανός should have a fundamentally different sense the first two times as compared with the last two, esp. as it is always in the sing.[217] The sky, which is as far as the disciples can see Him, is the margin of the heaven which receives and conceals the ascended Lord. The author saw here no contradiction with Ac. 2:32 ff., and rightly so, since the same concept is in the background there too. The primary sense of heaven is that of the incommensurable created cosmos, and this includes as its limit the firmament, by means of which it discharges its function of concealment. Throughout, however, there is also a reference to the direct sphere of God's sovereignty. Witness to this is borne by the quoting of ψ 109:1, which is applied to Christ. This also shows that the heavenly dominion is not yet thought to be consummated. The rule of salvation has still to come down from heaven and be set up on earth (... ἕως ἄν θῶ ..., Ac. 2:35, materially identical with ... ἄχρι χρόνων κτλ., 3:21). Since all speculative interest is set aside by the intense expectation of Christ, or the consummation of salvation history in Lk. and Ac., the determinative factor in the ascension story, too, is the understanding of οὐρανός sub specie dexterae Dei, cf. 1 Pt. 3:22; Mk. 16:19.[218]

> There is a distinctive formulation in Ac. 3:21: Χριστὸν 'Ιησοῦν, ὃν δεῖ οὐρανὸν ... δέξασθαι.[219] Jesus is here[220] the obj. of an activity of οὐρανός, which stands under the saving will of God.[221] The created cosmic heaven, as the upper world with no will of its own, has in virtue of its concealing function (ἄχρι χρόνων ἀποκαταστάσεως) to receive Christ, i.e., His lordship. This statement corresponds materially to the others. Gnostic ideas are quite remote.[222] Cf. Rev. 19:11.

A completely different idea of heaven is found in Eph. 4:9 f. The ἀναβαίνειν, which comes from the quotation of ψ 67:18,[223] is to be taken along with the preceding καταβαίνειν.[224] It is high above the many heavens, indeed, all the heavens (ὑπεράνω πάντων τῶν οὐρανῶν). The heavens are not the goal of the ascent; they are simply passed through in transit. Coming down from heaven means emerging from the heavenly zones, not the coming of the divine rule from heaven. The whole picture gives evidence of Gnostic influence; the plur. is not Semitic, but Hellenistic. The heavenly zones, originally the planetary spheres and regions of fixed stars, are thought to be dominated by powerful evil forces which determine destiny and bind man to the earth and to death. These hermetically seal off the earth from God and keep man captive in their prison. The journey to earth and

---

community which perhaps underlie the account in Ac. as well. Cf. Loh. Mk. on 16:19; πορευθείς Hell. as the journey of Christ in Kn. Pt., ad loc.

[217] This is true even though one argues that the two last refs. come from liturgical formulae whereas the first two belong to the psychologising depiction of the author.

[218] For the ascent to heaven cf. Rev. 11:12; for material cf. Kroll, passim; Loh. Apc., ad loc.

[219] Cf. esp. Bau. Ag., 66 f., who thinks that the basis is an ancient Elijah pericope.

[220] As against Luther. Cf. Wndt. Ag., ad loc.; δέχεσθαι means "to receive," → II, 51, 27 ff.

[221] δεῖ in this sense is Lucan: Ac. 1:21; 5:29; 9:16; 14:22 etc. → II, 22, 31.

[222] Though cf. 1 Pt. 3:22.

[223] The referring of the verse to Christ is a Scripture proof in midrash form. The Rabb. refer Ps. 68:18 to Moses. Cf. Str.-B., II, 596. Sukka, 5a, Bar.: "Nowhere has the Shekinah descended, but Moses and Elijah have ascended."

[224] Cf. H. Schlier, Christus u. d. Kirche im Eph. (1930), 3; G. P. Wetter, Der Sohn Gottes (1916), 82-101. Bu. J., 107, n. 5. For the expression cf. Dt. 30:11, 12; Prv. 30:4; Bar. 3:29; 4 Esr. 4:8; → καταβαίνειν, I, 523, 2. On the preceding καταβαίνειν v. πρῶτον in B it.

the ascent through the heavens is a cosmic shattering of the isolation imposed by these evil powers. This is the work of the Redeemer Christ (Eph. 4:9), who thus mounts up high above the heavens. [225] By disarming these powers He can fulfil the whole (τὰ πάντα = τὰ ἐπὶ [ἐν] τοῖς οὐρανοῖς καὶ τὰ ἐπὶ τῆς γῆς, Eph. 1:10, → 517, 6 ff.). The ascension is here the triumphant procession of the exalted Christ through all the cosmic zones of heaven which He has subjugated. [226] The same line of thought — ἀναβήσεται-καταβήσεται — shapes the similar rhetorical question in R. 10:6 f. [227]

In Jn. 3:13: καὶ οὐδεὶς ἀναβέβηκεν εἰς τὸν οὐρανὸν εἰ μὴ ὁ ἐκ τοῦ οὐρανοῦ καταβάς, the idea of descending and ascending, which is hinted at in Eph. 4:9, finds radical formulation. Only he who has come down from heaven can mount up to heaven, which is barred off from earth, Jn. 3:31. [228] In Jn. οὐρανός does not belong to the "κόσμος." It is ἐπάνω πάντων, 3:31. Yet it belongs to creation (1:3?). In Jn. only the saving will of God and the saving action of the Son of Man characterise the heaven from which Jesus comes [229] and to which He ascends again. [230] Hence this divine will and plan are called → ἐπουράνια in 3:12. According to the Gnostic view the heavenly prototype (εἰκών) of the redeemer remains in heaven even after the beginning of the earthly journey, [231] and he has to be reunited with it when he ascends again. [232] Similarly, the incarnation does not interrupt fellowship with the Father; heaven, which is normally closed, is open above the Son of Man, 1:51, → 530, 3. [233] This opening of heaven, which denotes Christ's redemptive work, is seen by the disciples in the form of the ἀναβαίνειν and καταβαίνειν of angels, which reflects this work. [234]

This continuing fellowship with God is differently expressed by 𝔎Θ lat syr [235] in the addition to Jn. 3:13: ὁ ὢν ἐν τῷ οὐρανῷ [236] (cf. Da. 7:13). Not the pre-existence or the post-existence but the true and proper existence of the Son of Man is in heaven. Heaven is where the continuity of existence is maintained for the Son of Man and for those who belong to Him, cf. Jn. 15:16, 19; 1 Jn. 4:6, → 541, 33 ff.

---

[225] Cf. Jn. 3:31: ἐπάνω πάντων ἐστίν (not D); R. 9:5: ὁ ὢν ἐπὶ πάντων θεός. In respect of the world there is thus equation of Christ with God. For the expression cf. Corp. Herm., XIII, 17: τῷ ἐπὶ τῶν οὐρανῶν μετεώρῳ.

[226] Kroll, 59: "The ascent through the closed spheres is a descent with the reverse sign." Cf. the enthroned Soter on the sarcophagus of Junius Bassus (3rd cent. A.D.), which shows the beardless Christ on the throne, His feet on the head of god Uranos, the veil stretched out above him as the vault of heaven, → 500, 10 ff.

[227] Cf. Ltzm. R., ad loc.; → I, 521, 24 ff.

[228] The fact that οὐρανός is used in Jn. only in the sing. indicates an absence of Gnostic and Jewish speculation about heaven. Indeed, it may indicate a basically anti-gnostic trend, even though there is an extensive use of Gnostic sources and vocabulary. The ἄρχων, or power opposed to God, is said to be τοῦ κόσμου, not in heaven, cf. Jn. 12:31; Eph. 2:2; 1:21.

[229] ἐρχόμενος in 3:31 is a Messianic title and denotes the One who has already come.

[230] The perf. is to be taken as a pres., Bu. J., 107, n. 3.

[231] Ibid., 74, n. 4.

[232] Ibid., 108, n. 4.

[233] This is not a Johannine form of the Synoptic baptism incident, Mt. 3:17; 4:11, so M. Goguel, Au seuil de l'Evangile. Jean Baptiste (1928), 289, 219, and on the other side Bu. J., 74, n. 4.

[234] Acc. to Bu. J., 68 an addition of the Evangelist to his source.

[235] Sys reads ὁ ὢν ἐκ τοῦ οὐρανοῦ, syc impf., so also Bau. J., ad loc.: "Who was in heaven," so that He is now in heaven as the exalted Lord.

[236] Acc. to Bu. J., ad loc. a gloss which indicates post-existence after the ascension, cf. 108, n. 4; also Bau. J., ad loc.

As the One who has come down from heaven (Jn. 6:42, 38) [237] Jesus manifests Himself as the true ἄρτος ὁ καταβαίνων (καταβάς) ἐκ τοῦ οὐρανοῦ (6:41, 50, 51). The originally adverbial ἐκ τοῦ οὐρανοῦ (Ex. 16:4) is now used adjectivally. [238] As concerns the meaning of οὐρανός in Jn., it is worth noting that this ἐκ τοῦ οὐρανοῦ is a negative expression of man's incapacity (6:32): οὐ Μωϋσῆς δέδωκεν, while positively it denotes God's work in salvation history according to an eschatological understanding: ἀλλ' ὁ πατήρ μου δίδωσιν (pres.). ὁ καταβαίνων ἐκ τοῦ οὐρανοῦ can thus be a simple alternative for τοῦ θεοῦ in v. 33. It serves to characterise the uniqueness and comprehensiveness of Christ as Revealer, like ἀληθινός in v. 32 and ζῶν in v. 51. He can thus be called also ὁ ἄρτος (ὁ ζῶν, ὁ ἀληθινός) ὁ ἐκ τοῦ οὐρανοῦ, with a reference to the Lord's Supper in v. 58. [239]

Hb., too, contains similar expressions resting on the thought of a heavenly journey. In these are combined two theological assertions, [240] first, Christ's exaltation to the right hand of majesty ἐν τοῖς οὐρανοῖς (8:1, cf. 1:3 ἐν ὑψηλοῖς), and secondly, the fulfilment of the high-priestly task of Jesus in the fact that, having gone through heaven (διεληλυθότα τοὺς οὐρανούς, 4:14), He has there become ὑψηλότερος τῶν οὐρανῶν (7:26). The σκηνή of 9:11 is also to be understood as heaven (the heavenly tent, → 514, 3; 533, 29). It is indeed the sanctuary [241] through which (διά) He has passed εἰς τὰ ἅγια. Hb. can also use heaven for this chief sanctuary, the holy of holies: εἰς αὐτὸν τὸν οὐρανόν (sing.), 9:24. Different ideas of heaven are to be found here. [242] οἱ οὐρανοί are equated with σκηνή. Of them it is said that they are the greater and more perfect tabernacle not made with hands. They do not belong to this κτίσις, cf. κτίσις in 4:13 with οὐρανοί in 4:14. The heavenly tent here is not cosmic. Hence these heavens do not pass away like those in 1:10-12 (12:26). They are thought of in eschatological and apocalyptic terms. It would be out of place to draw doctrinal conclusions from the fact that they do not belong to the impermanent κτίσις. In accordance with the concepts of Jewish apocalyptic (cf. Slav. En. 3 ff.; Test. L. 3; Asc. Is. 3) they are conceived of as filled with the liturgical ministries of angels. For this reason they are a forecourt which has to be traversed to reach the holy of holies, [243] in which, according to the sacrificial theology of Hb., the true offering is made. The spatial concept has to make way for the metaphysical understanding.

The traversing of heaven in Hb. stands in complete antithesis to Gnostic ideas, where the main point is liberation from the mortal threat to existence and redemption from absolute tragic lostness, → 501, 13. ὑψηλότερος τῶν οὐρανῶν in Hb. 7:26 has a radi-

---

[237] ἀπό (AD ἐκ), elsewhere ἐκ, though with no material distinction, suggests another author or, acc. to Bu. J., ad loc., the Evangelist as distinct from the source.
[238] So already ψ 77:24.
[239] ἐξ (for ἐκ τοῦ) οὐρανοῦ, hence a different author from the source.
[240] "Good Friday and Ascension Day become Christianity's great Day of Atonement," Mi. Hb.[8], 202.
[241] Cf. Rev. 4:1; 19:11, where heaven is also a sanctuary; in 11:19 the ναός τοῦ θεοῦ is in heaven and is opened, "the holy of holies of the heavenly temple." Loh. Apk., ad loc. (Rev. 14:17; 15:5; 16:17 vl. give evidence of a broad identity between heaven, temple and throne).
[242] Mi. Hb. on 9:11 distinguishes between 1. the created transitory heaven, 1:10-12; 2. the heaven through which Jesus passes = the tent which does not belong to this creation, 9:10-12; 3. heaven as the dwelling-place of God, 9:24, → 535, 9.
[243] Cf. Jos. Ant., 3, 123: The holy of holies as a type of heaven and like it inaccessible: "This division of the tabernacle is meant to represent the whole cosmos." As the sanctuary it does not belong to this κτίσις. Cf. Eisler, 603.

cally different sense from the ὑπεράνω πάντων τῶν οὐρανῶν of Eph. 4:10. For as distinct from the Gnostic idea of a complete sealing off of earth from God, and investment by the hostile powers of the zones, the heavens of Hb. are full of angels serving God. [244] There is thus no conflict as in Gnostic views. [245] Only formally is there a certain similarity to the Gnostic structure in so far as the true sanctuary (the place of light) is on the far side of heaven in Hb. too.

Traversing of heaven leads the great High-priest into the true heaven: εἰς αὐτὸν τὸν οὐρανόν (= τὰ ἅγια), 9:24. This is given its true and proper character by the πρόσωπον τοῦ θεοῦ. The figurative language does not clearly say whether one enters God's presence in this heaven or whether this heaven is in some sense identical with God's presence (cf. Rev. 12:10, → 533, 22). Before God's face there are no longer any δείγματα τῶν ἐν τοῖς οὐρανοῖς (Hb. 9:23); there is no type or shadow; there is no longer anything unreal. Here is fulfilment, so that only here can the priestly ministry of heaven be discharged for the community: ἐκάθισεν ἐν δεξιᾷ ... ἐν τοῖς οὐρανοῖς, 8:1 [246] (cf. 1:3). In Hb., then, God is high above the heavens, and yet He is in the heavens.

The def. suggested by the ascension stories, and also by Col. 3:1: τὰ ἄνω ... οὗ ὁ Χριστός ἐστιν ἐν δεξιᾷ τοῦ θεοῦ, namely, that heaven is where Christ is, [247] is, if we assume that τὰ ἄνω = ὁ (οἱ) οὐρανός (-οί), correct in so far as the estimation of heaven in the NT is based, not on what heaven is, but on the purpose it serves, which is to denote the right hand or throne of God. But the def. is in danger of harming the creatureliness and therewith the concept of the spatiality of heaven unless it finds the true sense in a combination of both aspects within God's saving action from heaven on behalf of the created world.

In connection with the preaching of the resurrection Paul contrasts the first man, who is ἐκ γῆς χοϊκός (Gn. 2:7 LXX: τὸν ἄνθρωπον χοῦν ἀπὸ τῆς γῆς) [248] with the δεύτερος ἄνθρωπος ἐξ οὐρανοῦ, 1 C. 15:47, [249] whom he then calls ὁ ἐπουράνιος, → 541, 29 ff. The sharp polemic of v. 46 and the total context make it clear — quite apart from the other typological Adam-Christ passages [250] — that Christ is for Paul the ἄνθρωπος ἐξ οὐρανοῦ (= ἔσχατος Ἀδάμ = πνεῦμα ζωοποιοῦν = ὁ δεύτερος ἄνθρωπος). But there is need to investigate the specific bearing of this expression, the character imparted by the ἐξ οὐρανοῦ, and therewith also the meaning of οὐρανός in this connection. The phrase ὁ οὐράνιος ἄνθρωπος used by Philo [251] (→ 502, 7 f.; 537,

---

[244] Cf. Asc. Is. 7:13 ff.; Test. L. 3 also refers only to ministering creatures in the seven heavens.

[245] Only on the margin of heaven (the firmament) is there in Asc. Is. 7:9 ff. a battle which typifies the war with evil on earth.

[246] Cf. v. 4, so that in some sense there is a use of the formula ἐν οὐρανοῖς ἐπὶ γῆς. He could not be a priest on earth, since God is absolutely above the heavens. The formula is used here to affirm an abs. antithesis.

[247] Barth, 511 (ET, 438).

[248] Cf. Bousset-Gressm., 253 f.; Clemen, 72 f.; Reitzenstein Hell. Myst., 345-350; Ltzm. K., Exc. after 15:46; → I, 142, 4 ff.

[249] Marcion has κύριος for ἄνθρωπος; A has both; G, anticipating v. 48, adds ὁ οὐράνιος.

[250] R. 5:12 ff.; 1 C. 15:22; → I, 141, 13 ff.

[251] Philo Op. Mund., 134: "There is a very gt. distinction between the man who was now (Gn. 2:7) formed and τοῦ κατὰ τὴν εἰκόνα θεοῦ γεγονότος πρότερον (Gn. 1:27)." He calls this man ὁ δὲ κατὰ τὴν εἰκόνα ἰδέα τις ἢ γένος ἢ σφραγίς, νοητός, ἀσώματος ... ἄφθαρτος φύσει, cf. Leg. All., I, 31: "There are two kinds of men: ὁ μὲν γάρ ἐστιν οὐράνιος ἄνθρωπος, ὁ δὲ γήϊνος· ὁ μὲν οὖν οὐράνιος" (on the basis of Gn. 1:27), ibid., 42: To him, the spirit created after God's image and the idea, there had to be assigned a share in the breath (πνεῦμα) of power, which is strength, as compared with the weak breathing allotted to him who was formed of matter. In Philo the first man is the idea, the spiritual heavenly man, the logos (Conf. Ling., 146), while the second is the historical Adam.

23 f.) is like Paul's. Both undoubtedly presuppose the Gnostic myth of the primal man. [252] The origin of this myth is wrapped in obscurity. [253] The resultant terminology became a common legacy. In Philo's οὐράνιος ἄνθρωπος it served to link a concept of man's first estate with the Platonic idea of man. Heaven was here the mythical primal state or the abs. ideal ἀρχή, → 502, 4. Paul, however, probably encountered the myth only in a Rabb. or apoc. version, esp. in the form of the Son of Man (Enoch). [254] He thus used the concept and phrase ἄνθρωπος ἐξ οὐρανοῦ, but in a completely altered sense. The sharp inversion in v. 46 is a safeguard against all myth, for in the context the emphasis rests on the σῶμα or corporeality, not on a fundamentally secondary position of the man from heaven. [255] In Paul, then, the ἄνθρωπος ἐξ οὐρανοῦ belongs, not to the primal age, but to the last time, [256] or, more accurately, to the eschatological present understood as the last time. It is worth noting that there is no exegesis of the ἄνθρωπος ἐξ οὐρανοῦ such as that advanced for the πρῶτος ἄνθρωπος from Gn. 2:7, → n. 251. Paul, then, is not speaking of a heavenly being or using οὐρανός mythically to express the primal state or pre-existence of the heavenly man. [257] He gives the phrase ἐξ οὐρανοῦ its content from the primitive *kerygma*. The train of thought in the chapter — resurrection (v. 20), quotation of ψ 109:1 (v. 25), πνεῦμα ζωοποιοῦν (v. 45), return (v. 52), with a continuing stress on the σῶμα — shows that the phrase is selected mainly from the standpoint of heavenly exaltation. [258] ἐξ οὐρανοῦ is basically and primarily controlled, not by the first time, eternity, pre-existence, but by the victory over θάνατος and σταυρός, the victory which enables the Victor to initiate His manifestation ἐξ οὐρανοῦ. Only from this standpoint, and hence secondarily, is there any ref. to pre-existence. One cannot, then, adopt the mythical scheme and say that Christ's story moves from heaven through the world to heaven. [259] One has to say that Christ is He who rose again in a σῶμα, who is awaited from heaven, and who is thus the ἄνθρωπος ἐξ οὐρανοῦ who already came from heaven in the incarnation. The thesis that He came from heaven has its meaning and origin in the expectation of His coming from heaven. Both statements about the ἐξ οὐρανοῦ are rooted in the resurrection as His heavenly exaltation. The ἄνθρωπος ἐξ οὐρανοῦ is the risen Lord. He is not the consummator but the "death of natural humanity," because, as the One ἐξ οὐρανοῦ, He is the Initiator of the aeon of resurrection.

4. Heaven Opened.

Integral to the story of the baptism of Jesus [260] is the statement: ἠνεῴχθησαν οἱ οὐρανοί, Mt. 3:16. [261] The opening of heaven, which is now closed, [262] cor-

---

[252] Cf. R. Bultmann, Art. "Paulus," RGG², IV, 1035; M. Dibelius, Art. "Christologie, I," RGG², I, 1600 f.

[253] Iranian (Mandaean?); cf. esp. Reitzenstein Hell. Myst., 168 f.; Ir. Erl., 107-110.

[254] Eth. En. 71; 48; v. Bousset-Gressm., 253 f.; cf. also similar ideas in respect of hypostatised wisdom, Prv. 8:22 f.; Wis. 7:25; En. 42.

[255] Cf. Col. 1:15, which refers Gn. 1:27 to Christ, → I, 142, 10 ff.

[256] Cf. W. Bousset, *Kyrios Christos²* (1921), 159.

[257] So E. Stauffer, *Die Theol. d. NT⁴* (1948), 97. Acc. to Jeremias (→ I, 143, 23 ff.) ἄνθρωπος is simply a form of the *bar nasha* which the Corinthians would understand.

[258] So Bousset, *op. cit.*, 184, n. 1; 158 f.; 159, n. 1.

[259] Cf. Dibelius, *op. cit.* (→ n. 252), 1600. So G. Bornkamm in G. Bornkamm, W. Klaas, "Mythos u. Evangelium," *Theologische Existenz heute*, NF, 26 (1951), 25.

[260] Cf. the Johannine form in 1:51, 32; this verse comes from a redactor acc. to Bu. J., 58, but not Bau. J., *ad loc.*

[261] Lk. 3:21: ἀνεῳχθῆναι τὸν οὐρανόν (sing.). Cf. Ez. 1:1: ἠνοίχθησαν οἱ οὐρανοί. Worth noting is the fact that what is here prophetic vision becomes the content of apocalyptic expectation: ἐὰν ἀνοίξῃς τὸν οὐρανόν, Is. 63:19c; Mk. 1:10 reads σχιζομένους τοὺς οὐρανούς (D lat ἠνοιγμένους), which follows the קרע of Is. 63:19 rather than the פתח of Ez. 1:1. With a ref. to 15:38 Loh. Mk. on 1:10 sets the holy of holies of the Jewish in temple parallelism with heaven. Cf. Rev. 11:19; Jos. Ant., 3, 123; on the similar thought in Hb. → 527, 19.

[262] Cf. also Lk. 4:25; Jm. 5:18; Rev. 11:6: The closing of heaven means drought in acc.

responds to eschatological expectation,[263] and implies that Jesus is the Messiah and His baptism the beginning of eschatological happenings : God (the kingdom of heaven) is here (in Him) at hand.[264] Thus Jesus says in Jn. 1:51 that heaven is always open over Him,[265] and as a commentary on Gn. 28:12 this means that Jesus, as Messiah, is Bethel, the house of God,[266] the gate of heaven (v. 17b) on earth. That opened heaven makes it possible for faith to see the δόξα of Jesus[267] corresponds in content to Ac. 7:56,[268] though here, in correspondence with the structure of the Synoptic Gospels and Rev.,[269] the thought is that of a real opening of the sky which conceals heaven.[270] Decisive is the point that the opening of heaven is grounded in the Messianic work of Jesus and also serves to bear testimony to it. On this basis the vision of open heaven in Rev. 19:11 is to be understood as the ἀποκάλυψις Ἰησοῦ Χριστοῦ in Rev. 1:1. Heaven is here a temple (cf. 11:19) to which the door has been opened[271] (Rev. 4:1; cf. 8:1; 11:15; 12:10; 19:1). From this opened Christ-heaven Peter, too, receives his vision, Ac. 10:11, 16; 11:5.

5. Heaven as the Starting-point of the Event of Revelation.

As Christ, the ἄνθρωπος ἐξ οὐρανοῦ, is awaited from heaven, God's revelations also come from heaven. At the baptism of Jesus there sounds forth the φωνὴ ἐκ τῶν οὐρανῶν, Mk. 1:11 and par. (Lk. 3:22 : ἐξ οὐρανοῦ. Cf. 2 Pt. 1:18).

ἐκ τοῦ οὐρανοῦ does not simply denote the pt. in space where the voice comes from. It is also a rendering of the Jewish tt. קוֹל בַּ.[272] The phrase is thus meant to denote the authoritative, because divine, character of the voice from heaven. In the story of the baptism ἐκ τοῦ οὐρανοῦ can even indicate God's own voice from open heaven, and therewith the commencement of the eschatological aeon.[273] The same applies to Jn. 12:28[274] (cf. Ac. 11:9; 2 Pt. 1:18), where the φωνὴ ἐκ τῆς νεφέλης (cf. Mk. 9:7 and par.) becomes a φωνὴ ἐκ τοῦ οὐρανοῦ, with a reminiscence of the divine saying repeated from the baptismal voice. As in Mk. 11:30 heaven here denotes divine con-

---

with the idea of the closing of the sluices of the heavenly ocean ; but behind is concealed the gracious action of God (blessing, fruitfulness). Heaven has always to be understood in this twofold way, → 542, 32.

[263] The basic ref. is Is. 63:19. Cf. S. Bar. 22:1; 3 Macc. 6:18; Volz Esch., 119, 410, 418. Cf. also Corp. Herm., XIII, 17: ἀνοίγητε οὐρανοί.

[264] So Loh. Mk., ad loc.; also G. Bornkamm, "Die nt.liche Lehre von der Taufe," ThBl, 17 (1938), 45.

[265] Note that in Mk. and Mt. the opened heaven is connected with an ἀναβαίνειν and καταβαίνειν (though of a different kind), → 525, 25.

[266] Cf. Gn. 28:17: וְזֶה שַׁעַר הַשָּׁמָיִם.

[267] So Bu. J., 75.

[268] One cannot with Bau. Ag., ad loc. adduce Gn. r., 68, 5 (Str.-B., III, 220) as a par., since here the ref. is not to the opening of heaven but to the divine indication of the reward for the esp. righteous just before death. In particular, Ac. 7:56 refers to the vision of eschatological consummation, not personal reward. The latter rests on the former.

[269] In the ἐν τῷ οὐρανῷ of Rev. 12:1, 3 (cf. v. 4) and 15:1 the ref. is to a vision in the heavens. Similarly, the vision of Rev. 12:7, 13 is seen in the sky (not heaven); cf. Asc. Is. 7:9 as against v. 13.

[270] ἀτενίζειν in Ac. 7:55 is a plastic term ; cf. 1:10. It is peculiar to Lk. Note the sing. in v. 55, the plur. in v. 56.

[271] → n. 240; v. Had. Apk., ad loc.

[272] Cf. Str.-B., I, 125 f.; II, 128; Schl. Mt., 93.

[273] Loh. Mk. on 1:9.

[274] So also Bau., Schl. J., ad loc., but not Bu. J., 328, who seeks an explanation in Mandaean texts, but wrongly, since the refs. adduced speak of a voice in heaven (though also in connection with thunder).

firmation and origin. In Rev. a φωνὴ ἐκ τοῦ οὐρανοῦ is often heard by the divine, 10:4, 8; 11:12; 14:13; 18:4; 21:3.[275] Whether in 10:4, 8; 14:13 this is a tt. for the direct voice of God is open to question.[276] 18:4; 21:3 certainly cannot be related to God's voice.[277] We have thus to think in terms of angels' voices — as in 14:2 — which the seer hears from heaven but which have divine authority. Hb. 12:25 is probably a veiled way of referring to God as the One who speaks from heaven. But the special form ἀπ' οὐρανῶν also bears witness to the preaching of the Gospel by Jesus Christ in heaven, and to its heavenly content,[278] cf. 1 Pt. 1:12.

Like the voice of God, τὸ πνεῦμα also comes from heaven in the story of the baptism in Mk. 1:10 (θεοῦ, Mt. 3:16; τὸ ἅγιον, Lk. 3:22),[279] cf. also Jn. 1:32. Since heaven is here presupposed to be torn apart or opened, the reference cannot be to endowment with the Spirit but to a specific possession of the Spirit.[280]

In 1 Pt. 1:12 the Holy Spirit is described as ἀποσταλέντι ἀπ' οὐρανοῦ. Though acquaintance with the account of Pentecost is unlikely here, it should be noted that at the beginning of the occurrence in Ac. 2:2 there is ref. to an ἦχος which comes ἐκ τοῦ οὐρανοῦ, which can hardly be the upper atmosphere in this instance.[281] From heaven denotes origin, i.e., from the dominion of Jesus, who ascended to heaven and is expected thence.[282] John's baptism was also from heaven, Mk. 11:30 and par. This origin denotes the divine dignity, validity and authority of the baptism, with special emphasis on its eschatological form. Though heaven here is not a direct synonym for God, it intimates God's saving action from heaven. Not perceiving that this heaven is in its significatory character something which has to be believed, the Pharisees ask for a sign ἀπὸ τοῦ οὐρανοῦ, (Mk. 8:11; Mt. 16:1 ἐκ τοῦ; Lk. 11:16 ἐξ). Again the φῶς ἐκ τοῦ οὐρανοῦ in Ac. 9:3 (ὑπὲρ τὴν λαμπρότητα τοῦ ἡλίου, 26:13) is not just from up above, → 542, 36. Under this symbolism it is heavenly. That is, it shines forth from the Kurios in heaven and is thus an illuminating light which leads to faith, knowledge and conversion. Jn. 3:27 says generally that it is impossible for a man to receive anything which is not given him ἐκ τοῦ οὐρανοῦ. The exclusive formulation ἐὰν μὴ ᾖ δεδομένον is typical in Jn. and denotes the exclusiveness of God's (saving) lordship, so Jn. 3:27; 6:65; cf. 19:11, where we have εἰ μὴ ἦν. Thus ἐκ τοῦ πατρός in 6:65 and ἄνωθεν in 19:11 may be adduced in elucidation of ἐκ τοῦ οὐρανοῦ. There is no simple equation of ἐκ τοῦ οὐρανοῦ with God as in Jewish usage, though this is close in 6:65. Worth noting is the difference in emphasis in the differing situations of 6:65 and 19:11. As ἄνωθεν (→ I, 378) is not just identical with God (or ἐκ or ἀπὸ τοῦ πατρός, cf. Jn. 3:3 with 5; Jm. 1:17; Job 3:4), neither is ἐκ τοῦ οὐρανοῦ. Hence it cannot be personified. It acquires a special sense as a function in God's action. Basically and absolutely all giving is from heaven, i.e., from the dominion of the Father of Jesus, which is beyond human control or influence (ἄνωθεν). Man is under heaven; in principle, then, he can be only a passive recipient. Heaven here denotes the action of God which embraces the whole world and which controls all men.

R. 1:18 tells us that the wrath of God is included in the event of revelation which goes forth from heaven. In a plain link with v. 17 (ἀποκαλύπτεται), ἀπ' οὐρανοῦ

---

[275] The ἄλλη of Rev. 18:4 distinguishes this voice from that of the angel in v. 2; in 21:3 ℜP sy have οὐρανοῦ, ℌ vg θρόνου; this shows the connection between the two terms, → 522, 5 f.

[276] Cf. the two plain statements about God's voice in Rev. 16:17; 21:6.

[277] Rev. 19:5; cf. Loh. Apk. on 18:4 and 19:5; also Had. Apk., ad loc.

[278] Cf. Mi. Hb.⁸ on 12:25; E. Käsemann, Das wandernde Gottesvolk (1939), 29.

[279] τὸ πνεῦμα in Mk. (also Jn. 1:32) was, acc. to Dalman, 166, unheard of for God's Spirit in the Jewish period. But "from heaven" is added to the plain designation, cf. Bultmann Trad., 268.

[280] Loh. Mk. on 1:10.

[281] ὥσπερ compares the noise to a wind, cf. Wdt. Ag., ad loc.

[282] Cf. Ac. 3:21; → 525, 19.

corresponds to the ἐν αὐτῷ (sc. εὐαγγελίῳ, v. 16). The saving power manifested in
the Gospel is contrasted with the wrath revealed from heaven, → 426, 30. It is not as
though the Gospel were not also from heaven, cf. 1 Pt. 1:12. But the wrath is not in
the Gospel. As "from heaven" indicated the going forth in revelation of the divine event
of salvation, so God's wrath is also shown by the repeated ἀποκαλύπτεται to be included in the revelation of salvation from heaven. OT figures of speech are adopted to
present God's wrath concretely (→ 399, 9 ff.), e.g., πῦρ ἀπὸ τοῦ οὐρανοῦ (Lk. 9:54;
17:29; Rev. 20:9 vl.; in antichristian imitation ἐκ, Rev. 13:13), θεῖον (Lk. 17:29), χάλαζα
(Rev. 16:21).[283] The closed heaven might also be mentioned here; this withholds the
blessing of rain and fruitfulness, Lk. 4:25; Jm. 5:18; Rev. 11:6.[284]

6. Heaven and the Blessings of Salvation.

As God's throne, the destination of the ascension and the point of departure of
the returning Christ, οὐρανός is an integrating focus for the present and future[285]
blessings of salvation in the new aeon.[286] The strongly sublimated concept of its
spatiality is a help in this connection.[287] The terms used for these blessings confirm
this : → πολίτευμα in Phil. 3:20,[288] → οἰκοδομή, οἰκία, οἰκητήριον[289] in 2 C.
5:1 f., → κληρονομία in 1 Pt. 1:4,[290] → μισθός[291] in Mt. 5:12 and par., → θησαυρός in Mt. 6:20 and par.,[292] also such verbs as ἔχειν in 2 C. 5:1,[293] θησαυρίζειν
in Mt. 6:20, τηρεῖν in 1 Pt. 1:4, ἀποκεῖσθαι in Col. 1:5,[294] ἐγγράφεσθαι, ἀπογράφεσθαι in Lk. 10:20; Hb. 12:23.[295] These blessings are in heaven, which means
with God or Christ,[296] but with the God or Christ with whom believers will also
be, or already are in faith. Heaven here is like a place, but there can be no asking
where it is situated, for such a question is opposed to the whole concept. Heaven
means concealment, and this implies incomprehensibility.[297] The same heavenly
concealment and reality is assumed for the New Jerusalem which the divine sees
coming down from heaven, Rev. 3:12; 21:2, 10.[298] The same applies to the God

---

[283] Gn. 19:24; Ex. 9:23 f.; 2 K. 1:10, 12; 2 Ch. 7:1; Job 1:16; Ep. Jer. 61.

[284] Lack of rain is an apocalyptic sign in Sib., III, 539 f.; Eth. En. 80:2; 100:11; Gr.
Bar. 27:6.

[285] In 2 C. 5:1 ff. ἐπιποθοῦντες is set alongside ἔχομεν to express the dialectical eschatological present indicated by the opened heaven.

[286] Paradise as a heavenly place will come down from heaven to earth at the end of the
days, cf. Bousset-Gressm., 284.

[287] Cf. Plat. Ap., 40c: μετοίκησις τῇ ψυχῇ τοῦ τόπου τοῦ ἐνθένδε εἰς ἄλλον τόπον.

[288] πολίτευμα has "also spatial significance," Loh. Gefbr., ad loc. "Christians belong to
a kingdom," Dib. Gefbr., ad loc.

[289] Cf. Ltzm. K., ad loc.; Wnd. 2 K., ad loc. οἰκοδομὴ ἐκ θεοῦ is here equated with
οἰκία ἐν οὐρανοῖς and οἰκητήριον ἐξ οὐρανοῦ. "From God" means concretely "from
heaven," and what is in heaven is significant as that which comes forth from it. Wnd.
2 K. n., ad loc. pts. out that οἰκοδομή has "greater solidity" than σκηνή.

[290] Used thus esp. in relation to the possession of land.

[291] Cf. Corp. Herm. Exc. 23, 17 (Scott, I, 466, 22): εὐσταθησάσαις μὲν οὖν ὑμῖν οὐρανὸς ὁ μισθός.

[292] The term implies saving, keeping, so S. Nu. § 135 on 27:12. Str.-B., I, 232, 429 f.

[293] ἔχειν lays special stress on the reality; we are thus to think of real possession.

[294] In the part. is "the thought of a substantiality," Loh. Gefbr., ad loc.; cf. Dib. Gefbr.,
ad loc., who pts. out that this is a tt. for the entering of worthy names in the state records.

[295] Cf. Ex. 32:32; Ps. 69:28; Da. 7:10; 12:1; Eth. En. 47:3; 104:1; 108:7; Jub. 30:20. Cf.
Str.-B., II, 169; Dalman, 169, 171.

[296] The pt. of the statement is that the goods are not accessible in their eternal state.
There is no ref. back to the inaccessibility of heaven or the question of its creatureliness,
which also means its transitoriness. Heaven here is defined in terms of the lordship of God
or Christ.

[297] Cf. Barth., 509 (ET, 437).

[298] 4 Esr. 7:26; (10:54) 13:36; cf. Str.-B., III, 796; Loh. Apk. on 21:2.

who speaks from heaven, from Mt. Zion, and from the New Jerusalem, Hb. 12:25, 22.[299] Cf. the temple in heaven in Rev. 11:19.

7. Heaven and the Angels.

Heaven (or the heavens) is served by innumerable angels, their hosts and families. It is the sphere of their existence, Mt. 18:10; Mk. 12:25; 13:32 and par.; Eph. 3:15; Rev. 12:7; 19:1 etc.[300] They come from heaven and return to it either individually (Mt. 28:2 and par.; Lk. 22:43; Gl. 1:8) or in hosts (Lk. 2:15). The seer of Rev. sees them in the heavens or in opened heaven, Rev. 10:1; 18:1; 20:1; 19:14. Their origin in heaven,[301] whose concealment and mystery they share, indicates their character as divine servants and their full authority as God's messengers. But evil powers also seem to live in heaven,[302] e.g., 1 C. 8:5; Ac. 7:42;[303] cf. → ἐπουράνιος, Eph. 3:10; 6:12; (2:2). Heaven here is to be understood as the atmosphere (Eph. 2:2 ἀήρ)[304] or firmament, cf. Asc. Is. 7:9. A pt. to be considered is whether this also applies to Satan, who fell from heaven (Lk. 10:18).[305] If so, the figure of speech is connected with the vision in Rev. 12:7 ff.,[306] where there is ref. to war ἐν τῷ οὐρανῷ, whose outcome is materially similar to the content of the saying of Jesus, since an unexpressed ἐξ οὐρανοῦ (cf. v. 12 κατέβη) corresponds to the ἐβλήθη εἰς τὴν γῆν of v. 9 f., 13. The idea of Satan in heaven is present already in later strata of the NT (→ II, 73, 36 ff.),[307] though, even if he had a τόπος ἐν οὐρανῷ (Rev. 12:8), there is no stress anywhere on his heavenly origin. His fall from heaven[308] — along with the proclamation of the kingdom of heaven — means that he can no longer stand ἐνώπιον τοῦ θεοῦ (Rev. 12:10), so that here "in heaven" means "in God's presence." The exemplary significance of the fact that God's will is done in heaven (→ 518, 34 f.) finds expression in the summons to the οὐρανοί to rejoice, Rev. 12:12 = Is. 49:13 LXX; cf. Rev. 18:20 (sing.), similarly Dt. 32:43; Is. 44:23. Here we have, not hypostatisation, but objectification in hymnic style. Strictly οἱ ἐν αὐτοῖς σκηνοῦντες (Rev. 12:12) are addressed, not angels, but those made perfect, esp. the martyrs.[309] For these are they who mount up into heaven (11:12) and over whom God sets His tent (7:15; cf. 21:3); the equation of tent and heaven is to be noted.[310] Here heaven, like the New Jerusalem, is defined in terms of the perfect service of God rendered by those who are perfected.

---

[299] Mi. Hb., ad loc.

[300] The τὰ ἐν οὐρανοῖς of Eph. 1:10; Col. 1:16, 20 should also be remembered here.

[301] Cf. the alternation of ἄγγελος κυρίου, ἄγγελος τοῦ θεοῦ and ἄγγελος τοῦ (τῶν) οὐρανοῦ (-ῶν).

[302] On the rise of the idea, esp. common in Gnosticism (→ 501, 12), that stars and evil powers are connected, cf. Bousset-Gressm., 322.

[303] ἀρχαί, ἐξουσίαι, 1 C. 15:24; Col. 1:16; 2:10, 15; Eph. 1:21; 3:10; 6:12; δυνάμεις, 1 C. 15:24; 1 Pt. 3:22; κυριότητες, Col. 1:16; Eph. 1:21; θρόνοι, Col. 1:16; κοσμοκράτορες, Eph. 6:12.

[304] Str.-B., IV, 1, 515.

[305] So Pr.-Bauer. In Rev. 12:3 ἐν τῷ οὐρανῷ means in heaven.

[306] Cf. Loh. Apk., ad loc. with instances of similar ideas.

[307] Job 1:6 ff.; Zech. 3:1; cf. 1 Ch. 21:1. To deduce from this that hell is in the midst of heaven corresponds nowhere to the NT view. But cf. Slav. En. 8, where hell is alongside Paradise in the third heaven.

[308] Cf. on this Lk. 10:18 ff., where the same fig. of speech is behind the saying, whose pt. is proclamation of the commencing new aeon. In the context of the gospel this v. is linked with the promise of the inscribing of names in heaven; the same proclamation underlies Rev. 12.

[309] Cf. Loh. Apk., ad loc.

[310] On the shechina of God cf. Str.-B., III, 805, 848.

8. Heaven as the Firmament.

Jesus and men lift up their eyes to this heaven, Mk. 6:41 and par.; 7:34 and Jn. 17:1; Lk. 18:13; Ac. 1:11; 7:55. They look up to the sky. This οὐρανός conceals God's throne and yet therewith it is also a sign of God's ruling presence above men. This is why the publican does not look upwards.³¹¹ The gesture of him who swears corresponds to that of the man who prays toward heaven as toward God, Rev. 10:5. To be man and to live on earth is to be ὑπὸ τὸν οὐρανόν, Ac. 2:5; 4:12; Col. 1:23.³¹² The common pagan expression takes on in Christian preaching the character of man's direction by God. Heaven is a sign of great height, Mt. 11:23; Rev. 18:5. There is also the thought of God's nearness.³¹³ As the atmosphere it becomes red, Mt. 16:2. The hypocrite does not discern that its face (πρόσωπον, Lk. 12:56) is a sign. There fly in it τὰ πετεινὰ τοῦ οὐρανοῦ. Mt. 6:26; 8:20 and par.; Mk. 4:32 and par.; Lk. 8:5; Ac. 10:12; 11:6.³¹⁴ On the other hand, νεφέλη in connection with οὐρανός is already a tt. for the halo, → IV, 905, 22; 909, 20).³¹⁵ The innumerable ἄστρα τοῦ οὐρανοῦ are affixed to heaven as the firmament, Hb. 11:12.³¹⁶ Their falling from heaven is an apocalyptic sign, the breaking up of the firmament,³¹⁷ Mk. 13:25; Mt. 24:29;³¹⁸ Rev. 6:13; 8:10; 9:1; 12:4. The final catastrophe, through it leaves the earth and men remarkably untouched,³¹⁹ is described as a collapse of the vault of heaven, which is awaited as the complete shattering of the δυνάμεις τῶν οὐρανῶν, Mt. 24:29; αἱ ἐν τοῖς οὐρανοῖς, Mk. 13:25.³²⁰

9. Heaven in the Plural.

Since there are many reasons for the use of the plur. οὐρανοί in the individual NT writings,³²¹ one cannot lay down a general rule which applies to the NT as a whole.³²² Paul speaks of the heavenly journey³²³ of his soul in 2 C. 12:2 : ἕως

---

³¹¹ Surprisingly there is little mention of the attitude of prayer, cf., e.g., ψ 122:1; 120:1; Δα. Θ 4:34; Jos. Ant., 11, 162; Str.-B., II, 246; also Lk. 21:28.

³¹² Qoh. 1:13; 3:1. In Lk. 17:24 γῆ or χώρα should be added to ἐκ τῆς and εἰς τήν. For non-bibl. use → 499, 7.

³¹³ Cf. 1 Εσδρ. 8:72; 4 Esr. 11:43. Cf. Hom. Od., 15, 329.

³¹⁴ Cf. Luther's "birds under heaven."

³¹⁵ In Rev. 11:12 the cloud is a means of ascent into heaven, as in Ac. 1:9. This idea of the cloud as a vehicle up to and down from heaven is a common one.

³¹⁶ vl. D it sy τῶν οὐρανῶν.

³¹⁷ On the catastrophe in nature cf. Eth. En. 80:4 ff.; 4 Esr. 5:4 f.; Bousset-Gressm., 250.

³¹⁸ Both verses combine Is. 13:10 LXX : ἀστέρες τοῦ οὐρανοῦ, and 34:4; the ἐκ τοῦ of Mk. becomes ἀπὸ τοῦ οὐρανοῦ (sing.) in Mt.

³¹⁹ Cf. Loh. Mk. on 13:24 ff.

³²⁰ vl. D it sy τῶν οὐρανῶν. Cf. Is. 34:4 : כָּל־צְבָא הַשָּׁמַיִם. Acc. to → II, 307, 16 ff. the ref. is to the spiritual forces behind the cosmic orders ; their disarming is an eschatological event.

³²¹ On plural heavens under the influence of Hell. Gnosticism cf. the material in A. Dieterich, Eine Mithrasliturgie (1903), 179-220; Str.-B., III, 531 f.

³²² Bl.-Debr. § 141, 1: "οὐρανοί = shamayim, though in most authors only in a looser sense as the divine seat (also sing.), while in the strict sense the sing. predominates, except where several heavens are distinguished acc. to the Jewish view." Loh.'s statement, op. cit. (→ n. 115), 78 also does not stand up to examination, e.g., plur. in connection with the earth at Mt. 16:19; 18:10; 24:29; Eph. 1:10; 3:15; Col. 1:16, 20 etc., but there are many instances to the contrary. His rule is that the sing. is used in connection with the earth, the plur. for heaven in its distinction from everything earthly and its orientation to God.

³²³ There are no essentially Gnostic traits here, since the ref. is not to a process of redemption but a special → ὀπτασία, → ἀποκάλυψις granted to him who is already in Christ and an apostle. On the heavenly journey of the soul as an ecstatic state cf. Rohde, II, 91 f.; Reitzenstein Hell. Myst., 221.

τρίτου οὐρανοῦ. In v. 3 f., in what are in part verbal repetitions, he describes this rapture as εἰς τὸν παράδεισον. [324] It is hardly possible to say anything more specific on the nature of the three heavens. [325] Even the first can hardly be regarded unreservedly as the firmament, cf. Asc. Is. 7:9 with v. 13. Only of the third can one say that Paradise and the throne of God are in it or in close proximity. [326] The heavenly function of concealment applies to what is heard there. These are ἄρρητα. That is, they may not and cannot be uttered, a tt. for the secret of the mysteries [327] and in mathematics for what is irrational. [328]

The various heavens of Hb., whose number is not given, are thought of as filled with hosts of ministering angels. If Hb. gives no support for detailed distinction, in terms of the divine action it is possible to classify these heavens under the concepts : κτίσις, σκηνή, ἅγια, [329] → 527, 21. On the heavens of Eph. → 525, 25.

E. The Post-Apostolic Fathers.

The use of οὐρανός in the post-apost. fathers is in general the same as that in the NT, and in the strong appeal to the OT in 1 Cl. it follows specifically that of the LXX. The quotations in 1 Cl. are always in the sing. except at 27,7 (LXX plur.). In 20, 1; 33, 3; 36, 2 the plur. shows the authorship and view of the writer. The heavens are moved by the διοίκησις of God, 20, 1. God has established the heavens by His power (οὐρανοὺς ἐστήρισεν, 33, 3). There are OT and even, at 20, 1, Stoic echoes in these statements about God's work as Creator and Sustainer. On the other hand, at 36, 2 we find popular gnosis in this very ungnostic and moralising author : διὰ τούτου ἀτενίζομεν εἰς τὰ ὕψη τῶν οὐρανῶν, [330] διὰ τούτου ἐνοπτριζόμεθα τὴν ... ὄψιν αὐτοῦ ... διὰ τούτου ἠθέλησεν ὁ δεσπότης τῆς ἀθανάτου γνώσεως ἡμᾶς γεύσασθαι. Barn. has OT quotations and also touches on the ascension : ἀνέβη εἰς οὐρανούς (plur.), 15, 9. In Herm. v., 1, 1, 4 heaven (sing.) opens, and at the end of the manifestation it closes again (v., 1, 2, 1, here plur., though obviously with no special significance). The unattainable height of heaven plays a role in m., 11, 18; v., 4, 1, 5. We find the phrase under heaven for on earth, m., 12, 4, 2; s., 9, 17, 4, → 534, 7. Man can also have honour in the heavens (plur., v., 1, 1, 8). In Did., 8, 2 we find heaven in the sing. in the Lord's Prayer (Mt. 6:9 plur.). In Did., 16, 6 ἐκπέτασις ἐν οὐρανῷ is an apocalyptic sign ; the ref. is to the opening of heaven. [331] Gnostic influences in 2 Cl., 1, 16, 3 (as distinct from 2 Pt. 3:12) are responsible for the restriction τινὲς τῶν οὐρανῶν at their consuming by fire. In Mart. Pol., 9, 1 Polycarp hears a φωνὴ ἐξ οὐρανοῦ; this is the voice of the Lord which none of the bystanders hears. In prayer he lifts up his glance to heaven, 14, 1. In Dg. οὐρανός occurs 12 times, esp. in the plur. Twice we find ἐπὶ γῆς — ἐν οὐρανοῖς, → 517, 4 f.; Christians pass their time on earth, but ἐν οὐρανῷ πολιτεύονται, 5, 9 (cf. Phil. 3:20), cf. 10, 7: τότε θεάσῃ τυγχάνων ἐπὶ γῆς, ὅτι θεὸς ἐν οὐρανοῖς πολιτεύεται. For Christians, who have an immortal soul in a mortal tent,

---

[324] For the setting of Paradise in heaven cf. Eth. En. 39:3; 70:3 etc.; Jos. Bell., 3, 374; 4 Esr. 7:36 ff.; Slav. En. 8. In the last verse the third heaven and Paradise are very close together, though it is not clear whether Paradise is in or directly over the third heaven, cf. Gk. Bar. 4, also Volz Esch., 374; Mi. Hb.⁸ on 4:14, and refs. in Wnd. 2 K. and Ltzm. K., ad loc.

[325] E.g., the first heaven, the sky ; the second, the heavenly ocean ; the third, God's throne. So Barth, 522 (ET, 448).

[326] Rev. 21:3; 7:15 : God in the midst of the elect and the martyrs ; cf. Eth. En. 61:12; 70:3 etc.

[327] Cf. Ltzm. K., ad loc.

[328] Plat. Resp., VIII, 546c.

[329] Cf. Mi. Hb. on 9:11.

[330] For the expression cf. 4 Esr. 4:21: ... τὰ ἐπὶ τοῦ ὕψους τῶν οὐρανῶν.

[331] So Pr.-Bauer,⁴ s.v. ἐκπέτασις.

await έν ούρανοῖς άφθαρσίαν, 6, 8. From heaven God sets the truth and the holy Logos among men. He sends the Creator of the heavens and not an angel or archon etc., one to whom the έν ούρανοῖς διοικήσεις are entrusted, 7, 2. In 10, 2 God's lordship is described as ή έν ούρανῷ βασιλεία, cf. Mart. Pol., 22, 3. The word occurs only twice (sing.) in Ign. We find the formula έπί — έν in Sm., 11, 2 : your work shall be perfect καί έπί γῆς καί έν ούρανῷ. In Eph., 19, 2 an άστήρ έν ούρανῷ cosmically reveals the incarnation of God τοῖς αἰῶσιν by its ineffable appearance.

† ούράνιος.

"Heavenly," [1] of "what dwells in heaven, comes out of or from it, or appears in it." [2] Like ούρανός (→ 497 f.) the word has a double ref. to the abode of the gods or the gods themselves, and also to the sky. It thus acquires two concrete meanings : a. "what is proper to deity," "deity," "God," "divine" (opp. άνθρώπινος, άνθρωπος, θνητός), [3] and b. "what is proper to the firmament or the atmosphere under it" (opp. έγγειος, Plat. Tim., 90a).

It denotes the immortal gods in probably the oldest instance, Hom. Hymn. Cer., 55 : τίς θεῶν ούρανίων ἠὲ θνητῶν άνθρώπων. So Aesch. Ag., 88 ff.: πάντων δὲ θεῶν ... τῶν ούρανίων, also Plat. Leg., VIII, 828c : τῶν χθονίων καί ὅσους αὖ θεοὺς ούρανίους έπονομαστέον. In particular, it characterises Zeus as Ζεὺς Ύψιστος Ούράνιος, cf. Hdt., VI, 56; Ps.-Aristot. Mund., 7, p. 401a, 25 etc. [4] But with him all the Olympian gods bear this name, [5] esp. Artemis (Eur. Hipp. 59), Eros (CIG, 3157), Hera (CIG, 7034) and Themis (Θέμιν ούρανίαν, Pind. Fr., 30, 1; cf. Soph. El., 1064), the daughters of Ούρανός (Hes. Theog., 135). [6] As such they are also called Όλύμπιοι (= οἱ ἄνω = οἱ ὕπατοι); for as Olympus is heaven, it can also be called ούράνιος Ὄλυμπος, Orph. (Abel) Fr., 104. In particular Aphrodite (Κύπρις) is called Ούρανία, Pind. Fr., 122, 4; Hdt., I, 105; this is a distinguishing name (opp. πάνδημος), Xenoph. Sym., VIII, 9; Plat. Symp., 180d. [7] Hes. Theog., 188-198 derives it by a strange development from the god Uranos. [8] ούράνιαι is also used generally for goddesses in the inscr. IG, V, 1, 40 : 'Αγαθοκλῆς ... γραμματεὺς ... καί ἱερεὺς Ούρανίων. [9] The proud saying of the Orphic initiate bears the same sense : Γῆς παῖς εἰμι καί Ούρανοῦ άστερόεντος, αὐτὰρ έμοὶ γένος ούράνιον. This is found on the gold plate of Petelia (4th-3rd cent. B.C.; Diels[5], I, 15, 26); the heavenly race is the divine race. [10] In a similar though weaker sense one can read in Aristot. Fr., 43, p. 1483a, 4 : ή άρμονία έστὶν ούρανία τὴν φύσιν έχουσα θείαν, where ούράνιος and θεῖος are equated. Cf. Aristoph. Ra., 1135 : ήμάρτηκεν ούράνιον ὅσον, also Aesch. Pers., 573.

In the pre-Socratics ούράνιος refers almost exclusively to heavenly phenomena. Thus the sun is φῶς ούράνιον, Emped. Fr., 44 (Diels[5], I, 330, 23); Soph. Ant., 944; the milky way, γάλα τ' ούράνιον, Parm. Fr., 11, 2 (Diels[5], I, 241, 22); the heavenly pole, ού-

---

ούράνιος. [1] Mostly with three, also with two, and in the NT only two, endings ; cf. Bl.-Debr., § 59, 2.

[2] Cf. Δ. Δημητράκου μέγα λεξικὸν τῆς έλληνικῆς γλώσσης (1933), s.v.

[3] Cf. Hom. Hymn. Cer., 55; v. also Philolaos Fr., 11 (Diels[5], I, 411, 10 f.), where we have the combination ... καί θείω καί ούρανίω βίω, and then the continuation καί άνθρωπίνω, i.e., divine and heavenly life, also human.

[4] U. v. Wilamowitz-Moellendorff, Der Glaube d. Hellenen, I (1931), 333 f.

[5] Cf. Aesch. Prom., 164 f.: ούρανίαν γένναν.

[6] On the notable non-Gk. god Αἴξ ούράνιος, cf. Wilamowitz, I, 130.

[7] Acc. to Hes. Theog., 78 Ούρανία is the name of one of the muses ; cf. Plat. Crat., 396bc; cf. also Eur. Phoen., 1729. A daughter of Oceanos also bore this name, Hom. Hymn. Cer., 423; Hes. Theog., 350.

[8] Cf. Wilamowitz, 95, esp. n. 5.

[9] Cf. Pind. Pyth., II, 38 f.

[10] On ούράνιον προκάλυμμα (Orph.) cf. R. Eisler, Weltenmantel u. Himmelszelt, I (1910), 51.

ράνιος πόλος, Aesch. Prom., 429; cf. Eur. Fr., 839, 11 (TGF, 633), and rain οὐράνια ὕδατα, Pind. Olymp., XI, 2; the star is ἀστὴρ οὐράνιος, Pind. Pyth., III, 75. The courses of the stars are called οὐράνια σημεῖα in Xenoph. Cyrop., I, 6, 2, and τὰ οὐράνια are phenomena in the heavens in Xenoph. Mem., I, 1, 11. οὐράνια πάθη are astronomical declensions and changes, Plat. Hi., I, 285c [11] (cf. on this Theophr. Metaphysica, 320b : ἐν τῷ οὐρανῷ καὶ τοῖς οὐρανίοις τὴν φορὰν ζητητέον).

Plato uses the term both scientifically : οὐράνιον ῥεῦμα, Tim. 23a; φυτὸν οὐκ ἔγγειον ἀλλὰ οὐράνιον, 90a, [12] and also popularly for the gods, Leg., VIII, 828c. But in him the term also takes on a sense connected with his doctrine of the ideas. Ἔρως is οὐράνιος, not so much as the descendant of Uranos and son of Urania (Symp., 180d; cf. CIG, 3157), but as the true and proper Eros, because he is determined by the virtue (Symp., 185b) which Socrates accepts as ἀληθές (212a), and this means by true being, the ὄντως ὄν, the idea ; cf. contemplation of supraheavenly space from the highest vault of heaven, Phaedr., 247b. It may thus be said : ὅτι τὰ ... οὐράνια καὶ θεῖα ἀγαπῶμεν, Critias, 107d.

In Gnosticism the οὐράνιοι are heavenly and divine intermediary beings furnished with a σῶμα. [13] Under εἱμαρμένη as the deus summus they stand in the πάντων οὐρανίων τάξις, cf. Corp. Herm., VIII, 4. In the pap. cf. esp. petitions and oaths which mention the tyche of the ruler : δέομαι τῆς οὐρανίου ὑμῶν τύχης, P. Lips., 35, 20; 34, 17 etc.; P. Masp., 97, II, 79 : κατὰ τοῦ ζῶντος θεοῦ οὐρανίου. The word occurs in the Lord's Prayer in BGU, III, 954, 16. It is a mathematical entity in Okkelos, Diels⁵, I, 440, 15.

Philo is acquainted with the οὐράνιος ἄνθρωπος who κατ' εἰκόνα δὲ τετυπῶσθαι θεοῦ, Leg. All., I, 31; he is the οὐράνιος Ἀδάμ, I, 90. By participation in him each man is an οὐράνιος, a dweller in heaven, since he draws close to the stars by his visual faculty, Op. Mund., 147. In Philo οὐράνιος is a term which is designed to express the philosophical concept of the idea and also that of divine origin. [14] As there is a heavenly and earthly man, so also heavenly and earthly virtue, Leg. All., I, 45, and a corresponding moral philosophy, Sacr. AC, 86. Heavenly or Olympian insights are free from αἴσθησις, Som., I, 84. Thus Philo can speak of an οὐράνιος λόγος, Plant., 52, of heavenly love, Cher., 20, a heavenly message, wisdom etc., οὐράνιος being oriented to the pure νοῦς, Gig., 60; Som., I, 146. There is no precise usage in Jos. The pagan gods (Ap., 1, 255) and the theme of philosophy (1, 14) are both οὐράνιος. The term also refers to astronomical processes, so that σοφία ἡ περὶ τὰ οὐράνια is without religious accent, Ant., 1, 69. But the χῶρος οὐράνιος is the heaven in which martyrs and righteous men are received, Bell., 3, 374; → 533, 28.

The term hardly found its way into the LXX, and there are few instances in the pseudepigr. When there is a Heb. or Aram. original we always find שמים or שמיא. There are thus the same distinctions of meaning as for οὐρανός (→ 497 f.; 509 f.). Instead of τὸν θησαυρὸν ..., τὸν οὐρανόν Dt. 28:12 A reads : τὸν θησαυρὸν ..., τὸν οὐράνιον in the same sense ; heaven is the storehouse from which rain and fruitfulness are promised. It is God Himself who opens the heavenly gates so that radiant angels may descend from heaven, 3 Macc. 6:18. "Heavenly" is thus used for the space in which the angels hold sway around God's throne. Their host can also be called οὐράνιος στρατός in 4 Macc. 4:11; cf. Lk. 2:13. As heaven can denote God (→ 521, 14), the same applies to οὐράνιος. Hence the God of Israel can also be called κύριος ὁ οὐράνιος, 1 Εσδρ. 6:14. The ἐξουσία ἡ οὐράνιος of Δα. ΘΒ 4:26 (Α ἐπουράνιος) refers to God's power. God's children bear the name οὐράνιοι παῖδες, 2 Macc. 7:34. [15] But this verse also shows that the concept "heavenly" = "divine" always carries with

---

[11] A work of Democrit. is called αἰτίαι οὐράνιαι, Diels⁵, II, 91, 13.
[12] There is a reading οὐράνιον ἀψῖδα for ὑπουράνιον, Phaedr., 247b.
[13] Dii celestes inhabitant summa celestia, Ascl., III, 38b (Scott, I, 362, 2).
[14] Cf. Op. Mund., 117; Abr., 69; Plant., 52.
[15] Cf. Rev. 11:12, where God camps among the martyrs.

it a spatial implication, for these children are the martyred brothers (cf. 7:36) who have entered the sphere of God's covenant promise to eternal life. [16] In 2 Macc. 9:10 οὐράνιος is controlled by the idea of the firmament as the boundary of the unattainable divine region.

In the NT οὐράνιος is used esp. in the formula in Mt. [17] ὁ πατὴρ ὑμῶν ὁ οὐράνιος (5:48; 6:14, 26, 32; 23:9) or ὁ πατήρ μου ὁ οὐράνιος (15:13; 18:35). [18] This is another rendering of the same Jud.-Aramaic expression elsewhere translated by the Matthean formula ὁ πατήρ μου (σου, ἡμῶν, ὑμῶν) ὁ ἐν τοῖς οὐρανοῖς, → 520, 17. The vl. at 5:48; 23:9 confirm this. In the context οὐράνιος seeks to emphasise two things. The first is the heavenly Father's openness and turning to man, the second His power to achieve it. The heavenly Father is He who from heaven brings the saving change of the aeons over all nations and to all men. [19] In Lk. 2:13 the στρατιά is called οὐράνιος. [20, 21] This is designed to show that the στρατιά consists of servants of God who from heaven proclaim on earth His saving action, the birth of the σωτήρ, → 533, 8. In Ac. 26:19 the ὀπτασία (→ 372, 26 ff.) which initiates Paul's conversion is called οὐράνιος. οὐράνιος here is par. to οὐρανόθεν in 26:13 or ἐκ τοῦ οὐρανοῦ in the other accounts in 9:3; 22:6. It denotes the place from which the appearance comes. The vision is from the κύριος (26:15), i.e., the risen Lord, and demonstrates His resurrection power. Cf. Ac. 26:16 f. [22]

In the post-apost. fathers the word occurs only in Mart. Pol., 22, 3, where the βασιλεία (of Jesus Christ) is called ἡ οὐράνιος, cf. Dg., 10, 2.

† ἐπουράνιος. [1]

ἐπ- here does not denote "upon" but "at," i.e., "in heaven," cf. ἐπι-θαλάσσιος "situated by the sea." a. It is used of the heavenly gods who dwell in heaven and come thence. It bears only this sense in Hom.: οὐκ ἂν ἔγωγε θεοῖσιν ἐπουρανίοισι μαχοίμην, Il., 6, 129; Od., 17, 484; Ζεὺς ἐπουράνιος, P. Flor., 296, 12 (6th cent. A.D.: Preisigke Sammelbuch, 4166); synon. with God : τὸν γάρ φασι μέγιστον ἐπουρανίων, Theocr. Idyll., 25, 5. [2] In the Orph. it is once said of the θεῖος λόγος, under Jewish-

---

[16] בְּנֵי שָׁמַיִם = ἐπουράνιοι, 1 C. 15:48, as a self-designation for a pious sect, → 299, n. 21.
[17] At Lk. 11:13 P⁴⁵ reads οὐράνιος for ἐξ οὐρανοῦ, → 521, 12; cf. the par. Mt. 7:11.
[18] At 5:48 Tert. D* and many others, and at 23:9 ℵ (DΘ) read ὁ ἐν τοῖς οὐρανοῖς for ὁ οὐράνιος, while at 18:35 CℜΘ read ἐπουράνιος. This shows that οὐράνιος and ἐπουράνιος are taken in the sense not only of ἐν τοῖς οὐρανοῖς but also of ἐκ τοῦ οὐρανοῦ, describing God's action as from heaven, → 521, 5.
[19] This, and with it the eschatological belief in Yahweh, is completely missed by v. Wilamowitz, op. cit., I, 334, who notes concerning Ζεὺς οὐράνιος, the lord of heaven as universal god : "Among the Jews it was the great accomplishment of the prophets that the old Yahweh, bound to earth and place, was set in heaven ... But Yahweh remained the national God, and the national gods of other nations remained gods alongside Him ..., whereas the God whom Jesus proclaims was really the Father of all men and could thus be fused very well with the god of the Hellenes."
[20] B* D* read οὐρανοῦ, so also Ac. 7:42, but with ref. to the stars worshipped as deities.
[21] Cf. 4 Macc. 4:11 οὐράνιος στρατός; 3 Βασ. 22:19 : וְכָל צְבָא הַשָּׁמַיִם; = πᾶσα ἡ στρατιὰ τοῦ οὐρανοῦ; cf. 2 Ch. 18:18. In the Rabb. all Israel or the tribe of Levi alone can be called heavenly hosts, cf. Str.-B., II, 116.
[22] οὐράνιος ἄνθρωπος corresponds to the philosophical term for the first or primal man, → 528, 33; 537, 21 f. In 1 C. 15:47 G has the materially equivalent οὐράνιος for ἐξ οὐρανοῦ. This shows that in the NT οὐράνιος is never controlled by the sense of "sky."
ἐπουράνιος. [1] In class. Gk. with three endings, in the NT with two.
[2] Cf. also Luc. Dialogi Deorum, 4, 3 : ἤδη γὰρ ἐπουράνιος εἶ.

Christian influence : ἔστι δὲ πάντῃ αὐτὸς ἐπουράνιος, καὶ ἐπὶ χθονὶ πάντα τελευτᾷ ἀρχὴν αὐτὸς ἔχων καὶ μέσσην ἠδὲ τελευτήν, Orph. Fr., 247, 33 ff. b. In the sense of "belonging to the divine heaven" : εὐσεβέων ἐπουράνιοι, Pind. Fr., 132, 3. [3] In Plato those who love in chastity traverse the ἐπουράνιος πορεία after death, Phaedr., 256d. They will see the truth, the ideas, there. c. It is used for the μετέωρα in Plat. Ap., 19b : τά τε ὑπὸ γῆς καὶ τὰ ἐπουράνια (vl. οὐράνια).

In the Herm. writings the θεός is called ἐπουράνιος. [4] Along with this general use the ἐπουράνια are more precisely defined as things *quae in caelo sunt*, or *deos ... qui supra ... sunt.* [5] They are also described by ἀσώματον, ἀγένητον, αὐτεξούσιον, and esp. as not ἀνάγκῃ ὑποκείμενα. [6] Abammonis calls them cosmic as distinct from supracosmic deities ; they are indeed among the ἐμπύριοι. [7] There is a similar use in the great Paris magic pap. (Jewish), P. Par., 574, 3042.

Philo can use the term in sense b.: the soul is properly nourished by the ἐπουρανίοις ἐπιστήμαις which consist in the λόγος (reason) θεοῦ συνεχής Leg. All., III, 168 f. He also has it in sense c.: Abram ═ ἄνθρωπος οὐρανοῦ because among the Chaldeans he was occupied with τὰ μετέωρα καὶ ἐπουράνια, Gig., 62, cf. Virt., 12.

The word is rare in the LXX ; it is sometimes an alternative for οὐράνιος. In ψ 67:14 it is a rendering of שַׁדַּי, elsewhere transl. παντοκράτωρ. For God it means the same as κύριος (θεός) ἐν τῷ οὐρανῷ or οὐρανοῦ, → 510, 38; 520, 8. In a second instance it is used for שַׁדַּי. In Δα. Θ 4:26 A (Mas. 4:23), also 4 Macc. 4:11; 11:3, it is a vl. for οὐρανός, with the same sense. In 2 Macc. 3:39 the divine name is paraphrased ὁ τὴν κατοικίαν ἐπουράνιον ἔχων. The context shows that it is meant to denote God's saving dominion over the whole earth and all nations so that it corresponds materially to παντοκράτωρ ἐπουράνιος in 3 Macc. 6:28 and ὁ ἐπουράνιος θεός in 7:6. There is an obvious spatial implication in 2 Macc. 3:39, where it is orientated to created heaven as God's throne. This spatial concept is never abandoned in principle.

In the NT ἐπουράνιος occurs in Jn. 3:12, and apart from that only in Paul, Eph., 2 Tm. and Hb. [8] It is used both as adjective and noun.

In Eph. we find the formula [9] ἐν τοῖς ἐπουρανίοις at 1:3, 20; 2:6; 3:10; 6:12. A comparison with par. verses shows the sense. Thus in Eph. 1:20 (cf. 2:6), as regularly in other citations of the same passage (cf. also the throne of God, → 522, 7), the καθίζειν ἐν δεξιᾷ αὐτοῦ of ψ 109:1 is represented as in οὐρανός. This is why the vl. Eph. 1:20 B can have ἐν τοῖς οὐρανοῖς in exactly the same sense. The ἀρχαὶ καὶ ἐξουσίαι which are ἐν τοῖς ἐπουρανίοις acc. to Eph. 3:10; 6:12 are thought of as dwelling in the οὐρανοί, Col. 1:16; cf. Eph. 3:15 etc. In all these passages ἐν τοῖς ἐπουρανίοις is materially a full equivalent of the simple ἐν τοῖς οὐρανοῖς. God Himself and Christ belong to this heavenly world, for the right hand of God, the throne, the government, is represented as ἐν τοῖς ἐπουρανίοις. Here the term, like οὐρανός, has a local nuance. [10] But in Eph. we find not only the OT idea of the throne of God in heaven but also the gnostically influenced view (→ 525, 25) acc. to which Christ, exalted high above the heavenly world, reigns as its conqueror and ruler, Eph. 4:10. This world itself is regarded

---

[3] Cf. Pind. Fr., 132, 1: ψυχαὶ ... ὑπουράνιοι.
[4] Exc. 12, 1 (Scott, I, 434, 9); Exc. 21, 2 (Scott, I, 454, 2).
[5] Ascl., III, 32b (Scott, I, 356, 20 f.).
[6] Fr. 26 (Scott, I, 544, 1 f.).
[7] Scott, IV, 32, 9.
[8] At Mt. 18:35 vl. C Θ read ἐπουράνιος for οὐράνιος in the same sense in the formula ὁ πατήρ μου ὁ οὐράνιος, → 538, 5 ff.
[9] Cf. Dib. Gefbr. on Eph. 1:3.
[10] Cf. in Phil. 3:20 πολίτευμα, "a solid place in heaven," and in 4 Macc. 17:5 ἐστήρισαι ἐν οὐρανῷ.

as filled with "non-transparent, incalculable, incomprehensible, superior, anonymous, spiritual potencies which dominate and constitute this sphere."[11] (3:10; 6:12).[12] The Church or Christians share in this dominion of Christ over the heavenly world (2:6) and are blessed with blessing in the heavenly world ἐν Χριστῷ,[13] 1:3. That they are set in a position to withstand the conflict against the powers in the heavens[14] means that they follow their Christ in His victorious traversing of the heavens, 4:9 f.[15] Herein the mystery of Christ in the world (the κόσμος) is manifest, 3:10. In these last two verses ἐν τοῖς ἐπουρανίοις sets the cosmic significance of the event of revelation in the foreground. The reason for this use of the plerophoric expression ἐν τοῖς ἐπουρανίοις, which is taken from the cultic vocabulary of paganism, is to be sought in a growing liturgical and apologetic interest. The same applies to the plur. οὐρανοί in Eph.

In Hb. ἐπουράνιος is given its stamp by the idea of the perfect heavenly sanctuary into which the heavenly High-priest, Christ, enters to finish His work, 8:5; 9:23.[16] A distinctive point here is that there is no specific mention of the heavenly things (or vessels?). So strictly are they related to the appearing of the High-priest Christ in the true heaven before God's face (→ 528, 7 ff.) that they seem to be absorbed therein. They are defined as ἀληθινά (8:2; 9:24) and μέλλοντα (9:11 vl.; 10:1; 11:20; 13:14).[17] The ἐπουράνια are what is truly real, what is eschatologically future. Since they stand for the consummation, they have no absolute opposite, as, e.g., in 1 C. 15:48 (χοϊκός), Jn. 3:12 ἐπίγεια. There is only comparison, Hb. 8:5; 9:23; 11:16; cf. 7:19, 22; 10:34; 11:35.[18] Thus everything in the OT is only σκιά, ὑπόδειγμα, ἀντίτυπος to τὰ ἐπουράνια, 8:5; 9:23. The essence of the ἐπουράνια, corresponding to the αὐτὸς ὁ οὐρανός of 9:24 (→ 528,

---

[11] H. Schlier, Die Kirche nach dem Brief an d. Epheser, Beiträge zur Kontroverstheologie, 1 (1949), 180 f. Cf. Col. 1:16; Eph. 2:2; M. Dibelius, Die Geisterwelt im Glauben d. Pls. (1909), 158-164.

[12] At Eph. 6:12 ℵ reads τοῦ αἰῶνος for ἐν τοῖς ἐπουρανίοις. The alteration is an attempt to interpret the concept of the heavenly world in OT or Jewish fashion solely in terms of the throne or right hand of God, i.e., His lordship. That πνεύματα τῆς πονηρίας are no longer in heaven is part of the most primitive Christian kerygma, Lk. 10:18; cf. Rev. 12:8. The attempt confirms the equation of ἐν τοῖς ἐπουρανίοις and ἐν τοῖς οὐρανοῖς.

[13] ἐν is to be taken here, as in 2:6, causally and instrumentally rather than somatically, as Schlier, op. cit. understands it.

[14] In view of Eph. 2:2 ὁ ἄρχων τῆς ἐξουσίας τοῦ ἀέρος, ἐν τοῖς ἐπουρανίοις in 6:12 might be construed as the atmosphere under God's heaven. But we have here two very different worlds of thought; the expression in 2:2 is also unique.

[15] Schlier, op. cit., takes a different view: "In this 'spiritual' sphere (formally speaking) the Church is to be found. In the sphere thus expounded the Christian stays in the Church."

[16] Cf. Mi. Hb.[8] on 8:1; 9:23.

[17] Ibid. on 8:1.

[18] The comparative relation of ἐπουράνια-ὑπόδειγμα, ἀντίτυπος caused Ltzm. Gl. Exc. on 4:26, in exposition of the heavenly Jerusalem, to misunderstand ἐπουράνια along Platonic lines: "... the heavenly city is the Platonic 'idea' Jerusalem." There are two formal pars., since Plato can use "heaven" and "heavenly" for the idea, → 537, 11, and the idea of heaven is also in heaven. Cf. Mi. Hb.[8] on 8:1: "The contrast between heavenly and earthly in Hb. is meant Hellenistically, but not philosophically." Thus in Hb. heaven, τὰ ἐπουράνια, perfection and the heavenly Jerusalem are ultimately identical; heavenly things, though naturally only as shadows, also have earthly antitypes and correspondences. Materially, however, the heavenly things represent all others as a Platonic idea. For in the correspondences of Hb. we are not dealing with a general principle, but with a specific sign in the ἐπουράνια which is set up only in salvation history and within the chosen people. Hence the perfection of heaven, and the ἐπουράνια are not an ontic magnitude. They are worked out in the course of the pro- and transgressus of Christ as High-priest.

8), is the future presence of God, from and to which alone there is reality, 9:24; cf. Rev. 12:10. To this degree is τὰ ἐπουράνια a strictly eschatological concept in Hb. When the κλῆσις is described as ἐπουράνιος in Hb. 3:1 (cf. Phil. 3:14 ἡ ἄνω κλῆσις), this denotes its source and goal; it is to and through the ἀρχιερεὺς τῆς ὁμολογίας ἡμῶν, who will rule τὰ ἐπουράνια. Similarly in Hb. 6:4 the δωρεά which we have tasted is called ἡ ἐπουράνιος. It stands in material relation to τὰ ἐπουράνια in 9:23. Hence it is to be understood as eschatological salvation (σωτηρία, 9:28).[19] The πατρίς of 11:16 and Jerusalem of 12:22 are also ἐπουράνιος. This characterises them as the final aim for God's community.[20] Hb. 12:22 paints a broad canvas. To the heavenly world belong tens of thousands of angels, the festal congregation, the community of the first-born, those who are written in heaven, the Judge, the God of all men, and the Mediator of the new covenant, Jesus.

In 2 Tm. 4:18 the βασιλεία of Christ is described as ἡ ἐπουράνιος[21] with emphasis on the consummated kingdom of God. The concept of lordship is no longer adequate here. This kingdom is not only in Christ but with Him in heaven.

In the hymn to Christ used by Paul in Phil. 2:6 ff., the πᾶν γόνυ from Is. 45:23 is liturgically broadened by the addition of ἐπουρανίων καὶ ἐπιγείων καὶ καταχθονίων.[22] This is not just a general topographical note (in heaven, earth and hell).[23] All three members[24] refer to ruling spiritual forces. ἐπουρανίων is used as a noun; whether it be masculine or neuter makes no difference. With powers on earth and under the earth those in the heavens (plur., Phil. 3:20) are also vanquished and incorporated into the all-encompassing dominion of Jesus Christ (Col. 1:20; Eph. 1:10). In Judaism these are angelic creatures (→ 527, 28 f.), whereas in the Gnostic Hellenistic world they are powers of fate, → 539, 8 ff. Similarly, though without theological emphasis, ἐπουράνια is used in 1 C. 15:40 in antithesis to ἐπίγεια to illustrate the difference in σώματα and their δόξα. In material relation to ἐπουράνια Paul goes on to speak of ἥλιος, σελήνη, ἀστήρ. The reference is not to heavenly bodies in our sense, but to the bodies of heavenly things, the stars being equated with angelic powers.[25] There is a very different use in 1 C. 15:48 f. In v. 47 Paul mentions the ἄνθρωπος ἐξ οὐρανοῦ, the risen, returning and hence pre-existent Christ (→ 528, 25), ὁ ἐπουράνιος (opp. χοϊκός). He is the πνευματικός of v. 46b;[26] in v. 47 vl. P46 He is this as ἄνθρωπος ἐξ οὐρανοῦ. In us the εἰκὼν τοῦ χοϊκοῦ is separated from that of the ἐπουρανίου. The subject

---

[19] Similarly Mi. Hb.[8] on 6:4, who refers to R. 5:15; 2 C. 9:15. This also brings out the connection with the μέλλων αἰών of 6:5. On the other hand, precisely this heavenly gift is present in once-for-all μετάνοια.

[20] For this concept cf. 4 Esr. 7:26; 8:52; 10:54; 13:36; S. Bar. 4:3-6 (v. also Eth. En. 53:6; 90:28 f.). Bibl. and examples in Bousset-Gressm., 239; Volz Esch., 334; R. Knopf, "Die Himmelsstadt," Nt.liche Studien, Festschr. G. Heinrici (1914), 213-219; Str.-B., III, 573.

[21] Cf. the combinations ἡ ἐν οὐρανῷ βασιλεία, Dg., 10, 2; ἡ οὐράνιος βασιλεία αὐτοῦ, Mart. Pol., 22, 3; ἡ ἐπουράνιος αὐτοῦ βασιλεία, Mart. Pol. Epil., 5 (20, 2 vl.).

[22] Cf. Ign. Tr., 9, 1 τῶν ἐπουρανίων καὶ ἐπιγείων καὶ ὑποχθονίων for the powers which are simply spectators of the cross. Obviously general Jewish ideas underlie this; cf. Preis. Zaub., IV, 3041 ff.: καὶ σὺ λάλησον ὁποῖον ἐὰν ᾖς ἐπουράνιον ἢ ἀέριον εἴτε ἐπίγειον εἴτε ὑπόγειον ἢ καταχθόνιον κτλ., and v. on this Deissmann LO, 220, 223, n. 11. Dib. Gefbr. pts. to P. Oxy., XI, 1380, 164 : δ[α]ίμονες ὑπήκοοι σοὶ [γ]ίνο[ν]ται.

[23] So Loh. Phil., ad loc.

[24] On the threefold division of the cosmos cf. E. Peterson, Εἷς θεός = FRL, NF, 24 (1926), 159.

[25] Cf. στρατιὰ τοῦ οὐρανοῦ → 512, 41 f.; cf. also Philo Op. Mund., 73; Plant., 12; Som., I, 135.

[26] Cf. J. Weiss, Der 1 K. (1910), 376.

does not change; it is we who bore and we who bear. But the identity of this subject does not lie in itself ; it resides in the οὐράνιος = Christ, whose εἰκών alone is determinative. ἐπουράνιος here denotes, not a general quality of life, but given membership in the ἐπουράνιος, the risen Christ.

In Jn. τὰ ἐπουράνια in 3:12 are to be explained in terms of vv. 13-16. They embrace the earthly journey and reunion of the Son of Man, grounded in the love and saving purpose of God and fulfilled by the obedience of Jesus.[27] They have formally the character of the concealment of the heavenly incurred by the world. In content, corresponding to the use of οὐρανός in Jn. (→ 526, 14), they express the divine secret of revelation in the Son.[28]

> In the post-apostolic fathers the plur. noun occurs only in Ign. in the sense of "heavenly spirits" (Sm., 6, 1 = archons and δόξα of angels, Tr., 5, 1 f. = τοποθεσίαι ἀγγελικαί κτλ.) whose nature is contention (Eph., 13, 2; cf. Pol., 2, 1). In 1 Cl., 61, 2 God is addressed as ἐπουράνιε βασιλεῦ τῶν αἰώνων, and similarly Jesus in Mart. Pol., 14, 3, also with αἰώνιος. Mart. Pol. Epil. 5, also 20, 2, vl., reads εἰς τὴν ἐπουράνιον αὐτοῦ βασιλείαν. 2 Cl., 20, 5 speaks of ἐπουράνιος ζωή.

† οὐρανόθεν.

> "From heaven,"[1] in the various senses of heaven. Common in Hom., of the gods, Il., 11, 184; 17, 545; but also of the αἰθήρ, 8, 558, the clouds, 23, 189, and night, Od., 5, 294; 9, 69; cf. Hes. Theog., 761: οὐρανόθεν καταβαίνων, Aristot. Mot. An., I, 4, p. 699b, 37 in a quotation from Hom. Elsewhere the word is comparatively rare. Since it soon became stereotyped, it needed a strengthening to bring out the sense, either ἀπό (Hom. Il., 21, 199; Od., 11, 18; Hes. Scutum Herculis, 384), or ἐξ (Hom. Il., 8, 19 and 21; 17, 548). In all these passages the ref., with no special emphasis, is to the dwelling-place of the gods which is in heaven. The term occurs only once in Philo in an allegorical exposition of Ex. 22:25, which is referred to the speech which God δι' ἔλεον τοῦ γένους ἡμῶν εἰς νοῦν τὸν ἀνθρώπινον οὐρανόθεν ἀποστέλλει, Som., I, 112.

> In the LXX the word is found only in 4 Macc. 4:10 : οὐρανόθεν ἔφιπποι προυφάνησαν ἄγγελοι. Here it refers to the (inner) heavenly place where the στρατός of angels (4:11) and the martyrs (17:5) are.

There are two instances in the NT, both in Ac. In 14:17 several meanings interfuse : a. the rain comes from God, which means concretely b. that it comes from His gracious lordship which opens the closed heavens to men ; c. the rain comes from the heavenly ocean, and hence d. it comes from up above, from the sky.[2] In the context the strongest emphasis lies on sense b. οὐρανόθεν is more precise than ἄνωθεν in Jm. 1:17, cf. Jn. 19:11; 3:27 (→ 514, n. 121; 531, 30). In 26:13 οὐρανόθεν is an alternative to the ἐκ τοῦ οὐρανοῦ of 9:3; 22:6 (→ 531, 25).

---

[27] The ref. is not to τὰ ἐν οὐρανοῖς, as in Wis. 9:16; cf. בשמיא in Sanh., 39a, which refers generally to what is in heaven, and what is hidden as such. Nor is a ref. to 4 Esr. 4:21 relevant : οἱ ἐπὶ τῆς γῆς κατοικοῦντες τὰ ἐπὶ γῆς συνιέναι μόνον δύνανται, καὶ οἱ ἐπὶ τῶν οὐρανῶν τὰ ἐπὶ τοῦ ὕψους τῶν οὐρανῶν. Bengel, ad loc., is right, though not very precise : interiores rationes regni Dei. Bau. J., ad loc. pts. to Lk. 16:11b, and rightly equates ἐπουράνια and ἀληθινά, → 520, n. 181; 540, 18. But ἀληθινά, too, is concrete, not abstract (cf. 6:32, → 527, 10).
[28] Cf. Bu. J., 105, n. 2, who pts. to the ἐπουράνια μυστήρια of Gnosticism.
ο ὐ ρ α ν ό θ ε ν.   [1] Cf. Bl.-Debr. § 104, 1.
[2] In the OT only ὑετοῦ τοῦ οὐρανοῦ, Dt. 11:11, though ἐπὶ τὴν γῆν is common, and this presupposes an ἐξ οὐρανοῦ or οὐρανόθεν.

Here, too, the meaning is complex. The light shines from the sky, but this is not described as its source. The οὐρανόθεν is designed to show that this is the light which shines forth from the Revealer. It is revelation, the halo of the κύριος, which pouring forth from Him pierces the firmament.

Traub

Οὐρίας → III, 1.

> οὖς, ὠτίον, ὠτάριον, ἐνωτίζομαι

† οὖς.

Contents : A. οὖς outside the NT : 1. The Greek Usage ; 2. The OT ; 3. Philo and Josephus ; 4. The Rabbis. B. οὖς in the NT : 1. The Synoptic Gospels and Acts ; 2. Paul's Epistles ; 3. The Catholic Epistles ; 4. Revelation.

A. Οὖς outside the NT.

1. The Greek Usage.

In Hom. the word bears the sense "ear," e.g., Ἄντιφον αὖ παρὰ οὖς ἔλασε ξίφει, Il., 11, 109, also "handle" of vessels, e.g., οὔατα δ' αὐτοῦ τέσσαρ' ἔσαν Il., 11, 633 f.; cf. 18, 378 f.[1] The word is common later for the ears of men and animals.[2] So Hdt., VII, 39 : ἐν τοῖσι ὠσὶ τῶν ἀνθρώπων οἰκέει ὁ θυμός, ὃς χρηστὰ μὲν ἀκούσας τέρψιος (with ease) ἐμπιπλέει τὸ σῶμα, ὑπεναντία δὲ τούτοισι ἀκούσας ἀνοιδέει (swells up).[3] For the ears of animals, Hdt., IV, 129 : ὀρθὰ ἱστάντες τὰ ὦτα. Charac-

---

ο ὖ ς. Thes. Steph., Pass., Liddell-Scott, Pr.-Bauer³, Moult.-Mill., H. v. Herwerden, Lexicon Graecum suppletorium² (1910), *s.v.*; G. Kittel, Art. ἀκούω, ἀκοή → I, 216 ff.; W. Michaelis, Art. ὁράω κτλ. → 315 ff.; M. Dibelius, "Wer Ohren hat zu hören, der höre," ThStKr, 83 (1910), 461-471; E. v. Dobschütz, "Die fünf Sinne im NT," JBL, 48 (1929), 378-411; G. Kittel, *Religionsgeschichte u. Urchr.* (1932), 95-106; K. L. Schmidt, "Die Verstockung des Menschen durch Gott ...," *Theol. Zeitschrift*, 1 (1945), 1-17; J. Jeremias, *Die Gleichnisse Jesu* (1947), 1-14; R. Bultmann, "Zur Geschichte der Lichtsymbolik im Altertum," Philol., 97 (1948), 1-36; O. Weinreich, "Θεοὶ ἐπήκοοι," *Ath. Mitt.*, 37 (1912), 1-68. Cf. also the bibl. on ἀκούω, ἀκοή, → I, 216 f., 221, and on μέλος → IV, 555. As concerns the etym. *v.* Boisacq, 730 f.; Walde-Pok., I, 18 : *aus-*; grammatically cf. Bl.-Debr. § 393, 6; 400, 2.

[1] Not in this sense in the NT. The forms which alongside οὖς (from this only ὠσίν) Hom. constructs from οὖας, including οὔατα, do not occur in the NT, only οὖς in the nom. and acc. sing. and ὦτα in the nom. and acc. plur., also ὠσίν. "In Hellenistic Gk. (but not the NT) we find ὧς (built back from the stem ὠτ-); Mayser, I¹, 5; I², 2, 48; Liddell-Scott, *s.v.* οὖς" [Debrunner].

[2] Also transf., e.g., proverbial, personified of the tale-bearers to the tyrant, Plut. De Curiositate, 16 (II, 522 f.): τὸ τῶν λεγομένων ὤτων καὶ προσαγωγέων γένος, cf. De Vitioso Pudore, 18 (II, 535 f. and 536a); humorously of the brilliant wing-cases of the beetle, Aristoph. Pax, 154-156 : διακινήσας φαιδροῖς ὠσίν, T. L. Agar, "Notes on the Peace of Aristoph.," *The Class. Quarterly*, 12 (1918), 196 f.

[3] Cf. also Plut. Aud., 2 (II, 38a): περὶ τῆς ἀκουστικῆς αἰσθήσεως, ἥν ὁ Θεόφραστος παθητικωτάτην εἶναί φησι πασῶν. The sense of hearing is mostly emotionally responsive, but is also a tool of reason in education : ἔστι δὲ λογικωτέρα μᾶλλον ἤ παθητικωτέρα ... τῇ δ' ἀρετῇ μία λαβὴ τὰ ὦτα τῶν νέων ἐστίν, ἄν ᾖ καθαρὰ καὶ ἄθρυπτα κολακείᾳ, *loc. cit.*

teristic in Gk. thought is the higher value of the eye, e.g., Heracl. Fr., 101a (Diels[5], I, 173, 15 f.): ὀφθαλμοὶ γὰρ τῶν ὥτων ἀκριβέστεροι μάρτυρες, and Hdt., I, 8 : ὦτα γὰρ τυγχάνει ἀνθρώποισι ἐόντα ἀπιστότερα ὀφθαλμῶν, with a cosmogonic basis in Aristoph. Thes., 16-18,[4] → 319, 13 ff. The expression εἰς (πρὸς) τὸ οὖς (τὰ ὦτα) λαλεῖν τι means "secretly to bring to the ears," "to whisper," so in the tragic dramatists, Eur. Or., 616 f.: ἐς οὖς ἀεὶ πέμπουσα μύθους etc., Soph. Ai., 148 f.: λόγους ψιθυροὺς πλάσσων εἰς ὦτα φέρει. A loud noise which strikes the ears is rendered in Soph. Ant., 1187 f.: καί με φθόγγος ... βάλλει δι' ὥτων, and in Aesch. Pers., 605 : βοᾷ ἐν ὠσὶ κέλαδος. We also find among others the phrases παρέχειν τὰ ὦτα, aures praebere, "to lend one's ears,"[5] and ἐπισχέσθαι τὰ ὦτα, "to stop up one's ears,"[6] both in Plat. Symp., 216a : εἰ ἐθέλοιμι παρέχειν τὰ ὦτα,[7] and ὥσπερ ἀπὸ τῶν Σειρήνων ἐπισχόμενος τὰ ὦτα, also ὦτα ἔχειν, "to hear," Plut. Col., 12 (II, 1113c): μέγα βοῶντός ἐστιν τοῖς ὦτα ἔχουσιν. Among the pre-Socratics Heracl. thinks eyes and ears are in special reciprocity with the ψυχή, Fr., 107 (Diels[5], I, 175, 1 f.): κακοὶ μάρτυρες ἀνθρώποισιν ὀφθαλμοὶ καὶ ὦτα βαρβάρους ψυχὰς ἐχόντων "so far as they have barbarian souls." The question is also raised how hearing comes about through the ears. Attention is drawn to the role played by the movement of air in the process, Diogenes of Apollonia in Theophr. De Sensu et Sensibilibus, 40 (cf. Diels[5], II, 55, 13 ff.): τὴν δ' ἀκοήν, ὅταν ὁ ἐν τοῖς ὠσὶν ἀὴρ κινηθεὶς ὑπὸ τοῦ ἔξω διαδῷ πρὸς τὸν ἐγκέφαλον κτλ. Aristot. tried to form a physical picture of the process,[8] and rejected pseudo-scientific and superstitious notions.[9] Epictetus, who exhorted his hearers to thank God for seeing and hearing, thinks man's will-power, and not simply the faculty of hearing, is the basis of the ability to close or open his ears, Diss., II, 23, 10 : τίς ἡ τὰ ὦτα ἐπικλείουσα καὶ ἀνοίγουσα (sc. δύναμις); ... ἡ ἀκουστική; οὐκ ἄλλη ἢ ἡ προαιρετικὴ δύναμις.[10]

Along with the more rational views of Aristot. and Epict. there is also among the Gks. an ultimate religious basis in the background. Thus the human ear can also be opened as the organ by which divine communications are received. In respect of the Orphic demand for purity here, and the synonymity of οὖς and ἀκοή in the sense of organ of hearing (→ I, 221, 17), note should be taken of Orph. Fr. (Kern), 249 :

Δεῦρό νυν οὔατά μοι καθαρὰς ἀκοάς τε πετάσσας
κέκλυθι τάξιν ἅπασαν, ὅσην τεκμήρατο Δαίμων.

---

[4] Bultmann, 16 f. On this whole question cf. also G. Rudberg, "Hell. Schauen," Classica et Mediaevalia, 5 (1942), 159-186; K. Kerényi, Die antike Religion (1940), 100-134. Also B. Snell, Die Entdeckung des Geistes[2] (1948), 15-19. Over against the theological statement of Xenophanes Fr., 24 (Diels[5], I, 135, 7): οὖλος ὁρᾶι. οὖλος δὲ νοεῖ, οὖλος δέ τ' ἀκούει (→ 320, n. 32), Epicharmos Fr. (I, 200, 16): νοῦς ὁρῆι καὶ νοῦς ἀκούει· τἆλλα κωφὰ καὶ τυφλά (→ 320, n. 30), sets an epistemological saying, with genuine eleatic paradox declaring in all seriousness "that only the νοῦς sees and hears and eye and ear do nothing at all" (cf. Parm. Fr., 4 [Diels[5], I, 232, 3 ff.]). R. Schottlaender, "Drei vorsokratische Topoi," Herm., 62 (1927), 437, n. 5 and generally 435-438.
[5] Cf. also Plut. De Vitioso Pudore, 18 (II, 535 f.): οἱ τὰ ὦτα τοῖς κολακεύουσι παραδιδόντες.
[6] Cf. Ac. 7:57: συνέσχον τὰ ὦτα αὐτῶν, and on this art. παρακοή, → I, 223, 23 ff.
[7] Cf. also Plat. Crat., 396d.
[8] An., II, 8, p. 420a, 3 ff. Cf. H. Bonitz, Index Aristotelicus (1870) s.v.
[9] Hist. An., I, 11, p. 492a, 14 : ἀναπνεῖν τὰς αἶγας κατὰ τὰ ὦτα, that goats breathe through the ears, cf. Diels[5], I, 212, 14 f. For other instances of such superstitious ideas in pseudo-scientific garb Wnd. Barn. on 10:6-8, e.g., of the weasel : διὰ γὰρ τῶν ὥτων συλλαμβάνει, τεκνοποιεῖ δὲ τῷ στόματι, Ep. Ar., 165 ff.; here the Mosaic command not to eat weasels (Lv. 11:29) is given a moral basis in the unclean character of the tale-bearer who receives through the ear and fashions through words. Cf. Plut. Is. et Os., 74 (II, 381a). Aristot. Gen. An., III, 6, p. 756b, 15 f. and 31 ff. advances a rational explanation for this error.
[10] Cf. 26 f.

Cicero Orator, 9, 28 also veers towards a religious view of the process of hearing. Here the specially acute ears of the Attic orator, attuned to catch the slightest nuance, are called *aures religiosae*. [11]

On inscr. οὖς (also → ὠτίον, → ὠτάριον) occurs also in records of consecrated objects, so in the Aesculapium at Athens, IG, II, 2, No. 835, 20 : οὖς κατάμακτον πρὸς πίνακι, ὃ ἀνέθηκεν Σπινθήρ, also line 17, 19, 42 etc., e.g., 86 : ὀφθαλμοὶ ἀργυροῖ δύο καὶ ὦτα ἐκ τοῦ αὐτοῦ. [12] Weinreich has made it clear that in a series of depictions of ears and the corresponding attestations on inscr. or otherwise we are to think of the ears of the gods, and that these ears imply a request for hearing on the part of the θεοὶ ἐπήκοοι — the ἀριήκοον οὖς of the deity is extolled [13] — though in individual cases one cannot always be sure whether these are votive ears reflecting sick ears which have been cured or simply a symbol of hearing on the part of the deity. [14] To be very close to the god, and thus to be heard more easily, the custom was to speak softly to statues, whispering in the ear, [15] so to Aphrodite Paus. in Eustath. Thessal. Comm. in Od. on 20, 8 : ᾿Αφροδίτη ... ἐκαλεῖτο δὲ ... ψίθυρος διὰ τὸ τὰς εὐχομένας αὐτῇ πρὸς τὸ οὖς λέγειν, [16] also to Hermes Agoraios in Pharai Paus., VII, 22 f.: ἐρωτᾷ πρὸς τὸ οὖς τὸν θεόν. [17] But in the rich material attesting the ears of deity and the epithet ἐπήκοος, "he who hears prayers," it is "surprising how few inscr. come from Greece proper ... there may be seen here the predominant influence of oriental cults." [18] Depictions of the ears of deity may be traced back to Egyptian stimuli. [19] To attach such significance to the ears of deity was alien to the original religious sense of the Gks. This is shown by the observation of Plut. on the ear-less statue of Zeus on Crete, Is. et Os., 76 (II, 381d): ἐν Κρήτῃ Διὸς ἦν ἄγαλμα μὴ ἔχον ὦτα· τῷ γὰρ ἄρχοντι καὶ κυρίῳ πάντων οὐδενὸς ἀκούειν προσήκει. [20]

As regards the Gnostic idea that the members of the cosmic god, including his ears, are in the cosmos, cf. the Sarapis oracle in Macrob. Sat., I, 20, 17: τὰ δ' οὔατ' ἐν αἰθέρι κεῖται, → III, 676, 24 ff.; IV, 557, 1 f.

In the pap. οὖς is common for the natural "ear," P. Petr., III, 19c, 15 : οὐλὴ ὑπ' ὦς δεξιόν, also P. Tebt., III, 793, XI : τὸν Δωρίωνος δεξιὸν ὦτα εἰς τέλος ἐξέτεμεν, [21] and P. Petr., III, 13, 18 : λοβοὶ ὤτων, [22] but also for "handle," here the diminutive ὠτίον, so P. Oxy., XIV, 1658, 13 : ὠτίον χαλκίου (handle on the kettle). [23] We also find the expression ὦτα παρέχω ἄνοα αὐτῷ, "I have deaf ears to him," P. Oxy., II, 237, VI, 22. Worth noting is the magical expectation that the ears should open to the direction of an invoked deity, cf. the formula in Preis. Zaub., VII, 329 f.: ἄνοιξόν μου τὰ ὦτα, ἵνα μοι χρηματίσῃς περὶ ὧν σε ἀξιῶ, ἵνα ἀποκριθῇς μοι. There

---

[11] Cf. here the basic meaning of *religiosus, religio, religere* : to listen with the ear to the external forms of the divine [Kleinknecht]. Cf. on this Kerényi, 122.

[12] Cf. Weinreich, 60, n. 1. On Weinreich's thesis v. B. Keil, "AKOAI," Herm., 45 (1910), 474-477; P. Wolters, "AKOAI," Herm., 49 (1914), 149-151; O. Weinreich, "Noch einmal AKOAI," Herm., 51 (1916), 624-629.

[13] Proclus to Aphrodite in Hymnus, II, 14 (Orph. [Abel], p. 279): πάντῃ γὰρ ἔχεις ἀριήκοον οὖσας, Weinreich, 55 and n. 2.

[14] Weinreich, 58.

[15] Censured by Seneca, Ep., 41, 1, cf. Weinreich, 56, n. 1.

[16] Weinreich, 56, n. 2.

[17] *Ibid.*, 56, n. 4.

[18] *Ibid.*, 25.

[19] *Ibid.*, 46-49.

[20] Whether the ears might have been lost in the course of time, so T. Hopfner, *Plut. über Is. u. Os.*, II (1941), 275 f., has no bearing on Plut.'s interpretation.

[21] Cf. M. Rostovzeff, "Οὖς δεξιὸν ἀποτέμνειν," ZNW, 33 (1934), 198.

[22] Further examples in Preisigke Wört. and Moult.-Mill., *s.v.* οὖς, ὠτίον, ὠτάριον; e.g., P. Oxy., I, 108, II, 17: ὠτίον α = 1 ear (of a slaughtered animal) in the accounts of a cook.

[23] Diminutive of οὖς → ὠτίον, 558, 12 f. and n. 1.

is a magical forcing of the ears in the admonition to use the formula, *ibid.*, XIII, 248 : ἐὰν ἐπείπῃς ἐπὶ παντὸς πετεινοῦ εἰς τὸ ὠτίον, τελευτήσει.

2. The OT.

Among the members of the body the "ear" is an important organ, Heb. אֹזֶן, dual אָזְנַיִם, so Ps. 115:4-7 (cf. 135:17), where dead idols are critically assessed in terms of the living human body, and the organs of speech and hearing are mentioned three times, that of seeing only once.

a. First אֹזֶן denotes the visible part of the body in men, e.g., Gn. 35:4; Ex. 21:6, and animals, e.g., Am. 3:12 : בְּדַל־אֹזֶן, tip of the ear, LXX λοβὸν ὠτίου ("lobe"), as the remains of the lion's booty, and ψ 57:4 : βυούσης τὰ ὦτα, of the adder which stops its ears.

The oriental loves to adorn the ear with pendants and rings, Gn. 35:4:הַנְּזָמִים אֲשֶׁר בְּאָזְנֵיהֶם τὰ ἐνώτια τὰ ἐν τοῖς ὠσὶν αὐτῶν, [24] cf. Ex. 32:2 f. Boring through the ear [25] of perpetual slaves with the awl at the door (Ex. 21:6 : τρυπήσει ... τὸ οὖς τῷ ὀπητίῳ, cf. Dt. 15:17) is a legal act symbolising willingness to become the permanent possession of the owner, and acceptance into the master's family. The original cultic significance of the act as something done at the doorpost, the seat of Elohim, the *penates*, protector of the home, [26] is lost in the legal custom [27] which God guarantees, Ex. 21:6 : προσάξει αὐτὸν ... πρὸς τὸ κριτήριον τοῦ θεοῦ). The boring through of the ear is still of special significance, however, for the bondage (*Hörigkeit*) of the slave who is bound to obedience for the whole of his life ; cf. the expression in Ex. 17:14 : שׂוּם בְּאָזְנֵי פ׳, "to command," lit. "to lay down in the ears."

b. The ear denotes not only the part of the body but also its function, the faculty or sense of hearing. This is never as such separated conceptually from the visible member, as shown by the common addition of בְּאָזְנֵי ἐν ὠτίοις to verbs of hearing and speaking, e.g., Gn. 20:8 דבר, Is. 49:20 אמר, Ex. 24:7 קרא, 2 S. 18:12 צוה etc. [28] The ears are regarded as the instrument by which speech and orders are noted, not the brain, as with us. Hence the ear is the seat of "insight." [29] In keeping is the LXX ἀνακαλύπτει νοῦν for יִגְלֶה אֹזֶן at Job 33:16. [30] The function of the ear is so important for the total picture of the person of a man that בְּאָזְנֵי פ׳, "before the ears," means "in the

---

[24] ἐνώτιον, "ear-ring," cf. Liddell-Scott, *s.v.*, is found from Aesch. Fr., 102 (TGF, 35 f.). For illustrations cf. K. Galling, *Bibl. Reallexikon* (1937), 398-402.

[25] Probably the right as in Lv. 8:23 f.; 14:14 ff.

[26] Cf. G. Beer-K. Galling, *Ex.* = *Handbuch z. AT*, I, 3 (1939), ad loc. as against R. Kittel, *Gesch. d. Volkes Israel*, II⁷ (1925), 52, who thinks an originally public religious ceremony in the sanctuary was changed by Dt. 15:17 into a private secular one in the house, with a symbolic fastening of the ear to the doorpost. But even if boring through the ear is simply a marking in token of slavery (*loc. cit.*), the question still arises why the ear was marked. There were other signs, e.g., slitting the nose. Cf. also A. Jeremias, *Handbuch d. altorientalischen Geisteskultur²* (1929), 93. On Ex. 21:6 : "From here the variant οὖς comes into the par. Dt. 15:17, where BO L rightly read ὠτίον" [Katz].

[27] A. Jeremias, *Das AT im Lichte d. alten Orients⁴* (1930), 437, 411 f., 799. H. Holzinger, *Ex.* (1900), ad loc.: "Pagan echoes whose point is no longer clear to them ..., but which they followed." G. Hoffmann-H. Gressmann, "Teraphim. Masken u. Winkorakel," ZAW, 40 (1922), 102. A. Dillmann-V. Ryssel, *D. Bücher Ex. u. Lv.³* (1880), ad loc., with examples of the piercing of the ears of slaves among oriental peoples. On the legal aspect of the ceremony cf. F. Horst, *Das Privilegrecht Jahves. Rechtsgeschichtliche Untersuchungen zum Dt.* (1930), 70-76.

[28] Cf. the list in Ges.-Buhl, *s.v.* אֹזֶן.

[29] This is in keeping with oriental anthropology. Cf. A. Jeremias, *op. cit.*, 93 f. and on the whole question L. Köhler, *Theol. d. AT²* (1947), 122 f., 128-131.

[30] Cf. also 12:11 (cf. 34:3): νοῦς BSA and 34:3 AV (→ n. 37).

presence." This brings out the significance of the presence of witnesses in Gn. 23:10. [31]

The biblical use thus begins with the natural ear and when hearing is in view always has this in mind rather than a concept of the phenomenon of hearing → μέλος, IV, 558, 7-14. Similarly, the formula בְּאָזְנֵי εἰς τὰ ὦτα or ἐν τοῖς ὠσί, which embraces both speech and hearing, gives to the spoken word the character of a concrete process; it is no mere expression of a thought, e.g., Gn. 20:8; Ex. 10:2; 24:7; Dt. 5:1; 2 S. 18:12; Is. 49:20. [32] In phrases which speak of the ears of the people, i.e., the קָהָל, the reference is not to abstract hearing but to realistically envisaged ears, e.g., Dt. 31:30; cf. 32:44. The expression λαλεῖν εἰς τὰ ὦτα, unlike the Gk. (→ 544, 4 ff.), often means loud and audible expression, so Dt. 31:11: ἀναγνώσεσθε ... εἰς τὰ ὦτα αὐτῶν etc., reading out loud, since the written word, too, is meant to be heard rather than seen, being destined for the ear, Ex. 17:14: κατάγραψον τοῦτο ... ἐν βιβλίῳ καὶ δὸς εἰς τὰ ὦτα 'Ιησοῖ, cf. 'Ιερ. 43:6 etc. Another distinctive phrase is גָּלָה אֹזֶן פ', "to uncover the ear of someone" so that something may be said to him, something important revealed. This is rendered ἀποκαλύπτειν τὸ οὖς or ὠτίον in the LXX, [33] cf. 1 S. 20:2: ἀποκαλύψει τὸ ὠτίον μου [34] (Rt. 4:4 τὸ οὖς). It is also used for God's act of revelation, e.g., 1 S. 9:15; 2 S. 7:27. To speech which must be punished like bloodguiltiness the ear of the righteous should be closed, Is. 33:15: אֹטֵם אָזְנוֹ, βαρύνων τὰ ὦτα, ἵνα μὴ ἀκούσῃ κρίσιν αἵματος, [35] cf. Sir. 27:14: ἐμφραγμὸς ὠτίων. Thus the ear has also a critical function. In its activity it becomes a subject, [36] Job 12:11: οὖς ... ῥήματα διακρίνει, [37] cf. 34:3: οὖς λόγους δοκιμάζει. [38]

c. Any psychological explanation of the process of hearing such as we find among the Gks. (→ 544, 16-25) is alien to the OT. This is content simply to affirm that Yahweh has created the ear, Ps. 94:9: הֲנֹטַע אֹזֶן = ψ 93:9: ὁ φυτεύσας τὸ οὖς, cf. Prv. 20:12: οὖς ἀκούει καὶ ὀφθαλμὸς ὁρᾷ· κυρίου ἔργα καὶ ἀμφότερα (יהוה עָשָׂה). [39] This is the basis of man's great responsibility for the proper use of his ears. Though a fleshly organ, the ears are permeated by God's living breath. From this breath the

---

[31] In comparison with v. 10: בְּאָזְנֵי בְנֵי־חֵת, "in the presence of the Hittites," it is worth noting that when the purchase of the burying ground has been completed and there is no further question of witness, since the ground is in Abraham's possession, v. 18 simply uses לְעֵינֵי, "in their presence"; cf. also v. 11, where the witnesses are to see what is being purchased. On this sense cf. also ἐν ὠσί, Lk. 4:21.

[32] For other refs. cf. Hatch-Redp., s.v. οὖς.

[33] So also the Hexapla translators at Job 36:10 for the Mas.: וַיִּגֶל אָזְנָם לַמּוּסָר, where the LXX completely alters the sense by rendering ἀλλὰ τοῦ δικαίου εἰσακούσεται, with a bigger stress on the antithesis between the righteous and the ungodly already found in the Mas. Cf. 33:16, where the LXX first puts νοῦς for οὖς and then departs from the Mas. by vowel changes [Bertram]. Cf. also Is. 50:5: פָּתַח־לִי אֹזֶן.

[34] Σ has here δηλώσῃ εἰς ἀκοήν; in 20:12 (no LXX) ἀκουστὸν ποιήσω [Bertram].

[35] אטם Heb. "to close," Aram. "to be heavy," Ges.-Buhl, s.v. Hence the LXX βαρύνω, but 'ΑΣΘ lit. βύων. Is. 33 is post-exilic acc. to H. Guthe in Kautzsch, ad loc.

[36] Cf. Schl. Mt. on 5:29 and Jk. on 5:4: "The member is the subj. of the activity," → IV, 567, 12-18.

[37] → n. 30. νοῦς for οὖς, cf. Epicharm. Fr., 12 (Diels⁵, I, 200, 16), → n. 4. The consequent spiritualising, which the LXX also seeks at Ιωβ 12:11; 34:3; 33:16, is not originally present in the doctrine of the nous in Anaxagoras [Bertram]. Acc. to the attempted reconstruction of the confused section Job 12:3-11 by G. Richter, Textstudien zum Buche Hiob (1927), 21 f., which alters אֹזֶן to אָזְנִי and puts v. 11 after v. 3a b, the whole context has also to be understood along the lines of the presupposition which is regarded as self-evident in v. 9 f.

[38] Acc. to G. Hölscher, Hiob, Handbuch z. AT, I, 17 (1937), ad loc. a quotation from 12:11. As distinct from the LXX the Mas. has אֹזֶן מִלִּין תִּבְחָן. in both verses.

[39] Cf. B. Gemser, Sprüche Salomos, Handbuch z. AT, I, 16 (1937), on 20:12.

organ has received the faculty of hearing and testing words, as Job 12:9-11 obviously means. [40] There is no thought here of the interrelation of two abstractly regarded entities, body and soul. Only when the LXX rendered נֶפֶשׁ by ψυχή was the way prepared for a Gk. understanding. [41]

The greatest thing that man can hear is דְּבַר יהוה; this comes in a special way to the prophet [42] — Is. 22:14 : נִגְלָה בְאָזְנֵי יהוה, "Yahweh revealed himself in my ears" [43] — but it is then proclaimed as Law to the whole people. The Son of Sirach gives expression in 17:13 to a tendency which leads to the domination of the Torah in Judaism: μεγαλεῖον δόξης εἶδον οἱ ὀφθαλμοὶ αὐτῶν, καὶ δόξαν φωνῆς αὐτοῦ [44] ἤκουσεν τὸ οὖς αὐτῶν. Revelation is especially to the ear of man. [45] On the precedence of hearing over seeing, of the ear over the eye, in receiving revelation cf. → 329, 1 ff. and I, 217-219. [46] Yet the natural ear is not in itself adequate to grasp the content of revelation. Even though it functions properly, it may be quite deaf to this, and come under the judgment of hardening, so Is. 6:9 f.: Ἀκοῇ ἀκούσετε καὶ οὐ μὴ συνῆτε ...· ἐπαχύνθη γὰρ ἡ καρδία τοῦ λαοῦ τούτου, καὶ τοῖς ὠσὶν αὐτῶν βαρέως ἤκουσαν ..., μήποτε ... τοῖς ὠσὶν ἀκούσωσιν. [47] Behind this riddle of inability to hear, for all the external hearing, stands the free sovereignty of God who Himself decides whether He will open the ear for faith and understanding, e.g., Is. 48:(6 f.)8 : οὔτε ἔγνως οὔτε ἠπίστω, οὔτε ἀπ' ἀρχῆς ἤνοιξά σου τὰ ὦτα. [48] When the Messianic age dawns, it is promised in Is. 35:5 : ὦτα κωφῶν ἀκούσονται. But now morning by morning Yahweh opens the disciple's ear, Is. 50:4 f.: προσέθηκέν μοι ὠτίον ἀκούειν· καὶ ἡ παιδεία κυρίου ἀνοίγει μου τὰ ὦτα, ἐγὼ δὲ οὐκ ἀπειθῶ. In the consecration of the priest there is a priestly parallel to this prophetic opening of the ear. Ears, not eyes, are with hands, the organs of priestly actions, and feet, which go up to the altar, the members which at consecration receive by smearing with sacrificial blood (ἐπὶ τὸν λοβὸν τοῦ ὠτός, עַל־תְּנוּךְ אֹזֶן, on the tip of the right ear, Ex. 29:20)

---

[40] → n. 37.

[41] Cf. Köhler, op. cit., 130.

[42] Cf. art. λόγος → IV, 94-100, esp. 94, 1 ff.; 12 ff., 20 f., n. 105; 96, 39 ff.; 99, 32.

[43] H. Guthe in Kautzsch reads ad loc. נִגְלָה for Mas. וְנִגְלָה; LXX : καὶ ἀνακεκαλυμμένα ταῦτά ἐστιν ἐν τοῖς ὠσὶν κυρίου completely alters the sense.

[44] As against BA αὐτῶν with Rahlfs, cf. V. Ryssel in Kautzsch Apkr. u. Pseudepigr., ad loc.: "Should δόξα (= כבוד) be put here to avoid an anthropomorphism ? — Cf., e.g., Ex. 20:22 and → II, 245, 20 ff. [Würthwein].

[45] LXX sometimes underlines revelation through the ear by using ἐν τοῖς ὠσίν σου or εἰς τὰ ὦτα πάσης ἐκκλησίας (1 Βασ. 3:17; Jos. 8:35 [= 9:2 f.]) for a simple אֵלֶיךָ or נֶגֶד. In the first instance the ref. is to God's revelation to the boy Samuel, in the second to the reading of the Law of Moses to the people. On the other hand, the LXX can also use abbreviated expressions, ἐναντίον in, e.g., Gn. 44:18, πρός, e.g., Is. 37:29, the dat. Ἰερ. 43(36):20 [Bertram].

[46] Cf. G. Kittel, Religionsgeschichte u. Urchr., 95-106. On the relation between revelation by image and word → IV, 94, 43 ff. Cf. also R. Bultmann, "Θεὸν οὐδεὶς ἑώρακεν πώποτε," ZNW, 29 (1930), 179 : "The way in which seeing and hearing God are related expresses plainly God's sovereignty over man and man's subjection to God." But cf. also F. Delitzsch, System d. bibl. Psychologie (1855), 190 f.: "Among them (sc. the five senses) seeing comes first ... All perception, whether mediated by the senses or not (like prophetic hearing and vision), from the most spiritual knowledge down to the experience which loses itself in unconsciousness, is understood and described by Scripture as seeing" [Würthwein].

[47] On the problem of hardening, esp. Is. 6:9 f., cf. K. L. Schmidt, 12-17.

[48] Cf. Is. 42:20; 43:8; Jer. 5:21; Ez. 12:2; Mi. 7:16; Dt. 29:3.

a sacred character for special ministry to Yahweh, to whom the same blood of sacrifice is offered. [49]

d. Since hearing and perceiving are so closely linked with the ear, it need cause no surprise that the OT often refers to the ears of God, e.g., Nu. 14:28; 1 S. 8:21; cf. also in the Ps., as at ψ 16:6 : κλῖνον τὸ οὖς σου ἐμοί; also Is. 59:1; Bar. 2:16. The ear of divine zeal hears all things, Wis. 1:10 : οὖς ζηλώσεως ἀκροᾶται τὰ πάντα. [50] Since idols with their ears are savagely ridiculed (e.g., ψ 134:17: ὦτα ἔχουσιν καὶ οὐκ ἐνωτισθήσονται), [51] it is plain that the desire in prayer for the most vivid possible phrase, even though it be anthropomorphic, is due to a wish to give strong expression to the certainty of being truly heard in this personal dialogue with the invisible God. All the same, the figurative nature of the anthropomorphism is plain enough here on man's side, as may be seen in ψ 93:9 : ὁ φυτεύσας τὸ οὖς οὐχὶ ἀκούει; [52] It is worth noting that the NT avoids all these anthropomorphic phrases about God's members, including His ears ; it uses them only when quoting the OT. [53]

3. Philo and Josephus.

a. The biblical pattern is still normative for Philo. He often speaks of the ear, even when a verbal form of ἀκούειν would do instead, [54] and sees that the ear is given by creation. He thus recalls ψ 93:9 : ἀκοὴν εἰς οὖς φυτεύσας "(God) planted hearing in the ear." In Poster. C., 35 f. he rejects as the view of the ungodly the principle of Protagoras that man is the measure of all things, for this would logically mean that everything is the gift of his own spirit : δωρεὰ τοῦ νοῦ τὰ πάντα, ὥστε ... κεχάρισται ... ὡσὶ τὸ ἀκούειν. This is an illusion of the soul, Cher., 57. Nevertheless, the Gk. view of an explanation by natural causes comes victoriously to the forefront. On the Stoic model the ear is explained teleologically in Fug., 182 : τὸ μὲν ὁρατικὸν πνεῦμα τείνοντος εἰς ὄμματα, τὸ δὲ ἀκουστικὸν εἰς οὖς, that is, the leading part of the soul (ἡγεμονικόν) causes the sense of hearing to stretch to the ear. [55] Sensual perception through the ears nourishes the νοῦς, Plant., 133 : τὸ τρέφον τὸν νοῦν ἡμῶν ἐστιν αἴσθησις, ... εὐτρεπίζουσα ... δι' ὤτων παντοδαπὰς τὰς τῶν φωνῶν ἰδιότητας ... But man should philosophise only practically on the organs of the body. Som., I, 55 : ἐπίσκεψαι ὀφθαλμούς, ὦτα, ... τὰ ἄλλα, ὅσα καὶ αἰσθήσεως ὄργανα, καὶ φιλοσόφησον ἀναγκαιοτάτην ... φιλοσοφίαν ἀνθρώπῳ, ζητῶν, τί ὅρασις, τί ἀκοή, ... τί τὸ ἀκούειν καὶ πῶς ἀκούεις. This investigating of the good and evil he has thus prepared in his own dwelling leads man to "Know thyself." Linked with this is the nature of the ethical and pedagogical assessment of the ear. Det. Pot. Ins., 101: δύναται δὲ καὶ τὸ οὖς πασῶν ἀντιλαμβάνεσθαι φωνῶν, ἀλλ' ἐνίων παρακούετω. μυρία γὰρ τῶν λεγομένων αἰσχρά, cf. Poster. C., 137. Like the Stoa, Philo does not say this without an ascetic concern in relation to the organs of sense, Agric., 35 : ὦτα

---

[49] Cf. H. Holzinger in Kautzsch, ad loc. and Lv. 8:22 ff. Also K. Galling in Beer-Galling, op. cit., 145 : "Thus the priest is consecrated by a rite which confers power, so that he can hear (cf. 1 S. 3:7), perform cultic actions, and enter the sanctuary without fault. The very ancient rite does not have expiatory significance here (though it does in Lv. 14:14)."

[50] The Messiah, unlike men, does not have to judge by what he hears, i.e., by what is said : Is. 11:3 Σ : οὐδὲ τῇ ἀκοῇ τῶν ὤτων αὐτοῦ (LXX : κατὰ τὴν λαλιὰν ἐλέγξει [Bertram].

[51] ἐνωτίζομαι (→ 559, 6 ff.) is a biblical construct of great significance for the LXX in this context.

[52] On the anthropomorphisms and their meaning cf. Köhler, 4-6 : "They represent God as personal"; "anthropomorphism does not mean making in man's image," 6.

[53] Schl. Jos., 20.

[54] Leisegang, s.v. οὖς. On this whole question cf. H. Schmidt, Die Anthropologie Philons v. Alexandreia (1933), 31-67.

[55] H. Leisegang on Poster. C., 104, n. 4 in L. Cohn-J. Heinemann, Die Werke Philos v. Alex., IV (1923), 29 f.: "... what is said about the artistic structure of the organs of speech and ear is naturally borrowed from Stoic teleology (probably Posidonius)."

καὶ ὀφθαλμοὺς χωρὶς ἡνιῶν ἐάσαντες φέρεσθαι, in such men the ears, hearing all kinds of sounds and never satisfied, [56] always yearning for the gratification of their busy curiosity, sometimes give themselves over to the most petty tittle-tattle, so that the manner of life is unhappily disrupted by eyes and ears : τὸν ἑαυτῶν οἱ δυστυχεῖς διά τε ὀφθαλμῶν καὶ ὤτων ἀνατρέποντες βίον.

The influence of Gk. models also betrays itself very clearly in the precedence given to the eye over the ear, Sacr. AC, 34 : ἀμάρτυρος πίστις ὀφθαλμοῖς ὤτων ἐναργεστέρῳ κριτηρίῳ (through a clearer means of perception) βεβαιουμένη. Philo never wearies of repeating this idea of Heraclitus (→ 544, 2), e.g., Spec. Leg., IV, 60 : ὦτα ... ὀφθαλμῶν ἀπιστότερα. [57] Biblical anthropology is already under pressure from the Gk. view of the soul, Det. Pot. Ins., 33 : οὐκ οἰκία ψυχῆς τὸ σῶμα; ... οὐκ ὀφθαλμοὶ καὶ ὦτα καὶ ὁ τῶν ἄλλων χορὸς αἰσθήσεων ψυχῆς ὥσπερ τινὲς δορυφόροι καὶ φίλοι; The ears themselves do not hear, but the spirit by means of them, Poster. C., 126 f.: τῶν αἰσθήσεων ἑκάστην ὥσπερ ἀπὸ πηγῆς τοῦ νοῦ ποτίζεσθαι ...; οὐδεὶς γοῦν ... εἴποι ἂν ὀφθαλμοὺς ὁρᾶν, ἀλλὰ νοῦν δι' ὀφθαλμῶν, οὐδ' ὦτα ἀκούειν, ἀλλὰ δι' ὤτων ἐκεῖνον. [58]

b. In Joseph., [59] too, the formulae of the ancient and uniform biblical view of human life, whereby actions are performed by the parts of the body, so that the ear hears and the heart thinks, are ousted by the Gk. idea of the soul which differentiates the inner life from the body as an independent sphere. [60] It is worth noting how Jos. in Ant., 3, 59 f. gives a much broader picture of the scene in Ex. 17:14 (→ 547, 11 ff.) with its δὸς εἰς τὰ ὦτα Ἰησοῖ, the command which Moses enjoins esp. on Joshua. OT formulae of this kind no longer fit in with his Hell. psychology, and are no longer found. [61] Instead of the ἐναντίον παντὸς Ισραηλ εἰς τὰ ὦτα αὐτῶν of Dt. 31:11 we find in the par. in Ant., 4, 210 concerning the laws : ταῖς ψυχαῖς ἐγγραφέντας καὶ τῇ μνήμῃ φυλαχθῆναι μηδέποτε ἐξαλειφθῆναι δυναμένους. Since the laws ταῖς ψυχαῖς ἐγγραψάντων (not, then, τοῖς ὠσίν) διὰ τῆς ἀκοῆς ἃ κελεύουσιν, ὥστ' εἶναι διὰ παντὸς ἔνδον αὐτοῖς τὴν προαίρεσιν αὐτῶν (ibid., 211), they have their will continually within. Prophetic inspiration no longer comes to the chosen man in the Word of Yahweh through eye and ear, but through the soul and its ability to interpret dreams. Thus Joseph. says of himself in prayer : τὴν ἐμὴν ψυχὴν ἐπελέξω (hast thou chosen) τὰ μέλλοντα εἰπεῖν, Bell., 3, 354.

4. The Rabbis.

For the Rabb. the biblical view of the significance of the ear is fundamental. As concerns the former revelation of Yahweh to the prophets (Is. 5:9), in Midr. Lam. Intr., 22 (34b) [62] Resh Laqish envisages the process very concretely and dramatically : As one shouts in the ears of one's neighbour, not just in one but in both. Scripture does, of course, use at times inadequate figures of speech for God's majesty in order that the weak ear of man may understand something of it : לְשַׁכֵּךְ הָאוֹזֶן, "to satisfy the ear," M. Ex., 19, 18 (72b). [63] It is now realised that this direct revelation into the ear has

---

[56] Cf. Qoh. 1:8 : οὐ πληρωθήσεται οὖς ἀπὸ ἀκροάσεως, "nor the ear filled with hearing." Cf. Ac. 17:20 f.

[57] Cf. Spec. Leg., IV, 137; Ebr., 82; Vit. Mos., I, 274; II, 213; Decal., 46 f.; Abr., 147-150; Fug., 208 → I, 217, 4-8. Cf. on this Leisegang, op. cit. (→ n. 55), III (1919), 228, n. 3, M. Adler, ibid., V, 35, n. 1. Cf. H. Schmidt, op. cit., 49-63.

[58] So it is also said that God grants revelation τοῖς ἀκοὰς ἔχουσιν ἐν τῇ ψυχῇ, Abr., 127. Cf. also Leisegang, IV, 36, n. 3 and Epicharm. Fr., 12 → n. 4.

[59] Examples, a. the natural ear, Ant., 14, 366 : Antigonos ἐπιτέμνει αὐτοῦ (Hyrcanus) τὰ ὦτα, to make him unfit for his high-priestly ministry ; b. the expression εἰς (πρὸς) οὖς. Ant., 6, 165 : πρὸς τὸ οὖς ἠρέμα λαλεῖ.

[60] Schl. Theol. d. Judt., 20 and in general 17-22; Schl. Jos., 22.

[61] Schl. Theol. d. Judt., 20.

[62] Str.-B., I, 604.

[63] Ibid., III, 138.

long since ceased, but the ear should be inclined to the Torah. Certain expressions show that success may be expected at once if there is an effort to use the ear aright in the understanding of Scripture. R. Eliezer (c. 90) in S. Lv., 7, 18 (159b): "Bow thine ears to hear," [64] cf. Midr. Cant., 1, 1 (79a). [65] The same applies to the exposition of a noted teacher, Chul., 89a : "Make thine ears like a funnel (that nothing be lost)." [66] R. Jehoshua b. Qarcha, at the beginning of his exposition of a passage of Scripture, expresses the wish in M. Ex., 19, 5 (70b): כדי שתבקע אוזן, that the ear of the hearers may split, i.e., open. [67] The greatest thing to which the righteous man may, like Moses, incline his ear, is the Torah. He who does this before reading or expounding Scripture may count upon it that his hearers will in the same way hear aright, so Dt. r., 10 (206b). [68]

Direct revelation through the Bath Qol, the echo of God's voice (→ I, 219, 10), retreats into the background. [69] Worth noting is the tradition that rabbis could not be torn away from the written revelation by a wonderful Bath Qol. Nevertheless, the Bath Qol is not an inner voice of mysticism. If use is to be made of it, it is the word, received with the ears, of real men, of a man, woman or even child, which is to be regarded as an omen, e.g., Meg., 32a. [70]

The way in which all human utterances are very closely linked to the ear may be seen from the expression : "May thine ears hear what thy mouth has spoken (speaks)," when someone needs to be smitten by his own words. [71] If with ear and nose (smell) the ear is one of the three members which a man does not have under his own control [72] (→ IV, 559, 27 ff.), the ear is in every sense under the judgment of the Law. One should not listen to unprofitable words with the ears, for they burn first of the members (in Gehinnom). Thus at Dt. 23:14 Ket., 5a Bar. Qaparra would read אָזְנֶךָ (ear) for אֲזֵנֶךָ (vessel). He then regards the finger as the plug. "If a man hears a word which is not seemly, he should put his finger in his ears like a plug," or, acc. to another version, "put his lobe in his ear." [73]

B. Οὖς in the NT.

1. The Synoptic Gospels and Acts.

a. In accordance with the ancient biblical view, NT proclamation thinks of the hearing process in terms of the physical ear. The ear is not referred to as though it were the symbol of a spiritual process abstracted as such from the part of the body. [74] The tradition tells of the healing of real ears by Jesus, Mk. 7:33; [75] Lk. 22:50 f. [76]

---

[64] *Ibid.*, I, 604.
[65] *Ibid.*, IV, 444.
[66] *Ibid.*, I, 604.
[67] *Ibid.*, I, 604.
[68] *Ibid.*, IV, 172.
[69] *Ibid.*, I, 125-135; II, 128.
[70] *Ibid.*, I, 134; II, 133 for further details.
[71] *Ibid.*, III, 35, 47, 120; IV, 524 for examples.
[72] *Ibid.*, III, 757.
[73] *Ibid.*, II, 684.
[74] "It is the Palestinian soul which ... wants certainty through seeing and hearing," not through visions and mysticism, Schl. Mt., 92.
[75] Cf. Mt. 15:30; *v.* also 11:5 and Lk. 7:22, in part also *s.v.* κωφός, Pr.-Bauer³. It is perhaps worth noting that in the saying about hewing off hand or foot or plucking out the eye in Mk. 9:43-47 and par. Mt. 18:8 f., cf. 5:29 f. — typically not in Lk. — there is nothing about maiming the ear. The ear is indispensable because of preaching.
[76] The healing of the ear of the high-priest's slave which had been cut off is narrated only by Luke the physician (Zn. J. on 18:10). Lk. "atticises" when he puts οὖς for → ὠτίον, Bl.-Debr. § 111, 3. Cf. also → 558, 14-20 and n. 3; Mt. 26:51; Jn. 18:10 vl.; 18:26; → ὠτάριον, Mk. 14:47 and Jn. 18:10.

b. The ear of the hearer is the most important organ for the proclamation of Jesus and hence for the process of faith. The message of Jesus does not come to the world's hearing merely as a timelessly valid truth which is of value no matter who it is that hears. Jesus seeks to strike the real ear of the hearer in his specific hour and situation. He is aware that His sending is fulfilled "to-day" : σήμερον πεπλήρωται ἡ γραφὴ αὕτη ἐν τοῖς ὠσὶν ὑμῶν, Lk. 4:21. His message is to-day an eschatological event inasmuch as it presses into the ears of the hearers. [77] This is why the Synoptic tradition gives so prominent a place to the challenging formula : [78] ὁ ἔχων ὦτα <ἀκούειν> [79] ἀκουέτω, Mt. 11:15; 13:43; Mk. 4:9 : ὃς ἔχει ὦτα ἀκούειν ἀκουέτω, [80] cf. also 4:23 : εἴ τις ἔχει ὦτα ... and 7:16; [81] Lk. 8:8; 14:35. [82] Yet the mere possession of good hearing is not what decides whether the Word of Jesus is heard aright. [83] The admonition ἀκουέτω (cf. θέσθε ὑμεῖς εἰς τὰ ὦτα ὑμῶν, Lk. 9:44) implies that the physical ear should be the organ for a true hearing which corresponds to the special content of the message.

c. It was again the fulfilment of a saying of Scripture, namely, Is. 35:5 f.: ὦτα κωφῶν ἀκούσονται ... καὶ τρανὴ ἔσται γλῶσσα μογιλάλων, which proved the determinative factor in the retention of the story of healing of the ear of the μογιλάλος in Mk. 7:31-37 with its special features. [84] The sick man could see Jesus, but could not hear His Word. If things were to be changed for him, his ear had first to be opened. He is thus a significant example for man in general, to whom a σωθῆναι cannot be given without opening of the ear by Jesus. In His pastoral dealing Jesus, unconcernedly making use of popular medicine, shows him on what members (fingers in the ears, spittle on the tongue) [85] he may expect a miracle of healing from above (Jesus looks up in prayer to heaven). The ἐφφαθά, [86] "be opened," implies more than a medical opening of the closed instrument of hearing (καὶ ἠνοίγησαν αὐτοῦ αἱ ἀκοαί, v. 35). [87] Is. 35:5 f. makes this plain.

---

[77] If the κωφοί corresponding to Is. 61:1 are not found in Lk. 4:18 (unless an original which spoke of the opening of the ears is concealed behind the Mas. פְּקַח־קוֹחַ; LXX and Lk. 4:18 took τυφλοῖς ἀνάβλεψιν to refer to the opening of the eyes), they are still implied in the σήμερον πεπλήρωται of the γραφή, as is shown by Lk. 7:22 (par. Mt. 11:5) with its echo of Is. 29:18; 35:5; 42:18. Cf. also K. Budde in Kautzsch on Is. 61:1.

[78] M. Dibelius, Die Formgeschichte d. Ev.² (1933), 248; also → Dibelius, 471. J. Schniewind Mk. (NT Deutsch), on 4:9; cf. Kl. Mk., ad loc. Whether the formula may be an addition in one or other of the passages (Bultmann Trad., 352) does not affect the significance of its content. Nor does the comparison with similar formulae in secular Gk., Wettstein, I, 383.

[79] On the inf. Bl.-Debr. § 393, 6. The inf. ἀκούειν does not occur in Mt. acc. to the best reading in 11:15; 13:43. On the formula in Rev. → 558, 1-10.

[80] The addition καὶ ὁ συνίων συνιέτω (qui intelligit intelligat) in D a b ff² i r robs the saying of its intentional sharpness, Wbg. Mk. on 4:9. On the use of the addition by the Gnostics cf. Kl. Mk., ad loc.

[81] Not in all MSS, but in 𝔎D pl it vg go syrutr arm aeth. Not in א BLΔ* 28. 102 cop. H. Soden and Wbg. Mk., ad loc. would retain it, also Schniewind Mk. (NT Deutsch), ad loc.: "The verse transcends the whole cultic legislation of the OT, and this is its secret."

[82] In Lk. 12:21 only in HUTΛ, elsewhere in the margin.

[83] Cf. Schl. Mt., 373 : In addition to the possession of the ear "an inner act is needed in order that there should be the hearing required of him to whom an ear is given."

[84] E. Hoskyns and F. N. Davey, The Riddle of the NT (1931), 117-123.

[85] Schl. Mk., ad loc. → γλῶσσα, I, 721, 1 ff. This pastoral action to release from demonic bondage (δεσμὸς τῆς γλώσσης, v. 35) is very different from magical action, → 545, 31 ff.

[86] Schl. Mk., ad loc.: "This looks more Heb. than Syr.," though cf. Pr.-Bauer³, s.v.

[87] It is quite evident here that οὖς and ἀκοή are synon.

"One who is shut up or bound is liberated." [88] This is a sign of the Messianic age of salvation.

d. The ears of the disciples can be called blessed (Mt. 13:16), [89] not because they have merely heard a Word of God — they had done so already in Scripture — but because proclamation of the inaugurated age of salvation has come into their ears. [90] But the mystery of this age of salvation is Jesus Himself. Hence Mt. 10:27: καὶ ὃ εἰς τὸ οὖς ἀκούετε, κηρύξατε ἐπὶ τῶν δωμάτων, has really preserved the original sense of the saying as compared with Lk. 12:3 : καὶ ὃ πρὸς τὸ οὖς ἐλαλήσατε ἐν τοῖς ταμιείοις, κηρυχθήσεται ἐπὶ τῶν δωμάτων, [91] since the reference is to Jesus Himself, not to the disciples. [92] Notwithstanding the proverbial ring, the original sense cannot be secular. It must have referred to the message of Jesus, and this means the mystery of His person. [93] Whether according to the version in Mt. Jesus is speaking of what He first caused the disciples to hear from ear to ear, but what would then be publicly proclaimed by them on the house-tops, [94] or whether according to the version in Lk. the confession of the disciples first spoken from ear to ear [95] is to become a published word, [96, 97] the ear of the disciples has in any case to be opened first ; they must become hearers of Jesus before they can be preachers. [98] The call to hear is also drawing attention to a particular secret in the mashal in Mt. 11:14 f. whereby the Baptist is interpreted as Elijah redivivus. [99] The warning of Lk. 9:44 with its emphatic OT style : θέσθε

---

[88] Schniewind, op. cit., ad loc. Cf. also Jeremias, 75-82.

[89] The macarism about the ὦτα is not found in the par. Lk. 10:23 f.

[90] Cf. Bultmann Trad., 114 and 137.

[91] On εἰς τὸ οὖς and πρὸς τὸ οὖς cf. Str.-B., I, 579 f.: 1. The reader whispers in the ear of his translator or speaker (amora) what the latter then transmits out loud to the worshipping congregation. 2. Certain esoteric doctrines are given (in a whisper) under four eyes to the pupils by the rabbis.

[92] With Kl. Mt., Schl. Lk., K. H. Rengstorf Lk. (NT Deutsch), Hck. Lk., ad loc. as against Bultmann Trad., 99. On the different versions of the sayings in the 4 Gospel verses (Mk. 4:22; Lk. 8:17; 12:2; Mt. 10:26) cf. Jeremias, 107 f., n. 289a : The saying is perhaps originally a proverb which Jesus takes eschatologically. It speaks of an eschatological reversal of relations. But the reference is not just to the material fact of the reversal. It is to the proclamation of Jesus in the personal relation to Him of the disciples who now hear and will then preach. With Jeremias we believe that this may also be indicated by Mk.'s understanding in 4:22 and possibly by the saying in P. Oxy., IV, 654, 5, behind whose general formulation οὐ γάρ ἐστιν κρυπτόν the Christ kerygma may be detected in ἐγερθήσεται.

[93] J. Schniewind Mt. (NT Deutsch), on 10:26, as against Bultmann Trad. Neither v. 26 nor 27 is originally profane. The decisive pt., however, is not whether a secular proverb is present, but by whom it is used, or by whom its use is transmitted. If it is used by Jesus, the important factor is not the introductory form, the first person sing. λέγω, but the relation of the use of the proverb to the one who uses it, the existential statement which Jesus makes with its help. Otherwise Jesus was simply proclaiming platitudes such as : "It will all come to light."

[94] Rooftops were used for public cultic proclamations in the Orient, cf. Str.-B., I, 580; Zn. Mt.⁴, 409, n. 46.

[95] Mt. 16:20 and par. Cf. also Jeremias, 105 f.

[96] Schl. Lk., 525 f. Rengstorf, op. cit., on Lk. 12:3 : "The power which is immanent in the word of the disciples and which presses for public proclamation."

[97] Lk. obviously reshaped the saying in the light of the historical development of missionary preaching, cf. Schl. Lk., ad loc.

[98] Along these lines, too, it should be noted that the pt. of ἀκοή is the "preaching of faith," → I, 221, 29 f., cf. 219, 25 f.

[99] Cf. Schniewind, op. cit., ad loc.: "The ear must be opened if the saying about Elijah is to be 'received' (v. 14). For if Elijah has come, 'the end' has begun."

ὑμεῖς εἰς τὰ ὦτα ὑμῶν,[100] also points to the mystery of the Messianic way of suffering whose intimation can be heard, and later understood in recollection, only with believing ears.[101] One can thus understand why in the infancy stories in Lk. the Holy Spirit opens the ear of Elisabeth to the true significance of the greeting of Mary in 1:44: ἐγένετο ἡ φωνὴ τοῦ ἀσπασμοῦ σου εἰς τὰ ὦτά μου (v. 41). Both women and their children are in the sphere of the operation of the Spirit. Hence a hearing ear is given them, and hence, too, they give a witness in the Spirit.

e. According to the view of the Synoptists, there is concealed in the mashal of Jesus which is heard only with the natural ears, in the parable of the sower and other παραβολαί whose symbolical character is fairly evident (Mk. 4:1-34 and par.), the true mystery (v. 11)[102] of the divine rule actualised in the Word of Jesus. To comprehend this with the ears is to believe. Worth noting is that the explanatory additions of the Evangelists in interpretation of the parable of the sower are attached to the verb ἀκούειν: in all three τὸν λόγον,[103] then also in Mk. 4:20 παραδέχεσθαι, Mt. 13:23: συνιέναι, Lk. 8:15: ἐν καρδίᾳ καλῇ καὶ ἀγαθῇ.[104] Thus the ear can be synonymous with the heart in the NT (→ III, 612, 27 ff.),[105] and faith and understanding remain connected with the act of hearing.[106] If Lk. 4:21 runs: πεπλήρωται ἡ γραφὴ αὕτη ἐν τοῖς ὠσὶν ὑμῶν, "in your ears" does not mean that the passage is still echoing in their ears but that it is fulfilled in the person of the One who now sets it in their ears[107] so that it should penetrate as a living word to the heart. The very fact that Jesus expresses the mystery given by the passage, and that they hear it, means that the Scripture is fulfilled in this act of being heard.[108] But it is still an open question whether this hearing brings belief or hardening. In the terrible fact that the great mass of hearers whose ears were touched by the proclamation of Jesus did not come to the hearing of faith the tradition saw, not an inexplicable contingent fact, but Jesus fulfilling a prophesied divine mystery.

For the theologoumenon of hardening the Gospels adduced a saying which is a free citation from Is. 6:9 f., Mk. 4:11-12 par. Mt. 13:11, 13-15 and Lk. 8:10[109] (cf. Jn. 12:40).

---

[100] On τίθεσθαι εἰς τὰ ὦτα (only here in the Bible) cf. materially Jer. 9:19; Ex. 17:14 (→ 546, 22) or the common → ἐνωτίζεσθαι, e.g., Is. 28:23. Lat r has in auribus vestris vel in corde vestro, vulg only in cordibus vestris, a "superfluous emendation," Zn. Lk., ad loc., n. 12. Cf. → 559, 11 ff.

[101] Hck. Lk., ad loc.

[102] For a criticism of this approach, and its danger, because as a theory it led to allegorising, cf. Jeremias, 5-67. Nevertheless, the mashal, broadly understood (ibid., 12 f., 75, n. 201), permeates all the preaching of Jesus, and the understanding which explains it in the ears of the first hearers of Jesus is the understanding of Jesus' own person. To this degree, even if with some one-sidedness, there is an element of truth in the Synoptic idea of the μυστήριον of παραβολαί. This may be seen in the discussion ibid., 75-114 with its conclusion that all the parables of Jesus are full of the mystery of the royal dominion of God, of the certainty of eschatology which is being realised (in His Word), 114.

[103] A term in missionary preaching.

[104] Biblical (Is. 6:10) and Hellen. elements come together in this formula.

[105] Cf. Ac. 7:51; 16:14; 2 C. 3:2 f.; 3:15; R. 2:15; cf. Ex. 17:14; Hb. 8:10.

[106] Cf. on → n. 80 the addition to Mk. 4:9. This reading with its καί is wholly Gk. The addition is superfluous for Palestinians. Cf. Pl. in R. 10:14 ff.

[107] As against Kl. and Hck. Lk., ad loc.

[108] The perf. πεπλήρωται denotes a state: is fulfilled, lives in the present in fulfilment of what was promised earlier [Debrunner].

[109] Jeremias, 8: "Mk. 4:11 f. is originally an independently preserved logion, and must be primarily exegeted without regard to its present context." It is not convincing to suggest

The Synoptists introduce this into the section composed of parables (Mk. 4:1-34 and par.), and thus refer it more narrowly to the question of the disciples as to the purpose of speaking in parables, [110] whereas Jn. understands the verse from the prophets more generally and thus expounds it as originally referring to all Jesus' preaching, so that it explains the fact of the rejection of this preaching by His contemporaries. [111] In the Synoptists the preceding challenge (Mk. 4:9 and par.): ὁ ἔχων ὦτα (→ n. 78), lays special stress on the ἵνα ἀκούοντες ἀκούωσιν καὶ μὴ συνιῶσιν, μήποτε ἐπιστρέψωσιν of the saying within the passage as a whole. The only question is how the saying about hardening is to be construed. If we do not start with a theory of hardening on the part of the Evangelists, but seek first the original meaning of the logion apart from the passage in which it is set, we will find in the μυστήριον τῆς βασιλείας (v. 11), not various insights which explain the parables, but the divine gift (ὑμῖν δέδοται) [112] of this μυστήριον, which consists in a single insight grounded in awareness of the present dawn of the divine lordship as this is set visibly and audibly before the men of the age by Him who proclaims it. [113] It is this awareness which distinguishes those who hear with understanding and faith from those who remain ἔξω, hearing only with their natural ears. If the original saying is expounded along the lines of contemporary exegesis, [114] the ἵνα will have to be taken as almost an abbreviation for ἵνα πληρωθῇ and translated "in order that," [115] and the μήποτε "unless perhaps," "unless perhaps they convert and God forgive them." [116] Though the prophecy of Is. 6:9 f. is so terribly serious, a possibility of grace and conversion is thus left open. For in the preaching of Jesus are fulfilled at one and the same time both judgment and grace, both salvation and perdition. [117]

God it is who must here open the ear for true and believing hearing, and yet the imperative of the challenge to hear maintains its full seriousness, if the physical

---

that the Evangelists themselves turned "the result of historical development, the separation of the community from the unconverted masses," into "a purpose of the divine Teacher," Meyer Ursprung, I, 108; cf. Bultmann Trad., 215, 351, n. 1, who thinks Mk. 4:10-12 is "quite secondary." How, then, could Jesus understand the failure of His preaching in His relation, attested elsewhere, to the Book of Is.? On Is. 6:9 f. and the problem of hardening cf. K. L. Schmidt and → n. 47, 48.

[110] Jeremias, 7-10; 8, n. 5c; 49-51; 59, n. 169 on the composition and esp. the exegesis of vv. 10-12.

[111] Cf. in Jn. 12:38 the preceding ref. to Is. 53:1, where ἀκοή is understood as preaching, Bu. J., ad loc., 347, n. 1.

[112] The pass. is for the divine name, Jeremias, 8, n. 5d.

[113] Jeremias, 8.

[114] Examples in Str.-B., I, 662 f., and cf. Jeremias, 9 f.; → n. 116.

[115] Because the free quotation follows ἵνα. Cf. Jn. 12:38 : ἵνα ὁ λόγος Ἠσαΐου τοῦ προφήτου πληρωθῇ, and Bu. J., ad loc., 346, n. 4; 347, n. 2.

[116] Jeremias, 9 f. The pass. ἀφεθῇ, like δέδοται, implies the divine name, ibid., 10, n. 12 → n. 112. Hence the μήποτε is not to be taken (cf. the LXX, ad loc.) as a transl. of פֶּן "in order that ... not," but along the lines of Rabb. exegesis like the דִּילְמָא of Tg. on Is. 6:10 in the sense "unless peradventure," ibid., 9. Jeremias in a letter says that he has found support for the conjecture (op. cit., p. 9) that Jesus was following the exegesis of His time : "Diverging from the Heb. וְרָפָא (10) and the LXX καὶ ἰάσομαι αὐτούς (cf. Σ ἰαθῇ), Mk. 4:12 says καὶ ἀφεθῇ αὐτοῖς. Exactly the same free rendering of the text is found in sypes : we ništebeq leh, and in the Tg.: weyištebeq lehon, so that here, too, we have "forgive" for "save," and the pass. for the divine name. Hence the quotation in Mk. 4:11 f. follows "the accepted version for synagogue purposes, a version which later was incorporated in the written Targum," T. W. Manson, The Teaching of Jesus [1948], 77. Jeremias, 9 f. thus transl. v. 11 f.: "To you God has given the mystery of the lordship of God ; but to those who are outside everything is enigmatic, so that, as it is written, they see and yet they do not see, they hear and yet they do not understand, unless perhaps they convert and God forgive them."

[117] Jeremias, 10; Schniewind, op. cit., ad loc. Also Schmidt, 6 f.

ear with its possibilities of hearing is to be set in the service of the most astonishing thing that a man can hear. The small circle of disciples who heard with faith[118] stands out like the remnant of Is. from the multitude of those who merely hear. The prophecy of hardening can be pronounced because the beatitude is also linked with it as an inseparable counterpart: μακάριοι οἱ ὀφθαλμοί ... καὶ τὰ ὦτα (ὑμῶν), ὅτι ἀκούουσιν, Mt. 13:16 (as compared with v. 14 f.). Nevertheless, even to the circle of disciples to whom this beatitude applies, and consequently to the community, no certainty of a proper and open use of the ears is guaranteed. The ὦτα ἔχοντες οὐκ ἀκούετε of Mk. 8:18[119] applies to the disciples themselves in the discussion of the mashal of the leaven;[120] their failure to understand Jesus sets them under the same saying of Is. in 6:9 f. as those who are without. It condemns their confidence in their own understanding. It sets them constantly, as hearers of Jesus, under a final seriousness.[121]

f. Similarly in Ac., which in general follows the biblical mode of expression,[122] uncircumcision of the ears in 7:51: ἀπερίτμητοι καρδίαις καὶ τοῖς ὠσίν,[123] is connected with the resistance of the enemies of Stephen to the work of the Holy Ghost: ἀντιπίπτετε. Herein is expressed the pagan mind (ἀπερίτμητοι) which resists Israel's vocation.[124] When they stop their ears (7:57: συνέσχον τὰ ὦτα αὐτῶν)[125] to intimate that they will not listen to any blasphemous words,[126] in reality they fight against the opening of their ears by the Spirit.[127] In Ac. 28:25 ff. the author intentionally sees the inspired prophetic saying of Is. 6:9 f. fulfilled not merely in the preaching of Jesus, cf. Lk. 8:10: ἵνα ... ἀκούοντες μὴ συνιῶσιν, but also at the conclusion of his writings (Ac. 28:26 f.) where Paul refers it to his own person and the result of his labours for the Judaism of the dispersion,[128] which were not literary but involved a wrestling from ear to ear: τοῖς ὠσὶν βαρέως ἤκουσαν ...· μήποτε ... τοῖς ὠσὶν ἀκούσωσιν καὶ τῇ καρδίᾳ συνῶσιν

---

[118] οἱ μαθηταί as against ἐκεῖνοι, λοιποί, οἱ ἔξω, Mk. 4:11 and par.

[119] Not in the par. Mt. 16:9 or Lk. 12:1.

[120] Form-critical questions as to the saying and the secondary form of the discussion (cf. Kl., Hck. Mk.; Schniewind, op. cit., ad loc.; Bultmann Trad., 139, 357) do not affect the interesting pt. here, namely, the significance of these testimonies to a comprehensive criticism of the disciples too in the tradition.

[121] Cf. Schniewind, ad loc. Cf. also M. Barth, Der Augenzeuge (1946), 54-58.

[122] Up to 7:57. Biblical expression may be seen in 2:14: ἐνωτίσασθε τὰ ῥήματά μου, v. Bau. Ag., ad loc. (→ 559, 12 ff.), and esp. clearly 11:22 in the pleonastic (Wdt., Ag., ad loc.) ἠκούσθη δὲ ὁ λόγος εἰς τὰ ὦτα τῆς ἐκκλησίας, cf. Is. 5:9. The ἐκκλησία (→ III, 504 ff.) is shown to be, not a conceptual magnitude, but a community of real hearing men.

[123] On the plur. cf. Zn. Ag., 258, n. 72. The figure of speech is based on Jer. 6:10 (cf. 4:4; 9:25), Wdt. Ag., ad loc. Cf. Bau. Ag., ad loc. Pr.-Bauer³, s.v. ἀπερίτμητος. Gn. r., 46 in Str.-B., II, 683 f.

[124] C. F. Noesgen, Commentar über die Ag. d. Lk. (1882), 171 f.

[125] συνέχειν lit. "to hold to(gether)," → II, 816, n. 1; cf. the refs. in Liddell-Scott under συνέχω 2 and 6, and Pr.-Bauer³, 2. For this elsewhere ἐπισχέσθαι τὰ ὦτα (→ n. 6) and βύειν, "to stop," cf. Pr.-Bauer⁴, s.v. and → n. 35, also 544, 10 ff. So ψ 57:4; Ign. Eph., 9, 1: βύσαντες τὰ ὦτα (from heresies); Luc. Charon, 21: ὡς μηδ' ἂν τρυπάνῳ ἔτι διανοιχθῆναι αὐτοῖς τὰ ὦτα· τοσούτῳ κηρῷ ἔβυσαν αὐτά (men from the knowledge that they must die); though cf. Luc. Tyr., 5: οὐκ ἐπακούουσί μου βεβυσμένοι τὰ ὦτα (on account of the hardness of hearing of old age). Cf. further Wettstein, II, 502 f., ad loc.

[126] H. J. Holtzmann, Handcomm. z. NT³, I (1901), Ag., ad loc.; Str.-B., II, 684; → 547, 16 ff.; 551, 21 ff.

[127] Antithesis in Ac. 16:14: ἧς ὁ κύριος διήνοιξεν τὴν καρδίαν, for which we might very well have ὦτα. Cf. Ac. 28:26 f.

[128] Zn. Ag., 857 f. Cf. Lk. 10:16.

καὶ ἐπιστρέψωσιν. But his preaching to the Gentiles is justified, v. 28 : αὐτοὶ καὶ ἀκούσονται.

2. Paul's Epistles.

In R. 11:8, in a quotation from the Torah (Dt. 29:3) supported, as often in Paul, by a prophetic saying (Is. 29:10), the sense especially of Is. 6:9 f. finds an echo. [129] The question which torments Paul, namely, why Israel does not hear the message of Jesus, is answered even more sharply by this mixed quotation. The stupefying of Israel in Is. 29:10: πνεῦμα κατανύξεως, [130] Mas. רוּחַ תַּרְדֵּמָה (deep sleep, drunkenness), which makes the ears of Israel deaf, [131] was foreseen by God Himself : [132] ἔδωκεν αὐτοῖς ὁ θεὸς πνεῦμα κατανύξεως, ... ὦτα τοῦ μὴ ἀκούειν. [133] In 1 C. 2:9 : ἃ ... οὓς οὐκ ἤκουσεν καὶ ἐπὶ καρδίαν ἀνθρώπου οὐκ ἀνέβη, one is rather to see an echo of Is. 64:3 and 65:17 or Jer. 3:16, which in that time had become proverbial, than a quotation from the apocryphal Apocalypse of Elias. [134] For τοῖς ἀγαπῶσιν [135] (τὸν θεόν) to know the Crucified, eye and ear and heart had first to be freed from the veil by the πνεῦμα (v. 10), since otherwise the human senses cannot apprehend the revelation of the divine mystery. [136] In the list of parts of the body in 1 C. 12:16 we find οὖς (→ μέλος, IV, 562, 31 ff.) with ὀφθαλμός, as often in biblical usage.

3. The Catholic Epistles.

In the Catholic Epistles there is reference to God's ears, but notably only in OT quotations. [137] Hence with emphatic solemnity we find a threat on the basis of Is. 5:9 (cf. ψ 17:6) in Jm. 5:4 : αἱ βοαὶ τῶν θερισάντων (whose reward is withheld by the rich) εἰς τὰ ὦτα κυρίου σαβαὼθ εἰσελήλυθαν. [138] Again, on the basis of ψ 33:15, 1 Pt. 3:12 : ὅτι ὀφθαλμοὶ κυρίου ἐπὶ δικαίους καὶ ὦτα αὐτοῦ εἰς δέησιν αὐτῶν, [139] provides a comforting foundation for the preceding exhortation. Assurance of being heard (→ 549, 5 ff.) is linked with calling (v. 9), but also with obedience (v. 8).

---

[129] Cf. E. v. Dobschütz, "Zum paulinischen Schriftbeweis," ZNW, 24 (1925), 306 f.

[130] → III, 626, 5 ff.

[131] The sensual organs (ears) are not just symbols for the organs of spiritual perception ; in them there actually takes place true hearing of God's summons or the reverse, as against B. Weiss, Der Brief an d. Römer⁸ (1891), ad loc.

[132] J. C. K. v. Hofmann, Die heilige Schrift NTs, III (1868), 471 f.

[133] "Such ears that they ..." Cf. for the inf. with art. Bl.-Debr. § 400, 2; 393, 6.

[134] From the time of Orig., who argued for an apocr. quotation, and Jerome, who assumed a canonical basis (Is. 64:3), explanation of the origin has in the main vacillated between these two views up to our own day. For details cf. Bchm. K., ad loc.; Str.-B., III, 327 ff. With Bchm., Schl. K., ad loc. and O. Schmitz, Urchr. Gemeindenöte (1939), 32 against Schürer, III⁴, 361-365, and Bau. J.³, 4 f., who champion a Gnostic derivation. On the quotation in the post-apost. fathers at 1 Cl., 34, 8; 2 Cl., 11, 7; Mart. Pol., 2, 3, ibid.

[135] So Paul distinctively for Is. 64:3 LXX ὑπομένουσιν ἔλεον, cf. Bengel, ad loc.

[136] So with Bchm. K., ad loc. Schl. K., ad loc., however, takes the saying eschatologically. It often occurs in the Rabb. in established use "as a proof of the inconceivable glory of the world to come," "neither eye nor ear ... is adequate to grasp what is to come."

[137] The NT generally refers to God's eye, mouth, or foot only in quotations Schl. Jos., 23, cf. → 549, 12 ff. and n. 53; 60.

[138] "The member is the subject of the activity. Hence the ear closes itself to the call, or opens itself thereto," Schl. Jk., ad loc. and → n. 36.

[139] Wnd., Wbg. Pt., ad loc. The OT words are here integrated into a much higher train of thought (eternal life), Hck. Jk., ad loc.

4. Revelation. [140]

In all its seven letters Rev. uses again the challenge [141] of the dominical sayings in the Synoptic tradition: ὁ ἔχων οὖς ἀκουσάτω τί τὸ πνεῦμα λέγει ταῖς ἐκκλησίαις. This sometimes comes before (2:7, 11, 17) and sometimes after (2:29; 3:6, 13, 22) the saying about those who overcome. [142] By the πνεῦμα the risen Lord causes the seer to reach the ear of the reader and hearer (1:3) for whom there dawns the truth of the message, which is for him personally as well as for the particular community. [143] In 13:9 the abbreviated formula εἴ τις ἔχει οὖς, ἀκουσάτω is designed to give special emphasis to the urgency of the warning and of the call to vigilance before the threatened ascent of the beast.

† ὠτίον.

ὠτίον is originally a diminutive of οὖς, lit. "lobe of the ear," "little ear," of the external ear; Hell. used like οὖς, "ear," so also LXX and NT. [1]

In the NT the word occurs only in the Gospels, and here only in the account of the cutting off of the ear at the arrest of Jesus, Mt. 26:51: εἷς ... πατάξας τὸν δοῦλον τοῦ ἀρχιερέως ἀφεῖλεν αὐτοῦ τὸ ὠτίον. Lk. in 22:50 atticises this to τὸ οὖς, [2] and also adds τὸ δεξιόν [3] (cf. Jn. 18:10: τὸ ὠτάριον τὸ δεξιόν). [4] In the next sentence he continues: ἁψάμενος τοῦ ὠτίου ἰάσατο αὐτόν. [5] "Contempt for force, love of enemies and saving power" [6] are emphasised in contrast to the attitude of the disciple, who has not grasped the hour, v. 53. [7]

---

[140] In the Joh. writings οὖς occurs neither in the Gospel (only 18:26 → ὠτίον) nor the Epistles, though we find ἀκούω (→ I, 220 f.) esp. here. On the relation between hearing and seeing → 544, 1 ff. and 548, 10 ff.; 550, 6 ff.; → v. Dobschütz, 400 f.

[141] Cf. Dibelius, 470 f.; Had. Apk. on 2:7.

[142] Zn. Apk., 226, n. 88 on 2:7.

[143] Cf. Zn. Apk., Loh. Apk., J. Behm Apk. (NT Deutsch) on 2:7. Also → 554, 6 ff.

ὠ τ ί ο ν. Liddell-Scott, Pass., Pr.-Bauer³, s.v.; bibl. → οὖς.

[1] The use of the diminutive for οὖς itself may come from the nursery or it may be due, as in other cases, to the avoidance of monosyllables and of words which are unusual in formation and inflection [Katz]. While οὖς and ἀκοή are used for the organ of hearing, ὠτίον and → ὠτάριον are among the diminutives for parts of the body which are comparatively rare in the NT, Bl.-Debr. § 111, 3. ὠτίον is rare in literary use elsewhere, but common in the pap., where it usually means "handle." Cf. the refs. in Moult.-Mill. and Preis. Wört., s.v., and → ὠτάριον, also → 545, 4 ff., 31, 546, 1 f. It does not occur in the sense "handle" in the NT, nor do we find it in Jos. or Philo (Schl. Mt., 755). Cf. also Moeris Lexicon Atticum, s.v. οὖς ἀττικῶς. ὠτίον ἑλληνικῶς.

[2] Cf. Bl.-Debr. § 111, 3. Only DK al aliq it (exc a c) vg have ὠτίον auriculam, → 551, n. 76.

[3] Rostovzeff, op. cit., thinks the wounding of the right ear is designed to shame rather than to kill. But against this view are Mt. 26:52 and Jn. 18:11. Bultmann Trad., 340 thinks the addition is "inoffensive" if also of interest methodically, since Mk. does not have it.

[4] At 18:26, however, only (without δεξιόν) συγγενὴς ὤν ("compatriot," Schl. J., ad loc.) οὗ ἀπέκοψεν Πέτρος τὸ ὠτίον.

[5] There are noteworthy deviations in D (οὖς) and a ff² d e l. Cf. Zn. Lk., ad loc., n. 82. "Only the doctor Lk." tells about the healing, Zn. J. on 18:10. It is idle to ask what was the nature of the healing, B. Weiss, Die Ev. d. Mk. u. Lk.⁹ (1901), Wellh., cf. Kl. Lk., ad loc.

[6] Hck. Lk., ad loc.

[7] Jesus censures, not the possession of a sword, but the wholly wrong reasons for which it is drawn by the disciple on the one side (v. 49) and His enemies on the other (v. 52).

† ὠτάριον.

ὠτάριον, a diminutive of οὖς "little ear," is in later Hellen. usage a simple synonym for οὖς, used of the outward ear.[1] It does not occur in the LXX, and the only NT instances are at Mk. 14:47: ἀφεῖλεν αὐτοῦ τὸ ὠτάριον,[2] and Jn. 18:10 : Πέτρος ... ἀπέκοψεν αὐτοῦ τὸ ὠτάριον[3] τὸ δεξιόν.[4]

† ἐνωτίζομαι.

Dep. mid., "to hear," "to listen," "to note."[1] It is a biblical construct (LXX),[2] mostly for אזן hi. It is esp. common in the Ps.[3] when prayer is made that God will hear, e.g., ψ 16:1 (54:1): ἐνώτισαι τῆς προσευχῆς[4] μου. But cf. also Gn. 4:23 (with acc.); Ex. 15:26 (dat.) etc.[5]

In the NT it is found only at Ac. 2:14 : καὶ ἐνωτίσασθε τὰ ῥήματά μου,[6] "listen to my words."[7] There is expressed here the same seriousness as in the challenge formula,[8] this time in connection with the answer to the charge of intoxication.[9]

Horst

> ὀφείλω, ὀφειλή, ὀφείλημα, ὀφειλέτης

ὀφείλω.

A. ὀφείλω outside the NT.

1. ὀφείλω, whose etym. derivation is obscure,[1] means first "to owe someone something," Hom. Il., 11, 688 : χρεῖός τινι. a. Of things, esp. money, Plat. Resp., I, 332a c d; ὀβολόν, BGU, III, 846, 16 (2nd cent. B.C.); ὁ ὀφείλων, "the debtor," BGU, II, 486, 10; τοὐφειλόμενον, "the sum owed," Xenoph. An., VII, 7, 34; esp. pl. "the loan owed," BGU, IV, 1149, 35 (1st cent. B.C.), "the rent owed," P. Oxy., VI, 910, 25 (2nd cent. A.D.); ὀφείλω τινί, "I have debts with someone," BGU, I, 36, 6 (2nd cent. A.D.). b. Of other things owed, including spiritual : τὴν ψυχὴν πᾶσιν, Ael. Var. Hist., 10, 5;

ὠ τ ά ρ ι ο ν. Bibl. cf. on → ὠτίον.
[1] Cf. → ὠτίον, n. 1.
[2] With אD pc against CאΘ pl : ὠτίον.
[3] With אC* LX it vg *auriculam* against אDΘ pl.
[4] Materially cf. → ὠτίον n. 3-7.

ἐ ν ω τ ί ζ ο μ α ι. [1] Pr.-Bauer[3], Liddell-Scott, Pass., *s.v.* Explained by Hesych., *s.v.* as ἐν ὠτίοις δέχεσθαι, Bl.-Debr. § 123, 2 : "But ἐν in such hypostatic compounds has in older fashion the sense of εἰς, cf. E. Schwyzer, *Gr. Grammatik (Handbuch AW,* II, 1), II (1950), 460, n. 3" [Debrunner].
[2] Hatch-Redp. has 37 instances, *s.v.*
[3] → 549, 7 f. and n. 51.
[4] τὴν προσευχήν SA.
[5] Abs. in Is. 1:2, cf. Barn., 9, 3.
[6] D* obviously a scribal error : ἐνωτίσατε (-σασθε).
[7] Cf. Bau. Ag., *ad loc.* and οὖς → n. 122.
[8] → 552, 7-11 and n. 78.
[9] Cf. Bengel, *ad loc.*

ὀ φ ε ί λ ω. *Beiträge zur kunde d. indogerm. sprachen,* Gen. Index (1907), 186; Class. Rev., 15 (1901), 147; 24 (1910), 218a; 25 (1911), 94b; Moult.-Mill., 468 f.; Dalman WJ, I, 334-344; J. Haussleiter, Art. "Vaterunser," RE[3], XX, 441-443; E. Lohmeyer, *Das Vaterunser*[2] (1947), 112-134.
[1] Boisacq, 731 f.; Walde-Pok., I, 15.

τοῖς θεοῖς χάριν, Soph. Ant., 331; P. Giess., 27, 9 (2nd cent. A.D.): τοῖς θεοῖς τὰς ὀφειλομένας σπονδὰς ἀποδιδόναι. Characteristically Gk. is Plat. Resp., I, 335e : τοῖς μὲν ἐχθροῖς βλάβην ὀφείλεσθαι παρὰ τοῦ δικαίου ἀνδρός, τοῖς δὲ φίλοις ὠφελίαν. c. With inf. "to be in debt," "to be under obligation," "to have to," "ought to," Polyb., 6, 37, 5 : τὸ αὐτὸ πάσχειν, P. Oxy., VII, 1021, 14 ff. (54 A.D.): θεοῖς εἰδέναι χάριτας, Plat. Leg., IV, 717b: οἷς θέμις ὀφείλοντα ἀποτίνειν τὰ πρῶτά τε καὶ μέγιστα ὀφειλήματα, Letter of Sempronius (Deissmann LO⁴, 160, line 27 f.): ὀφίλομεν σέβεσθε (= σέβεσθαι) τὴν τεκοῦσαν ὡς θε[όν]. — οὐκ ὀφείλειν, "should not."

ὀφείλειν, "to owe," is esp. common in relation to revenge and law.[2] In personal offences the transgressor is a debtor so far as the injured party is concerned. Only the injured party can remit revenge as a debt owed to him. In the transition from personal revenge to national law the guilty party becomes a debtor to the law.[3] The transgressor feels bound and obligated to suffer the punishment.[4] In ancient times punishments were in different degrees penances.[5] The malefactor owes (ὀφείλει) the injured party compensation. Alongside the secular payment is sacral penance. This has a stronger force, and is often pronounced for purely secular transgressions too. In this case the wrongdoer owes the penance to God.[6] God's benevolence also makes man a debtor and demands cultic payment. Hence the dying Socrates can admonish his friends : τῷ Ἀσκληπιῷ ὀφείλομεν ἀλεκτρυόνα, Plat. Phaed., 118. ὀφείλω, then, reaches over from the legal sphere into the moral, and from this into the religious. The negative concept of payment becomes the positive one of moral indebtedness and obligation. The idea of obligation as a particular affair arising out of special circumstances gives way to that of lasting commitment. The personal ὀφείλω is distinguished from the neutral καθῆκον, which is a leading ethical concept in Stoic philosophy, by the fact that the latter expresses what belongs to or is incumbent upon man by nature in his environment (→ III, 438, 17) whereas the former basically implies obligation to another. On the distinction from δεῖ → II, 21 ff.

2. In view of the copious number of examples in general Gk. literature it is surprising how rare ὀφείλειν is in the LXX. In the OT proper it occurs only 5 times, with a further 10 instances in the Apocrypha.

a. In the lit. sense of owing a sum of money it is used in Dt. 15:2 (χρέος) for the Heb. נָשָׁה,[7] another form of נָשָׁא, which is found (alongside δανείζων) in Is. 24:2.[8]

---

[2] Cf. R. Hirzel, Themis, Dike u. Verwandtes (1907), 191, 200, n. 2.
[3] Aesch. Choeph., 310 f.: τοὐφειλόμενον πράσσουσα Δίκη, Plat. Leg., X, 909a : δίκην; Jos. Ant., 7, 121.
[4] Eur. Andr., 360 : βλάβην ὀφείλω, Lys., 1, 32 : διπλῆν τὴν βλάβην, Plat. Crat., 400c : ἕως ἂν ἐκτείσῃ τὰ ὀφειλόμενα, Lys., 9, 10 : ζημίαν.
[5] K. Latte, Heiliges Recht (1920), 48-61.
[6] For violating the peace of God in Olympia a penance was laid on the Spartans to be paid partly to Zeus and partly to the community of Elis, Thuc., V, 49, 5; Ditt. Syll.³, 986, 10 ff.: πέντε στατῆρας ὀφειλέτω (sc. the transgressor of the law) ἀγνῶς πρὸς τὸ θεό, Hdt., III, 52 : ἱρὴν ζημίην τοῦτον (sc. the violator of the commandment) τῷ Ἀπόλλωνι ὀφείλειν, Demosth., 24, 22; Plat. Leg., VI, 774a. In a rather different sense — under the influence of oriental modes of thinking — trespass against a god is described in an inscr. from Asia Minor as the debt to be paid, Ditt. Syll.³, 1042, 15 : ἁμαρτίαν ὀφιλέτω Μηνὶ Τυράννωι, Latte, op. cit., 77; Deissmann NB, 52; Steinleitner, 83.
[7] From this the noun מַשָּׁאָה Dt. 24:10 (→ ὀφείλημα) and מַשָּׁא, Neh. 10:32 (2 Εσδρ. 20:32 ἀπαίτησις).
[8] Cf. E. Liebmann, "Der Text in Js. 24-27," ZAW, 22 (1902), 27 f.; as in Jer. 15:10 the translator confuses ὀφείλω with ὠφελέω, and thus changes the sense in Gk.

In Ez. 18:7 the aramaicising (cf. Da. 1:10) חוֹב (LXX ὀφείλοντος) is undoubtedly a textual error. [9] At 1 Macc. 10:43 βασιλικά, taxation owed to the state (cf. Jos. Ant., 13, 56 : βασιλικὰ χρήματα), in 1 Macc. 13:39 στέφανον, crown tax, [10] 13:15 ἀργύριον. Transf. Prv. 14:9 of the sacrifice of purification (καθαρισμόν) which fools (the ungodly) owe. [11] b. With the acc. of punishment regarded as the payment which the malefactor must make, Tob. 6:13 : ὀφειλήσει θάνατον, 4 Macc. 11:3 : περὶ πλειόνων ἀδικημάτων ὀφειλήσῃς τῇ οὐρανίῳ δίκῃ τιμωρίαν, Job 6:20 : αἰσχύνην; [12] pass. Wis. 12:20 : ὀφειλομένους θανάτῳ. c. With inf. in the sense "to be obliged," "to have to," Wis. 12:15 : τὸν μὴ ὀφείλοντα κολασθῆναι, 4 Macc. 11:15 ἀποθνήσκειν.

This review shows that only in the basic sense ("to be in debt for an amount") does the LXX have a Hebrew original. The infrequent occurrence in other senses finds an explanation, however, in the different mode of thought in the OT. The main idea here is not that of inner obligation, but of the Law and the divine will, God's imperious statutes, to which man must render obedience, Mi. 6:8; Ex. 20; Dt. 4:1 f. Partly by way of the cultus, partly by way of prophetic preaching, the OT developed with increasing force the thought that man's sin makes him a debtor before God. [13] We do not find, however, the later Jewish idea that man's acts can be calculated in relation to God, or the corresponding image of the sum which man owes and must pay to God as a business partner.

3. In distinction from the LXX Philo often follows general Gk. usage and speaks of ὀφείλειν as a positive duty and obligation of man. This is an indebtedness which proceeds partly from the relation to God, partly from the given facts of creation, and partly from the divine Law or sacred custom.

Thus the priest, inasmuch as he belongs to God, is under obligation to turn aside from everything created (ὀφείλει πάντων ἀλλοτριοῦσθαι τῶν ἐν γενέσει, Spec. Leg., I, 114). Cultic worship of the one God is a duty which the Gentiles have wrongly set aside (τὰς ὀφειλομένας λατρείας ἀποδεδράκασι, ibid., II, 167; cf. I, 209). Parents have a special obligation to maintain their children (σῴζειν ὀφείλοντες, III, 115), while children have a duty κληρονομεῖν ἔθη πάτρια and not just their parents' money and possessions, IV, 150. In contrast to the adulteress the innocent woman is to remain alive (ζῆν ὀφείλει, III, 59). Physical cleanness is an obligation as a sign of moral purity, I, 5. In accordance with Stoic influence, Philo sometimes argues from what is given by nature. As fire, if it is to warm, must be warm itself, so the judge must first be full of pure justice if he is to dispense justice, IV, 56. The use in Philo, which is not influenced by the Rabbinic-Aram. חוּב, leads from secular Gk. to NT and apostolic.

4. Later Judaism, which views the relation to God as a legal and business relation, often applies the metaphor of indebtedness to the ethical and religious relation between man and God. [14] Man is in arrears with his good works and thus falls into debt with God.

---

[9] This is either to be changed to שׁוֹב or eliminated altogether, cf. v. 12.

[10] S. Krauss, Talmudische Archäologie, II (1911), 374.

[11] The underlying Heb. can hardly be in good shape.

[12] ὀφειλήσουσιν with no Heb. original (בֹּשׁוּ); BHK³ conjectures לְבֹשׁוּ בֹשֶׁת.

[13] In this connection we constantly find the stem אָשַׁם, partly as noun (Gn. 26:10; Lv. 6:10; Nu. 5:7, 8; Jer. 51:5), partly as verb (Lv. 4:13, 22; Nu. 5:6, 7; Is. 24:6; Ps. 34:21 f.; Prv. 30:10).

[14] Perhaps verses like Ps. 50:14 : "Pay thy vows unto the most High," can be regarded as a point of contact in the OT [L. Rost].

The Aram. term for this is the verb חוּב (חִיב), which like ὀφείλω comprises both the sense of liability to punishment and also that of being under obligation, pi "to declare to be in debt," opp. זָכָה. חִיּוּב means "indebtedness," "obligation," "liability to punishment," and חַיָּב "debtor," "liable," "under penalty." In later Judaism the noun חוֹב, חוֹבָה ("debt," "guilt") becomes a common term for sin, → 565, 11 ff. It is typical of later Judaism that it should add this term from the world of law and business to the many others already present. Man's relation to God is that of a debtor to his creditor. [15] Each transgression means indebtedness to the God who has given the Law. In heaven men's acts are entered into an account book (שְׁטַר חוֹב), and the final reckoning decides whether the fulfilments of the Law or the transgressions are in the ascendancy. "Because the individual is judged by the majority (i.e., of his works) ..., man always appears to be in part righteous (זַכַּי) and in part guilty (חַיָּב). If he keeps a commandment, well with him, for he has ... inclined the scale on the side of merit ..." [16] Or we find the comparison with the population of a city which is in arrears in its payment of taxes to the king. God will finally remit a third in consideration of the fasting of those of high repute. [17] Akiba prays: "Our father, our king, according to thy great mercy remit our promissory notes (כָּל־שְׁטָרֵי חוֹבוֹתֵינוּ)." [18] The concept of the gracious God who remits debts is present here, but the accompanying presence of the idea of works and merits prevents it from being purely developed in later Judaism. There is also a tendency for the view of sin to be debased into a matter of calculation. As חוֹב sin is no longer rebellion against God (פֶּשַׁע), or missing the mark (חַטָּאת), or guilty deviation from the way (עָוֹן), or disobedience to God's commandments. It is a negative thing, arrears in payment, which can be made up by a corresponding payment. [19]

B. ὀφείλω in the NT.

The word group ὀφειλ- is common in the NT. [20] Unmistakably closest to later Jewish usage is that in Mt. Here the Aram. חַיָּב shines through strongly. On the other hand we do not find in Mt. the otherwise current Greek combination with the inf., though this is almost the only construction in the other books of the NT.

1. In a way which formally resembles later Judaism, Jesus speaks of man as a debtor to God, e.g., in the Lord's Prayer (Mt. 6:12; Lk. 11:4), the parable of the wicked servant (Mt. 18:23 ff.), that of the woman who sinned much (Lk. 7:41), the saying about the unprofitable servant (Lk. 17:10), and that about being bound by an oath to God (Mt. 23:16, 18). Only in Mt. 6:12 is sin defined as ὀφείλημα, as in later Judaism, → 565, 18 f. Jesus uses the metaphor of the debtor to explain man's situation in relation to God. [21] The figure of 10,000 talents shows how irretrievably great is man's indebtedness, Mt. 18:24. The same confession underlies the request for forgiveness in the Lord's Prayer, Mt. 6:12. For Jesus, who teaches His disciples to pray for remission, perceives how impossible is the way of compensating for bad deeds by good deeds after the manner of Pharisaic thinking. In

---

[15] Bacher Term., I, 58 f.; Dalman Wört., 138, 144; Levy Chald. Wört., I, 253; T. on Mal. 1:14; Tg. O. on Gn. 18:23 f.; Ex. 5:16; → Lohmeyer, 113. חוֹבָה, "duty," is in Halachic exegesis the antonym of רְשׁוּת, which denotes action according to free judgment.

[16] T. Qid., 1, 14 (§ 336) in Str.-B., IV, 11; Weber, 281 f.; Str.-B., III, 628; IV, 14.

[17] Tanch. אמור, 178a in Str.-B., I, 798 f.

[18] bTaan., 25b; cf. Str.-B., I, 421; also I, 800.

[19] Cf. Eichrodt Theol. AT, III, 81-89.

[20] It is absent only from Mk., 1 and 2 Pt., Jm., Jd. and Rev.

[21] The thought that God has given man everything, and that man owes all that he is and has to God, is wrongly imported into the context by Lohmeyer, 118.

the formally similar use of the same metaphor Jesus rises above Jewish thought materially by grounding the divine remission in the divine mercy. He does not speak of any underlying human achievements in the form of works, merits, sacrifices, fasts etc. Whereas in the OT remission of debt is as it were bought from God by the guilt offering etc., Jesus lifts the process right out of the cultic and legal sphere. ἀφιέναι, "to remit," becomes "to forgive." Forgiveness is a matter of grace. [22] From the experience of the divine remission of debt Jesus deduces a duty to act in the same way towards one's brother, Lk. 11:4; Mt. 6:14 f.; 18:23 ff. [23] The word σύνδουλος in Mt. 18:28 f. is a reminder of the binding interrelation of men and of their common and very serious subjection to the same Lord and Judge. If there is a refusal to remit the debt of one's brother, then God for His part will replace grace by the pitiless justice which casts one back quite hopelessly into the state of inability to pay. The related ὡς καὶ ἡμεῖς ἀφήκαμεν in the fifth petition of the Lord's Prayer (Mt. 6:12) is not to be regarded here as an appeal to our own action with its claim to remission by God. It is simply stating that no implacability of ours to a brother stands in the way of this petition to God. Similarly, the καὶ γὰρ αὐτοὶ ἀφίομεν in Lk. 11:4 states the reason why the petitioner takes courage to approach the holy God with the difficult request for remission of his debts. The appendix reminds him that his request for remission would be hopeless from the very first if he himself displayed no readiness to forgive. The aorist of Mt. (ἀφήκαμεν) expresses the seriousness of the desire for reconciliation by the completed act, whereas the present of Lk. (ἀφίομεν) expresses it by constant readiness to forgive. In Mt. 23:16, 18, where Jesus speaks of oaths which are binding or not binding according to the Pharisees, the use of חַיָּב may again be seen in the ὀφείλειν. By uttering the formula man is set under obligation to God to keep the oath. [24] The common Gk. phrase "to be obliged to do" (ὀφείλω with inf.) is used by Jesus in the Gospels only once each in Lk. (17:10, the duty of the servant towards his master, God) and Jn. (13:14, the duty of the disciple to serve his fellow-disciples). In general Jesus does not refer to human obligations. As the Lord who commands, He speaks in direct imperatives. His requirements acquire a stronger unconditional character thereby.

2. In other parts of the NT ὀφείλειν is used in Phlm. 18 in the literal sense, while in Jn. 19:7 ὀφείλει ἀποθανεῖν is equivalent to the ἔνοχος θανάτου of Mt. 26:66. [25] In Hb. 5:3 the word refers to the legal duty which the high-priest cannot evade by reason of his human weakness. [26] Hb. 2:17 (cf. ἔπρεπεν in v. 10) speaks of a more inward obligation and necessity incumbent on Christ the High-priest. In 1 C. 11:7, 10 there undoubtedly echoes in the ὀφείλει something of Paul's past under the Law. Covering the head in expression of her subjection to man was in Judaism the woman's duty according to the Halacha. Paul sees in the commandment a recognition of the custom grounded in the order of creation, so that it should not be disregarded in the Christian community. [27] In most of the apostolic

---

[22] Lohmeyer, 119, 123.

[23] For the τοῖς ὀφειλέταις ἡμῶν of Mt. 6:12, to which the literal sense clings overmuch, Lk. has παντὶ ὀφείλοντι ἡμῖν.

[24] Cf. Ned., 2, 3 in Str.-B., I, 932; ἔνοχος (→ II, 828, 16 ff.), which goes back to חַיָּב, corresponds materially.

[25] The Heb. חַיָּב מִיתָה corresponds to both; cf. Schl. Mt., 762.

[26] Rgg. Hb., 127; Mi. Hb.⁸ on 5:3; cf. Test. Jos. 14:6.

[27] Str.-B., III, 435 ff.; Schl. K., 314; S. Lösch, "Chr. Frauen in Korinth," Theol. Quart., 127 (1947), 216-261.

passages, almost always ὀφείλειν with infinitive, legal duty is transcended. In R. 13:8 Paul uses a pun on the twofold meaning of ὀφείλειν ("to owe" and "to be under obligation") in his admonition to Christians that they should not be in debt to anyone but that they owe love to one another in so high and broad and deep a measure that they can never be said fully to have discharged this duty.[28] According to R. 15:1 Christians have the duty of considerately upholding the weak, according to R. 15:27 they should repay the spiritual goods which they have received with material, and according to 2 Th. 1:3; 2:13 they are to give thanks for the growth of the community. 2 C. 12:14 is an admonition to parental duty, Eph. 5:28 to the duty of marital love, 1 Jn. 2:6 to that of sanctification, 3:16 to self-sacrifice, 4:11 to reciprocal brotherly love, and 3 Jn. 8 to hospitality.

These verses clearly reflect a certain shift as compared with the teaching of Jesus. Whereas Jesus the Lord speaks in imperatives, apostolic preaching, though it contains these, unfolds the obligations which follow from the basic Christian facts and total Christian thinking. In the main the obligation in these apostolic references is an obligation towards men which is deduced and which follows from the experienced or preceding act of God the Saviour. In many instances the sentence construction indicates the connection between human obligation and the experienced act of salvation.[29] From this it may also be seen that NT ὀφείλειν does not lead into externally imposed legalism, but that the Christian commitment, the NT imperative, develops out of salvation already known.

3. In some verses ὀφείλειν has the weaker sense of mere compulsion, e.g., Ac. 17:29; 1 C. 5:10; 9:10; 2 C. 12:11; Hb. 5:12.

† ὀφειλή.

This word is rare in secular literature,[1] common in the pap., "debt," esp. of money, so in the formula καθαρὰ ἀπό τε ὀφιλῆς καὶ ὑποθήκης καὶ παντὸς διεγγυήματος, BGU, I, 112, 11, cf. IV, 1158, 18; P. Masp., 95, 22 (6th cent. A.D.); it does not occur in the LXX.

In the NT it is used literally for a financial debt in Mt. 18:32,[2] more generally for obligations and taxes in R. 13:7 (φόρον, τέλος), transf. for the conduct which is an obligation in R. 13:7 (φόβον, τιμήν), and in a euphemism for the marital duty of co-habitation in 1 C. 7:3: τῇ γυναικὶ ὁ ἀνὴρ τὴν ὀφειλὴν ἀποδιδότω.[3] ὀφειλή corresponds here to the Rabb. חוֹבָה (→ 562, 4), which is distinguished from מִצְוָה.[4] The latter denotes an express commandment, the former an obligation which arises out of the law of custom in the Halacha. Paul naturally sets aside this legal distinction. The ὀφειλή of 1 C. 7:3 is the mutual obligation of spouses deriving from the order of creation.

---

[28] Cf., ad loc. A. Fridrichsen, "Exegetisches zu den Paulusbriefen," ThStKr, 102 (1930), 294-297.

[29] R. 15:3: καὶ γὰρ ὁ Χριστός ..., 15:27: εἰ γὰρ ... καὶ ..., Eph. 5:28: οὕτως ..., 1 Jn. 3:16: ἐκεῖνος ... καὶ ἡμεῖς ..., 4:11: εἰ οὕτως ὁ θεός ... καὶ ἡμεῖς ..., also Jn. 13:14: εἰ οὖν ἐγώ ... καὶ ὑμεῖς.

ὀ φ ε ι λ ή. [1] Johannes Zonaras Lexicon, p. 1489 in Thes. Steph., s.v.

[2] Deissmann B, 221; NB, 48.

[3] Cf. Str.-B., III, 368 f.; Er., 100b (the command to co-habit); the koine-text at 1 C. 7:3 has the euphemism τὴν ὀφειλομένην εὔνοιαν in the same sense.

[4] In Chul., 105a washing the hands before a meal is מִצְוָה, after a meal חוֹבָה.

† ὀφείλημα.

a. "Debt," "sum owed," *debitum,* "loan," not *culpa,* Plat. Leg., IV, 717b; Phryn., 463 : ὀφείλημα δὲ ὃ ἐδανείσατό τις, Pollux, 3, 84; Ditt. Or., 90, 13 (2nd cent. B.C.): βασιλικὰ ὀφειλήματα, obligations to the treasury. b. In a broader sense "obligation," Ditt. Syll.³, 1108, 11: ὀφειλήματ[ο]ς ἀπολυθείς (a common use), Thuc., II, 40, 4 : οὐκ ἐς χάριν, ἀλλ᾽ ἐς ὀφείλημα τὴν ἀρετὴν ἀποδώσων (cf. R. 4:4, → line 21 f.), Aristot. Eth. Nic., IX, 2, p. 1165a, 3.

It occurs twice in the LXX at Dt. 24:10 for "debt," Heb. נְשִׁי and מַשָּׁאת; also the Apocr. at 1 Macc. 15:8 : ὀφείλημα βασιλικόν, "debt to the exchequer" (→ 561, 2 ff.); 1 Εσδρ. 3:20 (forget all debts). It is not found in Jos. or Philo.

In later Judaism חוֹב is a common term for "sin." [1] This involves a change of outlook, → 562, 4. חוֹב means arrears to a creditor, and as such it can be made good by payments. God for His part can as creditor remit the debt ; ἀφιέναι is the corresponding term for this, e.g., Dt. 15:2. It is worth noting that this word, which intrinsically does not go too well with "sin," is fairly uncommon for God's forgiveness in the OT. [2] Innumerable instances in later Judaism show how lively was the sense of indebtedness to God here.

In the NT ὀφείλημα occurs only twice. In Mt. (6:12) — and notably only in Mt. — it is a translation of the Rabbinic חוֹב, "debt." [3] Lk. replaces this word, whose figurative religious sense was alien to the Gk. world, by its material equivalent ἁμαρτία. Paul then uses ὀφείλημα in the broader sense of obligation at R. 4:4 in the context of the doctrine of justification. Where there are real works a reward enters in by obligation, as something owed in return, and not simply by grace (cf. the same antithesis in Thuc., II, 40, 4, → *supra,* line 5 f.).

† ὀφειλέτης.

In profane use 1. The "debtor," Plat. Leg., V, 736d; with χρεώστης BGU, III, 954, 22 (6th cent. A.D.); 2. "someone under an obligation," also transf. in the moral field, Soph. Ai., 590 : οὐδὲν ἀρκεῖν εἴμ᾽ ὀφειλέτης ἔτι. The word does not occur in the LXX, Jos., or Philo ; En. 6:3 : ὀφειλέτης ἁμαρτίας μεγάλης, "the guilty man" who must atone for a great sin.

In the NT the term is used 1. for the "debtor" in Mt. 18:24 (μυρίων ταλάντων). In accordance with the later Jewish use of חוב (→ *supra*) ὀφειλέτης is one who is guilty of a fault. It is used thus in relation to men in the fifth petition of the Lord's Prayer according to Mt. 6:12 [1] (→ *supra*), and in relation to God in the same sense as "sinner" in, e.g., Lk. 13:4 (ἁμαρτωλός in 13:2). [2]

2. Figuratively it is used of various obligations and duties. Thus Paul, once a persecutor of the Gospel, is after his visitation and calling by Christ committed to be a messenger to all mankind, R. 1:14 : Ἕλλησίν τε καὶ βαρβάροις ... ὀφειλέτης εἰμί. He sees that Gentile Christians, who have received the spiritual blessing

---

ὀφείλημα. [1] Examples in Dalman WJ, I, 336 f.; very common in the Tg., e.g., Tg. O. on Nu. 14:19; Ex. 34:7; Is. 53:4, 12.

[2] Heb. counterparts נָשָׁא and סְלֹה, → I, 507, 4 ff.

[3] E. Lohmeyer, *Das Vater-unser*² (1947), 111-123; Schl. Mt., 213 f.; Str.-B., I, 421; Did., 8, 2 has τὴν ὀφειλὴν ἡμῶν.

ὀφειλέτης. [1] Lk. 11:4 has παντὶ ὀφείλοντι ἡμῖν for this expression, which would be odd for Gks.

[2] Lk. seems to use a Jewish Christian source, cf. P. Feine, *Eine vorkanonische Überlieferung des Lk.* (1891), 93-96.

of the Gospel from the mother community, are under obligation to give this community material support, R. 15:27. He emphasises that commitment to the whole Law is involved for those who accept the covenant sign of circumcision, Gl. 5:3. He realises that the prior obligation to the σάρξ is set aside by the relationship with Christ, R. 8:12.

Hauck

ὀφθαλμοδουλία → II, 280, 9 ff. ὀφθαλμός → 375, 25 ff.

| † ὄφις | → δράκων, → ἔχιδνα.

Contents. A. The Serpent in Antiquity : 1. The Serpent as an Animal ; 2. The Serpent in Religious History as a Hostile Animal ; 3. The Earthly Nature of the Serpent in Religious History ; 4. The Serpent as the Animal of Life ; 5. Summary. B. The Serpent in the OT : 1. Linguistic Data ; 2. The Nature of the Serpent ; 3. Gn. 3 ; 4. Nu. 21. C. The Serpent in Later Judaism : 1. The Serpent in the LXX Translation : a. Linguistic Data ; b. Material Data ; 2. The Serpent in the Apocrypha, Pseudepigrapha and Rabbis : a. The Serpent as Metaphor ; b. Echoes of Mythological Ideas ; c. The Serpent of Paradise ; d. Nu. 21; e. The Serpent and the Demonic. D. The Serpent in the NT : 1. The Serpent in Similitudes ; 2. The Serpent of Paradise ; 3. The Brazen Serpent. E. The Serpent in Gnosticism.

ὄφις is the term for "serpent" ("snake") as a member of the genus in distinction from δράκων ("dragon"), ἔχιδνα ("viper," "poisonous serpent"), ἀσπίς ("asp") and other terms for individual kinds. γένος μὲν γὰρ ὁ ὄφις, εἶδος δὲ ὁ δράκων καὶ ἔχις καὶ τὰ λοιπὰ τῶν ὄφεων. [1]

A. The Serpent in Antiquity.

1. The Serpent as an Animal.

Though snakes vary greatly among themselves in appearance, size and poisonous quality, the word "snake" or "serpent," ὄφις, *serpens,* נָחָשׁ etc. awakens among the

---

ὄ φ ι ς. W. Wundt, *Völkerpsychologie,* II (1909), esp. Part 3, 172-180; J. G. Frazer, *The Golden Bough*[3], IV, 1 (1922), 80-88; O. Schrader, *Reallexikon d. indogerm. Altertumskunde,* II[2] (1929), 319 f.; W. W. Graf v. Baudissin, "Drache zu Babel," RE[3], V, 3-12; also "Eherne Schlange," *ibid.,* XVII, 580-586; Chant. de la Saussaye, Index, *s.v.* "Schlange"; E. Ulbeck, "The Serpent in Myth and Scripture," Bibliotheca sacra, 90 (1933), 449-455; O. Keller, *Die antike Tierwelt,* II (1913), 284-305; W. W. Graf v. Baudissin, "Die Symbolik d. Schlange im Semitismus," *Studien zur semitischen Religionsgeschichte,* I (1876), 258-292; also *Adonis u. Esmun* (1911), 325-339; A. Jeremias, *Das AT im Lichte d. Alten Orients*[4] (1930), Index of Subjects, *s.v.* "Schlange"; also *Handbuch d. altorientalischen Geisteskultur*[2] (1929), Index, *s.v.* "Schlange"; B. Meissner, *Babylonien u. Assyrien,* II (1925), Index, *s.v.* "Schlange"; M. Jastrow, *Die Religion Babyloniens u. Assyriens,* I (1905), II (1912), Index, *s.v.* "Schlange"; A. Erman, *Die Religion d. Ägypter* (1934), Index, *s.v.* "Schlange"; H. Kees, *Der Götterglaube d. alten Ägypten* (1940), Index, *s.v.* "Schlange"; A. Wiedemann, *Das alte Ägypten* (1920), Index, *s.v.* "Schlange"; G. Roeder, *Urkunden zur Religion d. alten Ägypter, Religiöse Stimmen d. Völker,* 4 (1915), Index, *s.v.* "Schlange"; C. Frank, *Studien zur babylonischen Religion,* I (1911), 249-256; S. A. Cook, *The Religion of Ancient Palestine in the Light of Archaeology* (1930), Index, *s.v.* "Serpent"; L. M. Hartmann, J. Gossen, A. Steier, Art. "Schlange" in Pauly-W., 2. Reihe, II, 494-557; Rohde, Index, *s.v.* "Schlange"; M. P. Nilsson, *Gesch. d. gr. Religion,* I (1941), II (1950), Index, *s.v.* "Schlange(nkult)"; E. Küster, "Die Schlange in d. gr. Kunst u. Religion," RVV, XIII, 2 (1913); J. Kroll, *Gott u. Hölle* (1932), 185-190, 317, n. 3; A. Dieterich, *Abraxas* (1891), 12 f., 111-126; R. Eisler, *Weltenmantel u. Himmelszelt,* II (1910), 380-383; H. Gunkel, *Schöpfung u. Chaos* (1921), 29-114, 315-323.
[1] Schol. on Eur. Or., 479 (ed. E. Schwartz, I [1887]); Lat. cf. Servius in Vergilii Aeneidem, II, 204 : *angues angues aquarum sunt, serpentes terrarum, dracones templorum ... sed haec significatio plerumque confunditur.*

most varied peoples a series of essentially similar ideas. First, as a creeping animal without limbs it is different from man, and alien to him, in a special way. It is a child of the earth. [2] As it glides out unexpectedly from holes and caves, between leaves and foliage, it also disappears again thither, apparently into the very earth itself. Then it has a distinctive and often almost hypnotic stare : *cur in amicorum vitiis tam cernis acutum quam aut aquila aut serpens Epidaurius?*, asks Horace. [3] Esp. noted, too, is the fact that it sloughs its skin and therewith becomes new again. [4] The strange nature of its relatively fast forward movement also causes much surprise and leads to comparisons. [5] If not all snakes are poisonous, the concept of the snake awakens the idea of poison and of what is hostile to life ; [6] this is emphasised by the mentioning of specially poisonous snakes. [7] Widespread, too, is the idea of the cunning and malice of snakes as indicated in the expression "to nourish a snake in one's bosom," related proverbs, [8] and many phrases. [9] For the snake is not an animal which one can engage in open combat, like, e.g., the lion. It fights with poison from concealment, and its silent gliding in creeping movements strengthens the impression of malice and subtlety. [10] All these elements combine in a primitive feeling towards this animal which is common to mankind : "the snake is the sinister and peculiar animal *kat' exochen.*" [11] This sense of menace and

---

[2] Artemid. Oneirocr., II, 13 (p. 106, 15): γῆς γάρ ἐστι καὶ αὐτὸς [ὁ δράκων] παῖς, Ael. Arist. Or., 37, 9. The killing of the Python must be expiated before his mother Ge ; this was part of the content of the Pythian games, Küster 123. In Egyptian the serpent is the son of the earth, → n. 4.

[3] Sat., I, 3, 26 f. The ancients derived ὄφις from the stem ὀπ-, δράκων from δέρκομαι, Gossen-Steier, 495. Cornut. Theol. Graec., 20 : σμερδαλέον (horrible, dreadful) γὰρ ὁ δράκων δέδορκε, ibid., 33 : προσοχῆς ὁ δράκων σημεῖον. Cf. Hom. Il., 22, 95, Diod. S., III, 36, 6 and A. Otto, *Die Sprichwörter u. sprichwörtlichen Redensarten d. Römer* (1890), 319. Modern etym. has abandoned derivation from the stem *egh-*. On the other hand, a linguistic connection between ὄφις and ἔχις/ἔχιδνα, also Lat. *anguis,* is probable, cf. too the Sanskr. *ahi,* the *aži* ("serpent") of the Avesta, and the Arm. *iž* ("snake," "viper"). Walde-Pok., I, 63 ff.; J. Pokorny, *Indogerm. etym. Wörterbuch* (1948), 44 ff.; A. Walde-I. B. Hofmann, *Lateinisches etym. Wörterb.³*, I (1938), 48, 414 [Debrunner].

[4] Artemid. Oneirocr., II, 13 (p. 106, 4 ff.): δράκων ... σημαίνει ... χρόνον διὰ τὸ μῆκος καὶ διὰ τὸ ἀποδιδύσκεσθαι τὸ γῆρας καὶ πάλιν νεάζειν, Cornut. Theol. Graec., 33 : διὰ τοῦτο γὰρ δράκοντα αὐτῷ (sc. Ἀσκληπιῷ) παριστῶσιν, ἐμφαίνοντες ὅτι ὅμοιόν τι τούτῳ πάσχουσιν οἱ χρώμενοι τῇ ἰατρικῇ κατὰ τὸ οἱονεὶ ἀνανεάζειν ἐκ τῶν νόσων καὶ ἐκδύεσθαι τὸ γῆρας. Cf. the Egyptian Book of the Dead (Roeder, 266): "I (the dead person) am the son of the earth, whose years are stretched out, since I am born nightly. I am the son of the earth who lives in this earth ; I am born, renewed and rejuvenated every night." Cf. on this Wnd. 2 K., 153.

[5] Philo of Byblos in Eus. Praep. Ev., 1, 10, 46 (ed. W. Dindorf [1867]): τάχος ἀνυπέρβλητον ... χωρὶς ποδῶν τε καὶ χειρῶν ... καὶ ποικίλων σχημάτων τύπους ἀποτελεῖ (ὁ δράκων). Rabb.: Ex. r., 9 on 7:9 in Str.-B., I, 115 : "As the snake contorts itself, so the government contorts its ways."

[6] Artemid. Oneirocr., II, 13 : ὄφις νόσον σημαίνει καὶ ἐχθρόν. Otto, 25 : *odisse atque anguis* and other expressions ; Aesch. Choeph., 544 ff.; Hom. Il., 22, 93 ff.; 3, 33-37; Sir. 21:2 : ὡς ἀπὸ προσώπου ὄφεως φεῦγε ἀπὸ ἁμαρτίας.

[7] To denote the malice of wicked men Epictet. uses, not ὄφις, but ἔχις "viper," "poisonous snake," Diss., I, 28, 9; IV, 1, 127.

[8] *Tu viperam sub ala nutricas,* Petronius, 77, Lat proverb, Otto, 372.

[9] Soph. Ant., 531 f.: ὡς ἔχιδν' ὑφειμένη λήθουσά μ' ἐξέπινες, Aesch. Choeph., 928, 249; Menand. Monostichi, 201 and A. Meineke, *Menandri et Philemonis reliquiae* (1823), 363, v. Pauly-W., X, 529; Plut. in Apostolius, 13, 79a, v. Otto, 373 : ὄφιν τρέφειν καὶ πονηρὸν εὐεργετεῖν ταὐτόν ἐστιν· οὐδετέρου γὰρ ἡ χάρις εὔνοιαν γεννᾷ.

[10] Egyptian : "The spirits of the dead, they insinuate themselves like snakes," v. Chant. de la Saussaye, I, 575; Wundt, III, 174; T. Canaan, "Dämonenglaube im Lande d. Bibel," *Morgenland,* 21 (1929), 13 : "cunning," also "sly as the serpent." Plut. Pyth. Or., 27 (II, 408a): δράκων δόλιος, Plut. Them., 29 (I, 126b) a Persian to Themistocles : ὄφις Ἕλλην ὁ ποικίλος.

[11] G. van der Leeuw, *Phänomenologie d. Religion* (1933), 59.

malignity does not apply to the non-poisonous house-snake, which is almost a domestic pet. [12]

2. The Serpent in Religious History as a Hostile Animal.

The natural peculiarity of the serpent is the reason why it plays an extraordinarily large part in the religions of the peoples. [13] In the following pages we can only sketch the extension of its image in space, time and substance through religious history, esp. that of antiquity. It appears first as an animal which is hostile to life wherever there is an attempt to arouse the idea of fear and terror, esp. as an apotropaic means, [14] in descriptions of the underworld, [15] in the depiction of the Eumenides. [16] That the ref. is to the harmful effects of the snake may be seen from the animals mentioned along with it in such contexts. [17] As a fearsome animal, which "spits out a flame against the heads of the guilty" and "destroys and rends their bodies," [18] the Egyptian king carries the dangerous cobra in his head-band. [19] Before him goes the priest, burning incense to it that "its beautiful countenance may be gracious to the king this day." [20] From this it is only a step to the depiction of chaos withstanding the forces of order under the figure of a great serpent (Gk. δράκων). To the material given in → II, 281, 6 ff. we might add the Sumerian figure of Kur, [21] the Hittite Illuyankas, [22] and the Anat myth of Ras Shamra, in which there is an exact par. to the expression in Is. 27:1: לִוְיָתָן נָחָשׁ בָּרִחַ וְלִוְיָתָן נָחָשׁ עֲקַלָּתוֹן. [23] Perhaps in keeping with the use of the serpent in these myths is the fact that the primal sea encompasses the earth like a serpent, with an implication of the serpent's hostility. In Egypt esp. the serpent Apophis, as its name shows, is a symbol of evil and harm. [24]

---

[12] Nilsson, I, 183: "Acc. to the witness of folklore the house-snake is as common and almost more common than the deadly snake." Hartmann in Pauly-W., X, 518 refers to the fact that certain snakes live in symbiosis with men.

[13] This implies the widespread distribution of the snake on earth.

[14] The snake-element is seldom absent from apotropaic animal-combinations in Babylon, Meissner, 204 ff., 50 f., 72 (Jeremias, Handbuch, 285). In Egypt snakes keep the doors of the temple, Kees, 57. In Greece cf. snakes on shields, Küster, 49.

[15] For Egypt, Roeder, XXIX, 256. For Greece, Chant. de la Saussaye, II, 372; Aristoph. Ra., 143 f.: In the underworld are ὄφεις καὶ θηρί' ὄψει μυρία δεινότατα. The Chimaera is both lioness and snake, Hom. Il., 6, 181; snakes guard the head of Cerberus, Horat. Carmina, III, 11, 17 f.

[16] A. Rapp, Art. "Erinys," Roscher, I, 1330-1336; Aesch. Eum., 128; Horat. Carmina, II, 13, 35 f.

[17] In Babylon it is apparent at once that the menace of the snake is the determining factor. In Egypt the snake is accompanied by the scorpion esp., but also beasts like the crocodile and lion, Kees, 58 f.

[18] Roeder, 175.

[19] Kees, 53 f.

[20] H. Kees, Ägypten = Kulturgeschichte d. Alten Orients, I (Hndbch. AW, III, 1, 3) (1933), 177. Cf. also the symbol of the serpent in the Isis procession, Apul. Met., 11, 4 and 11, and J. Leipoldt, Die Religionen in d. Umwelt des Urchristentums (Haas, 9-11), No. 56 f.

[21] S. N. Kramer, Sumerian Mythology (1944), 78, though acc. to Kramer it is not quite certain that Kur has the form of a serpent.

[22] On the two forms of the myth cf. L. Delaporte, Les Hittites (1936), 250 f. On the relation between this myth and the Gk. Typhon saga cf. W. Porzig, "Illujankas u. Typhon," Kleinasiatische Forschungen, ed. F. Sommer and H. Ehelolf, I (1930), 379-386. To the same context belong myths about the snakes buried under volcanoes, e.g., Typhon, Pind. Pyth., I, 15-28; J. Winkler, Die Toba-Batak auf Sumatra (1925), 8.

[23] C. H. Gordon, Ugaritic Literature = Scripta pontificii instituti biblici, 98 (1949), 67, I, 1 (p. 38): "Because thou didst smite Lōtān, the writhing serpent, didst destroy the crooked serpent the accursed one of seven heads"; also Anat, III, 34-42 (p. 19 f.). Cf. Nock's addition to Corp. Herm., I, 4: σκότος ... ἦν ... ὡς <ὄφει> εἰκάσαι με (A. D. Nock and A. J. Festugière, Corp. Herm., I [1945]); Reitzenstein Poim., 329 has ὡς εἰκάσαι με <δράκοντι>.

[24] Apophis is called "opponent," "villain," "one to be warded off," "one worthy to be destroyed," Kees, 55.

In dualistic religions the serpent became the demonic animal in a narrower sense. Among the Persians it was one of the beasts of Ahriman.[25] In Palestine a jinn can be suspected in every snake.[26]

3. The Earthly Nature of the Serpent in Religious History.

One cannot fully understand the imagery last mentioned without taking into account the earthly nature of the serpent. This is the most important element in the whole symbolism. The snake is a chthonic animal. It is pre-eminently dedicated to the gods of the bowels of the earth. In Babylon it is a child of the earth-goddess Ka-di,[27] the sacred animal of Ningizzida, the par. to Aesculapius, and of Ereshkigal.[28] It is also connected with the god of the ocean depths, Ea.[29] If later in Egypt gods were given the sign of the falcon and goddesses that of the snake,[30] this may reflect the close connection between earth and the feminine.[31] In Greece the serpent was not originally linked with the Olympian gods,[32] but with earth-deities like Hecate, Demeter and Kore. Even the snake associated with Athena in her city points to the chthonic god Erechtheus,[33] and the god of healing, Aesculapius, whose constant attribute is the snake, was originally an earth-god of Thessaly.[34] Figures like Cychreus,[35] Sosipolis,[36] Cecrops[37] et al., which belong to a pre-Homeric and in part perhaps pre-Greek faith,[38] lead us to the widespread Gk. connecting of the serpent with the world of the dead.[39] This is attested, e.g., by Artemidor., who mentions as gods to whom the δράκων is holy Ζεὺς Σαβάζιος,[40] Ἥλιος, Δημήτηρ καὶ Κόρη, Ἑκάτη, Ἀσκληπιός, Ἥρωες.[41] There are examples of the same connection in Egypt,[42] and it may be observed in animism too.[43]

Through its relation to the earth[44] the serpent is in the ancient Orient,[45] and esp. in Greece,[46] the mantic animal: ἴδιον δὲ ἦν ἄρα τῶν δρακόντων καὶ ἡ μαντική.[47] The appearance of a snake in a dream or in real life is full of significance.[48] Certain snakes give oracles themselves; well-known are the serpent Glycon of Alexander of

---

[25] Chant. de la Saussaye, II, 241.
[26] Canaan, 13; H. Duhm, Die bösen Geister im AT (1904), 5 f.
[27] Frank, 250.
[28] Jeremias, Handbuch, 233; Meissner, 34.
[29] Frank, 250.
[30] Kees, 57.
[31] In Egypt, of course, the earth is masculine.
[32] E. Pottier, Art. "Draco," Daremb.-Saglio, II, 404.
[33] Küster, 99 f.; Hartmann, 511.
[34] Küster, 133 f.; Rohde, I, 141 f.; Hartmann, 511.
[35] Rohde, I, 196; Hartmann, 511; Paus., I, 36, 1.
[36] Paus., VI, 20, 4 f.
[37] Aristoph. Vesp., 438.
[38] Hartmann, 512.
[39] Theophr. Char., 16, 4: ἐὰν ἴδῃ [sc. ὁ δεισιδαίμων] ὄφιν ἐν τῇ οἰκίᾳ ..., ἐὰν δὲ ἱερόν, ἐνταῦθα ἡμῷον εὐθὺς ἱδρύσασθαι. Artemid. Oneirocr., IV, 79: δράκοντες οἱ μὲν εἰς ἄνδρας μεταβάλλοντες Ἥρωας σημαίνουσιν, οἱ δὲ εἰς γυναῖκας, Ἡρωίδας. Plut. De Cleomene, 39 (I, 824a): οἱ παλαιοὶ μάλιστα τῶν ζῴων τὸν δράκοντα τοῖς ἥρωσι συνῳκείωσαν. Wundt, II, 2, 269 calls the serpent the "universally dominant animal of souls." Chant. de la Saussaye, I, 137; II, 298; Hartmann, 514-517; Küster, 62-72; Rohde, I, 244, n. 4; Frazer, 80-88.
[40] Theophr. Char., 16, 4: ἐὰν ἴδῃ ὄφιν ἐν τῇ οἰκίᾳ, ἐὰν παρείαν, Σαβάζιον καλεῖν.
[41] Oneirocr., II, 13 (p. 106, 9 f.).
[42] Kees, 321.
[43] E. Johanssen, Geistesleben afrikanischer Völker im Lichte des Ev. (1931), 33 f.
[44] Γαῖα as πρωτόμαντις: Aesch. Eum., 2.
[45] Meissner, 261; Jeremias, Hndbch., 258.
[46] Küster, 121-137.
[47] Ael. Nat. An., XI, 16. Python is the "oracle demon of the pre-Apollonian earth oracle at Delphi," Hartmann, 510. Cf. also Rohde, I, 132-134; Küster, 121-124.
[48] Liv., 1, 56, 4 f.; 21, 22, 8 f.; Hom. Il., 2, 308-330; Aesch. Choeph., 527 ff.; Hartmann, 518.

Abonuteichos, [49] Trophonios, [50] and the role of the pythian δράκων at Delphi, → Πύθων.

4. The Serpent as the Animal of Life.

If in such contexts the serpent is no longer hostile, but simply belongs to the earth, it is given a wholly positive aspect by its association with the sources of the earth which are so important to life, [51] and also with the treasures of the underworld. [52] From this it is but a step to the serpent as the symbol of fertility. [53] In the Gk. mysteries it then becomes a phallic symbol. [54] Related is its appearance in birth legends. [55] The serpent thus comes to be connected with the sphere of life. The sloughing of its skin denotes rejuvenation and renewal. [56] Hence in the Orient [57] and in Egypt [58] it becomes the lord of life. In Greece the healing serpent represents the god in incubation dreams, [59] and elsewhere, too, its appearing denotes the coming of the divine. [60] The serpent itself is then regarded and worshipped as divine. Thus we find the serpent deity Sachan in Babylon, which had a cult in Der and was mentioned in oaths. [61] In Egyptian superstition we find a snake goddess. [62] Before the union of the kingdoms Buto was the deity of Lower Egypt. [63] Philo of Byblos quotes Sanchuniathon : τὴν μὲν οὖν τοῦ δράκοντος φύσιν καὶ τῶν ὄφεων αὐτὸς ἐξεθείασεν ὁ Ταυτός, καὶ μετ' αὐτὸν αὖθις Φοίνικές τε καὶ Αἰγύπτιοι. Πνευματικώτατον γὰρ τὸ ζῷον πάντων τῶν ἑρπετῶν καὶ πυρῶδες ὑπ' αὐτοῦ παρεδόθη. This is couched in Egyptian terms, for the Egyptians spoke of the scorching breath of the serpent, → 568, 11 f. Hence the serpent became for them a symbol of the fiery eye of Horus. [64] In many places a domestic snake is venerated. Snakes were kept in the temples in Babylon and Egypt, [65] and later every house or temple by the Nile had its snake. [66] We read of Rome : *nullus . . . locus sine genio,*

---

[49] Luc. Alex., 12-16.

[50] Rohde, I, 120, n. 2 on p. 121.

[51] In the Orient Frank, 253; Egypt, Kees, 56; Greece, Küster, 153-157.

[52] Artemid. Oneirocr., II, 13 (p. 106, 7 f.): (δράκων σημαίνει) καὶ πλοῦτον καὶ χρήματα διὰ τὸ ἐπὶ θησαυροὺς ἱδρύεσθαι. Cf. also the monsters which guard the fleece and the guardians of the apples of Hesperides, Küster, 120; J. H. Breasted-H. Ranke, *Gesch. Ägyptens* (1936, Phaidon ed.), 139; Kees, 56.

[53] Küster, 140-153.

[54] *Ibid.*, 149-153. Cf. the refs. in A. Dieterich, *Eine Mithrasliturgie* (1903), 123. The serpent in the Sabazios mysteries, Nilsson, II, 633 f. The snake as medication, e.g., against impotence, Meissner, 317. As a symbol of the libido, cf. C. G. Jung, *Wandlungen u. Symbole der Libido*[3] (1938), Index, *s.v.* "Schlange"; S. Strauss, "Zur Symbolik d. Schlange," *Psyche,* 1 (1947/48), 340-357.

[55] Suet. Aug., 94; W. Deonna, "La Légende d'Octave-Auguste," RHR, 42, Vol. 83 (1921), 167; Hartmann, 518; Keller, 286 f.

[56] Philo of Byblos in Eus. Prep. Ev., I, 10, 47 (→ n. 5): καὶ πολυχρονιώτατον δέ ἐστιν [sc. the ζῷον ὄφις] οὐ μόνον τε ἐκδυόμενον τὸ γῆρας νεάζειν, ἀλλὰ καὶ αὔξησιν ἐπιδέχεσθαι μείζονα πέφυκε.

[57] Sachan as lord of life an independent deity in Der, Meissner, 284, 36; Frank, 253.

[58] Roeder, 266.

[59] Ditt. Syll.[3], 1168, 115 ff.

[60] Plut. De Cleomene, 39 (I, 823e) → II, 282, n. 11.

[61] Frank, 250 f.

[62] Kees (→ n. 20), 333.

[63] Breasted, 37; Kees, 53.

[64] Kees, 54. Cf. the passage from Philo in Eus. Praep. Ev., I, 10, 46 (→ n. 5). The missionary Unger (J. Spieth, *Die Religion d. Eweer in Süd-Togo* [1911] 143) tells of a tribe which regards living serpents as holy, and when they meet a python they bow before it and kiss the earth close to their foreheads.

[65] Meissner, 66, 71; Frank, 251 f.; Roeder, 154 (a poisonous snake is kept in the temple).

[66] Kees, 57, 216, 301; Chant. de la Saussaye, I, 463.

qui per anguem plerumque ostenditur. [67] The worship of Ζεὺς Κτήσιος and Ζεὺς Μειλί-χιος under the form of serpents, also that of the sons of Zeus (Διὸς κοῦροι), goes back to the cult of the domestic god, and may finally have its roots in the Minoan period. [68] Finally, ref. should be made to the primal Egyptian snake Kneph. [69] In Orph. cosmogony the serpent plays a similar role. [70] Echoes are heard right on into the literature of magic. [71]

5. Summary.

The circle of the serpent symbol is thus complete. It leads from the serpent of primal chaos to the primal serpent. The duality of the symbol is hereby revealed. [72] In the last analysis this is the duality of nature itself as symbolised by the earth. Nature gives birth to life, but also swallows it up again. The twofold character of the serpent, as power of primal chaos and primal power, cannot be explained simply in terms of the distinction between poisonous snakes and non-poisonous. For it is the serpent's power to kill, its alien character, the total otherness of its appearance, its sinister quality, which gives it such a predominant role in the world of religions. In the light of the OT and NT, however, the elevation of this cunning, earthbound, harmful creature, which is so different from man, into a radiant symbol of the divine, is a sinister indication of the confused intermingling of God and the devil.

Foerster

B. The Serpent in the OT.

Snakes are plentiful in almost all the southern territories of Asia. This applies to the Near East too. In Palestine 33 kinds have been listed, [73] including some which are poisonous. Various kinds of snakes are given different names in the OT, though it is not possibly to say what is the precise zoological species in every instance. [74]

1. Linguistic Data.

Most common is the name of the species פֶּתֶן, [75] e.g., Dt. 32:33; Is. 11:8; Ps. 91:13. Par. are צִפְעֹנִי (Is. 11:8) [76] and אֶפְעֶה (Job 20:16), both used as par. to other words, e.g., in Jer. 8:17; Prv. 23:32 — Is. 30:6; 59:5. As hapax legomenon we find שְׁפִיפֹן (Gn. 49:17),

---

[67] Servius in Vergilii Aeneidem, V, 85; A. Nehring, Art. "Ahnenkultus," O. Schrader, *Reallexikon d. indogermanischen Altertumskunde,* I (1917-21), 23; G. Wissowa, *Religion u. Kultus d. Römer* (1912), 176 f.; Hartmann, 518 f.; Nilsson, I, 325, 387 f. The ἀγαθὸς δαί-μων as serpent, Nilsson, II, 205 f.

[68] Nilsson, I, 267 f., 378-388; Chant. de la Saussaye, II, 308, 322.

[69] Kees (→ n. 20), 330; Kees, 347, 349.

[70] Damascius De Principiis, 123 (in M. P. Nilsson, *Die Religion d. Griechen = Religionsgeschichtliches Lesebuch,* ed. A. Bertholet², 4 [1927], 51, No. 104); H. Leisegang, "Das Mysterium d. Schlange," *Eranos-Jbch.,* 8 (1940), 151-250.

[71] σὺ εἶ ὁ μέγας "Οφις ἡγούμενος τούτων τῶν θεῶν, ὁ τὴν ἀρχὴν τῆς Αἰγύπτου ἔχων καὶ τὴν τελευτὴν τῆς ὅλης οἰκουμένης, Preis. Zaub., IV, 1637-1642. On the snake which bites itself in the tail as a symbol of the Αἰών and the world, v. Nilsson, II, 479, n. 1, 481.

[72] Wundt, II, 3, 174 speaks of a "vacillation of frame of mind which is everywhere typical of the sphere of the demonic."

[73] H. B. Tristram, *The Fauna and Flora of Palestine = The Survey of Western Palestine,* 4 (1884), 140.

[74] Baudissin, *Symbolik,* 281 ff.; A. Socin, Art. "Schlange," BW; P. Thomsen, Art. "Schlange," M. Ebert, *Reallexikon der Vorgeschichte,* XI (1927/28), 264 f.

[75] In some cases the Heb. names may be equated with known species, but we shall not attempt any such equation here.

[76] Is. 14:29 צֶפַע.

עֲכְשׁוּב (Ps. 140:3) and קִפּוֹז (Is. 34:15). Of all these words which (apart from קִפּוֹז) denote various kinds of poisonous snakes, only אֶפְעֶה at Job 20:16 is rendered ὄφις by the LXX. [77]

The use of שָׂרָף for the serpent takes us out of the zoological sphere. In the story of the brazen serpent the dangerous serpents which bite the people are called הַנְּחָשִׁים הַשְּׂרָפִים in Nu. 21:6 (Dt. 8:15 : נָחָשׁ שָׂרָף), and simply נָחָשׁ in Nu. 21:7, 9. Similarly the image of a serpent made by Moses is שָׂרָף in v. 8, though נְחַשׁ נְחֹשֶׁת in v. 9. Nu. 21:4 ff., which contains no ref. to the supernatural character of the serpents, thus uses שָׂרָף for a poisonous snake of the desert (or its image) which can no longer be fixed with pre-cision. On the other hand the שָׂרָף מְעוֹפֵף (Is. 14:29; 30:6) is a zoologically unknown creature, a construct of popular thought such as is also found beyond the confines of Israel ; for there are no flying serpents in the world of nature. [78] The seraphim with six wings which encircle the throne of Yahweh (Is. 6:2, 6) are hybrids. The תַּנִּין, too, belongs to different spheres. In Dt. 32:33 and Ps. 91:13 it is mentioned along with פֶּתֶן, in Is. 27:1 and Ps. 74:13 f. along with לִוְיָתָן. In Gn. 1:21 (and Ps. 148:7 ?) it is a great fish, in Ex. 7:9 f., 12 a great poisonous serpent, in Job 7:12 a mythical sea-monster, a dragon hostile to God, and in Is. 51:9 (par. to רַהַב) etc. Egypt and its ruler. Similarly לִוְיָתָן (Is. 27:1 with תַּנִּין, and called a snake) is a mythical creature opposed to God, cf. Ps. 74:13 f.; Job 3:8. [79] In Ps. 104:26 and Job 40:25 לִוְיָתָן is a great beast of the sea (crocodile ?), but its mythical origin is not hereby refuted, → II, 281-283. [80]

The name for the genus is נָחָשׁ. This is sometimes used as a par. to names of species, e.g., Gn. 49:17; Ps. 58:4; 140:3; Prv. 23:32, and the combination with terms which are sometimes mythologically tinged shows that it belongs to both the zoological and also the religious sphere. Since the serpent was regarded as unclean in Israel, and was not a domestic animal as in the Gentile world (→ n. 12 and 570, 21 ff.), it could not be numbered among beasts available for sacrifice. The reason for the uncleanness of the serpent is that it was paid cultic honours by neighbouring peoples. The word ὄφις (→ 576, 5 f.), which the LXX uses 29 times for נָחָשׁ, is an almost perfect equivalent. The only difference is that the Gk. term refers only to land serpents. In Am. 9:3 and Job 26:13, where the ref. according to the context, or the view of the translator, is to a sea-serpent, δράκων is employed for נָחָשׁ.

2. The Nature of the Serpent.

In contrast to the often very fantastic ideas of the Gks. and Romans, the OT in the main observes the serpent with zoological exactitude. [81] It is here an esp. dangerous animal. Its mysterious progression on its belly is noted with aversion and alarm,

---

[77] The LXX can use ἀσπίς for almost all the Heb. names of species ; it also has βασι-λίσκος, δράκων, κεράστης, ἐχῖνος. שְׁפִיפֹן in Gn. 49:17 has no Gk. equivalent.

[78] The Arabs, e.g., assume that flying serpents exist in the desert ; they see in them demonic creatures.

[79] Cf. G. Hölscher, Hiob = Handbuch z. AT, I, 17 (1937), 15.

[80] Esp. plain is the derivation of Leviathan from non-Israelite mythology in Is. 27:1, where in the depiction of God's eschatological victory over the empires of the world we find — in the same sequence — the mythological terms also encountered in the Ugaritic myth of the death of Baal : לִוְיָתָן, נָחָשׁ בָּרִיחַ and נָחָשׁ עֲקַלָּתוֹן (cf. Syria, 15 [1934], 305 ff.): ltn (= lôtan from lwtn), bšn (= פֶּתֶן?), brh and bšn 'kltn. For לִוְיָתָן and תַּנִּין the LXX usually has δράκων, also once each κῆτος, while the transcription Δευιαθαν is common in 'Α, Σ and Θ.

[81] Our answer to the question whether the OT really believes the serpent eats dust depends on a lit. or fig. reading of Gn. 3:14 and Mi. 7:17 (cf. Is. 65:25). Possibly the idea rests on the observation that many species of snakes put spittle around their victims and thus get dust on their mouths [L. Rost, orally].

Gn. 3:14; Lv. 11:42. So are its sinister hissing (Jer. 46:22; cf. Wis. 17:9) and its surprising attacks on men and animals (Gn. 3:15; 49:17). Its dangerous bite and deadly poison are feared, Gn. 3:15; Nu. 21:6; Dt. 32:24, 33; Am. 5:19; Job 20:14 etc. Hence the Psalmist can depict God's protection vividly as His keeping of the righteous against the snake, Ps. 91:13. Because of its mysterious and cunning nature the snake is regarded as the most subtle beast;[82] it also stands under God's curse, and is man's mortal enemy, malicious and implacable, Gn. 3:1, 14 f. Thus comparison with the snake is used in depictions of the malignity of the ungodly, Dt. 32:33; Is. 59:5; Ps. 140:3 etc. Disciples of wisdom are warned to flee sin as they would a snake, Sir. 21:2. Serpents serve God as instruments of punishment in the correction of His people, Nu. 21:6; Dt. 32:24; Jer. 8:17; cf. Sir. 39:30. On the other hand, the climax of the prophet's description of the Messianic kingdom of peace is the ref. to peace between snake and man, Is. 11:8.

Grether/Fichtner

3. Gn. 3.

As already noted (→ n. 80), ideas about the serpent current in the religions and cults of Israel's neighbours left many traces in the OT, even if these are in part closely concealed.[83] In the story of the fall in Gn. 3 (→ I, 281 ff.) the serpent (הַנָּחָשׁ) is assigned an important function. Nevertheless, the story cannot be regarded as a serpent myth, since the serpent's role, though important, is still secondary. J wants it to be regarded as only an animal,[84] and expressly calls it God's creature.[85] Even when doomed to a shameful manner of life and to perpetual conflict with man, it is still for him an animal, though in some sense banished from the company of honourable beasts by the curse: אָרוּר אַתָּה... מִכֹּל חַיַּת הַשָּׂדֶה, Gn. 3:14.[86] It is to be noted, however, that in his picture of the nature and activity of the serpent the author uses colours not taken from the animal world. Its refined (satanic) skill in temptation, its knowledge of things hidden from man, and especially the intention brought to light by its action, namely, that of disrupting the harmony between Creator and creature, and of robbing man of the great gift of life — all these are traits which give indication of more than a mere animal.

Now in the mythologies of Israel's neighbours the serpent is on the one side a mantic animal, initiated into special mysteries (→ 569, 22 ff.), and on the other side a demonic creature hostile to God (→ 569, 1). To be sure, nowhere in the ancient Orient is there a literary par. to the biblical story of the fall, and the pictorial representation on the so-called Babylonian fall cylinder[87] bears no relation to Gn. 3.[88] There is also no assured connection between the name of the mother of the race, Eve (חַוָּה), and the Phoenician snake-goddess, Chavva.[89] But in many ancient oriental myths, as in Gn. 3,

---

[82] It is worth noting that the serpent is not called חָכָם but עָרוּם (subtle, crafty).

[83] A cult of snakes or even totemism can hardly be deduced from the personal names נָחָשׁ (1 S. 11:1 etc.), נַחְשׁוֹן (Rt. 4:20), or שָׂרָף (1 Ch. 4:22) (M. Noth, *Isr. Personennamen* [1929], 230), though place-names like עִיר נָחָשׁ (1 Ch. 4:12), עֵין הַתַּנִּין (Neh. 2:13) and אֶבֶן הַזֹּחֶלֶת (1 K. 1:9) probably pt. to a pre-Israelite, Canaanite serpent cult.

[84] "For him the serpent which speaks here is no other than the animal speaking in its animality, the mother of all snakes as Eve is the mother of all men," J. Hempel, "Gott, Mensch u. Tier im AT," ZSTh, 9 (1932), 229.

[85] Gn. 3:1: מִכֹּל חַיַּת הַשָּׂדֶה אֲשֶׁר עָשָׂה יְהוָה אֱלֹהִים.

[86] אָרוּר with מִן, "away from, separated from"; cf. also Gn. 4:11 (L. Köhler, Lexicon in Veteris Testamenti libros [1948 ff.], *s.v.* ארר).

[87] AOB, Ill. 603 and p. 168.

[88] Cf. B. Bonkamp, *Die Bibel im Lichte der Keilschriftforschung* (1939), 102.

[89] For a different view cf. L. Köhler, *Theol. d. AT* (1936), 239, n. 97; cf. M. Lidzbarski, "Neue Götter," *Festgabe f. T. Nöldeke* (1916), 90 f.

the serpent displays its hostility to God by destroying the harmony of God's creation, or seeking to prevent its realisation. [90] Again, in the Gilgamesh epic, as in the story of Paradise, the serpent deprives man of life. [91] Hence at many pts. in Gn. 3 one can detect the ancient mythical tradition which sets the figure of the serpent in an ambivalent light as both an animal and yet also a special being whose hostility to God is plain to see.

If J, on introducing the serpent in Gn. 3:1, sets it unequivocally in the animal kingdom, and if, in the concluding scene, the pronouncement of the curse in 3:14 f., he again presupposes its animal character, the reason can only be that in his proclamation he seeks to protect the sole deity of Yahweh. Intentionally, then, he dissociates himself from mythical ideas outside Israel which assume that there is a conflict between chaos deities in the form of the dragon or serpent and the creation deities whose work they threaten. For J there is only one God, (אֱלֹהִים) יהוה, the only Creator and Lord. All other beings are creatures. In tension with this principle is, of course, another insight of the biblical witness which one cannot with perspicuous logic bring into harmony with the belief in God's omnicausality, and which thus creates the ambivalence in which the whole story, and especially the figure of the serpent within it, stands. J realises that in his own existence, and in that of the world at large, the divinely planned harmony between Creator and creature is no longer present. Man lives at a distance from God, separated from his Creator. Gn. 3 tells how this rift came into God's creation. This chapter of the Bible is not a collection of ancient aetiologies. It deals with man's present existence and its primal basis in the loss of Paradise by apostasy from God. Decision for or against God is unquestionably set before man in Gn. 3. The theme is "man and his guilt." [92] Nevertheless, the fact that temptation comes from without is not due merely to the need to give outward expression to what goes on within man. [93] In veiled and enigmatic fashion J uses the more than animal features in the figure of the serpent to suggest a power inimical to God which helps to bring about man's apostasy from God and which presents a deadly threat to the life of man in every age. He does not equate the serpent with a demon or anti-god [94] — how could he when he is dissociating himself from the religions around him? But he suggests the mystery behind the insoluble question how evil could enter the world which God created. [95]

In connection herewith a word should be said about the so-called proto-gospel in Gn. 3:15. The alteration of the nature of the serpent as a result of the curse affects in the first instance its animal constitution (its way of moving and eating). But it also affects the relation of the serpent to man, which is changed by God

---

[90] Apophis among the Egyptians, Tiâmat and Labbu among the Babylonians, Illuyankas among the Hittites, Lôtan among the Phoenicians, and Aži Dahāka among the Iranians, → 568, 17 ff.

[91] Plate XI, AOT, 182 f.

[92] G. v. Rad, *Das erste Buch Mose Kp. 1-12:9, AT Deutsch* (1949), 70.

[93] So v. Rad, *op. cit.*, though he goes on to speak of the "antagonist of man" who "throughout history ..." remains "in a hardly definable incognito, not unmasked." Cf. also G. Quell, → I, 285, who does, of course, observe that by introducing the serpent J gives us to understand "that a kind of alien power comes over the man who sins." J. Coppens sees in the serpent of Gn. 3 a symbol of the vegetation deities of Canaan, and suggests that they are trying to bring into subjection to the earth deities ("La connaissance du bien et du mal et le péché du paradis," Analecta Lovaniensia Biblica et Orientalia, II, 3 [1948]).

[94] Let alone with Satan, who plays the role of God's adversary only much later, L. Köhler, *op. cit.*, 164 f.

[95] Cf. Hempel, *op. cit.*, 228 and Eichr. Theol. d. AT, III, 96, n. 1.

from apparently innocuous co-operation (against God) into the never-ending confrontation of mortal enmity. As a penal measure this divine decision applies to the snake, but it should also be noted that the curse on the snake alters the situation of man and speaks of a permanent and deadly threat to mankind. The point of this threat is not just that the life of the individual is menaced by snake-bites, [96] for this would hardly be in keeping with the theologically significant character of Gn. 3, which is explaining the totality of human existence, with its sufferings, sorrows and subjection to death, in terms of the guilt of man. The reference is rather to the more profound threat presented to man by the underlying power which is inimical to God, which continually tempts man to disobedience against Him, and which seeks thereby to deliver him up to death. [97] According to Gn. 3 there is no deliverance from this deadly threat in this fallen creation. Inasmuch as Gn. 3:15 sees no end to the confrontation between serpent and man [98] one can hardly regard the verse as proto-gospel. Nevertheless, in the new creation which God makes with the sending of His Son the hostile forces are vanquished by Him. To this degree one may commend the Christian preaching of Christ as the serpent's Conqueror.

4. Nu. 21.

The story of the brazen serpent (Nu. 21:4-9; cf. Dt. 8:15) is of clear theological import in its present form.[99] It is one of the many traditional stories of the time of the Exodus and the wilderness wandering which have as their theme the murmuring of the people against God's plan of salvation, the consequent judgment of God on the renegades, and then His gracious help. We find such stories in the most varied forms in all the Pentateuchal sources, [100] and in them the decisive role is always played by the miraculous coming of the covenant God to help His people. A distinctive feature in the story of the brazen serpent is perhaps that here, in contrast to the feeding with manna in Ex. 16:1-21 or the drawing of water out of the rock in Ex. 17:1-7; Nu. 20:2-13, the whole people is not helped unconditionally by a miraculous act. God's assistance is only for those who look at the symbol which is set up. On the other hand, one should not overlook the fact that in its present form the story does not emphasise the magical effect of looking at the brazen serpent. The stress is rather on the fact that this gracious means of help was ordained — one might almost say set up — by God as "a sign of salvation which could be seen by all and which was thus of help to all." [101]

One cannot be sure that the brazen serpent was the same as Moses' serpent rod in Ex. 4:2 ff.; 7:8 ff.; 17:8 ff. [102] Nor is there any express statement as to its con-

---

[96] Nor the general hostility between man and beast. Only in Gn. 9 (P) is there in primal history a basic alteration of the relationship established at creation between the race of man and the animal kingdom.

[97] Cf. Gn. 6:1-4 and 6:5 ff., and the many passages in the OT where there is a close connection between sin and death.

[98] The assumption that the condemnation to perpetual conflict between man and snake was for the ancient Orient shot through by the hope of a deliverer, the conqueror of the serpent, is not adequately grounded, though there is surely some intimation of it in the text.

[99] One cannot discuss here the question what religious ideas lie behind Nu. 21:4 ff. Sympathetic magic has been adduced as a par. (cf. H. Gressmann, Die Schriften des AT in Auswahl, I, 2 [1922], 99), and comparison has also been made with the serpent staffs of gods of healing, AOB, Ill., 367.

[100] Cf. Ex. 14:9 ff.; 15:22 ff.; 16:1 ff.; 17:1 ff. (par. Nu. 20:2 ff.); Nu. 11:1 ff., 31-34; 17:6 ff.

[101] L. Goppelt, Typos (1939), 220.

[102] Eichr. Theol. AT, I, 49 f. makes this identification, but he has to assume that in

nection with the נְחֻשְׁתָּן which Hezekiah removed from the temple in Jerusalem. [103]

Fichtner

C. The Serpent in Later Judaism.

1. The Serpent in the LXX Translation.

a. Linguistic Data. In 29 out of 32 refs. נָחָשׁ is rendered ὄφις (δράκων in Am. 9:3 and Job 26:13), while δράκων is the word used for תַּנִּין in 14 out of the 15 refs., and for לִוְיָתָן in 5 out of 7, and ἀσπίς in 4 of the 6 refs. for פֶּתֶן. אֶפְעֶה is twice ἀσπίς and once ὄφις. There are various terms for צֶפַע or צִפְעֹנִי (ἔκγονα ἀσπίδων, βασιλίσκος, κεράστης), also for שָׂרָף → II, 815, 33 ff. (ὄφις and ἀσπίς). ἐχῖνος occurs once for קִפּוֹד at Is. 34:15. רַהַב is rendered in many different ways, twice as κῆτος, once transcribed as Ρααβ, elsewhere very freely. κῆτος is also used at Gn. 1:21 for תַּנִּין and at Job 3:8 for לִוְיָתָן. In combinations with נָחָשׁ, we find ὄφις with part. (θανατῶν or δάκνων) for נָחָשׁ צִפְעֹנִי. at Jer. 8:17 and נָחָשׁ שָׂרָף What considerations led the LXX to change the rams (עַתּוּדִים) which preceded the flock at Jer. 50(27):8 into serpents (δράκοντες), we cannot tell. Sometimes ὄφις is used pleonastically in the LXX (Gn. 3:1; Nu. 21:8) where there is no Heb. original.

b. Material Data. The material question arises whether the LXX meant to take up a position *vis-à-vis* the mythological figures of chaos in its rendering. The allusion to the Rahab conflict is left out of the LXX at Is. 51:9, [104] and at Ps. 74(73):13a B does not have the half-verse referring to Leviathan, which is surely original in view of the many variants in the other MSS. At Job 9:13 the "helpers of Rahab" are rendered κήτη τὰ ὑπ' οὐρανόν. Here is one way of meeting myth, i.e., that of excision. A second way is that of leaving mythological names as they are, Ps. 87(86):4 Ρααβ. The third way is that of ethical and religious application. Thus נָחָשׁ בָּרִחַ (→ 568, 17-18) is certainly transl. ὄφις φεύγων at Is. 27:1, but at Job 26:13 we find δράκων ἀποστάτης, and Ps. 89(88):10 goes even further with its ὑπερήφανος for רַהַב. [105] The later translators adopt the same line. Σ always has ἀλαζονεία for רַהַב (Job 9:13; 26:12; Is. 51:9), and 'A has ὄρμημα at Is. 51:9. When Ps. Sol. has ὑπερηφανία τοῦ δράκοντος for Pompey's birth, here, too, the ancient nature myth of the serpent of chaos is linked with Lucifer or Antichrist motifs.

2. The Serpent in the Apocrypha, Pseudepigrapha and the Rabbis.

a. The Serpent as a Metaphor. With no allusion either to myth or to the special qualities of the serpent, Mordecai and Haman are compared to two δράκοντες about to do battle in 'Εσθ. 1:1e; 10:3d. The ὄφις appears as an animal bringing destruction to Nero in Sib., V, 29. For the Rabb. the serpent is not so much the specially clever

---

the E account in Nu. 21 the idea of the leader's staff has been suppressed or lost, *loc. cit.*, n. 9.

[103] It is true that 2 K. 18:4 describes the נְחֻשְׁתָּן as נָחָשׁ הַנְּחֹשֶׁת אֲשֶׁר עָשָׂה מֹשֶׁה, but it is not so certain that this is the original significance of the *nechushtan*. If it was a pagan cultic symbol which had been taken over like the other objects mentioned in the passage, it can be construed in many different ways, e.g., as chthonic deity, the heavenly serpent, or a totem animal. If it belonged to the Yahweh cult, it was certainly not a depiction of Yahweh (there is no support whatever for this) but a symbol of the gracious help of the covenant God whose power to save from death had constantly renewed the people from the Exodus onwards. Was Nu. 21:4 ff. meant to show the legitimacy of the symbol ?

[104] Θ has ἡ λατομήσασα πλάτος (= רַהַב), διαλύσασα δράκοντα (= תַּנִּין).

[105] Also worth noting is Ps. 104(103):26, where Leviathan, created to take his pastime in the sea, becomes the δράκων, ὃν ἔπλασας ἐμπαίζειν αὐτῷ ("to mock him"). Acc. to the Rabb. God plays with him every day, Str.-B., III, 160; IV, 1159.

animal (this is the fox), [106] though we do find in one Rabb. saying a contrast between the cleverness of the serpent and the harmlessness of the dove. [107] Sometimes the crooked ways of the serpent are compared to those of government, [108] and the serpent's cunning is emphasised : the devil found no beast so crafty in doing evil as the serpent. [109] The serpent is also an illustration of cunning temptation in 4 Macc. 18:8; Ps. Sol. 4:9. [110] The poison of dragons and venom of asps in Dt. 32:33 are referred to the kings of the Gentiles and Greece in Damasc. 8:9 ff.

b. Echoes of Mythological Ideas. Bel et Draco alludes to the temple snakes of Babylon, → 570, 21. Once ideas of Hades are presented, the snake appears as in paganism, → 568, 8 f. In Slav. En. the guardians of the gates of Hades are like great serpents ; Hades itself is portrayed in Gr. Bar. 4 [111] and Apc. Abr. 31:7 as a dragon (worm) which eats up evil, cf. Joseph and Asenath 12:11 (Riessler, 511 f.). When death shows its true figure, the attributes of the serpent are not wanting, Test. Abr. A 17. [112] OT echoes of the fight with the dragon of chaos are no longer understood in later Judaism. [113] Rahab is not mentioned, nor is Leviathan thought of as a serpent. [114] The last mythical remnant is the relating of Leviathan to the primal depth [115] and his fiery breath. [116] In the pseudepigr. and Rabb. Leviathan and Behemoth are mentioned only in connection with the Messianic age, when they will serve as food for the righteous. [117]

c. The Serpent of Paradise. With the development of the idea of Satan it was natural that light should be thrown on the mysterious serpent of Gn. 3 (→ 574, 14 ff.) by connecting it with the power which is hostile to God. To be sure, in the older pseudepigr. (Jub. 3:17 ff.; S. Bar. 48:42) and in Jos. (Ant., 1, 41), also to a large extent in the Rabb., [118] no link is forged between this serpent and the devil. Nevertheless, one can see clear evidence of thinking about the motives of the serpent. Behind Wis. 2:24 : φθόνῳ δὲ διαβόλου θάνατος εἰσῆλθεν εἰς τὸν κόσμον, are more explicit ideas on the relation between the serpent and the devil. Later the serpent is called the σκεῦος or ἔνδυμα of Satan, Apc. Mos. 16; [119] Gr. Bar. 9. [120] Finally, the two are fully equated. [121] In the Rabb. writings Lv. r., 26 on 21:4 preserves a tradition acc. to which Simon b. Yochai (c. 150 A.D.) equated the serpent and the angel of death, i.e., Satan. [122] In Ab. RN, 1 M the serpent is called the "evil one," a name for Satan, → II, 78, n. 42.

---

[106] Str.-B., II, 200 f.

[107] Ibid., I, 574 f.

[108] Ibid., I, 115.

[109] Ibid., IV, 1128.

[110] On the question whether the idea of a sexual temptation of Eve lies behind this passage v. A. Deissmann in Kautzsch Apkr. u. Pseudepigr. on 4 Macc. 18:8; Ltzm. and Wnd. 2 K. on 11:3.

[111] Furnished with the attributes of the Egyptian "devourer of the underworld."

[112] Ed. M. R. James in TSt, II, 2 (1892), 99, 17.

[113] Bousset-Gressm., 499 : "The original meaning was at all events completely forgotten."

[114] Leviathan was thought of as a fish with fins, Lv. r., 13 (114b), Str.-B., IV, 3 M.

[115] Pesikt. r., Suppl., 1, Str.-B., IV, 1160.

[116] BB, 75a, Str.-B., IV, 1128. Cf. S. Daiches, "Talmudische u. midraschische Par. zum babylonischen Weltschöpfungsmythus," Zschr. f. Assyriologie, 17 (1903), 394-399.

[117] Str.-B., IV, Index, s.v. "Livjathan"; Bousset-Gressm., Index, s.v. "Paradies"; Volz Esch., 389; Moore, 363 f.

[118] Schl. Theol. d. Judt., 36, 2.

[119] C. Tischendorf, Apocalypses apocryphae (1866), 8, line 2 from the bottom.

[120] Ed. M. R. James, TSt, V, 1 (1897), 91. Cf. PREl, 13a, Str.-B., I, 137 f.

[121] Vit. Ad. 16 (Kautzsch Apkr. u. Pseudepigr., II, 513 f.) and Lives of the Prophets, Hab. 14 (C. C. Torrey, The Lives of the Prophets = JBL Monograph Series, I [1946], 29): ἐν αὐτοῖς γνωσθήσεται ἐπὶ τέλει κύριος, ὅτι φωτίσουσι τοὺς διωκομένους ὑπὸ τοῦ ὄφεως ἐν σκότει ὡς ἐξ ἀρχῆς.

[122] "The serpent has broken through the hedge (the Law) of the world and has thus become the executioner for all who break through the hedge."

We need do no more than allude to speculations about an originally different and bigger form of the serpent. [123]

The account is more seriously altered by speculation as to the serpent's motives, as in Wis. 2:24 and also the Rabb. [124] Suggested are jealousy at Adam's good fortune, [125] esp. at the food prepared for him by ministering angels, [126] the desire for world dominion, [127] refusal to bow to Adam's rule, [128] or sexual desire. [129] Constantly the unfathomable root of evil is confused with one of its branches. Another dilution is when the temptation of Eve is regarded as sexual, acc. to the ancient use of the serpent symbol (→ 570, 7 ff.), cf. Gn. r., 22 on 4:1; 18 on 3:1 and perhaps Slav. En. 31:6. [130] Thus the serpent is supposed to have injected (הֵטִיל) Eve with filth (זֻהֲמָא). [131] The influence of this idea may be seen in Christian and Gnostic circles. [132] We also read that she was tempted to drink wine, [133] so that the tree of knowledge was a vine, or that Adam and Eve were seduced, [134] or that Adam arbitrarily extended the prohibition concerning the tree. [135] All these ideas decisively reduce the profundity of the biblical story.

The general Rabb. term for the serpent of Paradise is נָחָשׁ or הַנָּחָשׁ הַקַּדְמוֹנִי. [136] In later Jewish writings only Test. A. 7:3 alludes to the proto-gospel in Gn. 3:15 : ἕως οὗ ὁ ὕψιστος ἐπισκέψηται τὴν γῆν, καὶ αὐτὸς ἐλθών (ὡς ἄνθρωπος μετὰ ἀνθρώπων ἐσθίων καὶ πίνων) καὶ συντρίβων τὴν κάραν τοῦ δράκοντος ἐπὶ τοῦ ὕδατος, οὗτος σώσει τὸν Ἰσραὴλ καὶ πάντα τὰ ἔθνη (θεὸς εἰς ἄνθρωπον ὑποκρινόμενος); the words in parentheses are a Christian interpolation ; since καὶ αὐτὸς ἐλθὼν καὶ συντρίβων corresponds to a Hebrew construction, the rest might well be original. The Messianic name "son of the posterity of the mother of all living" in Eth. En. 62:7 etc. combines Da. 7:13 and Gn. 3:15.

d. Nu. 21. With ref. to the brazen serpent the late comm. Nu. r., 19 on 21:6 [137] displays all the artificiality of Rabb. exegesis and has nothing essential to offer. RH, 3, 8 [138] alone is important : "Could then the serpent slay or keep alive ? Rather, when Israel looks up, and when they subject their hearts to their Father in heaven, they get well again, and when they do not, they waste away." Here miracle and faith are associated. Wis. 16:6 f. with its σύμβολον σωτηρίας εἰς ἀνάμνησιν ἐντολῆς νόμου σου has the brazen serpent in view. Not it, but God delivered : ὁ γὰρ ἐπιστραφεὶς οὐ διὰ τὸ θεωρούμενον ἐσῴζετο, ἀλλὰ διὰ σὲ τὸν πάντων σωτῆρα.

2. The Serpent and the Demonic. For the Rabb. the serpent as a natural animal (not as a metaphor or symbol) stands close to the demonic and demons : Tg. J. I on

[123] The serpent originally four-footed and as big as a camel : Gn. r., 19 on 3:1 (R. Simeon b. Eleazar, c. 150 A.D.), cf. Str.-B., I, 137 f.; it was upright like a pole, loc. cit. (R. Hoshaya the Elder, first generation of the Amoraeans); it was to be king of all the beasts, bSota, 9b.

[124] Tanch. Buber מצורע § 7 (24a), Str.-B., IV, 747; Nu. r., 19 on 19:2; cf. A. Rappaport, Agada u. Exegese bei Flavius Josephus (1930), 81.

[125] Jos. Ant., 1, 41.

[126] bSanh., 59b.

[127] Slav. En. 29:4 f.; Nu. r., 8 on 5:6.

[128] Vit. Ad., 14 ff.

[129] Gn. r., 18 on 2:25 (R. Josua b. Qorcha, Tannaite).

[130] Bousset-Gressm., 408 f.

[131] bShab., 145b-146a par.; Weber, 219.

[132] Prot. Ev. Jc., 13; Hipp. Ref., V, 26, 22 f.; Epiph. Haer., 40, 5, 3, though it is doubtful whether the same thought has also influenced Just. Dial., 100, 4 f., since it is simply said here that Eve "received" the word of the serpent as did Mary that of the angel. Wnd. 2 K., 323 f.

[133] Nu. r., 10 on 6:3, Str.-B., III, 250 M, also n. 2.

[134] S. Dt. § 323 on 32:32 f.; Str.-B., I, 115.

[135] Ab. R. Nat., 1 M, cf. Gn. r., 19 on 3:2, Str.-B., I, 694 f.

[136] S. Dt. § 323 on 32:32 f.

[137] Str.-B., II, 425 f.

[138] Par. M. Ex. on 17:11 (62a), Str.-B., III, 192; II, 426 M.

Dt. 32:10, [139] demons and dragons howl in the desert; BQ, 16a, [140] the hyena, by way of various animals, last among them the snake, becomes a שֵׁד;; bQid, 29b, a dragon with seven heads (תַּנִּינָא) is the form in which an evil spirit (מַזִּיק) is manifested, one of the heads falling off every time the rabbi bends in prayer. [141] But these are only occasional statements and legends. In view of the prodigal use of the serpent in the pagan world it is natural that the Rabb. should have an esp. strong aversion for the figure of the snake. [142]

D. The Serpent in the NT.

1. The Serpent in Similitudes.

In the NT the serpent is in the first instance the dangerous and malevolent animal which one avoids and puts away: ὄφεις, γεννήματα ἐχιδνῶν, πῶς φύγητε ἀπὸ τῆς κρίσεως τῆς γεέννης; Mt. 22:33, → II, 815, 34 ff. In the non-authentic Marcan ending (16:17, 18) the signs which follow believers are the expulsion of devils, speaking with tongues, taking up serpents, drinking poison and healing the sick. The context rules out an understanding of the third and fourth members in v. 18 as forms of persecution. Exorcising demons and speaking with tongues are signs of God's inaugurated dominion. Hence there may be seen in the lives of believers something of the new creation which is intimated in Is. 11:8 and in which the deadly conflict of nature is ended. Related is Lk. 10:19. [143] To tread on snakes and scorpions without hurt was possible in the ark according to the Rabbis. [144] It is told of R. Chanina b. Dosa that a snake bit him while he was asleep, but he was not disturbed and did not suffer any harm, and his pupils found the snake dead in front of its hole. [145] But these are isolated statements. Jesus in His saying possibly has Ps. 91:13 in view. [146] According to the context the power to tread on serpents and scorpions is connected with the fall of Satan. But this does not mean that the animals are "half-demonic." [147] In the special Lucan material to which 10:19 belongs sickness is attributed to Satan (13:16). In other words, everything harmful in nature is connected with him. But even linguistically (cf. the use of ἐξουσία) this indirect destructive work of the enemy is differentiated from the direct operation of his δύναμις. That which menaces natural life and that which seeks to destroy personal life (→ II, 18, 45 ff.) are here viewed together as belonging to the kingdom of him who is a murderer from the very beginning.

In the parable on the answering of prayer we have in Mt. 7:10 and Lk. 11:11 two different versions which both contain the fish/serpent saying. [148] The version in Mt. is distinctive inasmuch as there is between the two members, for all the basic similarity, an unmistakable difference. A stone is useless, a serpent harmful.

---

[139] Str.-B., IV, 516.
[140] Ibid., 507.
[141] Ibid., 535.
[142] A. Schlatter, "Das AT in d. joh. Apk.," BFTh, 16 (1912), 68 (600), n. 1. On the command in AZ, 3, 3 not to bring an image of the dragon into the Dead Sea cf. H. Blaufuss, "Götter, Bilder u. Symbole nach den Traktaten über den fremden Dienst," Beilage zum Jahresberichte d. Königlichen Neuen Gymnasiums im Nürnberg f. das Schuljahr 1909/10 (1910), 40 ff.; also "Aboda zara," ibid. 1915/16 (1916), 67.
[143] Hck. Lk. and K. H. Rengstorf Lk. (NT Deutsch), ad loc.
[144] Midr. Ps. 91 § 8, Str.-B., II, 168 f.
[145] bBer., 33a (Tannaitic); T. Ber., 3, 20, Str.-B., I, 399 f.
[146] Zn. Lk. and Rengstorf Lk., ad loc. But this suggestion is by no means certain, since there is no mention of scorpions in the verse in the Ps.
[147] Kl. Lk., ad loc.
[148] At Lk. 11:11 א D Θ pm offer a certain assimilation to Mt., so that we have a kind of three-membered saying. The very form, however, shows that this is secondary.

Hence the second saying is sharper than the first. But there is no such difference in Lk. In fact, the second member is weaker, since the scorpion is less dangerous. Now in the double comparisons of Jesus it is common for the second member to have a slightly different nuance. This favours the view that Mt. offers the more original version. This conclusion is supported by the consideration that bread and fish were the staple diet of the simple people who lived by Lake Gennesaret, Mk. 6:38. The serpent, then, is the harmful animal which in appearance is not unlike a fish but which has very different effects. The point of the saying is not simply to summon to faith that prayer will be answered but to give the assurance that what is given in answer to prayer will really be good. In the life of faith it is not very clear how one can even remotely confuse bread and a stone or a fish and a serpent.

Concerning Mt. 10:16: γίνεσθε οὖν φρόνιμοι ὡς οἱ ὄφεις καὶ ἀκέραιοι ὡς αἱ περιστεραί, we may refer not merely to the Rabb. pars. adduced → 576, 35 f. but also to the modern proverbial saying in Palestine, "as cunning (or sly) as a serpent." [149] It is possible, though not certain, that the Rabbinic and Palestinian Mohammedan idea of the cleverness of the serpent goes back to Gn. 3. א* and Or (but only these) read ὡς ὁ ὄφις at Mt. 10:16. This would contain a reference to the serpent of Paradise, and the saying would thus be the more pointed. The fact that Gn. 3:1 also uses the adjective φρόνιμος lends support to the reading, but against it is the harsh alternation of the sing. ὄφις and plur. περιστεραί which is thereby caused. Ign. Pol., 2, 2 (φρόνιμος γίνου ὡς ὄφις ... καὶ ἀκέραιος ... ὡς ἡ περιστερά) also argues against a reference to the fall. The memorable and yet also the difficult feature in the admonition is the combination of the serpent's cunning with the dove's innocence. [150] The holding up of the unjust steward as an example offers a certain parallel.

In Rev. 9:19 it is said of the "horses" of the "Parthian" cavalry: ἡ γὰρ ἐξουσία τῶν ἵππων ... ἐστὶν καὶ ἐν ταῖς οὐραῖς αὐτῶν· αἱ γὰρ οὐραὶ αὐτῶν ὅμοιαι ὄφεσιν, ἔχουσαι κεφαλάς, καὶ ἐν αὐταῖς ἀδικοῦσιν. The sixth trumpet, which comes immediately before the end, introduces an even worse horror than the fifth. [151] If the fifth with the locusts brings demonic powers from the abyss to torment those who are without faith, the sixth brings hellish powers to destroy them. Hell is indicated by the fire, smoke and brimstone of vv. 17, 18, destruction by the serpents, who are the manes of the horses as compared with the scorpion-tails of the locusts. Whereas the sting of the scorpion is not fatal, that of a poisonous snake is. The scorpion and the serpent are related in their malevolent hostility, but differ in the degree of their effect. In their similarity and distinction they are thus an important element in the two plagues.

2. The Serpent of Paradise.

Rev. 12:9 and 20:2 use the Rabb. expression "the old serpent," → 578, 16 f. In the context they make the equation of the serpent of Paradise with Satan, which is rare in the Rabb. and occurs only after the NT period, → 577, 19 ff. The related terms → δράκων and ὄφις (12:14 f.) are used in Rev. with no obvious distinction. Paul also refers to the serpent of Paradise in 2 C. 11:3: φοβοῦμαι δὲ μή πῶς, ὡς ὁ ὄφις ἐξηπάτησεν Εὔαν ἐν τῇ πανουργίᾳ αὐτοῦ, φθαρῇ τὰ νοήματα ὑμῶν

---

[149] Canaan, op. cit., 14.

[150] To construe φρόνιμοι as "shy" (L. Köhler, Kleine Lichter [1945], 76 ff.) is linguistically unnatural and takes the sting out of the saying.

[151] Loh. Apk. on 9:17.

ἀπὸ τῆς ἁπλότητος τῆς εἰς Χριστόν. The image of the community as the bride of Christ controls v. 2, and is also echoed in the second part of v. 3. Hence it is a justifiable question whether Paul in alluding to the fall has in view the later Jewish idea of the sexual temptation of Eve, → 578, 8-12.

This exegesis cannot look to 1 Tm. 2:14 f. for support. For there Paul is alluding to Eve's receptivity to cunning arguments — the ἐξαπατηθεῖσα precedes the ἐν παραβάσει γέγονεν — which makes the woman unfit for teaching. She is thus referred to her natural sphere. By fulfilling her duties as a mother she will be saved if she abides in the faith, not by entering alien spheres such as that of teaching in congregational gatherings. In 2 C. 11:3 the choice of the not unexpected φθαρῇ might be explained by reading → φθείρειν as "to seduce." But νοήματα are the subj. of φθαρῇ. It would seem, then, that in the first clause Paul is not alluding to the idea of the sexual temptation of Eve. The addition ἐν τῇ πανουργίᾳ αὐτοῦ remains within the sphere of the biblical account.

Paul is thus saying that Eve listened to the subtle arguments of the serpent instead of rendering simple obedience. He is warning the community against a similar course.

Since Paul is alluding to Gn. 3:15 in R. 16:20 : ὁ δὲ θεὸς τῆς εἰρήνης συντρίψει τὸν σατανᾶν ὑπὸ τοὺς πόδας ὑμῶν ἐν τάχει, [152] he, too, equates the serpent of Paradise with Satan.

3. The Brazen Serpent.

Paul alludes to the introduction to the story of the brazen serpent in 1 C. 10:9. Perhaps he has in view the account and interpretation given in ψ 77:18. The story itself is used by Jesus in Jn. 3:14 f. to bring out the saving significance of His exaltation, → ὑψόω. As looking up to the serpent healed, so nothing but a saving look at Christ can save. [153] The reference to Christ distinguishes the use of the passage from that found in the Rabb., → 578, 25-32.

The NT, even in Rev. 12, [154] remains aloof from pagan myths. The serpent. which plays an ambivalent role in pagan religions, is in Rev. a symbol of the final force that presents a cunning threat to life. Nor does this dangerous power of the abyss have any divine splendour. Faith in Christ forbids worship of the serpent.

E. Gnosticism.

In Gnosticism the serpent plays a manifold and varied part, chiefly as a symbol of evil.

In the Act. Phil. there is ref. to the worship of ἔχιδνα in Asia Minor, [155] but there the δράκων is also a form in which Satan appears : ὁ ὄφις ὁ πονηρὸς δράκων ὁ ἀρχέκακος, and φεύγετε ἀπὸ τοῦ δράκοντος τοῦ Σατανᾶ. [156] In another passage [157] all κοσμοκράτορες and the πονηρὸς δράκων ὁ ἀντικείμενος ἡμῖν are mentioned together. In the third πρᾶξις of the Act. Thom. the δράκων is the tempter of Eve, Cain, Pharaoh, Herod and Caiaphas, related to the δράκων outside the ocean, whose tail is in its mouth ; it is also the demiurge. [158] There, too, Ὄφις is one of the devil's names. [159] In the Pearl Song, as in the related prayer of Kyriacos, [160] the δράκων is

---

[152] Zn. R. and Schl. R., ad loc.
[153] Goppelt, op. cit., 220.
[154] W. Foerster, "Die Bilder in Apk. 12 f. und 17 f.," ThStKr, 104 (1932), 280-288.
[155] Hartmann, 510.
[156] 111 (p. 43, 13 and 25 f. L/B).
[157] 144 (p. 86, 8).
[158] C. 32. Cf. on this G. Bornkamm, Mythos u. Legende (1933), 28-33.
[159] 52 (p. 168, 12).
[160] Reitzenstein Ir. Erl., 78.

matter, which drags man down. This animal is also connected with evil elsewhere in this lit., [161] in the Mandaean writings, [162] and in Od. Sol. 22:5 (the dragon with seven heads).

In the Gnostic sects the snake plays a varied role, partly as the embodiment of the evil principle, matter, partly as a symbol of the good. In Iren. Epid., I, 30, 5 νοῦς, wounded in the form of the serpent, is the leader of the evil principle, *ibid.*, I, 30, 7. Acc. to some Gnostics even Sophia itself is supposed to have become a serpent and as such to have opposed the demiurge in Paradise, I, 30, 15. This duality occurs elsewhere in Gnosticism. Thus in I, 30, 9 it is Michael and Sammael, → II, 79, 6 f., while among the Naassenes it is the chief principle, the mediator between the upper and lower world, and again in the Gnosis of Baruch Νάας is the adversary of Baruch. [163]

Foerster

| ὄχλος |

A. The Non-Biblical Usage.

ὄχλος [1] is found in Gk. lit. from the time of Pindar in the following senses.

1. "Crowd." a. In the first instance ὄχλος denotes a crowd of men milling around or closely pressed together, Pind. Pyth., IV, 85 : ἐν ἀγορᾷ πλήθοντος ὄχλου, cf. Soph. Trach., 423 f.; Aristoph. Eccl., 383. Philo uses it allegorically for "throng," "tumult," in Leg. All., II, 85 : τὸν ψυχικὸν ὄχλον σκεδάσαντος θεοῦ, "as God disperses the tumult of the soul." On the colourful composition of the ὄχλος cf. Aesch. Pers., 53 : πάμμεικτος ὄχλος. Athen., VII, 2 (p. 276c): παμμιγὴς ὄχλος. Xenophon Hist. Graec., II, 2, 21 refers to the mob streaming together : εἰσιόντας δ᾽ αὐτοὺς ὄχλος περιεχεῖτο πολύς, cf. I, 7, 13, also Plat. Phaedr. 229d, where an ὄχλος Γοργόνων καὶ Πηγάσων is mentioned. Polyb., IV, 7, 6 calls the gathering of many men a συναγωγὴ τῶν ὄχλων, cf. συναγωγαὶ ὄχλων, Ditt. Or., 383, 150 f. (1st cent. B.C.); συνελθόντων τῶν ὄχλων ἐν ἐκκλησίᾳ, Ditt. Syll.³, 814, 5 (67 A.D.). b. The ὄχλος is also the "public" as distinct from the private person or the small closed circle, Aristot. Pol., III, 15, p. 1286a, 31: κρίνει ἄμεινον ὄχλος πολλὰ ἢ εἷς ὁστισοῦν. Speaking in a small circle is differentiated from public appearance, Eur. Hipp., 986; in Xenoph. Mem., III, 7, 5 private talks,

---

[161] In Act. Joh., 94 (p. 197, 11 f.) the ἄνομος ὄφις is the instigator of the Jewish legislation.
[162] Cf. Lidz. Ginz., Index.
[163] On the symbol of the snake among the Ophites cf. H. Leisegang, *Die Gnosis* (1924), 111 ff., 167-180; Nilsson, II, 594 f.

ὄ χ λ ο ς. Liddell-Scott, Moult.-Mill., Pape, Pass., Pr.-Bauer³, Thes. Steph., *s.v.* On C. : S. Krauss, *Griech. u. lat. Lehnwörter*, II (1899), 18 f. On D. : P. Joüon, "ὄχλος au sens de 'peuple, population' dans le grec du NT et dans la lettre d'Aristée," *Recherches des Sciences Religieuses*, 27 (1937), 618 f.; J. Abrahams, 'Am ha-'Areç," in C. G. Montefiore, *The Synoptic Gospels*, II (1927), 647-669; Bousset-Gressm., 165, 187 f., 391; A. Büchler, *Der galiläische 'Am ha-Areṣ des 2. Jhdts.* (1906); S. Bialoblotzky, Art. "Am ha-Arez," EJ, II, 535-541; L. Finkelstein, *The Pharisees* (1938), *passim* ; A. Geiger, *Urschrift u. Übersetzungen d. Bibel²* (1928), 151; S. Hamburger, *Realencyclopädie f. Bibel u. Talmud*, II (1896), 54-56; J. A. Selbie, Art. "People," Hastings DB, III (1900), 742 f.; D. Eaton, "Pharisees," *ibid.*, 826 f.; K. Kohler, Jew. Enc., I, 484 f.; R. Meyer, "Der 'Am hā-'Āreṣ," Judaica, 3 (1947), 169-199; C. G. Montefiore, Hibbert Lectures (1892), 497-502; Moore, I, 60, 321; II, 72 f., 157-161; Schürer⁴, II, 454, 468-475 (with older bibl.); Str.-B., II, 494-519; E. Würthwein, "Der 'am ha-arez im AT," BWANT, 4 F., 17 H. (1936); 1, n. 1 bibl.

[1] Etym. most uncertain, *v.* Walde-Pok., I, 41, 147. Connection with ὀχλίζω ("laboriously move away," Hom.) and ὀχλέω ("roll along," Hom.) is probable, but obscure. ὀχλέω ("burden" class.) and ἐνοχλέω (from Aristot., also inscr., pap., LXX; Lk. 6:18; Hb. 12:15) are related. The basic meaning seems to be "press," "disorderly heap" [Debrunner].

ἴδιαι ὁμιλίαι, are contrasted with the public assembly. It is not decorous for girls to show themselves in public, ὄχλος, Eur. Or., 108; cf. Eur. Heracl., 43 f. There is ref. to a successful appearance before the ὄχλος, the great public, in Plat. Gorg., 458e, cf. 502c : πολὺς ὄχλος καὶ δῆμος, "wide public," Xenoph. Sym., 2, 18, ἐν ὄχλῳ, "before all the people." ἐν ὄχλῳ seems to have the same meaning in an Egyptian letter, P. Petr., II, 4, 6, 16 : δεινὸν γάρ ἐστιν ἐν ὄχλωι ἀτιμάζεσθαι (255/54 B.C.), and in a magic text requesting success in a race we read in P. Oxy., XII, 1478, 4 : δὸς νείκην ὁλοκληρίαν σ[τ]αδίου καὶ ὄχλου (3rd/4th cent. A.D.). c. With the broad public is contrasted the single aristocrat or the leading political or intellectual group. The ὄχλος denotes the anonymous mass as distinct from men of rank or officials, e.g., in a Ptolemaic war communiqué : ἄλλος ὄχ[λος ἐστεφ]ανωμένος (264 B.C.).[2] A judicial record speaks of the delivering up of a Phikion to the crowd by the governor Septimius Vegetus : ἄξιος μ[ὲ]ν ἧς μαστιγωθῆναι ... χαρίζομαι δέ σε τοῖς ὄχλοις (85 A.D.).[3] ὄχλος is often the "leaderless and rudderless mob," the "politically and culturally insignificant mass," cf. Plat. Leg., II, 670b, where the people is said to have no power of judgment : γελοῖος γὰρ ὅ γε πολὺς ὄχλος ἡγούμενος ἱκανῶς γιγνώσκειν τό τ᾽ εὐάρμοστον καὶ εὔρυθμον καὶ μή, Philo Praem. Poen., 20 with moral disparagement : ὅ τι γὰρ ἄτακτον, ἄκοσμον, πλημμελές, ὑπαίτιον, τοῦτο ὄχλος ἐστί.[4] Acc. to Vit. Mos., I, 197 the masses are fickle ; Jos., 58 ff. describes how the public, which buys over the statesman, ὠνούμενος τὸν πολιτικὸν ὄχλος, is in truth politically powerless, εὐνοῦχος; it follows its desire as a man runs after a woman : μνᾶται γὰρ ὄχλος ἐπιθυμίαν ὥσπερ ἀνὴρ γυναῖκα, ibid., 60. For its part the despised ὄχλος is indifferent to or even envious of the skill of the ruling clique, Herodian Hist., VII, 3, 5.

2. "Host," "troop," "army." Militarily ὄχλος is used a. for the lightly armed host, Thuc., IV, 56, 1: ὄχλος τῶν ψιλῶν, cf. VII, 84, 2 : ἄλλος ὄχλος alongside the cavalry. The ὄχλος is also b. the baggage-train, Thuc., VI, 64, 1; VII, 78, 2; Xenoph. Cyrop., IV, 2, 6. It also means c. the host of common soldiers, ὄχλος τῶν στρατιωτῶν, Xenoph. Cyrop., VI, 1, 26. With μισθοφόρος it means d. mercenaries, Thuc., III, 109, 2. For ὄχλος in the sense of "troops" cf. Ditt. Syll.[3], 700, 22 ff.: συνεπελθόντος ... Τίπα τοῦ τῶν Μαίδων δυνάστου μετ᾽ ὄχλ[ου π]λείονος (117 B.C.), also 709, 8 f.: Παλάκου δὲ τοῦ Σκυθᾶν βασιλέος αἰφνιδίως ἐπιβαλόντος μετὰ ὄχλου πολλοῦ (Chersones. c. 107 B.C.).[5] e. ὄχλος can also be an irregular armed mass, Thuc., IV, 126, 6 : οἱ τοιοῦτοι ὄχλοι, Herodian Hist., VI, 7, 1: ὄχλος μᾶλλον ἢ στρατός.

3. "People," "population." For "people" we find the plur. ὄχλοι, e.g., Ditt. Syll.[3], 700, 26 (→ supra): προελόμενος δὲ μένειν τοὺς ὄχλους ἐπὶ τῶν ἔργων, "since he preferred that the people should remain at work." An Egyptian in a letter refers to the ὄχλοι ("population") of Hermonthis :[6] πρὸς τὸ καταστεῖσαι[7] τοὺς ἐν Ἑρμώνθαι ὄχλους (131/130 B.C.). Cf. also an Egyptian deed of purchase : λιβὸς γῆ τῶν ὄχλων ἢ οἵ ἂν ὦσι γείτ[ονες], P. Lond., III, 1208, 12 (97 B.C.).[8]

4. A measure; ὄχλος means a great number, e.g., Eur. Iph. Aulis, 191: ἵππων ὄχλος,[9] also a Critias fragment : ἄκριτος ἄστρων ὄχλος.[10] Plat. Tim., 75e : ὁ τῶν σαρκῶν

---

[2] Mitteis-Wilcken, I, 2, 1, Col. III, 22 f.
[3] P. Flor., I, 61, 61; Deissmann LO, 229.
[4] Cf. also ῥυπαρώτατος ὄχλος, "filthiest rabble," Dion. Hal. Ant. Rom., IX, 44.
[5] Cf. also Preisigke Sammelbuch, 6949, 18 ff., where in the account of a victory from Aksum six minor kings with their troops, σὺν τῷ ὄχλῳ αὐτῶν, are mentioned (4th cent. A.D.).
[6] Mitteis-Wilcken, I, 2, 10, 8 ff.
[7] An error for καταστεῖλαι, "to put down," Mitteis-Wilcken, loc. cit. n. 10.
[8] Preisigke Wört., II, s.v. cautiously proposes "community field" for the not very clear γῆ τῶν ὄχλων; perhaps it means the land belonging to the people as distinct from γῆ βασιλική, that belonging to the king [Kleinknecht]. On problems of landed property in Egypt from the time of the Ptolemies cf. C. H. Becker, Islamstudien, I (1924), 220 f.
[9] Here the sense of "throng" is often in the background, e.g., ὄχλος τῶν νεῶν, "throng of ships," Thuc., I, 49, 3; VII, 62, 1.
[10] Fr., 19, 4 f. (Diels[5], II, 385, 2 f.).

ὄχλος, is taken up in Philo Rer. Div. Her., 56 : εὖ γε τὸ προσνεῖμαι τῷ σαρκῶν ὄχλῳ τὴν αἵματος ἐπιρροήν. Ref. might also be made to Isoc. Panathenaicus, 273b: ὄχλος πραχθέντων, Luc. Nec., 4, 461: ὄχλος ὀνομάτων, and Philo's περιττὸς ὄχλος for the great number of scribes, Flacc., 3. Philo often uses ὄχλος for the swarm of lower sense stimulations ; thus in Spec. Leg., IV, 188 the human νοῦς is tied to the host of sensual perceptions : ἐνδεδεμένος αἰσθήσεων ὄχλῳ τοσούτῳ. Ref. is made in Det. Pot. Ins., 71 to the vain multitude (μάταιος ὄχλος) of contradictory opinions.

5. "Unsettlement," "harassment." For this cf. Eur. Ion, 635. Philo says of διάνοια (→ IV, 964, 11 ff.): διὰ τὸ πλῆθος τῶν περὶ αὐτὴν ὄχλων καὶ θορύβων ἀνηκέστατα κακὰ τίκτει, Mut. Nom., 144. The combination ὄχλον παρέχειν is found e.g., in Eur. Or., 282; Hdt., I, 86, 5; Xenoph. An., III, 2, 27. On δι' ὄχλου εἶναι (γίγνεσθαι) "to inconvenience," cf. Thuc., I, 73, 2; Aristoph. Eccl., 888; Ps.-Plat. Alc., I, 103a; Joseph. Bell., 4, 496.

Meyer

B. The OT Usage.

ὄχλος is almost completely absent from older parts of the LXX. [11] There are three or more instances only in 1 and 2 Εσδρ., 1 and 2 Macc., Wis., Jer., Ez., Da. LXX and Θ. It is used for הָמוֹן, חַיִל, טַף, עַם, קָהָל, רַבִּים, מַאֲסֵף, קְהִלָּה. Where there is no textual corruption [12] and the sense intended by the translators can be decided [13] the following senses occur. [14]

---

[11] Only once in the Pentateuch (Nu. 20:20). In Jos. 6:13 the first occurrence is secondary and the second should read καὶ ὁ λοιπὸς ὄχλος ἅπαξ, for ἅπαξ with the doublet in bx S ; Is. 43:17; not in Ju., S., K. (originally), or Ps.

[12] Critical reconstruction of the text eliminates ὄχλος at Ιερ. 31(48):42 : ἀπὸ λαοῦ for מֵעָם, not ἀπὸ ὄχλου, cf. also 45(38):1 in א* † where ὄχλον is a scribal error for λαόν. In 2 Εσδρ. 14:4 Rahlfs correctly has καὶ ὁ χοῦς πολύς for וְהֶעָפָר הַרְבֵּה (Neh. 4:4); ὄχλος is a false reading of BאV (Bא*Vk correct). In the same v. τῶν ἐχθρῶν is also corrupt. Perhaps τῶν <νωτ>οφόρων is to be read with 2 Ch. 2:17; 34:13. F. Wutz, "Die Transkriptionen d. Septuaginta bis zu Hieronymus," BWAT, NF, 9 (1925/33), 34 and W. Rudolph (BHK³) on Ιερ. 39(32):24 propose ὁ χοῦς rather than ὄχλος for הַסֹּלְלוֹת ("ramparts," 'A προσχώματα). Finally, in 2 Macc. 13:15, ὄχλῳ, which is only in the Sixtina, should be ὄντι (materially v. A. Kamphausen in Kautzsch Apkr. u. Pseudepigr., ad loc.). In 2 Macc. 6:3 Rahlfs with most MSS reads τοῖς ὅλοις, "completely."

[13] Whereas earlier translators sought to follow the original, though occasionally with intentional modifications in a way reminiscent of the Targumim, so that they selected the most varied Gk. terms for the one Heb. word, there is in the later translators a tendency to keep to one Gk. word in order to allow of conclusions from the letter of the normative Heb. text quite irrespective of the sense or nonsense which resulted. Even the modifications mentioned above were now superfluous since responsibility was placed on expositors of the original text. This development culminates in Aquila who offers only one term for homonymous roots in the original (examples in P. Katz, *Philo's Bible* [1950], esp. 64 f., 148 f.). Hence in Aquila one can at most be sure only of the starting-point of his selection. Since he keeps to the choice without regard to the context, there is no point in asking what is the meaning in individual instances. For he is no longer translating. He is simply giving initiates, i.e., participants in Jewish worship who know Hebrew, an intelligible ref. to the original. It is enough to say, then, that in Aquila ὄχλος is used for הָמוֹן. By this one can test the readings in the Hexapla. If, e.g., codd 86 and 88 have καὶ τὸν ὄχλον for 'ΑΣ at Ιερ. 48(41):16, this is incorrect for 'A, since the Heb. is וְטַף. This 'A text, however, often made its way into LXX MSS, e.g., 3 Βασ. 21(20):13 (F. C. Burkitt, *Fragments of the Books of Kings according to the Translation of Aquila* [1897], 26 f.). Here πάντα τὸν ὄχλον (= הָמוֹן) is the 'A reading, while the original is τὸν ἦχον, now found for the most part only in the Lucianic group.

[14] Here and in the section on the Apocr. the enumeration is the same as in A. This makes it plain what senses do not occur in the Gk. Bible. Da. Θ is adduced for the sake of comparison with Da. LXX.

1. ὄχλος in the Canonical Books. a. "Crowd of people." Da. 3:4 LXX : ἐκήρυξε τοῖς ὄχλοις for קְרָא בְחָיִל ("cried aloud"), חַיִל being taken in the sense of "host" rather than "strength." [15] "Noisy crowd," Da. 10:6 Θ : ὡς φωνὴ ὄχλου (= קְקוֹל הָמוֹן, LXX ὡσεὶ φωνὴ θορύβου). "Popular assembly," "great public," Ιερ. 38(31):8 in a promise : τεκνοποιήσῃ ὄχλον πολύν(קָהָל גָּדוֹל). Less felicitously ὄχλοι (16:40; 23:47) and ὄχλος (23:46) are used for קָהָל in two related passages in Ez. The solemn קָהָל of the people, which acc. to Lv. 24:16 (συναγωγή) has the duty of stoning adulteresses, thus becomes a tumultuous mob. Sir. 7:7: μὴ καταβάλῃς σεαυτὸν ἐν ὄχλῳ (בְקָהְלָה), "do not lower yourself to the common public." "Masses," 2 Εσδρ. 3:12, of the great crowd at the dedication of the temple (רַבִּים, 1 Εσδρ. 5:61 πολλοί). b. "Camp-followers," for טַף = children, wives and children, families, those incapable of marching, [16] 2 Βασ. 15:22. For מְאַסֵּף, "rearguard" : ὁ λοιπὸς ὄχλος, Jos. 6:13. "Mercenaries," "troops" : Nu. 20:20 : ἐν ὄχλῳ βαρεῖ בְּעַם כָּבֵד; [17] Is. 43:17: ὄχλον ἰσχυρόν (חַיִל וְעִזּוּז, host and heroes); Ez. 17:17: (καὶ οὐκ ἐν δυνάμει μεγάλῃ) οὐδ' ἐν ὄχλῳ πολλῷ, "levy," "men" (וְלֹא בְחַיִל גָּדוֹל וּבְקָהָל רָב). In Da., where in 11:10-13:25 הָמוֹן and חַיִל singly or together (11:10) mean "army," the two transl. keep to the same divergent renderings ; הָמוֹן is συναγωγή in LXX, ὄχλος in Θ, while חַיִל is ὄχλος in LXX and δύναμις in Θ. [18] "Irregular armed mob" : here at the earliest we may include 2 Εσδρ. 16:12 f., where for "they had bribed him (the false prophet)" (Neh. 6:12) the LXX wrongly expands ἐμισθώσαντο ἐπ' ἐμὲ ὄχλον. c. As a measure ὄχλος can be used along with another noun, e.g., Ez. 23:24 : μετ' ὄχλου λαῶν = בְּקָהָל עַמִּים, "with a host of peoples," also Da. Θ 11:10 : ὄχλον δυνάμεων πολλῶν = הָמוֹן חֲיָלִים (LXX συναγωγὴν ὄχλου πολλοῦ).

2. ὄχλος in the Apocrypha. a. Crowd of people, 1 Εσδρ. 5:62; 8:88; Ep. Jer. 5; Sus. 48 LXX; Bel. 31 f. LXX; 2 Macc. 4:40; 11:6; 3 Macc. 1:28. "Public," Wis. 8:10; Sir. 26:5 : ἐκκλησία ὄχλου, "the banding together of the great masses." b. "Army," "troop," 1 Macc. 1:17, 20, 29; 2 Macc. 14:23, 43, 45 f.; 3 Macc. 2:7. "Camp-followers," Jdt. 7:18; 1 Macc. 9:35. c. "Population" of the land : ὄχλος τῆς χώρας, Bel. 30 LXX, as distinct from the Jews, cf. v. 28 : οἱ ἀπὸ τῆς χώρας. d. Measure : ἐπὶ ὄχλοις ἐθνῶν, Wis. 6:2 (par. πλῆθος).

Katz

C. ὄχλος as a Loan Word in Rabbinic Literature.

In the Rabb. ὄχλος is used as a loan word in both Heb. and Aram. forms. 1. For the crowd of people, T. Ber., VII, 2 : "He who sees a (Jewish) crowd of people אוכלוסין = ὄχλοι, let him say : Blessed be the wise one of mysteries, for their faces are not alike and their knowledge is not alike." R. Hamnuna in bBer., 58a contrasts the Jewish crowd

---

[15] At Da. 5:7 the LXX correctly has ἐφώνησε φωνῇ μεγάλῃ, at 4:11 simply ἐφώνησε. Da. Θ 3:4; 4:11; 5:7 ἐν ἰσχύι. The same confusion as in Da. LXX 3:4, with restriction to Aram. texts, occurs in Ezr. 4:23. For בְּאֶדְרַע וְחָיִל, "with arm and might," 1 Εσδρ. 2:25 already has μεθ' ἵππου καὶ ὄχλου παρατάξεως (doublet ?), cf. 2 Εσδρ. 4:23 : ἐν ἵπποις καὶ δυνάμει.

[16] Cf. L. Köhler, "Tapp = Nicht oder wenig Marschfähige," *Theol. Zschr.*, 6 (1950), 387 f. In Gn., Ex., Nu. טַף is rendered ἀποσκευή. This does not seem to be used elsewhere for groups of family members. Σ and Θ have ὄχλος for טַף, also anon. at Dt. 1:39. ὄχλος for παιδία at 2 Ch. 20:13 is from Lucian, who later, at the wrong place, adds καὶ (οἱ) υἱοὶ αὐτῶν.

[17] There can be no objection to ὄχλος in this fixed expression, as compared with the instances in Ιερ. mentioned in → n. 12.

[18] ἐν τῷ ὄχλῳ αὐτοῦ in Da. 11:43 LXX is a mistransl. of בְּמִצְעָדָיו, "in his train." In Θ ἐν τοῖς ὀχυρώμασιν αὐτῶν perhaps comes from 11:39 (= מִבְצָרִים, which Θ misreads as מִצְרַיִם Αἴγυπτον in 11:24).

אוכלוסי ישראל with the Gentile crowd אוכלוסי אומות העולם. That here, too, there is a sense of "press" may be seen from the saying of R. Eleazar bPedath (c. 270): "Where there is a crowd, אוכלוסין, there is a press," Pesikt., 108a. 2. For "army," "troop," "levy," "train" אוכלוסים = ὄχλοι occurs with חֲיָלוֹת in Gn. r., 39 on 12:1; cf. אוכלוסין = "host," ibid., 44 on 15:1. Pesikt., 186a has troops in mind, esp. those of Pharaoh (אוכלוסין של פרעה), while the Gk. army (האוכלוסין של יון) is mentioned in Ex. r., 15 on 12:1. The leader of the host is ריש אוכלוסי in Tg. on 1 Ch. 11:6, and Tg. on 1 Ch. 19:8 has אוכלוסי גבריא for צְבָא הַגִּבּוֹרִים, "army of professional soldiers." The loan word can also mean "men" e.g., S. Dt., 25 on 1:28; cf. also bBM, 108a, which refers to the troop (אוכלוסא) of compulsory workers. Finally, in a similitude of R. Acha the stars are called the "train" = אוכלוסא of the moon, Gn. r., 6 on 1:16. 3. ὄχλος is a measure in, e.g., jSanh., 29b, 8 : אוכלוסיא דתלמדיא "great hosts of pupils," cf. also the hyperbolical measure in bBer., 58a, where the אוכלוסא comprises no less than sixty myriads.

D. The NT Usage.

I. The Meanings. [19]

1. Crowd of People. a. ὄχλος (ὄχλοι), except for Rev. 7:9; 19:1, 6, occurs only in the Gospels and Acts. In the Gospels it denotes for the most part the anonymous background to Jesus' ministry. It runs together to see or hear Jesus, Mt. 13:2; Mk. 3:20; 9:25; Lk. 5:1; Jn. 11:42. It receives Jesus, or goes to Him, or seeks Him, Lk. 8:40; Jn. 12:9. It accompanies the Master, Mk. 5:27; Lk. 7:9; Mt. 21:9; Jn. 12:17. Various reasons are found for this by the Synoptists. Jesus calls the crowd to Himself to instruct it, Mk. 7:14; 8:34; Mt. 15:10. In many cases the motive is that of our Lord's pity for the ὄχλος, cf. esp. Mk. 6:34 : εἶδεν πολὺν ὄχλον καὶ ἐσπλαγχνίσθη ἐπ' αὐτοὺς ὅτι ἦσαν ὡς πρόβατα μὴ ἔχοντα ποιμένα. The crowd wants to see miraculous healings by Jesus, Lk. 6:19. It throngs and harasses Him so that He has a ship kept ready, Mk. 3:9, cf. Mk. 5:30 f.: βλέπεις τὸν ὄχλον συνθλίβοντά σε, καὶ λέγεις· τίς μου ἥψατο τῶν ἱματίων; [20] It thus seems that those who merely seek marvels or are simply curious are held at a distance. In this way tension is increased and the faith of true seekers underlined, cf. the role of the ὄχλος in the story of the sick of the palsy in Mk. 2:4 f., also Mt. 20:31 and Lk. 19:3 f. On the other hand, the ὄχλος is closer to the Master than His physical relatives, Mk. 3:31-35 and par. As the chorus which confirms Jesus' words and acts by joy, admiration, astonishment and fear, the crowd has an essential role in the Synoptists, [21] as at the end of the story of the man sick of the palsy in Mt. 9:8 : ἰδόντες δὲ οἱ ὄχλοι ἐφοβήθησαν καὶ ἐδόξασαν τὸν θεόν, or at the end of the Sermon on the Mount in Mt. 7:28 : ἐξεπλήσσοντο οἱ ὄχλοι ἐπὶ τῇ διδαχῇ αὐτοῦ.

b. After completing His acts or addresses Jesus withdraws from the public. Thus in Mt. 13:36, after the parable of the tares among the wheat, He leaves the people (ὄχλοι) and goes into the house (εἰς τὴν οἰκίαν) to give further instruction to the disciples. In Mt. 14:22 f. His withdrawal from the ὄχλοι (ὄχλος Mk.

---

[19] We do not find the sense of "unsettlement," "harassment" (→ 584, 8 ff.); only ὀχλέω pass., "to be tormented by evil spirits," Ac. 5:16 (cf. Tob. 6:8 : ἐάν τινα ὀχλῇ δαιμόνιον ἢ πνεῦμα πονηρόν), is found along with ἐνοχλέω, which is used like the simple form in Lk. 6:18, while in Hb. 12:15 it is abs. "to cause trouble" (quoting Dt. 29:17 LXX BA); cf. on this → n. 1. Acc. to P. Katz, ThLZ, 75 (1951), 537 ἐνοχλῇ is an error for ἐν χολῇ.
[20] Cf. Lk. 8:45 : οἱ ὄχλοι συνέχουσίν σε καὶ ἀποθλίβουσιν. Mt. 9:20 f., in a dogmatic correction of the ancient popular account, does not mention the motives of ignorance and affliction.
[21] On the form-critical problem cf. M. Dibelius, Formgeschichte² (1933), 50, 54 f., 64, 72.

6:45) after the feeding introduces the story of walking on the water, which is thus emphatically presented as an experience of the disciples. [22] Away from the multitude He heals the deaf mute in Decapolis in Mk. 7:33 : καὶ ἀπολαβόμενος αὐτὸν ἀπὸ τοῦ ὄχλου, obviously "to keep the healing process secret from the unauthorised." [23] The motive of separation is modified in Jn. 5:13, where the withdrawal comes after the healing. As the general public, the crowd speaks and argues about the person of Jesus. Thus Jesus asks in Lk. 9:18 : τίνα με οἱ ὄχλοι λέγουσιν εἶναι; [24] In the story of the entry in Mt. 21:1-11 the πλεῖστος ὄχλος [25] (v. 8) or the ὄχλοι [26] (v. 9) pay homage to the Lord as the Messiah entering the holy city. According to v. 10 Jerusalem is not ready for this entry, and when the people of Jerusalem ask about Jesus the ὄχλοι who accompany Him answer (v. 11): οὗτός ἐστιν ὁ προφήτης Ἰησοῦς ὁ ἀπὸ Ναζαρὲθ τῆς Γαλιλαίας. Here the multitude, which is elsewhere colourless, takes on the individual form of a crowd of Galilean pilgrims going up to the feast, → 588, 33 ff. [27] Jesus is also a cause of debate in Jn. 7:12, 43 (→ 588, 20 ff.). A distinctive point in Jn. is that Jesus prays to the Father for the crowd around Him, Jn. 11:42.

c. The masses are sometimes contrasted with the authorities, whose actions are determined by fear of popular opinion. Thus in Mt. 14:5 Herod Antipas does not dare to put the Baptist to death : ἐφοβήθη τὸν ὄχλον, ὅτι ὡς προφήτην αὐτὸν εἶχον. [28] In Mk. 15:15 Pilate is under pressure from the crowd : βουλόμενος τῷ ὄχλῳ τὸ ἱκανὸν ποιῆσαι. [29] The Jewish leaders in steps against Jesus are dependent on the mood of the mob, e.g., at the cleansing of the temple in Mk. 11:18, [30] or the question of John's baptism, Mt. 21:26; [31] cf. also Mk. 12:12. Jesus is called a seducer of the common people in Jn. 7:12 : πλανᾷ τὸν ὄχλον. The same charge is made against Paul, cf. Ac. 24:12, 18. The scorn of the ruling Jewish classes for the ὄχλος finds expression in Jn. 7:49, → 589, 19 ff. Fickle in mood and defenceless against clever propaganda, the ὄχλος is induced to condemn Jesus, Mk. 15:11; Mt. 27:20. On the crowd at the trial cf. Mk. 15:8 and par.; on its remorse when the evil deed was done, Lk. 23:48.

The relation of the crowd to the apostles corresponds in essentials to what has been said already, though there are fewer instances. The ὄχλοι want to hear the apostles, Ac. 8:6; 13:45. [32] Gentile ὄχλοι are inclined to worship men, Ac. 14:11,

---

[22] Cf. also Mk. 4:36, where the disciples leave the ὄχλος.

[23] Kl. Mk.[3], ad loc.; cf. Mk. 8:23.

[24] Mk. 8:27; Mt. 16:13 : οἱ ἄνθρωποι.

[25] Mk. 11:8 : πολλοί. Lk. 19:36 : 3rd person plur.

[26] Only Mt. has οἱ ὄχλοι.

[27] On Mt. 21:10b-11, which is peculiar to Mt., Kl. Mt.[3], ad loc., quoting K. L. Schmidt, Der Rahmen d. Geschichte Jesu (1919), 284, says : "To emphasise the significance of the manifestation of Jesus in Jerusalem, Mt. adds a description of the effect of the Messianic entry which is enhanced even further in Jn. 12:12, 18." But since the term προφήτης is also outside the framework (cf. v. 11 with 8 f.), like the astonished question of inhabitants of Jerusalem in v. 10b, it may be assumed that in 10b-11 Mt. was following a fixed tradition related to Jn. 12:12, 18. According to this the acclamation was that of a group of Galilean pilgrims in which Jerusalem had no part ; cf. W. Bousset, Kyrios Christos[2] (1921), 35 f.; R. Meyer, Der Prophet aus Galiläa (1940), 18 f.

[28] The motivation in Mk. 6:20 is different ; in its non-Messianic character it corresponds to Jos. Ant., 18, 117. On the problem cf. R. Meyer, op. cit., 90 f.

[29] Omitted at Mt. 27:25, softened in form and content at Lk. 23:24.

[30] Lk. 19:48 : ὁ λαὸς ἅπας, no motive in Mt.

[31] Mk. 11:32. Lk. 20:6 λαός.

[32] D sa : τὸ πλῆθος.

13 f., 18. It is no less easy to sway the fickle mob, Ac. 14:19; 17:8, 13; 19:26; 21:27, or to set it in an uproar, Ac. 16:22; 19:33, 35; 21:34 f.

2. "Host," "troop." ὄχλος means an armed body in the ὄχλος μετὰ μαχαιρῶν καὶ ξύλων of Mk. 14:43.

3. "People." As the context shows, the plur. ὄχλοι is used in Rev. 17:15 for "peoples," "hosts of peoples": τὰ ὕδατα ... οὗ ἡ πόρνη κάθηται, λαοὶ καὶ ὄχλοι εἰσὶν καὶ ἔθνη καὶ γλῶσσαι. [33]

4. As a measure, only in the Lucan writings, cf. Lk. 5:29: ὄχλος πολὺς τελωνῶν καὶ ἄλλων, also 6:17; Ac. 1:15; 6:7; 11:24, 26.

II. ὄχλος and 'Am ha-Areṣ.

1. The Johannine ὄχλος. The term ὄχλος acquires a special sense in John's Gospel. [34]

Thus we find the ὄχλος in Jn. 5:13 at a Jewish feast, cf. 5:1. Acc. to 6:2, 5, 22, 24 the ὄχλος is a Galilean crowd present at the miracle of feeding and the walking on the sea. [35] The word ὄχλος is esp. common in Jn. 7 and 12. In 7:11 Jesus is sought by the Jews at the Feast of Tabernacles; the Jews are the ὄχλοι in v. 12. What is meant in v. 11 f. is the Jewish public. [36] There is further ref. to the Jews in vv. 15-19, when they debate with Jesus, and in v. 20 ὄχλος is used again for the Jewish crowd. In 7:31 f., however, the Pharisees are contrasted with the multitude. Many of the crowd believe in Jesus, so that the high-priests and scribes are forced to take action against Him. Ref. is again made to this crowd in vv. 40-49 in connection with the speech which Jesus made on the last day of the Feast of Tabernacles. Some of the crowd regard Jesus as a prophet, some as the Messiah, whereas others doubt His Messiahship; hence we read in v. 43: σχίσμα οὖν ἐγένετο ἐν τῷ ὄχλῳ δι' αὐτόν. [37] Jn. 7:45 f. takes up again the reason for arresting Jesus given in v. 31 f., though the servants of the high-priests and Pharisees return unsuccessfully with the excuse: οὐδέποτε ἐλάλησεν οὕτως ἄνθρωπος, ὡς οὗτος λαλεῖ ὁ ἄνθρωπος. The servants thus take the same position as a great part of the crowd. Hence a Pharisee says in v. 48 f.: μή τις ἐκ τῶν ἀρχόντων ἐπίστευσεν εἰς αὐτὸν ἢ ἐκ τῶν Φαρισαίων; ἀλλὰ ὁ ὄχλος οὗτος ὁ μὴ γινώσκων τὸν νόμον ἐπάρατοί εἰσιν. Jn. thus differentiates the ἄρχοντες and Φαρισαῖοι, who radically reject Jesus, [38] from the wretched mob which does not know the Law. Acc. to the context this judgment applies both to participants in the feast and to the common people of Jerusalem. 11:55 refers esp. to the pilgrims, who are first called the "many from the country" (πολλοὶ ἐκ τῆς χώρας) and then in 12:12 ὁ ὄχλος πολὺς ὁ ἐλθὼν εἰς τὴν ἑορτήν. These pilgrims go to meet Jesus and hail Him as the Messianic king, vv. 12-19. The same motif occurs in the Synoptists except that here they are portrayed as being with Him from the outset when He enters Jerusalem, → 587, 7-14. [39] Finally, the ὁ ὄχλος πολὺς ἐκ τῶν Ἰουδαίων of Jn. 12:9 is the great company of Jews which

---

[33] Cf. Da. 3:4 LXX: ἔθνη καὶ χῶραι, λαοὶ καὶ γλῶσσαι, though not ὄχλοι, cf. Pr.-Bauer³, s.v.

[34] On what follows cf. Zn. J. on 7:14 ff.

[35] The Galilean ὄχλος is constantly with Jesus here, cf. Bau. J.³ on 6:2. This ὄχλος (here for ἄνθρωποι, v. 14 f.) also wants to make Jesus king after acknowledging Him as the prophet that should come into the world. Jn. shows that he is acquainted with Jewish dogmatics, for the feeding is a sign of the last time, → IV, 464, 23 ff.

[36] But cf. v. 13, also 5:15-18; 9:22; 18:12, where the word Ἰουδαῖοι is restricted to the ruling classes, Bau. J.³ on 1:19 and exc.

[37] On the problem of the same divided assessment of Jesus as reflected in the Synoptic Gospels cf. R. Meyer, op. cit., 10-40.

[38] Cf. on the other hand Jn. 3:1-21.

[39] Possibly an ancient Christian rite lies behind the version of the entry in Jn., cf. Bau. J.³ on 12:13.

six days before the Passover goes to Bethany to see Jesus and Lazarus. The ref. acc. to v. 11 is to the πολλοὶ τῶν Ἰουδαίων who on account of Lazarus believed in Jesus and were thus unfaithful to the high-priests, cf. v. 10. [40] It is hardly possible to establish a consistent usage in Jn. This is not surprising in view of the range of meaning of ὄχλος and the peculiar style of Jn. [41] As the term Ἰουδαῖοι (→ III, 377, 3 ff.) does not always refer to the upper stratum of the Jewish people, so ὄχλος does not in every case denote a particular stratum of society.

Nevertheless, for all the obscurities of usage, one may suspect that the author had a specific purpose in the striking employment of ὄχλος in Jn. 7 and 12. In the first instance the term refers to the pilgrims at the feast. It is also natural to suppose that the ὄχλος is made up of Galileans, very probably those who wanted to make Him king, cf. 6:14 f. But ὄχλος can also denote the common people of Jerusalem. Perhaps more emphatically than in the Synoptists, this is for the most part opposed to the ruling classes. The response which Jesus finds among the ὄχλος is by no means consistent. Along with those who see in Him the prophet or Messiah are others who reject Him altogether. For this, too, there are Synoptic parallels. In Jn. as in the Synoptic Gospels there are those of the crowd who fall away after first believing in Him and doing homage to Him.

2. The ʿAm ha-Areṣ. What gives the Johannine ὄχλος its particular stamp is the judgment of the Pharisees in 7:49: Cursed is the rabble which does not know the Law. This characterises the festal pilgrims and the common people of Jerusalem, who are impressed by the Messianic personality of Jesus, as a lawless *massa perditionis*. The statement also shows that Jn. knows the tensions in contemporary Judaism which one may reasonably well infer from Jewish sources and which are very closely bound up with the concept ʿAm ha-Areṣ. [42]

The term was not coined by the Rabb.; it is found already in the OT. In pre-exilic times it denotes the Jewish nobility as the ruling class in the southern kingdom, while in post-exilic times it denotes the landowners of Palestine who do not belong to the common Jewish body. [43] In post-exilic OT writings the term obviously denotes the distinction between the temple community, decisively controlled by the returned exiles, and the Samaritans. [44] In Rabb. writings, however, the original sociological sense was completely lost, and the term became an exclusively religious and political one among the Jews themselves. [45] As a slogan on the lips of the Pharisees it denotes the masses, or the individuals belonging to them, who in conduct do not live up to the nomistic ideal of the sanctification of all life; cf. in this connection the claim of Hillel (20 B.C.) in Ab., 2, 5: "An uneducated man does not fear sin, and an ʿAm ha-Areṣ is not pious." [46]

---

[40] In Jn. 12:17 the ὄχλος is the crowd present at the raising of Lazarus (11:42), while in v. 18 the ὄχλος has only heard of this. This difficulty is due to compression cf. Bau. J.³ on 12:17 f. In Jn. 12:29, as in 11:42 and often in the Synoptists, the ὄχλος has the supernumerary role of the chorus, → 586, 32 ff., while in 12:34 it is the opponent of Jesus.

[41] T. Zahn's all too summary assertion (→ n. 34): "Alongside the inhabitants of the capital (7:25) is the much more frequently mentioned ὄχλος (12:20, 31, 40, 43, 49), the masses of pilgrims from all parts of the country, which disappeared after the feast (8:12-10:21) and, apart from 11:42, were mentioned again only at the Passover (12:9 ff.)," does not correspond to the complicated usage.

[42] On what follows cf. Str.-B., II, 494-519 and R. Meyer, 169-199.

[43] Würthwein, 70.

[44] On the problem of the shift in meaning, which cannot be pursued in detail, cf. Würthwein, 70 f., n. 30.

[45] Only c. 200 A.D. does the Rabb. concept ʿAm ha-Areṣ acquire secondarily a sociological nuance, R. Meyer, 194.

[46] This is in fact the oldest example; on bSota, 48a, which Str.-B., II, 500; IV, 659, 664 puts in the time of Hyrcanus I, cf. R. Meyer, "Das angebliche Demai-Gesetz Hyrkans, I," ZNW, 38 (1939), 124-131.

Even programmatically a sharp differentiation is thus made from the 'Am ha-Areṣ without regard to the social position of those thus stigmatised. [47] In keeping is the consistent struggle of the Pharisees (→ Φαρισαῖος) — in the first instance only one religio-political party alongside others — to actualise their nomistic ideal, which finally, after the downfall of the older Jewish theocracy, was put into practice in the patriarchate and the all-comprehensive synagogue. In this bitter conflict, in which gradually, and not least as a result of the political events of 70-135 A.D., all the other groups were eliminated, Pharisaism, by virtue of its ideological and organisational superiority rather than its numerical strength, [48] subjugated the broad masses of the Jewish people, i.e., the 'Am ha-Areṣ, so that by the end of the 2nd century A.D. Rabbinism held undisputed sway. [49]

The context of Jn. 7:49 shows that the concept ὄχλος as used here is not fully co-extensive with the 'Am ha-Areṣ of Rabbinic literature, since it expresses social contempt as well as containing a religious judgment. This tension in usage is to be explained by the social situation of primitive Christianity and the perspective resulting therefrom. Within the 'Am ha-Areṣ, which embraced all classes, the ordinary people were those chiefly attracted by the message of Jesus. They were recruited in the main from Galileans with strong eschatological expectations on the one side [50] and a distaste for Pharisaic nomism on the other. [51] But when they joined Jesus they did so with hopes very different from those which He could fulfil on the basis of His mission. A glance at the various ideas about Jesus preserved at various points in the Gospels is adequate to show that these hopes moved predominantly in the sphere of national eschatology. [52] Since Jesus disappointed such hopes, which found expression in major and minor revolts right up to the disaster under Hadrian, it was inevitable that there should be a parting of the ways on this issue, and that Jesus' influence on the 'Am ha-Areṣ should be only an episode. For further discussion of Jesus and the 'Am ha-Areṣ → Φαρισαῖος.

Meyer

| † ὀχύρωμα |

In 2 C. 10:4 Paul says that the aim of his warfare is the destruction of ὀχυρώματα.

ὀχύρωμα is a military tt. for "fortified place." It is not used in a transf. sense in class. lit. or the pap. [1] But similar concepts are applied to God in the OT. Mostly the

---

[47] → R. Meyer, 177.

[48] Acc. to Jos. Ant., 17, 42 the number of organised Pharisees was only something over 6,000.

[49] On the struggle between the Pharisees and the 'Am ha-Areṣ in the 2nd cent. cf. R. Meyer, 185-195.

[50] → II, 884 f.; cf. G. Bertram, "Der Hellenismus in d. Urheimat des Ev.," ARW, 32 (1935), 265-281; R. Meyer, *op. cit.* (→ n. 27), 70-82.

[51] The attitude of the Galileans in the 1st cent. A.D. finds expression in a saying of Jochanan b. Zakkai, who for 18 yrs. before the destruction of the temple worked in the Upper Galilean place 'Arāb near Sepphoris ('Arrābet Baṭṭōf), and who in this long period had to give only two legal opinions : "Galilee, Galilee, thou hatest the Law, at the end thou wilt make common cause with those who impose taxes" (jShab., 15d, 61); R. Meyer, 180.

[52] Cf. R. Meyer, *op. cit.* (→ n. 27), 18-31.

ὀχύρωμα. [1] Moult.-Mill., *s.v.* ἐχυρός is common in the transf. sense : ἐν τῷ ἐχυρῷ εἶναι, "to be in safety," Thuc., VII, 77, 6 (of an army, but not in a fortress), ἐχυρὰ παρέχεσθαι, "to give tenable grounds," I, 32, 2 [Debrunner].

LXX brings out the theological point of comparison, καταφυγή for מְצוּדָה in ψ 30:3; 70:3 ('Α ὀχύρωμα), for מִשְׂגָּב Ps. 9:9 (Σ ὀχύρωμα), ἰσχύς for עֹז, Is. 49:5; Jer. 16:19; ·βοηθός for עֹז ψ 27:7; 58:17. This method of transl. may be regarded as a concession to Greek modes of thought, which find such comparisons strange. [2] In three instances, however, the LXX has a fig. sense (as compared with 70 instances of the lit.): at 2 Βασ. 22:2 for מְצוּדָה, at Job 19:6 for מָצוֹד, and with no Mas. requirement at Prv. 10:29 for עֹמֶן, cf. also ψ 70:3 : τόπος ὀχυρός (Heb. uncertain). The ref. is always to God, not to men, as in 2 C. 10:4. On the other hand, there is a ref. to men in Philo Conf. Ling., 129 f., where in a striking linguistic par. and material approximation to Paul ὀχύρωμα denotes the tower of Babel (Gn. 11:3) [3] or the tower at Penuel (Ju. 8:9), and vaunting reason is compared with this bastion : τὸ γὰρ κατεσκευασμένον ὀχύρωμα διὰ τῆς τῶν λόγων πιθανότητος οὐδενὸς ἕνεκα ἑτέρου κατεσκευάζετο ἢ τοῦ μετατραπῆναι καὶ μετακλιθῆναι διάνοιαν ἀπὸ τῆς τοῦ θεοῦ τιμῆς· οὗ τι ἂν γένοιτο ἀδικώτερον; ἀλλὰ πρός γε τὴν τοῦ ὀχυρώματος τούτου καθαίρεσιν ὁ πειρατὴς τῆς ἀδικίας καὶ φονῶν ἀεὶ κατ' αὐτῆς εὐτρέπισται ...

It is possible that Paul, too, is alluding to the tower of Babel. At any rate his usage corresponds to the LXX. The comparison is designed to bring out the suitability of his spiritual weapons and the apparent strength of the philosophical structure (vv. 4 ff.) and of the pretended repute of his opponents in Corinth (1 f., 7 ff.).

Heidland

---

† ὀψώνιον

Lit. "what is appointed for buying food," then "money," [1] then mostly a military tt. for "pay," originally including the maintenance allowance (i.e., ὀψώνιον = μισθός + σιτηρέσιον, Menand. Fr., 1051 [CAF, III, 259]), later just the pay given along with σῖτος and other allowances, e.g., P. Strassb., 103, 7 and 16. This narrow sense is also found in the 3 instances in the LXX (1 Εσδρ. 4:56; 1 Macc. 3:28; 14:32) and the loan word אַפְסַנְיָא in Rabb. lit. [2] Occasionally the term is used outside the military sphere for the salaries of state officials or for wages generally. But in any case the recipient has a legal right, often fixed by tariff, to the ὀψώνιον, which can be pleaded in court for, e.g., support of a child, P. Lond., III, 898, 31. Usually the ref. is not to a once-for-all

---

[2] Other figures of speech for God which express the idea of a sure refuge are also taken theologically by the translators. Only in later translators does a lit. rendering correspond to the ideal of philological exactitude. The LXX, on the other hand, follows the theological usage of the synagogal liturgy. Cf. G. Bertram, "Der Sprachschatz d. Septuaginta u. der des hebr. AT," ZAW, NF, 16 (1939), 85-101 [Bertram].

[3] Gn. 11:4 : עִיר וּמִגְדָּל, LXX πόλιν καὶ πύργον. ὀχύρωμα is not elsewhere used for these Heb. terms, but Philo paraphrases already in his quotation of Gn. 11:4 : ὀχυρωσώμεθα τὰ οἰκεῖα, Conf. Ling., 111, and βασίλειον ὀχυρώτατον, ibid., 113.

ὀψώνιον. Preisigke Fachwörter, *s.v.*; Mitteis-Wilcken, I, 1, 357, 411; J. Kromayer-G. Veith, *Heerwesen u. Kriegführung d. Griechen u. Römer = Hndbch. AW*, IV, 3, 2 (1928), 111.

[1] [Debrunner].

[2] Str.-B., III, 233.

payment or premium[3] but to pay over a period, at a daily rate,[4] by the month[5] etc. Since as the basic rate it is accompanied by allowances in cash and kind, it is not a reward corresponding to the work done (→ IV, 695, 19 ff.) but the minimal subsistence rate.

1. The Baptist when preaching to the soldiers in Lk. 3:14 (→ I, 465, 10 f.) warns them against abusing their armed power and also against trying to seize by force the "allowances" needed because their pay was so small. To be content with one's pay is thus to put one's own claims second to the commandments of God and to be satisfied with a modest standard of living.

2. When Paul uses ὀψώνιον for the support given him by the churches (2 C. 11:8; cf. 1 C. 9:7), there is both a reference to the metaphor of the *militia Christi* and also an emphasis on the legal claim implicit in the concept. Not claiming the ὀψώνιον is an act of freedom on the apostle's part in relation to the churches[6] and also a venture of faith, which refuses any assured basis of subsistence.[7] In the use of the term there may also be allusion to the thought that the support of the congregation never can or will be adequate compensation for the apostle's work but is "only" an ὀψώνιον.

3. In R. 6:23 (→ I, 309, 26 ff.; III, 17, 16 ff.) the context shows that three aspects are emphasised. a. Since ὀψώνια serve to defray the costs of subsistence, the first part of the verse contains a sharp contrast: "The subsistence which sin pays and offers is death." Sin is a deceiver; it promises life and gives death. b. Since ὀψώνιον is not a single payment but continuous, θάνατος cannot be simply the end of life or the final penalty, but is also the active shadow which this death projects on life.[8] As eternal life is already granted to the justified through the ἀρραβών of the Spirit, so sin already holds out to its servants deadly poison from the cup of death. c. Since the term is a legal one in contrast to χάρισμα (the special gift),[9] the relation of law[10] is set over against that of grace in the two halves of the verse. Man has rights only in relation to sin, and these rights become his judgment. When he throws himself on God without claim, salvation comes to him.[11]

Heidland

---

[3] P. Oxy., IV, 731, 10, where Grenfell has "present," Bachm. K. on 2 C. 11:8 "Trinkgeld," could well mean "travelling allowance." "Payment" is also possible *ibid.*, 744, 7 (Grenfell "present"). At P. Herm., 54, 7 the meaning is not "reward for victory" but "annuity" ("honorarium," *v.* Preisigke Wört., *s.v.*).

[4] Ditt. Syll.[3], 581, 34.

[5] P. Fay., 302.

[6] Inscr. Priene, 109, 94 emphasises that a certain στρατηγός rendered his service ἄτερ ὀψωνίου καὶ ἐλαίου.

[7] When citizens refused ὀψώνιον for honorary military service they received instead a higher σῖτος, Kromayer-Veith, 78. Paul's refusal obviously cannot be understood in this way. He uses ὀψώνιον comprehensively for any support in cash or kind.

[8] Note that θάνατος has no article.

[9] Zn. R., *ad loc.*

[10] P. Althaus R. (*NT Deutsch*), *ad loc.*

[11] Ign. also uses ὀψώνιον for the pay which God gives Christ's soldiers, Pol., 6, 2: ἀρέσκετε ᾧ στρατεύεσθε, ἀφ᾽ οὗ καὶ τὰ ὀψώνια κομίζεσθε.

παγίς, παγιδεύω

† παγίς.

The word means primarily "anything which fastens" or "holds fast" (πήγνυμι), esp. "noose," "snare," "net." In the Hell. period it can mean "mouse-trap." [1] In Anth. Pal., 6, 109 we find νευροτενεῖς παγίδες (snares with cords). The crafty and destructive aspect of παγίς is stated in Menand. Fab. Inc., 67: κεκρυμμένη κεῖται παγὶς τοῖς πλησίον. Worth noting is the expression παγίδας ἱστάναι in Aristoph. Av., 527 f.: ἴστησι βρόχους, παγίδας, ῥάβδους, ἕρκη, νεφέλας, δίκτυα, πηκτάς. Fig. the phrase παγίδας ἱστάναι τοῖς ἄρτοις, Alexis Fr., 66 (CAF, II, 319), in Athen., 3 (p. 109b) is very vivid for the idea of "snatching at bread." The metaphorical sense is most common in sayings relating to women as dangerous creatures who entice men. This is esp. true of the hetaerae, who seek to ensnare men and catch them in their nets. Amphis in Athen., 13 (p. 567 f) calls the hetaerae παγίδες τοῦ βίου. In Luc. Dialogi Meretricii, 11 a courtesan has the nickname Παγίς. In Anth. Pal., 5, 56, 4 the eyes of a girl are called παγίδες. The adornment of women is also called αἱ τῶν γυναικῶν παγίδες in Aristoph. Fr., 666 (CAF, I, 556). In Anth. Pal., 9, 152 the Trojan horse which trapped and destroyed the Trojans is called a δουρατέα (wooden) παγίς. With παγίς we find the synonym δίκτυον ("fishing-net," "hunter's net," "snare"). So Epigr. Graec., 421: δίκτυα λυγρὰ καὶ γοερὰς παγίδας προὔφυγον ἀμπλακίης. Anth. Pal., 5, 56, 4: δίκτυα καὶ παγίδες. Aristoph. Av., 194, 527 (→ supra). The idea of religious ensnarement, e.g., "to be caught in the net of Ate" (guilt, delusion, perdition), is also found in the Gk. world, though the word used in this common figure of speech is δίκτυον, not παγίς, Aesch. Prom., 1078. [2]

There is a rich fig. use of the word in the LXX. [3] To the fore is the concept of snares for birds or game. We find various figures of speech, that of the pit and net in ψ 68:22; snares, nets and traps in ψ 139:5; snares, nets and pits in Hos. 5:1 f. In Job 18:8 the par. to παγίδι is the fig. δικτύῳ. In Is. 24:17 f. the Gk. text either cannot or does not try to reproduce the Heb. paronomasia פחד ופחת ופח; it simply transl.: φόβος καὶ βόθυνος καὶ παγὶς ἐφ᾽ ὑμᾶς τοὺς ἐνοικοῦντας ἐπὶ τῆς γῆς. In the transf. use derived from the metaphorical the main emphasis is on the crafty and destructive aspect. The chief sense is "cause of ruin." A series of typical LXX expressions derives in part from the figure of speech and also agrees in part with non-biblical usage : παγίδας (συν)ἱστάναι (Jer. 5:26; ψ 140:9; Sir. 27:26), τιθέναι (ψ 118:110), κρύπτειν (Jer. 18:22; ψ 9:16; 30:4; 63:5; 139:5; 141:3). The destructive element is plainly expressed in the combinations διαφθορὰ παγίδος (ψ 34:7) and παγὶς θανάτου (Tob. 14:10; ψ 17:5; Prv. 14:27;

π α γ ί ς. [1] So in the Hell. work Batrachomyomachia, 117: ἣν παγίδα καλέουσι, μυῶν ὀλέτειραν ἐοῦσαν, ed. T. W. Allen, Homeri Opera, V (1912), 173.

[2] Hermes warns the daughters of Ocean who sympathise with Prometheus that when disaster strikes they cannot excuse themselves on the ground that they did not know and were caught suddenly and unawares in the net of Ate from which is no escape : εἰδυῖαι γὰρ κοὐκ ἐξαίφνης οὐδὲ λαθραίως εἰς ἀπέρατον (ἀπέραντον) δίκτυον ἄτης ἐμπλεχθήσεσθ᾽ ὑπ᾽ ἀνοίας [Kleinknecht].

[3] There is a detailed discussion of παγίς in the LXX by G. Stählin, Skandalon (1930), 98-104. His conclusions are in large part the basis of the treatment in this section. He also gives examples.

21:6). [4] Very frequently, esp. in Ps., the suddenness of the destruction which comes on men is underlined. [5] The concept gradually loses its vividness and becomes weak and stereotyped. If the field of usage is considered, two main groups stand out, the one relating to idolatry, the other to the "snares of the ungodly." The word is mostly used for the latter. This use brings us "into the sphere of the implacable contrast between the 'righteous' and the 'ungodly' which lasted for centuries." [6] The expression occurs already in Jer. (5:26; 18:22), but it is found chiefly in the Ps., then in Prv. and Sir. [7] (There is similar ref. to the snares of the harlot, Sir. 9:3.) We also find a special group in which παγίς is used. In the abs. it denotes destruction itself "in a distinctively comprehensive and sinister sense," [8] cf., e.g., Is. 24:17; Ιερ. 31(48):43 f. A further abs. sense in which the term is, of course, rationalised and ethicised, may be found in the Wisdom lit., in Prv. and Sir. e.g., Prv. 13:14; 29:6; Sir. 9:13; 27:29. παγίς is the "divine punishment" itself, and in ψ 10:6 the ungodly are punished with God's παγίδες.

Joseph. does not have παγίς, but we find πάγη in Ant., 16, 239. [9] This is used in secular Gk. from Aesch., but is not used in the NT. παγίς does not occur in Philo.

The term is comparatively rare in the NT. In Lk. 21:34 f. in the eschatological discourse of Jesus the disciples are warned to be on guard lest the last day should come on them suddenly like a snare. [10] Those who busy themselves with the things of the world will be overtaken by the destruction which that day brings with it. παγίς is most common in the letters to Timothy. In 1 Tm. 3:7 and 2 Tm. 2:25 f. there is ref. to the παγὶς τοῦ διαβόλου. Acc. to 1 Tm. 3:7 bad conduct on the bishop's part has two results: the ἐπίσκοπος is rightly despised by the people (→ ὀνειδισμός, 241, 20 ff.), and he is an easy prey for Satan, who thus gets him in his power and renders him unfit for service to the congregation. [11] Acc. to 2 Tm. 2:25 f. those who resist the Christian message are in the snare of the devil. The ultimate reason for their opposition is that he has deluded them and trapped them into doing his will.

The idea of the παγὶς τοῦ διαβόλου has an ancient mythological basis. In almost all religions, not merely among primitive peoples but also among the Sumerians, Baby-

---

[4] No trace remains of any mythological background. J. Scheftelowitz, "Das Schlingen-u. Netzmotiv," RVV, XII, 2 (1912), 10, finds in the metaphors "cords of death" and "snares of death" "the indestructible reflection of a mythological mode of thought which has remained even when its true significance was wholly lost." Stählin, op. cit., 99 takes a different view. On this whole question note should be taken of the very interesting 2nd section in Scheftelowitz, 3-12 ("Snare and Net as Weapons of the Gods").

[5] ψ 17:5; 34:7; 63:5; cf. ψ 56:6; also Job 22:10. Very graphic is ἐμπίπτειν εἰς παγίδα ("fall into the snare") in Tob. 14:10b; Prv. 12:13; Sir. 9:3.

[6] Stählin, op. cit., 101.

[7] Loc. cit.

[8] Ibid., 102.

[9] Cf. Schl. Lk., 420.

[10] Where ὡς παγίς should be put is debated. Most exegetes place it in v. 34 with אBD it: ἐπιστῇ ἡ ἡμέρα ἐκείνη ὡς παγίς. Others, so Blass, Merx, Zahn, favour v. 35 with A it syr: ὡς παγὶς ἐπεισελεύσεται. Cf. Kl. Lk., ad loc.

[11] Though cf. Wbg. Past., ad loc., who argues that through slanders on the part of the ἔξωθεν the wrongly calumniated bishop "may easily err in his faith and be unfaithful in the discharge of his office." "In such a situation Satan may with prospect of success cast a snare in his way by which he will come into Satan's power and fall away completely from the faith." Cf. also Dib. Past., ad loc.: " 'The snare of the devil' is easy to understand after the ref. to ὀνειδισμός: one should not give the old accuser even the appearance of a reason for complaint (in the form of calumnies by opponents)." H. J. Holtzmann, Hand-Commentar z. NT, III, 234 supplies τοῦ διαβόλου with εἰς ὀνειδισμόν and interprets the v. as follows: "The idea, then, is that a Christian can first fall under slander, then into captivity, and finally under the judgment of the devil." This is in itself a true thought, but it is not what the verse says.

Ionians and Persians, in India, Greece and Rome, we find the belief that gods and demons were equipped with snares and nets with which they overcame their enemies. [12] The NT reference to the παγὶς τοῦ διαβόλου is to be seen in this context. The devil is not just man's accuser. He is the demon which opposes God, which is equipped with weapons that bring destruction, which is at work in the world, and which seeks to capture men and destroy them.

1 Tm. 6:9 deals with the dangers which men incur when they strive after wealth. Such men are said to fall into a snare. The combination of the terms πειρασμός, παγίς and ἐπιθυμίαι suggests that here, too, we have the idea of the παγὶς τοῦ διαβόλου. The author of the temptation, snare and desires is the devil. In the great letters Paul uses παγίς only once at R. 11:9, and this is a quotation, Ps. 69:23. God's judgment of hardening has come on most of the people of Israel. God has made their table, i.e., "all that they live by and do," [13] into a snare, an offence, and a recompense: εἰς παγίδα καὶ εἰς θήραν καὶ εἰς σκάνδαλον καὶ εἰς ἀνταπόδομα.

The post-apost. fathers take up again the LXX phrase παγὶς τοῦ θανάτου. Did., 2, 4 uses it of double-dealing (the double tongue): παγὶς γὰρ θανάτου ἡ διγλωσσία. Barn., 19, 8 uses it of the mouth generally: παγὶς γὰρ τὸ στόμα θανάτου, cf. Prv. 11:9; 18:7.

† παγιδεύω.

This word occurs only in the LXX, Test. XII, and NT. It is thus newly minted by the *koine*. Indeed, since it has not been found on pap. either, it is perhaps coined directly by the LXX. παγιδεύειν [1] is strictly a hunting expression, "to lay a snare," "to set a trap," "to entice into or catch in a trap."

The LXX [2] uses it only twice at 1 Βασ. 28:9 and Qoh. 9:12. In the former it means "to set a trap." The witch of Endor sees a threat to her own life in the king's request to conjure up the ghost of Samuel from the underworld, since the king himself had set the death penalty for witchcraft. In Qoh. 9:12 the metaphor of being caught is used for being overtaken by misfortune.

In the other renderings 'Α has παγιδεύειν in Ez. 13:20, 21 for being enmeshed in magical snares, i.e., for the destruction of souls which are caught like birds by false prophets. Σ has παγιδεύεσθαι (παγιδευθήσονται καὶ συλληφθήσονται) at Is. 8:15. Israel and the people of Jerusalem are snared and caught by the gins and traps laid for them. The vivid metaphor refers to the destruction which comes from God. At Prv. 6:2 Σ uses παγιδεύεσθαι of the tongue: ἐπαγιδεύθης ἐν ῥήμασι στόματός σου. Θ has the word in a similar connection in Prv. 11:15: μισῶν παγιδευθῆναι πεποιθήσει, i.e., he will not willingly be caught in the snare of too great self-confidence.

In Test. XII cf. Test. Jos. 7:1: ἔτι δὲ ἡ καρδία αὐτῆς ἔκειτο εἰς τὸ κακὸν καὶ περιεβλέπετο ποίῳ τρόπῳ με παγιδεῦσαι.

The word occurs only once in the NT at Mt. 22:15. The Pharisees are trying to get Jesus in their power. They consult together how they can lay a trap with a (specific) saying and thus ensnare Him in His own words about paying taxes to the Roman state. Jesus will then be broken in this conflict with Rome. The phrase

---

[12] Cf. in detail Scheftelowitz, *op. cit.*, 3-12.

[13] P. Althaus, *Der Brief an die Römer* (*NT Deutsch*), ad loc.

π α γ ι δ ε ύ ω. [1] The -ευω of παγιδεύω is obviously from the group ἀγρεύω, θηρεύω, ἐπιβουλεύω, ἐνεδρεύω etc. Cf. E. Fraenkel, *Griech. Denominativa* (1906), 174-224 [Debrunner].

[2] Cf. on this G. Stählin, *Skandalon* (1930), 129 f.

ὅπως αὐτὸν παγιδεύσωσιν ἐν λόγῳ brings out very well the crafty and destructive aspects of the action.

J. Schneider

πάθημα, παθητός, πάθος → πάσχω.

---

† παιδεύω, † παιδεία, † παιδευτής,
† ἀπαίδευτος, † παιδαγωγός

Contents : A. The Orientation of the Concept in the Greek World : 1. Home Education among the Greeks : a. In the Time up to the Sophists ; b. The Concept of Education in the Classical Period and its Later Development ; 2. The Legislator and Paideia ; 3. ὑπὸ Διὸς παιδεύεσθαι. B. Education in the Old Testament : 1. God's Discipline by Law and Wisdom ; 2. God's Discipline in the Prophetic Revelation ; 3. The Reconstruction of the Concept in the Greek Translation of the OT : a. In the Wisdom Literature ; b. In the Psalms ; c. In the Prophetic Writings ; d. In the Presentation of History. C. The Paideia Concept in Hellenistic and Rabbinic Judaism : 1. παιδεία and νόμος in Philo ; 2. Jewish-Hellenistic Education in Josephus ; 3. Discipline through Suffering in Later Jewish Theology. D. The Paideia Concept in the New Testament : 1. Greek and Jewish Culture in the NT ; 2. The Law as Taskmaster ; 3. Education by God ; 4. Christian Discipline in the NT.

παιδεία, παιδεύειν, denotes the upbringing and handling of the child which is growing up to maturity and which thus needs direction, teaching, instruction and a certain measure of compulsion in the form of discipline or even chastisement. παιδεία is both the way of education and cultivation which has to be traversed and also the goal which is to be attained. Apart from the words in the title ref. might also be made to παίδευμα, παίδευσις, and various compounds belonging to the group. The basis is a relatively late development of παιδ- (παῖς), and in the first instance it is obviously as difficult as in the case of τρέφειν to distinguish between the senses "upbringing" (e.g., Soph. Fr., 433 [TGF, 235]) and "education." [1]

π α ι δ ε ύ ω κ τ λ. Liddell-Scott, II, 1286 ff.; Thes. Steph., VI, 28 ff.; Preisigke Wört., II, 220 f.; Moult.-Mill., 473 f.; Cr.-Kö., Pr.-Bauer, s.v.; W. Jaeger, Paideia, I-III (1934, 1944, 1947); J. Stenzel, Platon, der Erzieher (1928); C. N. Cochrane, Christianity and Classical Culture (1940); W. Jentsch, "Urchristliches Erziehungsdenken, die Paideia Kyriu im Rahmen d. hellenistisch-jüdischen Umwelt," BFTh, 45, 3 (1951); R. Marcus, Law in the Apocrypha (1927), 29-31; T. J. Haarhoff, Art. "Education," Oxford Classical Dictionary (1949), 305-307; H. v. Campenhausen, "Glaube u. Bildung nach d. NT," Studium Generale, 2 (1949), 182-194; L. Dürr, Das Erziehungswesen im AT u. antiken Orient (1932); G. Bertram, "Der Begriff d. Erziehung in d. gr. Bibel," Imago Dei, Festschr. Gustav Krüger (1932), 33-51; Trench, 66-69; H. Kraus, "Paedagogia Dei als theologischer Geschichtsbegriff," Evangelische Theol., 8 (1948/49), 515-597.

[1] παιδ-εύω means "to be intensively or professionally engaged with a child." Cf. E. Fraenkel, Griech. Denominativa (1906), 176, 194, who refers to ὀρφανεύειν and παρθενεύειν. The oldest instance of παιδεία (from παιδεύειν) is in Aesch. Sept. c. Theb., 18, still in the same sense as τροφή for bringing up children. Cf. Jaeger, I, 25; II, 367, n. 82. In every age παιδεία implies for the Gks. a process of growth, and there is always a relation between the words for education and nourishment, originally almost identical in meaning, ibid., II, 303 (though Debrunner disputes this in a letter). The sense of culture, esp. for adults or of the mind, develops only in the 2nd half of the 5th cent. παιδεία becomes "the sum-total of all ideal perfections of mind and body — complete kalokagathia — which was now consciously taken to include a genuine intellectual and spiritual culture. This new comprehensive conception was firmly established by the time of Isocrates and Plato," ibid., I, 364 (ET, I, 286). In Isoc. Panegyricus, 50 we find the statement that education, not heredity, makes the Greek. F. Bogner, "Die Judenfrage in d. griech.-römischer Welt," FJFr., I, 84 (1937).

A. The Orientation of the Concept in the Greek World.

The word group characterises Gk. culture. In retrospect Hesychius in the 5th century A.D. defines παιδεία as ἀγωγή and ὠφέλιμος διδαχή, thus giving the two possibilities of understanding whose mutual relationship is the theme of the history of the group.[2] Direction and teaching can develop into πεῖρα and νουθεσία. In this twofold sense παιδεία and related terms are used from the time of the tragic dramatists, in the Sophists, and in classical philosophy, to express all human culture. The concept of paideia remains an essential one for the rich development, and also for some of the limitations, of cultural striving in the West.

1. Home Education among the Greeks.

a. In the Time up to the Sophists.

The paideia concept is not so genuinely rooted in the Gk. world as one might think. Neither the term nor the thing is known to Homeric Greece. The principles of nobility and descent hold sway, Hom. Il., 6, 208 and 211; 9, 443. Arete is a gift of the gods, Il., 20, 242. τρέφειν is used for upbringing and education, and it is more vegetative than ethical in character. Pindar, in reaction against an overestimation of διδαχή, contrasts the value of what is inborn with the valuelessness of what is learned, Nem., 3, 40 ff.[3] Theognis, a champion of the aristocratic ideal, is of the conviction that no teaching can make a bad man good, 437 f. (Diehl, I, 139). Naturally there was always education in the sense of handing on uses, customs and laws from one generation to another, with variations according to birth, rank and calling. In contrast to the aristocratic view, however, the Sophists taught the equality of all men, Hippias of Elis in Plat. Prot., 337c. There thus arises the question of man's capacity for education, and the Sophists begin to give the Greek concept of paideia its distinctive orientation. Thus in the poet Eur., who was under Sophist influence, we read in Suppl., 913-917 (cf. 891): ἡ δ' εὐανδρία διδακτός, εἴπερ καὶ βρέφος διδάσκεται λέγειν ἀκούειν θ' ὧν μάθησιν οὐκ ἔχει· ἃ δ' ἂν μάθῃ τις, ταῦτα σῴζεσθαι φιλεῖ πρὸς γῆρας· οὕτω παῖδας εὖ παιδεύετε. Up to a certain degree, at least, culture can be acquired, Eur. Iph. Aul., 558-562. Soph. uses παιδεύειν generally for the influencing of belief and conduct, Ai., 595; Oed. Col., 562, 919; Trach., 451. In Phil., 1361 there is ref. to the formative power of evil influences.

b. The Concept of Education in the Classical Period and its Later Development.

For the ancients μουσική and γυμναστική παιδεία were related.[4] Plato[5] takes the same view (e.g., Resp., II, 376e, Leg., VII, 795d), and sets alongside them education in individual disciplines, παιδεία μαθημάτων (Leg., VII, 822d), though vocational training is not to be counted as παιδεία (Leg., I, 644a). In so far as education is a parental matter, parents should be made capable of it by enlightenment, Leg., VII, 788a. The goal is from the very first repudiation of what deserves repudiation and love for those

---

[2] Cf. also the Roman grammarian Gellius (c. 175 A.D.), Noctes Atticae, 13, 17: humanitatem appellarunt id propemodum, quod Graeci παιδείαν vocant, nos eruditionem institutionemque in bonas artes dicimus. Quas qui sinceriter percupiunt appetuntque hi sunt vel maxime humanissimi. → μανθάνω, IV, 390 ff., and → διδάσκω, II, 135 ff.

[3] Jaeger, I, 287, 366-377, 388-390.

[4] On Socrates cf. W. Kamlah, "Sokrates u. d. Paideia," Archiv f. Philosophie, 3 (1949), 277-315; W. Nestle, Vom Mythos zum Logos (1940), Index s.v. "Paideia."

[5] R. G. Bury, "Theory of Education in Plato's Laws," Revue des Études Grecques, 50 (1938), 304-317. Kant is influenced by Plato's view: "Man is the only creature which has to be educated. By education we mean tending (care, support), discipline and instruction along with cultivation of the spirit (Bildung)," Über Pädagogik, Einl., ed. Philosoph. Bibliothek, VIII, 193. The term Bildung is a mystical Pietist expression which was used for the development of a man's spiritual life only from the second half of the 18th century.

of love (μισεῖν-στέργειν). ἡδονή and λύπη are here educational factors, *ibid.*, II, 653c. [6] Aristotle [7] distinguishes the age-groups 7-14 and 14-21, Pol., VII, 17, p. 1336b, 38. Education is designed to fulfil natural presuppositions, physis, *ibid.*, p. 1337a, 2. It should combine harmoniously admonition and habit, VII, 15, p. 1334b, 8; VIII, 3, p. 1338b, 4 ff., and safeguard against sexual excesses, gluttony and their consequences, p. 1336b, 23. Along with gymnastics and music, language and writing are essential, VIII, 3, p. 1337b, 23. Musical education is free, noble, and a source of joy, VIII, 5, p. 1338a, 30. It is no game : μετὰ λύπης γὰρ ἡ μάθησις (VIII, 5, p. 1339a, 27), but fashions the ethos of the soul (p. 1340b, 6 f.) and endows with moderation, force and decorum, p. 1342b, 33. Personal education, whose aim is the good man, fits in with general education (Eth. Nic., V, 5, p. 1130b, 26 f.), since it makes no difference whether one or many are educated by written or unwritten laws. The father's authority is even greater than the lawgiver's, for it is grounded in blood relationship and parental concern, *ibid.*, X, 10, p. 1180b, 1-7. τρέφειν is a private affair, παιδεύειν a public, [8] Oec., I, 3, p. 1344a, 8. As the child must obey the direction of the pedagogue, so desire is subject to reason. The cultured soul brings happiness to itself and to the man to whom it belongs, Dialogi, 89, p. 1491b, 42.

Those who follow are nurtured by the educational thinking of the 4th century, the classical century of paideia. [9] The intellectualistic type of education develops into that of Stoic philosophy. Influential here is the self-critical attitude of Gk. tragedy. Under the Apollonian slogan Γνῶθι σαυτόν [10] the concern now is for the philosophical man, the Hellenistic cosmopolitan. That Roman legal thinking must have contributed to this type may be seen at once from the practical educational objectives of the Roman Empire. [11] Thus speculative Platonic thinking is replaced by the volitional educational goal of firmness of character. Musonius esp. recognises the family to be the decisive factor in education, and in this connection marriage is estimated as a life-fellowship, 11, 3 f., 67-75. Musonius also follows the Spartan system and warns against pampering. [12] σωφροσύνη and φρόνησις in a sober Stoic understanding are with ἀνδρεία and δικαιοσύνη the virtues of the educated man, 3, 11 ff.; 50, 9 ff. A heroic attitude to fate gives the philosophical man freedom in relation to the claims of the state as well, [13] since it holds all the good things of life in light esteem, and in the last resort makes possible an easy renunciation of life itself, Sen. Dial., VI, 20, esp. 2; XII, 4. This ataraxia of the sage as

---

[6] Aristot. Eth. Nic., II, 2, p. 1104b, 11 ff. refers to this : διὸ δεῖ ἦχθαί πως εὐθὺς ἐκ νέων, ὡς ὁ Πλάτων φησίν, ὥστε χαίρειν τε καὶ λυπεῖσθαι οἷς δεῖ· ἡ γὰρ ὀρθὴ παιδεία αὕτη ἐστίν, cf. also X, 1, p. 1172a, 20 f.: διὸ παιδεύουσι τοὺς νέους, οἰακίζοντες ἡδονῇ καὶ λύπῃ.

[7] O. Willmann, *Aristot als Pädagog u. Didaktiker* (1909).

[8] From the time of Aristot. παιδεία is an essential part of πολιτεία. Even to-day the modern Gk. concept of *politeuma* includes education, Jaeger, I, 511 f. Cf. Pol., IV, 12, p. 1296b, 17: ἔστι δὲ πᾶσα πόλις ἔκ τε τοῦ ποιοῦ καὶ ποσοῦ. λέγω δὲ ποιὸν μὲν ἐλευθερίαν πλοῦτον παιδείαν εὐγένειαν, ποσὸν δὲ τὴν τοῦ πλήθους ὑπεροχήν. But the state cannot be depicted in a specific number of constituent parts ; it is an organic whole. Cf. W. Dilthey, *Einl. in d. Geisteswissenschaften*, I (1922), 229.

[9] Jentsch, 25-85.

[10] Cf. also Ps.-Plat. Alc., I, 124a-c.

[11] Cf. O. Willmann, Art. "Griech. Erziehung," in W. Rein, *Enzyklopädisches Handbuch d. Pädagogik* (1909). The pedagogic wisdom of antiquity is summed up by the Roman orator Quintilian (35-96 A.D.) in the Institutio Oratoria. "Pedagogy and child psychology reach at this period a level which has hardly ever been surpassed," C. Schneider, "D. gr. Grundlagen der hell. Religionsgeschichte," ARW, 36 (1939), 319.

[12] In the 4th cent. the Spartan discipline became the ideal of the Philolaconian educational movement, Jaeger, I, 120-139. Even Socrates lauded the extent and degree of education among the Lacedaemonians, and mentioned the seven sages as their pupils, Plat. Prot., 342d-343a.

[13] The supreme power of the state over man, and the wresting of education in the exclusive service of the state, Aristot. excused by the momentous thought that the state consists in its constitution, its form, Pol., IV, 15, p. 1299b, 25. The masses are the material for the construction of the state, VII, 4, p. 1325b, 40. The politician is the artist who moulds the state out of this material, Dilthey, *op. cit.*, 231.

the ideal of education is taught also by the pupil of Musonius, Epictetus. It must impress itself on the πρόσωπον of the πεπαιδευμένος, Diss., IV, 3, 3; that is, it corresponds to the role which the man of culture (καλὸς καὶ ἀγαθός, φιλόσοφος, πεπαιδευμένος, Diss., III, 22, 69; I, 29, 57; IV, 3, 3) has come to play in this world. [14]

More in terms of the content than the concept of humanist education Plutarch, esp. with his parallel biographies, was of particular importance right on into the 19th cent. There has been preserved under his name the small work De Liberis Educandis, which, starting with family education, sums up once again the results of Gk. thought on education. As everywhere in antiquity, education is only for free men, Lib. Educ., 1 (II, 1a); 10 (II, 7c). [15] The poor, slaves, the masses and most women are excluded therefrom. The work of the farmer is an illustration of paideia. The natural ability of the child is like the earth waiting to receive the seed ; the teacher is like the farmer ; his words of admonition and instruction are like the seed, 4 (II, 2b). Attainment of virtue rests on ἔθη καὶ παιδείαι καὶ διδασκαλίαι καὶ βίων ἀγωγαί, 4 (II, 3a b). The first step in pedagogy relates to the τροφή, the care and support of the child. Boys are put in the hands of pedagogues, who must be carefully screened. These are slaves, who thus rule over free men, Plat. Lys., 208b, cf. 223a. The goal of education is jeopardised if against one's better judgment the most unserviceable, greedy and intemperate slaves are used. Plato (Resp., III, 390e etc.) held up Phoenix, the pedagogue of Achilles, as an example. [16] The pedagogue is like the private tutor of more recent days. Socrates in Ps.-Plat. Alc., I, 121e, 122a tells of the education of a prince at the Persian court. Four of the best pedagogues are chosen. The wisest of these gives instruction in the fear of God and in kingship, the most righteous in uprightness, the most prudent in inner freedom and self-discipline, the most manly in fearlessness. Plato himself demanded that pedagogues should be selected acc. to age and experience, Resp., V, 467d, cf. also Polit., 308d-e. Plut. grants to the pedagogue a broad influence on education and culture, and thus demands a blameless life and correct deportment as well as experience : πηγὴ γὰρ καὶ ῥίζα καλοκαγαθίας τὸ νομίμου τυχεῖν παιδείας, Lib. Educ., 7 (II, 4b). Plut. also appeals to Lacon, the proto-type of the Spartan educator : It is the teacher who τὰ καλά ... τοῖς παισὶν ἡδέα ποιῶ and ποιήσει τὸν παῖδα τοῖς καλοῖς ἥδεσθαι καὶ ἄχθεσθαι τοῖς αἰσχροῖς, Plut. An Virtus doceri possit, 2 (II, 439f); De Virtute Morali, 12 (II, 452d). Fathers themselves must be more concerned about education, for poor education leads to irregular living and baser diversions, Lib. Educ., 7 (II, 4d-5b) (cf. Socrates in Plat. Clit., 407a); 13 (II, 9c). εὐγένεια, πλοῦτος, κάλλος, ὑγίεια, ἰσχύς are not save possessions under man's control. In relation to them ἀγωγὴ σπουδαία καὶ παιδεία νόμιμος is the beginning, middle and end. Culture alone is immortal and divine ; even war, which catches up everything like a whirlpool, cannot take this away, 8 (II, 5c e f); 9 (II, 6, a): ἀδιάφθορος and ὑγιαίνουσα; 7 (II, 5a): ὑγιαίνων καὶ τεταγμένος βίος. The ἐγκύκλια παιδεύματα should all be gone through at least γεύματος ἕνεκεν. But philosophy is the main element in education, 10 (II, 7d). [17]

---

[14] Here is the non-Gk. view of human life as a puppet-theatre whose figures are manipulated by the gods, as only the poet perceives, Jaeger, III, 278; Plat. Leg., I, 644d-e; VII, 803c → παίζω.

[15] Epictet., a freed slave, dared to oppose this view, Diss., II, 1, 22 ff.: οὐ γὰρ τοῖς πολλοῖς περὶ τούτων πιστευτέον, οἳ λέγουσι μόνοις ἐξεῖναι παιδεύεσθαι τοῖς ἐλευθέροις, ἀλλὰ τοῖς φιλοσόφοις μᾶλλον, οἳ λέγουσι μόνους τοὺς παιδευθέντας ἐλευθέρους εἶναι. In Diss., III, 21, 15 it is said of the mysteries : ἐπὶ παιδείᾳ καὶ ἐπανορθώσει τοῦ βίου κατεστάθη πάντα ταῦτα ὑπὸ τῶν παλαιῶν. Here the tension between Plato's concern in Resp. to free παιδεία as culture as much as possible from παῖς, and the grounding of παιδεία in the education of the child in Leg. (e.g., II, 653a b), is resolved. At issue is παίδευσις ψυχῆς (Phaedr., 241c), self-education, ἑαυτὸν πλάττειν (Resp., VI, 500d; cf. also Resp., II, 377b; Leg., II, 671c), the dominion of man in man, the λόγος παιδαγωγός of which Epictet. speaks, cf. Jaeger, II, 268, 359, 418, n. 389, III, 87, 301, 304.

[16] Hdt., VIII, 75 tells of a confidential task which a certain Sikinnos, slave and pedagogue of the children of Themistocles, executed at the latter's request.

[17] Memory is the reservoir of culture, ibid., 13 (II, 9d-e).

Spiritual love of young people promotes education, develops talents of leadership, and fashions essential virtue, 15 (II, 11e). Finally, everything depends on a good example ; fathers must not be teachers of wrongdoing to their children.[18] Cf. on this Apophth. Lac. (II, 216d), where the son, appealing to his education, refuses to be led astray by his parents.

That education remained a privilege of the ruling classes is shown also by the non-literary tradition of the inscr. and pap. Thus we read in P. Oxy., II, 265, 24 (81-95 A.D.); τὴν πρέπουσαν ἐλευθέροις παισὶ παιδείαν, and an inscr. (Ditt. Syll.³, 578, 61, 2nd cent. B.C.) has : τὸ ἀργύριον τὸ ἐπιδοθὲν ... εἰς τὴν παιδείαν τῶν ἐλευθέρων παίδων.[19] Elsewhere παιδεία is used with ref. to the schools.[20] The comparatively important and esteemed position of the pedagogue is attested in a pap. in which a mother writes to her son, P. Oxy., VI, 930, 2nd/3rd cent. A.D.[21] παιδεύειν is often used in the general sense "to cultivate" or "to instruct." There is an important testimony to the sense "to chastise" in BGU, III, 846, 11 f. (2nd cent. A.D.) in a letter of a son to his mother : πεπαίδευμαι καθ' ὃν δεῖ τρόπον.[22] Disciplining by fate is the παιδεία ἐν λύπῃ to which the philosophers also refer.[23] But παιδεύειν for corporal punishment by the pedagogue is not yet attested in non-biblical Gk., though from the letter adduced above it seems to have been adopted in popular Hell. usage.

2. The Legislator and Paideia.

Even ideas about family education in the classical period are mostly presented as demands of the legislator. For strictly all education is a public affair.[24] It was for the sake of paideia that Plat. wrote his Polit. and Leg. Indeed, the state exists on its behalf. At issue in paideia is the relation of man to the *polis*, and the fate of Socrates indicates the indissoluble tension between man's freedom and the claim of society.[25]

Man is by nature ordained for paideia (culture),[26] and the measure of his development is not his own wish (ψυχή) but the nomos, Xenoph. Cyrop., I, 3, 18. παιδεία is δύναμις θεραπευτικὴ ψυχῆς, Ps.-Plat. Def., 416.[27] It thus has an individualistic orientation. Nevertheless, it is basic to the ideal state of Plato,[28] and to the security

---

[18] παιδαγωγός is often used in Plut. in a broader sense : παιδαγωγὸν τῆς τυραννίδος, Galb., 17 (I, 1060c); οὐ μόνον δημοκρατίας ἀλλὰ καὶ βασιλείας παιδαγωγός, Aratus, 48 (I, 1049e); cf. παιδευτὴς ἐλευθερίας, Lycurg., 12 (I, 46d); παιδαγωγία πρὸς τὸ θεῖον, Nomas, 15, 1 (I, 70b). In the question ἂν καλῶς ὑπὸ τοῦ λόγου παιδαγωγηθῇ τὸ πάθος, De Virtute Morali, 4 (II, 443d), the logos appears as pedagogue, → n. 15.

[19] Moult.-Mill., 474 *s.v.*, with further material.

[20] But cf. the Apollonian proverb of the Δελφικὰ παραγγέλματα in the inscr. Ditt. Syll.³, 1268, I, 10 : παιδείας ἔχου [Kleinknecht].

[21] In a letter a mother asks her son to apply with his pedagogue for a suitable teacher, and her greeting is : ἄσπασαι τὸν τειμιώτατον παιδαγωγόν σου "Ερωτα, Moult.-Mill., 474, *s.v.*; cf. also Jentsch, 171-174 for further instances.

[22] Deissmann LO, 154 f.: "I am suitably chastised." The letter bears witness to the conversion of a prodigal son.

[23] On παιδεία and λύπη in Plut. Ser. Num. Pun., 3 (II, 459c d) → IV, 317, n. 20.

[24] Cf. P. Natorp, Art. "Erziehung" in W. Rein, *Enzyklopädisches Handbuch d. Pädagogik* (1909): "Education is a social function and with other social orders it serves the purpose of social self-preservation." Cf. the def. in Plat. Leg., II, 659d : παιδεία μέν ἐσθ' ἡ παίδων ὁλκή τε καὶ ἀγωγὴ πρὸς τὸν ὑπὸ τοῦ νόμου λόγον ὀρθὸν εἰρημένον. The logos here is the law put in words. Aristotelian ethics is along the same lines, Jaeger, III, 443, n. 103.

[25] Jaeger, II, 138, 224.

[26] *Ibid.*, III, 300 παιδεία == culture.

[27] Thus the Ps.-Aristotelian def. of παιδεία no longer refers to the education of the body and mind, but only to that of the soul : καθάπερ γάρ ἐστι φυλακτικὸν σώματος ὑγίεια, οὕτω ψυχῆς φυλακτικὸν καθέστηκε παιδεία, Rhet. Al., 1, p. 1428a, 18.

[28] Plato's depiction of justice and its function in the best state reflects his doctrine of the soul and its parts, Jaeger, II, 280 f.

of this state, Leg., VI, 752c. The aim and purpose of education is integration of the child into the surrounding world as this is determined by law and experience, II, 659d. νομοφύλαξ [29] and παιδευτής go together, VII, 811d; VIII, 835a. The law itself is an educator, VII, 809a; V, 730b. From birth the laws order the education of the child, as of adults, both physically and mentally, Crito, 50d; 51c. Thus education is fully a matter for the state, Menex., 248d. The Gks. as ἐν νόμοις καὶ ἀνθρώποις τεθραμμένοι are distinguished by their culture from barbarians, who are without παιδεία and every other salutary impulsion to virtue (Prot., 327c d). Children should be as little without διδάσκαλοι and παιδαγωγοί as sheep without shepherds or slaves without masters : ὁ δὲ παῖς πάντων θηρίων δυσμεταχειριστότατον (hardest to handle), Leg. All., VII, 808d. We find the same comparison between man and animal in Resp., I, 335b-c, cf. III, 416a-c. If ἀρετή and ἦθος belong to φύσις, this destroys the sure distinction between man and beast. [30] But the word group παιδεία is used almost exclusively of man, and even the exceptions [31] involve a treatment of animals in human terms. A good education is of great profit to the state : παιδεία ... φέρει καὶ νίκην, νίκη δ᾽ ἐνίοτε ἀπαιδευσίαν, Leg., I, 641c; cf. VII, 803d; VIII, 832d. From this standpt. the Gks. constantly kept before them the Laconian or even the Persian system (cf. Xenoph. Cyrop.), and in this light Plato explains the shifting fortunes of the Persian rulers : ἀρετή and σωφροσύνη are smothered in riches and tyranny, Leg., III, 694-696. There thus arises for the Athenians the democratic ideal of education stated by Plato at the end of the Leg., XII, 969b-c : The ideal state will become a reality ἐὰν ἄρα ἡμῖν οἵ τε ἄνδρες ἀκριβῶς ἐκλεχθῶσι, παιδευθῶσί τε προηκόντως, παιδευθέντες ... φύλακες ἀποτελεσθῶσιν, οἵους ἡμεῖς οὐκ εἴδομεν ἐν τῷ πρόσθεν βίῳ πρὸς ἀρετὴν σωτηρίας γεγομένους, cf., 964c-e. [32] On the basis of his philosophy Plato attacks with particular sharpness the traditional method of education which starts with lying myths, Resp., II, 377a. These throw contempt on the gods and make children worse, 381e. This is certainly contrary to the general evaluation of Hom.: λέγουσιν ὡς τὴν Ἑλλάδα πεπαίδευκεν οὗτος ὁ ποιητής, Resp., X, 606e. But it seems to be a political necessity that public behaviour and the culture imparted to the young should be subject to strict pedagogical and ethical control. μάθησις and ἄσκησις constitute education, Resp., VII, 536b. For Plato's Socrates virtue is also culture, and man's happiness is dependent on παιδεία and δικαιοσύνη, Gorg., 470e. Natural disposition and education (training) bring about the moderation and restriction of desires in joy and suffering, Resp., IV, 431c. Culture also requires personal commitment. Philosophers must dedicate themselves to government and thus sacrifice their contemplative life for society, Resp., VII, 540b.

For Aristot. there can be no doubt that education is a political problem. It must apply to all children, and be regulated by the lawgiver. The content and aim are debated. Is the issue τὰ χρήσιμα πρὸς τὸν βίον ἢ τὰ τείνοντα πρὸς ἀρετήν, or something beyond ? (Pol., VIII, 1, 2, p. 1337a, 11 ff.). At any rate, common education should be the basis of political unity. Better to level the desires of men than their possessions, II, 7, p. 1266b, 30 ff.; cf. II, 5, p. 1263b, 37 and 1264a, 30. If a government is truly good, it will not merely have but also display in its acts true humanity, II, 9, p. 1270b, 37; 1271a, 1; cf. III, 16, p. 1287a, 25 and b, 25. By the same education and habit one becomes both a worthy man and a statesman and ruler, III, 18, p. 1288b, 1; cf. III, 13, p. 1283a, 25; IV, 11, p. 1295a, 27; 1296. In democracy as in aristocracy the eminent are

---

[29] The order of the watchers rests on the selection and esp. the education of a special military caste. It was of wide historical significance. For "in the last resort it is the source of the claim of the modern state authoritatively to regulate the education of its citizens." Cf. Jaeger, II, 282-285.

[30] There is an ἀρετή of dogs and horses, but not of the common man, Jaeger, I, 26.

[31] Though cf. Xenoph. Eq., X, 6. On the relation of training and discipline to παιδεία cf. Jaeger, III, 214.

[32] In the construction of the ideal state Plato demands the rule of the best, so that education of the ruler is for him a decisive concern. But in Aristot. this has direct political significance. The law shapes the ruler, Pol., III, 16, p. 1287a, 25, b, 25 : κρίνει γὰρ ἕκαστος ἄρχων πεπαιδευμένος ὑπὸ τοῦ νόμου καλῶς.

distinguished by wealth, birth, excellence, or culture, IV, 4, p. 1291b, 29; 8, p. 1293b, 37. Habit and education should not lead to the realisation of party desires but to the fulfilment of the existing form of state, V, 9, p. 1310a, 14 ff. As compared with the ruling class, the people is marked by humble origin, poverty and lack of culture, VI, 2, p. 1317b, 39. In Aristot. even more than Plato law is the true pedagogue. Political education is introduction into the political relations created by the legislator. Thus the state attains to radical superiority over the individual; even musical education is a goal of social teaching. [33]

3. ὑπὸ Διὸς παιδεύεσθαι.

The anthropocentric and also individualistic character of rational Greek thinking is comprehensively stated in the well-known principle of Protagoras : "Each man is for himself the measure of things, of those that are, that they are, and of those that are not, that they are not," Plat. Theaet., 152a. This finally stands behind all the paideia of the Greeks, and paideia as a task and goal of the state brings no basic change at this point. But Plato achieves a new and intentionally antithetical formulation : ὁ δὴ θεὸς ἡμῖν πάντων χρημάτων μέτρον ἂν εἴη μάλιστα, καὶ πολὺ μᾶλλον ἤ πού τις ... ἄνθρωπος, Leg., IV, 716c. Here neither individualism nor anthropocentrism is in the last resort abandoned. But a definitive and absolute claim replaces relativism. Thus the necessary transcendent orientation of paideia is discovered. Nevertheless, the introduction of theology, [34] with whose help pupils sought to understand the fundamental law of the Platonic state, did not really liberate Greek thinking from its human, earthly and physico-materialistic connection. [35]

Education for the good presupposes knowledge of the good, which is theology, Resp., II, 379a-c. This is an evident and very natural deduction from the Socratic equation of virtue and culture. [36] The theology of the visible gods (Tim., 40d) is linked with superstition. Thus in Tim., 23d it is said of the city of Athens that the deity ἔλαχε καὶ ἔθρεψε καὶ ἐπαίδευσε it. Nevertheless, professional, political and spiritual education in Plato is wholly rational. Above all human σωφροσύνη, however, stands divinely caused μανία, which μυρία τῶν παλαιῶν ἔργα κοσμοῦσα τοὺς ἐπιγιγνομένους παιδεύει, Phaedr., 245a. In Ps.-Plat. God is the true instructor in self-knowledge somewhat in the sense of the Socratic daemon. Thus the myth of Minos tells how he φοιτᾶν παιδευθησόμενον ὡς ὑπὸ σοφιστοῦ ὄντος τοῦ Διός, Ps.-Plat. Min., 319c; cf. d : ὑπὸ Διὸς πεπαιδεῦσθαι, and 320b : ἦν αὕτη ἡ συνουσία ... διὰ λόγων ἐπὶ παιδείᾳ εἰς ἀρετήν. The myth that the gods τέχνας πρώτους παιδευθησάμενοι established the life of men

---

[33] Three main problems of παιδεία are insoluble for the Gks.: 1. the socio-ethical problem of slavery, 2. the biologico-ethical problem of the family, i.e., the place of women and children, and 3. the theologico-ethical problem of freedom, or death. Nevertheless the Roman state, which inherited and represented Gk. culture, became the educator of mankind by its laws and ordinances.

[34] Plato creates the concept of theology, Jaeger, III, 21.

[35] The παιδεία of God embraces totality. The world soul, which is the divine in Leg., X, is, with its order, the ruling principle of the world. Leg., X, 897b : ψυχὴ ... νοῦν μὲν προσλαβοῦσα ἀεὶ θεὸν ὀρθῶς θεοῖς, ὀρθὰ καὶ εὐδαίμονα παιδαγωγεῖ πάντα. Cf. on this Jaeger, III, 321.

[36] Orientation to the good, which is the divine, establishes a fellowship among men which is stronger and more genuine than any other. Plat. Ep., VII, 334b : οὐ γὰρ διὰ βαναύσου φιλότητος ἐγεγόνει φίλος, διὰ δὲ ἐλευθέρας παιδείας κοινωνίαν, cf. ibid., 345b. This turning to the good and the divine is conversion in the Platonic sense. Thus Resp., VII, 518d speaks of the τέχνη ... τῆς περιαγωγῆς. Here too, then, the history of a Christian concept has its beginning in Plato, though with a material distinction, → μετάνοια IV, 979, 26-980, 11, cf. also 979, 9 ff., the ref. to Ceb. Tab., 11, 1. In the passage adduced from Plato may be seen the ultimate root of the pedagogic technique which gained ground increasingly in the Hellenistic-Roman period.

may also be found in the Platonic tradition (Menex., 238b), and finally there is a certain transcending of pedagogic rationalism : εἰ δ' ἐπὶ τὸ παιδεῦσαι δεῖ τινος, οὔτε ὁ παιδεύσων οὔτε οἱ παιδευθησόμενοι ... εἰσὶν ὑμῖν, ἀλλὰ τὸ λοιπὸν τοῖς θεοῖς εὔχεσθαι, Ep., XI, 359b. The linking of παιδεία, μαντεία and θεραπεία (Ps.-Plat. Epin., 988a) characterises this development. There is nothing more divine for men than deliberation on paideia, Ps.-Plat. Theag., 122b. Here basic instruction in γράμματα, κιθαρίζειν, παλαίειν καὶ τὴν ἄλλην ἀγωνίαν may be presupposed, 122e. But ultimately even in Plato himself the concern is for the nature and cultivation and even the eternal salvation of the soul. Thus we read in Phaed., 107d : οὐδὲν γὰρ ἄλλο ἔχουσα εἰς "Αιδου ἡ ψυχὴ ἔρχεται πλὴν τῆς παιδείας τε καὶ τροφῆς. But this view raises the question how far virtue may be taught. The question is posed in Menon, and the ultimate answer is that things do not depend on the pedagogic measures or on the teachers or parents, since even the best may fail in their attempts to educate their children, Men., 93d-e, 94a, 96d, 99e. But θείᾳ μοίρᾳ ἡμῖν φαίνεται παραγιγνομένη ἡ ἀρετὴ οἷς ἂν παραγίγνηται, 100b. For Aristot. theology has an assured place in the system of sciences, and hence also in paideia, Metaph., V, 1, p. 1026a, 19. In his successors culture becomes a quality which sets men on a level with the gods, for the fruit of paideia is rational planning : τὸ βουλεύεσθαι τῶν περὶ τὸν ἄνθρωπον θειότατόν ἐστιν, Ps.-Aristot. Rhet. Al., 1, p. 1420b, 19 f. For Plato, however, the experiment of Syracuse, where the ruler was to be brought up as a philosopher, showed only too plainly that only in conjunction with a divine dispensation can the ruler be a philosopher or the philosopher a ruler, Ep., VII, 326b, 327e, 336e; Resp., VI, 492a e; IX, 592a.

The παιδεία of the Gks. rounds out human nature, Aristot. Pol., VII, 16, p. 1337a, 2. It is the basis of all πολιτεία (ibid., 11-17), and it fulfils the true destiny of man by directing his strivings to the paradigm and measure of the good, i.e., God, Plat. Resp., VII, 540a; Leg., IV, 716c. [37] If Socrates in Athens and Plato in Syracuse failed in their educational attempts, this does not imply a deficiency in παιδεία but the perfecting of philosophy in necessary suffering face to face with a lack of understanding on the part of those around, Plat. Ep., VII, 350-352; cf. Ps.-Plat. Epin., 973d.

B. Education in the Old Testament.

1. God's Discipline by Law and Wisdom.

Originally the biblical tradition shows no acquaintance with the idea of man's education or religio-ethical development. [38] The people of Israel is chosen by God, and he who does not fall in with the resultant claim on God's part forfeits his life, Gn. 17:14; Ex. 12:15, 19; 31:14; Lv. 7:20, 21, 25, 27; cf. 10:2. Venial sins and offences, however, are expiated by sin and guilt offerings, Lv. 4-7, → III, 306, 24 ff.; 309, 33 ff. Inasmuch as the rules of purity involve specific ordinances, one might speak of habit and education. God is the Holy One, and the Israelite, a member of the chosen people, must be holy to Him, Lv. 20:26. [39] If the substance of education is in some sense present, there is no psychological exposition or development. Hence no pedagogic vocabulary is formed.

In so far as holiness was understood in moral as well as cultic terms, [40] keeping the moral commandment became an obligation for members of the covenant. Man is not alone at this pt., for God helps him. He gives him the commandments, punishes infringements, rewards obedience. God leads His people to the goal appointed by Him. Songs and stories magnifying God's acts, laws and prophetic sayings, stamp and fashion the people of the old covenant as no other people in history has ever been moulded. In

---

[37] Jaeger, III, 320 f., 333 f.

[38] L. Cordier, Evangelische Pädagogik, II, 1, "Die Jugenderziehung von der Christusfrage" (1938), 28 f., 68 f.

[39] The OT figures, esp. the patriarchs, are not educational examples. Only the secularised Judaism of the Hell. period made them such. Cf. G. Bertram, "Das antike Judt. als Missionsreligion," G. and F. Rosen-G. Bertram, Juden u. Phönizier (1929), 61.

[40] B. Stade-A. Bertholet, Bibl. Theol. d. AT, I (1905), 300 f.

particular the Law [41] is an educative force. Short summaries of the Law like the Decalogue (Ex. 20, 34), Torah liturgies (Ps. 15; 24:3-6; Mi. 6:6-8), and also the broader casuistical definition of the Law, regulate the life of the Israelite even to the minutest everyday details, and hedge him in with its ordering, limiting and keeping power (Ps. 119). In everyday life the father is the guardian of the Law. He is the responsible agent of tradition. He must instruct the younger generation, Gn. 18:19; Ex. 12:26; 13:14; Dt. 4:32; 6:7, 20. [42] Thus the Law survives, though in the new forms attested by the different sources, even when the kingdom and the temple are destroyed. The force which sustains and educates both people and individuals abides.

For God's chosen people, with whom He has made His covenant, the Law is the revealed standard of growth in discipline and order, in faith and confidence. There is no broad vocabulary of education. The Heb. OT has a whole series of words for teaching and direction, for chastisement and correction, but only the one word יסר and the derived מוסר can denote "to educate," "education." [43] This word certainly belongs to the same field and can itself denote "rearing" (in the moral, not the biological sphere) as "correction," but it can also take on a more intellectual sense and stand for "culture" in the sense of possession of wisdom, knowledge, and discernment. [44] The word refers to intra-personal action. God deals with men, or men with their fellows. It is not used of animals. In detail different spheres, relations and meanings have to be differentiated in its application, though these often overlap: the education of children which is training and which uses chastisement; the learning which includes intellectual culture; the moral and religious shaping of the righteous which embraces instruction in wisdom but finds its fulfilment in correction by suffering; and finally the training of the people, which has its basis and content in hearing, learning and obeying the divine commandments, but which must often be enforced by severe chastisements. One might also refer to the chastisement of a transgressor as a legal punishment, [45] disciplinary measures against slaves and subjects, [46] and instruction in the sense of imparting specific knowledge. Finally, censure, [47] admonition and warning play a great role in education, and the same root can be used in this special sense.

Acc. to the wisdom teaching preserved, e.g., in Prv., education cannot dispense with corporal punishment: "He that spareth his rod hateth his son: but he that loveth him

---

[41] A. Alt, Die Ursprünge des isr. Rechts (1934), 59-71; G. v. Rad, Das formgeschichtliche Problem des Hexateuchs (1938), 22 f.; M. Noth, Die Gesetze im Pentateuch (1940). The Law is God's claim on the people of His possession with whom He made the covenant. But the Law becomes a human rule of action with a claim to divine reward. Thus the concept of twofold retribution in reward and punishment becomes decisive for the righteous, and links up with the experience of chastisement by God. Hence arises the Jewish view of education developed in the LXX.

[42] Cf. J. Hempel, "Das Ethos d. AT," ZAW, Beih. 67 (1938), 19; J. Benzinger, Hbr. Archäologie³ (1927), 25 f., 129; J. Fichtner, "Zum Problem Glaube u. Geschichte in der isr.-jüdischen Weisheitsliteratur," ThLZ, 76 (1951), 149.

[43] Kraus, 520; L. Köhler, Lexicon in veteris testamenti libros (1950), avoids "educate" even for יסר, and suggests "to correct," "to guide aright," "to chastise," "to guide," etc.; also "chastisement," "training," "admonition" for מוּסָר.

[44] Related on the biological side are esp. גדל pi and אמן, and on the ethical ירה hi (intellectual) and יכח hi (volitional). On גדל pi (and רבה pi) cf. 2 K. 10:6; Is. 1:2; 23:4; 49:21; 51:18; Ez. 19:2; Hos. 9:12; Lam. 2:22; Da. 1:5. אֹמֵן means "guardian," Nu. 11:12; 2 K. 10:1, 5; Is. 49:23; 2 S. 4:4; Rt. 4:16; Est. 2:7. LXX usually has ἐκτρέφω for גְּדֵּל (τιθηνός for אֹמֵן) and only once at Da. 1:5 ἐκπαιδεύω.

[45] Cf. Dt. 21:18; 22:18.

[46] Cf. 1 K. 12:11, 14; 2 Ch. 10:11, 14. With ref. to the sanctions behind subjects it is perhaps said of God in Job 12:18: "He looseth the discipline of kings," unless we are to read מוֹסֵר "bond," "fetter" (from אסר), cf. Hos. 5:2.

[47] יִסּוֹר, from יסר, in the sense of "faultfinder," is used with מוכיחַ "accuser," with ref. to Job in God's reply, Job 40:2.

chasteneth him betimes," Prv. 13:24; cf. 29:15; Sir. 22:3. For correction keeps from
worse things, even death, 23:13. It gives hope of amendment, 19:18. But it must be in
love, not anger. It drives out folly, 22:15. It gives joy and refreshment to the educator
(29:17) and life to the one who receives it (4:13). These sayings bear witness to the
responsibility of the father and mother for their children. Thus Scripture admonishes at
the outset in Prv. 1:8 : "My son, hear the instruction of thy father, and forsake not the
law of thy mother." [48] The words of Lemuel in 31:1 are also traced back to the teaching
or training of his mother. Similarly, the mirror of the prince given there serves to train
a prince.

In the Wisdom literature of Israel and Judah, however, the ref. is not just to the
education of children but to the cultivation of the character of adults acc. to the norm
of *sapiens et eloquens pietas* which finally derives from this literature. Fear of God is
the beginning of knowledge, while fools despise wisdom and culture, Prv. 1:7; cf. 15:33.
The goal of instruction is "to learn wisdom and discipline, to understand intelligible
speech, to attain to wholesome discipline, righteousness, duty and integrity, to teach
cleverness to the simple, knowledge and circumspection to the boy. Let the wise man
hear and increase his wisdom, and the man of understanding find guidance," Prv. 1:2 ff. [49]
It is plain that the ref. is to practical moral training rather than purely intellectual education. The commandment is a lamp and wisdom a light, and training gives direction
on the way of life, 6:23; cf. 16:22; 10:17. The ref. here is undoubtedly to a discipline
and education voluntarily and independently accepted, 12:1; 13:1; 19:20, 27; 23:12;
15:32, 33. Only a fool will reject his father's advice, 15:5. For poverty and shame pursue
the despiser of instruction, 13:18. Thus the lazy man with his neglected property is a
warning to others, 24:32. מוסר is here commonly associated with other terms. In particular, תוכחת is often a par. in the sense of "correction," "censure." Culture and
knowledge are more costly than silver or gold, 8:10, cf. 8:33. There is certainly no
sense in wasting the work of education on despisers and transgressors, 9:7. The transgressor even rejects God's discipline.

All discipline comes ultimately from God. Its authority is grounded in Him. If this
theonomous character does not always emerge in Prv., this is linked with the history
of these Wisdom sayings. [50] The community of the old covenant understands them
increasingly of the saving work of its God. The verse in Prv. 3:11, which is so significant in the passion theology of both Judaism and Christianity, is only one plain example
of this. [51] Here, in accordance with the religious character of the practical wisdom of
Israel, the fear of Yahweh and trust in Him are said to be the basis and content of
all instruction, and an express warning is given against one's own reason and wisdom,
3:5 ff.; cf. Is. 5:21. The Ps. often speak of Yahweh's own discipline and correction. He
it is who admonishes through the conscience, Ps. 16:7. Chastisement corresponding to

---

[48] Cf. B. Gemser, *Sprüche Salomos* = *Handbuch z. AT*, I, 16 (1937) on Prv. 1:8.

[49] Cf. Gemser, *ad loc.* On the last clause cf. LXX κυβέρνησιν κτήσεται. תַּחְבֻּלוֹת is from
חֶבֶל "measure," and means "canon," "rule," "direction." The ref. is not to the direction
taken by the man of understanding, but to his direction by the words of God to which
he gives himself. The relation is that of grace, not law. The opp. is προαίρεσις πνεύματος, "self-will," Qoh. 1:14, 17; 2:11, 22, 26; 4:4, 6, 16; 6:9. Cf. on this G. Bertram, "Hebr.
u. gr. Qohelet. Ein Beitrag zur Theologie d. hell. Bibel," ZAW, NF, 22 (1951), esp. the
last section. In Wisdom teaching the education of children merges into adult culture.

[50] W. Baumgartner, *Isr. u. altorientalische Weisheit* (1933); also "Die isr. Weisheitsliteratur," ThR, NF, 5 (1933), 259-288. Wisdom, discipline and piety are contrasted with
folly, indiscipline and godlessness. God's will is the authority behind all admonition and
warning, Prv. 6:16 ff. W. Zimmerli, "Zur Struktur d. at.lichen Weisheit," ZAW, NF, 10
(1933), 177-204; J. Fichtner, *Die altorientalische Weisheit in ihrer israelitisch-jüdischen Ausprägung* (1933), 79-97.

[51] Humble acceptance of and subjection to the discipline of suffering is a mark of the
righteous, Ps. 118:21; 119:71 etc. On 119:75 cf. B. Heyne, "Zu Ps. 119:75 und 67," ZAW,
NF, 10 (1933), 312.

the sin would destroy man, Ps. 39:11. Hence the request : "Neither chasten me in thy hot displeasure," Ps. 6:1; 38:1; → 405, 7-20. And the righteous man confesses : "The Lord hath chastened me sore, but he hath not given me over unto death," Ps. 118:18. Thus it may finally be said : "Blessed is the man whom thou chastenest, O Lord, and teachest him out of thy law," 94:12. This is the view of Eliphaz the Temanite : "Happy is the man whom God correcteth (יכח); therefore despise not thou the chastening of the Almighty," Job 5:17. To Job, of course, the statements of his friends are insulting censure, since his guilt is presupposed, 20:3, cf. 36:10. [52] In the Ps. mentioned, as in Job, we thus find the same ideas about God's correction as in the wisdom sayings of Prv. God is the stern Judge who punishes and chastises. But He does so as a Father who in love severely disciplines His children. God's demanding and educating power also extends beyond the confines of the covenant people to the Gentile world : "He that chastiseth the heathen, shall not he correct, he that teacheth man knowledge ?" Ps. 94:10. [53] The same claim is to be seen in Ps. 2:10 : "Be instructed, ye judges of the earth."

2. God's Discipline in the Prophetic Revelation.

In the Wisdom writings, in keeping with the spirit of the works, discipline and correction are related to teaching and instruction. In the prophets, however, the ref. is to God's acts in the history of the people and peoples. Under God's discipline is not merely the individual, but the chosen people as a whole in all its chances and providences. Discipline is the point of the Law. In this light the essentials of the prophetic proclamation are to be understood. Thus Hosea already announces the people's chastisement by God, 10:10, cf. 7:12, 15. [54] In Hos. 10:12 the only possible meaning is : "Break up more broken ground . . ., until he comes to teach you righteousness." Here, then, the correction of the people by deportation seems to precede the teaching of Yahweh. But prophetic proclamation rests on Yahweh's direction, which gives the man of God a correct insight, opposed to all popular opinions and desires, into the course of historical events. This is the experience of Is. (8:11). The best introduction to his theology of history is the parable of the husbandman whom God instructs (28:26). [55] As the husbandman does not always do the same thing, so Yahweh's (educative) dealings with His people do not follow a single pattern. [56] To the pre-exilic period also belongs Zephaniah with his lament over Jerusalem, which will not receive instruction, 3:2, 7. [57] In a special way the word of correction is given impressive monitory force by such political events as the destruction of Jerusalem and the deportations. To the same effect is the historical understanding of a Jeremiah. The sin and apostasy of the people bring down chastisement and punishment upon it, 2:19. But all correction is futile in face of the resistance of those to whom it applies, 2:30; 5:3; 7:28; 17:23. Yahweh has untiringly given instruction to His people, but they have accepted no admonition, discipline, or correction, 32:33. Hence the warnings of the prophets have all been in vain, 6:8; 35:13. The prophet's

---

[52] Cf. G. Hölscher, Das Buch Hiob = Handbuch z. AT, I, 17 (1937), on 33:16.

[53] H. Gunkel, Die Ps.⁴ (1926), on 94:10 (415): "We are not to think in terms of true education, nor should the universalism of the saying be pressed or even compared with Paul" (R. 1:20; 2:14 f.), though cf. H. Schmidt, Die Ps. = Handbuch z. AT, I, 15 (1934), ad loc. On the wisdom of the Ps. cf. H. L. Jansen, D. spätjüdische Psalmendichtung (1937).

[54] Hos. 5:2 (→ supra), H. Guthe in Kautzsch reads מוֹסֵר "fetter" for מוּסָר. T. H. Robinson emends to מְיַסֵּר acc. to the LXX, T. H. Robinson-F. Horst, Die 12 kleinen Propheten, Handbuch z. AT, I, 14 (1938). For Amos cf. E. Würthwein, "Amos-Studien," ZAW, NF, 21 (1949/50), 40-49.

[55] On the so-called invention sagas → ἔργον, II, 648, 18 ff.

[56] From a later hand comes the saying Is. 26:16 in the so-called Isaianic apocalypse (24:27): "Yahweh, in the affliction of thy visitation were we afraid of the oppression of thy chastisement which smote us" (acc. to H. Guthe in Kautzsch).

[57] Though the juxtaposition of threat and promise in 3:1-20 is attributed to redaction (cf. F. Horst, ad loc.), the words themselves come from the prophet. Cf. also Jer. 7:28.

petition is too late : "O Lord, correct me, but with judgment ; not in thine anger, lest thou bring me to nothing," 10:24. For we read in 30:14 : "I have struck thee with the blow of an enemy, with cruel chastisement." There can be no question now of educative punishment nor of a father-son relation. Nevertheless, the promise is given in 30:11 (cf. 46:28): "For I am with thee, saith the Lord, to save thee : though I make a full end of all the nations whither I have scattered thee, yet will I not make a full end of thee : but I will correct thee in measure, and will not leave thee altogether unpunished." [58] But now Ephraim repents bitterly and renews his confession of Yahweh who corrected him, 31:18. In Ez. the word group occurs only twice at 5:15 [59] and 23:48 in the sense of "warning" and "to be warned." An important verse in the Ebed Yahweh songs is Is. 53:5 : [60] "The chastisement which brings us peace was upon him, and by his stripes there was healing for us." The ref. here is to vicarious chastisement, and the statement, taken up into the passion theology of Judaism, impressed itself on Jewish piety in the experience of believers during many a time of persecution, and finally found in Jesus Christ its fulfilment in salvation history.

The OT depiction of history shows how the prophetic admonitions and warnings about the chastisement of the people by God came into effect in the events of political history. The whole story of the people is presented here from the standpoint of education : As a father instructs his son so does Yahweh His people, Dt. 8:5; cf. Is. 1:2. The wilderness experiences esp. promoted this education, Dt. 11:2. [61] Yahweh Himself guided and tended His people from heaven, Dt. 4:36. Again and again He chastised the people for their sins, Lv. 26:18-28. The context shows that these are chastisements, while the miraculous deliverances in the desert are to be regarded as education acc. to Dt. 11:2. On this interpretation it should not be forgotten, however, that in the original the same word מוּסָר is used, as constantly in other places, so that one can hardly make a sharp distinction of meaning. Obviously the OT has chiefly in view the negative aspect of education, and only in Dt. is there even the beginning of a comprehensive subordination of the whole of salvation history to the concept of education.

Since Israel, in keeping with ancient oriental thought, is often depicted as an individual, there is no difficulty in applying the essentially individual concept of education to the people. God treats and educates His people with severity and yet also with kindness, as a father does his son. At the same time, there also apply to righteous individuals the views of education found in the ancient Wisdom literature, which was present in Israel from the days of Solomon, and which increasingly in the post-exilic period became a special feature of the moral and religious culture of the Jews. [62] In this connection, it was never forgotten on the soil of OT revelation that the reference is not to the individual in self-asserted autonomy, but to the individual as a member of the chosen people, to which are addressed God's promises and requirements, which hold up the holiness of God as a criterion of life for the children of Israel.

---

[58] F. Giesebrecht, *Das Buch Jeremia*², Handkomm. z. AT, III, 2, 1 (1907), ad loc.; cf. W. Rudolph, *Jer.*, Handbuch z. AT, I, 12 (1947), ad loc.

[59] In Ez. 5:15 the fate of Jerusalem should serve as a warning to the Gentiles ; in 23:48 the warning is to the women of the land, cf. A. Bertholet, *Hesekiel*, Handbuch z. AT, I, 13 (1936), ad loc.

[60] Cf. K. F. Euler, "D. Verkündigung vom leidenden Gottesknecht aus Js. 53 in d. griech. Bibel," BWANT, 4, F. 14 (1934), 63-65.

[61] Cf. on this K. Marti in Kautzsch : "The education of Yahweh is explained by the following objects : it consisted in the experiences which Israel had on the exodus from Egypt and in the desert, esp. also in the punishments for disobedience ; cf. a similar view of the significance of the wilderness journey in 8:2-6." But the miracles of salvation experienced by the people are also part of the education as well as the punishments. Thus the ref. is to education and not just to correction or chastisement ; cf. Kraus, op. cit., 521.

[62] L. Cordier, op. cit., 58, 67.

3. The Reconstruction of the Concept in the Greek Translation of the Old Testament.

Experience of the discipline and correction of both individual and people by Yahweh does not affect the theocentric character of the OT revelation. Nevertheless, in so far as Yahweh is now presented as the Educator of His people, in so far as He teaches and admonishes and warns through the prophets, the OT message acquires a more anthropocentric ref. [63] This applies everywhere in the OT where moral, social and pedagogic questions are raised. The many attempts to solve the problem of theodicy, in which suffering is viewed as punishment, testing, or a means of discipline and education, seem to lead away from the theocentric character of OT piety by raising anthropological questions. In this respect the irrational idea of testing does most justice to the mystery of God's rule, [64] whereas ideas of discipline, education and development tend to see God too readily in human terms. [65] Hence these notions belong materially to the margin of biblical piety, and the number and nature of the relevant statements indicate the secondary significance of these trains of thought, which were often so important in later Christianity. [66] Nevertheless, they find expression in the Gk. transl. of the OT, and the Gk. term παιδεία is the linguistic means which enables the translators to give a pedagogic interpretation of salvation history. The Gk. words παιδεία and παιδεύειν are mostly used for מוסר and יסר. Herewith the Gk. terms acquire a new and originally almost alien significance. παιδεία takes on the sense of discipline and chastisement. [67] On the other hand, the OT text is permeated by the intellectual element of culture, education and instruction to a much greater degree than may be said of the original.

a. In the Wisdom Literature. The setting for pedagogic thinking in the Wisdom literature is the discipline exercised by the father *vis-à-vis* his children and household. In detail, there are in the LXX many softenings as compared with the original. Thus at Prv. 17:21 a positive addition is made to the negative formulations of the Mas., though here, as at Sir. 42:5, παιδεία is to be rendered "correction." The Gk. term has fully adapted itself to the original. At Prv. 29:19 the LXX limits the principle that verbal instruction is not enough for a slave, to the obdurate slave : λόγοις οὐ παιδευθήσεται οἰκέτης σκληρός. Elsewhere, too, the LXX uses παιδεύειν for "to chastise," even when the HT does not demand it, as at Dt. 22:18; 2 Esr. 7:26, and with another word at the corresponding 1 Esr. 8:24, where the LXX introduces the punishment of chastisement. In the rules for sovereigns in Sir. 10:1 [68] and 37:23, however, παιδεύειν has more the sense of "education." This is esp. true in the second instance, esp. as נחכם is rendered παιδεύειν.

The religious use of παιδεία for chastisement by God corresponds fully to the secular use. What is said about God the Educator in the basic verse Dt. 8:5 is more broadly

---

[63] G. Bertram, "Der anthropozentrische Charakter d. Septuagintafrömmigkeit," *Forschungen u. Fortschritte*, 8 (1932), 219.

[64] A. Sommer, *Der Begriff d. Versuchung im AT u. im Judt.* (1935); J. H. Korn, *Peirasmos. Die Versuchung d. Gläubigen in d. griech. Bibel* (1937), 13, 48-88; W. Hasenzahl, *Die Gottverlassenheit d. Christus nach dem Kreuzeswort bei Mt. u. Mk. u. das christologische Verständnis des griech. Psalters* (1937), 102-148.

[65] G. Bertram, "Religion in der Bibel. Zur Vermenschlichung d. bibl. Offenbarung," *Kirche im Angriff*, 12 (1936), 89-103; also "Die Aufgabe einer bibl. Theologie beider Testamente," *ibid.*, 416-427.

[66] The root יסר occurs some 85 times in the HT. We find the verb 8 times in the Pentateuch and the noun once, the verb 12 times in the prophets and the noun 14 times, the verb 15 times in the hagiographa and the noun 36 times.

[67] The possibility of a change in meaning in the transl. Gk. of the OT was afforded by popular Hell. usage, cf. → 600, 13 ff.

[68] R. Smend, *Die Weisheit d. Jesus Sirach erklärt* (1906), 89, regards the Gk. text as original and corrects the HT accordingly.

developed in Prv. 3:11 f. [69] The LXX here presupposes education by suffering. Thus in place of the HT וּכְאָב ("and like a father") it reads a form of the root כאב in the hi ("to cause sorrow"), [70] which it renders by μαστιγοῦν. The parallelism of παιδεύει and μαστιγοῖ shows that παιδεία κυρίου in v. 11 unequivocally means the discipline of suffering. If the LXX is here propounding a basic concept of Jewish passion piety in contrast to the HT, the translator usually keeps to the HT and in Job, the Ps. and the few prophetic passages expresses the thought of the discipline or chastisement of individuals or the people by God. [71]

Nevertheless, under stronger Hell. influence the term brings in ideas of culture which are characteristic of Hell. Judaism [72] with its susceptibility to secularisation. Thus Judaism endorses foreign pagan culture when it ascribes it to Daniel (1:20) or Moses (Ac. 7:22). To be well brought up or educated in the secular sense is the ideal of many Wisdom sayings. Prv. and Sir. are permeated by constantly renewed praise of wisdom. Prv. introduces the παιδεία πατρός and admonishes the son to accept it, 1:8; 4:1, 13; 15:5; 19:20, 27; 28:7. The interest of the Gk. translators here is not in discipline or chastisement, but in intellectual instruction. [73]

The father is important only as the representative of tradition. Behind him stands the true authority, the almost mythical figure of wisdom. This is not identical with *ratio,* with human reason. It rests on revelation : "God has taught me wisdom, and I have attained to knowledge of the Holy One," Prv. 30:3 [74] LXX, presupposing וְאֵל לַמְּדֻנִי Culture and revelation are united, so that Sir. 1:27 can say : σοφία γὰρ καὶ παιδεία φόβος κυρίου, the meaning of φόβος κυρίου being "religion." [75] Here παιδεία is God's gift in the teaching of the Law and the education of life. Discipline and correction are integrated into and subordinated to the OT view of paideia, and it is possible to speak of correction through wisdom, [76] Sir. 4:17. Here is manifest the irrational and numinous element which in the OT is associated with sophia and also paideia. Acc. to the HT the first half of the verse refers to the attitude of wisdom, which initially disguises itself (hitp of נכר) so that it cannot be recognised. But acc. to the LXX the path of the disciples of wisdom is winding. Thus the way in which wisdom educates men corresponds to the wonderful dealings of God with men, which bring human wisdom to nothing, cf. Is. 29:14. [77]

At Sir. 23:2 [78] the LXX introduces παιδεία as the logical subj.; from it the scourge and chastisement come. The righteous man prays for παιδεία σοφίας. It is not wholly

---

[69] The verse Prv. 3:12 is quoted with ψ 117:18 and 140:4 in 1 Cl., 56, 3 and 4 : "Thus saith the holy word ..." Cf. E. Hatch, *Essays in Biblical Gk.* (1889), 207.

[70] So already H. Grotius, Annotationes in NT (ed. C. E. v. Windheim, II [1757]) on Hb. 12:6; cf. Job 5:18.

[71] Moore, II, 248-256.

[72] A. Wendel, *Säkularisierung in Israels Kultur* (1934), 330 ff., 387.

[73] With intellectualisation there may be detected a stronger legalistic emphasis, cf. C. H. Dodd, *The Bible and the Greeks* (1935), 79 f.

[74] Gemser, *op. cit.* emends the Mas. along the lines of the LXX. But there is no compelling reason for this. It is not even necessary to introduce v. 3b with a question (C. Steuernagel in Kautzsch, *ad loc.*). The meaning is that human understanding cannot attain to the nature and essence of God. But the LXX here appeals to God as the Teacher.

[75] Thus יִרְאַת אֱלֹהִים in Gn. 20:11 is rendered θεοσέβεια, → θεοσεβής, III, 124, 36 ff.

[76] On the relation between σοφία and παιδεία → 615, 13 ff.

[77] Cf. also Is. 28:21, and on this → ἔργον, II, 640, 44 ff. → βασανίζω, I, 562, 39 ff. echoes the basic meaning "to test the genuineness." Nevertheless, it is to be noted here, too, that paideia means sorrow, cf. → n. 51, Vulgate and exc. "Leiden als Züchtigung Gottes," Mi. Hb.⁸, 297 f.

[78] Acc. to Smend, *ad loc.* As may be seen from the Syr. transl., the HT had שבט מוסר. By putting παιδεία σοφίας for this, the LXX seems to presuppose the allegorical interpretation carried to such extreme lengths in Philo, → 614, 20 ff. If so, παιδεία σοφίας (as against V. Ryssel in Kautzsch Apkr. u. Pseudepigr., *ad loc.*) is to be taken always in the sense of correction, as in 4:17. Cf. Prv. 22:15 HT (LXX ῥάβδος δὲ καὶ παιδεία).

clear whether the request is that he be kept from sins or punished for them betimes. In the former case instruction is sought from wisdom, in the latter chastisement. From the time of the Maccabees (cf., e.g., 2 Macc. 6:12, 16; 7:33; 10:4; 4 Macc. 10:10) there is ref. to the discipline of suffering, i.e., to suffering as educative punishment. Wis. and Ps. Sol. offer examples. [79] The mercy of the father and the wrath of the judge and king combine in this concept of God. For the righteous, sufferings are an educative and purgative punishment. The one promotes amendment, the other is an anticipation of eschatological punishment. But in the actualities of life prior to the last judgment it is not easy to distinguish the chastisement of the righteous from judgment on the wicked : unenlightened (ἀπαίδευτοι) souls have fallen into error at this pt., Wis. 17:1. σοφία and παιδεία are necessary for right understanding. Thus in Wis. παιδεία sometimes has an intellectualistic sense, 7:14; 3:11. The term always denotes not only correction, but the pious understanding of disciplinary suffering. Thus we have in Wis. 6:17-19 the climax : ἀρχὴ γὰρ αὐτῆς (σοφίας) ἡ ἀληθεστάτη παιδείας ἐπιθυμία, φροντὶς δὲ παιδείας ἀγάπη, ἀγάπη δὲ τήρησις νόμων αὐτῆς, προσοχὴ δὲ νόμων βεβαίωσις ἀφθαρσίας, ἀφθαρσία δὲ ἐγγὺς εἶναι ποιεῖ θεοῦ. [80] Desire for teaching is rewarded by true education, 6:11. Wis. 1:5 speaks of ἅγιον πνεῦμα παιδείας in this sense. In general Wis. has adopted the cultural ideal of the Hell. world, but it has filled it out with experience of the divine discipline, and this has led it to a solution to the problem of theodicy : God, the merciful, becomes the Educator of His people.

b. In the Psalms. The ref. here is almost always to correction or education by God, or to instruction concerning His will. The LXX brings in the concept of paideia in the sense of chastisement in the well-known v. Ps. 2:12 : δράξασθε παιδείας. [81] Only an anon. transl. has the similar but more intellectualistic understanding : ἐπιλάβεσθε ἐπιστήμης. The Lat. rendering obviously follows the LXX. All the other transl. presuppose the Heb. In 2:10 σύνετε and παιδεύθητε ('Α ἐπιστημώθητε), the admonition to cleverness and that to discipline, are obviously combined intentionally. In ψ 17:34, cf. 2 Βασ. 22:36, the Gk. renderings in various ways replace the theological statement by one which is more anthropologically orientated. In Θ παιδεία has a more intellectualistic nuance. The verb, or words associated with it, can yield a similar intellectualistic understanding at Ps. 94(93):10, 12, cf. Job 5:17; Ps. 119(118):66; [82] Ps. 50(49):16, 17. In the Ps., too, the noun παιδεία is used more in the Hell. sense of culture and education, while the verb has more of the biblical sense of discipline and correction. In the main these verses may be grouped with the proverbial wisdom of the OT.

c. In the Prophetic Writings. There is often a more important difference between the LXX and the HT in the prophetic writings, where the word is introduced by the LXX at precisely the decisive pt. in relation to the problem of paideia. In the Gk. of Jer. παιδεύειν and παιδεία commonly have the sense of "to discipline," "discipline." More

---

[79] Cf. Moore, II, esp. 225, also Str.-B., III, 445 (with bibl.) and Bousset-Gressm., 385 f.: "As there (with much speaking and confession of grace) the heaping up of words and emphatic expression betray inner uncertainty, so the same uncertainty is displayed here in the many attempts to establish the relation between gentle mercy and almighty justice."

[80] On the chain syllogism cf. J. Fichtner, Weisheit Salomos, Handbuch z. AT II, 6 (1938), ad loc. (27). Wis. is an apocalyptic Wisdom book. The apoc. and chokmatic goals are related. By instruction (παιδεία) in wisdom the work seeks to protect readers against the last judgment. Cf. J. Fichtner, "Die Stellung der Sap. Sal. in d. Lit.- u. Geistesgeschichte ihrer Zeit," ZNW, 36 (1937), 127.

[81] F. Wutz, Die Ps. textkrit. untersucht (1925), 4, thinks the Heb. original is נשו דובר, The word דובר (disciplina, rectio, mores, ratio agendi) is deduced from the Syr. But the method of deducing unattested Heb. words from transcriptions is open to radical criticism, cf. G. Bertram, "Das Problem d. Umschrift u. d. religionsgeschichtliche Erforschung d. LXX," ZAW, Beih. 66 (1936), 101. If with A. Bertholet in Kautzsch and H. Schmidt, op. cit., we keep to the consonants of the HT, there is no explanation of the LXX text.

[82] παιδεία is used here for טעם, "taste," "sensibility," "understanding," which is rendered γεῦμα in 'Α and Σ, but in the Vulgate, obviously on the basis of the LXX, disciplina.

plainly even than the HT the LXX presents God's dealings with the people from the standpoint of correction. The Heb. phrase מוּסָר לָקַח is often slightly changed in the Gk. (Prv. 16:17; Sir. 32:14; 51:26; cf. Prv. 24:32). In Jer. we find in the first part (2:30; 5:3; 7:28; 17:23; cf. Zeph. 3:2, 7) δέξασθαι παιδείαν, in the second (39[32]:33; 42[35]:13) λαβεῖν παιδείαν. At Is. 53:5 the LXX transl. lit.: παιδεία εἰρήνης ἡμῶν ἐπ' αὐτόν. [83] This seems to have been influenced by the rendering of Is. 9:6, 7 in ΣΘ. παιδεία means "chastisement" here. The ref. is to the vicarious suffering of punishment, so that there can be no question of education. In Is. 53:5 LXX; Is. 9:6, 7 ΣΘ, the Gk. term takes on a sense alien to the Gk. spirit. It becomes a tt. for passion. In Ez. is used only once for מוּסָר at 5:15 Θ; the LXX uses it at 13:9 for סוֹד, "fellowship," "secret." [84] The LXX assumes that the task of the true prophet is to educate the people by means of the divine wisdom revealed to him. The prophets are thus grouped with the teachers of wisdom, cf. Mt. 23:34; Lk. 11:49. Acc. to Ez. 13:9 LXX the prophets have not fulfilled this task : "They have not shared in the education of my people." παιδεία is also used for סוֹד at Am. 3:7. The Mas. reads : "Surely the Lord God does nothing, unless he has revealed his secret (סוֹד) to his servants the prophets." [85] But the LXX thinks in terms of God's plan of education which is declared to the prophets. The content of revelation is thus concerned with the education of the people, though there is no thought of the education of the human race in this connection. Ref. may also be made to the correction of other nations, Ps. 2:12, also Ez. 28:3, where the LXX introduces the term in a sense hardly consonant with revelation. Fundamentally, however, the concept of education presupposes in the OT the belief in election. Education by God is a gift of grace allotted only to God's people.

The occasional use in the prophets (cf., e.g., Hos. 7:12, 14; 10:10) [86] shows that the view of history held by the transl. disposes them inwardly towards the concept of education. When used of God יסר can have such varied senses as "to warn," "to correct," "to chastise," "to educate." But the Gk. παιδεύειν always suggests the education of children even though the means can run the whole range from instruction to chastisement. Hence it occurs continually in the Law (Lv. 26:18, 23, 28; Dt. 4:36; 8:5), sometimes for other Heb. words. In using it thus, the LXX is simply following up the hint in the fundamental v. at Dt. 11:2 (→ n. 61). All the experiences of Israel after the exodus were thus gradually brought under the concept of παιδεία. The LXX finally states this plainly in Hos. 5:2 : ἐγὼ δὲ παιδευτὴς ὑμῶν. The Mas. has מוּסָר but, even though it defies the context and perhaps the original HT, [87] the LXX, displaying a creative understanding of the OT, expresses an influential concept of Jewish piety when it describes God as the Educator of His people.

d. In the Presentation of History. Here the thought naturally refers to God's dealings with His people, to all the varied happenings which befall the chosen people and righteous individuals. But the people of the teaching tradition, [88] of the Law and Wisdom

---

[83] Cf. Euler, op. cit., 24, 63 f., 116.

[84] סוֹד occurs 21 times in the HT, and 12 different words are used for it in the LXX. In 'A and Σ the transl. is more uniform, though other words are found here too. Acc. to H. Schmidt, Die grossen Propheten, Die Schriften des AT, II, 2² (1923), the Mas. at Ez. 13:9 runs : "I stretch out my hand against the prophets who see delusions and speak lies. They shall not be in the council of my people ..."

[85] Acc. to H. Guthe in Kautzsch. Apart from the tenses ("will do," "reveals") Robinson agrees, but not H. W. Robinson, Inspiration and Revelation in the OT (1946), 164-169. Perhaps LXX read another word for סוֹדוֹ, e.g., מִזְמֹר, cf. Schleusner, s.v. [T. W. Manson].

[86] Here and in Ps. 105(104):22 there is confusion of אסר and יסר.

[87] Robinson, ad loc. emends acc. to the LXX. But since מוֹסֵר fits the context better it is suggested for מוּסָר by O. Procksch in BHK³ and H. Guthe in Kautzsch.

[88] In the intr. to the section on the synagogue Moore, I, 281-289 underlines the gradually increasing emphasis on teaching in Jewish religion.

literature, could hardly avoid thinking of God as the Teacher, as the Author and Mediator of all these traditions. For Hell. Judaism the very content and meaning of the Gk. word for education involved the inclination toward a more intellectual understanding of the education of the Jewish people by God. Certainly the heavy blows in the period of the conflict of faith promoted the interpretation of history in the sense of paideia. But the happenings to the patriarchs kept alive in the tradition, and ultimately the Law itself and all the commandments contained therein or attached thereto, were for Judaism means of education received from the hand of God. The Law is the educator of the pious Jew and the Jewish community. Nevertheless, the Law is called this only once, and that in a passage in which Judaism vindicates itself to itself and the world by adapting itself to the forms of this world, 4 Macc. 5:34 : παιδευτὰ νόμε.

The Law became the basis of Jewish culture in both the spiritual and also the secular sense. The claim to culture in later Judaism is universalistic ; hence the Law is the book of education for all mankind. In respect of the Law Judaism confronts the world with a supreme claim to culture, Sir Prol. 3; 39:8; 4 Macc. 5:24; 13:22, 24. In the discipline of the Law Judaism finds life and bliss, Sir. 24:27: ὁ [νόμος] ἐκφαίνων ὡς φῶς παιδείαν. [89]

C. The Paideia Concept in Hellenistic and Rabbinic Judaism.

1. παιδεία and νόμος in Philo.

Philo's works are permeated by the thought of paideia. The word group is one of the many concepts which form for Hellenistic Judaism a bridge between OT revelation and Gk. culture. Philo is particularly concerned to sum up in the idea the intellectual content of the OT tradition for the educated man of his age, and therewith to make it accessible and intelligible. At the same time he uses the group to try to prove the unconditional superiority of the OT revelation, of the Mosaic legislation, and consequently of Judaism too. Even if only for propagandist reasons, he thus arrives at a theologico-philosophical form of the paideia concept which might well be described also in terms of salvation history. [90]

For Philo παιδεία is primarily the education and culture of the individual and people. He has in mind the general culture which transcends and gathers up specialised training

---

[89] In this classification our concern is material rather than chronological. Neither in the Heb. OT nor the LXX is there a discipline of the father without the Law, or of the Law without God. On the other hand, there is no ref. whatever to the power of the state, which is so decisive for the παιδεία of the Gks. Scribal learning, and therewith Jewish paideia, were independent even of the hierarchy of the post-exilic period. God's "mediator" is not the priest but the head of the house, who must become a scribe in order to fulfil his task of educating (cf. → 604, 5 ff.), develops the teacher, the rabbi. Among the Gks. it is hardly possible to distinguish education by the father from that by the law or divinity, since divinity is simply the human sublimated. For the Gks. education is the self-unfolding of the individual, and the *polis*, too, has only a ministering function. But since the state exists for education, this fact gives it the power ultimately to depress the individual to the level of the masses. In the OT God alone is the Educator. The head of the house and the Law are simply His instruments. Education is discipline under God's commandment. Only in the NT does tension arise between the limited human possibility of the earthly father and the sphere of the Law on the one side, and the divinely achieved consummation of creation by the revelation of the spirit of divine sonship on the other. The bridges between the OT and philosophical paideia were built by Hell. Judaism (Philo of Alex.). Here the Gk. idea of culture is carried over into the OT in the form of cultivation of the soul. The patriarchs of the OT become types of a specific attitude of soul.

[90] Philo is a politician because he is a Jew who believes in the Messiah. Cf. G. Bertram, "Zur Philoforschung," ThLZ, 64 (1939), 193-197.

and which consists in the moral establishment of character and the fulfilment of man's nature as *humanitas*. Then it is for him philosophical education, which combines basic knowledge, discernment, the search for a clear view of the world and God, and the resultant practical wisdom. In this connection he is concerned to present the OT righteous as representatives of paideia. Finally, he seeks spiritual as well as intellectual culture. παιδεία becomes a hypostasis, [91] and as such brings about the unfolding of the human spirit in both individuals and peoples. It is the grace and gift of God and reveals its secret only to the pious and purified spirit. Certainly in all this the intellectualistic character of the Gk. understanding of paideia seems to be dominant. In fact, however, there flows into the Gk. form the spirit of the OT, the will of God which calls and renews man, and which comprises Law and promise. Hence the concept is for Philo the agent and mediator of the OT revelation in the Gk. world. Only in Christianity, and even there only in the course of centuries, did this combination of OT content and Gk. form exert a historical influence. Thus Philo's ref. of the paideia concept to salvation history is a first form of the Christian, if not the NT, view of education. Judaism, however, rejected and denied his life-work right up to the threshold of the modern era.

In shaping education Philo borrowed from the traditions of the world around him. Parents are their children's benefactors. They have given them life and care for their τροφή and παιδεία ἡ κατά τε σῶμα καὶ ψυχήν, [92] Spec. Leg., II, 229. Since children are born in the house and their parents pay for their upkeep and education, for nurses, pedagogues etc., they belong to their parents like slaves. In this thesis (233) the patriarchal conditions of the OT are loosely combined with the principles of Hell. law. The authority of the father over the child, which in the OT is based upon and limited by the divine order of creation (Dt. 21:18-21), is here given the form of an autonomous right of human possession. Education is a human achievement rather than a divine gift. Education itself ends with coming of age : γένεσις, τροφή, παιδεία, ἀρχή, Vit. Mos., II, 1, cf. Flacc., 158. But παιδεία also embraces the cultivation and self-education of the adult, e.g., by foreign travel, Abr., 65, or even by keeping sheep [93] in preparation for a royal calling, Vit. Mos., I, 62. Possession of culture is man's pack on the way, Rer. Div. Her., 274. Education and culture are specifically for men in Philo, though the authorities should see that a suitable education is provided for girls too, Spec. Leg., II, 125.

Along with and prior to Gk. culture Philo is acquainted with that of the synagogue. [94] In spite of all attempts at adaptation and integration, however, this remains distinct. It is primarily education in εὐσέβεια and ὁσιότης. οἰκονομία and πολιτεία stand between δικαιοσύνη and ἐπιστήμη. The right must be chosen and the wrong avoided, and all from the three standpoints of love for God, virtue, and one's fellow-men, Omn. Prob. Lib., 83. This is what Philo means when he speaks of philosophical instruction in the Jewish synagogue at Rome, Leg. Gaj., 156. Philo has in view only cultured persons : οἱ ἀπὸ παιδείας (Op. Mund., 17), with whom οἱ παιδείας ἀμύητοι, "the uneducated," are contrasted in, e.g., Det. Pot. Ins., 77, cf. παιδείας ἄγευστοι, Spec. Leg., III, 163; Virt., 39; Omn. Prob. Lib., 4. [95] Formation of the personality takes place under the discipline (ἐλέγχειν) of ἀρετή and the instruction (παιδεύειν) of φρόνησις,

---

[91] As Dodd observes (*op. cit.*, 110), there is in Jewish Hellenism, and esp. Philo, a tendency in respect of heavenly essences to vacillate between abstract understanding and concrete presentation in the form of personal hypostases. This is also true of paideia.

[92] Anthropological dualism characterises Philo's mode of expression, cf. E. Hatch, *op. cit.*, 109-130.

[93] W. Jost, ποιμήν. *Das Bild vom Hirten in der bibl. Überlieferung u. seine christologische Bedeutung* (1939), 21 f.

[94] The fusion in Philo of older traditional Jewish material with secular Hell. material has been shown by W. Bousset, *Jüdisch-chr. Schulbetrieb in Alexandria u. Rom* (1915), esp. 43-83, 149-173.

[95] The restless urge for knowledge is undoubtedly a Gk. legacy, and it is no accident that there are constant Platonic echoes in Philo, as noted in this connection by W. Völker, *Fortschritt u. Vollendung bei Philo von Alex.* (1938), 170.

Congr., 179. It follows the rule of the ὀρθὸς λόγος and παιδεία [96] (Mut. Nom., 206, cf. 211), and corresponds to the λογικὴ φύσις (Som., I, 107). The man who wants to give up παιδεία hurts his most noble part, Ebr., 23. Paideia is our most valuable possession, peaceful by nature in contrast to all other earthly goods, for which there are continual wars, Poster. C., 118. But the individual wins through πεπαιδεῦσθαι τὸ ἐν καιρῷ κάλλιστον, ἡσυχίαν, Abr., 20. He attains to serenity of soul, Leg. All., III, 128. Hence παιδεία is a divine jewel of the divine soul, Cher., 93. Or, as stated in Leg. All., III, 167: φῶς δὲ ψυχῆς ἐστι παιδεία, cf. also δᾳδουχοῦσα, "bearing a torch," "bringing light," Ebr., 168; καθαρὰ παρθένος, Agr., 158; ψυχῆς νόμισμα, Som., II, 90. It is νηφόντων ἡγεμονίς in contrast to μεθυόντων ἔξαρχος ἀπαιδευσία, Ebr., 153. By it man becomes a king, and things are subject to him. [97] But γίνωσκε σαυτόν, the philosophical term for self-education, is for Philo simply the biblical πρόσεχε σεαυτῷ, Gn. 24:6; Ex. 34:12 etc. Hereby the requirement of apologetics is met on the one hand, [98] and on the other all self-education is brought back to the divine commandment which restrains and sustains, Migr. Abr., 8. The superiority of Jewish culture [99] may be seen in its content, [100] which is influenced by Stoicism and Dualism in many of its forms of expression (Spec. Leg., I, 176; II, 46), but which is finally concerned with the one God and Creator. [101] Parents, pedagogues and teachers, the laws and unwritten customs, teach this to children from their youth up, Leg. Gaj., 115, 210; cf. Virt., 220; Praem. Poen., 162. Thus paideia is for the Jews a staff which serves both to support and to correct. The staff mentioned in the law of the Passover (Ex. 12:11) signifies paideia in allegorical exposition ; [102] this is thus more firmly combined with discipline and chastisement, Leg. All., II, 89, 90; Sacr. AC, 63; Congr., 94; Fug., 150. Without this paideia by means of the stick it is impossible for many νουθεσίαν ἐνδέξασθαι καὶ σωφρονισμόν, Poster. C., 97. Thus the staff is a sign of νουθεσία, of σωφρονισμός and παιδεία. [103] As a sceptre it is a symbol of royal dominion, and therewith of God, the one King, who Himself stands behind all paideia, Mut. Nom., 135.

---

[96] The work of the Law is παιδεία, Ebr., 143. Platonic influence stands behind this and similar statements, Völker, op. cit., 65 f. The ὀρθὸς λόγος is the Jewish Law, cf. E. R. Goodenough, The Politics of Philo Judaeus (1938), 30 f.

[97] The essence of intellectual kingship is grounded in the fact that it exercises its dominion acc. to the law of nature, cf. Goodenough, 86-91.

[98] That Jews, too, shared Hell. culture is emphasised by Philo (Vit. Mos., II, 32) with express ref. to the translators of the LXX.

[99] For material cf. Schürer, III, 698 f. There has been research more recently into Philo's relation to the piety of the mysteries, J. Pascher, Ἡ βασιλικὴ ὁδός. Der Königsweg zur Wiedergeburt u. Vergottung bei Philon v. Alex. = Studien z. Geschichte d. Kultur des Altertums, 17, 3/4 (1931); E. R. Goodenough, By Light, Light. The Mystic Gospel of Hellenistic Judaism (1935).

[100] Jews are priests for the whole world, and the Law is a school for the priesthood, H. Wenschkewitz, "Die Spiritualisierung d. Kultusbegriffe," Angelos, 4 (1932), 131-134, 138 f.

[101] Philo is the first whom one can really call a theologian. Externally it might often appear otherwise, but this is due to his style. Goodenough thinks that behind the sheen and colour of Hell. Jewish paideia the Messianic faith of Judaism is the true essence of Philo. Hence Hell. influences should not be overestimated. Even the cosmology and cosmogony of the world around were only an external part of his cultural heritage. Cf. Bousset, op. cit., 14-43; Dodd, 111-144.

[102] Allegorical exposition of the staff passed over into Christian exegesis too. Thus the catena on Hb. 1:8 has a quotation from Basil : Ἔστι δὲ καὶ παιδευτική τις ἡ ῥάβδος τοῦ θεοῦ. παιδεύουσα δὲ εὐθείας καὶ οὐ παρατετραμμένας ἐπάγει τὰς κρίσεις. διὰ τοῦτο ῥάβδος εὐθύτητος ἡ ῥάβδος τῆς βασιλείας αὐτοῦ προσαγορεύεται. Cf. also Greg. Naz. Or. Theol., 45, 19 (MPG, 36, 649b c).

[103] Trench has examined the relation between the two concepts παιδεία and νουθεσία (66-69), but νουθεσία occurs also in the sense of "chastisement." Joseph. even has μάστιξιν νουθετεῖν (Ant., 8, 217) for the παιδεύειν of the LXX. He can appeal to πληγαῖς νουθετεῖν in Plut. Sertorius, 19 (I, 578d). Possibly he is intentionally replacing παιδεύειν, which was alien to the literary usage of Hellenism in this sense.

He it is who has also fashioned the prototypes of human culture in secret, Som., I, 173. Thus paideia brings salvation, σωτήριος, Plant., 144. It is healthy and heals, Ebr., 141. [104] Assuming a good natural disposition and an appropriate education, the soul can attain to health, power, and other good gifts only by means of continual exercise in the principles of virtue, Praem. Poen., 64. As indiscipline brings death, so discipline brings immortality, Ebr., 140. It is the property of law and culture, which is the unwritten law of conscience, to differentiate between unholy and holy, unclean and clean, whereas conversely lawlessness and ill-breeding (ἀπαιδευσία) confuse everything, Ebr., 143. Another metaphor for paideia is that of the source or well, Fug., 177, 183; Ebr., 113. The well is one that only kings and not ordinary mortals can dig. This is to be seen also as a ref. to the saving significance of paideia. But ultimately this is grounded in the goodness and clemency of God and in His promises to those who love His discipline. Discipline is the bond to which and by which God keeps the soul fast and pure (Nu. 19:15). [105] The Israelite is taught to look up to the manna, the divine logos, which is the incomparable food of the soul that yearns for vision, [106] Rer. Div. Her., 79. The eye of the soul alone is shaped (πεπαίδευται) for vision of God, Mut. Nom., 203; cf. Leg. Gaj., 5; Ps.-Philo Vit. Cont., 66. [107]

For Philo, then, paideia is a hypostasis in his metaphysical view of the world. His statements about it cannot be grouped conceptually in a system. [108] Acc. to Fug., 52 the daughter of God, [109] Sophia, as male principle and father begot in souls μάθησις, παιδεία, ἐπιστήμη, φρόνησις, καλαὶ καὶ ἐπαινεταὶ πράξεις. In the care of souls true reason is the father and average or general culture the mother. Paideia brings men under the positive law set up by individual states, lands and peoples, Ebr., 33, 34; cf. Som., II, 139; Fug., 188. This average paideia is only a handmaiden compared with the native citizen ἐπιστήμη καὶ σοφία καὶ ἀρετή, while the other disciplines are on the border between aliens and citizens, Congr., 22. Average paideia [110] is represented by Hagar (Congr., 12, 14, 20, 23, 28, 145, 156), while Sarah represents ἀρετὴ τελεία (Leg. All., III, 244; cf. Cher., 3, 6; Poster. C., 130, 137; Som., I, 239; Mut. Nom., 255). But average paideia is the most that a normal man can attain to. Its fruit is and remains healthy in all connections, for the good is by nature imperishable, Plant., 114, cf. 116. Paideia does not grow old. While other things perish with time, it marches on, constantly rejuvenated, blooming with eternal blossom, refreshed and renewed in unceasing endeavour, Agric., 171. With all this Philo has a clear view of the practical significance of paideia. [111] It means for him that life is led under the direction of God's word, the divine logos, from which all

---

[104] Philo gives 2 par. explanations of the law forbidding the Levites to take intoxicants (Lv. 10:8-10). The one quoted seems to be his own. Cf. Bousset, 93.

[105] The final task of all ethics is θεῷ μόνῳ ζῆσαι, Mut. Nom., 213. Philo's ethics is theocentric in character, Völker, op. cit., 206 f.

[106] Here the ref. is not to the average paideia which can be perfected by progress, but to the divinely given wisdom which can be fulfilled only at blessed moments in vision, cf. Völker, 281-289; Bousset, 134.

[107] F. C. Conybeare, Philo about the Contemplative Life or the Fourth Book of the Treatise concerning Virtues (1895), 258-358, defends the authenticity, and also seeks to establish a link with the genuine Philo at this pt. In so doing, however, he does not consider the paideia concept. Acc. to Vit. Cont., 2 education in reverence for being (neutral) is based on nature and the holy laws, cf. Som., I, 35.

[108] As here, so elsewhere in Philo the doctrine of intermediate beings is full of inner contradictions. It does not rest on a well thought out and well constructed system, but is only a means of exposition, cf. Völker, 193.

[109] Here, too, interpretation in terms of comparative religion would be wrong. The mythical garb is a form which can easily be doffed and replaced by another, cf. Völker, 164, n. 4.

[110] In the tractate Congr. the exclusive concern is the relation between philosophy and paideia. Cf. Bousset, 98-110. These are represented by Sarah and Hagar, and the friend of culture, Abraham, must move on from the one to the other, and therewith to perfection, cf. Völker, 172-175.

[111] παιδεία is the νόμος. Thus Gk. and biblical ideas jostle one another in Philo, Völker, 220 f., 234.

potentialities of culture and all wisdom eternally proceed: ῥῆμα θεοῦ καὶ λόγος θεῖος, ἀφ' οὗ πᾶσαι παιδεῖαι καὶ σοφίαι ῥέουσιν ἀένναοι, Fug., 137. [112]

2. Jewish-Hellenistic Education in Josephus.

Like his older contemporary Philo, Joseph. has a rich share in the OT and secular culture of Hell. Judaism. [113] Brought up with his brother (συμπαιδευόμενος) εἰς μεγάλην παιδείας προύκοπτον ἐπίδοσιν, as he tells us in Vit., II, 8, he raises a claim to culture acc. to his age, and knows the educational theory of the time quite well. He sees and champions the twofold nature of all education as teaching and practice, and for him the goal of all education is religion, *pietas,* in which all individual virtues unite as parts of the whole, Ap., II, 171. Among the Gks. either teaching or practice is neglected. The Lacedaemonians and Cretans [114] decided for practice, the Athenians and most other Gks. for teaching. Moses, on the other hand, has both. [115] For the Law, τὸ κάλλιστον καὶ ἀναγκαιότατον παίδευμα, combines the two, constant exercise, as demanded, e.g., by the dietary commandments, and the Sabbath hearing and ἐκμανθάνειν. The γράμματα παιδεύειν (Ap., II, 204) is the necessary presupposition of this. If Plato has similar educational measures, he is simply imitating Moses, Ap., II, 257. [116] But Moses, the Jewish lawgiver, has educated us in mildness and humanity: ἡμερότητα καὶ φιλανθρωπίαν ἡμᾶς ἐξεπαίδευσεν, [117] II, 213, cf. Ant., I, 6. How strongly influenced by Stoicism Joseph. is here in his depiction of Jewish paideia may be seen from the alleged utterances of the leader of the defenders of Masada, Eleazar, in support and defence of suicide: ἔδει μὲν οὖν ἡμᾶς οἴκοθεν πεπαιδευμένους ἄλλοις εἶναι παράδειγμα τῆς πρὸς θάνατον ἑτοιμότητος, Bell., 7, 351. Those outside realise, too, that obedience to law is the basis of Jewish education. Their deficiency in this respect is thus cast up against them as ἀπαιδευσία, Ant., 17, 316. Joseph., too, can give the term a volitional as well as an intellectual ref. [118] The superiority of Jewish culture over Gk. is emphasised in an account of the meeting of Aristot. with a Jew, in support of which Clearch. is adduced, [119] Ap., I, 176-181. Fundamentally, Joseph. accepts the Gk. norm of culture. This is shown by his remarks about the acceptance of the culture of the Oriental, Manetho, Ap., I, 73, also Berossus, I, 129. Nor does it worry him to have to ascribe lack of culture to Apion, II, 3, cf. 37, 38, 130. [120] In Ant., 4, 260 ff. he discusses the ruling about the rebellious son in Dt. 21:18. [121] Parental discipline con-

---

[112] Here the ref. is to the wisdom which rains down from heaven, and the logos appears as its mediator, Völker, 164, 281.

[113] Acc. to his own testimony Joseph. received a careful Rabb. training and became acquainted with the various trends in Judaism, which in the light of Hell. culture he described as philosophical schools, cf. Schürer, I, 74-106.

[114] These refs. relate Joseph. to the history of Gk. pedagogy, → n. 12.

[115] Philo basically associates teaching, nature and practice as ways to virtue. Thus in the tractate Abr., Abraham represents teaching, Isaac nature, and Jacob practice. But these are Platonic ideas, cf. Plat. Leg., VII, 536b, and on this → 601, 28 ff.

[116] Already in the middle of the 2nd cent. B.C. the Alexandrian Jewish philosopher Aristobulus maintains that the Gk. philosophers were dependent on Moses, and finally the pythagorising Neo-Platonist Numenius, who lived toward the end of the 2nd cent. A.D., is supposed to have said that Plato was no more than an Atticistic Moses, cf. Schürer, III, 512, 627.

[117] Cf. esp. the well-known passage Plat. Crito, 51c.

[118] On the other hand he turns the saying at the end of the biblical story of Joseph (Gn. 50:20), which contains the salvation history of the Bible *in nuce,* into a superficial assertion that the brothers were not ill-disposed to him by nature, but that the course of events was in accordance with God's will.

[119] Cf. H. Guthe, Art. "Judaea," RE³, 9, 558, 53 and Schürer, III, 12, 156, n. 24. The Jews are here represented as philosophers among the Syrians, Ap., I, 179. He was Gk. in soul as well as speech, *ibid.,* 180. Hence Aristot. has to vouch for the Gk. culture of the Jew.

[120] Ptolemy II Philadelphus proves his culture by his interest in the OT, Ant., 1, 10, → n. 98.

[121] Cf. Philo Spec. Leg., II, 233; Ebr., 15 ff. and on this Bousset, 85-98.

sists primarily in admonition, νουθεσία, with recollection of the παιδεία that the parents have bestowed on the son. If this succeeds no further punishment is needed. Only if all else fails should the death sentence be executed. [122] For Joseph., then, παιδεύειν and παιδεία have the sense of education and culture. He did not think that he could expect his readers to understand the specifically OT sense of discipline or correction.

3. Discipline through Suffering in Later Jewish Theology.

The Rabbis, as representatives of Jewish theology on the soil of the OT tradition, developed a doctrine of education in which education by God is essentially correction. In so doing they were influenced by the experiences of the Maccabean period and by the conceptual development of Jewish passion piety in that and the succeeding age. [123] God is the Father who in grace allots correction to His son, i.e., the chosen people, while the ungodly, the other nations, are left without grace in superficial earthly prosperity, marching on in success and triumph to certain ruin at the last. This view finds literary attestation on the margin of the OT and in the apocr. It is found esp. in the Wisdom literature. [124] But it wins ground in the apocal. of later Judaism as a vital and at times fanatical expression of eschatological expectation. It is then developed more doctrinally in Rabb. theology. From apocal. circles comes S. Bar., a work which had its origin in Palestine, or at least in an orthodox milieu. [125] We read in 13:10 : "Hence they (the Jews) were then chastised, that they might be purged from sin." [126] Another view is found in 4:13. Paideia is now, not chastisement, but discipline or education. For the sin of its children, who did not take the path of instruction in divine righteousness, Jerusalem must atone. The concept of education is personified in 4 Esr. 8:11 f.: "Thou dost further it (thy product from the mother's womb) by thy mercy and nourish it by thy knowledge." But it is a postulate of the author that God ought not to have allowed His people to be destroyed by His own enemies, but to appease His hatred He should have chastised it with His own hands, 4 Esr. 5:30. In this tension between mercy and hatred there is revealed all the inner insecurity of this passion theology, [127] which as a pious theory could not really solve the problem of theodicy. Even the promise in the concluding message of 4 Esr., which summons to self-discipline, cannot conceal this : "If now you establish your mind and discipline your hearts, you will be kept in life and achieve grace in death," 14:34. The Book of Tobit, which seems to be related in many ways to 4 Esr., proclaims in Tobit's song of praise, 13:2, 5, 10, 16 : "He will chastise us (μαστιγώσει) on account of our unrighteousness, and then be merciful again." Thus the word group is not used. The Shadrach Apc. follows similar trains of thought, just as it also has literary connections with the works mentioned. Here, too, the question is that of theodicy. God says in 3:7: "Man is my work and the product of my hands, and I instruct him as I see fit." Shadrach answers in 4:1: "Thy discipline consists in fire and pain." [128]

---

[122] → n. 103. Joseph. uses νουθεσία for fatherly correction in Ant., 3, 311. Here, too, he is not thinking of verbal admonition but of the punishment of 40 years of wandering in the desert. Thus the theological type is used in an apologetic presentation of history.

[123] H. W. Surkau, *Martyrien in jüdischer u. frühchristlicher Zeit* (1938), 57-65, 74-82.

[124] (→ 610, 2 ff.) and the bibl. under → n. 79.

[125] Volz Esch., 40-48.

[126] The temporally limited chastisement of the Jews is contrasted with the lasting chastisement of the Gentiles. Cf. H. Gressmann in B. Violet, *Die Apokalypsen des Esra u. des Baruch* = GCS, 32 (1924), *ad loc.*, 345.

[127] W. Wichmann, "Die Leidenstheologie," BWANT, 4 F. 2 (1930), 43-50 sees in S. Bar. an attempt to overcome the negative radicalism of 4 Esr.

[128] For later Judaism there is no more problem of suffering. Where the solutions of punishment, testing and vicarious suffering do not apply, it is God's incomprehensible and terrible wrath which causes men to suffer, or the devil and demons torment and torture men and corrupt the earth. But finally everything is subordinated to the belief in retribution as the basic dogma of later Judaism, cf. E. Balla, "Das Problem des Leides in d. isr.-jüd. Religion," *Eucharisterion f. H. Gunkel* (1923), 255.

There is no such remonstration in Rabb. theology. The academic tradition has worked out a solid solution to the problem of theodicy. [129] A statement of R. Akiba preserved in S. Dt., 73b on 6:2 gives evidence of clarification of the doctrine: "Dear are the chastisements." [130] The Jewish view of retribution is herewith given a new turn, but it only becomes the more severe. Chastisement presupposes guilt, Ber., 5b: [131] "Is the Holy One open to the suspicion ... of inflicting a punishment unjustly ?" Thus one may deduce from the nature of the chastisement the specific human fault, Shab., 33a, Bar. That there is no death without sin (Ez. 18:20), no chastisement without guilt (Ps. 89:32), is the teaching of R. Ammi (c. 300) acc. to Shab., 55a. The principle rules: Measure for measure, cf. T. Sota, 3, 1 (295) acc. to R. Meïr (c. 150), cf. Mt. 7:2. [132] The Talmud tractate Ber. deals expressly with chastisements. There Is. 53:10 is expounded accordingly: "In whom the Holy One ... finds good-pleasure, him he oppresses with chastisements." [133] In the same context (Ber., 5a) there is handed down a saying of R. Simon b. Yachai: "The Holy One gave three good gifts ... to Israel, but all were won only by chastisements. That is, the Torah, the land of Israel, and the future world." [134] Chastisements remain afar off from him who devotes himself to the Torah (cf. Ex. 15:26). If anyone sees chastisements falling on him, he should examine his acts, cf. Lam. 3:40. If he does so and finds nothing, he should ascribe them to neglect of the Torah, cf. Ps. 94:12. If he still finds no reason, they are surely chastisements of love. [135] Appeal is also made to Ex. 21:26 : The tooth and eye are only individual parts of a man. If nevertheless a slave may go out in freedom on their account, how much more effective are these chastisements which affect the whole body of a man. They allow a man to go out free from all the guilt of sin. Hence they are more efficacious even than sacrifices. [136] Abraham attained to the cancellation of sins by chastisements along these lines. [137]

The plenitude of examples, however, should not deceive us. The contradiction between God's justice and mercy still remains. Even the idea of chastisements of love cannot resolve it. To use the concept of education and chastisement as an answer to the question of suffering is to think in human terms, just as the concept of paideia itself is anthropologically, if not anthropocentrically, controlled. [138] Hence even on the presuppositions of Jewish apocalyptic and Rabb. theology it cannot be united with the theocentric view, i.e., with the claim of the OT revelation of God to be unconditional. [139]

---

[129] Cf. Bousset-Gressm., 386; Moore, II, 248-256.

[130] Str.-B., I, 484; II, 274 f. cf. Ber., 5a-b; L. Goldschmidt, *Der babylonische Talmud,* (1929), 15.

[131] Goldschmidt, *op. cit.,* 16.

[132] St.-B., I, 192, 495, cf. 444-446.

[133] Ber., 5a, Goldschmidt, 13.

[134] Str.-B., II, 274. For further material cf. II, 193.

[135] Ber., 5a, Goldschmidt, 13 f.

[136] Str.-B., II, 194; Bousset-Gressm., 386.

[137] E. Sjöberg, *Gott u. der Sünder im palästinischen Judt.* (1939), 67 f., 73. As the sufferings of chastisement sufferings are a safeguard against temptation, they serve as a means of expiating sins, they bring about conversion, and through this forgiveness, *ibid.,* 170-183.

[138] Wendel, *op. cit.,* 339 f.: "Critical reflection on the divine retribution arose for the first time, then, where the usual theory of retribution ... was recognised as no longer adequate. This criticism could lead to the unmasking of the belief in retribution as an attempt to force God's acts into categories of human and worldly thought." What is true of the theory of retribution is equally true of suffering viewed as chastisement and of all other attempts to solve the problem of suffering.

[139] The word "pedagogue" became a not unfamiliar loan word in Rabb. writings. It often has the broader sense of "supervisor," "supporter," "guardian." A parable in Gn. r., 31 (18d) refers to the pedagogue of a king's son. The equation of pedagogue and slave, which is taken for granted in the Hell. world, is not found in Judaism. The pedagogue has a different position here. Cf. Str.-B., III, 339 f., 557.

D. The Paideia Concept in the New Testament.

1. Greek and Jewish Culture in the NT.

Controlled merely by history, and without theological significance, are the two verses Ac. 7:22 and 22:3, where one finds the usage which Hellenistic biography developed and which Hellenistic Judaism correspondingly used in biographical observations concerning its great men.

Ac. 7:22 : ἐπαιδεύθη Μωυσῆς πάσῃ σοφίᾳ Αἰγυπτίων. It is part of the Moses story that Moses was nurtured in all the wisdom of Egypt, as in Luc. Philops., 34 [140] the same is reported of a ἱερογραμματεύς from Memphis, of whom he says : θαυμάσιος τὴν σοφίαν καὶ τὴν παιδείαν πᾶσαν εἰδὼς τῶν Αἰγυπτίων. Similarly, the tragic writer Ezekiel says of Moses (37 f.): τροφαῖσι βασιλικαῖσι καὶ παιδεύμασιν ἅπανθ' ὑπισχνεῖθ' ὡς ἀπὸ σπλάγχνων ἑῶν. [141] Thus the position of Moses is secured on the secular side. In Joseph., however, there is at the decisive pt. (Ant., 2, 238) no παιδευθείς with the γεννηθείς τε καὶ τραφείς, though these normally constitute almost a formula. [142] His ἀρετή here is not based on his Egyptian education. Philo expressly emphasises in Vit. Mos., I, 32 that, though the Moses of the story had prospects of the Egyptian throne : τὴν συγγενικὴν καὶ προγονικὴν ἐζήλωσε παιδείαν. The teacher of Moses was God Himself : ὑπὸ μόνου μόνος ἐπαιδεύετο (ibid., I, 80). This refers in the first instance to instruction in the miraculous acts, but it also has typical significance, for when Moses received the Ten Commandments during the 40 days on the mount, ἐμυσταγωγεῖτο παιδευόμενος τὰ κατὰ τὴν ἱερωσύνην πάντα (II, 71). If in the common formula we read of the γένεσις, τροφή and παιδεία of Moses (II, 1), Egyptian culture played no part in the παιδεία. Education for the office of lawgiver was a matter of tradition (I, 32). But the simpler opinion that Moses was initiated into the famous ancient culture of the Egyptians is also found alongside this critical theological position, and it finds uninhibited expression in Ac. 7:22. [143]

In Paul's account of himself as reported by the author of Ac. in 22:3, we find the three customary biographical elements concerning his youth : γεγεννημένος ἐν Ταρσῷ ..., ἀνατεθραμμένος (brought up) ἐν τῇ πόλει ταύτῃ, παρὰ τοὺς πόδας Γαμαλιὴλ πεπαιδευμένος (taught, or, according to D, παιδευόμενος [144] cultivating myself) κατὰ ἀκρίβειαν τοῦ πατρῴου νόμου, ζηλωτὴς ὑπάρχων τοῦ θεοῦ (vl. τοῦ νόμου). [145] Paul devoted himself to the study of the Law of the fathers according to the precise method of Rabbinic and Pharisaic exegesis. Hence he was zealous for God and the Law. From his youth up he was educated in the Law. He could thus understand the importance of such education for the pagan world. As a Christian and an apostle, however, he had to dispute the claim of the Jews to be παιδευτὴς ἀφρόνων. As it is the very life and essence of the Jew to ground himself in the Law, so there arises for him the never forgotten obligation to come forward as ὁδηγὸς τυφλῶν, φῶς τῶν ἐν σκότει, παιδευτὴς ἀφρόνων,

---

[140] Cf. Zn. Ag.³, 252, n. 58.

[141] Quoted by Grotius, ad loc. Transl. Riessler, 338.

[142] The ref. in Ant., 2, 232, 236, 237 is again simply to care or support or upbringing, not to education.

[143] H. Gressmann, Mose u. seine Zeit (1913), 6-16; Schürer, II, 405; Bousset-Gressm., 74, n. 4.

[144] A. C. Clark, The Acts of the Apostles, a Critical Edition (1933), ad loc., does not take note of this reading. Zn. Ag.³, 751: "The third statement does not refer to what we usually call education, but to the student days of a young man destined to be a future rabbi."

[145] Acc. to Zn. Ag.³, 752, n. 31 Jerome gave authority to a most incredible formulation in the West when he wrote : nutritus autem in ista civitate secus pedes Gamaliel, eruditus iuxta veritatem paternae legis, aemulator legis.

διδάσκαλος νηπίων, R. 2:19 f. [146] He has knowledge and truth in the palpable form of the Law. The expressions quoted do not refer, at least in the first instance, to an intellectual understanding or the consequent transmission of a doctrine. The reference is to the practical influencing of life and moral conduct which was necessarily and not at all arbitrarily bound to shine forth from the strictness and consistency of the Jewish mode of life into the morally insecure and religiously questing world around. [147] Example is decisive, and along with the more theoretical task of the διδάσκαλος the word παιδευτής, like παιδαγωγός elsewhere, suggests practical guidance and direction. [148] In this case → νήπιος is used for the one who is capable of culture, and ἄφρων (→ σώφρων) for the man who, having no sure or clear judgment, needs direction.

2. The Law as Taskmaster.

Jesus rejected the claim of the Jew to be a teacher of the Law and an educator for the world (Mt. 23:15), and Paul followed Him in this, quoting Is. 52:5; Ez. 36:20 (R. 2:24). [149] For Paul the Law itself had lost its comprehensive and unconditional significance. It had come between (R. 5:20; Gl. 3:19), and thus had limited validity up to Christ (Gl. 3:24). From the standpoint of salvation history, the age of the Law ended with Christ. [150] The historical significance of the Law lies in the fact that it was a pedagogue. Materially it is of less significance what particular nuance the idea of παιδεία through the Law has in the relevant passage. There is certainly nothing derogatory in the term pedagogue. Paul might equally well have used νόμος παιδευτής or διδάσκαλος [151] or ὑφηγητής (cf. Philo Spec. Leg., III, 182) or ἐπίτροπος which occurs with παιδαγωγός and διδάσκαλος in Philo Leg. Gaj., 27 with reference to the νήπιος-heir, or finally even παιδεία νόμου. Education through the Law ends with man's coming of age. Up to this time the minor needs pedagogues, teachers and supervisors. Though a son of the house, he is no different from the slaves. Indeed, he is under them, for the pedagogues, teachers and supervisors, including the stewards mentioned in Gl. 4:2, were normally domestic slaves. The supervision, confinement and servitude (Gl. 3:22, 23; 4:3) imply that those dominated by sin, the Law and the rudiments of the world are still children. [152] Only faith alters this situation. God makes us adults, causes us to come of age (πλήρωμα τοῦ χρόνου might mean this for mankind), by sending His Son. Sonship as immediacy to the Father is rather different from dependence on even the best pedagogue. That the pedagogue is inferior to the father is the decisive thing, not his special quality. In the world around the NT the unpleasant reality of a pedagogue who might only do harm was accompanied by the ideal picture of the teacher of youth. [153] When Paul speaks of the pedagogue, he is not referring to the nature of the pedagogue, [154] but to being shut up under sin and the Law,

---

[146] Cf. Bousset-Gressm., 74 f.

[147] Cf. Sib., III, 195: οἳ πάντεσσι βροτοῖσι βίου καθοδηγοὶ ἔσονται. Cf. I, 384 f.

[148] Str.-B., I, 924 ff.; III, 105 ff.

[149] Str.-B., III, 118; Rosen-Bertram, op. cit., 62-68, 132 f.

[150] Cf. Jentsch, 175, 179.

[151] Acc. to Chrysostom (Cramer Cat. on Gl. 3:24) pedagogues and teachers are not rivals, but work together; cf. 4 Macc. 5:34 and on this → 612, 12 ff.

[152] In this case "up to Christ" is an indication of time; otherwise "with a view to Christ" denotes the goal.

[153] → 599, 15 ff. and n. 21, 22, 139, 154.

[154] Oe. Gl. on 3:34 gives conflicting testimonies about the pedagogue of antiquity. Jentsch, 174-179 inclines to a negative estimation of the pedagogue of Gl. 3:24.

to the bondage of man to the Law and the elements. Though Paul associates the Law with sin and the rudiments, and though he limits the Law by Christ, he is not against the Law. In his discussions of congregational questions he constantly appeals to it. [155] In Marcion's Gl. text [156] 3:15-25 is omitted, so that κατάρα τοῦ νόμου and στοιχεῖα τοῦ κόσμου are almost directly associated. The saying that the Law is a taskmaster, which softens and even overrides this purely negative attitude to the Law, is left out by Marcion. But Paul, and with him and after him the Church, adopt the concept of education [157] as a means of interpreting the OT in the light of Christ. They thus use it continally for all its relativity and incipient riskiness.

3. Education by God.

In the story of the passion (Lk. 23:16, 22) παιδεύειν is twice used with reference to Christ in the sense of *castigare*. The meaning is "to chastise." The words λύπη [158] and δουλεία [159] had long since been used alongside παιδεία. Outside the Bible there is no instance of the concrete sense "to strike" or "to scourge." But in the Gk. world dealing with a child — and παιδεύειν means "to treat as a child" — included not only instruction but whipping too, as frequently attested (→ 600, 16). Hence this is not a special biblical usage. It is simply a popula: expression which was kept out of the language of letters, so that instances are not to be found. At Lk. 23:16, 22 the word refers to the independent punishment of scourging, which Pilate wished to inflict on Jesus so that he could then let Him go, but which was not carried out according to the Synoptic records. [160]

Hb. 12 speaks of the discipleship of suffering. It is seeking to explain the experience of suffering from the OT standpoint of the παιδεία κυρίου, which is παιδεία πατρός. ἔμαθεν ἀφ᾽ ὧν ἔπαθεν is true in spite of sonship (5:8), or, as it is now said, just because of it. The relation between father and son is shown to be a moral one by the education, discipline and correction which the father accords to the son in responsible love. Since the reference in Hb. 12 is to sinful men, who are not willing to recognise their sin, παιδεία is accompanied by the more judicial function of conviction and punishment (→ ἐλέγχω, II, 474, 30 ff.). For the Jewish world the father-son relation is in the first instance only a com-

---

[155] → νόμος IV, 1077, 15 f.

[156] A. v. Harnack, *Marcion* (1921), *Beilage* III, 70 f.

[157] Cordier, 115-370. German Idealism esp. developed a philosophy of history out of the concept of education. Thus G. E. Lessing in his *Education of the Human Race* (1780) coins the statement : "What education is to the individual man, revelation is to the whole human race. Education is revelation coming to the individual man ; and revelation is education which has come, and is still coming, to the human race" (§§ 1 and 2, ET, *Lessing's Theological Writings*, London, 1956, p. 82 f.).

[158] → 598, 1 f.; 598, 9 f.; n. 6, 23, 51, 77.

[159] → 599, 17 ff.: Plat. Lys., 208b. Ps.-Plat. Ax., 366d, 367.

[160] G. Bertram, "Die Leidensgeschichte Jesu u. der Christuskult," FRL, NF, 15 (1922), 69. The scourging prior to crucifixion is denoted by φραγελλοῦν (and μαστιγοῦν), → IV, 517, 1 ff. In Jn. 19:1 the scourging seems not to be a preliminary punishment but the independent one of μαστιγοῦν, and thus an execution of the plan indicated in Lk. 23:16, 22. It is carried out by the soldiers with mockery → ἐμπαίζειν, and is meant by Pilate to evoke pity. The μαστιγοῦν of Jn. thus corresponds to the παιδεύειν of Lk. Since Lk. 18:33 also has μαστιγοῦν in the prediction of the passion, the scourging is thought to have been carried out here too. It is certainly part of the oldest confession of the community, and is a primary part of the way of suffering for the disciples too, Mt. 10:17; 23:34. Cf. Jentsch, 143 f. Acc. to Hck. Lk., *ad loc.* Lk. avoids the Latinism (*flagrare* "burn," *flagrum, flagellum* "scourge," *flagrio* "slave").

parison, and in the LXX it is even less significant. [161] The LXX develops the idea of education by suffering in Gk. categories (→ 608, 8 ff.), and it thus influences the vocabulary of passion theology, with which παιδεία is connected. The NT relates the sufferings of the Christian to those of Christ. Hb. is not offering a theodicy such as that of Prv. 3:11, 12. There is no question of trying to overcome the power of suffering to disturb faith or to sow despair or uncertainty. The reference is to chastisement as a guarantee of sonship, and consequently of God's grace and forgiveness. [162] Hence it is not enough to say that παιδεία is a training which makes the athlete strong and unconquerable for the contests. [163] The experience of suffering at the Father's hand sets the Christian alongside Christ. It thus shows him plainly that he is the Father's child, loved by Him, received by Him as a son, Hb. 12:7 f. [164] The εἰς παιδείαν ὑπομένετε of 12:7 seems to suggest that the goal of the correction is Christian "culture," [165] the state of purified Christian personality. But it is hard to think that NT παιδεία signifies a state in this way. There is no completed Christian "culture" in the earthly sphere, cf. Phil. 3:12 → πληρόω, τελειόω. Christian perfection is a gift of the last time to which education by God is leading. Hence παιδεία can never be the goal, only the way. It is what God does to us [166] if we submit to Him. At Hb. 12:7 εἰ should be read for εἰς, as in many MSS. [167] Submission sets us alongside Christ, 12:2, 3. This is really fatherly correction, not → κόλασις (→ III, 816, 15 ff.) and τιμωρία. [168] Thus even the reading εἰς can yield a good sense: Endure for the purpose of education. [169] What is already valid in the human sphere according to God's will (the fifth commandment and household tables) becomes in man's relation to God a glad message of education by God, εὐαγγελικὴ παίδευσις as Cyril [170] puts it, an education which is better and stronger than the παιδεία νόμου in the OT. [171] Finally man comes to realise that his earthly father is an educator. But whereas human ideals are at issue in the father's earthly education, eternal life is at stake in obedience to the Father of spirits, 12:9. [172] God, however, exercises discipline

---

[161] On Prv. 3:11 f. → 605, 34 ff., 608, 38 ff.

[162] Mi. Hb.[8], 299, cf. Hb.[7], 201.

[163] So the cat., ad loc.

[164] Ideo ecclesia tempore martyrum erat florentissima, quia dilectissima, hoc est disciplinis Domini exercitatissima, Luther's Lectures on Hb. acc. to the Vatican MS, ed. E. Hirsch and H. Rückert (1929), gloss on Hb. 12:6 (p. 84).

[165] παιδεία is in Hb. 12:7 "both chastisement ... and also the goal of education attained by chastisement. In what follows Hb. expounds this twofold sense to show that God's chastisement is both intentional and necessary," Mi. Hb.[7], 197.

[166] The ref. is thus to an event, as Grotius says ad loc.: quo verbo significari solet institutio, quae factis fit, puta vinculis, legibus, poenis.

[167] Mi. Hb., ad loc. keeps to the traditional reading and regards the vl. as a softening in assimilation to the constr. which follows. On the other hand Jentsch, 163; Rgg. Hb.[3], 395 find in the traditional text an ancient scribal error.

[168] So the catenae tradition, ad loc. Cf. also Grotius, ad loc.: Nam si vere sunt Christiani, adversa talia illis non evenient, nisi ex decreto quodam Dei, et quidem in ipsos benevoli, nempe ut si quid sordis adhaeret, excoquatur, aut ut ipsi per patientiae exercitia reddantur meliores.

[169] The community itself would almost have to ask for this παιδεία, Mi. Hb., ad loc.

[170] Cf. Cramer Cat. on Hb. 2:4.

[171] God gave the Law as a help, but it meets only childish needs. The mysterium Christi does the rest, Glaphyron, Cramer Cat., ad loc.

[172] Cf. Wettstein on 12:10 : Patres castigant, donec puer ex ephebis excesserit ; Deus per totam vitam. At tempus castigationum Dei, ad vitam aeternam collatum, multo brevius est tempore castigationum paternarum cum vita hominis comparato. Cf. also Oecumenius of Tricca in K. Staab, Pauluskommentare aus der griech. Kirche (1933), 468 : οὔτε γὰρ

to our advantage, i.e., in such a way that we may partake of His holiness, Hb. 12:10; Mt. 5:48; Lv. 19:2. Certainly παιδεία and λύπη go together in Christianity too ; παιδεία does not in the first instance bring joy, but strenuous exercise. The fruit of all effort, however, is righteousness in peace, Hb. 12:11.

The view of education which derives from OT proverbial wisdom, and which is further developed by the practical piety of Judaism, fits smoothly into the context of eschatologically determined Christology. The son is educated for eternity ; the Christian is to share in the eternal worship of God in heaven. [173] In particular the admonitory letters of Rev. serve this goal. In Rev. 3:19 the basic principle of παιδεία κυρίου is adopted : ὅσους ἐὰν φιλῶ, ἐλέγχω καὶ παιδεύω, God Himself intervenes with educative punishments in the life of men because He loves them and can in this way kindle zeal for repentance. Since the verbs ἐλέγχειν and παιδεύειν have so many meanings, and as translations of יכח take over much of the content of this many-sided term, various renderings are possible. The context suggests that here the main emphasis should be on the use of the term for rousing or stirring. For all the sharpness — we do not find the father-son comparison — it is meant as the word of a friend (Jn. 15:14) full of admonitory earnestness. Testing and punishing, censuring and smiting, chastising and educating, all are expressed in the two words, which refer to God's dealings with man in contrast to all the moralising of legalistic religions or average middle-class ethics. [174]

As in Hb. and Rev. God's loving will as Father stands behind this use of paideia along the lines of OT proverbial wisdom, so the subject of the saying in Tt. 2:12 points in the same direction. This is the grace of God, which has shown itself to be to man's salvation and which subjects the Christian community to its education and discipline. There is no further reference to the means used in this. But in the Pastorals it is undoubtedly the ὑγιαίνουσα διδασκαλία, [175] the Word of God, which does its educative work by admonition, warning, correction and instruction. The goal is twofold, renunciation of ungodliness and the confident hope and expectation of the appearing of the glory of our great God and Saviour Jesus Christ ; παιδεία κυρίου aims at both.

In connection with self-examination at the Lord's Supper Paul takes up the idea of Jewish passion theology that the judgment of the Lord is for Christians chastisement, but not condemnation, as for the world, 1 C. 11:32. [176] Illnesses and other divine punishments warn Christians of their sins. [177] They are παιδεία κυρίου, the outflowing of His fatherly love. Paul made the same point in relation to his personal experience in the list of peristases in 2 C. 6:9. He sees a tension between the outward experiences of his life, which to himself and others necessarily have the appearance of dying, chastisement and sorrow, and the inner assurance of life, the victory over death and the joy. The second set of contrasting terms here

---

ἰσχύουσι δι' ὅλου παιδεύειν ἡμᾶς, ἵνα τελείους ἐργάσωνται, ὁ δὲ θεὸς ἀεὶ παιδεύων τελείους ποιεῖ.

[173] T. Arvedson, Das Mysterium Christi (1937), 150. Mi. Hb.⁸ on 12:11.

[174] Cf. Had. Apk., ad loc. On the concept of God's educative righteousness, which was widespread in later Judaism, cf. Bousset-Gressm., 384.

[175] Cf. Plut. Lib. Educ., 7 (II, 5b).

[176] Grotius, op. cit., ad loc.: κρίνεσθαι dixit de malis huius vitae et morte immatura ; κατακρίνεσθαι de poenis aeternis. Omnia mala, quae in hac vita eveniunt, fiunt νουθεσίαι sive παιδεύσεις, מוסרים si sequatur seria poenitentia et emendatio.

[177] Calvin on v. 30 : significat, morbis et reliquis Dei flagellis nos admoneri, ut de peccatis nostris cogitemus. Neque enim nos frustra affligit Deus, quia malis nostris non delectatur.

(παιδευόμενοι καὶ μὴ θανατούμενοι) [178] is influenced by Ps. 118:18. He has obviously experienced παιδευόμενοι, 2 C. 11:23 : ἐν πληγαῖς ὑπερβαλλόντως. But the point is, not what blows men or nature dealt to the apostle, but that this is the παιδεία κυρίου. Satan himself with the thorn in the flesh [179] must play his part in seeing that the apostle does not become proud. This, too, is a revelation of the grace which chastens us, 2 C. 12:9; Tt. 2:12.

4. Christian Discipline in the NT.

In the household table in Eph. 6:4 we find the formulation (not in the par. Col. 3:21): οἱ πατέρες ... ἐκτρέφετε αὐτὰ (τὰ τέκνα ὑμῶν) ἐν παιδείᾳ καὶ νουθεσίᾳ κυρίου. [180] Here the basic rule of all Christian education is stated. The gen. κυρίου is a subj. gen.; this is the education which the Lord gives through the father. To this end He uses all the means available for education in the secular realm too : exemplo, beneficiis, admonitionibus, verberibus denique. [181] There is, then, a hendiadys. Only if a gen. limitationis or qualitatis [182] were presupposed could one differentiate Christian discipline and admonition from one another. In this case the former would be education by act, the latter education by word. [183] In the Pastorals Paul's basic principle of evangelical paideia in the family is applied to the community. The significance of revealed Scripture is sketched along these lines ; it serves the purpose of teaching, correction, conversion and instruction in righteousness, 2 Tm. 3:16. The reference is to the understanding and use of the OT in the Christian community. It might almost seem that here, in contrast to Gl. 3:24, there is set up again a παιδεία νόμου even after Christ. But the author does not see, and certainly does not intend, any contradiction of Gl. 3:24 or of Paul generally. He has in view the Christian and his nurture. [184] Those in the congregation who have gone beyond the first instruction can progress on the right way only under the influence of the Holy Scriptures. [185] "Education in uprightness is designed to produce conduct whereby δικαιοσύνη is actualised as a sphere of life. [186] The concrete task of evangelical education is in the hands of the leaders of the community. [187] But neither in the NT age nor in that of the Apologists is the vocabulary of παιδεία developed further, e.g., under the influence

---

[178] The paired expressions indicate the contrast between what Paul is thought and appears to be to men and what he is in truth, what constitutes his life-orientation in the higher sense, what fills his life with its supreme content, Bchm. K., 281. Cf. also Grotius, ad loc.: viri summe pii, qui per ista testamenta semper meliores fiunt. The vl. πειραζόμενοι represented by the Western tradition cannot be considered seriously. It simply points to the relationship between πειρασμός and παιδεία in Jewish passion theology, → n. 64.

[179] Jentsch, 179 calls Satan a functionary of God, on 1 Tm. 1:20.

[180] → n. 103.

[181] Wettstein, ad loc.

[182] Jentsch, 144.

[183] Haupt Gefbr., ad loc.

[184] In 2 Tm. 3:16 παιδεία is the educative activity which promotes healthy development. The term really denotes education (rather than discipline), which is active in the sphere of the normal disposition well-pleasing to God, B. Weiss, ad loc., Die Briefe Pauli an Tm. u. Tt.⁷ (1902). The anthropological concept of personality, which is commonly misunderstood idealistically, was fashioned by Tertullian and Boethius into a theological concept in the framework of the doctrine of the Trinity.

[185] Grotius, ad loc.

[186] Wbg. Past., ad loc.

[187] In the NT communities we find at least the function, though not the office, of the pedagogue. Even παιδευτής in the NT denotes the function rather than an office-bearer. It is committed to apostles, bishops, presbyters etc., → Jentsch, 223, n. 3.

of Paul in 1 C. 4:15, nor indeed put to more common use. [188] According to 2 Tm. 2:25 Timothy is meekly to discharge the task of education in relation to opponents. The reference here is to a specific error, but no material debate is to be sought. The error is to be set aside and repudiated from the very first as → μωρός and ἀπαίδευτος, i.e., not adapted to promote spiritual development, 2:23. Thus all discussion is ruled out. The reference, then, is not to penal correction with words — this would be ἐλέγχειν — but to παιδεύειν, the exercising of an educative influence, which, if God permits, will bring about conversion to knowledge of the truth and therewith deliverance from the snares of the devil.

Finally παιδεύειν has no human subject in 1 Tm. 1:20. Delivering up to Satan (→ n. 179) implies chastisement, not definitive destruction. It may consist in sickness or misfortune. It is designed to prevent blasphemy and to lead back to faith, cf. 1 C. 5:5; 2 C. 12:7. παιδεύειν has here more the sense of punishment than education, and only inasmuch as this promotes amendment can one speak of παιδεία in the Christian sense. But the authority of discipline (Church discipline) is given to the Christian community for the purpose of its edification, Ac. 5:1-11; 13:6-12.   *Bertram*

παιδίον → παῖς, 636.

> παίζω, ἐμπαίζω, ἐμπαιγμονή, ἐμπαιγμός, ἐμπαίκτης

† παίζω.

παίζω, in class. times ἔπαισα, πέπαικα, πέπαισμαι — forms which agree in sound with those of παίειν, "to hit" — later ἔπαιξα, πέπαιχα, πέπαιγμαι, ἐπαίχθην, [1] means in virtue of its derivation from παῖς "to act in childlike or childish fashion,"

---

[188] In the age of the NT apocr. and post-apost. fathers the word group plays only a very minor role, though Pol., 4, 2 refers to women educating children in the fear of God. Nevertheless, it is in this period that the seeds of evangelical paideia begin to unfold with the practice of Christian education at home and in the community. When Cl. Al. wrote his Paidagogos, the conflict with ancient and Jewish Hell. ideas of education had been fully joined, and an individual Christian culture was arising and coming to its first flower, Jentsch, 265-285. As in the centuries before Christ "Greek-educated Jews presented the religion of Yahweh to the Greeks in much abbreviated and spiritualised form," so the Chr. Apologists, following Philo of Alex. in particular, offered Christianity as the supreme and absolute philosophy, Harnack Dg., I, 502. On the basis of Calvin's use of paideia in Institutes, II, 11, 2, Kraus seeks to understand the unity of the OT and NT along these lines. But παιδεία in the sense of education is not a concept with genuine OT roots, → 603, 32 f., and Gl. 4:1-7 specifically contrasts the rudiments (or the Law, 3:24), as supervisors (pedagogues), with God, the Father. Hence the Testaments are united, not by a pedagogic view of history, but inwardly by unconditional theonomy, G. Bertram, "Die Aufgaben einer Biblischen Theologie beider Testamente," *Kirche im Angriff*, 12 (1936), 425.

π α ι ζ ω. Hug, Art. "Spiele," Pauly-W., 2. Reihe, III, 1762-1774; R. Freiling, *Das heilige Spiel* (1925); K. Groos, *Die Spiele d. Tiere* (1908); also *Die Spiele d. Menschen* (1899); also *Der Lebenswert des Spieles* (1910); also "Das Spiel als Katharsis," *Zschr. f. pädagogische Psychologie u. experimentelle Pädagogik*, 12 (1911), 353-367; R. Guardini, *Vom Geist d. Liturgie*[12] (1922), 56-70; J. Huizinga, *Homo ludens* (1939).

[1] In Hell. Gk., unlike Attic, παίζειν has a guttural character. Similarly, the Doric of the *koine* is prominent in later constructs like ἐμπαίκτης, ἐμπαιγμός, ἐμπαιγμονή; it is strengthened by a concern to distinguish the forms of παίζειν from those of παίειν. Bl.-Debr.[7] § 71 App.; E. Schwyzer, *Griech. Grammatik* (*Handbuch AW*, II, 1), I (1939), 738.

"to play," "to dance," "to jest," "to mock." Related are the nouns παιδία, παιδιά, [2] also as a personification of erotic play, attested both on inscr. and in art, e.g., on a vase at Munich, Paidia, tossing the winged Himeros. [3] παιδιά means "play," "jest," παῖγμα, παιγνία "play," "jest," "mockery," παίγνιον "toy," "plaything," "rascal."

1. The Use of the Word by the Greeks.

In Hom. παίζω is used (Od., 6, 100-106; 7, 291) for the play (ball-games) of maidens or nymphs; in 8, 251 the verb means "to dance," cf. also 23, 147. Very commonly in secular Gk. the verb denotes lack of seriousness in something, e.g., attitude or conduct, Hdt., IV, 77: ὁ λόγος πέπαισται (vl. πέπλασται), i.e., the saga is lightly treated or invented. In the Platonic dialogues the question is often raised whether what Socrates says is meant seriously (σπουδάζειν, σπουδή) or is to be taken in jest (παίζειν, παιδιά), Gorg., 481b; Phaedr., 234 d. Xenoph. Mem., IV, 1, 1 argues to the contrary that even what Socrates says in jest is no less profitable to his friends than what is meant seriously, cf. also Plat. Phileb., 30e; Leg., I, 647d; II, 656c. Cf., too, Plut. Sept. Sap. Conv., 13 (II, 156d): ᾧ πλεῖστον ἡδονῆς ἅμα καὶ παιδιᾶς καὶ σπουδῆς ἔνεστιν, ἐγείρουσι τούτῳ (sc. the Muses) ... τὴν φιλοφροσύνην, Xenoph. Sym., I, 1: τὰ μετὰ σπουδῆς πραττόμενα ... καὶ τὰ ἐν ταῖς παιδιαῖς. The use of παιδιά in Plat. Resp., X, 602b shows disparagement of the term; it denotes what is of little account, what is not to be regarded as serious or significant, cf. Aesch. Prom., 314. The ship is a plaything of the winds, Secundus Sententiae, 17. Man is a plaything of fate, ibid., 7; cf. Luc. Nigrinus, 20; Anth. Pal., 10, 64, 6. Man is already presented as a plaything of deity in Plato (Leg., VII, 803c): ἄνθρωπον ... θεοῦ τι παίγνιον εἶναι μεμηχανημένον ... · τούτῳ δὴ δεῖν τῷ τρόπῳ συνεπόμενον καὶ παίζοντα ὅτι καλλίστας παιδιὰς πάντ' ἄνδρα καὶ γυναῖκα οὕτω διαβιῶναι (cf., 797b). The element of scorn is stronger in BGU, IV, 1024 VII 26 (4th cent. A.D.): ἔπεζεν (for ἔπαιζεν) αὐτὴν ἡ πεν[ε]ία. Finally, life in general is not taken seriously and the advice is given on burial inscr.: παῖσον, τρύφησον, ζῆσον, ἀποθανεῖν σε δεῖ (2nd/3rd cent. A.D.). [4] Thus jesting and mockery meet. A low view of this frivolous attitude from the standpoint of true culture is to be found esp. in Plat. Prot., 347d: ὅπου δὲ καλοὶ κἀγαθοὶ συμπόται καὶ πεπαιδευμένοι εἰσίν, οὐκ ἂν ἴδοις οὔτ' αὐλητρίδας οὔτε ὀρχηστρίδας οὔτε ψαλτρίας, ἀλλ' αὐτοὺς αὑτοῖς ἱκανοὺς ὄντας συνεῖναι ἄνευ τῶν λήρων τε καὶ παιδιῶν τούτων ... In the pap. παιδιά is used in the sense of "wantonness," also "folly," "stupidity." [5]

In philosophy and pedagogics the concept of play had an established place from the time of Plato. Aristot. is decisive here. He examines the place of music in education. He asks whether it belongs to education, to play, or to amusement, and concludes that it is to be put with all three, Pol., VIII, 5, p. 1339a, 11 ff., b, 9 ff. At b, 15 he says: ἥ τε γὰρ παιδιὰ χάριν ἀναπαύσεώς ἐστι. Cf. Eth. Nic., X, 6, p. 1176b, 27-35: οὐκ ἐν παιδιᾷ ἄρα ἡ εὐδαιμονία. καὶ γὰρ ἄτοπον τὸ τέλος εἶναι παιδιάν, καὶ πραγματεύεσθαι καὶ κακοπαθεῖν τὸν βίον ἅπαντα τοῦ παίζειν χάριν, ἅπαντα γὰρ ὡς εἰπεῖν ἑτέρου ἕνεκα αἱρούμεθα πλὴν τῆς εὐδαιμονίας· τέλος γὰρ αὕτη. σπουδάζειν δὲ καὶ πονεῖν παιδιᾶς χάριν ἠλίθιον φαίνεται καὶ λίαν παιδικόν. παίζειν δ' ὅπως σπουδάζῃ, κατ' Ἀνάχαρσιν, ὀρθῶς ἔχειν δοκεῖ· ἀναπαύσει γὰρ ἔοικεν ἡ παιδιά, ἀδυνατοῦντες δὲ συνεχῶς πονεῖν ἀναπαύσεως δέονται. That

---

[2] παιδία is "childishness," παιδιά "what belongs to the child," but the meanings overlap, cf. Luc. Toxaris, 36. The Gk. word group is not confined to the play of children, but it cannot have the comprehensive sense of play or sport as in other languages. The construction in Gk. maintains the connection with the child. Hence it is more or less unsuitable for higher forms of human play. Play is indeed a basic element in Gk. culture, and both Plato and Aristot. are concerned to understand it as such, cf. the quotations in the text. But Gk. uses many other terms as well as παιδιά, e.g., ἀγών "contest," διαγωγή "diversion," or σχολή "leisure," cf. Huizinga, 30-32, 48-50, 241-244, 256-259.
[3] Ill. in Roscher, s.v. "Paidia," III, 1251 f.
[4] Epigr. Graec., 362, 5.
[5] Preisigke Wört., II, 221.

play relaxes and refreshes is the determinative thought in Aristot.'s discussion, cf. also Pol., VIII, 3, p. 1337b, 33-42. Cf. further Eth. Nic., IV, 14, p. 1127b, 33 f., 1128a, 20 f.; VII, 8, p. 1150b, 17. As the more pleasant side of life play is contrasted with seriousness in Rhet., I, 11, p. 1370a, 14 ff.: διὸ αἱ ῥαθυμίαι καὶ αἱ ἀπονίαι καὶ αἱ ἀμέλειαι καὶ αἱ παιδιαὶ καὶ αἱ ἀναπαύσεις καὶ ὁ ὕπνος τῶν ἡδέων· οὐδὲν γὰρ πρὸς ἀνάγκην τούτων. καὶ οὗ ἂν ἡ ἐπιθυμία ἐνῇ, ἅπαν ἡδύ. Finally, there is the judgment of Pol., VIII, 3, p. 1337b, 33 ff.; though play is a means of relaxation and recreation, it is not a worthy use of leisure. It naturally maintains its universal significance in education of children, though certain requirements must be considered in relation to the kind of play. Aristot. speaks of these in Pol., VII, 17, p. 1336a, 33 f. διὸ τὰς παιδιὰς εἶναι δεῖ τὰς πολλὰς μιμήσεις τῶν ὕστερον σπουδαζομένων, cf. Pol., VIII, 5, p. 1339a, 31 ff. [6]

2. παίζω in the OT and LXX.

That play is devotion finds expression in the religious and cultic nature of games and dances in the primitive, the ancient oriental and the classical Gk. worlds alike. [7] The gods are venerated in games and dances, Plat. Leg., VII, 815d; cf. 796b : Κουρήτων ἐνόπλια παίγνια. In the cults of the world around the OT and NT we thus find many games and dances as means of expressing piety, and it is no more than natural that the people of Israel should share in this common phenomenological feature of religion. Thus in Ex. 15:20; Ju. 11:34 (cf. Jdt. 15:12) we read of religious dances on the occasion of victory celebrations. [8] In 1 K. 18:26 there is ref. to dancing around the altar of Baal. Ju. 21:21 bears testimony to dances in Yahweh worship at an annual feast (harvest ?). More orgiastic was the dancing before the ark in 2 S. 6:14-16. In the cultic psalms (e.g., 26:6; 42:4; 149:3; 150:4) what is meant is a more solemn dance as in processions.

If we consider the verb παίζειν alone, our first refs. are 2 Βασ. 6:5, 21; 1 Ch. 13:8; 15:29. [9] Here פחק is transl. παίζειν. ὀρχεῖσθαι is added at 2 Βασ. 6:21 with no Hb. original, and at 1 Ch. 15:29 with the original רקד. But the par. in Joseph. show that the meaning does not have to be dancing, for Joseph. either has ἐν κινύρᾳ παίζοντος καὶ κροτοῦντος (Ant., 7, 85), or παίζειν τε καὶ πολλάκις χορεῦσαι (7, 88), or he does not mention the dance at all, as in the par. to 1 Βασ. 18:7, where instead of the poorly attested παίζουσαι of the LXX (Lucian χορεύουσαι) and the χορεύουσαι παίζουσαι of the Hexapla he simply has μετὰ κυμβάλων καὶ τυμπάνων καὶ παντοίας χαρᾶς (6, 193). To the passages mentioned should be added the eschatological statements in Jer. 31:4 : "I will build thee again . . . O virgin of Israel ; adorn thee again with thy tabrets, and go forth in the dances of them that make merry" (μετὰ συναγω-γῆς παιζόντων), and 30:19 : "And out of them shall proceed again thanksgiving and the voice of them that make merry" (HT), for which the LXX (37:19) has : ἐξελεύ-

---

[6] Cf. W. Jaeger, *Paideia*, 3 (1947), 43 f. Aristot. is basic for the treatment of play and the impulse to play in the general history of culture as well as education, cf. Eth. Nic., X, 6, p. 1176b, 9. On Aristot. cf. Hug, 1763. Huizinga, 236-247 examines the forms of play in philosophy, esp. in relation to the Sophists. But for Aristot. παιδιά is the play of children or amusement, 257-259.

[7] F. Schiller, *Über die ästhetische Erziehung*, Letter 15 (1794) writes : "Man plays only when he is man in the full sense of the term, and he is fully man only when he plays." F. Frank, following Schleiermacher, tried to illustrate the nature of God by perfect play. Cf. J. Kaftan, *Dogmatik* (1909), 176; F. Kattenbusch, *Die deutsche evangelische Theol. seit Schleiermacher* (1924), 23.

[8] Cf. W. O. E. Oesterley, *The Sacred Dance* (1923); E. König, Art. "Spiele bei den Hebräern," RE³, 18, 633-636; A. Bertholet, Art. "Spiel," I, RGG², V, 691 f.; A. Jeremias, *Das AT im Lichte d. Alten Orients⁴* (1930), 521; J. Pedersen, *Israel Its Life and Culture²* (1947), Index, s.v. "Dance." For further information on the connection between cultus and play from ancient tragedy to the medieval mystery plays cf. G. Bertram, *Die Leidensgeschichte Jesu u. der Christuskult* (1922), 81 and Huizinga, 31.

[9] Luther deals with this v. and 2 S. 6:14 in the well-known letter to Provost G. Buchholzer of Berlin, Dec. 4, 1539, cf. Weimar ed., *Briefwechsel*, Vol. VIII (1938), 625, No. 3421. On the cultic ps. cf. H. Schmidt, *Die Ps. = Handbuch z. AT*, I, 15 (1934).

σονται ἀπ' αὐτῶν ᾄδοντες καὶ φωνὴ παιζόντων. [10] Also eschatological is Zech. 8:5 : The streets of Jerusalem shall again be full of children at play. With similar more than life-like colours the return of the exiles to Jerusalem under Darius is depicted as a joyous eschatological procession in 1 Εσδρ. 5:3.

In the story of Samson παίζειν means the playing of a musical instrument in Ju. 16:25, 27. The verb is used of the dancing at the worship of the golden calf in Ex. 32:6, → 629, 28 ff. The ref. in Gn. 21:9 is to innocent play and fun : Ishmael plays with Isaac. [11] The sense has to be dancing again in Is. 3:16. Here it is used for טפף, which means "to take small steps," "to trip," like children. It is hard to say whether the translator was thinking of an etym. correct and suitable rendering or whether the word was supposed to express a frivolous disposition. Just. Dial., 27, 3 quotes the v. in the context of ethical admonitions and warnings.

3. The Sense of Play, Scorn, Bravado.

Acc. to Wis. 15:12 the Gentiles regard life as a game, and in Sir. 32:12, where the HT is modified, we find an admonition which corresponds elsewhere to the Hell. view of things : [12] ἐκεῖ (at a feast) παῖζε καὶ ποίει τὰ ἐνθυμήματά σου καὶ μὴ ἁμάρτῃς λόγῳ ὑπερηφάνῳ (HT : "And there speak what comes into thy mind in the fear of God and not without understanding." [13] Jer. 15:17 HT refers to the merriness of those who jest ; the prophet, burdened by the revelation which fills him with horror at the sins of his people, cannot join in with them, → 394, 30 ff. The LXX no longer thinks of merriness in this sense. Its παίζοντες refers, not to innocent joking, but to an arrogance which scorns revelation, so that no righteous man can have any part in it. [14] Particularly

---

[10] Here, too, שׂחק is rendered παίζειν; the LXX thus emphasises one-sidedly the element of movement, of playing or dancing. It is true that the words mean much the same, but שׂחק can be used for simple laughter, and is originally a sound word like "giggle" or γελᾶν or "laugh," whereas παίζειν denotes the merry nature of the child expressed in sound and movement. A special OT use is at 2 Βασ. 2:14, where παίζειν = שׂחק denotes the joust, though this is in bloody earnest, cf. Aristot. Rhet., I, 11, p. 1370b, 35 ff. Huizinga, 67, 79 f., 144-170 finds here a connection between play and war in the culture of Semitic peoples too.

[11] Gn. 21:9 is quoted in Just. Dial., 56, 7. The conduct of Ishmael could be construed as a mocking of Isaac, → I, 659, n. 4. Cf. Gn. 26:8, where it is referred to sexual intercourse in a reading which could come from a scholiast (συνουσιάζειν). Acc. to Procop. it was a Jewish euphemism for this, cf. Field, ad loc., where Procop. is quoted in the cat. of Nicephorus. Philo takes the verse allegorically : τί γὰρ ἄλλο ἐμπρεπὲς ἔργον σοφῷ ἢ τὸ παίζειν καὶ γανοῦσθαι καὶ συνευφραίνεσθαι τῇ τῶν καλῶν ὑπομονῇ, Plant., 170. Among the patriarchs Isaac represents for him φυσικὴ ἀρετή, Abr., 52. In him τὸ εὐδαιμονεῖν is born. This is the signification of his name, which Philo also renders by γέλως and χαρά on the basis of Gn. 21:6 LXX : "Laughter has the Lord made for me ; for whoever hears it will rejoice with me," Leg. All., III, 218, 219 etc.

[12] Cf. the Hell. burial inscr., → n. 4, or "Eat, drink, be merry, come," and on this G. Bertram, "The Problem of Death in Popular Judaeo-Hell. Piety," Crozer Quarterly, 10 (1933), 267; also "Hebr. u. griech. Qohelet," ZAW, NF, 22 (1951), esp. on 11:10; 12:1, also the saying of Chrysogonos of Cos in the imperial period in R. Herzog, Koische Forschungen u. Funde (1899), 103 ff., No. 163; cf. Deissmann LO⁴, 251: "Drink, thou dost see death." Ltzm. K. on I, 15:32 has further examples from inscr., cf. the literary refs. in Wettstein, ad loc. Historical integration is attempted by F. Dornseiff, "D. Buch Prediger," ZDMG, NF, 14 (1935), 243-249, also G. Kittel, Die Religionsgeschichte u. das Urchr. (1931), 116 f. Hdt., II, 78 describes the Egypt. table custom of Memento mori. Cf. the corresponding account in Plut. Sept. Sap. Conv., 2 (II, 148a-b) concerning the ἄχαρις καὶ ἄωρος ἐπίκωμος. Where Hdt. has πίνε καὶ τέρπευ Plut. tries to spiritualise : We simply have the admonition πρὸς τὸ πίνειν καὶ ἡδυπαθεῖν ἀλλὰ πρὸς φιλίαν καὶ ἀγάπησιν ἀλλήλων. In the so-called Harper Song from the New Kingdom c. 1450 B.C. we find the same deipnosophy : "Celebrate the merry day and do not grow weary, lo, to none is it granted to take his goods with him ...," AOT, 29; cf. Is. 22:13.

[13] R. Smend. Die Weisheit d. Jesus Sirach erklärt (1906), ad loc.

[14] In Prv. 26:19 παίζων ἔπραξα is a foolish excuse for a wrong action.

significant is Prv. 8:30 f. Here the HT reads : "Then I was at his side as a small child (אָמוֹן); then I was all delight, daily playing before him the whole time, playing on his earth, taking my delight in the children of men (playing ‗ מְשַׂחֶקֶת)." [15]

If wisdom speculations and christological chains of thought attached themselves to this passage, Ps. 104:26 makes it possible to introduce the idea of play into the doctrine of God, into theology in the narrower sense. Here the Mas. tells us that God created Leviathan to play with him (לְשַׂחֶק־בּוֹ) or that He created Leviathan to play in it, i.e., the sea. That He made Leviathan as a plaything is the view of Rabb. tradition and also of the LXX, which writes : δράκων ... ὃν ἔπλασας ἐμπαίζειν αὐτῷ. [16] The Rabb. or LXX understanding is in keeping with the original text. Thus the question in Job 40:29, which emphasises the fact that man cannot play (שׂחק) with Leviathan, pre-supposes that the Creator can. B has παίζειν here. [17]

The group has a more ironical sense in sayings about God's attitude to men in their petty and ridiculous pretension. Thus we read in Hab. 1:10 : τύραννοι παίγνια αὐτοῦ (מִשְׂחָק לוֹ). [18] In other places, too, παίζειν and derivates can be used for "to scorn." Thus Wis. 12:26 refers to mocking punishments (παιγνία ἐπιτιμήσεως). But παιγνία, for תִּפְלֶצֶת ‗ "fear," "terror," [19] can also be used of the inner attitude of men who have fallen victim to hubris, 'Ιερ. 30:10, Mas. 49:16. 'ΑΣ have ἀλαζοσύνη or ἀλαζονεία here. The par. is ἰταμία ("insolence," Heb. זָדוֹן). Just as God confronts human bravado with superior scorn, so those who are on God's side may mock at enemies, temptations, dangers and the world, cf. 4 Βασ. 19:21. It is said esp. of David in Sir. 47:3 : ἐν λέουσιν ἔπαιξεν (שׂחק) ὡς ἐν ἐρίφοις. Thus behind παίζειν as used by the Gk. translators of the OT stands the whole range of play and mockery, of bravado and arrogance.

4. παίζω in the New Testament.

In the NT παίζειν occurs only once at 1 C. 10:7 in an OT quotation from Ex. 32:6. Here the OT verse naturally stands already under the whole weight of the repudiation of all pagan cultic forms by Judaism. R. Akiba (d. c. 135 A.D.) construed צחק as "to engage in idolatry." [20] There can be no doubt that Ex. 32:19 refers to cultic dances. As in Gn. 26:8 (cf. 39:14, 17) צחק has an erotic sense, so

---

[15] On the difficult exegetical problems of the v. cf. B. Gemser, Sprüche Salomos ‗ Hndbch. z. AT, I, 16 (1937), ad loc., and L. Köhler, Lexicon in Veteris Testamenti libros (1948 ff.), 59, s.v. אָמוֹן. For אָמוֹן ("small child") the Mas. has אָמוֹן ("master builder"). The LXX (ἁρμόζουσα) also sets aside the idea of play, but the Hexapla translations keep it.

[16] So also F. Baethgen, Die Ps. (1904), ad loc., and H. Schmidt, op. cit., also A. Bertholet in Kautzsch, ad loc., who alludes to the equation of this fabled creature with the crocodile in Job 40:25 ff., and Helbing, 271 (s.v. ἐμπαίζειν). On the other hand 'ΑΣ have αὐτῇ with ref. to the sea, also Jerome (ut inluderet ei), Luther, A.V. Hence the ref. is to an ordinary fish, not the mythical Leviathan. For Rabb. exegesis cf. bAZ, 3b, R. Jehuda in the name of Rab (d. 247 A.D.).

[17] Σ has ἐμπαίζειν at Job 40:29, also 'ΑΣ at Ps. 104:26. This makes the mythological background clearer : As victor over the ancient dragon Yahweh can play with him in mockery.

[18] The grammatical subj. in Hab. 1:10 is the people which carries out God's plan. God is the logical subj. The people enjoys His power and scornful supremacy, Ps. 2:4; the ref. then, is not to human arrogance as in Is. 10:8-16. Cf. also F. Horst and T. Robinson, Die 12 kleinen Proph. ‗ Hndbch. z. AT, I, 14 (1938), ad loc. (172): "For this people, called in by Yahweh, is the agent of His will, the executor of His judgment, and hence the embodiment of crushing penal force which causes fear and horror."

[19] As the many different renderings and par. concepts show, there is doubt as to the meaning of תִּפְלָצֶת. Cf. W. Rudolph, Jeremia ‗ Hndbch. z. AT, I, 12 (1947), ad loc.

[20] For further material, and the same view in Akiba's contemporary, R. Yishmael, cf. Str.-B., III, 410, 2.

צחק can denote both idolatry and also the cultic licentiousness often associated with it. Tertullian in De Jejunio, 6 speaks of *lusus impudicus* with ref. to the verse in Ex. 32:6. Along with the idea of idolatry he follows herewith a second Rabb. tradition which in accordance with the subsidiary erotic meaning of צחק sees a reference to shameless dances, T. Sota, 6, 6 (R. Eliezer b. Jose of Galilee, *c.* 150 A.D.). For the Corinthian Christians, too, the diversion of sacrificial feasts was a great temptation to idolatry.[21] Thus in Christian exegesis, esp. in respect of the meaning of παίζειν (1 C. 10:7), there is essential agreement: *Ludere aliquando lasciviam significat, aliquando saltationes impudicas, Judaeis idololatriam.*[22]

† ἐμπαίζω.

1. The Vocabulary of Mockery in the Greek OT.

ἐμπαίζειν means first "to play with," "to dance around," then "to take one's sport with someone," "to mock," "to mock someone," also "to deceive," "to defraud," e.g., Hdt., IV, 134: ὁρῶν αὐτοὺς ἐμπαίζοντας ἡμῖν, Soph. Ant., 799: ἄμαχος γὰρ ἐμπαίζει θεὸς Ἀφροδίτα, Anth. Pal., 10, 56, 2: τοῖς ἐμπαιζομένοις ἀνδράσι ταῦτα λέγω, also the pap.: ἐνέπεξέν (ἐνέπαιξέν) με.[1] It belongs to a large group of words[2] for the disparagement or low estimation of others, or indeed the world, creatures, and even deity, in word, attitude or act: contemptuous speech, scorn and insult, ridicule, speaking ill, turning up the nose (→ ἐκ-μυκτηρίζειν, IV, 796 f.), shaking the head (→ κινεῖν τὴν κεφαλήν, → III, 718, 20), clapping the hands as a sign of scorn (ἀνα-κροτεῖν), whistling (συρίζειν, συρισμός), spitting (ἐμπτύειν), finding fault (φαυλί-ζειν), tittle-tattling (κατα-φλυαρεῖν), dissecting, backbiting, dragging in the dust (δια-παρασύρειν), mocking (χλευάζειν), whispering, calumniating secretly (ψιθυρί-ζειν), ridiculing (καταχαίρειν, ἐκγελᾶν), disparaging (ἐξουδενεῖν), bantering (τω-θάζειν), making fun of (ἀθύρειν), disdaining (κατα-μωκᾶσθαι, κατειρωνεύεσθαι), deriding (γελοιάζειν). παίζειν belongs to this group along with its compounds, which include ἐκ-, κατα, προσ- and συμπαίζειν as well as ἐμπαίζειν. There may be a reason for the scorn, or there may not. It may be an exercise of constructive or even instructive criticism and express real superiority, or it may derive from foolish (→ μωρός) arro-gance (→ ὕβρις), basic hostility and aversion, so that in the last resort it can be a special manifestation of the enmity of evil against good. This attitude of basic hostility often finds expression in the fact that the wicked do not take the utterances of the righteous seriously, cf. Noah[3] and Lot (Gn. 19:14: Both sons-in-law think he is jesting), also the prophets, e.g., Is. 28:7 ff.

In Gk. as in Heb., the words in this group, which leads us into the broad sphere of sins of the tongue, are very numerous, though they do not always correspond in detail. The LXX often refers to scorn and mockery where the HT does not primarily refer either to the term or to the thing itself. In so doing the LXX is simply fitting a specific circumstance into its Jewish schema of piety. The main Heb. terms are a. לעג and תְּעַתֻּעִים. The verb is used esp. in a v. which is important in the passion piety of Judaism

---

[21] Bchm. K.[3], 332.

[22] Wettstein, *ad loc.*

ἐ μ π α ί ζ ω. [1] Preisigke, *Griech. Urkunden d. ägyptischen Museums zu Cairo* (1911), 3, 10 (362 A.D.). On the constr. cf. Helbing Kasussyntax, 271 f.

[2] Cf. F. Dornseiff, *Der deutsche Wortschatz nach Sachgruppen*[2] (1940), *s.v.* "Spott" etc.

[3] Utnapishtim, too, is questioned with open mockery by the people because he builds the chest, A. Jeremias, *Das AT im Lichte des Alten Orients*[4] (1930), 151. Cf. also Koran Sura, 11, 3: "Noah, then, made the ark, and whenever a crowd of his people went by, they laughed at him. But he said: 'You now mock at us; later we shall mock at you as you now mock at us.'" The Koran can also speak of the basic scorning of revelation, cf. 11, 4: "But then will be fulfilled what they laugh at now" (i.e., the revelation).

and Christianity, namely, 2 Ch. 36:16 = 1 Εσδρ. 1:49. [4] Joseph. has ὑβρίζειν in the corresponding Ant., 10, 103. For the hitp of זעע at Gn. 27:12, too, Σ has καταπαίζειν, LXX καταφρονεῖν, 'Α καταμωκᾶσθαι. Materially the ref. is to Jacob, who deals with his father as one who makes mock. The noun at Jer. 51:18 denotes idols as a subject of scorn; the LXX (28:18) has ἔργα μεμωκημένα, Σ the materially equivalent παιγνία. At Jer. 10:15, from which the text derives, the LXX has ἐμπεπαιγμένα, 'Α μεμωκημένα, and Σ χλευασμοῦ. b. קלס means in the hi and hitp "to ridicule," and various Gk. terms are regularly employed for it : 2 K. 2:23 καταπαίζειν, Hab. 1:10 : ἐντρυφᾶν, Σ ἐμπαίζειν, Ez. 22:5 ἐμπαίζειν. The ref. in Ez. 22:4 f. is to the contempt and scorn which Yahweh will bring on Jerusalem. Sir. 11:4 has ἐπαίρεσθαι, קלס being taken in the newer sense "to boast," so that the hubris motif replaces that of scorn. The nouns קלס and קלסה are rendered χλευασμός at Jer. 20:8, also the same or κατάγελως at ψ 43:12, χλευασμός at ψ 78:4, and ἐμπαιγμός at Ez. 22:4. c. More common are שׂחק and צחק, "to laugh," pi "to jest," and derivates ; these are rendered (ἐπι-, ἐγ-, ἐκ-, κατα-)γελᾶν, γελοιάζειν, (ἐν-)εὐφραίνειν, συγχαίρειν, ὀρχεῖσθαι, χαρμονὴν ποιεῖν, and usually for pi παίζειν and ἐμπαίζειν in 26 of 57 instances. [5] d. עלל "to insult someone," hitp "to act wantonly," is rendered ἐμπαίζειν in 6 of the instances in which it occurs in the hitp : Ex. 10:2; Nu. 22:29; Ju. 19:25 (Joseph. uses ὑβρίζειν, ὕβρις, καθυβρίζειν in his account of the story in Ant., 5, 145-148); 1 S. 6:6; 31:4; 1 Ch. 10:4; in the 7th at Ιερ. 45(38):19 καταμωκᾶσθαι is used. The derived תעלולים, "caprice," "knavishness," [6] the "fate which plays with someone," is in its two occurrences rendered ἐμπαῖκται by the LXX at Is. 3:4 ('Α ἐναλλάκται) and ἔμπαιγμα at Is. 66:4. The Mas. reads : "I will also choose for them a fate which will play them ill, and I will bring that which they dread upon them." Like תעלולים, then, ἔμπαιγμα is not something which men do but something which they suffer. It is the punishment which God brings on them. It might be a mocking punishment, as in Wis. 12:26, → 629, 16 ff. The mockery here, however, is in an act, not in words. In the 2nd half of the verse there is ref. to the sinful action which is the reason for the punishment, → I, 288, 30 ff. e. לעג and לַעַג are transl. 8 times → (ἐκ-)μυκτηρίζειν, also 6 times ἐκ- and καταγελᾶν, and once each καταμωκᾶσθαι, φαυλίζειν or φαυλισμός. In the free rendering of Job 11:3 תלעג is passed over, and ἀποστερεῖν is used at Sir. 4:1. For the noun לעג μυκτηρισμός is used 3 times (ψ 43:13; 78:4; Job 34:7), φαυλισμός at Hos. 7:16, ὄνειδος at ψ 122:4, καταπάτημα at Ez. 36:4, no LXX at Ez. 23:32. Only in the secondary tradition is the relevant part of verse added, Θ ἔσται εἰς γέλωτα καὶ εἰς μυκτηρισμόν. f. לעב, "to deride," is a hapax legomenon in the Mas. at 2 Ch. 36:16; the LXX has μυκτηρίζειν (1 Εσδρ. 1:49 ἐκ-). It is read as an emendation at Sir. 30:13; [7] the LXX has a different text. g. בון and בוה "to mock," are taken to imply despising or disparagement rather than actual mockery in the LXX, hence the usual renderings are ἐξουθενεῖν, καταφρονεῖν, φαυλίζειν, and only occasionally do we find μυκτηρίζειν (Prv. 11:12; 12:8; 15:20 → IV, 796, 8 f.) or καταγελᾶν (Gn. 38:23; Sir. 7:11), cf. also μυκτηρισμός at 2 Εσδρ. 13:36. h. There is also a series of Heb. words used only occasionally for mockery and derision, so בוס, which in Prv. 27:7 is rendered ἐμπαίζειν in the sense of "despise." i. גדף, "to deride," "blaspheme," is usually taken by the LXX in the latter sense, and is thus rendered βλασφημεῖν, ὀνειδίζειν etc. k. For הלל,

---

[4] For זעע the LXX has ἐμπαίζειν or ἐκπαίζειν. Cf. ἀτιμάζειν in Lk. 20:11; this is often used with the words for "scorn." It is the only term of this kind in Is. 53 ("to despise").

[5] In the story of Samson at Ju. 16:25 the Mas. and LXX B have ; "He played (an instrument) before them." A has : "They mocked him (ἐνέπαιζον αὐτῷ)," although παιξάτω ἐνώπιον ἡμῶν is uniform in all earlier traditions. Joseph. has (ἐν-)ὑβρίζειν in the corresponding Ant., 5, 314 f., Θ has παίξεται θηλάζον at Is. 11:8 too (LXX παιδίον νήπιον), cf. J. Ziegler, Septuaginta XIV, Isaias (1939), ad loc.

[6] Abstractum pro concreto like the translations, but the meaning is contested.

[7] Cf. Ges.-Buhl, s.v.

"to hit," ἐμπαίζειν is used in Prv. 23:35; in this way the LXX, which is materially right, expresses the element of scorn. The ἀνακροτεῖν of Θ refers to mock clapping of the hands. The LXX transl. intentionally chose ἐνέπαιξαν rather than the lit. ἐνέπαισαν to depict this aspect of the situation of the drunkard. [8] l. כְּלִמָּה, כלם, חֶרְפָּה, חרף are taken by the LXX in the sense of defamation rather than derision. m. The hapax legomenon מוק "to scorn" in Ps. 73:8 is referred by the LXX to the mind and rendered διενοήθησαν. n. Similarly at 1 K. 2:8; Mi. 2:10; Job 6:25; 16:3 the LXX did not recognise the use of מרץ for "to scorn," and rendered it by other terms. o. The double transl. of ענה pi "to treat badly" at Ju. 20:5 A by ἐταπείνωσαν καὶ ἐνέπαιξαν αὐτῇ (B only ἐταπείνωσαν) amplifies along the lines of 19:25. p. Like ענה, פֶּרֶךְ "mistreatment" at Ex. 1:13 in Θ [9] and at Lv. 25:43, 46 in an anon. translator, is rendered ἐμπαιγμός. Σ has ἐντρυφῶντες in the first ref., while the LXX transl. the word, which occurs only 6 times, by βία at Ex. 1:13, 14 and μόχθος at Lv. 25:43, 46-53; Ez. 34:4. Zech. 12:3 LXX is reminiscent of the ideas echoed in these verses. [10] The Mas. takes a different course : "And in that day I will make Jerusalem a burdensome stone for all people ; all that burden themselves with it shall be cut in pieces, [11] and all the people of the earth shall be gathered together against it." In contrast the LXX reads : "And it shall come to pass in that day that I will make Jerusalem for all peoples the stone which shall be trodden upon. Everyone who treads upon it in scorn shall himself receive scorn (ἐμπαίζων ἐμπαίξεται), and on him shall all the nations of earth gather." The LXX transl. seems to have had something of the same thought in Is. 33:4 when he renders שׁקק "to fall upon" (variously transl. in the LXX, only 6 times in the Mas.) by ἐμπαίζειν. [12] q. Sir. 13:6, 7 has several words from the group in Heb.: Unequal dealings lead to dissimulation. Flattery, jesting (שׂחק), the kindling of hopes, fine words, make a fool of him who is deceived by them : התל (μυκτηρίζειν at LXX 1 K. 18:27 [→ IV, 796, 8 f.], καυχᾶσθαι at Sir. 11:4 [→ III, 647, 10 f.], construed differently and rendered ἀποκενοῦν at Sir. 13:6 f.), ערץ "to outwit," "overreach" (?) [13] καταμωκᾶσθαι, [14] נוּעַ בְּרֹאשׁ κινεῖν τὴν κεφαλήν. התל is a secondary development from the hi of תלל "to deceive," "to defraud"; it is transl. καταπαίζειν in Jer. 9:4, 'Α παραλογίζεσθαι. It expresses in the LXX the fact that deceiving one's neighbour always implies disparagement. The noun הֲתֻלִּים ("mockeries") from תלל occurs only at Job 17:2. Here the LXX has a different text. Σ has παραλογίζεσθαι, "to be cheated," so that once again we have the same combination of deceiving and despising. r. Sir. 8:4 has προσπαίζειν for רגל. The HT reads : "Have no dealings (ל with fools, that he despise not those of noble disposition." The LXX reads : "Do not jest with the uneducated, that thy conduct be not reviled." This is consequently a weaker use in rules of life which are applied

---

[8] Here, as often, the LXX abandons the Heb. parallelism in favour of a progressive depiction. ἐμπαίειν does not occur in the Gk. OT, nor παίειν and compounds for הלם.

[9] Jos. Ant., 2, 202 has ἐνυβρίζειν. Elsewhere, too, Joseph. prefers the concept of hubris in the sense of bravado or arrogance, cf. Ant., 2, 54 on Gn. 39:17, צחק= ἐμπαίζειν LXX.

[10] In 2 Ch. 29:8 שְׁרֵקָה is transl. συρισμός. Yahweh gives Jerusalem εἰς ἔκστασιν καὶ εἰς ἀφανισμὸν καὶ εἰς συρισμόν. Cf. Mi. 6:16 (par. ὀνείδη λαῶν for וְחֶרְפַּת עַמִּי) Jer. 18:16; 19:8; 25:9, 18. Also συρίζειν for שׁרק in Jer. 3 times and Lam. 2:15.

[11] Mas. שׂרט, so lit. Θ.

[12] Sir. 27:28 contains a rule of wisdom which is pertinent here : ἐμπαιγμὸς καὶ ὀνειδισμὸς ὑπερηφάνῳ, unless we are to read ὑπερηφάνων and transl. "on the part of the arrogant." But in the context the dat. is more probable : "Scorn and contempt will be the portion of the arrogant." Cf. R. Smend, Die Weisheit des Jesus Sirach erklärt (1906), ad loc. V. Ryssel in Kautzsch Apkr. u. Pseudepigr., ad loc. prefers the second reading.

[13] Acc. to Smend, op. cit.

[14] Perhaps καταμωκᾶσθαι is used for the Heb. התל, and ἀποκενοῦν is supplied from v. 5, where it is a transl. of רשׁשׁ "to make poor."

differently in the Gk. and Heb., and which are to some degree textually uncertain. s. Fig. one might mention "to sharpen the tongue" in Ps. 64:3; 140:3. But the ref. here, perhaps, is to calumny or even magic and cursing [15] rather than mockery. Nah. 2:4 is hard to understand both in the Mas. and the LXX. [16] t. At Jer. 2:16 the transl. has attempted to render the fig. "to feed on the crown" by καταπαίζειν. The people is given up, defenceless and helpless, to the violence and mockery of its enemies. The double transl. ἔγνωσάν σε καὶ κατέπαιζόν σου rests on confusion of יְרָעוּךְ and יְדַעוּךְ (?). The former refers to the sexual delivering up of the subjugated. Hence the idea of mockery takes on a radical sense appropriate to the context.

2. The Motif of Mockery in the Martyr Piety of Judaism.

The word is common in those parts of the OT found only in Gk. or written in Gk. Indeed, there seems to be here a distinct vocabulary which developed in Jewish passion piety. At any rate, the nouns ἔμπαιγμα, ἐμπαιγμός, ἐμπαιγμονή, ἐμπαίκτης are found only in the LXX or NT. Only συμπαιγμός occurs also in profane Gk. on a pre-Christian pap. [17] The hubris of the mighty finds expression in Bar. 3:17. The ref. is to the commanders of the nations who defied the birds under heaven. The use in Wis. 17:7 is different. Here the mockery lies in an error called forth by magical arts. At Wis. 12:25 f., to which ref. has been made already (→ 631, 26), God is the subj. Acc. to the author He first sends only derisive punishments as upon unreasonable children. Acc. to 12:23, 24, 27 the plagues which came on the Egyptians (cf. 11:15-12:2) are obviously punishments of this kind. What ἐμπαιγμός means may be seen most plainly from the statement that "thou hast tormented them with their own abominations." [18] The mockery is a punishment for sin to those against whom it is directed. On the other hand, it is a test when the ungodly ridicule the righteous by inflicting torments. The word group is used in this sense in Macc. At 1 Macc. 9:26 we read that Bacchides took revenge and vented his scorn on the supporters of Judas, and this brought great affliction on Israel. In the par. account in Jos. Ant., 13, 4 it is worth noting that we find : ὁ δὲ βασανίζων πρῶτον αὐτοὺς καὶ πρὸς ἡδονὴν αἰκιζόμενος. This corresponds exactly to the presentation of persecutions in Jewish passion piety. In 2 Macc. 7:7, 10 the word is even used directly of the martyrdom of the seven brothers. In 2 Macc. 8:17 the ref. is to hubris against the temple, the despising and maltreatment of the city, and finally the removal of its constitution. This suggests shameful acts whereby those affected were humiliated. Similarly in 3 Macc. 5:22 terrible tortures are obviously to be inferred from the mockery.

Here, then, the word group is used in a special way. It has a place in the depiction of Gentile abominations against the Jews. The way is prepared for this usage in the LXX. The Heb. OT offers no specific linguistic basis for the group. It is the translator who according to his own conception classified certain data from the OT story of Jewish piety under the slogan of mockery. Obviously the ref. in many cases is to derision and ridicule not merely by words but also by action, namely, by humiliating tortures which can even lead to martyrdom. In this respect the group is to be differentiated esp. from μυκτηρίζειν and derivates, but also from ὑβρίζειν. The latter terms refer more to the subjective attitude towards the one derided, particularly as expressed in words.

---

[15] Cf. H. Schmidt, Die Ps. = Hndbch. z. AT, I, 15 (1934), ad loc., and esp. S. Mowinckel, Psalmenstudien, I : "Åwän u. d. individuellen Klagepsalmen" (1921), ad loc., who construes sins of the tongue largely as magic.

[16] Cf. H. Guthe in Kautzsch, ad loc.; with emendations F. Horst-T. H. Robinson, Die 12 kleinen Proph. = Hndbch. z. AT, I, 14 (1938), ad loc. On the constr. cf. Helbing, 271. Instead of the part. pu of תלע, "clothed in scarlet" (hapax legomenon) the transl. read a form of עלל, whose hitp is regularly transl. ἐμπαίζειν. Here, too, the idea of mocking brings us into the vicinity of pride and arrogance (→ ὕβρις).

[17] Moult.-Mill., s.v. ἐμπαιγμός : P. Tor., I, 1, VI, 15 (117/116 B.C.).

[18] → βασανίζειν, I, 562, 19 ff.; βάσανος also occurs in Wis. 2:19 (par with ὕβρις) in the sense of "derision."

3. ἐμπαίζω in the New Testament.

The word group ἐμπαίζειν is not very common in the NT. The verb ἐμπαίζειν occurs only in the Synoptic Gospels. At Mt. 2:16 Herod is outwitted by the wise men. This use in the sense of "to dupe" corresponds to that in Wis. 17:7. [19] Acc. to Lk. 14:29 the imprudent builder brings down on himself the ridicule of those around. The reference is to verbal ridicule of the inability of the builder to finish what he has begun. The person of the builder himself is herewith disparaged because of his weakness, whether this consists in lack of thought, in rash arrogance, or simply in the fact of failure. [20]

All the other passages refer to Jesus. The term occurs in predictions of the passion. [21] The third and most express intimation of the passion in Mt. 20:19 = Mk. 10:34 = Lk. 18:32 contains the word ἐμπαίζειν in all three Gospels. In Mt. μαστιγοῦν and σταυροῦν are used with it. Mk. has ἐμπαίζειν, ἐμπτύειν, μαστιγοῦν and ἀποκτείνειν; of these ἐμπτύειν and μαστιγοῦν might be regarded as elucidations of ἐμπαίζεν. Lk., however, has the pass. ἐμπαίζειν, ὑβρίζειν and ἐμπτύειν; ὑβρίζειν is to be taken as a synonym of ἐμπαίζειν, while spitting seems to be an individual form of derision. The scourging is related to the putting to death in the form of a part. aor., and the two go together. The mockery here is that of the Gentiles, into whose hands Jesus is delivered.

In the passion story itself there is a specific account of the mocking in Mk. 15:16-20 = Mt. 27:27-31. The acts of the soldiers, putting on a purple robe and a crown of thorns, saluting Him, smiting Him with a reed, spitting and bowing before Him, constitute the mockery. [22] Only Mt. says that the reed with which they smote Him served as a sceptre. The tradition does not expressly say that the crown of thorns was the specific form of torture it was later made out to be in Christian art. Nor do Mt. and Mk. say plainly what was the temporal and material relation of the scourging to the mockery. Jn. 19:1-3 is clearer on this point. [23] There it may be seen that the μαστιγοῦν (→ IV, 517) took the form of ἐμπαίζειν, that is, the soldiers did not simply carry out the punishment of scourging, but ridiculed and reviled the prisoner as they struck Him. This is the fact behind the Synoptic Gospels. [24] In what follows the scourging of Jn. 19:1 is then more precisely described as mockery with the ensuing blows. Whether

---

[19] Cf. J. Fichtner, Weisheit Salomos = Hndbch. z. AT, II, 6 (1938), ad loc., who translates "pretences" and refers to Mt. 2:16. B. Weiss, Mt.[9] (1898), ad loc. refers to Soph. Ant., 799 (→ 630, 13). Zn. Mt.⁴, 108 sees in the hypocritical promise to return, and the deception, a mocking of King Herod.

[20] A scholion of Hagios Maximos applies the parable to the tower of Christian gnosis. The acquisition of a certain item of knowledge is needed to complete this. The man who does not have the necessary requirements for this falls victim to the derision of men and demons. Cf. Cramer Cat. on Lk. 14:28.

[21] On the mocking of Jesus cf. J. G. Frazer, The Golden Bough³, III (1923), 226-229 (par. in religion and folklore); H. Reich, "Der König mit der Dornenkrone," N. Jbch. Kl. Alt., 7 (1904), 704-732; G. Bertram, Die Leidensgeschichte Jesu u. der Christuskult (1922), 72 f., 79-85; R. Delbrück, "Antiquarisches zu den Verspottungen Jesu," ZNW, 41 (1942), 124-145.

[22] Philo Flacc., 33-34 has the story of a mocking of King Agrippa I in Alexandria which is often adduced as a par. But this seems to have been an anti-semitic demonstration on the part of the city population, and there were no acts of violence.

[23] Cf. also Ev. Pt. The word ἐμπαίζειν does not occur in Jn. or Ev. Pt. μαστιγοῦν occurs in the intimations of the passion and the prediction of the fate of the disciples, Mt. 20:19; 10:17 etc. At Mt. 27:26 and Mk. 15:15 we find φραγελλοῦν, cf. φραγέλλιον in Jn. 2:15. παιδεύω → 621, n. 160.

[24] The Ebed Yahweh Song also distinguishes between scourging and smiting on the cheek, Is. 50:6.

the soldiers here observed a specific (religious) custom, whether they were following, e.g., the Persian practice of Sacaean sacrifice, or whether they were simply holding up the supposed King of the Jews to incidental ridicule, it is hardly possible to say with any certainty. The misunderstood Messianic claim of Jesus is certainly adequate to explain the scene.

Something similar is already recorded in Mt. 26:67 f.; Mk. 14:65; Lk. 22:63-65 concerning the hearing before the Jews. Here, too, details are mentioned: ἐμπτύειν, [25] κολαφίζειν (→ III, 819, 3), ῥαπίζειν (ῥαπίσμασιν λαβεῖν). Only Lk. uses ἐμπαίζειν as a comprehensive term for the whole incident. The obvious similarity with the mockery by the soldiers is hereby emphasised, though now the ridicule is against the Prophet rather than the King. [26] According to Lk., whose account deviates here in other ways from that of Mt. and Mk., the guards mock Him overnight to while away the time prior to the decisive morning meeting of the Sanhedrin. In Mt. and Mk. the hearing and condemnation precede the mocking, and it seems as if the very judges themselves express their contempt by scorn and derision. [27] Though the word ἐμπαίζειν is not used, we find the terms which characterise the martyrdom of the righteous as derision; Jesus is spat upon, maltreated, derided and smitten as a prophet. [28]

Finally, in the material peculiar to Lk. ἐμπαίζειν occurs at 23:11, this time with ἐξουθενεῖν. Herod and his soldiers mock Jesus. The robe with which they invest Him is for the purpose of ridicule, so that the whole incident seems to be "a prelude to the mockery and investiture by Pilate's soldiers, which is not recorded in Lk." [29]

The motif of mockery occurs for a third time in all the Synoptists at the actual crucifixion, Mk. 15:31; Mt. 27:41; Lk. 23:35 (ἐκμυκτηρίζειν, → IV, 798, 32 ff.). Mk. and Mt. use ἐμπαίζειν to describe the attitude and conduct of the high-priests and scribes. [30] The subject of their derision is the crucifixion of the innocent between two malefactors, the inscription on the cross, and the conduct of those at the cross. There is at any rate fulfilled here what the story of Jewish martyrdom had already taught (→ 633, 10 ff.): Martyrdom is ἐμπαιγμός, that is, the raw act of violence expresses a sinful attitude and disposition, the attitude of the mocker, towards the instrument of revelation. This explains the use of the word ἐμπαίζειν in the passion story of our Lord. Behind it, however, stands the development and specific application of the word in Jewish passion piety.

† ἐμπαιγμονή, † ἐμπαιγμός, † ἐμπαίκτης.

How important ἐμπαίζειν is in the NT may be seen from the fact that new terms are coined from the stem ἐμπαίζειν. From the OT ἐμπαιγμός (e.g., ψ 37:8; Ez. 22:4) and ἐμπαίκτης (Is. 3:4) are adopted. On the whole the word ἐμπαίζειν

---

[25] Cf. the spitting in Is. 50:6.

[26] Cf. the vl. of D at Mk. 14:65 and Wellh. Mk., ad loc., who thinks that the original pt. was that the soldiers wanted to stop Jesus prophesying by blows, so that the demand was ironic.

[27] In Mk. 14:65 the servants are explicitly mentioned as well as the indefinite "they."

[28] Cf. also Is. 50:6. βλασφημεῖν → I, 621 and δέρειν are also tt. for the passion of Jesus and His disciples.

[29] Zn. Lk., ad loc.

[30] Lk. 23:36 f. uses the term again when it remodels the drink motif into a mocking. In Mt. 27:34 the humane custom correctly recorded in Mk. 15:23 again seems to become a mocking under the influence of OT prophecy (Ps. 69:21). On the further development of the mockery motif cf. W. Bauer, Das Leben Jesu im Zeitalter der nt.lichen Apkr. (1909), 199-207.

is restricted to the passion narrative, and in the first instance is used neither of
the disciples and followers of the Lord nor of Christians generally. Nevertheless
the context and specific content of Hb. 11:36 show that the reference is to christologically defined martyr piety. The verse has in view the martyrdom of the OT
righteous, which in the light of Christ can be called ἐμπαιγμῶν καὶ μαστίγων
πεῖρα. The phrase is parallel to the ὀνειδισμὸς τοῦ Χριστοῦ of Hb. 11:26. The
terms ἐμπαιγμονή and ἐμπαῖκται occur only once or twice in the NT at Jd. 18
and 2 Pt. 3:3 (ἐμπαιγμονή is not in ℵ al and is materially of no significance).
The mockers referred to in Jd. 18 and the par. 2 Pt. 3:3 are possibly Gnostic
Libertines. [1] Their mockery seems to be directed against the delay in the *parousia,*
and consequently against the Church's eschatology in general. [2] Certainly 2 Pt.
understood Jd. 18 in this way. Originally the term might have had a more general
reference. The scoffer is the opposite of the righteous, and though each age and
ecclesiastical trend has its specific opponents, who are condemned, the designation
"mocker" does not mean that these opponents scoffed at specific Church views
or doctrines, but simply characterises the attitude of these men as hostile to revelation, or ungodly, as the examples adduced in Jd. 4 ff. show. In the NT mockers or
scoffers are enemies of the cross of Christ, Phil. 3:18; cf. Gl. 5:11; 6:12; also
1 C. 1:23. The enemies in Jd. are to be regarded as such, and even the special use
in 2 Pt. should not be isolated from this basic NT understanding. For it was in
this sense that the concept of mockery received its definitive biblical imprint in
the passion narratives.

Bertram

παῖς, † παιδίον, † παιδάριον, τέκνον, † τεκνίον, † βρέφος   → υἱός.

Contents : A. Lexical Data. B. The Child from the Natural and Ethico-Religious Standpoint : I. The Child in Antiquity : 1. Original Positive Estimation ; 2. Decline and Counter-
Measures from the Classical Period ; 3. The Rediscovery of the Child in Hellenism ;
4. Ethico-Religious Evaluation ; 5. The Child in the Cultus. II. The Child in the Old
Testament and Judaism : 1. The Religious Evaluation of Progeny ; 2. The Estimation of
the Child ; 3. The Participation of the Child in Religious Exercises. III. The Child in the
New Testament : 1. Affirmation of the Child as a Creature of God ; 2. Affirmation of the
Individuality of Children ? 3. The Child in God's Saving Counsel. IV. The Later Church
and the Child : 1. The Child as Creature of God ; 2. The Relation to the Child ; 3. The
Child in the Cultus : a. Clerical Functions; b. Infant Baptism and Communion. C. Divine
Sonship. I. Religio-Historical Connections. II. Divine Sonship in the New Testament.
III. Divine Sonship in the Church.

ἐ μ π α ι γ μ ο ν ή κ τ λ. [1] Wnd. Pt. on 2 Pt. 3:3.
[2] Wnd. Kath. Br. on Jd. 18.
π α ῖ ς κ τ λ. On A : Liddell-Scott, Walde-Pok., Pr.-Bauer, *s.v.* On B I : H. Preisker,
Nt.liche Zeitgeschichte (1938), 22; J. Leipoldt, *Das Kind in d. alten Welt* (no year); P.
Stengel, *D. griech. Kultusaltertümer*[3] (1920), 38, 209, 215, 228; I. v. Müller and A. Bauer,
D. griech. Privat- u. Kriegsaltertümer[2] (1893), 147, 154-184; H. Blümner, *D. römischen Privataltertümer* (1911), 304; O. Seeck, *Gesch. des Untergangs d. antiken Welt,* I[3] (1910), 337-
390; O. v. Allmen, *Das Kind in d. epischen Dichtung d. Griechen,* Diss. Berne (1923);
J. Overbeck, "Die Entdeckung des Kindes im 1. Jhdt. n. Chr.," N. Jbch. Kl. Alt., 27, Vol. 54
(1924), 1-8; J. Xirotyris, *Die Auffassung von Kind u. Kinderleben bei d. griech. Roman-
schriftstellern der Spätantike,* Diss. Munich (1936); D. Heubach, *Das Kind in d. griech.
Kunst,* Diss. Heidelberg (1903); M. Quatember, *Die Darstellung von Mutter u. Kind in d.
antiken Kunst,* Diss. Vienna (1948); H. Devrient, "Das Kind auf d. antiken Bühne," *Jahresbericht Weimar* (1904); O. Köhler, De Hautontimorumeni Terentianae compositione, Diss.

A. Lexical Data.

1. βρέφος, from Hom. and Pind., pap., means "young," "fruit of the body," as "embryo," of animals, Hom. Il., 23, 266, of men, Sir. 19:11; Lk. 1:41, 44; "small child," "infant," 1 Macc. 1:61; 2 Macc. 6:10; 4 Macc. 4:25; Jos. Bell., 6, 205; Lk. 2:12, 16; 18:15; Ac. 7:19. ἀπὸ βρέφους, "from a child," 2 Tm. 3:15; fig. 1 Pt. 2:2 : ὡς ἀρτιγέννητα βρέφη.

2. παῖς, strictly παϝις, on vases παῦς, from √ pŏu, pau, pu, "small," "little," cf. pauper, paucus, parvus, paulus, puer, pusus, pusillus, puella,[1] usually masc. "boy," in a settlement law from Locris opp. κόρα.[2] Hom. Il., 1, 20, 443 etc.: "girl," "daughter," Gn. 34:4 B (A παιδίσκη) for יַלְדָּה, Dt. 22:28 for נַעֲרָה, "maiden," Lk. 8:51, 54 of a 12 yr. old. a. The ref. of παῖς may be to age, "child," inscr., pap., ironically Hom. Or., 4, 665, non-ironically Prv. 1:4. It can be used for a boy of 7-14 as distinct from one not yet 7 (παιδίον) or the adolescent (μειράκιον) of 14-21, Hippocr. De Hebdomadibus, 5;[3] cf. Xenoph. Cyrop., VIII, 7, 6; LXX Prv. 1:4 (elsewhere with the more precise differentiation παιδίον, παιδάριον, νεανίσκος). In the NT of infants, Mt. 2:16; growing children, Mt. 17:18; 21:15; Lk. 9:42; Ἰησοῦς ὁ παῖς, the 12 yr. old, Lk. 2:43; youth, Ac. 20:12, cf. v. 9. b. Another ref. is to descent, "son," Hom. Il., 2, 205; Thuc., I, 4; inscr., pap.; LXX for בֵּן only Prv. 4:1; 20:7, for נַעַר Prv. 29:15; Job 29:5; = υἱός Jn. 4:51, cf. v. 46 f., 50; so also Mt. 8:6, 8, 13, though probably sense c. c. It can refer also to social position, "boy," "servant," "slave," not Hom.; Aesch. Choeph., 653; Aristoph. Ach., 395; Nu., 132 with παιδίον; Plut. Alcibiades, 4 (I, 193d); Adulat., 24 (II, 65c); 31 (II, 70e); Ditt. Syll.³, 96, 26; often pap.; predominant in the LXX, mostly for עֶבֶד, Aram. עֲבֵד, or נַעַר, not in 2-4 Macc. or Wis., though possibly Wis. 2:13 in the sense "servant of God" (→ 652, 12-654, 20), so also Bar. 2:28, 20 of Moses and prophets, though like Wis. 2:16,

---

Leipzig (1908), 21; K. Latte, "Schuld u. Sünde in d. griech. Religion," ARW, 20 (1920), 254, 282; G. van der Leeuw, Virginibus puerisque (1939), 13-24, 33; L. Deubner, Attische Feste (1932), 142, 199; A. Dieterich, "Sommertag," Kl. Schriften (1911), 324-352; also "Mutter Erde," ARW, 8 Beih. (1905); A. Oepke, "Ἀμφιθαλεῖς im griech. u. hell. Kult," ARW, 31 (1934), 42-56; E. Groag, Art. "Camillus" in Pauly-W., III, 1431 f.; C. G. Jung and K. Kerényi, Einführung in das Wesen d. Mythologie. Gottkindmythos. Eleusinische Mysterien (1941), 41-102 (1951 ed. not available); E. Norden, Die Geburt des Kindes = Studien d. Bibliothek Warburg, 3 (1924). On B II : J. Benzinger, Hbr. Archäologie³ (1927), 121-130; J. Hempel, Gott u. Mensch im AT,² BWANT, 3 F. 2 (1936), 193 f., 197 f., 234, 275; R. Meyer, Hellenistisches in d. rabb. Anthropologie (1937), esp. 87, 88, 103-114; Str.-B., Index s.v. "Kind." On B III : A. Oepke, "Jesus u. das Kind," AELKZ, 65 (1932), 33-36, 55-59, 74-78; J. Jeremias, Hat die Urkirche die Kindertaufe geübt ?² (1949) (with full bibl.). On B IV : R. B. Tollington, Clement of Alex. (1914), 270-302; J. Bingham, Origines sive Antiquitates ecclesiaticae. Lat. J. H. Grischovius, Ed. II (1725), 8, 34-35; III (1727), 48; IV (1727), 349-350; VI (1728), 391; F. J. Dölger, Sol salutis² (1925), 124, 86-97; J. Quasten, Musik u. Gesang in den Kulten d. heidnischen Antike u. chr. Frühzeit (1930), esp. 133-141. On C : J. Gottschick, Art. "Kindschaft Gottes," RE³, X, 291-304; E. Wissmann and S. Eck, Art. "Gotteskindschaft," RGG², II, 1394-1401; J. Hempel, Gott u. Mensch im AT² BWANT, 3 F. 2 H. (1936), 55, 170-178; Bousset-Gressm., 377 f.; Str.-B., I, 219 f., 371, 392-396; II, 49 f., 360 f.; III, 15-22; R. Gyllenberg, "Gott d. Vater im AT u. in d. Predigt Jesu," Studia Orientalia, I (1925), 51-60; J. Leipoldt, "Das Gotteserlebnis Jesu im Lichte d. vergleichenden Religionsgeschichte," Angelos Beih., 2 (1927), esp. 5, 15, 22, 28-32; A. Harnack, "Die Terminologie d. Wiedergeburt u. verwandter Erlebnisse in d. ältesten Kirche," TU, 42, 3 (1918); W. Grundmann, Die Gotteskindschaft in d. Gesch. Jesu u. ihre religionsgeschicht-lichen Voraussetzungen (1938); Oe. Gl., Index s.v. "Gotteskindschaft ;" also art. "Adoption" in RAC, I, 103-112, esp. 106-109; also "Jesus u. d. Gottesvolkgedanke," Luthertum (NkZ, NF), 53 (1942), 33-62. In the bibl. and the text we are indebted to H. Kleinknecht and others for suggestions which cannot be acknowledged in detail.

[1] Walde-Pok., II, 75 f.; A. Walde-J. B. Hofmann, Lat. etym. Wörterb.³, II (1950), 382 f., 392 f.

[2] U. v. Wilamowitz-Moellendorff, "Ein Siedlungsgesetz aus West-Lokris," SAB (1927), 7 (5th cent. B.C.).

[3] Ed. E. Littré, VIII (1853), 636, 20.

18 the ref. acc. to 9:4; 12:7; 19:6 might easily be to God's child; Lk. 7:7 = δοῦλος (cf. 2:3, 8, 10); also Mt. 8:6, 8, 13; Lk. 15:26; 12:45 with παιδίσκη. παῖδες of courtiers, hardly Diod. S., 17, 36, 76, where the ref. is to slaves, but Gn. 41:10, 37 f.; 1 Βασ. 16:15, 17; Ιερ. 43(36):31; 44(37):2 for עֲבָדִים, 1 Macc. 1:6, 8; Mt. 14:2. The word can denote membership of a category (παῖδες ῥητόρων, "orators," παῖδες Ἀσκληπιοῦ, "doctors," not Semitisms), or in the Bible the relation of men, angels, the elect, Christ to God, c. being predominant here, though the boundary between it and b. cannot always be fixed with abs. certainty, → παῖς θεοῦ. Sense b. is used fig. of intellectual products like works of literature or laws. Plat. Symp., 209d e sets these παῖδας σωτῆρας high above human children. Does a divine-child-myth lie behind this? (→ 640, 4-7).

3. παιδίον, diminutive of παῖς, "little child," a. in age, Hdt., II, 119; Aristoph. Pax, 50; inscr.; new-born child, Hdt., I, 110; Gn. 17:12; 21:8 יֶלֶד: Jn. 16:21; Mt. 2:8, 9, 11, 13 f., 20 f.; Lk. 1:59, 66, 76, 80; 2:17, 27, 40; Hb. 11:23; growing child, Hippocr. (→ supra; cf. Philo Op. Mund., 105) up to 7 yrs. of age; Gn. 45:19 טַף; Mt. 11:16 and par.; 14:21; 15:38; 18:2 ff. and par.; 19:13 f. and par.; Mk. 5:39 ff.; 7:28, 30; 9:24. b. Also with ref. to descent, Lk. 11:7; Jn. 4:49. Of the children of God or Christ, Hb. 2:13 f. (acc. to the NT understanding of Is. 8:18). c. With ref. to social position like παῖς (→ supra), Aristoph. Ra., 37; Nu., 132. Not the LXX (Ju. 19:19 vl.) or NT.

Fig. a. of undeveloped understanding, like νήπιος (→ IV, 917, 33 ff.), 1 K. 14:20 → 649, 33 f. b. As an affectionate address of the spiritual father to those committed to him: the risen Lord to His disciples in Jn. 21:5; the teacher to his hearers and readers, 1 Jn. 2:18; 3:7 vl. So also 1 Jn. 2:14; 2:12 vl., since the sequence παιδία, πατέρες, νεανίσκοι would be odd if the sense were a. (→ supra). The readers are first addressed as a body, and then distinguished into old and young men. [4] This use is peculiar to the NT and is found only in Jn.

4. παιδάριον, a further diminutive of παῖς, from Aristoph., Plat., inscr., pap., common in the LXX. a. It denotes age, "little boy," Aristoph. Av., 494; Pl., 536; ἐκ παιδαρίου, Plat. Symp., 207d; Mt. 11:16 textus receptus; "youngster," Gn. 37:30, a 7 yr. old (cf. v. 2); Tob. 6:2 f. So perhaps Jn. 6:9, otherwise sense b. b. It also denotes rank, young "slave," Aristoph. Pl., 823, 843; Athen., V, 32 (p. 200 f.); Xenoph. Ag., I, 21; 1 Βασ. 25:5; Rt. 2:5, 9; Mart. Pol., 6, 1; 7, 1.

5. τέκνον from √τεκ (cf. τίκτω "to beget," "to bear"), the child from the standpoint of origin (the embryo in Barn., 19, 5; Did., 2, 2). ἄλοχοι καὶ νήπια τέκνα Hom. Il., 2, 136; τέκνα καὶ γυναῖκες, Hdt., I, 164; II, 30; Ditt. Syll.³, 569, 10 (Cos, 3rd cent. B.C.); γυναῖκες καὶ τέκνα, Hdt., VI, 19; BGU, VIII, 1811, 5: πατρὸς σωφροσύνη μέγιστον τέκνοις παράγγελμα, Democr. Fr., 208 (Diels⁵, II, 187, 16 f.), cf. 222 (ibid., 190, 1 f.). In Attic prose it is less common than παῖς, but it occurs frequently in Xenoph., e.g., Resp. Lac., I, 8; Lys., 2, 74; Demosth. Or., 11, 9; also IG², IV (1), 122, 82 (Epidauros, 4th cent. B.C.); P. Petr., 3, p. 237 (3rd cent. B.C.). In Hom. the sing. is only an affectionate address to adults, with masc. attribute: φίλε τέκνον, Il., 22, 84; Od., 2, 363 etc. The following relative may be masc. or fem. In context the word may take on the sense "son," P. Gen., 74, 1 ff.; P. Amh., 136, 1 f.; P. Oxy., VI, 930, 18. In the LXX it answers to 11 Heb. words, though predominantly to בֵּן.

In the NT the word is used both generally and also in various specific senses. Mt. 7:11 and Lk. 11:13: τὰ τέκνα ὑμῶν, Mk. 7:27: ὁ ἄρτος τῶν τέκνων, Ac. 21:5: σὺν γυναιξὶ καὶ τέκνοις, 2 C. 12:14 (θησαυρίζειν) οἱ γονεῖς τοῖς τέκνοις. It means "son" in Mt. 21:28a; Rev. 12:5, also in affectionate address at Mt. 21:28b; Lk. 2:48; 15:31; fig. 1 Th. 2:11; 1 C. 4:14; 2 C. 6:13; Phil. 2:22. It can also mean "progeny": Ῥαχὴλ κλαίουσα τὰ τέκνα αὐτῆς, Mt. 2:18; 27:25; Ac. 2:39(?); 13:33, esp. Abraham's children, first his physical descendants, R. 9:8: τὰ τέκνα τῆς σαρκός, also in address (Lk. 16:25), then his spiritual progeny, Mt. 3:9; Lk. 3:8; Jn. 8:39; R. 9:7 (= υἱοὶ

---

[4] Cf. Bü. J. on 1 Jn. 2:12, 14; F. Hauck, Die Briefe d. Pt., Jak., Jud. u. Joh. (NT Deutsch) on 1 Jn. 2:12, as against Wnd. J. on 2:12-14.

Ἀβραάμ, Gl. 3:7; τοῦ Ἀβραάμ σπέρμα, Gl. 3:29). True Christian women are also children (daughters) of Sarah in 1 Pt. 3:6. τέκνον also goes beyond blood relationship when it is an intimate address to those not related, Mk. 2:5; Mt. 9:2, cf. θυγάτηρ in Mk. 5:34 and par., or when it is used for the relation of the spiritual child to the teacher or apostle (Preis. Zaub., IV, 475; τέκνον ἐν κυρίῳ, 1 C. 4:17; ἐν πίστει, 1 Tm. 1:2; κατὰ κοινὴν πίστιν, Tt. 1:4; plur. 3 Jn. 4), also in address (sing. Sir. 2:1; 4:1 etc.; Corp. Herm., XIII, 2a b; Preis. Zaub., XIII, 226, 233, 742, 755; 1 Tm. 1:18; 2 Tm. 2:1; Did., 3, 1 and 3-6; 4, 1; plur. Mk. 10:24; Barn., 15, 4). Here we have genealogy and analogy to ancient ideas of adoption which are partly oriental, also Jewish, and partly Gk., but which are reorientated by the Christian eschatological context. Both may be seen in the strong figurative expressions in Gl. 4:19; Phlm. 10 (cf. 1 C. 4:15; 1 Th. 2:7).[5] In the allegory in Gl. 4:21-31 the use of the word (v. 25, 27, 28, 31) is controlled by the text, though it is related to the description of members of a community as its children, as in 2 Jn. 1, 4, 13; Herm. v., 3, 9, 1 and 9. The relation to wisdom is portrayed under the same figure in Lk. 7:35; Mt. 11:19 vl., though also the relation to error or the false prophetess, Rev. 2:23. In Hebrew fashion the inhabitants of Jerusalem are called its τέκνα, Jl. 2:23; Zech. 9:13; Bar. 4:19, 21, 25; 1 Macc. 1:38; Mt. 23:37; Lk. 13:34; 19:44; Gl. 4:25. Expressions like τέκνα φωτός, Eph. 5:8; ὀργῆς, Eph. 2:3; ὑπακοῆς, 1 Pt. 1:14; κατάρας, 2 Pt. 2:14; ἀγάπης, Barn., 9, 7; ἀγάπης καὶ εἰρήνης, 21, 9; εὐφροσύνης, 7, 1; φωτὸς ἀληθείας, Ign. Phld., 2, 1 are also Hebraisms.

6. τεκνίον, a late and rare diminutive, is a nursery term for "little child." An anon. tragic or comic writer in P. Lond., I, 84; Epict., III, 22, 78; Heliodor. Aeth., VII, 12; P. Flor., 365, 15 (3rd cent. B.C.); P. Oxy., XIV, 1766, 14 (3rd cent. A.D.), not the LXX or the earliest Chr. lit. outside the NT. In the NT it occurs only in the vocative plur. as an affectionate address of Jesus or the apostles to their spiritual children. τεκνία, Jn. 13:33; 1 Jn. 2:12 (vl. παιδία, not children in the strict sense → 638, 22-25); 2:28; 3:7, 18; 4:4; 5:21. τεκνία μου: Gl. 4:19 vl.; 1 Jn. 2:1.

B. The Child from the Natural and Ethico-Religious Standpoint.

I. The Child in Antiquity.

1. Original Positive Estimation.

In the pre-Gk. Mediterranean world and the early Gk. world, in part even into the class. period, children, esp. sons, were desired to enhance the labour force, the defensive power and the glory of a house, Hom. Il., 2, 701; 6, 476 ff.; Aesch. Ag., 898; Eur. Iph. Taur., 57; Ion, 475 f. The god of Epidauros still grants them as desired.[6] Even in Hell. novels the birth of an eminent child is greeted in the city by a feast and in the neighbouring countryside by embassies bearing congratulations.[7] The Romans have similar feelings, though they are rarely personal. From Tertius or Quintus on sons are simply numbered. It has been hard to find even 18 Roman first names.[8]

2. Decline and Counter-Measures from the Classical Period.

Cultic motifs are involved in the ancient practice of exposing children.[9] This is also designed to weed out cripples and the unfit, often including girls simply as such. The main causes, however, were economic difficulties and sloth. Prevention of pregnancy,

---

[5] For details cf. A. Oepke, Art. "Adoption," RAC, I, 109.
[6] R. Herzog, Die Wunderheilungen von Epidauros (1931). In No. 34, 31, 42 the desire for a son is granted, in 2 the desire for a daughter.
[7] Chariton, III, 7, 7 (Erotici Scriptores Graeci, ed. Hercher, II [1859]).
[8] E. Bethe, Ahnenbild u. Familiengeschichte bei Griechen u. Römern (1935), 41.
[9] R. Tolles, Untersuchungen zur Kindesaussetzung bei d. Griechen, Diss. Breslau (1941), 78-91; B. Nyberg, Kind u. Erde (1931), 170-194 (bibl.). On the ritual and magic slaying of children cf. also F. J. Dölger, "Sacramentum infanticidii," Antike u. Christentum, IV (1934), 211-217.

abortion, and restriction to families with only one or two children led to depopulation, Hes. Op., 376; Polyb., 36, 17, 5 ff., esp. 7; Dio Chrys., 7, 34 ff. [10] The Roman need for grain sank from 14,600 hectolitres daily under Augustus to 6,600 under Severus. [11] The main reason is to be sought in a deficient understanding of childhood. The primitive glorifying of the divine child or youth in mythology [12] (Hes. Theog., 472, 478 : Zeus ; Hom. Hymn., 4 : Hermes ; Callim. Hymn., 3 : Artemis ; Theocr. Idyll., 24 : Heracliscos, the little Heracles) is set aside in a double sense ; childhood becomes merely a biographical stage. The child is a νήπιος, without power or significance. The question of the ultimate meaning of life remains unanswered, TGF Adespota, 111 (p. 862); the burial inscr. on which there are many variations : οὐκ ἤμην, γενόμην, οὐκ ἔσομ'. οὐ μέλει μοι· ὁ βίος ταῦτα, [13] Sen. ad Marciam, 23, 3; Cl. Al. Strom., III, 3, 22, 1-24, 3.

We find external counter-measures, partly by concessions for those with many children, partly by legal compulsion, cf. Liv., 39, 24, 3; Dio C., 43, 25, 2; Horat. Carmina, IV, 5, 21-24; Carmen Saeculare, 13-24; [14] Suet. Aug., 46. But these were more or less unsuccessful. So, too, were the inward counter-measures, Hippocr. De Jurejurando, 1, 3. Of the philosophers only Musonius definitely rejects the limitation of families, Fr., 12, 15 (p. 64, 1 f.; 77, 9 f.-81, Hense). Epictet. thinks the Cynic should not marry or have children (III, 22, 67-82), but he likes children (I, 23; II, 24, 18; I, 29, 31 etc.). Poetry, partly in conscious reaction to imperial reforms, magnifies the frivolous living for self of free love, of which a child is the least desirable consequence, Prop., II, 7, 7-14; Ovid Amores, III, 4, 37; Ars amatoria, I, 31 ff.; II, 157 f., 599 f.; III, 57 f.; Mart., VI, 3; IX, 11; V, 75; VI, 2, 7, 90; VIII, 31; IX, 6, 66. Along with jealousy (Xenophon Ephesius, V, 5), [15] adultery (Heliodor. Aeth., VII, 9), murder of wife or husband (Xenophon Ephesius, III, 12, 5), procuring (Heliodor., VII, 20), traffic in girls (Xenophon Ephesius, V, 5, 4 f.), and pederasty (ibid., III, 2, 4), the Hell. novel also speaks of the coy love which is not necessarily continent (Heliodor., X, 40), but which melts into sentimentality (Xenophon Ephesius, V, 8, 4; IV, 3, 3 f.; Heliodor., VIII, 12). The idea of continence even in marriage comes to the fore, Plot. Enn., III, 5, 2 : ὅτι μηδὲ ἐν οὐρανῷ γάμοι (not in the same sense as Mt. 22:30).

3. The Rediscovery of the Child in Hellenism.

Parental love continued. Though not without mistakes, provision is made for the welfare of children, Plut. Lib. Educ., 7 (II, 4a ff.); 13 (II, 9a ff.), prayer is made lest they be lost (M. Ant., IX, 40, 9), their loss is bewailed (CIL, III, 686, 1 f.), hope is held out of a blessed hereafter (ibid., 686, 17-20; the children's paradise of Octavia Paulina), [16] and consolation is thus found (Plut. Consolatio ad Uxorem, II, 608-612). Hellenism formally rediscovered the child. The promotion of the diminished rising generation only reached its climax from the 2nd cent. A.D. (CIL, V, 5262; Pliny the Younger, Ep., 7, 18; CIL, X, 6228; II, 1174; VIII, 1641; Ps.-Aurelius Victor Epitome De Caesaribus, 12, 4; Dio C., 68, 5, 4; Script. Hist. Aug., I Hadrian, 7, 8; ibid., III Antoninus Pius, 8, 1; ibid., IV Marcus Antoninus, 7, 8; ibid., XVIII, Alexander Severus, 57, 7; CIL, XI, 1147; IX, 1455). Poetry and art now begin (in part again) to acquire a closer relation to the child.

---

[10] Köhler, 21.

[11] Seeck, 345.

[12] For the cultic figure of a divine παῖς with plaything in both the Cabeiri mysteries and Orphism cf. O. Kern, Religion d. Griechen, I (1926), 129 f., 134, 241. This is only one form of the ancient Mediterranean child-god figure, which the emerging universe embodies mythologically ; M. P. Nilsson, Gesch. d. griech. Religion = Hndbch. AW, V, 2, I (1941), 293-302, Jung-Kerényi, 41-102; R. Enking, "Minerva Mater," Jbch. d. Archäologischen Instituts, 59/60 (for 1944/45, publ. 1949), 111, 118, 123.

[13] Rohde, II, 395, n. 2; cf. L. Friedländer, Darstellungen aus d. Sittengeschichte Roms[10], IV (1921), 396.

[14] P. Jörs, "Die Ehegesetze des Augustus," Festschr. T. Mommsen (1893), 1-65.

[15] Ed. R. Hercher, Erotici Scriptores Graeci, I (1858), 327 ff.

[16] G. Bendinelli, "Il concetto dell' oltretomba nel monumento di 'Octavia Paulina,'" Angelos, 1 (1925), 122-125.

Poetry had had this before, Hom. Il., 6, 404, 466 ff.; 482 ff.; [17] 22, 484 ff.; 9, 485 ff.; 16, 7 ff., 260 ff.; Od., 15, 450 ff.; 19, 399 ff. In Vergil's Ecl., 4 there are echoes of ancient mythical motifs of the divine child of the golden age, but with such new feeling that the Church could see here a prophecy of Christ and number the poet with the prophets. [18] The use of the child in drama was subject to technical limitations, [19] but we find boyish pranks in comedy, Aristoph. Eq., 417-426; Vesp., 248-257; Nu., 877-881; cf. Herond. Mim., 3. Plastic art is the last to make the link, and even then only in a limited way. The art of antiquity depicts the child as a small adult. [20] Kephisodotus and, in spite of progress, even Praxiteles create puppets rather than children. [21] Ancient vase painting wrestles hopelessly with the problem of corotrophos. [22] In Hellenism for the first time we find exquisite figures, the child with the fox, Boethos' goose-slayer, Hermes, Heracles or Solon as a boy. [23] The classic boy with the thorn [24] is travestied as a street arab. [25] The putti motif may be seen in the Nile swarming with 16 children. [26] We find a host of cupids standing, sitting or hovering, of children on horses, with torches, lyres, or horns of plenty. [27] On frescoes children imitate the doings of adults with ornate gravity. [28] The Dionysus child, Isis with Horus, Harpocrates alone, and the birth of Mithra [29] show art and religion competing for the child, and prepare the way for Christian art. But the taste is sentimental and perverse. The rich surround themselves with *deliciae*. These slave children amuse the carousing guests with impertinences, [30] smooth the churned up floor of the arena, and are even torn to pieces by beasts, Mart., II, 75; V, 31; Juv., IV, 122; Dio C., 72, 13. On the other hand, children can become emperors. [31]

4. Ethico-Religious Evaluation.

Antiquity speaks more rarely than one would expect of the innocence of the child, and in a different sense. [32] Juv., 14, 47 ff.: *maxima debetur puero reverentia, siquid | turpe paras, nec tu pueri contempseris annos, | sed peccaturo obstet tibi filius infans.* The child has no sexual complications; hence it can be used in the cultus and magic, → 643, 3-645, 21. In Rome it shares the *toga praetexta* with officials, not because it needs special protection, but as an expression of power. [33] For it has no inkling of joy or suffering, and

---

[17] W. Schadewaldt, "Homerische Szenen," 1, *Antike*, 11 (1935), 149.

[18] Norden, 1 f.; K. H. Schelkle, *Virgil in d. Deutung Augustins* (1939), 16-22.

[19] Devrient, *passim*. In the tragic poets cf. the dumb child and the children's chorus, Eur. Alc., 189 ff., 269-392; Med., 894-1080, but with considerable decline as compared with Hom., Soph. Ai., 529-595.

[20] Haas, 2/4 Bonnet (1924), Ill., 23; 13/14 Rumpf (1928), Ill. 193 and 194 (c. 400 B.C.), even Ill. 25 (c. 300); 7 Karo (1925), Ill. 72, though cf. 79; child among wild goats.

[21] H. Luckenbach, *Kunst u. Gesch.* (1913), Ill. 154 and 164.

[22] Heubach, 6-16; Quatember.

[23] W. Klein, *Vom antiken Rokoko* (1921), 130.

[24] Luckenbach, Fig., 172.

[25] Wendland Hell. Kult., Plate 3, 6.

[26] Vatican. Luckenbach, Fig. 169.

[27] F. Winter, *Die Typen d. figürlichen Terakotten*, II (1903), 237-373.

[28] Pompeii; T. Birt, *Aus dem Leben d. Antike* (1918), Plate 10 (esp. Whence come the Amoretti? 134); J. Leipoldt, *Dionysos* (1931), Plate 4.

[29] Haas, 13/14 Rumpf (1928), Ill. 72; Photo. Giraudon, 1840; Haas, 9-11 Leipoldt (1926), Ill. 37-42; Meyer, 112; Haas, 15 Leipoldt (1930), 29 f.

[30] Birt, *op. cit.* The *deliciae*, however, are not just models of the cupids whom art divinised. We seem to have two distinct phenomena here. H. Herter, "Das Kind im Zeitalter d. Hellenismus," *Bonner Jahrbücher d. Vereins von Altertumsfreunden im Rheinlande*, 132 (1927), 256.

[31] W. Hartke, *Römische Kinderkaiser* (1951), 190-242, esp. 197, 218, 227. But the term is taken very broadly, since Octavian at 19 was reckoned a child. And "nothing was more alien to the older Roman way than a child in the supreme position of empire," 219. In the main dynastic considerations were what counted, not the view of children.

[32] Schiller's soul of "childlike" purity is not in the original Aesch. Eum., 313-320.

[33] Van der Leeuw, 13, cf. W. Fowler, "The *toga praetexta* of Roman Children," *Roman Essays and Interpretations* (1920), 42.

is thus fortunate, Soph. Ai., 552 ff. Finally, it is unable to deceive, Artemid. Oneirocr., II, 69. But this is less a moral quality than an intellectual deficiency, Xenoph. Ag., I, 17; Sen. De Ira, II, 26, 6: the failings of children have *pro innocentia imprudentiam.*

The concept of the wonder child is esp. strong in Egypt. The 12 yr. old Si Usire is surpassed by no magician in Memphis in the reading of magical books. [34] But the idea occurs also in the West, Suet. Aug., 94, 6; Vergil Ecl., 4, 26 f.: the reading divine child. [35] The learning and teaching child is a candidate for felicity, and a guarantee of it, on the sarcophagi of children. [36]

On the margin, however, we also find ideas of inherited evil and sin. [37] The universality of guilt is often emphasised, Petronius Saturae, 75, 1: *nemo nostrum non peccat, homines sumus, non dei* ; cf. Sen. De Ira, II, 28. Acc. to Iambl. Vit. Pyth. Pythagoras is supposed to have said (18, 82): τί ἀληθέστατον λέγεται; ὅτι πονηροὶ οἱ ἄνθρωποι. This universality of imperfection is connected with human nature. Isoc., 5, 35 : ἀλλὰ γὰρ ἅπαντες πλείω πεφύκαμεν ἐξαμαρτάνειν ἢ κατορθοῦν, Eur. Fr., 810 (TGF, 623): μέγιστον ἄρ' ἦν ἡ φύσις· τὸ γὰρ κακὸν/οὐδεὶς τρέφων εὖ χρηστὸν ἂν θείη ποτέ, Muson. Diss., VI (p. 26, 17 ff.): διὰ τὴν ἀπὸ παίδων εὐθὺς γεγονυῖαν ἡμῖν διαφθορὰν καὶ τὴν ὑπὸ τῆς διαφθορᾶς συνήθειαν πονηράν we judge evils and goods wrongly, cf. also Thuc., III, 82, 2; 84, 2. Ceb. Tab. speaks of the all-bemusing drink of 'Απάτη, of σῴζεσθαι and ἀπόλλυσθαι, in notes which seem almost Christian, though harmonised differently, 5, 2; 6, 2; 14, 3; 19, 5. Orphism in particular sees an overriding nexus of evil which must be overcome by initiatory rites. Orph. Fr. (Kern), 232 speaks of λύσις προγόνων ἀθεμίστων, → I, 166, 22 f. Where the human race is thought to have its origins in the wild Titans, who were shattered by Zeus' lightning because of the tearing apart of Dionysus Zagreus, or where an equation is made between σῶμα and σῆμα, there the idea of innocent childhood can find no place in the strict sense. On the contrary, "the idea of original sin establishes itself in the Hell. world at this point." [38] Guilt is handed down to the generations to come. [39]

These ideas are only marginal. Antiquity primarily sees in the child the element of immaturity or childishness. This sense attaches, not to the words denoting descent, βρέφος and τέκνον, but exclusively to those denoting age, νήπιος (→ IV, 912, 14 ff.) and παῖς (→ 637, 7-12) with diminutives. Heracl. Fr., 79 (Diels[5], I, 169, 1 f.) has the profound saying : ἀνὴρ νήπιος ἤκουσε πρὸς δαίμονος ὅκωσπερ παῖς πρὸς ἀνδρός. Acc. to Plat. Prot., 342e the smallest Lacedaemonian could answer so readily ὥστε φαίνεσθαι τὸν προσδιαλεγόμενον παιδὸς μηδὲν βελτίω. To fear death is δεδιέναι τὸ τῶν παίδων. But perhaps a παῖς is actually in us, ὅστις τὰ τοιαῦτα φοβεῖται, Plat. Phaed., 77d e. The child lives only for the moment : κλαίωμεν καὶ πάλιν κροτῶμεν ὡς τὰ παιδία, Epict. Diss., III, 24, 8. It plays ball (M. Ant., VI, 57, 1), or pretends to be a wrestler, or trumpeter, or tragedian, or orator, or philosopher, or tax-gatherer, or imperial official, but never puts its whole soul in the game, Epict. Ench., 29, 3, 7. It can build contentedly with sand and ashes and then destroy again, Diss., III, 13, 18. Fundamentally it does not take anything seriously. Socrates called popular dogmas παιδίων δείματα, bogies to frighten children, M. Ant., XI, 23. Children are easily frightened, e.g., by clay masks, Epict. Diss., III, 22, 106. He who fears death παιδίον ἐστίν, M. Ant., II, 12, 3. τί ... ἐστὶ παιδίον; ἄγνοια ... ἀμαθία, Epict. Diss., II, 1, 16. There is hardly any word which better denotes the ancient estimation of children than *erudire.* Plut. Lib. Educ., II, 1-14 everywhere presupposes that only by strenuous educative effort, and only then with normal gifts and the right technique, can something be made of the raw material. Thus rationalistic optimism combines with a low estimation

---

[34] F. Griffith, *Stories of the High Priests of Memphis* (1900), 41-66.
[35] Norden, 134.
[36] F. Cumont, "Un Sarcophage d'enfant trouvé à Beyrouth," *Syria,* 10 (1929), 217.
[37] Latte, 254; K. Deissner, *Das Idealbild des stoischen Weisen* (1930), 7.
[38] Latte, 282.
[39] Steinleitner, No. 6.

of the child. There is no sense of the limitation of the educator, no regard for the developing personality, no profound love for the child, even in the later period. [40]

5. The Child in the Cultus.

a. In a way which the modern man finds hard to understand the child of antiquity took part in the general cultus. The family and tribe were an objective cultic fellowship in the ancient world. The newborn child was incorporated in this fellowship from the very first days of its life. In Greece this took place by laying the child in the wickerwork cradle, the licnon, which we know from the Eleusinian mysteries to have been a symbol of purification and fertility, and also by the *amphidromia*, at which a nurse or female relative would carry the child quickly around the hearth to place it under the protection of the household gods, [41] though in classical times there is direct attestation of this only in Athens. In Rome it took place by the *Dies lustricus*, [42] with which were connected sacrifice and the giving of a name. From the very first children, even infants, were present at adult cults. This is true of Egypt, [43] Greece, [44] and Rome. As the attendance of nurses shows, small children would not be absent from the monthly purifying bath of Deisidaimon, Theophr. Char., 16. They are lifted up to kiss the household gods like adults, Ambr. De Abraham., II, 11, 81; Prud. Contra Symmachum, I, 208 ff.

b. Children also have a place in the public cultus, which is an extension of that of the clan. Those who serve at sacrifices are in the first instance children of the priest. These are accompanied by children from other privileged families. *Camillus* and *camilla* were originally used for all freeborn boys and girls, [45] though later restricted to servers at the Flamen Dialis, the Flaminica, and the Curiones. For the sacrifice of the Decemviri *decem ingenui, decem virgines* were appointed (Liv., 37, 3, 6), for the offering to Zeus Sosipolis in Magnesia on the Maeander nine παῖδες καὶ παρθένοι (Ditt. Syll.³, 589, 20 ff. [196 B.C.]). Children sing at religious festivals. [46] In the Delphic sanctuary there is a school for ἱεροὶ παῖδες. [47] Under Trajan one such sets up a statue for his and Plutarch's friend L. Cassius Petraeus, Ditt. Syll.³, 825c. But already c. 227 B.C. a *chorodidascalos* was teaching these boys the paean, *ibid.*, 450, 5. Alexander of Abonuteichos turns the pious custom to scandalous ends, Luc. Alex., 41. Conscious or unconscious manticism was also ascribed to the child. The crowds of children who accompany Apis *repente lymphati futura praecinunt,* Plin. Hist. Nat., VIII, 46, 185. Anthia, seeking news of her lost husband in the temple of Apis, hears from the lips of children playing in front of the temple that she will soon find him again, Xenophon Ephesius, V, 4, 9-11. Plut. Is. et Os., 14 (II, 356e) has the aetiological legend that Isis, when seeking Osiris, received information from children. All the examples are from Egypt. [48] Inter-

---

[40] W. Jentsch, "Urchristliches Erziehungsdenken. Die Paideia Kyriu im Rahmen d. hellenistisch-jüdischen Umwelt," BFTh, 45, 3 (1951), 43-85.

[41] v. Müller, 161.

[42] Blümner, 304.

[43] Haas, 2-4 Bonnet (1924), Ill. 23.

[44] Bas-reliefs in the Louvre, Photo. Giraudon, 2040, 2042, Alinari, 22767.

[45] Macrob. Sat., V, 20, 18; Festus De Significatione Verborum, *s.v.* "Flaminius Camillus," "Flaminia," ed. W. M. Lindsay (1913), 82. The etym. seems to lead to a Semitic root קַדְמִיאֵל *ante deum* (Ezr. 2:40; 3:9; Neh. 7:43; 9:4 f.; 10:10; 12:8, 24, name of a Levite; for other suggestions cf. M. Noth, "Die isr. Personennamen im Rahmen d. gemeinsemitischen Namengebung," BWANT, 3 F. 10 [1928], 256). The *toga praetexta* which the *camillus* wears also pts. to the East, to Phoenicia, the land of purple (φοῖνιξ). This represents the blood of sacrifice which gives the wearer power, van der Leeuw, 13-24, cf. P. Berger, "Camillus," *Mémoires de la Société de Linguistique,* VI (1889), 140. It probably made its way to the West *via* the cult of the Cabeiri in Samothrace.

[46] Horat. Carmina, III, 1, 4; Carmen Saeculare, 6; cf. CIL, VI, 32323, 147 f.; Zosimus Historia Nova, II, 5, 12; Macrob. Sat., I, 6, 14; Dio C., 59, 7, 1; Ael. Arist. Or., 47, 30 (Keil).

[47] *Bulletin de Correspondance Hellénique,* 20 (1896), 719, 6.

[48] A. D. Nock, "A Vision of Mandulis Aion," HThR, 27 (1934), 69.

cessory processions by children are thought to be particularly efficacious, Liv., 27, 37, 7 and 12; 31, 12, 9. To turn aside the plague in Miletus the seer Branchos has the children sing a strange verse which, unintelligible to adults, contained twice all the letters of the alphabet, Cl. Al. Strom., V, 8, 48, 5. At the intercessory procession for Zeus Sosipolis in Magnesia on the Maeander children were mentioned just after the officiating priests and before the notables of the city as those who pray for the σωτηρία of the city, Ditt. Syll.³, 589, 21-31. The current reason is formulated by Iambl. (Vit. Pyth., 10, 51) as a saying of his hero : Children are esp. dear to the gods (θεοφιλεστάτους) and should thus pray for rain in time of drought, since the deity will usually answer them and them alone, because, being fully chaste (ἀγνεύουσιν) they have a full right ἐν τοῖς ἱεροῖς διατρίβειν. Catull., 34, 1-4 sketches the ministry of children in some fine lines :

> Dianae sumus in fide
> puellae et pueri integri :
> Dianam pueri integri
> puellaeque canamus.

A painting from Ostia shows a kind of choir (Vatican Library). [49]

The transition to priestly functions is almost imperceptible. In Epidauros a young πυρφορῶν obtains from those who seek healing a promise to give thanks, Ditt. Syll.³, 1168, 43 f. In the Olympian and Pythian games a boy with a golden knife cuts the victors' leaves from the sacred olive. [50] The young Daphnephoros in Thebes even acts as priest for a year, Paus., XI, 10, 4. In Rome the games were not rite facti unless the boy leading the tensa with the exuviae of the gods lost the reins, Arnobius Adversus Nationes, IV, 31 (CSEL, 4, 166). Freeborn boys and girls assisted the Vestal virgins at the Capitol lustration, Tac. Hist., IV, 53. The ministering child is called sacerdotula. [51] Many priestly colleges received children as regular members, e.g., the Salians, Script. Hist. Aug., IV Marcus Antonius, 4, 2. Appointment as a Vestal virgin had to take place between the sixth and tenth yr., Gellius Noctes Atticae, I, 12. To guarantee the chastity of divine ministers [52] priestly functions were discharged exclusively by children in many Gk. cults, Paus., X, 34, 8; VII, 24, 4; VIII, 47, 3; II, 33, 2; VII, 26, 5; VII, 19, 1. Care was taken that the children were in the possession of both parents, ἀμφιθαλεῖς, Lat. patrimi et matrimi. [53] The ministry of priestly children was highly esteemed. [54] The camilli wore a special dress : short sleeve-tunics with girdle, naked legs, on one shoulder the ricinium (small mantle with fringe), in the hand the acerra (censer). [55]

c. Children were not excluded even from secret cults. They take part in the processions of the gods of Eleusis [56] and of Isis, [57] cf. perhaps the child with the little carriage behind the married couple on the Orph. underworld vase of Canosa. [58] Parents dedicated children in tender or more advanced youth for consecration to the mystery

---

[49] B. Nogara, Le Nozze Aldobrandine etc. (Milan, 1907), Plate 47; Dieterich, "Sommertag," Plate I, 344-352.

[50] Pind. Olymp. Schol. on 3, 60, ed. A. B. Drachmann (1910). Cf. Eustath. Thessal. Comm. in Il., 22, 495; Procl. in Phot. Bibliotheca, 239 (MPG, 103, 1205a).

[51] Festus De Significatione Verborum, s.v. "Flaminia" etc., → n. 45.

[52] Children also represent the gods, e.g., a child at the head of the Stepterion procession in Delphi : Apollo, or two children in ancient Ionian garb in the chorus of the Oschophoria in Athens : Dionysus and Ariadne, M. P. Nilsson, Griech. Feste (1906), 152; A. Mommsen, Feste d. Stadt Athen (1898), 283.

[53] Oepke, ARW, 45.

[54] Inscr. from Thyatira, Bull. de Correspondance Hellénique, 10 (1886), 415; 11 (1887), 98.

[55] Pauly-W., III, 1432; Ill. Daremberg-Saglio, s.v. "Camillus," I, 859.

[56] K. Kuruniotes, "Ἐλευσινιακά" in Ἀρχαιολογικὸν Δελτίον, 8 (1923/1925), 164. On par. vase paintings cf. H. G. Pringsheim, Archäologische Beiträge zur Gesch. des eleusin. Kults, Diss. Bonn (1905), 16. A statuette of a boy with a bundle of myrtles from Eleusis, Ath. Mitt., 20 (1895), 357.

[57] Apul. Met., XI, 9; relief in Klein-Glienicke, Angelos 2 (1926), Plate 4.

[58] Haas, 9-11 Leipoldt (1926), 175.

deities, Xenophon Ephesius, III, 11; Liv., 39, 9. Initiation of children was customary in Samothrace. [59] Himerios had his son initiated into the Bacchic and Eleusinian mysteries soon after birth, Or., 23, 7, 8 and 18. The inscr. are esp. rewarding, CIG, III, 6238, Bacchus insignia, boy of 7 yrs. and 2 months, an initiate for 3 (yrs.?); Epigr. Graec., 153, Athens, Roman period, a seven-yr. old initiate of Eleusis, cf. CIL, III, 686; VI, 751b. Perhaps with tendentious exaggeration the Confessio Cypriani describes the pre-Christian life of its Antiochene hero : dedicated from earliest youth to Apollo, even as νήπιος received into the dramaturgy of the dragon, at barely 7 Mithras initiation, at 10 torch-bearer of Demeter etc. [60] Polygnotus's painting in Delphi already presupposes that children could treat the mysteries lightly, Paus., X, 31, 11. Two children's mummies with scenes from the Isis mysteries have been preserved. [61]

In the mysteries, too, children discharge cultic functions. A seven yr. old boasts on his burial inscr. (CIG, III, 6206) that he has been a priest of all gods, the Bona Dea, the Magna Mater, Dionysus etc. Demosthenes says of his opponent Aeschines that as a boy, when his mother, a base woman of poor repute, engaged in solemn rites, he read the ritual and went about among the intoxicated in the festal crowds, Or., 19, 199. On the other hand, the μυούμενοι and μυούμεναι ἀφ᾽ ἑστίας in Eleusis were taken from the leading families, and there were inscr. in their honour. [62] A boy is reading the ritual in the Dionysiac bridal ceremony depicted on the frieze of the Villa Item. [63] The Bacchic mysteries inscr. of Torre Nova introduces two amphithaleis into the middle of the list of priests. [64]

II. The Child in the Old Testament and Judaism.

1. The Religious Evaluation of Progeny.

In the OT increase is an order of creation, Gn. 1:28. To be without children is a sorrow and a religious vexation, Gn. 15:2; 1 S. 1:2. Children are a gift of God and a blessing, Ps. 127:3-5; 128:3 f. In them a man lives on, → 253, 31 ff. In the background is a strong affirmation of life. The high estimation of progeny is anchored in faith in God. "Woe unto him that striveth with his maker ... that saith unto his father, Why be-gettest thou? and to the woman, Why dost thou bring forth?" Is. 45:9 f.

Judaism develops and to some degree isolates this view with special ref. to the concept of the people of God. "If anyone does not engage in increase, it is as though he were to shed blood or to diminish God's image," bJeb., 63b. [65] There is more of popular wisdom in Ps.-Phocylides. [66] Those who die childless still have descendants by Levirate marriage. Contraception is esp. infamous, Gn. 38:8 ff. Elsewhere it is permissible only for young girls, those already pregnant, or nursing mothers, bNed., 35b; bJeb., 12b; bKet., 39a. That intercourse is not in lust but for the sake of children is emphasised (under philosophical influence?) in Tob. 8:7; Philo Spec. Leg., I, 112; Virt., 207 etc.; Jos. Ap., II, 199. Ascetic inclinations are found only among the Essenes, Therapeutae and a few others. The Test. XII are only occasionally ascetic, Test. R. 6; Jos. 9 ff. etc. Elsewhere they simply warn against whoring and immoderation in marriage, Test. Iss. 2.

---

[59] Aelius Donatus Commentarius in Terentii Phormionem, I, 1, 13 (ed. P. Wessner, II [1905]).

[60] Cyprian Op., ed. S. Baluze, Venice (1727), App. CCLXXVII.

[61] C. C. Edgar, "Graeco-Roman Coffins, Masks and Portraits" = Catalogue général des Antiquités Egypt. du Musée du Caire, 19 (1905), No. 33215, 33216. For child membership of cultic societies and colleges cf. Inscr. regni Neapolitani latinae, ed. T. Mommsen (1852), No. 6845; Ditt. Syll.³, 1109, 39 ff. and IG, IV, 824.

[62] Material in Oepke, ARW, 51 f. For sacral functions cf. Porphyr. Abst., IV, 5; for the lower degree of initiation perhaps Himerius Or., 22, 7.

[63] Photo. Anderson, 26380; A. Maiuri, La Villa dei Misteri (1931), Fig. 47, Plate I, II.

[64] F. Cumont, "La Grande Inscr. Bachique du Metropolitan Museum," American Journal of Archeology, 37 (1933), Plate 27, 250.

[65] Str.-B., II, 373.

[66] Diehl, I² (1936), LV, 175-179, 207-217.

A pure marriage is pleasing to God, even for the priest, Test. L. 9:10; 11 f. Abortion is pagan, bNidda, 30b; allowed in bBQ, 41b; bNidda, 44b; not to be sought in Jos. Ant., 4, 287. Exposure is occasionally attested (Ez. 16:5; Qid., 4, 1; bBM, 87a), but only as pagan depravity (cf. Ac. 7:19). The unusual fertility of the Jews is to be explained on these grounds.

2. The Estimation of the Child.

a. The OT bears witness to paternal love (Gn. 22:2; 37:35; 2 S. 12:15 ff. etc., fig. Ps. 103:13; Jer. 31:20 etc.) and maternal love (1 K. 3:26; 2 K. 4:18 ff., fig. Is. 49:15; 66:13). But beyond the self-evident duty of obeying and learning (Ex. 20:12; Dt. 11:19; Prv. 4:1 ff. etc.) it hardly pays any psychological, let alone philosophical or artistic, regard to the individuality of the child. The psalmist hears a magnifying and praising of Yahweh in the babbling of children and infants, Ps. 8:2. Though objectively intended, this shows understanding of the piety of children. Not children as such, but a few who are specially blessed, have the gift of prophecy, 1 S. 3:1-19. The high estimation of the Messianic child (cf. Is. 7:14 ff.; 9:5 f.; 11:1 ff. [?]) is not peculiar to the OT (cf. Vergil Ecl., 4). The general judgment is in the main negative. The child is without understanding and self-willed, Is. 3:4, 12(?); Qoh. 10:16; Wis. 12:24; 15:14. It inclines to naughtiness and needs sharp divine and human discipline, 2 K. 2:23 f.; Sir. 30:1-13. The imagination of man is evil from his youth up, Gn. 8:21 (J), half in exculpation ?; Ps. 58:3.

Except in so far as softened by Hell. sentimentality, Judaism has little understanding of the individuality of the child. The qatan is without understanding, like a fool or imbecile, BM, 7, 7; Ter., 1, 1. The many proverbs about the high estimation of esp. schoolchildren [67] are at root exalting the Torah rather than children. The nature of the rabbi is not at all childlike. At most an odd Talmud anecdote might tell of a scholar spending time with a child, but this is regarded as a waste of time, Ab., 3, 10 : R. Dosa b. Archinos said : "Morning sleep, mid-day wine, chattering with children and tarrying in places where men of the common people assemble, destroy a man." R. Jochanan has said : "Since the day the temple was destroyed prophecy has been taken from the prophets and given to fools and children," bBB, 12b. [68] Under Hell. influence we hear of the wonder child. Josephus says that he instructed the wise while still only 14 yrs. of age, Vit., 9.

b. The principle of the innocence of children is alien to the OT. Radical judgments and acts of revenge which do not spare the child hardly lead to reflections of this kind, Is. 13:16; Jer. 6:11; 44:7; Ps. 137:9. The idea of the national unit is at first predominant. But against a mechanical idea of retribution there arises an understanding of individual responsibility, Jer. 31:29 f.; Ez. 18:2 ff. Nevertheless, man is thought to be implicated from birth in a nexus of guilt and punishment which only God can break, Ps. 51:5; Gn. 3; Job 25:4.

Judaism, though it never contested or forgot individual responsibility, worked out a complete doctrine or original sin, guilt and punishment. The curse of Adam's deed is on all born of woman, and each affirms the deed afresh, S. Bar. 54:15. The tension between the two approaches may be seen throughout apocalyptic literature, but it does not result in an acceptance of the innocence of children, → I, 290 ff. Where this seems to be suggested later, the point is different or we simply have secondary tendencies. The expression that one may be "like a new-born child" can have a purely casuistical sense, bJeb., 62a, 97b, [69] and even where the moral sense is more apparent, as in bJeb., 48b etc., [70] it hardly envisages more than a new beginning in the sense of earlier lack of responsibility. The thesis of R. Jehoshua (c. 90) that the children of the ungodly in the land of Israel will attain to the future world [71] was contested by others. One cannot

---

[67] Str.-B., I, 780 f.
[68] Ibid., I, 607.
[69] Ibid., II, 423.
[70] Ibid., II, 423.
[71] Ibid., I, 786.

systematise the individual statements. The child is not yet responsible up to 1 yr. or even up to 9 yrs., and to that degree it is not sinful, Pesikt., 61b; Pesikt. r., 16 (84a); [72] Ket., 1, 2, 4; 3, 1; bJeb., 60b; Tanch. בראשית, 4b. [73] In its mother's womb [74] or even up to the age of 6 [75] it receives instruction in the Torah from an angel or even from God Himself. But the evil impulse is there from conception or birth ; it is 13 yrs. older than the good. [76] There is debate as to whether children sin already in the womb. [77] In such a context the principle of the innocence of children [78] can have at best only relative significance. It is strengthened when Jewish moralism combines with Hell. sentimentality, 2 Macc. 8:4 : τῶν ἀναμαρτήτων νηπίων παράνομος ἀπώλεια. But even Philo is divided : μὴ παίδων ἄκακον ἡλικίαν οἰκτισάμενοι, Flacc., 68, cf. Leg. Gaj., 234; up to the age of 7 the soul is ἀκραιφνής (integer), ἀμέτοχος ἀγαθοῦ τε καὶ κακοῦ, Leg. All., II, 53. On the other hand, it soon adopts the bad, ἅ τε ἐξ ἑαυτῆς εἴωθε γεννᾶν ψυχή, Rer. Div. Her., 295; evil is at the beginning, Sacr. AC, 14. The child is esp. open to sensual and even sexual desire, Op. Mund., 161. Even in Rabbinism the OT unity of soul and body is increasingly crowded out by Platonic dualism. As ἀπόσπασμα θεῖον (Philo Leg. All., II, 161) the soul is pure. But unwillingly or by its own fault, and certainly to its hurt, it is chained to matter. The unique Haggada Simlai (middle of the 3rd cent.) on the development of the child (Nidda, 30b) seems to be dependent on the one side on the Platonic myth of the soul (Resp., X, 614b-621d : Prior apportionment or choice, freedom of moral decision, complaint of the soul, accompanying daemon, forgetting and anamnesia), and on the other on the Horus myth (light on the head of the child, view of the world, blow on the mouth at birth). [79] Even here the innocence of the child is uncertain. By way of Hellenism there is renewed attachment to the idea of the curse. The myth of the divine child has no place in the OT or Judaism.

3. The Participation of the Child in Religious Exercises.

There can be no doubt that in historical time circumcision mediates the child's entry into the national and the co-extensive cultic fellowship. The firstborn son belongs to Yahweh, and must be presented to Him and redeemed by a sacrifice. In the OT children are present at family offerings, 1 S. 1:4; from weaning on (?), v. 22 ff. They are thus nurtured in the practice of religion. By way of supplement planned instruction is also given. In the first instance this is instruction in the historical foundations of Yahweh religion (Dt. 4:9), then in the related requirements of Yahweh (Dt. 11:19), and finally, not without alien influences, in practical religious and moral wisdom (Prv. 4:1 ff.). Hence the child's relation to religion is esp. close in Israel. Early dedication to the sanctuary is practised (1 S. 1:28), and this leads to a semi-priestly ministry (1 S. 2:18 ff.). But this is exceptional. Children were never priests in the true sense in Israel.

In Judaism, esp. after the destruction of the temple, there is a shift of emphasis from the cultus to knowledge and practice of the Torah. This involves a sharper differentiation between boys and girls. For only the man is obligated to keep the Torah in its full compass, and only he is justified in learning it, Sot., 3, 4; bSot., 21b; not without contradiction, also not without Gk. and Roman pars., → I, 777, 27 ff., 780, 6 ff., 781, 44 f. At puberty the Jewish boy becomes a בַּר מִצְוָה, cf. Jesus when He was 12. But instruction and practice begin much earlier. Joshua b. Gamla (high-priest c. 63-65) ordered that there should be teachers in every province and city, and that boys from the age of 6 or 7 should be brought to them, bBB, 21a. This was, however, an emergency provision because the religious education given by fathers had not always been suffi-

---

[72] Ibid., I, 773 f.
[73] Ibid., IV, 469.
[74] → R. Meyer, 87.
[75] Ibid., 88.
[76] Str.-B., IV, 468 f.
[77] Ibid., II, 528 f.
[78] Ibid., IV, 469.
[79] R. Meyer, 103-114.

cient. This education normally lasted for 13 yrs. (Gn. r., 63 [40a]), [80] so that it began very early, even from birth. The duties of shaking the festal straw, wearing the prayer cloak and phylacteries and learning the sacred language began as soon as there was ability to perform them. [81] In Jerusalem the boy who could take his father's hand (Hillel) or ride on his shoulders (Shammai) to the temple hill was under obligation to keep the great feasts. [82] "A child who no longer needs his mother has a duty to keep the feasts. When once the daughter of Shammai the Elder was confined (at the Feast of Taber-nacles), he came in and for the boy's sake (women, esp. minors, did not have to keep the feasts) set up a tabernacle roof over the bed," Sukk., 2, 8. [83] This very old example of scrupulosity in legal observance makes it particularly clear that the Jewish child belongs from the very first to the community. Circumcision is not strictly an act of reception but the first fulfilment of a duty to the newly born child, and a first sign of duty. The proselyte baptism which developed in pre-Christian times was a rite for re-ceiving "those not born in holiness" (→ I, 535 f.), and it applied to existing children as well as their parents. This is shown by the stereotyped ref. to "proselytes converted under three years and a day," Ket., 1, 2, 2; 1, 4; 3, 1; bKet., 11a; bJeb., 60b. It is very clear in bJeb., 78a : "Raba said : If a pregnant non-Jewess is converted, her son does not need baptism." For the foetus is part of the mother's body and is baptised with her. But if the son was born before the mother's baptism, he would be baptised too. In bKet., 11a we read that very small children, e.g., under three yrs. and a day, would either be baptised with their father if he were converted at this time, or, if they had no father, acc. to the judgment of the court. This passage [84] is of special interest because it shows that, while the problem of individual decision was felt, the traditional practice was maintained. The reason, based on a saying of R. Huna (Babylonian, d. 297), is that "an advantage may be conferred on a man without his knowledge (lit. in his absence)." It is then considered whether in certain circumstances, as a mitigation, it might not be better to remain a Gentile ; the ruling is that this is true only for an adult. Individual decision follows later. R. Joseph (Babylonian, d. 333) said : "Once of age, they can raise an objection (and return to paganism without being punished or treated as apostate Jews, Rashi)." But this objection is valid only when they attain their majority. Hence Judaism as a missionary religion practised infant baptism. [85] It is true that the attestation is later than the earliest attestation of the Christian practice. But it is highly improbable that we have here a Christian or syncretistic accretion. The baptising of the children of proselytes is wholly in line with what we know of the understanding of proselyte baptism.

III. The Child in the New Testament.

1. Affirmation of the Child as a Creature of God.

a. Jesus, though not with non-dialectical uniformity, adopts the OT belief in God, and therewith its knowledge of the Creator. This carries with it an affir-mation of human existence. He can find a place for the ascetic concerns which are stronger in Hellenism and only incidental in Judaism, but He does not identify Himself with them, Mt. 19:11, 12. Within the limits herewith laid down He affirms and sanctifies the love of parents, Mk. 5:36 and par.; 9:19b and par.; Mt. 7:9 ff. and par.

b. Between Jesus and the community a sharp distinction cannot always be made. But it may be assumed that the sayings which are handed down from Jesus

---

[80] Str.-B., II, 147.
[81] *Ibid.* II, 145 f.
[82] *Ibid.,* II, 146.
[83] *Ibid.,* II, 145.
[84] In detail it is variously translated and expounded. But the paraphrase given in the text correctly conveys the sense.
[85] Gerim, 2, 1 may not be quoted against this.

or set on His lips generally reflect the view of the community too. For it is plain from Mt. 24:19 and par. that the community regarded giving birth and giving suck as a normal part of life which would continue even into the days of the last tribulation. The community undertakes to support apostles and their wives who move about in missionary service, and this would presumably include their children too, 1 C. 9:5. Paul accepts this in principle, though he does not personally avail himself of it. Ascetic inclinations and interim ethics do not prevent him from regarding marriage and children as an order of creation, 1 C. 7 → I, 651, 20 ff. He, too, transcends both the Jewish and the Hellenistic schema, and apart from minor deviations keeps essentially to the same line as Jesus. The household tables also display a positive attitude to family life and the rearing of children, → I, 653, 15 ff. 1 Tm. 2:15, even if it is deutero-pauline, is still worth noting inasmuch as it shows what was also possible in primitive Christianity. It refers to being delivered διὰ τῆς τεκνογονίας. This certainly does not mean that bearing children is the only basis of salvation, nor that it is a penance for the original sexual fault of the woman. [86] What is meant is that child-bearing (including nurture?) can be called a work which promotes salvation and is well-pleasing to God. Rather strikingly, the myth of the divine child is without significance in the NT world of thought.

2. Affirmation of the Individuality of Children?

a. Jesus [87] opposed to the low estimation of children common among His people an emphatically high evaluation, Mt. 18:2 ff., 10; 19:13-15; 21:15 f. This can hardly be regarded as "the noblest expression of the current Hellenistic mood." [88] Such a strong dependence would be almost inconceivable in a Galilean, especially at so early a time. Jesus never speaks of the innocence of children, not even in the relative, let alone the absolute, sense. He refers rather to the fact that they are modest and unspoiled as compared with adults, who do not want anything given to them, Mt. 18:2 ff.; 19:13 ff. This is not a quality which belongs to the child and which might be discovered. The child's littleness, immaturity and need of assistance. though commonly disparaged, keep the way open for the fatherly love of God, whereas grown-ups so often block it.

b. Paul is closer to the current view. He makes one allusion to the innocence of the child, 1 C. 14:20, → 641, 23-26; 646, 31-37 and 40 ff. Elsewhere he sees in the child immaturity (→ 642, 28-46; 646, 15-21) in the sense of inferiority, 1 C. 3:1; 13:11; 14:20a; Gl. 4:1, 3; Eph. 4:14. The same is true at Hb. 5:13. The innocence of children is a subsidiary motif in the concept of regeneration. This is especially so in 1 Pt. 2:1 f. In the context of the biblical concepts of sin and perdition it is obvious that this was not taken in the absolute sense, cf. also Jn. 3:6a.

3. The Child in God's Saving Counsel.

a. Little needs to be said about the basic point that according to the general view of the NT children have a place in God's saving counsel. Jesus' attitude to them is explicable only from this standpoint, → 648, 38-44. Paul, too, takes the saving work of the Initiator of the new creation as objectively and universally as possible, R. 5:18 f.; 1 C. 15:22. Even election (Gl. 3:9; 6:16; 1 Th. 1:4; R. 8:29 f. etc.) ultimately pursues universal goals (R. 11:25: πλήρωμα τῶν ἐθνῶν, 11:26:

---

[86] Dib. Past., ad loc. διά instrumental.

[87] Oepke, AELKZ.

[88] Birt, op. cit., 140. Even greater dependence is suggested by J. Leipoldt, Jesu Verhältnis zu Griechen u. Juden (1941), 178 f.

πᾶς Ἰσραὴλ σωθήσεται, 11:32 : ἵνα τοὺς πάντας ἐλεήσῃ). That the child as such should be excluded from salvation is out of the question. The relation between salvation and faith does, of course, raise questions which are particularly pressing in respect of children. But fundamentally the situation in Paul is that faith does not effect salvation ; it receives it. That a community which handed on the infancy stories and the account of the blessing of the children by Jesus, and which also had an organic sense of the interrelatedness of the generations (Ac. 2:39), should take a different view, is highly improbable. At the very most we might suspect something of this in John, though even he gives a very objective turn to the thought of Mt. 18:2 ff. (Jn. 3:1-21). [89]

b. From what has been said, it is hardly surprising to find that children are generally numbered with the community. They take part in crucial events in the life of the community (Ac. 21:5), and at least when they reach years of discretion they are present at the services (Ac. 20:9, 12; Col. 3:20; Eph. 6:1-3). A later age pays particular regard to the faith and conduct of the children of leaders in the community (1 Tm. 3:4; 5:4; Tt. 1:6). In the light of ancient and oriental parallels it is even probable that at gatherings for worship infants would be present in their mothers' arms.

c. Did the primitive Church baptise infants ? Recent research [90] makes it fairly certain that when whole households joined the Church (Ac. 16:15, 33; 18:8; 1 C. 1:16; in sense also Ac. 10:48; 11:14) existing children would also be baptised. This is supported by all the religious analogies (→ 643, 3-645, 21), but especially by proselyte baptism of children (→ 648, 13-35) and also by the patristic testimony of the first centuries (→ 652, 5-11). Baptism takes the place of circumcision (Col. 2:11) and is an eschatological sealing according to Ez. 9:4, 6. All the members of God's people participate in it (1 C. 10:1 f.). The objections against it are not decisive. Primitive Christianity takes a view of the sacrament which, though not magical, is supremely objective. 1 C. 7:14c probably refers only to the children of mixed marriages who might be unbaptised. That children born in Christian wedlock should not be baptised, after the manner of the proselyte law, is most unlikely, since the efficacy of baptism is very different from that of the proselyte washing, and we know of no unbaptised Christians in the apostolic age or the subsequent history of the Church. Any change would certainly have had to take place prior to about 65 A.D. The story of the blessing of the children in Mk. 10:13-16 and par. might well be aimed against objections to infant baptism.

IV. The Later Church and the Child.

1. The Child as Creature of God.

In the Church the high estimation of children on the basis of the biblical belief in creation was soon counterbalanced in part by exaggerated eschatology (Hipp. in Danielem, IV, 19), asceticism (Act. Pt. 34; Act. Andr. 4 f.; Act. Thom. 117, 124; Act. Pl. 5; Act. Joh. 63, 113; Ev. Egypt.), [91] self-castration, formal marriage, and the hermit life and monasticism. Nevertheless, in some degree Christianity gave a new and vital impulse to declining antiquity. The Church protected marriage, fought licentiousness, and with stringent this-worldly sanctions forbade contraception, abortion and exposure of children, Did., 2, 2; Barn., 19, 5; Apc. Pt. 8:26. It also demanded simplicity and a readiness to serve.

---

[89] On 1 Jn. 2:12, 14 → 638, 19-25. τέκνα is used in a similar transf. sense in 2 Jn. 1:4, 13.
[90] Cf. esp. J. Jeremias, *op. cit.* (Bibl.).
[91] Hennecke, 58.

The union of the best in antiquity with the legacy of Christianity may be seen in Cl. Al. Cl. is never bitter, like Tert. (Exhort. ad Castitatem, 9; Ad Uxorem, 1, 5). He says rather that childlessness or the loss of children is a heavy burden and the possession of children a great blessing, Strom., III, 9, 67, 1; II, 23, 142, 1. The pessimism of antiquity (→ 640, 8-11) is a sin against the Creator, III, 3, 22, 1-25, 4; 12, 81, 6. One should marry for the sake of the nation as a whole, the children, and the συντελείωσις of the world, in so far as this is in our hands. In marriage intercourse is ἐπὶ μόνῃ παιδοποιίᾳ, III, 15, 92, 2; 98, 4; 18, 107, 5. Even the apostles married and had children, III, 7, 52, 5. Moderation is the true contraceptive, III, 3, 24, 2. Means of abortion are κακότεχνοι μηχαναί, Paed., II, 10, 96, 1. Exposing children is unnatural, barbarous and ungodly, Paed., III, 4, 30, 2; Strom., II, 18, 92, 3-93, 1; Ecl. Proph., 41, 1 f.

2. The Relation to the Child.

The simple depiction of the child Jesus in Lk. (2:40-52) was no longer enough for a later age. In the Ev. Thom. it is replaced by a highly baroque childhood story.[92] Youthful androgynous features characterise the teaching Christ in the Thermae Museum in Rome.[93] This is Gnostic. The Church emphasises esp. the innocence of the child; if in Ign. Tr., 5, 1 νήπιος == rudis, cf. Herm. s., 9, 24, 2 f.: ἄκακοι, 9, 29, 1-3: νήπια βρέφη without κακία, m., 2, 1; Barn., 6, 11. Aristid. says of a child which died young: sine peccato per mundum transivit, Apol., 15, 11. But the nexus of evil is not forgotten. The same Tert. who in Bapt., 18 rejects the baptism of innocens aetas later as a Montanist confesses belief in original sin, De Anima, 39-41. Distinctive again is the union of antiquity and Christianity in Cl. Al. In the style of antiquity Cl. uses νήπιος in the sense of "foolish," Strom., I, 23, 157, 2; 11, 53, 2; cf. II, 4, 21, 2; Paed., III, 2, 14, 1; II, 12, 118, 2; I, 5, 16, 2; Strom., VII, 11, 66, 3. But he is also concerned that there should be nothing in the concept to arouse contempt, Paed., I, 5, 6. The child is νε-ήπιος (fresh and friendly), ἀταλός and ἁπαλός (tender), ἁπλοῦς, ἄδολος, ἀνυπόκριτος, ὀρθός, Paed., I, 5, 19, 1-3. It is the opp. of σκληροκάρδιος, III, 12, 94, 1; I, 4, 12, 4. The simple praise ἀδόλως ἀκάκοις στόμασιν παίδων ἡγήτορα Χριστόν, III, 12, 101, 3; cf. V, 10, 31. But Cl. thinks of innocence in religious rather than moral terms. He sees an interconnection between ὑπομονή and the merry childish laughter of ἐν Χριστῷ παιδίων, Paed., I, 5, 21, 4. There is constant praise of the divine child, Christ, I, 5, 24, 2 f.: παῖς κρατερός, III, 12, 101, 3 hymn line 60,[94] τὸν νήπιον τοῦ πατρός, I, 5, 24, 4. Hell. distortion may be detected in the story of the play-baptisms of the child Athanasius recognised by the bishop, Rufinus, Hist. Ecclesiastica, I, 14 (MPL, 21, 487 B). Augustine is more biblical. In the story of his conversion there comes to him from a distance the voice of a prophesying child, Confessiones, VIII, 12. He has little sense of the innocence of children, ibid., I, 7: the sinful greed of the infant. But genuinely childlike features are not wholly absent, I, 9 and 14.

3. The Child in the Cultus.

a. Participation and Clerical Functions. The prayer of innocent children (→ 649, 32 f.) is thought to be particularly efficacious, Ps.-Clem. Recg., 5, 30; Greg. Naz. Or., 16, 13 (MPG, 35, 952 B). In contrast to yawning adults Basil lauds the zeal of παῖδες σμικρότατοι in song, In Famem et Siccitatem Homilia, 3 (MPG, 31, 309 C). In Jerusalem there were antiphonal choirs of boys acc. to Aetheria, CSEL, 39, 72. Zeal outside the Church

---

[92] At most the canonical Gospels have only faint echoes of non-biblical motifs, and these are really independent material pars., cf. G. van den Bergh van Eysinga, Indische Einflüsse auf evang. Erzählungen (1909), 63, 90, 91; H. Gressmann, Das Weihnachtsevangelium (1914); Clemen, 209; Hennecke, 13*, 11. The childhood miracles in Ev. Thom. are connected not only to Gk. themes (→ 640, 4-7) but possibly also to the childhood story of Krishna in the Vishnu-Puranas, Hennecke, 94.

[93] O. Thulin, "Die Christus-Statuette im Museo Nazionale Romano," Rom. Mitt., 44 (1929), 201-259; F. Gerke, Christus in d. spätantiken Plastik³ (1948), Ill. 56-59. For the Christus puer in art cf. esp. c. 2 of the latter work.

[94] Cf. Dölger, op. cit., 224.

carried the Church along with it. The Nestorians had choir schools even in villages. Julian gave prizes to the best boy singers. Boys served as lectors (from the 5th yr. ? CIL, VII, 453; Victor Vitensis, II, 29 [CSEL, 7, 34]), though this was regarded as an abuse. [95]

b. Infant Baptism and Communion. From a very early period infant baptism is said to be an apostolic tradition, Mart. Pol., 9, 3; Polycrates of Ephesus in Eus. Hist. Eccl., V, 24, 6; Just. Apol., 15, 6; Iren. Haer., II, 33, 2; Hipp. Church Order, 46: ... qui vero loqui non possunt ...; [96] Orig. Comm. in Epistulam ad Romanos, 5, 9. [97] Delaying baptism is found only from the 4th cent. A.D. (the beginnings of a rational defence occur in Greg. Naz. Or., 40, 28). For infant communion there is an unbroken chain of witnesses from Cyprian (De Lapsis, 9) to the 12th cent.

C. Divine Sonship.

The motif of divine sonship arises within this circle — → παῖς θεοῦ is only an apparent exception — almost exclusively in connection with the word τέκνον, which alone denotes close personal relationship. It is also found only in Paul and John. For source material → πατήρ, υἱός, υἱοθεσία.

I. Religio-Historical Connections.

Like most national religions, Gk. religion thinks of divine sonship in natural terms (mythological in respect of the θεῖος ἄνθρωπος). God and man are one by nature. In the mysteries, however, divine sonship comes only by initiation understood as regeneration or adoption. Possibly under oriental influence, a stronger sense of distance is hereby expressed. The goal, however, is not divine sonship; it is deification. In spite of the lofty prayers, e.g., in Hermes mysticism, the background is pantheistic. Philosophy starts with natural presuppositions, but lays greater stress on the claim implied in divine sonship.

The OT uses the thought of divine sonship in a strictly non-mythological way. The primary application is to God's people, Hos. 11:1 etc. Only indirectly is the ref. to individuals within the people, Dt. 14:1 etc. Salvation history controls the relation. The figure of the king is more prominent than that of the father, and the latter is thought of at first in predominantly authoritarian terms, cf. Mal. 1:6. Individualism and universalism (not to be confused with cosmopolitanism) gradually come to the fore. The partial strengthening of this aspect in Judaism is not due to syncretistic dilution, as the continuing ref. to the concept of God's people shows, but is a product of inner development. By emphasising the idea of merit, however, the Synagogue made a claim out of God's prevenient grace. Divine sonship is thus ensnared in casuistry and dogma. It is not at the heart of Jewish piety.

II. Divine Sonship in the New Testament.

1. Jesus is the first to set divine sonship in the centre. Its individual and universal character are fully brought out by Him. It rests entirely on the prevenient grace of God which has simply to be received with the unassuming mind of the child, Mk. 10:15 and par.: ὡς παιδίον. With no restriction, then, it stands under the banner of freedom. This is not to be taken non-dialectically however, as in natural theology, which entails the oversimplification that Jesus is proclaiming divine sonship to all who bear the face of man. Jesus certainly sees the original connection between divine sonship and creation, but this has been broken on man's side. There has to be reacceptance into sonship, and this involves a paradox.

---

[95] Concilium Toletanum, IV, Can. 20, J. D. Mansi, Sacrorum conciliorum collectio, X (1764), 625.
[96] Hennecke, 579.
[97] Cf. Jeremias, 29-37 for these and other testimonies.

The One who makes Himself known as Father is the Holy One of Israel. In view of the possibility of falling away from sonship again, the fear of God is a continuing control, Mt. 10:28b and par. The thought of God's people is of fundamental significance for Jesus too. Only self-conceit and bargaining with God are excluded. Jesus realises that He is fulfilling the OT, that He personally bears God's definitive offer. This is not because He enjoys divine sonship in archetypal force, and is to this degree a pioneer. It is because He has been eschatologically sent. In this capacity He finally gives His life as λύτρον ἀντὶ πολλῶν. Materially one may see already in the Synoptic Gospels the difference between His divine sonship and that of believers. Only later is this worked out linguistically. But never in the Synoptics is Jesus called τέκνον θεοῦ. τέκνον is used only to denote descent from Abraham as a pre-condition of divine sonship, Mk. 3:9 and par., or to indicate the latter in parables, Mk. 7:27 and par.; Mt. 21:28; Lk. 15:31. The term used is → υἱός, which in this connection is always in the plur., Mt. 5:9, 45 and par.; Lk. 20:36.

2. Paul speaks on the basis of the possession of divine sonship effected through the life, death and resurrection of Christ. Only in appearance has he changed the simple teaching of Jesus about God's fatherhood into a complicated dogma. By means of the concept of → υἱοθεσία he rules out all mythological ideas and also an oversimple deduction of sonship from creation. [98] By the same means he establishes a connection with the OT and the concept of the people of God, R. 9:4. Divine sonship is mediated by a correctly understood descent from Abraham, Gl. 3:6 ff.; R. 4; cf. Gl. 6:16; 1 C. 10:1, 18 etc. It is thus grounded in salvation history. Universalism is very strongly advocated, but this universalism has nothing whatever to do with religious cosmopolitanism. The status of son implies full freedom and adulthood as compared with legal servitude and restriction. It means freedom from all cosmic powers, Gl. 3:25 ff.; 4:1 ff., 9; R. 8:31 ff. The Christology of the apostle is still so free that he can call Christ the πρωτότοκος ἐν πολλοῖς ἀδελφοῖς, R. 8:29. υἱός is not yet reserved for Christ. But along with the plur. υἱοί, which is still used, we also find the term τέκνον or τέκνα [τοῦ] θεοῦ, which is again not applied to Christ, R. 8:16, 17, 21; 9:8; Phil. 2:15. Full υἱοθεσία is still an object of hope, R. 8:23.

3. In Jn. there is a consistent linguistic distinction between being a son of God and a child of God. Only Christ is now υἱός. In distinction from Him believers are exclusively τέκνα [τοῦ] θεοῦ, Jn. 1:12; 11:52; 1 Jn. 3:1, 2, 10; 5:2. In controversy with Gnosticism sonship is described in strongly realistic terms derived originally from mythology, e.g., being begotten or born from above, from God, Jn. 1:12 f.; 3:3 ff.; 1 Jn. 2:29; 3:9 etc. But these are given a specific sense. The reference is to communion with God rather than deification, to community religion rather than mystical individualism. [99] Though the concept of the people of God seems at a first glance to be eliminated, it often shines through (in connection with divine

---

[98] Ac. 17:28 naturally cannot be adduced against this. Even if we regard as exaggerated the thesis of M. Dibelius, "Pls. auf dem Areopag," SAH (1938/39), 2. Heft and M. Pohlenz, "Pls. u. d. Stoa," ZNW, 42 (1949), 69-104 (as opposed to W. Schmid, "Die Rede des Ap. Pls. vor den Philosophen u. Areopagiten in Athen," Philol., 95 [1943], 79-120), that the address is wholly outside the framework of the Pauline and even the NT kerygma, it may still be said that the detailed authenticity of the address is not wholly assured. And if Paul really used the quotation from Aratus, the reapplication is obvious. Thus Dio Chrys. Or., XII, 27 ff. deduces from the divine origin of men the permissibility of idol worship.

[99] Cf. E. Gaugler, Die Bedeutung der Kirche in den joh. Schriften, Diss. Berne (1925); D. Faulhaber, Das Johannesevangelium u. die Kirche (1938).

sonship, Jn. 11:51 f.). [100] Nor are genuine eschatological connections wholly absent from the Gospel. [101] They are perfectly clear in 1 Jn. (3:2 etc.). The status of the child is depicted as one of blessed possession and hope, to which externality and legalism are wholly alien, and which is victory over the world and death. Yet the driving out of fear is paradoxical (1 Jn. 4:18), and its presupposition, perfect love, is hardly attainable on earth. The child of God is engaged in constant flight from the accusations of his own heart to the One who is greater and who knows all things, 1 Jn. 3:19 f. [102] There is entailed brotherly love and an unconditional break with sin, 1 Jn. 3:9-24 etc. The connection is here so close that the thought can be reversed, 1 Jn. 5:2. Jn. gives us the most succinct and meaningful expression of the Christian concept of divine sonship in the whole of the NT.

4. The linguistic distinction between υἱός and τέκνον is peculiar to Jn. In the remaining NT writings the latter term is not used to denote the divine sonship of believers. In Jm. 1:18 and 1 Pt. 1:23, however, divine sonship is again brought into connection with regeneration.

III. Divine Sonship in the Church.

Early Church history offers us a remarkable spectacle, for, while sonship in the biblical sense was never wholly forgotten, it was very quickly and extensively overgrown by alien concepts, which were in part naturalistic, in part moralistic. Individual instances could be given only if greater space were available. [103]

Oepke

---

† παῖς θεοῦ

Contents : A. The עֶבֶד יהוה in the OT : I. The Profane Use of the Term עֶבֶד: 1. עֶבֶד as Slave ; 2. The עֶבֶד in Royal Service ; 3. עֶבֶד to Denote Political Subjection ; 4. עֶבֶד as a Humble Self-Designation ; 5. The Servants of the Sanctuary. II. The Religious Use

---

[100] Cf. A. Oepke, *Das neue Gottesvolk in Schrifttum, Schauspiel, bildender Kunst u. Weltgestaltung* (1950), 237.

[101] G. Stählin, "Zum Problem d. joh. Eschatologie," ZNW, 33 (1934), 225-259. If Bultmann takes a different view, this is in accordance with his total understanding.

[102] Cf. Bü. J., Exc. 10 on 1 Jn. 4:18.

[103] Cf. Oepke, *op. cit.* (→ n. 5), 108 f. and esp. RE³, X, 297-304.

π α ῖ ς θ ε ο ῦ. On A. I : W. W. Baudissin, "Zur Entwicklung des Gebrauchs von *ebed* in religiösem Sinne," *Festschrift K. Budde,* ZAW Beih., 34 (1920), 1-9; also *Kyrios als Gottesname,* III (1929), 176-242, 524-555; C. Lindhagen, *The Servant Motif in the OT* (1950). On A. II : B. Duhm, *Das Buch Js.⁴* (1922); P. Volz, *Js. II* = *Komm. z. AT,* IX, 2 (1932); H. Gressmann, "Die literarische Analyse Dtjs's," ZAW, 34 (1914), 254-297; L. Köhler, *Dtjs stilkritisch untersucht* (1937); K. Elliger, *Dtjs in seinem Verhältnis zu Tritjs.* = BWANT, 4. F., 11. H. (1933); K. Budde, *Die sog. Ebed-Jahve-Lieder u. d. Bedeutung des Knechtes Jahves in Js. 40-55* (1900); also *Das Buch Js. Kp. 40-66* in Kautzsch⁴; F. Giesebrecht, *Der Knecht Jahves d. Dtjs* (1902); H. Gressmann, *Der Ursprung der isr.-jüd. Eschatologie* (1905), 301-333; also "Der Messias" = FRL, NF, 26 (1929), 287-339 and Index, s.v. "Ebed Jahve"; L. Dürr, *Ursprung u. Ausbau der isr.-jüd. Heilandserwartung* (1925), 125-152; W. Rudolph, "Der exilische Messias," ZAW, 43 (1925), 90-114; E. Sellin, *Serubbabel* (1898); also *Mose u. seine Bedeutung f. d. isr.-jüd. Religionsgeschichte* (1922), 77-113; also "Die Lösung d. deuterojesajanischen Gottesknechtsrätsels," ZAW, 55 (1937), 177-217; S. Mowinckel, *Der Knecht Jahwäs* (1921); also "Die Komposition d. deuterojesajanischen Buches," ZAW, 49 (1931), 87-112, 242-260; J. Hempel, "Vom irrenden Glauben," ZSTh, 7 (1930), 631-660; J. Begrich, "Das priesterliche Heilsorakel," ZAW, 52 (1934),

of עֶבֶד 1. עֶבֶד as a Humble Self-Designation of the Righteous before his God ; 2. Servants of Yahweh in the Plural as a Term for the Righteous ; 3. עֶבֶד יהוה in the Singular as a Term for Israel ; 4. עֶבֶד יהוה as a Term to Denote especially Distinguished Figures : a. The Patriarchs ; b. Moses ; c. The King ; d. The Prophet ; e. Job ; 5. The Suffering Servant of God in Dt. Is. B. The LXX Translations : 1. Translations of עֶבֶד in the LXX ; 2. The Translation of the Servant of God Passages in Dt. Is. C. παῖς θεοῦ in Later Judaism in the Period after the LXX : I. The Twofold Meaning of παῖς θεοῦ : 1. παῖς θεοῦ == Child of God ; 2. παῖς θεοῦ == Servant of God. II. The Persistence of the OT Religious Use of עֶבֶד יהוה : 1. παῖς θεοῦ as a Self-Designation in Prayer ; 2. The Plural Servants of God ;

81-92; also "Studien z. Dtjs" == BWANT, 4. F., 25. H. (1938), esp. 131-151; O. Eissfeldt, *Der Gottesknecht bei Dtjs im Lichte der isr. Anschauung von Gemeinschaft u. Individuum* (1933); C. North, *The Suffering Servant in Deutero-Is.* (1948); A. Bentzen, *Messias, Moses redivivus, Menschensohn* == Abh. z. Theologie d. A u. NT, 17 (1948); J. J. Stamm, *Das Leiden d. Unschuldigen in Babylon u. Israel* (1946); H. W. Robinson, "The Hebrew Conception of Corporate Personality," in J. Hempel, *Werden u. Wesen d. AT* == ZAW Beih., 66 (1936), 49-62; I. Engnell, "The 'Ebed Yahweh Songs and the Suffering Messiah in 'Deutero-Isaiah," *Bulletin of the John Rylands Library*, Vol. 31, No. 1 (1948); N. H. Snaith, "The Servant of the Lord in Dt. Is.," *Studies in OT Prophecy*, Festschrift T. H. Robinson (1950), 187-200; H. W. Wolff, *Js. 53 im Urchr.*[2] (1950); E. Burrows, "The Servant of Jahweh in Isaiah," *The Gospel of the Infancy and other Biblical Essays* (1940). On B. : K. F. Euler, "Die Verkündigung vom leidenden Gottesknecht" == BWANT, 4. F., 14. H. (1934); J. Ziegler, *Untersuchungen zur LXX des Buches Isaias* (1934); also *Isaias* == Septuaginta, XIV (1939). On C. : Older bibl. in Schürer, II, 648, n. 92. A. Wünsche, יִסּוּרֵי הַמָּשִׁיחַ oder die Leiden d. Messias (1870); S. R. Driver and A. Neubauer, *The Fifty-third Chapter of Is. according to the Jewish Interpreters*, I and II (1876/7); G. Dalman, "Der leidende u. d. sterbende Messias d. Synagoge im ersten nachchr. Jahrtausend," *Schriften d.* Institutum Judaicum Berlin, 4 (1888) (quoted as Dalman I); P. Billerbeck, "Hat die alte Synagoge einen präexistenten Messias gekannt?" *Nathanael*, 21 (1905), 89-150; P. Humbert, "Le Messie dans le Targum des prophètes," *Revue d. Théol. et de Philosophie*, 43 (1910), 430-447; 44 (1911), 5-46; A. Schlatter, "Das AT in d. joh. Apk.," BFTh, 16, 6 (1912), 50 f.; Schürer, II, 648-651; G. Dalman, "Js. 53, das Prophetenwort vom Sühnleiden des Gottesknechtes"[2], *Schriften des* Institutum Judaicum Berlin, 13 (1914) (quoted as Dalman II); Str.-B., I, 481-485; II, 273-299; R. A. Aytoun, "The Servant of the Lord in the Targum," JThSt., 23 (1922), 172-180; Moore, I, 229, 549-551; III, 63, 166; G. Kittel, Art. "Menschensohn" in RGG[2], III, 2118-2121; H. Odeberg, *3 Enoch or the Hebrew Bk. of Enoch* (1928); J. Jeremias, "Erlöser u. Erlösung im Spätjudentum u. Urchr.," *Deutsche Theologie*, II (1929), 106-119; W. Staerk, "Soter," BFTh, 2. Reihe, 31. Bd. (1933), 72-84; K. F. Euler → *supra* under B.; J. Bonsirven, *Le Judaïsme Palestinien au temps de Jésus, Christ*, I (1934), 380-385; J. Jeremias, "'Αμνὸς τοῦ θεοῦ — παῖς θεοῦ," ZNW, 34 (1935), 115-123; P. Seidelin, "Der 'Ebed Jahwe u. d. Messiasgestalt im JsTg," ZNW, 35 (1936), 194-231; R. Bultmann, "Reich Gottes u. Menschensohn," ThR, NF, 9 (1937), 26-30; W. Staerk, *Die Erlösererwartung in d. östlichen Religionen* (1938), 406-408; J. J. Brierre-Narbonne, *Le Messie souffrant dans la littérature rabbinique* (1940); N. Johansson, Parakletoi (1940), 96-119; R. Otto, *Reich Gottes u. Menschensohn*[2] (1940), 118-209; W. Manson, *Jesus the Messiah* (1943), 99, 171 ff.; H. A. Fischel, "Die deuterojesajanischen Gottesknechtlieder in d. jüd. Auslegung," *Hebr. Union Coll.*, 18 (1943/4), 53-76; E. Sjöberg, "Der Menschensohn im äth. Henochbuch," Acta Regiae Societatis Humaniorum Litterarum Lundensis, Vol. 41 (1946), 116-139; H. Riesenfeld, "Jésus transfiguré," Acta Seminarii Neotestamentici Upsaliensis, Vol. 16 (1947), 81-96, 307-317; C. C. Torrey, "The Messiah Son of Ephraim," JBL, 66 (1947), 253-277; W. D. Davies, *Paul and Rabbinic Judaism* (1948), 274-284; I. Engnell → *supra* under A.; H. J. Schoeps, "Symmachusstudien," III, Biblica, 29 (1948), 31-51 (V, "Der aussätzige Messias," 38 f.); J. F. Stenning, *The Targum of Isaiah* (1949); M. Buber, "Jesus u. d. 'Knecht,'" Pro regno, pro sanctuario, Festschrift f. G. van der Leeuw (1950), 71-78 (republished in *Zwei Glaubensweisen* [1950], 103-116); H. H. Rowley, "The Suffering Servant and the Davidic Messiah," *Oudtestamentische Studiën*, VIII (1950), 100-136; H. Hegermann, *Js. 53 in Tg. u. Peschitta*, Diss. Göttingen (1951), quoted as Hegermann I; also *Js. 53 bei* 'A, Θ, u. Σ, quoted as Hegermann II. On D. : Dalman WJ, I, 226-229; W. Bousset, *Kyrios Christos*[2] (1921), 56 f., 69-74; C. F. Burney, *The Aramaic Origin of the Fourth Gospel* (1922), 104-108; F. C. Burkitt, *Christian Beginnings* (1924), 35-41; A. v. Harnack, "Die Bezeichnung Jesu als

3. The Collective Use; 4. παῖς θεοῦ as a Title of Honour for Important Instruments of God; 5. Servant of God as a Term for the Messiah. III. Interpretations of the Servant of God Passages in Dt. Is.: 1. Hellenistic Judaism; 2. Palestinian Judaism: a. The Collective Interpretation; b. Reference to the Prophet Isaiah; c. References to the Messiah: (a) Jesus Sirach; (b) Visionary Discourses of Eth. En.; (c) Peshitta; (d) NT; (e) Aquila; (f) Theodotion; (g) Tg. Is.; (h) The Rabbis; (i) Opposition to Christianity. D. παῖς θεοῦ in the NT: I. παῖς θεοῦ as a Title of Jesus: 1. The Provenance of the Title; 2. The Meaning of the Predication; 3. The Change of Meaning from Servant of God to Child of God. II. Christological Interpretations of the Deutero-Isaianic Servant of God in the NT: 1. The References: a. Pre-Pauline Tradition and Formulae; b. Pre-Synoptic Tradition and Formulae; c. Tradition and Formulae in Ac.; d. Primitive Formulae in 1 Pt.; Hb.; e. Primitive Formulae in the Johannine Writings; f. Paul, Matthew; 2. The Setting in the Primitive Church: a. Proof from Scripture; b. Christology of the Primitive Community; c. Liturgy; d. Early Christian Exhortation. III. Can Jesus Have Thought of Himself as the Servant of God of Dt. Is.?

A. The עֶבֶד יהוה in the OT.

I. The Profane Use of the Term עֶבֶד.

The noun עֶבֶד comes from the verb עָבַד, which originally means "to work." [1] In the noun, however, it is striking how weakened is the content of the root, [2] and to what degree it is replaced by a specific personal relation. The expressed or unexpressed and

'Knecht Gottes' u. ihre Gesch. in d. alten Kirche," SAB, 28 (1926), 212-238; E. Lohmeyer, "Kyrios Jesus," SAH, 1927/8, 4. Abh., 33-36, 42, 49, n. 4, 69; L. L. Carpenter, Primitive Christian Application of the Doctrine of the Servant (1929); J. H. Ropes, "The Influence of Second Isaiah on the Epistles," JBL, 48 (1929), 37-39; C. C. Torrey, "The Influence of Second Isaiah in the Gospels and Acts," JBL, 48 (1929), 24-36; H. J. Cadbury, "The Titles of Jesus in Acts," Jackson-Lake, I, 5 (1933), 364-370; K. F. Euler, → supra under B; J. Jeremias, "'Ἀμνὸς τοῦ θεοῦ — παῖς θεοῦ," → supra under C.; G. Kittel, "Jesu Worte über sein Sterben," DTh, 3 (1936), 166-189; V. Taylor, Jesus and His Sacrifice, A Study of the Passion-Sayings in the Gospels (1937); O. Procksch, "Jesus, der Gottesknecht," Abhandlungen d. Herder-Gesellschaft u. des Herder-Instituts zu Riga, VI, 3 (1938), 146-165; I. Zolli, Il Nazareno (1938), 228-233, 331-355; Bau. Ag. on 3:13, 26 and 4:27; J. Gewiess, "Die urapostolische Heilsverkündigung nach d. Ag.," Breslauer Studien z. historischen Theol., NF, 5 (1939), 38-57, 75-81; L. Goppelt, "Typos," BFTh, 2. Reihe, 43. Bd. (1939), 113-116, 120-127; G. Wiencke, "Pls. über Jesu Tod," BFTh, 2. Reihe, 42. Bd. (1939), 161-164; R. Otto → supra under C.; V. Taylor, The Atonement in NT Teaching² (1945); G. Sass, "Zur Bedeutung von δοῦλος bei Pls.," ZNW, 40 (1941), 24-33; H. W. Wolff, → supra under A.; E. Lohmeyer, "Gottesknecht u. Davidsohn," Symbolae Biblicae Upsalienses, 5 (1945); W. Michaelis, Herkunft u. Bedeutung des Ausdrucks "Leiden u. Sterben Jesu Christi" (1945); L. Cerfaux, "L'hymne au Christ-Serviteur de Dieu (Phil. 2:6-11 = Is. 52:13-53:12)," Miscellanea Historica in honorem A. de Meyer (Université de Louvain, Recueil de Travaux d'Histoire et de Philosophie, 3e série, 22e fascicule [1946], 117-130); R. Bultmann, Theol. d. NT (1948 ff.), 31 f., 47, 51 f.; O. Cullmann, Die Tauflehre d. NT, Abhandlungen zur Theol. d. A u. NT, 12 (1948), 11-16; also "Gesù, servo di Dio (Jesoûs Paîs Theoû)," Protestantesimo, 3 (1948), 49-58; J. Jeremias, "Das Lösegeld für Viele," Judaica, 3 (1948), 249-264; also Die Abendmahlsworte Jesu² (1949), 78, n. 8, 80 f., 91-93, 108-111; K. H. Schelkle, Die Passion Jesu in d. Verkündigung d. NT (1949), 60-194; O. Cullmann, Urchr. u. Gottesdienst², Abhandlungen zur Theol. d. A u. NT, 3 (1950), 64-66; M. Buber, → supra under C. [Note: At the request of J. Jeremias and with the kind permission of the S.C.M. Press his section of the art. has been presented according to the revised 1965 edition. Changes in the text or notes are marked by [1965].]

[1] T. Noeldeke, review of F. Delitzsch, Prolegomena eines neuen hbr.-aram. Wörterbuchs zum AT, ZDMG, 40 (1886), 741; W. J. Gerber, Die hbr. Verba denominativa (1896), 14-16; Lindhagen, op. cit., 41-42.

[2] It may still be detected in, e.g., Job 7:2, or 1 K. 9:22, where in an addition in Origen the OT נָתַן עֶבֶד is rendered by ἔδωκεν εἰς πρᾶγμα.

implied counterpart of עֶבֶד is not one who is inactive but אָדוֹן, the "master." [3] The עֶבֶד is the "worker who belongs to a master." The whole rich development of the עֶבֶד concept commences with this element of relationship. The suffix and construct combinations, also the rarer loose use with לְ, all refer, not to the object of the work, but to the master who orders it. [4] In detail, the following primary circles of use may be singled out in respect of the word עֶבֶד.

1. עֶבֶד as Slave. עֶבֶד means the "slave," the man whose chief characteristic is that he belongs to another. [5] The slave seems to be one who has become a mere chattel. One may see from OT law, however, that there were limits to this process in Israel. The slave has human rights. In distinction from, e.g., Babylonian law, an offence against a slave must be made good to him by manumission. [6] In the OT laws of slavery there is no punishment by mutilation. [7] The slave who has run away from another is not to be handed over. [8] One thing which contributed to the greater freedom of the slave was the fact that according to OT belief, with its orientation to the community and the people of God, the slave had a part in the cultic fellowship. [9] Again, Israel itself realised from the very first that it owed its whole existence to an act of deliverance from Egypt, the house of bondage, Ex. 20:2; Dt. 5:6; 6:12 etc. Lv. 25:42 is able to show how clearly the resultant allegiance of Israel to Yahweh can assure its bondslaves of at least the right to live. Gn. 24 tells the most beautiful slave story in the OT. It does not give the name of the hero; he is simply called עֶבֶד־אַבְרָהָם, or more briefly הָעֶבֶד. [10] What he does is wholly controlled by the cultic fellowship of the house of his master. God is for him "the God of my master Abraham," v. 12, 27, 42, 48. At this point, however, free service is possible. In this matter of wooing a bride for Abraham's son the עֶבֶד acts with just the same authority as if Abraham himself were there. He is the full representative of his lord, and yet he is still the unnamed and subordinate servant who does not even permit himself a humanly understandable rest at the place of his successful mission, vv. 54 ff.

2. The עֶבֶד in Royal Service. The need to repel the Philistines, who had a professionally trained army, made it necessary from the days of Saul onwards for the king, who originally had at his disposal only the general levy, to form a standing army of paid soldiers. [11] The man who joined this army left the natural tribal organisation and became עֶבֶד הַמֶּלֶךְ. [12] It would hardly be appropriate to speak of slavery in this connec-

---

[3] This is beautifully clear in Lv. 25, where v. 39 forbids that a fellow-countryman who has fallen into bondage should be made to do עֶבֶד work, though v. 40 regards it as self-evident that he will work (עבד).

[4] Thus one may speak verbally of a עֶבֶד אֲדָמָה (Gn. 4:2; Zech. 13:5; Prv. 12:11; 28:19), but never of a עֶבֶד אֲדָמָה in the sense of a worker on the land. The verb עבד in the sense "to serve" is to be regarded as a secondary derivation from עֶבֶד. On its use cf. Gerber. loc. cit. The palpable weakness in the work of Lindhagen (cf. esp. → n. 41) lies in the undetected confusion of the noun עֶבֶד and the verb עבד, which results in his misunderstanding of the עֶבֶד passages in the OT.

[5] This is most evident in, e.g., the lists of possessions in Gn. 20:14; 24:35; 30:43; 32:6 etc., or in the extremely unsentimental הוּא כַּסְפּוֹ of Ex. 21:21 (cf. on this Lv. 22:11 as well).

[6] Ex. 21:26 f., cf. Codex Hammurabi § 199, 213.

[7] Codex Hammurabi § 205, 282.

[8] Dt. 23:16, cf. Codex Hammurabi § 15-20.

[9] Sacrifice, Dt. 12:12, 18; Sabbath, Ex. 20:10; Dt. 5:14; Passover, Ex. 12:44; circumcision, Gn. 17:13, 27. Though עֶבֶד is not used in Lv. 22:11, the matter itself is plain.

[10] עֶבֶד אַבְרָהָם vv. 34, 52, 59; הָעֶבֶד, 5, 9, 10, 17 etc.; v. 2 represents him as עַבְדּוֹ זְקַן בֵּיתוֹ הַמּשֵׁל בְּכָל־אֲשֶׁר לוֹ. The reader of all the stories about Abraham now collected in the text will think of the Eliezer mentioned in Gn. 15:2.

[11] 1 S. 14:52; cf. esp. A. Alt, Die Staatenbildung der Israeliten in Palästina (1930), 33 f.; E. Junge, Der Wiederaufbau d. Heerwesens des Reiches Juda unter Josia (1937), 8-22.

[12] עַבְדֵי שָׁאוּל, 1 S. 18:5; 22:9 etc.; עַבְדֵי אִישׁ־בּשֶׁת בֶּן־שָׁאוּל, 2 S. 2:12; עַבְדֵי דָוִד, 2 S. 2:13, 15, 17 etc.

tion, for royal service was probably based on a firm agreement in which the king accepted reciprocal obligations. [13] עֶבֶד is used because here, too, a clear relationship of allegiance, which superseded previous relationships, determined the status of these royal servants. With the extension of monarchy to other fields and the creation of other groups of officials עֶבֶד came into wider use. All officials dependent on the king could be generally described as servants of the king. [14] Finally, the bearer of an important individual office at court, whose duties are unfortunately not made clear in the one reference to him in 2 K. 22:12 (par. 2 Ch. 34:20) (→ n. 92), seems to have borne the title עֶבֶד הַמֶּלֶךְ in a specialised sense. [15]

3. עֶבֶד to Denote Political Subjection. עֶבֶד is used more widely and imprecisely to denote political subjection in a very general sense. [16] Even kings can be called עֶבֶד in this connection, 2 S. 10:19, cf. 2 K. 18:24. But עֶבֶד always implies subjection and allegiance. There always lurks within it an expression of abasement which can once come out unawares in an obvious lament, Lam. 5:8.

4. עֶבֶד as a Humble Self-Designation. On the basis of court usage self-designation as עֶבֶד became a formal expression of humility in everyday politeness. [17] Here words may sometimes be added which overemphasise the element of humility. [18]

5. The Servants of the Sanctuary. Perhaps the servants of the sanctuary should be mentioned as a special group. Acc. to Jos. 9:23 Joshua condemns the Gibeonites to be

[13] 1 S. 22:7; the "king's right," with its obscure implications, pushes the voluntary character of the עֶבֶד into the background, though there is ref. to reward in 1 S. 8:14 f. Here and in what follows ref. may be made to the Arab. *baiʿ*-covenant, J. Pedersen, *Der Eid bei d. Semiten* (1914), 52-63. On the other hand it is hardly correct to describe the עֶבֶד relation, and hence every slave relation, as a ברית relationship of a *baiʿ* type, Lindhagen, 53. Though in Israel the religious עֶבֶד relation can be integrated into the ברית relation of Israel, the religious עֶבֶד statement being a special form, the עֶבֶד and ברית relations are originally different structures.

[14] Thus already in Saul's day a עֶבֶד seems to have had special charge of the flocks, 1 S. 21:8. 2 S. 9:2 (cf. v. 9) calls the steward Ziba עֶבֶד (is this a preliminary form of the עַל־הַבַּיִת of 1 K. 4:6; 16:9 ?). He himself again has עֲבָדִים at his disposal. Saul's advisers are called this in 1 S. 16:15. In 2 S. 11:9, 13 the circle of courtiers not involved in the war in David's time is called עֶבֶד, cf. also David's counsellors in 2 S. 15:34 and his ambassadors in 2 S. 10:2-4. Comparison of the par. texts 2 K. 19:23 and Is. 37:24 shows that מַלְאָךְ can be used instead of עֶבֶד. In 1 K. 11:26 Jeroboam, who is Solomon's labour overseer, is called עֶבֶד; cf. 2 Ch. 13:6.

[15] If the Jeroboam named in the inscr. of the fine seal found in Megiddo שמע עבד ירבעם is one of the kings of this name (AOB, Ill., 578, cf. K. Galling, "Beschriftete Bildspiegel d. 1. Jahrtausends," ZDPV, 64 [1941], 121-202, No. 17), and if עזיו and אחז in the seal inscr. Galling No. 85 and 125 or No. 1a refer to Uzziah and Ahaz, then perhaps we have further refs. to this court title, which is perhaps directly attested on the seal No. 43 (ליאוניהו עבד המלך). Cf. D. Diringer, *Le iscrizioni antico-ebraiche palestinesi* (1934), 229-231; Lindhagen, 36-39.

[16] Thus the Gibeonites come with the formula of subjection עֲבָדֶיכֶם אֲנַחְנוּ in Jos. 9:11, cf. 1 K. 20:32; 2 K. 10:5. For the fuller formula of a subjection which is seeking help cf. 2 K. 16:7: עַבְדְּךָ וּבִנְךָ אָנִי (→ II, 267, 13 ff.).

[17] L. Köhler, "Archäologisches," ZAW, 40 (1922), 43 f.; I. Lande, *Formelhafte Wendungen d. Umgangssprache im AT* (1949), 68-71; for politeness in diplomatic intercourse, → II, 267, n. 40-42. We find not only the polite self-designation but also the polite description of a third party as עֶבֶד by the speaker.

[18] Cf. Hazael in 2 K. 8:13 : "thy servant the dog," or Mephibosheth in 2 S. 9:8 : "What is thy servant, that thou shouldest turn to such a dead dog as I am ?" Cf. J. A. Knudtzon, *Die El-amarna-Tafeln* (1915), 60, 6 f.; 71, 17 f.; 85, 64. On the *ardu/amtu* of the Amarna letters cf. Lindhagen, 7-30. For other lands (→ n. 17), 74-76. The formula עבדך כלב in the Lachish letters 2, 5, 6 (ed. H. Torczyner, *The Lachish Letters* [1938], 36 f., 92 f., 104 f.).

עֶבֶד לְבֵית אֱלֹהַי. [19] When we view the OT as a whole, however, it is noticeable how plainly the ref. of עֶבֶד elsewhere is personal. Pars. to the formula often found in Carthaginian inscr.: עֶבֶד of the house of God,[20] do not occur in the OT.[21] This is important not merely in answering the question as to the rise of a temple capitalism but also in evaluating the use of עֶבֶד. עֶבֶד is a person who belongs to a person.

II. The Religious Use of עֶבֶד.

In religious use we find the same three constructions as in secular use, the construct formation עֶבֶד יהוה,[22] the suffix with all three persons, and less commonly the combination with לְ.[23]

1. עֶבֶד as a Humble Self-Designation of the Righteous before his God. The relation to secular usage is most plainly to be seen in the self-designation of the righteous before God. Just as the inferior, standing before his superior, refers to himself as "thy servant" in the third person, this mode of address is particularly appropriate when a man stands before the absolute Lord.[24] In this connection the term can bear different emphases. First, the predominant note in many passages may be that of a simple, humble confession of the lowliness of the speaker before his mighty Lord.[25] But then a claim can be heard arising from the word of humble submission. As on the lips of Ahaz the formula of subjection turned into

---

[19] Is the intervening "hewers of wood and drawers of water" a gloss or original? The ref. is probably to the sanctuary in Gilgal. Cf. M. Noth, *Das Buch Josua = Handbuch z. AT*, I, 7 (1938), 29-33.

[20] עבד בת צדתנת Corpus Inscr. Semiticarum, I, 1 (1881), No. 247-249; עבד בת אשמן, 252, cf. also 250 f., 253 f.

[21] In the list of sanctuary servants in Ezr. 2 and Neh. 7, where we should most have expected a ref. to such people, we have a group of בְּנֵי עַבְדֵי שְׁלֹמֹה in Ezr. 2:55, 58; Neh. 7:57, 60; 11:3. These must have been appointed to a specific ministry from the time of Solomon. It is significant, however, that even at this later date they are still called בְּנֵי עַבְדֵי שְׁלֹמֹה in accordance with their earlier personal relationship.

[22] So 21 times. Plur. עַבְדֵי יהוה. Only later when the name of Yahweh is suppressed do we find עֶבֶד הָאֱלֹהִים, 1 Ch. 6:34; 2 Ch. 24:9; Neh. 10:30; Da. 9:11. Once in an earlier passage we can see the introduction of the Father-God title: in Gn. 50:17 the brothers call themselves עַבְדֵי אֱלֹהֵי אָבִיךָ when in the presence of Joseph; in Aram. Da. 6:21 Darius once describes Daniel as עֶבֶד אֱלָהָא חַיָּא and in 3:26 the three friends are called עַבְדוֹהִי דִּי אֱלָהָא עִלָּיָא. In Aram. Ezr. 5:11, in the address to the Persian governor, the Jews style themselves עַבְדוֹהִי דִּי אֱלָהּ שְׁמַיָּא וְאַרְעָא.

[23] עַבְדִּי 62 times, עֲבָדַי 17 times, עַבְדְּךָ 92 times, עֲבָדֶיךָ 20 times, עַבְדּוֹ 23 times, עֲבָדָיו 16 times. With לְ: sing. Is. 44:21; 49:5 f.; plur. 56:6; Lv. 25:55.

[24] Cf. esp. Baudissin, *Kyrios*, III, 524-555. This similarity between the language of politeness and that of liturgy is strongest in passages where it is doubtful whether the speaker is aware of standing face to face with the divine Lord. In Gn. 18:3, 5 the meaning of the original seems to be that Abraham did not at first recognise Yahweh among the three men who came to visit him, so that initially he was simply using the language of courtesy. On the other hand, the HT by its vocalisation of אֲדֹנָי in v. 3 seeks to express already the fact that Abraham knows he is in God's presence. He obviously did not regard any change in style as necessary.

[25] Cf. Moses in Ex. 4:10; Nu. 11:11; Dt. 3:24. Rather oddly עֶבֶד is not used in Abraham's strong words of self-abasement in Gn. 18:27. If the emendation proposed by H. Torczyner at 2 S. 7:21 is right (בַּ עֲבוּר עַבְדְּךָ וְכַלְבֶּךָ), "Dunkle Bibelstellen," *Festschr. K. Marti = ZAW, Beih.* 41 [1925], 275), then we have here in the language of prayer the form of self-depreciation customary in secular speech: thy servant and dog. Since, however, this basically de-personalising self-abasement does not occur before God elsewhere in the OT — is this merely accidental? — doubts arise as to the correctness of Torczyner's reconstruction.

the petition : "I am thy servant and thy son : come up, and save me" (2 K. 16:7), so it may be before the divine Lord. He who confesses allegiance to a master withdraws from the dominion of all other possible masters, and with inner justification he can thus ask the master to whom he confesses allegiance to see to it for his part that his dominion is upheld and his servant protected. The honour of the divine Lord is also at stake. [26] If in this supplicatory approach man's own achievement stands emphatically to the fore (I am thy worshipper), the self-designation עֶבֶד acquires a strongly active ring. On the other hand, if the friendliness of God already experienced is emphasised, the name עֶבֶד suggests the attitude of grateful self-commitment. [27]

What has been said thus far is by no means peculiar to the OT. These aspects of pious self-designation as עֶבֶד (Babylonian *ardu*) are also to be found in the world surrounding Israel. Three further points are to be noted, however, which distinguish the OT encounter with God and which enable us to see why the OT understanding of עֶבֶד could undergo its own especially rich development.

a. OT faith arises out of encounter with Yahweh, the jealous Lord, Ex. 20:5; 34:14; Dt. 4:24; 5:9; 6:15; Jos. 24:19; Nah. 1:2. When Ashurbanipal calls himself the servant of Nebo, [28] but at the next New Year's feast again grasps the hands of Ashur, the god of his residence and land, and is again invested with his dominion by him, the self-designation as a servant of Nebo cannot be taken exclusively. In Israel, however, the self-designation of the righteous as עֶבֶד יהוה has something total about it. The principle that "no man can serve two masters" embraces not merely the moment of turning to the deity in worship, but the whole of life. Alongside it no other עֶבֶד status is conceivable. This seriousness is evident on both sides. Yahweh demands the total obedience of His servant, and the servant, even in the hour of affliction, may make full appeal to his allegiance to this one Lord.

b. OT faith is conscious of a primal turning of Yahweh to Israel on the basis of the free decision of Yahweh. As regards the development of the phrase עֶבֶד יהוה this means that this movement cannot be made definitively in the sphere of individual piety or even in that of a local cult. It stands related to the whole event of Israel. The individual can only become a servant of the Lord in so far as he is a member of Israel. For the will of Yahweh is orientated to Israel. In the exodus from Egypt and the ensuing conclusion of the covenant, of which Israel spoke even in its early period, this will of Yahweh for Israel was made manifest. The servant status of the righteous is a status in the sphere of this relationship which was not formed by man but effected by Yahweh, → n. 13.

c. OT faith perceives that Israel's encounter with Yahweh took place in history and that it also aims at a historical embodiment. Thus the term "servant" does not remain in the timeless sphere of individual prayer. It takes on special significance

---

[26] Ps. 143:11 f.: "Quicken me, O Lord, for thy name's sake ... destroy all them that afflict me : for I am thy servant." Cf. the Babylonian : "Quicken thy servant, he would exalt thy power, he would extol thy greatness among all men," W. Schrank, *Babylonische Sühnriten* (1908), 56.

[27] So, e.g., in the inscr. on a votive pillar in Malta : "To our Lord Melkart, the Lord of Tyre (the pillar) dedicated by thy servant (עבדך) Abdosir and my brother Osirshamar, the two sons of Osirshamar, the son of Abdosir, for he has heard their voice. May he bless them !" Corpus Inscr. Semiticarum, I, 1 (1881), No. 122.

[28] J. Pinckert, *Hymnen u. Gebete an Nebo* (1920), 16 f. The text is none too certain in line 5, but this does not affect the basic principle at issue here.

when Yahweh in His historical dealings with His people summons individuals to special service.

If we turn back again from these insights to the humble self-designation of the righteous as it is found in the OT we shall be able to understand the strong confidence implicit in it. The עֶבֶד status is not one to which the righteous has attained by his own achievement, nor does it rest solely on sacrifices or good works. The self-designation עַבְדְּךָ finds its security in the fact that it is aware of being an echo of a name which was first given by the mouth of Yahweh Himself. Thus in Nu. 12:7 f. Yahweh says of Moses in an emphatic and repeated affirmation : "My servant Moses." [29] The simple, unknown man of prayer can also say : "Let ... thy merciful kindness (חֶסֶד) be for my comfort, according unto thy word to thy servant," Ps. 119:76. On the basis of a saying of Yahweh known to him, the worshipper dares to draw near to Yahweh as a servant. The saying which is in his ears, however, continually becomes a word of command and direction from the covenant God. [30] "I have gone astray like a lost sheep : seek thy servant, for I do not forget thy commandments," Ps. 119:176, cf. v. 17, 23, 135, 140. The servant is he who is obedient to the command of Yahweh. But the עֶבֶד יהוה will also have foes who are especially sinister because they embody hostility to Yahweh too. Thus implicitly or explicitly the self-designation עַבְדְּךָ may be orientated to its opposite "my foes" (= thy foes, i.e., the foes of Yahweh). "Let them curse, but bless thou : when they arise, let them be ashamed ; but let thy servant rejoice," Ps. 109:28. [31]

2. Servants of Yahweh in the Plural as a Term for the Righteous. On account of its inner seriousness the term עֶבֶד יהוה is a very vital one in the OT. It breaks loose from the conventional formula for the righteous individual [32] and can be freely used in the plural for the righteous. [33]

The synonymity of par. statements will perhaps elucidate their inner content. The servants of Yahweh are those who "seek refuge in him" (Ps. 34:22) and who "love his name" (Ps. 69:36) — possession of the hereditary land is here promised to them. They are also "his saints" (= those bound to Him in חֶסֶד, Ps. 79:2). Most succinctly and comprehensively they are "his people" (Ps. 105:25; 135:14). Here a ref. to the divine election is plainly linked to the עֶבֶד concept. [34] In Tt. Is. the division of the community

---

[29] Cf. also Caleb in Nu. 14:24, David, Isaiah, Eliakim, Nebuchadnezzar etc. It is worth noting statistically that whereas עַבְדְּךָ occurs 92 times on the lips of the worshipper there are as many as 62 instances of עַבְדִּי on the lips of Yahweh (plur. עֲבָדֶיךָ 20 times and עֲבָדַי 17).

[30] E.g., Ps. 50 or the Torah Ps. 15 and 24.

[31] In this context there is no need to discuss the problem of the "enemies" in the Ps.

[32] In the ancient oriental world around the OT the chief setting of the designation עֶבֶד seems to have been this formula of humble self-description and the giving of names. The votive inscr. from Malta quoted in → n. 27 will perhaps convey some impression of the rigidity of this formula. Though two benefactors are named there, they do not venture to put the formula in the plur. but instead have the clumsy "thy servant and my brother." For the giving of names cf. esp. the rich material in Baudissin, *Kyrios*, III, 531-548. On Ras Shamra cf. Lindhagen, 30-31. On OT names cf. M. Noth, *Die isr. Personennamen im Rahmen der gemeinsemitischen Namengebung* (1928), 137-138. In Karatepe 'ztwd describes himself as עבד בעל, A. Alt, "Die phönizischen Inschr. v. Karatepe," *Die Welt d. Orients* (1949), 272-287.

[33] Ps. 113:1 and 135:1 f. mention the community worshipping in the temple, or the circle of priests. Ps. 134:1 refers to a vigil. Ps. 113:1 (παῖδες), ᾿ΑΣΘ (δοῦλοι) and 135:1 LXX (δοῦλοι) have "your servants" in the abs. through a failure to recognise the st. c. עַבְדֵי י (αἰνεῖτε, παῖδες, κύριον). There is no instance of the abs. use in the HT.

[34] Lindhagen, 153-155.

into the servants and enemies of Yahweh is strongly emphasised (65:13 ff.). The two poles of the עֶבֶד concept are also clear to see. Is. 56:6 calls obedience to the covenant statutes the basis of the עֶבֶד status, while 65:9 equates the servants of Yahweh with the elect and thus throws all the emphasis on the divine choice. These elect are the visible pledge of the gracious favour of Yahweh. "So will I do for my servants' sakes" runs His own gracious promise, Is. 65:8.

3. עֶבֶד יהוה in the Singular as a Term for Israel. From the humble self-designation of the individual a line may also be traced to the description of Israel in the singular as עֶבֶד יהוה. The first instance of this is probably in Dt. Is. [35] Dt. Is. formulates most of his promises of salvation in the style of the priestly oracle of deliverance. [36] The oracle given to the suppliant by the priest corresponds closely in style to the lament with which the suppliant approaches his God. [37] Thus the oracle takes up the liturgical confession of the suppliant which is customary in individual laments: "I am thy servant" (Ps. 116:16; 119:125) and embeds it in the wholly new context of the comforting divine promise: "But thou, Israel, art my servant, Jacob whom I have chosen, the seed of Abraham my friend, whom I have taken from the ends of the earth, and called thee from the chief men thereof, and said unto thee, Thou art my servant; I have chosen thee, and not cast thee away ..." [38] The designation עֶבֶד is changed on the lips of Yahweh. No longer does there stand in the foreground the humble confession of lowliness of the people crushed by the exile, whom Dt. Is. thinks of in wholly personal terms as a single individual. To the fore now is the powerful and gracious commandeering of this people by Yahweh. In sayings which far transcend the circle of the master-servant concept, and which are no longer harmonised among themselves, expression is given to the thought of total and gracious commitment to Yahweh. Israel, the עֶבֶד יהוה, has been created by Yahweh (44:2, 21), elected by Him (41:8 f.; 44:1; 45:4), brought from the ends of the earth (41:9). It is the seed of Abraham, the friend of God (41:8). In a formula found already in Babylonian oracles of redemption, it is summoned to fear not (44:2). Help is promised by Yahweh. Indeed, He promises the ransom [39] which is paid for the blood relation (48:20). Nothing is said about any action on the part of the servant Israel itself. If 42:19 refers to Israel, the servant is here stated to be totally blind, cf. 43:8. The witness to Yahweh's power which the people [40] is called upon to render is that of the passive recipient of a gift. "To convert" is the only activity which is expected from the people (44:22) — to convert in the light of the saving act accomplished by Yahweh alone. [41]

---

[35] If Jer. 30:10 (→ n. 41) is accepted as authentic, the beginning of this further development will be found in Jer. In this case, however, the paucity of testimony to the new use of עֶבֶד in Jer. is surprising. Did Jer. find it in a stream of prophetic utterance now unknown to us, and hence use it occasionally? The full vitality which the phrase "servant of the Lord" enjoys when applied to Israel in Dt. Is. seems to me to indicate that this is an original usage.

[36] Begrich, Heilsorakel, 81-92; also Studien, 6-19, 137, 140 f.

[37] H. Gunkel-J. Begrich, Einl. in die Ps. (1933) § 6, cf. also § 4.

[38] 41:8 f. Cf. also 44:1 f.; 45:4. In admonition 44:21. In a brief allusion, 48:20.

[39] J. J. Stamm, Erlösen und Vergeben im AT (1940), 27-45.

[40] 43:10. It is an open question whether the עֶבֶד here is Israel or an individual alongside the people.

[41] The usage of Dt. Is. is echoed in Jer. 30:10 (par. 46:27 f.), → n. 35. At Ez. 28:25 and 37:25 it is doubtful whether the patriarch Jacob or the people is the servant of Yahweh. In the analogous saying in Ps. 136:22, which uses the name Israel, the ref. is clearly to the people. It is here that Lindhagen is most dangerously misleading. Since he does not distinguish between the noun and verb in his investigation, he is unable to see how narrowly

4. עֶבֶד יהוה as a Term to Denote especially Distinguished Figures. Yahweh encountered His people Israel in history. He held this people firmly in history as the setting of His presence and the place of responsibility. It is not surprising, then, that OT faith continually finds in history figures whom it sees to be servants of Yahweh in a special way. We must now take note of these outstanding historical representatives of the עֶבֶד יהוה status. In so doing we must expect from the very outset to find traces of the influence of secular courtly usage, which is also familiar with the distinction of pre-eminent עֶבֶד figures as well as the general polite use of the term.

a. The Patriarchs. Israel finds the beginnings of its history summarised in the figures of the patriarchs. Their story expresses most limpidly [42] the gracious character of the story of Yahweh which began long before there was any people at all. We are thus given to understand that whenever there is reference to the patriarchs as the servants of Yahweh what comes first is quite unequivocally the gracious relationship to Yahweh. The patriarchs are pledges of the divine will to save. For the sake of Abraham His servant Yahweh promises blessing to Isaac. [43] In an hour of especial danger for the people Moses in his prayer to Yahweh reminds Him of the oath which He sware to the three patriarchs, His servants, who are mentioned by name, Ex. 32:13; Dt. 9:27.

b. Moses. On the threshold of the national history stands Moses. Forty times in the Mas. he is called עֶבֶד. Two pre-Deuteronomic passages give him this title with special emphasis. In Nu. 12:7 f. (E) Moses is differentiated by a divine declaration from the prophets who know God only in dreams or visions : "Not so is my servant Moses, who is faithful in all mine house. With him I speak mouth to mouth ... wherefore then were ye not afraid to speak against my servant Moses ?" Moses is the vizier, the faithful steward of Yahweh. We are reminded of the faithful servant of Abraham, → 657, 19 ff. Then in Ex. 14:31 (J), when Israel has been saved at the Red Sea under the leadership of Moses, we read : "Then they believed Yahweh and his servant Moses." Moses was only Yahweh's servant. But Yahweh was so patently present in what he did with such plenitude of power that the answering faith of the people bows to him, and in him to Yahweh. An essential feature of biblical revelation is expressed here. God's history is not a transcendent heavenly history. It stoops to earth and makes men with their works and words its signs. Moses, the servant of Yahweh, embodies in his works and words such a part of the divine history. Obedience or disobedience to Yahweh is decided by obedience or disobedience to Moses' word. Much more strongly than the patriarchs Moses is an active servant figure. He enjoins the Law (Jos. 1:2, 7; 2 K. 18:12; Mal. 3:22 etc.), gives specific orders concerning the conquest (Jos. 1:13, 15; 8:31 etc.), regulates cultic matters (2 Ch. 1:3; 24:6), promises future rest in the land (1 K. 8:53, 56). Behind it all, however, stands the choice of Yahweh which allots to him and to Aaron their ministry. [44]

---

restricted is the sphere in which the sing. עֶבֶד is used for Israel. The rich use of the verb עבד for Israel conceals this from him. In consequence the whole lay-out of his enquiry gives the impression that what is said about Israel as the servant of Yahweh comes first (the main section 82-233 is entitled "Israel as Yahweh's Servant"), and then only by derivation do righteous individuals bear the title עֶבֶד יהוה (pp. 233-262 deal with the group of righteous as עֶבֶד יהוה and pp. 262-288 with "The Servant as Individual Members of the People of Israel"). The real situation regarding the noun עֶבֶד is the exact opposite.

[42] So at least acc. to the popular tradition found esp. in Gn. For a different view in the prophets cf. Hos. 12:3 ff.; Jer. 9:3; Is. 43:27.

[43] Gn. 26:24, cf. Ps. 105:6, 42. Isaac is called the servant of Yahweh only in the speech of Abraham's servant, Gn. 24:14. When the name Jacob is used, the difficulty in any given instance is to distinguish between the patriarch and the people named after him, → n. 41. Cf. in 1 Ch. 16:13 the adapted quotation from Ps. 105:6.

[44] Cf. the par. in Ps. 105:26. In an echo of the story of Moses, Joshua, as the one who completes his work, is once called the servant of Yahweh (Jos. 24:29 = Ju. 2:8). On the

c. The King. The series of servants of Yahweh now divides quite unmistakably into two lines of development. On the one side is the king, who has to render a distinctive service in Israel. "By the hand of my servant David I will save my people Israel out of the hand of their enemies," is a saying on the lips of Yahweh in 2 S. 3:18, which is undoubtedly pre-Deuteronomic. The king is the servant of Yahweh with the special office of saving the people of God out of the hands of its enemies. But not every king, for there is a further development out of the promise of Nathan in 2 S. 7. Marked off by a special covenant of grace, David is the king of the saved people. Hence the blameless obedience of David is emphasised in the Deuteronomic history, in which the designation of David as עֶבֶד יהוה occupies a prominent place. Along with this there would seem to be a heavy stress on meritoriousness in respect of the office of servant. But this is only in appearance. The same history also underlines emphatically the genuinely basic fact of the divine election [45] which again shows the Davidic monarchy to be a pure gift of grace. 1 K. 11:34 combines the two aspects in a tension-filled duality : "David my servant, whom I chose because he kept my commandments and my statutes." The more the history leads into darkness the more powerfully OT faith clings to the divine servant David as a sign of promise. It waits for the day when David, the servant of Yahweh, will be king, Ez. 34:23 f.; 37:24 f. It reminds Yahweh in prayer of the oath which He sware to His chosen servant David, Ps. 89:3, cf. v. 20. It speaks of the unbreakable covenant which Yahweh has made with His servant David, Jer. 33:21 f., 26. [46] Directly after the exile we see the hope flare up again. The post-exilic successor of David, Zerubbabel, who in Zech. 3:8 is given the secret Messianic title צֶמַח, acquires both here and in Hag. 2:23, on the lips of Yahweh, the title of honour עַבְדִּי. [47] Jer. 25:9; 27:6; 43:10 show that the designation of a king as עֶבֶד יהוה can have a special use even in the sphere of the prophetic proclamation of judgment. [48] In Nebuchadnezzar the judicial holiness of Yahweh appointed, with a limited commission, a royal servant who was alien to Israel. Here, too, the divine will takes human form in the servant. Whoever resists Nebuchadnezzar resists Yahweh, Jer. 27-29.

d. The Prophet. Alongside the line of the king stands that of the prophet. The prophet is the messenger of the Word of Yahweh. The office of messenger is found in the royal service too. [49] The account of David's embassy to Hanun (2 S. 10:2 ff.) makes it clear how closely the honour of the envoy is bound up with the honour of his king. 1 K. 18:36 shows that the same applies to the servant of God. Elijah prays on Carmel : "Yahweh,

---

other hand, the thought of obedience is clearly emphasised in the case of Caleb, the man who brought back a faithful report (Nu. 14:24).

[45] 1 K. 11:13, 32 mentions both David and the chosen city of Jerusalem as pledges of the faithfulness of Yahweh. On the liturgical background to this association cf. H. J. Kraus, Die Königsherrschaft Gottes im AT (1951), 58 f. 1 K. 11:36 and 2 K. 8:19 refer to Yahweh's will to give David a lamp. 2 K. 19:34 and 20:6 formulate most strongly the significance of David as a divinely appointed sign of salvation : Yahweh will help "for my ... and for my servant David's sake."

[46] How closely the cause of Yahweh is bound up with that of His royal servant of the house of David is shown by what is said about the envoys of Sennacherib, who speak "against the Lord Yahweh, and against his servant Hezekiah" (2 Ch. 32:16; the Chronicler expresses this even more strongly, though without the use of עֶבֶד, in 1 Ch. 28:5; 29:23; 2 Ch. 13:18). Yahweh's honour is at stake in the affair of Hezekiah. Cf. what was said about Ex. 14:31 → 663, 26 ff.

[47] An unknown descendant of David Ps. 89:39, 50. Cf. also 1 K. 8:30, 36 (corrected text), 52, 59.

[48] But the pre-hexaplar LXX reads עַבְדִּי only in the second ref. (δουλεύειν αὐτῷ לְעָבְדוֹ). The statement about Nebuchadnezzar is so unusual, however, that it is unlikely to be a later development. Since it inwardly fits in best with the preaching of Jer., the most satisfactory solution is to assume that he was the one who first applied it in this novel fashion.

[49] For the alternation of עֶבֶד and מַלְאָךְ → n. 14. Is. 44:26 (corrected text) has a corresponding parallelism for the office of the prophetic messenger of God, and Job 4:18 for that of the heavenly messenger.

God of Abraham, Isaac, and of Jacob, let it be known this day that thou art God in Israel, and that I am thy servant, and that I have done all these things at thy word." The history of Yahweh is again present among men in the fully authorised messenger of His Word. Knowledge of God depends upon knowledge of His servant. In the Deuteronomic history the prophet takes on almost functional significance. His word thus shows the course of history to be a continual fulfilment of divine prophecy. [50] Along these lines Ahijah of Shiloh (1 K. 14:18; 15:29), Elijah (2 K. 9:36; 10:10) and Jonah ben Amittai (2 K. 14:25) — a prophet of salvation — are referred to as servants of Yahweh. [51] In the wider circle of Deuteronomic literature the general expression "my (thy, his) servants the prophets" becomes a stereotyped formula. It is a fixed phrase mostly used theologically in specific contexts. The messengers of the word are the great warners of the people, uninterruptedly sent by Yahweh. [52] In all these references prominence is given to a specific active mission of the servant. The parallel to a royal court is particularly clear in this respect. To the court of Yahweh belong the servants who fulfil His Word on earth. Job 4:18 also speaks of the heavenly messengers who fulfil His Word. [53]

In the older stories (esp. about Elisha) seer and prophet are frequently given the probably pre-Israelite [54] title אִישׁ הָאֱלֹהִים. [55] The obvious later replacement of this term by עֶבֶד was probably due to a desire not only to see the weaker אֱלֹהִים replaced by יהוה, [56] but even more so the non-commital אִישׁ by עֶבֶד, which expresses more sharply the full personal commitment [57] of the divine messenger. On the other hand, the older writing prophets unmistakably [58] avoid עֶבֶד as a term for their office. An attempt has been made to explain this by pointing out that "the word servant everywhere implies the bondage of one's own will to that of the master." The prophets, however, "demand a free decision for obedience to the will of Yahweh." [59] This explanation is highly improbable. It is better to see that the designation of self and others as עֶבֶד יהוה is rooted in the cultic language of the sanctuaries (the Psalms) and national piety, and that this in turn is shaped by the language of court. The older writing prophets, however, are strongly opposed to this piety and they avoid its vocabulary. [60] It is significant that this terminology then makes fresh gains in the Deuteronomic parts of Jer. and esp. in Dt. Is., [61] whose close affinity to popular prophecy and the piety of the Psalter is increasingly recognised to-day.

e. Job. In the prose sections of the book Job is often called "my servant" by Yahweh, 1:8; 2:3; 42:7 f. In the framework of a writing influenced by the Wisdom literature the

---

[50] G. v. Rad, *Deuteronomiumstudien* (1947), 55-58 (ET [1953], pp. 74 ff.). The thought is then taken up by Dt. Is. and made an important pillar in his argument against the idols of the Gentiles, Is. 41:22 f., 26 f.; 42:9 etc.

[51] Isaiah is also called "my servant" by Yahweh in Is. 20:3.

[52] 2 K. 9:7; 17:13, 23; 21:10; 24:2; Jer. 7:25; 25:4; 26:5; 29:19; 35:15; 44:4; Ez. 38:17; Am. 3:7 (probably a later addition); Zech. 1:6; Da. 9:6, 10; Ezr. 9:11.

[53] In 1 K. 22:19 ff. both circles of the divine court are distinctively associated. The title עֶבֶד is not mentioned here.

[54] Noth, *loc. cit.* (→ n. 32).

[55] LXX 2 Ch. 24:6 renders Moses' title עֶבֶד יהוה by ἄνθρωπος τοῦ θεοῦ.

[56] For later development → n. 23.

[57] אִישׁ can also express an impersonal relation, e.g., in the plur.: the men of Kirjath-jearim in 1 S. 7:1, of Jabesh in 1 S. 11:5, 10. With עֶבֶד such a use is inconceivable, cf. also → n. 21.

[58] Am. 3:7 is probably secondary; Is. 20:3 seems to be a report at third hand, cf. O. Procksch, *Js.* I (1930), 255; cf. 37:35, which comes from the Isaiah legend. There thus remains 22:20, if authentic.

[59] Baudissin, *Entwicklung*, 8.

[60] Cf. the terms "covenant," "election," "fathers."

[61] The passages in Is. and Ez. which use עֶבֶד religiously seem to come from groups of pupils.

writer here speaks quite uninhibitedly of a servant of Yahweh outside the confines of the people of Israel. Even though the name of Yahweh in avoided by Job himself, what is then concretely worked out in the fidelity of Job is thus the supreme biblical recognition of Yahweh's indissoluble relationship with His creation, cf., e.g., 14:13-15. Futhermore, strong emphasis is here laid on the aspect of active obedience on the part of the servant of God. Job's fear of God, which is powerfully depicted in the introduction, is demonstrated in loyal obedience. In spite of all the temptations of Satan he will not renounce God with cursing. Hence Yahweh also acknowledges Job. In spite of the calumniations of Satan (1:8; 2:3) and the over-righteous speeches of the friends (42:7 f.), He graciously claims Job by naming him his עֶבֶד.

5. The Suffering Servant of God in Dt. Is. The OT use of עֶבֶד יהוה comes to fulfilment in the suffering servant passages in Dt. Is.

Since Duhm in 1892 took the passages 42:1-4; 49:1-6; 50:4-9 and 52:13-53:12 out of their present context and ascribed them to a later age as songs dealing with the fate of an unknown teacher of the Torah, the question of the relationship of these songs to Dt. Is. has been much discussed. [62] Closer investigation has made it increasingly plain how closely the songs [63] are related to the rest of Dt. Is. in vocabulary, style, genre and structure. [64] This is least true of 52:13-53:12, where esp. the middle section (53:1-11a), which has the typical style of a community song of thanksgiving, stands out distinctively by reason of its vocabulary. [65] In content, too, it goes beyond what is said in the first songs. It is not possible, however, to detach it from the framework of the sayings of Yahweh (52:13-15; 53:11b, 12), which for their part cannot be separated from 49:7. Now 49:7 is more strongly Deutero-Isaianic, and it is not so different in thought from 50:4-9. Hence 52:13-53:12, whose final mystery has not yet been cleared up, seems to be firmly riveted to the whole cycle of songs, and with the other songs it is to be interpreted in the context of the preaching of Dt. Is.

a. How is the figure of the עֶבֶד to be understood? From early times the history of exposition has followed two main directions. Consideration of the present text of 49:3, and the predominant use of עֶבֶד elsewhere in Dt. Is. (→ 662, 7 ff.), necessarily suggest a collective reference to Israel. [66] To this is opposed the individual interpretation which would find a single person in the songs. [67] Investigation of the religious use of עֶבֶד in the OT cannot in itself help us to decide, for whereas an individual application is predominant elsewhere (→ A, II, 1, 2, 4), there can be no doubt as to the collective reference to Israel in Dt. Is. An individual interpretation seems to be suggested in 49:5 f. God is the speaker here, and in answer to the servant's complaint He refers to an originally more limited ministry of the עֶבֶד to Israel and its later extension to the Gentiles. This raises insuperable difficulties for a collective understanding. [68] In the יִשְׂרָאֵל of 49:3 we shall have

---

[62] North gives a full history of recent exposition in the first part of his book.

[63] We might add to these 42:5-9; 49:7, 8-13. Cf. Begrich, Studien, 74 f., 131-151.

[64] Gressmann, Analyse; Köhler; Begrich, Studien. Mowinckel, Komposition, argues against this, but he does not pay adequate attention to established data concerning style and genre.

[65] Even in recent times Elliger, Volz and Sellin have championed a separate origin for 52:13-53:12.

[66] Cf. already the textual emendation of the LXX at 42:1, → 676, 14 ff. In the Middle Ages the Jewish exegesis of Rashi, Ibn Ezra, Kimchi, later J. Wellhausen, Is. u. jüd. Gesch. (1894), 117-118; Giesebrecht; Budde, Ebed Jahve-Lieder, 34; Eissfeldt, 25 etc.

[67] The oldest instance is probably in Is. 61:1 ff., cf. W. Zimmerli, "Zur Sprache Tritjs's," Festschr. L. Köhler (1950), 69-71. The LXX at least for 52:13 ff. → 676, 26. Cf. also the question of the Ethiopian eunuch in Ac. 8:34. For recent examples → n. 70.

[68] The ruthless reconstruction of the text by Giesebrecht, 44 f. is as little convincing as the tortured reinterpretation of Budde (in Kautzsch), ad loc. Similarly, the more recent

to see an early, but in the text a secondary gloss [69] along the lines of collective interpretation. The original, however, can only be taken individually. What kind of an individual is meant? Apart from the reference to great figures of the past (the patriarchs, Moses), the use of עֶבֶד elsewhere in the OT suggests two main lines of development: the royal-messianic (→ 664, 1 ff.) and the prophetic (→ 664, 29 ff.). Attempts have been made to solve the riddle of עֶבֶד along both lines. [70] Closer study of features in the discharge of the servant's office, the organs needed for it according to the description in 50:4 f. (ear, tongue), and unmistakable similarities with the accounts of the call of both Jer. and Ez. all seem to speak in favour of the prophetic line. [71] Whatever suggests kingly action (execution of judgment, 42:1, 3 f., liberation of prisoners, 42:7; 49:9 and the sharp sword, 49:2) may also be ascribed to the prophet. [72]

b. What individual prophet might have determined the features of the עֶבֶד? The hypothesis strongly suggests itself that in the songs something of the office

---

attempts at a collective interpretation by Eissfeldt and H. W. Robinson, 58-62, while they have significant things to say about the conception of the people as a collective personality, do not deal properly with the text of Dt. Is. Finally, the claim that we ought not to be confronted with exclusive alternatives (e.g., A. Bentzen, *Introduction to the OT*, II [1949], 113: "'Ebed Jahweh is both the Messiah and Israel and Deutero-Isaiah and his band of disciples" etc.) seems to me to serve only to confuse the whole issue.

[69] For the possibility of such glosses cf. LXX on 42:1. That the MS Kennicott, 96, which does not have יִשְׂרָאֵל at 49:3, cannot be adduced in testimony to a sound ancient tradition, has been proved by J. A. Bewer, "The Text-critical Value of the Heb. Ms. Ken. 96 for Is. 49:3," *Jewish Studies in Memory of G. A. Kohut* (1935), 86-88, and "Textkritische Bemerkungen," *Festschr. A. Bertholet* (1950), 67-68. The gloss goes back behind all available textual evidence, cf. also M. Burrows, *The Dead Sea Scrolls of St. Mark's Monastery*, I = *The Isaiah Manuscript and the Habakkuk Commentary* (1950), Plate 40, line 30.

[70] The following have been suggested on the royal line: Uzziah (J. C. W. Augusti, "Über den König Usia, nebst einer Erläuterung Js. 53," *Magazin f. Religionsphilosophie, Exegese u. Kirchengeschichte*, 3 [1795], 282-299; K. Dietze, *Ussia, der Knecht Gottes* [1929]), Hezekiah (L. Itkonen, "Dtjs metrisch untersucht," *Annales Academiae Fennicae*, 14 [1916]), Jehoiachin (E. Sellin, *Studien z. Entstehungsgesch. d. jüd. Gemeinde*, I [1901], 284-287; also *Das Rätsel des deuterojesajanischen Buches* [1908], 144-150), Zerubbabel (Sellin, *Serubbabel*, 148-192), the Messiah (Gressmann, *Messias*, 337 ff.; J. Fischer, *Isaias 40-55 u. d. Perikopen vom Gottesknecht* [1916], 165) etc. On the prophetic line suggestions include: Moses (Sellin, *Mose*, 108-113), Isaiah (C. F. Stäudlin, *Neue Beiträge zur Erläuterung d. bibl. Propheten* [1791]), Jeremiah (C. J. Bunsen, *Vollst Bibelwerk f. d. Gemeinde*, Vol. 2 [1860], 438), Ezekiel (R. Krätzschmar, *Ez.* [1900]) etc. For the whole story of interpretation cf. North.

[71] Ref. has already been made to the fact that the high evaluation of the word of the prophets in illumination of history (Dt. Is. uses עֶבֶד for them in the corrected text of 44:26), is a point of similarity with the Deuteronomist, → n. 50.

[72] Whether the passion features may be claimed as royal traits which Dt. Is. took over from the ritual of the suffering and atoning king, or which penetrated into the whole genre of individual laments, is the subject of much debate, v. Dürr, Engnell, Bentzen. Gressmann, *Ursprung*, 329-333 argues from the Tammuz rite. Is it likely that the author would be influenced by these timeless traits of a ritual king-liturgy taken from the cultic life of Babylon, which Dt. Is. so passionately rejected? Is it not more probable from the OT standpoint that he should build on the prophetic confessions of Jer. (→ n. 75), which arose out of the afflictions of a specific historical mission? At individual pts. ancient cultic formulations might well have come down by way of the psalmody already present in Canaan and then cultivated in the age of the monarchy. One cannot rule out the possibility that these helped to shape the expression. Nevertheless, these formulae can hardly have been the real forces which moulded the image of the servant of the Lord in Dt. Is., who had such a passion for historical decision.

and experience of the prophet Dt. Is. has found an echo [73] and received an interpretation which transcends the empirical reality of his life and dares in faith to lay hold of ultimate insights, [74] → IV, 612, 46 ff. [75] The striking objectivity and yet also the anonymous concealment under the name of עֶבֶד יהוה may well indicate that the prophet does not wish to be misunderstood simply in subjective-biographical terms. [76] The figure is called עֶבֶד. As in the story of the slave in Gn. 24 (→ 657, 19) the absence of a proper name is designed to express the fact that the true essence of this figure is to be found in its belonging to another, in this instance Yahweh. [77] It thus becomes clear that the commitment is not to a cause but to a person, → 659, 5. The term "servant" mostly occurs in sayings of Yahweh which lay a personal claim, 42:1; 49:3, 6; 52:13; 53:11, only 49:5 in the third person. The servant has been fashioned by Yahweh (42:6; 49:5, 8) from his mother's womb (49:5, cf. v. 1). He is the elect (42:1) on whom Yahweh has focused His good-pleasure (42:1), and whom the hand of Yahweh has grasped (42:1). He has been called by Yahweh in truth (i.e., really, validly, 42:6; 49:1). His name has been named by Yahweh with all the solemnity of a cultic name-giving. [78] With the summons to service comes endowment for it. Yahweh equips His servant with His Spirit. [79] He awakens and prepares for him the organs which are especially important for his prophetic calling : the ear (50:4 f.) and the mouth (49:2; 50:4). [80]

c. In what does the content of the servant's office as a messenger consist ? In the words of introduction in 42:1-4, in which Yahweh presents His servant to a wider public and which represents an outward-looking summons of Yahweh to the prophet, [81] the word מִשְׁפָּט is used 3 times in the absolute to describe the content of the servant's preaching, 42:1, 3, 4. Our whole understanding of the servant's task will be decided by our understanding of this word. Is it here stated that the servant must propagate the truth, [82] "religion, the only religion there is, since Yahweh is the only God," [83] "the only Law in which the Spirit of Yahweh has

---

[73] First impressively demonstrated by Mowinckel in his *Knecht,* then rejected by Mowinckel himself in his *Komposition.*

[74] Cf. the analogy to the royal line, and on this G. v. Rad, "Erwägungen zu den Königspsalmen," ZAW, 58 (1940/41), 216-222.

[75] The parallelism to the confessions of Jer. pts. also in the same direction. These, too, are loosely integrated into the literary structure of the book and they bear witness to the inner vision of prophetic obedience to office, the inescapability of the prophet's commission, and above all the path of suffering which the prophets must tread. But what ends for Jer. in enigmatic night (20:14 ff.) becomes in Dt. Is. a distinctively final answer which is the culmination and conclusion of OT insight.

[76] That Jer.'s confessions, too, give evidence of a wrestling with his office has been shown by G. v. Rad, "Die Konfessionen Jeremias," *Evang. Theol.,* 3 (1936), 265-276.

[77] Is there not fully expressed herein something which Jeremiah stated differently in his confessions : "When I found thy words I did eat them, and thy word was unto me the joy and rejoicing of mine heart : for I am called by thy name, Yahweh," 15:16.

[78] 49:1. On הִזְכִּיר שֵׁם cf. Ex. 20:24; 23:13; Jos. 23:7 and → 255, 18 ff.

[79] 42:1. Here a link is forged with the older popular prophecy (e.g., 2 K. 2:9) which had been pushed into the background by the great writing prophets. Cf. P. Volz, *Der Geist Gottes* (1910), 24, 62-69. In the version of the saying in Tt. Is. (61:1 → n. 67) there is added the thought of the anointing of the prophet, of which there are instances in the older prophecy, cf. 1 K. 19:16.

[80] Cf. in this connection Jer. 1:9, also Is. 6:7; Ez. 3:1 ff.

[81] An analogy in the NT is the juxtaposition of the baptismal saying to Jesus Himself in Mk. 1:11 par. Lk. 3:22 and the address to the bystanders in Mt. 3:17, cf. even more expressly Mt. 17:5 Mk. 9:7 and Lk. 9:35.

[82] Volz, *ad loc.*

[83] Budde in Kautzsch, *ad loc.*

found perfect expression"? [84, 85] If so, the servant might well be regarded simply as a missionary whose task among the nations was to convert men to this true and timeless insight — a task which is hardly conceivable or practicable for a single individual, and against which the champions of the collective view rightly raise their objections. Is not the reference rather to a strictly historical instruction in right and judgment (in 42:4 מִשְׁפָּט is par. to תּוֹרָתוֹ) which is grounded in God's accompanying establishment of right in history? It cannot be denied that this second mode of understanding is far nearer to what we find elsewhere in prophecy than is the first line, which makes Deutero-Isaiah a teacher of religion in quite novel fashion.

What then is the history to which the proclamation of מִשְׁפָּט is orientated and in which it is rooted according to its content? In Is. 42:2 f. the content of this proclamation is intimated by three figures of speech which are probably taken from the sphere of legal symbolism, so that no doubt is left as to the setting in which the proclamation took place. By means of the image of the herald who contrary to custom does not cry aloud, of the bruised reed which symbolises the death sentence and which against expectation is not fully broken, and the flame which is almost out but not completely extinguished, the vv. express the fact that Yahweh establishes judgment in a surprising act of grace. [86] 42:7 speaks more plainly of the liberation of captives from prison, and 49:5 f. states quite openly that what is at issue is the restoration of the preserved of Israel, i.e., the exiles, and the gathering together of the people (in v. 5 read יִשְׂרָאֵל לוֹ יֵאָסֵף), 49:8 ff. depicts this restoration along the same lines as the joyful message of Dt. Is. elsewhere. It is a return through a wilderness which is now transformed and blessed with water. It is a repossession of the devastated land of inheritance. At the same time the point is evident that all this is not merely an external historical restitution. It is an establishment of right and justice which transforms Israel both outwardly and inwardly. Blind eyes are to be opened (42:7; cf. the blind people of 43:8). Darkness is to be lifted (49:9). Israel will again find its God and know His faithfulness (hence the call for conversion, 44:22). Thus Yahweh miraculously establishes right for a people which had complained of the loss of its right, 40:27.

But this is not the end of the matter. 49:5 f. speaks of a mighty extension of the task of the servant which is made clear to him at the very moment he despairs of the success of his efforts. [87] 42:1 f. already emphasises that the מִשְׁפָּט, whose primary reference is obviously to Israel, will be proclaimed in all the world among all peoples even to the farthest isles. [88] 49:5 f. makes of this incidental remark a full and direct statement: The servant is to be a light for the whole world of the

---

[84] W. Hertzberg, "Die Entwicklung des Begriffes משפט im AT," ZAW, 41 (1923), 41, n. 1.

[85] On מִשְׁפָּט cf. further → III, 932; J. Pedersen, *Israel, Its Life and Culture*, I-II (1946), 348-352. Rather strangely K. Fahlgren, ṣedākā, nahestehende und entgegengesetzte Begriffe im AT (1932), who deals with מִשְׁפָּט on pp. 120-138, does not discuss the passage Is. 42:1-4.

[86] The images of the sword and the arrow (49:2) are designed to show that the Word of God on the lips of the prophet has penetrating force, cf. Jer. 23:29. They should not be sentimentally set in antithesis to 42:2 f. (as against Volz, ad loc.).

[87] In a striking par. the despairing prophet in Jer. 12:1-6 is "comforted" by Yahweh's ref. to an increased burden.

[88] Here again one can hardly miss the par. to the call of Jer., who from the very first is ordained a prophet for the nations (1:5, 10), but who at first confines his ministry to Judah.

nations. [89] His work, which takes place against the background of the historical acquittal of Israel by Yahweh, [90] puts to shame the whole world of idols even though this still appears to triumph. [91] It magnifies the sole honour of Yahweh and thereby becomes light and salvation for the whole world. [92]

d. The sections 49:7; 50:4-9 and 52:13-53:12 make it plain that the servant has to suffer. The fate of Jeremiah is repeated in the servant of Yahweh. The sufferings of Jeremiah, however, are fully brought to light biographically in his own confessions and in the passion story probably written by Baruch. In contrast, the

---

[89] Cf. the אוֹר גּוֹיִם of 42:6, though this is not textually certain (Ziegler, *Untersuchungen*, 54). If the בְּרִית עָם, combined with it in 42:6, and also found in 49:8, is to be regarded as synonymous, then with the expansion of the covenant category of Israel's salvation history the reference to the servant is even fuller ; he becomes a בְּרִית for the peoples. The covenant is at this pt. viewed exclusively as a gift of grace, cf. J. Begrich, "*berith*," ZAW, 60 (1944), 1-11; → I, 34, n. 73. The concept of the covenant can hardly be pressed juridically here. It embraces two points : 1. that Yahweh's salvation reaches to the ends of the earth, and 2. that consequently every knee shall bow and every tongue confess the power of Yahweh, 45:23 f.

[90] This is the place to discuss the intimation concerning Cyrus. In a sense this announcement is a development of the declaration concerning the king-servant Nebuchadnezzar in Deuteronomic-Jeremianic circles. The only point is that in Dt. Is. the title עֶבֶד is replaced by the patently military and political title מָשִׁיחַ. In view of this it is unlikely that עֶבֶד is to be construed in a kingly-messianic sense. The substitution theories (e.g., Hempel), which find in the עֶבֶד preaching a substitute for disappointed hopes about Cyrus, rest on very uncertain ground at the decisive pt., the supposed experience of disappointment. It is equally impossible to view Cyrus expectation (cf. Begrich, *Studien,* 144 f.) as the meagre remnant of disappointed eschatological hope. It represents, not for logic but for daring faith in Yahweh, a valid historical embodiment of the saving presence of Yahweh. The same processes of historical embodiment may also be seen in Is. and Jer.

[91] The rebukes and judgments passed on idols in 41:1-5, 21-29; 43:8-13; 44:4-6 etc. are to be understood against the background of Yahweh's expected establishment of right and justice in history. They are not designed to proclaim static monotheistic insights timelessly divorced from history. They triumphantly magnify the truth which is soon to be enacted in the execution of judgment, which thereby assumes eschatological dimensions. That the salvation of the peoples will be accomplished through a judgment which smites both idols and idolaters may be seen in the address to the escaped of the nations, 45:20; cf. on this Begrich, *Studien,* esp. c. 3 : "Das Verhältnis Dtjs's zur religiösen Überlieferung."

[92] Begrich, *Studien, Beilage,* I, 161-166 translates הוֹצִיא מִשְׁפָּט in 42:1 by "to make known the judgment." He then finds in the servant the one who proclaims to the world Yahweh's gracious judgment on Israel, and he goes on to ask whether we are not to see in 42:1-4 the list of duties of the עֶבֶד הַמֶּלֶךְ mentioned above, → 657, 30 ff. This would then be a herald whose task is to publish the king's judgments under the symbolism apparent in 42:2 f. Acc. to Begrich the choice of the title עֶבֶד יהוה is thus to be understood by analogy to this office. Against this final hypothesis it must be objected that Begrich obviously does not take adequately into account the extent to which Dt. Is. is here dependent on older linguistic use in description of the prophets, so that he is in no sense coining a new vocabulary. Furthermore, Begrich's rendering of הוֹצִיא מִשְׁפָּט can hardly be justified. At a pinch this might be considered for the הוֹצִיא מִשְׁפָּט of 42:1, but it is utterly impossible for the synon. שִׂים מִשְׁפָּט of 42:4, and the parallelism of מִשְׁפָּט and תּוֹרָה rules it out completely. The ref. here is clearly to the establishment of universal divine justice which transcends the individual instance (cf. the מִשְׁפַּט הַמֶּלֶךְ of 1 S. 8 or the formula in 2 K. 17:27: הוֹרָה אֶת מִשְׁפַּט אֱלֹהֵי הָאָרֶץ, which is akin to Is. 42:4). At the same time, Begrich is surely right in closely relating this proclamation of judgment to the concrete historical judgment of grace on Israel, which Dt. Is. or the servant declares as a messenger of glad tidings, and hence in finding the living centre of the proclamation of salvation to the peoples in this experience of grace through which Israel is Yahweh's true witness, 43:10; 44:8.

record of Dt. Is. maintains a notably objective aloofness. In what does the servant's suffering consist? Was he persecuted by his fellow-countrymen? This seems to be suggested by the obvious opposition of the exiles to his announcement that Cyrus had been sent by Yahweh as the anointed one and the deliverer of Israel. Was the power of Babylon deployed against the proclaimer of the power of Yahweh? The phrase "servants of rulers," coined in antithesis to "servant of Yahweh" (49:7), and the reference in 49:7 and 52:15 to the coming astonishment of kings, seem to point in this direction. Did sickness smite the servant?[93] The songs are ambivalent here. As in the psalms of complaint, no more than hints are given in the various competing images. Even the question whether 53:8-10 refers to the death of the servant,[94] or whether it simply adopts the style of the lament and speaks of the imminent and ineluctable but not yet actualised necessity of death,[95] is veiled in an obscurity which it is impossible to pierce with certainty. This is connected with the further point that in 52:13-53:12, even though passing features were discernible in the earlier songs, the sphere of the biographical from which we sought to understand the servant's office is completely abandoned, and we are given a sketch of the true servant of Yahweh which transcends all individual experience. Hence it is neither by accident nor mistake that Is. 53 has constantly been regarded as pointing to the figure of one who is to come.[96]

This, then, is the point where was is said about the servant diverges from Jeremiah's account in his confessions and goes beyond these in two respects to deliver a final word on the office and promise of the true עֶבֶד יהוה. Jeremiah's confessions ended in darkest night.[97] In contrast, the servant of Yahweh finds rest in a recognition of the profound meaning of his suffering. His suffering is vicarious.[98] In the context of this recognition, which, straining language to its uttermost limits, is expressed not by the servant himself but by a great host of believers gripped by this event,[99] the servant's own reaction to his suffering is very

---

[93] Duhm, ad loc. takes the נָגוּעַ of 53:4 to imply leprosy.

[94] Elliger; Sellin, Lösung. In this case the writer must have been a disciple.

[95] Begrich, Studien.

[96] H. W. Wolff, 36 coins the concept of "prefiguration" (of one who is to come) to express this prophetic transcending of the description of personal office. G. v. Rad, " 'Gerechtigkeit' u. 'Leben' in den Ps.," Festschr. A. Bertholet (1950), 424 f., has shown that when the Psalmist speaks of the righteous we already have this kind of figure which transcends the empirical and which is ultimately ventured in faith. He refers to the "prototype" of the צַדִּיק. Along the royal-messianic line we might refer to the analogy of Ps. 2 (→ n. 74).

[97] In the last of his confessions the tormented messenger of God curses his own birth, 20:14 ff. The only ray of light in this darkness is the prophet's awareness that he does not suffer alone but that his suffering is a sharing in that of Yahweh. This is stated directly in the saying to Baruch in 45:4 f., and it may be seen indirectly in 12:7 ff.

[98] Stamm, 68-75: vicarious suffering. The use of the common sacrificial term אָשָׁם in 53:10, and the use of the image of the slaughtered animal, which is derived of course from Jer., are perhaps an indication that the idea of sacrifice is not far off. But here, too, everything is very imprecise. One may ask whether, in view of the obvious connections between Dt. Is. and the Deuteronomic material, there is not an allusion to Moses, the great servant of Yahweh, who was more than a prophet (Bentzen, 64-67, following H. S. Nyberg). Dt. tells of Moses, when he had prayed to be allowed to enter the land of Canaan: "But Yahweh was wroth with me for your sakes" (3:26). There is no mention here of Moses' own guilt as apparently implied in Nu. 20:12. Moses bears the anger of Yahweh against His people. There is no ref., however, to voluntariness on his part. On Ex. 32:30 cf. Stamm, 71.

[99] 53:1-11a is set in the framework of two divine sayings (52:13-15; 53:11b-12); the second of these takes up the theme of substitution from 53:1-11a.

different from that of Jeremiah. The עֶבֶד attitude finds fulfilment in the fact that the עֶבֶד יהוה bears in obedient surrender what has been ordained for him by Yahweh, 53:6, 10. In words which echo Ez. he confesses his unresisting obedience. [100] The image of the lamb led to the slaughter, which Jeremiah uses in his confessions and which in Jer. 11:19 is designed to express the unsuspecting innocence of the prophet in the midst of threats, [101] is now deepened by the servant to portray his quiet readiness for suffering, 53:7.

e. What is the source of this surrender? Is it really just the result of an insight into the hidden meaning of his own suffering? Or is it simply blind obedience? This is the second point at which Dt. Is. goes beyond Jeremiah. He wins through to the triumphant confession that Yahweh will confess His servant even beyond death and the tomb. Alongside the confession of unconditional subjection to the Lord, which is an integral part of the עֶבֶד consciousness of the OT, there now stands the liberated confession of faith in the ultimate faithfulness of Yahweh to the servant called by Him. To put it in the two concepts which occur in the servant's own confession of trust (49:4), the servant knows that he will receive from Yahweh his right (מִשְׁפָּט) and his reward (פְּעֻלָּה). Right is the key-word which controls 50:7 ff. In face of the obloquy which he has experienced, the servant here confesses Yahweh with steadfast confidence: "The Lord Yahweh will help me; therefore shall I not be confounded; therefore have I set my face like a flint, and I know that I shall not be ashamed." But then in a form which Dt. Is. favours elsewhere, that of the appeal of a defendant in court, [102] he bursts out: "He is near that justifieth me; who will contend with me? Let us stand together; who is mine adversary? Let him come near to me. Behold, they shall wax old as a garment; the moth shall eat them up." [103] As Yahweh's servant Job knows that his righteousness will finally be vindicated in spite of present attacks, so does the servant of Yahweh. On the other hand, in 52:13-53:12 we are led to the thought of Yahweh's reward for His servant. Externally, this whole line of thinking is given even greater emphasis by the fact that this final goal is not merely expressed in the confession of the servant's trust but in the words of Yahweh Himself, who after the community has spoken in 53:1-10a finally speaks Himself and makes the concluding promise to the servant. The image of the division of conquered booty [104] is used to express Yahweh's definitive acknowledgment of His servant beyond death and the tomb, 53:12. [105] Those who seek in Is. 53 a didactically constructed statement on what is involved in salvation from death, [106] which is obviously the subject here, will be disappointed. There is no such statement. What is said is concealed in a figure. On the other hand, there can be no mistaking the ratification of the promise that Yahweh Himself will confess His servant in face of death and

---

[100] 50:5. Is there here a side-glance at Jeremiah, who became a rebel in his prophetic suffering, 15:19? מרה occurs in the case of Ezekiel in the prophetic call in 2:8 etc.

[101] In a saying omitted from the LXX, this is used in Jer. 12:3 as a fierce word of revenge against enemies.

[102] Begrich, *Studien,* 19-42, 48-49.

[103] In Is. 51:8 the same image is used for Yahweh's eschatological vindication of right against His foes.

[104] 40:10 f. seems to connect the spoil with the reward. 9:2 also uses the illustration of the joy of sharing booty to depict the joy of the eschatological day of salvation.

[105] In 10b the astonished bystanders were already speaking of the granting of descendants to him who was obviously lost in death.

[106] On this whole group of problems cf. C. Barth, *Die Errettung vom Tode in den individuellen Klage- u. Dankliedern d. AT* (1947).

the tomb, and that He will prove thereby that the servant belongs inviolably to Him.

f. In all this, however, is it ultimately just a question of a private happening between two parties, the servant and His Lord? It is surprising how strongly the speech of Yahweh which introduces the final word (Is. 52:13 ff.) emphasises the effect of the happening between Yahweh and His servant on a wider public. Kings and the great men of the earth will be astonished at it (52:14 f.). 49:7 perhaps brings out what Yahweh finally intends by this public character of the happening between Himself and His servant. "Kings shall see and arise, princes also shall worship, because of the Lord that is faithful, because of the Holy One of Israel that hath chosen thee." This vindication and rewarding of the servant will also serve finally to promote Yahweh's honour and the fuller recognition of His faithfulness before the whole world. Herein the ministry of the servant is fulfilled.

B. The LXX Translations.

1. Translations of עֶבֶד in the LXX.

עֶבֶד occurs 807 times in the Mas. text. [107] The following equivalents may be found in the LXX: [108] παῖς (παιδίον, παιδάριον) 340 times (→ 637, 22 ff.); δοῦλος (δουλεία, [109] δουλεύων) 327 times (→ II, 265, 29 ff.); οἰκέτης (οἶκος) 36 times; θεράπων (θεραπεία, θεραπεύων) 46 times (→ III, 129, 7 ff.); υἱός once; → ὑπηρέτης once. Add 56 instances where there is no equivalent or the word is misunderstood or rendered very freely. The translation by different Gk. words does not follow the same principles in all the books of the OT. Different rules are observed in different places; this obviously points to the fact that there were several translators. Since the 272 instances in which עֶבֶד occurs in relation to Yahweh are not distinguished by any special mode of translation, we may review the renderings of all the עֶבֶד passages together.

a. A first great layer of translation is to be found in the books from Gn. to Jos. It is not that these books constitute a unity as regards the mode of translation. With striking clarity one may see that a different hand must have been at work in Gn. from that discernible in Ex. [110] παῖς predominates in Gn. Of 88 instances of עֶבֶד 79 are transl. by παῖς, while οἰκέτης occurs 5 times. In Ex., on the other hand, θεράπων prevails. Of 43 instances of עֶבֶד 23 are rendered by θεράπων, only 8 by παῖς and 6 by οἰκέτης. The Egyptian courtiers, called παῖδες in Gn., are here described as θεράποντες. [111] In the remaining writings of the Hexateuch we find a mixture of the distinctive terms used in Gn. and Ex.: Lv. 3 times παῖς, 4 οἰκέτης; Nu. 4 times θεράπων, 5 παῖς, 1 οἰκέτης; Dt. 9 times παῖς, 8 οἰκέτης, 4 θεράπων. Jos. alone shows a stronger preference for παῖς (13 times), though θεράπων (3) and οἰκέτης (3) also occur. The feature which unites all the books of the Hexateuch in spite of these distinctions, and which unmistakably differentiates them from the 5 historical books which follow, is the

---

[107] 800 times in the Heb., 7 in the Aram. text.

[108] Acc. to Rahlfs' text. In Ju. text B is used for the statistics, in Da. the LXX and not the Theodotion text of the great MSS. On Is. cf. Ziegler, Isaias.

[109] The numerous δουλία passages found in Swete are all judged to be itacism by Rahlfs and are thus written in the form δουλεία.

[110] The thesis of F. Baumgärtel (J. Herrmann-F. Baumgärtel, Beiträge zur Entstehungsgeschichte der Septuaginta [1923], 55) that "Gn. occupies a special position as compared with the rest of the Pentateuch" is thus fully supported by investigation of the translation of עֶבֶד.

[111] In Gn. the court of Pharaoh (פַּרְעֹה וַעֲבָדָיו) is rendered by Φαραω καὶ ἡ θεραπεία αὐτοῦ only at 45:16. In humble self-designation θεράπων is used with the concept "God of the fathers" at 50:17: τῶν θεραπόντων τοῦ θεοῦ τοῦ πατρός σου.

almost complete absence of δοῦλος. Not one of the 88 instances of עֶבֶד in Gn. or the 11 in Nu. is rendered by δοῦλος. Of ᵗhe 15 instances of δοῦλος in the other 4 books of the Hexateuch, 10 occur in the phrase "the house of bondage" (οἶκος δουλείας) for Egypt. In Lv. 25:44 the alien slave is called δοῦλος. The text of Ex. 21:7, which is misunderstood by the LXX, also seems to point in this direction. Dt. 32:36 belongs to the Song of Moses, which also gives evidence of distinctiveness in the Gk. translation at v. 43, where עֶבֶד occurs for the second time in the HT of this song, → infra. Jos. 24:29 (LXX v. 30) seems to be based on the par. in Ju. 2:8. There remains Jos. 9:23, where the word δοῦλος occurs in the curse on the Gibeonites. It is thus apparent that δοῦλος is used, very infrequently, when the emphasis is on especially severe bondage. Elsewhere in the law of slavery (for Ex. 21:7 → supra), and also in the formulae of subjection in Jos. 9:8 f., 11, παῖς (Ex. 21:2, 5, 20, 32) or οἰκέτης (Ex. 21:26 f.) is always used. παῖς also occurs in courtly use, Gn. 18:3, 5 etc.; οἰκέτης along with it in Ex. 5:16. It passes over from this into the language of abasement before Yahweh. Jacob calls himself the παῖς of Yahweh in Gn. 32:11, and Moses is His θεράπων in Ex. 4:10. Even where the title is used independently Moses, the servant of Yahweh, is His θεράπων (Ex. 14:31; Nu. 12:7 f.), the patriarchs are His οἰκέται (Ex. 32:13), and Caleb (Nu. 14:24), like Moses (Jos. 1:13; 12:6 etc.), is the παῖς κυρίου. Here again the really surprising thing is the complete avoidance of the term δοῦλος, though this attains to equally exclusive domination in the vocabulary of religion from Ju. to 4 Βασ.

Brief mention should be made of the Song of Moses. First, it is noteworthy that v. 36 is the only place in the Hexateuch where δοῦλος is used in a religious sense. On the other hand, v. 43 is the only place where עֶבֶד is translated by δοῦλος. The two elements in עֶבֶד (cf. also → II, 266, 29 ff.) are thus brought into curious tension. Had Dt. 32 the same history of translation as the rest of the Hexateuch ?

b. If the Hexateuch is a clearly defined group by reason of its negative features, we have to set alongside it another group which is equally clearly characterised by positive traits, namely, Ju. to 4 Βασ. Here only two words (παῖς and δοῦλος) are used to render עֶבֶד. One may also discern a careful distinction between them. παῖς is used only for freer servants of the king (soldiers, ministers, officials) who by their own choice enter his service, → 657, 30 ff. δοῦλος, on the other hand, is used for slavery proper. [112] The δοῦλος is an enforced vassal even though he be a king, 2 Βασ. 10:19. δοῦλος is, of course, used in the contemptuous speeches of a Saul (1 Βασ. 22:8) and even a Nabal (1 Βασ. 25:10) against David, though the ref. is to one whose status is objectively that of the παῖς. This leads us to the final pt. that δοῦλος is used in the wide sphere of courtly speech, whether with ref. to self or a third person. [113] When עֶבֶד הַמֶּלֶךְ in 4 Βασ. 22:12 is rendered δοῦλος τοῦ βασιλέως, this is probably an indication that this office is wrongly taken to be one of menial service. The distinction is usually observed so strictly throughout the 4 books that when there seems to be deviation from it one has to ask quite seriously whether the translator was trying to express in Gk. a slight nuance not apparent in the Heb., 2 Βασ. 12:18 f.; 15:34; possibly 21:22. In keeping with what has been said that in lowly self-abasement before God in prayer δοῦλος is always used. If δοῦλος is also used without exception for the gt. figures in Israel's history, for Moses and Joshua and royal personages, [114] this plainly shows that the translator desired these great men in the history of Yahweh to be understood not after the pattern of free kingly ministry but after that of the menial servant.

---

[112] The slaves of Ziba (2 Βασ. 9:10, 12; 19:18), himself a παῖς of the house of Saul in 9:2; the Egyptian slave of an Amalekite, 1 Βασ. 30:13.

[113] Ahimelech of the servants of Saul (1 Βασ. 22:14), who are called παῖδες in the objective narrative at v. 6 f., or Ziba in polite self-designation in 2 Βασ. 9:2 (παῖς in the same v.).

[114] The ref. 3 Βασ. 8:59 LXX (B), in which, as distinct from the Mas., Israel itself seems to be regarded as the servant, is to be adjudged an error through homoioteleuton, cf. Rahlfs.

c. The two literary groups Gn. to Jos. [115] and Ju. to 4 Βασ. enable us to pick out two phases in the history of the translation of the LXX. The second of these is plainly characterised by a desire for a more precise understanding of the facts in the rendering of עֶבֶד. This finds expression in the strict differentiation between παῖς and δοῦλος. The first phase is more difficult to interpret. It has been suggested that the rule of translation discernible here is that "an equivocal παῖς best corresponds to the equivocal עֶבֶד." [116] This purely linguistic explanation may well throw light on the situation in Gn. Nevertheless, it must be pointed out that the ambiguity of παῖς and עֶבֶד is in different directions, so that the correspondence is not one of material content. And what about θεράπων in Ex.? Why the patent avoidance of the harsh δοῦλος when interchangeable use of παῖς, οἰκέτης and θεράπων is the rule (Ex.-Jos.)? The fact that even when עֶבֶד is used religiously it is not transl. δοῦλος, but only παῖς, οἰκέτης and even θεράπων, which is not very close to the OT attitude, [117] may be explained if we assume that the transl. of the Hexateuch represents a first phase of Bible translation in Hell. Judaism, and that this phase was marked by a strong and uninhibited approximation to the Gk. sense of the nearness of God and man. [118] The rather later transl. of Ju.-4 Βασ. gives evidence of an awareness of the more specifically OT sense of the distance between God and man and of the fact that man belongs to God. In the exclusive use of the harsher term δοῦλος in religious speech the offence of the austere sovereignty of God is imported even into the view of man in the Gk. Bible. [119]

d. In the later books we no longer find as a rule the same uniform picture of two great literary complexes as at the beginning of the LXX. The types begin to fuse. In general it may be said that the transl. of עֶבֶד by θεράπων, the most daring rendering, and the furthest removed from the Heb., fades from the picture. Apart from the ref. in Is. 54:17, [120] it occurs only in Job, though it is again predominant there. [121] The harsher line of δοῦλος is followed by the Ps., where it occurs 53 times as compared with the 3 instances of παῖς. [122] All five of the religious instances of עֶבֶד in Ez. are rendered δοῦλος (David, Jacob, the prophets); so, too, are all five in the Minor Prophets (Moses, David, the prophets) and the 2 in Ezr. (the prophets, the Jerusalem community). [123] Is. takes a different course. In Is. all 3, and in Dt. Is. 14 of the 20 religious instances of עֶבֶד are rendered by παῖς (Is.: Isaiah, Eliakim and David; Dt. Is.: Israel, the prophetic servant, → 676, 14 ff.). [124] Da. goes the same way. παῖς is used in all 12 instances

---

[115] It may be accepted that Jos. belonged to the first group translated, and that the Hexateuch, which as a literary unity is beginning to be quite a problem in OT research (M. Noth, Überlieferungsgeschichtliche Studien, I [1943], 253), was already a collected sequence in the age of translation.

[116] [P. Katz.] That such rules are discernible has been shown by P. Katz, Philo's Bible (1950), 6, n. 1 and App. I, 141-146, with ref. to the rendering of שָׁמַיִם. On the use of παῖς and δοῦλος in Philo, ibid., 83-87.

[117] → III, 131, 34 ff.: "Intrinsically ... the term (θεραπεία) is more compatible with the usage of paganism than with that of the OT religion of revelation (cf. Ac. 17:25)."

[118] παῖς and οἰκέτης also express a stronger familiar relationship of the servant than δοῦλος.

[119] The later variants have δοῦλος even in the Hexateuch, e.g., Codex Ambrosianus on Jos. 1:1, 15; Alexandrinus on 14:7.

[120] In the form θεραπεύοντες (κύριον), which may indicate a verbal understanding of עַבְדֵי יהוה.

[121] 9 of the total 12 instances of עֶבֶד are transl. θεράπων; 5 of these predicate Job as the servant of God. Only 1:8 has παῖς in a religious sense. LXX (A) agrees here, while A with LXX (V) substitutes παῖς for θεράπων at 42:8 in the first of the 3 occurrences there.

[122] ψ 85:16 in humble self-designation in prayer; 112:1 in description of the worshipping community; 17, of David in the title.

[123] In both verses 1 Εσδρ. replaces δοῦλος by παῖς. Cf. 2 Εσδρ. 5:11; 9:11 with 1 Εσδρ. 6:12; 8:79.

[124] In a surprising way the transl. of Tr. Is. deviates into the use of δοῦλος alone. It might be argued (→ 661, 25 ff.) that in Is. 56-66 the distinction between the righteous who

(7 religious). [125] In Jer. the confusion of terms is esp. noticeable. While the formula "my servants the prophets" in the first half of the book (7:25; 25:4) is rendered by δοῦλος, we then find παῖς in 26(33):5; 35(42):15; 44(51):4. Jacob is δοῦλος in 46(26):27 and παῖς close by in 28. That there is a special problem in the relation of the LXX to Jer. [126] may be seen from the frequent absence of any word for the Heb. עֶבֶד in the older MSS. The later ones usually supply δοῦλος. The confusion of types is fullest in Neh. and Ch. Here it is no longer possible to pick out any rule of alternation. [127] Moses is God's παῖς in Neh. 1:7 f. (2 Εσδρ. 11:7 f.) and His δοῦλος in 9:14 (2 Εσδρ. 19:14). In Nehemiah's humble self-designation in the presence of God we find παῖς and δοῦλος together in the same v., 1:11 (2 Εσδρ. 11:11). All feeling for the specific content of the terms seems to have been lost. The rendering of עֶבֶד יהוה by ἄνθρωπος τοῦ θεοῦ in 2 Ch. 24:6 has already been mentioned in → n. 55.

2. The Translation of the Servant of God Passages in Dt. Is., → 666, 10 ff.

The wording of 42:1: Ιακωβ ὁ παῖς μου, ἀντιλήμψομαι αὐτοῦ· Ισραηλ ὁ ἐκλεκτός μου, προσεδέξατο αὐτὸν ἡ ψυχή μου, shows that the LXX takes the introductory words of the servant songs in the narrower sense to apply to the servant Israel, → n. 66. Since the addition of the proper names disrupts the double three metre clearly discernible in the Heb. up to v. 4, this is an argument against the LXX text being original. Yet the LXX text is important. For one thing, it shows quite unmistakably in what direction the passage was interpreted, and is thus an early witness to the collective understanding. For another, it is an instance of the secondary penetration of interpretative expansions into the text. In this light a similar penetration is at least possible in 49:3 as well, → n. 69. One may assume, then, that the LXX refers 42:1-4 (also 5-9) and 49:1-6 (with the ensuing 7, 8-13) to Israel. The rendering of 50:4-9 affords no obvious clue to the interpretation of the translator.

On the other hand, 52:13-53:12 in the LXX might well be taken to refer to an individual. [128] The יוֹנֵק of 53:2 is surprisingly transl. by παιδίον, which is familiar from the Messianic statement in 9:5 and par. to the correctly rendered ῥίζα, also reminiscent of the Messianic 11:1. This raises the question whether there may not be discerned in the LXX transl. a Messianic understanding. The reconstruction ἀνέτειλε [129] in 53:2 might well pt. in a similar direction. [130] If so, the LXX translator must have found in Is. 52:13-53:12 the description of a Messianic figure whose coming he awaits. This may be in-

---

obey God and the disobedient ungodly is strongly developed. Is there a connection in the fact that with the threefold δοῦλος (56:6; 63:17; 65:9) we find in the Gk. transl. 6 instances of δουλεύων, which lays even stronger emphasis on the active obedience of the servant (65:8, 13-15)? Only once is עֶבֶד rendered by σεβόμενος (66:14; in Orig and Luc φοβούμενος).

[125] Theodotion has δοῦλος 6 times (all עֶבֶד in the religious sense). Only at 3:28 (Δα. 3:95) do we find παῖς in this sense.

[126] P. Volz, Der Prophet Jer.[2] = Komm. z. AT, X (1928) L; W. Rudolph, Jer. = Handbuch z. AT, II, 12 (1947), XIX f.

[127] Comparison with the par. texts in 1-4 Βασ. enables us to recognise as a general tendency a strong penetration of παῖς. The clearly discernible distinction between παῖς and δοῦλος in Ju. to 4 Βασ. is here completely effaced, though this does not seem to be intentional. Cf., e.g., the promise of Nathan in 2 S. 7 with the version in 1 Ch. 17. In 7 of the 10 comparable texts παῖς replaces δοῦλος, which occurs only in 2 S. Then in the word of Yahweh concerning David we find hopelessly jumbled together τὸν παῖδά μου in 17:4 and τῷ δούλῳ μου in 17:7, or in humble self-designation before God τοῦ παιδός σου in 17:25 and τὸν δοῦλόν σου in 17:26. In 1 Ch. 18:6 f., where the par. 2 S. 8:6 f. makes a nice distinction between παῖς and δοῦλος, παῖς is uniformly used.

[128] Euler, 85-91.

[129] ἀνηγγείλαμεν, which appears in the tradition, is to be regarded as a Gk. textual corruption, cf. Ziegler, Isaias, ad loc. and 99; v. 2 should read: ἀνέτειλε μὲν ἐναντίον αὐτοῦ ὡς παιδίον. For an attempt to expound the traditional text cf. Euler, 22-23.

[130] ἀνατολή as a transl. of the Messianic צֶמַח, → I, 352 f.

dicated by the translation of 52:14 f. as a future,[131] which is a plain deviation from the HT. The scornful turning aside of many from the servant (v. 14) takes place in the future like the astonished turning to him of peoples and kings (v. 15). The perfects of the depiction of his suffering in 53:1 ff., into which the present tense has often penetrated in deviation from the HT,[132] may then be regarded as prophetic perfects. Moreover, one may ask whether the recurrent key-word δόξα (52:13, 14b, c; 53:2), for which there is no real Heb. equivalent, does not bear the fundamental mark of interpretation.[133] The ref. here is to a figure who possesses a secret δόξα in virtue of his childlike nearness to God. Before men, of course, the παῖς seems to be humiliated and without honour. Measured by human standards, he has no glory.[134] Through a word from God,[135] however, the παῖς achieves awareness, and more than awareness, of his glory. Through his lowliness and death in consequence of the ignorance of men God leads him to exaltation and glorification.[136] In this way knowledge is granted to a series of men so that they can apprehend the glory of the παῖς and the meaning of his passion. They express their new understanding in 53:1 ff. Against too strong an emphasis on the concept of δόξα it may be objected, of course, that the ὑψωθήσεται καὶ δοξασθήσεται of 52:13 is a common expression which occurs also in 10:15; 33:10 and which is not, therefore, to be overestimated. But the readoption and repetition of a word previously used to translate similar terms is a stylistic feature often found in Is. 53.[137] Hence δόξα is not to be regarded merely as an interpretative element in the LXX translation. It should be plainly recognised, however, that the LXX has in view a suffering of the παῖς which leads him to death.[138] The exaltation which follows this death, and which is described in the imagery of the HT,[139] goes beyond the HT, however, in its distinctive assertion that judgment is passed on the ungodly in retribution for the putting to death of the παῖς.[140] In contrast to the interpretation of the Tg., which also introduces the thought of judgment at this pt.,[141] judgment according to the LXX is executed by God Himself, not the παῖς.

Zimmerli

C. παῖς θεοῦ in Later Judaism in the Period after the LXX.[142]

παῖς (τοῦ) θεοῦ occurs only seldom in later Jewish lit. after 100 B.C.: Wis. 2:13; 9:4; 12:7, 20; 19:6; Bar. 1:20; 2:20, 24, 28; 3:37; Ps. Sol. 12:6; 17:21; 1 Εσδρ. (= 3 Esr.) 6:12, 26; 8:79; only once each in Philo[143] (Conf. Ling., 147) and Jos.[144] (Ant., 10, 215); finally in the later Gk. transl. of the OT (Is. 42:1 Θ vl. [→ 683, 21]; Jer. 30:10 Θ; Δα. 3:95 Θ; Dt. 34:5 Αλλ.).

---

[131] ὃν τρόπον ἐκστήσονται ... οὕτως ἀδοξήσει ... οὕτως θαυμάσονται ...
[132] v. 2 οὐκ ἔστιν εἶδος, v. 4 φέρει ... ὀδυνᾶται, v. 8 αἴρεται.
[133] So esp. Euler, 101-107.
[134] 52:14b: οὕτως ἀδοξήσει ἀπὸ ἀνθρώπων τὸ εἶδός σου καὶ ἡ δόξα σου ἀπὸ τῶν ἀνθρώπων.
[135] The LXX makes the whole of 52:14 a word of Yahweh to the servant.
[136] 52:13: συνήσει ... ὑψωθήσεται ... δοξασθήσεται.
[137] Cf. Ziegler, *Untersuchungen,* 24-25.
[138] 53:8b: ὅτι αἴρεται ἀπὸ τῆς γῆς ἡ ζωὴ αὐτοῦ, ἀπὸ τῶν ἀνομιῶν τοῦ λαοῦ μου ἤχθη εἰς θάνατον.
[139] The φῶς of 53:11 has now been confirmed in Heb., v. *The Dead Sea Scrolls* (→ n. 69), Plate 44, line 19.
[140] 53:9: καὶ δώσω τοὺς πονηροὺς ἀντὶ τῆς ταφῆς αὐτοῦ καὶ τοὺς πλουσίους ἀντὶ τοῦ θανάτου αὐτοῦ.
[141] Hegermann, I, 37.
[142] Towards the end of the 2nd cent. B.C. most of the OT was available in the LXX transl. This date is supported by both the Prologue to Sir. and Ep. Ar. In what follows an account is given of the development of παῖς θεοῦ from c. 100 B.C.
[143] Leisegang, 619.
[144] Schl. Theol. d. Judt., 50.

I. The Twofold Meaning of παῖς θεοῦ.

In most instances the context and usage enable us to say with certainty whether the meaning is "God's child" or "God's servant." Debatable are 2 Macc. 7:34 (→ lines 8 ff.) and Bar. 3:37 (→ lines 34 ff.).

1. παῖς θεοῦ = Child of God.

The plur. παῖδες θεοῦ in the sense "God's children" is found 4 times in Wis. for the people of Israel (12:7, 20; 19:6) or the righteous (9:4). [145] It bears the same meaning in the one place where it occurs in Philo, Conf. Ling., 147. [146] This [147] rather than "God's servants" [148] is also the probable meaning in 2 Macc. 7:34, where the Israelites are called οὐράνιοι παῖδες. The sing. παῖς θεοῦ in the sense of "child of God" is attested only once at Wis. 2:13. [149] Here the ungodly say of the righteous man : παῖδα κυρίου ἑαυτὸν ὀνομάζει. In the light of LXX usage (→ 673, 16 ff.) the most natural sense seems to be "God's servant." [150] But in the next v. it is said that the righteous boasts of God as his Father (2:16), and in 2:18 he is called the υἱὸς θεοῦ. [151] Since the plur. παῖδες θεοῦ and υἱοὶ θεοῦ also alternate in Wis. (→ n. 145), the meaning "child of God" would seem to be fairly certain in 2:12. [152] Now Wis. also depicts the righteous man in terms derived from Is. 52:13 ff., → 684, 11-19. This means that the suffering servant of God of Dt. Is. has become in Wis. — via the twofold sense of παῖς — the child of God who in spite of all affliction and disgrace knows that he is secure in his Father and glories in this. The infrequency of παῖς θεοῦ in the sense of "child of God" is only partially explained by the fact that Hell. Judaism prefers → υἱὸς τοῦ θεοῦ (occasionally τέκνον τοῦ θεοῦ) for "child of God"; the real reason is that later Judaism as a whole describes the relation of the individual or the people to God less commonly in the figure of childhood [153] than in that of servanthood. [154]

2. παῖς θεοῦ = Servant of God.

In the relevant period after 100 B.C. παῖς θεοῦ occurs more frequently in the sense of "servant of God." This is undoubtedly the meaning in Bar. 1:20; 2:28; Dt. 34:5 Αλλ, where Moses is called God's παῖς, since the description of Moses as the "servant of God" was by now a fixed usage, → n. 183. The same is true of the designation of the prophets in Bar. 2:20, 24; 1 Εσδρ. (= 3 Esr.) 8:79 by the stereotyped formula (→ n. 167) τῶν παίδων σου τῶν προφητῶν. When the three men in the burning fiery furnace are called God's παῖδες in Δα. 3:95 Θ, [155] δοῦλοι in 3:93 Θ, there can be no doubt that the meaning is "servants," and the context shows that the same holds good in 1 Εσδρ. (== 3 Esr.) 6:12 (δοῦλοι, 2 Εσδρ. 5:11), 26. The meaning of παῖς (of God) seems to be in doubt only in the passages mentioned in → n. 177, where the term is used

---

[145] The meaning "children of God" results from the interchangeability of παῖδές σου in 9:4; 12:20 and υἱοί σου in 9:7; 12:19, 21, and it is confirmed by what is said about 2:13, → lines 10-14.

[146] καὶ γὰρ εἰ μήπω ἱκανοὶ θεοῦ παῖδες νομίζεσθαι γεγόναμεν, so of his logos. The context makes it clear that the meaning is "children of God."

[147] So also Mi. Hb.[8] on 2:10.

[148] So the vl. οἱ δοῦλοι αὐτοῦ, cf. 7:33.

[149] We should possibly add Bar. 3:37, → lines 34 ff.

[150] So K. Siegfried, Kautzsch Apkr. u. Pseudepigr., I, 483; Wolff, 41.

[151] Cf. also 5:5 : πῶς κατελογίσθη (the righteous) ἐν υἱοῖς θεοῦ; ask sinners at the last judgment.

[152] So also the comm. of O. F. Fritzsche, Kurzgefasstes Handbuch z. d. Apkr. d. AT, 6 (1860), ad loc.; P. Heinisch, Das Buch d. Weisheit (1912), 51; F. Feldmann, Das Buch d. Weisheit (1926), ad loc.; J. Fichtner, Weisheit Salomos = Handbuch z. AT, II, 6 (1938), ad loc.; also Dalman, I, 31, n. 1; Bousset, 48, 54; Str.-B., I, 219; Dalman WJ, I, 228. Cf. the Syr. transl. of Wis. 2:13, 18 : ברה דאלהא == "son of God."

[153] For examples cf. Str.-B., I, 219 f., 371 f.

[154] Bousset, 54, Schl. Theol. d. Judt., 50.

[155] So also Jos. Ant., 10, 215.

collectively. But since παῖς θεοῦ always means "servant of God" elsewhere in Bar. (1:20; 2:20, 24, 28), this would also seem to be the sense in Bar. 3:37 (Ἰακωβ τῷ παιδὶ αὐτοῦ), and hence also in Ps. Sol. 12:6; 17:21; at Lk. 1:54 comparison with 1:69 leads to the same conclusion. This survey shows that in verses where παῖς θεοῦ means "servant of God" the OT use of עֶבֶד יהוה lives on with its various ramifications.

II. The Persistence of the OT Religious Use of עֶבֶד יהוה.

Since the OT עֶבֶד יהוה does not live on merely in the Gk. παῖς θεοῦ, the following survey — esp. in view of the great significance of the phrase עֶבֶד יהוה for the NT — must not be limited to παῖς θεοῦ but should also take into account the occurrence of (God's) עֶבֶד, טַלְיָא, [156] מְשָׁרֵת, שַׁמָּשׁ,[157] → διάκονος θεοῦ, [158] → δοῦλος θεοῦ, → θεράπων θεοῦ, [159] οἰκέτης θεοῦ, [160] → ὑπηρέτης θεοῦ, [161] ὑποδιάκονος θεοῦ. [162] Disregarding the fact that "my servant," which is so common on God's lips in the OT, now occurs only infrequently [163] because the age of revelation ended with the death of the last writing prophet, we may say that the OT use of עֶבֶד יהוה persisted with no essential change, though naturally with characteristic distinctions of emphasis.

1. παῖς θεοῦ as a Self-Designation in Prayer. The ancient humble self-designation as עַבְדְּךָ before God in prayer (→ 660, 11 ff.) continues to be used without change. [164] It is hardly an accident, however, that in the Gk. renderings after 100 B.C., in contrast to the LXX, which sometimes has παῖς, sometimes δοῦλος, there are no instances of (God's) παῖς, and only δοῦλος and διάκονος are attested, cf. → n. 166, 183, 184. The worshipper's sense of distance from God is unmistakably meant to be expressed herewith.

2. The Plural Servants of God. As in the OT (→ 661, 25 f.), [165] the plur. "servants of God" is still commonly used for the Israelites [166] and the prophets. [167] A new feature as compared with OT usage is that the righteous, who are called the "servants of

[156] Gn. 18:3 sy^{pal}; Jer. 30:10 sy^{pal}.
[157] On נַעַר → n. 194.
[158] Only in Jos. Bell., 3, 354.
[159] Only in Philo, Leisegang, 384.
[160] Only 1 Εσδρ. (= 3 Esr.) 4:59; Sir. 36:16 א A (→ n. 169).
[161] Only Philo, Leisegang, 802.
[162] Only Philo, Leisegang, 804.
[163] 4 Esr. 7:28 f.; 13:32, 37, 52; 14:9; S. Bar. 70:9, → 681, 15 ff. In each of these the ref. is to the Messiah as "my (God's) servant."
[164] δοῦλος (of God): Wis. 9:5; Δα. 3:33, 44 Θ (also LXX); 9:17 Θ (LXX παῖς); 2 Macc. 8:29. οἰκέτης (of God): 1 Εσδρ. (= 3 Esr.) 4:59, διάκονος (of God): Jos. Bell., 3, 354. Preserved only in Lat., Syr., Eth., Arab. and Armen. transl.: 4 Esr. 5:45, 56; 6:12; 7:75, 102; 8:6, 24; 10:37; 12:8; 13:14; only in Syr.: S. Bar. 14:15; 48:11; 54:6. עַבְדֶּיךָ (of God): Sir. 36:16 (22) and the 16th Beraka of the XVIII Benedictions (Pal. rec.); Shema benediction אֱמֶת וְיַצִּיב 1, W. Staerk, Altjüd. liturgische Gebete² = Kl. T., 58 (1930), 6. טַלְיָךְ in humble address to God: Gn. 18:3 sy^{pal} (Tg. O. J. I עבדך [Heb.], Samaritan Tg. [ed. A. Brüll, 1879]: שמשכן).
[165] Israelites: Lindhagen, 82 ff.; prophets: ibid., 277-280; → 665, 18 f.
[166] Jub. 23:30; S. Bar. 14:15. (God's) παῖδες: 1 Εσδρ. (= 3 Esr.) 6:12; Sib., V, 68 (on 2 Macc. 7:34 → 678, 9 ff.). (God's) δοῦλοι: 2 Macc. 7:34 vl.; 8:29; Philo Migr. Abr., 45. Acc. to Jos. Ant., 11, 101 the Jews are called δοῦλοι τοῦ θεοῦ (90 : τοῦ μεγίστου θεοῦ) in the Edict of Cyrus, though δοῦλος θεοῦ is rare in Jos., cf. Schl. Theol. d. Judt., 49 f. In both self-designation in prayer (→ n. 164) and the description of the Israelites as servants of God the predominance of δοῦλος is worth noting. (God's) עבדים: M. Ex. 22:20; S. Nu. 15:41 § 115; also in prayers, → n. 164. (God's) עבדיא: Tg. Is. 48:20. (God's) משרתים: M. Ex. 22:20.
[167] (God's) παῖδες: 1 Εσδρ. (= 3 Esr.) 8:79; Bar. 2:20, 24 (in all three verses τῶν παιδων σου [of God] τῶν προφητῶν as a formula: cf. Ιερ. 33:5; 42:15; 51:4). (God's) δοῦλοι: Da. 9:6, 10 Θ (LXX παῖδες θεοῦ) cf. Rev. 11:18. (God's) ὑπηρέται: Philo

Yahweh" comparatively seldom in the OT, and only in later writings, [168] are now described thus much more frequently. [169] After the OT pattern [170] the priests, too, are given this title. [171] Moreover proselytes can now be called this, [172] also parents [173] and angels. [174]

3. The Collective Use. The new collective use of the sing. עֶבֶד יהוה for Israel, first found for certain in Dt. Is. (→ 662, 7 ff.), [175] lives on after 100 B.C. in both Hell. and Palestinian Judaism. If, however, one excludes OT quotations and later translations of the OT, [176] examples are not common. [177]

4. παῖς θεοῦ as a Title of Honour for Important Instruments of God. As in common oriental and pre-exilic usage, παῖς θεοῦ is also used as a title of honour for important instruments of God, [178] → 663 ff., though apart from Scripture quotations [179] almost

---

Decal., 178. (God's) ὑποδιάκονοι, loc. cit. (God's) עבדיא: Tg. Is. 50:10. In the Dead Sea Scrolls, too, the prophets are often referred to, Dead Sea Scrolls, I, Plate 55, col. 2, line 9; Plate 58, col. 7, line 5; ibid., II, 2; Manual of Discipline (1951), col. 1, line 3.

[168] Lindhagen, 223-262.

[169] (God's) παῖδες : Jos. Ant., 10, 215 (of the three in the furnace as in 3:93, 95 LXX; 3:95 Θ). (God's) δοῦλοι : 2 Macc. 7:6 (== LXX Dt. 32:36), 33; 8:29; Ps. Sol. 2:37; 10:4; Philo Det. Pot. Ins., 146; Rer. Div. Her., 7; Jos. Ant., 11, 90 and 101; Δα. 3:85 Θ. (God's) θεράποντες : Philo Det. Pot. Ins., 62. (God's) עבדיא: Tg. Is. 42:19 (→ n. 219); 44:26 (→ n. 221). The designation of the righteous as οἰκέται (of God) in Sir. 36:16 (22) אA is original, as may be seen from the HT (עבדיך). The LXX ἱκετῶν (suppliants) for οἰκετῶν is a scribal error.

[170] Lindhagen, 107-120.

[171] (God's) θεράποντες : Philo Spec. Leg., I, 242; in 116 the high-priest is the ὑποδιάκονος (of God). λειτουργοὶ θεοῦ, ibid., IV, 191.

[172] (God's) עבדים: M. Ex., 22, 20. (God's) משרתים, loc. cit. LXX Is. 66:14 already has proselytes in view when it renders עֲבָדָיו (of God) by σεβόμενοι αὐτόν (אA) or φοβούμενοι αὐτόν (B).

[173] ὑπηρέται (of God): Philo Decal., 119.

[174] δοῦλοι (of God): Ps. Sol. 18:12. θεράποντες (of God): Philo Fug., 67. ὑπηρέται (of God): Philo Mut. Nom., 87; Som., I, 143. ὑποδιάκονοι (of God): Philo Spec. Leg., I, 66; Abr., 115. משרתים (of God): Hb. En. 1:8; 4:1; 6:2 f.; 19:6; 40:1. שמשין (of God): M. Ex. 20:23 par. bRH, 24b; Tg. Is. 6:2 etc. In Philo Spec. Leg., I, 31 the heavenly bodies are called ὑποδιάκονοι θεοῦ, and in bChul., 60a the sun is one of the שמשין of God.

[175] Is. 41:8, 9; 44:1, 2, 21 (twice); 45:4; 48:20; 49:3; there is a 10th instance in the LXX at Is. 42:1: Ιακωβ ὁ παῖς μου (Mas. only עֲבְדִי), → 684, 3 ff. Also outside Dt. Is. in the HT : Jer. 30:10 (no LXX, but Θ has παῖς); 46(26):27: δοῦλος, v. 28 : παῖς; Ps. 136:22 (ψ 135:22 LXX δοῦλος); on Ez. 28:25 and 37:25 → n. 41. With no Heb. equivalent cf. also LXX 3 Βασ. 8:34 BA; 16:2 A; ψ 134:12 אA (in all 3 δοῦλος). In all these instances Jacob and Israel have collective significance. Since there is no certain example of the use of these names for the people ("my servant Israel or Jacob" [collectively]) prior to Dt. Is., the influence of Dt. Is. on all these passages must be assumed, Bentzen, 63; → n. 35.

[176] E.g., Jer. 30:10 Θ : σὺ δὲ μὴ φοβοῦ, παῖς μου Ιακωβ (sypal טַלְיִי; Tg. עַבְדִּי). On the transl. and interpretation of the collective "servant of God" passages from Dt. Is. (→ n. 175) in Palestinian Judaism, → 684, 35. Here it may simply be noted that Tg. Is. (following the HT) keeps the phrase "servant of God" at 41:8, 9; 44:1, 2, 21 (twice); 45:4; 49:3, and refers it to Israel collectively ; only at 48:20 does the Tg. have a plur. for the HT sing.

[177] Bar. 3:37: Ιακωβ τῷ παιδὶ αὐτοῦ καὶ Ισραηλ τῷ ἠγαπημένῳ ὑπ' αὐτοῦ (cf. LXX Is. 44:2: παῖς μου Ιακωβ καὶ ὁ ἠγαπημένος Ισραηλ ὃν ἐξελεξάμην); Ps. Sol. 12:6 : Ισραηλ παῖδα αὐτοῦ (of God); 17:21: Ισραηλ παῖδά σου (of God); cf. Lk. 1:54 (allusion to Is. 41:8), → 700, 5 ff.; Rabb. examples → n. 213.

[178] G. Sass, "Zur Bdtg. von δοῦλος bei Pls.," ZNW, 40 (1941), 24-32, rightly emphasises that in both OT and NT the title "servant of God" expresses divine election. The decisive aspect is not the readiness for service of the man concerned, but the divine commission.

[179] S. Dt. § 27 on 3:24 has a long list of those called "servant of God" in the OT.

exclusively in ancient formulae, esp. prayers. Examples are not numerous. This usage does not occur in Philo at all. [180] In Jos. we find only Moses as δοῦλος θεοῦ [181] and the three in the fiery furnace as παῖδες τοῦ θεοῦ. [182] In the whole of the Mishnah the title "servant of God" occurs only three times, and then only in the three confessions of sin by the high-priest on the Day of Atonement ; each of the three has the formula ככתוב בתורת משה עבדך, Yoma, 3, 8 (T. Yoma, 2, 1) ; 4, 2 ; 6, 2. The title is solidly established only for Moses, [183] and next for David ; [184] it is used only occasionally for Noah, [185] Abraham, [186] Isaac, [187] Jacob (→ n. 186), Aaron, [188] Elijah [189] and the three men in the fiery furnace. [190] On the lips of non-Jews the title "servant of God" is used for Zerubbabel [191] and also, following biblical texts, for Daniel [192] and the three men in the fiery furnace. [193] In Hb. En. Metatron, the heavenly vice-gerent, bears the title עֶבֶד (of God). [194]

5. Servant of God as a Term for the Messiah. Servant of God is also found as a term for the Messiah. Already in the OT the Messiah is 5 times called "my servant" : Ez. 34:23 f. ; 37:24 f. (in all 4 verses עַבְדִּי דָוִד) ; Zech. 3:8 (עַבְדִּי צֶמַח). [195] Later one may add 4 Esr. 7:28 ; 13:32, 37, 52 ; 14:9 (always "my servant") ; 7:28 vl. 29 ; S. Bar. 70:9 ("my servant the Messiah") ; [196] Tg. Is. 42:1 ; 43:10 ; 52:13 ; Tg. Zech.

---

[180] It is typical of Philo that he replaces the phrase Αβρααμ τοῦ παιδός μου (LXX Gn. 18:17) by Αβρααμ τοῦ φίλου μου (Sobr., 56), cf. Katz, loc. cit.

[181] Ant., 5, 39.

[182] Ant., 10, 215.

[183] (God's) παῖς : Bar. 1:20 ; 2:28 (both in the same prayer of penitence), δοῦλος : Jos. Ant., 5, 39 (prayer), cf. Rev. 15:3, θεράπων : Wis. 10:16 (poetic praise of divine wisdom) ; cf. 1 Cl., 51, 3 and 5 ; 53, 5 ; Barn., 14, 4, עֶבֶד 4 Esr. 14:31 Syr. (Ezra's last words to the people) ; cf. also → line 6 (formula of confession of sin). The later Gk. translations call Moses God's δοῦλος : Ex. 4:10 ᾽Α ; Jos. 1:15 ᾽ΑΣΘ ; Da. 9:11 Θ ; only Dt. 34:5 ΑΛΛ has παῖς κυρίου.

[184] Except in later translations the description of David as God's servant occurs only in prayers : 1 Macc. 4:30 (τοῦ δούλου σου Δαυιδ) ; 4 Esr. 3:23 and the 15th Beraka of the XVIII Benedictions (Babyl. rec.) as vl. (+ עבדך) דוד ; ancient Musaf prayer interpolated on the days of the new moon into the 17th (16th) Benediction : זכרון משיח בן דוד עבדך (W. Heidenhein, שפת אמת [1886], 21 ; S. R. Hirsch, ישראל תפלות סדור, Israels Gebete [1921], 146, 274, 624) ; prayer וּבְמַקְהֵלוֹת, the Passover haggada before the 4th cup : דוד בן־ישי עבדך משיחך. Cf. Lk. 1:69 ; Ac. 4:25 ; Did., 9, 2 (in all 3 παῖς [of God]) ; these early Christian instances, too, are from prayers. The later Gk. transl. always call David δοῦλος (of God), 1 K. 11:36 ᾽ΑΣ ; 14:8 ᾽Α ; Ps. 36:1 ᾽ΑΣ ; Is. 37:35 ᾽ΑΣΘ.

[185] 4 Esr. 3:11 Armenian (prayer).

[186] 2 Macc. 1:2 : Αβρααμ καὶ Ισαακ καὶ Ιακωβ τῶν δούλων αὐτοῦ (of God) τῶν πιστῶν (blessing) ; S. Bar. 4:4 (God speaking).

[187] → n. 186 ; Δα. 3:35 Θ (= LXX) : διὰ Ισαακ τὸν δοῦλόν σου (prayer).

[188] Hb. En. 2:3 : משרת (of God).

[189] Third benediction after the reading of the prophets in worship : "Make us to rejoice, Yahweh, our God" באליהו הנביא עבדך, Hirsch, 342.

[190] Jos. Ant., 10, 215 : τοὺς παῖδας τοῦ θεοῦ, → n. 169.

[191] 1 Εσδρ. (= 3 Esr.) 6:26 : τὸν παῖδα τοῦ κυρίου Ζοροβαβελ, → n. 195.

[192] Da. 6:21 Θ (ὁ δοῦλος τοῦ θεοῦ τοῦ ζῶντος, vocative).

[193] Δα. 3:95 Θ (παῖδες of God) ; 3:93 Θ (δοῦλοι of God).

[194] 1:4 ; 10:3 ; 48 C 1, D 1 (17th of the 70 names), D 9. Metatron also retains the title עֶבֶד יהוה later, cf. Odeberg, 2, 28. If he is called נַעַר in Hb. En. 2:2 ; 3:2 ; 4:1 f., this word is the equivalent of עֶבֶד in the sense "servant," cf. Odeberg, 2, 173 for other instances. Cf. also → n. 256.

[195] Cf. also Hag. 2:23, where Zerubbabel is called עַבְדִּי (LXX τὸν δοῦλόν μου) and is given the promise that he will be "as a signet."

[196] In the passages mentioned from 4 Esr. the term for the Messiah varies in the different versions. The rival titles are "my son" (so consistently Lat. and Syr. ; also Eth. 13:52 ;

3:8 (in all 4 passages of the Tg. עבדי משיחא); Tg. Ez. 34:23 f.; 37:24 f. (in all 4 עבדי דוד). These are all the examples. Especially surprising is the complete absence of the term "servant of God" for the Messiah in the rest of Rabb. literature except in OT quotations. On the reason for this silence → 697, 19 ff. In the whole of the OT and later Jewish literature, then, the description of the Messiah as God's servant occurs only in the form "my servant" and only on the lips of God. We have here a biblical usage which persisted to the end of the 1st cent. A.D. and then disappeared, living on only in quotations from Scripture. As may be seen from the fact that it is restricted to God's own lips, "servant of God" was never at any time a true title of the Messiah in Judaism.

III. Interpretations of the Servant of God Passages in Dt. Is.

With reference to the NT it is of particular importance to consider how later Judaism interpreted the Ebed passages in Dt. Is. If we ignore the three verses where historical personages are called עַבְדִּי by God (Is. 20:3: Isaiah; 22:20: Eliakim; 37:35: David), the singular "servant of God" occurs in the whole of Is. only in 41-53, and here 19 times: 41:8, 9; 42:1, 19 (twice); 43:10; 44:1, 2, 21 (twice), 26 (though → n. 221); 45:4; 48:20; 49:3, 5, 6; 50:10; 52:13; 53:11. In investigating the later Jewish interpretation of these 19 instances it is essential that various widespread causes of error be avoided. First it should be noted that the modern isolation of the Servant Songs, like the division of the book into Proto-, Deutero- and Trito-Isaiah, was completely unknown in that day. Hence our enquiry cannot be restricted to these songs or to Is. 53. Secondly, one has to realise that in view of the atomistic character of the exegesis of the period a uniform interpretation of the Ebed cannot be presupposed. Thus Tg. Is. relates certain servant passages from Dt. Is. to the people, others to the prophets and others again to the Messiah, → 692, 18 ff. and n. 291. The concept of the Ebed found in modern research "does not exist at all in Jewish exposition." [197] One should not generalise, then, from individual interpretations. Thirdly, a careful distinction has to be made between mere allusions or the arbitrary relating of individual sayings to other contexts on the one side, and deliberate interpretation on the other. [198] Only the latter carries real weight. Finally, it should not be overlooked that the diaspora, partly as a result of divergent LXX readings, developed

---

14:9; Sahidic 13:32), "my child" (Arab., ed. G. H. A. Ewald [1863], 7:28), "my young man" (ibid., 13:32, 37, 52; 14:9; Arab. ed. J. Gildemeister [1877], 13:37; Eth. 13:37) and "my servant" (Arab., ed. Gildemeister, 13:32, 52; 14:9; Eth. 7:29). All these renderings go back to the παῖς of the Gk. which underlies all surviving translations of 4 Esr. Cf. B. Violet, Die Apokalypsen des Esr. u. des Bar. in deutscher Gestalt = GCS, 32 (1924), 74 f.: "A Christian would never have changed υἱός into παῖς, but might very easily have done the reverse." This conclusive argument has rightly found general acceptance, cf. Harnack, Die Bezeichnung Jesu als "Knecht Gottes," 212 f.; A. v. Gall, Βασιλεία τοῦ θεοῦ (1926), 417; Gressmann, Messias, 383 f.; J. Jeremias, Erlöser u. Erlösung, 110 f.; also Ἀμνὸς τοῦ θεοῦ, 120, n. 29; Buber, 77; Torrey, The Messiah, 260. Even earlier J. Drummond had correctly assessed the situation in The Jewish Messiah (1877), 285-289, and Bousset, 53 independently reached the same conclusion on the basis of the edition of 4 Esr. in B. Violet, Die Esra-Apokalypse, I (4 Esr.) = GCS, 18 (1910). The Messiah is called עַבְדִּי in S. Bar. 70:9; the Gk. underlying the Syr. probably read παῖς; this may be assumed in view of the situation in 4 Esr.

[197] Fischel, 54.

[198] Rightly emphasised by Moore, I, 229, 541; III, 166, n. 255 (on I, 551); cf. also Schlatter, BFTh, 16, 6 (1912), 50; K. G. Kuhn, S. Nu. = Rabb. Texte, 2nd Series, Tannaitische Midraschim (1933 ff.), 527; Sjöberg, 119. Fischel, 59, n. 24 tries to establish rules for distinguishing between mere allusion and deliberate interpretation.

its own traditions of interpretation. Hellenistic and Palestinian statements must not be put on the same level.

1. Hellenistic Judaism.

a. While the LXX mostly has παῖς [199] for the עֶבֶד יהוה of Dt. Is., but still uses δοῦλος in 3 instances, [200] δοῦλος later drops out of the picture altogether in connection with the servant of God passages in Dt. Is. In the period after the composition of the LXX the Ebed is always παῖς in Hell. Jewish literature. [201] This remains true up to 100 A.D. In virtue of the ambiguity of παῖς the phrase παῖς θεοῦ can be rendered either "servant of God" (LXX) or "child of God" (Wis., → 678, 5-20). The greater the distance from the original Heb. text the more strongly the second view ("child of God") prevailed in the Hell. Jewish understanding of Is. 40 ff.

Only from the beginning of the 2nd cent. did the picture change, but then radically. Aquila [202] (→ n. 203) always calls the servant of Dt. Is. δοῦλος. [203] The question as to what caused him to choose this word may be answered by stating that outside Is. 40 ff., too, he renders עֶבֶד by δοῦλος. Hence he is simply following his own strictly practised translation technique of always rendering Heb. roots by the same Gk. roots. [204] There is thus no pt. in trying to find for his transl. of עֶבֶד (of God) by δοῦλος (of God) any other reason than that of a desire for an accurate rendering of the Heb. term. [205] His example was normative for his successors. Theodotion, too, has δοῦλος for עֶבֶד, and he consequently calls the servant of God δοῦλος in all the extant passages in Is. 40 ff.: 41:8, 9; 42:1; 49:6; only at 42:1 do we find παῖς (= LXX) as a vl. [206] The transl. of the Jewish Christian Symmachus also calls the Ebed δοῦλος after the example of Aquila. [207]

b. A determinative factor in the interpretation of the servant of Dt. Is. in Hell. Judaism was the fact that the LXX had extended to other passages (→ 676, 19-25) the collective

---

[199] 41:8, 9; 42:1, 23 א; 43:10; 44:1, 2, 21 (twice), 26; 45:4; 49:6; 50:10; 52:13; cf. also the plur. οἱ παῖδές μου for the Heb. עֲבָדַי at 42:19a.

[200] 48:20; 49:3, 5; cf. the plur. οἱ δοῦλοι τοῦ θεοῦ for the Heb. עֶבֶד יהוה at 42:19b and δουλεύοντα for the Heb. עַבְדִּי at 53:11.

[201] Jeremias, Ἀμνὸς τοῦ θεοῦ, 118-121.

[202] Just. Dial. refers repeatedly to a new Gk. transl. of the OT which differs from the LXX and which his opponents accept, 120, 4; 124, 2 f.; 131, 1; 137, 3. He also alludes to their low opinion of the LXX, 43, 8; 67, 1; 68, 7; 71, 1-73, 5; 84, 3 f. A. Rahlfs, "Über Theodotion-Lesarten im NT u. Aquila-Lesarten bei Justin," ZNW, 20 (1921), 194-199 for Mi. 4:1 (quoted in Just. Dial., 109, 2), has tried to show that this new transl. was that of Aquila. Orig. ep. ad Julium Africanum, 2 (MPG, 11, 52 B) says of Aquila: φιλοτιμότερον πεπιστευμένος παρὰ Ἰουδαίοις ἡρμηνευκέναι τὴν γραφήν· ᾧ μάλιστα εἰώθασι οἱ ἀγνοοῦντες τὴν Ἑβραίων διάλεκτον χρῆσθαι, ὡς πάντων μᾶλλον ἐπιτετευγμένῳ (because he succeeded best of all).

[203] Preserved: Is. 41:8, 9; 42:1; 49:6; 52:13.

[204] Aquila practises this principle with such astonishing consistency that one is even led to assume that before beginning his transl. he prepared a Heb.-Gk. glossary, cf. Septuaginta, ed. A. Rahlfs (1935), I, p. X.

[205] The conjecture stated (with reservations) by Euler, 88, also Zolli, 229 f.; J. Jeremias, "Zum Problem der Deutung von Js. 53 im palästinischen Spätjudentum," Aux sources de la tradition chrétienne = Mélanges offerts à M. Goguel (1950), 115 f., that Aquila's disinclination to render עֶבֶד (of God) by παῖς is due to anti-Christian tendencies cannot, therefore, be sustained, Hegermann, II.

[206] So Q and the Syro-Hexaplarist transl. Acc. to Theodoret of Cyrus, however, Theodotion also had δοῦλος for עֶבֶד at Is. 42:1. An argument in favour of the correctness of the reading δοῦλος is that Theodotion always seems to have δοῦλος for עֶבֶד and that παῖς (acc. to Hatch-Redpath, s.v.) does not occur at all in the extant fragments of his work (except as a vl. at Is. 42:1).

[207] Preserved: Is. 41:8, 9; 42:1, 19 (twice); 49:6; 52:13.

understanding offered by the Heb. in 9 places (→ n. 175). Thus at Is. 42:19 the LXX rendered the sing. of the Heb. twice in the plur. (עֶבֶד = LXX οἱ παῖδές μου; עֶבֶד יהוה = LXX οἱ δοῦλοι τοῦ θεοῦ). [208] It proved to be particularly significant in its consequences that the LXX also took the "my servant" of 42:1 collectively and expressed this understanding by adding the word Ιακωβ : Ιακωβ ὁ παῖς μου (Heb. only עֶבֶדִּי). There thus arose a bifurcation in the interpretation of 42:1 ff. Following the LXX, Hell. Judaism refers the passage to the people Israel, [209] while Palestinian Judaism takes it to be wholly Messianic, → 687, 10 ff.; 689, 5 ff. and n. 262; 693, 1 ff.; 695, 19 ff. and n. 306.

Another very similar bifurcation may be noted in respect of Is. 53. So far as we know, Hell. Judaism interprets the suffering servant of God collectively, again in contrast to the Messianic understanding in Palestine. The collective interpretation of 53 is first found in Wis. This depicts the righteous man, whom it calls παῖς κυρίου "child of God" in 2:13 (→ 678, 11-16), and the fate of this man, along the lines of Is. 52:13 ff. This is esp. true of the scene at the last judgment (Wis. 4:20 ff.), where sinners confess with trembling that they have despised and misunderstood the righteous and erred from the way of truth. Here in one detail after another there is allusion to Is. 52:13 ff.; cf. Wis. 4:18 with Is. 53:3; 4:20; 5:3 with 52:15, 5:3 f. with 53:2-4, 5:5 (κλῆρος) with 53:12 (κληρονομήσει), 5:6 f. with 53:6, 5:15 f. with 53:10-12; also Wis. 2:13 with Is. 52:13; 53:11, 2:19 f. with 53:7 f. [210] In Wis., then, the παῖς θεοῦ of Is. 52:13 ff. is a type of the righteous. Obviously, then, the collective interpretation of Is. 53 was well-known to the author. [211] Origen gives us another example in Cels., I, 55, where he tells us that Jews with whom he came into contact took Is. 53 to refer collectively "to the people, understood as a single person, which had been dispersed and tormented." Whereas this collective understanding of the servant of God in Is. 53 was completely unknown to Palestinian Judaism during the first Christian millennium (it occurs for the first time in Rashi, d. 1105), [212] it was current in Hell. Judaism, as may be seen from Wis. One must assume, therefore, that those to whom Origen appeals were Hell. Jews.

To sum up, one may say that Hell. Judaism inclines to construe the παῖς θεοῦ of Dt. Is. as "child of God," and prefers the collective interpretation.

2. Palestinian Judaism.

In Palestinian Judaism during the first millennium we find three different interpretations of the servant of God in Dt. Is. An important pt. is that with some exceptions these three do not overlap. Each of them is restricted to certain of the 19 passages (→ 682, 16 f.) in which there is ref. to the servant.

a. The Collective Interpretation (Is. 41:8 f.; 42:19 [twice]; 44:1, 2, 21 [twice]; 45:4; 48:20; 49:3, 5 f. [?]; 50:10).

The collective ref. of the servant of God to Israel occurs in the Heb. original in 9 of the 19 passages in Dt. Is. (Is. 41:8 f.; 44:1, 2, 21 [twice]; 45:4; 48:20; 49:3, → 682, 16 f.). This fixed the application of these 9 verses to Israel during the period which followed, as may be seen from Tg. Is., → n. 176. [213] Under the influence of 49:3 ("My servant art thou, Israel") the Tg. also seems to have referred the servant of God to Israel in v. 5 and v. 6 as well. [214] In the older Rabb. tradition, as distinct from the Hell. (→ 683, 24-

---

[208] Cf. also Is. 44:26, where the LXX (A) renders עֲבָדוֹ (of God) in the plur. by παίδων αὐτοῦ, and Is. 48:20, where the LXX (A) has τὸν λαὸν αὐτοῦ Ιακωβ for עֲבְדּוֹ יַעֲקֹב.
[209] Just. Dial., 123, 8 f.; cf. Dalman, I, 32; Fischel, 59.
[210] Dalman, I, 32, n. 1.
[211] W. Staerk, "Zur Exegese von Js. 53 im Diasporajudentum," ZNW, 35 (1936), 308.
[212] Dalman, I, 34 f.; Str.-B., I, 481.
[213] The texts are referred to Israel in the following places as well as the Tg.: Is. 41:8 f.: Lk. 1:54; Gn. r., 44, 3 on 15:1; Is. 44:2 : Bar. 3:37 (→ n. 177); Midr. Ps. 111 § 1; Is. 49:3 : S. Dt. § 355 on 33:26 par. M. Ex., 15, 2; Lv. r., 2 on 1:2; Ex. r., 21 on 14:15 (for other examples relating to Is. 49:3 cf. Dalman, I, 97, n. 1).
[214] This is how Tg. Is. 49:5 f. is mostly taken: Dalman, I, 97, n. 1; Humbert, 25, n. 5; Str.-B., II, 330; Seidelin, 202. But in view of the alternation between sing. and plur. we

684, 29) no allusion was seen to Israel in the other servant passages. [215] In particular, Is. 53 was never referred to Israel by Palestinian Rabb. Judaism during the 1st Christian millennium (→ supra). In Rabb. literature the collective reference to Israel was strictly confined to those passages where it was demanded by the Heb. and supported by the context. [216]

As concerns the reference of individual servant sayings to the righteous, the prophets and the scribes, the following pts. may be made. We simply have allusions when Sir. 11:13 [217] applies a free quotation from Is. 52:15 to the suffering righteous (→ III, 31, n. 17) or Da. 12:3 [218] relates a phrase from Is. 53:11, in the plur., to the teachers of Israel. We have exegesis, however, when in Tg. Is. 42:19 (twice) the servant of God is related to penitent sinners [219] and in 50:10 to the prophets. [220, 221] In bBer., 5a (Rab Huna, d. 297) and Seder Eliyyahu r., 7 [222] Is. 53:10 is referred to penitent sufferers; in bYoma, 86a (Abbaye, d. 338/9) Is. 49:3, and in Seder Eliyyahu r., 14 and 25 [223] Is. 53:11 is applied to the upright teacher of the Torah. In these 5 instances, however, the words are taken out of context, so that no conclusions may be drawn as to the interpretation of the latter. [224] Only occasionally, then, did Palestinian Judaism apply the servant passages of Dt. Is. to the righteous, the prophets and the scribes. [225]

In the Qumran texts there is no conclusive evidence of a collective application of the servant to the Essene community [225a] [1965].

---

cannot be wholly certain to whom Tg. refers the "ministering servant" (Tg. Is. 49:5) and the "servants" of God; Fischel, 60, 74 is quite right to put a question mark against the ref. of Tg. Is. 49:5 f. to Israel. (On the construction and transl. of Tg. Is. 49:5 f. cf. the valuable observations of Humbert, 25, n. 5.) On the interpretation of Is. 49:6 in Rabb. writings → n. 305.

[215] Acc. to Fischel, 76 Is. 42:19 was also referred to Israel in Rabb. literature, but he gives no example. He probably had in view Tg. Is. 42:19, though the ref. here is to penitent sinners, → n. 219.

[216] The correct conclusion of Fischel that "in the Tannaitic and Amoraic period, apart from the reports of Just. and Orig., we find no ref. of 42:1 ff.; 50:4 ff. or 53 to Israel," may be extended to cover all the servant passages in Dt. Is. apart from the 9 mentioned → 684, 37 f.; as far as Palestinian Judaism is concerned we should also cut out the qualifying reference to Just. (→ n. 209) and Orig. (→ 684, 21-27).

[217] וְיתְמהוּ עָלָיו רבּים ("and many will be astonished at him"). This is the earliest ref. to Is. 52:13 ff. we have.

[218] מַצְדִּיקֵי הָרַבּים ("which have brought many to righteousness").

[219] Tg. Is. 42:19: "Will not the wicked, when they convert, be called 'my servant' (Heb. עַבְדִּי, so Tg.-Codd, only Cod Orientalis 1474 [British Museum] has the plur. עַבְדַּי)? ... If they convert, they will be called 'servants of God' (Heb. עֶבֶד יְהוָה, Tg. plur. עבדיא דיהוה)."

[220] The Tg. has עבדוהי נבייא for the Heb. עַבְדּו.

[221] On the other hand it is arguable whether Tg. Is. 44:26 belongs here. Certainly the Tg. renders the Heb. of this v. (עַבְדּו) by עבדוהי צדיקיא. But the parallelism makes it probable that the form עבדו was intended as a plur. (עֲבָדיו) in the original (so BHK², ³, ad loc.), and since the LXX construed the Heb. thus (παίδων αὐτοῦ) one may ask whether the Tg. did not also understand the original as a plur. If so, Tg. Is. 44:26 is not an example of the collective interpretation of the servant but of the use of the plur. to denote the righteous, → n. 169.

[222] Str.-B., I, 484. At the earliest, the 2nd half of the 5th cent.; acc. to Strack, Einl., 220 the 2nd half of the 10th cent.

[223] Str.-B., I, 484 f.

[224] Cf. the warning of Moore, III, 166, n. 255.

[225] For mediaeval authors who represent this understanding cf. Fischel, 61, 74-76.

[225a] For passages which seem to draw on the Servant Songs in wording or content cf. M. Black, "Servant of the Lord and Son of Man," Scottish Journal of Theology, 6 (1953), 4-8; W. H. Brownlee, "The Servant of the Lord in the Qumran Scrolls," Bull. of the American School of Oriental Research, 132 (Dec. 1953), 8-15; 135 (Oct. 1954), 33-38; F. F. Bruce, "Biblical Exegesis in the Qumran Texts," Exegetica, III, 1 (1959), 50-58. But these are at best allusions, and we do not find the concept of the Ebed in any of them [1965].

b. Reference to the Prophet Isaiah (Is. 49:5; 50:10).

It must have seemed quite obvious to understand some of the servant passages as statements of the prophet about himself ; this is esp. true of the description of suffering in the 1st person in 50:4 ff., which culminates in the summons to hear the voice of the servant of God, v. 10. In fact, Jerome's Comm. in Is. states expressly, with ref. to v. 10, that the Jews took this section to apply to the prophet himself. [226] 49:5, [227] which is also in the first person, was also referred sometimes to Isaiah. [228] There is no contemporary par., however, for the extension of this interpretation to Is. 53:7 f. in the question of the Ethiopian eunuch, Ac. 8:34. [229]

The recurrent applications of individual servant passages to individual figures are without significance. For such refs. as that of Is. 41:8 to the patriarch Jacob (S. Dt. § 27 on 3:24), of the עַבְדִּי of 43:10 to David (Midr. Ps. 51 § 3 on 51:4), of 44:26 to the angel who wrestled with Jacob (Gn. r., 78, 3 on 32:27 f., R. Levi c. 300), of 49:8 f. to Noah and his family who came out of the ark with him, [230] of 50:10 to Abraham (Gn. r., 60 on 24:12), [231] or of 53:12 to Moses' eschatological reward (S. Dt. § 355 on 33:21), the zealous deed of Phinehas (S. Nu. § 131 on 25:13), R. Akiba [232] or the men of the great synagogue (jSheq., 5, 1 [48c 48]) [233] — are all without exception refs. to individual verses which do not tell us how the rabbis concerned expounded the passages in context. [234] In particular, the connecting of Is. 53:12 with Moses' intercession (bSota, 14a) [235] has its source in R. Simlai (c. 250), who plays a part in the Palestinian tradition mainly because of his controversies with Christians. [236] By applying Is. 53:12 to Moses, he is probably trying to prevent Chr. apologists from appealing to the verse. [237] This is the more probable in that the same tendency with regard to Is. 53:12 already seems to have influenced Theodotion in the 2nd cent., → 693, 17 ff.

c. References to the Messiah (Is. 42:1; 43:10; 49:6; 52:13; 53:11).

The Messianic interpretation of certain servant passages in Dt. Is. can very probably be traced back to the pre-Christian period, → 677.

(a) Jesus Sirach. In Sir. 48:10 להכין שבטי ישראל is mentioned as one of the three tasks of the returning Elijah, → II, 931, 8 ff. The phrase is taken from Is. 49:6, where the Ebed receives the task of לְהָקִים אֶת־שִׁבְטֵי יַעֲקֹב. The reestablishment of the twelve tribes is a Messianic task, and its assignment to Elijah is meant to mark the latter as the coming

---

[226] MPL, 24, 496. In Lv. r., 10, 2 on 8:1 par. Pesikt., 125b (ed. S. Buber [1868]) R. Jehuda b. Simon (c. 330) refers Is. 50:6 to Isaiah. When Tg. Is. 50:10 renders Heb. עַבְדּוֹ by "his (God's) servants the prophets" (→ n. 220) this at least includes a ref. to Isaiah. Is. 50:4-10 was never taken Messianically in Judaism, Seidelin, 206, n. 28 and esp. Fischel, 63, 74 f.; → lines 14 f.

[227] S. Dt. § 27 on 3:24.

[228] Is. 49:1 is accordingly referred to Isaiah : Midr. Ps. 9 § 59 on 9:6, 43a; Pesikt. r., 129a.

[229] In particular, as Fischel pts. out (63), there is no ref. to the Ebed in the accounts of the martyrdom of Isaiah.

[230] Aggadat Bereshit, 7 (ed. A. Jellinek, Bet-ha-Midrasch, IV [1857], 12).

[231] Str.-B., II, 608.

[232] The author is R. Jona (c. 350).

[233] The last three texts in Str.-B., I, 483 f.

[234] Schlatter, Moore, Kuhn → n. 198. K. G. Kuhn, S. Nu. (1933 ff.), 527 correctly says of the ref. of Is. 53:12 to the zealous deed of Phinehas (S. Nu. § 131 on 25:13): "The explanation does not specify, then, that the prophecy in Is. 53:12 refers to Phinehas." For a different view cf. Fischel, 63, n. 51, who, appealing to Sir. 48:10 (→ 686, 28 ff.) and Mk. 9:13, finds in the ref. of Is. 53:12 to Phinehas more than an "incidental homiletical allusion." But the equation of Phinehas with Elijah, which Fischel thinks he sees in S. Nu. § 131, belongs only to the post-NT period (→ II, 933, 20 f.), and it is debatable whether it occurs in S. Nu. § 131. (K. G. Kuhn has doubts on this, as he has told me orally, though cf. Str.-B., IV, 463.)

[235] Str.-B., I, 483.

[236] Bacher Pal. Am., I, 555 f.

[237] Moore, III, 166, n. 254.

redeemer. [238] Since, however, only a free allusion is made to Is. 49:6, we cannot with full certainty infer a Messianic interpretation of the latter from Sir. 48:10 alone, [239] though → n. 305. In any case it is significant that Sir. took the servant of God of Is. 49:6 in an individual sense. [240]

(b) Visionary Discourses of Eth. En. [241] The next relevant source chronologically is the so-called Visionary Discourses [244] of Eth. En. (37-71), which are undoubtedly pre-Christian. [245] Here the Messiah is to a striking degree furnished with traits drawn from Dt. Is. Apart from the titles "Son of Man" (→ υἱὸς τοῦ ἀνθρώπου) and "Messiah," [246] he also bears constantly the name "Elect," [247] and occasionally elsewhere "Righteous One." [248] The "Elect," however, is a title of the servant of God in Is. 42:1, [249] as is also the "Righteous One" in Is. 53:11. [250] We are thus led at once to the two sections in Dt. Is. which we find to have been Messianically interpreted in the period which followed, namely, Is. 42:1 ff. and Is. 52:13 ff. [251]

---

[238] → II, 931, 12 ff. and n. 17; cf. also Dalman, I, 28; Str.-B., IV, 780.

[239] Similarly North, 7. Dalman, I, 28 is more confident in his judgment.

[240] The Qumran texts come after Sir. chronologically and are thought by some to combine refs. to the Messiah and the servant, and to identify the Teacher of Righteousness with this (Messiah-)servant figure, so esp. A. Dupont-Sommer, "Le livre des Hymnes découvert près de la Mer Morte," Semitica, 7 (1957), 64, n. 8, 10; Les écrits esséniens découverts près de la Mer Morte (1959), 377. Both these hypotheses are unacceptable, however, for the following reasons : (a) The Messianic passages contain no straightforward quotations of, nor allusions to, the servant texts of Dt. Is. (b) All that can be brought forward in favour of the identification of the Teacher of Righteousness with the servant are some uncertain and remote reminiscences of Dt. Is., the general description of the Teacher as a humble and humiliated person, and two quotations from Is. 50:4 (1 QH, 7, 10; 8, 35 f.). But there is no mention of vicarious suffering on the Teacher's part. The epithet of Ebed is used in connection with him, but only by himself in the accepted sense of a humble self-description of the worshipper → 679; it is never applied to him by somebody else, and is never combined with refs. to the servant songs (cf. the detailed discussion in G. Jeremias, Der Lehrer der Gerechtigkeit, 299-307, with bibl.) [1965].

[241] The original art. contained here a section on the Testament of Benjamin, but Jeremias has now dropped this on textual grounds, and the relevant notes (originally n. 240-243) are omitted [1965].

[244] The transl. "Visionary Discourses" is now established and is thus retained, but it is not quite exact. Eth. mĕsālē = Heb. מָשָׁל = Gk. παραβολή denotes in Eth. En. 37:5; 38:1; 45:1; 57:3; 58:1; 68:1; 69:29 three apocalyptic visions. Hence the word means here "teaching with a secret sense."

[245] The dating of the Discourses depends on the ref. to the Parthian invasion of Palestine (40 B.C.) in 56:5-7. They were composed shortly after this and a little later interwoven into En. The untenability of the view that the Discourses as a whole are Chr. or have been provided in part with Chr. interpolations has been shown by Sjöberg, 3-24. The main argument against this theory is the complete absence of anything specifically Christian.

[246] "The Anointed," En. 48:10; 52:4.

[247] En. 39:6; 40:5; 45:3 (vl.), 4; 49:2; 51:3, 5; 52:6, 9; 53:6; 55:4; 61:5, 8, 10; 62:1; cf. 46:3; 48:6; 49:4.

[248] En. 38:2 (vl. "righteousness," Sjöberg, 96, n. 48); 47:1, 4; 53:6 ("the Righteous and Elect"). Cf. also 39:6 : "the Elect of righteousness and faithfulness"; 46:3 : "the Son of Man who has righteousness, with whom righteousness dwells"; 71:14.

[249] Rightly, the allusion to Is. 42:1 is generally recognised. Cf. esp. En. 49:4 : "He has been chosen before the Lord of spirits as he has willed" (on the transl. v. Sjöberg, 122, n. 33) with Is. 42:1: "Mine elect, in whom my soul delighteth." Ps. 89:3, 19, where David is called "mine elect" (3) or "a chosen one" (19), cannot be considered as an OT prototype, since later Judaism consistently refers both vv. to the historical David, not the Messiah.

[250] The Messiah is also called righteous in Zech. 9:9 (cf. "righteous branch" : Jer. 23:5; 33:15). But in view of the many refs. to Dt. Is. only Is. 53:11 arises as the prototype of Eth. En., cf. Str.-B., I, 481.

[251] Str.-B., I, 481: "The Messianic interpretation (of Is. 53) is first (but cf. → 677, 686)

In En. 48:4 the Son of Man is then called the "light of the nations" — an attribute of the servant of God in Is. 42:6; 49:6. It is further said that "his name" was named before creation "in the presence of the Lord of spirits" (En. 48:3) — an exposition and amplification of Is. 49:1: ("he named my name when I was not yet born"). He was at first "hidden before him (God)" (En. 48:6; cf. 62:7) — a ref. to Is. 49:2 ("in the shadow of his hand he hid me"). [252] In the description of the manifestation of the Son of Man we constantly find in the Discourses the humbling of kings and mighty men before the Son of Man, with allusions to Is. 49:7; 52:15. [253] It is said that they will see him in glory (En. 55:4; 62:1, 3), rise up before him (46:4; 62:3) and bow down before him (48:10 vl.; 62:9; cf. 48:5), cf. Is. 49:7: "Princes and kings shall see and arise and worship." It is also said that their countenance will be cast down (En. 46:6; 48:8), cf. Is. 52:15 : "Kings shall shut their mouths at him." In particular En. 62:1 ff. depicts the conduct of kings, the mighty and the possessors of the earth in close connection with Is. 52:13 ff.: "They will be afraid (cf. Is. 52:14), they will cast down their eyes (Is. 52:15), and sorrow will grip them, when they shall see the Son of Man sitting on his glorious throne ; kings (cf. Is. 52:15), mighty men and all the possessors of the earth will praise, extol and magnify him who reigns over all (cf. Is. 52:13), who was hidden (cf. Is. 52:15)." [254] It is again the passages Is. 42:1 ff.; 52:13 ff. (→ 690, 9 ff.) which are interpreted Messianically, along with 49:1-2, 6-7. Finally, the following statements about the Son of Man carry loose allusions to Dt. Is. The Elect has the spirit of righteousness (En. 62:1 f., cf. [in addition to Is. 11:2, 4] 42:1: "Mine elect ... I have put my spirit upon him"). He judges (En. 41:9; 45:3; 49:4; 55:4; 61:9; 62:2 f.; 69:27, cf. Is. 42:4 'AΘ Tg.). En. 48:4b : "He shall be the light of the nations and the hope of the distressed," combines Is. 42:6 ("light of the nations") with the context (42:7: salvation of the blind and wretched). The Son of Man of the Discourses is thus very largely [255] furnished with traits borrowed from the servant sayings of Dt. Is. (42:1-7; 49:1 f., 6 f.; 52:13-15; 53:11).

The resultant combination of the Son of Man and the servant of God, though restricted to traits which exalt the servant's glory, [255a] was of decisive significance for Jesus' sense of mission. [256]

(c) Peshitta. The next source which possibly gives information on the interpretation of the Ebed sayings in later Judaism is the Peshitta, though it is uncertain whether this is of Jewish [257] and/or of Christian origin [1965]. The Peshitta takes Is. 53, including what is said about suffering, Messianically. [258] One may see this from the passages in which it reveals its understanding of Is. 53 by deviations from the Heb. text. Acc. to

espoused by the Visionary Discourses of En.," cf. Wolff, 38 f.; Fischel, 61; H. Kosmala, "Jom Kippur," Judaica, 6 (1950), 16.

[252] Cf. with Is. 49:2 ("in the shadow of his hand") En. 39:7: "I saw his dwelling under the pinions of the Lord of spirits." The concept of the hiddenness of the Messiah plays a gt. part in the period which follows, also in the NT (e.g., Mt. 24:26; Jn. 7:27; Rev. 12:5; cf. also Just. Dial., 8, 110, v. Dalman, I, 34). (Cf. Sjöberg, Der verborgene Menschensohn, 41-89 [1965].)

[253] Billerbeck, 108; Fischel, 61.

[254] That this passage takes up Is. 52:13 ff. is confirmed by the fact that it is understood, just as in contemporary exegesis (Wis. 4:20 ff.; 'A; Θ; Tg.), as a final judgment scene [1965].

[255] Billerbeck, 107: "almost exclusively." Cf. Staerk, Soter, 72-77, 82 f.

[255a] The suggestion that this combination in Eth. En. embraces the statements about the servant's humiliation as well (Str.-B., II, 282, n. 1; J. Jeremias, Erlöser u. Erlösung, 106 ff.; Staerk, Soter, 83, 86) is untenable [1965].

[256] Buber, 112 f. An echo of this combination of Son of Man and servant of God in Eth. En. may be seen in the fact that in Hb. En. Metatron, who bears many attributes of the Son of Man (Odeberg, 146), is called עֶבֶד (of God) or נַעַר, → n. 194. Cf. J. Bowman, "The Background of the Term 'Son of Man,' " Exp. T., 59 (1948), 288.

[257] P. Kahle, The Cairo Genizah² (1959), 265-273; also Hegermann, 22-27 [1965].

[258] Hegermann, I, 87 f.

these the Peshitta saw in the servant of God a figure awaited in the future (52:14) who shall "purify" many peoples (52:15); this figure is rejected (53:2), despised (53:3) and put to death (53:5), but he is exalted by God and (at the last judgment) will mediate forgiveness (53:5 : healing). These statements can refer only to the Messiah. [259]

(d) NT. At one pt. the NT, too, affords an example of Messianic interpretation of an Ebed saying on the part of later Judaism. According to Lk. 23:35 [259a] the ἄρχοντες mock the crucified Lord in the words : ἄλλους ἔσωσεν, σωσάτω ἑαυτόν, εἰ οὗτός ἐστιν ὁ χριστὸς τοῦ θεοῦ, ὁ ἐκλεκτός. In the present context the point is that it is the Jewish ἄρχοντες who here give the Messiah the title ὁ ἐκλεκτός. Christian influence on this formulation is unlikely, since elsewhere in the NT ὁ ἐκλεκτός occurs as a Christological predicate only in Jn. 1:34. [260, 261] We are already familiar with the title "Elect," however, from Eth. En., where it is a pre-Christian, Jewish predicate of the Messiah derived from Is. 42:1 → 687, 10 f. [262] Thus in Lk. 23:35 we have an echo of the Messianic understanding of Is. 42:1 in later Judaism. It may also be noted here, in confirmation of what has been said, that in the NT, too, Messianic interpretation of the servant sayings of Dt. Is. is confined to Is. 42:1-4, 6; 49:6 and 52:13-53:12, → 709, 9 ff.

(e) Aquila. At the beginning of the 2nd cent. A.D. [263] Aquila made in Palestine a new transl. of the OT into Gk. which was designed to replace the LXX, esp. since this offered Christians too much scope for the adducing of Christological proofs from Scripture. [264] How Aquila interpreted the servant of God in Is. 53 may be seen from his referring of

---

[259] *Loc. cit.*

[259a] From Luke's special source, J. Jeremias, "Perikopenumstellungen bei Lukas ?" *New Testament Studies,* 4 (1957/58), 115-119 [1965].

[260] The fact that the reading ὁ ἐκλεκτός offered by the oldest MSS at Jn. 1:34 is the most ancient reading, in spite of the small no. of witnesses (𝔓⁵ ℵ 77. 218 sy^sc a b e ff²), has been convincingly shown by A. v. Harnack, "Zur Textkritik u. Christologie der Schriften d. Joh.," SAB (1915), 552-556 = *Studien* I (= *Arbeiten zur Kirchengeschichte,* 19 [1931], 127-132). For all three linguistic areas of the early Church, Gk., Syr. and Lat., textual history unanimously begins with this reading. It was replaced by ὁ υἱός during the 4th cent. in the battle agains Adoptionist Christology.

[261] At Lk. 9:35 we find the divergent form ὁ ἐκλελεγμένος as the (probably original) reading. ὁ ἐκλεκτός does not occur at all for Christ in the post-apostolic fathers or Apologists.

[262] Elsewhere it occurs unequivocally as such only in Apc. Abr. 31:1. On the other hand Test. B. 11:4 καὶ ἔσται ἐκλεκτὸς θεοῦ ἕως τοῦ αἰῶνος (→ IV, 185, 9 ff.), as the text shows, is undoubtedly part of a Chr. interpolation (11:2b-5) and refers, not to Christ, but to the Benjamite Paul (Charles, *op. cit.,* 215 f. n. on c. XI).

[263] The dating of Aquila's transl. is fixed by the fact that he was a pupil on the one hand of R. Akiba (Jer. on Is. 8:11 ff. [MPL, 24, 119 A] : *Akibas quem magistrum Aquilae proselyti autumant* ; jQid., 1, 1 [59a, 9], and on the other of R. Eli'ezer b. Hyrcanos and R. Jehoshua' b. Chanania (jMeg., 1, 11 [71 c, 9]). The work of the last two reached its peak c. 90 A.D. But R. Jehoshua' had ministered in the temple as a Levite (bAr., 11b; S. Nu. § 116 on 18:3; T. Sheq., 2, 14). This means that he had reached the Levitical age of 20 prior to the destruction of the temple, so that he was born for certain before 50 A.D. R. Eli'ezer b. Hyrcanos was even older, for he began his studies only at the age of 22 or 28 (Pesikta R. Eli'ezer, 1; Gn. r., 42, 3 on 14:1; Ab. R. Nat., 6) and had pursued them for many yrs. prior to 70 A.D. with Rabban Jochanan b. Zakkai. Hence he must have been born between 30 and 40 (J. Klausner, *Jesus v. Nazareth* [1930], 46, cf. R. T. Herford, *Christianity in Talmud and Midrash* [1903], 142, n. 1; acc. to Klausner he was already of advanced age c. 80). As regards the date of his death, we know he died before R. Akiba, hence before 135 A.D. (bSanh., 68a). For some time before his death he was in exile and was avoided by his colleagues and students. Since Aquila read his transl. to R. Eli'ezer and R. Jehoshua' (jMeg., 1, 11 [71 c, 9]) it can hardly have been written after 110 A.D., and was probably earlier.

[264] *Septuaginta,* ed. A. Rahlfs (1935), I, p. VII f. [N. 265 excised, 1965].

53:8 f. to the judgment which the servant holds, as in the Tg.; this points to a Messianic understanding. [266] Moreover Aquila (acc. to Jerome) transl. the נָגוּעַ of Is. 53:4 by ἀφημένον ("leprous"), [267] cf. Vg quasi leprosum. This rendering is explained by the fact that the pass. part. of נגע in later Heb. (pu) and Aram. (pa) has the sense "leprous." In the present context this transl. is most significant, for we find the same inference of leprosy from Is. 53:4 in the Rabb. writings, and here with ref. to the Messiah. [268] We have in view two passages in bSanh., 98, which, along with a late saying in the Midrash, [269] are the only ones in the Talmud to preserve the strange idea of a leprous Messiah. [270] The one passage is bSanh., 98b, from c. 200. [271] In a list of Messianic titles we read here: "And the teachers said: 'The leper,' those of the house of Rabbi [272] said: 'The sick one' is his name; for it is written: 'Surely he hath borne our griefs, and carried our sorrows: yet we did esteem him stricken with leprosy (נָגוּעַ), smitten of God, and afflicted' (Is. 53:4)." [273] The other passage is bSanh., 98a (a supposed experience of R. Jehoshua' b. Levi, c. 250), which describes how the Messiah sits before the gates of Rome among the wretched who "bear sicknesses" (cf. Is. 53:4) [274] and is the only one among them who opens and binds up just one wound so that he may fulfil without delay the summons to redeem Israel.

Aquila's translation of Is. 53 enables us to trace back to 100 A.D. this reference of Is. 53:4 to the leprous Messiah. [275] Indeed, we must go back even further; the

---

[266] Hegermann, 42, 112; cf. 122 ff. for further observations, esp. on the agreement between Aquila and Tg.

[267] Jer. (in Is. 53:4 [MPL, 24, 507 A]): Pro eo quod Symmachus transtulit, ἐν ἀφῇ ὄντα, hoc est in lepra, Aquila posuit ἀφημένον, id est leprosum; quod multi non intelligentes putant relictum (ἀφειμένον), et alii legunt καθήμενον, id est sedentem. Acc. to Eus. (Ziegler, Isaias, ad loc.) Aquila transl. נָגוּעַ by τετραυματισμένον. But Jerome's ἀφημένον is unquestionably right, for the context of the reading given by Eus. rules out its derivation from Aquila (cf. J. Ziegler, "Textkritische Notizen zu d. jüngeren gr. Übers. d. Buches Is." = NGG Fachgruppe V, NF, I, 4 [1939], 97 f.). Furthermore, Aquila consistently rendered the Heb. stem נגע by the Gk. word group ἀφή/ἅπτεσθαι, and ἀφᾶσθαι is a pass. form which is not attested elsewhere in Gk. literature. It has been derived from ἀφή, which in Jewish Gk. had the specific connotation of "plague," "leprosy." There is no reason to doubt Jerome's statement that the perf. pass. part. ἀφημένος means "leprous" [1965].

[268] Euler's conjecture (31 f.) that Aquila has in mind a leprous priest is wide of the mark. His observations on Aquila suffer throughout from the fact that he does not appreciate Aquila's translation technique (→ 683, 15 ff.; Hegermann, II).

[269] Sepher Zerubbabel (ed. A. Jellinek, Bet-ha-Midrasch, II [1853/4], 54, 19 ff.; cf. Str.-B., II, 291). Comparison with bSanh., 98a shows that the "wounds" from which men hide their faces refer to leprosy.

[270] The essay by H. Gressmann, "Der aussätzige Messias," Chr. W., 34 (1920), 663-668 contains nothing helpful to our investigation.

[271] This date is derived from the introductory formula רבנן אמרי, Dalman, I, 37; cf. also Str.-B., II, 286.

[272] Rabbi is R. Jehuda, I (135-c. 217).

[273] Thus the text read by Raymundus Martini, Pugio fidei (after 1278 A.D., ed. D. J. de Voisin [1651]), 672, cf. Dalman, I, 36, n. 2, and rightly (→ n. 309) adopted by E. B. Pusey in Driver-Neubauer, II, p. XXXIV and by North, 14. The present text of bSanh., 98b: "And the teachers said: 'The leper of the house of Rabbi' is he called, for it is written: 'Surely he ... (Is. 53:4),'" certainly takes Is. 53:4 Messianically but it is an obvious corruption. Omission of the word cholya ("the sick one") has produced the meaningless Messianic title: "The leper of the house of Rabbi."

[274] Rashi expounds these words as follows: "Who are stricken with leprosy, and he too is leprous, see Is. 53:3, 4" (text, Wünsche, 58, n. 2). An indication of leprosy (see also Dalman, I, 39) is the number of wounds needing to be bound up, but esp. sitting before the gates (J. Jeremias, Jerusalem zur Zeit Jesu, II, A [1924], 33, n. 1): The law that walled cities are barred to lepers (Str.-B., IV, 751-757) is transferred to Rome.

[275] That the inferring of leprosy from Is. 53:4 attests a Messianic interpretation of the servant of God as early as the Tannaitic period has been shown by H. J. Schoeps, "Sym-

Messianic interpretation of Is. 53:4 in Aquila cannot have originated c. 100 A.D., for it is completely out of the question that the Jews should have begun to entertain a Messianic interpretation of the passion texts in Is. 53 at the very time when Christians were already appealing to Is. 53 as the decisive Christological proof from Scripture. [276]

(f) Theodotion. Aquila's transl. was followed in the 2nd cent. [277] by that of Theodotion. [278] Theodotion, too, understood Is. 53 Messianically. This may be seen most clearly from his rendering of the concluding sentence of the chapter. Is. 53 (Mas.) closes with the words : וְלַפֹּשְׁעִים יַפְגִּיעַ (53:12). The verb הִפְגִּיעַ/פָּגַע means "to have to do with someone" a. in bonam partem "to intercede for" or b. in malam partem "to attack." The context shows that the Heb. had in view the first meaning : "And he made intercession for the transgressors"; it is correctly understood by the NT (R. 8:34; Hb. 7:25; 1 Jn. 2:1 f.), Just., [280] Vg., [281] Tg., [282] bTalmud [283]; the very free rendering of the LXX : καὶ διὰ τὰς ἁμαρτίας αὐτῶν παρεδόθη, with its ref. to martyrdom, also took the word in bonam partem. The Peshitta is the first to take יַפְגִּיעַ in malam partem, [284] and it is followed by Aquila, who acc. to Ps.-Chrys. (→ n. 278) transl.: occurret irridentibus eum, and Symmachus : καὶ τοῖς ἀθετοῦσιν (contradicentibus Ps.-Chrys.) ἀντέστη (Cod 86), "and he withstood those who rejected him." This understanding in malam partem persists in Theodotion, though in the version: et impios torquebit (Ps.-Chrys.). In him, then, the chapter on the suffering servant of God concludes with the horrible picture of the servant torturing the ungodly. Unless we assume a gross misunderstanding on the part of the Ps.-Chrys. text, which has unfortunately been preserved only in Armen., the starting-point of interpretation will have to be the fact that LXX 'A Tg. agree in regarding Is. 53:9 as a depiction of the last judgment, [285] so that the "torture" of Theodotion is a ref. to eternal damnation. [286] The fact that he found in the servant the final Judge shows that he understood Is. 53 Messianically. [287]

Theodotion, unlike Aquila and Symmachus, did not make a new transl. He took the LXX, in use also among Christians, as his basis, and time and again improved it in accordance with the original. It is to be expected, then, that in some of his corrections he tried to exclude Christological interpretations which the LXX made possible. The passage already mentioned (53:12) suggests this. It is not surprising that Θ replaced the LXX text (καὶ διὰ τὰς ἁμαρτίας αὐτῶν παρεδόθη), for the LXX had translated

machusstudien," III, Biblica, 29 (1948), 38 f. = Aus frühchristlicher Zeit (1950), 108 f.
[276] F. Delitzsch, Der Messias als Versöhner (1885), 21; Schlatter, 50; Aytoun, 176; North, 11; cf. Riesenfeld, 84; Torrey, JBL, 66 (1947), 257.
[277] Acc. to Epiph. De mensuris et ponderibus, 17 (under Commodus, 180-192).
[278] Up to 1939 research had at its command only the collection of Hexapla material in F. Field, Origenis Hexaplorum quae supersunt (1875). For Is. we now have instead of this work the excellent Hexapla apparatus in Ziegler, Isaias. Though Field's work was outstanding for its time, Ziegler has been able to improve it from the MSS at many pts., and above all he adduces for the first time the Hexapla refs. found 1. in the comm. on Is. by Theodoret of Cyrus (ed. A. Möhle [1933]), 2. in a comm. on Is. which has come down in Armen. and is supposed to be by Chrys. (ed. Venice, 1880), and 3. in the comm. on Is. by Eus., which has not yet been edited and is preserved in the margin of the Florentine Cod. Laurentianus Pluteus, XI, 4. [N. 279 omitted, 1965].
[280] Just. Apol., 50, 2 : καὶ τοῖς ἀνόμοις ἐξιλάσεται ("he will make atonement," → III, 315, 24).
[281] Et pro transgressoribus rogavit.
[282] "And for his sake gainsayers will be forgiven."
[283] bSota, 14a : " 'He interceded for the transgressors' (Is. 53:12): for he implored mercy for the transgressors of Israel that they might return in penitence ; by this 'intercession' no other than prayer is meant."
[284] Hegermann, I, 82 f. on Is. 53:12 Peshitta.
[285] Ibid., I, 37 f., 56 f. on Is. 53:9 Tg.
[286] Hegermann, II compares Is. 66:24; Mt. 25:41, 46.
[287] Cf. the further observations, ibid., II. Symmachus supports a Messianic interpretation.

very freely here. But the fact that in place of the LXX statement about the substitutionary martyrdom of the servant he put an expression which in its offensive severity is not supported by the Heb. ("and he shall torture the ungodly") might well be due to opposition to the Chr. use of the LXX (cf. R. 4:25). Among the few fragments of the transl. of Is. 53 [287a] we also find a curious rendering of 53:12d : וְאֶת־פֹּשְׁעִים נִמְנָה, "and he was numbered with the transgressors." Here the LXX translates : καὶ ἐν τοῖς ἀνόμοις ἐλογίσθη, but Θ : καὶ τῶν ἀσεβῶν ἀπέσχετο (Cod 86), "and he held aloof from the ungodly." The surprising thing in this instance is that Θ replaces a perfectly accurate LXX rendering by its exact opposite ; the servant numbered among the transgressors (Heb., LXX, 'A, Σ) becomes in Θ the servant who holds aloof from them. [288] In this alteration anti-christian bias might again have played a part. Indeed the LXX already exhibits a tendency to modify or eliminate the passion texts of Is. 53, [288a] but it stops before 53:12 [1965]. 53:12d was esp. important for Christians (cf. Lk. 22:37) because it did not just refer generally to the servant's suffering but stated that he was vicariously (53; 12e) numbered among the transgressors. More plainly than anywhere else in Is. 53 they found here a prophecy of the scandal of the cross. By turning the text into its opposite Theodotion was perhaps seeking to make the Chr. interpretation impossible. [288b]

(g) Tg. Is. Chronologically the Aram. transl. of Is. must be considered next, for although the Tg. Is. [289] in its present form is no older than the 5th century A.D., the text was fixed long before. The history of the oral tradition of transl., whose result the Tg. represents, goes back to the pre-Chr. period. [290] In particular, it may be shown that

---

[287a] Careful analysis of the extant fragments by Hegermann, 45-52 [1965].

[288] Hegermann, 51. R. Brinker (London) made to the author the illuminating suggestion that Theodotion read נִמְנַע ("he held aloof") for נִמְנָה ("he was numbered").

[288a] 53:5b : instead of "he was bruised," μεμαλάκισται "he was sickly"; 53:8c : instead of "he was cut off," αἴρεται "(his life) was taken away," i.e., "lifted up" (Fascher, 8); 53:9ab : reinterpreted to mean that the verdict is passed upon the wicked and the rich ; 53:10a : "to bruise" becomes "to cleanse"; 53:10b : the Heb. text is corrupt, but it is clear that it contains a statement about the servant which the LXX evades by changing the subj. to the 2nd pers. plur. [1965].

[288b] Note that Theodotion does not eliminate the servant's passion and death in general, but only his dying ignominiously, Hegermann, 114 [1965].

[289] Editions : P. de Lagarde, Prophetae Chaldaice (1872) acc. to the Cod Reuchlini ; with apparatus Stenning (1949). The section Is. 52:13-53:12 has also been published by G. Dalman, Aram. Dialektproben² (1927), 10 f. The very creditable work of Seidelin reaches very debatable conclusions because he misses the distinction between Hell. Jewish and Palestinian Jewish exegesis of Is. 53, and in his evaluation of Rabb. material fails to differentiate between allusions to and interpretations of Is. 53. Furthermore, he does not realise the antiquity of Rabb. interpretations of Is. 53:4 and underrates the significance of anti-Christian polemic.

[290] An esp. clear example of the great age of the transl. tradition preserved in the Tg. is furnished by Is. 6:10. The HT reads : וְרָפָא לוֹ, LXX καὶ ἰάσομαι αὐτούς, Σ καὶ ἰαθῇ. The Tg. transl. very differently : וְיִשְׁתְּבֵיק לְהוֹן, "and they shall be forgiven"; רְפָא ("to heal") is confused with רָפָה ("to remit"), Schl. Mk. on 4:12. This version of the text is very old, for it appears in syP : ונשתבק לה and Mk. 4:12 : καὶ ἀφεθῇ αὐτοῖς (cf. T. W. Manson, The Teaching of Jesus [1948], 77; → 555, n. 116). As concerns Is. 53 in particular, it is easy with the help of LXX, Peshitta, 'A, Σ, Θ to give many instances of the antiquity of the text preserved in the Tg. A few examples may be offered : 1. Is. 52:13 : on the age of the expression עַבְדִי מְשִׁיחָא → 682, 2 ff. 2. Is. 53:3b is referred by the Tg. (not the Heb. or LXX) to the turning aside of the Shekinah, as already in 'A ; 3. Is. 53:4 : for חֳלָיֵנוּ "our sicknesses," Tg. has חוֹבָנָא, also LXX : ἁμαρτίας ἡμῶν. 4. Is. 53:5 : the LXX derives מְחֹלָל from חָלַל po, "to pierce" : ἐτραυματίσθη, but the Tg. derives it from חָלַל pu, "to be put to shame" : אִיתַּחַל "he was profaned," so already 'A : βεβηλωμένος. 5. Is. 53:7: LXX and Itala derive נגש from נָגַשׂ, "he was mistreated," but the Tg. derives it from נָגַשׁ "he drew near," so already Σ and Vg. 6. Is. 53:9 : the ref. to the judgment in Tg. is found already

the Messianic interpretation of the servant texts Is. 42:1 and 52:13 in Tg. Is. is old. Of the 19 Ebed Yahweh passages in the Heb. (→ 682, 16 f.) only 3 are construed Messianically in Tg. Is.: 42:1; 43:10; 52:13.[291] In all 3 the Heb. עַבְדִּי is rendered עבדי משיחא by the Tg.[292] Our findings thus far support the conclusion that the Messianic understanding of 42:1 and 52:13 rests on ancient tradition, → 686 ff.[293] We are led to the same conclusion by the fact that the description of the Messiah as the servant of God occurs only in the pre-Rabb. stratum of later Jewish literature (4 Esr., S. Bar. → 681, 15 ff.) but nowhere in Rabb. writings outside the Tg., → 682, 2 ff. In particular, the antiquity of the Messianic interpretation of Is. 52:13 in the Tg. is shown by the fact that Tg. Is. takes the whole of 52:13-53:12 Messianically; for the Messianic understanding of esp. 53:1-12 cannot, as we saw (→ 690, 19 f.), have arisen only in the Chr. period.

Tg. Is. 52:13-53:12 runs: "(52:13) Behold, my servant, the Messiah, will have success, will become very high, great and strong. (14) As the house of Israel hoped for him many days when their appearance was darkened in the midst of the peoples and their glory less than that of men, (15) so he will scatter many peoples; for his sake kings will be silent, will lay their hand on their mouth; for what they have not been told they see, and what they have never heard of they perceive. (53:1) Who believed this our message, and to whom was the strength of the arm of Yahweh thus[294] revealed? (2) And the righteous[295] shall be great before him, lo, as sprouting branches and as a tree which sends out its roots to brooks of water, so shall the holy generations increase in the land which needed him (the Messiah). His appearance is not like that of a profane thing, and the fear which he inspires is not an ordinary fear, but his radiance will be a holy radiance so that whoever sees him will gaze (fascinated) upon him. (3) Then he will be despised and will (cause to) cease[296] the glory of all kingdoms. They will be

---

in LXX, 'A and Θ, → 691, 23 f. 7. Is. 53:10: the LXX already has καθαρίσαι for דַּכְּאוֹ, Tg. מְצָרַף (cf. Hegermann, I, 54-58).

[291] Of the other 16 passages Tg. refers a. Is. 41:8, 9; 44:1, 2, 21 (twice); 45:4; 48:20; 49:3 to Israel, probably also 49:5, 6 (→ n. 214); b. 42:19 (twice) to penitent sinners (→ n. 219); c. 50:10 to the prophets (→ n. 220); d. it probably read the Heb. at 44:26 as a plur. (→ n. 221); e. at 53:11 (HT עַבְדִּי) it has an infin.: "to make servants of the law."

[292] There is textual uncertainty only at Tg. Is. 42:1. Here Cod Reuchlini (→ n. 289), Cod Nuremberg (Stenning, XXIX) and the Vilna ed. (1893) read עבדי משיחא, but Cod Orientalis 2211 (Brit. Museum) and others simply have עבדי. The reading עַבְדִּי משיחא, however, is supported by the fact that the whole Palestinian tradition — as distinct from the Hell., → 684, 2 ff. — from the pre-Chr. era onwards expounds Is. 42:1 ff. Messianically, → 699, 11 ff.

[293] The Messianic interpretation of Is. 43:10, possibly based on the Heb. עַבְדִּי on the lips of God as in 42:1 and 52:13 (Seidelin, 228), finds on the contrary no par. in other later Jewish writings: Midr. Ps. 51 § 3 on 51:4 refers Is. 43:10 to David. But Jerome in Is. 43:1-10 says that the Jews had interpreted the passage de secundo Salvatoris adventu, quando post plenitudinem gentium omnis salvandus sit Israel, Seidelin, 222, n. 79.

[294] כדין; ed. Venice (1517): כדון ("now"), probably a scribal error.

[295] צדיקיא (plur.); but Cod Reuchlini (→ n. 289), Biblia Hebraica Rabbinica (ed. J. Buxtorf the elder [1618/19]) and the Arab. transl. of Tg. J. I (1196 A.D., cf. Dalman, I, 48, n. 1) read the sing. צדיקא. The sing. is supported by the striking sing. of the immediately preceding and related verb וְיִתְרַבָּא. It could refer to the Messiah (cf. the Messianic interpretation of the v. by R. Berechiah [c. 340], which seems to have been removed from Talmudic literature, → n. 313). Yet a collective sing. was probably meant, so that there is no difference in sense between the better attested plur. and the sing. reading.

[296] The textual question which arises here is of gt. importance. There are two possible readings which are hardly distinguishable in writing but quite different in content. 1. Cod Orientalis 2211 (Brit. Museum), most MSS, also the Vilna ed. (1893) read יפסיק (aph'el: "he will cause to cease"); 2. But Cod Orientalis 1474 (Brit. Museum) reads יפסוק (qal: "it will cease"). In Cod Reuchlini יפסק is ambiguous on account of the missing mater

weak and pitiable — lo, as a man of sorrows and as one destined for sicknesses, and as when the *shekinah* turns its face from us, the despised and unesteemed. (4) Then he will make intercession for our transgressions, and for his sake our iniquities will be forgiven, though we were accounted stricken, smitten by Yahweh and afflicted. (5) But he will build up the sanctuary which was desecrated because of our transgressions and delivered up because of our sins, and through his teaching his peace [297] will be richly upon us, and when we gather around his words our transgressions will be forgiven. (6) We were all scattered as sheep, every one went his own way into exile ; but it was Yahweh's will to forgive the iniquities of us all for his sake. (7) When he prays, he receives an answer and he hardly opens his mouth before he finds a hearing. He will hand over the strong of the peoples to be slaughtered like a lamb, and as a ewe that is dumb before its shearers, and no one will (dare to) open his mouth and put in a word (sc. of advocacy). (8) He will bring back our exiles out of suffering and chastisement. Who can recount the wonders which will come upon us in his days ? For he will remove the dominion [298] of the peoples from the land of Israel ; he will lay on them [299] the transgressions of which my people was guilty. (9) And he will deliver up the ungodly to hell, and those who have enriched themselves by robbery to (eternal) destruction, so that those who commit sin may not be preserved and may not (any longer) speak deceitfully with their mouth. (10) And it pleased Yahweh to refine and purify the remnant of his people, to cleanse their soul from iniquities. They will see the royal dominion of their Messiah ; they will have many sons and daughters ; [300] they will live long, and those who keep the law of Yahweh will by his good pleasure prosper. (11) He will cause their soul to escape from the bondage of the nations ; they will see the chastisement of those that hate them, and will be satisfied with the plunder of their kings. By this wisdom he will pardon the innocent, to make many servants of the law. And for their transgressions he will make intercession. (12) Hereafter I will apportion to him the spoil of many people, and he will divide the possession of strong towns as booty, because he gave up [301] his soul to death, and subjugated gainsayers to the law. And he will make intercession for many transgressions, and gainsayers will be forgiven for his sake."

It may be seen how, step by step, Tg. Is. 52:13-53:12 depicts the glorious establishment of the Messianic rule over Israel. By consistent artificial reinter-

---

lectionis. The two readings presuppose different subjects. In the first (יְפַּסֵּיק) the Messiah is the subj. : "Then he will be despised and will cause to cease the glory of all kingdoms" (favoured by Wünsche, 41; Humbert, 445; 38, n. 1; Str.-B., I, 482; II, 284; Kittel, 179; Brierre-Narbonne, 99; North, 12). In the second (יְפַּסוּק) the subj. is "the glory of all kingdoms" and the transl. is : "Then the glory of all kingdoms will turn to shame and will cease" (favoured by Dalman, 10, n. 18; Seidelin, 207, 211 f.). The textual evidence plainly supports the first reading ; the weakly attested second reading also stands under the suspicion of being designed to set aside the suffering of the Messiah. Thus in Tg. Is. 53:3, in the saying : "Then he will be despised," it is highly probable that we have a trace of the Messianic passion in the Tg. text.

297 שלמיה; Cod Reuchlini, Cod N (→ n. 292) and Venice ed. (1517): שלמא (without suffix).

298 שולטן can also mean "ruler."

299 With Dalman, 11, n. 6 ימטי is to be read as aph'el == יַמְטֵי (Cod Orientalis 2211 [Brit. Museum]: יְמְטֵי).

300 With Dalman, 11, n. 9 יסגון is to be read as aph'el יַסְגּוּן (Cod Orientalis 2211 יִסְגּוּן).

301 As Dalman, I, 48, n. 3 has shown, it is not necessarily implied that death has taken place ; commitment to the danger of death might be intended (so also Str.-B., I, 482 f.; Seidelin, 215, n. 62). The text does not say on what occasion he "gave himself up to death." The ref. might be to the war preceding the Messianic age (Weber, 361; Seidelin, 215), or more probably, in acc. with the original, to death (or danger of death) from maltreatment, cf. Is. 53:7 f.

pretation the statements about the sufferings of the servant of God are so radically eliminated that only at two points do weak traces remain. [302] By reason of its freedom of paraphrase, which is unusual in the translation technique of the Tg., the section Tg. Is. 52:13-53:12 stands alone in the total context of Tg. Is. 40-66, which elsewhere keeps much more closely to the Heb. [303] Though we have already noted an earlier tendency of the LXX to attenuate the passion texts of Is. 53 [1965], there is only one possible explanation for this violent wresting of the chapter in the Tg., with its consistent reversal of the meaning, namely, that we have here an instance of anti-Christian polemic. [304] From the 2nd cent. at the latest Judaism sought in various ways to rescue Is. 53 from its use by Christians as a Christological proof from Scripture, → 697, 19 ff. The curious version of Is. 53 in the Tg. shows with what consistency this end was pursued. The whole section is expounded Messianically because the Messianic interpretation of Is. 52:13-53:12 was now so firmly established that Tg. Is. could not avoid it. In abrupt contrast with the original, however, the passion sayings were replaced by the current view of the Messiah. The fact that this radical process of reinterpretation was carried through in respect of the Gk. text (→ 691, 27 ff.) as well as the Aram. shows how firmly rooted the Messianic understanding was in Palestinian Judaism.

(h) The Rabbis. On the part of the Rabbis only two of the servant passages in Dt. Is. were in fact expounded Messianically: 42:1 ff. and 52:13 ff. [305] These are the two sections which we have thus far found to be constantly understood in a Messianic sense. As regards Is. 42:1 ff., it is essential to note that there is in Rabb. literature no instance of any other interpretation of the servant of God here than the Messianic. [306] As regards Is. 52:13-53:12 there is attestation in the Rabb. [307] for a Messianic interpretation of both the sayings about exaltation and also those about suffering. [308] In particular, the reference of the passion sayings of Is. 53 to the Messiah is to be found very early in several Rabbinic writings.

---

[302] There are 2 such pts. in Tg. Is.: 1. Tg. Is. 53:3: "He will be despised" יהי לבסרן → n. 296; 2. Tg. Is. 53:12: "He gave up his soul to death" מסר למותא נפשיה → n. 301; Humbert, 5; Bonsirven, I, 383; Fischel, 70.

[303] Aytoun, 172.

[304] This is generally acknowledged. Dalman, I, 43-49 tried to escape this conclusion but later had to accept it, G. Dalman, Jesus-Jeschua (1922), 156. The tendentious revision is plainly distinguishable from an older version, Hegermann, I, 48-54. Later, too, Jewish exegesis of Is. 53 was palpably controlled by opposition to the Christian interpretation, Fischel, 66 f.

[305] Whether Is. 49:6 should be mentioned as a third instance is extremely doubtful. Raymundus Martini, op. cit., 645 certainly read a Messianic interpretation of Is. 49:6 in Gn. maior on 41:44 (Dalman, I, 97, n. 1), and in the post-Talmudic period there is one instance of a Messianic interpretation of 49:8: Pesikt. r., 31, Seidelin, 218; Fischel, 62. This isolated interpretation might well have been influenced by an older tradition in view of Sir. 48:10 (→ 686, 28 ff.), the Visionary Discourses of Eth. En. (→ 688, 1 f.) and the NT (→ n. 403). But this is not certain. Tg. at any rate does not take 49:6 Messianically (→ n. 214), and there is no other support for the Rabb. interpretation of 49:6 apart from the two late texts mentioned.

[306] Midr. Ps. 2 § 9 on 2:7 (Str.-B., I, 483); 43 § 1 on 43:3 (ibid., I, 87); Pesikt. r., 36 (ibid., II, 288); Jalqut Shim'oni, II, 88d, 104d (Dalman, I, 97, n. 1); Seder Gan 'Eden (ed. A. Jellinek, Bet ha-Midrasch, III [1885], 133, 12). Cf. also Tg. Is., ad loc., → 693, 1-5.

[307] For a selection of Rabb. texts cf. Str.-B., I, 481-483; also 50 f.

[308] Rabb. refs. of the exaltation sayings of Is. 52:13 ff. to the Messiah are Tg. Is., ad loc. (→ 693, 13 ff.); Tanch. תולדות § 20 (70a Buber); Midr. Ps. 2 § 9 on 2:7. For further examples and pars. v. Wünsche, 76; Dalman, I, 84, n. 3; Str.-B., I, 483. Cf. Moore, III, 166.

Unfortunately the first witness is textually uncertain. Raymundus Martini (after 1278),[309] who usually proves to be trustworthy [1965],[310] read in S. Lv. a saying of R. Jose the Galilaean (before 135 A.D.) which interpreted Is. 53 in terms of the suffering and grieving King-Messiah who through his suffering justifies all peoples. This statement, which seeks to give information about "the merit of the King-Messiah and the recompense of the just," opens with a ref. to the fact that the one transgression of Adam caused innumerable sentences of death, and concludes from this by means of the axiom of God's two different measures:[311] If Adam's sin had already caused such punishment to fall upon him and his followers, though God punishes less than is deserved, "how much more then will the King, the Messiah, who suffers and sorrows for the godless, justify all mankind, as it is written: 'But he was wounded for our transgressions' (Is. 53:5). The same is meant by Is. 53:6: 'The Lord hath laid on him the iniquity of us all.'" In our S. Lv. texts there is a different form of this passage (S. Lv., 12, 10 on 5:17).[312] Here, the subject is limited to the "recompense of the just," not the "merit of the Messiah," and the contrast with Adam's sin is not the passion of the Messiah but the fulfilment of certain commandments by the just. Which reading is the original one? In the light of the severity with which Judaism opposed the Chr. interpretation of the passion texts of Is. 53, we must reckon with the possibility of textual excision, esp. since the Messianic interpretation of Is. 53 seems to have been eliminated in other places as well, cf. → n. 328a. In this part. instance, however, the Messianic form attested by Raymundus Martini is probably secondary. The idea of a Messiah who acquires merit by suffering for the ungodly fits poorly into an assertion which focuses on the "recompense of the just"; in fact, the whole context is concerned with those who fulfil or break the Law.[313] The reading preserved in the present text of S. Lv., which contrasts Adam and the righteous, the one who violated and the one who fulfils the commandment, appears to be original. — Next comes a witness from the middle of the 2nd cent. A.D., Justin's Dial. with Trypho. Just. tells us that Trypho[314] several times conceded quite explicitly that the Messiah was παθητός, 36, 1; 39, 7; 49, 2; 68, 9; 76, 6-77, 1; 89, 1-2; cf. esp. 90, 1: παθεῖν μὲν γὰρ καὶ ὡς πρόβατον ἀχθήσεσθαι (= Is. 53:7) οἴδαμεν. He also says that this was the opinion of the Jewish teachers (διδάσκαλοι) in general, 68, 9. Now the statements of an apologist are to be viewed with caution. On the other hand, they are not too be dismissed too lightly. The credibility of Justin's account of his dialogue with Trypho is strengthened by his frank admission that it was a failure. Therefore, his report seems to be trustworthy that the final parting of the ways occurred not over the preliminary question of whether the Messiah was παθητός, but over the Chr. doctrine that he had not only suffered, but died on the cross, a death upon which God had laid his curse.[315] Still, Justin's statements must not be pressed. It is to be noted that, acc. to him, Trypho and the other Jewish rabbis whom Just. quotes do not advance

---

[309] Op. cit. (→ n. 273), 675, Dalman, I, 79 f., 44, n. 2; text in Wünsche, 65 f.; Driver-Neubauer, II, 10 f. [For the rest of the original note → n. 310.]

[310] On the credibility of Raymundus Martini cf. L. Zunz, Die gottesdienstlichen Vorträge d. Juden historisch entwickelt² (1892), 301; H. L. Strack, art. "Raimundus Martin," RE³, 16, 414 f. On the soundness of his traditions, which has been brilliantly confirmed by a discovery in Prague (Dalman, II, 6), → n. 273; Driver-Neubauer, XXV-XXXV; L. Zunz, op. cit., 300-305; Strack Einl., 223 f. (bibl.).

[311] The axiom that God's measure of goodness is greater than that of punitive justice, i.e., that he punishes less but rewards more than is deserved (in addition to the ref. → supra cf. bYoma, 76a; bSanh., 100a; T. Sota, 4, 1; Midr. Qoh. 4:1 and cf. bSota, 11a; M. Ex. 12:12 par. 14:4 [1965]).

[312] First ed., Venice (1545), 15b; ed. Weiss (1862), 27a. [Originally n. 310.]

[313] Thus Dalman, I, 43, 81; Sjöberg, Der verborgene Menschensohn, 262 f. [1965].

[314] Trypho has often been identified with R. Tarphon (the most detailed presentation of this view is by T. Zahn, "Studien z. Justinus Mart.," Zschr. f. Kirchengeschichte, 8 (1885), 1-84, cf. 61-65. The evidence does not support this, as N. Hyldahl, "Tryphon u. Tarphon," Studia Theol., 10 (1956), 77-88, has conclusively shown [1965].

[315] Dial., 32, 1; 89, 2; 90, 1. Sjöberg, Der verborgene Menschensohn, 247-254 overstates his case in saying that Just.'s presentation at this pt. is just literary fiction [1965].

the idea of the Messiah's passion as part of their case, but concede it as Just. confronts them with Is. 53 [paragraph revised, n. 316 omitted, 1965].

The first incontestable quotation comes from the period c. 200, → n. 271. This is the naming of the Messiah as "the leper" and "the sick one," on the basis of Is. 53:4, in bSanh., 98b, → 690, 9 ff. We first find the idea that the servant is described as a leper (Is. 53:4) in Aquila, → 690, 2 ff. Aquila was a pupil of R. Akiba, → n. 263. It can hardly be an accident that R. Akiba himself taught a suffering of the Messiah, [317] and that R. Dosa (c. 180 A.D.), who for the first time in Rabb. literature expounds Zech. 12:12 with ref. to the slaying of the Messiah b. Joseph, [318] was reporting a saying of Akiba's pupil Jehuda b. El'ai. [319] R. Akiba, the most influential scholar of the first two centuries A.D., lived c. 50-135. [320] It was his school esp. which preserved the tradition of a Messianic interpretation of the passion sayings in Is. 53 [partly revised, 1965].

In the 3rd cent. R. Jochanan (c. 200-279), [321] and in the 4th R. Acha (c. 320), [322] refer Is. 53:5 : "He was wounded for our transgressions," to the sufferings of the Messiah. R. Berechiah (c. 340) follows with a Messianic interpretation of Is. 53:2. [323] In the post-Talmudic period examples are more numerous, [324] but on the whole they are still not too common. The paucity of testimony may be explained by the antithesis between this idea of the Messiah and the current view, and esp. by the opposition to Christianity.

(i) Opposition to Christianity. From the 2nd cent. A.D. the history of Jewish exposition of Is. 53 was increasingly affected by opposition to Christianity. [325] This process begins with the avoidance of such terms for the Messiah as "Servant of God" or "the Elect," which the pseudepigrapha had still used quite freely

---

[317] Str.-B., II, 284. Akiba deduced from the typology of the time of Moses and the time of the Messiah that the Messianic period would be one of 40 yrs. of affliction in the wilderness ; in support he appealed to Job 30:4 (Tanch. עקב, Vienna ed. [1863], 7b, → IV, 860, 26 ff.

[318] bSukka, 52a. The incidental nature of the ref. to Messiah b. Joseph and his death shows that this was a well-known idea, Moore, II, 370; → n. 243. The Messianic interpretation of Zech. 12:10 ff. is old : Jn. 19:37; Rev. 1:7 cf. Mt. 24:30; Tg. (Str.-B., II, 583 f.); Midr. (ibid., 298 f.). It may well go back to the original, → III, 849, 10 ff.; Torrey, JBL, 66 [1947], 253-277.

[319] Bacher Tannaiten, II, 389; Strack Einl., 131. It may be noted that two of Akiba's pupils, R. Jehuda and R. Nechemiah (both c. 150), took part in the oldest Rabb. discussion about the Messiah b. Joseph, Gn. r., 75 on 32:6.

[320] P. Benoit, "Rabbi Aqiba ben Joseph, sage et héros du Judaisme," Rev. Bibl., 54 (1947), 56.

[321] Rt. r., 5 on 2:14 (H. L. Strack, "Zur altjüd. Theol.," ThLBl, 2 [1881], 10 f.; Str.-B., I, 27; II, 285). As the name of the author one should read, with Yalqut Shim'oni, ad loc. § 603, R. Jochanan rather than R. Jonathan (Str.-B., I, 27; II, 285; Fischel, 62; Bacher Pal. Am., I, 312 already has the correct reading).

[322] Midr. Samuel, 19 § 1 (Str.-B., II, 287). On the vl. which gives R. Idi (I, c. 250) as the author cf. Dalman, I, 52, n. 1.

[323] Str.-B., I, 50 f.; → n. 313.

[324] Dalman, I, 53-84; Dalman, II, 3-18, and the comprehensive collection in Brierre-Narbonne, though this does not add materially to Dalman. Worthy of special note is the gt. depiction of the suffering of the Messiah in Pesikt. r., 34-37, which acc. to B. J. Bamberger, "A Messianic Document of the 7th Century," Hb. Un. Coll., 15 (1940), 425-431, was composed in Palestine in 632-637, but is based on much older materials. Is. 53, it is true, is here expressly quoted only in the form of the text in the Gn. r. maior of R. Moshe-ha-darshan (Wünsche, 79, n. 1 acc. to Raymundus Martini [→ n. 273], 664). But what is said about the vicarious punishment of the Messiah in Pesikt. r., 34-37 rests on the ideas expressed in Is. 53 (Dalman, I, 67), as is shown esp. by the allusion to Is. 53:11 in Pesikt. r., 37 (Moore, I, 552, n. 1). Pesikt. r., 34-37 tells how the Messiah, before he gloriously defeats Israel's enemies, is imprisoned and threatened with death until God comes to his rescue. Chr. influence is out of the question ; it is excluded, inter alia, by the fact that the Messiah is merely threatened with death, not killed (Fascher, 30 f.) [1965].

[325] There has as yet been no exhaustive treatment of the rich material on Judaism's anti-Chr. apologetic and polemic.

(→ 682, 2 ff.; n. 262), and also of the Messianic title "Son of Man" [326] and of the name Jesus, now a *nomen odiosum*, → III, 287, 11 ff. From the end of the 2nd cent. we find that apologetic weapons like textual alteration [327] and tendentious reinterpretation are used in the translation of Is. 53 in order to dull the force of passages which Christians might use in their proof from Scripture. This weapon is employed especially by Tg. Is., → 692 ff. A related form of apologetic is to be found in R. Simlai (c. 250), who refers Is. 53:12 to Moses, → n. 329. If possible, however, Is. 42:1 ff. and 53 are not used at all. [328] Indeed, it seems that Messianic interpretations of Is. 53 were sometimes expunged; in several instances there are at least grounds for suspecting this. [328a] These points are of great importance in assessing later Jewish exegesis of Is. 53. The widespread conclusion that the relative paucity of Messianic interpretations of Is. 53 in later Judaism shows that the latter was unfamiliar with the concept of a suffering Messiah fails to do justice to the sources, since it ignores the great part which — very understandably — the controversy with Christianity played in this matter.

The sparseness of the testimony is counterbalanced by the fact that a distinctly non-Messianic interpretation of Is. 53 is not to be found in the Rabb. literature of the first Christian millennium. [329] This is especially surprising when we consider

[326] As distinct from Eth. En., this does not occur in Slav. or Hb. En., nor in the whole of Rabb. literature (Str.-B., I, 959; there also the apparent exception in jTaan., 2, 1 [65b], 60).

[327] For an example of the changing of the Gk. text → 691, 27 ff.; for an example of the changing of the Aram. → n. 296.

[328] Fischel, 66, n. 67: "Probably the not very common use of 42:1 ff.; 50:4 ff. and 52:13 ff. in the Midrash is because of the great significance of these passages in Chr. exegesis."

[328a] Just. already accuses the Jewish teachers of having completely eliminated many passages of Scripture from the LXX (πολλὰς γραφὰς τέλεον περιεῖλον) which referred to the Crucified (Dial., 71, 2), though of the 4 mentioned by him (72, 1-73, 6; cf. 120, 5) 3 are obviously Chr. interpolations. At all events the rapid replacement of the LXX by Aquila (→ n. 202) shows that in the 2nd cent. the removal of unwanted texts was in fact a weapon in Judaism's conflict with Christianity. As regards Is. 53 in particular, "the single ref. of Is. 53 to the suffering Messiah in Sanh., 98b" shows that we have to reckon with textual abbreviations, Strack Einl., 79. This conclusion is supported by the report of mediaeval sources (Ibn Ezra, d. 1167 [or 1168]; acc. to Dalman, I, 40, n. 2 also מלחמת מצוה, composed 1240) that the section beginning with Is. 52:13 in Sota, 1. was referred to the Messiah. This interpretation does not occur in our texts of bSota, 1. Even Rashi (d. 1105) did not find a Messianic interpretation of Is. 52:13 ff. (apart from 53:4) in the Talmud; as he expressly says, he knew of it only from hearsay, Comm. on Is. 53 (text in Wünsche, 94). It is also surprising that a Messianic exposition of Is. 53 by R. Berechiah, who lived c. 340 (Str.-B., I, 49 f.), has come down to us only through the Christian Raymundus Martini (op. cit., 594), who wrote almost 1000 yrs. later (after 1278), while there is no trace of it in the older sources. The authenticity of the report that R. Berechiah interpreted Is. 53:2 Messianically is supported by the fact that this scholar championed the idea of the passion of the Messiah, Str.-B., II, 285 f.; cf. I, 86 f. Finally, the Messianic interpretation of Is. 53:5 by Moshe-ha-darshan (first half of the 11th cent.) in his work Gn. r. maior on 24:67 (text Dalman, II, 6 f. acc. to A. Epstein; Wünsche, 69 acc. to Raymundus Martini, 671, cf. Dalman, I, 79) is the only quotation by Raymundus from Gn. r. maior whose source cannot be found in the older literature, Dalman, I, 80 f. [1965; n. 313 in the original art.].

[329] It is very doubtful whether in the Palestinian Judaism of the first millennium (as distinct from Hell. Judaism, → 684, 9 ff.) there existed any other interpretation of Is. 53 than the Messianic, unless one takes into account bSota, 14a, where Is. 53:12 is referred by R. Simlai (c. 250) to Moses' intercession; this is, however, a reinterpretation on apologetic grounds, → 686, 19 ff. The passages collected by Str.-B. in the exc. "Js. 53 in der älteren Lit." (I, 481-485), under the heading "B. References to the Righteous" (I, 483-485), are refs. to individual texts taken out of context, → 684, 35 ff.; 686, 10 ff. The only Midr. example under "C. References to the People of Israel" (I, 485), namely, Nu. r., 13 on 13:2 (anonymous), is from a Midrash composed in the 12th cent.

Rabbinic sayings about the atoning power of death.[329a] This idea occupies a surprisingly large place in later Judaism. A criminal's death expiates his offence if he has made the expiatory vow, → n. 475; instruction in this vow was given to all the dying. Moreover later Judaism from pre-Christian times was familiar with the atoning power of the death of the high-priest, martyrs, the righteous, the patriarchs, and innocent children. It is remarkable that in this rich material there is no ref. to Is. 53.[330] For this there is only one possible explanation, namely, that already in the pre-Christian period Is. 53 was so firmly and exclusively connected with the Messiah in Palestinian Judaism that the linking of this chapter with the expiatory death of the righteous did not even come into consideration.[331]

To sum up, 1. the Messianic interpretation of the servant of Dt. Is. in Palestinian Judaism was confined to Is. 42:1 ff.;[332] 43:10;[333] 49:1 f., 6 f.;[334] and 52:13 ff.;[335] with this the NT evidence agrees.[336] 2. As far as Is. 42:1 ff. and 52:13 ff. are concerned, the Messianic understanding is constant from pre-Christian times. In this regard Is. 52:13 ff. is also taken to be a picture of the last judgment.[337] 3. As for the Messianic interpretation of the passion sayings in Is. 53:1-12, this can be traced back, if not with the same certainty, at least with a high degree of probability (→ esp. 90 f.), to the pre-Christian period.[338] Without exception right up to the Talmudic period the suffering of the Messiah is herewith regarded as coming

---

[329a] Lohse, 104-109; J. Jeremias, *Eucharistic Words,* 151 f. [1965].

[330] The one exception (R. Simlai, c. 250) is only apparent, → n. 329.

[331] I owe this important observation to E. Lohse. A note is needed on two objections to our conclusion. First, does not the repeated remark of the Evangelists that the disciples did not understand Jesus' predictions of the passion presuppose that the idea of Messianic suffering was completely unknown to them (cf. Rowley, 80-84 [1965])? Mk., however, records this lack of comprehension on the part of the disciples only after the second prediction of the passion (9:32 : οἱ δὲ ἠγνόουν τὸ ῥῆμα καὶ ἐφοβοῦντο αὐτὸν ἐπερωτῆσαι). This might well be a later variant of the very different objection of Peter (8:32 after the first prediction) whose antiquity is guaranteed by the sharpness of the reply of Jesus, which described Peter as Satan. Again, in Mk. the dullness of the disciples is by no means related only to the passion. It runs like a motif through the whole Gospel (4:13, 40 f.; 6:52; 7:18; 8:16-21; 9:32; 10:38), cf. W. Wrede, *Das Messiasgeheimnis in den Ev.* (1901), 93-114. Mk. has a remark on this dullness of the disciples in 6:52. 8:16-21, with its ref. to the doublet of the story of the feeding, is very plainly a literary composition. Lk. has a sharper version of the motif (cf. 9:45 with Mk. 9:32); he introduces it with no Marcan par. at 18:34. Finally, Jn. uses the motif in the form of constant and very extensive misunderstanding. Pars. in comparative religion make it probable that this is an epiphany motif, H. J. Ebeling, "Das Messiasgeheimnis u. d. Botschaft des Marcus-Evangelisten," ZNW Beih. 19 (1939), 167 f., 170. If this is correct, historical conclusions cannot be drawn. But even if not the lack of comprehension (ἀγνοεῖν in Mk. 9:32 can also mean "not to acknowledge") is understandable since the death and passion of the Messiah were in complete contradiction with popular Messianic expectation. Secondly, does not the offence which the Jews took at the preaching of the cross (1 C. 1:23) imply that the idea of a suffering Messiah was alien to them? In fact, the Messianic interpretation of Is. 53 seems to have been alien to Hell. Judaism, → 684, 9 ff. The more deeply, then, the manner of Jesus' death must have offended it ; the real scandal for Palestinian Judaism, too, was that death on the cross was accursed, Gl. 3:13; Just. Dial., 90.

[332] → 684, 7 f.

[333] Only in the Tg., ad loc. → 693, 2 ff. and n. 293.

[334] → 688, 1 ff. and n. 305 (cf. 686, 28 ff.).

[335] → 686-700.

[336] → 709, 9 ff. Only the Messianic interpretation of Is. 43:10 is not found in the NT.

[337] Hell. and Palestinian Judaism agree in referring Is. 52:13 ff. to the last judgment, Wis. 4:20 ff.; Eth. En. 46:4 f.; 48:8; 55:4; 62:1-9; 63:1-11, v. J. Jeremias, "Das Lösegeld für Viele," Judaica, 3 (1948), 263 f.

[338] This occurs in the Peshitta (→ 688, 30 ff., Aquila (→ 689, 21 ff.), Theodotion (→ 691, 6 ff.) and Rabb. texts (→ 697, 3 ff.), and there are probably traces in Tg. Is. 53 (→ 694,

before the definitive establishment or enforcement of his rule. [339] When the meaning of the Messiah's passion is discussed, the answer is that he suffers vicariously to expiate the sins of Israel. [340]

D. παῖς θεοῦ in the New Testament.

The expression παῖς (of God) [341] is rare in the NT, as in later Judaism (→ 677, 31-35): Mt. 12:18; Lk. 1:54, 69; Ac. 3:13, 26; 4:25, 27, 30. Of these 8 instances one refers to Israel (Lk. 1:54), 2 refer to David (Lk. 1:69; Ac. 4:25), and the other 5 to Jesus. [342] When the Magnificat says: ἀντελάβετο Ἰσραὴλ παιδὸς αὐτοῦ (Lk. 1:54), it is alluding to Is. 41:8 f.: σὺ δέ, Ἰσραήλ, παῖς μου Ἰακώβ, ὃν ἐξελεξάμην, σπέρμα Ἀβραάμ, ὃν ἠγάπησα, οὗ ἀντελαβόμην. The collective use corresponds to that of the OT (→ n. 175) and later Judaism (→ n. 177, 213). As in Ps. Sol. 12:6, righteous Israel is in view. Lk. 1:54 also has the same liturgical ring as Ps. Sol. 12:6; 17:21. The ref. to David as God's servant falls similarly within the framework of later Judaism. As there (→ n. 184), so in primitive Christianity the instances are in prayers: in the Benedictus at Lk. 1:69: ἐν οἴκῳ Δαυὶδ παιδὸς αὐτοῦ, in the prayer of the primitive Church after the release of the apostles at Ac. 4:25: ὁ τοῦ πατρὸς ἡμῶν διὰ πνεύματος ἁγίου στόματος Δαυὶδ παιδός σου εἰπών, [343] cf. also the eucharistic prayer over the cup in Did., 9, 2: εὐχαριστοῦμέν σοι, πάτερ ἡμῶν, ὑπὲρ τῆς ἁγίας ἀμπέλου Δαυὶδ τοῦ παιδός σου, "of whom David, thy servant, speaks" (i.e., in Ps. 80:8 ff.). [344] "David, thy servant," is thus a liturgical formula of later Judaism which primitive Christianity adopted.

The usage is also that of the OT and later Judaism when in 1 Cl., 39, 4 (= Job 4:18) angels, 5 Esr. 1:32; 2:1 (2nd cent. A.D.) the prophets, and 5 Esr. 2:18 Isaiah and Jeremiah are called servants of God (→ n. 174 on angels and n. 167 on the prophets).

I. παῖς θεοῦ as a Title of Jesus.

1. The Provenance of the Title.

Jesus is called παῖς θεοῦ in the NT with surprising infrequency, namely, in a quotation in Mt. (12:18 = Is. 42:1), and 4 times in Ac. (3:13, 26; 4:27, 30). In all 5 instances we have to do with early tradition.

In Mt. 12:18 this is clear from the mixed character of the quotation. Behind Mt. 12:18-20 (= Is. 42:1-3) lies the Heb. text, [345] but in the last v. of the quotation (12:21 =

---

31 ff.). Buber has argued very definitely (78, n. 6) against the theory that the Messianic interpretation of Is. 53 does not arise until the 2nd cent. A.D.

[339] Str.-B., II, 291.

[340] bSanh., 98b (also 98a → 690, 13 ff., cf. Str.-B., II, 286); Rt. r., 5 on 2:14, → n. 321; Midr. Samuel, 19 § 1, → n. 322; Pesikt r., 31 (Str.-B., II, 287); ibid., 36 (Str.-B., II, 288); Midr. Konen (Str.-B., II, 290). Cf. Str.-B., II, 291 f. Only acc. to the Peshitta does the Messiah suffer for the offences of many peoples, Hegermann, I, 69 on Is. 52:15. M. Rese, "Überprüfung einiger Thesen v. J. Jeremias zum Thema d. Gottesknechts im Judentum," ZTK, 60 (1963), 21-41, objects to my lines of argument → 684-700, but his art. is mainly based on secondary sources (this is esp. clear in his inadequate treatment of Tg. Is.), and adduces no new evidence. Nevertheless, this art. has drawn welcome attention to certain pts. at which my argument needed clarification [1965].

[341] In the NT always with possess. pronoun: ὁ παῖς μου (Mt. 12:18), σου (Ac. 4:25, 27, 30), αὐτοῦ (Lk. 1:54, 69; Ac. 3:13, 26), i.e., of God.

[342] Christians, on the other hand, are always → δοῦλοι (not παῖδες) θεοῦ.

[343] The text is over-full. The words πνεύματος ἁγίου are probably an ancient gloss.

[344] R. Eisler, "Das letzte Abendmahl," ZNW, 25 (1926), 6 f. has convincingly shown that this is the meaning of the apparently puzzling expression ἡ ἁγία ἄμπελος Δαυίδ.

[345] The wording of the Mt. text deviates most strongly from the LXX, whose collective understanding of παῖς in Is. 42:1 (→ 684, 3 ff.) would not allow of a ref. of the passage to Jesus. (As against the view of Kahle, op. cit., 167 that Mt. use an older lost Gk. transl. of Is., cf. P. Katz, "Das Problem des Urtextes der Septuaginta," Theologische Zeitschr., 5 [1949], 18.)

Is. 42:4d) the LXX is suddenly quoted.[346] Two hands are thus discernible,[347] and this suggests that the text has had an earlier history. That the first hand uses the Heb. pts. to the Semitic linguistic sphere. In the 4 refs. from Ac. (→ supra) the par. use of παῖς σου in 4:24-30 for David (v. 25) and for Jesus (27-30) shows that Luke is using archaic expressions which he has borrowed from the language of liturgical prayer, → 702, 26 ff.[348] The fact that he does not employ the formula except in his description of the primitive community of Jerusalem as given in Ac. 3 and 4 makes it clear that he was aware of its archaic character[348a] [1965].

It may be conjectured, however, that the designation of Jesus as παῖς θεοῦ underlies other NT passages as well. Esp. to be noted in this connection are the voice at the baptism (Mk. 1:11 and par.) and the voice at the transfiguration (Mk. 9:7 and par.).
Comparison of
Mk. 1:11 = Lk. 3:22[349] par. Mt. 3:17 with Is. 42:1 (quoted acc. to Mt. 12:18)

σὺ εἶ (οὗτός ἐστιν Mt.) ὁ υἱός μου   ἰδοὺ ὁ παῖς μου ὃν ᾑρέτισα,
     ὁ ἀγαπητός   ὁ ἀγαπητός μου
ἐν σοὶ (ᾧ Mt.) εὐδόκησα   ὃν εὐδόκησεν ἡ ψυχή μου·
(cf. Mk. 1:10 and par.: τὸ πνεῦμα ...   θήσω τὸ πνεῦμά μου ἐπ' αὐτόν
καταβαῖνον εἰς αὐτόν)

has long since raised the question whether the υἱός μου of the voice at the baptism and the transfiguration does not go back to παῖς μου (so LXX Is. 42:1). If so Mk. 1:11 and par.; 9:7 and par. are not mixed quotations from Ps. 2:7 and Is. 42:1, but originally only from the latter (HT), and the twofold παῖς μου (1. my servant, 2. my child) had even before Mk. been interpreted as υἱός θεοῦ in the Hell. sphere, where quite early the designation of Jesus as παῖς θεοῦ was avoided, → 702, 23 ff.[350]

The thesis that the voice at the baptism was originally based on Is. 42:1 alone is supported by many considerations. First, the heavenly voice in Mk. 1:11 is obviously designed to explain the impartation of the Spirit (1:10) as a fulfilment of Scripture.[351] As so often in OT quotations, e.g., in Rabb. literature, the continuation: θήσω[352] τὸ πνεῦμά μου ἐπ' αὐτόν (Is. 42:1 acc. to Mt. 12:18c), is implied but not directly cited. The voice from heaven is thus saying that the promise of the Spirit in Is. 42:1 has just been fulfilled. Secondly, when the text of the saying from heaven at the baptism and transfiguration vacillates between ἀγαπητός (Mk. 1:11 and par.; 9:7 par. Mt. 17:5 and Lk. 9:35 vl.; 2 Pt. 1:17) and ἐκλελεγμένος (Lk. 9:35), these are presumably alternative renderings of בָּחִיר in Is. 42:1, which is sometimes transl. ἐκλεκτός (LXX ΣΘ), some-

---

[346] The LXX has for לְתוֹרָתוֹ (Is. 42:4): ἐπὶ τῷ ὀνόματι αὐτοῦ, which must be a slip for ἐπὶ τῷ νόμῳ αὐτοῦ (Ziegler, Isaias, ad loc.), → 262, 5. The LXX error recurs in Mt. (τῷ ὀνόματι αὐτοῦ).

[347] Schl. Mt., 402. Mt. himself seems to be quoting from the LXX.

[348] J. C. O'Neill, The Theology of Acts in Its Historical Setting (1961), 135 (following M. J. Wilcox) [1965].

[348a] Ibid., 139 [1965].

[349] The Western reading at Lk. 3:22: υἱός μου εἶ σύ, ἐγὼ σήμερον γεγέννηκά σε (= LXX Ps. 2:7) is simply an assimilation of NT quotations to the OT original (supposed in this instance). The Western text often attempts this and it is one of its distinctive features, cf. Mk. 15:34 par. Mt. 27:46, where the Western replaces the Aram. quotation of Ps. 22:1 by the original Hebrew of the Bible.

[350] Dalman WJ, I, 227; Bousset, 57, n. 2; Lohmeyer, Gottesknecht, 9; Cullmann, Tauflehre, 11-13. There is a similar process at Jn. 1:34, where an original ὁ ἐκλεκτός becomes ὁ υἱός; the ref. is again to Is. 42:1.

[351] Dalman WJ, I, 227.

[352] The perf. of the Heb. is transl. as a future in Mt. 12:18.

times ἀγαπητός (Mt. 12:18). Thirdly, in Jn. 1:34 the voice from heaven at baptism [353] acc. to what seems to be the oldest text (→ n. 260) runs: οὗτός ἐστιν ὁ ἐκλεκτὸς τοῦ θεοῦ. But "the elect of God" is a Messianic title deriving from Is. 42:1, → 687 ff. Jn. 1:34 shows plainly that the voice at baptism must have been originally a uniform quotation from Is. 42:1. If so, this confirms the fact (→ 700, 27 ff.) that designation of Jesus as παῖς θεοῦ belongs to a very ancient (pre-Marcan) stratum of the tradition. [354]

Further indirect instances of παῖς θεοῦ predication and its antiquity are possibly furnished by the Johannine writings.

Our first ref. here is to Jn. 1:29, 36 : ἴδε ὁ ἀμνὸς τοῦ θεοῦ (+ v. 29 : ὁ αἴρων τὴν ἁμαρτίαν τοῦ κόσμου). It has been pointed out already (→ I, 338 f., 186, 1 ff.) that the phrase ὁ ἀμνὸς τοῦ θεοῦ contains both a material and a linguistic difficulty : 1. description of the Redeemer as a Lamb is unknown to later Judaism ; 2. the phrase ὁ ἀμνὸς τοῦ θεοῦ is a wholly unique gen. construction. Both difficulties are solved if we refer back to the Aram., where טַלְיָא means a. "lamb" and b. "boy," "servant." [355] The probable Aram. original of ὁ ἀμνὸς τοῦ θεοῦ is טַלְיָא דַאלְהָא (→ n. 164, 176) in the sense of עֶבֶד יהוה. [356] This conjecture is supported by the ref. of Jn. 1:29b (ὁ αἴρων τὴν ἁμαρτίαν τοῦ κόσμου) to the Ebed saying in Is. 53:12 (וְהוּא חֵטְא רַבִּים נָשָׂא), → I, 186, 7 ff. In the absence of any analogy in later Judaism the use of → ἀρνίον in Rev. (28 times) might well [357] derive from the same ambiguous טַלְיָא. [358] If this conjecture is right, then the use of παῖς θεοῦ for Jesus must have its origin in the Aram. speaking primitive Church.

Finally, the story of the predication in the early Church offers a surprising confirmation of its great antiquity. [359] Apart from 3 quotations [360] and Ac. the designation of Jesus as παῖς θεοῦ is found in Gentile Christian writings up to 170 A.D. only at 11 places and in 3 works.

It occurs 1. in the Did. in the ancient agape prayers (before the eucharist) [361] said before and after the meal (9, 2, 3; 10, 2, 3), and also in the anointing prayer (10, 7 Copt.); [362] in all 5 refs. we have the stereotyped formula διὰ Ἰησοῦ τοῦ παιδός

---

[353] Cullmann, Tauflehre, 13, 16; also Urchr.², 64 f.

[354] The implications of this are extraordinarily far-reaching. Not only is there no connection between the voice and enthronement, adoption etc., but in part. the question arises whether the designation παῖς θεοῦ does not play an essential role in the development of the Messianic title → ὁ υἱὸς τοῦ θεοῦ, which was unknown to later Judaism.

[355] For examples of טַלְיָא "servant" in West. Aram. dialects (Pal. Midrash, Pal. Talmud, Tg., Chr.-Pal. dialect) cf. Jeremias, Ἀμνὸς τοῦ θεοῦ, 116 f.

[356] C. J. Ball, "Had the Fourth Gospel an Aram. Archetype ?", Exp. T., 21 (1909/10), 92 f.; C. F. Burney, 107 f.; Loh. Apk., 52; Jeremias, Ἀμνὸς τοῦ θεοῦ, 115-123; Zolli, 228-233; W. F. Howard, Christianity acc. to St. Jn. (1943), 100 ff.; G. S. Duncan, Jesus, Son of Man (1947), 91, n. 4; Cullmann, Tauflehre, 16, n. 11; Gesù, 55; Urchr.², 65 f. Regarding the objection of C. H. Dodd in his review of the art. → ἀμνός in JThSt, 34 (1933), 285 that Tg. Is. renders עֶבֶד יהוה by עַבְדָּא, not טַלְיָא, we may refer back to what was said → 683, 12 ff., namely, that from c. 100 A.D. Gk.-speaking Judaism changes abruptly from παῖς θεοῦ to δοῦλος θεοῦ, and there is nothing against the assumption that Aram.-speaking Judaism made a similar change from טַלְיָא to עַבְדָּא. Furthermore, a text which uses טַלְיָא for the servant of God has now been found in Is. 52:13 syrpal → n. 156 [1965].

[357] Probably (in the absence of τοῦ θεοῦ) by way of ἀμνὸς τοῦ θεοῦ [K. G. Kuhn].

[358] → I, 339, 24-28; Loh. Apk., 52.

[359] This has been shown in exemplary fashion by the brilliant investigation of A. v. Harnack, op. cit. (Bibl.).

[360] Mt. 12:18; also Barn., who inserts παῖς κυρίου (6, 1) or παῖς μου (9, 2) into OT quotations.

[361] Jeremias, Abendmahlsworte², 66.

[362] Ed. C. Schmidt, "Das kopt. Didache-Fr. d. Brit. Museum," ZNW, 24 (1925), 85, cf. 94.

σου. [363] It occurs again 2. in the gt. prayer of the Roman church in 1 Cl., 59, 2-4. [364] It is also found 3. in the prayer of Polycarp, based on the eucharistic prayer of Smyrna, [365] in Mart. Pol., 14, 1-3, [366] and also in the closing doxology in Mart. Pol., 20, 2. [367] In all 11 instances, then, we have prayers, and except in the doxologies in 1 Cl., 59, 4 (→ n. 364) and Mart. Pol., 14, 1 (→ n. 366), the liturgical formula διὰ ᾽Ιησοῦ τοῦ παιδός σου is always used.

This simple formula is very old. [368] The very absence of Χριστός in the oldest examples of the formula (Ac. 4:30; Did., 9, 2 and 3; 10, 2, 3 and 7) shows this, [369] but especially the fact that διὰ Δαυὶδ τοῦ παιδός σου (Ac. 4:25) is a similar ancient Palestinian formula. [370] Furthermore, of the 4 passages in Ac., 2 are in a prayer (4:27, 30), and one of these has the formula διὰ ... τοῦ ... παιδός σου ᾽Ιησοῦ (4:30). Surveying the examples of the designation of Jesus as παῖς (θεοῦ), we may conclude 1. that in the Gentile Christian world the title παῖς (θεοῦ) never became a commonly accepted term for the Messiah (it does not occur at all in Paul), the titles κύριος, Χριστός, υἱὸς τοῦ θεοῦ being preferred in this sphere, and 2. that in the Gentile Church the title lived on only as a fixed liturgical formula anchored in the eucharistic prayer, the doxology and the confession. [371]

The period which followed confirms these conclusions. [372] παῖς (θεοῦ) remains infrequent. The title persists in prayers and doxologies, and elsewhere almost exclusively in solemn sacral speech. It does not make its way into dogmatic usage, but remains confined to the liturgy and lofty speech. From the 5th century παῖς disappears completely as a term for Christ. [373]

If our investigation thus far has pointed at every stage to the antiquity of the title and its Palestinian provenance, the report of Epiphanius that the Ebionites ἕνα θεὸν καταγγέλλουσι καὶ τὸν τούτου παῖδα ᾽Ιησοῦν Χριστόν [374] takes on added significance. Above all, however, the disappearance of the Messianic title "servant of God" in Palestinian Judaism (→ 682, 2 ff.) is indirect evidence that the designation of Jesus as God's servant was alive in Palestinian Christianity. The provenance of the title is thus to be sought in the earliest Palestinian community. [375] To the Gentile Church it was offensive from the very first because it did not seem to bring out the full significance of the majesty of the glorified Lord; [376]

---

[363] At Did., 10, 3 read ᾽Ιησοῦ with the Copt. transl.

[364] 1 Cl., 59, 2 : διὰ τοῦ ἠγαπημένου παιδὸς αὐτοῦ ᾽Ιησοῦ Χριστοῦ, 59, 3 : διὰ ᾽Ιησοῦ Χριστοῦ τοῦ ἠγαπημένου παιδός σου, 59, 4 : σὺ εἶ ὁ θεὸς μόνος καὶ ᾽Ιησοῦς Χριστὸς ὁ παῖς σου.

[365] Cf. v. Harnack, 221; Bousset, 56.

[366] Mart. Pol., 14, 1 : ὁ τοῦ ἀγαπητοῦ καὶ εὐλογητοῦ παιδός σου ᾽Ιησοῦ Χριστοῦ πατήρ, δι᾽ οὗ ... ; 14, 3 : διὰ ... ᾽Ιησοῦ Χριστοῦ, ἀγαπητοῦ σου παιδός.

[367] 20:2 : διὰ τοῦ παιδὸς αὐτοῦ τοῦ μονογενοῦς ᾽Ιησοῦ Χριστοῦ.

[368] v. Harnack, 235, n. 3 considers whether the common Pauline formula διὰ ᾽Ιησοῦ Χριστοῦ is based on διὰ ᾽Ιησοῦ τοῦ παιδός σου.

[369] v. Harnack, 219 f.

[370] Cf. 2 S. 3:18 : בְּיַד דָּוִד עַבְדִּי = LXX ἐν χειρὶ τοῦ δούλου μου Δαυίδ. 1 Macc. 4:30 : ἐν χειρὶ τοῦ δούλου σου Δαυίδ (with διά c. acc. Is. 37:35 : διὰ Δαυὶδ τὸν παῖδά μου, with δοῦλος : 3 Βασ. 11:13, 32, 34; 4 Βασ. 8:19; 19:34; 20:6, with ἕνεκεν, ψ 131:10).

[371] 1 Cl., 59, 4 : σὺ εἶ ὁ θεὸς μόνος καὶ ᾽Ιησοῦς Χριστὸς ὁ παῖς σου is a formula of confession.

[372] For materials cf. v. Harnack, 224-233.

[373] Ibid., 236-238.

[374] Epiph. Haer., 29, 7, 3. Cf. on this Bousset, 56, n. 2.

[375] Rightly noted by Bousset, 57. Cf. also → 709, 39 ff.

[376] C. Maurer, "Knecht Gottes u. Sohn Gottes im Passionsbericht d. Mk.-Ev.," ZTK, 50 (1953), 38; M. D. Hooker, Jesus and the Servant (1959), 109 [1965].

παῖς (θεοῦ), therefore, was already replaced by υἱὸς θεοῦ in the Hellenistic Jewish Christian Church, R. 1:3 → n. 354 [lines 1-2, 1965].

2. The Meaning of the Predication.

The fact that παῖς (θεοῦ) as a term for Jesus originally meant "servant (not child) of God" may be deduced already from the surprising reserve of the Gentile Church towards this predication — a reserve which can be due only to offence at the lowly character of the term. It may also be deduced, however, from the juxtaposition of David as the παῖς (of God) and Jesus as the παῖς (of God) in Ac. (David in 4:25, Jesus in 4:27, 30) and Did. (David in 9, 2, Jesus in 9, 2 and 3). For David is undoubtedly called God's servant here. [377] This juxtaposition of David and Jesus as "servants," which Ac. seems to find inadequate, [378] shows that παῖς is here a title of honour such as is applied to eminent men of God elsewhere (→ 680, 9 ff.) in later Judaism. [379] Still, when speaking of Jesus as παῖς (θεοῦ), the NT had to remember the servant passages of Dt. Is. sooner or later. This is demonstrated by the quotations Mt. 12:18, cf. Mk. 1:11 (→ 700 f.) as well as by the ref. to Is. 52:13 ff. in Ac. 3:13 ff. [380] [lines 13-16, 1965].

3. The Change of Meaning from Servant of God to Child of God.

In the sphere of Gentile Christianity παῖς (θεοῦ) as a term for Jesus acquired at the very latest in the 2nd century the meaning "child (of God)."

This shift in meaning is certainly to be seen in Mart. Pol., 14, 1: κύριε, ὁ θεὸς ὁ παντοκράτωρ, ὁ τοῦ ἀγαπητοῦ καὶ εὐλογητοῦ παιδός σου Ἰησοῦ Χριστοῦ πατήρ (as the combination of παῖς and πατήρ shows) and 20, 2: διὰ τοῦ παιδὸς αὐτοῦ τοῦ μονογενοῦς Ἰησοῦ Χριστοῦ (as the association with μονογενής shows). [382] It is probable [383] that the understanding of παῖς (θεοῦ) as "child (of God)" occurs already in 1 Cl., 59, 2 f., where Jesus Christ is called ὁ ἠγαπημένος παῖς. The formula σὺ εἶ ὁ θεὸς μόνος καὶ Ἰησοῦς Χριστὸς ὁ παῖς σου in 59, 4 also points to the sense "child of God." [384] On the other hand it is unlikely that Luke used παῖς (θεοῦ) at Ac. 3:13, 26; 4:27, 30 as a solemn expression for "Son (of God)," [385] considering that he undoubtedly understood it in the sense of "servant" in Ac. 4:25 [1965]. There can be no doubt that the change from servant of God to child of God was a gradual one,

---

[377] Furthermore παῖς θεοῦ in the sense of "child of God" is extremely rare in Hell. Judaism, → 678, 6-11.

[378] The fact that only at Ac. 4:27, 30 (not 3:13, 26) is the adj. ἅγιος found in connection with Jesus (ὁ ἅγιος παῖς σου Ἰησοῦς) could be due to the intention to make a distinction between the παῖς Jesus and the παῖς David (4:25).

[379] Thus esp. Cadbury, 367; E. Haenchen, Die Apostelgeschichte (Meyer, 3) on Ac. 3:13; Hooker, 109 f. [1965].

[380] Ac. 3:13: ὁ θεὸς ... ἐδόξασεν τὸν παῖδα αὐτοῦ Ἰησοῦν (cf. Is. 52:13: ὁ παῖς μου ... δοξασθήσεται), ὃν ὑμεῖς μὲν παρεδώκατε καὶ ἠρνήσασθε (cf. Is. 53:2 Peshitto; Eth. En. 48:10); 3:14: τὸν ἅγιον καὶ δίκαιον (cf. Is. 53:11: δίκαιον, → 687) ἠρνήσασθε; 3:18 (God) προκατήγγειλεν διὰ στόματος πάντων τῶν προφητῶν, παθεῖν τὸν χριστὸν αὐτοῦ. The ref. of Ac. 3:13 to Is. 52:13 also appears in the fact that Ac. 3:13 is the only text in the Synoptics and Ac. in which δοξάζειν has the meaning "transfigure" [1965]. [A short paragraph and n. 381 omitted here, 1965.]

[382] Cf. the ecstatic exclamation of the prophets mentioned by Celsus: ἐγὼ ὁ θεός εἰμι ἢ θεοῦ παῖς ἢ πνεῦμα, Or. Cels., 7, 9. The exclamation is modelled upon the Trinitarian formula, which shows that θεοῦ παῖς means "son of God" [1965].

[383] Dalman WJ, I, 228: "quite indisputable."

[384] We are taken back to an even earlier period if the conjecture is right that a παῖς μου lies behind the υἱός μου of the story of the baptism and the transfiguration (→ 701, 9 ff.) and that the title ὁ υἱὸς τοῦ θεοῦ developed out of ὁ παῖς τοῦ θεοῦ, → n. 354.

[385] Thus Haenchen, op. cit., on Ac. 3:13 [1965].

and that it did not take place everywhere at the same time. [386] The meaning "servant of God," as Did. shows (→ 704, 4-13), persisted most tenaciously in liturgical formulae.

How natural the understanding of παῖς θεοῦ as "child of God" must have been for Hell. sensibility is apparent from contemporary literature; for Hell. Judaism cf. what is said → 678, 17 ff.; 683, 9 ff., for Hell. paganism cf. Corp. Herm., XIII, 2: [387] ὁ γεννώμενος θεοῦ θεὸς παῖς, XIII, 4: ὁ τοῦ θεοῦ παῖς, ἄνθρωπος εἷς effects regeneration, XIII, 14: θεὸς πέφυκας καὶ τοῦ ἑνὸς παῖς. It may be added that there was something archaic and distinguished about the word παῖς, [388] so that, e.g., the emperor's son could be described as Καίσαρος παῖς. [389] Nevertheless, it should not be forgotten that παῖς always has a lowly ring as well; this is why παῖς θεοῦ was unable to establish itself in the Gentile Church in spite of the change of meaning from "servant of God" to "son of God," → 703, 13 ff.

II. Christological Interpretations of the Deutero-Isaianic Servant of God in the New Testament.

In our investigation of παῖς (θεοῦ) in later Judaism (→ 677 ff.) it has already become clear that purely linguistic enquiry, though an indispensable basis, does not lead us to the core of the problem of the servant of God. To get to this we have had to take up the question of the interpretation of the servant passages of Dt. Is. in later Judaism. The same holds good with respect to the NT. We reach the decisive question only when we ask 1. where christological interpretations of the servant passages of Dt. Is. are to be found in the NT, and 2. what is their setting in the primitive Church.

1. The References.

There are astonishingly few passages in the NT where a saying relating to the servant of God in Dt. Is. is applied to Jesus in express quotation: Mt. 8:17 (Is. 53:4); 12:18-21 (42:1-4); Lk. 22:37 (53:12); Jn. 12:38 (53:1); Ac. 8:32 f. (53:7 f.); [390] R. 15:21 (52:15). [391] Nevertheless, restriction to express quotations gives a false impression [392] and in this particular question even involves a serious error of method which has not always been avoided. [392a] If direct and indirect allusions are added to the quotations, the picture presented by the christological interpretations of the Deutero-Isaianic servant in the NT is as follows.

---

[386] The it cod. on Ac. 3:13, 26; 4:27, 30 give us a glimpse into the process, for in all 4 an original *puer* is gradually replaced by *filius*, v. Harnack, 218. There is vacillation in the cod. on this pt.; the Vg has *filius* at 3:13, 26; 4:30 but *puer* at 4:27 (under the influence of v. 25). In the Western Church the offence given by *puer* is "almost as old as the translation itself," v. Harnack, 218; Tert. already read *filius* at 4:27 in Bapt., 7; adv. Praxean, 28. The Syr. has בר in all 4 verses (3:13, 26; 4:27, 30). There is a similar vacillation on the part of the Chr. translator of 4 Esr. in the rendering of the Messianic designation παῖς μου, → n. 196 [conflating original n. 385 and n. 386, 1965].

[387] Corp. Herm., ed. A. D. Nock-A. J. Festugière, I and II = *Collections des Universités de France* (1945).

[388] v. Harnack, 225; he compares the German *Weib*, 237.

[389] Just. Epit., 2, 16; cf. Melito in Eus. Hist. Eccl., IV, 26, 7; Athenag. Suppl., 37, 1.

[390] In Ac. 13:47: τέθεικά σε εἰς φῶς ἐθνῶν τοῦ εἶναί σε εἰς σωτηρίαν ἕως ἐσχάτου τῆς γῆς (= Is. 49:6 LXX) one cannot say for certain whether the twofold σε refers to Jesus or the apostles. But the intr. (οὕτως γὰρ ἐντέταλται ἡμῖν ὁ κύριος) and comparison with Ac. 26:18 favour the second possibility.

[391] The christological ref. lies in περὶ αὐτοῦ.

[392] Rightly emphasised by Wolff, 69, 79, 85, 102, 106 etc. Even the usual restriction to Is. 53 and ignoring of the other servant passages foreshortens the picture.

[392a] Thus, by restricting the scope of her study to explicit quotations and to the idea of vicarious suffering as expressed in Is. 53, Miss Hooker is led to the conclusion that neither Jesus nor the early Church attached any particular christological significance to the servant texts of Dt. Is. Cf. against this Lohse², 220-224 [1965].

a. Pre-Pauline Tradition and Formulae. The first passage calling for mention here is the ancient kerygma in 1 C. 15:3-5, which contains Semitic features, [393] and whose κατὰ τὰς γραφάς (v. 3) must be referring to Is. 53 in view of the ὑπὲρ τῶν ἁμαρτιῶν ἡμῶν. [394] To the same pre-Pauline tradition belong the liturgically formulated [395] eucharistic sayings in 1 C. 11:23-25, [396] the christological formula of R. 4:25 [397] with its synthetic parallelism, the hymn to Christ in Phil. 2:6-11, [398] the confessional formula of R. 8:34, [399] the ransom saying in 1 Tm. 2:6 (→ n. 401), the ancient ὑπέρ formula with its variants (→ n. 435), very common in Paul, and finally the expression (παρ)έ-δωκεν ἑαυτόν which is in all instances connected with the ὑπέρ formula, Gl. 1:4; 2:20; Eph. 5:2, 25; 1 Tm. 2:6; Tt. 2:14. [399a] The refs. to Is. 53:12 and 11 contained in R. 5:16 (πολλοί), 19 (οἱ πολλοί) most probably are traditional too, as suggested by the fact that the Heb. text is in the background. [399b] That the use of Is. 53:1 (LXX) as quoted in R. 10:16 is pre-Pauline is confirmed by Jn. 12:38. [399c] Whether R. 8:32 is traditional cannot be determined with certainty, because Pl. refers to LXX. [399d] The only ref. to a servant passage which is undoubtedly due to Pl. himself is R. 15:21 where he grounds his missionary activity in Is. 52:15 LXX → 708, 31 ff. This means that all Pauline allusions to the Ebed Yahweh texts of Dt. Is. apart from R. 15:21 make use of ancient tradition.

b. Pre-Synoptic Tradition and Formulae. In the Synoptists, too, most of the refs. to the Ebed Yahweh sayings of Dt. Is. show that ancient tradition is used. The linguistic data make this plain in the case of the ancient eucharistic formula in Mk. 14:24 par. [400] and the λύτρον saying in Mk. 10:45 par. Mt. 20:28, [401] independence of the LXX proves it in the case of the voice at baptism in Mk. 1:11 par. ⊨ Is. 42:1, [402] the linguistic and stylistic character of the whole hymn Lk. 2:29-32 supports it in the case of Lk. 2:32, [403] the mixed character of the text argues in this direction in the case of Mt. 12:18-21 (= Is. 42:1-4) (→ 700, 29 ff.), and the relation to the HT pts. in the same direction in

---

[393] J. Jeremias, Abendmahlsworte², 96 f.
[394] Cf. Lohmeyer, Gottesknecht, 39; Cullmann, Gesù, 57 f.
[395] Jeremias, op. cit., 95-97.
[396] For the ref. to Is. 53 → n. 438 (παρεδίδοτο) and → 710, 11 ff. (ὑπέρ formula).
[397] παρεδόθη διὰ τὰ παραπτώματα ἡμῶν in R. 4:25a corresponds exactly to Is. 53:5b Tg. אֶתְמְסַר בַּעֲוָיָתַנָא; by contrast Is. 53:12 LXX (διὰ τὰς ἁμαρτίας αὐτῶν παρεδόθη) differs from R. 4:25 in vocabulary (ἁμαρτίας) and personal pronoun (αὐτῶν). For the pre-Pauline character of the formula cf. Ltzm. R., ad loc.; Stauffer Theol., 223; Bultmann Theologie, 47 [revised 1965].
[398] For the allusion to the Is. text (Heb.) → 711, 12 ff. Lohmeyer, Kyrios Jesus, has proved the pre-Pauline character of Phil. 2:6 ff.
[399] R. 8:34: ὃς καὶ ἐντυγχάνει ὑπὲρ ἡμῶν, takes up the end of Is. 53:12 (Heb.) → 710. The LXX differs. Cf. C. H. Dodd, According to the Scriptures (1952), 94 [1965].
[399a] The pre-Pauline age of the formula is shown by the translation variants → 710 [1965].
[399b] → πολλοί. Cf. S. Mowinckel, "Die Vorstellungen d. Spätjudentums vom heiligen Geist als Fürsprecher u. d. johanneische Paraklet," ZNW, 32 (1933), 121, n. 82; O. Cullmann, Christology of the NT² (1959), 77 [1965].
[399c] → 708, 24 ff. [1965].
[399d] R. 8:32: ὑπὲρ ἡμῶν πάντων παρέδωκεν αὐτόν, refers to Is. 53:6 LXX: καὶ κύριος παρέδωκεν αὐτὸν ταῖς ἁμαρτίαις ἡμῶν, → 710, 18 ff. [1965].
[400] For the ref. to Is. 53 cf. Jeremias, Abendmahlsworte², 108 ff., cf. 91-93. For the Palestinian character of the language, ibid., 88-94. For independence of the LXX (ὑπέρ does not occur in LXX Is. 53) → n. 434.
[401] For the ref. to Is. 53:10-12 Heb. cf. Jeremias, "Lösegeld," 262-264; also Abendmahlsworte², 92 f. For the Palestinian character, Jeremias, "Lösegeld," 260-262; Abendmahlsworte² 91-93.
[402] Cf. also → 701, 27 ff. on the antiquity of Mk. 1:11 and par. and 9:7 and par.
[403] The phrase in Lk. 2:32: φῶς εἰς ἀποκάλυψιν ἐθνῶν, is based on a servant text (לְאוֹר גּוֹיִם) which is literally the same in Is. 42:6 and 49:6, though the combination of Gentiles and Israel (Lk. 2:32a b) shows that Is. 49:6 is the closer.

respect of Lk. 22:37 (= Is. 53:12) [404] and Mt. 8:17 (= Is. 53:4 HT), → n. 347. The fact that the many general refs. to Scripture found in all three Synoptists in connection with the passion sayings of Jesus [405] are also — and probably even primarily — allusions to Is. 53 is demonstrated by the ancient [406] saying in Mk. 9:12 (ἐξουδενηθῇ cf. ἐξουδενωμένος in Is. 53:3 ᾽ΑΣΘ = נִבְזֶה) by the common παραδιδόναι formula (→ n. 437), and by Lk. 22:37. [407] That most of these refs. are pre-Synoptic is clear from, e.g., 1 C. 15:3 (→ 706, 1 ff.). The very slight role of the LXX in these Synoptic passages is quite astonishing ; whereas the influence of the Heb. may be seen in many of them, [408] that of the LXX is apparent only in the addition Mt. 12:21 (→ 700, 29 ff.) and Lk. 22:37 (→ n. 404). The result is similar to that in Paul. Almost all the refs. to the Ebed Yahweh sayings of Dt. Is. in the first three Gospels come from ancient tradition or formulae.

c. Tradition and Formulae in Acts. In Ac. we find at 8:32 f. a quotation from Is. 53:7 f. LXX which is applied to Jesus. It occurs in the traditional material relating to Philip, 8:5-40. [410] The antiquity of this is to be seen esp. from what is said about baptism in 8:12 ff., 36, 38 f. [411] The description of Jesus as παῖς, which is confined to Ac. 3 and 4, [412] is also part of a very old tradition, → 704, 4-10. Again, Jesus is three times called ὁ δίκαιος in Ac. (3:14; 7:52; 22:14). Since in all 3 instances there is an art. but no noun, this is a title, most probably the Messianic title "the Righteous One" which is known to us from Eth. En. (→ 689, 8 ff.) and which in the latter bears an allusion to Is. 53:11. Comparison of Ac. 22:13 f. with 9:17 (ὁ δίκαιος/ὁ κύριος) shows that ὁ δίκαιος is the older title. [413] Finally, in the addresses of Ac. the biblical passages quoted in connection with the passion and death of Jesus are so stereotyped [414] that we can only view them as a constituent part of the ancient kerygma. [415]

d. Primitive Formulae in 1 Peter ; Hebrews. In 1 Pt. 2:21-25 we find a whole series of free quotations from Is. 53 LXX (v. 22 : Is. 53:9; v. 24a : Is. 53:12; cf. 4, 11; v. 24b : Is. 53:5; v. 25 : Is. 53:6); these are used in part as formulae. Furthermore, in 1 Pt. 3:18

---

[404] Lk. 22:37: καὶ μετὰ ἀνόμων ἐλογίσθη, cf. Is. 53:12 : וְאֶת־פֹּשְׁעִים נִמְנָה; on the other hand LXX Is. 53:12 : καὶ ἐν τοῖς ἀνόμοις ἐλογίσθη. The words ἄνομοι and λογίζεσθαι are taken from the LXX ; the prep. μετά and the missing art., on the other hand, betray the influence of the HT [revised 1965].
[405] Mk. 8:31 par. (δεῖ); 9:12 par.; 14:21 par.; (γέγραπται); 14:49 par. (ἵνα πληρωθῶσιν αἱ γραφαί); Lk. 18:31 (τελεσθήσεται πάντα τὰ γεγραμμένα διὰ τῶν προφητῶν); cf. Mk. 10:32 par. (μέλλειν, so also Mt. 17:12, 22; Lk. 9:44); peculiar to Mt. 26:54 (πῶς οὖν πληρωθῶσιν αἱ γραφαί ... δεῖ) and peculiar to Lk. 13:33; 17:25; 24:7, 25-27, 44-46 (δεῖ); 9:31 (ἤμελλεν πληροῦν); 22:22 (κατὰ τὸ ὡρισμένον); 24:32 (διήνοιγεν ... τὰς γραφάς); 24:44 (δεῖ πληρωθῆναι πάντα τὰ γεγραμμένα), 46 (γέγραπται).
[406] Otto, 197-199; Michaelis, 8 f. The antiquity is clear from the imprecise form of the intimation of the passion and the fact that the four-membered statement in Mk. 8:31 is obviously a later extension of the two-membered statement in 9:12. H. Tödt, The Son of Man in the Synoptic Tradition (1965), 164 ff. finds in Mk. 9:12 an allusion to Ps. 118:22 because this v. is quoted in Ac. 4:11 as ὁ λίθος ὁ ἐξουθενηθείς. But this form of Ps. 118:22 is not attested elsewhere. It is probably due to Lk. who has also changed the following word οἰκοδομοῦντες (ψ 117[118]:22 LXX) to οἰκοδόμοι. Lk. likes to trim his scriptural quotations to shape. In addition he employs ἐξουθενέω in 18:9; 23:11 [revised, 1965].
[407] Cf. also Lk. 18:31: τὰ γεγραμμένα διὰ τῶν προφητῶν.
[408] Mk. 1:11 par. (cf. 9:7 par.); 9:12; 10:45; 14:24; Mt. 8:17; 12:18-20; Lk. 22:37.
[410] J. Jeremias, "Untersuchungen zum Quellenproblem d. Ag.," ZNW, 36 (1937), 215 f.
[411] 8:12 ff.: baptism without reception of the Spirit; 36, 38 f.: baptism without catechumenate.
[412] On the allusion to Is. 53 in Ac. 3:13 f. → n. 380.
[413] Jackson-Lake, I, 4 (1933) on Ac. 9:17 conclude from a comparison of this v. with 22:14 that ὁ δίκαιος = צַדִּיק was perhaps "the oldest title given to Jesus."
[414] 2:23 (τῇ ὡρισμένῃ βουλῇ καὶ προγνώσει τοῦ θεοῦ, cf. Is. 53:10); 3:18, cf. 7:52 (προκαταγγέλλειν); 13:27; 26:22 f. (οἱ προφῆται); 3:18, cf. 10:42 (plerophorically πάντες οἱ προφῆται); 4:28 (προορίζειν); 13:29 (πάντα τὰ ... γεγραμμένα); 17:2 (γραφαί), 3 (ἔδει).
[415] Dibelius, op. cit. (→ n. 381), 15.

περὶ ἁμαρτιῶν is probably an allusion to Is. 53:10, and δίκαιος to 53:11. Both in 1 Pt. 2:21-25 and 3:18 we find the ancient ὑπέρ formula (2:21; 3:18 → 710, 11 ff.). Both passages use traditional liturgical material, the former a hymn to Christ and the latter christological formulae. [416] In 1 Pt. 1:11 we find again the general scripture refs. relating to Christ's passion which are already familiar to us from the ancient *kerygma* (→ 706, 1 ff.), the Synoptists (→ 707, 1 ff.) and Acts (→ 707, 12 ff.). — Hb. makes use of LXX Is. 53:12 in 9:28 (εἰς τὸ πολλῶν ἀνενεγκεῖν ἁμαρτίας). The expression has a formal character, → 711, 1. This is also shown by the fact that the whole paragraph 9:27 f. "makes use of older catechetical material." [416a] On Christ's intercession (7:25, also 2:18; 9:24) → 710, 9. "The writer to the Hb. does not actually quote from Is. 53, but he takes it for granted and builds his own work upon it" [417] [section on Hb. 1965].

e. Primitive Formulae in the Johannine Writings. In the Johannine literature, too, the refs. to the Ebed Yahweh of Dt. Is. belong without exception to ancient tradition. We may mention first verses already discussed : 1:29 (ὁ ἀμνὸς τοῦ θεοῦ ὁ αἴρων τὴν ἁμαρτίαν τοῦ κόσμου) and 1:36 → 702, 9 ff.; 1:34 (ὁ ἐκλεκτός) → 702, 1 ff.; 3:14; 12:34 (δεῖ) → n. 405. On 1 Jn. 2:1, 29; 3:7 (δίκαιος) → 707, 17 ff., 26 ff.; on 2:2; 4:10 (ἱλασμός) → n. 431; on 3:5 (τὰς ἁμαρτίας αἴρειν) → 710, 34 ff.; on 3:5 (ἁμαρτία ἐν αὐτῷ οὐκ ἔστιν) → 711, 1 f.; on ἀρνίον in Rev. → 702, 18 ff. [418] The expression τιθέναι τὴν ψυχήν (Jn. 10:11, 15, 17, 18) also calls for notice. It is reminiscent of Is. 53:10 (Heb.); 53:12 (Aram.), and comparison with Mk. 10:45 and par. (διδόναι τὴν ψυχήν) and the ὑπέρ formula (→ 710, 11 ff.) shows that it is traditional. [419] Jn. 16:32 (σκορπισθῆτε ἕκαστος εἰς τὰ ἴδια), as ἕκαστος εἰς τὰ ἴδια shows, is a ref. to Is. 53:6; the Palestinian exegesis of the passage preserved in the Tg. (אתבדרנא "we were scattered") is used. [420] Finally, the striking thing in the quotation at Jn. 12:38 (= Is. 53:1 LXX) is that the quotation which immediately follows in v. 40 uses a different transl. technique ; [421] even the introductory formulae are different. Since the intr. to the second quotation (Jn. 12:40) is typically Johannine in style, [422] the first (12:38) could well be traditional in both form and content. [423] In fact R. 10:16 confirms the traditional character of the quotation from Is. 53:1.

f. Paul ; Matthew. In Paul, apart from the rich traditional material (→ 706, 1 ff.), the only christologically interpreted Ebed quotation is at R. 15:21 (→ Is. 52:15 LXX). It is worth noting, however, that the emphasis here is not on the christological interpretation (περὶ αὐτοῦ) but on the missionary task of preaching the Gospel where it has not yet been heard ; Paul finds a prefiguration of this task in the v. from Is. The situation is much the same in the Synoptists. Apart from the rich traditional material to be found there too (→ 706, 18 ff.), and with the exception of the addition Mt. 12:21 (→ 700, 29 ff.), the only certain allusion one may ascribe to any of the Evangelists personally is the general one at Mt. 26:54, which bears the distinctive linguistic stamp of Matthew. [424]

---

[416] R. Bultmann, "Bekenntnis- u. Liedfragmente im 1 Pt.," Coniectanea Neotestamentica, XI (1947), 1-14.

[416a] O. Michel, *Der Brief an die Hb.*[11] (1960), on Hb. 9:27 f. with detailed proof [1965].

[417] B. Lindars, *New Testament Apologetic* (1961), 83 [1965].

[418] On ὑψοῦν and δοξάζειν in Jn. → n. 441.

[419] → 710, 24 ff. The ὑπέρ also occurs elsewhere in Jn. → n. 435.

[420] Hegermann, I, 31 f.

[421] Jn. 12:38 follows the LXX against the HT, as the addition of κύριε shows ; 12:40, however, deviates completely from the LXX.

[422] Διὰ τοῦτο ... ὅτι cf. Bu. J., 346, n. 4; 177, n. 5.

[423] *Ibid.,* 346, where Jn. 12:37 f. is ascribed to the "σημεῖα source" used by the Evangelist. We have intentionally stated the matter more generally.

[424] Πῶς in a direct rhetorical question with a subj. following occurs in the NT only in Mt. (23:33; 26:54); πληροῦν (of Scripture) is a favourite word of Mt. (12 times as compared with 1 in Mk., 2 in Lk. and 8 in Jn., cf. Kl. Mt. on 1:22). On the other hand Mt. 8:17 can hardly be ascribed to the Evangelist himself (Schl. Mt., *ad loc.*), for here Is. 53:4 is quoted from the HT, whereas Mt. follows the LXX in his own quotations.

The absence of references to the Ebed in Jm., 2 and 3 Jn., Jd., 2 Pt. and Rev., [425] the remarkable paucity of such references in Paul, Hb. and Jn., and finally the circumstance that the many references are almost exclusively to be found in ancient traditional material and formulae, all lead to the same conclusion as that suggested by our survey of the expression παῖς θεοῦ (→ 703, 29 ff.), namely, that the christological interpretation of the servant of the Lord of Dt. Is. belongs to the most primitive age of the Christian community, and very soon came to be fixed in form. This finding is confirmed and made precise by a further observation. A review of all the Is. passages thus far mentioned shows that of the Ebed passages in Dt. Is. only Is. 42:1-4, 6; 49:6 and Is. 52:13-53:12 were expounded christologically in the NT. But these are the very passages which Palestinian Judaism, as distinct from Hellenistic (→ 683, 24 ff.), also expounded Messianically, → 699, 11 ff. From this it is to be deduced that the christological interpretation of these passages derives from the Palestinian, pre-Hellenistic stage of the primitive Church. [426]

2. The Setting in the Primitive Church.

Our conclusion thus far is further supported and made more concrete when we ask concerning the setting of the christological interpretation of the Ebed in the primitive Church.

a. Proof from Scripture. The original setting of the christological interpretation of the servant passages of Dt. Is. in the primitive community — if we disregard for the moment the transmission of the sayings of Jesus (→ 712, 19 ff.) — is that of proof from Scripture. The situation after the death of Jesus forced the community from the very outset to offer proof from Scripture that the crucifixion was divinely ordained and had vicarious force. That scriptural proof for the crucifixion belonged to the very earliest kerygma, and that it relied on the help of Is. 53, may be seen conclusively from 1 C. 15:3, → 706, 1 ff. Its importance may be gathered from the great number of references and the variety of formulae, → n. 405, 414. Whereas in most instances Is. 53 is presumed to be so well-known that a general reference to Scripture is enough, [427] Ac. 8:32 f. has a literal quotation from Is. 53:7b-8a according to the LXX. Ancient tradition (→ 707, 6; 700, 29 ff.) also finds in Is. 42 and 53 prophecies of details in the life of Jesus (Mt. 8:17 = Is. 53:4 HT: healing of the sick; Mt. 12:18-20 = Is. 42:1-3 HT: avoidance of public notice). An intimation of the unbelief of Israel is also perceived in Is. 53:1; in this connection the independent agreement between Paul and John is to be noted, R. 10:16; Jn. 12:38 → 708, 24 ff. Finally, in Is. 52:15 Paul found a prophetic indication of his own special missionary task of preaching Christ where nothing was yet known of Him, R. 15:21. [428]

b. Christology of the Primitive Community. The Ebed of Dt. Is. also influenced very strongly the development of the Christology of the primitive community. This is demonstrated by the great number of christological predicates and formal expressions based on Is. 42:1 ff. and Is. 52:13 ff.

[425] Rev. 1:16; 19:15 (sword out of the mouth) cannot be regarded as allusions to the Ebed, since the ref. here is to Is. 11:4. Is. 49:2 is only secondarily combined with Ps. 149:6, Schlatter, 37.
[426] C. H. Dodd, According to the Scriptures (1952), 94 with ref. to the "ubiquity" of the christological interpretation of Is. 53 in the NT [1965]. Cullmann, Gesù, 56: Ebed Yahweh Christology is "probabilmente la più antica cristologia."
[427] J. Dupont, Les problèmes du Livre d. Actes d'après les travaux récents (1950), 110.
[428] Cf. the related ref. to Is. 42:7, 16 in Ac. 26:18.

The following christological predicates should be noted : ὁ παῖς (of God) (→ 700, 24 ff.), perhaps connected with this ὁ υἱὸς τοῦ θεοῦ (→ 701, 13 ff.), ὁ ἀμνὸς τοῦ θεοῦ (→ 702, 9 ff.), τὸ ἀρνίον (→ 702, 18 ff.), also ὁ ἐκλεκτός (Jn. 1:34 → n. 261), ὁ ἐκλελεγμένος (Lk. 9:35), the interchangeable ὁ ἀγαπητός, [429] and finally ὁ δίκαιος, which, though it is not infrequent as a Messianic attribute in later Jewish literature (→ II, 186, 28 ff.), should perhaps, as a predicate of Jesus, be connected primarily with Is. 53:11, → 707, 16 ff., 26 f., 708, 24 f. [430] Moreover, the description of Jesus as ἱλασμὸς περὶ τῶν ἁμαρτιῶν ἡμῶν (1 Jn. 2:2; 4:10) seems to rest on Is. 53:10; [431] his description as intercessor (1 Jn. 2:1: παράκλητος; R. 8:34 and Hb. 7:25 : ἐντυγχάνειν) corresponds to Is. 53:12; [432] on φῶς εἰς ἀποκάλυψιν ἐθνῶν → n. 403.

Among christological formulae related to Is. 53 the ὑπέρ formula comes first even numerically. Its derivation from Is. 53 is clear from the link with the word πολλοί (ὑπὲρ πολλῶν, Mk. 14:24; περὶ πολλῶν, Mt. 26:28; ἀντὶ πολλῶν, Mk. 10:45; Mt. 20:28), which is a catchword of Is. 53, and also from 1 C. 15:3 : κατὰ τὰς γραφάς. The antiquity of the formula may be seen from its use in the primitive kerygma (1 C. 15:3) and the eucharistic sayings (Mk. 14:24 par.), [433] also from its independence of the LXX [434] and the pronounced variation in the prepositions, [435] which is due to varied renderings of the underlying Semitic text. [436] Another key-word which often carries a ref. to Is. 53 is (παρα-) διδόναι. Two different stages of association with Is. 53 may be distinguished, depending on whether the verb is construed in the act., the act. with a reflexive obj., or the pass. The reflexive use leads us back to Semitic-speaking circles. This follows from the fact that παραδιδόναι ἑαυτόν (Gl. 2:20; Eph. 5:2, 25) alternates with the simple διδόναι ἑαυτόν (Gl. 1:4; 1 Tm. 2:6; Tt. 2:14), the latter being a Gk. form of διδόναι τὴν ψυχήν (cf. Mk. 10:45; Mt. 20:28), which, on its part, is par. to the synon. τιθέναι τὴν ψυχήν (Jn. 10:11, 15; 15:17 f.; 15:13; 1 Jn. 3:16). All these forms are very probably different transl. of שִׂים נַפְשׁוֹ (Is. 53:10 HT) or מָסַר נַפְשֵׁהּ (53:12 Tg.). We are similarly led back to a Semitic-speaking environment by the pass. παραδίδοσθαι (the pass. being used to denote God's action). For in R. 4:25 παρεδόθη διὰ τὰ παραπτώματα ἡμῶν is an exact rendering of Is. 53:5b Tg. אִתְמְסַר בַּעֲוָיָתַנָא, → n. 397. On the other hand, the act. παραδιδόναι with God as subj., which is used in R. 8:32 : ὑπὲρ ἡμῶν πάντων παρέδωκεν αὐτόν, pts. to a Hell. background, for here Is. 53:6c LXX (καὶ κύριος παρέδωκεν αὐτόν) is referred to. In all the instances just quoted (παρα-) διδόναι is linked with the ὑπέρ formula and its variants. Finally, the use of the expression αἴρειν τὴν ἁμαρτίαν (Jn. 1:29; with plur. 1 Jn. 3:5), or ἀναφέρειν

---

[429] Mk. 1:11 par.; 9:7 par.; Mt. 12:18; Lk. 9:35 vl.; 2 Pt. 1:17. Cf. Eph. 1:6 : ὁ ἠγαπημένος.

[430] H. Dechent, "Der 'Gerechte' — eine Bezeichnung für den Messias," ThStKr, 100 (1927/8), 439-443.

[431] ἱλασμός = אָשָׁם Is. 53:10 (?); on περὶ τῶν ἁμαρτιῶν ἡμῶν cf. Is. 53:4-6; Wolff, 104 f.

[432] Mowinckel, 120 f. Note that Jesus is called δίκαιος in 1 Jn. 2:1 (cf. Is. 53:11).

[433] With regard to the Semitic linguistic character of both groups cf. Jeremias, Abendmahlsworte², 88-98. ὑπὲρ τῶν ἁμαρτιῶν ἡμῶν (1 C. 15:3) is shown to be pre-Pauline by the non-Pauline plur., ibid., 96.

[434] ὑπέρ does not occur in LXX Is. 52:13-53:12; there διά c. acc. (53:5 twice, 12) and περί c. gen. (53:4 cf. 10) are used.

[435] The following prep. alternate in statements about the death of Jesus : ἀντί, Mk. 10:45; Mt. 20:28; ὑπέρ c. gen.: Mk. 14:24; Lk. 22:19, 20; Jn. 6:51; 10:11, 15; 11:51 f.; 15:13; 17:19; 18:14; R. 5:6, 8; 8:32; 14:15; 1 C. 1:13; 5:7 vl.; 11:24; 15:3; 2 C. 5:14, 15 (twice), 21; Gl. 1:4; 2:20; 3:13; Eph. 5:2, 25; 1 Th. 5:10 vl.; 1 Tm. 2:6; Tt. 2:14; Hb. 2:9; 7:27; 10:12 (cf. 26); 1 Pt. 2:21; 3:18; 4:1 vl.; 1 Jn. 3:16; περί c. gen.: Mt. 26:28; R. 8:3; 1 C. 1:13 vl.; Gl. 1:4 vl.; 1 Th. 5:10; 1 Pt. 3:18; 1 Jn. 2:2; 4:10; διά c. acc.: R. 3:25; 4:25; 1 C. 8:11. It is no accident that in many of these passages there are other indications of the use of formulae. Furthermore, the preponderance of ὑπέρ over περί, which is more common in Hell. Gk., suggests antiquity, Lohse, 131, n. 4 [1965].

[436] For a particularly clear example of variants in transl. cf. Mk. 10:45 par. (ἀντὶ πολλῶν) and 1 Tm. 2:6 (ὑπὲρ πάντων). [Notes 437-439 omitted, 1965.]

ἁμαρτίας (Hb. 9:28; 1 Pt. 2:24) from Is. 53:12, [440] probably also ἁμαρτίαν οὐκ ἐποίη-σεν (1 Pt. 2:22), or ἁμαρτία ἐν αὐτῷ οὐκ ἔστιν (1 Jn. 3:5) from Is. 53:9b, [441] is formal in character. The variety in attempts to render the Heb. אָשָׁם (Is. 53:10) into Gk. is an indication of the early and vigorous influence of Is. 53 on the Christology of the primitive Church. [442]

c. Liturgy. Liturgy should also be mentioned. In the eucharist the πολλῶν of the liturgical sayings (Mk. 14:24 and par.) points to the servant of the Lord, and the ancient liturgical formula διὰ 'Ιησοῦ τοῦ παιδός σου lives on with great tenacity in the eucharistic prayer and the doxology, → 702, 22 ff. [443] Already from the pre-Pauline period (→ n. 398 on Phil. 2:6-11) Jesus is extolled in psalms as the servant of God (Phil. 2:6-11; 1 Pt. 2:22-25; Lk. 2:32; cf. R. 4:25).

The link between Phil. 2:6-11 and Is. 53 [444] is apparent once it is realised that, whereas the hymn follows the LXX in v. 10 f., in 6-9 it makes use of a christological terminology drawn from Is. 53 HT. Even the use of δοῦλος rather than παῖς in 2:7 is less jarring (→ n. 444) if viewed as a direct rendering of the Heb. עֶבֶד (Is. 52:13). The decisive proof of the thesis that the Christology of Phil. 2:6-9 is rooted in Is. 53 HT lies in the fact that the expression ἑαυτὸν ἐκένωσεν (Phil. 2:7), which is not attested elsewhere in Gk. and is grammatically extremely harsh, is an exact transl. of הֶעֱרָה... נַפְשׁוֹ (Is. 53:12). [445] Furthermore, we are referred to Is. 53 by other verbal echoes, [446] the

---

[440] Jn. 1:29; 1 Jn. 3:5 follow Is. 53:12 HT, while Hb. 9:28; 1 Pt. 2:24 follow the LXX; this accounts for the alternation between αἴρειν and ἀναφέρειν [1965].

[441] Cf. further τὸν μὴ γνόντα ἁμαρτίαν, 2 C. 5:21. One cannot say for certain whether the formal use of the verbs ὑψοῦν, Ac. 2:33; 5:31; Jn. 3:14; 8:28; 12:32, 34 and δοξάζειν, Ac. 3:13; Jn. 7:39; 12:16, 23; 17:1, 5 etc. is connected with Is. 52:13 LXX (so O. Michel, "Probleme d. nt.lichen Theologie," DTh, 9 [1942], 29; Wolff, 85; Cerfaux, 123, n. 1).

[442] λύτρον: Mk. 10:45; Mt. 20:28 (Dalman, op. cit. [→ n. 304], 110; Wolff, 61; Jeremias, "Lösegeld," 262) hellenised as ἀντίλυτρον, 1 Tm. 2:6; περὶ ἁμαρτίας (= LXX Is. 53:10) R. 8:3; perhaps also ἱλαστήριον; ἱλασμός → n. 431.

[443] Cf. also the eucharistic epiclesis of the Church Order of Hippolytus, v. Harnack, 227 f.; H. Lietzmann, Messe u. Herrenmahl (1926), 80 f.; also the as yet unedited liturgy of a Berlin pap. in which we read: "May the eucharist serve εἰς φάρμακον ἀθανασίας ... διὰ τοῦ ἠγαπημένου σου παιδός, Lietzmann, 257, n. 2.

[444] Accepted by, e.g., Lohmeyer, Kyrios Jesus, 32 f., 35 ff., 40-42; H. Windisch in his review of Lohmeyer, ThLZ, 54 (1929), 247; Kittel, → I, 224, 36 ff.; Euler, 45, 47 f., 101, 103, 118; H. Wheeler Robinson, loc. cit. (→ n. 445); Stählin → III, 353; Cerfaux, 117-124; G. S. Duncan, Jesus, Son of Man (1947), 193 f.; W. D. Davies, Paul and Rabb. Judaism (1948), 274; Cullmann, Gesù, 58; Schelkle, 95. The argument against such a link (K. H. Rengstorf → II, 278 f.; Gewiess, 56, n. 149) rests on the use of δοῦλος rather than the expected παῖς at Phil. 2:7, cf. also E. Käsemann, "Kritische Analyse v. Phil. 2:5-11," ZThK, 47 (1950), 313-360.

[445] Recognised by H. Wheeler Robinson, "The Cross of the Servant," in The Cross in the OT (1955), 57, 104 f.; also C. H. Dodd, JTS, 39 (1938), 292; According to the Scriptures (1952), 93; J. A. T. Robinson, The Body (Studies in Bibl. Theology, 5) (1952), 14, n. 1. The verb ערה means "to lay bare, expose" or "to pour out." In the latter sense the LXX and Hexapla versions usually render it by ἐκκενοῦν, LXX Gn. 24:20; 2 Ch. 24:11; Ps. 137:7; 'A Ps. 141:8; cf. Σ Jer. 51(28):58; cf. Dodd, JTS, 292. In 3 instances the LXX prefers a free rendering, viz. Is. 32:15 and in 2 places which mention a "pouring out of life," Is. 53:12 παρεδόθη εἰς θάνατον ἡ ψυχὴ αὐτοῦ and ψ 140:8: μὴ ἀντανέλῃς τὴν ψυχήν μου. It is to be noted, however, that 'A in this last instance has ἐκκενοῦν, thus confirming that this usual equivalent of ערה could also be used in this idiom. The use of Is. 53:12 shows that the expression ἑαυτὸν ἐκένωσεν implies the surrender of life, not the kenosis of the incarnation. G. Bornkamm, "Zum Verständnis des Christus-Hymnus Phil. 2:6-11," Studien zu Antike u. Urchr. (1959) (²1963), 180, objects to the idea of ἑαυτὸν ἐκένωσεν being a rendering of Is. 53:12 הֶעֱרָה לַמָּוֶת נַפְשׁוֹ, 1. that לַמָּוֶת is lacking, 2. that נַפְשׁוֹ, too, was left untransl., and 3. that Jesus' death is not referred to until v. 8b. I have tried to show in "Zu Phil. 2:7: Ἐαυτὸν ἐκένωσεν," Novum Testamentum, 6 (1963), 182-8 that these ob-

contrast between humiliation and exaltation, the willingness to be humbled, and the mention of obedience unto death. [447] The hymn to Christ in 1 Pt. 2:22-25 (→ 707, 24 ff.) almost seems to be a short summary of Is. 53. It shows how completely Jesus was viewed as the suffering servant. The song of Simeon in Lk. 2:29-32 takes up Is. 49:6 (→ n. 403) and refers this servant saying to Jesus.

d. Early Christian Exhortation. Finally, Is. 53 plays a considerable role in primitive Christian exhortation and the literature of martyrdom. Jesus as the Suffering Servant is, according to context, held up as an example of service (Mk. 10:45 and par.), unselfishness (Phil. 2:5-11), innocent and voluntary suffering (1 Pt. 2:21-25) and humility (1 Cl., 16, 1-17). The martyr especially is a perfect imitator of the servant of God, Ign. Eph., 10, 3; Eus. Hist. Eccl., V, 1, 23; V, 2, 2. [448]

There is no area of the primitive Christian life of faith which was not touched and stamped by the Ebed Christology. The impact on formal phrases, which is much the same in all areas, proves the antiquity and deep rootage of this Christology, and explains the paucity of express quotations, → 705, 24 ff.; 708, 30 ff. But if the christological interpretation of Is. 42:1 ff.; 49:6 and esp. 52:13 ff. belongs to the oldest Palestinian stage of the primitive Church, a further question arises to which we must now address ourselves.

III. Can Jesus Have Thought of Himself as the Servant of God of Dt. Is.?

The Gospels say so. In the following passages they have Jesus refer servant sayings from Dt. Is. to Himself.

Mk. 9:12 : ἐξουδενηθῇ, cf. Is. 53:3 : נִבְזֶה ('A, Σ, Θ ἐξουδενωμένος), → 706. [448a] Mk. 9:31 and par.; 10:33 and par.; 14:21, 41 and par.; Mt. 26:2; Lk. 24:7: παραδίδοται / παραδοθήσεται / παραδίδοσθαι / παραδοθῆναι, cf. Is. 53:5b Tg.: אִתְמְסַר. Mk. 10:45 par. Mt. 20:28 : διακονῆσαι καὶ δοῦναι τὴν ψυχὴν αὐτοῦ λύτρον ἀντὶ πολλῶν, cf. Is. 53:10 HT : נַפְשׁוֹ אָשָׁם תָּשִׂים-אִם; 53:11, 12 : רַבִּים; διακονῆσαι is an allusion to the servant ; λύτρον seems to be a free rendering of אָשָׁם (in the common [451] meaning "indemnification"). [452] Mk. 14:8 : Jesus expects a criminal's burial (without anointing), cf. Is. 53:9. Mk. 14:24 and par.: ἐκχυννόμενον ὑπὲρ πολλῶν, cf. Is. 53:12 : הֶעֱרָה . . .

_____

jections are unfounded. 1. Ps. 141:8 ("pour not my life out," i.e., "kill me not") proves that the idiom was used with (Is. 53:12) or without (Phil. 2:7) לָמָוֶת, the latter being no indispensable part of it. 2. That נַפְשׁוֹ was not transl. is a mistaken assumption. It is represented, quite accurately, by the reflexive pronoun ἑαυτόν, which often serves to transl. נֶפֶשׁ when it holds the place of a reflex. pron. lacking in Semitic. 3. To say that ἑαυτὸν ἐκένωσεν cannot take up Is. 53:12 because Phil. 2:7a does not yet speak of Jesus' death is begging the question. It can in fact be shown that the hymn consists of 3 four-line stanzas (vv. 6-7a, 7b-8, 9-11), the first 2 of which run par. in form and substance. Thus, far from precluding our interpretation of Phil. 2:7a, the very structure of the hymn suggests that this clause refers to Jesus' death as well as v. 8b [1965].

446 With μορφή (Phil. 2:6, 7) one should perhaps compare the rendering of תֹּאַר (Is. 52:14) by μορφή in 'A, (→ IV, 751, n. 53); with ἐταπείνωσεν ἑαυτόν (Phil. 2:8) cf. the transl. of מְעֻנֶּה (Is. 53:4) by ταπεινοῦν in 'ΑΣΘ. With ὑπήκοος (Phil. 2:8) cf. the rendering of נַעֲנֶה (Is. 53:7) by ὑπήκουσεν in Σ (acc. to Eus.); with διό (Phil. 2:9) cf. לָכֵן (Is. 53:12); with ὑπερύψωσεν (Phil. 2:9) cf. וְגָבַהּ מְאֹד וְנִשָּׂא יָרוּם (Is. 52:13).

447 Cf. Cerfaux, 117-124.

448 Cerfaux, 128 f. On the wide use of Is. 53 in post-NT writings, esp. Just., cf. Wolff, 108-142, also → III, 550 ff.

448a Tödt has objected that Mk. 9:12 refers rather to Ps. 118:22. Against this → n. 406 [1965]. [Notes 449, 450 omitted, 1965.]

451 Cf. K. G. Kuhn, "Die Abendmahlsworte," ThLZ, 75 (1950), 406, n. 2.

452 For the ref. to Is. 53 cf. Dalman, op. cit., 110; Wolff, 61; Jeremias "Lösegeld," 262.

רַבִּים. [453] Mk. 14:61 par. Mt. 26:63 : Jesus is silent before the Sanhedrin ; Mk. 15:5 par. Mt. 27:12, 14; Jn. 19:9 before Pilate ; Lk. 23:9 before Herod Antipas, cf. Is. 53:7 נֶאֱלָמָה. [454] Lk. 11:22 : καὶ τὰ σκῦλα αὐτοῦ διαδίδωσιν, cf. Is. 53:12 יְחַלֵּק שָׁלָל (LXX μεριεῖ σκῦλα) (?). [454a] Lk. 22:37: δεῖ τελεσθῆναι ἐν ἐμοί, τό καὶ μετὰ ἀνόμων ἐλογίσθη = Is. 53:12 וְאֶת־פֹּשְׁעִים נִמְנָה. (LXX καὶ ἐν τοῖς ἀνόμοις ἐλογίσθη). Lk. 23:34 : Jesus makes intercession, cf. Is. 53:12 HT. [455] Jn. 10:11, 15, 17 f.: τιθέναι τὴν ψυχήν, cf. Is. 53:10 HT : נַפְשׁוֹ ... תָּשִׂים. Finally we should mention the many refs. Jesus makes to Scripture (→ n. 405); on their connection with Is. 53 → 707, 1 ff. [revised, 1965].

Many of these passages are wholly or in part the work of the community. Thus the striking thing about the silence of Jesus before His judges (the Sanhedrin, Pilate, Herod) is that this is recounted more than once, → lines 2 ff. [458] Again, the predictions of the passion, when compared, display a secondary tendency to become more concrete and to accommodate themselves to the actual course of events. [459] Nevertheless, there are points in the texts which forbid us to say that all the references of Jesus to the Ebed are inauthentic. [460]

The assertion of the Gospels that Jesus expected a violent death has the strongest historical probability in its favour. First, the actual situation forced Jesus to think in these terms. The charge of βλασφημία (Mk. 2:7 and par.; Jn. 10:33-36, cf. 5:18) carried with it the threat of stoning [461] and the subsequent exposure of the body on a cross. [462] The same punishment (though without exposure of the body) was meted out for breaking the Sabbath ; [462a] of the 2 Sabbath stories in Mk. 2:23-3:7a the first reports the warning [463] after which any repetition would be deliberate and punishable ; consequently in 3:1 ff. Jesus risks His life (cf. 3:6) and has to save Himself by flight (3:7a :

---

[453] Jeremias, *Abendmahlsworte*², 108 ff. On Jesus' own comparison of Himself with the Paschal Lamb *(ibid.,* 105) cf. Is. 53:7.

[454] H. W. Surkau, *Martyrien in jüd. u. frühchr. Zeit* (1938), 87; J. Schniewind, *Mk.* *(NT Deutsch)* on 14:61. On Mk. 14:62 par. Mt. 26:64 ὄψεσθε cf. also Is. 52:15.

[454a] → III, 400, 17 ff. Yet it remains possible that in Lk. 11:21 f. par. there is present an image which is independent of the OT, so W. Bieder, *Die Vorstellung v. d. Höllenfahrt Jesu Christi* (1949), 35 [1965].

[455] This intercession is for those who sin unwittingly, cf. Is. 53:10 : אָשָׁם is the offering for unwitting sins. (Lk. 23:34a is missing in some of the MSS and seems to be an ancient addition resting on solid tradition.) [Notes 456, 457 omitted, 1965.]

[458] Wolff, 76, n. 316 (following J. Schniewind). A pt. in favour of authenticity is that if the feature were invented one would expect a ref. to Scripture (Is. 53:7). M. D. Hooker, *op. cit.,* 87-89 also pts. out that Jesus merely refused to answer the false accusations [1965].

[459] Thus Mk. at 8:31; 9:31; 10:34 has μετὰ τρεῖς ἡμέρας, while Mt. and Lk. in the pars. have independently of one another, and *ex eventu,* changed this to τῇ τρίτῃ ἡμέρᾳ (or τῇ ἡμέρᾳ τῇ τρίτῃ). Cf., too, the ἀποκτενοῦσιν of Mk. 10:34 with the σταυρῶσαι of Mt. 20:19. The so-called third prediction (more accurately the third version of the prediction) in Mk. 10:33 f. par. might well have been touched up *ex eventu* (as comparison with the first 2 versions in 8:31 and 9:31 suggests); nevertheless, it should not be overlooked that 10:33 f. does not contain any feature which one would not normally expect in capital proceedings against Jesus acc. to the legal practices and modes of execution at the time. This is a warning to be cautious with the judgment *"ex eventu."*

[460] Thus Lk. 11:22 pre-dates the theology of the community, since it connects the victory of Jesus over satanic and demonic powers, not with the crucifixion and resurrection, but with the temptation of Jesus, → III, 401, 16 ff. The relation of this v. to Is. 53, however, is uncertain, → n. 454a.

[461] Sanh., 7, 4; S. Lv., 24, 11 ff. (53a, 31 ff., Venice, 1545); Jn. 10:31, 33.

[462] Sanh., 6, 4 : "All who are stoned are hanged" — words of R. Eli'ezer (b. Hyrcanos [c. 90], the representative of the older tradition). Acc. to the Halakha *(ibid.)* this applies only to blasphemers and idolaters.

[462a] Sanh., 7, 4. 8 [1965].

[463] On the warning in later Jewish law and the NT cf. K. Bornhäuser, "Zur Perikope vom Bruch des Sabbats," NkZ, 33 (1922), 325-334; J. Jeremias, *op. cit.* (→ n. 410), 208-213. οὐκ ἔξεστιν in Mk. 4:24 is a warning formula, cf. Jn. 5:10.

ἀνεχώρησεν). [464] If Mk. 3:22b par.; Mt. 9:34 implies an accusation of sorcery, [464a] He is again charged with a crime which entails stoning. [464b] Finally, the false prophet (cf. Lk. 13:33) was threatened with capital punishment. [464c] The reports that Jesus repeatedly stood in direct danger of stoning [465] are quite in the realm of the possible, esp. in view of Mk. 2:23-3:7a. Secondly, history forced Jesus to expect a violent death. In words which represent esp. sound tradition, [466] Jesus regarded Himself as one of the prophets [467] and expected the fate of the prophets, namely, martyrdom, Lk. 13:33; Mt. 23:34-36 par., 37 par. [468] We know from the NT, [469] from Jewish legends concerning the prophets, [470] and from the growing custom of honouring the tombs of the prophets by expiatory monuments, [470a] to what a gt. extent, even in the days of Jesus, martyrdom was considered an integral part of the prophetic office. [471] Jesus Himself found in salvation history an unbroken series of martyrdoms of the just from Abel to Zechariah, Mt. 23:35 and par. Recent history, the fate of John the Baptist, prefigured His own destiny, Mk. 9:12 f. and par., cf. 6:16; Lk. 13:31. A third pt. may be added in favour of the historicity of the reports that Jesus expected a violent end. His predictions of the passion contain a number of features which never occurred. At times, perhaps on the basis of actual experience (→ lines 2 ff.), He seems to have considered the possibility of being stoned (Mt. 23:37 and par.) by the Jews as a false prophet (Lk. 13:33). This expectation, like that of being buried as a criminal (Mk. 14:8 and par.), was not fulfilled. The same is true of the expectation that some of the disciples would have to share His fate (Mk. 10:32-40 and par.; Lk. 14:25-33), or at least be brought into danger of death by His execution (22:36 f.); rather singularly the Jewish authorities were satisfied with the execution of Jesus and left His disciples unmolested [472] [revised 1965].

---

[464] Mk. 3:7a has a par. in Mt. 15:21 and might originally have been the conclusion of the pericope in Mk. 3:1-6.

[464a] Str.-B., I, 631. Cf. bSanh., 107b : "Jeshu has practised sorcery" [1965].

[464b] Sanh., 7, 4 and 11 [1965].

[464c] Sanh., 11, 1 [1965].

[465] Lk. 4:29; Jn. 8:59; 10:31-36; 11:8; *Unknown Gospel* fr. 1 recto, lines 23 f., cf. Mt. 23:37 par.

[466] R. Bernheimer, "Vitae prophetarum," *Journal of the American Oriental Soc., 55* (1935), 202 f.

[467] Similarly Jesus sets His disciples among the prophets, Mt. 5:12 par.

[468] The fact that only occasionally did the primitive Church set Jesus among the prophets is an argument for the authenticity of these sayings.

[469] Refs. to the killing of the prophets in the NT are : Mt. 21:35 f.; 22:6; 23:30-32 par., 34-36 par., 37 par.; Lk. 13:33; Ac. 7:51 f.; R. 11:3; 1 Th. 2:15; Hb. 11:35-38; Rev. 11:7; 16:6; 18:24; cf. Jm. 5:10.

[470] Prophetarum vitae fabulosae, ed. T. Schermann (1907); *The Lives of the Prophets*, ed. C. C. Torrey (JBL, Monograph Series, I [1946]); M. R. James, *The Lost Apocrypha of the OT (Translations of Early Documents*, Ser. I [1920]); Jos. Ant., 10, 38; Orig. Comm. series, 28 on Mt. 23:37-39 (GCS, 38, 50) and Cat. fr., 457, II on Mt. 23:29-35 (GCS, 41, 190); Tert. Scorpiace, 8 (MPL, 2, 137 B); Asc. Is. 2:16; 5:1-14; Paral. Jer. 9:21-32; Str.-B., I, 940-942; III, 747; H. Vincent-F. M. Abel, *Jérusalem*, II (1926), 855-874.

[470a] J. Jeremias, *op. cit.* (→ n. 471), *passim* [1965].

[471] A. Schlatter, "Der Märtyrer in den Anfängen d. Kirche," BFTh, 19, 3 (1915), 18-22; O. Michel, "Prophet u. Märtyrer," BFTh, 37, 2 (1932); H. J. Schoeps, *Die jüd. Prophetenmorde* = Symbolae Biblicae Upsalienses, 2 (1943); H. A. Fischel, "Prophet and Martyr," JQR, 37 (1947), 265-280, 363-386, esp. 279, 382.

[472] C. H. Dodd, *The Parables of the Kingdom*[7] (1946), 59. The despair of the disciples on Good Friday is not a cogent argument against the historicity of the predictions of Jesus' passion since it was essentially caused by the fact that the course of events did not measure up to the expectations held by the disciples on the basis of the intimations of Jesus. For, though they obviously expected passion and martyrdom both for Jesus and themselves (Mk. 10:39 par.; 14:29 par.), they also expected immediately after this a "corporate triumph" (Lk. 24:21; Ac. 1:6, cf. T. W. Manson, "The NT Basis of the Doctrine of the Church," *The Journ. of Ecclesiastical History*, 1 [1950], 6 and n. 3). On the disciples' lack of understanding → n. 331.

If, however, Jesus expected a violent death, then in view of the extraordinary significance which the theologoumenon of the atoning power of death had for later Judaism. [473] He must have reflected on the meaning and purpose of His death. The assertion of the sources that Jesus found the key to the necessity and meaning of His passion in Is. 53 also enjoys a high degree of historical probability. It may first be stated very generally that Is. 40 ff. had great significance for Jesus' sense of mission, cf. Mt. 11:5 and par.; 5:3 f.; Mk. 11:17; Lk. 4:18 ff.; → II, 708, 15 ff.; 718, 1 ff. The references to Is. 53 thus fit into the framework of His preaching and use of Scripture. If, then, we examine in detail the texts mentioned → 712, 22 ff., five considerations support their antiquity. First, we have here pre-Hellenistic tradition, for none of the passages apart from Lk. 22:37 (though → n. 404) shows any plain influence of the LXX; this is indeed ruled out so far as Mk. 9:12; 10:45; 14:8, 24; Lk. 23:34; Jn. 10:11, 15, 17 are concerned. Thus an older stratum of tradition emerges characterised by use of the HT of Is. 53:3, 9, 10-12. [473a] Mk. 9:31 has an Aram. play on words : בַּר נָשָׁא/בְּנֵי נָשָׁא; the non-Greek expression εἰς χεῖρας is a rendering of the Aram. prep. לִידֵי. The religious use of λύτρον in Mk. 10:45 and par. is Jewish ; [474] the expression δοῦναι τὴν ψυχήν (par. τιθέναι τὴν ψυχήν, Jn. 10:11, 15, 17 f.) points to a Semitic-speaking environment, → 710 f. Lk. 23:34 also presupposes Palestinian connections : for later Judaism the expiatory vow of the criminal is part of the execution ("May my death be an expiation for all my sins"), [475] but Jesus, like the Maccabean martyrs, [476] reverses this, transferring the atoning efficacy of His death to His tormentors, → n. 455. Secondly, several of the intimations of the passion are so general that they cannot have been touched up *ex eventu* ; invention *ex inventu* is incontestably ruled out in all those cases where intimations of what would happen were not borne out by the subsequent events. That applies not only to quite a few predictions of the passion (→ 714), but also to several predictions of the glorification. For repeatedly "the third day" is used to designate the moment, not of the resurrection, but of the "fulfilment" (Lk. 13:32, cf. Jn. 16:16) or of the appearance of the new temple (Mk. 14:58 and par.). We are entitled to conclude from this that Jesus talked in varying terms about God's triumph which was to occur "within three days" or "on the third day," i.e., "immediately," and that only secondary interpretation referred these three days to the period between crucifixion and resurrection. [476a] This means that the core, not only of the predictions of the passion, but also of the predictions of the glorification which interpret the passion, is pre-Easter tradition, not yet coloured by the historic course of events [1965]. Thirdly, some of the sayings are so anchored in the context that they cannot be detached from it. This is particularly true of Mk. 8:31, which is inseparably related to the sharp rebuke of Peter in 8:33 ; but the description of Peter as Satan cannot have been put on the lips of Jesus later. Again, the expectation of a criminal's burial without anointing (Mk. 14:8) is firmly embedded in the context. This is obvious once it is perceived that in the story in

---

[473] Lohse, 9-110; Jeremias, *Abendmahlsworte*², 110 f.

[473a] Cf. R. H. Fuller, *The Mission and Achievement of Jesus* (*Studies in Bibl. Theology*. 12) (1954), 55-59 [1965].

[474] J. Jeremias, "Lösegeld," 249-258. While the language of Mk. 10:42-45 is Palestinian, the par. Lk. 22:24-27 displays strong Hell. influence, *ibid.*, 258-262.

[475] Sanh., 6, 2; TSanh., 9, 5; bSanh., 44b; jSanh., 6, 4 (23b, 47), cf. A. Büchler, *Studies in Sin and Atonement* (1928), 170, n. 4; K. G. Kuhn, "R. 6:7," ZNW, 30 (1931), 306.

[476] 4 Macc. 6:29; 2 Macc. 7:37 f.

[476a] C. H. Dodd, *The Parables of the Kingdom*² (1936), 98-101 [passage revised and notes 477, 478 omitted, 1965].

Mk. 14:3-9 almsgiving (צְדָקָה, 14:5) and the work of love (גְּמִילוּת חֲסָדִים, 14:6),[479] which is more important, are set in antithesis, and that only the information (14:8) which of the works of love the woman has unwittingly performed for Jesus, namely, burial of the dead, gives us the key to an understanding of the whole incident.[480] Lk. 22:37 is similarly anchored in the context. This saying, which is based on the HT of Is. 53:12 (→ n. 404), stands between the two obviously ancient sayings about the swords in v. 36 and v. 38, of which the first (v. 36) intimates the imminent commencement of the time of eschatological tribulation and to this degree is an unfulfilled prophecy → 715. The reason given for this intimation in v. 37, namely, that because Jesus is to be expelled from the community of Israel as an ἄνομος, His disciples, too, will be treated as ἄνομοι and refused food and threatened with death,[481] is surely indispensable to the context. Mention should also be made of Mk. 9:12b in this connection. If, as is probable (→ II, 937, 20 ff.), the Elijah prophecy of Mal. 3:23 f. is adduced by the disciples in Mk. 9:11 as an objection to Jesus' intimation of His passion — the apocatastasis which Elijah accomplishes three days before the end makes the suffering of the Messiah unnecessary — then the passion saying in 9:12b is again indispensable to the context. Fourthly, in Mk. 9:31, a prediction of the passion which has a very archaic ring because of its conciseness, its enigmatic character and the word-play employed (→ 715), the passive is used periphrastically to describe God's action: ὁ υἱὸς τοῦ ἀνθρώπου παραδίδοται εἰς χεῖρας ἀνθρώπων, "God will deliver the man to the men." The same παραδίδοσθαι, which is an allusion to Is. 53:5b Tg. (→ 712), recurs in Mk. 10:33; 14:21, 41; Mt. 26:2; Lk. 24:7. Hence it is firmly rooted in the tradition. Representing God's action through the passive is a later Jewish mode of speech; but it is nowhere even remotely as frequent as in the words of Jesus, and must therefore be considered a token of His personal style [481a] [1965]. Fifthly, and finally, it is of decisive importance that at one point in the oldest and soundest tradition we come across Is. 53, namely, in the eucharistic sayings of Jesus (Mk. 14:24 and par.: ὑπὲρ πολλῶν). Paul received his version of the sayings, which he passed on to the Corinthians (1 C. 11:23-25) in 49/50 A.D., in the Hellenistic sphere,[482] possibly after 40 in Antioch.[483] Since the Synoptic versions are shown to be older than the Pauline Hellenistic version by, amongst other things, their many Semitic features,[484] they take us back to the thirties. Here, then, we have the bedrock of the tradition.

The fact that the number of passages in which Jesus refers Is. 53 to Himself is not great, and that there are none at all in the material peculiar to Mt. and Lk.,

---

[479] On almsgiving and works of love cf. Str.-B., IV, 536-610.

[480] J. Jeremias, "Die Salbungsgeschichte Mc. 14:3-9," ZNW, 35 (1936), 75-82. The authenticity of Mk. 14:8 is also supported by the fact that the prophecy is unfulfilled, → 712, 28 f., since Jesus was spared a dishonourable burial, Mk. 15:45 f.; Jn. 19:38 ff.

[481] Schl. Lk., 428.

[481a] Jeremias, Abendmahlsworte³ (1960), 194 f. [1965].

[482] Ibid.², 94.

[483] The relationship between the Pauline and Lucan versions (Lk. 22:19b-20a agrees almost word for word with 1 C. 11:24 f.) points to Antioch, ibid., 76.

[484] For Semitisms in Mk. 14:22-25 v. ibid., 88-94. For additional material considerations, ibid., 80-85. As regards the ὑπέρ phrase in particular, the Pauline ὑπὲρ ὑμῶν (1 C. 11:24) is undoubtedly secondary as compared with the ὑπὲρ πολλῶν of Mk. 14:24, for in Paul the Semitism πολλῶν (→ πολλοί) is avoided and under the influence of liturgical use the theological interpretation (in the 3rd person) has become a formula of distribution (in the 2nd person). Furthermore, the Pauline association of the ὑπέρ phrase with the bread is probably secondary as compared with the Marcan association with the cup, ibid., 82, 95 [revised 1965].

is probably connected with the fact that only in His esoteric and not His public preaching did Jesus declare Himself to be the Servant of God. [485] Only to His disciples did Jesus reveal the mystery that He regarded the fulfilment of Is. 53 as His divinely imposed task. [486] Only to them did He interpret His death as a vicarious dying for the countless multitude (→ πολλοί) of those who had come under the judgment of God, Mk. 10:45; 14:24. Because He goes to His death innocently, voluntarily, patiently, and in accordance with the will of God (Is. 53), His dying has unlimited atoning power. The life which He pours out is life from God and with God. [487]

J. Jeremias

πάλαι, παλαιός, παλαιότης, παλαιόω

† πάλαι.

πάλαι, [1] "earlier," "before," "once upon a time," also "long since," "for a long time," an adv. of time; the essential pt. in the meaning is antithesis to the present; it makes no difference whether the event in question took place hours or centuries before.

In the NT πάλαι is soundly attested 7 times. Just a short time before is meant in Mk. 15:44 (BD al read ἤδη) and 2 C. 12:19, [2] while a more distant event is at issue in 2 Pt. 1:9, and one which is very much earlier in Mt. 11:21 (= Lk. 10:13), Hb. 1:1 and Jd. 4.

† παλαιός.

1. παλαιός, "old," with no distinction between what once was and has now ceased to exist. and what has been there for a long time. It can also have the subsidiary sense of "antiquated," "dated," e.g., Soph. Oed. Tyr., 290: καὶ μὴν τά γ᾽ ἄλλα κωφὰ καὶ παλαί ἔπη, though also "venerable," e.g., Antiphon. Or., VI, 4: ἅπερ μέγιστα καὶ παλαιότατα τοῖς ἀνθρώποις, of contests etc. Between ἀρχαῖος and παλαιός there is the general distinction that the former has the predominant sense of original or venerable, whereas this is rare in the case of παλαιός, → I, 486, 21-30. (The main antonyms of παλαιός are καινός [→ III, 447-450] and νέος [→ IV, 896-899].) But in NT Gk. the distinction is no longer so sharp. Thus Paul can write in, e.g., 2 C. 5:17: τὰ ἀρχαῖα παρῆλθεν, ἰδοὺ γέγονεν καινά, and yet in Eph. 4:22-24 he can contrast the καινὸς ἄνθρωπος with the παλαιὸς ἄνθρωπος. In the NT, esp. in Paul, παλαιός has greater theological force than ἀρχαῖος, esp. in the phrase παλαιὸς ἄνθρωπος.

---

[485] Buber, 74; V. Taylor, The Life and Ministry of Jesus (1954), 145 [1965].

[486] Buber, 73 f.: "If we view the connexion rightly, Jesus understood himself, under the influence of the conception of Dt. Is., to be a bearer of the Messianic hiddenness"; ibid., 77: "The idea of the 'servant,' modified by the Apocalypses [through the combination with the Son of Man]," has entered "into the actual life-story" of Jesus.

[487] J. Schniewind, Mk. (NT Deutsch) on 10:45.

π ά λ α ι. V. the dict.

[1] Etym. πάλαι (Aeolic πήλυι) is related to τῆλε, "distant," "far away," cf. Walde-Pok., I, 517. Hence it orig. means "long ago," cf. Hom. Il., 9, 527; Soph. El., 1049; Plat. Theaet., 142a [Debrunner].

[2] 𝕻[45] D al add a πάλαι after ὀψίας γενομένης ἦν at Mk. 6:47 to show that the ship had already been in the middle of the lake for a long time.

2. The LXX uses παλαιός for various words, mostly יָשָׁן (Lv. 25:22; 26:10), which is occasionally rendered ἀρχαῖος (Is. 22:11). In the main the term is without theological significance. But this does not apply to the verb παλαιόω, used for בלה. בלה is a value concept to denote the lesser value or valuelessness of esp. clothes after prolonged use, cf. Dt. 8:4; 29:4; Neh. 9:21; Jos. 9:4, 5, 13, but also Jer. 38(45):11, 12. More important, however, is the fig. use, e.g., for the body, flesh and bones of man in their transitoriness and passibility, Ps. 32:3; 49:14; Gn. 18:12; Is. 50:9; Ez. 23:43; Job 13:28; Lam. 3:4; Sir. 14:17. The same is true of man's life and of the works of his hand, Job 21:13; Is. 65:22, also of the bodies of earth and heaven, which are like a garment to God, Is. 51:6; Ps. 102:26, and acc. to ΣΘ Ps. 72:7; Job 14:12. If in Gk. παλαιόω is mostly used for this, its temporal content is hereby eschatologically determined, → III, 449, 5 ff. The aging of man and the world is a final reality ordained by God. Translation by παλαιοῦν brings in this new content even where other Heb. roots lie behind it instead of בלה. עתק is rendered in this way with ref. to hills and rocks (Job 9:5; 14:18), or to men and their words (ψ 6:7; Job 32:15). The eschatological nuance is plain in the important v. at Da. 7:9 in an anon. rendering. [1] Here it is said of God that He causes the days, the time of the world, to grow old. This is a transl. of עַתִּיק יוֹמִין, which at 7:9, 13, 22 the LXX and Θ render by παλαιὸς ἡμερῶν. [2, 3]

3. παλαιός occurs in the Synoptic tradition only at Mk. 2:21 f. par. Mt. 9:16 f.; Lk. 5:36-38 and Lk. 5:39 in the sharp antithesis of old and new, and Mt. 13:52 with its similar antithesis. After the discussion of fasting the Synoptists add the proverbial sayings of Jesus concerning the incompatibility of old and new, Mk. 2:21 f. and par. The precise meaning depends on whether we take the verse more strictly in the context of the preceding discussion, so that there is esp. a polemic against John's disciples, [4] or whether we see an absolute expression of the certainty of Jesus, discernible in the antitheses of the Sermon on the Mount and many other passages, that the new thing which He brings can no more be united with what has been present thus far, the old, than a patch of unfulled material can be put on a new coat or new wine put in old skins. The whole character of the proclamation of Jesus inclines decisively towards the second and more general interpretation. His message is something completely new. In so far as the new replaces the old, there is further elucidation in Mt. 5:17: οὐκ ἦλθον καταλῦσαι ἀλλὰ πληρῶσαι. The new is the fulfilment of the old. [5] The saying in Lk. 5:39 is peculiar to Lk. and is related to the verse on the incompatibility of the old and the new. It is thus difficult to expound. Taken alone, it contradicts the preceding verses, since it advocates retention of the old. But it can be taken only in context, and hence it has to be regarded as a warning againt overvaluing the old. [6] Only Mt. 13:52 has at the end of the great discourse in parables the saying about the scribe who would be a disciple of the kingdom of heaven [7] and who thus like a householder brings forth out of his treasure things both new and old. The simplest explanation, namely, that he must set the new along with what he already had, [8] is hardly satisfying in the light of Mk. 2:21 f. and par. Furthermore, all the parables in Mt. 13

π α λ α ι ό ς. [1] Cf. Field, ad loc.
[2] It is surprising that this expression does not occur at all in the NT, not even in Rev., which is dependent on the descriptions in Da. at many other pts. It crops up again only in Just. Dial., 31, 2-3, 5; 32, 1; 79, 2.
[3] This paragraph, apart from the first two sentences, is by Bertram.
[4] Schl. Mt., 314 f., cf. also Loh. Mk., ad loc.
[5] → πίμπλημι. Cf. Hck. Mk., ad loc.; J. Schniewind Mk. (NT Deutsch), on 2:21 f.
[6] → 163, 12-20 and n. 6, 7; Hck. Lk., ad loc.
[7] On the Christian scribe → I, 742, 9-11 and the bibl. given there under n. 16.
[8] Kl. Mt., ad loc.

deal precisely with the one new thing presented by Jesus and His Word.[9] One must deal cautiously with proverbs of this kind, which are plainly supplementary in character (cf. Lk. 5:39). It is hard to say what would be the old things which the scribe of the kingdom of heaven is also to teach. One is tempted to refer to the fulfilment of the old along the lines of Mt. 5:17. That the new things are those brought by Jesus is plain to see.[10]

4. In Paul the antithesis of old and new is just as much emphasised as in the proclamation of Jesus. Indeed, Paul makes it even sharper by seeing in it the anti-thesis between evil and good. This is plain in the figurative 1 C. 5:6-8. The old leaven of malice and wickedness, which is the old nature, must give way to the unleavened bread of sincerity and truth, → II, 903, 9-905, 13. Paul is seeking to express the incompatibility between the previous life in sin and the newly begun Christian life. He does this by referring to the OT command that the old leaven must be put away prior to the Passover, Ex. 13:7. The thought is even more sharply put in the contrast between the old man and the new, R. 6:6; Col. 3:9; Eph. 4:22 (→ I, 365 f. and III, 449 f.). In R. 6 Paul says that he who is baptised is baptised into Christ's death (v. 3, 5); the old man he previously was has been crucified and put to death. The service of sin is no longer possible. He now has the gift and task of ἐν καινότητι ζωῆς περιπατεῖν (v. 4), of life ἐν καινότητι πνεύματος (7:6). The old and the new are mutually exclusive. The same is said in the horta-tory Col. 3:9 and the related Eph. 4:22. Christians are summoned to take seriously what is given them in baptism. They are to put off the old man and give place entirely to the new man, to put on this new man. Col. 3:5-8 describes the nature of the old man. He is characterised by a list of vices. But the mark of the new man is that he is created after God's image, Col. 3:10; Eph. 4:24. Paul is obviously thinking here of man's being made anew in baptism, which brings the old to a complete end. The similarity of the thought of Col. 3:11 to Gl. 3:27 f., where baptism is expressly mentioned, shows that this is the only possible interpretation. A further argument in favour of this understanding is to be found in 2 C. 5:14-17, where the thought of death (in baptism) leads to the victorious cry: "If any man be in Christ, he is a new creature: old things (τὰ ἀρχαῖα) are passed away; behold, all things are become new."[11]

The Law contributes nothing to this renewal of man. It is rather on the side of the old. Hence the covenant of the Law is called by Paul for the first time the παλαιὰ διαθήκη (2 C. 3:14, → II, 130, 18-29). It is characterised by the absence of the Spirit and the domination of the letter which kills, 3:6. In keeping with Paul's total view of the significance of the Law, he has in mind primarily the Pentateuch when he refers to the παλαιὰ διαθήκη. The reference to the reading of the Law in 2 C. 3:14 f. obviously forces us to assume that what is in view is public reading from the OT Scriptures in the synagogue.[12] But the old has passed away now that Christ has brought in the completely new. The old covenant brings judgment. The new, in contrast, brings righteousness. The new sets the old wholly

---

[9] J. Schniewind Mt. (*NT Deutsch*) on 13:52.

[10] The διὰ τοῦτο at the beginning of v. 52 may well relate to the whole of the preceding chapter.

[11] On the question of the origin of the metaphor of the old and new man → I, 366, n. 12, with bibl. So far no pre-Christian example of the Pauline usage has been found. There is no support for the thesis of Dib. Gefbr. on Col. 3:10 that παλαιός and νέος ἄνθρωπος are mystical terms ethically applied.

[12] Wnd. 2 K., *ad loc.*

to one side. They are incompatible. Nevertheless, the truth remains that the old covenant is significant, and is a covenant of God. [13]

5. In a way which is very different from that of Paul Jn. contrasts the ἐντολὴ καινή and the ἐντολὴ παλαιά, 1 Jn. 2:7. The whole context and the total presentation in Jn. shows that the ἐντολὴ παλαιὰ ἣν εἴχετε ἀπ᾽ ἀρχῆς does not refer to the OT commandment of love, which the world knew from its very origin (ἀπ᾽ ἀρχῆς). The allusion of ἀπ᾽ ἀρχῆς here is to the time of the conversion of the readers of the epistle, so that the meaning of the statement is : "I write to you the old commandment which you know so long as you are already Christians." Hence there is no theological antithesis between new and old at this point. Presumably when mentioning the old commandment Jn. had in view the commandment of love in Jn. 13:34 f., even if he only wrote the Gospel later. [14]

† παλαιότης.

παλαιότης, "age," "what is outdated." The word occurs in Eur., Plat., Aeschin., but is rare. [1] In the NT it is used only at R. 7:6 : ὥστε δουλεύειν [ἡμᾶς] ἐν καινότητι πνεύματος καὶ οὐ παλαιότητι γράμματος. In accordance with our earlier exposition (→ 719, 7-32) Paul is again emphasising the incompatibility of the old and the new. The service of God which consists only in observance of what is written is outmoded, and must be replaced by service in the power of the Spirit, → I, 766, 16-34.

† παλαιόω.

παλαιόω, [1] "to make old," "to declare to be obsolete." The term is found from Hippocr. and Plat., occurs in the pap., and is common in the LXX (= בָּלָה). Outside the Bible it is used only in the pass. In the NT it occurs in Hb. 1:11 in a quotation from ψ 101:26 : καὶ πάντες ὡς ἱμάτιον παλαιωθήσονται. Cf. Sir. 14:17: πᾶσα σὰρξ ὡς ἱμάτιον παλαιοῦται, and Jos. 9:13. In the NT also Lk. 12:33 : ποιήσατε ἑαυτοῖς βαλλάντια μὴ παλαιούμενα, "purses which do not grow old." On the use in the LXX → 718, 1 ff.

The word has theological significance only in Hb. 8:13, where it occurs twice. Without reference to historical events, and solely on the basis of his exposition of Jer. 31:31-34, the author argues in Hb. 8:13 that by setting up the new covenant God has declared the old to be outdated. God Himself cancels its validity. [2] The final conclusion is drawn in v. 13b, where it is said that what has become old and outmoded is (obviously) about to disappear (ἐγγὺς ἀφανισμοῦ). Thus we find here the same antithesis of new and old as in Jesus and Paul, though in the distinctive way determined by the exposition of Scripture in Hb.

Seesemann

---

[13] → IV, 1076, 9-43. It could well be that Paul coined the expression "old covenant" as a counterpart to the "new covenant" of Scripture (Jer. 31:31) and the eucharistic tradition (1 C. 11:25). In Pl., Jer. 31:31-34 is echoed only in R. 11:27 and is never quoted directly. On the other hand, it is expressly cited in Hb. 8:8-12. In explanation, however, Hb. normally calls the old covenant the "first" covenant, 8:7, 13; 9:1, 15, 18. The tabernacle is also called the "first" tent, 9:8. The greater and more perfect tabernacle is contrasted with it, 9:11.

[14] Cf. Wnd. Kath. Br., *ad loc.* and Bü. J., *ad loc.*

π α λ α ι ό τ η ς. [1] Cf. Pr.-Bauer, *s.v.*

π α λ α ι ό ω. [1] Cf. Pr.-Bauer, *s.v.*

[2] In v. 13a we find the rare act. παλαιόω, which occurs only in the LXX : Job 9:5 (of God): ὁ παλαιῶν ὄρη καὶ οὐκ οἴδασιν, cf. Is. 65:22; Lam. 3:4.

| † πάλη | → πανοπλία, 295-302.

This word, attested from the time of Hom., occurs in the NT only at Eph. 6:12, and here in the context of the metaphor of the Christian's armour.

Since πάλη (not in the LXX) [1] is primarily "wrestling," it seems at a first glance to be out of place in this passage. But Gk. tragedy had prepared the way for the more general sense of "conflict," Eur. Heracl., 159. [2] Philo, too, likes to speak of the wrestling of the ascetic, though he does not add other terms which go beyond the metaphor of actual wrestling, Leg. All., III, 190 : πάλην δ' οὐ τὴν σώματος ἀλλ' ἣν παλαίει ψυχὴ πρὸς τοὺς ἀνταγωνιστὰς τρόπους αὐτῆς πάθεσι καὶ κακίαις μαχομένη, Mut. Nom., 14 : μετὰ γοῦν τὴν πάλην, ἣν ὑπὲρ κτήσεως ἀρετῆς ὁ ἀσκητὴς ἐπάλαισε. Nevertheless, Philo may have no more than general "conflict" in view, as shown by a comparison with Abr., 243, which describes the armour in which the logos goes out to meet the same foe as the ascetic elsewhere (πάθη). The metaphor of the believer's warfare is naturally suggested whenever proclamation demands moral strictness, liberation from the chains of matter, endurance in the world etc. The Stoic [3] feels that he is a warrior, and so, too, does the devotee of the mysteries. [4] The Jewish sect of the Dead Sea Scrolls thinks of itself as the "children of light" engaged in battle with the "children of darkness," → 298-300. [5]

For the Christian this warfare has an eschatological dimension. His wrestling is part of the great final battle which has already begun and is intensifying. His opponents are the devil and demons, [6] his reward preservation and deliverance in the judgment. The same figure of speech is used by Paul elsewhere, cf. 1 Th. 5:8; R. 6:13; 13:12. [7]

Greeven

παλιγγενεσία → I, 686, 20 ff.

π ά λ η. J. Jüthner, Art. "Pale," Pauly-W., XVIII, 2, 82-89. Dib. Gefbr., Exc. on Eph. 6:10-17.

[1] The verb παλαίειν occurs in the LXX, e.g., for Jacob's wrestling at Gn. 32:25 (אבק) and also with ref. to the primal and eschatological cosmic conflict in 'A at Job 38:8, the sea (גיח), and LXX Est. 1:1e, the dragon (no Mas.), cf. also Ju. 20:33 A (גיח). In all these passages παλαίειν has the general sense "to fight" [Bertram].

[2] Cf. Thes. Steph., s.v. πάλη also means "conflict" in the Alexandra of Lycophron, 1358 etc., though this is perhaps not by the poet, but by a younger author b. 250-240 B.C., cf. K. J. Beloch, Griech. Geschichte², IV, 2 (1927), 568-574.

[3] E.g., Epict. Diss., III, 25, 2.

[4] Material in Dibelius.

[5] Cf. also K. G. Kuhn, "Die in Palästina gefundenen hbr. Texte u. d. NT," ZThK, 47 (1950), 202 f., 208.

[6] W. Bousset, "Die Himmelsreise d. Seele," ARW, 4 (1901), 144 conjectures that the ref. in Eph. is to demons hampering the soul on its heavenly journey.

[7] Closely related is the boxing metaphor (→ πυκτεύω) in 1 C. 9:26, which, as πάλη originally did, belongs to the fairly commonly adduced sphere of sporting contests. On the history of the metaphor of conflict in the early Church cf. A. Harnack, Militia Christi (1905), 93-114; H. v. Soden, "Μυστήριον u. sacramentum in den ersten 2 Jhdten. d. Kirche," ZNW, 12 (1911), 206-224; on the earlier history, H. Emonds, "Geistlicher Kriegsdienst. Der Topos der militia spiritualis in d. antiken Philosophie," Heilige Überlieferung, Festgabe J. Herwegen (1938), 21-50.

---

† πανήγυρις

πανήγυρις is composed of πᾶν + ἀγείρω, "gathering" of the whole people esp. on cultic occasions and at festivals : "festal assembly," Hom., e.g., Il., 16, 661. The word is found from Archiloch., Pind., Hdt. (II, 58 f.: πανηγύριας δὲ ἄρα καὶ πομπὰς καὶ προσαγωγὰς πρῶτοι ἀνθρώπων Αἰγύπτιοί εἰσι οἱ ποιησάμενοι ... πανηγυρίζουσι δὲ Αἰγύπτιοι οὐχ ἅπαξ τοῦ ἐνιαυτοῦ, πανηγύριας δὲ συχνάς ...), Thuc. (V, 50, 4 : δέος ἐγένετο τῇ πανηγύρει μέγα), also Philo (Flacc., 118), inscr., pap. It also occurs in the same sense in the LXX, mostly for sacrifices which are rejected by God because they are under pagan influence : Hos. 2:13 : καὶ ἀποστρέψω ... ἑορτὰς αὐτῆς καὶ τὰς νουμηνίας αὐτῆς καὶ τὰ σάββατα αὐτῆς καὶ πάσας τὰς πανηγύρεις αὐτῆς (here = מוֹעֵד). Cf. also Hos. 9:5; Ez. 46:11 (where it means the feast which God Himself has appointed). At Am. 5:21 it is used for עֲצָרָה, cf. Wis. 15:12. The verb πανηγυρίζειν is used at Is. 66:10 = גִּיל. In Ael. Var. Hist., III, 1 πανήγυρις ὀφθαλμῶν has the looser sense "pleasure," "delight."

In the NT the word πανήγυρις occurs only at Hb. 12:22 : ἀλλὰ προσεληλύθατε Σιὼν ὄρει καὶ πόλει θεοῦ ζῶντος, Ἰερουσαλὴμ ἐπουρανίῳ, καὶ μυριάσιν ἀγγέλων, πανηγύρει, (23) καὶ ἐκκλησίᾳ πρωτοτόκων. While the term itself causes no difficulties, since it can only have the common sense of "festal gathering," the grammatical order of the words is more difficult. It seems best, with most of the Greek fathers, [1] to take πανηγύρει in apposition to μυριάσιν ἀγγέλων : "you have come ... to myriads of angels, to the festal assembly, and to the company of the firstborn." The position of πανηγύρει is thus the same as that of the appositive Ἰερουσαλὴμ ἐπουρανίῳ. The independent datives in vv. 22-24 are usually linked by a καί. The punctuation of the ancient MSS[2] also supports this view. A description of this type of festal assembly may be found in the NT in Rev. 4. πανήγυρις never established itself as a Christian term.

Seesemann

πανοπλία → 295 ff.

---

† πανουργία, † πανοῦργος

A. πανουργία and πανοῦργος in Non-Biblical Usage.

Derivation from the stems παν- and εργ- gives the basic sense of "capable of all work," [1] and there is conscious recollection of this. [2] πανοῦργος is common from Aesch., derivates from Soph.

π α ν ή γ υ ρ ι ς. Cf. the dict. and Boisacq, *s.v.*
[1] Orig., Euseb., Bas. Cf. Mi. Hb., *ad loc.*
[2] A C L M P al. Cf. Rgg. Hb.[3] (1922), 415, n. 21. Cf. also the vl. of D : μυρίων ἀγίων πανηγύρει.

π α ν ο υ ρ γ ί α, π α ν ο ῦ ρ γ ο ς. Wnd. 2 K., 133; Liddell-Scott, *s.v.* Def.: Thom. Mag., Ecloge vocum atticarum, ed. F. Ritschl (1832), 303.
[1] πανττουργός (earlier only in Soph. Ai., 445) also goes back to the same two stems. Acc. to Kühner-Blass, II, 335, n. 9 πανοῦργος follows the analogy of παντουργός, but Debr. Griech. Wortb., 33, 61 and E. Schwyzer, *Griech. Gramm.*, I = Hndbch. *AW*, II, 1, 1 (1939), 437 give convincing reasons for analogous formation to that of κακοῦργος.
[2] E.g., in the complaint about the power of money, Soph. Ant., 300 f.: πανουργίας δ' ἔδειξεν ἀνθρώποις ἔχειν καὶ παντὸς ἔργου δυσσέβειαν εἰδέναι.

1. In the few instances in which the word group is positively meant to express all-round ability there is always the reservation of a certain degree of assumption. Man is inclined to regard himself as the πανουργότατον among all creatures. In truth, however, he is the εὐπαραλογιστότατον, the one "which most easily comes to a wrong self-evaluation, or concerning which a wrong estimation can most easily be made." [3]

It is worth noting that the judge with a disturbed past (πολλὰ αὐτὸς ἠδικηκώς) may think that he is better qualified by virtue thereof (καὶ πανοῦργός τε καὶ σοφὸς οἰόμενος εἶναι, Plat. Resp., III, 409c). Average men dominated by superficial rationalism, who think the whole idea of future consequences for present actions is an imaginary product of the ἀνόητοι, are in their own eyes, but only theirs, δεινοὶ καὶ πανοῦργοι, Plat. Theaet., 177a. In parody many things seem to be πανούργως, highly effective, which — by an added ὑποκριτικῶς — are shown to be more at home on the stage than on the stage of life, Athen., IX, 72 (p. 407a). The youthful worshipper of the Muses should not uncritically regard the εὑρησιλογίαι (sophistries) which he finds in the poets as κομψὸν καὶ πανοῦργον (fine and clever) (Plut. Aud. Poet., 8 [II, 28a]). That the positive use here is imposed upon the less assured, so that in some sense it stands in quotation marks, is shown by the sentences immediately preceding, in which Plutarch's own use emerges, for here seductive λόγοι are called πιθανοί and πανοῦργοι (plausible and cunning). [4]

2. The positive use, which is exceedingly limited and rare, seems to be secondary and not a direct development of the positive possibility implicit in the word. It is also attested only many centuries after the negative use, according to which πανοῦργος has the amoral sense of "capable of anything" (→ n. 2) and πανουργία that of "slyness," "cunning." [5] The idea that a man himself may have something of the πανοῦργος about him, and yet still be respected, might have some appeal to sophistical spirits whose mode of thought and speech is contested by the authorities cited above (→ lines 7-20), but if another man is called πανοῦργος the criticism decisively outweighs any respect.

The expression πανουργικὸν ξύλον is an example of the way in which the negative sense is rooted in the general linguistic sense. Since it is found in a magical direction for the detection of thieves, [6] it might suggest a piece of wood of general magical force, but what is really meant is a piece of wood from the place befitting a πανοῦργος, namely, the gallows. Antigone did not carry out as ὅσια πανουργήσασα pious acts of extraordinary efficacy. She simply observed a pious duty which was a transgression in the eyes of others, Soph. Ant., 74. The word group is used for wily animals, Aristot. Hist. An., VIII, 1, p. 588a, 23. Even though πανοῦργος can be a divine attribute, [7] the negative sense is self-evident. Aristot. Eth. Nic., VI, 13, p. 1144a, 23-29, 36 f., in a discussion of δεινότης, obviously uses both adj. and noun in the negative sense always found in him. δεινότης is ability truly to reach a set σκοπός, ἂν μὲν οὖν ὁ σκοπὸς ᾖ καλός, ἐπαινετή ἐστιν, ἂν δὲ φαῦλος, πανουργία· διὸ καὶ τοὺς φρονίμους δεινοὺς καὶ <τοὺς> πανούργους φαμὲν εἶναι. ἔστι δ᾽ ἡ φρόνησις οὐχ ἡ δεινότης, ἀλλ᾽ οὐκ ἄνευ τῆς δυνάμεως ταύτης ... ὥστε φανερὸν ὅτι ἀδύνατον φρό-

---

[3] [Kleinknecht]; Polyb., 5, 75, 2.

[4] Cf. G. v. Reutern, *Plutarchs Stellung zur Dichtkunst*, Diss. Kiel (1933), 38.

[5] Pass., *s.v.* δεινός goes too far when he says that in the moral sense δεινός is the same in the good as πανοῦργος is in the bad.

[6] Preis. Zaub., V, 74-75 (Liddell-Scott suggests there may be a scribal error). The pap. have πανοῦργος and πανουργία only in the bad sense, Preisigke Wört., *s.v.* If in Ps.-Callisth., II, 16 vl. the ref. of the puzzling ὅπλα πανουργικά is to an actualisation of the marshal's dream of universal weapons, then this is meant, of course, only in an ironical sense.

[7] Eur. Hipp., 1400 on the lips of Artemis with ref. to Aphrodite.

νιμον εἶναι μὴ ὄντα ἀγαθόν. If the goal is morally good, δεινότης is praiseworthy, but if not, it is πανουργία. Hence we call the φρόνιμοι and the πανοῦργοι δεινοί. φρόνησις is not itself the ability, but is not without it. [8]

The word group, then, can be synonymous to the κακουργία group (→ III, 484, 34 ff.) [9] and in the Attic sphere [10] it can even go further by reason of the incalculability of the παν-. [11,12] The fact that it is constructed after the manner of that group (→ n. 1), however, does not wholly explain the primarily negative signification, since παντουργός, which is constructed analogously to πανοῦργος, is not used negatively in the one known example from an earlier period (→ n. 1). Hence the true reason why the positive possibility immanent in the term was not developed in the first instance is to be found in the insight that this possibility is in truth no real possibility for man because of his physical and personal limitations; the very thought of such a possibility is already a step to ὕβρις. The man who by reason of intelligence and energy has the secret of success to any considerable degree will, according to experience, use it unscrupulously. Awareness of this introduces such reserve in the use of the word group that, though such use might seem natural, it is not even applied to deity in the positive sense (→ n. 7).

B. Πανουργία and πανοῦργος in the LXX and Philo.

1. In the LXX the word group is used 17 times for the Heb. group ערם, עָרוּם, עָרְמָה, [13] and only 3 times for other Heb. words, [14] while ערם is not rendered by πανουργ- 6 times. [15] The Heb. group corresponds to the Gk. inasmuch as it can mean "sly," "cunning," but there is tension to the degree that in Prv. it can have the unconditional positive sense of "clever," "prudent." Since the group is used esp. commonly in Prv., its meaning has in the main a notable tendency towards the positive side. In face of this shift in meaning it should be recalled that in Prv. negative ethico-religious concepts are preferably rendered by κακός (→ III, 476, 32 ff.), and that a word which obviously

---

[8] So E. Schlesinger, "Δεινότης," Philol., 91, NF, 45 (1936), 60. If the introduction of τούς before πανούργους is not regarded as certain, there might be criticism of a wrong positive use of the adj.: "Hence (in overhasty confusion of terms) we are wont to call the φρόνιμοι δεινοί and even πανοῦργοι." But such a use would take much too lightly the ethical quality attaching to the very essence of the φρόνιμος. Cf. on this Plat. Menex., 247a πᾶσά τε ἐπιστήμη χωριζομένη δικαιοσύνης καὶ τῆς ἄλλης ἀρετῆς πανουργία οὐ σοφία φαίνεται. Where, as among the Phoenicians and Egyptians, there is in instruction a failure to counterbalance formal ability to count by true education, there arises acc. to Plat. Leg., V, 747c α καλουμένη ... πανουργία ἀπτὶ σοφίας, cf. F. Zucker, "Athen u. Ägypten bis auf den Beginn der hell. Zeit," Aus Antike u. Orient = Festschr. f. W. Schubart (1950), 158 f.

[9] Ditt. Or., II, 515, 48. Cf. also the beginning of Schol. in Demosth. Or. adversus Leptinem, ed. F. A. Wolf (1789), 108 f.

[10] Cf. Schol. (ed. G. Dindorff, 4, 2 [1838]) on Aristoph. Ra., 35: τὸ δὲ "πανοῦργε" ἡμεῖς μὲν μετριώτερον φαμέν, Ἀττικοὶ δὲ ἐπὶ σφοδρᾶς βλασφημίας.

[11] Cf. Demosth. Or., 1, 3: πανοῦργος ὢν καὶ δεινὸς ἄνθρωπος ... τὰ μὲν εἴκων ... τὰ δὲ ἀπειλῶν ... τὰ δ᾽ ἡμᾶς διαβάλλων.

[12] Cf. → n. 2 and the unquestionably realistic chorus of knights in Aristoph. Eq., 247-250:
παῖε παῖε τὸν πανοῦργον καὶ ταραξιππόστρατον
καὶ τελώνην καὶ φάραγγα καὶ Χάρυβδιν ἁρπαγῆς,
καὶ πανοῦργον καὶ πανοῦργον· πολλάκις γὰρ αὔτ᾽ ἐρῶ.
καὶ γὰρ οὗτος ἦν πανοῦργος πολλάκις τῆς ἡμέρας.

[13] Jos. 9:4; 1 Βασ. 23:22; Prv. 1:4; 8:5; 12:16; 13:16; 14:8, 15, 18; 15:5; 19:25; 22:3; 27:12; Job 5:12; cf. Nu. 24:22, where the LXX reads עד־מה as ערמה, and Prv. 14:24, where it rightly reads ערמתם for עשרם. Finally ψ 82:3 κατεπανουργεύσαντο.

[14] Prv. 13:1; 21:11; 28:2.

[15] Gn. 3:1; Ex. 21:14; Prv. 8:12; 12:23; Job 5:13; 15:5.

did not have this negative sense in its root did not invite so much use in this way. [16] On the other hand, this hardly explains the abundant positive use. Nor does a popular development of Sophist use (→ 723, 25 ff.), which at the very most has only incidental significance. Nor does mere awkwardness in translation technique, for in 3 of the 6 instances where the Heb. has a negative content the LXX avoids transl. by πανουργ-, [17] while on the other hand it has πανουργ- on 3 occasions where in an emphatically positive sense the Heb. has the adj. חָכָם (Prv. 13:1) or the verbs חכם, בין, ידע (Prv. 21:11; 28:2). The essential reason why the LXX tends to evaluate the word group positively is thus to be sought in the Heb. text, but in the content rather than the letter. The content of the OT awakened a firm conviction that man might very well be able in the good sense to pursue successfully any work in the human sphere : "whatever he does prospers." The fear of God gives rise to → σοφία (Prv. 1:7) and closely related to this, though not identical, is sovereign practical wisdom (Prv. 14:24). [18] To express this in Gk. the word group naturally sprang to mind. With no ironical or pessimistic undertones it could be used in the sense which was proper to it by origin but which in practice had been left in statu nascendi, namely, that of "full ability." Its choice as a rendering of ערם was primarily suggested, not by the link with the possible negative use of ערם, but by its own potential positive signification. The admonition in Prv. 8:5 νοήσατε, ἄκακοι, πανουργίαν would have to be understood as an unequivocal temptation according to the current use (→ n. 23), but one need not be surprised that in the LXX the simple are hereby summoned to a supremely legitimate cleverness. Nor need one be surprised that in the LXX the υἱὸς πανοῦργος is held up as a model of obedience, Prv. 13:1; cf. 15:5. [19]

In Sir. the use of the group and the relation to the Heb. original correspond to our findings in respect of the Heb. Canon. [20] It is noteworthy that the σφραγὶς πανοῦργος which acc. to 22:27 should restrain the tongue is a prudent rather than a cunning seal. Nevertheless, it is even more evident in Sir. that the wisdom nourished by divine revelation is the primary thing and that πανουργία is derived, so that if it breaks free it becomes an evil, or πανουργία in the current sense : οὐ παιδευθήσεται, ὃς οὐκ ἔστιν πανοῦργος, ἔστιν δὲ πανουργία πληθύνουσα πικρίαν (much πανουργία, however, brings much bitterness with it), 21:12, cf. 19:23, 25. At Sir. 37:19 the Heb. has חָכָם for the unworthy teacher who in spite of striking success is inwardly empty. If the LXX has πανοῦργος here rather than σοφός, this is not because of the relation between the terms, as at Prv. 13:1, but because of the difference between them. There was no desire to say of the σοφός that he might be τῇ ἰδίᾳ ψυχῇ ἄχρηστος. [21]

2. Philo uses πανουργία in one place (Leg. All., II, 106 f.) in connection with manual τέχναι, so that it might well have the neutral sense of "skill" : τὰ γοῦν ποιητικὰ αὐτῆς (sc. ἡδονῆς) εὑρίσκεται διὰ πανουργίας πάσης, χρυσὸς ἄργυρος δόξα τιμαί ἀρχαί, αἱ ὗλαι τῶν αἰσθητῶν καὶ τέχναι αἱ βάναυσοι καὶ ὅσαι ἄλλαι κατασκευαστικαὶ ἡδονῆς πάνυ ποικίλαι. Just before, however, he says of ἡδονή that it, like the serpent in Paradise, τῶν πάντων πανουργότατόν ἐστιν, and directly after

---

[16] Cf. G. Bertram, "Das Problem d. Umschrift u. d. religionsgeschichtliche Erforschung d. LXX," ZAW Beih., 66 (1936), 107 f.

[17] Gn. 3:1 (as against ᾿ΑΣΘ); Ex. 21:14; Job 15:5 (not Σ). In the last ref. we have to reckon with the possibility that the selected rendering δυνάστης is meant positively for those are in a position to say something [Bertram].

[18] In this milieu one need not fear misunderstanding in the sense of amoral self-assertion, though in the transl. of other bibl. books we do not find a full emancipation from the current negative use, Nu. 24:22; Jos. 9:4; 1 Βασ. 23:22; Job 5:12; cf. Sir. 19:23, 25; 21:12b; 34(31):10; 37:19, → infra. Jdt. 11:8 is perhaps intentionally equivocal. Holofernes is not displeased to hear admiration of his πανουργία from the lips of the weak, but the reader has his own ideas, → 723, 25 ff.

[19] Cf. the other refs. from Prv. → n. 13, 14. On the puzzling πανοῦργος δὲ ἔρχεται εἰς μετάνοιαν in 14:15 → IV, 984, n. 44; 991, 1 ff.

[20] 1:6; 6:32; 19:23, 25; 21:12, 20; 22:27; 34:10; 37:19; 42:18.

[21] R. Smend, Die Weisheit d. Jesus Sirach (1906), 334.

ἡδονή is called the source of ἀδικήματα which οὐκ ἄνευ πανουργίας τῆς ἐσχάτης ἐστίν. Since, then, the negative sense of "cunning" or "extreme cunning" is unambiguous both before and after, the sentence in between, no matter how construed, obviously has a negative and critical bearing ; πανουργία means here "refinement" in the less reputable sense. Hence the passage is no exception to Philo's consistently negative use as distinct from that of the LXX. [22] The word group is for him ill-adapted to describe the quality of the wise man. On the contrary, designation of πανουργία as σοφία is a misuse, contrary to the truth, which ὁ νῦν ἀνθρώπων σοφιστικὸς ὅμιλος makes, ἔργῳ μοχθηρῷ θεῖον ἐπιφημίσαντες ὄνομα, Poster. C., 101 and → n. 8 Plato. If it is true of man that in some sense he is capable of all things, Philo sees primarily the tragedy which results from abuse of this ability. He would not speak of πανουργία in animals. The φοραί in which even irrational brutes share do not derive ἀπὸ κακίας πανούργου but from ἀμαθία. πανουργία on the other hand is ἑκούσιον ψυχῆς ἀρρώστημα, Sacr. AC, 47 f.; Cain already fell victim to it, Det. Pot. Ins., 165; cf. Jos. Ant., 1, 61. Allusion was made to its early history in Gn. 3, → 725, 41. Again, in Op. Mund., 156, after ref. to the serpent, we are told that the eating incited by it ἐξ ἀκακίας καὶ ἁπλότητος ἠθῶν εἰς πανουργίαν μετέβαλεν. [23] Philo has a sense of the satanic background of πανουργία. He mentions it not infrequently ; it is at the head of the long list of vices in Sacr. AC, 32, cf. Conf. Ling., 117.

C. πανουργία and πανοῦργος in the NT and the Later Period.

1. The NT uses the word group only negatively. At Lk. 20:23 the πανουργία of the opponents of Jesus is to be construed as "cunning" in the current sense. The same is true of the accusation which Paul denies in 2 C. 12:16 and perhaps also 2 C. 4:2, [24] though here some contribution is perhaps made by the motif of satanic cunning and the art of misrepresentation (v. 4 : ὁ θεὸς τοῦ αἰῶνος τούτου), as is probable in Eph. 4:14 [25] and certain in 2 C. 11:3. At 1 C. 3:19 Paul has πανουργία in an OT quotation where the LXX has a different rendering (Job 5:13, → n. 15). He is perhaps influenced by the Hebrew text or by recollection of Job 5:12.

Here, and in all our findings, it is evident how remote the NT is from the positive development in the LXX. Regard for the capacity of the hearers militated already against this development, for the LXX use was not the current one. Another factor was the significance of the idea of satanic πανουργία. In particular, however, the word group probably had an autonomous and self-righteous ring. On the NT view the way from OT πανουργία to βδέλυγμα was even shorter than on that of Sir. 19:23 (Sir. 21:12 → 725, 31 f.). In the non-biblical world regard for self-seeking had prevented the development of the positive possibilities immanent in the word group. Regard for self-righteousness, however, prevented the further development of the positive use found already in the LXX. The NT equivalent of the concern of the LXX is not expressed by this group but in other ways, cf. Mk. 9:23 or Phil. 4:13 : πάντα ἰσχύω ἐν τῷ ἐνδυναμοῦντί με.

2. In Herm., v., 3, 3, 1 Hermas is called πανοῦργος in a warning, though not with full seriousness, but probably (as the answer shows) in the sense that there are possibly

---

[22] As against I. Heinemann in L. Cohn, Die Werke Philos v. Alex. in deutscher Übersetzung, 3 (1919), 85, n. 1. Joseph., too, uses the word group only negatively.

[23] Cf. on this → 727, 18, Prv. 8:5.

[24] We have to take into account the possibility that the criticism was not meant as sharply as appears in the rejoinder. On the lips of opponents the adj. πανοῦργος possibly meant simply that Paul is so cunning, and can always find such effective ways to help himself, that his official refusal of support does not amount to very much.

[25] Cf. 4:14 πανουργία πρὸς τὴν μεθοδείαν τῆς πλάνης with 6:11 μεθοδείας τοῦ διαβόλου.

ulterior motives behind his pious curiosity, cf. s., 5, 5,1, where πανοῦργος stands alongside αὐθάδης (→ I, 508 f.). The sister word παντουργός (→ n. 1), which was always rarer and thus less loaded, came later to fulfil high functions in both the non-Christian [26] and the Christian sphere, Eustath. Comm. in Il., 29, 31: θεία ἐστίν ἡ λέξις; cf. the conclusion of the def. mentioned above.

Bauernfeind

παντοκράτωρ → III, 914, 13 ff.

παρά

Contents : A. παρά with the Genitive : 1. Spatial ; 2. To denote the Author : a. With a Specific Group of Verbs ; b. With Verbs in the Pass.; c. With Other Verbs and Verbal Concepts ; d. With Adjectival and Nominal Prepositional Expressions. B. παρά with the Dative : 1. Spatial : a. With Things ; b. With Persons ; 2. Forensically ; 3. Figuratively. C. παρά with the Accusative : 1. Spatial : a. The Question Whither ? b. The Question Where ? 2. Comparative : a. To Denote Preference ; b. In the Comparative Sense ; c. Exclusive ; 3. To Denote Difference ; 4. Adversative ; 5. Causal.

A. παρά[1] with the Genitive (Ablative).[2]

1. Spatial : from the proximity of a person, [3] "out of," "from beside," "from," [4] Mk. 16:9; [5] Lk. 6:19.

---

[26] Damascius Dubitationes et solutiones de primis principiis, 57 (ed. C. Ruelle, 1 [1889], 120).

π α ρ ά. Bl.-Debr.[7, 8] § 236-238, v. also § 185, 3; 245, 3; A. Robertson, *A Grammar of the Gk. NT*[3] (1919), 612-616; F. M. Abel, *Grammaire du grec biblique* (1927), 228 f.; P. F. Regard, *Contribution à l'étude des prépositions dans la langue du NT* (1918), 513-526; Johannessohn Kasus, 44; also Präpos., 226-235; Mayser, II, 2, 482-492; E. Schwyzer, *Griech. Grammatik,* II (*Hndbch. AW*, II, 1, 2 [1950]), 491-499. F. H. Rau, "De praepositionis παρά usu," *Studien z. gr. u. lat. Grammatik*, ed. G. Curtius, Vol. 3 (1870); A. R. Alvin, De usu praepositionis παρά apud Thuc. (Diss. Uppsala [1878]); W. Nawijn, De praepositionis παρά significatione atque usu apud Cassium Dionem (Diss. Amsterdam [1907]). For works on διά (→ II, 65 bibl.) and other prep. cf. Schwyzer, II, 417 f. Cf. also M. Zerwick, *Graecitas biblica exemplis illustratur*[2] (1949), 20-33; B. F. C. Atkinson, *The Theology of Prepositions* (1944); H. Widmann, *Beiträge z. Syntax Epikurs* (1935), 191-231; F. Krebs, *Die Präpos. bei Polybius* (1882); A. Rüger, *Die Präpos. bei Pausanias* (Diss. Erlangen [1897]); also *Studien zu Malalas : Präpos. u. Adverbien* (1895); also *Die Präpos. bei Johannes Antiochenus,* 1 (Gymnasial-Programm Münnerstadt [1895/96]); H. Mossbacher, *Präpositionen u. Präpositionsadverbien … bei Cl. v. Alex.* (Diss. Erlangen [1931]); F. Spohr, *Die Präp. bei M. Aurelius Antonin* (Diss. Erlangen [1890]); F. Rostalski, *Sprachliches zu d. apokryphen Apostelgeschichten,* 2 (Gymnasial-Programm Myslowitz [1910/11]); E. Seidel, De usu praepositionum Plotiniano quaestiones (Diss. Breslau [1886]); S. Linnér, *Syntaktische u. lexikalische Studien zur Historia Lausiaca des Palladios* (Diss. Uppsala [1943]), 27-77; J. Scheftlein, De praepositionum usu Procopiano (Diss. Erlangen [1893]); H. Rheinfelder, De praepositionum usu Zosimeo (Diss. Würzburg [1915]).

[1] Related first to πάρος, "earlier," then to περί, πρό, πρός, Lat. *per, prae, pro* : Boisacq[3] (1938), 772; Schwyzer, II, 492. As an adv. it means "near," "at hand." In compounds παρά as a prefix before verbs, nouns and adj. has the following senses in the NT : 1. "near," "beside," "at hand," as in παρακαθίζω, παραθαλάσσιος, πάροινος; 2. "comparative," e.g., παραβάλλω, παρομοιάζω; 3. "to," e.g., παραγίνομαι, παραδίδωμι; 4. "hither," e.g., παραδέχομαι, παραλαμβάνω; 5. "along," e.g., παράγω, παραπλέω; 6. "away," e.g., παραιτέω, παραφέρω; 7. "over," "crossing over the borders," "against," e.g., παραβαίνω, παρανομέω, παράδοξος; 8. "swerving from the right way," "wrongly," "secretly," e.g., παρεισάγω, παρεισέρχομαι; 9. "leaving out of account," e.g., παραβουλεύομαι, παρακούω, παροράω; 10. strengthening or factitive sense, e.g., παροξύνω,

2. To denote the Author. By transf. from the spatial sense it is used to denote the author, "from."

a. With a Specific Group of Verbs. [6]

(a) After verbs of asking or demanding ἠτήσατο ... παρ' Ἀθηναίων τριακοσίους ἱππέας, Xenoph. Hist. Graec., III, 1, 4; cf. P. Fay., 121, 13; τὰ μὲν ἔργα παρ' ὑμῶν αὐτῶν ζητεῖτε, τὰ δὲ βέλτιστα ἐπιστήμη λέγειν παρὰ τοῦ παριόντος, Demosth. Or., 8, 75. In the LXX the use of παρά in this and the next instances [7] corresponds in the main to the Heb. use of מִן, מֵעִם or מֵאֵת, also מִלִּפְנֵי, מִיַּד and מֵאֵצֶל, e.g., Ex. 3:22; 11:2; also Sir. 7:4; Tob. 4:18. (b) After verbs of taking, receiving and buying : παρὰ Μήδων τὴν ἀρχὴν ἐλάμβανον Πέρσαι, Xenoph. An., III, 4, 8 : λαβὼν ἐξουσίαν παρὰ σοῦ, Jos. Ant., 14, 167; Cf. P. Oxy., III, 504, 14; IV, 742, 2. ὠνέονται τὰς γυναῖκας παρὰ τῶν γονέων, Hdt., V, 6; P. Oxy., VII, 1149, 5; in the LXX, e.g., Gn. 21:30; Dt. 2:6; 2 Esr. 20:32; 1 Macc. 8:8; 11:34. (c) After verbs of hearing and answering : ἀκούσαντες πολλοὺς ἑτέρους λόγους παρὰ τῶν πρέσβεων, Demosth. Or., 6, 26; παρὰ θεῶν πυνθανόμενος, Xenoph. Cyrop., I, 6, 23; ὁμολογέουσι παρ' Αἰγυπτίων μεμαθηκέναι, Hdt., II, 104; cf. Jos. Ap., II, 176. In the LXX e.g., Ex. 18:15; Is. 21:10; 2 Ch. 32:31; Sir. 8:8, 9; 3 Macc. 1:1.

In the NT we find sense (a) at, e.g., Mt. 20:20; [8] Mk. 8:11; Jn. 5:44; [9] Jm. 1:5; sense (b) at, e.g., Mt. 18:19; Mk. 12:2; Ac. 7:16; Eph. 6:8; 2 Th. 3:8. With the message or commission the authority of the giver, acc. to Jewish tradition, [10] passes to the recipient : ταύτην τὴν ἐντολὴν ἔλαβον παρὰ τοῦ πατρός μου, Jn. 10:18 (cf. 5:34, 41, 44); παραλαμβάνειν παρά τινος, 1 C. 11:23 vl.; [11] Gl. 1:12; 1 Th.

παραπικραίνω, παράσημος. Cf. on this Schwyzer, II, 493, 498; Robertson, 613; W. Crönert, "Adnotamenta in Papyros Musei Britannici Graecas," Class. Rev., 17 (1903), 26; P. A. van der Laan, De παρά praepositionis vi apud Euripidem in compositione verborum (Diss. Amsterdam [1907]). Elision with παρά in the NT MS tradition mostly only before pron., e.g., παρ' αὐτῶν, παρ' ἡμῶν, παρ' οὐδενί though cf. also παρ' ἐλπίδα in R. 4:18 and παρ' ἀγγέλους in Hb. 2:9 (ψ 8:5), though there is probably more elision in the spoken word than the written, cf. Bl.-Debr. § 17. On πάρ and παρά in older speech cf. Schwyzer, II, 491 f., also P. Kretschmer, "Zur Gesch. d. griech. Dialekte," Glotta, 1 (1909), 35-37, 51 f.; F. Sommer, Zur griech. Prosodie, ibid., 178.

[2] The gen. is most common with παρά in the NT, also the LXX.

[3] Cf. the French de chez quelqu'un, also the Heb. מֵעִם in 2 S. 3:15; 24:21; Ps. 121:2, which the LXX renders by παρά and the gen.

[4] There are many instances in profane Gk. and the LXX, but this sense is rarer in the Hell. period, and in the NT occurs only with persons, not things.

[5] vl. ἀπό.

[6] In most verbs of this kind along with ἀπό, ἐκ, πρός τινος, cf. Bl.-Debr. § 210, 3. In the Hell. period ἀπό becomes esp. prominent in this connection.

[7] Johannessohn Präpos., 227 f.; Helbing Kasussyntax, 41; Abel, 228.

[8] vl. ἀπ' αὐτοῦ. Bl.-Debr. § 210, 3.

[9] Here the expression τὴν δόξαν τὴν παρὰ τοῦ μόνου θεοῦ is influenced by the controlling οὐ ζητεῖτε.

[10] Cf. παράδοσις → II, 172 f.; W. G. Kümmel, "Jesus u. d. jüdische Traditionsgedanke," ZNW, 33 (1934), 105-130; O. Cullmann, "Paradosis et Kyrios," Revue d'Histoire et de Philosophie Religieuses, 30 (1950), 12-30.

[11] ἐγὼ γὰρ παρέλαβον παρὰ κυρίου D, ἀπὸ τοῦ κυρίου in most MSS, ἀπὸ θεοῦ G. The reading παρὰ κυρίου is influenced by the use of παραλαμβάνειν παρά τινος elsewhere in Pl., the reading ἀπὸ θεοῦ is certainly not original. Linguistic pars. show that παρά usually denotes direct receiving of a tradition, whereas ἀπό is best construed as its mediation through a chain of human members, hence ἀπὸ τοῦ κυρίου, "from the Lord" (so esp. E. B. Allo, Komm. zu 1 K. [1935], 277, 309-316), and consequently not to be linked with the Damascus vision (so, e.g., Ltzm. K., ad loc.).

2:13; 4:1; 2 Th. 3:6. [12] We find sense (c) [13] at, e.g., Mt. 2:4, 7, 16; Jn. 1:40; 6:45; 8:26, 38; Ac. 24:8; 2 Tm. 1:13; 3:14.

b. With Verbs in the Passive. In class. Gk. certain verbs are used to denote the doer or logical subj. along with ὑπό and gen. or παρά and gen. This is esp. true of verbs of sending, giving and intellectual impartation, which suggest the pt. of origin ("from") as well as the activity. In the Hell. period παρά encroaches on other verbs too. [14]

So παρὰ θεῶν ἡ τοιαύτη μανία δέδοται, Plat. Phaedr., 245c; cf. Isoc., 4, 26; ὁ λόγος ὁ παρὰ σέο εἰρημένος, Hdt., VII, 103; τὰ παρὰ σοῦ λεγόμενα, Xenoph. Cyrop., VI, 1, 42; cf. I, 6, 2; [15] Polyb., 3, 34, 1; [16] Epict. Diss., IV, 10, 29. αἰτηθεὶς παρὰ τῶν στρατιωτῶν οὐκ ἔδωκε χρήματα, Dio C., 79, 3, 3; [17] τὸ παρὰ σου γραφὲν ἐπιστόλιον, P. Tebt., I, 12, 15; [18] in the LXX συντετέλεσται ἡ κακία παρὰ τοῦ πατρός μου, 1 Βασ. 20:9; cf. v. 33; 2 Macc. 11:17. [19]

In the NT cf. Lk. 1:45: τοῖς λελαλημένοις αὐτῇ παρὰ κυρίου, where the author of the promise is God but it comes to Mary from Him by way of the angel; [20] Jn. 1:6: ἄνθρωπος ἀπεσταλμένος παρὰ θεοῦ, Ac. 22:30 vl.: τί κατηγορεῖται παρὰ τῶν Ἰουδαίων. [21]

c. With Other Verbs and Verbal Concepts. The movement emphasises the starting-point, the action the doer.

Hdt., VIII, 140: ἀγγελίη ἥκει παρὰ βασιλέος, where the message does not simply come from the great king but is sent by him and at his command; Ditt. Or., I, 49, 5: τοὺς παρὰ τοῦ βασιλέως [παραγ]ινομένους, where coming from the king implies being sent by him; Plat. Symp., 179b: τοῦτο ὁ Ἔρως τοῖς ἐρῶσι παρέχει γιγνόμενον παρ᾽ αὐτοῦ, "deriving from him himself." [22] In the LXX cf. παρὰ κυρίου ἐξῆλθεν τὸ πρόσταγμα τοῦτο, Gn. 24:50; παρὰ κυρίου ἐγένετο αὕτη, "from the Lord," i.e., "through him," ψ 117:23. [23]

In the NT coming from someone denotes being sent by him at Mk. 14:43; Lk. 2:1; 8:49. The ref. may also be to the author of an event: παρὰ κυρίου ἐγένετο αὕτη, Mt. 21:42; Mk. 12:11 (in both cases ψ 117:23). With a negative verb παρά is used in an expression which is taken fairly literally from the LXX

---

[12] The thought of attainment is present in εὑρίσκειν (2 Tm. 1:18) and ἔχειν (Ac. 9:14).
[13] Bl.-Debr. § 173, 1.
[14] ἀπό expands even more in this sense, Bl.-Debr. § 210, 2.
[15] H. Richards, "The Minor Works of Xenophon (Cynegeticus)," Class. Rev., 12 (1898), 291, col. a.
[16] Krebs, 51.
[17] Nawijn, 92-106.
[18] Παμφίλῳ τῷ παρ᾽ ἡμῶν προκεχειρισμένῳ, New Classical Fragments and other Gk. and Lat. Pap., ed. B. P. Grenfell and A. S. Hunt (1897), II, 23, 18. Cf. also Mayser, II, 2, 485 f.
[19] Cf. the other examples in Johannessohn Präpos., 226 f.
[20] Bl.-Debr. § 237, 1; Zerwick, 21 f., where the less likely possibility of relating παρὰ κυρίου to ἔσται τελείωσις is considered.
[21] In the better MSS ὑπό. The prep. παρά is forensic here, "on the part of the plaintiff"; cf. Dion. Hal. Ant. Rom., XI, 10, 2: κατηγορίαι γίνονται ... παρὰ πολλῶν.
[22] Cf. Herm. s., 2, 3 παρ᾽ ἑαυτῆς φέρει καρπὸν καὶ παρὰ τῆς πτελέας "(the vine) bears fruit of which it is the author as well as the elm."
[23] Heb. מֵאֵת יהוה. Further examples in Johannessohn Präpos., 226. On the fem. αὕτη v. M. J. Lagrange, Komm. zu Mk. (1947), 310.

at Lk. 1:37:[24] οὐκ ἀδυνατήσει παρὰ τοῦ θεοῦ πᾶν ῥῆμα. In Jn. the coming forth of the Son from the Father is denoted by the following expressions : εἶναι παρὰ τοῦ πατρός (6:46; 7:29; 9:16, 33);[25] μονογενὴς παρὰ πατρός (1:14). The Son has come from the Father, and this means that He has been sent by Him, 16:27. For the procession of the Spirit cf. 15:26.[26] Everything that Jesus imparts to nen comes from God, 17:7.

d. In Adjectival and Nominal Prepositional Expressions.

(a) In adj. prepositional expressions οἱ πρέσβεις οἱ παρὰ βασιλέως, Aristoph. Ach., 61, where the verbal concept of going forth and being sent lies in the noun πρέσβεις. So also αἱ παρὰ τῶν ὑπάτων ἐντολαί, Polyb., 3, 106, 9; ἡ παρὰ τῶν ἐμπείρων ἀνδρῶν παράδοσις, 11, 8, 2; τὴν παρ' ἐμοῦ ἐπιστολήν, Ditt. Syll.[3], 543, 25. Sometimes simply for a subj. or possessive gen.:[27] τὴν παρὰ τῶν θεῶν εὔνοιαν, Lyc., 82; cf. Xenoph. Mem., II, 2, 12; οἱ παρὰ τῶν Καρχηδονίων ἡγεμόνες, Polyb., 8, 30, 4; Xenoph. Cyrop., V, 5, 13. (b) In nominal prepositional expressions, of things : <τὰ> παρὰ τῶν μαθηματικῶν, Polyb., 9, 19, 9; εἰ δεομένοις δωροῖο τὰ παρὰ σεαυτῆς, Xenoph. Mem., III, 11, 13; Jos. Ant., 8, 175;[28] of persons : οἱ παρ' ἡμῶν, Eur. Phoen., 1189; οἱ παρὰ Φιλίππου, Polyb., 22, 11, 2. Nevertheless, the use, esp. in the Hell. period, is freer.[29] It can denote those who belong to someone as well as those sent by him : οἱ παρ' αὐτοῦ, his soldiers, Polyb., 3, 69, 13.[30] In the pap.:[31] οἱ παρ' ἐμοῦ, οἱ παρά σου etc., servants, officials, Preisigke Sammelbuch, I, 4369b, 24; P. Oxy., VI, 910, 35; legal successors, heirs : P. Amh., II, 99b, 15; friends, neighbours : P. Oxy., II, 298, 37; P. Par., 51, 40; relatives, BGU, II, 385, 10; Preisigke Sammelbuch, I, 5238, 19. In the LXX this use seems to be limited to the parts which are not translations, e.g., τὰς παρ' ἡμῶν ἐπιστολάς, 1 Macc. 12:17; cf. ψ 151:7. The plur. of the art. with παρά and gen. to denote those around someone is found esp. in 1 Macc., e.g., ἦλθεν Νουμήνιος καὶ οἱ παρ' αὐτοῦ, 15:15; καὶ ᾤκει ἐκεῖ αὐτὸς καὶ οἱ παρ' αὐτοῦ, 13:52; cf. 9:12, 44, 58; Sus. 33.[32]

In the NT we find sense (a) at R. 11:37 (Is. 59:21):[33] ἡ παρ' ἐμοῦ διαθήκη, where the covenant does not come forth from God but is willed and established by Him, hence "my covenant." Sense (b) occurs to denote possession at Mk. 5:26 :[34] τὰ παρ' αὐτῆς, cf. Lk. 10:7; Phil. 4:18. οἱ παρ' αὐτοῦ in Mk. 3:21[35] is used for the relatives of Jesus ;[36] intrinsically the term might mean either close or more distant kinsmen, or even the disciples. In this case, we are to think in

---

[24] Gn. 18:14 → 733, 2 ff. Here most LXX MSS have the dat. παρὰ τῷ θεῷ, also a vl. at Lk. 1:37. The gen. with παρά is closer to the Heb. original : הֲיִפָּלֵא מֵיְהֹוָה דָּבָר (on the other hand ἀδυνατεῖν ἐνώπιόν τινος at Zech. 8:6). Cf. Johannessohn Präpos., 230, n. 3.
[25] Cf., however, ὑμεῖς ἐκ τοῦ πατρὸς τοῦ διαβόλου ἐστέ, Jn. 8:44.
[26] ἐξέρχεσθαι ἀπὸ θεοῦ, Jn. 13:3; 16:30; cf. 8:42. Bl.-Debr. § 210, 3.
[27] Rau, 28; Krebs, 52; Nawijn, 106.
[28] On τὸ παρά τινος for a sum of money to be raised by someone cf. Mayser, II, 1, 12; II, 2, 487.
[29] Schwyzer, II, 498 calls the gen. in this use a genuine gen. (not ablative) in place of the more common παρά with dat. Cf. also L. Radermacher on Ps.-Demetr. (1901), 82.
[30] Krebs, 52 f.; Mitteis-Wilcken, I, 2, 11 n. I, 22.
[31] Preisigke Wört., s.v.; Moult.-Mill. s.v.; Mayser, II, 1, 12. C. Rossberg, De praepositionum Graecarum in chartis Aegyptiis Ptolemaeorum aetatis usu (Diss. Jena [1909]), 52; W. Kuhring, De praepositionum Graecarum in chartis Aegyptiis quaestiones selectae (Diss. Bonn [1906]), 14 f.
[32] Cf. Jos. Ant., 1, 193 πάντες οἱ παρ' αὐτῷ. For further examples cf. Johannessohn Präpos., 229.
[33] Heb. בְּרִיתִי. παρά is used in the same sense as a subj. gen. in Ac. 26:12 vl., 22 vl.
[34] vl. τὰ παρ' ἑαυτῆς.
[35] Cf. on this the bibl. in Pr.-Bauer[4], s.v. παρά I, 4b β.
[36] Lat. sui.

terms of the group mentioned in 3:32, which consists of the mother, the brothers
(→ I, 144, 16 ff.) and the sisters of Jesus. Some expositors (and older translators)
have seen a difficulty in the fact that the charge ἐξέστη should be set on the lips
of this group. [37]

B. παρά with the Dative (Locative). [38]

1. Spatial: a. With Things: "beside," "by."

παρά with dat. of object (παρὰ νηΐ etc.) is common in Hom. but less so in the class.
and post-class period. In the Hell. age cf., e.g., ἐνκαθίσας παρὰ τῆι θύραι, P. Par., 22.
In the LXX παρὰ τῇ θύρᾳ, 2 Βασ. 10:8; 11:9; ἐποίησεν ... παρὰ ταῖς πανοπλίαις
πλοῖα ἐγγεγλυμμένα, 1 Macc. 13:29.

The only NT instance is at Jn. 19:25: εἱστήκεισαν παρὰ τῷ σταυρῷ τοῦ
Ἰησοῦ.

b. With Persons.

(a) Of direct proximity, "beside": πὰρ δέ οἱ ἑστήκει Σθένελος, Hom. Il., 4, 367.
(b) Of a wider circle, "with," "by": οὐ παρὰ μητρὶ σιτοῦνται οἱ παῖδες ἀλλὰ
παρὰ τῷ διδασκάλῳ, Xenoph. Cyrop., I, 2, 8; οἱ παρ' ἡμῖν ἄνθρωποι, our people,
Plat. Phaed., 64b; τοῖς παρ' ἡμῖν οὖσιν γράψον, "members of our household," P. Greci
e Latini, IV, 345, 5; οἱ παρ' ἐμοί, "the persons belonging to my household," Xenoph.
Mem., II, 7, 4; ἔχειν παρ' ἑαυτῷ, "to have with one," P. Hibeh, 73, 14; Ditt. Or.,
I, 90, 52. In the LXX the following prepositions are rendered by παρά and the dat.:
עִם ἀντὶ τῆς ἐργασίας ἧς ἐργᾷ παρ' ἐμοὶ ἔτι ἑπτὰ ἔτη, Gn. 29:27; אֶת ἰδοὺ τόπος
παρ' ἐμοί, Ex. 33:21; παρ' ᾧ ἂν εὑρεθῇ τὸ κόνδυ, Gn. 44:9, 10; בְּיַד 44:16, 17. Sometimes it is used for a Heb. gen.: ἐν τῷ οἴκῳ παρὰ τῷ κυρίῳ, "in the house of his
master," 39:2. [39] (c) Of the intellectual sphere, or the sphere of influence of a person
or group. It is common with verbs of asking or praying, where the topographical sense
of a personal visit or presence in the temple of the god is implied: φρουρὰν ᾐτήσαντο
παρὰ Ῥωμαίοις, Dio C., Fr., 40, 5 vl.; [40] εὐχόμεθά σοι παρὰ τῆι Ἀστάρτηι,
P. Greci e Latini, V, 531, 1; μνίαν σου ποιούμενος παρὰ τοῖς ἐνθάδε θεοῖς, BGU,
II, 632, 5 f. [41] In the LXX cf. 4 Macc. 11:7: εἴπερ ... ἐλπίδα εἶχες παρὰ θεῷ σωτηρίου, hope of salvation with God.

In the NT sense (a) occurs at Lk. 9:47: ἔστησεν αὐτὸ παρ' ἑαυτῷ. [42] For
sense (b) cf. 1 C. 16:2: παρ' ἑαυτῷ, "at home." [43] In Lk. 19:7 Jesus goes in to

---

[37] G. Hartmann, "Markus 3:20 f.," BZ, 11 (1913), 249-279 takes the view that the ref. is
to the disciples (αὐτόν and ἐξέστη = ὄχλος), but this runs into the difficulty that after
the collective ὄχλος one would expect the plur. On the possibility of an impersonal sense
of ἔλεγον ("it was said") cf. C. H. Turner, "Marcan Usage (The Impersonal Plural),"
JThSt, 25 (1924), 383 f., also Lagrange, op. cit., 70.

[38] παρά with the dat. is common in Hom., later less so than with the gen. and acc. In
the NT, as in the whole Hell. period, the dat. is the rarest case with παρά (only once with
an object). Nevertheless, it occurs in all the writers apart from Hb. and Jd. Instead of
παρά with dat. we find πρός with dat. and acc., περί and ἐπί. For details cf. Schwyzer,
II, 493; Rau, 35-37; A. Wifstrand, "Εἰκότα," Kungliga Humanistiska Vetenskaps-samfundet
i Lund (Årsberättelse, 1933-34), 60-65. On the difference between παρά with dat. and
παρά with acc. cf. J. Keelhoff, "Sur une construction de παρά," Revue de Philologie,
Nouvelle Série, 17 (1893), 187.

[39] Cf. Johannessohn Präpos., 229 ff.

[40] Cf. on this Nawijn, 23 f.

[41] Quoted in Deissmann LO, 150. The spatial concept is close here, cf. the examples in
Mayser, II, 2, 370, 18 f.; 488, 20 f.

[42] vl. ἑαυτόν D.

[43] Cf. Chrys. Hom. in 1 C. (MPG, 61, 368), ad loc.

men, παρὰ ἁμαρτωλῷ ἀνδρὶ εἰσῆλθεν καταλῦσαι (Lk. 19:7) and has meals in their houses, ὅπως ἀριστήσῃ παρ' αὐτῷ (11:37). The disciples move into the same quarters as He does, Jn. 1:39. We read of the entering in of the apostles in Ac. 9:43; 10:6; 18:3; 21:8, 16; 2 Tm. 4:13. Cf. παρ' ὑμῖν, "among you" (in Pergamon), Rev. 2:13; also Mt. 22:25; Jn. 4:40; Col. 4:16. Sense (c) is found at Jn. 8:38 : παρὰ τῷ πατρί, which denotes God's sphere, i.e., heaven, where the Son was in His pre-existence. Jesus promises the Spirit's abiding παρ' ὑμῖν, i.e., the disciples, Jn. 14:17, cf. v. 25. The rumour that the body of Jesus had been stolen spread abroad παρὰ 'Ιουδαίοις, wherever there were Jews, Mt. 28:15. In an expression which is in part fig. Jesus says of the Father and the Son : μονὴν παρ' αὐτῷ ποιησόμεθα, Jn. 14:23 : in the spiritual sphere of the man who loves Him, the presupposition of such fellowship. 1 C. 7:24 is to be taken in the same way : ἕκαστος ἐν ᾧ ἐκλήθη, ἐν τούτῳ μενέτω παρὰ θεῷ, in the sphere of God, and hence in fellowship with Him. 44

2. Forensically, with reference to the judge before whom the parties appear, "before." παρὰ Δαρείῳ κριτῇ, Hdt., III, 160; Demosth. Or., 18, 13; 27, 2; IG², I, 16, 9. 45 In the NT παρὰ κυρίῳ in 2 Pt. 2:11 means before God's judgment seat.

3. Figuratively, partly on the basis of the forensic sense, partly on that of the primary spatial sense, with no sharp dividing line.

a. With the person who evaluates something, "with" : 46 οὗτος παρ' ἐμοὶ τὸ οὔνομα τοῦτο ... δίκαιός ἐστι φέρεσθαι, Hdt., I, 32, 86; cf. Soph. Trach., 589. In the LXX φοβερὸς παρὰ τοῖς βασιλεῦσι τῆς γῆς, ψ 75:12. b. With the person with whom someone stands in favour, "with" : ὥστε παρὰ πᾶσιν ἀνθρώποις ἀγαπᾶσθαι, Isoc., 4, 46; εὐδοκιμέων παρὰ 'Αθηναίοισι, Hdt., VI, 132; μέγα γὰρ δύναται πότνι' 'Ερινὺς παρὰ τ' ἀθανάτοις ..., Aesch. Eum., 950 f.; P. Greci e Latini, IV, 435, 19; 1 Cl., 21, 8. In the LXX partly for the Heb. בְּעֵינַי et al.: 47 χάριν ἔχεις παρ' ἐμοί, Ex. 33:12, 16; Prv. 12:2; εἰ εὕρηκα ἔλεος παρὰ σοί, Nu. 11:15; μνήμη παρὰ τοῖς ἐσομένοις μετὰ ταῦτα, "with posterity," Qoh. 1:11 Σ; cf. also καὶ παρὰ θεῷ γινώσκεται καὶ παρὰ ἀνθρώποις, "virtue stands in esteem with ...," Wis. 4:1; τῷ ἐπαινουμένῳ παρὰ θεῷ λογισμῷ, 4 Macc. 13:3. c. With the person who possesses something or with whom something is a quality or characteristic, "with" : παρ' ὑμῖν οὐ σοφὸν τόδε, Eur. Heracl., 881, the attitude of a group of men. Of behaviour : τοῦτο δ' ἑώρων παρ' ἑαυτοῖς καὶ παρ' ἐμοί, παρὰ δ' ὑμῖν οὔ, Demosth. Or., 18, 287 f. Often of peoples and their customs, usages and institutions, e.g., παρὰ τοῖς "Ελλησιν, Dio C., 55, 12, 5; Cl. Al. Prot., IV, 48, 1. 48 With ref. to the gods or men in general : πῶς δ' ὑγίειαν δώσουσ' αὐτοῖς, οὖσαν παρὰ τοῖσι θεοῖσιν; Aristoph. Av., 603; Nu., 903; οὐδέ τις αἰδὼς ἔστι παρ' ἀνθρώποισιν, Quintus Smyrnaeus, XIV, 432 f.; 1 Cl., 30, 8. Sometimes the sense of παρά τινι approximates to that of a simple dative to describe the owner : εἰ δ' οὖν ἐστι καὶ παρ' ἐμοί τις ἐμπειρία τοιαύτη, Demosth. Or., 18, 277; ἡ δὲ πᾶσα τῆς ἀρχῆς δύναμις ἦν ... παρὰ 'Ρουφίνῳ, Zosimus, V, 1, 1;

---

44 F. Zorell, Lexicon Graecum Novi Testamenti² (1931), s.v. παρά II, 2. e : cum Deo unitus, a voluntate Dei non recedens, though cf. Ltzm. K., ad loc.; Allo, op. cit., ad loc.; Pr.-Bauer⁴, s.v. παρά, II, 2. e "vor" (coram), → infra. The forensic meaning, however, does not go too well with the verb, μενέτω. Cf. τῶν οὖν φοβουμένων αὐτὸν ... ἐκείνων ἡ ζωή ἐστι παρὰ τῷ θεῷ, Herm. m., 7, 5.

45 Cf. also Rau, 40 f.

46 In senses a. and b. παρά with passive verbs is often used like ὑπό with the gen. to denote the author, but the local sense shines through. Cf. on this R. Helbing, Die Präpositionen bei Herodot (1904), 128 f.; Rau, 42-44; Alvin, 20; Nawijn, 21 f.; Radermacher, op. cit., 81; Mayser, II, 2, 489.

47 Elsewhere mostly ἐναντίον τινός or ἐν ὀφθαλμοῖς τινος.

48 Cf. the examples in Helbing, loc. cit. and Nawijn, 16. Elsewhere usually ἐν, cf. Radermacher, 141.

cf. Hyperides Pro Euxenippo, 27. In the LXX : καλεῖται δὲ παρὰ τοῖς πολλοῖς Νεφθαι, 2 Macc. 1:36 : μὴ ἀδυνατεῖ παρὰ τῷ θεῷ ῥῆμα; is anything impossible with, i.e., for God ? Gn. 18:14, [49] where the Heb. is יָם; cf. the same expression in a free rendering at 2 Ch. 14:10 : οὐκ ἀδυνατεῖ παρὰ σοὶ σῴζειν ἐν πολλοῖς καὶ ἐν ὀλίγοις, also 1 Cl., 27, 2 : οὐδὲν γὰρ ἀδύνατον παρὰ τῷ θεῷ εἰ μὴ τὸ ψεύσασθαι. d. Reflexive, κρίνας τι παρὰ σαυτῷ, Plat. Theaet., 170d; Demosth. Or., 10, 17; 19, 4; λέγειν παρ᾽ ἑαυτῷ, M. Ant., III, 11, 1.

In the NT sense a. is used when the probing judgment of God decides the real truth : δίκαιοι παρὰ τῷ θεῷ, before God, R. 2:13; Gl. 3:11; 2 Th. 1:6. θρησκεία καθαρά … παρὰ τῷ θεῷ, Jm. 1:27; ἡ γὰρ σοφία τοῦ κόσμου τούτου μωρία παρὰ τῷ θεῷ ἐστιν, 1 C. 3:19; μία ἡμέρα παρὰ κυρίῳ ὡς χίλια ἔτη, in the eyes of God, 2 Pt. 3:8. It is presupposed that human judgment is misleading : ἵνα μὴ ἦτε παρ᾽ ἑαυτοῖς φρόνιμοι, R. 11:25; [50] 12:16; cf. Ac. 26:8. Sense b. is used for favour with God : εὗρες γὰρ χάριν παρὰ τῷ θεῷ, Lk. 1:30, an expression taken from the LXX; 1 Pt. 2:4, 20. Favour with men may be co-extensive with this, Lk. 2:52 : προέκοπτεν ἐν τῇ σοφίᾳ καὶ ἡλικίᾳ καὶ χάριτι παρὰ θεῷ καὶ ἀνθρώποις. More concretely this regard may be pictured as a reward : μισθὸν οὐκ ἔχετε παρὰ τῷ πατρὶ ὑμῶν, Mt. 6:1. Sense c. is used when omnipotence is seen as a feature of God in contrast to man : παρὰ ἀνθρώποις τοῦτο ἀδύνατόν ἐστιν, παρὰ δὲ θεῷ πάντα δυνατά, Mt. 19:26 (par. Mk. 10:27; Lk. 18:27). The preposition has a fluid meaning here. One may lay greater stress on the sphere which the relevant word controls : in the world of men, i.e., on earth — in the kingdom of God, i.e., in heaven. [51] Or emphasis may be placed on the personal ability, for men — for God. From what follows, which belongs to the sinful world, God is free : οὐ γάρ ἐστιν προσωπολημψία παρὰ τῷ θεῷ, R. 2:11; Eph. 6:9; μὴ ἀδικία παρὰ τῷ θεῷ; R. 9:14; παρ᾽ ᾧ οὐκ ἔνι παραλλαγή, Jm. 1:17. Of human characteristics : παρ᾽ οὐδενὶ τοσαύτην πίστιν ἐν τῷ Ἰσραὴλ εὗρον, Mt. 8:10; cf. 2 C. 1:17. For sense d. cf. Mt. 21:25 vl.: διελογίζοντο παρ᾽ ἑαυτοῖς λέγοντες. [52]

C. παρά with the Accusative.

1. Spatial. [53]

a. The Question Whither ? "to," "toward" : in older Gk. prose mostly of persons : πέμπει παρὰ Ξενοφῶντα τοὺς πελταστάς, Xenoph. An., IV, 3, 27, though poetically also of things : ἴτην παρὰ νῆας Ἀχαιῶν, Hom. Il., 1, 347. LXX for Heb. אֶל: ἐκοίμισεν τὰς καμήλους … παρὰ τὸ φρέαρ τοῦ ὕδατος, Gn. 24:11; Ex. 29:12. b. The Question Where ? (a) "beside," "on the margin of," "by," "with" : ὁ δὲ παρ᾽ ἐμὲ καθήμενος, Plat. Euthyd., 271b; ἐνταῦθα ἦν παρὰ τὴν ὁδὸν κρήνη, An., I, 2, 13 : παρὰ τὸ τοῦ Διὸς ἱερόν, pap. [54] Of the crocus, whose root loves to be trampled : δι᾽ ὃ καὶ παρὰ τὰς ὁδοὺς καὶ ἐν τοῖς κροτητοῖς κάλλιστος, Theophr. Hist. Plant., VI, 6, 10 : by paths, or on the borders of paths, where there is going to and fro. In the LXX : ἐκάθητο παρὰ τὴν πύλην, Gn. 19:1; cf. 25:11. (b) Of spatial extension, [55]

---

[49] Cf. → n. 24.

[50] vl. ἐν ἑαυτοῖς.

[51] So A. Fridrichsen, "Marc 10:27," Symb. Osl., 14 (1935), 44-46.

[52] So most MSS. The better reading is ἐν B L 33, cf. Mt. 16:8. πρὸς ἑαυτούς occurs in the same sense at Mk. 11:31. H. Pernot, Recherches sur le texte original des Évangiles (1938), 119 thinks παρά in Mt. 21:25 is an emendation.

[53] In the NT never directly with persons, though this is common in class. Gk., Kühner-Blass-Gerth, III, 511 f.

[54] Cf. Mayser, II, 2, 489, 33.

[55] In class. Gk. (rarer in Hell.) also for temporal extension, "during."

"along," "beside" : ἔπλεον παρὰ τὴν ἤπειρον, Hdt., VII, 193. In the LXX παρεπορεύοντο παρὰ τὸν ποταμόν, Ex. 2:5.

In the NT sense a. occurs in Mt. 15:30 : ἔρριψαν αὐτοὺς παρὰ τοὺς πόδας αὐτοῦ, and Lk. 8:41 (the gesture of supplication): πεσὼν παρὰ τοὺς πόδας Ἰησοῦ. [56] In the Parable of the Sower ἔπεσεν παρὰ τὴν ὁδόν in Mt. 13:4, 19 and par. may mean that that the seeds fell on a path running across the field, which would be ploughed up after sowing, or that they fell along a path or bigger road. [57] For sense b. (a) cf. Lk. 7:38 : στᾶσα ὀπίσω παρὰ τοὺς πόδας αὐτοῦ, "at his feet" ; also 8:35. [58] Of beggars : καθήμενοι παρὰ τὴν ὁδόν "by or on the road," Mt. 20:30 par. ἐκάθητο παρὰ τὴν θάλασσαν, Mt. 13:1 par. cf. Lk. 5:1, 2; Hb. 11:12. For b. (b) cf. Mt. 4:18 : περιπατῶν δὲ παρὰ τὴν θάλασσαν τῆς Γαλιλαίας, also 15:29.

2. Comparative. The comparative sense develops from the basic spatial sense of "beside," "beyond." Superiority over the thing denoted by παρά is expressed.

a. To denote preference. "Compared with," "more than," "before," [59] with emphasis on preference : παρὰ τὰ ἄλλα ζῷα ὥσπερ θεοὶ οἱ ἄνθρωποι βιοτεύουσι, "before other creatures," Xenoph. Mem., I, 4, 14. For the comparative : ἀνδρεῖος παρ᾽ ὁντινοῦν, "braver than any other," Plat. Theaet., 144a; θαυμασταί, παρ᾽ ὃ δεῖ, λόγων καὶ ἀνθρώπων, "beyond what is permissible," i.e., "beyond all bounds," Plut. Quomodo quis sentit profectum virtutis, 13 (II, 83 f.). This Gk. form of expression is used esp. in the LXX to render the Heb. מִן in a comparative sense : [60] μέγας κύριος παρὰ πάντας τοὺς θεούς, Ex. 18:11; Nu. 12:3. Also ἔκθυμος δὲ γενόμενος ὁ βασιλεὺς τούτῳ παρὰ τοὺς ἄλλους χειρίστως ἀπήντησεν, "treated him more cruelly than the others," 2 Macc. 7:39; ὑψώσει αὐτὸν παρὰ τοὺς πλησίον, "to set higher than," Sir. 15:5; cf. Da. 7:7. b. In the comparative sense, or with words like ἄλλος, "than." The use of the prep. is par. to the particle ἤ or the gen. comparationis, though often with a slight difference in sense. [61] χειμὼν ... μείζων παρὰ τὴν καθεστηκυῖαν ὥραν, Thuc., IV, 6, 1. With ἄλλος, ἕτερος etc. : οὐκ ἔχω παρὰ ταῦτα ἄλλα φάναι, Plat. Gorg., 507a; Xenoph. Hist. Graec., I, 5, 5; ἄλλο τι παρὰ τὸ γάλα, Cl. Al. Paed., I, 6, 37, 3. In the pap.: μείζοσι πέτροις παρὰ τὰ εὐσταθμα, P. Tebt., I, 5, 85. [62] c. Exclusive : "excluding," "except," "in place of." τῷ δελφῖνι παρὰ πάντα καὶ μόνῳ, "alone and to the exclusion of all others," Plut. De Sollertia Animalium, 36 (II, 984c); πάντες οἱ λοιποὶ παρ᾽ ἡμᾶς ἄνθρωποι, "all except us," Ep. Ar., 134; τὸν μόνον θεὸν ... σεβόμενοι παρ᾽ ὅλην τὴν κτίσιν, "in place of creation," 139; Ps. Sol. 9:9. [63]

In the NT the prep. is used in sense a., to denote that a preceding concept is to be emphasised as compared with that governed by the prep., at, e.g., Lk. 13:2 : ἁμαρτωλοὶ παρὰ πάντας τοὺς Γαλιλαίους, "greater sinners than all (the other) Galileans," cf. 13:4; R. 14:5 : ὃς μὲν κρίνει ἡμέραν παρ᾽ ἡμέραν, "one man lays greater weight on one day as compared with another, and thus esteems it more

---

[56] Elsewhere also πρὸς, εἰς, ἐπὶ τοὺς πόδας τινός.
[57] D. Haugg, "Das Ackergleichnis," Theol. Quart., 127 (1947), 168-173 thinks the sense in Mt. and Mk. is "on the way," whereas that in Lk. is "along the way."
[58] Elsewhere also πρὸς τοὺς πόδας, ἐνώπιον, or ἔμπροσθεν τῶν ποδῶν.
[59] Lat. praeter.
[60] For מִן in this sense we also find in the LXX ἀπό, ἐξ and ὑπέρ, and sometimes a comparative, e.g., δυνατώτερος ἡμῶν ἐγένου, Gn. 26:16. For details cf. Johannessohn Kasus, 44; Thackeray, 23.
[61] Cf. also ὑπέρ with acc., Lk. 16:8; cf. 1 Βασ. 1:8; Hag. 2:9; v. Bl.-Debr. § 185, 3; A. N. Jannaris, Historical Gk. Grammar (1897), 389.
[62] Modern Gk. ἀπό or παρά in place of ἤ or gen. comparationis.
[63] In distinction from this we find παρά for "beside" in the inclusive sense, e.g., Demosth. Or., 20, 160 : παρὰ πάντα δὲ ταῦτα ἐκεῖνο ἔτι ἀκούσατέ μου.

highly"; Hb. 2:7 (ψ 8:5): ἠλάττωσας αὐτὸν βραχύ τι παρ' ἀγγέλους, R. 12:3 : μὴ ὑπερφρονεῖν παρ' ὃ δεῖ φρονεῖν, "to transgress in thought the bounds of what is permissible." For sense b. cf. Lk. 3:13; Hb. 1:4; 3:3.[64] After ἄλλος, 1 C. 3:11. As regards c., comparison may lead to a choice where decision is made for one thing and the other is left out of account. Hence ἐλάτρευσαν τῇ κτίσει παρὰ τὸν κτίσαντα in R. 1:25 does not mean a false worship of God along with a true worship less perfectly fulfilled, but idolatry in place of the worship of God, the Creator being completely ignored. Similarly κατέβη οὗτος δεδικαιω-μένος ... παρ' ἐκεῖνον[65] in Lk. 18:14 does not say that the Pharisee, too, is justified, though to a lesser degree than the publican. The prep. here serves the interests of the paradox that (against expectation) this man went away justified instead of the other. ἔχρισέν σε ... παρὰ τοὺς μετόχους σου in Hb. 1:9 (ψ 44:7) says that God has preferred His Son — the king in the OT psalm — to all other men, and has thus anointed Him.

3. To Denote Difference. The basic sense of "beside," "beyond," can denote distance from and hence difference, a. "by," b. "with a difference of," "all but." "less."

a. "By" : παρὰ τοσοῦτον γιγνώσκω, "I judge by so great a difference," i.e., my judgment deviates by so much,[66] Thuc., VI, 37, 2. παρὰ μικρόν, "with a small differ-ence," "almost," Isoc., 7, 6; Herm. s., 8, 1, 14. παρά τι, "almost," Herm. s., 9, 19, 3; Vett. Val., 228, 6.[67] In the LXX: ἐμοῦ δὲ παρὰ μικρὸν ἐσαλεύθησαν οἱ πόδες, παρ' ὀλίγον ἐξεχύθη τὰ διαβήματά μου, ψ 72:2; cf. Ez. 16:47; Prv. 5:14. b. "With a difference of," "all but," "less." Κίμωνα παρὰ τρεῖς μὲν ἀφεῖσαν ψήφους τὸ μὴ θανάτῳ ζημιῶσαι, "with a difference of three voices," i.e., a majority of three, Demosth. Or., 23, 205; Thuc., VIII, 29, 2; P. Oxy., II, 264, 4. τετταράκοντ' ἐτῶν παρὰ τριάκονθ' ἡμέρας, 40 yrs. all but (less) 30 days, Jos. Ant., 4, 176; Ap., II, 265.[68]

In the NT cf. Lk. 5:7 vl.[69] for sense a. (παρά τι) and 2 C. 11:24 for sense b.: τεσσεράκοντα παρὰ μίαν ἔλαβον.

4. Adversative. The sense of "beside," "beyond," is also the point of departure for the adversative sense: "without regard for," "in spite of," "against."[70]

So παρὰ δύναμιν τολμηταὶ καὶ παρὰ γνώμην κινδυνευταί, Thuc., I, 70, 3; παρὰ τὸ δίκαιον, V, 90; παρὰ τὸν νόμον, Xenoph. Hist. Graec., I, 7, 14 (opp. κατὰ τοὺς νόμους); VI, 17, 1; παρὰ τὰ ἐκκείμενα προστάγματα, P. Tebt., I, 5, 205. In the LXX: ὃς δ' ἂν παρὰ ταῦτα ποιήσῃ ἢ ἀθετήσῃ τι τούτων, 1 Macc. 14:45; παρὰ λόγον, 2 Macc. 4:36; cf. 3 Macc. 7:8.

In the NT δύναμιν ... ἔλαβεν καὶ παρὰ καιρὸν ἡλικίας, Hb. 11:11 (the ability to bear children is in this case granted to Sarah without regard to the obstacle

---

[64] Cf. Bl.-Debr. § 185, 3.

[65] vl. ἢ ἐκεῖνος W, ἢ γὰρ ἐκεῖνος A P and minuscules, μᾶλλον παρ' ἐκεῖνον τὸν Φαρισαῖον D it. Acc. to J. Jeremias, Die Gleichnisse Jesu (1947), 87, n. 229 an exclusive Aram. מִן lies behind R. 1:25; Lk. 18:14; Hb. 1:9.

[66] H. Richards, "Dislocations in the Text of Thuc.," Class. Quarterly, 6 (1912), 223 f.; Kühner-Blass-Gerth, III, 514.

[67] Examples esp. in Nawijn, 153-156. The sense "beside" = "for," "as," is to be distin-guished here : λιτὰς ... παρ' οὐδὲν ... ἔθεντο, "to regard as nothing," Aesch. Ag., 227 ff.; παρ' ὀλίγον ἐποιοῦντο τὸν Κλέανδρον, Xenoph. An., VI, 6, 11; παρ' οὐδὲν ἡγούμενος, Mayser, II, 2, 491, 3.

[68] Cf. Nawijn, 147 f.; Jannaris, 390. Modern Gk. παρὰ τρίχα, "by a hair's breadth," A. Thumb, Handbuch d. neugriech. Volkssprache² (1910), 93.

[69] So D. There is nothing corresponding in the other MSS.

[70] The opp. is denoted by κατά and acc.

of age). [71] παρὰ φύσιν means "against nature," partly of the forbidden acts of men, R. 1:26 (opp. φυσικός, acts according to nature and hence according to creation), partly of the miraculous intervention of God, R. 11:24 (opp. κατὰ φύσιν, what takes place by nature). παρ' ἐλπίδα ἐπ' ἐλπίδι, against (human) hope in (believing) hope, R. 4:18; παρὰ τὸν νόμον Ac. 18:13; cf. παρὰ τὴν διδαχήν, against the norms set in (Christian) instruction, R. 16:17. ἐὰν ... εὐαγγελίσηται ὑμῖν παρ' ὃ εὐηγγελισάμεθα ὑμῖν, Gl. 1:8 f.: a preaching contrary to that previously commanded.

5. Causal. When it denotes contributory circumstances ("in keeping with," "corresponding to") the prep. takes on a causal sense, "on account of," "because of." [72]

So παρὰ τοῦτο γέγονεν τὰ τῶν Ἑλλήνων, Demosth. Or., 18, 232; παρὰ τὴν ἑαυτοῦ ἀμέλειαν, Thuc., I, 141, 7, cf. Demosth. Or., 4, 11. παρὰ τόδε, "consequently," Preisigke Sammelbuch, I, 4512, 79. [73] In the LXX, e.g., οὐ παρὰ τοῦτο τὸν λογισμὸν ἡμῶν γλωττοτομήσεις, 4 Macc. 10:19. παρὰ τό with infin. is often used here to denote the reason or cause, e.g., ἀπώλοντο παρὰ τὸ μὴ ἔχειν φρόνησιν, Bar. 3:28. [74]

In the NT: οὐ παρὰ τοῦτο οὐκ ἔστιν ἐκ τοῦ σώματος, it does not follow that the foot (or ear) is not of the body, 1 C. 12:15, 16: the foot and ear cannot, as they claim, separate themselves from the body. [75]

Riesenfeld

| παραβαίνω, παράβασις, παραβάτης, ἀπαράβατος, ὑπερβαίνω |

† παραβαίνω.

1. a. Intr. "to go by or beside," e.g., Hom. Il., 11, 522 Ἕκτορι παρβεβαώς, "standing by Hector on the chariot," cf. 13, 708 (παρβεβαῶτε). There is a special technical use in Aristoph. Ach., 629 etc.: παραβαίνειν πρὸς τὸ θέατρον, "to step forward." b. Trans. in transf. sense: "to overstep," "to transgress," "to offend," strictly "to pass by someone without noticing." With various objects, always with ref. to divine or human statutes and ordinances, gen. παραβαίνειν τινα δαιμόνων, "to sin against one of the gods by transgressing the law," Hdt., VI, 12, 3; cf. Dion. Hal. Ant. Rom., I, 23, 4: τίνα θεῶν ἢ δαιμόνων παραβάντες ..., specifically δίκην, Aesch. Ag., 789; θεοῦ νόμον, Eur. Ion, 230; τοὺς νόμους, Aeschin. Ktesiphon, 204; τὰ τεθέντα, Plat. Resp., IV, 714d; τὰ γεγραμμένα, Aeschin. Tim., 161; τοὺς ὅρκους, Aristoph. Thes., 357 f.; Thuc., I, 78 etc.; τὰς σπονδάς, treaty, Thuc., I, 123; IV, 16 and 123; τὰς συνθήκας, Polyb., 7, 5, 1; cf. Aeschin. Ktesiphon, 70. Most instructive Porphyr. Abst., II, 61 τοὺς τῆς φύσεως νόμους καὶ τὰς θείας παραγγελίας ... παραβαίνειν. Cf. also Andronicus Rhodius, De Passionibus, IX, 6 [1] τὸ παραβαίνειν τὰς ὁμολογίας καὶ τὰς πίστεις, treaties and pledges. In the moral sphere: τὸ παραβαίνειν τὰ πάτρια ἔθη, ibid., IX, 6. [2] Abs. "to break the law," "to sin," e.g., Aesch. Ag., 59: πέμπει παραβᾶσιν Ἐρινύν. c. "To pass over," "to let pass," "to let slip," like "to transgress," but with different objects,

---

[71] ἀφρόνως δόξαντα καὶ παρ' ἡλικίαν ἀπείρως τοῖς πράγμασι κεχρῆσθαι in Plut. Romulus, 25 (I, 33e) means "unskilful and clumsy by reason of age." παρά has here sense 5.
[72] Lat. propter.
[73] Cf. Schwyzer, II, 497; Kühner-Blass-Gerth, III, 513; Nawijn, 135-140; Mayser, II, 2, 491.
[74] This use is also found in the pap.; v. Mayser, II, 2, 491.
[75] Bl.-Debr. § 236, 5; cf. 402, 4, also Bengel, ad loc. Though one might put in a "nevertheless," it is not so natural; cf. Allo, ad loc.
π α ρ α β α ί ν ω. [1] Ed. K. Shuchhardt (1883), 30, 16.
[2] Ibid., 30, 14.

Soph. Trach., 499 τὰ μὲν θεῶν παρέβαν; Eur. Hec., 704 οὔ με παρέβα φάσμα ... "nothing escaped me"; Aristot. Oec., II, p. 1351b, 17 παρέβη τρεῖς ἡμέρας.

In the pap. the original spatial meaning "to step over" is comparatively rare, P. Hal., I, 87: τὸν ὅρον παραβαίνειν, "to step over the border of the plot of ground (in building)," cf. "to go away," P. Ryl., II, 77, 44 : εἰς τὴν κατεπείγο[υσα]ν ἀρχὴν παραβαίνειν. The usual ref. in the pap. is to legal provisions in public or private law. The word is commonly used for breaking the stipulations in agreements, also in penal clauses and wills : "not to regard public ordinances," Preisigke Sammelbuch, I, 5675, 5; cf. also BGU, II, 638, 16; "to violate legal statutes," P. Masp., I, 24, 58 and 59 νόμον; "to break sworn assurances," P. Par., 46, 12 τοὺς ὅρκους; gen. "to break one's word," P. Oxy., III, 526, 10 τὸν λόγον. In the sphere of private law, "to violate the terms of an agreement," P. Oxy., III, 491, 11: "to violate a will"; P. Oxy., III, 494, 28; P. Lond., I, 77, 47; P. Flor., I, 47, 15, "not to keep an exchange agreement"; P. Amh., II, 35, 30, "to break the terms of a promissory note," cf. also P. Par., 63, 9. Since in the language of the pap. παραβαίνειν [3] can mean "to break an agreement" even without obj., the one guilty of such violation is simply ὁ παραβάς, e.g., P. Oxy., IV, 725, 54; P. Flor., I, 51, 23, or ἡ παραβαίνουσα, e.g., P. Lond., II, 293, 23. [4, 5] ὁ παραβάς can also be, though infrequently, the one who violates a testamentary disposition, P. Oxy., I, 105, 7. Often in wills the one who acts contrary to the provisions of the law is called ὁ παραβησόμενος, P. Oxy., III, 491, 11 ff. In the Byzantine period there is a shift in terms. [6] τὸ παραβαῖνον μέρος is the one who is unfaithful to an agreement, P. Par., 20, 36; P. Lond., II, 483, 6; BGU, I, 315, 19 etc. [7] ὁ παραβαινόμενος is the offended party, P. Lond., I, 113, I, 60. A more general expression is ἅπαντα ὑπ[αλλάξας] καὶ πα[ρ]αβάς σου τὴν συνταγή[ν], "thou hast changed (pledged ?) everything and the agreement is broken." [8] In close connection with the legal use is the religious. In Ditt. Syll.[3], 989 we read in relation to the temple of Artemis in Ephesus: ὅς δ᾽ ἂν παραβαίνηι, αὐτὸς [αὐτὸν αἰτιάσεται]. Similarly in Ditt. Or., II, 569, 19 the words [τὴν τιμὴν] τὴν τοῖς θεοῖς ὀφειλομένην παραβαίνειν express the fact that the respect owed to the gods must be shown.

2. The usage found in the pap. and inscr. is plainly to be seen in the LXX, except that here there is little or no trace of the sphere of private law. Man becomes guilty in respect of God's commandments and ordinances, Ex. 32:8 : παραβαίνειν ἐκ τῆς ὁδοῦ, "to turn aside from the right way," cf. also Dt. 9:12, 16. More firmly related to the original spatial sense, and much more vivid, is the statement in Sir. 23:18 : ἄνθρωπος παραβαίνων ἀπὸ τῆς κλίνης αὐτοῦ, "to commit adultery." Sir. 42:10 takes the same direction : μετὰ ἀνδρὸς οὖσα, μήποτε παραβῇ, where the context shows quite plainly that παραβαίνειν has the sense of "to break the divine ordinance of marriage." That παραβαίνειν is sin against God is clearly expressed in 3 Macc. 7:10 : παραβαίνειν τὸν ἅγιον θεόν. In Is. 66:24 God calls those who have fallen away from Him οἱ παραβεβηκότες ἐν ἐμοί. Other relevant expressions found elsewhere are παραβαίνειν τὸ ῥῆμα κυρίου (Nu. 14:41 etc.; Dt. 1:43); τὸν λόγον κυρίου (1 Βασ. 15:24; Sir. 39:31); τὴν διαθήκην (Jos. 7:11 etc.; 4 Βασ. 18:12; Hos. 6:7; 8:1; often in Ez.); τὰ νόμιμα κυρίου (1 Εσδρ. 1:46); τὰ θεῖα προστάγματα (3 Macc. 7:11); τὴν ἐντολὴν τοῦ θεοῦ (4 Macc. 13:15; 16:24); τὰς ἐντολὰς (τοῦ θεοῦ) (Tob. 4:5; Sir. 10:19); also παραβαίνειν ἀπὸ τῶν ἐντολῶν (Dt. 17:20); ἀπὸ πάντων τῶν λόγων (Dt. 28:14); τὸν ὅρκον (Tob. 9:4). Characteristic of the books of Macc. is παραβαίνειν τοὺς πατρίους (ἡμῶν) νόμους or ἐντολάς (2 Macc. 7:2; 4 Macc. 9:1). The commands and statutes of an earthly king are also norms to which man is subject : τὸν

---

[3] παρασυγγραφεῖν also occurs along with παραβαίνειν.

[4] Plur. οἱ παραβάντες, P. Oxy., I, 34, III, 12.

[5] The one who keeps to the contract is ὁ ἐμμένων, P. Oxy., IV, 725, 55; P. Tebt., II, 383, 40 etc., or simply ὁ μένων, P. Tebt., II, 391, 24.

[6] A. Berger, Die Strafklauseln in den Papyrusurkunden (1911), 3; B. Olsson, Papyrusbriefe aus d. frühesten Römerzeit, 51, 3 (1935), 148.

[7] The opp. of τὸ παραβαῖνον μέρος is τὸ ἔμμενον μέρος.

[8] Cf. on this section Mayser, II, 2, 313.

νόμον (1 Εσδρ. 8:24); παραβαίνειν τὸν λόγον τοῦ βασιλέως (1 Εσδρ. 4:5). Here we find almost the same expressions as for transgressing the divine commandments : τὸν νόμον (1 Εσδρ. 8:24), τὰ προστάγματα (1 Εσδρ. 8:79), τὰς ἐντολάς (Da. 9:5 LXX). There is no fixed Heb. original for παραβαίνειν. It is used for 7 Heb. verbs, of which מָעַל occurs only once at Lv. 26:40. 5 times in Dt., and once each in Ex., Jos., 1 Βασ. and Da. παραβαίνειν is used for סור, mostly with ἀπό or ἐξ, so that the meaning is "to deviate from the way." It also has this sense for שָׂטָה, which is rendered by παραβαίνειν 4 times in Nu. מָרָה, "to be rebellious," is also transl. by παραβαίνειν once each in Nu. and Dt. The expression הֵפֵר בְּרִית (hi of פרר), which is peculiar to Ez. (16:59; 17:15, 16, 18, 19; 44:7), and which means "to break the covenant," is always transl. by παραβαίνειν (τὴν) διαθήκην in the LXX (so also for חִלֵּל בְּרִית in ψ 54:20 Σ). פָּשַׁע, "to be apostate," is rendered παραβαίνειν only once in Is. 66:24; the LXX usually has some other term for it. In sense παραβαίνειν corresponds closest to עָבַר. This verb denotes changes of place or position of every kind, stepping over set boundaries. In the fig. sense of "transgressing a command" it is the original of παραβαίνειν 10 times, also Da. 9:11 Θ and Σ ψ 72:6 in a more general sense, cf. also Σ ψ 54:20; 88:34. In general παραβαίνειν seems to be used more frequently and more generally in the other translations. In 'A it is regularly used for מָעַל. It can also be used, as in Sir., for other Heb. words than those mentioned, or it can even be introduced. Thus in Prv. 8:29 the Mas. simply refers to the water running over the border (Θ στόμα) of the sea, but Σ takes it fig. in the sense that the water must not transgress God's command (λόγον). Here, then, the Gk. brings in the idea of transgression in the moral sense. Σ also has καὶ παραβῆναι ὅρκον θεοῦ μὴ σπεύσῃς at Qoh. 8:2 where there is no Mas. original. [9]

3. We find the usage of the LXX in Joseph. too. Here παραβαίνειν means violating the commands of God or the king. Very typical in this respect is Ant., 11, 130 : παραβαίνῃ τὸν τοῦ θεοῦ νόμον ἢ τὸν βασιλικόν. In details the ref. is a. to transgression of the divine commandments. These are either the Law as a single entity or the individual commandments. In view is either the fact that these were given through the mediation of Moses or, as in Macc., that the individual stands in the religious and ethical tradition of the fathers. Thus we find the following statements : παραβαίνειν τὴν τοῦ θεοῦ πρόσταξιν (Ant., 1, 46); τὸν νόμον (Bell., 2, 174; Ap., II, 176); τοὺς νόμους (Ant., 8, 229; Ap., II, 214, 276); τὰ καλῶς νομοθετηθέντα (Ant., 1, 14); τοὺς παραβάντας τι τῶν ὁσίων (Ant., 8, 115); τοὺς Μωϋσέως νόμους (Ant., 8, 191; 10, 59; cf. Ant., 6, 151 τὰς ἐντολὰς τοῦ προφήτου); τοὺς πατρίους νόμους (Ant., 9, 243; 10, 214; cf. Ant., 4, 139 τὰ πάτρια; Ant., 20, 143 τὰ πάτρια νόμιμα). The ref. may also be b. to the political order : παραβαίνειν τὴν (πάτριον) πολιτείαν, "to harm the state," Ant., 11, 140; 13, 2.

4. Philo emphasises the penalty for transgressing the laws : τιμωρίαι κατὰ τῶν παραβαινόντων, Spec. Leg., II, 257; Vit. Mos., II, 49; cf. Decal., 176. Two refs. to the order of marriage are important. In Spec. Leg., III, 30 it is said of the divorced woman who enters into a new marital relation : θεσμοὺς παραβᾶσα τοὺς ἀρχαίους, "in so doing she has violated the ancient order of marriage." In Spec. Leg., III, 61 the words of the priest to the woman suspected of adultery are to the same effect : εἰ μὲν τοὺς ἐπὶ γάμοις θεσμοὺς οὐ παραβέβηκας, "if thou hast not transgressed the laws of marriage."

5. It is noticeable that the word is very rare in the NT. This is connected with the NT view of sin. Sin is not just transgression of the Law. In the first instance it is a demonic power, → I, 296, 11 ff. παραβαίνειν, which is used both trans. and intr., always occurs in religious and ethical sayings. Even Ac. 1:25 is to be taken in this way. Literally, of course, it simply states the fact that Judas has withdrawn from his apostolic office (ἀποστολή, ἀφ' ἧς παρέβη). [10] But the choice of the

---

[9] This paragraph is by G. Bertram.
[10] Cf. the OT use with ἀπό, ἐξ → 737, 32 ff.

word παρέβη carries an unmistakable reference to the guilt of Judas. In Mt. 15:2 f. the juxtaposition of παραβαίνειν τὴν παράδοσιν τῶν πρεσβυτέρων [11] (the charge of the Pharisees and scribes against the disciples of Jesus) and παραβαίνειν τὴν ἐντολὴν τοῦ θεοῦ διὰ τὴν παράδοσιν ὑμῶν (the charge of Jesus against the scribes and Pharisees) brings into the sharpest possible relief the battle of Jesus against Rabbinic theology and piety. [12] Transgression is sin only where there is disregard for the ἐντολή of God. Human tradition, though it purports to be plain exposition of the commandments of God, is in truth a sin against these commandments if the human ordinance obscures the pure and original will of God, and turns it into its opposite.

At 2 Jn. 9 ℵ sy read παραβαίνων for προάγων. προάγων is undoubtedly original. The meaning is that he who, like the "antichrists," does not abide in the teaching of Christ, but goes beyond this, has no fellowship with God. [13] παραβαίνων is a vl. which serves the interests of exposition. It changes the "going beyond" into a "transgression" of the limit set for the true Christian.

† παράβασις.

"Striding to and fro": παράβασις καὶ παράλλαξις τῶν σκελῶν, Plut. Philop., 6 (I, 359c). "Stepping over," "transgression" both spatially and fig., mostly with gen. in the moral sphere: τῶν νόμων, ὅρκων, δικαίων etc. [1] The abs. use is rare in secular Gk., e.g., Plut. Quaest. Conv., IX, 7 (II, 746c): ὅπου δὲ πολλαὶ πλημμέλειαι πολλαὶ δ' ἀμετρίαι καὶ παραβάσεις. In the pap. the term is often used in the sense of "contravention," "violation of an agreement." Only P. Flor., III, 313, 15 (5th cent., under Christian influence) is worth noting because of the association with κατάγνωσις. The pap. often have παραβασία instead of παράβασις. [2]

Joseph. uses the word with various gen.: παράβασις τῶν νόμων (Ant., 3, 218); τῶν ἐννόμων (19, 302); τοῦ πατρίου νόμου (18, 263); τῶν πατρίων νομίμων (8, 129). The plur. occurs once in Ant., 18, 81 κατηγορία παραβάσεων νόμων τινῶν. The ref. in Ant., 18, 304 (ἐπὶ παραβάσει τῶν ἐμῶν ἐντολῶν) is to the transgression of human commands. Philo has the word in the abs. at Leg. Gaj., 211, and with a gen. at Spec. Leg., II, 242 (ἐπὶ τῇ τούτων [sc. νόμων] παραβάσει) and Som., II, 123 (τῆς τῶν ὅλων παραβάσεως).

In the LXX παράβασις occurs with the object of transgression (τῶν ὅρκων) in 2 Macc. 15:10 and without it in ψ 100:3 (ποιοῦντες παραβάσεις) and Wis. 14:31 (ἡ τῶν ἀδίκων παράβασις). At 4 Βασ. 2:24 Cod. A, like Θ, has τέκνα παραβάσεως καὶ ἀργίας with no Heb. original (cf. also Σ Da. 11:14 υἱοὶ τῶν παραβάσεων). The word also occurs in, e.g., ᾽Α Lv. 5:15; Θ Gn. 3:18 (17) and Σ Job. 20:11.

In the NT the word denotes "sin in its relation to law, i.e., to a requirement or obligation which is legally valid or has legal force." [3] Paul in R. 2:23 alleges that the Jew dishonours God by transgressing the Law. [4] In R. 4:15 he declares that

---

[11] For Rabb. pars. cf. Schl. Mt., 477.

[12] Cf. the juxtaposition of the sayings of Jesus with the association of νόμιμα τὰ γεγραμμένα and τὰ ἐκ τῆς παραδόσεως τῶν πατέρων in Jos. Ant., 13, 297. Cf. Schl. Mt., 477.

[13] Cf. on this Bü. J., 96. Büchsel conjectures that προάγειν was a slogan of the antichrists "since it makes sense only in the light of their presuppositions, not those of Jn."

π α ρ ά β α σ ι ς. [1] Porphyr. Abst., II, 61 (Nauck, 186, 6 f.): παράβασις τοῦ νόμου.

[2] For details cf. Preisigke Wört., s.v. παραβασία.

[3] Cr.-Kö., 183.

[4] Ltzm., ad loc. rightly agrees with Lagrange that v. 23 is to be taken as a statement rather than a question. With v. 24 it constitutes a comprehensive conclusion.

there is transgression only where there is law. [5] But transgression of God's Law provokes God's wrath. νόμος is also correlative to παράβασις in R. 5:14. The command which Adam received and transgressed was that he should not eat of the tree of the knowledge of good and evil. Men who lived in the time between Adam and Moses sinned, but they were not guilty of transgression in the same way as Adam, → 195, 21 ff. For in this intervening period there was no express statement of God's commandment. Hence ἁμαρτία was present (→ I, 310, 8 ff.) but not παράβασις. [6] In Gl. 3:19 Paul says of the Law: "It was added because of transgressions, until the seed should come to whom the promise was made." The words τῶν παραβάσεων χάριν are a crisp formulation of what he says elsewhere (R. 5:20; 7:7 ff., 13; 8:3) about the Law and transgression. The Law is not added to the promise to prevent transgressions. [7] Jewish thought saw in the Law the "hedge of the world" which protects it against the invasion of chaos. [8] But Paul constantly emphasised that the task of the Law is to establish the fact that men's evil deeds are transgressions of the divine commandments and ordinances. [9]

In 1 Tm. 2:14 it is said that the woman rather than the man was deceived and seduced into acting contrary to God's commandment, thereby falling into transgression. [10]

παράβασις occurs twice in Hb. at 2:2 and 9:15. The thought in 2:2 is that under the old covenant each transgression of the ordinances of the Law, and each revolt against the will of God expressed in the Law, carried with it a penalty which had full recompense as its goal. [11] In 9:15 Christ is the mediator of the new covenant which is characterised by the full demonstration of God's grace in the remission of sins. In the language of Hb. this means that Christ's death serves to remit [12] the transgressions committed in the time of the old covenant. The παραβάσεις are acts of disobedience against the divine Law which were wittingly and willingly committed [13] and which have brought all Israel into guilt against God.

† παραβάτης.

In secular Gk. the word is used only seldom for "transgressor of laws," e.g., Polemon in Macrob. Sat., V, 19, 29 παραβάτης δὲ γενόμενος τῶν θεῶν ἐμποδῶν τελευτᾷ. Usually it just means "one who stands besides," "companion," "comrade," "helper." It is esp. a tt. for the warrior who stands in the chariot beside the charioteer, Hom. Il., 23, 132 (παραιβάται), Eur. Suppl., 677 (παραιβάτας); Xenoph. Cyrop., VII, 1, 29

---

[5] Lagrange, ad loc. suggests that for οὗ δέ (ℌ) we read οὗ γάρ with DG𝔎. Ltzm. accepts οὗ δέ, but thinks that "δέ is here used carelessly." Materially, then, he reaches the same result as Lagrange.

[6] Cf. on this section Trench, 157 f. Trench refers to the distinction which Augustine makes between peccatum (ἁμαρτία) and praevaricatio (παράβασις), Enarratio in Ps. 118, Serm. 25. Acc. to Augustine's usage the peccator is one who sins without standing under an express law, whereas the praevaricator is one who sins while in possession of such a law.

[7] Cf. W. Gutbrod, Die paul. Anthropologie (1934), 116. Cf. also H. Shears, The Gospel according to St. Paul (1920). In his first c. Shears investigates the connection between sin, law and transgression, cf. esp. pp. 2 ff., where Gl. 3:19 is discussed.

[8] Cf. the examples in Schlier Gl., 107, n. 2.

[9] Schlier Gl., 106.

[10] Cf. on this J. Jeremias, Tim. u. Tit. (NT Deutsch), ad loc.

[11] Rgg. Hb., 30, n. 79 notes concerning παράβασις and παρακοή that both terms "involve a deliberate rejection of the divine will."

[12] Rgg. Hb., 269, n. 28 rightly shows that ἀπολύτρωσις here means essentially the same as ἄφεσις.

[13] Rgg. Hb., 269.

(παραιβάτας), Diod. S., 5, 29, 1; 12, 70, 1; Strabo, XV, 1, 52 etc. In a similar use in Plut. Aem., 12 (I, 260e) παραβάται are foot-soldiers distributed among the cavalry whose task is to seize the horses of fallen riders, to sit on them, and to continue the battle as riders in place of those who have fallen.

Rather oddly the word does not occur at all in the pap., Joseph. or Philo. In the pap. the one who is guilty of a breach of contract is called ὁ παραβαίνων or παραβάς, cf. → 737, 14 ff. παραβάτης, the party to an agreement who does not fulfil his obligations, is attested in the Byzantine period only in P. Masp., II, 158, 30; III, 314, Fr. 3, 2.[1]

The LXX, like the koine generally, uses ὁ παραβαίνων, παραβάς, or παραβεβηκώς instead of the noun, sometimes also ἄνθρωπος παραβαίνων, e.g., Hos. 6:7 (8); v. also Sir. 23:18. Only Σ sometimes has παραβάτης, with no fixed Heb. original: ψ 16:4, ἐγὼ ἐφυλαξάμην ὁδοὺς παραβάτου (LXX ἐγὼ ἐφύλαξα ὁδοὺς σκληράς), for פָּרִיץ (Ps. 17:4); ψ 138:19 for רָשָׁע (Ps. 139:19 LXX ἁμαρτωλούς, 'Α ἀσεβῆ); Jer. 6:28 : ἄρχοντες παραβάται for סָרֵי סֹורְרִים (LXX ἀνήκοοι, 'Α ἄρχοντες ἐκκλίνοντες).

In the NT the παραβάτης is one who transgresses a specific divine commandment.[2] Paul in R. 2:25, 27 pricks the pride of the Jews. If the Gentiles ought to keep the Law, they have a right to judge Jews who are guilty of transgressing it.[3] In Gl. 2:18 Paul says : εἰ γὰρ ἃ κατέλυσα ταῦτα πάλιν οἰκοδομῶ, παραβάτην ἐμαυτὸν συνιστάνω. He is refuting the accusation that by preaching freedom from the Law he makes Christ an abettor of sin. He maintains that his negation of the Law is also a negation of sin. For the man who is justified by faith is no longer a sinner. Freedom from the Law is not freedom for sin. On the contrary, I become a sinner when I re-establish the Law, when I renew its validity, since the question of transgression arises only under the dominion of the Law. If Peter and the legalistic Jewish Christians in Antioch demand subjection to the dietary laws of the Torah, they subject themselves afresh to the power under which there is παράβασις, "for they again make themselves men who are under obligation to keep the Torah, and who transgress it."[4]

Jm. 2:9 castigates respect of persons. The man who is guilty of this sin is shown to be a transgressor by the Law,[5] which establishes deviation from the valid norm.[6] In Jm. 2:11 the man who transgresses one commandment (of the Decalogue) is called a παραβάτης νόμου.[7] Because all the commandments come from one

---

π α ρ α β ά τ η ς. [1] Cf. Preisigke Wört., s.v.

[2] So already Lk. 6:5 D : ... εἶπεν αὐτῷ· ἄνθρωπε, εἰ μὲν οἶδας τί ποιεῖς, μακάριος εἶ, εἰ δὲ μὴ οἶδας, ἐπικατάρατος καὶ παραβάτης εἶ τοῦ νόμου.

[3] Cf. on this Schl. R., 110 : "His sin acquires the severity of transgression by reason of Scripture and circumcision."

[4] Schlier Gl., 60. A. Oepke Gl., 47 takes v. 18 a little differently : The I of v. 18 is not strictly that of Pl. himself. For Pl. what is said in v. 18 arises only in a highly unreal sense. The first person must be construed as rhetorical. Pl. has in view the legalistic Jewish Christians in Antioch, and esp. Peter. Peter by deciding for Christ invalidated the Law. But in Antioch he accepted it again as a binding norm. He thus set himself in contradiction to his faith in Christ. In so doing he made himself a "transgressor of the divine ordinance, an offender against the divine will." A similar view is taken by W. Mundle, "Zur Auslegung von Gl. 2:17, 18," ZNW, 23 (1924), 152 f., who refers the words παραβάτην ἐμαυτὸν συνιστάνω to Jews rather than Christians, since transgression can arise only under the dominion of the Law.

[5] The ref. is to the whole Law, but one may still think esp. of Lv. 19:15 and Dt. 16:19.

[6] Cf. also J. B. Mayor, The Epistle of St. James (1897), 88. Cf. also with ref. to Jm. 2:9 the pertinent statement of Hauck (Jk., 109) that "παραβάτης knows no degrees. The man who is one is so totally."

[7] Jm. 2:11 A has ἀποστάτης for παραβάτης. This is a later ecclesiastical understanding of παραβάτης which restricts it to one field. Cf. the next paragraph.

author, transgression of one commandment is in God's eyes the same as disregard for all the commandments.

In later ecclesiastical literature (Byzantine) the word is commonly attested in the sense of "renegade," "apostate." [8]

† ἀπαράβατος.

1. This is a rare word found only in later Gk. Only very infrequently does it have the sense of "inviolable," Epict. Ench., 51, 2 νόμος ἀπαράβατος, also P. Ryl., II, 65, 18; P. Grenf., I, 60, 7. [1] Its usual sense is "unchangeable," "immutable." In this sense fate is said to be unconditionally fixed and subject to no change or alteration, Plut. De Fato, 1 (II, 568d): ἡ εἱμαρμένη, λόγος θεῖος ἀπαράβατος δι' αἰτίαν ἀνεμπόδιστον; De Placitis Philosophorum, I, 28, 4 (II, 885b): οἱ Στωϊκοὶ εἱρμὸν αἰτιῶν, τουτέστι τάξιν καὶ ἐπισύνδεσιν ἀπαράβατον; [2] M. Ant., XII, 14, 1: ἀνάγκη εἱμαρμένης καὶ ἀπαράβατος τάξις; ibid., 2: ἀπαράβατος ἀνάγκη. On the immutability of fate among the Stoics cf. v. Arnim, II, 265, 1: εἰ δὲ εἱμαρμένη εἱρμός τις οὖσα αἰτιῶν ἀπαράβατος (cf. also ibid., II, 293, 31). In the same sense the term is used with ref. to the fixed course of the stars, esp. their unchanging movement, Plut. Def. Orac., 3 (II, 410 f.). Acc. to Catal. Cod. Astr. Graec., VIII, 4, Cod. 82 (p. 215, 3) certain constellations produce ἀπαραβάτους μαθηματικούς, "infallible mathematicians." [3] This is not an isolated instance of ref. to men. In Jos. Ant., 18, 266, too, we read: ἀπαράβατοι μεμενηκότες. This does not mean that we have lived without transgression but that we have gone on without change, or remained immutable. [4] Cf. in this connection Epict. Diss., II, 15, 1: ἀπαραβάτως ἐμμένειν. The word is finally combined with terms which by their very nature imply steadfastness and immutability: νόμος (Plut. Quaest. Conv., IX, 14, 6 [II, 745d]) and εὐσέβεια (Jos. Ap., II, 293): τί γὰρ εὐσεβείας ἀπαραβάτου κάλλιον; "what is more beautiful than undeviating piety?" Cf. also Stob. Ecl., I, 49, 44 (966): ἀπαράβατος θεωρία, "perfectly sure observation." It is noteworthy that the word occurs neither in Philo nor the LXX.

2. In the sense "unchangeable" the word is a tt. in law. A judgment from the 1st cent. A.D. (P. Ryl., II, 65, 18) ends with the words: καὶ τἄλλα τὰ δι' αὐτῆ[ς δι]ωρισμένα μένειν καὶ ἀπαράβατα ("valid and unalterable"). From the 2nd cent. A.D. cf. P. Cattaoui, I : [5] ἕνια ἀπαράβατά ἐστιν, "there are things in which nothing can be altered." The legal usage obviously maintained itself tenaciously. We find it again only in 5th and 6th cent. agreements, P. Grenf., I, 60, 7 (581 A.D.) ἀπαραβάτῳ πράσει, P. Lond., III, 1015, 12 ἄτρωτα καὶ ἀσάλευτα καὶ ἀπαράβατα, "incorruptible, unshakable and unalterable"; BGU, IV, 1020, 9 : ἡ ἔγγραφός μου καὶ ἀπαράβατος ὁμολογία.

The adv. ἀπαραβάτως occurs 5 times in Vett. Val. [6] It is found also in P. Strassb., I, 40, 23 (569 A.D.) in the sense "inviolably." Cf. also v. Arnim, II, 279, 27 (ἀπαραβάτως = "unchangeably").

3. Hb. 7:24 says of Christ that because He remains to eternity He has an unchangeable and imperishable priesthood. [7] Instead of the pass. "unchangeable"

---

[8] For examples cf. Sophocles Lex., s.v. παραβάτης. Already in Eus. Hist. Eccl., V, 18, 9 παραβάτης is the equivalent of ἀποστάτης. The same applies in later ecclesiastical authors. ἀ π α ρ ά β α τ ο ς. [1] Cf. also Just. Apol., 1, 53.

[2] H. Diels, Doxographi Graeci² (1929), 324. The adv. ἀπαραβάτως can also express the same thing. Ar. Did. Epitomes Fr. physica, 29, 6 says of Zeus : πάντα διοικεῖ ἀπαραβάτως ἐξ ἀιδίου, προσονομάζεσθαι εἱμαρμένην, Diels, op. cit., 465, 2.

[3] Cf. also Ocellus Lucanus, 1, 15 : ἡ τῆς κινήσεως ἰδέα ἀπαράβατος.

[4] Cr.-Kö., s.v. ἀπαράβατος.

[5] Mitteis-Wilcken, II, 2, No. 372, V, 19.

[6] Kroll, Index, s.v.

[7] Cf. the transl. of Rgg. Hb., 207 f., and esp. n. 80. So also Mi. Hb.⁸, ad loc.

many expositors [8] suggest the act. sense "which cannot be transferred to another" : "Christ has a priesthood which cannot be transferred to anyone else." This is a natural interpretation [9] and yields a good sense, but it does not really fit the context. [10] We should keep to the rendering "unchangeable," the more so as the act. sense is not attested elsewhere.

† ὑπερβαίνω.

1. a. The basic meaning of the word is "to step over," so BGU, III, 1007, 10 ὑπερέβησαν εἰς τὴν αὐλήν μου. [1] This stepping over may be by force. Thus the word can mean "to break in," "to fall on something," P. Fay., 110, 9 : a deep ditch is dug around an oil press ἵνα μὴ εὖ ὑπερβατὸν ἦι τὸ ἐλαιουργῖον, cf. P. Ryl., II, 138, 16 : measures are taken against a robber to prevent him breaking into a farm (ἐξ ὑπερβατῶν). Of rivers, "to overflow," Hdt., II, 99, 3 : εἰ ἐθελήσει ὑπερβῆναι ὁ ποταμός. b. Transf. "to exceed the limit of a particular age," P. Greci e Latini, VI, 685, 6 : τὰ ἑξήκοντα ἔτη, the age limit, cf. P. Lond., I, 113, I, 23. c. "To transgress legal ordinances" : νόμους, Soph., Hdt., Aeschin.; τὰ ἐγγεγραμμένα, the provisions of an agreement, P. Lond., V, 1711, 76. Cf. also Demosth. Or., 11, 2 : τὰς πίστεις καὶ τοὺς ὅρκους, Plat. Resp., II, 373d : τὸν τῶν ἀναγκαίων ὅρον. ὑπερβαίνειν can also be used abs. in the sense "to err," "to sin," cf. esp. Plat. Resp., II, 366a : ὑπερβαίνειν καὶ ἁμαρτάνειν, also Hom. Il., 9, 501 : ὅτε κέν τις ὑπερβήῃ καὶ ἁμάρτῃ. d. In the pap. the word can also denote the share which "passes" or "falls" to someone, P. Monacensis, 9, 67 : [2] ἡ ὑπερβαίνουσά μοι ζημία, "the fine which falls on me." e. "To overlook something," "to leave unnoticed," esp. in Plato, e.g., Resp., VII, 528d. Esp. worth noting is Plut. De Amore Prolis, 4 (II, 496d), which says of motherly love : οὐχ ὑπερέβη τὸ νήπιον οὐδ᾽ ἔφυγεν. [3] "To pass over in speech," "to be silent," common in Plat., e.g., Crat., 415b c; Isoc. Or., 15, 320 (345c); Aeschin. Ktesiphon, 118 : τοὺς μὲν ἄλλους λόγους ὑπερβήσομαι.

2. The LXX has both the spatial and fig. use. a. Spatial, "to cross the threshold (of a house)," 1 Βασ. 5:5; 4 Macc. 18:7; "to leap over" a wall, 2 Βασ. 22:30 ⇒ ψ 17:29; "to climb over" the palisades, 4 Macc. 3:12; "to cross" a river, Prv. 9:18b (in all Cod. but BS*†); "to pass" in a race (2 Βασ. 18:23). Also "to step over a boundary," Job 24:2, cf. also 38:11 and Ιερ. 5:22. With ref. to time Job 14:5 : God has set a term for human life καὶ οὐ μὴ ὑπερβῇ. In a transf. sense also "to emulate," "surpass," someone, 3 Macc. 6:24 tyrants in cruelty (ὠμότητι). b. Theologically in the sense "to overlook," "to leave unnoticed," synon. παρέρχεσθαι, → II, 681: Job 9:11. In Mi. 7:18 ὑπερβαίνειν can even mean "to forgive" : τίς θεὸς ὥσπερ σύ; ἐξαίρων ἀδικίας καὶ ὑπερβαίνων ἀσεβείας (וְעֹבֵר עַל־פֶּשַׁע). It is striking that in the LXX there are no theological statements where ὑπερβαίνειν = παραβαίνειν. [4]

---

[8] So, e.g., Bengel, ad loc.: non transeuntem in successores. Schl. Erl., ad loc. translates : "a priesthood which does not pass away."
[9] Cf. in this connection Wnd. Hb., ad loc.
[10] Cf. Cr.-Kö., s.v. ἀπαράβατος.
ὑ π ε ρ β α ί ν ω. [1] Cf. also H. Diels, Doxographi Graeci² (1929), 656, 13 : κἀκεῖθεν ὑπερβαίνω πάλιν εἰς τρίτον κόσμον, εἶτα εἰς τέταρτον καὶ πέμπτον ...
[2] Ed. A. Heisenberg and L. Wenger, Byzantinische Pap. d. Kgl. Hof- u. Staatsbibliothek München (1914).
[3] H. Diels, op. cit., 613, 5 (Hermias, Irrisio Gentilium Philosophorum, 18): ἵνα μὴ τὸν τῆς εἰσαγωγῆς τρόπον ὑπερβαίνειν δοκῶμεν.
[4] Cr.-Kö., s.v. ὑπερβαίνω seeks to explain this fact as follows : ὑπερβαίνειν is not synon. with παραβαίνειν as a term for sin "because, being more consonant with the Gk. view that the essence of sin is ὕβρις, it seemed to the biblical sense of language to be less suitable than παράβασις, in accordance with the understanding of sin as παρακοή." This may well be, but the main pt. is the simple one that the non-biblical koine also preferred παραβαίνειν to ὑπερβαίνειν in the moral sphere, → 736, 26 ff.

'ΑΣΘ use ὑπερβαίνειν more than the LXX. At Prv. 20:2 they render מִתְעַבְּרוֹ (LXX ὁ δὲ παροξύνων) [5] by ὑπερβαίνων, and at Is. 31:5 פָּסֹחַ (LXX καὶ περιποιήσεται). Σ alone also has ὑπερβαίνειν in Lv. 13:8 ὑπερέβη (Mas. פָּשְׂתָה LXX μετέπεσεν); Prv. 19:11 καὶ ἀγλάϊσμα αὐτοῦ ὑπερβαίνειν ἀδίκημα (Mas. וְתִפְאַרְתּוֹ עֲבֹר, LXX τὸ δὲ καύχημα αὐτοῦ ἐπέρχεται παρανόμοις); Ez. 18:10 ὑπερβαίνοντα (Mas. פָּרִיץ, LXX Θ λοιμόν, 'Α ἁμαρτωλόν).

3. The word is more common in Philo than the Gk. OT. Philo, however, does not use it in the moral sense, but with the following meanings : a. "in discussion or knowledge to pass by certain things, to disregard them," in order to establish the facts which really matter, Deus Imm., 157; Abr., 122; Spec. Leg., I, 20; Deus Imm., 149; cf. also Op. Mund., 2 : Moses as lawgiver avoided both ordinances in an unadorned and simple form and also the concealment of the truth by mythical images. b. ὄρους ὑπερβαίνειν, "to cross the limits," Poster. C., 180 (the limits of selfishness and pleasure-seeking); Leg. All., III, 232 (the border [τὸν ὅρον] of the truth); Decal., 43 (the boundaries of nature); Sobr., 6 (the limits of the soul).

4. The word occurs only once in the NT at 1 Th. 4:6 : τὸ μὴ ὑπερβαίνειν καὶ πλεονεκτεῖν ... τὸν ἀδελφὸν αὐτοῦ. The question arises whether it has no object here — in which case it means "to sin" — or whether it is to be combined with τὸν ἀδελφὸν αὐτοῦ as object. The sense "to sin" hardly fits the general context of the passage. The word is rather used along the same lines as πλεονεκτεῖν. Both words are designed to emphasise the idea of "ruthless defrauding." [6, 7] The correct translation, then, is that one should not "act with force or cunning against one's brother (disregarding him) and overreach him in business."

Worth noting in exegesis of 1 Th. 4:6 and Gl. 2:18 (→ 741, 19 ff.) is a scholion of Eus. of Emesa on Gl. 2:18 : [8] Ἡ ἐκκλησία νόμον οὐ τηροῦσα, νόμου οὐ παραβαίνει, ἀλλὰ νόμον ὑπερβαίνει. ὁ λέγων ὅτι πεπλήρωται ὁ νόμος καὶ πέπαυται, κἂν μὴ τηρῇ νόμον, οὐ παρανομεῖ· ὁ δὲ ποτὲ μὲν ἐσθίων τὰ ἀπηγορευμένα ὑπὸ τοῦ νόμου, πάλιν δὲ μὴ ἐσθίων, τῷ μὴ ἐσθίειν μηνύει ὅτι ἰσχύει ὁ νόμος καὶ μένει εἰς ὃν ἀνατρέχει. οὐκοῦν ἐπειδὴ μένει ὁ νόμος, αὐτὸς δὲ παρὰ τὰ νόμιμα ἔφαγες, καλῶς ἀκούεις ταῦτα.

                                                                                            J. Schneider

---

παραβολή

Contents : A. Secular Greek. B. Old Testament, Septuagint, Later Judaism. C. New Testament : 1. Usage ; 2. Definition and Form of NT Parables ; 3. The Question of Authentic Transmission ; 4. The Meaning and Purpose of Parables in the Preaching of Jesus ; 5. The

[5] Cf. Cr.-Kö., s.v. ὑπερβαίνω.

[6] Loc. cit. Cf. the second possibility suggested by Cr.-Kö., namely, "that ὑπερβαίνειν (with πλεονεκτεῖν) seeks esp. to emphasise the ruthlessness involved in the sense of an act of violence against someone who by rank or circumstance cannot offer resistance, like a man who is wounded or dead on the field of battle."

[7] ὑπερβαίνειν is thus used as in P. Fay., 110, 9 and P. Ryl., II, 138, 16, → 743, 8 ff.

[8] K. Staab, Pauluskommentare aus d. griech. Kirche (1933), 48.

π α ρ α β ο λ ή. G. Gerber, Die Sprache als Kunst, II² (1885), 472-482; A. Jülicher, D. Gleichnisreden Jesu, I and II (1910); G. Heinrici, Art. "Gleichnisse Jesu," RE³, 6 (1899), 688-703, with older bibl.; 23 (1913), 560-562; E. König, Stilistik, Rhetorik, Poetik in bezug auf d. bibl. Lit. (1900), 77-110; H. Weinel, "Die Bildersprache Jesu in ihrer Bedeutung f. d. Erforschung seines inneren Lebens," Festschr. B. Stade (1900), 49-97; H. Wendt, D. Lehre Jesu (1901), 107-139; A. Loisy, Études évangéliques (1902), 1-121; C. A. Bugge, Die Hauptparabeln Jesu (1903), XV-XX, older bibl.; H. Weinel, Die Gleichnisse Jesu⁵ (1929); J. Ziegler, Die Königsgleichnisse d. Midrasch, beleuchtet durch d. römische Kaiserzeit (1903); P. Fiebig, Altjüdische Gleichnisse u. d. Gleichnisse Jesu (1904); L. Fonck, Die Parabeln d. Herrn im Ev.⁴ (1927); J. Z. Lauterbach, Art. "Parables," Jew. Enc., IX (1905), 512-514;

Message Proclaimed by the Parables; 6. Figurative Language in Paul, James and Revelation. D. Post-Apostolic Fathers.

A. Secular Greek.

1. We find the noun παραβολή in secular Gk. in the following senses : a. "Setting beside" (παραβάλλειν, "to set beside," "to compare"), "comparison," Polyb., 1, 2, 2 with σύγκρισις, Plat. Phileb., 33b : ἐν τῇ παραβολῇ τῶν βίων; Aristot. Pol., II, 5, p. 1264b, 4 f ἐκ τῶν θηρίων ποιεῖσθαι τὴν παραβολήν. In rhetoric the word is used technically for "similitude," "parable," Aristot. Rhet., II, 20, p. 1393a, 22-1394a, 18. b. "Standing beside," Polyb., 15, 2, 13 ἐκ παραβολῆς (νεῶν) ... προσμαχόμενοι. c. Astronomically the conjunction παραβολαὶ ἀλλήλων, Plat. Tim., 40c; Procl. in Tim., 3, 146 D. d. "Aberration" from the right way, "twist," Plut. Aratus, 22 (I, 1036 f.) δι' ἑλιγμῶν (windings) καὶ παραβολῶν, esp. the parabola as a conic section. e. Division as distinct from multiplication, Diophantus, 4, 22. f. Ditt. Or., I, 41, 5 in the sense of παρακαταβολή, "money deposited," esp. in trials.

2. In rhetoric, which tries to differentiate conceptually the forms of speech, παραβολή is a tt. Rhetoric distinguishes a. the short figure of speech introduced by a comparative particle (εἰκών, → II, 388, 27 ff., imago : "he fought like a lion"), b. the non-literal metaphor, which has no such particle (μεταφορά, translatio, "the lion Achilles"), catachresis, the comparison which has passed into common use (abusio : "wing of a door"), d. the comparison (ὁμοίωσις, → 190, 17 f. simile),[1] e. the παραβολή (collatio, similitudo) as a more or less developed comparison in which two things or processes from different fields are set side by side so that in

M. J. Lagrange, "La Parabole en dehors de l'Évangile," Rev. Bibl., NS, 6 (1909), 198-212; 342-367; also "Le but des paraboles d'après l'Évangile selon St. Marc," ibid.. 7 (1910), 1-35; P. Wendland, Die urchr. Literaturformen = Hndbch., I, 3 (1912), 287-292; P. Fiebig, Die Gleichnisreden Jesu im Lichte d. rabb. Gleichnisse d. nt.lichen Zeitalters (1912); O. Eissfeldt, "Der Maschal im AT," ZAW, Beih., 24 (1913); J. Kögel, "Der Zweck d. Gleichnisse Jesu," BFTh, 19, 6 (1915); G. Dalman, Jesus-Jeschua (1922), 200-214 : "Jüdische Sprichwörter u. Sentenzen"; C. Koch, Jesu Liknelser[3] (1923); P. Fiebig, "Der Erzählungsstil d. Ev.," UNT, 11 (1925), 32-76; Str.-B., IV, Index s.v. "Gleichnisse," esp. I, 653 f.; M. Winternitz-H. Gunkel-R. Bultmann, Art. "Gleichnis u. Parabel," RGG[2], II, 1238-1242; H. Pongs, Das Bild in der Dichtung, 1 (1927), 150-175, 437-455; T. Guttmann, Das Maschal-Gleichnis in tannaitischer Zeit, Diss. Frankfurt (1929); F. Torm, Hermeneutik d. NT (1930), 109-127; A. Skrinjar, "Le but des paraboles sur le règne ...," Biblica, 11 (1930), 291-321, 426-449; 12 (1931), 27-40; Bultmann Trad., 179-222; A. T. Cadoux, The Parables of Jesus, Their Art and Use (1931); T. W. Manson, The Teaching of Jesus (1931), 57-81; D. Buzy, "Les paraboles," Verbum Salutis, VI[16] (1948); I. M. Vosté, Parabolae selectae[2] (1933); also "De parabolarum fine," Angelicum, 7 (1930), 169-209; M. Dibelius, Die Formgeschichte des Ev.[2] (1933), 247-258; L. Haefeli, Sprichwörter u. Redensarten aus d. Zeit Christi (1934); C. H. Dodd, The Parables of the Kingdom[7] (1946); U. Holzmeister, "Vom angeblichen Verstockungszweck d. Parabeln des Herrn," Miscellanea biblica, I (1934), 201-244; J. K. Madsen, Die Parabeln der Ev. u. d. heutige Psychologie (1936); F. Gealy, "The Composition of Mk. 4," Exp. T., 48 (1936/37), 40-43; B. T. D. Smith, The Parables of the Synoptic Gospels (1937); W. O. E. Oesterley, The Gospel Parables in the Light of their Jewish Background[2] (1938); T. W. Manson, The Mission and Message of Jesus (1937), 320-327; E. Lohmeyer, "Der Sinn d. Gleichnisse Jesu," ZSTh, 15 (1938), 319-346; H. D. Wendland, "Von den Gleichnissen Jesu u. ihrer Botschaft," Die Theologin, 11 (1941), 17-29; J. Jeremias, "Eine neue Schau der Zukunftsaussagen Jesu" (on Dodd's book), ThBl, 20 (1941), 216-222; G. C. Morgan, Parables and Metaphors of our Lord (1943); J. Pirot, Allégories et Paraboles dans la vie et l'enseignement de Jésus Christ (1943); L. Cerfaux, "Le thème littéraire parabolique de l'Évangile de St. Jean," Coniectanea Neotestamentica, 11 (1947), 15-25; M. Hermaniuk, La parabole évangélique, Diss. Löwen (1947) (XIII-XXVIII, good bibl., esp. non-German); M. Albertz, Die Botschaft d. NT (1947), 74-83; J. Jeremias, Die Gleichnisse Jesu[2] (1952); E. Percy, "Liknelseteorien i Mk. 4:11 f. och kompositionen av Mk. 4:1-34," Svensk Exegetisk Årsbok, 12 (1947), 258-278; M. Meinertz, Die Gleichnisse Jesu[4] (1948); O. A. Piper, "The Mystery of the Kingdom of God ...," Interpretation, 1 (1947), 183-200.

[1] For the defs. of antiquity cf. K. Alewell, Über d. rhetorische παράδειγμα, Diss. Kiel (1913), 18-24; H. Lausberg, Elemente d. literarischen Rhetorik (1949), 15 f.

virtue of the similarity the unknown may be elucidated by the known.[2] Different from the parable, in which there is essentially one point of comparison, the *tertium comparationis*, is f. the allegory (ἀλληγορία, *inversio*), an integrated whole artificially constructed from a number of metaphors in which the individual members have to be given their real signification, → I, 260, 3 ff.[3]

3. Epic style, esp. that of Hom., is rich in similitudes in the Gk. sense.[4] They develop out of the poetic impulse to illustrate events, and the poet's joy in depiction gives them a certain independence in relation to the narrative. Along with their impressive illustrative power their evocative content is important to the poet. They can often serve to give an awareness of the spiritual which a lack of corresponding abstract terms makes it impossible to convey otherwise.[5] The more extended the similitude, the more value it usually has. Gnomic poetry also loves comparisons.[6] Plato's poetic speech is more or less rich in developed similitudes. For him they are instructive examples which confirm or underlie principles. In the main he uses typical actions or relations, and only less frequently extraordinary cases. In distinction from the comedians, who take their illustrations from the life of animals, he prefers, in keeping with the seriousness of his discussions, to take his examples from the broad sphere of human life, and sometimes from myth.[7] Usually his parables are interwoven stylistically into the flow of speech; they are not independent stylistic unities, as in the Gospels. The Stoic-Cynic diatribe, in consonance with its popular mode of instruction, is rich in illustrations, which, taken from the most varied spheres,[8] serve to clarify philosophical ideas. The principle is usually stated at the beginning, and it is then illustrated by a similitude, which is also used in many cases as the answer to an opponent's objection, showing that the view of the opponent is

---

[2] Quint. Inst. Orat., V, 11, 23: παραβολή, *quam Cicero collationem vocat*. Cic. De Inventione, I, 30, 49: *collatio est oratio rem cum re ex similitudine conferens*. Ps.-Cic. De Ratione Dicendi ad Herennium, IV, 45, 59: *similitudo est oratio traducens ad rem quampiam aliquid ex re dispari simile*. Cf. further Alewell, 20 f. Expressly on παραβολή Eustath. Comm. in Il., 176, 21-177, 46 (on 2, 87) and Index, *s.v.*; A. Hirzel, *Gleichnisse u. Metaphern im Rigveda in kulturhistorischer Hinsicht zusammengestellt u. verglichen mit den Bildern bei Hom., Hes., Aesch., Soph., Eur.* (1890); R. Volkmann, *Rhetorik d. Griechen u. Römer*[2], Hndbch. AW, II, 3 (1874), 189, 333, 379 f.; W. Schmid-O. Stählin, *Gesch. d. griech. Lit.*, I, 1, Hndbch. AW, VII, 1, 1 (1929), Index *s.v.*; Gerber, 474-482.

[3] H. Gunkel-H. Gressmann, Art. "Allegorie," RGG[2], I, 219 f.; Torm, 114 f.

[4] Cf. Hom. Il., 8, 555 ff.; 13, 492 ff., 178; 15, 624 ff.; 16, 297 ff. H. Fränkel, *Die homerischen Gleichnisse* (1921); Schmid-Stählin, *op. cit.*, 92; P. Cauer, *Grundfragen d. Homerkritik*[3] (1923), 459-481. On the path from the Homeric similitude to the academic and philosophical analogy cf. B. Snell, *Die Entdeckung d. Geistes*[2] (1948), c. 7: "Gleichnis, Vergleich, Metapher, Analogie, Die Entwicklung vom mythischen zum logischen Denken," pp. 181-216; W. Kranz, "Gleichnis u. Vergleich in d. frühgriech. Philosophie," Hermes, 73 (1938), 99-122 speaks of the reflective function of the image and similitude; this elucidates the specific nature of one thing only by another. K. Riezler, "Das homerische Gleichnis u. d. Anfänge d. Philosophie," Antike, 12 (1936), 253-271; W. Schadewaldt, *Von Homers Welt u. Werk*[2] (1951).

[5] Il., 2, 147 (joy); 3, 222 (volubility); 10, 5 (storm in the breast); 18, 109 (anger); 19, 233 (the heart as unyielding as brass).

[6] Theogn., 183 ff.; on the other hand similitudes are rare in the tragedians, e.g., Soph. Ai., 1142 ff., 1150 ff.; Ant., 712 ff. Schmidt-Stählin, 289, 495, 498.

[7] Plat. Leg., VI, 758a (ship of state); Phaed., 82e (body as a prison); 85e (harmony of the lyre); 87b (body as a garment); from the animal world, Ap., 30e (horse); Resp., II, 375a-376c (dog as watchman); cf. 404a; from myth, Soph., 246a (battle of the giants); Euthyd., 288b; 285c; cf. G. O. Berg, *Metaphor and Comparison in the Dialogues of Plato*, Diss. Baltimore (1903).

[8] Epict. Diss., I, 24, 19 f. (children); 14, 15 (soldiers who swear an oath of loyalty); II, 14, 21 f. (philosopher as physician); 16, 9 (constraint of the orator); III, 25, 6-10 (physician); IV, 1, 105-110 (life is like a divinely given festival); 7, 22 f. (quarreling children); 13, 11 f. (winecask); R. Bultmann, "Der Stil d. paul. Predigt u. die stoisch-kynische Diatribe," FRL, 13 (1910), 35-42; H. Fenstell, *De comparationibus Lucretianis*, Diss. Halle (1893); R. Rudberg, *Forschungen zu Poseidonios* (1918), 156 ff.

wide of the mark. Here again the custom is to use common events or conditions by way of illustration. As with Plato, these are not parables in the stricter NT sense. Aristotle, whose definitions were the most influential later, counts the παραβολή (Rhet., II, 20) among the examples (παραδείγματα) [9] which the orator uses in inductive or indirect proof (ἐπαγωγή) as a generally recognised means of demonstration and illustration (κοιναὶ πίστεις). There are according to him two kinds, the intrinsically more valuable story of true events taken from history, and the more easily invented example, like the fable (λόγος, ἀπόλογος) [10] or parable, e.g., the illustrations used by Socrates. [11] Unlike the fable, the parable has its material from observation of real life. The effectiveness of comparison, and hence also of the parable, rests on man's ability to see similarities. [12] In analogy lies a certain power to establish and to demonstrate. In many cases the *tertium comparationis* is not expressly mentioned. It must be grasped independently by the receptive and discerning mind of the hearer. In theory antiquity distinguishes between parable and allegory, but in practice they are often mixed, and Quintilian finds something attractive in this. [13] Seneca (Ep., 59, 6) commends to the orator who wishes to demonstrate something the use of *parabolae*, because they are *imbecillitatis nostrae adminicula*, and the hearer *in rem praesentem adducant*.

B. Old Testament, Septuagint, Later Judaism.

1. In the LXX παραβολή is with two exceptions [14] the rendering of מָשָׁל or of forms of the verb מָשַׁל. [15] As the analogy of other Semitic languages shows, the latter has the original sense "to be similar, like." [16] מָשָׁל is used for all expressions which contain a comparison, whether directly, or in such a way that they illustrate a general truth for comparison with other unmentioned cases. [17] מָשָׁל is a saying which indicates something, which has something at the back of it. [18] In the course of time the term came to have a considerable range.

a. In the oldest biblical example מָשָׁל is a proverb (1 S. 10:12). Proverbs often contain comparisons; in content they portray truth by example. [19]

---

[9] Alewell, 18-28.

[10] O. Crusius, Art. "Apologos," Pauly-W., II, 167-170; A. Hausrath, Art. "Fabel," VI, 1704-1736; E. Ebeling-H. Gunkel, Art. "Fabel," RGG², II, 489-491.

[11] Cf. Xenoph. Mem., I, 2, 9 (helmsman-statesman, where skill is needed, one cannot cast lots); cf. *ibid.*, II, 1, 21-34 (Hercules at the cross-roads); Plat. Theaet., 149a-151e (art of the midwife); Phaedr., 276b; Lys., 206a.

[12] Aristot. Rhet., II, 20, p. 1394a, 3; Theophr. De Sensu, 1, 1: αἴσθησις τῷ ὁμοίῳ and αἴσθησις τῷ ἐναντίῳ; Quint. Inst. Orat., VIII, 3, 72 : *Praeclare vero ad inferendam rebus lucem repertae sunt similitudines ; quarum aliae sunt, quae probationis gratia inter argumenta ponuntur, aliae ad exprimendam rerum imaginem compositae.*

[13] Quint. Inst. Orat., VIII, 6, 48 : *Illud vero longe speciosissimum genus orationis, in quo trium permixta est gratia, similitudinis, allegoriae, translationis* (with a ref. to Cic. Pro Murena, 17, 35).

[14] Qoh. 1:17 הוֹלֵלָה folly; Sir. 47:17 חִידָה. מָשָׁל for its part is sometimes rendered by a different word, 1 K. 9:7; Ez. 14:8 : εἰς ἀφανισμόν, Is. 14:4 : θρῆνος, Job 17:6 : θρύλημα, Prv. 1:1: παροιμία, 25:1: παιδεία, Job 27:1; 29:1: προοίμιον.

[15] In the kal "to cite a proverb" : מָשָׁל מָשַׁל, Ez. 12:23; 18:2 f.; "to tell a parable," Ez. 17:2; 24:3; pi : 21:5.

[16] Aram., Assyr., Eth.; in Arabic *maṯala* is "to portray," "to illustrate," *miṯl* "similitude," *miṯal* "model," *tiṃtal* "statue," "image," *maṯal* "similitude," "proverb." Hermaniuk, 62-96, 123 f. concludes from this that in Heb., too, the decisive sense is not "saying" as a literary form but the "living, concrete portrayal of a thing, symbol, typical instance." In Heb. מָשַׁל ni means "to be similar" at Is. 14:10; Ps. 28:1; 143:7; hi "to compare" at Is. 46:5. No original connection can be shown with מָשַׁל II "to rule," cf. Hermaniuk, 117, n. 137.

[17] Cf. H. Fuchs-J. Krengel, Art. "Maschal," Jüd. Lexikon, III, 1411-1415.

[18] So Kautzsch, II, 205, n. a.

[19] Cf. 1 S. 24:14; 2 S. 5:8; 20:18; 1 K. 12:10; 18:21; 20:11; Ez. 12:22; 18:2; Job 5:7. Hermaniuk, 70 on 1 S. 10:12 : Saul becomes a symbol.

b. The expression הָיָה לְמָשָׁל means "to become a popular proverb," "to come into the (mocking) speech of the people."[20] In Is. 14:4; Hab. 2:6 מָשָׁל is directly a song of mockery, a byword, in which someone is held up as a ridiculous or tragic example. מָשָׁל becomes a term for the author of such songs, Nu. 21:27; Is. 28:14.

c. From popular use מָשָׁל παραβολή then finds a place in Wisdom circles. In the sense of wise saying (proverb), it becomes a genre in Wisdom literature, and enjoys here a rich development. In form and content the wisdom of Israel is closely related to that of the ancient Orient, whose great centres were in Egypt (1 K. 5:10; Is. 19:11 f.) and Babylon-Assyria,[21] though it blossomed also in Edom and Arabia (Ob. 8; Jer. 49:7). The proverb in these circles contains examples from life, rules of prudence and courtesy, vocational advice, moral admonitions and religious directions. Many close parallels may be found to the wisdom sayings of the OT.[22] In the OT Solomon, the later model of the sage, is lauded for his ability to coin proverbs, 1 K. 5:12; Prv. 1:1; Sir. 47:14, 17 f. The proverbs about plants and animals to which ref. is made are similar to the fables and sentences beloved in Babylon.[23] The Book of Proverbs has a title (מִשְׁלֵי שְׁלֹמֹה, LXX παροιμίαι) which is used again for individual collections within the book, 1:1; 10:1; 25:1.[24] In content the proverbs are mostly sayings or sentences containing practical wisdom. Formally many of them use the comparative "as" (25:11-13; 26:18 f.; 27:15). In others a "but" is used, esp. 10:3-14:23. In others comparison is made by juxtaposition, 16:8; 15:16; 17:1 etc. According to the book as we now have it the comparative form is not characteristic of the *mashal*.[25] Parallelism, used in different ways, is predominant. Proverbs are often put in groups. Sir., too, consists in the main of short sentences, though other genres have made their way into this book (songs of lamentation and thanksgiving, prayers etc.).[26] As the eastern sage loves to use veiled expressions, so מָשָׁל-παραβολή is often a synon. of חִידָה (αἴνιγμα, → I, 178, 17 ff.), "riddle," Prv. 1:6; Ps. 49:4. In Ps. 78:2 the poet, when he calls his psalm a *mashal*, means a didactic poem which seeks to solve the dark riddles in the history of the people. Sir. in 39:3 speaks of αἰνίγματα παραβολῶν and in 47:15 of παραβολαὶ αἰνιγμάτων. Sir. shows that the glory of the sage is to find clever sayings, 3:29. They are, of course, the result of hard reflection, 13:26. By means of them the wise man shines in the assembly, while the saying of the fool finds no approval, 20:20; 21:16 f. Job, too, can turn angrily and disparagingly against the sayings of his comforters, which are like ashes, doing no justice to the real seriousness of life, 13:12.

d. The *mashal* is then found in the form of a developed comparison, the "similitude." This genre is attested early in Israel, though there are only a few examples of the kind

---

[20] Ps. 69:11; Dt. 28:37; here with שְׁנִינָה, "taunt," "mock," cf. "to make a byword" in Jer. 24:9 (נְתַן לְמָשָׁל) and Ps. 44:15 (שִׂים מָשָׁל).

[21] Cf. W. Baumgartner, *Isr. u. altorientalische Weisheit* (1933), 31-33 (bibl.); J. Fichtner, "Die altorient. Weisheit in ihrer isr.-jüd. Ausprägung," ZAW Beih., 62 (1933), 3-11. R. Anthes, "Lebensregeln u. Lebensweisheit d. alten Ägypter," AO, 32, 2 (1933); B. Meissner, "Das Märchen vom weisen Achikar," AO, 16, 2 (1917).

[22] E.g., Ps. 1; Prv. 22:17-23:10; 23:13 f. For details cf. Baumgartner, 11-19.

[23] Cf. Jos. Ant., 8, 44 : Solomon wrote ... παραβολῶν καὶ εἰκόνων βίβλους τρισχιλίους· καθ᾽ ἕκαστον γὰρ εἶδος δένδρου παραβολὴν ... καὶ περὶ κτηνῶν ... Ε. Ebeling, "Die babyl. Fabel u. ihre Bedeutung f. d. Literaturgeschichte," *Mitteilungen d. altorientalischen Gesellschaft*, II, 3 (1927); Baumgartner, 17 f.; A. Alt, "Die Weisheit Salomos," ThLZ, 76 (1951), 139-144 finds in the sayings and songs of Solomon in 1 K. 5:12 a continuation of the Sumerian-Accadian "science of cunning."

[24] Prv. 25:1 LXX παιδεῖαι Σαλωμῶντος; there is in the LXX nothing corresponding to the heading in 10:1.

[25] Cf. Hermaniuk, 96-101. Here, too, the *mashal* depicts typical instances or symbols of real practical wisdom.

[26] W. Baumgartner, "Die literarischen Gattungen in d. Weisheit d. Jesus Sir.," ZAW, 34 (1914), 161-198.

of parable found in the Rabb. and the NT, and — probably accidentally [27] — the word מָשָׁל is never found in association with them. The best-known example is that of Nathan in 2 S. 12:1-4. Other stories have a form very like that of the fable, Ju. 9:8-15; 2 K. 14:9 f. As the *mashal* in the form of proverb found its way into the Wisdom literature and underwent considerable development there, it is significant that as "parable" it becomes a very important form of proclamation in prophecy. The prophet may construct parables to make his preaching more impressive (Is. 28:23-29; Ez. 15:1 ff.), or they may be given him in visions (Am. 7:8). The most common example is the parable of the vineyard in Is. 5. The special feature of the OT parable is that it is not just an extended comparison but a story complete in itself, so that its real point can remain completely hidden from the hearer. This may first be seen in the relation which the story bears to persons or circumstances, 2 S. 12:7. In the song of the vineyard Is. himself gives the interpretation and application in v. 6b, 7. In hidden parabolic speech, which provokes reflection, the prophets convey to dull hearers the divine summons which seek to awaken their conscience or religious perception. In Ez. the word מָשָׁל-παραβολή is used for several allegories which, as Rabb. usage shows, are in Semitic thought simply a form of parabolic speech, Ez. 17:2; 24:3. [28] In content the מָשָׁל is here a word of divine revelation. As the complaint of the people concerning the obscure speech of the prophet shows (21:5), the term carries with it an element of the mysterious and enigmatic. A second word of revelation is required to show the meaning of the oracular saying (17:11 ff.; 24:6 ff.), which refers to God's judicial action in the future. We obviously have here a trend which is developed further in apocalyptic (4 Esr.; En.). [29] The obscure oracles which God sets on the lips of Balaam (Nu. 23:7, 18; 24:3, 15, 20-23) are also called מָשָׁל. [30] In Ps. 49:4, too, the poet speaks as a prophet. He has received as revelation from God a saying which solves the riddle of the incomprehensible prosperity of the wicked by the belief in a rapture of the righteous to Yahweh. In many cases we also find parabolic actions in the prophets. [31]

Thus מָשָׁל, passing from popular speech into Wisdom utterance and prophetic proclamation, took on a wide range of meaning in the OT. Of great linguistic significance is the fact that through the LXX this richly varied signification was transferred to παραβολή, so that in the Jewish-Hellenistic and primitive Christian sphere this word acquired a much enlarged content as compared with secular Greek. [32]

2. In apocalyptic מָשָׁל-παραβολή ("similitude") becomes a means of giving eschatological instruction. In 4 Esr. the angel uses similitudes from the sphere of nature and human life to enlighten the seer concerning God's world government, esp. His plan for history, and eschatological events (judgment and final salvation). Earthly events help to clarify divine and heavenly events, the events of the future and the world to come. The fable of the impossible war of the forests against the sea makes it plain to the seer that the dwellers on earth can perceive only earthly things, 4:12 ff. From the mother's womb, which bears one child after another, he comes to see the necessity of different generations making way for one another, 5:41 ff. In face of the terrible problem of the great number of the lost, the righteousness of God is brought out by a comparison:

---

[27] So Lagrange, "La parabole," 350, though cf. Hermaniuk, 119.

[28] Jüd. Lexikon, III, 1411-1415; there is a definitely artificial allegory in Qoh. 12:1-7. On the prophetic images cf. F. Haeussermann, "Wortempfang u. Symbol," ZAW Beih., 58 (1932).

[29] Cerfaux, 15-25.

[30] Eissfeldt, 28 considers the possibility that this sense developed only in the post-exilic period, but Hermaniuk, 80 thinks it was very early.

[31] Is. 20:2 ff.; Jer. 13:1 ff.; 18:1-5; 27:2 ff.; Ez. 4:4-8; 12:3-6. Cf. Haeussermann, 32 f.; A. van den Born, *De symbolische handelingen der Oud-Testamentische profeten* (1935).

[32] Cf. J. Wackernagel, "Griechisches u. Lateinisches," *Indogermanische Forschungen*, 31 (1912/13), 262-267.

"As the ground, so the sowing, as the labour, so the work, as the labourer, so the harvest," 9:17, so also 7:1 ff.; 8:41. Almost always an explanation is offered, and the insight which the comparison gives into the problem is stated (on the lips of the angel), 4:21, 42, 50; 5:40; 7:11, 105.

In En. מָשָׁל-παραβολή-similitudo is used for eschatological similitudes in which the seer — in a way very different from that of the NT parables — describes the apocalyptic visions which have been imparted to him, [33] cf. the general introduction in 1:2, 3, the introduction to the Messianic book of similitudes (37-71) in 37:5, [34] refs. in the first, second and third similitudes in 38:1; 45:1; 58:1, and the retrospective note in 68:1. [35] These are neither parables nor allegories, but visions of heavenly and future mysteries (judgment, the kingdom of God, resurrection, abodes of the blessed, angels, the world of the stars etc.) which are inaccessible to man without revelation, → 687, n. 244. Here again, when the seer asks the meaning of what he has seen, the angel tells him in a second revelation, 40:9; 43:4; 52:5 etc. In the מָשָׁל, or word of revelation, the cleft between man and the future, or the world to come, is bridged. [36]

3. Closest to the Synoptic parables are those of the Palestinian rabbis. [37] For them, too, מָשָׁל is often a short saying or proverb which illumines or establishes something, e.g., "Physician, heal thine own lameness" (cf. Lk. 4:23). [38] More commonly, the מָשָׁל is a more or less extended comparison, whether fable, allegory, or, as in most cases, parable after the Synoptic manner, with one pt. of comparison. Thus the term מָשָׁל is used for the fable of R. Akiba (c. 130 A.D.) about the fox and the fishes, [39] also for allegories like those of R. Jochanan b. Zakkai [40] about the worker and his tool, or that of Akiba: "Everything is given on credit, the net is cast over all lands, the chest is open, the merchant lends, the tablet is unsealed and the hand writes on it ..." [41] The pt. of this allegory is that man has received all his gifts and goods only as a loan from God, and will finally have to account for their use before God, cf. Mt. 21:33 ff. Short similitudes are most common in the Rabbis. It makes relatively little difference whether pure parables are distinguished from mixed ones [42] which are built around common metaphors, the king, [43] son, servant, vineyard, meal etc., and which thus contain allegorical elements. A parable of the first kind is that of R. Eleazar ben Azaria, 90-130

---

[33] "I saw," En. 39:7, 13; 40:1; 41:1 etc., cf. Hermaniuk, 127-141: The things and persons seen are symbols of divine mysteries inaccessible to man. Here, too, the *mashal* is the reflection of a very different reality.

[34] "Three similitudes (מְשָׁלֵי, παραβολαί) were imparted to me."

[35] "Then my grandfather Enoch gave me in a book the signs (teaching?) of all mysteries, and the similitudes which were given him, and collected them for me in the words of the book of the similitudes" (= c. 37-71).

[36] In Philo, who expounds the OT allegorically, and whose abstract nature has no taste for comparisons, παραβολή plays no role. Conf. Ling., 99 ἐν παραβολῆς εἴδει, "in the figure of a comparison."

[37] They value the parable highly as a form of instruction. Cf. Midr. Cant., 1, 1 (79a), Str.-B., I, 653 f.: "... Let not the parable be lowly in thine eyes, for through a parable one can attain to an understanding of the words of the Torah." It is worth noting that the role of the parable is less prominent in the Babyl. rabbis than the Palestinian, Str.-B., I, 654 f.; cf. Jer. in Mt. 18:23 (MPL, 26, 132 C): *Familiare est Syris et maxime Palaestinis, ad omnem sermonem suum parabolas jungere: ut quod per simplex praeceptum teneri ab auditoribus non potest, per similitudinem exemplaque teneatur.*

[38] Gn. r., 23 on Gn. 4:23 אסיא אסי חיגרתך, cf. Fiebig, *Gleichnisreden*, 164 ff.; G. Dalman, *Aram. Dialektproben*[2] (1927), 38; also Fiebig, *Altjüd. Gleichnisse*, 52 ff.; M. Lewin, *Aram. Sprichwörter u. Volkssprüche*, Diss. Erlangen (1895).

[39] bBer., 61b, Fiebig, *Gleichnisreden*, 79 f.

[40] Ab. R. Nat., 67 (ed. S. Schechter [1887]), Fiebig, 35 f.

[41] Ab., 3, 16, Fiebig, 76 ff.

[42] Fiebig, 224-233.

[43] Ziegler, Introd. XXVI f.

A.D. [44] He wants to show that the future redemption is greater than that out of Egypt: "How is this? It is like a man wanting children. When a daughter was born he took vows by her life. But when a son was born he left the daughter and took vows by his son's life." An example of a mixed parable is that of Hillel when he is seeking to show that earth was created before heaven: "A parable. It is like a king building a palace. Only when he had built the first storey did he build the second. Thus (says Scripture in Gn. 2:4) in the day when God made heaven and earth." [45] With no hesitation — and this is important in relation to the NT too — the term מָשָׁל is used by the Rabb. for pure and mixed parables, and for allegories as well. The Rabb. parables, which usually come in the context of scholarly discussion, seek to explain or establish a statement, esp. polemically. Usually, in keeping with the work of the Rabb., they are designed to expound the Law, and often individual verses. Eschatological parables are very rare. From the names of the Rabb. who are said to be the authors it may be seen that parables are already an established rhetorical and didactic form in the NT period. They are one of the rhetorical devices used by the Rabb. It does not appear that they were used in the interests of esoteric teaching.

Formally, too, they are very similar to the NT parables. They are usually marked off from the general context by an introductory formula. This will often be: "A parable. [46] To what is the matter like?," and the dat. will then be used in continuation (cf. Mk. 4:30; Lk. 13:18; Mt. 11:16), or: "A parable was told; what is it like?", or: "A parable of such and such," or simply: "Like a man (king)." [47] The pt. of comparison, and even the interpretation, is often stated in the final sentence, introduced by a "so". [48] Sometimes parables are antithetical, as the use of "but" before the final clause shows. [49] In keeping with Jewish brevity the introductory saying is often so short that it is not properly connected to the parable and the connection has to be supplied. Thus the beginning of the parable of R. Jochanan b. Zakkai [50] is: "A parable. This is like a king who invited his servants to a feast," while the main point of the parable is the conduct of the servants. As a rule the explanatory sentence directs attention to one pt. of comparison. But in the very nature of things an action has several features which may become subordinate pts. of comparison. [51] Among Rabb. parables there are some with two climaxes, [52] which makes the comparison more complicated. There is no doubt that these parables are designed to elucidate difficult matters, but this does not rule out the fact that they sometimes have an oracular form, since the Semitic sage loves to speak in not wholly clear comparisons as a spur to the perspicacity of his hearers.

C. New Testament.

1. Usage.

In the NT παραβολή is used only in the Synoptic Gospels (48 times) and Hb. (twice). The synon. → παροιμία is used 3 times in Jn. (10:6; 16:25, 29) and once in 2 Pt. (2:22). The Synoptic use of παραβολή corresponds fully to the broad use of מָשָׁל-παραβολή in the OT and Rabb. literature.

---

[44] M. Ex., 13, 2, Fiebig, 71 f., cf. on this R. Meyer, "Hellenistisches in d. rabb. Anthropologie," BWANT, IV, 22 (1937), 72 f.

[45] Midr. Gn. r., 1, Fiebig, 101 f. On pp. 7-82 Fiebig gives 20 examples of Rabb. parables from the time of Hillel to c. 130 A.D., and on pp. 94-103 further anonymous parables from the NT age. On the chronology of Jewish parables cf. Fiebig, Altjüd. Gleichnisse, 107-124.

[46] משל is here an abbreviation for מָשְׁלוֹ מָשָׁל, "tell him a parable," W. Bacher, Die exegetische Terminologie der jüd. Traditionsliteratur, II (1905), 121.

[47] Cf. Str.-B., I, 653 f.; Fiebig, Erzählungsstil, 32-76; Jeremias, Gleichnisse, 78 f.

[48] Cf. Fiebig, Altjüd. Gleichnisse, No. 8, 9, 10, 11 etc.

[49] Ibid., No. 17, 46, 47 etc.

[50] Shab., 153a, Fiebig, Gleichnisreden, No. 3a and 234-237.

[51] Cf. Fiebig, Altjüd. Gleichnisse, 92-95.

[52] Cf. Fiebig, Gleichnisreden, No. 3a (R. Jochanan b. Zakkai).

In the Synoptics παραβολή means a. a short saying which is combined with a comparison or figure of speech, so Mt. 15:15 (Mk. 7:17) in relation to the saying in v. 11 οὐ τὸ εἰσερχόμενον εἰς τὸ στόμα κοινοῖ τὸν ἄνθρωπον κτλ. It also means b. a proverbial saying, Lk. 4:23. [53] But in the main it is c. a parable, Mt. 13:3, 18, 24, 31, 33, 53; 21:45; Mk. 3:23; 4:2, 10, 13, 30; Lk. 6:39; 8:4, 9, 11; 12:16 etc.

In Hb. παραβολή means "counterpart" or "type," Hb. 9:9 : The former tabernacle is a figurative intimation of the heavenly tabernacle. According to Hb. 11:19 the returning of Isaac to Abraham was a likeness pointing beyond itself. It represented future awakening from the dead. [54]

2. Definition and Form of NT Parables.

The NT parable is more than a mere metaphor (leaven of the Pharisees, Mt. 16:6) or simile (clever as serpents, Mt. 10:16, shine as the sun, 13:43). It is an independent similitude in which an evident or accepted truth from a known field (nature, human life) is designed to establish or illustrate a new truth in the preaching of Jesus (kingdom of God, God's nature and action, piety). [55] Formally one might differentiate a. true parables, which are distinguished from figures of speech and similes only by the more extended development of the image, [56] and which may sometimes grow out of metaphors (Mt. 18:12-14; 24:43 f.), sometimes out of similes (Mt. 13:31 f., 33, 44, 45 f.). The obvious truth which all may know and which is set forth in the parable constitutes its power to convince ; hence οὐδείς, πᾶς, οὐ δύναται, μήτι is often found in the formulation. Then there are b. parables which consist of a story, often with subsidiary details, to which the comparative material is adapted. The story is in the past tense, Mk. 4:3-9; Mt. 21:39; 22:2; 25:1. The experience of one (indefinite art.) rather than all is now the parable. The distinction between b. and a. is fluid, but the characteristic narrative form is plain to see, e.g., in Mk. 4:3-9; Lk. 11:5-8; 13:6-9; 18:1-8. [57] Then we have c. illustrative stories in which the idea is presented without figurative garb. Lk. alone offers this type of parable in the 4 passages 10:30-37; 12:16-21; 16:19-31; 18:9-14. [58] Jesus takes the material for His parables partly from nature (Mk. 4:26-29; 13:28 f.; Lk. 12:54-56 etc.) and partly from the manifold relationships of human life as He knew them from His Palestinian background (householder, servant, money-lender, merchant, friend, widow, shepherd, housewife, judge, bridegroom, house-building etc.). In part He uses regular occurrences (leaven, grain of mustardseed), in part typical incidents (quarrelling children, sower), in part exceptional situations (the workers in the vineyard, Mt. 20:1-16). [59] Like the Rabbis, Jesus

---

[53] Various sayings attributed to Jesus may be proverbs used by Him, cf. Mt. 24:28; 6:24; 7:12. Bultmann Trad., 102, 111 f., 219, n. 1.

[54] Rgg. Hb., 365 f. ἐν παραβολῇ here does not just mean "as it were." The order and context are against this, cf. Dt. 28:37. L. Goppelt, "Typos," BFTh, II, 43 (1939), 212.

[55] For definitions cf. Jülicher, I, 80; Bultmann Trad., 184; Torm, 117; Manson, *Teaching*, 80 f.; Albertz, 88 f. W. Straub, *Die Bildersprache d. Ap. Pl.* (1937), 16 f. rightly contests the view of W. Stählin (*Das Gottesjahr* [1936], 58; *Vom Sinn des Leibes³* [1952], 90-100), who on the basis of modern symbolical thinking extends the definition to cover the whole Bible.

[56] Bultmann Trad., 184 on the basis of Jülicher's division. By metaphors Bultmann means sayings in which image and object are not linked by a comparative particle, as, e.g., Sir. 3:25 : "Where there is no apple of the eye, there is no light, and where there is no understanding, there is no wisdom," *ibid.*, 181.

[57] Jülicher, I, 92; Bultmann Trad., 188 ff.

[58] Jülicher, I, 114; Bultmann Trad., 192.

[59] Dibelius, 250 f. differentiates 1. parables in which the comparison is in the present (grain of mustard-seed), 2. those in which it is in the past (leaven), 3. short didactic stories

often incorporates stock metaphors in His parables, the king, the servant, the vineyard, the fig-tree, etc. But these do not become allegories, a point of some importance in interpretation. The parable of the husbandmen in Mk. 12:1-9 is close to an allegory. [60] It is possible that Jesus sometimes uses a current story in His parables. [61] It can hardly be assumed that He borrows from the Rabbis [62] or they from Him. [63] Both the Rabbis and Jesus take their parables from the same relationships and customs. [64]

Even independently of our evaluation of Mk. 4:11 f. (→ 757, 1 ff.) the question of a correct understanding of the parables arises. Already in the NT period there commenced a movement towards allegorical interpretation. With the centuries this became the dominant and accepted mode of exposition. [65] In opposition to this mistaken understanding modern scholarship has rightly worked out a fundamental distinction between parable and allegory, → 746, 1 ff. [66] On the other hand one should not press too far the theory that there can only be one *tertium comparationis*. [67] For some parables have more than one climax, → 751, 30 f.; Lk. 15:11 ff.; 16:19 ff. Again, the story in a parable is an organism. The main relation between figure and object can break up into a number of subordinate points of comparison (the sower, the four types of soil). Correct exposition must seek to relate these subsidiary features as closely as possible to the main thought (constructive interpretation). [68] Misunderstanding can also arise when the most general statement possible is worked out as the connecting thought. [69] Jesus was not a humanist or a philosopher trying to illustrate general truths. He was a preacher of the kingdom of God. Thus the connecting statement is to be sought in its living context within the theme of Jesus' preaching. The parables are thus to be understood and expounded in terms of the concrete situation of the proclamation of Jesus. [70]

In form the Synoptic parables [71] are in complete correspondence with the Rabbinic. They are often introduced by an initial announcement, e.g., Lk. 5:36 : ἔλεγεν δὲ καὶ παραβολὴν πρὸς αὐτούς, Mt. 13:18 : ὑμεῖς οὖν ἀκούσατε τὴν παραβολὴν τοῦ

(building, Mt. 7:24-27), 4. narratives worked out with greater poetic fulness. From the standpoint of material he differentiates parables whose "fable" contains 1. normal, 2. typical, 3. extraordinary, 4. constructed events. He puts Mt. 13:24-30 (wheat and tares) in the last group. Cf. also Wendt, 112 f.; Bugge, 61-65, who distinguishes between illustrative and argumentative parables.

[60] Jülicher, II, 385-406; Bultmann Trad., 191; for authenticity, Dodd, 124 ff., since the details are too slightly related to the fulfilment to constitute a *vaticinium ex eventu*. In interpretation cf. E. Lohmeyer, "Das Gleichnis von den bösen Weingärtnern," ZSTh, 18 (1941), 243-259.

[61] Dibelius, 251 f.; perhaps also the parable of the rich man, Lk. 16; cf. H. Gressmann, "Vom reichen Mann u. armen Lazarus," AAB (1918), No. 7, 1-8.

[62] So A. Drews, *Christusmythe*, II (1911), 390, but cf. Fiebig, *Gleichnisreden*, 222 f., 268 f.

[63] So Jülicher, I, 169.

[64] There are instances of interrelated motifs, e.g., Mt. 18:12-14; 20:1-16; 22:1-14, v. Bultmann Trad., 219 f. On the chronology of the Jewish parables and the originality of those of Jesus cf. Fiebig, *Altjüd. Gleichnisse*, 107-163.

[65] For the history of exposition of the parables cf. Jülicher, I, 203-322. On παραβολή in Cl. Al. and Orig. cf. Hermaniuk, 366-455.

[66] This is the permanent contribution of Jülicher.

[67] Jülicher, I, 70.

[68] Torm, 125; Dibelius, *Formgeschichte*, 253 ff.; Jülicher, I, 58-68.

[69] Cf. Jülicher, II, 188, 201, 266, 361, 442, 457, 481. Dodd, 24 is guilty of exaggeration, however, when he says that this is done consistently by Jülicher.

[70] Esp. emphasised by Cadoux, Dodd, Jeremias.

[71] For a penetrating analysis cf. Bultmann Trad., 193-222; Fiebig, *Erzählungsstil*, 32-77, also *Gleichnisreden*, 251-269.

σπείραντος, the story then beginning in the nominative. In many cases, too, a word like ὡς, ὥσπερ will serve as introduction, Mk. 4:31; Mt. 25:14, or we may find ὁμοία ἐστὶν ἡ βασιλεία τῶν οὐρανῶν ..., Mt. 13:31, 33, 44, or the question τίνι ὁμοία ἐστὶν ἡ βασιλεία τοῦ θεοῦ; Lk. 13:18, or τίνι ὁμοιώσω τὴν γενεὰν ταύτην; Mt. 11:16, or ὡμοιώθη ἡ βασιλεία τῶν οὐρανῶν ..., 13:24, or ὁμοιωθήσεται ἡ βασιλεία τῶν οὐρανῶν ..., 25:1, with a dat. as in the Rabbis, → 751, 19. Often a relative clause will follow, as in the Rabb., cf. Mk. 4:31; Mt. 7:24; 11:16; 13:33 etc., or, in a Gk. recasting, a part., Mk. 13:34; Mt. 13:24 etc. The introduction, as with the Rabb., may take the form of a question designed to stimulate the judgment of the listeners, Mk. 2:19; 4:21; Mt. 7:9 etc. The pt. is often given emphasis by (ἀμὴν) λέγω ὑμῖν, Mt. 18:13; 21:31; Lk. 14:24 etc. The parables may often close without application, Mk. 4:26-29; Lk. 11:5-8; 13:6-9 etc. Sometimes the parable may end with a question to the audience, Lk. 7:42; 10:36; Mt. 21:31. The hearers themselves are thus invited to state the conclusion. Very often, as in the Rabb., an application is appended, and this is introduced by οὕτως, Mt. 13:49; 18:14, 35; 20:16, etc., and impressed upon the listeners by an added imperative, Mk. 4:9, 23; 13:29; Mt. 25:13; Lk. 10:37. Sometimes, as in Jewish parables, the application is antithetical, Lk. 12:40, 56. This brief review of the forms enables us to see already that the aim is undoubtedly to clarify rather than to obscure the message. In His development of the form Jesus is much superior to the Rabbis, whether in the wealth of imagination, the power of short and realistic depiction, or the spiritual force of the ideas presented. His parables express His disturbing new thinking as compared with Judaism.

3. The Question of Transmission.

To discuss the original purpose of the parables one has first to tackle the question of the historical fidelity with which they have been transmitted. In the main, one may say that the degree of fidelity is very high. [72] In the three Synoptic Gospels the parables are given so much in the characteristic style and manner of thought of Jesus, and they carry so strongly the imprint of the Palestinian setting of the Gospel, that we are obviously very close to the actual words of Jesus. On the other hand, Synoptic criticism shows that there are slight differences between the different witnesses, and that certain alterations have been made. Comparison shows that some additions are secondary. Thus a reference to the destruction of Jerusalem may be seen plainly in Mt. 22:6 f. Fundamental enquiry must be made into the standpoints from which the alterations were made. Reference has rightly been made [73] to the twofold setting of the parables. On the one side they belong to the preaching of Jesus, on the other to that of the primitive community. Almost inevitably greater or smaller changes were occasioned by the situation of the community, its experiences, conflicts, goals and expectations. These must be reversed if we are to get back to the parables of Jesus in their original form. [74] In detail, of course, the subjective factor of the scholar will unavoidably enter into the picture here. Nevertheless, certain fundamental principles may be stated.

Through the change in audience [75] some parables originally addressed to opponents are now applied to believers. Thus the parable of the labourers was originally designed to show to self-righteous Pharisees how great is God's loving-kindness. But the appended saying in Mt. 20:16 makes it a warning to believers.

---

[72] Cf. the individual analyses in Bultmann Trad., 184-193; Jülicher, I, 1-24 (on the authenticity of the parables), 183-206 (a catalogue of the parables).

[73] Jeremias, Gleichnisse, 16.

[74] M. Dibelius, "Rabb. u. evangelische Erzählungen," ThBl (1932), 5, refers to "overshadowings of one interest by another in the tradition," and asks (8): "How are the first concerns of the story, which brought it to birth, related to those which underlie the present tradition?" Dodd, 148 speaks of a certain tendency to make general maxims out of sayings which were coined for a specific situation. Jeremias, op. cit., 17-19 refers to "embellishments."

[75] Jeremias, 19-28.

Similarly the parable of the lost sheep is in Mt. 18 (vv. 12-14) part of the teaching addressed to the community. It thus becomes an admonition to exemplary pastoral care, though originally it expressed the great joy of God at the conversion of a sinner. [76] In general the parables are made to serve the needs of ecclesiastical exhortation. [77] Thus the eschatological parable in Lk. 12:58 f. becomes an admonition to readiness for reconciliation in Mt. (5:25 f.). The situation of the Church, [78] with its successful Gentile missions, causes Lk. 14:23 to add a second invitation as compared with Mt. 22:9 f., while the Jewish Christian Evangelist for his part (Mt. 22:11-13) adds what seems to be originally an independent parable with the warning not to appear at the banquet of God's kingdom without the adornment of good works. [79] In eschatological parables especially the tarrying of the *parousia* and concentrated expectation of the coming again of Christ led to changes. What was originally a summons to the multitude becomes an admonition to the community (Mt. 25:1-13), and allegorical interpretation has given the parable a christological edge. [80] Allegory almost unavoidably invades eschatological parables. [81] The man of Lk. 14:16 becomes a king in Mt. 22:2, and the king is the heavenly Christ; cf. the thief of Mt. 24:43 and the householder of Mk. 13:35. The words of the returning merchant in Mt. 25:21, 23, 30 have perhaps been changed somewhat already to become words of the Christ of the *parousia*. But a theoretical desire to get stylistically pure parables in no way justifies us in attributing all allegorical features to the community. [82] In relation to the total understanding of the parable it is important that, in marked distinction from the eschatological parables of Mt., those peculiar to Lk. contain almost no allegorical features. It seems natural to deduce the basic form of the parables of Jesus from this. [83]

> As the settings of narratives and addresses are often to be attributed to the Evangelists, so it is with the parables (cf. Lk. 12:41; 14:7; cf. 8:4 with Mk. 4:1 f. etc.). The same applies to their integration into a context (Mk. 9:50; Mt. 5:25 f.; 18:12-14, 23; Lk. 6:39 f.), the interrelating of many parables (Mk. 4; Mt. 13), and the statements about the listeners (Lk. 15:1 f.; 16:1 etc.). Lk. esp. has settings which he seems to have constructed himself in view of the linguistic peculiarities. [84] In the application features often occur which do not appear to fit in properly with the parables, thus betraying their secondary nature. Thus Lk. 14:33 uses οὕτως οὖν to introduce an application which certainly contains an authentic saying of Jesus but which does not really make the same point as the preceding parable. [85]

The question of authenticity is particularly urgent in the two interpretations which are given by the Evangelists and set on the lips of Jesus Himself, Mk. 4:13-20

---

[76] *Ibid.*, 26.

[77] *Ibid.*, 28-33. Dibelius, 257: The tendency to get as much exhortation as possible out of the sayings of Jesus affected the transmission of the parables.

[78] Jeremias, 33-50.

[79] Bultmann Trad., 189, 218, 220 : It may be that a fragment from a Jewish parable has lodged in Mt. 22:11-13; cf. Str.-B., I, 878 f.

[80] Jeremias, *Gleichnisse*, 38-40; Bultmann Trad., 190 f.; Dibelius, 256.

[81] Jeremias, 50-70.

[82] Jülicher undoubtedly goes too far at this pt. Dibelius rightly perceives in the vacillation between parable and allegory something esp. distinctive of the oriental spirit.

[83] Jeremias, 69.

[84] Cf. Lk. 8:4; 15:1 ff.; 18:1, 9; 19:11. The setting in Lk. 10:25-37 is the question as to the greatest commandment (vv. 25-28 par. Mk. 12:28-31). At the end (v. 36) there is a ref. back to this introduction, though not in quite the same form, Bultmann Trad., 192.

[85] Cf. Bultmann Trad., 184. 18:6-8 may well be secondary too, Jülicher, II, 283 ff.; Bultmann Trad., 189; cf. also 12:21, Jülicher, II, 613 f.; Bultmann Trad., 193, and 16:8, Jülicher II, 509 f.; Bultmann Trad., 190 etc.

(Mt. 13:18-23; Lk. 8:11-15, the sower), and Mt. 13:36-43 (the wheat and the tares). According to Mk. 4:10 and Mt. 13:36 the interpretations are given at the request of the disciples, and are for this smaller circle alone. They are perhaps connected with the idea that even in their original context the parables need an interpretation as riddles need to be solved, Mk. 4:34 ἐπέλυεν. The allegorical nature of the interpretations is used as an argument against their authenticity. [86] Closer stylistic analysis of Mk. 4:13-20 also shows that it contains several expressions which are alien to Jesus' style but common to that of the community. [87] Similarly, the interpretation in Mt. 13:36-43 is shot through by the linguistic peculiarities of Mt. [88] Both interpretations would seem to belong to the second "setting" of the parables.

4. The Meaning and Purpose of the Parables in the Preaching of Jesus. [89]

According to Mk. 4:33 f. Jesus made considerable use of parables in His preaching. [90] This was adapted to the deficient understanding of the simple people (4:33 : καθὼς ἠδύναντο ἀκούειν). [91] As with the Rabb., the parables were designed to make explicitly intellectual concepts easier to understand by means of concrete illustrations from familiar fields. [92] This is particularly so in the case of Jesus because He realised that He was called at the most critical hour in the people's history to be God's messenger to arouse them to seize the hour (Lk. 12:54-56) and to make the required decisions (17:26-30). If His cries of warning were to be effective, they had to be clear (1 C. 14:8). He is a prophet seeking to kindle a fire (Lk. 12:49), not an apocalyptist speaking obscurely. In the primary situation, i.e., in the original context of the preaching, the parables were directly apprehensible and needed no interpretation, as is also true of the Rabbinic use of parables. On the other hand, the understanding of parables presupposes listeners who are willing to accompany the speaker in His thinking and who are capable of grasping the similarity between image and reality. [93] At this point we come up against an unmistakable frontier, the more so as Jesus' ideas on the coming kingdom and the nature of God were quite different from those current in Judaism. The parable may fail if there is no spiritual power to grasp its heart or if the revelation of God which it contains is rejected. Jesus experienced both these things. Nor does acceptance of the principle that Jesus used the parables as an aid to understanding rule out the fact that He sometimes used this form of speech to express His thoughts in a veiled manner, Mt. 21:33-46. It is rather a different matter that parables, when detached from their original setting, become riddles [94] because the point of contact, which was plain in the original situation, is lost.

---

[86] In part, of course, this may be traced back to the mode of thought of the primitive community, which is not at home with the abstract and expresses the relation between figure and reality by simple equations, cf. Bultmann Trad., 214.

[87] For details cf. Jeremias, Gleichnisse, 59-62; cf. also Schniewind, ad loc.

[88] For details cf. Jeremias, 63-66.

[89] Cf. Jülicher, I, 118-148; Lagrange, 1-35; Kögel; Hermaniuk, 1-32, 302-350.

[90] The statement in v. 34 that Jesus spoke only in parables which He then explained to the narrower circle of the disciples is related to the theory in 4:11 f.

[91] E. Molland ("Zur Auslegung v. Mk. 4:33," Symbolae Osloenses, VIII [1929], 83-91) construes δύνασθαι ἀκούειν as "to be able to bear hearing," (Jn. 6:60; 8:43; Epict. Diss., II, 24, 11; III, 1, 24; 2, 3 etc.), and in a way which is not very convincing he takes this to mean : as the people could listen to His preaching in the vivid and captivating form of parables.

[92] Wendt, 123, 128 f., refers to the principle of the greatest clarity in the shortest way — a way which Jesus followed precisely by speaking in parables.

[93] Wellh. Mk., 31.

[94] Mt. 7:6 ? 24:28 ? Mk. 9:49 ?

The view that the parables may be understood quite easily is contradicted by the much debated saying in Mk. 4:11 f. (→ IV, 817, 21 ff.) that by preaching in parables Jesus deliberately intended (Mk., Lk. : ἵνα) [95] to conceal the knowledge of salvation from those outside the circle of the disciples in order that (μήποτε κτλ.) this might lead to a hardening of the people, which would make it ripe for God's judgment.

The saying in Mk., which is surprising in the context of 4:10 ff., is not really isolated in Mk., since c. 3 describes how there is a great division among the people, and only a small circle emerges as the true brothers and sisters of Jesus, 3:31-35. Later in c. 4, at v. 24 f., Mk. also has the saying about true hearing with its threat, and in 4:34 (→ 756, 5) he says that the parables are riddles which demand interpretation. Mt., who follows the Markan order in his interrelating of the parables in c. 13, weaves the saying of Mk. 4:25 (Mt. 13:12) directly into the statement about the significance of preaching in parables in 13:10-13. The true reason here (ὅτι, v. 13) is found in the dullness of the multitude, and, quoting Is. 6:9 f. (exactly acc. to the LXX), he describes it theologically as a fulfilment (ἀναπληροῦται) of the OT prophecy. At the end of the address in parables (v. 35) he adds a further quotation from Ps. 78:2. [96] The preaching in parables is thus portrayed, in fulfilment of the OT saying, as a revelation of things concealed from the beginning of creation, and the μυστήρια τῆς βασιλείας in v. 11 is the present actualisation in Jesus of God's eternal plan of salvation. Lk., who shares the theological concern neither of Mk. nor Mt., summarises the whole pericope in the simplified statement : ὑμῖν δέδοται γνῶναι τὰ μυστήρια τῆς βασιλείας τοῦ θεοῦ, τοῖς δὲ λοιποῖς ἐν παραβολαῖς, ἵνα βλέποντες μὴ βλέπωσιν καὶ ἀκούοντες μὴ συνιῶσιν, 8:10.

In the looser structure of Mk. 4 [97] v. 11 f. obviously stands apart from vv. 3-9 and 13-20. Both v. 11 and v. 13 have their own introductory formulae. V. 13 is a continuation of v. 10, and it answers the question of the disciples. V. 11 f. is an interpolation. Two views esp. are possible in relation to this much debated saying. The critical understanding (→ IV, 817 f.) sees in it a later construction which echoes the theology of the community rather than Jesus Himself. The historical result, namely, that Israel remained aloof in unbelief, is regarded by the community as the intention of Jesus. [98] The community was beset by the problem of the defeat of Jesus, and it solved it by having recourse to the concept of predestination, Is. 6:9 f. cf. Ac. 28:25-27; Jn. 12:39 f. On the other hand, a conservative understanding (→ 554 f.) regards the saying as an authentic saying of Jesus Himself. On this view it is a very serious saying based on Jesus' own painful experience of His calling. Two groups have emerged : the disciples, who have seen the importance of the present hour, the mystery which God has granted them [99]

---

[95] A causal view of ἵνα is possible acc. to later *koine* usage, and in this case the ὅτι of Mt. would be an intentional clarification, but one can hardly adopt this interpretation here, → III, 323 ff.; Bl.-Debr.[8] § 369, 2 App.

[96] He calls the author of the Ps. a prophet because he sees in the saying a prediction of Christ. The reading Ησαΐου א*Θ is secondary.

[97] K. L. Schmidt, *Der Rahmen d. Gesch. Jesu* (1919), 126-135; Percy, 258-278; Gealy, 40-43.

[98] Meyer Ursprung, I, 108; Well. Mk., 31; Jülicher, I, 120-148; A. Merx, *Die 4 kanon. Ev.*, II, 2 (1905), 46; Kl. Mk., ad loc.; Bultmann Trad., 215; H. J. Ebeling, "Das Messiasgeheimnis u. d. Botschaft d. Mk.," ZNW *Beih.*, 19 (1939), 179-193, who thinks the interpolation embraces vv. 10-25, and who sees in the theory about parables in the c. a serious warning against frivolous hearing and hardening of heart. On the other hand A. Schweitzer, *Gesch. d. Leben-Jesu-Forschung*[4] (1926), 400-405 thinks Mk. 4:11 f. represents Jesus' own view ; cf. also his *Messianität u. Leidensgeheimnis*[2] (1929), 24 ff. Cf. also ad loc. M. Goguel, *Leben Jesu* (1934), 178-182; Stauffer Theol., 36.

[99] → IV, 817, 20 ff. It is a fact that nowhere else in the Synoptics does Jesus refer to this apocalyptic concept (Da. 2:18 f., 27 ff.; En. 41:1, 3 etc.; Rev. 1:20, which was also used by the Rabb. for esoteric doctrines, → IV, 817, 1-18. Ebeling, *op. cit.*, 184 f. sees in μυστήρια a link with Hell. gnosis. The mystery theory is continued and developed by the Gnostics. Cl. Al. Exc. Theod., 66 (GCS, 17, 128); Iren. Haer., II, 27, 2. R. Liechtenhan, *Die Offenbarung im Gnosticismus* (1901), 45-50.

being insight into the fact that the kingdom of God is now dawning ; and the unbelieving masses (οἱ ἔξω), [100] who do not have this insight, and for whom the events of the present are thus a complete enigma. [101] Jesus judges that there is here fulfilled [102] what Is. stated prophetically on the basis of his own painful experience. Divine judgment is threatened against unbelieving rejection of revelation. From this original stage of the saying is to be distinguished a second stage, its incorporation by Mk. into the chapter on parables, where the ἐν παραβολαῖς (v. 11) is erroneously referred to the use of parables, which as obscure utterance brings down the judgment of hardening according to the will of Jesus or God. This secondary use in Mk. 4, which in contrast to their obvious character regards them as a judgment on the stupid multitude, clearly constitutes a theological concept in the total structure of his gospel. In a general statement (τὰ πάντα, → IV, 817, 30 f.) a theory is advanced concerning the preaching of Jesus in parables. [103] But obviously a distinction has to be made between the theology of Mk. and the original meaning and purpose of the preaching in parables.

5. The Message Proclaimed by the Parables.

In content the parables of Jesus are elucidations of the great themes of His preaching : the kingdom of God, the nature and work of God, the being and destiny of man. This means already that many of the parables will have an eschatological character. It also means, however, that by no means all the parables will be eschatological. [104] In this respect an immediate distinction arises between the parables of Jesus and those of the Rabbis, which in general are so similar to them. In keeping with the main concern of the Rabb., their parables deal primarily with the Law and its elucidation and exposition, while eschatology is secondary. In Jesus, however, eschatology is a dominant theme. Yet the eschatological parables of Jesus are not apocalyptic revelations like those of En. or on occasion 4 Esr. (→ 749, 34 ff.). As regards the question of disclosure or concealment one has to differentiate between parables which, like those of the Rabb., are interwoven into

---

[100] → II, 575 f., though the phrase οἱ ἔξω for unbelievers would seem to belong to a period of more developed church life than that of Jesus, when everything was still fluid, cf. P. Feine, "Zur synpt. Frage," Jbch. pr. Theol., 14 (1888), 412.

[101] R. Otto, Reich Gottes u. Menschensohn (1934), 110-117, conjectures an original לִמְשָׁלִים, "everything will be a puzzle, or puzzling, to unbelievers," which under the influence of a later esoteric theory of parables became בִּמְשָׁלִים (ἐν παραβολαῖς). Cf. Jeremias, Gleichnisse, 7-12, who thinks (10, n. 3) that γίνεσθαι ἐν, like εἶναι ἐν, depicts a state which we would usually express adjectivally, cf. Pr.-Bauer⁴ (1950), 407. J. Schniewind Mk. (NT Deutsch), 76 f., who keeps "in parables" for ἐν παραβολαῖς, sees in the enigmatic form of parables, which provokes thought, an instrument to serve the content of the mystery of the divine lordship and its presence in Jesus. In favour of the antiquity of the saying Manson, Teaching, 75-81, shows that the quotation of Is. in Mk. 4:12 agrees with the Targum current in Palestine, cf. F. Horst, → 554, 29 ff., esp. n. 116. The ἵνα is to be traced back to the Aram. דְּ, which is not necessarily final, though not simply relative (Gk. οἵ). On μήποτε cf. → 555, n. 116; Pr.-Bauer⁴, s.v. μήποτε. Hermaniuk, 302-350 finds in Mk. 4:11 f. Jesus' intention of disclosing the mystery of the kingdom of God only in stages, fully to the apostles, in veiled form to the masses. In general his interpretation of ἀφεθῇ αὐτοῖς, 331 f., that the mystery is "not delivered or handed over to them," is quite erroneous.

[102] The softer reading of ἵνα in the sense of ἵνα πληρωθῇ (so Lagrange, "Le but," 28 f.; cf. Pr.-Bauer⁴, s.v. ἵνα; → IV, 818, 14 f.) is an illegitimate alleviation of the difficulty, Hermaniuk, 315.

[103] Acc. to W. Wrede, Das Messiasgeheimnis (1901), 54-59, this is linked with the theologoumenon of Mk. On the similar view of the παραβολή in Hermas → 761, 17 ff.

[104] Manson, Teaching, 69 f. distinguishes between parables relating to human conduct (ethical types, appeals to the conscience) and those illustrating God's action (religious types, appeals to the faith of the hearers). Lohmeyer, 325 distinguishes between eschatological and paradigmatic parables.

a didactic context, [105] and those which are not bound to a given theme (Mk. 4:3-9 ? 12:1-11?) but in which the speaker by veiled speech stirs the audience to note and detect the statement concealed behind the veil, 4:9 → 554, 9 ff. By far the majority of the parables of Jesus seem to belong to the first group ; the sources do not allow us to make precise distinction.

Many of the parables of Jesus seek to clarify for the hearers the nature and coming of the kingdom of God, to impress vividly on them the new thoughts of Jesus concerning this kingdom, and even more so to stir them to make the appropriate resolves. Thus Jesus speaks in parables about the imminent establishment of God's kingdom (the fig-tree, Mk. 13:28 f., Lk. 21:29-31), its sudden coming (the thief, Mt. 24:43 f.; Lk. 12:39 f.). Indeed, the present hour is so great and decisive just because the kingdom of God is already dawning. [106] The present is the time of joy at the dawn of the last time. This is why the bridal party cannot fast, Mk. 2:19. The old aeon has run its course ; this is why patching it is useless, Mk. 2:21 f. The demons must yield to the stronger man who binds them, Mk. 3:27. An invitation is now given to enter the kingdom of God, 2:17. Without man's co-operation the harvest will ripen, Mk. 4:26-29. In spite of every failure in work for the kingdom of God, the harvest will be great, Mk. 4:3-9. In spite of small beginnings it will finally be world-embracing (the grain of mustard-seed, Mk. 4:31 f.). It will permeate the whole world (the leaven, Mt. 13:33). But the kingdom of God also carries with it the supreme crisis of history. It summons men to unconditional decision for God and God's kingdom. Man has to choose between the goods (and service) of the world and the kingdom of God, Mt. 6:24. Unfortunately men are blind and undiscerning in relation to the signs of the times, Lk. 12:54-56. The turning-point threatens to come like the disaster of the flood and the judgment on Sodom and Gomorrah, Lk. 17:26-29. The end will entail separation (the wheat and the tares, Mt. 13:24-30; the drag-net, 47-50). The man who now finds security in earthly goods is a fool, Lk. 12:16-20. Those who are unfruitful stand under threat (the fig-tree, Lk. 13:6-9). False disciples will then be trampled underfoot like useless salt, Mt. 5:13; Lk. 14:34 f. It is advisable to put one's affairs in order before the judgment, Lk. 12:58 f. Watchfulness is the great requirement of the hour (the servant, Mk. 13:33-37; the virgins, Mt. 25:1-13). Only the hearer who becomes a doer of the Word will stand in the last judgment (the house on the rock, Mt. 7:24-27). The decisive question will be whether one is worthy of the confidence reposed (the servant, Mt. 24:45-51). In the kingdom of God there will be a balancing out of earthly circumstances (Lazarus, Lk. 16:19-26), and no extraordinary miracle is needed to believe God's call, 27-31.

Other parables depict God's nature and action, partly in connection with the eschatological theme, partly in independence of it. God is kind like a father who gives only good gifts to his children, Mt. 7:9-11. As man rejoices when he finds again something he had lost, so God rejoices at the conversion of a sinner (the lost sheep, Mt. 18:12-14). As the human father receives back with love a son who comes home again repentant, even more so does God receive the sinner who returns to Him, Lk. 15:11-32; the hard and self-righteous scribes and Pharisees must learn this lesson. As the lazy friend yields to the request of his friend, much more so does the God who is rich in love answer human petitions (Lk. 11:5-8), and as

---

[105] Mt. 7:3-5, 9-11; 11:16 f.; 24:32 f., 42-44; Lk. 7:41 f. etc.

[106] So correctly Jeremias, 162; Jeremias, ThBl., 216-222. In contrast to Dodd's exaggerated idea that the reality of Jesus is "realised eschatology" (132 f., 98) Jeremias prefers to speak of eschatology in process of realisation.

even a hard and unjust judge does not close his ears to a pleading widow, much more so the Judge who is kind and righteous will not do so (Lk. 18:1-8). The man who repents finds God's forgiveness, while the self-righteous man goes away empty (the Pharisee and the publican, Lk. 18:9-14). To repent and do God's will is what matters (the two sons, Mt. 21:28-32). So generous is God that He gives the same share in the kingdom of God even to him who has done little (the labourers in the vineyard, Mt. 20:1-16). God repays the faithful servant superabundantly, Mt. 25:14-30.

Several parables deal with the nature and duty of man, especially in relation to God. Like capricious children with their playmates, men criticise God and God's acts, Mt. 11:16-19. Self-examination is needed before decision for God's kingdom (the tower, Lk. 14:28-32). The present hour demands resolute and prudent action (the steward, Lk. 16:1-8). Like a labourer in the service of his master, man has with God no claim to reward, Lk. 17:7-10. The disciple can expect no better fate than his master, Mt. 10:24 f. He must shine out like a city on the hill, Mt. 5:14b. He must let his light shine, 5:16. Blindness is bad, especially in the present hour (the eye, Mt. 6:22 f.). The one who knows forgiveness overflows with gratitude (the woman who sinned much, Lk. 7:36-50). This and other parables are plainly aimed at opponents whom Jesus describes as blind leaders of the blind, Mt. 15:14. True uncleanness is not in the body, but in the inward man, Mt. 15:10 ff. The tree is known by its fruit, Mt. 7:16-20. God demands humility (the publican, Lk. 18:9-14). God will give His vineyard to other husbandmen, Mk. 12:1-11. Some parables refer to man's dealings with his fellows. The man who is shown mercy by God must be merciful towards his brethren (the wicked servant, Mt. 18:23-35). The love of neighbour which God demands recognises no limits set by men (the good Samaritan, Lk. 10:30-37).

On the parables in Jn. → παροιμία.

6. Figurative Language in Paul, James and Revelation.

Paul does not use the word παραβολή. But his speech, too, is rich in comparisons drawn from the most varied spheres of life. The figurative world of this city dweller and Hellenist is, of course, a very different one from that of Jesus. [107] He often uses metaphors (R. 13:12 : armour of light ; 1 C. 5:8 : leaven of wickedness) and comparisons, e.g., R. 6:13 f.: the members as weapons, 6:16 f.: sin as service, 1 C. 3:2 : milk as a first food, 6:19 : the body as a temple, 7:22 : believers as Christ's freedmen, 13:12 : present knowledge like seeing in an unclear mirror, 2 C. 5:1: the body as an earthly tabernacle etc. Paul is also found of extended comparisons, e.g., R. 7:1 ff.: the legal status of the married woman in comparison with man's bondage to the Law, 1 C. 3:5 ff.: the community as a crop, 9:24-27: the Christian life as a contest in the arena, 12:12 ff.: the unity and multiplicity of the bodily organism as a picture of the community, Gl. 3:15 ff.: God's word of promise and a human testament, 1 C. 15:35 ff.: the earthly and resurrection bodies like the seed and plant, Eph. 6:10 ff.: the Christian's armour. Sometimes his comparisons are not consistent (1 C. 3:11 ff.; 2 C. 3:2 f.) or they are wide of the mark materially (R. 11:17 ff.). There are no true parables after the manner of Jesus.

The language of Jm. is rich in figures, like that of Palestine, but he, too, has no real parables. Rev., in accordance with its apocalyptic style, has a plenitude of visions, allegories and symbols, but no parables. [108]

---

[107] W. Straub, *Die Bildersprache d. Ap. Pl.* (1937), 105-113 lists 28 "parables" in Pl. in the sense of extended comparisons. Form-critically he concludes that these are neither parables (stories) nor rounded off comparisons ; they stand between the Jewish and the Gk. tradition (112 f.). Cf. R. Bultmann, *op. cit.* (→ n. 8), 35-42, 88-94; R. Eidem, *Pauli Bildvärld*, I (1913), which is unfinished and deals only with sporting and military images.

[108] Bss. Apk., 1-19 on the literary style of Rev.; Had. Apk., 8 f., Exc. 1 on the formal

D. Post-Apostolic Fathers.

In the post-apost. fathers παραβολή occurs only in Barnabas and Hermas.

It occurs twice in Barn. in connection with the allegorical interpretation of the OT. In 6, 10, with ref. to Ex. 33:1-3, mentioned just before, it means a "riddle" which is to be allegorically referred to Christ. The παραβολή, which contains a hidden deeper sense, is an aid to understanding of the mystery of God, though only for him who like the author (v. 10 ἐν ἡμῖν) has the requisite γνῶσις (v. 9; cf. Mt. 13:11; Lk. 8:10 γνῶναι). For this (v. 10) he praises the Lord who such σοφίαν καὶ νοῦν θέμενος ἐν ὑμῖν τῶν κρυφίων αὐτοῦ. [109] In his own work he interprets the provisions of the OT Law as allegories of Christ, and then in conclusion (17, 2) he says that due to their lack of understanding (οὐ μὴ νοήσητε) he will not write about the future, since this is shut up in "riddles" (διὰ τὸ ἐν παραβολαῖς κεῖσθαι). He again means sayings which have a hidden, allegorical sense, and which thus contain mysterious intimations of the divinely ordained future. [110]

The third part of Herm. has the title παραβολαὶ ἃς ἐλάλησεν μετ' ἐμοῦ. [111] The first five of these are extended comparisons built up on current metaphors (esp. 1 and 5). They are like the Synoptic parables in basic character. Interpretations are appended; these are partly parabolical (3, 3; 4, 2 ff.) and partly (esp. 5) a mixture between the parabolical (5, 3) and the allegorical (5, 4, 1-6, 8). Each of the first five contains a revelation by figure. Because of the obscurity of the theme, there follows a request for explanation (ἐπιλύω 5, 3, 1), sometimes with an asseveration that understanding is otherwise impossible (5, 3, 1; 4, 2). The request is followed by the solution of the riddle (5, 5, 1 ἐπίλυσις), which Herm. is to pass on to others (ἵνα γνωστὰ πᾶσιν ποιήσῃς αὐτά). The Shepherd gives this in Herm., as Jesus does in Mk. In part it consists of equations, like the explanations in the Synoptists. Admonitions are closely interwoven into it. The view of parables in Herm. is very like that of Mk. 4:11 f. (Mt. 13; Lk. 8). One cannot say for certain that it is dependent on this alone. Perhaps Mk. 4:11 f. and Herm. both derive from an existing understanding that differs from the use of parables seen in Jesus, which is similar to that in the Rabb. In 6-10, as distinct from 1-5, the parables are visions which impart divine revelations to Herm. in figures of speech. Herm. again confesses his lack of understanding (9, 14, 4), whereupon the interpreting angel yields to his request and explains the allegories (8, 3, 2 and 6, 4; 9, 11, 9-31, 2).

Hauck

---

† παραγγέλλω, † παραγγελία

A. The General Greek Usage.

Acc. to the dict. [1] the verb παραγγέλλω, and with it the noun παραγγελία, embraces a wealth of meaning and shades of meaning which it would be superfluous to enumerate. On the basis of the original sense "to pass on an announcement" [2] they all

---

elements in apoc. literature; C. Clemen, "Die Bildlichkeit d. Apk.," *Festschr. J. Kaftan* (1920), 25-43; K. L. Schmidt, "D. Bildersprache in d. Joh.-Apk.," *Theol. Zschr.,* 3 (1947), 161-177.

[109] Cf. *ad loc.,* H. Windisch, *Hndbch.,* Suppl. III, "Die Apost. Vät." (1923), 334 f.; Hermaniuk, 353-357.

[110] Cf. Iren. Haer., V, 26, 2 διὰ τὸ ἐν παραβολαῖς καὶ ἀλληγορίαις κεῖσθαι (from Barn. ?); Asc. Is. 4:20: "The rest of the vision of the Lord, lo, it is set forth in similitudes in my words, in that which is written in the book, which I have openly proclaimed."

[111] Cf. Dib. Herm., esp. 560-577; Hermaniuk, 357-365.

π α ρ α γ γ έ λ λ ω. [1] Cf., e.g., Pape, II, 473; Liddell-Scott, 1306.

[2] In keeping with the sense of παρα- as "along" (E. Schwyzer, *Griech. Gramm.* [*Handbuch AW,* II, 1], II [1950], 493) the basic meaning of παραγγέλλειν is "to pass an

have to do with "intimation." The only sense to appear in the NT, though with much modification, is simply that of "order" or "direction." Rather oddly the special use of the verb for the "military order," which is so common in Hdt.,[3] Thuc.,[4] Xenoph.,[5] and Polyb.,[6,7] does not occur at all (though cf. Ac. 4:18; 5:28, 40; 16:23). Similarly the so-called official use (common in the pap.)[8] of both verb and noun for a "summons to court" is not to be found. It is thus no surprise that the fairly common use, esp. in Plut.,[9] for "running for an office" is alien to the NT. On the other hand, in relation to NT usage it is worth noting that Plat.[10] has παραγγέλλειν for the "orders" of God (Resp., III, 415b), the "laws" (Leg., IX, 860a; cf. Resp., IV, 429c) and "heads of state" (ἄρχοντες, Leg., VI, 764a). The ref. is to regulations of practical conduct. In Aristot., too, παραγγελία is once used for "direction" or "statute," Eth. Nic., II, 2, p. 1104a, 7. Closest to NT usage, though not with the same content, is that of Epict., though he does not use the noun.[11] He has the verb for the recommendations or directions of philosophers[12] (Diss., IV, 4, 18), esp. in connection with the Γνῶθι σεαυτόν of the "ancients" (I, 18, 17) or "philosophers" (II, 9, 13) in the sense "to lay down," "to command."[13] Worthy of special mention is the common use of παραγγελίαι for "astrological rules" in Vett. Val. (156, 21; 221, 7; 273, 32; 308, 26).

The difference between παραγγέλλειν and κελεύειν is instructive. Since the former originally denoted passing on a communication from one to the other,[14] it is chosen when the one concerned is to be addressed and committed personally, while the latter has rather the actual command in view.[15]

B. The Hellenistic Jewish Usage.

1. The noun does not occur in the LXX.[16] The verb[17] is mostly used of "military orders," Ju. 4:10; 1 S. 15:4; 23:8; 1 K. 15:22; Ιερ. 27(50):29; 28(51):27; 1 Macc. 5:58; 9:63; 3 Macc. 1:1, esp. those of the commander, Jdt. 7:1; 2 Macc. 15:10, cf. also Jos. 6:7.

announcement along (the ranks)," "to give an order." Since it is obvious that an order has to be passed on, one can easily see how the word came to have the more general sense "to order" (in the first instance with application to a group) [Debrunner].

[3] Cf. J. E. Powell, A Lexicon to Herodotus (1938), s.v.

[4] Cf. E. A. Bétant, Lex. Thucydideum, II (1847), s.v.

[5] Cf. F. W. Sturz, Lex. Xenophonteum, III (1801), s.v.

[6] Cf. I. Schweighäuser, Lex. Polybianum (1822), s.v. Polyb. also has παραγγελία for a military order.

[7] In inscr. παραγγέλλειν is often used with ref. to the orders of the στρατηγός. Cf. Ditt. Syll.³, IV, 489.

[8] Cf. Moult.-Mill., 480 f.; Preisigke Wört., II, 235; on the construction cf. Mayser, II, 1, 158, 160 f., 255, 309, 315, 338 f.

[9] Cf. K. Jacobitz and E. E. Seiler, Handwörterbuch d. gr. Sprache, II, 1 (1843), 563.

[10] Cf. F. Astius, Lex. Platonicum, III (1838), 30.

[11] Instead παράγγελμα at Diss. Fr., I, lines 13/14 (Schenkl).

[12] Diss., I, 7, 9 for the rules and requirements of philosophical enquiry.

[13] Cf. Diss. Fr., I, line 16, where προσέχειν τῇ προστάξει corresponds to παραγγέλλειν.

[14] Cf. Plat. Resp., VIII, 556d ἄλλον ἄλλῳ παραγγέλλειν ... Similarly παραγγελία can express the passing on of a command from man to man.

[15] There is a fine instance of this distinction in Xenoph. Hist. Graec., II, 1, 3 : παραγγέλλειν ἐκέλευσε. In the main the two verbs are more or less par. in sense, cf. Xenoph. An., I, 5, 13 παραγγέλλει εἰς τὰ ὅπλα, Hist. Graec., II, 3, 20 κελεύσαντες ἐπὶ τὰ ὅπλα, also An., IV, 3, 17; Thuc., II, 84, 3 and Ditt. Or., II, 669, 52.

[16] παράγγελμα occurs in 1 S. 22:14, where a captain of the guard becomes an ἄρχων παντὸς παραγγέλματος of the king [Bertram].

[17] For the Heb. equivalents cf. Hatch-Redp., II, 1056. Only 13 times does παραγγέλλειν have a Heb. original in the LXX, 6 times for שמע, twice for אמר, twice for עבר hi, and once each for זעק, יעץ and צעק, also in Σ once for קרא and in an anon. transl. once for צדה. There is no fixed original, and the term takes on its distinctiveness only in the Gk. Bible [Bertram].

It is once used for "summoning" the people to an assembly, 1 S. 10:17. A special use is when a royal command is publicly proclaimed, 2 Ch. 36:22; 2 Εσδρ. 1:1; Δα. 3:4. παραγγέλλειν also has the character of "official proclamation" in Ιερ. 26(46):14, where it is used synon. to ἀναγγέλλειν for the word of the Lord to the prophet which is to be heard in Egypt. In Δα. 2:18 it is used for the "religious direction" which Daniel gives his companions [18] (cf. also 2 Macc. 13:10). Though the last two refs. pt. in the direction of the NT, they give little evidence of any specifically biblical use.

2. The picture is the same in Philo. He uses παράγγελμα for "precept," esp. "legal statute," [19] while παραγγελία is found for "demand." [20] The verb is used for God's orders [21] or the admonition of the hierophant Moses, [22] though also for the dietary rules of athletes, Leg. All., I, 98. Once, in Leg. All., III, 80, παραγγέλλειν is contrasted with the ἐπιτάττειν of the tyrant and approximates to πείθειν, but it does not lose the character of laying down rules. [23] On the whole Philo's use here is closer to the NT than the LXX.

C. The Usage of the New Testament.

1. In the Synoptic Gospels [24] παραγγέλλειν is used only of Jesus. It denotes His word of command in His authority as the Christ. It may be in the form of the instructions given to the disciples when He sends them out (introducing direct speech in Mt. 10:5, with a ἵνα clause in Mk. 6:8), [25] or it may be a command to the unclean spirit to depart (Lk. 8:29 with inf.), [26] or an injunction to the disciples to keep silence (Lk. 9:21), the command to the cleansed leper (Lk. 5:14), the command to Jairus and his family (Lk. 8:56), and the instruction to the hungry multitude to be seated (Mk. 8:6; Mt. 15:35). [27] Worth noting is Luke's liking for the word (cf. Lk. 5:14 with Mk. 1:44 and Mt. 8:4; Lk. 8:56 with Mk. 5:43 διεστείλατο; Lk. 9:21 with Mk. 8:30 and Mt. 16:20 ἐπετίμησεν).

2. This observation is confirmed by the use in Ac., where the verb is relatively common. The reference is always to a "directive from an authoritative source." It may be the command of the risen Lord to the disciples to remain in Jerusalem (Ac. 1:4), or the task of proclamation laid upon them (10:42), [28] or the summons which in the name of Jesus Christ Paul issues at Philippi to the spirit of soothsaying to leave the girl (16:18), or the binding of Gentile Christians to the Law of Moses, which is urged upon the apostles by Pharisaic Jewish Christians (15:5), or the command of the council to Peter and John that they should refrain from

---

[18] καὶ παρήγγειλε νηστείαν καὶ δέησιν καὶ τιμωρίαν ζητῆσαι παρὰ τοῦ κυρίου τοῦ ὑψίστου περὶ τοῦ μυστηρίου τούτου.

[19] Leisegang, II, 623.

[20] Flacc., 141. Joseph. has παραγγελία for "order" (Ant., 16, 241) and παραγγέλλειν for "to decree" (19, 311).

[21] Poster. C., 29; also Leg. All., I, 100, 102, where παραγγέλλειν is so used as to embrace command and prohibition, admonition and warning.

[22] Leg. All., III, 151; cf. also Test. Jud. 21 for παραγγέλλειν in the sense "to admonish": καὶ νῦν, τέκνα μου, ἀγαπᾶτε τὸν Λευί ...

[23] Comparison of Mk. 6:39 and 8:6 shows how close παραγγέλλειν can be to ἐπιτάττειν.

[24] The noun does not occur, nor does the verb in the Johannine writings.

[25] The short Marcan ending has πάντα τὰ παρηγγελμένα for the charge which the young man in white garments gives to the women at the tomb.

[26] For the construction cf. Bl.-Debr.³ § 392, 1d; 397, 3; 409, 1. Worth noting is the transition from indirect to direct speech in Mk. 6:8 f.; Lk. 5:14; Ac. 1:4 f.; 23:22.

[27] If Lk. does not have the παραγγέλλειν of Mk. 8:6; Mt. 15:35 this is because there is no second feeding in Lk.

[28] D has ἐνετείλατο for παρήγγειλεν. One might also mention 17:30 if the reading παραγγέλλει is original (instead of ἀπαγγέλλει).

preaching (4:18), or the similar command to the apostles generally (5:28, [29] 40), or the command of the magistrates of Philippi to the prison warden that he should keep Paul and Silas securely (16:23), [30] or the injunction of the captain Lysias to Paul's nephew that he should keep silent concerning the communication made to him (23:22), or his order to the accusers of Paul to present their case before Felix, the governor (23:30). Neither in the Synoptic Gospels nor Ac. is there any sign of a specific Christian use of the verb. The word receives its special NT sense, whether used of Jesus or Paul, only in virtue of the supreme authority of Jesus as the Christ, an authority which is imparted to the apostle too (Ac. 16:18). [31]

3. The same point is to be seen in the Pauline Epistles, which alone in the NT use the noun as well as the verb. Here the reference is always to the Christian walk. Even in 1 Tm. 1:3, where Timothy is given the task of issuing a sharp prohibition against the false teachers, [32] παραγγελία has according to 1:5 the positive goal of "love out of a pure heart, and a good conscience, and faith unfeigned." [33] For Paul, too, the decisive authority is the word of the Lord, from which (1 C. 7:10) he emphatically differentiates his own pastoral counsel in the question of separation. In general, however, his instructions, including that concerning women covering their heads at divine service, have the character of authoritative apostolic ordinances, behind which stands the full authorisation of Christ Himself. Thus when he beseeches and admonishes the Thessalonians Paul can refer to the directions which were given "by the Lord Jesus" at the founding of the church, 1 Th. 4:2; [34] cf. 2 Th. 3:10. Again, when he renews these παραγγελίαι in a letter with reference to those who are disorderly (2 Th. 3:12), and when he commands withdrawal from "every brother that walketh disorderly" (2 Th. 3:6), this takes place "in the name of the Lord Jesus Christ" or "in the Lord Jesus Christ." In the apostle's saying, then, the readers have to do with the Lord Himself, even though, as in 1 C. 7:10, Paul cannot quote any traditional saying of Jesus.

---

[29] On the strengthening of the verb by repetition in the dat. (παραγγελία παρηγγείλαμεν), in imitation of the Heb. inf. abs., cf. Bl.-Debr.³ § 198, 6; Radermacher², 128 f.

[30] The noun is used for this injunction in v. 24.

[31] Moulton, 194 refers to the great force of aor. presents such as παραγγέλλω here.

[32] Tm. can παραγγέλλειν because "as Paul's representative he acts in his name," cf. Schl. Past., 29.

[33] Schl. Past., 39 rightly assumes that ἡ παραγγελία in 1:5 takes up again the ἵνα παραγγείλῃς of 1:3, though God does not cease hereby to be the one who commands. Hence one cannot with Dib. Past.², 11 (cf. also Pr.-Bauer³, 1021) relate the παραγγελία of 1:5 to Christian preaching in general. It means rather "the concrete direction of the ecclesiastical office," cf. O. Michel, "Grundfragen d. Past.," Auf dem Grunde d. Apostel u. Propheten, Festschr. T. Wurm (1948), 88 f. When Michel speaks of "a Hell. word" "which obviously occurs again in the same sense in Christian and non-Christian official speech," he can certainly give examples from non-Christian usage (→ 762, 4 ff.), but it should be remembered that "office" means "ministry" in the NT, including the Past., e.g., 1 Tm. 1:12.

[34] Dob. Th., 158: "Instead of the παρεδώκαμεν corresponding to παρελάβετε, Paul uses παραγγελίας ἐδώκαμεν, a very common alternative in Hell. Gk., in order to give greater force to what is demanded." Wbg. Th.², 88, n. 1 observes not unjustly concerning the use of the noun and verb in Pl.: "There are intermingled in it the two senses of loud and public announcement (Aesch. Ag., 279, 284, 306 [= 289, 294, 316, Wilamowitz], intimation of the destruction of Troy by the glare of fire) and the giving of an order, esp. by an officer to his soldiers (Aesch. Pers., 469; Xenoph. Cyrop., I, 2, 5; VI, 3, 27)." W. Neil (The Moffatt NT Commentary, 1 and 2 Th. [1950], 77) says concerning the meaning of παραγγελία here: "The word here for 'instruction' (παραγγελία) means significantly enough a word of command given by a superior officer to be passed down to others (e.g., Ac. 16:24)."

In 1 Tm. παραγγέλλειν is one of the special tasks of the recipient of the letter. The apostle authorises him to discharge this ministry to the community (4:11; 5:7). He acts on this commission (1:18). He is to command, esp. false teachers (1:3 f. → n. 32, 33), widows (5:7), and those who are rich in this world (6:17). [35] In so doing, however, he must himself be under the apostle's order "to keep the commandment" in such a way that he is without spot or blame "until the appearing of our Lord Jesus Christ," 6:13 f. This order of the apostle does not rest on his own authority. It is given in the sight of God, who calls all things to life, and also in that of Christ Jesus, who witnessed a good confession before Pontius Pilate. With great seriousness all genuine παραγγέλλειν is thus referred back to its origin in the saving Messianic work of the Creator. It is thus distinguished radically from all religious or ethical injunctions which do not have their roots in the soil of the saving events of the NT. [36]

Schmitz

παράγω → I, 129, 32 ff.
παραδειγματίζω → II, 32, 4 ff.

| † παράδεισος | → ᾅδης, I, 146, 33 ff. |

Contents : A. History of the Word : 1. In Greek ; 2. In Hebrew and Aramaic. B. Paradise in the Later Judaism of the NT Period : 1. Paradise in the First Age ; 2. The Return of Paradise in the Last Age ; 3. The Hiddenness of Paradise in the Present Time ; 4. The Identity of the Paradise of the First Time, the Last Time, and the Intervening Time. C. Paradise in the New Testament : 1. The First, Hidden, and Last Paradise in the NT ; 2. Paul's Rapture into the Hidden Paradise (2 C. 12:4); 3. Fellowship with Christ in Paradise (Lk. 23:43); 4. Paradise and Hades in the Christological Statements of the NT ; 5. Jesus, the One who Brings Back Paradise.

A. History of the Word.

1. παράδεισος is a loan word from old Persian, where the *pairi-daēza-* (read *pari-daiza-* or *-dēza-*) of the Avesta denotes an enclosure, then the park surrounded by a wall. [1] In Gk. it occurs first in Xenoph. for the parks of the Persian king and nobility. [2]

---

[35] W. M. Ramsay, "The Greek of the Early Church and the Pagan Ritual," Exp. T., 10 (1898/99), 159 compares with παραγγέλλω in 1 Tm. 6:17 and also on the other hand the use of the verb in the inscr. of Dionysopolis : παραγγέλλω πᾶσιν μὴ καταφρονεῖν τοῦ θεοῦ ...

[36] This rootage is missing already in the use of παραγγέλλειν in 1 Cl., 1, 3; 27, 2 (the παραγγελίαι of 1 Cl., 42, 3 are "a part of the apostolic tradition," cf. O. Michel, *op. cit.* [→ n. 33], 89), but it may still be seen in Ign. Pol., 5, 1. In Just. Dial., 14, 3; 112, 1 the verb is used of God's commands, or those of Moses, in the Law, and in 133, 6 of Christ's command in the Sermon on the Mount that we are to love our enemies. Here, too, one misses the note of salvation characteristic of the NT.

π α ρ ά δ ε ι σ ο ς. Str.-B., I, 207-214; III, 533 f.; IV, 892 f., 965-967, 1020 f., 1118-1165 (basic). Also Deissmann B, 146; Ide Vuippens, *Le paradis terrestre au troisième ciel* (1925); Volz Esch., 395 f., 412-419; J. B. Frey, "La vie de l'au-delà dans les conceptions juives au temps de Jésus-Christ," Biblica, 13 (1932), 129-168; O. Michel, "Der Mensch zwischen Tod u. Gericht," *Theologische Gegenwartsfragen,* ed. O. Eissfeldt (1940), 6-28; E. Langton, *Good and Evil Spirits* (1942), Index, *s.v.* "Paradise"; K. Galling, Art. "Paradeisos," Pauly-W., 18, 2 (1949), 1131-1134; J. Jeremias, "Zwischen Karfreitag u. Ostern," ZNW, 42 (1949), 194-201; J. Daniélou, Sacramentum futuri (1950), 3-52; H. Bietenhard, *D. himmlische Welt im Urchr. u. im Spätjudt.* (= *Wissenschaftliche Untersuchungen z. NT,* 2 [1951]), 161-191.

[1] *Pari-daiza*-corresponds etym. to a (non-attested) Gk. περίτοιχος, and belongs to the Indo-Europ. root *dheigh-* "to knead" (cf. Gk. τεῖχος, τοῖχος, Germ. "Teig," Lat. *fingo*),

Already by the 3rd cent. B.C. it can then be used generally for a "park." [3] In Jewish Gk., from the LXX on, it is used esp. for the garden of God in the creation story (LXX Gn. 2:8-10, 16 etc.). [4] More exactly God's garden as distinct from secular parks is ὁ παράδεισος τοῦ θεοῦ (LXX Gn. 13:10; Ez. 28:13; 31:8; cf. ὡς παράδεισος κυρίου, Is. 51:3) [5] or ὁ παράδεισος τῆς τρυφῆς (LXX Gn. 2:15 vl.; 3:23 f.; Is. 51:3 vl.; Ez. 31:9; cf. ὡς παράδεισος τρυφῆς, Jl. 2:3; ὡς κῆπος τρυφῆς, Ez. 36:35). [6] This involves a notable shift in meaning; the LXX has moved the term from the profane sphere to the religious. Test. L. 18:10 (→ n. 16) was then the first to give the simple word the technical sense of "Paradise." [7] This religious use is in the pseudepigr. extended to the intervening hidden Paradise (→ 767, 15 ff.) and the eschatological reappearance (→ 767, 3 ff.) of Paradise. In Jewish Gk. it seems to have led to the replacement of παράδεισος in the secular sense by κῆπος. [8]

2. The Persian term was adopted in Heb. and Aram. too (Heb. פַּרְדֵּס, Aram. פַּרְדֵּיסָא)·
Here, however, it kept its profane sense and was used for "garden," "park." [9] Only once [10] does פַּרְדֵּס have a transf. sense in older Rabb. literature. In this instance it is used for metaphysical Gnostic speculations which are cosmogonic in content, [11] but the exception is due to Jewish Gk. influence. The consistent Rabb. term for the Paradise of the first, the intervening, and the last time is Heb. גַּן עֵדֶן, Aram. גִּנְּתָא דְעֵדֶן. [12]

B. Paradise in the Later Judaism of the New Testament Period. [13]

1. Paradise in the First Age.

The exclusive starting-point of all later Jewish statements about the Paradise of the first age is the Paradise story in Gn. 2 f. If this alone offered rich materials for imagina-

---

v. Boisacq, 746 f.; J. Pokorny, *Indogermanisches etym. Wörterbuch* (1949 ff.), 244 f.; E. Kieckers in *Indogerm. Forschungen*, 38 (1917/20), 212 f.; παρα- instead of the etym. corresponding περι- is an assimilation of the Iranian *pari-* to the Gk. prep. παρα- [Debrunner].
[2] Instances in Liddell-Scott, *s.v.*; also once in LXX at 2 Εσδρ. 12:8 (Neh. 2:8).
[3] Pap. inscr., LXX (Nu. 24:6; Qoh. 2:5 etc.); Apcr. Ez. (in Epiph. Haer., 64, 70, 5-17); Philo; Jos. (Schl. Lk., 451: only in this sense).
[4] Equivalent in the Heb. OT גַן, occasionally עֵדֶן as a name for Paradise (Sir. 40:27; Is. 51:3 LXX vl. Σ).
[5] Fig. the righteous are ὁ παράδεισος τοῦ κυρίου, τὰ ξύλα τῆς ζωῆς (Ps. Sol. 14:3).
[6] τρυφή is a rendering of the Heb. עֵדֶן. The LXX (except Sir. 40:27, where παράδεισος) usually has τρυφή for עֵדֶן, only at Gn. 2:8, 10; 4:16, where the Heb. indicates by prepositions that Eden is meant to be a place-name, does its have the transcription Εδεμ.
[7] As against Deissmann B, 146, who thinks the first use as a tt. is in Paul (2 C. 12:4).
[8] In the NT the garden is always κῆπος, Lk. 13:19; Jn. 18:1, 26; 19:41 (twice), never παράδεισος.
[9] In the OT only 3 late vv.: Cant. 4:13; Qoh. 2:5 (= park); Neh. 2:8 (forest of the Persian king in Palestine). Later T. Sukka, 2, 3; T. Jom tob, 1, 10; T. Taan., 4, 7 (twice); T. Ar., 2, 8; bSanh., 91a b; bAr., 14a etc. Aram.: Tg. J. I, Gn. 14:3; J. II, Gn. 21:33; Tg. Ju. 4:5; Tg. Qoh. 2:5; Tg. Job 2:11; bBM, 73a, 103a etc.
[10] Str.-B., IV, 1119 β.
[11] T. Chag., 2, 3 par. jChag., 2, 1 (77b); bChag., 14b; Midr. Cant. on 1:4. Cf. Bacher Tannaiten, I², 332 f.; Str.-B., IV, 1119; M. Abraham, *Légendes juives apocryphes sur la vie de Moïse* (1925), 23, n. 2.
[12] Cf. Gn. 2:15 (3:23 f.).
[13] Near Eastern ideas of Paradise (cf. A. Jeremias, *Das AT im Lichte des alten Orients*⁴ [1930], 79-98), and Gk. ideas of the golden age, the isles of the blessed, the Elysian fields and the garden of Hesperides (cf. on the historico-religious significance of the garden in the Gk. and Hell. world C. Schneider, "Die griech. Grundlagen d. hell. Religionsgeschichte," ARW, 36 [1939], 324 f. [Kleinknecht]), exerted no direct influence on the NT. The same applies to Philo's allegorical interpretation of Paradise (Daniélou, 45-52), towards which there are tendencies already in Sir. 24:12-33; 40:17, 27 and Ps. Sol. 14:3 (→ n. 5); cf. also → *supra*.

tive adornment, [14] this tendency was increased even further by the combination of Paradise with the eschatological hope.

2. The Return of Paradise in the Last Age.

The hope of a future time of bliss, which is commonly attested in the OT, may be traced back to long before the Exile. The depiction of this age uses Paradise motifs. [15] The last time is like the first. Ez. is the first explicitly to compare the expected time of salvation with the Paradise of the first age, 36:35; Is. 51:3. Only in pre-Christian apocalyptic, however, do we find the idea that the Paradise of the last age is identical with that of the first, [16] that the Paradise of the first age reappears in that of the last. The site of reopened Paradise [17] is almost without exception the earth, [18] or the new Jerusalem. [19] Its most important gifts are the fruits of the tree of life, [20] the water and bread of life, [21] the banquet of the time of salvation, [22] and fellowship with God. [23] The belief in resurrection gave assurance that all the righteous, even those who were dead, would have a share in reopened Paradise.

3. The Hiddenness of Paradise in the Present Time.

Identification of the Paradise of the first age with that of the second necessarily carried with it the further idea that Paradise exists now in hidden form. This hidden Paradise is first mentioned in Eth. En. Throughout apocalyptic it is the present abode of the souls of the departed patriarchs, [24] the elect and the righteous, [25] and Enoch

---

[14] Str.-B., IV, 1118 f., 1120-1130.

[15] Great fruitfulness: Hos. 2:24; Am. 9:13; Is. 7:15; Jl. 3:18, esp. abundant water: Is. 35; 41:18 f.; Ez. 47:1-12; Ps. 46:4; Zech. 14:8, peace between the nations: Is. 2:4; 9:6; Mi. 5:9 f., also between animals: Is. 11:6 f., and between men and animals: Is. 11:8, cf. Hos. 2:20, longevity: Is. 65:20, 22; no disease: Zech. 8:4, no death: Is. 25:8; 26:19, fellowship with God: Hos. 2:21 f.; Jer. 31:31-34. Cf. H. Gunkel, *Schöpfung u. Chaos* (1921), 368; Bousset-Gressm., 282-285; A. Bentzen, *Messias, Mose redivivus, Menschensohn* (1948), 37 ff.; Daniélou, 4 f.

[16] Test. L. 18:10 f.: "He himself (the priestly Messiah) will open the gates of Paradise, take away the sword which threatened Adam, and give the saints to eat of the tree of life; then will the spirit of holiness rest upon them"; Test. D. 5:12; Eth. En. 25:4 f.: The tree of life will be planted in the temple; cf. Slav. En. 65:9 A, 10 B; 4 Esr. 7:36, 123; 8:52; Apc. Mos. 13 etc. Rabb. writings are hesitant and restrained here (Str.-B., IV, 892 f.); this is connected with the Rabb. injunction to treat eschatological statements as *arcanum* (*ibid.*, 1151g).

[17] For this cf. Test. L. 18:10; 4 Esr. 8:52, cf. Sib., 3, 769 f.

[18] Only S. Bar. and Slav. En. put the final consummation in heaven. This is because these two works do not distinguish between the present and the last form of its manifestation, Str.-B., IV, 1145, 1150 f.

[19] Eth. En. 25:4 (→ n. 16); 4 Esr. 7:36 (as distinct from γέεννα); for further examples cf. Str.-B., IV, 1151h. Cf. also Rev. 21 f.

[20] Test. L. 18:10 f. (→ n. 16); Eth. En. 24:4-25:7; 4 Esr. 7:123; 8:52; Apc. Mos. 28:4 etc.

[21] The water of life: Slav. En. 8:5 f. A; Str.-B., III, 854-856; the bread of life, Sib. prooem., 87.

[22] Eth. En. 62:14, cf. 60:7 f.; Str.-B., IV, 1146 f., 1154-65.

[23] Apc. Mos. 13:4; Str.-B., IV, 1146, 1153 f. Cf. also Slav. En. 65:9 A: "From then on there will be among them neither toil nor pain nor suffering nor waiting nor distress nor violence nor night nor darkness, but the great light will be among them (and) a great indestructible wall and great incorruptible Paradise; for everything corruptible will pass away, but the incorruptible will come, and it will be the shelter of an eternal dwelling" (based on the transl. of Bonwetsch).

[24] Eth. En. 70:4; Apc. Mos. 37:5; Test. Abr. 20 A (→ n. 37). With Enoch, Abel in Paradise (Test. Abr., 10 B, ed. M. R. James, TSt, II, 2 [1892], 114) holds a judgment of souls after death, *ibid.* 11 B, James, *op. cit.*, 115 f.

[25] Eth. En. 60:7 f., 23; 61:12; 70:4; cf. 32:3; Slav. En. 9:1; 42:3 A; Apc. Abr. 21:6 f.; Moses in Gan Eden after death, bTem., 16a; Shadrach's soul after death ἐν τῷ παραδείσῳ μετὰ τῶν ἁγίων ἁπάντων, Apc. Shadrach 16, ed. M. R. James, TSt, II, 3 (1893), 137.

and Elijah, who were translated thither during their lifetime. [26] Whereas according to the older view *sheol* received the souls of all the dead, only the ungodly were now sought in *sheol* and the righteous in Paradise, → I, 147, 11-16. Hell. ideas about the future life played a normative part in this reconstruction of the concept of the intermediate state (→ n. 13). It should be noted, however, that both old and new ideas were still current in the NT period. Either Hades or Paradise (→ I, 147, 22-30) is here the abode of the souls of the righteous after death. This duality is important for an understanding of the statements about what happened to Jesus between Good Friday and Easter Day, → 771, 37 ff.

Pre-Christian apocalyptic has no consistent answer to the question where this hidden Paradise is to be found. a. The older view seeks it on earth, usually in the extreme East (cf. Gn. 2:8), [27] also the North (Eth. En. 61:1-4; 77:3; cf. Is. 14:13) or Northwest (Eth. En. 70:3 f.), or the extreme West, [28] or on a high mountain reaching up to heaven, cf. Ez. 28:13 f. [29] b. Closely related to the notion of a high mountain whose peak reaches into heaven is the idea, found from the 1st cent. A.D., that after Adam's fall Paradise was translated to God (S. Bar. 4:3, 6), and that since then it has been in heaven, [30] or more precisely in the third heaven. [31] Conceptually statements about the delights of the intervening [32] and the eschatological Paradise [33] merge into one another, though the former are not so strong, esp. in apocalyptic literature.

4. The Identity of the Paradise of the First Time, the Last Time, and the Intervening Time.

That we do not have three distinct entities in the Paradise of the first, the last, and the intervening time, but one and the same garden of God, may be seen quite indubitably from both the terminology and the content of the relevant statements. As regards the terms, Paradise in all three ages is παράδεισος in the Gk., עֵדֶן גַּן in the Heb., גִּנְּתָא דְעֵדֶן in Aram. [34] As regards the content, identity is proved esp. by the common mention of the tree of life in statements about the intervening and the eschatological Paradise. [35]

---

[26] Enoch : Eth. En. 60:8; 70:3; 87:3 f.; 89:52; Jub. 4:23; Test. Abr. 11:3, cf. 10:2. Elijah : Eth. En. 89:52. Other righteous men who were translated into Paradise while yet alive are enumerated in *Däräk 'äräc zutta,* 1 (ed. A. Tawrogi, Diss. Königsberg [1885], 8 f.).

[27] Eth. En. 32:2 f.; Jub. 8:16; cf. 4:26; Slav. En. 42:3 f. A (→ n. 34); bBB, 84a (the sun is red at morning because it passes over Gan Eden and reflects the gleam of its roses); Midr. Konen, ed. A. Jellinek, *Bet ha-Midrasch,* II (1853), 28, 8.

[28] So the Essenes : Jos. Bell., 2, 155 f. ("beyond the ocean"), and perhaps also 4 Esr. 14:9 (the Messiah comes out of Paradise) compared with 13:3 (out of the sea).

[29] Eth. En. 24:3 f.; 25:3 cf. 87:3; Jub. 4:26, → 483, 11 ff.

[30] 4 Esr. 4:7 f.; Vit. Ad. 25:3; Test. Abr. 10 B, M. R. James, *op. cit.,* 114. It cannot be said for certain whether bBer., 28b (Rabban Jochanan b. Zakkai, d. c. 80 A.D.) refers to the intermediate Paradise in heaven (Str.-B., IV, 1034, 1131) or the eschatological Paradise on earth. bChag., 15b (cf. Str.-B., IV, 1119) and Gn. r., 65 on 27:27 par. Midr. Ps. 11 § 7 (*ibid.,* 1130 f.) are the first definite attestations of the idea of a heavenly Paradise in Rabb. literature.

[31] Apc. Mos. 37:5; Slav. En. 8:1 (Str.-B., IV, 1137 f.); Gr. Bar. 4:8 (→ 512, 5 ff.). There is a combination of an earthly and a heavenly location of Paradise in Slav. En. 42:3 A : the intervening Paradise is in the East, but is opened to the third heaven.

[32] Str.-B., IV, 1130-1144.

[33] → 767, 10 ff.; Str.-B., IV, 1144-1165.

[34] Str.-B., IV, 1118-1120, 1130 f. has an excellent review of the terminology, though the statement on 1118 is mistaken : "The older Synagogue knows a threefold Paradise"; more precisely the ref. ought to be to three stages or forms of the one Paradise. Vit. Ad. distinguishes between the "Paradise of righteousness" (25:3) and the "Paradise of visitation and the command of God" (28:3), but the ref. is really to two different spheres of Paradise rather than two Paradises ; the former is the abode of God and the latter the smaller portion of Paradise allotted to the first man, Str.-B., IV, 1119. Slav. En. 8:1-6 A; 42:3 A (Str.-B., IV, 1137 f.) is to be taken in the same way.

[35] Str.-B., IV, 1132, 1143 (intervening Paradise); 1146, 1152 k (eschatological Paradise). Acc. to Eth. En. the tree of life is now on the loftiest of seven hills (24:3 f.) and after the judgment of the world it will be planted toward Jerusalem (25:4 f.).

C. Paradise in the New Testament.

In the NT the word παράδεισος — and this can hardly be accidental (→ 772, 33 ff.) — occurs only three times (Lk. 23:43; 2 C. 12:4; Rev. 2:7), though the thing itself is more common.

1. The First, Hidden, and Last Paradise in the New Testament.

The Paradise of the first age is not mentioned under the term παράδεισος but there are in the NT repeated refs. to the story of Paradise, → I, 141 ff. In his paradisial state Adam had δόξα (R. 3:23); sin and death were unknown (R. 5:12; 8:20); there was no divorce (Mt. 19:8b).

In its present concealment Paradise is according to Lk. 23:43 the abode of the souls of the redeemed in the intermediate state between death and resurrection. Elsewhere, however, the word παράδεισος is used for the hidden Paradise only in 2 C. 12:4. As later Judaism had no consistent view of the intermediate state of the righteous, but used many other figures of speech as well as גַּן עֵדֶן,[36] so the NT has other expressions as well as παράδεισος for the state of the redeemed after death: table fellowship with Abraham (ἐν τοῖς κόλποις Ἀβραάμ, Lk. 16:23),[37] being with the Lord (2 C. 5:8), σὺν Χριστῷ εἶναι (Phil. 1:23 cf. Ac. 7:59; Jn. 12:26), the heavenly kingdom (2 Tm. 4:18), the heavenly Jerusalem (Hb. 12:22), abiding-places in the Father's house (Jn. 14:2).[38] As concerns the location of the hidden Paradise, it appears from Mk. 13:27 that Jesus sought it in the heavenly world, for the assembling of the elect from the four winds from the point of earth to the point of heaven is the assembling of the living and the dead (who dwell in Paradise), → 516, 18 ff.[39]

Paradise as now concealed points beyond itself to its eschatological return. The first saying to the victors in Rev. 2:7 refers to this: Τῷ νικῶντι δώσω αὐτῷ φαγεῖν ἐκ τοῦ ξύλου τῆς ζωῆς,[40] ὅ ἐστιν ἐν τῷ παραδείσῳ τοῦ θεοῦ, → 766, 3 f. That it is really speaking of the eschatological Paradise may be seen from the fact that all the victor sayings in the seven letters of Rev.[41] have an eschatological character, and also from the fact that the gift of enjoyment of the fruit of the

---

[36] Str.-B., II, 264-269 mentions the world to come, heaven, the domain of God, the heavenly academy, the throne of God, the treasure house, the covenant of the living, the land of the living, with the angels, in Abraham's bosom.

[37] That Lk. 16:22-31 refers to the state after death and not after the last judgment may be seen from the use of the word → ᾅδης in 16:23 (not → γέεννα) and also from comparison with the Egyptian and later Jewish story which Jesus uses, cf. H. Gressmann, "Vom reichen Mann u. armen Lazarus," AAB (1918), No. 7, 32; cf. also Test. Abr., 20 A (M. R. James, op. cit., 103 f.), where God says to the angels after Abraham's death: "Lead my friend Abraham into Paradise where the tabernacles of my righteous are and the dwellings of my saints, Isaac and Jacob ἐν τῷ κόλπῳ αὐτοῦ." That the righteous and the ungodly may look across to one another in the intermediate state (Lk. 16:23) is a common idea in later Judaism, 4 Esr. 7:85, 93; cf. Str.-B., II, 228 and IV, 1040 for Rabb. examples.

[38] Cf. also the verses which speak esp. of the martyrs, 6:9; 7:9-17; 14:13.

[39] Cf. Schl. Mk., ad loc. Whether the abode of Lazarus with Abraham (Lk. 16:23b) is on account of the "gt. gulf" (16:26) to be sought in the underworld is not so certain as I assumed in → I, 147, 18 f.; 148, 34 ff. in the light of Eth. En. 22 (a bright place with a source of water in the underworld) and in company with Str.-B., IV, 1019 f. Older and later ideas seem to interfuse in Lk. 16:23-26 (→ I, 147, 7-15). It is certainly true that later Judaism never set גַּן עֵדֶן in sheol, → n. 52.

[40] עֵץ הַחַיִּים, Gn. 2:9 = the tree of life whose fruit confers eternal life.

[41] 2:7, 11, 17, 26-28; 3:5, 12, 21.

tree of life is an established attribute of the Paradise of the last time. [42] Even though the word "paradise" is not used, the garden of God is in Rev. the epitome of the glory of the consummation. The Jerusalem of the last time is depicted as Paradise when ref. is made to the trees of life by the water of life (22:1 f., cf. 14, 19), to the destruction of the old serpent (20:2 cf. 10), and to freedom from suffering, affliction and death (21:4). According to 21:2, 10 the eschatological Paradise is centred on the Jerusalem of the renewed earth.

2. Paul's Rapture into the Hidden Paradise (2 C. 12:4).

In writing which has all the force of an experience whose strange character is expressed by the use of the third person, Paul mentions in 2 C. 12:4 a rapture into Paradise, that is, acc. to established usage (→ 767, 18 ff.), the place of the righteous departed. [43] The reserve which leads him to make only a brief reference distinguishes his account from the fantastic descriptions of heavenly journeys by contemporary Hellenistic mystics and Jewish apocalyptists. [44] Since we cannot say for certain whether the rapture to the third heaven in 12:2 is the same as that into Paradise in v. 4, [45] we do not know whether Paul located Paradise in the third heaven (→ 534, 25 ff.; 768, 17) or in some other place (→ 768, 10 ff.). All that can be said for certain is that ineffable revelations (ἄρρητα ῥήματα) were granted to him in Paradise.

Since Pl. says in the introductory words that he is going to tell about visions of Christ (ὀπτασίας ... κυρίου, 2 C. 12:1), one is tempted to conclude that he saw Christ among the departed in Paradise. [46] But against this is the cogent consideration that 14 years before writing 2 C. Paul still had no specific Christian pronouncement to make on the intermediate state, → 771, 22 ff. Hence ὀπτασίας κυρίου is to be taken as a gen. auct. (not obj.), → 357, 19 ff.

3. Fellowship with Christ in Paradise (Lk. 23:43).

According to Lk. the penitent thief prayed to Jesus: "Be graciously mindful of me (→ IV, 677, 6 ff.) when thou comest again [47] as king," [48] i.e., at the last judgment [49] (23:42). The answer of Jesus: ἀμήν σοι λέγω, σήμερον [50] μετ᾽ ἐμοῦ ἔσῃ ἐν τῷ παραδείσῳ (23:43), goes beyond what is asked, for it promises the

---

[42] Test. L. 18:10 f. (→ n. 16); Eth. En. 25:4 f.; 4 Esr. 8:52; Apc. Mos. 13:2 f.; 28:4; Rev. 22:2, 14, 19. It should be noted, however, that in "conscious interpenetration" (Loh. Apk., 27) Rev. uses eschatological ideas proleptically to depict the intermediate state of the martyrs (e.g., 6:11), so that intermediate and eschatological statements are intermingled in what is said about the martyrs.

[43] Schl. K., ad loc.

[44] Cf. Wnd. 2 K., ad loc. The closest par. is bChag., 14b : ערבעה נכנסו לפרדס (→ n. 11).

[45] The comm. are divided. One experience (because only one ref. to time) is assumed by Bchm., Ltz. K., ad loc., Wnd. 2 K., ad loc., Bietenhard, 164 f., H. Traub, → 535, 1 f.; Schl. and H. D. Wendland (NT Deutsch), ad loc. favour two.

[46] Schl. K. on 2 C. 12:4.

[47] The Semitism frequently does not express the nuance "again" when it is indispensable in other languages.

[48] Read ἐν τῇ βασιλείᾳ σου (אACΘ𝔐) = בְּמַלְכוּתָךְ = "as king" (Dalman WJ, I, 109). The reading εἰς τὴν βασιλείαν σου (only BL lat) arose when the Semitism was no longer understood and βασιλεία was mistakenly regarded as a spatial kingdom.

[49] The vl. ἐν τῇ ἡμέρᾳ τῆς ἐλεύσεώς σου D confirms that the petition refers to the parousia.

[50] To obviate contradiction of the doctrine of a descent into Hades (→ 771, 37 ff.) the σήμερον has occasionally been dropped or related to what precedes (cf. Zn. Lk., ad loc.), though on the latter view it is superfluous. The D reading θάρσει, σήμερον κτλ. confirms its relation to what follows.

thief that already to-day he will enjoy fellowship with Jesus in Paradise. Paradise is here the place which receives the souls of the righteous departed after death, → 767, 18 ff. [51] It is thus the hidden (intervening) Paradise. [52] But in the eschatological → σήμερον there is also expressed the *hic et nunc* of the dawn of the age of salvation. In the promise of forgiveness the "one day" becomes the "to-day" of fulfilment. Paradise is opened even to the irredeemably lost man hanging on the cross. He is promised fellowship with the Messiah. This shows how unlimited is the remission of sins in the age of forgiveness which has now dawned. [53]

In the martyr stories of later Judaism a recurrent feature is that converted Gentiles who (voluntarily or otherwise) share the destiny of the martyrs will also share their reward. Thus, when the fate of the martyr Chananiah b. Teradyon (c. 135 A.D.), who was condemned to be burned to death, was announced to a philosopher, he said: "Tomorrow my portion will be with this man in the future world," S. Dt. on 32:4 § 307. It has thus been concluded that the promise to the malefactor represents a special privilege, [54] i.e., ordination to be a companion of the Messiah, [55] cf. 4 Esr. 14:9: "Thou thyself wilt be translated, and henceforth thou wilt be with my servant (the Messiah, → 681, 16 ff.) and with those like thee, until the times are at an end," cf. 7:28. But closer to the saying to the thief is Eth. En. 39:4 ff.; 70:1-4, where the Son of Man is with the righteous departed. The other NT statements about the intermediate state, which extend the promise of fellowship with Christ after death to all believers, are against a restrictive interpretation which would isolate Lk. 23:43.

The NT consistently represents fellowship with Christ after death as the distinctively Christian view of the intermediate state. Stephen prays: κύριε 'Ιησοῦ, δέξαι τὸ πνεῦμά μου (Ac. 7:59). Paul in the older epistles has no authority to pronounce on the intermediate state, [56] but he expects the union of the dead with Christ only after the *parousia*, 1 Th. 4:17. When he does speak of the intermediate state, however, fellowship with Christ is its sole content, 2 C. 5:8; Phil. 1:23; 2 Tm. 4:18; cf. R. 8:38 f.; 14:7-9. The σὺν Χριστῷ of Phil. 1:23 is simply the μετ' ἐμοῦ of Lk. 23:43 in the third person. Though Paul was obviously acquainted with the Paradise traditions (→ 770, 8 ff.), he ignores them and refers the hope directly to Christ. In exactly the same way Jn. 12:26; 14:2 f. and Rev. 7:9-17 set fellowship with Christ in the centre. This assurance entails a radical refashioning of ideas about the future by faith in Christ. All fantastic speculations concerning the hidden Paradise and its delights are set aside.

4. Paradise and Hades in the Christological Statements of the New Testament. [57]

In the NT statements concerning what happens to Jesus directly after death we find two different views, namely, that of descent and that of ascent. On the one side the

---

[51] Str.-B., III, 534; Zn. Lk., ad loc.; Schl. Lk., ad loc.

[52] Lk. 23:43 says nothing about its location. It simply rules out any idea that, to avoid contradiction with the doctrine of the descent, one can seek it in Hades, so H. H. Wendt, *Die Lehre Jesu*² (1901), 153; Gan Eden is never set in Hades, Str.-B., II, 227.

[53] The ref. of the word παράδεισος to the hidden Paradise in which Jesus stays until the *parousia* certainly corresponds to the view of Lk. The question is whether an older, purely eschatological sense lies behind it. If so, παράδεισος is the eschatological Paradise and the thief is promised a share in the imminent new creation. The σήμερον, after the analogy of the "three days" of Mk. 14:58, is then fig.

[54] M. Dibelius, *Die Formgeschichte d. Ev.*² (1933), 204, n. 1; Dib. Ph.³, 69.

[55] Michel, 13, 20 f.

[56] Dib. Ph.³, 68. Argument from silence, for otherwise he would not have given the disturbed Thessalonian church the teaching about the departed in 1 Th. 4:13-18.

[57] Jeremias, 194-201 (with bibl.).

saying to the thief implies the entry of Jesus into Paradise (Lk. 23:43, cf. v. 46). The Christology of Hb. also gives us a depiction of Jesus offering His blood in the heavenly sanctuary (Hb. 7:26 f.; 9:11-14). Similarly, the → ὑψοῦσθαι sayings in Jn. (3:14; 8:28; 12:32) interrelate the lifting up on the cross and the exaltation to the heavenly world. [58] On the other side we have statements about the sojourn in → ᾄδης (R. 10:7; Ac. 2:27, 31; Mt. 12:40) and the redemptive work there (1 Pt. 3:19 f.; 4:6; cf. Rev. 1:18). [59] The two conceptions arose independently. Those which imply ascent are linked to apocalyptic ideas like those in Eth. En. 39:4 ff.; 70:3 f., while those which imply descent are based on Ps. 16:8-11 (Ac. 2:25-28). The decisive pt. is that the context of both groups of sayings expresses the same assurance of faith, though in different garb. This is the certainty that the atoning efficacy of Christ's death is unique, unrestricted, and universal. [60]

5. Jesus, the One Who Brings Back Paradise. [61]

In the victor saying in Rev. 2:7 the exalted Lord promises that He will give to eat of the fruit of the tree of life in the Paradise of God. He is thus shown to be the awaited Messiah who "will open the gates of paradise, remove the sword which threatened Adam, and give the saints to eat of the tree of life," Test. L. 18:10 f. The new thing as compared with the OT and later Judaism, however, is the fact that the message of the Gospels goes much further when it says that the return of Paradise has come already with the coming of Jesus. Jesus Himself declared this when in Mt. 11:5 (par. Lk. 7:22) He showed by word and deed that His proclamation is a fulfilment of the depiction of Paradise in Is. 35:5 f. and when He accordingly made the divine will in Paradise binding again upon His disciples, Mk. 10:2-12 and par. The Marcan version of the temptation also depicts Jesus as the one who brings back the garden of God (ἦν μετὰ τῶν θηρίων, καὶ οἱ ἄγγελοι διηκόνουν αὐτῷ, Mk. 1:13), [62] and the chorus in Mk. 7:37 extols Him in quotations from Gn. 1:31 and Is. 35:5 f. According to Jn. Jesus offered in His own person both the bread and the water of life, the ancient symbols of Paradise. [63] All these passages express the certainty that Jesus is already the one who brings back Paradise. [64]

In the 2nd century one can see an invasion of Christian writings by sayings about Paradise from Jewish apocalyptic, cf. the (inauthentic) agraphon which Papias (c. 130) quotes and which has Jesus depict in fantastic terms the fruitfulness of the last time. [65] This relapse perhaps explains why the term "paradise" is so rare in the NT; it could so easily divert attention to the external aspects. For Jesus and the primitive Church the garden is not important as an independent

---

[58] G. Bertram, "Die Himmelfahrt Jesu vom Kreuz aus u. der Glaube an seine Auferstehung," *Festschr. A. Deissmann* (1927), 187-217. But for the sake of clarity one should not speak of an "ascension" from the cross, since Lk. 23:43 (unlike Ac. 1:9) does not refer to a physical ascent.

[59] J. Kroll, *Gott u. Hölle* (1932).

[60] Jeremias, 201.

[61] J. Jeremias, *Jesus als Weltvollender* (1930), esp. 19-21, 52 f., 68 f., 74.

[62] → I, 141, 14 ff.; Daniélou, 8 f.

[63] The bread of life, Jn. 6; the water of life, Jn. 4:10-14; 7:37. Probably one should also refer to Mk. 7:27-29 in this connection : The Syrophoenician woman is not approved by Jesus because she is quick witted, but because in her answer (7:28) she accepts the fact that Jesus dispenses the bread of life. It is an open question whether comparison with Jn. 6 justifies the conclusion that the one bread of Mk. 8:14 is Jesus, the bread of life.

[64] Pl. uses the Adam/Christ typology (→ I, 141 ff.) to depict the concept of the restitution of creation by Christ which the Gospels express with the help of the symbolism of the garden of God.

[65] Iren. Haer., V, 33, 3 f.; cf. J. Jeremias, *Unbekannte Jesusworte* (1951), 15. The closest par. is in S. Bar. 29:5, though it goes much beyond this.

entity. What really matters is not the felicity of Paradise but the restoration of the communion with God which was broken by Adam's fall.

Joachim Jeremias

παραδίδωμι → II, 169, 18 ff.

παράδοξος → II, 255, 5 ff.

παράδοσις → II, 172, 5 ff.

παραζηλόω → II, 877, n. 1.

παραθήκη → τίθημι.

παραιτέομαι → I, 195, 1 ff.

| παρακαλέω, † παράκλησις | → παραμυθέομαι.

Contents : A. The Common Greek Usage : 1. "To call to"; 2. "To beseech"; 3. "To exhort"; 4. "To comfort." B. παρακαλέω and παράκλησις in Greek Judaism : 1. The Hebrew Equivalents and Their Influence on the Meaning of the Word ; 2. The Word Group in the LXX Without Hebrew Original ; 3. The Word Group in the Extra-Canonical Writings. C. Comfort and Comforters in Non-Biblical Antiquity : I. Comfort and Admoni-

παρακαλέω, παράκλησις. Pass., Liddell-Scott, Preisigke Wört., Moult.-Mill., Pr.-Bauer, Cr.-Kö., Hatch Redp., *s.v.* J. A. C. Heusdius, Diatribe in locum philosophiae moralis qui est de consolatione apud Graecos (1840); P. Albert, *Les consolateurs, variétés morales et littéraires* (1879), 1-63; A. Gercke, "De consolationibus," Tirocinium philologum sodalium regii seminarii Bonnensis (1883), 28-70; K. Buresch, "Consolationum a Graecis Romanisque scriptarum historia critica," *Leipziger Studien z. klass. Philologie*, IX, 1 (1886) (= Buresch I); É. Boyer, *Les consolations chez les Grecs et les Romains*, Diss. Montauban (1887); W. Schaeffer, Argumenta consolatoria quae apud veteres Graecorum scriptores inveniuntur, Diss. Göttingen (1922), summary in *Jbch. d. Philosophischen Fakultät d. Georg August-Universität zu Göttingen* (1922), 2nd Half, 12-16; Rohde[9], [10], II, 379-396; F. Cumont, Lux Perpetua (1949); A. Giesecke, De philosophorum veterum quae ad exilium spectant sententiis, Diss. Leipzig (1891); K. Ziegler, Art. "Plutarch v. Chaironeia," Pauly-W., XXI, 1, 792-801; R. Herkenrath, "Studien zu d. griech. Grabschriften," *5. Jahresbericht d. Privatgymnasiums Stella Matutina in Feldkirch* (1895/96), 3-56; K. Buresch, "D. griech. Trostbeschlüsse," *Rheinisches Museum f. Philologie*, 49 (1894), 424-460 (= Buresch II); M. Galdi, "Influssi letterarii sulla composizione degli ψηφίσματα παραμυθητικά?" *Mélanges P. Thomas* (1930), 312-326; O. Gottwald, "Zu d. griech. Trostbeschlüssen," Commentationes Vindobonenses, 3 (1937), 5-19; E. Martha, *Études morales sur l'antiquité*[3] (1896); B. Lier, "Topica carminum sepulcralium latinorum," Philol., 62 (1903), 445-477, 563-603; 63 (1904), 54-65; A. A. T. Ehrhardt, "Unsterblichkeitsglaube u. Politik im Römerreich," *Theol. Zschr.*, 2 (1946), 418-437, esp. 425 ff.; J. v. Wageningen, De Ciceronis Libro Consolationis (1916); G. Radbruch, *Gestalten u. Gedanken* (1944), 7-27 (Cicero, for Tullia); F. Skutsch, Art. "Consolatio ad Liviam," Pauly-W., IV, 933-947; O. Schantz, De incerti poetae Consolatione ad Liviam deque carminum consolatoriorum apud Graecos et Romanos historia, Diss. Marburg (1889); T. Birt, "Seneca," *Pr. Jhrb.*, 144 (1911), 282-307, esp. 289; J. Dartigue-Peyrou, Quae sit apud Senecam consolationum disciplina vis ratioque, Diss. Paris (1897); A. Siegmund, "De Senecae consolationibus," *Programm d. Staatsgymnasiums Böhmisch-Leipa* (1912); J. F. Schinnerer, "Über Senecas Schrift an Marcia," *Programm d. Gymnasiums Hof* (1889); W. Kaiser, "Beiträge zur Erläuterung v. Senecas Trostschrift an Marcia," *Progr. d. Askanischen Gymnas. Berlin* (1914); C. Favez, "Le sentiment dans les consolations de Seneca," *Mélanges P. Thomas* (1930), 262-270 (= Favez I); P. Papinii Statii Silvarum libri, ed. and expounded by F. Vollmer (1898), esp. 316 f.; Consolatio ad Liviam, ed. F. Vollmer, Poetae Latini Minores, II, 2 (1923); Carmina Latina Epigraphica, ed. F. Buecheler, rev. E. Engström (1912); Fragmenta Philosophorum Graecorum, 3 Vols., ed. F. W. A. Mullach (1860/81), I, 514; III, 146-150; W. Nestle, "Die Überwindung des Leids in d. Antike," *Das Gymnasium*, 53 (1942), 6-27; G. Stählin, "Trost u. Trostlosigkeit in d. Umwelt d. NT," Viva Vox Evangelii = *Festschr. H. Meiser* (1951), 308-323. T. Hermann, Art. "Trost, Tröster, trösten," Calwer Bibellex.[4] (1924), 776; P. Billerbeck, "Die Tröstung d. Trauernden," Str.-B., IV, 1, 592-607; P. Wendland, "Philo u. d. kynisch-stoische Diatribe," P. Wendland-O. Kern, *Beiträge z. Gesch. d. griech. Philosophie u. Religion* (1895), 1-75;

tion. II. Comforters. III. Ways and Means of Comfort. IV. Reasons for Comfort : 1. In Epicurus ; 2. Common Reasons ; 3. The Thought of Immortality. D. Comfort and Comfortlessness in the OT : I. Human Comfort : 1. Bearers ; 2. Means ; 3. Self-comforting. II. Divine Comfort : 1. Comfortlessness ; 2. Comfort ; 3. Metaphors ; 4. Mediators. E. Human and Divine Comfort in Judaism : I. Human Comfort : 1. Occasions ; 2. The Duty of Comforting ; 3. Forms of Comforting ; 4. Reasons ; 5. Presuppositions of the Ability to Comfort ; 6. Self-comforting. II. Divine Comfort. F. παρακαλέω and παράκλησις in the New Testament : 1. Asking for Help ; 2. Exhortation ; 3. Consoling Help ; 4. Comforting by Men and as God's Act ; 5. Conclusion.

A. Common Greek Usage.

It is not our present task to give a history of the two words and their meaning in the Gk. world. On the other hand, certain preliminary remarks must be made on the common Gk. use of the words. We begin by noting that the manifold linguistic use of this strengthening compound of καλεῖν and of the derived noun all goes back to the sense "to call someone to oneself," not "to call to (someone)," cf. ἐπικαλεῖν, "to call to" and "to call (a name)," → III, 496, 28 ff. The difference is whether the calling, which is always addressed to another, refers back from the very first to the one who calls, so that the one called is led to the one who calls, or whether the calling to is more or less subordinate to the actual calling on another, which produces the sense of asking, encouraging or comforting according to the nature of the call, whether a request for help or a word of exhortation or consolation. With the help of typical examples the actual use may be discussed within this basic scheme, which is capable of a great deal of variation.

1. "To call to." The word means this lit. in, e.g., Xenoph. An., III, 1, 32 τὸν στρατηγόν, Thuc., V, 31, 2; Polyb., 2, 20, 1, and more or less fig. in Plat. Resp., IV, 425c : ἢ οὐκ ἀεὶ τὸ ὅμοιον ὂν ὅμοιον παρακαλεῖ, Xenoph. Oec., 93, where a place calls for, i.e., demands certain equipment, Xenoph. Cyrop., VII, 5, 23, where pitch and bundles of tow quickly call forth, i.e., stir up, a great flame ; Epict. Diss., I, 11, 9, where a means of proof is called in, i.e., summoned in aid, or used. παρακαλεῖν is used in the sense of summoning to help in Hdt., VII, 158 : σύμμαχον παρακαλεῖν τινα, Plat. Ep., VII, 329a : ἦλθες δήπου ἄν μοι βοηθός, ἐφ' ἅ σε παρεκάλουν, Epict. Diss., I, 27, 16 : calling in a legal adviser, III, 21, 12 : in prayer calling in the gods as helpers (βοηθούς). παρακαλεῖν contains a request for coming to aid with ref. to the physician. Thus Epict. Diss., II, 15, 15 uses it in the sense "to have called or fetched." III, 23, 27 f. speaks with biting irony of this invitation of the physician when it becomes the summons of the physician or philosopher to visit his consulting-room. Cf. also the noun : κομψὴ παράκλησις. The verb can mean invitation in the common sense in, e.g., Xenoph. Cyrop., IV, 6, 3 εἰς θήραν ; Epict. Fr., 17, 2 εἰς συμπόσιον (cf. Ench., 25, 4), though also fig. in Ench., 33, 2 : καιροῦ παρακαλοῦντος εἰς τὸ λέγειν, "when the moment invites speech." Here one might transl. "requires." This is the sense in, e.g., Plat. Ep., VII, 324d : co-operation ; Ditt. Syll.³, 485, 10 : sacrifice ; Ditt. Or., 339, 53 : παρακληθείς to become a gymnasiarch ; Epict. Diss., IV, 13, 10 : to tell his secrets. In many cases "to call on" is better than "to summon," e.g., Ditt. Syll.³, 90, 40; 434, 20; Epict.

G. Delling, "Speranda futura, Jüdische Grabinschriften Italiens über das Geschick nach dem Tode," ThLZ, 76 (1951), 521-526; N. Brüll, "Die talmudischen Traktate über Trauer um Verstorbene," Jbch. f. jüdische Gesch. u. Lit., 1 (1874), 1-57; J. Z. Lauterbach, Art. "Semahot," Jew. Enc., XI, 180-182; M. Jouisse, Père, fils et paraclet dans le milieu ethnique palestinien (1948). E. Stauffer, Theol. d. NT³ (1947), 327-330 (VI on parting scenes and discourses); also art. "Abschiedsreden," RAC, I, 29-35; H. Schlier, "Vom Wesen d. apost. Ermahnung nach R. 12:1-2," Christus des Gesetzes Ende ; Beiträge z. Evangelischen Theol., 1 (1940), 50-68; J. Schniewind, "Theologie u. Seelsorge," Evangelische Theol., 6 (1946/47), 363-367. J. Bauer, Die Trostreden d. Gregorios v. Nyssa in ihrem Verhältnis zur antiken Rhetorik, Diss. Marburg (1892), esp. 14 f., 21-29; C. Favez, La consolation latine chrétienne (1937) (= Favez II); also "Die Trostbriefe d. heiligen Augustin," Museum Helveticum, 1 (1944), 65-68 (= Favez III).

Diss., I, 16, 21: ἐπὶ τὴν αὐτὴν ταύτην ᾠδὴν παρακαλῶ, namely, ὑμνεῖν τὸν θεόν. The noun has the sense of "summons" to revolt, Polyb., 1, 72, 4, to a feast, Ditt. Syll.³, 695, 42 (after 129 B.C.): κατευχὴν καὶ παράκλησιν παντὸς τοῦ πλήθους ποιεῖσ<θαι τήν>δε : παρακαλῶ ... ¹ The legal use of παρακαλεῖν is instructive ("to summon"), P. Tebt., II, 297, 5 (2nd cent. A.D.). ² The phrase κατὰ παράκλησιν should be mentioned here ("on request"), ibid., II, 392, 26 and 36 (2nd cent. A.D.). The sense is close to that of asking.

2. "To beseech." The word is common in this sense, e.g., Epict. Diss., I, 9, 30; 10, 10; II, 7, 11; 24, 2; III, 33, 28; IV, 13, 15 and 18, often with ἀξιοῦν, Ditt. Syll.³, 346, 30; 590, 30. Cf. also ἀξιώσεις καὶ παρακλήσεις, Polyb., 1, 67, 10 : μετ' ἀξιώσεως καὶ παρακλήσεως, 22, 7, 2. Ibid., 30, 4, 5 tells us that in supreme national emergencies men were brought κατὰ τὰς παρακλήσεις μηκέτι παρακαλεῖν μηδ' ἀξιοῦν τοὺς φίλους ἀλλὰ δεῖσθαι μετὰ δακρύων. ³ συγγνώμη and παράκλησις occur together in Strabo, 13, 1, 1. In the magic pap. this asking (Preis. Zaub., LI, 1) ⁴ is supplication, with ἐξορκίζειν (XXXV, 24 f.) or ἐπικαλεῖσθαι and ἐξορκίζειν (XXXV, 35). This leads to the use with the acc. for calling on the gods or God in prayer, with a suggestion of the original sense of invoking divine help, e.g., Plat. Leg., XI, 917b and 931c. In a healing inscr. from Epidauros we read : καὶ γὰρ περὶ τούτου παρεκάλεσα τὸν θεόν, ⁵ and in a pap. letter from the 3rd cent. A.D. : τὸν μέγαν θεὸν Σάραπιν παρακαλῶ περὶ τῆς ζωῆς ἡμῶν, P. Oxy., VII, 1070, 8 f. παράκλησις is used for invocation of the gods in prayer in Iambl. Myst., 4, 3 and 4. If the one who asks has authority over the one asked, the requests are proposals, e.g., Polyb., 4, 29, 3 : ῥᾳδίως ἔπεισε συγχωρεῖν τοῖς παρακαλουμένοις. In this case the asking is close to exhortation.

3. "To exhort." This sense occurs in Xenoph. An., V, 6, 19; Ditt. Syll.³, 426, 35; 613, 25. In military contexts it is common for encouragement of soldiers, e.g., Philo Byzantius, ⁶ and often in Polyb. in the phrase παρακαλοῦντες σφᾶς αὐτούς, 1, 61, 1; 3, 19, 4; 4, 58, 6; 5, 71, 1; 18, 6, 6; cf. also 3, 84, 10. In Isoc., 3, 12 it occurs with προτρέπειν. The noun has the sense of "encouragement" in Ps.-Plat. Def., 415e : ὀργὴ παράκλησις τοῦ θυμικοῦ εἰς τὸ τιμωρεῖσθαι, P. Grenf., I, 32, 7: διὰ τὰς ἡμῶν παρακλήσεις. ⁷ The admonition, esp. when there is ref. to a παρακαλεῖν ἐπὶ τὰ κάλλιστα ἔργα = ἐξορμᾶν ἐπὶ τὴν ἀρετήν, as in Xenoph. An., III, 1, 24, may consist in both ἐπαινεῖν καὶ τιμᾶν of the good and λοιδορεῖν καὶ κολάζειν of the bad. ⁸ In Plat. Ep., VII, 350c παρακαλεῖν is used for winning over for a plan of revenge. ⁹

---

¹ The summons is by public proclamation, introduced by an "I summon all the inhabitants of the city etc."

² Cf. Preisigke Wört., II, 245 and Mitteis-Wilcken, II, 2, 71, 5. Other legal examples may be found in Liddell-Scott, II, 1311, 2a.

³ A. Debrunner pts. out the distinction between παρακαλεῖν and syn.; thus Hermogenes De Methodo, 3 (ed. H. Rabe = Rhetores Graeci, VI [1913], 415 f.) combats the use of ἐρωτῶ and παρακαλῶ for δέομαι. As he sees it, δέομαι means "ask for supply of a lack" (δέω "lack"), ἀξιόω "claim as a right, as equitable" (ἄξιος "fitting"), αἰτέω "demand" (→ I, 91), and παρακαλέω "call in or on to help or to do something" [Debrunner]. On the distinction from παραμυθέομαι → 820, 32 ff.

⁴ Pap. examples of ἐρωτᾶν and παρακαλεῖν in the sense of asking are to be found in Moult.-Mill., 484; cf. also παρακληθείς = "please."

⁵ Deissmann LO, 261 compares with this 2 C. 12:8. Cf. also Deissmann's helpful reconstruction ἐμοῦ δὲ παρακαλέσαντος τὸν θεὸν Σαράπιδα in the letter of the minister of Sarapis, Zoilos, 258/257 B.C., LO, 121.

⁶ Philonis Mechanicae Syntaxis libri quartus et quintus, ed. R. Schöne (1893), 101, 38; 98, 35. For the λόγος παρακλητικός as the commander's word of encouragement and admonition before a battle cf. J. Albertus, Die παρακλητικοί in d. gr. u. röm. Lit., Diss. Strassburg (1908), 1-16 [Kleinknecht].

⁷ Cf. Mayser, II, 1, 36.

⁸ Cf. Philo Byzantius, 111, 38.

⁹ Plato, 350d declines personally in the words κακὰ δὲ ἕως ἂν ἐπιθυμῆτε, ἄλλους παρακαλεῖτε, "but so long as you make your evil intentions clear, attract others" (E. Howald, Die Briefe Platons [1923], 111). The meaning is "to seek to persuade."

4. "To comfort." From friendly encouragement [10] it is only a step to comfort, esp. in times of grief. Yet it is noticeable how few and often only tentative are the instances of παρακαλεῖν for "to comfort." παράκλησις in the sense of "comfort" is found in a Phalaris letter : [11] It is made clear to the children of Stesichorus that there is no better comfort in sorrow than the ἀρετή τοῦ γονέως on account of which they experience it. No less philosophical is the παράκλησις of Charidemus in Dio Chrys., 30, 6. [12] The παρακαλεῖν used in sorrow also amounts to an admonition to stand firm in Teles : [13] ἐν στενοχωρίᾳ καὶ ἀπορίᾳ μὴ δυσκολαίνειν μηδὲ ἀβίωτον τὸν βίον νομίζειν κτλ. It is also no more than philosophical consolation when in Plut. Otho., 16, 2 (I, 1074a) the dying emperor exhorts his young nephew "to be brave (θαρρεῖν) and not to fear Vitellius." In the rare instances in which the verb and noun mean "to comfort" or "comfort" in ordinary Gk. usage, the consolation is mostly at the level of exhortation or encouragement to those who sorrow.

B. παρακαλέω and παράκλησις in Greek Judaism.

1. The Hebrew Equivalents and Their Influence on the Meaning of the Word.

When we turn from ordinary usage to the translation Gk. of the LXX, it is worth noting that the concordances list not only the common נחם but also 14 other Hebrew words as originals of παρακαλεῖν. [14] A few others are also found in Sir. [15] παρακαλεῖν is also used in many verses with no Heb. equivalent, so that we either have a free rendering or a new sense is introduced through deficient understanding of the basic Heb. [16] As regards the many Heb. equivalents, most of them are transl. by παρακαλεῖν

---

[10] Cf. the emotion in the noun in Isoc., 1, 5: οὐ παράκλησιν εὑρόντες ἀλλὰ παραίνεσιν γράψαντες.

[11] Phalaris Ep., 103 in Epistolographi Graeci, ed. R. Hercher (1873), 438 f.

[12] Cf. Buresch I, 123 with ref. to Dio Chrys.: παράκλησις ... is παραμυθία.

[13] Stob. Ecl., V, 990, 16 f. and O. Hense, Teletis reliquiae² (1909), 60, 11 f.

[14] Cf. Hatch-Redp., 1060, though רחם does not really belong, since in Is. 49:13 παρεκάλεσεν is used for נחם; the transl. simply changed round the two synon. verbs in the parallelism.

[15] Sir. 30:23 : παρακάλει τὴν καρδίαν σου, "speak to thine heart," HT piel of פול "to comfort," "to refresh." Cf. R. Smend, Die Weisheit d. Jes. Sir. erklärt (1906), 271; also Die Weisheit d. Jes. Sir. hbr. u. deutsch (1906), 76. At Sir. 35:17 (= 32:17; in Smend 32:21) the Gk. παρακληθῇ represents a basic תנוה from נוח "to find rest," "to be satisfied," cf. Smend's comm., 315 and Smend's ed., 61. At 17:24 and 49:10, where there is no Heb., Smend conjectures that παρεκάλεσεν or παρεκάλεσαν corresponds to hiphil forms of חלם, "to heal," cf. his comm., 160 and 144 (on 15:20).

[16] At 1 S. 22:4 the LXX confused וַיַּנְחֵם "he carried them away" (so BHK³ for וַיַּנְחֵם) with וַיְנַחֵם from נחם, and thus transl. παρεκάλεσεν. At ψ 125:1, through confusion of חלם II and I [G. Bertram], LXX has ἐγενήθημεν ὡς παρακεκλημένοι for the Heb. "as though we dreamed." At Prv. 1:10 παρακαλεῖν is used for enticing speech, no Heb. There is also no Heb. for the ματαία παράκλησις of Is. 28:29 and 30:7. παρακληθῆναι is a curious rendering for the mourning custom of putting a seal over the lips in Ez. 24:17, 22. Summoning by the hand lies behind the use of παρακαλεῖν (τῇ χειρί) for the pi or hi of נוף ("to stretch out the hand threateningly against") in Is. 10:32 and 13:2. This is also possible in 41:27, where there is originally an εἰς ὁδόν behind παρακαλέσω. An appeal to idols seems to be in view at 57:5, no Heb. R. R. Ottley, The Book of Is. (1904), Vol. 2 on 10:32, also I, 50, and J. Ziegler, Untersuchungen zur LXX des Buches Is. (1934), show that the transl., who had little exegetical tradition or Heb. scholarship, padded out the text with favourite expressions when he did not understand the original. παρακαλεῖν is one of the terms thus used [P. Katz].

only once. [17] Slight exceptions occur in the case of נָהַל[18] and קָרָא.[19] But the gt. exception is נחם, which is the Heb. equivalent in most of the LXX instances of παρακαλεῖν. [20] παράκλησις, which is much less common, is correspondingly used for nouns derived from נחם.[21] Only once (Ιερ. 38[31]:9) is it used for תַּחֲנוּן.[22]

The true significance of these observations concerning the LXX use only emerges, however, when one considers the meaning which παρακαλεῖν thus acquires in the LXX. [23] The primary pt. is that in the instances mentioned, [24] and also in the many verses in which נחם is the Heb. original, "to comfort" is by far the outstanding sense. The same applies to παράκλησις. To be sure, παρακαλεῖν, or rather the pass. παρακαλεῖσθαι, is often used for נחם when this means "to be sorry," not in the sense of comforting, but in that of the sympathy which relents or repents. But in the main these are simply exceptions which confirm the rule. [25]

---

[17] So the pi of אָמַץ in Dt. 3:28 : "to encourage," or אָמַר in Is. 35:4. Is. 38:16 refers to being comforted by God, παρακληθείς for the hi of חָלַם, "to be made well." At Is. 21:2 παρακαλέσω ἐμαυτόν ("to comfort") is used for the hi of שָׁבַת, "to make an end." This might also be the sense in Is. 66:12 where the word is used for שָׁעַע pilpel "to be fondled," though in a context which immediately (v. 13, cf. v. 11) goes on to speak of being comforted by God. A meaning related to "exhortation" is to be seen in Job 4:3, where παρακαλεῖν is used for חָזַק pi. The synon. νουθετεῖν certainly shows that exhortation or encouragement is in view. Dt. 13:7 refers to encouragement in the bad sense ; παρακαλεῖν is here used for the hi of סות, "to entice," "seduce," and the ref. is to being secretly seduced into serving idols. At Is. 33:7, where מַלְאָךְ is the original and ἀξιοῦν a synon., the meaning is "to ask."

[18] Ex. 15:13; Is. 40:11; 51:18. Cf. also Is. 57:18, where another word for "to lead" (נָחָה hi) is transl. by παρακαλεῖν. The ref. in Is. 40:11 is to divine comfort, and this is suggested in 57:18 by the continuation : καὶ ἔδωκα αὐτῷ παράκλησιν ἀληθινήν (נִחֻמִים). "To comfort" fits the sense best in Is. 51:18. In Ex. 15:13 the context demands "to summon." Cf. Ziegler, op. cit.

[19] In Is. 40:2 the powerful παρακαλεῖτε, παρακαλεῖτε τὸν λαόν μου of v. 1 affects the rendering of "call to her" by παρακαλέσατε αὐτήν, though παρακαλεῖν has the sense "to call to" when used for קָרָא in Prv. 8:4. The S* reading παρακαλέσατε for πατέρα καλέσατε at Jer. 3:19 is certainly not original ; it arose out of the abbreviation π̅ρακαλεσατε for πατερα καλεσατε [T. W. Manson].

[20] Conversely נחם is mostly rendered παρακαλεῖν. It occurs 108 times in the Mas. and 3 in Sir., with 11 instances of derived nouns. For the verb παρακαλεῖν is used 61 times and 3 in Sir. (for pi in 42 of 51 instances in the Mas.), also παράκλησις twice, παρακλήτωρ once at Job 16:2, also παράκλητος in ᾽ΑΘ, the only occurrences of these two terms in the Gk. OT. For derived nouns παράκλησις and cognates are used 8 times, μεταμέλεια once at Hos. 11:8. The LXX reinterprets Job 6:10; 15:11. Of the 44 instances of נחם where παρακαλεῖν is not the transl. μετανοεῖν is used 15 times for the ni ; apart from the doubtful Is. 46:8 (שׁוּב), this is used only for נחם in the LXX. μεταμέλειν also occurs 7 times for the ni. παύειν, διαναπαύειν, ἀναπαύειν and ἐλεεῖν are used 10 times (+ vl. 2) [G. Bertram].

[21] Cf. Hatch Redp., 1061. παράκλησις occurs at Na. 3:7 where the HT has the verb.

[22] The ref. here is to the fervent prayer of the returning people. The LXX ἐν παρακλήσει ἀνάξω αὐτούς suggests the divine comfort in contrast with the κλαυθμός with which they went out, unless the translator has in mind the invocation (παράκλησις) of God in prayer.

[23] The three later translators always have παρακαλεῖν for נחם [P. Katz].

[24] When παρακαλεῖν is not used for נחם (→ n. 14-19), apart from the sense of encouragement, enticement (Prv. 1:10), or exhortation (Job 4:3), we find only the rather doubtful meanings "to call" (Ex. 15:13; Is. 10:32; 13:2; 41:27), "to ask" (Is. 33:7) and "to call upon with a request" (1 S. 22:4; Is. 57:5, cultically).

[25] Thus παρεκλήθη is used for God's sympathy in Ju. 2:18, παρεκλήθησαν or ὁ λαὸς παρεκλήθη for the sympathy of the Israelites with the tribe of Benjamin in Ju. 21:6, 15,

The LXX refers first to comfort in bereavement, Gn. 24:67; 37:35; 38:12 (παρακληθείς = when the time of mourning was over); 2 S. 12:24; 1 Ch. 7:22; Job 29:25; Sir. 38:17, 23; Ιερ. 38(31):15 A (cf. Mt. 2:18); 16:7 (παράκλησις). παρακαλεῖν can then mean "to give expression to one's sympathy," 2 S. 10:2 f. 1 Ch. 19:2 f., cf. also Job 42:11. But like the noun it is also used for words of comfort in any human grief, Jdt. 6:20 (with ἐπαινεῖν); Job 2:11 (with ἐπισκέψασθαι); 7:13; 21:2 (παράκλησις); Qoh. 4:1, often synon. with λαλεῖν εἰς τὴν καρδίαν, Gn. 50:21; Rt. 2:13; cf. Sir. 30:23 : παρακάλει τὴν καρδίαν σου, also more generally for "encouragement" (Dt. 3:28 with κατισχύειν) or "friendly exhortation," Est. 5:1e, 2b, with no ref. to distress.

παρακαλεῖν is esp. used, and sometimes also παράκλησις, to promise and to testify to the comfort of God which is to be given to His people when under divine judgment, or to the individual in time of temptation, → 789, 17 ff.

2. The Word Group in the LXX Without Hebrew Original.

If one compares the use of παρακαλεῖν and παράκλησις in the translation Gk. of the LXX, which concentrates on divine and human comfort, with the use of the same terms in those parts of the LXX which are not translations of the sacred books, it is at once apparent that this meaning is almost completely absent. The verb is never used in this way, the noun only in 1 Macc. 12:9, where it is said of the sacred books that the people of the Jews had them as comfort (παράκλησις) in their hands. This is in a work which is not part of the translation but which rests on translation. When 2 Macc. 15:11 contrasts τὴν ἐν τοῖς ἀγαθοῖς λόγοις παράκλησιν with confidence in shields and spears (cf. also v. 9), this trust consists in a strengthening of the morale of the troops by encouragement (παραμυθέομαι → 818, 12 ff.) from the Law and the prophets and by recollection of past battles. What we have here, then, is encouragement and exhortation rather than true comfort in distress, just as παρεκάλει obviously means exhortation in v. 8. When παράκλησις is used elsewhere in this part of the LXX it means either "request" (1 Macc. 10:24) or "assurance" (2 Macc. 7:24). The verb often means "to encourage," 1 Macc. 5:53; 12:50; 13:3; 2 Macc. 13:12; 3 Macc. 1:6; 3:8, "to beseech" only at 1 Macc. 9:35 and 4 Macc. 4:11, also once in the original Gk. prologue to Sir. (Prol. 15). Esp. instructive is the way in which we often have the sense "to exhort" in 2, 3 and 4 Macc., though strangely enough never in 1 Macc.;[26] this is a meaning which is practically never found in the translation Gk. of the LXX. An impression of the great fluidity of the use of παρακαλεῖν, which embraces many larger and smaller nuances, may be gained from 2 Macc., though even here the wealth of

and παρακλήθητι for "have pity" in the prayer of ψ 89:13. Would the LXX readers understand it thus? As regards this pt. the following observation is instructive. In Dt. 32:36 (cf. ψ 134:14) παρακληθήσεται is used for God's pitying sympathy. The v. is quoted in 2 Macc. 7:6 on the lips of the martyr brothers, who when they saw the torments of the first brother encouraged one another (παρεκάλουν) with the words : "The Lord our God sees it and unquestionably has pity on us (παρακαλεῖται)." Since 2 Macc. is not translating from the Heb., παρακαλεῖσθαι in the sense of pitying sympathy must have made its way from the LXX into Jewish Gk. usage to some degree. This is the more remarkable in view of the fact that the same word occurs just before (v. 5) in the common Gk. sense of exhortation, cf. also v. 21. A further instance of this sense, though it does not occur elsewhere, is to be found in the curious gloss of Gk. Sir. at Sir. 16:9 (cf. on this Kautzsch Apkr. u. Pseudepigr., I, 309, n. c), which reads : καὶ ἐπὶ πλήθει ἁγίων αὐτοῦ οὐ παρεκλήθη, "even at the multitude of his saints he did not yield (in sympathy)." This is an allusion to Hos. 13:14 : παράκλησις κέκρυπται ἀπὸ ὀφθαλμῶν μου, "my eyes know no pity." It is the only instance in which a noun derived from נחם, which is rendered παράκλησις, does not mean "comfort" but the "sympathy" which relents (נחם). This leads us to instances in which παρακαλεῖσθαι connotes a sympathy which repents : 1 S. 15:11 (παρακέκλημαι); 2 S. 24:16 (παρεκλήθη). This sense of נחם is more commonly expressed by μεταμέλεισθαι (cf. Hatch-Redp., 916), which is remarkably used for "to be comforted" at Ez. 14:22, while παρακαλεῖν means "to comfort" in the following verse.

[26] Cf. 2 Macc. 2:3; 6:12; 7:5, 21; 8:16; 9:26; 12:42; 13:14; 15:8, 17; 3 Macc. 1:4; 5:36; 4 Macc. 8:17; 10:1; 12:6; 16:24.

meaning of the verb is by no means exhausted. In this work παρακαλεῖν can mean "to exhort" (→ n. 26), "to encourage" (13:12), "to cheer" (4:34; 6:21), "to speak good words" (13:23), "to enliven" (13:3; 14:25), "to strengthen" (15:17), "to propose" (11:15), "to reassure" (11:32), "to invite" (12:3). Some form of address is always implied. In view of this wealth of meaning it is the more striking that in these portions of the LXX there is never the sense of divine or human consolation found in the LXX as a translation.

3. The Word Group in the Extra-Canonical Writings.

The usage of Ep. Ar. corresponds fully to the picture already gained. παρακαλεῖν means "to ask" in 123, 309, 318 and 321, "to admonish" in 220, "to summon" in 301, "to command" in 184, "to beseech" in 245, "to exhort" in 229, 235, "to recognise" in 238, 264. Along the same lines one never finds the typical OT usage in the few passages in Philo. [27] In both Op. Mund., 157 and Poster. C., 138 the verb means "to summon" or "to invite," and in Vit. Cont., 12 the noun is synon. with παραίνεσις in the sense of "encouraging summons." This usage occurs also in Joseph. Vit., 87, though in Ant.,1, 272 and 3, 22 παράκλησις with εὐχαί or ἱκετεία means "invocation" of God in prayer, [28] as also παρακαλεῖν in, e.g., Ant., 1, 274; 3, 78; 6, 25; 6, 143; 11, 144. With "calling on God is combined the thought of the worshipper calling in God," [29] Ant., 1, 268 f.; 4, 194; 17, 195; cf. 4, 40 and 46. In the sense "to ask" παρακαλεῖν also occurs with ἀξιοῦν in Ant., 11, 338. Bell., 1, 667 uses παρακαλεῖν in the two successive senses of "to exhort" and "to comfort" (in face of death).

If Hell. Judaism outside the transl. Gk. of the OT never uses παρακαλεῖν for divine comfort in the OT sense, things are rather different in Test. XII. Here the verb has, with the senses "to call in" (R. 4:9 vl. perhaps Jud. 8:2) and "to exhort" (N. 9:1), the sense also of comforting (R. 4:4 and Jos. 17:4, cf. also the difficult A. 6:6 with the vl. παραμυθεῖσθαι). Indeed, it can be used twice for God's comfort in Jos. 1:6 : μόνος ἤμην καὶ ὁ θεὸς παρεκάλεσέν με (with many synon. expressions like ὁ κύριος ἐπεσκέψατό με and ὁ σωτὴρ ἐχαρίτωσέ με) and Jos. 2:6, where it is said of God : ἐν διαφόροις τρόποις παρακαλεῖ. If God's comfort is here simply related to the destiny of the righteous individual, in 4 Esr., esp. the 4th vision, the central ref. is to the fate of the city, i.e., its destruction. Zion is fig. represented as a woman mourning for her son ; her neighbours seek to console her in vain (10:2), but she should be comforted by the sorrow of Jerusalem (10:19, cf. v. 24). When Ezra begins to comfort her in her misfortune (10:40, 49), he is himself to some degree consoled by the vision of the glory of Zion as the city of God, into which the woman suddenly transforms herself. But then after the terrible 5th vision he prays : "Comfort my soul fully" (12:8), and it is explained to him that God's annihilating judgment will fall on the 4th world empire through the Christ, who will graciously redeem the remnant of the people and grant it joy until the final decision. The Messianic salvation itself, however, is not called "comfort" in 4 Esr. But one can plainly detect here the background of this Rabb. usage (→ 792, 18 ff.).   *Schmitz*

C. Comfort and Comforters in Non-Biblical Antiquity. [30]

I. Comfort and Admonition.

The imperative element in παρακαλέω ("to admonish") is always more or less plainly accompanied by the indicative ("to console") and *vice versa*. To this degree

---

[27] Cf. Leisegang's Index, 626 f., though Leisegang overlooks Omn. Prob. Lib., 64, where the verb means "to implore" : ἱκέτας καθεζομένους παρακαλεῖν, ἵνα κτλ.
[28] Cf. παράκλησιν δέχεσθαι, 2 C. 8:17.
[29] Schl. Theol. d. Judt., 112, cf. 109, 2. Cf. also Schl. Jos., 74 : "Normally παρακαλεῖν is so used as simply to suggest God's summons to an act."
[30] Materially paragraphs C-E belong to παρακαλέω κτλ. as well as παραμυθέομαι κτλ. Hence in what follows the material is related to both groups.

there is reflected in this key term and its pattern of meaning the twofold character of the "Word," in which the imperative of exhortation constantly grows out of the indicative of the *kerygma*.

Theoretically distinction is made between consolation and admonition, as in the division, traced back to Posidonius and given by Seneca (Ep., 95, 65), into *praeceptio, suasio, consolatio* and *exhortatio*, which is adopted in a Christianised form in Cl. Al. (Paed., I, 1 f.): διδασκαλικός (sc. λόγος), ὑποθετικός, παραμυθητικός, προτρεπτικός. [31] In practice, however, consolation and exhortation often merge ; μῦθοι παραμυθητικοί often become words of admonition rather than comfort. Hence the reasons for consolation dealt with → *infra* (784, 12 ff.) not infrequently have the form of the imperative — a further sign of the fact that the thinking of antiquity is oriented to law. In popular as in philosophical consolation the exhortation to stop crying and lamenting is the final word of wisdom. This is common comfort ; hence the emperor Julian, in a letter of condolence to Himerius (Amerius ?), [32] whose young wife had died, says that to another he would offer the usual consolations, τό τε συμβὰν ὡς ἀνθρώπινον καὶ τὸ φέρειν ὡς ἀναγκαῖον καὶ τὸ μηδὲν ἐκ τοῦ μᾶλλον ἀλγεῖν ἔχειν πλέον κτλ., but not to him, cf. also Plut. Cons. ad Apoll., 32 (II, 118b-c): "We normally comfort relatives and friends with the exhortation (παραμυθούμενοι καὶ πείθοντες) τὰ κοινὰ τοῦ βίου συμπτώματα κοινῶς φέρειν καὶ τὰ ἀνθρώπινα ἀνθρωπίνως. Even the other platitudes : "Lamenting is useless," [33] "one must set an example to others" (Sen. Dialogi, XI, 5, 4), "think of your distinguished position" (Consolatio ad Liviam, 345 ff., Sen. Dial., XI, 6, 1-5), always have as their conclusion : "Therefore stop lamenting." This will not, of course, surprise those who recognise that the comfort of antiquity, unlike that of primitive Christianity (→ 797, 31 ff.), is often designed simply to silence weeping, so that the heart is as little consoled as it was before (cf. Plut. Cons. ad Apoll., 19 [II, 111 f, 112a]). But even though consolation be understood as the setting aside of grief and the quieting of sorrow (πένθους κουφισμός, CIG, 4000, 11 f.), the *levare dolorem maerentium* (Cic. Tusc., III, 23, 55; 31, 75; cf. Plut. Cons. ad Apoll., 1 [II, 102b]: ... πρὸς ἄνεσιν τῆς λύπης καὶ παῦλαν τῶν πενθικῶν καὶ ματαίων ὀδυρμῶν), [34] the comforter often gives moral and rational admonition in acc. with Plato's ideals concerning the conquest of grief (cf. Plat. Resp., X, 604b-c, also Jul. Ep., 201 [412d]: The comforter will σωφρονίζειν καὶ παιδεύειν those who are not capable of this themselves, cf. Plut. Consolatio ad Uxorem [II, 608-612]). [35]

II. Comforters.

Nevertheless antiquity worked out a whole art of consolation with variations acc. to the various classes in need of it. Among these are above all the bereaved, esp. those who have lost children, or others who have died early, [36] or the fallen. But comfort is also given to the dying, [37] the elderly, [38] those left behind at separation, [39] exiles, for

[31] Cf. also Dio Chrys. Or., 12, 40. παρακλητικός does not occur here, since it had become a tt. for the commander's address to his troops, → n. 6.

[32] Jul. Ep., 201 (412c).

[33] This first in Archiloch. Fr., 7 (Diehl², I, 3, 7 f.). Expression is also given to the general human experience that mourning itself can assuage grief and thus has consoling power, Schaeffer Auszug, 12 f. On what follows cf. Skutsch, 938.

[34] Thus in antithesis to "to console" one finds μεῖζον τὸ πένθος παρασκευάζω, Ps.-Dion. Hal. Art. Rhet., VI, 4 (ed. H. Usener [1895], p. 29, 5 f.).

[35] Cf. W. v. Christ-W. Schmid-O. Stählin, Gesch. d. gr. Lit.⁶ = Hndbch. AW, VII, 2, 1 (1920), 493, n. 5; Ziegler, 792 f. Scholars are not agreed as to how much genuine feeling there is in this *consolatio* of Plut.

[36] ὁ ἄωρος θάνατος (Plut. Cons. ad Apoll., 16 [II, 110e]) plays a gt. part in the consolations of antiquity, → 787, 22 ff.

[37] Cf. Ps.-Plat. Ax., 364b ff.; Jos. Bell., 6, 183.

[38] Cf. Cic. Cato Maior de Senectute (→ n. 54); Stob. Ecl., V, 927-948, 954-956; also F. Boll, "Die Lebensalter," N. Jbch. Kl. Alt., 16 (1913), 94 with n. 1.

[39] Cf. Jul. Or., 8 ἐπὶ τῇ ἐξόδῳ τοῦ ἀγαθωτάτου Σαλουστίου παραμυθητικὸς εἰς ἑαυτόν. where the emperor consoles himself on separation from his fatherly friend Salustius.

whom a special genre of consolatory literature arose,[40] the victims of injustice,[41] and those afflicted by all kinds of misfortunes (blindness, defeat, the overthrow of their country, slavery etc.).

Intrinsically everyone is called upon to comfort those in need of consolation, for in pagan antiquity, too, the duty of consoling neighbours was generally appreciated. In particular, however, the philosopher has the *officium consolandi* in relation to his fellows (Cic. Tusc., III, 76). He goes like a doctor to those who mourn[42] or receives them in his infirmary, → 783, 9 ff. Alongside the philosopher is the poet, who writes consoling poems for himself and others, cf. Plut. Cons. ad Apoll., 16 (II, 110e f), 9 (106b), → 782, 3 f. and n. 54. Both expected and received rewards for their skill (cf. Aeschin. Or. in Ctesiphontem, 242), as did also the paid mourning men and women, → III, 842, 35 ff.

But the dying and even the dead could also be comforters, the dying in their carefully recorded parting discourses,[43] the dead in many consolatory writings,[44] poems,[45] and inscr.[46] in which they figured as supposed comforters.[47] On the stones set up for them they constantly exhort to cease lamenting, sometimes on a Platonic basis, namely, that they are in heaven, among the blessed gods, or even deified themselves: *desine flere deum!* Carmina Latina Epigraphica, 1109, 16 (→ 788, 2 ff.), sometimes on an Epicurean: Enjoy this life, eat and drink, *quare post obitum nec risus nec lusus nec ulla voluptas erit, ibid.,* 186; *hic summa est severitas, ibid.,* 85. ταῦτα φίλοις λέγω· παῖσον, τρύφησον, ζῆσον· ἀποθανεῖν σε δεῖ, Epigr. Graec., 362, 4 f., → 626, 25 ff.

Esp. numerous are the instances of mourners seeking to console themselves. This was thought to be a moral obligation, for only he who can console himself can be an example to others[48] and give them real comfort.[49] Hence each should comfort himself on the same grounds as those on which he is accustomed to console others.[50] Undoubtedly many of the consolatory writings of antiquity had their origin in the fact that the authors were seeking above all to comfort themselves.[51] Cicero[52] boasts that he was the first to try to do this. The final work of this kind in antiquity was the De Consolatione

---

[40] Cf., e.g., Plut. De Exilio (II, 599-607); Muson. Dissertationes, IX; Teles De Fuga, in O. Hense, *op. cit.* (→ n. 13), 21-32; Dio C., 38, 18, 5. Cf. also Giesecke; Christ-Schmid-Stählin, 509, n. 5; Stählin, 312, n. 6.

[41] Cf. Dio C., 56, 41, 6 (→ 819, 14); the laws which provide punishments for malefactors offer consolation here.

[42] Cf. Ps.-Plat. Ax., 364c; Plut. Cicero, 41 (I, 882a): καὶ συνῆλθον ... ἐπὶ τὴν παραμυθίαν (on the death of his daughter Tullia) τῷ Κικέρωνι πανταχόθεν οἱ φιλόσοφοι. Cf. also Plut. Superst., 7 (II, 168c): ὠθεῖται μὲν ἔξω νοσοῦντος (sc. τοῦ δεισιδαίμονος) ὁ ἰατρός, ἀποκλείεται δὲ πενθοῦντος ὁ νουθετῶν καὶ παραμυθούμενος φιλόσοφος, Mulierum Virtutes, Intr. (II, 242 f.).

[43] E.g., Plut. Otho., 15 (I, 1073); Tac. Agricola, 45; Dio Chrys. Or., 30, 6; cf. Stauffer Abschiedsreden; also Schaeffer Auszug, 14 (XIa).

[44] Sen. Ad Marciam de Consolatione, 26; cf. Plut. Cons. ad Apoll., 37 (II, 121 f.).

[45] Cons. ad Liviam, 445 ff., 467 f.; Statius Silvae, II, 6, 93 ff. etc.

[46] Cf. the inscr. of Amorgos in P. H. Menoud, *Le sort des trépassés d'après le NT* (1945), 16; Preisigke Sammelb., I, 4313, 5 ff. and many examples in Epigr. Graec. (e.g., 298, 333a, 588, 735) and Carmina Latina Epigr. (e.g., 507, 1274, 1533).

[47] Cf. Vollmer on Statius Silvae, II, 1, 226; 6, 93; Skutsch, 939 f.; Lier, 594 ff., 600 f., 55 ff.

[48] Cf. Apollonius Tyanensis Ep., 58, 6; 55, 2; Philostrati Opera, ed. C. L. Kayser, I (1870), 358 f., 359 ff.

[49] Cf. Sen. Ad Helviam Matrem de Consolatione, 1, 4: *quia possum instar efficacissimae consolationis esse ipse consolator;* Wnd. 2 K., 39.

[50] Cf. Plut. Cons. ad Apoll., 32 (II, 118b c); Statius Silvae, V, 5, 45 ff.; Buresch, I, 98 f.

[51] Seneca's cons. for his mother Helvia was conceived strictly as a consolation for his own exile to Corsica, and Julian's 8th address was entitled παραμυθητικὸς εἰς ἑαυτόν, though written in the 2nd person to his friend.

[52] Only fragments (C. F. W. Müller, M. T. Ciceronis Scripta, IV, 3 [1879], 332-338) of Cic.'s Liber Consolationis remain; cf. v. Wageningen, 2; Buresch, I, 95; R. Philippson, Art. "M. Tullius Cicero," Pauly-W., 2nd Ser., VII, 1123-1125; but cf. Cic. Fam., IV, 6.

Philosophiae which Boethius wrote in the last yrs. before his execution in prison [53] and in which, though a Christian, he sought to console himself with Neo-platonist rather than Christian ideas of the pursuit of happiness in God. Many poets also wrote to comfort themselves. [54] It may also be said of most of the burial inscr. of antiquity that they are designed to minister comfort to those responsible for them. In inscr. on statues it is constantly said in stereotyped expressions that they are set up by relatives παρα-μυθίας ἕνεκεν, e.g., IG, IX, 2, 227; XII, 1, 1064. [55] In antiquity the one in search of consolation also tried other sources of comfort, or these were at least recommended to him, e.g., the reading of works of consolation or academic studies. Thus many in search of comfort read Plato's Phaedo (cf. Plut. Cato Minor, 68 [I, 792e]; Luc. Philopseudes, 27), Panaetius advised Quintus Tuberus to learn by heart the consolation of Crantor, Cic. Academica Priora, II Lucullus, 44, 135; cf. Fin., IV, 9, 23. Rational and philosophical considerations can have a consoling effect, cf. Luc. Nigrinus, 7, → 783, 20 f., also Philo Abr., 257, → 792, 8 ff. So, too, can the recounting of one's own troubles (Plut. Quaest. Conv., 2, 1 [II, 630c]), or the fulfilling of duty (cf. Apollonius Tyanensis Ep., 58 → n. 48) or praising and loving those who wrong us (cf. Plat. Prot., 346b), or the sense of having lived a pure and righteous life (Xenoph. Ap., 5). Also advised were singing (Statius Silvae, II, 1, 33 f.), remarriage (after the death of a wife, Apoll. Tyanensis Ep., 55), or suicide, which characterises the predominantly hopeless and cheerless outlook of antiquity (cf. Cons. ad Liviam, 420 ff.; Statius Silvae, II, 1, 25; V, 1, 199). [56] Ref. is made to the hope of a life with the blessed after death (e.g., Plat. Phaed., 115d). Nevertheless, in spite of all the means of consolation both recommended and often tried, attempts at self-consolation were often unsuccessful; hence it was not regarded as unworthy to receive comfort from another. [57]

III. Ways and Means of Comfort.

How did one try to comfort the afflicted in antiquity? The means were in the main those still used or recommended to-day : the personal presence of someone who can console and cheer (e.g., Jos. Bell., 3, 194); esp., then, visits to offer sympathy, which in both East and West were conventional from the very earliest times (for the Graeco-Roman world cf., e.g., Aeschin. Tim., 145, to Achilles; Luc. De Luctu, 24). [58] From those who paid such visits there was expected esp. a lively expression of sympathy and participation, e.g., Jos. Bell., 6, 183, including joining in the laments of the sorrowing like the choruses in tragedy. [59] A letter might take the place of a personal visit, cf. several letters of Cicero (ad Brutum, 17 [I, 9]; Fam., V, 16; VI, 3), of Seneca (esp. 63, 93, 99), of Apollonius of Tyana (55 and 58), of Julian (201), and of Jerome (23, 39, 60, 66, 75,

---

[53] Cf. M. Manitius, Gesch. d. lat. Lit. d. MA, I = Hndbch. AW, IX, 2, 1 (1911), 32 f.; F. Klingner, "De Boëthii cons. philosophiae," Philologische Untersuchungen, H. 27 (1921); also Einführung z. d. Übers. v. K. Büchner (Boethius, Trost d. Philosophie, Sammlung Dieterich, 33 [1939]), VII-L; H. R. Patch, The Tradition of Boethius (1935).

[54] So Plut. Cons. ad Apoll., 9 (II, 106b). Examples of similar works : Xenoph. Cyrop., VIII, 7, 6-28; Ap., 5 f., 8, 28; Ep., 3 (supposed self-consolation on the death of his son Gryllus); Luc. Pro Lapsu inter Salutandum, 1; Jul. Or., 8. Cf. also in some sense Cato Maior as a work in which Cicero consoles himself and his friend and companion Atticus on the afflictions of growing old and esp. the proximity of death; cf. Buresch, I, 107 f.; → n. 38.

[55] Cf. Gottwald, 6 f., who has many other examples.

[56] Cf. R. Hirzel, "Der Selbstmord," ARW, 11 (1908), 75 ff.; J. Leipoldt, Der Tod bei Griechen u. Juden (1942), 19-40, cf. on p. 23 Hegesias of Cyrene, nicknamed πεισιθάνατος, "the one who persuades to die."

[57] Cf. Dio C., 38, 18, 5 : ... οὐ γάρ που καὶ ἀπαξιώσεις παραμυθίου τινὸς παρ' ἑτέρου τυχεῖν.

[58] In these two passages the comforter tries to persuade those who have fasted for a long time to take food, cf. → 788, 29 ff.; 791, 16 ff.; 821, 28 ff.

[59] Plut. De Exilio, 1 (II, 599b). Plut. rejects this means of comfort in favour of the proof that all lamentation is useless and foolish, though cf. R. 12:15 and on this Schaeffer Aus-zug, 12 f.

77 etc.).[60] A development of the letter of condolence is the consolatory writing, the παραμυθητικὸς λόγος (cf. Plut. Cons. ad Apoll., 1 [II, 102b]), of which we have many examples, e.g., Plat. Phaedo, *generis humani magna consolatio,*[61] and Ps.-Plat. Axiochus, while many others, e.g., that of Crantor, the model for many later writers,[62] have perished. Both the form and also the motifs of the consolatory writing, esp. paradigms from myth and history, come down through the centuries.[63] There is a whole genealogy of consolations from Plato to Jerome which follow the same path in plan and method.[64] There were also comforters who invited those in need of consolation to come to them and who treated them in a kind of clinic,[65] e.g., the orator Antiphon, who not only wrote a τέχνη ἀλυπίας,[66] but also undertook to cure the sorrowing of their grief by oral statements, ὥσπερ τοῖς νοσοῦσιν ἡ παρὰ τῶν ἰατρῶν θεραπεία ὑπάρχει. If this account is historical,[67] one may justly say that Antiphon was a forerunner of modern psychotherapists.

In these various ways of comforting the sorrowing certain specific means were used: the exhortations already mentioned (→ 780, 11 ff., 30 ff.);[68] the rational considerations which showed the futile and even harmful nature of grief or which sought to stop lamentation in other ways;[69] esp. the Stoic λογισμός which even Philo (→ 782, 13 f.; n. 144) commended; the doctrines of philosophy, cf. Plat. Phaed., 83a: ἡ φιλοσοφία ... τὴν ψυχὴν ἠρέμα παραμυθεῖται, Plut. Mulierum Virtutes, Intr. (II, 242 f.); Superst., 7 (II, 168c) (→ n. 42); Luc. Nigrinus, 7: "If I repeat the teachings of wisdom from memory, οὐ μικρὰν ἔχω παραμυθίαν." Consolations of a different kind are wine (e.g., Theophr. Fr., 120 in Athen., XI, 8 [p. 463c]; cf. → 788, 30 ff.)[70] and music, both called sweet solaces for terrible vexation in Horat. Epodi, 13, 17 f.: *illic omne malum vino cantuque levato, deformis aegrimoniae dulcibus adloquiis;* also diversions like riddles[71] and fairy-stories,[72] but esp. sleep, which effects πάσης λύπης ἱερὸν παραμύθιον (Orph. [Abel], 85, 6) and is thus called παραμύθιον ταλαιπωρούντων (Secundus Sententiae, 13 [Fragmenta Philosophorum Graecorum, I, 514]) and also falsehoods

---

[60] For further examples cf. Buresch, I, 71; → 791, 24 ff.; 822, 16 ff.

[61] Buresch, I, 20 f.

[62] Cf. H. v. Arnim, Art. "Krantor," Pauly-W., XI, 1587; Buresch, I, 38 ff.; Lier, 450; Stählin, 312, n. 5; some fragments in Gr. Philosophorum Graecorum, III, 146-150.

[63] Cf., e.g., Sen. Dialogi, XII, 1, 2; Buresch, I, 51, 109 f.; Lier, 446 f. etc.; Skutsch, 940; Stählin, 311 f. Special forms of *consolatio* are the burial poems on inscr. or in literature (λόγοι ἐπιτάφιοι) often put on the lips of the dead (→ 781, 12 ff. and n. 46), and also the resolutions of communities (ψηφίσματα παραμυθητικά), usually on inscr., which are as it were public addresses of sympathy, esp. in dirges, in honour of the dead and for the comfort of the bereaved, e.g., Tituli Asiae Minoris, III, 550, 6; μνῆμα φίλου παιδὸς πατρὶ παρηγορία, cf. Buresch II, Gottwald. Corresponding to these Gk. public resolutions are the funeral orations of Rome, cf. Liv., 5, 50; Cic. de Oratore, II, 11 [44 ff.]; Plut. Mulierum Virtutes Intr. [II, 242 f.].

[64] Cf. Ps.-Dion. Hal. Art. Rhet., VI, 4 (→ n. 34).

[65] Here, then, the common image of the physician for the comforter is more than a figure of speech, cf. Plut. Cons. ad Apoll., 32 (II, 118c); Philo Som., I, 112; Jul. Ep., 201 (412c); Cl. Al. Paed., I, 1, 2.

[66] The very title (fr. preserved in Stob. in Oratores Attici, ed. J. G. Baiter and H. Sauppe, II [1845/50], 149-151) is worth noting: To console is to put an end to sorrow, → 780, 26 ff.

[67] Plut. Vit. Dec. Orat., I, 18 (II, 833c d):... ἐν Κορίνθῳ ... κατεσκευασμένος οἴκημά τι παρὰ τὴν ἀγορὰν προέγραψεν ὅτι δύναται τοὺς λυπουμένους διὰ λόγων θεραπεύειν· καὶ πυνθανόμενος τὰς αἰτίας παρεμυθεῖτο τοὺς κάμνοντας. Cf. also Philostr. Vit. Soph., I, 15; Phot. Bibliotheca, ed. I. Bekker (1824), p. 486a, 18-22; Buresch, I, 72 ff.

[68] E.g., Plut. Cons. ad Apoll., 32 (II, 118b c), → 780, 17 ff.

[69] E.g., Plut. Sertorius, 16 (I, 575 f.): παραμυθεῖσθαι διὰ λόγων; for individual reasons cf. → 784, 20 ff.

[70] Cf. Schaeffer Auszug, 14.

[71] Cf. the instance from Historia Apollonii Regis Tyri in E. Rohde, *Der griech. Roman u. seine Vorläufer*[2] (1900), 439, 442 with n. 1; Buresch, I, 124 f.

[72] Cf. the end of the development of the meaning of παραμύθι(ον) in modern Gk.: the fairy-story told by mothers and nurses to comfort and settle children, → 819, n. 17.

(Eur. Iph. Aul., 1617; Philo Deus Imm., 65, the untrue consolations [παρηγορία] of doctors). We find a final group of means in the religion of antiquity : myths with a pt. which consoles or silences grief, so Plut. Cons. ad Apoll., 19 (II, 111 f.-112a), *ibid.*, 17 (II, 111b); (Thracian magical) sayings which heal the soul, cf. Plut. Charm., 156b-157c; Jul. Or., 8 (244a); the rites and ideas of the mysteries, cf. Pind. Fr., 137;[73] Plat. Phaed., 69c; Plut. Consolatio ad Uxorem, 10 (II, 611d e). These give assurance of immortality (→ 782, 20 f.; 785, 20 ff.) and promise the initiate pre-eminence in the world to come (Ps.-Plat. Ax., 371d) and a life of bliss with the gods (hence the anonymous author of Ax. recommends fairly directly that initiation take place in good time before death, 371d-e). A final ref. may be made to prayer, which is called the ἀτυχίας πάσης καὶ κακοπραγίας παραμύθιον, Plut. Coriolanus, 35 (I, 230e).

IV. Reasons for Comfort.

A whole literature of consolation offers to the sorrowing and to comforters a host of reasons for comfort varying from the most naive and trivial to the most exalted philosophical considerations.[74] Whatever myth and history, philosophy and common sense, popular piety and the wisdom of the mysteries can offer in the way of reasons for comfort is set in the service of the pagan office of consolation.[75] The authors, of course, go their different ways in their consolations acc. to their different philosophies.

1. In Epicurus. Epicurus and his followers found their purely immanent reasons for comfort chiefly in Epicurean anthropology.[76] The starting-point of most of their consoling thoughts is the conviction that death is the absolute end and that it consequently means a cessation of all feeling, Ps.-Plat. Ax., 365d-e; 369e-370a. As birth took place out of non-existence, so death leads to non-existence : οὐκ ἤμην, γενόμην· ἤμην, οὐκ εἰμι· τοσαῦτα, Epigr. Graec., 1117a.[77] Hence there is no need to grieve for death abroad. The deceased has no sense of his mortal remains resting in alien earth, Philodem. Philos. De Morte, col. 25, 38 ff., → n. 76. There is also no need to grieve at the gloating of opponents (col. 20, 3), or at the childlessness of the deceased. The esteem of his pupils and followers will outlive him, col. 22, 9-25, 2. All positive consolation, however, is focused on this life. Remember that each day is thy last, and then every new hour will be a gift, Horat. Ep., I, 4, 12-14; the beautiful past can never be taken away from thee, Cic. Tusc., III, 15, 33; Sen. Ep., 99, 4 f. On these grounds the Epicureans rejected the current consolations of others, e.g., that it is best not to be born at all, and if so, to die as young as possible, Epic. Men. in Diog. L., X, 126; cf. Philodem. Philos. De Morte, col. 17, 3 → 787, 16 f.

2. Common Reasons. There were many common reasons which all the schools could use acc. to their various premisses. To find comfort in death and other afflictions there is recollection a. of the happiness of what was once enjoyed (e.g., Cons. ad Liviam, 371 ff.),[78] whether it be the riches of a long life (e.g., Sen. Ep., 99, 3) or the exploits of a short one (e.g., Cons. ad Liviam, 285 f., 339 f.; Sen. Dialogi, VI, 24, 1: *incipe virtutibus illum, non annis numerare* ; Ep., 93, 2 : *longa est vita, si plena est* ; also 77, 4 and Plut. Cons. ad Apoll., 17 [II, 111d]: μέτρον γὰρ τοῦ βίου τὸ καλόν, οὐ τὸ τοῦ χρόνου μῆκος).[79] There is also recollection b. of the good things remaining to the bereaved

---

[73] Poetae Lyrici Graeci, ed. T. Bergk⁴, I (1878), 429.

[74] Buresch, II, 444.

[75] Cf. Hier. Ep., 60, 5 (CSEL, 54, 553 ff.); cf. Lier, 450; Stählin, 311.

[76] We know the consolations of Epicurus chiefly from their faithful reproduction by his disciples, e.g., in Philodem. Philos. De Morte, ed. S. Mekler (1886), and D. Bassi, Voluminum Herculanensium collectio tertia I (1914), also W. Scott, Fragmenta Herculanensia (1885). Cf. Buresch I, 143 ff.; R. Philippson, Art. "Philodemos (Diatriben)," Pauly-W., XIX, 2467-2474, esp. 2473 f.

[77] This is also common on Lat. inscr.: *Non fui, fui, non sum, non curo* ; how common was the thought may be seen from the use of the abbreviation NFFNSNC, Lier, 590 f.

[78] Cf. Skutsch, 938; Kaiser, 11.

[79] Skutsch, 940; v. Wageningen, 7; also the ref. from Phalaris (→ 776, 3 ff. and n. 11).

even after their painful loss (→ n. 144, No. 3), e.g., the other son (Cons. ad Liviam, 411 ff., 469 ff.), but esp. inner values, *innata et insita,* as distinct from *res adventiciae* which are received only as a gift and may be revoked at any time, cf. Sen. Dialogi, VI, 10, 1 f.[80] Again, there is recollection c. of the duration and yet also the corruptibility of the universe. As compared with the time of the universe each human life is only στιγμή τις ἀόριστος, a moment which cannot be fixed or measured, *puncti instar* (→ n. 144, No. 6). Thus there is no special reason to grieve at a short life, e.g., Sen. Ep., 99, 31.[81] As compared with the transitory nature of the universe, however, individual suffering is petty, Sen. Dialogi, XI, 1 [20], 2; Statius Silvae, II, 1, 209 ff.[82] d. In particular, however, the thought of the universality, the κοινὸς νόμος of death, the *non tibi hoc soli* (Cic. Tusc., II, 33, 79), is handed on as a *consolatio maxime pervulgata* (Fam., V, 16, 2) from lip to lip, writing to writing and inscr. to inscr.:[83] εὐψύχει (θάρσει), οὐδεὶς ἀθάνατος, "be comforted — no-one is immortal."[84] In constantly new variations this truism is commended as a ground of consolation acc. to the principle : *solamen miseris socios habuisse malorum,*[85] e.g., τὸ(ν?) λυπούμενον ἀλλοτρίοις κακοῖς παραμυθοῦ, Apollonius in Stob. Ecl., V, 1133, 9. Consolation is found esp. in the fact that the same fate befalls the sons of the gods (e.g., Epigr. Graec., 298, 7 f.;[86] Anth. Pal., VII, 8, 7 f.), kings (e.g., Horat. Carmina, II, 14, 9-12) etc. These ideas recur to the pt. of satiation in the most varied literary and non-literary attempts at consolation.

3. The Thought of Immortality. The decisive presupposition of all the profounder consolation of antiquity is the concept of the immortality of the soul :[87] the good are not dead.[88] The strongest pillars of the concept are the mysteries (→ 784, 7 ff.).[89] When Attis or Dionysus or Orpheus or Alkestis is depicted on inscr. or sarcophagi, this is a fig. expression of the hope or consolation of the immortality conferred by the mysteries. Death can be regarded as birth to never-ending life, and the day of death as *natalis aeterni,* cf. Sen. Dialogi, VI, 23. Or again, all earthly life can be thought of as simply a transition from eternal pre-existence to eternal post-existence (not from nothingness to nothingness, as in Epicurus, → 784, 22 ff. and n. 77). Or again, there is ref. to a heavenly journey of the dead, e.g., Anth. Pal., VII, 587, 2.[90] Death is simply a returning home,[91] a journey back to the heavenly heights from whence the soul came into the

---

[80] Buresch I, 158 f.; Skutsch, 939; Stählin, 315.

[81] Buresch I, 62. The thought occurs already in Crantor and Epicurus, also Philo (Jos., 24; → n. 144, No. 11); cf. also Seneca De Brevitate Vitae.

[82] Skutsch, 938.

[83] Rohde, II, 394 f.; Schaeffer Auszug, 14; Stählin, 313 f.

[84] This saying comes at the end of many burial inscr. (e.g., Epigr. Graec., 609, 9, also in simple transcription on Lat. inscr.: *eupsychi tecnon, udis athanatos,* CIL, VI, 10889, Lier, 569), also among Jews as well as Gentiles (*v.* J. B. Frey, Corpus Inscr. Judaicarum, I [1936], No. 314, 335, 380, 401, 450, 544; Delling, 521). On the development of the thought on Gk. and Rom. inscr. cf. Lier, 563-574.

[85] The formulation of this familiar thought (cf. G. Büchmann, *Geflügelte Worte*[28] [1937], 361) is medieval but the thought is ancient, cf. Sen. Dialogi, XI, 12, 2 : *est autem hoc ipsum solacii loco, inter multos dolorem suum dividere* ; with ref. to death, *ibid.,* 1, 4 : *maximum solacium est cogitare id sibi accidisse quod ante se passi sunt omnes omnesque passuri ... crudelitatem Fati consolatur aequalitas.* De Remediis Fortuitorum, 2, 3 : *morieris nec primus nec ultimus ; multi me antecesserunt, omnes sequentur.*

[86] τῆς ἐπ' ἐμοὶ λύπης παραμύθιον ἐμφρεσὶ θέσθε τοῦτον· καὶ μακάρων παῖδες ἔνερθεν ἔβαν, Gottwald, 18.

[87] E.g., Plat. Gorg., 523 ff.; Men., 81; Phaedo *passim* ; Plut. Cons. ad Apoll., 36 (II, 120d-121e). Rohde, II, 379-396; A. J. Festugière, *L'idéal religieux des Grecs et l'Evangile* (1932), 143-169; Schaeffer Auszug, 16; Ehrhardt, 430 ff.

[88] Cf. Ehrhardt, 432; Epigr. Graec., 259, 3 f.

[89] Cf. Buresch I, 12-20; Schaeffer Auszug, 16.

[90] That these thoughts were not worked out thoroughly or taken seriously is shown by the fact that, though incompatible in detail, they are often brought into direct proximity to one another, e.g., Sen. Dialogi, VI, 24 f.; Stählin, 318.

[91] Cf. Ps.-Plat. Ax., 365e; also Philo (→ n. 144, No. 9).

prison of the body. [92] Life is just a visit (παρεπιδημία τίς ἐστιν ὁ βίος, Ps.-Plat. Ax., 365b). On this view, for all its good things, it is a grievous exile. [93] The world is evil, [94] the earth a vale of tears, [95] the body a heavy burden on the soul (pondus animae, Sen. Ep., 65, 16), a prison, a fetter of the spirit (Sen. Dialogi, XII, 11, 7). Hence death is a joyous liberation, [96] and even if there were no hope of a hereafter it would be a sweet sleep (→ III, 14, n. 60; 436, 26 ff.) and the grave a welcome place of rest. [97] On the other hand, the suffering of earth has its good side, for it is the ineluctable presupposition for the reception of blessedness in the hereafter : ut ad illa venias, per illa exeundum est, Sen. Dialogi, VI, 18, 8. [98] Comforters delight to dwell on the better hereafter into which the one for whom we mourn has entered. He has a close view of divine things and can look down from above on the affairs of men, Sen. Dialogi, XI, 9 (27), 3. He receives a heavenly reward for his good life : τοῖς εὐσεβέσι τῶν μεταλλαξάντων ἔστι τις τιμὴ καὶ προεδρία καὶ χῶρός τις ἀποτεταγμένος ... ἐν ᾧ διατρίβουσιν αἱ τούτων ψυχαί, Plut. Cons. ad Apoll., 34 (II, 120b). There are many refs. to this heavenly choir. It is composed of the great men of the past, of the righteous of earlier days, [99] and esp. of one's own forefathers, though all are related there, Sen. Dialogi, VI, 25, 2. The wise man finds excellent masters there (Plat. Phaed., 63c), and the soul lives the life of the blessed, in the house of the blessed, on the isles of the blessed, in fellowship with the blessed gods themselves : πολιτεύεται μετὰ τῶν θεῶν, Menander De Laudationibus, II, 11, 294; [100] cf. Plut. Cons. ad Apoll., 37 (II, 121 f.). [101]

Refs. to God or the gods are the exception at this pt. in these consolatory letters. [102] Now and then instead of the truism "to die is human" we find "so the gods will." This was the consolation of Achilles to Priam, Hom. Il., 24, 525; cf. Plut. Cons. ad Apoll., 7 (II, 105b). In particular, providence fixes the time of death (Sen. Dialogi, VI, 10, 2), esp. an early death, [103] and it is a friendly act on God's part to cause someone to die ἐν καιρῷ τῆς ἡλικίας (Xenoph. Ap., 7). [104] For such favourites of the gods all is well among those who have fetched them thus early, e.g., Anth. Pal., VII, 483; Hyperides in Stob. Ecl., V, 1133, 3 f., → n. 106. Hence grief for them is an ἀσεβεῖν τὸν θεόν, Apollonius Tyanensis Ep., 58, 6, → n. 48. To those left behind it is said in consolation that God will not abandon those whom He has taken under His protection, Jul. Or., 8 (249a-250c; cf. 252b-d). Otherwise hardly any deity is mentioned as a comforter, for there was in antiquity no deity whose function and nature was consolation. Little comfort is won

---

[92] Sen. Dialogi, VI, 24 f.; Kaiser, 21.

[93] Sen. Dial., XII, 5; Kaiser, 14.

[94] Cf. the fine account in Ps.-Plat. Ax., 366a-369b, also Sen. Dial., VI, 22, 8 : iniqua tempora ; cf. Ep., 8, 8 : munera ista fortunae insidiae sunt.

[95] E.g., Plut. Cons. ad Apoll., 6 (II, 104c); cf. v. Wageningen, 7; Rohde[9, 10], II, 200.

[96] E.g., Carmina Latina Epigraphica, 783 : corporeo laetae (sc. animae) gaudent se carcere solvi ; Lier, 602 f.

[97] Cf. Herkenrath, 25 ff.

[98] The thought is not Seneca's own but Posidonius'; cf. Reitzenstein Poim., 254 f.

[99] Sen. Dialogi, VI, 25, 1: excepit illum coetus sacer, Scipiones Catonesque etc.

[100] Rhet. Graec., III (1856), 421, 16 f.

[101] Further examples of this train of thought may be found in Cons. ad Liviam, 329 ff.; Ovid Amores, III, 9, 59 ff.; Statius Silvae, II, 1, 194 ff.; 7, 107 ff.; cf. Skutsch, 938 (under no. 1); Vollmer on P. Papinii Statii Silvarum libri, V, 1, 253; E. Badstuebner, Beiträge z. Erklärung u. Kritik d. philosophischen Schriften Senecas (1901), 4.

[102] Cf. Gercke, 68 f. In popular philosophy and its sphere there is in the field of consolation, too, consistent ref., now to God, now to the gods.

[103] A late death can even be called a sorry fate (cf. Buresch I, 29 ff.), though it can also be lauded as a special privilege because the deceased has enjoyed life to the full and seen his children and grandchildren, Ps.-Dion. Hal. Art. Rhet., VI, 5, p. 30, 22 (→ n. 34); Epigr. Graec., 44, 67; Carmina Latina Epigraphica, 387; Lier, 596 f.

[104] ὅσσους γὰρ φιλέουσι θεοί, θνήσκουσιν ἄωροι, Epigr. Graec., 340, 8. For further examples cf. Buresch I, 32, n. 4; Lier, 596; e.g., Anth. Pal., VII, 574, 11 f.:

ἔμπης ὄλβιος οὗτος, ὃς ἐν νεότητι μαρανθεὶς
ἔκφυγε τὴν βιότου θᾶσσον ἀλιτροσύνην.

from the rule, provision, or friendliness of the gods, though cf. → 784, 2 ff. Ancient man has a greater sense of the envy of the gods than of their consoling sway.[105]

The disturbing thing about many of the more hopeful statements quoted above is that so often they are either explicitly or tacitly set under a doubting εἰ ἀληθής (Plut. Cons. ad Apoll., 34 [II, 120b]) or under the doubting condition : εἴ γε ὁ μετηλλαχὼς θειότερόν τινα βίον μετείληφεν, ibid., 25 (II, 114d) etc.[106] Uncertainty is equally clearly revealed by the τάχα που[107] or fortasse[108] of many comforters, and esp. the unreality of many statements.[109] Even for the best of them the thought of eternal life was hardly more than a comforting metaphysical hypothesis.[110]

For all the consoling descriptions there is at bottom a profound lack of hope or comfort in the world of antiquity. The dead are called blessed whether there is ascribed to them a new life or an eternal sleep or total annihilation.[111] But in fact most of the usual reasons for comfort sound cold and comfortless, as, e.g., the emperor Julian himself realises, → 780, 13 ff. Everything is transitory. All mourning is foolish and useless. Εἱμαρμένη is ἀπαραίτητος.[112] Vitam regit fortuna, non sapientia (→ n. 144, No. 2). Time and again the saying of Theognis is repeated :[113] "Best of all for mortals is never to have been born, but for those who have been born to die as soon as possible." Thus we read already in Eur. Fr., 449 (TGF, 498): "In respect of the newly born one must weep for all the evils into which he is plunged, but the dead one must send hence with joy and thanksgiving as one who is liberated from all distress," and Crantor (in Plut. Cons. ad Apoll., 27 [II, 115b]): "Many wise men regard life as a punishment, and the birth of man esp. as his greatest misfortune." Nevertheless, the death of those snatched away early is bewailed particularly : ἠϊθέων δακρυτὸς ἅπας μόρος, "the fate of those who die unmarried deserves nothing but tears," Alcaios in Anth. Pal., VII, 495, 5. For their death seems to be pointless, and hence their birth completely futile. Another inscr. has a dead youth himself lament μάτην ἐγενόμην, ibid., 558, 4. There is a cynical note in the verses in Ps.-Epicharm.[114] Fr., 64 (Diels, I⁶, 210; T. Bergk. op. cit. [→ n. 73], II, 239; Diehl², I, 64): εἰμὶ νεκρός, νεκρὸς δὲ κόπρος, γῆ δ' ἡ κόπρος ἐστιν· | εἰ

---

[105] On the attitude of the man of antiquity to death cf. Leipoldt, op. cit.; A. Brelich, Aspetti della morte nelle iscrizioni sepolcrali dell' Impero Romano, Budapest (1937). On the attitude of the sage, and on the Jewish attitude to the tomb, cf. G. Bertram, "The Problem of Death in Popular Judaeo-Hellenistic Piety," Crozer Quarterly, 10 (1933), esp. 267-271.

[106] Cf. also Hyperides in Stob. Ecl., V, 1133, 3 ff.: εἰ δ' ἔστιν αἴσθησις ἐν ᾅδου καὶ ἐπιμέλεια παρὰ τοῦ δαιμονίου, ὥσπερ ὑπολαμβάνομεν, εἰκὸς ... πλείστης κηδεμονίας ὑπὸ τοῦ δαιμονίου τυγχάνειν. Tac. Agricola, 46 : si, ut sapientibus placet, non cum corpore extinguuntur magnae animae ... Cf. also Rohde⁹, ¹⁰, II, 393 and n. 3; Ehrhardt, 435; Skutsch, 940; Lier (III), 54 f.; Cumont, 133.

[107] E.g., Menander De Laudationibus, II, 9, 283; (Rhet. Graec., III [→ n. 100], 414, 19-21).

[108] E.g., Statius Silvae, II, 6, 99, cf. v. 101; also Ehrhardt, 434.

[109] E.g., IG, IX, 2, 429 : εἰ δ' ἦν τοῖς ἀγαθοῖς ἀνάγειν, πάλιν ἦλθες ἂν εἰς φῶς ἐκπρολιπὼν ἀδύτους Περσεφόνης θαλάμους. In view of all this uncertainty it is the more surprising and also the more noteworthy with what emphasis the hopeless teaching of Epicurus is proclaimed, e.g., Epigr. Graec., 1117a, 2 (→ 784, 22 f.): ... εἰ δέ τις ἄλλο ἐρέει, ψεύσεται· οὐκ ἔσομαι.

[110] Cf. Cumont, 133.

[111] Cf. L. Friedländer, Sittengeschichte Roms, III⁹ (1920), 324.

[112] E.g., Jul. Or., 8 (246b): ἀπαραίτητον γάρ ἐστι τὸ λεγόμενον ζυγὸν τῆς ἀνάγκης, cf. Gottwald, 13.

[113] Elegia, I, 425-428; cf. Rohde⁹, ¹⁰, II, 200, esp. n. 4; Bacchyl., 5, 160 ff.; Plut. Cons. ad Apoll., 27 (II, 115c-e); cf. E. Rohde, op. cit. (→ n. 71), 219 f.; Hirzel (→ n. 56), 86; Lier, 465 f.; Schaeffer Auszug, 15; Sen. Dialogi, VI, 22, 3 : si felicissimum est non nasci, proximum est, puto, brevi aetate defunctos cito in integrum restitui ; cf. Kaiser, 19. The same thought is echoed in Qoh. 4:2 f.: "Happier are the dead than those still living, and happier than both the unborn."

[114] The true Epicharm. says : γᾶ μὲν εἰς γᾶν, πνεῦμα δ' ἄνω (in Plut. Cons. ad Apoll., 15 [II, 110a]).

δ' ἡ γῆ θεός ἐστ', οὐ νεκρός, ἀλλὰ θεός, [115] and in an epigram of Callimachus (15 [13] 3 f.), where the deceased gives information on the questions of the living: "How is it in the underworld? Deep darkness. How about return to us? All a lie. And Pluto? A myth. So we are lost." Perhaps is it just a naiver, or possibly a more cynical, expression of this profound lack of consolation when the grave is called a θάλαμος and death *nuptiae perpetuae*, [116] or when comfort is sought in the "resurrection" of the dead in the spring flowers on their graves, or in the idea of their transfiguration into stars or diffusion in the air, cf. Eur. Suppl., 531-536. [117] As in the poetic images, so, too, in many sculptures on steles and sarcophagi, some of which are still found to-day even in the Christian world (e.g., the extinguished torch, the broken column, the flawed rose, the winged hour-glass, [118] the weeping genius etc.), the hopelessness of antiquity finds expression. The same message is proclaimed by depictions of Endymion and Ariadne asleep, or of sleeping cupids etc. Even the noblest consolation of antiquity ends finally with hopeless capitulation to the majesty of death. [119]

At this point pagan antiquity shows "classically" how far man's own insights and resources can take him. His attitude is noble in face of the superiority of the powers which determine his life and make it a realm of suffering. It is petty and pitiable, however, in relation to the heavenly comfort of God in Christ to which the men and writings of the NT bear witness. With the consolation of Christ something completely new came into the world. [120]

Stählin

D. Comfort and Comfortlessness in the OT. [121]

I. Human Comfort.

1. Bearers. In the OT not only relatives and friends are called upon to give comfort (Job 2:11), but also those who are more distant (cf. 2 Βασ. 10:2), for it is a great honour for a man to be called "one who consoles the sorrowing" (Job 29:25). There are also many poor or awkward comforters who basically do the opposite, Job 16:2. [122] But to the praise and honour of the genuine comforter those consoled by him surround him as do warriors their king, Job 29:25.

2. Means. Visits are customary in the biblical world too, [123] → 782, 27 ff.; cf. Gn. 37:35; Job 2:11; 42:11. [124] At these bread and a cup are offered as well as consola-

---

[115] Cf. the Lat. inscr., Carmina Latina Epigraphica, 1532, 2 : *mortua hic ego sum et sum cinis, is cinis terra est | sin est terra dea, ego sum dea, mortua non sum* ; Lier, 449, 589 f.; Ehrhardt, 428; Stählin, 319.

[116] Lier, 563 f. and n. 2.

[117] Cf. Ehrhardt, 429; Lier, 600; P. H. Menoud, *op. cit.* (→ n. 46). Ancient mystery belief (Egyptian ?) lies behind the idea of transfiguration into stars, cf. Reitzenstein Hell. Myst.[1] (1910), 170 f.

[118] Cf. G. Bertram, *op. cit.*, 268.

[119] Cf. Stählin, 320, and on this whole chapter Cumont, 131 ff. with many examples.

[120] These concluding remarks were inspired by H. Kleinknecht.

[121] In general sections D and E present only insights and facts which distinguish the OT and Jewish world from the rest of the pre-NT world.

[122] Here the LXX has παρακλήτωρ. 'A and Θ have παράκλητος in the act. sense in distinction from the NT use in Jn. 14 ff.; 1 Jn. 2:1; cf. E. Y. Mullins, Art. "Comforter" in *The International Standard Bible Encyclopaedia*, II (1925), 679; Bu. J., 437 f.; → 801, n. 10; 801, 21-23.

[123] Letters can take the place of a personal visit, cf. 2 Βασ. 10:2 = 1 Ch. 19:2 f. But the formulation in Σ : ἀπέστειλεν Δαυὶδ παραμυθούμενος αὐτόν (sc. the king of Ammon) shows that David was himself the comforter in the person of his ambassadors acc. to the principle (→ I, 415, 19 ff.; V, 259, 9 ff.; Str.-B., III, 2) that the envoy of a man is as the man himself.

[124] The ref. here is to a visit of congratulation rather than condolence. One might almost take παρακαλέω in the sense "to congratulate," though, as the Heb. נוד shows, expression

tions, cf. Jer. 16:5, 7. The association of bread and wine as means of comfort is one of the oldest combinations of the two elements, though cf. Gn. 14:18; → I, 477 f.; V, 162 ff. Wine alone, at least acc. to a later understanding of Gn. 5:29, [125] is the oldest of all solaces in the Bible, for the interpretation of the name of Noah as "comforter" bears obvious ref. to the vineyard which he planted on the ground that had been cursed for Adam's sake, i.e., to the gladdening wine which he thus won as a consolation for the curse. [126] But for the men of the Bible as for those of non-biblical antiquity (cf. Theophr. Fr., 120 in Athen., XI, 8 [p. 463c], → 783, 22 f.) wine is also a solace because it enables us to forget trouble and affliction, [127] cf. Prv. 31:6 f.

3. Self-comforting. In the OT, too, the address of the comforter is often an exhortation to self-consolation (παρακάλει τὴν καρδίαν σου, Sir. 30:23). Sir. frequently recommends (38:17-23; cf. 30:21 ff.) brief mourning and rapid consolation on the grounds 1. that nothing can be altered and 2. that lamentation is wasteful, → 783, 15 f. The Bible can speak of a corrupt and futile comfort, e.g., confidence in riches and similar goods, cf. Job 31:24. [128] Nevertheless, in the biblical sphere, too, alms can be a great comfort before God, Tob. 4:11.

II. Divine Comfort.

The true consolation (παράκλησις ἀληθινή, Is. 57:18) [129] of the heart comes from God alone. In comparison with this all other is ματαία παράκλησις, Is. 28:29; cf. Zech. 10:2; Job 21:34. Apart from God, man, nation and world are without comfort.

1. Comfortlessness. The comfortlessness of the individual is expressed esp. in Ps., e.g., ψ 68:20. It can be so great that the soul is closed to all consolation, ψ 76:2. The comfortlessness of the people finds moving expression in Lam. (1:2, 9, 16, 21; 2:13 : τίς σώσει σε καὶ παρακαλέσει σε; cf. also Is. 22:4 etc.). That of mankind is bemoaned by Ecclesiastes (4:1): καὶ οὐκ ἔστιν αὐτοῖς παρακαλῶν. The true depth of this desolation lies in the fact that it comes from God Himself as a judgment, to-day in history (Is. 51:19; Na. 3:7), to-morrow at the Last Judgment (Wis. 3:18).

2. Comfort. Comforting is God's proper work. He turns earlier desolation into perfect consolation both in individuals (again esp. the Ps., e.g., ψ 22:4; 70:21; [130] 85:17; 93:19; particularly 118) and also in the people of God, cf. Is. 54:11 ff.; 51:19 ff. In this sense there is given in the second part of Is. God's great consoling promise to Israel : "Comfort, comfort my people, saith your God. Priests, speak to the heart of Jerusalem and comfort it. For its humiliation has reached its goal and its sin is remitted" (Is. 40:1 ff. LXX). In the time of salvation which now dawns God Himself will comfort Zion. He will console all its ruins by making them a παράδεισος κυρίου, Is. 51:3. ἐγώ εἰμι, ἐγώ εἰμι ὁ παρακαλῶν σε, Is. 51:12; cf. also Ez. 14:23; Bar. 4:30 : θάρσει, Ἰερουσαλήμ, παρακαλέσει σε

---

of sympathy after the suffering ends is really intended (cf. Ges.-Buhl, s.v. נוד). The many senses of "address" appear in the verbs παρακαλέω and παραμυθέομαι. Cf. A. Alt, "Zur Vorgeschichte d. Buches Hiob," ZAW, 55 (1937), 267 f.

[125] Cf. Ges.-Buhl, s.v. נחם.

[126] Cf. K. Budde, Bibl. Urgeschichte (1883), 307 ff.; H. Gunkel, Gn. (Handkommentar z. AT, I, 1⁵ [1922]) on Gn. 5:29.

[127] In the ancient saga of Helen this effect of wine is enhanced by the interfusion of magic, Hom. Od., 4, 220 ff.

[128] Cf. T. Hermann, Art. "Trost, Tröster, trösten," Calwer Bibellex., II⁴ (1924), 775.

[129] Here we have ἰᾶσθαι and παρακαλεῖν together (→ n. 65). P. Katz pts. out that "the Gk. text arises here only through two errors in transl. (ואנחמו for ואנחהו, Aquila rightly καθωδήγησα) and אֲבֵל (2 K. 4:14 "verily") for אבל "to mourn" (Ottley, op. cit. [→ n. 16], II, 358)" [Katz].

[130] In the LXX the assurance of the original is already fulfilled : καὶ ἐπιστρέψας παρεκάλεσάς με.

ὁ ὀνομάσας σε, and esp. ψ 125:1, where the LXX has "those that are comforted" for the "those that dream" of the original.

3. Metaphors. Two metaphors give vivid expression to the divine comfort. The first is that of the shepherd (Is. 40:11; Ιερ. 38[31]:9), the second that of the mother, which is sometimes used for God Himself (Is. 66:13), sometimes for Jerusalem, which, being comforted, becomes a comforter [131] (cf. 2 K. 1:4): All who love Jerusalem shall suck and be satisfied at the breast of her consolation (Is. 66:11). This figure of speech is then carried further, for the children of Jerusalem shall be comforted on her knees (v. 12). Being comforted is a characteristic of God's people in the future.

4. Mediators. God's comfort does not come directly. It reaches man through many mediators and channels. The first of these is His Word, esp. in ψ 118, where consoling help in the ταπείνωσις of the Psalmist is traced back to the quickening divine word of promise (λόγιον), [132] cf. v. 52, 76, 82. Another is Scripture (cf. 2 Macc. 15:9; → 818, 12 ff.), [133] and there is also wisdom, Wis. 8:9. The most important human bearers of divine comfort are the prophets. To give comfort is their finest calling. [134] Since they speak in God's stead, they do, of course, comfort and judge at the same time. Sometimes the two callings appear at different periods in their lives and are thus found in two different sections of their books (cf. Ez. 4-24 with 33-48); sometimes they are associated (cf. Jer. 31:18-20; Is. 43:22-28). In the memory of later generations, however, they are predominantly comforters, cf. Sir. 48:24; 49:10. [135] The greatest comforter on God's behalf is His Servant, [136] one of whose main tasks is to bring the good news to the poor and therewith παρακαλέσαι πάντας τοὺς πενθοῦντας, Is. 61:2. [137]

God's comfort, like the comfortlessness which He causes, is ultimately an eschatological reality. In the absolute it is deliverance in judgment, just as perdition is absolute desolation, cf. Wis. 3:18.

E. Human and Divine Comfort in Judaism. [138]

I. Human Comfort.

1. Occasions. In Judaism comfort is given to bereaved relatives, to the teachers of pupils who have died young [139] (though not to the masters of deceased slaves), [140] and

---

[131] In another way, by comforting comparison with those who suffer much or even more (→ 785, 13 ff. and n. 144, No. 4), Jerusalem plays the role of the comforter in 4 Esr. 10:20 : "Be comforted by the sorrow of Jerusalem."

[132] For this sense of λόγιον cf. T. W. Manson's study of λόγιον in the Gk. Bible, Bulletin of the John Rylands Library, Manchester, 29 (1945/46), 411-428, esp. 414 f.

[133] Cf. in this connection the role of Plato's Phaedo and Crantor's περὶ πένθους as sources of comfort (→ 782, 9 f.), also Dio C., 43, 11, 3.

[134] Cf. H. Gunkel (Kautzsch Pseudepigr.) on 4 Esr. 10:41; cf. v. 49.

[135] Cf. Smend, Sirach erklärt, op. cit. (→ n. 15), 473.

[136] Cf. the later Messianic name Menachem (→ 793, 4 ff.). It is not impossible that Jesus alludes to prior stages of this name not now known to us when He regards Himself as the παράκλητος in Jn. 14:16; cf. 1 Jn. 2:1 and when He promises another παράκλητος, → 800, n. 1, though cf. Bu. J., 439, n. 4.

[137] Rather strangely these words are omitted in Lk. 4:18. With the intimation of a day of divine vengeance they were either not read by Jesus or left out by Lk. (cf. Zn. Lk., ad loc.), though they would have gone well with the other infinitives which describe the task of Jesus. On the other hand, they probably underlie Mt. 5:4, cf. Str.-B., I, 195.

[138] Palestinian and Hell. Judaism are here considered together because, in spite of many differences, it is plain in this respect how much they share in common even apart from the biblical legacy, not least in their borrowing from the Hell. world, → n. 144.

[139] "For the pupil is as dear to the teacher as a son," jBer., 2, 5b, 65 (Str.-B., IV, 588).

[140] "For in the case of slaves one does not say : God comfort thee, but, as on the loss of domestic animals : God make good thy loss," bBer., 16b, Bar., Str.-B., IV, 595.

also on such occasions as assaults on the conscience (comfort through intercession, Test. R. 4:4) etc. (→ 778, 5 ff.).

2. The Duty of Comforting. The duty of comforting falls on close relatives (Jos. Ant., 15, 61; Bell., 1, 627), on pupils and colleagues (cf. T. Chull., 2, 24; Ab. R. Nat., 14; bBQ, 38a), on teachers (cf. bKet., 8b) and neighbours (cf. 4 Esr. 10:2), and in the case of prominent figures on leading citizens (cf. Philo Abr., 260) and even the whole nation (j Demai, 22a). In consequence of the predominant principle of retribution and merit Judaism emphasises more strongly than the OT (→ 788, 24 ff.) that to give comfort (תַּנְחוּמֵי אֲבֵלִים) is a good work incumbent on all (bSanh., 70b; cf. also Str.-B., IV, 595b-d) even in relation to the Goyim (jAZ, 1, 39c, 49 Bar.; Str.-B., IV, 595). In comparison with the world around an equally new thought is that of the μίμησις θεοῦ as a spur to comforters. God Himself has provided an example : "He has comforted those that mourn, as it is said : After the death of Abraham God spoke a word of consolation concerning Isaac (Midr. on Gn. 25:11) — and so do thou comfort those that mourn," bSota, 14a; Str.-B., IV, 561.

3. Forms of Comforting. As regards the various acts and forms of comforting the Rabb. developed a precise code of etiquette, e.g., for visits (cf. bKet., 8b) and at burials, when comfort should be given on the way home from the grave [141] and finally in the house of mourning, [142] culminating in the בִּרְכַּת אֲבֵלִים: "Our brothers, the Lord of consolations console you ! Blessed be the comforter of them that mourn," with the response : "Our brothers, the Lord of goodness recompense your goodness ! Blessed be thou, rewarder of goodness" (cf. Lv. r., 23 [121d]; Midr. Cant. 2:2 [95b, 29]). Sometimes the prayer : "Comfort my soul fully" (cf. 4 Esr. 10:8) was interwoven. When distance made a personal visit impossible, a letter was sent, e.g., S. Bar. 78-86. This important section is also an instance of a special custom in Judaism which may be explained as an analogy and development of consoling addresses on parting (→ 781, 12 f. and n. 153), namely, that of concluding books with a work of consolation and blessing, cf. also S. Nu. § 131 on 35:34. [143] This is a custom which was contined in Christianity, → 822, 16 ff.

4. Reasons. The reasons for comfort in Judaism are partly the same as those in the surrounding pagan world, [144] partly of biblical derivation, [145] and partly specifically Jewish. [146]

---

[141] Cf. the instances in Str.-B., IV, 592 ff. with 597 f. (k-m).

[142] Ibid., 603 for examples.

[143] Cf. K. G. Kuhn, S. Nu., 690, n. 69.

[144] In both Hell. and Pal. Judaism we find the usual consolations in both content and formulation. 1. Death is the lot of all (cf. Philo Abr., 257 and 259 with S. Bar. 83:10 ff.; bKet., 8b, though cf. the rejection of this thought as a consolation of the Babylonians and a blaspheming of God in bBQ, 38a → 785, 9 ff.; Lier, 564 ff.). On Jewish burial inscr. it is often found in the typical pagan form θάρσει οὐδεὶς ἀθάνατος, → 785, 12 f. 2. Life is a constant alternation of joy and sorrow, hence do not grieve, but hope (Philo Vit. Mos., I, 8; Buresch I, 59). 3. Something remains to all even after severe loss (Philo Abr., 196, → 784, 42 ff.). 4. The grief of others is even greater than one's own (S. Bar. 80:7), and yet many have been consoled (but cf. the rejection of this thought in Ab. R. Nat., 14 [5b]; Str.-B., IV, 604). 5. Many share our sorrow (bMQ, 28b; → lines 3 ff.). Cf. the consolations on the death of young men. 6. Compared with eternity there is no distinction between a long life and a short one (Philo Jos., 24; Wendland, 61; → 785, 4 ff.). 7. An early death spares a man much possible suffering (Schaeffer Auszug, 16). Judaism gives this a theological ref., namely, that if God had more good things for the deceased He would not have let him die so soon (bBQ, 38a; cf. the note on this in Str.-B., IV, 605). The same can apply to the old. 8. Death is like the snuffing out of a spent candle or the falling of ripe fruit, cf. Qoh. r., 5, 11 with Cic. Cato Maior, 19 and on this A. Wünsche, Die Bildersprache d. AT [1906], 39; Lier, 583 f. 9. Death is the returning home of the soul, Philo Abr., 258; Wendland, 60; → 785, 29 ff. 10. What we lose is corruptible, what we gain is incorruptible, S. Bar. 85:5. We also find the philosophical argument 11. that what is right is a golden mean of sorrow between πάθος and ἀπάθεια (Schaeffer Auszug, 13), attainable by the consolations of λογισμός (often in Philo, e.g., Som., I, 110 ff.; Wendland, 56 ff.), e.g., the consoling thought that in death φύσις exacts its οἰκεῖον ὄφλημα (Philo Jos., 24) or χρέος (Philo Abr., 257) (Stählin, 314).

5. Presuppositions of the Ability to Comfort. In Judaism more serious enquiry was made than in paganism into the presuppositions of the ability to comfort. The most important are knowledge of Scripture (cf. the examples in Str.-B., IV, 604 ff.) and being comforted oneself, for only he who is comforted can truly comfort, cf. Philo Vit. Mos., I, 137; → 790, 6 ff.

6. Self-comforting. For this reason Judaism, too, cultivates the ideal of self-comforting, both in Rabb. writings (cf. jSanh., 6, 23d, 60 in Str.-B., IV, 605 f.; Semachoth, 8 [16c], ibid., 588) and also in Hell. works (cf. Philo Abr., 257: Abraham as the prototype of philosophical self-consolation, and Jos., 23-27: the inconsolable Jacob as a countertype).

II. Divine Comfort.

With the OT, and unlike the world around, Judaism extols God as the only true comforter (cf. Test. Jos. 1:6; 2:6; 4 Esr. 12:8; 10:24), as the Lord of consolations (bKet., 8b, → n. 132). But here Palestinian and Hell. Judaism part company in respect of the means of divine comfort, for while the latter speaks of a native hope (συμφυὲς παραμύθιον, Philo Praem. Poen., 72) which God has sown in the human race, [147] the former, like the OT (→ 790, 12 ff.), refers to various mediators of God's comfort, first the divine word of promise (S. Bar. 87:7; cf. 83:1 ff.; → 790, 14 ff.), then the prophets (81:4), the angels (Test. A. 6:6), and the Messiah, [148] whose time of salvation is called the consolation of God, since the consolation of Israel, i.e., the resurrection, will then be a reality. [149]

The searching of the Scriptures (Jn. 5:39) by the teachers of Israel was what led to the use of the word נֶחָמָה, "comfort," "consolation," as a comprehensive term for the Messianic salvation. [150] Reflected here is the influence of the great OT promise of comfort in Is. 40:1 ff. [151] In this sense one reads of the "consolation of Zion," [152] the

---

[145] Suffering is a divine chastisement (S. Bar. 78:5), a judgment (loc. cit.; cf. jSanh., 6, 23d, 60 in Str.-B., IV, 605 f.), an expiation (bKet., 8b). But God Himself puts an end to suffering (S. Bar. 85:8; 78:7) and gives comfort (→ 789, 29 ff.; → lines 11 ff.).

[146] E.g., the consolation of the people in the consolatory epistle of S. Bar. The present suffering of the people is to salvation, for because of it the people will not come into judgment (78:6) as their enemies will (cf. 83:22; 82:2 ff. with the seven consoling pictures of the destruction of enemies). The conclusion is also worth noting (84 f.): If we repent, we shall regain all that we have lost and much better, attaining incorruptible things for corruptible (85:4 f.). With national consolation there is also that of the individual, e.g., Ab. R. Nat., 14, with three reasons: 1. "With the death of thy son thou hast given back intact to God what He loaned" (on this cf. Wendland, 59, esp. n. 1 with further examples; → n. 144). 2. "Thy son read the Holy Scriptures in his life." 3. "He departed this life without sin, hence thou mayest be sure of a favourable destiny as his reward." The self-consolation of R. Akiba is along similar lines: "I am comforted; for ... I know that one is a son of the future world because he has led many to righteousness" (Semachoth, 2 [16c]; Str.-B., IV, 588). This consolation of a good life was also proclaimed in the Gk. world, esp. in the mysteries with their belief in compensating justice in the kingdom of souls; cf., e.g., Eur. Fr., 311, 852 (TGF, 452 and 637); Plut. Cons. ad Apoll., 34 (II, 120b c): ... τοῖς εὐσεβέσι ... ἔστι τις τιμὴ καὶ προεδρία.

[147] The expression ἀνθρώπων γένει κατέσπειρεν is perhaps an antithetical allusion to the comfortless Gk. myth of Pandora's box from which all ills were scattered among mankind while hope alone remained inside, Hes. Op., 94-101.

[148] In virtue of his office as comforter Noah is a kind of precursor of the Messiah. His name "comfort" (→ 789, 4 f.) is taken in different ways by the Rabb., cf. Ju. 9:13; Gn. r., 25 (16c), Str.-B., IV, 964.

[149] → 793, 3 f. and n. 155.

[150] Str.-B., II, 125.

[151] Examples, ibid., 124 f.; cf. also Tanch. on Dt. 1:1 § 1 (ed. Horeb [1927], 617): כָּל-הַנֶּחָמוֹת שֶׁאָמַר יְשַׁעְיָהוּ in Schl. Lk., 198. Here, "in the framework of a haggada with the theme of the correspondence between the ideal time in the wilderness and the Messianic future there is ref. to all the consolations which Is. spoke" [Meyer].

[152] S. Bar. 44:7.

"days of consolation," the "years of consolation," the "consolation of Jerusalem." [153] Messianic salvation, the supreme earthly joy, is in view when oaths are taken by the consolation of Israel. [154] Thus the נֶחָמַת יִשְׂרָאֵל of Is. 40:1 f. embraces "the whole hope ; in Palestine the term could finally denote no less than 'resurrection'." [155] It is rightly assumed "that the name Menachem = Comforter, which the Messiah will bear acc. to some scholars ..., is also linked with this train of thought." [156] It comes from a later period, and was originally a symbolical designation rather than a proper name. [157] But it is no accident that the impulse towards it came from the desolate statement of Lam. 1:16, which in the LXX reads : ἐμακρύνθη ἀπ' ἐμοῦ ὁ παρακαλῶν με. Thus Rabb. Judaism still waited for the consolation of Israel even after the cry had gone out : ἤγγικεν ἡ βασιλεία τῶν οὐρανῶν, Mt. 3:2.

Schmitz-Stählin

F. παρακαλέω and παράκλησις in the NT.

A survey of the use of παρακαλεῖν and παράκλησις in the NT [158] shows that both verb and noun are absent from the Johannine writings and Jm., though the materials offered opportunities of using them. This absence can hardly be fortuitous ; it is linked with the spiritual structure and style of the authors. In Jn., of course, we do not find the stories in which those in need of help pray to Jesus acc. to the Synoptic tradition. Jm. is one long παράκλησις, but he does not use the term ; his admonition is pitched in the key of ἐπιτάσσειν or παραγγέλλειν rather than παρακαλεῖν. Worth noting also is the absence of the terms from Gl. The unparalleled tension in the situation seems to forbid the quiet (conventional) παρακαλῶ οὖν ὑμᾶς. All the greater, then, is the actual παράκλησις, especially in the last chapters.

The words receive their content [159] preponderantly from the NT event of salvation. There is, of course, a series of passages, esp. in Ac., where the verb does not in the least transcend the limits of ordinary usage. Thus παρακαλεῖν in Ac. 28:20 simply means "to call for," "to summon," in 28:14 "to invite," [160] in 16:39 "to placate," in 19:31; 27:33 f. "to exhort," in 24:4 "to pray," 25:2 "to beseech someone," in 8:31; 9:38; 13:42; 16:9, 15; 21:12 "to ask," though here the asking is always in some way related to the proclamation of salvation, cf. esp. 8:31; 13:42; 16:9. The same is true of the "summoning by admonition" of 2 C. 8:6; 9:5; 12:18. Like παράκλησις in the sense of "summons" in 2 C. 8:4, 17, παρακαλεῖν does not have here any specifically religious note, [161] though

---

[153] Examples in Str.-B., II, 125 f.; cf. also jBer., 8d, where on Elijah's last journey he and Elisha spoke of the consolations of Jerusalem, Schl. Lk., 198 (this is a discussion of the last words of Elijah from the later Palestinian Amorean age [Meyer]). The day of consolation is one of the 7 things hidden from men and is in this context apparently distinguished from the returning dominion of the house of David, denoting the blessedness of the world to come, Str.-B., II, 126, 412; cf. Schl. Lk., 198.

[154] Examples in Str.-B., II, 126, also for the consolation of the community as a more general term for "each salvation which follows a time of disaster."

[155] Schl. Mt., 135.

[156] Str.-B., I, 195; cf. 66, 83, esp. a. Cf. also Dalman WJ, I, 89 f.; Bousset-Gressm., 227.

[157] Cf. Moore, II, 348 and Str.-B., I, 66 (n), where it is pointed out that the word has the same numerical value as the "branch" of Jer. 23:5. But for R. Meyer Menachem is from the very first a highly significant historical figure from the time of the Jewish War, who then took on legendary proportions and was changed into the returning Messiah. Cf. R. Meyer, Der Prophet aus Galiläa (1940), 76-79, 113, 152, n. 183.

[158] Schlier, 51, n. 1: "παρακαλεῖν occurs 103 times in the NT, 54 times in Paul; παράκλησις 29 times in the NT, 20 in Paul."

[159] For the various possibilities of grammatical construction cf. Pr.-Bauer⁴, 1123 ff.

[160] Ibid., 1123 transl. παρακαλεῖν as "to invite" at Ac. 8:31; 9:38; 16:15 as well ; this is perhaps possible at 8:31, though "to ask" is better. "To invite" is also too weak at Lk. 8:41, but it is plainly the meaning at Mt. 20:28 D (παρακληθέντες δειπνῆσαι).

[161] At 1 C. 16:12 ordinary address and religious exhortation merge into one another. The same applies to "to charge" in 1 Tm. 1:3.

the terms are used in relation to the collection which Paul represents as a distinctively liturgical matter.

Often the words are only moving towards a fixed use for a specific NT content. Thus when prayer is made to Jesus for help, this is in the first instance just a request like any other. Nevertheless, this asking, since it is addressed to Jesus in the light of His manifested power to save, acquires a distinctive tone and content. Even more fixed is the use of παρακαλεῖν and παράκλησις for exhortation on the basis of the Gospel. But under OT or LXX influence the most distinctive usage of the verb and especially the noun is one which is related to Rabbinic modes of speech, namely, the use for eschatological consolation or comfort. In other instances the meaning "to comfort" is closer to the secular sense : "to comfort in earthly trouble" (e.g., Ac. 20:12; 1 Th. 3:7; 4:18; 2 C. 2:7). Even here, however, the comfort and comforting are on the ground of the Gospel. In general παρακαλεῖν, in its usage as determined in some way by the NT event of salvation, has three senses. Since in the NT the original sense "to summon" is far less prominent than the idea of turning to another in speech, these may all be brought under the common sense of "address." [162] They do, of course, bear distinctive nuances. At the same time, in these three modes of using παρακαλεῖν there are instructive transitions from the one sense to the other, and even within the three groups of meaning there are finer shades of sense according to the particular context in which the words are used. The noun as well as the verb shares in the second and especially the third sense.

1. Asking for Help.

παρακαλεῖν in the sense of asking for help, especially in face of the manifested power of Jesus to save, occurs particularly in the Synoptic tradition, where those in need of aid turn to Jesus with their requests. [163] Thus the centurion in Mt. 8:5, the elders of the Jews in Lk. 7:4, the healed demoniac in Mk. 5:18, [164] the sick in Mt. 14:36; Mk. 6:56, the leper in Mk. 1:40, Jairus in Mk. 5:23; Lk. 8:41, the guides of the deaf mute in Mk. 7:32 and the blind man in Mk. 8:22 all ask for help. This is always a beseeching whose urgency is emphasised by the addition of πολλά (Mk. 5:10, 23) or σπουδαίως (Lk. 7:4) or by falling at His feet (Mk. 1:40; Lk. 8:41). It is presupposed that the suppliant has come into the sphere of Jesus' saving power. παρακαλεῖν is also used in Mt. 26:53 for calling on God in affliction ; [165] Jesus here shows that a request to the Father for the protection of angels is an open possibility, though He does not avail Himself of it. This may be compared with 2 C. 12:8, where Paul tells us that three times he called on the risen Lord in vain for deliverance from the angel of Satan.

2. Exhortation.

παρακαλεῖν occurs especially in Ac. and Pl. for exhortation by the Word proclaimed in the power of the Holy Ghost. This use is distinguished from that

---

[162] Cf. J. C. K. v. Hofmann, *Der Schriftbeweis*, II², 2 (1860), 13, who argues that παρακαλεῖν is used for any kind of address which aims at a certain effect.

[163] In connection with the healing of the possessed we have requests which resist and reject Jesus, cf. the request of the demons in Mt. 8:31; Mk. 5:10, 12; Lk. 8:31 f., also of the demoniac in Mt. 8:34; Mk. 5:17, where Lk. 8:37 has ἐρωτᾶν instead of παρακαλεῖν.

[164] Lk. 8:38 has δεῖσθαι, cf. also 5:12 and Mk. 1:40.

[165] In the request of the wicked servant in Mt. 18:32 παρακαλεῖν is in the first instance an ordinary request (cf. also v. 29), but in the parable this request for remission of an earthly debt symbolises the prayer for divine forgiveness.

of asking for help by the fact that the address does not proceed from the person who seeks help but from one who speaks with almighty power in the name of God. Thus παρακαλεῖν is used for the wooing proclamation of salvation in the apostolic preaching. Particularly worth noting here is 2 C. 5:20 : ὡς τοῦ θεοῦ παρακαλοῦντος δι' ἡμῶν. According to the rendering of Weizsäcker this means : "As though God entreated through us," but Schlatter suggests : "As though God exhorted through us," and this is to be preferred, since what is at issue is the weight of supreme authority at work in the preacher's word of admonition, cf. 2 C. 6:1. But the parallel δεόμεθα ὑπὲρ Χριστοῦ shows that there is a note of entreaty in the expression. [166] Only once elsewhere does Paul use the substantive for missionary proclamation. This is in 1 Th. 2:3, where Paul describes his telling of the Gospel of God (v. 2) as ἡ παράκλησις ἡμῶν. We are reminded of Ac. 9:31, where the Palestinian community is increased by ἡ παράκλησις τοῦ ἁγίου πνεύματος. [167] In this sense of the authoritative offer of salvation the verb also occurs in Peter's sermon at Pentecost (Ac. 2:40 with διαμαρτύρεσθαι). This usage obviously expresses the obligation inherent in the message of salvation. This is eloquently attested in Lk. 3:18. Here the παρακαλεῖν of the Baptist is called the means whereby he brought the glad tidings to the people. What is meant is the proclamation of salvation in so far as this claims the will and deed of man.

Since this παρακαλεῖν of the Baptist includes preaching to classes (Lk. 3:10-14), it leads us to the use of παρακαλεῖν and παράκλησις for the admonition which is addressed to those already won and which is designed to lead them to conduct worthy of the Gospel. The following observation will show how closely the two usages are related. The λόγος παρακλήσεως expected of the apostles in Ac. 13:15 offers them an opportunity to present the message of salvation, with its serious summons to decision, for the very first time to their fellow-countrymen in Pisidian Antioch, v. 32, 40 f. But the same term is used in Hb. for the "word of exhortation" (13:22) to men of long standing in the faith, though in danger of growing weary. The authors of 1 Pt. (5:12) and Jd. (3) also understand their letters as παρακαλεῖν. Within the NT epistles, too, we constantly see this παράκλησις (Phil. 2:1) at work, especially in the later sections of Paul's epistles. These exhortations are often introduced by παρακαλῶ, e.g., R. 12:1; [168] 2 C. 10:1; 1 Th. 4:1; Phil. 4:2; Eph. 4:1; 1 Tm. 2:1; 1 Pt. 2:11; 5:1. The admonition is "in Christ" (Phil. 2:1), "in the Lord Jesus" (1 Th. 4:1, cf. 2 Th. 3:12), "by the name of our Lord Jesus Christ" (1 C. 1:10), "by our Lord Jesus Christ and the love of the Spirit" (R. 15:30), "by the meekness and gentleness of Christ" (2 C. 10:1), "by the mercy of God" (R. 12:1). The exhortation is distinguished from a mere moral appeal by this reference back to the work of salvation as its presupposition and basis. We also

---

[166] Where παρακαλεῖν is used of the proclamation of salvation "the elements of supplication, exhortation and consolation are always interwoven ... so that it is hardly possible to separate the one sense from the other," Cr.-Kö., 571. That παρακαλεῖν has the note of entreaty even when it means "to admonish" may be seen from Phlm. 8 f., where it is expressly distinguished from ἐπιτάσσειν and is an outflowing of love. Instructive for the fluidity of the usage is Lk. 15:28, where the παρακαλεῖν of the father in relation to the elder son means "to ask" in the sense of friendly encouragement or exhortation. "To invite" (Pr.-Bauer⁴, 1123, though cf. 1125) is much too weak here. On the synonyms cf. Schlier, 51 ff.

[167] "The call for repentance and the Gospel, addressed in the power of the Spirit with a personal offer to individuals, brought in new members who perceived that here God's Word applied to them and God's Spirit was calling them to Jesus," Schl. Erl., I (1908), 910.

[168] Cf. the whole essay of Schlier, though in this the "apostolic grace" from which exhortation proceeds is carried to the pt. at which "Christ's passion continues in the sacrifice of the apostles," 62.

find that the apostle requires of his fellow-workers that they should discharge this ministry of exhortation, 1 Tm. 5:1; 6:2; 2 Tm. 4:2; Tt. 2:6, 15 (cf. 1:9). Hb. more than once summons readers to help one another by mutual exhortation (3:13; 10:25). [169]

In all these admonitions, as in missionary proclamation, we have demonstrations of the power of the Holy Spirit. One might even speak of a charisma of pastoral exhortation (R. 12:8). [170] This παράκλησις or παρακαλεῖν belongs indeed to the sphere of προφητεύειν, 1 C. 14:3, 31. The admonition in the letter of the first community to the brethren in Antioch also has a spiritual character, Ac. 15:31, cf. 15:28. It is supported by the oral exhortation of Judas and Silas, who are both expressly described as prophets, 15:32. Ac. often refers to this oral exhorting of disciples who need strengthening, 11:23; 14:22; 16:40; 20:1 f. On Paul's commission Timothy is to fulfil a similar ministry of encouragement and exhortation among the Thessalonians (1 Th. 3:2), whom Paul himself on his first visit to Thessalonica had admonished as does a father his children (2:12). If it is here assumed at once that this exhortation is in the power of the Spirit (R. 15:19), in Ac. 11:24 it is emphasised that Barnabas could give this pastoral help as a man who was full of the Holy Ghost and faith.

Here and elsewhere the words used with παρακαλεῖν or παράκλησις (παραμυθεῖσθαι, 1 Th. 2:12, στηρίζειν, 1 Th. 3:2; 2 Tm. 2:17, [171] ἐπιστηρίζειν, Ac. 14:22; 15:32, ἐρωτᾶν, 1 Th. 4:1, οἰκοδομεῖν, 1 Th. 5:11, παραμύθιον ἀγάπης, Phil. 2:1, παραμυθία, 1 C. 14:3, οἰκοδομή, 1 C. 14:3, ὑπομονή, R. 15:4, 5) show that there is nothing sharp, polemical, or critical in the expressions. [172] If on the other side terms like μαρτύρεσθαι (1 Th. 2:12), ἐπιμαρτυρεῖν (1 Pt. 5:12), διαμαρτύρεσθαι (Ac. 2:40), ἐλέγχειν (2 Tm. 4:2), ἐπιτιμᾶν (2 Tm. 4:2), παραγγέλλειν (2 Th. 3:12), διδάσκειν (1 Tm. 6:2; cf. 4:13) are mentioned in the same breath with παρακαλεῖν, it is also clear how serious and urgent the word of admonition spoken in the power of the Holy Ghost can be. [173] The fact that παρακαλεῖν is the proper expression for "to comfort" pts. in the same direction. There are cases when it is hard to distinguish between exhortation and comfort. In 2 C. 13:11 παρακαλεῖσθε embraces "both the word which consoles the sufferer and the word which admonishes the slack and weary." [174]

3. Consoling Help.

Apart from a few instances in Mt. and Lk., παρακαλεῖν is used for consoling help through God's present and future salvation especially in the Pauline Epistles

---

[169] Cf. Schlier, 54. Mutual consolation is envisaged in 1 Th. 4:18. In 5:11 we have παρακαλεῖν with οἰκοδομεῖν (cf. 1 C. 14:3), and here we might follow Weizsäcker rather than Schlatter and translate "admonish," though it should be noted that the Gk. word is the same in the two instances.

[170] Diodore of Tarsus, of course, writes concerning R. 12:8 : παράκλησις δέ ἐστιν ἡ προτροπὴ δι' ἧς τοὺς ἔτι ἐν ἀγνοίᾳ εἰς τὴν τοῦ Χριστοῦ πίστιν παρακαλοῦμεν, cf. K. Staab, Pauluskomm. aus d. griech. Kirche (1933), 106.

[171] E. G. Selwyn, The First Epistle of St. Pt. (1946) considers the bearing of the linking of παρακαλεῖν and στηρίζειν in Th. and 1 Pt. (5:10, 12, cf. also Ac. 15:32) on the question of authorship (Silas).

[172] → 821, 4 ff.; cf. Phlm. 8 f. and 1 C. 4:13 δυσφημούμενοι παρακαλοῦμεν whether one translates "to console," "to admonish," or "to speak good words." Theodore Mops. has the last of these for παρακαλοῦμεν at 1 C. 4:13, Staab, 177.

[173] The rendering "to enjoin," which Pr.-Bauer⁴, 1124 (though cf. 1125) proposes for Lk. 3:18; 1 Tm. 6:2; Tt. 2:15, does not have the right emphasis. What is meant is "urgently to impress on," though it is best to keep to Schlatter's rendering, "to admonish."

[174] Schl. K., 681, cf. also the fine summing-up in Schlier, 68 : "Apostolic exhortation is a concerned and urgent address to the brethren which combines supplication, comfort and admonition."

and Hb. In Hb. one may see again the connection between exhortation and comfort, for in 12:5 it refers to the biblical verse Prv. 3:11 as a word of consolation and exhortation, [175] and in 6:18 it testifies to the strong encouragement to be found in the promise which God has confirmed by an oath. Similarly the ἰσχυρὰ παρά-κλησις of 6:18 is not so much exhortation as the powerful encouragement and consolation which resists all assaults and temptations to doubt. [176] The meaning is the same when in R. 15:4, with reference to OT Scripture, Paul speaks of the comfort which the written Word gives. [177] This is the consolation which we need as those who hope. [178] If in this connection God is called the God of all constancy and consolation who as such gives the community its spiritual unity, this refers us back to the ultimate source of all genuine comfort. The connection between this comfort and the loving act of God in Christ, and the orientation of this comfort to the eschatological goal which it has precisely as God's present help, are per-fectly plain in the apostle's prayer in 2 Th. 2:16 f.: "He himself, our Lord Jesus Christ, and God our Father, who has loved us and given us eternal consolation and good hope through grace, comfort your hearts and establish them by every good work and word." [179] This comforting of the heart is an object of Paul's inner wrestling for churches not known to him personally (Col. 2:2). The sending of Tychicus (Col. 4:8, cf. Eph. 6:22) is for this purpose. The background of this need for comfort is the severe pressure of the present aeon. In particular the apostle, on whom the fulness of Christ's sufferings lies, needs and continually experiences this consoling and encouraging help from God. [180] A kind act of Philemon's, concerning which we have no more precise information, brings him great joy and consolation (Phlm. 7). The glad news that Timothy could bring about the faith of the church in Thessalonica and its relation to the apostle com-forted him in all his afflictions and distresses, 1 Th. 3:7. The coming of Titus and his good news about brighter developments in Corinth were for him a consolation of the God who comforts the lowly, 2 C. 7:6, 13. The consolation with which Titus was comforted among the Corinthians was an integral part of the comfort which the apostle received so superabundantly, 2 C. 7:4, 7, 13.

4. Comforting by Men and as God's Act.

Here as elsewhere [181] consolation is by men, but it is real comfort only because God is finally and essentially the Comforter. In the great chapter of comfort in

---

[175] Rgg. Hb.[2, 3], 394.

[176] Rgg. Hb.[2, 3], 175.

[177] Cf. Schlatter's rendering.

[178] For the reason why Pl. speaks of hope here cf. Schl. R., 381: "As in 8:24 Pl. again calls it the precious possession and essential mark of the community. It keeps them through its enduring and sustaining power and through the admonition and consolation of the words which are made holy by the fact that they have become Scripture."

[179] Cf. Schlatter's rendering.

[180] When παρακαλεῖν and παράκλησις are used for "to comfort," "consolation," "comfort," it is important to catch also the note of encouragement. This applies to the rendering of Βαρναβᾶς as υἱὸς παρακλήσεως in Ac. 4:36. For the apostles whose witness had brought him to faith he was an encouragement like the son who is a real comfort to his father by his being and nature," Zn. Ag.[3], 184. On the question of the origin and cor-rectness of this interpretation of the name, cf. ibid., 181-188, and the bibl. given there. Cr.-Kö., 573 links υἱὸς παρακλήσεως with the prophetic gift of παρακαλεῖν which Barnabas enjoyed in special measure.

[181] Cf. also the συμπαρακληθῆναι ἐν ὑμῖν of R. 1:12 which stands alongside στηριχθῆ-ναι and which Schlatter renders: "also be encouraged with you." At 2 C. 7:6 Didymus of Alex. explains the παρακαλεῖν by παραμυθίαν ὀρέγειν or παραμυθεῖσθαι, cf. Staab, op. cit., 34.

the NT God is thus extolled as the God of all comfort "who comforteth us in all our tribulation, that we may be able to comfort them which are in any trouble, by the comfort wherewith we ourselves are comforted of God," 2 C. 1:3 f. [182] Thus the fellowship of suffering between the apostle and the church becomes a fellowship of comfort, and both in rich measure, 2 C. 1:5-7. It is significant that παράκλησις and σωτηρία are used together here, and that the perseverance of the Corinthians in affliction, in which the consolation is at work, fills the apostle with sure hope for them. [183] In other words, although the reference is to consoling help through the present salvation of God, this consolation stands in the light of future deliverance. [184] It is not for nothing that παράκλησις and ἐλπίς are related here, as in 2 Th. 2:16 and R. 15:4. Being thus bathed in the divine comfort, Paul advises the Corinthians to pardon and console the man who wronged him, 2 C. 2:7. In all these cases the counteraction of comfort against affliction is by words, as expressly stated in 1 Th. 4:18. But consoling παρακαλεῖν, as distinct from beseeching or exhorting παρακαλεῖν, can be by events as well as words, [185] e.g., the coming of Titus (2 C. 7:6), the deliverance of Paul from great danger of death (cf. 2 C. 1:3 ff. with 1:8-11), and the restoration of Eutychus to life (Ac. 20:12).

When comfort is promised in Mt. 5:4 with the coming of the final salvation, the ref. is not to human words of comfort, but simply to the eschatological act of God, no matter what may be the suffering of those to whom the prospect of comfort is held out. This eschatological comfort already reaches into the present time to the degree that the πενθοῦντες who stand under the promise are already μακάριοι. [186] Conversely, the rich of Lk. 6:24 have already received their consolation in their riches, so that they cannot look for the consolation of God in the world to come. [187] When Lk. 2:25 refers to the company of those who wait for the consolation of Israel, this is the Palestinian usage which on the basis of Is. 40:1 f. speaks of the Messianic age as the divine consolation of the people of salvation. [188] This consolation comes about through the redemption of Jerusalem, Lk. 2:38. Al-

---

[182] Cf. the transl. of Schlatter. Schl. K., 464, n. 1 compares bKet., 8b בַּעַל נֶחָמוֹת יְנַחֵם אֶתְכֶם, "may he who has consolations comfort you." God comforts διὰ τοῦ Χριστοῦ (v. 5) "by causing Christ, the risen Lord and bearer of all salvation (2 C. 13:4) to show Himself to be a source of joy and strength to those visited by Him," Bchm. 2 K., 31. On θεὸς πάσης παρακλήσεως cf. R. 15:5: ὁ ... θεὸς τῆς ὑπομονῆς καὶ τῆς παρακλήσεως.

[183] Pl. in one case links deliverance with comfort "because strengthening in tribulation prepares them for the coming deliverance," and in the other he links perseverance with comfort "because the sufferings of the apostle arise not only from his special office but from his Christianity, and thus become the experience of the community," Schl. K., 465. On the textual question cf. Wnd. 2 K., 42.

[184] When Wnd. 2 K., 43 suggests that here "by way of exception the ref. is not specifically eschatological and soteriological, but to deliverance from any distress, cf. ῥύεσθαι in v. 10," it should be remembered that for the apostle all such deliverances are provisional and are to be regarded as σωτηρία only in the light of the definitive deliverance.

[185] Bchm. K., II⁴, 27 has on this the excellent note : "Even such experiences, however, are a means for divine παρακαλεῖν simply by the fact that they speak a language which goes to the heart, so that there is maintained the concept of encouragement suggested for παρακαλεῖν by the etymon (to call) and by usage (in the LXX, e.g., synon. with λαλεῖν εἰς τὴν καρδίαν τινός = דִּבֶּר עַל־לֵב, Gn. 50:21; Is. 40:2), and this is indeed an inner encouragement which establishes the spirit and has no need of outward demonstration."

[186] For examples of the interrelation between παρακαλεῖν and πενθεῖν in linguistic usage cf. Schl. Mt., 135.

[187] Cf. Schl. Lk., 243.

[188] → 792, 21 ff.

ready when Lazarus is carried by the angels into Abraham's bosom it is said of him: νῦν δὲ ὧδε παρακαλεῖται, Lk. 16:25. It is worth noting that while the apostolic community keeps this usage it does not, to the best of our knowledge, cultivate it. [189] But it does set God's consoling help through present salvation more fully in the light of the coming consummation. God finally comforts when He definitively removes all suffering by His glorious presence among men, Rev. 21:3-5. This consolation, which is given already as a good hope, is thus called an eternal consolation, 2 Th. 2:16.

5. Conclusion.

In retrospect the NT use of παρακαλεῖν and παράκλησις may be summed up as follows. The possibilities presented by the wealth of meanings of παρακαλεῖν are very freely set in the service of testimony to the NT event of salvation. The sense "to call in" fades completely into the background. Of the three uses in which one who calls addresses another, the sense "to ask," which is very common elsewhere, is used predominantly for turning to Jesus with requests for help during His earthly life and within the account of the primitive Christian mission. It is striking how seldom the word occurs for calling on God or the risen Christ in prayer. The noun means either "request" or "invocation in prayer." The use of παρακαλεῖν for "to exhort," which is common in both the Greek and Hellenistic Jewish world, though almost completely absent from the translation Greek of the LXX, serves in the NT to denote missionary proclamation and also as a kind of formula to introduce pastoral admonition. For both forms of exhortation, which include both the element of beseeching and also that of encouraging, apostolic usage has the noun too. The meaning "to comfort," "comfort," "consolation," which is rare in both the Greek world and Hellenistic Judaism, but the more common in the translation Greek of the LXX, is influenced by the OT, and especially by Is. (and the Ps.) when the reference is to salvation history (cf. the "consolation of Israel" in later Judaism). It expresses the divine aid which is already lavishly granted to the members of the suffering community of Jesus by present exhortation and encouraging events, and which will reach its goal when the NT people of God is delivered out of all its tribulations.

If "asking" presupposes that the salvation of God is manifested in Jesus, "exhortation," being effected by the Spirit, is based on the salvation already accomplished, and "comfort" or "consolation" takes place through the present and future act of God Himself to salvation. Hence it is hardly too much to say that, as defined by the NT act of salvation, παρακαλεῖν and παράκλησις may be traced back to the saving work of the triune God which leads those in need of help as suppliants to the Son of God, which is preached as exhortation in the power of the Spirit of God, and which carries with it already in this time the eternal comfort of God the Father.

Schmitz

παράκειμαι → III, 656, 4 ff.

---

189 Paul Gerhardt is echoing this usage when in his hymn "I am a guest on earth" he refers to the home where "my Father will grant me consolations without measure."

| † παράκλητος | → παρακαλέω, 773, 7 ff. |

Contents: A. The Linguistic Problem: 1. Use outside the NT: a. In Greek; b. In the LXX; c. In the Rabbis; d. In Philo; e. In Early Christian Literature. 2. The Meaning in the NT. B. The Historico-Religious Background of the NT Concept: 1. The Helper: a. In Mandaean Writings; b. In the Odes of Solomon. 2. The Advocate: a. In the OT; b. In the Apocrypha and Pseudepigrapha; c. In the Rabbis; d. In the NT. C. The NT Concept.

In the NT this word is peculiar to the Johannine writings. In 1 Jn. 2:1 the epithet παράκλητος is applied to the exalted Jesus Christ. Four times in the Parting Discourses of the Fourth Gospel (14:16 [cf. 17], 26; 15:26; 16:7 [cf. 13]) the → πνεῦμα which is to be imparted to the disciples after Jesus goes, the Holy Spirit or Spirit of truth, is described as παράκλητος. The expression ἄλλον παράκλητον in 14:16 shows that the Evangelist uses the predicate primarily for Jesus Himself as the One sent by God to the earth. [1]

A. The Linguistic Problem.

1. Use Outside the NT.

a. In Gk. As a verbal adj. παράκλητος has a pass. sense, corresponding to παρακεκλημένος, [2] so perhaps BGU, II, 601, 11 f. (2nd cent. A.D.): τὸν ἀραβῶνα τοῦ

π α ρ ά κ λ η τ ο ς. G. C. Knapp, "De Spiritu sancto et Christo Paracletis," Scripta varii argumenti, I² (1823), 115-152; H. Usener, "Precator," Archiv f. lat. Lexikographie, 2 (1885), 228-232; J. B. Lightfoot, On a Fresh Revision of the English NT³ (1891), 56; Liddell-Scott, s.v.; Pr.-Bauer⁴, 1126 f.; Moult.-Mill., 485; Sophocles Lex., s.v.; Cr.-Kö., 571-573; J. Hastings, Art. "Paraclete," Hastings DB, III, 665-668; Zn. J.⁵, ⁶, 563-572; A. E. Brooke, The Johannine Epistles, ICC (1912), 23-27; Str.-B., II, 560-562; Deissmann LO, 285 f.; H. Sasse, "Der Paraklet im Joh.-Ev.," ZNW, 24 (1925), 260-277; F. Büchsel, Der Geist Gottes im NT (1926), 497-504; H. Windisch, "Die fünf johann. Parakletsprüche," Festschr. A. Jülicher (1927), 110-137; Schl. J., 297 f.; R. Asting, "'Parakleten' i Johannes-evangeliet," Teologi og kirkeliv. Avhandlinger til den eksegetiske forening "Syvstjernen"s 60-årsjubileum (1931), 85-98; S. Mowinckel, "Die Vorstellungen d. Spätjudentums vom heiligen Geist als Fürsprecher u. d. joh. Paraklet," ZNW, 32 (1933), 97-130; Bau. J.³, 182 f.; M. J. Lagrange, Évangile selon St. Jean⁵ (1936), 381-385; Eichr. Theol. AT, III (1939), 129 f.; Bu. J., 437-440; N. Johansson, Parakletoi (1940); cf. W. G. Kümmel, Svensk exegetisk Årsbok, 6 (1941), 120-130; N. H. Snaith, "The Meaning of the 'Paraclete,'" Exp. T., 57 (1945), 47 ff.; H. Michaelis, "Zur Herkunft d. joh. Paraklet-Titels," Coniectanea Neotestamentica, 11 (1947), 147-162; G. Bornkamm, "Der Paraklet im Joh.-Ev.," Festschr. R. Bultmann (1950), 12-35; N. H. Snaith, Distinctive Ideas of the OT (1944), 180 f.; C. K. Barrett, "The Holy Spirit in the Fourth Gospel," JThSt, New Series, 1 (1950), 1-15; C. H. Dodd, The Johannine Epistles (1946), 24 f.

[1] The difficulty of this odd description of the historical Jesus cannot be solved by excising the ἄλλον (cf. Windisch, 114 as against J. Wellhausen, Das Ev. Joh. [1908], 65 and F. Spitta, Das Joh.-Ev. [1910], 346). Michaelis, too, doubts whether Jesus is the first paraclete in Jn. 14:16 (152 f.); he thinks ἄλλος might be used pleonastically in the sense that "at my request the Father will give you another, i.e., as paraclete (or another, namely, the paraclete)." But this forced explanation, foreshadowed in part in E. W. Hengstenberg, Das Ev. d. heiligen Joh. erläutert, III² (1870), 43 or C. E. Luthardt, Das joh. Ev., II² (1876), 330, is difficult to harmonise with John's style (though A. Debrunner in a letter takes a different view) and is not in accord with the exegesis of the Gk. fathers, cf. Chrys. Hom. in Joh., 75 (MPG, 59, 403-410) or Greg. Nyss. Eunom., II (ibid., 45, 552). (More recently Bornkamm has argued for a parallelism between Jesus and the ἄλλος παράκλητος similar to the relation between the Baptist and Jesus: as the Baptist is the precursor of Jesus, so is Jesus of the Spirit. But 1 Jn. 2:1 is against this. Cf. also Bu. J., Ergänzungsheft [1950], 41 [Seesemann]).

Σαραπίωνος παρακλος (= παράκλητος, "summoned") [3] δέδωκα αὐτῷ. [4] The use as noun, attested in secular Gk. from the 4th cent. B.C. in the sense of a "person called in to help, summoned to give assistance," gives us the meaning of "helper in court," [5] Demosth. Or., 19, 1: αἱ ... τῶν παρακλήτων ... δεήσεις καὶ σπουδαὶ τῶν ἰδίων πλεονεξιῶν εἵνεκα γίγνονται, [6] Mimus Fr. in the British Museum, No. 1984, line 7 f. (2nd cent. A.D.), [7] where one actor says: οὐ χρῶμαί σοι οὔτε κριτῇ <οὔτε> παρα-κρήτῳ, and another emends to παρακλήτῳ (as advocate). Even when there is no ref. to a representative in court, the idea is still more or less clearly legal, e.g., Diog. L., IV, 50, where Bion shakes off a persistent petitioner with the decision: τὸ ἱκανόν σοι ποιήσω, ἐὰν παρακλήτους (representative) πέμψῃς καὶ αὐτὸς μὴ ἔλθῃς, or Heracl. Hom. All., 59e, which calls Priam's pathetic saying to Achilles about the body of Hector τῆς ἱκετείας παράκλητον (advocate). There is no instance of παράκλητος, like its Lat. equivalent advocatus, being used as a tt. for the professional legal adviser or defender of an accused person in the same sense as σύνδικος or συνήγορος. [8] But the use of παράκλητος for representative is to be understood in the light of legal assistance in court, the pleading of another's case, Dion. Hal. Ant. Rom., XI, 37, 1: τῶν τὰ δίκαια λεγόντων παράκλητοι. [9] The act. element brought to expression here derives from the functions of such a παράκλητος. We are debarred from seeing a link with the act. παρακαλεῖν, [10] at least in profane Gk., by the actual use of παράκλητος in a sense which is quite alien to the act. of the verb.

b. In the LXX. παράκλητος does not occur in the LXX. At Job 16:2 'A and Θ have παράκλητοι for מְנַחֲמִים (LXX παρακλήτορες, Σ παρηγοροῦντες); they this take the word act. for "comforters," but this is unusual in Jewish usage too. [11] Josephus [12] does not have παράκλητος, but has the compounds ἀπαράκλητος and δυσπαρά-κλητος, which he takes pass. [13] (Bell., 6, 190: a suffered loss πρὸς καιρὸν μὲν 'Ρω-μαίοις ἐνεποίησεν ἀθυμίαν, πρὸς δὲ τὸ μέλλον ὅμως ἀπαρακλήτους κατεσκεύα-σεν, Ant., 16, 151: [a characterisation of Herod the Gt.] τὸ σκληρὸν καὶ τὸ δυσπαρά-κλητον [14] ["difficult to placate," "unyielding"] τοῦ τρόπου). The thought of God as

---

[2] Cf., e.g., Aeschin. Tim., 1, 173.

[3] Corresponding to the gerundive παρακλητέος, Plut. Suav. Viv. Epic., 24 (II, 1104a); Luc. Pseudolog., 4.

[4] For a development of the use of παράκλητος in the early Church which deviates from the etym. → n. 36.

[5] On παράκλητοι in Gk. law cf. K. F. Hermann-V. Thumser, Lehrbuch d. gr. Staats-altertümer, I[6] (1889), 597 f., and on similar ideas in Hell. law cf. L. Mitteis, Reichsrecht u. Volksrecht in den östlichen Provinzen d. röm. Kaiserreiches (1891), 150, 189-196, also bibl. in Deissmann LO, 286.

[6] The fr. from the Attic orator Lyc., contemporary of Demosth., in Phot. Lex., II, 56. παράκλητος ὡς ἡμεῖς εἴρηκεν Λυκοῦργος, is no help.

[7] APF, 6 (1920), 4 f., cf. Deissmann LO, 285, n. 9.

[8] Still the word for a legal advocate in modern Gk.

[9] The use of παράκλητοι in Dio C., 46, 20, 1 for the noisy partisans with whom Cicero as consul packed the forum and capitol seems to be a caricature.

[10] So Snaith, "Meaning," 50. Zn. J.[5, 6], 564 f. postulates a fusion of the ideas of παρα-καλεῖν and παράκλητος in general linguistic feeling, with apparent theoretical justification, v. Kühner-Blass, II, 289, but in practice there is not the attestation present from classical times on for παρακλητικός, παρακλήτωρ, παρακλήτρια = παρακαλῶν v. Thes. Steph., Pass., Pape, Liddell-Scott, s.v. One would expect a παρακλήτης in the act., but (acc. to Liddell-Scott) this does not exist [Debrunner].

[11] On Zech. 1:13 LXX λόγους παρακλητικούς, "comforting words," → n. 10.

[12] Cf. Schl. J., 297.

[13] In keeping with general usage (Liddell-Scott and Moult.-Mill., s.v.), e.g., Plut. Pyth. Or., 19 (II, 403b): καὶ παρακαλούμενος καὶ ἀπαράκλητος, Ditt. Or., 248, 25 (2nd cent. B.C.); Jn. Mosch. (MPG, 87, 2905 B). ἀπαραίτητος is used similarly, e.g., Plut. Pyrrhus, 16, 3 (I, 392e); Poplicola, 3, 5 (I, 98e).

[14] vl. δυσπαραίτητον. On δυσπαράκλητος, "one with whom nothing can be achieved by asking," v. Schol. on Soph. Oed. Tyr., 334, where ἀτελεύτητος, "one with whom nothing can be effected," is explained by it, cf. Scholia in Soph. Tragoedias vetera, ed. P. N. Papageorgius (1888), 181 [C. Kappus].

one who may be called in to help (Ant., 1, 268 : τὸν θεὸν ταῖς εὐχαῖς ... παρα-
κεκλημένον, v. previously σύμμαχον ... καὶ συνεργόν) suggests that Jos. understood
παράκλητος analogously.

c. In the Rabbis. In the Heb. or Aram. of the Rabbis, in their religious vocabulary,
פְּרַקְלִיט (or פְּרַקְלֵיט) or פְּרַקְלִיטָא (or פְּרַקְלִיטָא) became a common loan word [15] in the
sense of "advocate," related in meaning to סְנִיגוֹר (or סָנֵיגוֹר) = συνήγορος, "counsel,"
"defender" (antonym קַטֵיגוֹר [or קַטֵיגוֹר] or קַטֵיגוֹרָא = κατήγορος, κατήγωρ → III,
636, 15 f. and n. 2, "accuser"). It always denoted an advocate before God, e.g., Ab.,
4, 11a (R. Eliezer b. Jaaqob): הָעוֹשֶׂה מִצְוָה אֶחָת קָנָה לוֹ פְּרַקְלִיט אֶחָד וְהָעוֹבֵר עֲבֵרָה אֶחָת קָנָה לוֹ
קַטֵיגוֹר אֶחָד תְּשׁוּבָה וּמַעֲשִׂים טוֹבִים כִּתְרִיס לִפְנֵי הַפֻּרְעָנוּת ("as a shield in the judgment"); Ex. r.,
18, 3 (on 12:29): Moses a פְּרַקְלִיט טוֹב; bShab., 32a : "If someone is led to the place of
judgment to be judged, he can be saved if he has great advocates (פְּרַקְלִיטִין גְּדוֹלִין), and
these are the פְּרַקְלִיטִין of a man : conversion and good works"; bBB, 10a (R. Eleazar
b. R. Jose): "All the benevolences and good works which the Israelites do in this
world ... are great advocates between the Israelites and their Father in heaven
(פְּרַקְלִיטִין גְּדוֹלִין בֵּין יִשְׂרָאֵל לַאֲבִיהֶן שֶׁבַּשָּׁמַיִם); S. Lv., 277a on 14:19 f. (R. Shimon): The sin-
offering is like the פְּרַקְלִיט, which comes forward to appease (sc. the judge)"; Tg.
Job 33:23 : "If a man has merits, an angel intervenes as advocate among 1000 accusers
(חֲדָא פְּרַקְלִיטָא מִן בֵּינִי אֶלֶף קַטֵיגוֹרַיָּא); ibid., 16:20 : פְּרַקְלִיטֵי חַבְרַיי, "my advocates my friends"
etc. [16]

d. In Philo. The word also means "advocate" consistently in Philo. [17] Here advocates
in the strict legal sense are those who speak before rulers on behalf of the accused,
Flacc., 13, 151, 181, cf. 22 : δεῖ δὴ παράκλητον ἡμᾶς εὑρεῖν δυνατώτατον, ὑφ' οὗ
Γάϊος ἐξευμενισθήσεται, [18] Jos., 239 : μηδενὸς ἑτέρου δεῖσθε παρακλήτου, says
Joseph to his brothers to show them his pardoning magnanimity. Fig. the idea serves in
Philo Op. Mund., 165 to portray the psychological process in sinning. The senses extend
to reason the gifts with which desire has bemused them as servants do to their master,
παράκλητον ἐπαγόμεναι πειθώ (the art of persuasion), that it may not decline them.
Applying the spiritualised conception to man's situation before God's judgment throne,
Philo speaks esp. of παράκλητοι in the religious sense, of advocates for sinners before
God. In Exsecr., 166 (τρισὶ χρησάμενοι παρακλήτοις τῶν πρὸς τὸν πατέρα καταλ-
λαγῶν) these are God's pardoning lovingkindness, the pious intercessions of the patriarchs of the people, and the conversion of sinners themselves. Acc. to Spec. Leg.,
I, 237 (ἐπαγόμενος παράκλητον οὐ μεμπτὸν τὸν κατὰ ψυχὴν ἔλεγχον) the penitent
cheat, who seeks forgiveness for his sins in the sanctuary, brings the accusations of his
conscience as advocates against whom no objection can be lodged. In Vit. Mos., II, 134
the advocate of the high-priest when he officiates in the temple in search of remission
of sins and felicity is the rich adornment of his garment, which symbolises the whole
universe, God's perfect son : ἀναγκαῖον γὰρ ἦν τὸν ἱερωμένον τῷ τοῦ κόσμου

[15] The word must have been much more common in everyday Hell. use than its literary
use would lead one to suppose, v. Deissmann LO, 286, n. 4.

[16] Cf. S. Krauss, Gr. u. lat. Lehnwörter in Talmud, Midrasch u. Targum (1898/99),
I, 210; II, 496; Dalman Gr., 185; J. Buxtorf-B. Fischer, Lex. chaldaicum, talmudicum et
rabbinicum (1869 ff.), 916; Levy Wört.², IV, 139; Levy Chald. Wört., II, 300; Dalman
Wört.³ (1938), 353; Str.-B., II, 560-562; M. Jastrow, A Dict. of the Targumim etc. (1926),
1241.

[17] On the material in Philo cf. Bu. J., 438 and Johansson, 286-295. In Philo παραιτητής
is synon. with παράκλητος, → IV, 617, 31, for examples cf. Bu. J., 438, n. 4; cf. παραιτούμενος, Test. L. 5:6; D. 6:2.

[18] Ibid., 23 : ὁ δὲ παράκλητος ... παρακλητεύσει. The verb "to be, to come forward
as, an advocate" seems to have been coined in the koine for the activity of the advocate.
It occurs on an inscr. of Thuria (50 B.C.-50 A.D.), line 3, ed. N. S. Valmin, "Inscr. de la
Messénie," Kungliga Humanistiska vetenskapssamfundet i Lund, Årsberättelse (1928/29),
123-127.

πατρὶ παρακλήτῳ χρῆσθαι τελειοτάτῳ τὴν ἀρετὴν υἱῷ πρός τε ἀμνηστίαν ἁμαρτημάτων καὶ χορηγίαν ἀφθονωτάτων ἀγαθῶν. [19] Even in Op. Mund., 23, which refers to the equipment of nature with rich and lavish gifts by God's free grace without the co-operation of any παράκλητος (οὐδενὶ παρακλήτῳ — τίς γὰρ ἦν ἕτερος; — μόνῳ δὲ αὐτῷ χρησάμενος ὁ θεός), the idea of the advocate is dominant in sublimated form. There can be no doubt as to the unequivocal meaning which the word παράκλητος had for Philo. [20]

e. In Early Christian Literature. In early Christian literature, so far as it was not influenced by the paraclete passages in the NT, παράκλητος is understood in just the same way as in later Judaism. Acc. to Did., 5, 2 = Barn., 20, 2 (the doctrine of the two ways — of Jewish origin?) there are on the way of death πλουσίων παράκλητοι, πενήτων ἄνομοι κριταί, those who act anti-socially in legal matters, advocates who help the rich, [21] but judge the poor unjustly. For Cl. Al. συνήγορος and παράκλητος are related in meaning, Quis Div. Salv., 25, 7 → 805, 3-5. In Eus. Hist. Eccl., V, 1, 10 (Letter of the Churches of Lyons and Vienne) it is said of Epagathos, who defended the persecuted brethren before the governor: παράκλητος Χριστιανῶν χρηματίσας. [22] 2 Cl., 6, 9: τίς ἡμῶν παράκλητος ἔσται, ἐὰν μὴ εὑρεθῶμεν ἔργα ἔχοντες ὅσια καὶ δίκαια; is an exact par. to bShab., 32a, → 802, 11-13.

Thus the history of the term in the whole sphere of known Greek and Hellenistic usage outside the NT yields the clear picture of a legal adviser or helper or advocate in the relevant court. The passive form does not rule out the idea of the παράκλητος as an active speaker "on behalf of someone before someone," [23] nor is there any need of recourse to the active of παρακαλέω in this connection. [24] That in one instance the rendering of the Hebrew OT into Greek produces the subsidiary sense of "comforter" for παράκλητος is an exception which the history of the word alone can hardly explain, [25] → 801, 21 ff.

2. The Meaning in the NT.

The use of the term παράκλητος in the NT, though restricted to the Johannine writings, [26] does not make any consistent impression, nor does it fit smoothly into the history of the word as described → 800-803. In 1 Jn. 2:1, where Jesus Christ is called the παράκλητος of sinning Christians before the Father, the meaning is obviously "advocate," and the image of a trial before God's court determines the meaning. In Jn. 16:7-11 (cf. 15:26) we again find the idea of a trial in which the Paraclete, the Spirit, appears (16:8-11). The Spirit, however, is not the defender

---

[19] For an understanding of the passage cf. L. Cohn, Die Werke Philos v. Alex. in deutscher Übers., I (1909), 329, n. 1, also P. Feine, Theol. d. NT[7] (1936), 353, and Dodd, 24.

[20] Cf. esp. Johansson, 286-295. The same insight in Bu. J., 438 is weakened by consideration of the meaning "mediator" (par. to μεσίτης → IV, 617, 8-42 and διαλλάκτής) or "helper," which does not contain the essential thought of παράκλητος, that of speaking on someone's behalf. The general sense of "adviser" favoured in some cases by Pr.-Bauer, Zn. J. and Lagrange is not in accord with the basic legal conception.

[21] Lat. divitum advocati.

[22] Rufinus: advocatus Christianorum.

[23] Bu. J., 438; Mowinckel, 118: "The one who represents and helps another with words."

[24] Mowinckel, 118, n. 75: "It is philologically unjustifiable to define the living sense of a current word by the customary and not even the etym. meaning of the underlying verb; in innumerable cases verbs and nouns have gone their separate ways."

[25] May one conclude with Bu. J., 438 that the twofold definition of the structure of the παράκλητος concept is sometimes abandoned under the influence of the sense "to comfort" for παρακαλεῖν?

[26] Jn. and 1 Jn., the only works in question, are treated here as a literary unity in terms of usage and understanding. Problems of sources and literary criticism are not considered except in so far as demanded by the task in hand.

of the disciples before God [27] but their counsel in relation to the world. Nor is the legal metaphor adhered to strictly. [28] What is said about the sending, activity and nature of this paraclete (16:7, 13-15; 15:26; 14:16 f., 26) belongs to a very different sphere, and here (cf. Jesus in 14:16) παράκλητος seems to have the broad and general sense of "helper." [29] The only thing one can say for certain is that the sense of "comforter," favoured by, e.g., Wycliffe, Luther and the A.V. in John's Gospel, [30] does not fit any of the NT passages. [31] Neither Jesus nor the Spirit is described as a "comforter." [32] There is no sign in the texts that παράκλητος is taken to be equivalent to παρακαλῶν. παρακαλέω and παράκλησις do not occur in the vocabulary of Jn. (including Rev.) (→ 793, 14-17). [33]

---

[27] Nor the advocate of God or Christ before men (Cr.-Kö., 571 f.), which involves an unwarranted shift of thought.

[28] The interpretation of Schlatter and Büchsel that in Jn. 14 ff. the disciples are the accused whose life and work are shot through by dispute with the world, but who always have counsel at their side in this dispute (Schl. J., 298, cf. Schl. Gesch. d. Chr.[1], 460 f., Schl. Theol. d. Ap., 152, 177 and F. Büchsel, *Der Geist Gottes im NT* [1926], 498, n. 8 and *NT Deutsch* on Jn. 14:16 etc.) is exaggerated.

[29] To say that this is the exclusive sense in the Fourth Gospel (e.g., Bau. J. on 14:16 and Bu. J., 437-440) is to leave out of account one aspect of the Johannine understanding.

[30] Calvin on Jn. 14:16 (In Joh. Comm., ed. A. Tholuck, III [1833], 274) tried to combine the meanings *consolator* and *patronus*. The attempt of Snaith "Meaning" to give to παράκλητος in Jn. the new sense of "convincer" ("he who convinces men of the things of God, and accomplishes in them a change of heart") is neither semasiologically nor exegetically tenable.

[31] Lagrange, 382 f. and Büchsel, 499 n. have made this abundantly clear. Nevertheless it should be remembered that Luther was influenced by the older concrete meaning of *Trost*. The root is the same as that of *Treue* and *Trotz*, and corresponds to the English "trust." At bottom is an Indo-European *deru* or *dreu*, which is etym. related to the Gk. δρῦς ("oak"), and the Gothic *triu*, and which thus means "strong, firm, hard, lasting as a tree" (cf. also the English "comfort" as distinct from "consolation"). The original content, then, is that of one who gives protection, help or security, with concrete ref. to an act or intervention for someone. In this sense the group is often used in law for the "security" and more rarely for the "advocate." In the religious sphere the word *Trost* was used c. 700 in S. W. German missionary circles for *consolatio, solamen*, etc., since there was no real equivalent. Only gradually did it make its way northward against the words chosen by Heliand and the German Tatian (*frôfra, frôfor, frôbra*), and not until the Reformation period did it hold sway in the whole Germanic world, including the North. There *Trost* often has the sense of strength or help (cf. "comfort"), and is frequently personified, esp. with ref. to Jesus. In Luther we often find the religious combination *Trost und Trotz*, in the sense of "confidence and strength," "refuge and might" etc. One can even find in Luther the idea of *Trost* against something. Thus he says that the Holy Spirit gives strength and comforts the shy and weak and timid conscience against the accusations and assaults of sins. Only in New High German usage does the term cease to denote an action and come to be used almost exclusively to express varied emotions in the manifold spheres of human life and experience. Acc. to the older meaning of the group the *nomen agentis* "comforter" denotes the helper or support in the legal sense of "guarantor" or more rarely "advocate," "representative." It can thus be used for God or Christ, but more esp. for the Holy Spirit on the basis of Jn. 14:16, 26; 15:26; 16:7. Cf. J. W. Grimm, *Deutsches Wörterb.*, XI, 1 (1937), 901-943, *s.v.* "Trost"; F. Kluge, and A. Götze, *Etym. Wörterb. d. deutschen Sprache*[15] (1951), 809 [Bertram].

[32] The Johannine Paraclete bears no relation to the later Jewish Messianic title מְנַחֵם "comforter" (Str.-B., I, 66; W. Staerk, *Soter* [1933], 113), as against Bousset-Gressm., 227; (cf. H. Gressmann, *Der Messias* [1929], 460 f.); *v.* Bu. J., 439, n. 4.

[33] Hence the view in Zn. J. that the παράκλητος is one who gives encouragement, the teacher of the heart and conscience (→ 806, 8-11; cf. T. Zahn, *Grundriss d. nt.lichen Theol.* [1928], 49, also Feine, *op. cit.*, 369) hardly does justice to the Johannine passages, whether linguistically or materially. The same is true of the assumption of Asting that the word means "proclaimer," "preacher" in Jn. in keeping with the act. of παρακαλέω.

The history of the word in early Christian usage as this is influenced by the employment of the term in the NT is very complicated. [34] On the basis of 1 Jn. 2:1 the Gk. fathers understood Christ as παράκλητος in the sense of "advocate." The idea of legal counsel persists in Cl. Al. Quis Div. Salv., 25, 7: τὸν τῆς σῆς συνήγορον καὶ παράκλητον ψυχῆς. [35] In Orig. Princ., II, 7, 4 (GCS, 22, 151) παράκλητος = deprecator acc. to the transl. of Rufinus. New in Orig. is the act. sense for Christ's intercessory work, v. Orat., 10, 2 (GCS, 3, 320): πρὸς τὸν πατέρα "παράκλητός" ἐστιν ὁ υἱὸς τοῦ θεοῦ, εὐχόμενος ὑπὲρ τῶν εὐχομένων καὶ συμπαρακαλῶν τοῖς παρακαλοῦσιν, Comm. in Joh., I, 33 (GCS, 10, 42): τὴν περὶ ἡμῶν πρὸς τὸν πατέρα προστασίαν αὐτοῦ δηλοῖ, παρακαλοῦντος ὑπὲρ τῆς ἀνθρώπων φύσεως ... ὡς "ὁ παράκλητος" or Princ., II, 7, 4 (GCS, 22, 152): in salvatore nomen "paracleti" pro deprecatore intelligendum videtur; deprecari enim patrem „pro peccatis nostris" dicitur. [36] In the oldest Gk. witness, the story of the martyrs in S. Gaul in 177/178 (Eus. Hist. Eccl., V, 1, 10) the Spirit's title παράκλητος in Jn. means "advocate." Concerning the brother who voluntarily represented the brethren at their trial, and who was thus called the παράκλητος Χριστιανῶν (→ 803, 14 ff.), it is said immediately after in a play on words: ἔχων δὲ τὸν παράκλητον ἐν ἑαυτῷ, τὸ πνεῦμα τοῦ Ζαχαρίου [37] (cf. Lk. 1:67). But many Gk. fathers take παράκλητος in Jn. in the sense of "comforter" on the basis of the act. of the verb. Cf. first Eus. De Ecclesiastica Theologia, III, 5, 11 f.: τὸ πνεῦμα τῆς ἀληθείας τὸ παράκλητον [38] πρὸς τὸ παρακαλεῖν αὐτοὺς καὶ παραμυθεῖσθαι ... καὶ πρὸς τὸ διδάξαι αὐτοὺς πᾶσαν τὴν ἀλήθειαν ... τῆς καινῆς διαθήκης, where obviously the understanding rests not merely on detailed functions of the Johannine Paraclete but on the general aim of the Parting Discourses to comfort the disciples as their Master leaves them (cf. Jn. 14:1-3, 18 f., 27 f.; 16:1-4, 20-23, 33). [39] Cf. also Chrys. Hom. in Joh., 75 (MPG, 59, 403): ἐπειδὴ γὰρ οὐδέπω αὐτὸν ἐγνωκότας εἰκὸς ἦν σφόδρα ἐπιζητεῖν τὴν συνουσίαν ἐκείνην, τὰ ῥήματα, τὴν κατὰ σάρκα αὐτοῦ παρουσίαν, καὶ μηδεμίαν δέχεσθαι παραμυθίαν ἀπόντος·

---

[34] Cf. Zn. J.[5, 6], 564-567; Bau. J. on 14:16; Brooke, 25 f.; Lagrange, 381-385; Bu. J., 437-440.

[35] Cf. Iren. Haer., III, 17, 3: ubi accusatorem habemus, illic habeamus et paracletum, though with ref. to the Spirit (unlike the NT).

[36] So also later writers like Oecumenius on 1 Jn. 2:1 (MPG, 119, 629 D): παράκλητον ... τὸν ὑπὲρ ἡμῶν φησι τὸν πατέρα παρακαλοῦντα. Ps.-Bas. Hom. adv. Calumniam Sanctae Trinitatis (MPG, 31, 1493 A) even explains the Spirit's title παράκλητος as follows: ὁ περὶ σοῦ παρακαλῶν. παράκλητος may be the name of an aeon in Valentinian Gnosticism (Iren. Haer., I, 1, 2; Hipp. Ref., VI, 30, 5, cf. on this K. Müller, "Beiträge zum Verständnis d. valentinianischen Gnosis," NGG [1920], 217-219), but this is not certain. Cf. also F. Sagnard, La Gnose Valentinienne (1947). Montanus, Mani, Mohammed etc., in claiming to be the promised Paraclete, took the title from Jn. or the tradition influenced by Jn. without any explanation of the term. Nor do we know what is meant by addressing Jesus as παράκλητος in prayer (P. Oxy., VI, 850, 10, 4th cent. A.D.; Fr. from Act. Joh., text defective), or by παράκλητος as applied to the Christ child which appears to Matthew, Mart. Mt., 2 (ed. R. A. Lipsius-M. Bonnet, Acta Apostolorum Apocr., II, 1 [1898], 219, 2). Nor can one say what Paraqlitos means as a magical name in an Abyssinian magic text, v. W. H. Worrell, "Studien z. abessinischen Zauberwesen," Zeitschrift f. Assyriologie, 24 (1910), 94.

[37] Rufinus: ille vero habens in se advocatum pro nobis Jesum. As distinct from the original, this makes the saying a christological statement.

[38] The adj. use of παράκλητος (→ 800, 16 f.) in the sense "comforting," as found already in the expression τὸ παράκλητον πνεῦμα in Hipp. Ref., VIII, 19, 1 (cf. also Mak. Hom., 6, 6 [MPG, 34, 521 C]: ἔπεμψε ... τὸ πνεῦμα τὸ παράκλητον εἰς τοὺς δώδεκα ἀποστόλους), is obviously a development of ecclesiastical speech on the basis of Jn. 14:16 f.; 15:26.

[39] Cf. Theod. Mops. Comment. in Ev. Joh. (Syr. text, ed. J. B. Chabot [1897], 307 f.). Since in all Gk. lit. παράκλητος is taken in the sense of "comforter" only in patristic exegesis of Jn., and here on plausible material grounds, there is much to be said for the conjecture of Hastings, 666 (cf. also Cr.-Kö., 572) that 'A and Θ were influenced by ancient Johannine exegesis when they rendered מְנַחֲמִים by παράκλητοι at Job 16:2 (→ 801, 21-23).

τί φησιν "ἐρωτήσω τὸν πατέρα καὶ ἄλλον παράκλητον δώσει ὑμῖν" (Jn. 14:16)·
τουτέστιν ἄλλον ὡς ἐμέ, or Greg. Nyss. Eunom., II (MPG, 45, 552 B): διπλῆς δὲ
οὔσης τῆς τοῦ "παρακαλεῖν" σημασίας ..., τῶν καθ' ἑκάτερον σημαινομένων
ἐπίσης ἡ ἁγία γραφὴ προσμαρτυρεῖ τῇ θείᾳ φύσει τοῦ παρακλήτου τὴν ἔννοιαν.
In Cyr. Cat. Myst., XVI, 20 (MPG, 33, 948 A): Παράκλητος ... καλεῖται διὰ τὸ
παρακαλεῖν καὶ παραμυθεῖσθαι καὶ συναντιλαμβάνεσθαι τῆς ἀσθενείας ἡμῶν·
... δῆλον δέ, ὅτι πρὸς τὸν θεόν, the meanings "comforter" and "advocate" are interfused. Theod. Mops. In Joh. on 14:16 (MPG, 66, 777 A) equates παράκλητος and
διδάσκαλος, a view echoed in Euthymius Zig. (MPG, 129, 1400 A), but along with the
idea of support: παράκλητος = παραινέτης καὶ ἀλείπτης ἐν τοῖς ἄθλοις τῆς
ἀρετῆς, καὶ ψυχαγωγία ἐν ταῖς θλίψεσι καὶ ἀντίληψις.

For the Latin fathers παράκλητος is often *advocatus* in the technical sense, e.g.,
Tert. De Ieiunio, 13: *paracletus id est advocatus ad exorandum judicem*; Adv. Praxeam,
9: "*alium advocatum*" ... *sic alium a se paracletum*; Hilarius De Trinitate, VIII, 19:
cum venerit advocatus ille. But *consolator* is equally common, [40] e.g., Hilarius Tractatus
super Psalmos, 125, 7: *mittet vobis et alium consolatorem*, Jer. Ep. ad Hedibiam, 120, 9:
qui appellatur consolator. Rufinus in his transl. of Orig. Princ., II, 7, 4 (GCS, 22, 151 f.)
has: "*Paracletus*" ... *quod dicitur spiritus sanctus, a consolatione dicitur* (παράκλησις
enim latine consolatione appellatur) ... *Videtur de salvatore "paracletus" dici deprecator, utrumque enim significat in graeco "paracletus" et "consolator" et "deprecator,"*
cf. the observation of Aug. In Joh. Ev. Tract., 94, 2 (on 16:4): *consolator ergo ille vel
advocatus (utrumque enim interpretatur quod est graece paracletus).*

Of early NT translations [41] the Codd. of Vetus Latina, if they do not keep to the Gk.
forms *paracletus* or *paraclitus*, usually have *advocatus*, though also *consolator.* The Vg
has *paracletus* in Jn, *advocatus* in 1 Jn. All East Syr. versions have the transcription
פרקליטא.[42] In the Palestinian Syr. of Jn. we find מנחמן, "comforter." [43] Also in the
Coptic texts (Bohairic and Sahidic) the alien παράκλητος is used consistently; only at
1 Jn. 2:1 does the Sahidic have "the one who prays for us." [44]

Neither semasiological investigation of the term nor the attempt to reach a
conclusion from its understanding in the early Church leads to any assured results.
One has to ask, therefore, whether the solution to the riddle lies in the history
of thought. [45] Are there in the religious history of the world surrounding the NT
ideas which explain the use of the epithet παράκλητος for Christ and the Spirit
in the NT ?

B. The Historico-Religious Background of the NT Concept.

Opinions differ as to the genealogy of the religious ideas which the Johannine
writings associate with the word παράκλητος. [46] On the one side the figures of
heavenly helpers, which play a notable role in Gnosticism, namely, in the Mandaean

---

[40] Cf. *advocator* in Tert. Marc., IV, 15: (God) *divitum aspernatorem ... mendicorum
advocatorem*, cf. *ibid.*, 14: *advocare languentes* for παρακαλέσαι τοὺς πενθοῦντας (Is.
61:2). On *advocare* = παρακαλεῖν, *advocatio* = παράκλησις v. H. Rönsch, *Itala u.
Vulgata*[2] (1875), 348; 305; on *advocare*, H. Rönsch, *Semasiologische Beiträge zum lat.
Wörterb.*, H. 3 (1889), 6, *advocator, ibid.*, H. 1 (1888), 6. Cf. also Thes. Ling. Lat., I
(1900), 890, 72 ff.; 891, 9 ff.; 892, 45 ff. [Debrunner].

[41] On the versions in general cf. Hastings, 667.

[42] Occasionally the sense of "comforter" may be found in exegetes (Ephraem etc.), v.
Zn. J.[5, 6], 564, n. 30; Bau. J., on 14:16.

[43] Cf. Zn. J.[5, 6], 565, n. 34.

[44] [H. Grapow.]

[45] Mowinckel, 118, n. 75: "The problem of the Paraclete is ... not lexicographical ...;
it is a problem of the history of religion."

[46] Hence one cannot consider remote and uncertain analogies such as those taken by
J. Grill, *Untersuchungen über d. Entstehung d. 4. Ev.*, II (1923), 334-337, from the Avesta,
or by Clemen, 282 from Gk. manticism.

writings and the Odes of Solomon, are regarded as the ancestors of the Johannine Paraclete. [47] On the other the Paraclete is inserted into the long list of human advocates before God found in the OT testimonies and later Jewish religion. [48]

1. The Helper.

a. In Mandaean Writings. Helpers sent down from heaven to souls on earth are part of the fixed stock of religious ideas in the Mandaean writings. [49] There are many helpers, both named and unnamed, who come to the anxious soul and establish, instruct and redeem it, e.g., Lidz. Ginza, 328:30 ff.: "... the great (life) sent me a lofty helper, he sent me a man as guardian. He sent me a gentle assistant who came and redeemed me from each thing. He spoke to me in living speech and redeemed me from the world. He called with a soft voice and caused my heart to rest on his support. He taught me concerning praise, so that I forgot the persecution of the Tibil" (cf. also 346, 19 ff.; 456, 19 ff.; 477, 23 ff.; 593, 9 ff.; Lidz. Joh., 69, 3 ff.; cf. 60, 15 ff.). In 316 ff. Jōkabar-Kuštā brings instruction and encouragement as well as revelations of the past and future to "men of proved uprightness" and says : "I was their helper" (320, 1), "whosoever shines and is clear, to him I will be a helper, a helper and support from the place of darkness to the place of light," 322, 11 ff. In Lidz. Liturg., 134 f. the very first, the son of the first great life, is extolled : "A helper, guide and leader wert thou to the great stem of life. Thou didst integrate him into fellowship with the life, thou didst build him into the great building of truth, and thou didst bring him forth to the great place of light and the shining abode." At 195 a man sent from above, a man of proved uprightness, says to his friends : "Bear the persecution of the world with a true believing heart. Honour me in degree, that I may install myself and be for you a helper, a helper and support from the place of darkness to the place of light." Mandā d Haije is called a "helper" of his disciples or friends, Lidz. Liturg., 107, 139, 52 ; Ginza, 284, 28 : "Helper, support, redeemer and deliverer"; ibid., 285, 8 : "A helper and support in this world of the wicked." In Lidz. Liturg. a righteous man praises him : "Yes, I have come to love my lord Mandā d Haije, (and hope) that I will have in him a helper, a helper and support from the place of darkness to the place of light." One of the supreme beings in the Mandaen pantheon is Jawar (the name means "helper"). He is associated or even identified with Mandā d Haije. [50] He is the helper κατ᾿ ἐξοχήν. [51] In the heavenly abode which he established [52] men of proved uprightness find a permanent home, Lidz. Liturg., 204, cf. 243; Ginza, 302, 30 ff.; Joh., 208, 6 ff. Thus Mandaean Gnosis called revealers from the upper world helpers. Nor is this merely a title for divine beings which bring encouragement, instruction and other heavenly gifts to men on earth. It is elevated to be the proper name of one of the supreme Uthras. The religious idea of the "helper" is in Mandaean writings so elastic, however, that it can also apply to those sent down to earth, so Lidz. Ginza, 295, 17 ff.: "The great (life) called, commissioned and equipped me, me, Anōš, the great Uthra, the son, the mighty ... He created for me helpers ... gentle, firm Uthras," ibid., 296, 37 ff.: (Words of the great life to Anōš): "Do not be troubled or afraid, and do not say : I am alone. If trouble befalls thee, we will all be with thee. We will all go to thee and be helpers to thee." Other heavenly beings are also called helpers. Lidz. Ginza, 301, 19 ff.: "(The great) ... equipped me (sc. Hibil) by his word, and created helpers for me ... helpers ... wondrous and without number." Even human piety can be called a helper, Lidz. Liturg., 107: "To each who gives alms, almsgiving will be a helper."

---

[47] Cf. Bau. J. on 14:19 etc., also Windisch, 136 f. and esp. Bu. J., 437-440. Whether the Fourth Gospel is dependent on Gnostic ideas directly or by way of sources makes no essential difference in assessing the intellectual relation.

[48] Mowinckel, 118-122 and Johansson, passim (summary, 296-302).

[49] Cf. Lidz. Ginza, Index, s.v. "Helfer," also Liturg. and Joh., Index, s.v. "Jawar," also the examples in Bau. J. on 14:19; Bu. J., 439 f. and 322, n. 8, also Michaelis, 150-162.

[50] For examples v. Bu. J., 440.

[51] Cf. the material in Bu. J., 440.

[52] "Between the two mountains" : sun and moon. Cf. on this Lidz. Joh., 189, n. 4.

b. In the Odes of Solomon. The Odes of Solomon,[53] whose monotheistic Gnosis is very different from Mandaean, do not link the concept of helper to that of revealer,[54] but to God Himself. The poet, freed from his bonds, praises God : "Thou wert the right hand of salvation and my helper" (25:2), or : "I lifted up my arms to the height of the grace of the Lord (מריא) because he struck off my chains from me and my helper lifted me up to his grace and redemption" (21:1 f., cf. v. 5).[55] The call to the righteous to praise the Lord, i.e., God (8:1 ff.) is on the basis that "the right hand of the Lord is with you, and he will be a helper to you" (v. 7). In the song of the new way of blessedness to God the poet has the bold image : "My way is beautiful; for it is for me a helper to the Lord" (7:3). Thus the thought of divine help is on a different level here from that of the Mandaean writings, and it can hardly be compared with the concept of the Paraclete in John.

The "helper" concept in Mandaean Gnosis has some of the features of the Johannine Paraclete : sending from the upper world, impartation of revelation concerning past and future by means of the instruction and exhortation of believers, leading to salvation, confirmation in moral conduct. But important aspects of the concept of the Johannine Paraclete are not to be found in the Mandaean description of the nature and work of the helpers. The plurality of the Mandaean helpers, who stand alongside one another autonomously and without inter-relation, is in marked contrast to the two paracletes of Jn., Jesus and the Spirit, of whom the latter follows the former, is linked to Him, represents Him, and is dependent on Him.[56] Nothing in the depiction of the Mandaean helpers corresponds to the forensic traits in the figure of the Johannine Paraclete, → 813, 10-18. In the two supposed chief representatives of the same idea, the Jawar of the Mandaeans and the Spirit-Paraclete of Jn., one would expect a greater degree of conceptual similarity if they were genealogically related.[57] Comparison of the Mandaean "helper" concept with the Johannine understanding of the Paraclete does not lead to anything more than a kinship in general type.[58]

It may be added that the attempt to explain παράκλητος as the transl. of a title borne by the figure of the revealer (or revealers) in the Gnosis to which the Mandaean writings and the O. Sol. bear witness,[59] has been unsuccessful.[60] In the Mandaean writings the word meaning "helper," used as a proper name for Jawar (יאואר), → 807, 28-32, is not a current appellative in the sense of "helper." The Mandaeans have 3 words for "helper," used interchangeably and with no apparent distinction of meaning : אהיד עדא ,אדיאורא (orig. "holder of the hand") and more rarely אצבא (orig. "planter").[61]

---

[53] Ed. W. Bauer, Kl. T., 64² (1933).
[54] As Bu. J., 440 thinks.
[55] God is also the Helper in 22:6, i.e., in overcoming the dragon.
[56] The thesis of Bu. J., 437: "The Paraclete is ... a par. figure to Jesus Himself," is exaggerated, since the divergent aspects are not considered. The question whether Mandaean Gnosis belongs to the circle of thought "in which revelation ... was apportioned to several successive figures, or repeated in them" (loc. cit.), can hardly be answered in the affirmative in the present state of research. In W. Staerk's religio-historical equiries into mediators of revelation as "aeonically recurring figures," or into the change of form or multiple form of the redeemer God ("Die sieben Säulen d. Welt u. d. Hauses der Weisheit," ZNW, 35 [1936], 232-261, cf. also his Die Erlösererwartung in d. östlichen Religionen [1938], 40-46, 91-97), it is worth noting that there are practically no Mandaean examples at all.
[57] Further arguments against Bultmann's derivation of the Johannine concept of the Paraclete from Mandaean Gnosis may be found in Michaelis, 150-162.
[58] Johansson, 285 rightly says : "The characteristic and constitutive features of the Johannine Paraclete find no counterpart in Mandaean thought."
[59] Cf. Bu. J., 439 f.
[60] For proof of this cf. Michaelis, 150-162.
[61] Examples in Michaelis.

Even if the three terms could be allotted to three different portions or strata of the Mandaean tradition, for which there are no solid grounds, there was no set title for the revealer(s) as helper(s) among the Mandaeans, and there is thus no certain original for the transl. of such a title by παράκλητος. In O. Sol. the word for "helper" is always מעדריא (from עדר "to help," the verb, e.g., 22:6). This is not a title for those who bring revelation (→ 807, 5-45), and so there is no reason to see connections with the Johannine Paraclete, the less so as παράκλητος was not the obvious transl. of מעדריא [62] and Syr., at least ecclesiastical Syr., had the loan word פרקליטא. Thus the linguistic data resist rather than support a derivation of the Johannine title of Paraclete from the Gnostic, and more particularly the Mandaean, world of thought. [63]

2. The Advocate.

a. In the OT. Advocates for man before God play a specific role in the OT. [64] The idea, widespread in religious history and in the ancient Orient, [65] that man can be represented before deity by a superior "holy" being, who comes forward as helper, defender and advocate, and speaks for him etc., found expression in Israel in a manner in keeping with the distinctive nature of the OT. Men of God like Abraham (Gn. 18:23-33; 20:7, 17), Moses (Ex. 32:11-14, 32; 34:8 f.; Nu. 14:13-19), and Samuel (1 S. 7:8 f.; 12:19, 23; 15:11), prophets like Amos (7:2, 5 f.) or Jeremiah (e.g., 14:7-9, 13, 19-22) intercede with Yahweh for others in guilt or distress, whether it be individuals or the people. As defenders at the bar (cf. Jer. 5:28; Job 29:16) they address Yahweh on behalf of those under their protection, though they can also become accusers (Nu. 16:15; Jer. 18:20-23). It is also the task of these men to declare to men the will of Yahweh and to show how it is to be done (1 S. 12:23 etc.). An advocate of higher rank is the מַלְאַךְ מֵלִיץ of Job 33:23, who intercedes with God for the sinner smitten with sickness, so that God forgives and heals him (cf. vv. 19-25): the interceding angel (מֵלִיץ = "interpreter," "mediator," "advocate"), [66] to whom there is ref. in Job 5:1 and perhaps also 16:19-22 and 19:25-27. [67] The angel, one of thousands (not a single professional advocate), has pity on man in his distress and stands at his side as defender and helper before the judgment seat of God when Satan acts as accuser, Job 1:6-12, → III, 636, 23 ff. But he also shows man his duty, corrects him, and calls him to repentance, 33:23 f. That the advocate and friend in heaven seeks to vindicate man against God (16:19-22) brings out clearly the legal character of the idea of the interceding angel. [68] The nature and

---

[62] Rather βοηθός, also ἀντιλήμπτωρ, cf. O. Sol. 7:3, W. Frankenberg, "Das Verständnis d. O. Sal.," ZAW Beih. 21 (1911), 9.

[63] Also regarded as improbable by Kümmel, 129.

[64] Cf. P. A. H. de Boer, Die Voorbede in het OT = Oudtestamentische Studiën, III (1943), 157-170, who as compared with Johansson emphasises more strongly the cultic background of the intercession [Würthwein]. Cf. also F. Hesse, Die Fürbitte im AT, Diss. Erlangen (1949), 95-101.

[65] Babylonia: protective deities; Persia: Fravashis. Cf. Chant. de la Saussaye, I, 552, 569, 584; II, 211 f., 229 etc.; H. Zimmern, Vater, Sohn u. Fürsprecher in d. babylon. Gottesvorstellung (1896), 13, in. 1 etc.; M. Jastrow, Die Religion Babyloniens u. Assyriens, II, 1 (1912), 92-105; Mowinckel, 111 f.; in general G. van der Leeuw, Phänomenologie d. Religion (1933), 123-129, 277 f.

[66] Cf. E. König, Das Buch Hiob (1929), 343 f.; G. Hölscher, Das Buch Hiob = Hndbch. z. AT, I, 17² (1952), 87 f.; Mowinckel, 109; Johansson, 25-27. The authenticity of "advocate" as a rendering of מֵלִיץ is proved by the use of פרקליטא for it in the Tg. (Johansson, 25).

[67] If Mowinckel's reconstruction and interpretation is right (110, cf. his "Hiobs go'el u. Zeuge im Himmel," Marti-Festschr. = ZAW Beih., 41 [1925], 207-212). The fact that the Tg. (→ n. 66) has פרקליטא for מֵלִיץ on 16:20 and also 33:23 supports a close connection of thought between the two passages.

[68] In the legal vocabulary of the OT the concept of the witness (עֵד) embraces all who in a trial speak for or against the accused, including defending and prosecuting counsel as well as witnesses for the prosecution or the defence, cf. Mowinckel, 103. Job, of course, speaks directly to God Himself (16:20); there is nothing here about a mediator [Fichtner].

work of such angels is described in Zech. 1:12; 3:1-10 in a way similar to that found in Job ; [69] the accusations of Satan are again resisted in 3:1-10.

b. In the Apocrypha and Pseudepigrapha. Here we find the same thoughts in established and extended form. Judaism is proud of being able to look back to a long history in which righteous men and prophets stood at the side of the fathers in advocacy before God, [70] as helpers (מעדריא, S. Bar. 85:1 f.), with the functions of the *defensor, qui ferat eis preces domino*, like the *magnus nuntius Moses, qui singulis horis diebus et noctibus habebat genua sua infixa in terra, orans ...*, Ass. Mos. 11:17. If the previous rule was : *oraverunt, qui potuerunt, pro invalidis* (4 Esr. 7:112), it is now felt to be incumbent on all who fear God to pray for one another, e.g., 2 Macc. 1:2-6; 8:14 f.; 12:39-45. Even stronger, however, is the sense that the people and pious individuals need and have superhuman, heavenly helpers : the blessed righteous (Eth. En. 39:5; Enoch, 83:10; 13:4-7; 15:2 f.; Slav. En. 64:5), and esp. angels (Eth. En. 47:2; 104:1). [71] The true office of the interceding angel, who does not merely mediate human prayers to God (Eth. En. 99:3) but is the advocate of the community and its members before God's judgment throne (Test. L. 6:5 : ὁ ἄγγελος ὁ παραιτούμενος τὸ γένος Ισραήλ), [72] rests in the hands of the supreme angels (Tob. 12:15; Eth. En. 40:6 f.; Test. L. 3:5), esp. Michael (Gr. Bar. 11 ff.; Eth. En. 68:4; Test. N. [Heb.] 9:2 : מליצכם במרום "your advocate on high"). [73] They can both defend and prosecute, in heaven they bring forth both the good and evil in a man's life (Jub. 30:20; 28:6, cf. 4:6; Eth. En. 9:3-11; 89:76; 99:3). That the advocate is also the teacher and adviser of those committed to his protection may be seen, e.g., in Eth. En. 81:5 f. (Jub. 4:15 ?). New and distinctive is the listing of the Spirit, the → πνεῦμα τῆς ἀληθείας, in the ranks of advocates in Test. Jud. 20:1: δύο πνεύματα σχολάζουσι τῷ ἀνθρώπῳ, τὸ τῆς ἀληθείας καὶ τὸ τῆς πλάνης, v. 5 : καὶ τὸ πνεῦμα τῆς ἀληθείας μαρτυρεῖ πάντα καὶ κατηγορεῖ πάντων, [74] καὶ ἐμπεπύρισται ὁ ἁμαρτωλὸς ἐκ τῆς ἰδίας καρδίας καὶ ἆραι πρόσωπον πρὸς τὸν κριτὴν οὐ δύναται, → 811, 15 ff. Features of the interceding angel are transferred to the hypostatised Spirit of God : acting before God's judgment seat and witness (→ 809, 28), combined with the role of accuser (→ 809, 29). The judicial action in heaven is reflected (Wis. 1:5-10) in the conscience of man (→ συνείδησις). [75] From this it is only a step to the idea of the ministry of intercession which the voice of conscience itself discharges in the sinner's prayer for forgiveness, cf. Philo (Spec. Leg., I, 237, → 802, 33 ff.), whose theological statements concerning παράκλητοι (→ 802, 21-803, 7) are simply a development or reconstruction of OT and Jewish ideas in accordance with his own way of thinking. [76]

c. In the Rabbis. The idea of the advocate is vigorously maintained in the Rabb. Their terms are סניגור and פרקליט → 802, 4-11. These are fully interchangeable, though the latter is rather less common. A new feature is the listing of the personified Torah

---

[69] In this context we cannot discuss the constructive attempt of Johansson, 49-62 to understand the Ebed Yahweh of Dt. Is. in terms of the concept of advocate (48 : "The Ebed Yahweh is the most striking intercessory figure in OT religion," 57: "Intercessory angels are the most important formal models for the Ebed Yahweh").

[70] Cf. B. Stade-A. Bertholet, *Bibl. Theol. d. AT*, II (1911), and Johansson, 65-95.

[71] It has not been proved that the Son of Man is also an advocate in Eth. En. (Johansson, 97-119), cf. Kümmel, 124. Gr. En. 104:1 (ed. C. Bonner, *The Last Chapters of Enoch in Greek = Studies and Documents*, 8 [1937]).

[72] The unclear statement about the ἄγγελος ὁ παραιτούμενος ὑμᾶς in Test. D. 6:2 : οὗτός ἐστι μεσίτης θεοῦ καὶ ἀνθρώπων (→ IV, 617, 17-20) does not make any solid contribution to our understanding of the concept of the advocate.

[73] Cf. W. Lueken, *Michael* (1898), 7-12.

[74] Text acc. to β A (Charles).

[75] Cf. P. Volz, *Der Geist Gottes* (1910), 160 f., 184 f.; Bousset-Gressm., 348 f., 403; esp. Mowinckel, 98-109, 115-118.

[76] Cf. also the observation of Mowinckel, 108 f.

among the heavenly advocates, Cant. r., 8, 17 on 8:14.[77] Also new is the idea that sacrifices and works of piety are advocates at God's judgment seat, S. Lv. on 14:19, (277a), → 802, 16 ff.; jBer., 7b, 32 (the two lambs which are to be offered daily acc. to Nu. 28:3): "two advocates daily"; Pesikt., 191b (S. Levi): "There are no better advocates than sacrifices" etc.; conversion and good works, bShab., 32a, → 802, 11-13 (with appeal to Job 33:23); cf. Ab., 4, 11a, → 802, 8-10; benevolence and works of charity, bBB, 10a, → 802, 13-16 etc.[78] Other advocates are again the righteous of earlier days, esp. Moses, whose intercession for Israel after the apostasy with the golden calf (Ex. 32:11) is constantly regarded as the great act by which he saved the people from destruction by God's anger, e.g., Ex. r., 43, 1 on 32:11: "R. Chama b. Chanina spoke: The good advocate comes forward at the trial with friendliness. Moses was one of the two advocates who arose and made speeches in defence of Israel."[79] Among the interceding angels who represent man before God (e.g., jRH, 57b, 13-19; Ex. r., 31, 15 on 22:26;[80] there is often allusion to Job 33:23-30),[81] Michael is again the chief, "the סניגור of Israel," Midr. Rt. on 1:1 (122b),[82] cf. Ex. r., 18, 5 on 12:29.[83] The idea that the Spirit is an advocate (→ 810, 22 ff.) was also maintained and developed (the word is סניגור). In exposition of Prv. 24:28 Lv. r., 6, 1 on 5:1 quotes this saying of R. Acha: "This holy Spirit conducted the defence (סניגוריא) on both sides: He said to Israel: 'Do not be in vain a witness against thy friend (i.e., God),' and he then said to God (Prv. 24:29): 'Do not say, as he has done to me, so will I do to him.' "[84] Here the Holy Spirit as סניגור has the twofold function of pleading with God for grace to His people and of reminding Israel of its duty to God.[85] The related Dt. r., 3, 12 on 9:1[86] has the Spirit exercise His intercessory office in connection with that of Moses. In Cant. r., 8, 11 on 8:10, where the Bath-Qol, the meagre remnant of the Spirit still to be found after the quenching of prophecy, is called a סניגור of Israel during its dispersion among the nations, the basic idea is that of the intercessory Spirit. The offices of defender and accuser are now very largely distinct (Ex. r., 15, 29 on 12:12 etc.).[87] That the advocate is not just a representative in the court of heaven but has also to warn men on earth and keep them on the right way, is shown esp. clearly by what is said about the advocacy of the Spirit, → supra.[88]

d. In the NT. The idea of the advocate in the OT and later Judaism is linked directly to the thought in 1 Jn. 2:1 (Jesus Christ a paraclete of sinful Christians before the Father). Dominant is the same forensic idea of the judgment of God before which sinners are arraigned and where they need an advocate. In the Paraclete sayings in the Gospel there are many features for which analogies may be found in the advocates of Israel and Judah. The Paraclete is an authoritative teacher of believers (14:26, cf. v. 16; 15:26; 16:7, 13 f.), a witness of revelation (15:26), a speaker in the trial of the world before the forum of God (16:8-11). In the religious heritage of later Judaism parallels may also be found for the idea

---

[77] Johansson, 174 f.
[78] For further examples cf. ibid., 175-178; Str.-B., II, 561 f.
[79] Str.-B., I, 141 f.; Johansson, 163 f. For further source materials cf. also Str.-B., II, 561; Johansson, 162-166.
[80] Johansson, 148 f.
[81] jQid., I, 10, 61d, 32 etc., v. Str.-B., II, 560 f.; Johansson, 146-150.
[82] Str.-B., IV, 1206.
[83] Johansson, 149 f., cf. also Lueken, 22-27, 48 for more material.
[84] Str.-B., II, 138, 562 (with textual emendation acc. to Jalqut Shim'oni, 2 § 961 on Prv. 24:28), cf. Johansson, 157 f.
[85] Mowinckel, 99-104.
[86] Johansson, 159 f.
[87] Ibid., 150-152.
[88] Cf. also in Heb. En. the figure of the Metatron as preacher and proclaimer of secrets, v. Johansson, 133-138.

of the Holy Spirit or Spirit of truth as Paraclete (14:16 f., 26; 15:26). The varying statements that the office of advocacy is exercised both in the court of heaven and also among men on earth are common to the OT and Jewish sources and to the NT material. The fact that they are linked in the former helps to overcome the difficulty of cleavage in the latter (between 1 Jn. and Jn.). In this heaping up of conceptual relationships agreement in the use of the term παράκλητος = פְּרַקְלִיט (or — more commonly — the synonymous סָנֵיגוֹר) strongly supports the thesis that there is a historico-religious connection between the concept of advocacy in the OT and Jewish world and the concept of the παράκλητος in the NT. Even on this answer certain difficulties still remain in connection with the origin of the concept παράκλητος. For instance, how does the title "advocate" tally with the functions of the one who bears this title in Jn., and how did Jesus come to be called paraclete (Jn. 14:16)? But these are not insuperable problems (→ C).

If it is asked whether the ideas which the NT connects with the word παράκλητος have their root in the "helper" idea of Mandaean Gnosis or the "advocate" concept of the OT and Judaism, there is a very strong probability that in the last analysis our decision must be in favour of the ancient biblical tradition. [89]

C. The NT Concept.

1. Of the various ideas linked with the word παράκλητος in the NT the most clearly etched is that of the advocate at the bar of God in heaven. [90] In place of the many advocates which Judaism found to defend the righteous before the forum of the heavenly Judge, primitive Christianity recognises only one advocate with the Father, Jesus Christ, who as the Righteous can intercede for sinners (1 Jn. 2:1). The thought is common to primitive Christianity even though the word παράκλητος does not occur in the non-Johannine writings (a caprice of tradition?). The living Christ intercedes at the right hand of the Father (R. 8:34: → ἐντυγχάνω). In intercession He places His incorruptible life at the service of His people (Hb. 7:25). [91] The advocacy of Jesus is also presupposed in Jn. 16:26. One may also see from Mt. 10:32 f. and par. (cf. Mk. 8:38 and par.) that when Jesus looked ahead to the end of the days He not merely claimed for Himself the office of Judge of the world (→ υἱός, ὁ υἱὸς τοῦ ἀνθρώπου) but was also conscious of being the defender of those who confess Him (and the accuser of those who deny Him) at the judgment seat of the Father. The Christian concept of a transcendent eschatological Paraclete, traces of which may be found throughout the NT, [92] goes back to Jesus.

---

[89] Acc. to the formula of Stauffer Theol., 5.

[90] The figure of the adversary, the κατήγωρ, the devil (→ III, 636, 23-27), is unequivocally found in the NT only at Rev. 12:10.

[91] In the picture of the exalted Christ in 1 Jn. 2:1 f. and Hb. 7:23-25 (cf. 9:24; 4:14-16; 2:17), also in 1 Cl., 36, 1, the forensic idea of the office of the Paraclete is very closely connected with the cultic conception of the (high-)priestly office (→ III, 278-282), v. also Mi. Hb.[8], 176; O. Moe, "Das Priestertum Christi im NT ausserhalb d. Hb.," ThLZ, 72 (1947), 338. But in accordance with the word "paraclete" the special feature of Christ as such is His coming forward with the Word. This also sets the limit to combinations of the Pauline "through Christ" and the Johannine παράκλητος (cf. A. Schettler, Die paul. Formel "durch Christus" [1907], 28 f., also Deissmann LO, 286), → II, 68, 36-69, 6. The same applies to the relation between μεσίτης (→ IV, 620-624 etc.) and παράκλητος in NT Christology.

[92] As in other early Chr. texts, it is probably echoed in P. Oxy., VI, 850, 10 (→ n. 36), but the state of the text does not allow us to say for certain.

2. More richly developed if more difficult to define is the idea, expressly attested only in Jn., of a Paraclete at work in the world both in and for the disciples. [93] Jesus Himself is regarded as such during His earthly ministry (14:16). [94] The only description, however, is that of the ἄλλος παράκλητος who after the departure of Jesus will continue His work and remain for ever with and in the disciples (14:16 f., 26; 16:7, 13 f.). This is the Spirit (→ πνεῦμα). [95] Sent by God or Jesus to the disciples (14:16, 26; 15:26; 16:7) — not to the world, which has no organ for Him (14:17) — He teaches with all-embracing authority and yet with strict adherence to Jesus and His message, maintaining, expanding and completing the work of Jesus, leading the disciples into all truth (14:26; 15:26; 16:13 f.). His witness to Jesus (15:26), [96] however, is also an accusation of the world before God's judgment seat : He convicts the world in respect of sin, righteousness and judgment. That is, He shows that sin is on the side of the world, right and triumph on that of Jesus (16:8-11). [97] The puzzle of the combination of kerygmatic and forensic features in the picture of the Spirit-Paraclete [98] is solved if we trace back the tradition historically to the OT and Jewish idea of the advocate (→ 809, 12- 810, 2) in which there is reference already to an advocacy of the divine Spirit for man in the here and now of his earthly life (→ 810, 20-30). [99] But the idea of the Spirit as παράκλητος is not unfamiliar to the rest of the NT even if the word is not used. Paul is aware that as the believer wrestles in prayer for assurance of the consummation of salvation the Spirit comes to aid him in his weakness and represents him before God by the babbling of glossolalia (R. 8:26 f.; → I, 376, 4 ff., συναντιλαμβάνω, → ἐντυγχάνω, ὑπερεντυγχάνω). Jesus promised His disciples that when they had to give an account before earthly powers the Spirit would speak for them at the decisive moment, Mk. 13:11 and par. The picture of the intercessory Jesus in the Synoptic and Johannine tradition (Lk. 13:6-9; 22:32; [23:34]; Jn. 17) may be added to these testimonies to the advocacy of the Spirit in the world. It would seem, then, that the idea of a Paraclete in the earthly life of the disciples goes back ultimately to Jesus Himself.

If Jesus took the concept from the OT and Jewish world and found in it a term well adapted to express certain aspects of His own self-awareness, one can under-

---

[93] Johansson is wide of the mark here (181-256). Cf. also Kümmel, 125 ff.

[94] P. Oxy., VI, 850, 10 (→ n. 92) may be cited in this connection, since the tenor of the prayer does not allow us to conclude that the address ὁ παράκλητος refers to the historical Jesus or the risen Christ.

[95] Since our concern is only with the predicate παράκλητος and its meaning, not the subject of whom it is used, we cannot discuss the understanding of πνεῦμα in Jn. 14-16, nor take up what is said by others (e.g., Sasse, 275-277 or R. Eisler, "Das Rätsel d. J.," Eranos-Jahrbuch [1935], esp. 391-422, also Windisch, 130-137 and Bu. J., 437-440) about figures to whom the designation παράκλητος might originally and properly apply.

[96] Cf. Bu. J., 426 f.

[97] On ἐλέγχειν (→ II, 474, 4 ff.) and the meaning of 16:8-11 cf. Bau. J., 196 f.; Lagrange, 418-420; Bu. J., 432-437.

[98] It is, however, a very moot pt. whether the Spirit is herewith described as a revealer, and thus as a par. figure to Jesus Himself (Bu. J., 437). On the other hand a purely forensic view : "defender of the disciples in their fight for right and truth before the judgment of men" (v. Schl. J., 298, cf. Theol. d. Ap., 152), or "advocate of the disciples esp. in conflict with the world" (F. Büchsel J., NT Deutsch, on 14:16), does not do justice to the Johannine predicate παράκλητος.

[99] The attempt of C. K. Barrett to ignore derivation from the religious world around and to find the background of the Johannine use of παράκλητος simply in apostolic proclamation is not very convincing in view of the wealth of comparative material available [Seesemann].

stand the concealed reference to Himself as παράκλητος put on His lips in Jn. (14:16), and the Greek word may well recall the term used by Jesus Himself in His mother tongue : פרקליטא.[100]

As regards the translation of παράκλητος in Jn., the history of the word and concept shows that in the course of religious history subsidiary senses were interwoven into the primary sense of "advocate," so that no single word can provide an adequate rendering. [101] If we are to avoid the alien Paraclete, favoured by many translators and exegetes both old and new (→ 806, 23 ff.), "supporter" [102] or "helper" is perhaps the best, though the basic concept and sustaining religious idea is that of "advocate."

Behm

παρακοή → I, 223, 1 ff.
παρακολουθέω → I, 215, 24 ff.
παρακούω → I, 223, 1 ff.

---

† παρακύπτω

1. παρακύπτω, based on the simple κύπτω, "I bend," [1] means "I stoop to see." The bent over (or forward, cf. παρα-) position may be modified by the situation of the observer (e.g., ἐκ θυρίδος, ἐκ σπηλαίου) or by that of what he is trying to see (e.g., κατ᾽ ἄντρον). As emphasised by the παρα-, it applies to a quick, fleeting, stolen look, [2] though it does make possible an accurate consideration. A verb of seeing may be specifically added, though this is unusual (cf. other compounds of κύπτω which refer to seeing). [3] It is not surprising that the simple and compounds are not common in inscr., [4] but in the pap. we find ἀνακύπτω, διακύπτω "I bend out" (of the window), P. Magd., 24, 4 (3rd cent. B.C.), ἐγκύπτω "I glance at" (a writing ; late), ἐκκύπτω, "I peep," P. Petr., II, 1, 16 (3rd cent. B.C.), also παρακύπτω : [5] P. Oxy., III, 475, 23 (182 B.C.), of a slave who bends over the edge of the flat roof to catch a glimpse of musicians playing in the courtyard : βουληθεὶς ἀπὸ τοῦ δώματος τῆς αὐτῆς οἰκίας παρακῦψαι, P. Lips., 29, 10 (295 B.C.): μηδὲ παρακύπτειν ᾡτινιοῦν πράγματι διαφέροντί μοι. [6]

2. In the LXX we find κύπτω (with προσκυνέω in 7 out of 18 instances), also several compounds (ἀνα-, δια-, διεκ-, ἐγ-, εἰς-, ἐκ-, κατα-, κατεπι-, προσ-, συγ-). παρακύπτω occurs 8 times, usually for Heb. שׁקף ni and hi, Cant. 2:9 שׁגח hi (both

---

[100] Cf. Zn. J.[5, 6], 564. F. Delitzsch, ספר הברית החדשה (1877) has פְּרַקְלִיט for παράκλητος in Jn., מֵלִיץ in 1 Jn. 2:1.
[101] Mowinckel, 130, also Lagrange, 383.
[102] So H. Strathmann J. (*NT Deutsch*[4] [1951]) on 14:16 f., 26; 15:26.

π α ρ α κ ύ π τ ω. [1] κύπτω is very rare in the NT. Only Mk. (1:7) uses it to depict the attitude in untying the shoe-latchets (this addition has no theological significance, cf. E. Lohmeyer, *Johannes d. Täufer* [1932], 186 f.). In Jn. 8:6, 8 it is said of Jesus when, sitting (8:2), He writes on the ground : κάτω κύψας (8:8 vl. κατακύψας). To this corresponds the use of ἀνακύπτω (8:7, 10) which occurs also in Lk. 13:11 (with συγκύπτω) and 21:28, → n. 12.
[2] So also Aristoph. Eccl., 202 : σωτηρία παρέκυψε (a weak prospect of deliverance appeared).
[3] Cf. Pass. and Liddell-Scott, *s.v.*; also Wettstein, I, 823 on Lk. 24:12.
[4] The indexes in Ditt. Syll.[3] and Ditt. Or. have nothing to offer. In an account of healing at Epidauros (4th cent. B.C.) in Ditt. Syll.[3], 1168, 91 we find : ὑπερέκυπτε εἰς τὸ ἄβατον.
[5] Preisigke Wört., II, 248, *s.v.*
[6] Cf. also Moult.-Mill., 486, *s.v.*

verbs are transl. also by other compounds and by βλέπω, ἐπιβλέπω, καταβλέπω, κατεῖδον). At 1 K. 6:4, in a description of the temple of Solomon, the difficult Heb. (שְׁקֻפִים) is rendered by the pass., which is not attested elsewhere : θυρίδας παρακυπτο-μένας (vl. διακρυπτομένας, δεδικτυωμένας). [7] In all other cases the ref. is to looking out of the window (διὰ τῆς θυρίδος, Gn. 26:8; Ju. 5:28 B; 1 Ch. 15:29; διὰ τῶν θυρί-δων, Cant. 2:9; ἀπὸ θυρίδος, Prv. 7:6), or looking in at the window (διὰ τῶν θυρίδων, Sir. 14:23; ἄφρων ἀπὸ θύρας παρακύπτει εἰς οἰκίαν, ἀνὴρ δὲ πεπαιδευμένος ἔξω στήσεται, Sir. 21:23). A verb of seeing is used at Gn. 26:8; 7 Ch. 15:29; Prv. 7:6. Quite apart from the question whether the windows are barred or not, [8] it is hard to say how intensive παρακύπτειν is meant to be in a given instance. If the ref. is to (barred) windows of the harem (Ju. 5:28; 1 Ch. 15:29; Prv. 7:6; Cant. 2:9), παρακύπτειν denotes a stolen and even forbidden, though steadfast glance. Joseph. does not have παρα-κύπτω. [9] In Gr. En. 9:1 it is said of the 4 great angels : παρέκυψαν ἐπὶ τὴν γῆν.

3. Jn. 20:5 tells us that when the beloved disciple came to the tomb on Easter morning : παρακύψας βλέπει κείμενα τὰ ὀθόνια, οὐ μέντοι εἰσῆλθεν. What is meant is looking in from outside through the apparently low entrance. That he did not go in denotes the awe felt by him. [10] That he gave only a fleeting glance [11] is no more suggested by παρακύψας than when it is said of Mary Magdalene in 20:11: παρέκυψεν εἰς τὸ μνημεῖον, and she sees (20:12) two angels with whom she enters into conversation. Related to Jn. 20:5 is the Peter tradition in Lk. 24:12, which says : παρακύψας βλέπει τὰ ὀθόνια μόνα. [12]

παρακύπτω is used fig. in Jm. 1:25 and 1 Pt. 1:12. In Jm. 1:25 : ὁ δὲ παρα-κύψας εἰς νόμον τέλειον τὸν τῆς ἐλευθερίας (→ II, 502, 8 ff.), the addition καὶ παραμείνας makes it clear that this is not a fleeting glance. [13] On the other hand,

---

[7] K. Galling, Art. "Fenster," Biblisches Reallex. = Hndbch. z. AT, I, 1 (1937), 164 f. pts. to the Assyr. sakkapu or askuppatu, "door-post" or "threshold," and suggests the "window of the side of the door." We obviously have a tt. which puzzled all the older translators, cf. Field, I, 602, ad loc. When שְׁקֻפִים occurs again at 1 K. 7:4 Σ has παρα-κύψεις, LXX μέλαθρα, 'Α ἀποβλέπτας.
[8] The bars are mentioned in Cant. 2:9 (τὰ δίκτυα, cf. Ju. 5:28 A; 1 K. 6:4 vl.). The primary function of windows was to let in light and air, cf. S. Krauss, Talmudische Archäol., I (1910), 42. In 2 K. 9:30 (διακύπτω) the ref. is to the outside window in the king's palace, cf. Galling, op. cit., 165.
[9] So expressly Schl. Jk., 150, n. 1. Cf. ἀνακύπτω, Jos. Ant., 6, 250; 19, 346; transf. Bell., 6, 401, ἐπανακύπτω, 1, 603, κατακύπτω, 2, 224. Leisegang does not list παρακύπτω for Philo. Cf. ἀνακύπτω, Leg. All., II, 34; fig. Flacc., 160, διακύπτω, Ebr., 167; Omn. Prob. Lib., 21; ὑπερκύπτω, Det. Pot. Ins., 100; Praem. Poen., 30; Spec. Leg., II, 166. Ep. Ar.: ἀνακύπτω, 233, διακύπτω, 19, ἐγκύπτω, 140, κατακύπτω, 91.
[10] Zn. J.[5, 6], 673 and Büchsel J. (NT Deutsch), ad loc.
[11] So Bau. J., ad loc., who alleges βλέπει (in supposed antithesis to the θεωρεῖ of 20:6, though cf. → 343, 11 f.; 346, 5; 346, 12 f.).
[12] The authenticity of the verse, questioned by B. Weiss, Mk. u. Lk. (Kritisch-exege-tischer Komm. über d. NT, ed. H. A. W. Meyer[9] [1901]), ad loc.; Zn. Lk.[3, 4], 714, n. 46; Kl. Lk., ad loc. etc., is perhaps to be accepted ; cf. J. Schniewind, Die Parallelperikopen bei Lk. u. J. (1914), 88 f. (the verse was struck out later because not fully par. to Jn. 20:5 or 20:3 ff.), Hck. Lk., ad loc. (the absence in D due to the influence of Tat), and K. H. Rengstorf Lk. (NT Deutsch), ad loc. If the verse is genuine, this is a real pt. of contact between Lk. and Jn., as shown to a lesser degree by the use of ἀνακύπτω, → n. 1.
[13] παραμείνας simply underlines this ; παρακύψας, as usage elsewhere shows, denotes penetrating absorption. Hck. Jk., ad loc.: "The stretched forward attitude of the body in-dicates tension and curiosity." Even better Schl. Jk., ad loc.: "παρακύψας seems to suggest the attitude of the attentive and zealous reader who stoops over the roll of the Torah." So also A. Meyer, "Das Rätsel d. Jk.," ZNW Beih. 10 (1930), 155, though he can find no par. in the later Jewish writings quoted. E. Stauffer, "Das 'Gesetz d. Freiheit' in d. Ordens-regel von Jericho," ThLZ, 77 (1952), 527-532, pts. out that not only the "law of liberty" but other motifs in Jm., including the principle of deeper knowledge expressed in παρα-κύψας, may be found in the Jericho rule (DSM = M. Burrows, The Dead Sea Scrolls of

when 1 Pt. 1:12 says of the sufferings of Christ and His ensuing δόξαι, or (cf. also → III, 43, n. 7) of the grace therein contained for Christians (1:10): εἰς ἃ ἐπιθυμοῦσιν ἄγγελοι παρακῦψαι (→ I, 85, 43 ff.; III, 170, 27 and n. 31), this might be inquisitive peeping, unless a desire for genuine perception [14] is in view. [15]

Michaelis

παραλαμβάνω → IV, 11, 15 ff.
παραμένω → IV, 577, 22 ff.

| † παραμυθέομαι, † παραμυθία, † παραμύθιον | → παρακαλέω, παράκλησις 773, 8 ff. |

Contents : A. Meaning : 1. Structure and Basic Meaning ; 2. Derivations from the Basic Meaning "To Admonish" ; 3. Derivations from the Basic Meaning "To Reassure," "To Console"; 4. Special Meanings of παραμυθία and παραμύθιον. B. The Word Group in the Old Testament. C. The Word Group in the New Testament : 1. Usage ; 2. Comfort and Comforters : a. Traditional Rites and the Comfort of Jesus ; b. Recipients ; c. Bearers ; d. The Chief Motif in NT Comfort.

A. Meaning.

1. Structure and Basic Meaning.

παραμυθέομαι is made up of the adv. παρά in the sense "towards" (as in παρ-έρχεσθαι etc.) [1] and μυθέομαι (→ IV, 766, n. 13); derived are παραμυθία, παρα-

---

St. Mark's Monastery, II, 2 [1951]). But this ref., worth noting in many respects, is to be accepted only with certain reservations. The "law of liberty" in DSM, 10, 6. 8. 11, if it denotes the "freely accepted special rule of the Jericho order" (529), is more a formal than a material par. (even if we do not simply have a contrasting par.), and the examples which Stauffer (530) adduces for the deeper knowledge analogous to παρακύψας (esp. DSM, 11, 3 ff. and 17, using נבט or הִבִּיט; cf. 530, n. 3 f.) are in DSM used in another context than that of the law of liberty. Thus, remarkable though it is if these par., acc. to Stauffer, refer to examination of a secret statute which goes beyond the Torah, the exposition given by Stauffer seems to lack complete cogency.

[14] This would certainly be so if the author were saying that the wish of the angels was granted, so Wbg. Pt., *ad loc.*, who quotes Eph. 3:10. But when Wbg. comments : "as through a barred window," this may be in keeping with OT usage (→ 815, 8 ff.), but it is not very felicitous (esp. if the window is that of a harem). Any topographical suggestion (e.g., the angels look down "from their sphere," Wbg.) is out of place, and is not even supported by a more external par. such as that of Gr. En. 9:1 (→ 815, 13). That the basis is a saying of Jesus (A. Resch, "Agrapha, Ausserkanonische Evangelienfragmente," TU, 5, 4 [1889], 301) has been rightly disproved by J. H. Ropes, "Die Sprüche Jesu," TU, 14, 2 (1896), 50 f. T. W. Manson, JThSt, 47 (1946), 220, considers a connection with Lk. 10:24 : ἄγγελοι = מלאכים for βασιλεῖς = מלכים, but it is unlikely that prophets and angels would have been associated in the original at Lk. 10:24, and such a misreading would hardly have been possible at the time when 1 Pt. was written (the prophets do occur in 1 Pt. 1:10 ff., but in a different connection).

[15] Post-apost. fathers : ἐγκύπτω (→ 814, 24) Pol., 3, 2 (of immersion in Paul's epistles), also 1 Cl., 40, 1; 45, 2; 53, 1; 62, 3. Cf. Pr.-Bauer, *s.v.* and Kn. Cl., *ad loc.* We do not find the simple or other compounds.

π α ρ α μ υ θ έ ο μ α ι κτλ.   Pass., Liddell-Scott, Preisigke Wört., Moult.-Mill., Pr.-Bauer⁴, *s.v.*; Cr.-Kö., 570-574 *s.v.* παρακαλέω κτλ. ; Joh. W. 1 K., 322, n. 2; E. Schwyzer, *Griech. Grammatik* (Hndbch. AW, II, 1), I (1939), 470; II (1950), 493; cf. also the bibl. under παρακαλέω, → 779, n. 30.

[1] Cf. Schwyzer, II, 493; also Cr.-Kö., 570, *s.v.* παρακαλέω; J. C. K. v. Hofmann, *Der Schriftbeweis*, II, 2 (1855), 13 f.; Schl. K., 681 on 2 C. 13:11.

μύθιον. [2] The basic meaning is thus "to speak to someone," or "to speak to someone, coming close to his side." [3] Closely related in structure and sense are → παραγγέλλω, παραθαρρύνω, παρορμάω etc., also the Lat. synon. *alloquor*. [4] Common to all is the favourable sense [5] of a friendly relation, as also esp. to groups very closely related to παραμυθέομαι, [6] namely, → παρακαλέω (παράκλησις), παρηγορέω (παρηγορία), [7] παραινέω (παραίνεσις), [8] in which it is almost impossible to separate the elements of petition, admonition and consolation. [9] In contrast the similarly constructed παρατηρέω means "to watch someone by keeping close to him." παραμυθέομαι first takes the dat. and inf. ("to summon, order, advise someone to do something," e.g., Hom. Il., 9, 417), [10] then the acc. and inf. (e.g., Plat. Leg., II, 666a), then the simple acc. (*ibid.*, I, 625b). [11]

The basic sense "to speak to someone in a friendly way" [12] (e.g., Plat. Phaed., 83a; Leg., X, 899d; similarly παραμυθία "friendly address," e.g., Plat. Resp., V, 450d) can develop along two main lines : with ref. to what ought to be done, "to admonish to something," and with ref. to what has happened, "to console about something." [13]

---

[2] παραμυθία refers originally to the act, παραμύθιον to the content, cf. Schwyzer, I, 470, also Phryn. Parerga, 1 § 10 (ed. C. A. Lobeck [1820], 517). In what follows there are also refs. to ἀπαραμύθητος (→ 819, 7 f.), εὐπαραμύθητος (→ 819, 8), παραμυθητικός (→ 818, 32 f.), παραμυθιακός (→ 818, 26 f.), προσπαραμυθέομαι (→ 818, 8).

[3] Another less probable meaning of the παρα- is given by H. C. G. Moule, *Cambridge Greek Testament* (with ref. to Horat. Epod., 13, 18, *v.* Moult-Mill., *s.v.*): "conversation which takes away any point from anxiety" (παρα- = "to draw aside").

[4] Cf. Varro De Lingua Latina, VI, 57 (ed. H. Goetz and F. Schoell [1910]): *adlocutum mulieres ire aiunt, cum eunt ad aliquam locutum consolandi causa. Alloquor and allocutio* already have this sense in Catull. (38, 5 and 7) and Seneca (Dialogi, VI, 1, 6; XII, 1, 3; Ep., 98, 9; 121, 4), and are used in the Vg OT for παραμυθέομαι (2 Macc. 15:9), παραμυθία (Wis. 19:12) and παραμύθιον (Wis. 3:18), also παραίνεσις (Wis. 8:9), though in the NT Vg uses *consolor* and derivates for "to console," and *alloqui* (Ac. 20:11; 21:40; 28:20) for "to speak to someone." Only in the Itala NT (Cod. f) is *alloquor* once used for παραμυθέομαι in the sense "to comfort" (Jn. 11:31). Cf. Thes. Ling. Lat., I, 1691, 67 ff.; 1696, 70 ff.

[5] Cf. P. Joüon, "Explication de la nuance méliorative des verbes tels que *alloquor* παραμυθέομαι," *Recherches de science religieuse*, 28 (1938), 311-314. But there are exceptions, e.g., LXX Est. 8:12e (→ 818, 18 f.); Plut. Praecepta de Tuenda Sanitate, 22 (II, 134a; → n. 15) can even speak once of μιαρά παραμύθια (though παραμύθια is to be put in quotation marks). There are similar exceptions in the case of παρακαλέω, which can mean "to seduce" (LXX Dt. 13:7), while ἀπατάω in Sir. 30:23 can be given a favourable sense by its proximity to παρακαλέω ("to comfort").

[6] The mid. can express (friendly) emotion, cf. Schwyzer, II, 228 f.

[7] παρηγορέω and παρηγορία are in very different spheres synon. with παραμυθέομαι and παραμυθία, i.e., in Gk. condolences (Epigr. Graec., 502, 4), in the transl. of the OT (e.g., the Hexapla tradition at Qoh. 4:1: LXX παρακαλῶν, Σ παρηγορῶν, ᾿Αλλ παραμυθούμενος), in the NT (Col. 4:11) and in Philo (Vit. Mos., I, 137), → n. 29.

[8] E.g., Wis. 8:9; Ac. 27:9 (here both admonition and consolation, Vg. *consolabatur*; → 817, 12 ff.).

[9] Cf. Cr.-Kö., 571; also F. Ast, Lex. Platonicum, III (1936), *s.v.* → n. 8.

[10] Cf. Schwyzer, II, 247 and 374.

[11] It is uncertain whether we have a constr. with the dat. alone, cf. P. Fay, 19, 6.

[12] Since the address can be very strong (cf. under 2. c-e), the friendly intent is sometimes esp. emphasised, e.g., by ἠρέμα in Plat. Phaed., 83a; Luc. Nec., 6, or ἐν τοῖς ἀγαθοῖς λόγοις, cf. also Plat Resp., V, 476e. But in general there is a note of reassurance in παραμυθέομαι κτλ., as often in παρακαλέω, e.g., Lk. 15:28; 1 C. 4:13; cf. Joh. W. 1 K., 112 f.

[13] The specific nuances are often hard to fix ; we are helped by the largely synon. or supplementary verbs and nouns, which are for this reason often mentioned in what follows ; cf. also the list in Joh. W. 1 K., 322, n. 2.

2. Derivations from the Basic Meaning "To Admonish."

a. "To urge," to do or not to do something, Plat. Menex., 247c : πατέρας ... καὶ μητέρας ἀεὶ χρὴ παραμυθεῖσθαι ὡς ῥᾶστα φέρειν τὴν συμφοράν, with (ἀνα)-πείθω, Aristoph. Vesp., 115, with δέομαι and προσεύχομαι, Plat. Euthyd., 288c, with προστρέπω, P. Fay., 19, 6 (2nd cent. A.D.); similarly παραμυθία "friendly admonition," though to free men, not slaves, for whom an ἄνευ παραμυθίας προστάττειν is fitting and customary, Philo Vit. Mos., II, 50. b. "To win over someone for something," Plat. Leg., II, 666a, cf. προσπαραμυθέομαι, Ditt. Syll.³, 762, 29 f. (48 B.C.). c. "To encourage," "to spur on," "to admonish," Hom. Il., 9, 417 (cf. 684), with πείθω (Plut. Cons. ad Apoll., 32 [II, 118b c]); παραμυθία "stimulus," Luc. Nigrinus, 7, παραμύθιον "admonition" Plat. Leg., VI, 773e, with πειθώ, ibid., IV, 720a, "warning," IX, 880a. d. "To inspire with courage," e.g., in the one LXX instance of παραμυθέομαι at 2 Macc. 15:9 : (ὁ Μακκαβαῖος) παραμυθούμενος αὐτοὺς ἐκ τοῦ νόμου καὶ τῶν προφητῶν ... προθυμοτέρους αὐτοὺς κατέστησεν, with παραθαρρύνω, Plat. Critias, 108c, with ἐπελπίζω, Dio C., 43, 15, 2; παραμυθία and παραμύθιον, "encouragement," Plat. Euthyd., 272b: παραμύθιον τοῦ μὴ φοβεῖσθαι, Resp., V, 450d (here taking up the directly preceding παραθαρρύνω). e. "To persuade" sometimes with evil intent, so παραμυθία in LXX Est. 8:12e : πολλοὺς τῶν ἐπ' ἐξουσίαις τεταγμένων ... παραμυθία μεταιτίους αἱμάτων ἀθῴων καταστήσασα περιέβαλε συμφοραῖς ἀνηκέστοις. f. "To convince," Plut. Gen. Socr., 20 (II, 589c): παραμυθεῖται τοὺς ἀπιστοῦντας. παραμυθία "power of persuasion," Plat. Phaed., 70b: τοῦτο δὴ ἴσως οὐκ ὀλίγης παραμυθίας δεῖται καὶ πίστεως ("proof").

3. Derivations from the Basic Meaning "To Reassure," "To Console."

a. "To cheer" (in words), Plat. Leg., I, 625b, cf. also παραμυθία, Plat. Soph., 224a. b. "To refresh," "to tend" (not necessarily with words), Aristoph. Fr., 45 (CAF, I, 403) in Athen., IX, 35 (p. 385 f.); esp. of tending plants, Geoponica, III, 5, 4, ¹⁴ cf. [π]αραμυθιακὴ ἐργασία, "solicitous tending," P. Oxy., XIV, 1631, 13; παραμυθία "refreshing," "vivifying," so perhaps LXX Wis. 19:12, also παραμύθιον Plut. Lucull., 44 (I, 521b); Brutus (I, 986e): Brutus as the refreshing or healing of his province when smitten by misfortune. c. "To mitigate," "to palliate," Luc. Dialogi Mortuorum, 28, 3; De Domo, 7 (παραμυθέομαι τὸ ἐνδέον, "to make up for the deficiency"), Theophr. Fr., 120 in Athen., XI, 8 (p. 463c); Geoponica, XII, 13, 11 (→ n. 14), cf. παραμυθητικός "able to soothe and even heal," Sext. Emp. Pyrrh. Hyp., I, 70 and παραμύθιον "alleviation," Theocr. Idyll., 23, 7; Plat. Critias, 115b (freely quoted in Athen., XIV, 46 [p. 640e] and Dio C., 65, 4, 3): μεταδόρπια as παραμύθια πλησμονῆς, ¹⁵ a "means of alleviation for the feeling of surfeit." d. "To weaken," "lessen," esp. shocks (e.g., at myths, Plut. Mulierum Virtutes, II, 248b), at what is unusual and strange, Plut. De Animae Procreatione in Timaeo Platonis, 5 (II, 1014a), at hated concepts like that of monarchy, Plut. Cleomenes, 11 (I, 809e), at contradictions in a presentation, Simpl. in Aristot. Phys., IV, 12, p. 729, 35; III, 3, p. 444, 15 f. (τὴν ἀπορίαν). ¹⁶ e. "To resolve" or "explain" (a contradiction), Plut. Praec. Ger. Reip., 13 (II, 808d, with διδάσκω), Eus. Praep. Ev., XV, 6 (p. 802b), often in Simpl. in Aristot. Phys., e.g., I, 1, p. 9, 32 f. (→ n. 16); παραμυθία "explanation," Plut. De Animae Procreatione in Tim. Plat., 1 (II, 1012b); Fac. Lun., 17 (II, 929 f); Pyth. Or., 3 (II, 395 f; with ἐπῳδή "reassurance by magical means"; the imagery of a means of appeasing thus plays some part in the concept, → 819, 4 f.). f. The sense of friendly exhortation or verbal reassurance leads to further shades of meaning, "to excuse," Strabo, 13, 1, 64; Simpl. in Aristot. Phys., I, 2,

---

¹⁴ Geoponica sive Cassiani Bassi Scholastici de re rustica eclogae, ed. H. Beckh (1895).

¹⁵ In Athen. ἡδονῆς, to be taken as a gen. qual. Elsewhere, with ref. to the decadent pleasure-seeking of imperial Rome, Plut. (Praecepta de Tuenda Sanitate, 22 [II, 134a]) uses the Platonic expression which had now become a household word : emetics and purgatives are for him μιαρὰ παραμύθια πλησμονῆς.

¹⁶ Simplicius in Aristot. Phys. (ed. H. Diels, Commentaria in Aristotelem Graeca, IX [1882] and X [1895]).

p. 38, 2; παραμυθία, "excuse," *ibid.*, I, 2, p. 37, 30; VIII, 10, p. 1341, 2 (→ n. 16). g. "To calm," "to appease," Luc. Toxaris, 33 (by compensation), with διαλλάττομαι Plat. Prot., 346b, with πραΰνω Plut. Cicero, 37 (I, 879c), with καταπραΰνω and προσλαλέω, Plut. Praec. Coniug., 37 (II, 143c), with τιθασεύω ("to tame") Dio C., 41, 15, 3, with κήλησις ("charming," "appeasing," "soothing") Plat. Euthyd., 290a; παραμυθία "means of soothing," Plut. Them., 22 (I, 123b; with κουφισμός), also παραμύθιον, Plut. Quaest. Conv., I, 10, 3 (II, 629a; with παραίνεσις), shortly after ἀπαραμύθητος "implacable" (the opp. is εὐπαραμύθητος, "easy to placate," e.g., Plat. Leg., X, 885b). h. "To pacify," Thuc., III, 75, 4; Plut. Sertorius, 16 (I, 575 f), with ἰσχναίνω Eur. Or., 298, with κηλέω and πραΰνω, Plat. Polit., 268b, with ἐπᾴδω and παύω Plut. Maxime cum Principibus Viris Philosopho esse Disserendum, 4 (II, 779a); παραμύθιον "pacification" Plat. Leg., IV, 704d, 705a. [17] i. "To satisfy," perhaps Aristoph. Fr., 45 (→ 818, 25) and LXX Wis. 19:12 (→ 818, 28): παραμυθία, "satisfying of a demand." j. "To give satisfaction," "to atone," attested only for παραμύθιον "satisfaction," Dio C., 56, 41, 6, "means of expiation," Plut. Def. Orac., 14 (II, 417c; with μειλίχια "expiatory offering").

The most important sense in this second group is "to console." [18] In this many of the previous lines intersect, especially the basic meaning of παραμυθεῖσθαι, for, to comfort someone, I instinctively draw close to him in a friendly way. Also implied, however, are the further senses "to exhort" — for comfort often consists in the admonition to bear what is suffered in a calm and cheerful spirit (→ 780, 8 ff.) — and "to alleviate" — for often the chief aim of comfort is to lessen the grief [19] (→ 780, 26 ff.).

4. Special Meanings of παραμυθία and παραμύθιον.

In the case of the nouns there is a whole series of special meanings in addition to the predominant sense of "comfort." a. In the epistolary style of antiquity παραμυθία is sometimes used as a formal address, e.g., P. Oxy., X, 1298, 2 (4th cent. A.D.). b. "Means of comfort," Plut. Cons. ad Apoll., 9 (II, 106b); the poet Antimachos παραμύθιον τῆς λύπης αὐτῷ ἐποίησε τὴν ἐλεγείαν τὴν καλουμένην Λύδην. c. "Sign of comfort," often of grave-stones, so Preisigke Sammelbuch, I, 4313, 11 (1st/2nd cent. A.D.): παραμυθία συνζοίης στοργῆς μοι τριετοῦς εὐσεβίην θεμένης, Epigr. Graec., 951, 4 : a bust for a youth who died young should πατρὸς καὶ μητρὸς Στρατόλας παραμύθιον εἶναι. Finally the two words are surprisingly used in the financial world with all kinds of nuances : d. "compensation," lit., e.g., BGU, IV, 1024, VII, 12 ff. (4th/5th cent. A.D.) [20] or fig. P. Flor., III, 332, 20 (2nd cent. A.D.); Ps.-Luc. Syr. Dea, 22; Plut. Quaest. Conv., II, 1, 2 (II, 630c): χάριν ... καὶ παραμυθίαν, "thanks and compensation." e. "Compensation or return for a loan," "interest" (παραμυθία τοῦ χρέους), e.g., P. Grec. e Lat., I, 48, 2, 5, 21 f. (6th/7th cent. A.D.); P. Flor., III, 300, 11 etc.; P. Masp., III, 309, 31; III, 314, 4; II, 167, 9, 16, 22; BGU, IV, 1020, 7 (6th cent. A.D.): ὑπὲρ παραμυθίας "as rent"; Preisigke Sammelbuch, I, 5285, 35 of a right of use ἀντὶ τῆς παραμυθίας τοῦ αὐτοῦ χρέους, "in place of interest on the said loan." On the other hand, in P. Lond., V, 1781, 2 (6th cent. A.D.) παραμυθία seems to mean a special reimbursement paid

---

[17] Later developments of this line in modern Gk. are παραμυθέομαι "to pacify (children) by storytelling," then simply "to tell a fairy-tale," and παραμύθι(ον) "fairy-tale," "fable"; possibly the use of μῦθος for "fairy-tale" had some influence here, → IV, 767, 11 ff. and n. 42.

[18] On other words for "comfort" and "to comfort" in antiquity cf. Exc. I in K. Buresch, Consolationum a Graecis Romanisque scriptarum historia critica = Leipziger Studien z. class. Philologie, IX, 1 (1886), 123-125. παραμυθέομαι "to console" sometimes takes a double as well as a single acc., e.g., Luc. Saturnalia, 30, and later it can also be used in a pass. sense (cf. παρακαλέομαι often in the LXX and NT, e.g., Gn. 37:35; ψ 125:1; Mt. 2:18; 5:4 etc.), "to be comforted"; cf. the refs. in H. v. Herwerden, Lex. Graecum suppletorium et dialecticum, II (1910), *s.v.*

[19] Cf. Plut. Cons. ad Apoll., 32 (II, 118c), also the quotations, *ibid.*, 2 (II, 102b c).

[20] Cf. the observations and refs. in Moult.-Mill., *s.v.*

in addition to rent. f. The (small) "pension" paid as solatium for age and poverty, e.g., P. Masp., III, 314, 29 of a yearly pension which sons had to pay their mother; Or., 7029 [21] of a παραμυθία which a vineyard yields a widow and her children. g. "Tip," e.g., P. Lond., IV, 1452, 12 and 32; 1497, 10 (709 A.D.), perhaps also V, 1785, 5.

B. The Word Group in the Old Testament.

.ταραμυθέομαι and derivates do not occur in the transl. Gk. of the LXX, but only in books where the LXX is the original : [22] παραμυθέομαι "to encourage," 2 Macc. 15:9 (→ 778, 20 ff.; 818, 12 f.); παραμυθία "refreshing" or "satisfying," Wis. 19:12 (→ 818, 28; 819, 13); παραμύθιον, "comfort," Wis. 3:18. The use here is thus limited to the sense "to soothe," "to comfort," whereas παρακαλέω in these books is used only in the sense "to admonish," though in transl. Gk., which does not have παραμυθέομαι etc., it can also mean "to comfort" (→ 777, 5 ff.; 778, 14 ff.).

The group does not occur in later Jewish translators except in Symmachus (2 Βασ. 10:2; Job 2:11; [42:11 cj Field]; Is. 40:2; 52:9; 66:13; Jer. 31:13; ψ 70:21; Is. 66:11) and occasionally in anon. pieces (Qoh. 4:1; Job 42:11; ψ 65:12). Here the main sense is "to comfort," and in most instances the ref. is to the divine consolations (→ 778, 10 ff.; 789, 29 ff.). [23]

C. The Word Group in the New Testament.

1. Usage.

παραμυθέομαι and derivates occur only half a dozen times in the NT, twice in Jn. (11:19, 31) and 4 times in Pl. The nouns occur only once each, παραμυθία in 1 C. 14:3, παραμύθιον in Phil. 2:1. Since the Johannine refs. are concerned only with Jewish practice (→ 821, 23-822, 15), we are faced by the astounding fact that Jn. has no term for the sphere of Christian παραμυθία, for the group παρακαλέω κτλ., apart from the special use of παράκλητος (→ 800 ff.), is also alien to him, → 793, 14 ff. In Paul, however, παράκλησις is so central a concept that παραμύθια always seems to be just supplementary; at any rate, when he uses the group παραμυθέομαι, the two terms always seem to be combined in some way : 1 Th. 2:12 : παρακαλοῦντες ὑμᾶς καί παραμυθούμενοι, [24] 5:14 : παρακαλοῦμεν ... ὑμᾶς, ἀδελφοί ... παραμυθεῖσθε τοὺς ὀλιγοψύχους, 1 C. 14:3 : ... λαλεῖ οἰκοδομὴν καὶ παράκλησιν καὶ παραμυθίαν, [25] Phil. 2:1: εἴ τις οὖν παράκλησις ἐν Χριστῷ, εἴ τι παραμύθιον ἀγάπης. [26]

It is natural to seek a distinction between παρακαλέω and παραμυθέομαι, [27]

---

[21] Quoted in a footnote to P. Lond., IV, 1497, 10.

[22] The attempt to reconstruct a Heb. original for one of these, namely, Wis. 1-5 (9) (F. Focke, "Die Entstehung d. Weisheit Salomos," FRL, NF, 5 H. [1913] etc.) has to be called a failure, cf. J. Fichtner, "Der AT-Text d. Sap. Sal.," ZAW, 57 (1939), 155-192, esp. 170.

[23] In most of the above refs. the Heb. is נחם. This originally denotes gestures as well as speech, just as the German Trost (cf. Eng. "trust") is more than speech. Hence at Qoh. 4:1 the conjecture מנקם for מנחם is unnecessary if with Luther we see in the term active help and not just verbal comfort (→ 804, n. 31). That the two belong together and are implied in one another may be seen from Is. 40:11, where the LXX has παρακαλεῖν for נהל "to lead" (→ 777, 1 and n. 18), but esp. from the comfort which Jesus gives (→ 822, 3 ff.). This special sense applies also to מנחם and its equivalent παράκλητος (→ 803 ff.). Cf. also the rendering of Job 2:11 in LXX and Σ [Bertram].

[24] Here a triad is formed by adding παραμυθέομαι to παρακαλέω and μαρτύρομαι (cf. Ac. 2:40, also 1 Pt. 5:12); cf. Dob. Th., ad loc.

[25] Here again a triad is formed by combination with παρακαλέω and οἰκοδομέω (cf. 1 Th. 5:11).

[26] In this case we have a tetrad.

[27] Thus J. C. K. v. Hofmann, Die heilige Schrift neuen Testaments, I² (1869), 183 sought

but difficult to find a convincing criterion by which to draw any sharp line of demarcation. Both are characterised by the twofoldness of admonition and comfort, nor can one show that in the NT the element of comfort is the more pronounced in the case of παραμυθέομαι κτλ. [28] For in all the relevant passages other meanings might be seen with at least the same right, e.g., "to encourage" at 1 Th. 2:12, "to strengthen" at 5:14, "encouragement" at 1 C. 14:3, "friendly word" at Phil. 2:1. In the NT, however, the close relation between admonition and consolation in the two groups [29] has a very different basis from that in secular usage. In the secular world consolation only too often takes the form of moral exhortation, → 780, 8 ff. In the NT, however, admonition becomes genuine comfort and *vice versa,* so that it is hard to separate or distinguish between the two, cf. Col. 2:2; 4:8; 1 Th. 5:11; Phil. 2:1; 1 C. 14:3. The unity of admonition and consolation is rooted in the Gospel itself, which is both gift and task. It is one of the forms which expresses the dialectical interrelation of indicative and imperative in the NT. Nevertheless, παρακαλέω and παραμυθέομαι are not fully interchangeable in the NT. It may be an accident, but it is certainly a fact that in the NT παραμυθέομαι κτλ. is never used directly for God's comfort, but at most only for the divine comfort mediated through prophecy (1 C. 14:3), or through the love which derives from God (Phil. 2:1). Nor does παραμυθέομαι ever denote eschatological comfort, as παρακαλέω so often does (→ 796, 33 ff.; 797, 8 ff.; 798, 8 ff.). It is always the comfort granted in this present earthly sphere.

2. Comfort and Comforters.

a. Traditional Rites and the Comfort of Jesus. The first and only Johannine occurrence of παραμυθέομαι in the NT refers to the typical Jewish custom of a visit of condolence, which is one of the most important works of love, → 791, 7 ff. Jn. 11:19: πολλοὶ δὲ ἐκ τῶν Ἰουδαίων ἐληλύθεισαν πρὸς τὴν Μάρθαν καὶ Μαριάμ, ἵνα παραμυθήσωνται αὐτὰς περὶ τοῦ ἀδελφοῦ, cf. v. 31.

> What we find here corresponds to Jewish rules about comforting ; comforters always stayed as near as possible to the sorrowing, and if possible in the house of mourning. They also accompanied them wherever they went, so as not to leave them alone in their grief and in the particular perils of the first days of sorrow (v. 31, 33). The period of consolation extended to the first seven days after death. [30] We do not know what words of comfort were spoken on such occasions. The pres. παραμυθούμενοι may relate to other things besides speech. These would include lamentation and weeping (v. 33). [31] Refs. to the same customs may be found in the stories of raising to life again in the Synoptic Gospels, Mk. 5:38; Lk. 7:12. [32] The throngs of mourners and comforters

---

to link παρακαλέω with the will and παραμυθέομαι with the mind. Cr.-Kö. and Trench do not go into the question.

[28] So Joh. W. 1 K., 322.

[29] A third group, used only once in the NT at Col. 4:11, displays the same duality of meaning. This is παρηγορέω-παρηγορία (→ n. 7), which is used for "exhortation" at 4 Macc. 5:12; 6:1 and for "comfort" at Col. 4:11 and Philo Som., I, 112, though the two often overlap, e.g., Philo Deus Imm., 65; Plut. De Exilio, 1 (II, 599b).

[30] Cf. Str.-B., IV, 596, → III, 842, 9 ff. The conjecture of J. Wellhausen (*Das Ev. J.* [1908], 52) and R. Bultmann (Bu. J., 305, n. 9) is thus erroneous when they suggest that the weeping Jews were originally only those of the procession on the day of burial, and that the four days (v. 39) were a secondary addition. H. J. Holtzmann J. = *Hand-Comm. z. NT,* 4³ (1908) on v. 19 is more reliable here.

[31] Cf. MQ, 25a Bar.; bShab., 105b; both in Str.-B., IV, 595; on this whole question κοπετός, → III, 844, 21-845, 15.

[32] Since we know nothing about relatives of Tabitha, we cannot say whether the widows who wept at her death-bed (Ac. 9:39) were simply lamenting or also offering comfort.

here correspond to what we read in Rabb. sources, MQ, 23a Bar.; jMQ, 3, 82b, 28; cf. Str.-B., IV, 596. In each case these well-meaning but often miserable comforters stand in sharp contrast to Jesus Himself as the one true comforter. Jesus does, of course, begin with words of comfort which do not categorically go beyond what is customary in Jewish consolation, Lk. 7:13 : μὴ κλαῖε, Mk. 5:36 : μὴ φοβοῦ, μόνον πίστευε (καὶ σωθήσεται, Lk. 8:50), Jn. 11:23 : ἀναστήσεται ὁ ἀδελφός σου (for the ref. to the hope of the resurrection is also found in the Rabb., cf. Gn. r., 14 (10c) in Str.-B., I, 895 f.; bKet., 8b, 9, ibid., IV, 606. Similarly, the saying to Jairus, esp. with the Lucan expansion, is to be construed as a consoling ref. to the ἔσχατα. In fact, however, all these sayings pt. forward to the active comfort which immediately follows. In Jesus one may see in a unique way that true comfort does not consist only in words but embraces active help as well, → n. 23, also → 797, 22 ff.; 798, 14 ff., 18 ff.; 799, 34 ff. The comfort of Jesus is the deed which He alone can perform and which alone comforts ; for all comfort which leaves the power of death unbroken is incomplete and unsatisfying. Hence true comfort can be given only by Him who is Himself the resurrection and the life, → 792, 18 f., 793, 3 f.

Other Jewish custom are to send letters of condolence (→ 791, 24 f.; cf. also 782, 33 ff.) and to conclude books with a word of consolation (→ 791, 26 ff.). The NT offers both in a completely new form, the one in 2 C., whose first part may be called the consolatory epistle κατ' ἐξοχήν in the NT (→ 798, 1 ff.), the other at the end of Mt. 28. [33]

b. Recipients. The recipients of comfort in the NT are in the first instance all those in need of consolation, whether or not they belong to the band of disciples or the Christian community : all who sorrow (cf. R. 12:15b), the sick and prisoners (Mt. 25:36, 43), orphans and widows (Jm. 1:27) — even if in these cases the terms are not used. Among comforted prisoners the apostle himself, isolated and condemned to inactivity, is especially emphasised (Col. 4:11), and when the word group παραμυθέομαι κτλ. is used, the ref. is to Christians : 1 Th. 2:12 : the apostle encourages those who are called into God's glorious kingdom ; 1 C. 14:3 : it is said of the primitive Christian prophet that he certainly edifies, exhorts and comforts men, but in the next v. these men are specifically called the ἐκκλησία; Phil. 2:1 deals unambiguously with the loving encouragement which one brother extends to another within the congregation. In the Church ὀλιγόψυχοι are esp. singled out as needing comfort (1 Th. 5:14), i.e., those who either lose heart in present afflictions [34] or are troubled by the thought of the parousia. [35]

c. Bearers. The bearers of Christian comfort are in the first instance the prophets in the NT community (1 C. 14:3), who in this respect are heirs of the OT prophets from the Exilic period (→ 789, 17 ff.). The charisma of παράκλησις καὶ παραμυθία, which is not a special office but part of the work of prophesying, is the proof of their spiritual authority. In 1 Th. 2:11 f. the apostle Paul describes his apostolic work in the individual cure of souls : ὡς πατὴρ τέκνα ἑαυτοῦ παρακαλοῦντες ... καὶ παραμυθούμενοι καὶ μαρτυρόμενοι εἰς τὸ περιπατεῖν ὑμᾶς ἀξίως τοῦ θεοῦ κτλ. (cf. also 2 C. 1:3 ff.; 2:1 ff.; 7:2 ff.). Paul lays strong emphasis here on the personal character of this work (ἕνα ἕκαστον ὑμῶν), as also in Col. 1:28 (3 times πάντα ἄνθρωπον) and Ac. 20:20. [36] It is a moot point whether the leaders of the community are addressed in 1 Th. 5:14. Early exegesis usually took it in this way, [37] but modern expositors mostly think in terms of the concern of the members for each other. In fact both views are tenable. If the latter be accepted, one may link it with the saying in Phil. 2:1, which speaks of the mutual

---

[33] Cf. O. Michel, "Der Abschluss d. Mt.-Ev.," Evangelische Theol., 10 (1950/51), 21 f.
[34] Wbg. Th., ad loc.
[35] Dob. Th., ad loc.
[36] Cf. Wbg. Th.², 56.
[37] Theod. Mops., ad loc.: vertit suum sermonem ad doctores (ed. H. B. Swete, II [1882], 36 f.).

consolation of Christians : εἴ τις οὖν παράκλησις ἐν Χριστῷ, εἴ τι παραμύθιον ἀγάπης, εἴ τις κοινωνία πνεύματος, εἴ τις σπλάγχνα καὶ οἰκτιρμοί ... It is true that the comfort of love might be the comfort received in Christ through God's love. But since all the other terms refer to the interrelations of Christians, and the whole list has the unity of the congregation as its goal, what is meant is surely the comfort that one brother gives another through the love of God shed abroad in our hearts by the Holy Ghost. This mutual work of consolation is one of the basic features of the community life of primitive Christianity. It makes the Christian fellowship of suffering into a fellowship of consolation, → 798, 3 ff. All consolations on the part of Christians have their model and source in the other world. Above all earthly comforters stands the one heavenly comforter who effects all genuine comfort on earth : ὁ θεὸς πάσης παρακλήσεως, 2 C. 1:3; cf. R. 15:5; → 797, 32 ff.

d. The Chief Motif in NT Comfort. Like all other gifts of the Gospel, its comfort, too, may be expressed in a single name, that of Jesus Christ. As compared with the multiplicity of inadequate motifs of consolation in the world around (→ 783 ff.; 791, n. 144), the NT offers this one efficacious and abiding comfort. All thoughts of comfort in the NT are in some way orientated to Christ. Even if the γραφαί, i.e., the OT, are adduced as a source of comfort and hope (R. 15:4), this is only because they are read in the light of the Gospel. The comfort which God Himself and the Holy Spirit give is bound up with the consoling deed of God in Christ. There are two main afflictions for which the NT offers comfort. 1. The first is death, for which comfort is sought more than for anything else in the world (→ 780, 36 ff.). The NT has the only genuine comfort for this in the promise of final resurrection, and this rests wholly and utterly on the testimony to the resurrection of Christ (1 C. 15). Jesus Himself, when He gave comfort in Jn. 11:23, said this when He distinctively identified His own person with the resurrection, v. 24 f. 2. The second is the suffering of Christians which they accept for Christ's sake and for which there is already valid and effective comfort in Christ. Christian suffering is fellowship with the suffering of Christ (2 C. 1:5; 1 Pt. 4:13). Recognition of this fact equips for the office of consolation (2 C. 1:4), and the suffering itself prepares for eternal glory (4:17). All the comfort which the apostle (1 Th. 2:12), the prophets (1 C. 14:3) and Christians themselves (1 Th. 5:14; Phil. 2:1) give is drawn from the Gospel. For the content of NT prophecy is the revelation of the mystery of Christ, the power of Christian comfort rests in the love of Christ (Phil. 2:1), and apostolic comfort is based on the fact that God has called us in Christ into His kingdom and glory (1 Th. 2:12).

Stählin

παρανομέω → IV, 1091, 1 ff.

παρανομία → IV, 1090, 27 ff.

παραπικραίνω, παραπικρασμός → πικρός.

παραπίπτω, παράπτωμα → πίπτω.

παρατηρέω, παρατήρησις → τηρέω.

παρατίθημι → τίθημι.

πάρειμι → παρουσία.

---

† παρεισάγω, † παρείσακτος

παρεισάγω, from Isoc., a rare word, relatively common in Polyb., has the neutral sense "I bring forward," "I present," "I introduce" (e.g., of prisoners of war or introduction at court), but mostly with a suggestion of the unlawful and furtive (e.g., letting enemies into a city) or at least the unexpected (e.g., introducing strange gods : ξένα παρεισάγων δαιμόνια [of Socrates], Plut. Alex. Fort. Virt., I, 5 [II, 328d]). [1] Cf. the other compounds with παρεισ-, which are very numerous (some 25) but sparsely attested, obviously because they involve words composed by spontaneous expansion with εἰσ- and specifically designed to express what is illegal, secret or unobserved. [2] παρεισάγω does not occur on inscr. [3] but is found in the pap., though only once : προσεφέρετο ἀλλότριον εἶναι τὸ παρεισαγόμενον ὑπ' αὐτοῦ, P. Tor., I, 8, 4 (117 B.C.) in the sense of secretly introducing. [4]

The term does not occur in the LXX, [5] nor apparently in Philo [6] or Joseph., [7] but we find it in Ep. Ar., 20 : The king wants to release Jews who came to Egypt in the time of his father but also οἵτινες προῆσαν ἢ μετὰ ταῦτα παρεισήχθησαν εἰς τὴν βασιλείαν. Here the προῆσαν shows that παρεισήχθησαν, too, is meant in a neutral sense, though those concerned did not come voluntarily but were settled in Egypt by force, so that the cogency of this ref. should not be exaggerated. [8] The usage elsewhere shows that the use in malam partem predominates rather than the neutral sense (cf. the instances of other παρεισ- compounds in → n. 4-7).

The drift found in non-biblical use is maintained in the single NT occurrence of παρεισάγω. When 2 Pt. 2:1 tells of the appearance of ψευδοδιδάσκαλοι, οἵτινες παρεισάξουσιν αἱρέσεις ἀπωλείας, the point is that such αἱρέσεις (→ I, 183, 16 ff.) have no business in the Christian community, that they have been able

---

π α ρ ε ι σ ά γ ω κ τ λ. [1] Cf. Pass. and Liddell-Scott, s.v.
[2] Cf. Pass. and Liddell-Scott, whose lists are much the same (Pass. alone has the terms παρεισακούω, παρείσβασις, παρειστρέχω found in the fathers). Cf. also Wettstein, II, 703 on 2 Pt. 2:1.
[3] The Indexes to Ditt. Syll.³ and Ditt. Or., which list, of course, only the res et verba notabiliora, do not have any other words with παρεισ-.
[4] So Mayser, I, 3² (1935), 246. Moult.-Mill., 492, s.v. (Preisigke Wört. does not have the word, since he refers only occasionally to P. Tor.) assures us that in this case παρα- "does not convey any idea of secrecy or stealth," though the same tendency is in Moult.-Mill. wrongly noted in respect of παρείσακτος (→ n. 15), παρεισέρχομαι (→ n. 6; II, 682, 30 ff.) and παρεισφέρω.
[5] Of compounds with παρεισ- only παρεισπορεύομαι at 2 Macc. 8:1: Judas Maccabaeus and his confederates go λεληθότως (the meaning of the verb is hereby emphasised, not extended) into the villages to gain supporters.
[6] Of compounds with παρεισ- Leisegang lists only παρεισέρχομαι, Op. Mund., 150; Abr., 96 and παρεισφθείρομαι, Agric., 15. Is the meaning in Op. Mund., 150 really the weaker one "to enter," "to creep in" (so → II, 682, n. 1)? Philo is referring to the entry of weakness, sickness and passion, which disturbs the power of thought and which he regards as undesirable ; the context is much the same in Abr., 96. Agric., 15 refers to the walling around of a field to protect the plants and fruits against τοὺς ἐπὶ τῷ σίνεσθαι παρεισφθείρεσθαι βουλομένους, → n. 7. In the Philo ref. in Eus. Praep. Ev., 8, 14 προσεισέρπω means "I worm my way in secretly."
[7] ἐπείσακτος Ant., 8, 194; 15, 332; Bell., 4, 661. Other compounds with παρεισ- are παρεισκομίζω at Bell., 2, 169 (statues of the emperor are hidden and brought into Jerusalem at night); 5, 497 (provisions are brought λάθρᾳ into the besieged town); παρεισπέμπω, 5, 100 (with ref. to a cunning stroke); παρεισφθείρομαι (→ n. 6), 4, 84 and 135 (of robber bands who settle in or break into the city).
[8] H. G. Meecham, The Letter of Aristeas (1935), 192 accepts too easily the view of Moult.-Mill. (→ n. 4). παρεισέρχομαι Test. Jud. 16:2; Test. Sol. 11:2.

to enter it only by illegal ways, and that they show themselves to be ψευδοδιδάσκαλοι by the manner in which they carry out their designs, though conversely
one can expect only παρεισάγειν of ψευδοδιδάσκαλοι, → II, 160, 5 ff. In the par.
in Jd. 4, which uses a verbal compound with παρεισ-, it is said of these heretics :
παρεισεδύησαν γάρ τινες ἄνθρωποι, "they have insinuated themselves (into the
community)." [9]

The verbal adjective παρείσακτος, used by Paul in Gl. 2:4, is to be taken in
the same sense. A neutral meaning is ruled out both by the context and also by
the flavour of the passage. παρεισάκτους as well as the ψευδαδέλφους are both
disparaging terms for the opponents of the Gentile mission and its freedom from
the Law. The detailed sense of παρεισάκτους here is apparently brought out more
clearly by the relative clause, for παρεισῆλθον takes up again the παρεισάκτους, [10] and both words relate to the way in which the Judaizing disturbers of the
peace have found a way into the Gentile Christian churches (or the church at
Antioch, cf. Ac. 15:1 ff.). [11]

παρείσακτος is very rare outside the Bible. Older than Gl. 2:4 is Strabo, 17, 1, 8,
where Ptolemy IX Alexander I is described as ὁ Κόκκης καὶ Παρείσακτος ἐπικλη-
θεὶς Πτολεμαῖος. It is not apparent from the context to what the nickname Παρείσακτος refers. Perhaps the pt. is that Cleopatra III first chose her elder son Ptolemy VIII
as co-ruler, and only when she had removed him did she call the younger Ptolemy IX
to the throne, so that the latter attained to power only against expectation and contrary
to the original wishes of the people. [12] The lexicographers of antiquity also mention the
term, and Hesych., Phot. and Suid., s.v. all agree : παρείσακτον· ἀλλότριον. [13] It
thus seems that παρείσακτος was no longer understood in a pass. or mid. sense, but
simply felt to be an adj. [14] ἀλλότριος (→ I, 265, 4 ff.) here is not just an assertion but

---

[9] παρεισδύω occurs only here in the NT, παρείσδυσις is found in Barn., 2, 10; 4, 10.
Cf. Pr.-Bauer, s.v.

[10] Hence παρείσακτος is not to be taken in the pass. sense, as against Zn. Gl.³, 87
who imputes a pass. understanding and concludes therefrom that the word does not so
much refer to the reprehensible conduct of these men but is rather censuring those who
either brought or let them in.

[11] So rightly Ltzm. Gl., ad loc., whereas Zn. Gl.³, 87 f. separates the two expressions
and refers παρείσακτος to general admission to the Church, i.e., the attainment of baptism.
The fact that παρεισάγω was later used of heretics does not permit us, more esp. as there
is here and in 2 Pt. 2:1 an acc. obj. (Hegesipp. in Eus. Hist. Eccl., IV, 22, 5 : ἰδίαν δόξαν;
Hipp. Ref., V, 17, 13 [GCS, 26, 116, 10]: μυστήρια; VII, 29, 1 [GCS, 26, 210, 8]: καινόν
τι), to conclude that "the term παρείσακτος is a suitable one for what a later age usually
called heretical" (so A. Hilgenfeld, "Paulus u. d. Urapostel usw.," ZwTh, 3 [1860], 126 n.).

[12] The word is still taken as a pass. on this view. That it was a nickname given by the
people is the more likely in that Κόκκη, "the Red," was probably also a nickname given
to Cleopatra III, cf. F. Stähelin, Art. "Kleopatra, 16" in Pauly-W., XI, 1, 747. Did παρείσακτος have to be a word in current use to be a nickname ? Rare words, or words specially
coined, may serve as nicknames, though cf. RGG, IV, 1651.

[13] Cf. also J. Zonaras, Lexicon, ed. J. A. H. Tittmann (1808), 1504 : παρεισάκτους·
ἀλλοτρίους; 1510 : παρεισάκτους (as fem.)· ἀλλοτρίας, ξένας.

[14] So rightly Oe. Gl., ad loc. That the word might not have been all that uncommon (cf.
also Vita Epiphanii, 36 [MPG, 51, 69 C], which was not influenced by Gl. 2:4) is to be
seen from the fact, noted already by C. F. A. Fritzsche, De nonnullis Pauli ad Galatas
epistolae locis commentatio, I, in Fritzschiorum Opuscula Academica (1838), 181, that
Hesych. as well as Suid. uses παρείσακτος to elucidate other words. Vg has introducunt
at 2 Pt. 2:1, but subintroducti at Gl. 2:4, the latter obviously to underline the illegitimacy.
Cf. virgines subintroductae in the 5th cent. (= συνείσακτοι; John of Damascus, De Haere-
sibus, 100 [MPG, 94, 761 B] has παρείσακτος once in this sense : συνοικοῦσι γὰρ
γυναιξὶ προφανῶς, καὶ παρεισάκτους συνάγουσιν).

also contains a note of censure. The one concerned does not belong where he is at work as an alien body ; he has wormed his way in. [15]

Michaelis

παρεισέρχομαι → II, 682, 31 ff.
παρεπίδημος → II, 64, 30 ff.
παρέρχομαι → II, 681, 16 ff.
πάρεσις → I, 509, 11 ff.

---

† παρθένος

Contents : A. Non-Biblical and Non-Jewish Use : 1. Use of παρθένος; 2. The "Virgin" in Religion : a. The Cultic Honouring of the Divine Virgin ; b. The "Virgin" as the Mother of the Divine Child ; 3. Virginity in Cultic Practice and Magic. B. The Old Testament and Judaism : 1. The Mother of Immanuel ; 2. The Meaning of παρθένος in the Septuagint ; 3. The Allegorical Use in Philo. C. παρθένος in the New Testament : 1. The More General Use ; 2. The Virginity of Mary ; 3. παρθένος in the Ascetic Sense ; 4. The Figurative Use.

---

[15] As against Moult.-Mill., *s.v.*, where Suid. is quoted in favour of the view that παρείσακτος "need not necessarily have a sinister reference, but may simply mean that the brethren are 'alien' to the body into which they have introduced themselves" (the rare noun παρεισαγωγή seems to be used more in the neutr. sense, cf. Pass., Liddell-Scott, *s.v.*). There is another example in Pr.-Bauer[4], *s.v.*: "In some MSS the prologue to Sir. is called πρόλογος παρείσακτος ἀδήλου, though this ref. is misleading inasmuch as the prologue is not by the Gk. translator of Sir., and is not therefore an instance of ancient usage, but is an inauthentic prologue to the book, identical with the preface (falsely ascribed to Athanasius) to Synopsis Scripturae Sacrae (D. Hoeschel, *Sapientia Sirachi sive Ecclesiasticus* [1604], 313) and found in LXX MS 248 (Codex Vaticanus graecus 346), which belongs to the 13th cent. From this it made its way into the Complutensian Polyglot, and from this into several editions of the LXX. E. Klostermann, *Analecta zur Septuaginta, Hexapla u. Patristik* (1895), 16 f. gives a copy of it. A title was added to the inauthentic prologue only in 1557 in the Bible ed. by R. Stephanus (*alia incerti authoris praefatio*), and this was transl. into Gk. in 1597 (Πρόλογος παρείσακτος ἀδήλου). This translator is thus responsible for the παρείσακτος.

π α ρ θ έ ν ο ς. On A : E. Fehrle, "Die kultische Keuschheit im Altertum," RVV, 6 (1910); R. Franckh, "Die Geburtsgeschichte Jesu Christi im Lichte d. altorientalischen Weltanschauung," *Philotesia = Festschr. P. Kleinert* (1907), 201-221; W. Gundel, Art. "Parthenos," Pauly-W., XVIII, 2, 1936-1957; G. Herzog-Hauser, Art. "Παρθένοι," Pauly-W., XVIII, 2, 1904-1912; A. Jeremias, *Babylonisches im NT* (1905); C. G. Jung-K. Kerényi, "Das göttliche Mädchen," Albae Vigiliae, 8/9 (1941); A. Klinz, 'ΙΕΡΟΣ ΓΑΜΟΣ, Diss. Halle (1933); H. Leisegang, "PNEUMA HAGION," *Veröffentlichungen d. Forschungsinstituts f. vergleichende Religionsgeschichte an d. Universität Leipzig*, 4 (1922), 14-72; E. Norden, "Die Geburt d. Kindes," *Studien d. Bibliothek Warburg*, 3 (1924); H. Strathmann, *Die Askese in d. Umgebung d. werdenden Christentums* (1914). On B : A. v. Bulmerincq, "Die Immanuelweissagung (Js. 7) im Lichte d. neueren Forschung," Acta et Commentationes Universitatis Tartuensis (Dorpatensis), B. 37, 1 (1935); H. Gressmann, "Der Messias," FRL, NF, 26 (1929), esp. 235-242; S. Gutknecht, *Das Motiv d. Jungfrauengeburt in religionsgeschichtlicher Beleuchtung*, Diss. Greifswald (1952); R. Kittel, "Die hell. Mysterienreligion u. d. AT," BWANT, NF, 7 (1924), 1-36, 43-45, 64-72; K. Rückert, "Die Begriffe παρθένος u. ἀπαρχή in Apk. 14:4, 5," Theol. Quart., 68 (1886), 391-448; 69 (1887), 105-132; A. Schulz, " 'Almā," BZ, 23 (1935/36), 229-241; J. J. Stamm, "La Prophétie d'Emmanuel," *Revue de Théol. et de Philosophie*, NS, 32 (1944), 97-123. On C : H. v. Baer, "Der Heilige Geist in d. Lukasschriften," BWANT, 3. F., 3. H. (1926), 48-54, 113-131; C. K. Barrett, *The Holy Spirit and the Gospel Tradition* (1947), 5-24; K. Barth K.D., I, 2³ (1945), 189-221 (C.D., I, 2 [1956], 172-202); K. Bornhäuser, "Die Geburts- u. Kindheitsgeschichte Jesu," BFTh, 2. R., 23. Bd. (1930), 38-45, 82-87; F. Büchsel, *Der Geist Gottes im NT* (1926), 191-201; G. Delling, "Paulus' Stellung zu Frau u. Ehe," BWANT, 4. F., 5. H. (1931), esp. 85-91, 115 f.; M. Dibelius, "Jungfrauensohn u. Krippenkind," SAH (1931/32), 4; A. Drews, *Die Marienmythe* (1928); D. Edwards, *The Virgin Birth in History and Faith* (1943); M. S. Enslin, "The Christian Stories of the Nativity," JBL, 59 (1940), 317-338,

A. Non-Biblical and Non-Jewish Use.

1. Use of παρθένος.

Since the etym. is uncertain, [1] the semasiological development can be deduced only from the literary examples. The term obviously means a "mature young woman" (→ n. 11) already in Hom., with ref. to one who is not married (Il., 2, 513 f.: οὓς τέκεν ... παρθένος αἰδοίη, hence παρθένιος, the son of a maiden, 16, 180); cf. then Aristoph. Nu., 530 f.: a παρθένος is not allowed to have a child; and on the other side Soph. Trach., 148 f.: ἕως τις ἀντὶ παρθένου γυνὴ κληθῇ (with her worries about husband and child). In the sense of "maiden" the emphasis, acc. to context, is either on the sex (Plat. Leg., VIII, 834d : παῖδας ἢ παρθένους, cf. VII, 794c), or age (Aristoph. Ra., 950 in contrast to old woman), or both (in Soph. Trach., 1071 f. Heracles says : ὥστε παρθένος βέβρυχα κλαίων), or on status (opp. of widow, Paus., II, 34, 12). The ref. in these instances is in fact usually to virgins, but there is no more stress on this than when we speak of a "girl" or "young woman" (which is in innumerable instances the best rendering). So Plut. (Mulierum Virtutes, 20 [II, 257e]): someone married someone as a young girl; Praec. Coniug., 2 [II, 138e]: the girlish whims of the young wife); hence it can be said of a young woman : παρθένων ... τῶν ἐν Λακεδαίμονι εἶναι ... αἰσχίστην (!), Paus., III, 7, 7. The word then went through an obvious process of narrowing down (cf. the German juncfrouwa, orig. "young lady") and παρθένος came to be used for the "virgin." So Aristoph. Eq., 1302 (παρθένοι for unused ships); Xenoph. Mem., I, 5, 2 : θυγατέρας παρθένους διαφυλάξαι, Cornut. Theol. Graec., 34 παρ-θένος = ἄχραντος (unspotted) and ἀγνός (of Artemis); adj. Eur. Hipp., 1006 : παρθένον ψυχὴν ἔχων (Hippolyt. is free from all erotic desire even of the eyes); Jos. Ant., 1, 34 : παρθένος γῆ (from which Adam is formed); hence παρθενεύειν διὰ βίου of the Vestals, Dio C., 7, 8, 11.

The various nuances intermingle in the refs., so that it is not possible to assign a specific meaning to each occurrence. In Plat. Hi., I the primary thought is that of virgin freshness when he uses the beauty of the παρθένος as a striking instance of the beautiful in general (287e-297d). But there can also be a sense of the special spiritual charac-teristics of the girl, e.g., primarily on the basis of external appearance, Xenoph. Ag., 6, 7: When there is the possibility of attacks by the enemy, he holds the army as close together as he can, ὡς ἡσύχως δ' ὥσπερ ἂν παρθένος ἡ σωφρονεστάτη προβαίνοι. From physical purity a connecting line is drawn to spiritual : The Pythia enters into relation with the god ἄπειρος ... καὶ παρθένος ὡς ἀληθῶς τὴν ψυχήν (Plut. Pyth. Or., 22 [II, 405c]).

2. The "Virgin" in Religion.

a. The Cultic Honouring of the Divine Virgin.

The multiplicity of content is not clarified when the term παρθένος is used in the religious sphere. To some degree it cannot really be said which of the various nuances is really predominant here. This is, of course, connected with the fact that female deities had to take over the manifold characteristics of the goddesses whom they replaced. In

---

esp. 320-329; G. Erdmann, "Die Vorgeschichten d. Lukas- u. Matthäus-Evangeliums," FRL, NF, 30 (1932); H. Gressmann, Das Weihnachts-Evangelium (1914); F. Kattenbusch, "Die Geburtsgeschichte Jesu als Haggada d. Urchristologie," ThStKr, 102 (1930), 454-474; M. J. Lagrange, "La conception surnaturelle du Christ d'après Saint Luc," Rev. Bibl., 23 (1914), 60-71, 188-208; S. Lösch, Deitas Jesu u. Antike Apotheose (1933), 81-105; J. G. Machen, The Virgin Birth of Christ² (1932), → Kattenbusch : H. Sahlin, "Der Messias u. d. Gottes-volk," Acta Seminarii Neotestamentici Upsaliensis, 12 (1945), 98, 104-113, 117-136; K. L. Schmidt, "Die jungfräuliche Geburt Jesu Christi," ThBl, 14 (1935), 289-297; A. Steinmann, Die jungfräuliche Geburt d. Herrn³ (1926); V. Taylor, The Historical Evidence for the Virgin Birth (1920). Cf. also the bibl. in Pr.-Bauer⁴, 1141 f.
[1] Herzog-Hauser, 1910 favours the suggestion in Boisacq, 747, namely, a connection with -θεν- "to swell," "to bloom."

the last resort the epithet παρθένος could not be ascribed to them unless it carried a varied meaning.

Artemis, for instance, is emphatically παρθένος. She is identified with various goddesses. [2] She protects chaste young men and women, and punishes offences. [3] But she is also a nature goddess. Agriculture, the raising of cattle, youth, marriage and birth all belong to her domain. [4] Again — and this leads us back to the thought of the virgin goddess in the narrower sense — she is the guardian of oaths. [5] There is a similar fusion of apparent opposites in astrological religion. The Virgin in heaven is on the one hand the giver of fruitfulness [6] and on the other the strict mistress of law. [7] The Virgin of astrological religion, esp. in the Hell. sphere, apparently contributed to the further fusion of opposites in the concept of the divine παρθένος. In the first instance the Virgin in heaven was simply a symbol of woman set among the constellations. She comprised in herself the various characteristics of woman (ancient Babylonian influences are perhaps to be seen here).

Now for the Gks. there is already a connection between the apparent opposites; παρθένος represents young and budding life and strict innocence. In both is a power which is understood in religious terms. Where they are present together, special powers are at work. This thought finds expression in the fact that Gk. myth tells of individual virgins or groups of virgins whose sacrifice or self-sacrifice had a particular effect on the gods. [8] Their sacrifice had special force because they surrendered their lives in a state of youthful freshness on the one side and in that of innocence on the other. They thus became σώτειραι and were invoked as helpers in distress. [9] This idea of the particular power of the girl by reason of youth on the one side and virginity on the other obviously underlies the cultic honouring of the more famous Παρθένοι of myth. We also find various cults which worship an anonymous goddess as Παρθένος. Thus a cult of this kind persisted for many centuries in Sebastopol; it included epiphanies, miracles, and an era named after the goddess (βασιλευούσας Παρθένου). [10] In this case it is quite possible that the term παρθένος primarily denotes unfading freshness. This is also true when the word is used at times for goddesses of love (Aphrodite and her oriental cousins), cf. the idea that Hera becomes a παρθένος again after each union with Zeus. [11]

The concept takes a particular form in Athene. [12] It is true that Athene had to take

---

[2] K. Wernicke, Art. "Artemis," Pauly-W., II, 1, 1375, 1396.

[3] Ibid., 1352 (cf. G. Wentzel, Art. "Aktaion," Pauly-W., I, 1210).

[4] Wernicke, 1342-1348; Cornut. Theol. Graec., 34, brings out the apparent contradictions in Artemis; cf. also Plat. Crat., 406b: The name Artemis means τὸ ἀρτεμές (the inviolate) ... καὶ τὸ κόσμιον, διὰ τὴν τῆς παρθενίας ἐπιθυμίαν.

[5] Wernicke, 1351.

[6] Gundel, 1949, 1956.

[7] Ibid., 1945, 1957. Arat. Phaen., 100-136: Δίκη, who dwelt on earth in the golden age and had dealings with men only rarely in the silver age, went to heaven as the constellation of the Virgin in the bronze age. Cf. Vergil Ecl., 4, 6: iam redit et Virgo, the age of righteousness (cf. H. Hommel, Theologia Viatorum, 2 [1950], 188 f., n. 6. The interpretation of Gressmann, Messias, 468, 470, 475 — the mother of him who brings salvation — is impossible in the context). Cf. already Hes. Op., 256 for Δίκη as παρθένος in the narrower sense.

[8] Herzog-Hauser. Eur. took up the theme in several tragedies, ibid., 1909; cf. J. Schmitt, "Freiwilliger Opfertod bei Eur.," RVV, 17, 2 (1921), esp. 78-84 ("Der ritueller Sprachgebrauch in d. Devotionsszenen"): "It is ritual purity ... which makes the sacrifice of the virgin so well adapted to placate the divine powers," also the beauty of the παρθένος (81).

[9] Herzog-Hauser, 1904, 1910 etc.

[10] Ditt. Syll.³, 360, 1. 51; 709, 23 f. 52; Strabo, 7, 4, 2; E. Diehl, Art. "Parthenos," Pauly-W., XVIII, 2, 1959; cf. also Herzog-Hauser, 1911.

[11] Paus., II, 38, 2; L. Ziehen, Art. "Parthenios," Pauly-W., XVIII, 2, 1892; Fehrle, 201 ff. Klinz, 104 suggests there might be a link with the worship of Hera as a goddess of vegetation; she becomes young again each spring.

[12] Fehrle, 196-201.

on a series of maternal characteristics. [13] But for intellectual strata in the Gk. world, as expressed in art, she is the epitome of the unapproachable and self-contained maiden ; in the everyday world the thought of the chaste Athene is expressed in a statement like that in Artemid. Oneirocr., II, 35 (p. 133, 17 f.): (ʼΑθηνᾶ) γυναιξὶ δὲ ἑταίραις καὶ μοιχευομέναις πονηρά, ἔτι καὶ γυναιξὶ γήμασθαι προῃρημέναις· παρθένος γὰρ ἡ θεός. [14] With the figure of the Παρθένος Athene is linked esp. the idea of non-sexual origin ; she is without either father or mother (to the Gk. the exclusion of the female rather than the male element is important here). This notion then plays a role in speculative philosophy, and here it is explained in detail : Athene springs from the head of Zeus, and so does Nike, Philolaos (?) Fr. 20 (Diels⁶, I, 416, 15 f.), the παρθένος ἀμήτωρ, with whom the number seven is compared because it is formed of no other number but one (line 22). And now follows a list of important predicates : ἔστι γὰρ ἡγεμὼν καὶ ἄρχων ἁπάντων, θεός, εἷς, ἀεὶ ὤν, μόνιμος, ἀκίνητος, αὐτὸς ἑαυτῷ ὅμοιος, ἕτερος τῶν ἄλλων (line 23 f.). For the Gk., then, the word has the implication of immutability, self-sufficiency and separation. It comprises something divine and establishes superiority. Perhaps one might say that παρθένος mythicises αὐτάρκεια, which is so important to the Gk. It is a symbol of the personality which is independent, self-derived and self-contained. The image of Athene already carries related features in Hom., [15] though we do not find the terms παρθένος and αὐτάρκεια for her. This helps us to see why the word Παρθένοι is used for the goddesses who watch incorruptibly over law (Nemesis and Dike as well as Artemis); [16] these have to be unapproachable.

b. The "Virgin" as the Mother of the Divine Child.

In the world of religion around the Bible there is frequent reference to a "virgin" who bears a divine child. Nevertheless, one has to ask in each case what specific ideas are bound up with the statement.

For one thing, the meaning of "virgin" is at issue. In the sphere of Gk. religion παρθένος may simply denote the bloom of youth, the pt. of transition from girl to woman. When used in the narrower sense, the word lays particular stress on virginity by nature, [17] which certainly includes unapproachability, but does not stress physical chastity. When a woman is called "virgin," however, one has to ask whether the emphasis is on strict virginity (παρθένος and κόρη, e.g., are to a large extent interchangeable terms), [18] i.e., whether a "virgin" mother is called this because the child is conceived without intercourse, or because she was a virgin up to the time of conception, or even because of her youthful bloom. In many areas in the world of antiquity the statements are so short or formal that it is hard to answer this question. Thus in Egypt the concept of virginity has no religious significance. [19] If Isis is called παρθένος, one may see here the influence of astral religion. [20] Generalisations [21] do not contribute to an elucidation of the NT statements.

---

[13] Fehrle, 169-195.
[14] Cf. Plut. Demetr., 26 (I, 901a). F. Höfer, "Parthenos," Roscher, III, 1, 1663. For poetic examples cf. C. F. H. Bruchmann, Epitheta deorum quae apud poetas Graecos leguntur (1893), 13 f.
[15] Fehrle, 195 f.
[16] Herzog-Hauser, 1912.
[17] This is plain in the work of Jung-Kerényi, → Bibl. n.
[18] This is not sufficiently noted in Kittel, 24, 45 with relation to Persephone, cf. 39. Thus in Epiph. Haer., 51, 22, 10 (GCS, 31, 286, 6), is not τουτέστιν ἡ παρθένος an elucidation of Epiph., who wished to demonstrate "virgin birth" in pagan religions ? The child of Persephone was begotten by Zeus (F. Höfer, Art. "Jakchos," Roscher, II, 1, 3). Cf. Fehrle, 21 f.; Clemen, 119; Franckh, 213 f. ("a vague development" of the concept of virginity).
[19] H. Gressmann, "Götterkind u. Menschensohn," DLZ, 47 (1926), 1920; Gressmann, Messias, 470 f. (cf. 392 and → 830, 16 ff. on Plut. Numa, 4). Cf. Clemen, 120.
[20] F. Boll, Sphaera (1903), 209-216.
[21] Jeremias, 47: "The redeemer king appears everywhere as the virgin's son" (cf. 36 f., 47 f., but also Franckh, 205-214). Cf. Kittel, 24, 70-72 (64 f. etc.); Gressmann, Weihnachts-

Again, one has to ask what is implied by the conception of the divine child. The idea of the ἱερὸς γάμος is widespread in the ancient world. [22] The deity may come in his own form, in a changed form, or in a dream, though in every case antiquity regards the process as a natural one. There is no question of parthenogenesis in the strict sense even when no man is present and conception is simply by a sperm or equivalent. [23] There is, however, a sublime idea of extraordinary conception (though not by a virgin) in one Egyptian reference, if the Greek witness understood it aright.

Plut. Quaest. Conv., VIII, 1, 2 (II, 717d) mentions the myth of the (sexual) begetting of Plato by Apollo, but this is rejected as incompatible with the incorruptibility of God (begetting implies change, 1, 3 [II, 717e]). Plut. gives it a fresh turn by suggesting that, as in the creation of the world, the god activates a principle of becoming (ἀρχή, → I, 479 f.) in matter (ὕλη), not after the manner of human begetting, but by certain contacts δι' ἑτέρων ... ὑποπίμπλησι θειοτέρας γονῆς τὸ θνητόν (718a). Plut. is borrowing the idea from the Egyptians, who maintain that Apis was conceived by a touch (ἐπαφῇ) of the moon (cf. Is. et Os., 43 [II, 368c]: a ray of light from the moon). This whole question has some significance for Plut.; it is found again in Numa, 4 (I, 62). He can well understand that a divine being may incline in friendly fashion to a noble man, 4, 4 (I, 62b). The idea of physical contact leading to conception is more difficult, 4, 5 (I, 62b). "And yet the Egyptians seem not incredibly to maintain that it is not impossible," γυναικὶ ... πνεῦμα πλησιάσαι ("approaches") θεοῦ καί τινας ἐντεκεῖν ἀρχὰς γενέσεως, ἀνδρὶ δ' οὐκ ἔστι σύμμειξις πρὸς θεὸν οὐδ' ὁμιλία σώματος, 4, 6 (I, 62c). Here, and in what follows, one may detect a certain criticism of the Egyptian view; the final sentence, which finds a par. in Quaest. Conv., VIII, 1, 3 (II, 718b), apparently shows that, as attested elsewhere, the Egyptians held the (to him) intolerable concept of sexual intercourse between God and women. He had obviously heard, however, of the idea of a less crude origin of divine children, and he uses this to form his own theory in Quaest. Conv., VIII, 1. One cannot be sure as to the exact meaning of what is said about the Egyptian view in Numa, 4 (I, 62). [24] The verb πλησιάσαι, esp. in contrast to what follows (ἀνδρί), is surprising. Perhaps in respect of πνεῦμα we are to think of a divine emanation. At any rate, in these passages in Plut. the divine operation is presented in terms which suggest immediacy, though through very refined matter. [25]

3. Virginity in Cultic Practice and Magic.

Various motifs seem to be conjoined in the requirement of celibacy laid permanently or temporarily on priests or participants in the cultus (also magicians). [26] The lifelong sexual abstinence demanded of priests and priestesses by certain deities [27] carries with it in the first instance the thought that virginity conveys a special religious power. But in the case of a priestess the main idea in chastity may be simply that she lives in marital relation to the god. [28] If priests and other participants in the cultus have to

---

Ev., 43 is rightly more cautious about emphasising the predicate "virgin" is respect of Ištar etc., cf. Clemen, 118; Gressmann, Messias, 476: "not attested from Babylonian texts in the case of Ištar." In keeping is the presentation in Jeremias, 27-30; Gressmann, op. cit. (→ n.19), 1926 f. Gutknecht concludes that in the ancient Orient one cannot find examples of the virgin mother-goddess. The mother-goddess is not virgin, and the virgin Anat in Ras Shamra is not a mother-goddess [A. Jepsen].

[22] → I, 653, 26 ff.; Fehrle, 3-12, 20-22, 216-218; Reitzenstein Poim., 228 f.; Klinz (quotes and discusses the texts); Gressmann, Messias, 476 f.

[23] Clemen, 117; Fehrle, 22.

[24] Reitzenstein Poim., 230 calls it an explanation of the theogamy of the wives of the Egyptian kings etc.

[25] The substantial view of πνεῦμα also lies behind the examples which, e.g., Norden, 77 gives under πνεῦμα.

[26] Fehrle, 157.

[27] Ibid., 75-112; Strathmann, 172-180; for non-priestly assistants, Fehrle, 112-125; for laity, 126-154; Strathmann, 201-204 etc.

[28] Fehrle, 42 etc.

abstain from sex relations for a few days before (e.g., Ps.-Demosth. Or., 59, 78), the reason is obviously to be found in the statement: τὰ ἀφροδίσια μιαίνει (Porphyr. Abst., IV, 20), which is naturally to be understood only ritually, not ethically. [29] It is conceivable that the idea of demonic infection through sexual intercourse also played some part. [30] Cf. also → II, 765, 25 ff. The philosophically grounded, lifelong celibacy of an Apollonius of Tyana (Philostr. Vit. Ap., I, 13 [p. 13]; VI, 11 [p. 218]) is not in the last resort for religious reasons.

Application of the predicate of "virgin" to the magic goddess Hecate-Selene was probably influenced by the thought of the religious power of virginity (Preis. Zaub., IV, 2255, 2265, 2287 etc. in address). This is certainly the main concept when the use of the lymph of a (dead) girl is prescribed in magical acts (IV, 2577; cf. 2876 f.; the "uncorrupted youth" also plays a role, II, 56; V, 375 f.; here physical virginity is obviously important as such), or when a living virgin averts disease by a certain action, Plin. Hist. Nat., 26, 9 (60).

B. The Old Testament and Judaism.

1. The Mother of Immanuel.

The word עַלְמָה, which occurs 9 times in the OT, obviously means an unmarried woman in 3 instances (esp. clearly Gn. 24:43; Ex. 2:8; probably Ps. 68:25, and perhaps, if עַל־עֲלָמוֹת is to be derived from עַלְמָה, Ps. 46:1 and 1 Ch. 15:20). The same may be assumed in Cant. 1:3, and the par. "daughter" in Cant. 6:9 [31] suggests that girl is the meaning in v. 8 (court ladies and maids). The meaning is uncertain at Prv. 30:19 (LXX ἐν νεότητι for בְּעַלְמָה). [32] In the light of the use elsewhere it probably has the same sense as παρθένος had originally, namely, the young woman who has just reached maturity (and thus at Prv. 30:19 concretely the bride who has just been brought home). Certainly there is no emphasis on virginity in עַלְמָה. [33] It seems likely that the meaning at Is. 7:14 is the same as at Prv. 30:19.

The broader interpretation of Is. 7:14 depends on our understanding of the context. [34] Is הָעַלְמָה an individual (the wife of the prophet, [35] of Hezekiah, or an anonymous woman, unknown to Is. too), or (with a general art.) is she the totality of all the women pregnant at that time in the nation? Again, is Immanuel the name of a future personage (the Messiah; along with Is. 8:8, 10?), or the name of many born at the time? Are milk and honey the only food that will be left for all in the coming time of tribulation, [36] or the divine food of the promised One? Do we have a sign of salvation or a sign of judgment?

The latter is obviously meant in vv. 15-17. Yahweh keeps to the promise of vv. 4-7, but He answers the unbelief of Ahaz by threatening ruin in place of the sign of salvation given earlier (the distress indicated in v. 17 confirms the authority of the prophet for the demand of v. 11). The name Immanuel, however, is to be taken only as a sign of salvation; it pts. mysteriously beyond the time of affliction primarily referred to in the

---

[29] We are to see an attack on the usual view when the supposed wife of Pythagoras, asked the question when a woman became pure from a man, replied: "In relation to her husband at once, but never in relation to another man," Stob., IV, 587, 1 f.

[30] For this view cf. Strathmann, 213 f.

[31] Cf. the comm.; Schulz, 232.

[32] On this basis Schulz, 238 et al. conjecture a Heb. "in youth."

[33] As against v. Bulmerincq, 12. The ref. in Gn. 24:43 is not to Rebekah (who is called בְּתוּלָה in v. 16), but generally to the maiden promised to Eliezer (in v. 14 the par. is הַנַּעֲרָ) On cognates of עַלְמָה in other Semitic languages cf. Stamm, 110 and Schulz, 230, though with divergent conclusions.

[34] Cf. v. Bulmerincq, 7-14; Stamm, 102-109.

[35] Stamm, 116 f.

[36] So, e.g., Stamm, 114, who pts. first to the importance of these products in Israel.

context of v. 12 f. The sign of immediate promise in v. 11 is changed into a sign of threat in v. 13 f. ("therefore"), but the promise remains intact in the name Immanuel with its ref. to the more distant future, though no precise interpretation is given, and exposition is thus difficult. Is the name to be connected with the significant naming of the sons of Is. in 7:3; 8:3, or is it to be listed with the Messianic epithets of 9:5? An argument against the former view is that the name in 8:3 is given by the father; the term in 7:14 is also an unusual one for the prophet's wife [37] (עַלְמָה is not normally used for the mother of a son who has long since been able to walk, 7:3). Since Immanuel can hardly be a son of Hezekiah, [38] the only other possibility is that he is the son (presumably the first) [39] of an unknown woman. There is thus an element of mystery both for Is. and also for those to whom Is. 7:14 is addressed; the same is true of the promised child of Is. 9:5; 11:1. Whether the young bride is of the house of David (Is. 11:1) is intentionally left obscure in 7:14. The promised son stands directly under God's protection and direction; hence the father is not named, and the name is perhaps given by the mother for this reason. The decisive pt. is that the son of the young woman is the one who is commissioned by God to bring salvation (as the bearer of God's Spirit, Is. 11:2). The name "God with us" emphasises the fact that Yahweh is acting through him. [40]

On this view it is unlikely that the reference is to a divine child. [41] The idea of divine generation seems to be incompatible with the OT belief in God, while parthenogenesis would seem to require בְּתוּלָה rather than עַלְמָה. [42] This is still true even if the art. before the noun points "to the well-known figure of the virgin in the oriental world of thought." [43] The "known" figure of "the" virgin is an abstraction of religious history. In the age of Is. goddesses bearing the name of virgin exist only in specific religions (e.g., astral religion) with specific features. That Is. should have set a goddess alongside Yahweh is, however, quite incompatible with his view of God. It is equally incredible that he should have expected the birth of the Saviour from a pagan goddess.

2. The Meaning of παρθένος in the Septuagint.

In the LXX παρθένος has much the same sense as בְּתוּלָה for which it is used in the great majority of instances (בְּתוּלִים, Lv. 21:13). In many verses it simply means "girl," esp. when the plur. is set alongside νεανίσκοι etc., cf. Dt. 32:25; Ez. 9:6; Lam. 1:4; Ep. Jer. 8 (φιλοκόσμῳ), [44] though the chastity of the παρθένος is usually included as self-evident even in more general use, cf. Jer. 2:32 (par. νύμφη). In some instances virginity is specially emphasised, e.g., Lv. 21:13 f. (the priest may marry only a virgin, Ez. 44:22); Dt. 22:23, 28; Ju. 19:24 (ἡ θυγάτηρ μου ἡ παρθένος); 21:11, 12 (νεάνιδας παρθένους); 2 Βασ. 13:2, 18 etc.

---

[37] On these pts. cf. Stamm, 116 f.; cf. the prophetess in Is. 8:3.

[38] For objections cf. Stamm, 114 f.

[39] This is suggested by the word עַלְמָה and also by the importance of the firstborn in the OT and elsewhere ("virgin's son").

[40] Cf. Stamm, 120 as opposed to H. Schmidt, Der Mythos v. wiederkehrenden König im AT² (1933), 12 f. (" god in our midst").

[41] v. Bulmerincq, 14; milk and honey do not prove this, cf. Stamm, 114.

[42] Stamm, 109.

[43] v. Bulmerincq, 12; Kittel, 71: Is. is recalling the "well-known divine wife." On the other hand, Gressmann, op. cit. (→ n. 19), 1926 argues that "the oldest testimony" to the name "'virgin' for the queen of heaven" "is Is. 7."

[44] For this reason, to emphasise virginity quite unequivocally, a combination with ἄφθορος is once selected for בְּתוּלָה (Est. 2:2). In keeping on the other side is the fact that παρθένος is used 5 times in Gn. for נַעֲרָה or נַעַר. In Gn. 24:16 παρθένος is used once for נַעֲרָה, also once for בְּתוּלָה, though the original distinguishes plainly between young woman and virgin.

The idea of not being forced seems to be primarily in view when παρθένος is combined with place-names, esp. in adjectival use in the formula παρθένος θυγάτηρ (Βαβυλῶνος, Is. 47:1; Αἰγύπτου, Ιερ. 26[46]:11); so also παρθένος θυγάτηρ Σιων, Is. 37:22, cf. Am. 5:2. Obviously the idea of the love between Yahweh and His people can also stand behind the combination, Ιερ. 38(31):4 : Ισραηλ; [45] Lam. 1:15. [46] The people of Yahweh is the virgin who does not forfeit her purity by idolatry, Jer. 18:13-15; on Israel as bride → IV, 1101, 25 ff.

Only twice is παρθένος used for עַלְמָה, which is only rarely transl. νεᾶνις (normally for בְּתוּלָה or נַעֲרָה). The Gk. would give παρθένος the intrinsic meaning of both בְּתוּלָה and עַלְמָה. In the LXX, however, there is usually differentiation which strongly develops the one line of non-biblical usage for παρθένος; thus בְּתוּלָה implies virginity more forcefully. Nevertheless, one may see from Gn. 24:43 that παρθένος can have the sense of עַלְמָה: "a young woman ready for marriage," → 831, 17 f. In a special instance παρθένος can even be a girl who has been raped, Gn. 34:3 for נַעֲרָה; παρθένος is also used for this word at Sir. 30:20. This review (cf. also → n. 44) makes it plain that on purely lexical grounds it is impossible to say whether the translator is expressing true virginity when he uses παρθένος at Is. 7:14. The total picture of LXX usage demands no more than the sense of a "woman untouched by a man up to the moment of the conception (of Immanuel)." The other Gk. renderings have νεᾶνις here (Eus. Dem. Ev., VII, 1, 32 f.; Hist. Eccl., V, 8, 10). In itself this is in keeping with the meaning of עַלְמָה, though it may be suspected that the word was chosen in opposition to the Christian interpretation. One may compare the polemical Rabb. exegesis of OT statements which Christianity understood Messianically (→ 695, 5 ff.; 697, 19 ff.; → II, 949, 16 ff.). νεᾶνις is not shown to be used consistently for עַלְמָה.

On the basis of LXX usage it is also possible that the translator of Is. 7:14 envisaged a non-sexual origin of the virgin's son. Historically, even in his narrow circle, this might arise if historical value can be accorded to the stricter statements of Plut. (→ 830, 25 ff.) about Egypt.

3. The Allegorical Use in Philo.

The OT tells us that certain women, after a long period of waiting, were finally granted children by the special act of God. There is never any thought of the exclusion of the man. Rabbinic exegesis is to the same effect. By His wonderful intervention God creates in the bodies of these women the presupposition of conception, which then takes place through the husband. [47] Supernatural generation of the child is never intended. This understanding of Gn. 21:1 f.; 25:21; 29:31 contradicts Philo's attitude to the sensual world, Cher., 40. [48] Consequently Philo interprets the refs. allegorically. Sarah, Rebekah and Leah "are women only acc. to the letter, but in fact virtues," Cher., 41. God is ὁ σπείρων ἐν αὐταῖς (the virtues) τὰ καλά, He, the One who begets all things, Cher., 44. Man's soul has become womanly through the senses, Cher., 50. The woman, allegorically, denotes sensuality, αἴσθησις, → I, 187, 32 ff.; Cher., 41. But God has fellowship only with the soul which remains aloof from the emotions of the sensual world ; for it alone is ἀγνή and παρθένος, Spec. Leg., II, 30. Hence God makes the soul παρθένος again by freeing it from desire and endowing it with virtues ; for it befits Him to hold converse only with the "unspotted and pure nature, the true virgin," [49]

---

[45] Cf. W. Rudolph, Jeremia = Hndbch. z. AT, I, 12 (1947) on Jer. 31:4.

[46] Cf. W. Rudolph, Die Klagelieder = Komm. z. AT, 16, 3 (1939), ad loc.

[47] For a pagan analogy (the curing of a barren woman by Aesculapius and conception through her husband), cf. Ditt. Syll.³, 1169, 60 ff. (Dibelius, 36 f., though it seems to me that the ref. in the inscr. lines 129 ff. is to a theogamy, while lines 116 ff. are uncertain). On the Jewish attitude to marital affairs cf. Strathmann, 21-24.

[48] Cf. Strathmann, 125-147.

[49] The allegorical use of παρθένος in Philo is not formally consistent. Instead of a defiling union with αἴσθησις and its πάθη, he can speak of virtues contracting a marriage

Cher., 50; cf. Exsecr., 159 : [ψυχὴ] γίνεται ... ἀγνὴ παρθένος, also Migr. Abr., 224 f.
Special emphasis is here laid on the fact that in Jer. 3:4 God is called "the husband ...
not of the virgin" (the individual who can fall away again to the sensual world) but
"of virginity (τῆς παρθενίας, LXX), the idea which always remains exactly the same,"
Cher., 51. There is here demarcation even from the idea of a mystical conception in the
soul (which might seem to be suggested in 46). Not even polemically is there presupposed
an interpretation of the sayings about the wives of the patriarchs along the lines of
divine begetting. [50] Philo is led to expound the passages allegorically only because he
finds a literal understanding of the texts quite intolerable.

C. παρθένος in the New Testament.

1. The More General Use. The more general sense may be found at Mt. 25:1,
7, 11 (only in allegorical interpretation is this taken more specifically, cf. Herm. s.,
9, 1, 2-13, 8; → IV, 843, n. 91). On its scope → IV, 842 ff.; II, 706; the thought of
joy at the consummation is implied, → I, 654, 25 ff. In Ac. 21:9 the adj. παρθένοι,
used of the daughters of Philip, [51] may simply mean "unmarried." [52]

2. The Virginity of Mary. Mary's virginity prior to the birth of Jesus [53] (Mt.
1:23; Lk. 1:27) [54] is obviously not asserted by the NT for ascetic reasons. That
Mary continued to live as a virgin even after the birth of Jesus is a view which the
Western Church adopted only after 350. The concept of the virgin birth of Jesus
is not meant to disparage the marriage bond. [55] Its reference is to Jesus, not Mary.
It does not exclude the man as a basis for the sinlessness of Jesus. [56] If it did, then
Mary would have to be sinless too — a conclusion logically pressed for the first
time in Roman Catholic dogma. The process of birth does not cease to be natural;

(ἁρμόζεσθαι, Som., I, 200) with the ψυχὴ παρθένος, though they are elsewhere described
as παρθένοι, Praem. Poen., 53; Poster. C., 134; Mut. Nom., 196; the χάριτες θεοῦ are
also παρθένοι, Poster. C., 32). This shows us again that Philo is speaking in purely
allegorical fashion.
    [50] As against Norden, 78 f. Cf. Deus Imm., 3 as a counterpart to Cher., 46-52. Against
misinterpretation of Philo's statements cf. also Lösch, 91 f.; Franckh, 217. In Paul the ref.
at Gl. 4:29 is not to a spiritual, supernatural generation of Isaac (as against Dibelius, 29 f.);
v. 23 speaks of birth ("generation" is unlikely here) of the free woman διὰ τῆς ἐπαγγελίας. In R. 4:19 Paul plainly accepts begetting by Abraham, v. Baer, 121; Loesch, 86-88.
Hence the conclusions of Dibelius (32-34) in relation to Philo fall to the ground.
    [51] On these cf. Zahn Forsch., VI (1900), 165-174.
    [52] Against the background, though with no NT attestation, it is possible that the author
thought celibacy might be helpful in the prophetic ministry, cf. 1 C. 7:5 : ἵνα σχολάσητε
τῇ προσευχῇ.
    [53] The inexactitude only too common in this question contributes to an essential lack of
clarity. We have to distinguish 3 possibilities : 1. That considered → 829, 33 ff.; this is not
strictly a "virgin birth"; 2. birth without violation of virginity (→ n. 55), which alone
justifies the use of the term "virgin birth"; 3. conception without fertilisation (→ 833, 25 ff.),
which is strictly only a "virgin conception."
    [54] Sahlin, 107 maintains that παρθένος here simply "contains an emphasis on youth";
he conjectures an original "thou art pregnant" at v. 31 in Proto-Lk., 104-113. The excisions
and artificial interpretations in v. 34 (120 f.) and v. 35 (126 f., 131-136) are connected with
this. Cf. E. Hirsch, Frühgeschichte d. Ev., II (1941), 188 f., 191, 171 f.
    [55] H. Koch, Adhuc virgo, Mariens Jungfrauenschaft u. Ehe in d. altkirchlichen Über-
lieferung bis z. Ende d. 4. Jhdts. (1929), 28, 42 f. On the question of the virginitas post
partum cf. esp. P. R. Botz, D. Jungfrauschaft Mariens im NT u. in d. nachapostolischen Zeit,
Diss. Tübingen (1935). The first western witness is to be found in Prot. Ev. Jc. 17:1 (Joseph
has sons from a first marriage); 19:3-20:1 (virginity was not impaired even by the process
of birth). For the NT cf. Lk. 2:7 (πρωτότοκον; Koch, 37); → I, 144, 16 ff.
    [56] v. Baer, 115-118 introduces the thought of original sin on the basis of the OT and
Judaism, but he himself pts. out that in Judaism sinfulness was primarily traced back to
the woman, 117.

docetic features are completely absent from the narratives. In the infancy stories of the NT we are dealing neither with an ethical nor a physical demi-god. Neither His freedom from sin nor His miraculous power is explained here along natural-supernatural lines, just as the concept Son of God (→ υἱός) is not elucidated in this fashion in the rest of the NT. [57]

According to Luke, the events leading to the birth of Jesus are plainly distinguished from those leading to the birth of the Baptist. The experience of Elisabeth is similar to that of Sarah. The grief of barrenness (1:25) is taken from her in old age. If no description is given of God's miraculous intervention, there obviously lies behind 1:24 a view which corresponds basically to the Rabbinic concept of God's work in the wives of the patriarchs, especially Sarah. To be sure, the age of Zacharias is also an obstacle, 1:7, 18. But the very fact that this is mentioned shows that the process of conception was regarded as completely natural, cf. 1:13. In contrast is the understanding of Mary's experience. She is a young [58] woman engaged to be married, 1:27. While still a virgin (1:27, [59] 34) she is given the promise that she will conceive a son exclusively by the creative act of God, 1:31, 35. [60] The fulfilment of the promise is not as such described. [61] Nor is there any indication that it took place, e.g., during the visit of the angel.

The miracle of virgin conception, which is presented with such modest restraint, [62] seems to be understood similarly in Mt. in all essentials, though Lk. describes it in fuller and less unequivocal phrases (→ II, 300, 20 ff.; 681, 4 ff. → ἐπισκιάζειν). The thought of generation ἐκ πνεύματος ἁγίου is especially emphasised in Mt., 1:18, 20. [63] The reference to the Spirit is not to be regarded as a mythical statement about a divine begetting. Nothing is said regarding a mechanical operation on the body of Mary. Rather, there is reminiscence of Gn. 1:2. As the Spirit of God hovered over formless matter when the miracle of creation took place, so there is a new creative act of God when Jesus is born [64] (cf. the title βίβλος γενέσεως in Mt. 1:1). Thus expression is given to the uniqueness of Jesus even from the physical standpoint.

What has been said shows that in any attempt to find a genealogy of the virgin conception of Mary in the history of religions, there is no place for the concept of the ἱερὸς γάμος. [65] For the Palestinian the very fact that the "Spirit" is feminine makes

---

[57] It certainly seems as if we have something of this in Lk. 1:35d, but the statement does not have to contain more than an attempt to trace back Jesus' possession of the Spirit to the very first moments of His life.

[58] Acc. to the Rabb. view a girl was usually affianced at 12-12½, Str.-B., II, 374.

[59] Mt. 1:18. Between engagement and marriage there is normally something over a year, Str.-B., II, 394, 397. The legal position of the fiancée is the same as that of the married woman, ibid., 393. But the consummatio matrimonii is not included. By custom, at least in Galilee, it is virtually impossible, ibid., I, 45 f.

[60] τὸ γεννώμενον is simply "the child," A. Fridrichsen, "Randbemerkungen zur Kindheitsgeschichte bei Lukas," Symb. Osl., 6 (1928), 33-36 (with non-Christian examples). Cf. Lagrange, 191.

[61] Cf. Büchsel, 197.

[62] Büchsel, 191-193.

[63] The reading of syr[sin] at Mt. 1:16 is no true witness to the original, Dibelius, 57, n. 1; cf. n. 2, also Schmidt, 293, though Taylor takes a different view, 105-114.

[64] As against Enslin, 325 f. The thought of the author of a new race is at first an independent one. Paul links it with the obedience and resurrection of Jesus rather than His birth, R. 5:15 ff.; 1 C. 15:21 ff., 45 ff.

[65] In spite of Leisegang, 20-22 (in opposition to him cf. v. Baer, 113-115, 119, 123 f., 131; Büchsel, 193 f.).

it impossible to attribute the role of the man to the πνεῦμα. [66] Obviously, too, the supposedly Egyptian idea of the remote begetting of a child forms no true parallel. [67] There remains only the OT and Jewish analogy of a pure creation miracle which God accomplishes (cf. the barren women of the OT, except that in their case what is effected is the ability to conceive, in that of Mary conception itself).

It is naturally surprising that the virgin conception of Mary is not explicitly mentioned anywhere else in the NT. [68] The other statements adduced in this connection (e.g., Jn. 1:13, 14, 45; 6:42; R. 1:3; Gl. 4:4; Hb. 7:3; also the Son of David passages) speak plainly neither for nor against it. The silence of Paul, of whose Christology we have, of course, no compendious account, might be explained by saying that the idea had not yet made its way in his time, but it could hardly have remained unknown to the author of the Fourth Gospel. Did he feel that, in the form at least in which it was expressed in the infancy stories, it did not adequately express his true concern? Or did he presuppose it as self-evident? Mt. himself has no further reference to the mystery of the birth of Jesus. Are we to conclude from this that the infancy stories in Mt. were added later? Or is it a sign that the mystery was known, but not perverted into an event which can be manipulated and controlled by human recollection and demonstration? [69]

3. παρθένος in the Ascetic Sense. παρθένος seems to have a specific ascetic sense in 1 C. 7:34, 36-38 and also in v. 25 (perhaps of both women and men) and v. 28. [70] The reference is to women in the community who have agreed to set up house with a man in order that they may achieve the ideal of Christian asceticism in economic independence. Almost insuperable philological difficulties prevent us from seeing here a reference to unmarried daughters. [71] The literal ascetic sense is possible in Rev. 14:4 (especially if ἀπαρχή is used precisely). [72]

4. The Figurative Use. The context suggests that this sense is more likely at Rev. 14:4, → IV, 736 f. It is based on the more specific meaning "virgin pure," and refers to the host of the redeemed, whom the divine proleptically sees as perfected, as those who have remained pure when tempted to fall away (idolatry as pollution and licentiousness, → IV, 731, 1 ff.; 734, 37 ff.). In this case παρθένος is the opposite of πόρνη, which in Rev. is used only fig. (for the world). [73]

---

[66] Lagrange, 70. Mt. and Lk. obviously derived their account of the virgin conception of Jesus from Palestinian Christianity. It has been noted again and again that the infancy story in Lk. goes back to Jewish Christian tradition in style and structure, v. Baer, 114 f. P. Humbert, "Der bibl. Verkündigungsstil u. seine vermutliche Herkunft," *Archiv f. Orientforschung,* 10 (1935/36), 77-80 (on Lk. 1:31 f.; for 1:31 models are found not only in Is. 7:14 but also Gn. 16:11; cf. Ju. 13:3, 7). The μέγας predicate in Lk. 1:32 is richly attested in the OT and Judaism, → IV, 538, 32-539, 9; cf. also Ex. 11:3 (Moses), Lösch, 97-100. The expressions used for the Messiah and His kingdom in Lk. 1 f. also come from the sphere of Palestinian Christianity, → II, 950, n. 42.

[67] Though cf. Büchsel, 195. Yet Mt. 2:15 hardly forms a basis for the possibility of "a causal connection."

[68] Taylor, 1-21.

[69] Acc. to Schmidt, 295; cf. the whole passage. Lagrange, 206 f.

[70] J. Weiss, 1 K. (*Kritisch-exeget. Komm. über d. NT,* ed. H. A. W. Meyer[10] [1925]), ad loc. Cf. Pr.-Bauer⁴, 1142, s.v. 2.

[71] Delling, 86-91, also bibl. → I, 652, n. 24. But cf. A. Oepke, "Irrwege in d. neueren Paulusforschung," ThLZ, 77 (1952), 449-452. Cf. Pr.-Bauer⁴, 1142, s.v. 1.

[72] → I, 486, 2 ff.; cf. Loh. Apk., ad loc.; Pr.-Bauer⁴, 1142, s.v. 2.

[73] Rückert, 394, 400 f., esp. 405. The difficult expression μετὰ γυναικῶν οὐκ ἐμολύνθησαν is then elucidated by παρθένοι ... (there is a corresponding direct use of a figuratively meant word in Jm. 4:4, → IV, 734, 40 ff.).

In 2 C. 11:2 the community is emphatically called παρθένος as the bride of Christ [74] (→ IV, 1104, 32 ff.). Paul by his missionary work has affianced it to Christ, and he now watches over it jealously (→ II, 881, 15 ff.) so that he may present it for marriage at the *parousia*. In keeping with OT usage (→ 833, 5-7), virginity symbolises exclusive attachment to the Christ proclaimed by Paul, to whom it is unfaithful (ἑνὶ ἀνδρί) if it binds itself to another Jesus, v. 4. [75]

Delling

παρίημι → I, 509, 12 ff.

| † παρίστημι, παριστάνω |

The NT has in the pres. only the later form παριστάνω, R. 6:13, 16. This is found in the LXX and in non-biblical Gk., esp. after the 2nd cent. B.C. : Ditt. Syll.³, 589, 46 (196 B.C.); Polyb., 3, 96, 3; 11, 3, 8.

A. Non-Biblical Greek.

In non-biblical Gk. the following senses are the most important for the NT : a. trans. (pres., impf., fut., aor. I act.) in general "to present," more exactly "to place" : τοὺς ἱππεῖς ἐφ' ἑκάτερον παρέστησε τὸ κέρας, "he set the cavalry on both wings," Polyb., 3, 72, 9 ; "to place at disposal" : τᾷ μὲν ... Ἐλείθυιαν παρέστασέν τε Μοίρας, Pind. Olymp., 6, 41 f.; πᾶσι λαμπτηροφόρους παῖδας παρέστησε, Athen., IV, 29 (p. 148b); "to bring" someone before the magistrate or judge (class. mid., later also act.): μάρτυρας παρίστανται, Isaeus Op., 4, 13; [1] "to offer," e.g., sacrifices : παραστησάμενος δύο ἱερεῖα, Xenoph. An., VI, 1, 22; ταύρους καὶ κριοὺς παραστῆσαι, Jos. Ant., 4, 113; also of spiritual presentation : τὸ δεινὸν παραστῆσαι τοῖς ἀκούουσιν, Demosth. Or., 21, 72; "to demonstrate" : ὅταν παραστήσῃς τινὶ τοῦτο, Xenoph. Oec., 13, 1; [2] "to make ready," "set up," or simply "to make" (cf. καθίστημι, → III, 445, 1 ff.): (ἡ πίσσα) τὸν οἶνον εὔποτον παρίστησι, Plut. Quaest. Conv., V, 1 (II, 676c). [3] Many special meanings like the mid. "to bring to one's side," e.g., παρίστασαι (πόλιν) βίᾳ, Soph. Oed. Col., 916 are of less account in the NT b. Intr. (pres., impf., fut. mid.; aor. II, perf. and pluperfect act.; aor. pass.): "to come beside," "to approach" : τὸν παρισταμένη, Hom. Od., 24, 516; παραστὰς τάφῳ, Soph. Ant., 1215; "to place oneself at the disposal," "to assist," "to wait on" : ἀμφίπολος ... οἱ κεδνὴ ἑκάτερθε παρέστη, "a good servant waited on her on both sides," Hom. Od., 1, 335 (of respectful attendance on a superior, commonly expressed in the LXX [4] and NT by intr. παριστάνω, though very uncommon in non-biblical Gk.); "to aid," "to help" : οὐ παρέστη πώποτε οὐδ' ἐβοήθησε, Demosth. Or., 45, 64; "to stand by," "to be present," often subst. : οἱ παρεστηκότες, P. Petr., II, 4, 6, 13; "to be close" : ἄγχι παρέστηκεν θάνατος, Hom.

---

[74] The essential features of the church both local and universal are the same for Paul in other passages. On the later development of the idea cf. F. C. Conybeare, "Die jungfräuliche Kirche u. d. jungfräuliche Mutter," ARW, 8 (1905), 373-389; 9 (1906), 73-86.

[75] The link with v. 3 does not justify us in drawing conclusions as to a true ascetic understanding of virginity ; the par. to Eve simply consists in the corruption of the νοήματα (the ref. is to the loss, not of παρθενία, but of ἁπλότης).

π α ρ ί σ τ η μ ι. Pass., III, 751 f.; Moult.-Mill., 494 f.; Liddell-Scott, II, 1340 f.; Pr.-Bauer⁴, 1142 ff.; Δ. Δημητράκος, Μέγα Λέξικον τῆς Ἑλληνικῆς Γλώσσης, VII (1949), 5552-5554.

[1] Cf. further → Δημητράκος, 5553 § 11.

[2] For further examples cf. Liddell-Scott, 1340 § A.

[3] Cf. Δημητράκος, 5553 § 10.

[4] On the OT cf. C. Lindhagen, *The Servant Motif in the OT* (1950), 40, n. 1; 101 f.

II., 16, 853; "to happen" : δόξα μοι παρεστάθη, Soph. Oed. Tyr., 911; "to be on hand" : τὸ χρῶμα τὸ παρεστηκός, Aristoph. Eq., 399.

Reicke

B. Septuagint.

In the Gk. transl. of the OT, too, παριστάναι is one of the terms which can have many senses within the basic meaning. With the help of it many statements can be made about persons or things to express simple "presence" (e.g., Jdt. 13:1: the guests), "serving," "helping," "being at someone's disposal to save," [5] and even "to be ready, complete, ripe." In sum, however, the word is used only about 100 times in the LXX, in 70 instances with a clear, though not always the same, Heb. original ; another 7 examples are to be found in Σ. [6] Heb. verbs of standing or setting are naturally to the fore, esp. עמד, which is 31 times the original of παριστάναι. This no. seems small, however, when one considers how often עמד occurs in the Mas., and how embracing its content is. Of verbs of standing יצב hitp and נצב ni and hi may also be mentioned. A special meaning of עמד is respectful standing or service. This idea is transferred to παριστάναι, so that it, too, can be used for "to serve" (→ IV, 219, 42 ff.), and an occasional Semitism [7] results. In such cases the reader may easily keep to the lit. Gk. sense. Thus παριστάναι with συνιστάναι in Gn. 40:4 can hardly mean that Joseph served his fellow-prisoners. For the Gk. translator, too, Joshua was more likely the assistant of Moses than his servant, Ex. 24:13; Nu. 11:28; cf. Dt. 1:38. The reader of Is. 60:10 : "Their (the Gentiles') kings will stand at thy (Israel's) service," will certainly not think in terms of personal service but of political subjection. The use of παριστάναι is very different in ψ 2:2. There it means "to oppose," "to oppress" (Σ συνιστάναι), and in Sir. 51:2 the part. means "opponent" for קום, cf. also Is. 5:29. When the context demands, the Gk. παριστάναι can also denote a relationship of service, cf. Gehazi and Elisha in 4 Βασ. 5:25, also Prv. 22:29; 3 Βασ. 10:8; 2 Ch. 9:7. These passages speak of men who stand before kings, i.e., serve them. In many such instances "servant" is more of an honorary title and can have the sense of "minister." These men all have the privilege of access to the king. The same applies to the queen in Est. 8:4; ψ 44:9.

Only with the help of the particular relation of the servant to the king can one understand the religious and cultic use of παριστάναι in the OT. This servant relation is a privilege and confers dignity, although according to oriental law and court ceremonial it presupposes absolute dependence on the monarch and subjection to him. It is thus that the angels, the heavenly forces, the winds, stand before God's throne, Tob. 12:15 S; Job 1:6; 2:1; Da. 7:10, 13; 2 Ch. 18:18 A; Zech. 6:5. In this connection only the simple form is used at Is. 6:2 and Rev. 7:9. 4 Macc. 17:18 can say the same about the martyrs. It can also be said about men during their life on earth. Thus the Levites (to their dignity cf. Nu. 16:9) and the priests, on the basis of special election, serve at the altar in the presence of God, Dt. 10:8; 17:12; 18:5, 7; 21:5; Ju. 20:28 (before the ark, Luther "before him, i.e., God"). Even when we read of the institution of priests by the king,

---

[5] The senses merge into one another, cf. 1 Βασ. 2:22 vl. for צבא of the temple ministry of the Levites, which is regarded as a kind of *militia sacra*, cf. Nu. 8:24 Σ παρίστασθαι; here of women who ministered at the entrance to the sanctuary ; 1 Βασ. 4:20 for נצב ni of women who served as midwives. "To place at disposal," "to pay a sum of money" for שקל at Est. 4:7 vl. With no Heb. at Job 37:20 : μὴ βίβλος ἢ γραμματεύς μοι παρέστηκεν;

[6] Even the constr. of the verb pts. to the plurality of meanings ; it is used with the inf., the dat. and acc., and no less than 12 different prepositions, with differing grammatical connections, often very loose : εἰς, ἐξ, ἐν, ἔναντι, ἐνώπιον, ἐπί, κατά, μετά, παρά, πρό, πρός, ὑπό.

[7] A. Deissmann, "Hellenistisches Griechisch," RE³, 7, 637 distinguishes between occasional and common Semitisms. The former occur in transl. and may easily be misunderstood by the reader.

the verb is used, 3 Βασ. 12:32. What is true of the priests is also true of the prophets. Thus Elijah and Elisha, in their prophetic utterances, appeal to the God in whose service they stand (3 Βασ. 17:1; 18:15; 4 Βασ. 3:14; 5:16). This is the basis of their authority. The same is obviously true in Zech. 4:14. [8] The right of direct access to God gives the pious the right of interceding with God for others, as Jeremiah can say in 15:11 acc. to the LXX. [9] Finally the position of the national community as described by the verb in Ex. 19:17 or 2 Ch. 6:3 is to be understood not just as presence on the mount or at the temple dedication or even before the king, but as inner readiness to receive God's message. The verb can go even further in ψ 5:3 and express the urgent prayer of the righteous man : τὸ πρωὶ παραστήσομαί σοι καὶ ἐπόψομαι, though the meaning of the Mas. is different.

παριστάναι can also be used of God, so that it does not as such imply subordination. The LXX sometimes refers παριστάναι directly to God, e.g., at Ex. 34:5 for יצב hitp, though in the Mas. Moses is the subject. Wis. 10:11 is unequivocal both materially and formally. Here it is said of wisdom : "She set herself at his side (παρέστη) and made him rich." The statement corresponds to what is said about God's particular concern for the poor, e.g., in ψ 108:31: παρέστη ἐκ δεξιῶν πένητος, "God stood at the side of the poor man." The trans. is also used of God : He sets the righteous always before His face, ψ 40:12 Σ : παραστήσεις (נצב hi) με ἔμπροσθέν σου δι᾽ αἰῶνος, i.e., He grants him access to Himself and gives him assurance (LXX ἐβεβαίωσάς με) and confidence. If the ref. here is to the gracious God, ψ 49:21 speaks of the wrathful God who will set man's sins before his eyes (παραστήσω = ערך).

The meaning "to make ready" has the least support in the Mas., and occurs esp. when there is no Heb. original. Ref. might be made to Ep. Jer. 36 A : τυφλὸν εἰς ὅρασιν, 1 Macc. 6:35 : εἰς πόλεμον, 2 Macc. 8:21: εὐθαρσεῖς αὐτοὺς παραστήσας, Jl. 3:13 : παρέστηκεν τρύγητος for בשל, "to ripen"; Ex. 9:31: κριθὴ παρεστηκυῖα for הַשְּׂעֹרָה אָבִיב (cf. Mk. 4:29). This sense occurs in a theological statement at Jdt. 9:6 : παρέστησαν ἃ ἐβουλεύσω, [10] of God's counsel.

Bertram

C. The New Testament.

First, the NT has some sentences in which παριστάνω bears the familiar secular meanings. Then there are verses in which the verb is linked to a particular theological mode of thinking.

1. Trans. "to place at the disposal" : κτήνη παραστῆσαι, Ac. 23:24; "to furnish" : παραστήσει μοι ... πλείω δώδεκα λεγιῶνας, Mt. 26:53 (military expressions); "to show" : παρέστησεν ἑαυτὸν ζῶντα, Ac. 1:3; παρέστησεν αὐτὴν ζῶσαν, 9:41; "to prove" : οὐδὲ παραστῆσαι δύνανταί σοι περὶ ὧν νυνὶ κατηγοροῦσίν μου, Ac. 24:13.

2. Intr.: "to approach" : παρέστησαν αὐτῷ, Ac. 9:39; of the revelation of an angel, Ac. 27:23; of hostile approach : παρέστησαν οἱ βασιλεῖς τῆς γῆς (Ps. 2:2), Ac. 4:26; "to stand by" : εἷς παρεστηκὼς τῶν ὑπηρετῶν, Jn. 18:22; οἱ παρεστῶτες, Lk. 19:24; Ac. 23:2, 4; "to assist" : ἵνα ... παραστῆτε αὐτῇ, R. 16:2; ὁ κύριός μοι παρέστη, 2 Tm. 4:17; "to be there," "to be present," with adv. or in the abs.: ὁ κεντυρίων ὁ παρεστηκὼς ἐξ ἐναντίας αὐτοῦ, Mk. 15:39; τὸν μαθητὴν παρεστῶτα, Jn. 19:26; ἄνδρες δύο παρειστήκεισαν αὐτοῖς, Ac. 1:10; παρέστηκεν ἐνώπιον ὑμῶν ὑγιής, Ac. 4:10; as a noun οἱ παρεστηκότες or οἱ παρεστῶτες,

---

[8] F. Horst in T. H. Robinson and F. Horst, *Die zwölf kleinen Propheten* = Hndbch. z. AT, I, 14 (1938), ad loc.

[9] Cf. Jer. 21:2 and on this F. Giesebrecht, *Das Buch Jer.* = Handkomm. z. AT, III, 2, 1 (1894), on Jer. 15:11.

[10] Cf. Ps. 33:9 and 148:5, 6.

"those present," Mk. 14:47, 69 f.; 15:35; "to be at hand," "to be there" : παρέστηκεν ὁ θερισμός, Mk. 4:29.

3. The NT verses which have theological significance (trans. and intr.) use the verb along with various concepts of religious service (→ 837, 17 ff., 29 ff. "to place or stand at the disposal," "to assist," "to serve," and cf. esp. the notes on the LXX → 838, 15-839, 11). In the NT, as in the Orient generally, there is assumed a certain analogy between religion and court ceremonial; this is particularly apparent in Rev. [11] At all events, in the content of the NT belief in the *Kurios* παριστάνω is often linked with the idea of serving or proffering. An "official" tendency may thus be detected. Thus the angel in Lk. 1:19 says : "I am Gabriel, who waits on God" (→ 838, 30 ff.). Such ideas of service are found especially in the Pauline literature. Sin is no longer to have dominion, yet Christians must not (any longer) place their members as weapons of unrighteousness in the service of sin (παριστάνετε) but (now) they should set them in the service of God (παραστήσατε), R. 6:12 f., cf. 19. The question is, then, at whose disposal one sets oneself as a servant to obey (ᾧ παριστάνετε ἑαυτοὺς δούλους εἰς ὑπακοήν), v. 16. There also seems to be a hint of court procedure in the thesis of Paul in 1 C. 8:8 : βρῶμα ἡμᾶς οὐ παραστήσει τῷ θεῷ, "food will not bring us close to God." In 2 C. 4:14 God Himself effects a corresponding setting of believers before His throne at the last day : "He will raise us up and present us with you." In neither of these two references is there any thought of judgment, so that a forensic interpretation is not so likely. [12] Another form of court ceremonial can explain 2 C. 11:2. Paul as conductor of the bride (→ IV, 1104, 32 ff. νυμφίος) wants to present the community as a pure virgin to Christ. Behind this image there probably lies the solemn presentation of a royal bride, as in Ps. 45. According to Eph. 5:27 Christ Himself will see to the tasks necessary here : "That he might present the church to himself (as a bride) in glory." Another official allusion may be seen in the forensic statement in R. 14:10 : "We shall all stand before the judgment seat of God (or Christ vl.)." For God, as Judge, is Ruler and King, as emphasised in v. 11: "Every knee shall bow to me." In view of its religious character this saying cannot be fully equated, of course, with purely forensic expressions such as we find in Ac. 23:33 : "They presented Paul also before him (the governor)," or Ac. 27:24 : "Thou must appear before Caesar (for trial)." Yet in these sayings, too, the verb obviously has an official setting. In other verses the reference is to the earthly temple, though here again God is to be presupposed as the Ruler on His throne. Thus Lk. 2:22 uses παραστῆσαι τῷ κυρίῳ

---

[11] New knowledge of the ancient Orient, and investigations such as those of E. R. Goodenough, "The Political Theory of Hellenistic Kingship," Yale Class. Studies, 1 (1928), 55-102, "Kingship in Early Israel," JBL, 48 (1929), 169-205, mean that the NT scholar can no longer study the "close connection between the god and the ruler" (→ III, 442, 5 f. κάθημαι) with exclusive ref. to Hellenism, but has to take into account the whole Near East and the OT too. Cf. H. Gressmann, *Der Messias* (1929), 1-63 (on court style in Israel); I. Engnell, *Studies in Divine Kingship* (1943), 174-177; C. J. Gadd, *Ideas of Divine Rule in the Ancient East* (1948), 1-62. This principle is not affected by debatable issues, e.g., whether the whole of the Near East is controlled by a specific ritual schema, or whether Israel regarded its kings as divine, which is denied, perhaps too sceptically, by H. Frankfort, *Kingship and the Gods* (1948), 341; M. Noth, "Gott, König, Volk im AT," ZThK, 47 (1950), 157-191. Our present concern is simply with the fact that ancient religious ideas were influenced in various ways by court traditions, and that this may be seen also in the NT, cf. T. Arvedson, *Das Mysterium Christi* (1937), 21-35, 115-136 etc. and H. Riesenfeld, *Jésus transfiguré* (1947), 9-14 etc.

[12] Pr.-Bauer⁴, 1143 § 1e.

in connection with the presentation of Jesus in the temple, and we best understand this in terms of the presentation of a sacral minister to his master. The author would seem to mean that like Samuel or a Nazirite Jesus is basically set in and dedicated to the service of God. [13] In this Messianic sense the law of the consecration of the firstborn (Ex. 13:2, 12-15) is here fulfilled, v. 23. The narrator is not implying, then, that this kind of presentation is normal for all Israelites. [14] Finally, the motif of presenting someone to God to give evidence of ritual cleanness (cf. the lepers who in Lk. 17:14 were told to show themselves to the priests) may underlie certain figurative expressions such as Col. 1:22 : "Christ died to present you holy and unblameable and unreproveable to himself," or v. 28 : Paul preaches the Gospel that he may "present every man perfect in Christ," or 2 Tm. 2:15 : Timothy must be zealous to "shew himself approved unto God." In another figurative use of the temple setting the verb can also mean "to bring as an offering": "I exhort you ... to present your bodies ... as a living sacrifice" (also defined as an allegorical service of God), R. 12:1. In religious connections, too, one may thus detect official and sacrificial modes of thought in the NT use of παριστάνω.

D. The Post-Apostolic Fathers.

In the post-apost. fathers the verb is used in the following verses, which are closely related to the NT (both trans. and intr.): παραστήσω σε κατὰ πρόσωπόν σου (ψ 49:21 with the addition of σέ), "I will set thee before thine eyes (unmask)," 1 Cl., 35, 10; πάντας δεῖ παραστῆναι τῷ βήματι τοῦ Χριστοῦ (= R. 14:10 vl.), Pol., 6, 2: (ἄγγελοι) λειτουργοῦσιν παρεστῶτες ... μύριαι μυριάδες παρειστήκεισαν αὐτῷ (Da. 7:10), 1 Cl., 34, 5 f.; παρεστάθην αὐτῷ, "I went up to him," Herm. s., 8, 4, 1; παρεστὼς ὁ κύριος ὡμίλει αὐτοῖς, Mart. Pol., 2, 2; σταφυλὴ παρεστηκυῖα, "a ripe cluster," 1 Cl., 23, 4; 2 Cl., 11, 3 (→ 837, 24 f.).

Reicke

---

† πάροικος, † παροικία, † παροικέω

Contents : A. Profane Greek. B. The Old Testament : 1. The Terms παροικία and παροικέω; 2. The Attitude of Israel to the πάροικος; 3. The People of Israel as πάροικος. C. Hellenistic and Rabbinic Judaism : 1. Philo and Josephus ; 2. Rabbinic Judaism. D. The New Testament. E. The Early Church.

---

[13] J. Weiss, *Lk. in Schr. NT*, I (1906), ad loc.; Hck. Lk., ad loc.; H. Sahlin, *Der Messias u. das Gottesvolk* (1945), 245.

[14] In other cases the firstborn were redeemed, Ex. 13:13; 34:20; Str.-B., II, 120-123. Jesus, however, was not redeemed, as Billerbeck seems to think (120). The offerings in Lk. 2:24 are for the purification of the mother acc. to Lv. 12:6 ff.

π ά ρ ο ι κ ο ς κτλ. Preliminary Note. Owing to sickness K. L. Schmidt could not prepare for press the art. which he had composed, and this has been done for him by his son M. A. Schmidt.

G. Gilbert, *Handbuch d. griech. Staatsaltertümer*, II (1885), 294-296; J. B. Lightfoot, *The Apostolic Fathers*, I : St. Clement of Rome, 2 (1890), 5 f.; A. Bertholet, *Die Stellung d. Israeliten u. der Juden zu den Fremden* (1896); Deissmann NB, 54; E. v. Dobschütz, Art. "Proselyten, 2 : Die Gerim im AT," RE³, 16, 113-115; G. Busolt-H. Swoboda, *Griech. Staatskunde³*, I = Hndbch. AW, IV, 1, 1 (1920), 292; P. de Labriolle, "Paroecia," *Recherches de science religieuse*, 18 (1928), 60-72; G. Rosen, *Juden u. Phönizier*, revised by F. Rosen and G. Bertram (1929), 39-48 (Bertram on "Die religiöse Bedeutung d. at.lichen Fremdgesetzgebung u. d. Fremdlingstypologie d. Septuaginta," quoted as Bertram); T. J. Meek, "The Translation of ger in the Hexateuch and its Bearing on the Documentary Hypothesis," JBL, 49 (1930), 172-180; R. Frick, "Not, Verheissung u. Aufgabe der Diaspora nach dem

A. Profane Greek.

πάροικος, adj. and (esp. later) noun, means a. gen. "neighbouring," "neighbour" (so first Hdt., Aesch., Soph., Thuc.); b. specifically a tt. (first in Aristot., common in inscr.),[1] like μέτοικος as earlier used in this sense, and replacing it : "non-citizen," like ξένος (→ 1 ff.), though in distinction from this furnished with special rights, mostly conferred for payment. The πάροικος is not a παρεπίδημος (→ II, 64, 30 ff.), who lives in a place for only a short time, but a resident alien, who has his domicile[2] with or among the natives, having no civic rights but living under the common protection.[3] The noun παροικία occurs only in biblical and ecclesiastical authors ; it derives from the technical sense of the adj.[4] The verb παροικεῖν means a. "to dwell beside," so Thuc., I, 71, 2 : πόλει ὁμοίᾳ παροικοῦντες, cf. III, 93, 2; Isoc. Or., 4, 162 : ἀπὸ Κνίδου μέχρι Σινώπης Ἕλληνες Ἀσίαν παροικοῦσιν, "dwell along the coast of Asia," and b., from the technical sense, "to be a resident alien," of a foreigner who dwells somewhere without national rights, so Diod. S., 13, 47, 4 : οἱ παροικοῦντες ξένοι.

B. The Old Testament.

1. The Terms παροικία and παροικέω.

a. The noun denotes the state, position or fate of a resident alien, "dwelling abroad" without civil or native rights :[5] ψ 118:54 for מְגוּרִם; 119:5 for a form of גּוּר; also Jdt. 5:9; 3 Macc. 7:19; Wis. 19:10; Sir. Prologue 34;[6] 16:8;[7] 41:5;[8] Ps. Sol. 17:17 (here more a

---

bibl. Zeugnis," *Monatschrift f. Pastoraltheologie,* 32 (1936), 261-272; V. Monod, "Le voyage, le déracinement de l'individu hors du milieu natal constituent-ils un des éléments déterminant de la conversion religieuse ?" *Revue d'histoire et de la philosophie religieuses,* 16 (1936), 385-399; K. L. Schmidt, "Israels Stellung zu den Fremdlingen u. Beisassen u. Israels Wissen um seine Fremdling- u. Beisassenschaft," *Judaica,* 1 (1945-1946), 269-296; E. G. Selwyn, *The First Epistle of St. Peter* (1946), 118; H. G. Meecham, *The Epistle to Diognetus* (1949), 109; v. also → 1 f., ξένος, Bibl. n.

[1] Cf. the indexes to Ditt. Or. and Ditt. Syll.[3]

[2] This is not to say that he can acquire a house or a piece of land, which was forbidden to the *metoikoi* in Athens.

[3] Cf. Gilbert, 294-296; Lightfoot, 5 f.; Busolt-Swoboda, 292; Deissmann NB, 54; de Labriolle, 60-72; Selwyn, 118; Meecham, 109.

[4] Cf. Cr.-Kö., Moult.-Mill. and Pr.-Bauer[4], s.v.

[5] For the individual Jew the situation changes only when he acquires citizenship abroad, so Paul in Ac. 21:39; 22:26; cf. 16:37 (→ πολιτεία). A Jewish city community like that in Egyptian Alexandria may also be regarded politically as an alien colony, though city Jews with their drive for assimilation seem to feel that alien residence is more easily linked with smaller patriarchal relations. Apart from this, as Judaism sees it the political fact of παροικία is to be understood theologically as well as sociologically, so that what counts is not quantity and the external circumstances, but the quality of the Jewish community before God, the claim to be God's people and consequently pilgrims in the world.

[6] Here esp., as in other places, παροικία might simply be taken as an equivalent of → διασπορά, with the same implied questions and ideas, → II, 98 ff.

[7] οὐκ ἐφείσατο περὶ τῆς παροικίας Λωτ. A more likely transl. of this than that of V. Ryssel in Kautzsch Apkr. u. Pseudepigr., *ad loc.* is : "He did not spare (the Sodomites) on account (in spite) of the residence of Lot among them" [A. Debrunner]. The HT (cf. R. Smend, *Die Weisheit d. Jesus Sirach, hbr. u. deutsch* [1906]) has מְגוּרֵי לוֹט. Smend has : "He also spared not the dwelling-place of Lot," and comments in *Die Weisheit d. Jesus Sir., erklärt* (1906), *ad loc.* that מְגוּרֵי means "place of residence as in Job 18:19."

[8] τέκνα βδελυρὰ γίνεται τέκνα ἁμαρτωλῶν καὶ συναναστρεφόμενα παροικίαις ἀσεβῶν, "who have dealings with the πάροικοι of the ungodly" [A. Debrunner]. The HT (Smend, *op. cit.*) runs : גּוּרֵי רשׁע [לֹהם] אוי ונכד רעים דבר נמאס גין. Smend thus supplies גּוּרֵי רָשָׁע, "the whelps of the ungodly." As he sees it in his commentary (*op. cit.*), *ad loc.* the LXX reads מְגוּרִים here.

concrete fellowship of persons). Also for גּוֹלָה "banishment": 1 Εσδρ. 5:7 (Ezr. 2:1); [9] 2 Εσδρ. (Ezr.) 8:35. [10] All these verses, at most with the exception of Sir. 41:5, refer to Israel or its members. The righteous Israelite in particular regards himself as a resident alien (→ lines 37 ff.; 846, 32 ff.): "I praise thy statutes in song in the house (ἐν τόπῳ for בְּבֵית) of my παροικία" [11] (ψ 118:54). [12] The παροικία τῶν ἀσεβῶν in Sir. 41:5 is the opposite of this pious exile.

The verb as a tt. ("to live as a resident alien" where one is not a citizen, abroad) corresponds to גּוּר. Non-Israelite παροικοῦντες are the Beerothites in 2 Βασ. 4:3 and the outcasts of Moab in Is. 16:4. More commonly the ref. is to the Israelites, e.g., Abraham in Egypt in Gn. 12:10, in Canaan in 17:8; Lot in Sodom in 19:9; Abraham in Gerar in 20:1; in the land of the Philistines in 21:34; Isaac in Canaan in 26:3; Abraham and Isaac, and then Jacob, in Hebron in 35:27; the sons of Jacob in Egypt in 47:4; Abraham, Isaac and Jacob in Canaan in Ex. 6:4; a Levite from Bethlehem-Judah in Ephraim in Ju. 17:7-9; Elimelech and his family in Moab in Rt. 1:1; the Shunammite whose son Elisha had raised from the dead and who might go wherever she would in 4 Βασ. 8:1 f.; the remnant of Judah in Egypt in Ιερ. 51(44):14. In Jdt. 5:7, 8, 10 the stay of the patriarchs in Mesopotamia is described as παροικεῖν, but they are brought there simply as "this people" (v. 6).

With the thought of residence abroad there is intertwined in the OT that of inhabiting and possessing the promised land. If on the one side the final dwelling in Canaan is increasingly felt to be a permanent relation of sojourning vis-à-vis God (→ 846, 12-847, 21), on the other hand alien residence belongs to the past, esp. in passages which extol God's dealings with His people. Thus in Ps. 105:11 ff., in an account of God's miracles to the fathers, we read: "Unto thee will I give the land of Canaan, the lot of your inheritance (נַחֲלָה, LXX κληρονομία), when they were but a few men in number; yea, very few, and strangers in it (גֵּרִים, LXX πάροικοι), when they went from one nation to another ..." Cf. also Ps. 78:55: "He cast out the heathen also before them, and divided them an inheritance (נַחֲלָה, LXX κληροδοσία) by line, and made the tribes of Israel to dwell in their tents." [13] This explains why the LXX can sometimes use κατοικεῖν when one would expect παροικεῖν. 1 Ch. 29:15 Cod B has κατοικοῦντες for παροικοῦντες, the rendering of תּוֹשָׁבִים elsewhere. If this reading is to be explained simply by the fact that יָשַׁב is generally transl. κατοικεῖν, and if it is to be preferred in view of the preceding πάροικοί ἐσμεν, the LXX text brings to light a surprising fact in Jer. 29-51, for here the q of גּוּר is 9 times rendered κατοικεῖν, but several alternatives (οἰκεῖν, ἐνοικεῖν, παροικεῖν, μετοικεσία) make it plain that this transl. was felt to be not quite accurate.

The verb is no longer directly a tt. when the Psalmist prays in ψ 60:4: παροικήσω (אָגוּרָה) ἐν τῷ σκηνώματί σου εἰς τοὺς αἰῶνας, σκεπασθήσομαι ἐν σκέπῃ τῶν

---

[9] οἱ ἀναβάντες ἐκ τῆς αἰχμαλωσίας τῆς παροικίας, הָעֹלִים מִשְּׁבִי הַגּוֹלָה. 2 Εσδρ. 2:1 has for this: οἱ ἀναβαίνοντες ἀπὸ τῆς αἰχμαλωσίας τῆς ἀποικίας.

[10] οἱ ἐλθόντες ἀπὸ τῆς αἰχμαλωσίας υἱοὶ τῆς παροικίας, הַבָּאִים מֵהַשְּׁבִי בְּנֵי־הַגּוֹלָה. Elsewhere 1 Εσδρ. usually has αἰχμαλωσία for גּוֹלָה, 2 Εσδρ. ἀποικία, ἀποικεσία.

[11] Cf. H. Gunkel, Die Ps. = Handkomm. z. AT, II, 2 (1926), ad loc.: "The 'house of his pilgrimage' is his own house, in which the author feels that he is not a permanent resident but only a 'guest' for a short time ..." Here, then, in his exposition of the OT Hebrew text he finds a thoroughly NT-Gk. idea (→ 851, 22-853, 8) which is to be regarded as biblical and eschatological, whereas the LXX text might be Greek-dualistic or even mystical; → n. 33; 47.

[12] In this connection the thought of redemption is that of deliverance from exile, cf. ψ 33:4 Cod B: ἐκ πασῶν τῶν παροικιῶν μου ἐρρύσατό με. Here παροικία is used for מְגוּרָה, which, from גּוּר "to fear" (v. L. Koehler-W. Baumgartner, Lex. in Veteris Testamenti libros [1948 ff.], s.v.), means "fear"; thus Cod S A have θλίψεων, while B has in mind a derivate of גּוּר "to be foreign."

[13] → κλῆρος, κληρονομία, esp. III, 759-776.

πτερύγων σου. Cf. also 14:1: κύριε, τίς παροικήσει (יָגוּר) ἐν τῷ σκηνώματί σου, καὶ τίς κατασκηνώσει ἐν τῷ ὄρει τῷ ἀγίῳ σου; In both passages the parallelism suggests that what is expressed is not alien residence in the strict sense, but dwelling with God, which is possible only for the righteous. It is much, indeed, it is everything, to be God's guest, and hence simply to be with Him. Yet in the background is also the thought that the righteous man has to regard his life on earth as a sojourning, a true παροικία, → 847, 9-21.

When παροικεῖν is used in its original sense and in a secular context, it is once the equivalent of גּוּר: Δαν ἵνα τί παροικεῖ (יָגוּר) πλοίοις; Ju. 5:17a, but elsewhere we find other words. Thus Ju. 5:17b Cod A: Ασηρ παρῴκησεν (יָשַׁב) παρ᾿ αἰγιαλόν, 17:11: παροικεῖν (יָשַׁב) παρὰ τῷ ἀνδρί, ψ 93:17: παρὰ βραχὺ παρῴκησεν (כְנָה, שׁ [14] the usual word for "to dwell").

2. The Attitude of Israel to the πάροικος. [15]

πάροικος, "the alien who stands in close connection with, who is accepted by Israel," peregrinus as hospes, is used by the LXX for Heb. גֵּר or תּוֹשָׁב, whereas the alien who has no relation and is rejected, peregrinus as hostis, is usually denoted by terms derived from ἄλλος, e.g., ἀλλότριος (→ I, 265, 3 ff.), ἀπηλλοτριωμένος, ἀλλογενής (→ I, 266, 10 ff.), ἀλλόφυλος (→ I, 267, 14 ff.), corresponding to the Heb. זָר or נָכְרִי. [16] The rather subtle distinction between גֵּר and תּוֹשָׁב (→ 848, 11-16 and n. 35) may be discerned from the fact that the former is commonly rendered either πάροικος or → προσήλυτος, the latter only πάροικος (→ 8, 21-26 ξένος). The πάροικος then, is the resident alien in relation to whom certain legal and social rights developed in Israel, but who as such is to be distinguished as a non-Israelite from the member of God's people or the resident. The related Edomite and the non-related Egyptian may both count as πάροικος, and Israel itself was once πάροικος in Egypt, cf. Dt. 23:8; → 846, 14-23. Saul was killed by an Amalekite πάροικος (גֵּר), 2 Βασ. 1:13. A resident alien cannot share in certain cultic rights and duties. Thus a πάροικος (תּוֹשָׁב) ἢ μισθωτός cannot eat the paschal lamb, Ex. 12:45. The πάροικος (תּוֹשָׁב) or μισθωτός of a priest may not eat of dedicated things or sacrificial gifts, Lv. 22:10. On the other hand, it is not permitted the Israelite, but only τῷ παροίκῳ (גֵּר) τῷ ἐν ταῖς πόλεσίν σου, to eat the flesh of a fallen beast, Dt. 14:21.

Other passages show that the resident alien had the same right of protection as the Israelite and was assimilated into the cultic life of God's people to a limited degree. The same right of asylum was granted as to the children of Israel, Nu. 35:15. The πάροικος (תּוֹשָׁב) was also to be helped in the same way as a poor Israelite and vice versa, Lv. 25:35. The fruits of the sabbatical year were to be granted also τῷ παροίκῳ (תּוֹשָׁב) τῷ προσκειμένῳ πρὸς σέ, Lv. 25:6. The Israelite who became so poor that he had to sell himself to another was not to serve as a slave, but "as a μισθωτὸς ἢ πάροικος (תּוֹשָׁב) he shall be with thee," v. 40; he is also to go free the next year of jubilee. This account of the position of the resident alien presupposes that a πάροικος (תּוֹשָׁב) might become well-to-do, Lv. 25:47.

The positive and negative aspects are brought out even more vividly when we consider the refs. in which → προσήλυτος is used for the noun גֵּר instead of πάροικος.

---

[14] Cr.-Kö., 781 mistakenly has יָשַׁב.

[15] Cf. Bertholet; v. Dobschütz; Meek, 172-180; Monod, 385-399; also → ξένος, 1 f. Bibl. n.; K. L. Schmidt, 279 f., n. 16. On πάροικος as well as → ξένος note should be taken of M. Weber's treatment of "Die gerim u. die Erzväterethik" in his collected essays on religious sociology, III: Das antike Judt.² (1923) = Archiv f. Sozialwissenschaft, Vol. 44 (1917), 34-76. Weber's strictly sociological thesis that the Jews are a "pariah people" (1-8) is subjected to equally strict theological assessment by W. Vischer, Das Christuszeugnis d. AT, I⁶ (1943), 151-155.

[16] → 1, 20-4, 3: "The Tension in the ξένος Concept," and → 8, 15-35, on the various OT terms for "foreign."

Here again natives and aliens are put under the same law of protection, [17] and in addition the law of the burnt offerings (Nu. 15:14) and the passover (Nu. 9:14) is to be the same for both. In this connection the statement of 9:14b is emphasised by formal and almost literal repetition in Nu. 15:15 f. on the one side and Ex. 12:49 on the other : "Ye shall have one ordinance, both for the stranger (προσήλυτος) and for him that was born in the land (τῷ αὐτόχθονι τῆς γῆς)." But what does this one ordinance imply in respect of the passover ? That on both sides no uncircumcised may eat it, cf. Ex. 12:48b. Only if the alien has himself and his house circumcised, may he eat the passover, v. 48a. Otherwise he is under the law that no ἀλλογενής (v. 43) and no πάροικος ἢ μισθω-τός (v. 45) may eat it. Circumcision, then, is the last barrier which prevents the resident alien from entering into full cultic fellowship. It is not an insuperable barrier, however, for the alien may desire circumcision and thus becomes a full-fledged Israelite from the cultic standpoint.

In distinction from natives [18] on the one side and temporary residents [19] (e.g., mer-chants) or foreign slaves on the other, πάροικοι (or → προσήλυτοι) have their own legal status. The individual alien who for some reason leaves his own land and race and thus forfeits both country and legal standing may still acquire in Israel, under certain conditions, both the right of protection and a better social position. As μισθωτός he is distinguished from slaves (→ IV, 696, 43 ff.; 697, 41 ff.; 701, 10 ff.). If he is frequently oppressed or exploited, humane social laws protect him increasingly in the Book of the Covenant and esp. Dt. and the Holiness Code (→ 9, 17-10, 13 ξένος), and the way to wealth (844, 39 ff.) is not barred to him. [20] In P, however, one may detect a strong tendency to define more precisely and to restrict as narrowly as possible the cultic position of the resident alien, which was undoubtedly very fluid in the pre-deuteronomic period with its various sanctuaries, → 11, 13-25 ξένος.

This attempt is followed up by the LXX translators when in many places they make favourable additions to the older regulations. Thus at the beginning of H in Lv. 17:3, in a directive to Israel concerning the proper way of slaughtering animals, the LXX adds after τῶν υἱῶν Ἰσραηλ (בֵּית־יִשְׂרָאֵל) the words ἢ τῶν προσηλύτων τῶν προσκει-μένων ἐν ὑμῖν, which are not in the Heb. and which would run אוֹ מִן־הַגֵּר הַגָּר בְּתוֹכְכֶם. [21] At Dt. 12:18, in a law concerning the place of worship, we even find that the LXX has changed the HT הַלֵּוִי אֲשֶׁר בִּשְׁעָרֶיךָ into ὁ προσήλυτος ὁ ἐν ταῖς πόλεσιν ὑμῶν. [22] Is this a ref. to proselytes in the later sense ? [23] But even earlier the process could work in favour of aliens. It is no alteration but simply a confirmation of what was said about the passover and circumcision (→ 844, 42 ff.) if in Ez. 47:22 f. a full equation of Israelites and resident aliens is promised : "Ye shall divide it (the holy land) by lot for an inheritance unto you, and to the strangers that sojourn among you, which shall beget children among you ; and they shall be unto you as born in the country among the children of Israel ; they shall have inheritance with you among the tribes of Israel. And ... in what tribe the stranger sojourneth, there shall ye give him his inheritance,

---

[17] Cf. Jos. 20:9 for the right of asylum, and esp. Jer. 7:6; Zech. 7:10, acc. to which widows, orphans and strangers are not to be oppressed. On the other hand the Wisdom literature refers only to widows and orphans, not strangers, cf. J. Fichtner, *Altorientalische Weisheit in ihrer israelitisch-jüd. Ausprägung* (1933), 31.

[18] אֶזְרָח, αὐτόχθων, *indigena*, e.g., Nu. 9:14; 15:30; also ἐγχώριος, Ex. 12:49.

[19] נָכְרִי, בֶּן־נֵכָר, ἀλλότριος (→ I, 265, 3 ff.), ἀλλογενής (→ I, 266, 10 ff.), *alienigena*.

[20] There was always some fluidity here. Thus distinction is made between aliens under private protection and those under royal protection ; cf. Bertholet, 27-45.

[21] Cf. BHK³, *ad loc.*

[22] This not unimportant deviation of the LXX is not noted in BHK³. It is influenced by similar formulae in Ex. 20:10; Dt. 5:14; 14:21; 16:14; 31:12. Λευίτης is kept by the LXX at Dt. 14:27 and 16:11, with προσήλυτος in the later verse. Similarity of characters (גר for לוי) enters into the question as well as material similarity [Bertram].

[23] Cf. E. Meyer, *Die Entstehung d. Judts.* (1896), 227-234.

saith the Lord God." Later the trend toward an enforced circumcising of strangers gains increasingly in strength, cf. 1 Macc. 2:46. [24]

Legally the alien resident (cf. the Gk. *metoikoi* and Roman *peregrini*) [25] is acc. to the current view sacrosanct as a guest. [26] In virtue of his weakness he enjoys the divine favour which the laws of Israel also assert on behalf of weak compatriots. His alien blood does not definitively place him outside the people of God. Nevertheless, he ought to accept the covenant sign of circumcision by which the covenant God recognises a man to be a member of His covenant people. The attitude of Israel to the resident alien will not become fully clear, however, until we have considered its attitude to itself as "inhabitant" and "owner" and yet also as "resident alien" in its own land, → 846, 25-848, 16.

3. The People of Israel as πάροικος. [27]

We remain within the confines of what has been said thus far in 2. when we find that πάροικος is also used for Israelites in a foreign land. Thus Moses confesses in Midian : πάροικός (גֵּר) εἰμι ἐν γῇ ἀλλοτρίᾳ, Ex. 2:22; cf. 18:3. Similarly, all the people were resident aliens in Egypt. With this, however, ideas are already combined which finally lead us to a new aspect of the problem.

That Israel was a stranger in Egypt is not just asserted as a historical fact. It gives occasion for reflections and admonitions as to the present attitude of these former aliens to those who are now strangers among them in Canaan : "Thou shalt not abhor an Edomite, for he is thy brother ; thou shalt not abhor an Egyptian, because thou wast a stranger (πάροικος, גֵּר) in his land. The children that are begotten of them shall enter into the congregation of the Lord in their third generation," Dt. 23:8 f. The fact that Israel itself once lived as a πάροικος among strangers is a warning that in God's sight all nations are resident aliens, not possessors. When one looks back to the past and forward to the eschatological future (cf. Is. 19), the Israelite is in almost exactly the same position as the Egyptian who now comes to Canaan as a foreigner. Nevertheless, present possession of the promised land is something which being a sojourner before God cannot overthrow. The divine Word was given to the forefather Abraham · πάροικον (גֵּר) ἔσται τὸ σπέρμα σου ἐν γῇ οὐκ ἰδίᾳ, Gn. 15:13. He keeps this awareness of his nature, and approaches the Hittites accordingly in Gn. 23:4 : πάροικος καὶ παρεπίδημος (גֵּר וְתוֹשָׁב) ἐγώ εἰμι. Does this alien status confessed by Abraham last for his descendants only so long as the land does not definitively belong to them, so that the post-Mosaic period marks the limit of the promise of Gn. 15:13 ? On the contrary, it seems evident that the patriarch as a resident alien is a τύπος in whom the people of Israel sees its own true nature reflected rather than a single social instance of a specially conditioned rather than a more general sojourning. Throughout his wanderings Abraham accepted his alien status as a sign of faith and obedience towards God, as an example of the modesty which the people must always observe in face of God when it asks concerning its being under His promise. Abraham is regarded as a πάροικος in this sense in Hb. 11:8 f. (→ 851, 23-28). This alien status is confirmed in the NT community. Indeed, it is emulated, since circumcision is no longer demanded. "Neither Jew nor Greek ... For ye are all one in Christ Jesus," Gl. 3:28. "No Greek nor Jew, no circumcision [28] nor uncircumcision, no barbarian, Scythian, bond nor free, but Christ all and in all," Col. 3:11. [29]

---

[24] For details → περιτομή.

[25] → 4, 6-7, 14 ξένος, esp. n. 28; also → n. 3.

[26] → 17, 1-25, 30 ξένος : "The Custom of Hospitality," cf. K. L. Schmidt, 294-296.

[27] Cf. the bibl. under → n. 15, also Frick, 261-272.

[28] The antithesis between circumcision and Christ is found also in Barn., 9, though Barn. disregards the fact that Christ Himself was circumcised : γενόμενος ὑπὸ νόμον, Gl. 4:4.

[29] Though certain formal pars. may be found in the Humanistic philosophy of the Stoa (cf. Ltzm. Gl. and Dib. Gefbr., *ad loc.*), neither this nor strict Judaism (→ 850, 6-851, 11; cf. also → 11, 32-14, 20 ξένος) leads to Gl. 3:28 and Col. 3:11, but exclusively God's act

In face of the impending overthrow of Jerusalem the prophets hammer home the fact that one can appeal neither to the land, the temple, nor Yahweh Himself as a possession. The sovereignty of God's grace is displayed in the fact that Yahweh would not let Himself be tied to "His" land. As Ez. sees the going forth of the כְּבוֹד־יְהוָה from the sanctuary (8-11), so Jer. cries, or has the people cry : "Hope of Israel, its Saviour in the time of trouble, why art thou as a stranger in the land (כְּגֵר בָּאָרֶץ, ὡσεὶ πάροικος ἐπὶ τῆς γῆς) and as a traveller (כְּאֹרֵחַ, LXX ὡς αὐτόχθων, as a native) who stops (only) for the night ?" Jer. 14:8. Acc. to v. 9 Yahweh is like one who is asleep and cannot help. This awareness of the sovereignty of God towards His people, which will not be bound by blood, soil, or tradition, is maintained in the post-exilic community, which, in addition to the traditional Abraham typology, is mindful also of recent exile as both judgment and grace. Thus in Chronicles David, Israel's king *par excellence*, speaks of the national community as it is in God's sight : "For we are πάροικοι (גֵרִים) before thee . . . as were all our fathers ; our days on the earth are as a shadow, without hope," 1 Ch. 29:15. ψ 38:12 is to the same effect : "A πάροικος (גֵר) am I with thee, and a παρεπίδημος (תּוֹשָׁב), as all my fathers were." This awareness of being an alien may be combined with a prayer for grace : "I am a πάροικος (גֵר) in the earth ; hide not thy commandments from me," ψ 118:19. This religious understanding of alien status has its implications in the legal and cultic sphere : "The land shall not be sold for ever : for the land is mine ; ye are προσήλυτοι καὶ πάροικοι (גֵרִים וְתוֹשָׁבִים) with me (HT), before me (LXX)," Lv. 25:23. [30]

One is tempted to reverse the sequence of the data thus depicted, so that originally Yahweh, as God and Lord of the land, is in relation to Israel what the individual owner is in relation to resident aliens, and this originally legal and cultic concept is then given a religious application later (cf. 1 Ch. 29:15 with v. 14 and v. 16). In this case the site of the cultus is the place where the Israelite has concretely the status of an alien before God, and ψ 38:12 is saying that the righteous is an alien before God irrespective of his position *vis-à-vis* the world. In keeping is the fact that acc. to the common Semitic concept of God the relation between God and people is that of master and slave, [31] and that the πάροικος is often a μισθωτός (though not a δοῦλος), → 845, 18 f. In the light of 2 K. 17:24 ff. ψ 118:19 can then be interpreted : The גֵר must recognise the commandments of the god in whose land he dwells. [32] We shall also have to reckon with a development from the view of the HT to that of the LXX. [33] It certainly seems

---

of redemption towards His people, whose members live as πάροικοι in the world, → 851, 34-853, 8. Cf. the relativising of Jewish restrictions in Mt. 3:9 par. Lk. 3:8; Mt. 8:10 ff.; 15:28; Lk. 7:9; 9:51-55; 10:29-37; 17:11-19 and Jn. 4.

[30] Cf. Frick, 262 : "Even when nationally independent, Israel retains its alien status, not in relation to a foreign overlord, but in relation to God, by whose will and patience alone it lives. To be guest, stranger, alien is an affliction, not the ideal of national pride. But to be alien and guest with God is also a situation big with promise . . ."

[31] Cf. W. W. Graf Baudissin, *Kyrios als Gottesname im Judt. u. seine Stelle in d. Religionsgeschichte*, III (1929), 554 f.: "The Psalmist too, who in 39:12 calls himself a guest . . . and alien before Yahweh, dare not go beyond the concept of a remote relation of attachment to God." On this view the idea of the worshipper as a stranger did not just come in later, as against W. R. Smith, *The Religion of the Semites* (1899), 55. Cf. on this debate Bertram, 139 f. On Ps. 39:12, *ibid.*, 46.

[32] Cf. A. Bertholet in Kautzsch[4], *ad loc.* אֶרֶץ would here as elsewhere be the land of Canaan as Yahweh's possession. But it might also, as elsewhere, be the earth (so Kautzsch[3] on the same verse), which is certainly the sense of the LXX γῆ.

[33] → n. 32 on ψ 118:19. At ψ 38:12 Cod B *et al.* have for גֵר אָנֹכִי עִמָּךְ πάροικος ἐγώ εἰμι ἐν τῇ γῇ (from ψ 118:19), Cod S A *et al.* παρὰ σοί. Here, too, there might be at least a hint of the thought of being a stranger *on earth* in the HT. On the thesis that the LXX Bible Hellenises the original materially as well as linguistically (so A. Deissmann, "Die Hellenisierung des semitischen Monotheismus," N. Jbch. Kl. Alt., 6 [1903], 161-177), cf. in relation to παροικία Bertram, 141 and n. 51, 54, 55. In Philo, Gnosticism and the

that Lv. 25:23 is an original cultic claim of Yahweh to the land in the sense of a right of ownership which in the sacral sphere is recognised afresh at every 7th harvest feast.

In all this it should not be forgotten, however, that Yahweh is more than the owner of His land like any other god. He is the Creator, and hence the owner of the whole world, cf. Ps. 24:1. We may also refer again in this connection to what was said earlier about Jer. 14:8, → 847, 1-9. What is true of God as Father is also true of God as Owner. The anthropomorphism is not in the last resort a transferring of human relations to the idea of God. It is to be derived rather from God's personal claim to lordship over human relations. [34] God creates and posits human relations ; human relations do not make or fashion the God of Israel.

Before God's claim the more or less important distinctions of human law between ξένος (→ 1 ff.), παρεπίδημος (→ II, 64, 29 ff.), πάροικος and → προσήλυτος, גֵּר and תּוֹשָׁב, lose their force. The Heb. equivalents to the Gk. terms have been given in what precedes because this shows that the overlapping in the transl. cannot finally be explained on linguistic or lexical grounds. [35] It is noteworthy that often, as in Gn. 23:4; Lv. 25:23, 35, 47; Nu. 35:15, [36] the terms גֵּר and תּוֹשָׁב form a single concept.

C. Hellenistic and Rabbinic Judaism.

1. Philo and Josephus.

As later more and more Jews came to live in the *diaspora*, this was bound to affect Israel's consciousness of its alien status, on the one side by enhancing it, on the other by diminishing it. Whereas eschatological and apocalyptic Judaism, followed by primitive Christianity, brought the dispersion into connection with recollection of the Babylonian captivity and therefore directly with the land of Palestine, Hellenistic Judaism went its own way and increasingly weakened the historical bond. [37]

a. Philo, too, uses πάροικος, παροικία, παροικεῖν to express the fact that the righteous man is a stranger on earth. But what he has in view is distance from the heavenly home. Cf. Cher., 120 (with ref. to Lv. 25:23): ἕκαστος γὰρ ἡμῶν ὥσπερ εἰς ξένην πόλιν ἀφῖκται τόνδε τὸν κόσμον, ἧς πρὸ γενέσεως οὐ μετεῖχε, καὶ ἀφικόμενος παροικεῖ, μέχρις ἂν τὸν ἀπονεμηθέντα τοῦ βίου χρόνον διαντλήσῃ. *Ibid.*, 121 (on the same v.): μόνος κυρίως ὁ θεὸς πολίτης ἐστί, πάροικον δὲ καὶ ἐπήλυτον τὸ γενητὸν ἅπαν. In Philo these statements are embedded in his total view

---

Mandaean writings the importation of anthropological and cosmological dualism is palpable, → 849, 24-850, 1. But in the LXX one must be cautious and decide from case to case. Bertram, n. 51 (following Gunkel, *op. cit.*) regards Ps. 119 as fairly late (cf. also Kautzsch[3], *ad loc.*). He thus thinks that there has been some penetration of dualistic thought into the original. Whether there is really an antithesis between παροικία in the land and on earth is a question which cannot be answered by a simple affirmative. Thus on the one side the earth — heaven dualism may not just be of Platonic origin, but may correspond to the biblical eschatological antithesis of present and future (Bertram, n. 55), while on the other the land and Jerusalem, as a sign of God's faithfulness to His history, are in eschatological hope refined, sublimated and spiritualised as the heavenly city, yet not without actual connections (→ πόλις). Cf. → n. 11 and n. 47.

[34] Cf. K. L. Schmidt, 288 f.

[35] → 844, 18 ff. On the difference between גֵּר and תּוֹשָׁב cf. K. L. Schmidt, 279, n. 15, which refers to J. D. Michaelis, *Mosaisches Recht* § 138, Vol. 2 (1771), 427-429; M. Weber, *op. cit.*, 32 f. n.; Bertholet, 156-159; O. Procksch, *Gn.-Komm. z. AT*[2, 3] (1924), on 23:4. It may at least be said that גֵּר, is more general (every תּוֹשָׁב is a גֵּר but not *vice versa*, Bertholet, 159) and older, while תּוֹשָׁב is more specific and later, the former belonging to nomadic culture, the latter to rural and urban (Procksch, 528).

[36] For לַגֵּר וְלַתּוֹשָׁב LXX Cod B* has here τῷ προσηλύτῳ τῷ παροίκῳ, B[c] puts καί (which the other MSS have) in the wrong place.

[37] → II, 98-104; also → 847, 32 f. and n. 33.

of the conflict of man against the πάθη and the world with its treasures. [38] The body is νεκρὸν καὶ τεθνηκὸς ἀεί, and hence the soul is νεκροφοροῦσα, Leg. All., III, 69; Agric., 25. The body (σῶμα) is regarded as the tomb (σῆμα) of the soul, Leg. All., I, 108. Man has as his task τὸ ἐξαγαγεῖν ἐκ τῆς σωματικῆς χώρας τὸν ὁρατικὸν καὶ φιλοθεάμονα νοῦν, Mut. Nom., 209. Hence, as is said with ref. to Gn. 47:4, where both terms occur, man must only παροικεῖν and not κατοικεῖν; in Conf. Ling., 77 f. the followers of Moses are contrasted with the builders of the tower, who wanted to settle down in firm possession : διὰ τοῦτο οἱ κατὰ Μωϋσῆν σοφοὶ πάντες εἰσάγονται παροικοῦντες· αἱ γὰρ τούτων ψυχαὶ ... πατρίδα μὲν τὸν οὐράνιον χῶρον ἐν ᾧ πολιτεύονται, ξένην δὲ τὸν περίγειον ἐν ᾧ παρῴκησαν νομίζουσαι ... Gn. 47:9; 26:2; Ex. 2:22 are then named as examples. In the last of these Philo has γιώρας (= "immigrant"), not πάροικος (LXX). [39] The goal of this ethical teaching is reached by the man who has no needs, of whom it is said : ἀπροσδεὴς εἰκότως ἐστὶν ἄλλων, Agric., 54.

The contemporary background of this psychological interpretation of man's alien status in the world [40] is the Cynic-Stoic diatribe, e.g., in Muson. and Epictet, [41] and Platonising Stoicism in general. Seneca (Dial., VI, 24, 5) calls the body a *vinculum animi.* By way of these Stoics and by direct acquaintance Philo's flight from and negation of the world goes back to Plato (esp. Phaed.). [42]

Philo, however, sets his stranger-typology not merely in a psychological context but also in the cosmological-Gnostic context of his *logos* philosophy. The *logos* itself, like the individual soul, is to be regarded as a stranger. [43] In the Gnostic sphere the mythological background is esp. plain in the Mandaean and Manichean traditions. [44] Mani laments : "I an a king's son ... and I have become a stranger from the great glory." [45] Here, then, the myth of the redeemer god is clothed in the typology of the stranger. For the redeemer to accept alien status entails suffering. [46] In this respect he is like the soul, which is also alien in this world. This idea can be illustrated from the Mandaean texts : "A poor man am I ..., an alien in the world who comes from afar ..., whom the uthras make strange to the world ; they brought me out of the dwelling of the good. Alas, they caused me to dwell in the abode of the wicked," Lidz. Liturg., 223 f.; "I saw the great house of the father in which my brothers dwell," Lidz. Ginza, 577; "I will set

---

[38] Cf. on this W. Völker, "Fortschritt u. Vollendung bei Philo v. Alex.," TU, 49, 1 (1938), 126-154, esp. 137-142, where rich materials are assembled and expounded.

[39] Here Philo uses this fairly rare word because he wants to explain the name of the son of Moses and Zipporah, Gershom. At Ex. 12:19; Is. 14:1; Lv. 19:34 Cod A has γιώρας for גֵּר. Cf. the details in P. Katz, *Philo's Bible* (1950), 73 f.

[40] So correctly Bertram, 48.

[41] Cf. P. Wendland, "Philo u. d. kynisch-stoische Diatribe," P. Wendland and O. Kern, *Beiträge z. Gesch. d. griech. Philosophie u. Religion* (1895), 1-75.

[42] On the debated question whether and how Philo, for all his Hellenism, also combats it on the ground of his Jewish belief in God, cf. W. Völker, *op. cit.,* 139-145. Philo's was a "divided nature ... to which one cannot apply any logical standard but which one must view in its contradictory fulness, and expound accordingly," 153.

[43] At the conclusion of his discussion of the stranger-typology in Mandaean and Manichean texts (→ lines 20 ff.), where the house of the soul is portrayed as a tent, Bertram, 47 f. says : " 'He tabernacled among us,' Jn. 1:14. This saying in Jn. finds a par. in Philo, for whom also the *logos* was a stranger." Cf. Bu. J., 10 with ref. to the *logos* in the world of Gnosticism : "Here the main interest centres on the question of man, who feels his being in the world is an exile, and whc believes that he originally belongs to the divine sphere." → σκηνόω on Jn. 1:14; *v.* Bu. J. on 1:14.

[44] Even though the Mandaeans come after Christianity, and must be regarded as dependent on it, this does not mean that we cannot regard as pre-Christian certain Mandaean ideas. Cf. Bertram, 142, n. 58.

[45] Cf. F. W. K. Müller, *Handschriftenreste in Estrangelo-Schrift aus Turfan, Chinesisch-Turkestan,* II (AAB, 1904), 29 and 108 (in Bertram, 142, n. 59).

[46] Cf. on this also H. Preisker, "Urchr. u. mandäischer Erlösungsglaube," ThBl, 7 (1928), 143-151, esp. 146 f.

forth and go to my father's house, I will not return to my house here," *ibid.*, 560. [47]

b. Joseph. has the technical sense when he says in Ant., 8, 59, with ref. to the men whom Solomon brought for his building work : ἦσαν δ' ἐκ τῶν παροίκων οὓς Δαυίδης καταλελοίπει. [48]

K. L. and M. A. Schmidt

2. Rabbinic Judaism.

a. Proselyte, Godfearer, Resident Alien. [49] The Rabb. divide aliens who stand in religious and social relation to Israel as follows : the full proselyte [50] (→ προσήλυτος), the half-proselyte or godfearer [51] (→ φοβούμενος, σεβόμενος τὸν θεόν), and the resident alien [52] (גֵּר תּוֹשָׁב, תּוֹשָׁב). Full proselytes have been accepted into the Jewish community by a rite of initiation. [53] Godfearers are the wider missionary community of Judaism. Both these are found in the dispersion as well as Palestine. Not so the resident alien. This is an immigrant who has settled in Israel and works [54] there while remaining a non-Jew. [55] If the Rabb. demand certain concessions from the resident alien, this is because as πάροικος he is economically and socially dependent on his Jewish environment and is thus a kind of client. [56]

b. Duties of the Resident Alien. The first aim of the Rabbinic conditions is to set up a basis which makes it possible to have relations with the alien without cultic difficulty. Acc. to bAZ, 64b he is obliged to keep the so-called Noachic commands. [57] These bring resident aliens under Jewish law and forbid idolatry, cursing God, licentiousness, shedding blood, stealing, and eating a member torn from a living animal, [58] cf. TAZ, 9, 4 ff. (473) par. There are, of course, other views. Thus R. Meïr (c. 150 A.D., bAZ, 64b) says that anyone can become a resident alien if he promises before three chaberim publicly to avoid idolatry, though in the same passage the more difficult duty is laid on the resident alien, not merely of eating meat which is ritually slaughtered, but also of keeping all the commandments which are mentioned in the Torah. [59] In jJeb., 8d, 30 ff. Amorean scholars go even further and demand an official repudiation of pagan worship.

---

[47] On the basis of this idea, in combination with ψ 38:12 Cod B (→ n. 33), Bertram, 48 stresses the related assimilation of Judaism to the surrounding world, which provided the possibility of missionary work, and adds on p. 142 f., n. 66 : "It is well known, and thus needs no proof, that the typology of the stranger is still to be found in modern Jewish and Christian piety." These observations are undoubtedly correct to the degree that the ultimately dualistic view of the Gk. world has found a place in both Judaism and Christianity. It should be emphasised, however, that OT and NT eschatology, in terms of which the stranger typology of the NT is to be expounded, cannot be combined with this Gk. view of the other world, → n. 11 and 33.

[48] On the whole one finds more secular modes of expression in Joseph. He speaks of emigration and immigration, but the religious concept of the alien does not occur in him [Bertram].

[49] Str.-B., II, 715-723.

[50] Moore, I, 332, 338, 339 f.

[51] Cf. 2 Ch. 5:6 LXX, the oldest instance. The φοβούμενος τὸν θεόν originates in the dispersion but is found in Palestine, since here, too, Judaism dwelt largely "in dispersion" even in the time of its greatest extension of power. Cf. the φοβούμενοι τὸν θεόν = יִרְאֵי שָׁמַיִם, M. Ex., 22, 20 (101b) par.; also jMeg., 3, 74a, 25 ff. par.

[52] Moore, I, 339 f.

[53] Cf. J. Leipoldt, *Die urchr. Taufe im Lichte d. Religionsgeschichte* (1928), 2-8.

[54] Tg. O. on Lv. 25:47.

[55] Cf., e.g., BM, 5, 6; 9, 12.

[56] Schürer[4], III, 177 f.; Moore, I, 339 f.

[57] Cf. on this Str.-B., III, 737; also Moore, I, 274 f., 453, 462.

[58] It is possible that behind this prohibition stands a rejection of cultic orgies, e.g., those of Dionysiac origin, cf. J. Leipoldt, *Dionysos* (1931), 39.

[59] Since acceptance of a part of the Torah is for the יְרֵא שָׁמַיִם not the pagan גֵּר תּוֹשָׁב, it seems likely that there is a confusion of resident alien and godfearer in this last requirement.

c. The Historical Value of Rabbinic Statements. Aliens settling as private persons in Palestine undoubtedly had to pay regard to the religious customs of the Jews — even Romans did this for reasons of state. Nevertheless, one can hardly say that postexilic Palestine offered the necessary presuppositions for an alien colony in the strict sense. This was true only after the destruction of the temple and the revolt under Hadrian. In essence, then, what the Rabbis have to say about resident aliens is mostly to be regarded as religious legal theory which did not have to be put into practice. [60] Thus a pupil of R. Meïr, Simon b. Eleazar, obviously with ref. to the actual situation of his Jewish contemporaries, rightly says in bAr., 29a that the גֵּר תּוֹשָׁב could be found only up to the commencement of the Babylonian exile.

Meyer

D. The New Testament.

In the NT πάροικος occurs 4 times, παροικία twice, παροικέω twice; it is a restricted and emphatic tt. except perhaps in Lk. 24:18.

a. The close connection with ideas present in the OT may be seen in the fact that in all the NT refs. there is either quotation of the OT or allusion to it. With ref. to Israel's history, which Stephen recounts in Ac. 7, Gn. 15:13 is quoted in v. 6 : ἔσται τὸ σπέρμα αὐτοῦ (Abraham) πάροικον ἐν γῇ ἀλλοτρίᾳ (Egypt) (→ 846, 29 f.), and Ex. 2:15 in v. 29: ἔφυγεν δὲ Μωϋσῆς ... καὶ ἐγένετο πάροικος ἐν γῇ Μαδιάμ (→ 846, 15). In the introduction to his address at Pisidian Antioch Paul in Ac. 13:16 ff. recalls the παροικία of Israel in Egypt : καὶ τὸν λαὸν ὕψωσεν ἐν τῇ παροικίᾳ ἐν γῇ Αἰγύπτου καὶ (cf. Ex. 6:1, 6) μετὰ βραχίονος ὑψηλοῦ ἐξήγαγεν αὐτοὺς ἐξ αὐτῆς, v. 17. Of the remaining passages Hb. 11:9 is particularly important. Among the great heroes of faith in the OT Abraham is mentioned because on the basis of Gn. 23:4 (→ 846, 30 ff.) and 26:3 (→ 843, 10) it can be said of him : πίστει παρῴκησεν εἰς γῆν τῆς ἐπαγγελίας ὡς ἀλλοτρίαν, ἐν σκηναῖς κατοικήσας, μετὰ Ἰσαὰκ καὶ Ἰακὼβ τῶν συγκληρονόμων τῆς ἐπαγγελίας τῆς αὐτῆς. The reason is then given in v. 10 : ἐξεδέχετο γὰρ τὴν τοὺς θεμελίους ἔχουσαν πόλιν, ἧς τεχνίτης καὶ δημιουργὸς ὁ θεός. Because he will one day be a citizen of the heavenly city, he is a resident alien on earth. Cf. Hb. 11:13, where it is said of OT believers : πόρρωθεν αὐτὰς (sc. τὰς ἐπαγγελίας) ἰδόντες καὶ ἀσπασάμενοι, καὶ ὁμολογήσαντες ὅτι (cf. ψ 38:12, → 847, 15 f.) ξένοι καὶ παρεπίδημοί εἰσιν ἐπὶ τῆς γῆς. [61]

b. What is true of ancient Israel is applied by the apostle to the new Israel, the ἅγιοι, the Church of God in Jesus Christ. Christians were once strangers and sojourners, but now they are this no longer (ἄρα οὖν οὐκέτι ἐστὲ ξένοι καὶ πάροικοι); they are fellow-citizens of the saints and members of God's household (ἀλλὰ ἐστὲ συμπολῖται τῶν ἁγίων καὶ οἰκεῖοι τοῦ θεοῦ, Eph. 2:19). [62] But what they are no longer, they still are in a different form, namely, in relation to

---

[60] Cf. also Moore, III, 112 and n. 104.

[61] This v. from the Ps. is also quoted in 1 Pt. 2:11 (→ 852, 2-4), though here with πάροικοι (not ξένοι), as in the LXX.

[62] Dib. Gefbr. Eph., ad loc., rightly says : "Here nothing depends on the distinction between ξένοι and πάροικοι," though equally correctly he then goes on to translate and expound both words as tt. Unfortunately many translators both ancient and modern do not display the same exactitude and balance, without which there can be no clear grasp of the idea. This applies not only to the LXX in relation to the Heb. original, but also in some measure to the Vg, in which the NT words are often incorrectly rendered, and are thus set in dissonance with the passages quoted from the OT. Even Luther is at fault here. The revised Zurich Bible does better when, e.g., it renders παροικία at 1 Pt. 1:17 by "pilgrimage" in place of the colourless "walk" (*Wandel*) of Luther.

the earth, on which they still wander, and to the σάρξ, in which they still live. Hence they can be admonished in 1 Pt. 2:11: ἀγαπητοί, παρακαλῶ ὡς παροίκους καὶ παρεπιδήμους ἀπέχεσθαι τῶν σαρκικῶν ἐπιθυμιῶν, αἵτινες στρατεύονται κατὰ τῆς ψυχῆς. Christians, then, are to understand their life, their ἀναστρέφεσθαι on earth as a παροικία, and they must pay heed to the exhortation : ἐν φόβῳ τὸν τῆς παροικίας ὑμῶν χρόνον ἀναστράφητε, 1 Pt. 1:17.

The NT Church is ἐκκλησία and παροικία, or, more accurately, as ἐκκλησία it is also παροικία. [63] The Church applies to itself two antithetical tt. from political law, the one with reference to God, the other to the world, the one with ref. to the "now already" (and consequently the "no longer"), the other to the "still." The character of the Church as παροικία comes out particularly clearly in Hb. 13:14, which says : "For here have we no continuing city, but we seek one to come." [64] In this respect the fact of the dispersion of Israel takes on particular significance. Christians are παρεπίδημοι διασπορᾶς (1 Pt. 1:1) and the δώδεκα φυλαὶ ἐν τῇ διασπορᾷ (Jm. 1:1; → II, 102 ff.). Special importance attaches to the integration of Christians into two political or civil spheres. [65] The Church as diaspora, which it is not merely in the so-called dispersion but in general, has

---

[63] Cf. on what follows K. L. Schmidt, "Das Gegenüber von Kirche u. Staat in der Gemeinde d. NT," ThBl, 16 (1937), 12 f. and 15 f. (Exc. II : "Die Kirche als Beisassenschaft").

[64] Hb. as a whole, esp. in its christological concepts, is to be understood in terms of the idea of pilgrimage. In the background is Hellen. dualism in the form given it by Philo (→ 848, 25 ff.) — cf. the study of J. Pascher, Η ΒΑΣΙΛΙΚΗ ΟΔΟΣ. Der Königsweg z. Wiedergeburt u. Vergottung bei Philon v. Alex. (1931), though this is one-sidedly dominated by Hellen. mysticism, also the world of Mandaean thought (→ 849, 22 ff.), and the type of the heavenly journey of the soul developed in Gnosticism. Particular pars. are the pearl hymn in Act. Thom., 108 ff. and the Prayer of Kyriakos (cf. H. Gressmann, "Das Gebet d. Kyriakos," ZNW, 20 [1921], 23-35). The Son of God Himself becomes a stranger on this earth, suffers all its sorrows, assaults and temptations as we do (Hb. 2:17 f.; 4:15), strides, unknown, from the unknown to the unknown like Melchisedec (7:3), cf. the Johannine Christ (Jn. 7:27, 34; 8:14, 21 ff., 42; 13:33 → σκηνοῦν), or even the prodigal son of the parable (Lk. 15:13, 18), who experienced the alienation of extreme distance from God as Jesus did on the cross (Mk. 15:34 par.; Hb. 2:9 with the vl. χωρὶς θεοῦ; 5:7 with Harnack's conjecture οὐκ εἰσακουσθείς). The prodigal is indeed a reflection of man going astray in the alien world until he finds rest (Hb. 4:1, 3) in the Father's house (3:4, 6; Eph. 2:19). Externally, then, the Christ of Hb. is the primal man of Gnosticism, the redeemed Redeemer. This mythical understanding of Christ's destiny justifies the High-priest of the NT against the OT and Judaism, and at the same time safeguards the Christian community against superficial historical dogmatism. Nevertheless, Hb. clings fast to the uniqueness of the story of Jesus (Hb. 7:27; 9:12, 28). If the pilgrim piety of the Chr. community refers back to the experiences of the OT people of God, it finds a new fulfilment in the pilgrim destiny of Jesus Himself (Mt. 8:20; Lk. 9:58; cf. 2 C. 8:9; Mt. 25:35 → 16, 8-15 ξένος). The prophetic conflict with localised religion (cf. in this connection esp. Jer. 14:8 → 847, 1-9) finds fulfilment in the παροικία of the NT community, whose piety can be regarded only as a piety of pilgrimage even from the standpoint of the religion of cultic law. This is the view of Hb., and it has been suggested that even the title indicates it, for "Hebrews" are the righteous wandering homelessly over the earth, seeking the heavenly home. Cf. E. Lehmann, Stället och vägen (1917); V. Burch, The Epistle to the Hebrews (1936), 113-148; E. Käsemann, "Das wandernde Gottesvolk. Eine Untersuchung zum Hebräerbrief," FRL, NF, 37 (1939), esp. 5-19 [Bertram].

[65] Cf. in this connection the graphic account in W. Weber, Römische Kaisergesch. u. Kirchengesch. (1929), 55; also Harnack Miss., 421 f.: "He who belonged to the Church no longer had citizenship on earth, but instead a sure citizenship in heaven. This transcendent meaning of the term became very significant in the 2nd century, but less and less so in the 3rd." Cf. also the footnote : "The self-designation of Christians as 'pilgrims and paroikoi' became almost technical in the first century (v. the Pauline Epistles, 1 Pt. and Hb., though not yet Lk.); but παροικία (and παροικεῖν) becomes really technical to denote the individual churches living in the world ..." → 853, 25 ff.

according to the biblical testimony a specific affliction, promise and task, wherewith it is given its eschatological definition and destiny. On this understanding, to be a stranger and sojourner is not something definitive, but provisional. The proleptic statement of Eph. 2:19 can be made with reference to the present only because it is at once added that Christians are fellow-citizens of the saints and members of the household of God. And 1 Pt., which admonishes Christians strongly to remember their παροικία in their conduct, lays upon them with this burden the most impressive titles in the OT, cf. 1 Pt. 2:5-10.

c. By way of appendix we might refer to the one passage where perhaps the use of παροικεῖν is non-technical. In Lk. 24:18 one of the disciples on the road to Emmaus asks the risen Lord, as yet unknown to them : σὺ μόνος παροικεῖς Ἰερουσαλὴμ (less well attested ἐν Ἰερουσαλήμ) καὶ οὐκ ἔγνως τὰ γενόμενα ἐν αὐτῇ ...; here παροικεῖν might simply mean "to live," though possibly there is a ref. to the Jewish *diaspora,* or to the fact that Jesus does not belong to Jerusalem, so that we might paraphrase : "Among the countless Jews from abroad residing in Jerusalem, or the foreign pilgrims temporarily staying in Jerusalem, are you the only one who has no knowledge of the things which have just taken place ?" [66]

E. The Early Church.

Even after the NT period the Church still regards itself as an alien colony. Dg., 5, 5 impressively portrays it as such : πατρίδας οἰκοῦσιν ἰδίας, ἀλλ' ὡς πάροικοι· μετέχουσι πάντων ὡς πολῖται, καὶ πάνθ' ὑπομένουσιν ὡς ξένοι· πᾶσα ξένη πατρίς ἐστιν αὐτῶν, καὶ πᾶσα πατρὶς ξένη. In 2 Cl., 5, 1 παροικία is used as in 1 Pt. 1:17: ὅθεν, ἀδελφοί, καταλείψαντες τὴν παροικίαν τοῦ κόσμου τούτου ποιήσωμεν τὸ θέλημα τοῦ καλέσαντος ἡμᾶς, καὶ μὴ φοβηθῶμεν ἐξελθεῖν ἐκ τοῦ κόσμου τούτου. Acc. to Eus. Hist. Eccl., V, 24, 14 Irenaeus calls the Chr. churches παροικίαι; so, too, does the anti-Montanist Apollonius acc. to V, 18, 9. Similarly Mart. Pol. prooem sends greetings πάσαις ταῖς κατὰ πάντα τόπον τῆς ἁγίας καὶ καθολικῆς ἐκκλησίας παροικίαις. This plur. use is a further development. Thus far παροικία had denoted a state of the people of God or the NT community, or the situation of each member of this ἐκκλησία, and consequently the existence of this ἐκκλησία as that of a παροικία (→ 852, 7 f.), but now it is used as a par. of ἐκκλησία for the individual congregation, so that as the NT speaks of ἐκκλησίαι (e.g., Gl. 1:22; Rev. 1:20) we now have the παροικίαι of the one "holy and catholic" ἐκκλησία, so that ἐκκλησία comes to be used with increasing exclusiveness for the whole Church, and παροικία becomes a tt. for the individual congregation within it. [67] In this connection it is worth remembering that παροικία, Lat. *paroecia* (so still Codex iuris canonici) or *parochia,* Eng. "parish," denotes a Christian society of strangers or aliens whose true state or citizenship is in heaven. In the introductory greeting to Mart. Pol. this meaning is still palpable when the verb παροικεῖν is used of the individual congregations here called ἐκκλησίαι : ἡ ἐκκλησία τοῦ θεοῦ ἡ παροικοῦσα Σμύρναν τῇ ἐκκλησίᾳ τοῦ θεοῦ τῇ παροικούσῃ ἐν Φιλομηλίῳ. Polycarp addresses the Philippian church in the same way (prooem). So does the Roman church the church at Corinth in 1 Cl., prooem. Finally, ref. should be made to Dg., 6, 8 : Χριστιανοὶ παροικοῦσιν ἐν φθαρτοῖς, τὴν ἐν οὐρανοῖς ἀφθαρσίαν προσδεχόμενοι, "Christians dwell as aliens in the corruptible world, awaiting heavenly incorruptibility."

K. L. and M. A. Schmidt

---

[66] Cf. Kl. Lk., *ad loc.*; also Pr.-Bauer⁴, *s.v.,* who suggests a rhetorical phrase : "Are you alone so strange in Jerusalem ?"

[67] Cf. Harnack Miss., 421 f. (→ n. 65).

---

† παροιμία

A. The Word outside the New Testament.

1. The word παροιμία[1] expresses by construction an essential aspect of the "proverb." It is not used independently, but is a sentence accompanying (παρά), amplifying or summing up what is said (cf. Lat. *adagio,* Eng. "by-word").[2] Of the essence of the proverb, too, is that it should be of popular derivation, ancient and widespread. It states an experienced truth of popular wisdom in short and pointed form. Since it embodies a generally recognised truth, it serves as a cogent argument or provides easy popular orientation in dubious cases. Often a concrete instance is set forth as typical, serving to represent the abstract thought contained in it.[3] Since it only alludes to the example, the proverb can be rather enigmatic for those not acquainted with it.[4] The concept is a common one in Gk. The border is fluid between the proverb and the maxim (gnome or aphorism), which is the more artistic and deliberate saying of the thinker, and which serves as a judgment in the higher strata of the people.[5] Since proverbs are often fig., Aristot. classifies them as metaphors.[6] Since they refer frequently to nature and the animal world, antiquity sees a relation between the proverb and the fable.[7] Being timeless and popular, the proverb is distinct from the apophthegm, which arises out of a specific historical situation and which is handed down with the occasion that produced and interprets it, and does not seek to express truth of universal validity.[8] Even in

---

π α ρ ο ι μ ί α. → 744 f. παραβολή Bibl. n. R. Volkmann, *Die Rhetorik d. Griechen u. Römer*[2] (1885), 417, 435; G. Gerber, *Die Sprache als Kunst,* II, 2 (1885), 166-182; E. Hatch, *Essays in Biblical Greek* (1889), 64-71; P. Martin, "Studien auf dem Gebiet d. griech. Sprichwortes," *Programm d. Gymnasiums Plauen* = Diss. Erlangen (1889), E. König, *Stilistik, Rhetorik, Poetik in bezug auf d. bibl. Lit.* (1900), 77-110; E. Geisler, "Beiträge z. Gesch. d. griech. Sprichwortes," *Programm d. Friedrichs-Gymnasiums Breslau* (1908); E. v. Prittwitz-Gaffron, "Das Sprichwort im griech. Epigramm," Diss. München (1912); W. Schmid-O. Stählin, *Gesch. d. griech. Lit.,* I, 1 = *Hndbch. AW,* VII, 1, 1 (1929), Index *s.v.* "Sprichwort"; Str.-B., IV, Index *s.v.* "Sprichwörter"; Jüd. Lex., V, *s.v.* "Sprichwort"; L. Bieler, "Die Namen d. Sprichwörter in den klass. Sprachen," *Rheinisches Museum,* NF, 85 (1936), 240-253; M. Thilo, *5000 Sprichwörter aus Palästina, aus dem Arab. übersetzt* (1937); K. Rupprecht, Art. παροιμία in Pauly-W., XVIII, 2 (1949), 1707-1735; Art. "Paroimiographoi," *ibid.,* 1735-1778.

[1] Etym. from (οἶμος) οἴμη "way," then transf. "song," "narrative," cf. Walde-Pok., II, 509 f.

[2] So Rupprecht, 1708 f. as against Bieler, 240 ff. (a word which accompanies the hearer along the way, admonition), who appeals to Apostolius Συναγωγὴ παροιμιῶν praef., 4 (CPG, II, 234 f.): παροιμία ἐστὶ διήγημα παροδικὸν, ἢ ῥῆμα τετριμμένον ἐν τῇ χρήσει τῶν γε πολλῶν.

[3] Bas. Homilia, 12, 2 (MPG, 31, 388 B): τὸ τῶν παροιμιῶν ὄνομα ἐπὶ τῶν δημωδεστέρων λόγων, Apostolius praef., 4 (CPG, II, 235): παροιμία ἐστὶ λόγος ὠφέλιμος, ἤτοι βιωφελής, ἐπικρύψει μετρίᾳ πολὺ τὸ χρήσιμον ἔχων ἐν ἑαυτῷ· ἢ λόγος προτρεπτικὸς παρὰ πᾶσαν τοῦ βίου τὴν ὁδὸν χρησιμεύων. Aristot. Fr., 2, p. 1474 b, 5: ... (αἱ παροιμίαι) ... παλαιᾶς φιλοσοφίας ... ἐγκαταλείμματα. Cf. F. Seiler, *Deutsche Sprichwörterkunde* = *Hndbch. d. deutschen Unterrichts an höheren Schulen,* IV, 3 (1922), 150.

[4] Cf. Apostolius praef., 4 (→ n. 2, 3); Cyrillus Alex. Comm. in Ev. Joh., XI, 2 on Jn. 16:25 (MPG, 74, 461 C); Suid., *s.v.:* ... ἢ παροιμία ἐστὶ λόγος ἀπόκρυφος, δι' ἑτέρου προδήλου σημαινόμενος. But Suid., and after him Hesych., seem to be influenced also by Johannine usage.

[5] Cf. Aristot. Rhet., II, 21, p. 1395a, 17: ἔνιαι τῶν παροιμιῶν καὶ γνῶμαί εἰσιν.

[6] Aristot. Rhet., III, 11, p. 1413a, 14 : αἱ παροιμίαι μεταφοραὶ ἀπ' εἴδους ἐπ' εἶδός εἰσιν, cf. Prittwitz-Gaffron, 3.

[7] Quint. Inst. Orat., V, 11, 21: *cui (fabulae) confine est* παροιμίας *genus illud, quod est velut fabella brevior et per allegoriam accipitur.*

[8] Cf. Plut. Apophth. prooem, Alexandros (II, 172b-e; 179d-181 f).

higher Gk. literature the proverb is interwoven into speeches and esp. letters. [9] In poetry popular proverbs are given poetic form. [10] Short introductory formulae are used to indicate the proverbial nature of such sayings. [11] In time we find collections of proverbs : Aristotle, Clearches, Zenobius, Diogenian, the last two under Hadrian.

2. The Heb. term for proverb is מָשָׁל. The very common use of this word is to be seen from → παραβολή, which is also used for it, → 747, 26 f.; 748, 17. The true Gk. word, παροιμία, does not occur in the LXX in the historical books, the prophets, Ps., Job etc., and only twice in Prv. (1:1; 26:7; 25:1 vl.) and 5 times in Sir. (6:35; 8:8; 18:29; 39:3; 47:17). [12] Like מָשָׁל παροιμία can also mean "profound saying," → 748, 5 ff. [13] The title of Prv. in 1:1 describes as such all the sayings that follow, which in the same title are attributed to Solomon, the model sage. Where popular proverbs are concealed behind the sayings of Prv. — and this seems to be frequently the case — they are still interwoven into the parallelism. [14] In Sir. the original of παροιμία at 6:35; 47:17 is מָשָׁל, at 8:8 חִידָה. For both words Sir. also has παραβολή (→ 748, 25); they are thus synon. For Sir., too, παροιμίαι are "wisdom sayings" devised or composed by the wise (8:8; 18:29; 39:3), esp. Solomon (47:17). For the most part they contain practical wisdom, sometimes in obscure form, 8:8 חִידָה). In 39:3 (ἀπόκρυφα παροιμιῶν, ἐν αἰνίγμασι παραβολῶν) [15] and 47:17 παραβολαί and παροιμίαι are par., and the aspect of hidden wisdom is stressed in both.

3. Philo uses παροιμία often for "proverb." [16] In Rabb. and Talmudic works proverbs are frequently employed in elucidation and proof. [17] Normally an introductory formula is used when they are quoted. [18]

B. The New Testament.

1. παροιμία occurs in the sense of "proverb" in the NT only at 2 Pt. 2:22. In the manner of Greek literary usage two common sayings [19] are here employed in graphic disparagement of the conduct of the Gnostic heretics. Jn. 4:37 also adduces in elucidation a proverb attested elsewhere, and a common introductory formula is used (ἐν τούτῳ ὁ λόγος ἐστὶν ἀληθινός), [20] though it is not expressly called a παροιμία. [21] The warning formula in 1 C. 15:33 (μὴ πλανᾶσθε) introduces the statement of Menander which is also found in other places. [22] Pl. uses the same

---

[9] Cf. R. Sollert, "Die Sprichwörter bei Synesios v. Kyrene, I," *Programm d. Gymnasiums St. Stephan Augsburg* (1909), 12.

[10] Martin, 8; cf. Theogn., 537; Aristoph. Thes., 928.

[11] Cf. Plat. Lys., 216c : κατὰ τὴν ἀρχαίαν παροιμίαν, Crat., 384a : παλαιὰ παροιμία, Polit., 264b : κατὰ τὴν παροιμίαν, Euthyd., 307c : τὸ λεγόμενον, Anth. Pal., V, 5 (ed. Dübner : 6), 3 : λέγουσιν ἀληθέα, Soph. Ai., 664 : ἀλλ' ἔστ' ἀληθὴς ἡ βροτῶν παροιμία, Trach., 1.

[12] Σ Ez. 12:22; 16:44 παροιμία.

[13] LXX never has γνώμη for this.

[14] Cf., e.g., Prv. 10:6, 9, 15; 11:2, 13, 16, 21; 12:14; 13:24; Sir. 2:5; 13:1, 17; 27:26; Qoh. 10:8.

[15] There is no Heb. at Sir. 18:29; 39:3. V. Ryssel in Kautzsch has "parables" at both.

[16] Vit. Mos., I, 22, 156; II, 29 etc.

[17] Str.-B., IV, Index s.v. "Sprichwörter u. Gleichnisse," esp. I, 653 f.

[18] E.g., "People are wont to say"; "this is as people say"; "the proverb says"; "it is said in the proverb."

[19] Cf. for the first proverb Prv. 26:11; Apostolius (→ n. 2), 10, 30; 17, 75 (CPG, II, 492 f., 705); Str.-B., III, 773; Wnd. Kath. Br., ad loc.; G. Dalman, *Jesus-Jeschua* (1922), 212.

[20] Cf. → n. 11.

[21] For attestation elsewhere cf. Zenobius, I, 65 (CPG, I, 25); Apostolius (→ n. 2), 2, 51 (CPG, II, 276); → Martin, 21; W. Freytag, Arabum proverbia, 1 (1838), 570, No. 166. Bu. J., ad loc.

[22] Menand. (Thais) Fr., 218 (CAF, III, 62); Eur. Fr., 1013 (TGF, 683); H. Koch, "Quaestiones de proverbiis apud Aesch., Soph., Eur. II," *Programm d. Gymnasiums Bartenstein* (1892), 10.

formula to introduce the proverbial statement in Gl. 6:7.²³ The saying in Lk. 4:23 is shown to be a proverb by the use of → παραβολή.²⁴ The saying of the voice in Ac. 26:14 is also proverbial,²⁵ and the quotation in Tt. 1:12 rests on a proverb.²⁶ Undoubtedly there are among the Synoptic sayings of Jesus some which were already current as popular proverbs and which He adopted and combined with the truth of His message. This is shown by the transmission of such sayings partly in the Talmudic, partly in the Aramaic and Arabic, and partly in the Hellenistic Greek legacy of proverbs. The following sayings certainly seem to be proverbial : Mt. 5:14; 6:21, 24a, 34; 7:5, 7, 12, 15, 16; 8:20; 12:30; 19:24; 20:16; 22:14; Mk. 4:24 f.; 8:37; 9:40; Lk. 12:2, 48b; 14:34.²⁷

2. In John's Gospel παροιμία occurs 3 times at 10:6 and 16:25, 29. In keeping with the sense which among others מָשָׁל and the Synoptic → παραβολή may have, παροιμία in Jn. means "hidden, obscure speech" which stands in need of interpretation. As Jesus according to Mk. 4:10-12 (→ 757, 1 ff.) intentionally speaks in parables which are difficult to understand, so the Johannine Christ speaks ἐν παροιμίαις. Thus 10:6 retrospectively calls the allegory of the shepherd a concealing speech of this kind, and in retrospective summary 16:25 describes all Jesus' words up to the Parting Discourses as obscure speech which can only imperfectly indicate supraterrestrial truth in human words. Later — the reference is not to Easter or Pentecost, but to the *parousia* — this will be replaced by unconcealed revelation (ἐν παρρησίᾳ, → 881, 2 ff.) which will be for the first time fully objective speech concerning heavenly things.²⁸ It is as it were a dawning of this new and welcome state of affairs when the disciples are given as a clear revelation His saying about the Father and His going to Him, 16:29 → 881, 6 f. His life's task has now reached its goal. He who came to proclaim God can now leave the earth and return to the world of God.²⁹

Hauck

παρομοιάζω → 199, 6 ff.

παρόμοιος → 198, 30 ff.

---

²³ 4 Esr. 9:17 (Str.-B., III, 578). Cf. Plat. Phaedr., 260d : καρπὸν ὧν ἔσπειρε θερίζειν, Gregorius Cyprius, II, 57 (CPG, I, 363); A. Otto, *Die Sprichwörter d. Römer* (1890), 1104, No. 221; *ut sementem feceris, ita metes* (Cic. De Orat., II, 65, 261).

²⁴ → παραβολή, 752, 4.

²⁵ → III, 664, 33 ff.; 665 f.; Pind. Pyth., 2, 94 f.; Aesch. Ag., 1624. Eur. Ba., 795; Zenobius, V, 70 (CPG, I, 148); Apostolius (→ n. 2), 8, 90 f.; 14, 100 (CPG, II, 457 and 628); A. Otto, *op. cit.*, 331, No. 1693; Wettstein, *ad loc.*; Lib. Ep., 1190; E. Salzmann, *Sprichwörter u. sprichwörtliche Redensarten bei Lib.*, Diss. Tübingen (1910), 75; Zn. Ag., *ad loc.*; Bau. Ag., 269 f.; M. Dibelius, "Die Reden d. Ag.," *Aufsätze zur Ag.*, FRL, NF, 42 (1951), 120-162. For the fact that a Bat-qol can be given in the form of a proverb cf. Str.-B., I, 134, 127.

²⁶ Dib. Past., *ad loc.*; Anth. Pal., VII, 275, 6 : Κρῆτες ὅπου ψεῦσται . . . ; Callim. Hymn., I, 8 f. (ed. O. Schneider, I [1870], cf. p. 138): Κρῆτες ἀεὶ ψεῦσται καὶ γὰρ τάφον, ὧ ἄνα, σεῖο Κρῆτες ἐτεκτήναντο, σὺ δ' οὐ θάνες. κρητίζειν = "to lie," Zenobius, IV, 62 (CPG, I, 101); A. Otto, *op. cit.*, 98, No. 463; *mendax Creta* (Ovid Ars Amatoria, I, 298): Polyb., 8, 19, 5 : πρὸς Κρῆτα κρητίζειν. C. Wunderer, *Polybios-Forschungen*, 1 (1898), 95, 111, 116.

²⁷ Cf. Bultmann Trad., Index *s.v.* "Sprichwörter"; Str.-B., Index *s.v.* "Sprichwörter"; Dalman, *op. cit.*, 200-214 (Jewish proverbs and sayings).

²⁸ Cf. Nu. 12:8 LXX.

²⁹ E. Lohmeyer, "Vom Sinn d. Gleichnisse Jesu," ZSTh, 15 (1938), 319-346, esp. 320 f.; H. Strathmann J. (*NT Deutsch* [1951]), *ad loc.*; P. Fiebig, *Altjüdische Gleichnisse u. d. Gleichnisse Jesu* (1904), 164-167. E. Schweizer, "Ego eimi," FRL, NF, 38 (1939), 112-124; Bu. J., 452-454; W. Wrede, *Das Messiasgeheimnis in den Evangelien*² (1913), 191-206, 249 f.

† παροξύνω, † παροξυσμός

ὀξύνω, orig. "to sharpen" (→ ὄξος, 288 f.), but transf. like the composite παροξύνω, "to spur on," "to stimulate," pass. "to be provoked"; Xenoph. Mem., III, 3, 13; Isoc. Or., 1, 46. The word usually means "to stir to anger," pass. "to be irritated," "incensed"; Eur. Alc., 674 : πατρὸς μὴ παροξύνῃς φρένας. The word is common in this sense in the LXX, while the more neutral sense is almost completely absent. [1] It is normally used with ref. to God : Nu. 14:11: εἶπεν κύριος ... ἕως τίνος παροξύνει με ὁ λαὸς οὗτος; [2] The pass. is very common, Dt. 1:34: κύριος ... παροξυνθεὶς ὤμοσεν [3] (→ 395, 34-397, 4).

The noun παροξυσμός is rare. A neutral sense of "incitement" is found neither in secular Gk. nor the LXX, but the word is used for "provocation," "irritation" in Demosth. Or., 45, 14 : ἢ παροξυσμὸς ἢ φιλονικία, Dt. 29:27: ... ἐν θυμῷ καὶ ὀργῇ καὶ παροξυσμῷ μεγάλῳ, cf. Ιερ. 39:37.

In the NT the verb occurs at Ac. 17:16; it is said of Paul that when he saw pagan Athens παρωξύνετο τὸ πνεῦμα αὐτοῦ ἐν αὐτῷ, "his spirit was provoked or incensed in him." [4] The expression seeks to emphasise the honest anger of the apostle, and can hardly suggest that he was stirred or stimulated to preach or to win converts. [5] 1 C. 13:5 says of love : οὐ παροξύνεται, "it does not let itself be provoked." Pl. uses this expression with a conscious eye on the tensions in the church at Corinth, where there had been a good deal of provocation. [6]

The noun παροξυσμός is found in the usual sense of "irritation" at Ac. 15:39, which tells of the quarrel between Paul and Barnabas. An unusual occurrence is at Hb. 10:24 : κατανοῶμεν ἀλλήλους εἰς παροξυσμὸν ἀγάπης καὶ καλῶν ἔργων, where παροξυσμός, in keeping with the first meaning of the verb, can only have the sense of "incitement," "stimulation." [7] Perhaps the author is intentionally suggesting the idea of spurring on or stimulation to give special force to his summons to love and good works. [8]

Seesemann

παροργίζω, παροργισμός → 382 ff.

παροξύνω κτλ. E. Schwyzer, Griech. Grammatik, II (Hndbch. AW, II, 1, 2 [1950]), 492 f.

[1] Prv. 6:3 : παρόξυνε τὸν φίλον σου, "pester thy friend."

[2] Cf. also Nu. 16:30; 20:24; Dt. 9:7, 8, 22; 31:20; ψ 9:25 etc.

[3] Cf. also Dt. 9:19; 32:19; Hos. 8:5; Zech. 10:3 : παρωξύνθη ὁ θυμός μου.

[4] Cf. Is. 63:10 : αὐτοὶ δὲ ... παρώξυναν τὸ πνεῦμα τὸ ἅγιον αὐτοῦ.

[5] Cf. Pr.-Bauer⁴, s.v.

[6] Cf. Joh. W. 1 K., ad loc.

[7] Cf. Wnd. Hb., ad loc. and Jos. Ant., 16, 125 : δύνασθαι δὲ τὴν μετάνοιαν ... παροξῦναι ... τὴν εὔνοιαν (= "to stimulate" goodwill).

[8] Cf. Mi. Hb.³ and W. Loew, Der Glaubensweg d. Neuen Bundes, Eine Einführung in den Brief an d. Hebräer = Die urchr. Botschaft, 18 (1931), ad loc.

→ ἐπιφάνεια.

→ ἔρχομαι, II, 666, 4-684.

† παρουσία, πάρειμι   → ἥκω, II, 926, 29-928, 25.

→ ἡμέρα, II, 943, 21-953, 27.

→ μαραναθά, IV, 466, 13-472, 10.

Contents: A. The General Meaning: 1. Presence; 2. Appearing. B. The Technical Use
of the Terms: I. In Hellenism: 1. The Visit of a Ruler; 2. The Parousia of the Gods;
3. The Sacral Meaning of the Word in Philosophy. II. OT Presuppositions for the Technical Use of the Terms in the NT: 1. The Coming of God in Direct Self-Attestation and
in the Cultus; 2. The Coming of God in History; 3. The Coming of Yahweh as World
King; 4. The Coming of the Messiah. III. Progress and Regress in Judaism: 1. Palestinian
Judaism: a. Expectation of the Coming of God; b. Expectation of the Messiah (and other
Saviours); 2. Hellenistic Judaism: a. Greek Translations of the Bible; b. Philo; c. Josephus.
IV. The Technical Use of πάρειμι and παρουσία in the NT: 1. The Historical Place
of the Concept of the Parousia in the NT; 2. The Detailed Development of the Concept:
a. The Synoptic Jesus; b. The Primitive Community; c. Paul; d. Deutero-Paulinism:
e. The Epistles of James, Peter and Jude; f. Revelation; g. John's Gospel and Epistles;
3. Theological Summary. V. πάρειμι and παρουσία in Ecclesiastical Usage.

π ά ρ ε ι μ ι, π α ρ ο υ σ ί α. In general and on A.: Liddell-Scott, Cr.-Kö., Moult.-Mill.,
Pr.-Bauer⁴, *s.v.* On B. I: Preisigke Wört. (also III, 11, *s.v.*) and Fachwörter, *s.v.*; Ostraka,
I, 274 ff.; Mitteis-Wilcken, I, 1, 356 f.; Deissmann LO⁴, 100 f., 314-320, 368, 370; M. P.
Nilsson, *Gesch. d. gr. Religion,* II = *Hndbch. AW,* V, 2, 2 (1950), esp. 373, 431; W. Weber,
Untersuchungen z. Gesch. d. Kaisers Hadrianus (1907), esp. 81, 93, 109, 115, 125 f., 130,
150, 185, 197 f., 201, 227, 247; W. Otto, *Priester u. Tempel im hell. Ägypten,* II (1908),
63 f.; E. Biedermann, *Studien zur ägypt. Verwaltungsgeschichte* (1913), 85 f.; E. Norden,
Die Geburt d. Kindes = *Studien z. Bibliothek Warburg,* 3 (1924), esp. 116-128. On B. II
and III: H. Stade-A. Bertholet, *Bibl. Theol. d. AT* (1905/11), *passim*; Eichr. Theol. AT,
passim; Bousset-Gressm., esp. 213-301; Moore, II, 323-395; H. Gressmann, "Der Messias,"
FRL, NF, 26 (1929), *passim*; Volz Esch., *passim*; W. Staerk, *Soter, Die bibl. Erlösererwartung in d. östlichen Religionen* (1938), *passim*; E. Bréhier, *Les idées philosophiques et
religieuses d. Philon d'Alexandrie* (1908), 5-10, 22; Schl. Theol. d. Judt., 252-263; Str.-B.,
esp. IV, 764-1015; B. Murmelstein, "Adam, ein Beitrag zur Messiaslehre," WZKM, 35
(1928), 242-275; 36 (1929), 51-86. On B. IV: H. J. Holtzmann, *Nt.liche Theol.*² (1911),
Index *s.v.* "Parusie": P. Feine, *Theol. d. NT*⁸ (1950), esp. 120 f., 283-285, 367-369, 378 f.,
416-420; H. Weinel, *Bibl. Theol. d. NT*⁴ (1928), Index *s.v.* παρουσία; R. Bultmann, *Theol.
d. NT* (1948 ff.), 2-9, 38-54, 75-82, 404-405, 421-439; W. Bousset, *Kyrios Christos*³ (1926),
Index *s.v.* "Parusie"; H. E. Weber, *"Eschatologie" u. "Mystik" im NT* (1930), *passim*;
P. Althaus, *Die letzten Dinge*⁵ (1949), esp. 241-246; Kl., Hck., Loh. Mk. on c. 13; Zn.,
Bau. J., esp. on 14:1 ff.; 16:16 ff.; Bu. J., Index "Eschatologie"; Joh. W., Bchm. 1 K. on
15:23 ff., 50 ff.; Wnd., Bchm. 2 K. on 5:1 ff.; Dob., Dib. Th. on 1 Th. 2:19 f.; 4:13 ff.; 5:1 ff.;
2 Th. 2:1 ff.; Bss., Had., Loh. Apk. on 14:14 ff; 19:11 ff.; E. v. Dobschütz, "Zur Eschatologie
d. Evangelien," ThStKr, 84 (1911), 1-20 Eng. "The Eschatology of the Gospels," Exp.,
Ser. 7, Vol. 9 (1910), 97-117; A. Schweitzer, *Gesch. d. Leben-Jesu-Forschung*⁵ (1933), 390-
443, esp. 407-414; W. Michaelis, *Täufer, Jesus, Urgemeinde* (1928), esp. 55-58, 88-91, 95 f.,
100-103, 119; R. Otto, *Reich Gottes u. Menschensohn*² (1939), 118-191; F. Busch, "Zum
Verständnis d. synpt. Eschatologie," *Nt.liche Forschungen,* IV, 2 (1938); H. Riesenfeld,
Jésus transfiguré (1947), 247, 293-299; P. L. Schoonheim, *Een semasiologisch onderzoek van
PAROUSIA met betrekking tot het gebruik in Mattheüs 24,* Diss. Utrecht (1953); J. Gewiess,
Die urapostolische Heilsverkündigung nach d. Ag. (1939), esp. 31-38; F. Tillmann, *Die
Wiederkunft Christi nach d. paul. Briefen* (1909); A. Schweitzer, *Die Mystik d. Ap. Pl.*
(1930), Index *s.v.* "Parusie Jesu"; F. Guntermann, *Die Eschatologie d. heiligen Pls.* (1932);
A. Oepke, "Die Eschatologie d. Pls.," AELKZ, 60 (1927), 458-462, 482-489, 509-513, 530-
536; B. Brinkmann, "Die Lehre v. d. Parusie beim heiligen Pls. u. im Hen.," *Biblica,* 13
(1932), 315-334, 418-434; J. Kiss, "Zur eschatologischen Beurteilung d. Theol. des Ap.
Pls.," ZSTh, 15 (1938), 379-416. E. Haack, "Eine exegetisch-dogmatische Studie zur
Eschatologie über 1 Th. 4:13-18," ZSTh, 15 (1938), 544-569; A. Meyer, *Das Rätsel d. Jk.-
Briefes* = ZNW Beih., 10 (1936), Index *s.v.* "Parusie," esp. 159-161; G. Bornkamm, "Die

παρουσία, an abstract term based on πάρειμι, is found from Aesch., first in a very general sense. It is formed from παροντ-ία as ἐξουσία is from ἐξοντ-ία and γερουσία from γεροντ-ία.

A. The General Meaning.

1. Presence.

πάρειμι, "to be present," is used of persons (Jn. 11:28) and also of impersonal things, e.g., evil in Prv. 1:27; τὰ παρόντα, "possessions," Hb. 13:5 (cf. 2 Pt. 1:8 vl.). παρουσία denotes esp. active presence, e.g., in legal documents (BGU, IV, 1127, 37; 1129, 27; P. Gen., 68, 11 f.; P. Masp., 126, 15; P. Oxy., VI, 903, 15), of representatives of the community, 1 C. 16:17; Paul himself, Phil. 2:12; ἡ παρουσία τοῦ σώματος, 2 C. 10:10 (opp. letters); also income, Plato Comicus Fr., 177 (CAF, I, 650), or troops, Thuc., VI, 86, 3.

2. Appearing.

πάρειμι, "to have come," 1 Macc. 12:42, vl. 45; 2 Macc. 3:9; Mt. 26:50; Ac. 10:21; 17:6,[1] or "to come," Lk. 13:1. παρουσία, "arrival," Thuc., I, 128, 5: τῇ προτέρᾳ παρουσίᾳ, "during the first 'invasion' "; so also 2 Macc. 8:12. Of the arrival of Titus (2 C. 7:6 f.) or Paul himself (Phil. 1:26). The absence of the word from the LXX in the books originally written in Heb. may be explained by the fact that the Semite speaks more concretely.

B. The Technical Use of the Terms.

I. In Hellenism.

1. The Visit of a Ruler. There is no sharp distinction between profane and sacral use. When Demetrius Poliorketes entered Athens after driving out Demetrius of Phaleron (307 B.C.), he was greeted by a paean which even an ancient author felt to be insipid flattery, Athen., VI, 62-63 (p. 253d-f) = Diehl², II, 6, p. 104 f. As the greatest of the gods of the city draw near (πάρεισιν, line 2), he is present laughing (πάρεστι, line 8). The other gods hold aloof or do not exist: σὲ δὲ παρόνθ' ὁρῶμεν, line 18. He, the θεὸς ἀληθινός, is to bring peace and destroy the sphinx. παρουσία, which at every simple meal denotes the presence of the gods,[2] is used technically for the visit of a ruler or high official, 3 Macc. 3:17. In general, however, the technical use arises first through the addition of a gen. or pronouns or verbal phrases: παρουσία τῆς βασιλίσσης, Ostraka, 1481, 2; Germanicus: εἰς τὴν ἐμὴν παρουσίαν, Preisigke Sammelbuch, I, 3924, 3 f.; of Ptolemy Philometor and Cleopatra: καθ' ἃς ἐποιεῖσθ' ἐν Μέμφει παρουσίας, P. Par., 26, I, 18.

Komposition der apokalyptischen Visionen in d. Offenbarung Johannis," ZNW, 36 (1937/38), 132-149; E. Schwartz, "Aporien im vierten Evangelium," NGG, 1907 (1907), 342-372; 1908 (1908), 115-188, 497-560, esp. 160, n. 1, 557; R. Bultmann, "Die Eschatologie d. J.," Glauben u. Verstehen (1933), 134-152; K. Kundsin, "Die Wiederkunft Jesu in den Abschiedsreden d. J.," ZNW, 33 (1934), 210-215; G. Stählin, "Zum Problem d. joh. Eschatologie," ZNW, 33 (1934), 225-259. On the delay in the parousia: W. Michaelis, Der Herr verzieht nicht die Verheissung. Die Aussagen Jesu über die Nähe d. Jüngsten Tages (1942); O. Cullmann, "Die Hoffnung d. Kirche auf die Wiederkunft Christi," Verhandlungen d. schweizerischen reformierten Pfarrervereins, 83 (1942); also "Le retour de Christ. Espérance de l'église selon le NT," Cahiers théologiques de l'actualité protestante, I (1943); also "Das wahre durch d. ausgebliebene Parusie gestellte nt.liche Problem," Theol. Zschr., 3 (1947), 177-191; J. Schildenberger, "Weissagung u. Erfüllung," Biblica, 24 (1943), 205-230; also Vom Geheimnis d. Gotteswortes (1950), 189-196; W. G. Kümmel, "Verheissung u. Erfüllung," Abhandlungen zur Theol. d. AT u. NT, 6 (1945); T. F. Glasson, The Second Advent (1945); G. Bornkamm, "Die Verzögerung d. Parusie," In memoriam E. Lohmeyer (1951), 116-126. On B. V: W. Caspari, "Advent," RE³, 1, 188-191.
[1] Bl.-Debr. § 322.
[2] F. Dölger, "Zu den Zeremonien d. Messliturgie," Antike u. Christentum, II (1930), 190-221, esp. 216. Cf. the Roman "Dii propitii" when the Lares are placed on the table.

The customary honours on the *parousia* of a ruler are : flattering addresses, Menand. Rhetor. (Rhet. Graec., III, 368), tributes (Ditt. Syll.³, 495, 9. 84 f.), delicacies, asses to ride on and for baggage, improvement of streets (P. Petr., II, 18a, 4 ff. [258-253 B.C.]), golden wreaths *in natura* or money (Callixeinos in Athen., V, 35 [p. 203b], 2239 talents and 50 minas), and feeding of the sacred crocodiles, P. Tebt., I, 33. These and other honours had to be paid for by the population of the district favoured by the *parousia* of the king or his ministers, and if voluntary gifts were not enough a forced levy was made, which led to much complaint, Ditt. Or., 139, esp. line 9. Understanding rulers repeatedly tried to make redress (P. Tebt., I, 5, esp. lines 178-187; Preisigke Sammelbuch, I, 3924), but with little success (CIG, III, 4956). The imperial period with its world ruler or members of his household, if it did not increase the cost, certainly invested the *parousia* of the ruler with even greater magnificence. This could be done by the inauguration of a new era, inscr. of Tegea : ἔτους εθ᾽ (69) ἀπὸ τῆς θεοῦ ῾Αδριανοῦ τὸ πρῶτον εἰς τὴν ῾Ελλάδα παρουσίας,³ or a holy day in Didyma : ἱερὰ ἡμέρα τῆς ἐπιδημίας τοῦ Αὐτοκράτορος,⁴ or by buildings : Hadrian's gate in Athens, the Olympieion in Delos : νέα ᾽Αθηνᾷ ῾Αδριανά, or by the minting of advent coins, e.g., in Corinth on the coming of Nero : *Adventus Augusti,* or the like.⁵ Hadrian's travels produced such coins in most provinces.⁶ That the *parousia* of the ruler could sometimes be a ray of hope for those in trouble may be seen from the complaints and requests made on such occasions, e.g., that of the priestesses of Isis in the Sarapeion at Memphis (163/162 B.C.) to the "gods" Ptolemy Philometor and Cleopatra, P. Par., 26, 29.

2. *The Parousia of the Gods.* This applies esp. to the helpful *parousia* of the gods in the narrower sense. Aesculapius heals a woman who has a miscarriage on her way home : τάν τε παρουσίαν τὰν αὐτοῦ παρενεφάνιζε (declared), Ditt. Syll.³, 1169, 34. Diod. S., 4, 3, 3 depicts the cultic παρουσία of Dionysus in the Theban mysteries, which took place at three year intervals. Ael. Arist. in a dream experiences the παρουσία of Aesculapius Soter at the same time as a temple warden. Though this raises his hair on end, it causes tears of joy and lays on him an inexpressible burden of knowledge, Ael. Arist. Or. Sacr., II, 30-32 (ed. B. Keil [1898], II, 401).⁷

3. *The Sacral Meaning of the Word in Philosophy.* In philosophy, too, παρουσία increasingly takes on a sacral sense. Plato still uses it in the profane sense as a synon. of μέθεξις, "participation," Phaed., 100d.⁸ It is not particularly prominent in Stoicism, and the same is true of πάρειμι, though this is common in Epict. Things are different, however, in Hermes mysticism and Neo-platonism. In the former παρουσία is still neutral, Stob. Hermes Excerpt., IVa, 7 (Scott, I, 404, 19 f.). But the sacral sense shines through plainly when Nous says of its dwelling with the righteous : ἡ παρουσία μου γίνεται <αὐτοῖς> βοήθεια, Corp. Herm., I, 22. Acc. to Porphyr.⁹ Egyptian priests exorcised demons by the blood of animals and lashing the air, ἵνα τούτων ἀπελθόντων παρουσία τοῦ θεοῦ γένηται. In Iambl. Myst. the word is common and always sacral, cf. V, 21 of the invisible "presence" of the gods at sacrifices, or III, 11 in spontaneous

---

³ BCH, 25 (1901), 275. On the other hand, the Cos inscr. in Deissmann LO, 318, n. 4 (*The Inscr. of Cos,* ed. W. R. Paton and E. L. Hicks [1891], No. 391) refers to the beginning of Caligula's rule (ἐπιφάνεια).

⁴ T. Wiegand, "Bericht VII über Milet," AAB, 1911 (1911), App. 54.

⁵ Weber, 164 and 93.

⁶ *Ibid.,* 81 (Rome), 109 (Britain), 115 (Spain), 125 f. (Bithynia), 130 (Asia), 150 (Moesia), 155 (Macedonia), 197 (Sicily), 198 (Italy), 201 (Mauretania), 227 (Phrygia), 247 (Alexandria).

⁷ A primitive Egypt. theologoumenon, the *parousia* of a new god in the heavenly circle, is reflected in the ritual of enthronement, and may still be detected in Vergil Ecl., IV, 15 ff. (Norden, 116-124). Related is Corp. Herm., I, 26a (of the ascent of the soul to deification): συγχαίρουσι δὲ οἱ παρόντες (sc. spirits which have already reached the 8th step) τῇ τούτου παρουσίᾳ.

⁸ J. D. Mabbot, "Aristot. and the ΧΩΡΙΣΜΟΣ of Plato," *Class. Quarterly,* 20 (1926), 72-79, esp. 76 f.

⁹ Porphyr., De Philosophia ex Oraculis Haurienda, II (ed. G. Wolff [1856], 148).

ecstasy; cf. also III, 6 of the *parousia* of divine fire. V, 21 reminds us vaguely of descriptions of the *parousia* in the NT: before the παρουσία (coming) of the gods when they wish to visit earth, all subject powers are set in motion and precede and accompany them. II, 8: the ἀρχάγγελοι emit a radiance which is not intolerable for the better. αἱ τῶν ἀγγέλων παρουσίαι make the air bearable so that it does not harm the priests.

II. OT Presuppositions for the Technical Use of the Terms in the NT.

Since Semitic forms of speech are more concrete, there are no words for "presence" and "coming" in Heb. For the verbs "to be present" and "to come," however, there are several other terms in addition to אָתָה and בּוֹא, → 864, 21. These all have a predominantly secular sense, though they can sometimes have a numinous echo. The word of the seer comes (1 S. 9:6), the time (appointed by God) is present, the end is near (Lam. 4:18), evil comes (Prv. 1:27), the day of recompense (Dt. 32:35) or of Yahweh (Jl. 2:1) comes, and the year of redemption will also come (Is. 63:4). In particular God is everywhere present (Ps. 139:8); He is there when His people cry to Him (Is. 58:9). The OT saint can also experience the coming of God more specifically as follows.

1. The Coming of God in Direct Self-Attestation and in the Cultus.

These are closely related. Places of grace become cultic sites and *vice versa*, Gn. 16:13 f.; 28:18; Ju. 6:11-24; 2 S. 24:25, also 1 S. 3:10; 1 K. 8:10. This is reflected already in primitive history and the stories of the patriarchs, cf. Gn. 4:4; 8:20 f.; 15:17. [10] Later the — older — idea of coming in the cultus is attested first (c. 950 B.C. ?) in the Book of the Covenant, Ex. 20:24, 26; → 255, 14-21. The cover of the ark is, at least from the time of P, the chariot throne of Yahweh, [11] so that the entry of the ark is His coming, 1 S. 4:6 f.; 2 S. 6:9, 16; 2 Ch. 8:11. Ps. 24:7 ff. might well be a song for such occasions. [12] אֹהֶל מוֹעֵד, "the tent of meeting," should be mentioned in the same connection. [13] Yahweh, however, is never tied to specific media in His self-declaration. He can come in dreams (Gn. 20:3; 28:13), in more or less veiled theophanies (Gn. 18:1 ff.; 32:25 ff.; Ex. 3:2 ff.; 24:10 ff.; 34:6 ff.; Ps. 50:3), in the cloud (→ IV, 905, 5-18, 905, 31-906, 2), and esp. also in visions at the calling of the prophets (Is. 6:1 ff.; Jer. 1:4 ff.; Ez. 1:4 ff.), in the storm, in the quiet breath (1 K. 19:12 f.), in His Spirit (Nu. 24:2; Ju. 3:10; 11:29; 1 S. 11:6; 19:20), with His hand (1 K. 18:46), in His Word (Nu. 22:9; 2 S. 7:4; 1 K. 17:2 etc.) etc.; cf. also the common נְאֻם יהוה, Am. 6:8; Is. 1:24.

2. The Coming of God in History.

The Song of Deborah extols the victory over Sisera as a theophany, Ju. 5:4 f. The coming of Yahweh means victory over the enemies of Israel (Egypt, Is. 19:1; Assyria, Is. 30:27; the nations, Hab. 3:3 ff., 13). [14] For His apostate and disobedient people, too, esp. its rebellious members, His coming is terrible, His anger fearful (Am. 5:18-20; Zeph. 1:15-18; 2:2; 2 S. 24:15 f.; Jer. 23:19, 30 ff.; Mal. 3:5; → 398, 1-409, 3). To the fore, however, is His appearing to bring freedom from tyranny (Ex. 3:8; Ps. 80:2), to conclude the covenant (Ex. 19:18, 20). The liberation from exile is regarded as almost an exact equivalent of the redemption out of Egypt, Is. 35:2, 4; 40:3 ff., 10; 59:20; 60:1; 62:11. The coming age of salvation leads to the eschaton.

3. The Coming of Yahweh as World King.

Within the story of Moses Yahweh is lauded as king in Jeshurun, who came from Sinai and shone forth from Seir, to whom none is like (Dt. 33, 2. 5. 26 ff.). In the Balaam

---

[10] A. Alt, *Der Gott d. Väter* (1929), esp. 49-73.
[11] H. Schmidt, "Kerubenthron u. Lade," *Eucharisterion f. H. Gunkel,* I (1923), 120-144.
[12] A. Weiser Ps., I (*AT Deutsch*), *ad loc.* suggests this interpretation.
[13] G. v. Rad, *Deuteronomium-Studien²* (1948), 27.
[14] The genre of oracles on the nations arose among the prophets of salvation but was then adopted by prophets of judgment like Is., cf. Gressmann. 140.

songs the name of a god Melekh is perhaps transferred to Yahweh, Nu. 23:21. In the Song of the Red Sea Yahweh is called King "for ever and ever," Ex. 15:18. The more the concept of Yahweh's kingship expanded, the more all existing demonstrations of it were felt to be provisional. At the end of the days (בְּאַחֲרִית הַיָּמִים, Is. 2:2; Mi. 4:1 etc.; analogously בַּיּוֹם הַהוּא, Is. 2:11; Jer. 4:9, בַּיָּמִים הָהֵם, Jer. 3:16, 18, בָּעֵת הַהִיא, Is. 18:7; Mi. 3:4, הִנֵּה יָמִים בָּאִים, Is. 39:6), Yahweh will enter into His kingship in full power and majesty. This is prefigured in the festival of Yahweh's enthronement. [15] Then the promises of salvation, which progressively increase after the exile, [16] will be fulfilled. In Tt. Is. the prospect of the coming of Yahweh as world king is combined with the cosmic perspective of the creation of a new heaven and earth, Is. 66:15, cf. v. 22 and 65:17. All creatures will rejoice before Yahweh, Ps. 47; 93; 95-99. Universal peace will reign among men and beasts, Is. 2:2-4; 11:6-9. All suffering will be overcome, Is. 65:21 ff. Happiness and rejoicing will hold sway, and from Gentile lands glorious gifts and the dispersed will be brought as offerings to Yahweh, Is. 60:1 ff.; 66:10 ff., 20.

4. The Coming of the Messiah.

The anointed one sent by Yahweh may take His place. In this connection בּוֹא is first used in Gn. 49:10. [17] Courtly style, which gives evidence of foreign influences, contributed much to the transcending of the empirical. Expectation of a hero and a prince of peace [18] involves no self-contradiction, for world peace is the goal of the Messianic war. In the OT, however, the main function of the Messiah is not to conquer but to execute peace, Zech. 9:9 f. [19] The discipline of Yahweh religion prevents the hope of salvation from becoming a selfish fantasy. The coming is in the first instance regarded as a coming in history, though not without eschatological impulses. Da. 7:13 [20] is the starting-point of a new development. In contrast to the beasts (the world empires) from the abyss, we have the man (the people of God). The ref. is not yet to the personal pre-existence and historical *parousia* of the Messiah. It is understandable, however, that the ensuing age should put the personal interpretation to the forefront and take from the text both the concept of pre-existence and also the colours in which to portray the *parousia*. One should not overestimate the significance of the Messiah in the OT and the later period. In the Ps. the whole emphasis is on the coming of Yahweh.

III. Progress and Regress in Judaism.

In Judaism the progressive uprooting of the cultus and the increasing elimination of the direct revelation of God even in present history strengthen the orientation of religion to the future. On the other hand, Hellenistic influences retard or spiritualise eschatology. There is only a relative distinction between Palestinian and Hellenistic Judaism.

---

[15] S. Mowinckel, "Das Thronbesteigungsfest Jahwes u. d. Ursprung d. Eschatologie," *Psalmenstudien,* II (1922); H. J. Kraus, *Die Königsherrschaft Gottes im AT* (1951).

[16] Jer. 31:31 ff.; Ez. 36:23 ff.; Dt. Is. *passim* ; Zech. 12:14 etc., with ever present threatening, Ez. 7:2; Jl. 1:15; 2:1, 31; Zech. 14:5. The earlier elimination of all concluding promises from the pre-exilic prophets of judgment is no longer regarded as tenable to-day, cf. Am. 9:11-15; Hos. 14:5-9 etc.

[17] The difficult passage : "The sceptre shall not depart from Judah, nor the ruler's staff from between his legs" עַד כִּי־יָבֹא שִׁילֹה וְלוֹ יִקְּהַת עַמִּים   is best interpreted with the help of Giesebrecht's conjecture (H. Gressmann, "Der Ursprung d. isr.-jüd. Eschatologie," FRL, 6 [1905], 263): מֹשְׁלוֹ (his ruler), an allusion to Solomon acc. to H. Gunkel, Art. "Schilo," RGG², V, 162. Acc. to L. Dürr, *Ursprung u. Ausbau der isr.-jüd. Heilandserwartung* (1925), 59, the expression "the coming one" was already generally understood, so that no more than an allusion was necessary.

[18] Together in e.g., Is. 9:1 ff.; 11:1 ff.; Mi. 4 and 5.

[19] Here again בּוֹא, cf. also Ez. 21:32. The fact that Yahweh brings the Messiah explains the rare occurrence. Cf. Zech. 3:8 : הִנְנִי מֵבִיא.

[20] Cf. Volz, 11 ff.

1. **Palestinian Judaism.**

a. **Expectation of the Coming of God.**

Apocalyptic is saturated by close expectation of the end. Concealed [21] or direct refs. [22] are made to God's coming. Sometimes παρουσία is used (→ infra and n. 23), though it is hard to say whether the original is the noun מְטִיתָא, which came to be used in Syr., or a verbal expression (Test. Jud. 22:2 : καὶ ἐν ἀλλοφύλοις συντελεσθήσεται ἡ βασιλεία μου, ἕως τοῦ ἐλθεῖν τὸ σωτήριον τοῦ Ἰσραήλ, [ἕως τῆς παρουσίας θεοῦ τῆς δικαιοσύνης]). [23] In an undoubted interpolation Ass. Mos. 10:12 has a phrase which is still original : usque ad adventum illius (God). Slav. En. Longer Redaction 32:1; 42:5 distinguishes between God's first coming in creation and a second or final coming, but it also uses the term half numinously of the return of Enoch to the earth, 38:2 f. [24] Wis. 5:17-22 (→ 297, 21-26) has a vivid depiction of God's parousia in full panoply, cf. also Ass. Mos. 10:1-7; Sib., V, 344-360, where ref. is also made to His thundering voice. Cf. also Eth. En. 1:4, 9; 25:3. Ps. Sol. 15:12 esp. refers to judgment.

The Rabb. have fewer direct refs. to God's coming, but He is still the Goel of Israel, Tanch. במדבר (Buber), 16 (7b): [25] In this world I have made you banners (דְּגָלִים) ..., but in the future world I spring in (מְדַלֵּג, play on words) ... and redeem you (Cant. 2:8)." Pirqe of R. Eliezer, 11 (6c) [26] of the final world ruler : "We shall see him eye to eye, as is written in Is. 52:8." This is usually set in the Messianic time, seldom in the other world, and the concept is predominantly spatial. The idea is more that of manifestation than coming. The main theme is the coming of the righteous individual to God. [27]

b. **Expectation of the Messiah (and other Saviours).**

Up to 70 A.D. there is a confused interrelating of political Messianism, expectation of the Son of Man, and hope of the other aeon. But the idea of coming is still a vital one. Whether 4 Esr. consciously distinguishes between the parousia of the Messiah who dies after 400 yrs. (7:28 ff.) and that of the Messiah who remains (12:31 ff., cf. 11:37) is not wholly clear. S. Bar. 30:1 has παρουσία in the Gk. (Syr. מְטִיתָא, "arrival"). But the text is incontestably a Chr. interpolation. [28] In the vision of the clouds the ref. of the lightning (53:8 ff.) to the Messiah (72:1 f.) is originally intended [29] (an isolated par. to Mt. 24:27). [30] Parousia notions are esp. combined with the Elect and the Son of Man (→ υἱὸς τοῦ ἀνθρώπου), cf. Eth. En. 38:2; 49:4; 51:3; 52:9; 62:5 ff.; 69:27, 29; 71:16 f. Similar colours are used in 4 Esr. 13 to paint the coming of the man out of the sea who flies with clouds. Test. S. 6 f. has undergone Chr. revision, [31] similarly Sib., V, 256, though Sib., V, 414 ff. may be Jewish.

---

[21] Shining forth of majesty, Damasc. 20:26; coming of the glory of God, Sib., III, 47 f.; Kaddish Prayer, cf. Volz, 52.

[22] Test. S. 6:5 : κύριος ὁ θεὸς φαινόμενος ἐπὶ τῆς γῆς ἥξει. The text has come down in various forms. ὡς ἄνθρωπος is undoubtedly a Chr. interpolation. Cf. Test. Zeb. 9:8 and Test. D. 5:1, 13.

[23] The words in the parentheses [] do not occur in the Armen. but can hardly be a Chr. interpolation. Both Armen. versions read παρουσία at Test. L. 8:11. παρουσία means "presence" at Test. L. 8:15.

[24] For the refs. from Slav. En. cf. N. Bonwetsch, Die Bücher d. Geheimnisse Henochs = TU, 44, 2 (1922), 30, 39, 34 f. Test. Abr., which goes back to a Jewish original but has undergone Chr. revision, speaks of a parousia of Abel and Michael (Rec. A 13:2, TSt, II, 2 [1893], 92, 11; 78, 26).

[25] Str.-B., IV, 860.

[26] Ibid., III, 472.

[27] Volz, 131.

[28] Volz, 43 f.

[29] Against the substitution of water for lightning at 72:1 (R. H. Charles, The Apocrypha and Pseudepigrapha, II [1913], 518, n. ad loc.) cf. B. Violet, Die Apokalypsen d. Esra u. d. Baruch = GCS, 32 (1924), 309, n. ad loc. The ref. is to the Messiah, Volz, 44.

[30] Cf. Pesikt. r., 36 (162a), Str.-B., I, 954.

[31] In spite of E. Lohmeyer, "Kyrios Jesus," SAH, 1927/28, 4. Abh. (1928), 69.

Judaism speaks also of the coming of other saviours more or less akin to the Messiah, e.g., Abel, Enoch, Michael (→ I, 7, 35-8, 3; line 11 f.; n. 24), Elijah (→ II, 931, 5 ff.), the priest king to whom all the words of the Lord are to be revealed. His star will rise like that of a king, and he will radiate light and knowledge (Chr. ?). There will then be peace on earth, and the spirit of understanding and glory will rest on him. He will open the gates of Paradise, and the Lord will rejoice over His children, Test. L. 18. The appearing (παρουσία) of the priest king, for whom a Maccabean (John Hyrcanus ?) might have served as a model, but to whom eschatological expectations were transferred, is "highly esteemed as a prophet of the Most High" (*munus triplex*), Test. L. 8:15. [32] → προφήτης; 'Αδάμ, I, 141 ff.; Μωϋσῆς, IV, 848 ff.; 'Ηλίας, II, 928 ff.; 'Ενώχ, II, 556 ff.; 'Ιερεμίας, III, 218 ff.; 'Ιησοῦς, III, 284 ff. (Joshua as Taheb also → I, 388, 22 ff.).

Rabb. Judaism rejects apocalyptic and asks : "When will the Son of David come ?" bSanh., 98a. He is expected at a time of great tribulation and dereliction (→ ὠδίν), *ibid.*, 97a, 98a; Sot., 9, 15. On the other hand, the cleansing of the people from sin is regarded as a precondition. His coming is awaited with fear. One might not see him, or at most sitting in the shadow of the dung of his ass, bSanh., 98b. → υἱὸς Δαυίδ.

2. Hellenistic Judaism.

a. Greek Translations of the Bible.

πάρειμι occurs in the LXX, in Aquila, Symmachus and Theodotion, over 70 times, mostly for בּוֹא also אָתָה, חוּשׁ and הִגָּה, Aram. מְטָה and קְרֵב aphel. It thus means "to come," and this affects παρουσία accordingly. The context sometimes gives it numinous overtones (→ 861, 9 ff.), though it is never technical. παρουσία occurs only in works originally written in Gk.: [33] Jdt. 10:18; 2 Macc. 8:12; 15:21; 3 Macc. 3:17, always in a profane sense. But the very occurrence of the word is significant. Hell. Judaism took it from its environment. That it also found its way into religious usage may be seen from Test. XII (→ 863, 4 f.). The technical sense does not seem to have been normative at first. But one may assume that it soon exerted an influence. [34]

b. Philo.

It might be accidental that παρουσία does not occur in Philo. [35] In his world of thought, however, Hell. influences almost completely obliterated the expectation of a coming of Yahweh or the Messiah, let alone other saviours. [36] There is in Praem. Poen. c. 16 (91-97) a single ref. to the coming man (Nu. 24:7) who will bring universal peace, and tame man and beast (95). This ideal has, however, a Hell. flavour.

c. Josephus.

Jos. uses the verb for God's presence to help, [37] παρουσία being the Shekinah, Ant., 3, 80 and 202. Elisha asked God to display His δύναμις and παρουσία to his servant, 4 Βασ. 6:17; Ant., 9, 55. God also revealed it to the pagan governor Petronius, Ant., 18, 284. [38] Hellenism does not exert such a strong levelling influence on the

---

[32] On the question of Chr. interpolation cf. W. Bousset, "Die Test. XII," ZNW, 1 (1900), 172 f.; Volz, 191 f.; Schoonheim, 186-195. F. Schnapp in Kautzsch Apkr. u. Pseudepigr., *ad loc.* undoubtedly goes too far in assuming interpolation.

[33] 2 'Εσδρ. 12:6 (= Neh. 2:6) has παρουσία only in A. The πορεία of the other witnesses is both better attested and more pertinent, so that it is probably original. Yet παρουσία, too, comes from a Jewish hand, so that the reading testifies to the penetration of the word into Hell. Judaism.

[34] One might have expected a greater use of the word in the LXX. We cannot say that it was regarded as too pagan (considered but rejected by Schoonheim, 145-158). The reason is to be sought in the literalness of the translation.

[35] παρεῖναι is common.

[36] Cf. Bréhier 5.

[37] For instances cf. Schlatter, 30 f.

[38] Reading παρουσία against Niese with lat.

Palestinian Jos. His rejection of apocalyptic is Rabbinic, and politically opportunist. The temporally limited (Ant., 10, 267) prophecy of Da. concerning the son of Man he refers in non-Zealot fashion to Vespasian (Bell., 6, 313) if not to the period of Antiochus Epiphanes (Ant., 10, 276; 12, 322). [39] In Da. 2 the iron represents the Roman Empire, Ant., 10, 209. Jos. was not ready, however, to ascribe eternal duration (κρατήσει εἰς ἅπαντα?) to this. He cleverly avoids interpreting the stone of Da. 2:34, 44 f., [40] regarding it as his task simply to record the past and what has taken place, Ant., 10, 210. The referring of the Messianic hope to Vespasian, though not revoked, is only penultimate. In the background there is expectation of another ruler who on his coming will begin to rule the world from Jerusalem and give dominion to the Jewish people. [41] Without apocalyptic passion, however, this belief loses all formative power. A Hell. layer of microcosmic eschatology emerges. The concept of the *parousia* is in ruins. The Chr. interpretation of Da. 7:13 is even more remote from Jos. than the interpretation of the Zealots.

IV. The Technical Use of πάρειμι and παρουσία in the NT.

1. The Historical Place of the Concept of the Parousia in the NT.

Primitive Christianity waits for the Jesus who has come already as the One who is still to come. The hope of an imminent coming of the exalted Lord in Messianic glory is, however, so much to the fore that in the NT the terms are never used for the coming of Christ in the flesh, and παρουσία never has the sense of return. The idea of more than one *parousia* is first found only in the later Church, → 871, 1 ff. A basic prerequisite for understanding the world of thought of primitive Christianity is that we should fully free ourselves from this notion, which, so far as the NT is concerned, is suspect both philologically and materially.

In the NT generally παρεῖναι is not a tt. Only in certain passages does it take on the familiar (→ 861, 9 ff.; 864, 22 f.) numinous quality, though now with ref. to Christian data, so more or less in Jn. 11:28; 1 C. 5:3; 2 C. 13:10 with a personal subj., Jn. 7:6: Col. 1:6; Hb. 12:11; 2 Pt. 1:12 with a non-personal. Hence in what follows our concern will be only with the noun.

παρουσία as a tt. for the "coming" of Christ in Messianic glory seems to have made its way into primitive Christianity with Paul. The older designation ἡμέρα τοῦ κυρίου or the like (→ II, 945, 1-947, 3; 951, 6-953, 5) occurs in the Synoptists and Jn., and is also used a dozen times or so in Paul as compared with 7-8 instances of παρουσία (1 C. 1:8 vl.; 15:23; 1 Th. 2:19; 3:13; 4:15; 5:23; 2 Th. 2:1; 2:8). In the Past. παρουσία is replaced by → ἐπιφάνεια, which is even more influenced by Hellenism. In the Gospels we find it only in Mt., who has it 4 times in the apocalyptic discourse or its setting. [42] Jn. has the word only at 1 Jn. 2:28, but we find it 3 times in the strongly Hellenising 2 Pt. (1:16; 3:4, 12) and twice

---

[39] Schlatter, 252.

[40] The Rabb. usually expounded the stone as the Messiah, Tanch. תְּרוּמָה (Buber) § 6 (46b), Str.-B., I, 69, 877. The eloquent silence of Jos. seems to indicate that he shared this view.

[41] The spread of this idea among the Jewish people is attested not merely by Jos. himself (Bell., 6, 312 f.) but also by Tacitus Hist., V, 13, and Sueton. Vespasian, 4, though perhaps both these drew their information from Jos. Cf. Schürer, II, 604.

[42] Mt. 24:3 (Mk. 13:4 and Lk. 21:7 paraphrase), 27 (Q, Lk. 17:24: ὁ υἱὸς τοῦ ἀνθρώπου ἐν τῇ ἡμέρᾳ αὐτοῦ), 37 (Q, Lk. 17:26: ἐν ταῖς ἡμέραις τοῦ υἱοῦ τοῦ ἀνθρώπου), 39 (not in Q or Lk.). Schoonheim (2) made this the starting-point for his extensive investigation. Whether the thesis that Mt. is Palestinian in origin and emphasis needs revision in the light of it, is a question which cannot be pursued in this context.

in Jm. (5:7 f.). These data leave us in no doubt as to the historical place of the technical use of παρουσία in the NT. The term is Hellenistic. In essential content, however, it derives from the OT, Judaism, and primitive Christian thinking. [43]

2. The Detailed Development of the Concept.

a. The Synoptic Jesus.

Apart from the actual occurrence of the word, the whole thinking of Jesus is permeated by ideas of *parousia*. This is true in all strata of the Synoptic tradition. It is already apparent in Mk., at least from the time of the exchange at Caesarea, Mk. 8:38 and par. To His Jewish judges Jesus holds out the threat of His coming even during their lifetime, [44] Mk. 14:62 and par.; Lk. emphasises only the session at the right hand of God. If Q warns against seeing in Jesus an apocalyptist or even a fanatic, [45] this is unintelligible apart from the concept of the *parousia*. [46] The same is true of passages peculiar to Mt. (25:1-13, [47] 14-30 [?], 31-46) and Lk. (12:35-38, 49 [?]; 22:29 f. [?]). So far as can be seen, the *parousia* concept is one of the original stones in the Synoptic tradition concerning Jesus. It is present in fully developed form in the *parousia* address in Mk. 13 and par., which, strongly influenced though it is by Jewish and primitive Christian apocalyptic, has crystallised around genuine dominical sayings. [48] Here all the Evangelists distinguish

---

[43] The older debate between Cremer and Deissmann is only of historical interest. Both were one-sided. Cremer, perhaps overlooking the true facts, or arbitrarily restricting the secular concept to the Attic, argues that παρουσία is seldom used for "coming" in profane Gk. (with some correction in Cr.-Kö.). Deissmann (LO⁴, 314-320) acutely applies Hell. pars. to the NT, but in the joy of discovery overestimates their significance. In Christianity too (→ 859, 29-33) the technical use rests, not on the word itself, but on the added genitives. Hence independent parallel development remains a possibility. The Syr. מָאתִיתָא and later Heb. בִּיאָה show that the noun is not wholly non-Semitic. Even verbal forms are best rendered by παρουσία in Gk. Pl. is still acquainted with the everyday use, → 859, 10 f., 16. If there was an early sense of the similarity to the ruler *parousia*, the contrast was also felt, though it can hardly be reduced to the formula that whereas rulers demand gifts, Jesus brings them (cf. Deissmann, 315). The oldest instance of a consciously drawn par. seems to be in a pap. belonging to the 6th cent. A.D., which is, however, referring to the descent into Hades (APF, 5 [1913], 284): Villagers affirm that they await the arrival of their lord with as much yearning as spirits in Hades await that of Christ, and that they pray day and night to be worthy of his *parousia*.
[44] Against the objections of H. Lietzmann ("Der Prozess Jesu," SAB, 1931, No. 14 [1931]) to the historicity of the trial of Jesus before the Sanhedrin one may refer to several acute discussions in ZNW, 30 (1931) — 33 (1934); cf. also J. Jeremias, "Zur Geschichtlichkeit d. Verhörs Jesu vor dem Hohen Rat," ZNW, 43 (1950/51), 145-150. For older bibl. cf. A. Oepke, "Ein Jahrzent Jesusliteratur," ThLBl, 50 (1929), 273-282, 289-297, esp. 292 f., and for a broader review cf. A. Oepke, "Probleme d. vorchr. Zeit des Pls.," ThStKr, 105 (1933), 387-424 and J. Blinzler, *Der Prozess Jesu* (1951).
[45] A. Harnack, "Sprüche u. Reden Jesu," *Beiträge z. Einleitung in d. NT,* II (1907), 173.
[46] Mt. 23:39 par. Lk. 13:35; Mt. 24:26 f. par. Lk. 17:23 f.; Mt. 24:28, 37-41 par. Lk. 17:26 f., 35, 37; Mt. 24:42-51 par. Lk. 12:39-46. So also Harnack, *op. cit.,* 165 and Dobschütz, 3.
[47] In spite of J. Jeremias, *Die Gleichnisse Jesu²* (1952), 38-40.
[48] A Jewish apocalypse from the time of Caligula (Schürer, I, 503-506) has been sifted out by G. Hölscher, "Der Ursprung d. Apk. Mk. 13," ThBl, 12 (1933), 193-202 (v. 7 f., 12, 14-20, 24-27). For older attempts cf. Busch, 1-14, 54-59. But the argument that v. 7 f., 12 depict only what is past is not convincing. Hck. Mk., *ad loc.* distinguishes similarly between the basic material and sayings of the disciples (v. 5 f., 9-11, 13, 23), but he thinks that even the former was under Chr. influence (that of Jesus?). Loh. Mk., *ad loc.* thinks it is impossible to distinguish sharply between source and additions, though his detailed analysis is artificial. How strongly the views of critics influence their judgment may be seen by comparing E. Winkel, *Das Ev. nach Mk.* (1937), 73 f.; R. Thiel, *Jesus Christus u. d. Wissen-*

between the judgment on Jerusalem and the *parousia*. How far Jesus Himself made this distinction, how far He even made a clear distinction between His resurrection and His *parousia*, it is no longer possible to say with certainty. [49] He does seem to have envisaged an interval between the first and the definitive restoration, a time of the community. Otherwise there would be no space for the conversion of the Gentiles, and such conversion without the preaching of repentance would be contrary to His basic principles. He probably thought His *parousia* was imminent. This is supported by many sayings which are hard to interpret in any other sense and which can hardly derive from the theology of the community, Mk. 9:1 and par.; 13:24-30 and par.; 14:62 and par. [50] etc. The tremendous tension which permeates Jesus' whole world of thought would also be inexplicable otherwise. If Jesus also enjoins endurance (Mt. 24:13 and par.; 24:22-27 and par.; 25:1-13 [51] etc.), there are pastoral reasons for this, and it also corresponds to the basic attitude of NT eschatology, that of both concentrated and extended expectation at one and the same time, → 868, 10 f. Mk. 13:32 and par. [52] does not stand in contradiction to this. It simply contests Jesus' knowledge of the exact time, and condemns human attempts to calculate it, though without giving any right, historically speaking, to interpose thousands of years at will. Jesus, however, undoubtedly divests Jewish eschatology of its political and literal character. [53] He sets the active and ethical element in the foreground, Mt. 25:14-30 and par.; 25:31-46.

b. The Primitive Community.

Though the word does not occur in Ac., and the primitive community perhaps had no equivalent for it, the central significance of belief in the *parousia* is incontestable. Apart from the Synoptic Gospels, Ac. itself bears witness to this. 1:11 gives us the original interpretation of the Easter faith. [54] Christ is expected from heaven, 3:20 f. → I, 387, 16 ff., esp. 391, 24 ff. The *parousia* of the world ruler is found mostly in the *kerygma*, 10:42; 13:33 intimated by Ps. 2:7; even 17:31. "Son of Man" is a title of Jesus in the primitive community, though it occurs only once at Ac. 7:56. It is impossible to

---

schaft (1938), 314; also "Drei Mk.-Evangelien," *Arbeiten z. Kirchengeschichte,* 26 (1938), 59, 111, 180, 213 f. and E. Hirsch, *Frühgeschichte d. Ev.,* I² (1951), 139-142, 256-258. Though their source criticism and exegesis vary, they all arrive at the same result, namely, the elimination of the *parousia* of the Son of Man from the original preaching of Jesus.

[49] The statement of Michaelis (101): "The resurrection does not compete with the *parousia*; it is the *parousia*," goes too far, at least in the positive thesis. The view of Schweitzer (407 f.) that Jesus expected the *parousia* even before the return of the disciples from their preaching mission, i.e., without the death and resurrection, is shattered by the fact that it appeals to portions of the commission in Mt. 10 which are taken from the address in Mk. 13 and the related tradition, so that the ref. is to the period after the death of Jesus. Cf. Mt. 10:17-23 with Mk. 13:9-13 and par.

[50] The conjecture of A. Debrunner, Coniectanea Neotestamentica, 11 = In honorem Antonii Fridrichsen (1947), 48 that one should read ἀπαρτί ("verily") for ἀπ᾽ ἄρτι ("from henceforth," Lk. 22:69 : ἀπὸ τοῦ νῦν) is more likely in respect of Rev. 14:13 than Mt. 26:64.

[51] Jeremias, 38-40 thinks the exhortations to watchfulness here and elsewhere were added because of the delay in the *parousia,* but this is unlikely.

[52] Dalman WJ, I, 159 regards the saying about the Son and the Father as a later addition, but Loh. Mk., ad loc. maintains its authenticity. Who would have dared invent such a saying?

[53] In a way which is suspect methodologically Busch uses the variations in historical criticism to discredit it altogether. He himself would banish all temporal ideas from the *parousia* concept and reduce the content of the discourse on the *parousia* to the *kerygma* of the passion of Christ, 50, 52, 60 f., 97-109, 112, 133-135, 146, though he finally admits "the naïvety of imminent expectation," 149.

[54] Gewiess, 31.

say for certain whether the standing at the right hand of God simply denotes majesty or is a position of readiness either to receive the martyr or for the *parousia*. [55] Activity with a view to the *parousia* is certainly included. [56]

c. Paul.

In Paul there is the first palpable beginning of a christology which includes pre-existence, but this does not alter in the slightest the emphasis on the future. Paul always uses παρουσία with the gen. It is used of men (1 C. 16:17; 2 C. 7:6 f.; 10:10; Phil. 1:26; 2:12), once of antichrist (2 Th. 2:9), elsewhere of Christ (1 C. 15:23; 1 Th. 2:19; 3:13; 4:15; 5:23; 2 Th. 2:1, 8; 1 C. 1:8 vl.). Technical significance is not attached to the word (more to ἀπάντησις? → I, 380, 25-381, 5). Both lexically and materially it is important in the Thessalonian Epistles. Once again expectation is both concentrated (1 Th.) and extended (2 Th.), → 867, 14 f. The reason, however, is pastoral, and no contradiction is involved. Paul rejects all attempts at calculation, 1 Th. 5:1 ff.; 2 Th. 2:2. There are colourful depictions of the *parousia* not only in 1 Th. 4:13-18 and 2 Th. 1:7-2:8, but also in 1 C. 15:22-28, 50-55. Paul believes that he and most of his readers will experience the *parousia*, 1 Th. 4:15; 1 C. 15:51. Even in 2 C. 5:1-10 there is no shift of attention to the interim period and microcosmic eschatology, → II, 318, 1-321, 10. Romans is fully orientated to the older concept, 8:19, 23; 13:11 etc. Only with the prospect of martyrdom does the σὺν Χριστῷ εἶναι receive greater stress, Phil. 1:23. But this does not mean that hope of the *parousia* is abandoned, Phil. 3:20 f.; 4:5; Col. 3:4; Eph. 4:30. Though possession of salvation is now seen to be inward and spiritual, this hope is still the indissoluble core.

d. Deutero-Paulinism.

In the Past. the synon. → ἐπιφάνεια is once used for the manifestation of Christ in the flesh, 2 Tm. 1:10; cf. 1 Th. 3:16. This paves the way for a similar use of παρουσία and *adventus* later (→ 870, 35-871, 20). The older expectation survives, but already there is the beginning of establishment in the world, 2 Tm. 3:16; Tt. 2:12 etc. 1 Tm. 4:1 and 2 Tm. 3:1 are weaker statements than one finds in Pl. Neither word nor subject seems to be present in Hb. The focus here is, not the coming Christ, but Christ already come and perfected by suffering, 10:7; 9:11; 4:14; 2:10 etc. The coming reign of God is replaced by the entry of believers into rest (4:11; 9:27; a microcosmic eschatology). 2:8b is more of a protest and a transition than a reference. Nevertheless, the concept lives on, 12:26; 9:28; 10:37, 13; 6:2. There is need to endure and to be prepared, 10:25. The thought of a double *parousia* is to be found already in Hb. In spite of Gl. 4:4 and R. 8:3, the ἐκ δευτέρου of 9:28 is not Pauline.

e. The Epistles of James, Peter and Jude.

Jm. 5:7 f. (originally of God's coming?) [57] is a ref. to Christ's *parousia*. 1:12 and 2:12 could be taken microcosmically. Expectation of the *parousia* is much more dynamic in 1 Pt., though the term does not occur: πάντων τὸ τέλος ἤγγικεν, 4:7. The Messianic tribulation has already come upon the world, and primarily upon the community, 4:13, 17; 5:8, 10. The idea of a first advent of Christ at the end of the times is to be found in 1:20. The descent into Hades is also presented as a *parousia* in 3:19; 4:6, → n. 43. The decisive → ἀποκάλυψις Ἰησοῦ Χριστοῦ is immediately at hand, 1:5, 7, 13. In the light

---

[55] For standing deities alongside seated cf. Haas Lfrg., 9/11, Leipoldt (1929), Ill. 151, 175-177, 191.

[56] Bau. Ag., *ad loc.*

[57] Meyer Jk., 159: The ἐν ἡμέρᾳ σφαγῆς of 5:5 is to be taken in the light of ἐν ἐσχάταις ἡμέραις in 5:3. The exposition of Wnd. Kath. Br., *ad loc.*: "Day of terror when the rich will be spared," is not convincing in view of Jer. 12:3. Cf. Meyer, 172.

of it believers are strangers and sojourners, [58] 1:17; 2:11. In Jude there are only weak traces of the earlier expectation.

2 Peter meets doubt by reinterpretation. The message is not a fable, 1:16. Mockers (3:3 f.) are wrong. As once the world perished by water, so it will perish by fire, 3:5 ff. But for the longsuffering God a thousand years are as a day, 8 f. The day will come like a thief. Believers should hasten towards the παρουσία τῆς τοῦ θεοῦ (vl. κυρίου) ἡμέρας, 3:12. In the first instance παρουσία has here the general sense of "coming" or "arrival," but there is a suggestion of the technical meaning too.

f. Revelation.

The word does not occur in Rev., but from the ἐν τάχει of 1:1 and ὁ καιρὸς ἐγγύς of 1:3 to the ἔρχου κύριε 'Ιησοῦ of 22:20 the book is full of ardent hope of the parousia. The dreadful Messianic afflictions, depicted in visions, issue in lofty portrayals of the parousia in 14:14-20 and 19:11-16, and this in turn is followed by further eschatological events to give us the fullest sketch we have of primitive Chr. eschatology. The time-sequence, which seems to lead to a doubling of the parousia, should neither be taken too literally nor dismissed as a mechanical theory of recapitulation. The decisive factor is the prophetic aim of impressing the eschatological hope upon the harassed community by increasingly urgent depictions. [59]

g. John's Gospel and Epistles.

Patent in Rev., the Jewish element is in the other Johannine writings interfused with so many syncretistic trends that the question arises whether eschatology, and with it the concept of the parousia, have not been abandoned altogether. [60] Both are found (1 Jn. 2:28; 3:2; Jn. 21:22 f.), but are they alien bodies? Johannine religion is a religion of timeless possession. Jesus gives His people eternal life in time, 6:68; 17:3; 14:9; 11:25 f.; 5:25. The κρίσις takes place now, inwardly, 5:24; 3:18; 12:31; 9:39; 1 Jn. 3:14; Jn. 3:17; 8:15; 12:47; 5:45. The victory has been won, 1 Jn. 5:4. In this flood all eschatological concepts seem to be lost for ever. Similarly, in the Parting Discourses the coming of the risen Lord, the coming of the Spirit and the coming at the end of the days flow into one another. [61] Nevertheless, we constantly find genuine eschatological expressions: ἐσχάτη ἡμέρα, which is peculiar to Jn.: [11:24]; 6:39, 40, 44, 54; 12:48; ἐσχάτη ὥρα, 1 Jn. 2:18 twice. [62]

It is no more possible to eliminate this "contradiction" critically [63] than to reduce it to a Jewish remnant or a concession to community thinking. [64] It is also impossible to refer everything to the eschatologically conceived coming of the Logos in the flesh as the parousia of Him who is eschatologically sent. [65] This involves as its basis an axiological view of eschatology which is not compatible with the Johannine understanding. Deeply rooted in John's world of thought is the fact that there is much unrealised eschatology as

---

[58] W. Weber, Römische Kaisergeschichte u. Kirchengeschichte (1929), 53 f.

[59] Bornkamm.

[60] Bultmann and Bu. J., Index s.v. "Eschatologie"; Stählin.

[61] More exact exegesis does not support the attempt at sharp distinction made in Zn. J.

[62] The ἐρχόμενον ἐν σαρκί of 2 Jn. 7 is to be referred to the historical Jesus with → II, 674, 4 ff., Wnd. Kath. Br. and Bu. J., ad loc. and against Stählin, 242.

[63] Acc. to Schwartz, J. Wellhausen, Das Ev. Johannis (1908), ad loc. and H. H. Wendt, Die Schichten im 4. Ev. (1911), 23-25, also Bu. J., 196, who ascribes 5:28 f. to a redactor balancing v. 24 f. with traditional eschatology. For 1 Jn. cf. R. Bultmann, "Die kirchliche Redaktion des 1. Johannesbriefes," In memoriam E. Lohmeyer (1951), 189-201.

[64] So H. J. Holtzmann, Nt.liche Theol.², II (1911), though cf. A. Schweitzer, Die Mystik d. Ap. Pls. (1930), 358. "Inverted eschatology" is the phrase used by v. Dobschütz, 18; cf. also W. Heitmüller, Schr. NT on Jn. 5.

[65] Bultmann, 144: "The parousia has taken place already." Bu. J., Index s.v. "Eschatologie," also Theol. d. NT (1953), 404.

well as realised. For all the revelation, the judging and saving work of Christ has about it much that is concealed and provisional. So, too, does the believer's experience of salvation. This demands consummation when death has been definitively defeated, and indeed after a cosmic eschatology. [66] Without this, realised eschatology would be untrue. Hellenisation is not the whole story. Research has begun to concern itself with the Jewish and primitive Christian foundations of Johannine theology. [67] Johannine religion, too, is set in the tension of possession and hope. It is characterised only by a stronger inwardness which puts the accent more firmly on possession. Thus φανεροῦσθαι becomes an alternative for παρουσία, 1 Jn. 2:28; 3:2; cf. Col. 3:4.

3. Theological Summary.

As in the individual writings, so in the NT as a whole the concept of the parousia defies exact systematisation. Powerful antitheses exist. Jesus and Paul take a middle line, John and Rev. are at the extreme edges. Thus the NT itself urges us to consult the significance rather than the letter. Jesus rejected Jewish particularism. Even Rev. parts company with Judaism in its universalism and its encouragement to passive resistance, 13:10. The sensual element is reduced, fully so in Jn., and in the Synoptists, Paul and even Rev. at least to the degree that the external fulfilment is not awaited for its own sake but as an accompanying circumstance leading to full fellowship with God. The strict preservation of transcendence overcomes any abstract opposition between the present and future aspects of God's rule. If παρουσία is not used for the incarnation, it becomes increasingly clear that with the life, death and resurrection of Jesus — invisibly and for faith — the turning point of the aeons has been passed. The parousia is the definitive manifestation of what has been effected already as an eschatological reality. The NT itself prepares the way inwardly for the crisis which threatens with the delay of the parousia, so that this is fairly easily surmounted. The parousia, in which history is anchored, is not a historical event, nor does it merely give history its goal and meaning. It is rather the point where history is mastered by God's eternal rule. [68] The significance of the NT parousia concept is that the tension between nonfulfilment and fulfilment, between this world and the world to come, between hope and possession, between concealment and manifestation, between faith and sight, should be resolved, and that the decisive contribution towards this has already been made in Christ. Cf. the bibl.

V. πάρειμι and παρουσία in Ecclesiastical Usage.

παρεῖναι is mostly used in its lit. sense in the earlier writings of the Church, and it has no theological role, though Just. Dial., 54, 1 says that Christ is present in believers and will be present (παρέσται) at the second parousia. παρουσία is used in the profane sense (the coming of Danaos to the Peloponnese), Tat. Or. Graec., 39, 3. The technical eschatological sense of παρουσία occurs in the post-apost. fathers only at Dg., 7, 6 [69] and Herm. s., 5, 5, 3, cf. also Act. Thom. 28. In Ign. Phld., 9, 2 there is ref. to the earthly coming of Jesus : The Gospel has as its chief content τὴν παρουσίαν τοῦ σωτῆρος ... τὸ πάθος αὐτοῦ καὶ τὴν ἀνάστασιν. [70] In Just. the term occurs only infrequently for the coming in power and glory (Dial., 49, 8; 31, 1; 35, 8; 51, 2). It is used more often for the earthly coming (Dial., 88, 2; cf. 120, 3; Apol., 48, 2; 54, 7). Mostly the two are set

---

[66] So Stählin, 239; H. E. Weber, 195-197.

[67] For a basic discussion cf. esp. A. Schlatter, Sprache u. Heimat des vierten Evangelisten (1902); also Der Evangelist Joh. (1930).

[68] Althaus, 241-246.

[69] Dg., 7, 9 : presence (of God).

[70] Cf. Act. Pt. in Cl. Al. Strom., VI, 15, 128, 1: ... εὕρομεν καὶ τὴν παρουσίαν αὐτοῦ καὶ τὸν θάνατον καὶ τὸν σταυρὸν ... καὶ τὴν ἔγερσιν ...

in juxtaposition as δύο παρουσίαι, πρώτη and δευτέρα, ἄδοξος and ἔνδοξος παρουσία (Apol., 52, 3; Dial., 14, 8; 49, 2, 7; 53, 1; 54, 1 etc.). There is a hint of the idea of the coming again of Christ (Dial., 35, 8; 118, 2). The eschatological emphasis is stronger in Iren. In the Gk. of Haer., I, 10, 1 (MPG, 7, 549) — if we are to read τὴν ἔλευσιν with the Lat. — he seems to be distinguishing between ἔλευσις and παρουσία. But in the Lat., which is all we have for the other passages, he speaks repeatedly of the twofold coming, IV, 22, 1 and 2 (MPG, 7, 1046 f.); 33, 11 f. (1079 f.), illustrated by the twofold coming in Gethsemane. Hippolyt. speaks similarly of δύο παρουσίαι, ἄτιμος and ἔνδοξος. [71] On the other hand, Cl. Al., in his 41 refs. to the παρουσία, almost without exception has the earthly life in view. Here παρουσία occurs frequently without gen., Strom., III, 12, 90, 4; VI, 17, 159, 9. In Strom., V, 6, 38, 6 the ref. seems to be to the discernible presence in the Church (αἰσθητὴ παρουσία). Once in an obscure context, perhaps under alien influence, we find the ancient formula of a twofold coming, Ecl. Proph., 56, 1. The eschatological sense seems to be almost forgotten. We are pointed in the same direction by a Pap. Fr. from Cairo [72] which in line 10 calls Jn. the Baptist the forerunner of the παρουσία of Christ. This complete de-eschatologising is, however, the exception. The further history of the term in the West comes to be connected esp. with the word adventus. Later an adventus triplex or quadruplex was distinguished. Liturgists and preachers sought such distinctive formulations as adventus ad homines, in homines, contra homines, or in carnem, in mentem, in morte, in maiestate. [73]

Oepke

---

† παρρησία, † παρρησιάζομαι

Contents : A. παρρησία, παρρησιάζομαι in the Greek World and Hellenism : 1. In the Political Sphere ; 2. In the Private Sphere ; 3. Particularly as a Moral Concept. B. The Septuagint and Hellenistic Jewish Literature : 1. LXX ; 2. Hellenistic Jewish Literature ; 3. Ethiopian Enoch. C. The New Testament : 1. The Johannine Writings ; 2. Acts ; 3. The Pauline Corpus ; 4. Hebrews. D. παρρησία, παρρησιάζομαι in Ancient Ecclesiastical Literature : 1. The Apostle in NT Apocrypha ; 2. The Martyr Literature ; 3. The Connection between παρρησία and Prayer.

A. παρρησία, παρρησιάζομαι in the Greek World and Hellenism.

1. In the Political Sphere. The term, which occurs first in Eur. and Aristoph. and is of Attic development, [1] belongs to the political sphere of the Gk. polis. It is an essential mark of Gk. democracy, the sign of the freedom obtaining therein. Polyb., 2, 38, 6 : ἰσηγορία καὶ παρρησία καὶ καθόλου δημοκρατία ἀληθινή, (Ps.-)Demosth. Or., 60, 26 : αἱ δὲ δημοκρατίαι πολλά τ' ἄλλα καὶ καλὰ καὶ δίκαι' ἔχουσιν, ὧν τὸν

---

[71] De Antichristo, ed. P. A. de Lagarde (1858), p. 21.

[72] Catalogue général des antiquités égypt. du Musée du Caire, X (1903), No. 10735 acc. to the reconstruction of the text in Deissmann LO, 368-371.

[73] Caspari, 189. The number of Sundays in Advent, which fluctuated for some time, was fixed at 4 in the 11th century.

π α ρ ρ η σ ί α κτλ. Bibl. In general E. Peterson, "Zur Bedeutungsgeschichte von παρρησία," Festschr. f. R. Seeberg, I (1929), 283-297. On A : M. Radin, "Freedom of Speech in Ancient Athens," The American Journal of Philology, 48 (1927), 215-220. On C : H. Boerner, De παρρησία fidelium in die iudicii (1724); P. Joüon, "Divers sens de παρρησία dans le NT," Recherches de science religieuse, 30 (1940), 239-241.

[1] Acc. to W. Schmid-O. Stählin, Gesch. d. gr. Lit. = Hndbch. AW, VII, 1, 4 (1946), 39, n. 3, with ref. to Plat. Gorg., 461e, from παν and root ῥη- "to speak," probably directly as a "hypostatising," not by way of a (non-attested) παν-ρητος. Cf. E. Schwyzer, Gr. Grammatik, I = Hndbch. AW, II, 1, 1 (1939), 437, 469. Perhaps the synon. ἐξουσία influenced the formation [Debrunner].

εὖ φρονοῦντ' ἀντέχεσθαι δεῖ, καὶ τὴν παρρησίαν ἐκ τῆς ἀληθείας ἠρτημένην οὐκ ἔστι τἀληθὲς δηλοῦν ἀποτρέψαι. Precisely for love of genuine παρρησία Isoc. can say bitterly in Or., 8, 14 "that in spite of the rule of the people there is no full freedom of speech (ὅτι δημοκρατίας οὔσης οὐκ ἔστι παρρησία) except for the most rash and foolish and for dramatists in the theatre." Attic democracy in particular is acknowledgeably distinguished for παρρησία. Eur. Hipp., 421 ff.: ἀλλ' ἐλεύθεροι παρρησίᾳ θάλλοντες οἰκοῖεν (sc. my children) πόλιν κλεινῶν 'Αθηνῶν, Ion, 670 ff.: εἰ δ' ἐπεύξασθαι χρεών, ἐκ τῶν 'Αθηνῶν μ' ἡ τεκοῦσ' εἴη γυνή, ὥς μοι γένηται μητρόθεν παρρησία. Demosth. Or., 9, 3 : ἀξιῶ δ', ὦ ἄνδρες 'Αθηναῖοι, ἄν τι τῶν ἀληθῶν μετὰ παρρησίας λέγω, μηδεμίαν μοι διὰ τοῦτο παρ' ὑμῶν ὀργὴν γενέσθαι. σκοπεῖτε γὰρ ὡδί. ὑμεῖς τὴν παρρησίαν ἐπὶ μὲν τῶν ἄλλων οὕτω κοινὴν οἴεσθε δεῖν εἶναι πᾶσι τοῖς ἐν τῇ πόλει, ὥστε καὶ τοῖς ξένοις καὶ τοῖς δούλοις αὐτῆς μεταδεδώκατε, καὶ πολλοὺς ἄν τις οἰκέτας ἴδοι παρ' ἡμῖν μετὰ πλείονος ἐξουσίας ὅ τι βούλονται λέγοντας ἢ πολίτας ἐν ἐνίαις τῶν ἄλλων πόλεων, ἐκ δὲ τοῦ συμβουλεύειν παντάπασιν ἐξεληλάκατε. Cf. also Plat. Gorg., 461d/e, where the substance is there though not the word : τί δέ ; οὐκ ἐξέσται μοι λέγειν ὁπόσ' ἄν βούλωμαι ; (Socrates' answer :) Δεινὰ μέντ' ἄν πάθοις, ὦ βέλτιστε, εἰ 'Αθήναζε ἀφικόμενος, οὗ τῆς 'Ελλάδος πλείστη ἐστὶν ἐξουσία τοῦ λέγειν. Polyb., 2, 38, 6; cf. 2, 42, 3; Stob. Ecl., III, 459, 3. The presupposition of παρρησία is that one should be a full citizen of a Gk. polis. At the height of Gk. democracy the full citizen alone has the right to say anything publicly in the ἐκκλησία. Aristoph. Thes., 540 f.: οὔσης παρρησίας κᾆξὸν λέγειν ὅσαι πάρεσμεν ἀσταί. Aliens and slaves have no such right. Eur. Ion, 673 ff.: ξένος, κἄν τοῖς λόγοισιν ἀστὸς ᾖ, τό γε στόμα δοῦλον πέπαται (possesses) κοὐκ ἔχει παρρησίαν, Phoen., 391 f.: The φυγάς lacks ἓν μὲν μέγιστον, οὐκ ἔχει παρρησίαν. Answer : δούλου τόδ' εἶπας, μὴ λέγειν ἅ τις φρονεῖ, Teles., 15, 16 : οὐκ ἄρχουσι (the φυγάδες), οὐ πιστεύονται, οὐ παρρησίαν ἔχουσιν. For this reason there is no higher possession than παρρησία and no greater loss than to lose it, Demosth. Fr. 21 (ed. H. Sauppe): οὐδὲν ἄν εἴη τοῖς ἐλευθέροις μεῖζον ἀτύχημα τοῦ στέρεσθαι τῆς παρρησίας. It is regarded as a typical characteristic, and also as a reason for the fall of the Gk. polis, that παρρησία is the privilege of all who live in the polis. This is attested by Demosth. Or., 9, 3 (→ supra) and 58, 68 : μετασχεῖν τῆς καὶ τοῖς ξένοις δεδομένης παρρησίας. Acc. to Isoc. Or., 7, 20 it is a consequence of bad political education ἡγεῖσθαι τὴν μὲν ἀκολασίαν δημοκρατίαν, τὴν δὲ παρανομίαν ἐλευθερίαν, τὴν δὲ παρρησίαν ἀνομίαν, τὴν δ' ἐξουσίαν τοῦ πάντα ποιεῖν εὐδαιμονίαν. As regards the phenomenon of παρρησία itself this extension of the right to say anything implies uprooting from the concrete political presuppositions and an exaltation of the thing as such. "If all men have παρρησία, the concept is destroyed." [2] It necessarily takes on also a different sense. The right to say anything becomes a complete lack of restraint or restriction, Plat. Resp., VIII, 557b : ἐλευθερίας ἡ πόλις μεστὴ καὶ παρρησίας γίγνεται, καὶ ἐξουσία ἐν αὐτῇ ποιεῖν ὅ τί τις βούλεται. At this pt. one might mention already that the meaning of παρρησία does in fact change ; the word acquires the sense of "shamelessness." [3]

In the political sphere the word may be understood from three angles and it is thus used with three shades of meaning which more or less persist in its later development. a. The element of the right to say anything may be emphasised in παρρησία. The full citizen of the Gk. polis has the objective right to manifest himself in the logos. Cf. Aristoph. Thes., 540 f. (→ supra); Demosth., 9, 3 (→ supra); Plat. Gorg., 461d/e; Isoc. Or., 2, 3 : ἡ παρρησία καὶ φανερῶς ἐξεῖναι. παρρησία here is close to ἐξουσία. [4] b. But stress may be placed on the fact that in παρρησία the actuality of things is

---

[2] Peterson, 289.

[3] Ibid., 285, transl. the τῆς παρρησίας of Menand. Epit., 667 (ed. C. Jensen [1929]) by "What shamelessness !" Cf. W. Jaeger, Paideia, I (1934), 458.

[4] Peterson, 285 pts. out that in the Byzantine period, in the stories of Justinian, παρρησία is used directly for ἐξουσία. But cf. also Vett. Val., 6, 3 : γίνονται βασιλικοί, ζωῆς καὶ θανάτου παρρησίαν ἔχοντες.

stated, so that there is a close relation to truth (→ ἀλήθεια, I, 238, 15 ff.). Eur. in Stob. Ecl., III, 454, 2 : καλὸν γ' ἀληθὴς κἀτενὴς παρρησία. Demosth. Or., 6, 31: τἀληθῆ μετὰ παρρησίας ἐρῶ πρὸς ὑμᾶς καὶ οὐκ ἀποκρύψομαι, cf. 10, 53 and 54; 23, 204; 37, 55; (Ps.-)Demosth. Or., 60, 26 (→ 871, 34 ff.); Demosth. Or., 4, 51: ἃ γιγνώσκω πάνθ' ἁπλῶς οὐδὲν ὑποστειλάμενος πεπαρρησίασμαι, Aeschin. Fals. Leg., 70 : προῄρημαι γὰρ παρρησιάσασθαι καὶ ἐλευθέρως ἅμα καὶ τἀληθῆ λέγων σῴζεσθαι, Stob. Ecl., III, 466, 8 f.: παρρησίη ἀπὸ γνώμης ἐλευθέρης καὶ ἀληθείην ἀσπαζομένη προέρχεται. In such contexts παρρησία takes on the sense of openness to truth. This openness is controlled by the object and by one's relation to the object to which one turns, and it resists the tendency of things to conceal themselves, and man's tendency to conceal them from himself. This is why the Persians are taken as examples in Plat. Leg., III, 694b: καὶ εἴ τις αὖ φρόνιμος ἦν ἐν αὐτοῖς καὶ βουλεύειν δυνατός, οὐ φθονεροῦ τοῦ βασιλέως ὄντος, διδόντος δὲ παρρησίαν καὶ τιμῶντος τοὺς εἴς τι δυναμένους συμβουλεύειν, κοινὴν τὴν τοῦ φρονεῖν εἰς τὸ μέσον παρείχετο δύναμιν, καὶ πάντα δὴ τότε ἐπέδωκεν αὐτοῖς δι' ἐλευθερίαν τε καὶ φιλίαν καὶ νοῦ κοινωνίαν. c. The term παρρησία may also have in view the fact that to the right and openness of full freedom of speech obstacles may be posed by those to whom παρρησία applies. In face of such obstacles παρρησία is the courage of openness, i.e., candour. This candour opposes all those who would limit the right to reveal the truth or hamper the unveiling of the truth, esp. the τύραννος, who in some circumstances may threaten to destroy δημοκρατία in the form of the δῆμος. The gt. orators claim to exercise such παρρησία by defending the right and duty of openness. Cf. again Demosth. Or., 9, 3 (→ 872, 9 ff.). But cf. too Isoc. Or., 2, 28: πιστοὺς ἡγοῦ μὴ τοὺς ἅπαν ὅ τι ἂν λέγῃς ἢ ποιῇς ἐπαινοῦντας, ἀλλὰ τοὺς τοῖς ἁμαρτανομένοις ἐπιτιμῶντας. δίδου παρρησίαν τοῖς εὖ φρονοῦσιν, ἵνα περὶ ὧν ἂν ἀμφιγνοῇς ἔχῃς τοὺς συνδοκιμάσοντας. διόρα καὶ τοὺς τέχνῃ κολακεύοντας καὶ τοὺς μετ' εὐνοίας θεραπεύοντας ..., Aristot. Ἀθηναίων Πολιτεία, 16, 6 : ὁ δὲ Πεισίστρατος ἡσθεὶς διὰ τὴν παρρησίαν καὶ τὴν φιλεργίαν ἀτελῆ πάντων ἐποίησεν αὐτόν (excused him all taxes). From a later period cf. Dio C., 62, 13 : οὕτω γάρ πως ἐρρωμένως τῇ παρρησίᾳ ἐχρῆτο ὥστε ... εἶπεν ... (Burrus and Nero). Dio Chrys., 32, 26 f.: κολακεία κἀπάτη κρατεῖ παρ' αὐτοῖς (sc. tyrants). ὁμοίως δὲ καὶ δῆμος ὁ μέν τις εὐγνώμων καὶ πρᾷος καὶ γαληνὸς ὄντως, οἷος γεύσασθαι παρρησίας καὶ μὴ πάντα ἐθέλειν τρυφᾶν ... The quotations make it clear that the opposite of such candid speech is the κολακεύειν and τρυφᾶν whose consequences are so dangerous for the *polis,* whereas παρρησία simply serves political society. By defending the right to say anything, notwithstanding the anger of the tyrant, it keeps the reality of things open in candid objectivity.

2. In the Private Sphere. The words παρρησία and παρρησιάζομαι also play a role in the private sphere. They came into this from the political arena. The doctrine of φιλία esp. is the place where the term παρρησία occurs. Aristot. Eth. Nic., IX, 2, p. 1165a, 29 f.: To each his own, and different honour to parents and the gods, to the sage and the general : πρὸς ἑταίρους δ' αὖ καὶ ἀδελφοὺς παρρησίαν καὶ ἁπάντων κοινότητα. Acc. to Plat. Gorg., 487a-e the friend should be able to show ἐπιστήμην, εὔνοια and παρρησία, παρρησία being the opp. of (too gt.) αἰσχύνη, → I, 170, 9 ff. But παρρησία which does not fear αἰσχρόν and therewith δόξα (→ I, 170 f.) is a sign of friendship for the very reason that it is not afraid to censure a friend. Hence παρρησία is defined in Isoc. Or., 2, 3 as τὸ φανερῶς ἐξεῖναι τοῖς τε φίλοις ἐπιπλῆξαι καὶ τοῖς ἐχθροῖς ἐπιθέσθαι ταῖς ἀλλήλων ἁμαρτίαις. παρρησία serves the truth and is thus profitable. Socrates is a good example of this παρρησία. Cf. Plat. Lach., 188e : αὐτὸν ηὗρον ἄξιον ὄντα λόγων καλῶν καὶ πάσης παρρησίας. The κόλαξ differs from the φίλος (→ line 26 f. and III, 817, 14 ff.). His παρρησία is unhelpful. For this reason he should be avoided. Cf. Stob. Ecl., III, 469, 9 f. (Zeno): Ἔλεγχε σαυτὸν ὅστις εἶ, [καὶ] μὴ πρὸς χάριν ἄκου', ἀφαιροῦ δὲ κολάκων παρρησίαν.

Quite apart from its use in the doctrine of φιλία, παρρησία has in private usage the predominant sense of candour. Plat. Gorg., 491e : ὃ ἐγώ σοι νῦν παρρησιαζόμενος λέγω, Charm., 156a : μᾶλλον γάρ σοι παρρησιάσομαι περὶ τῆς ἐπῳδῆς, Xen.

Cyrop., V, 3, 8 : πολλά ... ἔγωγε κἀκεῖνος ἐπαρρησιασάμεθα πρὸς ἀλλήλους, Diod. S., 12, 63; 14, 66 : παρρησίαν ἄγειν, Plut. Praec. Ger. Reip., 6 (II, 802 f): ἀλλ' ἤθους ἀπλάστου καὶ φρονήματος ἀληθινοῦ καὶ παρρησίας πατρικῆς καὶ προνοίας καὶ συνέσεως κηδομένης ὁ λόγος ἔστω μεστός, P. Oxy., VIII, 1100, 15 : In face of oppression by officials one should bring complaints to the prefect μετὰ παρρησίας ("without fear"). [5] The verb παρρησιάζεσθαι can often take on here the weaker sense of simply speaking, e.g., Plut. Aud., 12 (II, 43e): ἄν ... ὁ φιλόσοφος ... παρρησιάζηται περὶ τῶν διαφερόντων. It is worth noting that sometimes παρρησία can abandon the connection with λόγος and acquire the sense of "liberality." Thus Ditt. Or., 323, 10 (2nd cent. B.C.): κεκόσμηκε τὸν αὐτοῦ βίον τῇ καλλίστῃ παρρησίᾳ. It should also be noted that in general usage παρρησία can denote the abuse of free speech in the sense of "impudence" (Plat. Symp., 222c, where the παρρησία of Alkibiades provokes laughter) "or insolence" (Plat. Phaedr., 240e : παρρησίᾳ κατακορεῖ καὶ ἀναπεπταμένῃ χρῆσθαι) or "shamelessness." παρρησίαι εἰς τοὺς θεούς (Isoc. Or., 11, 40) are βλασφημίαι and signs of ἀσέβεια. An example of importunate and even insolent prayer is that of Timon in Luc. Tim., 11: οἷον ἦν τὸ μέγα κεκραγέναι καὶ ὀχληρὸν εἶναι καὶ θρασύν· οὐ τοῖς δικαιολογοῦσι (advocates) μόνοις, ἀλλὰ καὶ τοῖς εὐχομένοις τοῦτο χρήσιμον· ἰδού γέ τοι αὐτίκα μάλα πλούσιος ἐκ πενεστάτου καταστήσεται (= γενήσεται) ὁ Τίμων βοήσας καὶ παρρησιασάμενος ἐν τῇ εὐχῇ καὶ ἐπιστρέψας τὸν Δία (drew the attention of Zeus to him)· εἰ δὲ σιωπῇ ἔσκαπτεν ἐπικεκυφώς, ἔτι ἂν ἔσκαπτεν ἀμελούμενος.

3. Particularly as a Moral Concept. παρρησία shares the same destiny as ἐξουσία (→ II, 487 ff.). When adopted by popular Hell. philosophy of all schools, esp. Cynicism, it becomes primarily a moral rather than a political concept. In so doing it does not abandon its formal structure or sense, but its content changes. This is apparent at two pts. a. The presupposition of παρρησία, while formally the same, changes significantly in content. The transition may be traced in Aristot., who on the one side still maintains that παρρησία is a virtue of the εὐγενής, but on the other sees such a one in the μεγαλόψυχος : Nic. Eth., IV, 3, p. 1124b, 29. Luc. Calumniae non Temere Credendum, 23 also speaks of the ἐλεύθερον καὶ παρρησιαστικόν of the γενναῖοι. Above all, παρρησία and ἐλευθερία are now closely related. Thus we read in Democr. Fr., 226 (Diels[6], II, 190, 15 f.): οἰκήιον ἐλευθερίης παρρησίη, κίνδυνος δὲ ἡ τοῦ καιροῦ διάγνωσις. Cf. Luc. Demon., 3 : ὁ ... Δημῶναξ ... ὅλον ... παραδοὺς ἑαυτὸν ἐλευθερίᾳ καὶ παρρησίᾳ διετέλεσεν αὐτός τε ὀρθῷ καὶ ὑγιεῖ καὶ ἀνεπιλήπτῳ βίῳ χρώμενος καὶ τοῖς ὁρῶσι καὶ ἀκούουσι παράδειγμα παρέχων τὴν ἑαυτοῦ γνώμην καὶ τὴν ἐν τῷ φιλοσοφεῖν ἀλήθειαν. Acc. to Luc. Dialogi Mortuorum, 11, 3 Antisthenes bequeaths to Diogenes σοφίαν, αὐτάρκειαν, ἀλήθειαν, παρρησίαν, ἐλευθερίαν, cf. 10, 9. [6] These are the highest goods, and ἐλευθερία and παρρησία in particular are the distinguishing marks of Cynicism. [7] Diog. L., VI, 69 tells of Diogenes: ἐρωτηθεὶς τί κάλλιστον ἐν ἀνθρώποις, ἔφη, παρρησία, and cf. VI, 71: μηδὲν ἐλευθερίας προκρίνων. It is obvious that the ἐλευθερία so closely connected with παρρησία is moral freedom rather than political, and that the presupposition of παρρησία, too, has changed accordingly. The man who is morally free has παρρησία. It is still an open question who this is. But on the lips of the man dominated by the passions παρρησία simply means "shamelessness." His παρρησία implies only λοιδορεῖν "to insult." Cf. Luc. Pergr. Mort., 18 : ὁ φιλόσοφος, διὰ τὴν παρρησίαν καὶ τὴν ἄγαν ἐλευθερίαν ἐξελαθείς, Ael. Arist., II, 401 (ed. Dindorf): τὴν μὲν ἀναισχυντίαν ἐλευθερίαν νομίζοντες, τὸ δ' ἀπεχθάνεσθαι παρρησιάζεσθαι, τὸ δὲ λαμβάνειν φιλανθρωπεύεσθαι (sc. the philosophers tackled by him, whom he understands as Cynics). b. Though the concept retains the public character appertaining to political speech, [8] the public aspect in view is not now that of the *polis* and its representative

---

[5] Cf. O. Eger, *Rechtsgeschichtliches zum NT* (1919), 41 f.
[6] Peterson, 286, n. 4.
[7] Cf. J. Bernays, *Lukian u. d. Kyniker* (1898), 101 f.
[8] Peterson, 288.

the δῆμος or even the τύραννος, but that of the *cosmopolis* and its rulers. He who has παρρησία leads a public life. This is an abiding mark of the philosopher, who now exercises παρρησία. Diogenes is the ideal here.[9] Cf. M. Ant., XI, 6, also Philo Spec. Leg., I, 321, which in its use of the image shows the formal connection between the moral concept and the political : οἱ μὲν γὰρ τὰ βλαβερὰ πράττοντες αἰσχυνέσθωσαν καὶ ... ἐπικρυπτέσθωσαν ...· τοῖς δὲ τὰ κοινωφελῆ δρῶσιν ἔστω παρρησία (almost "publicity") καὶ μεθ᾿ ἡμέραν διὰ μέσης ἴτωσαν ἀγορᾶς ... φύσις, too, does not conceal its works.

B. The Septuagint and Hellenistic Jewish Literature.

1. LXX. παρρησία is rare in the LXX. We first find the Gk. and Hellen. aspects already mentioned. παρρησία is a mark of the free man as distinct from the δοῦλος, Lv. 26:13, the only ref. in the Pentateuch : ἐγώ εἰμι κύριος ὁ θεὸς ὑμῶν ὁ ἐξαγαγὼν ὑμᾶς ἐκ γῆς Αἰγύπτου ὄντων ὑμῶν δούλων καὶ συνέτριψα τὸν δεσμὸν τοῦ ζυγοῦ ὑμῶν καὶ ἤγαγον ὑμᾶς μετὰ παρρησίας. The ἤγαγον ὑμᾶς μετὰ παρρησίας is a transl. of וָאוֹלֵךְ אֶתְכֶם קוֹמְמִיּוּת "and made you go upright."[10] παρρησία as open and candid speech is distinctively ascribed to divine σοφία in Prv. 1:20 f.: Σοφία ἐν ἐξόδοις ὑμνεῖται, ἐν δὲ πλατείαις παρρησίαν ἄγει ... ἐπὶ δὲ πύλαις πόλεως θαρροῦσα λέγει. παρρησίαν ἄγειν is here a notable interpretation of the general concept תִּתֵּן קוֹלָהּ, cf. Cant. 8:10 AS :[11] ἡ νύμφη παρρησιάζεται. ἐλέγχειν μετὰ παρρησίας is set over against ἐννεύειν ὀφθαλμοῖς μετὰ δόλου in Prv. 10:10. 4 Macc. 10:5 refers to the παρρησία of the martyr : οἱ δὲ πικρῶς ἐνέγκαντες τὴν παρρησίαν τοῦ ἀνδρός. παρρησία is displayed in the witness which under threat of death confesses the νόμος of the fathers. There is a suggestion of unrestrained (impudent) speech in the verb at Sir. 6:11: καὶ ἐν τοῖς ἀγαθοῖς σου ἔσται ὡς σὺ (the friend in good days) καὶ ἐπὶ τοὺς οἰκέτας σου παρρησιάσεται.[12] The public aspect is to be seen in Est. 8:12 s : τὸ δὲ ἀντίγραφον τῆς ἐπιστολῆς ταύτης ἐκθέντες ἐν παντὶ τόπῳ μετὰ παρρησίας ἐᾶν τοὺς ᾿Ιουδαίους χρῆσθαι τοῖς ἑαυτῶν νομίμοις, cf. 8:13 : τὰ δὲ ἀντίγραφα ἐκτιθέσθωσαν ὀφθαλμοφανῶς ἐν πάσῃ τῇ βασιλείᾳ, ἑτοίμους τε εἶναι ..., cf. 1 Macc. 4:18; 3 Macc. 4:1. παρρησία is used for ἐξουσία in Sir. 25:25 : μὴ δῷς ὕδατι διέξοδον μηδὲ γυναικὶ πονηρᾷ παρρησίαν (B⁺ ἐξουσίαν),[13] cf. also in this connection 3 Macc. 7:12 : ἔδωκεν αὐτοῖς ἄδειαν πάντων, ὅπως τοὺς παραβεβηκότας τοῦ θεοῦ τὸν νόμον ἐξολεθρεύσωσιν κατὰ πάντα τὸν ὑπὸ τὴν βασιλείαν αὐτοῦ τόπον μετὰ παρρησίας ἄνευ πάσης βασιλικῆς ἐξουσίας καὶ ἐπισκέψεως.

The LXX goes beyond the Hellenistic senses in passages where it is stated that God gives the people παρρησία and that divine σοφία has παρρησία.[14] The influence of OT faith is especially to be seen, however, when there is reference to παρρησία towards God or to the παρρησία of God Himself. Particularly significant are two passages from Job, 27:9 f.: ἢ τὴν δέησιν αὐτοῦ (sc. ἀσεβοῦς)

---

[9] Plut. De Exilio, 16 (II, 606c) asks : τί δέ; Διογένης οὐκ εἶχε παρρησίαν, ὃς εἰς τὸ τοῦ Φιλίππου στρατόπεδον παρελθών ... ὡς κατάσκοπος, ᾿ναί, κατάσκοπος᾿ ἔφη, ᾿τῆς ἀπληστίας ἀφῖχθαι αὐτοῦ καὶ τῆς ἀφροσύνης ...᾿ This anecdote has symbolical historical significance. To the destroyer of Attic democracy Diogenes comes as the radical representative of the ideal of παρρησία who carries over the political demand of the Gk. *polis* into the moral world of the Hell. κοσμόπολις, Peterson, 288.

[10] Later anon. translators have ἀνισταμένους (Mᵐᵍ) and ὀρθῶς (Vᵐᵍ) [Bertram].

[11] Not in the text but in the *distinctiones actorum* (A. Rahlfs, *Septuaginta,* II [1935], 270 f.).

[12] One finds it in the same sense in ψ 30:13 ᾿Α for יסר ni (LXX ἐπισυναχθῆναι, Σ συσκέπτεσθαι) and acc. to Swete in Ez. 16:30 Θ.

[13] R. Smend, *Die Weisheit d. Jesus Sirach erklärt* (1906), 232 thinks ἐξουσία is correct, cf. 30:11 and the refs. he gives there (276).

[14] The παρρησία of the martyrs springs out of a specifically Jewish situation.

εἰσακούσεται κύριος; ἢ ἐπελθούσης αὐτῷ ἀνάγκης μὴ ἔχει τινά παρρησίαν ἔναντι αὐτοῦ; ἢ ὡς ἐπικαλεσαμένου αὐτοῦ εἰσακούσεται αὐτοῦ; and 22:23-27: ἐὰν δὲ ἐπιστραφῇς καὶ ταπεινώσῃς σεαυτὸν ἔναντι κυρίου, πόρρω ἐποίησας ἀπὸ διαίτης σου τὸ ἄδικον ... ἔσται οὖν σου ὁ παντοκράτωρ βοηθὸς ἀπὸ ἐχθρῶν, καθαρὸν δὲ ἀποδώσει σε ὥσπερ ἀργύριον πεπυρωμένον. εἶτα παρρησιασθήσῃ ἔναντι κυρίου ἀναβλέψας εἰς τὸν οὐρανὸν ἱλαρῶς· εὐξαμένου δέ σου πρὸς αὐτὸν εἰσακούσεταί σου, δώσει δέ σοι ἀποδοῦναι τὰς εὐχάς. παρρησία here is "freedom" or "free and joyful standing before God," including open access to Him with no more let or hindrance. [15] Wis. 5:1, where παρρησία is used in the absolute and with an eschatological orientation, confirms this sense, though along with 5:5 and 5:15 f. it also indicates that this free standing before God is manifested in the δόξα of him who stands therein. Cf. Wis. 5:1 f.: τότε (in the judgment) στήσεται ἐν παρρησίᾳ πολλῇ ὁ δίκαιος κατὰ πρόσωπον τῶν θλιψάντων αὐτὸν καὶ τῶν ἀθετούντων τοὺς πόνους αὐτοῦ. ἰδόντες ταραχθήσονται φόβῳ δεινῷ ... v. 5 : πῶς κατελογίσθη ἐν υἱοῖς θεοῦ καὶ ἐν ἁγίοις ὁ κλῆρος αὐτοῦ ἐστιν; ... v. 15 f.: δίκαιοι δὲ εἰς τὸν αἰῶνα ζῶσιν, καὶ ἐν κυρίῳ ὁ μισθός, καὶ ἡ φροντὶς αὐτῶν παρὰ ὑψίστῳ. διὰ τοῦτο λήμψονται τὸ βασίλειον τῆς εὐπρεπείας καὶ τὸ διάδημα τοῦ κάλλους ἐκ χειρὸς κυρίου, ὅτι τῇ δεξιᾷ σκεπάσει αὐτοὺς καὶ τῷ βραχίονι ὑπερασπιεῖ αὐτῶν. The presupposition of παρρησία is "righteousness." The δίκαιος, not the ἀσεβής, has it. The δίκαιος is also the σοφός, [16] so that the Hellen. view, which ascribes *parrhesia* to the philosopher, returns here in a new form corresponding to the Jewish orientation to the Law. The same combination of παρρησία and δίκαιος may be seen in Prv. 13:5 : λόγον ἄδικον μισεῖ δίκαιος, ἀσεβὴς δὲ αἰσχύνεται καὶ οὐχ ἕξει παρρησίαν, cf. Prv. 20:9 : τίς καυχήσεται ἁγνὴν ἔχειν τὴν καρδίαν; ἢ τίς παρρησιάσεται [17] καθαρὸς εἶναι ἀπὸ ἁμαρτιῶν; This παρρησία of the righteous finds expression in prayer, as is plainly shown by the texts already quoted from Job. ἐπικαλεῖσθαι and εὔχεσθαι draw close to παρρησιάζεσθαι. The philosopher, too, prays to God as a free man, and in the attitude of a free man. But though there is similarity between what is said about the attitude of prayer in Job 22:26 (→ line 5 f.) and the statement in Epict. Diss., II, 17, 29 : ἀνατεῖναι τὸν τράχηλον πρὸς τὰ πράγματα ὡς ἐλεύθερον καὶ εἰς τὸν οὐρανὸν ἀναβλέπειν ὡς φίλον τοῦ θεοῦ, the refs. in the LXX do not expressly base this attitude on a doctrine of φιλία, nor do the Hellenistic texts contain either here or anywhere a concept of παρρησία towards the gods or God, though the thing itself is present and there is reference to the example of θαρρεῖν in such contexts, Plut. Tranq. An., 1 (II, 465b): θαρροῦντες αὐτοὺς (sc. the gods) παρακαλῶμεν ὡς εὐμενεῖς ὄντας ἤδη καὶ φίλους. [18] παρρησία as the freedom of the righteous towards God expressed in prayer contains joy within itself. παρρησία (παρρησιάζεσθαι) is in Job the rendering of ענג hitp, "to have delight, joy in something," which is trans-

---

[15] Chrys. in Expositio in Ps. ψ 137:1 (MPG, 55, 407), where the LXX has καὶ ἐναντίον ἀγγέλων ψαλῶ σοι, quotes an anon. transl. which reads παρρησίᾳ, ὁ θεός, ᾄσω σε [Bertram].

[16] Cf. J. Fichtner, "Die Stellung d. Sap. in der Lit.- u. Geistesgeschichte ihrer Zeit," ZNW, 36 (1937), 118.

[17] Here, as in Prv. 1:20, παρρησιάζεσθαι is used for a mere *verbum dicendi,* i.e., for אמר, supplied by the LXX from the first half of the verse.

[18] Probably "the difference in the Jewish and pagan concepts of God shaped the difference in usage." "Though the Stoic sage might also feel that he was a friend of God, the Stoic God was not of a kind to manifest himself to a 'friend' and thus to give this friend the possibility of παρρησία," Peterson, 291, 292, cf. on the whole question 290 ff.

lated by κατατρυφᾶν in LXX ψ 36:4, 11 and by τρυφᾶν in Is. 66:11, to stress the element of the dawn or blossoming of joy, while in Is. 58:14 we read: καὶ ἔσῃ πεποιθὼς ἐπὶ κύριον. This joy which is linked with *parrhesia* towards God displays clearly the difference between the OT view of God in the LXX and the Hellenistic view in the philosophers. The God to whom the righteous have access in freedom, so that they can pray to Him and their prayer is heard, manifests Himself as the gracious Judge and thus fulfils their freedom in joy. Of the two verses which speak of God's own παρρησία, ψ 93:1 is unequivocal: ὁ θεὸς ἐκδικήσεων κύριος, ὁ θεὸς ἐκδικήσεων ἐπαρρησιάσατο. παρρησιάζεσθαι is a rendering of יפע hi, "to shine forth," "to appear in brightness." This word is specially used in relation to Yahweh. It is rendered ἐμφαίνεσθαι at ψ 79:1 and ἐπιφαίνεσθαι at Dt. 33:2. [19] What is meant may be seen from ψ 49:1-3: θεὸς θεῶν κύριος ἐλάλησεν καὶ ἐκάλεσεν τὴν γῆν ἀπὸ ἀνατολῶν ἡλίου καὶ μέχρι δυσμῶν. ἐκ Σιὼν ἡ εὐπρέπεια τῆς ὡραιότητος αὐτοῦ, ὁ θεὸς ἐμφανῶς ἥξει, ὁ θεὸς ἡμῶν, καὶ οὐ παρασιωπήσεται· πῦρ ἐναντίον αὐτοῦ καυθήσεται, καὶ κύκλῳ αὐτοῦ καταιγὶς σφόδρα. יפע is here a term for the radiant epiphany of the God who speaks out of His silence. In some circumstances, then, παρρησιάζεσθαι could be chosen as a translation, since it contains within it the two aspects of appearing or manifestation (or shining forth, cf. Wis. 5:1 and 16, → 876, 16 f.) and speech or word. In ψ 11:5: Ἀπὸ τῆς ταλαιπωρίας τῶν πτωχῶν καὶ ἀπὸ τοῦ στεναγμοῦ τῶν πενήτων νῦν ἀναστήσομαι, λέγει κύριος, θήσομαι ἐν σωτηρίᾳ, παρρησιάσομαι ἐν αὐτῷ, the original text is uncertain. It is possible, however, that παρρησιάσομαι ἐν αὐτῷ, as a par. to ἀναστήσομαι (→ n. 10) and θήσομαι ἐν κυρίῳ, should be rendered "to shine forth on him," cf. ψ 93:1.

2. Hellenistic Jewish Literature. Hell. Jewish literature, which is chiefly represented by Philo and Joseph., is marked as Hellenistic by the fact that it adopts for the most part the Gk. and Hell. understanding of παρρησία. Hence we find "candour" repeatedly and as a matter of course, cf. Philo Sacr. AC, 12, 35, opp. οὐδὲν ὑποστειλαμένη ... λέξω, 66; Agric., 64; Plant., 8; Flacc., 4 etc.; Jos. Ant., 2, 116; 15, 37 etc. In Jos. Ant., 9, 226 παρρησία is used for ἐξουσία: ὁ δ' (sc. βασιλεύς) ὑπ' αἰσχύνης τε τοῦ συμβεβηκότος δεινοῦ καὶ τοῦ μηκέτ' αὐτῷ παρρησίαν εἶναι τὸ κελευόμενον ἐποίει ... The connection between παρρησία and φιλία may be seen in Ep. Ar., 125. There is a link between παρρησία and εὐγένεια in Philo Leg. Gaj., 63, cf. Omn. Prob. Lib., 126: ἔχουσι γάρ τι βασιλικὸν αἱ εὐγενεῖς ψυχαί ... ἀλαζονείᾳ παρρησίαν ἀντιτάττον, cf. 95, where παρρησία corresponds to moral ἐλευθερία: γέμων μὲν παρρησίας ὁ λόγος, πολὺ δὲ μᾶλλον ἐλευθερίας ὁ νοῦς. The need for παρρησία towards οἰκέται is stressed in Stoic fashion with a ref. to their equality with their master which is guaranteed them by natural laws, Philo Spec. Leg., III, 138; cf. also IV, 74: μήτ', εἴ τις ἔνδοξος, ὑψηλὸν αἴρων αὐτὸν αὐχείτω φρυαττόμενος, ἀλλ' ἰσότητα τιμήσας μεταδιδότω παρρησίας τοῖς ἀδόξοις. That an ἄκαιρος παρρησία is foolish and causes harm is realised by the ἀστεῖος as a θεωρὸς of all the things of the cosmos, and for this reason he exercises εὐλάβεια (= caution), as shown in Som., II, 81 ff. The same antithesis between παρρησία and αὐθάδεια, also between παρρησία and κολακεία (→ 873, 33 ff.), is emphasised by Philo Jos., 73: ἐάν τε βουλεύω (sc. as a good πολιτικός), γνώμας εἰσηγήσομαι τὰς κοινωφελεῖς, κἂν μὴ πρὸς ἡδονὴν ὦσιν· ἐάν τε ἐκκλησιάζω, τοὺς θῶπας λόγους (flattering speeches) ἑτέροις καταλιπὼν τοῖς σωτηρίοις χρήσομαι καὶ συμφέρουσιν, ἐπιτιμῶν, νουθετῶν, σωφρονίζων, οὐκ αὐθάδειαν μανιώδη καὶ παράφορον ἀλλὰ νήφουσαν παρρησίαν ἐπιτετηδευκώς. In Jos., 77 one may see the relation of this παρρησία to ἀλήθεια:

---

[19] In 'A it is the rendering of יסד ni, "to come together for consultation," in ψ 30:13 and 2:2 (here acc. to the retranslation by Field), and in Θ it is used at Ez. 16:30 for שׁלֶּטֶת, "having power," from שׁלט, where the LXX presupposes a different text [Bertram].

τεθνάναι μᾶλλον ἂν ἑλοίμην ἢ πρὸς ἡδονήν τι φθεγξάμενος ἐπικρύψαι τὴν ἀλήθειαν καὶ τοῦ συμφέροντος ἀμελῆσαι. Also genuinely (Gk.-)Hell. is the link between παρρησία and αἰδώς (→ I, 170, 5 f.), Jos., 107: ὁ δὲ τάξίωμα τοῦ λέγοντος οὐδὲν καταπλαγεὶς ὥσπερ ὑπηκόῳ βασιλεύς, ἀλλ᾽ οὐχ ὑπήκοος βασιλεῖ, παρρησίᾳ σὺν αἰδοῖ χρώμενος διελέγετο, cf. 222.

Nevertheless, OT Jewish motifs are just as apparent here as in the LXX. The LXX view of παρρησία is found also in Jewish Hell. texts. The presupposition of παρρησία here is fulfilment of the Law, righteousness, piety. Yet this is again taken Hell., of course, inasmuch as the concept of συνείδησις (τὸ συνειδός) occurs. Cf. Philo Spec. Leg., I, 203 f.: βούλεται γὰρ τοῦ θύοντος πρῶτον μὲν τὸν νοῦν ὡσιῶσθαι γνώμαις ἀγαθαῖς καὶ συμφερούσαις ἐνασκούμενον, ἔπειτα δὲ τὸν βίον ἐξ ἀρίστων συνεστάναι πράξεων, ὡς ἅμα τῇ τῶν χειρῶν ἐπιθέσει δύνασθαί τινα παρρησιασάμενον ἐκ καθαροῦ τοῦ συνειδότος τοιαῦτα εἰπεῖν· αἱ χεῖρες αὗται οὔτε δῶρον ἐπ᾽ ἀδίκοις ἔλαβον οὔτε ... αἵματος ἀθῴου προσήψαντο ... ἀλλ᾽ ὑποδιάκονοι πάντων ἐγένοντο τῶν καλῶν καὶ συμφερόντων, ἃ παρὰ σοφίᾳ καὶ νόμοις καὶ σοφοῖς καὶ νομίμοις ἀνδράσι τετίμηται. The ἀσεβής has no παρρησία, Test. XII R. 4:2 f.: ὅτι ἄχρι τελευτῆς τοῦ πατρός μου οὐκ εἶχον παρρησίαν ἀτενίσαι εἰς τὸ πρόσωπον αὐτοῦ, ἢ λαλῆσαί τινι τῶν ἀδελφῶν μου, διὰ τοὺς ὀνειδισμούς. Καὶ ἕως νῦν ἡ συνείδησίς μου συνέχει με περὶ τῆς ἀσεβείας μου. How common is the connection between *parrhesia* and a good conscience may be seen in Jos. Ant., 2, 131: οὐδὲν γὰρ αὐτοῖς συνειδότες ἦγον παρρησίαν, ὡς ἐδόκουν, ἀκίνδυνον, and 2, 52 : τῆς δὲ πρὸς τὸν ἄνδρα κοινωνίας ἀπόλαυσιν ἐχούσης ἀκίνδυνον καὶ προσέτι πολλὴν τὴν ἀπὸ τοῦ συνειδότος καὶ πρὸς τὸν θεὸν παρρησίαν καὶ πρὸς τοὺς ἀνθρώπους.

The last ref. shows that these writings speak of παρρησία towards God. One might also adduce Ant., 5, 38 : βλέπων δὲ οὕτως ὁ Ἰησοῦς τήν τε στρατιὰν καταπεπληγυῖαν καὶ περὶ τῶν ὅλων πονηρὰν ἤδη τὴν ἐλπίδα λαμβάνουσαν παρρησίαν λαμβάνει πρὸς τὸν θεόν. παρρησία expresses itself in prayer. There is a longer discussion of παρρησία towards God in Philo Rer. Div. Her., 5-29. Here all the aspects are combined, and Jewish elements are characteristically fused with Hellenistic. εὐτολμία and ἡ ἐν τῷ δέοντι παρρησία πρὸς τοὺς ἀμείνους are ἀρεταί, ibid., 5. An οἰκέτης has παρρησία towards his master, ὅταν ἠδικηκότι μὲν ἑαυτῷ μηδὲν συνειδῇ, πάντα δ᾽ ὑπὲρ τοῦ κεκτημένου καὶ λέγοντι καὶ πράττοντι, ibid., 6. Hence also ἐλευθεροστομεῖν πρὸς τὸν ἑαυτοῦ τε καὶ τοῦ παντὸς ἡγεμόνα καὶ δεσπότην is only suitable ὅταν ἁμαρτημάτων καθαρεύῃ καὶ τὸ φιλοδέσποτον ἐκ τοῦ συνειδότος κρίνῃ, to be God's servant is his greatest joy and he carries out each command of the master obediently, 7 and 9. παρρησία is, of course, possible only for the σοφός who in contrast to the ἀμαθής has learned silence and listening with the soul, 10 ff. τοῖς μὲν οὖν ἀμαθέσι συμφέρον ἡσυχία, τοῖς δὲ ἐπιστήμης ἐφιεμένοις καὶ ἅμα φιλοδεσπότοις ἀναγκαιότατον ἡ παρρησία κτῆμα, 14. These ἔρωτι σοφίας θείῳ πεπιστευκότες (= οἱ σοφοί, 19) should then not simply speak but cry, and not merely with the lips and tongue ἀλλὰ τῷ παμμούσῳ καὶ μεγαλοφωνοτάτῳ ψυχῆς ὀργάνῳ, οὗ θνητὸς μὲν ἀκροατὴς οὐδὲ εἷς, ὁ δὲ ἀγένητος καὶ ἄφθαρτος μόνος 14. The *parrhesia* of the σοφός, typified by Moses (and Abraham), finds expression in mystical speech : τοσαύτη δ᾽ ἄρα χρῆται παρρησίᾳ ὁ ἀστεῖος, ὥστε οὐ μόνον λέγειν καὶ βοᾶν, ἀλλ᾽ ἤδη καὶ καταβοᾶν ἐξ ἀληθοῦς πίστεως καὶ ἀπὸ γνησίου τοῦ πάθους θαρρεῖ, 19. Yet it is not just audacity, but boldness in a good sense (not τόλμα but εὐτολμία), διότι οἱ σοφοὶ πάντες φίλοι θεοῦ, καὶ μάλιστα κατὰ τὸν ἱερώτατον νομοθέτην. παρρησία δὲ φιλίας συγγενές· ἐπεὶ πρὸς τίνα ἄν τις ἢ πρὸς τὸν ἑαυτοῦ φίλον παρρησιάσαιτο; Moses, however, is called the φίλος θεοῦ (Ex. 33:11) ... θρασύτης μὲν γὰρ αὐθάδους, φίλου δὲ θαρραλεότης οἰκεῖον 21. Thus παρρησιάζεσθαι or θαρρεῖν is in harmony with εὐλάβεια, 22 ff. — a development of the Stoic paradox of the unity of εὐλάβεια and θάρσος (→ II, 752, 11 f.; 752, 52 ff.). ἀπλήστως οὖν εὐωχοῦμαι τοῦ κράματος, ὅ με ἀναπέπεικε μήτε ἄνευ εὐλαβείας παρρησιάζεσθαι μήτε ἀπαρρησιάστως εὐλαβεῖσθαι, 29. That in prayer, which Philo puts on Moses' lips in this connection (24 ff.), God Himself is called ἡ παρρησία shows wherein παρρησία has its origin : ἀλλὰ σύ μοι, δέσποτα, ἡ πατρίς, σὺ ἡ συγγένεια, σὺ ἡ πατρῴα ἑστία, σὺ ἡ ἐπιτιμία, ἡ παρρησία, ὁ μέγας καὶ ἀοίδιμος καὶ ἀναφαίρετος πλοῦτος, 27.

3. Ethiopian Enoch. In an eschatological context παρρησία occurs repeatedly in Eth. En. The ref. is always to the reward of the open standing of the righteous before the throne of God or the Messiah, to the radiance given therewith, to the integration into the joy expressed in praise. The antithesis is the position of sinners, who cannot stand yet have to stand in the revelation of judgment, who are in darkness, who lower their glances for fear and shame and sorrow, who engage in useless beseeching and bewailing. Cf. 47:2 ff.; 48:8; 51:5; 61:3 ff., 9 ff.; 62:3-5 : "And in those days will all kings and mighty men and lofty ones ... rise up, and they shall see and know him, that he sits on the throne of his glory, and that judgment is exercised by him in righteousness ... Then sorrow will come on them ..., and they will be afraid and cast their glances to the ground, and sorrow will seize them ..." v. 10 : "But that Lord of spirits will press them, that they go out quickly from his presence, and their faces will be full of shame, and darkness will be heaped on their faces ..." v. 15 : "And the righteous and elect will have lifted up themselves from the earth and will cease to look down to the earth and will be invested with the robe of glory ... and your glory will not perish before the Lord of spirits." 63:1 ff.; 69:26 : "And there held sway among them a great joy, and they praised and lauded and extolled that the name of the Son of Man was revealed to them ..." 104:1 ff., esp. v. 4 : "... to you will great joy be given like (that of) the angels in heaven ... you will not need to hide in the day of the great judgment ..." παρρησία is used in this eschatological sense in 4 Esr. 7:98 ff.: "The seventh joy of the righteous, greater than all mentioned, is that they may rejoice with confidence (with boldness), that they may be confident and exult without fear, for they hasten to see the countenance of him whom they have served in life and from whom they shall receive praise (ἔνδοξος) and reward ... For seven days they have freedom (opportunity) to behold in these seven days that whereof I have spoken ; then they will be assembled in their chambers." The opposite of the seventh joy had been mentioned already in 7:87: "The seventh torment, worse than all mentioned, that they waste away for shame, that they are consumed by anxiety, that they languish for fear of having to see the glory of the Most High before whom they have sinned in life and by whom they shall be judged in the last judgment." Here the *parrhesia* of the righteous who have served God is not merely the antithesis of the shame or anxiety of the ungodly; it is also the freedom to hasten to God and see His face, a freedom combined with confidence, fearlessness and above all joy. The OT meaning of *parrhesia* found in Job is thus continued.

By way of appendix it might be pointed out that παρρησία occurs in Rabb. writings [20] as a loan word (פַּרְהֶסְיָא), though it plays no special role. It is used 1. for "in an open, loud voice" as distinct from בְּלְחִישָׁה, "in a whisper," Dt. r., 2 (199c); 2. for "publicly," בפרהסיא, in express distinction from בצנעא, Taan., 16, or במטמוניות T. Dᵉmai, 2, 9 (48), בחשאי, Gn. r., 17 (12a), בסתר, Ab., 4, 4, "secretly," or with no express antithesis, M. Ex., 12, 31 (17a) etc.; 3. for "candidly" or "with cheerfulness," S. Dt. § 76 on 12:23 (90b).

C. The New Testament.

1. The Johannine Writings. In the Gospel παρρησία is distinctively linked with the work of Jesus and has a place in the Johannine dialectic of the revelation of Jesus. A mark of Jesus as Revealer is that He works publicly, Jn. 18:20 f.: ἐγὼ παρρησίᾳ λελάληκα τῷ κόσμῳ· ἐγὼ πάντοτε ἐδίδαξα ἐν συναγωγῇ καὶ ἐν τῷ ἱερῷ, ὅπου πάντες οἱ Ἰουδαῖοι συνέρχονται, καὶ ἐν κρυπτῷ ἐλάλησα οὐδέν ... ἴδε οὗτοι οἴδασιν ἃ εἶπον ἐγώ. This public sphere is the cosmos represented by the Jews, whether in synagogue or temple. The opposite is ἐν κρυπτῷ,

---

[20] Str.-B., II, 18 f., 485 f.

"not publicly, in a corner." It is thus emphasised that the preaching of Jesus is "not secret doctrine, and his society is not a sect." [21] The statement in 18:20 is confirmed in 7:25 f.: οὐχ οὗτός ἐστιν ὃν ζητοῦσιν ἀποκτεῖναι; καὶ ἴδε παρρησίᾳ λαλεῖ, καὶ οὐδὲν αὐτῷ λέγουσιν, which suggests the knowledge of the authorities, and 7:26b: μήποτε ἀληθῶς ἔγνωσαν οἱ ἄρχοντες ὅτι οὗτός ἐστιν ὁ Χριστός; 11:54 tells how Jesus withdrew from the public eye: ὁ οὖν ᾽Ιησοῦς οὐκέτι παρρησίᾳ περιεπάτει ἐν τοῖς ᾽Ιουδαίοις, ἀλλὰ ἀπῆλθεν ἐκεῖθεν εἰς τὴν χώραν ἐγγὺς τῆς ἐρήμου, εἰς ᾽Εφραίμ λεγομένην πόλιν, κἀκεῖ ἔμεινεν μετὰ τῶν μαθητῶν. Notwithstanding this παρρησίᾳ λαλεῖν or περιπατεῖν, Jesus in another sense remains concealed. His brothers think that His ἐν παρρησίᾳ εἶναι will follow at once from appearing in Judaea (7:4), and that His works will be perceived and acknowledged by a φανεροῦν ἑαυτὸν τῷ κόσμῳ. But they can think this only because they do not understand the hidden significance of His works, their character as σημεῖα, and because they do not believe in Him, 7:5. The public nature of His work should not be confused with His manifestation. The Evangelist, though he tells us that Jesus went to Jerusalem (7:10) and appeared publicly (7:14, cf. 7:26), can thus say: καὶ αὐτὸς ἀνέβη, οὐ φανερῶς ἀλλὰ [ὡς] [22] ἐν κρυπτῷ, 7:10. As he understands it, Jesus went up in hidden form if openness is the same as manifestation. Open manifestation begins for the cosmos only with the eschatological event commencing with Jesus' ascension to the Father. This is confirmed by what is said about the καιρός in 7:6 ff. (→ III, 460, 13 ff.), where the Evangelist adopts and adapts the Greek and Hellenistic relating of παρρησία to the καιρός doctrine, → 874, 32; 877, 40 ff. The "decisive, irrevocable moment" [23] of the *parrhesia* of Jesus has not yet come, is not yet fulfilled, 7:8, since it is the eschatological moment of His exaltation, which, taking place within this time, is not a possibility of this time, and which, though fixed by God, is yet in the freedom of the Son, who does the will of the Father.

How little the public nature of the work of Jesus as perceived and understood by the cosmos is the *parrhesia* of the Revealer may be seen from the fact that the public work of Jesus is hidden from the Jews as a Messianic work: ἐκύκλωσαν οὖν αὐτὸν οἱ ᾽Ιουδαῖοι καὶ ἔλεγον αὐτῷ· ἕως πότε τὴν ψυχὴν ἡμῶν αἴρεις; εἰ σὺ εἶ ὁ Χριστός, εἰπὸν ἡμῖν παρρησίᾳ. ἀπεκρίθη αὐτοῖς ὁ ᾽Ιησοῦς· εἶπον ὑμῖν, καὶ οὐ πιστεύετε· τὰ ἔργα ἃ ἐγὼ ποιῶ ... ταῦτα μαρτυρεῖ περὶ ἐμοῦ, 10:24 f. They would like to be able to lay hold of Jesus in direct self-witness. But they receive from Him the answer that open witness is given in His works. This witness is grasped, however, only by faith, which recognises the eschatological character of His works. Faith alone understands the figurative speech of Jesus, which is the result and reflection of His revelation. Jesus says in 11:11: Λάζαρος ὁ φίλος ἡμῶν κεκοίμηται. But according to the direct statement of the author the disciples misunderstand Him, 11:12 f. Hence we read in 11:14: τότε οὖν εἶπεν αὐτοῖς ὁ ᾽Ιησοῦς παρρησίᾳ· Λάζαρος ἀπέθανεν ... This παρρησίᾳ λέγειν means concretely "to speak non-figuratively," "openly," "without concealment." The misunderstanding of the disciples is not based, of course, on misunderstanding of the image as such, but on misunderstanding of the matter, since, in spite of the presence of Jesus, they do not realise that death is only sleep. They do not believe in Him who is the resurrection and the life. This concealment is radically

---

[21] Schl. J., 334.
[22] This is not in ℵ D pc it^var syr, and is an interpretation which keeps in view the distinction between "public" and "manifest." Jesus' open journey to Jerusalem is at the same time concealed.
[23] Bu. J., 220, n. 2.

bound up with the life of Jesus right up to the coming again in the Paraclete. His speech is now in metaphor and riddle. In that day Jesus will proclaim παρρησία, 16:25 ff. This is the day when the disciples will pray in the name of Jesus and on the basis of their love and faith they will receive directly from God. It is the day when the πνεῦμα τῆς ἀληθείας comes, 16:13. The *parrhesia* of Jesus is thus given with the presence of the risen Lord in the Spirit. That the believer can pierce the concealment by the → παροιμίαι may be seen from the continuation in 16:29 ff.

In Mk. 8:32 παρρησίᾳ is the opp. of ἐν παραβολαῖς and means "open." The ref. is to the plain teaching given to the disciples, as distinct from the public (Mk. 2:9), on the life, death and resurrection of Jesus. The appended Peter story (8:32b f.) shows that the very openness hides Jesus from His disciples (cf. Mk. 9:32; 10:32). In Mk., too, Jesus can ἐν παρρησίᾳ εἶναι only for faith.

παρρησία is significant in another respect in the Johannine corpus. It is used in 1 Jn. for man's openness to God. [24] In this connection we find a series of Hellenistic and Jewish traits in the Johannine understanding. παρρησία to God, found already in Hellenistic Jewish writings and in the LXX, denotes in 1 Jn. our present standing before God, 3:21; 5:14. It presupposes a good conscience, cf. 3:21: ἀγαπητοί, ἐὰν ἡ καρδία μὴ καταγινώσκῃ, παρρησίαν ἔχομεν πρὸς τὸν θεόν ... [25] The basis of this good conscience is that we τὰς ἐντολὰς αὐτοῦ τηροῦμεν καὶ τὰ ἀρεστὰ ἐνώπιον αὐτοῦ ποιοῦμεν, v. 22. But His commandment relates to the fact that we πιστεύσωμεν τῷ ὀνόματι τοῦ υἱοῦ αὐτοῦ Ἰησοῦ Χριστοῦ καὶ ἀγαπῶμεν ἀλλήλους καθὼς ἔδωκεν ἐντολὴν ἡμῖν, v. 23. *Parrhesia* to God thus presupposes faith in Jesus Christ, the Son of God, and love of one's neighbour. Good conscience is here qualified in such a way that it arises with fulfilment of the commandment of Jesus by faith in Him and the related love of one's neighbour. A further distinctive aspect of παρρησία may be seen, however, in v. 24. It is given with the presence of the πνεῦμα in us. The Spirit, whom God gives, points us to the fact that God is in us and that we abide in Him and thus keep His commandment. A good conscience, and therewith παρρησία, presupposes not only keeping the commandments of Jesus but also with this the presence of God in the Spirit. *Parrhesia* to God is to be found where God indwells by the Spirit those who keep the commandments of Jesus. This παρρησία finds expression in prayer to God which God hears (3:22;) 5:14 f.: καὶ αὕτη ἐστὶν ἡ παρρησία ἣν ἔχομεν πρὸς αὐτόν, ὅτι ἐάν τι αἰτώμεθα κατὰ τὸ θέλημα αὐτοῦ ἀκούει ἡμῶν. καὶ ἐὰν οἴδαμεν ὅτι ἀκούει ἡμῶν ὃ ἐὰν αἰτώμεθα, οἴδαμεν ὅτι ἔχομεν τὰ αἰτήματα ἃ ᾐτήκαμεν ἀπ' αὐτοῦ. This again is a Hellenistic Jewish (or OT) view. The only thing is that these verses emphasise the point that prayer is according to God's will. This will is naturally not the same as it is taken to be in Jewish Hellenism. παρρησία, freedom towards God, the right and power to say anything to God, is to be found where a man, taught by the Spirit to obey the commandments of Jesus, and at one with the will of God, opens his heart to God in prayer.

1 Jn. distinguishes between present παρρησία and the future παρρησία which Christians have in the last day, at the coming of Christ, before God, the judge

---

[24] In Jn. 7:13: οὐδεὶς μέντοι παρρησίᾳ ἐλάλει περὶ αὐτοῦ (sc. Jesus) διὰ τὸν φόβον τῶν Ἰουδαίων, the primary meaning of παρρησία is "publicly." But since the public is hostile, παρρησίᾳ λαλεῖν about Jesus also has the sense of speaking with candour. The ὄχλος referred to here is already seen to be different from those who as martyrs give witness to Jesus. It does not have the mark of the *parrhesia* of witnesses, namely, fearlessness.

[25] Cf. Prv. 20:9, → 876, 25 f.

and righteous δεσπότης, 2:28; 4:17. There had been references to this eschatological παρρησία in Wis. 5:1 and especially 4 Esr. 7:98 ff. (→ 876, 12 ff.; 879, 23 ff.). As in 4 Esr. 7:98 ff. and Eth. En., so here we find the antithesis between παρρησία and αἰσχύνη or παρρησία and φόβος. παρρησία is openness to God in the further sense that he who has παρρησία need not be ashamed before the coming Judge, will not be put to shame by Him, and has no fear of punishment. For παρρησία is simply a reflection of the fulness of the love of God for us in which we abide. Abiding in the love of God, which knows no fear because it keeps the commandments, is brought to light in the future judgment in the fact that we have access and openness, i.e., *parrhesia*, to God.

2. Acts. Acts has παρρησία and παρρησιάζεσθαι only towards man. Παρρησία is so closely related to the λαλεῖν or διδάσκειν (4:29, 31; 9:27 f.; 18:25 f.) of the apostles that παρρησιάζεσθαι almost takes on the sense "to preach," cf. 9:27 f.; 14:3; 18:26; 19:8. The forum before which it applies consists either of the Jews in general (2:29; 9:27 f.; 13:46; 18:26; 19:8), the Jewish authorities in particular (4:13; 26:26; cf. 4:5 ff.), Jews and Gentiles (14:3, cf. 14:2 [28:31]), or Gentiles and Jews along with their political representatives, 4:29, 31, cf. v. 27. It is the forum of the public and of political or judicial authorities. This public is always regarded as hostile : ἔπιδε ἐπὶ τὰς ἀπειλὰς αὐτῶν, 4:29. Public speaking is thus open or candid speaking. In all instances, then, παρρησία might be rendered "candour" and παρρησιάζεσθαι "to speak with candour or boldness," though the public aspect is not forgotten, e.g., 4:29, 31; 28:31; 9:27 f.; 14:3; 18:26; 19:8. In Ac. the meaning of παρρησία is basically controlled by the situation of confession. But a third element has also to be taken into account. According to Ac. 4:13 the Jewish authorities are surprised by the παρρησία of the apostles Peter and John because they ἄνθρωποι ἀγράμματοί εἰσιν καὶ ἰδιῶται. Their *parrhesia*, then, is not that of men whose training has given them rhetorical ability. Theirs is a different power. Here, then, παρρησία means rhetorical skill, and this aspect is emphasised. The κύριος gives such παρρησία to his servants. In Ac. 4:29 one finds again, in Christian form, the thought that the δοῦλος as such has no παρρησία. The παρρησία of the apostles is, of course, ἐπὶ τῷ κυρίῳ τῷ μαρτυροῦντι ἐπὶ τῷ λόγῳ τῆς χάριτος αὐτοῦ, διδόντι σημεῖα καὶ τέρατα γίνεσθαι διὰ τῶν χειρῶν αὐτῶν, 14:3. The κύριος Jesus Himself confirms the open preaching of His apostles by signs and wonders, and this witness by signs and wonders belongs to the eloquent preaching, the παρρησιάζεσθαι, cf. 4:29 f.: καὶ τὰ νῦν, κύριε, ἔπιδε ἐπὶ τὰς ἀπειλὰς αὐτῶν, καὶ δὸς τοῖς δούλοις σου μετὰ παρρησίας πάσης λαλεῖν τὸν λόγον σου, ἐν τῷ τὴν χεῖρα ἐκτείνειν σε εἰς ἴασιν καὶ σημεῖα καὶ τέρατα γίνεσθαι διὰ τοῦ ὀνόματος τοῦ ἁγίου παιδός σου Ἰησοῦ. That this power of bold and open speech, which is given by God and confirmed by the κύριος, is in the situation of confession made possible for the servants of God, the apostles, only by the Spirit, may be seen from the continuation of the passage just quoted in 4:31: καὶ δεηθέντων αὐτῶν ἐσαλεύθη ὁ τόπος ἐν ᾧ ἦσαν συνηγμένοι, καὶ ἐπλήσθησαν ἅπαντες τοῦ ἁγίου πνεύματος, καὶ ἐλάλουν τὸν λόγον τοῦ θεοῦ μετὰ παρρησίας. Peter also speaks πλησθεὶς πνεύματος ἁγίου in 4:8. The same connection may be seen again in 18:25 f. Of Apollos, who ζέων τῷ πνεύματι ἐλάλει καὶ ἐδίδασκεν ἀκριβῶς τὰ περὶ τοῦ Ἰησοῦ, it is said : οὗτός τε ἤρξατο παρρησιάζεσθαι ἐν τῇ συναγωγῇ. The *parrhesia* of the apostle who preaches openly and eloquently to a hostile world is a *charisma*.

3. The Pauline Corpus. In the Pauline corpus, too, there is emphasis on Christian and especially apostolic *parrhesia*. This represents a prominent aspect

of Christian and especially apostolic life, Phil. 1:20; Eph. 3:12. It is to be found in connection with preaching the Gospel, Eph. 6:19 f. παρρησία is openness towards God (2 C. 3:12; [Phil. 1:20;] Eph. 3:12) and also towards men (2 C. 3:12; Eph. 6:20; 1 Th. 2:2; 2 C. 7:4; 1 Tm. 3:13; Phlm. 8). But it also includes openness in the Gospel, Eph. 6:19 f.; 1 Th. 2:2 ff. Above all the discussion in 2 C. 3:12 ff. shows [26] that for Paul παρρησία to God — the uncovered face of Paul looking towards Him, 3:18 — implies an uncovered face which men can see as Israel could not see the covered face of Moses, 3:13. He who lifts up his face uncovered to God also turns uncovered to men. This openness of apostolic life, however, has its basis in the gift of the Gospel and its ministry, the διακονία τοῦ πνεύματος and τῆς δικαιοσύνης, 3:7 ff. The apostle can lift up his face openly to God and men because he serves incorruptible δόξα and kindles unshakable hope, 3:7 ff. Thus παρρησία is negatively a law of non-concealment and positively a reflection of abiding glory grasped in hope. The openness of apostolic life makes this life a mirror of the δόξα κυρίου in which it is increasingly transformed by the πνεῦμα, 3:18. The aspects of παρρησία found in 2 C. 3 are in part confirmed by other statements of Paul. In Eph. 3:12 : ἐν ᾧ ἔχομεν τὴν παρρησίαν καὶ προσαγωγὴν ἐν πεποιθήσει διὰ τῆς πίστεως αὐτοῦ, the juxtaposition of παρρησία and προσαγωγή shows plainly that παρρησία has the character of openness to God. [27] He who is in Christ has found again freedom towards God and can approach God with confidence. He can stand before the Ruler and Judge free and erect, not lowering his head, able to bear His presence. Openness towards men is in view in Phil. 1:20; Eph. 6:19 f.; 1 Th. 2:2. παρρησία is used in rather a different sense in 2 C. 7:4, where Paul's openness or freedom towards the Corinthians, which is based on the right disposition of his heart to them, is almost "affection." In Phlm. 8, however, we have an instance of παρρησία in much the same sense as ἐξουσία. The reference in 1 Tm. 3:13 is to παρρησία towards God and men. If we are to expound παρρησία here with reference to that wherein it finds expression, then it is the "unhampered and joyful word, both in prayer and in dealings with men." [28] It presupposes καλῶς διακονεῖν and is grounded ἐν πίστει τῇ ἐν Χριστῷ Ἰησοῦ. That we have such παρρησία in Christ was mentioned already in Eph. 3:12 (→ lines 12 ff.); that the reference is to a παρρησιά-ζεσθαι ἐν τῷ θεῷ ἡμῶν may be seen in 1 Th. 2:2; and that the πνεῦμα Χριστοῦ Ἰησοῦ effects this παρρησία is intimated in Phil. 1:19 f.: οἶδα γὰρ ὅτι τοῦτό μοι ἀποβήσεται εἰς σωτηρίαν διὰ τῆς ὑμῶν δεήσεως καὶ ἐπιχορηγίας τοῦ πνεύματος Ἰησοῦ Χριστοῦ, κατὰ τὴν ἀποκαραδοκίαν καὶ ἐλπίδα μου ὅτι ἐν οὐδενὶ αἰσχυνθήσομαι, ἀλλ' ἐν πάσῃ παρρησίᾳ ὡς πάντοτε καὶ νῦν μεγαλυν-θήσεται Χριστὸς ἐν τῷ σώματί μου, εἴτε διὰ ζωῆς εἴτε διὰ θανάτου. [29] These sentences indicate once again the nature of παρρησία. It embraces here openness to both God and men. It stands opposed to the shame in which man perishes, and represents the glory in which he is great. Distinctive in this passage is the presupposition of the union between Christ and the apostle. If the apostle is not put to shame, Christ Himself in His body will be great in all openness or freedom.

The only reference to the παρρησία of Christ Himself as the risen Lord is in Col. 2:15. Christ exposes the powers to the cosmos in public triumph. Since, how-

---

[26] Cf. Wnd. 2 K., 118 f.
[27] Acc. to Peterson, 292 we are to imagine a court scene ; this is already presupposed in Eth. En.
[28] Schl. 1 Tm., 108.
[29] Cf. Loh. Phil., ad loc. (547).

ever, δειγματίζειν already contains the idea of public display (→ II, 31, 36 ff.), it may be asked whether ἐν παρρησίᾳ does not emphasise, not openness or boldness, but rather the superiority or ἐξουσία of Christ.

4. Hebrews. In Hb. παρρησία plays a relatively important part. [30] It connotes a distinctive mode of being on the part of the Christian. As has been correctly observed, [31] παρρησία has "a peculiarly objective character." One has it, not as a subjective attitude, but as the appropriation of something already there. One keeps it by holding fast, not merely oneself as a believer, but the presupposition of faith in the promise. παρρησία is thus posited objectively with the object of hope, and it is worked out in a life which is commensurate with and has entered into this openness. Hb. 3:6 contains the admonition to hold fast παρρησία and τὸ καύχημα τῆς ἐλπίδος. In 3:14 we read : τὴν ἀρχὴν τῆς ὑποστάσεως μέχρι τέλους βεβαίαν κατασχεῖν. ὑπόστασις is the formal term for παρρησία and the καύχημα which we have in hope. We have only its ἀρχή. In content παρρησία is freedom of access to God, authority to enter the sanctuary, openness for the new and living way which Jesus has restored for us, 10:19. This παρρησία is given with the blood of Jesus (10:19) and is grounded in His high-priestly way (4:14 f.). The saving work of Jesus, which penetrates all the heavens, has created *parrhesia* and made its fulfilment possible. *Parrhesia* works itself out in the confidence and openness which need not be ashamed when it stands before the Judge, 4:16. It is preserved by patience in tribulation, 10:34 ff. It demands an ἀληθινὴ καρδία ἐν πληροφορίᾳ πίστεως, and presupposes purifying of the conscience and baptism, 10:22. Since it is freedom on the way to God, it contains a reward, the attainment of hope. If it is kept open, there is already achieved, with saving participation in Christ, redeeming membership of His house, 3:14, 6.

D. παρρησία, παρρησιάζομαι in Ancient Ecclesiastical Literature.

It is obvious that so important a concept as παρρησία could not simply fade from the scene in the early Church. In fact there is a whole series of established senses and typical connections in which it may be found. To take a few examples, one reads of the παρρησία of the λόγος in Dg., 11, 2, cf. Orig. Comm. in Joh., 13, 16 (GCS, 10, 240, 24 f.) etc. One also finds the antithesis between παρρησία and μυστήριον in Dg., 11, 2. Cf. παρρησία and καιρός in Act. Thom., 46; Act. Joh., 22, παρρησία and public in Act. Phil., 116, παρρησία and joy, *ibid.*, 7, παρρησία and λαμπρότης, Chrys. Hom. in Eph., 1 (MPG, 62, 14), παρρησία and αἰδώς, Act. Thom., 43. In the post-apost. fathers the most important instance is at 1 Cl., 34, 1 ff. Here, as in Philo, παρρησία towards God is illustrated by the relation between servant and master. Only the δοῦλος who may be confident because of his work has παρρησία towards his δεσπότης. The παρρησία of the Christian, however, stands in the Lord. [32] It is also the Lord's gift, and as a condition requires obedience to Him. Its consequence and expression is the accordant prayer which grants participation in the promise. Similarly in 2 Cl., 15, 3 παρρησία has the presupposition : ἐμμείνωμεν οὖν ἐφ' οἷς ἐπιστεύσαμεν δίκαιοι καὶ ὅσιοι, ἵνα μετὰ παρρησίας αἰτῶμεν τὸν θεὸν τὸν λέγοντα· "Ετι λαλοῦντός σου ἐρῶ· ἰδοὺ πάρειμι. Its expression here is prayer to God. It is also worked out in the θεράπων Moses, esp. in intercession for the people — a new motif well worth noting (1 Cl., 53, 5).

Nevertheless, so far as I can see, παρρησία has an assured place in this literature

---

[30] Cf. on what follows Mi. Hb.[8], *ad loc.*
[31] E. Käsemann, *Das wandernde Gottesvolk* (1938), 23.
[32] Transferred to other relations, this δοῦλος motif still plays a role in Const. Ap., II, 28, 6. Cf. also Act. Thom., 81.

only 1. in the portrait of the apostle in the apocryphal writings, 2. in the martyr literature, and 3. in the doctrine of prayer.

1. The Apostle in NT Apocrypha. Here there is a significant change as compared with the NT. Though one finds the connection between παρρησία and λόγος (Act. Phil., 97 and 144), the close link between λόγος and mighty acts leads to greater stress on the connection between παρρησία and ἐξουσία. The term παρρησία comes to mean almost the "power to work miracles" or the "freedom to do mighty acts." Cf. Act. Thom., 81: ὁ τὴν ἑαυτοῦ δύναμιν ἐμπνέων ἡμῖν καὶ παραθαρσύνων ἡμᾶς καὶ παρέχων παρρησίαν ἐν ἀγάπῃ τοῖς ἰδίοις σου δούλοις· δέομαί σου ἰαθεῖσαι αἱ ψυχαὶ ἀναστήτωσαν … In Act. Joh., 22 παρρησία is confidence in Christ, but this confidence finds expression and confirmation in miraculous power, cf. Act. Joh., 30 and 33; Act. Thom., 46 of the demon which was driven out and which now says : καὶ αὐτὸν (sc. the apostle) μὲν ἐπιλήσῃ, ἐμοὶ δὲ καιρὸς καὶ παρρησία γενήσεται, cf. Act. Phil., 110.

2. The Martyr Literature. This speaks of παρρησία in 3 ways. a. The martyr shows it towards his persecutors. This continues the Jewish Hellenistic and NT strand. [33] Mart. Pol., 10, 1: εἰ κενοδοξεῖς, ἵνα ὀμόσω τὴν Καίσαρος τύχην, ὡς σὺ λέγεις, προσποιεῖ δὲ ἀγνοεῖν με, τίς εἰμι, μετὰ παρρησίας ἄκουε· Χριστιανός εἰμι, Eus. Hist. Eccl., V, 1, 18 : τὴν ὁμολογίαν παρρησιάσασθαι, ibid., V, 2, 4 : καὶ τὴν μὲν δύναμιν τῆς μαρτυρίας ἔργῳ ἐπεδείκνυντο, πολλὴν παρρησίαν ἄγοντες πρὸς πάντα τὰ ἔθνη, καὶ τὴν εὐγένειαν διὰ τῆς ὑπομονῆς καὶ ἀφοβίας καὶ ἀτρομίας φανερὰν ἐποίουν, τὴν δὲ πρὸς τοὺς ἀδελφοὺς τῶν μαρτύρων προσηγορίαν παρῃτοῦντο, ἐμπεπλησμένοι φόβου θεοῦ, Mart. Andreae, 8; Mart. Pionii, IV, 9 : λέγουσιν (sc. the Jews) ὅτι καιροὺς παρρησίας ἔχομεν. Acc. to Orig. Hom. in Luc., 27 (GCS, 30, 170, 3); Cels., II, 45 (GCS, 2, 167, 25; 168, 4) Jn. the Baptist and the apostles are models here. Even yet it is still realised that this παρρησία of the martyrs is a charisma. Cf. Eus. Hist. Eccl., V, 1, 49 : Ἀλέξανδρός τις … γνωστὸς σχεδὸν πᾶσιν διὰ τὴν πρὸς τὸν θεὸν ἀγάπην καὶ παρρησίαν τοῦ λόγου (ἦν γὰρ καὶ οὐκ ἄμοιρος ἀποστολικοῦ χαρίσματος). b. Above all, however, the martyr has παρρησία toward God in heaven. The idea of heavenly parrhesia is still found elsewhere, e.g., in connection with the ascent of the soul in Act. Thom., 103 : καὶ αὐτός σοι σύνοδος γένηται ἐν τῇ φοβερᾷ λεωφόρῳ, καὶ αὐτός σε ὁδηγήσει εἰς τὴν βασιλείαν αὐτοῦ· εἰσάξει δέ σε εἰς τὴν αἰωνίαν ζωήν, παρέχων σοι τὴν παρρησίαν τὴν μὴ παρερχομένην μήτε ἀλλασσομένην, cf. 148; Act. Joh., 109 (?). With ref. to martyrs it has a special emphasis, Act. Justini, 5, 6 : δι' εὐχῆς ἔχομεν διὰ τὸν κύριον ἡμῶν Ἰησοῦν Χριστὸν τιμωρηθέντες σωθῆναι, ὅτι τοῦτο ἡμῖν σωτηρία καὶ παρρησία γενήσεται ἐπὶ τοῦ φοβεροῦ καὶ παγκοσμίου βήματος τοῦ δεσπότου ἡμῶν καὶ σωτῆρος, Orig. Exhortatio ad Martyrium, 28 (GCS, 2, 24, 7): ὁποῖον δ' ἐστὶ τὸ μαρτύριον καὶ πόσην παρρησίαν ἐμποιοῦν πρὸς τὸν θεόν, καὶ ἐντεῦθεν ἔστι καταμαθεῖν, Chrys. in Sanctos Martyres Bernicen et Prosdocen, 7 (MPG, 50, 640) of the souls of the martyrs : πολλὴν γὰρ ἔχουσι παρρησίαν οὐχὶ ζῶσαι μόνον, ἀλλὰ καὶ τελευτήσασαι, καὶ πολλῷ μᾶλλον τελευτήσασαι. νῦν γὰρ τὰ στίγματα φέρουσι τοῦ Χριστοῦ, Chrys. Adversus Judaeos, 8, 6 (MPG, 48, 937): καταφύγῃς … πρὸς τοὺς φίλους (!) αὐτοῦ, τοὺς μάρτυρας, τοὺς ἁγίους, καὶ τοὺς εὐηρεστηκότας αὐτῷ καὶ πολλὴν ἔχοντας πρὸς αὐτὸν παρρησίαν. [34] As may be seen from these texts, this παρρησία is grounded in martyrdom itself. [35] It applies to the δεσπότης whose φίλος the martyr became. It expresses itself in intercession made for those who pray and above all for others, cf.

---

[33] Cf. the formulation in the literary phrase in Athenag. Suppl., 11, 1 f.: ἐπιτρέψατε ἐνταῦθα τοῦ λόγου ἐξακούστου μετὰ πολλῆς κραυγῆς γεγονότος ἐπὶ παρρησίαν ἀναγαγεῖν, ὡς ἐπὶ βασιλέων φιλοσόφων ἀπολογούμενον.

[34] For this and other refs. cf. Peterson, 294, who also emphasises how stereotyped was the mention of the παρρησία of the martyrs in later literature.

[35] His works, faith, temptations and resultant patience gave him παρρησία, as Photius of Constantinople says in exposition of Hb. 10:35. Cf. K. Staab, Pauluskommentare aus d. griech. Kirche = Nt.liche Abhandlungen (1933), 649.

Asterios Hom., 10 : In Sanctos Martyres (MPG, 40, 317 C): πρεσβευτὰς αὐτοὺς τῶν εὐχῶν καὶ αἰτημάτων, διὰ τὸ ὑπερβάλλον τῆς παρρησίας, ποιοῦμεν (sc. the martyrs). ἐντεῦθεν πενίαι λύονται, καὶ ἰατρεύονται νόσοι, καὶ ἀρχόντων ἀπειλαὶ κοιμίζονται· πασῶν δὲ τῶν ταραχῶν καὶ χειμώνων τοῦ βίου λιμένες εἰσὶν εὔδιοι, οἱ ἱεροὶ τῶν μαρτύρων σηκοί. c. παρρησία to God is, however, enjoyed already by the living martyr or confessor, as stressed by Chrys. In Sanctos Martyres Bern. et Prosdoc., 7 (→ *supra*). In this he is not alone. He is accompanied by the saint or ascetic or mystic. [36] "He who has seen God alone can truly pray to God ; he can thank Him sincerely ; he may ask Him, indeed, he should ask Him for all things ; he has free access, παρρησία, to God, and can speak to Him as friend to friend," says Holl [37] of the ascetic mystic, and he gives a list of examples of which we may quote two : Symeon, the new theologian, Or. 15 : [38] χρὴ οὖν πρότερον πιστεῦσαι καὶ καταλλαγῆναι θεῷ καὶ τότε ψάλλειν αὐτῷ, συγγνώμην αἰτοῦντος πρότερον τοῦ ψάλλοντος, ὧν ἥμαρτεν, in connection with Ethica, 13 C folium 316 recto : [39] κατὰ γὰρ τὴν ἀναλογίαν τῆς μετανοίας ἀναλογοῦσαν εὑρίσκει τὴν πρὸς θεὸν παρρησίαν καὶ οἰκειότητα πᾶς ἄνθρωπος καὶ ταύτην γνωστῶς καὶ ἐναργῶς καὶ ὡς εἴ τις φίλος πρὸς φίλον καὶ προσομιλεῖ αὐτῷ προσώπῳ πρὸς πρόσωπον καὶ ὁρᾷ αὐτὸν νοεροῖς ὀφθαλμοῖς.

3. The Connection between παρρησία and Prayer. This is maintained and deepened. At one pt. it is the subject of special discussion. Acc. to Orig. Orat., 22, 1 (GCS, 3, 346, 18 f.) a specific NT παρρησία is expressed when God is called Father. This does not occur in the old covenant. Hence the Lord's Prayer is prefaced in the Liturgy of James by sentences containing prayer for this *parrhesia* : καὶ καταξίωσον ἡμᾶς, δέσποτα φιλάνθρωπε, μετὰ παρρησίας, ἀκατακρίτως, ἐν καθαρᾷ καρδίᾳ, ψυχῇ συντετριμμένῃ, ἀνεπαισχύντῳ προσώπῳ, ἡγιασμένοις χείλεσι τολμᾶν ἐπικαλεῖσθαί σε τὸν ἐν τοῖς οὐρανοῖς ἅγιον Θεὸν Πατέρα καὶ λέγειν. [40] Every prayer demands παρρησία, but esp. that in which a filial relationship is expressed. οἵας γὰρ τῷ λέγοντι χρεία ψυχῆς ! ὅσης τῆς παρρησίας ! οἵας τῆς συνειδήσεως !, to say Father when one has known God, Greg. Nyss. De Oratione Dominica, Or., 2 (MPG, 44, 1140 C).

Schlier

πᾶς, ἅπας

Contents : A. Linguistic Data on πᾶς and ἅπας in the NT : 1. πᾶς as Adjective : a. With Article ; b. Without Article ; 2. πᾶς as Noun : a. With Article ; b. Without Article ; 3. ἅπας. B. Material Aspects : 1. God as Creator and Ruler of All Things according to the OT ; 2. πᾶς in the LXX ; 3. πᾶς in the World of Greek and Hellenistic Thought : 4. πᾶς in the NT.

---

[36] Cf. the examples in Peterson, 295.
[37] K. Holl, *Enthusiasmus u. Bussgewalt beim griech. Mönchtum* (1898), 73 ff.
[38] Holl, *op. cit.*, 73 f. In the Lat. transl. of Pontanus, MPG, 120, 388 AB.
[39] Holl, 74.
[40] M. A. Brightman, *Liturgies Eastern and Western*, I (1896), 59, 28 ff.; cf. the Liturgy of Mark, *ibid.*, 135, 31 ff.; of Basil, 410, 26 f.; of Chrys., 339, 20 f. Cf. Peterson, 296.
π ᾶ ς, ἅ π α ς. K. W. Krüger, *Griech. Sprachlehre*[5] (1875) § 50, 11, 8-13; K. Brugmann, *Die Ausdrücke f. d. Begriff d. Totalität in d. indogerm. Sprachen* (1893/4), 2 f., 53, 60-64; Winer-Schmiedel § 20, 11; A. N. Jannaris, *An Historical Gk. Grammar* (1897) § 1239 f.; K. Meisterhans-E. Schwyzer, *Grammatik d. attischen Inschr.* (1900), 233 f.; Kühner-Blass-Gerth, II, 1 § 465, 6 (p. 631-634); B. L. Gildersleeve, *Syntax of Classical Gk. from Homer to Demosthenes*, II (1911) § 642-652; A. T. Robertson, *A Grammar of the Gk. NT*[4] (1923), 771-774; Radermacher[2], 112 f., 117; Mayser, II, 2, 96-102; J. M. Bover, "Uso del adjetivo singular πᾶς en San Paolo," *Biblica*, 19 (1938), 411-434; Bl.-Debr., § 164, 1, 275, 413; P. Chantraine, *Morphologie historique du grec* (1945) § 60, II and 66, II; Pr.-Bauer[4] (1952), 148, 1149-1153.

A pronominal adj. and pronoun, "whole," "all," "each," current from the time of Hom. *παντ- was formed from *k̥u̯ā-nt- "increasing," "strengthening," and is related to κύω, κύριος and the Doric πέπαμαι, "to possess." ἅπας is a subsidiary form strengthened by ἅ- (*sm̥). It may be compared with σύμπας, found in the LXX but not in the NT. [1]

A. Linguistic Data on πᾶς and ἅπας in the NT.

1. πᾶς as Adjective.

πᾶς as adjective can have very different meanings acc. to its use with article or without article, predicatively or attributively (cf. words like αὐτός, μόνος, ἄκρος, μέσος, ἔσχατος). [2] The use of the art. normally depends on whether or not the simple noun would be with or without art. [3] As regards the art. and noun one has to distinguish between an individual or demonstrative and a generic or indefinite function. In particular one may speak of a summative, implicative and distributive signification of πᾶς as the term embraces either a totality or sum as an independent entity (summative), an inclusion of all individual parts or representatives of a concept (implicative), or extension to relatively independent particulars (distributive). If the reference is to the attainment of the supreme height or breadth of a concept, we have an elative (or amplificative) significance.

a. With Article.

Predicative Position. With the demonstr. art., implicative significance. Sing. "all," "whole" : πᾶσα ἡ Ἰουδαία, Mt. 3:5; πᾶσα ἡ ἀλήθεια, Mk. 5:33; after, and thereby emphasised : ἡ κρίσις πᾶσα, "in its whole scope," Jn. 5:22. In such cases ὅλος might also be used, → 174 f. The art. may be omitted with geographical names, πᾶσα Ἱεροσόλυμα, Mt. 2:3; πᾶς οἶκος Ἰσραήλ (OT), Ac. 2:36; ἐπὶ παντὸς προσώπου τῆς γῆς (OT), 17:26. Plur. "all" : πᾶσαι αἱ γενεαί, Mt. 1:17; πάντα τὰ ῥήματα ταῦτα, Lk. 1:65. Also with part. as noun : πάντα τὰ γενόμενα, Mt. 18:31 and with a substantive prepositional expression : πάντες οἱ ἐν τῇ οἰκίᾳ, Mt. 5:15; πάντες οἱ σὺν αὐτῷ, Lk. 5:9; with pronoun, but without art.: πάντες ἡμεῖς, Ac. 2:32; πάντες οὗτοι, Ac. 2:7; ἐπὶ πᾶσιν τούτοις, Col. 3:14. With generic art., distributive significance, with part. "whoever," "all possible" (cf. πᾶς ὅστις), e.g., πᾶς ὁ ὀργιζόμενος, Mt. 5:22; πᾶν τὸ πωλούμενον, 1 C. 10:25; πάντες οἱ κακῶς ἔχοντες, Mt. 4:24; and in prepositional phrases : πάντες οἱ εἰς μακράν, Ac. 2:39. πᾶς is here a strengthening of the generic art. With elative (amplificative) significance, "all" : πᾶσα ἡ γνῶσις, πίστις, 1 C. 13:2; ἐπὶ πάσῃ τῇ θλίψει ἡμῶν, 2 C. 1:4; εὐχαριστῶ ἐπὶ πάσῃ τῇ μνείᾳ ὑμῶν, "for all your remembrance (of me)," [4] Phil. 1:3; πᾶσαν τὴν μέριμναν ὑμῶν, 1 Pt. 5:7.

Attributive Position. By this close connection with the noun, the content of the whole is emphasised in its totality, [5] so that the word has summative significance : "whole," "as a whole," "generally," e.g., τὸν πάντα χρόνον, Ac. 20:18; ὁ πᾶς νόμος, Gl. 5:14; οἱ σὺν ἐμοὶ πάντες ἀδελφοί, Gl. 1:2.

---

[1] For the etym. of πᾶς cf. Brugmann, 61 ff.; Walde-Pok., I (1930), 366 f.; Boisacq³ (1938), 748; J. B. Hofmann, Etym. Wörterbuch des Griechischen (1949/50), 254; on ἅπας cf. Brugmann, 10, 26, 63; Boisacq, 67; E. Schwyzer, Griech. Grammatik, I = Hndbch. AW, II, 1, 1 (1939), 433.

[2] Jannaris § 1239.

[3] Kühner-Blass-Gerth, II, 1, p. 631, 633; Gildersleeve § 642-652.

[4] Pr.-Bauer⁴, 1150 renders like many others : "with every mention of you," equivalent to "whenever I mention you" (950, s.v. μνεία). But this is not linguistically satisfying, since the art. is not normally used when the meaning is "every." On μνεία in the sense of "remembrance" = "assistance" cf. R. 12:13 vl. (→ IV, 679, n. 1).

[5] Mayser, II, 2, 100.

b. Without Article.

Elative Significance : "full," "supreme," "total," "pure," in the NT only with abstract nouns : πᾶσα ἐξουσία, Mt. 28:18; μετὰ παρρησίας πάσης, Ac. 4:29; ἐν πάσῃ ἀσφαλείᾳ, probably "with full favour [6] on the part of men as our goal," 2 C. 4:2; ἐν παντὶ πάντοτε πᾶσαν αὐτάρκειαν ἔχοντες (strong emphasis), 2 C. 9:8; also 12:12; Eph. 4:2; ἐν πάσῃ προσκαρτερήσει καὶ δεήσει, "with all perseverance in prayer," Eph. 6:18; Phil. 1:20 etc. [7] In profane Gk. this sense is found also with material objects, e.g., πᾶς χαλκός, πᾶν ἀργύριον, "pure." [8]

Distributive Significance : "each." Generic : "each one" in a group (though not with such stress on the individual as ἕκαστος, "each apart"); [9] in the plur. "all" : πᾶσα φάραγξ, πᾶν ὄρος (on earth), Lk. 3:5; πᾶσα σάρξ (OT) "each being," Lk. 3:6; εἰς πάντα τόπον τῆς περιχώρου, Lk. 4:37; πᾶς ἄνθρωπος (in the world), Jn. 1:9; 2:10; πάντες ἄνθρωποι, Ac. 22:15; πάντες ἄγγελοι, Hb. 1:6; πᾶσα ἀρχὴ καὶ πᾶσα ἐξουσία (there is), 1 C. 15:24; πᾶσα γραφή, 2 Tm. 3:16. Also indefinite : "each," "any," "all possible," πᾶν δένδρον μὴ ποιοῦν καρπόν, Mt. 3:10; Lk. 3:9; πᾶσα νόσος καὶ πᾶσα μαλακία (which might occur), Mt. 4:23; πᾶν ἁμάρτημα, 1 C. 6:18; πᾶν ἔργον ἀγαθόν, Tt. 1:16; 3:1; πᾶς ἄνεμος τῆς διδασκαλίας, Eph. 4:14. Rarely with part.: παντὸς ἀκούοντος, "each who hears," Mt. 13:19; παντὶ ὀφείλοντι, Lk. 11:4. In some instances everything general is set aside and the individual is intended : "whoever," "whatever," ἐὰν συμφωνήσωσιν ... περὶ παντὸς πράγματος, Mt. 18:19; κατὰ πᾶσαν αἰτίαν, "for whatever reason," Mt. 19:3; μὴ παντὶ πνεύματι πιστεύετε, 1 Jn. 4:1 etc. [10] As in secular Gk. πᾶς in privative phrases means "any," e.g., ἄνευ παντὸς [ὑπ]ολόγου, "without any deduction," P. Leid. P, 32, [11] so in the NT, under Heb. influence (בָּל-לֹא), one finds an even more strongly restrictive πᾶς along with οὐ or μή, [12] usually with the sense of "none at all" : οὐ πᾶν ῥῆμα, "nothing at all," Lk. 1:37; οὐδέποτε ἔφαγον πᾶν κοινόν, "never anything," Ac. 10:14; πᾶς λόγος σαπρός ... μὴ ἐκπορευέσθω, Eph. 4:29. By analogy a similar πᾶς occurs in Mk. 4:13 predicatively with art.: πῶς πάσας τὰς παραβολὰς γνώσεσθε; "how will you understand any parables?" (here one might also think in terms of πάντως). Cf. in all these instances the class. ὁστισοῦν, not found in the NT.

2. πᾶς as Noun.

a. With Article.

Implicative Significance. The art. is usually demonstrative, and only with the plur.: οἱ πάντες, "they all," Mk. 14:64; R. 11:32; 1 C. 9:22; 10:17; 2 C. 5:14; Phil. 2:21 (the context shows who are meant); τὰ πάντα, "all things," 2 C. 4:15; Phil. 3:8; Col. 3:8 (but "they all" in 1 C. 12:19, where several neutral subst. are comprised). Sometimes the art. is half generic : ζωὴ καὶ πνοὴ καὶ τὰ πάντα, "and all such things," Ac. 17:25; σὺν αὐτῷ τὰ πάντα ἡμῖν χαρίσεται, "he will with him (the Son) give us all these things" (i.e., the things associated herewith), R. 8:32. "All these things" (in the world) is formally used for "all things," "all creatures," "the universe," R. 11:36; 1 C. 8:6; 15:28; Gl. 3:22; Eph. 1:10; 3:9; 4:10; Phil. 3:21; Col. 1:16 f., 20; 1 Tm. 6:13; Hb. 1:3; 2:10; Rev. 4:11.

---

[6] Not "to or before the conscience," for → πρός with acc. has a final sense, and this does not go with "conscience." If, as more than once elsewhere in the NT, συνείδησις is linked with σύνοιδά τινι (instead of ἐμαυτῷ), and transl. "assent" or the like, the phrase makes sense. B. Reicke, The Disobedient Spirits and Christian Baptism (1946), 175 f., 180.

[7] Pr.-Bauer⁴, 1150 § 1 a δ. Cf. also Bover, op. cit., 419-423.

[8] Mayser, II, 2, 97.

[9] Ibid., 2, 96 takes a different view : πᾶς "any," ἕκαστος "each." But this is hardly possible at, e.g., Lk. 4:37: εἰς πάντα τόπον τῆς περιχώρου, "to each." It thus seems better to see in ἕκαστος the distinctive sense of "each apart," cf. Schwyzer, I, 630, n. 4.

[10] Pr.-Bauer⁴, 1149 § 1 a γ.

[11] Mayser, II, 2, 97.

[12] Bl.-Debr. § 302, 1.

Summative Significance. In explanatory apposition to a noun οἱ πάντες etc. are used half adverbially for "in all," "all together," esp. with numbers : [13] ἦσαν οἱ πάντες ἄνδρες ὡσεὶ δώδεκα, "they were in all about twelve men," Ac. 19:7; ἤμεθα αἱ πᾶσαι ψυχαί 276, "we were in all 276 souls," Ac. 27:37 (such phrases would be open to misunderstanding without the art.); but also without numbers : μέχρι καταντήσωμεν οἱ πάντες, "until we all attain," Eph. 4:13. Neutr. plur. in a similar function or as acc. of relation : ὑμῖν τὸ μυστήριον δέδοται ... ἐκείνοις δὲ τοῖς ἔξω ἐν παραβολαῖς τὰ πάντα γίνεται (note the order), "to those without all things are done in parables," Mk. 4:11; αὐξήσωμεν εἰς αὐτὸν τὰ πάντα, "grow up to him in all things," Eph. 4:15 (πάντα without art. means "in every connection," → infra).

b. Without Article.

Distributive Significance, generic or indefinite acc. to context. Sing. "each" : πᾶς, "each man," Lk. 16:16; πᾶς ἐξ ὑμῶν, "each," 14:33; after prep. → lines 25-30. Plur. "all"; πάντες, "all men," Mt. 10:22; "all present," 14:20; 15:37; "all Jews," 21:26 etc. πάντα, "all things," the extent and content being decided by the context : πάντα μοι παρεδόθη, Mt. 11:27; Lk. 10:22; πάντα ἀποδώσω σοι, Mt. 18:26; πάντα ἕτοιμα, Mt. 22:4; πάντα δι᾽ αὐτοῦ ἐγένετο, Jn. 1:3; ὁ ὢν ἐπὶ πάντων θεός, "God who rules over all (sc. all creatures)," R. 9:5; πάντα ὑμῶν, "all that you do," 1 C. 16:14 etc.

Adverbial Phrases. A partitive gen. πάντων is used adverbially in superlatives : "of all," cf. ὕστερον or ἔσχατον πάντων, "last of all," Mt. 22:27; Mk. 12:22; πρῶτον πάντων, "first of all," 1 Tm. 2:1; it is independent of the gender of the main noun : ποία ἐντολὴ πρώτη πάντων, "the first commandment of all," Mk. 12:28 (πλεῖον πάντων in Lk. 21:3 might similarly mean "the most of all," though "more than all" is more likely in view of Mk. 12:43). πάντα is also used adverbially as an acc. of relation : "in every respect," Ac. 20:35; 1 C. 9:25 etc. With prep.: διὰ παντός (sc. χρόνου), "always," Mt. 18:10 etc.; εἰς πάντα, "in every respect," 2 C. 2:9; ἐν παντί, "in everything," 1 C. 1:5 etc.; ἐν πᾶσιν "in all parts," Eph. 1:23; "in all things," 1 Tm. 3:11 etc.; ἐν παντὶ καὶ ἐν πᾶσιν μεμύημαι, Phil. 4:12 (repetition for the sake of emphasis); [14] κατὰ πάντα, "in every respect," Ac. 17:22 etc.; περὶ πάντων, "in all things," 3 Jn. 2; πρὸ πάντων, "above all," Jm. 5:12; 1 Pt. 4:8. The adv. πάντως in general means "in all circumstances." This explains the various special senses, e.g., "certainly": πάντως φονεύς ἐστιν, Ac. 28:4; "generally" : πάντως οἱ πόρνοι, "fornicators generally," 1 C. 5:10.

3. ἅπας.

Etym. → 887, 3 f. In Attic ἅπας was used after consonants, πᾶς after vowels. This distinction is not always observed in the NT (cf. ἄνωθεν πᾶσιν, Lk. 1:3; [15] ἤρξαντο ἅπαν τὸ πλῆθος, 19:37; similarly Ac. 5:16; 25:24), but ἅπας is preferred when something impressive is to be said, esp. with implicative meaning, though usually after a consonant, and chiefly in the Lucan writings. Otherwise ἅπας is used in exactly the same way as πᾶς : ἅπας ὁ λαός, "the whole people," Lk. 3:21; τὴν ἐξουσίαν ταύτην ἅπασαν, Lk. 4:6; ἅπαν τὸ πλῆθος τῆς περιχώρου, Lk. 8:37; ἅπαντες, "all," Mt. 24:39; Lk. 5:26 etc.; ἅπαντα, "everything," Mk. 8:25; Ac. 2:44; 4:32 vl. etc. As apposition and with summative significance : ἤρξαντο ἅπαν τὸ πλῆθος τῶν μαθητῶν χαίροντες αἰνεῖν, "they began," i.e., the whole company of the disciples (as one man), Lk. 19:37.

B. Material Aspects.

1. God as Creator and Ruler of All Things according to the OT.

In the OT belief in the God of Israel as Creator and Ruler of all things is of fundamental significance. There is in the OT no uniform, abstract concept of

---

[13] Mayser, II, 2, 101 f.
[14] D. Tabachovitz, Études sur le grec de la basse époque (1943), 39.
[15] Bl.-Debr. § 275.

the totality of things in the sense of the cosmos or universe, → I, 678, 22 ff. Instead, the OT uses "heaven and earth," Gn. 1:1 etc.; "the earth and the fulness thereof," Ps. 24:1. The idea of the totality is often present, however, in concrete forms, and sometimes the adjective כֹּל ("all," "each") is used in this connection. The constant reference is to the fact that God, since He has created everything, is also the Lord of all creatures. Here are some examples : "The heaven and the heaven of heavens is the Lord thy God's, the earth also, with all that therein is," Dt. 10:14; "Under **all heaven (all) these things are mine**," Job 41:3; "The earth is the Lord's, and the fulness thereof ; the world, and they that dwell therein," Ps. 24:1 (quoted by Paul in 1 C. 10:26; cf. Ps. 50:12; 89:11; Jer. 10:12; 51:15). There are particularly detailed depictions of the omnipotence of the Creator God in Job 38-41 and Ps. 104. Emphasis is also laid on the fact that the God of Israel, as Lord of creation, is also Lord of world history : "I have made the earth ... and I give it to whom it seems meet to me," Jer. 27:5; "The most High ruleth in the kingdom of men, and giveth it to whomsoever he will," Da. 4:32; cf. also what is said about Assyria in Is. 7:18 ff.; 10:5. With regard to the human race, it was a unity after the flood (Gn. 9:19; 11:1, 6), but was scattered after the building of the tower of Babel (Gn. 11:7, 9). The fellowship between man and God established at creation was broken by the fall, and can now be restored only by God's saving dealings with Israel, Gn. 12:3; Is. 60 etc. Consequently belief in creation is basically related to belief in salvation, [16] in which Israel occupies a key position. As Creator and Ruler of the whole world, the God of the chosen people declares : "I am the first, and I am the last," Is. 44:6; 48:12. This means that He is all-embracing, and yet He is always Yahweh, the God of Israel. He never becomes an abstraction. He does not lose His personal character. His link with history is unbroken. In this respect it should be noted that the origin of many of the comprehensive statements is perhaps to be sought in the hymnic style of the Orient.

The firm conviction that the God of Israel is the Creator and Ruler of all things, all peoples, and all history is one of the constitutive ideas of the OT. In general the reference is to a universalism tied to Israel and Zion ; only in Jonah, Job and the Wisdom literature is the emphasis not on Israel. Later the universalism of Israel is developed and extended by the LXX and NT. The Greek πᾶς is variously used in this connection.

Reicke

2. πᾶς in the LXX.

Along with and after κύριος, which occurs some 8000 times in the Greek OT, πᾶς with 6-7000 instances is in the Greek Bible the most commonly used term with intellectual significance. It is true that many passages which speak of totality are psychologically conditioned by the popular nature of the tradition, by the narrow horizon of the narrators, by the desire for comprehension or the tendency to exaggerate. They may be intended rhetorically or derive from liturgical plerophory, Da. 3:57-90. Hence many passages, taken in isolation, have little material importance. In the context of biblical revelation, however, they correspond to the universal and total claim of the Word of God, which does not know or recognise any exceptions, which in its statements embraces all cases, which has general validity and which fully and completely describes the facts. If in about 10% of the LXX instances there is no Hebrew original (e.g., Da. 4 and 5), this merely

---

[16] G. v. Rad, "Das theologische Problem d. at.lichen Schöpfungsglaubens," *Werden u. Wesen d. AT* = ZAW, Beih. 66 (1936), 138-147. G. Lindeskog, *Studien zum nt.lichen Schöpfungsgedanken*, I = Acta Universitatis Upsaliensis, 1952, 11 (1952), 15-133.

indicates the inwardly necessary development and extension of the universal claim in the Greek Bible. The *via eminentiae* is with the *via causalitatis* and the *via negationis* one of the ways in which man can speak about God. In this light one may also understand those totality sayings in the biblical tradition which are not directly theological.

In accordance with the election of the people Israel, the OT revelation applies in the first instance quite exclusively to this people, Ex. 19:5; 23:22 LXX; 33:16; 34:10; Lv. 20:24, 26; Dt. 7:6; 14:2 etc. The universal God who has made all things, and in whose hand the souls and spirits of all men lie (Job 12:9, 10), has chosen Israel exclusively and is invoked by Israel alone (Nu. 16:22; 27:16). Either way the LXX understands the concept of God along the lines of cosmological speculation. God is the God of spirits and all flesh. Israel is subject to the Law and must accept all its rights, commandments and statutes, obeying all that is written, Lv. 18:5; Dt. 6:2; Jos. 1:8; 2 Ch. 33:8; 35:19 LXX; Neh. 8:13; 10:29 etc. The sacrificial law is also of general validity, Lv. 1 ff. The scapegoat takes away all sins, Lv. 16:21. Elsewhere, too, expiation is total, 2 Ch. 29:16, 24; 30:19. The cultic legislation raises a claim to universal validity, Lv. 5:17; 11:46; Nu. 3:12 etc. This claim is transferred to Jerusalem and its temple, Lam. 2:15; Is. 56:7. All who do not obey God, and all the enemies of Israel, fall victim to wrath and destruction, Dt. 4:3; Jos. 11:11, 14; 24:18; Ju. 5:31; 2 Βασ. 7:9.

The history of Israel is God's revelation to all peoples, 3 Βασ. 9:7; 8:43, 60; 1 Ch. 16:23. The works and miracles of God are to be declared, 1 Ch. 16:9. His judgments extend to the whole world, 1 Ch. 16:14; Job 11:10 LXX; Is. 66:16. He is the one God above all the kingdoms of the earth, 4 Βασ. 19:15; cf. 5:15. He is unique on the whole earth (Ex. 9:14), great over all gods (Ex. 18:11). Frequently in the historical narration of the OT there is ref. to the whole land as the theatre of revelation. In the light of the universalistic concept of God, and under the influence of expressions like 3 Βασ. 2:2; Gn. 19:31, it is easy for the Gk. reader to make this into the whole earth. The statements about God refer to this, or to the cosmos generally: He is Creator, Judge, King and Lord of the whole earth, all nations, all men, the universe, Gn. 18:25; Job 8:3 (HT שַׁדַּי elsewhere usually παντοκράτωρ or κύριος); Ez. 18:4. He is the Saviour in all troubles, 1 Βασ. 10:19. All His ways are mercy and truth, Ps. 25:10; ψ 118:64. His salvation and forgiveness are for all believers, Ps. 2:12; 5:12; 25:3, 18; cf. ψ 144:13; 2 Βασ. 23:5. Indeed, they are for the whole earth, Ps. 98:3; ψ 103:28 (only the LXX). His wrath smites all the wicked, all enemies of the righteous, Ps. 3:7; 5:12; 6:7, 10. He knows all things, Bar. 3:32. He tries all hearts, 1 Ch. 28:9. He knows all thoughts, ψ 138:2 vl. He sees all things, Job 34:23 LXX. He can do all things, Job 10:13 LXX. If the primary ref. is always to Israel, to the righteous as the elect, to the land of Canaan as the land of promise, so that the universalism is limited by the particularity of salvation history, the concept of totality itself finally helps to give these statements a universalistic extension. Revelation is for all men. God's salvation, like His judgment, affects all men. This universalistic tendency, which is implicit in the very essence of OT revelation, comes out even in passages which relate exclusively to Israel, e.g., in the prayer of Solomon in 3 Βασ. 8:37-43, which tells us in v. 43 that all nations are to come to the knowledge and fear of God. In many respects the content of the prayer has universal significance. Hence in v. 38 the LXX omits the ref. to the whole people of Israel. Validity for all men is thus maintained, and the predication in 39b takes on a broader material significance. Hence real assertions of omnipotence grow out of Israel's experiences of salvation. Even when a particularism of salvation becomes widespread, as in later Judaism (cf. 1 Βασ. 3:21; 3 Βασ. 8:53 with 3 Macc. 6:26), the universalism of belief in the almightiness of God persists. God is Ruler of all things, 1 Ch. 29:11, 12; Jdt. 2:5 etc.; Est. 4:17b-d; Job 5:8; 28:24 LXX; Ps. 47:7 etc.

Fundamentally this universalism of the concept of God explains the universal sayings about man and human reason even when secularisation sets in and ungodly forces raise a totalitarian claim, cf. Prv. 6:16 LXX. God has placed all creation under man, Gn. 1:26; 2:19; 9:3; Ps. 8:6; Job 27:17 LXX. But all men are corrupt and subject to death, Gn. 6:5.

12, 13; Job 15:20; ψ 145:4; 38:5. OT wisdom frequently expresses the general validity of its sayings. Here, too, the LXX goes beyond the Mas., cf. Prv. 1:7, 33; 3:7, 12, 18, 23, 26, 32 etc. In Qoh. universalistic sayings are already common in the HT. The LXX frequently uses σύμπας, which is rare elsewhere. In the assimilating of this remarkably Semitic transl. to Gk. this comes in through combining σύν (for the nota acc. אֵת) with the πᾶς which follows. At Qoh. 3:11; 4:2 πᾶς is added to make the text smoother. [17]

Bertram

3. πᾶς in the World of Greek and Hellenistic Thought.

The Greeks had a developed concept of the universe from the time of the pre-Socratics, [18] and ideas as to the origin of all things are found as early as Hom.: Ὠκεανοῦ, ὅς περ γένεσις πάντεσσι τέτυκται, Il., 14, 246. In pre-Socratic philosophy there was an avid search for the basic substance of the universe, as Aristot. Metaph., I, 3, p. 983b, 6 f., 10 f. emphasises : τῶν δὴ πρώτων φιλοσοφησάντων οἱ πλεῖστοι τὰς ἐν ὕλης εἴδει μόνας ᾠήθησαν ἀρχὰς εἶναι πάντων ... τοῦτο στοιχεῖον καὶ ταύτην ἀρχήν φασιν εἶναι τῶν ὄντων. Thus Thales suggested water, ibid., 20 f.; Anaximander argued that all things came from ἄπειρον, Aetius Placita, I, 3, 3; [19] Anaximenes derived all things from air, ibid., 4; [20] Heraclitus (Fr. 30 [Diels⁶, I, 157, 11 ff.]) dissolved the traditional concept of substance and made eternally mutable fire the inner essence of the universe. The Pythagoreans, however, represented more abstract thought and saw numbers at the basis of their picture of the cosmos, cf. Philolaos Fr. 4 (Diels⁶, I, 408, 4 f.): πάντα ... τὰ γιγνωσκόμενα ἀριθμὸν ἔχοντι.

In the cosmogony of this philosophy there was no place for a personal Creator God. Even sayings like the πάντα πλήρη θεῶν of Thales in Aristot. An., I, 5, p. 411a, 8 are very different from the biblical belief in God. It is true that later in Plato, Stoicism (for all its atheistic basis) and other Hellen. schools one finds the belief in a personal Creator or Demiurge (in the good sense) who is equated either with Zeus or some other god. But this god was always more of a philosophical idea, and never enjoyed fulness of life, might and power like the God of Israel. Cf. τὸν μὲν οὖν ποιητὴν καὶ πατέρα τοῦδε τοῦ παντὸς εὑρεῖν τε ἔργον καὶ εὑρόντα εἰς πάντας ἀδύνατον λέγειν, Plat. Tim., 28c; περὶ τὸν πάντων βασιλέα πάντ' ἐστὶ καὶ ἐκείνου ἕνεκα πάντα, καὶ ἐκεῖνο αἴτιον ἁπάντων τῶν καλῶν, Ps.-Plat. Ep., II, 312e; Χρύσ[ι]ππος ... [ἐν μὲ]ν τῷ πρώτ[ῳ περὶ θεῶ]ν Δία φη[σὶν εἶναι τὸ]ν ἅπαντ[α διοικοῦν]τα λόγον ... Δία (καλεῖσθαι) [ὅ]τι πάντων αἴτ[ι]ος [καὶ κύ]ριος, Philodem. Philos. De Pietate, 11 (v. Arnim, II, 315, 3 ff.); (Zeus) πάσης ἐπώνυμος ὢν φύσεώς τε καὶ τύχης, ἅτε πάντων αὐτὸς αἴτιος ὤν, Ps.-Aristot. Mund., 7, p. 401a, 26 f. Philo more than once speaks of God as πατὴρ τοῦ παντός and the like, but he also makes the term πᾶς a logical symbol of perfection, e.g., τὸ κατὰ μέρος νοητὸν ἀτελὲς ὂν οὐ πᾶν, τὸ δὲ γενικὸν ἅπαν, ἅτε πλῆρες ὄν, Leg. All., I, 24; similar speculations concerning πᾶς are common in his works. [21]

In the mysteries, as in Gnosticism, there developed in connection with Greek-Hellen. philosophy a more or less consistent pantheism, e.g., ἕν ἐστι τὰ πάντα, καὶ μάλιστα [τὰ] νοητὰ σώματα, Corp. Herm., XII, 8; τοῦτο (τὸ θεῖον) γάρ ἐστι τὸ πᾶν, καὶ ἐξ αὐτοῦ τὸ πᾶν, καὶ δι' αὐτοῦ τὸ πᾶν, Zosimus Alchimista, IX, 1; [22] una quae es omnia dea Isis, CIL, X, 3800. These pantheistic trends are also found in hymnic predications. Cf. Ζεύς ἐστιν αἰθήρ, Ζεὺς δὲ γῆ, Ζεὺς δ' οὐρανός, Ζεύς τοι τὰ πάντα,

---

[17] Cf. G. Bertram, "Hbr. u. gr. Qoh. Ein Beitrag zur Theologie d. hell. Bibel," ZAW, 64 (1952), 26-49.

[18] πᾶς is common in the pre-Socratics, cf. Diels⁶, III, Index s.v. (337-341), where one may also find many instances of πᾶν and πάντα for universe.

[19] H. Diels, Doxographi Graeci (1879), 277.

[20] Ibid., 278.

[21] Leisegang, II, 633 f., s.v.

[22] M. Berthelot-C. E. Ruelle, Collection des anciens alchimistes grecs, Texte grec (1888), X, 143, 20 f.

Aesch. Fr., 70 (TGF, 24); Ζεῦ, φύσεως ἀρχηγέ, νόμου μέτα πάντα κυβερνῶν, χαῖρε· σὲ γὰρ πάντεσσι θέμις θνητοῖσι προσαυδᾶν ... σοὶ δὴ πᾶς ὅδε κόσμος ... πείθεται, Cleanthes' Hymn to Zeus, Fr. 537 (v. Arnim, I, 121, 35 f.; 122, 3 f.): ἐκ σέο γὰρ πάντ' ἐστὶ καὶ εἷς [σ'], αἰών[ι]ε, πάντα τελευτᾷ, Orphic hymn to Selene in the great Paris magic pap., Preis. Zaub., IV, 2838 f.; [23] cf. the Isis hymn of Kyme [24] and the Carpocrates hymn of Chalkis. [25] We have here doxologies and aretalogies such as are found also in the Orient and the OT (e.g., Ps. 104). For all their inspiration, however, they do not presuppose the strict monotheistic thinking of the OT but for the most part derive from an intentional juxtaposition of the worship of many gods. [26] To some degree the NT authors used similar doxologies to magnify God or Christ. Cf. the ἐξ αὐτοῦ καὶ δι' αὐτοῦ καὶ εἰς αὐτὸν τὰ πάντα of R. 11:36 with the ἐκ σοῦ (said of the cosmos) πάντα, ἐν σοὶ πάντα, εἰς σὲ πάντα of M. Ant., IV, 23. Both probably go back to the same Stoic and generally Hellen. formulations, and in this respect we should not forget pre-Pauline Jewish Hellenism. [27] But Paul's personal belief in God constitutes a decisive difference, so that the dependence is purely formal. How sharply the biblical writers drew the line against pantheism may be seen, e.g., from Sir. 43:1-33, esp. vv. 26 ff.: ἐν λόγῳ αὐτοῦ σύγκειται τὰ πάντα ... τὸ πᾶν ἐστιν αὐτὸς ... αὐτὸς γὰρ ὁ μέγας παρὰ πάντα τὰ ἔργα αὐτοῦ.

4. πᾶς in the NT.

a. In the NT as in the LXX it is striking how common πᾶς is. It occurs 1228 times, to which should be added 32 instances of ἅπας. [28] This shows a liking for the concept of totality. This inclination is in part objectively determined by the universality of the concept of God and the proclamation of redemption (→ 893, 38-896, 1), and in part subjectively by the joy of salvation (→ 896, 2-9). These reasons are, of course, very closely related. In content many points of agreement with the OT may be noted (→ 889, 47-890, 33). Similar thoughts about the creation and redemption of all things are also to be found, however, in the religious and philosophical literature of the contemporary non-biblical world (→ 892, 8-893, 18). On the other hand, the uniqueness of the NT view is that here all ideas of totality relate to a specific history of creation and salvation. As compared with the OT, the NT is distinguished especially by a richer soteriology. The oriental and Hellenistic systems of religious or philosophical cosmology and anthropology fall short of the NT concept of totality above all in respect of the historical and personal factors. In the NT there is no abstract interest in the foundations of existence such as we find in cosmological apocalyptic, mysticism, gnosis and philosophy. The interest of the NT focuses exclusively on the personal God and personal salvation.

b. 1 C. 8:6 states the basic NT position towards the universe. There is for us only one God, the Father, ἐξ οὗ τὰ πάντα καὶ ἡμεῖς εἰς αὐτόν, and one Lord, Jesus Christ, δι' οὗ τὰ πάντα καὶ ἡμεῖς δι' αὐτοῦ. All creation is God's work. Hence there is no independent power beside Him. In particular, there is no demiurge through whom the world is fundamentally evil. Nor is there any independent demonic power whom one must fear. Greek and Gnostic speculations inclined to a cleavage of deity along these lines. In contrast, Paul clings fast to the OT belief

---

[23] Cf. other Orphic hymns in W. Quandt, Orphei hymni (1941), 75, s.v. πᾶς.

[24] W. Peek, Der Isishymnus v. Andros u. verwandte Texte (1930), 122-125.

[25] R. Harder, "Karpokrates v. Chalkis u. d. memphitische Isispropaganda," AAB, 1943, Abh. 14 (1944), 8.

[26] Many of the texts cited here are taken from E. Norden, Agnostos Theos (1913), 240-250, 347-354; a few others were passed on by H. Kleinknecht.

[27] Norden, loc. cit.

[28] There may be some fluctuation in the figures acc. to textual variants.

in a personal Creator. Yet even when, as here, he emphasises God's role as universal Creator (cf. also R. 11:36; Eph. 3:9; 1 Tm. 6:13), his chief concern is not to advance an explanation of the world. Nor is his aim doxology, though the relevant statements contain doxological forms, acclamations and predications such as are to be found in the Orient, in the OT, and, *mutatis mutandis,* in Greek and Hellenistic syncretism, → 893, 6-18. Equally remote from the apostle is the pantheism to which Hellenistic mysticism was inclined, → 892, 40 ff. Precisely to the contrary, he stresses the fact that all creatures are dependent on God and that for this reason they must be subject to Him. God is above all creatures, R. 9:5. He gives them all life and breath and all things, and allows them to dwell on earth that they might seek Him, Ac. 17:25 ff. Hence in 1 C. 8:6 Paul says ἡμεῖς εἰς αὐτόν as well as ἐξ οὗ τὰ πάντα. We belong to God and should fear Him in order that the union with Him which was purposed in creation and restored in Christ may be realised individually. This does not mean for the cosmos the flowing out and back again of a quasi-divine substance, as in mysticism and Gnosticism. The reference here is to personal dependence, to the ordination of angels, men and all things to obedience and subjection. This is what is meant in R. 11:36: "For of him, and through him, and to him, are all things"; it should be remembered in this connection that Paul has just been speaking of the redemption of Israel. If formally such predications may perhaps be traced back to Greek traditions, in content they are in harmony with the personal and ethical concept of God found in the OT, e.g., at Is. 44:24: "I am the Lord who has made all things."

c. Even the NT transferring of the belief in the Creator to Christ goes back to the OT by way of Messianic interpretation. Thus in Ps. 8:6 it is said of the "son of man": "Thou madest him to have dominion over the works of thy hands: thou hast put all things under his feet." Furthermore, acc. to Prv. 8:22-31; Sir. 24:3-5, 9; Wis. 9:9, wisdom had a part in creation. Strictly, too, creation was by means of the word in Gn. 1:1 ff. Hence it was only a short step to the NT doctrine of Christ as the firstborn of creation, which was accomplished through Him alone. This theme occurs again in 1 C. 8:6 (→ 893, 38 ff.): δι' οὗ (Christ) τὰ πάντα καὶ ἡμεῖς δι' αὐτοῦ. The meaning is, not only that all things came into being through the Firstborn, but that all things are born anew through Him. The first creation in the Son points forward to the new creation in the Redeemer, and the original dependence of all things on the Son is thus a basis for his later seizure of power and for redemption in Him. This is how we are to construe other statements concerning the role of the Son in creation, e.g., Jn. 1:3: "All things were made by him (sc. the Logos)," or Col. 1:15-18: "The firstborn of all creation; in him were all things created, that are in heaven, and that are in earth ... all things were created by him, and for him; and he is before all things, and by him all things consist"; He is also "the firstborn from the dead, that in all things he himself might be the first" — the cosmogony is here organically related to the soteriology, the protology to the eschatology.

The universe, however, refuses to recognise its dependence on the Creator. This is especially true of man (R. 1:18-25), for the fall has clouded his judgment. Hence all the world is guilty before God (R. 3:19) and has fallen victim to vanity (R. 8:20). It sighs for redemption (8:22), but Scripture has concluded all under the bonds of sin (Gl. 3:22). The original unity and totality is destroyed by this blindness and disharmony, [29] which finds expression in idolatry (R. 1:18-23) and

---

[29] S. Hanson, *The Unity of the Church in the NT* (1946), 8-16, 25-27, 60-65.

which leads to sin, perversity, and the dominion of the flesh and the devil (R. 1:24-32; 7:7-23; Mt. 12:29 f. par. Lk. 11:21 ff.). The only way out of this situation is the victory of Christ and the reconciliation accomplished thereby (R. 7:24 f.; → καταλλάσσω, I, 255-259).

The incarnate Logos is invested with cosmic authority even here on earth, Jn. 3:35; 13:3: the Father has put all things in His hands; 17:2: He has given Him power over all flesh. The debated Mt. 11:27 par. Lk. 10:22 is probably to be understood along these lines: "All things are delivered unto me of my Father, and no man knoweth the Son ..."[30] Though the continuation speaks of knowledge, the "all things" obviously include more than knowledge. Hence the verse is to be construed, not along the lines of Jn. 21:17 or 1 C. 2:10, but along the lines of Jn. 3:35; 13:3; 17:2: "all power," which includes knowledge as well. Elsewhere, however, it is said of the Redeemer during His earthly life that He has laid aside His power and appeared in lowliness and humility, Mt. 11:29; 12:18-21; 2 C. 8:9; Phil. 2:5-8, → κενόω III, 661, 13-28, cf. the temptation of Jesus, Mt. 4:8 f. par. Lk. 4:5 f. Thus, when the full power of Jesus is occasionally mentioned during the time of His humiliation, it is merely a proleptic fact.

A new situation is brought into being with the crucifixion and resurrection. The Chosen One seizes the full power which He had from the beginning of the world, Mt. 28:18: "All power is given unto me in heaven and in earth." Cf. the proclamations of the heavenly King in Rev., e.g., concerning Alpha and Omega, → I, 1-3. Investiture with royal power is especially depicted by quotations from Ps. 8:6 and 110:1.[31] The chief point in the Epistles is that the risen Lord is exalted above all angelic beings, R. 8:38; Eph. 1:21; Phil. 2:9 ff.; Col. 2:10, 15; 1 Pt. 3:22. In Eph. and Col. this thought is combined with that of fulness (→ πλήρωμα) and recapitulation (→ ἀνακεφαλαιόομαι, III, 681 f.). This is here the cosmological aspect of reconciliation.

d. Since most men do not confess this principial power of Christ, mission is needed to actualise it in detail, → ἀποστέλλω, I, 403-406, 420-447; εὐαγγελίζομαι, II, 717 ff., 727 ff. The Church is also needed, → ἐκκλησία, III, 504-536. In this ecclesiological connection the word πᾶς has a special function. All flesh is to see salvation. Lk. 3:6. The house of Israel will do so first (Ac. 2:36), but then the whole world or all creation (Mk. 16:15; Col. 1:6, 23). In this way the original totality or fulness of Christ as decisive Head will be worked out in the Church as dependent body, so that He will be all in all (Eph. 1:22 f.; 3:19; 4:16; Col. 1:19 f.; 2:9 f., 19; 3:11),[32] all creatures in the universe will do homage to Him (Rev. 5:13), and He will finally present His all-embracing kingdom to the Father (1 C. 15:24). But this also means that all things will be made new, Rev. 21:5. Until then all creation is at the disposal of Christians so long as they use it only with pure and humble hearts: "All things are yours ..., the world, or life, or death, or things present, or things to come; all are yours; and ye are Christ's," 1 C. 3:21 ff.; "For every creature of

---

[30] Bibl. in Pr.-Bauer⁴, 1152.

[31] Mt. 22:44 par.; Ac. 2:34 f.; 1 C. 15:25 ff.; Eph. 1:20 ff.; Hb. 1:13; 2:8; 10:12 f. In many of these refs. there is emphasis on the "all."

[32] On Eph. and Col. cf. F. R. Montgomery-Hitchcock, "The Pleroma as the Medium of the Self-Realisation of Christ," Exp., VIII, 24 (1922), 135-150 (on Eph. 1:23); also "The Pleroma of Christ," *The Church Quarterly Review*, 125 (1937), 1-18; H. Schlier, *Christus u. d. Kirche im Eph.* = *Beiträge z. historischen Theol.*, 6 (1930), 55, n. 1; Hanson, *op. cit.*, 106-161; O. Perels, "Kirche u. Welt nach dem Epheser- u. Kolosserbrief," ThLZ, 76 (1951), 391-400, esp. 396 f.

God is good ... it is sanctified by the word of God and prayer, 1 Tm. 4:4 f. [33]

e. All NT proclamation is full of abounding joy at the universality of Christ. This is expressed by the common use of πᾶς, which is often found even when a critical view could not be quite satisfied at such an enthusiastic piling up of the term, e.g., Eph. 1:22 f.: πάντα ὑπέταξαν ... κεφαλὴν ὑπὲρ πάντα ... τὸ πλήρωμα τοῦ τὰ πάντα ἐν πᾶσιν πληρουμένου. This emotional exuberance, however, simply corresponds to the fact that in the first instance the Gospel means personal commitment. At the same time there is an OT model for this expressive mode of utterance in the prophets, Is. 2:2 etc.

f. On the other hand, not every appearance of πᾶς in the NT is in cosmological and soteriological contexts, nor is the word always controlled by the theme presented. There are many verses in which it simply corresponds to popular narrative style with the exaggeration still common to-day. A few examples should suffice. Thus we read of "all Jerusalem" in Mt. 2:3, "all Judaea" in Mt. 3:5, "all (ὅλη) Syria" and "all (πάντες) the sick" in Mt. 4:24. Here πᾶς is not to be taken strictly. It is simply a popular way of denoting a great number.

Reicke

| † πάσχα | → κλάω, III, 731-743. |

Contents : 1. The Feast of the Passover in the NT ; 2. The Passover Meal ; 3. Christ the Passover Lamb ; 4. The Passover in the Primitive Church.

πάσχα (indeclinable, neuter) [1] is a transcription of the Aram. אחספ, which is pronounced phasha. [2] Whereas LXX, Philo, NT, 'Α, Σ, Θ always have πάσχα, we

[33] On the creation theology of the NT (→ III, 868 f., 883-895, κόσμος, and III, 1000 f., 1028-1035, κτίζω) and its connection with Christology cf. J. Jeremias, "Jesus als Weltvollender," BFTh, 33, 4 (1930), 8-12, 64-69 etc.; M. Teschendorf, "Der Schöpfungsgedanke im NT. Zur Logosfrage," ThStKr, 104 (1932), 337-372; G. Bornkamm, *Gesetz u. Schöpfung im NT* = Sammlung gemeinverständlicher Vorträge, 175 (1934), 12-28; W. Gutbrod, "Die paul. Anthropologie," BWANT, IV, 15 (1934), 9-18; H. M. Biedermann, "Die Erlösung d. Schöpfung beim Apostel Pl.," Cassiciacum, 8 (1940), 49-104; R. Bultmann, "Das Verständnis v. Welt u. Mensch im NT u. im Griechentum," ThBl, 19 (1940), 1-14; E. Stauffer, *Die Theol. d. NT*[4] (1948), 34-46, 100-109, 120-123, 201-211; M. Meinertz, *Theol. d. NT*, II (1950), 67 f., 98, 307; Lindeskog, *op. cit.*, 163-272.

π ά σ χ α. E. Schwartz, "Osterbetrachtungen," ZNW, 7 (1906), 1-33; H. L. Strack, P°sahim = *Schriften d. Institutum Judaicum*, 40 (1911); G. Beer, Pesachim = *Giess. Mischna*, ed. G. Beer and O. Holtzmann, II, 3 (1912); G. Dalman, *Jesus-Jeschua* (1922), 80-166; Str.-B., I, 985, 987 ff.; II, 812, n. 1; IV, 41-76; H. Laible, "Die drei Sprachen Jesu," ThLBl, 44 (1923), 115 f.; K. Holl, "Ein Bruchstück aus einem bisher unbekannten Brief d. Epiph.," *Festgabe f. A. Jülicher* (1927), 159-189 (= Gesammelte Aufsätze, II [1928], 204-224, from which it is quoted here); Moore, II, 40-43; I. Elbogen, "Die Feier d. drei Wallfahrtsfeste im zweiten Tempel," *46. Bericht d. Hochschule f. d. Wissenschaft des Judts.* (1929), 25-48; J. Jeremias, "Die Passahfeier d. Samaritaner," ZAW Beih. 59 (1932); O. Casel, "Art u. Sinn d. ältesten chr. Osterfeier," *Jbch. f. Liturgiewissenschaft*, 14 (1938), 1-78; F. Bussby, "A Note on πάσχα in the Synoptic Gospels," Exp. T., 59 (1948), 194 f.; J. Jeremias, *Die Abendmahlsworte Jesu*[2] (1949); P. J. Heawood, "The Time of the Last Supper," JQR, 42 (1951), 37-44; H. Schürmann, "Die Anfänge chr. Osterfeier," *Theol. Quartalschrift*, 131 (1951), 414-425 ; B. Lohse, *Das Passafest d. Quartadecimaner*, Diss. Göttingen (1952).

[1] Bl.-Debr.[7, 8] § 58. πάσχα is always neut. except in Jos.: διαδέχεται τὴν πάσχα (sc. ἑορτὴν) ἡ τῶν ἀζύμων ἑορτή, Ant., 3, 249; τὴν φάσχα (sc. ἑορτὴν) ἑώρταζον, Ant., 5, 20 [Debrunner].

[2] On pronunciation in Aram.: 1. Witness to the breathing with the initial פ is to be found in Jos. Ant., 5, 20; 9, 271; 14, 21 vl.; 17, 213; Bell., 2, 10 (φάσκα) and this is confirmed by the consistent transcription of the Heb. חספ by φασεκ/φασεχ (LXX 18 times in 2 Ch. 30, 35 and 'Ιερ. 38[31]:8; Philo Leg. All., III, 94; 'Α Jos. 5:10; Σ Ex. 12:11, 27;

occasionally find φάσκα (→ n. 2) in Joseph.; both forms arose through dissimilation of the impossible Gk. sequence φ-χ to either φ-κ (φάσκα) or π-χ (πάσχα),[3] and so they point us back to phasḥa as the underlying Aram. pronunciation. The Gk. pronunciation πάσχα, already current in the Synagogue at the time of the LXX,[4] is not then an irregular assimilation to πάσχειν.[5] The Aram. פסחא (unlike the Heb. פסח) should not be reproduced with a final h in German.[6]

In the NT τὸ πάσχα denotes a. the (seven-day) Jewish feast of the Passover. b. Only rarely does it have a narrower sense and on the basis of OT usage denote the actual Passover (held on the night of the 15th Nisan).[7] c. As in the OT it may then be used for the Passover lamb slain at mid-day on the 14th Nisan in the forecourt of the temple at Jerusalem and then eaten after sundown.[8] d. In Christian usage Easter is called πάσχα,[9] and figuratively (from the time of Lk. 22:15 f.) the term can also be used for the "eschatological banquet," (from the time of Marcion) for the "Lord's Supper,"[10] and (from the time of Dg.) for the parousia.[11] The discussion which follows is based on these four senses.

Nu. 9:2; Jos. 5:10) or φεσε ('A Dt. 16:1) and by phase (vg). This breathing is not a "dialectical variation" (Bussby, 195) but is regular, since Pal. Aram. in the time of Jesus (apart from a few loan words) does not have p even at the beginning of a syllable (K. Siegfried, "Die Aussprache d. Hebräischen bei Hier.," ZAW, 4 [1884], 63; Dalman Gr., 67 f.; Ges.-K.[29], 39 f.; Laible, 115; F. Diening, Das Hebräische bei d. Samaritanern = Bonner Orient. Studien, 24 [1938], 15; P. Kahle, The Cairo Geniza [1947], 103). 2. The vocalisation with i (פיסחא) in jTalmud, Tg. and Midr. is shown to be late by LXX, Philo, NT, Joseph. (πάσχα), cf. Jeremias, Abendmahlsworte, 10, n. 1.
[3] Bl.-Debr.[7, 8] § 39, 2 and 3 with App.
[4] [Debrunner].
[5] Dalman Gr., 138, n. 2; Laible, 115.
[6] O. Procksch, "Passa u. Abendmahl," Vom Sakrament des Altars, ed. H. Sasse (1941), 11, n. 1.
[7] In the NT only Mk. 14:1: ἦν δὲ τὸ πάσχα καὶ τὰ ἄζυμα μετὰ δύο ἡμέρας and the phrase ποιεῖν τὸ πάσχα, "to keep the passover," at Mt. 26:18; Hb. 11:28; with an OT basis (LXX Ex. 12:48; Nu. 9:2-14; Dt. 16:1; Jos. 5:10; 4 Βασ. 23:21; 2 Ch. 30:1, 2, 5; 35:1, 16-18; 1 Ἐσδρ. 1:6; 2 Ἐσδρ. 6:19; Rabb. examples in Schl. Mt., 739). In Judaism, too, this OT use is rare. 1 Ἐσδρ. 1:17: καὶ ἠγάγοσαν ... τὸ πασχα καὶ τὴν ἑορτὴν τῶν ἀζύμων ἡμέρας ἑπτά, Jub. 49:1, 22; constantly in Philo : Spec. Leg., II, 149, cf. 145; Vit. Mos., II, 224; Decal., 159 etc.; in Joseph. only when he reproduces biblical statements, Ant., 3, 249 : πέμπτη δὲ καὶ δεκάτη διαδέχεται τὴν πάσχα ἡ τῶν ἀζύμων ἑορτὴ ἑπτὰ ἡμέρας οὖσα, 2, 312 f. (Heawood, 40 f.). Except in the Tg. (Str.-B., I, 988c) there seem to be no Rabb. examples (ibid., 985). πάσχα can include the 14th Nisan, as in Philo Spec. Leg., II, 145 : the sacrifice of lambs at the Passover.
[8] τὸ πάσχα θύειν, "to slay the paschal lamb," Mk. 14:12; Lk. 22:7; 1 C. 5:7; cf. LXX Ex. 12:21; Dt. 16:2, 5 f.; 2 Ch. 30:15, 17; 35:1, 6, 11; 1 Ἐσδρ. 1:1, 6; 7:12; Philo Leg. All., III, 165; Jos. Ant., 3, 248; 9, 271. ἑτοιμάζειν τὸ πάσχα, "to prepare the paschal lamb," Mk. 14:16; Mt. 26:19; Lk. 22:8, 13, cf. LXX 2 Ch. 35:6, 14 f. (ἑτοιμάζειν = הֵכִין, said of the paschal lamb). φαγεῖν τὸ πάσχα, "to eat the paschal lamb," Mk. 14:12, 14; Mt. 26:17; Lk. 22:8, 11, 15; Jn. 18:28, cf. LXX 2 Ch. 30:18; 2 Ἐσδρ. 6:21; Philo Rer. Div. Her., 255.
[9] → n. 43.
[10] Epiph. Haer., 42, 11, 15 (GCS, 31, 149, 8 f.) opposes Marcion : καὶ μὴ λέγε ὅτι ὃ ἔμελλε μυστήριον (= the Lord's Supper) ἐπιτελεῖν, τοῦτο προωνόμαζε λέγων· θέλω μεθ' ὑμῶν φαγεῖν τὸ Πάσχα (Lk. 22:15), cf. Zn. Lk. on 22:15. Ep. Apostolorum, 15 Eth. (cf. H. Duensing, Kl. T., 152 [1925], p. 14) speaks of "drinking the passover" (though only in the Eth. text). [Orig. in Mt. Comm., 79 (GCS, 38, 189, 28): celebramus pascha (= the Lord's Supper) Christo nobiscum coëpulante ; In Jer. Hom., 19, 13 (GCS, 6, 169, 31): ἵνα ἑορτάσῃς τὸ πάσχα. J. Betz.] Eus. Περὶ τῆς τοῦ Πάσχα ἑορτῆς, 7 (MPG, 24, 701 n.): ἡμεῖς (in distinction from the Jews who killed the paschal lamb only once a year) ... ἐφ' ἑκάστης Κυριακῆς ἡμέρας τὸ ἑαυτῶν Πάσχα τελοῦντες.
[11] Dg., 12, 9 : τὸ κυρίου πάσχα προέρχεται, "the Lord's Passover draws on". (c. 11 f. were added later and belong to the late 2nd [Melito of Sardis ?] or early 3rd cent. [Hippolyt. of Rome ?]).

1. The Feast of the Passover in the NT.

The Passover feast [12] derives from the nomadic days of Israel. [13] A yearling lamb of the sheep or goats (Ex. 12:5) was slain by the head of the house at sundown on the 14th Nisan (12:6). Its blood was sprinkled on the entrance to the tent, and after the settlement on the doorposts and lintel of the house (12:7, 22-27). The flesh was roasted and eaten by the family during the night of the 14th-15th Nisan (12:8 f.). Only in Canaan did the Passover merge into the seven-day Mazzot feast (on this → II, 902, 8-17). After the cultic reforms of Josiah (621 B.C.) the killing and eating of the Passover took place in Jerusalem, Dt. 16:5-7; 2 K. 23:21-23; 2 Ch. 35:1. The blood was now sprinkled, not on the entrance to the house, but on the altar of burnt offering, 2 Ch. 35:11; Jub. 49:20; Pes., 5, 6. The removal of the feast to Jerusalem, which took place only gradually, [14] resulted in the feast becoming a pilgrimage. The basic features of the liturgy used during the meal (Pes., 10, 2 ff.; → 899, 14-16; 900, 14 f.) were already emerging during the pre-Christian period. [15]

Whereas the OT distinguishes between the Passover, which was celebrated on the night of the 14th-15th Nisan, and the feast of unleavened bread, held from the 15th to the 21st Nisan, [16] in later Judaism the two were popularly combined and "passover" was generally used for both. [17] This is the predominant usage in the NT (Lk. 22:1: ἤγγιζεν δὲ ἡ ἑορτὴ τῶν ἀζύμων ἡ λεγομένη πάσχα, cf. also Mt. 26:2; Lk. 2:41; Jn. 2:13, 23; 6:4; 11:55 [twice]; 12:1; 13:1; 18:39; 19:14; Ac. 12:4). The feast was one of the three pilgrimages [18] and as such was a high point of the year. With its recollection of the deliverance from Egypt it awakened national feelings and hope of the coming redemption. [19]

The Passover of the exodus from Egypt, with which Moses established the feast as a permanent institution, [20] is mentioned in Hb. 11:28. This first observance of the rites is for Hb. a demonstration of the faith of Moses, because he showed thereby how firmly he believed the promise that God would spare the firstborn of Israel for the sake of the paschal blood. [21]

---

[12] On the history of the Passover cf. H. Guthe, "Das Passahfest nach Dt. 16," *Abhandlungen zur semitischen Religionskunde u. Sprachwissenschaft* = ZAW Beih., 33 (1918), 217-232; also "Zum Passah d. jüd. Religionsgemeinde," ThStKr, 96/97 (1925), 144-171; N. M. Nicolsky, "Pascha im Kulte d. jerusalemischen Tempels," ZAW, 45 (1927), 171-190, 241-253; Jeremias, *Passahfeier*, 53-106; J. Pedersen, "Passahfest u. Passahlegende," ZAW, 52 (1934), 161-175.

[13] L. Rost, "Weidewechsel u. altisraelitischer Festkalender," ZDPV, 66 (1943), 205-216, conjectures that the Passover was originally kept on the departure for new pastures at the beginning of the dry season. Up to the present day the Samaritans have preserved nomadic techniques in the preparation of paschal lambs, Jeremias, *op. cit.,* 93, also Ill. 29-44.

[14] Jeremias, *op. cit.,* 67-72.

[15] Jeremias, *Abendmahlsworte,* 48 f.

[16] Lv. 23:5 f.; Nu. 28:16 f.; Ez. 45:21 conjecture ; 2 Ch. 35:1, 17; Ezr. 6:19-22.

[17] Jos. Ant., 14, 21: κατὰ τὸν καιρὸν τῆς τῶν ἀζύμων ἑορτῆς, ἣν πάσχα λέγομεν, 17, 213; 18, 29; 20, 106; Bell., 2, 10. Pes., 9, 5 : פֶּסַח דּוֹרוֹת נוֹהֵג כָּל־שִׁבְעָה, "the passover of (later) generations will be celebrated for seven days" (as distinct from the Egypt. Passover); Chag., 1, 3 : the 15th Nisan is יוֹם טוֹב הָרִאשׁוֹן שֶׁל פֶּסַח; for other Rabb. passages cf. Str.-B., I, 985.

[18] With Pentecost and Tabernacles.

[19] Jeremias, *Abendmahlsworte,* 101, 124, n. 1.

[20] πεποίηκεν τὸ πάσχα in Hb. 11:28 is a perf. of effect on the object, Bl.-Debr.[7, 8] § 342, 4. On ποιεῖν τὸ πάσχα → n. 7.

[21] πίστει πεποίηκεν τὸ πάσχα καὶ τὴν πρόσχυσιν τοῦ αἵματος, ἵνα μὴ ὁ ὀλεθρεύων τὰ πρωτότοκα θίγῃ αὐτῶν. The phrase ἡ πρόσχυσις τοῦ αἵματος, "pouring out the blood," does not fit in with the smearing of the doorposts and lintel at the exodus (Ex. 12:7). It is explained by the later rite. After the centralisation at Jerusalem the blood of the paschal lamb was sprinkled on the base of the altar in the temple, → *supra* and cf. Rgg. Hb., 374, n. 68.

In the Gospels the Passover is the setting of several stories. The boy Jesus visits the temple during the Passover pilgrimage, Lk. 2:41-51. Underlying the feeding of the multitude (Mk. 6:32-44 and par.; 8:1-9 and par.) there probably lies a meeting between Jesus and a procession of Galilean pilgrims. [22] The violence exerted by Pilate against Galilean visitors to the temple (Lk. 13:1-3) took place on the occasion of one of the three pilgrimages, [23] probably the Passover. In particular, the background of the Passover is essential for an understanding of the passion narrative. [24] Finally, it was during the Passover that both James the son of Zebedee (Ac. 12:1-4, 44 A.D.) and James the Lord's brother [25] suffered martyrdom in Jerusalem. [26]

2. The Passover Meal.

The Passover meal, which in distinction from ordinary meals began only after sunset and lasted long into the night, had to be eaten within the walls of Jerusalem. It was enframed in a liturgy whose core was the Passover prayer of the head of the house and the recitation of the Hallel (Ps. 113-118; cf. Mk. 14:26 par. Mt. 26:30 : ὑμνήσαντες), → III, 732 f. [27] As to the important question whether the Last Supper was a Passover meal the Gospels do not give consistent information. The Synoptists say that it was (Mk. 14:12-16 and par.; Lk. 22:15), but Jn. seems to place the Last Supper on the night of 13th-14th Nisan, 18:28, cf. 19:14.

In Jn. 18:28 it is said of the Jewish accusers of Jesus : καὶ αὐτοὶ οὐκ εἰσῆλθον εἰς τὸ πραιτώριον, ἵνα μὴ μιανθῶσιν ἀλλὰ φάγωσιν τὸ πάσχα. Since φαγεῖν τὸ πάσχα is a fixed term (→ n. 8) for eating the paschal lamb, this had still to be eaten early on Good Friday. Attempts have been made to avoid discrepancy with the Synoptic chronology by saying that φαγεῖν τὸ πάσχα, on the basis of 2 Ch. 30:22, means "celebrating the (seven-day) Passover-Mazzot feast," [28] or that, on the basis of Talmudic statements, it means "eating the festive offerings." [29] But in 2 Ch. 30:22 the reading וַיֹּאכְלוּ is corrupt (cf. LXX συνετέλεσαν = וַיְכַלּוּ), while the use of פֶּסַח for the paschal offerings (חֲגִיגָה) made during the whole feast is isolated and unmistakable in the context, [30] so that the reader of Jn. would hardly glean this from the simple text of Jn. 18:28. [31] One has thus to acknowledge the difficulty posed by the Johannine and Synoptic datings.

The objections which on the basis of the Rabb. Halaka are raised against the Synoptic identification of the Last Supper with the Passover are for the most part

---

[22] Cf. Jn. 6:4 : ἦν δὲ ἐγγὺς τὸ πάσχα. In keeping is the fact that the χλωρὸς χόρτος of Mk. 6:39 indicates spring.

[23] The procurator, who resided in Caesarea Maris, came to Jerusalem only for the great feasts except for special reasons such as taking office (Ac. 25:1), cf. Schürer, I, 457 f.; Schl. Gesch. Isr., 278; F. M. Abel, Histoire de la Palestine, I (1952), 425; P. Benoit, "Prétoire, Lithostraton et Gabbatha," Rev. Bibl., 59 (1952), 540.

[24] Jn. 2:13-22 incorrectly (or due to confusion of pages ?) puts the cleansing of the temple during an earlier Passover, so that there are three Passovers in Jn. (1. Jn. 2:13, 23; 2. 6:4; 3. 11:55; 12:1; 13:1; 18:28, 39; 19:14).

[25] Hegesipp. in Eus. Hist. Eccl., II, 23, 10-18 (GCS, 9, 168 ff.): c. 62 A.D.

[26] Passovers are also mentioned in Ac. 20:6 and 1 C. 5:8 (ἑορτάζωμεν).

[27] On the rite at the meal cf. Strack ; Beer ; Dalman, 98-166; Jeremias, Passahfeier ; Abendmahlsworte, 47-49.

[28] So, e.g., Zahn Einl.[3], II (1907), 523, 534-536; Zn. J., 631-633; C. C. Torrey, "The Date of the Crucifixion acc. to the Fourth Gospel," JBL, 50 (1931), 239 f.

[29] So J. Lightfoot, Opera omnia, II (1686), 670 f.; C. Schoettgen, Horae hebraicae et talmudicae (1733), 400 f.; C. C. Torrey, op. cit., 237-239; also "In the Fourth Gospel the Last Supper was the Paschal Meal," JQR, 42 (1951/52), 242 ff.

[30] Str.-B., II, 837 f.

[31] Dalman, 81 f.; Str.-B., II, 837-840; Jeremias, Abendmahlsworte, 13. Further bibl. → II, 693, n. 31.

founded on erroneous presuppositions. [32] The main argument is that condemnation of Jesus by the Sanhedrin on the night of the Passover would be against the prohibition of capital trials on feast days. [33] To this, however, one may reply that in Dt. 17:13 (par. 13:12; 21:21) the Torah ordains that in the case of particularly serious offences, among which the Halaka numbers false prophecy, the execution should serve as a deterrent and hence "all Israel should hear it," which in Rabb. exegesis is taken to mean that it should be on one of the pilgrimage feasts. [34] To carry out this provision in the case of Jesus it was thus necessary that He should be condemned immediately after arrest. [35] At the same time a whole series of points incidentally mentioned in the narratives both in the Synoptic Gospels and Jn. display the paschal character of the Last Supper. [36] For instance, the unusual circumstance that Jesus clothes His words and gift in the form of an interpretation of bread and wine can hardly be explained except in terms of the Passover ritual. The interpretation of detailed elements in the meal [37] is a fixed part of the Passover liturgy conducted by the head of the house. If the Last Supper is advanced 24 hours in Jn., this is perhaps due to the widespread comparison of Jesus with the paschal lamb (→ infra), which led to a fixing of the death of Jesus at the same time as the slaying of the lambs during the afternoon of the 14th Nisan.

3. Christ the Passover Lamb.

The casual way in which Paul says : τὸ πάσχα (→ n. 8) ἡμῶν ἐτύθη Χριστός, 1 C. 5:7, suggests that this comparison was already familiar to the Corinthian church. [38] It is indeed common in the NT (1 Pt. 1:19; Jn. 1:29, 36; → I, 338-340; cf. Rev. 5:6, 9, 12; 12:11) and probably goes back to Jesus Himself, for, since σῶμα/αἷμα = בִּשְׂרָא/דְּמָא [39] are, like ἐκχύννεσθαι, sacrificial terms, one may conclude that in the sayings at the Lord's Supper (Mk. 14:22-24 and par.) Jesus was comparing Himself with the paschal lamb, and calling His death a sacrifice. [40] This comparison is the core of a rich Passover typology in the primitive Church. This is found in three forms. a. In Lk. 22:16 (ἕως ὅτου πληρωθῇ ἐν τῇ βασιλείᾳ τοῦ θεοῦ) Jesus calls the banquet of the age of salvation a fulfilment of the

[32] Dalman, 86-98; Str.-B., II, 815-834; Jeremias, Abendmahlsworte, 34-44, esp. 42-44.
[33] Yom ṭobh, 5, 2; T. Yom ṭobh, 4, 4 (207, 15); Philo Migr. Abr., 91; cf. Str.-B., II, 815-820 and Ac. 12:4.
[34] T. Sanh., 11, 7 (432, 1-3); Jeremias, op. cit., 44.
[35] That Jesus was condemned by the council as a false prophet may be seen from the nature of the mockery after condemnation (Mk. 14:65 par.: προφήτευσον).
[36] → III, 732-734; Jeremias, op. cit., 18-34.
[37] E.g., the lamb, unleavened bread, bitter herbs.
[38] Joh. W. 1 K., ad loc.
[39] J. Bonsirven, "Hoc est corpus meum," Biblica, 29 (1948), 205-219; Jeremias, op. cit., 103-106.
[40] R. H. Kennett, The Last Supper, its Significance in the Upper Room (1921), 38; A. Schweitzer, Die Mystik d. Ap. Pls. (1930), 245; W. Niesel, "Vom heiligen Abendmahl Jesu Christi," Abendmahlsgemeinschaft? (1937), 47; I. Zolli, Il Nazareno (1938), 232; O. Procksch, "Passa u. Abendmahl," Vom Sakrament d. Altars, ed. H. Sasse (1941), 24; H. Sasse, "Das Abendmahl im NT," ibid., 44, 70, 75; A. Oepke, "Jesus u. d. Gottesvolkgedanke," Luthertum, 53 (1942), 49; M. Barth, Das Abendmahl, Passamahl, Bundesmahl u. Messiasmahl (1945), 13; F. J. Leenhardt, Le sacrement de la Sainte Cène (1948), 31, 37; R. Stählin, "Die nt.liche Lehre vom Heiligen Abendmahl," Evangelisch-lutherische Kirchenzeitung, 2 (1948), 62; Jeremias, Abendmahlsworte, 105; G. Walther, Jesus, das Passalamm des Neuen Bundes (1950), 38-91; A. J. B. Higgins, The Lord's Supper in the NT (1952), 49 ff. It should be noted that the Passover liturgy was pronounced by Jesus as head of the house prior to the words of interpretation, which were spoken at the prayer before and after the main meal. This liturgy included an interpretation of the paschal lamb, → 900, 14 f. and n. 37. The disciples were thus prepared for the comparison in the eucharistic sayings.

Passover. b. In 1 C. 5:7 f. the community for which Christ was sacrificed as the paschal lamb is called the unleavened dough. This expresses the fact that to be in Christ is to be already in the fulfilled Passover.[41] c. In 1 Pt. 1:13-21 the baptised are compared to the people of God which, redeemed by the blood of the lamb without spot or blemish (v. 18 f.),[42] sets forth on its pilgrimage (v. 17) with loins girded (v. 13). In both 1 C. and 1 Pt. the typology is set in the service of admonition, to the purifying of the congregation and the heart on the one side, to sanctification and walking in fear on the other.

4. The Passover in the Primitive Church.

Rather oddly, the Church took over only two of the great feasts in the Jewish calendar, namely, the Passover and Pentecost, but not Tabernacles. In distinction from Pentecost (→ πεντηκοστή), Easter was given the Aram. title found also in the Jewish dispersion.[43] The oldest accounts of a Christian Paschal feast take us back to the apostolic period.[44] The NT tells us nothing about the details, but the gaps may be filled in from accounts of the Quartodecimans,[45] since their Easter, as we now know, was a direct continuation of that of the primitive Church.[46]

[41] Behind this there probably stands a primitive Christian Passover liturgy, → II, 903, 12 f., cf. Jeremias, op. cit., 32 f.

[42] 1 Pt. 1:18 : ἐλυτρώθητε; in Ex. the same verb denotes the redemption out of Egypt (LXX Ex. 15:13; cf. Dt. 7:8); cf. J. Daniélou, Sacramentum Futuri (1950), 141, who pts. out that there is a continuation of Ex. typology in what follows : 1 Pt. 2:4 (the rock which gives water), 9 (quotation from Ex. 19:5 f.).

[43] Jn. 2:13; 6:4; 11:55 : τὸ πάσχα (6:4 + ἡ ἑορτὴ) τῶν Ἰουδαίων, obviously distinguishes the Jewish Passover from the Christian; Ep. Apostolorum, 15 (middle of the 2nd cent.); Melito of Sardis, Περὶ τοῦ πάσχα Fr. (quoted in Eus. Hist. Eccl., IV, 26, 3 [GCS, 9, 382, 13]), Polycrates of Ephesus (quoted Eus. Hist. Eccl., V, 24, 6), → n. 44. At the first it would seem that the title "Feast of Unleavened Bread" was also kept, cf. Ac. 12:3; 20:6 : αἱ ἡμέραι τῶν ἀζύμων. This Jewish title is striking in so Hell. a work as Ac. (cf. Jackson-Lake, I, 4 [1933] on Ac. 20:6) and presupposes that it was in use in the Gentile congregations.

[44] Acc. to Iren. (quoted in Eus. Hist. Eccl., V, 24, 16 [GCS, 9, 496, 10-13]) Polycarp of Smyrna affirmed that he had personally celebrated the Paschal feast with Jn. and other apostles; cf. also Polycrates of Eph. (after 190) in his letter to Victor of Rome (Eus. Hist. Eccl., V, 24, 2-7 [GCS, 9, 490 ff.]), who maintained that Jn. and Philip celebrated the feast in Asia Minor. That the Ebionites kept it as an annual feast may be seen from Epiph. Haer., 30, 16, 1 → n. 54; cf. Casel, 6, n. 8. Even in the NT one can find traces of a Christian festival, cf. Ac. 20:6 (→ n. 43); 1 C. 5:7 f. (→ n. 41); Jn. 2:13; 6:4; 11:55 (→ n. 43); Schürmann, 420-425 (though what he says about the Quartodecimans [414-420] stands in need of correction).

[45] The most important sources for a Quartodeciman Passover are Eus. Hist. Eccl., V, 23-25 (GCS, 9, 488-498); Ep. Apostolorum (→ n. 10), 15 Copt. par. Eth.; Epiph. Haer., 50, 70 (GCS, 31, 244-248; 37, 232-249). The basic account of Eus. is valuable because he gives the documents relating to the Easter controversy; his own comments should be read critically, cf. N. Zernov, "Eusebius and the Paschal Controversy at the End of the Second Century," Church Quarterly Review, 116 (1933), 24-41; Lohse, passim, esp. 81-83. Bibl.: W. Bauer, Das Leben Jesu im Zeitalter d. nt.lichen Apkr. (1909), 158-163; Schwartz; Holl; H. Lietzmann, Gesch. d. Alten Kirche, II (1936), 129-132; for a good review of the lit. cf. Lohse, 9-19; 88-96. Right up to our own day research into the Quartodeciman Paschal feast has been confused by erroneous views as to the terms, → n. 53.

[46] Schwartz, 10 f.; Holl, 214; Lohse, 53-67. The accounts of Iren. and Polycrates (→ n. 44) agree that the ap. Jn. kept the Passover in Asia Minor acc. to the Quartodeciman custom. The Quartodecimans also claimed that they had received their rite from the primitive Church; they appealed to Jn. as sponsor for their tradition. The keeping of the Jewish term and the connections between their rite and the Passover (→ n. 54) show that this was a justifiable claim. "The principle for which Asia Minor later fought so passionately, namely, that Easter should be celebrated with the Jews, could only have arisen in the primitive community," Holl, 214.

The paschal feast thus took place in the primitive Church at the same time as the Jewish Passover, that is, on the night of the 15th Nisan, and by the date rather than the day. The feast had, however, a very different character from the Jewish Passover, though without denying its derivation from this. If Judaism was already awaiting the coming of the Messiah on the Passover night, [47] expectation of the *parousia* lay at the heart of the primitive Christian festival, [48] and this soon came to have a profound effect on its course. It is true that at first the Jerusalem church seems to have taken part in the slaying of the Passover lamb, [49] but later — unfortunately we do not know exactly when [50] — the festival was radically reconstructed, and the paschal vigil replaced the Passover meal. The accompanying fast, which ancient traditions call a vicarious fast for Israel, [51] originally prepared the community to receive its *Kurios*. During the fast, the story of the exodus (Ex. 12) was read and expounded typologically, with particular emphasis on the fact that the lamb points to Christ. [52] At cock-crow the fast was broken by the celebration of the sacred meal which unites the community with the Lord. [53] Hence the original Christian Easter, as we have come to know and deduce it from Quartodeciman sources, shared with the Jewish Passover not only the time and details

---

[47] For examples cf. Jeremias, *op. cit.,* 101.

[48] → n. 53. It is the merit of Lohse's work (45-52, cf. 63-66) to have made this likely and thus to have dispelled a host of erroneous ideas concerning the Quartodecimans and the paschal feast of the primitive Church. Hier. Comm. in Mt., IV on 25:6 (MPL, 26, 184 f.) still calls it an apostolic tradition *ut in die vigiliarum Paschae ante noctis dimidium populos dimittere non liceat, exspectantes adventum Christi.*

[49] This is supported by an interpretation of the Passover lamb which goes back to before the destruction of the temple and which Just. attributes to Ezra, though it is in fact Chr.: τοῦτο τὸ πάσχα ὁ σωτὴρ ἡμῶν καὶ ἡ καταφυγὴ ἡμῶν, Just. Dial., 72, 1. The words presuppose that the speaker had the lamb in front of him and was expounding it in the framework of the Passover haggada, cf. A. Schlatter, "Die Kirche Jerusalems vom Jahre 70-130," BFTh, 2, 3 (1898), 77.

[50] At the latest the destruction of the temple in 70 A.D., for the Chr. fast reaches back as far as we can follow Easter, K. Holl, "Die Schriften d. Epiph. gg. die Bilderverehrung," *Gesammelte Aufsätze,* II (1928), 374; it is possible that Mk. 2:20 : τότε νηστεύσουσιν ἐν ἐκείνῃ τῇ ἡμέρᾳ, has the paschal fast in view.

[51] Epiph. Haer., 70, 11, 3 (GCS, 37, 244, 9 ff.): "When they (the Jews) feast, we should mourn for them with fasting," cf. also Didasc., ed. H. Achelis-J. Flemming, TU, NF, 10, 2 (1904), p. 114, 10-14; Const. Ap., V, 13, 3 f.; Schwartz, 18; Holl, 210 f.; Lohse, 36-39. This interpretation is Jewish Christian and thus ancient.

[52] This may be seen from the newly discovered (edited 1940) paschal homily of the Quartodecimam bishop Melito of Sardis, cf. *The Homily on the Passion by Melito Bishop of Sardis,* ed. C. Bonner, *Studies and Documents,* 12 (1940); Lohse, 44 f. Cf. already 1 C. 5:7, → n. 41. The opening sentence of Melito's homily : ἡ μὲν γραφὴ τῆς Ἑβραϊκῆς ἐξόδου ἀνέγνωσται, καὶ τὰ ῥήματα τοῦ μυστηρίου διασεσάφηται, probably refers to the reading of the original of Ex. 12 and its transl. into Gk., cf. G. Zuntz, "On the Opening Sentence of Melito's Paschal Homily," HThR, 36 (1943), 299; T. W. Manson, *Dominican Studies,* 2 (1949), 191 f.

[53] Ep. Apostolorum (→ n. 10), 15. The constantly recurring assertion in works on the Quartodecimans that they broke the fast at the third hour on the afternoon of the 14th Nisan (the hour of the death of Jesus acc. to Jn.) is a product of mid-nineteenth cent. fantasy for which there is no support in the sources, Lohse, 24. More momentous than the assertion itself were its results, for it was deduced that the Quartodecimans championed the Johannine chronology of the passion and that their paschal feast was originally remembrance of the passion. As against this the Ep. Apostolorum (ed. C. Schmidt, TU, 43) proves that in fact the fast was broken at cock-crow on the morning of the 15th Nisan (so correctly Lietzmann, 130; Casel, 5), and this time shows that the original Quartodeciman feast was not, like that of the 2nd cent., a remembrance of the passion but expectation of the *parousia* (in the early Church the resurrection was not an annual festival but was celebrated each Sunday, cf. O. Cullmann, *Urchr. u. Gottesdienst*[2] [1950], 14). Thus the Quartodecimans did not espouse the Johann. chronology of the passion. On the contrary, in so far as they took sides, they supported the Synoptic dating, cf. Bauer, 160 f.

of the rite [54] but also expectation of the Messiah. The difference is that for it expectation of the *parousia* gave the feast its true meaning, so that very early a fast concluding with the eucharist replaced the Passover meal. A pt. of particular importance is that this primitive paschal celebration shows how strongly expectation of the *parousia* controlled the life of the Church in the earliest period.

Later in the 2nd cent. the course of the Chr. feast was everywhere changed in essence. [55] Lights were now solemnly kindled at the commencement. [56] Baptism preceded the breaking of the fast at cock-crow. [57, 58] Leavened bread had long since replaced unleavened. [59] Though the rite itself had been subjected to only minor deviations and developments in the 2nd cent., it was a more serious matter that the feast had been given a new meaning. Even among the Quartodecimans [60] it was generally related to recollection of the passion; [61] in favour of this appeal was made to the (etym. erroneous) derivation of πάσχα from πάσχειν. [62]

If there was general agreement in the Church as to the course and meaning of the paschal feast, differences developed regarding its date. In Asia, and partly also in Rome, Cilicia, Syria and Mesopotamia, [63] the Church kept to the primitive custom and observed the paschal fast on the night of 15th Nisan at the same time as the Jewish Passover. Elsewhere in the East, however, other days were kept (→ n. 66), and in Rome, Palestine, Egypt, Greece, Pontus, Gaul etc. the feast was held on the night of the Sunday following the Jewish Passover. [64] The first assured ref. to a Sunday Easter is in 155 A.D., [65] but it was probably much older than this. [66] The difference in date led c. 190 to the

---

[54] E.g., reading the story of the exodus, → 902, 11 f. Acc. to 1 C. 5:8 unleavened bread also seems to have been used at the Lord's Supper on the Passover night, H. Lietzmann, *Messe u. Herrenmahl* (1926), 211, n. 1: "an ancient Jewish Chr. custom." The ancient practice was kept up by the Ebionites, who used unleavened cakes each year at the paschal eucharist, cf. Epiph. Haer., 30, 16, 1 (GCS, 25, 353, 10-12): μυστήρια δὲ δῆθεν τελοῦσι κατὰ μίμησιν τῶν ἁγίων ἐν τῇ ἐκκλησίᾳ ἀπὸ ἐνιαυτοῦ εἰς ἐνιαυτὸν διὰ ἀζύμων καὶ τὸ ἄλλο μέρος τοῦ μυστηρίου δι' ὕδατος μόνου, "obviously in imitation of the sacred festivals in the (great) church they celebrate mysteries (the Eucharist) annually with unleavened bread and the other half of the mystery (the cup) only with water." In East Syria, too, it was the custom to eat unleavened bread at Easter, Aphraates Demonstratio, 12, 8 (Patrologia Syriaca, I, 1, p. 521, 14 f.), cf. Lietzmann. Orig. Hom. in Jer. 12:13 (GCS, 6, 100, 4 f.) attacks Christians who use unleavened bread at Easter. For details cf. O. Michel, Art. "Azyma," RAC, I, 1058-1062.
[55] As regards the rite there is no difference between the Quartodecimans and the rest of the Church, Casel, 13, 21.
[56] Eus. Hist. Eccl., VI, 9, 1 ff. (GCS, 9, 538, 2-15), from the time of Narcissos of Jerusalem, 180-192; Dg., 12, 9 (where we are to read with the MS: καὶ κηροὶ συνάγονται καὶ μετὰ κόσμου ἁρμόζεται [read ἁρμόζονται], "and wax candles were brought forth and tastefully arranged"). Cf. K. Schmaltz, "Das heilige Feuer in der Grabeskirche im Zshg. mit d. kirchlichen Liturgie u. den antiken Lichtriten," PJB, 13 (1917), 53-99, esp. 55 f., 57, 92. That lights were lit at the beginning may be seen from the description of Easter night in an ancient Armen. lectionary, cf. Schmaltz, 55 f.
[57] Cl. Al. Περὶ τοῦ πάσχα Fr. (GCS, 17, p. LIII, 18 f.); *Church Order of Hippolyt.*, 16, 1 (ed. F. X. Funk, *Didask. et Const. Ap.*, II [1905], p. 109, 15) and on this Casel, 23. Attested as a Roman custom in Dionys. of Alex. Ep. ad Basilidem, MPG, 10, 1272 f.
[58] Oldest instance, Tert. Bapt., 19 (CSEL, 20, 217, 1-6); Hippolyt., → n. 57.
[59] Distinction was made from Judaism in other respects, Did., 8, 1; → n. 64. Only the Ebionites kept to unleavened bread at Easter, → n. 54.
[60] Ep. Apostolorum, 15.
[61] Tert. Bapt., 19 (CSEL, 20, 217, 1 f.); Ps.-Tert., Adv. Iudaeos, 10 (*ibid.*, 70, 309, 145 f.).
[62] Melito, 46; Iren. Haer., IV, 10, 1 (MPG, 7, 1000 B); Tert., → n. 61.
[63] Lohse, 32-35.
[64] Cf. the inclination to break away from Judaism.
[65] Eus. Hist. Eccl., V, 24, 16 (GCS, 9, 496, 7-15): Easter debates regarding the visit of Polycarp of Smyrna to Anicetus of Rome c. 155 A.D.
[66] Iren. (quoted in Eus. Hist. Eccl., V, 24, 14 [GCS, 9, 494, 28-496, 2]) traces the Roman Sunday-Easter back to Xystus (c. 120), though he is not giving a time for the introduction of the paschal feast to Rome. It is probable that in Rome, too, the feast goes right back to

controversy between the churches of Rome and Asia Minor, Eus. Hist. Eccl., V, 23-25
(GCS, 9, 488-498), in which, after a protracted struggle, Rome finally prevailed.

J. Jeremias

πάσχω, παθητός, προπάσχω, συμπάσχω, πάθος, πάθημα, συμπαθής,
συμπαθέω, κακοπαθέω, συγκακοπαθέω, κακοπάθεια, μετριοπαθέω,
ὁμοιοπαθής, πραϋπάθεια

---

† πάσχω.

Contents : A. The Greek and Hellenistic World. B. The LXX and Judaism : 1. The LXX;
2. Philo and Josephus; 3. Pseudepigrapha and Rabbinism. C. The New Testament: 1. General;
2. The Suffering of Christ : a. The Synoptic Gospels and Acts ; b. Hb. and 1 Pt.; 3. The
Sufferings of Christians : a. Ac. 9:16; b. Paul ; c. 1 Pt. D. The Post-Apostolic Fathers.

A. The Greek and Hellenistic World.

1. πάσχω, [1] used from Hom. on, means basically "to experience something" which
comes from without and which has to be suffered : "something encounters me," "comes
upon me" etc. Often, also in philosophy, the antonym of verbs of free action like ἔρξαι,
Hom. Od., 8, 490; Aesch. Ag., 1564, ῥέζειν, Pind. Nem., 4, 32, δρᾶν, Aesch. Choeph., 313:
Gorg. Fr., 11, 7 (Diels[6], II, 290, 13 f.), ἐνεργεῖν, Corp. Herm., XII, 11 (Scott, I, 228, 34),
→ II, 652, 23 ff.; cf. also πάσχειν as the pass. of ποιεῖν, Aristot. Cat., 4, p. 2a, 4; Metaph.,
IV, 7, p. 1017a, 26 etc. Originally πάσχω is not a *vox media*. [2] The use in Hom. shows
plainly that its original sense was "to suffer evil." This was perhaps given with the
etym., → n. 1. Later, with appropriate additions, it could be used for experiencing anything
that might come.

Additions would show whether the use was *in malam* or *bonam partem*. Cf. on the one
side κακῶς πάσχειν, "to be in bad case," Hom. Od., 16, 275, ὑπό τινος (as with a
genuine pass.), Aesch. Prom., 1041, and on the other εὖ πάσχειν, "to be in a good
position," Pind. Pyth., 1, 99; Democr. Fr., 248 (Diels[6], II, 195, 1), "to experience good,"
Soph. Oed. Col., 1489; Thuc., II, 40; Ditt. Syll.[3], 317, 50 (318/7 B.C.), ὑπό τινος, Plat.
Gorg., 519c. Also with adj. : κακόν τι, Xenoph. Hier., II, 13, ἀγαθά, Hdt., II, 37,

---

the founding of the church, Casel, 14. If Mk. 2:20 refers to the Passover fast (→ n. 50),
this would be a proof. Certainly in the 2nd cent. there were not churches with the paschal
feast and churches without, but in various parts of the Church in the 2nd/3rd cent. the date
was fixed very differently (14th Nisan, the Sunday after, the equinox on March 25, the
Sunday after April 6, Schwartz, 10-16; Lohse, 76 f.). It was more or less an accident that
the dispute arose between Asia Minor (the evening of the 14th Nisan) and Rome (the
Sunday after).

π ά σ χ ω. Cr.-Kö., 840 f.; Loh. Mk., 164-167; W. Wichmann, "Die Leidenstheologie.
Eine Form d. Leidensdeutung im Spätjudentum," BWANT, 4. F., 2. H. (1930); F. K. Euler,
"Die Verkündigung vom leidenden Gottesknecht aus Js. 53 in der griech. Bibel," BWANT,
4. F., 14. H. (1934); H. Braun, "Das Leiden Christi. Eine Bibelarbeit über den 1 Pt.,"
Theologische Existenz heute, 69 (1940); K. H. Schelkle, *Die Passion Jesu in d. Verkündigung
d. NT* (1949); C. Maurer, "Knecht Gottes u. Sohn Gottes im Passionsbericht d. Mk.-Ev.,"
ZThK, 50 (1953), 1-38.

[1] πάσχω (stem πενθ-, πονθ-, παθ-) agrees phonetically with the Indo-Eur. *bhend*
(Germ. *binden*, Eng. "bind"), but can hardly be related in sense, so that other etymologies
have been sought (Walde-Pok., I, 513). H. Pedersen, "Zwei Fälle eines irrtümlich als
labiovelar aufgefassten π," *Revue des études indoeuropéennes*, 1 (1938), 193 assumes an
original intr. use of πάσχω (accusative always acc. of content) and thus arrives at the
meaning "to be bound, hampered entangled" [Debrunner].
[2] As against Pr.-Bauer[4], *s.v.*

τερπνόν τι, Soph. Ai., 521. Very common with acc. of object : ἄλγεα, Hom. Il., 20, 297, κήδεα, Od., 17, 555 (mostly thus in Hom., adv. only Od., 16, 275, → 904, 24 f.); often in fig. etym. πάθημα πάσχειν : χαῖρε παθὼν τὸ πάθημα, Orph. Fr., 32 f., 3 (Kern) (= Diels⁶, I, 17, 12; IG, XIV, 642, 3). Cf. also later the widespread use in the pap. for verbs, esp. where the mid. and pass. cannot be distinguished, e.g., βίαν πάσχειν, P. Amh., II, 78, 4 (184 A.D.); Mitteis-Wilcken, I, 2, No. 461, 12 = βιάζεσθαι (pass.), [ὕβριν] πάσχειν, P. Oxy., VIII, 1120, 1 (3rd cent. A.D.) = ὑβρίζεσθαι. In this development the basic sense "to suffer evil" exerts an influence at least to the degree that the use with additions *in bonam partem* remained much less frequent than that with additions *in malam partem*. Moreover there is a rich use of πάσχω with additions of another kind which always tend to be *in malam partem*. In particular, the abs. use is always *sensu malo*. Hence the word is used *sensu bono* only when there is an addition to this effect or, very rarely, the context makes it sufficiently plain. ³ There are many ways of indicating the opposite. Already very common in Hom. (Il., 5, 567; 11, 470 etc.) is the expression πάσχω τι, "some evil overtakes me," also the euphemism παθεῖν τι, "to die," ⁴ esp. in the form ἀνθρώπινόν τι παθεῖν etc. ⁵ The question τί (γὰρ) πάθω; expresses expectation of the worst, e.g., Hom. Il., 11, 404; Od., 5, 465; Hdt., IV, 118; τί πάσχεις; Aristoph. Nu., 798; Av., 1044; cf. also the common Att. introduction τί παθών; (already Hom. Od., 24, 106 : τί παθόντες ἐρεμνὴν γαῖαν ἔδυτε;) → IV, 392, 15 ff.

2. Comparatively old ⁶ is also the forensic use of πάσχω in the sense "to suffer punishment," "to be punished." It is combined with verbs of action in Aesch. Ag., 1564 : παθεῖν τὸν ἔρξαντα, Choeph., 313 : δράσαντι παθεῖν, also Lys., 20, 30 (cf. κακῶς ἀκούειν καὶ πάσχειν, "to have a bad reputation and to be punished," Democr. Fr., 265 [Diels⁶, II, 200, 1]); ἢν δέ τις [τὴν στήλην] ἀφαν[ίζηι ἢ τὰ γράμματα], πασχέτω ὡς ἱερόσυλος, Ditt. Syll.³, 1016, 7 f. (4th cent. B.C.), 194, 8 ff. (357/6 B.C.); Ditt. Or., 218, 115 f. (3rd cent. B.C.). In the phrase παθεῖν ἢ ἀποτίνειν in Plat. Polit., 299a; IG, I², 65, 50; Ditt. Syll.³, 663, 25 (c. 200 B.C.) ἀποτίνειν refers to a fine and παθεῖν to corporal or capital punishment (though the ref. in such connections is not exclusively to execution and hence παθεῖν does not mean "to suffer death" as a penalty).

3. In the main πάσχω in the sense "to suffer," "to undergo," "to experience" means having to suffer misfortune, blows of fate, the disfavour of men or gods. It is used abs. in this sense (cf. ὁ παθών, "the one hurt" [affected by the ἁμάρτημα of another], Plat. Leg., V, 730a), but also with other constr. Along with → πάθος and → πάθημα, also → θλίβω, θλῖψις, → λύπη etc., it is the term at hand when the Greek or Hellenistic world wants to express or discuss the problem of suffering. In keeping with the wide range of πάθος in the sense of "suffering" (→ 926, 23 ff.) πάσχω embraces the multiplicity of experiences which can overtake a man. In the first instance, more descriptively, it has here the sense "to experience," "to undergo," with no thought of painful feeling. In so far as it is used of sickness, ⁷ it means, not to suffer under an illness, but to suffer from it, to be sick. In the statement in Isoc. Or., 3, 61: ἃ πάσχοντες ὑφ' ἑτέρων ὀργί-

---

³ This, then, is how we are to take the examples of the sense "to experience" ("of enjoyable, pleasant experiences") in Pr.-Bauer⁴, *s.v.* 1 (cf. Cr.-Kö., 840). Oe. Gl. incorrectly says that "πάσχειν is used in a good sense" at 3:4. He refers esp. to Jos. Ant., 3, 312, but here the preceding context, not the εὐεργεσίαι which only follows, fixes the meaning. In Dion. Hal., 7, 51 a good sense is plainly prejudged by the context. P. Oxy., XVI, 1855, 8, 10, 14 : πάσχω ἀπόκρισιν, is late (6th/7th cent. A.D.), and ἀπόκρισις is obviously used *in bonam partem* ("favourable report," "acceptance").

⁴ The oldest instance is Callinus Elegicus (7th cent. B.C.). Fr., 1, 17 (Diehl³, I, 1 [1949], 2).

⁵ Many instances from pap. from the 3rd cent. B.C. on may be found in Preisigke Wört., I, 124 f., *s.v.* ἀνθρώπινος. Cf. P. M. Meyer, Juristische Pap. (1920), Index, *s.v.* πάσχω.

⁶ The examples do not prove that this use is part of the early history of the meaning of πάσχω.

⁷ Since πάθος (→ 926, 26) is attested much earlier in the sense of "sickness" etc., the abs. use of πάσχειν for "to be sick," "suffering," though attested comparatively late (e.g., Gal., 16, 583; ὁ πάσχων = ὁ κάμνων, "the patient," Preis. Zaub., IV, 3017 [4th cent. A.D.]), may well be old. Also constr. with acc. of respect (as with the pass. cf. Bl. Debr. § 159, 3; 160): τοὺς πόδας, P. Greci e Lat., IV, 293, 23 (3rd cent. A.D.).

ζεσθε, ταῦτα τοὺς ἄλλους μὴ ποιεῖτε, the relation between πάσχω and ποιέω shows plainly that πάσχω, as distinct from ὀργίζομαι, has little to do with the emotional life. Unlike, e.g., λύπη, it is predominantly objective (cf. the difference between the German *Leid* and *Leiden*). Naturally πάσχω (cf. πάθος in the sense of "mood," "spiritual state," "emotion," "passion" → 926, 27 ff.) is also used for emotional states, [8] but when used thus it should be rendered "to be in a mood," "to be affected by," rather than "to suffer," "to undergo." Cf. σώφρων ὁ μὴ πάσχων, "he who is free from passion," Aristot. Eth. M., II, 6, p. 1203b, 21; πάσχειν τι πρός τινα, "to be swept into a feeling against someone," Xenoph. Sym., 4, 11 (→ n. 20).

As regards the purpose of suffering, many answers were given. Already acc. to Hes. Op., 218 it can and should increase experience and give a better insight into things : παθὼν δέ τε νήπιος ἔγνω, cf. Soph. Oed. Tyr., 403. This is most impressively stated by Gk. tragedy, [9] esp. Aesch. : Δίκα δὲ τοῖς μέν παθοῦσιν μαθεῖν ἐπιρρέπει, Ag., 249 f., esp. 176 ff.: τὸν φρονεῖν βροτοὺς ὁδώσαντα, τὸν [10] πάθει μάθος θέντα κυρίως ἔχειν. Plainly this learning through suffering is not just a later understanding of the salutary purpose of individual sufferings or a growing wise through painful experiences, as in Hes. It is a deeper view of human existence in its totality, → I, 298, 32 ff.: III, 72, 18 ff.: IV, 394, 13 ff. [11] The striking play on words (πάθει μάθος) kept this insight alive, → 909, 47 f.; 917, 20; 926, 25; IV, 410, n. 147 f.; cf. παθήματα/μαθήματα, Hdt., I, 207; → IV, 400, n. 82; → 908, 18 ff. and n. 26.

In Stoicism the sphere of πάσχειν was broadened to embrace the whole cosmos. Only deity is exempt from πάσχειν and possesses ἀπάθεια. Outside deity, life is not conceivable without πάσχειν. [12] The use of πάσχω is here fully influenced by the developed doctrine of → πάθη. [13] The Stoic himself accepts the ideal of ἀπάθεια or ἀταραξία. He finds freedom in the negation of πάθη (cf. → III, 139, 40 ff. and esp. II, 495, 15-496, 29), [14] which can be defined as freedom from πάθη. At this pt. one may see the rationalistic nature of Stoic philosophy. [15]

In the Herm. writings, too, everything created is subject to πάθη and condemned to πάσχειν. Only God does not suffer and has no πάθη. The ἄνοια and ἀγνωσία of πάθη αὐτῷ περιτιθέντες are violently attacked, Corp. Herm., XIV, 8 (Scott, I, 260,

---

[8] Cf. Pass., *s.v.*, 3b and Liddell-Scott, *s.v.*, II, 1.

[9] The suffering of others is also a lesson, → IV, 316, 13 ff.

[10] τόν is conjectured for τῷ. Cf. the transl. in E. Tièche, "Die Griechen," *Mensch u. Gottheit in den Religionen*[2] (1942), 150 : "He (Zeus) it is who has assigned man to self-reflection and established the eternally valid principle : learn through suffering."

[11] Cf. W. Nestle, "Die Überwindung d. Leids in d. Antike," *Gr. Weltanschauung in ihrer Bedeutung f. d. Gegenwart* (1946), 414-440. Acc. to G. Nebel, *Weltangst u. Götterzorn* (1951), 115 f. the problem of suffering is grasped more profoundly in tragedy than in the philosophical ethics of antiquity, since tragedy shows, "not in theoretical generality but in actual disaster, that through suffering we learn who we are and what befalls us." The passage in Plat. Resp., II, 361e-362a, which is a starting-point for E. Benz, "Der gekreuzigte Gerechte bei Plat., im NT u. in d. alten Kirche," *Abh. der Mainzer Akademie d. Wissenschaften u. d. Lit., Geistes- u. sozialwissenschaftliche Klasse*, 1950 (1950), 1029-1074 (cf. also "Christus u. Sokrates in d. alten Kirche," ZNW, 43 [1950/51], 195-224), certainly uses πάσχω, but it is not a leading concept and forms no true par. to what is said in the NT, → IV, 613, 33 ff. It is worth noting that Prometheus, himself both a god and a benefactor of humanity, is also a figure of suffering. His last words in Aesch. Prom., 1094 are : ἐσορᾷς μ᾽ ὡς ἔκδικα πάσχω.

[12] Cf. J. Kroll, *Die Lehren d. Herm. Trismegistos* (1914), 125, 194 ff. On ἀνάγκη (→ I, 345, 7 ff.) and πρόνοια (→ IV, 1012, 26 ff.) cf. *ibid.*, 222 f.; cf. also H. Jonas, "Gnosis u. spätantiker Geist, I," FRL, NF, 33 (1934), 160.

[13] Cf., e.g., the distinctive Stoic constr. of πάσχω with ὅτι in the sense "to think," "to imagine" (the opinions in view are dependent on external impressions).

[14] Cf. also → IV, 480, 18 ff.

[15] Cf. R. Liechtenhan, "Die Überwindung des Leides bei Pls. und in d. zeitgenössischen Stoa," ZThK, NF, 3 (1922), 372, 390 ff.

16 f.).[16] In the highest regions of heaven suffering is unknown, Stob. Excerpt, VI, 6 (Scott, I, 412, 28 f.). Elsewhere the rule holds good : οὐδὲν ἀπαθές, πάντα δὲ παθητά, Corp. Herm., XII, 11 (Scott, I, 228, 32 f.). Even of the νοῦς it is said : καὶ ὁ νοῦς ἄρα παθητός (Scott; MS πάθος) ἐστι, συγχρωματίζων (Scott συγχρωτίζων) τοῖς πάθεσιν, ibid., XII, 10 (Scott, I, 228, 22 f.; cf. II, 351). The deduction is : <ὥστε καὶ ὁ νοῦς, ἐν σώματι μὲν ὤν, παθητός ἐστιν> (as correctly amplified by Scott) ἀπηλλάγη δὲ τοῦ σώματος, ἀπηλλάγη καὶ τοῦ πάθους, ibid., XII, 11 (I, 228, 30 ff.). The initiate transitorily experiences this liberation in ecstasy and he enjoys it definitively after death. This οὐσιώδης ἄνθρωπος knows no πάσχειν : ἀθάνατος γὰρ ὢν καὶ πάντων τὴν ἐξουσίαν ἔχων, ibid., I, 15 (I, 122, 6 f.).[17] Hence one does not learn through suffering, as in tragedy, nor hold πάθη at bay by ἀπάθεια, as in Stoicism. One is snatched away from πάσχειν by redemption and deification.

B. The LXX and Judaism.

1. The LXX.

In the LXX πάσχω occurs only 21 times.[18] There is a Heb. original in only 5 instances. For ὅσα πεπόνθασι, "all they had had to go through," in Est. 9:26 we find מֶה־רָאוּ, → 325, 5 f. In Am. 6:6 וְלֹא נֶחְלוּ עַל־שֵׁבֶר יוֹסֵף is rendered καὶ οὐκ ἔπασχον οὐδὲν ἐπὶ τῇ συντριβῇ Ιωσηφ; for חלה ni ("to be afflicted," only here)[19] πάσχω is suitably used in the sense "to be oppressed by" or "to suffer under."[20] We find the same constr. and sense in Zech. 11:5 (חמל). In Ez. 16:5 the noun חֶמְלָה (only here), from חמל, is used in the expression לְחֶמְלָה עָלַיִךְ, "to have sympathy for thee"; the transl. is τοῦ παθεῖν τι ἐπὶ σοί, "to show oneself (sympathetically) moved towards thee." At Da. 11:17 וְלֹא תַעֲמֹד is fittingly rendered καὶ οὐ μὴ παραμείνῃ by Θ (cf. also Prv. 12:7), but the LXX has οὐ πείσεται (slip for στήσεται ? Cf. 11:16).

Since Heb. has no word for passivity (πάσχω) as distinct from action,[21] the use of πάσχω in the LXX, in so far as it corresponds to the Heb., is no standard by which to judge the significance and range of OT thinking about suffering.[22] Neither the statements on the problem of suffering in Job, the many sayings about

---

[16] ἀπάθεια is not ascribed to God directly in Corp. Herm. Cf. XIV, 9 (Scott, I, 260, 19): ὁ γὰρ θεὸς ἓν μόνον ἔχει πάθος, τὸ ἀγαθόν ("God has only one passion, the good"), while elsewhere it is said : ὅπου δὲ πάθος, οὐδαμοῦ τὸ ἀγαθόν· ὅπου δὲ τὸ ἀγαθόν, οὐδαμοῦ οὐδὲ ἓν πάθος, VI, 2a (Scott, I, 166, 18 ff.).

[17] Cf. Jonas, op. cit., 181 f., 346; cf. Scott, II, 44 f.

[18] Cf. also πάθωσιν in Job 41:9 א*, a slip for ἀποσπασθῶσιν.

[19] Cf. Ryssel on Sir. 49:2 (Kautzsch Apkr. u. Pseudepigr., I, 465).

[20] Cr.-Kö., 841 refers to the constr. with πρός τινα (→ 906, 8 f.). But this means "to be led into a feeling against someone," whereas ἐπί and dat. in Am. 6:6 refers to the cause or reason.

[21] πάσχω does not occur, then, in 'ΑΘΣ, which in the main try to stick closer to the HT. Antitheses with δρᾶν etc. and πάσχειν cannot be constructed in Heb. and do not occur in the LXX. Many of the functions of πάσχω are approximately discharged by words like כְּאֵב, עָמָל, עָנָה, but their LXX equivalents can only be limited synon. of πάσχω. Cf. עָמָל κοπιάω, Ju. 5:26 B, μοχθέω, Qoh. 2:18 etc., עָנָה κακόομαι, Zech. 10:2, ταπεινόομαι, ψ 115:1; 118:67; כְּאֵב ἀλγέω 68:29; Job 14:22, πονέω, Sir. 13:5. In many cases an original Gk. version would probably have chosen πάσχω. In a passage like 3 Βασ. 2:26 : ἐκακουχήθης ἐν ἅπασιν οἷς ἐκακουχήθη ὁ πατήρ μου, this is confirmed by the use of πάσχω in the par. Wis. 18:11 (κακουχέω, in the LXX elsewhere only at 3 Βασ. 11:39 in the act., is common in 'Α, also κακουχία, cf. → n. 55.

[22] Suffering in the OT is dealt with for the most part in other arts.: → I, 32, 19 ff. (God's suffering love in Hos. and Jer.); 345, 38 ff. (ἀνάγκη); 359, 22 ff. (ἀνέχω); 440, 2 ff. (Jeremiah's prophetic sense of mission and suffering); 555, 3 ff. (βάρος/δόξα); 562, 19 ff. (βάσανος); → II, 229, 18 ff. (διώκω); 257, 21 ff. (δοκιμάζω); → III, 140, 12 ff.; 142, 14 ff. (θλῖψις; cf. πολλαὶ αἱ θλίψεις [רָעוֹת] τῶν δικαίων, "the righteous must suffer many

the sufferings of the righteous in the Psalter, nor the interpretation of the suffering of the ʾEbed Yahweh in Dt. Is. are related to the word πάσχω (or → πάθος, πάθημα) in the LXX. [23]

b. In the apocr. πάσχω also occurs twice in passages where a Heb. original has to be taken into account : Ep. Jer. 33 and Sir. 38:16 (both good Gk.). But the most important refs. are in works originally composed in Gk., i.e., Wis. and 2 and 4 Macc. [24] The πάσχοντες of Wis. 12:27 refers to the sufferings of the enemies of Israel, cf. also 18:1, 11, 19; 19:13. Indirectly, however, πάσχειν refers also to the sufferings of the people Israel — if the aim of 12:19-27 is to show the different purpose behind the one set of sufferings as compared with the other. The sufferings of Israel's ἐχθροί are a divine punishment, though it is added that God seeks to warn by sufferings (12:26) and to grant χρόνους καὶ τόπον δι' ὧν ἀπαλλαγῶσι τῆς κακίας (12:20). In the case of the sufferings of the παῖδες of God, however, there is much stronger emphasis on the fact that, though God must punish them for ἁμαρτήματα and send them sufferings, yet for the sake of the promises given to the fathers He proceeds very circumspectly (μετὰ πάσης ἀκριβείας, 12:21) in order that He may lead them through sufferings to μετάνοια (12:19) and educate them (12:22 : παιδεύων). There is an obvious difference as compared with the πάθει μάθος of Gk. tragedy (→ 906, 13 ff.). In Wis. (and the biblical writings generally) the interpretation of suffering as a means of instruction is orientated, not anthropocentrically, ethically and philosophically, but soteriologically, religiously and theologically. What is at issue is not self-reflection (φρονεῖν, Aesch. Ag., 176), [25] but μετάνοια, readiness for God's ἔλεος (Wis. 12:22). [26] It should also be noted that from 11:15 on the theme is God's clemency even towards the Egyptians, Canaanites etc. [27]

In 2 Macc. 6:30, where (ταῦτα) πάσχω is par. to the preceding ὑποφέρω, it is not a tt. for martyrdom. Similarly, the ref. in 7:18, 32 is to the sufferings of the Jewish people generally. Though Antiochus IV is responsible for these (7:18, 32), and will be called to account by God (in 9:28 πάσχειν refers plainly to the sufferings preceding death), the sufferings are still regarded as a divine chastisement, though, seeing that the merited punishment has been meted out, they are positively estimated as transitory, cf. 7:33. [28] If acc. to 7:36 the one whom God must punish for sin is again in possession of the promise after punishment, the idea could grow that the one who suffers for his faith or even dies as a martyr may expect a special reward. [29] In 4 Macc., which stands

---

things," ψ 33:19); 200, 30 ff. (ἰάομαι); 302-310 (suffering and atonement); 816, 18 ff. (κό-λασις); 828, 21 ff. (κόπος); → IV, 317 f. (λύπη); 485, 3 ff. (suffering of the ʾEbed Yahweh); 584, 19 ff., 36 ff. (ὑπομένω); 612, 39 ff., 46 ff.; 613, 26 ff.; 614, 16 ff. (suffering mediation : Moses, ʾEbed Yahweh etc., cf. 858, 7 ff.); 706-712 (belief in retribution); 1096, 14 ff. (sickness of the suffering Servant of God); → V, 115, 12 ff. (ὀδύνη); 608, 8 ff.; 609, n. 77; 610, 2 ff.; 617, 6 ff.; 621, 23 ff.; 623, 5 ff. (παιδεύω); 666, 10 ff.; 682, 11 ff. (παῖς θεοῦ), → ταπεινόω etc.

[23] Cf. E. Balla, "Das Problem des Leids in d. Gesch. d. isr.-jüd. Religion," *Eucharisterion* H. Gunkel, = FRL, NF, 19 (1923), I, 214-260; Wichmann, *passim* ; Euler, esp. 114-119 on the vocabulary of suffering in Is. 53; J. J. Stamm, *Das Leiden des Unschuldigen in Babylon u. Israel* (1946); R. Bultmann, *Das Urchr. im Rahmen d. antiken Religionen* (1949), 25 f.; M. Buber, *Zwei Glaubensweisen* (1950), 146-158; Mi. Hb.[8], Exc. on 12:5 f. (297 f.).

[24] Other words are used to express the problem of suffering in the apocr., → n. 22. Cf. also → I, 136, 7 ff. (ἀγών); III, 187, 6 ff. (θύω).

[25] But cf. Nebel, *op. cit.* (→ n. 11).

[26] For πάθει μάθος cf. ψ 118:71: ἀγαθόν μοι ὅτι ἐταπείνωσάς με ὅπως ἂν μάθω τὰ δικαιώματά μου.

[27] Cf. J. Fichtner, "Weisheit Salomos," *Handbuch z. AT*, II, 6 (1938), 45-49. Also G. Bertram, "Der Begriff d. Erziehung in d. gr. Bibel," *Imago Dei* (1932), 43.

[28] There is even a hint of vicarious suffering in 7:37 f. (→ III, 314, n. 56). → 909, 10 f. On the difference between this (also 4 Macc.) and Is. 53 and the NT cf. Maurer, 20 ff.

[29] In 2 Macc. 6:12-17, which may be regarded as the oldest instance of what is called passion theology (cf. Wichmann, 18-21), πάσχω is not used (→ IV, 45, n. 75). Cf. H. W. Surkau, "Martyrien in jüd. u. frühchristl. Zeit," FRL, NF, 36 (1938), 9 ff., 13, 57-65.

on the border between apocr. and pseudepigr., and which is so important as regards the rise and development of the martyr concept (→ IV, 488, 9 ff.), πάσχω is not a tt. for martyrdom as death and passion. In 14:9 it can even mean "to experience for oneself," "to undergo." Nor does it mean death as such in 4:25, but the suffering of this fate (the τοῦτο refers to death). Again, in 10:10 the martyrdom of the seven is indicated by ταῦτα, which corresponds to βασάνους, while πάσχω is par. to καρτερέω. In the clause in 9:8 : δι' ὃν (sc. θεὸν) καὶ πάσχομεν, πάσχω is used in the abs., but the preceding διὰ τῆσδε τῆς κακοπαθείας (→ 936, 30 f.) καὶ ὑπομονῆς makes this possible ; πάσχω is not a fixed tt. Significant though 4 Macc. is for the appraisal of suffering (cf. the singularly clear concept of vicarious suffering in 6:29, cf. also 1:11; 17:20 ff.), the term πάσχω is not here a vehicle for the idea of martyrdom (cf. the word μάρτυς etc., → IV, 487, 32 ff.). Hence in 13:17 preference should be given to the reading θανόντας rather than παθόντας (Cod A), not only on textual grounds, but also in virtue of the use elsewhere in 4 Macc. [30] παθεῖν no more means θανεῖν in 4 Macc. than in 2 Macc. The reading παθόντας rests on the preceding παθοκράτεια in 13:16, though this has reference to the domination of πάθη, → IV, 487, 14 f. [31] Nevertheless, at at later time, when the concept of suffering came to be taken for granted, the πάσχω refs. in 4 Macc., including the vl. at 13:17, might well have broken away from the original use and influenced the development of the word as a tt. for "to suffer (as a martyr)" = "to die."

2. Philo and Josephus.

a. Philo uses πάσχω some 150 times, [32] often in the usual combinations : with κακῶς, e.g., Spec. Leg., IV, 3; Placc., 124; more commonly (since πάσχω without addition tends in malam partem for Philo too) with εὖ, Spec. Leg., I, 298; II, 226 f.; Det. Pot. Ins., 52 (par. ἵνα εὖ σοι γένηται, Ex. 20:12 LXX). παθεῖν ἢ ἀποτεῖσαι (905, 26 ff.) also occurs : Spec. Leg., III, 145, 148; cf. μηδὲν παθεῖν, "to go unpunished," I, 192; Praem. Poen., 69. We often run across the thought that one experiences oneself the fate prepared for others : Jos., 156; Vit. Mos., I, 218; Spec. Leg., III, 84 f.; IV, 103, 222; Fug., 191 etc. Cf. on the other side the quotation from Philo in Eus. Praep. Ev., VIII, 7: ἃ τις παθεῖν ἐχθαίρει, μὴ ποιεῖν αὐτόν. In by far the majority of cases πάσχω denotes passivity as distinct from free action ; anton. δρᾶν, e.g., Conf. Ling., 6; Abr., 263; Vit. Mos., I, 297; Spec. Leg., II, 52; IV, 197; Agr., 163; more rarely ποιεῖν, Migr. Abr., 219; Dec., 30 f. In Det. Pot. Ins., 49 f. there is ref. to the Stoic concept of what are called unitary beings, ἡνωμένα, for whom action and suffering are the same, cf. Leg. All., III, 33; the ψυχή is among them. In general Philo's usage is very much under the influence of the terminology and outlook of Gk.-Hell. philosophy, → 906, 21 ff. Sensual impressions are regarded as πάσχειν, whereas to νοῦς (as distinct from ψυχή and γνώμη, Mut. Nom., 94, 161, 243) δρᾶν is ascribed, Leg. All., II, 38; cf. 39 ff. Ultimately action is for God alone ; everything creaturely is passive, Cher., 77; Leg. All., I, 49. Hence man can rely neither on αἴσθησις nor νοῦς; these can hold out before him only a very deceptive freedom, Cher., 71 ff.: he thinks he acts, but fundamentally he is merely passive (πάνθ' ὅσα δράσειν ἐνενόησε παθὼν ἀνὰ κράτος, 75). In this connection Philo raises the question how man can bear νόσους, γῆρας, θάνατον and the great number of other evils, and his judgment here too is : ὁ νομίζων καταλαμβάνειν ἢ κρατεῖν καταλαμβάνεται καὶ κρατεῖται, Cher., 75. Everywhere his treatment of the problem of suffering is embedded, both in form and content, in the Gk.-Hell. doctrine of pathos, cf. → III, 815, 21 ff. Even in instances in which παθεῖν and μαθεῖν occur together (e.g., Fug., 138; Rer. Div. Her., 73, there is only a remote influence of the bitter-strong saying πάθει μάθος (→ 906, 12 ff.), → IV, 411, n. 148.

---

[30] As against A. Deissmann in Kautzsch Apkr. u. Pseudepigr., II, 168, who (with Swete) adopts the reading παθόντας; Rahlfs chooses θανόντας.

[31] πάθος, which is so common in 4 Macc. (→ 927, 7 ff.), means "emotional state," not "suffering."

[32] Acc. to Leisegang, II, s.v.

b. Joseph. uses πάσχω very commonly, esp. in Ant., not so much in other works. [33] We find most of the meanings, and the word is used more generally than in Philo. The pass. nature of πάσχω is very plain even in the constr. (ὑπό τινος, e.g., Ant., 7, 209, 270; 9, 252), and the main sense is "to experience," "to undergo" (with no special influence of the pathos doctrine). But the idea of retribution, which is very important for Jos., is often implied : "to suffer punishment." The word often has this meaning, either in the abs. or with additions, Ant., 2, 291; 5, 166. The punishment may be death, but this depends on the context ; πάσχω alone simply means "to suffer," "to suffer punishment" : Ant., 4, 270, 279 (cf. 280); 6, 267 etc. The same applies to other instances of suffering death. Cf. the euphemistic use : παθεῖν ἀνθρώπινόν, Ant., 9, 43, πάσχειν τι, 15, 204; 17, 83, παθεῖν τι χεῖρον, Ap., I, 259; Vit., 404. In Ant., 4, 322 αὐτὸ πάσχοντες means death, but refers back to ἐπὶ μελλούσῃ τελευτῇ, cf. also 6, 16; 9, 86; 14, 167 and 170 etc. In 17, 240 the ref. is to those who have suffered a violent death, but οἱ πεπονθότες can only mean "those affected," "the victims," so also 17, 309; cf. Bell., I, 35. The πολλὰ παθών of Ant., 13, 268 obviously refers to the torments preceding death. The boast of the pious Jew that he would rather die than give up the Law (cf. Ant., 17, 152; 18, 59; → IV, 487, 16 ff.) is put in the phrases πρὸ τοῦ νόμου πάσχειν ἑτοίμως ἔχειν (Bell., 2, 196); περὶ τοῦ μηδὲ ῥῆμα φθέγξασθαι παρὰ τὸν νόμον πάντα παθεῖν γενναίως προείλοντο (Ap., II, 219), but in these instances πάσχω alone can hardly mean "to die." On Ant., 3, 312 → n. 3.

3. Pseudepigrapha and Rabbinism.

a. In the pseudepigr. so far as they were written or preserved in Gk. πάσχω is rare. In Ep. Ar., 214 the meaning is "to have an impression," "to be impressed"; in Test. XII "to suffer punishment" (B. 7:4; Jud. 15:2 [Charles]; S. 4:3; but also R. 3:9; 4:1; G. 5:11; S. 4:1). [34] In the Jewish sections of Sib. πάσχω occurs at 3, 529; 11, 282; 4, 209 for the suffering of severe tribulations. πάσχω does not occur in Gk. En. [35] As concerns pseudepigr. not preserved in Gk., one can presuppose πάσχω in the Gk. version at, e.g., Jub. 23:9 (cf. 12 f.). τὰ κακὰ ἃ πεπόνθαμεν is possible at 4 Esr. 12:43 (cf. Est. 9:26), but also ἃ εἴδομεν or ἃ εὗρεν ἡμᾶς etc. (cf. ψ 89:15; Gn. 44:34). In 4:12 the daughter transl. based on the Gk. point to πάσχω; on 7:126 cf. the Arab., and on the other hand 7:128. [36] Acc. to S. Bar. 78:6 — 52:6 is less plain ; cf. also 84:6 — present sufferings are an anticipation of future punishment, and acc. to the law of compensation they are thus the best guarantee of future felicity.

b. This interpretation is found also in Rabbinism, i.e., in the passion theology which developed esp. after the destruction of Jerusalem. [37] Even earlier (cf. also Lk. 13:2, 4; Jn. 9:2) the principle was propounded that sin brings penal sufferings "measure for measure," and that sufferings may be traced back to specific sins. [38] These sufferings should induce penitence [39] and they have atoning force. [40] Vicarious sufferings obviously do not come on the individual as a result of his own offences. But there may be other sufferings which involve no guilt, which serve rather to test and to educate, and which increase merit if borne steadfastly ("chastisements of love"). [41] One of the roots of

---

[33] Bell. is a transl. from Aram.; cf. 1, 3 and Ap., I, 50.
[34] On Test. Jos. 20:6 → συμπάσχω, 925, n. 2.
[35] Eth. En. 96:3 "you suffering," "you sick," would be οἱ πάσχοντες in Gk.
[36] On 8:44 (III, 25, 3 Violet) cf. H. Gunkel in Kautzsch Apkr. u. Pseudepigr., III, 382, n. a.
[37] The author of S. Bar. is influenced by it (Wichmann, 32-42). On Ps. Sol. cf. H. Braun, "Vom Erbarmen Gottes über den Gerechten. Zur Theol. d. Ps. Sal.," ZNW, 43 (1950/51), 6 f., 16, 24, 33.
[38] Cf. Str.-B., I, 444-446, 495, 815; II, 193-197, 527-529.
[39] *Ibid.,* II, 274-282. One should thus be glad of sufferings and thank God for them, *ibid.,* 274, 277; III, 221 f.
[40] *Ibid.,* I, 169, 417 f., 636; II, 274-292; IV, 847; → III, 312, 27 ff., 40 ff.; 313, 31 ff.; Wichmann, 7.
[41] Str.-B., II, 275, 279-282; → III, 313, 17 ff. In particular the death of the righteous and martyrs is regarded as achievement (→ IV, 488, 4 ff.), as a vicarious expiatory suffering.

passion theology is the application of the idea of the atoning power of sufferings to retribution in the world to come. Strong emphasis was laid on this atoning power of sufferings when the sacrificial cultus was ended and its possibilies of expiation were thus lost. [43] Even though immeasurable sufferings fell on the Jewish people, the idea of rejection by God was met [44] by the thought that the possibility of purification and expiation which God had given even in this aeon was in fact a sign of election. Even more frequently this explanation of suffering is applied to the individual. The ungodly are spared sufferings because God will give them no chance of expiation, whereas the righteous can be certain of acceptance by God precisely because God allows them to suffer. [45] The great significance of this view [46] in later Rabb. Judaism can hardly be contested. [47] But the weaknesses of the term "passion theology" are apparent. [48] It does not rest on any terms corr. to πάσχω or πάθημα. [49] The words actually used are יִסּוּרִין ("chastisements") or צָרוֹת ("afflictions"). [50] The OT offers no special word for sufferings, [51] though there is a definite understanding of these if they are viewed in part as afflictions and in part as divinely imposed chastisements. [52] The term "passion theology" unavoidably but unjustifiably narrows the gap between the Rabbinic understanding and the statements of the NT. [53] Even what is said about the suffering and death of the Messiah, if not formulated in a very different way, does not rest on a tt. whose Gk. equivalent would be πάσχω. [54]

---

[42] Str.-B., II, 193 f., 275; → I, 41, 33 ff.; III, 201, 14 ff. Acc. to Buber 139 the suffering of love was regarded as proceeding from the love of God and also as endured in the most inward spontaneity of love for God.

[43] Cf. also H. J. Schoeps, "Die Tempelzerstörung des Jahres 70 in d. jüd. Religionsgeschichte," Coniectanea Neotestamentica, 6 (1942), 33 ff.

[44] On various other suggestions cf. Schoeps, 14-17 and → I, 41, 36 ff.

[45] Wichmann, 9-15. Cf. Str.-B., I, 390; II, 227 f.; III, 140 f.

[46] Acc. to Wichmann, 10 Volz Esch.¹, 155 (cf. ², 126) was the first to speak of a theology of suffering with ref. to this development.

[47] Cf. the Tannaite and Amoraean examples in Wichmann, 51-78; for a later period cf. 78-80.

[48] → 617, 24 ff.; Wichmann, 13, 79; E. Gaugler, "Das Spätjudentum," Mensch u. Gottheit in den Religionen² (1942), 302.

[49] Cf. esp. the appendix in Wichmann, 81-97 (texts of passion theology) and the instances in Str.-B., → n. 38-42.

[50] Str.-B., II, 274. יִסּוּרִין can also mean "corrections" by censure, not suffering, e.g., S. Dt. § 32 on 6:5 (73b); rendering of Prv. 6:23 (Mas. מוּסָר; LXX παιδεία). Even when יִסּוּרִין are sufferings, these are viewed as chastisements.

[51] Though one might mention צָרוֹת, → III, 143, 7 ff.

[52] The meaning "chastisements (coming from God)" favours the idea that suffering is a (divine, not human) means of expiation. On the other hand the Rabb. took יִסּוּרִין very broadly and applied it to all kinds of mischances, thus emptying it of content, cf. Str.-B., III, 245; Wichmann, 84, 57, n. 10.

[53] In this respect cf. the concept of martyrdom, → IV, 487, n. 35; 495, 19 ff.

[54] This is no place for an express discussion of the age and spread of expectation of a suffering Messiah (cf. the art. παῖς θεοῦ, → 654 ff., esp. 682-700). That a Messianic interpretation of Is. does not prove of itself that later Judaism even kept to the statements about suffering in the c. is emphasised by J. Jeremias, "Js. 53 im Spätjudentum," Aux sources de la tradition chrétienne. Mélanges offerts à M. Goguel (1950), 118, n. 6. The NT itself bases its case for the suffering of the Messiah on a direct appeal to the OT (→ II, 22, 46 ff.; 24, 13 ff., cf. also → I, 758, 26 ff.). As concerns suffering in the Rabb. statements about the Messiah as the second Moses (→ IV, 863, 7 ff.), none of the Dt. refs (→ IV, 863, n. 184; 612, 38 ff.) and certainly no Rabb. example speaks as plainly as Ass. Mos. 3:11, where Moses is called the one "who suffered much in Egypt, at the Red Sea, and 40 years in the wilderness" (→ IV, 853, 11 f.; Lat. fr. qui multa passus est; cf. passi sunt, Ass. Mos. 9:3). But this passage must be dated after the death of Herod the Gt.; O. Stählin, Die hell.-jüd. Lit. (1921), 580 even puts it in 131 or 132. The later Jewish tradition which Jeremias (→ II, 939, 24 ff.) takes from Apc. El. concerning the martyrdom of Elijah redivivus in the last time (→ IV, 863, n. 189; Stauffer Theol.⁴, 255 n. 267, 292 n. 703) does not use a passion

C. The New Testament.

1. General.

πάσχω is found 42 times in the NT. Most of the refs. are to the sufferings of Christ Himself (→ 913, 3 ff.) and to the sufferings of Christians for His sake (→ 919, 13 ff.). In keeping with the sparse use in the HT or LXX (→ 907, 14 ff.), πάσχω is never used in OT quotations or allusions. The word occurs neither in Jn. nor the Johannine Epistles. In the Catholic Epistles it is found only in 1 Pt., and there are only 7 instances in Pl. Paul does not use it in the lists of sufferings in 1 C. 4:11 ff.; 2 C. 6:4 ff.; 11:23 ff.; 4:8 ff. It is not found in Hb., [55] and even the NT Book of Martyrs (→ IV, 495, n. 61), Rev., can get along without it (cf. only 2:10, → n. 58). Certain common uses do not occur, partly for material reasons, e.g., the favourite non-biblical euphemism παθεῖν τι (ἀνθρώπινον) for "to die" (→ 905, 15 ff.; 910, 10 ff.). πάσχω is not found in plain antithesis to verbs of action (→ 904, 15 ff.; 909, 30 ff.). [56] If κακῶς ἔχει is the original reading in Mt. 17:15 א BΘ etc., it can hardly mean "he is sick" (cf. 4:24 etc.), but, in accordance with the reading κακῶς πάσχει CDℜ, "he is in sorry case." ἔπαθεν οὐδὲν κακόν in Ac. 28:5 refers to the fact that there is damage to health, though possibly, in view of 28:4, there is an implication of "not being punished (by the gods)," → 905, 20 ff.

The question of Gl. 3:4 : τοσαῦτα ἐπάθετε εἰκῆ; refers to the violent and beneficial experiences implied by the τοσαῦτα, though πάσχω itself is not used in a good sense. [57] The sense in Lk. 13:2 : ὅτι ταῦτα πεπόνθασιν (cf. Est. 9:26) is the general one "to experience," "to undergo," "to meet with." [58] πάσχω could mean "to suffer punishment" here only if we had a mere repetition of the Jewish evaluation. Pilate's wife (Mt. 27:19) possibly dreamed that she would be punished for the wrong done by her husband to an innocent man, though it may be that she simply suffered anguish and pangs of conscience in the dream. [59] When Mk. 5:26 says of the woman with a flux : πολλὰ παθοῦσα ὑπὸ πολλῶν ἰατρῶν, [60] the ref. is not perhaps exclusively to painful or unnecessarily troublesome treatments, [61] but rather to the varied and contradictory treatments which she had to undergo. The meaning is that she had already been much doctored by many physicians. [62] In 1 C. 12:26 the pass. sense and antithetical δοξάζεται

---

term and is no help in explaining the NT data, Mk. 9:4 f. par.; 9:12 f. par.; Rev. 11:3 ff. Cf. J. Munck, "Pt. u. Pls. in d. Offenbarung Johannis," *Publications de la Société des Sciences et des Lettres d'Aarhus, Série de Théologie,* 1 (1950), 113-118 (the criticism on 118 ff. of attempts to document the idea of a suffering Moses is also illuminating).

[55] Can one regard κακουχέομαι in Hb. 11:37 (cf. 13:3 and συγκακουχέομαι in 11:25; → n. 21) as a substitute ? All the πάσχω refs. in Hb. are to the passion of Christ, → 917, 5 ff.

[56] On Mt. 17:12 → 914, 1 ff. In 1 Pt. 2:20 ἀγαθοποιέω and πάσχω, esp. in view of κακοποιέω (→ III, 485, 32 ff.; 1 Pt. 3:17) and κακοπαθέω (→ 936, 18 ff.), can hardly be a play on words. In non-Christian negative versions of the Golden Rule of Mt. 7:12 (e.g., Isoc. Or., 3, 61 → 905, 40 ff.; Philo → 909, 29 f.), sometimes also in patristic repetitions, πάσχειν or *pati* is used (= γίνεσθαι c. dat. Ac. 15:29 D; Did., 1, 2). Cf. G. Resch, "Das Aposteldekret nach seiner ausserkanonischen Textgestalt," TU, NF, 13, 3 (1905), 132-141.

[57] Cf. → n. 3. Neither the context nor the contents of the epistle support the idea of suffering under persecution (so Zn. Gl.³, 146).

[58] On the other hand in Rev. 2:10 the context suggests the sense "to suffer, to be persecuted (for Christ's sake)," cf. → 918, 14 ff.

[59] Cf. → 235, 6 and n. 49; M. Dibelius, *Die Formgesch. d. Ev.²* (1933), 113 f., 197; Bultmann Trad., 305, n. 2; E. Fascher, "Das Weib des Pilatus," *Hallische Monographien,* 20 (1951), 5-31. The sense "to be punished" may also be present in the saying of the thief in Ev. Pt. 13 : οὕτω πεπόνθαμεν (cf. δικαίως ... ἀπολαμβάνομεν, Lk. 23:41).

[60] The more choice expression (paronomasia ; cf. Bl.-Debr. § 488, 1a) hardly pts. to a later revision of the original Mk. (cf. Wbg. Mk., 161, n. 24).

[61] Cf. Heracl. Fr., 58 (Diels⁶, I, 163, 11 f.).

[62] Wbg. Mk., 161. On the constr. with ὑπό (in the NT only elsewhere at Mt. 17:12 and 1 Th. 2:14) cf. Bl.-Debr. § 315; πάσχω is not, however, a true pass. in the sense "to be (medically) treated."

show that the meaning of πάσχει is *in malam partem*: "to suffer harm," "to be un-favourably influenced." [63]

2. The Suffering of Christ.

a. The Synoptic Gospels and Acts.

Apart from the Synoptic Gospels and Acts, πάσχω is used of the suffering of Christ only in Hb. and 1 Pt. The examples in the Synoptics and Ac. divide plainly into two groups.

(a) In Lk. 22:15; 24:26, 46; Ac. 1:3; 3:18; 17:3 there is a special and uniform sense to the degree that πάσχω is here abs. (on Lk. 24:26 → n. 64) and manifestly means "to die," as in Hb. and 1 Pt., → 917, 5 ff. This is evident, esp. in view of the preceding παρέστησεν ἑαυτὸν ζῶντα, in Ac. 1:3 : μετὰ τὸ παθεῖν αὐτόν, and in the corresponding phrase in Lk. 22:15 : πρὸ τοῦ με παθεῖν. Nor is it less evident in the two-membered phrases in which παθεῖν is mentioned along with the resurrection in Lk. 24:26, 46; [64] Ac. 17:3 (cf. also 26:23, → 924, 10 ff.). Hence also the παθεῖν τὸν χριστὸν αὐτοῦ of Ac. 3:18 refers to the death of Jesus (3:15a), which was followed by His resurrection (3:15b), not to the details of the passion mentioned in 3:13 f. By virtue of its combination with the act. εἰσελθεῖν of Lk. 24:26 and the intr. but not pass. ἀναστῆναι of 24:46; Ac. 17:3, [65] πάσχω takes on a more active nuance in the statements of this group. If in Lk. 22:15 ff. we have an older tradition than the par. one in Mk. and Mt., [66] and if the saying in Lk. 22:15 merits greater attention, [67] we have here an example of the fact that παθεῖν, or the Aram. equivalent, is used by Jesus Himself in the sense "to die." [68]

(b) A second group is composed by Mk. 8:31 par. Mt. 16:21 and Lk. 9:22; Mk. 9:12 par. Mt. 17:12; Lk. 17:25.

---

[63] Though 12:26 is still fig. (cf. Bchm. 1 K., 386 f.), the meaning is not "to be sick" (→ n. 7). "To be harassed, troubled," is possible in view of the συγχαίρει of 12:26b (cf. also → IV, 564, 3 ff.), but very unlikely, particularly since συμπάσχω in 12:26a means "to be drawn into fellow-suffering," → 925, 8 ff.

[64] In Lk. 24:26 παθεῖν is not, of course, used abs. but with ταῦτα. But the association with the resurrection and the par. 24:46 show that it is a fixed term for the fate of Jesus. This may be seen esp. in 24:46 if the οὕτως there is to be related, not to παθεῖν (Kl. Lk., *ad loc.*; Cr.-Kö., 840), but to γέγραπται (cf. the transl. in Hck. Lk., *ad loc.*; Zn. Lk.³, ⁴, 729).

[65] Cf. Bl.-Debr. § 97, 1.

[66] Cf. Bultmann Trad., 286 f., 300, 303; E. Gaugler, *Das Abendmahl im NT* (1943), 21.

[67] Gaugler, *op. cit.*, 18, n. 1 finely sees that the Semitic ἐπιθυμίᾳ ἐπεθύμησα (Bl.-Debr. § 198, 6) proves the fidelity of the tradition. J. Jeremias, *Die Abendmahlsworte Jesu*² (1949), 86, n. 3, also shows that Lucan style does not form an argument for Lucan invention. Since πάσχα also occurs in Lk. 22:15, it may be noted that it is most improbable that πάσχα with π is an "irregular echo of πάσχω" (so Jeremias, 10, n. 1 following Dalman Gr., 138, n. 2). The LXX, which has the oldest instances of πάσχα, cannot support this conjecture, since the pres. and impf. of πάσχω (the similarity disappears in the other tenses) are very rare here (only 13 times). Nor in the case of Philo and Joseph. does the similarity prove that they took over the spelling from the LXX. In the NT the pres. of πάσχω occurs 15 times, but in the Synoptists, where alone there can be any question of influence on the spelling of πάσχα, only at Mt. 17:12, 15. → 897, 3 ff.

[68] While the deviations from Mk. 8:31; 9:12 in Mt. 16:21; 17:12 may denote a Jewish Christian outlook, the Lucan παθεῖν "to die" is shown by its perpetuation in Hb. and 1 Pt. not to be a Gentile Christian peculiarity. This is also supported by the fact that Lk. is employing an older usage. If παθεῖν means execution in the phrase παθεῖν ἢ ἀποτεῖσαι (→ 905, 26 ff.), it should be considered (E. Haenchen in a letter) whether the Lucan pre-ference of παθεῖν for "to die" was not influenced by non-biblical usage. But παθεῖν ἢ ἀποτεῖσαι does not have this restricted sense.

In Mt. 17:12b : οὕτως καὶ ὁ υἱὸς τοῦ ἀνθρώπου μέλλει πάσχειν ὑπ᾽ αὐτῶν, the constr. with ὑπό shows how strongly here πάσχω is felt to be pass. The preceding ἐποίησαν ἐν αὐτῷ ὅσα ἠθέλησαν in 17:12a does not provide the occasion for this use, [69] esp. as there is in the Marcan version very little connection between πολλὰ πάθῃ in 9:12 and ἐποιήσαν in 9:13. [70] At 16:21 Mt. leaves out the ἀποδοκιμασθῆναι of Mk. 8:31 and construes with πολλὰ παθεῖν the related [71] ὑπὸ τῶν πρεσβυτέρων κτλ. of Mk.; in 17:12 he does not take over the ἐξουδενεῖσθαι of Mk. 9:12 and simply has the παθεῖν. As he sees it, παθεῖν is the decisive term. [72] Constr. with ἀπό or ὑπό, it must have for him very much the same sense as the ἀποδοκιμασθῆναι or ἐξουδε- νεῖσθαι, so that it can take over without difficulty the function of these terms. The activity of the opponents of Jesus within the word παθεῖν is nowhere so prominent as in Mt. (even more so with the ὑπό of 17:12 than the ἀπό of 16:21).

In Mk. 8:31 and Lk. 9:22 πολλὰ παθεῖν is not a master concept at the head of a four-membered statement, as though what followed were a development of the πολλά. Neither in Mk. 9:31 par. nor 10:33 f. par. is it used to describe the whole of the passion, nor can it be a master concept for ἀναστῆναι. [73] On the other hand, it cannot refer exclusively to the death of Jesus. The πολλά alone forbids this, and esp. the separately mentioned ἀποκτανθῆναι. Nor can the πολλὰ παθεῖν be related to the accompanying circumstances of ἀποκτανθῆναι, i.e., to the suffering in dying, since the two sayings are separated by ἀποδοκιμασθῆναι κτλ. Purely linguistically, though there is no other instance of this in the NT, [74] πολλὰ παθεῖν might refer to the events preceding a violent death (rough treat- ment etc.), cf. 2 Macc. 9:28, → 908, 28 f. and Jos. Ant., 13, 268, → 910, 14 f. But in this case the events would have to precede the ἀποδοκιμασθῆναι κτλ. They would thus be, not the mocking and scourging, but at most the arrest and trial, and possibly the treachery of Judas and denial of Peter. Probably neither πολλὰ παθεῖν nor ἀποδοκιμασθῆναι originally had this sense. [75] πολλὰ παθεῖν καὶ ἀποδοκιμασθῆναι might have been an older independent combination representing an earlier stage of the intimation of the passion in Mk. 8:31 par. [76] This is suggested by Lk. 17:25 : πρῶτον δὲ δεῖ αὐτὸν πολλὰ παθεῖν καὶ ἀποδοκιμασθῆναι ἀπὸ τῆς γενεᾶς ταύτης. If the present form of the saying is secondary, [77] the saying itself may well be very old, at least as regards the combining of πολλὰ παθεῖν and ἀποδοκιμασθῆναι. [78] In Mk. 9:12 πολλὰ παθεῖν is again combined with a

---

[69] Cf. → n. 56; Bl.-Debr. § 315.

[70] Only Loh. Mk. on 8:31 and Schelkle, esp. 66, 73-75 pay any gt. attention to the use of πάσχω. Cf. H. v. Campenhausen, Die Idee d. Martyriums in d. alten Kirche (1936), 62 f. → n. 137.

[71] Cf. also Lk. 9:22.

[72] Kl. Mt. on 16:21 rightly notes that "καὶ ἀποδοκιμασθῆναι is omitted as superfluous," but he wrongly asks whether εἰς ᾽Ιεροσόλυμα ἀπελθεῖν (cf. 20:18 par.) is substituted for καὶ ἀποδοκιμασθῆναι.

[73] Loh. Mk., 167, who simply sees in ἀποκτανθῆναι and also in ἀναστῆναι "an ex- plication of what is involved in suffering many things," uses Lk. 24:26, 46 and Ac. 1:3 as a basis for including ἀναστῆναι, and adds that the only instance where ἀναστῆναι is not expressly added, namely, Lk. 17:25, makes no difference. But Mk. 9:12 should be mentioned as well as Lk. 17:25, and πολλά is not used in Lk. 24:26, 46 and Ac. 1:3.

[74] Loh. Mk., 164.

[75] Loc. cit. Cf. also Buber, op. cit., 103 f.

[76] Loh. Mk., 165 thinks the original form of the prophecy is : δεῖ τὸν υἱὸν τοῦ ἀν- θρώπου πολλὰ παθεῖν καὶ ἀποδοκιμασθῆναι (cf. Lk. 17:25).

[77] Cf. Kl. Lk., ad loc.; Bultmann Trad., 353 and Theol. d. NT (1953), 30.

[78] Kl. Lk., ad loc. regards the saying as "a repetition of 9:22," "but with the general ἀπὸ τῆς γενεᾶς ταύτης comprehensively for the authorities mentioned there." It seems more likely, however, that the enumeration of the authorities in 9:22 par. is a secondary

synonym of ἀποδοκιμασθῆναι, i.e., ἐξουδενηθῆναι (without further addition). [79] Though the other members of the first intimation of the passion do not have to be of late origin, [80] πολλὰ παθεῖν καὶ ἀποδοκιμασθῆναι must be accepted as an ancient two-membered expression. Now in the first instance ἀποδοκιμασθῆναι does not denote a single action. It acquires this sense only through the addition ὑπὸ τῶν πρεσβυτέρων κτλ., while the ἀπὸ τῆς γενεᾶς ταύτης of Lk. 17:25 is even more general, → n. 78. ἀποδοκιμασθῆναι is a more comprehensive description of the rejection of the Son of Man by men. To express in a similar saying the divine meaning and purpose of this event, [81] only πολλὰ παθεῖν remains, and this seems in fact to be its task. The explanation of the two members is thus as follows: on God's side the fate of Jesus is a πολλὰ παθεῖν, on man's an ἀποδοκιμασθῆναι.

Since the NT πάσχω is sometimes rendered saibar in Syr., which means "to bear," "to endure," and which is also an equivalent of ἀνέχομαι, ἀντέχομαι and ὑπομένω, [82] it may be asked whether the סָבַל of Is. 53:4, 11 lies behind it. To be sure, neither LXX nor 'ΑΘΣ use πάσχω in these verses. But πολλὰ παθεῖν may still be related to them. [83] Perhaps, on the basis of Is. 53:4, 11, the ref. of the πολλά is to the fulness or totality [84] of the human guilt which the Son of Man is to bear. For its part, παθεῖν or the Aram. original is firmly attested in the sense "to bear," cf. also → 936, n. 4. Both parts of the formula πολλὰ παθεῖν καὶ ἀποδοκιμασθῆναι might thus stand under the influence of Is. 53, → n. 79. The formula as a whole consequently has an enhanced effect. Even the sense "to die" for παθεῖν, whose age is proved by Lk. 22:15 (→ 913, 19 ff.), is no material departure from the prior history of the term, for, though the verses underlying the πολλὰ παθεῖν do not speak of death, this is the plain ref. of 53:8 f., 12. [85] πολλὰ παθεῖν is already changed and weakened in the first intimation of the passion, and it

---

extension on the basis of the actual role of the Sanhedrin in the historical course of events. Acc. to W. G. Kümmel, *Verheissung u. Erfüllung*² = *Abh. z. Theol. d. AT u. NT*, 6 (1953), 64 "there is no well-founded objection to the assumption that Lk. 17:25 is an old and reliable tradition."

[79] Cf. the rendering of ψ 117:22 on the one hand in Mk. 12:10 par.; 1 Pt. 2:7 (ἀπεδοκί-μασαν, so LXX) and on the other in Ac. 4:11 (ἐξουθενηθείς). Does the ἐξουδενηθῆναι of Mk. 9:12 indicate a ref. to Is. 53:3? 'A and Σ have ἐξουδενωμένος there (cf. Euler, 29, 33, 140). Cf. Maurer, 28.

[80] On ἀποκτείνω cf. Loh. Mk., 165; Schelkle, 27, n. 15; 65, n. 11, 74; Dib. Th.³ (1937) on 1 Th. 2:14. In intimations of the passion ἀποκτείνω is older than σταυρόω, Mt. 20:19 (cf. 26:2), but as compared with πολλὰ παθεῖν καὶ ἀποδοκιμασθῆναι it is a development, like ἀναστῆναι.

[81] Loh. Mk., 165.

[82] Cf. O. Klein, *Syr.-Gr. Wörterbuch z. d. 4 kanon. Ev.*, ZAW Beih., 28 (1916), 72. At Mk. 5:26; Hb. 5:8 we even find sᵉbal. The Syr. verbs do not seem to be related.

[83] → I, 596, n. 1. Of the 7 instances of סָבַל q 5 are in Dt. Is. F. Delitzsch, who elsewhere has עָנָה for πάσχω in his Heb. rendering of the NT, uses סָבַל at Lk. 17:25; 24:26. סָבַל q is transl. ἀνέχομαι and ἀναλαμβάνομαι in the LXX at Is. 46:4, ὑπέχω at Lam. 5:7, and πονέω at Gn. 49:15. The rendering is free at Is. 53:4 (though cf. βαστάζω in the quotation in Mt. 8:17), and ἀναφέρω is used in v. 11 ('A ὑπομένω at v. 4, βαστάζω v. 11; Σ ὑπο-μένω v. 4, ὑποφέρω v. 11; Θ ὑποφέρω v. 11). → I, 186, 7 ff.

[84] Cf. the use of (οἱ) πολλοί = πάντες, e.g., Is. 53:12 and in the NT. On this cf. J. Jeremias, *op. cit.*, 91 ff.; O. Cullmann, " Ὑπὲρ (ἀντὶ) πολλῶν," *Theol. Zschr.*, 4 (1948), 471 ff., → n. 109. Cf. Jn. 1:29 (τοῦ κόσμου).

[85] As in Heb. (→ 907, 25 f.), so in Aram. there is no direct equivalent for πάσχω, cf. J. Jeremias, 87 and n. 12; also ThLZ, 75 (1950), 35. Was Aram. סָבַל the bridge? But perhaps πολλὰ παθεῖν and παθεῖν "to die" were not linguistically related in Aram. as in the Gk. transl. On the other hand derivation from Is. 53 is the more sure the more the idea of the Suffering Servant of God controls the oldest, pre-Marcan passion narrative, Maurer, 10, 23 etc.

does not occur again in the NT. [86] On the other hand the rendering "to die" had a further history, → 917, 5 ff.; 918, 19 ff.; 922, 20 ff.; 923, 2 f., 5 ff. [87] In so far as Is. 53 contributed the idea of vicarious expiatory suffering (cf. also → IV, 612, 46 ff.; 621, 29 ff.; V, 671, 23 ff.), the abs. use of παθεῖν is no reason why this παθεῖν should not have saving significance ὑπὲρ ἡμῶν. In particular there derives from Is. 53 the activist view which characterises the sayings about the passion of Jesus. [88] In the πολλὰ παθεῖν, and esp. the παθεῖν "to die," what men do to Jesus has no prominence, → 915, 11 f. Jesus is the acting subject of a παθεῖν understood actively. [89] In the light of Is. 53 His πολλὰ παθεῖν is also an obedient suffering in execution of a divine commission. The link with Is. 53 shows how mistaken is the view that Jesus tried to force the will of God by an arbitrary death, as the so-called consistent eschatology would have it. [90] The 'Ebed Yahweh whom God ordains to suffer stands in the strongest possible contrast to the possibility that Jesus, on the basis of Is. 53, thought it scriptural that even against God's will He should bring in the kingdom of God by a death which He Himself sought.

The uniqueness of the passion of Jesus is reflected in the fact that παθεῖν occurs only in sayings of Jesus relating to His own person. Neither the persecutions of the prophets (e.g., Mt. 5:12 par.; 23:37 par.), the fate of John the Baptist (Mk. 9:12 f. par.), [91] nor the sufferings of the disciples (e.g., Mk. 8:34 ff. par.; Mt. 10:17 ff. par.; 23:34 par.) are called παθεῖν, though there may be agreement in respect of other terms. [92] The uniqueness of our Lord's passion is brought out by the choice of this word παθεῖν whose prior history had prepared it to express this content (→ 904, 12 ff. and 904, 17 ff.) but which had not yet been used in this way even in the LXX. This is especially true of the more specific sense "to die," → 908, 25 ff., 33 ff. [93]

b. Hebrews and 1 Peter.

When the later period used παθεῖν in relation to the passion of Christ, it followed for the most part the use noted in Lk. and Ac., where the meaning is "to die." In the NT itself this applies only to Hb. and 1 Pt.

If πάσχω is not used for the death of Jesus in Jn., this is not so much because Jn. does not use the word, but rather because the death of Jesus is here evaluated in such distinctively Johannine categories as δοξασθῆναι (→ II, 249, 17 ff.) and ὑψωθῆναι

---

[86] → n. 108. πολλὰ παθεῖν occurs again only in Barn., 7, 11a, though here with ref. to the suffering discipleship of the community, → 923, 27 f.

[87] The expression "death and passion" is found only after the post-apost. fathers (→ 923, n. 138; 926, n. 9). It can hardly go back to Mk. 8:31 par., for here ἀποκτανθῆναι means "to be put to death," and πολλά is an integral part. The phrase refers either to the suffering accompanying death (no NT ref.; on Hb. 2:9 → 934, 11 ff.), the preceding details of the passion story (some basis in the usage of the first intimation of the passion), or the scene in Gethsemane (no NT ref.; on Hb. 5:8 → 917, 18 ff.). "Suffered" was not in the Roman Creed in its original form; it was added to "crucified" only later. Cf. the review in H. Lietzmann, "Symbolstudien, I-VII," ZNW, 21 (1922), 16 f.; also Messe u. Herrenmahl = Arbeiten z. Kirchengesch., 8 (1926), 50-53, 61, 62, n. 1 (with express emphasis on Const. Ap., VIII, 12, 38); W. Michaelis, "Herkunft u. Bdtg. des Ausdrucks 'Leiden u. Sterben Jesu Christi'" (1945), 4 f., 11 f., 13 f., n. 5 f.; Schelkle, 74 f., 247 ff.

[88] Cf. → 913, 16 ff.; 915, 18 ff., but also δοῦναι τὴν ψυχήν, Mk. 10:45 par.

[89] Schelkle, 78-81. R. Bultmann, Theol. d. NT (1953), 400 is wrong when he argues that this is so for the first time only when πάσχω is abandoned by Jn.

[90] Cf. A. Schweitzer, Das Messianitäts- u. Leidensgeheimnis² (1929), 81-89.

[91] Even in the original of Ac. 3:18 ff., if Bau. Ag., 66 ff. reconstructs it correctly, we do not have a saying of Jesus.

[92] Cf. → διώκω, II, 229, 33 ff.; → μαστιγόω, IV, 516 f., → σταυρόω etc. ἀποθνήσκω, too, is not used about the future destiny of the disciples in dominical sayings (though we find ἀποκτείνω, → n. 80). On Mt. 10:38; 16:24 par. → I, 214, 15 ff.

[93] On Ac. 26:23 (adduced → 913, 14) → 924, 10 ff.

(→ 711, n. 441). Jn. makes only sparing use of ἀποθανεῖν. Except in Jewish sayings at 11:50 (cf. 18:14; 19:7 and comments of the author at 11:51; 12:33; 18:32, the word is used of Jesus' death only in the figure of the corn of wheat which dies and brings forth much fruit, 12:24 (→ III, 616, 1 f.; 811, 18 ff.).

(a) Though the author of Hb. could use ἀποθανεῖν for death, including violent death (7:8; 9:27; 10:28; 11:4, 13, 21, 37), he never uses this for the death of Jesus (though he does have θάνατος, → 918, 15), but speaks of the παθεῖν of Jesus. In 13:12 ἔπαθεν, if it refers to what took place ἔξω τῆς πύλης, can only denote the death of Jesus (cf. διὰ τοῦ ἰδίου αἵματος), not the preceding events in the city (the trial, mocking etc.). The fact that 2:18 : ἐν ᾧ γὰρ πέπονθεν αὐτὸς πειρασθείς, δύναται τοῖς πειραζομένοις βοηθῆσαι, does not refer to temptations prior to the passion (cf. Lk. 22:28) may be seen from 2:9 ff. where 2:9 speaks of the πάθημα τοῦ θανάτου (= γεύσασθαι θανάτου, loc. cit.), → 934, 11 ff. 2:18 is speaking rather[94] of the passion. In this He suffered under temptation.[95] The author is not thinking of Gethsemane,[96] as the expression πάθημα τοῦ θανάτου in 2:9 shows,[97] and as may be seen also from 5:7 ff. In 2:18 πέπονθεν πειρασθείς refers exclusively to the death of Jesus.

5:7 for its part refers to what took place in Gethsemane.[98] If τελειωθείς in v. 9 also suggests Gethsemane,[99] the whole section from v. 7 to τελειωθείς in v. 9, including ἔμαθεν ἀφ᾽ ὧν ἔπαθεν τὴν ὑπακοήν in v. 8 (→ 906, 15 ff.; IV, 410, 36 ff.) has the same ref. But this explanation founders on the ἐγένετο πᾶσιν τοῖς ὑπακούουσιν αὐτῷ αἴτιος σωτηρίας αἰωνίου attached to τελειωθείς (cf. 2:10).[100] 5:9 is not, of course, exclusively oriented to the resurrection of Jesus.[101] Otherwise 5:8 would necessarily refer to the death of Jesus, since this is not mentioned otherwise. But there is a ref. to the death, too, in 5:9 (→ III, 276, 8 f.; 279, 26 ff.).[102] There are three reasons why 5:8, like 5:7, cannot refer only to Gethsemane : first, εἰσακουσθείς in v. 7 takes us already to the end of the Gethsemane incident ;[103] secondly, ὑπακοή, in view of Phil. 2:8 and R. 5:19, refers to the death, though not exclusively ; thirdly, the use of παθεῖν elsewhere in Hb. is against it. One can hardly put the ἔμαθεν in the Gethsemane incident and then think generally of the approaching death with ref. to ἔπαθεν ;[104] the ἔμαθεν is at the same time as the ἔπαθεν. There would be no NT par. for referring the παθεῖν exclusively to the struggle in Gethsemane as such. Either ἔμαθεν, like ἔπαθεν, relates

---

[94] Rgg.[2,3], 120; Mi. Hb.[8] on 4:15 (122 f.). On the secondary reading πεπειραμένον, cf. J. H. Korn, "ΠΕΙΡΑΣΜΟΣ," BWANT, 4. F., 20. H. (1937), 30 f. → 936, 2 ff.

[95] On the relation of πέπονθεν and πειρασθείς cf. Rgg. Hb., 64, n. 63, on ἐν ᾧ, ibid., n. 64; Mi. Hb.[8] on 2:18 (92).

[96] Mi. Hb.[7], ad loc. (38) states this without further ado on the basis of the link between πάθος and πειρασμός, but Mi. Hb.[8], ad loc. (92) is more cautious. Hb. does not have πάθος, and elsewhere in the NT this never means "suffering" (→ 928, 4 ff.). The Gethsemane incident is not described as πειρασμός in the Synoptics (Mk. 14:38 par. has the disciples in view).

[97] Here "the suffering cannot be confined to the moment of death" (Rgg. Hb., 63, n. 62), but does the expression include "all the painful accompaniments leading up to it" ? (loc. cit.)

[98] Cf. Rgg. Hb., 130-137; Mi. Hb.[8], ad loc. (133 f.).

[99] Wnd. Hb., ad loc.: The perfecting consisted in the Son's wrestling through to submission to the will of God, i.e., to suffering.

[100] Cf. also Rgg. Hb., 138; E. Käsemann, "Das wandernde Gottesvolk," FRL, NF, 37 (1939), 86, n. 4.

[101] So Mi. Hb.[7], ad loc. (62): "The 'perfecting' of Jesus is obviously identical with His exaltation."

[102] Cf. also Rgg. Hb., 138.

[103] Even if there should be an οὐκ before εἰσακουσθείς (→ II, 753, 26 ff., though cf. Mi. Hb.[8], ad loc. [134 f.]; → IV, 412, 20 ff.), the ref. in 5:8 does not have to be to Gethsemane.

[104] So, e.g., Rgg. Hb., 136 f.

to the individual stages of the passion beginning with Gethsemane and ending with the death, [105] or it relates exclusively to the death. The use of παθεῖν in 13:12 favours the second possibility. The ref. to obedience brings 5:8 into the closest proximity to Phil. 2:8, [106] and τελειωθείς in 5:9 denotes the death and esp. the resurrection as the installation of Jesus into His high-priestly office (cf. his installation into the high office of κύριος in Phil. 2:9 ff.).

In 9:26, too, the context supports an exclusive reference to the death of Christ, [107] for the contrast between πολλάκις in 9:25 f. and ἅπαξ in 9:26, 28 shows that something is indicated by the παθεῖν which did not merely happen ἅπαξ de facto, but which also could not possibly have happened πολλάκις, cf. R. 6:9 f. [108]

Though in Hb. παθεῖν is never combined with ὑπὲρ ἡμῶν etc. (cf. 1 Pt. 2:21; 3:18), this thought is implied (cf. simply 10:12; 13:12). As in Paul θάνατος does not embrace the whole story of the passion (in R. 5:10 it is identical with the αἷμα of v. 9; cf. also Col. 1:20 with 1:22; → I, 174, 18 ff.; in Phil. 2:8 it is defined as θάνατος σταυροῦ), so the παθεῖν of Hb. is related to the use which the author makes of θάνατος (cf. 2:9, 14; 5:7; 9:15 f.), αἷμα (e.g., 9:12, 14; → I, 175, 22 ff.) and σταυρός (only 12:2). [109] The relationship between Hb. and Lk. (→ IV, 411, n. 150) also finds expression in the use of παθεῖν. [110]

(b) At 1 Pt. 2:21: εἰς τοῦτο γὰρ ἐκλήθητε, ὅτι καὶ Χριστὸς ἔπαθεν ὑπὲρ ὑμῶν κτλ., we find in א Min syᵖ etc. the reading ἀπέθανεν. [111] This imports ἀπέθανεν, which is common in Paul (cf. also the vl. at 3:18, → 919, 1 ff.), whereas the author of 1 Pt. — irrespective of its other use, e.g., for the sufferings of Christians in 2:19 f. (→ 921, 8 ff.) — employs πάσχω here with ref. to the death of Jesus. This is unequivocally the sense in 2:23 as well.

While 2:22 (cf. Is. 53:9) is a general characterisation (cf. also 3:9; → IV, 294, 17 f.), the λοιδορούμενος οὐκ ἀντελοιδόρει of 2:23a refers to the passion (→ IV, 294, 12 ff.; cf. also R. 15:3). Then in 2:24 we have an exposition of the meaning of the crucifixion, cf. Is. 53:4, 12; → I, 315, 3 ff.). The exemplary (2:21) conduct of Jesus at the cross, which is hardly at issue in 2:24, can then be expressed only in the πάσχων οὐκ ἠπείλει of 2:23b (and 2:23c). [112, 113]

The ref. in the Χριστοῦ οὖν παθόντος of 4:1 is also to the crucifixion. The ὁ παθὼν σαρκί (→ 922, 20 ff.) which follows, and which applies to the Christian,

---

[105] Cf. Rgg. Hb., 137 and n. 62 for a similar interpretation.

[106] → IV, 411, 29 ff.; Mich. Ph., 38 f.; W. Michaelis, *Zur Engelchristologie im Urchr.* (1942), 46 ff.; J. Bieneck, *Sohn Gottes als Christusbezeichnung d. Synpt.* = Abh. z. Theol. d. AT u. NT, 21 (1951), 58-69.

[107] Hence προσφέρειν ἑαυτόν cannot refer merely to the self-giving of the exalted Lord (Rgg. Hb., 287, n. 81).

[108] The arrest, trial, mocking etc., also Gethsemane, are unique events, but since a πολλάκις cannot be ruled out in principle in these cases, they do not have the ἅπαξ of the παθεῖν. Cf. also the correspondence between the ἅπαξ ἀποθανεῖν appointed for men (9:27) and the ἅπαξ προσενεχθείς of Christ (9:28). The juxtaposition of ἀποθανεῖν in 9:27 and παθεῖν in 9:26 works out the singularity of the death of Jesus. The weakly attested vl. ἀποθανεῖν for παθεῖν blurs this distinction. The vl. πολλά for πολλάκις in Cod D is a slip rather than a reminiscence of the Synoptic πολλὰ παθεῖν. Cf. Rgg. Hb., 287, n. 80.

[109] The plur. in ἀφ' ὧν at 5:8 does not have to refer to the details (→ IV, 411, 15 ff.). Similarly the πολλά of Mk. 9:12; Lk. 17:25 means *multum*, not *multa*.

[110] Since the origin of the use of παθεῖν in Hb. is apparent, there is no need to postulate Gnostic influence.

[111] Cf. Wbg. Pt., 77.

[112] Ibid., 79.

[113] There is no ref. to a special feature such as might perhaps fit λοιδορούμενος, → IV, 294, 14. The arrest is at issue in Mt. 26:53 f.

supports this view, as does the par. θανατωθεὶς μὲν σαρκί in 3:18. In א AC Min the beginning of 3:18 runs: ὅτι καὶ Χριστὸς ἅπαξ περὶ ἁμαρτιῶν ἀπέθανεν, while Bℜ have ἔπαθεν. The latter reading is surely original; [114] its alteration into ἀπέθανεν was influenced by Pauline usage with the addition περὶ ἁμαρτιῶν etc. [115] In any case 2:21, 23; 4:1 show that the author stands in the tradition which uses παθεῖν for the death of Jesus. [116]

> 1 Pt., too, attests that this death took place περὶ ἁμαρτιῶν (3:18) or ὑπὲρ ὑμῶν (2:21), cf. the vl. ὑπὲρ ἡμῶν at 4:1. It also emphasises the once-for-all character of the death (ἅπαξ, 3:18), its unity with the resurrection (cf. 3:21 f. between 3:18 and 4:1), and the link between παθήματα and δόξαι, 1:11 → 934, 25 ff. Distinctive of 1 Pt. is the great stress on the exemplary nature of the παθεῖν of Christ for the πάσχειν of Christians.

3. The Sufferings of Christians.

When Jesus speaks of the way of suffering which His disciples must tread He does not use πάσχω, → 916, 18 f. Elsewhere in the NT, however, the word is used to denote the sufferings of Christians, i.e., in Ac. 9:16; Rev. 2:10 (→ n. 58), Paul and 1 Pt.

a. Ac. 9:16. If βαστάσαι τὸ ὄνομα in Ac. 9:15 is to be referred to the propagation of the Gospel and rendered: "to bear my name to nations and kings and the children of Israel," [117] then the ὅσα δεῖ αὐτὸν ὑπὲρ τοῦ ὀνόματός μου παθεῖν of v. 16 refers to the totality of Paul's missionary sufferings, after the manner of the list in 2 C. 11:23 ff. On the other hand, if we are to translate: "before nations and kings etc." (cf. also → IV, 179, 6 f.), then the meaning of ὅσα . . . παθεῖν is just as specific as that of βαστάσαι τὸ ὄνομά μου, cf. → I, 596, 16 ff. Since 9:16 underlies 9:15, the βαστάσαι τὸ ὄνομά μου is made possible only by the ὑπὲρ τοῦ ὀνόματός μου παθεῖν. The παθεῖν does not refer to phenomena accompanying the βαστάσαι; on the contrary, only he who suffers for the name is its bearer. In this case, the δεῖ of v. 16 does not indicate the unavoidability of the resultant or accompanying phenomena without which the apostolic ministry is inconceivable. [118] It states the law that only παθεῖν validates the apostle as σκεῦος ἐκλογῆς, cf. 2 C. 11:23 ff., where διάκονοι Χριστοῦ are shown to be such by their sufferings. The apostle has to show that he is a bearer of Christ, [119] and he does this by his sufferings, cf. Gl. 6:17; → 932, n. 16; I, 596, 13 ff. [120] The active

---

[114] The א reading is suspect since א obviously prefers ἀποθανεῖν to παθεῖν, cf. ἀπέθανεν at 2:21 and in א* ἀποθανόντος at 4:1. Hb. 9:26, 28 as a par. in no way favours ἀπέθανεν (→ I, 381, 31 ff.), for we have ἅπαξ προσενεχθείς in 9:28 and παθεῖν in 9:26.

[115] Schelkle, 73, n. 21, 251; R. Bultmann, "Bekenntnis- u. Liedfr. im 1 Pt.," Coniectanea Neotestamentica, 11 (1947), 2, n. 4.

[116] This παθεῖν for Christ is not just "almost synon." (Braun, 22) but fully synon. to ἀποθανεῖν in 1 Pt. Cf. B. Reicke, "The Disobedient Spirits and Christian Baptism. A Study of 1 Pt. 3:19 and Its Context," Acta Seminarii Neotestamentici Upsaliensis, 13 (1946), 214. Acc. to W. Bieder, "Grund u. Kraft d. Mission nach dem 1 Pt.," Theol. Studien, 29 (1950), 23, n. 33 παθεῖν (in 4:1) denotes "the climax of suffering in death," though cf. ibid., 14, n. 11.

[117] So Bau. Ag., 134, also Zn. Ag., 326; cf. also → 278, 17 f.

[118] Zn. Ag., 327.

[119] Cf. G. Bertram, "Paulus Christophorus," Stromateis (1930), esp. 34-38; J. Schneider, "Die Passionsmystik d. Pls.," UNT, 15 (1929), 14-21.

[120] H. Windisch, "Pls. u. Christus," UNT, 24 (1934), 138 writes on Ac. 9:15 f.: "A Christ motif, or more accurately a Synoptic Son of Man motif, is present in the conclusion of the directions: I will show him ὅσα δεῖ αὐτὸν ὑπὲρ τοῦ ὀνόματός μου παθεῖν, cf. Lk. 9:22 par.; 17:25 par.; 24:26, 46. Paul is here described as the divinely chosen suffering servant

sense which παθεῖν has in Ac. too when applied to Christ Himself (1:3; 3:18; 17:3) is specifically expressed in 9:16 by the definition ὑπὲρ τοῦ ὀνόματός μου and by the link with βαστάσαι τὸ ὄνομά μου in 9:15. The reference is not to patient endurance of hostile attacks and persecutions, but to representing the cause of Christ by παθεῖν.

b. Paul. Most of the instances of πάσχω in Paul relate to his readers, i.e., Christians in general. Only rarely does Paul use πάσχειν of himself, though cf. → πάθημα. He does not use πάσχω at all in enumerating his missionary sufferings. → 912, 8 f. In 2 Tm. 1:12 : δι' ἣν αἰτίαν καὶ ταῦτα πάσχω the δι' ἣν αἰτίαν shows that πάσχειν results from discharging the high office of herald, apostle and teacher, cf. 1:11. But the proclamation of the Gospel is also forwarded by suffering, cf. 1:8; 2:3; → 937, 34 f., and the καί, particularly as it goes with οὐκ ἐπαισχύνομαι, [121] shows how necessary and almost natural suffering is. 1 Th. 2:14 is the only Pauline instance of a plainly pass. use of πάσχω. [122] That πάσχω can have a very act. ring in Paul[123] is shown by Phil. 1:30, where the τὸ ὑπὲρ αὐτοῦ πάσχειν of v. 29 is elucidated by τὸν αὐτὸν ἀγῶνα ἔχοντες. [124] πάσχειν thus means "to fight," perhaps "to fight an enforced fight" (cf. the ἀντικείμενοι in v. 28), not "to be helplessly exposed or subject to alien pressure," but "to struggle manfully" (cf. also the συναθλοῦντες of v. 27) [125] and "to prevail" (cf. στήκετε). According to Phil. 1:29 παθεῖν is not a privilege of the apostle or a select few but is of the very essence of Christianity as such. All the same, it is a privilege, a special grace (ὑμῖν ἐχαρίσθη) which surpasses even the grace of being able to believe in Christ. The ὑπὲρ αὐτοῦ, towards which the τὸ ὑπὲρ Χριστοῦ at the very beginning of the sentence is already orientated, [126] sets Phil. 1:29 in close relationship to the ὑπὲρ τοῦ ὀνόματός μου of Ac. 9:16 (→ 919, 18 ff.), and the active, positive sense of πάσχειν is plainly apparent. Since tne ὑπέρ refers to Christ or His name (the kingdom of God in 2 Th. 1:5), it can hardly be the apostle's intention to speak of a soteriological significance of the sufferings of Christians. Christ, His name and the kingdom of God cannot be the subject of soteriological effort.

The ref. of πάσχειν to Christ, which is plain in the ὑπὲρ Χριστοῦ of Phil. 1:29 (→ I, 139, 20 ff.), may be seen in another form in the fact that the παθήματα of the apostle and of Christians count as παθήματα τοῦ Χριστοῦ (→ 931, 20 ff.) acc. to

---

of God of Is. 53, a second servant of God and son of man after Jesus (and in His service)." But only on the assumption that the OT intimations have found their supreme fulfilment in the person of Jesus Christ is Ac. 9:16 possible, since it is primarily based on this and not on Is. 53. Paul must suffer, not as a second servant of God or even son of man, but as an apostle of Him who is alone the Servant of God and Son of Man. The δεῖ of 9:16 does not mean "according to the Scriptures," as in Lk. 9:22; 24:26, 46. It means that apostolic suffering is entailed by conformity to Christ.

[121] Cf. Wbg. Past., 281.

[122] Constr. with ὑπό (→ n. 62). The act. element is not wholly absent, → IV, 667, 1 ff. Acc. to G. Wiencke, "Pls. über Jesu Tod," BFTh, II, 42 (1939), 127 Pl. in 1 Th. 2:14 f. sets in a series "the sufferings of the prophets, of Jesus, of the churches of Judaea, and of the church of Thessalonica." The constr. and terminology show that this is only partly true.

[123] 1 Th. 2:2 might also be adduced as an example, → 924, 35 ff.

[124] Cf. also ἐν πολλῷ ἀγῶνι in 1 Th. 2:2 (on this Wbg. Th., 43, and for a different view Dib. Th., ad loc.; → I, 137, 9 ff.).

[125] One cannot divide the συναθλέω of Phil. 1:27; 4:3 into passion and action (cf. → I, 167, 27 ff.), since the passion is action.

[126] Cf. Mich. Ph., 30.

2 C. 1:5 ff. (in 1:6 we find [παθήματα] πάσχειν par. θλίβεσθαι). The eschatological goal of these sufferings, which is also apparent in the mention of σωτηρία in 2 C. 1:6 (cf. Phil. 1:28), is plainly stated in the ref. to the βασιλεία τοῦ θεοῦ in 2 Th. 1:5. The connection between suffering and glory is explicitly stated in R. 8:17: εἴπερ συμπάσχομεν ἵνα καὶ συνδοξασθῶμεν. Only here (→ 925, 13 ff.) and in Phil. 3:10 (→ 932, 1 ff.) is there in Paul any urgent question as to the relation between the sufferings of Christians and the suffering of Christ.

c. 1 Pt. If in Paul the question of the relation between the sufferings of Christians and the death of Jesus is very secondary, a first glance at 1 Pt. might give the impression that the author heavily stresses this relation when in 2:19 f.; 3:14, 17; 4:1, 15, 19; 5:10 he takes the word πάσχω, which he uses for the death of Jesus (→ 918, 19 ff.; he never has ἀποθανεῖν, θάνατος or σταυρωθῆναι, σταυρός) and applies it to Christians (cf. also his use of πάθημα, → 934, 23 ff.). Yet πάσχω never means "to die" in this use, except fig. at 4:1. πάσχω occurs first in 2:19 f. The connection with v. 18 shows that πάσχω refers to the treatment of a Christian slave by a master who is σκολιός. This is brought out even more plainly in v. 20. 2:20a shows that the maltreatment is in punishment for faults, → III, 819, 6 ff. Hence ἀγαθοποιοῦντες καὶ πάσχοντες in 2:20b (par. 2:19) refers to the opposite situation, i.e., that slaves who have faithfully done their duty are undeservedly, ἀδίκως (→ I, 152, 37 f.) punished. It is true that πάσχω could have the more general sense "to be treated badly" (with ref. to scolding, blows, poor food etc.). The relation to κολαφίζεσθαι, however, supports the sense "to suffer punishment," → 905, 20 ff.; 912, 17 f., 23 f., esp. as we find in 4:15 too the saying: μὴ γάρ τις ὑμῶν πασχέτω ὡς (→ 905, 25) φονεὺς ἢ κλέπτης (→ III, 755, 22 ff.) ἢ κακοποιὸς (ibid., 485, 33, 38 ff.) ἢ ὡς ἀλλοτριεπίσκοπος (→ II, 620, 42 ff.). 4:15 refers to the possibility of Christians being punished by the public courts as thieves, murderers etc. In 4:16, esp. as πάσχω has to be supplied from v. 15, the εἰ δὲ ὡς Χριστιανός also suggests public condemnation and punishment, though, as in 4:19,[127] it might refer to all the sufferings to which Christians were probably exposed in the days of 1 Pt., i.e., abuse (cf. 4:14, → 240, 14 ff.), threats, assaults, disadvantages at work, persecutions etc.

The slight change in sense which there is in this case between 4:15 and 4:16 should not surprise us, for the meaning "to suffer punishment" in 2:19 f. does not affect the πάσχω sayings in 2:21, 23 nor is the use in 2:19 f. orientated in advance to 2:21, 23.[128] The link between the verses is not by way of πάσχω but via the thoughts contained in ἀδίκως and ὑποφέρειν in v. 19 and ὑπομένειν in v. 20 : Though Christ undoubtedly had to die ἀδίκως, He did so on our account (2:21, 24), not His own (2:22). He willingly accepted this, and so His death can be an example to ἀγαθοποιοῦντες, 2:20b, → I, 215, 12 ff.; 773, 8 ff.; III, 404, 1 ff. We find exactly the same relation between 3:14, 17 and 3:18.

The saying in 3:14 : ἀλλ᾽ εἰ καὶ πάσχοιτε διὰ δικαιοσύνην, μακάριοι (→ IV, 368, 4 and 11), since the διά can hardly be modal (→ II, 69, 16 ff.), goes further than the ἀδίκως of 2:19 and the ἀγαθοποιοῦντες of 2:20; 3:17. If on the one hand there is punishment in spite of the performance of duty, here the thought is

---

[127] On the relation of 4:15 and 4:19 to 4:16 f. cf. Wbg. Pt., 142, ad loc.; → III, 59, 16 ff.; 461, 9 ff.; 939, 15 f.

[128] Similarly κολαφιζόμενοι in 2:20 is not controlled by regard for 2:21 ff., since Christ is not called κολαφιζόμενος in what follows, and a reminiscence of Mk. 14:65 par. can hardly be inserted as a connecting member. Cf. → III, 819, 3 ff. and K. L. Schmidt, "Ἰησοῦς Χριστὸς κολαφιζόμενος," Aux sources de la tradition chrétienne. Mélanges offerts à M. Goguel (1950), 221 f.

that of suffering on account of doing what is right (→ II, 199, 29 f.; cf. suffering ὡς Χριστιανός, 4:16). 3:17, which is more general than 3:14, is in its whole tenor related to 2:20. [129] As 2:19 is followed by the reference to Christ in 2:21 ff., so it is with 3:14-17 and 3:18, → 919, 1 ff. The characterisation δίκαιος ὑπὲρ ἀδίκων (→ II, 189, 9 ff.) is more than an elucidation of the περὶ ἁμαρτιῶν. It, and not just the παθεῖν of Christ as such, shows how far Christ is an obligatory example for Christians when they have to suffer διὰ δικαιοσύνην (3:14) and as ἀγαθο-ποιοῦντες (3:17). The sufferings indicated by πάσχω in 5:10 and by παθήματα in 5:9 (→ 934, 34 f.) are not fundamentally different from those referred to else-where in 1 Pt. The only point is that here at the conclusion there is greater em-phasis on their extent and seriousness, cf. already 4:12. [130] The thought of their eschatological termination, expressed by the aor. παθόντας in 5:10, [131] is also present in 1:6 f. and 4:12 f. (cf. also 5:1). The saying in 4:13 : καθὸ κοινωνεῖτε τοῖς τοῦ Χριστοῦ παθήμασιν, reminds us only formally of the κοινωνία παθη-μάτων αὐτοῦ of Phil. 3:10 (→ 932, 1 ff.). The sufferings of Christians are not here derived from the passion of Christ or the necessity of participating in this. What is stated is rather that Christians as πάσχοντες (4:19) do in fact follow in His steps (2:21). The verse is closer to 2 C. 1:5 ff. (→ 931, 20 ff.) than Phil. 3:10.

In 4:1: Χριστοῦ οὖν παθόντος σαρκὶ καὶ ὑμεῖς τὴν αὐτὴν ἔννοιαν ὁπλίσασθε, ὅτι ὁ παθὼν σαρκὶ πέπαυται ἁμαρτίας, the ὅτι clause is to be regarded as parenthetical. [132] At any rate, in so far as it applies to Christians, it should not be referred to their sufferings (3:14, 17). [133] In analogy to Christ's παθεῖν σαρκί, which is mentioned just before and in which παθεῖν means "to die" (cf. also 3:18; → 917, 34 ff.), it refers to their death, i.e., in baptism (cf. 3:21). [134] The similarity to R. 6:7: ὁ γὰρ ἀποθανὼν δεδικαίωται ἀπὸ τῆς ἁμαρτίας, and to the context of this v., is very plain. [135] In dying, Christ, too, accepted the will of God (cf. 4:2). [136] If Christians arm themselves with the same ἔννοια, they, too, will in the future live only to God, R. 6:11.

This transf. use of παθεῖν (σαρκί) with ref. to baptism is found only here in 1 Pt. or the NT generally. It is possible only on the basis of the usage παθεῖν = "to die." [137]

---

[129] On κρεῖττον in 3:17 cf. κλέος and χάρις in 2:20 (though χάρις in 2:19 f. does not have the force of ἐχαρίσθη in Phil. 1:29, → 920, 21 ff.).

[130] A division such as that proposed by Bieder (→ n. 116), 11 is superfluous and in-practicable. Acc. to Bieder a new writing begins in 4:12. But in both 3:17 and 4:19 suffering is subject to God's will. Again, 5:8 does not say that the διάβολος is the author of suffering. What is meant is that he uses the occasion of suffering to make Christians more pliable to himself.

[131] Cf. Wbg., Pt., 154.

[132] Cf. also A. Kirchgässner, *Erlösung u. Sünde im NT* (1950), 237 f. → IV, 971, n. 18.

[133] As against Braun, 47. Schelkle (73, 235, n. 62) wrongly considers whether there might not even be a ref. to martyrs.

[134] Wbg. Pt., 121 rightly emphasises that παθών is used, not πάσχων. The vl. ἐν σαρκί is influenced by βιῶσαι ἐν σαρκί (as against Wbg., *loc. cit.*, n. 88).

[135] Cf. → IV, 971, 19 ff.; Kirchgässner, *op. cit.*; Reitzenstein Hell. Myst., 259, n. 3. Quite wrongly R. Perdelwitz, "Die Mysterienreligion u. d. Problem d. 1 Pt.," RVV, XI, 3 (1911), 85 relates the saying to the fact that the initiate must undergo certain physical sufferings and torments before he attains σωτηρία.

[136] In this connection it is also said of Him : πέπαυται ἁμαρτίας, → I, 315, 5 ff.

[137] The age and constancy of this meaning are overlooked by Wnd. Pt. on 1 Pt. 4:1: "Perhaps παθών already = ἀποθανών in Ign. Sm., 2; Barn., 7, 11." The conjecture of Reitzenstein Hell. Myst., 161: "The use seems to be late Jewish," finds no confirmation, → 910, 21 ff.

Moreover, it is difficult to explain unless we assume the influence of the thought of R. 6, which Paul regarded as common to primitive Christianity.

D. The Post-Apostolic Fathers.

There is no great use of πάσχω in the post-apost. fathers (c. 50 times). Worth noting is the fact that the sense "to die" comes strongly to the fore, whether for the death of Jesus or for the martyr's death. πάσχω does not occur in Did. 1 Cl., 6, 1 f.; 45, 5 refer to martyrdom, though πάσχω with an acc. obj. means "to suffer." Ign., on the other hand, always uses πάσχω abs. except in Sm., 2, where, with ref. to the πάθος (→ 929, 1 ff.) of 1, 2, which plainly denotes the death of Jesus, and also in orientation to the birth, baptism and resurrection (1, 1 f.), we read : ταῦτα γὰρ πάντα ἔπαθεν δι' ἡμᾶς ἵνα σωθῶμεν. The meaning is the general "to undergo" (only here in Ign.); there is no thought of an extension of the παθεῖν of the passion to the birth etc. Yet just after παθεῖν is used of the passion : καὶ ἀληθῶς ἔπαθεν, ὡς καὶ ἀληθῶς ἀνέστησεν ἑαυτόν, and then again in the rejection of the Docetic view : τὸ δοκεῖν αὐτὸν πεπονθέναι, cf. the par. Tr., 10. In the saying about the σάρξ of Jesus Christ in the eucharist in Sm., 7, 1: τὴν ὑπὲρ τῶν ἁμαρτιῶν ἡμῶν παθοῦσαν ἣν τῇ χρηστότητι ὁ πατὴρ ἤγειρεν, παθεῖν again means "to suffer" in the sense "to die." The other refs. relate to Ign. himself, i.e., to his prospective martyrdom : R., 4, 3; 8, 3; Tr., 4, 2; Pol., 7, 1. [138] The sense "to die" may also be seen in the use of συμπάσχω in Ign. (→ 926, 9 ff.). Whether πάσχειν means this with ref. to Christians in Polycarp Ep., 8, 2 depends on how we are to construe the preceding μιμηταί (→ IV, 674, 27 f.). In Barn. 11 of the 14 instances of πάσχω refer to the death of Jesus, and though we find the constr. with ὑπό (→ n. 122) in 5, 5; 7, 5, the colouring is usually active : 5, 5 (1st instance); 5, 13 (ἐπὶ ξύλου); 6, 7 (in this v. also the only use of πάθος for "death" in Barn., → 929, 28 ff.); 7, 2 and 10; 12, 2 (→ σταυρός) and 5. Whether there is an allusion to the πάσχειν of Jesus in 6, 9 (cf. 6, 7): ἄνθρωπος γὰρ γῆ ἐστιν πάσχουσα, is an open question. [139] In an exposition of Lv. 16:21 f. as a τύπος Ἰησοῦ meant for the community, we read in 7, 11: He who would take away the wool (from the bush) δεῖ αὐτὸν πολλὰ παθεῖν (→ n. 86) on account of the terrible thorns καὶ θλιβέντα κυριεῦσαι αὐτοῦ (sc. τοῦ ἐρίου). οὕτω, φησίν (sc. Jesus), οἱ θέλοντές με ἰδεῖν καὶ ἅψασθαί μου τῆς βασιλείας ὀφείλουσιν θλιβέντες καὶ παθόντες λαβεῖν με (→ III, 143, 27 f.). [140] In Herm. v., 3, 1, 9; 2, 1; 5, 2; s., 8, 3, 6 f.; 9, 28, 2-6 [141] παθεῖν refers to martyrdom, [142] as shown esp. by the distinction between παθεῖν and θλιβῆναι in s., 8, 3, 6 f. (→ III, 144, n. 7). [143] In s., 6, 3, 6 πάσχω means "to suffer punishment," cf. also 6, 5, 4 and 6. πάσχειν is combined with ὑβρίζεσθαι in 6, 3, 4 (cf. 1 Th. 2:2; → 924, 28 ff.). On τί παθεῖται in 2 Cl., 7, 5 cf. → 905, 16 ff.; 2 Cl., 1, 2 reminds us of Barn., 5, 5. παθόντα

---

[138] Ign. also uses ἀποθνήσκω both of Christ's death (e.g., Tr., 2, 1; R., 6, 1) and his own (e.g., R., 4, 1; 6, 2). Yet Ign. can hardly have contributed to the later use of παθεῖν with ἀποθανεῖν for "to suffer and to die" (→ n. 87). Cf. also → 930, n. 35.

[139] The thesis of M. Werner, Die Entstehung d. chr. Dogmas (1941), 486 that the ref. is to the sacramental use of milk and honey and to the origin of the eucharist in Christ's death can hardly be sustained in view of the interpretation in terms of faith and word in 6, 17. Cf. also Wnd. Barn. on 6, 17; → I, 647, 13 f.; IV, 558, n. 29.

[140] On the question of an agraphon cf. Wnd. Barn., ad loc. Cf. Ac. 14:22.

[141] On the tradition at s., 8, 10, 4 cf. Dib. Herm., ad loc. Pap. Michigan (ed. C. Bonner [1934]) has παθοῦνται (a gap follows).

[142] This is not refuted by the fact that καὶ παρέδωκαν τὰς ψυχὰς αὐτῶν is added in s., 9, 28, 2, since this is tautological. On s., 9, 28, 5 (cf. 8, 10, 3 → I, 596, n. 7) cf. Ac. 9:16 → 919, 18 ff.

[143] It is obvious that this must have been influenced by the NT use of παθεῖν even though the author does not use this for the death of Jesus ; in fact, he never speaks of this expressly (cf., e.g., s., 5, 6, 2 f.).

is used of the death of Jesus in Mart. Pol., 17, 2 (vl. ἀποθανόντα): ὡς οὐδὲν πεπονθώς, "as though nothing had befallen him." [144]

† **παθητός.**

1. Verbal adj. of πάσχω. From examples and construction it is later. It means "open to external impressions" or more particularly "subject to external impressions" (opp. ἀπαθής). Common in Plut., sometimes with θνητός. [1] It then means "subject to the πάθη," → 926, 27 ff. In Philo Op. Mund., 8 f. it is the opp. of δραστήριος, cf. Spec. Leg., III, 180 opp. δρᾶν. Cf. also Sacr. AC, 70; Ebr., 73. παθητός does not occur in the LXX, cf. also → 368, n. 4.

2. It occurs in the NT only at Ac. 26:23. The phrase εἰ παθητὸς ὁ χριστός does not ask whether Christ can suffer, whether His sufferings are conceivable. The starting-point is that He has to suffer according to Scripture, and that Jesus had to do so for the same reason. Since Ac. 26:23 is closely related to Lk. 24:26, 46; Ac. 3:18; 17:3, the meaning of παθητός is defined by the use of παθεῖν there. Suffering in the sense of dying is in view, and the term also shares the active sense peculiar to the verses mentioned and to those dealt with → 913, 3 ff. Hence the meaning is, not "exposed, subject to πάσχειν," [2] but "ordained for, charged with πάσχειν." Cf. → 916, n. 93.

3. Post-Apostolic Fathers. The word occurs only in Ign. Eph., 7, 2 and Ign. Pol., 3, 2, in both instances with ref. to Christ (opp. ἀπαθής), though post-existence is in view in Eph., pre-existence in Pol., → 370, 9 f. παθητός here hardly denotes the One who entered the world of πάθη, but the One who could die, cf. the use of πάσχω, → 923, 5 ff. and πάθος → 929, 2 ff. in Ign. [3]

† **προπάσχω.**

From Soph. and Hdt., partly abs. (as in Paul), e.g., Hdt., VII, 11; Thuc., III, 82, 7, partly with acc. obj.: [1] "to be under previous influence" (usually *in malam partem*), "to suffer before," e.g., Jos. Bell., 6, 219.

The only NT instance is at 1 Th. 2:2, where the reference of Paul's προπαθόντες καὶ ὑβρισθέντες καθὼς οἴδατε ἐν Φιλίπποις is to the events at Philippi recorded in Ac. 16, cf. Phil. 1:30. [2] In keeping with the use of πάσχω in Paul (→ 920, 6 ff.) προπάσχω means "to suffer before." Only here does Paul use πάσχω with a related verb to constitute a pair (cf. Herm. s., 6, 3, 4 → 923, 32 f.; materially the προ applies also to ὑβρισθέντες). [3] The combining of πολλὰ παθεῖν with ἐξουδενηθῆναι or ἀποδοκιμασθῆναι in Mk. 9:12; Lk. 17:25 (→ 914, 27 ff.) is no direct analogy. Yet it is possible that προπαθόντες, in distinction from the passive ὑβρισθέντες, lays greater stress on the active side of the matter, since πάσχω, too, can have this nuance in Paul, → 920, 14 ff.; 920, 25 ff.

---

[144] In the Apologists, too, there is an influence of the use of πάσχω for the death of Jesus. Cf. Tat. Or. Graec., 13, 3, also Just., in whom over half the 50 or so refs. are to the death of Jesus. Cf. → παθητός, n. 3; 930, n. 35.

π α θ η τ ό ς. For bibl. → πάσχω.
[1] Cf. Cr.-Kö., 841 and Pr.-Bauer, *s.v.*
[2] So Pr.-Bauer, *s.v.*
[3] In Ign. the meaning is "to be subject to suffering" (= θνητός), while ἀπαθής means "not exposed to suffering," "incapable of suffering." Cf. Just., who uses the word a good deal, e.g., Dial., 85, 2 : παθητοῦ γενομένου ἀνθρώπου par. to the preceding διὰ παρθένου γεννηθέντος. On the relation to Is. 53 cf. Euler, 133, 135; → 696, 27 ff.

π ρ ο π ά σ χ ω. [1] Cf. Pass. and Liddell-Scott, *s.v.*
[2] Cf. the use of διωγμοί and παθήματα in 2 Tm. 3:11, → 932, n. 12.
[3] On this cf. E. Schwyzer, *Griech. Grammatik,* II (1950), 422 [Debrunner].

† συμπάσχω.

1. From Plat. in the sense "to suffer at the same time," "to suffer with or the same as." [1] Very rarely in the sense "to sympathise" (which is usually → συμπαθέω), e.g., Polyb., 4, 7, 3; 15, 19, 4; Diod. S., 17, 36. The LXX does not have συμπάσχω (Αλλ. 1 Βασ. 22:8). Philo only Spec. Leg., III, 194 etc. in the sense "to suffer with." This is also the meaning at Test. Zeb. 6:5; 7:3 ("to sympathise" is in the context expressed by σπλαγχνίζομαι). [2]

2. The only use in the NT is at R. 8:17; 1 C. 12:26. In the similitude of the body and its members (1 C. 12:12, 14 ff.) συμπάσχειν in 12:26a means "also to suffer," "to be involved in fellow-suffering." [3] When applied to the community 12:26a does not mean that when a member suffers harm all the members share the loss emotionally. [4] What it means is that in this case they all suffer the loss too. In R. 8:17: εἴπερ συμπάσχομεν, ἵνα καὶ συνδοξασθῶμεν (→ II, 250, 11 f.; III, 804, 29 ff.; 806, 6 ff., 20 ff.), the whole context makes it plain that συμπάσχω cannot be meant in the sense "to sympathise." It may also be seen from the preceding συγκληρονόμοι Χριστοῦ that the συν- in συμπάσχω does not refer to a fellowship of suffering among Christians, but has in view a relation to Christ. The meaning is not "to suffer likewise," though the word can have this sense. For Paul, who does not use παθεῖν for the death of Christ in the special sense "to die," [5] never speaks of a πάσχειν of Christ. [6] This undermines the possibility that συμπάσχομεν might denote a common participation of Christ and Christians in a common suffering, → III, 806, 19 f. No such idea of common suffering is found anywhere else in Paul, → 933, n. 20. Christians are called συγκληρονόμοι Χριστοῦ because they are set by Christ in the position of sons and heirs, → III, 782, 2 ff., 35 f. συνδοξασθῶμεν also includes the thought that they have received the heavenly δόξα through Him, cf. Phil. 3:21; Col. 1:27; → II, 250, 9 f., 13. Similarly συμπάσχομεν means that Christ has set them in this suffering. The reference is to a suffering διὰ 'Ιησοῦν (cf. 2 C. 4:11), to a ὑπὲρ αὐτοῦ πάσχειν (Phil. 1:29), to παθήματα τοῦ Χριστοῦ in this sense, → 932, 25 ff.

R. 8:18 shows plainly that συνδοξασθῆναι is not to be expected directly after the συμπάσχειν, but only at the resurrection, just as in Lk. 24:26 etc. (→ 913, 12 ff.; cf. also 1 Pt. 1:11, → 934, 23 ff.) entry into δόξα followed Christ's παθεῖν at the resurrection. Unlike the συνήγειρεν of Eph. 2:6 or the ἐδόξασεν of R. 8:30, the συνδοξασθῆναι relates to the time when Christ Himself appears ἐν δόξῃ and acc. to Col. 3:4 believers are also to be manifested ἐν δόξῃ either σὺν αὐτῷ or through Him. As the συνδοξασθῶμεν is contemporaneous with Christ, so is the συμπάσχομεν. If the above explanation is correct, then the συν- in συμπάσχομεν refers neither to the fact that Christians are made contemporaneous with Christ's death by a — mystical or some

---

σ υ μ π ά σ χ ω. For bibl. → πάσχω.

[1] Cf. Pass. and Liddell-Scott, s.v. Only late in inscr. and pap.; cf. Preisigke Wört., II, 514 and Moult.-Mill., 612, s.v.

[2] On the other hand the meaning is "to sympathise" in Test. Jos. 20:6 : τοῖς Αἰγυπτίοις ὡς ἰδίοις μέλεσι συνέπασχεν. But Charles reads : ὡς μέλος ἔπασχεν.

[3] It is unnecessary and even erroneous to assume a link with Stoic teaching, with Joh. W. 1 K., 307. Cf. Str.-B., III, 448 f.; → 913, n. 63.

[4] The emotional aspect comes out only in συγχαίρει, perhaps in transition to the application to the community.

[5] There can certainly be in συμπάσχομεν no parallelism between the πάσχειν of Christians and the death of Jesus, and the saying cannot be restricted to martyrdom.

[6] One may refer only to the πάθημα of Phil. 3:10. Even this stands alone in the instances of πάθημα (→ 932, 1 ff.), and hence it gives no guidance as to the understanding of πάσχω and compounds in Paul.

other — κοινωνία (even Phil. 3:10 does not mean this, → 932, 1 ff.), nor to the fact that their union with Christ, which is general and which finds expression in their ἐν Χριστῷ εἶναι (cf. → 934, n. 26), makes their πάσχειν at once a συμπάσχειν.

The εἴπερ of R. 8:17 makes the συμπάσχειν not merely an indispensable condition of future συνδοξασθῆναι (cf. 2 Tm. 2:12) but also a presupposition of the fact that there is genuine Christianity, fellowship with Christ and divine sonship, R. 8:14 ff. The πάσχειν of Christians is a συμπάσχειν because Christ leads them to suffering. [7]

3. Post-Apostolic Fathers. In Ign. Sm., 42 : εἰς τὸ συμπαθεῖν αὐτῷ (sc. Christ) πάντα ὑπομένω the ref. is certainly not to suffering in general but to death. This is not surprising in view of the fact that Ign. normally uses πάσχειν for "to die," → 923, 5 ff. This is also an argument for the sense "to die with" when συμπάσχω occurs in Ign. Pol., 6, 1. If in the list there συγκοιμᾶσθε and συνεγείρεσθε mean death and resurrection, [8] this is, of course, an obstacle to construing συμπάσχετε (sc. ἀλλήλοις) as death. Nevertheless, the six members are grouped in pairs : at the beginning συγκοπιᾶτε and συναθλεῖτε, at the end συγκοιμᾶσθε and συνεγείρεσθε, and in the middle συντρέχετε and συμπάσχετε. Thus these two can refer to fellowship in life (as a journey to martyrdom) and in death, while the last two, death and resurrection, carry the thought further. [9] Pol., 9, 2 says of Ign. and other martyrs who are now παρὰ τῷ κυρίῳ : ᾧ καὶ συνέπαθον. The meaning is obviously "to die with," → 923, 18 ff. Elsewhere [10] συμπάσχω occurs only in 2 Cl., 4, 3 in the sense "to sympathise." The word is not to be found in the Apologists.

† πάθος.

1. πάθος, used from the tragic poets, [1] is a noun which shares the history of πάσχω. → 904, 4 ff. It first denotes an "experience": πάθει μάθος Aesch. Ag., 177 (→ 906, 15 ff.): τὸ συντυχὸν πάθος, Soph. Ai., 313. Even without addition it is used in malam partem for "misfortune," "mishap," "defeat," "sickness" etc. The meaning "mood," "feeling," "emotion" etc. is very common in both a good sense and a bad ; cf. the def. in Aristot. Eth. Nic., II, 4, p. 1105b, 19 ff.: τὰ ἐν τῇ ψυχῇ γινόμενα τρία ἐστι, πάθη δυνάμεις ἕξεις ... λέγω δὲ πάθη μὲν ἐπιθυμίαν (→ III, 168, 22 f. and n. 6), ὀργήν (→ 385, 1) φόβον, θράσος, φθόνον, χαράν, φιλίαν, μῖσος, πόθον, ζῆλον, ἔλεον (→ II, 478, 14 ff.), ὅλως οἷς ἕπεται ἡδονὴ (→ II, 913, 4 ff.; → IV, 315, 7 ff.) ἢ λύπη. This meaning is often in malam partem : "passion," "impulse." [2] Cf. ἐκτὸς τοῦ πάθους εἶναι, Teles, p. 56 (Hense) or ἔξω τῶν παθῶν γίνεσθαι, Dio C., 60, 3 as the Cynic-Stoic ideal of ἀπάθεια or ἀταραξία, cf. also → II, 495, 21 ff. Under Pythagorean

---

[7] When 8:18 speaks of παθήματα τοῦ νῦν καιροῦ, no fundamentally different motivation of suffering is offered, → 934, 4 ff.

[8] So rightly Pr.-Bauer, s.v., though Bau. Ign., ad loc. translates "sleep, awake."

[9] H.-W. Bartsch, "Gnostisches Gut u. Gemeindetradition bei Ign. v. Antiochien," BFTh, II, 44 (1940), 124 tries to relate all 6 words, esp. the last 3, to the cultus: "There they suffered and died with Christ to be raised again with Him." But παθεῖν is never used by Ign. for suffering as distinct from death. The combination of συμπάσχετε and συγκοιμᾶσθε forms no basis for the expression "to suffer and to die," → 916, n. 87; 923, n. 138.

[10] Pr.-Bauer⁴, s.v. mistakenly refers also to Ign. R., 6, 3, → 936, 14 ff.

π ά θ ο ς. For bibl. → πάσχω. Cr.-Kö., 841 f.; A. Vögtle, "Die Tugend- u. Lasterkataloge im NT," Nt.liche Abh., XVI, 4/5 (1936); H. Schlier, "Religionsgeschichtliche Untersuchungen zu d. Ignatiusbriefen," ZNW Beih., 8 (1929); H.-W. Bartsch, "Gnost. Gut u. Gemeindetradition bei Ign. v. Ant.," BFTh, II, 44 (1940).

[1] πάθος for the Homeric → πένθος, which took on the meaning "sorrow," formed from ἔπαθον. Cf. E. Schwyzer, Gr. Grammatik, I (1939), 512.

[2] Rare in inscr.: σπουδαίῳ πάθει, "with passionate zeal," Ditt. Syll.³, 810, 20 f. (55 A.D.); of sicknesses, ibid., 1239, 22 f. (2nd cent. A.D.); pap. in Preisigke Wört., II, 220, s.v. only from the 2nd cent. on for "sickness" (cf. Preis. Zaub., III, 287; XII, 305), also BGU, II, 588, 4 (2nd/3rd cent. A.D.): ἔργον καὶ πάθος ἔχειν, "to have toil and vexation."

influence is the use of πάθος for "changes," "modifications," "processes," Plat. Resp., X, 612a; τὰ περὶ τὸν οὐρανόν τε καὶ τὴν γῆν πάθη, Phaed., 96b c; also "attribute" (opp. οὐσία): ἔστι καὶ ἀριθμοῦ ἴδια πάθη, οἷον περιττότης, ἀρτιότης, Aristot. Metaph., I, 2, p. 985b, 29. As a rhetorical tt. for emotional expression : "pathos," cf. πάθος ποιεῖν in Aristot. Rhet., III, 17, p. 1418a, 12. [3]

2. In the LXX πάθος occurs in writings with an original Heb., apart from Job 30:31, where πένθος AR (so also ᾽ΑΘΣ) is a better reading than πάθος אB (Mas. אֲבָל "complaint"), only at Prv. 25:20 with ref. to "sickness." [4] Elsewhere it is found only in 4 Macc., though here 63 times (only 1:14, 24; 13:4 sing.). The whole work is meant to be a φιλοσοφώτατος λόγος on the theme εἰ αὐτοδέσποτός ἐστιν τῶν παθῶν ὁ εὐσεβὴς λογισμός, 1, 1 (→ IV, 286, 21 ff.). The πάθη here are emotions, not as pura naturalia, [5] but as bad impulses (opp. ἀρεταί, 1:30). Cf. → II, 916, 30 ff. [6]

3. Philo uses πάθος much more often than → πάθημα, some 400 times. [7] In the vast majority of instances the meaning is "emotion" in the sense of the Stoic doctrine of πάθη, cf. Spec. Leg., IV, 79. God alone is παντὸς πάθους ἀμέτοχος, Abr., 202; cf. Deus Imm., 52 etc. [8] The 4 Platonic and Stoic emotions (Leg. All., II, 102; III, 139; Det. Pot. Ins., 119 etc.), ἡδονή and ἐπιθυμία (→ III, 170, 4 ff.), λύπη (→ IV, 319, 19 ff.) and φόβος are often listed in this or some other order. [9] For Philo ἡδονή esp. is πάθος, → II, 917, 11 ff.: τῶν ἄλλων παθῶν χείρων εἶναι δοκεῖ, Leg. All., III, 113. [10] The emotions are closely related to αἴσθησις, → I, 187, 32 ff.; [11] on the other side νοῦς, διάνοια, λόγος, λογισμός are ready to support man in battle against the πάθη. [12] Cf. also → II, 341, 8 ff. and 924, 19 ff. Philo emphatically champions the demand for ἀπάθεια (noun rare, ἀπαθής more common, → III, 273, 38 f.). But we also find another more Jewish view [13] acc. to which the πάθη are simply to be bridled. Here εὐπάθεια (37 times) is more typical than → μετριοπαθέω, μετριοπάθεια. Joseph., too, uses πάθος more often than → πάθημα, mostly for an "(unhappy) event," "misfortune," also "illness." πάθος does not mean "death" when used alone, cf. Ant. 4, 320; 5, 360; 19, 212. Rarely of emotions, more often libido, Ant., 2, 43, 46, 53, 252; 4, 136; 7, 169; Bell., 4, 562. There is no discernible influence of the Gk. concept of emotion (ἀπαθής, Ant., 1, 284, 327; 2, 152; 4, 50 etc. simply means "without hurt," "unmolested"). [14] In Test. XII the word means "vice" in Jud. 18:6; D. 3:5; 4:5 (text α Charles); B. 5:1. On the other hand, "(sexual) passion" is more the sense in Jos. 7:8, → 928, 19 ff. There is no special

---

[3] Cf. further on πάθος in Pass. and Liddell-Scott, s.v.

[4] Since v. 20a LXX is another version of v. 20, is πάθος used for "trouble" par. λύπη in v. 20a ? Or does it have the same Heb. original as βλάπτει in v. 20a (πάθος = βλάβη)? At Job 16:4 Σ adds πάθη and thus objectifies the statement (as distinct from the LXX) [Bertram].

[5] As against Cr.-Kö., 842, s.v.

[6] Also παθοκράτεια in 13:5, 16 (→ 909, 14 ff.), παθοκρατέομαι 7:20, ἡδυπάθεια 2:2, 4 "delight in impulses and pleasures" (cf. 2 Cl., 16, 2; 17, 7). On the other hand, in 4 Macc. → κακοπάθεια, → συμπαθής and → συμπαθέω are not related to πάθος in the sense of "emotion."

[7] Cf. Leisegang, 611-616 for the refs. in 10 sections.

[8] Ibid., 615, No. 7, also 366 f., s.v. θεός, No. 1, 2d. → 909, 38 ff.

[9] Ibid., 611, No. 1b.

[10] Ibid., 611 f., No. 1d. Rarely referred to the sexual area : "inclination," Spec. Leg., III, 67, 80, 173, libido, Virt., 110; Spec. Leg., III, 44; Dec. 129.

[11] Ibid., 612, No. 2.

[12] Cf. W. Völker, "Fortschritt u. Vollendung bei Philo v. Alex.," TU, 49, 1 (1938), 126-154.

[13] Cf. Völker, 87 ff., 134-137, 266 ff.

[14] With → συμπαθ-, → κακοπαθ-, μετριοπαθ- there is a whole series of other combinations with παθ- : περιπαθέω, Ant., 15, 86, ὑπερπαθέω, Bell., 6, 124, δεινοπαθέω, Ant., 1, 312, ἐνθηλυπαθέω, Bell., 4, 561, ἀναξιοπάθεια, Ant., 15, 37 and 283; 18, 47, ἐκπαθῶς, Bell., 2, 471, ἐμπαθῶς, Ant., 16, 100.

relation to the concept of emotion in Test. XII. [15] In the Rabb. world there is no term equivalent to πάθος in the sense of "emotion," "passion," → 911, n. 50; II, 917, 41 ff.; III, 170, 15 ff.

4. In the NT πάθος occurs only in Pl., plur. R. 1:26, sing. Col. 3:5; 1 Th. 4:5. The πάθη ἀτιμίας of R. 1:26a are the scandalous vices of homosexuality, 1:26b, 27. If ἀκαθαρσία, elsewhere (including Col. 3:5) used for sexual impurity, is more general in 1:24 (→ III, 428, 21 ff.), πάθος is the latest point for transition to the depiction of sexual perversion, and it thus denotes erotic passion. [16] When Col. 3:5 adds to the demand: νεκρώσατε οὖν τὰ μέλη τὰ ἐπὶ τῆς γῆς (→ II, 924, n. 90; IV, 894, 33 ff.; 565, 22 ff.) the clarifying list: πορνείαν, ἀκαθαρσίαν, πάθος, ἐπιθυμίαν κακήν, appending also the clause καὶ τὴν πλεονεξίαν ἥτις ἐστὶν εἰδωλολατρία (→ II, 380, 8 ff.), 4 closely related concepts are contrasted with the final πλεονεξία. [17] Since πορνεία and ἀκαθαρσία (→ III, 429, 2 ff.) already have a sexual reference, πάθος here cannot mean "passion" or "feeling" in general, but denotes "erotic passion."

This use leads us back to Jewish writings. In Ps.-Phocylides, 194 (Poetae Lyrici Graeci, ed. T. Bergk, II [1882]): οὐ γὰρ ἔρως θεός ἐστι, πάθος δ' ἀΐδηλον ἁπάντων, one may detect a contribution made by the Hell. concept. But apart from Philo (→ n. 9) we must refer esp. to Joseph. (→ supra) and Test. Jos. 7:8 (→ supra), esp. as πάθος and ἐπιθυμία πονηρά (= κακή, Col. 3:5) occur together here, so that πάθος seems to be an erotic urge which is first given active expression as sin by ἐπιθυμία πονηρά. This would give a well-planned climax in Col. 3:5 too. [18]

Since R. 1:26 and Col. 3:5 are not oriented to the Stoic πάθος concept, [19] the same applies to 1 Th. 4:5, → III, 171, 14 f. πάθος ἐπιθυμίας does not mean ἐπιθυμία as πάθος in the Stoic sense but πάθος as sexual passion which is combined with or grows out of (gen. of origin, not quality as in R. 1:26) ἐπιθυμία, → lines 20 ff. [20]

5. In the post-apost. fathers, πάθος, always sing., refers to the evil of adultery or bad temper in Herm. m., 4, 1, 6; s., 6, 5, 5, → IV, 1091, 30 f. Elsewhere, however, it always

---

[15] ἐπὶ τῷ πάθει τοῦ ὑψίστου in Test. L. 4:1 is a Chr. interpolation — perhaps Patripassian? cf. R. Seeberg, Lehrbuch d. Dogmengesch., I² (1908), 476, n. 2; W. Bieder, "Die Vorstellung v. d. Höllenfahrt Christi," Abh. z. Theol. d. AT u. NT, 19 (1949), 162. But cf. the use of the Armen. version in W. Bousset, "Die Testamente d. Zwölf Patriarchen," ZNW, 1 (1900), 163 f. here obviously means death; cf. also J. Kroll, Gott u. Hölle (1932), 354, n. 5. Sib. Prol., line 20 (GCS, 8, 2) is Chr.: πάθος is the passion of Jesus; cf. also 8, 250: ὁ παθὼν ἔνεχ' ἡμῶν. On τὸ πάθος τοῦ βεβαμμένου καὶ ἠρημένου in Epict. Diss., II, 9, 19 f. cf. → I, 535, 32 ff.; R. Reitzenstein, Die Vorgeschichte d. chr. Taufe (1929), 232 f.; A. Seeberg, Das Ev. Christi (1905), 101; G. Polster, "Der kleine Talmudtraktat über d. Proselyten," Angelos, 2 (1926), 21, n. 1.

[16] The transl. "sufferings which are a disgrace" (Schl. R., 68) is certainly wrong, esp. as πάθος means "(evil) passion," "vice," elsewhere in Paul. Acc. to M. Pohlenz, "Pls. u. d. Stoa," ZNW, 42 (1949), 82 the phrase πάθη ἀτιμίας is not at all Stoic. Cf. → n. 18.

[17] In 3:8 one cannot speak of a "repeated list of five vices" alongside 3:5, of a second list "competing with the first," Dib. Gefbr., ad loc. The grouping in five occurs for the first time in 3:8 and is continued in 3:12, while 3:5 has to be expounded in terms of its own presuppositions. Cf. Cr.-Kö., 842, s.v.; Loh. Kol., 137 f.; → IV, 565, 34 ff. and n. 80.

[18] Vögtle, 209 f. The construing of πάθος as homosexuality is too specific here (even in R. 1:26 the word as such does not mean this); there is no instance to support it. The Lat. pathicus (Loh. Kol., 137, n. 2) refers only to the pass. type of homosexual (the μαλακοί, 1 C. 6:9, not the ἀρσενοκοῖται). Cf. Vögtle, 24; Jos. Ap., II, 215.

[19] Cf. Cr.-Kö., 842; Vögtle, 208 f., 211 f., 217; Pohlenz, 81 f.; A. Bonhöffer, "Epiktet u. d. NT," RVV, X (1911), 124 f.

[20] If 4:4 f. refers to married life (Dob. Th., 167), πάθος ἐπιθυμίας is an exaggeration or perversion of the sexual aspect, but if 4:4 f. refers to sex relations generally (Dib. Th.³, 21 Exc. σκεῦος) πάθος is rather par. to πορνεία in 4:3, cf. Col. 3:5.

means "suffering" "death," with ref. to the death of Jesus, Barn., 6, 7 (→ 923, 22 f.) and 15 times in Ign. There is no support for the view that Ign. also has it in a broader sense covering the whole work of salvation. [21] Unmistakable in this regard is the association of Christ's πάθος with His ἀνάστασις, Eph., 20, 1; Mg., 11, 1; Phld. inscriptio ; 9, 2; Sm., 7, 2; 12, 2. In Tr. inscriptio ἀνάστασις refers to the resurrection of Christians, but there can be no doubt as to the ref. of πάθος to the death of Jesus (cf. also Paul in R. 5:1; Eph. 2:14; Col. 1:20), unless the eucharist is in view. [22] When Sm., 5, 3 speaks of the conversion of heretics εἰς τὸ πάθος ὅ ἐστιν ἡμῶν ἀνάστασις, then, no matter whether this implies abandonment of docetic ideas or a new attitude to the eucharist, [23] the specific description of true Christianity as an ἀνάστασις effected by Christ's πάθος is possible only if the exclusive ref. of πάθος is to death. [24] Pregnant in a different sense is the ἀποθανεῖν εἰς τὸ αὐτοῦ πάθος of Mg., 5, 2, but here esp. (cf. Paul in R. 6:3 f.) the ref. of the πάθος of Jesus to death is beyond cavil, as also in R., 6, 3, which deals with martyrdom : ἐπιτρέψατέ μοι μιμητὴν εἶναι τοῦ πάθους τοῦ θεοῦ μου. [25] Moreover, the sense of death is supported in Sm., 1, 2 by the nailing of Jesus to the cross and in Tr., 11, 2 by mention of the upright of the cross. [26] The emphasis on the πάθος ἀληθινόν in Eph. inscriptio is directed against a docetic misunderstanding of the death of Jesus, cf. also Phld., 3, 3 [27] with special ref. to the eucharist. When acc. to Eph., 18, 2 Christ ἐβαπτίσθη ἵνα τῷ πάθει τὸ ὕδωρ καθαρίσῃ, this gives us no reason to relate πάθος to anything but the passion. [28] We thus conclude that πάθος always denotes the death of Jesus in Ign. This fits in with his use of πάσχω [29] and παθητός. [30]

Since Gnosticism, in so far as it spoke of a πάθος or πάσχειν of the redeemer, completely overlaid the historical fact of the death of Jesus by mythological speculations, sometimes even to the pt. of introducing the Gk. doctrine of πάθος, [31] the impressive stress on the πάθος of Jesus in Ign. is certainly part of the original tradition of the community. [32] It is true that the use of the noun πάθος as a tt. for the death of Jesus seems to be the invention of Ign. himself, since it is not attested elsewhere. [33] But it is a further development of the basic use of παθεῖν in the sense "to die," which Ign. had

---

[21] Schlier, 70, but cf. H. v. Campenhausen, Die Idee des Martyriums in d. alten Kirche (1936), 74, n. 4, cf. 63, n. 2.

[22] Cf. Bartsch, 119 f.; Schlier, 70 relates πάθος to the whole work of salvation.

[23] Cf. Bau. Ign., 192 f.; Schlier, 167 f.; Bartsch, 122.

[24] As against Schlier, 70.

[25] Schlier, 70 (not 158 f.) relates this again to the whole work of salvation. Cf. → IV, 674, 7 ff.; Bartsch, 83, 124, 126 f.; J. Schneider, "Die Passionsmystik d. Pls.," UNT, 15 (1929), 130.

[26] Cf. Schlier, 107 f. (not 70).

[27] Ibid., 70, 108, 167 f.; Bartsch, 35 f., 101.

[28] Even a ref. to the whole work of salvation (Schlier, 70; cf. 43-48, 102 ff.) hardly lessens the striking nature of the thought. To separate the ἵνα clause from the baptism of Jesus, and thus to take it as an early instance of the idea of a creation of the sacraments by the death of Jesus (M. Werner, Die Entstehung d. chr. Dogmas [1941], 485) is hardly possible, though water is meant as the element used in baptism, → I, 543, 34 f. Against a conjectured πάτῳ (Bartsch, 139) is the fact that πάτος does not occur in the LXX, NT, or post-apost. fathers (and in the Apologists only at Just. Dial., 3, 1).

[29] → 923, 5 ff. Schlier, 70 wrongly calls Tr., 10 and Sm., 7, 1 examples of a ref. to the whole work of salvation. Even if πάσχω has in Sm., 7, 1 the general sense "to suffer," which semasiologically precedes "to die," this use is not to be regarded as a subsequent extension of πάσχω (with its ref. to the death) to the whole work of salvation.

[30] → 924, 19 ff., as against Schlier, 70.

[31] Cf. also Schlier, 107 and n. 2, also H. Jonas, "Gnosis u. spätantiker Geist, I," FRL, NF, 33 (1934), 189, 165 f., 369 f.

[32] Bartsch, 127 f.

[33] It is true that the combination of πάθος and ἀνάστασις (→ lines 4 ff.) can have some "formal" influence (Bartsch, 50), but it is worth noting that in Ign., as distinct from the NT : Lk. 24:46 etc., this combination hardly finds a par. in verbal form. Cf. only Sm., 2 (but not 7, 1; R., 6, 1; Phld., 8, 2; Tr., 9, 1 f.), also R., 4, 3.

already adopted, → 923, 5 ff. Though he never describes his own martyrdom directly as πάθος, [34] he could hardly have attained to this use apart from the overwhelming significance which the death and resurrection must have had for him as he faced his own approaching death. [35]

† πάθημα.

1. Used from the time of the tragedians, πάθημα, [1] like → πάθος, though less common, [2] shared the history of → πάσχω. It first denotes that which befalls a man and has to be accepted by him. It is mostly used in malam partem, "misfortune," "suffering" (often plur.). In punning combination with μάθημα it denotes what is experienced as distinct from what is learned, e.g., Xenoph. Cyr., III, 1, 17; Aristoph. Thes., 199, → 906, 19; IV, 316, 12 ff. It also refers to the bodily or spiritual condition induced by external events, usually in malam partem : "state of suffering," "sorrowful mood," "sorrow," "grief." Rarely (from Aristot.) syn. of πάθος for "emotions." [3]

2. It does not occur in the LXX (or other transl.), nor in Ep. Ar., Test. XII, Gr. En. There are only 7 instances in Philo : for alterations in the cosmos in Abr., 2; Vit. Mos., II, 126, esp. the air, Op. Mund., 70; Cher., 88; Spec. Leg., I, 210, also "sickness," Gig., 10; Conf. Ling., 23. It is very rare in Joseph.: Ant., 1, 156 of cosmic processes ; "sickness" in 6, 10; 7, 325; 8, 115, → 928, 1 f.

3. In the NT πάθημα, always plur. except at Hb. 2:9, has the rare meaning "passion," "impulse" (→ line 13) at Gl. 5:24; R. 7:5, but its main sense is "suffering," cf. Paul in R. 8:18; 2 C. 1:5-7; Phil. 3:10; Col. 1:24; 2 Tm. 3:11, also Hb. 2:9 f.; 10:32 and 1 Pt. 1:11; 4:13; 5:1-9.

a. Gl. 5:24 : οἱ δὲ τοῦ Χριστοῦ Ἰησοῦ τὴν σάρκα ἐσταύρωσαν σὺν τοῖς παθήμασιν καὶ ταῖς ἐπιθυμίαις, reminds us of Col. 3:5, → 928, 8 ff. It does not refer only to the sexual field, however, but embraces all that is mentioned in 5:19-21. While ἐπιθυμίαι makes plain how resolute the desires are, the dependence of man is expressed in παθήματα. [4] παθήματα are emotions in malam partem,

---

[34] At most indirectly in Mg., 5, 2; R., 6, 3 (παθήματα is used in Sm., 5, 1 → 935, 1 f.). This reserve, though Ign. does use παθεῖν of himself (→ 923, 15 ff.), should prevent us from overexaggerating the idea that the martyr undergoes the πάθος of the Redeemer and becomes identical with Him, Schlier, 158 ff.; Bartsch, 80-90.

[35] Apologists : In Just. the sing. πάθος (except at Apol., 3, 1; 5, 1 "passion") always refers to the death of Jesus : 22, 4; 32, 7; Dial., 30, 3; 31, 1; 40, 3; 41, 1 (of the Lord's Supper : εἰς ἀνάμνησιν τοῦ πάθους); 74, 3; 89, 2; 97, 3; 105, 2; 114, 2; 117, 3; 125, 5 (Schlier, 71). The plur., used for "vice," "passion," "sickness" etc., has in Just. Apol., 22, 4, as shown by the addition τοῦ θανάτου, the general sense of "fates" (the ref. is to the ways in which the sons of Zeus die). In Dial., 103, 8 Just. speaks of the πάθη of Jesus in Gethsemane ; this plur. cannot be the direct starting-point for the phrase "death and passion," → 916, n. 87. The Lat. passio, a noun only from Apul., later came to be used for the passion of Jesus and martyrs. Cf. also H. Dörrie, "Machabaei Passio SS Machabaeorum, Die antike lat. Übers. d. 4 Macc.," AGG, 3, F., 22 (1938), 31-35; also W. Elert, "Die Theopaschitische Formel," ThLZ, 75 (1950), 195-206; uncritically Kroll, op. cit., 15 f.

π ά θ η μ α. For bibl. → πάσχω and → πάθος; J. Schneider, "Die Passionsmystik d. Pls.," UNT, 15 (1929); G. Kittel, "Kol. 1:24," ZSTh, 18 (1941), 186-191; G. Wiencke, "Pls. über Jesu Tod," BFTh, II, 42 (1939).

[1] The same constr. as μάθημα, though while in the case of μανθάνω the forms μαθήσομαι and μεμάθηκα sufficiently explain the development of μάθημα (alongside μάθος from ἔμαθον), πάσχω has no corresponding forms. Perhaps πάθημα arose by analogy because of the play on words πάθος/μάθος, μάθημα/πάθημα (→ line 9 f.; 926, 25) [Debrunner].

[2] No instances in Ditt. Syll.[3] and Or., pap. (acc. to Preisigke Wört. and Moult.-Mill.) or Corp. Herm.

[3] For further examples cf. Cr.-Kö., 841, s.v.; → II, 478, n. 13.

[4] Oe. Gl., ad loc.: "that he is completely passive," better : "completely subdued." Cf. Cr.-Kö., 841, s.v.

i.e., "impulses," "passions." Gl. 5:24 is simply emphasising that the παθήματα, with their basis the σάρξ, are crucified and overcome in Christians ; this has taken place in baptism, cf. R. 6:6. But in the light of 5:25 and the hortatory context this carries with it the admonition that the παθήματα are still to be put to death, cf. Col. 3:5; R. 8:13. [5] Similarly, in R. 7:5 the παθήματα are a feature of the ἐν τῇ σαρκὶ εἶναι of the pre-Christian period. When Paul writes : τὰ παθήματα τῶν ἁμαρτιῶν τὰ διὰ τοῦ νόμου ἐνηργεῖτο ἐν τοῖς μέλεσιν ἡμῶν, this implies, not that the παθήματα have their seat in the members, but that they work through the members, → IV, 562, 9, 12 f. But this means that, if we rule out the sense of "passions" (as in Gl. 5:24), we can hardly construe παθήματα as "sufferings," or "sufferings which result from ἁμαρτίαι." [6] For this would mean that sins have παθήματα as their result, and that only their operation brings to maturity the fruit of death. The subj. of ἐνεργεῖσθαι, however, is a more active entity than mere results or unhappy conditions could ever be, → II, 654, 13 f. τῶν ἁμαρτιῶν does not name the author of παθήματα but simply describes in a general way their nature, [7] though this does not mean that πάθημα becomes vox media or that the παθήματα are identical with the ἐπιθυμίαι. [8] The relation between the Law and passions (διὰ τοῦ νόμου) corresponds to that between the Law and sin (or desire) in 7:7 ff. [9]

b. In 2 C. 1:5 Paul calls his sufferings παθήματα τοῦ Χριστοῦ, while in 1:6 f. he speaks more briefly only of παθήματα (par. θλῖψις in 1:4, 8; cf. θλίβεσθαι in 1:6 par. [παθήματα] πάσχειν). In 1:7 the Corinthians are then called κοινωνοί of the apostle's παθήματα, → III, 143, 38 ff.; 806, 29 ff. κοινωνοί in 1:7 does not just refer to a general fellowship of suffering which is possible, mystically or otherwise, without any suffering of one's own. According to 1:6 the Corinthians themselves, both then and at other times, were subject in fact to specific παθή-ματα. The τὰ αὐτὰ παθήματα does not mean that the circumstances were exactly the same (thus the θλῖψις of 1:8 ff., which is included already in 1:4, obviously finds no direct analogy in the παθήματα of the Corinthians). These are the same afflictions because for both Paul and the Corinthians they are the παθήματα τοῦ Χριστοῦ. The statement in 1:6 : εἴτε δὲ θλιβόμεθα, ὑπὲρ τῆς ὑμῶν παρακλήσεως καὶ σωτηρίας, is not then — by interpolation of a false understanding of Col. 1:24 (→ 933, 8 ff.) — to be taken to mean that the afflictions of the apostle, because they take something from the common pool of Christian suffering, → III, 806, 32 ff., bring consolation to the Corinthians and effect deliverance for them. On the contrary, when a Christian has to suffer, then, because suffering is of the esse of Christianity and a gift of grace according to Phil. 1:29 (→ 920, 20 ff.), this is not only for himself, but according to Phil. 1:28 for all the rest (cf. also 2 Tm. 2:10), an ἔνδειξις ... σωτηρίας.

These παθήματα are called παθήματα τοῦ Χριστοῦ. In 2 C. 1:5 this is not a subj.

---

[5] Cf. Oe. Gl., ad loc. Vögtle, 211 rightly emphasises that for Paul "the crucifixion of passions and desires" does not mean, as for the Stoa, "the attainment of moral freedom" (in ἀπάθεια), "but only the presupposition for this," since this freedom is fulfilled "in devotion to one's neighbour."

[6] → IV, 862, 10 : "states of passion" in the sense of "disturbances," "devastating consequences," Schl. R., 228 f.

[7] → II, 497, 14 ff.: "sinful affections." Perhaps also "the passions which come to light in sins" (Ltzm. R., ad loc.).

[8] As against Zn. R., 334, n. 67.

[9] → I, 310, 32 ff.; II, 497, 15 f.; IV, 562, 11. C. Maurer, Die Gesetzeslehre d. Pls. (1941), 43; E. Gaugler, Der R., I (1945), 192 f. But cf. Schl. R., 229.

gen.; hence the reference is not to Christ's passion. Things are different, however, in Phil. 3:10 (the αὐτοῦ with τῆς ἀναστάσεως and παθημάτων, also τῷ θανάτῳ, naturally denotes the same relation to Christ). Since Paul does not use παθεῖν for the death of Jesus, it might seem that he has in view, not the death, but the other sufferings of Jesus ; [10] this conjecture is supported by the plur. Nevertheless, the chiastic construction in 3:10 f. shows plainly that the παθήματα of Christ are the same as His θάνατος. That the plur. παθήματα [11] can be used as a term for the death of Jesus is shown not merely by 1 Pt. 1:11, where the plur. even leads on to δόξαι as a word for the resurrection (→ 934, 25 ff.), but esp. by Hb. 2:10 (→ 934, 18 ff.). The phrase συμμορφιζόμενος τῷ θανάτῳ αὐτοῦ in Phil. 3:10 means being fashioned into likeness by sufferings, whether these involve death or not. But the κοινωνία παθημάτων αὐτοῦ is then actualised only in the sufferings of the apostle himself. [12] This shows that here too (→ 931, 23 ff.) there can be no idea of a fellowship of suffering in the sense of true passion mysticism accessible to all at all times. [13] The statement in Phil. 3:10 f. is shown, of course, by both wording and context to refer primarily only to the apostle Paul in person, [14] and it is certainly no accident that it is to be found in Phil., which is so rich in personal confessions, just as the saying which relates his sufferings to the death of Jesus occurs in the very personal epistle 2 C. (4:10).

2 C. 4:10 f. is also instructive inasmuch as the ζωὴ τοῦ Χριστοῦ here corresponds to what Phil. 3:10 calls the δύναμις τῆς ἀναστάσεως αὐτοῦ. On the other hand the νέκρωσις τοῦ ᾿Ιησοῦ of 2 C. 4:10 (→ IV, 895, 9 ff.), which is synon. with θάνατος or παθήματα αὐτοῦ in Phil. 3:10, finds in the εἰς θάνατον παραδιδό-μεθα διὰ ᾿Ιησοῦν of v. 11 an elucidation which is a strong barrier against an exclusively mystical interpretation. [15] Hence one has also to consider whether the τοῦ Χριστοῦ in the παθήματα τοῦ Χριστοῦ of 2 C. 1:5 is not to be construed along the same lines as the διὰ ᾿Ιησοῦν of 2 C. 4:11. [16] Cf. also the ὑπὲρ αὐτοῦ πάσχειν of Phil. 1:29 (→ 920, 23 ff.) and the συμπάσχειν of R. 8:17 (→ 925, 13 ff.; 925, 36 ff.). The gen. τοῦ Χριστοῦ does not, then, denote a relation of the παθή-ματα of the apostle (or of the Corinthians or any Christians) to the παθήματα

---

[10] Cf. Wiencke, 126 f.

[11] In 2 C. 1:5 ff. etc. Paul speaks of his own παθήματα only in the plur.; perhaps this habit caused him to use the plur. in Phil. 3:10 too.

[12] Experience of the power of the resurrection of Jesus (3:10) is not to be related only to certain special operations but to the new life of the apostle (3:8 f.) in its totality. Yet Paul says that his sufferings, too, fill his whole life, cf. ἐν παντί, 2 C. 4:8, πάντοτε, 4:10, ἀεί, 4:11. On the other hand, there are for Paul certain situations of particular affliction as well, e.g., the imprisonment which was the setting of Phil., the θλῖψις of 2 C. 1:8, the διωγμοί or παθήματα during the first missionary journey, 2 Tm. 3:11 (cf. also προπαθόν-τες in 1 Th. 2:2, → 924, 28 ff. and the instances of πάσχω in Paul, → 920, 6 ff.).

[13] The "mystical" content of Phil. 3:10 (→ I, 710, 22 ff.; III, 806, 14 ff.) is subdued by the real character of the apostle's sufferings and of the awaited resurrection (3:11).

[14] Schelkle, 264 presses the verse much too far when he refers it to the fellowship of all believers with Christ.

[15] As against Schneider, 54, n. 2. A sacramental understanding (→ IV, 895, 7 f.) is not likely inasmuch as the description of sufferings as νέκρωσις is on a different level from dying with Christ in baptism, R. 6:2 ff. Cf. also Wiencke, 128. Furthermore, Phil. 3:10 and παθήματα τοῦ Χριστοῦ in 2 C. 1:5 are not meant sacramentally.

[16] If the στίγματα τοῦ ᾿Ιησοῦ of Gl. 6:17 refers to scars suffered in persecution (the use of σῶμα does not restrict this to the purely physical field; cf. 2 C. 4:10 with 8 f.; → III, 147, 29 f.), the gen. τοῦ ᾿Ιησοῦ simply means that Paul "received them in the service of Jesus" (Oe. Gl., ad loc.) or that they mark him as the property of Jesus ; it does not have to mean that "his sufferings are a visible representation of the sufferings of Jesus Christ," Schneider, 51.

of Christ Himself, whether by analogy, or as a continuation (→ III, 144, 4 ff.), or as a mystical (→ III, 144, 15 ff.) or non-mystical imitation.[17] The necessity of Christian suffering is not based on the fact that there has to be analogy, continuation or imitation, but on the fact that Jesus — because there are necessarily παθήματα τοῦ νῦν καιροῦ (R. 8:18; → 934, 4 ff.), and hence the way to the kingdom of God is through tribulation (Ac. 14:22) — holds out before His disciples the prospect of afflictions[18] (cf. also the ὑποδείξω of Ac. 9:16, → 919, 18 ff.).

When we read in Col. 1:24 : νῦν χαίρω ἐν τοῖς παθήμασιν ὑπὲρ ὑμῶν καὶ ἀνταναπληρῶ τὰ ὑστερήματα τῶν θλίψεων τοῦ Χριστοῦ ἐν τῇ σαρκί μου ὑπὲρ τοῦ σώματος αὐτοῦ, ὅ ἐστιν ἡ ἐκκλησία, the θλίψεις τοῦ Χριστοῦ here are identical with the παθήματα τοῦ Χριστοῦ, since παθήματα and θλίψεις are synon., as also in 2 C. 1:4 ff. 2 C. 1:4 ff. thus suggests (as distinct from Phil. 3:10) that in the phrase θλίψεις τοῦ Χριστοῦ the gen. is not to be taken as a subj. gen. (→ III, 143, 42 ff.; 144, 30 f.). On the other hand, even without the vl. μου, there is no doubt but that the παθήματα of Col. 1:24 are the sufferings of the apostle. If the ὑπὲρ ὑμῶν is to be taken non-vicariously along the lines of 2 C. 1:6 (→ 931, 35 ff.),[19] then the ὑπὲρ τοῦ σώματος αὐτοῦ, which is an extension of the ὑπὲρ ὑμῶν (the Colossians) to the whole ἐκκλησία, is also to be construed non-vicariously. The θλίψεις τοῦ Χριστοῦ are thus par. to the παθήματα or afflictions of the apostle, and any attempt to expound the whole saying (→ III, 143, 38 ff.; 806, 18 ff.; IV, 1097, 32 ff.) must be based on these presuppositions.[20] The idea that θλίψεις or παθήματα are necessary is common in the apostle, cf. 1 Th. 3:3 f.;[21] Ac. 14:22; also 9:16, → 919, 18 ff.; → III, 143, 22 ff. Whatever may be the reason for this necessity (→ lines 2 ff.), it is simply given with the fact that Jesus holds it out as a sure prospect for all disciples.[22] Sayings like Mt. 5:11; 10:17 f. were

---

[17] For him the sufferings do not have to stand "in the closest connection with the passion of Christ," Schneider, 49. It is not unimportant to note that not only does Paul's use of πάσχω (→ 920, 6 ff.) not stand under the influence of παθεῖν = "to die" for the death of Jesus, but also that in proximity to or in connection with his πάσχω sayings we do not find such terms as ἀποθανεῖν, θάνατος, σταυρός, αἷμα referring to the death of Jesus, → n. 18. The only exception, apart from 2 C. 4:10 f., is Phil. 3:10 f., and here it is permissible to maintain that there is "a spiritual union between Paul and the crucified Lord in the full sense," O. Schmitz, "Die Christus-Gemeinschaft des Pls. im Lichte seines Genetivgebrauchs," Nt.liche Forschungen, I, 2 (1924), 197.

[18] → 933, 21 ff. is worth noting is the observation of Kittel, 189 that when Jesus speaks of the disciples being persecuted, scorned and hated, He does not link this primarily with His death, but with the fact that He, too, is persecuted, scorned and hated.

[19] One can hardly relate ὑπὲρ ὑμῶν generally to χαίρω, cf. also Eph. 3:13.

[20] Cf. also Schneider, 54-59; Schmitz, op. cit., 190-196; A. Schweitzer, Die Mystik d. Ap. Pls. (1930), 127; Dib. Kol., ad loc.; Schelkle, 264 f. Cogent objections to a mystical interpretation may be found in Loh. Kol., 77. Better, though unconvincing, is the view of C. Bonnard, "L'Épître de Saint Paul aux Colossiens," Commentaire du NT, X (1950), 110 : These θλίψεις of Jesus (cf. 110, n. 6 : subj. gen.) are not, of course, identical with the "acte rédempteur de Dieu en Christ" in the death of Jesus (and the resurrection, cf. n. 5); nevertheless, one may speak of a lack in them because "le but de l'oeuvre du Christ" is reached only when the Gospel is preached to all the nations, and this is the task of the apostle, a task which entails suffering, so that "ces souffrances apostoliques doivent s'ajouter à celles du Christ," 111. In Phil. 2:30; 1 C. 16:17 the word ὑστέρημα, when used with ἀνταναπληρόω, does not denote a quantitative difference as compared with some future measure, but refers to a present religious and ethical obligation. The idea of a foreordained amount of suffering which has to be met is present neither in Paul (→ 931, 31 ff.) nor elsewhere in the NT, nor is it suggested by contemporary assumptions, Kittel, 188.

[21] Acc. to 3:4 the intimation of sufferings is a constituent part of Paul's missionary preaching.

[22] This is very strongly emphasised by Kittel, 189 f. All the same, the ἀνταναπληρῶ of Col. 1:24 is too strongly orientated to the word ὑστέρημα to permit the understanding

for Paul and his congregations the presupposition for the fact that suffering is normal and that the absence of it is to be regarded as ὑστερήματα, Col. 1:24. ἀνταναπληρόω thus means the elimination of this deficiency by the presence of sufferings. In spite of the severity of afflictions R. 8:18 is true : ὅτι οὐκ ἄξια τὰ παθήματα τοῦ νῦν καιροῦ πρὸς τὴν μέλλουσαν δόξαν ἀποκαλυφθῆναι εἰς ἡμᾶς. The concept ὁ νῦν καιρός is synon. with ὁ αἰὼν οὗτος, → I, 205, 40 f.; 206, 25 ff. Afflictions here are those which necessarily arise from the antithesis between the Christ event and the nature of this aeon. Hence the παθήματα τοῦ νῦν καιροῦ are no different from the παθήματα or θλίψεις τοῦ Χριστοῦ, 2 C. 1:5; Col. 1:24. At their end is συνδοξασθῆναι, R. 8:17, → 925, 30 ff.

c. In the phrase διὰ τὸ πάθημα τοῦ θανάτου in Hb. 2:9, the addition διὰ παθημάτων in v. 10 rules out the sense of "bearing" or "undergoing." [23] The reference is not to sufferings as a special form or accompaniment of the death of Jesus, [24] but to the suffering which consists in death, as shown by the γεύσηται θανάτου which follows. Since in Hb. παθεῖν means "to die" (→ 917, 5 ff.), πά- θημα τοῦ θανάτου is tautology used by the author to give special stress to this first mention of the death of Jesus. The sing. πάθημα (only here in the NT) is an assimilation to the sing. θάνατος (cf. the converse in 1 Pt. 1:11, → lines 25 ff.). The plur. παθήματα in 2:10 refers to the total process of the crucifixion, cf. also διὰ τοῦ θανάτου in 2:14 and the use of τελειῶσαι in 2:10 in relation to 5:8 f., → 917, 18 ff. In 10:32 παθήματα is used in connection with the sufferings of Christians, → I, 138, 15 ff., 167, 30 ff.; IV, 411, n. 149.

The author of 1 Pt., like the author of Hb., has παθεῖν for "to die" with re- ference to the death of Jesus, → 918, 19 ff. He uses παθήματα in the same way. It is said of the Spirit indwelling the OT prophets (1:11) that He declared in advance (→ IV, 512, 36 ff.) τὰ εἰς Χριστὸν παθήματα καὶ τὰς μετὰ ταῦτα δόξας. Quite apart from the pars. in Lk. 24:26 and Hb. 2:9 it is quite evident that the reference is to the death and resurrection of Jesus. [25] The plur. παθήματα, which is the fixed use abandoned for special reasons (→ lines 17 ff.) only at Hb. 2:9, is plerophoric. [26] In 5:1 (cf. → IV, 494, 22 ff.; III, 806, 24 f.) the author describes himself as μάρτυς τῶν τοῦ Χριστοῦ παθημάτων. He is referring, not to the fact that he is an eye-witness of the passion, but, as shown by the continuation ὁ καὶ τῆς μελλούσης ἀποκαλύπτεσθαι δόξης κοινωνός (cf. 5:10; Rev. 1:9), [27] to his own share (→ IV, 494, 32 ff.; 495, 1 f.) in the παθήματα (τοῦ Χριστοῦ) which according to 4:13; 5:9 are laid on all Christians. The meaning is thus the same as in 2 C. 1:5, → 931, 20 ff.

which Kittel suggests (190), namely, that it is part of the πληρῶσαι τὸν λόγον τοῦ θεοῦ (v. 25) fulfilled in the life and work of Paul."

[23] This sense is extremely rare, cf. Pass., s.v. 3.

[24] So apparently Rgg. Hb. ², ³, 43 : "The painful suffering of death."

[25] The attempt of Wbg. Pt., 21-28 to refer 1:10 ff. to the NT prophets and to under- stand the παθήματα and δόξαι as the sufferings and glories set forth in prospect for the community runs into severe difficulties. Cf. Wnd. Pt. on 1:11; → II, 86, 36 f.; III, 585, 16 ff.

[26] The possibility that εἰς may sometimes be used for ἐν (Bl.-Debr. § 205 f.) cannot be adduced in support of an equation of τὰ εἰς Χριστὸν παθήματα with παθήματα ἐν Χριστῷ, Schneider, 122, esp. since we never find παθήματα (or even πάσχειν) ἐν Χριστῷ in the NT; in any case 1 Pt. makes only sparing use of ἐν Χριστῷ. This is an εἰς of relation, → IV, 512, 39 f., also → II, 432, 25 ff. Cf. Cr.-Kö., 841, s.v.: "what Christ should suffer"; Pr.-Bauer⁴, 1097, s.v. 1.

[27] The συν- in συμπρεσβύτερος also affects the μάρτυς, which is linked to it by the same article ; the author is not the only one who can call himself μάρτυς τῶν τοῦ Χριστοῦ παθημάτων. Cf. 4:13. → 924, προπάσχω, n. 3.

4. παθήματα occurs twice in the post-apost. fathers. The ref. in Ign. Sm., 5, 1 is to the sufferings of Christians, esp. martyrdom (cf. 4, 2), [28] while in 1 Cl., 2, 1 (cf. Gl. 3:1) we have a use, rare in the NT, for the death of Jesus (cf. Phil. 3:10; Hb. 2:9 f.; 1 Pt. 1:11). In the Apologists παθήματα means "destinies" in Athenag. Suppl., 28, 4; its only other occurrence is as a vl. in Just. Epit., 2, 16.

† συμπαθής, † συμπαθέω.

1. The adj. συμπαθής, formed from σύν and πάθος like συγγενής from σύν and γένος (he who has the same γένος), is from the time of Aristot. used first for him "who has the same πάθος," "who is affected like another by the same sufferings, impressions, emotions," or "who suffers, experiences etc. the same as another," later one "who has fellow-feeling, sympathy with another." From συμπαθής, συμπαθέω : "to suffer with, alongside, the same as" (more common than → συμπάσχω, with which it is synon.), "to sympathise." [1] For cosmic interactions the noun συμπάθεια esp. is the common term from the days of Epic. [2]

2. In the LXX we find συμπαθής (apart from the vl. in Job 29:25 A) 3 times in 4 Macc.: 13:23 (twice); 15:4 (the reading τῶν παθῶν is obviously a slip based on τῶν πατέρων) in the sense "feeling with one another." συμπαθέω, except as a vl. at 13:23, occurs only in 5:25 : The divine lawgiver ἡμῖν συμπαθεῖ, not, acc. to 5:26, "he has sympathy," but "he has the best in view." συμπάθεια at 6:13; 14:13 f., 18, 20; 15:7, 11 also means "fellow-feeling" rather than "sympathy."

3. Philo uses συμπαθέω only in Spec. Leg., II, 115 with ἔλεος. συμπαθής occurs in Leg. Gaj., 273; Vit. Mos., II, 228; Spec. Leg., IV, 202 of fellow-feeling and mutual participation, Leg. All., I, 8 cosmic movements (like συμπάθεια in Philo). [3] In Joseph. the group means "fellow-feeling," "participation," "sympathy": συμπαθής, Ant., 16. 102, 329; 19, 330; Bell., 6, 211; Adv. Ant., 7, 252; συμπαθέω, 6, 341; 16, 404; Bell., 2, 579; συμπάθεια, Ant., 13, 233. Cf. also Test. XII : συμπαθέω, B. 4:4; S. 3:6; συμπάθεια, Zeb. 7:4; ἀσυμπαθής, S. 2:4.

4. There is little use of the group in the NT. For sympathy or fellow-feeling such words as ἐλεέω, ἔλεος (→ II, 482, 15 ff.), οἰκτίρω κτλ. (→ 161, 5 ff.) and → σπλάγχνα, σπλαγχνίζομαι are available. συμπαθής occurs only in the short list of virtues in 1 Pt. 3:8. Since εὔσπλαγχνοι follows, συμπαθεῖς does not denote active sympathy with those in distress, [4] but understanding and sympathetic participation in the destiny of others in all situations. [5] At Hb. 4:15 συμπαθῆσαι ταῖς ἀσθενείαις ἡμῶν is given as the motive which led the pre-existent Son to take flesh, but the meaning here is neither "to sympathise" nor "to suffer the same," "to suffer with," in orientation to the destiny or conduct of the incarnate Lord, cf. also → III, 279, n. 58. The reference is rather to the heavenly High-priest

---

[28] The Gospel previously mentioned can hardly be, as Bartsch (100) suggests, "the cultic myth belonging to the sufferings of martyrdom."

σ υ μ π α θ ή ς κ τ λ. For bibl. → πάθος.

[1] For details cf. Pass., Liddell-Scott, Pr.-Bauer, Cr.-Kö., 842 f., s.v. On the meaning "to favour someone," "to sympathise with someone," for συμπαθέω cf. the examples in the pap., Preisigke Wört., II, 512, s.v. (8th cent. A.D.). Only later does the idea of "sympathy" come to be associated with the group.

[2] Cf. → II, 389, 24-32; C. F. Heinrici, Die Hermes-Mystik u. d. NT (1918), 81 f., 99, 113. Esp. on Pos. cf. K. Reinhardt, Kosmos u. Sympathie (1926); M. Pohlenz, Die Stoa, I (1948), Index II, s.v. "Sympathie."

[3] Cf. Reinhardt, 52, n. 2, 129, n. 2; F. Cumont, Die orientalischen Religionen im römischen Heidentum³ (1931), 157, 296, n. 41; W. Völker, "Fortschritt u. Vollendung bei Philo v. Alex.," TU, 49, 1 (1938), 181 ff.

[4] As against Wbg. Pt., 94 f.

[5] Cf. Vögtle, 47, 188. R. 12:15 sheds a clearer light than 1 C. 12:26 (cf. Cr.-Kö., 842, s.v.).

(cf. 4:14, 16), the exalted Lord, though naturally in union with the Crucified, cf. 5:1 ff.; 7:27; 8:1 ff. As compared with the τοῖς πειραζομένοις βοηθῆσαι of 2:18 (→ 917, 10 ff.) συμπαθῆσαι — related herein to the ἐλεήμων of 2:17 — denotes disposition rather than act, i.e., fellow-feeling with the ἀσθένειαι, → I, 492, 24 f. As the One who during His life on earth was tempted καθ' ὁμοιότητα, Jesus learned to know ἀσθένειαι in all their greatness and as our fault, though He Himself remained χωρὶς ἁμαρτίας. His συμπαθῆσαι is not a sympathetic understanding which condones everything — even ἀσθένειαι is not a weakening — but a fellow-feeling which derives from full acquaintance with the seriousness of the situation and which can take in the guilt concealed from us.[6] As a reason for 10:33b sharing the lot of imprisoned brothers in the faith (Hb. 10:34 : τοῖς δεσμίοις συνεπαθήσατε) embraces more than μνημονεύειν (cf. Col. 4:18); the reference is to help given by both word and deed.[7]

5. In the post-apost. fathers we simply find συμπαθέω at Ign., R., 6, 3. What is meant is fellow-feeling in the sense that Ign. asks the Roman Christians for understanding of his motives and his urge for martyrdom. There is no need to combine the term with the preceding μιμητής τοῦ πάθους, → IV, 674, 7 ff.[8]

† κακοπαθέω, † συγκακοπαθέω, † κακοπάθεια.

1. As συμπαθέω and συμπάθεια are related to the adj. συμπαθής, so are κακοπαθέω and κακοπάθεια to the very rare adj. κακοπαθής.[1] The meaning of κακοπαθέω is generally "to suffer misfortune," "to be in sorry case," etc., e.g., Thuc., I, 78, 3; Xenoph. Mem., II, 1, 17. A rare meaning is "to endure evil," "to know how to bear evil," e.g., Aristot. Eth. Nic., X, 6, p. 1176b, 29. In keeping with this κακοπάθεια can have not only the more common pass. sense of "misfortune," "suffering," "trouble" (e.g., Thuc., VII, 77, 1; Isoc. Or., 6, 55) but also the act. sense of "enduring suffering, toil, exertion" (e.g., Polyb., 3, 42, 9; 4, 8, 3).[2] Similarly the noun κακοπαθία (in inscr. from the 3rd cent. B.C. on).[3] συγκακοπαθέω is not found prior to the NT.

2. In the LXX κακοπαθέω occurs in Jon. 4:10 in the sense "to go to pains," "to exert oneself" (Mas. עָמַל). κακοπάθεια means "trouble" in Mal. 1:13 (Mas. תְּלָאָה) also in 2 Macc. 2:26 f., though in 4 Macc. 9:8 (→ 909, 7 ff.; 927, n. 6) the meaning seems to be the "enduring of afflictions."[4] Σ also has both words. In Ep. Ar. we find κακο-

---

[6] There can be no missing the "strongly emotional tinge" here (E. Käsemann, "Das wandernde Gottesvolk," FRL, NF, 37 [1939], 152 on ἔλεος in 4:16), cf. also συμπαθῆσαι. But it is going too far to speak of a "doctrine of redemption fundamentally alien to Christianity," ibid., 151. συμπαθέω is not just a Stoic term, loc. cit., n. 5. Cf. also Mi. Hb.[8], 91 on 2:16; 122 on 4:15 : "not psychological, but existential," and 131 on 5:2.

[7] → III, 807, 35 ff.; Rgg. Hb. [2],[3], 332; Mi. Hb.[8] on 10:33 (239 and n. 5).

[8] As against Schlier, esp. 163 f.; cf. Bartsch, 124. In Ign. one has to differentiate between συμπάσχω (→ 926, 9 ff.) and συμπαθέω (cf. also Act. And., 9). The Apologists : συμπαθέω, "to sympathise," Just. Dial., 38, 2, συμπάθεια as cosmic influence, Athenag. Suppl., 7, 1; 22, 7; 25, 3.

κ α κ ο π α θ έ ω κτλ. [1] Cf. Pass., s.v.

[2] For further details cf. Pass. and Liddell-Scott, s.v.; Preisigke Wört., I, 724; Moult.-Mill., 316.

[3] -παθία for -πάθεια rests on the pre-Atticistic confusion of -ία (from adj. in -ος) and -εια (from adj. in -ης). Later the constructions were merged by itacism (apart from the accent, where the MS tradition is naturally unreliable) [Debrunner]. Cf. Bl.-Debr. § 23; Winer (Schmiedel) § 5, 13c.

[4] G. Björck, "Quelques cas de ἓν διὰ δυοῖν dans le NT et ailleurs," Coniectanea Neotestamentica, 4 (1940), 3, n. 1 would (with ref. to Jm. 5:10 → n. 7) take 4 Macc. 9:8 too as hendiadys, so that only ὑπομονή means "enduring," and κακοπάθεια means "affliction." But cf. ὑπομονή and μακροθυμία in Col. 1:11 (→ IV, 384, n. 82), and ἐκτένεια and κακοπάθεια in an Aegean inscr. (2nd cent. B.C.) in Deissmann NB, 91 f.

παθέω in 241 and κακοπάθεια in 92, 208, 259, always "trouble." [5] κακοπαθέω in Philo Spec. Leg., II, 60 perhaps means "(successfully) to take pains," or "to exert oneself," as in Virt., 88, 130; Sacr. AC, 38; Som., II, 105, 181; Cher., 88, cf. ἄνευ κακοπαθείας, Cher., 87. The noun also occurs in Decal., 117; Leg. All., III, 135; Vit. Mos., I, 154; Jos., 26, 223; Exsecr., 128. The meaning is always "trouble," "difficulty," except at Vit. Mos., I, 154 (plur. in a list of virtues) "enduring of trouble." Jos. often has κακοπαθέω for "to run into misfortune or difficulties," esp. military, Ant., 1, 185; 2, 74, 103, 211 etc.; Ap., I, 278; Bell., 1, 148, 159; 6, 37; "to be able to endure trouble" only Ant., 10, 220 par. Ap., I, 135. κακοπάθεια for "trouble" is very much less frequent, Ant., 15, 251, 312; 17, 347.

3. In the NT the noun κακοπάθεια occurs only in Jm. 5:10 : ὑπόδειγμα λάβετε, ἀδελφοί, τῆς κακοπαθείας καὶ τῆς μακροθυμίας τοὺς προφήτας. The combination with μακροθυμία (→ IV, 385, 25 ff.), dependence on ὑπόδειγμα (→ II, 33, 31 f.) and mention of ὑπομονή in v. 11 (→ IV, 587, 21 ff.) give κακοπάθεια or κακοπαθία B*D (→ n. 3) the sense of "enduring affliction." [6] The meaning "suffering" or "affliction" [7] is not supported even by the fact that κακοπαθέω in v. 13 means "to be smitten by a misfortune or evil," for 5:13 belongs to a new section. In 5:13, as shown by the antithetical parallel εὐθυμέω, the κακοπαθέω suggests, not so much the distressing situation as such, but the spiritual burden which it brings with it, and which drives us to prayer. Hence the prayer is more for the giving of strength than the removal of the situation. [8]

In 2 Tm. 2:9 : ἐν ᾧ κακοπαθῶ μέχρι δεσμῶν ὡς κακοῦργος the ἐν ᾧ perhaps refers back to the Ἰησοῦ Χριστοῦ of v. 8. In the requirement of 4:5 : κακοπάθησον, the word obviously means "to accept suffering, affliction, adversity," not to be overcome by them, to endure them, cf. ὑπομένω in 2:10. Already Timothy has been exhorted to συγκακοπαθεῖν in 1:8 and 2:3. The reference in 2:3 is not to a spiritual sharing of the present distress of the apostle but to the fact that Timothy, too, must suffer and enter the fellowship of those who, like Paul himself, endure as true soldiers of Jesus Christ, holding out in the afflictions appointed for them, and thus wrestling through to victory, → I, 138, 13 f. [9] Cf. συγκακοπάθησον in 1:8. The addition τῷ εὐαγγελίῳ ... θεοῦ (cf. 2:9 : οὐ δέδεται) is not representing the Gospel itself as a suffering entity with which one has to suffer also. [10] Nor can it mean that the sufferings are caused by the Gospel. This is a dat. commodi : the sufferings of Paul and Timothy will prosper the cause of the Gospel,

---

[5] Though cf. Pr.-Bauer⁴, s.v. (92, 259 "exertion"); P. Wendland in Kautzsch Apkr. u. Pseudepigr. (92 "exertion"); H. G. Meecham, The Letter of Aristeas (1935), 68 (208 "suffering," 92, 259 "toil").

[6] Cf. Wnd. Jk., ad loc.: "patience in affliction"; Deissmann NB, 91; Cr.-Kö., 844, s.v.; Pr.-Bauer⁴, 720, s.v.

[7] So apparently Schl. Jk., 275, esp. as in n. 2 he refers to Jos. Ant., 17, 347, where the meaning is "misfortune." But Jos. has the plur., and one would expect this in Jm. 5:10 as well if the meaning were "affliction." Hck. Jk., 227 combines a pass. and act. sense, but there can surely be only the one meaning. More correctly Cr.-Kö., 844 s.v. says with ref. to 4 Macc. 9:8 and Jm. 5:10 : "κακοπάθεια refers to the fact that affliction is endured, ὑπομονή and μακροθυμία to the manner." There is no reason to assume hendiadys ("prenez pour exemple de patience dans les afflictions les prophètes," Björck, op. cit., 3).

[8] Schl. Jk., 279 relates κακοπαθέω esp. to "want, poverty, imprisonment, flight, maltreatment, mutilation," but there is nothing else in the section (cf. 5:7 ff.) to suggest persecution.

[9] κακοπαθέω itself does not refer (fig.) to the hardships of military service, cf. Cr.-Kö., 844. B. Weiss, Die Briefe Pauli an Tim. u. Tit.⁷ (1902), 263 is quite mistaken when he relates the συν- "to those to whom he has entrusted the preaching of sound doctrine (v. 2)."

[10] Though cf. Schl. Past., 222. The simple in the act. sense, however, underlies the compound συγκακοπαθέω.

→ 920, 11 f.; Phil. 1:27. Ability to hold out has its root in the δύναμις θεοῦ, → II, 317, 24 ff.

4. In the post-apost. fathers κακοπαθέω is used in 2 Cl., 19, 3 par. to ταλαιπωρέω in 19, 4 for being beset by the afflictions of this world. The group is not found in the Apologists.

† μετριοπαθέω.

1. Deriv. from the adj. μετριοπαθής. This is ascribed by Diog. L., V, 31 to Aristot., but its attestation is late. [1] It denotes one who has moderate πάθη, or who knows how to moderate his πάθη. Presupposed is the development of πάθος to the sense of "passion," → 926, 27 ff. Hence μετριοπαθέω means "to exercise moderation in emotions or passions," cf. Sext. Emp. Pyrrh. Hyp., III, 235 f.

2. The group does not occur in the LXX. Philo has the adj. in Spec. Leg., III, 97 (par. ἐπιεικής), and the verb and noun 3 or 4 times. [2] Acc. to Abr., 255 f. Abraham, on the death of his wife, followed λογισμός in all his λύπη; that is (257), he neither grieved πλέον τοῦ μετρίου nor gave way to ἀπάθεια, but chose the mean between the two extremes (τὸ δὲ μέσον πρὸ τῶν ἄκρων ἑλόμενον), and exerted himself to keep a balance (μετριοπαθεῖν πειρᾶσθαι). Cf. also Jos., 26 and Virt., 195 (noun). On the other hand, in Leg. All., III, 129 Moses is represented as οὐ μετριοπάθειαν ἀλλὰ συνόλως ἀπάθειαν ἀγαπῶν who οὐδὲ μετριοπαθεῖν βούλεται ἀλλ' ἐκ περιουσίας ὅλα τὰ πάθη ἀπέκοψεν, 134, cf. also 132 and 144 (in both cases the noun). [3] Joseph. in Ant., 12, 128 praises the μετριοπαθεῖν of Vespasian and Titus on the conclusion of peace. Cf. also μετριάω in 5, 256. The adj. is also used in Ep. Ar., 256.

3. In the NT we find only the verb in the hapax legomenon in Hb. 5:2, where it is said of the OT high-priest: μετριοπαθεῖν δυνάμενος τοῖς ἀγνοοῦσιν καὶ πλανωμένοις, ἐπεὶ καὶ αὐτὸς περίκειται ἀσθένειαν, cf. 7:28, → I, 491, 36 f.; 492, 23 ff. The thought of his own weakness and sin makes him moderate in his (justifiable) displeasure and anger at the sins of the people. Materially, μετριοπαθεῖν is closely related to the συμπαθῆσαι of 4:15 (→ 935, 33 ff., → III, 279, 10 f.), but they are not identical. [4]

4. We do not find the group in either the post-apost. fathers or the Apologists. [5]

† όμοιοπαθής.

1. The adj. όμοιοπαθής denotes "one who finds himself in the same or similar relations," "whose attitude or feeling is the same or similar," etc. Cf. Plat. Tim., 45c; Resp., III, 409b; Theophr. Hist. Plant., V, 7, 2. Derived from the adj. are the verb όμοιοπαθέω (e.g., Aristot. Eth. Nic., I, 3, p. 1095b, 22) and the noun όμοιοπάθεια. [1] The adj. occurs twice in the LXX. In Wis. 7:3 the earth is called όμοιοπαθής, with the same meaning as κοινός bears when used just before of the air, i.e., the same for all men. [2] In 4 Macc. 12:13 the tyrant ἄνθρωπος ὤν is compared with his victims as

μετριοπαθέω. [1] Cf. Pass. and Liddell-Scott, s.v., also esp. Cr.-Kö., 843.
[2] Acc. to Leisegang, s.v., who does not note the adj.
[3] This vacillation in Philo may be attributed to regard for his basic OT sources, cf. W. Völker, "Fortschritt u. Vollendung bei Philo v. Alex.," TU, 49, 1 (1938), 134 and 266. Hence his occasional espousing of metriopathy is not a decisive counterbalance to his usual emphasis on apathy, → 927, 22 ff.
[4] As against Cr.-Kö., 843.
[5] But cf. μέτρια νοεῖν in 1 Cl., 1, 3 and μέτριος, "moderate," "modest," in Athenag. Suppl., 11, 2; 12, 1; 37, 1.
όμοιοπαθής. [1] Cf. Pass. and Liddell-Scott, s.v.
[2] The transl. of J. Fichtner, "Weisheit Sal.," Handbuch z. AT, II, 6 (1938), ad loc.: "fell on the earth on which all suffer the same," is not quite correct. What is meant is that "I (Solomon) fell (as a child) on the same earth (as all children fall on)."

ὁμοιοπαθεῖς, which is amplified by ἐκ τῶν αὐτῶν γεγονότες στοιχείων, so that ὁμοιοπαθής does not have just the general sense "of the same kind," but the more specialised sense "feeling precisely so." Philo in Conf. Ling., 7 uses τὸ ὁμοιότροπον καὶ ὁμοιοπαθές for similarity in mode of life and feelings among both men and beasts, or for the same manner and way of life. Joseph. does not use the word.

2. The term appears in the NT only at Ac. 14:15 and Jm. 5:17 in the general sense "similar," "in the same situation." In Ac. 14:15 Barnabas and Paul protest against being regarded as θεοὶ ὁμοιωθέντες ἀνθρώποις (14:11): καὶ ἡμεῖς ὁμοιοπαθεῖς ἐσμεν ὑμῖν ἄνθρωποι, "we are only men exactly like yourselves." [3] When it is said of Elijah in Jm. 5:17: ἄνθρωπος ἦν ὁμοιοπαθὴς ἡμῖν, this is again a protest against the view that Elijah might have had superhuman powers. [4] Hence the efficacy of his prayer in 5:17 f. supports what is said about the righteous man in v. 16, and the reader is encouraged to like prayer. [5] In neither passage is there any special theory of the equality of all men.

3. The word does not occur in the post-apost. fathers, but it is common in the Apologists, with ref. to the incarnate Christ in Just. Epit., 10, 8; Dial., 48, 3; 57, 3. Cf. also Eus. Hist. Eccl., I, 2, 1.

† πραϋπάθεια.

1. A late construct, related to the adj. πραϋπαθής ("gentle"), which occurs in Philo Spec. Leg., IV, 93 and may be conjectured in Leg. Gaj., 335 (for πρᾳοπαθής, cf. Fug., 6). The noun is used in Philo Abr., 213 (vl. πρᾳότης) for the "gentleness" of Abraham. [1]

2. The only instance in the NT is at 1 Tm. 6:11 at the end of a list of virtues. [2] The meaning is not so much "meekness" in the sense of "tractability" but "composure" (cf. the preceding ὑπομονή) which can take wrongs calmly. [3]

3. In the post-apost. fathers it is in Ign. Tr., 8, 1 a virtue which the community must acquire. [4] The word does not occur in the Apologists.

Michaelis

† πατάσσω

The intr. "to knock loudly" (Hom. Il., 7, 216) does not occur in the NT. The trans. "to strike," "to hit" (Aristoph. Ra., 54; Plat. Gorg., 527c; Demosth. Or., 21, 33) is more common and can also be used for a fatal blow, Demosth. Or., 23, 77; Polyb., 7, 29 (31), 8.

The word is very common (over 400 times) in the LXX, usually for נכה hi. In keeping with the original πατάσσειν means here "to hit," "to strike," sometimes fatally. Ex.

---

[3] Hardly a special ref. to the fact that "they are moved by their πάθη" (Bau. Ag., 183), for gods who have become men will also have πάθη. The word supports neither the rendering "weak as you" (*ibid.*, 181) nor the transl. "mortal men" (Pr. Ag., ad loc.). Cf. Zn. Ag., 476, n. 89.

[4] The word does not particularly emphasise the fact that our nature is passively determined, Hck. Jk., 237. Wnd. Jk., ad loc. incorrectly refers to "the bodily weakness and limitation of the prophet," and thus suggests the transl.: "(only) a man who shares our human weaknesses."

[5] R. Bohren, *Das Problem d. Kirchenzucht im NT* (1952), 90.

π ρ α ϋ π ά θ ε ι α. For bibl. → πάθος.

[1] Leisegang does not list πραϋπάθεια.

[2] πραϋπαθία ℵ* A etc. is either a phonetic vl. for πραϋπάθεια or is to be read as πραϋπαθία, cf. Pr.-Bauer, *s.v.* and → 936, n. 3. A common vl. in the NT is πραϋτης ℵᶜD* 31 or πρᾳότης DᶜKL.

[3] Schl. Past., 166. Cf. also Wbg. Past., 210. But cf. Vögtle, 172; also 178.

[4] Schlier, 157 wrongly contrasts this v. with 4, 2 : while Ign. has still to exercise himself in πρᾳότης, the community, being perfected, has πραϋπάθεια already (but cf. the ἀναλαβόντες with imp. in 8, 1).

21:12 : ἐὰν δὲ πατάξῃ τίς τινα καὶ ἀποθάνῃ, 2:12 : Μωϋσῆς ... πατάξας τὸν Αἰγύπτιον. In most instances, however, πατάσσειν is used of God and it usually denotes His educative, judicial or penal "smiting"; Lv. 26:24 : καὶ πατάξω ὑμᾶς κἀγὼ ἑπτάκις ἀντὶ τῶν ἁμαρτιῶν ὑμῶν. Cf. also Dt. 32:39; Jer. 2:30 etc. πατάσσειν is used in the description of the plagues of Egypt, Ex. 7:20, 25; 8:12 f.; 9:15; 12:12, 23, 27, 29. Cf. 1 Βασ. 4:8 and other passages, esp. in Ps., in which there is recollection of the plagues. Rarely πατάσσειν denotes destruction by God, cf. Gn. 8:21: οὐ προσθήσω οὖν ἔτι πατάξαι πᾶσαν σάρκα ζῶσαν. Cf. also Nu. 33:4.

There is nothing distinctive about the NT use. πατάσσειν occurs 10 times, 3 in OT quotations : Ac. 7:24 = Ex. 2:12; Mk. 14:27; Mt. 26:31 = Zech. 13:7.[1] When Jesus is arrested, Mt. 26:51 and Lk. 22:49, 50 refer to the πατάσσειν of an unnamed disciple : καὶ πατάξας τὸν δοῦλον ...; Mk. 14:47, like Jn. 18:10, uses the equivalent παίω. Ac. 12 twice speaks of a πατάσσειν of the angel of the Lord. In v. 7 Peter in prison is awakened by a blow from the angel, and in v. 23 it is said of the death of Herod, who would not give God the glory : παραχρῆμα δὲ ἐπάταξεν αὐτὸν ἄγγελος κυρίου. In both cases we have a description of God's intervention in human life through an angel. The NT, like the OT, is convinced that God directs human destiny and that He intervenes both to help and to smite as He himself decides. Finally, the word is found twice in Rev. 11:6 with reference to the two witnesses : ἐξουσίαν ἔχουσιν ... καὶ πατάξαι τὴν γῆν ἐν πάσῃ πληγῇ.[2] The echo of the description of the first plague of Egypt in Ex. 7:19, 20 provides the key to an understanding of πατάσσειν here.[3] The two witnesses receive from God the same power in the discharge of their office as Moses received. Nevertheless, one cannot say for certain in what the πατάσσειν consists. It is plainly a judicial or penal, and perhaps a fatal, smiting, Rev. 19:15 says of the Logos as universal Judge : καὶ ἐκ τοῦ στόματος αὐτοῦ ἐκπορεύεται ῥομφαία ὀξεῖα, ἵνα ἐν αὐτῇ πατάξῃ τὰ ἔθνη. The OT verse which the author has in mind (Is. 11:4) is the clue to the meaning of πατάξῃ here. It is there said of the Messiah : καὶ πατάξει γῆν τῷ λόγῳ τοῦ στόματος αὐτοῦ, καὶ ... ἀνελεῖ ἀσεβῆ. Similarly, Rev. 19:15 refers not merely to the judging and punishing of the nations of the earth, but to their total destruction. The universal Judge definitively extirpates all hostility to God on the earth.[4]

Seesemann

┌───┐
│ † πατέω, † καταπατέω, περιπατέω, † ἐμπεριπατέω   │
└───┘

A. πατέω and Compounds in General Greek Usage.

1. πατέω means intr. "to go," "to walk," trans. "to tread" (Gospel Fr., P. Oxy., V, 840, 12 ff.: τίς ἐπέτρεψέν σοι πατ[εῖν] τοῦτο τὸ ἁγνευτήριον); "to tread with the feet," often in a transf. sense : "to treat disparagingly," even "to maltreat," "to despoil," Heliodor. Aeth., IV, 19 : πατεῖν πόλιν.

π α τ ά σ σ ω.   [1] For the LXX reading πατάξατε Mk. and Mt. have πατάξω, cf. Kl. Mk., ad loc.; cf. also Barn., 5, 12.
[2] Cf. D. Haugg, "Die zwei Zeugen," Nt.liche Abh., XVII, 1 (1936), 20.
[3] Cf. Bss. Apk., ad loc.
[4] Cf. Had. Apk., ad loc.: "The victory is complete." Loh. Apk. refers to Wis. 18:22 and Eth. En. 62:2. The latter is unquestionably dependent on Is. 11:4.

π α τ έ ω κτλ. Cf. the dict. On the etym. (πάτος-πατέω) E. Schwyzer, Griech. Gramm., I = Handbuch AW, II, 1, 1 (1939), 457, 1; 458, 3; 726, 2; Boisacq, 752, 803; H. Frisk, "Zur griech. Wortkunde," Eranos, 38 (1940), 43-46 [Debrunner].

2. καταπατέω is a strengthened form which in distinction from the simple πατέω denotes "treading down," "trampling," Hdt., II, 14 : ἐπεὰν δὲ καταπατήσῃ τῇσι ὑσὶ τὸ σπέρμα ... Here again the fig. sense "to treat contemptuously," "to despise," is common, Plat. Leg., IV, 714a : καταπατήσας τοὺς νόμους.

3. περιπατέω means "to walk around," "to stay" (Demosth. Or., 54, 7: περιπατεῖν ἐν ἀγορᾷ). Alien to class. Gk. is the transf. sense "to walk" = "to conduct the walk of life"; this is echoed in Philodem. Philos. De Liberate, 23, 3, where περιπατεῖν means generally "to live"; only in the LXX, however, is it common in this sense, → 942, 45 ff.

4. ἐμπεριπατέω is found only at a later period in general Gk. usage, i.e., from Plut., Luc., Achill. Tat. It means "to walk about in," "to walk."

Seesemann

B. πατέω and Compounds in the LXX.

1. In the LXX we find not only the simple πατέω but also the compounds κατα-, συμ-, περι- and the double compound ἐμπεριπατέω.[1] The word does not denote purposeful movement, but the treading of the feet, which includes moving to and fro or around, but also treading on something (e.g., the winepress). The πατοῦντες τὴν γῆν are the dwellers on earth, Is. 42:5; cf. περιπατοῦντες ὑπὸ τὸν ἥλιον, Qoh. 4:15. One treads a land to take possession of it, Dt. 11:24; cf. 2:5 Allos. The variety in Heb. originals[2] points to a certain independence on the part of the translator in his choice of words, esp. as the Hebrew terms for their part are also rendered in very different ways in the Gk. The group does not belong to the linguistic field of the stranger or alien (→ 1, 1 ff.; 842, 16 ff.; II, 64, 29 ff.) or to the realm of the wandering people of God. περιπατεῖν denotes the righteous walk, the living of life in the sight of God.

2. Negatively πατέω, κατα- and συμπατέω denote esp. God's judgments in history. In the language of vine-growers the word is a tt. (→ ληνός, IV, 254, 12) in its original and transf. sense ; treading the winepress is an early activity of peaceful men engaged in agriculture and the cultivation of the vine (2 Esr. 23:15, desecration of the Sabbath). Judgment can also be depicted under the image of the winepress, Jl. 3:13; Is. 63:2, 3, 6. Threshing is a similar metaphor. The corn is trodden by oxen. πατεῖν (דוש) ἐν ἁμάξαις in Is. 25:10 means "to work over with the threshing sled,"[3] cf. Am. 2:13 HT. In historical narrative we often find the idea of trampling (κατα- or συμπατεῖν) with no ref. to the image of the harvest. The foot of war or of the conqueror treads down or destroys a land (Mas. רמס); in the strict sense "to crush," "to trample," 4 Βασ. 7:17, 20; 9:33; 14:9; 2 Ch. 25:18 (the parable of the thistle or thornbush which aspired high but was trampled down by a wild beast; cf. also Jos. 19:48 vl. κατῴκησαν, Mas. ירש and ישב). Fig. the destruction of a land (Mas. שׁסה, שׁסס): 1 Βασ. 14:48; 17:53; 23:1. Prophetic warning takes up the image of crushing or treading down (Mas. מִרְמָס): Mi. 7:10; Is. 5:5; 7:25; 10:6; cf. 16:4 (רמס), 8 (הלם); 25:10 (דוש); 28:18; Is. 14:25; 18:2, 7; 22:5 (מבוסה, בוס); 22:18 (no Heb.). Is. 41:25 uses another image for the crushing of princes, namely, that of the potter who treads clay. Lam. 2:8 (בלע) refers to the κατα-πάτημα of the wall of the daughter of Zion by the hand of the Lord. Is. 28:28 reads : οὐδὲ φωνὴ τῆς πικρίας μου (θεοῦ) καταπατήσει ὑμᾶς. The righteous can be instruments of God for the treading down of the ungodly, Mal. 3:21 (4:3); Is. 26:6; cf. ψ 43:5 ʼΑΣ; Zech. 10:5. ψ 90:13 was taken Messianically. Here the Messiah is depicted as victor over the powers of hell, which are represented as lions and dragons. In another sense salvation is intended when it is said that Yahweh causes the blind to tread ways that they know not, Is. 42:16. The threat that the temple will be destroyed (Is. 63:18) is found more than once in OT history. In Da. 8:13 LXX we read : τὰ ἅγια ἐρημωθή-σεται εἰς καταπάτημα (Θ συμπατηθήσεται), cf. 1 Macc. 3:45, 51; 4:60. The ref. in 2 Macc. 8:2 is to the people of God: τὸν ὑπὸ πάντων καταπατούμενον λαόν.

---

[1] ἀποπατεῖν occurs only once in Σ at 1 Βασ. 24:4 ("to tread down").

[2] καταπατεῖν is used for 16 Heb. terms, cf. Hatch-Redpath, s.v.

[3] K. Galling, Bibl. Reallexikon = Handbuch z. AT, I, 1 (1937), 138, s.v. "Dreschen."

3 Macc. 2:18 combines the motif of the treading down of the sanctuary by the Gentiles with that of ungodly hubris : οἱ παράνομοι ... ἐν ὑπερηφανίᾳ ... λέγοντες : ἡμεῖς κατεπατήσαμεν τὸν οἶκον τοῦ ἁγιασμοῦ (→ ὕβρις). This is a common combination. Cf. Job 28:8 LXX. The generation of the flood trod a wrong path, Job 22:15. Acc. to Zech. 12:3 Jerusalem will be a trampled stone for all nations : ὁ καταπατῶν αὐτὴν ἐμπαίζων ἐμπαίξεται; he who crushes it vents his pride in derision over it, → 632, 17-20. Here, too, the LXX introduced the combination of trampling and deriding. In many cases these are terms for war. As such they denote on the one hand the position of the vanquished, who are to be trodden underfoot. On the other side, however, treading, treading down, trampling, is the characteristic attitude of the conqueror. When the victors are Israel's enemies — and hence God's enemies acc. to popular belief in Israel — πατεῖν and compounds are tt. for an ungodly and arrogant attitude. Thus Am. 2:7 LXX is directed against the ungodly who tread down the poor and lowly (שאף "to trample underfoot"). Cf. also Am. 4:1; 5:12; Is. 59:8 Σ; Jer. 12:10 'ΑΣ; 4 Βασ. 19:26 πάτημα along with the perishable grass, though cf. Is. 37:27 (ἄγρωστις). In Ez. 36:4 (לעג) ("mocking," → 631, 29-35) is rendered καταπάτημα by the LXX along the lines of this combination of ideas, and in Ez. 34:18 men of arrogance are contrasted with men of humility as those who exercise πατεῖν on the one side and those who are πατήματα on the other. The group is also used to portray the attitude of the ungodly in Ez. 26:11 (the hooves of horses) and 32:2 (Pharaoh under the figure of a monster from the Nile). Cf. also the portrayal of the 4th beast or he-goat in Da. 7:7, 19, 23 Θ; 8:10 (LXX pass. κατεπατήθη, Θ act. συνεπάτησεν).[4] The Psalmist, too, sees himself confronted by proud enemies who tread him down, ψ 7:5; 55:1, 2; 56:3. In ψ 138:11 σκότος is a fig. term for the hostile power which, the righteous fears, will tread him down (καταπατήσει με). The LXX, of course, takes a path different here from that of the Mas. tradition, which is correctly understood by Σ and an anon. transl.: σκότος ἐπισκεπάσει (καλύψει) με.

3. περιπατέω and ἐμπεριπατέω are closely related in LXX usage. περιπατέω, for the root הלך (usually hitp) except at Job 9:8, means "to go around," and in the first instance denotes aimless moving to and fro in a specific place, e.g., outside Ex. 21:19; in the house 2 Βασ. 11:2; around the court Est. 2:11; in the garden Sus. 7:13, 36; on the wall Da. 4:26; in the fire Da. 3:25, cf. Wis. 19:21 (ἐμπεριπατεῖν). It is the natural and necessary expression of human life, Ex. 21:19; 1 Βασ. 17:39. It may be in exploration of a land (Ju. 18:9), or, like Satan, one may go to and fro on the earth to get to know men (Job 1:6, 7; 2:2). In 'Α ἐμπεριπατέω can be used to describe the sphere in which one lives, Ez. 19:6; 28:14. A special use is for God walking to and fro, e.g., in Paradise (Gn. 3:8, 10),[5] in the camp (Dt. 23:15, cf. Lv. 26:12 → 945, n. 27; 2 Βασ. 7:6 and 1 Ch. 17:6 Allos). God walks where man cannot go, Job 9:8; 38:16; ψ 103:3, cf. also the way of wisdom acc. to Sir. 24:5, also that of the mythical crocodile in Job 41:24. Very different are the helpless idols which cannot walk, ψ 113:15; 134:17. Prv. 6:28 contains a proverbial fig. of speech (to walk on hot coals); cf. also 30:31 (the cock among the hens). The word occurs in Δα. 4:33b for "to waste away," "to vegetate," cf. also Prv. 23:31. By way of exception Ju. 21:24 expresses a change of place, while the ref. in Is. 8:7 is to hostile power, cf. Job 20:25.

The terms are frequently used, however, not in the spatial sense, but to express man's religious and ethical walk.[6] This is in keeping with the basic concept of piety in the

---

[4] Since the angels and the power of God are on the side of the stars, the pass. is quite possible, cf. A. Bentzen, Da. = Handbuch z. AT, I, 19² (1952), ad loc.

[5] Cf. Philo Leg. All., III, 51: ἐπειδὴ γὰρ ᾠήθης τὸν θεὸν ἐν τῷ παραδείσῳ περιπατεῖν. Phil. regards a lit. understanding of the Paradise story as μυθοποιία, Leg. All., I, 43.

[6] A. Kuschke, "Die Menschenwege u. der Weg Gottes im AT," Studia Theologica, V, 2 (1951), 106-118; E. Eidem, Det Kristna levet enligt Paulus, I (1927), 49; G. Eingren, "Weg, Wanderung u. verwandte Begriffe," Studia Theol., III, 1-2 (1949), 111-123; → ὁδός, 49, 37 ff.

OT. Man as the creature of God always walks before God on the earth, Gn. 17:1. The LXX often avoids a lit. rendering of this idea, obviously because it found it too naïve. Thus in the passage quoted and elsewhere in Gn. and Ps. it has εὐαρεστέω for הלך hitp. [7] On the other hand 'A often has (ἐμ-)περιπατέω, Gn. 5:22 (Enoch); 6:9 (Noah); ψ 114:9 (so also Σ); cf. also 1 Βασ. 2:35. Acc. to Prv. 8:20 wisdom walks in righteousness, and in 6:22 man is admonished to keep the commandments of the fathers wherever he walks. The king appeals to a righteous walk of this kind in the prayer of 4 Βασ. 20:3. The same is in view in Qoh. 11:9 (ἄμωμος) and with slight variations also in Prv. 28:6 'ΑΣΘ (ἐν ἁπλότητι, LXX πορευόμενος ἐν ἀληθείᾳ); ψ 85:11 'Α ἐν ἀληθείᾳ. In contrast is walking in darkness, which is to be taken mythically at first, but which is then meant ethically and psychologically: Is. 59:9 (LXX 'ΑΣΘ); ψ 90:6 ('Α reads דֶבֶר, ῥῆμα, LXX πρᾶγμα for דֶבֶר, Σ λοιμός). [8] Cf. also ψ 72:9 Σ and σκυθρωπὸς περιπατεῖν in ψ 37:6 Σ; cf. 41:9. In all these refs. there is a hint of the contrast between light and darkness in the ethical sense. A dualistic usage is thus adopted which had been developed in the surrounding world from the Persian period, and which was taken up later by certain Jewish sects. [9] We also catch an echo of the motif of the two ways. [10] Since there is no orientation to a goal, the terms are particularly well adapted to indicate the sphere of life in which the life of the righteous or the ungodly is lived. This fig. usage came to be accepted in the Gk. Bible, though less in the LXX than in later renderings. [11] It is an open question how far NT usage, esp. that of Paul, may be traced back to the use in the Gk. OT.

Bertram

C. πατέω and Compounds in the NT.

1. πατέω occurs only 5 times in the NT. In all instances the use is fixed by the LXX. When the seventy return to Jesus, He says to them in Lk. 10:19: ἰδοὺ δέδωκα ὑμῖν τὴν ἐξουσίαν τοῦ πατεῖν ἐπάνω ὄφεων καὶ σκορπίων. The expression πατεῖν ἐπάνω ὄφεων recalls ψ 90:13, → 941, 44 f. Jesus is thus referring to the protection which He as Messiah has granted His disciples against every power of Satan. [12] They trod over snakes and scorpions on the way, → 579, 7 ff. On Lk. 21:24: καὶ Ἰηρουσαλὴμ ἔσται πατουμένη ὑπὸ ἐθνῶν, cf. esp. Zech. 12:3, also Da. 8:13, → 941, 48 f. The same expression is to be found in Rev. 11:2: (τὰ ἔθνη) τὴν πόλιν τὴν ἁγίαν πατήσουσιν μῆνας τεσσεράκοντα καὶ δύο. Like καταπατεῖν in the LXX passages, πατεῖν has here the sense of "destroying," "plundering," though one might go further and render "to plunder and desecrate," since plundering the holy city (including the temple) is necessarily equivalent to its desecration. [13] In Rev. 14:20 and 19:15 we have the OT image of πατεῖν the winepress for the judgment of divine wrath. [14] Here πατεῖν means "to tread," "to trample."

---

[7] εὐαρεστεῖν, which occurs only 14 times in the LXX, is used 11 times for הלך hitp, 9 times for walking before God, once (ψ 25:3) for walking in truth, and only once for "to walk" (ψ 34:14).

[8] The LXX, when it correctly identified דֶבֶר, usually transl. it by θάνατος, 'Α and Σ by λοιμός.

[9] There thus arises a distinctive state of conflict, cf. → πανοπλία, 298, 25-300, 27.

[10] Cf. the intr. to the Didache: "There are two ways, one to life and one to death..."

[11] Philo, too, makes only occasional use of περιπατεῖν.

[12] Cf. in Test. L. 18 the promise for the age of salvation: πατεῖν ἐπὶ τὰ πονηρὰ πνεύματα. Cf. Hck. Lk., ad loc. and Str.-B., II, 168 f.

[13] Cf. Had. Apk., 118 ad loc.; Hck. Lk., 255 ad loc.

[14] Cf. Jl. 3:13: εἰσπορεύεσθε, πατεῖτε, διότι πλήρης ἡ ληνός. Cf. also Is. 63:2-6; → ληνός, IV, 255, 18-257, 11.

2. καταπατέω is used 4 times in the lit. sense "to tread underfoot" : Mt. 5:13; 7:6; Lk. 8:5; 12:1. It appears in a transf. sense in Hb. 10:29. In the section on the ἑκουσίως ἁμαρτάνοντες the author speaks with horror of the καταπατήσας τὸν υἱὸν τοῦ θεοῦ. The severest punishment is to be expected by him who "tramples underfoot," "denies," "despises" the Son of God. [15]

3. περιπατέω is first used in the NT quite commonly in the simple original sense "to walk around." Thus in the accounts of the healing of lame folk we repeatedly find περιπατεῖν, Mk. 2:9 par.; Jn. 5:8-12; Ac. 3:6-12. Mk. 5:42 says of Jairus' daughter: ἀνέστη τὸ κοράσιον καὶ περιεπάτει. In Lk. 24:17 Jesus asks the disciples on the way to Emmaus what they were talking about περιπατοῦντες, i.e., as they walked. 1 Pt. 5:8 speaks of the devil, who περιπατεῖ ("roams around") like a λέων ὠρυόμενος. There is nothing distinctive about this use of the word.

περιπατεῖν, however, is found especially in Paul, who uses it for the walk of life, more particularly in the moral sense. Almost always precision is given to the word by the addition of κατά, ἐν, ἀξίως or a dat. [16] Even though instances of this use are less common in the LXX than in later OT translations, it is impossible that Paul should have taken it from any other source. [17] There are no parallels in classical Greek. In Gl. 5:16 Paul puts to his readers the requirement : λέγω δέ, πνεύματι περιπατεῖτε καὶ ἐπιθυμίαν σαρκὸς οὐ μὴ τελέσητε. He is here calling on them to live their lives as a walk in the Spirit. [18] The lists of vices and virtues which follow are rounded off in 5:25 by the admonition πνεύματι καὶ στοιχῶμεν, στοιχεῖν being simply another word sometimes used by Paul for περιπατεῖν. A similar demand is often found in Paul's epistles : περιπατεῖν ὑμᾶς ἀξίως τοῦ θεοῦ, 1 Th. 2:12; περιπατῆσαι ἀξίως τοῦ κυρίου, Col. 1:10; ἀξίως περιπατῆσαι τῆς κλήσεως, Eph. 4:1; ὡς τέκνα φωτὸς περιπατεῖτε, 5:8; cf. also 2:10; 5:2, 15; Col. 4:5; R. 14:15; 2 C. 4:2; Phil. 3:17 f. [19] Acc. to 1 Th. 4:1 Paul left the newly baptised directions τὸ πῶς δεῖ ὑμᾶς περιπατεῖν καὶ ἀρέσκειν θεῷ. Though the whole walk of life could not be regulated by such precepts, some general rules must have been given. [20] These are to be found in 1 Th. 4:2-12. The baptised have to learn by specific examples what it means εὐσχημόνως περιπατεῖν (4:12; cf. R. 13:13). Similarly, Col. 2:6 : ὡς οὖν παρελάβετε τὸν Χριστὸν Ἰησοῦν τὸν κύριον, ἐν αὐτῷ περιπατεῖτε, points to traditional rules for walking "in Christ." [21] Keeping these rules is mandatory ; in 2 Th. 3:6, 11 Paul issues a warning against all who, being baptised, were ἀτάκτως περιπατοῦντες; he demands that there should be withdrawal from such. These men themselves are to come back again to an orderly course of life and quietly to take up their work. In 1 C. 7:17 there is the similar injunction that each ὡς κέκληκεν ὁ θεός, οὕτως περιπατείτω. Faith does not mean social reshuffling. But there is to be a radical change in the walk. It is impossible to become a Christian and to continue to walk as a pagan, Eph. 4:17. For Paul the beginning of the new walk is closely related to baptism. Baptism makes us participators in the death and resurrection of Jesus, → I, 541, 13-542, 12. It puts an end to the walk in sins, Col. 3:7; cf. Eph. 2:2. It gives victory over κατὰ

---

[15] Cf. Mi. Hb., ad loc., and the OT refs. there.
[16] Paul uses the word 33 times (incl. Eph. and Col.); it does not occur in the Past.
[17] → 942, 45-943, 21 and the bibl. in n. 6.
[18] R. Bultmann, Theologie d. NT (1953) § 38 deals with the question of freedom from sin in Paul under the heading "The Walk in the Spirit."
[19] On Phil. 3:18 cf. Loh. Phil., 152, n. 2 (ad loc.).
[20] H. Preisker, Das Ethos d. Urchr.² (1949), 168-195, esp. 169 f.
[21] A "Christian Halakah." → παραλαμβάνειν, IV, 13, 26-14, 29 and the bibl. there.

ἄνθρωπον περιπατεῖν, 1 C. 3:3. It sets κατὰ σάρκα περιπατεῖν in the past, R. 8:4; 2 C. 10:2 f. This is true even though Paul has to ascribe ἐν σαρκὶ περιπατεῖν (= humanity) to himself and all the baptised, 2 C. 10:3. For the σάρξ is no longer the lord of the baptised. The force which controls them is the Spirit, Gl. 5:16; cf. 2 C. 12:18. Through baptism we have not only the ability but also the possibility ἵνα ἐν καινότητι ζωῆς περιπατήσωμεν, R. 6:4. This must be the goal of the baptised. 2 C. 5:7 stands apart : διὰ πίστεως γὰρ περιπατοῦμεν, οὐ διὰ εἴδους. It is the only instance of περιπατεῖν with the prep. διά, which denotes, not the nature, but the accompanying circumstance of the walk (here "life" in a more general sense). Faith alone, not sight, is called the mark of the Christian life. [22]

περιπατεῖν is also used more than once by Jn. to denote the "walk." Jn. has the non-fig. sense of "going" (Jn. 11:9 f.; 21:18), but the word has a deeper meaning for him : ὁ ἀκολουθῶν μοι οὐ μὴ περιπατήσῃ ἐν τῇ σκοτίᾳ, ἀλλ᾽ ἕξει τὸ φῶς τῆς ζωῆς, Jn. 8:12. In distinction from the predominantly hortatory use in Paul the use in Jn. is more general. It refers not merely to practical conduct but to the whole stance of the believer or of faith itself, [23] cf. Jn. 12:35 : περιπατεῖτε ὡς τὸ φῶς ἔχετε, ἵνα μὴ σκοτία ὑμᾶς καταλάβῃ, also 1 Jn. 1:6 f.; 2:11, and the admonition in 2:6, which is based on the example of Christ's walk : ὁ λέγων ἐν αὐτῷ μένειν ὀφείλει καθὼς ἐκεῖνος περιεπάτησεν καὶ αὐτὸς οὕτως περιπατεῖν. [24] Only a few verses in the minor letters of Jn. correspond to Paul's use under the influence of the OT translations, cf. 2 Jn. 4; 3 Jn. 3 f.: περιπατεῖν ἐν ἀληθείᾳ, "to act uprightly," [25] 2 Jn. 6 : ... ἵνα περιπατῶμεν κατὰ τὰς ἐντολὰς αὐτοῦ.

In the other NT writings there are only odd instances of the fig. use : Mk. 7:5; Ac. 15:1 (D); 21:21; Hb. 13:9; Rev. 21:24 (cf. Is. 60:3, though the LXX has πορεύσονται here).

4. ἐμπεριπατέω occurs only once in 2 C. 6:16, where it is taken from Lv. 26:12 : ἐνοικήσω ἐν αὐτοῖς (obviously added by Paul or taken from an unknown transl.) καὶ ἐμπεριπατήσω καὶ ἔσομαι αὐτῶν θεός. The thought of God's dwelling in the righteous is elsewhere alien to Paul. If the section 2 C. 6:14-7:1 is by Paul, [26] v. 16b is to be interpreted in the context of the apostle's theology, and it can be regarded only as a statement about God's redeeming presence in His community. [27]

Seesemann

πατήρ, πατρῷος, πατριά, ἀπάτωρ, πατρικός

† πατήρ.

Contents : A. The Father Concept in the Indo-European World and Graeco-Roman Antiquity : I. The Use of πατήρ; II. The Ancient Indo-European Concept and Its Influence

---

[22] Cf. the exposition by G. Kittel, *ad loc*. → II, 374, cf. also Barn., 10, 11 and 2 C. 10:3.
[23] Cf. Bu. J., 261, n. 1.
[24] *Ibid*. on 1:6 (18).
[25] Cf. 4 Βασ. 20:3; → I, 242, 26-36 and V, 943, 7 f.
[26] Cf. on this Wnd. 2 K., 18 f.
[27] Lv. 26:12 often plays a part in Philo, e.g., Mut. Nom., 266; Som., I, 148 f.; II, 248; Praem. Poen., 123 f. But the Philo passages are not to be taken mystically, cf. W. Völker, "Fortschritt u. Vollendung bei Philo v. Alex.," TU, 49, 1 (1938), *passim*, and on this G. Bertram, "Philo als politisch-theologischer Propagandist des spätantiken Judts.," ThLZ, 64 (1939), 193-199 [Bertram].

π α τ ή ρ κ τ λ. Cr.-Kö., Liddell-Scott, Pape, Pass., Pr.-Bauer, *s.v.*; A. Bertholet, Art. "Vatername Gottes," RGG, V, 1442 ff.; F. Heiler, *Das Gebet*[4] (1921), Index, *s.v.* "Kind-on the Mediterranean World; III. The Father among the Greeks: 1. The Father as Head of the House and Teacher; 2. Piety towards the Father; IV. The Influence of the Roman *patria potestas* on the Hellenistic World; V. The Religious Use of the Father Image: 1. The Ancient Indo-Iranian Basis of the Idea of God as Father; 2. Zeus the Father and Ruler; 3. The Father in the Mysteries; VI. Philosophical and Gnostic Forms of Belief in the Father: 1. The Father in Plato's Cosmology; 2. The Father as Begetter and the Synthesis of King and Father in Stoicism; 3. The Father Concept in Philo: a. The Greek Influence; b. Jewish Factors; 4. The Father in Hermes Mysticism. B. The Father Concept in the Old Testament: 1. πατήρ and Other Terms for אָב in the LXX; 2. אָב as a Primary

---

schaftsverhältnis"; N. Söderblom, *Das Werden des Gottesglaubens*[2] (1926), 146-149, 192; W. Schmidt, *Ursprung u. Werden d. Religion* (1930), 259, 261; G. van der Leeuw, *Phänomenologie d. Religion* (1933), 161-166, 225-232, 492 f.; K. Prümm, *Der chr. Glaube u. d. altheidnische Welt*, I (1935), 91-96, 450; K. Kerényi, "Archetypisches u. Kulturtypisches in d. gr. u. römischen Religion," *Paideuma*, 5 (1951), 98-102. On A, I: Walde-Pok., II, 4; B. Delbrück, "Die indogermanischen Verwandtschaftsnamen," ASG, 11, 5 (1890), 446-452, 573-578; P. Kretschmer, *Einl. in d. Geschichte d. gr. Sprache* (1896), 335-346; O. Jespersen, *Die Sprache, ihre Natur, Entwicklung u. Entstehung* (1925), 135-141; W. Wundt, *Völkerpsychologie*, I, 2[3] (1912), 3rd Chapter; III[3] (1919), 326; W. Oehl, "Das Lallwort in der Sprachschöpfung," *Rectoral Address at Fribourg, 1932* (1933). On A, II: J. Kohler, "Allg. Rechtsgeschichte," in P. Hinneberg, *Die Kultur der Gegenwart*, II, 7, 1 (1914), 102; U. v. Wilamowitz-Moellendorff, "Staat u. Gesellschaft d. Griechen," *ibid.*, II, 4, 1[2] (1923), 217 f.; G. Ipsen, "Der alte Orient u. d. Indogermanen," *Festschr. f. W. Streitberg* (1924), 223-237; E. Meyer, "Die Volksstämme Kleinasiens, das erste Auftreten d. Indogermanen in d. Gesch. u. die Probleme ihrer Ausbreitung," SAB, 1925, No. 18 (1925), 244-260; W. Weber, *Die Staatenwelt d. Mittelmeers in d. Frühzeit des Griechentums* (1925); E. Kornemann, "Die Stellung d. Frau in d. vorgriech. Mittelmeerkultur," *Orient u. Antike*, 4 (1927). On A, III: A. Bonhöffer, *Die Ethik des Stoikers Epiktet* (1894), 90-92; K. Prächter, *Hierokles der Stoiker* (1901), 45-54, 134 f. On A, IV: R. Leonhard, Art. "Familia" in Pauly-W., VI, 1980-1984; H. Blümner, *Die römischen Privataltertümer* (1911), 302; R. Taubenschlag, "Die patria potestas im Recht d. Pap.," *Zschr. der Savigny-Stiftung f. Rechtsgeschichte, 37, Romanistische Abteilung* (1916), 177-230; L. Wenger, "Hausgewalt u. Staatsgewalt im römischen Altertum," *Miscellanea f. F. Ehrle*, II (1924), 1-55; H. F. Jolowicz, *Historical Introduction to Roman Law* (1932), 118-120. On A, V, 1: J. Wackernagel-A. Debrunner, *Altindische Grammatik*, III (1930), 221 f.; L. v. Schroeder, *Arische Religion*, I (1914), 309-315; Chant. de la Saussaye[4] (1925), II, 13. On A, V, 2: A. Zinzow, "Ζεὺς πατήρ u. θεὸς πατήρ," ZWL, 3 (1882), 189-224; G. M. Calhoun, "Zeus the Father in Homer," *Transactions and Proceedings of the American Philological Association*, 66 (1935), 1-17; H. Hommel, "Der allgegenwärtige Himmelsgott," ARW, 23 (1926), 195-206; M. P. Nilsson, "Vater Zeus," ARW, 35 (1938), 156-171; also *Gesch. d. gr. Religion*, I = *Handbuch AW*, V, 2, 1 (1941), 314, 364 ff. On A, V, 3: A. Dieterich, *Eine Mithrasliturgie*[3] (1923), 134-156; Reitzenstein Hell. Myst., 27, 117; L. Dürr, "Heilige Vaterschaft im antiken Orient," *Heilige Überlieferung, Festschr. f. J. Herwegen* (1938), 1-20; K. Kerényi, *Töchter d. Sonne, Betrachtungen über gr. Gottheiten* (1944), 9-61. On A, VI, 1: U. v. Wilamowitz-Moellendorff, *Platon*, I[2] (1920), 589, 606; R. Reitzenstein and H. H. Schaeder, *Studien zum antiken Synkretismus* (1926), 142 ff.; E. Wechssler, *Hellas im Evangelium* (1936), 305-308. On A, VI, 2: A. Bonhöffer, *Epiktet u. d. Stoa* (1890), 76-80; H. Binder, *Dio Chrys. u. Poseidonios*, Diss. Tübingen (1905), 86. On A, VI, 3: F. Wendland, *Philos Schrift über die Vorsehung* (1892), 10; J. Heinemann, *Philons gr. u. jüdische Bildung* (1932), 231-261. On B: A. Alt, *Der Gott d. Väter* (1929), 16-32 *Kleine Schriften zur Gesch. d. Volkes Israel* (1953), 13-29; also Art. "Familie" in *Reallex. der Vorgeschichte*, 3 (1925), 181; also "Die Ursprünge d. isr. Rechts," *Bericht über die Verhandlungen d. sächsischen Akademie d. Wissenschaften zu Leipzig, Philosophisch-historische Klasse*, 86, 1 (1934), 54-58 = *Kleine Schriften* (1953), 319-322; W. Baudissin, *Kyrios als Gottesname*, III (1929), 309-379; also *Adonis u. Ešmun* (1911), 39-52; P. Baur, "Gott als Vater im AT," *ThStKr*, 72 (1899), 483-507; A. Bertholet, *Kulturgeschichte Israels* (1919), 82-86, 110; G. Buchanan Gray, *Studies in Hebrew Proper Names* (1896), 22-34; A. Bertholet-H. Seeger, Art. "Vatername" in RGG, V (1931), 1442-1445; K. Galling, Art. "Patriarchat," *Reallex. d. Vorgeschichte*, 10 (1927), 62 f.; O. Eissfeldt, *El im ugaritischen Pantheon* (1951), 61-64; J. Hempel, *Gott u. Mensch im AT*[2] (1936), 170-178; also *Das Ethos d. AT* (1938), 67-73; A. Lods, *Israël des origines au milieu du*

Word ; 3. אָב as a Basic Element in the Family Concept ; 4. Basic Features of Patriarchy ; 5. The Myth of the Father of the Gods ; 6. Father and Other Terms of Relationship in the Tribal Religion ; 7. Father as a Theophorous Element in the Proper Names of Israel ; 8. Father as a Metaphor ; 9. Father as a Concept of Authority ; 10. The Trend Towards Universality in the Designation of God as Father. C. The Father Concept in Later Judaism : I. The Earthly Father : 1. Piety towards the Father ; 2. Parents as Instruments and Representatives of God ; 3. The Duties of the Father. II. The Fathers in Judaism ; 1. The Concept ; 2. The Importance of the Fathers for the Jews. III. Father as a Title for the Teacher ; IV. God as Father in Judaism : 1. Distinction from Greek Cosmology : a. Not the Begetter of the World, but the Protector of the National Community ; b. Father and Lord ; 2. The Father in the Heavens ; 3. Invocation of the Father in Prayer ; 4. The Relation to Other Names for God in the Synagogue, and the Limitations of the Jewish Understanding of God as Father. D. Father in the New Testament : I. Father according to the Jesus of the Synoptists : 1. Honouring of the Earthly Father and Its Limits ; 2. The Religious Use of πατήρ : a. The Presupposition of Patriarchy ; b. Invocation of God as Abba ; c. The Father in the Heavens : (a) The Question of Sources and the Historical Problem ; (b) The Meaning of the Formula ; d. My Father and Your Father : (a) The Question of Sources ; (b) The Distinction between "My Father" and "Your Father" ; (c) The Christological Confession ; e. The Absolute πατήρ ; f. God the Father of All Men ? g. The Heavenly Father as the Absolute Authority ; Fatherly Authority and Fatherly Care ; h. The Significance of Belief in the Father for the Disciples : (a) The Christological Form of Belief in an Authoritative Father ; (b) The Cry of Jubilation in Mt. 11:25-30; Lk. 10:21 f.; (c) The Christological Message concerning the Father in Lk. 15:11-32; i. The Unity of Father, King and Judge : (a) Father and Judge ; (b) Father and Ruler ; II. Father in John : 1. The Usage ; 2. The Concept of Father and Patriarchy ; 3. The Concept of Revelation ; 4. The Harmony of Father and Son ; 5. The Conflict with the Jews for the Truth of the Father ; 6. The Father and Prayer ; III. Father in Other Apostolic Writings : 1. The Earthly Father ; 2. The Application of the Metaphor of Father to Men in Paul : a. Abraham as Father ; b. The Apostle as the Father of the Community ; 3. God as Father : a. The Basic Significance of the Cry Abba ; b. The Use of πατήρ : (a) θεὸς πατήρ; (b) θεὸς ὁ πατήρ; (c) θεὸς καὶ πατήρ; (d) ὁ πατήρ; (e) πατήρ, θεός, υἱός, κύριος; c. The Content of the Father Concept : (a) The Fatherhood of God as Lordship ; (b) The Gift of Grace through the Father ; d. The Influence of the Surrounding Greek World : (a) The Christian Answer to Belief in the Father of All in 1 C. and Eph.; (b) Some Exceptions to the Rule.

VIIIᵉ siècle (1930), 217-219; E. Meyer, Gesch. d. Altertums, I, 1⁵ (1925), 21-35; I. Morgenstern, "Beena Marriage. Matriarchate in Ancient Israel and Its Historical Implications," ZAW, NF, 5 (1929), 91-110; also "Additional Notes," ZAW, NF, 8 (1931), 46-58; J. D. Michaelis, Mosaisches Recht (1777), II, 73-77; VI, 77-80; M. Noth, "Die isr. Personennamen im Rahmen d. gemeinsemitischen Namengebung," BWANT, 3 F. 10 (1928), 66-75; J. Pedersen, Israel, I/II (1926), 46-54; W. R. Smith, The Religion of the Semites (1956 ed.), 28 ff.; J. L. Saalschütz, Das Mosaische Recht nebst den vervollständigenden talmudisch-rabb. Bestimmungen² (1853), 816-820; J. Zobel, Der bildliche Gebrauch d. Verwandtschaftsnamen im Hbr. mit Berücksichtigung d. übrigen semitischen Sprachen, Diss. Halle (1932), 7-16. On C, I : Moore, II, 119-140; C. G. Montefiore and H. Loewe, A Rabb. Anthology (1938), 500-506. On C, IV : Str.-B., I, 392-396; W. Bousset, Die Religion d. Judts.³ (1926), 376-378; Moore, II, 201-211; A. Marmorstein, The Old Rabbinic Doctrine of God (1927), 56-62; Dalman WJ, I², 155-159; Volz Esch., 99, 106, 166; Schl. Jos., 14 f.; Schl. Theol. d. Judt., 24 f., 47. On D, I : C. A. Bernoulli, "Le Dieu-Père de Jésus d'après les Synoptiques," Actes du Congrès international d'histoire des religions, 1923, II (1925), 211-224; R. Gyllenberg, "Gott d. Vater im AT u. in d. Predigt Jesu," Studia orientalia, I (1926), 3-140; H. Weinel, Bibl. Theol. d. NT⁴ (1928), 122-131; T. W. Manson, The Teaching of Jesus (1931), 89-115; P. Feine, Theol. d. NT⁸ (1951), 18 f.; W. Grundmann, Die Gotteskindschaft in d. Gesch. Jesu u. ihre religionsgeschichtlichen Voraussetzungen (1938); W. Twisselmann, "Die Gotteskindschaft d. Christen nach d. NT," BFTh, 41, 1 (1939); W. Manson, Bist du, der da kommen soll ? (1952), 81-85, 125-133; S. V. McCasland, "Abba Father," JBL, 72 (1953), 79-91. Bibl. on D, I, 2, i → n. 299; on D, II → n. 305.

A. The Father Concept in the Indo-European World and Graeco-Roman Antiquity.

I. The Use of πατήρ.

πατήρ, Sanskr. *pitár*, nom. *pitā*, Lat. *pater*, Avestan *pitar*, Old Persian *pitar*, is, like μήτηρ, of primitive Indo-Europ. origin. Along with the part -τηρ it contains the natural childish stammer originally heard as *pa* (or *ma*) and then interpreted by adults. [1] πάππα is another such word, Hom. Od., 6, 57, cf. παππάζειν in Il., 5, 408, also ἄττα, 9, 607 and τέττα, 4, 412. Here, too, there is great similarity throughout the Indo-European family and even far beyond. On πάτερ and ἀββᾶ ὁ πατήρ → n. 251. In ordinary Gk. use πατήρ means first the father of the family. Very occasionally the grandfather, who is usually πάππος (Jos. Ant., 7, 180; Bell., 1, 556) can be called πατήρ (Jub. 23:3; Philo Som., I, 166), also the great-grandfather, Hb. 7:10. This use is possible because πατήρ, even in the sing., can reach further back and be used for "forefather," "progenitor," cf. Wis. 10:1 of Adam : πρωτόπλαστος πατὴρ κόσμου, 1 Cl., 6, 3 : "our father," Just. Dial., 119, 4 of Noah : πατὴρ ... παντὸς ἀνθρώπων γένους, 4 Macc. 2:19 : Jacob, Mk. 11:10; Lk. 1:32; Ac. 4:25 : David as the royal forefather of Israel or the Messiah ; also Ishmael in Just. Dial., 119, 4; Simeon Jdt. 9:2; Aaron 4 Macc. 7:11; Phinehas 1 Macc. 2:54. Forefather can then be taken spiritually as the initiator of an occupation, trend, or group, Gn. 4:20 f. πατήρ, then, does not have to denote blood relationship and its projection into the past. The word can also be used of the representative of a stage of life : "the old or honourable man." He can be called "father" because he reminds us of our physical father, Hom. Il., 24, 503 f., whose contemporary he is, Ps.-Phocylides, V, 221. Thus πατήρ is a term of respect in addressing the aged and honourable, Hom. Od., 7, 28; Il., 24, 362. The plur. occurs in 1 Jn. 2:13 f., and with ἀδελφοί in Ac. 7:2; 22:1. There is a link here with the Jewish custom of saying Abba to teachers, → 977, 18 ff. The plur. πατέρες is comparatively rare for "parents," Hb. 11:23, cf. Plat. Leg., VI, 772e, 773a; Diod. S., 21, 17; Dion. Hal. Ant. Rom., 2, 26. For the most part it means "ancestors," Hom. Od., 24, 508; Il., 6, 209; Aristoph. Nu., 968; Jos. Ant., 19, 248 of the Romans, Jdt. 5:7 of the Chaldeans. Cf. the "fathers" in Israel, → 970, 18 ff.; 976, 1 ff.

II. The Ancient Indo-European Concept and Its Influence on the Mediterranean World.

The ancient Indo-Europ. concept, as the basic sense of *pitar* shows, is in the first instance genealogical. [2] But *pótis* as a legal and sociological term plainly denotes the head of the family. The Gk. πόσις like the Sanskr. *pátiš* (stem *páti-*) denotes both the husband and the head of the house. δεσπότης throws light on his position. [3] The head of the house with his unlimited power of command is the supreme authority whose monarchical rule includes the right of judicial punishment. He rules with royal power over both the free and unfree who belong to his house. To be sure, benevolent care and provision are combined with the right of command. [4] But the kindness is mixed with severity. [5] The movement of the Indo-Europeans to Asia Minor and the Mediterranean, which took place before and after 2000 B.C., affected the cultural foundations

---

[1] On *pitar* Walde-Pok., II, 4. For father and mother as childish lispings cf. Delbrück, Kretschmer, Wundt, Jespersen, Oehl. Cf. L. Köhler, "Hbr. Vokabein, ii," ZAW, NF 14 (1937), 168-172 (אָב and אֵם).

[2] In Vedic Sanskr. the dual of *pitar* or *mātar* alone can denote both parents. Cf. J. Wackernagel, *Altindische Gramm.*, II, 1 (1905), 151; E. Schwyzer, *Gr. Gramm.*, II, *Handbuch AW*, II, 1, 2 (1950), 50 f. The terms father and mother are thus closely related. Cf. Hom.: μήτηρ ἠδὲ πατήρ. Furthermore, both are related to "child" [Debrunner].

[3] "Head of the house" : Sanskr. *pátir dán* or *dámpati*. Cf. A, Wackernagel-Debrunner, I, 243 f.; Schwyzer, I (1939), 547 f. [Debrunner].

[4] Cf. Rigveda, I, 31, 10 provider as well as father ; IV, 17, 17 protector. He is kind, a friend, carries on the arm, holds to the breast. Cry is made to him in distress, Delbrück, 447.

[5] On the father acc. to the law-book of Narada cf. J. Jolly, "Recht u. Sitte (der Inder)," *Grundriss d. Indoarischen Philologie u. Altertumskunde*, II, 8 (1896), 78.

of the peoples which received this influx. It promoted a social order organised on strictly patriarchal lines. [6]

III. The Father Among the Greeks.

1. The Father as Head of the House and Teacher.

Patriarchal control in house and family is found among the Gks. too. In Hom. it is to be seen in the concept of the οἴκοιο ἄναξ καὶ δμώων, Od., 1, 397 f. Τὸ ἀνάγκη corresponds the naming of close relatives and adherents (slaves) of the house as ἀναγκαῖοι, Od., 24, 210. The οἴκοιο ἄναξ unites the family group religiously by an oath, Il., 3, 107; 22, 119. The jurisdiction of the father of the house is typified here. A patriarchal feature is the fact that the gods stand before father Zeus, Il., 1, 533. The sons and daughters begotten by him have to obey his fatherly authority without qualification, Il., 15, 197 ff. His despotic threats enhance the picture. The same fundamental concept of household authority is to be found in Heracl., Plat. and Aristot. When Heracl. Fr., 53 (Diels⁶, I, 162, 7 ff.) says of war : πόλεμος πάντων μὲν πατήρ ἐστι, πάντων δὲ βασιλεύς, he explains this as follows, that war sifts and clarifies and orders all things, selecting but also restoring. The linking of father and king is worth noting here. The def. is basically determined by the idea of the controlling lordship of the father. Plat. Leg., III, 690a also emphasises the γονέας ἐκγόνων ἄρχειν, cf. γονεῖς and ἄρχοντες in XI, 917a. Aristot. Pol., I, 7, p. 1255b, 19 speaks of the οἰκονομικὴ μοναρχία of the house and *ibid.*, I, 12, p. 1259b, 11 he calls parental power ἀρχὴ βασιλική. [7] In Stoicism parental authority finds classical expression in Epict. Diss., II, 10, 7 (a par. to Lk. 15:31): "To be a son is to regard all one's possessions as the property of the father, to obey the father in all things, never to blame him before anyone, to support him with all one's power." Sen., too, speaks of the *imperium durum* of parents which is rightly appreciated only in riper age, Ben., III, 38, 2, cf. V, 5, 2. The strictly patriarchal father concept in Philo is influenced by the Gk. model. Acc. to Spec. Leg., II, 226 ff. children are subject to parents as elders, benefactors, superiors and lords. Love is not enjoined, since it is self-understood, Spec. Leg., II, 240. [8] Acc. to Philo's anthropology the woman is below the man in rank. For him the mother symbolises αἴσθησις (sensuality), the father νοῦς, Leg. All., III, 81, cf. II, 51; III, 22, 5; Det. Pot. Ins., 52; Poster. C., 175 etc. The virtues are manly. But along with this emphasis on fatherly authority one should not overlook the motif of heartfelt love in the Gk. world. Cf. Eur. Herc. Fur., 634; Iph. Aul., 1220; Suppl., 530. Touching traits of fatherly love are also to be found in Epict. Diss., I, 11; III, 22, 71; III, 7, 3.

Democr. with his ref. to the inner aspect of fatherly instruction [9] leads on to the basic principles of Plato, Leg. All., V, 729b c, cf. Prot., 324d-325a. Plato regards education as the visible practice of example. Plut. Lib. Educ., 20 (II, 14a): Sons must be able to see the walk of their fathers as in a mirror, → 600, 2 ff. In Philo the physiological aspect strongly affects the father concept, but one may see from the allegory in Spec. Leg., II, 29 that the ideal of good education is that the father should engender good resolves and brave actions and uphold these by gentle doctrines of discipline and wisdom. Acc. to Sacr. AC, 68 he is to be imitated in good works.

2. Piety towards the Father.

The view of the mother can hardly be described as uniform among the Gk. moralists. [10] But the question of piety and esp. of honouring the father reveals unanimity in the ethical statements of the Gk. world. Cf. Cleobulus (Diels⁶, I, 63, 2) with his πατέρα δεῖ

---

[6] On this whole question → Bibl. on A, II.

[7] Acc. to Attic law the husband is also κύριος of his wife, cf. J. H. Lipsius, *Das Attische Recht u. Rechtsverfahren* (1905), 482 → κύριος, III, 1042, 34 ff., 41 ff.

[8] Cf. Sen. Ben., IV, 17, 2 : *supervacuum est enim.*

[9] σωφροσύνη as the supreme admonition, Fr., 208 (Diels⁶, II, 187, 16 f.).

[10] Cf. → μήτηρ, IV, 642 ff. Heinemann, 252, n. 3.

αἰδεῖσθαι. For piety in Plat. *v.* Leg., IV, 717b ff.; Ep., VII, 331c. The Stoics regard this
as a duty recognised by all thinking people. Love of children is κατὰ φύσιν, Epict.
Diss., I, 11, 17, cf. I, 23, 3. To command love of parents is superfluous, → 949, 27 f. If
these statements display a certain "ideal imprecision and generality,"[11] a greater
profundity may be seen in the thesis that only philosophical education makes possible a
true love of parents in the ἐλεύθερος, Epict. Diss., III, 24, 59 ff., 85. The φαῦλοι do
not have it, Diog. L., VII, 120 = Chrysipp. Fr., 731 (v. Arnim, III, 183, 22 ff.). Stoicism
is also characterised by the fact that it finds a deeper religious root for piety. The order
of rank — first the gods, then parents — is the same as elsewhere. Aristot. Topica, I, 11,
p. 105a, 5 f., in Stoicism Epict. Diss., II, 22, 16; III, 7, 26; in Diog. L., VII, 120, we read
that the Stoics championed honouring of parents ἐν δευτέρᾳ μοίρᾳ μετὰ θεούς. But
popular Stoic philosophy goes much further when it calls parents δεύτεροι θεοί, ἐμ-
φανεῖς ἐπίγειοι θεοί.[12] Plato already in Leg., XI, 931a d could call aged parents in
the house living images of the gods. Aristot., too, in Eth. Nic., IX, 2, p. 1165a, 24 emphasises τιμὴν δὲ γονεῦσι καθάπερ θεοῖς. But Stoicism developed systematically the
concept that state, government and family are a reflection of deity. The idea that the
gods may be seen in parents is not to be confused with ancestor worship, in which
parents are themselves gods. What is meant is that divine reason finds expression in
human societies. Hence the universe may be compared to a house or state.[13] Philo is
influenced at this pt. by the surrounding world of philosophy. Cf. Decal., 107 ff., 119 f.;
Spec. Leg., II, 225 ff.[14]

On the question of religious conflict with parents Stoicism laid down the principle that
the ἀγαθόν takes precedence of father and mother, Epict. Diss., III, 3, 6 ff. Thus if there
is cutting across the command of the κοινὸς ἁπάντων πατὴρ ἀνθρώπων καὶ θεῶν,
the decision goes against the earthly father, Muson., XVII (ed. O. Hense [1905], 86,
18 ff.; 87, 2). If the latter forbids φιλοσοφεῖν, Zeus commands it. He who does τὰ
προσήκοντα, τὰ συμφέροντα obeys his parents in the true sense. Cf. Ac. 5:29.

IV. The Influence of the Roman *patria potestas* in the Hellenistic World.

What was prefigured in the ancient Indo-European household found in the culture
of antiquity distinctive development and enhancement in civil law, i.e., in the Latin-
Roman order of the *pater familias* and the *patria potestas*.[15] The concept is linked to
dominium in domo. It denotes the authority and power of the head of the house, which
go hand in hand with his marital power. Legally this sets the wife in strict subjection.
Sacral law is the basis. The head of the house is also the household priest. This *dominica
potestas* extends not only to all children at all ages, including adopted children, but also
to grown-up married sons and their issue. It lasts until the death of the father. It also
embraces other members of the household, the slaves. It includes the *jus vitae necisque*
and the right to expose children. The father has disciplinary and penal power. He can
marry and divorce his children as he sees fit. He can give in adoption and emancipate.
Acc. to ancient Roman law the son earns income only for the father. Relaxation of
paternal control comes only with the Justinian Code.[16]

---

[11] Bonhöffer, *Ethik*, 90.

[12] Cf. Prächter, 45-54; H. v. Arnim, *Hierokles' ethische Elementarlehre, Berliner Klassiker-
texte*, 4 (1906), 56, 57, 13 ff.

[13] Cf. Wendland, 10, n. 1, 2.

[14] For a discussion of natural law in Philo cf. E. R. Goodenough, *The Jurisprudence of
the Jewish Courts in Egypt and Legal Administration by the Jews under the Early Roman
Empire as Described by Philo Judaeus* (1929); Heinemann, 231 ff.

[15] → Bibl. on A, IV. For the later period cf. W. Kroll, *Die Kultur der ciceronianischen
Zeit*, I (1933), 35 f.; II, 112; for connections with the Indo-European world cf. B. W. Leist,
Altarisches Jus civile, II (1896), 159.

[16] In spite of the legal severity, the Roman period bears witness to much tender love,
cf. Kroll, *op. cit.*, II, 112.

Already in the 1st century A.D. one may detect the influence of Roman ideas on Gk. law.[17] This influence extends to the whole sphere of the Hell. world. Even Jewish parents who were Roman citizens laid claim to the Roman *patria potestas*. Acc. to Philo (Spec. Leg., II, 227, 233, cf. Decal., 165) parents not only have ἀρχή and ἡγεμονία, but also δεσποτεία. With ref. to the birth of children and the related monetary offerings he does not shrink from using the metaphor of slavery. Simpl. has the same par. in Epict., 37, p. 199b (Dübner).[18]

V. The Religious Use of the Father Image.

1. The Ancient Indo-Iranian Basis of the Idea of God as Father.

Invocation of deity under the name of father is one of the basic phenomena of religious history. It is found among both primitive and culturally elevated peoples, both around the Mediterranean and in Assyria and Babylon.[19] The concept of the author of being, which is clothed in the name father, is found already in the form *Dyaús pitá*, father heaven (cf. Gk. Ζεὺς πατήρ, Δειπάτυρος,[20] Lat. Juppiter[21]) in the ancient documents of Indian religion.[22] The assumption that we have here an Indo-European belief in the person of a supreme heavenly God (called father heaven, not father in heaven) is rejected by the majority of students in spite of the many ethnological pars.[23] But even if this view is unlikely, there can be no doubt that in ancient India vegetation (rain = seed), and the life which it made possible, was thought to have arisen by conception from heaven and earth. To *Dyaús*, the father, corresponds the earth (*Prthivī*) as mother,

---

[17] Cf. L. Mitteis, *Reichsrecht u. Volksrecht* (1891). J. Juster, *Les Juifs dans l'empire romain*, II (1914), 55; Taubenschlag, 177-230; H. Kreller, *Erbrechtliche Untersuchungen auf Grund der graeco-ägypt. Pap.-Urkunden* (1919).

[18] The father concept has gt. influence on political life. The first traces of government in the ancient Indo-Europ. world are patterned on household rule. The Gk. state, too, grows out of the family and clan. Plat. Leg., III, 680e (πατρονομούμενοι, βασιλευόμενοι) theoretically develops patriarchal monarchy as the earliest and most just form of government. In Rome (cf. Wenger) the influence of the power of the *pater familias* on the understanding of governmental authority finds expression in the emperor's title *pater patriae*. Cf. the Gk. title πατὴρ τῆς πόλεως. In Sen. De Clementia, I, 14 the concept of fatherly provision fills out the title. In Jewish works cf. 1 Macc. 2:65; Jos. Ant., 20, 11. Cf. Just. Apol., 68, 3. T. Mommsen, *Römisches Staatsrecht*, II, 2³ (1887), 779 f., 785; III, 2 (1888), 1187; E. Skard, "Pater patriae," *Festskr. til Halvdan Koht* (1933), 42-70; A. Alföldi, "Die Geburt d. kaiserlichen Bildsymbolik, 3, parens patriae," *Museum Helveticum*, 9 (1952), 204-243.

[19] For the Babylonians cf. Baudissin, *Kyrios*, III, 310 f.

[20] Δειπάτυρος is Illyrian, P. Kretschmer, "Dyaus, Ζεύς Diespiter u. d. Abstrakta im Indogermanischen," *Glotta*, 13 (1924), 113.

[21] Juppiter is originally vocative (= Ζεῦ πάτερ). This shows how common was the invocation of father heaven. The ancient *Diēs* (= Ζεύς, Sanskr. *Dyaús*) is also found as a divine name in Lat. only with *pater* (Diespiter). When *pater* is used for the Roman gods it is worth noting that even the ancient native gods bear the designation. On *pater* for Roman deities cf. J. B. Carter, Epitheta deorum quae apud poetas latinos leguntur = Suppl., II to Roscher (1902); for bibl. cf. H. Herter, "De Priapo" = RVV, 23 (1932), 201 f.; A. Zinzow, "Der Vaterbegriff bei den römischen Gottheiten," *Gymnasialprogramm Pyritz* (1887), 3 ff.; C. Koch, *Der röm. Juppiter* = Frankfurter Studien z. Religion u. Kultur d. Antike, 14 (1937), 31, 42, 45.

[22] E.g., Rigveda, I, 71, 5: "To the gt. father *Dyaús*." Also *Dyaús pitá* in Brahmana texts. Ritual texts often echo the Rigveda, so that they prove little as to the continued life of *Dyaús pitá*. Mantra acc. to Jaim B, 1, 129 seems, however, to be more independent: "I rely on father heaven." In post-Vedic religion *Dyaús pitá*, who is invoked only rarely in the Veda, completely disappears. In class. Sanskr. *dyaús* even became a fem.; it is sometimes fem. even in Rigveda, though this is secondary. Cf. Wackernagel-Debrunner, 221.

[23] Cf. v. Schroeder, I, 309-313; also Konow in Chant. de la Saussaye, II, 13, who rejects the semi-personal form of the idea among the Indians and gives *Dyaús pitá* the sense of primary Deva (man) or radiant heaven. For a rebuttal of the latter interpretation cf. Nilsson, *Vater Zeus*, 156-171.

and *Dyaúš pitā* is called *janitā,* begetter.[24] The Gks. speak similarly of Ζεὺς πατὴρ γενετήρ (or γενέτης) and the Romans of *Diovis pater genitor.* But this idea of the divine progenitor develops and spreads in many different ways and forms.[25] We find it not merely among the Mediterranean peoples but also, e.g., in ancient Egypt. There the ruler cult gives rise to the idea that the king is God's son in the sense of physical descent, → υἱός.

2. Zeus the Father and Ruler.

In Hom. Zeus as πατὴρ ἀνδρῶν τε θεῶν τε [26] (Od., 1, 28; Il., 1, 544) is exalted as universal god. The word father controls all persons, both human and divine. Here is a central doctrine of the Gk. world.[27] This epithet cannot be regarded as original. The idea of the progenitor and ancestor in this sense does not correspond to the general findings of mythology.[28] Even in the Rigveda *Dyaúš pitā* is not the father of gods and men, though other deities are.[29] The formula is secondary, and the only explanation is that many older traditions are transferred to Zeus.[30] In Hom. πατὴρ Ζεύς or Ζεὺς πατήρ already bears a specific sense. Invocation of Zeus in prayer is found in all ages in the Gk. world.[31] In concert with Indo-Europ. patriarchalism, fatherhood and monarchy meet in the Homeric view of Zeus, Od., 1, 45; Il., 8, 31: ὕπατε κρειόντων. It is true that in Il. and Od. Zeus is never called βασιλεύς. But he is ἄναξ.[32] He rules over both

---

[24] On *Dyaúš pitā janitā* cf. Rigveda, I, 164, 33; IV, 1, 10; V, 43, 2; VI, 51, 5. In the Avesta, too, the view of the marriage of heaven and mother earth exerts a remote influence. In Gk. mythology Zeus is correlative to mother Gaia, cf. Paus., X, 12, 3.

[25] Cf. Rigveda, X, 82, 3 of the creator of the world Vishva-Karman : "Who is our father, progenitor, creator." The gt. gods of Hinduism, Vishnu and Shiva, can also be called father, begetter, ancestor. Among the Scythians (Hdt., IV, 59) παπαῖος is used for the supreme God, among the Bithynians and Phrygians πάπας (Diod. S., 3, 58, 4).

[26] Acc. to Calhoun, 15, n. 30 Hom. speaks of Zeus as father more than 100 times, mostly in Il. Here, too, there are early oriental pars., cf. the ancient Sumerian Enlil, father of the gods, Baudissin, *Kyrios,* III, 323.

[27] This is proved by the fact that later Just. Apol., 22, 1 and Athenag. Suppl., 21, 2; 29, 1 from the standpoint of Chr. apologetics discuss this concept, which demands distinction and division when the new confession puts the name of father at the centre.

[28] The gods whose father Zeus is, come from elsewhere, or are at most of Minoan origin. The ancient Gk. gods are Zeus' brethren (Poseidon, Hades). Nor in very early Gk. mythology is Zeus the father as the creator of men. Cf. Nilsson, *Vater Zeus,* 156-171; *Gesch. d. gr. Religion,* I, 314, 364-400; Calhoun, 1-17; also "Classes and Masses in Hom.," *Class. Philol.,* 29 (1934), 197 f.

[29] We also find "father of the gods" in ancient Sumerian texts. Rigveda, II, 26, 3 calls Brahmanaspati father of all the gods, while in V, 4, 2 Agni, the god of fire, is the "father of men."

[30] In later interpretation of the formula the concept of generation is even stronger, Critias Fr., 16, 7 (Diels⁶, II, 383, 6): Hercules begotten of Zeus. On Epict. → 955, 25 ff.; Plut. Apophth. Alexandri, 15 (II, 180d → n. 54); Jos. Ant., 12, 22; Sib., III, 278 vl. alongside Cod A.

[31] Calling on Zeus in prayer : Ζεῦ πάτερ, Hom. Od., 4, 341; 20, 201 f.; Il., 1, 503; 3, 365 f. etc.; Archiloch. Fr., 94 (Diehl³, I, 3, 41); Hes. Fr., 161, 1; Pind. Pyth., 4, 194; Nem., 8, 35; 9, 31; Isthm., 6, 39; Soph. Oed. Col., 1268; Trach., 275; Eur. Hel., 1441; Aristoph. Ach., 224.

[32] On the other hand Zeus is called βασιλεύς in the Homeric hymns, Cer., 358; Thebais Fr., 3; Cypria Fr., 6. In particular, he is king of gods and men in Hes. Op., 668; Theog., 886, 923. He is also invoked as ruler in Theogn., 373, cf. 803 f. and Soph. Oed. Col., 1085; Oed. Tyr., 904. An emphatic use of father and king together occurs in Hes. Theog., 71: πατήρ and ἐμβασιλεύειν; Fr., 4 : "father and ruler (σημάντωρ)"; Hipponax., 34 (Diehl³, I, 3, 90). Then Aristot. Pol., I, 12, p. 1259b, 2 can say : "Hom., when he calls Zeus the father of men and gods, describes him as their king." The combination of father and king occurs also in the Stoic hymn of Cleanthes, Fr., 537 (v. Arnim, I, 122, 10, 30 f.). Plut. Ser. Num. Pun., 4 (II, 550a) expounds the Δωδωναῖε μεγάσθενες, ἀριστότεχνα πάτηρ of Pind. Fr., 57: ἄρχοντα καὶ κύριον ἁπάντων θεόν.

mortals and immortals, Od., 20, 112; Il., 12, 242. Zeus is also the divine original of the head of the household. He is, as it were, the apotheosis of the master of the house. This corresponds again to the Indo-Europ. father concept. Later writers expressed it in the name Ζεὺς πατρῷος. [33] In Plat. Leg., IX, 881d : Διὸς ὁμογνίου καὶ πατρῴου, this means that he protects the rights of relatives and parents, cf. Epict. Diss., III, 15. [34] Thus Zeus is the father *par excellence* in the family sense. How strongly the human concept influences and sustains the religious idea may be seen from all the distinctive attributes of the head of the house which are attributed to Zeus. Even that which has continually and correctly been called unethical in Hom. grows from these roots. The capriciousness, scolding and blustering of the Olympian is a one-sided depiction of his *patria potestas*. If none is so terrible as he (Hom. Od., 20, 201 f.), if he feels no sympathy even with his own children (Il., 3, 365 f.; 17, 546), it is not too much to say that in these sayings we see something of an unrestrained rebellion against the severity of paternal authority. There is a despotic aspect to this view of the father. He exercises penal power, Soph. Trach., 275; Hes. Fr., 125. The fact that Zeus is portrayed in human terms is the reason why μοῖρα and εἱμαρμένη, τύχη and πότμος, νόμος, θέμις and δίκη are set over him or made equal to him. Cf. Hes. Theog., 901 f.; Op., 242, 256.

3. The Father in the Mysteries.

God is commonly addressed as father in the mystery cults, e.g., Ἄττε πάππα in the cult of Cybele. [35] In the Isis cult Serapis (Osiris) is father. Mithras is the father of believers, and Helios is also called father. [36] He is, of course, the υἱὸς μονογενής of Mithras and the μεσίτης between him and the cultic community. Nevertheless, as a revered god, he is also πατήρ. Different motifs coalesce in this concept of the father. The idea of the "generating" sun is very old. [37] The notion of regeneration [38] through the father, which mediates divinisation, is at the centre. Invocation of the gods as πατέρες, which is common in the cults, corresponds here esp. to the need to express inward relationship to the specific deity. But generation by the father declares his good-will, love, friendship and power to bless, which grants thought, word and knowledge, Preis. Zaub., III, 583 ff. The mystical concept of the father unites, however, with the domestic. This is plain in the exploitation of the thought of the family. The πατήρ makes the initiates not only υἱοί but also ἀδελφοί. He welds them into a φρατρία or φράτρα.

---

[33] Other names for Zeus like ἑρκεῖος "protector of the house," Hom. Od., 22, 335, cf. Il., 11, 772-775; ξείνιος, "guardian of hospitality," Il., 13, 624 f.; Od., 9, 270 f.; ἱκετήσιος, "sponsor of those who seek protection," Od., 13, 213 f. are all related to the house and thus underline this πατρῷος.

[34] On the form of the saying in Epict. Diss., III, 15 cf. Hom. Od., 14, 57. For further epithets cf. Dio Chrys., 1, 39.

[35] Cf. H. Graillot, *Le culte de Cybèle* (1912), Index, s.v. Πάππας.

[36] F. Cumont, *Textes et monuments figurés relatifs aux mystères de Mithra*, I (1896), 345; II (1899), 16, 40. Dieterich, 53, 68, 135. On this cf. Porphyr. Antr. Nymph., 5, 6 : πάντων ποιητοῦ καὶ πατρὸς Μίθρου. Mithras liturgy in Dieterich, 6, line 12 f.: "The way of the visible gods will appear through the solar disk" πατρός μου θεοῦ. In Preis. Zaub., IV, 1181 f. Helios is invoked : ἥλιε πάτερ κόσμου.

[37] The Mithras cult has its roots in the Indo-Europ. world. But in, e.g., the Rigveda the sun god Sûrya is never called father, but the son of heaven. Long before the arrival of the worship of sol invictus there is found in the Gk. sphere, on the basis of purely natural experience, the obvious designation of the sun as life-giving father and of the earth as mother. Anaxag. in Aristot. De Plantis, I, 2, p. 817a, 23 calls Helios πατήρ; in Aesch. Choeph., 984 f. Helios is both the original and model of earthly fatherhood ; in Soph. Fr., 1017, 3 (TGF, 355) he is πατὴρ πάντων. Cf. Philo Som., I, 73. The idea of the sun as a demiurge is found in Pos. under the influence of the Syr. cult of the sun, cf. K. Reinhardt, *Kosmos u. Sympathie. Neue Untersuchungen über Pos.* (1926), 365-376. In the Orphic Fr. (Kern), 236, 4 Helios is called παγγενέτωρ. On the sun god as tribal father in ancient Latium cf. C. Koch, *Gestirnverehrung im alten Italien* (1933), 111-113; also *Der röm. Jupiter* (→ n. 21), 50.

[38] On regeneration Dieterich, 4, lines 8, 11 ff.; 14, lines 31 ff.

This is true of the Isis cults as well as of those of Attis, Dionysus and Mithras. [39] The family motive may be seen also in the commonly attested use of πατήρ as a cultic office [40] or title for the spiritual fatherhood of the teacher or pastor of adepts. Ref. is rightly made to the hereditary nature of oriental priesthood. The physical son receives instruction from his father. [41] In orientally influenced rites the descent from father to son lives on in the form of spiritual descent. The domestic element is present here too ; the father transmits religious instruction to the son. In a wider sense the family character is strengthened by the fact that the cultic title was also affected by the significance of the *patronus,* the *pater collegii,* in societies. Possibly linked with this [42] is the thought that the priestly father takes the place of the divine father and receives novices in his name. This also corresponds to the ancient view that the father of the family is a reflection of deity and exercises his office in the sacral sphere.

VI. Philosophical and Gnostic Forms of Belief in the Father.

1. Father in the Cosmology of Plato.

Plato calls the idea of the good, the ultimate and supreme thing standing over all being (Resp., VI, 509b), πατήρ (*ibid.,* 506e, cf. VII, 517b c; Hi., I, 297b). [43] The good streams into the world ; though it remains in the world beyond, it still becomes visible and active, Resp., VI-VII, 504-517. [44] This father concept is then given cosmological form in the creation myth in Tim. [45] An uncommonly powerful idea was thus introduced into the ancient world of thought. If in the first instance it simply served to explain the world, it prepared the way for a spread of the religious father concept. In so doing it also prepared the way for the influence of the witness of Jesus to the Father, though it differs profoundly from this. As a synon. of γεννητήρ, πατήρ describes the relation of God to the world as Creator. In Tim., 28c God is called ποιητής καὶ πατὴρ τοῦ παντός. The concept of the author of being is also present in 37c : ὁ γεννήσας πατήρ, cf. 34b. God has made this world (41a) as δημιουργὸς πατήρ τε ἔργων. Father and architect (cf. already Resp., VI, 507c; X, 596d, 597d for this) are thus identical here. The cosmos is καλός (Tim., 29a) because its architect is ἀγαθός (cf. 29e). Acc. to a well-considered plan it was created πρὸς τὸ ἀίδιον, incomparable as a reflection of the eternal gods, 29a, 34a, 37c. Having through God's πρόνοια become a besouled and rational ζῷον (so already Polit., 269d), a single, visible and wholly perfect entity, it is a blessed, sensually perceptible god (the μονογενής : 30b d, 33a, 34b, 92c. [46] This myth is carried even further in Ep., VI, 323d, where ὁ τῶν πάντων θεὸς ἡγεμών (= δημιουργός) is distinguished from the πατὴρ κύριος τοῦ τε ἡγεμόνος καὶ αἰτίου. Here, too, πατήρ corresponds to what Plato elsewhere calls the idea of the good. The distinction is perhaps a last effort on the part of the aged thinker to differen-

---

[39] Dieterich, 149.

[40] On ἀππᾶς, πατρομύσται, πατὴρ συνόδου, πατὴρ τῶν ἱερέων, *parens, pater sacrorum, pater patrum* — in Mithraism "father" is the highest of the seven degrees of initiation — cf. Dieterich, 146-149; Reitzenstein, 27 f.; E. Ziebarth, *Das gr. Vereinswesen* (1896), 51, 154; F. Poland, *Gesch. d. gr. Vereinswesens* (1909), 161, n. 2; 247; 357; 397; W. Otto, *Priester u. Tempel im hell. Ägypten,* I (1905), 130.

[41] Diod. S., 2, 29, 4 of the Chaldeans, where φιλοσοφία (astrology, priestly ministry) παραδέδοται καὶ παῖς παρὰ πατρὸς διαδέχεται; cf. 1, 73, 5.

[42] Dieterich, 135, 150.

[43] Cf. Plot. Enn., V, 1, 8 : πατέρα φησὶ τἀγαθόν, καὶ τὸ ἐπέκεινα νοῦ καὶ ἐπέκεινα οὐσίας.

[44] Plat. (*loc. cit.*) makes this plain in the similitude of the sun. But he calls the ἥλιος, the author of light and life, ἔκγονος τοῦ ἀγαθοῦ rather than father, Resp., VI, 506e.

[45] On Plat. Tim. *v.* Reitzenstein-Schaeder, 142 ff.; v. Wilamowitz-Moellendorff, 424, 605, 626, 707, n. 2.

[46] Already in Heracl. Fr., 50 (Diels⁶, I, 161, 14 ff.) we find the pantheistic formula that the cosmos both begets and is begotten, πατὴρ υἱός. Acc. to Diels this is a Chr. addition ; but the μονογενής of Plat. seems to be in view.

tiate between visible nature as the work of creation and the far side of all being and becoming, the ideas of the good (= deity). But what we have here is hardly more than the figurative language of personification.

The conception of God as father of the world is very old.[47] In a way which is undoubtedly fig., it uses the thought of generation.[48] The influence of the myth in Tim. cannot be rated too highly. From the time of Pos. there are many commentaries on the work by Peripatetics and Neo-Platonists up to Procl. The main ideas, i.e., cosmic generation, the parallelism of πατήρ, ποιητής, and δημιουργός, become the common legacy of culture. Philo makes use of these terms, as do also Corp. Herm., Dio Chrys., Chr. authors, esp. the Apologists and above all Cl. Al., → n. 49. Numenios further develops religious father speculation.[49] He calls the first God the grandfather of the cosmos, and thinks of the godhead in three stages: the chief principle (νοῦς), the demiurge and the cosmos, Procl. in Tim., 93a. Procl. himself (in Tim., I, 303, 27) adopts the triad πατήρ, δημιουργός, κόσμος. Plot. in Eus. Praep. Ev., XI, 17, 6 strongly emphasises γεννᾶν. Porphyr. Abst., II, 46 calls the cosmos: ὁ τοῦ πατρὸς νεώς. In Chr. Gnostic systems, as in Neo-Platonism, the demiurge is distinguished from the supreme God. The demiurge νοῦς is the second god. A common term in cosmological father speculation is the father of all: πατὴρ τῶν ὅλων or πάντων or τοῦ παντός (alongside δημιουργὸς πάντων, ποιητὴς τῶν ὅλων). Precisely acc. to this catchword one can measure the degree of Hell. influence. In particular, it is to be found in all writings coloured by Gnosticism.

2. The Father as Begetter and the Synthesis of King and Father in Stoicism.

Ancient Stoicism was already using the myth of the ἱερὸς γάμος of Zeus and Hera in its natural philosophy.[50] Hence the origin of the world can be traced back to divine begetting. The λόγοι σπερματικοί are a philosophical term for this.[51] The ἐκ σοῦ γὰρ γένος ἐσμέν in the hymn of Cleanthes[52] is anchored here. So also Epict. Diss., I, 9, 4: "From God the seed fell not only on my father and grandfather, but on all that propagates or plants itself on the earth, though esp. on rational creatures." Dio Chrys., 36, 55 calls ἔρως, cosmogonically said of God, the ὁρμὴ ἐπὶ τὸ γεννᾶν.[53] The first sections of Epict. Diss. (I, 3 and 9) consider the question what follows from the fact that God is the father of gods and men and that man is συγγενὴς τῷ θεῷ (I, 9, 22

---

[47] On the father of all among primitive peoples cf. Söderblom, 118. Rigveda, VI, 49, 10 calls Rudra (later Shiva) the father of the world (*bhúvanasya pitáram*); Bhagavad Gîtâ, 11 (theophany), 43 extols Vishnu-Krishna as father of the world.

[48] Aristot. Metaph., XII, 10, p. 1086 f. does not go beyond the idea of the father of the house. On the other hand Plut. Quaest. Plat. (II, 1001b) considers how far πατήρ is only a metaphor here. His finding is that as Creator of the body God is a demiurge, but in relation to the soul, which is part of Himself, He shows Himself to be begetter. Cf. Stoicism → 955, 22 ff.

[49] In Judaism God is not originally called the Father of the cosmos but of Israelites who do His will. Rabb.: Ex. r., 46 (101c), Str.-B., I, 467. For "father and maker" cf. Is. 64:7. On the other hand, He is Father of all in Jos. Ant., 7, 380, where David calls God πατέρα τε καὶ γένεσιν τῶν ὅλων ἀπὸ καλῶν καὶ δημιουργὸν ἀνθρωπίνων καὶ θείων. On Philo → 956, 27 ff.; on Corp. Herm., → 958, 9 ff. Cf. Dio Chrys., 36, 60. In Chr. writings we find "Father of all" in 1 Cl., 35, 3; Just. Apol., 10, 6; Dial., 7, 3; Athenag. Suppl., 27, 2; Cl. Al. Strom., IV, 13, 92, 1; VIII, 9, 29, 3-6. In Gnostic authors: Iren. Haer., I, 30, 1; Ep. of Ptolemaeus to Flora in Epiph. Haer., 33, 3, 7; 7, 4; 7, 7 (GCS, 25, 452, 456 f.). On this cf. A. v. Harnack, "Der Brief d. Ptol. an die Flora," SAB (1902), 524 f., with text as app. I, pp. 536-541. Other metaphors which give evidence of drawing on this sphere are to be found in Test. Job 8:10; Apc. Mos. 35:36.

[50] Cf. Orig. Cels., IV, 48 (GCS, 2, 321, 9) of Chrysipp.

[51] Apart from Orig. (→ n. 50) on Zeno Kitieus: Diog. L., VII, 136 (v. Arnim, I, 28, 26); Gal. Definitiones Medicae, 29 (ed. C. G. Kühn [1830], 350): The soul is moved of itself κατὰ σπερματικοὺς λόγους. Cf. also Aetius, Procl., Stob. Ecl. in v. Arnim, Index, *s.v.*

[52] Stob. Ecl., I, 25, 3 ff. (v. Arnim, I, 121 37 ff.).

[53] On divine relationship in Stoicism cf. Bonhöffer, 76-80.

and 25), indeed, that he is related to God as ὁ ἴδιος υἱός (I, 19, 9). The answer is that man thereby shares in God's λόγος and γνώμη, Diss., I, 3, 3. With this high sense of his relationship to Zeus man cannot think ignobly of himself and lives always with awareness of this dignity, I, 3, 1-3; II, 14, 27. This basic attitude gives freedom from worry and fear, I, 9, 7. It does not allow man to do anything unworthy of God's father-hood, II, 8, 18. It gives a right relationship to related brethren (I, 12, 3) who also have Zeus as progenitor (πρόγονον). At root, however, only the sage is aware of this re-lation. Hence it is only a step to the more limited view that God is father only of the good. Sen. De Providentia, I, 5; 2, 5 f. shows that Deity is a stern father precisely for the *bonus vir.* Dio Chrys., 31, 58 calls the good alone θεοφιλεῖς. In 4, 22 he denies that the φαῦλοι have any right to call God the father of gods and men. The gods as our relatives and ancestors desire their own to be virtuous, and so they do not love bold sinners, 33, 28; 39, 2. Hence what is said about divine sonship leads to ethical teaching. [54] Later Stoicism lays particular stress on God's authority as ruler. [55] In Epict. the inter-relation of father and king is set in the service of the concept of providence. ποιητής, πατήρ and κηδεμών ("provider," "supporter") are associated in Epict. Diss., I, 9, 7, cf. III, 11, 5. The total view shows that πρόνοια does not relate only to natural require-ments, since these do not represent a real good. The limit is the Stoic attitude to the natural. The emphasis is on the fact that God as a good king and true father grants us freely available powers in the struggle against adversities, I, 6, 40. In such connections the father is envisaged as the head of the house ruling as a king. [56] In Dio Chrys. (Or., 1, 39) the synthesis of father and king is presented for the most part in philosophical and political terms, cf. Or. 1-4. Here the monarchical rule of the king is set in the frame-work of the royal sway of Zeus, the μέγας βασιλεὺς βασιλέων [57] (Or., 2, 75), who holds all things in a firmly constituted universal harmony.

3. The Father Concept in Philo. [58]

a. The Greek Influence.

Philo undoubtedly made a strong contribution to speaking of God as Father, [59] Leg. All., I, 64; II, 67; cf. Rer. Div. Her., 62. The abs. "the Father," which is not just Johannine, is also common in Philo, Op. Mund., 46, 89, 156; Spec. Leg., II, 59; Abr., 118 etc. He has a liking for epithets of majesty; as distinct from the γεννητὸς πατήρ God is ὁ ἀΐδιος, Jos., 265; cf. Virt., 204; ὁ γνήσιος, Som., II, 273; Aet. Mund., 83; ἀληθὴς πατήρ, in face of whom the polytheist is blind, Migr. Abr., 69. [60]

The term as used by Philo comes from many sources. Homer's chief formula for Zeus (→ 952, 8) had some influence, also esp. Plat. Tim. [61] The intersection of these motifs is

---

[54] The restrictive distinction becomes an occasion of boasting in the statement attributed to Alexander the Gt., Plut. Apophth. Alexandri, 15 (II, 180d): Zeus is φύσει the father of all, but ἑαυτοῦ ... ποιεῖται τοὺς ἀρίστους. Plut. Alex., 27 (I, 681a) has the same with κοινὸς πατήρ. On this formula cf. Epict. Diss., III, 22, 82; Dio Chrys., 12, 74.

[55] Cf. J. Kroll, *Die Lehren d. Herm. Trismeg.* (1914), 31; Wendland, 51, n. 2; H. Binder, *Dio Chrys. u. Pos.,* Diss. Tübingen (1905), 86.

[56] Worth noting are the warm-hearted statements about the relation of Odysseus to Zeus as father in Epict. Diss., III, 24, 15 f.

[57] βασιλεὺς βασιλέων (Rev. 17:14; 19:16) occurs also in Philo Decal., 41. Zeus is al-ready the heavenly counterpart of the earthly monarch in Xenoph. An., III, 1, 12.

[58] Cf. E. Bréhier, *Les idées philosophiques et religieuses de Philon d'Alex.* (1907), 74, n. 3.

[59] ὁ πατὴρ θεός, Corp. Herm., I, 30; O. Sol. 9:5; ὁ θεὸς καὶ πατήρ, Corp. Herm., I, 21: "The Father" abs. Test. Job 40:2.

[60] "Eternal Father": Rigveda, V, 4, 2 of the god of fire Agni; Mahâbhârata, XIII, 149 of Vishnu: "the eternal father of all beings." In Plato → 954, 29 f. of the cosmos; Corp. Herm., → n. 69. πατὴρ γνήσιος, Corp. Herm., XIV, 4. "Great Father," Rigveda, I, 71, 5, → n. 22. On the Manichean "Father of greatness" cf. H. H. Schaeder in Reitzenstein-Schaeder, 243, 277. Sib., III, 296. "Holy Father": Test. Jud. 24:2; O. Sol. 31:5; cf. Jn. 17:11.

[61] In Aet. Mund., 15 Philo has πατήρ, ποιητής, δημιουργός together. He has ὁ τοῦ κόσμου πατήρ in Decal., 134; Vit. Mos., II, 134; countless times ποιητὴς καὶ πατήρ,

to be seen in Spec. Leg., II, 165. But Philo goes beyond Plato, for under Stoic influence, though more intensively, he develops the thought of the generation of the cosmos and the soul. While Jos., who in Ant., 7, 380 (→ n. 49) has a related formula, elsewhere speaks of divine γεννᾶν [62] only in respect of the Law, Philo makes considerable use of ὁ γεννήσας or γεννητὴς πατήρ (Spec. Leg., III, 189; II, 30 f.; Op. Mund., 84) in relation to creation, whether with ref. to the stars, man, the soul, or the ὀρθὸς λόγος. He carries this terminology as far as possible. He even describes τὸ πᾶν expressly as the son, Spec. Leg., I, 96; Ebr., 30; Vit. Mos., II, 134. How highly Philo estimates the image is shown by the fact that he sometimes uses "husband" along with "father" (Det. Pot. Ins., 147, because God makes possible the conception and birth of all things). But He is also Spouse and Father of the soul, Som., II, 273; Mut. Nom., 205. The main idea here is the ethical one that virtues are begotten in her. Spiritual and ethical teaching is still Philo's main concern in relation to the birth of children to the patriarchs, Cher., 41, 44, 46, 50, 52; Ebr., 20; Det. Pot. Ins., 124. Hence in Poster. C., 68 he can call the norm of the ὀρθὸς λόγος the father and the soul a child of the ὀρθὸς λόγος, cf. Conf. Ling., 43; Som., II, 135. [63] On the basis of Gn. 18:17 the picture is rather different in Sobr., 56. The wise man, in a genuinely Stoic sense, is here adopted by God as a son, so that for the first time he truly has God as Father, [64] → υἱοθεσία. [65]

Along with the basic concepts of generation and building, other terms used to elucidate fatherhood are ἡγεμών, ἐπίσκοπος, ἐπίτροπος, again with ref. to the cosmos, Op. Mund., 135; Decal., 90; Ebr., 74. These words describe the πρόνοια of the Father, His rule and provision with a view to sustaining His work. His sons are deemed worthy of this care, Spec. Leg., I, 318; cf. Migr. Abr., 193; Op. Mund., 10. σωτὴρ τοῦ κόσμου (Spec. Leg., II, 198) also expresses the idea of the upholding of the cosmos. The phrase is also used for God's fatherly pity, Praem. Poen., 39. Acc. to Spec. Leg., II, 247 God is no σιδήριος πατήρ, par. Mt. 7:9. He is not the author of evil for His children, Op. Mund., 75. As the Father of good He is φιλόδωρος, Fug., 62. If we catch here an echo of the religious understanding of the concept of the head of the house, full justice is not done to this aspect. The intellectualism, dualism and truncation of the historical side do not permit this.

b. Jewish Factors.

Philo seldom uses βασιλεύς along with πατήρ, Flacc., 3; Op. Mund., 144. When he wants to express the idea of authority, he prefers κύριος and δεσπότης. We find the kingly side, however, when he speaks of the two basic powers of God, Vit. Mos., II, 99; Cher., 27; Plant., 86; Sobr., 55; Rer. Div. Her., 166. The motifs associated with the father concept relate to the first of these, the ποιητικὴ δύναμις, which is called ἀγαθότης, also χαριστική, εὐεργετική. The name θεός corresponds to it. It denotes the creative power by which God summons all things into being and orders all things. The other basic power is βασιλικὴ δύναμις, His power as ruler, also called κολαστική, whereby He exercises ἐξουσία as κύριος and δεσπότης. This division corresponds to the tradition of the Synagogue, which earnestly discussed the relation between the divine attributes of mercy and justice. Philo finds the solution between the two powers in the idea of the *logos*. In this, the vehicle of transcendent deity, all powers find their common and comprehensive centre. By it God is Ruler and yet also kind (= the Father, Cher., 27). The σπερματικὸς καὶ τεχνικὸς ... λόγος (Rer. Div. Her., 119) belongs to the

---

Rer. Div. Her., 98; Praem. Poen., 24 etc. He esp. likes ὁ ποιητὴς καὶ πατὴρ τῶν ὅλων, Rer. Div. Her., 236; Fug., 84 etc.; or πάντων τοῦ παντός, τοῦ γεγονότος, τῶν ὄντων, or very often πατὴρ τῶν ὅλων alone.

[62] On γεννᾶν in Jos. cf. Schl. Jos., 15.

[63] In Ebr., 81 the father is ὀρθὸς λόγος and the mother παιδεία, a couple subordinate to θεός and σοφία.

[64] We have here two figures of speech : he takes God as patron (as aliens in Athens had to have a sponsoring citizen); εἰσποιητός, however, means adopted.

[65] Cf. Wendland, *Philos Schrift* ..., 50 f.

Father. [66] But it is also the first-begotten son whom the Father of all brought into being. [67] He used it in creation. He thus validates His fatherly χαριστικὴ δύναμις (cf. Cher., 127; Rer. Div. Her., 205), but no less so His ruling authority. In this sense God remains εἷς ὢν ὁ μέσος, Sacr. AC, 59.

4. The Father in Hermes Mysticism. [68]

Though not a true unity, but a mixture of philosophical and mythological elements, some pantheistic and some monotheistic, Corp. Herm. still pursues a main theme, that of knowing the world. Platonic ideas from Tim. [69] have a big influence, along with which we also find Stoic features. In this mystical confusion the Father of all, the supreme God in the highest world of νοῦς, is also the one fixed pole. In spite of His exaggerated transcendence He has a central relation to all things. The name "father" contains something distinctive and inalienable. But this mysticism is γνωρίζειν the Father (Corp. Herm., XIV, 4), [70] which is linked with self-knowledge (XIII, 22a). [71] God as Father is αὐτὸς ἑαυτοῦ αἴτιος, VIII, 2; cf. Jn. 5:26. The meaning of father is defined by ποιεῖν, here understood as begetting, II, 17a; X, 2. In this sense the true ἔργον of God is τὸ πατέρα εἶναι, V, 9. In its concentration on the concept of generation Corp. Herm. goes even further than Philo, XII (II), 15b; VIII, 5. In XI (I), 5; II, 17a ποιεῖν is identical with τίκτειν. What is meant is the sowing of ποιά (qualities) by the Father, VIII, 3. The cosmogonic myth in I, 12 ff.; XIII, 10 f.; XI, 6-8 also treats of the primal man begotten of the Father of all. Hermaphrodite like the Father, [72] he receives from Him light and life, I, 21. The Father of all allows him to create, I, 12. When he breaks through the spheres and mates with φύσις, this is a fall, but it is made possible by that privilege. [73] Exultation at the birth of children (II, 17a), [74] which is hardly consonant with the demand to hate the flesh in IV, 6, is simply a deduction from what is originally meant by calling God Father. [75] There is a liking for triads, [76] e.g., θεός, ποιητής,

---

[66] Though rarely, he can thus call the logos "father," Conf. Ling., 41 (ἄνθρωπος θεοῦ = father). Cf. in the Chr. world 2 Cl., 1, 4; Dg., 9, 6; Cl. Al. Paed., III, 12, 101, 1 (GCS, 12, 290, 30).

[67] A second series of logos statements refers to God as its father and σοφία as its mother, Fug., 108 f.; Det. Pot. Ins., 54; cf. Ebr., 30 (ἐπιστήμη τοῦ πεποιηκότος for σοφία). Carried over into the Chr. sphere, the idea that God begets the Logos is very important in the Apologists, Just. Dial., 61, 1, 3; 62, 4; 128, 4; 129, 4; Tat. Or. Graec., 5, 1; Cl. Al. Quis Div. Salv., 37, 2 (GCS, 17, 184, 3); O. Sol. 41:9 f.

[68] On this cf. J. Kroll, Die Lehren d. Herm. Trismeg. (1914); C. F. G. Heinrici, Die Hermesmystik u. d. NT (1918).

[69] Platonic elements: God as father of the cosmos, IX, 8; father of all, I, 21, 27, 31; V, 9, 10a; XIII, 21; Ascl., I, 9; Stob. Excerpt., 26, 9 (Scott, I, 520, 7 ff. = Stob. Ecl., I, 466, 22 ff.); begetting, → lines 15 ff.; the world eternal and immortal through the eternal father, VIII, 2; X, 10; XI, 2, 3, 15; after his image a second god, VIII, 1b, 2, 5; the cosmos God's son, IX, 8; hence the world good.

[70] Cf. Heb. En. 48 C : 7 (Odeberg, p. 169).

[71] Cf. the saying of Jesus in P. Oxy., IV, 654 (= Kl. T., 8 [1910], 17 f.): ἑαυτοὺς γνώσεσθαι [καὶ εἰδήσετε ὅτι υἱοὶ] ἐστε ὑμεῖς τοῦ πατρός.

[72] Cf. O. Sol. 14:2; 19:2 ff.: the breasts of the Father.

[73] In the Naassene hymn in Hipp. Elenchos, V, 10, 2 this is referred to Jesus who asks the Father for permission to come down and who redemptively goes the same way as the primal man.

[74] For a pessimistic counterpart cf. S. Bar. 56:6.

[75] The relation of πατήρ to νοῦς is ambivalent. νοῦς can be used in many ways. There is identification in I, 6, cf. I, 12; Stob. Ecl., I, 34, 5. The unity of νοῦς as Father-God and as Logos is life and light, I, 12, 21. But if the two are equated here, they are differentiated in II, 13. In I, 9 the demiurge who creates the seven planetary gods, and in XIII, 8 the πρωτόγονος θεός, is equated with νοῦς. Everything which derives from the world of the Father is determined by νοῦς.

[76] On the triad cf. E. Norden, Agnostos Theos (1913), 353.

πατήρ, XIV, 2-6, esp. 4. Another triad is ὁ θεὸς καὶ πατὴρ καὶ τὸ ἀγαθόν, Χ, 1b, 2, 9; cf. XIV, 4.[77] God as the author of all being is good. He who receives nothing and gives everything embraces the good wholly in Himself, Χ; VI; II, 12. Here, too, the work of creating and begetting is in view. πατήρ and ἀγαθόν, closely related as in Plato and Philo, are incontestably proper to Him in the abs. sense and thus describe His nature, II, 14 ff.; 17a. If the meaning of this nomenclature is accessible only to γνῶσις and not to αἴσθησις (Χ, 9), if the names — pantheistically intended — are predicated of the One who bears every name and is at the same time nameless (V, 10a; Ascl., III, 20a; Apul. Asclepius, XX [ed. P. Thomas, III, p. 55]), πατήρ is still an indispensable characterisation.[78]

The Father is said to exercise a saving rule. By His θέλημα and βουλή (XIII, 9; → III, 54, 3 ff.) He fixes the destiny of men. He is impelled by His ἔλεος (XIII, 3, 10). The initiate is ἐλεηθείς. The Father is the ἐπόπτης and ἐπίσκοπος of favoured souls (cf. 1 Pt. 2:25). πατὴρ τῶν ψυχῶν, XVIII, 12. Mysticism is sanctification in the fellowship of the Father, I, 32.[79] In this man is helped by the νοῦς, which leads to true self-knowledge, to the abhorring of the senses (I, 20-26, esp. 22), to μιμεῖσθαι of the Father (Χ, 21;[80] → IV, 662, n. 4). This knowledge is imparted to the ἔννους ἄνθρωπος, the initiate, I, 21. Already in virtue of his origin he has a share in νοῦς, which is both a gift (I, 22) and a prize (IV, 3). The thought of fatherly provision is completely absent from Corp. Herm. The Father is also τροφή for the cosmos (Χ, 3), but His concern for the whole life of His τέκνα (Jesus) is crowded out by intellectual Gnostic factors, and is as little evident as in Stoicism or Philo. Everything is orientated to the process of redemption, the ἄνοδος to the transcendent world of νοῦς, which is a return to the Father, I, 24-26; cf. XIII, 15. Sensual nature and evil impulses are gradually discarded during this ascent in order that the goal of deification may be reached. But in deifying regeneration through ecstasy (XIII, esp. 13 f.) as in the orientation of the ἄνοδος use is made of the father concept at the decisive pt. The regenerate belongs to the πατρικὸν γένος, XIII, 3. Through γενεσιουργία (XIII, 21)[81] the Father is the One who begets in a twofold sense.[82] The community of initiates is that which prays to the Father. "Father" is the final word of prayer on which solemn emphasis falls, I, 27; 30-32; V, 2; XIII, 18, 21. After supreme vision and instruction on the constitution of the universe the initiate extols Him, I, 27. In the fulness of the glory of the Hermes hymn there is ascent to this invocation, XIII, 21. But the ultimate goal is absorption into the all (XIII, 11), initiates becoming δυνάμεις ἐν θεῷ (I, 26).

Schrenk

B. The Father Concept in the Old Testament.

1. πατήρ and Other Terms for אָב in the Old Testament.

In the LXX πατήρ is used almost exclusively for אָב. The only exception, οἱ πατέρες σου for רָאשֹׁנִים at Dt. 19:14, is perhaps due to an error, since Cod. A rightly has πρότεροι. Sometimes for the sake of precision phrases with πατήρ are used for the degrees of relationship דּוֹד and דּוֹדָה, e.g., Lv. 25:49 דֹּדוֹ אוֹ בֶן־דֹּדוֹ = ἀδελφὸς πατρὸς αὐτοῦ ἢ

---

[77] Stob. Exc., 23, 37 (Scott, I, 476, 23 = Stob. Ecl., I, 396, 19 f.): δέσποτα καὶ πάτηρ καὶ ποιητά. Kore Kosmu likes epithets of rule along with father, Stob. Exc., 23, 58 (Scott, I, 488, 19 ff. = Stob. Ecl., I, 404, 10 ff.): πάτερ, βασιλεῦ, δέσποτα. Acc. to Iren. Haer., I, 5, 1 "Father and King of all things" is Gnostic.

[78] This paradox seems here to endanger the father concept as little that of V, namely, that God as the invisible is the most visible thing in creation.

[79] Cf. the eternal goal in O. Sol. 8:23 ff.

[80] On the other hand God is ἀμίμητος acc. to Corp. Herm., VI, 5.

[81] Corp. Herm. has this in common with the mysteries. On the begetting and birth of the initiate through deity cf. Dieterich, 134 f.

[82] Cf. Cl. Al. Paed., I, 6, 41, 2 (GCS, 12, 114, 28).

υἱὸς ἀδελφοῦ πατρός (cf. Lv. 10:4; Ιερ. 39:7 etc.; Est. 2:7, 15), and Ex. 6:20 : דֹּדָתוֹ
= θυγάτηρ τοῦ ἀδελφοῦ τοῦ πατρὸς αὐτοῦ. The involved expression with the fem.
is probably designed to prevent a ref. to the definition of דֹּדָה in Lv. 18:14, which would
involve transgression of the marriage law of Lv. 20:20.

The other renderings of אָב yield no particularly significant results. Along with adj.
phrases instead of the gen. such as πατρῷος in Prv. 27:10, πατρικός in Sir. 42:10 or
ὁμοπάτριος in Lv. 18:11, we find attempts either at greater precision or extension,
e.g., ἀρχιπατριώτης in Jos. 21:1, πατριάρχης in 1 Ch. 24:31, also for רֹאשׁ הָאָבוֹת
in 2 Ch. 19:8; 26:12. We also find elegant Gk. terms like γονεῖς for אָב וָאֵם in Est. 2:7
(also surprisingly only for אֵם in Prv. 29:15) or πρόπαππος for אֲבֹתֶיךָ אֲבוֹת in Ex. 10:6.
δύναμις for בֵּית אָבוֹת in Nu. 1:45 is also a typical softening. At Jos. 24:32 οἱ κατοικοῦντες ἐν Σικιμοις for אֲבִי שְׁכֶם is a typical adaptation of the fig. genealogical wording
for Gks.: Shechem is no longer a man but a city. When the city Kirjath-arba in Jos. 15:13
is called the father of Anak, the rendering μητρόπολις Ενακ is an interpretation along
the same lines. [83]

2. אָב as a Primary Word.

אָב is a primary word, one of the isolated nouns [84] connected with no stems. In distinction from the Egypt. 'it, which like most of its Coptic modifications means "father" as
well as "barley," [85] אָב has only one meaning, and no alien note can be detected in it.
It possibly has its origin in childish speech, [86] though this thesis is true only in so far
as precedence is given to the secular use, as is undoubtedly correct. The situation is
presumably similar in respect of אָח "brother" and חָם "father-in-law," which are related
in nature and use.

There are practically no synon. Whether אָב is genuinely related to אוֹב ("spirit of
the dead") is open to question. Perhaps there never was any such connection. The
part. hi הַמּוֹלִיד, which occurs only once in Is. 66:9, refers to the Creator and can be
brought only into very loose connection with the sacral father concept. Inadequately
supported, too, is the thesis [87] that the noun פַּחַד in the famous crux פַּחַד יִצְחָק (Gn. 31:42,
53) has a synon. function to "kinsman" or "ancestor." Relationship to a second and not
unambiguous פחד, which in the description of the crocodile in Job 40:17 as in the Arabic
faḥid, means "thigh," is given weight by the fact that the Arabic word can also mean
the sub-division of a tribe, [88] and also by the fact that in Palmyrenian inscr. [89] from
the Roman period the sense "clan" is frequently attested for פחד. The Ugaritic phd
"herd" [90] seems at least not to be in contradiction with this conclusion. Nevertheless,
this does not constitute a bridge, but a leap is still demanded, from clan to the chief of
a clan, and consequently to the exegetical right to replace the "fear" of Isaac by the
"ancestor" or even the "kinsman" of Isaac. [91] In these circumstances one can have no
confidence that the thesis is proved, though the impression remains undiminished that
better justice is done to the problem of this combination as a name of God by the

---

[83] אַבְרֵךְ in Gn. 41:43, which the LXX ignores, has nothing to do with אָב, but is the
transcription of an Egypt. acclamation with more than one possible meaning.

[84] J. Barth, Die Nominalbildung in d. semitischen Sprachen (1889), § 1.

[85] A. Erman-A. Grapow, Wörterbuch d. ägypt. Sprache, I (1926), 141 f.

[86] So Zobel, 9, n. 1 with ref. to the form אַבָּא. On childish words cf. Köhler, op. cit., 171 f.

[87] W. F. Albright, Von d. Steinzeit zum Christentum (1949), 248 f., 434, n. 84; Eng.
(1946), 188 f.

[88] So H. Wehr, Arabisches Wörterbuch, II (1952), 625b.

[89] M. Lidzbarski, Handbuch d. nordsemitischen Epigraphik, I (1898), 350.

[90] Albright, op. cit., 434, n. 84.

[91] The Targumic פחדין in the sense of "testicles" (Dalman Wört.³, 330b with ref. to
Lv. 21:20) cannot serve as a bridge, and there is no other possibility.

conjectured meaning than by the idea of the "fear of Isaac," which always seems to be a forced solution.

3. אָב as a Basic Element in the Family Concept.

The socio-legal order of family life, and the influence of this order on the emotions, determined the later Heb. use of the word father in all its modifications even up to logical metaphors.[92] The circle of experience of the son, whether as adult or child, brings out the vital elemental motifs of the usage in reciprocity with that of the loving and suffering father. The Heb. family is בֵּית־אָב, the father's house, the household community subordinate to the supreme degree of male relationship. This is the Accadian *bit abi*, which is found already in suffix constructions in the Amarna letters,[93] and since house in this connection can have the basic sense of building (Gn. 24:23), it pts. plainly to an urban culture as the soil on which it arose. The term denotes and recognises the legal supremacy of the father. Yet it is an open question whether and how far more than the physical father is in view. Usually in polygamous marriage the sons[94] and daughters of the same father and his wives and concubines constitute with these and others the בֵּית־אָב or merely the בַּיִת, Jos. 24:15. But the marriages of the sons and the new בֵּית־אָבוֹת which arise therefrom complicate the concept "house" and give rise to the מִשְׁפָּחָה "tribe," in which the authority of the father yields to a sense of brotherly relationship with a democratic tendency. How fluid the border is may be seen from the procedure in Jos. 7:14, 17: the tribe is drawn, then the family, then the house, then the man. This גֶּבֶר is the father of a family and no longer נַעַר under paternal authority. The house is an intervening member, not yet the family but more than the basic household. It is similar to the community of brethren in Ps. 133:1, and possibly this broader concept of the בֵּית־אב as the greater family is earlier. We have certainly to reckon with the use of אָב for "forefather," as is sufficiently shown by the genealogical stories in Gn. and as may be seen also from the noteworthy plur. בֵּית־אָבוֹת "father's house" for an aggregate of households or larger family. The phrase "God of the fathers" (Ex. 3:13 etc.) also teaches us that the term "fathers" did not normally carry with it any relic of numinous content, since the fathers could not be characterised more plainly as men who worshipped God than by a gen. of this kind.[95] How long the sense of belonging to a forefather can persist through the generations depends on the amount of love and pride which a figure of the past could attract. Abraham — also David — could be regarded as the father of all, and "fathers" is still found in Paul (R. 4:12 etc.), the Gospels (Lk. 1:73; 16:24; Jn. 8:53 etc.) and long after.

4. Basic Features of Patriarchy.

The family laws of ancient Israel which were codified or which may be discerned in the stories have to be distinguished according to time and place, but one may easily perceive in all of them the primacy of the father, whether the physical father or the forefather, in all family decisions, esp. in matters of property and inheritance. The development of these relations prior to the rise of the greater national federation must have been the same as everywhere else in the primitive period. It may be clarified at least to the degree that in the pre-historic nomadic groups which constituted the core of

---

[92] Cf. אָב בִּנְיַן "raising up of a family (בֵּית־אָב)" for "logical deduction" in the Tannaites, one of the 7 middot of Hillel; cf. Strack Einl.[5], 97 f.

[93] For examples cf. J. A. Knudtzon, *Die El-Amarna-Tafeln*, II (1915), 1393. The meaning of *bit abia* in 189, 10 is undoubtedly "district."

[94] Where we have the appositional "thy brother, thy mother's son" (Gn. 27:29; Dt. 13:7), descent from the same father is taken for granted. Only the mother is mentioned because there were several mothers in the father's house, and there were thus groups among the children. The ref. is to a full brother rather than half-brother. "Sister" is daughter of the father "or" of the mother, Lv. 20:17.

[95] "Father of nomads, musicians and smiths" (Gn. 4:20-22) means "patron" rather than "ancestor."

the people of Israel we have to reckon with different social forms until finally the patriarchy which dominated the picture was able to establish itself. Patriarchy, which rests on the principle that the clan continues in the male line, is the antithesis of matriarchy, according to which the children of a man are incorporated into the tribe of the mother, and only the children of the sister can be heirs. [96] Matriarchy probably persisted for a long time in small relationships, which we can now grasp only schematically, under the undisputed validity of the tribal constitution. In the larger development which began for Israel with the acceptance of the cult of Yahweh, however, it could not continue. One of the reasons is very probably to be sought in the cultic requirements of Yahweh religion, which expected certain sacral functions from the head of the clan, and which also excluded women from the cultus. [97]

There seem to be some noteworthy if not primary arguments for the conjecture that the precedence of male heads of families and clans in the early nomadic period rested very largely in the sacral dignity which prior to the acceptance of Yahweh religion they had to an even higher degree than later. The first argument is to be found in the story in Ju. which tells how the tribe of Dan took over a private sanctuary, Ju. 17 f. There a נַעַר, an unmarried man still young in years, when appointed priest at what was first a family and then a tribal sanctuary, was given the title "father" (Ju. 17:10; 18:19). We are surely justified in concluding, [98] therefore, that this remarkable term, used to denote priestly authority, is connected with a tradition whereby the discharge of priestly ministry is thus incumbent on the actual head of the family, so that whoever functions in his place acquires the dignity of father. The young man was called "father" because he did what the father was required to do. If this were a pagan cult one might concede the possibility that in the case of this priest of Dan an alien etiquette was adopted acc. to which, as in the religions of Egypt and Mesopotamia, [99] a title borrowed from the mythical world was conferred on the priest. In spite of its attraction, however, the idea that the priest has a place in any kind in myth is not consonant with the ministry of Yahweh. At a pinch one can only turn to the late account (predominantly P) of the first pesach-maṣṣot feast in Ex. 12:1-14, 21-28. This feast is to be observed in the house by families. [100] The whole assembly of the congregation of Israel (v. 6) is to slay and eat the lamb by families. This veiled form of expression may be taken to mean that the priest is the head of the house, the one who decides, like Joshua : "I and my house,

---

[96] Judgment varies as to what relics of matriarchy are to be seen in the OT tradition. In particular, the septs named after women (Leah, Rachel, Bilhah and Zilpah, Gn. 29 f.) call for notice, also the giving of the name by the mother, and perhaps the equal mention of father and mother, as in the Decalogue and other texts, cf. Ex. 20:12; Dt. 5:16; Gn. 2:24; Ex. 21:15, 17; Lv. 19:3; 20:9; Ps. 27:10; → 964, 24 ff. Legally this equal mention may presuppose a tribal law in which both sexes claimed primacy, and it can be regarded as a compromise between patriarchy and matriarchy on the principle of equity. On the other hand the commonly adduced saying in Gn. 2:24, that a man leaves father and mother and cleaves to his wife, is an aetiological statement which does not deal with the legal relationship of marriage but simply with its common presupposition in the fact that the impulse towards the wife is stronger than other bonds of relationship.

[97] In Yahwism the woman exercises only charismatic authority as a prophetess or a mother in Israel" (Deborah, Ju. 5:7). There is no ref. to institutional or sacral authority. Women had undefined tasks in the sanctuary, certainly at Shiloh, though in the Mosaic tent probably only acc. to a theory of P or a glossator, 1 S. 2:22; Ex. 38:8.

[98] Bertholet, Kulturgeschichte, 256. That the title "father" was widely used in sacral circles is perhaps shown by a fuller predicate like אֲבִי־עַד in Is. 9:5, which could be a priestly title, though its significance is obscure.

[99] A link with the Egypt. wb' nśw:t "king's attendant" (Erman-Grapow, 292), an official title from the 19th dynasty, is not very likely. Nor does the priestly title it nṯr "father of the gods" call for consideration. A. Erman, Die Religion d. Ägypter (1934), 188 calls its origin an enigma. On "father" as a term for Babylonian priests cf. K. Frank, Studien z. babylonischen Religion, I (1911), 4.

[100] M. M. Nicolsky, "Pascha im Kulte d. jerusalemischen Tempels," ZAW, NF, 4 (1927), 180.

we serve Yahweh" (Jos. 24:15), and who also imparts the sacral tradition to his children (Ex. 12:26 f.). This priestly head of the house transfers his dignity as father to priestly officials who do not belong to the tribe, then to the prophets, who are called "father" by their pupils (2 K. 2:12) or the king (2 K. 6:21), and finally to administrators, [101] those who bear trustworthy authority, or benefactors, the "fathers of the poor," Job 29:16. [102]

Along with the sacral aspect we find that other basic features are transferred with the term father to non-tribal positions and persons. Thus the figure of the father is a kind of ideal when it represents the side of the priestly office which should evoke respect, or when it stands for the even higher authority of the prophet with its demand for unconditional acknowledgment. It would also appear that supreme family rank was freely and spontaneously accorded, not merely in address but in official usage, to esp. the high-ranking administrator as one who discharges his office by commanding with loving concern. It could be that this is mere etiquette, a type of speech which has no basis in reality, and which owes its origin to love of flattery. Nevertheless, it might be argued equally well that the authority of the father concept is shown to be predominant by this courtly figure of speech. It is certainly possible to place the accent differently in such statements. This may be seen also in the legal material which lies behind the usage.

The right of the father is given its distinctive character by the principle of inheritance that sons and daughters are born into the clan of the father and remain in it. The sons are heirs [103] of the father no matter who their mother may be, unless she is a "strange woman" (Ju. 11:2). They keep the clan alive, whereas daughters, when they marry, increase the material possessions of the father through the bringing of the מֹהַר on the part of the son-in-law. [104] The authority of the father thus extends to both sons and daughters, though to differing degrees. Due to contingent factors associated with the fragmentary nature of the sources, and also perhaps with the limited amount of business material, we learn more about the law pertaining to daughters (Ex. 21:9) than to sons. The casuistical law of the book of the covenant discusses the case of a man selling his daughter as a bond-servant (Ex. 21:7). [105] Acc. to Gn. 38:24 Judah as judge pronounces or proposes — the situation is not wholly clear [106] — the sentence of death on his daughter-in-law Tamar because of her unchastity as revealed in pregnancy. Difficult to assess is the ruling in Dt. 21:18-21 on the duty of parents to report their own son. This is possibly a case designed to give instruction in a very severe view of law. The prin-

---

[101] Gn. 45:8 : Joseph as Pharaoh's minister ; Is. 22:21: Eliakim b. Hilkiah as the substitute for a political leader ; 1 Macc. 11:31 f.: Lasthenes, also called συγγενής, an official of Demetrius II.

[102] Irrelevant here is the fact that David calls Saul "my father" in 1 S. 24:12, since David was related to the king by marriage. On Ps. 68:5 : "father of the fatherless," → n. 118.

[103] This principle, though not formulated, is everywhere presupposed, Saalschütz, 820 f.

[104] On the open question of a connection with the Accad. maḫiru, "purchase-price," cf. H. Zimmern, Akkadische Fremdwörter als Beweis f. babylonischen Kultureinfluss (1914), 18.

[105] It is a mistake to adduce the emergency of Neh. 5:2 in interpretation, the more so as the decisive word has to be conjectured there. More to the pt. is the use of property law (financial loss) as a ground for the decision of Ex. 21:21: "He is thy money," with ref. to the maltreatment of a slave and his master as the one responsible. In this type of legal thinking the daughter and wife as well as the slave can be regarded as chattels.

[106] Cf. Dt. 13:9 : "And thou (the father) shalt surely kill him (the one who leads astray into idolatry); thine hand shall be first upon him . . . and afterwards the hand of all the people." The procedure is not very clear ; either "thou shalt surely kill him" alone is original, or one must assume that there has been a serious mistake and conjecture ἀναγγέλλων ἀναγγελεῖς περὶ αὐτοῦ with the LXX. Obscure, too, is the ref. in Zech. 13:3 to parents in the last time putting their son to death because he comes forth as a prophet. In Gn. 31:32 Jacob promises his father-in-law Laban that anyone in his house who has stolen Laban's gods will be put to death. Is this meant to show that he has a legitimate paternal right of life and death so far as all those belonging to him are concerned ? Hardly, for like Zech. 13:3 this passage has a rhetorical flavour ; cf. also Reuben's offer to his father in Gn. 42:37: "Slay my two sons," which is a particularly solemn oath with no suggestion of a right or of psychological probability or even possibility.

ciple is advocated that law has little time for feelings and is concerned only to eradicate evil. Evil must not find a refuge even in one's own son. The father, supported by the mother, can accuse his son. This painful aspect of judicial practice kindles heroic passion in the recognition of a higher law, though it is, of course, coloured by doctrinaire theory. [107]

As social forms changed with cultural development, the acknowledgment of paternal authority as something to be respected in all circumstances was affected only to the degree that communal justice restricted the judicial powers of heads of houses and families to certain areas of penal and personal law. In the tribal court of the elders the influence of heads of families was probably considerable, though we know little about the composition of these colleges. The possibility of the father being such a tormentor and tyrant that the only remedy was to flee from home finds no support in the tradition unless we view the flight of Hagar in this light. [108] Some rulings on brutal actions in the Law (Ex. 21:11, 20 f., 26 f.) show that there could be abuse of paternal authority. In the account of the judgment executed by the Levites on their own people (Ex. 32:27) we are simply told that they killed with the sword brothers, fellow-countrymen and neighbours, but fathers are not mentioned among their victims. [109] There is no instance of patricide in the OT. Even maltreatment of father or mother is punished by death, [110] and only a law like this, or the annexed law about cursing (Ex. 21:17), prevents us from assuming a father taboo. There is, however, no precedent for this in the nations around Israel. On the contrary Canaan is cursed because, unlike his brothers, he ceases to pay to his father, so soon as occasion seemed to warrant, the respect which is taken for granted. [111]

It is, of course, undoubtedly much more than a contingency of legal enactment that in the law and ethos of the OT, regardless of the march of time, there is everywhere tacitly presupposed a basic norm which the Decalogue sets forth in the commandment : "Honour thy father and thy mother." The idea of honouring is an emotional one, as shown by its hymnic use. Hence it does not fit in too well in legal speech. It corresponds, not to a precise sense of law, but to an impulse which underlies this, which brings out for the first time the genuine intention of the law, and which safeguards it against the danger of formalistic stiffening. If from this standpoint the mother, who is legally weaker, is unreservedly associated with the father, this may be connected with ancient tensions in tribal law, → 962, 2 ff. At any rate, there is herewith found in the object of respect a human element which, along with the non-legal concept of honouring, expresses emotion far more strongly than thought. The book of the covenant categorically threatens with death anyone who smites his father or mother (Ex. 21:15) or who curses his father or

---

[107] V. 21 is the law, not part of the complaint. Formally the parents are not acting as judges. They simply present their son and describe his a-social tendencies. But since a complaint carries with it the proposed punishment, the complaint would probably not be made when the complainants knew the ruling. Sanh., 8, 1-5 has an effective clause to cover the worst cases. Cod. Hammurabi § 168 provides only for disinheritance, and in § 169 there is pardon for a first offence.

[108] Gn. 16:6. Neither the father nor the mother is responsible for the intolerable situation, but the psychologically absurd legal notion which ties the knot. Even one who leaves his family, saying of his father : "I know him not" (Dt. 33:9), does so only for the sake of priestly ministry. The formula is very old in address to deity. Gudea says to a goddess : "I have no mother, thou art my mother. I have no father, thou art my father," A. Jirku, Altorientalischer Komm. z. AT (1923), 125; cf. A. Jeremias, Handbuch z. altorient. Geisteskultur² (1929), 352, 361 f.

[109] Similarly Dt. 13:7 mentions only brothers, sons, daughters, wives and aliens among those who are to be put to death for leading astray into idolatry.

[110] Ex. 21:15. In acc. with customary use מַכֵּה cannot here mean "who slays" as elsewhere (cf. Ex. 2:12). This sense would demand וָמֵת in supplementation, as in v. 12. "And" in "father and mother" has the force of "or" both here and in v. 17, since it links two terms which are introduced conditionally.

[111] Gn. 9:20-27. On the fragmentary character of the story v. H. Gunkel, Gn.⁵ (1922), ad loc. Canaan has done something we are not told (v. 24).

mother (21:17). By making both father and mother the object, the two statements join hands with the commandment, the only material difference being that they refer to a specific offence and prescribe a specific penalty, whereas the commandment is a basic summons with no precise application. The idea behind the commandment is that it is better to inculcate a positive norm of conduct than to threaten crude outbursts of hate and contempt with the direst penalties. The question whether the father is worthy of respect is silenced by the impressive nature of the divine command. When the word is transferred to priests, prophets and officials, an ideal type is set up which must be ready to accept correction. But here "thy father" and "thy mother" are to be honoured. It is God's ordinance that man has a father. Hence this is a good ordinance. Along these lines the OT authors are certain that we find in fatherly dignity a source of the genuine humanity which is born of God. The father motifs are recognised to be one of the strongest safeguards against ethical degeneration. For there is something divine in the father, seeing that there is something fatherly in God. [112]

5. The Myth of the Father of the Gods.

From the standpoint of the history of religion, the word father is interesting in the OT when it is used in speaking to God and about God. If the canonical writings make only comparatively sparing use of this powerful and fruitful motif, this is not surprising, for in Yahweh religion trust in God is expressed less in the language of perception and feeling than in that of thought. It is possible that the concept of the covenant, which proved very adaptable as an intellectual definition of the relation between God and man, worked to the detriment of the father motif, which was alien to it and more closely related to myth. For the father motif is quite independent of the covenant concept. Indeed, it rules it out by describing the relation to Yahweh in its own naïve and much more emotional way.

Israel shares the description of God as Father with its closest neighbours, esp. the Aramaeans and the Semitic group of peoples which before it were partially or totally resident in Palestine. The most important proof of this kinship is to be found in theophorous proper names, among which those containing the element אָב form a considerable percentage. It is not so clear, however, whose father God is supposed to be. To take a simple example, does אֲבִיאֵל "father is 'ēl," mean that 'ēl is the father of the one who bears the name, of his tribe, or even of others, including gods ? We shall speak later of the first possibility, → 969, 18 ff. The last must be ruled out since the one who bears the name is a man and it would hardly be suitable to make a purely mythological statement into a proper name. At most one might think in terms of a father of the tribe, [113] but the larger notion of a father of the gods, which was current among the Sumerians and Babylonians, seems to be out of place in the simple sphere of proper names.

There are, of course, hints of the myth in the language of the OT. The only thing is that the interwoven mythological complex of the father of the gods has been transformed almost beyond recognition, except perhaps at Dt. 32:8 f., and even here the Mas. has been able to conceal the image, so that it reappears only in the LXX reading. The pt. is that the number of the peoples corresponds to the number of the sons of God, so that with the division of the earth, described with legal exactitude as the apportionment of an inheritance, each people is given not only its own precise territory but also its own god, to which it owes service. Acc. to the LXX (v. 9): καὶ ἐγενήθη μερὶς κυρίου ὁ λαὸς αὐτοῦ, one may legitimately ask whether the Most High who gives the peoples and the lands to the gods is identical with Yahweh or whether Yahweh is one of the sons of God, a member of the family which makes up the pantheon. [114] The

---

[112] The basis of honouring parents is sometimes sought in ancestor worship (G. Hölscher, Gesch. d. isr. u. jüd. Religion [1922], 31, n. 5). But the actual statement does not support this, for the concept of honouring is perhaps the latest element in the sentence, and in any case כבד pi, though it can have a special hymnic sense, hardly bears the general meaning "to worship cultically."

[113] Noth, 73; → 969, 32 ff.

[114] Cf. K. Budde, JBL, 40 (1921), 41 f.

exhortation in Dt. 4:19 corrects the ambivalent picture by omitting the idea of a distribution to sons and by clearly showing that Yahweh is the subject of the allocation (חלק) of stars to the nations, cf. also the Mas. of the Song of Moses. [115]

The pagan mythologoumenon of the divine family has left several discernible traces in the canonical Psalter, sometimes with and sometimes without express retention of the figure of the father. In Ps. 82:6 f. we again have the equivocal "sons of the most High"; the ref. is undoubtedly to gods in contrast to men. [116] But again it is hard to say whether Yahweh is the Most High. May it be that the author has in view the same myth as that which the Mas. removed from the Song of Moses? Weaker is the image of the בְּנֵי אֵלִים or בְּנֵי אֱלֹהִים without mention of the father, Ps. 29:1; 89:6 etc. These constitute the chorus of praise which clad in sacred festal raiment sings the hymn for Yahweh, a fellowship of gods but under the supreme rule of Yahweh. In such phrases one may easily see that the word "sons" has only formal significance. As "son of man" denotes an individual man, so "sons of the gods" denotes beings belonging to the divine species, [117] whether gods or demons. The concept of the father has been eliminated. One can interpret along the lines of Ps. 97:7, which is a simplified variation on 29:1: "All gods sink down in worship before him." The sons of the gods are gods.

The mythologoumenon of the father of the gods, which could not be transferred to Yahweh without friction, is thus no more than a stylistic intermezzo, a poetic formulation, which abandons the mythological concept in both the Song of Moses and Ps. 82. Elsewhere in the OT what is said about God as Father refers to His relation to men, and chiefly to His own people, not to other gods.

6. Father and Other Terms of Relationship in the Tribal Religion.

As a preliminary glance at proper names has shown already (→ 965, 31), the concept of God as Father remains even when the motif of the divine family is eliminated. The content of sayings concerning the Father God consists of general human feelings rooted in blood relationship, feelings of trust, respect, or even love for the Head of the race. Nevertheless, Yahweh could be given a place as Father only with some violence in the cultic community made up of the tribal federation, or even in the national religion, since the father-son relationship seems to correspond less to so broadly based a collective sense than to the religious capacity of smaller blood groups. At any rate, the natural community sense of the family, sept or tribe provided a foundation for the increasingly important term father in biblical religion, though the beginnings of metaphorical use are not yet discernible. The thought of the Father God is certainly very old, possibly much older than the amphictyonic cultic order, for the El of Ugarit is already the "father of mankind" in the 14th cent. In Moab, the people of Chemosh, the god had also revealed himself to his sons and daughters as a helping father, Nu. 21:29. The idea had had a place among agricultural and pastoral tribes long before it was applied with reservations to the God of Israel. This must have taken place in the time of J, the narrator of Ex. 4:22, who speaks of all Israel as the firstborn of Yahweh. Perhaps the tradition concerning the beginnings of Yahweh religion gave the word "father" so minor a place because it was strongly freighted with the ancient mythological content of the tribal religions and could thus give rise very easily to erroneous pagan ideas. Only the proper names of confessors of Yahweh like אֲבִיאֵל, אֲבִיָּה etc. show that belief in the Father could not have been so rare in Israel as one might suspect from its mention in historical and poetic texts, where it is essentially restricted to the ideology of kingship. [118]

---

[115] Cf. the echo in Dt. 29:25c.

[116] Attempts to understand the sons of the gods as men are unconvincing in the light of v. 7.

[117] Cf. Ges.-K. § 128 v.

[118] On אב אדם in Ugaritic cf. O. Eissfeldt, 35, 56 f. On Ps. 89:27 f. cf. 2 S. 7:14; Ps. 2:7. For the hymnic motif "father of the fatherless" in Ps. 68:5 an origin in the world of Egypt. officialdom may be assumed, H. Gunkel, Die Ps.[4] (1926), ad loc., → n. 101.

The origin of the designation of the tribal deity as father is to be sought in a specific view of the rise of blood ties. All human life arises by generation. Similarly, the mysterious beginning of the sequence of generations plainly lies in a propagation of the power of life, not by a man, but by a god. On the soil of Israel there are traces of this myth in the tribe of Gad if reality corresponds to appearances and the divine name Gad (cf. Is. 65:11) is related to the designation of the tribe as the sons of Gad (Nu. 1:24). [119] It is possible that a similar explanation is to hand for the tribe of Asher, [120] though the limits of the knowable are closely drawn when it comes to combinations relating to the origin of the patriarchs in the tribal myth. [121] There is certainly no sure ground in the biblical tradition for the intrinsically not wholly improbable idea that ancestor worship is the root and basis of the concept of a god as the father of the tribe and its members. Even if it can be shown that the departed fathers were regarded as divine powers (1 S. 28:13) to whom there was an inclination to offer gifts (Dt. 26:14), and even though the description of the spirits of the dead as אֹבוֹת gives us a remarkably similar word to אָבוֹת ("fathers"), [122] this merely shows that investigation of the origins of belief in the Father takes us back to mere hints of trains of thought which may well be part of the rudimentary sub-structure of the religion of Israel, but which no longer have any organic connection with belief in Yahweh.

This all goes to show that the father concept did not proceed from genuine belief in Yahweh but was imported into it and received by it. To describe God as Father is to emphasise very strongly by means of a biological concept the fact that fellowship with deity is a generative blood relationship. The sense of distance between Creator and creature is hereby notably diminished, for it is simply construed in terms of the legal and social position of the father as the ruler and lord.

All the same, this distance is more strongly safeguarded by the word "father" than by the concept of the deity as "mother," which can be used only as a comparison in Israel, [123] or by analogous terms of relationship (cf. proper names) like אָח "brother," עַם "member of the tribe," דּוֹד "uncle," in which the suspicious familiarity of the terminology is enhanced, at least for non-nomads, by the diminution of the element of authority. It is true, of course, that "father" belongs to the same series, as may be seen from 'Abirām, 'Aḥirām, 'Amrām, (Jehorām), and the question of Israel's use of the term "father" in speaking about deity, and of the corresponding use of the term "son" or "child," cannot be isolated from the total question of the religious employment of terms of relationship. [124] The problem is whether the more or less close blood relationship denoted by these terms was thought of literally as a direct relationship transmitted through the generations and experienced by each individual, or whether it was meant metaphorically and stated only for the sake of its emotional content.

In view of the strong emphasis on motifs of distance in prophetic religion, and of the distinction between the divine and the human which is always plain even in older Yahwism (→ III, 83), there is obviously no pt. in pursuing the first possibility beyond certain clear rudimentary findings. As the idea of brotherhood is not only a sustaining motif in the covenant concept but one of its earliest components (→ II, 115), so the idea of a relationship with deity based on begetting or birth is an element of nature religion preserved in the religious heritage of Israel, and even though it inevitably tends to obscure the distinction between God and man it is found acceptable in the tradition, esp.

---

[119] Cf. R. Kittel, Gesch. d. Volkes Israel, I⁵ (1923), 275 on Gn. 30:11; W. Baudissin, Art. "Gad," RE³, 6, 333, 41 ff.

[120] Kittel, loc. cit.

[121] Cf. esp. E. Meyer, Die Israeliten u. ihre Nachbarstämme (1906), 249-271.

[122] Cf. F. Schwally, Das Leben nach dem Tode (1892), 47; P. Torge, Seelenglaube u. Unsterblichkeitshoffnung im AT (1909), 69.

[123] Cf. Hempel, Gott u. Mensch, 170, n. 2.

[124] It is a mistake to deduce from this material the recognition of different deities or divine families in the same tribal fellowship, Noth, 73-75.

the liturgical tradition. The author of the Song of Moses can with poetic licence speak uninhibitedly and very effectively of the "rock which bare (or begot), thee, the people," and of the "God which brought thee forth in travail" (Dt. 32:18). These atavistic mythologoumena do not make a Baal of the God whom he has speak in this way. [125] Ps. 2:7 can make God speak similarly of the begetting of the king by Him, though here we obviously have a formula [126] which is often found in legal usage both in and outside the Bible, and which must be interpreted as adoption. It might even be asked whether the expression "this day have I borne thee" would not come more suitably from a goddess rather than a god, though this contributes nothing to our total understanding. In Dt. 32:4 the rock motif is quite freely referred to Yahweh, though the prophet Jeremiah sees and says that it is pagan and unworthy of a man who knows Yahweh, 2:27. The harsh dissonance between the idea of a mother goddess in birth pangs [127] and the very definitely masculine concept of the sovereign God in the OT also lends support to the idea that atavistic formulae are adopted.

To what degree, however, these mythical views were current at times even in culturally mature circles may be seen from the fact that Jeremiah finds them amongst priests and prophets as well as nobles, men who say "to a stock, Thou art my father; and to a stone, Thou hast brought me forth" (2:26 f.). The worshippers of Yahweh who speak in this way have a bad conscience, for the God to whom they thus dedicate themselves is very different from the One proclaimed to them as the God of Israel. Even Ezekiel tends to slip here in his polemic against pagan inclinations, for in a broad and barely tolerable variation on the theme of the marriage of Yahweh first introduced by Hosea [128] he has Yahweh beget sons and daughters in the form of the symbolic figures Aholah and Aholibah (23:4, cf. 16:8). Remnants of a myth of ἱερὸς γάμος are also to be found in Ps. 19:5 where the sun comes forth as a bridegroom out of his chamber.

J uses the myth of divine begetting in Gn. 6:4, though the redactor abbreviates considerably. Ps. 90 clearly puts the whole complex in the setting of nature religion when it calls the earth the mother which bears the mountains (v. 2), whereas the Lord is God from everlasting to everlasting. A view which logically corresponds to the thought of mother earth, namely, that God is the father of nature, is ruled out by the simple and for that very reason eloquent emphasis on the deity of God. God, because He is God, does not beget His servants; He is their sovereign Lord. They are His work (v. 16) and may see His kingly glory. His way is not the physical propagation of His kind. It is the creation of things by the Word which establishes reality. [129] Nevertheless the power of this theistic proclamation, which finds further expression in the creation story of P, had to contend against severe obstacles, as may be seen from the fact that the Song of Moses (Dt. 32), which must belong to much the same period as P, can still use the thought of birth from deity as well as creation as a motif in exhortation, and can do so in a way which is effective not only artistically but also religiously.

Vital and genuine though the motifs are, there is every reason to doubt whether it is right to take such statements, or the explicit saying in Dt. 32:6 : "Is not he thy father that hath created thee?" or the ref. to Yahweh's "sons and daughters" in v. 19, as

---

[125] Hempel, op. cit., 173 n.

[126] 2:7 f.. For comparative material cf. Gunkel, 6 f. H. J. Kraus, Die Königsherrschaft Gottes im AT. Beiträge zur historischen Theol., 13 (1951), 69 f. tries to establish a connection between Ps. 2:7 and 2 S. 7.

[127] There is possibly a scattered trace of a thought intrinsic to this myth in Nu. 11:12 (J); Moses asks Yahweh : "Have I conceived this people, have I borne it?" On the other hand, there is no mythical basis for Is. 45:10 : "Since a man says to a father, What begettest thou? or to a woman, What dost thou bring forth?" for it is not God Himself who makes the accusation of v. 9 f. On this whole problem cf. A. Bertholet, Das Geschlecht der Gottheit (1934), 15.

[128] Hos. 3:3 seems to be abbreviated, cf. J. Wellhausen, Skizzen u. Vorarbeiten, 5 (1893), 102.

[129] Ps. 33:9. In Job 38:4-8, too, one may see the contrast between the founder of the earth and the earth as mother.

illustrations of belief in a blood relationship between the people of Yahweh and their Father. [130] In their desire for a wealth of living colour the poets and prophets of Yahweh make use of their mythical heritage, but their only purpose is to depict the reality of fellowship with God as vividly as possible.

7. Father as a Theophorous Element in the Proper Names of Israel.

Ancient and fairly common proper names — at least in early times and possibly in the whole pre-exilic period — force us to take more seriously the basic vitality of motifs proper to nature and tribal religions even in the community of Yahweh.

A name like יוֹאָב, or in the reverse form אֲבִיָּה, is a nominal statement: "Yahweh is Father," or, with a simple alteration in emphasis: "Father is Yahweh." There is an exact equivalent in the Samar. ostraka of the 8th century, namely, אבבעל: "Father is Baal." More central is the biblical אֱלִיאָב or אֲבִיאֵל or אֲבִיָּה: "God is Father." The assertion is so objective that it makes no difference whether the bearer of the name is a man (1 S. 8:2) or a woman (2 Ch. 29:1). At issue is a confession whereby the bearer of the name acknowledges the fatherhood of Yahweh, Baal, or some other god who can be described as father. Names like אֲבִירָם, אֲבִינָדָב etc. are thus theophorous. So, too, are אֲחִיָּהוּ and other names formed with אָח: אֲחִירָם, אֲחִיקָם etc. [131]

The confession is to be regarded personally as that of the son when there is a 1st person pronominal suffix as in אֲבִיָּה or אֲבִיאֵל. "My Father is Yahweh." [132] Nevertheless, when names with אָב and אָח apply to one and the same person in both forms, [133] with and without ī, e.g., אֲבִישָׁלוֹם or אַבְשָׁלוֹם, אֲבִינֵר or אַבְנֵר, one may conjecture that the ī is of no gt. significance and can hardly be a pronominal suffix. Since in these instances it also cannot serve to indicate, as often elsewhere, [134] a st. c., because this would give an impossible sense, we can only regard it as analogous to a secondary syllable which has phonetic but no grammatical significance. The idea of a case ending [135] creates difficulties, since ī would suggest the gen. Again, ḥireq compaginis, [136] with a few doubtful exceptions, [137] is usually reserved for the st. c., and furthermore it is in most cases emphasised.

But in spite of the grammatical uncertainty and the general nature of a form without the difficult ī like יוֹאָב: "Father (abs.) is Yahweh," the confession contained in the name has still to be taken as personal. The person thus named lets it be known that Yahweh is his father. [138] The only pt. is that indifference as to the form of the statement leads to the question previously mentioned (→ 967, 1 ff.) whether kinship is a natural basis for the development of the father concept in religion, and it allows us to conclude with some degree of probability that there is a collective sense in such names: a feeling of relationship to blood brothers in the father's house gives rise to the confession that God as Head of the blood fellowship is Father to each member of the union. Similarly, in the case of אֲחִיָּהוּ etc. God is a member of the tribe. [139] The name is thus no less a confession of blood relationship than of the God who creates, protects and blesses.

---

[130] Even the ref. to the sons and daughters of the Moabite god Chemosh in the old song in Nu. 21:29 is not clear enough. On Mal. 2:10 → 973, 7 ff. and I, 34, 39 ff.

[131] Noth, 69 f.

[132] So E. König, Hbr. u. aram. Wörterbuch z. AT [6, 7] (1936), 1; H. Bauer-P. Leander, Historische Grammatik d. hbr. Sprache (1922), § 65g. For a basic discussion of ī between nominal elements cf. Noth, 33-36.

[133] In 1 S. 25:18 אבוגיל ī is put in only by qerē.

[134] E.g., in עַבְדִּיאֵל: "servant of God."

[135] Noth, 35.

[136] Baudissin, Kyrios, III, 353 f.

[137] Ges.-K. § 90 n.

[138] The pt. made by Smith (28) that the individual Israelite had no right to regard himself as a son of Yahweh needs to be stated less sharply in view of this possibility.

[139] → 967, 27 ff. and Noth, 75.

8. Father as a Metaphor.

Though it may well be true that God is genealogically related to the tribe along the lines of nature myth, e.g., in refs. to the God who bears or begets (→ 968, 1 ff., 24), nevertheless the centre of constructive belief is hardly to be sought in such complexes. Mythology, however naïve and simple, is theoretically expounded religion, and cannot give rise to piety. In Israel an image of God which was not much more than a heightened image of man was always contested. Hence, when the term father occurs, it is fundamentally applied to God only in a metaphorical sense, and if we are to understand it everything depends on finding the right point of comparison.

For the Hebrews with their strong sense of family "father" is a distinctly ethical term which had had to prove itself in the sphere of law and justice and which in virtue of its rich content could be used to describe a relation of authority even when the reference was to God. It was never recognised as adequate, however, to describe the nature of God or the manner of His relationship to man. When thought of or used in this way, it always found opponents who instinctively felt that this would lead back to worship of the ancient gods which had been abolished from the days of Joshua (Jos. 24:23). Along with this concern lest there should be relapse into outmodel religious forms the term "God of the fathers" (→ 961, 27 ff.), which had been used emphatically from primitive times, effectively prevents the wild spread of the father concept in the field of biological consciousness by very obviously giving the pre-eminence to God. It is worth noting that the name "sons of Yahweh" occurs only once in this solemn form (Dt. 14:1). It could not establish itself; the people came to be called the children of Israel. Only in the last days, says Hosea, "shall it be said unto them, Ye are the sons of the living God" (1:10).

Necessary though it is to take the metaphor literally and therefore mythologically if we are to understand the hesitation of the OT to use this phrase, one cannot really do adequate justice to the traditional material along these lines. Proclamation of Yahweh as God of the people and as God generally did not take over the intrinsically unclear and disputable appellation "father" without adjusting and modifying it by bringing out the true and constructive point of comparison. Men spoke of Yahweh as of a father, and in the Hellenistic period they spoke to Him as though to a father, Sir. 23:1, → 971, 44 ff. The *tertium comparationis* was found in the sociological significance of the father as an unconditionally recognised and trustworthy authority and, from the father's standpoint, in his inner attitude to his household. "Like as a father pitieth his children, so Yahweh pitieth them that fear him," says Ps. 103:13. As a father corrects his beloved son, so God brings up those whom He chastises, Prv. 3:12; Dt. 8:5. Much stronger than these pedagogic utterances are the words of Is. 1:2 f., where God Himself is speaking to the readers. [140] Full of sorrow, the Father complains to the court of dumb nature because He has been rejected by the children whom He raised up with love. The point of comparison between God and the father is nowhere more tenderly revealed than in this outburst of bottled up feelings which seek fellowship but do not find it. The prophet is expressing the fact that, even though the word is not used, love is the basic feeling in God's dealings with Israel. Hosea, in a statement of great pregnancy, introduces the same theme when God elegiacally recalls the youth of Israel, His son, 11:1; → n. 145. Even in the ideology of kingship, for all its political structure (→ n. 126), the element of love is present when the word "son" is used. The author of Ps. 27 in his personal distress borrows from this the

---

[140] Jer. 4:22, which is almost too innocuous as compared with Is., is perhaps modelled on this poem.

concept of adoption (v. 10, → 974, 3 f.), and in 2 S. 7:14 f., though not in Chronicles, God's relation to the king is stated as follows: "I will be his father"; His position is the same as if He were a physical father. If we have here the mythologoumenon which is so graphically expressed in Ps. 2:7: "This day have I begotten thee," and which is then strongly spiritualised and reduced to a simple figurative core of meaning in Ps. 89: "He shall cry unto me, Thou art my father," other statements which are not expressly put in the form of comparisons must be construed in the same way. In fact most of the material serves only to set forth the greatness and loving concern of God.

9. Father as a Concept of Authority.

From the official and semi-official secular mode of expression one may indirectly draw the conclusion that predominantly, and sometimes even exclusively, Israel regarded the father relationship as one of authority. At any rate, it is noticeable that the emotional relationship of the son to the father is expressed with far greater restraint than the delight of the father in the son. [141] This applies to sayings from very different ages and situations. The tone is set by the commandment that the son should honour the father (→ 964, 26 ff.), and a definite limit is set by the respect which must always be shown to the father, Ex. 20:12; Dt. 5:16; Gn. 37:10. Rebellion against one's father is a capital crime, Dt. 21:18, 21, → 963, 29 ff., and to treat one's father with mockery merits cursing (Gn. 27:12) and an unworthy end (Prv. 30:17). The formula of subjection in the embassy of Ahaz to Tiglathpileser (2 K. 16:7) is eloquent: "I am thy servant and thy son," as though the two words were synonymous.

In all this the basic chord is struck which may be heard in all statements concerning the filial relation of Israel to God. [142] These may even serve on occasion to impress on men the duty to obey by reminding them of God's free and unrestricted sovereignty. This is certainly in view in Dt. 14:1: "You are the children of Yahweh, your God," which serves to introduce legal regulations, and which is at once interpreted in terms of the election by which God's act of will has made this people His possession. A later prophet makes the same point even more forcefully when he takes up the great saying of Jer. 18:6 f.: "As the clay is in the potter's hand, so are ye in mine hand," which sharply expresses the fact of passive dependence on the divine will, and, not without some wresting of the father motif, enlarges it: "Thou, Yahweh, art our father; we are the clay, and thou art our potter; and we are all the work of thy hand," Is. 64:8. The point of the mixed metaphor is not creation or providence but the power of the educator who fashions imperfect men as though they were a shapeless mass upon whom even the slightest touch can make an impress. It is foolish, the metaphor teaches, to resist the formative grip of God. It is just as foolish and frivolous as to ask one's father: "Why didst thou beget me?" (Is. 45:9 f.). Even if God is not mentioned in this question to the father, He is there between the lines, for in v. 11 Yahweh says: "Would you command me concerning the work of my hands?" All this goes to show how natural it was for the individualistic piety of the Jewish age to adopt the ruler motif in interpretation of the father motif. An address like that of the prayer of

---

[141] That petitioners used the address: "My father," cannot be deduced from אָבִי in Job 34:36. אָבִי was never a particle of wishing with its own root.

[142] On the rather different content of the mother metaphor (Is. 49:15; 66:13) cf. Hempel, *Gott u. Mensch*, 185, n. 1.

Sir. 23:1: κύριε, πάτερ καὶ δέσποτα ζωῆς μου, [143] may be regarded as in its own way a mature exposition of the OT belief in the Father, since love leads to respect.

10. The Trend Towards Universality in the Designation of God as Father.

As one might gather from the instances already given, the word "father" can serve to express God's greatness and power even when the reference is to the creation of the world. The theological value of such statements is that they provide a logical presupposition for extension of the father concept beyond the confines of national religion, though this does not prove that in each instance the author himself made this extension. The Song of Moses may again be cited in this connection, though its crude mythological colouring and passionate nationalism would not lead one to expect this theme : "Thou foolish and unwise people," asks Dt. 32:6, "is he not thy father who hath created thee, he who hath made and established thee ?" The father concept is couched in national terms, but the creation which is brought into the closest relation to it is not thought of as begetting along the lines of the old tribal religion, as in, e.g., v. 18. For the key words קנה, עשׂה and כונן do not belong to the complex of ideas whose core is the word "father" biologically understood. On the contrary, they presuppose as subject the God who works in cosmic miracle and who fashions as an architect. They are the same words as those normally used in statements about the creation of the world. If we are told that "Yahweh, the father, has created the people" (cf. also v. 15c), does this mean, then, that He created only the people ? This question is undoubtedly too doctrinaire. Nevertheless, the first note of the whole poem : "Hear, ye heavens," leads us to Is. 1:2 as a model, where the same distinctive summons introduces God's complaint about His children who, devoid of the natural instinct with which even animals are endowed, set themselves against their Father. "They" (וְהֵם), i.e., Israel, have done this. Are they alone God's children ? For Isaiah a question of this kind hardly arises within the sphere of the father concept, though he does speak about "strangers" in the poem which follows immediately, 1:7. Jeremiah is the first to think of raising this particular question. It is true that even here the relevant statement (3:19) [144] may be taken as a purely figurative formula which does not have the breadth suggested by the context. Nevertheless, the breadth is apparent.

Israel is portrayed as the wife or daughter [145] of Yahweh. God says to her : "Among the [146] children will I put thee, and give thee a goodly land as a heritage. Then thou shalt [147] call me 'my father' in thanksgiving and love." The saying refers to the rise of nationhood and the transition to a settled state. Logically Jer. is thus thinking of children apart from Israel, of sons with a hereditary title, i.e., nations already settled in their territories. [148] Yahweh will now give His daughter a title among these sons, and "put

---

[143] We do not have the original. The variation κύριε, πάτερ καὶ θεὲ ζωῆς μου occurs in v. 4.

[144] W. Rudolph, Jer. = Hndbch. z. AT, I, 12 (1947), ad loc. interprets 3:19 in the light of 32:27: "I, Yahweh, am the God of all flesh."

[145] There is no fixed figure ; Israel is sometimes portrayed as a daughter and sometimes as a son (Hos. 11:1).

[146] For some unknown reason the art. has been questioned from the time of F. Hitzig, Jer.² (1866), ad loc.

[147] In spite of difficulties the ketib "you will" is perhaps to be preferred (God addressing mankind).

[148] So LXX B, which is undoubtedly right. Even if בָּנִים is doubted, which is unnecessary, אָבִי in v. 19c shows that God's fatherly sentiment is the basic thought in 3:19.

her among the children." [149] One is tempted to relate this saying to that about Israel as Yahweh's firstborn, which in Ex. 4:22 and Jer. 31:9 denotes the election, for fundamentally it is meaningful to speak of the firstborn only when there are other children or when others may be expected. To make an inference from the logical connection between the two groups of sayings is justifiable in the light of the mode of expression, which in both instances is drawn from the sphere of family law. [150] Materially, however, the connection is too evidently accidental to serve as an impregnable exegetical foundation. Similarly, Mal. 2:10 will serve only if the questions : "Have we not all one father ? Hath not one God created us ?" vary in form alone and not also in theme. On stylistic grounds, however, it is hardly likely that Abraham or Jacob [151] is first meant as father and then God as Creator. Hence we must accept the view that in trying to stir the divided community to moral action parallel to the message of creation, the prophet sets before his people the unity of men as children of one divine Father, so that the form used is that of the rhetorical question.

In general, then, it is reserved for a living divine unrest to bring out clearly the true motif in the national father concept, namely, the paternal feeling embodied in God's person, → I, 30 ff. The urgency of such statements increases under the pressure of the harsh destiny of the nation. "Generation of thy children" is such a phrase in time of crisis (Ps. 73:15). In his prayer the author coins it for the living and the dead who have proved themselves under the assault of affliction and distress. There is a certain echo of this in the liturgy in Jer. 3 (v. 22): "Return, ye backsliding children," cries God, "and I will heal your backslidings," and they answer Him : "Yes, we come unto thee ; for thou, Lord, art our God." Though the word "father" is not used, those who return confess God as Father, and in the later poem in Jer. 31:18-20, where the sons of Ephraim are now the son, one may clearly perceive the original of the parable of the prodigal, → 994, 7 ff. [152] Ephraim comes back home out of affliction, full of shame and remorse : "Cause me to turn, and I shall turn ; for thou art the Lord, my God." It is again striking that he does not say "my Father," as though the author were afraid of the word. [153] But the Father's heart is moved, there is no place for doubt : "I must have mercy upon him." Hosea, who is perhaps to be regarded as the inspirer of these sayings, states in this connection the classical basis of the Father's love (→ I, 32, 9 ff.): "For I am God, and not man," 11:9. Tt. Is., who belonged to a heavily embattled generation of believers, was also prepared, on the basis of the saying that Ephraim is God's dear child, to raise in prayer the urgent question : "Where is thy zealous love, thy heart's beat ?" (cf. Jer. 31:20), though he then goes on to invoke God with the confession : "But thou art our father." He is conscious of the full greatness of the divine fatherhood. The fathers after the flesh, Abraham and Israel, are not redeemers who bring saving help. Father is a name which in truth belongs from the very first to God alone, Is. 63:15 f.

---

[149] "To set someone among others" is to give him rights which they already have, cf. 2 S. 19:29. The equality of the daughters of Job with his sons is mentioned in Job 42:15 to show how affluent he was.

[150] Jer. 31:9 : "I am a father to Israel," also reminds us of kingship.

[151] Cf. F. Horst in T. H. Robinson-F. Horst, *Die 12 kleinen Propheten = Hndbch. z. AT,* I, 14 (1938), *ad loc.* One can hardly speak of the oneness of Jacob, however, and then suddenly mention the "covenant of our fathers" in a third question based on the answer to the first two. There were at least three fathers.

[152] In opposition to Rudolph's attempted differentiation (167) it should be noted that Jn. 3:16 is based no more and no less than Jer. 31:18-20 on the belief in election.

[153] Is. 66:13 uses the analogous image of the mother, which is perhaps more suitable pastorally : "As a man's mother comforts him, so will I comfort you."

It is no big step from national motifs to personal and universal concerns. Nevertheless, in the individual songs of complaint in the canonical Psalter we do not find the address "father" — the same reserve as noted in the liturgy of Jer. 31:18-20. Yahweh is, however, given the ancient title "father of the fatherless" in Ps. 68:5 (→ n. 118), so that when God is called "father" it is realised that this means far more than the analogy of human experience can of itself suggest. "My father and my mother have forsaken me, but Yahweh takes me up" (Ps. 27:10) [154] is the strongest expression of this motif of comfort. The adoption is adoption to sonship as in Ps. 2:7. In post-canonical psalms the theme lives on, though in barely recognisable form, in the prayer "from the very gates of hell" when one who is condemned to die goes far beyond mere reminiscence of Ps. 89:26 and calls upon God: "Yahweh, thou my father, [155] my God and hero, who helps me," Sir. 51:10. Here at least reserve is conquered. In this spontaneous declaration of trust in God's person the confession of God as Father, which developed from so small a root, serves now to express the supreme insight of biblical faith.

Quell

C. The Father Concept in Later Judaism.

I. The Earthly Father.

1. Piety towards the Father.

The Rabb. paid considerable attention to the fact that in the Decalogue honouring the father comes before honouring the mother (→ 964, 27 ff.), but then the order is reversed in Lv. 19:3 (cf. 21:2). Philo Spec. Leg., II, 293 ff. follows the LXX here; [156] influenced by the dominant *patria potestas* it changed the order. Philo thus champions a strongly patriarchal view, being also influenced to some degree by Gk. law. On the other hand M. Ex. 20:12 (77b); Ker., 6, 9, cf. S. Lv. on 19:3 (343a) [157] try to explain the OT order, instructively playing it down on the ground that while both parents are worthy of honour, the mother also owes respect to the father. [158] In one case she can come first because she gives the child good advice. A man should honour his father more, however, because it is his father who teaches him the Torah. In later Judaism the injunction to honour parents is an important head of instruction, Sir. 7:27; 23:14; Tob. 4:3-5; Ep. Ar., 238; Menander Prv., 16, 34 f. If Sir. 30:1-13, cf. 41:17 treats of the responsibility of paternal instruction in a way which shows how severe and non-pampering it was, there is in comparison, esp. in Hell. Judaism, an unmistakable difference in emotional expression. In Joseph. one finds the glorification of parents and a tendency towards the eudaemonistic, sentimental and affectedly ethical. [159] In Jub. and Test. XII there is much greater tenderness. [160] The Synagogue, with its liking for codification of duties, lays

---

[154] It is hard to see any real relationship of motif between this saying and the innocuous statements from El Amarna letters quoted in Jirku, *op. cit.*, 225.

[155] The LXX πατέρα κυρίου μου is a highly singular expression perhaps based on Ps. 110:1

[156] So also Pesh. and Vg.

[157] Str.-B., I, 706.

[158] Acc. to Philo Quaest. in Gn., I, 27 on Gn. 2:22 the wife must honour her husband as a father.

[159] In Jos. Ant., 1, 229 the brave Isaac is most unnatural in the way he acts towards his father prior to his offering up. Cf. also 1, 233 and 266 (diplomatic); 1, 272 and 281 (eudaemonistic); 1, 280 (glorification of the father); 2, 148 ff. (wordy and moralistic).

[160] Jub. 22:26: The relations of the patriarchs cannot be regarded as too close; Jacob sleeps with his grandfather, hence an exact transmission of injunctions. 35:6 Rebekah's judgment on the perfect Jacob. Cf. also 31:8; Test. N. 7; Test. B. 3 Jacob kisses Joseph; Test. Abr. 6:1-3; Test. Isaac 3:5 f.; 9:4 ff.; Joseph and Asenath 22:9, though cf. 12:8. Comparison with expressions of paternal love in ancient Greece (e.g., Hom. Il., 1, 98: Chryses) is instructive; things are much more restrained there.

down minute rules for honouring the father, Qid., 31b, 32a, Bar. [161] It should be noted that the son is not to contradict his father openly, nor should he censure even transgression of the Law by his father. [162] The Synagogue took it that the fifth commandment demanded that grown-up sons should care for their aged parents, and not merely that small children must respect their parents. [163]

2. Parents as Instruments and Representatives of God.

The subtle Rabb. discussions whether the fifth commandment is severe (jPea, 1, 15d, 13) [164] are less important than the preceding and far more profound question whether honouring God takes precedence. On a consistently monotheistic view it would seem that the answer is simple, [165] Jeb., 5b, Bar., cf. also Menander Prv. 4; Sib., III, 594; Ps.-Phocylides, V, 8; Jos. Ap., II, 206; Philo Spec. Leg., II, 235. Nevertheless, there is danger in the view of Pea, 1, 1 that study of the Torah counts more than honouring parents, and that the teacher takes precedence of the father. [166] In an echo of popular Stoicism there is also in Rabb. sources a kind of equation of parents with God inasmuch as parents can be called God's partners in reproduction, S. Lv., 19, 2; T. Qid., 30b; Gn. r., 8, 9. Philo, too, calls parents instruments of divine generation, Rer. Div. Her., 171. [167] The connection between divine and earthly fatherhood means that God counts honour paid to parents as honour given to Him, while He avenges offences against parents as offences against Himself, Qid., 30b, Bar.; Jos. Bell., 3, 375; Ant., 4, 262. [168]

3. The Duties of the Father.

Among the obvious paternal duties of provision as enumerated by the Rabb. [169] one of the most important to which pre-eminence is given is that the father should instruct his son in the Torah, cf. Jub. 8:2; 11:16. This gives a deeper significance to the phrase "God of the father." Acc. to Jub. 12:1-7 there is a religious discussion between Terah and his son Abraham, idolatry being one of the subjects. It is always the father who imparts religious instruction. On the father as educator → παιδεύω, 613, 17 ff. Submissive children imitate their parents acc. to Philo Sacr. AC, 68. As to the limits of parental authority, there is consensus that immoral precepts are not to be obeyed, S. Lv., 19, 3, cf. Philo Spec. Leg., II, 236. [170] On punishment by parents → 613, 22 ff.; 614, 21 ff. If the Rabb. weakened Dt. 21:18 ff. by provisos (e.g., Sanh., 71 bBar.), [171] in Jos. (Ant., 4, 260-264; 3, 311) and Philo (Spec. Leg., II, 224-262) parental authority is enhanced as compared with the Torah and the Synagogue; this is due to the influence of Roman law, cf. Leg. Gaj., 28. Even in relation to the OT penalties prescribed for those who dishonour their parents by curses or blows (Ex. 21:15; Lv. 20:9, → 964, 18 ff.), later Synagogue exposition gives evidence of humane softening, whereas Jos. and Philo make the patria potestas even more severe. [172]

---

161 Str.-B., I, 709.
162 Par.: Plut. De Vitioso Pudore, 15 (II, 534d-e) Agesilaos and his father.
163 Cf. J. Jeremias, Die Pastoralbriefe, NT Deutsch on 1 Tm. 1:9.
164 Str.-B., I, 705, 902, cf. 903.
165 Sanskr. par.: The first commandment is to honour the gods, the second to honour parents, Leist, I, 183.
166 Cf. BM, 2, 11; Hor., 13a, Bar. (Str.-B., I, 587).
167 Cf. Moore, II, 132; Goodenough, Jurisprudence, 67, 128; Heinemann, 254.
168 On God and the earthly father cf. also Jos. Ant., 2, 152; 1, 232.
169 Nu. r., 17, cf. T. Qid., 1, 11 (336), Str.-B., I, 394; Qid., 29b Bar., ibid., I, 778.
170 In later Stoicism Muson., XVI (Hense): "Whether unrestricted obedience is owed to parents."
171 Cf. D. Hoffmann, Midrasch Tannaim zum Dt. II (1909), 10; M. Guttmann, Eine Untersuchung über den Geltungsumfang d. mosaischen Gebote. Wissenschaftliche Beilage z. Jahresbericht d. jüd. Seminars (1931), 25.
172 Cf. Sanh., 7, 8 (Str.-B., I, 709 on Mt. 15:4); Sanh., 11, 1 (ibid., I, 710); M. Ex. on 21:17 (88a), though cf. Jos. Ap., II, 206; Philo Spec. Leg., II, 243.

II. The Fathers in Judaism. [173]

1. The Concept.

The meaning is not always explicitly "patriarchs," though this sense predominates. Fathers may be a. simply earlier generations, Israel's forefathers. [174] In the sequence of generations emphasis often falls b. on the Israel which was tested in Egypt or brought out thence, or the people of the wilderness age, which is singled out as the generation which experienced the decisive divine redemption. [175] c. The term can also include all the outstanding men of God in Scripture and right up to the present time. [176] d. The first in this long series, however, are the patriarchs Abraham, Isaac and Jacob, [177] to whom the title is given in a special sense. In Judaism this is the most solemn and yet also an incredibly overworked sense. The patriarchs are also called "fathers of the world." [178] Among the three patriarchs Abraham is regarded as the father in the full and supreme sense. He is the father of fathers, [179] the "great one of the world." [180] Usually the Synagogue says: "our father Abraham." [181] The expression occurs countless times in all traditions and in every age. [182] But even without "our," Abraham is the father; the title becomes part of his name. [183] Acc. to Gn. 17:4 he is also the father of nations. [184] Compared with him Isaac as a patriarch is much less prominent. [185] On the other hand, Jacob or Israel appears as father on innumerable occasions. [186]

---

[173] Cf. Alt, *Gott d. Väter.*

[174] 1 'Εσδρ. 1:12; 4:60; very common in Jos.: Ant., 4, 143; 7, 342 etc. λατρεία πατέρων, 1 Macc. 2:19; MSS of the fathers, Slav. En. 33:12; 35:2; Jos. Ant., 11, 24 (βιβλία). In the NT: Mt. 23:30, 32; Lk. 6:23, 26; 11:47 f.; Ac. 5:30; 13:36; 15:10; 28:25; Hb. 1:1. The Samaritan forefathers, Jn. 4:20. The Christian fathers, understood spiritually, 2 Pt. 3:4.

[175] Ab., 5, 4; Jeb., 46a Bar. (Str.-B., I, 106); LXX Bar. 1:19 f.; 1 Macc. 4:9 f.; 4 Esr. 14:29. Jos. Ap., I, 232, 280; Bell., 5, 382 ff. In the NT: The fathers in Egypt, Ac. 7:19; 13:17; Hb. 8:9. The wilderness generation: Jn. 6:31, 49, 58; Ac. 7:38 f., 44 f.; 1 C. 10:1; Hb. 3:9. In Stephen's address there is alternation between "our fathers" (Ac. 7:44 f.) and "your fathers" (7:51 f.). The latter are the gainsayers.

[176] In the hymn in Sir. 44:1-50:26 the πατέρες extend from Enoch (but cf. also Adam, Shem and Seth in 49:16) to the high-priest Simon. Cf. Derekh Erez zuta, 1 (Str.-B., II, 26), where Moses, Phinehas and David are mentioned after the patriarchs. In 4 Macc. 13:17 we find καὶ πάντες οἱ πατέρες after the patriarchs. The idea of all the righteous of the OT is common when the formula is used in the post-apost. fathers and Apologists, Barn., 5, 7; 14, 1; 1 Cl., 62, 2; 2 Cl., 19, 4; Just. Dial., 57, 2; 67, 8; 136, 3 etc.

[177] On d. cf. Str.-B., I, 918. Cf. in Jewish Hell. writings Bar. 2:34; Test. L. 15:4; Jos. Ant., 11, 169; Test. Isaac 1:6. If acc. to Ber., 16b Bar. there are strictly only three fathers, this is a later restriction which is not adhered to.

[178] Pesikt. r., 37 (162b) (Str.-B., II, 289). For further examples cf. Str.-B., I, 284, 918; II, 335. In general, *ibid.,* I, 918. In Wis. 10:1 Adam is called the father of the world, which is logical but does not accord with the thinking of Israel. In the NT τοὺς πατέρας ἡμῶν in Lk. 1:55 means Abraham and his seed, cf. 1:72. Jn. 7:22 and Ac. 3:25 also have Abraham in view. For the 3 patriarchs cf. Ac. 3:13; 7:32. Paul, too, speaks of the patriarchs in R. 9:5; 11:28, though his ref. is always to Abraham. The promise to the fathers: Ac. 13:32; 26:6; R. 15:8; Barn., 5, 7. διαθήκη πατέρων: 1 Macc. 2:20; Ass. Mos. 11:17.

[179] Test. Isaac 10:9 f.

[180] S. Dt. § 38 on 11:10 (77a) (Str.-B., I, 516).

[181] Ab., 5, 2, 3, 22; Jochanan b. Zakkai (d. 80) in Chag. 14b (Str.-B., I, 664); also T. Chag., 2, 1 (234) (Str.-B., I, 189). Further examples, Str.-B., I, 116.

[182] In Hell. Judaism: 4 Macc. 16:20; 4 Esr. 2:6; 3:10; Test. N. Heb. 8:3; Jos. Ant., 1, 158. In the NT: Lk. 1:73; Ac. 7:2; Jm. 2:21; cf. later 1 Cl., 31, 2.

[183] 4 Macc. 17:6; Jos. Ant., 1, 222, 242, 346. Jos. interprets the term for his readers in Ant., 14, 225; Bell., 5, 380; Ant., 8, 155. Just. Dial., 100, 3. In the NT: Proud boasting of the fathers Mt. 3:8 f.; Lk. 3:8. The rich man in the afterworld cries: "Father Abraham," Lk. 16:24, 30, cf. 27. On "Abraham's bosom," in v. 22 cf. Str.-B., II, 225 and I, 119. 4 Macc. 5:37 cf. 13:17; 18:23: the fathers receive the martyrs to themselves.

[184] Sir. 44:19; Jub. 15:6 f.; Jos. Ant., 1, 193; Just. Dial., 11, 5.

[185] R. 9:10, cf. jBer., 4, 7a, 50 (Str.-B., II, 699 f.); 4 Macc. 16:20.

[186] Gn. r., 78 (50c) (Str.-B., I, 84). In the NT: Jn. 4:12. Then 1 Cl., 4, 8; Just. Apol., 32, 14; the sons of Jacob as πατέρες, Ac. 7:11 f., 15.

2. The Importance of the Fathers for the Jews.

The use of fathers for ancestors, found also in the Gk. world, takes on unique significance in Judaism. The fathers are the rock whence the Israelites are hewn. [187] For the Synagogue they embody the principle of tradition acc. to the classical exhortation in Sir. 8:9. Pharisaism busies itself with the παράδοσις τῶν πατέρων. [188] This view gives rise to formulations like : "we have a tradition from our fathers." Moreover, the fathers guarantee the grace of the divine covenant. To them above all peoples the Lord gave the Law. [189] As Yahweh recalls His mercies to the fathers [190] He is and remains the God of the people. The merits of the fathers, mediated by physical descent, lead the people. Israel relies upon them. [191] They blot out the sins of those who come after [192] and bring pardon in the judgment. [193] Acc. to popular belief their intercession is always successful, [194] for their own prayers were effectual and their works beyond compare. [195] Hence invocation of the God of the fathers is in liturgical prayer a characteristic expression of this religion of the fathers. Here we find the constantly recurring form : "Yahweh, our God and the God of our fathers," or, less frequently : "My God and the God of my fathers." [196] This liturgical invocation found an echo in Jewish Hell. writings too, [197] and the use of the formula elsewhere was influenced by the liturgical practice.

III. Father as a Title for the Teacher.

"Father" is a general title of honour. [198] It is used esp. for the rabbi. This use of אָב, det. אַבָּא, bears no relation to the "fathers of the people Israel" (→ 976, 1 ff.) but is a title of esteem. The use of the word for, e.g., the prophet is an OT model, → 963, 2 ff. The πατέρων ὕμνος in Sir. 44-50 also contains the name of the high-priest Simon (→ n. 176). If occasionally Shammai, Hillel, R. Jishmael and Akiba are called "fathers of the world," [199] this is an exaggerated glorification. [200] The title of the tractate Abot simply implies that the general title of honour is given esp. to the respected teacher, unless Pirke Abot means principal sayings. The word does not occur in this sense as an address אֲבִי Aram. אַבָּא. [201] The title, closely linked with the name of the teacher, is given to many. [202] In 4 Macc. 7:1, 5, 9 Eleazar is called "father" as an example of

---

[187] Ex. r., 15 (76c) (Str.-B., I, 733).

[188] Jos. Ant., 13, 297. Cf. Slav. En. 52:9 f.: principles, commands and decisions of the fathers.

[189] S. Bar. 77:3, cf. 84:9.

[190] Prayer of 18 Petitions, 1, Babylonian rec.

[191] Cf. Str.-B., I, 119; Tg. J. II on Nu. 23:9 (Str.-B., I, 29 f.); Lv. r., 36 (133b); Ex. r., 44 (99d) (Str.-B., I, 117). Cf. also Str.-B., II, 278.

[192] Jos. Ant., 8, 278; Midr. Cant. on 1:5 (87b) (Str.-B., I, 118).

[193] Pesikt., 153b; Lv. r., 29 (127b) (Str.-B., I, 118).

[194] Slav. En. 53:1; S. Bar. 85:12 f.

[195] Jos. Ant., 6, 89; Bell., 5, 377.

[196] Of several examples Ab., 5, 20 jBer., 4, 7d, 28 (Str.-B., I, 741); ibid., 4, 8b, 22 (Str.-B., II, 54); jJoma, 5, 42c, 7 (Str.-B., II, 694). Cf. the eulogy of R. Akiba after the Hallel associated with the 2nd cup : Pes., 10, 6. 1st Benediction in the Prayer of 18 Petitions, Pal. rec.: "Extolled be thou, Yahweh, our God and the God of our fathers ... our shield and the shield of our fathers"; ibid., 17, the thanksgiving.

[197] 1 Ἐσδρ. 4:62; Tob. 8:5; Wis. 9:1; 3 Macc. 7:16; 4 Macc. 12:17; in the NT esp. Ac.: 3:13; 5:30; 7:32; 22:14.

[198] → 948, 23. In 2 Macc. 14:37 a person kindly disposed to the people is called a "father of the Jews." Cf. Jos. Ant., 17, 45 : πατὴρ καὶ εὐεργέτης (the king). Polycarp is later called by the crowd ὁ πατὴρ τῶν Χριστιανῶν, Mart. Pol., 12, 2.

[199] Ed., 1, 4; cf. Str.-B., I, 918.

[200] Cf. bBer., 16b → n. 177.

[201] Str.-B., I, 919.

[202] For examples ibid., I, 287, cf. 919.

glorious endurance in martyrdom for correct observance of the Law. The form of speech is not distinctively Jewish. [203]

IV. God as Father in Judaism. [204]

Even in Judaism prior to Jesus, in the 2nd and 1st centuries B.C., it is apparent (→ n. 209, 210) that God is commonly addressed as Father, not merely in the collective but also in the individual sense. That Hellenistic culture contributed to the strengthening of this concept in Judaism is not surprising when one considers the great influence of Plato's Timaeus as this may be seen also in Justin. The only difference, as remains to be shown, is that in Palestine the accent is not cosmic and genealogical (as in Philo) but theocratic and national. [205] If from the end of the 1st century A.D. the religious use of "Father" becomes more common in the Synagogue, this seems to be even more true from the 2nd century to the 4th. Modern Jewish liturgies reflect this influence. In this respect there may well be mutual interaction between Judaism and Christianity. The question which had the greater right to the use necessarily arises, especially as primitive Christianity filled the word with new content.

1. Distinction from Greek Cosmology.

a. Not the Begetter of the World, but the Protector of the National Community.

The most important difference as compared with the Gk. world and antiquity generally is that the true Jew orientated to the OT does not speak of the "father of the world"; when he uses the term "Father" he has in view the relation of God to the covenant people. This is a wholly personal relationship to the national community and its individual members. [206] Of OT sayings, as we learn from Rabb. exegesis, Dt. 32:6 and Is. 63:16 in particular promoted the religious use of the name "Father." [207] What is meant is not God's begetting, let alone God as an abstract cosmic principle, but His fatherhood as a disposition, attitude and action. [208] There is specific ref. to His protective care for His people, 3 Macc. 7:6. Whenever Judaism speaks of God as "Father of all," Hell. influence has been at work, e.g., Jos. (→ n. 49). The exception in Midr. Prv., 10, 1: "Father of the whole world," simply confirms the rule, which is generally valid for the Synagogue. It is true that in other expressions the Rabb. bring out forcefully God's relation to the world, but in such cases the phrase is "Lord of the world" or "He who spake and the world came into being" or "omnipotence." When the image of the father is used an emotional complex is introduced alongside these others. The added pronominal adjectives "our," "your," "my," "thy," "his" distinctly express the very

---

[203] Among the Pythagoreans, too, the teacher is the father and the pupil the child, cf. Iambl. in Diels⁶, I, 471, 25. Acc. to Epict. Diss., III, 22, 82 the Cynic chides the people as a father and brother and servant of the κοινὸς πατήρ Zeus. As spiritual adviser in Pl. → 1005, 22 ff. In Just. and Cl. Al. the founder of a philosophical school or Gnostic system is called πατὴρ τοῦ λόγου, τῆς αἱρέσεως, Just. Dial., 2, 2; 35, 6; Cl. Al. Prot., 5, 66, 4 (GCS, 12, 50, 28); cf. 2, 13, 5 (GCS, 12, 12, 16).

[204] Cf. Dalman WJ, I, 150-159, 296-304; Moore, II, 201-211; Str.-B., I, 392-396; Marmorstein, 56-62.

[205] With this qualification the observation of E. Wechssler, Hellas im Ev.² (1947), 324 f. is pertinent.

[206] God the Father of Israel the son is a common theme in the Targumim and Midrashim: Tg. J. I on Dt. 32:6 (Str.-B., I, 393); Tg. Jer. 31:9 (ibid., III, 15); M. Ex. on 12:1 (2a) (ibid., I, 643); Midr. Cant., 2, 16 (102b) (ibid., I, 394); Dt. r., 2 (199c) (ibid., II, 29); Nu. r., 17 (ibid., I, 394); Ex. r., 32 (93c) (ibid., I, 393). Cf. Moore, II, 203 f. The same theme is to be found in Jub. 1:24 f., 28; 2:20; 19:29; 3 Macc. 7:6; Jos. Ant., 5, 93.

[207] On Dt. 32:6 cf. Tg. O., ad loc. (Str.-B., I, 393); bBer., 35a (ibid., I, 686); on Is. 63:16 Shab., 89b (Str.-B., I, 120 f). The truth "God as our Father" in Jewish Hell. writings: Tob. 13:4; Sib., III, 726; Apc. Mos. 35; Apc. Sedrach 9:2.

[208] Cf. Gyllenberg, 55 f.

personal content. How far it may still become a stereotyped formula depends, like all religious utterance, on the attitude of those who use the word and on the real vitality which it is given. In both the Rabbis and Jewish Hell. writings "Father" is used predominantly as a predicate of God and an address to Him. It is used directly for God only in Philo, O. Sol., Corp. Herm. apart from the one exception in Test. Jud. 24:2. The other pseudepigr. do not have this usage. This may be explained again by the Gk. origin of ὁ πατήρ which in its generality, with no pronominal adj. to relieve the abstraction, simply expresses the cosmic-genealogical universal principle. The mode of expression in Jn. (→ 996, 21 ff.) is close to this world of thought. It is characterised, however, by a concern to fill the Hell. concept with wholly new content. The Rabb. take a different course. The earliest known instances come from the end of the 1st cent. The phrase used is almost always "the Father in the heavens."

b. Father and Lord.

The synthesis "Father and Lord (King)" is a fully developed one in later Judaism. It is prefigured in the OT at Mal. 1:6. In Sir. there is a strong link between κύριος and πατήρ even in invocation. [209] The phrase also occurs in Tob., 3 Macc. and Wis. [210] In Jos. δέσποτα is the most common address to God, but we find πατὴρ καὶ δεσπότης for God. [211] In the Synagogue "our Father, our King" is a fixed formula in liturgical prayers; it gives eloquent expression to the understanding of God. [212] The fact that the synthesis is also found in later Stoicism and Gnosticism simply helped to foster the liking for it in later Judaism. Combination of the two, always with a strict national ref., keeps Judaism from the weakening of the religious father concept which always accompanies a failure to recognise God's holiness. A mawkish expression like that used in address to God in Joseph and Asenath, 12 is quite isolated.

2. The Father in the Heavens. [213]

אָב שֶׁבַּשָּׁמַיִם is not attested in apocal. and other pseudepigr. On the other hand it is a common, though not the most common, term for God in the Palestinian Synagogue. It is attested from the end of the 1st cent. A.D. Through the influence of Mt. on the Church it becomes a binding link between the Synagogue and primitive Christianity. Tradition has Rabbis using the phrase c. 70. "Israel and its Father in heaven" [214] is a particularly common form. Even the individual "my Father in heaven" in prayer is put

---

[209] Sir. 23:1, 4; 51:10. In Sir. 23:1 κύριε πάτερ is followed by καὶ δέσποτα ζωῆς μου. For δέσποτα A⁺ has θεέ, also at 23:4 (Rahlfs): κύριε πάτερ καὶ θεὲ ζωῆς μου. Acc. to P. Katz, Philo's Bible (1950), 152 θεέ is always secondary here. On Sir. 51:10: ἐπεκαλεσάμην κύριον πατέρα κυρίου μου cf. R. Smend, Die Weisheit d. Jesus Sirach erklärt (1906), 500 f.; N. Peters, Sir. (1913), ad loc. Smend (unlike Dalman WJ, I, 151) does not read the acc. like the LXX and Syr. but the vocative אָבִי; he refers to Ps. 89:26 as the basis. (If there is a ref. to Ps. 110:1 it is only by Chr. interpretation and hence secondarily. The simplest tradition is κύριον [P. Katz].)

[210] Tob. 13:4 πατήρ with κύριος and θεός; 3 Macc. 5:7 with παντοκράτωρ κύριος and ἐλεήμων θεός; Wis. 11:10: In the wilderness period God was πατὴρ νουθετῶν, to the ungodly ἀπότομος βασιλεύς.

[211] On the def. of δεσπότης cf. Hdt., VII, 104. On πατὴρ καὶ δεσπότης in Jos. Ant. prooem, 20; Ant., 5, 93; Ap., II, 174 cf. Schl. Jos., 15; Theol. d. Judt., 24 f. Just. often has the same combination: Apol., 12, 9; 32, 10; 36, 2 etc. cf. Dial., 139, 4. Also Mart. Pol., 14, 1; 19, 2; Cl. Al. Strom., VII, 3, 16, 6 (GCS, 17, 12, 21): ὁ πανβασιλεὺς καὶ παντοκράτωρ πατήρ.

[212] Shemone Esre, Bab. rec., Petition 5. In 4 and 6 the Pal. rec. has אָבִינוּ (W. Stärk, Altjüd. liturgische Gebete [1930], 12) also the Bab. rec., 6. In bBer., 11b the benediction Ahaba rabba (Stärk, 6): אָבִינוּ מַלְכֵּנוּ. Cf. esp. the common "our Father, our King" in the New Year prayer Abinu malkenu (Stärk, 27-29, cf. Str.-B., I, 10, 175, 421). Akiba (d. c. 135) pronounces the beginning of this prayer at a service of fasting acc. to bTaan., 25b (Str.-B., I, 421). Father and King are combined already in the prayer of Eleazar in 3 Macc. 6:2-4.

[213] For bibl. → n. 204.

[214] Cf. M. Ex., 12, 2 (3b); bSanh., 42a; Midr. Est. Intr. (82a); T. Shab., 13, 5 (129); Sota, 9, 15 (Str.-B., I, 207, 219, 367, 396).

on the lips of a contemporary. [215] What is meant by "in the heavens"? The expression does not contain speculation on the remote God of transcendence. In the first instance it simply rules out confusion with the earthly father and describes the divine Father as exalted and also as standing above all earthly fatherhood. This is shown by S. Dt. § 48 on 11:22 [216] with its distinction between "his father on earth" and "his father who is in heaven." But this traditional and correct interpretation [217] needs amplification. The expression, which comes in strongly after 70, shows itself to be well adapted to emphasise that what is in heaven can now serve as a true substitute for what is destroyed on earth, → n. 215. But this temporally coloured understanding was not uniform. [218] Nevertheless, it always seems that the expression is taken to be a counterpart to the earthly situation; thus in political bondage an antithesis and consolation is sought by looking to the Father in the heavenly world. [219] The basic structure of the use of the formula is still provided by the idea of "Israel and its father in heaven," → n. 214. Fundamental expression is given to this collective sense by Abaje (d. 338/339) in bBer., 29b: "In his prayers a man should always fuse with the whole body." But we also find the individual version: "My, thy, his Father in heaven," [220] in every age at least after the time that this type of individual saying appears in Sir., → n. 209. Nevertheless, these instances are in a minority compared with the wide use of "our Father." The personal form is found esp. in relation to men who have a particular role in the history of revelation [221] or who keep the law to an outstanding degree, [222] so that they are said to enjoy a specially close relation to God. [223] But it also occurs in passages where this does not apply. Certainly the individual version of relationship to the heavenly Father does not appear for the first time in Jesus, though there can be no question as to its unparalleled content when used by Him. The justification for transferring what is implied in the term "Father" from the community to the individual is provided by OT statements. [224] Naturally the individual can participate herein only as a member of the covenant people.

---

[215] R. Jochanan b. Zakkai (d. c. 80) in M. Ex. on 20:25 (81a) (Str.-B., I, 283): "The stones (of the altar, Dt. 27:6) establish peace between Israel and its Father in heaven." R. Çadoq (c. 70) in Seder Elijjahu r., 28 (149) (Str.-B., I, 394): "My Father who art in heaven, thou hast destroyed thy city and burnt thy temple and remainest untroubled and calm." R. Eliezer (c. 90) in Sota, 9, 15 (Str.-B., I, 395 f.): "Since the temple was destroyed, the scribes are ... ashamed and cover their heads ... On whom shall we rely? On our Father in heaven."

[216] Str.-B., I, 395.

[217] Cf. Dalman WJ, I, 152; Moore, II, 205; Str.-B., I, 393; Schl. Jos., 14 f. This is how Ign. R. prooem and Cl. Al. Paed., III, 12, 101, 3 (GCS, 12, 291, 18) took πατὴρ ὕψιστος.

[218] Thus R. Eleazar (c. 270) in bBer., 32b (Str.-B., I, 456) can even say later: "From the day the sanctuary was destroyed an iron wall forms a partition between Israel and its Father in heaven."

[219] Lv. r., 23 (122a) (Str.-B., I, 771): "Though dues in kind and forced labour are exacted from the Israelites their heart is set on their Father in heaven." Cf. Moses at prayer looking into the upper world, RH, 3, 8 (Str.-B., I, 395).

[220] Examples of this which are ascribed to Rabb. between 70 and 200: "My Father in heaven": R. Cadoq (c. 70) → n. 215; S. Lv., 20, 26 (374a), Str.-B., I, 176 (c. 100); M. Ex., 20, 6 (75b), ibid., I, 345 (c. 100). "Thy Father in heaven": Ab., 5, 20, ibid., I, 395 (before 200). "His Father in heaven": T. Chul., 2, 24 (503), ibid., I, 36 (c. 90); S. Dt. § 48 on 11:22 (84b) → 980, 4 f.; Kil., 9, 8 (c. 190), Dalman WJ, I, 154.

[221] Cf. Machzor Vitry (1893-1897), 342, Dalman loc. cit.

[222] Examples in Str.-B., I, 394 f. In Wis. 2:16 (cf. 2:13, 18) God is the Father of the righteous man who is described as παῖς κυρίου, υἱὸς θεοῦ, which the ungodly construes as boasting. Cf. Plut. → n. 54. In both cases we have an ethics of merit.

[223] The question whether to say "my" or "our God" was discussed by the pupils of Gamaliel II (c. 90), cf. Bacher Tannaiten², I, 94, 2 (Str.-B., I, 410a). They think the former should be used. In the v. from Sir → n. 209 the righteous says πάτερ in distinction from the ungodly.

[224] The Babylonians already think in terms of an individual relation to deity, cf. Baudissin, Kyrios, III, 360.

A common phrase is: "Before the Father in heaven," which expresses the attitude of Israel in prayer. [225] Another favourite phrase is: "To direct one's heart to the Father in heaven," "to subject one's heart to Him." [226]

3. Invocation of the Father in Prayer.

That this was an actual practice in Judaism is proved by the Jewish Hell. writings and esp. by the liturgy of the Synagogue, → n. 212. It is reflected in Sir. (→ n. 209), in the πάτερ of Wis. 14:3, in the fr. of the Apocryphon of Ez. in Cl. Al. Paed., I, 9, 91, 2, [227] in 3 Macc. 6:3, 8 and even in so Hell. an invocation (Abraham's) as that in Test. Isaac 8:10. The simple πάτερ, in Heb. "our Father," recurs constantly. The common address "our Father" [228] in prayer is based on OT sayings like Is. 63:16; 64:7. In 1 Ch. 29:10 HT David prays: "Thou God of our father Israel," but the LXX has: κύριε, ὁ θεὸς ᾽Ισραήλ, ὁ πατὴρ ἡμῶν. Here, too, we catch an echo of the later liturgy with its אָבִינוּ → n. 212. "Our Father in heaven" is, however, less frequent in prayer. At this pt. the possibility that the Lord's Prayer exerted some influence cannot be ruled out. Cf. Seder Elijjahu, 7 (33); Tanna debê Elijjahu, 21. [229] The only instance of "my Father (in heaven)" used in prayer seems to be that of R. Çadoq, → n. 215. [230]

4. The Relation to Other Names for God in the Synagogue, and the Limitations of the Jewish Understanding of God as Father.

Apart from expressions which denote God's power over the world (→ 978, 30 ff.) the Rabbis more commonly use phrases like "the Holy One, blessed be He," "He who causes His name to dwell in His house," or, in addition to "almightiness," "the merciful One," or substitutes like "heaven," "the place," "the dwelling," "the speaking," "the word." All such terms lay stronger emphasis on the holiness, dominion, power and presence of God than on His fatherliness. In spite of the synthetic formula "Father/King" there is usually a certain abruptness if the two are put together. The Rabbis do not normally speak in one breath of the Lord of the world or the Almightiness on the one side and the Father in heaven on the other. Even in the Synagogue the latter is the most affectionate name for God. [231] Nevertheless, the affectionate use has no great profundity in detail. A statement like that in Sota, 9, 15 (→ n. 215) is rare. A living (and saving) understanding of fatherly care such as that of 3 Macc. 6:2-4 will be found only occasionally. In Kil., 9, 8 R. Shimeon b. Eleazar (c. 190) says: He who wears garments of mixed weave "turns aside and causes his Father in heaven to turn aside from him." As punctilious fulfilment of the demands of the Law was in the last resort still linked up with this name, so, too, was belief in merit, T. Pea, 4, 21 (24): [232] "Beneficence and works of love are advocates and peacemakers between Israel and its Father in heaven." Indeed, the destroyed temple can separate Israel from the Father, bBer., 32b, → n. 218. The term lacks vitality because it does not express a radical appreciation of the fatherliness of God. It seems to be confined within the very different system of a legalism which contradicts fatherly freedom. What Israel possesses in this name looks ahead

---

[225] T. J. I on Ex. 1:19 (Str.-B., I, 396); Qaddish, II, 3a; Qaddish of the Rabb., 3b, Stärk, op. cit., 31.

[226] Ber., 5, 1; Yom., 76a (Str.-B., I, 421). On the phrase "to do the will of the Father in heaven" → III, 54, 22 ff.

[227] GCS, 12, 143, 21, cf. K. Holl, "Das Apokryphon Ez.," Aus Schrift u. Geschichte = Theol. Abh. f. A. Schlatter (1922), 88-98.

[228] "Our Father" for God is naturally no new thing in religion. Cf. Rigveda, I, 90, 7 of Dyaúš pitá: "Heaven our father"; ibid., VI, 73, 1 of Brihaspati, the lord of prayer or magical power; also of Indra in the Vālakhilya hymns of Rigveda, IV, 5.

[229] Str.-B., I, 410.

[230] Ibid., II, 50. "You shall call me 'my Father'" in Tanch. משפטים 97b (ibid., I, 393) refers to Israel.

[231] Cf. the characteristic gloss in Ex. r., 46 (101b) (ibid., II, 216): "When you find yourselves in affliction, call me 'our Father'."

[232] Str.-B., II, 561 f.

to a view which goes incomparably deeper, which transcends mere formality, which is no longer tied to the idea of merit, which no longer thinks in terms of the privilege of an elite or of respected teachers, which is not even evoked by the pressure of affliction or the loss of cultic guarantees. The materials are there, but the spirit of true faith in the Father is still lacking.

D. Father in the New Testament.

I. Father according to the Jesus of the Synoptists.

1. Honouring of the Earthly Father and Its Limits.

In opposition to a complicated casuistry which so easily promotes untruth (→ II, 548 ff.), Jesus gives force to the original divine meaning of the Torah. Hence He says emphatically that the commandment to honour parents is obligatory, Mk. 10:19 and par. If an ordinance cuts across this normative requirement, it is hypocrisy and transgression, Mk. 7:10-13; Mt. 15:4-7; [233] → κορβᾶν III, 865 f. For further evidence of tender regard for the relationship between parents and children cf. Mk. 5:40 par. Lk. 8:51; Mk. 9:14-29 par. Mt. 17:14-21 and Lk. 9:37-43 (cf. Jn. 4:46-53).

Only in appearance is there a contradiction between this unconditional affirmation of the fifth commandment and those sayings which set the discipleship owed to Jesus above all the duties of piety. The interrelating of the two may be described indeed as the distinctive thing in Jesus' teaching. He does not release His disciples from the unparalleled tension which is kept from becoming a poor compromise only by true regard for the righteousness of the rule of God. Affirmation of the fifth commandment protects the disciples from a loveless and fanatical truncation of the elementary will of God. The demand for discipleship prevents anyone from evading decision for Christ through false piety. The fact that Jesus claims the primary love of the disciples above all family ties is the common denominator in all sayings of this second group. On ἄξιος in Mt. 10:37 → I, 379, 25 ff. Sometimes a man has to leave his father ἕνεκεν τοῦ ἐμοῦ ὀνόματός, Mt. 19:29 cf. Mk. 10:29. This carries with it an unexpected promise. In Mk. 10:29 f. the present blessing is more strongly accented than the effect on eternal destiny. As in Mk. 10:7; Mt. 19:5 a new order of life is set up when a man leaves his father and mother to get married (Gn. 2:24), [234] so discipleship, if it entails leaving father and mother, is established as a higher order above the natural order, though without abrogating the latter. If this involves a truncating of the rights of parents, this is very different from cunning, pseudo-religious truncation (the misuse of Corban). It is demanded by a special calling. At this point, however, an eschatological outlook is essential, → 983, 10 ff. The same applies in Mt. 8:21 f.; Lk. 9:59 f. What is at issue when Jesus does not allow the disciples to escape discipleship by appealing to filial piety is more than a convention; it is the proclamation of the βασιλεία, Lk. 9:60. The choice is not between showing piety or not; burying the dead means neglecting the message. [235] The stringency of this demand, which in face of Jewish sensibility [236]

---

[233] Quoted in Mk. 10:19 from the Decalogue acc. to Dt. 5:16 (≡ Ex. 20:12) LXX, in Mk. 7:10 par. Mt. 15:4 acc. to Ex. 21:16 LXX, cf. Lv. 20:9 the divine punishment of κακολογεῖν against parents. The weaker ἀτιμάζειν of Dt. 27:16 is not used.

[234] Cf. Loh. Mk. on 10:7.

[235] In 1 K. 19:20 f. Elisha is trusted to come back and follow Elijah after the death of his parents. In Mt. 8:21 f. and par., however, it is tacitly assumed that the temporiser will not come back.

[236] Cf. Schl. Mt., 288 and Str.-B., I, 487-489. Burying the dead is an unconditional obligation of piety — even the priest must bury his father. The strictest Rabb. provisions are made

brusquely ignores custom where it might imperil allegiance to Jesus, cannot be softened. The most severe saying in Lk. 14:26 demands of the disciple a μισεῖν of his father, of all his relatives, and even of his own life. In accordance with the meaning of שָׂנֵא (→ IV, 690, 18 ff.) this figure of speech is to be interpreted as "to set aside for." [237] But the great severity derives from the experience of parting. Since μισεῖν refers to one's own life also, it is plain that Jesus is not demanding the renunciation of family in the form of a vow or a special achievement. What is required is the total and irreversible denial of everything earthly with a view to discipleship. [238]

The directions of the second group have to be related to this call to prophecy as found in Mt. 10:35 (διχάσαι): Mi. 7:6; Zech. 13:3. In some circumstances families and generations may be torn apart by the Son of Man. A mark of persecution in the last time is that the father will deliver up the son to death and that children will rise up against their parents, Mk. 13:12; Mt. 10:21. The shaking of the family relationship corresponds to Jewish eschatological expectation, [239] except that now the crisis is simply brought on by confession of Jesus. Lk. 1:17, however, presents a reconciling aspect; by the Baptist's work the hearts of the fathers will be turned again to the children. [240] There is interwoven a healing of family disruption and of the disobedient.

2. The Religious Use of πατήρ.

a. The Presupposition of Patriarchy.

A specific view of the nature of fatherhood underlies each religious use of the term "father." In so far as we can catch the sociological basis in the Synoptists and John (→ 997, 1 ff.), we constantly encounter the ancient patriarchal authority of the Jews in the context of a domestic social order. It is an unusual thing to leave father and fishing boat and to follow Jesus, Mt. 4:22. Ordinarily the son follows the same trade or work as the father. [241] Acc. to Mt. 21:28 all sons are under obligation to work in the vineyard as the father wills. [242] The same holds good with respect to the property of the father in Lk. 15:17. τέκνον, σὺ πάντοτε μετ' ἐμοῦ εἶ, καὶ πάντα τὰ ἐμὰ σά ἐστιν in v. 31 bears witness to this popular background of patriarchy. By zealously observing domestic law (δουλεύω σοι, v. 29) the elder son acts as is proper and not to his own disadvantage, for he thereby makes sure of his share of the property. In spite of the διεῖλεν of v. 12 [243] he still regards this property as belonging to his father (cf. also

---

concerning the dead who leave no relatives behind. These apply even to the high-priest and Nazirite who would not otherwise defile themselves with the corpse of their father. Study of the Torah and divine service come second at this pt., Meg., 3b, Str.-B., I, 488e.

[237] Cf. Gn. 29:31, 33; Wellh. Mt. on 6:24; S. Dt. § 32 on 6:5 (73a) in Schl. Mt., 350.

[238] Epict. Diss., III, 3, 5-7 demands similar resolution from the Stoic standpoint. There precedes all relationship : οὐδὲν ἐμοὶ καὶ τῷ πατρί, ἀλλὰ τῷ ἀγαθῷ. If the father says : πατήρ σου εἰμί, one must answer : ἀλλ' οὐκ ἀγαθόν. Here a philosophical abstraction takes precedence, i.e., the good, whereas in Christianity one has to follow Christ.

[239] Eth. En. 99:5; 100:1 f.; Jub. 23:16; S. Bar. 70:6; Sanh., 97a. Cf. Wellh. Mk., 109.

[240] Cf. Schl. Lk., 153 : Conditions among youth at the end of the Herodian period.

[241] Mk. 1:20 says less drastically that the sons of Zebedee left their father and the hired workers.

[242] On φυτεύειν, φυτεία (in the father's vineyard or garden) in Mt. 15:13 cf. Ign. Phld., 3, 1; Tr., 11, 1.

[243] On the Rabb.-Talmudic law of inheritance cf. Str.-B., III, 545-553 (esp. from the standpoint of the will); S. Krauss, Talmud. Archäologie, III (1912), 189; M. Bloch, Mosaischtalmud. Erbrecht (1890); M. Guttmann, Mafteach ha-Talmud, I (1906), 33 f.; S. Bialoblocki, Art. "Erbrecht im Talmud," EJ, VI, 703-711. Philo and inheritance (cf. Spec. Leg., II, 133 f.):

v. 30 : σου τὸν βίον). So long as the father lives, the sons have nothing of their own. With his brusque demand the younger son violates this basic view. His request counts on an exception. His δός μοι τὸ ἐπιβάλλον μέρος τῆς οὐσίας (v. 12) overlooks the father's right to enjoyment of the children's goods. His offence is that of arbitrary emancipation, of frivolous departure from the fellowship of the household. [244] He lightly makes the father's τὰ ἐμά (v. 31) into τὰ σά. All interpretations rest on this basis. Sin is a leaving of the father's house in wantonness and selfishness with what is freely given at the father's expense. [245] Conversion is returning to the father's fellowship in the family and in work.

Whenever the NT uses the image of the "father" it always builds on this concept of patriarchy. The fundamental characteristics of totality and authority demand that the Father's will be done in obedience, Mt. 7:21. Israel never isolated the "mine" of the Father as "its own." To stay in fellowship with the Father is the gift on which all else rests. Jesus can sum up everything in the word "Father" only because the lordship of God is always implied in His fatherhood. If we remain only at the emotional level, the concept of the Father becomes a matter of mere religious enthusiasm. [246]

b. Invocation of God as Abba, → I, 5 f.

The authentic term for God in the teaching of Jesus has been preserved in the original Aramaic. The term Jesus used was אַבָּא. Mk. 14:36, [247] cf. Gl. 4:6; R. 8:15 prove that this address was not forgotten but highly esteemed in primitive Christianity.

I. Heinemann, *Philons gr. u. jüd. Bildung* (1932), 320-329; E. R. Goodenough, *The Juris-prudence of the Jewish Courts in Egypt as described by Philo Judaeus* (1929). On in-heritance in the pap.: L. Mitteis, *Reichsrecht u. Volksrecht* (1891); H. Kreller, *Erbrechtliche Untersuchungen auf Grund d. Paryrusurkunden* (1919). On Lk. 15:12 Kreller, *op. cit.*, 205-208, 214; J. C. Naber, "Observatiunculae de iure Romano," Mnemosyne, NS, 34 (1906), 64-72, esp. 66; P. Rabel, "Elterliche Teilung," *Festschr. zur 49. Versammlung deutscher Philologen u. Schulmänner* (1907), 521 ff., 532. The διεῖλεν of Lk. 15:12 obviously denotes a disposition of the property during the father's lifetime as in the case of the voluntary endowment מַתָּנָה, Aram. מַתְּנָא, אַמַתְּנָא. But such dispositions are realisable only on the death of the donor. Up to his death the donor has full enjoyment. In Lk. 15, however, a Galilean farm is partly sold in order that the younger son may have his share in cash. The father thus renounces his right of enjoyment. Even so, the conduct of the elder son and the ruling of v. 31 show that the patriarchal economy is still emphasised. We should prefer the view (Naber, Rabel, Kreller) that here we have Gk.-Jewish popular law which cannot be wholly explained by Rabb. pars. Already in enchoric law there is found a division or prior transfer of one portion with immediate effect, though such agreements were usually restricted by reservation of usufruct. Thus the father in the parable takes the exceptional course. He renounces the right of enjoyment on the relinquished piece of land which the younger son sells. The elder son is not put in a new position so long as his father is alive. There is a par. from the 6th/7th cent. in P. Oxy., I, 131 where in his lifetime the father assigns to his younger son David the mother's land. When he dies he declares that the son was in large measure apportioned therewith.

[244] Consideration whether the father's yielding to the younger son was pedagogically correct lies outside the sphere of legitimate hermeneutics. The parable is at this pt. deter-mined by the meaning : God in the first instance allows the sinner to go his own way, and if he sins with what is freely granted to him God cannot stop him.

[245] Cf. Apc. Sedrach 6:4 of Adam : "He took what was mine and became alien to me." In 6:4-7 four times : "to leave the father in the lurch."

[246] Cf. Bernoulli, 222. Discussion of "Father and Lord" in Jesus is continually cut short by the fact that the starting-point in the ancient understanding of the father is ignored.

[247] The ἀββᾶ ὁ πατήρ of Mk. 14:36 is also meant vocatively in the Gk. part. Cf. Mt. 11:26; Lk. 10:21; Jn. 17:21, 24. The double form can hardly be due to incidental transl. by Mk. and Pl. It may well reflect the liturgical use of the nationally mixed primitive community. Cf. Loh. Mk. on 14:36.

אַבָּא is not (→ I, 5, 3) a determination of אַב but the vocative form. [248] Acc. to a linguistic process for which there are numerous analogies, however, the vocative is easily generalised and carried over into other cases. [249] The linguistic evidence corresponds to the finding that 'abba is the babbling of an infant like the Gk. πάππα, [250] → 948, 6 f. If the asking of a child corresponds to the cry of urgent distress in Gethsemane, in Paul, too, explanation of the term is controlled solely and simply by the image of the childish cry, → 1006, 12 ff.

This word is always the original of πατήρ in the prayers of the Gospels. [251] The new thing in the usage is that an everyday infant sound is applied without inhibition to God. To Jewish sensibility this is too familiar. For Jesus it is the simplest and sincerest conceivable term to express God's attitude and it also implies a rejection of all religious pretension. Hence 'abba is a basic word of faith in the revelation of Jesus and the confession of His community. Yet it does not imply a banal self-assurance which takes things for granted, → 1006, 17. This basic word tells us that God is not a distant Ruler in transcendence but One who is intimately close. Unconditional faith in the Father is thus taken seriously. The term alone, however, does not carry the whole message. The right of sonship is within the limits of the βασιλεία. The synthesis Father/Judge, Father/Lord makes any lack of respect impossible by imposing submission to His holy rule, → 995, 10 ff.

c. The Father in the Heavens, → 520, 17 ff.

(a) The Question of Sources and the Historical Problem. Was it just Mt. who wrote the longer "Father in the heavens," whereas Jesus Himself probably did not normally use this? [252] Research in Q makes this judgment dubious. It is obvious that Lk. sometimes cuts down the longer "Father in the heavens" as a Jewish expression. Suspect is υἱοὶ ὑψίστου in Lk. 6:35, [253] where Mt. 5:45 has: υἱοὶ τοῦ πατρὸς ὑμῶν τοῦ ἐν

---

[248] G. Kittel abandoned the opinion expressed in → I, 5, 3, which is shared by Str.-B., II, 49; cf. Kittel's Die Religionsgesch. u. d. Urchr. (1932), 73, 92-95, 146, n. 214; also "Lexicographia Sacra," DTh, 5 (1938), 97 f. For further bibl. Dalman WJ, I, 154, 157, 302; Dalman Gr.² § 14, 7d f (90 f., 90, n. 1, 198); Zn. R., 396, n. 93; C. H. Turner, The Oldest Manuscript of the Vulgate Gospels (1931), XXXV f.; T. W. Manson, Bulletin of John Rylands Library, 26 (1941), 114-116; also "Entry into Membership of the Early Church," JThSt, 48 (1947), 29; J. Jeremias in Kennzeichen der ipsissima vox Jesu argues that there is in all Jewish lit. no earlier instance of 'abba without suffix and without the addition "in the heavens." Tg. Job, 34, 36, MS of the year 1238 (Levy Chald. Wört., I, 1; cf. Str.-B., II, 50) → I, 5, n. 5 is a late variant; the addition Lv. r., 32 on 24:10 → I, 5, n. 6 is also late. Cf. Dalman WJ, I, 154.

[249] Cf. E. Littmann, "Anredeformen in erweiterter Bdtg.," NGG, 1916 (1916), 94-111.

[250] On 'abba as childish lisping cf. bTaan., 23b (1st cent. B.C.) in J. Leipoldt, Jesu Verhältnis zu Juden u. Griechen (1941), 136 f. On this J. Jeremias, → n. 248. Cf. also bBer., 40a; bSanh., 70b, cf. Dalman WJ, I, 302.

[251] The invocation πάτερ or ἀββᾶ, (ὁ) πατήρ, πάτερ μου occurs 19 times on the lips of Jesus in the 4 Gospels, including pars. In the cry of jubilation πάτερ Mt. 11:25; Lk. 10:21, where there is also a ὁ πατήρ. In Gethsemane Mk. 14:36 ἀββᾶ ὁ πατήρ; Mt. 26:39 πάτερ μου (λ Orig.); 26:42 πάτερ μου; Lk. 22:42 πάτερ. On the cross Lk. 23:34, 46 twice πάτερ. In Jn. the same 5 times: 11:41; 12:27, 28; 17:1, 5. With ἅγιε 17:11, twice πατήρ as an address: 17:21, 24. The same with δίκαιε: 17:25. πάτερ alone corresponds to the way a Gk. son addresses his father. Cf. Epict. Diss., I, 26, 5; Tob. 5:1; Jos. Ant., 6, 127; 16, 105; Bell., 1, 621. We do not find ὦ πάτερ in the NT, cf. Bl.-Debr. § 146, 1 and 3. It is very common in the Hell. sphere, Jos. Ant., 16, 119; Bell., 4, 628. Very common in Corp. Herm., e.g., IV, 3; X, 5; XII, 7.

[252] Dalman WJ, 157 doubts whether Jesus used this expression in prayer. Weinel, 124 attributes it to Mt. alone. So does Grundmann, who thinks there is adaptation to Jewish usage in Mt.

[253] ὑψίστου is related to οὐρανοί, cf. Lk. 2:14; 19:38; Mk. 11:10; Mt. 21:9. Lk. is also fond of this solemn designation elsewhere, 1:32, 35, 76; Ac. 7:48.

οὐρανοῖς. Lk. 11:13 : ὁ πατὴρ ὁ ἐξ οὐρανοῦ δώσει [254] (Mt. 7:11: ὁ πατὴρ ὑμῶν ὁ ἐν τοῖς οὐρανοῖς δώσει) gives us even more reason to suppose that here the original Q is better preserved in Mt. It is probable that Lk. made changes consonant with his purpose of writing for the Gk. world. That the traditional "your Father in the heavens" was known to Mk. may be seen from 11:25. Here the formula was retained as a stubborn part of the tradition. [255] Elsewhere it may be stated that when Luke found "Father" in Q he did not cut it our or replace it. He made radical changes only in respect of "Father in the heavens." It is possible that Mt. in 10:29 par. Lk. 12:6 and 6:26 par. Lk. 12:24 put "Father" for "God." He does not usually do this when he finds θεός in Q or Mk. This important controlling observation prevents us from arguing purism on Mt.'s part in applying the heaven formula. By way of supplement we may refer to another group of sayings where Mt. uses "Father" more frequently as compared with Markan sayings. [256] But only in one instance does he here add the heaven formula, 12:50. The decisive phrase here is always πατήρ μου. The question raised → 985, 21 f. is thus to be answered as follows. From Mt. himself it may be shown that the word "Father" on the lips of Jesus is not always accompanied by the addition. Mt. conforms most closely to the usage of the Jewish Christian community. He and his sources, esp. Q, found a place for this form. The Evangelists who worked among the Gks., on the other hand, were not greatly concerned, if at all, about the addition, though they did not diminish at all the implied truth of fatherhood. It is probable, however, that both Mk. and Lk. knew the expression. In Mt. we have to reckon not merely with Jewish assimilation but also with real elements of authentic tradition. Without attempting to solve the problem in pedantic biographical style, we might say that Jesus used both "Father" and "Father in the heavens." How often it is authentic in the texts there can be no saying. We certainly find a true father theology in Mt. Mt. has a consistent line of proclamation as well as a consistent style. But he is orientated to a basic understanding of the message of Jesus to which he as a Palestinian stands in close relation. [257]

(b) The Meaning of the Formula. In "Father in the heavens" as used by Mt. the distinction between heaven and earth is strongly implied (cf. Mt. 18:19 on earth — Father in the heavens). The formula is not a substitute for God or a periphrasis, → 520, 21 ff. It is a deeper form of personal designation. It does not express transcendence as distance, → 520, 12 ff. It certainly suggests the apartness of the One who is absolutely superior and who reigns in sovereignty. But nearness is also emphasised, for perfect fatherhood is predicated of the transcendent God and the status of sonship is fully affirmed by the pronominal adjectives ὑμῶν, ἡμῶν, μου. If one has regard to the intentions behind "your Father in the heavens," one cannot speak of a relapse into Judaism. The key is to be found in the Lord's Prayer in Mt. 6:9. [258] Here "Our Father in the heavens" stands at the head. The

[254] This "whence for where" (Bl.-Debr. § 437) is not to be explained as Marcionite (A. Merx, *Die 4 kanonischen Evangelien nach ihrem ältesten bekannten Texte*, II, 2 : "Die Ev. Mk. u. Lk." [1905], 286) but as an attack on the misunderstanding of placid transcendence. Lk. also avoided βασιλεία τῶν οὐρανῶν and used (32 times) βασιλεία τοῦ θεοῦ. He was not afraid of the Semitic use of οὐρανός (-οί) as such but saw an active correspondence between heaven and earth, Lk. 2:14, 15 (the chief motif in the trilogy) → II, 749, 25 ff.; V, 518, 32 ff.; 520, 3. Though Lk. does not have the word, he brings to full material expression the concern manifested in the special sections in Mt., → lines 28 ff.

[255] In Mk. 11:25 f. only v. 26 may be differentiated as an intrusion from Mt. (cf. Schl., Hauck, Loh. Mk., *ad loc.*, though not Kl. Mk., *ad loc.*).

[256] Mt. 12:50 par. Mk. 3:35; Mt. 26:29 par. Mk. 14:25; Mt. 20, 23 par. Mk. 10:40. These are extraordinary instances in contrast to the indulgent treatment of Mk.'s θεός elsewhere in Mt.

[257] Later there is occasional addition, so Just. Dial., 101, 2, who cites Mk. 10:17 f. par. in this form.

[258] Bibl. J. Haussleiter, Art. "Vaterunser" in RE³, 20, 431-445; v. Harnack, *op. cit.*, 524; also "Einige Worte Jesu, die nicht in d. Kanon. Ev. stehen," SAB, 1904 (1904), 195 ff.;

concern of the prayer may be seen from the direction of the earthly by the ὄνομα, βασιλεία and θέλημα of the Father, the normative control of earth by heaven, 6:10; → 518, 32 ff. What is perfect in heaven is to be actualised on earth as the kingdom of God. Along the same lines we read in the Sermon on the Mount that he who wants a display of religion before men loses his Father in heaven. The Father seeks to regulate our piety. The original saying about the use of the title Abba in Mt. 23:9 (→ n. 286) also shows that the πατὴρ οὐράνιος normatively fixes the deepest meaning of "Father." Cf. also Mt. 18:10, 14; 5:16; Mk. 11:25; Mt. 10:32 f. This common denominator is continually used to proclaim, not rigid transcendence and otherworldliness, but final orientation from the heavenly sphere, the direction of earth by the reality which is above earth, the correspondence of the heavenly and the earthly. He who is lifted up is also near and intimate. Thus this, too, is a genuine word of revelation, nor does it differ from 'abba.

d. My Father and Your Father.

(a) The Question of Sources. In Mk. "my Father" is never used in such a way that Jesus speaks of His Father to others. Nevertheless the cry in 14:36 and the τοῦ πατρὸς αὐτοῦ of 8:38 display the same view as is common to all the sources. "My" is not too surely attested in Q, [259] but materially this weak attestation makes no difference, since the text is solidly grounded in the cry of jubilation, → 992, 40 ff. We enter a broader sphere when we come to the special materials in Mt. and Lk. In both the sayings have a stronger Semitic colouring and the use is more common. [260] Esp. is this true of the material peculiar to Mt. There can be no disputing the fact that on this basis Mt. notably changes the Mk. tradition at this pt. [261] "Your Father" is found in Mk. only at 11:25. Q also uses it only with respect to the disciples. [262] This is again the use in Lk. 12:32 (peculiar to Lk.). It is possible that Mt. in his use of Q has "your Father" more often ; he seems to lay stress on it. [263]

(b) The Distinction between "My Father" and "Your Father." In sayings which have "your Father" the thesis cannot be sustained that the content is the same as that in sayings with "my Father." [264] If one starts with expressions of this kind in Mk. and Q, which will take in a good deal of the material in Mt. and Lk. as well [265] (though Mt. may have increased the number), it is evident that these sayings are simply directions concerning true discipleship, → 991, 12 f. The special Lucan material is in accord with this. It is not explicitly emphasised that the "my"

J. A. Hutton, "When ye pray, say, Our Father !" Exp. T., 36 (1924/25), 121-124; J. Jeremias, "Das Gebetsleben Jesu," ZNW, 25 (1926), 123-140; P. Fiebig, Das Unservater (1927); E. Lohmeyer, Das Vater Unser³ (1952); E. F. Scott, The Lord's Prayer : Its Character, Purpose and Interpretation (1951). The categories Q and special Matthean material break down here because we have a community prayer handed down orally. Such a piece is of more value as a source than what has gone through the reflective process of a Hell. Evangelist. The testimony of the fact that Jesus also said "Father in heaven" in this prayer of the primitive community is important. Did., 8, 2 shows that the addition (here sing.) was customary.

[259] Because Lk. 6:46 reproduces in very abbreviated form what is found in Mt. 7:21. It is probable that where Lk. 12:8 f. concurs with Mt. 10:32 f. Q had "my."

[260] Lk. 2:49; 22:29; 24:49. Cf. the increase in sayings on the cross containing πάτερ, → n. 251. In Mt.: 15:13; 16:17; 18:10, 19, 35. Without the heaven formula : 20:23; 25:34; 26:29, 53.

[261] Cf. Mk. 3:35 par. Mt. 12:50; Mk. 10:40 par. Mt. 20:23; Mk. 14:25 par. Mt. 26:29.

[262] This is shown by Lk. 12:30 par. Mt. 6:32; Lk. 6:36 par. Mt. 5:48.

[263] So perhaps Mt. 10:20 par. Lk. 12:12; Mt. 10:29 par. Lk. 12:6.

[264] So Weinel, 125.

[265] Mk. 11:25; Mt. 5:45 par. Lk. 6:35; Mt. 5:48 par. Lk. 6:36; Mt. 6:32 par. Lk. 12:30; Mt. 7:11 par. Lk. 11:13; Mt. 10:20 par. Lk. 12:12; Mt. 10:29 par. Lk. 12:6.

gives authoritative force to the "your."[266] Only in appearance, however, do the "your Father" sayings, especially in Mt., have any autonomy in relation to "my Father." If we are to examine the relationship between the two groups of sayings properly we cannot assume that only an express connection in place and setting constitutes valid proof. In the Synoptic Gospels there is no "your Father" which does not stand in relationship to Jesus, not even when there is no explicit christological qualification as in Mt. 23:8, 9. The most intimate relationship to the Christ reality should never be overlooked. The admonitions to the disciples are not just moral exhortations; they derive their special force from the gift of the kingdom and from the fact that Jesus Himself embodies what this kingdom is.[267] The truth of fatherhood is thus the revelation of the Son, so that only through Him is it a truth for the disciples. From the sources, however, it is impossible to trace development from a more general form of the idea of God as Father to this christological version consciously emphasised in Mt. That which later leads Paul to the corresponding formula: "The Father of our Lord Jesus Christ," is materially decisive already in the earliest tradition.

(c) The Christological Confession. According to Mt. Jesus taught His disciples to pray: "Our Father." But in the Synoptists, even in traces of the earliest sources, we never find that He associated Himself with the disciples in this "our."[268] The "my" expresses a relationship to God which cannot be transferred. Wherever it appears a special sense of sonship may also be seen. But the term also has a further effect in shaping primitive Christology, the faith confessed by the community. Mt. of all the Evangelists plays the biggest part in this. The first beginnings are already present, however, in Mk. and Q. In this connection the material peculiar to Mt. finds important parallels, especially in special Lucan passages. These, which are plainly Palestinian in origin like those of Mt., testify to the christological precision of the deliberate "my Father." According to Lk. 2:49 this saying on the lips of the boy Jesus can even presuppose a sense of His unique relation to the Father.[269] Cf. also in Lk. 23:34, 46 the greater use of πάτερ on the cross as compared with the other Evangelists. Mt., however, took the "my/your Father" found in the other sources and developed it consistently and even systematically. At every point one may see in him a christological evaluation and confessional development. Mt. 16:17 is not just Peter's confession. It is the acceptance of this confession by "the Church of Mt." Mt. 18:19 shows how the Jewish Christian community is expressing the presence of the exalted Lord in this mode

---

[266] The old and valuable saying in Lk. 12:32 which promises assurance of the βασιλεία to the little flock ("your Father") may be compared with Lk. 22:29, where "my Father" appoints the kingdom for Jesus, cf. the Johannine par.: the gift of the kingdom to His own. This is in agreement with the parallel "kingdom of my Father" and "kingdom of your Father," Mt. 26:29 (a revision of Mk.), cf. Mt. 13:43; 25:34 — except that here the correspondence, though not accidental, is in separated passages. The same is true of sayings about forgiveness: Mt. 6:14 f. (your Father) and 18:35 (my Father). These are interchangeable. In only one instance, when dealing with the μικροί, is it possible that Mt. uses the order to express the fact that the Son stands warranty for the lowly, the "my" of 18:10 being changed into "your" in 18:14 to give emphasis to the pt.

[267] This is the element of truth in the christological interpretation of the Sermon on the Mount in E. Thurneysen, Die Bergpredigt = Theologische Existenz heute, 46 (1936). Cf. on this O. Schmitz, Jbch. d. Theol. Schule Bethel, IX (1938), 17-36.

[268] Acc. to Weinel, 125 the avoidance of this is overdone.

[269] ἐν τοῖς τοῦ πατρός μου links the house of God and the Word of God. On the Messiah's unique knowledge of God cf. Str.-B., II, 152.

of expression.[270] In Mt. one might describe "my Father" as a catchword for his Christology of the Revealer. It may be divided into the following main groups: 1. God is the Father who reveals Himself in the Son;[271] 2. Decision is made in Him who is one with the Father;[272] 3. The suffering Jesus is perfectly fulfilling the will of the Father;[273] 4. As He who is united with the Father He grants salvation and promises His followers that their prayers will be heard, Mt. 18:10, 19. 5. The promise orientated to consummation crowns the statements which use "my Father."[274]

e. The Absolute ὁ πατήρ.[275]

The abs. ὁ πατήρ is uncommon, but we find it in all strata. Always on the lips of Jesus, it usually[276] occurs alongside "the Son" or "the Son of Man." It appears already in Q (Mt. 11:27; Lk. 10:22), and also in Mk. 13:32, a saying which is shown to be ancient and authentic by the limitation ascribed to Jesus (par. Mt. 24:36 with μόνος). The formula Father/Son, like Son and Son of Man, belongs inseparably to apocalyptic contexts.

A firm basis has been constantly sought in the vision in Da. 7:13 f. The combination of the Ancient of days and bar nasha in Da. (which was combined with Ps. 2:7 and 110:1) undoubtedly demanded the interrelating of Father and Son.[277] This vision was well adapted to express both the sovereignty of the Father and also the commission of the Son as these may be seen esp. in what the Synoptists have to say about the parousia, judgment, and glory, → n. 300.[278] In Mt. 28:19 the abs. ὁ πατήρ occurs in the Trinitarian baptismal formula.[279] It recurs in a revision of the Marcan text in Lk. 9:26. In

---

[270] Cf. the related Jewish saying about the Shechinah, Ab., 3, 2 ff. (Str.-B., I, 794 f.).

[271] Mt. 16:17, cf. 15:13. "My Father" occurs already in the cry of jubilation taken from Q, Mt. 11:27 (Lk. 10:22) → 993, 5 f.

[272] Mt. 7:21; 10:32 f.; 12:50; 18:35; cf. 16:27 par. Mk. 8:38 (of his Father); Lk. 9:26 (of the Father).

[273] Mt. 26:42 (cf. 53) par. Mk. 14:36. Cf. Lk. 23:34, 46.

[274] Mt. 20:23; 25:34; 26:29. Cf. Lk. 24:49.

[275] "The father" is good Palestinian in familiar usage. It also corresponds to class. Gk., Bl.-Debr. § 278. Cf. the commandment, Mt. 15:4; 19:19. For Rabb. examples cf. Schl. Mt., 383. But the use of the abs. אַבָּא for God is highly exceptional, cf. M. Ex., 12, 1 (Schl. Mt., 384), where it is controlled by its counterpart בֵּן (Israel), → 979, 28 f.

[276] An exception is Lk. 11:13, a revision of Q (cf. Mt. 7:11), though it is relevant here only in the version in א 700 (without ὁ).

[277] In Eth. En. 46 ff. God is not called Father but the Lord of spirits, though also the Ancient of days, before whom the Son of Man is mentioned (48:2), who stands before Him (49:2). 105:2: "I and my Son," is, as the whole c. shows, a Chr. interpolation, cf. J. Jeremias, "Ἀμνὸς τοῦ θεοῦ — παῖς θεοῦ (Jn. 1:29, 36)," ZNW, 34 (1935), 123, n. 42.

[278] Son alternates with Son of Man: Before the high-priest the question about the Son of God (Mk. 14:61 f.; Mt. 26:63 f.; Lk. 22:69) is answered in terms of the Da. saying about the Son of Man, so that the two are identified. In Mk. 13:26, too, "Son of Man" bears an express ref. to Da. 7:13. To this synon. use corresponds the use of Father and Father of the Son of Man in Mk. and Mt. In Mk. 8:38 the Son of Man comes to judge in the δόξα of His Father. Mt. 16:27 adopts both without difficulty, and in Mt. 25:31, 34, which is peculiar to this Gospel, a statement of the Son of Man speaks of "my Father." Lk. at 9:26, in distinction from Mt., changes the Marcan version (8:38) into the simple τοῦ πατρός, but this goes to show that Father of the Son of Man and the abs. Father are felt to be one and the same. In Mt. 25:31, too, the combining of Son of Man with "his Father" is in keeping with the pt. of the pericope. "Father of the Son of Man," like "Father/Son," is apocalyptically conditioned and thus belongs to the earliest part of the tradition. Hence it may be regarded as an integral part of the preaching of Jesus Himself. → υἱός and υἱὸς τοῦ ἀνθρώπου.

[279] This liturgical v. reflects Jewish Chr. baptismal practice c. 80 A.D. On its feasibility in this form cf. J. Leipoldt, Die urchr. Taufe im Lichte d. Religionsgeschichte (1928), 33 f.

Alexandrian mysticism and Hell. Gnosticism the expression is speculative and it is best rendered "universal Father" in this world of thought. [280] The term shares with the world around only the transferring of God's absoluteness to His title as Father. This is the only pt. of contact. But the personal statements of Jesus about the Father are elevated in a radical way by this brief formulation. It is thus particularly well adapted to serve in ecclesiastical confessions of faith with a dogmatic character.

f. God the Father of All Men? [281]

The Stoic belief in providence accepted the rational idea that God is the Father of all men as a self-evident truth, → 955, 23 ff. The European Enlightenment modernised the Stoic interpretation and read universal fatherhood into the Sermon on the Mount. In Judaism, on the other hand, the individual is regarded as a member of the people which is chosen as God's son by election and salvation, → 978, 21 ff. That Jesus shared the OT view is emphasised wherever the original position of privilege is in question. [282] This limits the activity of Jesus to concentration on Israel. In Mt. 21:28-31, as in Lk. 15:11-32, the ref. is to Israel's relation to the Father, except that in both cases the sonship of Israel is divided into the main types of legal and non-legal. If in Mt. 21 the question is : Does Israel really do the will of the Father?, in Lk. 15 it is : Does it affirm His mercy to the world of sinners? Hence the sonship of Israel is not just a national privilege or even an occasion for pride in election. The decision as to Israel's relation to the Father rests on its encounter with the Revealer of the Father.

Did Jesus go beyond this and think of God as the Father of all men? [283] According to Mt. 5:43-45 His goodness as Creator extends to all. But this is not fatherhood. Hence the decisive question is posed : Do we want to be God's sons or not? There is no reference to a general sonship by nature or estate. When the word "Father" is used, it puts the disciple over against the Father, who (through Jesus) issues a demand for love. In this encounter the truth of fatherhood is established. Thus in the teaching about the fowls of the air and the lilies in

---

That the Trinitarian formula was customary is also shown by Did., 7, 1 and 3 and Just. Apol., 61, 3. F. C. Conybeare, "The Eusebian Form of the Text Mt. 28:19," ZNW, 2 (1901), 275-288 conjectures that Eusebius did not find it in Mt. because he often has only ἐν τῷ ὀνόματί μου. But cf. E. Riggenbach, "Der trinitarische Taufbefehl Mt. 28:19 nach seiner urspr. Textgestalt u. seiner Authentie untersucht," BFTh, 7, 1 (1903); also "Der trinitarische Taufbefehl Mt. 28:19 bei Orig.," BFTh, 8, 4 (1904); Zn. Mt., 722, n. 7. The Trinitarian text is attested already at the beginning of the 2nd cent.; in the West there is no other form from the time of Tert.

[280] Plato, → 954, 25; 955, 18. Philo → 956, n. 61; Corp. Herm. → 958, 9.

[281] At two pts. source criticism has tried to find an older universal use of "Father" in Jesus. Weinel, 125 speaks of a progressive restriction of "your Father" among the disciples. It was originally broader in his view. But neither in Q, Mk., nor the special material in Mt. and Lk. is "your Father" a general truth of reason. It is always a truth of revelation related to Jesus. Again, the sing. "thy Father" in Mt. 6:4, 6, 18 has been referred to the Jews : "It sounds the most ancient." Weinel, 125. The form is found in Palestine, Ab., 5, 20; Tg. O. Dt., 23, 6. But the conjecture of form criticism that it is a Chr. form of the Jewish expression sounds more convincing. Cf. M. Albertz, Die synpt. Streitgespräche (1921), 150 : a didactic poem. So also Grundmann, 61; Bultmann Trad., 141: a catechetical piece. The "Thou" is here controlled by the context : The individual is rescued from a false collectivising of piety by a new understanding of the truth of fatherhood.

[282] Cf. Mk. 7:27 par. Mt. 15:26; Mt. 8:12 : τέκνα, υἱοὶ τῆς βασιλείας and the antithesis.

[283] Dob. Th. on 1 Th. 1:1 thinks that the "Father of Christians" in Pl. is a narrowing of the "Father of men" in Jesus. Cf. Weinel, 126 : "It is plain that Jesus really regarded God as the Father of all men, i.e., strictly as the Father of the Jews …, but He is thinking, not of their Jewishness, but of their human need … and obligation." J. Leipoldt, Jesu Verhältnis zu Griechen u. Juden (1941), 140 regards the question as doubtful and exegetically insecure. K. Bornhäuser, "Die Bergpredigt" BFTh, II, 7 (1923), 129-137, referring to the christological "my Father/your Father," rejects the Enlightenment view. Cf. also Lofthouse, op. cit., 291 f.

Mt. 6:26 ff., which is directed against anxiety, the message of fatherhood is part of the message of eschatological salvation (v. 33 : the kingdom and its righteousness). If the persecuted disciple is told to consider such natural illustrations as the sparrow and the hairs of the head (Mt. 10:29-31; Lk. 12:6 f. without "father"), and if the reference here is again to the generosity of the Creator under which all men stand, we are not actually told that God is ὁ πατὴρ τῶν ὅλων. [284] The word "father" is for those who accept the teaching of Jesus about "your Father." This is true even when the starting-point is the analogy of the experience of fatherhood, Mt. 7:9-11; Lk. 11:11-13 (Q), → 992, 2 ff. Even when a wider circle is suggested (Lk. 6:27; Mt. 23:1), the hearers are not given in this truth of fatherhood a universal truth. A new sense is imparted which includes discipleship, Lk. 6:35 f.; Mt. 23:8 f. The concern in Jesus' preaching of fatherhood is always to instruct the disciples about the βασιλεία. The reference to creation is always related closely to a reference to the rule of the commanding and gracious God whom Jesus declares in His call to repentance and in His message. Like the reference to the guidance of Israel (→ 990, 14 f.) it has as its ultimate implication the lordship of God. [285]

g. The Heavenly Father as the Absolute Authority; Fatherly Authority and Fatherly Care.

In His impartial goodness the πατὴρ ὁ οὐράνιος is a norm and paradigm, → 990, 22. Cf. → τέλειος-τέλειοι, Mt. 5:48; Lk. 6:35 f. God exercises His perfection and totality supremely in His forgiveness, through which He seeks to impress the same character on His υἱοί, Mt. 5:45. In keeping with the presuppositions of the imagery (→ 983, 21 ff.), His love is united with effective discipline. The greatest gift becomes at once the strongest claim and demands decision, Mk. 11:25; Mt. 6:14 f.; 18:35; cf. Lk. 15:25 ff. The reality of fatherhood seeks to correct the practice of religion, Mt. 6:1 ff. Piety before men and a reward with the Father cancel one another out, → IV, 699, 32 ff. Belief in the Father means that God is regarded as unconditioned and unique (Father always equals Lord). [286] He who penetrates all things regulates worship, Mt. 6:4, 6, 18. Pharisaic control is replaced by direct disclosure to the Father. If everything in conduct is so totally referred to Him, the only possible aim is to glorify Him, Mt. 5:16. Belief in the Father is a spur to sanctification of life.

Commanding power is united with the motif of solicitude. This embraces all earthly needs right up to final salvation. God's εἰδέναι precedes our prayer,

---

[284] Did Lk. occasionally replace "father" in Q by θεός because he wanted to avoid the wrong Gk. idea of the πατὴρ τῶν ὅλων? The Gk. set the "Father" above nature as the Jew set Him above the people.

[285] Synoptic proclamation does not work out the idea that human fatherhood is a reflection of original divine truth, but that the original father concept is choked and deformed in the Gentile world and thus needs to be corrected by the "my Father" of the Redeemer. This — systematic — answer to our question would have to part company both with the universal Father and also with the idea of universal truth.

[286] In Mt. 23:9 God is called εἷς ὁ πατὴρ ὁ οὐράνιος in opposition to the Rabbinate, which claims sovereignty in matters of religion, law and custom. The honorary title "father" granted to the rabbi, and the legal bondage which makes dependent on the teacher, is rejected by the disciples as an attitude and custom. "Nor shall you call any one of you on earth father." The Western reading ὑμῖν (Aramaism for ὑμᾶς) is preferred by Wellh. and Klostermann Mt., ad loc., but it is best to follow F. Schulthess, "Zur Sprache d. Evangelien," ZNW, 21 (1922), 226, who suggests that τινὰ ἐξ should be supplied. In this rejection by Jesus of a magnifying of the teaching office (→ 977, 17 ff.), the name of the Father and the authoritative claim to lordship are both treated as equally essential. For God's ability to see what is hidden cf. Jos. Ant., 6, 263; 9, 3; Bell., 5, 413, cf. Schl. Mt., 203.

Mt. 6:8, 32; Lk. 12:30. βατταλογεῖν (→ I, 597, 1 ff.) in Mt. 6:7 implies mechanical praying and magical pressure which fails to recognise His willingness. In Mt. 7:9-11 and Lk. 11:11-13 (Q, → 991, 7 ff.) the use of the image of the earthly father reaches its climax. There is no anxious strain in the appeal to human experience. Even the πονηρός is not without fatherly goodness. The innocent man of prayer who will not deceive his own son may count on his heavenly Father with a πόσῳ μᾶλλον. [287] The main thought of provision is carried a stage further when the Father arms and protects in persecution and conflict. The parallelism of Mt. 6:26 and 10:29 (→ 990, 26 ff.) confirms the unbroken unity for both the inward and the outward. The persecuted experience supreme provision through His Spirit who endows with the word of witness, Mt. 10:20. Fatherly care for the μικροί (→ n. 266) includes their eternal destiny and keeps them from perishing, Mt. 18:14. There is a solemn appeal to this final court: Father. Thus the "your Father" is shown to be definitively all-encompassing. The power of the Lord and care of the Father, uniform and total, provide for all needs both temporal and eternal.

h. The Significance of Belief in the Father for the Disciples.

(a) The Christological Form of Belief in an authoritative Father. The vivid power of the natural image of the patriarchal norm gives life even to what is said about the relationship between Jesus and His Father. Already in the Synoptics this is a total determination of His will by the Father, a total commitment to Him in the work of salvation. Obedient subjection also implies limitation — a renunciation of any greater knowledge or power than that given to the Son. Mk. 13:32 par. Mt. 24:36 deals with ignorance of the date of the *parousia*. Mt. 20:23 (Mk. 10:40 without "father") shows that Jesus is limited in respect of further forms of service in the βασιλεία. Fatherhood carries with it dominion over the Son, and it is the task of the Son to affirm these limits in perfect union with the will of the Father. The prayer in the passion maintains this subjection, Mk. 14:36 and par. The superior (Mk.: πάντα δυνατά σοι) and solely normative will of the Father is affirmed in face of all self-will. In conformity with this is the attitude according to Mt. 26:53 f. Again, the sayings concerning the revelation and declaration of the Father in the Son are not fully intelligible to us to-day unless we remember the relation of father and son in patriarchy: whatever authority the son has he receives from the father. It is the gift of the Father which the Son distributes; He stands wholly in the Father's service. In Mt. 16:17 it is thus the Father who reveals the truth of the Son to those who make confession. If in the future gift of the kingdom He unites His people with Himself at table, this is again based on household fellowship. The cry of jubilation and the parable of the prodigal and his elder brother (Lk. 15) bring us to the supreme point of the message of the Father as Christology.

(b) The Cry of Jubilation in Mt. 11:25-30. The mystery of the Son is an integral part of the cry of jubilation (Mt. 11:25-30; Lk. 10:21 f.) [288] as the self-witness of

---

[287] The analogy of the human father may be traced again in the idea of the father seeing his child and knowing his needs, or in the father's ἀποδώσει (his response to filial love).

[288] For older bibl. to 1911 cf. esp. H. Schumacher, "Die Selbstoffenbarung Jesu bei Mt. 11:27 (Lk. 10:22)," *Freiburger Theol. Studien,* H. 6 (1912), IX-XVI. For textual questions cf. also T. Zahn, *Forschungen zur Gesch. d. nt.lichen Kanons u. d. altkirchlichen Lit.,* I (1881), 148 f.; also *Gesch. d. nt.lichen Kanons,* I (1888), 555-557; II (1890), 470; A. Merx, *Die 4 kanonischen Ev. nach ihrem ältesten bekannten Texte,* II, 1: *Das Ev. Mt.* (1902), 199-202; A. v. Harnack, *Sprüche u. Reden Jesu* (1907), 189-216; also *Marcion*[2] (1924), 206; J. Chapman, ThSt, 10 (1909), 552-566. On interpretation outside the comm.:

Jesus. [289] As the bearer of the unique revelation of the Father He is in His own person completely independent of success or failure. [290] His only source of power is the fellowship with the Father from which He draws His authority, and which involves mutual knowledge. [291] From this proceeds the whole declaration of the Father in indissoluble co-operation. In Mt. esp. the saying, taken from Q, [292] is adapted like nothing else in the economy of the Gospel to give the "my Father" its ultimate root. The fact that Mt. like Lk. could so use a saying which derives from the Johannine sphere [293] is worth pondering. For here the Synoptic and the Johannine proclamation is fused at a decisive

D. F. Strauss, "Jesu Weheruf über Jerusalem u. die σοφία τοῦ θεοῦ, Mt. 23:34-39; Lk. 11:49-51; 13:34 f.," ZwTh, 6 (1863), 92; R. Seydel, "Miscelle zu Mt. 11:27; Lk. 10:22," Jbch. pr. Th., 7 (1881), 761 f.; W. Brandt, Die ev. Gesch. u. d. Ursprung des Christentums (1893), 561 f., 576; Dalman WJ, I, 158 f., 231-233; P. W. Schmiedel, "Die 'joh.' St. bei Mt. u. Lk.," Pr. M., 4 (1900), 1-22; also Das 4. Ev. gegenüber d. drei ersten (1906), 48-52; O. Pfleiderer, Das Urchr., I² (1902), 435-437; A. Loisy, L'Évangile et l'Église⁴ (1908), 77 f.; H. J. Holtzmann, Lehrbuch d. Nt.lichen Theol., I² (1911), 345-348; W. Heitmüller, Art. "Jesus Christus," RGG¹, III, 374 (= Jesus [1913], 70-89); A. Schweitzer, Gesch. d. Leben-Jesu-Forschung² (1913), 411; E. Norden, Agnostos Theos (1913), 75 ff., 277-308; J. Weiss, "Das Logion Mt. 11:25-30," Nt.liche Studien f. G. Heinrici (1914), 120-129; W. Bousset, Kyrios Christos² (1921), 45-51; T. Häring, "Mt. 11:28-30," Aus Schrift u. Geschichte. Theol. Abh. f. A. Schlatter (1922), 3-15; E. Meyer, Ursprung u. Anfänge d. Christentums, I (1924), 280-291; D. A. Frövig, "Das Sendungsbewusstsein Jesu u. d. Geist," BFTh, 29, 3 (1924), 228-232; Clemen, 77 f.; C. F. Burney, The Poetry of our Lord (1925), 133, 144 f., 171 f.; J. Schniewind, "Zur Synoptikerexegese," ThR, NF, 2 (1930), 169 f.; Bultmann Trad., 171 f.; L. de Grandmaison, Jésus Christ, II⁶ (1931), 60 ff.; M. Dibelius, Die Formgeschichte d. Ev.² (1933), 279-284; T. Arvedson, "Das Mysterium Christi. Eine Studie z. Mt. 11:25-30," Arbeiten u. Mitteilungen aus d. Nt.lichen Seminar zu Uppsala, 7 (1937); on this J. Jeremias, ThBl, 18 (1939), 135 f.

[289] The psalm-like hymn of Mt. consists of three parts which are very different in metre and style : 11:25 f. (I), 27 (II), 28-30 (III). There is no doubt as to the Semitic character of I and III, cf. Str.-B., I, 606 f.; Schl. Mt., 381-389; Bultmann Trad., 172; Hck. Lk., J. Schniewind Mt. (NT Deutsch), ad loc. The relation of II to the OT and Jewish world is contested. The term ἀποκαλύπτειν (which gathers up 25 f. and 27 in a kind of slogan, Jeremias, 135) is not necessarily a word taken from Hell. mysticism, cf. Sir. 3:19 f. Heb.; Mt. 16:17; → III, 569 f., 580 ff. Best attested in the text is ἐπιγινώσκει (with ἔγνω, gnomic aor.) in Mt. and γινώσκει in Lk., corresponding to the Heb. יָדַע. In favour of Hell. Gnosticism are Bousset, op. cit., 48 f., 50, n. 1; J. Weiss, op. cit., 125; Dibelius, op. cit., 280, n. 2; Bultmann Trad., 172; cf. → I, 713, 28 (Chr. proclamation in Gnostic terms); Arvedson, op. cit. (liturgy of a mystery feast); against it is J. Jeremias, op. cit., 135 f. To be rejected is double knowing in the sense of identification mysticism, also παραδιδόναι as the transmission of secret teaching (so first Seydel, 761, then H. J. Holtzmann, Die Synoptiker = Hand-Comm. z. NT, I, 1³ [1901], ad loc.; Wellh. Mt., ad loc.; Heitmüller, 375; J. Weiss, 123; Norden, 292). The ref. here is rather to the transmission of power: Da. 7:14 LXX; Mt. 28:18; 1 C. 15:24; → II, 171, 1-13. On "to transmit" and "all things" in the Rabb. cf. Schl. Mt., 383 f. Knowledge and fulness of power are related, Schweitzer, 411. The goal is the act of revelation.

[290] This is how Mt. took it, ἐπιγινώσκειν being contrasted with the failure to recognise Jesus, Mt. 11:1-6, 11, 18 f., 20-24; c. 12 ff. The extolling of the Father takes place against this background. Cf. Schl. Mt., 384; Schniewind, op. cit. on 11:25.

[291] Already in the 2nd cent. — Marcion, Just., Tat. — we often find the order: "No one knows the Father but the Son, and no one knows the Son but the Father." The Father is put first for dogmatic reasons, but this disturbs the train of thought, which is that the Son knows and reveals. For express refs. cf. Schumacher, op. cit., 50-100.

[292] Mt. 11:28-30, however, is from a special source. III is not an unimportant appendix; it develops further the contents of I and II. The heavy-laden yoke are like the νήπιοι. Here, too, one may see the antithesis to the σοφοί (their burdensome yoke). As anaw Jesus promises the aniyyim Messianic menucha. But anaw (as the content of v. 29) interprets υἱός. Cf. esp. Häring, op. cit., 13 f.

[293] The Johannine form of Mt. 11:27 is incontestable. Cf. the πάντα παρεδόθη, the abs. "the Father," "the Son," the self-witness of Jesus, the secret of His nature, the mutual knowledge in correspondence, the theme of revelation. On παρεδόθη cf. διδόναι in Jn., where it is linked with πάντα or πᾶσα σάρξ and with πατήρ: Jn. 3:35; 13:3; 17:2.

pt. by the Evangelists themselves. That Q had this element shows that striving for confessional formulation was known in this stratum too. The question of formal authenticity can be answered in respect of the cry of jubilation only as in respect of Jn. Spiritual truth concerning the nature of Jesus is here given kerygmatic form. The assumption that genuine sayings of Jesus are developed in this way is supported by the consideration that expression is thus given to the mystery of the Son of Man.

c. The Christological Message concerning the Father in Lk. 15:11-32. Lk. 15:11-32 proclaims the christological message concerning the Father. [294] Fatherly love shows mercy with direct force, not demanding a time of strict punishment. [295] Here again (→ 984, n. 244) the ref. is not to pedagogic casuistry but to the central question of true conversion. If this is present, grace is freely given. With tender tact this seals the penitent's lips and grants unlimited restoration. The father's zealous attempt in the second part to win approval for his action [296] and also to put across a new concept of co-operation is a further climax. Reception of the prodigal is extended to winning the elder brother into the same circle of blessing. But the elder brother opposes the truth of fatherhood by refusing to have pity and by spoiling the father's gift with his idea of rewards. The father's will is not just to be done as a command but by acceptance of his mercy. Like the conversion of the prodigal, that of the elder brother will mean the restoration of a true relation to the father. The father wants to be truly one with both his sons. Hence the joyous feast [297] is not meant to be the exaggerated pampering of one group, but a rejoicing together of the whole household.

Everything here stands in very close relation to the work of Jesus. The father of the parable embodies the action of the heavenly Father no less than of Jesus Himself. Lk. 15 refers to the Father inasmuch as He is the main person in the work of Jesus. Jesus' approach to the two attitudes is a manifestation of heaven. He shows both groups the Father who opens His doors to the guilty and seeks to overcome legalistic hardness. Christology, then, consists in action which the Father has appointed and by which He unites in a new fellowship the community which has been divided into unrighteous and righteous. What is presented is not just the abstract idea: "You have a loving Father." The gracious work of Jesus displays the whole Christ-content in living deeds.

---

[294] Bibl. apart from comm. and expositions of the parables (cf. bibl. in J. Jeremias, *Die Gleichnisse Jesu*[2] [1952], 5): W. M. Macgregor, "The Parable of the Two Sons," Exp. T., 38 (1926/27), 498-501; A. Schlatter, "Jesu Gleichnis v.d. beiden Söhnen," *Jbch. d. Theol. Schule Bethel*, 2 (1931), 35-63; J. Schniewind, *Das Gleichnis vom verlorenen Sohn* (1940); T. W. Manson, *The Sayings of Jesus* (1949), 284-290; J. Jeremias and E. Schweizer, "Zum Gleichnis vom verlorenen Sohn. Lk. 15:11-32," *Theol. Zschr.*, 5 (1949), 228-233; J. A. Findlay, *Jesus and His Parables* (1950), 72-77. On Lk. 15 and the death of Jesus: Jülicher Gl. J., II, 364 f.; E. Cremer, "Die Gleichnisse Lk. 15 u. das Kreuz," BFTh, 8, 4 (1904), 69 ff.; Schlatter, *op. cit.*, 51 f.

[295] In the Indian Saddharma Pundarika Sutra the prodigal is restored to his inheritance only after 50 yrs. of probation and on the death of his father. Cf. R. Seydel, *Die Buddhalegende u. d. Leben Jesu nach d. Ev.*[2] (1897): D. G. A. van den Bergh v. Eysinga, *Indische Einflüsse auf evangelische Erzählungen* (1904).

[296] The pt. made in → n. 243 throws light on the conduct of the father in 3 ways: 1. His agreement to the division is an exercise of sovereign power. This opening must have given offence to the legalistic sensibilities of the Pharisees. In interpretation it strengthens the element of free and generous power of disposal. 2. This element is enriched by the fact that the father is the most affected and that he twice renounces ownership and usufruct. 3. The conversation with the legalistic elder brother thus takes place against a special background. The father, who makes the greatest self-sacrifice and loses the most, exhorts the elder brother: As I have done, go out of your way in pity instead of insisting on the letter of the law.

[297] This is not just the starting-point of the story (Lk. 15:1 f.) but a paradigm of the joy of the creative work of Jesus.

The thesis that the understanding of the death of Jesus as a saving act bears no relation to Lk. 15 and is shown to be superfluous thereby isolates His death from His total work. What brings Jesus to the cross, however, is that He seeks to unite the sundered people in the Father. Lk. himself shows that He loves the two sons even to death itself, for He forgives the thief and prays for the self-righteous. His death is the crown and centre of His whole life, for He who thus preaches and acts fulfils on the cross the truth of fatherhood which dominates His ministry. On the other hand, there is, of course, no explicit theology of the cross here.

i. The Unity of Father, King and Judge.

(a) Father and Judge. In the thinking of antiquity there is no antithesis between fatherly provision and judicial power. A feature of the most primitive patriarchy is that the father discharges a judicial function in the home. Mt. 7:21-23 (cf. 15:13) deals with the attitude to the will of the Father as the norm in judgment, and Mt. 18:23-35 (v. 35) with the judicial activity of the Father. Here we have the synthesis of the Father (= King) and Judge, cf. 1 Pt. 1:17, → 1010, 28 ff. In Mt. 25:31, 34, 41 the Son of Man judges in the name of His Father. [298]

(b) Father and Ruler. [299] The very concept of father entails full and true lordship without any need for additional support or borrowing. In the preaching of Jesus, however, this element of command in "father" is strengthened by the link with the βασιλεία. This is yet another check against any weakening of the concept. The one is always related to the other, and the two merge into one another in harmonious proclamation. [300] One may thus speak of a unity between Father and Ruler, for the primary sense of *malkut* emphasises the divine kingship. [301] The fusing of Father and *malkut* might be described as the leading principle in the whole proclamation of Jesus. It is thus impossible to set the divine King and the divine Father in antithesis the one to the other. Attempts have been made to distinguish between the *abinu malkenu* in the Prayer of Eighteen Petitions and Akiba (→ 979, n. 212) and what Jesus has in view. The synagogal form of address certainly does not occur in Jesus. Yet in the cry of jubilation (→ 992, 40 ff.) we read : [302] πάτερ, κύριε τοῦ οὐρανοῦ καὶ τῆς γῆς, Mt. 11:25; Lk. 10:21. Only if one diminishes the primary significance of the divine lordship can one fail to see the God-King motif in Jesus. Certainly the sparing use of βασιλεύς for God in the Synoptic Gospels stands

---

[298] Grundmann's view (127-234) that the thought of God as Judge is not intrinsic to Jesus, and that the idea of Jesus as world Judge is secondary (155 f.), is untenable in the light of the imposing support for both in Q, Mk. and the material peculiar to Mt. For Jesus there is no βασιλεία or fatherhood of God without the proclamation of judgment.

[299] On the divine king and father in oriental and Gk. thought cf. J. Leipoldt, *War Jesus Jude?* (1923), 25 f.; also "Der Sieg d. Christentums über d. antiken Religionen," *Ephémerides Orientales*, No. 27 (1925), 8 ff.; also "Das Gotteserlebnis Jesu im Lichte d. vergleichenden Religionsgeschichte," *Angelos Beih.*, 2 (1927), 11-16; also *Jesu Verhältnis z. Griechen u. Juden* (1941), 124-144; Grundmann, 117 ff.; G. Kittel, *Die Religionsgeschichte u. d. Urchr.* (1931), 153, n. 334. That the Jew of Jesus' day could not separate *malkut* from *mäläk* is shown by the fact that the Rabb. principle : "To take on oneself the yoke of the *malkut*," meant confession of the one God.

[300] Father and kingdom are expressly related in all strata. They are already interwoven in Q, Mt. 6:32 f.; Lk. 12:30 f. Their combination is fundamental to an understanding of the Lord's Prayer, Mt. 6:9 f. Possibly Mt. has helped to shape Mt. 7:21, but the passages from the special sources in Mt. 13:41-43; 25:31, 34; Lk. 12:32; 22:29 show again (→ 989, 16 ff.) how closely the *malkut* concept from Da. 7 is bound up with the preaching of the Father.

[301] Cf. J. Weiss, *Die Predigt Jesu vom Reiche Gottes²* (1900); R. Bultmann, "Reich Gottes u. Menschensohn," ThR, NF, 9 (1937), 1-35.

[302] We also find κύριος for God on the lips of the Synoptic Jesus. In OT quotations Mk. 12:11 par. Mt. 21:42; Mk. 12:29 f.; Mt. 4:7, 10 par. Lk. 4:8, 12; Lk. 4:19. Though cf. also Mk. 5:19; 13:20; Lk. 20:37 and Mt. 9:38 par. Lk. 10:2.

in need of some explanation. [303] The reason for the infrequency is to be sought in the transferring of Χριστός and κύριος to Jesus Himself ; when the Gospels were written this use was just as established as that of θεὸς ὁ πατήρ for God. On the basis of the unity of πατήρ and βασιλεία Jesus summons to conversion from all pseudo-theocracy. The kingly rule of God in the sense of the dawning age of salvation is also the fatherly rule of grace. There can be no room for doubt that in *malkut* Jesus maintains the divine rule, for His whole witness breathes personal theocentricity. If in a new comprehension and with a new depth and dynamism He prefers the word "father," He nevertheless combines the father motif with the ruler motif. He puts an end to any legalistic restriction of such terms as "Lord," "King" and "Judge." These strong elements are not ruled out as Jewish or transitory. This would promote only a mollusc-like use of the father concept. The astonishing novelty that in early Chr. worship πατήρ is preferred to Yahweh, *adonai, kurios* or *theos* is not the fruit of a teaching movement but the living experience of Him who as the definitive Revealer is wholly rooted in the Father. Thus a term which in Judaism is related to Israel becomes universal and world-wide. Accumulated terms for God give way to a simplicity previously unknown. Whereas in Judaism awe of the Holy One led to fear of the very name of God, [304] both cult and fear, both accumulation and concealment of names, are now overcome by the one word "father."

II. πατήρ in John. [305]

1. The Usage.

In John's Gospel θεός, except when referred to Jesus (→ n. 346), occurs 73 times, κύριος is used for God only once in the quotation in 12:13, and πατήρ appears 115 times as a term for God (ὁ πατήρ, [306] ὁ πατήρ μου, [307] πάτερ, πατήρ in prayer). The number is not too certain because of textual variants. The *koine* text likes to put a μου with πατήρ. But the abs. easily predominates. Only at 6:27 do we find ὁ πατήρ ... ὁ θεός. [308] "Our Father" does not occur in Jn. and "your Father" only once, though in the decisive verse 20:17 where it denotes the new status of the disciples after the resurrection, → 1001, 6 ff. Avoidance of "your Father" as a Jewish confession is clarified by the controversy. [309] It is also striking that "Father in the heavens" does not appear, though we do find "Son of Man" and "kingdom of God." The author, however, is not concerned about fidelity to the formal usage of Jesus. He does not encumber the thematic revelational term "father" by the addition. Elsewhere he stresses the antithesis between the heavenly and the earthly, though in this connection he uses a different terminology from the authentically Jewish. [310]

---

[303] The king who forgives the debt in Mt. 18 (cf. v. 23 with 35) and then judges the unforgiving servant is the heavenly "Father." We find βασιλεία = βασιλεύς in Mt. 22:2-14, again with the thought of judgment. The Son of Man is King in Mt. 25:34, 40, → 995, 14 f.

[304] This fear, extended to κύριος, may be seen in Jos., cf. Schl. Theol. d. Judt., 24-26, 60; Schl. J., 35.

[305] Bibl.: W. F. Lofthouse, *The Father and the Son* (1934); also "Fatherhood and Sonship in the Fourth Gospel," Exp. T., 43 (1931), 442-448 (Germ. ThBl, 11 [1932], 289-300); Bu. J., 36 f.

[306] The abs. "the Father" is adopted esp. by the Did., Apologists, Cl. Al.; Did., 1, 5; Just. Dial., 74, 1; 76, 3; 86, 2 etc.; Cl. Al. Prot., 10, 94, 3 (GCS, 12, 69, 11); Cl. Al. Exc. Theod., 30, 1 (GCS, 17, 116, 27); cf. O. Sol. 19:2, 4.

[307] On "my Father" cf. O. Sol. 10:4; "his Father" 41:11. The first-born son says of God "my Father" in Apc. Sedrach 9:5.

[308] 2 Jn. 3 may be compared with the liturgical blessings in Pl. except that in the battle against heretics τοῦ υἱοῦ τοῦ πατρός approximates to dogmatic formulation. 1 and 2 Jn. share the fixed ὁ πατήρ with Jn. In Rev. πατήρ, always with αὐτοῦ or μου, is related solely to Christ, 1:6; 2:28; 3:5, 21; 14:1.

[309] In Jn. 8:38 the ὑμῶν, if original, refers to Abraham. In 8:42 πατὴρ ὑμῶν is called in question when used with ref. to God, → 1002, 12 ff.

[310] The epithet in ὁ ζῶν πατήρ (Jn. 6:57) arises out of the context. On πάτερ ἅγιε in 17:11 cf. Test. Jud. 24:2; Did., 10, 2. From the standpoint of comparative religion the

2. The Concept of Father and Patriarchy.

The idea of begetting (→ 955, 23 ff.) is not related by Jn. to the name "father," [311] though he does use the illustration of the head of the household to explain the christological mystery. The Father is unconditionally (→ 983, 22 ff.) ὁ μείζων (Jn. 14:28). He takes precedence. His character as Lord is expressed in His authoritative giving, 6:32. The Son knows His will, obeys Him, recognises Him and honours Him. For all the inner harmony (10:30) there can be no doubt that the Son's love implies obedience, and that it is only as He obeys that He is continually loved. According to modern ideas an adult son totally dependent on his father in all his acts is quite inconceivable. Without analogies from folklore the figure of speech is hardly intelligible. Only on these presuppositions can the full dependence of the Revealer on Him who ultimately reveals find expression in the symbolism of father and son. There is a genuine patriarchal feature in 8:35 : The Son remains for ever in the Father's house and fellowship. According to 16:15; 17:10 everything the Father has is His, cf. Lk. 15:31, → 983, 28 f. In virtue of His hereditary position He has influence as a mediator and advocate and can gain a hearing with His Father for the servants under His protection, 8:35. 14:2 is also based on the idea of patriarchal rule. He who goes to the Father prepares a place there for those who belong to Him. He establishes them as members of the Father's household. He makes His home accessible to them as a final place of residence. [312]

3. The Concept of Revelation.

Though other points of connection are to be noted, one has to say of Jn. that his proclamation of the Father is possible only on a Synoptic foundation. In adopting the message of Jesus concerning the divine fatherhood, however, he developed it as an interpretation of the concept of revelation. In him, therefore "father" has a special sense determined by the relation of the Revealer to God. "Father" has a purely christological and soteriological foundation. In keeping is the absolute use, though this does not differ from ὁ πατήρ μου. In the Synoptists, too, the father concept is not a general religious idea (→ 990, 21 ff.) but is controlled by "my Father" as used by Jesus. No less, and quite indisputably, Jn. differs from the Greek world by taking as his point of departure, not a veneration of the πατήρ τῶν ὅλων, but solely and simply the truth that the Son, who is sent, is uniquely related to the Father and is the first to say πατήρ in the full sense. [313]

---

radius here is very broad : Rigveda, VII, 52, 3 : "The great Father who is worthy of sacrifice" (of Varuna). Cf. also Bu. J., 384, n. 4; on πατήρ δίκαιε in Jn. 17:25 ibid., 399, n. 3.

[311] The children of God are certainly said to be begotten or born of Him : Jn. 1:13; 3:3 ff., even more strongly 1 Jn. 2:29; 3:9; 5:18, cf. also 5:1, 4. But none of these statements is in explanation of ὁ πατήρ. Nor does Jesus ever say in Jn. that the Father begot Him. The Nicene γεννηθέντα is not in view in Johannine Christology ; the idea of eternal preexistence would seem to preclude it. This thought is not necessarily connected with the μονογενής of 1:14, 18; 3:16, 18, since this word, used in many different ways, had become so formal that there is no emphasis on -γενής in the sense of origin by begetting. The stress is placed on His unique sonship. What concerns Jn. is the present outworking of the Father-Son relation rather than the Gnostic problem of generation. For μονογενής cf. Bu. J., 47, n. 2. While Schl. J., 26; Lofthouse, Exp. T., 43 and Bu. J. ("Revealer") decide in favour of unique sonship, F. Büchsel (→ IV, 741, 24 ff.) takes the word to denote "only-begotten" in the Nicene sense.

[312] On Jn. 14:1-7: O. Schäfer, "Der Sinn d. Rede Jesu von den vielen Wohnungen in seines Vaters Hause u. von dem Weg zu ihm (Jn. 14:1-7)," ZNW, 32 (1933), 210-217.

[313] The cosmological speculation that God as Father brought forth the cosmos as His son, endowed it with fulness of power, and loves it (→ 954, 23 ff.; 958, 9 ff.), is quite alien to Jn.'s proclamation, as may be seen from the difference in substance between this cos-

4:21, 23 (→ 1003, 25 ff.) is also christologically rooted. There is no more radical rejection of the idea of universal fatherhood than this treatment of the question purely on the basis of Messianic actuality. That the issue is always the divine reality of the primary meaning and process of revelation and its ultimate foundations may be seen already in the Prologue in Jn. 1:14, 18, where the oneness of Father and Son is a main theme. The Father is the author and giver of revelation, the Son is the Revealer. The invisible God is manifested through Him who is in the most intimate fellowship with Him (1:18) and who comes in the name (→ 273, 22 ff.), i.e., on the commission, of the Father (5:43), whose θέλημα (→ III, 55 f.) stands behind Him and sustains the whole saving event. [314] The Father as authoritative Giver gives Him in person as the true bread from heaven, 6:32. He bore witness to Him already in the Scriptures, 5:37 ff. If Israel rejects Him, Moses himself will be its accuser πρὸς τὸν πατέρα, 5:45, → 1002, 27.

Profundity is added by the concept of pre-existence. Jn. is the first to give the inner divine relationship the accent of eternity. [315] Only He who is beyond all human comparison and has always been most intimate with the Father can declare the Father, 1:1, 18. The ὁ ὢν εἰς τὸν κόλπον τοῦ πατρός does not refer to a single stage (prae, post) but to what has always been and always is. [316] The Father's love for Him (→ 999, 30 ff.) is from the foundation of the world, 17:24. Because Jesus has seen the Father, He can declare Him, 6:46. [317, 318]

What has been said already enables us to see why "sending" is a key word for the work of revelation, → I, 404, 25 ff. [319] One may speak of an alternation between "father" and "sender." The one elucidates the other. This use exercises a predominant control over the father concept inasmuch as it shows that the Father is

---

mology and Jn.'s concept of revelation. Bu. J., 119, esp. n. 3, 188, n. 3, cf. 190, n. 2, 294, n. 4 champions the view that Jn. uses the concepts of Gnostic myth in interpretation. He abandons the mythology but he retains the terms, which enable him to go beyond the OT concept of prophecy in his characterisation of the person and word of Jesus. Now there can be no doubt that in his attempt to speak to Gnosticism Jn. uses such forms without himself becoming Gnostic. The only pt. is that the cosmic mythology becomes quite unrecognisable in his presentation. Nor should one overlook the primary connection with Da. 7 in respect of ἐξουσία and the transfer of power, → n. 289.

[314] On Jesus as the One who does His Father's θέλημα cf. Jn. 4:34; 5:30; 6:38-40, cf. 7:17. Cf. Just. Dial., 85, 1; 113, 4; Cl. Al. Paed., III, 1, 2, 1 (GCS, 12, 236, 28). Acc. to Prot., 12, 120, 4 (GCS, 12, 85, 6 f.) He is in person the will of the Father.

[315] Materially cf. esp. 8:58 and all the sayings about His coming into the world, coming from above, descent from heaven, coming forth from God, though the term "father" is not always used in this connection, e.g., Jn. 1:9; 3:13, 19; 6:33, 38, 41 f., 46, 50 f., 58; 8:14, 42; 13:3; 16:28, 30.

[316] On Jn. 1:18 cf. H. Windisch, "Angelophanien um den Menschensohn auf Erden," ZNW, 30 (1931), 223.

[317] This art. does not deal expressly with the imparted ἐξουσία or the transfer of power to the Son, nor is any emphasis given to explicit statements about the Son. In view of the theme in → 999, 17 ff. it has naturally not been possible to adhere rigidly to this distinction. The sayings about authority which include the basis in eternity (Jn. 3:34 f.; 13:3; 17:2 → υἱός) tell us many important things about the meaning of πατήρ, not only in respect of the foundation in the Father's love (Jn. 3:35 f., → 999, 30 f.), but also in respect of the insight that He is sealed (= confirmed) by the Father, that from Him He has life in Himself, and that only thus does He fulfil His commission right on to the eschata, Jn. 5:22-30, cf. 6:40.

[318] The eternity saying in 1 Jn. 1:2, which is secondary in form, is based on Jn. 1:2, πατήρ being added.

[319] In this sense πέμπειν is used 24 times and ἀποστέλλειν 18. There is a full statement in Jn. 5:23: "The Father has sent the Son." The idea is linked directly with πατήρ 11 times: Jn. 5:23, 36 f.; 6:44, 57; 8:16, 18; 10:36; 12:49; 14:24; 20:21.

the One who authoritatively commissions the Son to be the instrument of His will (→ 997, 5 f.; → III, 55 f.) and the doer of His work (→ 1000, 8 ff.). The Son has no other purpose. He is the bearer of His ἐντολή, 12:49 f. → II, 553, 20 ff. The mission is most impressively described in 10:36 as a consecration to sacred ministry. [320]

Does the emphasis always fall on the process of revelation, [321] and not also on the fact that "father" itself is a word of revelation? In the declaration according to the Synoptic Gospels the name of "father" is inseparable from the process. So, too, Jn. 17:6, 26: ἐφανέρωσα or ἐγνώρισα ... τὸ ὄνομά σου, [322] sums up the whole work of Jesus. According to 17:11 this name is the keeping power in which the disciples are protected, cf. 17:12. Precisely by this name which cannot be disregarded Jesus makes God known, cf. 12:28. [323] What is made known cannot be anything higher than the Father, cf. 14:28. Whatever Jesus may proclaim to the disciples, it will ultimately have only one content; it will be declaration περὶ τοῦ πατρός, 16:25. To be sure, this is not just a theoretical father concept. It is not a self-grounded father theology. It is certainly not the mere veneration of a holy verbal symbol. Revelation is never separated from the saving work of the Son. It is given in and with this event, which is always the content of the witness to the Father, 6:41 ff. To know or see the Son is to know or see the Father, 14:7-10, cf. 8:19; 12:45. Acceptance or rejection of the Revealer is also a final attitude vis-à-vis the Father who reveals Himself, 8:42; 15:23 f. Finally, then, the process of revelation is explicitly a declaration of the Father. One cannot object that there is nothing new in calling God "Father," for as definitive revelation is given by Jesus this very word πατήρ is filled with new content in the decisive Now. [324]

4. The Harmony of Father and Son, → υἱός.

The whole event of salvation is anchored in the most intimate union between Father and Son. This is the core of Johannine proclamation. [325] What, then, does it imply for the πατήρ concept in Jn. that the Son lives only on the basis of the Father (6:57), that He is one with Him (10:30), and that He has unlimited participation in Him (16:15; 17:10, → 997, 14 f.)? The main accent falls on the simple basic statement: "The Father loves the Son," 3:35 (→ I, 52, 39 ff.). [326] This is not meant emotionally or mystically. It is always very closely bound up with the commissioned work of the Son, 8:16, 29; cf. 5:20. Love, then, is the deepest expression of the relation between the One who reveals Himself and His instrument,

---

[320] The Father is also Sender in 1 Jn. 4:14.

[321] Bu. J., 188 f., 374, 453 takes this view. But justice must be done to the revelation expressly given in the name "father."

[322] The name of God is no longer a mystery enveloped in silence as in the Synagogue. Cf. Schl. J., 319 f.

[323] In 5:43; 10:25, however, name means commission.

[324] Liturgically the greeting in 2 Jn. 3 presents the same view more pregnantly → n. 368.

[325] In the Johannine Epistles, too, the inseparable unity of Father and Son is basic (1 Jn. 1:3; 2:22 f.; 2 Jn. 9), also in Rev. in all πατήρ sayings, → n. 308.

[326] For Gnostic pars. to the fact that the Son is not separated from the Father cf. Bu. J., 212, n. 2, cf. 269, n. 23. Referring back to mythological terminology from the time of Plat. Tim. (→ 954, 19 ff.), which is developed in cosmological speculation, Bu. J. (119, 190, 293, 397, 400, 415 f.) argues that the meaning of loving is that God the Creator and Redeemer gives Himself form in His Son and is thus present and active in Him as in an image. The dignity of the Revealer is also expressed herewith. The par. has historical significance; the only pt. is that the purely mythological element is laid aside in Jn. and the meaning of loving is controlled by the reality of salvation as primitive Christianity understood it.

15:9; 17:23 f., 26. [327] That ἀγαπᾶν is used in the preterite as well as the present corresponds yet again to its foundation in pre-temporal being. Mutual γινώσκειν and εἰδέναι (8:55; 10:15, → 993, 3 f.) are unconditional characteristics of the loving. This is also the presupposition of the commission and sending, cf. 7:29; 8:55; 17:25. [328] Even though the love can be described as a being [329] of the Father in the Son or *vice versa* (→ υἱός; 10:38; 14:11; 17:21), action is always the decisive feature. This unity finds expression in the fact that the Father determines what the Son does and says (ποιεῖν, 5:19, cf. 8:28; λαλεῖν, 7:17 f., cf. 12:49). The Father gives the Son a work to complete, 17:4. The ἔργα are done in His name (→ II, 642, 37 ff.), 10:25. They are ἐκ τοῦ πατρός, 10:32. Indeed, they are works of the Father Himself, 10:37 f. The main point at issue in the words, too, is the λόγος τοῦ πατρός, 14:24, cf. 3:34 f. The word is taught (8:28) and commanded (12:49) by the Father, indeed, it is first spoken by Him to the Son (12:50). Words and works are so closely connected that they can be alternated (14:10) and treated as synonymous (8:28). They bear witness to both the Sender and the Sent (10:25). In both the basis in eternity is emphasised by the concept of pre-existence. [330] Anchored thus, the total fellowship of giving produces the dramatic act of revelation. The giving of the Father ordains everything up to the resurrection and glory, 6:39, 44. The whole state of salvation is impregnably grounded in this "being given by the Father" as an ultimate statement, 10:29 f.; 17:24; cf. 6:37; → 1003, 9 ff. [331] The unity of Father and Son finds perfect expression in the sacrifice of life. The expression "to go to the Father," [332] however, means more than dying. [333] It embraces the whole future which awaits the Son from the passion to the yielding up of the spirit and its implications. [334] The unbroken harmony, the οὐκ εἰμὶ μόνος

---

[327] For Mandaean and Manichean pars. to the theme of the Revealer as an instrument cf. R. Bultmann, "Die Bdtg. der neuerschlossenen mandäischen u. manichäischen Quellen f. d. Joh.-Ev.," ZNW, 24 (1925), 100-146.

[328] Bultmann (Bu. J., 187) rightly emphasises that the unity of Jesus with God is not merely at the level of moral will and action, but that the authoritative claim of mission is always at issue. It is important, however, that the unity is worked out ethically and not mystically.

[329] The term "of one substance," which derives from οὐσία speculation, does not really accord with what is stated in Jn. 10:30, 38; 14:10 f., 20 f., for in Jn. we do not have a static view of being or a metaphysical statement corresponding to Gk. thought but a statement of pure action and relation. The unity (*nomen actionis*) is living and active. It is no mere subject of consideration in and for itself, but a constant process of salvation. Cf. Schl. J., 242, 245; Bu. J., 186 f., 290 f., 392 f., n. 2, 470; Lofthouse, ThBl, 293; E. Gaugler, "Das Christuszeugnis des Joh.," *Jesus Christus im Zeugnis d. heiligen Schrift u. d. Kirche* (1936), 43, 55 f.

[330] Cf. Jn. 3:34 f.; 5:36; 8:26, 28; 12:49 f.; 17:4. Jn. normally uses the preterite, esp. the perf., to establish the basis in eternity. Jn. 5:19 again means the situation created by pre-existence and not the process of guidance. Cf. Schl. J., 153 ("not mantic inspiration and dictation"); Bu. J., 191, n. 5 (as against L. Brun, "Die Gottesschau d. joh. Christus," Symb. Osl., 5 [1927], 1-22; W. Lütgert, *Die joh. Christologie*² [1916], 25-36; F. Büchsel, *Das Ev. nach Joh.*² [*NT Deutsch*, 1937], 15 f.).

[331] In support of the view that this "given" contains a stress on eternity cf. διδόναι in the perf.: Jn. 6:39; 10:29; 17:24. In 17:2 the most comprehensive word of authority is linked with the fact that believers are "given."

[332] Jn. 16:28 gives a full development of stages, for this going presupposes coming, descent, being sent. The way of the Revealer assumes ἐξῆλθον, 16:28; 17:8, cf. 16:30 (→ II, 680, 3 ff., → υἱός). Other verses which contain "to go to the Father" are 13:1, 3; 14:12, 28; 16:10, 17, 28. The risen Lord has an illuminating closing word on this in 20:17, → 1001, 11 f.

[333] So Ign. R., 17, 2 for the goal of the martyr: δεῦρο πρὸς τὸν πατέρα.

[334] Cf. Bu. J., 102, n. 1, 210 f., 224, 354, 371 for coming and going as terms in Gnostic myth. That Jesus knows His whence and whither simply means that He appeals to His

(8:16, 29), is not disrupted by the passion, 16:32. Everything finds its focus here: the giving, for the Father gives Him the cup of suffering to drink (18:11 perfect, cf. Mk. 14:36 par.; Mt. 20:22); the loving as the Father's innermost assent to the self-offering (10:17); the obeying as the extreme demonstration that the ἐντολή is kept (10:17 f., cf. 14:31); the glorifying of the Father as the final goal (13:31; 14:13; 17:1 ff.). [335] There is a marked distinction between Jn. and the Synoptists in that the "your Father" in its one occurrence in Jn. is a word of the risen Lord with a specific meaning, namely, that only now does the Lord make His Father and God in the full sense the Father and God of His "brothers" (only here in Jn.) as well, 20:17. [336] This amplifies and fulfils 14:6, i.e., that the Son is personally and definitively the only way to the Father. [337] The Paraclete brings a full outworking of the Father-Son relation in His followers as a gift which lasts for ever, 14:18-21, 23, cf. 16:15: [338] The primordial divine fellowship is a paradigm of the life of the community. Leading concepts in the prototype like knowing and recognising (10:14 f., cf. 17:25), loving (15:9 f., cf. 14:21; 17:23, 26; 14:23 cf. 21), unity [339] (14:20; 17:4, 21), sending and glorifying (17:18; 20:21) have a fundamental and normative force for the Church. This is brought out by the use of καθώς and ὥσπερ in analogical inferences and reciprocity formulae. It is present figuratively in the address on the vine, 15:1 ff. [340]

5. The Conflict with the Jews for the Truth of the Father.

In 2:16 Jn. has Jesus say that the Jews corrupt "the house of my Father" (a significant change as compared with the Synoptists) by their mercenary spirit. The real conflict takes place, however, in the key incidents in the controversy about the relation of Jesus to the Father. Jesus is accused not only of desecrating

---

authorisation by and union with the Father. In Jn., however, one must insist that the real point is that a statement of faith is made about real coming whence and going whither.

[335] On the pt. that the ἐξουσία motif also culminates in the way of suffering (13:3 f., cf. 17:2) → υἱός.

[336] On the preparation of μοναί in the Father's house (14:2) → 997, 18 ff.

[337] 1 Jn. rests on what is promised in the Gospel, which is now seen to be fulfilled, namely, fellowship with the Father and the Son (1 Jn. 1:3). The τέκνα in the community have known the Father, cf. Jn. 14:7, 20. πατέρες and παιδία stand under the reality of the Father (1 Jn. 2:13 f.). Hence there can be ref. not only to abiding in the Son but also to abiding in the Father, 1 Jn. 2:24, cf. 4:12, 15 f. This extension of the formula again derives from the experience of fulfilled promise. Acc. to 1 Jn. 2:24 (cf. Jn. 5:38; 8:31; 15:7) this abiding means that what was heard from the beginning abides with them, cf. 2 Jn. 9 (διδαχή). In the struggle against heresy true doctrine is valued as an expression of the knowledge of fellowship with the Father and the Son. If acc. to Jn. 1:12 f. (cf. 11:52) the Logos gives ἐξουσία τέκνα θεοῦ γενέσθαι, so 1 Jn. 3:1 extols with joy the direct relation to the Father who in His love makes us τέκνα θεοῦ. Hence the developments in 1 Jn. are all seen to be deductions from the resurrection truth in 20:17, → 1001, 7 f.

[338] The variations regarding the question who sends the Spirit or from whom He proceeds (14:26; 15:26; 14:16; 16:7) simply propagate the basic fact of the fellowship between Father and Son. Emphasis is placed on the truth that the Spirit so proceeds from the Father that He attains His goal through the Son. Here, too, the Father is always the ultimate basis of revelation.

[339] Ign. Phld., 7, 2 tends to moralise this Joh. motif. In Eph., 5, 1, under the influence of κοινωνία in 1 Jn. 1:3, Ign. uses ideas of unity to strengthen the episcopate. On the other hand he shows a genuine understanding of Jn. 17 in Mg., 1, 2, where he desires the unity of the Church with the Father and the Son. Athenag. Suppl., 10, 2; 12, 2 also deals with the ἑνότης and κοινωνία between Father and Son. Cf. Cl. Al. Paed., I, 5, 24, 3 (GCS, 12, 104, 14); I, 7, 53, 1 (GCS, 12, 121, 26).

[340] Worth noting is the further development of both concept and expression in Rev. 2:26 ff.; 3:21; 14:1.

the Sabbath but also (5:18) of arrogant self-deification because He claims God as πατέρα ἴδιον. Even after the answer in 5:19-47 this is still the theme of the debate in c. 6, and it is continued especially in c. 8. The truth of fatherhood as the basic relation of Jesus to God is thus at the very heart of the conflict. According to 5:18 (cf. 19:7) Jesus has to die for this. The fundamental distinction is that He knows the Father and they know neither Him nor the Father. [341] The cleavage is brought out very clearly by the opponents' question: "Where is thy Father?" (8:19). The Jews want to compare Him to a mere man, and they place Him in the house of His earthly father (6:42) in order to invalidate the distinctiveness of His mission. [342] The appeal of the Jews to the εἷς πατὴρ ὁ θεός in 8:41 (based on Mal. 2:10) intentionally contains the basic monotheistic confession wherewith they hope to refute the charge that they are bastards. This dogma that God is their Father is contested because they do not prove it by recognition of the Father and the Son, 8:54 f. The controversy offers a significant explanation of Jn.'s avoidance of "your Father." The challenge in 8:42 (εἰ ὁ θεὸς πατὴρ ὑμῶν ἦν) gives striking proof of Jn.'s resolute concentration on a christologically controlled "father." Even the future persecution prophesied for the disciples stands under the same judgment of 17:25 (16:3, cf. 15:21). [343] But the conflict goes deeper. The battle for the mission and the truth of fatherhood is repeated in the convincing of the cosmos by the Paraclete (16:8-11, esp. v. 10). The antithesis between the Jews and Jesus is traced back to a difference in fatherhood (8:38; the devil is called their father in v. 44). [344] The reference is to spiritual relationship, not to birth. The child learns all that is decisive from his father (→ 975, 21 ff.). He imitates him (cf. the eloquent example of Abraham, → line 30 or Jn. 8:41: ποιεῖν τὰ ἔργα τοῦ πατρός). They derive from the devil the mainsprings of volition (τὰς ἐπιθυμίας τοῦ πατρὸς ποιεῖν, 8:44). As a murderer and liar from the beginning he is also the father of the liar. [345] The patriarchs Abraham and Moses are brought in as witnesses, cf. 5:45, → 998, 12 f. They claim Abraham as their father, but only their basic attitude can prove this claim, 8:39, 53, 56. Here, too, the decisive point is that the child of Abraham does τὰ ἔργα τοῦ Ἀβραάμ, → line 24.

6. The Father and Prayer.

The more suffering enters the picture, the more Jesus is depicted in Jn. as the One who prays to the Father, 11:41 f.; 12:27 ff.; 17. [346] Giving thanks at the tomb of Lazarus, He reveals in a lofty and impressive way the basic aspect of His unity

---

[341] This negative of γινώσκειν and εἰδέναι (→ 1001, 2 f.) occurs throughout the Gospel: 5:37; 7:28; 8:19, 54 f.; 15:21, 23 f. (μισεῖν); 16:3; 17:25.

[342] The contrast between κόσμος and πατήρ is given a rather different form in 1 Jn. (2:15-17). ἐκ τοῦ πατρός is a spiritual counterpart to ἐκ τοῦ κόσμου, which also occurs in Jn. In the meditation, which shows advance on the Gospel, emphasis is laid on tendencies which do not derive from the Father. Acc. to 2:22 f. antichrist denies both Father and Son. New here is the concept of antichrist and the use of ἀρνεῖσθαι (opp. ὁμολογεῖν) in the battle against heresy. The correspondence between Father and Son is taken from the Gospel.

[343] Cf. Just. Apol., 63, 14.

[344] In 8:44 "father of the devil" is grammatically possibly but materially unnecessary. Bu. J., 241 thinks that Jn. has incorrectly transl. a Semitic text which read: ἐκ τοῦ πατρὸς ὑμῶν, τοῦ διαβόλου (appos.). On Gnostic ideas of birth from the devil and on the father of the devil cf. Zn. J., 425, n. 33; Bau. J., ad loc.; Bu. J., 241, n. 1.

[345] Cf. Jub. 10:5; the angels as fathers of demons; Joseph and Asenath, 12, 9 f.: the devil as the father of the Egypt. gods.

[346] With ref. to consubstantiality (→ n. 329) in 11:41 Bau. J. objects that the Christ of Jn. could not really pray. But the Logos, who is certainly predicated as θεός in Jn. 1:1; 20:28 (cf. 5:18; 10:33), can still pray as the One who is obedient in the flesh, in the world.

with the Father, who here as always is exalted by Him. He thus marches on to suffering. The missionary form of prayer in 11:41 f., which is designed to produce faith in His mission, is unique. But according to the plan of the Gospel it simply states the goal of His whole life. In 12:27 ff. prayer as address and answer depicts the attitude in spiritual conflict. Like the Synoptic prayer in Gethsemane it ends, not with a request for deliverance from existence and suffering, but with magnifying of the Father. The heavenly voice gives a confirmatory promise. Here, as in 11:41, prayer is not an isolated end in a static Father/Son communion, but a fulfilment of mission (v. 30 : δι' ὑμᾶς). In particular, the parting prayer in c. 17 stands under the two watchwords resulting from the primary basis of revelation, namely, given by the Father (v. 2, 4, 6, 7, 8, 9, 11, 14, 22, 24) and glorifying of the Father (v. 1, 4, 24).

The consummation of Jesus brings the disciples direct access to the Father, which is experienced as the hearing of prayer. But the directness of the relationship is always controlled by faith in the Son. It is not a vision of God which eliminates the original fellowship, → 999, 26 ff. Hence the new praying in the name of the Son involves appeal to Him and agreement with Him. One may be certain of reaching the Father in this name, 14:13; 15:16; 16:23; → 276, 20 ff. No special intercession need be made by the Son, 16:26 f. Through the Revealer a direct relation to the Father is assured as a definitive gift, cf. 14:6; → 1001, 10 ff. The γνωρίσω of 17:26, however, shows that revelation is experienced as something vital and progressive which can now take place from this point on, cf. ἀπ' ἄρτι in 14:7; "at that day" in 14:20; 16:23. Finding and knowledge of the Father is the ripe fruit of the whole work of salvation, cf. 16:27 and the basis in 16:23. [347] The sayings in Samaria (4:21-26) tally with the Parting Discourses for they are full of promise, show that the absolute πατήρ is the final goal of prayer, and also speak of worship in the Spirit. Here, however, the directness of this worship through ἀληθινοὶ προσκυνηταί whom the Father seeks is contrasted with cultic localisation, whether on Zion or Gerizim. The same basic view (→ 998, 1) is assured by the ἐγώ εἰμι testimony. [348] Yet these sayings, though true to the situation, do not anticipate instruction in the passion. If the Synoptists, esp. Mt., set the disciples' prayer to the Father, which Jesus taught and mediated, within His whole activity, in Jn. this prayer is the fruit of His completed work of salvation. [349]

---

[347] Because prayer and the work which now begins are inseparable from the promise of the Paraclete, the points mentioned in → 999, 26 ff. are found again in the promise, the original divine fellowship being worked out in the disciples, 14:13; 20; 16:27 f. Here, too, we read that the Father "gives," 15:16; 16:23. Because prayer leads to fruitfulness which glorifies the Father (15:8, cf. v. 7) it is bound up with the new work. It goes further than anything earlier because Jesus goes to the "greater." His relationship to God enables His disciples to do greater works, 14:12-28.

[348] This is missed by H. Windisch, "Jesus u. d. Geist im Joh.-Ev.," Amicitiae Corolla = Festschr. R. Harris (1933), 309. Cf. on this Bu. J., 140.

[349] As regards Trinitarianism in Jn. there is no express doctrine of the Trinity in the metaphysical sense of oneness of essence and substance. The Father, Son and Paraclete are formally inter-related only in the non-authentic comma Johanneum in 1 Jn. 5:7 f.: ὁ πατήρ, ὁ λόγος καὶ τὸ ἅγιον πνεῦμα. Cf. A. v. Harnack, "Zur Textkritik u. Christologie der Schriften d. Joh., Anh. B," SAB, 1915 (1915), 572 f.; E. Riggenbach, "Das Comma Johanneum," BFTh, 31 (1928); Bü. 1 J., 82 f.; J. Chaine, "Les Épîtres Catholiques," Études Bibliques (1939), 126-137; T. A. Marazuela, "Nuevo estudio sobre el 'Comma Ioanneum,'" Biblica, 28 (1947), 83-112, 216-235 shows that it is not part of the original text of the Vg. Vg Clem : quoniam tres sunt, qui testimonium dant in caelo : Pater, Verbum et Spiritus Sanctus et hi tres unum sunt. Priscillianus, Liber Apologeticus, 4 (CSEL, 18, 6, 7 ff.) (c. 380): tria sunt quae testimonium dicunt in caelo : pater, verbum et spiritus et haec tria unum sunt in Christo Iesu.

III. Father in Other Apostolic Writings.

1. The Earthly Father.

The household tables [350] in Col. 3:18-4:1; Eph. 5:22-6:9 [351] give explicit instruc-tions to fathers. Here we find Jewish-Hellenistic tradition and agreement with popular custom. The OT and common practice — cf. the par. in Menander, → n. 350 — teach much the same. But the general and natural elements in Col. and Eph. are given profundity by the reference to the κύριος. This is the determinative point here. [352] The measure and control are to be found in the new relationship of faith. This is the basis of the commandment in Col. 3:20 : εὐάρεστόν ἐστιν ἐν κυρίῳ. The same is called δίκαιον in Eph. 6:1-3 and strengthened by ἐντολὴ πρώτη ἐν ἐπαγγελίᾳ, → II, 552, 33 ff. [353] Col. 3:21 and Eph. 6:4 are directed against a capricious and brutal corruption of the patria potestas. Primitive Christian pedagogy, however, does not scorn the rational and psychological, as the reasoning in Col. 3:21 shows. [354] On παιδεία in Eph. 6:4 → 624, 8 ff. In what is said about earthly fathers in Hb. 12:4 ff. chastisement — as a figure of the divine use of affliction — is so treated, on the basis of Prv. 3:11 f., that the temporal limits of the father's power are brought out, → 621, 23 ff. Discipline will characterise the father, however, because it shows loving interest in the son. This passage, which is used in the service of a theology of suffering, may also be regarded as a Christian acceptance of the patria potestas and yet also as a criticism of its earthly form — sub specie patris coelestis. It is worth noting that in a mixed marriage Paul in 1 Cor. 7:14 does not give the decisive vote to the father, but to the believing partner. The unbelieving partner and the children are consecrated by the believing partner (ἁγιασθῆναι, → I, 112, 26 ff.). This divine fact is viewed as superior to all human elements. [355] Elsewhere in Paul there is nothing of essential significance

---

[350] Bibl. on the household tables : Dib. Kol. Exc. on 3:18-4:1; Loh. Kol. on 3:18 ff. (153-157); Kn. Did. on 4:9-11; G. Klein, Der älteste chr. Katechismus u. d. jüd. Propagandalit. (1909), 137 ff.; K. Weidinger, Die Haustafeln (1928), 62. Similar admonitions : Menander in Stob. Ecl., IV, 650 f. Cf. the aphorisms, IV, 651: ἡδὺς πατὴρ φρόνησιν ἀντ' ὀργῆς ἔχων, line 11; υἱὸς δ' ἀμείνων ἐστὶν εὐνοίᾳ πατρός, line 13; ὡς ἡδὺ πρᾶος καὶ νεάζων τῷ τρόπῳ πατήρ, lines 15 f.; οὐ λυποῦντα δεῖ παιδάριον ὀρθοῦν, ἀλλὰ καὶ πείθοντά τι, lines 17 ff. On the Jewish Hell. tradition Ps.-Phokylides, 175-228 in J. Bernays, Über d. phokylideische Gedicht (1856), and Gesammelte Abh., I (1885), 259 f. Cf. Philo Decal., 165-167. On later Stoicism K. Prächter, Hierokles der Stoiker (1901), 7-90.

[351] Cf. the further tables in 1 Pt. 2:18-3:7, where relationship to the father is not con-sidered ; 1 Jn. 2:12 ff., where τεκνία and παιδία refer to the whole community, each group being addressed acc. to its spiritual state (πατέρες and νεανίσκοι); Did., 4, 9-11 and Barn., 19, 5 and 7 ("thy son," "thy daughter"), which give instruction in the fear of God (1 Cl., 21, 8 : ἡ ἐν Χριστῷ παιδεία).

[352] Both passages are dominated by this : Col. 3:18, 20, 22-25, 4:1; Eph. 5:22-25 ff.; 6:1, 4, 6, 9.

[353] Cf. Ep. Ar., 228 : ἐντολὴν μεγίστην.

[354] Cf. Dib. Kol., ad loc.

[355] Cf. Ltzm. K., ad loc.; A. Robertson-A. Plummer, A Critical and Exegetical Comm. on the First Epistle of St. Paul to the Corinthians (1911), ad loc.; H. Windisch, "Zum Problem d. Kindertaufe im Urchr.," ZNW, 28 (1929), 121; A. Oepke, "Urchr. u. Kindertaufe," ZNW, 29 (1930), 85-87; J. Jeremias, Hat die älteste Christenheit die Kindertaufe geübt? (1938), 22 f. In Jewish proselyte law the conversion of the father is warranty for the child, Ket., 11a (Str.-B., I, 111), but children conceived and born prior to conversion are unholy, 4, 3 (Str.-B., III, 374). We do not find this kind of casuistry in Paul. Oepke, op. cit., 85 and 87 ascribes a material and ritual view of holiness to Paul here, but not so Schl. K., 222 f. On patristic exegesis of the v. cf. Oepke, 84.

concerning earthly fathers. Respect for old age (1 Tm. 5:1 f.) [356] is both ancient and Jewish.

2. The Application of the Metaphor of Father to Men in Paul.

a. Abraham as Father.

In R. 4:1 Paul takes as his starting-point the Jewish view that Abraham is the father of the race. [357] In him, however, the formula "father Abraham" is given a completely new sense, for the patriarch is brought in as a witness to justification. If Abraham is important only as a believer, it is only as such that he is also the father. All believers, whether circumcised or not, are his sons, R. 4:11 f., 16 f., 18, cf. 13; Gl. 3:7 → I, 9, 12 ff. Thus Paul achieves a universal understanding. The πίστις of the προπάτωρ prior to his circumcision (Gn. 15 comes before 17) shows with respect to the Gentiles that even in the OT itself blood-relationship is not the decisive thing. What counts for both Israel and non-Israel is a genealogy of faith which goes back to Abraham. [358] He is πατὴρ πάντων τῶν πιστευόντων δι' ἀκρο-βυστίας, R. 4:11. [359] But he is also πατὴρ περιτομῆς in so far as Israel believes as he did, 4:12. πατήρ here does not mean only model or prototype. It is not just that we should believe as he did, but also that we can believe because he did. Cf. 4:12 : τοῖς στοιχοῦσιν τοῖς ἴχνεσιν ... [360] The reference is to a spiritual descent in all nations (cf. σπέρμα in 4:18). This is more real than any physical descent.

b. The Apostle as the Father of the Community.

In his dealings with the churches and instruction of helpers Paul likes to make pastoral use of the father metaphor ; indeed, he refers expressly to birth, 1 C. 4:15; cf. Gl. 4:19; Phlm. 10. As Jesus called the disciples children (Mk. 10:24; Jn. 13:33) and 1 Jn. has τεκνία, παιδία (→ 638, 20 ff.; 653, 33 ff.), so Timothy is called τέκνον, τέκνον ἀγαπητόν in 1 C. 4:17; 2 Tm. 1:2 and Titus γνήσιον τέκνον in Tt. 1:4; cf. 1 Pt. 5:13 : Mark ὁ υἱός μου. In 1 C. 4:15 the one father is distinguished from the many teachers, though in Paul the idea of begetting is restricted by "in Christ Jesus through the Gospel." πατήρ is not used as a title as among the Rabbis, → 977, 19 ff. There are no references to suggest that the apostles were addressed as fathers. What is denoted by πατήρ is the fact of mediation of life. Phil. 2:22 gives evidence of a teacher/pupil relation different from that of the Rabbis ; father and child are inter-related in common δουλεύειν εἰς τὸ εὐαγγέλιον, → II, 733, 40 ff., whereas in Judaism the domination of the teacher entails legal dependence. Cf. such additions as ἐν πίστει etc. in 1 Tm. 1:2; Tt. 1:4; 1 C. 4:17. Apostolic authority and common dependence on Christ are interwoven. If the churches are described as τέκνα, 1 Th. 2:11 ff. expounds fatherly action in terms of παρα-καλεῖν, παραμυθεῖσθαι, μαρτύρεσθαι and 1 C. 4:14 describes it as νουθετεῖν.

---

[356] Cf. Schl. Past., 134 f. For pars. from moral philosophy cf. Dib. Past., ad loc. When 1 Tm. calls the rise of patricide and matricide a mark of the last time this is in keeping with Jewish apocalyptic tradition, cf. Volz Esch., 156 f.

[357] Cf. Jos. Bell., 5, 380 : προπάτωρ ἡμέτερος. At 4:1 we are to read with ACDG bo sah d g vg Ambrosiast : τί οὖν ἐροῦμεν εὑρηκέναι 'Αβραὰμ τὸν προπάτορα ἡμῶν κατὰ σάρκα; To relate κατὰ σάρκα to εὑρηκέναι is materially impossible — we are simply told that he found justification. This rules out the reading in KLP syᵖ Chrys Thdrt (ℜ): εὑρηκέναι after ἡμῶν, which would support the error. B 1908 Ath Or do not have εὑρηκέναι (simplification). Cf. Ltzm. R., ad loc.

[358] This goes beyond even the Rabb. "father of proselytes and all men," Str.-B., III, 195, 211, → 976, 16.

[359] Cf. Barn., 13, 7.

[360] On Abraham as the "author of life," Schl. R., 166.

The ancient oriental custom of calling the teacher and pastor "father" (→ 954, 1 ff.), and of viewing this spiritual fatherhood as controlled by the word already in the teacher of wisdom, is not mediated in Paul by the παράδοσις of the ἱερὸς λόγος or by consecration as spiritual birth through the *pater sacrorum.* [361] On the contrary, Rabbinic parallels which speak of the begetting of the pupil by the rabbi, the Torah being the means, are so impressive that one must assume an adoption of the Jewish figure of speech in Christian form, → I, 665, 29 ff.; 667, 40 ff. [362]

3. God as Father.

a. The Basic Significance of the Cry Abba, → 984, 17 ff.

The common Christian practice of calling on the Father is confirmed not merely by Paul but also by 1 Pt. 1:17 and the use of the Lord's Prayer. What Paul says in Gl. 4:6 and R. 8:15, however, is certainly not to be restricted to the opening words of the Lord's Prayer. [363] The cry Abba is here regarded as an experience of fundamental significance. It goes beyond the use of a particular liturgical formula. Paul views it as the working of the Spirit of adoption given in the heart. That the community is here reminded of its innermost experience of the Spirit agrees with the observation that elsewhere in Paul πατήρ is the proper and determinative word in prayer. The constant doxologies in Paul show that this invocation of the Father involves a permanent attitude. It is significant, however, that the expression of experience in Gl. 4 and R. 8 goes hand in hand with more crystallised liturgical formulae. Paul find the particularity of κράζειν, not in enthusiasm or ecstasy, [364] but in childlike and joyous assurance as contrasted with the attitude of the servant, → III, 902, 32 ff. In antithesis to δουλεία or φόβος is sonship, inheritance, maturity, Gl. 4:1 ff.; R. 8:15 ff. The cry Abba is thus the very opposite of nomism. It puts an end to this, for it includes the achieved προσαγωγή of faith, cf. R. 5:2. By meditation on the Scriptures Paul established and deepened this insight derived from Jesus. He took the OT promise of the Father out of its immediate context and saw its fulfilment in Christ. Cf. the mosaic of quotations in 2 C. 6:14 ff., where the final link in the chain of promises is the promise of fatherhood. [365]

b. The Use of πατήρ. [366]

(a) θεὸς πατήρ.

θεὸς πατήρ, without art., in asyndetic agreement, [367] with or without ἡμῶν, is found in blessings, extended salutations, and final greetings. The salutations at the beginning

---

[361] Cf. the spiritual father in monasticism, where one may see a fusion of primitive Chr. expressions and the influence of the mysteries.

[362] Schl. K., 162 f. On this whole subject cf. Str.-B., III, 240 f.

[363] So Zn. R., 396, n. 93 acc. to Ephr. in his comm. on Gl. 4:5 (in Armenian) and Jer. (Vallarsi), *ad loc.* Cf. the Boh. transl. of 1 Pt. 1:17, which has "our Father."

[364] Zn. Gl., 206: "as with natural force"; Oe. Gl. on 4:6 alludes to 1 C. 12:3 and c. 14. Schl. R., 265 takes a different view: "In contrast the speech of servants is the kind of murmuring prayer prescribed by Jewish custom." κράζειν is often used for religious acclamation in worship, cf. E. Peterson, ΕΙΣ ΘΕΟΣ = FRL, NF, 24 (1926), 191-193, 226.

[365] Cf. Wnd. 2 K., *ad loc.* What is said about David's son in 2 Βασ. 7:14, cf. 1 Ch. 22:10; 28:6: καὶ αὐτὸς ἔσται μοι εἰς υἱόν, is with the help of Ιερ. 38(31):9: ὅτι ἐγενόμην τῷ Ισραηλ εἰς πατέρα, transferred to the Christian community in the words: καὶ ἔσομαι ὑμῖν εἰς πατέρα. In closer keeping with the text Hb. 1:5 interprets Messianically the conjunction of father and son in 2 Βασ. 7:14.

[366] E. Lohmeyer, "Probleme paul. Theologie, I," ZNW, 26 (1927), 158-173.

[367] Par. πατὴρ θεός, Wis. 2:16; ὁ πατὴρ θεός, Philo Leg. All., I, 64; πατὴρ ὁ πάντων θεός, Rer. Div. Her., 62. If Philo, too, can sometimes relate θεός and πατήρ, in him this is never such a fixed formula as in the apostolic greetings.

of Paul's letters take the form χάρις ὑμῖν καὶ εἰρήνη ἀπὸ θεοῦ πατρὸς ἡμῶν καὶ κυρίου Ἰησοῦ Χριστοῦ in Gl. 1:3; 1 C. 1:3; 2 C. 1:2; R. 1:7; Phil. 1:2; Phlm. 3; Eph. 1:2. This occurs also in the concluding greeting in Eph. 6:23, cf. Ign. Eph., 21, 2. Whether Paul adopted the formula is open to question — before Gl. one may see an earlier stage in 1 Th. 1:1. Paul thus developed it gradually. We already find θεὸς πατήρ without art. in 1 and 2 Th. But only from Gl. 1:3 onwards do we have the above form. The distinctive feature in Pl. is that θεὸς πατήρ never occurs without κύριος after it. This form of address with θεὸς πατήρ and Jesus Christ (with His own predicates) becomes a common legacy of the Church, though with individual variations at times. [368] Omission of the article emphasises the rhythmic correspondence, pregnancy and loftiness of effect; it gives "father" almost the appearance of a proper name. Liturgical use was promoted by reading the Epistles, which was certainly congregational. [369] The blessing takes the form of prayer. The confessional content is crystallised liturgically. If the divine designation finds sonorous expression herewith, this emphasises the significance of the combination of θεὸς πατήρ and κύριος.

The other verses which use θεὸς πατήρ (without ἡμῶν) confirm the loftiness of setting and requirement. Thus the concluding sentence in Phil. 2:11 owes its terseness to hymnic rhythm; other doxologies (cf. Gl. 1:4 f.; 2 C. 11:31) have the form θεὸς καὶ πατήρ. What is said about εὐχαριστεῖν in Col. 3:17, where ὁ θεὸς πατήρ is the exception, is in keeping with the same solemnity of style. θεὸς πατήρ is used in greetings, ὁ θεὸς καὶ πατήρ in thanksgivings, cf. also Eph. 5:20. It is no accident that Col. and Eph. show certain deviations. Finally 2 Pt. 1:17 makes it plain that θεὸς πατήρ without article later came into common use as a dogmatic formulation, cf. Ign. Mg., 3, 1.

(b) θεὸς ὁ πατήρ (apposition). [370]

This form, which is close to both ὁ πατήρ and θεὸς πατήρ, is found in this terse form only in 1 C. 8:6 : εἷς θεὸς ὁ πατήρ, → III, 101, 12 ff. and V, 1008, 28 f. with n. 379. This is a lofty confessional expression with an intentional liturgical ring.

(c) ὁ θεὸς καὶ πατήρ. [371]

ὁ θεὸς καὶ πατὴρ ἡμῶν, esp. in the early epistles 1 Th. and Gl., is the formula of doxology in thanksgiving or introduction, though also in other prayers. From it there develops later the formula mentioned → 1007, 2 f. [372] In 1 Th. 1:2 f. it represents, with ἔμπροσθεν, the basic attitude of prayer. 1 Th. 3:11 is shaped by the implied petition. 1 Th. 3:13 uses the language of prayer with OT echoes. [373] The formula is here always accompanied by κύριος, though without a genitive. In 1 Th. 3:11 (cf. 2 Th. 2:16) it is linked to ὁ κύριος by καί; the twofold ἡμῶν strengthens the parallelism and sense of unity. καί is also used as a link in Gl. 1:4. Phil. 4:20 is doxological. [374] It occurs without ἡμῶν in 1 C. 15:24, where it is set above and related to the αὐτὸς ὁ υἱός of v. 28, → 1010, 3.

ὁ θεὸς καὶ πατὴρ τοῦ κυρίου ἡμῶν Ἰησοῦ Χριστοῦ. The use of καί as a link is preferred esp. with the asyndetic version when there is a gen. with πατήρ. It is

---

[368] In the Past. there is relationship to the Pauline formulation, but with certain differences. Cf. also 2 Jn. 3; Jd. 1; 1 Pt. 1:2; Mart. Pol. Inscr.; Ign. Mg. Inscr.; Phld. Inscr.

[369] Cf. Loh. Kol. on 1:2.

[370] Linguistic par. 1 Ch. 29:10 : κύριε ὁ θεὸς Ισραηλ, ὁ πατὴρ ἡμῶν, O. Sol. 9:5 : "Become rich in God the Father"; Philo Leg. All., II, 67, cf. Jos. Ant., 2, 152 (with πάντων).

[371] θεός and πατήρ are already linked by καί in Judaism : 3 Macc. 5:7, cf. Jm. 1:27. Related is Jm. 3:9 : εὐλογοῦμεν τὸν κύριον καὶ πατέρα. Both statements in Jm. are in the first instance good Jewish sayings, but they can be filled with Chr. content. It cannot be contested that in Jm. the use of "father" for God is more independent of faith in Christ than elsewhere, so also Dib. Jk. and Wnd. Jk., ad loc., though not Schl. Jk., 228.

[372] This understanding is not far off in 1 Th. 1:3; 3:11, 13, cf. 2 Th. 2:16 (instead of καί : ὁ θεὸς ὁ πατὴρ ἡμῶν, appos.).

[373] ψ 111:8; Sir. 6:37; cf. G. Harder, Pls. u. das Gebet (1936), 70, n. 4. On αὐτὸς δέ in 1 Th. 3:11; 2 Th. 2:16, which corresponds to σὺ δὲ ὁ αὐτὸς εἶ in ψ 101:27, cf. Harder, 63, n. 3 and 26, n. 2 and 3.

[374] On the final statements of the missive, which throw light on suffering, cf. Loh. Phil., ad loc.

usually found in thanksgivings at the beginning and end of epistles. If θεὸς πατήρ is developed in greeting, this form is a more explicit presentation of the content in the designation of God. πατὴρ τοῦ κυρίου adds to and defines θεός. But there is always something lofty about the double name, and it is of liturgical derivation. The question arises, however, whether (1) the relationship to Christ is at issue in θεός as well as πατήρ (the God and Father of the κύριος), or (2) θεός is independent and only "father" is related to Jesus. [375] In view of the link between θεός and πατήρ already present in Judaism (→ n. 370, 371) (2) is to be preferred ; the combination has a specific sense even prior to Paul. The apostle is thus stressing the divine glory when he uses θεός and the revelation in Christ when he speaks of the "Father of the Kurios." All statements of this category contain praise in the style of prayer, cf. introduction by εὐλογητός in 2 C. 1:3; Eph. 1:3; 1 Pt. 1:3. [376] They are εὐχαριστεῖν in Col. 1:3; Eph. 1:17, δοξάζειν in R. 15:6. If it is only a question of giving solemn force in 2 C. 11:31, the transition to doxology is still a feature there. [377] Appeal to the Father of Jesus Christ is always an occasion for the exposition of salvation and blessing, not just in express εὐλογήσας, Eph. 1:3. This form of expression was adopted by others as well as Paul, 1 Pt. 1:3.

ὁ θεὸς καὶ πατήρ (without ἡμῶν) occurs in confessional statements, 1 C. 15:24; Eph. 4:5 f. (→ 1007, 37; → 1012, 21). In Eph. 5:20 we find it in an admonition which suggests the whole attitude of prayer. The terseness is well suited to praise in divine worship.

ὁ θεὸς καὶ πατήρ, developed in an added gen., occurs in 2 C. 1:3 : πατὴρ τῶν οἰκτιρμῶν καὶ θεὸς πάσης παρακλήσεως (Semitic expressions). [378] ὁ πατὴρ τῆς δόξης in Eph. 1:17 is distinctive inasmuch as it occurs in apposition to ὁ θεὸς τοῦ κυρίου ἡμῶν Ἰησοῦ Χριστοῦ. Here, then, θεός, not πατήρ, is linked with κύριος. The gen. describes the Father as Him who is transcendent in glory.

(d) ὁ πατήρ.

The abs. ὁ πατήρ (apart from the vocative cry → 1006, 10 ff.) is to be found in the Pauline corpus only in Col. and Eph. [379] These writings, like the Johannine works, give evidence for the most part of conflict with Gnosticism, whose terminology they also employ. [380] Col. 1:12 f. links ὁ πατήρ and ὁ υἱός (τῆς ἀγάπης αὐτοῦ) with solemn

---

[375] Gk. expositors already differed, cf. Ew. Gefbr., ad loc. (66). Jer., Theod. Mops. and Theophylactus favoured (1). The most decided among the moderns are Ew. Gefbr. on Eph. 1:3; J. Weiss, Das Urchr. (1917), 363 (the creatureliness of Christ). Cf. J. Schmid, Der Eph. d. Ap. Pls. (1928), 208, n. 2. Wnd. 2 K., Ltzm. K. on 2 C. 1:3 think (1) worth considering, but incline to (2), though the reverse is true of Kn. 1 Pt. on 1:3. The main proponents of (2) are Haupt Gefbr. on Eph. 1:3; P. W. Schmiedel, Die Briefe an die Thessal. u. an d. Korinther, Hand-Commentar z. NT, II (1891), 175 on 2 C. 1:3. The common art. proves nothing, Winer (Schmiedel) § 18, 17a.

[376] On εὐλογητός (= בָּרוּךְ) in the LXX → II, 764, 10 ff., in the prayer of the Synagogue → II, 760, 9 ff.

[377] That elsewhere, too, the word "father" leads to doxology may be seen from Gl. 1:4; Phil. 4:20. But doxologies with θεός are more numerous (cf. Judaism).

[378] The Semitism "Father of mercy" (rachamim), e.g., in the benediction Ahaba rabba (Str.-B., I, 397). Cf. τῶν οἰκτιρμῶν σου ψ 24:7 and materially ψ 102:13 ("father"). On "God of all comfort" cf. Ket., 8b (Str.-B., III, 494). He dispenses mercy and comfort.

[379] 1 C. 8:6 (→ 1007, 26) is not a true example. In R. 6:4 τοῦ πατρός, as the context shows, is an abbreviation for "his, namely, Christ's Father." In the Cath. Ep. (apart from Jn.) the abs. does not occur. In Jm. 1:17 and Hb. 12:9 (→ 1013, 22 f.; 1014, 6 ff.) the expansive genitives express fatherly sovereignty over a sphere, with no ref. to Christ.

[380] The Johannine element in the use of πατήρ in Col. and Eph. is not restricted simply to the abs. catchword. Cf. also Eph. 1:17 with Jn. 20:17; Rev. 1:6; 3:12 and for δόξα : δοξάζειν in Jn. The Father of glory dispenses the Spirit. The prayer to the Father in the name of the κύριος (Jn.: υἱός) in Col. 3:17; Eph. 5:20 reminds us of Jn. 14:13 f. There is a similar connection in Ac. 1:4, 7, where an abs. πατήρ with the promise of the Spirit and an emphasis on fatherhood is put on the lips of the risen Lord, cf. Jn. 20:17.

εὐχαριστεῖν. The abs. formula here fits both the ὑμᾶς of v. 12 and the αὐτοῦ of v. 13. In Eph. 2:18 there is similarity to John not only in ὁ πατήρ but also in the emphasis on universal προσαγωγή in the Spirit after overcoming all barriers, cf. Jn. 4:23 f. On Eph. 3:14 → πατριά, 1017, 20 ff. [381]

(e) πατήρ, θεός, υἱός, κύριος.

As a rule Paul uses θεός. [382] He can put the new content in this term and combine it with what is presented as the core of revelation through the Lord. Important statements can be made about God and His Son without the use of the name "Father." πατήρ is, properly, used in prayer. θεός and πατήρ are indissolubly linked, θεός as the name which denotes God's power as Creator, His omnipotence and His transcendent glory, Father as the starting-point, centre and goal of redemption. [383] The linking of the names leads to the reciprocal influence of the one on the other. In 2 C. 1:3 the mercy of the Father carries with it an interpretation of θεός as the God of comfort, while in Eph. 1:17 ὁ πατήρ τῆς δόξης takes over the characteristic features of θεός, → 1008, 23 ff. Paul does not, like Judaism, combine κύριος or δεσπότης with πατήρ. [384] With primitive Christianity he splits and assigns the names. Jesus is called κύριος [385] (→ III, 1088, 27 ff.) and God is the Father of the κύριος. [386] The rule is scrupulously observed that υἱός should occur with θεός rather than πατήρ. [387] This is true even in a text like Gl. 4:6 where there is an express relating of υἱός τοῦ θεοῦ to "Father." This sober usage is the more surprising in view of the fact that πατήρ is always in the background. Why is the great complex of father-sayings linked to κύριος and not to υἱός? The only possible answer is that κύριος is the confession of the community ("our Lord") while υἱός denotes the relation of Jesus to the Father ("His Son"). κύριος is also closely connected with the view of the Son of Man in Daniel, which includes a relationship to υἱός. [388] In Paul, too, it is always plain that God, as the Father of Jesus Christ, is also our Father. The distinction from Jn. (→ 997-1003) is that there the relation of the Father to the Son stands in the centre as a paradigm of revelation. The Pauline formula corresponding to the Johannine πατήρ/υἱός, namely, ὁ υἱός τοῦ θεοῦ, is relatively less common [389] because his message chiefly

---

[381] The many readings with πατήρ at Col. 2:2 f. (τοῦ θεοῦ [καὶ] πατρὸς τοῦ Χριστοῦ, τοῦ θεοῦ πατρὸς καὶ τοῦ Χριστοῦ, τοῦ θεοῦ καὶ πατρὸς καὶ τοῦ Χριστοῦ) should all be regarded as expansions of the difficult original 𝔓 46 B Hilar : εἰς ἐπίγνωσιν τοῦ μυστηρίου τοῦ θεοῦ, Χριστοῦ (apposition). Cf. J. B. Lightfoot, St. Paul's Epistles to the Colossians and to Philemon⁸ (1886), ad loc. (250 f.). They seek to restore the text dogmatically and are instructive as early expressions in the christological conflict.

[382] θεός occurs 498 times (44 in the Past), and another 33 times in combination with πατήρ. Incl. the Past. (3 times) πατήρ occurs only 42 times in Pl., and in 33 instances it is combined with θεός.

[383] Cf. Schl. R., 382; Schl. K., 657.

[384] Cf. Is. 63:16; 1 Ch. 29:10; Sir. 23:1, 4; Jos. Ant., 1, 20; 5, 39; cf. Jm. 3:9; → n. 371; Herm. v., 3, 9, 10.

[385] In Pl. κύριος is used of Jesus 225 times (perhaps God in some OT quotations), 22 times in the Past. πατήρ occurs with κύριος in an explicit formula 27 (28) times. In other verses where it occurs with πατήρ the ref. to Christ is always indisputable.

[386] κύριος for God is rare, occurring only in OT quotations, cf. 2 C. 6:18 : κύριος παντοκράτωρ, R. 9:29 : κύριος Σαβαώθ. Pl. does not use the κύριος θεός of the LXX. It occurs infrequently in Hb. and Rev.

[387] Cf. 1 Th. 1:9 f.; Gl. 1:15 f. (αὐτοῦ of θεός, who is not mentioned, though cf. ℌℜD pl); 2:20; 4:4; 1 C. 1:9; R. 1:1-4, 9; 5:10; 8:3, 29, 31 f.; Eph. 4:13.

[388] → n. 289; Lohmeyer, op. cit. (→ n. 366), 166-169; also "Kyrios Jesus. Eine Untersuchung z. Phil. 2:5-11," SAH, 1927/28, 4 Abh. (1928), 68 f.

[389] υἱός is used of Christ 16 times in Pl.

develops what is given to the community in the Father and its κύριος. This is made particularly clear by exceptions which are closer to Jn., e.g., Col. 1:12 f. (→ 1008, 31) and esp. 1 C. 15:24-28, which occupies a special place. [390] More explicit, and already formulated dogmatically, is the combination of θεός πατήρ and ὁ υἱός μου ὁ ἀγαπητός μου in 2 Pt. 1:17 (the baptism of Jesus).

c. The Content of the Father Concept.

Our review of the usage shows that in Paul and elsewhere in primitive Christianity mention of the Father is not just a dogmatic statement of faith. It is a supreme doxological statement. As the brevity of formulation proves, it is always emphatic. Hence the word "father" is not weakened. It is reserved in the main for benediction, praise and prayer. The sonorous "Father of our Lord Jesus Christ" (→ 1007, 38 ff.), which corresponds best to Paul's proclamation, is also prayer. Confessions like 1 C. 8:6; Eph. 4:6 bear quite naturally the same character of acclamation. But what is the content of this linking of deity with the father concept?

(a) The Fatherhood of God as Lordship. The constant filling out of πατήρ by linking it with θεός makes it clear that the fatherhood of God means sovereignty. Primitive Christianity is not to blame for the elimination of this aspect. The will of the Father, which determines all things in the work of salvation (Gl. 1:4), shows that He is Ruler. In the witness of the apostles statements concerning the divine lordship are combined with this word. The election of the Father is His overruling of the community, 1 Pt. 1:2. The thanksgiving "always for all things" (Eph. 5:20; cf. Col. 3:17) is made possible by His power, which controls and governs all life. The emphasis thus falls on obedience to the Father's will. The gift of the Father is a serious summons to sanctification, 2 C. 6:14 ff., cf. 18; 7:1, [391] → n. 365; Hb. 12:10; 1 Cl., 56, 16. The Father sanctifies the community by leading it to obedience, 1 Pt. 1:2. The goal of sanctification in the parousia sets it before the face of the Father as Judge, 1 Th. 3:13. [392] The unity of Father and Judge is most impressively presented as a motive of sanctification in 1 Pt. 1:17 ff., → 995, 10 ff. On the basis of this synthesis, taken together with the sacrificial death of Christ, there is here again an emphasis on the sovereignty of the divine fatherhood which demands obedience. [393] The relating of πατήρ and βασιλεία → n. 300, which strengthens this aspect, occurs not only in Col. 1:12 f., where the power of redemption is described in terms of an exchange of lordship. It is also found eschatologically in 1 C. 15:24 ff., where Christ at the end of the Messianic interim hands over the

---

[390] The exposition in v. 23 f. divides persons and groups. Χριστός occurs once without art. In keeping are the terse nouns without possessive pronouns: ὁ θεὸς καὶ πατήρ, 28: αὐτὸς ὁ υἱός.

[391] The continuation in 2 C. 7:1 shows that commitment to ἁγιωσύνη is perceived in the OT promise of the Father.

[392] The ἔμπροσθεν τοῦ θεοῦ καὶ πατρὸς ἡμῶν which expresses the attitude of prayer in 1 Th. 1:2 f. (→ 1007, 31) refers here to the parousia, cf. ἔμπροσθεν τοῦ βήματος in 2 C. 5:10 with the ἔμπροσθεν used for the judicial act in Mt. 10:33; Lk. 12:8; Mt. 25:32; Lk. 21:36 (Herm. v., 3, 9, 10: κατέναντι τοῦ πατρός).

[393] The unity of Father and Judge is a divinely purified use of the image of the ancient patria potestas as echoed, e.g., in Jos. Ant., 4, 260 (οἱ πατέρες): αὐτάρκεις γὰρ ἐφ' υἱάσιν οὗτοι δικασταί. The linking of motifs corresponds to the unity of grace and law in Pauline justification, → II, 204, 23 ff. Materially the basic elements in this belief in justification are to be found in 1 Pt. 1:17 ff., esp. as the crucifixion is here interwoven with the Father/Judge synthesis.

βασιλεία τῷ θεῷ καὶ πατρί in order that God may be all in all. Belief in the Father is thus connected with the ultimate goal of the rule of God, as in the last sentence of the hymn to Christ in Phil. 2:10 f., cf. πατὴρ τῆς δόξης, Eph. 1:17. It is worship of the κύριος, however which finds utterance in this extolling of the Father. [394] The unity of Father and Ruler is thus definitively revealed in the fact that God is the Father of the Kurios. Christ as such is also Ruler and Judge. When primitive Christianity makes this predication, the believing reader of the LXX is bound to see that God does not herewith surrender His dignity as Ruler but as the Father of the Kurios reveals the dominion which leads to the final consummation. In the apostolic documents the use of "Father" for God is always, with few exceptions (→ 1013, 22 ff.; 1014, 8 ff.), controlled by the revelation in Christ. There is convincing proof that the basis of the use of πατήρ in both Mt. (→ 990, 21 ff.) and Jn. (→ 997, 22 ff.) is christological. πατήρ became a term of revelation in Christianity. In salutations and thanksgivings the reference back to the Father as the supreme authority always carries with it an emphasis on His sovereign superiority. Christ's subordination to the Father is clearly expressed. Hence mention of the κύριος does not imply ditheistic Jesulatry, → III, 104, 1 ff. It is this Lord, however, who first makes possible true belief in the Father.

(b) The Gift of Grace through the Father. The Father dispenses χάρις supplemented by ἀγάπη, ἔλεος, παράκλησις, εἰρήνη, 2 Th. 2:16 f.; 2 C. 1:3; 1 Pt. 1:3. Since God is Father in the Kurios, the χάρις of the Giver is an ongoing part of the redemption leading to the consummation. In Eph. 1:3 εὐλογεῖν is shown to be a fulfilment of the whole counsel of salvation. Everything has its goal in this comforting dispensation of grace, 2 Th. 2:16. Even the cry Abba (→ 1006, 10 ff.) is explained, not emotionally, but in terms of salvation history. Hence in apostolic proclamation "Father" always embraces the gift of salvation, direct προσαγωγὴ εἰς τὴν χάριν, Eph. 2:18, cf. R. 5:2. This benefit, which brings universal unity, is far above all subjectivity. There is not absent, of course, an emphasis on the leading of the Spirit, who makes us sons (R. 8:14), and this leading can be individual, 1 Th. 3:11. In 1 and 2 Th. 1:1, however, non-mystical concealment in (ἐν) the Father by faith is said about the whole ἐκκλησία, which according to Jd. 1 consists of ἐν θεῷ πατρὶ ἠγαπημένοι. [395]

---

[394] On Phil. 2:6-11 cf. Lohmeyer, 61 on v. 10 f. ὅτι introduces the eschatological acclamation: E. Peterson, "Die Einholung d. Kyrios," ZSTh, 7 (1929/30), 698; also op. cit. (→ n. 364), 171, 371. It is not a ὅτι of logical discussion (Calvin, ad loc.) on which εἰς δόξαν θεοῦ πατρός depends. It is open to question whether the words are true acclamation. They are appended explanation. Cf. K. Barth, Erklärung d. Phil.³ (1936), 62: "God has found His glory therein." O. Sol. 10:2: "I became strong and mighty and captured the world. This took place to the glory of the Most High, God, my Father."

[395] For the first beginnings of Trinitarian formulation → n. 349 and III, 107, 1 ff. The elements of triadic interrelationship are to be found in πατήρ, κύριος and πνεῦμα. As a rule, however, there is no need at all to relate these triadically. Cf. esp. 1 C. 8:6, where only God the Father and the Kurios are mentioned. To be sure, there is in Pl. a whole series of kerygmatic observations in which θεός (rarely πατήρ), κύριος (or Χριστός, rarely υἱός) and πνεῦμα are fairly closely associated. Even these, however, are not deliberately triadic. The only Trinitarian formula in Pl. is at 2 C. 13:13 (κύριος, θεός, πνεῦμα), which does not have πατήρ. In this order it gives evidence of no particular didactic concern; it is soteriologically and ecclesiologically orientated, and spoken out of the experience of the community. Hence this version is genuinely liturgical. The strongest Trinitarian impulse is to be seen in 1 Pt. 1:2 (θεὸς πατήρ, πνεῦμα, Ἰησοῦς Χριστός). Here, too, everything is soteriological, and formalism is avoided. Nowhere is there any suggestion of a contemplation of God's intertrinitarian being.

d. The Influence of the Surrounding Greek World.

(a) The Christian Answer to Belief in the Father of All in 1 C. and Eph. [396] In 1 C. 8:4 ff. confession of the Father is set in antithesis to polytheism. [397] If ὁ πατὴρ πάντων is widely accepted in that sphere, Paul here makes use of τὰ πάντα in a way which involves its removal from Greek cosmology and refashioning according to the biblical belief in creation, → 893, 38 ff. To the θεοὶ λεγόμενοι is opposed εἷς θεὸς ὁ πατήρ, to the κύριοι εἷς κύριος ᾿Ιησοῦς Χριστός, → III, 101, 7 ff.; 1091, 13 ff. This is the faith of the community (ἀλλ᾽ ἡμῖν and the twofold ἡμεῖς, v. 6). εἷς and θεός belong together as acclamation. "For us there is one God, the Father." ἐξ οὗ τὰ πάντα describes Him as the author of all creation, while ἡμεῖς εἰς αὐτόν shows that the unity of θεός and πατήρ leads to a unity of creation and redemption. The added statement about the κύριος, however, makes it plain that this would be impossible without Him. [398] This correction of belief in the universal Father is the more impressive in that Stoic-pantheistic expressions [399] are used, but given a new and completely different sense.

In Eph. τὰ πάντα, οἱ πάντες do not refer to God's relation to the universe. [400] On the contrary they link the concept of the community with what is said about the Father. After the wall is broken down the universal ἐκκλησία has in one Spirit through Christ προσαγωγή to the Father, 2:18, cf. vv. 11-17. In vv. 19 ff. this is elucidated by the image of the father, which is in no sense Gnostic here. Access creates οἰκεῖοι τοῦ θεοῦ. This is yet another contribution to the popular understanding of πατήρ (→ 997, 2 ff.). Household rights are enjoyed with the ἅγιοι; there is access in one Spirit to the Father. The unity of the Church is then developed in the exhortation of 4:1-6. [401] The list of what is held in common is crowned by εἷς θεὸς καὶ πατὴρ πάντων, ὁ ἐπὶ πάντων καὶ διὰ πάντων καὶ ἐν πᾶσιν. We have here a remarkable linguistic mixing of OT phrases (Dt. 6:4; Mal. 2:10) with the Stoic formula of unity. [402] This can hardly be a purely stylistic

---

[396] Bibl.: E. Norden, Agnostos Theos (1913), 240-250, 253, 347 f.; J. Weiss, Der 1 K.[10] (1925) on 8:4 ff.; Ltzm. R. on 11:36; Dib. Gefbr. on Eph. 4:1 ff.; also "Die Christianisierung einer hell. Formel," N. Jbch. kl. Alt., 35 (1915), 224-236; Peterson, op. cit. (→ n. 364), 255 f.; H. Schlier, Religionsgeschichtliche Untersuchungen zu d. Ignatiusbr. (1929); also Christus u. d. Kirche im Eph. (1930); E. Käsemann, Leib u. Leib Christi (1933), 137-186.

[397] If in ὅτι οὐδὲν εἴδωλον ἐν κόσμῳ there is no express ref. to the deification of the cosmos, deifications are contested. "As there are many gods and lords" in v. 5 refers to demons (cf. 1 C. 10:20 f.), so ad loc. J. Weiss; W. Bousset, 1 u. 2 K., Schr. NT, II[3]; Ltzm. K.; H. D. Wendland, Die Briefe an d. Kor. (NT Deutsch), or angelic powers, P. W. Schmiedel, 110, with a possible ref. to emperor worship, Schl. K., 253 f.

[398] The relating of εἷς θεὸς ὁ πατήρ to the relative clauses implies distinction as well as comprehension.

[399] Pl. uses the imagery in 2 ways. As regards τὰ πάντα, he uses this for his own message without fearing its pantheistic use. He then employs the formula with various prepositions which are not merely found with physical and philosophical definitions but are often imbued with the religious feelings of the pagan world. Oppian Halieutica, I, 409 (200 A.D.) has εἰς and ἐκ with ref. to father Zeus. Cf. the three-membered form in M. Ant., IV, 23 (→ 893, 11 f.). If in R. 11:36 (→ 893, 11) Pl. uses ἐκ, διά and εἰς with πάντα, the distinction in 1 C. 8:6 is due to the fact that Kurios is used along with the Father. The reading δι᾽ ὄν B eth Noet in Epiph. Haer., 57, 5,1 is a reminiscence. So, e.g., Chrysipp. in Stob. Ecl., I, 31, 14 (= v. Arnim, II, 312, 23): of Zeus δι᾽ αὐτὸν πάντα; Philo Cher., 125 f.: δι᾽ ὅ with ref. to God as author. The rhet. variation of prep. also occurs esp. in Eph. 4:6.

[400] Cf. Schlier, Christus u. d. Kirche, 55, n. 1.

[401] On ἑνότης, ἕνωσις, Schlier, Ignatiusbriefe, c. 6.

[402] Cf. M. Ant., VII, 9: κόσμος τε γὰρ εἷς ἐξ ἁπάντων καὶ θεὸς εἷς διὰ πάντων καὶ οὐσία μία καὶ νόμος εἷς, λόγος κοινὸς πάντων τῶν νοερῶν ζῴων, καὶ ἀλήθεια μία.

or formal matter; the aim is the polemical one of demarcation. Whereas on the one side the way leads from the harmonious unity of the cosmos to what is said about the universal God, on the other εἷς θεὸς καὶ πατήρ creates the new unity of the united redeemed people. The religious slogan of the day is thus given a new sense. What is comprehensively embraced is the universal Christian community because it has the one Father. Belief in the Father promotes concentration on the εἷς θεός. [403] It is a dynamic ἑνότης: "over all, through all, in all."

(b) Some Exceptions to the Rule. It may be allowed that many sayings go beyond the limits of what we have hitherto found to be the NT father concept, though not in such a way as significantly to change the basic structure of the main findings. These sayings are, as it were, marginal to the total picture.

In 1 Pt. 1:3 ἀναγεννᾶν [404] is used of the θεὸς καὶ πατὴρ τοῦ κυρίου. If this refers to begetting, the combination of "father" with this forms an exception to NT usage. But elsewhere "to be born anew" (→ n. 311) is not expressly linked with the name "father." Perhaps the most appropriate translation is: "He has effected regeneration in us." [405]

Jm. 1:18 appends to a saying about the πατήρ (τῶν φώτων, → lines 22 ff.) an utterance concerning regeneration: βουληθεὶς ἀπεκύησεν [406] ἡμᾶς λόγῳ ἀληθείας (on the continuation ἀπαρχή, → I, 485, 37 ff.). Here ἀποκυεῖν has a soteriological reference to the new birth, not a cosmological reference to the whole of creation [407] (on βουληθείς → I, 632, 2 ff.). The statement: "Every good gift and every perfect gift is from above," [408] is strengthened in 1:17, where we read that the Giver is the "Father of lights." [409] It may be assumed that the reference is to

---

[403] For reflections on the monotheistic significance of ὁ πατὴρ μόνος, εἷς πατήρ, cf. Just. Dial., 68, 4; Cl. Al. Paed., III, 12, 101, 2 (GCS, 12, 291, 9 ff.); Paed., I, 6, 42, 1 (12, 115, 10 ff.); Strom., VII, 10, 58, 4 (17, 43, 3). The use of the father concept to combat polytheism is also found in Lact. Inst., IV, 3, 11 ff. (CSEL, 19, 279, 17 ff.): *Quod sic natura non patiatur, ut sint unius hominis multi patres (ex uno enim procreatur), ergo deos enim multos colere contra naturam est contraque pietatem.* The scorn poured by Lucilius Fr., 9 on many *patres* (Neptune, Liber, Saturn etc.) as well as Jupiter is quoted there (CSEL, 19, 280, 4 ff.).

[404] On γεννάω → I, 665, 20 ff.; ἀναγεννάω, → I, 673, 1 ff.; A. Fridrichsen, "Randbemerkungen zur Kindheitsgeschichte bei Lucas," Symb. Osl., 6 (1928), 33; C. M. Edsman, "Schöpferwille u. Geburt Jac. 1:18," ZNW, 38 (1939), 13. ἀναγεννᾶν occurs only here in the NT. When used later it is always in the pass., so Just. Apol., 61, 3 f.; Dial., 138, 3; Cl. Al. Paed., I, 6, 27. 2 f. (GCS, 12, 106, 8 and 16). Since γεννᾶν can be used neutrally of both sexes, there is no linguistic obstacle to the rendering "He has begotten us" (so H. v. Soden, *Die Kath. Br., Hand-Commentar z. NT,* III³ [1899], 129; Kn. Pt., Wnd. Kath. Br., ad loc.; Pr.-Bauer⁴, s.v.).

[405] So H. Gunkel in *Schr. NT,* III³, ad loc. The Gk. fathers also construed it thus.

[406] On ἀπεκύησεν Corp. Herm., I, 9 and 12; Philo Ebr., 30. A. Meyer, *Das Rätsel des Jk.* (1930), 269 finds an etym. of the name Reuben in "willing he begot." Schl. Jk., 138 emphasises the implied thrust against Jewish synergism. In the Synagogue the divine work is described by the function of the mother, e.g., Tanch. שמות, 18, 10. H. Schammberger, *Die Einheitlichkeit des Jk. im antignostischen Kampf* (1936), 59 refers to the male-female principle in Gnosticism. Edsman, 11-44 works this out rather more profoundly. He gives several instances of ἀποκυέω. The question of Gnostic derivation is thus to the fore.

[407] So also J. B. Mayor, *The Epistle of St. James³* (1910), ad loc.; Dib. Jk., Hck. Jk., Wnd. Kath. Br., ad loc.; Schl. Jk., 136 f. For a cosmological understanding cf. F. Spitta, *Der Brief d. Jk., Zur Geschichte u. Lit. d. Urchr.,* II (1896), 45; Edsman, 11 f.

[408] Conjecture is needed to explain the saying which follows. For modern attempts cf. C. Könnecke, "Emendationen zu St. d. NT," BFTh, 12, 1 (1908), 12 f.; Hck. Jk., 67 f., ad loc. (acc. to 𝔓 23); Dib. Jk., ad loc. The most convincing is the last: παραλλαγὴ τροπῆς ἢ ἀποσκιάσματος, "with whom is no alteration through turning or shadow."

[409] Thus far "Father of lights" has been found only at Apc. Mos. 36 and 38 in the Armen. transl., A. Ceriani, Monumenta sacra et profana, V, 1 (1868), 23; cf. R. H. Charles, *The*

besouled stars. [410] We find the same train of thought in Philo as here. [411] In this use of πατήρ with reference to the cosmos Jm. stands in encounter with Hellenistic piety and shows himself to have been influenced by πατήρ τῶν ὅλων — though only in an incidental aphoristic use of this common phrase.

Hb. uses πατήρ very sparingly even in Christology. Apart from the quotation from 2 S. 7:14 in 1:5, which is taken Messianically, we find "father" for God only in 12:9. The "Father of spirits" [412] is contrasted with τῆς σαρκὸς ἡμῶν πατέρες. Here, too, the concept refers to creation. It is not controlled by the main christological theme of the epistle, but stands close to Greek thought. In this respect the verse differs from the usual NT restriction to a soteriological "Father of Jesus Christ."

† πατρῷος.

1. πατρῷος means a. "what belongs to the father" : τέμενος πατρώιον, Hom. Il., 20, 391; μῆλα ... πατρώϊα, Od., 12, 136; πατρώϊα, "patrimony," Od., 17, 80; πατρῷος οἶκος, Philo Spec. Leg., I, 129. Transf. to God : Som., I, 256 : εἰς τὸν πατρῷον οἶκον

Apocrypha and Pseudepigr. of the OT, II (1913), 15 f., ad loc. But this source shows signs of Chr. redaction and is thus questionable. In Test. Abr. Rec. B, VII, 11 (ed. M. R. James, TSt, II, 2 [1892], 111) we find πατὴρ τοῦ φωτός for the angel of light. "Prince of lights," Damasc., 5, 17 f. (ed. S. Schechter, Documents of Jewish Sectaries, I [1910], in R. H. Charles, op. cit., 7, 19 [p. 811]), refers to an archangel (so E. Meyer, "Gemeinde d. Neuen Bundes im Lande Damaskus. Jüd. Schrift aus der Seleukidenzeit," SAB, 1919, No. 9 [1919], 36), not to God (so Dib. Jk., 96).

[410] The heavenly lights in apocalyptic : En. 41; 72; 73-75. The fact that they have souls, and the identification of angels and stars, are common motifs. "The leaders of the stars" in En. 72:3; 75:1; 82:4; 18:13-16 are fallen angels. Cf. also S. Bar. 51:10. See Hck. Jk., 66, n. 6.

[411] In Jm. the train of thought is as follows : If God is also the Father of stars He is distinguished from all changes and shadowings in this sphere by the fact that He remains unchanged as the Giver of good and perfect gifts. We find the same conjunction of ideas in Philo : πατὴρ τοῦ κόσμου (→ n. 61) and ἀγαθός together, Op. Mund., 21; Spec. Leg., I, 209; the motif of the unchangeable God and changing creation, Deus Imm., 22; Poster. C., 23, 27 f., 29 f.; Leg. All., II, 33; Cher., 19; this as the basis of faith, Leg. All., II, 89. One might also consider the combination of πατήρ and the contemplation of the stars in Op. Mund., 56 f.; Som., I, 73, and the linking of the star motif with the immutability of God in Poster. C., 19.

[412] The formula is a development of Nu. 16:22; 27:16 : "God of the spirits of all flesh," cf. T. J. I on Nu. 16:22; Jub. 10:3. Synagogal anthropology believes that by creation there is a direct relation between God and the spirit, Nidda, 31a, Str.-B., III, 748. This creationist view, however, is linked with traducianism. The LXX transl. of the verse in Nu. is : θεὸς τῶν πνευμάτων καὶ πάσης σαρκός. The separation opens a way for the Jewish doctrine of angels to seize on the v.: 2 Macc. 3:24; Vengeance prayer of Rheneia, Delos (c. 100 B.C.), Ditt. Syll.³, 1181, 2 : κύριον τῶν πνευμάτων. On this A. Deissmann, "Die Rachegebete v. Rheneia," Philol., 61 (1902), 252-265; also LO, 351-362, esp. 355; cf. also Preis. Zaub., V, 467. 1 Cl., 59, 3b perhaps tends in this direction. But Hb. 12:9 is also influenced by the "Lord of spirits" in En. 37-71. Here God is called the Lord of all who have spirit

---

of those above the earth and on earth. In the light of this prior history of the formula we may say that in Hb. the superiority of the divine Father over earthly fathers means that the former is the author of all πνεύματα both on earth and above it, whereas the latter are simply the means to transmit σάρξ to us. The changing of θεός to πατήρ is due to the context (παιδεία, υἱοί). In modern exegesis the following favour a ref. to human spirits : Schl. Erl., ad loc.; Wnd. Hb., ad loc.; H. Strathmann, Der Brief an d. Hebräer (NT Deutsch), ad loc., while Pr.-Bauer, s.v. champions a ref. to angels, and Rgg. Hb., 397; Mi. Hb.⁸, ad loc. to both. On patristic exegesis cf. Rgg. Hb., 397, n. 61.

π α τ ρ ῷ ο ς. Ps.-Ammon., Suid., Liddell-Scott, s.v.; Roscher, III, 1684. On πατρῷος, πατρικός, πάτριος J. Wackernagel, "Über einige lat. u. gr. Ableitungen aus den Verwandtschaftswörtern," Festgabe f. A. Kaegi (1919), 40-54, esp. 49-52. On πατρῷος and πατρῷοι θεοί : H. Bolkestein, "Theophrastos' Charakter d. Deisidaimonia als religionsgeschichtliche Urkunde," RVV, XXI, 2 (1929), 46-50.

ἐπανελθεῖν for returning to God from abroad (cf. Jn. 8:35; 14:2). b. "What comes or is inherited from the father," LXX Prv. 27:10 : φίλον πατρῷον. Philo Leg. Gaj., 54 : γένος τό τε πατρῷον καὶ μητρῷον, Jos. Ant., 7, 382; 8, 53 : the throne or dominion handed down from the father. c. Zeus is called πατρῷος as the protector of paternal rights, Aristoph. Nu., 1468; Plat. Leg., IX, 881 f, → 953, 3 f. The πατρῷοι θεοί are the protective deities of the family or people, the household gods, Soph. Phil., 933. Cf. the patrii dii of the Romans (the protective deities of house and state, the penates).

2. In the LXX and Joseph. we find a special use of πατρῷος for what derives from the fathers acc. to the view of Israel. So already πατρῷος τάφος, "sepulchre of the fathers," 2 Macc. 5:10; plur. 2 Macc. 12:39. Esp., however, the Law, 3 Macc. 1:23; 4 Macc. 16:16 : ὑπὲρ τοῦ πατρῴου νόμου. Also with τιμαί, ἑορταί, 2 Macc. 4:15; 6:6. Joseph. — though rarely — has πατρῷος for πάτριος in this sense (→ lines 17 ff.). So of the Pharisees in Ant., 13, 408 : κατὰ τὴν πατρῴαν παράδοσιν. The term can be used for Judaism, Ant., 9, 256 : ὁ πατρῷος καὶ ἀληθῶς θεός, cf. Ant., 2, 278, also 4 Macc. 12:17: τὸν πατρῷον θεόν, and also for pagan statues and gods in a broader sense than → lines 4 ff., Ant., 18, 198, 328.

3. The favourite word of Joseph., however, corresponding to his basic tendency to express the uniqueness of Judaism, is πάτριος. The LXX also has this at 2 Macc. 6:1; 7:2 οἱ πάτριοι νόμοι or 4 Macc. 9:1 αἱ πάτριοι ἐντολαί. It is worth noting, however, that in these verses in the LXX we constantly find readings with πατρῷος. While Joseph. has πατρικός only about 4 times (→ 1021, 29 ff.) and πατρῷος about 48 times, he uses πάτριος about 213 times.[1] He has it for the Law, for native customs and practices, for tradition, national characteristics, the soil of Palestine, the language (cf. here 2 Macc. 7:27), the constitution etc. The emphasis falls on the νόμος (Ant., 19, 349) and ἔθη (14, 213) of Judaism. ὁ πάτριος θεός occurs in Ant., 10, 58. Though the word can be used of other nations, its primary reference as a catchword is to Israel. It is a Hell. term for "handed down from the fathers" in Heb. There are many pars. in Philo : ἔθη πάτρια, Vit. Mos., I, 31; Spec. Leg., IV, 150; Ebr., 193 etc.

4. In Ac. 22:3 Paul tells the people about his upbringing κατὰ ἀκρίβειαν τοῦ πατρῴου νόμου (→ lines 10 f.). In Ac. 24:14 he bears witness before Felix that he serves τῷ πατρῴῳ θεῷ (lines 13 f., 25). Finally, in Ac. 28:17 he tells the leading Jews in Rome that he has done nothing against τοῖς ἔθεσι τοῖς πατρῴοις.[2] This uniform usage in Ac., which prefers the sonorous πατρῷος to the more common πάτριος (esp. with νόμος and ἔθη), bears reference to the Law, God, and customs handed down from the fathers of Israel.

† πατριά.

A. πατριά outside the New Testament.

1. The Meaning.

Already in Hdt. πατριά means the family as derived from the father. It is used specifically for the father's family tree, III, 75; II, 143. But πατριαί can also mean tribes in I, 200 (= φυλαί). Elsewhere it is used for πάτρα, which can mean not only "country" or "native city" but also "house," "tribe," "family." So Pind. Pyth., 8, 38;

---

[1] πάτριος was a common word in Attic prose to express inherited customs, habits, and institutions. So already Thrasymachus Fr., 1 (Diels⁶, II, 324, 1); Aristoph. Ra., 1533. Also esp. with νόμος and ἔθη, Xen. Hell., II, 3, 1 f.; Iambl. Vit. Pyth., 176 (Diels⁶, I, 469, 16); Democr. Fr., 259 (ibid., II, 198, 2 f.).

[2] Par. Just. Dial., 63, 5; for ἔθη πάτρια in Jos. and Philo, → line 25, 28.

π α τ ρ ι ά. J. Wackernagel, "Über einige lat. u. gr. Ableitungen aus d. Verwandtschafts-wörtern," Festg. f. A. Kaegi (1919), 57 f. M. Scheller, Die Oxytonierung d. gr. Subst. auf -ιᾱ, Diss. Zurich (1951), 71 f. E. Schwyzer, Gr. Grammatik, I = Hndbch. AW, II, 1, 1 (1939), 469.

Nem., 6, 36 : "tribe," "race." The central pt. is always derivation from the same father or ancestor no matter whether the ref. be to nation, tribe, caste, or family. It should be noted that by linguistic formation πατριά is collective and thus concrete, not abstract.

2. πατριά in the LXX.

The word is common in the LXX, esp. in 1 and 2 Ch. It is used more often than the Heb. demands, cf. also 'ΑΣΘ. This proves that it was a favourite word. a. The organisation of the tribal life of the Hebrews is based on the primary cell of the family with the father as head. The union of several families (1 Ch. 23:11) forms the "father's house" as a sept, the בֵּית־אָב, pl. בֵּית־אֲבוֹת, shortened אָבוֹת, 1 Ch. 7:11. [1] Cf. the stereotyped לְבֵית אֲבֹתָם. Nu. 1:2 etc. This tt. "father's house" is rendered οἶκος πατριᾶς or πατριῶν in the LXX. The formula לְבֵית אֲבֹתָם is almost without exception transl. κατ' οἴκους πατριῶν αὐτῶν, Nu. 2:2, 32; 4:2; 2 Ch. 35:12 etc. b. But the bigger union, the clan (מִשְׁפָּחָה) [2] into which the septs combine as a military organisation (אֲלָפִים ideal number), can also be rendered in the LXX by πατριά, οἶκοι πατριᾶς (Ex. 6:17, 19) as well as δῆμος (Nu. 2:34; 4:22). [3] Sometimes, then, when we find מִשְׁפָּחוֹת with אָב in the Mas., obscurity can arise in the LXX through the twofold use of πατριαί, 1 Ch. 6:4. The heads of fathers' houses, Heb. נְשִׂיאִים, רָאשִׁים, שָׂרִים, are mostly οἱ ἄρχοντες (αὐτῶν) κατ' οἴκους πατριῶν, so Nu. 17:17, though sometimes also ἀρχηγοὶ οἴκων πατριῶν, e.g., Ex. 6:14, and about the same number of times ἡγούμενοι πατριῶν, e.g., 2 Ch. 5:2; [4] Ex. 6:25 : ἀρχαὶ πατριᾶς. Other terms are used on occasion. The ministering classes, the main divisions of the priesthood of Israel, can also be called בֵּית־אָבוֹת = οἶκοι πατριῶν in Ch.: 1 Ch. 24:4; 2 Ch. 31:17; 2 Εσδρ. 22:12, abbreviated אָבוֹת (πατριαί). c. If these senses, which also apply to the Levites, stand within the framework of the tribal division of Israel, there is in the LXX a further usage which applies to the nations. The Mas. מִשְׁפָּחָה, which can be used in so many different ways, can also denote the races or peoples, and in this sense it is rendered πατριά in ψ and Jer. Thus it means races without differentiation in ψ 106(107):41. Esp. important, however, is αἱ πατριαὶ τῶν ἐθνῶν τῆς γῆς (always for מִשְׁפָּחוֹת) in the sense of the "nations" or "races." Already in Jer. 25:9; Ez. 20:32 Θ the ref. is to the Gentiles. Worth noting because of its eschatological hope is the missionary saying about the πᾶσαι αἱ πατριαὶ τῶν ἐθνῶν (כָּל־מִשְׁפְּחוֹת גּוֹיִם) in ψ 21(22):27 and ψ 95(96):7, with the call to the πατριαὶ τῶν ἐθνῶν (מִשְׁפְּחוֹת עַמִּים) to give honour to the κύριος, esp. as these verses, taken from ψ 28(29):1 f., refer there to the angels בְּנֵי אֵלִים υἱοὶ θεοῦ. The enthronement psalm 95, which is influenced by Dt. Is., made a deep impression on Israel through its liturgical use. This is shown by its employment in 1 Ch. 16:23-33, v. 28 : πατριαὶ τῶν ἐθνῶν (מִשְׁפְּחוֹת עַמִּים.) This branch of the use of πατριά in the LXX is significant in relation to Eph. 3:14 f. (→ 1018, 2 ff.). [5]

B. πατριά in the New Testament.

1. In the sense of "father's house" or "kindred" (→ lines 8 ff.) πατριά occurs in Lk. 2:4. Joseph is ἐξ οἴκου καὶ πατριᾶς Δαυίδ, cf. Lk. 1:27. Does ἐξ οἴκου

---

[1] Cf. L. Rost, "Vorstufen v. Kirche u. Synagoge im AT," BWANT, 4 F., 24 H. (1938), 56-59.

[2] There is some vacillation even in the Mas. Thus בֵּת־אָבוֹת means the household in Ex. 12:3 and the clan in Ex. 6:14.

[3] Joseph. also uses πατριά in the sense of "clan" in Ant., 11, 68 and 81. πατριά is used along with "tribe" in Ant., 6, 51 and 62.

[4] Cf. Jos. Ant., 11, 84 : τοῖς ἡγουμένοις τῶν πατριῶν, 11, 86 : οἱ τῶν πατριῶν ἡγεμόνες cf. 67. The 24 priestly classes are πατριαί in 7, 365 f.

[5] Cf. Just. Dial., 73 for a similar regard for ψ 95 and 1 Ch. 16 in quotations.

πατριᾶς come from a source used by the author? Even if not, it is readily explicable. "House of David" implies "house of the ruler." [6] It is thus in place to add πατριά (with καί) in order to make it clear that the reference is simply to ancestral descent. [7] The phrase also carries with it a reminiscence of οἶκος πατριᾶς and approximation to it. Ac. 3:25 is related to the other branch of LXX usage, → 1016, 23 ff. This πᾶσαι αἱ πατριαὶ τῆς γῆς = "nations" in Peter's address, though it refers to the promise to Abraham, agrees neither with Gn. 12:3 מִשְׁפְּחֹת (φυλαί) nor Gn. 18:18; 22:18 גּוֹיִם (ἔθνη). It is a further and perhaps independent extension of the customary LXX rendering of מִשְׁפָּחֹות by πατριαί. It again substantiates the influence of the liturgical parts of the Psalter which were of missionary significance and which found a home in the community's vocabulary of prayer. This prepares the way for an understanding of Eph. 3:14 f. by showing how open primitive Christianity was to this meaning of πατριαί in the LXX.

2. Eph. 3:14 f.: τούτου χάριν κάμπτω τὰ γόνατά μου πρὸς τὸν πατέρα, ἐξ οὗ πᾶσα πατριὰ ἐν οὐρανοῖς καὶ ἐπὶ γῆς ὀνομάζεται. [8] It cannot be contested that the paronomasia is important to the author. [9] There is no par. for ὀνομάζεται ἐκ in the LXX. If regard is had to the etymological play on words and the ἐξ [10] ("to bear someone's name," "to be named after him"), we see that the meaning is, not that God is the name-giver [11] (→ 282, 16 ff.), but that every πατριά is so named after the πατήρ. But for the true Father who precedes all such naming, one could not speak of any πατριαί. The reference is to the origin and orientation of every such πατριά, which by its very name is referred back to the Father and forward to the goal. Also implied is that the revelation of the Father is there for all when the very name reminds us of Him. [12] πατριά is in no sense abstract: a fatherly relation or disposition. [13] Here, too, the tt. has a concrete sense; it refers to the family group (→ 1016, 8 ff.) or people (→ 1016, 27 ff.) named after the Father. The author, who is well versed in the LXX, possibly had both senses in view. [14]

---

[6] Cf. 2 S. 3:6, 10; 1 K. 13:2; 14:8; 2 K. 17:21; Is. 7:2, 13; 22:22; Jer. 21:12; Zech. 12:7 f., 10; Lk. 1:69.

[7] In Zech. 12:12, too, מִשְׁפַּחַת is put before בֵּית־דָּוִיד in the st. c. because the ref. is to the family in the strict sense (cf. what follows). Acc. to 1 Εσδρ. 5:5 Shealtiel comes genealogically ἐκ τοῦ οἴκου τοῦ Δαυιδ. But cf. Sir. 48:16: ἄρχων ἐν τῷ οἴκῳ Δαυιδ.

[8] On Eph. 3:14 f. cf. H. Frick, "Ideogramm, Mythologie u. d. Wort," *Marburger Theol. Studien,* 3 (1931), 16 ff.

[9] Cf. J. C. K. Hofmann, *Die heilige Schrift NTs,* IV, 1 (1870), 130 f.; Ew. Gefbr., *ad loc.*; Dib. Gefbr., *ad loc.* Since we have here a pregnant statement about God's fatherhood, one may not assume that in the text there is an equation of πατήρ and πατριά acc. to their structure.

[10] Calvin, Beza and other Reformed fathers, accepting the longer ℜ text in v. 14, related ἐξ οὗ to Christ and saw in πᾶσα πατριά the *tota ecclesia* (→ n. 15).

[11] So Ew. Gefbr., *ad loc.* (following Hofmann, 130 f.), also Dib. Gefbr., *ad loc.*; Pr.-Bauer, *s.v.*; → 282, 18 f. On this view the question what name is in view is left undecided. Hofmann and Ew. suggest the special name which God gives each πατριά acc. to its descent.

[12] Hofmann and Ew. reject this interpretation only because it has been linked with the idea that each πατριά accepts the connection between its name and the divine Father. But this is not said. What is meant is that the true Father stands secretly behind the term.

[13] Vg has *paternitas.* But πατριά is not the same as the late Gk. πατρότης. Luther transl. *paternitas* freely: "who is the true father above all that is called father in heaven and earth" (*Das Newe Testament Deutzsch* [1922]).

[14] On the relation between πᾶσα πατριά and εἰς πάσας τὰς γενεάς (races, generations) in Eph. 3:15, cf. v. 21: 1 Εσδρ. 5:37; Est. 9:27.

πᾶσα without art. means "each." [15] The primary ref. is not to the Church, though this is the centre and goal of everything in Eph. [16] The whole world of nations is in view. Each πατριά on earth means Israel and the ἔθνη, mentioned 3 times since 3:1. According to the total Hebrew understanding the question of the nations is viewed from the standpoint of the family and the father. ἐν οὐρανοῖς precedes ἐπὶ γῆς. [17] If πᾶσα πατριά ἐν οὐρανοῖς is referred only to the perfected community of salvation (Hb. 12:22 f.) and not to the angels, [18] we miss the significance of creation and redemption for heaven and earth according to Col. and Eph., → 518, n. 159. The heavenly and the earthly are constantly inter-related, and there is express emphasis on the angelic powers [19] (Eph. 1:10; 3:10, cf. Col. 1:16, 20); the ἀνακεφαλαιώσασθαι τὰ πάντα ἐν Χριστῷ (→ III, 682, 35 ff.) and the uniting of Jews and Gentiles in the ἐκκλησία (the mystery) are linked together on this view. Here we have something similar. From the Father of Jesus Christ our gaze is directed to every πατριά which finds the motive power of unity in this Father.

When it is argued that God is the original or prototype underlying the copy or reflection of all πατριαί, [20] this goes beyond what is said in the text. It is true

---

[15] Beza, Annotationes (1594), p. 365 : πᾶσα is used here for ὅλη (tota familia in caelis et in terra); A. T. Robertson, A Grammar of the Gk. NT (1914), 772 also regards this as possible. But ὅλη πατριά would mean "a whole πατριά." Cf. in the LXX ὅλη ἡ πατριά, 2 Βασ. 14:7 (with art.), 1 Ch. 4:27: πᾶσαι αἱ πατριαὶ αὐτῶν.

[16] The final concern in Eph. (cf. 3:10, 21 and the intervening verses) is always with the ἐκκλησία. That each πατριά comes into consideration for the ἐκκλησία is implied in the prayer in 3:15-19 and corresponds to the main theme. Each πατριά in heaven (cf. 3:10) receives γνωρισθῆναι through the ἐκκλησία.

[17] If this did not come first, and if the angelic powers were not so expressly noted in Col. and Eph., one might ask whether this was not just a "polar mode of expression." Cf. materially W. Havers, Handbuch d. erklärenden Syntax = Indogermanische Bibliothek, I, 1, 20 (1931), § 128y; Schwyzer, II (1950), 704; D. Tabachovitz, Études sur le grec de la basse époque = Skrifter Humanistiska Vetenskapsamfundet, Uppsala, 36, 3 (1943), 37-39. In this case heaven and earth would mean "everywhere," and one need not ask concerning the precise meaning of either [Debrunner].

[18] Cr.-Kö., 851.

[19] When the angels are called a family, it is natural to assume that πατριά is used fig. for a "group," since Judaism spoke of classes of angels (Rabb. כִּתּוֹת). Hence there need be no implication of descent. More important, however, is comparison with the Rabb. idea of an upper and lower פְּמַלְיָא ("ministry") in which Israel is the counterpart to the angelic world, Sanh., 98b, 99b (Str.-B., I, 744); Ber., 16b (ibid., III, 594). So H. Grotius, Annotationes in Novum Testamentum, II, 1, p. 618 (ed. E. v. Windheim, II, 1 [1756]; H. St. J. Thackeray, The Relation of St. Paul to Contemporary Jewish Thought (1900), 148 f.; H. Odeberg, "The View of the Universe in the Epistle to the Eph.," Lunds Universitets Årsskrift, 29, 6 (1934), 20, → 282, n. 1. If what is meant is that God is head of the house (בַּעַל הַבַּיִת) rather than begetter (Ab., 2, 15; Sota, 35a in Str.-B., III, 594), this simply corresponds to the observation that in Judaism the father concept was understood in terms of patriarchy, → 978, 18 ff. H. J. Holtzmann, Kritik d. Epheser- u. Kolosserbr. (1872), 301 f.; O. Everling, Die paul. Angelologie u. Dämonologie (1898), 105 saw in Eph. 3:15 the Gnostic Hell. idea of descent through conception among the angels. M. Dibelius, Die Geisterwelt im Glauben d. Pls. (1909), 58 has reservations, and P. Ewald, "Darum soll das Weib eine Macht auf dem Haupte haben um der Engel willen," NkZ, 11 (1900), 507-513 firmly rejects the idea. Appeal to En. 6:1; 7:2; 9:9; 10:9, 15; 12:5; 39:1; 69:4; 71:1; 106:5; Jub. 4:1, 5 is not adequate, on this thesis, to explain satisfactorily the primitive Chr. differentiation acc. to Mk. 12:25; Mt. 22:30.

[20] So Luther, cf. Ew. Gefbr., 165, n. 3, and with a strong Platonic accent Haupt Gefbr., 111-113. Cf. also W. Lueken, Der Brief an d. Eph., Schr. NT, II, ad loc.; also E. Percy, Die Probleme d. Kol.- u. Epheserbr. (1946), → 282, n. 1. But cf. M. Dibelius, op. cit. (→ n. 19), 158.

that a connecting line is drawn from the Father to each πατριά. But this is not specifically in terms of original and copy. All the same, the relationship of creation stands in the background. Do we then have the thought of God as the Father of all, so that God is presented as the Father of the world, [21] of all things on earth and in heaven? This formulation is not found elsewhere in the Pauline corpus. The fact that creation and redemption are conjoined, however, corresponds to the finding that θεός and πατήρ are interwoven in other Pauline homologoumena, → 1012, 16 ff. [22] The πατριαί are created (3:9 : ἐν τῷ θεῷ τῷ τὰ πάντα κτίσαντι) by Him who is Father in Christ, and they are ordained for this Father. In Eph., however, this Father is always the Father of Jesus Christ. [23] The difference, then, is that this passage does not look aside from the Father of Jesus Christ, whereas belief in the Father of all does. [24] Hence one can speak of a correction of this ὁ πατὴρ τῶν ὅλων. It is not as the primal father in the Greek sense, but as the revealed Father in Christ, that God has a relation to every πατριά, → 518, 12 ff.

† ἀπάτωρ.

A. ἀπάτωρ outside the New Testament.

On the formation cf. as a par. ἄπαις in Jos. Ant., 18, 137 and 139 and ἄτεκνος in Ant., 18, 131. ἀπάτωρ alongside ἀμήτωρ, Eur. Ion, 109; Nonnus Dionys., 41, 53.

1. Of Men.

a. "Orphan." Materially Lam. 5:3; Est. 2:7: אֵין לָהּ אָב וָאֵם. [1] Linguistically Soph. Trach., 300, cf. Hdt., IV, 154 (ἀμήτωρ). b. "Foundling" — who does not know his father or mother. Eur. Ion, 109, cf. Qid., 4, 1-3. [2] c. "Illegitimate" (σκότιος, spurius), esp. pap. [3] P. Hamb., 36, 4 (2nd cent. A.D.); cf. Epiph. Haer., 55, 7: υἱὸν εἶναι πόρνης. d. "From an unequal marriage," Eur. Ion, 837: as the son of a female slave ἀμήτωρ, ἀναρίθμητος. e. "Son publicly disowned by his father" (filius abdicatus), Plat. Leg., XI, 928e; Soph. Oed. Col., 1383: ἀπάτωρ ἐμοῦ. None of these meanings can apply to Hb. 7:3. On the other hand, this is not true of f. "of non-noble, unknown or unnamed origin," with the loss of certain rights. Dio Cass., 76, 9, 4 : Severus, previously ἀπάτωρ, finds a πατήρ by adoption into the gens Marcia. Judaism too, is familiar with this meaning of "without father." Thus we read in bJeb., 98a (cf. Pesikt. r., 23-24) [4] אֵין אָב לְגוֹי, i.e., when a pagan comes over to Judaism, he has no father so far as Jewish law is concerned.

---

[21] Cf. E. Lohmeyer, "Kyrios Jesus," SAH, 1927/28, 4 Abh. (1928), 61.
[22] Cf. Cl. Al. Strom., VI, 7, 59, 1 (GCS, 17, 461, 20): ὡς οὖν ἐπὶ τὸν ποιητὴν τὸν θεὸν πᾶσα ἀνατρέχει πατριά.
[23] Cf. Eph. 1:2, 3-14 (v. 5), 17; 3:17 (after v. 15); 4:4-6, cf. 5:1, 8, 20; 6:23.
[24] For the pure belief of antiquity in the Father of all cf. Jos. Ant., 4, 262 : ὅτι καὶ αὐτὸς πατὴρ τοῦ παντὸς ἀνθρώπων γένους ἐστί.
ἀ π ά τ ω ρ. Wettstein, Liddell-Scott, Pr.-Bauer, Cr.-Kö., s.v.; Str.-B., III, 693 f.; IV, 452-465 Exc.: "Der 110. Ps. in der altrabb. Lit." P. Billerbeck, "Psalmen in altrabb. Lit.," Nathanael, 26 (1910), 21-29, 33-35. Rgg., Wnd. (bibl. 63), Mi. Hb., ad loc.; → Μελχισεδέκ, IV, 568 ff. with bibl., also Mi. Hb.[8], 160, n. 2; cf. H. H. Rowley, "Melchizedek and Zadok," Festschr. f. A. Bertholet (1950), 461-472.
[1] Str.-B., III, 693.
[2] Ibid., I, 1.
[3] There are many examples from the 2nd and 3rd cent. in Preisigke Wört., 159; Fachwörter, s.v.; K. Wessely, Karanis u. Soknopaiu Nesos, Denkschr. d. kaiserlichen Akademie d. Wissenschaften in Wien, 47, 4 (1902), 30; J. Nietzold, Die Ehe in Ägypten zur ptolemäischen u. römischen Zeit (1903), 18 f.; J. H. Moulton and G. Milligan, "Lexical Notes from the Pap.," VII, Exp. 7th Ser., VI (1908), 89.
[4] I owe this ref. to K. G. Kuhn.

Cf. Midr. Est. on 2:7 (93b). In the Mas. Esther is simply called an orphan (→ *supra*).
But here "without father" is taken to mean "unknown, unnamed." [5] In the same sense
Midr. Lam. on 5:3 (69b, 78a) applies the term to the nameless redeemer.

2. Of the Gods and God.

a. Of Athena, Hephaistos, Aphrodite. Mythologically ἀπάτωρ, ἀμήτωρ can mean
"having entered into life without father or mother." Athena is called "motherless" because she sprang from the head of Zeus. Hephaistos is "fatherless" as the direct son of
Hera, Poll. Onom., III, 2, 4. The two deities are inter-related in Hes. Theog., 924-928. [6]
ἀμήτωρ is used of Aphrodite in Plat. Symp., 180d. b. Of God in Orphic, mystic and
Gnostic works. [7] In the Rabb., too, we read of God in Ex. r., 29 (88d): [8] "I have no
father," in exposition of Is. 44:6. In Gnosticism and the mystery literature influenced
by Orphism this is a favourite mode of expression with ref. to God or the demiurge. In
these circles ἀπάτωρ is used with such terms as αὐτοπάτωρ, αὐτομήτωρ, μονο-
πάτωρ, προπάτωρ, αὐτόγονος, μονογενής, Orph. (Abel), 10, 10; Iambl. Myst., 8, 7;
Iren. Haer., I, 5, 1 (the Valentinians of the demiurge); Lact. Inst., I, 7, 1 f. (CSEL, 19, 25,
15 ff.); IV, 8, 5 (*ibid.*, 296, 6); 13, 2 (316, 13). The meaning is confirmed by the positive
formulae : He has no origin, is uncreated, is *ex se et per se* (cf. Lact., *loc. cit.* and
Epitome, 4, 4 [CSEL, 16, 679, 17]). [9] In the same vein is the address to God in Apc.
Abr. 17: "Without father, without mother, unbegotten."

3. Philo's Allegorising.

Only ἀμήτωρ occurs in Philo. Sarah is ἡ ἀμήτωρ ἀρχή, the motherless principle,
Rer. Div. Her., 62. This idea, which rests on allegorical punning, is purely psychological
and has nothing whatever to do with any divine exaltation of the historical person of
Sarah or the like. Similarly, when Fug., 108 f. says that the high-priest is not a man
but the divine *logos* there is no intention of deifying the Jewish high-priest. The ἀρχιε-
ρεύς is set above human νοῦς and sensation. His father is God and his mother *sophia*.
One might think of this as a higher qualification conferred by his office, cf. the myth of
the king in Babylon, where the viceroy is called the son of the goddess : "I have no
mother, you are my mother. I have no father, you are my father." [10] ἀπάτωρ etc. in
Hb. 7:3 can thus mean "of heavenly origin" only if the figure of Melchisedec is understood in thoroughly Gnostic terms. [11]

---

[5] Cf. Str.-B., I, 50.
[6] Cf. also Eur. Phoen., 666; Hes. Theog., 886 ff.; Plat. Critias, 109c-d, 112b; Leg., XI,
920d.
[7] Cf. J. Kroll, *Die Lehren d. Herm. Trismegistos* (1914), 10; R. Raabe, "Die Apologie d.
Aristides, aus dem Syr. übersetzt," TU, IX, 1 (1893), 65; G. Wobbermin, *Religionsgeschichtliche Studien* (1896), 80 f., 85.
[8] Str.-B., II, 542.
[9] G. N. Bonwetsch, *Studien zur Geschichte d. Theol. u. Kirche*, I, 1 (1897), 28.
[10] Cf. F. Thureau-Dangin, *Die sumerischen u. akkadischen Königsinschriften*, *Vorder-
asiatische Bibliothek*, I, 1 (1907), 93. On this cf. Wnd. Hb., *ad loc.* and P. Feine, *Der Ap.
Pl.* (1927), 455.
[11] On the mythological-Gnostic interpretation of Hb. 7:3 → IV, 570, n. 8. It might be
added that in the books of Adam there is no trace of a legendary tradition concerning the
ἀπάτωρ which might have influenced Hb. Acc. to the version of the story in *Treasure
Cave* (22:4; 23:8, 25) Melchizedek had a father, Malach, the son of Arphaxad (cf. C. Bezold,
Die Schatzhöhle, syr. u. deutsch [1883], II, *syr. Text mit arab. Übers.* [1888]). The *Chr.
Book of Adam in the East* lays even greater stress on the question of lineage. A. Dillmann
gave it this title in his transl. of the book from the Eth. (the original is Arabic), *Jahrbücher
d. bibl. Wissenschaft*, 5 (1853), 1-144. Here Melchizedek's father is the frequently mentioned
Canaan, 102 etc. Special value is placed on his genealogy, 110, 116. It is the same as that of
Shem, who accompanies him on his procession with the corpse of Adam. Melchizedek is the
grandson of Arphaxad and the brother of Methuselah. The genealogies play a considerable
role in the book, 124 ff., 133 f. The Chr. Church has had a hand here, of course, for
Melchizedek dispenses the consecrated elements, cf. Dillmann, 139, n. 43, also *Treasure Cave,*

B. The Interpretation of Hb. 7:3.

The statements concerning Melchisedec fall into two groups : what Scripture says about him, and what it does not say. The silence of Scripture was regarded as a noteworthy hermeneutical principle not only by Philo but after him by the Greek fathers. [12] One may rightly ask why it is that in Gn., which is so fond of genealogies, this priest-king appears and disappears so abruptly, and nothing is said about his parents or lineage. [13] The three terms in Hb. 7:3 : ἀπάτωρ, ἀμήτωρ, ἀγενεαλόγητος, are arranged climactically, [14] and they show that since Melchisedec had no priestly genealogy, *sub specie juris sacerdotalis* he is stamped as disqualified from a Levitical ministry by this lacuna in the Gn. narrative. [15] This is how syP took it, → n. 11. Hb. has to be interpreted here in the light of its main theme. The author takes the same course as Paul does when he argues that the ἐπαγγελία precedes the νόμος in order to show that the latter has no eternal validity as a way of salvation. As in Paul the reference of the promise is to Christ, so in Hb. the reference of the original priesthood of Melchisedec is to the high-priesthood of Jesus. [16]

† πατρικός.

1. πατρικός can denote a. "fatherly nature or relation," applied politically in Aristot. Eth. Nic., X, 4, p. 1160b, 26 f.: monarchy as a πατρικὴ ἀρχή, cf. Pol., II, 2, p. 1253b, 10 as πατρικὴ οἰκονομία. b. The adj. is associated with the activities and qualities of the father, Aristot. Eth. Nic., IX, 12, p. 1180a, 19 πατρικὴ πρόσταξις, "paternal command," Thuc., VII, 69, 5 : τὰς πατρικὰς ἀρετάς of the virtues of individual fathers whose sons are addressed ; Polyb., 31, 25, 1 (32, 11) πατρικὴ αἵρεσις, "fatherly affection." c. In the LXX it is often used with οἰκία, οἶκος, father's house, Gn. 50:8; Jos. 6:25; 1 Ch. 12:29; Sir. 42:10 (τὰ πατρικά); 4 Macc. 18:7. d. There is esp. a thought of inheritance in the word : τὸ πατρικόν, "patrimony," P. Par., 22, 33 (163 B.C.), πατρικοὶ κλῆροι, P. Tebt., II, 382, 3 (1st cent. B.C.). Thus land is given εἰς τὸ πατρικόν, P. Tebt., 5, 12 (2nd cent. B.C.); συγγραφὴ πατρική "agreement deriving from the father," Preisigke Sammelbuch, 4638, 23 (2nd cent. B.C.). Joseph. uses πατρικός consistently for the legacy of the physical father transmitted to the ruler, Ant., 10, 225; Ap., I, 109, 138, 140. It is very often used with φίλος, ξένος, ἐχθρός, ἔχθρα, also inherited. πατρικὴ φιλία, P. Tebt., 159, 7 (c. 100 B.C.) — cf. Polyb., I, 18, 1: πατρικὴ σύστασις — can be one which is inherited from the father, whether transmitted by him or first

---

28:11 ff. ἀπάτωρ cannot refer to the fact that Melchizedek disappears in the middle of the earth, that he then comes to Abraham, and that he reckons his parents to be dead because Shem veils himself when he returns (in both versions). In the Syr. church the correction of the legend that he had no father is to the effect (*Treasure Cave*) that his parents are not listed in the genealogies in Mt. and Lk., 30:15 f. Cf. Hb. 7:3 in syP : *cuius neque pater neque mater scribuntur in generationibus.*

[12] On the silence of Scripture in patristic exegesis cf. Rgg. Hb., 184, n. 2. For examples from Philo cf. C. Siegfried, *Philo v. Alexandrien* (1875), 179 f. sub 19.

[13] On the genealogical proof of priestly lineage cf. Rgg. Hb., 184 and the examples from Philo and Joseph. in n. 3.

[14] Cf. Cr.-Kö., 855.

[15] Str.-B., III, 693.

[16] On the difficulty of applying all three terms (→ lines 7 f.) to Christ in the fathers cf. W. M. L. de Wette, *Kurzgefasstes exegetisches Handbuch zum NT,* II, 5³ (rev. W. Moeller, 1867); Rgg. Hb., ad loc.; Cr.-Kö., 854.

π α τ ρ ι κ ό ς. J. Wackernagel, "Über einige lat. u. gr. Ableitungen aus den Verwandtschaftswörtern," *Festgabe A. Kaegi* (1919), 40-54. Preisigke Wört., *s.v.*

beginning with him. The father passes it on and is the last link in the chain. Here we have plenty of refs. to the one father. Thus in Plat. La., 180e πατρικὸς φίλος is followed later by ὁ σὸς πατήρ; Ditt. Or., 227, 9 (c. 246 B.C.): παραθέντων ἡμῖν τῶν πατρικῶν φίλων is explained by τοῦ πατρός (one's own father) in 227, 2.[1] The same is true in Ditt. Syll.[3], 456, 18 (c. 240 B.C.), cf. 456, 10 and 20.[2] When Cratinus Fr., 116 (CAF, I, 50) (4th cent. B.C.) speaks of πατρικοὶ νόμοι in the sense of rules of play, these are also among the things passed on from father to son. In the Jewish Hell. sphere, however, πατρικός is not used of laws, institutions or customs of the fathers or people. πατρῷος is used for these (→ 1015, 8 ff.) and esp. πάτριος (→ 1015, 17 ff.).[3]

2. The Gnostic use, with special ref. to the father, also shows how the Gk. is inclined to use the term for one's own father in particular. So Corp. Herm., XIII, 3 : The regenerate belongs to the πατρικὸν γένος, Just. Dial., 61, 1 with βουλήματι of the will of the divine Father. Cl. Al. uses the adj. very frequently to express the relation of the Logos to the Father, Strom., VII, 2, 5, 6 (GCS, 17, 6, 4); Exc. Theod., 7, 1 (108, 4); 12, 1 (110, 25).

3. There are also exceptions, however, where the ref. is to the fathers. None too clear is the occasional LXX use of οἶκοι πατρικοί for πατριᾶς in 1 Ch. 7:4; 7:7 AB; 26:6 — for the father's house as a sept goes back to one father. In the transl. of Lv. 25:41; Nu. 36:8, however, the ref. is plainly to "fathers," for here πατρικός is a rendering of the specific Mas. אֲבֹתָיו (possession, inheritance of the fathers).

4. In Gl. 1:14 πατρικός denotes the religious inheritance of the father's house (→ 1021, 29 f.), with a specific reference to the immediate father. Cf. Ac. 23:6 and by way of supplement Phil. 3:5; 2 Tm. 1:3; Ac. 22:3; 26:5. The μου strengthens this understanding.[4]

Schrenk

| παχύνω, πωρόω (πηρόω), πώρωσις (πήρωσις), σκληρός, σκληρότης, σκληροτράχηλος, σκληρύνω | σκληροκαρδία → III, 613, 25 ff. |

This group of words, which come from different stems, has to do with the so-called hardening[1] of unbelievers, of enemies of the chosen people Israel, then of Israel itself, also of Jews as opposed to Christians, and finally of Christians themselves. The somewhat archaic word "to harden" has become especially at home,

---

[1] Cf. C. B. Welles, *Royal Correspondence in the Hell. Period* (1934), 106.
[2] Comm. in Welles, *op. cit.,* 120.
[3] Zn. Gl., 104 gives an excellent summary of the data.
[4] So, in addition to Zn. Gl., 61, Pr.-Bauer, s.v., but cf. F. Sieffert, Gl., Kritisch-exegetischer Komm. über d. NT, VII[9] (1899), Ltzm. Gl., Oe. Gl., ad loc. Also Schlier Gl., ad loc., though he adds that the "refined sense" more or less includes the father as well as a mediator.

π α χ ύ ν ω κτλ. Preliminary Note : K. L. Schmidt was prevented by sickness from preparing for press the art. which he had written, and so his son M. A. Schmidt did this for him. Bibl.: K. L. Schmidt, "Die Verstockung des Menschen durch Gott. Eine lexikologische u. bibl.-theologische Studie," *Theol. Zschr.,* 1 (1945), 1-17.

[1] Along with OT and NT theologies and works of Chr. dogmatics cf. the arts. on "Verstockung" by R. Knopf in RGG[1], V, 1663 f. and esp. by O. Schmitz in RGG[2], V, 1573-1575. Cf. also F. Hesse, "Das Verstockungsproblem im AT," *Beih. zur ZAW,* 74 (1954). On patristic exegesis of R. 9-11 cf. K. H. Schelkle, "Erwählung u. Freiheit im Römerbrief nach der Auslegung d. Väter," *Theol. Quart.,* 131 (1951), 17-31, 189-207. → 1024, 33 ff. and n. 13.

and has remained so, in this sphere of God's dealings with His people as the ἐκκλησία, → III, 501, 20 ff. [2]

> While the simple intr. "to harden" is common in a concrete sense, esp. physiological and medical, the intensive and mostly trans. "to harden" with its derivates is most familiar in Bible translation and with a transf. spiritual meaning. It can also be used in pedagogical and psychological circles. [3] We thus find, if less directly, the same connection between the physiological and the psychological, the medical and the ethical use, as in the Gk. equivalents.

Luther uses "to harden" or "hardening" for the above group of words and their derivates with a consistency which is hardly true of any other translation either in German or any other language : [4] so παχύνω at Mt. 13:15 and Ac. 28:27, πωρόω at Jn. 12:40; R. 11:7; 2 C. 3:14; cf. also Mk. 3:5 (πώρωσις), σκληρύνω Ac. 19:9; R. 9:18; Hb. 3:8, 13, 15; 4:7; also R. 2:5 (σκληρότης). [5] Most of the passages are OT quotations. Luther is justified in using a single word for many Greek stems by the fact that the material reference is the same, as the many variations in the textual tradition show.

Thus in Jn. 12:40 ἐπώρωσεν is based on Is. 6:10 ἐπαχύνθη, and cod. ℵ reads ἐπή-ρωσεν, → 1027, 32 ff. At Ac. 28:27 we find an ἐβαρύνθη as well as ἐπαχύνθη. βαρύνω or βαρέω at Lk. 21:34 (Luther "beschweren") perhaps refers to the process of hardening (like many OT verses) with ref. to Pharaoh, → I, 559, 5-10 and n. 2 σκληρύνω is most common in the LXX and NT for the process ; in the LXX it corresponds to חזק q "to be firm," pi "to make firm," or קשה q "to be hard," pi "to harden," though in the LXX we also find κατισχύω [6] both trans. and intr. corresponding to חזק q or אמץ pi, "to strengthen." In Dt. 2:30 we find both קשה hi = σκληρύνω and אמץ pi = κατισχύω, cf. 2 Ch. 36:13. In Hos. 13:8 סְגוֹר לִבָּם ("closing of the heart") is transl. συγκλεισμὸς καρδίας αὐτῶν in the LXX, Luther "verstocktes Herz." The fact that Luther uses "blindness" rather than "hardening" (Zurich Bible etc.) at R. 11:25 and Eph. 4:18 is connected with the occurrence of the vl. πήρωσις for πώρωσις both here and elsewhere, → 1027, 42 ff.

Other Heb. words or related concepts which come within the sphere of hardening are already transl. by milder or less precise terms in the LXX. Thus for שְׁרִירוּת "firmness," "hardness" in Dt. 29:18; Jer. 3:17 etc.; Ps. 81:12 we find πλάνη, ἀποπλάνησις, even ἐπιτηδεύματα, ἐπιθυμήματα, ἐνθυμήματα ἀρεστά etc. (Luther, "thoughts," "thoughts of the heart" etc.). [7] Is this an attempt to soften the offence of a divinely effected hardening by throwing greater stress on man's part and on the punishment which he has merited (→ 1025, 15 ff.)? But the human psychological side of hardening is already

---

[2] For the German word "Verstockung" cf. J. and W. Grimm, *Deutsches Wörterbuch*, XII, 1, *s.v.* "verstocken," "Verstocktheit," "Verstockung." The smaller Germ. dict. usually refer primarily to the Luther Bible. Rather surprisingly F. Kluge and A. Götze, *Etym. Wörterbuch d. deutschen Sprache*[15] (1951) do not have either noun or verb. *Der grosse Duden*[13] (1953), *s.v.* has only "verstocken," "Verstocktheit," and Calwer's *Bibelkonkordanz*[3] (*Bibelkonkordanz u. bibl. Handwörterbuch*, ed. Calwer Verlagsverein[3] [1922]) only "verstocken."

[3] → n. 2. But cf. also "hardened leather," "hardened washing."

[4] Cf. K. L. Schmidt, 2 f., 8. Luther uses "verstocken" 13 times in the NT (→ *infra*) and 25 times in the OT (also "verhärten" 9 times in the OT). → n. 5.

[5] In special instances (R. 11:25 and Eph. 4:18 → *infra*, Mk. 3:5 → *infra*) Luther had "verstarreten" for "verstockten" in some editions. On Mk. 6:52 and 8:17 → 1026, 9 ff. and n. 2.

[6] In the NT this verb occurs only intr. in the sense "to be strong," → III, 398, 17-26.

[7] The Zurich Bible almost always has "Verstocktheit" or "Starrsinn" here.

in view in the HT, cf. Is. 6:10 and 29:10, the former quoted in Mt. 13:15 and Ac. 28:27, [8] the latter in R. 11:8 (immediately after the ref. to the hardening of the Jews in v. 7b). Even at Is. 6:10 the LXX decisively softens the HT, and this is not reversed in Mt. 13:15 or Ac. 28:27, though it is in the freer citation in Jn. 12:40, → 1026, 14.

Even though the toning down of the process of hardening is often linked with a concern to soften the harsh thought of predestination ("God has hardened"), it always carries with it a sharper insight into the measure of human guilt and misery. This is particularly plain when hardening is related to death, cf. Mk. 3:5, where for πώρωσις we have the vl. νέκρωσις on this first occasion that Jesus is said to be troubled by the hardening of the Jews. [9]

The complicated interrelations of the words connected with the process of hardening thus display mildness, balance and severity in combination, antithesis and synthesis. The self-hardening of man as his hardening by God, the guilt and responsibility of man as self-judgment and yet also God's judgment, is so complex a matter, affecting the whole man, that there are hardly enough terms to give an adequate spiritual portrayal of the reality of his inner condition. [10] A genuine softening of the concept is to be seen, however, in the fact that in the biblical sphere the reference is never to the hardening of men as such within the framework of a general *praedestinatio gemina*, but always to the hardening of specific types, whether Pharaoh and his Egyptians against Israel, Israel against its true leaders and prophets, or finally the rejected Jews against Christians as the true Israel. What has the last word is not a theory of predestination but the divine history of salvation in the elect people, a history which just because it is so serious can become a history of judgment and rejection, yet in such a way that finally God in His freedom remains faithful to the rejected and the elect are constantly admonished not to slip back into the way of the rejected, → 1027, 1 ff. In what is said about hardening it is worth noting that there is always, even linguistically, a fear of saying either too much or too little. If we seem to have here a kaleidoscope of harsher and softer colours, the basic colour is clearly the beautiful one of the δόξα θεοῦ. Any theory which overhastily encloses man's sin in the divine action will either run into Gnostic dualism in its attempt to avoid an intolerable monism, or commend a quietistic withdrawal in which man finds excuse for his impotence. [11]

On the hardening of unbelievers in God's plan of salvation, which has always been a necessary concern of Christian dogmaticians, [12] the various refs. in *TWNT* to the gracious divine decree are materially relevant and should be consulted. [13]

---

[8] In many MSS ἐβαρύνθη for ἐπαχύνθη. In the LXX βαρύνω or βαρέω (with heart, eyes or ears) is very commonly used for the process of hardening. There is a good review of the various Heb. words and their use in the Pentateuchal sources in Hesse, *op. cit.*; cf. also → I, 559, n. 2.

[9] → 1027, 40 f. Cf. Loh. Mt., *ad loc.* On νέκρωσις v. R. 4:19 and 2 C. 4:10.

[10] K. L. Schmidt, 16.

[11] *Loc. cit.*

[12] → n. 1. On the debate about hardening cf. R. H. Grützmacher, Art. "Terminismus u. terministischer Streit," RE[3], 19, 524-527.

[13] → βουλή I, 635, 29 ff.; → προγινώσκω, πρόγνωσις, I, 715, 23 ff.; → εὐδοκέω, εὐδοκία II, 738-751, esp. 741 ff.; → θέλω, θέλημα, III, 47-61, esp. 52, 17 ff.; 55 f.; → καλέω, κλῆσις, κλητός, III, 487-496, esp. 495, 1 ff.; → ἐκλέγομαι, ἐκλογή, ἐκλεκτός, IV, 144-192, esp. 175, 29 ff.; 192, 1 ff.; → ὁρίζω, V, 452 f.; → προορίζω, V, 456, 12 ff.; → προτίθημι, πρόθεσις.

† παχύνω.

1. Derived from παχύς, "thick," "fat," "firm," τὸ πάχος, "thickness,"[1] παχύνω properly means "to thicken," "to fatten," and occurs in this sense from the time of Aesch., finding a special medical use from the time of Hippocr.: παχύνομαι (pass.) "to swell" (a tumour); so P. Tebt., II, 273, 31 (2nd/3rd cent. A.D.): πρὸς πεπαχυ[σμέν]α ...[2] In the general non-medical sense it occurs in early Chr. lit. only in 1 Cl., 3, 1: ἔφαγεν καὶ ἔπιεν καὶ ἐπλατύνθη καὶ ἐπαχύνθη καὶ ἀπελάκτισεν ὁ ἠγαπημένος (a free quotation from Dt. 32:15).

2. Fig. παχύνω means "to make impervious (lit. to water), insensitive, dull." So twice in the NT (obj. καρδία), Mt. 13:15: ἐπαχύνθη γὰρ ἡ καρδία τοῦ λαοῦ τούτου (vg: incrassatum est cor), cf. Ac. 28:27.[3] In both passages we have a quotation from Is. 6:10 with its more precise explanation of the hardening of Israel, on which no appeal for repentance can make any further impression, → 554, 29-555, 23; 1023, 36 ff.; 1026, 33 ff.

3. In Is. 6:10 this OT use corresponds to the hi of שׁמן "to make fat": הַשְׁמֵן לֵב־הָעָם הַזֶּה. In the HT, then, the prophet is ordered by God to make the heart of the people fat, to harden it. The LXX text is milder, for it ignores the fact that God has commanded this, and simply describes the hardening as a fact,[4] → 1023, 30 ff. In the context of a passage which speaks of a stiff neck and hardening, παχύνω also occurs in Job 15:27 ᾿ΑΣ.[5] Apart from Is. 6:10 the LXX also uses the verb in a literal sense in Dt. 32:15 (→ lines 6 ff.) for שׁמן q (cf. עבה q, "to be fat"); Is. 34:6 for דשׁן hotpael, "to become fat"; Qoh. 12:5 for סבל hitp, "to proceed with difficulty"; 2 Βασ. 22:12: ἐπάχυνεν ἐν νεφέλαις ἀέρος, "he was invisible," has no Heb. original. παχύνω does not occur in Philo.

† πωρόω (πηρόω), † πώρωσις (πήρωσις).

1. Derived from ὁ πῶρος, the "tuff-stone" (Poll., 7, 123), medically "hardening," hardened swelling of the bone, also jelly thickening out of the bone (Aristot. Hist. An., III, 19, p. 521a, 21), callus (callum),[1] through which the parts of a broken bone are knit

---

π α χ ύ ν ω. [1] On the derivation v. Walde-Pok., II, 151; E. Fraenkel, Gr. Denominativa (1906), 65, 31, 37; A. Debrunner, "Zu den konsonantischen io-Präsentien im Griech.," Indogermanische Forschungen, 21 (1907), 77; Debr. Gr. Wortb. § 226 (-ύνω in gen.). τὸ πάχος occurs, e.g., in Job 15:26, → n. 5.

[2] Cf. Preisigke Wört., Moult.-Mill., Pr.-Bauer⁴, s.v.

[3] On the vl. ἐβαρύνθη → 1024, n. 8.

[4] Perhaps we are to see here a certain correction on the part of the LXX in an attempt to make the concept of God as little anthropomorphic as possible. On Is. 6:9 f. in Rabb. lit. cf. Str.-B., I, 662 f. The passages quoted there show that the ancient Synagogue did not find in Is. 6:10 a divine judgment of hardening on Israel but thought that the prophet misunderstood God and turned His words into their opposite. Cf. Kl. Mt., ad loc.; K. L. Schmidt, 12 f., n. 18; → 554, 29 ff. Hesse has an exc. "Zur Nachgeschichte von Is. 6:9, 10," → 1022, n. 1.

[5] The HT (cf. G. Hölscher, Das Buch Hiob = Handbuch z. AT, I, 17² [1952], 38) describes the ungodly as follows: "... because he stretched out his hand against God and boasted before the Almighty, ran against him with a stiff neck, with the force of his embossed shield, because he covered his face with fat and smeared grease on his loins." The LXX (supplemented from Θ) has in v. 26: ἐν πάχει νώτου, and in v. 27 ᾿ΑΣ read: ἐπάχυνε πιμελὴν κατὰ τῆς ψόας. Here, too, hardening and a stiff neck go together. The verb τραχηλιάω in v. 25 is in the context to be construed as "to resist" (HT גבר hitp, "to behave arrogantly") [Bertram].

π ω ρ ό ω κ τ λ. Bibl.: Zn. R., 619-621 (exc. on πωροῦν, πώρωσις and πηροῦν, πήρωσις following P. de Lagarde, "De novo testamento ad versionum orientalium fidem edendo," Gesammelte Abhandlungen [1866], 101 and J. A. Robinson, "ΠΩΡΩΣΙΣ and ΠΗΡΩΣΙΣ," JThSt, 3 [1902], 81-93); Cr.-Kö., 969 f., s.v.; Wnd. 2 K. on 3:14a.

[1] Cf. Pape, s.v.; Fränkel, op. cit. (→ παχύνω, n. 1), 153, 149.

together again and the healing of the break is promoted, M. Ant., IX, 36. Hence πωρόω "to harden," medically of a hard swelling, though the word can also mean "to heal," i.e., to knit together parts of bone by callus, Hippocr. De Fracturis, 47, transf. "to make dull or insensitive," physically, Nymphis Fr., 16 (FHG, III, 16) or mentally.

2. The verb occurs in the LXX only twice at Job 17:7 (= כהה, "to become weak," of the eyes ; vl. πεπήρωνται) and Prv. 10:20 A, though with no thought of "hardening." We do not find the verbal noun in the LXX.

3. The verb occurs 5 times in the NT and is always fig., usually of the heart. It refers to the hardening of the Jews in Jn. 12:40; R. 11:7; 2 C. 3:14, and in Mk. 6:52; 8:17 to that of the disciples, whose misunderstanding is presented as a relapse into Jewish modes of thought, → 1027, 23 ff. [2] The verbal noun occurs 3 times with reference to the hardening of the Jews or Gentiles (Mk. 3:5 : τῇ πωρώσει τῆς καρδίας, also Eph. 4:18; [3] also R. 11:25).

In Jn. 12:40 God is expressly called the author of hardening. Other passages, even though they are imprecise, must be understood in the light of this. Nevertheless, the hardening by God is also a self-hardening of the unbeliever who does not obey God, → 1027, 1 ff. Though in this mystery man cannot escape the sovereignty of the divine action, this does not absolve him from personal responsibility. The admonition against hardening oneself (Ps. 95:8 = Hb. 3:8, 15; 4:7, → 1030, 10 ff.) applies even when the situation is hopeless from man's standpoint. The possibility and ineluctability of human responsibility are enclosed in God's dealings.

> Hence the OT prophet has to summon Israel to repentance even though he knows that it will not listen. [4] In this situation the call can only mean : "Make you a new heart and a new spirit" (Ez. 18:31). But who can make this new heart except God Himself (Ez. 11:19; 36:26 f.; cf. Jer. 31:33; 32:39)? Fear of a judgment which is no less ineluctable than merited, and hope of a new grace which is no less real than outside man's power, cannot be combined in an impersonal functional way ; they can be attested only as the Thus and Nevertheless of the personal God. The remorse which arises out of fear of impending punishment cannot be accepted as a restitution which restores the ancient relation (this is refuted in Jer. 14:1-12). The sin which derives from man's will must be worked out wholly and utterly in the sphere of his will. Sin and unbelief are the punishment of sin and unbelief. [5] The people which will not hear, which is deaf to the divine admonitions (Is. 1:2-5), will have this obduracy as its penalty and judgment (Is. 6:9 f.). There is no more hope of amendment or instruction. The only remaining possibility is that of complete renewal, of new creation after the destruction of the old, Is. 6:11-13.

---

[2] When Luther and others use a different word here to differentiate the disciples from the Jews (→ 1023, 9-13) they are not tackling the problem of hardening objectively. Cf. K. L. Schmidt, 10.

[3] πώρωσις τῆς καρδίας in Mk. 3:5 and Eph. 4:18 corresponds exactly, both in language and sense, to the very common Essene שרירות לב (in the OT → 1023, 30 f.): Book of Sects 1:6; 2:14, 16; 3:3; 5:4; 7:19, 24; 9:10; Hymns C 11 [Kuhn].

[4] E.g., Jer. 7:27; 18:12. Cf. M. Schmidt, Prophet u. Tempel (1948), 78-80.

[5] Eichr. Theol. AT, III³ (1950), 108 : "... that Yahweh punishes sin by a destructive power set in it, and thus evens things out justly ... Often it is expressly stressed that Yahweh Himself controls this abandonment to the sinful process, that He thus punishes sin with sin, and disaster indivertibly follows" (ref. is then made to Ex. 10:20, 27; 1 S. 2:25; Ju. 9:23 f.; Dt. 2:30; Jos. 11:20; 1 K. 12:15). On this whole problem in the OT cf. Hesse. The same problem arises in respect of παραδιδόναι. On the one side God has given up man to sin (R. 1:24 ff.); on the other side men have given up themselves to sin (Eph. 4:19). Cf. on this important usage, esp. as it concerns the hardening of Judas, K. L. Schmidt, "Der Todesprozess des Messias Jesus," Judaica, 1 (1945/46), 18-20. On R. 9-11 cf. → 1027, 1 ff.

Paul in R. 9-11 neither softened nor explained this prophetic message of hardening; he simply repeated and underlined it. According to 11:25 hardening happened in part to Israel. The meaning is, then, not only that this Israel was hardened by God (11:7-10) but also that on its own responsibility it chose the wrong path (9:30-10:3). To this Israel, however, the Christian Church, the true Israel, can boast only of the grace which it has received and not of the works which it has performed. The full force of this boasting is deployed only when it includes hope for the conversion of hardened Israel (11:33-36). This conversion is again hoped for both as a human decision ("if they do not persist in unbelief," 11:23) and also as a sovereign divine act (11:15: life from the dead; 11:17-24: the metaphor of ingrafting). In face of this ultimate eschatological aspect of the mystery (11:25, → IV, 822, 30-823, 5) one cannot raise the question which comes first and which second. This aspect, however, does not prevent Paul from being concerned even now for the salvation of the hardened Israelites (11:14), and in this zeal, which is nourished by a final hope, he warns the community not to be hardened itself, not to boast against ancient Israel and thereby to set itself in opposition to the depths of grace, of the riches and wisdom and knowledge of God (11:33), not to fall from grace to works and thus to return to the way of Israel's hardening (9:30-10:13; 11:19-22).

Connected with the fact that hardening by God is also the self-hardening of unbelievers is the exposition of 2 C. 3:14: ἐπωρώθη τὰ νοήματα αὐτῶν, in 4:4: ὁ θεὸς τοῦ αἰῶνος τούτου (the devil) ἐτύφλωσεν τὰ νοήματα τῶν ἀπίστων.[6] If in Mk. 6:52; 8:17 the reference is to the καρδία πεπωρωμένη of the disciples, and the disciples are thus grouped with the Jews, the hardening here cannot be regarded as not a full hardening, and thereby softened. According to the testimony of the NT, Christians are not completely kept from hardening. In the light of the history of the ancient covenant they can only be warned most urgently not to do as ancient Israel did, → 1024, 24 ff.; 1027, 14 ff. This means, then, that the disciples of Jesus are not immune to the danger of falling into the attitude of the people which did not recognise its Messiah but rejected Him, though we are not perhaps to think more narrowly of the instance of Judas.[7]

4. In almost all the verses mentioned we find for πωρόω the variant πηρόω, "to maim," "to wound," "to cripple," esp. in the members or sense organs, hence "to blind," also transf. Similarly πήρωσις ("maiming," esp. "blindness") can be used for πώρωσις.[8] The verb occurs in Mk. 8:17 D (with ω written over η; vg callatum; in some it MSS, however, obtusum or plur.; sy⁸ מעור, "blinded," but sy^P קשׁיא "hard"); Jn. 12:40 אWП and minuscules (but Lat. induravit); R. 11:7 C etc. (Lat. excaecati; sy^P אתעורו "were blinded"). There are no Gk. variants at Mk. 6:52 and 2 C. 3:14, but at both the meaning of πηρόω is assumed in ancient translations (Mk. 6:52 obcaecatum vg, also עויר sy⁸; 2 C. 3:14 sy^P). πήρωσις occurs at Mk. 3:5 in some minuscules (Lat. caecitate[m]; D has νεκρώσει [→ 1024, n. 9]; cf. מיתות sy⁸, but קשׁיות "hardness" sy^P). At R. 11:25 and Eph. 4:18 there are no Gk. variants, but cf. again the ancient translations (R. 11:25 caecitas Lat., also עוירות "blindness" sy^P; Eph. 4:18 caecitatem Lat., also sy^P). πηρός, "maimed," "crippled," "weakened," is very often used for spiritual blindness and incapacity. So 2 Cl., 1, 6: πηροὶ ὄντες τῇ διανοίᾳ, "blind in understanding"; cf.

---

[6] On the other hand Jos. Bell., 5, 343 says of the besieged Jews who had grown somewhat arrogant: ἐπεσκότει γὰρ αὐτῶν ταῖς γνώμαις διὰ τὰς παρανομίας ὁ θεός.

[7] On Mk. 6:52; 8:17 → n. 2. On Judas → n. 5.

[8] On the etym. of πηρός v. Boisacq, s.v. πῆμα, Walde-Pok., II, 8: root pē- "to do hurt," "to harm," cf. → ταλαίπωρος.

Philo Omn. Prob. Lib., 55 : διὰ λογισμοῦ πήρωσιν. M. Ant., II, 13, 3 compares this spiritual πήρωσις with the physical inability to distinguish black from white. In this fig. use the word does, of course, approximate to the biblical use of πωρόω, πώρωσις. This explains the uncertainty of copyists and translators in the relevant texts.

It may be added that the better attested πωρ- is a comparatively rare stem, whereas πηρ-, which replaces it, is very common. Substitution would naturally suggest itself where the ref. in the context is to "blindness," "not seeing," cf. Mk. 8:17 f.; Jn. 12:40 (τετύφλωκεν is par. to ἐπώρωσεν); R. 11:7 f. The occurrence of πηρ- in some MSS and translations does not mean that this is original. The most that one may deduce from it is that there was no longer any awareness of the difference in meaning between the two stems πωρ- and πηρ-. [9]

† σκληρός.

1. The adj. derives from the stem *sqel-* "to dry (up)," "to desiccate," with which "skeleton" is connected ; it means "dry," "arid," "hard," "rough," "unyielding." [1] It is found in Hes., also inscr., pap., Philo.

2. In the NT it occurs 6 times : a. of things in a transf. sense : σκληρός ἐστιν ὁ λόγος οὗτος, "hard," "unpleasant," "intolerable," Jn. 6:60; περὶ πάντων τῶν σκληρῶν (vl. + λόγων), Jd. 15; ὑπὸ ἀνέμων σκληρῶν, "strong," "rough," "contrary" winds, Jm. 3:4; b. of persons : ὅτι σκληρὸς εἶ ἄνθρωπος, a "harsh," "hard," "austere," "strict," "unmerciful" man, Mt. 25:24 (the par. in Lk. 19:21 has αὐστηρός, "unfriendly," "stern"). [2] The phrase σκληρόν σοι (Ac. 26:14), which uses the neuter, means "it is hard for thee"; it occurs in some MSS at Ac. 9:4, and is presupposed in some ancient translations.

3. Some of the NT passages mentioned plainly show traces of connections with the LXX and other Gk.-Jewish writings. [3] Thus Jd. 15 is a reminiscence of Gk. En. 1:9. [4] Jm. 3:4 recalls Is. 27:8 : τῷ πνεύματι (wind) τῷ σκληρῷ, בְּרוּחוֹ הַקָּשָׁה. Like Mt. 25:24, 1 Βασ. 25:3; Is. 19:4, cf. 48:4 speak of σκληροὶ ἄνθρωποι. The Heb. root קשׁה is presupposed here. σκληρός occurs over 50 times in the LXX and usually corresponds to the Heb. word just mentioned.

4. In the sphere of Hell. pars. we also find the usage in the post-apost. fathers : [5] λίθοι σκληροί, Herm. s., 9, 6, 8; 8, 6; ῥάβδος σκληρά, "knobbed stick," 6, 2, 5 : σκληρά, "hard words," v., 1, 4, 2 (with χαλεπός); Barn., 9, 5 has σκληροκαρδία in a quotation from Dt. 10:16, [6] → 1031, 8 f.

† σκληρότης.

1. This verbal noun occurs in the NT only at R. 2:5 : [1] κατὰ δὲ τὴν σκληρότητά σου καὶ ἀμετανόητον καρδίαν, where it denotes hardness as a human quality, in this instance characterising self-righteous and impenitent Jews (Luther : "according to thy hardened and impenitent heart").

---

[9] Hesych., Suid., and Etym. Gud. relate the stems etym. as well as materially.
σ κ λ η ρ ό ς. [1] Cf. Walde-Pok., II, 597. On the history of the word *v.* K. Dieterich, "Bedeutungsgeschichte gr. Worte," *Rheinisches Museum,* NF, 60 (1905), 236-240.
[2] Cf. Pr.-Bauer[4], *s.v.* αὐστηρός.
[3] Cr.-Kö., *s.v.* σκληρός.
[4] Kautzsch Apkr. u. Pseudepigr., II, 237.
[5] Pr.-Bauer[4], *s.v.* σκληρός.
[6] → σκληροκαρδία III, 613, 25 ff., where Barn., 9, 5 is not mentioned.
σ κ λ η ρ ό τ η ς. [1] Cf. Pr.-Bauer[4] and Cr.-Kö., *s.v.* σκληρότης.

2. It occurs for the first time in Antiphon Or., which speaks of the σκληρότης τοῦ δαίμονος, 3, 3 and 4. Cf. Plat. and Aristot.

3. We find it 4 times in the LXX. In Dt. 9:27 Moses prays : μὴ ἐπιβλέψῃς ἐπὶ τὴν σκληρότητα (קְשִׁי) τοῦ λαοῦ τούτου καὶ τὰ ἀσεβήματα καὶ τὰ ἁμαρτήματα αὐτῶν. In 2 Βασ. 22:6 David speaks of the σκληρότητες θανάτου which come over him (HT מֹקְשֵׁי מָוֶת, "snares" of death from יקשׁ, which is obviously linked with קשׁה in the LXX). In Is. 4:6 the prophet promises protection to purified Zion : ἀπὸ σκληρότητος καὶ ὑετοῦ (HT different). Is. 28:27 contains the threat of judgment : οὐ γὰρ μετὰ σκληρότητος (HT חָרוּץ, "threshing drum," from חרץ "to cut to a point," "to cut up," not understood by the LXX) [2] καθαίρεται τὸ μελάνθιον.

4. Philo uses the word in a more physiological sense. Thus in Op. Mund., 62 the sense of taste experiences μαλακότητας δὲ καὶ σκληρότητας, "softness and hardness." Psychologically Sacr. AC, 116 : διὰ σκληρότητα φύσεως, "on account of the aridity or unfruitfulness of the natural disposition." The idea of hardening is developed in Spec. Leg., I, 304 f.: Men are of uncircumcised hearts, as the Law puts it (Lv. 26:41), and on account of the hardness of their minds (διὰ σκληρότητα τρόπων) they throw off the reins and gallop along proudly and rowdily. The Law reproves such by saying : Circumcise the hardness of your hearts (περιτέμνεσθε τὴν σκληροκαρδίαν). [3]

5. In the post-apost. fathers the word occurs only in Herm. m., 5, 2, 6 : τὸ τρυφερὸν ... πνεῦμα, μὴ ἔχον συνήθειαν μετὰ πονηροῦ πνεύματος κατοικεῖν μηδὲ μετὰ σκληρότητος, "the tender Spirit who is not accustomed to dwell with an evil spirit and with hardness."

† σκληροτράχηλος.

1. This construct [1] means "stiff-necked," "obdurate," "recalcitrant." It occurs in the NT only at Ac. 7:51, where Stephen addresses the hardened Jews as σκληροτράχηλοι καὶ ἀπερίτμητοι (ταῖς) καρδίαις καὶ τοῖς ὠσίν. [2]

2. The LXX use is so developed that one might even trace the origin of the word here. [3] In Ex. 33:3 (→ n. 2) the HT runs : קְשֵׁה עֹרֶף, "hard in neck," cf. also 33:5; 34:9; Dt. 9:6, 13; Ex. 32:9 (no LXX). Cf. Dt. 31:27: עָרְפְּךָ הַקָּשֶׁה τὸν τράχηλόν σου τὸν σκληρόν, 10:16 : תַקְשׁוּ עֹוד לֹא וְעָרְפְּכֶם τὸν τράχηλον ὑμῶν οὐ σκληρυνεῖτε ἔτι, similarly 2 K. 17:14; Jer. 7:26; 17:23; 19:15; Neh. 9:16 f., 29; 2 Ch. 30:8; 36:13. In Prv. 29:1 σκληροτράχηλος corresponds to עֹרֶף מַקְשֶׁה, but in view of the LXX this should be emended to עֹרֶף מַקְשֶׁה. There is no Heb. at Sir. 16:11. In Prv. 29:19 we find both οἰκέτης σκληρός and οἰκέτης σκληροτράχηλος (HT only עֶבֶד). Philo does not use the term.

3. It occurs in the post-apost. fathers only in 1 Cl., 53, 3 quoting Dt. 9:13. [4]

---

[2] Acc. to Cr.-Kö. the LXX renders the concrete חָרוּץ abstractly.

[3] → III, 613, 29 f., cf. the ref. to the fact that we find σκληροτραχηλία as well as σκληροκαρδία, Test. S. 6:2 (vl.).

σ κ λ η ρ ο τ ρ ά χ η λ ο ς. [1] Listed in Cr.-Kö. only in the alphabetical glossary. For examples cf. Str.-B., II, 683 f.

[2] In Nestle's text the phrase is printed as a conflation of OT quotations, with a ref. to Ex. 33:3.

[3] C. L. W. Grimm, Lexicon Graeco-Latinum in Libros NT⁴ (1903), s.v.: apud profanos non legitur.

[4] Cf. also the use of עורף קשׁי in the Dead Sea Scrolls : Book of the Sects 4:11; 6:26; War of the Children of Light 12:17; also קשׁה עורף in Book of the Sects 5:5, 26 [Kuhn].

† σκληρύνω.

1. The verb σκληρύνω (the later σκληρόω does not occur in the NT), meaning "to make firm," "to harden," [1] is primarily a medical word, Hippocr., also Aristot., Galen, P. Leid., X, II, 28.

2. It occurs 6 times in the NT, always fig., Ac. 19:9; R. 9:18; Hb. 3:8, 13, 15; 4:7, with exactly the same sense as πωρόω. [2] In Ac. 19:9 it is said of the unbelieving Jews of the synagogue: ἐσκληρύνοντο καὶ ἠπείθουν κακολογοῦντες τὴν ὁδόν, which shows that hardening was equated with unbelief. In R. 9:18 we read of God: ὃν δὲ θέλει σκληρύνει. God punishes by delivering up to sin, cf. R. 1:24, 26, 28, → 1026, n. 5. On the other hand, in Hb. 3:8 Christians are admonished: μὴ σκληρύνητε τὰς καρδίας ὑμῶν ὡς ἐν τῷ παραπικρασμῷ (cf. 3:13), and this is repeated in v. 15 and 4:7. Even more plainly than verses which use πωρόω (→ 1026, 8 ff.) those which have σκληρύνω bring out the combination and interrelation between hardening by God and self-hardening, the punishment of sin by sin, and the fact that Christians for their part are admonished against hardening.

3. Both in Pl. and Hb. we have OT quotations. In R. 9:18 there is a reminiscence of Ex. 4:21; 9:12; 14:4, 8, 17 (חזק pi); 7:3 (קשׁה hi); 7:22; 8:15; 9:35 (חזק q), always with ref. to the hardening of Pharaoh. God's σκληρύνειν takes place along with and in contrast to His ἐλεεῖν. [3] In Hb. 3:8 etc. there is allusion to the story of the bitter water (Ex. 15:23; 17:7; Nu. 20:2-5). ψ 94:8 is quoted literally (= קשׁה hi). σκληρύνω occurs some 30 times in this sense in the LXX. In the forefront is the σκληρύνεσθαι of Pharaoh. Along with the verses mentioned ref. should also be made to Ex. 10:1 (כבד hi, vl. ἐβάρυνα, → 1024, n. 8). [4] Dt. 2:30 speaks of the hardening of Sihon king of Heshbon, who would not let Israel through his land. But Israel, too, is hardened. In 4 Βασ. 17:14 we read of the Israelites, i.e., the ten tribes: ἐσκλήρυναν τὸν νῶτον αὐτῶν ὑπὲρ τὸν νῶτον τῶν πατέρων αὐτῶν, cf. Neh. 9:16 f., 29 (the same with τὸν τράχηλον); Jer. 7:26; 17:23; 19:15. This process is a special theme of prophetic preaching. In Is. 63:17 the prophet complains to God: τί ... ἐσκλήρυνας (HT קשׁה hi rather than the usual קשׁה) ἡμῶν τὰς καρδίας τοῦ μὴ φοβεῖσθαί σε; In 2 Ch. 30:8 we have the admonition to Israel: καὶ νῦν μὴ σκληρύνητε τὰς καρδίας (A τοὺς τραχήλους) ὑμῶν· δότε δόξαν κυρίῳ τῷ θεῷ. 2 Ch. 36:13 depicts the hardening of Zedekiah; cf. 1 Εσδρ. 1:46 (48). Cf. Dt. 10:16, also ψ 94:8, which is quoted in Hb. 3:8, → supra. On this theme in the prophets → 1026, 23 ff.

The LXX, however, can use the word without the thought of hardening. Already in Sir. 30:12 there is a softening of the more specialised use; it is there said to the son under instruction: μήποτε σκληρυνθεὶς ἀπειθήσῃ σοι. σκληρύνω is used in the following verses with no emphasis on the theme of hardening: Gn. 49:7, where Jacob curses his sons Simeon and Levi because their μῆνις ... ἐσκληρύνθη (קשׁה q); Ju. 4:24, which refers to the hand of Israel resting heavily on its enemies (χεὶρ ... σκληρυνομένη); 2 Βασ. 19:44, where ἐσκληρύνθη ὁ λόγος means the same as σκληρός ἐστιν

σ κ λ η ρ ύ ν ω. [1] Fraenkel, op. cit. (→ 1025, n. 1), 66 (36, 37, 41); Debrunner (→ 1025, n. 1), 81 and 84; Debr. Griech. Wortb. § 226.

[2] Hence in the list of synonyms in Cr.-Kö., 1206.

[3] → II, 484, 12 ff.; also Zn. R., 453-456; for older exegesis of the σκληρύνειν of R. 9:18 in the context of the doctrine of predestination cf. the critical commentaries of H. A. W. Meyer, *Der Brief an d. Röm.*[3] (1859), 347-349 and B. Weiss, *Der Br. an d. Röm.*[6] (1881), 459-461; [9] (1899), 415 f.

[4] On the exegesis of Ex. 10:1 in the Rabbis in controversy with the Minim (Christians?) cf. Str.-B., III, 269.

ὁ λόγος (→ 1028, 16 ff.); 4 Βασ. 2:10 : ἐσκλήρυνας τοῦ αἰτήσασθαι, "thou hast asked a hard thing"; 2 Ch. 10:4 : ἐσκλήρυνεν τὸν ζυγὸν ἡμῶν, "he has made our yoke heavy"; ψ 89, 6 : σκληρυνθείη καὶ ξηρανθείη, of dried up grass (σκληρ- = ξηρ-); 1 Macc. 2:30 : ἐσκληρύνθη (vl. ἐπληθύνθη) ἐπ' αὐτοὺς τὰ κακά, "evil came ever more heavily upon them." Philo does not use the word.

4. In some passages in the post-apost. fathers we find the biblical use. In 1 Cl., 51, 3 there is a plain ref. to the process of hardening in Nu. 16:31 ff. In 1 Cl., 51, 5 the hardening of Pharaoh is at issue. Finally we should mention Barn., 9, 5 : τὸν τράχηλον ὑμῶν οὐ σκληρυνεῖτε (→ 1028, 32 f.), which quotes Dt. 10:16.

K. L. and M. A. Schmidt